LAROUSSE

DICTIONNAI...
DE POCHE

FRANÇAIS
ANGLAIS

ANGLAIS
FRANÇAIS

LAROUSSE

21, rue du Montparnasse 75283 Paris Cedex 06

© Larousse, 2007,
21, rue du Montparnasse
75283 Paris Cedex 06, France

ISBN 978-2-03-541016-0
Sales: Houghton Mifflin Company, Boston
Library of Congress CIP Data
has been applied for.

LAROUSSE

**POCKET
DICTIONARY**

**FRENCH
ENGLISH**

**ENGLISH
FRENCH**

LAROUSSE

21, rue du Montparnasse 75283 Paris Cedex 06

Sommaire

Contents

Au lecteur

Ce DICTIONNAIRE LAROUSSE français-anglais, anglais-français est un ouvrage spécialement conçu pour ceux qui apprennent l'anglais.

Avec 55 000 mots et expressions et 80 000 traductions, il couvre l'ensemble de l'anglais contemporain.

Par le traitement clair et détaillé du vocabulaire général, les exemples de constructions grammaticales, les tournures idiomatiques, les indications de sens soulignant la traduction appropriée, le DICTIONNAIRE LAROUSSE français-anglais, anglais-français permet de s'exprimer sans hésiter et sans faire de contresens.

Offrir un outil pratique et pédagogique à tous ceux qui apprennent l'anglais, tel est le but que nous nous sommes fixé avec le DICTIONNAIRE LAROUSSE français-anglais, anglais-français.

L'Éditeur

To our readers

This DICTIONARY has been designed as a reliable and user-friendly tool for use in all language situations. It provides accurate and up-to-date information on written and spoken French and English as they are used today.

Its 55,000 words and phrases and 80,000 translations give you access to French texts of all types. The dictionary aims to be as comprehensive as possible in a book of this size, and includes many proper names and abbreviations, as well as a selection of the most common terms from computing, business and current affairs.

Carefully constructed entries and a clear page design help you to find the translation that you are looking for fast. Examples (from basic constructions and common phrases to idioms) have been included to help put a word in context and give a clear picture of how it is used.

The publisher

Abbreviations

Abréviations

abbreviation	*abbr/abr*	abréviation
adjective	*adj*	adjectif
administration, administrative	ADMIN	administration
adverb	*adv*	adverbe
aeronautics, aviation	AERON/AÉRON	aéronautique
agriculture, farming	AGR(IC)	agriculture
anatomy	ANAT	anatomie
archaeology	ARCHAEOL/ARCHÉOL	archéologie
architecture	ARCHIT	architecture
slang	*arg*	argot
article	*art*	article
astrology	ASTROL	astrologie
astronomy	ASTRON	astronomie
automobile, cars	AUT(OM)	automobile
auxiliary	*aux*	auxiliaire
before noun	*avant n*	avant le nom
– indicates that the translation is always used directly before the noun which it modifies		– appliqué à la traduction d'un adjectif français, indique l'emploi d'un nom anglais avec valeur d'adjectif; souligne aussi les cas où la traduction d'un adjectif est nécessairement antéposée
biology	BIOL	biologie
botany	BOT	botanique
chemistry	CHEM/CHIM	chimie
cinema, film-making	CIN(EMA)	cinéma
commerce, business	COMM	commerce
compound	*comp*	nom anglais utilisé en apposition
comparative	*compar*	comparatif
computers, computer science	COMPUT	informatique
conjunction	*conj*	conjonction
construction, building trade	CONSTR	construction, bâtiment
continuous	*cont*	progressif
sewing	COUT	couture
culinary, cooking	CULIN	cuisine, art culinaire
definite	*def/déf*	défini
demonstrative	*dem*	démonstratif
juridical, legal	DR	juridique
ecology	ÉCOL	écologie
economics	ECON/ÉCON	économie
electricity	ELEC/ÉLECTR	électricité
electronics	ELECTRON/ÉLECTRON	électronique
especially	*esp*	particulièrement
exclamation	*excl*	interjection
feminine	*f*	féminin
informal	*fam*	familier
figurative	*fig*	figuré

VII

finance, financial	FIN	finances
formal	*fml*	soutenu
soccer	FTBL	football
generally, in most cases	*gen/gén*	généralement
geography, geographical	GEOGR/GÉOGR	géographie
geology, geological	GEOL/GÉOL	géologie
geometry	GEOM/GÉOM	géométrie
grammar	GRAM(M)	grammaire
history	HIST	histoire
humorous	*hum*	humoristique
industry	IND	industrie
indefinite	*indef/indéf*	indéfini
informal	*inf*	familier
infinitive	*infin*	infinitif
inseparable	*insep*	non séparable

– shows that a phrasal verb is inseparable, e.g. **look after**, e.g. *I looked after him* but not *I looked him after*

– indique qu'un verbe anglais à particule (« phrasal verb ») ne peut pas être séparé de sa particule, par exemple, *I looked after him* et non *I looked him after*

computers, computer science	INFORM	informatique
exclamation	*interj*	interjection
interrogative	*interr*	interrogatif
invariable	*inv*	invariable
ironic	*iro/iron*	ironique
linguistics	LING	linguistique
literal	*lit/litt*	littéral
phrase(s)	*loc*	locution(s)
adjectival phrase	*loc adj*	locution adjectivale
adverbial phrase	*loc adv*	locution adverbiale
conjunctive phrase	*loc conj*	locution conjonctive
prepositional phrase	*loc prép*	locution prépositionnelle

– adjectives, adverbs and prepositions consisting of more than one word, e.g. **d'affilée, par dépit**

– adjectifs, adverbes et prépositions composés de plusieurs mots, **d'affilée, par dépit,** par exemple

masculine	*m*	masculin
mathematics	MATH(S)	mathématiques
medicine	MED/MÉD	médecine
weather, meteorology	METEOR/MÉTÉOR	météorologie
military	MIL	domaine militaire
music	MUS	musique
mythology	MYTH	mythologie
noun	*n*	nom
nautical, maritime	NAUT/NAVIG	navigation
numeral	*num*	numéral
oneself	*o.s.*	
pejorative	*pej/péj*	péjoratif
personal	*pers*	personnel
pharmacology, pharmaceutics	PHARM	pharmacologie
philosophy	PHILO	philosophie

photography	PHOT	photographie
phrase(s)	*phr*	locution(s)
physics	PHYS	physique
plural	*pl*	pluriel
politics	POL(IT)	politique
possessive	*poss*	possessif
past participle	*pp*	participe passé
present participle	*ppr*	participe présent
preposition	*prep/prép*	préposition
pronoun	*pron*	pronom
psychology, psychiatry	PSYCH(OL)	psychologie
past tense	*pt*	passé
	qqch	quelque chose
	qqn	quelqu'un
registered trademark	®	nom déposé
railways	RAIL	rail
relative	*rel*	relatif
religion	RELIG	religion
someone, somebody	*sb*	
school	SCH/SCOL	scolarité
Scottish English	*Scotland*	anglais écossais
separable	*sep*	séparable
– shows that a phrasal verb is separable, e.g. **let in**, **help out**: *I let her in, he helped me out*		– indique qu'un verbe anglais à post-position (« phrasal verb ») peut être séparé de sa particule, par exemple *I let her in, he helped me out*
singular	*sg*	singulier
slang	*sl*	argot
sociology	SOCIOL	sociologie
formal	*sout*	soutenu
stock exchange	ST EX	Bourse
something	*sthg*	
subject	*subj/suj*	sujet
superlative	*superl*	superlatif
technology, technical	TECH(NOL)	domaine technique et technologique
telecommunications	TELEC/TÉLÉCOM	télécommunications
very informal	*tfam*	très familier
television	TV/TÉLÉ	télévision
printing, typography	TYPO	typographie
uncountable noun	*U*	substantif non comptable
– i.e. an English noun which is never used in the plural or with "a" or "an"; used when the French word is or can be a plural, e.g. **applause** *n* (*U*) applaudissements *mpl*, **battement** *nm* beat, beating (*U*)		– désigne en anglais les noms qui ne sont jamais utilisés au pluriel, lorsque le terme français est un pluriel, ou peut être mis au pluriel, par exemple **applause** *n* (*U*) applaudissements *mpl*, **battement** *nm* beat, beating (*U*)
British English	*UK*	anglais britannique
university	UNIV	université
American English	*US*	anglais américain
usually	*usu*	habituellement

link verb followed by a predicative adjective or noun	*v attr*	verbe suivi d'un attribut
verb	*vb/v*	verbe
veterinary science	VETER	médecine vétérinaire
intransitive verb	*vi*	verbe intransitif
impersonal verb	*v impers*	verbe impersonnel
very informal	*v inf*	très familier
pronominal verb	*vp*	verbe pronominal
transitive verb	*vt*	verbe transitif
vulgar	*vulg*	vulgaire
zoology	ZOOL	zoologie
cultural equivalent	≃	équivalence culturelle
introduces a new part of speech within an entry	◇	introduit une nouvelle catégorie grammaticale dans une entrée
introduces a sub-entry, such as a plural form with its own specific meaning or a set phrase containing the headword (e.g. a phrasal verb or adverbial phrase)	◆	introduit une sous-entrée, par exemple une forme plurielle ayant un sens propre, ou une locution (locution adverbiale, verbe pronominal, etc.)

The symbol ['] has been used to represent the French "h aspiré", e.g. **hachis** ['aʃi].

Le symbole ['] représente le « h aspiré » français, e.g. **hachis** ['aʃi].

The symbol ['] indicates that the following syllable carries primary stress and the symbol [ˌ] that the following syllable carries secondary stress.

Les symboles ['] et [ˌ] indiquent respectivement un accent primaire et un accent secondaire sur la syllabe suivante.

The symbol [ʳ] in English phonetics indicates that the final "r" is pronounced only when followed by a word beginning with a vowel. Note that it is nearly always pronounced in American English.

Le symbole [ʳ] indique que le « r » final d'un mot anglais ne se prononce que lorsqu'il forme une liaison avec la voyelle du mot suivant ; le « r » final est presque toujours prononcé en anglais américain.

A phonetic transcription has been given where appropriate after every French headword (the main word which starts an entry). All one-word English headwords similarly have phonetics. For English compound headwords, whether hyphenated or of two or more words, phonetics are given for any element which does not appear elsewhere in the dictionary as a headword in its own right.

Une transcription phonétique – quand elle a été jugée nécessaire – suit chaque libellé (terme-vedette de l'entrée) français, ainsi que chaque libellé anglais écrit en un seul mot. Pour les mots composés anglais (avec ou sans trait d'union, et composés de deux éléments ou plus), la phonétique est présente pour ceux des éléments qui n'apparaissent pas dans le dictionnaire en tant que libellé à part entière.

Phonetic Transcription Transcription Phonétique

English Vowels

[ɪ]	pit, big, rid
[e]	pet, tend
[æ]	pat, bag, mad
[ʌ]	putt, cut
[ɒ]	pot, log
[ʊ]	put, full
[ə]	mother, suppose
[iː]	bean, weed
[ɑː]	barn, car, laugh
[ɔː]	born, lawn
[uː]	loop, loose
[ɜː]	burn, learn, bird

Voyelles françaises

[i]	fille, île
[e]	pays, année
[ɛ]	bec, aime
[a]	lac, papillon
[ɑ]	tas, âme
[o]	drôle, aube
[ɔ]	botte, automne
[u]	outil, goût
[y]	usage, lune
[ø]	aveu, jeu
[œ]	peuple, bœuf
[ə]	le, je

English Diphthongs

[eɪ]	bay, late, great
[aɪ]	buy, light, aisle
[ɔɪ]	boy , foil
[əʊ]	no, road, blow
[aʊ]	now, shout, town
[ɪə]	peer, fierce, idea
[eə]	pair, bear, share
[ʊə]	poor, sure, tour

Nasales françaises

[ɛ̃]	limbe, main
[ɑ̃]	champ, ennui
[ɔ̃]	ongle, mon
[œ̃]	parfum, brun

Semi-vowels

you, spaniel	[j]	
wet, why, twin	[w]	
	[ɥ]	

Semi-voyelles

yeux, lieu
ouest, oui
lui, nuit

Consonants

English		French
pop, people	[p]	prendre, grippe
bottle, bib	[b]	bateau, rosbif
train, tip	[t]	théâtre, temps
dog, did	[d]	dalle, ronde
come, kitchen	[k]	coq, quatre
gag, great	[g]	garder, épilogue
chain, wretched	[tʃ]	
jig, fridge	[dʒ]	
fib, physical	[f]	physique, fort
vine, livid	[v]	voir, rive
think, fifth	[θ]	
this, with	[ð]	
seal, peace	[s]	cela, savant
zip, his	[z]	fraise, zéro
sheep, machine	[ʃ]	charrue, schéma
usual, measure	[ʒ]	rouge, jabot
how, perhaps	[h]	
metal, comb	[m]	mât, drame
night, dinner	[n]	nager, trône
sung, parking	[ŋ]	
	[ɲ]	agneau, peigner
little, help	[l]	halle, lit
right, carry	[ʀ]	arracher, sabre

Conjugaisons françaises

1. **avoir :** ind prés ai, as, a, avons, avez, ont ; imparfait avais, avais, avait, avions aviez, avaient ; ind fut aurai, auras, aura, aurons, aurez, auront ; subj prés que j'aie, que tu aies, qu'il ait, que nous ayons, que vous ayez, qu'ils aient ; imp aie, ayons ; pprés ayant; pp eu

2. **être :** ind prés suis, es, est, sommes, êtes, sont ; imparfait étais, étais, était, étions, étiez, étaient ; ind fut serai, seras, sera, serons, serez, seront; subj prés que je sois, que tu sois, qu'il soit, que nous soyons, que vous soyez, qu'ils soient ; imp sois, soyons ; pprés étant ; pp été

3. **chanter :** ind prés chante, chantes, chante, chantons, chantez, chantent ; imparfait chantais, chantais chantait, chantions, chantiez, chantaient ; ind fut chanterai, chanteras, chantera, chanterons, chanterez, chanteront ; subj prés que je chante, que tu chantes, qu'il chante, que nous chantions, que vous chantiez, qu'ils chantent ; imp chante, chantons ; pprés chantant; pp chanté

4. **baisser :** ind prés baisse, baissons ; imparfait baissais ; ind fut baisserai ; subj prés que je baisse ; imp baisse, baissons ; pprés baissant ; pp baissé

5. **pleurer :** ind prés pleure, pleurons ; imparfait pleurais ; ind fut pleurerai ; subj prés que je pleure ; imp pleure, pleurons ; pprés pleurant ; pp pleuré

6. **jouer :** ind prés joue, jouons ; imparfait jouais ; ind fut jouerai ; subj prés que je joue ; imp joue, jouons ; pprés jouant ; pp joué

7. **saluer :** ind prés salue; saluons ; imparfait saluais ; ind fut saluerai ; subj prés que je salue ; imp salue, saluons ; pprés saluant ; pp salué

8. **arguer :** ind prés argue, arguons imparfait arguais ; ind fut arguerai ; subj prés que j'argue ; imp argue, arguons ; pprés arguant ; pp argué

9. **copier :** ind prés copie, copions ; imparfait copiais ; ind fut copierai ; subj prés que je copie ; imp copie, copions ; pprés copiant ; pp copié

10. **prier :** ind prés prie, prions ; imparfait priais ; ind fut prierai ; subj prés que je prie ; imp prie, prions ; pprés priant ; pp prié

11. **payer :** ind prés paie, payons, paient ; imparfait payais ; ind fut paierai ; subj prés que je paie ; imp paie, payons ; pprés payant ; pp payé

12. **grasseyer :** ind prés grasseye, grasseyons ; imparfait grasseyais ; ind fut grasseyerai ; subj prés que je grasseye ; imp grasseye, grasseyons ; pprés grasseyant ; pp grasseyé

13. **ployer :** ind prés ploie, ployons, ploient ; imparfait ployais ; ind fut ploierai ; subj prés que je ploie ; imp ploie, ployons ; pprés ployant ; pp ployé

14. **essuyer :** ind prés essuie, essuyons, essuient ; imparfait essuyais ; ind fut essuirai ; subj prés que j'essuie, que nous essuyions ; imp essuie, essuyons ; pprés essuyant; pp essuyé

15. **créer :** ind prés crée, créons ; imparfait créais ; ind fut créerai ; subj prés que je crée ; imp crée, créons ; pprés créant ; pp créé

16. **avancer :** ind prés avance, avançons, avancent ; imparfait avançais ; ind fut avancerai ; subj prés que j'avance ; imp avance, avançons ; pprés avançant ; pp avancé

17. **manger :** ind prés mange, mangeons ; imparfait mangeais ; ind fut mangerai ; subj prés que je mange ; imp mange, mangeons ; pprés mangeant ; pp mangé

18. **céder :** ind prés cède, cédons, cèdent ; imparfait cédais ; ind fut céderai ; subj prés que je cède ; imp cède, cédons ; pprés cédant ; pp cédé

19. **semer :** ind prés sème, semons sèment ; imparfait semais ; ind fut sèmerai ; subj prés que je sème ; imp sème, semons ; pprés semant ; pp semé

20. **rapiécer :** ind prés rapièce, rapiéçons, rapiècent ; imparfait rapiéçais ; ind fut rapiécerai ; subj prés que je rapièce ; imp rapièce, rapiéçons ; pprés rapiéçant ; pp rapiécé

21. acquiescer : ind prés acquiesce, acquiesçons, acquiescent ; imparfait acquiesçais ; ind fut acquiescerai ; subj prés que j'acquiesce ; imp acquiesce, acquiesçons ; pprés acquiesçant; pp acquiescé

22. siéger : ind prés siège, siégeons, siègent ; imparfait siégeais ; ind fut siégerai ; subj prés que je siège ; imp siège, siégeons ; pprés siégeant ; pp siégé

23. déneiger : ind prés déneige, déneigeons ; imparfait déneigeais ; ind fut déneigerai ; subj prés que je déneige ; imp déneige, déneigeons ; pprés déneigeant ; pp déneigé

24. appeler : ind prés appelle, appelons, appellent ; imparfait appelais ; ind fut appellerai ; subj prés que j'appelle ; imp appelle, appelons ; pprés appelant ; pp appelé

25. peler : ind prés pèle, pelons, pèlent ; imparfait pelais ; ind fut pèlerai ; subj prés que je pèle ; imp pèle, pelons ; pprés pelant ; pp pelé

26. interpeller : ind prés interpelle, interpellons ; imparfait interpellais ; ind fut interpellerai ; subj prés que j'interpelle ; imp interpelle, interpellons ; pprés interpellant ; pp interpellé

27. jeter : ind prés jette, jetons, jettent; imparfait jetais ; ind fut jetterai ; subj prés que je jette ; imp jette, jetons ; pprés jetant ; pp jeté

28. acheter : ind prés achète, achetons, achètent ; imparfait achetais ; ind fut achèterai ; subj prés que j'achète ; imp achète, achetons ; pprés achetant ; pp acheté

29. dépecer : ind prés dépèce, dépeçons, dépècent ; imparfait dépeçais ; ind fut dépècerai ; subj prés que je dépèce ; imp dépèce, dépeçons ; pprés dépeçant ; pp dépecé

30. envoyer : ind prés envoie, envoyons, envoient ; imparfait envoyais ; ind fut enverrai ; subj prés que j'envoie ; imp envoie, envoyons ; pprés envoyant ; pp envoyé

31. aller : ind prés vais, allons, vont ; imparfait allais ; ind fut irai ; subj prés que j'aille ; imp va, allons ; pprés allant ; pp allé

32. finir : ind prés finis, finis, finit, finissons, finissez, finissent ; imparfait finissais, finissais, finissait, finissions, finissiez, finissaient; ind fut finirai, finiras, finira, finirons, finirez, finiront ; subj prés que je finisse, que tu finisses, qu'il finisse, que nous finissions, que vous finissiez, qu'ils finissent ; imp finis, finissons ; pprés finissant ; pp fini

33. haïr : ind prés je hais, haïssons ; imparfait haïssais ; ind fut haïrai ; subj prés que je haïsse ; imp hais, haïssons ; pprés haïssant ; pp haï

34. ouvrir : ind prés ouvre, ouvrons ; imparfait ouvrais ; ind fut ouvrirai ; subj prés que j'ouvre ; imp ouvre, ouvrons ; pprés ouvrant ; pp ouvert

35. fuir : ind prés fuis, fuyons, fuient ; imparfait fuyais ; ind fut fuirai ; subj prés que je fuie ; imp fuis, fuyons ; pprés fuyant ; pp fui

36. dormir : ind prés dors, dormons ; imparfait dormais ; ind fut dormirai; subj prés que je dorme ; imp dors, dormons ; pprés dormant; pp dormi

37. mentir : ind prés mens, mentons ; imparfait mentais ; ind fut mentirai; subj prés que je mente ; imp mentais ; pprés mentant ; pp menti

38. servir : ind prés sers, servons ; imparfait servais ; ind fut servirai ; subj prés que je serve ; imp sers, servons ; pprés servant; pp servi

39. acquérir : ind prés acquiers, acquérons, acquièrent ; imparfait acquérais ; ind fut acquerrai ; subj prés que j'acquière ; imp acquiers, acquérons ; pprés acquérant ; pp acquis

40 venir : ind prés viens, venons, viennent ; imparfait venais ; ind fut viendrai ; subj prés que je vienne ; imp viens, venons ; pprés venant ; pp venu

41. cueillir : ind prés cueille, cueillons ; imparfait cueillais ; ind fut cueillerai ; subj prés que je cueille ; imp cueille, cueillons ; pprés cueillant ; pp cueilli

42. mourir : ind prés meurs, mourons, meurent ; imparfait mourais ; ind fut mourrai ; subj prés que je meure ; imp meurs, mourons ; pprés mourant; pp mort

43. partir : ind prés pars, partons ; imparfait partais ; ind fut partirai ; subj prés que je parte ; imp pars, partons ; pprés partant; pp parti

44. revêtir : ind prés revêts, revêtons ; imparfait revêtais ; ind fut revêtirai ; subj prés que je revête ; imp revêts, revêtons ; pprés revêtant ; pp revêtu

45. courir : ind prés cours, courons ; imparfait courais ; ind fut courrai ; subj prés que je coure ; imp cours, courons ; pprés courant; pp couru

46. faillir : ind prés faillis, faillissons ; imparfait faillissais ; ind fut faillirai ; subj prés que je faillisse ; pprés faillissant ; pp failli

47. défaillir : ind prés défaille, défaillons ; imparfait défaillais ; ind fut défaillirai ; subj prés que je défaille ; imp défaille, défaillons ; pprés défaillant ; pp défailli

48. bouillir : ind prés bous, bouillons ; imparfait bouillais ; ind fut bouillirai ; subj prés que je bouille ; imp bous, bouillons ; pprés bouillant ; pp bouilli

49. gésir : ind prés gis, gisons ; imparfait gisais ; pprés gisant

50. saillir : ind prés il saille, ils saillent; imparfait il saillait ; ind fut il saillera; subj prés qu'il saille, qu'ils saillent ; pprés saillant ; pp sailli

51. ouïr : ind prés ouïs, ouïssons ; imparfait ouïssais ; ind fut ouïrai ; subj prés que j'ouïsse ; imp ouïs, ouïssons ; pprés oyant ; pp ouï

52. recevoir : ind prés reçois, recevons ; reçoivent ; imparfait recevais ; ind fut recevrai ; subj prés que je reçoive ; imp reçois, recevons ; pprés recevant; pp reçu

53. devoir : ind prés dois, devons, doivent ; imparfait devais ; ind fut devrai ; subj prés que je doive; pprés devant ; pp dû

54. mouvoir : ind prés meus, mouvons, meuvent ; imparfait mouvais ; ind fut mouvrai ; subj prés meuve, mouvions, meuvent ; imp meus, mouvons ; pprés mouvant; pp mû

55. émouvoir : ind prés émeus, émouvons, émeuvent ; imparfait émouvais ; ind fut émouvrai ; subj prés que j'émeuve ; imp émeus, émouvons ; pprés émouvant ; pp ému

56. promouvoir : ind prés promeus, promouvons, promeuvent ; imparfait promouvais ; ind fut promouvrai ; subj prés que je promeuve ; imp promeus, promouvons ; pprés promouvant ; pp promu

57. vouloir : ind prés veux, voulons, veulent ; imparfait voulais ; ind fut voudrai ; subj prés que je veuille, que nous voulions, qu'ils veuillent ; imp veuille, veuillons ; pprés voulant; pp voulu

58. pouvoir : ind prés peux, pouvons, peuvent ; imparfait pouvais ; ind fut pourrai ; subj prés que je puisse ; pprés pouvant ; pp pu

59. savoir : ind prés sais, savons ; imparfait savais ; ind fut saurai ; subj prés que je sache ; imp sache, sachons ; pprés sachant ; pp su

60. valoir : ind prés vaux, valons ; imparfait valais ; ind fut vaudrai ; subj prés que je vaille ; imp vaux, valons ; pprés valant ; pp valu

61. prévaloir : ind prés prévaux, prévalons ; imparfait prévalais ; nd fut prévaudrai ; subj prés que je prévale ; imp prévaux, prévalons ; pprés prévalant ; pp prévalu

62. voir : ind prés vois, voyons, voient ; imparfait voyais ; ind fut verrai ; subj prés que je voie ; imp vois, voyons ; pprés voyant ; pp vu

63. prévoir : ind prés prévois, prévoyons, prévoient ; imparfait prévoyais ; ind fut prévoirai ; subj prés que je prévoie ; imp prévois, prévoyons ; pprés prévoyant ; pp prévu

64. pourvoir : ind prés pourvois, pourvoyons, pourvoient ; imparfait pourvoyais ; ind fut pourvoirai ; subj prés que je pourvoie ; imp pourvois, pourvoyons ; pprés pourvoyant; pp pourvu

65. asseoir : ind prés assieds, asseyons, assoient ; imparfait asseyais ; ind fut assiérai ; subj prés que j'asseye ; imp assieds, asseyons ; pprés asseyant ; pp assis

66. surseoir : ind prés sursois, sursoyons, sursoient ; imparfait sursoyais ; ind fut surseoirai ; subj prés que je surseoie ; imp sursois, sursoyons ; pprés sursoyant ; pp sursis

67. seoir : ind prés il sied, ils siéent ; imparfait il seyait ; ind fut il siéra ; subj prés qu'il siée, qu'ils siéent ; pprés seyant

68. pleuvoir : ind prés il pleut ; imparfait il pleuvait ; ind fut il pleuvra ; subj prés qu'il pleuve ; pprés pleuvant ; pp plu

69. falloir : ind prés il faut ; imparfait il fallait ; ind fut il faudra ; subj prés qu'il faille ; pp fallu

70. échoir : ind prés il échoit, ils échoient ; imparfait il échoyait ; ind fut il échoira ; subj prés qu'il échoie ; pprés échéant ; pp échu

71. déchoir : ind prés déchois, déchoyons, déchoient ; ind fut déchoirai ; subj prés que je déchoie, qu'ils déchoient ; pp déchu

72. choir : ind prés je chois, ils choient ; ind fut choirai ; pp chu

73. vendre : ind prés vends, vends, vend, vendons, vendez, vendent ; imparfait vendais, vendais, vendait, vendions, vendiez, vendaient ; ind fut vendrai, vendras, vendra, vendrons, vendrez, vendront ; subj prés que je vende, que tu vendes, qu'il vende, que nous vendions, que vous vendiez, qu'ils vendent ; imp vends, vendons ; pprés vendant ; pp vendu

74. répandre : ind prés répands, répandons ; imparfait répandais ; ind fut répandrai ; subj prés que je répande ; imp répands, répandons ; pprés répandant ; pp répandu

75. répondre : ind prés réponds, répondons ; imparfait répondais ; ind fut répondrai ; subj prés que je réponde ; imp réponds, répondons ; pprés répondant ; pp répondu

76. mordre : ind prés mords, mordons ; imparfait mordais ; ind fut mordrai ; subj prés que je morde ; imp mords, mordons ; pprés mordant ; pp mordu

77. perdre : ind prés perds, perdons ; imparfait perdais ; ind fut perdrai ; subj prés que je perde ; imp perds, perdons ; pprés perdant ; pp perdu

78. rompre : ind prés romps, rompons ; imparfait rompais ; ind fut romprai ; subj prés que je rompe ; imp romps, rompons ; pprés rompant ; pp rompu

79. prendre : ind prés prends, prenons, prennent ; imparfait prenais ; ind fut prendrai ; subj prés que je prenne ; imp prends, prenons ; pprés prenant ; pp pris

80. craindre : ind prés crains, craignons ; imparfait craignais ; ind fut craindrai ; subj prés que je craigne ; imp crains, craignons ; pprés craignant ; pp craint

81. peindre : ind prés peins, peignons ; imparfait peignais ; ind fut peindrai ; subj prés que je peigne ; imp peins, peignons ; pprés peignant ; pp peint

82. joindre : ind prés joins, joignons ; imparfait joignais ; ind fut joindrai ; subj prés que je joigne ; imp joins, joignons ; pprés joignant ; pp joint

83. battre : ind prés bats, battons ; imparfait battais ; ind fut battrai ; subj prés que je batte ; imp bats, battons ; pprés battant ; pp battu

84. mettre : ind prés mets, mettons ; imparfait mettais ; ind fut mettrai ; subj prés que je mette ; imp mets, mettons ; pprés mettant ; pp mis

85. moudre : ind prés mouds, moulons ; imparfait moulais ; ind fut moudrai ; subj prés que je moule ; imp mouds, moulons ; pprés moulant ; pp moulu

86. coudre : ind prés couds, cousons ; imparfait cousait ; ind fut coudrai ; subj prés que je couse ; imp couds, cousons ; pprés cousant ; pp cousu

87. absoudre : ind prés absous, absolvons ; imparfait absolvais ; ind fut absoudrai ; subj prés que j'absolve ; imp absous, absolvons ; pprés absolvant ; pp absous

88. résoudre : ind prés résous, résolvons ; imparfait résolvais ; ind fut résoudrai ; subj prés que je résolve ; imp résous, résolvons ; pprés résolvant ; pp résolu

89. suivre : ind prés suis, suivons ; imparfait suivais ; ind fut suivrai ; subj prés que je suive ; imp suis, suivons ; pprés suivant ; pp suivi

90. vivre : ind prés vis, vivons ; imparfait vivais ; ind fut vivrai ; subj prés que je vive, que nous vivions ; imp vis, vivons ; pprés vivant ; pp vécu

91. paraître : ind prés parais, paraissons ; imparfait paraissais ; ind fut paraîtrai ; subj prés que je paraisse ; imp parais, paraissons ; pprés paraissant ; pp paru

92. naître : ind prés nais, naissons ; imparfait naissais ; ind fut naîtrai ; subj prés que je naisse ; imp nais, naissons ; pprés naissant ; pp né

93. croître : ind prés croîs, croissons ; imparfait croissait ; ind fut croîtrai ; subj prés que je croisse ; imp croîs, croissons ; pprés croissant ; pp crû

94. accroître : ind prés accrois, accroissons ; imparfait accroissait ; ind fut accroîtrai ; subj prés que j'accroisse ; imp accrois, accroissons ; pprés accroissant ; pp accru

95. rire : ind prés ris, rions ; imparfait riais ; ind fut rirai ; subj prés que je rie ; imp ris, rions ; pprés riant ; pp ri

96. conclure : ind prés conclus, concluons ; imparfait concluais ; ind fut conclurai ; subj prés que je conclue ; imp conclus, concluons ; pprés concluant ; pp conclu

97. nuire : ind prés nuis, nuisons ; imparfait nuisais ; ind fut nuirai ; subj prés que je nuise ; imp nuis, nuisons ; pprés nuisant ; pp nui

98. conduire : ind prés conduis, conduisons ; imparfait conduisais ; ind fut conduirai ; subj prés que je conduise ; imp conduis, conduisons ; pprés conduisant ; pp conduit

99. écrire : ind prés écris, écrivons ; imparfait écrivais ; ind fut écrirai ; subj prés que j'écrive ; imp écris, écrivons ; pprés écrivant ; pp écrit

100. suffire : ind prés suffis, suffisons ; imparfait suffisais ; ind fut suffirai ; subj prés que je suffise ; pprés suffisant ; pp suffi

101. confire : ind prés confis, confisons ; imparfait confisais ; ind fut confirai ; subj prés que je confise ; imp confis, confisons ; pprés confisant ; pp confit

102. dire : ind prés dis, disons ; imparfait disais ; ind fut dirai ; subj prés que je dise ; imp dis, disons ; pprés disant ; pp dit

103. contredire : ind prés contredis, contredisons ; imparfait contredisais ; ind fut contredirai ; subj prés que je contredise ; imp contredis, contredisons ; pprés contredisant ; pp contredit

104. maudire : ind prés maudis, maudissons ; imparfait maudissais ; ind fut maudirai ; subj prés que je maudisse ; imp maudis, maudissons ; pprés maudissant ; pp maudit

105. bruire : ind prés bruis ; imparfait bruyais ; ind fut bruirai ; pp bruit

106. lire : ind prés lis, lisons ; imparfait lisais ; ind fut lirai ; subj prés que je lise, que nous lisions ; imp lis, lisons ; pprés lisant ; pp lu

107. croire : ind prés crois, croyons, croient ; imparfait croyais ; ind fut croirai ; subj prés que je croie ; imp crois, croyons ; pprés croyant ; pp cru

108. boire : ind prés bois, buvons, boivent ; imparfait buvais ; ind fut boirai ; subj prés que je boive ; imp bois, buvons ; pprés buvant ; pp bu

109. faire : ind prés fais, faisons, font ; imparfait faisais ; ind fut ferai ; subj prés que je fasse ; imp fais, faisons, faites ; pprés faisant ; pp fait

110. plaire : ind prés plais, plaisons ; imparfait plaisais ; ind fut plairai ; subj prés que je plaise ; imp plais, plaisons ; pprés plaisant ; pp plu

111. taire : ind prés tais, taisons ; imparfait taisais ; ind fut tairai ; subj prés que je taise ; imp tais, taisons ; pprés taisant ; pp tu

112. extraire : ind prés extrais, extrayons, extraient ; imparfait extrayais ; ind fut extrairai ; subj prés que j'extraie ; imp extrais, extrayons ; pprés extrayant ; pp extrait

113. clore : ind prés clos, closons ; ind fut clorai ; subj prés que je close ; imp clos ; pprés closant ; pp clos

114. vaincre : ind prés vaincs, vainquons ; imparfait vainquais ; ind fut vaincrai ; subj prés que je vainque ; imp vaincs, vainquons ; pprés vainquant ; pp vaincu

115. frire : ind prés fris ; ind fut frirai ; imp fris ; pp frit

116. foutre : ind prés fous, foutons ; imparfait foutais ; ind fut foutrai ; subj prés que je foute ; imp fous, foutons ; pprés foutant ; pp foutu

Verbes Irréguliers

Première catégorie

Le prétérit et le participe passé de ces verbes ont la même forme. En voici quelques-uns parmi les plus fréquents :

bend	→	bent	bind	→	bound
bleed	→	bled	breed	→	bred
bring	→	brought	build	→	built
burn[1]	→	burnt	buy	→	bought
catch	→	caught	cling	→	clung
creep	→	crept	deal	→	dealt
dig	→	dug	dream[1]	→	dreamt
dwell[1]	→	dwelt	feed	→	fed
feel	→	felt	fight	→	fought
find	→	found	flee	→	fled
fling	→	flung	foretell	→	foretold
grind	→	ground	have	→	had
hear	→	heard	hold	→	held
keep	→	kept	kneel[1]	→	knelt
lay	→	laid	lead	→	led
lean[1]	→	leant	leap[1]	→	leapt
learn[1]	→	learnt	leave	→	left
lend	→	lent	light[1]	→	lit
lose	→	lost	make	→	made
mean	→	meant	meet	→	met
pay	→	paid	read	→	read
say	→	said	seek	→	sought
sell	→	sold	send	→	sent
shoot	→	shot	sit	→	sat
sleep	→	slept	slide	→	slid
sling	→	slung	smell[1]	→	smelt
speed	→	sped	spell[1]	→	spelt
spend[1]	→	spent	spill[1]	→	spilt
spit	→	spat	spoil[1]	→	spoilt
stand	→	stood	stick	→	stuck
sting	→	stung	strike	→	struck
sweep	→	swept	swing	→	swung
teach	→	taught	tell	→	told
think	→	thought	understand	→	understood
weep	→	wept	win	→	won
wind	→	wound	withhold	→	withheld
wring	→	wrung			

Première catégorie :
En anglais américain, les verbes suivis du chiffre[1] peuvent avoir des formes régulières en **-ed** (**burned**, **spoiled** …)

Deuxième catégorie :
1 **Ate** (prétérit de **eat**) se prononce [et] en anglais britannique et [eɪt] en anglais américain.
2 En anglais américain, une des formes du participe passé de **get** est **gotten**.
3 Ces verbes peuvent avoir des formes régulières dans certains sens (**show**, **showed**, **showed**).

Deuxième catégorie

Le prétérit et le participe passé ont des formes différentes. Voici une liste non exhaustive de ces verbes :

Base v.	Prétérit	Part. Passé	Base v.	Prétérit	Part. Passé
be	was	been	bear	bore	borne
beat	beat	beaten	become	became	become
begin	began	begun	bite	bit	bitten
blow	blew	blown	break	broke	broken
choose	chose	chosen	come	came	come
do	did	done	draw	drew	drawn
drink	drank	drunk	drive	drove	driven
eat	ate[1]	eaten	fall	fell	fallen
fly	flew	flown	forbid	forbade	forbidden
forego	forewent	foregone	foresee	foresaw	foreseen
forget	forgot	forgotten	forgive	forgave	forgiven
freeze	froze	frozen	get	got	got[2]
give	gave	given	go	went	gone
grow	grew	grown	hang[3]	hung	hung
hide	hid	hidden	know	knew	known
lie	lay	lain	mistake	mistook	mistaken
mow[3]	mowed	mown	ride	rode	ridden
ring	rang	rung	rise	rose	risen
run	ran	run	see	saw	seen
shake	shook	shaken	shine[3]	shone	shone
show[3]	showed	shown	shrink	shrank/shrunk	shrunk
sing	sang	sung	sink	sank	sunk
speak	spoke	spoken	spin	span/spun	spun
spring	sprang	sprung	steal	stole	stolen
stink	stank/stunk	stunk	stride	strode	stridden
swear	swore	sworn	swell[3]	swelled	swollen
swim	swam	swum	take	took	taken
tear	tore	torn	throw	threw	thrown
tread	trod	trodden	wake[3]	woke	woken
wear	wore	worn	weave	wove	woven
withdraw	withdrew	withdrawn	write	wrote	written

Troisième catégorie

Ces verbes, d'une seule syllabe, se terminent par **-d** ou **-t** et ont une même forme pour la base verbale, le prétérit et le participe passé :

bet	hit	set
bid	hurt	shut
burst	let	slit
cast (*also* forecast)	put	split
cost	quit	spread
cut	rid	thrust

Comment utiliser le dictionnaire ?

Comment trouver le mot ou l'expression que l'on recherche ?

Il faut d'abord se poser plusieurs questions :
- S'agit-il d'un mot isolé, d'un mot à trait d'union ou d'une abréviation ?
- S'agit-il d'un nom composé ?
- S'agit-il d'une expression ou d'une locution ?
- S'agit-il d'un verbe pronominal ?
- S'agit-il d'un verbe à particules anglais ?
- S'agit-il d'une forme irrégulière ?

Mots isolés, mots à trait d'union et abréviations

En règle générale, on trouve le mot recherché à la place qui lui correspond dans l'ordre alphabétique.

Les entrées commençant par une *majuscule* apparaissent après celles qui s'écrivent de la même façon mais commencent par une minuscule.
Si le mot avec majuscule et le mot avec minuscule sont liés du point de vue du sens, on trouvera la version avec majuscule sous son équivalent avec minuscule, après un losange noir (◆). Il s'agit d'un type de « sous-entrée » (voir plus bas).

> **réunion** [reynjɔ̃] *nf* - **1.** [séance] meeting - **2.** [jonction] union, merging.
>
> **Réunion** [reunjɔ̃] *nf*: (l'île de) la ~ Réunion.

> **congress** ['kɒŋgres] *n* [meeting] congrès *m*. ◆ **Congress** *n Am* POL le Congrès.

Dans certains cas, l'entrée est suivie d'un chiffre en *exposant*. Ceci veut dire que, juste avant ou juste après, figure une autre entrée, elle aussi suivie d'un chiffre, qui s'écrit de la même façon mais a un sens ou une prononciation totalement différents.

> **tear**[1] [tɪəʳ] *n* larme *f*.
>
> **tear**[2] [teəʳ] (*pt* **tore**, *pp* **torn**) *vt* [rip] déchirer.

Ce sont ce que l'on appelle des homographes. Il faut s'assurer que l'on ne se trompe pas d'entrée. Faisons donc bien attention à la catégorie grammaticale et à la prononciation. Dans l'exemple ci-dessus, les deux mots « tear » n'ont pas la même phonétique ; il faut par ailleurs se demander si l'on recherche un nom (n) ou un verbe transitif (vt).

Les mots comportant un *trait d'union*, un *point* ou une *apostrophe* viennent après ceux qui s'écrivent de la même façon mais sans aucun de ces signes.

> **second hand** ['sekənd-] *n* [of clock] trotteuse *f*.
>
> **second-hand** ['sekənd-] *adj* [goods, shop] d'occasion.

Les entrées portant un *accent* se trouvent après celles qui s'écrivent de la même façon mais sans accent.

ou [u] *conj* [indique une alternative, une approximation] or.
où [u] *pron rel* [spatial] where.

Certains mots sont traités en sous-entrée, précédés d'un losange noir (◆). Il s'agit notamment, comme on l'a vu plus haut, de formes avec majuscule sous la forme équivalente sans majuscule, ou bien de noms placés sous un adjectif.

animal, e, aux [animal, o] *adj* - **1.** [propre à l'animal] animal *(avant n)* - **2.** [instinctif] instinctive. ◆ **animal** *nm* [bête] animal.

Si l'on cherche un nom qui, au *pluriel*, a un sens différent de celui du singulier (comme *glass/glasses* en anglais), c'est sous la forme au singulier qu'on le trouvera : le mot au pluriel y figure en sous-entrée.

glass [glaːs] ◇ *n* - **1.** [gen] verre *m* - **2.** *(U)* [glassware] verrerie *f*. ◇ *comp* [bottle, jar] en OR de verre ; [door, partition] vitré(e). ◆ **glasses** *npl* [spectacles] lunettes *fpl*.

Certains noms apparaissent directement au pluriel dans la liste alphabétique, soit parce qu'ils n'existent pas au singulier, soit parce que ce dernier est rare (*scissors* en anglais, *abats* en français).

Noms composés

Un nom composé est une expression dotée d'une signification globale, mais constituée de plusieurs mots (p. ex. *homme d'affaires* ou *joint venture*). Dans la partie français-anglais, on trouve ces composés dans le dictionnaire à l'entrée correspondant au premier élément. Ainsi, *homme d'affaires* sera sous *homme*. Au sein d'une entrée, les différents noms composés sont classés par ordre alphabétique, sans tenir compte de la préposition médiane ; dans l'entrée *café*, par exemple, *café au lait* vient après *café glacé* et *café en grains*.

Certains composés français dont le sens est éloigné du mot d'entrée figurent dans l'article après un losange noir (◆).

fuseau, x [fyzo] *nm* - **1.** [outil] spindle - **2.** [pantalon] ski-pants *(pl)*. ◆ **fuseau horaire** *nm* time zone.

Du côté anglais, les noms composés apparaissent comme des entrées à part entière.
Il existe aussi des composés dont les deux éléments sont séparés par un

blood donor *n* donneur *m*, -euse *f* de sang.
bloodshot ['blʌdʃɒt] *adj* [eyes] injecté(e) de sang.

trait d'union. Ils figurent dans le dictionnaire en entrée, par exemple *train-spotter* ou *time-sharing*.

Expressions et locutions

Par « expression » on entend un groupe de mots qui se manifestent toujours dans le même ordre et qui ont un sens global (*prendre part à qqch, to do sb credit*). C'est notamment le cas des expressions figurées et idiomatiques, ainsi que des proverbes (*avoir un chat dans la gorge, to pull sb's leg*).

Toutes les expressions sont à chercher sous le premier nom dont elles se composent (*prendre part à qqch* sous *part, to do sb credit* sous *credit*). S'il n'y a pas de nom dans l'expression, on cherchera sous le verbe.

Certaines expressions très figées ayant une valeur grammaticale globale (locutions) sont traitées en sous-entrée sous le premier élément signifiant, précédées du symbole ◆,

> **part** [par] *nf* [de gâteau] portion ; [de bonheur, d'héritage] share ; [partie] part.
> ◆ **d'autre part** *loc adv* besides, moreover.

de façon à mettre en relief la différence de sens et de fonction grammaticale entre la locution et l'entrée à laquelle elle se rattache.

Verbes pronominaux

La plupart des verbes pronominaux sont placés en sous-entrée sous la forme principale qui leur correspond après le symbole ◆.

> **cacher** [3] [kaʃe] *vt* - **1.** [gén] to hide ; **je ne vous cache pas que ...** to be honest, ... - **2.** [vue] to mask. ◆ **se cacher** *vp* : se ~ **(de qqn)** to hide (from sb).

Verbes à particules anglais

Les verbes à particules anglais figurent en sous-entrée sous la forme principale du verbe.

> **get** [get] (*Br pt & pp* got, *Am pt* got, *pp* gotten) *vt* [cause to do] : **to ~ sb to do sthg** faire faire qqch à qqn. ◆ **get along** *vi* - **1.** [manage] se débrouiller - **2.** [progress] avancer, faire des progrès - **3.** [have a good relationship] s'entendre. ◆ **get up** ◇ *vi* se lever. ◇ *vt fus* [petition, demonstration] organiser.

Formes irrégulières

Les formes irrégulières des noms, adjectifs et verbes sont données en entrée dans le dictionnaire.

> **belle** [bɛl] *adj & nf* ▷ **beau**.

En outre, une liste des verbes irré-guliers anglais avec leurs différentes formes figure en annexe.

> **went** [went] *pt* ⊳ **go**.

Comment trouver la bonne traduction anglaise

Une fois que l'on aura localisé en français le mot ou l'expres-sion recherchés, il apparaîtra peut-être qu'il existe plusieurs traductions possibles. Qu'à cela ne tienne, on trouvera dans le dictionnaire tous les éléments nécessaires pour identifier la bonne traduction.

Comment fonctionne une entrée de dictionnaire ? Examinons l'entrée sauter.

Les losanges blancs (◇) introduisent une catégorie grammaticale lors-qu'un même mot peut en avoir plu-sieurs - ici, *vi* (verbe intransitif) puis *vt* (verbe transitif). Voir la liste des abréviations p. VII-X.

> **sauter** [3] [sote] ◇ *vi* - **1.** [bondir] to jump, to leap ; ~ **à la corde** to skip ; ~ **de joie** *fig* to jump for joy ; ~ **au cou de qqn** *fig* to throw one's arms around sb - **2.** [explo-ser] to blow up ; [fusible] to blow - **3.** [être projeté - bouchon] to fly out ; [- serrure] to burst off ; [- bouton] to fly off - **4.** *fam* [em-ployé] to get the sack. ◇ *vt* - **1.** [fossé, obs-tacle] to jump ou leap over - **2.** *fig* [page, re-pas] to skip.

Chaque catégorie grammaticale est alors divisée en catégories de sens, introduites par des chiffres en gras (-1., -2.), lorsque le mot a plusieurs sens. Des indicateurs entre crochets ([bondir]) per-mettent d'identifier le sens recherché.

Imaginons que l'on veuille traduire *tu as sauté une page*.

La phrase à traduire comporte un verbe dont nous savons qu'il peut être soit intransitif, soit transitif ; ici, c'est le verbe transitif qui nous intéresse (◇ vt) puisqu'il y a un complément d'objet dans la phrase.

Examinons le sens du verbe : le contexte étant celui d'un livre, c'est dans la catégorie -2. que l'on trouvera la traduction souhaitée, qui est *to skip*.

Examinons à présent l'entrée *page*.

La catégorie grammaticale qui nous intéresse est la première ◇ nf : « page » en tant que substantif féminin. Ensuite, c'est sous la pre-mière division sémantique, suivie de

> **page** [paʒ] ◇ *nf* - **1.** [feuillet] page ; ~ **blanche** blank page ; **mettre en ~s** TYPO to make up (into pages) ; ~ **d'accueil** INFORM home page - **2.** *loc* : **être à la** ~ to be up-to-date. ◇ *nm* page (boy).

l'indicateur [feuillet], que l'on trouvera la bonne traduction : *page*.

Il ne reste plus qu'à combiner les mots trouvés pour traduire la phrase, en mettant bien sûr le verbe *to skip* au temps et à la forme voulus : *you have skipped a page*.

How to use the dictionary

Finding the word or phrase you are seeking

First you can ask yourself some basic questions:
- Is it a single word, a hyphenated word or an abbreviation?
- Is it a compound noun?
- Is it a phrase or an idiom?
- Is it a phrasal verb?
- Is it a reflexive verb?
- Is it an irregular form?

Single words, hyphenated words and abbreviations

As a general rule, you will find the word you are seeking in its alphabetical order in the dictionary. If you wish to translate a French word into English, look in the French-English section. If you seek the meaning of an English term, look in the English-French section.

Words in **bold type** that begin an article are known as "entries". Words that are written with an *initial capital letter* appear as separate entries and are placed after words spelled the same way but beginning with a small letter.

> **china** ['tʃaɪnə] *n* porcelaine *f*.
> **China** ['tʃaɪnə] *n* Chine *f*.

Words with a *hyphen*, a *full stop* or an *apostrophe* come after those spelled the same way but without any of these punctuation marks.

> **am** [æm] ⊳ be.
> **a.m.** (*abbr of* **ante meridiem**) : at 3 ~ à 3h (du matin).

French *accented words* come after entries spelled in the same way but unaccented.

> **ou** [u] *conj* [indique une alternative, une approximation] or.
> **où** [u] *pron rel* [spatial] where.

Some entries are followed by a *superscript number*. These are homographs: words that are spelled in the same way but that have distinct meanings or pronunciations. You must be careful to identify correctly the entry you need.

> **mine**[1] [maɪn] *poss pron* le mien (la mienne), les miens (les miennes) (*pl*) ; **that money is** ~ cet argent est à moi ...
> **mine**[2] [maɪn] ◇ *n* mine *f*. ◇ *vt* - **1.** [coal, gold] extraire ...

On the French-English side of the dictionary, you will find certain words preceded by a black diamond (◆) and called "subentries". The

> **animal, e, aux** [animal, o] *adj* - **1.** [propre à l'animal] animal (*avant n*) - **2.** [instinctif] instinctive. ◆ **animal** *nm* [bête] animal.

main entry has a masculine and a feminine form; the subentry has only one of these forms.

If you are looking for a noun which in the plural has its own distinct meaning, you will find it under the singular form as a subentry.

> **glass** [glɑ:s] ⬦ n - 1. [gen] verre m - 2. (U) [glassware] verrerie f. ⬦ comp [bottle, jar] en OR de verre ; [door, partition] vitré(e).
> ➽ **glasses** npl [spectacles] lunettes fpl.

Some plural nouns appear as headwords when they are never or rarely used in the singular, e.g. *sneakers* in English or *abats* in French.

Irregular plurals appear as entries with cross-references to the headword in the singular.

> **man** [mæn] (pl men [men]) n homme m.
> **men** [men] pl ⟼ man.

Compound nouns

A compound noun is a word or expression which has a single meaning but is made up of more than one word, e.g. *gardien de but*. When a French compound noun is made up of several words separated by spaces, you will find it in the dictionary under the first element of the compound (e.g. *gardien de but* under *gardien*).

Some English compound nouns such as kiss of life or virtual reality are presented as separate entries in their alphabetical order in the dictionary.

Phrases and idioms

On the French-English side of the dictionary, phrases and idioms are to be found under the first noun element of the phrase. If there is no noun, you should look under the adjective or else under the verb. On the English-French side, look for the most important word; e.g. in *to fancy doing sthg, to take a fancy to* or *fancy that!*, the most important word is *fancy*.

> **fancy** ['fænsɪ] ... ⬦ n [desire, liking] envie f, lubie f ; **to take a ~ to sb** se prendre d'affection pour qqn ; **to take a ~ to sthg** se mettre à aimer qqch ; ... ⬦ vt - 1. inf [want] avoir envie de ; **to ~ doing sthg** avoir envie de faire qqch - 2. inf [like] : **I ~ her** elle me plaît - 3. [imagine] : **~ that!** ça alors !

Some very fixed phrases such as bien entendu or at home appear under the most important element as subentries after the black diamond (➽).

English phrasal verbs

English phrasal verbs (e.g. *to put off, to fork out*) are entered under the main form as subentries.

> **fork** [fɔ:k] ⬦ n - 1. [for eating] fourchette f - 2. [for gardening] fourche f - 3. [in road] bifurcation f ; [of river] embranchement m. ⬦ vi bifurquer. ➽ **fork out** inf ⬦ vt fus allonger, débourser. ⬦ vi : **to ~ out (for)** casquer (pour).

French reflexive verbs

French reflexive verbs are entered under the main form after the symbol ➡.

> **rappeler** [24] [raple] *vt* - **1.** [gén] to call back ... ➡ **se rappeler** *vp* to remember.

Irregular English verbs

If you are unsure of the infinitive of a verb, refer to pages XII-XIII.

> **caught** [kɔːt] *pt* & *pp* ▷ **catch**.

Irregular forms also appear in the dictionary as entries that are cross-referenced to the main form.

Finding the right translation

Once you have found the word or phrase you are seeking, you will have to identify the right translation. Some entries may have only one translation, but others may be subdivided into different grammatical categories and these in turn may be subdivided into different sense categories. If a word has more than one part of speech, each grammatical category is separated and indicated by a white diamond (◇).

Let us say that you want to translate the sentence *he has skipped a page*.

You must first decide what part of speech *skip* is in this instance. It is a verb with a direct object and therefore you must look for the translation under the transitive verb category, marked "vt" (see pages VII-X for the list of abbreviations). To further reassure you that this is the right category, you will find the noun "page" along with other nouns that are used typically with the verb *skip* in square brackets before the translation. So the translation you need here is *sauter*.

> **skip** [skɪp] ◇ *n* - **1.** [jump] petit saut *m* - **2.** *Br* [container] benne *f*. ◇ *vt* [page, class, meal] sauter. ◇ *vi* - **1.** [gen] sauter, sautiller - **2.** *Br* [over rope] sauter à la corde.

Now look at the word *page*.

Again you must decide what part of speech the word is. Here it is a noun. You will notice that the noun cate-

> **page** [peɪdʒ] ◇ *n* - **1.** [of book] page *f* - **2.** [sheet of paper] feuille *f*. ◇ *vt* [in airport] appeler au micro.

gory is divided again into several senses. When a word has several meanings within one part of speech, these are separated into numbered categories. To choose the right numbered category, you must use the information provided in the brackets to pinpoint the exact meaning of the word in its context.

In this case, we may assume that it is a page in a book rather than a single sheet of paper so the correct translation is *page*. After the translation you will notice the letter "f" in italics, indicating that the French noun is feminine.

You can translate the sentence, once you have conjugated the verb (see conjugation tables on pages XII-XIII), as: *il a sauté une page*.

a¹, A [a] *nm inv* a, A ; **de A à Z** from beginning to end.

a²1. [conjugaison] ➤ **avoir - 2.** [unité de mesure] *(abr écrite de* **are**) a.

à [a] *(contraction de "à + le" =* **au**, *contraction de à + les =* **aux**) *prép* **1.** [introduisant un complément d'objet indirect] to ; **parler à qqn** to speak to sb ; **donner qqch à qqn** to give sthg to sb, to give sb sthg - **2.** [introduisant un complément de lieu - situation] at, in, on ; [- direction] to ; **être à la maison/au bureau** to be at home/at the office ; **il habite à Paris/à la campagne** he lives in Paris/in the country ; **aller à Paris/à la campagne/au Pérou** to go to Paris/to the country/to Peru ; **un voyage à Londres/aux Seychelles** a journey to London/to the Seychelles - **3.** [introduisant un complément de temps] : **à onze heures** at eleven o'clock ; **au mois de février** in the month of February ; **à lundi!** see you (on) Monday! ; **à plus tard!** see you later! ; **de huit à dix heures** from eight to ten o'clock ; **se situer à une heure/à 10 kilomètres de l'aéroport** to be situated an hour/10 kilometres (away) from the airport - **4.** [introduisant un complément de manière, de moyen] : **à haute voix** out loud, aloud ; **rire aux éclats** to roar with laughter ; **agir à son gré** to do as one pleases ; **acheter à crédit** to buy on credit ; **à pied/cheval** on foot/horseback - **5.** [indiquant une caractéristique] with ; **une fille aux cheveux longs** a girl with long hair ; **l'homme à l'imperméable** the man with the raincoat - **6.** [introduisant un chiffre] : **ils sont venus à dix** ten of them came ; **un livre à 10 euros** a 10-euro book, a book costing 10 euros ; **la vitesse est limitée à 50 km à l'heure** the speed limit is 50 km per ou an hour ; **un groupe de 10 à 12 personnes** a group of 10 to 12 people, a group of between 10 and 12 people ; **deux à deux** two by two - **7.** [marque l'appartenance] : **c'est à moi/toi/lui/elle** it's mine/yours/his/hers ; **ce vélo est à ma sœur** this bike is my sister's ou belongs to my sister ; **une amie à moi** a friend of mine - **8.** [introduit le but] : **coupe à champagne** champagne goblet ; **le courrier à poster** the mail to be posted ; **appartement à vendre/louer** flat for sale/to let.

AB¹ *(abr écrite de* **assez bien**) fair grade (as assessment of schoolwork), ≃ B-.

AB² *(abr écrite de* **agriculture biologique**) *food label guaranteeing that a product is made from at least 95% organic ingredients (100% in the case of a single ingredient).*

abaisser [4] [abese] *vt* **1.** [rideau, voile] to lower ; [levier, manette] to push ou pull down - **2.** [diminuer] to reduce, to lower. ➤ **s'abaisser** *vp* **1.** [descendre - rideau] to fall, to come down ; [- terrain] to fall away - **2.** [s'humilier] to demean o.s. ; **s'abaisser à faire qqch** to lower o.s. to do sthg.

abandon [abɑ̃dɔ̃] *nm* **1.** [désertion, délaissement] desertion ; **à l'abandon** [jardin, maison] neglected, in a state of neglect - **2.** [renonciation] abandoning, giving up - **3.** [nonchalance, confiance] abandon.

abandonner [3] [abɑ̃dɔne] *vt* **1.** [quitter - femme, enfants] to abandon, to desert ; [- voiture, propriété] to abandon - **2.** [renoncer à] to give up, to abandon - **3.** [se retirer de - course, concours] to withdraw from - **4.** [céder] : **abandonner qqch à qqn** to leave sthg to sb, to leave sb sthg.

abasourdi, e [abazurdi] *adj* stunned.

abat-jour [abaʒur] *nm inv* lampshade.

abats [aba] *nmpl* [d'animal] offal *(U)* ; [de volaille] giblets.

abattement [abatmɑ̃] *nm* **1.** [faiblesse physique] weakness - **2.** [désespoir] dejection - **3.** [déduction] reduction ; **abattement fiscal** tax allowance *US*, exemption *US*.

abattis [abati] *nmpl* giblets.

abattoir [abatwar] *nm* abattoir, slaughterhouse.

abattre [83] [abatr] *vt* **1.** [faire tomber - mur] to knock down ; [- arbre] to cut down, to fell ; [- avion] to bring down - **2.** [tuer -

gén] to kill ; [- dans un abattoir] to slaughter - **3.** [épuiser] to wear out ; [démoraliser] to demoralize.

abbaye [abei] *nf* abbey.

abbé [abe] *nm* **1.** [prêtre] priest - **2.** [de couvent] abbot.

abc [abese] *nm* basics *pl.*

abcès [apsɛ] *nm* abscess.

abdiquer [3] [abdike] <> *vt* [renoncer à] to renounce. <> *vi* [roi] to abdicate.

abdomen [abdɔmɛn] *nm* abdomen.

abdos [abdo] *nmpl* **1.** [muscles] abs, stomach muscles - **2.** [exercices] stomach exercises, abs (exercises) ; **faire des abdos** to do stomach exercises ou abs.

abeille [abɛj] *nf* bee.

aberrant, e [abɛrɑ̃, ɑ̃t] *adj* absurd.

abîme [abim] *nm* abyss, gulf.

abîmer [3] [abime] *vt* [détériorer - objet] to damage ; [- partie du corps, vue] to ruin. **s'abîmer** *vp* [gén] to be damaged ; [fruits] to go bad.

abject, e [abʒɛkt] *adj* despicable, contemptible.

aboiement [abwamɑ̃] *nm* bark, barking (U).

abolir [32] [abɔlir] *vt* to abolish.

abominable [abɔminabl] *adj* appalling, awful.

abondance [abɔ̃dɑ̃s] *nf* **1.** [profusion] abundance - **2.** [opulence] affluence.

abondant, e [abɔ̃dɑ̃, ɑ̃t] *adj* [gén] plentiful ; [végétation, chevelure] luxuriant ; [pluie] heavy.

abonder [3] [abɔ̃de] *vi* to abound, to be abundant ; **abonder en qqch** to be rich in sthg ; **abonder dans le sens de qqn** to be entirely of sb's opinion.

abonné, e [abɔne] *nm, f* **1.** [à un journal, à une chaîne de télé] subscriber ; [à un théâtre] season-ticket holder - **2.** [à un service public] consumer.

abonnement [abɔnmɑ̃] *nm* **1.** [à un journal, à une chaîne de télé] subscription ; [à un théâtre] season ticket - **2.** [au téléphone] rental ; [au gaz, à l'électricité] standing charge.

abonner [3] [abɔne] **s'abonner** *vp* : **s'abonner à qqch** [journal, chaîne de télé] to take out a subscription to sthg ; [service public] to get connected to sthg ; [théâtre] to buy a season ticket for sthg.

abord [abɔr] *nm* : **être d'un abord facile/difficile** to be very/not very approachable. **abords** *nmpl* [gén] surrounding area *sg* ; [de ville] outskirts. **d'abord** *loc adv* **1.** [en premier lieu] first - **2.** [avant tout] : **(tout) d'abord** first (of all), in the first place.

abordable [abɔrdabl] *adj* [lieu] accessible ; [personne] approachable ; [de prix modéré] affordable.

aborder [3] [abɔrde] <> *vi* to land. <> *vt* **1.** [personne, lieu] to approach - **2.** [question] to tackle.

aborigène [abɔriʒɛn] *adj* aboriginal. **Aborigène** *nmf* (Australian) aborigine.

abouti, e [abuti] *adj* [projet, démarche] successful.

aboutir [32] [abutir] *vi* **1.** [chemin] : **aboutir à/dans** to end at/in - **2.** [négociation] to be successful ; **aboutir à qqch** to result in sthg.

aboyer [13] [abwaje] *vi* to bark.

abrasif, ive [abrazif, iv] *adj* abrasive.

abrégé, e [abreʒe] *adj* abridged.

abréger [22] [abreʒe] *vt* [visite, réunion] to cut short ; [discours] to shorten ; [mot] to abbreviate.

abreuvoir [abrœvwar] *nm* [lieu] watering place ; [installation] drinking trough.

abréviation [abrevjasjɔ̃] *nf* abbreviation.

abri [abri] *nm* shelter ; **à l'abri de** sheltered from ; *fig* safe from ; **se mettre à l'abri** to shelter, to take shelter ; **abri de jardin** garden shed.

Abribus® [abribys] *nm* bus shelter.

abricot [abriko] *nm & adj inv* apricot.

abricotier [abrikɔtje] *nm* apricot tree.

abriter [3] [abrite] *vt* **1.** [protéger] : **abriter qqn/qqch (de)** to shelter sb/sthg (from) - **2.** [héberger] to accommodate. **s'abriter** *vp + prép* : **s'abriter (de)** to shelter (from).

abroger [17] [abrɔʒe] *vt* to repeal.

abrupt, e [abrypt] *adj* **1.** [raide] steep - **2.** [rude] abrupt, brusque.

abruti, e [abryti] *fam nm, f* moron.

abrutir [32] [abrytir] *vt* **1.** [abêtir] : **abrutir qqn** to deaden sb's mind - **2.** [accabler] : **abrutir qqn de travail** to work sb silly.

abrutissant, e [abrytisɑ̃, ɑ̃t] *adj* **1.** [bruit, travail] stupefying - **2.** [jeu, feuilleton] moronic.

absence [apsɑ̃s] *nf* **1.** [de personne] absence - **2.** [carence] lack.

absent, e [apsɑ̃, ɑ̃t] <> *adj* **1.** [personne] : **absent (de)** [gén] away (from) ; [pour maladie] absent (from) - **2.** [regard, air] vacant, absent - **3.** [manquant] lacking. <> *nm, f* absentee.

absenter [3] [apsɑ̃te] **s'absenter** *vp* : **s'absenter (de la pièce)** to leave (the room).

absinthe [apsɛ̃t] *nf* [plante] wormwood ; [boisson] absinth.

absolu, e [apsɔly] *adj* [gén] absolute ; [décision, jugement] uncompromising.

absolument [apsɔlymɑ̃] *adv* absolutely.

absorbant, e [apsɔrbɑ̃, ɑ̃t] *adj* **1.** [matière] absorbent - **2.** [occupation] absorbing.

absorber [3] [apsɔrbe] *vt* **1.** [gén] to absorb - **2.** [manger] to take.

abstenir [40] [apstənir] ➤ **s'abstenir** *vp* **1.** [ne rien faire] : **s'abstenir (de qqch/de faire qqch)** to refrain (from sthg/from doing sthg) - **2.** [ne pas voter] to abstain.

abstention [apstɑ̃sjɔ̃] *nf* abstention.

abstentionnisme [apstɑ̃sjɔnism] *nm* abstaining.

abstinence [apstinɑ̃s] *nf* abstinence.

abstraction [apstraksjɔ̃] *nf* abstraction ; **faire abstraction de** to disregard.

abstrait, e [apstre, et] *adj* abstract.

absurde [apsyrd] *adj* absurd.

absurdité [apsyrdite] *nf* absurdity ; **dire des absurdités** to talk nonsense (U).

abus [aby] *nm* abuse ; **abus de confiance** breach of trust ; **abus de pouvoir** abuse of power.

abuser [3] [abyze] *vi* **1.** [dépasser les bornes] to go too far - **2.** [user] : **abuser de** [autorité, pouvoir] to overstep the bounds of ; [femme] to take advantage of ; [temps] to take up too much of ; **abuser de ses forces** to overexert o.s.

abusif, ive [abyzif, iv] *adj* **1.** [excessif] excessive - **2.** [fautif] improper.

acabit [akabi] *nm* : **du même acabit** *péj* of the same type.

acacia [akasja] *nm* acacia.

académicien, enne [akademisjɛ̃, ɛn] *nm, f* academician ; [de l'Académie française] member of the French Academy.

académie [akademi] *nf* **1.** SCOL & UNIV ≃ regional education authority *UK*, ≃ school district *US* - **2.** [institut] academy ; **l'Académie française** the French Academy *(learned society of leading men and women of letters)*.

acajou [akaʒu] *nm & adj inv* mahogany.

acariâtre [akarjatr] *adj* bad-tempered, cantankerous.

acarien [akarjɛ̃] *nm* [gén] acarid ; [de poussière] dust mite.

accablant, e [akablɑ̃, ɑ̃t] *adj* **1.** [soleil, chaleur] oppressive - **2.** [preuve, témoignage] overwhelming.

accabler [3] [akable] *vt* **1.** [surcharger] : **accabler qqn de** [travail] to overwhelm sb with ; **accabler qqn d'injures** to shower sb with abuse - **2.** [accuser] to condemn.

accalmie [akalmi] *nf litt & fig* lull.

accéder [18] [aksede] ➤ **accéder à** *vt* **1.** [pénétrer dans] to reach, to get to - **2.** [parvenir à] to attain - **3.** [consentir à] to comply with.

accélérateur [akseleratœr] *nm* accelerator.

accélération [akselerasjɔ̃] *nf* [de voiture, machine] acceleration ; [de projet] speeding up.

accélérer [18] [akselere] ◇ *vt* to accelerate, to speed up. ◇ *vi* AUTO to accelerate.

accent [aksɑ̃] *nm* **1.** [signe graphique] accent ; **accent aigu/grave/circonflexe** acute/grave/circumflex (accent) - **2.** [intonation] tone ; **mettre l'accent sur** *litt* to stress.

accentuation [aksɑ̃tɥasjɔ̃] *nf* [d'une lettre] accenting ; [en parlant] stress.

accentuer [7] [aksɑ̃tɥe] *vt* **1.** [insister sur, souligner] to emphasize, to accentuate - **2.** [intensifier] to intensify - **3.** [à l'écrit] to put the accents on ; [en parlant] to stress. ➤ **s'accentuer** *vp* to become more pronounced.

acceptable [akseptabl] *adj* satisfactory, acceptable.

acceptation [akseptasjɔ̃] *nf* acceptance.

accepter [4] [aksepte] *vt* to accept ; **accepter de faire qqch** to agree to do sthg ; **accepter que** (+ *subjonctif*) : **accepter que qqn fasse qqch** to agree to sb doing sthg ; **je n'accepte pas qu'il me parle ainsi** I won't have him talking to me like that.

acception [aksepsjɔ̃] *nf* sense.

accès [akse] *nm* **1.** [entrée] entry ; **avoir/donner accès à** to have/to give access to ; **'accès interdit'** 'no entry' - **2.** [voie d'entrée] entrance - **3.** [crise] bout ; **accès de colère** fit of anger.

accessible [aksesibl] *adj* [lieu, livre] accessible ; [personne] approachable ; [prix, équipement] affordable.

accession [aksesjɔ̃] *nf* : **accession à** [trône, présidence] accession to ; [indépendance] attainment of.

accessoire [akseswar] ◇ *nm* **1.** [gén] accessory - **2.** [de théâtre, cinéma] prop. ◇ *adj* secondary.

accident [aksidɑ̃] *nm* accident ; **par accident** by chance, by accident ; **accident de la route/de voiture/du travail** road/car/industrial accident.

accidenté, e [aksidɑ̃te] ◇ *adj* **1.** [terrain, surface] uneven - **2.** [voiture] damaged. ◇ *nm, f* (gén pl) **accidenté de la route** accident victim.

accidentel, elle [aksidɑ̃tɛl] *adj* accidental.

acclamation [aklamasjɔ̃] *nf* (gén pl) cheers *pl*, cheering (U).

acclamer [3] [aklame] *vt* to cheer.

acclimatation [aklimatasjɔ̃] *nf* acclimatization.

acclimater [3] [aklimate] *vt* to acclimatize ; *fig* to introduce. ➤ **s'acclimater** *vp* : **s'acclimater à** to become acclimatized to.

accolade [akɔlad] *nf* **1.** TYPO brace - **2.** [embrassade] embrace.

accommodant, e [akɔmɔdã, ãt] *adj* obliging.

accommodement [akɔmɔdmã] *nm* compromise.

accommoder [3] [akɔmɔde] *vt* CULIN to prepare.

accompagnateur, trice [akɔ̃paɲatœr, tris] *nm, f* **1.** MUS accompanist - **2.** [guide] guide.

accompagnement [akɔ̃paɲmã] *nm* MUS accompaniment.

accompagner [3] [akɔ̃paɲe] *vt* **1.** [personne] to go with, to accompany - **2.** [agrémenter] : **accompagner qqch de** to accompany sthg with - **3.** MUS to accompany.

accompli, e [akɔ̃pli] *adj* accomplished.

accomplir [32] [akɔ̃plir] *vt* to carry out. **s'accomplir** *vp* to come about.

accomplissement [akɔ̃plismã] *nm* [d'apprentissage] completion ; [de travail] fulfilment.

accord [akɔr] *nm* **1.** [gén] agreement - **2.** LING agreement, concord - **3.** MUS chord - **4.** [acceptation] approval ; **donner son accord à qqch** to approve sthg. **d'accord** *loc adv* OK, all right. *loc adj* : **être d'accord (avec)** to agree (with) ; **tomber** OU **se mettre d'accord** to come to an agreement, to agree.

accordéon [akɔrdeɔ̃] *nm* accordion.

accorder [3] [akɔrde] *vt* **1.** [donner] : **accorder qqch à qqn** to grant sb sthg - **2.** [attribuer] : **accorder qqch à qqch** to accord sthg to sthg ; **accorder de l'importance à** to attach importance to - **3.** [harmoniser] to match - **4.** GRAMM : **accorder qqch avec qqch** to make sthg agree with sthg - **5.** MUS to tune. **s'accorder** *vp* **1.** [gén] : **s'accorder (pour faire qqch)** to agree (to do sthg) ; **s'accorder à faire qqch** to be unanimous in doing sthg - **2.** [être assorti] to match - **3.** GRAMM to agree.

accoster [3] [akɔste] *vt* **1.** NAUT to come alongside - **2.** [personne] to accost. *vi* NAUT to dock.

accotement [akɔtmã] *nm* [de route] shoulder ; **accotement non stabilisé** soft verge UK, soft shoulder US.

accouchement [akuʃmã] *nm* childbirth ; **accouchement sans douleur** natural childbirth ; **accouchement sous X** *a woman's right to anonymity in childbirth*.

accoucher [3] [akuʃe] *vi* : **accoucher (de)** to give birth (to).

accouder [3] [akude] **s'accouder** *vp* to lean on one's elbows ; **s'accouder à** to lean one's elbows on.

accoudoir [akudwar] *nm* armrest.

accouplement [akupləmã] *nm* mating, coupling.

accourir [45] [akurir] *vi* to run up, to rush up.

accouru, e [akury] *pp* accourir.

accoutré, e [akutre] *adj péj* : **être bizarrement accoutré** to be oddly got up.

accoutrement [akutrəmã] *nm péj* getup.

accoutumer [3] [akutyme] *vt* : **accoutumer qqn à qqn/qqch** to get sb used to sb/sthg ; **accoutumer qqn à faire qqch** to get sb used to doing sthg. **s'accoutumer** *vp* : **s'accoutumer à qqn/qqch** to get used to sb/sthg ; **s'accoutumer à faire qqch** to get used to doing sthg.

accréditer [3] [akredite] *vt* [rumeur] to substantiate ; **accréditer qqn auprès de** to accredit sb to.

accro [akro] *fam* *adj* : **accro à** hooked on. *nmf* : **c'est une accro de la planche** she's a windsurfing freak.

accroc [akro] *nm* **1.** [déchirure] tear - **2.** [incident] hitch.

accrochage [akrɔʃaʒ] *nm* **1.** [accident] collision - **2.** *fam* [dispute] row.

accroche [akrɔʃ] *nf* COMM catch line.

accrocher [3] [akrɔʃe] *vt* **1.** [suspendre] : **accrocher qqch (à)** to hang sthg up (on) - **2.** [déchirer] : **accrocher qqch (à)** to catch sthg (on) - **3.** [attacher] : **accrocher qqch (à)** to hitch sthg (to). **s'accrocher** *vp* **1.** [s'agripper] : **s'accrocher (à)** to hang on (to) ; **s'accrocher à qqn** *fig* to cling to sb - **2.** *fam* [se disputer] to row, to have a row - **3.** *fam* [persévérer] to stick at it.

accroissement [akrwasmã] *nm* increase, growth.

accroître [94] [akrwatr] *vt* to increase. **s'accroître** *vp* to increase, to grow.

accroupir [32] [akrupir] **s'accroupir** *vp* to squat.

accru, e [akry] *pp* accroître.

accueil [akœj] *nm* **1.** [lieu] reception - **2.** [action] welcome, reception.

accueillant, e [akœjã, ãt] *adj* welcoming, friendly.

accueillir [41] [akœjir] *vt* **1.** [gén] to welcome - **2.** [loger] to accommodate.

accumulateur [akymylatœr] *nm* accumulator, battery.

accumulation [akymylasjɔ̃] *nf* accumulation.

accumuler [3] [akymyle] *vt* to accumulate ; *fig* to store up. **s'accumuler** *vp* to pile up.

accusateur, trice [akyzatœr, tris] *adj* accusing. *nm, f* accuser.

accusation [akyzasjɔ̃] *nf* **1.** [reproche] accusation - **2.** DR charge ; **mettre en accusation** to indict ; **l'accusation** the prosecution.

accusé, e [akyze] *nm, f* accused, defendant. ➤ **accusé de réception** *nm* acknowledgement (of receipt).

accuser [3] [akyze] *vt* **1.** [porter une accusation contre] : **accuser qqn (de qqch)** to accuse sb (of sthg) - **2.** DR : **accuser qqn de qqch** to charge sb with sthg.

acerbe [asɛrb] *adj* acerbic.

acéré, e [asere] *adj* sharp.

achalandé, e [aʃalɑ̃de] *adj* [en marchandises] : **bien achalandé** well-stocked.

acharné, e [aʃarne] *adj* [combat] fierce ; [travail] unremitting.

acharnement [aʃarnəmɑ̃] *nm* relentlessness.

acharner [3] [aʃarne] ➤ **s'acharner** *vp* **1.** [combattre] : **s'acharner contre** OU **après** OU **sur qqn** [ennemi, victime] to hound sb ; [suj: malheur] to dog sb - **2.** [s'obstiner] : **s'acharner (à faire qqch)** to persist (in doing sthg).

achat [aʃa] *nm* purchase.

acheminer [3] [aʃmine] *vt* to dispatch. ➤ **s'acheminer** *vp* : **s'acheminer vers** [lieu, désastre] to head for ; [solution, paix] to move towards OU toward *US*.

acheter [28] [aʃte] *vt litt & fig* [cadeau, objet, produit] to buy ; **acheter qqch à** OU **pour qqn** to buy sthg for sb, to buy sb sthg.

acheteur, euse [aʃtœr, øz] *nm, f* buyer, purchaser.

achevé, e [aʃve] *adj sout* : **d'un ridicule achevé** utterly ridiculous.

achèvement [aʃɛvmɑ̃] *nm* completion.

achever [19] [aʃve] *vt* **1.** [terminer] to complete, to finish (off) - **2.** [tuer, accabler] to finish off. ➤ **s'achever** *vp* to end, to come to an end.

achoppement [aʃɔpmɑ̃] ➤ **pierre.**

acide [asid] ◇ *adj* **1.** [saveur] sour - **2.** [propos] sharp, acid - **3.** CHIM acid. ◇ *nm* CHIM acid.

acidité [asidite] *nf* **1.** CHIM acidity - **2.** [saveur] sourness - **3.** [de propos] sharpness.

acidulé, e [asidyle] *adj* slightly acid.

acier [asje] *nm* steel ; **acier inoxydable** stainless steel.

aciérie [asjeri] *nf* steelworks *sg*.

acné [akne] *nf* acne.

acolyte [akɔlit] *nm péj* henchman.

acompte [akɔ̃t] *nm* deposit.

à-côté [akote] (*pl* **à-côtés**) *nm* **1.** [point accessoire] side issue - **2.** [gain d'appoint] extra.

à-coup [aku] (*pl* **à-coups**) *nm* jerk ; **par à-coups** in fits and starts.

acoustique [akustik] *nf* **1.** [science] acoustics (*U*) - **2.** [d'une salle] acoustics *pl*.

acquéreur [akerœr] *nm* buyer.

acquérir [39] [akerir] *vt* [gén] to acquire.

acquiescement [akjɛsmɑ̃] *nm* approval.

acquiescer [21] [akjese] *vi* to acquiesce ; **acquiescer à** to agree to.

acquis, e [aki, iz] ◇ *pp* ➤ **acquérir.** ◇ *adj* **1.** [caractère] acquired - **2.** [droit, avantage] established. ➤ **acquis** *nmpl* [connaissances] knowledge (*U*).

acquisition [akizisjɔ̃] *nf* acquisition.

acquit [aki] *nm* receipt ; **pour acquit** COMM received ; **faire qqch par acquit de conscience** *fig* to do sthg to set one's mind at rest.

acquittement [akitmɑ̃] *nm* **1.** [d'obligation] settlement - **2.** DR acquittal.

acquitter [3] [akite] *vt* **1.** DR to acquit - **2.** [régler] to pay - **3.** [libérer] : **acquitter qqn de** to release sb from.

âcre [akr] *adj* **1.** [saveur] bitter - **2.** [fumée] acrid.

acrobate [akrɔbat] *nmf* acrobat.

acrobatie [akrɔbasi] *nf* acrobatics (*U*).

acrylique [akrilik] *adj & nm* acrylic.

acte [akt] *nm* **1.** [action] act, action ; **faire acte d'autorité** to exercise one's authority ; **faire acte de candidature** to submit an application - **2.** THÉÂTRE act - **3.** DR deed ; **acte d'accusation** charge ; **acte de naissance/de mariage/de décès** birth/marriage/death certificate ; **acte de vente** bill of sale - **4.** RELIG certificate ; **faire acte de présence** to put in an appearance ; **prendre acte de** to note, to take note of. ➤ **actes** *nmpl* [de colloque] proceedings.

acteur, trice [aktœr, tris] *nm, f* actor (*f* actress).

actif, ive [aktif, iv] *adj* [gén] active ; **la population active** the working population. ➤ **actif** *nm* FIN assets *pl* ; **avoir qqch à son actif** to have sthg to one's credit.

action [aksjɔ̃] *nf* **1.** [gén] action ; **sous l'action de** under the effect of - **2.** [acte] action, act ; **bonne/mauvaise action** good/bad deed - **3.** DR action, lawsuit - **4.** FIN share.

actionnaire [aksjɔnɛr] *nmf* FIN shareholder, stockholder *US*.

actionner [3] [aksjɔne] *vt* to work, to activate.

activement [aktivmɑ̃] *adv* actively.

activer [3] [aktive] *vt* to speed up. ➤ **s'activer** *vp* to bustle about.

activiste [aktivist] *adj & nmf* activist.

activité [aktivite] *nf* [gén] activity ; **en activité** [volcan] active.

actualisation [aktualizasjɔ̃] *nf* [d'un texte] updating.

actualiser [3] [aktualize] *vt* to bring up to date.

actualité [aktualite] *nf* **1.** [d'un sujet] topicality - **2.** [événements] : **l'actualité sportive/politique/littéraire** the current sports/political/literary scene. ➤ **actualités** *nfpl* : **les actualités** the news *sg*.

actuel, elle [aktuɛl] *adj* [contemporain, présent] current, present ; **à l'heure actuelle** at the present time.

actuellement [aktuɛlmɑ̃] *adv* at present, currently.

acuité [akyite] *nf* acuteness.

acupuncture, acuponcture [akypɔ̃ktyr] *nf* acupuncture.

adage [adaʒ] *nm* adage, saying.

adaptateur, trice [adaptatœr, tris] *nm, f* adapter. ➤ **adaptateur** *nm* ÉLECTR adapter.

adaptation [adaptasjɔ̃] *nf* adaptation.

adapter [3] [adapte] *vt* **1.** [gén] to adapt - **2.** [fixer] to fit. ➤ **s'adapter** *vp* : **s'adapter (à)** to adapt (to).

additif [aditif] *nm* **1.** [supplément] rider, additional clause - **2.** [substance] additive.

addition [adisjɔ̃] *nf* **1.** [ajout, calcul] addition - **2.** [note] bill, check *US*.

additionner [3] [adisjɔne] *vt* **1.** [mélanger] : **additionner une poudre d'eau** to add water to a powder - **2.** [chiffres] to add up.

adepte [adɛpt] *nmf* follower.

adéquat, e [adekwa, at] *adj* suitable, appropriate.

adhérence [aderɑ̃s] *nf* [de pneu] grip.

adhérent, e [aderɑ̃, ɑ̃t] *nm, f* : **adhérent (de)** member (of).

adhérer [18] [adere] *vi* **1.** [coller] to stick, to adhere ; **adhérer à** [se fixer sur] to stick ou adhere to ; *fig* [être d'accord avec] to support, to adhere to - **2.** [être membre] : **adhérer à** to become a member of, to join.

adhésif, ive [adezif, iv] *adj* sticky, adhesive. ➤ **adhésif** *nm* adhesive.

adhésion [adezjɔ̃] *nf* **1.** [à une idée] : **adhésion (à)** support (for) - **2.** [à un parti] : **adhésion (à)** membership (of).

adieu [adjø] ⬦ *interj* goodbye!, farewell! ; **dire adieu à qqch** *fig* to say goodbye to sthg. ⬦ *nm* (*gén pl*) farewell ; **faire ses adieux à qqn** to say one's farewells to sb.

adipeux, euse [adipø, øz] *adj* [tissu] adipose ; [personne] fat.

adjectif [adʒɛktif] *nm* GRAMM adjective.

adjoint, e [adʒwɛ̃, ɛ̃t] ⬦ *adj* deputy (*avant n*), assistant (*avant n*). ⬦ *nm, f* deputy, assistant ; **adjoint au maire** deputy mayor.

adjonction [adʒɔ̃ksjɔ̃] *nf* addition.

adjudant [adʒydɑ̃] *nm* [dans la marine] warrant officer.

adjuger [17] [adʒyʒe] *vt* : **adjuger qqch (à qqn)** [aux enchères] to auction sthg (to sb) ; [décerner] to award sthg (to sb) ; **adjugé! sold!**

admettre [84] [admɛtr] *vt* **1.** [tolérer, accepter] to allow, to accept - **2.** [autoriser] to allow - **3.** [accueillir, reconnaître] to admit.

administrateur, trice [administratœr, tris] *nm, f* **1.** [gérant] administrator ; **administrateur judiciaire** receiver - **2.** [de conseil d'administration] director - **3.** INFORM : **administrateur de site (Web)** webmaster.

administratif, ive [administratif, iv] *adj* administrative.

administration [administrasjɔ̃] *nf* **1.** [service public] : **l'Administration** ≃ the Civil Service - **2.** [gestion] administration.

administrer [3] [administre] *vt* **1.** [gérer] to manage, to administer - **2.** [médicament, sacrement] to administer.

admirable [admirabl] *adj* **1.** [personne, comportement] admirable - **2.** [paysage, spectacle] wonderful.

admiratif, ive [admiratif, iv] *adj* admiring.

admiration [admirasjɔ̃] *nf* admiration.

admirer [3] [admire] *vt* to admire.

admis, e [admi, iz] *pp* ➤ **admettre**.

admissible [admisibl] *adj* **1.** [attitude] acceptable - **2.** SCOL eligible.

admission [admisjɔ̃] *nf* admission.

ADN (*abr de* acide désoxyribonucléique) *nm* DNA.

ado [ado] (*abr de* adolescent) *nmf fam* teen.

adolescence [adɔlesɑ̃s] *nf* adolescence.

adolescent, e [adɔlesɑ̃, ɑ̃t] *nm, f* adolescent, teenager.

adonner [3] [adɔne] ➤ **s'adonner** *vp* : **s'adonner à** [sport, activité] to devote o.s. to ; [vice] to take to.

adopter [3] [adɔpte] *vt* **1.** [gén] to adopt - **2.** [loi] to pass.

adoptif, ive [adɔptif, iv] *adj* [famille] adoptive ; [pays, enfant] adopted.

adoption [adɔpsjɔ̃] *nf* adoption ; **d'adoption** [pays, ville] adopted ; [famille] adoptive.

adorable [adɔrabl] *adj* adorable, delightful.

adoration [adɔrasjɔ̃] *nf* **1.** [amour] adoration - **2.** RELIG worship.

adorer [3] [adɔre] *vt* **1.** [personne, chose] to adore - **2.** RELIG to worship.

adosser [3] [adose] vt : **adosser qqch à qqch** to place sthg against sthg. ➤ **s'adosser** vp : **s'adosser à** ou **contre qqch** to lean against sthg.

adoucir [32] [adusir] vt **1.** [gén] to soften - **2.** [chagrin, peine] to ease, to soothe. ➤ **s'adoucir** vp **1.** [temps] to become ou get milder - **2.** [personne] to mellow.

adoucissant, e [adusisɑ̃, ɑ̃t] adj soothing. ➤ **adoucissant** nm softener.

adoucisseur [adusisœr] nm : **adoucisseur d'eau** water softener.

adresse [adrɛs] nf **1.** [gén & INFORM] address ; **adresse électronique** e-mail address - **2.** [habileté] skill.

adresser [4] [adrese] vt **1.** [faire parvenir] : **adresser qqch à qqn** to address sthg to sb - **2.** [envoyer] : **adresser qqn à qqn** to refer sb to sb. ➤ **s'adresser** vp : **s'adresser à** [parler à] to speak to ; [être destiné à] to be aimed at, to be intended for.

Adriatique [adriatik] nf : **l'Adriatique** the Adriatic.

adroit, e [adrwa, at] adj skilful UK, skillful US.

ADSL (abr de **asymmetric digital subscriber line**) nm ADSL ; **passer à l'ADSL** to switch ou upgrade ou go over to ADSL.

aduler [3] [adyle] vt to adulate.

adulte [adylt] nmf & adj adult.

adultère [adylter] ◇ nm [acte] adultery. ◇ adj adulterous.

advenir [40] [advənir] v impers to happen ; **qu'advient-il de...?** what is happening to...? ; **qu'est-il advenu de...?** what has happened to ou become of...?

advenu [advəny] pp ➤ **advenir**.

adverbe [advɛrb] nm adverb.

adversaire [adverser] nmf adversary, opponent.

adverse [advers] adj [opposé] opposing ➤ **parti**.

adversité [adversite] nf adversity.

aération [aerasjɔ̃] nf [circulation d'air] ventilation ; [action] airing.

aéré, e [aere] adj **1.** [pièce] well-ventilated ; **mal aéré** stuffy - **2.** fig [présentation] well-spaced.

aérer [18] [aere] vt **1.** [pièce, chose] to air - **2.** fig [présentation, mise en page] to lighten.

aérien, enne [aerjɛ̃, ɛn] adj **1.** [câble] overhead (avant n) - **2.** [transports, attaque] air (avant n) ; **compagnie aérienne** airline (company).

aérobic [aerɔbik] nm aerobics (U).

aérodrome [aerɔdrom] nm airfield.

aérodynamique [aerɔdinamik] adj streamlined, aerodynamic.

aérogare [aerɔgar] nf **1.** [aéroport] airport - **2.** [gare] air terminal.

aéroglisseur [aerɔglisœr] nm hovercraft.

aérogramme [aerɔgram] nm aérogramme, aerogram US, air letter.

aéronautique [aerɔnotik] nf aeronautics (U).

aéronaval, e, als [aerɔnaval] adj air and sea (avant n).

aérophagie [aerɔfaʒi] nf abdominal wind.

aéroport [aerɔpɔr] nm airport.

aéroporté, e [aerɔpɔrte] adj airborne.

aérosol [aerɔsɔl] nm & adj inv aerosol.

aérospatial, e, aux [aerɔspasjal, o] adj aerospace (avant n). ➤ **aérospatiale** nf aerospace industry.

affable [afabl] adj **1.** [personne] affable, agreeable - **2.** [parole] kind.

affaiblir [32] [afeblir] vt litt & fig to weaken. ➤ **s'affaiblir** vp litt & fig to weaken, to become weaker.

affaire [afer] nf **1.** [question] matter - **2.** [situation, polémique] affair - **3.** [marché] deal ; **faire une affaire** to get a bargain ou a good deal - **4.** [entreprise] business - **5.** [procès] case ; **avoir affaire à qqn** to deal with sb ; **vous aurez affaire à moi!** you'll have me to deal with! ; **faire l'affaire** to do nicely. ➤ **affaires** nfpl **1.** COMM business (U) - **2.** [objets personnels] things, belongings - **3.** [activités] affairs.

affairé, e [afere] adj busy.

affairer [4] [afere] ➤ **s'affairer** vp to bustle about.

affairisme [aferism] nm racketeering.

affaisser [4] [afese] ➤ **s'affaisser** vp **1.** [se creuser] to subside, to sink - **2.** [tomber] to collapse.

affaler [3] [afale] ➤ **s'affaler** vp to collapse.

affamé, e [afame] adj starving.

affecter [4] [afɛkte] vt **1.** [consacrer] : **affecter qqch à** to allocate sthg to - **2.** [nommer] : **affecter qqn à** to appoint sb to - **3.** [feindre] to feign - **4.** [émouvoir] to affect, to move.

affectif, ive [afɛktif, iv] adj emotional.

affection [afɛksjɔ̃] nf **1.** [sentiment] affection ; **avoir de l'affection pour** to be fond of - **2.** [maladie] complaint.

affectionner [3] [afɛksjone] vt to be fond of.

affectueusement [afɛktyøzmɑ̃] fectionately.

affectueux, euse [afɛkty... tionate.

affichage [afiʃaʒ] nm **1.** [d'un...

avis] putting up, displaying - **2.** ÉLECTRON : **affichage à cristaux liquides** LCD, liquid crystal display.

affiche [afiʃ] *nf* [gén] poster ; [officielle] notice.

afficher [3] [afiʃe] *vt* **1.** [liste, poster] to put up ; [vente, réglementation] to put up a notice about - **2.** [laisser transparaître] to display, to exhibit.

affilée [afile] ◆ **d'affilée** *loc adv* : **trois jours d'affilée** three days running.

affiler [3] [afile] *vt* to sharpen.

affiner [3] [afine] *vt litt & fig* to refine.

affinité [afinite] *nf* affinity.

affirmatif, ive [afirmatif, iv] *adj* **1.** [réponse] affirmative - **2.** [personne] positive. ◆ **affirmative** *nf* : **dans l'affirmative** if yes, if the answer is yes ; **répondre par l'affirmative** to reply in the affirmative.

affirmation [afirmasjɔ̃] *nf* assertion.

affirmer [3] [afirme] *vt* **1.** [certifier] to maintain, to claim - **2.** [exprimer] to assert.

affliction [afliksjɔ̃] *nf* affliction.

affligeant, e [afliʒɑ̃, ɑ̃t] *adj* **1.** [désolant] saddening, distressing - **2.** [lamentable] appalling.

affliger [17] [afliʒe] *vt sout* **1.** [attrister] to sadden, to distress - **2.** [de défaut, de maladie] : **être affligé de** to be afflicted with.

affluence [aflyɑ̃s] *nf* crowd, crowds *pl*.

affluent [aflyɑ̃] *nm* tributary.

affluer [3] [aflye] *vi* **1.** [choses] to pour in, to flood in - **2.** [personnes] to flock - **3.** [sang] : **affluer (à)** to rush (to).

afflux [afly] *nm* **1.** [de liquide, dons, capitaux] flow - **2.** [de personnes] flood.

affolement [afɔlmɑ̃] *nm* panic.

affoler [3] [afɔle] *vt* [inquiéter] to terrify. ◆ **s'affoler** *vp* [paniquer] to panic.

affranchir [32] [afrɑ̃ʃir] *vt* **1.** [lettre - avec timbre] to stamp ; [- à la machine] to frank - **2.** [esclave] to set free, to liberate.

affreux, euse [afrø, øz] *adj* **1.** [repoussant] horrible - **2.** [effrayant] terrifying - **3.** [détestable] awful, dreadful.

affriolant, e [afrijɔlɑ̃, ɑ̃t] *adj* enticing.

affront [afrɔ̃] *nm* insult, affront.

affrontement [afrɔ̃tmɑ̃] *nm* confrontation.

affronter [3] [afrɔ̃te] *vt* to confront.

affubler [3] [afyble] *vt péj* : **être affublé de** to be got up in.

affût [afy] *nm* : **être à l'affût (de)** to be lying in wait (for) ; *fig* to be on the lookout (for).

~ fûter [3] [afyte] *vt* to sharpen.

~hanistan [afganistɑ̃] *nm* : **l'Afghanistan** ~nistan.

afin [afɛ̃] ◆ **afin de** *loc prép* in order to. ◆ **afin que** *loc conj* (+ *subjonctif*) so that.

a fortiori [aforsjori] *adv* all the more.

africain, e [afrikɛ̃, ɛn] *adj* African. ◆ **Africain, e** *nm, f* African.

Afrique [afrik] *nf* : **l'Afrique** Africa ; **l'Afrique du Nord** North Africa ; **l'Afrique du Sud** South Africa.

agacer [16] [agase] *vt* to irritate.

âge [aʒ] *nm* age ; **quel âge as-tu?** how old are you? ; **prendre de l'âge** to age ; **l'âge adulte** adulthood ; **l'âge ingrat** the awkward ou difficult age ; **âge d'or** golden age ; **le troisième âge** [personnes] the over-sixties, senior citizens.

âgé, e [aʒe] *adj* old, elderly ; **être âgé de 20 ans** to be 20 years old ou of age ; **un enfant âgé de 3 ans** a 3-year-old child.

agence [aʒɑ̃s] *nf* agency ; **agence immobilière** estate agent's *UK*, real estate agency *US* ; **agence matrimoniale** marriage bureau ; **Agence nationale pour l'emploi** ≃ job centre *UK* ; **agence de publicité** advertising agency ; **agence de voyages** travel agent's, travel agency.

agencer [16] [aʒɑ̃se] *vt* to arrange ; *fig* to put together.

agenda [aʒɛ̃da] *nm* diary.

agenouiller [3] [aʒnuje] ◆ **s'agenouiller** *vp* to kneel.

agent [aʒɑ̃] *nm* agent ; **agent de change** stockbroker ; **agent de police** police officer ; **agent secret** secret agent.

agglomération [aglɔmerasjɔ̃] *nf* [ville] conurbation.

aggloméré [aglɔmere] *nm* chipboard.

agglomérer [18] [aglɔmere] *vt* to mix together.

agglutiner [3] [aglytine] *vt* to stick together. ◆ **s'agglutiner** *vp* [foule] to gather, to congregate.

aggraver [3] [agrave] *vt* to make worse. ◆ **s'aggraver** *vp* to get worse, to worsen.

agile [aʒil] *adj* agile, nimble.

agilité [aʒilite] *nf litt & fig* agility.

agios [aʒjo] *nmpl* FIN bank charges.

agir [32] [aʒir] *vi* **1.** [faire, être efficace] to act - **2.** [se comporter] to behave - **3.** [influer] : **agir sur** to have an effect on. ◆ **s'agir** *v impers* : **il s'agit de...** it's a matter of... ; **de quoi s'agit-il?** what's it about?

agissements [aʒismɑ̃] *nmpl péj* schemes, intrigues.

agitateur, trice [aʒitatœr, tris] *nm, f* POLIT agitator.

agitation [aʒitasjɔ̃] *nf* agitation ; [politique, sociale] unrest.

agité, e [aʒite] *adj* **1.** [gén] restless ; [enfant, classe] restless, fidgety ; [journée, atmosphère] hectic - **2.** [mer] rough.

agiter [3] [aʒite] *vt* **1.** [remuer - flacon, objet] to shake ; [- drapeau, bras] to wave - **2.** [énerver] to perturb. ➭ **s'agiter** *vp* [personne] to move about, to fidget ; [mer] to stir ; [population] to get restless.

agneau [aɲo] *nm* **1.** [animal, viande] lamb - **2.** [cuir] lambskin.

agonie [agɔni] *nf* [de personne] mortal agony ; *fig* death throes *pl*.

agoniser [3] [agɔnize] *vi* [personne] to be dying ; *fig* to be on its last legs.

agrafe [agraf] *nf* **1.** [de bureau] staple - **2.** MÉD clip.

agrafer [3] [agrafe] *vt* [attacher] to fasten.

agrafeuse [agraføz] *nf* stapler.

agrandir [32] [agrɑ̃dir] *vt* **1.** [élargir - gén & PHOTO] to enlarge ; [- rue, écart] to widen - **2.** *fig* [développer] to expand. ➭ **s'agrandir** *vp* **1.** [s'étendre] to grow - **2.** *fig* [se développer] to expand.

agrandissement [agrɑ̃dismɑ̃] *nm* **1.** [gén & PHOTO] enlargement - **2.** *fig* [développement] expansion.

agréable [agreabl] *adj* pleasant, nice.

agréé, e [agree] *adj* [concessionnaire, appareil] authorized.

agréer [15] [agree] *vt sout* **1.** [accepter] : veuillez agréer mes salutations distinguées ou l'expression de mes sentiments distingués yours faithfully - **2.** [convenir] : agréer à qqn to suit ou please sb.

agrégation [agregasjɔ̃] *nf* competitive examination for secondary school and university teachers.

agrégé, e [agreʒe] *nm, f* holder of the agrégation.

agrément [agremɑ̃] *nm* **1.** [caractère agréable] attractiveness - **2.** [approbation] consent, approval.

agrès [agrɛ] *nmpl* SPORT gym apparatus (U).

agresser [4] [agrese] *vt* **1.** [suj: personne] to attack - **2.** *fig* [suj: bruit, pollution] to assault.

agresseur [agresœr] *nm* attacker.

agressif, ive [agresif, iv] *adj* aggressive.

agression [agresjɔ̃] *nf* attack ; MIL & PSYCHO aggression.

agricole [agrikɔl] *adj* agricultural.

agriculteur, trice [agrikyltœr, tris] *nm, f* farmer.

agriculture [agrikyltyr] *nf* agriculture, farming.

agripper [3] [agripe] *vt* **1.** [personne] to cling ou hang on to - **2.** [objet] to grip, to clutch.

agroalimentaire [agroalimɑ̃ter] <> *adj* : industrie agroalimentaire food-processing industry ; les produits agroalimentaires processed foods ou foodstuffs. <> *nm* : l'agroalimentaire the food-processing industry.

agronomie [agrɔnɔmi] *nf* agronomy.

agrume [agrym] *nm* citrus fruit.

aguets [agɛ] ➭ **aux aguets** *loc adv* : être/rester aux aguets to be ou keep on the lookout.

ahuri, e [ayri] *adj* : être ahuri (par qqch) to be taken aback (by sthg).

ahurissant, e [ayrisɑ̃, ɑ̃t] *adj* astounding.

ai [ɛ] ➭ avoir.

aide [ɛd] *nf* **1.** [gén] help ; appeler (qqn) à l'aide to call (to sb) for help ; venir en aide à qqn to come to sb's aid, to help sb ; aide ménagère home help UK, home helper US - **2.** [secours financier] aid ; aide sociale social security UK, welfare US. ➭ **à l'aide de** *loc prép* with the help ou aid of.

aide-éducateur, trice [ɛdedykatœr, tris] *nm, f* SCOL teaching assistant.

aide-mémoire [ɛdmemwar] *nm inv* aide-mémoire ; [pour examen] revision notes *pl*.

aider [4] [ede] *vt* to help ; aider qqn à faire qqch to help sb to do sthg. ➭ **s'aider** *vp* **1.** [s'assister mutuellement] to help each other - **2.** [avoir recours] : s'aider de to use, to make use of.

aide-soignant, e [ɛdswaɲɑ̃, ɑ̃t] *nm, f* nursing auxiliary UK, nurse's aide US.

aie, aies *etc* ➭ avoir.

aïe [aj] *interj* [exprime la douleur] ow!, ouch!

aïeul, e [ajœl] *nm, f sout* grandparent, grandfather (f grandmother).

aïeux [ajø] *nmpl* ancestors.

aigle [ɛgl] *nm* eagle.

aigre [ɛgr] *adj* **1.** [gén] sour - **2.** [propos] harsh.

aigre-doux, aigre-douce [ɛgrədu, ɛgrədus] *adj* **1.** CULIN sweet-and-sour - **2.** [propos] bittersweet.

aigrelet, ette [ɛgrəlɛ, ɛt] *adj* **1.** [vin] vinegary - **2.** [voix] sharpish.

aigreur [ɛgrœr] *nf* **1.** [d'un aliment] sourness - **2.** [d'un propos] harshness. ➭ **aigreurs d'estomac** *nfpl* heartburn (U).

aigri, e [egri] *adj* embittered.

aigu, uë [egy] *adj* **1.** [son] high-pitched - **2.** [objet, lame] sharp ; [angle] acute - **3.** [douleur] sharp, acute - **4.** [intelligence, sens] acute, keen. ➭ **aigu** *nm* high note.

aiguillage [eguija3] *nm* [RAIL - manœuvre] shunting *UK*, switching *US* ; [- dispositif] points *pl UK*, switch *US*.

aiguille [eguij] *nf* **1.** [gén] needle ; **aiguille à tricoter** knitting needle ; **aiguille de pin** pine needle - **2.** [de pendule] hand.

aiguiller [3] [eguije] *vt* **1.** RAIL to shunt *UK*, to switch *US* - **2.** [personne, conversation] to steer, to direct.

aiguilleur [equijœr] *nm* **1.** RAIL pointsman *UK*, switchman *US* - **2.** AÉRON : **aiguilleur du ciel** air-traffic controller.

aiguiser [3] [egize] *vt litt & fig* to sharpen.

ail [aj] (*pl* **ails** ou **aulx** [o]) *nm* garlic *(U)* ; **ail des bois** *Québec* wild leek.

aile [ɛl] *nf* [gén] wing.

aileron [ɛlrɔ̃] *nm* **1.** [de requin] fin - **2.** [d'avion] aileron.

ailier [elje] *nm* winger.

aille, ailles *etc* ► **aller.**

ailleurs [ajœr] *adv* elsewhere, somewhere ou someplace *US* else ; **nulle part ailleurs** nowhere ou noplace *US* else ; **partout ailleurs** everywhere ou everyplace *US* else. ► **d'ailleurs** *loc adv* moreover, besides. ► **par ailleurs** *loc adv* moreover.

aimable [ɛmabl] *adj* kind, nice.

aimablement [ɛmabləmɑ̃] *adv* kindly.

aimant¹, e [ɛmɑ̃, ɑ̃t] *adj* loving.

aimant² [ɛmɑ̃] *nm* magnet.

aimer [4] [eme] *vt* **1.** [gén] to like ; **aimer bien qqch/qqn** to like sthg/sb, to be fond of sthg/sb ; **aimer bien faire qqch** to (really) like doing sthg ; **aimer (à) faire qqch** to like to do sthg, to like doing sthg ; **j'aime à croire que...** I like to think that... ; **elle aime qu'on l'appelle par son surnom** she likes being called by her nickname ; **je n'aime pas que tu rentres seule le soir** I don't like you coming home alone at night ; **j'aimerais (bien) que tu viennes avec moi** I'd like you to come with me ; **j'aimerais bien une autre tasse de café** I wouldn't mind another cup of coffee ; **aimer mieux qqch** to prefer sthg ; **aimer mieux faire qqch** to prefer doing ou to do sthg - **2.** [d'amour] to love. ► **s'aimer** *vp (emploi réciproque)* to love each other ; **s'aimer bien** to like each other.

aine [ɛn] *nf* groin.

aîné, e [ene] ◇ *adj* [plus âgé] elder, older ; [le plus âgé] eldest, oldest. ◇ *nm, f* [plus âgé] older ou elder child, older ou eldest son/daughter ; [le plus âgé] oldest ou eldest child, oldest ou eldest son/daughter ; **elle est mon aînée de deux ans** she is two years older than me.

aînesse [ɛnɛs] ► **droit.**

ainsi [ɛ̃si] *adv* **1.** [manière] in this way, like this - **2.** [valeur conclusive] thus ; **et ainsi de suite** and so on, and so forth ; **pour ainsi dire** so to speak. ► **ainsi que** *loc conj* [et] as well as.

air [ɛr] *nm* **1.** [gén] air ; **en plein air** (out) in the open air, outside ; **en l'air** [projet] (up) in the air ; *fig* [paroles] empty ; **air conditionné** air-conditioning - **2.** [apparence, mine] air, look ; **il a l'air triste** he looks sad ; **il a l'air de bouder** it looks as if he's sulking ; **il a l'air de faire beau** it looks like a nice day - **3.** MUS tune ; [à l'opéra] aria.

Airbag® [ɛrbag] *nm* airbag.

aire [ɛr] *nf* [gén] area ; **aire d'atterrissage** landing strip ; **aire de jeu** playground ; **aire de repos** lay-by *UK*, rest area *US* ; **aire de stationnement** parking area.

aisance [ɛzɑ̃s] *nf* **1.** [facilité] ease - **2.** [richesse] : **il vit dans l'aisance** he has an affluent lifestyle.

aise [ɛz] *nf sout* pleasure ; **être à l'aise** ou **à son aise** [confortable] to feel comfortable ; [financièrement] to be comfortably off ; **mettez-vous à l'aise** make yourself comfortable ; **mettre qqn mal à l'aise** to make sb feel ill at ease ou uneasy. ► **aises** *nfpl* : **aimer ses aises** to like one's (home) comforts ; **prendre ses aises** to make o.s. comfortable.

aisé, e [eze] *adj* **1.** [facile] easy - **2.** [riche] well-off.

aisselle [ɛsɛl] *nf* armpit.

ajourner [3] [aʒurne] *vt* **1.** [reporter - décision etc] to postpone ; [- réunion, procès] to adjourn - **2.** [candidat] to refer.

ajout [aʒu] *nm* addition.

ajouter [3] [aʒute] *vt* to add ; **ajouter foi à qqch** *sout* to give credence to sthg. ► **s'ajouter** *vp* : **s'ajouter à qqch** to be in addition to sthg.

ajuster [3] [aʒyste] *vt* **1.** [monter] : **ajuster qqch (à)** to fit sthg (to) - **2.** [régler] to adjust - **3.** [vêtement] to alter - **4.** [tir, coup] to aim. ► **s'ajuster** *vp* to be adaptable.

alarme [alarm] *nf* alarm ; **donner l'alarme** to give ou raise the alarm.

alarmer [3] [alarme] *vt* to alarm. ► **s'alarmer** *vp* to get ou become alarmed.

albanais, e [albanɛ, ɛz] *adj* Albanian. ► **albanais** *nm* [langue] Albanian. ► **Albanais, e** *nm, f* Albanian.

Albanie [albani] *nf* : **l'Albanie** Albania.

albâtre [albatr] *nm* alabaster.

albatros [albatros] *nm* albatross.

albinos [albinos] *nmf & adj inv* albino.

album [albɔm] *nm* album ; **album (de) photo** photo album.

alchimiste [alʃimist] *nmf* alchemist.

alcool [alkɔl] *nm* alcohol ; **alcool à brûler** methylated spirits *pl* ; **alcool à 90 degrés** surgical spirit.

alcoolique [alkɔlik] *nmf & adj* alcoholic.

alcoolisé, e [alkɔlize] *adj* alcoholic.

alcoolisme [alkɔlism] *nm* alcoholism.

Alc(o)otest® [alkɔtɛst] *nm* ≃ Breathalyser® *US*, ≃ Breathalyzer® *UK*.

alcôve [alkov] *nf* recess.

aléatoire [aleatwar] *adj* **1.** [avenir] uncertain - **2.** [choix] random.

alentour [alɑ̃tur] *adv* around, round about. ➡ **alentours** *nmpl* surroundings ; **aux alentours de** [spatial] in the vicinity of ; [temporel] around.

alerte [alɛrt] ◇ *adj* **1.** [personne, esprit] agile, alert - **2.** [style, pas] lively. ◇ *nf* alarm, alert ; **donner l'alerte** to sound ou give the alert ; **alerte à la bombe** bomb scare.

alerter [3] [alɛrte] *vt* to warn, to alert.

algèbre [alʒɛbr] *nf* algebra.

Alger [alʒe] *npr* Algiers.

Algérie [alʒeri] *nf*: **l'Algérie** Algeria.

algérien, enne [alʒerjɛ̃, ɛn] *adj* Algerian. ➡ **Algérien, enne** *nm, f* Algerian.

algue [alg] *nf* seaweed (U).

alibi [alibi] *nm* alibi.

aliénation [aljenasjɔ̃] *nf* alienation ; **aliénation mentale** insanity.

aliéné, e [aljene] ◇ *adj* **1.** MÉD insane - **2.** DR alienated. ◇ *nm, f* MÉD insane person.

aliéner [18] [aljene] *vt* to alienate.

alignement [aliɲmɑ̃] *nm* alignment, lining up.

aligner [3] [aliɲe] *vt* **1.** [disposer en ligne] to line up, to align - **2.** [adapter] : **aligner qqch sur** to align sthg with, to bring sthg into line with. ➡ **s'aligner** *vp* to line up ; **s'aligner sur** POLIT to align o.s. with.

aliment [alimɑ̃] *nm* [nourriture] food (U).

alimentaire [alimɑ̃tɛr] *adj* **1.** [gén] food (avant n) ; **c'est juste un travail alimentaire** I'm doing this job just for the money - **2.** DR maintenance (avant n).

alimentation [alimɑ̃tasjɔ̃] *nf* **1.** [nourriture] diet ; **magasin d'alimentation** food store - **2.** [approvisionnement] : **alimentation (en)** supply ou supplying (U) (of).

alimenter [3] [alimɑ̃te] *vt* **1.** [nourrir] to feed - **2.** [approvisionner] : **alimenter qqch en** to supply sthg with.

alinéa [alinea] *nm* **1.** [retrait de ligne] indent - **2.** [dans un document officiel] paragraph.

aliter [3] [alite] *vt* : **être alité** to be bedridden. ➡ **s'aliter** *vp* to take to one's bed.

allaitement [alɛtmɑ̃] *nm* [d'enfant] breastfeeding ; [d'animal] suckling.

allaiter [4] [alete] *vt* [enfant] to breast-feed ; [animal] to suckle.

allé, e [ale] *pp* ➡ **aller**.

alléchant, e [aleʃɑ̃, ɑ̃t] *adj* mouth-watering, tempting.

allécher [18] [aleʃe] *vt* : **il a été alléché par l'odeur/la perspective** the smell/prospect made his mouth water.

allée [ale] *nf* **1.** [dans un jardin] path ; [dans une ville] avenue - **2.** [trajet] : **allées et venues** comings and goings - **3.** *Québec* [golf] fairway.

allégé, e [aleʒe] *adj* [régime, produit] lowfat.

alléger [22] [aleʒe] *vt* **1.** [fardeau] to lighten - **2.** [douleur] to soothe.

allégorie [alegɔri] *nf* allegory.

allègre [alɛgr] *adj* **1.** [ton] cheerful - **2.** [démarche] jaunty.

allégresse [alegrɛs] *nf* elation.

alléguer [18] [alege] *vt* : **alléguer une excuse** to put forward an excuse ; **alléguer que** to plead (that).

Allemagne [almaɲ] *nf* : **l'Allemagne** Germany ; **l'(ex-)Allemagne de l'Est** (former) East Germany ; **l'(ex-)Allemagne de l'Ouest** (former) West Germany.

allemand, e [almɑ̃, ɑ̃d] *adj* German. ➡ **allemand** *nm* [langue] German. ➡ **Allemand, e** *nm, f* German ; **un Allemand de l'Est/l'Ouest** an East/a West German.

aller [31] [ale] ◇ *nm* **1.** [trajet] outward journey - **2.** [billet] single ticket *UK*, one-way ticket *US*. ◇ *vi* **1.** [gén] to go ; **allez!** come on! ; **vas-y!** go on! ; **allons-y!, on y va!** let's go!, off we go! - **2.** (+ *infinitif*) **aller faire qqch** to go and do sthg ; **aller chercher les enfants à l'école** to go and fetch the children from school ; **aller travailler/se promener** to go to work/for a walk - **3.** [indiquant un état] : **comment vas-tu?** how are you? ; **je vais bien** I'm very well, I'm fine ; **comment ça va? ça va** [santé] how are you? fine ou all right ; [situation] how are things? fine ou all right ; **aller mieux** to be better - **4.** [convenir] : **ce type de clou ne va pas pour ce travail** this kind of nail won't do ou isn't suitable for this job ; **aller avec** to go with ; **aller à qqn** to suit sb ; [suj: vêtement, taille] to fit sb ; **ces couleurs ne vont pas ensemble** these colours don't go well together - **5.** [mener - véhicule, chemin] to go - **6.** [fonctionner - machine] to go, to run ; [- moteur] to run ; [- voiture, train] to go ; **cela va de soi, cela va**

sans dire that goes without saying ; **il en va de... comme...** the same goes for... as... ; **il en va de même pour lui** the same goes for him. ◇ *v aux (+ infinitif)* [exprime le futur proche] to be going to, will ; **je vais arriver en retard** I'm going to arrive late, I'll arrive late ; **nous allons bientôt avoir fini** we'll soon have finished. ◆ **s'en aller** *vp* **1.** [partir] to go, to be off ; **allez-vous-en!** go away! - **2.** [disparaître] to go away.

allergie [alɛrʒi] *nf* allergy.

allergique [alɛrʒik] *adj* : **allergique (à)** allergic (to).

aller-retour [aleretur] *nm* return *UK* ou round trip *US* (ticket).

alliage [aljaʒ] *nm* alloy.

alliance [aljɑ̃s] *nf* **1.** [union - stratégique] alliance ; [- par le mariage] union, marriage ; **cousin par alliance** cousin by marriage - **2.** [bague] wedding ring.

allié, e [alje] ◇ *adj* : **allié (à)** allied (to). ◇ *nm, f* ally. ◆ **Alliés** *nmpl* : **les Alliés** the Allies.

allier [9] [alje] *vt* [associer] to combine. ◆ **s'allier** *vp* to become allies ; **s'allier qqn** to win sb over as an ally ; **s'allier à qqn** to ally with sb.

alligator [aligatɔr] *nm* alligator.

allô [alo] *interj* hello!

allocation [alɔkasjɔ̃] *nf* **1.** [attribution] allocation - **2.** [aide financière] : **allocation chômage** unemployment benefit *(U) UK* ou compensation *(U) US* ; **allocation logement** housing benefit *(U) UK*, rent subsidy *(U) US* ; **allocations familiales** child benefit *(U) UK*, welfare *(U) US*.

allocs [alɔk] *(abr de allocations familiales) fam nfpl* : **les allocs** social security *UK*, welfare *US*.

allocution [alɔkysjɔ̃] *nf* short speech.

allongé, e [alɔ̃ʒe] *adj* **1.** [position] : **être allongé** to be lying down ou stretched out - **2.** [forme] elongated.

allonger [17] [alɔ̃ʒe] *vt* **1.** [gén] to lengthen, to make longer - **2.** [jambe, bras] to stretch (out) - **3.** [personne] to lay down. ◆ **s'allonger** *vp* **1.** [gén] to get longer - **2.** [se coucher] to lie down.

allopathique [alɔpatik] *adj* allopathic.

allumage [alymaʒ] *nm* **1.** [de feu] lighting - **2.** [d'appareil électrique] switching ou turning on - **3.** [de moteur] ignition.

allume-cigares [alymsigar] *nm inv* cigar lighter.

allume-gaz [alymgaz] *nm inv* gas lighter.

allumer [3] [alyme] *vt* **1.** [lampe, radio, télévision] to turn ou switch on ; **allume**

dans la cuisine turn the kitchen light on - **2.** [gaz] to light ; [cigarette] to light (up) - **3.** *fam* [personne] to turn on.

allumette [alymɛt] *nf* match.

allumeuse [alymøz] *nf fam péj* tease.

allure [alyr] *nf* **1.** [vitesse] speed ; **à toute allure** at top ou full speed - **2.** [prestance] presence ; **avoir de l'allure** to have style - **3.** [apparence générale] appearance.

allusion [alyzjɔ̃] *nf* allusion ; **faire allusion à** to refer ou to allude to.

almanach [almana] *nm* almanac.

aloi [alwa] *nm* : **de bon aloi** [mesure] of real worth ; **de mauvais aloi** [gaîté] not genuine ; [plaisanterie] in bad taste.

alors [alɔr] *adv* **1.** [jadis] then, at that time - **2.** [à ce moment-là] then - **3.** [exprimant la conséquence] then, so ; **et alors, qu'est-ce qui s'est passé?** so what happened? ; **il va se mettre en colère [---] et alors?** he'll get angry [---] so what? - **4.** [emploi expressif] well (then) ; **alors, qu'est-ce qu'on fait?** well, what are we doing? ; **ça alors!** well fancy that! ◆ **alors que** *loc conj* **1.** [exprimant le temps] while, when - **2.** [exprimant l'opposition] even though ; **elle est sortie alors que c'était interdit** she went out even though it was forbidden ; **ils aiment le café alors que nous, nous buvons du thé** they like coffee whereas we drink tea.

alouette [alwɛt] *nf* lark.

alourdir [32] [alurdir] *vt* **1.** [gén] to weigh down, to make heavy - **2.** *fig* [impôts] to increase.

aloyau [alwajo] *nm* sirloin.

Alpes [alp] *nfpl* : **les Alpes** the Alps.

alphabet [alfabɛ] *nm* alphabet.

alphabétique [alfabetik] *adj* alphabetical.

alphabétiser [3] [alfabetize] *vt* : **alphabétiser qqn** to teach sb (how) to read and write ; **alphabétiser un pays** to eliminate illiteracy from a country.

alpin, e [alpɛ̃, in] *adj* alpine.

alpinisme [alpinism] *nm* mountaineering.

Alsace [alzas] *nf* : **l'Alsace** Alsace.

altérer [18] [altere] *vt* **1.** [détériorer] to spoil - **2.** [santé] to harm, to affect ; [vérité, récit] to distort. ◆ **s'altérer** *vp* **1.** [matière - métal] to deteriorate ; [- aliment] to go off, to spoil - **2.** [santé] to deteriorate.

alternance [altɛrnɑ̃s] *nf* **1.** [succession] alternation ; **en alternance** alternately - **2.** POLIT change of government party.

alternatif, ive [altɛrnatif, iv] *adj* **1.** [périodique] alternating - **2.** [parallèle] alternative. ◆ **alternative** *nf* alternative.

alternativement [alternativmɑ̃] *adv* alternately.

alterner [3] [alterne] *vi* [se succéder] : **alterner (avec)** to alternate (with).

altier, ère [altje, ɛr] *adj* haughty.

altitude [altityd] *nf* altitude, height ; **en altitude** at (high) altitude.

alto [alto] *nm* [MUS - voix] alto ; [- instrument] viola.

alu [aly] *fam* <> *nm* [métal] aluminium *UK*, aluminum *US* ; [papier] aluminium *UK* OU aluminum *US* foil, tinfoil. <> *adj* : **papier alu** aluminium *UK* OU aluminum *US* foil, tinfoil.

aluminium [alyminjɔm] *nm* aluminium *UK*, aluminum *US*.

alvéole [alveɔl] *nf* **1.** [cavité] cavity - **2.** [de ruche, poumon] alveolus.

amabilité [amabilite] *nf* kindness ; **avoir l'amabilité de faire qqch** to be so kind as to do sthg.

amadouer [6] [amadwe] *vt* [adoucir] to tame, to pacify ; [persuader] to coax.

amaigrir [32] [amegrir] *vt* to make thin OU thinner.

amaigrissant, e [amegrisɑ̃, ɑ̃t] *adj* slimming *(avant n)* *UK*, reducing *(avant n)* *US*.

amaigrissement [amegrismɑ̃] *nm* loss of weight.

amalgame [amalgam] *nm* **1.** TECHNOL amalgam - **2.** [de styles] mixture - **3.** [d'idées, de notions] : **il ne faut pas faire l'amalgame entre ces deux questions** the two issues must not be confused.

amalgamer [3] [amalgame] *vt* to combine.

amande [amɑ̃d] *nf* almond.

amandier [amɑ̃dje] *nm* almond tree.

amant [amɑ̃] *nm* (male) lover.

amarre [amar] *nf* rope, cable.

amarrer [3] [amare] *vt* **1.** NAUT to moor - **2.** [fixer] to tie down.

amas [ama] *nm* pile.

amasser [3] [amase] *vt* **1.** [objets] to pile up - **2.** [argent] to accumulate.

amateur [amatœr] *nm* **1.** [connaisseur - d'art, de bon café] : **amateur de lover of** - **2.** [non-professionnel] amateur ; **faire qqch en amateur** to do sthg as a hobby - **3.** *péj* [dilettante] amateur.

amazone [amazon] *nf* horsewoman ; **monter en amazone** to ride sidesaddle.

Amazonie [amazoni] *nf* : **l'Amazonie** the Amazon (Basin).

amazonien, enne [amazonjɛ̃, ɛn] *adj* Amazonian ; **la forêt amazonienne** the Amazon rain forest.

ambassade [ɑ̃basad] *nf* embassy.

ambassadeur, drice [ɑ̃basadœr, dris] *nm, f* ambassador.

ambiance [ɑ̃bjɑ̃s] *nf* atmosphere.

ambiant, e [ɑ̃bjɑ̃, ɑ̃t] *adj* : **température ambiante** room temperature.

ambidextre [ɑ̃bidɛkstr] *adj* ambidextrous.

ambigu, uë [ɑ̃bigy] *adj* ambiguous.

ambiguïté [ɑ̃biguite] *nf* ambiguity.

ambitieux, euse [ɑ̃bisjø, øz] *adj* ambitious.

ambition [ɑ̃bisjɔ̃] *nf* **1.** *péj* [arrivisme] ambitiousness - **2.** [désir] ambition ; **avoir l'ambition de faire qqch** to have an ambition to do sthg.

ambivalent, e [ɑ̃bivalɑ̃, ɑ̃t] *adj* ambivalent.

ambre [ɑ̃br] *nm* **1.** [couleur] amber - **2.** [matière] : **ambre (gris)** ambergris.

ambré, e [ɑ̃bre] *adj* [couleur] amber.

ambulance [ɑ̃bylɑ̃s] *nf* ambulance.

ambulant, e [ɑ̃bylɑ̃, ɑ̃t] *adj* travelling *UK*, traveling *US (avant n).*

âme [ɑm] *nf* **1.** [esprit] soul ; **avoir une âme de comédien** to be a born actor - **2.** [personne] : **âme sœur** soulmate - **3.** [caractère] spirit, soul.

amélioration [ameljɔrasjɔ̃] *nf* improvement.

améliorer [3] [ameljɔre] *vt* to improve. ➡ **s'améliorer** *vp* to improve.

amen [amɛn] *adv* amen.

aménagement [amenaʒmɑ̃] *nm* **1.** [de lieu] fitting out - **2.** [de programme] planning, organizing.

aménager [17] [amenaʒe] *vt* **1.** [pièce] to fit out - **2.** [programme] to plan, to organize.

amende [amɑ̃d] *nf* fine.

amendement [amɑ̃dmɑ̃] *nm* POLIT amendment.

amender [3] [amɑ̃de] *vt* **1.** POLIT to amend - **2.** AGRIC to enrich. ➡ **s'amender** *vp* to mend one's ways.

amener [19] [amne] *vt* **1.** [mener] to bring - **2.** [inciter] : **amener qqn à faire qqch** [suj : circonstances] to lead sb to do sthg ; [suj : personne] to get sb to do sthg - **3.** [occasionner, préparer] to bring about.

amenuiser [3] [amənɥize] *vt* **1.** [rendre plus petit] : **ses cheveux amenuisent son visage** her hair makes her face look thinner - **2.** [réduire] to diminish, to reduce. ➡ **s'amenuiser** *vp* to dwindle, to diminish.

amer, ère [amɛr] *adj* bitter.

américain, e [amerikɛ̃, ɛn] *adj* American. ➡ **américain** *nm* [langue] American English. ➡ **Américain, e** *nm, f* American.

américanisme [amerikanism] *nm* Americanism.

Amérique [amerik] *nf*: **l'Amérique** Amerique ; **l'Amérique centrale** Central America ; **l'Amérique du Nord** North America ; **l'Amérique du Sud** South America ; **l'Amérique latine** Latin America.

amertume [amɛrtym] *nf* bitterness.

améthyste [ametist] *nf* amethyst.

ameublement [amœbləmɑ̃] *nm* [meubles] furniture ; [action de meubler] furnishing.

ami, e [ami] <> *adj* friendly. <> *nm, f* 1. [camarade] friend ; **petit ami** boyfriend ; **petite amie** girlfriend - 2. [partisan] supporter, friend.

amiable [amjabl] *adj* [accord] friendly, informal. ◆ **à l'amiable** *loc adv & loc adj* out of court.

amiante [amjɑ̃t] *nm* asbestos.

amibe [amib] *nf* amoeba.

amical, e, aux [amikal, o] *adj* friendly. ◆ **amicale** *nf* association, club *(for people with a shared interest)*.

amicalement [amikalmɑ̃] *adv* 1. [de façon amicale] amicably, in a friendly way - 2. [dans une lettre] Yours (ever) Best wishes.

amidon [amidɔ̃] *nm* starch.

amidonner [3] [amidɔne] *vt* to starch.

amincissant, e [amɛ̃sisɑ̃, ɑ̃t] *adj* slimming.

amiral, aux [amiral, o] *nm* admiral.

amitié [amitje] *nf* 1. [affection] affection ; **prendre qqn en amitié** to befriend sb - 2. [rapports amicaux] friendship ; **faire ses amitiés à qqn** to give sb one's good ou best wishes.

ammoniac, aque [amɔnjak] *adj* CHIM ammoniac. ◆ **ammoniac** *nm* ammonia. ◆ **ammoniaque** *nf* ammonia (water).

amnésie [amnezi] *nf* amnesia.

amniocentèse [amnjosɛ̃tɛz] *nf* amniocentesis.

amnistie [amnisti] *nf* amnesty.

amnistier [9] [amnistje] *vt* to amnesty.

amoindrir [32] [amwɛ̃drir] *vt* to diminish.

amonceler [24] [amɔ̃sle] *vt* to accumulate.

amont [amɔ̃] *nm* upstream (water) ; **en amont de** [rivière] upriver ou upstream from ; *fig* prior to.

amoral, e, aux [amɔral, o] *adj* 1. [qui ignore la morale] amoral - 2. *fam* [débauché] immoral.

amorce [amɔrs] *nf* 1. [d'explosif] priming ; [de cartouche, d'obus] cap - 2. [à la pêche] bait - 3. *fig* [commencement] beginnings *pl*, germ.

amorcer [16] [amɔrse] *vt* 1. [explosif] to prime - 2. [à la pêche] to bait - 3. *fig* [commencer] to begin, to initiate.

amorphe [amɔrf] *adj* [personne] lifeless.

amortir [32] [amɔrtir] *vt* 1. [atténuer - choc] to absorb ; [- bruit] to deaden, to muffle - 2. [dette] to pay off - 3. [achat] to write off.

amour [amur] *nm* [gén] love ; **faire l'amour** to make love. ◆ **amours** *nfpl* [vie sentimentale] love-life.

amoureux, euse [amurø, øz] <> *adj* 1. [personne] in love ; **être/tomber amoureux (de)** to be/fall in love (with) - 2. [regard, geste] loving. <> *nm, f* 1. [prétendant] suitor - 2. [passionné] : **amoureux de** lover of ; **un amoureux de la nature** a nature lover.

amour-propre [amurprɔpr] *nm* pride, self-respect.

amovible [amɔvibl] *adj* [déplaçable] detachable, removable.

ampère [ɑ̃pɛr] *nm* amp, ampere.

amphétamine [ɑ̃fetamin] *nf* amphetamine.

amphi [ɑ̃fi] *nm fam* lecture hall ou theatre *UK* ; **cours en amphi** lecture.

amphibie [ɑ̃fibi] *adj* amphibious.

amphithéâtre [ɑ̃fiteatr] *nm* 1. HIST amphitheatre - 2. [d'université] lecture hall ou theatre *UK*.

ample [ɑ̃pl] *adj* 1. [vêtement - gén] loose-fitting ; [- jupe] full - 2. [projet] extensive ; **pour de plus amples informations** for further details - 3. [geste] broad, sweeping.

amplement [ɑ̃pləmɑ̃] *adv* [largement] fully, amply.

ampleur [ɑ̃plœr] *nf* 1. [de vêtement] fullness - 2. [d'événement, de dégâts] extent.

ampli [ɑ̃pli] *nm* amp.

amplificateur, trice [ɑ̃plifikatœr, tris] *adj* ÉLECTR amplifying ; **un phénomène amplificateur de la croissance** *fig* a phenomenon which increases growth. ◆ **amplificateur** *nm* 1. [gén] amplifier - 2. PHOTO enlarger.

amplifier [9] [ɑ̃plifje] *vt* 1. [mouvement, son] to amplify ; [image] to magnify, to enlarge - 2. [scandale] to increase ; [événement, problème] to highlight.

amplitude [ɑ̃plityd] *nf* 1. [de geste] fullness - 2. [d'onde] amplitude - 3. [de température] range.

ampoule [ɑ̃pul] *nf* 1. [de lampe] bulb - 2. [sur la peau] blister - 3. [médicament] ampoule, phial.

amputation [ɑ̃pytasjɔ̃] *nf* MÉD amputation.

amputer [3] [ɑ̃pyte] *vt* MÉD to amputate ; *fig* [couper] to cut (back ou down) ; **son article a été amputé d'un tiers** his article was cut by a third.

amulette [amylɛt] *nf* amulet.

amusant, e [amyzɑ̃, ɑ̃t] *adj* [drôle] funny ; [distrayant] amusing ; **c'est très amusant** it's great fun.

amuse-gueule [amyzgœl] *nm inv fam* cocktail snack, (party) nibble.

amusement [amyzmɑ̃] *nm* amusement (U).

amuser [3] [amyze] *vt* to amuse, to entertain. ◆ **s'amuser** *vp* to have fun, to have a good time ; **s'amuser à faire qqch** to amuse o.s. (by) doing sthg.

amygdale [amidal] *nf* tonsil.

an [ɑ̃] *nm* year ; **avoir sept ans** to be seven (years old) ; **en l'an 2000** in the year 2000 ; **le nouvel an** the New Year.

anabolisant [anabɔlizɑ̃] *nm* anabolic steroid.

anachronique [anakrɔnik] *adj* anachronistic.

anagramme [anagram] *nf* anagram.

anal, e, aux [anal, o] *adj* anal.

analgésique [analʒezik] *nm & adj* analgesic.

anallergique [analɛrʒik] *adj* hypoallergenic.

analogie [analɔʒi] *nf* analogy.

analogique [analɔʒik] *adj* analogue, analog US.

analogue [analɔg] *adj* analogous, comparable.

analphabète [analfabɛt] *nmf & adj* illiterate.

analyse [analiz] *nf* **1.** [étude] analysis - **2.** CHIM & MÉD test, analysis - **3.** [psychanalyse] analysis (U) - **4.** INFORM analysis.

analyser [3] [analize] *vt* **1.** [étudier, psychanalyser] to analyse UK, to analyze US - **2.** CHIM & MÉD to test, to analyse UK, to analyze US.

analyste [analist] *nmf* analyst.

analyste-programmeur, euse [analist-prɔgramœr, øz] *nm, f* systems analyst.

analytique [analitik] *adj* analytical.

ananas [anana(s)] *nm* pineapple.

anarchie [anarʃi] *nf* **1.** POLIT anarchy - **2.** [désordre] chaos, anarchy.

anarchique [anarʃik] *adj* anarchic.

anarchiste [anarʃist] *nmf & adj* anarchist.

anatomie [anatɔmi] *nf* anatomy.

anatomique [anatɔmik] *adj* anatomical.

ancestral, e, aux [ɑ̃sɛstral, o] *adj* ancestral.

ancêtre [ɑ̃sɛtr] *nmf* [aïeul] ancestor ; *fig* [forme première] forerunner, ancestor ; *fig* [initiateur] father (*f* mother).

anchois [ɑ̃ʃwa] *nm* anchovy.

ancien, enne [ɑ̃sjɛ̃, ɛn] *adj* **1.** [gén] old - **2.** *(avant n)* [précédent] former, old - **3.** [qui a de l'ancienneté] senior - **4.** [du passé] ancient.

anciennement [ɑ̃sjɛnmɑ̃] *adv* formerly, previously.

ancienneté [ɑ̃sjɛnte] *nf* **1.** [d'une tradition] oldness - **2.** [d'un employé] seniority.

ancre [ɑ̃kr] *nf* NAUT anchor ; **jeter l'ancre** to drop anchor ; **lever l'ancre** to weigh anchor ; *fam* [partir] to make tracks.

ancrer [3] [ɑ̃kre] *vt* [bateau] to anchor ; *fig* [idée, habitude] to root.

Andes [ɑ̃d] *nfpl* : **les Andes** the Andes.

Andorre [ɑ̃dɔr] *nf* : **(la principauté d')Andorre** (the principality of) Andorra.

andouille [ɑ̃duj] *nf* **1.** [charcuterie] *type of sausage made of chitterlings (pig's intestines eaten cold)* - **2.** *fam* [imbécile] prat, twit.

âne [an] *nm* **1.** ZOOL ass, donkey - **2.** *fam* [imbécile] ass.

anéantir [32] [aneɑ̃tir] *vt* **1.** [détruire] to annihilate ; *fig* to ruin, to wreck - **2.** [démoraliser] to crush, to overwhelm.

anecdote [anɛkdɔt] *nf* anecdote.

anecdotique [anɛkdɔtik] *adj* anecdotal.

anémie [anemi] *nf* MÉD anaemia UK, anemia US ; *fig* enfeeblement.

anémié, e [anemje] *adj* anaemic UK, anemic US.

anémique [anemik] *adj* anaemic UK, anemic US.

anémone [anemɔn] *nf* anemone.

ânerie [anri] *nf fam* [parole, acte] : **dire/faire une ânerie** to say/do something stupid.

ânesse [anɛs] *nf* she-ass, she-donkey.

anesthésie [anɛstezi] *nf* anaesthesia UK, anesthesia US ; **anesthésie locale** local anaesthetic UK ou anesthetic US ; **anesthésie générale** general anaesthetic UK ou anesthetic US.

anesthésier [9] [anɛstezje] *vt* to anaesthetize UK, to anesthetize US.

anesthésique [anɛstezik] *nm & adj* anaesthetic UK, anesthetic US.

anesthésiste [anɛstezist] *nmf* anaesthetist UK, anesthetist US.

anfractuosité [ɑ̃fraktɥozite] *nf* crevice.

ange [ɑ̃ʒ] *nm* angel ; **ange gardien** guardian angel ; **être aux anges** *fig* to be in seventh heaven.

angélique [ɑ̃ʒelik] *adj* angelic.

angélus [ɑ̃ʒelys] *nm* [sonnerie] angelus (bell).

angine [ɑ̃ʒin] *nf* [pharyngite] pharyngitis ; [amygdalite] tonsillitis.

anglais, e [ãglɛ, ɛz] *adj* English. ➤ **anglais** *nm* [langue] English. ➤ **Anglais, e** *nm, f* Englishman (*f* Englishwoman) ; **les Anglais** the English. ➤ **anglaises** *nfpl* ringlets.

angle [ãgl] *nm* **1.** [coin] corner - **2.** MATH angle ; **angle droit/aigu/obtus** right/acute/obtuse angle - **3.** [aspect] angle, point of view.

Angleterre [ãglətɛr] *nf* : **l'Angleterre** England.

anglican, e [ãglikã, an] *adj & nm, f* Anglican.

anglophone [ãglɔfɔn] <> *nmf* English-speaker. <> *adj* English-speaking, anglophone.

anglo-saxon, onne [ãglosaksɔ̃, ɔn] *adj* Anglo-Saxon. ➤ **anglo-saxon** *nm* [langue] Anglo-Saxon, Old English. ➤ **Anglo-Saxon, onne** *nm, f* Anglo-Saxon.

angoisse [ãgwas] *nf* anguish.

angoisser [3] [ãgwase] *vt* [effrayer] to cause anxiety to. ➤ **s'angoisser** *vp* **1.** [être anxieux] to be overcome with anxiety - **2.** *fam* [s'inquiéter] to fret.

anguille [ãgij] *nf* eel.

anguleux, euse [ãgylø, øz] *adj* angular.

anicroche [anikrɔʃ] *nf* hitch.

animal, e, aux [animal, o] *adj* **1.** [propre à l'animal] animal *(avant n)* - **2.** [instinctif] instinctive. ➤ **animal** *nm* [bête] animal ; **animal sauvage/domestique** wild/domestic animal.

animateur, trice [animatœr, tris] *nm, f* **1.** RADIO & TV presenter *UK* - **2.** [socioculturel, sportif] activities organizer.

animation [animasjɔ̃] *nf* **1.** [de rue] activity, life ; [de conversation, visage] animation - **2.** [activités] activities *pl* - **3.** CINÉ animation.

animé, e [anime] *adj* [rue] lively ; [conversation, visage] animated ; [objet] animate.

animer [3] [anime] *vt* **1.** [mettre de l'entrain dans] to animate, to liven up - **2.** [présenter] to present - **3.** [organiser des activités pour] to organize activities for. ➤ **s'animer** *vp* **1.** [visage] to light up - **2.** [rue] to come to life, to liven up.

animosité [animozite] *nf* animosity.

anis [ani(s)] *nm* BOT anise ; CULIN aniseed.

ankylosé, e [ãkiloze] *adj* [paralysé] stiff ; [engourdi] numb.

annales [anal] *nfpl* **1.** [d'examen] past papers *UK* - **2.** [chronique annuelle] chronicle *sg*, annals.

anneau, x [ano] *nm* **1.** [gén] ring - **2.** [maillon] link.

année [ane] *nf* year ; **souhaiter la bonne**

année à qqn to wish sb a Happy New Year ; **année bissextile** leap year ; **année scolaire** school year.

année-lumière [anelymjɛr] *(pl* **années-lumière)** *nf* light year.

annexe [anɛks] <> *nf* **1.** [de dossier] appendix, annex(e) - **2.** [de bâtiment] annex(e). <> *adj* related, associated.

annexer [4] [anɛkse] *vt* **1.** [incorporer] : **annexer qqch (à qqch)** to append ou annex sthg (to sthg) - **2.** [pays] to annex.

annexion [anɛksjɔ̃] *nf* annexation.

annihiler [3] [aniile] *vt* [réduire à néant] to destroy, to wreck.

anniversaire [aniversɛr] <> *nm* [de mariage, mort, événement] anniversary ; [de naissance] birthday ; **bon** ou **joyeux anniversaire!** happy birthday! <> *adj* anniversary *(avant n).*

annonce [anɔ̃s] *nf* **1.** [déclaration] announcement ; *fig* sign, indication - **2.** [texte] advertisement ; **petite annonce** classified advertisement, small ad *UK*, want ad *US*.

annoncer [16] [anɔ̃se] *vt* **1.** [faire savoir] to announce - **2.** [prédire] to predict.

annonciateur, trice [anɔ̃sjatœr, tris] *adj* : **annonciateur de qqch** heralding sthg.

annoter [3] [anɔte] *vt* to annotate.

annuaire [anɥɛr] *nm* annual, yearbook ; **annuaire téléphonique** telephone directory, phone book.

annuel, elle [anɥɛl] *adj* **1.** [tous les ans] annual, yearly - **2.** [d'une année] annual.

annuité [anɥite] *nf* **1.** [paiement] annual payment, annual instalment *UK* ou installment *US* - **2.** [année de service] year (of service).

annulaire [anɥlɛr] *nm* ring finger.

annulation [anylasjɔ̃] *nf* **1.** [de rendez-vous, réservation] cancellation - **2.** [de mariage] annulment.

annuler [3] [anyle] *vt* **1.** [rendez-vous, réservation] to cancel - **2.** [mariage] to annul - **3.** INFORM to undo. ➤ **s'annuler** *vp* to cancel each other out.

anoblir [32] [anɔblir] *vt* to ennoble.

anodin, e [anɔdɛ̃, in] *adj* **1.** [blessure] minor - **2.** [propos] harmless - **3.** [détail, personne] insignificant.

anomalie [anɔmali] *nf* anomaly.

ânon [anɔ̃] *nm* young donkey ou ass.

ânonner [3] [anɔne] *vt & vi* to recite in a drone.

anonymat [anɔnima] *nm* anonymity.

anonyme [anɔnim] *adj* anonymous.

anorak [anɔrak] *nm* anorak.

anorexie [anɔrɛksi] *nf* anorexia.

anormal, e, aux [anɔrmal, o] <> adj **1.** [inhabituel] abnormal, not normal - **2.** [intolérable, injuste] wrong, not right - **3.** [arriéré] (mentally) subnormal. <> nm, f mental defective.

ANPE (abr de **Agence nationale pour l'emploi**) nf French national employment agency, ≃ job centre UK.

anse [ãs] nf **1.** [d'ustensile] handle - **2.** GÉOGR cove.

antagoniste [ãtagɔnist] adj antagonistic.

antan [ãtã] ▸ **d'antan** loc adj litt of old, of yesteryear.

antarctique [ãtarktik] adj Antarctic ; **le cercle polaire antarctique** the Antarctic Circle. ▸ **Antarctique** nm **1.** [continent] : **l'antarctique** Antarctica - **2.** [océan] : **l'antarctique** the Antarctic (Ocean).

antécédent [ãtesedã] nm (gén pl) [passé] history sg.

antenne [ãtɛn] nf **1.** [d'insecte] antenna, feeler - **2.** [de télévision, de radio] aerial UK, antenna ; **antenne parabolique** dish aerial OU antenna US, satellite dish - **3.** [succursale] branch, office.

antenne-relais (pl **antennes-relais**) [ãtɛnrəlɛ] nf TÉLÉCOM mobile phone mast.

antérieur, e [ãterjœr] adj **1.** [dans le temps] earlier, previous ; **antérieur à** previous OU prior to - **2.** [dans l'espace] front (avant n).

antérieurement [ãterjœrmã] adv earlier, previously ; **antérieurement à** prior to.

anthologie [ãtɔlɔʒi] nf anthology.

anthracite [ãtrasit] <> nm anthracite. <> adj inv charcoal grey UK OU gray US.

anthropologie [ãtrɔpɔlɔʒi] nf anthropology.

anthropophage [ãtrɔpɔfaʒ] nmf cannibal.

antiacarien [ãtiakarjɛ̃, ɛ] <> adj antimite ; **traitement** OU **shampooing antiacarien** anti-mite treatment OU shampoo. <> nm anti-mite treatment.

antialcoolique [ãtialkɔlik] adj : **ligue antialcoolique** temperance league.

antibactérien, enne [ãtibakterjɛ̃, ɛn] adj antibacterial.

antibiotique [ãtibjɔtik] nm & adj antibiotic.

antibrouillard [ãtibrujar] nm & adj inv : **(phare** OU **feu) antibrouillard** fog lamp UK, foglight US.

antichambre [ãtiʃãbr] nf antechamber ; **faire antichambre** fig to wait patiently (to see somebody).

anticipation [ãtisipasjɔ̃] nf LITTÉR : **roman d'anticipation** science fiction novel.

anticipé, e [ãtisipe] adj early.

anticiper [3] [ãtisipe] <> vt to anticipate. <> vi : **anticiper (sur qqch)** to anticipate (sthg).

anticonformiste [ãtikɔ̃fɔrmist] adj & nmf [gen] non-conformist.

anticorps [ãtikɔr] nm antibody.

anticyclone [ãtisiklon] nm anticyclone.

antidater [3] [ãtidate] vt to backdate.

antidémarrage [ãtidemaraʒ] adj inv : **système antidémarrage** immobilizer.

antidépresseur [ãtidepresœr] nm & adj m antidepressant.

antidopage [ãtidɔpaʒ], **antidoping** [ãtidɔpiŋ] adj inv : **contrôle antidopage** dope test, drugs test.

antidote [ãtidɔt] nm antidote.

antigel [ãtiʒɛl] nm inv & adj inv antifreeze.

antillais, e [ãtijɛ, ɛz] adj West Indian. ▸ **Antillais, e** nm, f WestIndian.

Antilles [ãtij] nfpl : **les Antilles** the West Indies.

antilope [ãtilɔp] nf antelope.

antimilitariste [ãtimilitarist] nmf & adj antimilitarist.

antimite [ãtimit] adj inv : **boule antimite** mothball.

anti-mondialisation [ãtimɔ̃djalizasjɔ̃] adj inv anti-globalization.

anti-mondialiste [ãtimɔ̃djalist] adj antiglobalization.

antipathie [ãtipati] nf antipathy, hostility.

antipathique [ãtipatik] adj unpleasant ; **elle m'est antipathique** I dislike her, I don't like her.

antipelliculaire [ãtipelikyler] adj : **shampooing antipelliculaire** anti-dandruff shampoo.

antiquaire [ãtiker] nmf antique dealer.

antique [ãtik] adj **1.** [de l'antiquité - civilisation] ancient ; [- vase, objet] antique - **2.** [vieux] antiquated, ancient.

antiquité [ãtikite] nf **1.** [époque] : **l'Antiquité** antiquity - **2.** [objet] antique.

antirabique [ãtirabik] adj : **vaccin antirabique** rabies vaccine.

antiraciste [ãtirasist] adj & nmf antiracist.

antirides [ãtirid] adj inv anti-wrinkle.

antirouille [ãtiruj] adj inv [traitement] rust (avant n) ; [revêtement, peinture] rustproof.

antisèche [ãtiseʃ] nf arg scol crib, cheat sheet US, pony US.

antisémite [ãtisemit] <> nmf anti-Semite. <> adj anti-Semitic.

antiseptique [ãtiseptik] nm & adj antiseptic.

antisismique [ãtisismik] *adj* earthquake-proof.

antislash [ãtislaʃ] *nm* INFORM backslash.

antithèse [ãtitɛz] *nf* antithesis.

antitranspirant, e [ãtitrãspirã, ã] *adj* anti-perspirant.

antiviral, aux [ãtiviral, o] *nm* antivirus.

antivirus [ãtivirys] *nm* INFORM anti-virus software.

antivol [ãtivɔl] *nm inv* anti-theft device.

antre [ãtr] *nm* den, lair.

anus [anys] *nm* anus.

anxiété [ãksjete] *nf* anxiety.

anxieux, euse [ãksjø, øz] ⇔ *adj* anxious, worried ; **être anxieux de qqch** to be worried OU anxious about sthg ; **être anxieux de faire qqch** to be anxious to do sthg. ⇔ *nm, f* worrier.

aorte [aɔrt] *nf* aorta.

août [u(t)] *nm* August ; *voir aussi* **septembre.**

apaisement [apɛzmã] *nm* **1.** [moral] comfort - **2.** [de douleur] alleviation - **3.** [de tension, de crise] calming.

apaiser [4] [apeze] *vt* **1.** [personne] to calm down, to pacify - **2.** [conscience] to salve ; [douleur] to soothe ; [soif] to slake, to quench ; [faim] to assuage. ⇔ **s'apaiser** *vp* **1.** [personne] to calm down - **2.** [besoin] to be assuaged ; [tempête] to subside, to abate ; [douleur] to die down ; [scrupules] to be allayed.

apanage [apanaʒ] *nm sout* privilege ; **être l'apanage de qqn/qqch** to be the prerogative of sb/sthg.

aparté [aparte] *nm* **1.** THÉÂTRE aside - **2.** [conversation] private conversation ; **prendre qqn en aparté** to take sb aside.

apartheid [aparted] *nm* apartheid.

apathie [apati] *nf* apathy.

apathique [apatik] *adj* apathetic.

apatride [apatrid] *nmf* stateless person.

APEC [apɛk] (*abr de* **Association pour l'emploi des cadres**) *nf* employment agency for professionals and managers.

apercevoir [52] [apɛrsəvwar] *vt* [voir] to see, to catch sight of. ⇔ **s'apercevoir** *vp* : **s'apercevoir de qqch** to notice sthg ; **s'apercevoir que** to notice (that).

aperçu, e [apɛrsy] *pp* ▶ **apercevoir.** ⇔ **aperçu** *nm* general idea.

apéritif, ive [aperitif, iv] *adj* which whets the appetite. ⇔ **apéritif** *nm* aperitif ; **prendre l'apéritif** to have an aperitif, to have drinks (*before a meal*).

apesanteur [apəzãtœr] *nf* weightlessness.

à-peu-près [apøprɛ] *nm inv* approximation.

aphone [afɔn] *adj* voiceless.

aphrodisiaque [afrɔdizjak] *nm & adj* aphrodisiac.

aphte [aft] *nm* mouth ulcer.

apiculteur, trice [apikyltœr, tris] *nm, f* beekeeper.

apitoyer [13] [apitwaje] *vt* to move to pity. ⇔ **s'apitoyer** *vp* to feel pity ; **s'apitoyer sur** to feel sorry for.

ap. J.-C. (*abr écrite de* **après Jésus-Christ**) AD.

aplanir [32] [aplanir] *vt* **1.** [aplatir] to level - **2.** *fig* [difficulté, obstacle] to smooth away, to iron out.

aplatir [32] [aplatir] *vt* [gén] to flatten ; [couture] to press flat ; [cheveux] to smooth down.

aplomb [aplɔ̃] *nm* **1.** [stabilité] balance - **2.** [audace] nerve, cheek. ⇔ **d'aplomb** *loc adv* steady.

APN *nm abr de* **appareil photo numérique.**

apocalypse [apɔkalips] *nf* apocalypse.

apogée [apɔʒe] *nm* ASTRON apogee ; *fig* peak.

apolitique [apɔlitik] *adj* apolitical, unpolitical.

apologie [apɔlɔʒi] *nf* justification, apology.

apoplexie [apɔplɛksi] *nf* apoplexy.

apostrophe [apɔstrɔf] *nf* [signe graphique] apostrophe.

apostropher [3] [apɔstrɔfe] *vt* : **apostropher qqn** to speak rudely to sb.

apothéose [apɔteoz] *nf* **1.** [consécration] great honour UK OU honor US - **2.** [point culminant - d'un spectacle] grand finale ; [- d'une carrière] crowning glory.

apôtre [apotr] *nm* apostle, disciple.

apparaître [91] [aparɛtr] ⇔ *vi* **1.** [gén] to appear - **2.** [se dévoiler] to come to light. ⇔ *v impers* : **il apparaît que** it seems OU appears that.

apparat [apara] *nm* pomp ; **d'apparat** [dîner, habit] ceremonial.

appareil [aparɛj] *nm* **1.** [gén] device ; [électrique] appliance - **2.** [téléphone] phone, telephone ; **qui est à l'appareil?** who's speaking? - **3.** [avion] aircraft. ⇔ **appareil digestif** *nm* digestive system. ⇔ **appareil photo** *nm* camera ; **appareil photo numérique** digital camera.

appareillage [aparɛjaʒ] *nm* **1.** [équipement] equipment - **2.** NAUT getting under way.

appareiller [4] [apareje] ⇔ *vt* [assortir] to match up. ⇔ *vi* NAUT to get under way.

apparemment [aparamã] *adv* apparently.

apparence [aparãs] *nf* appearance. ⇔ **en apparence** *loc adv* seemingly, apparently.

apparent, e [aparã, ãt] *adj* **1.** [superficiel, illusoire] apparent - **2.** [visible] visible.

apparenté, e [aparãte] *adj* : **apparenté à** [personne] related to ; *fig* [ressemblant] similar to ; [affilié] affiliated to.

appariteur [aparitœr] *nm* porter *UK (in university).*

apparition [aparisjɔ̃] *nf* **1.** [gén] appearance - **2.** [vision - RELIG] vision ; [- de fantôme] apparition.

appart [apart] *(abr de* **appartement)** *nm fam* flat *UK,* apartment *US.*

appartement [apartəmã] *nm* flat *UK,* apartment *US.*

appartenir [40] [apartənir] *vi* **1.** [être la propriété de] : **appartenir à qqn** to belong to sb - **2.** [faire partie de] : **appartenir à qqch** to belong to sthg, to be a member of sthg - **3.** *fig* [dépendre de] : **il ne m'appartient pas de faire...** *sout* it's not up to me to do...

appartenu, e [apartəny] *pp inv* ▶ **appartenir.**

apparu, e [apary] *pp* ▶ **apparaître.**

appâter [3] [apate] *vt litt & fig* to lure.

appauvrir [32] [apovrir] *vt* to impoverish. ▶ **s'appauvrir** *vp* to grow poorer, to become impoverished.

appel [apɛl] *nm* **1.** [gén] call ; **faire appel à qqn** to appeal to sb ; **faire appel à qqch** [nécessiter] to call for sthg ; [avoir recours à] to call on sthg ; **appel (téléphonique)** (phone) call - **2.** DR appeal ; **faire appel** DR to appeal ; **sans appel** final - **3.** [pour vérifier - gén] roll-call ; SCOL registration - **4.** COMM : **appel d'offres** invitation to tender - **5.** [signe] : **faire un appel de phares** to flash *OU* blink *US* one's headlights.

appelé [aple] *nm* conscript, draftee *US.*

appeler [24] [aple] *vt* **1.** [gén] to call - **2.** [téléphoner] to ring *UK,* to call - **3.** [faire venir] to call for. ▶ **s'appeler** *vp* **1.** [se nommer] to be called ; **comment cela s'appelle?** what is it called? ; **il s'appelle Patrick** his name is Patrick, he's called Patrick - **2.** [se téléphoner] : **on s'appelle demain?** shall we talk tomorrow?

appendice [apɛ̃dis] *nm* appendix.

appendicite [apɛ̃disit] *nf* appendicitis.

appentis [apãti] *nm* lean-to.

appesantir [32] [apəzãtir] *vt* [démarche] to slow down. ▶ **s'appesantir** *vp* **1.** [s'alourdir] to become heavy - **2.** [insister] : **s'appesantir sur qqch** to dwell on sthg.

appétissant, e [apetisã, ãt] *adj* [nourriture] appetizing.

appétit [apeti] *nm* appetite ; **bon appétit!** enjoy your meal!

applaudir [32] [aplodir] ⬦ *vt* to applaud.

⬦ *vi* to clap, to applaud ; **applaudir à qqch** *fig* to applaud sthg ; **applaudir à tout rompre** *fig* to bring the house down.

applaudissements [aplodismã] *nmpl* applause *(U),* clapping *(U).*

applicable [aplikabl] *adj* : **applicable (à)** applicable (to).

application [aplikasjɔ̃] *nf* [gén & INFORM] application.

applique [aplik] *nf* wall lamp.

appliquer [3] [aplike] *vt* [gén] to apply ; [loi] to enforce. ▶ **s'appliquer** *vp* **1.** [s'étaler, se poser] : **cette peinture s'applique facilement** this paint goes on easily - **2.** [se concentrer] : **s'appliquer (à faire qqch)** to apply o.s. (to doing sthg).

appoint [apwɛ̃] *nm* **1.** [monnaie] change ; **faire l'appoint** to give the right money - **2.** [aide] help, support ; **d'appoint** [salaire, chauffage] extra ; **lit d'appoint** spare bed.

appointements [apwɛ̃tmã] *nmpl* salary *sg.*

apport [apɔr] *nm* **1.** [gén & FIN] contribution - **2.** [de chaleur] input.

apporter [3] [apɔrte] *vt* **1.** [gén] to bring ; **ça m'a beaucoup apporté** *fig* I got a lot from it - **2.** [raison, preuve] to provide, to give - **3.** [mettre - soin] to exercise ; [- attention] to give.

apposer [3] [apoze] *vt* **1.** [affiche] to put up - **2.** [signature] to append.

apposition [apozisjɔ̃] *nf* GRAMM apposition.

appréciable [apresjabl] *adj* **1.** [notable] appreciable - **2.** [précieux] : **un grand jardin, c'est appréciable!** I/we really appreciate having a big garden.

appréciation [apresjasjɔ̃] *nf* **1.** [de valeur] valuation ; [de distance, poids] estimation - **2.** [jugement] judgment - **3.** SCOL assessment.

apprécier [9] [apresje] *vt* **1.** [gén] to appreciate - **2.** [évaluer] to estimate, to assess.

appréhender [3] [apreãde] *vt* **1.** [arrêter] to arrest - **2.** [craindre] : **appréhender qqch/de faire qqch** to dread sthg/doing sthg.

appréhension [apreãsjɔ̃] *nf* apprehension.

apprendre [79] [aprãdr] *vt* **1.** [étudier] to learn ; **apprendre à faire qqch** to learn (how) to do sthg - **2.** [enseigner] to teach ; **apprendre qqch à qqn** to teach sb sthg ; **apprendre à qqn à faire qqch** to teach sb (how) to do sthg - **3.** [nouvelle] to hear of, to learn of ; **apprendre que** to hear that, to learn that ; **apprendre qqch à qqn** to tell sb of sthg.

apprenti, e [aprãti] *nm, f* [élève] apprentice ; *fig* beginner.

apprentissage [aprɑ̃tisaʒ] *nm* **1.** [de métier] apprenticeship - **2.** [formation] learning.

apprêter [4] [aprete] *vt* to prepare. ◆ **s'apprêter** *vp* **1.** [être sur le point] : **s'apprêter à faire qqch** to get ready to do sthg - **2.** [s'habiller] : **s'apprêter pour qqch** to dress up for sthg.

appris, e [apri, iz] *pp* ▶ **apprendre**.

apprivoiser [3] [aprivwaze] *vt* to tame.

approbateur, trice [aprɔbatœr, tris] *adj* approving.

approbation [aprɔbasjɔ̃] *nf* approval.

approchant, e [aprɔʃɑ̃, ɑ̃t] *adj* similar.

approche [aprɔʃ] *nf* [arrivée] approach ; **à l'approche des fêtes** as the Christmas holidays draw near ; **il a pressé le pas à l'approche de la maison** he quickened his step as he approached the house.

approcher [3] [aprɔʃe] ◇ *vt* **1.** [mettre plus près] to move near, to bring near ; **approcher qqch de qqn/qqch** to move sthg near (to) sb/sthg - **2.** [aborder] to go up to, to approach. ◇ *vi* to approach, to go/come near ; **approchez!** come nearer! ; **n'approchez pas!** keep ou stay away! ; **approcher de** [moment, fin] to approach. ◆ **s'approcher** *vp* to come/go near, to approach ; **s'approcher de qqn/qqch** to approach sb/sthg.

approfondir [32] [aprɔfɔ̃dir] *vt* **1.** [creuser] to make deeper - **2.** [développer] to go further into.

approprié, e [aprɔprije] *adj* : **approprié (à)** appropriate (to).

approprier [10] [aprɔprije] *vt* **1.** [adapter] to adapt - **2.** *Belgique* to clean. ◆ **s'approprier** *vp* [s'adjuger] to appropriate.

approuver [3] [apruve] *vt* [gén] to approve of.

approvisionnement [aprɔvizjɔnmɑ̃] *nm* supplies *pl*, stocks *pl*.

approvisionner [3] [aprɔvizjɔne] *vt* **1.** [compte en banque] to pay money into - **2.** [magasin, pays] to supply.

approximatif, ive [aprɔksimatif, iv] *adj* approximate, rough.

approximation [aprɔksimasjɔ̃] *nf* approximation.

approximativement [aprɔksimativmɑ̃] *adv* approximately, roughly.

appt *abr écrite de* **appartement**.

appui [apɥi] *nm* [soutien] support.

appui-tête [apɥitɛt] (*pl* **appuis-tête**) *nm* headrest.

appuyer [14] [apɥije] ◇ *vt* **1.** [poser] : **appuyer qqch sur/contre qqch** to lean sthg on/against sthg, to rest sthg on/against

sthg - **2.** [presser] : **appuyer qqch sur/contre** to press sthg on/against - **3.** *fig* [soutenir] to support. ◇ *vi* **1.** [reposer] : **appuyer sur** to lean ou rest on - **2.** [presser] to push ; **appuyer sur** [bouton] to press - **3.** *fig* [insister] : **appuyer sur** to stress - **4.** [se diriger] : **appuyer sur la** ou **à droite** to bear right. ◆ **s'appuyer** *vp* **1.** [se tenir] : **s'appuyer contre/sur** to lean against/on, to rest against/on - **2.** [se baser] : **s'appuyer sur** to rely on.

âpre [apr] *adj* **1.** [goût, discussion, combat] bitter - **2.** [ton, épreuve, critique] harsh - **3.** [concurrence] fierce.

après [aprɛ] ◇ *prép* **1.** [gén] after ; **après avoir mangé, ils...** after having eaten ou after they had eaten, they... ; **après cela** after that ; **après quoi** after which - **2.** [indiquant l'attirance, l'attachement, l'hostilité] : **soupirer après qqn** to yearn for sb ; **aboyer après qqn** to bark at sb. ◇ *adv* **1.** [temps] afterwards ; **un mois après** one month later ; **le mois d'après** the following ou next month - **2.** [lieu, dans un ordre, dans un rang] : **la rue d'après** the next street ; **c'est ma sœur qui vient après** my sister's next. ◆ **après coup** *loc adv* afterwards, after the event. ◆ **après que** *loc conj* (+ *indicatif*) after ; **je le verrai après qu'il aura fini** I'll see him after ou when he's finished ; **après qu'ils eurent dîné,...** after dinner ou after they had dined,... ◆ **après tout** *loc adv* after all. ◆ **d'après** *loc prép* according to ; **d'après moi** in my opinion ; **d'après lui** according to him. ◆ **et après** *loc adv* (*employée interrogativement*) **1.** [questionnement sur la suite] and then what? - **2.** [exprime l'indifférence] so what?

après-demain [apredmɛ̃] *adv* the day after tomorrow.

après-guerre [apreger] *nm* post-war years *pl* ; **d'après-guerre** post-war.

après-midi [apremidi] *nm inv* & *nf inv* afternoon.

après-rasage [aprerazaʒ] *nm* & *adj inv* aftershave.

après-ski [apreski] *nm* [chaussure] snowboot.

après-soleil [apresɔlɛj] *adj inv* after-sun (*avant n*).

après-vente [aprevɑ̃t] ▶ **service**.

à-propos [apropo] *nm inv* [de remarque] aptness ; **faire preuve d'à-propos** to show presence of mind.

APS (*abr de* **Advanced Photo System**) *nm* APS.

apte [apt] *adj* : **apte à qqch/à faire qqch** capable of sthg/of doing sthg ; **apte (au service)** MIL fit (for service).

aquagym [akwaʒim] *nf* aquarobics (*U*).

aquarelle [akwarɛl] *nf* watercolour *UK*, watercolor *US*.

aquarium [akwarjɔm] *nm* aquarium.

aquatique [akwatik] *adj* [plante, animal] aquatic ; [milieu, paysage] watery, marshy.

aqueduc [akdyk] *nm* aqueduct.

aqueux, euse [akø, øz] *adj* watery.

aquilin [akilɛ̃] ➤ **nez**.

arabe [arab] <> *adj* [peuple] Arab ; [désert] Arabian. <> *nm* [langue] Arabic. ➤ **Arabe** *nmf* Arab.

arabesque [arabɛsk] *nf* **1.** [ornement] arabesque - **2.** [ligne sinueuse] flourish.

Arabie [arabi] *nf* **:** l'Arabie Arabia ; l'Arabie Saoudite Saudi Arabia.

arabophone [arabɔfɔn] <> *adj* Arabic-speaking. <> *nmf* Arabic speaker.

arachide [araʃid] *nf* **1.** [plante] groundnut - **2.** [graine] peanut, groundnut *UK*.

araignée [arɛɲe] *nf* spider. ➤ **araignée de mer** *nf* spider crab.

arbalète [arbalɛt] *nf* crossbow.

arbitrage [arbitraʒ] *nm* **1.** [SPORT - gén] refereeing ; [- au tennis, cricket] umpiring - **2.** DR arbitration.

arbitraire [arbitrɛr] *adj* arbitrary.

arbitre [arbitr] *nm* **1.** [SPORT - gén] referee ; [- au tennis, cricket] umpire - **2.** [conciliateur] arbitrator.

arbitrer [3] [arbitre] *vt* **1.** [SPORT - gén] to referee ; [- au tennis, cricket] to umpire - **2.** [conflit] to arbitrate.

arbre [arbr] *nm* **1.** *fig & BOT* tree ; **arbre généalogique** family tree - **2.** [axe] shaft.

arbrisseau, x [arbriso] *nm* shrub.

arbuste [arbyst] *nm* shrub.

arc [ark] *nm* **1.** [arme] bow - **2.** [courbe] arc ; **arc de cercle** arc of a circle - **3.** ARCHIT arch.

arcade [arkad] *nf* **1.** ARCHIT arch ; arcades arcade *sg* - **2.** ANAT : **arcade sourcilière** arch of the eyebrows.

arc-bouter [3] [arkbute] ➤ **s'arc-bouter** *vp* to brace o.s.

arceau, x [arso] *nm* **1.** ARCHIT arch - **2.** [objet métallique] hoop.

arc-en-ciel [arkɑ̃sjɛl] (*pl* **arcs-en-ciel**) *nm* rainbow.

archaïque [arkaik] *adj* archaic.

arche [arʃ] *nf* ARCHIT arch.

archéologie [arkeɔlɔʒi] *nf* archaeology.

archéologique [arkeɔlɔʒik] *adj* archaeological.

archéologue [arkeɔlɔg] *nmf* archaeologist.

archet [arʃɛ] *nm* MUS bow.

archevêque [arʃəvɛk] *nm* archbishop.

archipel [arʃipɛl] *nm* archipelago.

architecte [arʃitɛkt] *nmf* architect ; **architecte d'intérieur** interior designer.

architecture [arʃitɛktyr] *nf* architecture ; *fig* structure.

archives [arʃiv] *nfpl* [de bureau] records ; [de musée] archives.

archiviste [arʃivist] *nmf* archivist.

arctique [arktik] *adj* Arctic ; **le cercle polaire arctique** the Arctic Circle. ➤ **Arctique** *nm* : l'arctique the Arctic.

ardemment [ardamɑ̃] *adv* fervently, passionately.

ardent, e [ardɑ̃, ɑ̃t] *adj* **1.** [soleil] blazing - **2.** [soif, fièvre] raging ; [passion] burning.

ardeur [ardœr] *nf* **1.** [vigueur] fervour *UK*, fervor *US*, enthusiasm - **2.** [chaleur] blazing heat.

ardoise [ardwaz] *nf* slate.

ardu, e [ardy] *adj* [travail] arduous ; [problème] difficult.

are [ar] *nm* 100 square metres.

arène [arɛn] *nf* arena. ➤ **arènes** *nfpl* [romaines] amphitheatre *UK*, amphitheater *US sg* ; [pour corridas] bullring *sg*.

arête [arɛt] *nf* **1.** [de poisson] bone - **2.** [du nez] bridge.

argent [arʒɑ̃] *nm* **1.** [métal, couleur] silver - **2.** [monnaie] money ; **argent liquide** (ready) cash ; **argent de poche** pocket money *UK*, allowance *US*.

argenté, e [arʒɑ̃te] *adj* silvery, silver.

argenterie [arʒɑ̃tri] *nf* silverware.

Argentine [arʒɑ̃tin] *nf* : l'Argentine Argentina.

argile [arʒil] *nf* clay.

argileux, euse [arʒilø, øz] *adj* clayey.

argot [argo] *nm* slang.

argotique [argɔtik] *adj* slang (*avant n*), slangy.

argument [argymɑ̃] *nm* argument.

argumentation [argymɑ̃tasjɔ̃] *nf* argumentation.

argus [argys] *nm* : **coté à l'argus** rated in the guide to secondhand car prices.

aride [arid] *adj* *litt & fig* arid ; [travail] thankless.

aristocrate [aristɔkrat] *nmf* aristocrat.

aristocratie [aristɔkrasi] *nf* aristocracy.

arithmétique [aritmetik] *nf* arithmetic.

armateur [armatœr] *nm* ship owner.

armature [armatyr] *nf* **1.** *fig & CONSTR* framework - **2.** [de parapluie] frame ; [de soutien-gorge] underwiring.

arme [arm] *nf* *litt & fig* weapon ; **arme blanche** blade ; **arme à feu** firearm. ➤ **armes** *nfpl* **1.** [armée] : **les armes** the army

- **2.** [blason] coat of arms sg ; **partir avec armes et bagages** to leave taking everything.

armée [arme] nf army ; **l'armée de l'air** the air force ; **l'armée de terre** the army. ➤ **Armée du salut** nf : **l'Armée du salut** the Salvation Army.

armement [arməmɑ̃] nm [MIL - de personne] arming ; [- de pays] armament ; [- ensemble d'armes] arms pl ; **la course aux armements** the arms race.

Arménie [armeni] nf : **l'Arménie** Armenia.

armer [3] [arme] vt **1.** [pourvoir en armes] to arm ; **être armé pour qqch/pour faire qqch** fig [préparé] to be equipped for sthg/to do sthg - **2.** [fusil] to cock - **3.** [appareil photo] to wind on - **4.** [navire] to fit out.

armistice [armistis] nm armistice.

armoire [armwar] nf [gén] cupboard UK, closet US ; [garde-robe] wardrobe ; **c'est une armoire à glace!** fam fig he's built like a tank! ; **armoire à pharmacie** medicine cabinet.

armoiries [armwari] nfpl coat of arms sg.

armure [armyr] nf armour UK, armor US.

armurier [armyrje] nm [d'armes à feu] gunsmith ; [d'armes blanches] armourer UK, armorer US.

arnaque [arnak] nf fam rip-off.

arnaquer [3] [arnake] vt fam to do UK, to swindle ; **se faire arnaquer** to be had.

aromate [arɔmat] nm [épice] spice ; [fine herbe] herb.

arôme [arom] nm **1.** [gén] aroma ; [de fleur, parfum] fragrance - **2.** [goût] flavour UK, flavor US.

arpège [arpɛʒ] nm arpeggio.

arpenter [3] [arpɑ̃te] vt [marcher] to pace up and down.

arqué, e [arke] adj **1.** [objet] curved - **2.** [jambe] bow (avant n), bandy ; [nez] hooked ; [sourcil] arched.

arr. abr écrite de **arrondissement**.

arrache-pied [araʃpje] ➤ **d'arrache-pied** loc adv : **travailler d'arrache-pied** to work away furiously.

arracher [3] [araʃe] vt **1.** [extraire - plante] to pull up ou out ; [- dent] to extract - **2.** [déchirer - page] to tear off ou out ; [- chemise, bras] to tear off - **3.** [prendre] : **arracher qqch à qqn** to snatch sthg from sb ; [susciter] to wring sthg from sb - **4.** [soustraire] : **arracher qqn à** [milieu, lieu] to drag sb away from ; [lit, sommeil] to drag sb from ; [habitude, torpeur] to force sb out of ; [mort, danger] to snatch sb from.

arrangeant, e [arɑ̃ʒɑ̃, ɑ̃t] adj obliging.

arrangement [arɑ̃ʒmɑ̃] nm **1.** [gén] arrangement - **2.** [accord] agreement, arrangement.

arranger [17] [arɑ̃ʒe] vt **1.** [gén] to arrange - **2.** [convenir à] to suit - **3.** [régler] to settle - **4.** [améliorer] to sort out - **5.** [réparer] to fix. ➤ **s'arranger** vp to come to an agreement ; **s'arranger pour faire qqch** to manage to do sthg ; **arrangez-vous pour être là à cinq heures** make sure you're there at five o'clock ; **cela va s'arranger** things will work out.

arrdt. abr de **arrondissement**.

arrestation [arɛstasjɔ̃] nf arrest ; **être en état d'arrestation** to be under arrest.

arrêt [arɛ] nm **1.** [d'un mouvement] stopping ; **à l'arrêt** [véhicule] stationary ; [machine] (switched) off ; **tomber en arrêt devant qqch** to stop dead in front of sthg - **2.** [interruption] interruption ; **sans arrêt** [sans interruption] non-stop ; [sans relâche] constantly, continually ; **être en arrêt maladie** to be on sick leave ; **arrêt du travail** stoppage - **3.** [station] : **arrêt (d'autobus)** (bus) stop - **4.** DR decision, judgment.

arrêté [arete] nm ADMIN order, decree.

arrêter [4] [arete] ➤ vt **1.** [gén] to stop - **2.** INFORM [ordinateur] to shut down - **3.** [cesser] : **arrêter de faire qqch** to stop doing sthg ; **arrêter de fumer** to stop smoking - **4.** [voleur] to arrest. ➤ vi to stop. ➤ **s'arrêter** vp to stop ; **s'arrêter à qqch** : **il ne s'arrête pas à ces détails** he's not going to dwell on these details ; **s'arrêter de faire** to stop doing.

arrhes [ar] nfpl deposit sg.

arrière [arjɛr] ➤ adj inv back, rear ; **roue arrière** rear ou back wheel ; **marche arrière** reverse gear. ➤ nm **1.** [partie postérieure] back ; **à l'arrière** at the back UK, in back US - **2.** SPORT back. ➤ **en arrière** loc adv **1.** [dans la direction opposée] back, backwards ; **faire un pas en arrière** to take a step back ou backwards - **2.** [derrière, à la traîne] behind ; **rester en arrière** to lag behind.

arriéré, e [arjere] adj [mentalité, pays] backward. ➤ **arriéré** nm arrears pl.

arrière-boutique [arjɛrbutik] (pl arrière-boutiques) nf back shop.

arrière-garde [arjɛrgard] (pl arrière-gardes) nf rearguard.

arrière-goût [arjɛrgu] (pl arrière-goûts) nm aftertaste.

arrière-grand-mère [arjɛrgrɑ̃mɛr] (pl arrière-grands-mères) nf great-grandmother.

arrière-grand-père [arjɛrgrɑ̃pɛr] (pl arrière-grands-pères) nm great-grandfather.

arrière-pays [arjɛrpei] nm inv hinterland.

arrière-pensée [arjɛrpɑ̃se] (*pl* **arrière-pensées**) *nf* [raison intéressée] ulterior motive.

arrière-plan [arjɛrplɑ̃] (*pl* **arrière-plans**) *nm* background.

arrière-saison [arjɛrsɛzɔ̃] (*pl* **arrière-saisons**) *nf* late autumn.

arrière-train [arjɛrtrɛ̃] (*pl* **arrière-trains**) *nm* hindquarters *pl*.

arrimer [3] [arime] *vt* **1.** [attacher] to secure - **2.** NAUT to stow.

arrivage [arivaʒ] *nm* [de marchandises] consignment, delivery.

arrivée [arive] *nf* **1.** [venue] arrival - **2.** TECHNOL inlet.

arriver [3] [arive] ◇ *vi* **1.** [venir] to arrive ; **j'arrive!** (I'm) coming! ; **arriver à Paris** to arrive in OU reach Paris ; **l'eau m'arrivait aux genoux** the water came up to my knees - **2.** [parvenir] : **arriver à faire qqch** to manage to do sthg, to succeed in doing sthg ; **il n'arrive pas à faire ses devoirs** he can't do his homework. ◇ *v impers* to happen ; **il arrive que** (+ *subjonctif*) : **il arrive qu'il soit en retard** he is sometimes late ; **il arrive à tout le monde de se décourager** we all get fed up sometimes ; **il arrive à tout le monde de se tromper** anyone can make a mistake ; **il lui arrive d'oublier quel jour on est** he sometimes forgets what day it is ; **quoi qu'il arrive** whatever happens.

arrivisme [arivism] *nm péj* ambition.

arrobas, arobas [arɔbas] *nf* [dans une adresse électronique] at.

arrogance [arɔgɑ̃s] *nf* arrogance.

arrogant, e [arɔgɑ̃, ɑ̃t] *adj* arrogant.

arroger [17] [arɔʒe] ▸ **s'arroger** *vp* : **s'arroger le droit de faire qqch** to take it upon o.s. to do sthg.

arrondi [arɔ̃di] *nm* [de jupe] hemline.

arrondir [32] [arɔ̃dir] *vt* **1.** [forme] to make round - **2.** [chiffre - au-dessus] to round up ; [- en dessous] to round down.

arrondissement [arɔ̃dismɑ̃] *nm* ADMIN arrondissement (*administrative division of a département or city*).

arroser [3] [aroze] *vt* **1.** [jardin] to water, to spray - **2.** *fam* [célébrer] to celebrate.

arrosoir [arozwar] *nm* watering can.

arsenal, aux [arsənal, o] *nm* **1.** [de navires] naval dockyard - **2.** [d'armes] arsenal.

arsenic [arsənik] *nm* arsenic.

art [ar] *nm* art ; **le septième art** cinema. ▸ **arts** *nmpl* : **arts et métiers** *state-funded institution offering vocational courses by correspondence or evening classes* ; **arts martiaux** martial arts.

art. *abr écrite de* **article.**

Arte [arte] *npr Franco-German cultural television channel.*

artère [arter] *nf* **1.** ANAT artery - **2.** [rue] arterial road *UK*, main road *US*.

artériel, elle [arterjɛl] *adj* arterial.

artériosclérose [arterjoskleroz] *nf* arteriosclerosis.

arthrite [artrit] *nf* arthritis.

arthrose [artroz] *nf* osteoarthritis.

artichaut [artiʃo] *nm* artichoke.

article [artikl] *nm* **1.** [gén] article ; **article de fond** feature - **2.** [sujet] point ; **à l'article de la mort** at death's door.

articulation [artikylasjɔ̃] *nf* **1.** ANAT & TECHNOL joint - **2.** [prononciation] articulation.

articuler [3] [artikyle] *vt* **1.** [prononcer] to articulate - **2.** ANAT & TECHNOL to articulate, to joint.

artifice [artifis] *nm* **1.** [moyen astucieux] clever device ou trick - **2.** [tromperie] trick.

artificiel, elle [artifisjɛl] *adj* artificial.

artillerie [artijri] *nf* MIL artillery.

artisan, e [artizɑ̃, an] *nm, f* craftsman (*f* craftswoman).

artisanal, e, aux [artizanal, o] *adj* craft (*avant n*).

artisanat [artizana] *nm* [métier] craft ; [classe] craftsmen.

artiste [artist] *nmf* **1.** [créateur] artist ; **artiste peintre** painter - **2.** [interprète] performer.

artistique [artistik] *adj* artistic.

as¹ [a] ▸ **avoir.**

as² [as] *nm* **1.** [carte] ace - **2.** [champion] star, ace.

ascendant, e [asɑ̃dɑ̃, ɑ̃t] *adj* rising. ▸ **ascendant** *nm* **1.** [influence] influence, power - **2.** ASTROL ascendant.

ascenseur [asɑ̃sœr] *nm* **1.** [in a building] lift *UK*, elevator *US* - **2.** INFORM scroll bar.

ascension [asɑ̃sjɔ̃] *nf* **1.** [de montagne] ascent - **2.** [progression] rise. ▸ **Ascension** *nf* : **l'Ascension** Ascension (Day).

ascète [asɛt] *nmf* ascetic.

asiatique [azjatik] *adj* **1.** [de l'Asie en général] Asian - **2.** [d'Extrême-Orient] oriental. ▸ **Asiatique** *nmf* Asian.

Asie [azi] *nf* : **l'Asie** Asia ; **l'Asie du Sud-Est** Southeast Asia.

asile [azil] *nm* **1.** [refuge] refuge - **2.** POLIT : **demander/accorder l'asile politique** to seek/to grant political asylum - **3.** *vieilli* [psychiatrique] asylum.

asocial, e, aux [asɔsjal, o] ◇ *adj* antisocial. ◇ *nm, f* social misfit.

aspect [aspɛ] *nm* **1.** [apparence] appearance ; d'aspect agréable nice-looking ; cette couleur donne à la pièce un aspect terne this colour makes the room look dull - **2.** LING aspect.

asperge [aspɛrʒ] *nf* [légume] asparagus.

asperger [17] [aspɛrʒe] *vt* : asperger qqch de qqch to spray sthg with sthg ; asperger qqn de qqch [arroser] to spray sb with sthg ; [éclabousser] to splash sb with sthg.

aspérité [asperite] *nf* [du sol] bump.

asphalte [asfalt] *nm* asphalt.

asphyxier [9] [asfiksje] *vt* **1.** MÉD to asphyxiate, to suffocate - **2.** *fig* [économie] to paralyse *UK*, to paralyze *US*.

aspic [aspik] *nm* [vipère] asp.

aspirant, e [aspirã, ãt] *adj* : hotte aspirante cooker hood *UK*, extractor hood ; pompe aspirante suction pump. ➤ **aspirant** *nm* [armée] ≃ officer cadet ; [marine] ≃ midshipman.

aspirateur [aspiratœr] *nm* Hoover® *UK*, vacuum cleaner ; passer l'aspirateur to do the vacuuming ou hoovering *UK*.

aspiration [aspirasjɔ̃] *nf* **1.** [souffle] inhalation - **2.** TECHNOL suction. ➤ **aspirations** *nfpl* aspirations.

aspirer [3] [aspire] *vt* **1.** [air] to inhale ; [liquide] to suck up - **2.** TECHNOL to suck up, to draw up - **3.** [désirer] : aspirer à qqch/à faire qqch to aspire to sthg/to do sthg.

aspirine [aspirin] *nf* aspirin.

assagir [32] [asaʒir] *vt* to quieten down.

assaillant, e [asajɑ̃, ɑ̃t] *nm, f* assaillant, attacker.

assaillir [47] [asajir] *vt* to attack, to assault ; assaillir qqn de qqch *fig* to assail ou bombard sb with sthg.

assainir [32] [asenir] *vt* **1.** [logement] to clean up - **2.** [eau] to purify - **3.** ÉCON to rectify, to stabilize.

assaisonnement [asezɔnmã] *nm* [sauce] dressing ; [condiments] seasoning.

assaisonner [3] [asezɔne] *vt* [salade] to dress ; [viande, plat] to season.

assassin, e [asasɛ̃, in] *adj* provocative. ➤ **assassin** *nm* [gén] murderer ; POLIT assassin.

assassinat [asasina] *nm* [gén] murder ; POLIT assassination.

assassiner [3] [asasine] *vt* [tuer - gén] to murder ; POLIT to assassinate.

assaut [aso] *nm* [attaque] assault, attack ; prendre d'assaut [lieu] to storm ; [personne] to attack.

assécher [18] [aseʃe] *vt* to drain.

ASSEDIC, Assedic [asedik] (*abr de* Association pour l'emploi dans l'industrie et le commerce) *nfpl French unemployment insurance scheme* ; toucher les ASSEDIC to get unemployment benefit *UK* ou welfare *US*.

assemblage [asɑ̃blaʒ] *nm* [gén] assembly.

assemblée [asɑ̃ble] *nf* **1.** [réunion] meeting - **2.** [public] gathering - **3.** ADMIN & POLIT assembly ; l'Assemblée nationale *lower house of the French parliament*.

assembler [asɑ̃ble] *vt* **1.** [monter] to put together - **2.** [réunir - objets] to gather (together) - **3.** [personnes - gén] to bring together, to assemble. ➤ **s'assembler** *vp* to gather.

assener [19] [asəne], **asséner** [18] [asene] *vt* : assener un coup à qqn [frapper] to strike sb, to deal sb a blow.

assentiment [asɑ̃timã] *nm* assent.

asseoir [65] [aswar] ⟨⟩ *vt* **1.** [sur un siège] to put - **2.** [fondations] to lay - **3.** *fig* [réputation] to establish. ⟨⟩ *vi* : faire asseoir qqn to seat sb, to ask sb to take a seat. ➤ **s'asseoir** *vp* to sit (down).

assermenté, e [asɛrmãte] *adj* [fonctionnaire, expert] sworn.

assertion [asɛrsjɔ̃] *nf* assertion.

assesseur [asesœr] *nm* assessor.

assez [ase] *adv* **1.** [suffisamment] enough ; assez grand pour qqch/pour faire qqch big enough for sthg/to do sthg ; assez de enough ; assez de lait/chaises enough milk/chairs ; en avoir assez de qqn/qqch to have had enough of sb/sthg, to be fed up with sb/sthg - **2.** [plutôt] quite, rather.

assidu, e [asidy] *adj* **1.** [élève] diligent - **2.** [travail] painstaking - **3.** [empressé] : assidu (auprès de qqn) attentive (to sb).

assiduité [asidyite] *nf* **1.** [zèle] diligence - **2.** [fréquence] : avec assiduité regularly. ➤ **assiduités** *nfpl péj & sout* attentions.

assiéger [22] [asjeʒe] *vt litt & fig* to besiege.

assiette [asjɛt] *nf* **1.** [vaisselle] plate ; assiette creuse ou à soupe soup plate ; assiette à dessert dessert plate ; assiette plate ou plate dinner plate - **2.** [d'impôt] base - **3.** CULIN : assiette anglaise assorted cold meats *pl UK*, cold cuts *pl US*.

assigner [3] [asiɲe] *vt* DR : assigner qqn en justice to issue a writ against sb.

assimiler [3] [asimile] *vt* **1.** [aliment, connaissances] to assimilate - **2.** [confondre] : assimiler qqch (à qqch) to liken sthg (to sthg) ; assimiler qqn à qqn to compare sb to ou with sb.

assis, e [asi, iz] ⟨⟩ *pp* ➤ asseoir. ⟨⟩ *adj* sitting, seated ; place assise seat.

assise *nf* [base] seat, seating. ◆ **assises** *nfpl* **1.** DR : **(cour d')assises** crown court *UK*, circuit court *US* - **2.** [congrès] conference *sg.*

assistance [asistɑ̃s] *nf* **1.** [aide] assistance ; **l'Assistance publique** *French authority which manages the social services and state-owned hospitals* - **2.** [auditoire] audience.

assistant, e [asistɑ̃, ɑ̃t] *nm, f* **1.** [auxiliaire] assistant ; **assistante sociale** social worker - **2.** UNIV assistant lecturer.

assister [3] [asiste] ◇ *vi* : **assister à qqch** to be at sthg, to attend sthg. ◇ *vt* to assist.

association [asɔsjasjɔ̃] *nf* **1.** [gén] association - **2.** [union] society, association ; **association humanitaire** charity organization ; **association sportive** sports club - **3.** COMM partnership.

associé, e [asɔsje] ◇ *adj* associated. ◇ *nm, f* **1.** [collaborateur] associate - **2.** [actionnaire] partner.

associer [9] [asɔsje] *vt* **1.** [personnes] to bring together - **2.** [idées] to associate - **3.** [faire participer] : **associer qqn à qqch** [inclure] to bring sb in on sthg ; [prendre pour partenaire] to make sb a partner in sthg. ◆ **s'associer** *vp* **1.** [prendre part] : **s'associer à qqch** [participer] to join ou participate in sthg ; [partager] to share sthg - **2.** [collaborer] : **s'associer à** ou **avec qqn** to join forces with sb.

assoiffé, e [aswafe] *adj* thirsty ; **assoiffé de pouvoir** *fig* power-hungry.

assombrir [32] [asɔ̃brir] *vt* **1.** [plonger dans l'obscurité] to darken - **2.** *fig* [attrister] to cast a shadow over. ◆ **s'assombrir** *vp* **1.** [devenir sombre] to grow dark - **2.** *fig* [s'attrister] to darken.

assommer [3] [asɔme] *vt* **1.** [frapper] to knock out - **2.** [ennuyer] to bore stiff.

Assomption [asɔ̃psjɔ̃] *nf* : **l'Assomption** the Assumption.

assorti, e [asɔrti] *adj* [accordé] : **bien assorti** well-matched ; **mal assorti** ill-matched ; **une cravate assortie au costume** a tie which matches the suit.

assortiment [asɔrtimɑ̃] *nm* assortment, selection.

assortir [32] [asɔrtir] *vt* [objets] : **assortir qqch à qqch** to match sthg to ou with sthg.

assoupi, e [asupi] *adj* [endormi] dozing.

assoupir [32] [asupir] *vt sout* [enfant] to send to sleep. ◆ **s'assoupir** *vp* [s'endormir] to doze off.

assouplir [32] [asuplir] *vt* **1.** [corps] to make supple - **2.** [matière] to soften - **3.** [règlement] to relax.

assourdir [32] [asurdir] *vt* **1.** [rendre sourd] to deafen - **2.** [amortir] to deaden, to muffle.

assouvir [32] [asuvir] *vt* to satisfy.

assujettir [32] [asyʒetir] *vt* **1.** [peuple] to subjugate - **2.** [soumettre] : **assujettir qqn à qqch** to subject sb to sthg.

assumer [3] [asyme] *vt* **1.** [fonction - exercer] to carry out - **2.** [risque, responsabilité] to accept - **3.** [condition] to come to terms with - **4.** [frais] to meet.

assurance [asyrɑ̃s] *nf* **1.** [gén] assurance - **2.** [contrat] insurance ; **assurance maladie** health insurance ; **assurance tous risques** AUTO comprehensive insurance ; **assurance-vie** life assurance *UK*, life insurance *US*.

assuré, e [asyre] *nm, f* policy holder ; **assuré social** National Insurance contributor *UK*, Social Security contributor *US*.

assurément [asyremɑ̃] *adv sout* certainly.

assurer [3] [asyre] *vt* **1.** [promettre] : **assurer à qqn que** to assure sb (that) ; **assurer qqn de qqch** to assure sb of sthg - **2.** [permanence, liaison] to provide - **3.** COMM to insure. ◆ **s'assurer** *vp* **1.** [vérifier] : **s'assurer que** to make sure (that) ; **s'assurer de qqch** to ensure sthg, to make sure of sthg - **2.** COMM : **s'assurer (contre qqch)** to insure o.s. (against sthg) - **3.** [obtenir] : **s'assurer qqch** to secure sthg.

astérisque [asterisk] *nm* asterisk.

asthme [asm] *nm* MÉD asthma.

asticot [astiko] *nm* maggot.

astiquer [3] [astike] *vt* to polish.

astre [astr] *nm* star.

astreignant, e [astrɛɲɑ̃, ɑ̃t] *adj* demanding.

astreindre [81] [astrɛ̃dr] *vt* : **astreindre qqn à qqch** to subject sb to sthg ; **astreindre qqn à faire qqch** to compel sb to do sthg.

astreint, e [astrɛ̃, ɛ̃t] *pp* ► **astreindre**.

astringent, e [astrɛ̃ʒɑ̃, ɑ̃t] *adj* astringent.

astrologie [astrɔlɔʒi] *nf* astrology.

astrologue [astrɔlɔg] *nm* astrologer.

astronaute [astronot] *nmf* astronaut.

astronautique [astronotik] *nf* astronautics (U).

astronomie [astronɔmi] *nf* astronomy.

astronomique [astronɔmik] *adj* astronomical.

astrophysicien, enne [astrofisisjɛ̃, ɛn] *nm, f* astrophysicist.

astuce [astys] *nf* **1.** [ruse] (clever) trick - **2.** [ingéniosité] shrewdness (U).

astucieux, euse [astysjø, øz] *adj* **1.** [idée] clever - **2.** [personne] shrewd.

asymétrique [asimetrik] *adj* asymmetric, asymmetrical.

atelier [atəlje] *nm* **1.** [d'artisan] workshop - **2.** [de peintre] studio.

athée [ate] ◇ *nmf* atheist. ◇ *adj* atheistic.

Athènes [atɛn] *npr* Athens.

athlète [atlɛt] *nmf* athlete.

athlétisme [atletism] *nm* athletics (U) UK, track and field US.

atlantique [atlɑ̃tik] *adj* Atlantic. ▬ **Atlantique** *nm* : l'Atlantique the Atlantic (Ocean).

atlas [atlas] *nm* atlas.

atmosphère [atmɔsfɛr] *nf* atmosphere.

atome [atom] *nm* atom.

atomique [atɔmik] *adj* 1. [gén] nuclear - 2. CHIM & PHYS atomic.

atomiseur [atɔmizœr] *nm* spray.

atone [atɔn] *adj* [inexpressif] lifeless.

atout [atu] *nm* 1. [carte] trump ; atout cœur/pique/trèfle/carreau hearts/spades/clubs/diamonds are trumps - 2. *fig* [ressource] asset, advantage.

âtre [atr] *nm litt* hearth.

atroce [atrɔs] *adj* 1. [crime] atrocious, dreadful - 2. [souffrance] horrific, atrocious.

atrocité [atrɔsite] *nf* 1. [horreur] atrocity - 2. [calomnie] insult.

atrophier [9] [atrɔfje] ▬ **s'atrophier** *vp* to atrophy.

attabler [3] [atable] ▬ **s'attabler** *vp* to sit down (at the table).

attachant, e [ataʃɑ̃, ɑ̃t] *adj* lovable.

attache [ataʃ] *nf* [lien] fastening. ▬ **attaches** *nfpl* links, connections.

attaché, e [ataʃe] *nm, f* attaché ; attaché de presse [diplomatique] press attaché ; [d'organisme, d'entreprise] press officer.

attaché-case [ataʃekɛz] (*pl* attachés-cases) *nm* attaché case.

attachement [ataʃmɑ̃] *nm* attachment.

attacher [3] [ataʃe] ◇ *vt* 1. [lier] : attacher qqch (à) to fasten ou tie sth (to) ; *fig* [associer] to attach sth (to) - 2. [paquet] to tie up - 3. [lacet] to do up ; [ceinture de sécurité] to fasten. ◇ *vi* CULIN : attacher (à) to stick (to). ▬ **s'attacher** *vp* 1. [émotionnellement] : s'attacher à qqn/qqch to become attached to sb/sth - 2. [se fermer] to fasten ; s'attacher avec ou par qqch to do up ou fasten with sth - 3. [s'appliquer] : s'attacher à qqch/à faire qqch to devote o.s. to sth/to doing sth, to apply o.s. to sth/to doing sth.

attaquant, e [atakɑ̃, ɑ̃t] *nm, f* attacker.

attaque [atak] *nf* [gén & MÉD] attack ; *fig* : attaque contre qqn/qqch attack on sb/sth.

attaquer [3] [atake] *vt* 1. [gén] to attack - 2. [DR - personne] to take to court ; [- jugement] to contest - 3. *fam* [plat] to tuck into. ▬ **s'attaquer** *vp* 1. [combattre] : s'attaquer à qqn to attack sb - 2. *fig* : s'attaquer à qqch [tâche] to tackle sth.

attardé, e [atarde] *adj* 1. [idées] outdated - 2. [passants] late - 3. [enfant] backward.

attarder [3] [atarde] ▬ **s'attarder** *vp* : s'attarder sur qqch to dwell on sth ; s'attarder à faire qqch to stay on to do sth, to stay behind to do sth.

atteindre [8] [atɛ̃dr] *vt* 1. [situation, objectif] to reach - 2. [toucher] to hit - 3. [affecter] to affect.

atteint, e [atɛ̃, ɛ̃t] ◇ *pp* ▬ atteindre. ◇ *adj* [malade] : être atteint de to be suffering from. ▬ **atteinte** *nf* 1. [préjudice] : porter atteinte à to undermine ; hors d'atteinte [hors de portée] out of reach ; [inattaquable] beyond reach - 2. [effet] effect.

attelage [atlaʒ] *nm* [chevaux] team.

atteler [24] [atle] *vt* [animaux, véhicules] to hitch up ; [wagons] to couple.

attelle [atɛl] *nf* splint.

attenant, e [atnɑ̃, ɑ̃t] *adj* : attenant (à qqch) adjoining (sth).

attendre [73] [atɑ̃dr] ◇ *vt* 1. [gén] to wait for ; le déjeuner nous attend lunch is ready ; attendre que (+ subjonctif) : attendre que la pluie s'arrête to wait for the rain to stop ; faire attendre qqn [personne] to keep sb waiting - 2. [espérer] : attendre qqch (de qqn/qqch) to expect sth (from sb/sth) - 3. [suj: surprise, épreuve] to be in store for. ◇ *vi* to wait ; attends! hang on! ▬ **s'attendre** *vp* : s'attendre à to expect. ▬ **en attendant** *loc adv* 1. [pendant ce temps] meanwhile, in the meantime - 2. [quand même] all the same.

attendrir [32] [atɑ̃drir] *vt* 1. [viande] to tenderize - 2. [personne] to move. ▬ **s'attendrir** *vp* : s'attendrir (sur qqn/qqch) to be moved (by sb/sth).

attendrissant, e [atɑ̃drisɑ̃, ɑ̃t] *adj* moving, touching.

attendu, e [atɑ̃dy] *pp* ▬ attendre. ▬ **attendu que** *loc conj* since, considering that.

attentat [atɑ̃ta] *nm* attack ; attentat à la bombe bomb attack, bombing.

attentat-suicide [atɑ̃tasɥisid] (*pl* attentats-suicides) *nm* suicide attack ; [à la bombe] suicide bombing.

attente [atɑ̃t] *nf* 1. [période] wait ; en attente in abeyance - 2. [espoir] expectation ; répondre aux attentes de qqn to live up to sb's expectations.

attenter [3] [atɑ̃te] *vi* : attenter à [liberté,

droit] to violate ; **attenter à ses jours** to attempt suicide ; **attenter à la vie de qqn** to make an attempt on sb's life.

attentif, ive [atɑ̃tif, iv] *adj* [auditoire] : **attentif (à qqch)** attentive (to sthg).

attention [atɑ̃sjɔ̃] <> *nf* **1.** [concentration] attention ; **faire attention** to pay attention to - **2.** [prudence] attention ; **à l'attention de** for the attention of ; **faire attention à** be careful of. <> *interj* watch out!, be careful!

attentionné, e [atɑ̃sjɔne] *adj* thoughtful.

attentivement [atɑ̃tivmɑ̃] *adv* attentively, carefully.

atténuer [7] [atenɥe] *vt* [douleur] to ease ; [propos, ton] to tone down ; [lumière] to dim, to subdue ; [bruit] to quieten. **s'atténuer** *vp* [lumière] to dim, to fade ; [bruit] to fade ; [douleur] to ease.

atterrer [4] [atere] *vt* to stagger.

atterrir [32] [aterir] *vi* to land ; **atterrir dans qqch** *fig* to land up in sthg.

atterrissage [aterisaʒ] *nm* landing.

attestation [atɛstasjɔ̃] *nf* [certificat] certificate.

attester [3] [atɛste] *vt* **1.** [confirmer] to vouch for, to testify to - **2.** [certifier] to attest.

attirail [atiraj] *nm fam* [équipement] gear.

attirance [atirɑ̃s] *nf* attraction.

attirant, e [atirɑ̃, ɑ̃t] *adj* attractive.

attirer [3] [atire] *vt* **1.** [gén] to attract - **2.** [amener vers soi] : **attirer qqn à/vers soi** to draw sb to/towards one - **3.** [provoquer] : **attirer des ennuis à qqn** to cause trouble for sb. **s'attirer** *vp* : **s'attirer qqch** to bring sthg on o.s.

attiser [3] [atize] *vt* **1.** [feu] to poke - **2.** *fig* [haine] to stir up.

attitré, e [atitre] *adj* **1.** [habituel] usual - **2.** [titulaire - fournisseur] by appointment ; [- représentant] accredited.

attitude [atityd] *nf* **1.** [comportement, approche] attitude - **2.** [posture] posture.

attouchement [atuʃmɑ̃] *nm* caress.

attractif, ive [atraktif, iv] *adj* **1.** [force] magnetic - **2.** [prix] attractive.

attraction [atraksjɔ̃] *nf* **1.** [gén] attraction - **2.** [force] : **attraction magnétique** magnetic force. **attractions** *nfpl* **1.** [jeux] amusements - **2.** [spectacle] attractions.

attrait [atrɛ] *nm* **1.** [séduction] appeal - **2.** [intérêt] attraction.

attrape-nigaud [atrapnigo] (*pl* **attrape-nigauds**) *nm* con.

attraper [3] [atrape] *vt* **1.** [gén] to catch - **2.** *fam* [gronder] to tell off - **3.** *fam* [avoir] to get.

attrayant, e [atrɛjɑ̃, ɑ̃t] *adj* attractive.

attribuer [7] [atribɥe] *vt* **1.** [tâche, part] : **attribuer qqch à qqn** to assign OU allocate sthg to sb, to assign OU allocate sb sthg ; [privilège] to grant sthg to sb, to grant sb sthg ; [récompense] to award sthg to sb, to award sb sthg - **2.** [faute] : **attribuer qqch à qqn** to attribute sthg to sb, to put sthg down to sb. **s'attribuer** *vp* **1.** [s'approprier] to appropriate (for o.s.) - **2.** [revendiquer] to claim (for o.s.)

attribut [atriby] *nm* **1.** [gén] attribute - **2.** GRAMM complement.

attribution [atribysjɔ̃] *nf* **1.** [de prix] awarding, award - **2.** [de part, tâche] allocation, assignment - **3.** [d'avantage] bestowing. **attributions** *nfpl* [fonctions] duties.

attrister [3] [atriste] *vt* to sadden. **s'attrister** *vp* to be saddened.

attroupement [atrupmɑ̃] *nm* crowd.

attrouper [3] [atrupe] **s'attrouper** *vp* to form a crowd, to gather.

au [o] **>** à.

aubade [obad] *nf* dawn serenade.

aubaine [obɛn] *nf* piece of good fortune.

aube [ob] *nf* [aurore] dawn, daybreak ; **à l'aube du jour** *fig* at the dawn of.

aubépine [obepin] *nf* hawthorn.

auberge [obɛrʒ] *nf* [hôtel] inn ; **auberge de jeunesse** youth hostel.

aubergine [obɛrʒin] *nf* **1.** BOT aubergine *UK*, eggplant *US* - **2.** *péj* [contractuelle] traffic warden *UK*, meter maid *US*.

aubergiste [obɛrʒist] *nmf* innkeeper.

auburn [obœrn] *adj inv* auburn.

aucun, e [okœ, yn] <> *adj indéf* **1.** [sens négatif] : **ne... aucun** no ; **il n'y a aucune voiture dans la rue** there aren't any cars in the street, there are no cars in the street ; **sans faire aucun bruit** without making a sound - **2.** [sens positif] any ; **il lit plus qu'aucun autre enfant** he reads more than any other child. <> *pron indéf* **1.** [sens négatif] none ; **aucun des enfants** none of the children ; **aucun d'entre nous** none of us ; **aucun (des deux)** neither (of them) - **2.** [sens positif] : **plus qu'aucun de nous** more than any of us.

aucunement [okynmɑ̃] *adv* not at all, in no way.

audace [odas] *nf* **1.** [hardiesse] daring, boldness - **2.** [insolence] audacity - **3.** [innovation] daring innovation.

audacieux, euse [odasjø, øz] *adj* **1.** [projet] daring, bold - **2.** [personne, geste] bold.

au-dedans [odədɑ̃] *loc adv* inside. **au-dedans de** *loc prép* inside.

au-dehors [odəɔr] *loc adv* outside. **au-dehors de** *loc prép* outside.

au-delà [odəla] ◇ *loc adv* **1.** [plus loin] beyond - **2.** [davantage, plus] more. ◇ *nm* : l'au-delà the hereafter, the afterlife. ➤ **au-delà de** *loc prép* beyond.

au-dessous [odəsu] *loc adv* below, underneath. ➤ **au-dessous de** *loc prép* below, under.

au-dessus [odəsy] *loc adv* above. ➤ **au-dessus de** *loc prép* above, over.

au-devant [odəvã] *loc adv* ahead. ➤ **au-devant de** *loc prép* : aller au-devant de to go to meet ; aller au-devant du danger to court danger.

audible [odibl] *adj* audible.

audience [odjãs] *nf* **1.** [public, entretien] audience - **2.** DR hearing.

Audimat [odimat] *nm* audience rating, ≃ Nielsen® ratings *US*.

audionumérique [odjɔnymerik] *adj* digital audio.

audiovisuel, elle [odjɔvizɥɛl] *adj* audiovisual. ➤ **audiovisuel** *nm* TV and radio.

audit [odit] *nm* audit.

auditeur, trice [oditœr, tris] *nm, f* listener. ➤ **auditeur** *nm* **1.** UNIV : **auditeur libre** *person allowed to attend lectures without being registered* auditor *US* - **2.** FIN auditor.

audition [odisjɔ̃] *nf* **1.** [fait d'entendre] hearing - **2.** DR examination - **3.** THÉÂTRE audition - **4.** MUS recital.

auditionner [3] [odisjɔne] *vt & vi* to audition.

auditoire [oditwar] *nm* [public] audience.

auditorium [oditɔrjɔm] *nm* [de concert] auditorium ; [d'enregistrement] studio.

auge [oʒ] *nf* [pour animaux] trough.

augmentation [ogmãtasjɔ̃] *nf*: **augmentation (de)** increase (in) ; **augmentation (de salaire)** rise *UK* ou raise *US* (in salary).

augmenter [3] [ogmãte] ◇ *vt* to increase ; [prix, salaire] to raise ; [personne] to give a rise to *UK*, to give a raise to *US*. ◇ *vi* to increase, to rise ; **le froid augmente** it's getting colder ; **la douleur augmente** the pain is getting worse.

augure [ogyr] *nm* [présage] omen ; **être de bon/mauvais augure** to be a good/bad sign.

aujourd'hui [oʒurdɥi] *adv* today.

aulx ➤ ail.

aumône [omon] *nf* : **faire l'aumône à qqn** to give alms to sb.

auparavant [oparavã] *adv* **1.** [tout d'abord] first (of all) - **2.** [avant] before, previously.

auprès [oprɛ] ➤ **auprès de** *loc prép* **1.** [à côté de] beside, next to - **2.** [comparé à] compared with - **3.** [en s'adressant à] to.

auquel [okɛl] ➤ lequel.

aurai, auras *etc* ➤ avoir.

auréole [oreɔl] *nf* **1.** ASTRON & RELIG halo - **2.** [trace] ring.

auriculaire [orikylɛr] *nm* little finger.

aurore [orɔr] *nf* dawn.

ausculter [3] [oskylte] *vt* MÉD to sound.

auspice [ospis] *nm* (*gén pl*) sign, auspice ; **sous les auspices de qqn** under the auspices of sb.

aussi [osi] *adv* **1.** [pareillement, en plus] also, too ; **moi aussi** me too ; **j'y vais aussi** I'm going too ou as well - **2.** [dans une comparaison] : **aussi... que** as... as ; **il n'est pas aussi intelligent que son frère** he's not as clever as his brother ; **je n'ai jamais rien vu d'aussi beau** I've never seen anything so beautiful ; **aussi incroyable que cela paraisse** incredible though ou as it may seem. ➤ **(tout) aussi bien** *loc adv* just as easily, just as well ; **j'aurais pu (tout) aussi bien refuser** I could just as easily have said no. ➤ **aussi bien... que** *loc conj* as well... as ; **tu le sais aussi bien que moi** you know as well as I do.

aussitôt [osito] *adv* immediately. ➤ **aussitôt que** *loc conj* as soon as.

austère [ostɛr] *adj* **1.** [personne, vie] austere - **2.** [vêtement] severe ; [paysage] harsh.

austérité [osterite] *nf* **1.** [de personne, vie] austerity - **2.** [de vêtement] severeness ; [de paysage] harshness.

austral, e [ostral] (*pl* australs ou austraux [ostro]) *adj* southern.

Australie [ostrali] *nf* : l'Australie Australia.

australien, enne [ostraljɛ̃, ɛn] *adj* Australian. ➤ **Australien, enne** *nm, f* Australian.

autant [otã] *adv* **1.** [comparatif] : **autant que** as much as ; **ce livre coûte autant que l'autre** this book costs as much as the other one ; **autant de (... que)** [quantité] as much (... as) ; [nombre] as many (... as) ; **il a dépensé autant d'argent que moi** he spent as much money as I did ; **il y a autant de femmes que d'hommes** there are as many women as men - **2.** [à un tel point, en si grande quantité] so much ; [en si grand nombre] so many ; **autant de patience** so much patience ; **autant de gens** so many people ; **il ne peut pas en dire autant** he can't say the same ; **en faire autant** to do likewise - **3.** [il vaut mieux] : **autant dire la vérité** we/you *etc* may as well tell the truth. ➤ **autant que** *loc conj* : **(pour) autant que je sache** as far as I know. ➤ **d'autant** *loc adv* accordingly, in proportion. ➤ **d'autant mieux** *loc adv* all the better ; **d'autant mieux que** all the better since. ➤ **d'autant que** *loc conj* : **d'autant (plus) que** all the more so since ; **d'autant moins que** all the less so since. ➤ **pour autant** *loc adv* for all that.

autel [otɛl] *nm* altar.

auteur [otœr] *nm* **1.** [d'œuvre] author - **2.** [responsable] perpetrator.

authentique [otɑ̃tik] *adj* authentic, genuine.

autiste [otist] *adj* autistic.

auto [oto] *nf* car.

autobiographie [otɔbjɔgrafi] *nf* autobiography.

autobronzant, e [otɔbrɔ̃zɑ̃, ɑ̃t] *adj* self-tanning.

autobus [otɔbys] *nm* bus.

autocar [otɔkar] *nm* coach UK, bus US.

autochtone [otɔktɔn] *nmf & adj* native.

autocollant, e [otɔkɔlɑ̃, ɑ̃t] *adj* self-adhesive, sticky. ◆ **autocollant** *nm* sticker.

autocouchettes [otɔkuʃɛt] *adj inv* : train autocouchettes ≃ Motorail® train.

autocritique [otɔkritik] *nf* self-criticism.

autocuiseur [otɔkɥizœr] *nm* pressure cooker.

autodéfense [otɔdefɑ̃s] *nf* self-defence UK, self-defense US.

autodétruire [98] [otɔdetrɥir] ◆ **s'autodétruire** *vp* **1.** [machine] to self-destruct - **2.** [personne] to destroy o.s.

autodidacte [otɔdidakt] *nmf* self-taught person.

auto-école [otɔekɔl] (*pl* auto-écoles) *nf* driving school.

autofinancement [otɔfinɑ̃smɑ̃] *nm* self-financing.

autofocus [otɔfɔkys] *nm & adj inv* auto-focus.

autogestion [otɔʒɛstjɔ̃] *nf* workers' control.

autographe [otɔgraf] *nm* autograph.

automate [otɔmat] *nm* [robot] automaton.

automatique [otɔmatik] ◇ *nm* **1.** [pistolet] automatic - **2.** TÉLÉCOM ≃ direct dialling UK ou dialing US. ◇ *adj* automatic.

automatisation [otɔmatizasjɔ̃] *nf* automation.

automatisme [otɔmatism] *nm* **1.** [de machine] automatic operation - **2.** [réflexe] automatic reaction, automatism.

automédication [otɔmedikasjɔ̃] *nf* self-medication.

automne [otɔn] *nm* autumn, fall US ; **en automne** in the autumn, in the fall US.

automobile [otɔmɔbil] ◇ *nf* car, automobile US. ◇ *adj* [industrie, accessoires] car (avant n), automobile (avant n) US ; [véhicule] motor (avant n).

automobiliste [otɔmɔbilist] *nmf* driver, motorist UK.

autonettoyant, e [otɔnɛtwajɑ̃, ɑ̃t] *adj* self-cleaning.

autonome [otɔnɔm] *adj* **1.** [gén] autonomous, independent - **2.** [appareil] self-contained.

autonomie [otɔnɔmi] *nf* **1.** [indépendance] autonomy, independence - **2.** [véhicule] range - **3.** POLIT autonomy, self-government.

autonomiste [otɔnɔmist] *nmf & adj* separatist.

autoportrait [otɔpɔrtrɛ] *nm* self-portrait.

autopsie [otɔpsi] *nf* post-mortem, autopsy.

autoradio [otɔradjo] *nm* car radio.

autorail [otɔraj] *nm* railcar.

autorisation [otɔrizasjɔ̃] *nf* **1.** [permission] permission, authorization ; **avoir l'autorisation de faire qqch** to be allowed to do sthg - **2.** [attestation] pass, permit.

autorisé, e [otɔrize] *adj* [personne] in authority ; **milieux autorisés** official circles.

autoriser [3] [otɔrize] *vt* to authorize, to permit ; **autoriser qqn à faire qqch** [permission] to give sb permission to do sthg ; [possibilité] to permit ou allow sb to do sthg.

autoritaire [otɔritɛr] *adj* authoritarian.

autorité [otɔrite] *nf* authority ; **faire autorité** [ouvrage] to be authoritative ; [personne] to be an authority.

autoroute [otɔrut] *nf* motorway UK, highway US, freeway US ; **autoroute de l'information** INFORM information highway ou superhighway.

auto-stop [otɔstɔp] *nm* hitchhiking.

auto-stoppeur, euse [otɔstɔpœr, øz] (*mpl* auto-stoppeurs, *fpl* auto-stoppeuses) *nm, f* hitchhiker, hitcher.

autour [otur] *adv* round UK, around. ◆ **autour de** *loc prép* **1.** [sens spatial] round UK, around - **2.** [sens temporel] about, around.

autre [otr] ◇ *adj indéf* **1.** [distinct, différent] other, different ; **je préfère une autre marque de café** I prefer another ou a different brand of coffee ; **l'un et l'autre projets** both projects ; **autre chose** something else - **2.** [supplémentaire] other ; **tu veux une autre tasse de café?** would you like another cup of coffee? - **3.** [qui reste] other, remaining ; **les autres passagers ont été rapatriés en autobus** the other ou remaining passengers were bussed home. ◇ *pron indéf* : **l'autre** the other (one) ; **un autre** another (one) ; **les autres** [personnes] the others ; [objets] the others, the other ones ; **l'un à côté de l'autre** side by side ; **d'une semaine à l'autre** from one week to the next ; **aucun autre, nul autre, personne**

d'autre no one else, nobody else ; **quelqu'un d'autre** somebody else, someone else ; **rien d'autre** nothing else ; **l'un et l'autre sont venus** they both came, both of them came ; **l'un ou l'autre ira** one or other (of them) will go ; **ni l'un ni l'autre n'est venu** neither (of them) came.

autrefois [otrəfwa] *adv* in the past, formerly.

autrement [otrəmɑ̃] *adv* **1.** [différemment] otherwise, differently ; **je n'ai pas pu faire autrement que d'y aller** I had no choice but to go ; **autrement dit** in other words - **2.** [sinon] otherwise.

Autriche [otriʃ] *nf* : **l'Autriche** Austria.

autrichien, enne [otriʃjɛ̃, ɛn] *adj* Austrian. ➡ **Autrichien, enne** *nm, f* Austrian.

autruche [otryʃ] *nf* ostrich.

autrui [otrɥi] *pron indéf inv* others, other people.

auvent [ovɑ̃] *nm* canopy.

aux [o] ➡ **à**.

auxiliaire [oksiljɛr] ◇ *nmf* [assistant] assistant. ◇ *nm* GRAMM auxiliary (verb). ◇ *adj* **1.** [secondaire] auxiliary - **2.** ADMIN assistant *(avant n)*.

auxquels, auxquelles [okɛl] ➡ **lequel**.

av. *abr écrite de* avenue.

avachi, e [avaʃi] *adj* **1.** [gén] misshapen - **2.** [personne] listless ; **il était avachi dans un fauteuil** he was slumped in an armchair.

aval [aval] *(pl* -als*) nm* backing *(U)*, endorsement. ➡ **en aval** *loc adv litt & fig* downstream.

avalanche [avalɑ̃ʃ] *nf litt & fig* avalanche.

avaler [3] [avale] *vt* **1.** [gén] to swallow - **2.** *fig* [supporter] to take ; **dur à avaler** difficult to swallow.

avance [avɑ̃s] *nf* **1.** [progression, somme d'argent] advance - **2.** [distance, temps] lead ; **le train a dix minutes d'avance** the train is ten minutes early ; **le train a une avance de dix minutes sur l'horaire** the train is running ten minutes ahead of schedule ; **prendre de l'avance (dans qqch)** to get ahead (in sthg). ➡ **avances** *nfpl* : **faire des avances à qqn** to make advances towards sb. ➡ **à l'avance** *loc adv* in advance. ➡ **d'avance** *loc adv* in advance. ➡ **en avance** *loc adv* : **être en avance** to be early ; **être en avance sur qqch** to be ahead of sthg. ➡ **par avance** *loc adv* in advance.

avancement [avɑ̃smɑ̃] *nm* **1.** [développement] progress - **2.** [promotion] promotion.

avancer [16] [avɑ̃se] ◇ *vt* **1.** [objet, tête] to move forward ; [date, départ] to bring forward ; [main] to hold out - **2.** [projet,

travail] to advance - **3.** [montre, horloge] to put forward - **4.** [argent] : **avancer qqch à qqn** to advance sb sthg. ◇ *vi* **1.** [approcher] to move forward - **2.** [progresser] to advance ; **avancer dans qqch** to make progress in sthg - **3.** [faire saillie] : **avancer (dans/sur)** to jut out (into/over), to project (into/over) - **4.** [montre, horloge] : **ma montre avance de dix minutes** my watch is ten minutes fast - **5.** [servir] : **ça n'avance à rien** that won't get us/you anywhere. ➡ **s'avancer** *vp* **1.** [s'approcher] to move forward ; **s'avancer vers qqn/qqch** to move towards *ou* toward *US* sb/sthg - **2.** [s'engager] to commit o.s.

avant [avɑ̃] ◇ *prép* before. ◇ *adv* before ; **quelques jours avant** a few days earlier *ou* before ; **tu connais le cinéma? ma maison se situe un peu avant** do you know the cinema? my house is just this side of it. ◇ *adj inv* front ; **les roues avant** the front wheels. ◇ *nm* **1.** [partie antérieure] front - **2.** SPORT forward. ➡ **avant de** *loc prép* : **avant de faire qqch** before doing sthg ; **avant de partir** before leaving. ➡ **avant que** *loc conj* (+ *subjonctif*) **je dois te parler avant que tu (ne) partes** I must speak to you before you leave. ➡ **avant tout** *loc adv* above all ; **sa carrière passe avant tout** his career comes first. ➡ **en avant** *loc adv* forward, forwards.

avantage [avɑ̃taʒ] *nm* [gén & TENNIS] advantage ; **se montrer à son avantage** to look one's best.

avantager [17] [avɑ̃taʒe] *vt* **1.** [favoriser] to favour *UK*, to favor *US* - **2.** [mettre en valeur] to flatter.

avantageux, euse [avɑ̃taʒø, øz] *adj* **1.** [profitable] profitable, lucrative - **2.** [flatteur] flattering.

avant-bras [avɑ̃bra] *nm inv* forearm.

avant-centre [avɑ̃sɑ̃tr] *(pl* avants-centres*) nm* centre *UK* *ou* center *US* forward.

avant-coureur [avɑ̃kurœr] ➡ **signe**.

avant-dernier, ère [avɑ̃dɛrnje, ɛr] *(mpl* avant-derniers, *fpl* avant-dernières*) adj* second to last, penultimate.

avant-garde [avɑ̃gard] *(pl* avant-gardes*) nf* **1.** MIL vanguard - **2.** [idées] avant-garde.

avant-goût [avɑ̃gu] *(pl* avant-goûts*) nm* foretaste.

avant-hier [avɑ̃tjɛr] *adv* the day before yesterday.

avant-première [avɑ̃prəmjɛr] *(pl* avant-premières*) nf* preview.

avant-projet [avɑ̃prɔʒɛ] *(pl* avant-projets*) nm* draft.

avant-propos [avɑ̃prɔpo] *nm inv* foreword.

avant-veille [avɑ̃vɛj] (*pl* avant-veilles) *nf* : l'avant-veille two days earlier.

avare [avar] <> *nmf* miser. <> *adj* miserly ; **être avare de qqch** *fig* to be sparing with sthg.

avarice [avaris] *nf* avarice.

avarie [avari] *nf* damage (U).

avarié, e [avarje] *adj* [aliment] rotting, bad.

avatar [avatar] *nm* [transformation] metamorphosis. ◆ **avatars** *nmpl fam* [mésaventures] misfortunes.

avec [avɛk] <> *prép* **1.** [gén] with ; **avec respect** with respect, respectfully ; **c'est fait avec du cuir** it's made from leather ; **et avec ça?, et avec ceci?** *fam* [dans un magasin] anything else? - **2.** [vis-à-vis de] to, towards, toward *US*. <> *adv fam* with it/him *etc* ; **tiens mon sac, je ne peux pas courir avec!** hold my bag, I can't run with it!

Ave (Maria) [ave(marja)] *nm inv* Hail Mary.

avenant, e [avnɑ̃, ɑ̃t] *adj* pleasant. ◆ **avenant** *nm* DR additional clause. ◆ **à l'avenant** *loc adv* in the same vein.

avènement [avɛnmɑ̃] *nm* **1.** [d'un roi] accession - **2.** *fig* [début] advent.

avenir [avnir] *nm* future ; **avoir de l'avenir** to have a future ; **d'avenir** [profession, concept] with a future, with prospects. ◆ **à l'avenir** *loc adv* in future.

Avent [avɑ̃] *nm* : **l'Avent** Advent.

aventure [avɑ̃tyr] *nf* **1.** [gén] adventure - **2.** [liaison amoureuse] affair.

aventurer [3] [avɑ̃tyre] *vt* [risquer] to risk. ◆ **s'aventurer** *vp* to venture (out) ; **s'aventurer à faire qqch** *fig* to venture to do sthg.

aventureux, euse [avɑ̃tyrø, øz] *adj* **1.** [personne, vie] adventurous - **2.** [projet] risky.

aventurier, ère [avɑ̃tyrje, ɛr] *nm, f* adventurer.

avenu, e [avny] *adj* : **nul et non avenu** DR null and void.

avenue [avny] *nf* avenue.

avérer [18] [avere] ◆ **s'avérer** *vp* : **il s'est avéré (être) à la hauteur** he proved (to be) up to it ; **il s'est avéré (être) un musicien accompli** he proved to be an accomplished musician.

averse [avɛrs] *nf* downpour ; **averse de neige** snowflurry.

averti, e [averti] *adj* **1.** [expérimenté] experienced - **2.** [initié] : **averti (de)** informed OU well-informed (about).

avertir [32] [avɛrtir] *vt* **1.** [mettre en garde] to warn - **2.** [prévenir] to inform ; **avertissez-moi dès que possible** let me know as soon as possible.

avertissement [avɛrtismɑ̃] *nm* **1.** [gén] warning - **2.** [avis] notice, notification.

avertisseur, euse [avɛrtisœr, øz] *nm* **1.** [Klaxon] horn - **2.** [d'incendie] alarm.

aveu, x [avø] *nm* confession.

aveugle [avœgl] <> *nmf* blind person ; **les aveugles** the blind. <> *adj litt & fig* blind.

aveuglement [avœgləmɑ̃] *nm* blindness.

aveuglément [avœglemɑ̃] *adv* blindly.

aveugler [5] [avœgle] *vt litt & fig* [priver de la vue] to blind.

aveuglette [avœglɛt] ◆ **à l'aveuglette** *loc adv* : **marcher à l'aveuglette** to grope one's way ; **avancer à l'aveuglette** *fig* to be in the dark.

aviateur, trice [avjatœr, tris] *nm, f* aviator.

aviation [avjasjɔ̃] *nf* **1.** [transport aérien] aviation - **2.** MIL airforce.

avide [avid] *adj* **1.** [vorace, cupide] greedy - **2.** [désireux] : **avide (de qqch/de faire qqch)** eager (for sthg/to do sthg).

avidité [avidite] *nf* **1.** [voracité, cupidité] greed - **2.** [passion] eagerness.

avilir [32] [avilir] *vt* [personne] to degrade. ◆ **s'avilir** *vp* **1.** [personne] to demean o.s. - **2.** [monnaie, marchandise] to depreciate.

aviné, e [avine] *adj* **1.** [personne] inebriated - **2.** [haleine] smelling of alcohol.

avion [avjɔ̃] *nm* plane, aeroplane *UK*, airplane *US* ; **en avion** by plane, by air ; **par avion** [courrier] airmail ; **avion à réaction** jet (plane).

aviron [avirɔ̃] *nm* **1.** [rame] oar - **2.** SPORT : **l'aviron** rowing.

avis [avi] *nm* **1.** [opinion] opinion ; **changer d'avis** to change one's mind ; **être d'avis que** to think that, to be of the opinion that ; **à mon avis** in my opinion - **2.** [conseil] advice (U) - **3.** [notification] notification, notice ; **sauf avis contraire** unless otherwise informed ; **avis de recherche** [d'un criminel] wanted (person) poster ; [d'un disparu] missing person poster.

avisé, e [avize] *adj* [sensé] sensible ; **être bien/mal avisé de faire qqch** to be well-advised/ill-advised to do sthg.

aviser [3] [avize] <> *vt* [informer] : **aviser qqn de qqch** to inform sb of sthg. <> *vi* to reassess the situation. ◆ **s'aviser** *vp* **1.** *sout* [s'apercevoir] : **s'aviser de qqch** to notice sthg - **2.** [oser] : **s'aviser de faire qqch** to take it into one's head to do sthg ; **ne t'avise pas de répondre!** don't you dare answer back!

av. J.-C. (*abr écrite de* **avant Jésus-Christ**) BC.

avocat, e [avɔka, at] *nm, f* DR barrister *UK*, attorney-at-law *US* ; **avocat de la défense** counsel for the defence *UK*, defense counsel *US* ; **avocat général** ≃ counsel for the prosecution *UK*, ≃ prosecuting attorney *US*.

avocat *nm* [fruit] avocado.

avoine [avwan] *nf* oats *pl*.

avoir ¹ *nm* **1.** [biens] assets *pl* - **2.** COMM & FIN credit note ; [en comptabilité] credit (side) ; **avoir fiscal** tax credit.

avoir ² [1] [avwar] ⟨⟩ *v aux* to have ; **j'ai fini** I have finished ; **il a attendu pendant deux heures** he waited for two hours. ⟨⟩ *vt* **1.** [posséder] to have (got) ; **il a deux enfants/les cheveux bruns** he has (got) two children/brown hair ; **la maison a un grand jardin** the house has (got) a large garden - **2.** [être âgé de] : **il a 20 ans** he is 20 (years old) ; **il a deux ans de plus que son frère** he is two years older than his brother - **3.** [obtenir] to get - **4.** [éprouver] to have ; **avoir du chagrin** to feel sorrowful ; **avoir de la sympathie pour qqn** to have a liking for sb ; **se faire avoir** *fam* to be had ou conned ; **en avoir assez (de qqch/de faire qqch)** to have had enough (of sthg/of doing sthg) ; **j'en ai pour cinq minutes** it'll take me five minutes ; **en avoir après qqn** to have (got) it in for sb. ; ▶ **faim, peur, soif** *(etc)* ▶ **avoir à** *v + prép* [devoir] : **avoir à faire qqch** to have to do sthg ; **tu n'avais pas à lui parler sur ce ton** you had no need to speak to him like that, you shouldn't have spoken to him like that ; **tu n'avais qu'à me demander** you only had to ask me ; **tu n'as qu'à y aller toi-même** just go (there) yourself, why don't you just go (there) yourself? ▶ **il y a** *v impers* **1.** [présentatif] there is/are ; **il y a un problème** there's a problem ; **il y a des problèmes** there are (some) problems ; **qu'est-ce qu'il y a?** what's the matter?, what is it? ; **il n'y a qu'à en finir** we'll/you'll *etc* just have to have done (with it) - **2.** [temporel] : **il y a trois ans** three years ago ; **il y a longtemps de cela** that was a long time ago ; **il y a longtemps qu'il est parti** he left a long time ago.

avoisinant, e [avwazinã, ãt] *adj* **1.** [lieu, maison] neighbouring *UK*, neighboring *US* - **2.** [sens, couleur] similar.

avortement [avɔrtəmã] *nm* MÉD abortion.

avorter [3] [avɔrte] *vi* **1.** MÉD : **(se faire) avorter** to have an abortion - **2.** [échouer] to fail.

avorton [avɔrtɔ̃] *nm péj* [nabot] runt.

avouer [6] [avwe] *vt* **1.** [confesser] to confess (to) - **2.** [reconnaître] to admit.

avril [avril] *nm* April ; *voir aussi* **septembre**.

axe [aks] *nm* **1.** GÉOM & PHYS axis - **2.** [de roue] axle - **3.** [prolongement] : **dans l'axe de** directly in line with.

axer [3] [akse] *vt* : **axer qqch sur qqch** to centre *UK* ou center *US* sthg on sthg ; **axer qqch autour de qqch** to centre *UK* ou center *US* sthg around sthg.

axiome [aksjom] *nm* axiom.

ayant [ɛjã] *p prés* ▶ **avoir**.

azalée [azale] *nf* azalea.

azimut [azimyt] ◀ **tous azimuts** *loc adj* [défense, offensive] all-out.

azote [azɔt] *nm* nitrogen.

azur [azyr] *nm litt* **1.** [couleur] azure - **2.** [ciel] skies *pl*.

B

b, B [be] *nm inv* b, B. ▶ **B** (*abr écrite de* **bien**) *good grade (as assessment on schoolwork)*, ≃ B+.

BA (*abr de* **bonne action**) *nf fam* good deed.

babiller [3] [babije] *vi* to babble.

babines [babin] *nfpl* chops.

bâbord [babɔr] *nm* port ; **à bâbord** to port, on the port side.

babouin [babwɛ̃] *nm* baboon.

baby-sitter [bebisitœr] (*pl* **baby-sitters**) *nmf* baby-sitter.

baby-sitting [bebisitiŋ] *nm* baby-sitting ; **faire du baby-sitting** to baby-sit.

bac [bak] (*abr de* **baccalauréat**) *nm* **1.** SCOL : **bac +** *level of studies after the baccalauréat* - **2.** [bateau] ferry - **3.** [de réfrigérateur] : **bac à glace** ice tray ; **bac à légumes** vegetable drawer ; [d'imprimante, de photocopieuse] : **bac à papier** paper tray.

BAC [bak] (*abr de* **brigade anticriminalité**) *nf police squad specializing in patrols to combat crime.*

baccalauréat [bakalɔrea] *nm school-leaving examinations leading to university entrance qualification.*

bâche [baʃ] *nf* [toile] tarpaulin.

bachelier, ère [baʃəlje, ɛr] *nm, f holder of the baccalauréat.*

bacille [basil] *nm* bacillus.

bâcler [3] [bakle] *vt* to botch.

bactérie [bakteri] *nf* bacterium.

badaud, e [bado, od] *nm, f* stroller.

badge [badʒ] *nm* badge.

badgeuse [badʒøz] *nf* swipe card reader.

badigeonner [3] [badiʒɔne] *vt* [mur] to whitewash.

badiner [3] [badine] *vi sout* to joke ; **ne pas badiner avec qqch** not to treat sthg lightly.

badminton [badmintɔn] *nm* badminton.

baffe [baf] *nf fam* slap.

baffle [bafl] *nm* speaker.

bafouiller [3] [bafuje] *vi & vt* to mumble.

bâfrer [3] [bafre] *fam vi* to guzzle.

bagage [bagaʒ] *nm* **1.** *(gén pl)* [valises, sacs] luggage *(U)*, baggage *(U)* ; **faire ses bagages** to pack ; **bagages à main** hand luggage - **2.** [connaissances] (fund of) knowledge ; **bagage intellectuel/culturel** intellectual/cultural baggage.

bagagiste [bagaʒist] *nmf* [chargement des avions] baggage handler ; [à l'hôtel etc] porter ; [fabricant] travel goods manufacturer.

bagarre [bagar] *nf* brawl, fight.

bagarrer [3] [bagare] *vi* to fight. ◆ **se bagarrer** *vp* to fight.

bagatelle [bagatɛl] *nf* **1.** [objet] trinket - **2.** [somme d'argent] : **acheter qqch pour une bagatelle** to buy sthg for next to nothing ; **la bagatelle de X euros** *iron* a mere X euros - **3.** [chose futile] trifle.

bagnard [baɲar] *nm* convict.

bagne [baɲ] *nm* [prison] labour *UK* ou labor *US* camp.

bagnole [baɲɔl] *nf fam* car.

bague [bag] *nf* **1.** [bijou, anneau] ring ; **bague de fiançailles** engagement ring - **2.** TECHNOL : **bague de serrage** clip.

baguer [3] [bage] *vt* [oiseau, arbre] to ring.

baguette [bagɛt] *nf* **1.** [pain] French stick *UK*, baguette *US* - **2.** [petit bâton] stick ; **baguette magique** magic wand ; **baguette de tambour** drumstick ; **mener qqn à la baguette** to rule sb with a rod of iron - **3.** [pour manger] chopstick - **4.** [de chef d'orchestre] baton.

bahut [bay] *nm* **1.** [buffet] sideboard - **2.** *arg scol* [lycée] secondary school.

baie [bɛ] *nf* **1.** [fruit] berry - **2.** GÉOGR bay - **3.** [fenêtre] : **baie vitrée** picture window.

baignade [bɛɲad] *nf* [action] bathing *(U)* *UK*, swimming *(U)* ; **'baignade interdite'** 'no bathing/swimming'.

baigner [4] [beɲe] ◇ *vt* **1.** [donner un bain à] to bath *UK*, to bathe *US* - **2.** [tremper, remplir] to bathe ; **baigné de soleil** bathed in sunlight. ◇ *vi* : **baigner dans son sang** to lie in a pool of blood ; **les tomates baignaient dans l'huile** the tomatoes were

swimming in oil. ◆ **se baigner** *vp* **1.** [dans la mer] to go swimming, to swim - **2.** [dans une baignoire] to have *UK* ou take a bath.

baigneur, euse [bɛɲœr, øz] *nm, f* bather *UK*, swimmer. ◆ **baigneur** *nm* [poupée] baby doll.

baignoire [bɛɲwar] *nf* bath *UK*, bathtub.

bail [baj] *(pl* baux [bo]*)* *nm* DR lease.

bâillement [bajmɑ̃] *nm* yawning *(U)*, yawn.

bâiller [3] [baje] *vi* **1.** [personne] to yawn - **2.** [vêtement] to gape.

bailleur, eresse [bajœr, bajrɛs] *nm, f* lessor ; **bailleur de fonds** backer.

bâillon [bajɔ̃] *nm* gag.

bâillonner [3] [bajɔne] *vt* to gag.

bain [bɛ̃] *nm* **1.** [gén] bath ; **prendre un bain** to have *UK* ou take a bath ; **bain moussant** foaming bath oil ; **bain à remous** spa bath, whirlpool bath ; **bains-douches** public baths - **2.** [dans mer, piscine] swim ; **bain de mer** sea bathing *UK* ou swimming ; **prendre un bain de soleil** to sunbathe.

bain-marie [bɛ̃mari] *(pl* bains-marie*)* *nm* : **au bain-marie** in a bain-marie.

baïonnette [bajɔnɛt] *nf* **1.** [arme] bayonet - **2.** ÉLECTR bayonet fitting.

baiser [4] [beze] *nm* kiss.

baisse [bɛs] *nf* [gén] : **baisse (de)** drop (in), fall (in) ; **en baisse** falling ; ÉCON falling off ; **la tendance est à la baisse** there is a downward trend.

baisser [4] [bese] ◇ *vt* [gén] to lower ; [radio] to turn down. ◇ *vi* **1.** [descendre] to go down ; **le jour baisse** it's getting dark - **2.** [santé, vue] to fail - **3.** [prix] to fall. ◆ **se baisser** *vp* to bend down.

bajoues [baʒu] *nfpl* jowls.

bal [bal] *nm* ball ; **bal masqué/costumé** masked/fancy-dress ball ; **bal populaire** ou **musette** popular old-fashioned dance accompanied by accordion.

balade [balad] *nf fam* stroll.

balader [3] [balade] *vt* **1.** *fam* [traîner avec soi] to trail around - **2.** [emmener en promenade] to take for a walk. ◆ **se balader** *vp fam* [se promener - à pied] to go for a walk ; [- en voiture] to go for a drive.

baladeur, euse [baladœr, øz] *adj* wandering. ◆ **baladeur** *nm* walkman.

balafre [balafr] *nf* **1.** [blessure] gash - **2.** [cicatrice] scar.

balafré, e [balafre] *adj* scarred.

balai [balɛ] *nm* **1.** [de nettoyage] broom, brush - **2.** *fam* [an] : **il a 50 balais** he's 50 years old.

balai-brosse [balɛbrɔs] *nm* (long-handled) scrubbing *UK* ou scrub *US* brush.

balance [balɑ̃s] *nf* 1. [instrument] scales *pl* - 2. COMM & POLIT balance. ➤ **Balance** *nf* ASTROL Libra.

balancer [16] [balɑ̃se] *vt* 1. [bouger] to swing - 2. *fam* [lancer] to chuck - 3. *fam* [jeter] to chuck out. ➤ **se balancer** *vp* 1. [sur une chaise] to rock backwards and forwards - 2. [sur une balançoire] to swing - 3. *fam* se balancer de qqch not to give a damn about sthg.

balancier [balɑ̃sje] *nm* 1. [de pendule] pendulum - 2. [de funambule] pole.

balançoire [balɑ̃swar] *nf* [suspendue] swing ; [bascule] seesaw.

balayage [balɛjaʒ] *nm* [gén] sweeping ; TECHNOL scanning.

balayer [11] [baleje] *vt* 1. [nettoyer] to sweep - 2. [chasser] to sweep away - 3. [suj: radar] to scan ; [suj: projecteurs] to sweep (across).

balayette [balɛjɛt] *nf* small brush.

balayeur, euse [balɛjœr, øz] *nm, f* road-sweeper *UK*, street cleaner *US*. ➤ **balayeuse** *nf* [machine] roadsweeper *UK*, street cleaner *US*.

balbutier [9] [balbysje] ◇ *vi* [bafouiller] to stammer. ◇ *vt* [bafouiller] to stammer (out).

balcon [balkɔ̃] *nm* 1. [de maison - terrasse] balcony ; [- balustrade] parapet - 2. [de théâtre, de cinéma] circle.

balconnet [balkɔnɛ] *nm* : soutien-gorge à balconnet half-cup bra.

baldaquin [baldakɛ̃] *nm* ➤ lit.

baleine [balɛn] *nf* 1. [mammifère] whale - 2. [de corset] whalebone - 3. [de parapluie] rib.

balise [baliz] *nf* 1. NAUT marker (buoy) - 2. AÉRON runway light - 3. AUTO road sign - 4. INFORM tag.

baliser [3] [balize] *vt* to mark out.

balivernes [balivɛrn] *nfpl* nonsense *(U)*.

Balkans [balkɑ̃] *nmpl* : les Balkans the Balkans.

ballade [balad] *nf* ballad.

ballant, e [balɑ̃, ɑ̃t] *adj* : les bras ballants arms dangling.

ballast [balast] *nm* 1. [chemin de fer] ballast - 2. NAUT ballast tank.

balle [bal] *nf* 1. [d'arme à feu] bullet ; balle perdue stray bullet - 2. [de jeu] ball - 3. [de marchandises] bale.

ballerine [balrin] *nf* 1. [danseuse] ballerina - 2. [chaussure] ballet shoe.

ballet [balɛ] *nm* [gén] ballet ; *fig* [activité intense] to-ing and fro-ing.

ballon [balɔ̃] *nm* 1. [jeux & SPORT] ball ; ballon de football football *UK*, soccer ball *US* - 2. [montgolfière, de fête] balloon - 3. AÉRON (hot-air) balloon - 4. CHIM round-bottomed flask.

ballonné, e [balɔne] *adj* : avoir le ventre ballonné, être ballonné to be bloated.

ballot [balo] *nm* 1. [de marchandises] bundle - 2. *vieilli* [imbécile] twit.

ballottage [balɔtaʒ] *nm* POLIT second ballot ; en ballottage standing for a second ballot *UK*, running in the second round *US*.

ballotter [3] [balɔte] ◇ *vt* to toss about. ◇ *vi* [chose] to roll around.

ballottine [balɔtin] *nf* : ballottine de foie gras *type of galantine made with foie gras*.

ball-trap [baltrap] *nm* clay pigeon shooting.

balluchon = baluchon.

balnéaire [balneɛr] *adj* : station balnéaire seaside resort.

balourd, e [balur, urd] *adj* clumsy.

balte [balt] *adj* Baltic. ➤ **Balte** *nmf* native of the Baltic states.

Baltique [baltik] *nf* : la Baltique the Baltic (Sea).

baluchon, balluchon [balyʃɔ̃] *nm* bundle ; faire son baluchon *fam* to pack one's bags (and leave).

balustrade [balystrad] *nf* 1. [de terrasse] balustrade - 2. [rambarde] guardrail.

bambin [bɑ̃bɛ̃] *nm* kiddie.

bambou [bɑ̃bu] *nm* [plante] bamboo.

ban [bɑ̃] *nm* [de mariage] : publier ou afficher les bans to publish ou display the banns ; être/mettre qqn au ban de la société to be outlawed/to outlaw sb (from society) ; le ban et l'arrière-ban the whole lot of them.

banal, e, als [banal] *adj* commonplace, banal.

banaliser [3] [banalize] *vt* : voiture banalisée unmarked police car.

banalité [banalite] *nf* 1. [caractère banal] banality - 2. [cliché] commonplace.

banane [banan] *nf* 1. [fruit] banana - 2. [sac] bum-bag *UK*, fanny bag *US* - 3. [coiffure] quiff *UK*.

bananier, ère [bananje, ɛr] *adj* banana (avant n). ➤ **bananier** *nm* 1. [arbre] banana tree - 2. [cargo] banana boat.

banc [bɑ̃] *nm* [siège] bench ; le banc des accusés DR the dock ; banc d'essai test-bed ; être au banc d'essai *fig* to be at the test stage ; banc de sable sandbank.

bancaire [bɑ̃kɛr] *adj* bank (avant n), banking (avant n).

bancal, e, als [bɑ̃kal] *adj* **1.** [meuble] wobbly - **2.** [théorie, idée] unsound.

bandage [bɑ̃daʒ] *nm* [de blessé] bandage.

bande [bɑ̃d] *nf* **1.** [de tissu, de papier] strip ; **bande dessinée** comic strip - **2.** [bandage] bandage ; **bande Velpeau**® crepe bandage - **3.** [de billard] cushion ; **par la bande** *fig* by a roundabout route - **4.** [groupe] band ; **en bande** in a group - **5.** [pellicule de film] film - **6.** [d'enregistrement] tape ; **bande magnétique** (magnetic) tape ; **bande originale** CINÉ original soundtrack ; **bande vidéo** video (tape) - **7.** [voie] : **bande d'arrêt d'urgence** hard shoulder - **8.** RADIO : **bande de fréquence** waveband - **9.** NAUT : **donner de la bande** to list.

bande-annonce [bɑ̃danɔ̃s] *nf* trailer.

bandeau, x [bɑ̃do] *nm* **1.** [sur les yeux] blindfold - **2.** [dans les cheveux] headband.

bandelette [bɑ̃dlɛt] *nf* strip (of cloth).

bander [3] [bɑ̃de] <> *vt* **1.** MÉD to bandage ; **bander les yeux de qqn** to blindfold sb - **2.** [arc] to draw back - **3.** [muscle] to flex. <> *vi vulg* to have a hard-on.

banderole [bɑ̃drɔl] *nf* streamer.

bande-son [bɑ̃dsɔ̃] *(pl* **bandes-son)** *nf* soundtrack.

bandit [bɑ̃di] *nm* [voleur] bandit.

banditisme [bɑ̃ditism] *nm* serious crime.

bandoulière [bɑ̃duljɛr] *nf* bandolier ; **en bandoulière** across the shoulder.

banlieue [bɑ̃ljø] *nf* suburbs *pl.*

banlieusard, e [bɑ̃ljøzar, ard] *nm, f person living in the suburbs.*

bannière [banjɛr] *nf* [étendard] banner.

bannir [32] [banir] *vt* : **bannir qqn/qqch (de)** to banish sb/sthg (from).

banque [bɑ̃k] *nf* **1.** [activité] banking - **2.** [établissement, au jeu] bank ; **Banque centrale européenne** European Central Bank - **3.** INFORM : **banque de données** data bank - **4.** MÉD : **banque d'organes/du sang/du sperme** organ/blood/sperm bank.

banqueroute [bɑ̃krut] *nf* bankruptcy ; **faire banqueroute** to go bankrupt.

banquet [bɑ̃kɛ] *nm* (celebration) dinner ; [de gala] banquet.

banquette [bɑ̃kɛt] *nf* seat.

banquier, ère [bɑ̃kje, ɛr] *nm, f* banker.

banquise [bɑ̃kiz] *nf* ice field.

baptême [batɛm] *nm* **1.** RELIG baptism, christening - **2.** [première fois] : **baptême de l'air** maiden flight.

baptiser [3] [batize] *vt* to baptize, to christen.

baquet [bakɛ] *nm* [cuve] tub.

bar [bar] *nm* **1.** [café, unité de pression] bar - **2.** [poisson] bass.

baraque [barak] *nf* **1.** [cabane] hut - **2.** *fam* [maison] house - **3.** [de forain] stall, stand.

baraqué, e [barake] *adj fam* well-built.

baraquement [barakmɑ̃] *nm* camp *(of huts for refugees, workers etc).*

baratin [baratɛ̃] *nm fam* smooth talk ; **faire du baratin à qqn** to sweet-talk sb.

baratiner [3] [baratine] *fam* <> *vt* [femme] to chat up UK, to sweet-talk US ; [client] to give one's sales pitch to. <> *vi* to be a smooth talker.

barbare [barbar] <> *nm* barbarian. <> *adj* **1.** *péj* [non civilisé] barbarous - **2.** [cruel] barbaric.

barbe [barb] *nf* beard ; **se laisser pousser la barbe** to grow a beard ; **barbe à papa** candyfloss UK, cotton candy US ; **quelle** OU **la barbe!** *fam* what a drag!

barbelé, e [barbəle] *adj* barbed. **barbelé** *nm* barbed wire *(U).*

barbiche [barbiʃ] *nf* [barbe] goatee.

barbiturique [barbityrik] *nm* barbiturate.

barboter [3] [barbɔte] *vi* to paddle.

barboteuse [barbɔtøz] *nf* rompersuit.

barbouillé, e [barbuje] *adj* : **être barbouillé, avoir l'estomac barbouillé** to feel sick UK OU nauseous US.

barbouiller [3] [barbuje] *vt* [salir] : **barbouiller qqch (de)** to smear sthg (with).

barbu, e [barby] *adj* bearded. **barbu** *nm* bearded man.

bardé, e [barde] *adj* : **il est bardé de diplômes** he's got heaps of diplomas.

barder [3] [barde] <> *vt* CULIN to bard. <> *vi fam* **ça va barder** there'll be trouble.

barème [barɛm] *nm* [de référence] table ; [de salaires] scale.

baril [baril] *nm* barrel.

bariolé, e [barjɔle] *adj* multicoloured UK, multicolored US.

barjo(t) [barʒo] *adj inv fam* nuts.

barmaid [barmɛd] *nf* barmaid.

barman [barman] *(pl* **barmans** OU **barmen** [barmɛn]) *nm* barman UK, bartender US.

baromètre [barɔmɛtr] *nm* barometer.

baron, onne [barɔ̃, ɔn] *nm, f* baron *(f baroness).*

baroque [barɔk] *adj* **1.** [style] baroque - **2.** [bizarre] weird.

barque [bark] *nf* small boat.

barquette [barkɛt] *nf* **1.** [tartelette] pastry boat - **2.** [récipient de fruits] punnet UK, basket US ; [- de crème glacée] tub.

barrage [baraʒ] *nm* **1.** [de rue] roadblock - **2.** CONSTR dam.

barre [bar] *nf* **1.** [gén & DR] bar ; **barre fixe** [gymnastique] high bar ; **barre des témoins**

DR witness box UK ou stand US - **2.** NAUT helm - **3.** [trait] stroke - **4.** INFORM : **barre d'espacement** space bar ; **barre de défilement** scroll bar ; **barre d'état** status bar.

barreau [baro] nm bar ; **le barreau** DR the Bar.

barrer [3] [bare] vt **1.** [rue, route] to block - **2.** [mot, phrase] to cross out - **3.** [bateau] to steer. ➡ **se barrer** vp fam to clear off.

barrette [baret] nf [pince à cheveux] (hair) slide UK, barrette US.

barreur, euse [barœr, øz] nm, f NAUT helmsman ; [à l'aviron] cox.

barricade [barikad] nf barricade.

barrière [barjer] nf litt & fig barrier.

barrique [barik] nf barrel.

baryton [baritɔ̃] nm baritone.

bas, basse [ba, bas] (prononcé [baz] devant un nm commençant par voyelle ou 'h' muet) adj **1.** [gén] low - **2.** péj [vil] base, low - **3.** MUS bass. ➡ **bas** ⟨⟩ nm [partie inférieure] bottom, lower part ; **avoir/connaître des hauts et des bas** to have/go through ups and downs. ⟨⟩ adv low ; **à bas...!** down with...! ; **parler bas** to speak in a low voice, to speak softly ; **mettre bas** [animal] to give birth. ➡ **en bas** loc adv at the bottom ; [dans une maison] downstairs. ➡ **en bas de** loc prép at the bottom of ; **attendre qqn en bas de chez lui** to wait for sb downstairs. ➡ **bas de gamme** ⟨⟩ adj downmarket. ⟨⟩ nm bottom of the range.

basalte [bazalt] nm basalt.

basané, e [bazane] adj tanned.

bas-côté [bakote] nm [de route] verge UK, shoulder US.

bascule [baskyl] nf [balançoire] seesaw.

basculer [3] [baskyle] ⟨⟩ vi to fall over, to overbalance ; [benne] to tip up ; **basculer dans qqch** fig to tip over into sthg. ⟨⟩ vt to tip up, to tilt.

base [baz] nf **1.** [partie inférieure] base - **2.** [principe fondamental] basis ; **à base de** based on ; **une boisson à base d'orange** an orange-based drink ; **de base** basic ; **sur la base de** on the basis of - **3.** INFORM : **base de données** database. ➡ **base de loisir** nf (outdoor) leisure ou sports complex.

baser [3] [baze] vt to base. ➡ **se baser** vp : **sur quoi vous basez-vous pour affirmer cela?** what are you basing this statement on?

bas-fond [bafɔ̃] nm [de l'océan] shallow. ➡ **bas-fonds** nmpl fig **1.** [de la société] dregs - **2.** [quartiers pauvres] slums.

basilic [bazilik] nm [plante] basil.

basilique [bazilik] nf basilica.

basique [bazik] adj basic.

basket [basket] ⟨⟩ nm = **basket-ball**. ⟨⟩ nf [chaussure] trainer UK, sneaker US ; **lâche-moi les baskets!** fam fig get off my back!

basket-ball [basketbol] nm basketball.

basque [bask] ⟨⟩ adj Basque ; **le Pays basque** the Basque country. ⟨⟩ nm [langue] Basque. ⟨⟩ nf [vêtement] tail (of coat) ; **être toujours pendu aux basques de qqn** fam fig to be always tagging along after sb. ➡ **Basque** nmf Basque.

bas-relief [barəljef] nm bas-relief.

basse [bas] ⟨⟩ adj ➡ **bas**. ⟨⟩ nf MUS bass.

basse-cour [baskur] nf **1.** [volaille] poultry - **2.** [partie de ferme] farmyard.

bassement [basmɑ̃] adv despicably.

basset [base] nm basset hound.

bassin [basɛ̃] nm **1.** [cuvette] bowl - **2.** [pièce d'eau] (ornamental) pond - **3.** [de piscine] : **petit/grand bassin** children's/main pool - **4.** ANAT pelvis - **5.** GÉOL basin ; **bassin houiller** coalfield ; **le Bassin parisien** the Paris basin.

bassine [basin] nf bowl, basin.

bassiste [basist] nmf bass player.

basson [basɔ̃] nm [instrument] bassoon ; [personne] bassoonist.

bastide [bastid] nf traditional farmhouse or country house in southern France ; walled town (in south-west France).

bastingage [bastɛ̃gaʒ] nm (ship's) rail.

bastion [bastjɔ̃] nm litt & fig bastion.

baston [bastɔ̃] nf tfam punch-up.

bas-ventre [bavɑ̃tr] nm lower abdomen.

bataille [bataj] nf **1.** MIL battle - **2.** [bagarre] fight - **3.** [jeu] : **la bataille** ≃ beggar-my-neighbour UK ; **en bataille** [cheveux] dishevelled UK, disheveled US.

bataillon [batajɔ̃] nm MIL battalion ; fig horde.

bâtard, e [batar, ard] ⟨⟩ adj **1.** [enfant] illegitimate - **2.** péj [style, solution] hybrid. ⟨⟩ nm, f illegitimate child. ➡ **bâtard** nm **1.** [pain] short loaf of bread - **2.** [chien] mongrel.

batavia [batavja] nf Webb lettuce UK, iceberg lettuce.

bateau [bato] nm **1.** [embarcation - gén] boat ; [- plus grand] ship ; **bateau à voile/moteur** sailing/motor boat ; **bateau de pêche** fishing boat ; **mener qqn en bateau** fig to take sb for a ride - **2.** [de trottoir] driveway entrance (low kerb) - **3.** (en apposition inv) [sujet, thème] well-worn ; **c'est bateau!** it's the same old stuff!

bateau-bus [batobys] (*pl* **bateaux-bus**) *nm* riverbus ; **prendre le bateau-bus** to take the riverbus.

bateau-mouche [batomuʃ] (*pl* **bateaux-mouches**) *nm* riverboat (*on the Seine*).

bâti, e [bati] *adj* **1.** [terrain] developed - **2.** [personne] : **bien bâti** well-built. ◆ **bâti** *nm* **1.** COUT tacking - **2.** CONSTR frame, framework.

batifoler [3] [batifɔle] *vi* to frolic.

bâtiment [batimɑ̃] *nm* **1.** [édifice] building - **2.** [dans l'industrie] : **le bâtiment** the building trade - **3.** NAUT ship, vessel.

bâtir [32] [batir] *vt* **1.** CONSTR to build - **2.** *fig* [réputation, fortune] to build (up) ; [théorie, phrase] to construct - **3.** COUT to tack.

bâtisse [batis] *nf* house.

bâton [batɔ̃] *nm* **1.** [gén] stick ; **bâton de ski** ski pole - **2.** *fam fig* 10,000 francs ; **mettre des bâtons dans les roues à qqn** to put a spoke in sb's wheel ; **à bâtons rompus** [conversation] rambling ; **parler à bâtons rompus** to talk of this and that.

bâtonnet [batɔnɛ] *nm* rod.

batracien [batrasjɛ̃] *nm* amphibian.

battage [bataʒ] *nm* : **battage (publicitaire ou médiatique)** (media) hype.

battant, e [batɑ̃, ɑ̃t] ◇ *adj* : **sous une pluie battante** in the pouring ou driving rain ; **le cœur battant** with beating heart. ◇ *nm, f* fighter. ◆ **battant** *nm* **1.** [de porte] door (*of double doors*) ; [de fenêtre] half (*of double window*) - **2.** [de cloche] clapper.

battement [batmɑ̃] *nm* **1.** [mouvement - d'ailes] flap, beating (*U*) ; [- de cœur, pouls] beat, beating (*U*) ; [- de cils, paupières] flutter, fluttering (*U*) - **2.** [intervalle de temps] break ; **une heure de battement** an hour free.

batterie [batri] *nf* **1.** ÉLECTR & MIL battery ; **recharger ses batteries** *fig* to recharge one's batteries - **2.** [attirail] : **batterie de cuisine** kitchen utensils *pl* - **3.** MUS drums *pl* - **4.** [série] : **une batterie de** a string of.

batteur [batœr] *nm* **1.** MUS drummer - **2.** CULIN beater, whisk - **3.** [SPORT - de cricket] batsman ; [- de base-ball] batter.

battre [83] [batr] ◇ *vt* **1.** [gén] to beat ; **battre en neige** [blancs d'œufs] to beat until stiff - **2.** [cartes] to shuffle. ◇ *vi* [gén] to beat ; **battre des cils** to blink ; **battre des mains** to clap (one's hands). ◆ **se battre** *vp* to fight ; **se battre contre qqn** to fight sb.

battu, e [baty] ◇ *pp* ▶ **battre**. ◇ *adj* **1.** [tassé] hard-packed ; **jouer sur terre battue** TENNIS to play on clay - **2.** [fatigué] : **avoir les yeux battus** to have shadows under one's eyes. ◆ **battue** *nf* **1.** [chasse] beat - **2.** [chasse à l'homme] manhunt.

baume [bom] *nm litt & fig* balm ; **mettre du baume au cœur de qqn** to comfort sb.

baux ▶ **bail**.

bavard, e [bavar, ard] ◇ *adj* talkative. ◇ *nm, f* chatterbox ; *péj* gossip.

bavardage [bavardaʒ] *nm* **1.** [papotage] chattering - **2.** (*gén pl*) [racontar] gossip (*U*).

bavarder [3] [bavarde] *vi* to chatter ; *péj* to gossip.

bave [bav] *nf* **1.** [salive] dribble - **2.** [d'animal] slaver - **3.** [de limace] slime.

baver [3] [bave] *vi* **1.** [personne] to dribble - **2.** [animal] to slaver - **3.** [limace] to leave a trail - **4.** [stylo] to leak ; **en baver** *fam* to have a hard ou rough time of it.

bavette [bavɛt] *nf* **1.** [bavoir, de tablier] bib - **2.** [viande] flank ; **tailler une bavette (avec qqn)** *fam* to have a chinwag (with sb).

baveux, euse [bavø, øz] *adj* **1.** [bébé] dribbling - **2.** [omelette] runny.

bavoir [bavwar] *nm* bib.

bavure [bavyr] *nf* **1.** [tache] smudge - **2.** [erreur] blunder.

bayer [3] [baje] *vi* : **bayer aux corneilles** to stand gazing into space.

bazar [bazar] *nm* **1.** [boutique] general store - **2.** *fam* [désordre] jumble, clutter.

bazarder [3] [bazarde] *vt fam* to chuck out, to get rid of.

BCBG (*abr de* **bon chic bon genre**) *nmf & adj* term used to describe an upper-class lifestyle reflected especially in expensive and conservative clothes.

BCE (*abr de* **Banque centrale européenne**) *nf* ECB.

bcp *abr écrite de* **beaucoup**.

bd *abr écrite de* **boulevard**.

BD, bédé [bede] (*abr de* **bande dessinée**) *nf* : **une BD** a comic strip.

beach-volley [bitʃvɔle] (*pl* **beach-volleys**) *nm* beach volleyball ; **jouer au beach-volley** to play beach volleyball.

béant, e [beɑ̃, ɑ̃t] *adj* [plaie, gouffre] gaping ; [yeux] wide open.

béat, e [bea, at] *adj* [heureux] blissful.

beau, belle, beaux [bo, bɛl] *adj* (**bel** [bɛl] *devant voyelle ou 'h' muet*) **1.** [joli - femme] beautiful, good-looking ; [- homme] handsome, good-looking ; [- chose] beautiful - **2.** [temps] fine, good - **3.** (*toujours avant le n*) [important] fine, excellent ; **une belle somme** a tidy sum (of money) - **4.** *iron* [mauvais] : **une belle grippe** a nasty dose of the flu ; **c'est du beau travail!** a fine mess this is! - **5.** (*sens intensif*) **un beau jour** one fine day ; **elle a beau jeu de dire ça** it's easy ou all very well for her to say that.

beau <> *adv* : **il fait beau** the weather is good ou fine ; **j'ai beau essayer...** however hard I try..., try as I may... ; **j'ai beau dire...** whatever I say... <> *nm* : **être au beau fixe** to be set fair ; **avoir le moral au beau fixe** *fig* to have a sunny disposition ; **faire le beau** [chien] to sit up and beg. **belle** *nf* **1.** [femme] lady friend - **2.** [dans un jeu] decider. **de plus belle** *loc adv* more than ever.

Beaubourg [bobur] *npr* name commonly used to refer to the Pompidou Centre.

beaucoup [boku] <> *adv* **1.** [un grand nombre] : **beaucoup de** a lot of, many ; **il y en a beaucoup** there are many ou a lot (of them) - **2.** [une grande quantité] : **beaucoup de** a lot of ; **beaucoup d'énergie** a lot of energy ; **il n'a pas beaucoup de temps** he hasn't a lot of ou much time ; **il n'en a pas beaucoup** he doesn't have much ou a lot (of it) - **3.** *(modifiant un verbe)* a lot ; **il boit beaucoup** he drinks a lot ; **c'est beaucoup dire** that's saying a lot - **4.** *(modifiant un adjectif comparatif)* much, a lot ; **c'est beaucoup mieux** it's much ou a lot better ; **beaucoup trop vite** much too quickly. <> *pron inv* many ; **nous sommes beaucoup à penser que...** many of us think that... **de beaucoup** *loc adv* by far.

beauf [bof] *nm* **1.** *péj* stereotype of average French man with narrow views - **2.** *fam* [beau-frère] brother-in-law.

beau-fils [bofis] *nm* **1.** [gendre] son-in-law - **2.** [de remariage] stepson.

beau-frère [bofrɛr] *nm* brother-in-law.

beau-père [boper] *nm* **1.** [père du conjoint] father-in-law - **2.** [de remariage] stepfather.

beauté [bote] *nf* beauty ; **de toute beauté** absolutely beautiful ; **en beauté** [magnifiquement] in great style ; *sout* [femme] ravishing.

beaux-arts [bozar] *nmpl* fine art *sg*. **Beaux-Arts** *nmpl* : **les Beaux-Arts** French national art school.

beaux-parents [boparɑ̃] *nmpl* **1.** [de l'homme] husband's parents, in-laws - **2.** [de la femme] wife's parents, in-laws.

bébé [bebe] *nm* baby.

bébé-bulle [bebebyl] *(pl* bébés-bulles*)* *nm* bubble baby.

bébé-éprouvette [bebeepruvɛt] *(pl* bébés-éprouvette*)* *nm* test-tube baby.

bébête [bebɛt] *adj* silly.

bec [bɛk] *nm* **1.** [d'oiseau] beak - **2.** [d'instrument de musique] mouthpiece - **3.** [de casserole] lip ; **bec de gaz** [réverbère] gaslamp *(in street)* ; **bec verseur** spout - **4.** *fam* [bouche] mouth ; **ouvrir le bec** to open one's mouth ; **clouer le bec à qqn** to shut sb up.

bécane [bekan] *nf fam* **1.** [moto, vélo] bike - **2.** [ordinateur etc] machine.

bécasse [bekas] *nf* **1.** [oiseau] woodcock - **2.** *fam* [femme sotte] silly goose.

bec-de-lièvre [bɛkdəljɛvr] *(pl* becs-de-lièvre*)* *nm* harelip.

bêche [bɛʃ] *nf* spade.

bêcher [4] [beʃe] *vt* to dig.

bécoter [3] [bekɔte] *vt fam* to snog *UK* ou smooch with. **se bécoter** *vp* to snog *UK*, to smooch.

becquée [beke] *nf* : **donner la becquée à** to feed.

becqueter, béqueter [27] [bɛkte] *vt* to peck at.

bedaine [bədɛn] *nf* potbelly.

bédé = **BD**.

bedonnant, e [bədɔnɑ̃, ɑ̃t] *adj* potbellied.

bée [be] *adj* : **bouche bée** open-mouthed.

bégayer [11] [begeje] <> *vi* to have a stutter ou stammer. <> *vt* to stammer (out).

bégonia [begɔnja] *nm* begonia.

bègue [bɛg] <> *adj* : **être bègue** to have a stutter ou stammer. <> *nmf* stutterer, stammerer.

béguin [begɛ̃] *nm* : **avoir le béguin pour qqn** *fam* to have a crush on sb.

beige [bɛʒ] *adj & nm* beige.

beignet [bɛɲɛ] *nm* fritter.

bel [bɛl] **beau**.

bêler [4] [bele] *vi* to bleat.

belette [bəlɛt] *nf* weasel.

belge [bɛlʒ] *adj* Belgian. **Belge** *nmf* Belgian.

Belgique [bɛlʒik] *nf* : **la Belgique** Belgium.

bélier [belje] *nm* **1.** [animal] ram - **2.** [poutre] battering ram. **Bélier** *nm* ASTROL Aries.

belladone [beladɔn] *nf* deadly nightshade.

belle [bɛl] *adj & nf* **beau**.

belle-famille [bɛlfamij] *nf* **1.** [de l'homme] husband's family, in-laws *pl* - **2.** [de la femme] wife's family, in-laws *pl*.

belle-fille [bɛlfij] *nf* **1.** [épouse du fils] daughter-in-law - **2.** [de remariage] step-daughter.

belle-mère [bɛlmɛr] *nf* **1.** [mère du conjoint] mother-in-law - **2.** [de remariage] stepmother.

belle-sœur [bɛlsœr] *nf* sister-in-law.

belligérant, e [beliʒerɑ̃, ɑ̃t] *adj & nm, f* belligerent.

belliqueux, euse [belikø, øz] *adj* [peuple] warlike ; [humeur, tempérament] aggressive.

belvédère [bɛlvedɛr] *nm* **1.** [construction] belvedere - **2.** [terrasse] viewpoint.

bémol [bemɔl] *adj & nm* MUS flat.

bénédiction [benediksjɔ̃] *nf* blessing.

bénéfice [benefis] *nm* **1.** [avantage] advantage, benefit ; **au bénéfice de** in aid of - **2.** [profit] profit.

bénéficiaire [benefisjɛr] <> *nmf* [gén] beneficiary ; [de chèque] payee. <> *adj* [marge] profit *(avant n)* ; [résultat, société] profit-making.

bénéficier [9] [benefisje] *vi* : **bénéficier de** [profiter de] to benefit from ; [jouir de] to have, to enjoy ; [obtenir] to have, to get.

bénéfique [benefik] *adj* beneficial.

Bénélux, Benelux [benelyks] *nm* : **le Bénélux** Benelux.

benêt [bənɛ] *nm* clod.

bénévole [benevɔl] <> *adj* voluntary. <> *nmf* volunteer, voluntary worker.

bénin, igne [benɛ̃, iɲ] *adj* [maladie, accident] minor ; **une forme bénigne de rougeole** a mild form of measles ; [cancer] benign.

bénir [32] [benir] *vt* **1.** [gén] to bless - **2.** [se réjouir de] to thank God for.

bénitier [benitje] *nm* holy water font.

benjamin, e [bɛ̃ʒamɛ̃, in] *nm, f* [de famille] youngest child ; [de groupe] youngest member.

benne [bɛn] *nf* **1.** [de camion] tipper - **2.** [de téléphérique] car - **3.** [pour déchets] skip *UK*, dump truck.

benzine [bɛ̃zin] *nf* benzine.

béotien, enne [beɔsjɛ̃, ɛn] *nm, f* philistine.

BEP, Bep *(abr de brevet d'études professionnelles) nm technical school diploma (taken at age 16).*

BEPC, Bepc *(abr de brevet d'études du premier cycle) nm former school certificate (taken at age 16).*

béquille [bekij] *nf* **1.** [pour marcher] crutch - **2.** [d'un deux-roues] stand.

berceau, x [bɛrso] *nm* cradle.

bercer [16] [bɛrse] *vt* [bébé, bateau] to rock.

berceuse [bɛrsøz] *nf* **1.** [chanson] lullaby - **2.** *Québec* [fauteuil] rocking chair.

béret [berɛ] *nm* beret.

berge [bɛrʒ] *nf* **1.** [bord] bank - **2.** *fam* [an] : **il a plus de 50 berges** he's over 50.

berger, ère [bɛrʒe, ɛr] *nm, f* shepherd (f shepherdess). ➤ **berger allemand** *nm* Alsatian *UK*, German shepherd.

bergerie [bɛrʒəri] *nf* sheepfold.

berk [bɛrk] *interj fam* ugh, yuk.

Berlin [bɛrlɛ̃] *npr* Berlin.

berline [bɛrlin] *nf* saloon (car) *UK*, sedan *US*.

berlingot [bɛrlɛ̃go] *nm* **1.** [de lait] carton - **2.** [bonbon] boiled sweet.

berlue [bɛrly] *nf* : **j'ai la berlue!** I must be seeing things!

bermuda [bɛrmyda] *nm* bermuda shorts *pl*.

berne [bɛrn] *nf* : **en berne** ≃ at half-mast.

berner [3] [bɛrne] *vt* to fool.

besogne [bəzɔɲ] *nf* job, work *(U)*.

besoin [bəzwɛ̃] *nm* need ; **avoir besoin de qqch/de faire qqch** to need sthg/to do sthg ; **au besoin** if necessary, if need ou needs be. ➤ **besoins** *nmpl* [exigences] needs ; **faire ses besoins** to relieve o.s.

bestial, e, aux [bɛstjal, o] *adj* bestial, brutish.

bestiole [bɛstjɔl] *nf* (little) creature.

bétail [betaj] *nm* cattle *pl*.

bête [bɛt] <> *nf* [animal] animal ; [insecte] insect ; **bête de somme** beast of burden. <> *adj* [stupide] stupid.

bêtise [betiz] *nf* **1.** [stupidité] stupidity - **2.** [action, remarque] stupid thing ; **faire/dire une bêtise** to do/say something stupid.

béton [betɔ̃] *nm* [matériau] concrete ; **béton armé** reinforced concrete.

bétonnière [betɔnjɛr] *nf* cement mixer.

betterave [bɛtrav] *nf* beetroot *UK*, beet *US* ; **betterave sucrière** ou **à sucre** sugar beet.

beugler [5] [bøgle] *vi* [bovin] to moo, to low.

beurk [bœrk] *fam* = **berk**.

beurre [bœr] *nm* [aliment] butter.

beurrer [5] [bœre] *vt* to butter.

beurrier [bœrje] *nm* butter dish.

beuverie [bœvri] *nf* drinking session.

bévue [bevy] *nf* blunder.

Beyrouth [berut] *npr* Beirut.

biais [bjɛ] *nm* **1.** [ligne oblique] slant ; **en** ou **de biais** [de travers] at an angle ; *fig* indirectly - **2.** COUT bias - **3.** [moyen détourné] expedient ; **par le biais de** by means of.

biaiser [4] [bjeze] *vi fig* to dodge the issue.

bibande [bibɑ̃d] *adj* dual-band.

bibelot [biblo] *nm* trinket, curio.

biberon [bibrɔ̃] *nm* baby's bottle.

bible [bibl] *nf* bible.

bibliographie [biblijɔgrafi] *nf* bibliography.

bibliophile [biblijɔfil] *nmf* book lover.

bibliothécaire [biblijɔtekɛr] *nmf* librarian.

bibliothèque [biblijɔtɛk] *nf* **1.** [meuble] bookcase - **2.** [édifice, collection] library ; **la Bibliothèque nationale de France** the French national library.

biblique [biblik] *adj* biblical.

bicarbonate [bikarbɔnat] *nm* : bicarbonate (de soude) bicarbonate of soda.

biceps [biseps] *nm* biceps.

biche [biʃ] *nf* ZOOL hind, doe.

bicolore [bikɔlɔr] *adj* two-coloured *UK*, two-colored *US*.

bicoque [bikɔk] *nf péj* house.

bicorne [bikɔrn] *nm* cocked hat.

bicyclette [bisiklɛt] *nf* bicycle ; **rouler à bicyclette** to cycle.

bide [bid] *nm fam* **1.** [ventre] belly - **2.** [échec] flop.

bidet [bidɛ] *nm* **1.** [sanitaire] bidet - **2.** *hum* [cheval] nag.

bidon [bidɔ̃] *nm* **1.** [récipient] can - **2.** *fam* [ventre] belly - **3.** *(en apposition inv) fam* [faux] phoney, phony *US*.

bidonville [bidɔ̃vil] *nm* shantytown.

bielle [bjɛl] *nf* connecting rod.

bien [bjɛ̃] <> *adj inv* (**mieux** *est le comparatif et le superlatif de* **bien**) **1.** [satisfaisant] good ; **il est bien comme prof** he's a good teacher ; **il est bien, ce bureau** this is a good office - **2.** [en bonne santé] well ; **je ne me sens pas bien** I don't feel well - **3.** [joli] good-looking ; **tu ne trouves pas qu'elle est bien comme ça?** don't you think she looks good ou nice like that? - **4.** [à l'aise] comfortable - **5.** [convenable] respectable. <> *nm* **1.** [sens moral] : **le bien et le mal** good and evil - **2.** [intérêt] good ; **c'est pour ton bien** I'm telling you this for your own good - **3.** [richesse, propriété] property, possession ; **faire du bien à qqn** to do sb good ; **dire du bien de qqn/qqch** to speak well of sb/sthg ; **mener à bien** to bring to fruition, to complete. <> *adv* **1.** [de manière satisfaisante] well ; **on mange bien ici** the food's good here ; **il ne s'est pas bien conduit** he didn't behave well ; **tu as bien fait** you did the right thing ; **tu ferais bien d'y aller** you would be wise to go ; **c'est bien fait!** it serves him/her etc right! - **2.** [sens intensif] quite, really ; **bien souvent** quite often ; **en es-tu bien sûr?** are you quite sure (about it)? ; **j'espère bien que...** I do hope that... ; **on a bien ri** we had a good laugh ; **il y a bien trois heures que j'attends** I've been waiting for at least three hours ; **c'est bien aimable à vous** it's very kind ou good of you - **3.** [renforçant un comparatif] : **il est parti bien plus tard** he left much later ; **on était bien moins riches** we were a lot worse off ou poorer - **4.** [servant à conclure ou à introduire] : **bien, je t'écoute** well, I'm listening - **5.** [en effet] : **c'est bien lui** it really is him ; **c'est bien ce que je disais** that's just what I said. <> *interj* : **eh bien!** oh well! ; **eh bien, qu'en penses-tu?** well, what do you think? <> **biens** *nmpl* property (*U*) ; **biens de consommation** consumer goods. <> **bien de, bien des** *loc adj* : **bien des gens sont venus** quite a lot of people came ; **bien des fois** many times ; **il a bien de la chance** he's very ou really lucky ; **il a eu bien de la peine à me convaincre** he had quite a lot of trouble convincing me. <> **bien entendu** *loc adv* of course. <> **bien que** *loc conj* (+ *subjonctif*) although, though. <> **bien sûr** *loc adv* of course, certainly.

bien-aimé, e [bjɛ̃neme] (*mpl* **bien-aimés**, *fpl* **bien-aimées**) *adj & nm, f* beloved.

bien-être [bjɛ̃nɛtr] *nm inv* [physique] well-being.

bienfaisance [bjɛ̃fəzɑ̃s] *nf* charity.

bienfaisant, e [bjɛ̃fəzɑ̃, ɑ̃t] *adj* beneficial.

bienfait [bjɛ̃fɛ] *nm* **1.** [effet bénéfique] benefit - **2.** [faveur] kindness.

bienfaiteur, trice [bjɛ̃fɛtœr, tris] *nm, f* benefactor.

bien-fondé [bjɛ̃fɔ̃de] (*pl* **bien-fondés**) *nm* validity.

bienheureux, euse [bjɛ̃nœrø, øz] *adj* **1.** RELIG blessed - **2.** [heureux] happy.

bientôt [bjɛ̃to] *adv* soon ; **à bientôt!** see you soon!

bienveillance [bjɛ̃vɛjɑ̃s] *nf* kindness.

bienveillant, e [bjɛ̃vɛjɑ̃, ɑ̃t] *adj* kindly.

bienvenu, e [bjɛ̃vny] <> *adj* [qui arrive à propos] welcome. <> *nm, f* : **être le bienvenu/la bienvenue** to be welcome ; **soyez le bienvenu!** welcome! <> **bienvenue** *nf* welcome ; **souhaiter la bienvenue à qqn** to welcome sb.

bière [bjɛr] *nf* **1.** [boisson] beer ; **bière blonde** lager ; **bière brune** brown ale ; **bière pression** draught *UK* ou draft *US* beer - **2.** [cercueil] coffin.

bifidus [bifidys] *nm* bifidus ; **yaourt au bifidus bio** yogurt, yogurt containing bifidus.

bifteck [biftɛk] *nm* steak.

bifurcation [bifyrkasjɔ̃] *nf* [embranchement] fork ; *fig* new direction.

bifurquer [3] [bifyrke] *vi* **1.** [route, voie ferrée] to fork - **2.** [voiture] to turn off - **3.** *fig* [personne] to branch off.

bigamie [bigami] *nf* bigamy.

bigoudi [bigudi] *nm* curler.

bijou, x [biʒu] *nm* **1.** [joyau] jewel - **2.** *fig* [chef-d'œuvre] gem.

bijouterie [biʒutri] *nf* [magasin] jeweller's *UK* ou jeweler's *US* (shop).

bijoutier, ère [biʒutje, ɛr] *nm, f* jeweller *UK*, jeweler *US*.

Bikini® [bikini] *nm* bikini.

bilan [bilɑ̃] *nm* **1.** FIN balance sheet ; **déposer**

son bilan to declare bankruptcy - **2.** [état d'une situation] state of affairs ; **faire le bilan (de)** to take stock (of) ; **bilan de santé** checkup.

bilatéral, e, aux [bilateral, o] adj **1.** [stationnement] on both sides (of the road) - **2.** [contrat, accord] bilateral.

bile [bil] nf bile ; **se faire de la bile** fam to worry.

biliaire [biljɛr] adj biliary ; **calcul biliaire** gallstone ; **vésicule biliaire** gall bladder.

bilingue [bilɛ̃g] adj bilingual.

billard [bijar] nm **1.** [jeu] billiards (U) - **2.** [table de jeu] billiard table.

bille [bij] nf **1.** [d'enfant] marble - **2.** [de bois] block of wood.

billet [bijɛ] nm **1.** [lettre] note - **2.** [argent] : **billet (de banque)** (bank) note, bill US ; **un billet de 100 euros** a 100-euro note - **3.** [ticket] ticket ; **billet de train/d'avion** train/plane ticket ; **billet de loterie** lottery ticket.

billetterie [bijɛtri] nf **1.** [à l'aéroport] ticket desk ; [à la gare] booking office ou hall - **2.** BANQUE cash dispenser UK, ATM US.

billion [biljɔ̃] nm billion UK, trillion US.

bimensuel, elle [bimɑ̃sɥɛl] adj fortnightly UK, twice monthly. ➤ **bimensuel** nm fortnightly review UK, semimonthly US.

bimoteur [bimɔtœr] nm twin-engined plane.

binaire [binɛr] adj binary.

biner [3] [bine] vt to hoe.

binocle [binɔkl] nm pince-nez. ➤ **binocles** nmpl fam vieilli specs.

bio [bjo] adj inv organic ; **aliments bio** organic food.

biocarburant [bjɔkarbyrɑ̃] nm biofuel.

biochimie [bjɔʃimi] nf biochemistry.

biodégradable [bjɔdegradabl] adj biodegradable.

biographie [bjɔgrafi] nf biography.

biologie [bjɔlɔʒi] nf biology.

biologique [bjɔlɔʒik] adj **1.** [sciences] biological - **2.** [naturel] organic.

biopsie [bjɔpsi] nf biopsy.

biorythme [bjɔritm] nm biorhythm.

bioterrorisme [bjɔtɛrɔrism] nm bioterrorism.

bip [bip] nm **1.** [signal] tone, beep ; **parlez après le bip (sonore)** please speak after the beep ou tone - **2.** [appareil] bleeper UK, beeper US.

biréacteur [bireaktœr] nm twin-engined jet.

bis¹, e [bi, biz] adj greyish-brown ; **pain bis** brown bread.

bis² [bis] adv **1.** [dans adresse] : **5 bis** 5a - **2.** [à la fin d'un spectacle] encore.

bisannuel, elle [bizanɥɛl] adj biennial.

biscornu, e [biskɔrny] adj **1.** [difforme] irregularly shaped - **2.** [bizarre] weird.

biscotte [biskɔt] nf toasted bread sold in packets and often eaten for breakfast.

biscuit [biskɥi] nm **1.** [sec] biscuit UK, cookie US ; [salé] cracker - **2.** [gâteau] sponge.

bise [biz] nf **1.** [vent] north wind - **2.** fam [baiser] kiss ; **grosses bises** love and kisses.

biseau, x [bizo] nm bevel ; **en biseau** bevelled UK, beveled US.

bison [bizɔ̃] nm bison.

bisou [bizu] nm fam kiss.

bissextile [bisɛkstil] ➤ **année.**

bistouri [bisturi] nm lancet.

bistrot, bistro [bistro] nm fam cafe, bar.

bit [bit] nm INFORM bit.

bivouac [bivwak] nm bivouac.

bivouaquer [3] [bivwake] vi to bivouac.

bizarre [bizar] adj strange, odd.

bizutage [bizytaʒ] nm practical jokes played on new arrivals in a school or college.

black-out [blakawt] nm blackout.

blafard, e [blafar, ard] adj pale.

blague [blag] nf [plaisanterie] joke.

blaguer [3] [blage] fam vi to joke.

blagueur, euse [blagœr, øz] fam ◇ adj jokey. ◇ nm, f joker.

blaireau, x [blɛro] nm **1.** [animal] badger - **2.** [de rasage] shaving brush - **3.** fam péj [homme] ≃ Essex man UK, ≃ Joe Sixpack US ; [femme] ≃ Essex girl UK.

blâme [blam] nm **1.** [désapprobation] disapproval - **2.** [sanction] reprimand.

blâmer [3] [blame] vt **1.** [désapprouver] to blame - **2.** [sanctionner] to reprimand.

blanc, blanche [blɑ̃, blɑ̃ʃ] adj **1.** [gén] white - **2.** [non écrit] blank - **3.** [pâle] pale. ➤ **blanc** nm **1.** [couleur] white - **2.** [personne] white (man) - **3.** [linge de maison] : **le blanc** the (household) linen - **4.** [sur page] blank (space) - **5.** [de volaille] white meat - **6.** [vin] white (wine) ; **chauffé à blanc** white-hot. ➤ **blanche** nf **1.** [personne] white (woman) - **2.** MUS minim UK, half note US. ➤ **blanc d'œuf** nm egg white.

blancheur [blɑ̃ʃœr] nf whiteness.

blanchir [32] [blɑ̃ʃir] ◇ vt **1.** [mur] to whitewash - **2.** [linge, argent] to launder - **3.** [légumes] to blanch - **4.** [sucre] to refine ; [décolorer] to bleach. ◇ vi [d'émotion] : **blanchir (de)** to go white (with).

blanchissage [blɑ̃ʃisaʒ] nm [de linge] laundering.

blanchisserie [blɑ̃ʃisri] *nf* laundry.

blasé, e [blaze] *adj* blasé.

blason [blazɔ̃] *nm* coat of arms.

blasphème [blasfɛm] *nm* blasphemy.

blasphémer [18] [blasfeme] *vt & vi* to blaspheme.

blatte [blat] *nf* cockroach.

blazer [blazɛr] *nm* blazer.

blé [ble] *nm* **1.** [céréale] wheat, corn *UK* - **2.** *fam* [argent] dough.

blême [blɛm] *adj* : **blême (de)** pale (with).

blennorragie [blenɔraʒi] *nf* gonorrhoea.

blessant, e [blesɑ̃, ɑ̃t] *adj* hurtful.

blessé, e [blese] *nm, f* wounded ou injured person.

blesser [4] [blese] *vt* **1.** [physiquement - accidentellement] to injure, to hurt ; [- par arme] to wound ; **ses chaussures lui blessent les pieds** his shoes make his feet sore - **2.** [moralement] to hurt. ◆ **se blesser** *vp* to injure o.s., to hurt o.s. ; **elle s'est blessée au bras** she injured ou hurt her arm.

blessure [blesyr] *nf litt & fig* wound.

blet, blette [blɛ, blɛt] *adj* overripe.

bleu, e [blø] ◇ *adj* **1.** [couleur] blue - **2.** [viande] very rare. ◇ *nm, f fam* [novice - généralement] newcomer ; [- à l'armée] raw recruit ; [- à l'université] freshman, fresher *UK*. ◆ **bleu** *nm* **1.** [couleur] blue - **2.** [meurtrissure] bruise - **3.** [fromage] blue cheese - **4.** [vêtement] : **bleu de travail** overalls *pl*, coveralls *pl US*.

bleuet [bløɛ] *nm* cornflower ; *Québec* [fruit] blueberry.

bleuir [32] [bløir] *vt & vi* to turn blue.

bleuté, e [bløte] *adj* bluish.

blindé, e [blɛ̃de] *adj* [véhicule] armoured *UK*, armored *US* ; [porte, coffre] armour-plated *UK*, armor-plated *US*. ◆ **blindé** *nm* armoured car *UK* ou armored car *US*.

blinder [3] [blɛ̃de] *vt* [véhicule] to armour *UK*, to armor *US* ; [porte, coffre] to armour-plate *UK*, to armor-plate *US*.

blizzard [blizar] *nm* blizzard.

bloc [blɔk] *nm* **1.** [gén] block ; **faire bloc avec/contre qqn** to stand (together) with/against sb - **2.** [assemblage] unit ; **bloc opératoire** [salle] operating theatre *UK* ou room *US* ; [locaux] surgical unit ; **bloc sanitaire** toilet block.

blocage [blɔkaʒ] *nm* **1.** ÉCON freeze, freezing *(U)* - **2.** [de roue] locking - **3.** PSYCHO (mental) block.

blockhaus [blɔkos] *nm* blockhouse.

bloc-notes [blɔknɔt] *nm* notepad, scratchpad *US*.

blocus [blɔkys] *nm* blockade.

blond, e [blɔ̃, blɔ̃d] ◇ *adj* fair, blond. ◇ *nm, f* fair-haired ou blond man, fair-haired ou blonde woman. ◆ **blond** *nm* : **blond cendré/vénitien/platine** ash/strawberry/platinum blond. ◆ **blonde** *nf* **1.** [cigarette] Virginia cigarette - **2.** [bière] lager.

blondeur [blɔ̃dœr] *nf* blondness, fairness.

bloquer [3] [blɔke] *vt* **1.** [porte, freins] to jam ; [roues] to lock - **2.** [route, chemin] to block - **3.** [personne] : **être bloqué** to be stuck - **4.** [prix, salaires, crédit] to freeze - **5.** PSYCHO : **être bloqué** to have a (mental) block. ◆ **se bloquer** *vp* [se coincer] to jam.

blottir [32] [blɔtir] ◆ **se blottir** *vp* : **se blottir (contre)** to snuggle up (to).

blouse [bluz] *nf* [de travail, d'écolier] smock.

blouson [bluzɔ̃] *nm* blouson *US*, bomber jacket.

blue-jean [bludʒin] (*pl* **blue-jeans** [bludʒins]) *nm* jeans *pl*.

blues [bluz] *nm inv* blues.

bluffer [3] [blœfe] *vi & vt fam* to bluff.

blush [blœʃ] *nm* blusher.

BNF *nf abr de* **Bibliothèque nationale de France**.

boa [bɔa] *nm* boa.

bobard [bɔbar] *nm fam* fib.

bobine [bɔbin] *nf* **1.** [cylindre] reel, spool - **2.** ÉLECTR coil.

bobo [bɔbo] (*abr de* **Bourgeois bohème**) *fam nmf* bobo.

bobsleigh [bɔbslɛg] *nm* bobsleigh *UK*, bobsled *US*.

bocage [bɔkaʒ] *nm* GÉOGR bocage.

bocal, aux [bɔkal, o] *nm* jar.

body-building [bɔdibildiŋ] *nm* : **le body-building** body building *(U)*.

bœuf [bœf] (*pl* **-s** [bø]) *nm* **1.** [animal] ox - **2.** [viande] beef ; **bœuf bourguignon** beef stew in a red-wine sauce.

bof [bɔf] *interj fam* [exprime le mépris] so what? ; [exprime la lassitude] I don't really care.

bogue [bɔg], **bug** [bʌg] *nm* INFORM bug ; **le bogue de l'an 2000** the millennium bug.

bohème [bɔɛm] *adj* bohemian.

bohémien, enne [bɔemjɛ̃, ɛn] *nm, f* **1.** [tsigane] gipsy - **2.** [non-conformiste] bohemian.

boire [108] [bwar] ◇ *vt* **1.** [s'abreuver] to drink - **2.** [absorber] to soak up, to absorb. ◇ *vi* to drink.

bois [bwa] ◇ *nm* wood ; **en bois** wooden. ◇ *nmpl* **1.** MUS woodwind *(U)* - **2.** [cornes] antlers.

boisé, e [bwaze] *adj* wooded.

boiserie [bwazri] *nf* panelling (U) UK, paneling (U) US.

boisson [bwasɔ̃] *nf* [breuvage] drink.

boîte [bwat] *nf* 1. [récipient] box ; **boîte de conserve** tin UK, can ; **boîte aux lettres** [pour la réception] letterbox ; [pour l'envoi] postbox UK, mailbox US ; **boîte à musique** musical box UK, music box US ; **boîte postale** post office box ; **en boîte** tinned UK, canned - 2. AUTO : **boîte à gants** glove compartment, glove box ; **boîte de vitesses** gearbox UK, transmission US - 3. INFORM : **boîte aux lettres électronique** electronic mailbox ; **boîte vocale** voice mail - 4. *fam* [entreprise] company, firm ; [lycée] school - 5. *fam* [discothèque] : **boîte (de nuit)** nightclub, club.

boiter [3] [bwate] *vi* [personne] to limp.

boiteux, euse [bwatø, øz] *adj* 1. [personne] lame - 2. [meuble] wobbly - 3. *fig* [raisonnement] shaky.

boîtier [bwatje] *nm* 1. [boîte] case - 2. TECHNOL casing.

bol [bɔl] *nm* 1. [récipient] bowl - 2. [contenu] bowl, bowlful ; **prendre un bol d'air** to get some fresh air.

bolet [bɔlɛ] *nm* boletus.

bolide [bɔlid] *nm* [véhicule] racing UK ou race US car.

Bolivie [bɔlivi] *nf* : **la Bolivie** Bolivia.

bombance [bɔ̃bɑ̃s] *nf fam* **faire bombance** to have a feast.

bombardement [bɔ̃bardəmɑ̃] *nm* bombardment, bombing (U).

bombarder [3] [bɔ̃barde] *vt* 1. MIL to bomb - 2. [assaillir] : **bombarder qqn/qqch de** to bombard sb/sthg with.

bombardier [bɔ̃bardje] *nm* 1. [avion] bomber - 2. [aviateur] bombardier.

bombe [bɔ̃b] *nf* 1. [projectile] bomb ; *fig* bombshell ; **bombe atomique** atomic bomb ; **bombe à retardement** time bomb - 2. [casquette] riding hat - 3. [atomiseur] spray, aerosol.

bombé, e [bɔ̃be] *adj* bulging, rounded.

bomber [bɔ̃bœr] *nm* bomber jacket.

bon, bonne [bɔ̃, bɔn] *adj* (**meilleur** *est le comparatif et le superlatif de* **bon**) 1. [gén] good - 2. [généreux] good, kind - 3. [utilisable - billet, carte] valid - 4. [correct] right - 5. [dans l'expression d'un souhait] : **bonne année!** Happy New Year! ; **bonne chance!** good luck! ; **bonnes vacances!** have a nice holiday UK ou vacation! ; **être bon pour qqch/pour faire qqch** *fam* to be fit for sthg/for doing sthg ; **tu es bon pour une contravention** you'll end up with ou you'll get a parking ticket ; **bon à** (+ *infinitif*) fit to ; **c'est bon à**

savoir that's worth knowing. ► **bon** ◇ *adv* : **il fait bon** the weather's fine, it's fine ; **sentir bon** to smell good ; **tenir bon** to stand firm. ◇ *interj* 1. [marque de satisfaction] good! - 2. [marque de surprise] : **ah bon!** really? ◇ *nm* 1. [constatant un droit] voucher - 2. FIN : **bon du Trésor** FIN treasury bill ou bond - 3. (*gén pl*) [personne] : **les bons et les méchants** good people and wicked people. ► **pour de bon** *loc adv* seriously, really.

bonbon [bɔ̃bɔ̃] *nm* 1. [friandise] sweet UK, piece of candy US - 2. Belgique [gâteau] biscuit.

bonbonne [bɔ̃bɔn] *nf* demijohn.

bonbonnière [bɔ̃bɔnjɛr] *nf* [boîte] sweetbox UK, candy box US.

bond [bɔ̃] *nm* [d'animal, de personne] leap, bound ; [de balle] bounce ; **faire un bond** to leap (forward).

bonde [bɔ̃d] *nf* 1. [d'évier] plug - 2. [trou] bunghole - 3. [bouchon] bung.

bondé, e [bɔ̃de] *adj* packed.

bondir [32] [bɔ̃dir] *vi* 1. [sauter] to leap, to bound ; **bondir sur qqn/qqch** to pounce on sb/sthg - 2. [s'élancer] to leap forward.

bonheur [bɔnœr] *nm* 1. [félicité] happiness - 2. [chance] (good) luck, good fortune ; **par bonheur** happily, fortunately ; **porter bonheur** to be lucky, to bring good luck.

bonhomme [bɔnɔm] (*pl* **bonshommes** [bɔ̃zɔm]) *nm* 1. *fam péj* [homme] fellow - 2. [représentation] man ; **bonhomme de neige** snowman.

bonification [bɔnifikasjɔ̃] *nf* 1. [de terre, de vin] improvement - 2. SPORT bonus points *pl*.

bonjour [bɔ̃ʒur] *nm* hello ; [avant midi] good morning ; [après midi] good afternoon.

bonne [bɔn] ◇ *nf* maid. ◇ *adj* ► **bon**.

bonnet [bɔnɛ] *nm* 1. [coiffure] (woolly) hat ; **bonnet de bain** swimming cap - 2. [de soutien-gorge] cup.

bonneterie [bɔnɛtri] *nf* [commerce] hosiery (business ou trade).

bonsoir [bɔ̃swar] *nm* [en arrivant] hello, good evening ; [en partant] goodbye, good evening ; [en se couchant] good night.

bonté [bɔ̃te] *nf* 1. [qualité] goodness, kindness ; **avoir la bonté de faire qqch** *sout* to be so good ou kind as to do sthg - 2. (*gén pl*) [acte] act of kindness.

bonus [bɔnys] *nm* [prime d'assurance] no-claims bonus.

booléen, enne [buleɛ̃, ɛn] *adj* Boolean.

booster [3] [buste] *vt* to boost.

bord [bɔr] *nm* 1. [de table, de vêtement]

edge ; [de verre, de chapeau] rim ; **à ras bords to the brim** - **2.** [de rivière] bank ; [de lac] edge, shore ; **au bord de la mer at the seaside** - **3.** [de bois, jardin] edge ; [de route] edge, side - **4.** [d'un moyen de transport] : **passer par-dessus bord to fall overboard.** ➤ **à bord de** *loc prép* : **à bord de qqch on board sthg.** ➤ **au bord de** *loc prép* at the edge of ; *fig* on the verge of.

bordeaux [bɔrdo] ◇ *nm* **1.** [vin] Bordeaux - **2.** [couleur] claret. ◇ *adj inv* claret.

bordel [bɔrdɛl] *nm vulg* **1.** [maison close] brothel - **2.** [désordre] shambles *sg*.

border [3] [bɔrde] *vt* **1.** [vêtement] : **border qqch de to edge sthg with** - **2.** [être en bordure de] to line - **3.** [couverture, personne] to tuck in.

bordereau, x [bɔrdəro] *nm* **1.** [liste] schedule - **2.** [facture] invoice - **3.** [relevé] slip.

bordure [bɔrdyr] *nf* **1.** [bord] edge ; **en bordure de** on the edge of - **2.** [de fleurs] border.

borgne [bɔrɲ] *adj* [personne] one-eyed.

borne [bɔrn] *nf* **1.** [marque] boundary marker - **2.** [limite] limit, bounds *pl* ; **dépasser les bornes to go too far** ; **sans bornes boundless** - **3.** *fam* [kilomètre] kilometre *UK*, kilometer *US*.

borné, e [bɔrne] *adj* [personne] narrow-minded ; [esprit] narrow.

borner [3] [bɔrne] *vt* [terrain] to limit ; [projet, ambition] to limit, to restrict. ➤ **se borner** *vp* : **se borner à qqch/à faire qqch** [suj: personne] to confine o.s. to sthg/to doing sthg.

bosniaque [bɔsnjak] *adj* Bosnian. ➤ **Bosniaque** *nmf* Bosnian.

Bosnie [bɔsni] *nf* : **la Bosnie** Bosnia.

bosquet [bɔskɛ] *nm* copse.

bosse [bɔs] *nf* **1.** [sur tête, sur route] bump - **2.** [de bossu, chameau] hump.

bosser [3] [bɔse] *vi fam* to work hard.

bossu, e [bɔsy] ◇ *adj* hunchbacked. ◇ *nm, f* hunchback.

bot [bo] ➤ **pied.**

botanique [bɔtanik] ◇ *adj* botanical. ◇ *nf* : **la botanique** botany.

botte [bɔt] *nf* **1.** [chaussure] boot - **2.** [de légumes] bunch - **3.** [en escrime] thrust, lunge.

botter [3] [bɔte] *vt* **1.** [chausser] : **être botté de cuir** to be wearing leather boots - **2.** *fam* [donner un coup de pied à] to boot - **3.** *fam vieilli* [plaire à] : **ça me botte** I dig it.

bottier [bɔtje] *nm* [de bottes] bootmaker ; [de chaussures] shoemaker.

Bottin® [bɔtɛ̃] *nm* phone book.

bottine [bɔtin] *nf* (ankle) boot.

bouc [buk] *nm* **1.** [animal] (billy) goat ; **bouc émissaire** *fig* scapegoat - **2.** [barbe] goatee.

boucan [bukɑ̃] *nm fam* row, racket.

bouche [buʃ] *nf* **1.** [anatomie] mouth - **2.** [orifice] : **bouche d'incendie** fire hydrant ; **bouche de métro** metro entrance ou exit.

bouché, e [buʃe] *adj* **1.** [en bouteille] bottled - **2.** *fam* [personne] dumb, thick.

bouche-à-bouche [buʃabuʃ] *nm inv* : **faire du bouche-à-bouche à qqn** to give sb mouth-to-mouth resuscitation.

bouchée [buʃe] *nf* mouthful.

boucher¹ [3] [buʃe] *vt* **1.** [fermer - bouteille] to cork ; [- trou] to fill (in ou up) - **2.** [passage, vue] to block.

boucher², ère [buʃe, ɛr] *nm, f* butcher.

boucherie [buʃri] *nf* **1.** [magasin] butcher's (shop) - **2.** *fig* [carnage] slaughter.

bouche-trou [buʃtru] (*pl* **bouche-trous**) *nm* **1.** [personne] : **servir de bouche-trou** to make up (the) numbers - **2.** [objet] stopgap.

bouchon [buʃɔ̃] *nm* **1.** [pour obturer - gén] top ; [- de réservoir] cap ; [- de bouteille] cork - **2.** [de canne à pêche] float - **3.** [embouteillage] traffic jam.

boucle [bukl] *nf* **1.** [de ceinture, soulier] buckle - **2.** [bijou] : **boucle d'oreille** earring - **3.** [de cheveux] curl - **4.** [de fleuve, d'avion & INFORM] loop.

bouclé, e [bukle] *adj* [cheveux] curly ; [personne] curly-haired.

boucler [3] [bukle] *vt* **1.** [attacher] to buckle ; [ceinture de sécurité] to fasten - **2.** [fermer] to shut - **3.** *fam* [enfermer - voleur] to lock up ; [- malade] to shut away - **4.** [encercler] to seal off - **5.** [terminer] to finish.

bouclier [buklije] *nm litt & fig* shield.

bouddhiste [budist] *nmf & adj* Buddhist.

bouder [3] [bude] ◇ *vi* to sulk. ◇ *vt* [chose] to dislike ; [personne] to shun ; **elle me boude depuis que je lui ai fait faux bond** she has cold-shouldered me ever since I let her down.

bouder, euse [budœr, øz] *adj* sulky.

boudin [budɛ̃] *nm* CULIN blood pudding *UK* ou sausage *US*.

boue [bu] *nf* mud.

bouée [bwe] *nf* **1.** [balise] buoy - **2.** [pour flotter] rubber ring ; **bouée de sauvetage** lifebelt.

boueux, euse [buø, øz] *adj* muddy.

bouffe [buf] *nf fam* grub.

bouffée [bufe] *nf* **1.** [de fumée] puff ; [de parfum] whiff ; [d'air] breath - **2.** [accès] surge ; **bouffées délirantes** mad fits.

bouffer [3] [bufe] *vt fam* [manger] to eat.

bouffi, e [bufi] *adj* : **bouffi (de)** swollen (with).

bouffon, onne [bufõ, ɔn] *adj* farcical. ▸ **bouffon** *nm* **1.** HIST jester - **2.** [pitre] clown.

bouge [buʒ] *nm péj* **1.** [taudis] hovel - **2.** [café] dive.

bougeoir [buʒwar] *nm* candlestick.

bougeotte [buʒɔt] *nf* : **avoir la bougeotte** to have itchy feet.

bouger [17] [buʒe] ◇ *vt* [déplacer] to move. ◇ *vi* **1.** [remuer] to move - **2.** [changer] to change - **3.** [s'agiter] : **ça bouge partout dans le monde** there is unrest all over the world.

bougie [buʒi] *nf* **1.** [chandelle] candle - **2.** [de moteur] spark plug, sparking plug *UK*.

bougon, onne [bugõ, ɔn] *adj* grumpy.

bougonner [3] [bugɔne] *vt & vi* to grumble.

bouillant, e [bujã, ãt] *adj* **1.** [qui bout] boiling - **2.** [très chaud] boiling hot.

bouillie [buji] *nf* baby's cereal ; **réduire en bouillie** [légumes] to puree ; **réduire en bouillie** [personne] to reduce to a pulp.

bouillir [48] [bujir] *vi* [aliments] to boil ; **faire bouillir** to boil.

bouilloire [bujwar] *nf* kettle.

bouillon [bujõ] *nm* **1.** [soupe] stock - **2.** [bouillonnement] bubble ; **faire bouillir à gros bouillons** to bring to a rolling boil.

bouillonner [3] [bujɔne] *vi* **1.** [liquide] to bubble - **2.** [torrent] to foam - **3.** *fig* [personne] to seethe.

bouillotte [bujɔt] *nf* hot-water bottle.

boul. *abr écrite de* **boulevard**.

boulanger, ère [bulãʒe, ɛr] *nm, f* baker.

boulangerie [bulãʒri] *nf* **1.** [magasin] baker's (shop) - **2.** [commerce] bakery trade.

boule [bul] *nf* [gén] ball ; [de loto] counter ; [de pétanque] bowl ; **boule de neige** snowball. ▸ **boules** *nfpl* **1.** [jeux] *game played on bare ground with steel bowls* - **2.** *tfam* **avoir les boules** [être effrayé] to be scared stiff ; [être furieux] to be pissed off *tfam* ; [être déprimé] to be feeling down.

bouleau, x [bulo] *nm* silver birch.

bouledogue [buldɔg] *nm* bulldog.

boulet [bulɛ] *nm* **1.** [munition] : **boulet de canon** cannonball - **2.** [de forçat] ball and chain - **3.** *fig* [fardeau] millstone (round one's neck).

boulette [bulɛt] *nf* **1.** [petite boule] pellet - **2.** [de viande] meatball.

boulevard [bulvar] *nm* **1.** [rue] boulevard - **2.** THÉÂTRE light comedy *(U)*.

bouleversant, e [bulvɛrsã, ãt] *adj* distressing.

bouleversement [bulvɛrsəmã] *nm* disruption.

bouleverser [3] [bulverse] *vt* **1.** [objets] to turn upside down - **2.** [modifier] to disrupt - **3.** [émouvoir] to distress.

boulgour [bulgur] *nm* **1.** bulgar ou bulgur wheat.

boulier [bulje] *nm* abacus.

boulimie [bulimi] *nf* bulimia.

boulon [bulõ] *nm* bolt.

boulonner [3] [bulɔne] ◇ *vt* to bolt. ◇ *vi fam* to slog (away).

boulot [bulo] *nm fam* **1.** [travail] work - **2.** [emploi] job.

boum [bum] *nf fam vieilli* party.

bouquet [bukɛ] *nm* **1.** [de fleurs - gén] bunch (of flowers) - **2.** [de vin] bouquet - **3.** [de feu d'artifice] crowning piece - **4.** TV : **bouquet de programmes** multi-channel package ; **bouquet numérique** channel package, channel bouquet.

bouquin [bukẽ] *nm fam* book.

bouquiner [3] [bukine] *vi & vt fam* to read.

bouquiniste [bukinist] *nmf* secondhand bookseller.

bourbier [burbje] *nm* [lieu] quagmire, mire ; *fig* mess.

bourde [burd] *nf fam* [erreur] blunder.

bourdon [burdõ] *nm* [insecte] bumblebee.

bourdonnement [burdɔnmã] *nm* [d'insecte, de voix, de moteur] buzz *(U)*.

bourdonner [3] [burdɔne] *vi* **1.** [insecte, machine, voix] to buzz - **2.** [oreille] to ring.

bourgeois, e [burʒwa, az] ◇ *adj* **1.** [valeur] middle-class - **2.** [cuisine] plain - **3.** *péj* [personne] bourgeois. ◇ *nm, f* bourgeois.

bourgeoisie [burʒwazi] *nf* ≃ middle classes *pl*.

bourgeon [burʒõ] *nm* bud.

bourgeonner [3] [burʒɔne] *vi* to bud.

Bourgogne [burgɔɲ] *nf* : **la Bourgogne** Burgundy.

bourlinguer [3] [burlẽge] *vi fam* [voyager] to bum around the world.

bourrade [burad] *nf* thump.

bourrage [buraʒ] *nm* [de coussin] stuffing. ▸ **bourrage de crâne** *nm fam* **1.** [bachotage] swotting *UK*, cramming - **2.** [propagande] brainwashing.

bourrasque [burask] *nf* gust of wind.

bourratif, ive [buratif, iv] *adj* stodgy.

bourreau, x [buro] *nm* HIST executioner.

bourrelet [burlɛ] *nm* [de graisse] roll of fat.

bourrer [3] [bure] *vt* **1.** [remplir - coussin] to stuff ; [- sac, armoire] to cram ; **bourrer qqch (de)** to cram sthg full (with) - **2.** *fam* [gaver] : **bourrer qqn (de)** to stuff sb (with).

bourrique [burik] *nf* **1.** [ânesse] she-ass - **2.** *fam* [personne] pigheaded person.

bourru, e [bury] *adj* [peu aimable] surly.

bourse [burs] *nf* **1.** [porte-monnaie] purse - **2.** [d'études] grant ; [au mérite] scholarship. **Bourse** *nf* [marché] stock exchange, stock market ; **la Bourse de Paris** the Paris Stock Exchange ; **jouer en Bourse** to speculate on the stock exchange ou stock market ; **Bourse de commerce** commodity market.

boursier, ère [bursje, ɛr] *adj* **1.** [élève] on a grant ou scholarship - **2.** FIN stock-exchange, stock-market *(avant n)*.

boursouflé, e [bursufle] *adj* [enflé] swollen.

bousculade [buskylad] *nf* **1.** [cohue] crush - **2.** [agitation] rush.

bousculer [3] [buskyle] *vt* **1.** [faire tomber] to knock over - **2.** [presser] to rush - **3.** [modifier] to overturn.

bouse [buz] *nf* : **bouse de vache** cow dung.

bousiller [3] [buzije] *vt fam* [abîmer] to ruin, to knacker *UK*.

boussole [busɔl] *nf* compass.

bout [bu] *nm* **1.** [extrémité, fin] end ; **au bout de** [temps] after ; [espace] at the end of ; **d'un bout à l'autre** [de ville etc] from one end to the other ; [de livre] from beginning to end - **2.** [morceau] bit ; **être à bout** to be exhausted ; **à bout portant** at point-blank range ; **pousser qqn à bout** to drive sb to distraction ; **venir à bout de** [personne] to get the better of ; [difficulté] to overcome.

boutade [butad] *nf* [plaisanterie] jest.

boute-en-train [butɑ̃trɛ̃] *nm inv* live wire ; **il était le boute-en-train de la soirée** he was the life and soul of the party.

bouteille [butɛj] *nf* bottle.

boutique [butik] *nf* [gén] shop ; [de mode] boutique.

bouton [butɔ̃] *nm* **1.** COUT button ; **bouton de manchette** cuff link - **2.** [sur la peau] spot *UK*, pimple *US* - **3.** [de porte] knob - **4.** [commutateur] switch - **5.** [bourgeon] bud.

bouton-d'or [butɔ̃dɔr] *(pl* **boutons-d'or)** *nm* buttercup.

boutonner [3] [butɔne] *vt* to button (up).

boutonneux, euse [butɔnø, øz] *adj* spotty *UK*, pimply *US*.

boutonnière [butɔnjɛr] *nf* [de vêtement] buttonhole.

bouton-pression [butɔ̃presjɔ̃] *(pl* **boutons-pression)** *nm* press-stud *UK*, snap fastener *US*.

bouture [butyr] *nf* cutting.

bovin, e [bɔvɛ̃, in] *adj* bovine. **bovins** *nmpl* cattle.

bowling [buliŋ] *nm* **1.** [jeu] bowling - **2.** [lieu] bowling alley.

box [bɔks] *(pl* **boxes)** *nm* **1.** [d'écurie] loose box - **2.** [compartiment] cubicle ; **le box des accusés** the dock - **3.** [parking] lockup garage *UK*.

boxe [bɔks] *nf* boxing.

boxer[1] [bɔkse] <> *vi* to box. <> *vt fam* to thump.

boxer[2] [bɔksɛr] *nm* [chien] boxer.

boxeur [bɔksœr] *nm* SPORT boxer.

boyau [bwajo] *nm* **1.** [chambre à air] inner tube - **2.** [corde] catgut - **3.** [galerie] narrow gallery. **boyaux** *nmpl* [intestins] guts.

boycotter [3] [bɔjkɔte] *vt* to boycott.

BP *(abr de* **boîte postale)** *nf* PO Box.

bracelet [braslɛ] *nm* **1.** [bijou] bracelet - **2.** [de montre] strap.

bracelet-montre [braslɛmɔ̃tr] *nm* wristwatch.

braconner [3] [brakɔne] *vi* to go poaching, to poach.

braconnier [brakɔnje] *nm* poacher.

brader [3] [brade] *vt* [solder] to sell off ; [vendre à bas prix] to sell for next to nothing.

braderie [bradri] *nf* clearance sale.

braguette [bragɛt] *nf* flies *pl UK*, fly *US*.

braille [braj] *nm* Braille.

brailler [3] [braje] *vi* to bawl.

braire [112] [brɛr] *vi* [âne] to bray.

braise [brɛz] *nf* embers *pl*.

bramer [3] [brame] *vi* [cerf] to bell.

brancard [brɑ̃kar] *nm* **1.** [civière] stretcher - **2.** [de charrette] shaft.

brancardier, ère [brɑ̃kardje, ɛr] *nm, f* stretcher-bearer.

branchage [brɑ̃ʃaʒ] *nm* branches *pl*.

branche [brɑ̃ʃ] *nf* **1.** [gén] branch - **2.** [de lunettes] arm.

branché, e [brɑ̃ʃe] *adj* **1.** ÉLECTR plugged in, connected - **2.** *fam* [à la mode] trendy.

branchement [brɑ̃ʃmɑ̃] *nm* [raccordement] connection, plugging in.

brancher [3] [brɑ̃ʃe] *vt* **1.** [raccorder & INFORM] to connect ; **brancher qqch sur** ÉLECTR to plug sthg into - **2.** *fam* [orienter] to steer ; **brancher qqn sur qqch** to start sb off on sthg - **3.** *fam* [plaire] to appeal to.

branchies [brɑ̃ʃi] *nfpl* [de poisson] gills.

brandir [32] [brɑ̃dir] *vt* to wave.

branlant, e [brɑ̃lɑ̃, ɑ̃t] *adj* [escalier, mur] shaky ; [meuble, dent] wobbly.

branle-bas [brɑ̃lba] *nm inv* pandemonium *(U)*.

braquage [braka3] *nm* **1.** AUTO lock - **2.** [attaque] holdup.

braquer [3] [brake] <> *vt* **1.** [diriger] : **braquer qqch sur** [arme] to aim sthg at ; [regard] to fix sthg on - **2.** *fam* [attaquer] to hold up. <> *vi* to turn (the wheel). **se braquer** *vp* [personne] to take a stand.

bras [brɑ] *nm* **1.** [gén] arm ; **bras droit** right-hand man ou woman ; **bras de fer** [jeu] arm wrestling ; *fig* trial of strength ; **avoir le bras long** [avoir de l'influence] to have pull - **2.** [de cours d'eau] branch ; **bras de mer** arm of the sea.

brasier [brazje] *nm* [incendie] blaze, inferno.

bras-le-corps [brɑlkɔr] **à bras-le-corps** *loc adv* bodily.

brassage [brasa3] *nm* **1.** [de bière] brewing - **2.** *fig* [mélange] mixing.

brassard [brasar] *nm* armband.

brasse [bras] *nf* [nage] breaststroke ; **brasse papillon** butterfly (stroke).

brassée [brase] *nf* armful.

brasser [3] [brase] *vt* **1.** [bière] to brew - **2.** [mélanger] to mix - **3.** *fig* [manier] to handle.

brasserie [brasri] *nf* **1.** [usine] brewery - **2.** [café-restaurant] brasserie.

brasseur, euse [brasœr, øz] *nm, f* [de bière] brewer.

brassière [brasjɛr] *nf* **1.** [de bébé] (baby's) vest *UK* ou undershirt *US* - **2.** *Québec* [soutien-gorge] bra.

bravade [bravad] *nf* : **par bravade** out of bravado.

brave [brav] <> *adj* **1.** *(après n)* [courageux] brave - **2.** *(avant n)* [honnête] decent - **3.** [naïf et gentil] nice. <> *nmf* : **mon brave** my good man.

braver [3] [brave] *vt* **1.** [parents, règlement] to defy - **2.** [mépriser] to brave.

bravo [bravo] *interj* bravo! **bravos** *nmpl* cheers.

bravoure [bravur] *nf* bravery.

break [brɛk] *nm* **1.** [voiture] estate (car) *UK*, station wagon *US* - **2.** *fam* [pause] break ; **faire un break** to take a break - **3.** SPORT : **faire le break** [tennis] to break service ; *fig* to pull away.

brebis [brəbi] *nf* ewe ; **brebis galeuse** black sheep.

brèche [brɛʃ] *nf* **1.** [de mur] gap - **2.** MIL breach.

bredouiller [3] [brəduje] *vi* to stammer.

bref, brève [brɛf, brɛv] *adj* **1.** [gén] short, brief ; **soyez bref!** make it brief! - **2.** LING short. **bref** *adv* in short, in a word. **brève** *nf* PRESSE brief news item.

brelan [brəlɑ̃] *nm* : **un brelan** three of a kind ; **un brelan de valets** three jacks.

Brésil [brezil] *nm* : **le Brésil** Brazil.

Bretagne [brətaɲ] *nf* : **la Bretagne** Brittany.

bretelle [brətɛl] *nf* **1.** [d'autoroute] access road, slip road *UK* - **2.** [de pantalon] : **bretelles** braces *UK*, suspenders *US* - **3.** [de bustier] strap.

breuvage [brœva3] *nm* [boisson] beverage.

brève ➤ **bref**.

brevet [brəvɛ] *nm* **1.** [certificat] certificate ; **brevet de secouriste** first-aid certificate - **2.** [diplôme] diploma ; **brevet des collèges** *school certificate taken after four years of secondary education* - **3.** [d'invention] patent.

breveter [27] [brəvte] *vt* to patent.

bréviaire [brevjɛr] *nm* breviary.

bribe [brib] *nf* [fragment] scrap, bit ; *fig* snippet ; **bribes de conversation** snatches of conversation.

bric [brik] **de bric et de broc** *loc adv* any old how.

bric-à-brac [brikabrak] *nm inv* bric-a-brac.

bricolage [brikɔla3] *nm* **1.** [travaux] do-it-yourself, DIY *UK* - **2.** [réparation provisoire] patching up.

bricole [brikɔl] *nf* **1.** [babiole] trinket - **2.** [chose insignifiante] trivial matter.

bricoler [3] [brikɔle] <> *vi* to do odd jobs (around the house). <> *vt* **1.** [réparer] to fix, to mend *UK* - **2.** [fabriquer] to make, to knock up *UK*.

bricoleur, euse [brikɔlœr, øz] *nm, f* home handyman (*f* handywoman).

bride [brid] *nf* **1.** [de cheval] bridle - **2.** [de chapeau] string - **3.** COUT bride, bar - **4.** TECHNOL flange.

bridé [bride] ➤ œil.

brider [3] [bride] *vt* [cheval] to bridle ; *fig* to rein (in).

bridge [brid3] *nm* bridge.

briefer [3] [brife] *vt* to brief.

briefing [brifiŋ] *nm* briefing.

brièvement [brijɛvmɑ̃] *adv* briefly.

brièveté [brijɛvte] *nf* brevity, briefness.

brigade [brigad] *nf* **1.** [d'ouvriers, de soldats] brigade - **2.** [détachement] squad ; **brigade volante** flying squad.

brigand [brigɑ̃] *nm* [bandit] bandit.

brillamment [brijamɑ̃] *adv* [gén] brilliantly ; [réussir un examen] with flying colours *UK* ou colors *US*.

brillant, e [brijɑ̃, ɑ̃t] *adj* **1.** [qui brille - gén] sparkling ; [- cheveux] glossy ; [- yeux] bright - **2.** [remarquable] brilliant. **brillant** *nm* [diamant] brilliant.

briller [3] [brije] *vi* to shine.

brimer [3] [brime] *vt* to victimize, to bully.

brin [brɛ̃] *nm* **1.** [tige] twig ; **brin d'herbe** blade of grass **- 2.** [fil] strand **- 3.** [petite quantité] : **un brin (de)** a bit (of) ; **faire un brin de toilette** to have a quick wash.

brindille [brɛ̃dij] *nf* twig.

bringuebaler, brinquebaler [3] [brɛ̃gbale] *vi* [voiture] to jolt along.

brio [brijo] *nm* [talent] : **avec brio** brilliantly.

brioche [brijɔʃ] *nf* **1.** [pâtisserie] brioche **- 2.** *fam* [ventre] paunch.

brioché, e [brijɔʃe] *adj* [pain] brioche-style.

brique [brik] *nf* **1.** [pierre] brick **- 2.** [emballage] carton **- 3.** *fam* [argent] *10,000 francs*.

briquer [3] [brike] *vt* to scrub.

briquet [brike] *nm* (cigarette) lighter.

briquette [briket] *nf* [conditionnement] carton.

brisant [brizɑ̃] *nm* [écueil] reef. ◆ **brisants** *nmpl* [récif] breakers.

brise [briz] *nf* breeze.

brise-glace(s) [brizglas] *nm inv* [navire] icebreaker.

brise-lames [brizlam] *nm inv* breakwater.

briser [3] [brize] *vt* **1.** [gén] to break **- 2.** *fig* [carrière] to ruin ; [conversation] to break off ; [espérances] to shatter. ◆ **se briser** *vp* **1.** [gén] to break **- 2.** *fig* [espoir] to be dashed ; [efforts] to be thwarted.

briseur, euse [brizœr, øz] *nm, f* : **briseur de grève** strike-breaker.

britannique [britanik] *adj* British. ◆ **Britannique** *nmf* British person, Briton ; **les Britanniques** the British.

broc [bro] *nm* jug.

brocante [brɔkɑ̃t] *nf* **1.** [commerce] second-hand trade **- 2.** [objets] secondhand goods *pl*.

brocanteur, euse [brɔkɑ̃tœr, øz] *nm, f* dealer in secondhand goods.

broche [brɔʃ] *nf* **1.** [bijou] brooch **- 2.** CULIN spit ; **cuire à la broche** to spit-roast **- 3.** ÉLECTR & MÉD pin.

broché, e [brɔʃe] *adj* **1.** [tissu] brocade (*avant n*), brocaded **- 2.** TYPO : **livre broché** paperback (book).

brochet [brɔʃe] *nm* pike.

brochette [brɔʃet] *nf* **1.** [ustensile] skewer **- 2.** [plat] kebab **- 3.** *fam fig* [groupe] string, row.

brochure [brɔʃyr] *nf* [imprimé] brochure, booklet.

broder [3] [brɔde] *vt & vi* to embroider.

broderie [brɔdri] *nf* **1.** [art] embroidery **- 2.** [ouvrage] (piece of) embroidery.

bromure [brɔmyr] *nm* bromide.

bronche [brɔ̃ʃ] *nf* bronchus ; **j'ai des problèmes de bronches** I've got chest problems.

broncher [3] [brɔ̃ʃe] *vi* : **sans broncher** without complaining, uncomplainingly.

bronchite [brɔ̃ʃit] *nf* bronchitis (U).

bronzage [brɔ̃zaʒ] *nm* [de peau] tan, suntan.

bronze [brɔ̃z] *nm* bronze.

bronzé, e [brɔ̃ze] *adj* tanned, suntanned.

bronzer [3] [brɔ̃ze] *vi* [peau] to tan ; [personne] to get a tan.

brosse [brɔs] *nf* brush ; **brosse à cheveux** hairbrush ; **brosse à dents** toothbrush ; **avoir les cheveux en brosse** to have a crew cut.

brosser [3] [brɔse] *vt* **1.** [habits, cheveux] to brush **- 2.** [paysage, portrait] to paint. ◆ **se brosser** *vp* : **se brosser les cheveux/les dents** to brush one's hair/teeth.

brouette [bruet] *nf* wheelbarrow.

brouhaha [bruaa] *nm* hubbub.

brouillard [brujar] *nm* [léger] mist ; [dense] fog ; **brouillard givrant** freezing fog ; **être dans le brouillard** *fig* to be lost.

brouille [bruj] *nf* quarrel.

brouillé, e [bruje] *adj* **1.** [fâché] : **être brouillé avec qqn** to be on bad terms with sb ; **être brouillé avec qqch** *fig* to be hopeless ou useless at sthg **- 2.** [teint] muddy **- 3.** ►œuf.

brouiller [3] [bruje] *vt* **1.** [désunir] to set at odds, to put on bad terms **- 2.** [vue] to blur **- 3.** [RADIO - accidentellement] to cause interference to ; [- délibérément] to jam **- 4.** [rendre confus] to muddle (up). ◆ **se brouiller** *vp* **1.** [se fâcher] to fall out ; **se brouiller avec qqn (pour qqch)** to fall out with sb (over sthg) **- 2.** [se troubler] to become blurred **- 3.** MÉTÉOR to cloud over.

brouillon, onne [brujɔ̃, ɔn] *adj* careless, untidy. ◆ **brouillon** *nm* rough copy, draft.

broussaille [brusaj] *nf* : **les broussailles** the undergrowth ; **en broussaille** *fig* [cheveux] untidy ; [sourcils] bushy.

brousse [brus] *nf* GÉOGR scrubland, bush.

brouter [3] [brute] ◇ *vt* to graze on. ◇ *vi* **1.** [animal] to graze **- 2.** TECHNOL to judder *UK*, to shudder *US*.

broutille [brutij] *nf* trifle.

broyer [13] [brwaje] *vt* to grind, to crush.

bru [bry] *nf sout* daughter-in-law.

brugnon [bryɲɔ̃] *nm* nectarine.

bruine [bruin] *nf* drizzle.

bruissement [bruismɑ̃] *nm* [de feuilles, d'étoffe] rustle, rustling (U) ; [d'eau] murmur, murmuring (U).

bruit [brui] *nm* **1.** [son] noise, sound ; **bruit de fond** background noise **- 2.** [vacarme &

TECHNOL] noise ; **faire du bruit** to make a noise ; **sans bruit** silently, noiselessly - **3.** [rumeur] rumour *UK*, rumor *US* - **4.** [retentissement] fuss ; **faire du bruit** to cause a stir.

bruitage [brɥitaʒ] *nm* sound effects *pl.*

brûlant, e [brylɑ̃, ɑ̃t] *adj* **1.** [gén] burning (hot) ; [liquide] boiling (hot) ; [plat] piping hot - **2.** *fig* [amour, question] burning.

brûle-pourpoint [brylpurpwɛ̃] ➞ **à brûle-pourpoint** *loc adv* point-blank, straight out.

brûler [3] [bryle] ◇ *vt* **1.** [gén] to burn ; [suj: eau bouillante] to scald ; **la fumée me brûle les yeux** the smoke is making my eyes sting - **2.** [feu rouge] to drive through ; [étape] to miss out, to skip. ◇ *vi* **1.** [gén] to burn ; [maison, forêt] to be on fire - **2.** [être brûlant] to be burning (hot) ; **brûler de** *fig* to be consumed with ; **brûler de faire qqch** to be longing ou dying to do sthg ; **brûler de fièvre** to be running a high temperature. ➞ **se brûler** *vp* to burn o.s.

brûlure [brylyr] *nf* **1.** [lésion] burn ; **brûlure au premier/troisième degré** first-degree/third-degree burn - **2.** [sensation] burning (sensation) ; **avoir des brûlures d'estomac** to have heartburn.

brume [brym] *nf* mist.

brumeux, euse [brymø, øz] *adj* misty ; *fig* hazy.

brun, e [brœ̃, bryn] ◇ *adj* brown ; [cheveux] dark. ◇ *nm, f* dark-haired man (*f* woman). ➞ **brun** *nm* [couleur] brown. ➞ **brune** *nf* **1.** [cigarette] cigarette made of dark tobacco - **2.** [bière] brown ale.

brunir [32] [brynir] *vi* [personne] to get a tan ; [peau] to tan.

Brushing® [brœʃiŋ] *nm* : **faire un Brushing à qqn** to give sb a blow-dry, to blow-dry sb's hair.

brusque [brysk] *adj* abrupt.

brusquement [bryskəmɑ̃] *adv* abruptly.

brusquer [3] [bryske] *vt* to rush ; [élève] to push.

brusquerie [bryskəri] *nf* abruptness.

brut, e [bryt] *adj* **1.** [pierre précieuse, bois] rough ; [sucre] unrefined ; [métal, soie] raw ; [champagne] extra dry ; **(pétrole) brut** crude (oil) - **2.** *fig* [fait, idées] crude, raw - **3.** ÉCON gross. ➞ **brute** *nf* brute.

brutal, e, aux [brytal, o] *adj* **1.** [violent] violent, brutal - **2.** [soudain] sudden - **3.** [manière] blunt.

brutaliser [3] [brytalize] *vt* to mistreat.

brutalité [brytalite] *nf* **1.** [violence] violence, brutality - **2.** [caractère soudain] suddenness.

Bruxelles [bry(k)sɛl] *npr* Brussels.

bruyamment [brɥijamɑ̃] *adv* noisily.

bruyant, e [brɥijɑ̃, ɑ̃t] *adj* noisy.

bruyère [bryjɛr] *nf* [plante] heather.

BT *nm* (*abr de* **brevet de technicien**) *vocational training certificate (taken at age 18).*

BTP (*abr de* **bâtiment et travaux publics**) *nmpl building and public works sector.*

BTS (*abr de* **brevet de technicien supérieur**) *nm advanced vocational training certificate (taken at the end of a 2-year higher education course).*

bu, e [by] *pp* ➞ boire.

buanderie [bɥɑ̃dri] *nf* laundry.

buccal, e, aux [bykal, o] *adj* buccal.

bûche [byʃ] *nf* [bois] log ; **bûche de Noël** Yule log ; **prendre** ou **ramasser une bûche** *fam* to fall flat on one's face.

bûcher¹ [byʃe] *nm* **1.** [supplice] : **le bûcher** the stake - **2.** [funéraire] pyre.

bûcher² [3] [byʃe] *fam* ◇ *vi* to swot *UK*, to grind *US*. ◇ *vt* to swot up *UK*, to grind *US*.

bûcheron, onne [byʃrɔ̃, ɔn] *nm, f* forestry worker.

bûcheur, euse [byʃœr, øz] ◇ *adj* hard-working. ◇ *nm, f fam* swot *UK*, grind *US*.

bucolique [bykɔlik] *adj* pastoral.

budget [bydʒɛ] *nm* budget.

budgétaire [bydʒetɛr] *adj* budgetary ; **année budgétaire** financial *UK* ou fiscal *US* year.

buée [bɥe] *nf* [sur vitre] condensation.

buffet [byfɛ] *nm* **1.** [meuble] sideboard - **2.** [repas] buffet - **3.** [café-restaurant] : **buffet de gare** station buffet.

buffle [byfl] *nm* [animal] buffalo.

bug [bʌg] *nm* = **bogue**.

buis [bɥi] *nm* box(wood).

buisson [bɥisɔ̃] *nm* bush.

buissonnière [bɥisɔnjɛr] ➞ **école**.

bulbe [bylb] *nm* bulb.

bulgare [bylgar] *adj* Bulgarian. ➞ **bulgare** *nm* [langue] Bulgarian. ➞ **Bulgare** *nmf* Bulgarian.

Bulgarie [bylgari] *nf* : **la Bulgarie** Bulgaria.

bulldozer [byldozer] *nm* bulldozer.

bulle [byl] *nf* **1.** [gén] bubble ; **bulle de savon** soap bubble - **2.** [de bande dessinée] speech balloon - **3.** INFORM : **bulle d'aide** pop-up text, tooltip.

bulletin [byltɛ̃] *nm* **1.** [communiqué] bulletin ; **bulletin (de la) météo** weather forecast ; **bulletin de santé** medical bulletin - **2.** [imprimé] form ; **bulletin de vote** ballot paper - **3.** SCOL report *UK*, report card *US* - **4.** [certificat] certificate ; **bulletin de salaire** ou **de paye** pay slip.

bulletin-réponse [byltɛ̃repɔ̃s] (*pl* **bulletins-réponse**) *nm* reply form.

buraliste [byralist] *nmf* [d'un bureau de tabac] tobacconist *UK*.

bureau [byro] *nm* **1.** [gén] office ; **bureau d'aide sociale** social security office ; **bureau de change** [banque] bureau de change, foreign exchange office ; [comptoir] bureau de change, foreign exchange counter ; **bureau d'études** design office ; **bureau de poste** post office ; **bureau de tabac** tobacconist's *UK* ; **bureau de vote** polling station - **2.** [meuble] desk - **3.** INFORM desktop.

bureaucrate [byrokrat] *nmf* bureaucrat.

bureaucratie [byrokrasi] *nf* bureaucracy.

bureautique [byrotik] *nf* office automation.

burette [byrɛt] *nf* [de mécanicien] oilcan.

burin [byrɛ̃] *nm* [outil] chisel.

buriné, e [byrine] *adj* engraved ; [visage, traits] lined.

burlesque [byrlɛsk] *adj* **1.** [comique] funny - **2.** [ridicule] ludicrous, absurd - **3.** THÉÂTRE burlesque.

bus [bys] *nm* bus.

busqué [byske] ► **nez**.

buste [byst] *nm* [torse] chest ; [poitrine de femme, sculpture] bust.

bustier [bystje] *nm* [corsage] strapless top ; [soutien-gorge] longline bra.

but [byt] *nm* **1.** [point visé] target - **2.** [objectif] goal, aim, purpose ; **errer sans but** to wander aimlessly ; **il touche au but** he's nearly there ; **à but non lucratif** DR non-profit-making *UK*, non-profit *US* ; **aller droit au but** to go straight to the point ; **dans le but de faire qqch** with the aim OU intention of doing sthg - **3.** SPORT goal ; **marquer un but** to score a goal ; **de but en blanc** point-blank, straight out.

butane [bytan] *nm* : **(gaz) butane** butane ; [domestique] Calor gas® *UK*, butane.

buté, e [byte] *adj* stubborn.

buter [3] [byte] <> *vi* [se heurter] : **buter sur/contre qqch** to stumble on/over sthg, to trip on/over sthg ; *fig* to run into/come up against sthg. <> *vt tfam* [tuer] to do in, to bump off. ► **se buter** *vp* to dig one's heels in ; **se buter contre** *fig* to refuse to listen to.

butin [bytɛ̃] *nm* [de guerre] booty ; [de vol] loot ; [de recherche] finds *pl*.

butiner [3] [bytine] *vi* to collect nectar.

butte [byt] *nf* [colline] mound, rise ; **être en butte à** *fig* to be exposed to.

buvard [byvar] *nm* [papier] blotting-paper ; [sous-main] blotter.

buvette [byvɛt] *nf* [café] refreshment room, buffet.

buveur, euse [byvœr, øz] *nm, f* drinker.

C

c¹, C [se] *nm inv* c, C. ► **C** (*abr écrite de* celsius, centigrade) C.

c² *abr de* centime.

c' ► **ce**.

CA *nm abr de* chiffre d'affaires.

ça [sa] *pron dém* **1.** [désignant un objet - éloigné] that ; [- proche] this - **2.** [sujet indéterminé] it, that ; **comment ça va?** how are you?, how are things? ; **ça ira comme ça** that will be fine ; **ça y est** that's it ; **c'est ça** that's right - **3.** [renforcement expressif] : **où ça?** where? ; **qui ça?** who?

çà [sa] *adv* : **çà et là** here and there.

caban [kabɑ̃] *nm* reefer (jacket), pea jacket.

cabane [kaban] *nf* [abri] cabin, hut ; [remise] shed ; **cabane à lapins** hutch.

cabanon [kabanɔ̃] *nm* **1.** [à la campagne] cottage - **2.** [sur la plage] chalet - **3.** [cellule] padded cell - **4.** [de rangement] shed.

cabaret [kabarɛ] *nm* cabaret.

cabas [kaba] *nm* shopping bag.

cabillaud [kabijo] *nm* (fresh) cod.

cabine [kabin] *nf* **1.** [de navire, d'avion, de véhicule] cabin - **2.** [compartiment, petit local] cubicle ; **cabine d'essayage** fitting room ; **cabine téléphonique** phone box *UK*, phone booth *US*.

cabinet [kabinɛ] *nm* **1.** [pièce] : **cabinet de toilette** ≃ bathroom - **2.** [local professionnel] office ; **cabinet dentaire/médical** dentist's/doctor's surgery *UK*, dentist's/doctor's office *US* - **3.** [de ministre] advisers *pl*. ► **cabinets** *nmpl* toilet *sg*.

câble [kabl] *nm* cable ; **(télévision par) câble** cable television.

câblé, e [kable] *adj* TV equipped with cable TV.

cabosser [3] [kabɔse] *vt* to dent.

cabotage [kabɔtaʒ] *nm* coastal navigation.

caboteur [kabɔtœr] *nm* [navire] coaster.

cabrer [3] [kabre] ► **se cabrer** *vp* **1.** [cheval] to rear (up) ; [avion] to climb steeply - **2.** *fig* [personne] to take offence *UK* OU offense *US*.

cabri [kabri] *nm* kid.

cabriole [kabrijɔl] *nf* [bond] caper ; [pirouette] somersault.

cabriolet [kabrijɔlɛ] *nm* convertible.

CAC, Cac [kak] (*abr de* **Compagnie des agents de change**) *nf* : **l'indice CAC-40** *the French stock exchange shares index.*

caca [kaka] *nm fam* pooh *UK*, poop *US* ; **faire caca** to do a pooh *UK* ou poop *US* ; **caca d'oie** greeny-yellow.

cacahouète, cacahuète [kakawɛt] *nf* peanut.

cacao [kakao] *nm* **1.** [poudre] cocoa (powder) - **2.** [boisson] cocoa.

cachalot [kaʃalo] *nm* sperm whale.

cache [kaʃ] <> *nf* [cachette] hiding place. <> *nm* [masque] card *(for masking text etc)*.

cache-cache [kaʃkaʃ] *nm inv* : **jouer à cache-cache** to play hide-and-seek.

cachemire [kaʃmir] *nm* **1.** [laine] cashmere - **2.** [dessin] paisley.

cache-nez [kaʃne] *nm inv* scarf.

cache-pot [kaʃpo] *nm inv* flowerpot holder.

cacher [3] [kaʃe] *vt* **1.** [gén] to hide ; **je ne vous cache pas que...** to be honest,... - **2.** [vue] to mask. ➤ **se cacher** *vp* : **se cacher (de qqn)** to hide (from sb).

cachet [kaʃɛ] *nm* **1.** [comprimé] tablet, pill - **2.** [marque] postmark - **3.** [style] style, character ; **avoir du cachet** to have character - **4.** [rétribution] fee.

cacheter [27] [kaʃte] *vt* to seal.

cachette [kaʃɛt] *nf* hiding place ; **en cachette** secretly.

cachot [kaʃo] *nm* [cellule] cell.

cachotterie [kaʃɔtri] *nf* little secret ; **faire des cachotteries (à qqn)** to hide things (from sb).

cachottier, ère [kaʃɔtje, ɛr] *nm, f* secretive person.

cactus [kaktys] *nm* cactus.

c.-à-d. (*abr écrite de* **c'est-à-dire**) i.e.

cadastre [kadastr] *nm* [registre] ≃ land register ; [service] ≃ land registry, ≃ land office *US*.

cadavérique [kadaverik] *adj* deathly.

cadavre [kadavr] *nm* corpse, (dead) body.

Caddie® [kadi] *nm* [chariot] trolley *UK*, shopping cart *US*.

cadeau, x [kado] <> *nm* present, gift ; **faire cadeau de qqch à qqn** to give sthg to sb (as a present). <> *adj inv* : **idée cadeau** gift idea.

cadenas [kadna] *nm* padlock.

cadenasser [3] [kadnase] *vt* to padlock.

cadence [kadɑ̃s] *nf* **1.** [rythme musical] rhythm ; **en cadence** in time - **2.** [de travail] rate.

cadencé, e [kadɑ̃se] *adj* rhythmical.

cadet, ette [kadɛ, ɛt] *nm, f* **1.** [de deux enfants] younger ; [de plusieurs enfants] youngest ; **il est mon cadet de deux ans** he's two years younger than me - **2.** SPORT junior.

cadran [kadrɑ̃] *nm* dial ; **cadran solaire** sundial.

cadre [kadr] *nm* **1.** [de tableau, de porte] frame - **2.** [contexte] context - **3.** [décor, milieu] surroundings *pl* - **4.** [responsable] : **cadre moyen/supérieur** middle/senior manager - **5.** [sur formulaire] box.

cadrer [3] [kadre] <> *vi* to agree, to tally. <> *vt* CINÉ, PHOTO & TV to frame.

caduc, caduque [kadyk] *adj* **1.** [feuille] deciduous - **2.** [qui n'est plus valide] obsolete.

cafard [kafar] *nm* **1.** [insecte] cockroach - **2.** *fig* [mélancolie] : **avoir le cafard** to feel low ou down.

café [kafe] *nm* **1.** [plante, boisson] coffee ; **café crème** *coffee with frothy milk* ; **café en grains** coffee beans ; **café au lait** white coffee *UK*, coffee with milk *US* (*with hot milk*) ; **café moulu** ground coffee ; **café noir** black coffee ; **café en poudre** ou **soluble** instant coffee - **2.** [lieu] bar, café.

caféine [kafein] *nf* caffeine.

cafétéria [kafeterja] *nf* cafeteria.

café-théâtre [kafeteatr] *nm* ≃ cabaret.

cafetière [kaftjɛr] *nf* **1.** [récipient] coffeepot - **2.** [électrique] coffeemaker ; [italienne] percolator.

cafouiller [3] [kafuje] *vi fam* **1.** [s'embrouiller] to get into a mess - **2.** [moteur] to misfire ; TV to be on the blink.

cafter [3] [kafte] *vi fam* to sneak, to snitch.

cafteur, euse [kaftœr, øz] *nm, f fam* sneak, snitch.

cage [kaʒ] *nf* **1.** [pour animaux] cage - **2.** [dans une maison] : **cage d'escalier** stairwell - **3.** ANAT : **cage thoracique** rib cage.

cageot [kaʒo] *nm* [caisse] crate.

cagibi [kaʒibi] *nm* boxroom *UK*, storage room *US*.

cagneux, euse [kaɲø, øz] *adj* : **avoir les genoux cagneux** to be knock-kneed.

cagnotte [kaɲɔt] *nf* **1.** [caisse commune] kitty - **2.** [économies] savings *pl*.

cagoule [kagul] *nf* **1.** [passe-montagne] balaclava - **2.** [de voleur, de pénitent] hood.

cahier [kaje] *nm* **1.** [de notes] exercise book *UK*, notebook ; **cahier de brouillon** rough book *UK*, notebook *US* ; **cahier de textes** homework book *UK* - **2.** COMM : **cahier des charges** specification.

cahin-caha [kaɛ̃kaa] *adv* : **aller cahin-caha** to be jogging along.

cahot [kao] *nm* bump, jolt.

cahoter [3] [kaɔte] *vi* to jolt around.

cahute [kayt] *nf* shack.

caille [kaj] *nf* quail.

caillé, e [kaje] *adj* [lait] curdled ; [sang] clotted.

caillot [kajo] *nm* clot.

caillou, x [kaju] *nm* **1.** [pierre] stone, pebble - **2.** *fam* [crâne] head.

caillouteux, euse [kajutø, øz] *adj* stony.

caïman [kaimã] *nm* cayman.

Caire [kɛr] *npr* : Le Caire Cairo.

caisse [kɛs] *nf* **1.** [boîte] crate, box ; **caisse à outils** toolbox - **2.** TECHNOL case - **3.** [guichet] cash desk, till ; [de supermarché] checkout, till ; **caisse enregistreuse** cash register - **4.** [recette] takings *pl* - **5.** [organisme] : **caisse d'allocation** ≃ social security office ; **caisse d'épargne** [fonds] savings fund ; [établissement] savings bank ; **caisse de retraite** pension fund.

caissier, ère [kesje, ɛr] *nm, f* cashier.

caisson [kɛsɔ̃] *nm* **1.** MIL & TECHNOL caisson - **2.** ARCHIT coffer.

cajoler [3] [kaʒɔle] *vt* to make a fuss of, to cuddle.

cajou [kaʒu] ▶ **noix**.

cake [kɛk] *nm* fruitcake.

cal¹ [kal] *nm* callus.

cal² (*abr écrite de* **calorie**) cal.

calamar [kalamar], **calmar** [kalmar] *nm* squid.

calamité [kalamite] *nf* disaster.

calandre [kalɑ̃dr] *nf* **1.** [de voiture] radiator grille - **2.** [machine] calender.

calanque [kalɑ̃k] *nf* rocky inlet.

calcaire [kalker] ⬦ *adj* [eau] hard ; [sol] chalky ; [roche] limestone *(avant n)*. ⬦ *nm* limestone.

calciner [3] [kalsine] *vt* to burn to a cinder.

calcium [kalsjɔm] *nm* calcium.

calcul [kalkyl] *nm* **1.** [opération] : **le calcul** arithmetic ; **calcul mental** mental arithmetic - **2.** [compte] calculation - **3.** *fig* [plan] plan - **4.** MÉD : **calcul (rénal)** kidney stone.

calculateur, trice [kalkylatœr, tris] *adj péj* calculating. ⬤ **calculateur** *nm* computer. ⬤ **calculatrice** *nf* calculator.

calculer [3] [kalkyle] ⬦ *vt* **1.** [déterminer] to calculate, to work out - **2.** [prévoir] to plan ; **mal/bien calculer qqch** to judge sthg badly/well. ⬦ *vi* [dépenses] [dépenser avec parcimonie] to budget carefully, *péj* to count the pennies.

calculette [kalkylɛt] *nf* pocket calculator.

cale [kal] *nf* **1.** [de navire] hold ; **cale sèche** dry dock - **2.** [pour immobiliser] wedge.

calé, e [kale] *adj fam* [personne] clever, brainy ; **être calé en** to be good at.

calèche [kalɛʃ] *nf* (horse-drawn) carriage.

caleçon [kalsɔ̃] *nm* **1.** [sous-vêtement masculin] boxer shorts *pl*, pair of boxer shorts - **2.** [vêtement féminin] leggings *pl*, pair of leggings.

calembour [kalɑ̃bur] *nm* pun, play on words.

calendrier [kalɑ̃drije] *nm* **1.** [système, agenda, d'un festival] calendar - **2.** [emploi du temps] timetable *UK*, schedule *US* - **3.** [d'un voyage] schedule.

cale-pied [kalpje] (*pl* **cale-pieds**) *nm* toe-clip.

calepin [kalpɛ̃] *nm* notebook.

caler [3] [kale] ⬦ *vt* **1.** [avec cale] to wedge - **2.** [stabiliser, appuyer] to prop up - **3.** *fam* [remplir] : **ça cale (l'estomac)** it's filling. ⬦ *vi* **1.** [moteur, véhicule] to stall - **2.** *fam* [personne] to give up.

calfeutrer [3] [kalføtre] *vt* to draughtproof *UK*. ⬤ **se calfeutrer** *vp* to shut o.s. up ou away.

calibre [kalibr] *nm* **1.** [de tuyau] diameter, bore ; [de fusil] calibre ; [de fruit, d'œuf] size - **2.** *fam fig* [envergure] calibre.

calibrer [3] [kalibre] *vt* **1.** [machine, fusil] to calibrate - **2.** [fruit, œuf] to grade.

Californie [kaliforni] *nf* : la Californie California.

califourchon [kalifurʃɔ̃] ⬤ **à califourchon** *loc adv* astride ; **être (assis) à califourchon sur qqch** to sit astride sthg.

câlin, e [kalɛ̃, in] *adj* affectionate. ⬤ **câlin** *nm* cuddle.

câliner [3] [kaline] *vt* to cuddle.

calleux, euse [kalø, øz] *adj* calloused.

call-girl [kolgœrl] (*pl* **call-girls**) *nf* call girl.

calligraphie [kaligrafi] *nf* calligraphy.

calmant, e [kalmɑ̃, ɑ̃t] *adj* soothing. ⬤ **calmant** *nm* [pour la douleur] painkiller ; [pour l'anxiété] tranquillizer, sedative.

calmar [kalmar] = **calamar**.

calme [kalm] ⬦ *adj* quiet, calm. ⬦ *nm* **1.** [gén] calm, calmness - **2.** [absence de bruit] peace (and quiet).

calmer [3] [kalme] *vt* **1.** [apaiser] to calm (down) - **2.** [réduire - douleur] to soothe ; [- inquiétude] to allay. ⬤ **se calmer** *vp* **1.** [s'apaiser - personne, discussion] to calm down ; [- tempête] to abate ; [- mer] to become calm - **2.** [diminuer - douleur] to ease ; [- fièvre, inquiétude, désir] to subside.

calomnie [kalɔmni] *nf* [écrits] libel ; [paroles] slander.

calorie [kalɔri] *nf* calorie.

calorique [kalɔrik] *adj* calorific.

calot [kalo] *nm* [bille] (large) marble.

calotte [kalɔt] *nf* **1.** [bonnet] skullcap - **2.** GÉOGR : **calotte glaciaire** ice cap.

calque [kalk] *nm* **1.** [dessin] tracing - **2.** [papier] : **(papier) calque** tracing paper - **3.** *fig* [imitation] (exact) copy.

calquer [3] [kalke] *vt* **1.** [carte] to trace - **2.** [imiter] to copy exactly ; **calquer qqch sur qqch** to model sthg on sthg.

calvaire [kalvɛr] *nm* **1.** [croix] wayside cross - **2.** *fig* [épreuve] ordeal.

calvitie [kalvisi] *nf* baldness.

camaïeu [kamajø] *nm* monochrome.

camarade [kamarad] *nmf* **1.** [compagnon, ami] friend ; **camarade de classe** classmate ; **camarade d'école** schoolfriend - **2.** POLIT comrade.

camaraderie [kamaradri] *nf* **1.** [familiarité, entente] friendship - **2.** [solidarité] comradeship, camaraderie.

Cambodge [kãbɔdʒ] *nm* : **le Cambodge** Cambodia.

cambouis [kãbwi] *nm* dirty grease.

cambré, e [kãbre] *adj* arched.

cambriolage [kãbrijɔlaʒ] *nm* burglary.

cambrioler [3] [kãbrijɔle] *vt* to burgle *UK*, to burglarize *US*.

cambrioleur, euse [kãbrijɔlœr, øz] *nm, f* burglar.

camée [kame] *nm* cameo.

caméléon [kameleɔ̃] *nm litt & fig* chameleon.

camélia [kamelja] *nm* camellia.

camelote [kamlɔt] *nf* [marchandise de mauvaise qualité] junk, rubbish *UK*.

caméra [kamera] *nf* **1.** CINÉ & TV camera - **2.** [d'amateur] cinécamera.

cameraman [kameraman] (*pl* **cameramen** [kameramɛn] OU **cameramans**) *nm* cameraman.

Cameroun [kamrun] *nm* : **le Cameroun** Cameroon.

Caméscope® [kameskɔp] *nm* camcorder.

camion [kamjɔ̃] *nm* lorry *UK*, truck *US* ; **camion de déménagement** removal van *UK*, moving van *US*.

camion-citerne [kamjɔ̃sitɛrn] *nm* tanker *UK*, tanker truck *US*.

camionnage [kamjɔnaʒ] *nm* road haulage *UK*, trucking *US*.

camionnette [kamjɔnɛt] *nf* van.

camionneur [kamjɔnœr] *nm* **1.** [conducteur] lorry-driver *UK*, truckdriver *US* - **2.** [entrepreneur] road haulier *UK*, trucker *US*.

camion-poubelle (*pl* **camions-poubelles** [kamjɔ̃pubɛl]) *nm* dustcart, (dust)bin lorry *UK*, garbage truck *US*.

camisole [kamizɔl] ➤ **camisole de force** *nf* straitjacket.

camouflage [kamuflaʒ] *nm* [déguisement] camouflage ; *fig* [dissimulation] concealment.

camoufler [3] [kamufle] *vt* [déguiser] to camouflage ; *fig* [dissimuler] to conceal, to cover up.

camp [kã] *nm* **1.** [gén] camp ; **camp de concentration** concentration camp - **2.** SPORT half (of the field) - **3.** [parti] side.

campagnard, e [kãpaɲar, ard] *adj* **1.** [de la campagne] country (*avant n*) - **2.** [rustique] rustic.

campagne [kãpaɲ] *nf* **1.** [régions rurales] country ; **à la campagne** in the country - **2.** MIL campaign - **3.** [publicité & POLIT] campaign ; **faire campagne** to campaign ; **campagne d'affichage** poster campaign ; **campagne électorale** election campaign ; **campagne de presse** press campaign ; **campagne publicitaire** OU **de publicité** advertising campaign ; **campagne de vente** sales campaign.

campement [kãpmã] *nm* camp, encampment.

camper [3] [kãpe] ◇ *vi* to camp. ◇ *vt* **1.** [poser solidement] to place firmly - **2.** *fig* [esquisser] to portray.

campeur, euse [kãpœr, øz] *nm, f* camper.

camphre [kãfr] *nm* camphor.

camping [kãpiŋ] *nm* **1.** [activité] camping ; **faire du camping** to go camping - **2.** [terrain] campsite.

Canada [kanada] *nm* : **le Canada** Canada.

canadien, enne [kanadjɛ̃, ɛn] *adj* Canadian. ➤ **canadienne** *nf* [veste] sheepskin jacket. ➤ **Canadien, enne** *nm, f* Canadian.

canaille [kanaj] ◇ *adj* **1.** [coquin] roguish - **2.** [vulgaire] crude. ◇ *nf* **1.** [scélérat] scoundrel - **2.** *hum* [coquin] little devil.

canal, aux [kanal, o] *nm* **1.** [gén] channel ; **par le canal de qqn** *fig* [par l'entremise de] through sb - **2.** [voie d'eau] canal - **3.** ANAT canal, duct. ➤ **Canal** *nm* : **Canal+** *French TV pay channel.*

canalisation [kanalizasjɔ̃] *nf* [conduit] pipe.

canaliser [3] [kanalize] *vt* **1.** [cours d'eau] to canalize - **2.** *fig* [orienter] to channel.

canapé [kanape] *nm* [siège] sofa.

canapé-lit [kanapeli] *nm* sofa bed.

canaque, kanak [kanak] *adj* Kanak. ➤ **Canaque** *nmf* Kanak.

canard [kanar] *nm* **1.** [oiseau] duck - **2.** [fausse note] wrong note - **3.** *fam* [journal] rag.

canari [kanari] *nm* canary.

cancan [kãkã] *nm* **1.** [ragot] piece of gossip - **2.** [danse] cancan.

cancer [kãser] *nm* MÉD cancer. **Cancer** *nm* ASTROL Cancer.

cancéreux, euse [kãserø, øz] <> *adj* **1.** [personne] suffering from cancer - **2.** [tumeur] cancerous. <> *nm, f* [personne] cancer sufferer.

cancérigène [kãseriʒɛn] *adj* carcinogenic.

cancre [kãkr] *nm fam* dunce.

cancrelat [kãkrəla] *nm* cockroach.

candélabre [kãdelabr] *nm* candelabra.

candeur [kãdœr] *nf* ingenuousness.

candi [kãdi] *adj* : **sucre candi** (sugar) candy.

candidat, e [kãdida, at] *nm, f* : **candidat (à)** candidate (for).

candidature [kãdidatyr] *nf* **1.** [à un poste] application ; **poser sa candidature pour qqch** to apply for sthg - **2.** [à une élection] candidature *UK*, candidacy *US*.

candide [kãdid] *adj* ingenuous.

cane [kan] *nf* (female) duck.

caneton [kantõ] *nm* (male) duckling.

canette [kanɛt] *nf* **1.** [de fil] spool - **2.** [petite cane] (female) duckling - **3.** [de boisson - bouteille] bottle ; [- boîte] can.

canevas [kanva] *nm* COUT canvas.

caniche [kaniʃ] *nm* poodle.

canicule [kanikyl] *nf* heatwave.

canif [kanif] *nm* penknife.

canin, e [kanɛ̃, in] *adj* canine ; **exposition canine** dog show. **canine** *nf* canine (tooth).

caniveau, x [kanivo] *nm* gutter.

canne [kan] *nf* **1.** [bâton] walking stick ; **canne à pêche** fishing rod - **2.** *fam* [jambe] pin. **canne à sucre** *nf* sugar cane.

cannelle [kanɛl] *nf* [aromate] cinnamon.

cannelure [kanlyr] *nf* [de colonne] flute.

cannibale [kanibal] *nmf & adj* cannibal.

canoë [kanɔe] *nm* canoe.

canoë-kayak [kanɔekajak] *nm* kayak.

canon [kanõ] *nm* **1.** [arme] gun ; HIST cannon - **2.** [tube d'arme] barrel - **3.** MUS : **chanter en canon** to sing in canon - **4.** [norme & RELIG] canon.

canoniser [3] [kanɔnize] *vt* to canonize.

canot [kano] *nm* dinghy ; **canot pneumatique** inflatable dinghy ; **canot de sauvetage** lifeboat.

canopée [kanɔpe] *nf* [écologie] canopy.

cantatrice [kãtatris] *nf* prima donna.

cantine [kãtin] *nf* **1.** [réfectoire] canteen *UK*, cafeteria *US* - **2.** [malle] trunk.

cantique [kãtik] *nm* hymn.

canton [kãtõ] *nm* **1.** [en France] ≃ district - **2.** [en Suisse] canton.

cantonade [kãtɔnad] **à la cantonade** *loc adv* : **parler à la cantonade** to speak to everyone (in general).

cantonais, e [kãtɔnɛ, ɛz] *adj* Cantonese ; **riz cantonais** egg fried rice. **cantonais** *nm* [langue] Cantonese.

cantonner [3] [kãtɔne] *vt* **1.** MIL to quarter, to billet *UK* - **2.** [maintenir] to confine ; **cantonner qqn à** OU **dans** to confine sb to.

cantonnier [kãtɔnje] *nm* roadman.

canular [kanylar] *nm fam* hoax.

canyon, cañon [kanjɔn, kanjõ] *nm* canyon.

canyoning [kanɔniŋ] *nm* canyoning.

caoutchouc [kautʃu] *nm* **1.** [substance] rubber - **2.** [plante] rubber plant.

caoutchouteux, euse [kautʃutø, øz] *adj* rubbery.

cap [kap] *nm* **1.** GÉOGR cape ; **le cap de Bonne-Espérance** the Cape of Good Hope ; **le cap Horn** Cape Horn ; **passer le cap de qqch** *fig* to get through sthg ; **passer le cap de la quarantaine** *fig* to turn forty - **2.** [direction] course ; **changer de cap** to change course ; **mettre le cap sur** to head for. **Cap** *nm* : **Le Cap** Cape Town.

CAP (*abr de* **certificat d'aptitude professionnelle**) *nm* vocational training certificate (taken at secondary school).

capable [kapabl] *adj* **1.** [apte] : **capable (de qqch/de faire qqch)** capable (of sthg/of doing sthg) - **2.** [à même] : **capable de faire qqch** likely to do sthg.

capacité [kapasite] *nf* **1.** [de récipient] capacity - **2.** [de personne] ability - **3.** UNIV : **capacité en droit** [diplôme] qualifying certificate in law gained by examination after 2 years' study.

cape [kap] *nf* [vêtement] cloak ; **rire sous cape** *fig* to laugh up one's sleeve.

CAPES, Capes [kapɛs] (*abr de* **certificat d'aptitude au professorat de l'enseignement du second degré**) *nm* secondary school teaching certificate.

capharnaüm [kafarnaɔm] *nm* mess.

capillaire [kapiler] <> *adj* **1.** [lotion] hair (*avant n*) - **2.** ANAT & BOT capillary. <> *nm* **1.** BOT maidenhair fern - **2.** ANAT capillary.

capillarité [kapilarite] *nf* PHYS capillarity.

capitaine [kapitɛn] *nm* captain.

capitainerie [kapitɛnri] *nf* harbour *UK* OU harbor *US* master's office.

capital, e, aux [kapital, o] *adj* **1.** [décision, événement] major - **2.** DR capital. **capital** *nm* FIN capital ; **capital santé** *fig* reserves *pl* of health ; **capital social** authorized OU share capital. **capitale** *nf* [ville, lettre] capital. **capitaux** *nmpl* capital *(U)*.

capitaliser [3] [kapitalize] <> *vt* FIN to capitalize ; *fig* to accumulate. <> *vi* to save. **capitaliser sur** *v + prép* to cash in on, to capitalize on.

capitalisme [kapitalism] *nm* capitalism.

capitaliste [kapitalist] *nmf & adj* capitalist.

capiteux, euse [kapitø, øz] *adj* [vin] intoxicating ; [parfum] heady.

capitonné, e [kapitɔne] *adj* padded.

capituler [3] [kapityle] *vi* to surrender ; **capituler devant qqn/qqch** to surrender to sb/sthg.

caporal, aux [kapɔral, o] *nm* **1.** MIL lance corporal - **2.** [tabac] caporal.

capot [kapo] *nm* **1.** [de voiture] bonnet UK, hood US - **2.** [de machine] (protective) cover.

capote [kapɔt] *nf* **1.** [de voiture] hood UK, top US - **2.** *fam* [préservatif] : **capote (anglaise)** condom.

câpre [kapr] *nf* caper.

caprice [kapris] *nm* whim.

capricieux, euse [kaprisjø, øz] <> *adj* [changeant] capricious ; [coléreux] temperamental. <> *nm, f* temperamental person.

capricorne [kaprikɔrn] *nm* ZOOL capricorn beetle. **Capricorne** *nm* ASTROL Capricorn.

capsule [kapsyl] *nf* **1.** [de bouteille] cap - **2.** ASTRON, BOT & MÉD capsule.

capter [3] [kapte] *vt* **1.** [recevoir sur émetteur] to pick up - **2.** [source, rivière] to harness - **3.** *fig* [attention, confiance] to gain, to win.

captif, ive [kaptif, iv] <> *adj* captive. <> *nm, f* prisoner.

captivant, e [kaptivã, ãt] *adj* [livre, film] enthralling ; [personne] captivating.

captiver [3] [kaptive] *vt* to captivate.

captivité [kaptivite] *nf* captivity.

capture [kaptyr] *nf* **1.** [action] capture - **2.** [prise] catch - **3.** INFORM : **capture d'écran** [image] screenshot ; [action] screen capture.

capturer [3] [kaptyre] *vt* to catch, to capture.

capuche [kapyʃ] *nf* (detachable) hood.

capuchon [kapyʃɔ̃] *nm* **1.** [bonnet - d'imperméable] hood - **2.** [bouchon] cap, top.

capucine [kapysin] *nf* [fleur] nasturtium.

caquet [kake] *nm péj* [bavardage] : **rabattre le caquet à** OU **de qqn** to shut sb up.

caqueter [27] [kakte] *vi* **1.** [poule] to cackle - **2.** *péj* [personne] to chatter.

car¹ [kar] *nm* coach UK, bus US.

car² [kar] *conj* because, for.

carabine [karabin] *nf* rifle.

caractère [karakter] *nm* [gén] character ; avoir du caractère to have character ; avoir mauvais caractère to be bad-tempered ; en petits/gros caractères in small/large print ; caractères d'imprimerie block capitals.

caractériel, elle [karakterjel] *adj* [troubles] emotional ; [personne] emotionally disturbed.

caractérisé, e [karakterize] *adj* [net] clear.

caractériser [3] [karakterize] *vt* to be characteristic of. **se caractériser** *vp* : se caractériser par qqch to be characterized by sthg.

caractéristique [karakteristik] <> *nf* characteristic, feature. <> *adj* : caractéristique (de) characteristic (of).

carafe [karaf] *nf* [pour vin, eau] carafe ; [pour alcool] decanter.

caraïbe [karaib] *adj* Caribbean. **Caraïbes** [karaib] *nfpl* : les Caraïbes the Caribbean.

carambolage [karãbɔlaʒ] *nm* pileup.

caramel [karamel] *nm* **1.** CULIN caramel - **2.** [bonbon - dur] toffee UK, taffy US, caramel ; [- mou] fudge.

carapace [karapas] *nf* shell ; *fig* protection, shield.

carapater [3] [karapate] **se carapater** *vp fam* to scarper, to hop it UK, to skedaddle.

carat [kara] *nm* carat UK, karat US ; **or à 9 carats** 9-carat gold.

caravane [karavan] *nf* [de camping, de désert] caravan.

caravaning [karavaniŋ] *nm* caravanning UK.

carbone [karbɔn] *nm* carbon ; **(papier) carbone** carbon paper.

carbonique [karbɔnik] *adj* : **gaz carbonique** carbon dioxide ; **neige carbonique** dry ice.

carboniser [3] [karbɔnize] *vt* to burn to a cinder.

carburant [karbyrã] *nm* fuel.

carburateur [karbyratœr] *nm* carburettor UK, carburetor US.

carcan [karkã] *nm* HIST iron collar ; *fig* yoke.

carcasse [karkas] *nf* **1.** [d'animal] carcass - **2.** [de bâtiment, navire] framework - **3.** [de véhicule] shell.

cardiaque [kardjak] *adj* cardiac ; **être cardiaque** to have a heart condition ; **crise cardiaque** heart attack.

cardigan [kardigã] *nm* cardigan.

cardinal, e, aux [kardinal, o] *adj* cardinal. **cardinal** *nm* **1.** RELIG cardinal - **2.** [nombre] cardinal number.

cardiologue [kardjɔlɔg] *nmf* heart specialist, cardiologist.

cardio-vasculaire   [kardjɔvaskylɛr] (*pl* cardio-vasculaires) *adj* cardiovascular.

Carême [karɛm] *nm* : le Carême Lent.

carence [karɑ̃s] *nf* [manque] : carence (en) deficiency (in).

carène [karɛn] *nf* NAUT hull.

caressant, e [karɛsɑ̃, ɑ̃t] *adj* affectionate.

caresse [karɛs] *nf* caress.

caresser [4] [karese] *vt* 1. [personne] to caress ; [animal, objet] to stroke - 2. *fig* [espoir] to cherish.

cargaison [kargɛzɔ̃] *nf* [transports] cargo.

cargo [kargo] *nm* 1. [navire] freighter - 2. [avion] cargo plane.

caricature [karikatyr] *nf* 1. [gén] caricature - 2. *péj* [personne] sight.

carie [kari] *nf* MÉD caries.

carillon [karijɔ̃] *nm* 1. [cloches] bells *pl* - 2. [d'horloge, de porte] chime.

carlingue [karlɛ̃g] *nf* 1. [d'avion] cabin - 2. [de navire] keelson.

carmin [karmɛ̃] *adj inv* crimson.

carnage [karnaʒ] *nm* slaughter, carnage.

carnassier [karnasje] *nm* carnivore.

carnaval [karnaval] *nm* carnival.

carnet [karnɛ] *nm* 1. [petit cahier] notebook ; carnet d'adresses address book ; carnet de notes SCOL report card - 2. [bloc de feuilles] book ; carnet de chèques cheque book UK, checkbook US ; carnet de tickets book of tickets ; carnet de timbres book of stamps.

carnivore [karnivɔr] <> *adj* carnivorous. <> *nm* carnivore.

carotte [karɔt] *nf* carrot.

carpe [karp] *nf* carp.

carpette [karpɛt] *nf* 1. [petit tapis] rug - 2. *fam péj* [personne] doormat.

carquois [karkwa] *nm* quiver.

carré, e [kare] *adj* [gén] square ; 20 mètres carrés 20 square metres. ◆ **carré** *nm* 1. [quadrilatère] square ; élever un nombre au carré MATH to square a number - 2. [jeux de cartes] : un carré d'as four aces - 3. [petit terrain] patch, plot.

carreau, x [karo] *nm* 1. [carrelage] tile - 2. [vitre] window pane - 3. [motif carré] check ; à carreaux [tissu] checked ; [papier] squared - 4. [cartes à jouer] diamond.

carrefour [karfur] *nm* [de routes, de la vie] crossroads *sg*.

carrelage [karlaʒ] *nm* [surface] tiles *pl*.

carrément [karemɑ̃] *adv* 1. [franchement] bluntly - 2. [complètement] completely, quite - 3. [sans hésiter] straight.

carrière [karjɛr] *nf* 1. [profession] career ; faire carrière dans qqch to make a career (for o.s.) in sthg - 2. [gisement] quarry.

carriériste [karjerist] *nmf péj* careerist.

carriole [karjɔl] *nf* 1. [petite charrette] cart - 2. *Québec* [traîneau] sleigh.

carrossable [karɔsabl] *adj* suitable for vehicles.

carrosse [karɔs] *nm* (horse-drawn) coach.

carrosserie [karɔsri] *nf* [de voiture] bodywork, body.

carrossier [karɔsje] *nm* coachbuilder UK.

carrure [karyr] *nf* [de personne] build ; *fig* stature.

cartable [kartabl] *nm* schoolbag.

carte [kart] *nf* 1. [gén] card ; carte d'abonnement season ticket ; carte d'anniversaire birthday card ; carte d'électeur polling card UK, voter registration card US ; carte d'étudiant student card ; carte à gratter scratch card ; carte grise ≃ logbook UK, ≃ car registration papers US ; carte d'identité identity card ; Carte Orange season ticket *(for use on public transport in Paris)* ; carte postale postcard ; carte à puce smart card ; carte de séjour residence permit ; Carte Vermeil *card entitling senior citizens to reduced rates in cinemas, on public transport etc* ; carte de vœux New Year greetings card ; carte de visite visiting card UK, calling card US ; donner carte blanche à qqn *fig* to give sb a free hand - 2. BANQUE & COMM : carte bancaire cash card UK, bank card ; carte de crédit credit card - 3. INFORM & TÉLÉCOM : carte graphique graphics board ; carte à mémoire memory card ; carte son soundcard ; carte téléphonique phonecard - 4. [de jeu] : carte (à jouer) (playing) card - 5. GÉOGR map ; carte d'état-major ≃ Ordnance Survey map UK, ≃ Geological Survey map US ; carte routière road map - 6. [au restaurant] menu ; à la carte [menu] à la carte ; [horaires] flexible ; carte des vins wine list - 7. INFORM card.

cartilage [kartilaʒ] *nm* cartilage.

cartomancien, enne [kartɔmɑ̃sjɛ̃, ɛn] *nm, f* fortune-teller *(using cards)*.

carton [kartɔ̃] *nm* 1. [matière] cardboard - 2. [emballage] cardboard box ; carton à dessin portfolio - 3. FOOTBALL : carton jaune yellow card ; carton rouge red card.

cartonné, e [kartɔne] *adj* [livre] hardback.

carton-pâte [kartɔ̃pat] *nm* pasteboard.

cartouche [kartuʃ] *nf* 1. [gén & INFORM] cartridge - 2. [de cigarettes] carton.

cas [ka] *nm* case ; au cas où in case ; en

aucun cas under no circumstances ; **en tout cas** in any case, anyway ; **en cas de** in case of ; **en cas de besoin** if need be ; **le cas échéant** if the need arises, if need be ; **cas de conscience** matter of conscience ; **cas limite** borderline case ; **cas social** person with social problems.

casanier, ère [kazanje, ɛr] *adj & nm, f* stay-at-home.

casaque [kazak] *nf* **1.** [veste] overblouse - **2.** [équitation] blouse.

cascade [kaskad] *nf* **1.** [chute d'eau] waterfall ; *fig* stream, torrent - **2.** CINÉ stunt.

cascadeur, euse [kaskadœr, øz] *nm, f* CINÉ stuntman (*f* stuntwoman).

cascher = kas(c)her.

case [kaz] *nf* **1.** [habitation] hut - **2.** [de boîte, tiroir] compartment ; [d'échiquier] square ; [sur un formulaire] box.

caser [3] [kaze] *vt* **1.** *fam* [trouver un emploi pour] to get a job for - **2.** *fam* [marier] to marry off - **3.** [placer] to put. ➤ **se caser** *vp fam* **1.** [trouver un emploi] to get (o.s.) a job - **2.** [se marier] to get hitched.

caserne [kazɛrn] *nf* barracks.

cash [kaʃ] *nm* cash ; **payer cash** to pay (in) cash.

casier [kazje] *nm* **1.** [compartiment] compartment ; [pour le courrier] pigeonhole - **2.** [meuble - à bouteilles] rack ; [- à courrier] set of pigeonholes - **3.** [à la pêche] lobster pot. ➤ **casier judiciaire** *nm* police record ; **casier judiciaire vierge** clean (police) record.

casino [kazino] *nm* casino.

casque [kask] *nm* **1.** [de protection] helmet - **2.** [à écouteurs] headphones *pl*. ➤ **Casques bleus** *nmpl* : **les Casques bleus** the UN peace-keeping force, the blue berets.

casquette [kaskɛt] *nf* cap.

cassant, e [kasɑ̃, ɑ̃t] *adj* **1.** [fragile - verre] fragile ; [- cheveux] brittle - **2.** [dur] brusque.

cassation [kasasjɔ̃] ➤ **cour**.

casse [kas] ⬦ *nf* **1.** *fam* [violence] aggro *UK* - **2.** [de voitures] scrapyard. ⬦ *nm fam* [cambriolage] break-in.

casse-cou [kasku] *nmf* [personne] daredevil.

casse-croûte [kaskrut] *nm inv* snack.

casse-noisettes [kasnwazɛt], **casse-noix** [kasnwa] *nm inv* nutcrackers *pl*.

casse-pieds [kaspje] *fam* ⬦ *adj inv* annoying. ⬦ *nmf* pain (in the neck).

casser [3] [kase] ⬦ *vt* **1.** [briser] to break - **2.** DR to quash - **3.** COMM : **casser les prix** to slash prices. ⬦ *vi* to break. ➤ **se casser** *vp* **1.** [se briser] to break - **2.** [membre] : **se casser un bras** to break one's arm ; **se casser**

la figure *fam* OU **gueule** *tfam* [personne] to come a cropper *UK*, to take a tumble ; [livre, carafe] to crash to the ground ; [projet] to bite the dust, to take a dive.

casserole [kasrɔl] *nf* [ustensile] saucepan.

casse-tête [kastɛt] *nm inv* **1.** *fig* [problème] headache - **2.** [jeu] puzzle.

cassette [kasɛt] *nf* **1.** [coffret] casket - **2.** [de musique, vidéo] cassette.

cassis [kasis] *nm* **1.** [fruit] blackcurrant ; [arbuste] blackcurrant bush ; [liqueur] blackcurrant liqueur - **2.** [sur la route] dip.

cassure [kasyr] *nf* break.

caste [kast] *nf* caste.

casting [kastiŋ] *nm* [acteurs] cast ; [sélection] casting ; **aller à un casting** to go to an audition.

castor [kastɔr] *nm* beaver.

castrer [3] [kastre] *vt* to castrate ; [chat] to neuter ; [chatte] to spay.

cataclysme [kataklism] *nm* cataclysm.

catadioptre [katadjɔptr], **Cataphote**® [katafɔt] *nm* **1.** [sur la route] cat's eye *UK*, highway reflector *US* - **2.** [de véhicule] reflector.

catalogue [katalɔg] *nm* catalogue, catalog *US*.

cataloguer [3] [kataloge] *vt* **1.** [classer] to catalogue, to catalog *US* - **2.** *péj* [juger] to label.

catalyseur [katalizœr] *nm* CHIM & *fig* catalyst.

catalytique [katalitik] ➤ **pot**.

catamaran [katamarɑ̃] *nm* [voilier] catamaran.

Cataphote® = catadioptre.

cataplasme [kataplasm] *nm* poultice.

catapulter [3] [katapylte] *vt* to catapult.

cataracte [katarakt] *nf* cataract.

catarrhe [katar] *nm* catarrh.

catastrophe [katastrɔf] *nf* disaster, catastrophe ; **catastrophe naturelle** natural disaster ; [assurances] act of God.

catastrophé, e [katastrɔfe] *adj* shocked, upset.

catastrophique [katastrɔfik] *adj* disastrous, catastrophic.

catch [katʃ] *nm* wrestling.

catéchisme [kateʃism] *nm* catechism.

catégorie [kategɔri] *nf* **1.** [gén] category - **2.** [de personnel] grade - **3.** [de viande, fruits] quality - **4.** ÉCON : **catégorie socioprofessionnelle** socio-economic group.

catégorique [kategɔrik] *adj* categorical.

cathédrale [katedral] *nf* cathedral.

cathodique [katɔdik] ➤ **tube**.

catholicisme [katɔlisism] nm Catholicism.

catholique [katɔlik] adj Catholic.

catimini [katimini] ◆ **en catimini** loc adv secretly.

cauchemar [koʃmar] nm litt & fig nightmare.

cauchemardesque [koʃmardɛsk] adj nightmarish.

cause [koz] nf **1.** [gén] cause ; **à cause de** because of ; **pour cause de** on account of, because of - **2.** DR case ; **être en cause** [intérêts] to be at stake ; [honnêteté] to be in doubt ou in question ; **remettre en cause** to challenge, to question.

causer [3] [koze] ◇ vt : **causer qqch à qqn** to cause sb sthg. ◇ vi [bavarder] : **causer (de)** to chat (about).

causerie [kozri] nf talk.

caustique [kostik] adj & nm caustic.

cautériser [3] [koterize] vt to cauterize.

caution [kosjɔ̃] nf **1.** [somme d'argent] guarantee - **2.** [personne] guarantor ; **se porter caution pour qqn** to act as guarantor for sb.

cautionner [3] [kosjone] vt **1.** [se porter garant de] to guarantee - **2.** fig [appuyer] to support, to back.

cavalcade [kavalkad] nf **1.** [de cavaliers] cavalcade - **2.** [d'enfants] stampede.

cavalerie [kavalri] nf MIL cavalry.

cavalier, ère [kavalje, ɛr] nm, f **1.** [à cheval] rider - **2.** [partenaire] partner. ◆ **cavalier** nm [aux échecs] knight.

cavalièrement [kavaljɛrmɑ̃] adv in an offhand manner.

cave [kav] ◇ nf **1.** [sous-sol] cellar - **2.** [de vins] (wine) cellar. ◇ adj [joues] hollow ; [yeux] sunken.

caveau, x [kavo] nm **1.** [petite cave] small cellar - **2.** [sépulture] vault.

caverne [kavɛrn] nf cave.

caviar [kavjar] nm caviar.

cavité [kavite] nf cavity.

CB (abr de citizen's band, canaux banalisés) nf CB.

cc (abr écrite de charges comprises) ► charge.

CCP (abr de compte chèque postal, compte courant postal) nm post office account, ≃ Giro UK.

CD nm (abr de compact disc) CD.

CDD nm (abr écrite de contrat à durée déterminée) ► contrat.

CDI nm **1.** (abr de centre de documentation et d'information) school library - **2.** abr de contrat à durée indéterminée.

ce, cette [sə, sɛt] (pl **ces** [se]) (le masculin **ce** devient **cet** [sɛt] devant une voyelle ou un 'h' muet) ◇ adj dém [proche] this, these pl ; [éloigné] that, those pl ; **ce mois, ce mois-ci** this month ; **cette année, cette année-là** that year. ◇ pron dém inv (**c'** devant le verbe être 3ième personne singulier) : **c'est** it is, it's ; **ce sont** they are, they're ; **c'est mon bureau** this is my office, it's my office ; **ce sont mes enfants** these are my children, they're my children ; **c'est à Paris** it's in Paris ; **qui est-ce ?** who is it? ; **ce qui, ce que** what ; **ils ont eu ce qui leur revenait** they got what they deserved ; **..., ce qui est étonnant ...**, which is surprising ; **vous savez bien ce à quoi je pense** you know exactly what I'm thinking about ; **faites donc ce pour quoi on vous paie** do what you're paid to do.

CE ◇ nm **1.** abr de comité d'entreprise - **2.** (abr de cours élémentaire) **CE1** second year of primary school ; **CE2** third year of primary school. ◇ nf (abr de Communauté européenne) EC.

ceci [səsi] pron dém inv this ; **à ceci près que** with the exception that, except that.

cécité [sesite] nf blindness.

céder [18] [sede] ◇ vt **1.** [donner] to give up ; **'cédez le passage'** 'give way UK', yield US ; **céder le passage à qqn** to let sb through, to make way for sb - **2.** [revendre] to sell. ◇ vi **1.** [personne] : **céder (à)** to give in (to), to yield (to) - **2.** [chaise, plancher] to give way.

cédérom [sederɔm] nm INFORM CD-ROM.

CEDEX, Cedex [sedɛks] (abr de courrier d'entreprise à distribution exceptionnelle) nm accelerated postal service for bulk users.

cédille [sedij] nf cedilla.

cèdre [sɛdr] nm cedar.

CEI (abr de Communauté d'États Indépendants) nf CIS.

ceinture [sɛ̃tyr] nf **1.** [gén] belt ; **ceinture de sécurité** safety ou seat belt - **2.** ANAT waist.

ceinturon [sɛ̃tyrɔ̃] nm belt.

cela [səla] pron dém inv that ; **cela ne vous regarde pas** it's ou that's none of your business ; **il y a des années de cela** that was many years ago ; **c'est cela** that's right ; **cela dit...** having said that... ; **malgré cela** in spite of that, nevertheless.

célèbre [selɛbr] adj famous.

célébrer [18] [selebre] vt **1.** [gén] to celebrate - **2.** [faire la louange de] to praise.

célébrité [selebrite] nf **1.** [renommée] fame - **2.** [personne] celebrity.

céleri [sɛlri] nm celery.

céleste [selɛst] adj heavenly.

célibat [seliba] nm celibacy.

célibataire [selibatɛr] ◇ adj single,

unmarried ; **père** ou **mère célibataire** single parent. <> *nmf* single person, single man (*f* woman).

celle ► celui.

celle-ci ► celui-ci.

celle-là ► celui-là.

celles ► celui.

celles-ci ► celui-ci.

celles-là ► celui-là.

cellier [selje] *nm* storeroom.

Cellophane® [seləfan] *nf* Cellophane®.

cellulaire [selylɛr] *adj* **1.** BIOL & TÉLÉCOM cellular - **2.** [destiné aux prisonniers] : **régime cellulaire** solitary confinement ; **voiture cellulaire** prison van.

cellule [selyl] *nf* **1.** [gén & INFORM] cell - **2.** [groupe] unit.

cellulite [selylit] *nf* cellulite.

celte [sɛlt] *adj* Celtic. ► **Celte** *nmf* Celt.

celui, celle [səlɥi, sɛl] (*mpl* **ceux** [sø] , *fpl* **celles** [sɛl]) *pron dém* **1.** [suivi d'un complément prépositionnel] the one ; **celle de devant** the one in front ; **ceux d'entre vous qui...** those of you who... - **2.** [suivi d'un pronom relatif] : **celui qui** [objet] the one which ou that ; [personne] the one who ; **c'est celle qui te va le mieux** that's the one which ou that suits you best ; **celui que vous voyez** the one (which ou that) you can see, the one whom you can see ; **ceux que je connais** those I know.

celui-ci, celle-ci [səlɥisi, sɛlsi] (*mpl* **ceux-ci** [søsi], *fpl* **celles-ci** [sɛlsi]) *pron dém* this one, these ones *pl*.

celui-là, celle-là [səlɥila, sɛlla] (*mpl* **ceux-là** [søla], *fpl* **celles-là** [sɛlla]) *pron dém* that one, those ones *pl* ; **celui-là... celui-ci** the former... the latter.

cendre [sɑ̃dr] *nf* ash.

cendré, e [sɑ̃dre] *adj* [chevelure] : **blond cendré** ash blond.

cendrier [sɑ̃drije] *nm* **1.** [de fumeur] ashtray - **2.** [de poêle] ashpan.

cène [sɛn] *nf* (Holy) Communion. ► **Cène** *nf* : **la Cène** the Last Supper.

censé, e [sɑ̃se] *adj* : **être censé faire qqch** to be supposed to do sthg.

censeur [sɑ̃sœr] *nm* **1.** SCOL ≃ deputy head *UK*, ≃ vice-principal *US* - **2.** CINÉ & PRESSE censor.

censure [sɑ̃syr] *nf* **1.** [presse & CINÉ] [- contrôle] censorship ; [- censeurs] censors *pl* - **2.** POLIT censure - **3.** PSYCHO censor.

censurer [3] [sɑ̃syre] *vt* **1.** CINÉ, PRESSE & PSYCHO to censor - **2.** [juger] to censure.

cent [sɑ̃] <> *adj num inv* one hundred, a hundred. <> *nm* **1.** [nombre] a hundred - **2.** [mesure de proportion] : **pour cent** percent ; *voir aussi* **six**.

centaine [sɑ̃tɛn] *nf* **1.** [cent unités] hundred - **2.** [un grand nombre] : **une centaine de** about a hundred ; **des centaines (de)** hundreds (of) ; **plusieurs centaines de** several hundred ; **par centaines** in hundreds.

centenaire [sɑ̃tnɛr] <> *adj* hundred-year-old (*avant n*) ; **être centenaire** to be a hundred years old. <> *nmf* centenarian. <> *nm* [anniversaire] centenary *UK*, centennial *US*.

centiare [sɑ̃tjar] *nm* square metre *UK* ou meter *US*.

centième [sɑ̃tjɛm] *adj num inv, nm & nmf* hundredth ; *voir aussi* **sixième**.

centigrade [sɑ̃tigrad] ► **degré**.

centilitre [sɑ̃tilitr] *nm* centilitre *UK*, centiliter *US*.

centime [sɑ̃tim] *nm* cent.

centimètre [sɑ̃timɛtr] *nm* **1.** [mesure] centimetre *UK*, centimeter *US* - **2.** [ruban, règle] tape measure.

central, e, aux [sɑ̃tral, o] *adj* central. ► **central** *nm* [de réseau] : **central téléphonique** telephone exchange. ► **centrale** *nf* **1.** [usine] power plant ou station ; **centrale hydroélectrique** hydroelectric power station ; **centrale nucléaire** nuclear power plant ou station - **2.** ÉCON : **centrale d'achat** COMM buying group ; [dans une entreprise] central purchasing department.

centraliser [3] [sɑ̃tralize] *vt* to centralize.

centre [sɑ̃tr] *nm* [gén] centre *UK*, center *US* ; **centre aéré** outdoor centre *UK* ou center *US* ; **centre antipoison** poison centre *UK* ou center *US* ; **centre d'appels** call centre *UK* ou center *US* ; **centre commercial** shopping centre *UK* ou mall *US* ; **centre culturel** arts centre *UK* ou center *US* ; **centre de gravité** centre *UK* ou center *US* of gravity ; **centre nerveux** nerve centre *UK* ou center *US*.

centrer [3] [sɑ̃tre] *vt* to centre *UK*, to center *US*.

centre-ville [sɑ̃trəvil] *nm* city centre *UK* ou center *US*, town centre *UK* ou downtown *US*.

centrifuge [sɑ̃trifyʒ] ► **force**.

centrifugeuse [sɑ̃trifyʒøz] *nf* **1.** TECHNOL centrifuge - **2.** CULIN juice extractor.

centuple [sɑ̃typl] *nm* : **être le centuple de qqch** to be a hundred times sthg ; **au centuple** a hundredfold.

cep [sɛp] *nm* stock.

cèpe [sɛp] *nm* cep.

cependant [səpɑ̃dɑ̃] *conj* however, yet.

céramique [seramik] *nf* [matière, objet] ceramic.

cerceau, x [sɛrso] *nm* hoop.

cercle [sɛrkl] *nm* circle ; **cercle vicieux** vicious circle.

cercueil [sɛrkœj] *nm* coffin.

céréale [sereal] *nf* cereal.

cérémonial, als [seremɔnjal] *nm* ceremonial.

cérémonie [seremɔni] *nf* ceremony.

cérémonieux, euse [seremɔnjø, øz] *adj* ceremonious.

cerf [sɛr] *nm* stag.

cerf-volant [sɛrvɔlɑ̃] *nm* [jouet] kite.

cerise [səriz] <> *nf* cherry. <> *adj inv* cherry.

cerisier [sərizje] *nm* [arbre] cherry (tree) ; [bois] cherry (wood).

cerne [sɛrn] *nm* ring.

cerné [sɛrne] ➡ œil.

cerner [3] [sɛrne] *vt* 1. [encercler] to surround - 2. *fig* [sujet] to define.

certain, e [sɛrtɛ̃, ɛn] <> *adj* certain ; **être certain de qqch** to be certain ou sure of sthg ; **je suis pourtant certain d'avoir mis mes clés là** but I'm certain ou sure I left my keys there. <> *adj indéf (avant n)* certain ; **il a un certain talent** he has some talent ou a certain talent ; **un certain temps** for a while ; **avoir un certain âge** to be getting on, to be past one's prime ; **c'est un monsieur d'un certain âge** he's getting on a bit ; **un certain M. Lebrun** a Mr Lebrun. ➡ **certains** (*fpl* **certaines**) *pron indéf pl* some.

certainement [sɛrtɛnmɑ̃] *adv* [probablement] most probably, most likely ; [bien sûr] certainly.

certes [sɛrt] *adv* of course.

certificat [sɛrtifika] *nm* [attestation, diplôme] certificate ; **certificat médical** medical certificate.

certifié, e [sɛrtifje] *adj* : **professeur certifié** qualified teacher.

certifier [9] [sɛrtifje] *vt* 1. [assurer] : **certifier qqch à qqn** to assure sb of sthg - 2. [authentifier] to certify.

certitude [sɛrtityd] *nf* certainty.

cerveau [sɛrvo] *nm* brain.

cervelle [sɛrvɛl] *nf* 1. ANAT brain - 2. [facultés mentales, aliment] brains *pl*.

cervical, e, aux [sɛrvikal, o] *adj* cervical.

ces ➡ ce.

CES *nm* 1. (*abr de* **collège d'enseignement secondaire**) *former* secondary school - 2. *abr de* **Contrat emploi-solidarité**.

césarienne [sezarjɛn] *nf* caesarean (section).

cesse [sɛs] *nf* : **n'avoir de cesse que** (+ *subjonctif*) *sout* not to rest until. ➡ **sans cesse** *loc adv* continually, constantly.

cesser [4] [sese] <> *vi* to stop, to cease. <> *vt* to stop ; **cesser de faire qqch** to stop doing sthg.

cessez-le-feu [seselføf] *nm inv* cease-fire.

cession [sɛsjɔ̃] *nf* transfer.

c'est-à-dire [setadir] *conj* 1. [en d'autres termes] : **c'est-à-dire (que)** that is (to say) - 2. [introduit une restriction, précision, réponse] : **c'est-à-dire que** well..., actually...

cet ➡ ce.

cétacé [setase] *nm* cetacean.

cette ➡ ce.

ceux ➡ celui.

ceux-ci ➡ celui-ci.

ceux-là ➡ celui-là.

cf. (*abr écrite de* **confer**) cf.

CFC (*abr de* **chlorofluorocarbone**) *nm* CFC.

chacal [ʃakal] *nm* jackal.

chacun, e [ʃakœ̃, yn] *pron indéf* each (one) ; [tout le monde] everyone, everybody ; **chacun de nous/de vous/d'eux** each of us/you/them ; **chacun pour soi** every man for himself ; **tout un chacun** every one of us/them.

chagrin, e [ʃagrɛ̃, in] *adj* [personne] grieving ; [caractère, humeur] morose. ➡ **chagrin** *nm* grief ; **avoir du chagrin** to grieve.

chagriner [3] [ʃagrine] *vt* 1. [peiner] to grieve, to distress - 2. [contrarier] to upset.

chahut [ʃay] *nm* uproar.

chahuter [3] [ʃayte] <> *vi* to cause an uproar. <> *vt* 1. [importuner - professeur] to rag, to tease ; [- orateur] to heckle - 2. [bousculer] to jostle.

chaîne [ʃɛn] *nf* 1. [gén] chain ; **chaîne de montagnes** mountain range - 2. [dans l'industrie] : **chaîne de fabrication/de montage** production/assembly line ; **travail à la chaîne** production-line work ; **produire qqch à la chaîne** to mass-produce sthg - 3. TV channel ; **chaîne câblée** cable channel ; **chaîne cryptée** pay channel *(for which one needs a special decoding unit)* ; **une chaîne payante** a subscription TV channel ; **chaîne à péage** ou **à la séance** pay TV channel ; **chaîne de télévision** television channel, TV channel ; **chaîne thématique** specialized channel - 4. [appareil] stereo (system) ; **chaîne hi-fi** hi-fi system. ➡ **chaînes** *nfpl fig* chains, bonds.

chaînon [ʃɛnɔ̃] *nm litt & fig* link.

chair [ʃɛr] *nf* flesh ; **avoir la chair de poule** to have goose pimples ou gooseflesh, to have goosebumps *US*.

chaire [ʃɛr] *nf* **1.** [estrade - de prédicateur] pulpit ; [- de professeur] rostrum - **2.** UNIV chair.

chaise [ʃɛz] *nf* chair ; **chaise longue** deckchair.

châle [ʃal] *nm* shawl.

chalet [ʃalɛ] *nm* **1.** [de montagne] chalet - **2.** *Québec* [maison de campagne] (holiday) cottage.

chaleur [ʃalœr] *nf* heat ; [agréable] warmth.

chaleureux, euse [ʃalœrø, øz] *adj* warm.

challenge [ʃalɑ̃ʒ] *nm* **1.** SPORT tournament - **2.** *fig* [défi] challenge.

chaloupe [ʃalup] *nf* rowing boat *UK*, rowboat *US*.

chalumeau [ʃalymo] *nm* TECHNOL blowlamp *UK*, blowtorch *US*.

chalutier [ʃalytje] *nm* [bateau] trawler.

chamailler [3] [ʃamaje] ➤ **se chamailler** *vp fam* to squabble.

chambranle [ʃɑ̃brɑ̃l] *nm* [de porte, fenêtre] frame ; [de cheminée] mantelpiece.

chambre [ʃɑ̃br] *nf* **1.** [où l'on dort] : chambre (à coucher) bedroom ; **chambre à un lit, chambre pour une personne** single room ; **chambre pour deux personnes** double room ; **chambre à deux lits** twin-bedded room ; **chambre d'amis** spare room ; **chambre d'hôte** bed and breakfast - **2.** [local] room ; **chambre forte** strongroom ; **chambre froide** cold store ; **chambre noire** darkroom - **3.** DR division ; **chambre d'accusation** court of criminal appeal - **4.** POLIT chamber, house ; **Chambre des députés** ≃ House of Commons *UK*, ≃ House of Representatives *US* - **5.** TECHNOL chamber ; **chambre à air** [de pneu] inner tube.

chambrer [3] [ʃɑ̃bre] *vt* **1.** [vin] to bring to room temperature - **2.** *fam* [se moquer] : **chambrer qqn** to pull sb's leg, to wind sb up *UK*.

chameau, x [ʃamo] *nm* [mammifère] camel.

chamois [ʃamwa] *nm* chamois ; [peau] chamois (leather).

champ [ʃɑ̃] *nm* **1.** [gén] field ; **champ de bataille** battlefield ; **champ de courses** racecourse - **2.** [étendue] area.

champagne [ʃɑ̃paɲ] *nm* champagne.

champêtre [ʃɑ̃pɛtr] *adj* rural.

champignon [ʃɑ̃piɲɔ̃] *nm* **1.** BOT & MÉD fungus - **2.** [comestible] mushroom ; **champignon vénéneux** toadstool.

champion, onne [ʃɑ̃pjɔ̃, ɔn] ➤ *nm, f* champion. ➤ *adj fam* brilliant.

championnat [ʃɑ̃pjɔna] *nm* championship.

chance [ʃɑ̃s] *nf* **1.** [bonheur] luck *(U)* ; **avoir de la chance** to be lucky ; **ne pas avoir de**

chance to be unlucky ; **porter chance** to bring good luck - **2.** [probabilité, possibilité] chance, opportunity ; **avoir des chances de faire qqch** to have a chance of doing sthg.

chanceler [24] [ʃɑ̃sle] *vi* [personne, gouvernement] to totter ; [meuble] to wobble.

chancelier [ʃɑ̃səlje] *nm* **1.** [premier ministre] chancellor - **2.** [de consulat, d'ambassade] secretary.

chanceux, euse [ʃɑ̃sø, øz] *adj* lucky.

chandail [ʃɑ̃daj] *nm* (thick) sweater.

Chandeleur [ʃɑ̃dlœr] *nf* Candlemas.

chandelier [ʃɑ̃dəlje] *nm* [pour une bougie] candlestick ; [à plusieurs branches] candelabra.

chandelle [ʃɑ̃dɛl] *nf* [bougie] candle.

change [ʃɑ̃ʒ] *nm* **1.** [troc & FIN] exchange - **2.** [couche de bébé] disposable nappy *UK*, diaper *US*.

changeant, e [ʃɑ̃ʒɑ̃, ɑ̃t] *adj* **1.** [temps, humeur] changeable - **2.** [reflet] shimmering.

changement [ʃɑ̃ʒmɑ̃] *nm* change.

changer [17] [ʃɑ̃ʒe] ➤ *vt* **1.** [gén] to change ; **changer qqch contre** to change ou exchange sthg for ; **changer qqn en** to change sb into - **2.** [modifier] to change, to alter ; **ça me/te changera** that will be a (nice) change for me/you - **3.** ÉCON : **changer des euros en dollars** to change euros into dollars, to exchange euros for dollars ; **changer son fusil d'épaule** to have a change of heart. ➤ *vi* **1.** [gén] to change ; **changer d'avis** to change one's mind ; **ça changera!** that'll make a change! ; **changer de direction** to change direction ; **changer de place (avec qqn)** to change places (with sb) ; **changer de train (à)** to change trains (at) ; **pour changer** for a change - **2.** [modifier] to change, to alter ; **changer de comportement** to alter one's behaviour *UK* ou behavior *US*.

chanson [ʃɑ̃sɔ̃] *nf* song ; **c'est toujours la même chanson** *fig* it's the same old story.

chansonnier, ère [ʃɑ̃sɔnje, ɛr] *nm, f* cabaret singer-songwriter.

chant [ʃɑ̃] *nm* **1.** [chanson] song, singing *(U)* ; [sacré] hymn - **2.** [art] singing.

chantage [ʃɑ̃taʒ] *nm litt* & *fig* blackmail ; **faire du chantage** to use ou resort to blackmail ; **faire du chantage à qqn** to blackmail sb.

chanter [3] [ʃɑ̃te] ➤ *vt* **1.** [chanson] to sing - **2.** *litt* [célébrer] to sing ou tell of ; **chanter les louanges de qqn** to sing sb's praises. ➤ *vi* [gén] to sing ; **faire chanter qqn** to blackmail sb ; **si ça vous chante!** *fam* if you feel like ou fancy it *UK*!

chanteur, euse [ʃɑ̃tœr, øz] *nm, f* singer.

chantier [ʃɑ̃tje] *nm* **1.** CONSTR (building)

site ; [sur la route] roadworks *pl* ; **chantier naval** shipyard, dockyard - **2.** *fig* [désordre] shambles *sg*, mess.

Chantilly [ʃɑ̃tiji] *nf* : **(crème) Chantilly** *stiffly whipped cream sweetened and flavoured*.

chantonner [3] [ʃɑ̃tɔne] *vt & vi* to hum.

chanvre [ʃɑ̃vr] *nm* hemp.

chaos [kao] *nm* chaos.

chap. (*abr écrite de* **chapitre**) ch.

chaparder [3] [ʃaparde] *vt fam* to steal.

chapeau, x [ʃapo] *nm* **1.** [coiffure] hat - **2.** PRESSE introductory paragraph.

chapeauter [3] [ʃapote] *vt* [service] to head ; [personnes] to supervise.

chapelet [ʃaple] *nm* **1.** RELIG rosary - **2.** *fig* [d'injures] string, torrent.

chapelle [ʃapɛl] *nf* [petite église] chapel ; [partie d'église] choir.

chapelure [ʃaplyr] *nf* (dried) breadcrumbs *pl*.

chapiteau, x [ʃapito] *nm* [de cirque] big top.

chapitre [ʃapitr] *nm* [de livre & RELIG] chapter.

chaque [ʃak] *adj indéf* each, every ; **chaque personne** each person, everyone ; **j'ai payé ces livres 100 euros chaque** I paid 100 euros each for these books.

char [ʃar] *nm* **1.** MIL : **char (d'assaut)** tank - **2.** [de carnaval] float - **3.** *Québec* [voiture] car.

charabia [ʃarabja] *nm* gibberish.

charade [ʃarad] *nf* charade.

charbon [ʃarbɔ̃] *nm* [combustible] coal ; **charbon de bois** charcoal.

charcuter [3] [ʃarkyte] *vt fam péj* to butcher.

charcuterie [ʃarkytri] *nf* **1.** [magasin] pork butcher's - **2.** [produits] pork meat products.

charcutier, ère [ʃarkytje, ɛr] *nm, f* [commerçant] pork butcher.

chardon [ʃardɔ̃] *nm* [plante] thistle.

charge [ʃarʒ] *nf* **1.** [fardeau] load - **2.** [fonction] office - **3.** [responsabilité] responsibility ; **être à la charge de** [personne] to be dependent on ; **les travaux sont à la charge du propriétaire** the owner is liable for the cost of the work ; **prendre qqch en charge** [payer] to pay (for) sthg ; [s'occuper de] to take charge of sthg ; **prendre qqn en charge** to take charge of sb - **4.** ÉLECTR, DR & MIL charge. ➡ **charges** *nfpl* **1.** [d'appartement] service charge - **2.** ÉCON expenses, costs ; **charges patronales** employer's contributions ; **charges sociales** ≃ employer's contributions.

chargé, e [ʃarʒe] ⬦ *adj* **1.** [véhicule, personne] : **chargé (de)** loaded (with) - **2.** [responsable] : **chargé (de)** responsible (for) - **3.** [occupé] full, busy. ⬦ *nm, f* : **chargé d'affaires** chargé d'affaires ; **chargé de mission** head of mission.

chargement [ʃarʒəmɑ̃] *nm* **1.** [action] loading - **2.** [marchandises] load.

charger [17] [ʃarʒe] *vt* **1.** [gén & INFORM] to load - **2.** ÉLECTR, DR & MIL to charge - **3.** [donner une mission à] : **charger qqn de faire qqch** to put sb in charge of doing sthg. ➡ **se charger** *vp* : **se charger de qqn/qqch** to take care of sb/sthg, to take charge of sb/sthg ; **se charger de faire qqch** to undertake to do sthg.

chargeur [ʃarʒœr] *nm* **1.** ÉLECTR charger - **2.** [d'arme] magazine.

chariot [ʃarjo] *nm* **1.** [charrette] handcart - **2.** [à bagages, dans un hôpital] trolley *UK*, cart *US* - **3.** [de machine à écrire] carriage.

charisme [karism] *nm* charisma.

charitable [ʃaritabl] *adj* charitable ; [conseil] friendly.

charité [ʃarite] *nf* **1.** [aumône & RELIG] charity - **2.** [bonté] kindness.

charlatan [ʃarlatɑ̃] *nm péj* charlatan.

charmant, e [ʃarmɑ̃, ɑ̃t] *adj* charming.

charme [ʃarm] *nm* **1.** [séduction] charm - **2.** [enchantement] spell - **3.** [arbre] ironwood, hornbeam.

charmer [3] [ʃarme] *vt* to charm ; **être charmé de faire qqch** to be delighted to do sthg.

charmeur, euse [ʃarmœr, øz] ⬦ *adj* charming. ⬦ *nm, f* charmer ; **charmeur de serpents** snake charmer.

charnel, elle [ʃarnɛl] *adj* carnal.

charnier [ʃarnje] *nm* mass grave.

charnière [ʃarnjɛr] ⬦ *nf* hinge ; *fig* turning point. ⬦ *adj* [période] transitional.

charnu, e [ʃarny] *adj* fleshy.

charogne [ʃarɔɲ] *nf* [d'animal] carrion (U).

charpente [ʃarpɑ̃t] *nf* **1.** [de bâtiment, de roman] framework - **2.** [ossature] frame.

charpentier [ʃarpɑ̃tje] *nm* carpenter.

charretier, ère [ʃartje, ɛr] *nm, f* carter.

charrette [ʃarɛt] *nf* cart.

charrier [9] [ʃarje] ⬦ *vt* **1.** [personne, fleuve] to carry - **2.** *fam* [se moquer de] : **charrier qqn** to take sb for a ride. ⬦ *vi fam* [exagérer] to go too far.

charrue [ʃary] *nf* plough *UK*, plow *US*.

charte [ʃart] *nf* charter.

charter [ʃarter] *nm* chartered plane.

chartreuse [ʃartrøz] *nf* **1.** RELIG Carthusian monastery - **2.** [liqueur] Chartreuse.

chas [ʃa] *nm* eye (of needle).

chasse [ʃas] *nf* **1.** [action] hunting ; **chasse à courre** hunting *(on horseback with hounds)* - **2.** [période] : **la chasse est ouverte/fermée** it's the open/close season - **3.** [domaine] : **chasse gardée** private hunting ou shooting preserve ; *fig* preserve - **4.** [poursuite] chase ; **faire la chasse à qqn/qqch** *fig* to hunt (for) sb/sthg, to hunt sb/sthg down ; **prendre qqn/qqch en chasse** to give chase to sb/sthg - **5.** [des cabinets] : **chasse (d'eau)** flush ; **tirer la chasse** to flush the toilet. ➤ **chasse au trésor** *nf* treasure hunt.

chassé-croisé [ʃasekwaze] *nm* toing and froing.

chasse-neige [ʃasnɛʒ] *nm inv* snowplough *UK*, snowplow *US*.

chasser [3] [ʃase] *vt* **1.** [animal] to hunt - **2.** [faire partir - personne] to drive ou chase away ; [- odeur, souci] to dispel.

chasseur, euse [ʃasœr, øz] *nm, f* hunter. ➤ **chasseur** *nm* **1.** [d'hôtel] page, messenger, bellhop *US* - **2.** MIL : **chasseur alpin** *soldier specially trained for operations in mountainous terrain* - **3.** [avion] fighter.

châssis [ʃasi] *nm* **1.** [de fenêtre, de porte, de machine] frame - **2.** [de véhicule] chassis.

chaste [ʃast] *adj* chaste.

chasteté [ʃastəte] *nf* chastity.

chasuble [ʃazybl] *nf* chasuble.

chat¹, chatte [ʃa, ʃat] *nm, f* cat.

chat² [tʃat] *nm* INFORM chat.

châtaigne [ʃatɛɲ] *nf* **1.** [fruit] chestnut - **2.** *fam* [coup] clout.

châtaignier [ʃatɛɲe] *nm* [arbre] chestnut (tree) ; [bois] chestnut.

châtain [ʃatɛ̃] *adj & nm* chestnut, chestnut-brown.

château, x [ʃato] *nm* **1.** [forteresse] : **château (fort)** castle - **2.** [résidence - seigneuriale] mansion ; [- de monarque, d'évêque] palace ; **château gonflable** [jeu de plage, attraction] bouncy castle ; **château de sable** sandcastle ; **les châteaux de la Loire** the Châteaux of the Loire - **3.** [réservoir] : **château d'eau** water tower.

châtiment [ʃatimɑ̃] *nm* punishment.

chaton [ʃatɔ̃] *nm* **1.** [petit chat] kitten - **2.** BOT catkin.

chatouiller [3] [ʃatuje] *vt* **1.** [faire des chatouilles à] to tickle - **2.** *fig* [titiller] to titillate.

chatoyant, e [ʃatwajɑ̃, ɑ̃t] *adj* [reflet, étoffe] shimmering ; [bijou] sparkling.

châtrer [3] [ʃatre] *vt* to castrate ; [chat] to neuter ; [chatte] to spay.

chatte ➤ chat.

chaud, e [ʃo, ʃod] *adj* **1.** [gén] warm ; [de température très élevée, sensuel] hot - **2.** *fig*

[enthousiaste] : **être chaud pour qqch/pour faire qqch** to be keen on sthg/on doing sthg. ➤ **chaud** ◇ *adv* : **avoir chaud** to be warm ou hot ; **il fait chaud** it's warm ou hot ; **manger chaud** to have something hot (to eat). ◇ *nm* heat ; **rester au chaud** to stay in the warm.

chaudement [ʃodmɑ̃] *adv* warmly.

chaudière [ʃodjɛr] *nf* boiler.

chaudron [ʃodrɔ̃] *nm* cauldron.

chauffage [ʃofaʒ] *nm* [appareil] heating (system) ; **chauffage central** central heating.

chauffant, e [ʃofɑ̃, ɑ̃t] *adj* heating ; **plaque chauffante** hotplate.

chauffard [ʃofar] *nm péj* reckless driver.

chauffe-eau [ʃofo] *nm inv* waterheater.

chauffer [3] [ʃofe] ◇ *vt* [rendre chaud] to heat (up). ◇ *vi* **1.** [devenir chaud] to heat up - **2.** [moteur] to overheat - **3.** *fam* [barder] : **ça va chauffer** there's going to be trouble.

chauffeur [ʃofœr] *nm* AUTO driver.

chaume [ʃom] *nm* [paille] thatch.

chaumière [ʃomjɛr] *nf* cottage.

chaussée [ʃose] *nf* road, roadway ; **'chaussée déformée'** 'uneven road surface'.

chausse-pied [ʃospje] *(pl* chausse-pieds*) nm* shoehorn.

chausser [3] [ʃose] ◇ *vt* [chaussures, lunettes, skis] to put on. ◇ *vi* : **chausser du 39** to take size 39 (shoes). ➤ **se chausser** *vp* to put one's shoes on.

chaussette [ʃosɛt] *nf* sock.

chausson [ʃosɔ̃] *nm* **1.** [pantoufle] slipper - **2.** [de danse] ballet shoe - **3.** [de bébé] bootee - **4.** CULIN turnover ; **chausson aux pommes** apple turnover.

chaussure [ʃosyr] *nf* **1.** [soulier] shoe ; **chaussure basse** low-heeled shoe, flat shoe ; **chaussure de marche** [de randonnée] hiking ou walking boot ; [confortable] walking shoe ; **chaussure à scratch** shoe with Velcro® fastenings ; **chaussure de ski** ski boot ; **chaussures à talon** (shoes with) heels - **2.** [industrie] footwear industry.

chauve [ʃov] *adj* [sans cheveux] bald.

chauve-souris [ʃovsuri] *nf* bat.

chauvin, e [ʃovɛ̃, in] *adj* chauvinistic.

chaux [ʃo] *nf* lime ; **blanchi à la chaux** whitewashed.

chavirer [3] [ʃavire] *vi* **1.** [bateau] to capsize - **2.** *fig* [tourner] to spin.

chef [ʃɛf] *nm* **1.** [d'un groupe] head, leader ; [au travail] boss ; **en chef** in chief ; **chef d'entreprise** company head ; **chef d'État** head of state ; **chef de famille** head of the family ; **chef de file** POLIT (party) leader ; [catégorie, produit] category leader ; **chef de**

gare stationmaster ; **chef d'orchestre** conductor ; **chef de rayon** departmental manager ou supervisor ; **chef de service** ADMIN departmental manager - **2.** [cuisinier] chef. **chef d'accusation** *nm* charge, count.

chef-d'œuvre [ʃedœvr] (*pl* **chefs-d'œuvre**) *nm* masterpiece.

chef-lieu [ʃefljø] *nm* ≃ county town UK, ≃ county seat US.

cheik [ʃɛk] *nm* sheikh.

chemin [ʃəmɛ̃] *nm* **1.** [voie] path ; **chemin d'accès** path ; **chemin vicinal** byroad, minor road - **2.** [parcours] way ; *fig* road ; **en chemin** on the way. **chemin de fer** *nm* railway UK, railroad US.

cheminée [ʃəmine] *nf* **1.** [foyer] fireplace - **2.** [conduit d'usine] chimney - **3.** [encadrement] mantelpiece - **4.** [de paquebot, locomotive] funnel.

cheminement [ʃəminmɑ̃] *nm* [progression] advance ; *fig* [d'idée] development.

cheminer [3] [ʃəmine] *vi* [avancer] to make one's way ; *fig* [idée] to develop.

cheminot [ʃəmino] *nm* railwayman UK, railroad man US.

chemise [ʃəmiz] *nf* **1.** [d'homme] shirt ; **chemise de nuit** [de femme] nightdress, nightgown - **2.** [dossier] folder.

chemisette [ʃəmizɛt] *nf* [d'homme] short-sleeved shirt ; [de femme] short-sleeved blouse.

chemisier [ʃəmizje] *nm* [vêtement] blouse.

chenal, aux [ʃənal, o] *nm* [canal] channel.

chêne [ʃɛn] *nm* [arbre] oak (tree) ; [bois] oak.

chenet [ʃənɛ] *nm* firedog.

chenil [ʃənil] *nm* [pour chiens] kennel.

chenille [ʃənij] *nf* **1.** [insecte] caterpillar - **2.** [courroie] caterpillar track.

chèque [ʃɛk] *nm* cheque UK, check US ; **faire un chèque** to write a cheque UK ou check US ; **toucher un chèque** to cash a cheque UK ou check US ; **chèque (bancaire)** (bank) cheque UK ou check US ; **chèque barré** crossed cheque UK ou check US ; **chèque postal** post office cheque UK ou check US ; **chèque sans provision** bad cheque UK ou check US ; **chèque de voyage** traveller's cheque UK, traveler's check US.

chèque-cadeau [ʃɛkkado] *nm* gift token.

chèque-repas [ʃɛkrəpa] (*pl* **chèques-repas**), **chèque-restaurant** [ʃɛkrɛstərɑ̃] (*pl* **chèques-restaurant**) *nm* luncheon voucher.

chèque-vacances (*pl* **chèques-vacances**) [ʃɛkvakɑ̃s] *nm* voucher that can be used to pay for holiday accommodation, activities, meals, etc.

chéquier [ʃekje] *nm* chequebook UK, checkbook US.

cher, chère [ʃɛr] ⬦ *adj* **1.** [aimé] : **cher (à qqn)** dear (to sb) ; **Cher Monsieur** [au début d'une lettre] Dear Sir ; **Chère Madame** [au début d'une lettre] Dear Madam - **2.** [produit, vie, commerçant] expensive. ⬦ *nm, f hum* : **mon cher** dear. **cher** *adv* : **valoir cher, coûter cher** to be expensive, to cost a lot ; **payer cher** to pay a lot ; **je l'ai payé cher** *litt & fig* it cost me a lot. **chère** *nf* : **aimer la bonne chère** *sout* to like to eat well.

chercher [3] [ʃɛrʃe] ⬦ *vt* **1.** [gén] to look for - **2.** [prendre] : **aller/venir chercher qqn** [à un rendez-vous] to (go/come and) meet sb ; [en voiture] to (go/come and) pick sb up ; **aller/venir chercher qqch** to (go/come and) get sth. ⬦ *vi* : **chercher à faire qqch** to try to do sth.

chercheur, euse [ʃɛrʃœr, øz] *nm, f* [scientifique] researcher.

chéri, e [ʃeri] ⬦ *adj* dear. ⬦ *nm, f* darling.

chérir [32] [ʃerir] *vt* [personne] to love dearly ; [chose, idée] to cherish.

chétif, ive [ʃetif, iv] *adj* [malingre] sickly, weak.

cheval, aux [ʃəval, o] *nm* **1.** [animal] horse ; **à cheval** on horseback ; **être à cheval sur qqch** [être assis] to be sitting astride sth ; *fig* [siècles] to straddle sth ; *fig* [tenir à] to be a stickler for sth ; **cheval d'arçons** horse *(in gymnastics)* - **2.** [équitation] riding, horseriding ; **faire du cheval** to ride.

chevalerie [ʃəvalri] *nf* **1.** [qualité] chivalry - **2.** HIST knighthood.

chevalet [ʃəvalɛ] *nm* [de peintre] easel.

chevalier [ʃəvalje] *nm* knight.

chevalière [ʃəvaljɛr] *nf* [bague] signet ring.

chevauchée [ʃəvoʃe] *nf* [course] ride, horse-ride.

chevaucher [3] [ʃəvoʃe] *vt* [être assis] to sit ou be astride. **se chevaucher** *vp* to overlap.

chevelu, e [ʃəvly] *adj* hairy.

chevelure [ʃəvlyr] *nf* [cheveux] hair.

chevet [ʃəvɛ] *nm* head *(of bed)* ; **être au chevet de qqn** to be at sb's bedside.

cheveu, x [ʃəvø] *nm* [chevelure] hair ; **se faire couper les cheveux** to have one's hair cut.

cheville [ʃəvij] *nf* **1.** ANAT ankle - **2.** [pour fixer une vis] Rawlplug®.

chèvre [ʃɛvr] ⬦ *nf* [animal] goat. ⬦ *nm* [fromage] goat's cheese.

chevreau, x [ʃəvro] *nm* kid.

chèvrefeuille [ʃɛvrəfœj] *nm* honeysuckle.

chevreuil [ʃəvrœj] nm **1.** [animal] roe deer - **2.** CULIN venison.

chevronné, e [ʃəvrɔne] adj [expérimenté] experienced.

chevrotant, e [ʃəvrɔtɑ̃, ɑ̃t] adj tremulous.

chevrotine [ʃəvrɔtin] nf buckshot.

chewing-gum [ʃwiŋɡɔm] (pl chewing-gums) nm chewing gum (U).

chez [ʃe] prép **1.** [dans la maison de] : **il est chez lui** he's at home ; **il rentre chez lui** he's going home ; **il va venir chez nous** he is going to come to our place ou house ; **il habite chez nous** he lives with us - **2.** [en ce qui concerne] : **chez les jeunes** among young people ; **chez les Anglais** in England - **3.** [dans les œuvres de] : **chez Proust** in (the works of) Proust - **4.** [dans le caractère de] : **ce que j'apprécie chez lui, c'est sa gentillesse** what I like about him is his kindness.

chez-soi [ʃeswa] nm inv home, place of one's own.

chic [ʃik] <> adj (inv en genre) **1.** [élégant] smart, chic - **2.** vieilli [serviable] nice. <> nm style. <> interj : **chic (alors)!** great!

chicorée [ʃikɔre] nf [salade] endive UK ; [à café] chicory.

chien [ʃjɛ̃] nm **1.** [animal] dog ; **chien de chasse** [d'arrêt] gundog ; **chien de garde** guard dog - **2.** [d'arme] hammer ; **avoir un mal de chien à faire qqch** to have a lot of trouble doing sthg ; **en chien de fusil** curled up.

chiendent [ʃjɛ̃dɑ̃] nm couch grass.

chien-loup [ʃjɛ̃lu] nm Alsatian (dog).

chienne [ʃjɛn] nf (female) dog, bitch.

chiffe [ʃif] nf : **c'est une chiffe molle** he's spineless, he's a weed UK.

chiffon [ʃifɔ̃] nm [linge] rag.

chiffonné, e [ʃifɔne] adj [visage, mine] worn.

chiffre [ʃifr] nm **1.** [caractère] figure, number ; **chiffre arabe/romain** Arabic/Roman numeral - **2.** [montant] sum ; **chiffre d'affaires** COMM turnover UK, sales revenue US, volume of sales ; **chiffre rond** round number ; **chiffre de ventes** sales figures pl.

chiffrer [3] [ʃifre] <> vt **1.** [évaluer] to calculate, to assess - **2.** [coder] to encode. <> vi fam to mount up.

chignole [ʃiɲɔl] nf drill.

chignon [ʃiɲɔ̃] nm bun (in hair) ; **se crêper le chignon** fig to scratch each other's eyes out.

Chili [ʃili] nm : **le Chili** Chile.

chimère [ʃimɛr] nf **1.** MYTHOL chimera - **2.** [illusion] illusion, dream.

chimie [ʃimi] nf chemistry.

chimiothérapie [ʃimjɔterapi] nf chemotherapy.

chimique [ʃimik] adj chemical.

chimiste [ʃimist] nmf chemist.

chimpanzé [ʃɛ̃pɑ̃ze] nm chimpanzee.

Chine [ʃin] nf : **la Chine** China.

chiné, e [ʃine] adj mottled.

chiner [3] [ʃine] vi to look for bargains.

chinois, e [ʃinwa, az] adj Chinese. **chinois** nm **1.** [langue] Chinese - **2.** [passoire] conical sieve. **Chinois, e** nm, f Chinese person ; **les Chinois** the Chinese.

chiot [ʃjo] nm puppy.

chipie [ʃipi] nf vixen péj.

chips [ʃips] nfpl : **(pommes) chips** (potato) crisps UK, (potato) chips US.

chiquenaude [ʃiknod] nf flick.

chiquer [3] [ʃike] <> vt to chew. <> vi to chew tobacco.

chirurgical, e, aux [ʃiryrʒikal, o] adj surgical.

chirurgie [ʃiryrʒi] nf surgery.

chirurgien [ʃiryrʒjɛ̃] nm surgeon.

chiure [ʃjyr] nf : **chiure (de mouche)** flyspecks pl.

chlore [klɔr] nm chlorine.

chloroforme [klɔrɔfɔrm] nm chloroform.

chlorophylle [klɔrɔfil] nf chlorophyll.

choc [ʃɔk] nm **1.** [heurt, coup] impact - **2.** [conflit] clash - **3.** [émotion] shock - **4.** (en apposition) **images-chocs** shock pictures ; **prix-choc** amazing bargain.

chocolat [ʃɔkɔla] <> nm chocolate ; **chocolat au lait/noir** milk/plain chocolate ; **chocolat à cuire/à croquer** cooking/eating chocolate. <> adj inv chocolate (brown).

chœur [kœr] nm **1.** [chorale] choir ; fig [d'opéra] chorus ; **en chœur** fig all together - **2.** [d'église] choir, chancel.

choisi, e [ʃwazi] adj selected ; [termes, langage] carefully chosen.

choisir [32] [ʃwazir] <> vt : **choisir (de faire qqch)** to choose (to do sthg). <> vi to choose.

choix [ʃwa] nm **1.** [gén] choice ; **le livre de ton choix** any book you like ; **au choix** as you prefer ; **avoir le choix** to have the choice - **2.** [qualité] : **de premier choix** grade ou class one ; **articles de second choix** seconds.

choléra [kɔlera] nm cholera.

cholestérol [kɔlesterɔl] nm cholesterol.

chômage [ʃomaʒ] *nm* unemployment ; **au chômage** unemployed ; **être mis au chômage technique** to be laid off.

chômeur, euse [ʃomœr, øz] *nm, f* : **les chômeurs** the unemployed.

chope [ʃɔp] *nf* tankard.

choper [3] [ʃɔpe] *vt fam* **1.** [voler, arrêter] to nick UK, to pinch - **2.** [attraper] to catch.

choquant, e [ʃɔkã, ãt] *adj* shocking.

choquer [3] [ʃɔke] *vt* **1.** [scandaliser] to shock - **2.** [traumatiser] to shake (up).

choral, e, als OU **aux** [kɔral, o] *adj* choral. **chorale** *nf* [groupe] choir.

chorégraphie [kɔregrafi] *nf* choreography.

choriste [kɔrist] *nmf* chorister.

chose [ʃoz] *nf* thing ; **c'est (bien) peu de chose** it's nothing really ; **c'est la moindre des choses** it's the least I/we can do ; **de deux choses l'une** (it's got to be) one thing or the other ; **parler de choses et d'autres** to talk of this and that.

chou, x [ʃu] ⬦ *nm* **1.** [légume] cabbage - **2.** [pâtisserie] choux bun. ⬦ *adj inv* sweet, cute.

chouchou, oute [ʃuʃu, ut] *nm, f* favourite UK, favorite US ; [élève] teacher's pet.

choucroute [ʃukrut] *nf* sauerkraut.

chouette [ʃwɛt] ⬦ *nf* [oiseau] owl. ⬦ *adj fam* great. ⬦ *interj* : **chouette (alors)!** great!

chou-fleur [ʃuflœr] *nm* cauliflower.

choyer [13] [ʃwaje] *vt sout* to pamper.

chrétien, enne [kretjẽ, ɛn] *adj & nm, f* Christian.

chrétienté [kretjẽte] *nf* Christendom.

Christ [krist] *nm* Christ.

christianisme [kristjanism] *nm* Christianity.

chrome [krom] *nm* CHIM chromium.

chromé, e [krome] *adj* chrome-plated ; **acier chromé** chrome steel.

chromosome [krɔmozom] *nm* chromosome.

chronique [krɔnik] ⬦ *nf* **1.** [annales] chronicle - **2.** PRESSE : **chronique sportive** sports section. ⬦ *adj* chronic.

chronologie [krɔnɔlɔʒi] *nf* chronology.

chronologique [krɔnɔlɔʒik] *adj* chronological.

chronomètre [krɔnɔmɛtr] *nm* SPORT stopwatch.

chronométrer [18] [krɔnɔmetre] *vt* to time.

chrysalide [krizalid] *nf* chrysalis.

chrysanthème [krizãtɛm] *nm* chrysanthemum.

chuchotement [ʃyʃɔtmã] *nm* whisper.

chuchoter [3] [ʃyʃɔte] *vt & vi* to whisper.

chut [ʃyt] *interj* sh!, hush!

chute [ʃyt] *nf* **1.** [gén] fall ; **chute d'eau** waterfall ; **chute de neige** snowfall ; **la chute du mur de Berlin** the fall of the Berlin Wall - **2.** [de tissu] scrap.

ci [si] *adv (après n)* **ce livre-ci** this book ; **ces jours-ci** these days.

ci-après [siaprɛ] *adv* below.

cible [sibl] *nf litt & fig* target.

cicatrice [sikatris] *nf* scar.

cicatriser [3] [sikatrize] *vt litt & fig* to heal.

ci-contre [sikɔ̃tr] *adv* opposite.

ci-dessous [sidəsu] *adv* below.

ci-dessus [sidəsy] *adv* above.

cidre [sidr] *nm* cider UK, hard cider US.

Cie (*abr écrite de* **compagnie**) Co.

ciel *nm* **1.** (*pl* **ciels** [sjɛl]) [firmament] sky ; **à ciel ouvert** open-air - **2.** (*pl* **cieux** [sjø]) [paradis, providence] heaven. **cieux** *nmpl* heaven *sg*.

cierge [sjɛrʒ] *nm* RELIG (votive) candle.

cigale [sigal] *nf* cicada.

cigare [sigar] *nm* cigar.

cigarette [sigarɛt] *nf* cigarette.

ci-gît [siʒi] *adv* here lies.

cigogne [sigɔɲ] *nf* stork.

ci-inclus, e [siɛ̃kly, yz] *adj* enclosed. **ci-inclus** *adv* enclosed.

ci-joint, e [siʒwɛ̃, ɛ̃t] *adj* enclosed. **ci-joint** *adv* : **veuillez trouver ci-joint...** please find enclosed...

cil [sil] *nm* ANAT eyelash, lash.

ciller [3] [sije] *vi* to blink (one's eyes).

cime [sim] *nf* [d'arbre, de montagne] top ; *fig* height.

ciment [simã] *nm* cement.

cimenter [3] [simãte] *vt* to cement.

cimetière [simtjɛr] *nm* cemetery.

ciné [sine] *nm fam* cinema UK, movies US.

cinéaste [sineast] *nmf* film-maker.

ciné-club [sineklœb] (*pl* **ciné-clubs**) *nm* film club.

cinéma [sinema] *nm* **1.** [salle, industrie] cinema UK, movies US - **2.** [art] cinema, film ; **un acteur de cinéma** a film star.

cinémathèque [sinematɛk] *nf* film archive.

cinématographique [sinematɔgrafik] *adj* cinematographic.

cinéphile [sinefil] *nmf* movie OU film UK buff.

cinglé, e [sẽgle] *fam adj* nuts, nutty.

cingler [3] [sɛ̃gle] *vt* to lash.

cinq [sɛ̃k] <> *adj num inv* five. <> *nm* five ; *voir aussi* **six**.

cinquantaine [sɛ̃kɑ̃tɛn] *nf* **1.** [nombre] : **une cinquantaine de** about fifty - **2.** [âge] : **avoir la cinquantaine** to be in one's fifties.

cinquante [sɛ̃kɑ̃t] *adj num inv & nm* fifty ; *voir aussi* **six**.

cinquantième [sɛ̃kɑ̃tjɛm] *adj num inv, nm & nmf* fiftieth ; *voir aussi* **sixième**.

cinquième [sɛ̃kjɛm] <> *adj num inv, nm & nmf* fifth. <> *nf* SCOL ≃ second year OU form *UK*, ≃ seventh grade *US* ; *voir aussi* **sixième**.

cintre [sɛ̃tr] *nm* [pour vêtements] coat hanger.

cintré, e [sɛ̃tre] *adj* COUT waisted.

cirage [siraʒ] *nm* [produit] shoe polish.

circoncision [sirkɔ̃sizjɔ̃] *nf* circumcision.

circonférence [sirkɔ̃ferɑ̃s] *nf* **1.** GÉOM circumference - **2.** [pourtour] boundary.

circonflexe [sirkɔ̃flɛks] ➡ **accent**.

circonscription [sirkɔ̃skripsjɔ̃] *nf* district.

circonscrire [99] [sirkɔ̃skrir] *vt* **1.** [incendie, épidémie] to contain - **2.** *fig* [sujet] to define.

circonspect, e [sirkɔ̃spɛ, ɛkt] *adj* cautious.

circonstance [sirkɔ̃stɑ̃s] *nf* **1.** [occasion] occasion - **2.** *(gén pl)* [contexte, conjoncture] circumstance ; **circonstances atténuantes** DR mitigating circumstances.

circonstancié, e [sirkɔ̃stɑ̃sje] *adj* detailed.

circonstanciel, elle [sirkɔ̃stɑ̃sjɛl] *adj* GRAMM adverbial.

circuit [sirkɥi] *nm* **1.** [chemin] route - **2.** [parcours touristique] tour - **3.** SPORT & TECHNOL circuit ; **en circuit fermé** [en boucle] closed-circuit *(avant n)* ; *fig* within a limited circle.

circulaire [sirkylɛr] *nf & adj* circular.

circulation [sirkylasjɔ̃] *nf* **1.** [mouvement] circulation ; **mettre en circulation** to circulate ; **circulation (du sang)** circulation - **2.** [trafic] traffic.

circuler [3] [sirkyle] *vi* **1.** [sang, air, argent] to circulate ; **faire circuler qqch** to circulate sthg - **2.** [aller et venir] to move (along) ; **on circule mal en ville** the traffic is bad in town - **3.** [train, bus] to run - **4.** *fig* [rumeur, nouvelle] to spread.

cire [sir] *nf* **1.** [matière] wax - **2.** [encaustique] polish.

ciré, e [sire] *adj* **1.** [parquet] polished - **2.** ➡ **toile**. ➡ **ciré** *nm* oilskin.

cirer [3] [sire] *vt* [chaussures] to polish ; **j'en ai rien à cirer** *fam* I don't give a damn.

cirque [sirk] *nm* **1.** [gén] circus - **2.** GÉOL cirque - **3.** *fam fig* [désordre, chahut] chaos *(U)*.

cirrhose [siroz] *nf* cirrhosis *(U)*.

cisaille [sizaj] *nf* shears *pl*.

cisailler [3] [sizaje] *vt* [métal] to cut ; [branches] to prune.

ciseau, x [sizo] *nm* chisel. ➡ **ciseaux** *nmpl* scissors.

ciseler [25] [sizle] *vt* **1.** [pierre, métal] to chisel - **2.** [bijou] to engrave.

Cisjordanie [sizʒɔrdani] *nf* : **la Cisjordanie** the West Bank.

citadelle [sitadɛl] *nf litt & fig* citadel.

citadin, e [sitadɛ̃, in] <> *adj* city *(avant n)*, urban. <> *nm, f* city dweller.

citation [sitasjɔ̃] *nf* **1.** DR summons *sg* - **2.** [extrait] quote, quotation.

cité [site] *nf* **1.** [ville] city - **2.** [lotissement] housing estate *UK* OU project *US* ; **cité universitaire** halls *pl* of residence.

citer [3] [site] *vt* **1.** [exemple, propos, auteur] to quote - **2.** DR [convoquer] to summon - **3.** MIL : **être cité à l'ordre du jour** to be mentioned in dispatches.

citerne [sitɛrn] *nf* **1.** [d'eau] water tank - **2.** [cuve] tank.

cité U [sitey] *nf fam abr de* **cité universitaire**.

citoyen, enne [sitwajɛ̃, ɛn] *nm, f* citizen.

citoyenneté [sitwajɛnte] *nf* citizenship.

citron [sitrɔ̃] *nm* lemon ; **citron pressé** fresh lemon juice ; **citron vert** lime.

citronnade [sitrɔnad] *nf* (still) lemonade.

citronnier [sitrɔnje] *nm* lemon tree.

citrouille [sitruj] *nf* pumpkin.

civet [sivɛ] *nm* stew ; **civet de lièvre** jugged hare.

civière [sivjɛr] *nf* stretcher.

civil, e [sivil] <> *adj* **1.** [gén] civil - **2.** [non militaire] civilian. <> *nm, f* civilian ; **dans le civil** in civilian life ; **policier en civil** plain-clothes policeman *(f* policewoman*)* ; **soldat en civil** soldier in civilian clothes.

civilement [sivilmɑ̃] *adv* : **se marier civilement** to get married at a registry office.

civilisation [sivilizasjɔ̃] *nf* civilization.

civilisé, e [sivilize] *adj* civilized.

civiliser [3] [sivilize] *vt* to civilize.

civique [sivik] *adj* civic ; **instruction civique** civics *(U)*.

civisme [sivism] *nm* sense of civic responsibility.

cl *(abr écrite de* **centilitre***)* cl.

clair, e [klɛr] *adj* **1.** [précis, évident] clear ; **c'est clair et net** there's no two ways about it - **2.** [lumineux] bright - **3.** [pâle - couleur, teint] light ; [- tissu, cheveux] light-coloured

UK, light-colored US. ➤ **clair** ◇ *adv* :
voir clair (dans qqch) *fig* to have a clear
understanding (of sthg). ◇ *nm* : mettre ou
tirer qqch au clair to shed light upon sthg.
➤ **clair de lune** (*pl* clairs de lune) *nm*
moonlight (U). ➤ **en clair** *loc adv* TV
unscrambled (*esp of a private TV channel*).

clairement [klɛrmɑ̃] *adv* clearly.

claire-voie [klɛrvwa] ➤ **à claire-voie**
loc adv openwork (*avant n*).

clairière [klɛrjɛr] *nf* clearing.

clairon [klɛrɔ̃] *nm* bugle.

claironner [3] [klɛrɔne] *vt fig* [crier] :
claironner qqch to shout sthg from the
rooftops.

clairsemé, e [klɛrsəme] *adj* [cheveux] thin ;
[arbres] scattered ; [population] sparse.

clairvoyant, e [klɛrvwajɑ̃, ɑ̃t] *adj* perceptive.

clamer [3] [klame] *vt* to proclaim.

clameur [klamœr] *nf* clamour UK, clamor
US.

clan [klɑ̃] *nm* clan.

clandestin, e [klɑ̃dɛstɛ̃, in] ◇ *adj* [jour-
nal, commerce] clandestine ; [activité] covert. ◇ *nm* [étranger] illegal immigrant ou
alien ; [voyageur] stowaway.

clapier [klapje] *nm* [à lapins] hutch.

clapoter [3] [klapɔte] *vi* [vagues] to lap.

claquage [klakaʒ] *nm* MÉD strain ; se faire
un claquage to pull ou to strain a muscle.

claque [klak] *nf* 1. [gifle] slap - 2. THÉÂTRE
claque.

claquer [3] [klake] ◇ *vt* 1. [fermer] to
slam - 2. : faire claquer [langue] to click ;
[doigts] to snap ; [fouet] to crack - 3. *fam*
[gifler] to slap - 4. *fam* [dépenser] to blow.
◇ *vi* [porte, volet] to bang.

claquettes [klakɛt] *nfpl* [danse] tap dancing (U).

clarifier [9] [klarifje] *vt litt & fig* to clarify.

clarinette [klarinɛt] *nf* [instrument] clarinet.

clarté [klarte] *nf* 1. [lumière] brightness
- 2. [netteté] clarity.

classe [klas] *nf* 1. [gén] class ; classe touriste
economy ou coach US class - 2. SCOL : aller
en classe to go to school ; classe de neige
skiing trip (*with school*) ; classe préparatoire
*school preparing students for Grandes Écoles
entrance exams* ; classe verte field trip (*with
school*) - 3. MIL rank ; faire ses classes MIL to
do one's training.

classé, e [klase] *adj* [monument] listed UK.

classement [klasmɑ̃] *nm* 1. [rangement] fil-
ing - 2. [classification] classification - 3. [rang
- SCOL] position ; SPORT placing - 4. [liste
- SCOL] class list ; SPORT final placings *pl*.

classer [3] [klase] *vt* 1. [ranger] to file
- 2. [plantes, animaux] to classify - 3. [cata-
loguer] : classer qqn (parmi) to label sb (as)
- 4. [attribuer un rang à] to rank. ➤ **se
classer** *vp* to be classed, to rank ; se classer
troisième to come third.

classeur [klasœr] *nm* 1. [meuble] filing
cabinet - 2. [d'écolier] ring binder.

classification [klasifikasjɔ̃] *nf* classification.

classique [klasik] ◇ *nm* 1. [auteur] classical author - 2. [œuvre] classic. ◇ *adj*
1. ART & MUS classical - 2. [sobre] classic
- 3. [habituel] classic ; ça, c'est l'histoire
classique! it's the usual story!

clause [kloz] *nf* clause.

claustrophobie [klostrɔfɔbi] *nf* claus-
trophobia.

clavecin [klavsɛ̃] *nm* harpsichord.

clavicule [klavikyl] *nf* collarbone.

clavier [klavje] *nm* keyboard.

clé, clef [kle] ◇ *nf* 1. [gén] key ; la clé du
mystère the key to the mystery ; mettre
qqn/qqch sous clé to lock sb/sthg up ; clé de
contact AUTO ignition key - 2. [outil] : clé
anglaise ou à molette adjustable spanner UK
ou wrench US, monkey wrench - 3. MUS
[signe] clef ; clé de sol/fa treble/bass clef.
◇ *adj* : industrie/rôle clé key industry/
role. ➤ **clé de voûte** *nf litt & fig* keystone.

clément, e [klemɑ̃, ɑ̃t] *adj* 1. [indulgent]
lenient - 2. *fig* [température] mild.

clémentine [klemɑ̃tin] *nf* clementine.

cleptomane = **kleptomane**.

clerc [klɛr] *nm* [assistant] clerk.

clergé [klɛrʒe] *nm* clergy.

Clic-Clac® [klikklac] *nm* pull-out sofa bed.

cliché [kliʃe] *nm* 1. PHOTO negative - 2. [ba-
nalité] cliché.

client, e [kliɑ̃, ɑ̃t] *nm, f* 1. [de notaire,
d'agence] client ; [de médecin] patient
- 2. [acheteur] customer - 3. [habitué] regular
(customer).

clientèle [kliɑ̃tɛl] *nf* 1. [ensemble des
clients] customers *pl* ; [de profession libérale]
clientele - 2. [fait d'être client] : accorder sa
clientèle à to give one's custom to.

cligner [3] [kliɲe] *vi* : cligner de l'œil to
wink ; cligner des yeux to blink.

clignotant, e [kliɲɔtɑ̃, ɑ̃t] *adj* [lumière]
flickering. ➤ **clignotant** *nm* AUTO indicator UK, turn signal US.

clignoter [3] [kliɲɔte] *vi* 1. [yeux] to blink
- 2. [lumière] to flicker.

climat [klima] *nm litt & fig* climate.

climatisation [klimatizasjɔ̃] *nf* air-conditioning.

climatisé, e [klimatize] *adj* air-conditioned.

clin [klɛ̃] ⬥ **clin d'œil** *nm* : **faire un clin d'œil (à)** to wink (at) ; **en un clin d'œil** in a flash.

clinique [klinik] ⬥ *nf* clinic. ⬥ *adj* clinical.

clip [klip] *nm* **1.** [vidéo] pop video - **2.** [boucle d'oreilles] clip-on earring.

cliquable [klikabl] *adj* clickable ; **plan cliquable** sensitive map.

cliquer [3] [klike] *vi* INFORM to click ; [bouton gauche] to left-click ; [bouton droit] to right-click.

cliqueter [27] [klikte] *vi* **1.** [pièces, clés, chaînes] to jingle, to jangle - **2.** [verres] to clink.

clivage [klivaʒ] *nm fig* [division] division.

clochard, e [klɔʃar, ard] *nm, f* tramp.

cloche [klɔʃ] ⬥ *nf* **1.** [d'église] bell - **2.** *fam* [idiot] idiot, clot *UK*. ⬥ *adj fam* **ce qu'elle peut être cloche, celle-là!** she can be a right idiot!

cloche-pied [klɔʃpje] ⬥ **à cloche-pied** *loc adv* hopping ; **sauter à cloche-pied** to hop.

clocher [klɔʃe] *nm* [d'église] church tower.

clochette [klɔʃɛt] *nf* **1.** [petite cloche] (little) bell - **2.** [de fleur] bell.

clodo [klɔdo] *nmf fam* tramp.

cloison [klwazɔ̃] *nf* [mur] partition.

cloisonner [3] [klwazɔne] *vt* [pièce, maison] to partition (off) ; *fig* to compartmentalize.

cloître [klwatr] *nm* cloister.

clonage [klɔnaʒ] *nm* cloning ; **clonage thérapeutique** therapeutic cloning.

clopiner [3] [klɔpine] *vi* to hobble along.

cloporte [klɔpɔrt] *nm* woodlouse.

cloque [klɔk] *nf* blister.

clore [113] [klɔr] *vt* to close ; [négociations] to conclude.

clos, e [klo, kloz] ⬥ *pp* ▶ **clore.** ⬥ *adj* closed.

clôture [klotyr] *nf* **1.** [haie] hedge ; [de fil de fer] fence - **2.** [fermeture] closing, closure - **3.** [fin] end, conclusion.

clôturer [3] [klotyre] *vt* **1.** [terrain] to enclose - **2.** [négociation] to close, to conclude.

clou [klu] *nm* **1.** [pointe] nail ; **clou de girofle** CULIN clove - **2.** [attraction] highlight.

clouer [3] [klue] *vt* [fixer - couvercle, planche] to nail (down) ; [- tableau, caisse] to nail (up) ; *fig* [immobiliser] : **rester cloué sur place** to be rooted to the spot.

clouté, e [klute] *adj* [vêtement] studded.

clown [klun] *nm* clown ; **faire le clown** to clown around, to act the fool.

club [klœb] *nm* club.

cm (*abr écrite de* **centimètre**) cm.

CM *nm* (*abr de* **cours moyen**) **CM1** *fourth year of primary school* ; **CM2** *fifth year of primary school.*

CNAM [knam] (*abr de* **Conservatoire national des arts et métiers**) *nm science and technology school in Paris.*

CNRS (*abr de* **Centre national de la recherche scientifique**) *nm national scientific research organization.*

coaguler [3] [kɔagyle] *vi* **1.** [sang] to clot - **2.** [lait] to curdle.

coalition [kɔalisjɔ̃] *nf* coalition.

coasser [3] [kɔase] *vi* [grenouille] to croak.

cobaye [kɔbaj] *nm litt & fig* guinea pig.

cobra [kɔbra] *nm* cobra.

co-branding [kɔbrandiŋ] *nm* co-branding.

Coca® [kɔka] *nm* [boisson] Coke®.

cocaïne [kɔkain] *nf* cocaine.

cocaïnomane [kɔkainɔman] *nmf* cocaine addict.

cocarde [kɔkard] *nf* **1.** [insigne] roundel - **2.** [distinction] rosette.

cocardier, ère [kɔkardje, ɛr] *adj* [chauvin] jingoistic.

cocasse [kɔkas] *adj* funny.

coccinelle [kɔksinɛl] *nf* **1.** [insecte] ladybird *UK*, ladybug *US* - **2.** [voiture] Beetle.

coccyx [kɔksis] *nm* coccyx.

cocher[1] [kɔʃe] *nm* coachman.

cocher[2] [3] [kɔʃe] *vt* to tick (off) *UK*, to check (off) *US*.

cochon, onne [kɔʃɔ̃, ɔn] ⬥ *adj* dirty, smutty. ⬥ *nm, f fam péj* pig ; **un tour de cochon** a dirty trick. ⬥ **cochon** *nm* pig.

cochonnerie [kɔʃɔnri] *nf fam* **1.** [nourriture] muck (U) - **2.** [chose] rubbish (U) - **3.** [saleté] mess (U) - **4.** [obscénité] dirty joke, smut (U).

cochonnet [kɔʃɔnɛ] *nm* [jeux] jack.

cocktail [kɔktɛl] *nm* **1.** [réception] cocktail party - **2.** [boisson] cocktail - **3.** *fig* [mélange] mixture.

coco [kɔko] *nm* **1.** ▶ **noix** - **2.** *péj* [communiste] commie.

cocon [kɔkɔ̃] *nm fig & ZOOL* cocoon.

cocorico [kɔkɔriko] *nm* [du coq] cock-a-doodle-doo.

cocotier [kɔkɔtje] *nm* coconut tree.

cocotte [kɔkɔt] *nf* **1.** [marmite] casserole (dish) - **2.** [poule] hen - **3.** *péj* [courtisane] tart.

Cocotte-Minute® [kɔkɔtminyt] *nf* pressure cooker.

cocu, e [kɔky] *nm, f & adj fam* cuckold.

code [kɔd] *nm* **1.** [gén] code ; **code-barres**

bar code ; **code postal** postcode *UK*, zip code *US* - **2.** ÉCON : **code secret** PIN number - **3.** [phares] : **code** dipped headlights *pl UK*, dimmed headlights *pl US* - **4.** DR : **code pénal** penal code ; **code de la route** highway code *UK*.

coder [3] [kɔde] *vt* to code.

coefficient [kɔefisjɑ̃] *nm* coefficient.

coéquipier, ère [kɔekipje, ɛr] *nm, f* teammate.

cœur [kœr] *nm* heart ; **au cœur de l'hiver** in the depths of winter ; **au cœur de l'été** at the height of summer ; **au cœur du conflit** at the height of the conflict ; **de bon cœur** willingly ; **de tout son cœur** with all one's heart ; **apprendre par cœur** to learn by heart ; **avoir bon cœur** to be kind-hearted ; **avoir mal au cœur** to feel sick ; **s'en donner à cœur joie** [prendre beaucoup de plaisir] to have a whale of a time ; **manquer de cœur, ne pas avoir de cœur** to be heartless ; **soulever le cœur à qqn** to make sb feel sick.

coexister [3] [kɔɛgziste] *vi* to coexist.

coffre [kɔfr] *nm* **1.** [meuble] chest - **2.** [de voiture] boot *UK*, trunk *US* - **3.** [coffre-fort] safe.

coffre-fort [kɔfrəfɔr] *nm* safe.

coffret [kɔfrɛ] *nm* **1.** [petit coffre] casket ; **coffret à bijoux** jewellery *UK* ou jewelry *US* box - **2.** [de disques] boxed set.

cogner [3] [kɔɲe] *vi* **1.** [heurter] to bang - **2.** *fam* [donner des coups] to hit - **3.** [soleil] to beat down. ⏹ **se cogner** *vp* [se heurter] to bump o.s. ; **se cogner à** ou **contre qqch** to bump into sthg ; **se cogner la tête/le genou** to hit one's head/knee.

cohabiter [3] [kɔabite] *vi* **1.** [habiter ensemble] to live together - **2.** POLIT to cohabit.

cohérence [kɔerɑ̃s] *nf* consistency, coherence.

cohérent, e [kɔerɑ̃, ɑ̃t] *adj* **1.** [logique] consistent, coherent - **2.** [unifié] coherent.

cohésion [kɔezjɔ̃] *nf* cohesion.

cohorte [kɔɔrt] *nf* [groupe] troop.

cohue [kɔy] *nf* **1.** [foule] crowd - **2.** [bousculade] crush.

coi, coite [kwa, kwat] *adj* : **rester coi** *sout* to remain silent.

coiffe [kwaf] *nf* headdress.

coiffé, e [kwafe] *adj* : **être bien/mal coiffé** to have tidy/untidy hair ; **être coiffé d'une casquette** to be wearing a cap.

coiffer [3] [kwafe] *vt* **1.** [mettre sur la tête] : **coiffer qqn de qqch** to put sthg on sb's head - **2.** [les cheveux] : **coiffer qqn** to do sb's hair. ⏹ **se coiffer** *vp* **1.** [les cheveux] to do one's hair - **2.** [mettre sur la tête] : **se coiffer de** to wear, to put on.

coiffeur, euse [kwafœr, øz] *nm, f* hairdresser. ⏹ **coiffeuse** *nf* [meuble] dressing table.

coiffure [kwafyr] *nf* **1.** [chapeau] hat - **2.** [cheveux] hairstyle.

coin [kwɛ̃] *nm* **1.** [angle] corner ; **au coin du feu** by the fireside - **2.** [parcelle, endroit] place, spot ; **dans le coin** in the area ; **un coin de ciel bleu** a patch of blue sky ; **coin cuisine** kitchen area ; **le petit coin** *fam* the little boys'/girls' room - **3.** [outil] wedge.

coincer [16] [kwɛse] *vt* **1.** [bloquer] to jam - **2.** *fam* [prendre] to nab ; *fig* to catch out *UK* - **3.** [acculer] to corner, to trap.

coïncidence [kɔɛ̃sidɑ̃s] *nf* coincidence.

coïncider [3] [kɔɛ̃side] *vi* to coincide.

coing [kwɛ̃] *nm* [fruit] quince.

coït [kɔit] *nm* coitus.

col [kɔl] *nm* **1.** [de vêtement] collar ; **col roulé** polo neck *UK*, turtleneck *US* - **2.** [partie étroite] neck - **3.** ANAT : **col du fémur** neck of the thighbone ou femur ; **col de l'utérus** cervix, neck of the womb - **4.** GÉOGR pass.

coléoptère [kɔleɔptɛr] *nm* beetle.

colère [kɔlɛr] *nf* **1.** [irritation] anger ; **être/se mettre en colère** to be/get angry - **2.** [accès d'humeur] fit of anger ou rage ; **piquer une colère** to fly into a rage.

coléreux, euse [kɔlerø, øz], **colérique** [kɔlerik] *adj* [tempérament] fiery ; [personne] quick-tempered.

colimaçon [kɔlimasɔ̃] ⏹ **en colimaçon** *loc adv* spiral.

colique [kɔlik] *nf* **1.** (*gén pl*) [douleur] colic (U) - **2.** [diarrhée] diarrhoea *UK*, diarrhea *US*.

colis [kɔli] *nm* parcel *UK*, package *US*.

collaborateur, trice [kɔlabɔratœr, tris] *nm, f* **1.** [employé] colleague - **2.** HIST collaborator.

collaboration [kɔlabɔrasjɔ̃] *nf* collaboration.

collaborer [3] [kɔlabɔre] *vi* **1.** [coopérer, sous l'Occupation] to collaborate - **2.** [participer] : **collaborer à** to contribute to.

collant, e [kɔlɑ̃, ɑ̃t] *adj* **1.** [substance] sticky - **2.** *fam* [personne] clinging, clingy. ⏹ **collant** *nm* tights *pl UK*, panty hose *pl US*.

colle [kɔl] *nf* **1.** [substance] glue - **2.** [question] poser - **3.** [SCOL - interrogation] test ; [- retenue] detention.

collecte [kɔlɛkt] *nf* collection.

collectif, ive [kɔlɛktif, iv] *adj* **1.** [responsabilité, travail] collective - **2.** [billet, voyage] group (*avant n*). ⏹ **collectif** *nm* **1.** [équipe] team - **2.** LING collective noun - **3.** FIN : **collectif budgétaire** collection of budgetary measures.

collection [kɔlɛksjɔ̃] *nf* **1.** [d'objets, de livres, de vêtements] collection ; **faire la collection de** to collect - **2.** COMM line.

collectionner [3] [kɔlɛksjɔne] *vt litt & fig* to collect.

collectionneur, euse [kɔlɛksjɔnœr, øz] *nm, f* collector.

collectivité [kɔlɛktivite] *nf* community ; **les collectivités locales** ADMIN the local communities ; **collectivité territoriale** ADMIN (partially) autonomous region.

collège [kɔlɛʒ] *nm* **1.** SCOL ≃ secondary school - **2.** [de personnes] college.

collégien, enne [kɔleʒjɛ̃, ɛn] *nm, f* schoolboy (*f* schoolgirl).

collègue [kɔlɛg] *nmf* colleague.

coller [3] [kɔle] ◇ *vt* **1.** [fixer - affiche] to stick (up) ; [- timbre] to stick - **2.** [appuyer] to press - **3.** INFORM to paste - **4.** *fam* [mettre] to stick, to dump - **5.** SCOL to give (a) detention to, to keep behind. ◇ *vi* **1.** [adhérer] to stick - **2.** [être adapté] : **coller à qqch** [vêtement] to cling to sthg ; *fig* to fit in with sthg, to adhere to sthg. **se coller** *vp* [se plaquer] : **se coller contre qqn/qqch** to press o.s. against sb/sthg.

collerette [kɔlrɛt] *nf* [de vêtement] ruff.

collet [kɔlɛ] *nm* **1.** [de vêtement] collar ; **être collet monté** [affecté, guindé] to be straitlaced - **2.** [piège] snare.

collier [kɔlje] *nm* **1.** [bijou] necklace - **2.** [d'animal] collar - **3.** [barbe] *fringe of beard along the jawline.*

colline [kɔlin] *nf* hill.

collision [kɔlizjɔ̃] *nf* [choc] collision, crash ; **entrer en collision avec** to collide with.

colloque [kɔlɔk] *nm* colloquium.

colmater [3] [kɔlmate] *vt* **1.** [fuite] to plug, to seal off - **2.** [brèche] to fill, to seal.

colo [kɔlo] *nf fam* children's holiday camp *UK*, summer camp *US*.

colocataire [kɔlɔkatɛr] *nmf* ADMIN cotenant ; [gen] flatmate.

colombe [kɔlɔ̃b] *nf* dove.

Colombie [kɔlɔ̃bi] *nf* : **la Colombie** Colombia.

colon [kɔlɔ̃] *nm* settler.

côlon [kɔlɔ̃] *nm* colon.

colonel [kɔlɔnɛl] *nm* colonel.

colonial, e, aux [kɔlɔnjal, o] *adj* colonial.

colonialisme [kɔlɔnjalism] *nm* colonialism.

colonie [kɔlɔni] *nf* **1.** [territoire] colony - **2.** [d'expatriés] community ; **colonie de vacances** holiday *UK* ou summer camp *US*.

colonisation [kɔlɔnizasjɔ̃] *nf* colonization.

coloniser [3] [kɔlɔnize] *vt litt & fig* to colonize.

colonne [kɔlɔn] *nf* column. **colonne vertébrale** *nf* spine, spinal column.

colorant, e [kɔlɔrɑ̃, ɑ̃t] *adj* colouring *UK*, coloring *US*. **colorant** *nm* colouring *UK*, coloring *US*.

colorer [3] [kɔlɔre] *vt* [teindre] to colour *UK*, to color *US*.

colorier [9] [kɔlɔrje] *vt* to colour in *UK*, to color in *US*.

coloris [kɔlɔri] *nm* shade.

colorisation [kɔlɔrizasjɔ̃] *nf* CINÉ colourization *UK*, colorization *US*.

coloriser [3] [kɔlɔrize] *vt* CINÉ to colourize *UK*, to colorize *US*.

colossal, e, aux [kɔlɔsal, o] *adj* colossal, huge.

colporter [3] [kɔlpɔrte] *vt* [marchandise] to hawk ; [information] to spread.

coltiner [3] [kɔltine] **se coltiner** *vp fam* to be landed with.

coma [kɔma] *nm* coma ; **être dans le coma** to be in a coma.

comateux, euse [kɔmatø, øz] *adj* comatose.

combat [kɔ̃ba] *nm* **1.** [bataille] battle, fight - **2.** *fig* [lutte] struggle - **3.** SPORT fight.

combatif, ive [kɔ̃batif, iv] *adj* [humeur] fighting (*avant n*) ; [troupes] willing to fight.

combattant, e [kɔ̃batɑ̃, ɑ̃t] *nm, f* [en guerre] combatant ; [dans bagarre] fighter ; **ancien combattant** veteran.

combattre [83] [kɔ̃batr] ◇ *vt litt & fig* to fight (against). ◇ *vi* to fight.

combattu, e [kɔ̃baty] *pp* **combattre**.

combien [kɔ̃bjɛ̃] ◇ *conj* how much ; **combien de** [nombre] how many ; [quantité] how much ; **combien de temps?** how long? ; **ça fait combien?** [prix] how much is that? ; [longueur, hauteur etc] how long/high etc is it? ◇ *adv* how (much). ◇ *nm inv* : **le combien sommes-nous?** what date is it? ; **tous les combien?** how often?

combinaison [kɔ̃binɛzɔ̃] *nf* **1.** [d'éléments] combination - **2.** [de femme] slip - **3.** [vêtement - de mécanicien] boiler suit *UK*, overalls *pl UK*, overall *US* ; [- de ski] ski suit - **4.** [de coffre] combination.

combine [kɔ̃bin] *nf fam* trick.

combiné [kɔ̃bine] *nm* receiver.

combiner [3] [kɔ̃bine] *vt* **1.** [arranger] to combine - **2.** [organiser] to devise. **se combiner** *vp* to turn out.

comble [kɔ̃bl] ◇ *nm* height ; **c'est un** ou **le comble!** that beats everything! ◇ *adj* packed. **combles** *nmpl* attic *sg*, loft *sg*.

combler [3] [kɔ̃ble] vt **1.** [gâter] : **combler qqn de** to shower sb with - **2.** [boucher] to fill in - **3.** [déficit] to make good ; [lacune] to fill.

combustible [kɔ̃bystibl] <> nm fuel. <> adj combustible.

combustion [kɔ̃bystjɔ̃] nf combustion.

comédie [kɔmedi] nf **1.** CINÉ & THÉÂTRE comedy ; **comédie musicale** musical - **2.** [complication] palaver.

comédien, enne [kɔmedjɛ̃, ɛn] nm, f [acteur] actor (f actress) ; fig & péj sham.

comestible [kɔmɛstibl] adj edible.

comète [kɔmɛt] nf comet.

comique [kɔmik] <> nm THÉÂTRE comic actor. <> adj **1.** [style] comic - **2.** [drôle] comical, funny.

comité [kɔmite] nm committee ; **comité d'entreprise** works council UK (also organizing leisure activities).

commandant [kɔmɑ̃dɑ̃] nm commander.

commande [kɔmɑ̃d] nf **1.** [de marchandises] order ; **passer une commande** to place an order ; **sur commande** to order ; **disponible sur commande** available on request - **2.** TECHNOL control - **3.** INFORM command ; **commande numérique** digital control.

commander [3] [kɔmɑ̃de] <> vt **1.** MIL to command - **2.** [contrôler] to operate, to control - **3.** COMM to order. <> vi to be in charge ; **commander à qqn de faire qqch** to order sb to do sthg.

commanditer [3] [kɔmɑ̃dite] vt **1.** [entreprise] to finance - **2.** [meurtre] to put up the money for - **3.** [tournoi] to sponsor.

commando [kɔmɑ̃do] nm commando (unit).

comme [kɔm] <> conj **1.** [introduisant une comparaison] like ; **il sera médecin comme son père** he'll become a doctor (just) like his father - **2.** [exprimant la manière] as ; **fais comme il te plaira** do as you wish ; **comme prévu/convenu** as planned/agreed ; **comme bon vous semble** as you think best ; **comme ci comme ça** fam so-so - **3.** [tel que] like, such as ; **les arbres comme le marronnier** trees such as ou like the chestnut - **4.** [en tant que] as - **5.** [ainsi que] : **les filles comme les garçons iront jouer au foot** both girls and boys will play football ; **l'un comme l'autre sont très gentils** the one is as kind as the other, they are equally kind - **6.** [introduisant une cause] as, since ; **comme il pleuvait, nous sommes rentrés** as it was raining we went back. <> adv excl [marquant l'intensité] how ; **comme tu as grandi!** how you've grown! ; **comme c'est difficile!** it's so difficult! ; **regarde comme il nage bien!** (just) look what a good swimmer he is!, (just) look how well he swims!

commémoration [kɔmemɔrasjɔ̃] nf commemoration.

commémorer [3] [kɔmemɔre] vt to commemorate.

commencement [kɔmɑ̃smɑ̃] nm beginning, start.

commencer [16] [kɔmɑ̃se] <> vt [entreprendre] to begin, to start ; [être au début de] to begin. <> vi to start, to begin ; **commencer à faire qqch** to begin ou start to do sthg, to begin ou start doing sthg ; **commencer par faire qqch** to begin ou start by doing sthg.

comment [kɔmɑ̃] <> adv interr how ; **comment?** what? ; **comment ça va?** how are you? ; **comment cela?** how come? <> nm inv > **pourquoi**.

commentaire [kɔmɑ̃tɛr] nm **1.** [explication] commentary - **2.** [observation] comment.

commentateur, trice [kɔmɑ̃tatœr, tris] nm, f RADIO & TV commentator.

commenter [3] [kɔmɑ̃te] vt to comment on.

commérage [kɔmeraʒ] nm péj gossip (U).

commerçant, e [kɔmɛrsɑ̃, ɑ̃t] <> adj [rue] shopping (avant n) ; [quartier] commercial ; [personne] business-minded. <> nm, f shopkeeper UK.

commerce [kɔmɛrs] nm **1.** [achat et vente] commerce, trade ; **commerce de gros/détail** wholesale/retail trade ; **commerce électronique** electronic commerce, e-commerce ; **commerce équitable** fair trade ; **commerce extérieur** foreign trade - **2.** [magasin] business ; **le petit commerce** small shopkeepers pl.

commercial, e, aux [kɔmɛrsjal, o] <> adj [entreprise, valeur] commercial ; [politique] trade (avant n). <> nm, f marketing man (f woman).

commercialiser [3] [kɔmɛrsjalize] vt to market.

commère [kɔmɛr] nf péj gossip.

commettre [84] [kɔmɛtr] vt to commit.

commis, e [kɔmi, iz] pp > **commettre**. <> **commis** nm assistant ; **commis voyageur** commercial traveller UK ou traveler US.

commisération [kɔmizerasjɔ̃] nf sout commiseration.

commissaire [kɔmisɛr] nm commissioner ; **commissaire de police** (police) superintendent UK, (police) captain US.

commissaire-priseur [kɔmisɛrprizœr] nm auctioneer.

commissariat [kɔmisarja] nm : **commissariat de police** police station.

commission [kɔmisjɔ̃] nf **1.** [délégation]

commission, committee - 2. [message] message. ➡ **commissions** *nfpl* shopping *(U)* ; **faire les commissions** to do the shopping.

commissure [kɔmisyr] *nf* : **la commissure des lèvres** the corner of the mouth.

commode [kɔmɔd] <> *nf* chest of drawers. <> *adj* **1.** [pratique - système] convenient ; [- outil] handy - **2.** [aimable] : **pas commode** awkward.

commodité [kɔmɔdite] *nf* convenience.

commotion [kɔmɔsjɔ̃] *nf* MÉD shock ; **commotion cérébrale** concussion.

commun, e [kɔmœ̃, yn] *adj* **1.** [gén] common ; [décision, effort] joint ; [salle, jardin] shared ; **avoir qqch en commun** to have sthg in common ; **faire qqch en commun** to do sthg together - **2.** [courant] usual, common. ➡ **commune** *nf* town.

communal, e, aux [kɔmynal, o] *adj* [école] local ; [bâtiments] council *(avant n)*.

communauté [kɔmynote] *nf* **1.** [groupe] community - **2.** [de sentiments, d'idées] identity - **3.** POLIT : **la Communauté européenne** the European Community.

commune ➡ **commun**.

communément [kɔmynemɑ̃] *adv* commonly.

communiant, e [kɔmynjɑ̃, ɑ̃t] *nm, f* communicant ; **premier communiant** *child taking first communion*.

communication [kɔmynikasjɔ̃] *nf* **1.** [gén] communication - **2.** TÉLÉCOM : **communication (téléphonique)** (phone) call ; **être en communication avec qqn** to be talking to sb ; **obtenir la communication** to get through ; **recevoir/prendre une communication** to receive/take a (phone) call ; **communication interurbaine** long-distance (phone) call.

communier [9] [kɔmynje] *vi* RELIG to take communion.

communion [kɔmynjɔ̃] *nf* RELIG communion.

communiqué [kɔmynike] *nm* communiqué ; **communiqué de presse** press release.

communiquer [3] [kɔmynike] *vt* : **communiquer qqch à** [information, sentiment] to pass on ou communicate sthg to ; [chaleur] to transmit sthg to ; [maladie] to pass sthg on to.

communisme [kɔmynism] *nm* communism.

communiste [kɔmynist] *nmf & adj* communist.

commutateur [kɔmytatœr] *nm* switch.

compact, e [kɔpakt] *adj* **1.** [épais, dense] dense - **2.** [petit] compact. ➡ **compact** *nm* [disque laser] compact disc, CD.

compagne ➡ **compagnon**.

compagnie [kɔ̃paɲi] *nf* **1.** [gén & COMM] company ; **tenir compagnie à qqn** to keep sb company ; **en compagnie de** in the company of - **2.** [assemblée] gathering.

compagnon [kɔ̃paɲɔ̃], **compagne** [kɔ̃paɲ] *nm, f* companion. ➡ **compagnon** *nm* HIST journeyman.

comparable [kɔ̃parabl] *adj* comparable.

comparaison [kɔ̃parɛzɔ̃] *nf* [parallèle] comparison ; **en comparaison de, par comparaison avec** compared with, in ou by comparison with.

comparaître [91] [kɔ̃parɛtr] *vi* DR : **comparaître (devant)** to appear (before).

comparatif, ive [kɔ̃paratif, iv] *adj* comparative.

comparé, e [kɔ̃pare] *adj* comparative ; [mérites] relative.

comparer [3] [kɔ̃pare] *vt* **1.** [confronter] : **comparer (avec)** to compare (with) - **2.** [assimiler] : **comparer qqch à** to compare ou liken sthg to.

comparse [kɔ̃pars] *nmf péj* stooge.

compartiment [kɔ̃partimɑ̃] *nm* compartment.

comparu, e [kɔ̃pary] *pp* ➡ **comparaître**.

comparution [kɔ̃parysjɔ̃] *nf* DR appearance.

compas [kɔ̃pa] *nm* **1.** [de dessin] pair of compasses, compasses *pl* - **2.** NAUT compass.

compassion [kɔ̃pasjɔ̃] *nf* sout compassion.

compatible [kɔ̃patibl] *adj* : **compatible (avec)** compatible (with).

compatir [32] [kɔ̃patir] *vi* : **compatir (à)** to sympathize (with).

compatriote [kɔ̃patrijɔt] *nmf* compatriot, fellow countryman (*f* countrywoman).

compensation [kɔ̃pɑ̃sasjɔ̃] *nf* [dédommagement] compensation.

compensé, e [kɔ̃pɑ̃se] *adj* built-up.

compenser [3] [kɔ̃pɑ̃se] *vt* [perte] to compensate ou make up for.

compétence [kɔ̃petɑ̃s] *nf* **1.** [qualification] skill, ability - **2.** DR competence ; **cela n'entre pas dans mes compétences** that's outside my scope.

compétent, e [kɔ̃petɑ̃, ɑ̃t] *adj* **1.** [capable] capable, competent - **2.** ADMIN & DR competent ; **les autorités compétentes** the relevant authorities.

compétitif, ive [kɔ̃petitif, iv] *adj* competitive.

compétition [kɔ̃petisjɔ̃] *nf* competition ; **faire de la compétition** to go in for competitive sport.

compil [kɔ̃pil] *nf* fam compilation album.

complainte [kɔ̃plɛ̃t] *nf* lament.

complaisant, e [kɔ̃plɛzɑ̃, ɑ̃t] *adj* **1.** [aimable] obliging, kind - **2.** [indulgent] indulgent.

complément [kɔ̃plemɑ̃] *nm* **1.** [gén & GRAMM] complement - **2.** [reste] remainder.

complémentaire [kɔ̃plemɑ̃tɛr] *adj* **1.** [supplémentaire] supplementary - **2.** [caractères, couleurs] complementary.

complet, ète [kɔ̃plɛ, ɛt] *adj* **1.** [gén] complete - **2.** [plein] full. ➤ **complet(-veston)** *nm* suit.

complètement [kɔ̃plɛtmɑ̃] *adv* **1.** [vraiment] absolutely, totally - **2.** [entièrement] completely.

compléter [18] [kɔ̃plete] *vt* [gén] to complete, to complement ; [somme d'argent] to make up.

complexe [kɔ̃plɛks] ⬦ *nm* **1.** PSYCHO complex ; **complexe d'infériorité/de supériorité** inferiority/superiority complex - **2.** [ensemble] complex ; **complexe multisalle** multiplex (cinema). ⬦ *adj* complex, complicated.

complexé, e [kɔ̃plɛkse] *adj* hung up, mixed·up.

complexifier [kɔ̃plɛksifje] *vt* to make (more) complex.

complexité [kɔ̃plɛksite] *nf* complexity.

complication [kɔ̃plikasjɔ̃] *nf* intricacy, complexity. ➤ **complications** *nfpl* complications.

complice [kɔ̃plis] ⬦ *nmf* accomplice. ⬦ *adj* [sourire, regard, air] knowing.

complicité [kɔ̃plisite] *nf* complicity.

compliment [kɔ̃plimɑ̃] *nm* compliment.

complimenter [3] [kɔ̃plimɑ̃te] *vt* to compliment.

compliqué, e [kɔ̃plike] *adj* [problème] complex, complicated ; [personne] complicated.

compliquer [3] [kɔ̃plike] *vt* to complicate.

complot [kɔ̃plo] *nm* plot.

comploter [3] [kɔ̃plɔte] *vt & vi litt & fig* to plot.

comportement [kɔ̃pɔrtəmɑ̃] *nm* behaviour UK, behavior US.

comportemental, e, aux [kɔ̃pɔrtəmɑ̃tal, o] *adj* behavioural UK, behavioral US.

comporter [3] [kɔ̃pɔrte] *vt* **1.** [contenir] to include, to contain - **2.** [être composé de] to consist of, to be made up of. ➤ **se comporter** *vp* to behave.

composant, e [kɔ̃pozɑ̃, ɑ̃t] *adj* constituent, component. ➤ **composant** *nm* component. ➤ **composante** *nf* component.

composé, e [kɔ̃poze] *adj* compound. ➤ **composé** *nm* **1.** [mélange] combination - **2.** CHIM & LING compound.

composer [3] [kɔ̃poze] ⬦ *vt* **1.** [constituer] to make up, to form - **2.** [créer - musique] to compose, to write - **3.** [numéro de téléphone] to dial ; [code] to key in. ⬦ *vi* to compromise. ➤ **se composer** *vp* [être constitué] : **se composer de** to be composed of, to be made up of.

composite [kɔ̃pozit] *adj* **1.** [disparate - mobilier] assorted, of various types ; [- foule] heterogeneous - **2.** [matériau] composite.

compositeur, trice [kɔ̃pozitœr, tris] *nm, f* **1.** MUS composer - **2.** TYPO typesetter.

composition [kɔ̃pozisjɔ̃] *nf* **1.** [gén] composition ; [de roman] writing, composition - **2.** SCOL test - **3.** [caractère] : **être de bonne composition** to be good-natured.

composter [3] [kɔ̃pɔste] *vt* [ticket, billet] to date-stamp.

compote [kɔ̃pɔt] *nf* compote ; **compote de pommes** stewed apple, apple sauce.

compréhensible [kɔ̃preɑ̃sibl] *adj* [texte, parole] comprehensible ; *fig* [réaction] understandable.

compréhensif, ive [kɔ̃preɑ̃sif, iv] *adj* understanding.

compréhension [kɔ̃preɑ̃sjɔ̃] *nf* **1.** [de texte] comprehension, understanding - **2.** [indulgence] understanding.

comprendre [79] [kɔ̃prɑ̃dr] *vt* **1.** [gén] to understand ; **je comprends!** I see! ; **se faire comprendre** to make o.s. understood ; **mal comprendre** to misunderstand - **2.** [comporter] to comprise, to consist of - **3.** [inclure] to include.

compresse [kɔ̃prɛs] *nf* compress.

compresser [4] [kɔ̃prese] *vt* [gén] to pack (tightly) in, to pack in tight ; [informatique] to compress.

compresseur [kɔ̃presœr] ➤ **rouleau**.

compression [kɔ̃presjɔ̃] *nf* [de gaz] compression ; *fig* cutback, reduction.

comprimé, e [kɔ̃prime] *adj* compressed. ➤ **comprimé** *nm* tablet ; **comprimé effervescent** effervescent tablet.

comprimer [3] [kɔ̃prime] *vt* **1.** [gaz, vapeur] to compress - **2.** [personnes] : **être comprimé dans** to be packed into.

compris, e [kɔ̃pri, iz] ⬦ *pp* ➤ **comprendre**. ⬦ *adj* **1.** [situé] lying, contained - **2.** [inclus] : **service (non) compris** (not) including service, service (not) included ; **tout compris** all inclusive, all in ; **y compris** including.

compromettre [84] [kɔ̃prɔmɛtr] *vt* to compromise.

compromis, e [kɔ̃prɔmi, iz] *pp* ➤ **compromettre**. ➤ **compromis** *nm* compromise.

compromission [kɔ̃prɔmisjɔ̃] *nf péj* base action.

comptabilité [kɔ̃tabilite] *nf* [comptes] accounts *pl* ; [service] : **la comptabilité** accounts, the accounts department.

comptable [kɔ̃tabl] *nmf* accountant.

comptant [kɔ̃tɑ̃] *adv* : **payer** ou **régler comptant** to pay cash. ● **au comptant** *loc adv* : **payer au comptant** to pay cash.

compte [kɔ̃t] *nm* **1.** [action] count, counting *(U)* ; [total] number ; **faire le compte (de)** countdown ; **compte à rebours** countdown - **2.** BANQUE & COMM account ; **ouvrir un compte** to open an account ; **compte bancaire** ou **en banque** bank account ; **compte courant** current account *UK*, checking account *US* ; **compte créditeur** account in credit ; **compte de dépôt** deposit account ; **compte d'épargne** savings account ; **compte d'exploitation** operating account ; **compte joint** joint account ; **compte postal** post office account ; **avoir son compte** to have had enough ; **être/se mettre à son compte** to be/become self-employed ; **prendre qqch en compte, tenir compte de qqch** to take sthg into account ; **se rendre compte de qqch** to realize sthg ; **s'en tirer à bon compte** to get off lightly ; **tout compte fait** all things considered. ● **comptes** *nmpl* accounts ; **comptes de résultats courants** above-the-line accounts ; **faire ses comptes** to do one's accounts.

compte-chèques, compte chèques [kɔ̃tʃɛk] *nm* current account *UK*, checking account *US*.

compte-gouttes [kɔ̃tgut] *nm inv* dropper.

compter [3] [kɔ̃te] ◇ *vt* **1.** [dénombrer] to count - **2.** [avoir l'intention de] : **compter faire qqch** to intend to do sthg, to plan to do sthg. ◇ *vi* **1.** [calculer] to count - **2.** [être important] to count, to matter ; **compter parmi** [faire partie de] to be included amongst, to rank amongst ; **compter pour** to count for ; **compter avec** [tenir compte de] to reckon with, to take account of ; **compter sur** [se fier à] to rely ou count on. ● **sans compter que** *loc conj* besides which.

compte rendu, compte-rendu [kɔ̃trɑ̃dy] *nm* report, account.

compteur [kɔ̃tœr] *nm* meter.

comptine [kɔ̃tin] *nf* nursery rhyme.

comptoir [kɔ̃twar] *nm* **1.** [de bar] bar ; [de magasin] counter - **2.** HIST trading post - **3.** *Suisse* [foire] trade fair.

compulser [3] [kɔ̃pylse] *vt* to consult.

comte [kɔ̃t] *nm* count.

comtesse [kɔ̃tɛs] *nf* countess.

con, conne [kɔ̃, kɔn] *tfam* ◇ *adj* bloody *UK* ou damned stupid. ◇ *nm, f* stupid bastard (*f* bitch).

concave [kɔ̃kav] *adj* concave.

concéder [18] [kɔ̃sede] *vt* : **concéder qqch à** [droit, terrain] to grant sthg to ; [point, victoire] to concede sthg to ; **concéder que** to admit (that), to concede (that).

concentration [kɔ̃sɑ̃trasjɔ̃] *nf* concentration.

concentré, e [kɔ̃sɑ̃tre] *adj* **1.** [gén] concentrated - **2.** [personne] : **elle était très concentrée** she was concentrating hard - **3.** ► **lait**. ● **concentré** *nm* concentrate ; **concentré de tomates** CULIN tomato purée.

concentrer [3] [kɔ̃sɑ̃tre] *vt* to concentrate. ● **se concentrer** *vp* **1.** [se rassembler] to be concentrated - **2.** [personne] to concentrate.

concentrique [kɔ̃sɑ̃trik] *adj* concentric.

concept [kɔ̃sɛpt] *nm* concept.

conception [kɔ̃sɛpsjɔ̃] *nf* **1.** [gén] conception - **2.** [d'un produit, d'une campagne] design, designing *(U)*.

concernant [kɔ̃sɛrnɑ̃] *prép* regarding, concerning.

concerner [3] [kɔ̃sɛrne] *vt* to concern ; **être/se sentir concerné par qqch** to be/feel concerned by sthg ; **en ce qui me concerne** as far as I'm concerned.

concert [kɔ̃sɛr] *nm* MUS concert.

concertation [kɔ̃sɛrtasjɔ̃] *nf* consultation.

concerter [3] [kɔ̃sɛrte] *vt* [organiser] to devise (jointly). ● **se concerter** *vp* to consult (each other).

concerto [kɔ̃sɛrto] *nm* concerto.

concession [kɔ̃sesjɔ̃] *nf* **1.** [compromis & GRAMM] concession - **2.** [autorisation] rights *pl*, concession.

concessionnaire [kɔ̃sesjɔnɛr] *nmf* **1.** [automobile] (car) dealer - **2.** [qui possède une franchise] franchise holder.

concevable [kɔ̃səvabl] *adj* conceivable.

concevoir [52] [kɔ̃səvwar] *vt* **1.** [enfant, projet] to conceive - **2.** [comprendre] to conceive of ; **je ne peux pas concevoir comment/pourquoi** I cannot conceive how/why.

concierge [kɔ̃sjɛrʒ] *nmf* caretaker *UK*, superintendent *US*, concierge.

conciliation [kɔ̃siljasjɔ̃] *nf* **1.** [règlement d'un conflit] reconciliation, reconciling - **2.** [accord & DR] conciliation.

concilier [9] [kɔ̃silje] *vt* [mettre d'accord, allier] to reconcile ; **concilier qqch et** ou **avec qqch** to reconcile sthg with sthg.

concis, e [kɔ̃si, iz] *adj* [style, discours] concise ; [personne] terse.

concision [kɔ̃sizjɔ̃] *nf* conciseness, concision.

concitoyen, enne [kɔ̃sitwajɛ̃, ɛn] *nm, f* fellow citizen.

conclu, e [kɔ̃kly] *pp* ▶ conclure.

concluant, e [kɔ̃klyɑ̃, ɑ̃t] *adj* [convaincant] conclusive.

conclure [96] [kɔ̃klyr] ⬥ *vt* to conclude ; **en conclure que** to deduce (that). ⬥ *vi* : **les experts en ont conclu à la folie** the experts concluded he/she was mad.

conclusion [kɔ̃klyzjɔ̃] *nf* **1.** [gén] conclusion - **2.** [partie finale] close.

concombre [kɔ̃kɔ̃br] *nm* cucumber.

concordance [kɔ̃kɔrdɑ̃s] *nf* [conformité] agreement ; **concordance des temps** GRAMM sequence of tenses.

concorder [3] [kɔ̃kɔrde] *vi* **1.** [coïncider] to agree, to coincide - **2.** [être en accord] : **concorder (avec)** to be in accordance (with).

concourir [45] [kɔ̃kurir] *vi* **1.** [contribuer] : **concourir à** to work towards ou toward *US* - **2.** [participer à un concours] to compete.

concours [kɔ̃kur] *nm* **1.** [examen] competitive examination - **2.** [compétition] competition, contest - **3.** [coïncidence] : **concours de circonstances** combination of circumstances.

concret, ète [kɔ̃krɛ, ɛt] *adj* concrete.

concrétiser [3] [kɔ̃kretize] *vt* [projet] to give shape to ; [rêve, espoir] to give solid form to. ⬥ **se concrétiser** *vp* [projet] to take shape ; [rêve, espoir] to materialize.

conçu, e [kɔ̃sy] *pp* ▶ concevoir.

concubinage [kɔ̃kybinaʒ] *nm* living together, cohabitation.

concupiscent, e [kɔ̃kypisɑ̃, ɑ̃t] *adj* concupiscent.

concurremment [kɔ̃kyramɑ̃] *adv* jointly.

concurrence [kɔ̃kyrɑ̃s] *nf* **1.** [rivalité] rivalry - **2.** ÉCON competition.

concurrent, e [kɔ̃kyrɑ̃, ɑ̃t] ⬥ *adj* rival, competing. ⬥ *nm, f* competitor.

concurrentiel, elle [kɔ̃kyrɑ̃sjɛl] *adj* competitive.

condamnation [kɔ̃danasjɔ̃] *nf* **1.** DR sentence - **2.** [dénonciation] condemnation.

condamné, e [kɔ̃dane] *nm, f* convict, prisoner.

condamner [3] [kɔ̃dane] *vt* **1.** DR : **condamner qqn (à)** to sentence sb (to) ; **condamner qqn à une amende** to fine sb - **2.** *fig* [obliger] : **condamner qqn à qqch** to condemn sb to sthg - **3.** [malade] : **être condamné** to be terminally ill - **4.** [interdire] to forbid - **5.** [blâmer] to condemn - **6.** [fermer] to fill in, to block up.

condensation [kɔ̃dɑ̃sasjɔ̃] *nf* condensation.

condensé [kɔ̃dɑ̃se] ⬥ *nm* summary. ⬥ *adj* ▶ lait.

condenser [3] [kɔ̃dɑ̃se] *vt* to condense.

condescendant, e [kɔ̃desɑ̃dɑ̃, ɑ̃t] *adj* condescending.

condiment [kɔ̃dimɑ̃] *nm* condiment.

condisciple [kɔ̃disipl] *nm* fellow student.

condition [kɔ̃disjɔ̃] *nf* **1.** [gén] condition ; **se mettre en condition** [physiquement] to get into shape - **2.** [place sociale] station ; **la condition des ouvriers** the workers' lot. ⬥ **conditions** *nfpl* **1.** [circonstances] conditions ; **conditions de vie** living conditions - **2.** [de paiement] terms. ⬥ **à condition de** *loc prép* providing ou provided (that). ⬥ **à condition que** *loc conj* (+ *subjonctif*) providing ou provided (that). ⬥ **sans conditions** ⬥ *loc adj* unconditional. ⬥ *loc adv* unconditionally.

conditionné, e [kɔ̃disjɔne] *adj* **1.** [emballé] : **conditionné sous vide** vacuum-packed - **2.** ▶ air.

conditionnel, elle [kɔ̃disjɔnɛl] *adj* conditional. ⬥ **conditionnel** *nm* GRAMM conditional.

conditionnement [kɔ̃disjɔnmɑ̃] *nm* **1.** [action d'emballer] packaging, packing - **2.** [emballage] package - **3.** PSYCHO & TECHNOL conditioning.

conditionner [3] [kɔ̃disjɔne] *vt* **1.** [déterminer] to govern - **2.** PSYCHO & TECHNOL to condition - **3.** [emballer] to pack.

condoléances [kɔ̃dɔleɑ̃s] *nfpl* condolences.

conducteur, trice [kɔ̃dyktœr, tris] ⬥ *adj* conductive. ⬥ *nm, f* [de véhicule] driver. ⬥ **conducteur** *nm* ÉLECTR conductor.

conduire [98] [kɔ̃dɥir] ⬥ *vt* **1.** [voiture, personne] to drive - **2.** PHYS [transmettre] to conduct - **3.** *fig* [diriger] to manage - **4.** *fig* [à la ruine, au désespoir] : **conduire qqn à qqch** to drive sb to sthg. ⬥ *vi* **1.** AUTO to drive - **2.** [mener] : **conduire à** to lead to. ⬥ **se conduire** *vp* to behave.

conduit, e [kɔ̃dɥi, it] *pp* ▶ conduire. ⬥ **conduit** *nm* **1.** [tuyau] conduit, pipe - **2.** ANAT duct, canal. ⬥ **conduite** *nf* **1.** [pilotage d'un véhicule] driving ; **avec conduite à droite/gauche** right-hand/left-hand drive - **2.** [comportement] behaviour (U) *UK*, behavior (U) *US* - **3.** [canalisation] : **conduite de gaz/d'eau** gas/water main, gas/water pipe.

cône [kon] *nm* GÉOM cone.

confection [kɔ̃fɛksjɔ̃] *nf* **1.** [réalisation] making - **2.** [industrie] clothing industry.

confectionner [3] [kɔ̃fɛksjɔne] *vt* to make.

confédération [kɔ̃federasjɔ̃] *nf* **1.** [d'états] confederacy - **2.** [d'associations] confederation.

conférence [kɔ̃ferɑ̃s] *nf* **1.** [exposé] lecture - **2.** [réunion] conference ; **conférence de presse** press conference.

conférencier, ère [kɔ̃ferɑ̃sje, ɛr] *nm, f* lecturer.

conférer [18] [kɔ̃fere] *vt* [accorder] : **conférer qqch à qqn** to confer sthg on sb.

confesser [4] [kɔ̃fese] *vt* **1.** [avouer] to confess - **2.** RELIG : **confesser qqn** to hear sb's confession. ➤ **se confesser** *vp* to go to confession.

confession [kɔ̃fesjɔ̃] *nf* confession.

confessionnal, aux [kɔ̃fesjɔnal, o] *nm* confessional.

confetti [kɔ̃feti] *nm* confetti *(U)*.

confiance [kɔ̃fjɑ̃s] *nf* [foi] confidence ; **avoir confiance en** to have confidence ou faith in ; **avoir confiance en soi** to be self-confident ; **en toute confiance** with complete confidence ; **de confiance** trustworthy ; **faire confiance à qqn/qqch** to trust sb/sthg.

confiant, e [kɔ̃fjɑ̃, ɑ̃t] *adj* [sans méfiance] trusting.

confidence [kɔ̃fidɑ̃s] *nf* confidence.

confident, e [kɔ̃fidɑ̃, ɑ̃t] *nm, f* confidant (*f* confidante).

confidentiel, elle [kɔ̃fidɑ̃sjɛl] *adj* confidential.

confier [9] [kɔ̃fje] *vt* **1.** [donner] : **confier qqn/qqch à qqn** to entrust sb/sthg to sb - **2.** [dire] : **confier qqch à qqn** to confide sthg to sb. ➤ **se confier** *vp* : **se confier à qqn** to confide in sb.

confiné, e [kɔ̃fine] *adj* **1.** [air] stale ; [atmosphère] enclosed - **2.** [enfermé] shut away.

confins [kɔ̃fɛ̃] *nmpl* : **aux confins de** on the borders of.

confirmation [kɔ̃firmasjɔ̃] *nf* confirmation.

confirmer [3] [kɔ̃firme] *vt* [certifier] to confirm. ➤ **se confirmer** *vp* to be confirmed.

confiscation [kɔ̃fiskasjɔ̃] *nf* confiscation.

confiserie [kɔ̃fizri] *nf* **1.** [magasin] sweet shop *UK*, candy store *US*, confectioner's - **2.** [sucreries] sweets *pl UK*, candy *(U) US*, confectionery *(U)*.

confiseur, euse [kɔ̃fizœr, øz] *nm, f* confectioner.

confisquer [3] [kɔ̃fiske] *vt* to confiscate.

confiture [kɔ̃fityr] *nf* jam.

conflit [kɔ̃fli] *nm* **1.** [situation tendue] clash, conflict - **2.** [entre États] conflict.

confondre [75] [kɔ̃fɔ̃dr] *vt* **1.** [ne pas distinguer] to confuse - **2.** [accusé] to confound - **3.** [stupéfier] to astound.

confondu, e [kɔ̃fɔ̃dy] *pp* ➤ confondre.

conformation [kɔ̃fɔrmasjɔ̃] *nf* structure.

conforme [kɔ̃fɔrm] *adj* : **conforme à** in accordance with.

conformément [kɔ̃fɔrmemɑ̃] ➤ **conformément à** *loc prép* in accordance with.

conformer [3] [kɔ̃fɔrme] *vt* : **conformer qqch à** to shape sthg according to. ➤ **se conformer** *vp* : **se conformer à** [s'adapter] to conform to ; [obéir] to comply with.

conformiste [kɔ̃fɔrmist] <> *nmf* conformist. <> *adj* **1.** [traditionaliste] conformist - **2.** [Anglican] Anglican.

conformité [kɔ̃fɔrmite] *nf* [accord] : **être en conformité avec** to be in accordance with.

confort [kɔ̃fɔr] *nm* comfort ; **tout confort** with all mod cons *UK*, with all modern conveniences *US*.

confortable [kɔ̃fɔrtabl] *adj* comfortable.

confrère, consœur [kɔ̃frer, kɔ̃sœr] *nm, f* colleague.

confrontation [kɔ̃frɔ̃tasjɔ̃] *nf* [face à face] confrontation.

confronter [3] [kɔ̃frɔ̃te] *vt* [mettre face à face] to confront ; *fig* : **être confronté à** to be confronted ou faced with.

confus, e [kɔ̃fy, yz] *adj* **1.** [indistinct, embrouillé] confused - **2.** [gêné] embarrassed.

confusion [kɔ̃fyzjɔ̃] *nf* **1.** [gén] confusion - **2.** [embarras] confusion, embarrassment.

congé [kɔ̃ʒe] *nm* **1.** [arrêt de travail] leave *(U)* ; **congé (de) maladie** sick leave ; **congé de maternité** maternity leave - **2.** [vacances] holiday *UK*, vacation *US* ; **en congé** on holiday *UK* ou vacation *US* ; **congés payés** paid holiday *(U)* ou holidays ou leave *(U) UK*, paid vacation *US* ; **une journée/semaine de congé** a day/week off - **3.** [renvoi] notice ; **donner son congé à qqn** to give sb his/her notice ; **prendre congé (de qqn)** *sout* to take one's leave (of sb).

congédier [9] [kɔ̃ʒedje] *vt* to dismiss.

congé-formation [kɔ̃ʒefɔrmasjɔ̃] *(pl* congés-formation*) nm* training leave.

congélateur [kɔ̃ʒelatœr] *nm* freezer.

congeler [25] [kɔ̃ʒle] *vt* to freeze.

congénital, e, aux [kɔ̃ʒenital, o] *adj* congenital.

congère [kɔ̃ʒer] *nf* snowdrift.

congestion [kɔ̃ʒɛstjɔ̃] *nf* congestion ; **congestion pulmonaire** pulmonary congestion.

Congo [kɔ̃go] *nm* [pays] : **le Congo** the

Congo ; **la République démocratique du Congo** the Democratic Republic of Congo ; [fleuve] : **le Congo** the Congo.

congratuler [3] [kɔ̃gratyle] *vt* to congratulate.

congrégation [kɔ̃gregasjɔ̃] *nf* congregation.

congrès [kɔ̃grɛ] *nm* [colloque] assembly.

conifère [kɔnifɛr] *nm* conifer.

conjecture [kɔ̃ʒɛktyr] *nf* conjecture.

conjecturer [3] [kɔ̃ʒɛktyre] *vt & vi* to conjecture.

conjoint, e [kɔ̃ʒwɛ̃, ɛt] <> *adj* joint. <> *nm, f* spouse.

conjonction [kɔ̃ʒɔ̃ksjɔ̃] *nf* conjunction.

conjonctivite [kɔ̃ʒɔ̃ktivit] *nf* conjunctivitis *(U)*.

conjoncture [kɔ̃ʒɔ̃ktyr] *nf* ÉCON situation, circumstances *pl*.

conjugaison [kɔ̃ʒygɛzɔ̃] *nf* 1. [union] uniting - 2. GRAMM conjugation.

conjugal, e, aux [kɔ̃ʒygal, o] *adj* conjugal.

conjuguer [3] [kɔ̃ʒyge] *vt* 1. [unir] to combine - 2. GRAMM to conjugate.

conjuration [kɔ̃ʒyrasjɔ̃] *nf* 1. [conspiration] conspiracy - 2. [exorcisme] exorcism.

connaissance [kɔnɛsɑ̃s] *nf* 1. [savoir] knowledge *(U)* ; **à ma connaissance** to (the best of) my knowledge ; **en connaissance de cause** with full knowledge of the facts ; **prendre connaissance de qqch** to study sthg, to examine sthg - 2. [personne] acquaintance ; **faire connaissance (avec qqn)** to become acquainted (with sb) ; **faire la connaissance de** to meet - 3. [conscience] : **perdre/reprendre connaissance** to lose/regain consciousness.

connaisseur, euse [kɔnɛsœr, øz] <> *adj* expert *(avant n)*. <> *nm, f* connoisseur.

connaître [91] [kɔnɛtr] *vt* 1. [gén] to know ; **connaître qqn de nom/de vue** to know sb by name/sight - 2. [éprouver] to experience. ➡ **se connaître** *vp* 1. : **s'y connaître en** [être expert] to know about ; **il s'y connaît** he knows what he's talking about/doing - 2. [soi-même] to know o.s. - 3. [se rencontrer] to meet (each other) ; **ils se connaissent** they've met each other.

connecter [4] [kɔnɛkte] *vt* to connect.

connexion [kɔnɛksjɔ̃] *nf* connection.

connu, e [kɔny] <> *pp* ➤ **connaître**. <> *adj* [célèbre] well-known, famous.

conquérant, e [kɔ̃kerɑ̃, ɑ̃t] <> *adj* conquering. <> *nm, f* conqueror.

conquérir [39] [kɔ̃kerir] *vt* to conquer.

conquête [kɔ̃kɛt] *nf* conquest.

conquis, e [kɔ̃ki, iz] *pp* ➤ **conquérir**.

consacrer [3] [kɔ̃sakre] *vt* 1. RELIG to consecrate - 2. [employer] : **consacrer qqch à** to devote sthg to. ➡ **se consacrer** *vp* : **se consacrer à** to dedicate o.s. to, to devote o.s. to.

conscience [kɔ̃sjɑ̃s] *nf* 1. [connaissance & PSYCHO] consciousness ; **avoir conscience de qqch** to be aware of sthg - 2. [morale] conscience ; **bonne/mauvaise conscience** clear/guilty conscience ; **conscience professionnelle** professional integrity, conscientiousness.

consciencieux, euse [kɔ̃sjɑ̃sjø, øz] *adj* conscientious.

conscient, e [kɔ̃sjɑ̃, ɑ̃t] *adj* conscious ; **être conscient de qqch** [connaître] to be conscious of sthg.

conscription [kɔ̃skripsjɔ̃] *nf* conscription, draft *US*.

conscrit [kɔ̃skri] *nm* conscript, recruit, draftee *US*.

consécration [kɔ̃sekrasjɔ̃] *nf* 1. [reconnaissance] recognition ; [de droit, coutume] establishment - 2. RELIG consecration.

consécutif, ive [kɔ̃sekytif, iv] *adj* 1. [successif & GRAMM] consecutive - 2. [résultant] : **consécutif à** resulting from.

conseil [kɔ̃sɛj] *nm* 1. [avis] piece of advice, advice *(U)* ; **donner un conseil ou des conseils (à qqn)** to give (sb) advice - 2. [personne] : **conseil (en)** consultant (in) - 3. [assemblée] council ; **conseil d'administration** board of directors ; **conseil de classe** staff meeting ; **conseil de discipline** disciplinary committee.

conseiller[1] [4] [kɔ̃seje] <> *vt* 1. [recommander] to advise ; **conseiller qqch à qqn** to recommend sthg to sb - 2. [guider] to advise, to counsel. <> *vi* [donner un conseil] : **conseiller à qqn de faire qqch** to advise sb to do sthg.

conseiller[2]**, ère** [kɔ̃seje, ɛr] *nm, f* 1. [guide] counsellor *UK*, counselor *US* - 2. [d'un conseil] councillor *UK*, councilor *US* ; **conseiller municipal** town councillor *UK*, city councilman (*f* councilwoman) *US*.

consensuel, elle [kɔ̃sɑ̃sɥel] *adj* : **politique consensuelle** consensus politics.

consentement [kɔ̃sɑ̃tmɑ̃] *nm* consent.

consentir [37] [kɔ̃sɑ̃tir] *vi* : **consentir à qqch** to consent to sthg.

conséquence [kɔ̃sekɑ̃s] *nf* consequence, result ; **ne pas tirer à conséquence** to be of no consequence.

conséquent, e [kɔ̃sekɑ̃, ɑ̃t] *adj* 1. [cohérent] consistent - 2. *fam* [important] sizeable, considerable. ➡ **par conséquent** *loc adv* therefore, consequently.

conservateur, trice [kɔ̃sɛrvatœr, tris] ◇ *adj* conservative. ◇ *nm, f* **1.** POLIT conservative - **2.** [administrateur] curator.
➤ **conservateur** *nm* preservative.

conservation [kɔ̃sɛrvasjɔ̃] *nf* **1.** [état, entretien] preservation - **2.** [d'aliment] preserving.

conservatoire [kɔ̃sɛrvatwar] *nm* academy ; **conservatoire de musique** music college.

conserve [kɔ̃sɛrv] *nf* tinned UK ou canned food ; **en conserve** [en boîte] tinned UK, canned ; [en bocal] preserved, bottled.

conserver [3] [kɔ̃sɛrve] *vt* **1.** [garder, entretenir] to keep - **2.** [entreposer - en boîte] to can ; [- en bocal] to bottle.

considérable [kɔ̃siderabl] *adj* considerable.

considération [kɔ̃siderasjɔ̃] *nf* **1.** [réflexion, motivation] consideration ; **prendre qqch en considération** to take sthg into consideration - **2.** [estime] respect.

considérer [18] [kɔ̃sidere] *vt* to consider ; **tout bien considéré** all things considered.

consigne [kɔ̃siɲ] *nf* **1.** (*gén pl*) [instruction] instructions *pl* - **2.** [entrepôt de bagages] left-luggage office UK, checkroom US, baggage room US ; **consigne automatique** left-luggage lockers *pl* UK - **3.** [somme d'argent] deposit.

consigné, e [kɔ̃siɲe] *adj* returnable.

consistance [kɔ̃sistɑ̃s] *nf* [solidité] consistency ; *fig* substance.

consistant, e [kɔ̃sistɑ̃, ɑ̃t] *adj* **1.** [épais] thick - **2.** [nourrissant] substantial - **3.** [fondé] sound.

consister [3] [kɔ̃siste] *vi* : **consister en** to consist of ; **consister à faire qqch** to consist in doing sthg.

consœur ➤ confrère.

consolation [kɔ̃sɔlasjɔ̃] *nf* consolation.

console [kɔ̃sɔl] *nf* **1.** [table] console (table) - **2.** INFORM : **console de jeux** games console ; **console de visualisation** VDU, visual display unit.

consoler [3] [kɔ̃sɔle] *vt* [réconforter] : **consoler qqn (de qqch)** to comfort sb (in sthg).

consolider [3] [kɔ̃sɔlide] *vt litt & fig* to strengthen.

consommateur, trice [kɔ̃sɔmatœr, tris] *nm, f* [acheteur] consumer ; [d'un bar] customer.

consommation [kɔ̃sɔmasjɔ̃] *nf* **1.** [utilisation] consumption ; **faire une grande** ou **grosse consommation de** to use (up) a lot of - **2.** [boisson] drink.

consommé, e [kɔ̃sɔme] *adj sout* consummate. ➤ **consommé** *nm* consommé.

consommer [3] [kɔ̃sɔme] ◇ *vt* **1.** [utiliser] to use (up) - **2.** [manger] to eat - **3.** [énergie] to consume, to use. ◇ *vi* **1.** [boire] to drink - **2.** [voiture] : **cette voiture consomme beaucoup** this car uses a lot of fuel.

consonance [kɔ̃sɔnɑ̃s] *nf* consonance.

consonne [kɔ̃sɔn] *nf* consonant.

conspirateur, trice [kɔ̃spiratœr, tris] *nm, f* conspirator.

conspiration [kɔ̃spirasjɔ̃] *nf* conspiracy.

conspirer [3] [kɔ̃spire] ◇ *vt* [comploter] to plot. ◇ *vi* to conspire.

constamment [kɔ̃stamɑ̃] *adv* constantly.

constant, e [kɔ̃stɑ̃, ɑ̃t] *adj* constant.

constat [kɔ̃sta] *nm* **1.** [procès-verbal] report - **2.** [constatation] established fact.

constatation [kɔ̃statasjɔ̃] *nf* **1.** [révélation] observation - **2.** [fait retenu] finding.

constater [3] [kɔ̃state] *vt* **1.** [se rendre compte de] to see, to note - **2.** [consigner - fait, infraction] to record ; [- décès, authenticité] to certify.

constellation [kɔ̃stelasjɔ̃] *nf* ASTRON constellation.

consternation [kɔ̃stɛrnasjɔ̃] *nf* dismay.

consterner [3] [kɔ̃stɛrne] *vt* to dismay.

constipation [kɔ̃stipasjɔ̃] *nf* constipation.

constipé, e [kɔ̃stipe] *adj* **1.** MÉD constipated - **2.** *fam fig* [manière, air] ill at ease.

constituer [7] [kɔ̃stitɥe] *vt* **1.** [élaborer] to set up - **2.** [composer] to make up - **3.** [représenter] to constitute.

constitution [kɔ̃stitysjɔ̃] *nf* **1.** [création] setting up - **2.** [de pays, de corps] constitution.

constructeur [kɔ̃stryktœr] *nm* **1.** [fabricant] manufacturer ; [de navire] shipbuilder - **2.** [bâtisseur] builder.

construction [kɔ̃stryksjɔ̃] *nf* **1.** [dans l'industrie] building, construction ; **construction navale** shipbuilding - **2.** [édifice] structure, building - **3.** *fig & GRAMM* construction.

construire [98] [kɔ̃strɥir] *vt* **1.** [bâtir, fabriquer] to build - **2.** [théorie, phrase] to construct.

construit, e [kɔ̃strɥi, it] *pp* ➤ construire.

consulat [kɔ̃syla] *nm* [résidence] consulate.

consultation [kɔ̃syltasjɔ̃] *nf* **1.** [d'ouvrage] : **de consultation aisée** easy to use - **2.** MÉD & POLIT consultation.

consulter [3] [kɔ̃sylte] ◇ *vt* **1.** [compulser] to consult - **2.** [interroger, demander conseil à] to consult, to ask - **3.** [spécialiste] to consult, to see. ◇ *vi* [médecin] to take ou hold surgery UK, to see patients US ; [avocat] to be available for consultation.
➤ **se consulter** *vp* to confer.

contact [kɔ̃takt] *nm* **1.** [gén] contact ; **le contact du marbre est froid** marble is cold to the touch ; **au contact de** on contact with - **2.** [relations] contact ; **prendre contact avec** to make contact with ; **rester en contact (avec)** to stay in touch (with) - **3.** AUTO ignition ; **mettre/couper le contact** to switch on/off the ignition.

contacter [3] [kɔ̃takte] *vt* to contact.

contagieux, euse [kɔ̃taʒjø, øz] *adj* MÉD contagious ; *fig* infectious.

contagion [kɔ̃taʒjɔ̃] *nf* MÉD contagion ; *fig* infectiousness.

contaminer [3] [kɔ̃tamine] *vt* [infecter] to contaminate ; *fig* to contaminate, to infect.

conte [kɔ̃t] *nm* story ; **conte de fées** fairy tale.

contemplation [kɔ̃tɑ̃plasjɔ̃] *nf* contemplation.

contempler [3] [kɔ̃tɑ̃ple] *vt* to contemplate.

contemporain, e [kɔ̃tɑ̃pɔrɛ̃, ɛn] *nm, f* contemporary.

contenance [kɔ̃tnɑ̃s] *nf* **1.** [capacité volumique] capacity - **2.** [attitude] : **se donner une contenance** to give an impression of composure ; **perdre contenance** to lose one's composure.

contenir [40] [kɔ̃tnir] *vt* to contain, to hold, to take. ◆ **se contenir** *vp* to contain o.s., to control o.s.

content, e [kɔ̃tɑ̃, ɑ̃t] *adj* [satisfait] : **content (de qqn/qqch)** happy (with sb/sthg), content (with sb/sthg) ; **content de faire qqch** happy to do sthg.

contentement [kɔ̃tɑ̃tmɑ̃] *nm* satisfaction.

contenter [3] [kɔ̃tɑ̃te] *vt* to satisfy. ◆ **se contenter** *vp* : **se contenter de qqch/de faire qqch** to content o.s. with sthg/with doing sthg.

contentieux [kɔ̃tɑ̃sjø] *nm* [litige] dispute ; [service] legal department.

contenu, e [kɔ̃tny] *pp* ▶ **contenir**. ◆ **contenu** *nm* **1.** [de récipient] contents *pl* - **2.** [de texte, discours] content.

conter [3] [kɔ̃te] *vt* to tell.

contestable [kɔ̃tɛstabl] *adj* questionable.

contestation [kɔ̃tɛstasjɔ̃] *nf* **1.** [protestation] protest, dispute - **2.** POLIT : **la contestation** anti-establishment activity.

conteste [kɔ̃tɛst] ◆ **sans conteste** *loc adv* unquestionably.

contester [3] [kɔ̃tɛste] ◇ *vt* to dispute, to contest. ◇ *vi* to protest.

conteur, euse [kɔ̃tœr, øz] *nm, f* storyteller.

contexte [kɔ̃tɛkst] *nm* context.

contigu, uë [kɔ̃tigy] *adj* : **contigu (à)** adjacent (to).

continent [kɔ̃tinɑ̃] *nm* continent.

continental, e, aux [kɔ̃tinɑ̃tal, o] *adj* continental.

contingence [kɔ̃tɛ̃ʒɑ̃s] *nf* MATH & PHILO contingency.

contingent [kɔ̃tɛ̃ʒɑ̃] *nm* **1.** MIL national service conscripts *pl* UK, draft US - **2.** COMM quota.

continu, e [kɔ̃tiny] *adj* [ininterrompu] continuous.

continuation [kɔ̃tinɥasjɔ̃] *nf* continuation.

continuel, elle [kɔ̃tinɥɛl] *adj* **1.** [continu] continuous - **2.** [répété] continual.

continuellement [kɔ̃tinɥɛlmɑ̃] *adv* continually.

continuer [7] [kɔ̃tinɥe] ◇ *vt* [poursuivre] to carry on with, to continue (with). ◇ *vi* to continue, to go on ; **continuer à** OU **de faire qqch** to continue to do ou doing sthg.

continuité [kɔ̃tinɥite] *nf* continuity.

contorsionner [3] [kɔ̃tɔrsjɔne] ◆ **se contorsionner** *vp* to contort (o.s.), to writhe.

contour [kɔ̃tur] *nm* **1.** [limite] outline - **2.** *(gén pl)* [courbe] bend.

contourner [3] [kɔ̃turne] *vt litt & fig* to bypass, to get round UK OU around.

contraceptif, ive [kɔ̃trasɛptif, iv] *adj* contraceptive. ◆ **contraceptif** *nm* contraceptive.

contraception [kɔ̃trasɛpsjɔ̃] *nf* contraception.

contracter [3] [kɔ̃trakte] *vt* **1.** [muscle] to contract, to tense ; [visage] to contort - **2.** [maladie] to contract, to catch - **3.** [engagement] to contract ; [assurance] to take out.

contraction [kɔ̃traksjɔ̃] *nf* contraction ; [état de muscle] tenseness.

contractuel, elle [kɔ̃traktɥɛl] *nm, f* traffic warden UK.

contradiction [kɔ̃tradiksjɔ̃] *nf* contradiction.

contradictoire [kɔ̃tradiktwar] *adj* contradictory ; **débat contradictoire** open debate.

contraignant, e [kɔ̃trɛɲɑ̃, ɑ̃t] *adj* restricting.

contraindre [80] [kɔ̃trɛ̃dr] *vt* : **contraindre qqn à faire qqch** to compel ou force sb to do sthg ; **être contraint de faire qqch** to be compelled ou forced to do sthg.

contraire [kɔ̃trɛr] ◇ *nm* : **le contraire** the opposite ; **je n'ai jamais dit le contraire** I have never denied it. ◇ *adj* opposite ; **contraire à** [non conforme à] contrary to ;

[nuisible à] harmful to, damaging to. ➤ **au contraire** *loc adv* on the contrary. ➤ **au contraire de** *loc prép* unlike.

contrairement [kɔ̃trɛrmɑ̃] ➤ **contrairement à** *loc prép* contrary to.

contrarier [9] [kɔ̃trarje] *vt* **1.** [contrecarrer] to thwart, to frustrate - **2.** [irriter] to annoy.

contrariété [kɔ̃trarjete] *nf* annoyance.

contraste [kɔ̃trast] *nm* contrast.

contraster [3] [kɔ̃traste] *vt & vi* to contrast.

contrat [kɔ̃tra] *nm* contract, agreement ; contrat d'apprentissage apprenticeship contract ; contrat à durée déterminée/indéterminée fixed-term/permanent contract ; Contrat emploi-solidarité *government-sponsored contract for the unempoyed involving professional training.*

contravention [kɔ̃travɑ̃sjɔ̃] *nf* [amende] fine ; contravention pour stationnement interdit parking ticket ; dresser une contravention à qqn to fine sb.

contre [kɔ̃tr] <> *prép* **1.** [juxtaposition, opposition] against - **2.** [proportion, comparaison] : élu à 15 voix contre 9 elected by 15 votes to 9 - **3.** [échange] (in exchange) for. <> *adv* [juxtaposition] : prends la rampe et appuie-toi contre take hold of the rail and lean against it. ➤ **par contre** *loc adv* on the other hand.

contre-attaque [kɔ̃tratak] (*pl* contre-attaques) *nf* counterattack.

contrebalancer [16] [kɔ̃trəbalɑ̃se] *vt* to counterbalance, to offset.

contrebande [kɔ̃trəbɑ̃d] *nf* [activité] smuggling ; [marchandises] contraband.

contrebandier, ère [kɔ̃trəbɑ̃dje, ɛr] *nm, f* smuggler.

contrebas [kɔ̃trəba] ➤ **en contrebas** *loc adv* (down) below.

contrebasse [kɔ̃trəbas] *nf* [instrument] (double) bass.

contrecarrer [3] [kɔ̃trəkare] *vt* to thwart, to frustrate.

contrecœur [kɔ̃trəkœr] ➤ **à contrecœur** *loc adv* grudgingly.

contrecoup [kɔ̃trəku] *nm* consequence.

contre-courant [kɔ̃trəkurɑ̃] ➤ **à contre-courant** *loc adv* [d'un cours d'eau] against the current.

contredire [103] [kɔ̃trədir] *vt* to contradict. ➤ **se contredire** *vp* **1.** *(emploi réciproque)* to contradict (each other) - **2.** *(emploi réfléchi)* to contradict o.s.

contredit, e [kɔ̃trədi, it] *pp* ▶ **contredire.**

contrée [kɔ̃tre] *nf* [pays] land ; [région] region.

contre-espionnage [kɔ̃trɛspjɔnaʒ] *nm* counterespionage.

contre-exemple [kɔ̃trɛgzɑ̃pl] (*pl* contre-exemples) *nm* example to the contrary.

contre-expertise [kɔ̃trɛkspertiz] (*pl* contre-expertises) *nf* second (expert) opinion.

contrefaçon [kɔ̃trəfasɔ̃] *nf* [activité] counterfeiting ; [produit] forgery.

contrefaire [109] [kɔ̃trəfɛr] *vt* **1.** [signature, monnaie] to counterfeit, to forge - **2.** [voix] to disguise.

contrefort [kɔ̃trəfɔr] *nm* **1.** [pilier] buttress - **2.** [de chaussure] back. ➤ **contreforts** *nmpl* foothills.

contre-indication [kɔ̃trɛ̃dikasjɔ̃] (*pl* contre-indications) *nf* contraindication.

contre-jour [kɔ̃trəʒur] ➤ **à contre-jour** *loc adv* against the light.

contremaître, esse [kɔ̃trəmɛtr, ɛs] *nm, f* foreman (*f* forewoman).

contremarque [kɔ̃trəmark] *nf* [pour sortir d'un spectacle] pass-out ticket *UK.*

contre-offensive [kɔ̃trəfɑ̃siv] (*pl* contre-offensives) *nf* counteroffensive.

contre-ordre = contrordre.

contrepartie [kɔ̃trəparti] *nf* **1.** [compensation] compensation - **2.** [contraire] opposing view. ➤ **en contrepartie** *loc adv* in return.

contre-performance [kɔ̃trəperfɔrmɑ̃s] (*pl* contre-performances) *nf* disappointing performance.

contrepèterie [kɔ̃trəpɛtri] *nf* spoonerism.

contre-pied [kɔ̃trəpje] *nm* : prendre le contre-pied de to do the opposite of.

contreplaqué, contre-plaqué [kɔ̃trəplake] *nm* plywood.

contrepoids [kɔ̃trəpwa] *nm litt & fig* counterbalance, counterweight.

contre-pouvoir [kɔ̃trəpuvwar] (*pl* contre-pouvoirs) *nm* counterbalance.

contrer [3] [kɔ̃tre] *vt* **1.** [s'opposer à] to counter - **2.** [jeux de cartes] to double.

contresens [kɔ̃trəsɑ̃s] *nm* **1.** [erreur - de traduction] mistranslation ; [- d'interprétation] misinterpretation - **2.** [absurdité] nonsense (U). ➤ **à contresens** *loc adv litt & fig* the wrong way.

contresigner [3] [kɔ̃trəsiɲe] *vt* to countersign.

contretemps [kɔ̃trətɑ̃] *nm* hitch, mishap. ➤ **à contretemps** *loc adv* MUS out of time ; *fig* at the wrong moment.

contrevenir [40] [kɔ̃trəvnir] *vi* : contrevenir à to contravene, to infringe.

contribuable [kɔ̃tribɥabl] *nmf* taxpayer.

contribuer [7] [kɔ̃tribɥe] *vi* : contribuer à to contribute to ou towards.

contribution [kɔ̃tribysjɔ̃] *nf* : contribution (à) contribution (to) ; mettre qqn à contribution to call on sb's services. ➡ **contributions** *nfpl* taxes ; contributions directes/indirectes direct/indirect taxation.

contrit, e [kɔ̃tri, it] *adj* contrite.

contrôle [kɔ̃trol] *nm* **1.** [vérification - de déclaration] check, checking *(U)* ; [- de documents, billets] inspection ; contrôle d'identité identity check ; contrôle parental parental control - **2.** [maîtrise, commande] control ; perdre le contrôle de qqch to lose control of sthg ; contrôle des naissances birth control ; contrôle des prix price control - **3.** SCOL test.

contrôler [3] [kɔ̃trole] *vt* **1.** [vérifier - documents, billets] to inspect ; [- déclaration] to check ; [- connaissances] to test - **2.** [maîtriser, diriger] to control - **3.** TECHNOL to monitor, to control.

contrôleur, euse [kɔ̃trolœr, øz] *nm, f* [de train] ticket inspector ; [d'autobus] (bus) conductor (*f* conductress) ; contrôleur aérien air traffic controller.

contrordre, contre-ordre (*pl* contre-ordres) [kɔ̃trɔrdr] *nm* countermand ; sauf contrordre unless otherwise instructed.

controverse [kɔ̃trɔvɛrs] *nf* controversy.

controversé, e [kɔ̃trɔvɛrse] *adj* [personne, décision] controversial.

contumace [kɔ̃tymas] *nf* DR : condamné par contumace sentenced in absentia.

contusion [kɔ̃tyzjɔ̃] *nf* bruise, contusion.

convaincant, e [kɔ̃vɛ̃kɑ̃, ɑ̃t] *adj* convincing.

convaincre [114] [kɔ̃vɛ̃kr] *vt* **1.** [persuader] : convaincre qqn (de qqch) to convince sb (of sthg) ; convaincre qqn (de faire qqch) to persuade sb (to do sthg) - **2.** DR : convaincre qqn de to find sb guilty of, to convict sb of.

convaincu, e [kɔ̃vɛ̃ky] <> *pp* ➡ convaincre. <> *adj* [partisan] committed ; d'un ton convaincu, d'un air convaincu with conviction.

convainquant [kɔ̃vɛ̃kɑ̃] *p prés* ➡ convaincre.

convalescence [kɔ̃valesɑ̃s] *nf* convalescence ; être en convalescence to be convalescing ou recovering.

convalescent, e [kɔ̃valesɑ̃, ɑ̃t] *adj & nm, f* convalescent.

convenable [kɔ̃vnabl] *adj* **1.** [manières, comportement] polite ; [tenue, personne] decent, respectable - **2.** [acceptable] adequate, acceptable.

convenance [kɔ̃vnɑ̃s] *nf* : à ma/votre convenance to my/your convenience. ➡ **convenances** *nfpl* proprieties.

convenir [40] [kɔ̃vnir] *vi* **1.** [décider] : convenir de qqch/de faire qqch to agree on sthg/to do sthg - **2.** [plaire] : convenir à qqn to suit sb, to be convenient for sb - **3.** [être approprié] : convenir à ou pour to be suitable for - **4.** *sout* [admettre] : convenir de qqch to admit to sthg ; convenir que to admit (that).

convention [kɔ̃vɑ̃sjɔ̃] *nf* **1.** [règle, assemblée] convention - **2.** [accord] agreement ; convention collective collective agreement.

conventionné, e [kɔ̃vɑ̃sjɔne] *adj* ≃ National Health *(avant n)* UK.

conventionnel, elle [kɔ̃vɑ̃sjɔnɛl] *adj* conventional.

convenu, e [kɔ̃vny] <> *pp* ➡ convenir. <> *adj* [décidé] : comme convenu as agreed.

convergent, e [kɔ̃vɛrʒɑ̃, ɑ̃t] *adj* convergent.

converger [17] [kɔ̃vɛrʒe] *vi* : converger (vers) to converge (on).

conversation [kɔ̃vɛrsasjɔ̃] *nf* conversation.

converser [3] [kɔ̃vɛrse] *vi sout* : converser (avec) to converse (with).

conversion [kɔ̃vɛrsjɔ̃] *nf* [gén] : conversion (à/en) conversion (to/into).

convertible [kɔ̃vɛrtibl] *nm* [canapé-lit] sofa bed.

convertir [32] [kɔ̃vɛrtir] *vt* : convertir qqn (à) to convert sb (to) ; convertir qqch (en) to convert sthg (into). ➡ **se convertir** *vp* : se convertir (à) to be converted (to).

convexe [kɔ̃vɛks] *adj* convex.

conviction [kɔ̃viksjɔ̃] *nf* conviction.

convier [9] [kɔ̃vje] *vt* : convier qqn à to invite sb to.

convive [kɔ̃viv] *nmf* guest *(at a meal)*.

convivial, e, aux [kɔ̃vivjal, o] *adj* **1.** [réunion] convivial - **2.** INFORM user-friendly.

convocation [kɔ̃vɔkasjɔ̃] *nf* [avis écrit] summons *sg*, notification to attend.

convoi [kɔ̃vwa] *nm* **1.** [de véhicules] convoy - **2.** [train] train.

convoiter [3] [kɔ̃vwate] *vt* to covet.

convoitise [kɔ̃vwatiz] *nf* covetousness.

convoquer [3] [kɔ̃vɔke] *vt* **1.** [assemblée] to convene - **2.** [pour un entretien] to invite - **3.** [subalterne, témoin] to summon - **4.** [à un examen] : convoquer qqn to ask sb to attend.

convoyer [13] [kɔ̃vwaje] *vt* to escort.

convoyeur, euse [kɔ̃vwajœr, øz] *nm, f* escort ; convoyeur de fonds security guard.

convulsion [kɔ̃vylsjɔ̃] *nf* convulsion.

cookie [kuki] *nm* **1.** [petit gâteau] cookie *US*, biscuit *UK* - **2.** INFORM cookie.

coopération [kɔɔperasjɔ̃] *nf* **1.** [collaboration] cooperation - **2.** [aide] : **la coopération** ≈ overseas development.

coopérer [18] [kɔɔpere] *vi* : **coopérer (à)** to cooperate (in).

coordination [kɔɔrdinasjɔ̃] *nf* coordination.

coordonnée [kɔɔrdɔne] *nf* **1.** LING coordinate clause - **2.** MATH coordinate. **coordonnées** *nfpl* **1.** GÉOGR coordinates - **2.** [adresse] address and phone number, details.

coordonner [3] [kɔɔrdɔne] *vt* to coordinate.

copain, ine [kɔpɛ̃, in] <> *adj* matey *UK* ; **être très copains** to be great pals. <> *nm, f* [ami] friend, mate *UK* ; [petit ami] boyfriend (*f* girlfriend).

copeau, x [kɔpo] *nm* [de bois] (wood) shaving.

Copenhague [kɔpənag] *npr* Copenhagen.

copie [kɔpi] *nf* **1.** [double, reproduction] copy - **2.** [SCOL - de devoir] fair copy ; [- d'examen] paper, script - **3.** INFORM : **copie d'écran** screenshot.

copier [9] [kɔpje] <> *vt* [gén & INFORM] to copy. <> *vi* : **copier sur qqn** to copy from sb.

copier-coller [kɔpjekɔle] *nm inv* INFORM copy and paste.

copieux, euse [kɔpjø, øz] *adj* copious.

copilote [kɔpilɔt] *nmf* copilot.

copine copain.

coproduction [kɔprɔdyksjɔ̃] *nf* co(-)production.

copropriété [kɔprɔprijete] *nf* co-ownership, joint ownership, condominium *US*.

coq [kɔk] *nm* cock, cockerel, rooster *US* ; **coq au vin** *chicken cooked with red wine, bacon, mushrooms and shallots* ; **sauter** OU **passer du coq à l'âne** to jump from one subject to another.

coque [kɔk] *nf* **1.** [de noix] shell - **2.** [de navire] hull.

coquelicot [kɔkliko] *nm* poppy.

coqueluche [kɔklyʃ] *nf* whooping cough.

coquet, ette [kɔkɛ, ɛt] *adj* **1.** [vêtements] smart, stylish ; [ville, jeune fille] pretty - **2.** *(avant n) hum* [important] : **la coquette somme de 100 livres** the tidy sum of £100. **coquette** *nf* flirt.

coquetier [kɔktje] *nm* eggcup.

coquetterie [kɔkɛtri] *nf* [désir de plaire] coquettishness.

coquillage [kɔkijaʒ] *nm* **1.** [mollusque] shellfish - **2.** [coquille] shell.

coquille [kɔkij] *nf* **1.** [de mollusque, noix, œuf] shell ; **coquille de noix** [embarcation] cockleshell - **2.** TYPO misprint.

coquillettes [kɔkijɛt] *nfpl* pasta shells.

coquin, e [kɔkɛ̃, in] <> *adj* [sous-vêtement] sexy, naughty ; [regard, histoire] saucy. <> *nm, f* rascal.

cor [kɔr] *nm* **1.** [instrument] horn - **2.** [au pied] corn. **à cor et à cri** *loc adv* : **réclamer qqch à cor et à cri** to clamour *UK* OU clamor *US* for sthg.

corail, aux [kɔraj, o] *nm* **1.** [gén] coral - **2.** RAIL : **train corail** ≈ express train.

Coran [kɔrɑ̃] *nm* : **le Coran** the Koran.

corbeau, x [kɔrbo] *nm* **1.** [oiseau] crow - **2.** [délateur] writer of poison-pen letters.

corbeille [kɔrbɛj] *nf* **1.** [panier] basket ; **corbeille à papier** wastepaper basket - **2.** INFORM trash (can) - **3.** THÉÂTRE (dress) circle - **4.** [de Bourse] stockbrokers' enclosure *(at Paris Stock Exchange)*.

corbillard [kɔrbijar] *nm* hearse.

cordage [kɔrdaʒ] *nm* **1.** [de bateau] rigging *(U)* - **2.** [de raquette] strings *pl*.

corde [kɔrd] *nf* **1.** [filin] rope ; **corde à linge** washing line *UK*, clothesline *US* ; **corde à sauter** skipping rope *UK*, jump rope *US* - **2.** [d'instrument, arc] string - **3.** ANAT : **cordes vocales** vocal cords - **4.** [équitation] rails *pl* ; [athlétisme] inside (lane).

cordée [kɔrde] *nf* [alpinisme] roped party *(of mountaineers)*.

cordial, e, aux [kɔrdjal, o] *adj* warm, cordial.

cordon [kɔrdɔ̃] *nm* string, cord ; **cordon ombilical** umbilical cord ; **cordon de police** police cordon.

cordon-bleu [kɔrdɔ̃blø] *nm* cordon bleu cook.

cordonnerie [kɔrdɔnri] *nf* [magasin] shoe repairer's, cobbler's.

cordonnier, ère [kɔrdɔnje, ɛr] *nm, f* shoe repairer, cobbler.

Corée [kɔre] *nf* Korea.

coriace [kɔrjas] *adj litt & fig* tough.

cormoran [kɔrmɔrɑ̃] *nm* cormorant.

corne [kɔrn] *nf* **1.** [gén] horn ; [de cerf] antler - **2.** [callosité] hard skin *(U)*, callus.

cornée [kɔrne] *nf* cornea.

corneille [kɔrnɛj] *nf* crow.

cornemuse [kɔrnəmyz] *nf* bagpipes *pl*.

corner¹ [3] [kɔrne] *vt* [page] to turn down the corner of.

corner² [kɔrnɛr] *nm* FOOTBALL corner (kick).

cornet [kɔrne] *nm* **1.** [d'aliment] cornet *UK*, cone - **2.** [de jeu] (dice) shaker.

corniaud, corniot [kɔrnjo] *nm* **1.** [chien] mongrel - **2.** *fam* [imbécile] twit.

corniche [kɔrniʃ] *nf* **1.** [route] cliff road - **2.** [moulure] cornice.

cornichon [kɔrniʃɔ̃] *nm* **1.** [condiment] gherkin, pickle *US* - **2.** *fam* [imbécile] twit.

corniot = corniaud.

Cornouailles [kɔrnwaj] *nf* : **la Cornouailles** Cornwall.

corollaire [kɔrɔlɛr] *nm* corollary.

corolle [kɔrɔl] *nf* corolla.

coron [kɔrɔ̃] *nm* [village] mining village.

corporation [kɔrpɔrasjɔ̃] *nf* corporate body.

corporel, elle [kɔrpɔrɛl] *adj* [physique - besoin] bodily ; [- châtiment] corporal.

corps [kɔr] *nm* **1.** [gén] body - **2.** [groupe] : **corps d'armée** (army) corps ; **corps enseignant** [profession] teaching profession ; [d'école] teaching staff.

corpulent, e [kɔrpylɑ̃, ɑ̃t] *adj* corpulent, stout.

correct, e [kɔrɛkt] *adj* **1.** [exact] correct, right - **2.** [honnête] correct, proper - **3.** [acceptable] decent ; [travail] fair.

correcteur, trice [kɔrɛktœr, tris] <> *adj* corrective. <> *nm, f* **1.** [d'examen] examiner, marker *UK*, grader *US* - **2.** TYPO proof-reader. ⬥ **correcteur orthographique** *nm* spell-checker.

correction [kɔrɛksjɔ̃] *nf* **1.** [d'erreur] correction - **2.** [punition] punishment - **3.** TYPO proofreading - **4.** [notation] marking - **5.** [bienséance] propriety.

corrélation [kɔrelasjɔ̃] *nf* correlation.

correspondance [kɔrɛspɔ̃dɑ̃s] *nf* **1.** [gén] correspondence ; **cours par correspondance** correspondence course - **2.** [transports] connection ; **assurer la correspondance avec** to connect with.

correspondant, e [kɔrɛspɔ̃dɑ̃, ɑ̃t] <> *adj* corresponding. <> *nm, f* **1.** [par lettres] penfriend *UK*, pen pal *US*, correspondent - **2.** [par téléphone] : **je vous passe votre correspondant** I'll put you through - **3.** PRESSE correspondent.

correspondre [75] [kɔrɛspɔ̃dr] *vi* **1.** [être conforme] : **correspondre à** to correspond to - **2.** [par lettres] : **correspondre avec** to correspond with.

corridor [kɔridɔr] *nm* corridor.

corrigé [kɔriʒe] *nm* correct version.

corriger [17] [kɔriʒe] *vt* **1.** TYPO to correct, to proofread - **2.** [noter] to mark - **3.** [guérir] : **corriger qqn de** to cure sb of - **4.** [punir] to give a good hiding to. ⬥ **se corriger** *vp* [d'un défaut] : **se corriger de** to cure o.s. of.

corroborer [3] [kɔrɔbɔre] *vt* to corroborate.

corroder [3] [kɔrɔde] *vt* [ronger] to corrode ; *fig* to erode.

corrompre [78] [kɔrɔ̃pr] *vt* **1.** [soudoyer] to bribe - **2.** [dépraver] to corrupt.

corrosion [kɔrozjɔ̃] *nf* corrosion.

corruption [kɔrypsjɔ̃] *nf* **1.** [subornation] bribery - **2.** [dépravation] corruption.

corsage [kɔrsaʒ] *nm* **1.** [chemisier] blouse - **2.** [de robe] bodice.

corsaire [kɔrsɛr] *nm* **1.** [navire, marin] corsair, privateer - **2.** [pantalon] pedal-pushers *pl*.

corse [kɔrs] <> *adj* Corsican. <> *nm* [langue] Corsican. ⬥ **Corse** <> *nmf* Corsican. <> *nf* : **la Corse** Corsica.

corsé, e [kɔrse] *adj* [café] strong ; [vin] full-bodied ; [plat, histoire] spicy.

corset [kɔrsɛ] *nm* corset.

cortège [kɔrtɛʒ] *nm* procession.

corvée [kɔrve] *nf* **1.** MIL fatigue (duty) - **2.** [activité pénible] chore.

cosmétique [kɔsmetik] *nm & adj* cosmetic.

cosmique [kɔsmik] *adj* cosmic.

cosmonaute [kɔsmɔnot] *nmf* cosmonaut.

cosmopolite [kɔsmɔpɔlit] *adj* cosmopolitan.

cosmos [kɔsmɔs] *nm* **1.** [univers] cosmos - **2.** [espace] outer space.

cossu, e [kɔsy] *adj* [maison] opulent.

Costa Rica [kɔstarika] *nm* : **le Costa Rica** Costa Rica.

costaud, e OU **costaud** [kɔsto, od] *adj* sturdily built.

costume [kɔstym] *nm* **1.** [folklorique, de théâtre] costume - **2.** [vêtement d'homme] suit.

costumé, e [kɔstyme] *adj* fancy-dress *(avant n)*.

costumier, ère [kɔstymje, ɛr] *nm, f* THÉÂTRE wardrobe master (*f* mistress).

cotation [kɔtasjɔ̃] *nf* FIN quotation.

cote [kɔt] *nf* **1.** [marque de classement] classification mark ; [marque numérale] serial number - **2.** FIN [valeur] quotation - **3.** [popularité] rating - **4.** [niveau] level ; **cote d'alerte** [de cours d'eau] danger level ; *fig* crisis point.

côte [kot] *nf* **1.** ANAT & BOT [de bœuf] rib ; [de porc, mouton, agneau] chop ; **côte à côte** side by side - **2.** [pente] hill - **3.** [littoral] coast ; **la Côte d'Azur** the French Riviera.

côté [kote] *nm* **1.** [gén] side ; **être couché sur le côté** to be lying on one's side ; **être aux côtés de qqn** *fig* to be by sb's side ; **d'un côté..., de l'autre côté...** on the one hand..., on the other hand... ; **et côté finances, ça va?** *fam* how are things moneywise? - **2.** [endroit, direction] direction, way ; **de quel côté est-il parti?** which way did he go? ; **de l'autre côté de** on the other side of ; **de tous côtés** from all directions ; **du côté de** [près de] near ; [direction] towards, toward *US* ; [provenance] from. ➞ **à côté** *loc adv* **1.** [lieu - gén] nearby ; [- dans la maison adjacente] next door - **2.** [cible] : **tirer à côté** to shoot wide (of the target). ➞ **à côté de** *loc prép* **1.** [proximité] beside, next to - **2.** [en comparaison avec] beside, compared to - **3.** [en dehors de] : **être à côté du sujet** to be off the point. ➞ **de côté** *loc adv* **1.** [se placer, marcher] sideways - **2.** [en réserve] aside.

coteau [kɔto] *nm* **1.** [colline] hill - **2.** [versant] slope.

Côte-d'Ivoire [kotdivwar] *nf* : **la Côte-d'Ivoire** the Ivory Coast.

côtelé, e [kotle] *adj* ribbed ; **velours côtelé** corduroy.

côtelette [kotlɛt] *nf* [de porc, mouton, d'agneau] chop ; [de veau] cutlet.

coter [3] [kɔte] *vt* **1.** [marquer, noter] to mark - **2.** *FIN* to quote.

côtier, ère [kotje, ɛr] *adj* coastal.

cotisation [kɔtizasjɔ̃] *nf* [à un club, un parti] subscription ; [à la Sécurité sociale] contribution.

cotiser [3] [kɔtize] *vi* [à un club, un parti] to subscribe ; [à la Sécurité sociale] to contribute. ➞ **se cotiser** *vp* to club together.

coton [kɔtɔ̃] *nm* cotton ; **coton (hydrophile)** cotton wool *UK*, (absorbent) cotton *US*.

Coton-Tige® [kɔtɔ̃tiʒ] *nm* cotton bud *UK*, Q-tip® *US*.

côtoyer [13] [kotwaje] *vt* *fig* [fréquenter] to mix with.

cou [ku] *nm* [de personne, bouteille] neck.

couchant [kuʃɑ̃] <> *adj* ▶ **soleil.** <> *nm* west.

couche [kuʃ] *nf* **1.** [de peinture, de vernis] coat, layer ; [de poussière] film, layer - **2.** [épaisseur] layer ; **couche d'ozone** ozone layer - **3.** [de bébé] nappy *UK*, diaper *US* - **4.** [classe sociale] stratum. ➞ **fausse couche** *nf* miscarriage.

couché, e [kuʃe] *adj* : **être couché** [étendu] to be lying down ; [au lit] to be in bed.

couche-culotte [kuʃkylɔt] *nf* disposable nappy *UK* ou diaper *US*.

coucher¹ [3] [kuʃe] <> *vt* **1.** [enfant] to put to bed - **2.** [objet, blessé] to lay down. <> *vi* **1.** [passer la nuit] to spend the night - **2.** *fam* [avoir des rapports sexuels] : **coucher avec** to

sleep with. ➞ **se coucher** *vp* **1.** [s'allonger] to lie down - **2.** [se mettre au lit] to go to bed - **3.** [astre] to set.

coucher² [kuʃe] *nm* **1.** [d'astre] setting ; **au coucher du soleil** at sunset - **2.** [de personne] going to bed.

couchette [kuʃɛt] *nf* **1.** [de train] couchette - **2.** [de navire] berth.

coucou [kuku] <> *nm* **1.** [oiseau] cuckoo - **2.** [pendule] cuckoo clock - **3.** *péj* [avion] crate. <> *interj* peekaboo!

coude [kud] *nm* **1.** [de personne, de vêtement] elbow - **2.** [courbe] bend.

cou-de-pied [kudpje] (*pl* **cous-de-pied**) *nm* instep.

coudre [86] [kudr] *vt* [bouton] to sew on.

couette [kwet] *nf* **1.** [édredon] duvet *UK* - **2.** [coiffure] bunches *pl UK*.

couffin [kufɛ̃] *nm* [berceau] Moses basket.

couille [kuj] *nf* (*gén pl*) *vulg* ball.

couiner [3] [kwine] *vi* **1.** [animal] to squeal - **2.** [pleurnicher] to whine.

coulée [kule] *nf* **1.** [de matière liquide] : **coulée de lave** lava flow ; **coulée de boue** mudslide - **2.** [de métal] casting.

couler [3] [kule] <> *vi* **1.** [liquide] to flow ; **faire couler un bain** to run a bath - **2.** [beurre, fromage, nez] to run - **3.** [navire, entreprise] to sink. <> *vt* **1.** [navire] to sink - **2.** [métal, bronze] to cast.

couleur [kulœr] <> *nf* **1.** [teinte, caractère] colour *UK*, color *US* - **2.** [linge] coloureds *pl UK*, coloreds (*pl*) *US* - **3.** [jeux de cartes] suit. <> *adj inv* [télévision, pellicule] colour (*avant n*) *UK*, color (*avant n*) *US*.

couleuvre [kulœvr] *nf* grass snake.

coulisse [kulis] *nf* [glissière] : **fenêtre/porte à coulisse** sliding window/door. ➞ **coulisses** *nfpl* *THÉÂTRE* wings.

coulisser [3] [kulise] *vi* to slide.

couloir [kulwar] *nm* **1.** [corridor] corridor - **2.** *GÉOGR* gully - **3.** *SPORT* [transports] lane.

coup [ku] *nm* **1.** [choc - physique, moral] blow ; **coup de couteau** stab (*with a knife*) ; **un coup dur** *fig* a heavy blow ; **donner un coup de fouet à qqn** *fig* to give sb a shot in the arm ; **coup de grâce** *litt & fig* coup de grâce, death blow ; **coup de pied** kick ; **coup de poing** punch - **2.** [action nuisible] trick - **3.** [SPORT - au tennis] stroke ; [- en boxe] blow, punch ; [- au football] kick ; **coup franc** free kick - **4.** [d'éponge, de chiffon] wipe ; **un coup de crayon** a pencil stroke - **5.** [bruit] noise ; **coup de feu** shot, gunshot ; **coup de tonnerre** thunderclap - **6.** [action spectaculaire] : **coup d'État** coup (d'état) ; **coup de théâtre** *fig* dramatic turn of events - **7.** *fam* [fois] time ; **avoir un coup de barre/de pompe** *fam* to feel shattered *UK* ou pooped US, I feel tired all of a sudden ; **boire un coup** to have a drink ; **tenir le coup** to hold out ; **valoir le coup** to be well worth it. ➤ **coup de fil** *nm* phone call. ➤ **coup de foudre** *nm* love at first sight. ➤ **coup du lapin** *nm* AUTO whiplash *(U)*. ➤ **coup de soleil** *nm* sunburn *(U)*. ➤ **coup de téléphone** *nm* telephone OU phone call ; **donner** OU **passer un coup de téléphone à qqn** to telephone OU phone sb. ➤ **coup de vent** *nm* gust of wind ; **partir en coup de vent** to rush off. ➤ **à coup sûr** *loc adv* definitely. ➤ **du coup** *loc adv* as a result. ➤ **coup sur coup** *loc adv* one after the other. ➤ **sur le coup** *loc adv* **1.** [mourir] instantly - **2.** [à ce moment-là] straightaway, there and then ; **je n'ai pas compris sur le coup** I didn't understand immediately OU straightaway. ➤ **sous le coup de** *loc.prép* **1.** [sous l'action de] : **tomber sous le coup de la loi** to be a statutory offence *UK* OU offense *US* - **2.** [sous l'effet de] in the grip of. ➤ **tout à coup** *loc adv* suddenly.

coupable [kupabl] ◇ *adj* **1.** [personne, pensée] guilty - **2.** [action, dessein] culpable, reprehensible ; [négligence, oubli] sinful. ◇ *nmf* guilty person OU party.

coupant, e [kupã, ãt] *adj* **1.** [tranchant] cutting - **2.** *fig* [sec] sharp.

coupe [kup] *nf* **1.** [verre] glass - **2.** [à fruits] dish - **3.** SPORT cup - **4.** [de vêtement, aux cartes] cut ; **coupe (de cheveux)** haircut - **5.** [plan, surface] (cross) section - **6.** [réduction] cut, cutback.

coupé, e [kupe] *adj* : **bien/mal coupé** well/badly cut.

coupe-ongles [kupɔ̃gl] *nm inv* nail clippers.

coupe-papier [kuppapje] *(pl inv* OU **coupe-papiers)** *nm* paper knife.

couper [3] [kupe] ◇ *vt* **1.** [gén & INFORM] to cut - **2.** [arbre] to cut down - **3.** [pain] to slice ; [rôti] to carve - **4.** [envie, appétit] to take away - **5.** [vin] to dilute - **6.** [jeux de cartes - avec atout] to trump ; [- paquet] to cut - **7.** [interrompre, trancher] to cut off - **8.** [traverser] to cut across. ◇ *vi* [gén] to cut. ➤ **se couper** *vp* **1.** [se blesser] to cut o.s. - **2.** [se croiser] to cross - **3.** [s'isoler] : **se couper de** to cut o.s. off from.

couper-coller *nm inv* INFORM : **faire un couper-coller** to cut and paste.

couperet [kuprɛ] *nm* **1.** [de boucher] cleaver - **2.** [de guillotine] blade.

couperosé, e [kuproze] *adj* blotchy.

couple [kupl] *nm* [de personnes] couple ; [d'animaux] pair.

coupler [3] [kuple] *vt* [objets] to couple.

couplet [kuplɛ] *nm* verse.

coupole [kupɔl] *nf* ARCHIT dome, cupola.

coupon [kupɔ̃] *nm* **1.** [d'étoffe] remnant - **2.** [billet] ticket.

coupon-réponse [kupɔ̃repɔ̃s] *(pl coupons-réponse)* *nm* reply coupon.

coupure [kupyr] *nf* **1.** [gén] cut ; [billet de banque] : **petite coupure** small denomination note ; **coupure de courant** ÉLECTR power cut ; INFORM blackout - **2.** *fig* [rupture] break.

cour [kur] *nf* **1.** [espace] courtyard, yard - **2.** [du roi, tribunal] court ; *fig & hum* following ; **Cour de cassation** Court of Appeal ; **cour martiale** court-martial.

courage [kuraʒ] *nm* courage ; **bon courage!** good luck! ; **je n'ai pas le courage de faire mes devoirs** I can't bring myself to do my homework.

courageux, euse [kuraʒø, øz] *adj* **1.** [brave] brave - **2.** [audacieux] bold.

couramment [kuramã] *adv* **1.** [parler une langue] fluently - **2.** [communément] commonly.

courant, e [kurã, ãt] *adj* **1.** [habituel] everyday *(avant n)* - **2.** [en cours] present. ➤ **courant** *nm* **1.** [marin, atmosphérique, électrique] current ; **courant d'air** draught *UK*, draft *US* - **2.** [d'idées] current - **3.** [laps de temps] : **dans le courant du mois/de l'année** in the course of the month/the year. ➤ **au courant** *loc adv* : **être au courant** to know (about it) ; **mettre qqn au courant (de)** to tell sb (about) ; **tenir qqn au courant (de)** to keep sb informed (about) ; **se mettre/se tenir au courant (de)** to get/keep up to date (with).

courbature [kurbatyr] *nf* ache.

courbaturé, e [kurbatyre] *adj* aching.

courbe [kurb] ◇ *nf* curve ; **courbe de niveau** [sur une carte] contour (line). ◇ *adj* curved.

courber [3] [kurbe] ◇ *vt* **1.** [tige] to bend - **2.** [tête] to bow. ◇ *vi* to bow. ➤ **se courber** *vp* **1.** [chose] to bend - **2.** [personne] to bow, to bend down.

courbette [kurbɛt] *nf* [révérence] bow ; **faire des courbettes** *fig* to bow and scrape.

coureur, euse [kurœr, øz] *nm, f* SPORT runner ; **coureur cycliste** racing cyclist.

courge [kurʒ] *nf* **1.** [légume] marrow *UK*, squash *US* - **2.** *fam* [imbécile] dimwit.

courgette [kurʒɛt] *nf* courgette *UK*, zucchini *US*.

courir [45] [kurir] ◇ *vi* **1.** [aller rapidement] to run - **2.** SPORT to race - **3.** [se précipiter, rivière] to rush - **4.** [se propager] : **le bruit court que...** rumour *UK* OU rumor *US* has it that... ; **faire courir un bruit** to spread a rumour *UK* OU rumor *US*. ◇ *vt* **1.** SPORT to run in - **2.** [parcourir] to roam (through) - **3.** [fréquenter : bals, musées] to do the rounds of.

couronne [kurɔn] *nf* **1.** [ornement, autorité] crown - **2.** [de fleurs] wreath - **3.** [monnaie - d'Islande] krona ; [- de Norvège] krone ; [- de la République tchèque] crown.

couronnement [kurɔnmɑ̃] *nm* **1.** [de monarque] coronation - **2.** *fig* [apogée] crowning achievement.

couronner [3] [kurɔne] *vt* **1.** [monarque] to crown - **2.** [récompenser] to give a prize to.

courre [kur] ▸ chasse.

courriel [kurjɛl] *Québec nm* INFORM e-mail.

courrier [kurje] *nm* mail, letters *pl* ; **courrier du cœur** agony column *UK*, Dear Abby *US*.

courroie [kurwa] *nf* TECHNOL belt ; [attache] strap ; **courroie de transmission** driving belt ; **courroie de ventilateur** fanbelt.

courroucer [16] [kuruse] *vt litt* to anger.

cours [kur] *nm* **1.** [écoulement] flow ; **cours d'eau** waterway ; **donner** OU **laisser libre cours à** *fig* to give free rein to - **2.** [déroulement] course ; **au cours de** during, in the course of ; **en cours** [année, dossier] current ; [affaires] in hand ; **en cours de route** on the way - **3.** FIN price ; **avoir cours** [monnaie] to be legal tender - **4.** [leçon] class, lesson ; **donner des cours (à qqn)** to teach (sb) ; **cours particuliers** private lessons - **5.** [classe] : **cours élémentaire** *years two and three of primary school* ; **cours moyen** *last two years of primary school* ; **cours préparatoire** ≃ first-year infants *UK*, ≃ nursery school *US*.

course [kurs] *nf* **1.** [action] running (*U*) ; **au pas de course** at a run - **2.** [compétition] race - **3.** [en taxi] journey - **4.** [mouvement] flight, course - **5.** [commission] errand ; **faire des courses** to go shopping.

coursier, ère [kursje, ɛr] *nm, f* messenger.

court, e [kur, kurt] *adj* short. ▸ **court** ⟨⟩ *adv* : **être à court d'argent/d'idées/d'arguments** to be short of money/ideas/arguments ; **prendre qqn de court** to catch sb unawares ; **tourner court** to stop suddenly. ⟨⟩ *nm* : **court de tennis** tennis court.

court-bouillon [kurbujɔ̃] *nm* court-bouillon.

court-circuit [kursirkɥi] *nm* short circuit.

courtier, ère [kurtje, ɛr] *nm, f* broker.

courtisan, e [kurtizɑ̃, an] *nm, f* **1.** HIST courtier - **2.** [flatteur] sycophant. ▸ **courtisane** *nf* courtesan.

courtiser [3] [kurtize] *vt* **1.** [femme] to woo, to court - **2.** *péj* [flatter] to flatter.

court-métrage [kurmetraʒ] *nm* short (film).

courtois, e [kurtwa, az] *adj* courteous.

courtoisie [kurtwazi] *nf* courtesy.

couru, e [kury] ⟨⟩ *pp* ▸ **courir**. ⟨⟩ *adj* popular.

couscous [kuskus] *nm* couscous *traditional North African dish of semolina served with a spicy stew of meat and vegetables.*

cousin, e [kuzɛ̃, in] *nm, f* cousin ; **cousin germain** first cousin.

coussin [kusɛ̃] *nm* [de siège] cushion.

cousu, e [kuzy] *pp* ▸ **coudre**.

coût [ku] *nm* cost.

coûtant [kutɑ̃] ▸ **prix**.

couteau, x [kuto] *nm* **1.** [gén] knife ; **couteau à cran d'arrêt** flick knife *UK*, switchblade *US* - **2.** [coquillage] razor shell *UK*, razor clam *US*.

coûter [3] [kute] ⟨⟩ *vi* **1.** [valoir] to cost ; **ça coûte combien?** how much is it? ; **coûter cher à qqn** to cost sb a lot ; *fig* to cost sb dear OU dearly - **2.** *fig* [être pénible] to be difficult. ⟨⟩ *vt fig* to cost. ▸ **coûte que coûte** *loc adv* at all costs.

coûteux, euse [kutø, øz] *adj* costly, expensive.

coutume [kutym] *nf* [gén & DR] custom.

couture [kutyr] *nf* **1.** [action] sewing - **2.** [points] seam - **3.** [activité] dressmaking ; **haute couture** designer fashion.

couturier, ère [kutyrje, ɛr] *nm, f* couturier.

couvée [kuve] *nf* [d'œufs] clutch ; [de poussins] brood.

couvent [kuvɑ̃] *nm* [de sœurs] convent ; [de moines] monastery.

couver [3] [kuve] ⟨⟩ *vt* **1.** [œufs] to sit on - **2.** [dorloter] to mollycoddle - **3.** [maladie] to be sickening for *UK*, to be coming down with *US*. ⟨⟩ *vi* [poule] to brood ; *fig* [complot] to hatch.

couvercle [kuverkl] *nm* [de casserole, boîte] lid, cover.

couvert, e [kuver, ert] ⟨⟩ *pp* ▸ **couvrir**. ⟨⟩ *adj* **1.** [submergé] covered ; **couvert de** covered with - **2.** [habillé] dressed ; **être bien couvert** to be well wrapped up - **3.** [nuageux] overcast. ▸ **couvert** *nm* **1.** [abri] : **se mettre à couvert** to take shelter - **2.** [place à table] place (setting) ; **mettre** OU **dresser le couvert** to set OU lay the table. ▸ **couverts** *nmpl* cutlery (*U*).

couverture [kuvertyr] *nf* **1.** [gén] cover - **2.** [de lit] blanket ; **couverture chauffante** electric blanket - **3.** [toit] roofing (*U*).

couveuse [kuvøz] *nf* **1.** [poule] sitting hen - **2.** [machine] incubator.

couvre-chef [kuvrəʃef] (*pl* **couvre-chefs**) *nm hum* hat.

couvre-feu [kuvrəfø] (*pl* **couvre-feux**) *nm* curfew.

couvreur [kuvrœr] *nm* roofer.

couvrir [34] [kuvrir] *vt* **1.** [gén] to cover ; **couvrir qqn/qqch de** *litt & fig* to cover sb/sthg with - **2.** [protéger] to shield. ◆ **se couvrir** *vp* **1.** [se vêtir] to wrap up - **2.** [se recouvrir] : **se couvrir de feuilles/de fleurs** to come into leaf/blossom - **3.** [ciel] to cloud over - **4.** [se protéger] to cover o.s.

covoiturage [kɔvwatyraʒ] *nm* car sharing, car pooling ; **pratiquer le covoiturage** to belong to a car pool.

CP *nm abr de* **cours préparatoire.**

CQFD (*abr de* **ce qu'il fallait démontrer**) QED.

crabe [krab] *nm* crab.

crachat [kraʃa] *nm* spit (*U*).

cracher [3] [kraʃe] ◇ *vi* **1.** [personne] to spit - **2.** *fam* [dédaigner] : **ne pas cracher sur qqch** not to turn one's nose up at sthg. ◇ *vt* [sang] to spit (up) ; [lave, injures] to spit (out).

crachin [kraʃɛ̃] *nm* drizzle.

crachoir [kraʃwar] *nm* spittoon.

craie [krɛ] *nf* chalk.

craindre [80] [krɛ̃dr] *vt* **1.** [redouter] to fear, to be afraid of ; **craindre de faire qqch** to be afraid of doing sthg ; **je crains d'avoir oublié mes papiers** I'm afraid I've forgotten my papers ; **craindre que** (+ *subjonctif*) to be afraid (that) ; **je crains qu'il oublie** OU **n'oublie** I'm afraid he may forget - **2.** [être sensible à] to be susceptible to.

craint, e [krɛ̃, ɛ̃t] *pp* ► **craindre.**

crainte [krɛ̃t] *nf* fear ; **de crainte de faire qqch** for fear of doing sthg ; **de crainte que** (+ *subjonctif*) for fear that ; **il a fui de crainte qu'on ne le voie** he fled for fear that he might be seen OU for fear of being seen.

craintif, ive [krɛ̃tif, iv] *adj* timid.

cramoisi, e [kramwazi] *adj* crimson.

crampe [krɑ̃p] *nf* cramp.

crampon [krɑ̃pɔ̃] *nm* [crochet - gén] clamp ; [- pour alpinisme] crampon.

cramponner [3] [krɑ̃pɔne] ◆ **se cramponner** *vp* [s'agripper] to hang on ; **se cramponner à qqn/qqch** *litt & fig* to cling to sb/sthg.

cran [krɑ̃] *nm* **1.** [entaille, degré] notch, cut - **2.** (*U*) [audace] guts *pl.*

crâne [kran] *nm* skull.

crâner [3] [krane] *vi fam* to show off.

crânien, enne [kranjɛ̃, ɛn] *adj* : **boîte crânienne** skull ; **traumatisme crânien** head injury.

crapaud [krapo] *nm* toad.

crapule [krapyl] *nf* scum (*U*).

craquelure [kraklyr] *nf* crack.

craquement [krakmɑ̃] *nm* crack, cracking (*U*).

craquer [3] [krake] ◇ *vi* **1.** [produire un bruit] to crack ; [plancher, chaussure] to creak - **2.** [se déchirer] to split - **3.** [s'effondrer - personne] to crack up - **4.** *fam* [être séduit par] : **craquer pour** to fall for. ◇ *vt* [allumette] to strike.

crasse [kras] *nf* **1.** [saleté] dirt, filth - **2.** *fam* [mauvais tour] dirty trick.

crasseux, euse [krasø, øz] *adj* filthy.

cratère [krater] *nm* crater.

cravache [kravaʃ] *nf* riding crop.

cravate [kravat] *nf* tie.

crawl [krol] *nm* crawl.

crayon [krɛjɔ̃] *nm* **1.** [gén] pencil ; **crayon à bille** ballpoint (pen) ; **crayon de couleur** crayon - **2.** TECHNOL pen ; **crayon optique** light pen.

créancier, ère [kreɑ̃sje, ɛr] *nm, f* creditor.

créateur, trice [kreatœr, tris] ◇ *adj* creative. ◇ *nm, f* creator. ◆ **Créateur** *nm* : **le Créateur** the Creator.

créatif, ive [kreatif, iv] *adj* creative.

création [kreasjɔ̃] *nf* creation.

créativité [kreativite] *nf* creativity.

créature [kreatyr] *nf* creature.

crécelle [kresɛl] *nf* rattle.

crèche [krɛʃ] *nf* **1.** [de Noël] crib UK, crèche US - **2.** [garderie] crèche UK, day-care center US.

crédible [kredibl] *adj* credible.

crédit [kredi] *nm* **1.** COMM credit ; **faire crédit à qqn** to give sb credit ; **accorder/obtenir un crédit** to grant/to obtain credit ; **acheter/vendre qqch à crédit** to buy/sell sthg on credit - **2.** *fig & sout* influence.

crédit-bail [kredibaj] (*pl* **crédits-bails**) *nm* leasing.

créditeur, trice [kreditœr, tris] ◇ *adj* in credit. ◇ *nm, f* creditor.

crédule [kredyl] *adj* credulous.

crédulité [kredylite] *nf* credulity.

créer [15] [kree] *vt* **1.** RELIG [inventer] to create - **2.** [fonder] to found, to start up.

crémaillère [kremajɛr] *nf* **1.** [de cheminée] trammel ; **pendre la crémaillère** *fig* to have a housewarming (party) - **2.** TECHNOL rack.

crémation [kremasjɔ̃] *nf* cremation.

crématoire [krematwar] ► **four.**

crème [krɛm] <> nf **1.** [produit de beauté] cream ; **crème hydratante** moisturizer - **2.** CULIN cream ; **crème anglaise** custard UK. <> adj inv cream.

crémerie [krɛmri] nf dairy.

crémier, ère [krɛmje, ɛr] nm, f dairyman (f dairywoman).

créneau, x [kreno] nm **1.** [de fortification] crenel - **2.** [pour se garer] : **faire un créneau** to reverse into a parking space - **3.** [de marché] niche - **4.** [horaire] window, gap.

créole [kreɔl] adj & nm creole.

crêpe [krɛp] <> nf CULIN pancake. <> nm [tissu] crepe.

crêperie [krɛpri] nf pancake restaurant.

crépi [krepi] nm roughcast.

crépir [32] [krepir] vt to roughcast.

crépiter [3] [krepite] vi [feu, flammes] to crackle ; [pluie] to patter.

crépon [krepɔ̃] <> adj ➤ **papier**. <> nm seersucker.

crépu, e [krepy] adj frizzy.

crépuscule [krepyskyl] nm [du jour] dusk, twilight ; fig twilight.

crescendo [kreʃɛndo, kreʃēdo] <> adv crescendo ; **aller crescendo** fig [bruit] to get OU grow louder and louder ; [dépenses, émotion] to grow apace. <> nm inv MUS & fig crescendo.

cresson [kresɔ̃] nm watercress.

Crète [krɛt] nf : **la Crète** Crete.

crête [krɛt] nf **1.** [de coq] comb - **2.** [de montagne, vague, oiseau] crest.

crétin, e [kretɛ̃, in] fam <> adj cretinous, idiotic. <> nm, f cretin, idiot.

creuser [3] [krøze] vt **1.** [trou] to dig - **2.** [objet] to hollow out - **3.** fig [approfondir] to go into deeply.

creux, creuse [krø, krøz] adj **1.** [vide, concave] hollow - **2.** [période - d'activité réduite] slack ; [- à tarif réduit] off-peak - **3.** [paroles] empty. ➤ **creux** nm **1.** [concavité] hollow - **2.** [période] lull.

crevaison [krəvɛzɔ̃] nf puncture UK, flat (tire) US.

crevant, e [krəvɑ̃, ɑ̃t] adj fam [fatigant] exhausting, knackering UK.

crevasse [krəvas] nf [de mur] crevice, crack ; [de glacier] crevasse ; [sur la main] crack.

crevé, e [krəve] adj **1.** [pneu] burst, punctured, flat US - **2.** fam [fatigué] dead, shattered UK.

crève-cœur [krɛvkœr] nm inv heartbreak.

crever [19] [krəve] <> vi **1.** [éclater] to burst - **2.** tfam [mourir] to die ; **crever de** fig [jalousie, orgueil] to be bursting with. <> vt **1.** [percer] to burst - **2.** fam [épuiser] to wear out.

crevette [krəvɛt] nf : **crevette (grise)** shrimp ; **crevette (rose)** prawn.

cri [kri] nm **1.** [de personne] cry, shout ; [perçant] scream ; [d'animal] cry ; **pousser un cri** to cry (out), to shout ; **pousser un cri de douleur** to cry out in pain - **2.** [appel] cry ; **le dernier cri** fig the latest thing.

criant, e [krijã, ãt] adj [injustice] blatant.

criard, e [krijar, ard] adj **1.** [voix] strident, piercing - **2.** [couleur] loud.

crible [kribl] nm [instrument] sieve ; **passer qqch au crible** fig to examine sthg closely.

criblé, e [krible] adj riddled ; **être criblé de dettes** to be up to one's eyes in debt.

cric [krik] nm jack.

cricket [krikɛt] nm cricket.

crier [10] [krije] <> vi **1.** [pousser un cri] to shout (out), to yell - **2.** [parler fort] to shout - **3.** [protester] : **crier contre** OU **après qqn** to nag sb, to go on at sb. <> vt to shout (out).

crime [krim] nm **1.** [délit] crime - **2.** [meurtre] murder ; **crimes contre l'humanité** crime against humanity.

criminalité [kriminalite] nf crime.

criminel, elle [kriminɛl] <> adj criminal. <> nm, f criminal ; **criminel de guerre** war criminal.

crin [krɛ̃] nm [d'animal] hair.

crinière [krinjɛr] nf mane.

crique [krik] nf creek.

criquet [krikɛ] nm locust ; [sauterelle] grasshopper.

crise [kriz] nf **1.** MÉD attack ; **crise cardiaque** heart attack ; **crise de foie** bilious attack - **2.** [accès] fit ; **crise de nerfs** attack of nerves - **3.** [phase critique] crisis.

crispation [krispasjɔ̃] nf **1.** [contraction] contraction - **2.** [agacement] irritation.

crispé, e [krispe] adj tense, on edge.

crisper [3] [krispe] vt **1.** [contracter - visage] to tense ; [- poing] to clench - **2.** [agacer] to irritate. ➤ **se crisper** vp **1.** [se contracter] to tense (up) - **2.** [s'irriter] to get irritated.

crisser [3] [krise] vi [pneu] to screech ; [étoffe] to rustle.

cristal, aux [kristal, o] nm crystal ; **cristal de roche** quartz.

cristallin, e [kristalɛ̃, in] adj **1.** [limpide] crystal clear, crystalline - **2.** [roche] crystalline. ➤ **cristallin** nm crystalline lens.

critère [kritɛr] nm criterion.

critique [kritik] <> adj critical. <> nmf critic. <> nf criticism.

critiquer [3] [kritike] *vt* to criticize.

croasser [3] [krɔase] *vi* to croak, to caw.

croate [krɔat] *adj* Croat, Croatian. **Croate** *nmf* Croat, Croatian.

Croatie [krɔasi] *nf* : **la Croatie** Croatia.

croc [kro] *nm* [de chien] fang.

croche [krɔʃ] *nf* quaver *UK*, eighth (note) *US*.

croche-pied [krɔʃpje] (*pl* **croche-pieds**) *nm* : **faire un croche-pied à qqn** to trip sb up.

crochet [krɔʃɛ] *nm* **1.** [de métal] hook ; **vivre aux crochets de qqn** to live off sb - **2.** [tricot] crochet hook - **3.** TYPO square bracket - **4.** [boxe] : **crochet du gauche/du droit** left/right hook.

crochu, e [krɔʃy] *adj* [doigts] claw-like ; [nez] hooked.

crocodile [krɔkɔdil] *nm* crocodile.

croire [107] [krwar] <> *vt* **1.** [chose, personne] to believe - **2.** [penser] to think ; **tu crois?** do you think so? ; **il te croyait parti** he thought you'd left ; **croire que** to think (that). <> *vi* : **croire à** to believe in ; **croire en** to believe in, to have faith in.

croisade [krwazad] *nf* HIST & *fig* crusade.

croisé, e [krwaze] *adj* [veste] double-breasted. **croisé** *nm* HIST crusader.

croisement [krwazmɑ̃] *nm* **1.** [intersection] junction, intersection - **2.** BIOL crossbreeding.

croiser [3] [krwaze] <> *vt* **1.** [jambes] to cross ; [bras] to fold - **2.** [passer à côté de] to pass - **3.** [chemin] to cross, to cut across - **4.** [métisser] to interbreed. <> *vi* NAUT to cruise. **se croiser** *vp* [chemins] to cross, to intersect ; [personnes] to pass ; [lettres] to cross ; [regards] to meet.

croisière [krwazjɛr] *nf* cruise.

croisillon [krwazijɔ̃] *nm* : **à croisillons** lattice (*avant n*).

croissance [krwasɑ̃s] *nf* growth, development ; **croissance économique** economic growth OU development.

croissant, e [krwasɑ̃, ɑ̃t] *adj* increasing, growing. **croissant** *nm* **1.** [de lune] crescent - **2.** CULIN croissant.

croître [93] [krwatr] *vi* **1.** [grandir] to grow - **2.** [augmenter] to increase.

croix [krwa] *nf* cross ; **en croix** in the shape of a cross ; **croix gammée** swastika.

Croix-Rouge [krwaruʒ] *nf* : **la Croix-Rouge** the Red Cross.

croquant, e [krɔkɑ̃, ɑ̃t] *adj* crisp, crunchy.

croque-mitaine [krɔkmitɛn] (*pl* **croque-mitaines**) *nm* bogeyman.

croque-monsieur [krɔkməsjø] *nm inv* toasted cheese and ham sandwich.

croque-mort [krɔkmɔr] (*pl* **croque-morts**) *nm fam* undertaker.

croquer [3] [krɔke] <> *vt* **1.** [manger] to crunch - **2.** [dessiner] to sketch. <> *vi* to be crunchy.

croquette [krɔkɛt] *nf* croquette.

croquis [krɔki] *nm* sketch.

cross [krɔs] *nm* [exercice] cross-country (running) ; [course] cross-country race.

crotte [krɔt] *nf* [de lapin etc] droppings *pl* ; [de chien] dirt.

crottin [krɔtɛ̃] *nm* [de cheval] (horse) manure.

crouler [3] [krule] *vi* to crumble ; **crouler sous** *litt* & *fig* to collapse under.

croupe [krup] *nf* rump ; **monter en croupe** to ride pillion.

croupier [krupje] *nm* croupier.

croupir [32] [krupir] *vi litt* & *fig* to stagnate.

croustillant, e [krustijɑ̃, ɑ̃t] *adj* [croquant - pain] crusty ; [- biscuit] crunchy.

croûte [krut] *nf* **1.** [du pain, terrestre] crust - **2.** [de fromage] rind - **3.** [de plaie] scab - **4.** *fam péj* [tableau] daub.

croûton [krutɔ̃] *nm* **1.** [bout du pain] crust - **2.** [pain frit] crouton - **3.** *fam péj* [personne] fuddy-duddy.

croyance [krwajɑ̃s] *nf* belief.

croyant, e [krwajɑ̃, ɑ̃t] <> *adj* : **être croyant** to be a believer. <> *nm, f* believer.

CRS (*abr de* **Compagnie républicaine de sécurité**) *nm member of the French riot police.*

cru, e [kry] <> *pp* ► **croire.** <> *adj* **1.** [non cuit] raw - **2.** [violent] harsh - **3.** [direct] blunt - **4.** [grivois] crude. **cru** *nm* [vin] vintage, wine ; [vignoble] vineyard ; **du cru** *fig* local ; **de son propre cru** *fig* of one's own devising.

crû [kry] *pp* ► **croître.**

cruauté [kryote] *nf* cruelty.

cruche [kryʃ] *nf* **1.** [objet] jug *UK*, pitcher *US* - **2.** *fam péj* [personne niaise] twit *UK*, nitwit.

crucial, e, aux [krysjal, o] *adj* crucial.

crucifix [krysifi] *nm* crucifix.

crudité [krydite] *nf* crudeness. **crudités** *nfpl* crudités.

crue [kry] *nf* rise in the water level.

cruel, elle [kryɛl] *adj* cruel.

crustacé [krystase] *nm* shellfish, crustacean ; **crustacés** shellfish (*U*).

crypter [kripte] *vt* to encrypt ; **chaîne cryptée** encrypted channel.

Cuba [kyba] *npr* Cuba.

cubain, aine [kybɛ̃, ɛn] *adj* Cuban. **Cubain, aine** *nm, f* Cuban.

cube [kyb] *nm* cube ; **4 au cube = 64** 4 cubed is 64 ; **mètre cube** cubic metre *UK* ou meter *US*.

cueillette [kœjɛt] *nf* picking, harvesting.

cueilli, e [kœji] *pp* ▶ **cueillir**.

cueillir [41] [kœjir] *vt* [fruits, fleurs] to pick.

cuillère, cuiller [kɥijɛr] *nf* [instrument] spoon ; **cuillère à café** coffee spoon ; CULIN teaspoon ; **cuillère à dessert** dessertspoon ; **cuillère à soupe** soup spoon ; CULIN tablespoon.

cuillerée [kɥijere] *nf* spoonful ; **cuillerée à café** CULIN teaspoonful ; **cuillerée à soupe** CULIN tablespoonful.

cuir [kɥir] *nm* leather ; [non tanné] hide ; **cuir chevelu** ANAT scalp.

cuirasse [kɥiras] *nf* [de chevalier] breastplate ; *fig* armour *UK*, armor *US*.

cuirassé [kɥirase] *nm* battleship.

cuire [98] [kɥir] <> *vt* [viande, œuf] to cook ; [tarte, gâteau] to bake. <> *vi* **1.** [viande, œuf] to cook ; [tarte, gâteau] to bake ; **faire cuire qqch** to cook/bake sthg - **2.** *fig* [personne] to roast, to be boiling.

cuisine [kɥizin] *nf* **1.** [pièce] kitchen - **2.** [art] cooking, cookery ; **faire la cuisine** to do the cooking, to cook.

cuisiné, e [kɥizine] *adj* : **plat cuisiné** ready-cooked meal.

cuisiner [3] [kɥizine] <> *vt* **1.** [aliment] to cook - **2.** *fam* [personne] to grill. <> *vi* to cook ; **bien/mal cuisiner** to be a good/bad cook.

cuisinier, ère [kɥizinje, ɛr] *nm, f* cook. ▶ **cuisinière** *nf* cooker *UK*, stove *US* ; **cuisinière électrique/à gaz** electric/gas cooker *UK* ou stove *US*.

cuisse [kɥis] *nf* **1.** ANAT thigh - **2.** CULIN leg.

cuisson [kɥisɔ̃] *nf* cooking.

cuit, e [kɥi, kɥit] <> *pp* ▶ **cuire**. <> *adj* : **bien cuit** [steak] well-done.

cuivre [kɥivr] *nm* [métal] : **cuivre (rouge)** copper ; **cuivre jaune** brass. ▶ **cuivres** *nmpl* : **les cuivres** MUS the brass.

cuivré, e [kɥivre] *adj* [couleur, reflet] coppery ; [teint] bronzed.

cul [ky] *nm* **1.** *tfam* [postérieur] bum *UK*, ass *US* - **2.** [de bouteille] bottom.

culbute [kylbyt] *nf* **1.** [saut] somersault - **2.** [chute] tumble, fall.

cul-de-sac [kydsak] (*pl* **culs-de-sac**) *nm* dead end.

culinaire [kyliner] *adj* culinary.

culminant [kylminɑ̃] ▶ **point**.

culot [kylo] *nm* **1.** *fam* [toupet] cheek, nerve ; **avoir du culot** to have a lot of nerve - **2.** [de cartouche, ampoule] cap.

culotte [kylɔt] *nf* [sous-vêtement féminin] knickers *pl UK*, panties *pl*, pair of knickers *UK* ou of panties.

culotté, e [kylɔte] *adj* [effronté] : **elle est culottée** she's got a nerve.

culpabilité [kylpabilite] *nf* guilt.

culte [kylt] *nm* **1.** [vénération, amour] worship - **2.** [religion] religion.

cultivateur, trice [kyltivatœr, tris] *nm, f* farmer.

cultivé, e [kyltive] *adj* [personne] educated, cultured.

cultiver [3] [kyltive] *vt* **1.** [terre, goût, relation] to cultivate - **2.** [plante] to grow.

culture [kyltyr] *nf* **1.** AGRIC cultivation, farming ; **les cultures** cultivated land - **2.** [savoir] culture, knowledge ; **culture physique** physical training - **3.** [civilisation] culture.

culturel, elle [kyltyrɛl] *adj* cultural.

culturisme [kyltyrism] *nm* bodybuilding.

cumin [kymɛ̃] *nm* cumin.

cumuler [3] [kymyle] *vt* [fonctions, titres] to hold simultaneously ; [salaires] to draw simultaneously.

cupide [kypid] *adj* greedy.

cure [kyr] *nf* (course of) treatment ; **faire une cure de fruits** to go on a fruit-based diet ; **cure de désintoxication** [d'alcool] drying-out treatment ; [de drogue] detoxification treatment ; **cure de sommeil** sleep therapy ; **faire une cure thermale** to take the waters.

curé [kyre] *nm* parish priest.

cure-dents [kyrdɑ̃] *nm inv* toothpick.

curer [3] [kyre] *vt* to clean out.

curieux, euse [kyrjø, øz] <> *adj* **1.** [intéressé] curious ; **curieux de qqch/de faire qqch** curious about sthg/to do sthg - **2.** [indiscret] inquisitive - **3.** [étrange] strange, curious. <> *nm, f* busybody.

curiosité [kyrjozite] *nf* curiosity.

curriculum vitae [kyrikylɔmvite] *nm inv* curriculum vitae, résumé *US*.

curry [kyri], **carry** [kari], **cari** [kari] *nm* **1.** [épice] curry powder - **2.** [plat] curry.

curseur [kyrsœr] *nm* cursor.

cutané, e [kytane] *adj* cutaneous, skin (*avant n*).

cutiréaction, cuti-réaction (*pl* **cuti-réactions**) [kytireaksjɔ̃] *nf* skin test.

cuve [kyv] *nf* **1.** [citerne] tank - **2.** [à vin] vat.

cuvée [kyve] *nf* [récolte] vintage.

cuvette [kyvɛt] *nf* **1.** [récipient] basin, bowl - **2.** [de lavabo] basin ; [de W.-C.] bowl - **3.** GÉOGR basin.

CV *nm* **1.** (*abr de* **curriculum vitae**) CV, résumé *US* - **2.** (*abr écrite de* **cheval-vapeur**) hp ; [puissance fiscale] *classification of former car tax.*

cyanure [sjanyr] *nm* cyanide.

cybercafé [siberkafe] *nm* cybercafé, internet café.

cybercommerce [siberkɔmers] *nm* e-commerce.

cybercrime [siberkrim] *nm* INFORM e-crime.

cyberespace [siberespas], **cybermonde** [sibermɔ̃d] *nm* cyberspace.

cybernaute [sibernot] *nm* (net) surfer, cybersurfer, cybernaut.

cyclable [siklabl] ▶ **piste.**

cycle [sikl] *nm* **1.** [série] cycle - **2.** [formation] cycle ; **second cycle** UNIV ≃ final year *UK*, ≃ senior year *US* ; SCOL upper school *UK*, high school *US* ; **troisième cycle** UNIV ≃ postgraduate year OU years.

cyclique [siklik] *adj* cyclic, cyclical.

cyclisme [siklism] *nm* cycling.

cycliste [siklist] *nmf* cyclist.

cyclone [siklon] *nm* cyclone.

cygne [siɲ] *nm* swan.

cylindre [silɛ̃dr] *nm* **1.** AUTO & GÉOM cylinder - **2.** [rouleau] roller.

cymbale [sɛ̃bal] *nf* cymbal.

cynique [sinik] *adj* cynical.

cynisme [sinism] *nm* cynicism.

cyprès [sipre] *nm* cypress.

cyrillique [sirilik] *adj* Cyrillic.

D

d, D [de] *nm inv* d, D.

d' ▶ **de.**

d'abord [dabɔr] ▶ **abord.**

d'accord [dakɔr] *loc adv* : **d'accord!** all right!, OK! ; **être d'accord avec** to agree with.

DAB [deabe, dab] (*abr de* **distributeur automatique de billets**) *nm* ATM.

dactylo [daktilo] *nf* [personne] typist ; [procédé] typing.

dactylographier [9] [daktilɔgrafje] *vt* to type.

dada [dada] *nm* **1.** [cheval] gee-gee *UK*, horsie *US* - **2.** *fam* [occupation] hobby - **3.** *fam* [idée] hobbyhorse - **4.** ART Dadaism.

dahlia [dalja] *nm* dahlia.

daigner [4] [deɲe] *vi* to deign.

daim [dɛ̃] *nm* **1.** [animal] fallow deer - **2.** [peau] suede.

dallage [dalaʒ] *nm* [action] paving ; [dalles] pavement.

dalle [dal] *nf* [de pierre] slab ; [de lino] tile.

dalmatien, enne [dalmasjɛ̃, ɛn] *nm, f* dalmatian.

daltonien, enne [daltɔnjɛ̃, ɛn] *adj* colour-blind *UK*, color-blind *US*.

dame [dam] *nf* **1.** [femme] lady - **2.** [cartes à jouer] queen. ◆ **dames** *nfpl* draughts *UK*, checkers *US*.

damier [damje] *nm* **1.** [de jeu] draught board *UK*, checkerboard *US* - **2.** [motif] : **à damier** checked.

damné, e [dane] *adj fam* damned.

damner [3] [dane] *vt* to damn.

dancing [dɑ̃siŋ] *nm* dance hall.

dandiner [3] [dɑ̃dine] ◆ **se dandiner** *vp* to waddle.

Danemark [danmark] *nm* : **le Danemark** Denmark.

danger [dɑ̃ʒe] *nm* danger ; **en danger** in danger ; **courir un danger** to run a risk.

dangereux, euse [dɑ̃ʒrø, øz] *adj* dangerous.

danois, e [danwa, az] *adj* Danish. ◆ **danois** *nm* **1.** [langue] Danish - **2.** [chien] Great Dane. ◆ **Danois, e** *nm, f* Dane.

dans [dɑ̃] *prép* **1.** [dans le temps] in ; **je reviens dans un mois** I'll be back in a month OU in a month's time - **2.** [dans l'espace] in ; **dans une boîte** in OU inside a box - **3.** [avec mouvement] into ; **entrer dans une chambre** to come into a room, to enter a room - **4.** [indiquant un état, une manière] in ; **vivre dans la misère** to live in poverty ; **il est dans le commerce** he's in business - **5.** [environ] : **dans les...** about... ; **ça coûte dans les 30 euros** it costs about 30 euros.

dansant, e [dɑ̃sɑ̃, ɑ̃t] *adj litt & fig* dancing ; **soirée dansante** dance ; **thé dansant** tea dance.

danse [dɑ̃s] *nf* **1.** [art] dancing - **2.** [musique] dance.

danser [3] [dɑ̃se] ◇ *vi* **1.** [personne] to dance - **2.** [bateau] to bob ; [flammes] to flicker. ◇ *vt* to dance.

danseur, euse [dɑ̃sœr, øz] *nm, f* dancer.

dard [dar] *nm* [d'animal] sting.

date [dat] *nf* **1.** [jour+mois+année] date ; **date de naissance** date of birth - **2.** [moment] event.

dater [3] [date] ◇ *vt* to date. ◇ *vi*

1. [marquer] to be ou mark a milestone - **2.** *fam* [être démodé] to be dated. ➡ à - **dater de** *loc prép* as of ou from.

datte [dat] *nf* date.

dattier [datje] *nm* date palm.

dauphin [dofɛ̃] *nm* **1.** [mammifère] dolphin - **2.** HIST heir apparent.

daurade [dɔrad] *nf* sea bream.

davantage [davɑ̃taʒ] *adv* **1.** [plus] more ; **davantage de** more - **2.** [plus longtemps] (any) longer.

de [də] (formes contractées de : 'de + le' = du, 'de + les' = des) ◇ *prép* **1.** [provenance] from ; **revenir de Paris** to come back ou return from Paris ; **il est sorti de la maison** he left the house, he went out of the house - **2.** [avec à] : **de... à** from... ou ; **de Paris à Tokyo** from Paris to Tokyo ; **de dix heures à midi** from ten o'clock to ou till midday ; **il y avait de quinze à vingt mille spectateurs** there were between fifteen and twenty thousand spectators - **3.** [appartenance] of ; **la porte du salon** the door of the sitting room, the sitting room door ; **le frère de Pierre** Pierre's brother - **4.** [indique la détermination, la qualité] : **un verre d'eau** a glass of water ; **un peignoir de soie** a silk dressing gown ; **un appartement de 60 m²** a flat 60 metres square ; **un bébé de trois jours** a three-day-old baby ; **une ville de 500 000 habitants** a town with ou of 500,000 inhabitants ; **le train de 9 h 30** the 9.30 train. ◇ *art partitif* **1.** [dans une phrase affirmative] some ; **je voudrais du vin/du lait** I'd like (some) wine/(some) milk ; **boire de l'eau** to drink (some) water ; **acheter des légumes** to buy some vegetables - **2.** [dans une interrogation ou une négation] any ; **ils n'ont pas d'enfants** they don't have any children, they have no children ; **avez-vous du pain?** do you have any bread?, have you got any bread? ; **voulez-vous du thé?** would you like some tea?

dé [de] *nm* **1.** [à jouer] dice, die - **2.** COUT : **dé (à coudre)** thimble.

DEA (abr de **diplôme d'études approfondies**) *nm* postgraduate diploma.

dealer¹ [dile] *vt* to deal.

dealer² [dilœr] *nm fam* dealer.

déambuler [3] [deɑ̃byle] *vi* to stroll (around).

débâcle [debɑkl] *nf* [débandade] rout ; *fig* collapse.

déballer [3] [debale] *vt* to unpack ; *fam fig* to pour out.

débandade [debɑ̃dad] *nf* dispersal.

débarbouiller [3] [debarbuje] *vt* : **débarbouiller qqn** to wash sb's face. ➡ **se débarbouiller** *vp* to wash one's face.

débarcadère [debarkadɛr] *nm* landing stage.

débardeur [debardœr] *nm* **1.** [ouvrier] docker - **2.** [vêtement] slipover.

débarquement [debarkəmɑ̃] *nm* [de marchandises] unloading.

débarquer [3] [debarke] ◇ *vt* [marchandises] to unload ; [passagers & MIL] to land. ◇ *vi* **1.** [d'un bateau] to disembark - **2.** MIL to land - **3.** *fam* [arriver à l'improviste] to turn up ; *fig* to know nothing.

débarras [debara] *nm* junk room ; **bon débarras!** *fig* good riddance!

débarrasser [3] [debarase] *vt* **1.** [pièce] to clear up ; [table] to clear - **2.** [ôter] : **débarrasser qqn de qqch** to take sthg from sb. ➡ **se débarrasser** *vp* : **se débarrasser de** to get rid of.

débat [deba] *nm* debate.

débattre [83] [debatr] *vt* to debate, to discuss. ➡ **se débattre** *vp* to struggle.

débattu, e [debaty] *pp* ▶ **débattre**.

débauche [deboʃ] *nf* debauchery.

débaucher [3] [deboʃe] *vt* **1.** [corrompre] to debauch, to corrupt - **2.** [licencier] to make redundant *UK*, to lay off *US*.

débile [debil] ◇ *nmf* **1.** [attardé] retarded person ; **débile mental** mentally retarded person - **2.** *fam* [idiot] moron. ◇ *adj fam* stupid.

débit [debi] *nm* **1.** [de marchandises] (retail) sale - **2.** [magasin] : **débit de boissons** bar ; **débit de tabac** tobacconist's *UK*, tobacco shop *US* - **3.** [coupe] sawing up, cutting up - **4.** [de liquide] (rate of) flow - **5.** [élocution] delivery - **6.** FIN debit ; **avoir un débit de 100 euros** to be 100 euros overdrawn.

débiter [3] [debite] *vt* **1.** [marchandises] to sell - **2.** [arbre] to saw up ; [viande] to cut up - **3.** [suj: robinet] to have a flow of - **4.** *fam fig* [prononcer] to spout - **5.** FIN to debit.

débiteur, trice [debitœr, tris] ◇ *adj* **1.** [personne] debtor (avant n) - **2.** FIN debit (avant n), in the red. ◇ *nm, f* debtor.

déblayer [11] [debleje] *vt* [dégager] to clear ; **déblayer le terrain** *fig* to clear the ground.

débloquer [3] [debloke] ◇ *vt* **1.** [machine] to get going again - **2.** [crédit] to release - **3.** [compte, salaires, prix] to unfreeze. ◇ *vi fam* to talk rubbish *UK*.

déboires [debwar] *nmpl* **1.** [déceptions] disappointments - **2.** [échecs] setbacks - **3.** [ennuis] trouble *(U)*, problems.

déboiser [3] [debwaze] *vt* [région] to deforest ; [terrain] to clear (of trees).

déboîter [3] [debwate] ◇ *vt* **1.** [objet] to dislodge - **2.** [membre] to dislocate.

◇ *vi* AUTO to pull out. ◆ **se déboîter** *vp* **1.** [se démonter] to come apart ; [porte] to come off its hinges - **2.** [membre] to dislocate.

débonnaire [debɔnɛr] *adj* good-natured, easy-going.

déborder [3] [debɔrde] *vi* [fleuve, liquide] to overflow ; *fig* to flood ; **déborder de** [vie, joie] to be bubbling with.

débouché [debuʃe] *nm* **1.** [issue] end - **2.** (*gén pl*) COMM outlet - **3.** [de carrière] prospect, opening.

déboucher [3] [debuʃe] ◇ *vt* **1.** [bouteille] to open - **2.** [conduite, nez] to unblock. ◇ *vi* : **déboucher sur** [arriver] to open out into ; *fig* to lead to, to achieve.

débourser [3] [deburse] *vt* to pay out.

debout [dəbu] *adv* [gén] : **être debout** [sur ses pieds] to be standing (up) ; [réveillé] to be up ; [objet] to be standing up ou upright ; **mettre qqch debout** to stand sthg up ; **se mettre debout** to stand up ; **debout!** get up!, on your feet! ; **tenir debout** [bâtiment] to remain standing ; [argument] to stand up ; **il ne tient pas debout** he's asleep on his feet.

déboutonner [3] [debutɔne] *vt* to unbutton, to undo.

débraillé, e [debraje] *adj* dishevelled UK, disheveled US.

débrayage [debrɛjaʒ] *nm* [arrêt de travail] stoppage.

débrayer [11] [debreje] *vi* AUTO to disengage the clutch, to declutch UK.

débris [debri] ◇ *nm* piece, fragment. ◇ *nmpl* [restes] leftovers.

débrouillard, e [debrujar, ard] *fam adj* resourceful.

débrouiller [3] [debruje] *vt* **1.** [démêler] to untangle - **2.** *fig* [résoudre] to unravel, to solve. ◆ **se débrouiller** *vp* : **se débrouiller (pour faire qqch)** to manage (to do sthg) ; **se débrouiller en anglais/math** to get by in English/maths ; **débrouille-toi!** you'll have to sort it out (by) yourself!

débroussailler [3] [debrusaje] *vt* [terrain] to clear ; *fig* to do the groundwork for.

débuguer [3] [debyge] *vt* to debug

début [deby] *nm* beginning, start ; **au début** at the start ou beginning ; **au début de** at the beginning of ; **dès le début** (right) from the start.

débutant, e [debytã, ãt] *nm, f* beginner.

débuter [3] [debyte] *vi* **1.** [commencer] : **débuter (par)** to begin (with), to start (with) - **2.** [faire ses débuts] to start out.

déca [deka] *nm fam* decaff.

deçà [dəsa] ◆ **deçà delà** *loc adv* here and

there. ◆ **en deçà de** *loc prép* **1.** [de ce côté-ci de] on this side of - **2.** [en dessous de] short of.

décacheter [27] [dekaʃte] *vt* to open.

décadence [dekadãs] *nf* **1.** [déclin] decline - **2.** [débauche] decadence.

décadent, e [dekadã, ãt] *adj* decadent.

décaféiné, e [dekafeine] *adj* decaffeinated. ◆ **décaféiné** *nm* decaffeinated coffee.

décalage [dekalaʒ] *nm* gap ; *fig* gulf, discrepancy ; **décalage horaire** [entre zones] time difference ; [après un vol] jet lag.

décaler [3] [dekale] *vt* **1.** [dans le temps - avancer] to bring forward ; [- retarder] to put back - **2.** [dans l'espace] to move, to shift.

décalquer [3] [dekalke] *vt* to trace.

décamper [3] [dekãpe] *vi fam* to clear off.

décapant, e [dekapã, ãt] *adj* **1.** [nettoyant] stripping - **2.** *fig* [incisif] cutting, caustic. ◆ **décapant** *nm* (paint) stripper.

décaper [3] [dekape] *vt* to strip, to sand.

décapiter [3] [dekapite] *vt* **1.** [personne - volontairement] to behead ; [- accidentellement] to decapitate - **2.** [arbre] to cut the top off - **3.** *fig* [organisation, parti] to remove the leader ou leaders of.

décapotable [dekapɔtabl] *nf & adj* convertible.

décapsuler [3] [dekapsyle] *vt* to take the top off, to open.

décapsuleur [dekapsylœr] *nm* bottle opener.

décédé, e [desede] *adj* deceased.

décéder [18] [desede] *vi* to die.

déceler [25] [desle] *vt* [repérer] to detect.

décembre [desãbr] *nm* December ; *voir aussi* septembre.

décemment [desamã] *adv* **1.** [convenablement] properly - **2.** [raisonnablement] reasonably.

décence [desãs] *nf* decency.

décennie [deseni] *nf* decade.

décent, e [desã, ãt] *adj* decent.

décentralisation [desãtralizasjɔ̃] *nf* decentralization.

décentrer [3] [desãtre] *vt* to move off-centre UK ou off-center US.

déception [desɛpsjɔ̃] *nf* disappointment.

décerner [3] [deserne] *vt* : **décerner qqch à** to award sthg to.

décès [desɛ] *nm* death.

décevant, e [desəvã, ãt] *adj* disappointing.

décevoir [52] [desəvwar] *vt* to disappoint.

déchaîné, e [deʃene] *adj* **1.** [vent, mer] stormy, wild - **2.** [personne] wild.

déchaîner [4] [defene] vt [passion] to unleash ; [rires] to cause an outburst of. ➤ **se déchaîner** vp **1.** [éléments naturels] to erupt - **2.** [personne] to fly into a rage.

déchanter [3] [defɑ̃te] vi to become disillusioned.

décharge [defarʒ] nf **1.** DR discharge - **2.** ÉLECTR discharge ; **décharge électrique** electric UK ou electrical US shock - **3.** [dépotoir] rubbish tip UK ou dump UK, garbage dump US.

déchargement [defarʒəmɑ̃] nm unloading.

décharger [17] [defarʒe] vt **1.** [véhicule, marchandises] to unload - **2.** [arme - tirer] to fire, to discharge ; [- enlever la charge de] to unload - **3.** [soulager - cœur] to unburden ; [- conscience] to salve ; [- colère] to vent - **4.** [libérer] : **décharger qqn de** to release sb from.

décharné, e [defarne] adj [maigre] emaciated.

déchausser [3] [defose] vt : **déchausser qqn** to take sb's shoes off. ➤ **se déchausser** vp **1.** [personne] to take one's shoes off - **2.** [dent] to come loose.

déchéance [defeɑ̃s] nf [déclin] degeneration, decline.

déchet [defɛ] nm [de matériau] scrap. ➤ **déchets** nmpl refuse (U), waste (U).

déchiffrer [3] [defifre] vt **1.** [inscription, hiéroglyphes] to decipher ; [énigme] to unravel - **2.** MUS to sight-read.

déchiqueter [27] [defikte] vt to tear to shreds.

déchirant, e [defirɑ̃, ɑ̃t] adj heartrending.

déchirement [defirmɑ̃] nm [souffrance morale] heartbreak, distress.

déchirer [3] [defire] vt [papier, tissu] to tear up, to rip up. ➤ **se déchirer** vp **1.** [personnes] to tear each other apart - **2.** [matériau, muscle] to tear.

déchirure [defiryr] nf tear ; fig wrench ; **déchirure musculaire** MÉD torn muscle.

déchu, e [defy] adj **1.** [homme, ange] fallen ; [souverain] deposed - **2.** DR : **être déchu de** to be deprived of.

décibel [desibɛl] nm decibel.

décidé, e [deside] adj **1.** [résolu] determined - **2.** [arrêté] settled.

décidément [desidemɑ̃] adv really.

décider [3] [deside] vt **1.** [prendre une décision] : **décider (de faire qqch)** to decide (to do sthg) - **2.** [convaincre] : **décider qqn à faire qqch** to persuade sb to do sthg. ➤ **se décider** vp **1.** [personne] : **se décider (à faire qqch)** to make up one's mind (to do sthg) - **2.** [choisir] : **se décider pour** to decide on, to settle on.

décilitre [desilitr] nm decilitre.

décimal, e, aux [desimal, o] adj decimal. ➤ **décimale** nf decimal.

décimer [3] [desime] vt to decimate.

décimètre [desimɛtr] nm **1.** [dixième de mètre] decimetre - **2.** [règle] ruler ; **double décimètre** ≃ foot rule.

décisif, ive [desizif, iv] adj decisive.

décision [desizjɔ̃] nf decision.

décisionnaire [desizjɔnɛr] nmf decisionmaker.

déclamer [3] [deklame] vt to declaim.

déclaration [deklarasjɔ̃] nf **1.** [orale] declaration, announcement - **2.** [écrite] report, declaration ; [d'assurance] claim ; **déclaration de naissance/de décès** registration of birth/death ; **déclaration d'impôts** tax return ; **déclaration de revenus** statement of income.

déclarer [3] [deklare] vt **1.** [annoncer] to declare - **2.** [signaler] to report ; **rien à déclarer** nothing to declare ; **déclarer une naissance** to register a birth. ➤ **se déclarer** vp **1.** [se prononcer] : **se déclarer pour/contre qqch** to come out in favour of/against sthg - **2.** [se manifester] to break out.

déclenchement [deklɑ̃fmɑ̃] nm [de mécanisme] activating, setting off ; fig launching.

déclencher [3] [deklɑ̃fe] vt [mécanisme] to activate, to set off ; fig to launch. ➤ **se déclencher** vp [mécanisme] to go off, to be activated ; fig to be triggered off.

déclic [deklik] nm **1.** [mécanisme] trigger - **2.** [bruit] click.

déclin [deklɛ̃] nm **1.** [de civilisation, population, santé] decline - **2.** [fin] close.

déclinaison [deklinɛzɔ̃] nf GRAMM declension.

décliner [3] [dekline] ◇ vi [santé, population, popularité] to decline. ◇ vt **1.** [offre, honneur] to decline - **2.** GRAMM to decline ; fig [gamme de produits] to develop.

décoder [3] [dekɔde] vt to decode.

décoiffer [3] [dekwafe] vt [cheveux] to mess up.

décoincer [16] [dekwɛ̃se] vt **1.** [chose] to loosen ; [mécanisme] to unjam - **2.** fam [personne] to loosen up.

décollage [dekɔlaʒ] nm litt & fig takeoff.

décoller [3] [dekɔle] ◇ vt [étiquette, timbre] to unstick ; [papier peint] to strip (off). ◇ vi litt & fig to take off.

décolleté, e [dekɔlte] adj [vêtement] lowcut. ➤ **décolleté** nm **1.** [de personne] neck and shoulders pl - **2.** [de vêtement] neckline, neck.

décolonisation [dekɔlɔnizasjɔ̃] *nf* decolonization.

décolorer [3] [dekɔlɔre] *vt* [par décolorant] to bleach, to lighten ; [par usure] to fade.

décombres [dekɔ̃br] *nmpl* debris (U).

décommander [3] [dekɔmɑ̃de] *vt* to cancel.

décomposé, e [dekɔ̃poze] *adj* 1. [pourri] decomposed - 2. [visage] haggard ; [personne] in shock.

décomposer [3] [dekɔ̃poze] *vt* [gén] : **décomposer (en)** to break down (into). ➤ **se décomposer** *vp* 1. [se putréfier] to rot, to decompose - 2. [se diviser] : **se décomposer en** to be broken down into.

décomposition [dekɔ̃pozisjɔ̃] *nf* 1. [putréfaction] decomposition - 2. *fig* [analyse] breaking down, analysis.

décompresser [4] [dekɔ̃prese] ◇ *vt* TECHNOL to decompress, to uncompress. ◇ *vi* to unwind.

décompression [dekɔ̃presjɔ̃] *nf* decompression.

décompte [dekɔ̃t] *nm* [calcul] breakdown (of an amount).

déconcentrer [3] [dekɔ̃sɑ̃tre] *vt* [distraire] to distract. ➤ **se déconcentrer** *vp* to be distracted.

déconcerter [3] [dekɔ̃sɛrte] *vt* to disconcert.

déconfiture [dekɔ̃fityr] *nf* collapse, ruin.

décongeler [25] [dekɔ̃ʒle] *vt* to defrost.

décongestionner [3] [dekɔ̃ʒɛstjɔne] *vt* to relieve congestion in.

déconnecter [4] [dekɔnɛkte] *vt* to disconnect.

déconseillé, e [dekɔ̃seje] *adj* : **c'est fortement déconseillé** it's extremely inadvisable.

déconseiller [4] [dekɔ̃seje] *vt* : **déconseiller qqch à qqn** to advise sb against sthg ; **déconseiller à qqn de faire qqch** to advise sb against doing sthg.

déconsidérer [18] [dekɔ̃sidere] *vt* to discredit.

décontaminer [3] [dekɔ̃tamine] *vt* to decontaminate.

décontenancer [16] [dekɔ̃tnɑ̃se] *vt* to put out.

décontracté, e [dekɔ̃trakte] *adj* 1. [muscle] relaxed - 2. [détendu] casual, laid-back.

décontracter [3] [dekɔ̃trakte] *vt* to relax. ➤ **se décontracter** *vp* to relax.

décor [dekɔr] *nm* 1. [cadre] scenery - 2. THÉÂTRE scenery (U) ; CINÉ sets *pl*, décor.

décorateur, trice [dekɔratœr, tris] *nm, f* CINÉ & THÉÂTRE designer ; **décorateur d'intérieur** interior decorator.

décoratif, ive [dekɔratif, iv] *adj* decorative.

décoration [dekɔrasjɔ̃] *nf* decoration.

décorer [3] [dekɔre] *vt* to decorate.

décortiquer [3] [dekɔrtike] *vt* [noix] to shell ; [graine] to husk ; *fig* to analyse UK ou analyze US in minute detail.

découcher [3] [dekuʃe] *vi* to stay out all night.

découdre [86] [dekudr] *vt* COUT to unpick.

découler [3] [dekule] *vi* : **découler de** to follow from.

découpage [dekupaʒ] *nm* 1. [action] cutting out ; [résultat] paper cutout - 2. ADMIN : **découpage (électoral)** division into constituencies.

découper [3] [dekupe] *vt* 1. [couper] to cut up - 2. *fig* [diviser] to cut out.

découpure [dekupyr] *nf* [bord] indentations *pl*, jagged outline.

découragement [dekuraʒmɑ̃] *nm* discouragement.

décourager [17] [dekuraʒe] *vt* to discourage ; **décourager qqn de qqch** to put sb off sthg ; **décourager qqn de faire qqch** to discourage sb from doing sthg. ➤ **se décourager** *vp* to lose heart.

décousu, e [dekuzy] ◇ *pp* ▶ **découdre**. ◇ *adj fig* [conversation] disjointed.

découvert, e [dekuvɛr, ɛrt] ◇ *pp* ▶ **découvrir**. ◇ *adj* [tête] bare ; [terrain] exposed. ◇ **découvert** *nm* BANQUE overdraft ; **être à découvert (de 1 000 euros)** to be (1,000 euros) overdrawn. ➤ **découverte** *nf* discovery ; **aller à la découverte de** to explore.

découvrir [34] [dekuvrir] *vt* 1. [trouver, surprendre] to discover - 2. [ôter ce qui couvre, mettre à jour] to uncover.

décrasser [3] [dekrase] *vt* to scrub.

décret [dekre] *nm* decree.

décréter [18] [dekrete] *vt* [décider] : **décréter que** to decide that.

décrire [99] [dekrir] *vt* to describe.

décrit, e [dekri, it] *pp* ▶ **décrire**.

décrocher [3] [dekrɔʃe] ◇ *vt* 1. [enlever] to take down - 2. [téléphone] to pick up - 3. *fam* [obtenir] to land. ◇ *vi fam* [abandonner] to drop out.

décroître [94] [dekrwatr] *vi* to decrease, to diminish ; [jours] to get shorter.

décrypter [3] [dekripte] *vt* to decipher.

déçu, e [desy] ◇ *pp* ▶ **décevoir**. ◇ *adj* disappointed.

déculotter [3] [dekylɔte] *vt* : **déculotter qqn** to take sb's trousers off.

dédaigner [4] [dedeɲe] *vt* 1. [mépriser - personne] to despise ; [- conseils, injures] to scorn - **2.** [refuser] : **dédaigner de faire qqch** *sout* to disdain to do sthg ; **ne pas dédaigner qqch/de faire qqch** not to be above sthg/ above doing sthg.

dédaigneux, euse [dedɛɲø, øz] *adj* disdainful.

dédain [dedɛ̃] *nm* disdain, contempt.

dédale [dedal] *nm litt & fig* maze.

dedans [dədɑ̃] *adv & nm* inside. ➡ **de dedans** *loc adv* from inside, from within. ➡ **en dedans** *loc adv* inside, within. ➡ **en dedans de** *loc prép* inside, within ; *voir aussi* **là-dedans**.

dédicace [dedikas] *nf* dedication.

dédicacer [16] [dedikase] *vt* : **dédicacer qqch (à qqn)** to sign ou autograph sthg (for sb).

dédier [9] [dedje] *vt* : **dédier qqch (à qqn/à qqch)** to dedicate sthg (to sb/to sthg).

dédire [103] [dedir] ➡ **se dédire** *vp sout* to go back on one's word.

dédommagement [dedɔmaʒmɑ̃] *nm* compensation.

dédommager [17] [dedɔmaʒe] *vt* **1.** [indemniser] to compensate - **2.** *fig* [remercier] to repay.

dédouaner [3] [dedwane] *vt* [marchandises] to clear through customs.

dédoubler [3] [deduble] .*vt* to halve, to split ; [fil] to separate.

déduction [dedyksjɔ̃] *nf* deduction.

déduire [98] [dedɥir] *vt* : **déduire qqch (de)** [ôter] to deduct sthg (from) ; [conclure] to deduce (from).

déduit, e [dedɥi, it] *pp* ➡ **déduire.**

déesse [deɛs] *nf* goddess.

défaillance [defajɑ̃s] *nf* **1.** [incapacité - de machine] failure ; [- de personne, organisation] weakness - **2.** [malaise] blackout, fainting fit.

défaillant, e [defajɑ̃, ɑ̃t] *adj* [faible] failing.

défaillir [47] [defajir] *vi* [s'évanouir] to faint.

défaire [109] [defɛr] *vt* [détacher] to undo ; [valise] to unpack ; [lit] to strip. ➡ **se défaire** *vp* **1.** [ne pas tenir] to come undone - **2.** *sout* [se séparer] : **se défaire de** to get rid of.

défait, e [defɛ, ɛt] <> *pp* ➡ **défaire.** <> *adj fig* [épuisé] haggard. ➡ **défaite** *nf* defeat.

défaitiste [defetist] *nmf & adj* defeatist.

défaut [defo] *nm* **1.** [imperfection - gén] flaw ; [- de personne] fault, shortcoming ; **défaut de fabrication** manufacturing fault - **2.** [manque] lack ; **à défaut de** for lack ou want of ; **l'eau fait (cruellement) défaut** there is a serious water shortage.

défaveur [defavœr] *nf* disfavour *UK*, disfavor *US* ; **être en défaveur** to be out of favour *UK* ou favor *US* ; **tomber en défaveur** to fall out of favour *UK* ou favor *US*.

défavorable [defavɔrabl] *adj* unfavourable *UK*, unfavorable *US*.

défavorisé, e [defavɔrize] *adj* disadvantaged, underprivileged.

défavoriser [3] [defavɔrize] *vt* to handicap, to penalize.

défection [defɛksjɔ̃] *nf* **1.** [absence] absence - **2.** [abandon] defection.

défectueux, euse [defɛktɥø, øz] *adj* faulty, defective.

défendeur, eresse [defɑ̃dœr, rɛs] *nm, f* defendant.

défendre [73] [defɑ̃dr] *vt* **1.** [personne, opinion, client] to defend - **2.** [interdire] to forbid ; **défendre qqch à qqn** to forbid sb sthg ; **défendre à qqn de faire qqch** to forbid sb to do sthg ; **défendre que qqn fasse qqch** to forbid sb to do sthg. ➡ **se défendre** *vp* **1.** [se battre, se justifier] to defend o.s. - **2.** [nier] : **se défendre de faire qqch** to deny doing sthg - **3.** [thèse] to stand up.

défendu, e [defɑ̃dy] <> *pp* ➡ **défendre.** <> *adj* : **il est défendu de jouer au ballon** 'no ball games'.

défense [defɑ̃s] *nf* **1.** [d'éléphant] tusk - **2.** [interdiction] prohibition, ban ; **'défense de fumer/de stationner/d'entrer'** 'no smoking/parking/entry' ; **'défense d'afficher'** 'stick *UK* ou post no bills' - **3.** [protection] defence *UK*, defense *US* ; **prendre la défense de** to stand up for ; **légitime défense** *DR* self-defence *UK*, self-defense *US*.

défenseur [defɑ̃sœr] *nm* [partisan] champion.

défensif, ive [defɑ̃sif, iv] *adj* defensive. ➡ **défensive** *nf* : **être sur la défensive** to be on the defensive.

déférence [deferɑ̃s] *nf* deference.

déferlement [defɛrləmɑ̃] *nm* [de vagues] breaking ; *fig* surge, upsurge.

déferler [3] [defɛrle] *vi* [vagues] to break ; *fig* to surge.

défi [defi] *nm* challenge.

défiance [defjɑ̃s] *nf* distrust, mistrust.

déficience [defisjɑ̃s] *nf* deficiency.

déficit [defisit] *nm* FIN deficit ; **être en déficit** to be in deficit.

déficitaire [defisiter] *adj* in deficit.

défier [9] [defje] *vt* [braver] : **défier qqn de faire qqch** to defy sb to do sthg.

défigurer [3] [defigyre] *vt* **1.** [blesser] to disfigure - **2.** [enlaidir] to deface.

défilé [defile] *nm* **1.** [parade] parade - **2.** [couloir] defile, narrow pass.

défiler

défiler [3] [defile] vi **1.** [dans une parade] to march past - **2.** [se succéder] to pass. ➤ **se défiler** vp fam to back out.

défini, e [defini] adj **1.** [précis] clear, precise - **2.** GRAMM definite.

définir [32] [definir] vt to define.

définitif, ive [definitif, iv] adj definitive, final. ➤ **en définitive** loc adv in the end.

définition [definisjɔ̃] nf definition ; **à haute définition** high-definition.

définitivement [definitivmɑ̃] adv for good, permanently.

défiscaliser [3] [defiskalize] vt exempt from taxation.

déflationniste [deflasjɔnist] adj deflationary, deflationist.

défoncer [16] [defɔ̃se] vt [caisse, porte] to smash in ; [route] to break up ; [mur] to smash down ; [chaise] to break.

déformation [defɔrmasjɔ̃] nf **1.** [d'objet, de théorie] distortion - **2.** MÉD deformity ; **déformation professionnelle** mental conditioning caused by one's job.

déformer [3] [defɔrme] vt to distort. ➤ **se déformer** vp [changer de forme] to be distorted, to be deformed ; [se courber] to bend.

défouler [3] [defule] vt fam to unwind. ➤ **se défouler** vp fam to let off steam, to unwind.

défricher [3] [defriʃe] vt [terrain] to clear ; fig [question] to do the groundwork for.

défunt, e [defœ̃, œ̃t] ◇ adj [décédé] late. ◇ nm, f deceased.

dégagé, e [degaʒe] adj **1.** [ciel, vue] clear ; [partie du corps] bare - **2.** [désinvolte] casual, airy - **3.** [libre] : **dégagé de** free from.

dégager [17] [degaʒe] ◇ vt **1.** [odeur] to produce, to give off - **2.** [délivrer - blessé] to free, to extricate - **3.** [bénéfice] to show - **4.** [pièce] to clear - **5.** [libérer] : **dégager qqn de** to release sb from. ◇ vi fam [partir] to clear off. ➤ **se dégager** vp **1.** [se délivrer] : **se dégager de qqch** to free o.s. from sthg ; fig to get out of sthg - **2.** [émaner] to be given off - **3.** [émerger] to emerge.

dégarnir [32] [degarnir] vt to strip, to clear. ➤ **se dégarnir** vp [vitrine] to be cleared ; [arbre] to lose its leaves ; **sa tête se dégarnit, il se dégarnit** he's going bald.

dégât [dega] nm litt & fig damage (U) ; **dégâts matériels** structural damage ; **faire des dégâts** to cause damage.

dégel [deʒɛl] nm [fonte des glaces] thaw.

dégeler [25] [deʒle] ◇ vt [produit surgelé] to thaw. ◇ vi to thaw.

dégénéré, e [deʒenere] adj & nm, f degenerate.

dégénérer [18] [deʒenere] vi to degenerate ; **dégénérer en** to degenerate into.

dégivrer [3] [deʒivre] vt [pare-brise] to de-ice ; [réfrigérateur] to defrost.

dégonfler [3] [degɔ̃fle] ◇ vt to deflate, to let down UK. ◇ vi to go down. ➤ **se dégonfler** vp **1.** [objet] to go down - **2.** fam [personne] to chicken out.

dégouliner [3] [deguline] vi to trickle.

dégourdi, e [degurdi] adj clever.

dégourdir [32] [degurdir] vt **1.** [membres ankylosés] to restore the circulation to - **2.** fig [déniaiser] : **dégourdir qqn** to teach sb a thing or two. ➤ **se dégourdir** vp **1.** [membres] : **se dégourdir les jambes** to stretch one's legs - **2.** fig [acquérir de l'aisance] to learn a thing or two.

dégoût [degu] nm disgust, distaste.

dégoûtant, e [degutɑ̃, ɑ̃t] adj **1.** [sale] filthy, disgusting - **2.** [révoltant, grossier] disgusting.

dégoûter [3] [degute] vt to disgust.

dégoutter [3] [degute] vi : **dégoutter (de qqch)** to drip (with sthg).

dégradé, e [degrade] adj [couleur] shading off. ➤ **dégradé** nm gradation ; **un dégradé de bleu** a blue shading. ➤ **en dégradé** loc adv [cheveux] layered.

dégrader [3] [degrade] vt **1.** [officier] to degrade - **2.** [abîmer - bâtiment] to damage - **3.** fig [avilir] to degrade, to debase. ➤ **se dégrader** vp **1.** [bâtiment, santé] to deteriorate - **2.** fig [personne] to degrade o.s.

dégrafer [3] [degrafe] vt to undo, to unfasten.

dégraissage [degrɛsaʒ] nm **1.** [de vêtement] dry-cleaning - **2.** [de personnel] trimming, cutting back.

degré [dəgre] nm [gén] degree ; **degrés centigrades** ou **Celsius** degrees centigrade ou Celsius ; **prendre qqn/qqch au premier degré** to take sb/sthg at face value.

dégressif, ive [degresif, iv] adj : **tarif dégressif** decreasing price scale.

dégringoler [3] [degrɛ̃gɔle] fam vi [tomber] to tumble ; fig to crash.

déguenillé, e [degənije] adj ragged.

déguerpir [32] [degɛrpir] vi to clear off.

dégueulasse [degœlas] tfam ◇ adj **1.** [très sale, grossier] filthy - **2.** [très mauvais - plat] disgusting ; [- temps] lousy. ◇ nmf scum (U).

dégueuler [5] [degœle] vi fam to throw up.

déguisement [degizmɑ̃] nm disguise ; [pour bal masqué] fancy dress.

déguiser [3] [degize] vt to disguise. ➤ **se**

déguiser *vp* : **se déguiser en** [pour tromper] to disguise o.s. as ; [pour s'amuser] to dress up as.

dégustation [degystasjɔ̃] *nf* tasting, sampling ; **dégustation de vin** wine tasting.

déguster [3] [degyste] ◇ *vt* [savourer] to taste, to sample. ◇ *vi fam* [subir] : **il va déguster!** he'll be in for it!

déhancher [3] [deɑ̃ʃe] ◆ **se déhancher** *vp* [en marchant] to swing one's hips ; [en restant immobile] to put all one's weight on one leg.

dehors [dəɔr] ◇ *adv* outside ; **aller dehors** to go outside ; **dormir dehors** to sleep out of doors, to sleep out ; **jeter** *ou* **mettre qqn dehors** to throw sb out. ◇ *nm* outside. ◇ *nmpl* : **les dehors** [les apparences] appearances. ◆ **en dehors** *loc adv* outside, outwards, outward *US*. ◆ **en dehors de** *loc prép* [excepté] apart from.

déjà [deʒa] *adv* **1.** [dès cet instant] already - **2.** [précédemment] already, before - **3.** [au fait] : **quel est ton nom déjà?** what did you say your name was? - **4.** [renforce une affirmation] : **ce n'est déjà pas si mal** that's not bad at all.

déjeuner [5] [deʒœne] ◇ *vi* **1.** [le matin] to have breakfast - **2.** [à midi] to have lunch. ◇ *nm* **1.** [repas de midi] lunch - **2.** *Québec* [dîner] dinner.

déjouer [6] [deʒwe] *vt* to frustrate ; **déjouer la surveillance de qqn** to elude sb's surveillance.

delà [dəla] ▶ **au-delà.**

délabré, e [delabre] *adj* ruined.

délacer [16] [delase] *vt* to unlace, to undo.

délai [delɛ] *nm* **1.** [temps accordé] period ; **sans délai** immediately, without delay ; **délai de livraison** delivery time, lead time - **2.** [sursis] extension (of deadline).

délaisser [4] [delese] *vt* **1.** [abandonner] to leave - **2.** [négliger] to neglect.

délassement [delasmɑ̃] *nm* relaxation.

délasser [3] [delase] *vt* to refresh. ◆ **se délasser** *vp* to relax.

délation [delasjɔ̃] *nf* informing.

délavé, e [delave] *adj* faded.

délayer [11] [deleje] *vt* [diluer] : **délayer qqch dans qqch** to mix sthg with sthg.

délecter [4] [delɛkte] ◆ **se délecter** *vp* : **se délecter de qqch/à faire qqch** to delight in sthg/in doing sthg.

délégation [delegasjɔ̃] *nf* delegation ; **agir par délégation** to be delegated to act.

délégué, e [delege] ◇ *adj* [personne] delegated. ◇ *nm, f* [représentant] : **délégué (à)** delegate (to).

déléguer [18] [delege] *vt* : **déléguer qqn (à qqch)** to delegate sb (to sthg).

délester [3] [delɛste] *vt* **1.** [circulation routière] to set up a diversion on, to divert *UK*, to detour *US* - **2.** *fig & hum* [voler] : **délester qqn de qqch** to relieve sb of sthg.

délibération [deliberasjɔ̃] *nf* deliberation.

délibéré, e [delibere] *adj* **1.** [intentionnel] deliberate - **2.** [résolu] determined.

délibérer [18] [delibere] *vi* : **délibérer (de** *ou* **sur)** to deliberate (on *ou* over).

délicat, e [delika, at] *adj* **1.** [gén] delicate - **2.** [exigeant] fussy, difficult.

délicatement [delikatmɑ̃] *adv* delicately.

délicatesse [delikates] *nf* **1.** [gén] delicacy - **2.** [tact] delicacy, tact.

délice [delis] *nm* delight.

délicieux, euse [delisjø, øz] *adj* **1.** [savoureux] delicious - **2.** [agréable] delightful.

délié, e [delje] *adj* [doigts] nimble.

délier [9] [delje] *vt* to untie.

délimiter [3] [delimite] *vt* [frontière] to fix ; *fig* [question, domaine] to define, to demarcate.

délinquance [delɛ̃kɑ̃s] *nf* delinquency.

délinquant, e [delɛ̃kɑ̃, ɑ̃t] *nm, f* delinquent.

délirant, e [delirɑ̃, ɑ̃t] *adj* **1.** MÉD delirious - **2.** [extravagant] frenzied - **3.** *fam* [extraordinaire] crazy.

délire [delir] *nm* MÉD delirium ; **en délire** *fig* frenzied.

délirer [3] [delire] *vi* MÉD to be *ou* become delirious ; *fam fig* to rave.

délit [deli] *nm* crime, offence *UK*, offense *US* ; **en flagrant délit** red-handed, in the act.

délivrance [delivrɑ̃s] *nf* **1.** [libération] freeing, release - **2.** [soulagement] relief - **3.** [accouchement] delivery.

délivrer [3] [delivre] *vt* **1.** [prisonnier] to free, to release - **2.** [pays] to deliver, to free ; **délivrer de** to free from ; *fig* to relieve from - **3.** [remettre] : **délivrer qqch (à qqn)** to issue sthg (to sb) - **4.** [marchandise] to deliver.

déloger [17] [delɔʒe] *vt* : **déloger (de)** to dislodge (from).

déloyal, e, aux [delwajal, o] *adj* **1.** [infidèle] disloyal - **2.** [malhonnête] unfair.

delta [dɛlta] *nm* delta.

deltaplane, delta-plane (*pl* delta-planes) [dɛltaplan] *nm* hang glider.

déluge [delyʒ] *nm* **1.** RELIG : **le Déluge** the Flood - **2.** [pluie] downpour, deluge ; **un déluge de** *fig* a flood of.

déluré, e [delyre] *adj* [malin] quick-witted ; *péj* [dévergondé] saucy.

démagogie [demagɔʒi] *nf* pandering to public opinion, demagogy.

demain [dəmɛ̃] <> *adv* **1.** [le jour suivant] tomorrow ; **demain matin** tomorrow morning - **2.** *fig* [plus tard] in the future. <> *nm* tomorrow ; **à demain!** see you tomorrow!

demande [dəmɑ̃d] *nf* **1.** [souhait] request - **2.** [démarche] proposal ; **demande en mariage** proposal of marriage - **3.** [candidature] application ; **demande d'emploi** job application ; **'demandes d'emploi'** 'situations wanted' - **4.** ÉCON demand.

demandé, e [dəmɑ̃de] *adj* in demand.

demander [3] [dəmɑ̃de] <> *vt* **1.** [réclamer, s'enquérir] to ask for ; **demander qqch à qqn** to ask sb for sthg ; [appeler] to call ; **on vous demande à la réception/au téléphone** you're wanted at reception/on the telephone - **3.** [désirer] to ask, to want ; **je ne demande pas mieux** I'd be only too pleased (to), I'd love to - **4.** [exiger] : **tu m'en demandes trop** you're asking too much of me - **5.** [nécessiter] to require. <> *vi* **1.** [réclamer] : **demander à qqn de faire qqch** to ask sb to do sthg ; **ne demander qu'à...** to be ready to... - **2.** [nécessiter] : **ce projet demande à être étudié** this project requires investigation ou needs investigating. **se demander** *vp* : **se demander (si)** to wonder (if ou whether).

demandeur, euse [dəmɑ̃dœr, øz] *nm, f* [solliciteur] : **demandeur d'asile** asylum-seeker ; **demandeur d'emploi** job-seeker.

démangeaison [demɑ̃ʒɛzɔ̃] *nf* [irritation] itch, itching *(U)* ; *fam fig* urge.

démanger [17] [demɑ̃ʒe] *vi* [gratter] to itch ; **ça me démange de...** *fig* I'm itching ou dying to...

démanteler [25] [demɑ̃tle] *vt* [construction] to demolish ; *fig* to break up.

démaquillant, e [demakijɑ̃, ɑ̃t] *adj* make-up-removing *(avant n)*. **démaquillant** *nm* make-up remover.

démaquiller [3] [demakije] *vt* to remove make-up from. **se démaquiller** *vp* to remove one's make-up.

démarche [demarʃ] *nf* **1.** [manière de marcher] gait, walk - **2.** [raisonnement] approach, method - **3.** [requête] step ; **faire les démarches pour faire qqch** to take the necessary steps to do sthg.

démarcheur, euse [demarʃœr, øz] *nm, f* [représentant] door-to-door salesman *(f saleswoman)*.

démarquer [3] [demarke] *vt* **1.** [solder] to mark down - **2.** SPORT not to mark. **se démarquer** *vp* **1.** SPORT to shake off one's marker - **2.** *fig* [se distinguer] : **se démarquer (de)** to distinguish o.s. (from).

démarrage [demaraʒ] *nm* starting, start ; **démarrage en côte** hill start.

démarrer [3] [demare] <> *vi* **1.** [véhicule] to start (up) ; [conducteur] to drive off - **2.** *fig* [affaire, projet] to get off the ground. <> *vt* **1.** [véhicule] to start (up) - **2.** *fam fig* [commencer] : **démarrer qqch** to get sthg going.

démarreur [demarœr] *nm* starter.

démasquer [3] [demaske] *vt* **1.** [personne] to unmask - **2.** *fig* [complot, plan] to unveil.

démêlant, e [demɛlɑ̃, ɑ̃t] *adj* conditioning *(avant n)*. **démêlant** *nm* conditioner.

démêlé [demele] *nm* quarrel ; **avoir des démêlés avec la justice** to get into trouble with the law.

démêler [4] [demele] *vt* [cheveux, fil] to untangle ; *fig* to unravel. **se démêler** *vp* : **se démêler de** *fig* to extricate o.s. from.

déménagement [demenaʒmɑ̃] *nm* removal.

déménager [17] [demenaʒe] <> *vt* to move. <> *vi* to move, to move house *US*.

déménageur [demenaʒœr] *nm* removal man *UK*, mover *US*.

démence [demɑ̃s] *nf* MÉD dementia ; [bêtise] madness.

démener [19] [demne] **se démener** *vp litt & fig* to struggle.

dément, e [demɑ̃, ɑ̃t] <> *adj* MÉD demented ; *fam* [extraordinaire, extravagant] crazy. <> *nm, f* demented person.

démenti [demɑ̃ti] *nm* denial.

démentiel, elle [demɑ̃sjɛl] *adj* MÉD demented ; *fam* [incroyable] crazy.

démentir [37] [demɑ̃tir] *vt* **1.** [réfuter] to deny - **2.** [contredire] to contradict.

démesure [deməzyr] *nf* excess, immoderation.

démettre [84] [demɛtr] *vt* **1.** MÉD to put out (of joint) - **2.** [congédier] : **démettre qqn de** to dismiss sb from. **se démettre** *vp* **1.** MÉD : **se démettre l'épaule** to put one's shoulder out (of joint) - **2.** [démissionner] : **se démettre de ses fonctions** to resign.

demeurant [dəmœrɑ̃] **au demeurant** *loc adv* all things considered.

demeure [dəmœr] *nf* sout [domicile, habitation] residence. **à demeure** *loc adv* permanently.

demeuré, e [dəmœre] <> *adj* simple, half-witted. <> *nm, f* half-wit.

demeurer [5] [dəmœre] *vi* **1.** *(v aux : être)* [habiter] to live - **2.** *(v aux : être)* [rester] to remain.

demi, e [dəmi] *adj* half ; **un kilo et demi** one and a half kilos ; **il est une heure et demie** it's half past one ; **à demi** half ;

dormir à demi to be nearly asleep ; **ouvrir à demi** to half-open ; **faire les choses à demi** to do things by halves. ➤ **demi** *nm* **1.** [bière] beer, ≃ half-pint *UK* - **2.** FOOTBALL midfielder. ➤ **demie** *nf* : **à la demie** on the half-hour.

demi-cercle [dəmisɛrkl] (*pl* **demi-cercles**) *nm* semicircle.

demi-douzaine [dəmiduzɛn] (*pl* **demi-douzaines**) *nf* half-dozen ; **une demi-douzaine (de)** half a dozen.

demi-finale [dəmifinal] (*pl* **demi-finales**) *nf* semifinal.

demi-frère [dəmifrɛr] (*pl* **demi-frères**) *nm* half-brother.

demi-gros [dəmigro] *nm* : **(commerce de) demi-gros** cash and carry.

demi-heure [dəmijœr] (*pl* **demi-heures**) *nf* half an hour, half-hour.

demi-journée [dəmiʒurne] (*pl* **demi-journées**) *nf* half a day, half-day.

démilitariser [3] [demilitarize] *vt* to demilitarize.

demi-litre [dəmilitr] (*pl* **demi-litres**) *nm* half a litre *UK* ou liter *US*, half-litre *UK*, half-liter *US*.

demi-mesure [dəmiməzyr] (*pl* **demi-mesures**) *nf* **1.** [quantité] half a measure - **2.** [compromis] half-measure.

demi-mot [dəmimo] ➤ **à demi-mot** *loc adv* : **comprendre à demi-mot** to understand without things having to be spelled out.

déminer [3] [demine] *vt* to clear of mines.

demi-pension [dəmipɑ̃sjɔ̃] (*pl* **demi-pensions**) *nf* **1.** [d'hôtel] half-board - **2.** [d'école] : **être en demi-pension** to take school dinners *pl*.

démis, e [demi, iz] *pp* ➤ **démettre**.

demi-sœur [dəmisœr] (*pl* **demi-sœurs**) *nf* half-sister.

démission [demisjɔ̃] *nf* resignation.

démissionner [3] [demisjɔne] *vi* [d'un emploi] to resign ; *fig* to give up.

demi-tarif [dəmitarif] (*pl* **demi-tarifs**) ◇ *adj* half-price. ◇ *nm* **1.** [tarification] half-fare - **2.** [billet] half-price ticket.

demi-tour [dəmitur] (*pl* **demi-tours**) *nm* [gén] half-turn - ; MIL about-turn ; **faire demi-tour** to turn back.

démocrate [demɔkrat] *nmf* democrat.

démocratie [demɔkrasi] *nf* democracy.

démocratique [demɔkratik] *adj* democratic.

démocratiser [3] [demɔkratize] *vt* to democratize.

démodé, e [demɔde] *adj* old-fashioned.

démographique [demɔgrafik] *adj* demographic.

demoiselle [dəmwazɛl] *nf* [jeune fille] maid ; **demoiselle d'honneur** bridesmaid.

démolir [32] [demɔlir] *vt* [gén] to demolish.

démolition [demɔlisjɔ̃] *nf* demolition.

démon [demɔ̃] *nm* [diable, personne] devil, demon ; **le démon** RELIG the Devil.

démoniaque [demɔnjak] *adj* [diabolique] diabolical.

démonstratif, ive [demɔ̃stratif, iv] *adj* [personne & GRAMM] demonstrative. ➤ **démonstratif** *nm* GRAMM demonstrative.

démonstration [demɔ̃strasjɔ̃] *nf* [gén] demonstration.

démonter [3] [demɔ̃te] *vt* **1.** [appareil] to dismantle, to take apart - **2.** [troubler] : **démonter qqn** to put sb out. ➤ **se démonter** *vp fam* to be put out.

démontrer [3] [demɔ̃tre] *vt* **1.** [prouver] to prove, to demonstrate - **2.** [témoigner de] to show, to demonstrate.

démoralisant, e [demɔralizɑ̃, ɑ̃t] *adj* demoralizing.

démoraliser [3] [demɔralize] *vt* to demoralize. ➤ **se démoraliser** *vp* to lose heart.

démordre [76] [demɔrdr] *vt* : **ne pas démordre de** to stick to.

démotiver [3] [demɔtive] *vt* to demotivate.

démouler [3] [demule] *vt* to turn out of a mould, to remove from a mould.

démunir [32] [demynir] *vt* to deprive. ➤ **se démunir** *vp* : **se démunir de** to part with.

dénaturer [3] [denatyre] *vt* **1.** [goût] to impair, to mar - **2.** TECHNOL to denature - **3.** [déformer] to distort.

dénégation [denegasjɔ̃] *nf* denial.

dénicher [3] [deniʃe] *vt* *fig* **1.** [personne] to flush out - **2.** *fam* [objet] to unearth.

dénigrer [3] [denigre] *vt* to denigrate, to run down.

dénivelé [denivle] *nm* difference in level ou height.

dénivellation [denivɛlasjɔ̃] *nf* **1.** [différence de niveau] difference in height ou level - **2.** [pente] slope.

dénombrer [3] [denɔ̃bre] *vt* [compter] to count ; [énumérer] to enumerate.

dénominateur [denɔminatœr] *nm* denominator.

dénomination [denɔminasjɔ̃] *nf* name.

dénommé, e [denɔme] *adj* : **un dénommé Robert** someone by the name of Robert.

dénoncer [16] [denɔ̃se] *vt* **1.** [gén] to

denounce ; **dénoncer qqn à qqn** to denounce sb to sb, to inform on sb - **2.** *fig* [trahir] to betray.

dénonciation [denɔ̃sjasjɔ̃] *nf* denunciation.

dénoter [3] [denɔte] *vt* to show, to indicate.

dénouement [denumɑ̃] *nm* **1.** [issue] outcome - **2.** [d'un film, d'un livre] denouement.

dénouer [6] [denwe] *vt* [nœud] to untie, to undo ; *fig* to unravel.

dénoyauter [3] [denwajote] *vt* [fruit] to stone *UK*, to pit *US*.

denrée [dɑ̃re] *nf* [produit] produce *(U)* ; **denrées alimentaires** foodstuffs.

dense [dɑ̃s] *adj* **1.** [gén] dense - **2.** [style] condensed.

densité [dɑ̃site] *nf* density.

dent [dɑ̃] *nf* **1.** [de personne, d'objet] tooth ; **faire ses dents** to cut one's teeth, to teethe ; **dent de lait** milk *UK* ou baby *US* tooth ; **dent de sagesse** wisdom tooth - **2.** GÉOGR peak.

dentaire [dɑ̃tɛr] *adj* dental.

dentelé, e [dɑ̃tle] *adj* serrated, jagged.

dentelle [dɑ̃tɛl] *nf* lace *(U)*.

dentier [dɑ̃tje] *nm* [dents] dentures *pl*.

dentifrice [dɑ̃tifris] *nm* toothpaste.

dentiste [dɑ̃tist] *nmf* dentist.

dentition [dɑ̃tisjɔ̃] *nf* teeth *pl*, dentition.

dénuder [3] [denyde] *vt* to leave bare ; [fil électrique] to strip.

dénué, e [denye] *adj sout* : **dénué de** devoid of.

dénuement [denymɑ̃] *nm* destitution *(U)*.

déodorant, e [deɔdɔrɑ̃, ɑ̃t] *adj* deodorant. ➡ **déodorant** *nm* deodorant.

déontologie [deɔ̃tɔlɔʒi] *nf* professional ethics *pl*.

dépannage [depanaʒ] *nm* repair ; **service de dépannage** AUTO breakdown service *UK*.

dépanner [3] [depane] *vt* **1.** [réparer] to repair, to fix - **2.** *fam* [aider] to bail out.

dépanneur, euse [depanœr, øz] *nm, f* repairman (*f* repairwoman). ➡ **dépanneuse** *nf* [véhicule] (breakdown) recovery vehicle *UK*, tow truck *US*, wrecker *US*.

dépareillé, e [depareje] *adj* [ensemble] non-matching ; [paire] odd.

départ [depar] *nm* **1.** [de personne] departure, leaving ; [de véhicule] departure ; **les grands départs** the holiday exodus *sg* - **2.** *fig* & SPORT start. ➡ **au départ** *loc adv* to start with.

départager [17] [departaʒe] *vt* **1.** [concurrents, opinions] to decide between - **2.** [séparer] to separate.

département [departəmɑ̃] *nm* **1.** [territoire] *territorial and administrative division of France* - **2.** [service] department.

départemental, e, aux [departəmɑ̃tal, o] *adj of a French département.* ➡ **départementale** *nf* secondary road, ≃ B road *UK*.

dépassé, e [depase] *adj* **1.** [périmé] old-fashioned - **2.** *fam* [déconcerté] : **dépassé par** overwhelmed by.

dépassement [depasmɑ̃] *nm* [en voiture] overtaking *UK*, passing *US*.

dépasser [3] [depase] ⋄ *vt* **1.** [doubler] to overtake, to pass *US* - **2.** [être plus grand que] to be taller than - **3.** [excéder] to exceed, to be more than - **4.** [durer plus longtemps que] : **dépasser une heure** to go on for more than an hour - **5.** [aller au-delà de] to exceed - **6.** [franchir] to pass. ⋄ *vi* : **dépasser (de)** to stick out (from).

dépayser [3] [depeize] *vt* **1.** [désorienter] to disorientate *UK*, to disorient *US* - **2.** [changer agréablement] to make a change of scene for.

dépecer [29] [depəse] *vt* **1.** [découper] to chop up - **2.** [déchiqueter] to tear apart.

dépêche [depɛʃ] *nf* dispatch.

dépêcher [4] [depeʃe] *vt sout* [envoyer] to dispatch. ➡ **se dépêcher** *vp* to hurry up ; **se dépêcher de faire qqch** to hurry to do sthg.

dépeindre [81] [depɛ̃dr] *vt* to depict, to describe.

dépeint, e [depɛ̃, ɛ̃t] *pp* ➤ **dépeindre**.

dépénaliser [3] [depenalize] *vt* to decriminalize.

dépendance [depɑ̃dɑ̃s] *nf* **1.** [de personne] dependence ; **être sous la dépendance de** to be dependent on - **2.** [à la drogue] dependency - **3.** [de bâtiment] outbuilding.

dépendre [73] [depɑ̃dr] *vi* **1.** [être soumis] : **dépendre de** to depend on ; **ça dépend** it depends - **2.** [appartenir] : **dépendre de** to belong to.

dépens [depɑ̃] *nmpl* DR costs ; **aux dépens de qqn** at sb's expense ; **je l'ai appris à mes dépens** I learned that to my cost.

dépense [depɑ̃s] *nf* **1.** [frais] expense - **2.** *fig* & FIN expenditure *(U)* ; **les dépenses publiques** public spending *(U)*.

dépenser [3] [depɑ̃se] *vt* **1.** [argent] to spend - **2.** *fig* [énergie] to expend. ➡ **se dépenser** *vp litt* & *fig* to exert o.s.

dépensier, ère [depɑ̃sje, ɛr] *adj* extravagant.

déperdition [deperdisjɔ̃] *nf* loss.

dépérir [32] [deperir] *vi* **1.** [personne] to waste away - **2.** [santé, affaire] to decline - **3.** [plante] to wither.

dépeupler [5] [depœple] vt **1.** [pays] to depopulate - **2.** [étang, rivière, forêt] to drive the wildlife from.

déphasé, e [defaze] adj ÉLECTR out of phase ; fam fig out of touch.

dépilatoire [depilatwar] adj : **crème dépilatoire** depilatory cream.

dépistage [depista3] nm [de maladie] screening ; **dépistage du SIDA** AIDS testing.

dépister [3] [depiste] vt **1.** [gibier, voleur] to track down - **2.** [maladie] to screen for.

dépit [depi] nm pique, spite. **en dépit de** loc prép in spite of.

déplacé, e [deplase] adj **1.** [propos, attitude, présence] out of place - **2.** [personne] displaced.

déplacement [deplasmɑ̃] nm **1.** [d'objet] moving - **2.** [voyage] travelling (U) UK, traveling (U) US.

déplacer [16] [deplase] vt **1.** [objet] to move, to shift ; fig [problème] to shift the emphasis of - **2.** [muter] to transfer. **se déplacer** vp **1.** [se mouvoir - animal] to move (around) - [- personne] to walk - **2.** [voyager] to travel - **3.** MÉD : **se déplacer une vertèbre** to slip a disc UK OU disk US.

déplaire [110] [depler] vt **1.** [ne pas plaire] : **cela me déplaît** I don't like it - **2.** [irriter] to displease.

déplaisant, e [deplezɑ̃, ɑ̃t] adj sout unpleasant.

dépliant [deplijɑ̃] nm leaflet ; **dépliant touristique** tourist brochure.

déplier [10] [deplije] vt to unfold.

déploiement [deplwamɑ̃] nm **1.** MIL deployment - **2.** [d'ailes] spreading - **3.** fig [d'efforts] display.

déplorer [3] [deplɔre] vt [regretter] to deplore.

déployer [13] [deplwaje] vt **1.** [déplier - gén] to unfold ; [- plan, journal] to open ; [ailes] to spread - **2.** MIL to deploy - **3.** [mettre en œuvre] to expend.

déplu [deply] pp ► **déplaire**.

déportation [depɔrtasjɔ̃] nf **1.** [exil] deportation - **2.** [internement] transportation to a concentration camp.

déporté, e [depɔrte] nm, f **1.** [exilé] deportee - **2.** [interné] prisoner (in a concentration camp).

déporter [3] [depɔrte] vt **1.** [dévier] to carry off course - **2.** [exiler] to deport - **3.** [interner] to send to a concentration camp.

déposé, e [depoze] adj : **marque déposée** registered trademark ; **modèle déposé** patented design.

déposer [3] [depoze] <> vt **1.** [poser] to put down - **2.** [personne, paquet] to drop

- **3.** [argent, sédiment] to deposit - **4.** DR to file ; **déposer son bilan** FIN to go into liquidation - **5.** [monarque] to depose. <> vi DR to testify, to give evidence. **se déposer** vp to settle.

dépositaire [depoziter] nmf **1.** COMM agent - **2.** [d'objet] bailee ; **dépositaire de** fig person entrusted with.

déposition [depozisjɔ̃] nf deposition.

déposséder [18] [deposede] vt : **déposséder qqn de** to dispossess sb of.

dépôt [depo] nm **1.** [d'objet, d'argent, de sédiment] deposit, depositing (U) ; **verser un dépôt (de garantie)** to put down a deposit ; **dépôt d'ordures** (rubbish) dump UK, garbage dump US - **2.** ADMIN registration ; **dépôt légal** copyright registration - **3.** [garage] depot - **4.** [entrepôt] store, warehouse - **5.** [prison] ≃ police cells pl.

dépotoir [depɔtwar] nm [décharge] (rubbish) dump UK, garbage dump US ; fam fig dump, tip UK.

dépouille [depuj] nf **1.** [peau] hide, skin - **2.** [humaine] remains pl.

dépouillement [depujmɑ̃] nm [sobriété] austerity, sobriety.

dépouiller [3] [depuje] vt **1.** [priver] : **dépouiller qqn (de)** to strip sb (of) - **2.** [examiner] to peruse ; **dépouiller un scrutin** to count the votes.

dépourvu, e [depurvy] adj : **dépourvu de** without, lacking in. **au dépourvu** loc adv : **prendre qqn au dépourvu** to catch sb unawares.

dépoussiérer [18] [depusjere] vt to dust (off).

dépravé, e [deprave] <> adj depraved. <> nm, f degenerate.

dépréciation [depresjasjɔ̃] nf depreciation.

déprécier [9] [depresje] vt **1.** [marchandise] to reduce the value of - **2.** [œuvre] to disparage. **se déprécier** vp **1.** [marchandise] to depreciate - **2.** [personne] to put o.s. down.

dépressif, ive [depresif, iv] adj depressive.

dépression [depresjɔ̃] nf depression ; **dépression nerveuse** nervous breakdown.

déprimant, e [deprimɑ̃, ɑ̃t] adj depressing.

déprime [deprim] nf fam **faire une déprime** to be (feeling) down.

déprimé, e [deprime] adj depressed.

déprimer [3] [deprime] <> vt to depress. <> vi fam to be (feeling) down.

déprogrammer [3] [deprɔgrame] vt to remove from the schedule ; TV to take off the air.

dépuceler [24] [depysle] *vt fam* **dépuceler qqn** to take sb's virginity.

depuis [dəpɥi] <> *prép* **1.** [à partir d'une date ou d'un moment précis] since ; **je ne l'ai pas vu depuis son mariage** I haven't seen him since he got married ; **il est parti depuis hier** he's been away since yesterday ; **depuis le début jusqu'à la fin** from beginning to end - **2.** [exprimant une durée] for ; **il est malade depuis une semaine** he has been ill for a week ; **depuis 10 ans/longtemps** for 10 years/a long time ; **depuis toujours** always - **3.** [dans l'espace] from ; **depuis la route, on pouvait voir la mer** you could see the sea from the road. <> *adv* since (then) ; **depuis, nous ne l'avons pas revu** we haven't seen him since (then). **depuis que** *loc conj* since ; **je ne l'ai pas revu depuis qu'il s'est marié** I haven't seen him since he got married.

député [depyte] *nm* [au parlement] member of parliament *UK*, representative *US*.

déraciner [3] [derasine] *vt litt & fig* to uproot.

déraillement [derajmɑ̃] *nm* derailment.

dérailler [3] [deraje] *vi* **1.** [train] to leave the rails, to be derailed - **2.** *fam fig* [mécanisme] to go on the blink - **3.** *fam fig* [personne] to go to pieces.

dérailleur [derajœr] *nm* [de bicyclette] derailleur.

déraisonnable [derezɔnabl] *adj* unreasonable.

dérangement [derɑ̃ʒmɑ̃] *nm* trouble ; **en dérangement** out of order.

déranger [17] [derɑ̃ʒe] <> *vt* **1.** [personne] to disturb, to bother ; **ça vous dérange si je fume?** do you mind if I smoke? - **2.** [plan] to disrupt - **3.** [maison, pièce] to disarrange, to make untidy. <> *vi* to be disturbing. **se déranger** *vp* **1.** [se déplacer] to move - **2.** [se gêner] to put o.s. out.

dérapage [derapaʒ] *nm* [glissement] skid ; *fig* excess.

déraper [3] [derape] *vi* [glisser] to skid ; *fig* to get out of hand.

déréglementer [3] [dereglǝmɑ̃te] *vt* to deregulate.

dérégler [18] [deregle] *vt* [mécanisme] to put out of order ; *fig* to upset. **se dérégler** *vp* [mécanisme] to go wrong ; *fig* to be upset ou unsettled.

dérider [3] [deride] *vt fig* : **dérider qqn** to cheer sb up.

dérision [derizjɔ̃] *nf* derision ; **tourner qqch en dérision** to hold sthg up to ridicule.

dérisoire [derizwar] *adj* derisory.

dérivatif, ive [derivatif, iv] *adj* derivative. **dérivatif** *nm* distraction.

dérive [deriv] *nf* [mouvement] drift, drifting (U) ; **aller** ou **partir à la dérive** *fig* to fall apart.

dérivé [derive] *nm* derivative.

dériver [3] [derive] <> *vt* [détourner] to divert *UK*, to detour *US*. <> *vi* **1.** [aller à la dérive] to drift - **2.** *fig* [découler] : **dériver de** to derive from.

dermatologie [dermatɔlɔʒi] *nf* dermatology.

dermatologue [dermatɔlɔg] *nmf* dermatologist.

dernier, ère [dernje, ɛr] <> *adj* **1.** [gén] last ; **l'année dernière** last year - **2.** [ultime] last, final - **3.** [plus récent] latest. <> *nm, f* last ; **ce dernier** the latter. **en dernier** *loc adv* last.

dernièrement [dernjɛrmɑ̃] *adv* recently, lately.

dernier-né, dernière-née [dernjene, dernjɛrne] *nm, f* [bébé] youngest (child).

dérobade [derɔbad] *nf* evasion, shirking (U).

dérobé, e [derɔbe] *adj* **1.** [volé] stolen - **2.** [caché] hidden. **à la dérobée** *loc adv* surreptitiously.

dérober [3] [derɔbe] *vt sout* to steal. **se dérober** *vp* **1.** [se soustraire] : **se dérober à qqch** to shirk sthg - **2.** [s'effondrer] to give way.

dérogation [derɔgasjɔ̃] *nf* [action] dispensation ; [résultat] exception.

déroulement [derulmɑ̃] *nm* **1.** [de bobine] unwinding - **2.** *fig* [d'événement] development.

dérouler [3] [derule] *vt* [fil] to unwind ; [papier, tissu] to unroll. **se dérouler** *vp* to take place.

déroute [derut] *nf* MIL rout ; *fig* collapse.

dérouter [3] [derute] *vt* **1.** [déconcerter] to disconcert, to put out - **2.** [dévier] to divert *UK*, to detour *US*.

derrière [derjɛr] <> *prép* behind. <> *nm* **1.** [partie arrière] back ; **la porte de derrière** the back door - **2.** [partie du corps] bottom, behind.

des [de] <> *art indéf* **un.** <> *prép* **de.**

dès [de] *prép* from ; **dès son arrivée** the minute he arrives/arrived, as soon as he arrives/arrived ; **dès l'enfance** since childhood ; **dès 1900** as far back as 1900, as early as 1900 ; **dès maintenant** from now on ; **dès demain** starting ou from tomorrow. **dès que** *loc conj* as soon as.

désabusé, e [dezabyze] *adj* disillusioned.

désaccord [dezakɔr] *nm* disagreement.

désaccordé, e [dezakɔrde] *adj* out of tune.

désaffecté, e [dezafɛkte] *adj* disused.

désaffection [dezafɛksjɔ̃] *nf* disaffection.

désagréable [dezagreabl] *adj* unpleasant.

désagréger [22] [dezagreʒe] *vt* to break up. ▪ **se désagréger** *vp* to break up.

désagrément [dezagremɑ̃] *nm* annoyance.

désaltérant, e [dezalterɑ̃, ɑ̃t] *adj* thirst-quenching.

désaltérer [18] [dezaltere] ▪ **se désaltérer** *vp* to quench one's thirst.

désamorcer [16] [dezamɔrse] *vt* [arme] to remove the primer from ; [bombe] to defuse ; *fig* [complot] to nip in the bud.

désappointer [3] [dezapwɛ̃te] *vt* to disappoint.

désapprobation [dezaprɔbasjɔ̃] *nf* disapproval.

désapprouver [3] [dezapruve] ◇ *vt* to disapprove of. ◇ *vi* to be disapproving.

désarmement [dezarməmɑ̃] *nm* disarmament.

désarmer [3] [dezarme] *vt* to disarm ; [fusil] to unload.

désarroi [dezarwa] *nm* confusion.

désastre [dezastr] *nm* disaster.

désastreux, euse [dezastrø, øz] *adj* disastrous.

désavantage [dezavɑ̃taʒ] *nm* disadvantage.

désavantager [17] [dezavɑ̃taʒe] *vt* to disadvantage.

désavantageux, euse [dezavɑ̃taʒø, øz] *adj* unfavourable *UK*, unfavorable *US*.

désavouer [6] [dezavwe] *vt* to disown.

désaxé, e [dezakse] ◇ *adj* [mentalement] disordered, unhinged. ◇ *nm, f* unhinged person.

descendance [desɑ̃dɑ̃s] *nf* [progéniture] descendants *pl*.

descendant, e [desɑ̃dɑ̃, ɑ̃t] *nm, f* [héritier] descendant.

descendre [73] [desɑ̃dr] ◇ *vt (v aux : être)* **1.** [escalier, pente] to go/come down ; **descendre la rue en courant** to run down the street - **2.** [rideau, tableau] to lower - **3.** [apporter] to bring/take down - **4.** *fam* [personne, avion] to shoot down. ◇ *vi (v aux : être)* **1.** [gén] to go/come down ; [température, niveau] to fall - **2.** [passager] to get off ; **descendre d'un bus** to get off a bus ; **descendre d'une voiture** to get out of a car - **3.** [être issu] : **descendre de** to be descended from - **4.** [marée] to go out.

descendu, e [desɑ̃dy] *pp* ▶ **descendre**.

descente [desɑ̃t] *nf* **1.** [action] descent - **2.** [pente] downhill slope ou stretch - **3.** [irruption] raid - **4.** [tapis] : **descente de lit** bedside rug.

descriptif, ive [dɛskriptif, iv] *adj* descriptive. ▪ **descriptif** *nm* [de lieu] particulars *pl* ; [d'appareil] specification.

description [dɛskripsjɔ̃] *nf* description.

désemparé, e [dezɑ̃pare] *adj* [personne] helpless ; [avion, navire] disabled.

désendettement [dezɑ̃dɛtmɑ̃] *nm* degearing *UK*, debt reduction.

désenfler [3] [dezɑ̃fle] *vi* to go down, to become less swollen.

désensibiliser [3] [desɑ̃sibilize] *vt* to desensitize.

déséquilibre [dezekilibr] *nm* imbalance.

déséquilibré, e [dezekilibre] *nm, f* unbalanced person.

déséquilibrer [3] [dezekilibre] *vt* **1.** [physiquement] : **déséquilibrer qqn** to throw sb off balance - **2.** [perturber] to unbalance.

désert, e [dezer, ert] *adj* [désertique - île] desert *(avant n)* ; [peu fréquenté] deserted. ▪ **désert** *nm* desert.

déserter [3] [dezerte] *vt & vi* to desert.

déserteur [dezertœr] *nm* MIL deserter ; *fig & péj* traitor.

désertion [dezersjɔ̃] *nf* desertion.

désertique [dezertik] *adj* desert *(avant n)*.

désespéré, e [dezespere] *adj* **1.** [regard] desperate - **2.** [situation] hopeless.

désespérément [dezesperemɑ̃] *adv* **1.** [sans espoir] hopelessly - **2.** [avec acharnement] desperately.

désespérer [18] [dezespere] ◇ *vt* **1.** [décourager] : **désespérer qqn** to drive sb to despair - **2.** [perdre espoir] : **désespérer que qqch arrive** to give up hope of sthg happening. ◇ *vi* : **désespérer (de)** to despair (of). ▪ **se désespérer** *vp* to despair.

désespoir [dezespwar] *nm* despair ; **en désespoir de cause** as a last resort.

déshabillé [dezabije] *nm* negligee.

déshabiller [3] [dezabije] *vt* to undress. ▪ **se déshabiller** *vp* to undress, to get undressed.

désherbant, e [dezerbɑ̃, ɑ̃t] *adj* weed-killing. ▪ **désherbant** *nm* weedkiller.

déshérité, e [dezerite] ◇ *adj* **1.** [privé d'héritage] disinherited - **2.** [pauvre] deprived. ◇ *nm, f* [pauvre] deprived person.

déshériter [3] [dezerite] *vt* to disinherit.

déshonneur [dezɔnœr] *nm* disgrace.

déshonorer [3] [dezɔnɔre] *vt* to disgrace, to bring disgrace on.

déshydrater [3] [dezidrate] *vt* to dehydrate. ▪ **se déshydrater** *vp* to become dehydrated.

désigner [3] [dezine] vt **1.** [choisir] to appoint - **2.** [signaler] to point out - **3.** [nommer] to designate.

désillusion [dezilyzjɔ̃] nf disillusion.

désincarné, e [dezɛ̃karne] adj **1.** RELIG disembodied - **2.** [éthéré] unearthly.

désinfectant, e [dezɛ̃fɛktɑ̃, ɑ̃t] adj disinfectant. ➤ **désinfectant** nm disinfectant.

désinfecter [4] [dezɛ̃fɛkte] vt to disinfect.

désinflation [dezɛ̃flasjɔ̃] nf disinflation.

désinstaller [3] [dezɛ̃stale] vt INFORM to uninstall.

désintégrer [18] [dezɛ̃tegre] vt to break up. ➤ **se désintégrer** vp to disintegrate, to break up.

désintéressé, e [dezɛ̃terese] adj disinterested.

désintéresser [4] [dezɛ̃terese] ➤ **se désintéresser** vp: se désintéresser de to lose interest in.

désintoxication [dezɛ̃tɔksikasjɔ̃] nf detoxification.

désinvolte [dezɛ̃vɔlt] adj **1.** [à l'aise] casual - **2.** péj [sans-gêne] offhand.

désinvolture [dezɛ̃vɔltyr] nf **1.** [légèreté] casualness - **2.** péj [sans-gêne] offhandedness.

désir [dezir] nm **1.** [souhait] desire, wish - **2.** [charnel] desire.

désirable [dezirabl] adj desirable.

désirer [3] [dezire] vt **1.** sout [chose] : désirer faire qqch to wish to do sthg ; vous désirez? [dans un magasin] can I help you? ; [dans un café] what can I get you? - **2.** [sexuellement] to desire.

désistement [dezistəmɑ̃] nm : désistement (de) withdrawal (from).

désister [3] [deziste] ➤ **se désister** vp [se retirer] to withdraw, to stand down.

désobéir [32] [dezɔbeir] vi : désobéir (à qqn) to disobey (sb).

désobéissant, e [dezɔbeisɑ̃, ɑ̃t] adj disobedient.

désobligeant, e [dezɔbliʒɑ̃, ɑ̃t] adj sout offensive.

désodorisant, e [dezɔdɔrizɑ̃, ɑ̃t] adj deodorant. ➤ **désodorisant** nm air freshener.

désœuvré, e [dezœvre] adj idle.

désolation [dezɔlasjɔ̃] nf **1.** [destruction] desolation - **2.** sout [affliction] distress.

désolé, e [dezɔle] adj **1.** [ravagé] desolate - **2.** [contrarié] very sorry.

désoler [3] [dezɔle] vt **1.** [affliger] to sadden - **2.** [contrarier] to upset, to make sorry. ➤ **se désoler** vp [être contrarié] to be upset.

désolidariser [3] [desɔlidarize] vt **1.** [choses] : désolidariser qqch (de) to disengage ou disconnect sthg (from) - **2.** [personnes] to estrange. ➤ **se désolidariser** vp : se désolidariser de to dissociate o.s. from.

désopilant, e [dezɔpilɑ̃, ɑ̃t] adj hilarious.

désordonné, e [dezɔrdɔne] adj [maison, personne] untidy ; fig [vie] disorganized.

désordre [dezɔrdr] nm **1.** [fouillis] untidiness ; en désordre untidy - **2.** [agitation] disturbances pl, disorder (U).

désorganiser [3] [dezɔrganize] vt to disrupt.

désorienté, e [dezɔrjɑ̃te] adj disoriented, disorientated UK.

désormais [dezɔrmɛ] adv from now on, in future.

désosser [3] [dezɔse] vt to bone.

despote [dɛspɔt] nm [chef d'État] despot ; fig & péj tyrant.

despotisme [dɛspɔtism] nm [gouvernement] despotism ; fig & péj tyranny.

desquels, desquelles [dekɛl] ► lequel.

DESS (abr de diplôme d'études supérieures spécialisées) nm postgraduate diploma.

dessécher [18] [deseʃe] vt [peau] to dry (out) ; fig [cœur] to harden. ➤ **se dessécher** vp [peau, terre] to dry out ; [plante] to wither ; fig to harden.

desserrer [4] [desere] vt to loosen ; [poing, dents] to unclench ; [frein] to release.

dessert [desɛr] nm dessert.

desserte [desɛrt] nf **1.** [transports] (transport) service - **2.** [meuble] sideboard.

desservir [38] [desɛrvir] vt **1.** [transports] to serve - **2.** [table] to clear - **3.** [désavantager] to do a disservice to.

dessin [desɛ̃] nm **1.** [graphique] drawing ; dessin animé cartoon (film) ; dessin humoristique cartoon (drawing) - **2.** fig [contour] outline.

dessinateur, trice [desinatœr, tris] nm, f artist, draughtsman (f draughtswoman) UK, draftsman (f draftswoman) US.

dessiner [3] [desine] ◇ vt [représenter] to draw ; fig to outline. ◇ vi to draw.

dessous [dəsu] ◇ adv underneath. ◇ nm [partie inférieure - gén] underside ; [- d'un tissu] wrong side. ◇ nmpl [sous-vêtements féminins] underwear (U). ➤ **en dessous** loc adv underneath ; [plus bas] below ; ils habitent l'appartement d'en dessous they live in the flat below ou downstairs.

dessous-de-plat [dəsudpla] nm inv tablemat.

dessus [dəsy] ◇ adv on top ; faites attention à ne pas marcher dessus be careful not to walk on it. ◇ *nm* **1.** [partie supérieure] top - **2.** [étage supérieur] upstairs ; **les voisins du dessus** the upstairs neighbours ; **avoir le dessus** to have the upper hand ; **reprendre le dessus** to get over it. ➡ **en dessus** *loc adv* on top.

dessus-de-lit [dəsydli] *nm inv* bedspread.

déstabiliser [3] [destabilize] *vt* to destabilize.

destin [dɛstɛ̃] *nm* fate.

destinataire [dɛstinatɛr] *nmf* addressee.

destination [dɛstinasjɔ̃] *nf* **1.** [direction] destination ; **un avion à destination de Paris** a plane to ou for Paris - **2.** [rôle] purpose.

destinée [dɛstine] *nf* destiny.

destiner [3] [dɛstine] *vt* **1.** [consacrer] : **destiner qqch à** to intend sthg for, to mean sthg for - **2.** [vouer] : **destiner qqn à qqch/à faire qqch** [à un métier] to destine sb for sthg/to do sthg ; [sort] to mark sb out for sthg/to do sthg.

destituer [7] [dɛstitɥe] *vt* to dismiss.

destructeur, trice [dɛstryktœr, tris] ◇ *adj* destructive. ◇ *nm, f* destroyer.

destruction [dɛstryksjɔ̃] *nf* destruction.

désuet, ète [dezɥɛ, ɛt] *adj* [expression, coutume] obsolete ; [style, tableau] outmoded.

désuni, e [dezyni] *adj* divided.

détachable [detaʃabl] *adj* detachable, removable.

détachant, e [detaʃɑ̃, ɑ̃t] *adj* stain-removing. ➡ **détachant** *nm* stain remover.

détaché, e [detaʃe] *adj* detached.

détachement [detaʃmɑ̃] *nm* **1.** [d'esprit] detachment - **2.** [de fonctionnaire] secondment UK - **3.** MIL detachment.

détacher [3] [detaʃe] *vt* **1.** [enlever] : **détacher qqch (de)** [objet] to detach sthg (from) ; *fig* to free sthg (from) - **2.** [nettoyer] to remove stains from, to clean - **3.** [délier] to undo ; [cheveux] to untie - **4.** ADMIN : **détacher qqn auprès de** to second sb to UK. ➡ **se détacher** *vp* **1.** [tomber] : **se détacher (de)** to come off ; *fig* to free o.s. (from) - **2.** [se défaire] to come undone - **3.** [ressortir] : **se détacher sur** to stand out on - **4.** [se désintéresser] : **se détacher de qqn** to drift apart from sb.

détail [detaj] *nm* **1.** [précision] detail - **2.** COMM : **le détail** retail. ➡ **au détail** *loc adj & loc adv* retail. ➡ **en détail** *loc adv* in detail.

détaillant, e [detajɑ̃, ɑ̃t] *nm, f* retailer.

détaillé, e [detaje] *adj* detailed.

détailler [3] [detaje] *vt* **1.** [expliquer] to give details of - **2.** [vendre] to retail.

détaler [3] [detale] *vi* **1.** [personne] to clear out - **2.** [animal] to bolt.

détartrant, e [detartrɑ̃, ɑ̃t] *adj* descaling. ➡ **détartrant** *nm* descaling agent.

détaxe [detaks] *nf* : **détaxe (sur)** [suppression] removal of tax (from) ; [réduction] reduction in tax (on).

détecter [4] [detɛkte] *vt* to detect.

détecteur, trice [detɛktœr, tris] *adj* detecting, detector *(avant n)*. ➡ **détecteur** *nm* detector.

détection [detɛksjɔ̃] *nf* detection.

détective [detɛktiv] *nm* detective ; **détective privé** private detective.

déteindre [81] [detɛ̃dr] *vi* to fade.

déteint, e [detɛ̃, ɛ̃t] *pp* ➤ **déteindre**.

dételer [24] [detle] *vt* [cheval] to unharness.

détendre [73] [detɑ̃dr] *vt* **1.** [corde] to loosen, to slacken ; *fig* to ease - **2.** [personne] to relax. ➡ **se détendre** *vp* **1.** [se relâcher] to slacken ; *fig* [situation] to ease - [atmosphère] to become more relaxed - **2.** [se reposer] to relax.

détendu, e [detɑ̃dy] ◇ *pp* ➤ **détendre**. ◇ *adj* **1.** [corde] loose, slack - **2.** [personne] relaxed.

détenir [40] [detnir] *vt* **1.** [objet] to have, to hold - **2.** [personne] to detain, to hold.

détente [detɑ̃t] *nf* **1.** [de ressort] release - **2.** [d'une arme] trigger - **3.** [repos] relaxation - **4.** POLIT détente.

détenteur, trice [detɑ̃tœr, tris] *nm, f* [d'objet, de secret] possessor ; [de prix, record] holder.

détention [detɑ̃sjɔ̃] *nf* **1.** [possession] possession - **2.** [emprisonnement] detention.

détenu, e [detny] ◇ *pp* ➤ **détenir**. ◇ *nm, f* prisoner.

détergent, e [detɛrʒɑ̃, ɑ̃t] *adj* detergent *(avant n)*. ➡ **détergent** *nm* detergent.

détérioration [deterjɔrasjɔ̃] *nf* [de bâtiment] deterioration ; [de situation] worsening.

détériorer [3] [deterjɔre] *vt* **1.** [abîmer] to damage - **2.** [altérer] to ruin. ➡ **se détériorer** *vp* **1.** [bâtiment] to deteriorate ; [situation] to worsen - **2.** [s'altérer] to be spoiled.

déterminant, e [detɛrminɑ̃, ɑ̃t] *adj* decisive, determining. ➡ **déterminant** *nm* LING determiner.

détermination [detɛrminasjɔ̃] *nf* [résolution] decision.

déterminé, e [detɛrmine] *adj* **1.** [quantité] given *(avant n)* - **2.** [expression] determined.

déterminer [3] [detɛrmine] *vt* **1.** [préciser] to determine, to specify - **2.** [provoquer] to bring about.

déterrer [4] [detere] *vt* to dig up.

détestable [detɛstabl] *adj* dreadful.

détester [3] [detɛste] *vt* to detest.

détonateur [detɔnatœr] *nm* TECHNOL detonator ; *fig* trigger.

détoner [3] [detɔne] *vi* to detonate.

détonner [3] [detɔne] *vi* MUS to be out of tune ; [couleur] to clash ; [personne] to be out of place.

détour [detur] *nm* 1. [crochet] detour - 2. [méandre] bend ; **sans détour** *fig* directly.

détourné, e [deturne] *adj* [dévié] indirect ; *fig* roundabout *(avant n)*.

détournement [deturnəmɑ̃] *nm* diversion UK, detour US ; **détournement d'avion** hijacking, skyjacking, **détournement de fonds** embezzlement ; **détournement de mineur** corruption of a minor.

détourner [3] [deturne] *vt* 1. [dévier - gén] to divert UK, to detour US ; [- avion] to hijack, to skyjack - 2. [écarter] : **détourner qqn de** to distract sb from, to divert sb from - 3. [la tête, les yeux] to turn away - 4. [argent] to embezzle. **se détourner** *vp* to turn away ; **se détourner de** *fig* to move away from.

détraquer [3] [detrake] *vt fam* [dérégler] to break ; *fig* to upset. **se détraquer** *vp fam* [se dérégler] to go wrong ; *fig* to become unsettled.

détresse [detrɛs] *nf* distress.

détriment [detrimɑ̃] **au détriment de** *loc prép* to the detriment of.

détritus [detrity(s)] *nm* detritus.

détroit [detrwa] *nm* strait ; **le détroit de Bering** the Bering Strait ; **le détroit de Gibraltar** the Strait of Gibraltar.

détromper [3] [detrɔ̃pe] *vt* to disabuse.

détrôner [3] [detrone] *vt* [souverain] to dethrone ; *fig* to oust.

détruire [98] [detrɥir] *vt* 1. [démolir, éliminer] to destroy - 2. *fig* [anéantir] to ruin.

détruit, e [detrɥi, it] *pp* ▶ **détruire**.

dette [dɛt] *nf* debt.

DEUG, Deug [dœg] *(abr de* **diplôme d'études universitaires générales)** *nm university diploma taken after two years of humanities-oriented courses.*

deuil [dœj] *nm* [douleur, mort] bereavement ; [vêtements, période] mourning *(U)* ; **porter le deuil** to be in ou wear mourning.

DEUST, Deust [dœst] *(abr de* **diplôme d'études universitaires scientifiques et techniques)** *nm university diploma taken after two years of science courses ; voir aussi* **DEUG.**

deux [dø] <> *adj num inv* two ; **ses deux fils** both his sons, his two sons ; **tous les**

deux jours every other day, every two days, every second day. <> *nm* two ; **les deux** both ; **par deux** in pairs ; *voir aussi* **six.**

deuxième [døzjɛm] *adj num inv, nm & nmf* second ; *voir aussi* **sixième.**

deux-pièces [døpjɛs] *nm inv* 1. [appartement] two-room flat UK ou apartment US - 2. [bikini] two-piece (swimming costume).

deux-points [døpwɛ̃] *nm inv* colon.

deux-roues [døru] *nm inv* two-wheeled vehicle.

dévaler [3] [devale] *vt* to run down.

dévaliser [3] [devalize] *vt* [cambrioler - maison] to ransack ; [- personne] to rob ; *fig* to strip bare.

dévaloriser [3] [devalɔrize] *vt* 1. [monnaie] to devalue - 2. [personne] to run ou put down. **se dévaloriser** *vp* 1. [monnaie] to fall in value - 2. *fig* [personne] to run ou put o.s. down.

dévaluation [devalɥasjɔ̃] *nf* devaluation.

dévaluer [7] [devalɥe] *vt* to devalue. **se dévaluer** *vp* to devalue.

devancer [16] [dəvɑ̃se] *vt* 1. [précéder] to arrive before - 2. [anticiper] to anticipate.

devant [dəvɑ̃] <> *prép* 1. [en face de] in front of - 2. [en avant de] ahead of, in front of ; **aller droit devant soi** to go straight ahead ou on - 3. [en présence de, face à] in the face of. <> *adv* 1. [en face] in front - 2. [en avant] in front, ahead. <> *nm* front ; **prendre les devants** to make the first move, to take the initiative. **de devant** *loc adj* [pattes, roues] front *(avant n)*.

devanture [dəvɑ̃tyr] *nf* shop window.

dévaster [3] [devaste] *vt* to devastate.

développement [devlɔpmɑ̃] *nm* 1. [gén & ÉCON] development ; **développement durable** sustainable development - 2. PHOTO developing.

développer [3] [devlɔpe] *vt* to develop ; [industrie, commerce] to expand ; PHOTO to develop ; **faire développer des photos** to have some photos developed. **se développer** *vp* 1. [s'épanouir] to spread - 2. ÉCON to grow, to expand.

développeur [devlɔpœr] *nm* [INFORM - entreprise] software development ou design company ; [- personne] software developer ou designer.

devenir [40] [dəvnir] *vi* to become ; **que devenez-vous?** *fig* how are you doing?

devenu, e [dəvny] *pp* ▶ **devenir.**

dévergondé, e [devɛrgɔ̃de] <> *adj* shameless, wild. <> *nm, f* shameless person.

déverser [3] [devɛrse] *vt* 1. [liquide] to pour out - 2. [ordures] to tip (out) UK - 3. *fig* [injures] to pour out.

déviation [devjasjɔ̃] nf 1. [gén] deviation - 2. [d'itinéraire] diversion UK, detour US.

dévier [9] [devje] ◇ vi : dévier de to deviate from. ◇ vt to divert UK, to detour US.

devin, devineresse [dəvɛ̃, dəvinrɛs] nm, f : je ne suis pas devin! I'm not psychic!

deviner [3] [dəvine] vt to guess.

devinette [dəvinɛt] nf riddle.

devis [dəvi] nm estimate ; faire un devis to (give an) estimate.

dévisager [17] [devizaʒe] vt to stare at.

devise [dəviz] nf 1. [formule] motto - 2. [monnaie] currency. ➡ **devises** nfpl [argent] currency (U).

dévisser [3] [devise] ◇ vt to unscrew. ◇ vi [alpinisme] to fall (off).

dévoiler [3] [devwale] vt to unveil ; fig to reveal.

devoir [53] [dəvwar] ◇ nm 1. [obligation] duty - 2. SCOL homework (U) ; faire ses devoirs to do one's homework. ◇ vt 1. [argent, respect] : devoir qqch (à qqn) to owe (sb) sthg - 2. [marque l'obligation] : devoir faire qqch to have to do sthg ; je dois partir à l'heure ce soir I have to ou must leave on time tonight ; tu devrais faire attention you should be ou ought to be careful ; il n'aurait pas dû mentir he shouldn't have lied, he ought not to have lied - 3. [marque la probabilité] : il doit faire chaud là-bas it must be hot over there ; il a dû oublier he must have forgotten - 4. [marque le futur, l'intention] : devoir faire qqch to be (due) to do sthg, to be going to do sthg ; elle doit arriver à 6 heures she's due to arrive at 6 o'clock ; je dois voir mes parents ce week-end I'm seeing ou going to see my parents this weekend - 5. [être destiné à] : il devait mourir trois ans plus tard he was to die three years later ; cela devait arriver it had to happen, it was bound to happen. ➡ **se devoir** vp : se devoir de faire qqch to be duty-bound to do sthg ; comme il se doit as is proper.

dévolu, e [devɔly] adj sout : dévolu à allotted to. ➡ **dévolu** nm : jeter son dévolu sur to set one's sights on.

dévorer [3] [devɔre] vt to devour.

dévotion [devɔsjɔ̃] nf devotion ; avec dévotion [prier] devoutly ; [soigner, aimer] devotedly.

dévoué, e [devwe] adj devoted.

dévouement [devumɑ̃] nm devotion.

dévouer [6] [devwe] ➡ **se dévouer** vp 1. [se consacrer] : se dévouer à to devote o.s. to - 2. fig [se sacrifier] : se dévouer pour qqch/pour faire qqch to sacrifice o.s. for sthg/to do sthg.

dévoyé, e [devwaje] adj & nm, f delinquent.

devrai, devras etc ➡ devoir.

dextérité [dɛksterite] nf dexterity, skill.

dézipper [3] [dezipe] vt to unzip.

diabète [djabɛt] nm diabetes (U).

diabétique [djabetik] nmf & adj diabetic.

diable [djabl] nm devil.

diabolique [djabɔlik] adj diabolical.

diabolo [djabɔlo] nm [boisson] fruit cordial and lemonade ; diabolo menthe mint (cordial) and lemonade.

diadème [djadɛm] nm diadem.

diagnostic [djagnɔstik] nm MÉD diagnosis.

diagnostiquer [3] [djagnɔstike] vt MÉD & fig to diagnose.

diagonale [djagɔnal] nf diagonal.

dialecte [djalɛkt] nm dialect.

dialogue [djalɔg] nm discussion.

dialoguer [3] [djalɔge] vi 1. [converser] to converse - 2. INFORM to interact.

diamant [djamɑ̃] nm [pierre] diamond.

diamètre [djamɛtr] nm diameter.

diapason [djapazɔ̃] nm [instrument] tuning fork.

diapositive [djapozitiv] nf slide.

diarrhée [djare] nf diarrhoea UK, diarrhea US.

dictateur [diktatœr] nm dictator.

dictature [diktatyr] nf dictatorship.

dictée [dikte] nf dictation.

dicter [3] [dikte] vt to dictate.

diction [diksjɔ̃] nf diction.

dictionnaire [diksjɔnɛr] nm dictionary.

dicton [diktɔ̃] nm saying, dictum.

dièse [djɛz] ◇ adj sharp ; do/fa dièse C/F sharp. ◇ nm sharp ; [symbole] hash ; appuyez sur la touche dièse press the hash key.

diesel [djezɛl] adj inv diesel.

diète [djɛt] nf diet ; [jeûne] to be fasting.

diététicien, enne [djetetisjɛ̃, ɛn] nm, f dietician.

diététique [djetetik] ◇ nf dietetics (U). ◇ adj [considération, raison] dietary ; [produit, magasin] health (avant n).

dieu, x [djø] nm god. ➡ **Dieu** nm God ; mon Dieu! My God!

diffamation [difamasjɔ̃] nf [écrite] libel ; [orale] slander.

différé, e [difere] adj recorded. ➡ **différé** nm : en différé TV recorded ; INFORM off-line.

différence [diferɑ̃s] nf [distinction] difference, dissimilarity.

différencier [9] [diferɑ̃sje] *vt* : **différencier qqch de qqch** to differentiate sthg from sthg. ◆ **se différencier** *vp* : **se différencier de** to be different from.

différend [diferɑ̃] *nm* [désaccord] difference of opinion.

différent, e [diferɑ̃, ɑ̃t] *adj* : **différent (de)** different (from).

différer [18] [difere] ◇ *vt* [retarder] to postpone. ◇ *vi* : **différer de** to differ from, to be different from.

difficile [difisil] *adj* difficult.

difficilement [difisilmɑ̃] *adv* with difficulty.

difficulté [difikylte] *nf* **1.** [complexité, peine] difficulty - **2.** [obstacle] problem.

difforme [difɔrm] *adj* deformed.

diffuser [3] [difyze] *vt* **1.** [lumière] to diffuse - **2.** [émission] to broadcast - **3.** [livres] to distribute.

diffuseur [difyzœr] *nm* **1.** [appareil] diffuser - **2.** [de livres] distributor.

diffusion [difyzjɔ̃] *nf* **1.** [d'émission, d'onde] broadcast - **2.** [de livres] distribution.

digérer [18] [diʒere] ◇ *vi* to digest. ◇ *vt* **1.** [repas, connaissance] to digest - **2.** *fam fig* [désagrément] to put up with.

digestif, ive [diʒestif, iv] *adj* digestive. ◆ **digestif** *nm* liqueur.

digestion [diʒestjɔ̃] *nf* digestion.

digital, e, aux [diʒital, o] *adj* **1.** *fam* TECHNOL digital - **2.** ▶ **empreinte.**

digne [diɲ] *adj* **1.** [honorable] dignified - **2.** [méritant] : **digne de** worthy of.

dignité [diɲite] *nf* dignity.

digression [digresjɔ̃] *nf* digression.

digue [dig] *nf* dike.

dilapider [3] [dilapide] *vt* to squander.

dilater [3] [dilate] *vt* to dilate.

dilemme [dilɛm] *nm* [gén] dilemma.

diligence [diliʒɑ̃s] *nf* diligence.

diluant [dilɥɑ̃] *nm* thinner.

diluer [7] [dilɥe] *vt* to dilute.

diluvien, enne [dilyvjɛ̃, ɛn] *adj* torrential.

dimanche [dimɑ̃ʃ] *nm* Sunday ; *voir aussi* **samedi.**

dimension [dimɑ̃sjɔ̃] *nf* **1.** [mesure] dimension - **2.** [taille] dimensions *pl*, size - **3.** *fig* [importance] magnitude. ◆ **à deux dimensions** *loc adj* two-dimensional. ◆ **à trois dimensions** *loc adj* three-dimensional.

diminuer [7] [diminɥe] ◇ *vt* [réduire] to diminish, to reduce. ◇ *vi* [intensité] to diminish, to decrease.

diminutif, ive [diminytif, iv] *adj* diminutive. ◆ **diminutif** *nm* diminutive.

diminution [diminysjɔ̃] *nf* diminution.

dinde [dɛ̃d] *nf* **1.** [animal] turkey - **2.** *péj* [femme] stupid woman.

dindon [dɛ̃dɔ̃] *nm* turkey ; **être le dindon de la farce** *fig* to be made a fool of.

dîner [3] [dine] ◇ *vi* to dine. ◇ *nm* dinner.

dingue [dɛ̃g] *fam* ◇ *adj* **1.** [personne] crazy - **2.** [histoire] incredible. ◇ *nmf* loony.

dinosaure [dinozɔr] *nm* dinosaur.

diplomate [diplɔmat] ◇ *nmf* [ambassadeur] diplomat. ◇ *adj* diplomatic.

diplomatie [diplɔmasi] *nf* diplomacy.

diplomatique [diplɔmatik] *adj* diplomatic.

diplôme [diplom] *nm* diploma.

diplômé, e [diplome] ◇ *adj* : **être diplômé de/en** to be a graduate of/in. ◇ *nm, f* graduate.

dire [102] [dir] *vt* : **dire qqch (à qqn)** [parole] to say sthg (to sb) ; [vérité, mensonge, secret] to tell (sb) sthg ; **dire à qqn de faire qqch** to tell sb to do sthg ; **il m'a dit que...** he told me (that)... ; **c'est vite dit** *fam* that's easy (for you/him *etc*) to say ; **c'est beaucoup dire** that's saying a lot ; **la ville proprement dite** the actual town ; **dire du bien/du mal (de)** to speak well /ill (of) ; **que dirais-tu de...?** what would you say to...? ; **qu'en dis-tu?** what do you think (of it)? ; **on dirait que...** it looks as if... ; **on dirait de la soie** it looks like silk, you'd think it was silk ; **et dire que je n'étais pas là!** and to think I wasn't there! ; **ça ne me dit rien** [pas envie] I don't fancy that ; [jamais entendu] I've never heard of it. ◆ **se dire** *vp* **1.** [penser] to think (to o.s.) - **2.** [s'employer] : **ça ne se dit pas** [par décence] you mustn't say that, [par usage] people don't say that, nobody says that - **3.** [se traduire] : **'chat' se dit 'gato' en espagnol** the Spanish for 'cat' is 'gato'. ◆ **cela dit** *loc adv* having said that. ◆ **dis donc** *loc adv fam* so ; [au fait] by the way ; [à qqn qui exagère] look here! ◆ **pour ainsi dire** *loc adv* so to speak. ◆ **à vrai dire** *loc adv* to tell the truth.

direct, e [dirɛkt] *adj* direct. ◆ **direct** *nm* **1.** [boxe] jab - **2.** [train] nonstop train - **3.** RADIO & TV : **le direct** live transmission (U) ; **en direct** live.

directement [dirɛktəmɑ̃] *adv* directly.

directeur, trice [dirɛktœr, tris] ◇ *adj* **1.** [dirigeant] leading ; **comité directeur** steering committee - **2.** [central] guiding. ◇ *nm, f* director, manager ; **directeur général** general manager, managing director *UK*, chief executive officer *US*.

direction [dirɛksjɔ̃] *nf* **1.** [gestion, ensemble des cadres] management ; **sous la direction**

de under the management of - **2.** [orientation] direction ; **en** OU **dans la direction de** in the direction of - **3.** AUTO steering.

directive [dirɛktiv] *nf* directive.

directrice ▶ **directeur**.

dirigeable [diriʒabl] *nm* : **(ballon) dirigeable** airship.

dirigeant, e [diriʒɑ̃, ɑ̃t] <> *adj* ruling. <> *nm, f* [de pays] leader ; [d'entreprise] manager.

diriger [17] [diriʒe] *vt* **1.** [mener - entreprise] to run, to manage ; [- orchestre] to conduct ; [- film, acteurs] to direct ; [- recherches, projet] to supervise - **2.** [conduire orienter] to steer - **3.** [pointer] : **diriger qqch sur** to aim sthg at ; **diriger qqch vers** to aim sthg towards OU toward US. ➤ **se diriger** *vp* : **se diriger vers** to go towards OU toward US, to head towards OU toward US.

discernement [disɛrnəmɑ̃] *nm* [jugement] discernment.

discerner [3] [disɛrne] *vt* **1.** [distinguer] : **discerner qqch de** to distinguish sthg from - **2.** [deviner] to discern.

disciple [disipl] *nmf* disciple.

disciplinaire [disipliner] *adj* disciplinary.

discipline [disiplin] *nf* discipline.

discipliner [3] [discipline] *vt* [personne] to discipline ; [cheveux] to control.

disco [disko] *nm* disco (music).

discontinu, e [diskɔ̃tiny] *adj* [ligne] broken ; [bruit, effort] intermittent.

discordant, e [diskordɑ̃, ɑ̃t] *adj* discordant.

discorde [diskord] *nf* discord.

discothèque [diskɔtɛk] *nf* **1.** [boîte de nuit] night club - **2.** [de prêt] record library.

discourir [45] [diskurir] *vi* to talk at length.

discours [diskur] *nm* [allocution] speech.

discréditer [3] [diskredite] *vt* to discredit.

discret, ète [diskrɛ, ɛt] *adj* [gén] discreet ; [réservé] reserved.

discrètement [diskrɛtmɑ̃] *adv* discreetly.

discrétion [diskresjɔ̃] *nf* [réserve, tact, silence] discretion.

discrimination [diskriminasjɔ̃] *nf* discrimination ; **sans discrimination** indiscriminately.

discriminatoire [diskriminatwar] *adj* discriminatory.

disculper [3] [diskylpe] *vt* to exonerate. ➤ **se disculper** *vp* to exonerate o.s.

discussion [diskysjɔ̃] *nf* **1.** [conversation, examen] discussion - **2.** [contestation, altercation] argument.

discutable [diskytabl] *adj* [contestable] questionable.

discuter [3] [diskyte] <> *vt* **1.** [débattre] : **discuter (de) qqch** to discuss sthg - **2.** [contester] to dispute. <> *vi* **1.** [parlementer] to discuss - **2.** [converser] to talk - **3.** [contester] to argue.

diseur, euse [dizœr, øz] *nm, f* : **diseur de bonne aventure** fortune-teller.

disgracieux, euse [disgrasjø, øz] *adj* **1.** [sans grâce] awkward, graceless - **2.** [laid] plain.

disjoncter [disʒɔ̃kte] *vi* **1.** ÉLECTR to short-circuit - **2.** *fam* [perdre la tête] to flip, to crack up.

disjoncteur [disʒɔ̃ktœr] *nm* trip switch, circuit breaker.

disloquer [3] [disloke] *vt* **1.** MÉD to dislocate - **2.** [machine, empire] to dismantle. ➤ **se disloquer** *vp* [machine] to fall apart OU to pieces ; *fig* [empire] to break up.

disparaître [91] [disparɛtr] *vi* **1.** [gén] to disappear, to vanish ; **faire disparaître** [personne] to get rid of ; [obstacle] to remove - **2.** [mourir] to die.

disparité [disparite] *nf* [différence - d'éléments] disparity ; [- de couleurs] mismatch.

disparition [disparisjɔ̃] *nf* **1.** [gén] disappearance - **2.** [d'espèce] extinction ; **en voie de disparition** endangered - **3.** [mort] passing.

disparu, e [dispary] <> *pp* ▶ **disparaître**. <> *nm, f* dead person, deceased.

dispatcher [3] [dispatʃe] *vt* to dispatch, to despatch.

dispensaire [dispɑ̃ser] *nm* community clinic UK, free clinic US.

dispense [dispɑ̃s] *nf* [exemption] exemption.

dispenser [3] [dispɑ̃se] *vt* **1.** [distribuer] to dispense - **2.** [exempter] : **dispenser qqn de qqch** [corvée] to excuse sb sthg, to let sb off sthg ; **je te dispense de tes réflexions!** *fig* spare us the comments!, keep your comments to yourself!

disperser [3] [disperse] *vt* to scatter (about OU around) ; [collection, brume, foule] to break up ; *fig* [efforts, forces] to dissipate, to waste. ➤ **se disperser** *vp* **1.** [feuilles, cendres] to scatter ; [brume, foule] to break up, to clear - **2.** [personne] to take on too much at once, to spread o.s. too thin.

dispersion [dispersjɔ̃] *nf* scattering ; [de collection, brume, foule] breaking up ; *fig* [d'efforts, de forces] waste, squandering.

disponibilité [disponibilite] *nf* **1.** [de choses] availability - **2.** [de fonctionnaire] leave of absence - **3.** [d'esprit] alertness, receptiveness.

disponible [disponibl] *adj* [place, personne] available, free.

disposé, e [dispoze] *adj* : **être disposé à**

faire qqch to be prepared ou willing to do sthg ; **être bien disposé envers qqn** to be well-disposed towards ou toward US sb.

disposer [3] [dispoze] <> vt [arranger] to arrange. <> vi : **disposer de** [moyens, argent] to have available (to one), to have at one's disposal ; [chose] to have the use of ; [temps] to have free ou available.

dispositif [dispozitif] nm [mécanisme] device, mechanism.

disposition [dispozisjɔ̃] nf 1. [arrangement] arrangement - 2. [disponibilité] : **à la disposition de** at the disposal of, available to. ▸ **dispositions** nfpl 1. [mesures] arrangements, measures - 2. [dons] : **avoir des dispositions pour** to have a gift for.

disproportionné, e [dispropɔrsjɔne] adj out of proportion.

dispute [dispyt] nf argument, quarrel.

disputer [3] [dispyte] vt 1. [SPORT - course] to run ; [- match] to play - 2. [lutter pour] to fight for. ▸ **se disputer** vp 1. [se quereller] to quarrel, to fight - 2. [lutter pour] to fight over ou for.

disquaire [disker] nm record dealer.

disqualifier [9] [diskalifje] vt to disqualify.

disque [disk] nm 1. MUS record ; [vidéo] videodisc ou US videodisk US ; **disque compact** ou **laser** compact disc - 2. ANAT disc UK, disk US - 3. INFORM disk ; **disque dur** hard disk - 4. SPORT discus.

disquette [disket] nf diskette, floppy disk ; **disquette système** system diskette.

dissection [diseksjɔ̃] nf dissection.

dissemblable [disãblabl] adj dissimilar.

disséminer [3] [disemine] vt [graines, maisons] to scatter, to spread (out) ; fig [idées] to disseminate, to spread.

disséquer [18] [diseke] vt litt & fig to dissect.

dissertation [disertasjɔ̃] nf essay.

dissident, e [disidã, ãt] adj & nm, f dissident.

dissimulation [disimylasjɔ̃] nf 1. [hypocrisie] duplicity - 2. [de la vérité] concealment.

dissimuler [3] [disimyle] vt to conceal. ▸ **se dissimuler** vp 1. [se cacher] to conceal o.s., to hide - 2. [refuser de voir] : **se dissimuler qqch** to close one's eyes to sthg.

dissipation [disipasjɔ̃] nf 1. [dispersion] dispersal, breaking up ; fig [de malentendu] clearing up ; [de craintes] dispelling - 2. [indiscipline] indiscipline, misbehaviour UK, misbehavior US.

dissiper [3] [disipe] vt 1. [chasser] to break up, to clear ; fig to dispel - 2. [distraire] to lead astray. ▸ **se dissiper** vp 1. [brouillard, fumée] to clear - 2. [élève] to misbehave - 3. fig [malaise, fatigue] to go away ; [doute] to be dispelled.

dissocier [9] [disosje] vt [séparer] to separate, to distinguish.

dissolution [disolysjɔ̃] nf 1. DR dissolution - 2. [mélange] dissolving - 3. sout [débauche] dissipation.

dissolvant, e [disolvã, ãt] adj solvent. ▸ **dissolvant** nm [solvant] solvent ; [pour vernis à ongles] nail varnish remover.

dissoudre [87] [disudr] vt : **(faire) dissoudre** to dissolve. ▸ **se dissoudre** vp [substance] to dissolve.

dissous, oute [disu, ut] pp ▸ dissoudre.

dissuader [3] [disɥade] vt to dissuade.

dissuasion [disɥazjɔ̃] nf dissuasion ; **force de dissuasion** deterrent (effect).

distance [distãs] nf 1. [éloignement] distance ; **à distance** at a distance ; [télécommander] by remote control ; **à une distance de 300 mètres** 300 metres away - 2. [intervalle] interval - 3. [écart] gap.

distancer [16] [distãse] vt to outstrip.

distant, e [distã, ãt] adj 1. [éloigné] : **une ville distante de 10 km** a town 10 km away ; **des villes distantes de 10 km** towns 10 km apart - 2. [froid] distant.

distendre [73] [distãdr] vt [ressort, corde] to stretch ; [abdomen] to distend. ▸ **se distendre** vp to distend.

distendu, e [distãdy] pp ▸ distendre.

distiller [3] [distile] vt [alcool] to distil UK, to distill US ; [pétrole] to refine ; [miel] to secrete ; fig & litt to exude.

distinct, e [distɛ̃, ɛ̃kt] adj distinct.

distinctement [distɛ̃ktəmã] adv distinctly, clearly.

distinctif, ive [distɛ̃ktif, iv] adj distinctive.

distinction [distɛ̃ksjɔ̃] nf distinction.

distingué, e [distɛ̃ge] adj distinguished.

distinguer [3] [distɛ̃ge] vt 1. [différencier] to tell apart, to distinguish - 2. [percevoir] to make out, to distinguish - 3. [rendre différent] : **distinguer de** to distinguish from, to set apart from. ▸ **se distinguer** vp 1. [se différencier] : **se distinguer (de)** to stand out (from) - 2. [s'illustrer] to distinguish o.s.

distraction [distraksjɔ̃] nf 1. [inattention] inattention, absent-mindedness - 2. [passetemps] leisure activity.

distraire [112] [distrer] vt 1. [déranger] to distract - 2. [divertir] to amuse, to entertain. ▸ **se distraire** vp to amuse o.s.

distrait, e [distre, ɛt] <> pp ▸ distraire. <> adj absent-minded.

distribuer [7] [distribɥe] *vt* to distribute ; [courrier] to deliver ; [ordres] to give out ; [cartes] to deal ; [coups, sourires] to dispense.

distributeur, trice [distribytœr, tris] *nm, f* distributor. ➡ **distributeur** *nm* **1.** AUTO & COMM distributor - **2.** [machine] : **distributeur (automatique) de billets** BANQUE cash machine, cash dispenser UK, ATM US ; [transports] ticket machine ; **distributeur de boissons** drinks machine.

distribution [distribysjɔ̃] *nf* **1.** [répartition, diffusion, disposition] distribution ; **distribution des prix** SCOL prize-giving - **2.** CINÉ & THÉÂTRE cast.

dit, dite [di, dit] ⬦ *pp* ▶ **dire.** ⬦ *adj* **1.** [appelé] known as - **2.** DR said, above - **3.** [fixé] : **à l'heure dite** at the appointed time.

divagation [divagasjɔ̃] *nf* wandering.

divaguer [3] [divage] *vi* to ramble.

divan [divɑ̃] *nm* divan (seat).

divergence [divɛrʒɑ̃s] *nf* divergence, difference ; [d'opinions] difference.

diverger [17] [divɛrʒe] *vi* to diverge ; [opinions] to differ.

divers, e [divɛr, ɛrs] ⬦ *adj* **1.** [différent] different, various - **2.** [disparate] diverse - **3.** (avant n) [plusieurs] several, various ; **en diverses occasions** on several ou various occasions ; **à usages divers** multipurpose (avant n). ⬦ *adj indéf pl* POLIT others ; **les divers droite/gauche** other right/left-wing parties.

diversifier [9] [divɛrsifje] *vt* to vary, to diversify. ➡ **se diversifier** *vp* to diversify.

diversion [divɛrsjɔ̃] *nf* diversion.

diversité [divɛrsite] *nf* diversity.

divertir [32] [divɛrtir] *vt* [distraire] to entertain, to amuse. ➡ **se divertir** *vp* to amuse o.s., to entertain o.s.

divertissement [divɛrtismɑ̃] *nm* [passetemps] form of relaxation.

divin, e [divɛ̃, in] *adj* divine.

divinité [divinite] *nf* divinity.

diviser [3] [divize] *vt* **1.** [gén] to divide, to split up - **2.** MATH to divide ; **diviser 8 par 4** to divide 8 by 4.

division [divizjɔ̃] *nf* **1.** MATH division - **2.** [fragmentation] splitting, division, partition - **3.** [désaccord] division, rift - **4.** FOOTBALL division - **5.** MIL division.

divorce [divɔrs] *nm* **1.** DR divorce - **2.** *fig* [divergence] gulf, separation.

divorcé, e [divɔrse] ⬦ *adj* divorced. ⬦ *nm, f* divorcee, divorced person.

divorcer [16] [divɔrse] *vi* to divorce.

divulguer [3] [divylge] *vt* to divulge.

dix [dis] *adj num inv* & *nm* ten ; *voir aussi* **six.**

dix-huit [dizɥit] *adj num inv* & *nm* eighteen ; *voir aussi* **six.**

dix-huitième [dizɥitjɛm] *adj num inv, nm* & *nmf* eighteenth ; *voir aussi* **sixième.**

dixième [dizjɛm] *adj num inv, nm* & *nmf* tenth ; *voir aussi* **sixième.**

dix-neuf [diznœf] *adj num inv* & *nm* nineteen ; *voir aussi* **six.**

dix-neuvième [diznœvjɛm] *adj num inv, nm* & *nmf* nineteenth ; *voir aussi* **sixième.**

dix-sept [disɛt] *adj num inv* & *nm* seventeen ; *voir aussi* **six.**

dix-septième [disɛtjɛm] *adj num inv, nm* & *nmf* seventeenth ; *voir aussi* **sixième.**

dizaine [dizɛn] *nf* **1.** MATH ten - **2.** [environ dix] : **une dizaine de** about ten ; **par dizaines** [en grand nombre] in their dozens.

DJ [didʒi, didʒe] (abr de disc-jockey) *nm* DJ.

DM (abr écrite de deutsche Mark) DM.

do [do] *nm inv* MUS C ; [chanté] doh.

doc [dɔk] (abr de documentation) *nf* literature, brochures *pl*.

doc. (abr écrite de document) doc.

docile [dɔsil] *adj* [obéissant] docile.

dock [dɔk] *nm* **1.** [bassin] dock - **2.** [hangar] warehouse.

docker [dɔker] *nm* docker, longshoreman US, stevedore US.

docteur [dɔktœr] *nm* **1.** [médecin] doctor - **2.** UNIV : **docteur ès lettres/sciences** ≃ PhD.

doctorat [dɔktɔra] *nm* [grade] doctorate, PhD US.

doctrine [dɔktrin] *nf* doctrine.

document [dɔkymɑ̃] *nm* document.

documentaire [dɔkymɑ̃tɛr] *nm* & *adj* documentary.

documentaliste [dɔkymɑ̃talist] *nmf* [d'archives] archivist ; PRESSE & TV researcher.

documentation [dɔkymɑ̃tasjɔ̃] *nf* **1.** [travail] research - **2.** [documents] paperwork, papers *pl* - **3.** [brochures] documentation.

documenter [3] [dɔkymɑ̃te] *vt* to document. ➡ **se documenter** *vp* to do some research.

dodo [dɔdo] *nm fam* beddy-byes ; **faire dodo** to sleep.

dodu, e [dɔdy] *adj fam* [enfant, joue, bras] chubby ; [animal] plump.

dogme [dɔgm] *nm* dogma.

dogue [dɔg] *nm* mastiff.

doigt [dwa] *nm* finger ; **un doigt de** (just) a drop ou finger of ; **montrer qqch du doigt** to point at sthg ; **doigt de pied** toe.

dois ▶ **devoir.**

doive ▶ **devoir.**

dollar [dɔlar] *nm* dollar.

domaine [dɔmɛn] *nm* **1.** [propriété] estate - **2.** [secteur, champ d'activité] field, domain.

dôme [dom] *nm* **1.** ARCHIT dome - **2.** GÉOGR rounded peak.

domestique [dɔmɛstik] <> *nmf* (domestic) servant. <> *adj* family *(avant n)* ; [travaux] household *(avant n)*.

domestiquer [3] [dɔmɛstike] *vt* **1.** [animal] to domesticate - **2.** [éléments naturels] to harness.

domicile [dɔmisil] *nm* [gén] (place of) residence ; **travailler à domicile** to work from OU at home ; **ils livrent à domicile** they do deliveries.

dominant, e [dɔminɑ̃, ɑ̃t] *adj* [qui prévaut] dominant.

domination [dɔminasjɔ̃] *nf* **1.** [autorité] domination, dominion - **2.** [influence] influence.

dominer [3] [dɔmine] <> *vt* **1.** [surplomber, avoir de l'autorité sur] to dominate - **2.** [surpasser] to outclass - **3.** [maîtriser] to control, to master - **4.** *fig* [connaître] to master. <> *vi* **1.** [régner] to dominate, to be dominant - **2.** [prédominer] to predominate - **3.** [triompher] to be on top, to hold sway. **se dominer** *vp* to control o.s.

Dominique [dɔminik] *nf*: **la Dominique** Dominica.

domino [dɔmino] *nm* domino.

dommage [dɔmaʒ] *nm* **1.** [préjudice] harm *(U)* ; **dommages et intérêts, dommages-intérêts** damages ; **quel dommage!** what a shame! ; **c'est dommage que** (+ *subjonctif*) it's a pity OU shame (that) - **2.** [dégâts] damage *(U)*.

dompter [3] [dɔ̃te] *vt* **1.** [animal, fauve] to tame - **2.** *fig* [maîtriser] to overcome, to control.

dompteur, euse [dɔ̃tœr, øz] *nm, f* [de fauves] tamer.

DOM-TOM [dɔmtɔm] (*abr de* **départements d'outre-mer/territoires d'outre-mer**) *nmpl French overseas départements and territories.*

don [dɔ̃] *nm* **1.** [cadeau] gift - **2.** [aptitude] knack.

donateur, trice [dɔnatœr, tris] *nm, f* donor.

donation [dɔnasjɔ̃] *nf* settlement.

donc [dɔ̃k] *conj* so ; **je disais donc...** so as I was saying... ; **allons donc!** come on! ; **tais-toi donc!** will you be quiet!

donjon [dɔ̃ʒɔ̃] *nm* keep.

donné, e [dɔne] *adj* given ; **étant donné que** given that, considering (that). **donnée** *nf* **1.** INFORM & MATH datum, piece of data ; **données numériques** numerical data - **2.** [élément] fact, particular.

donner [3] [dɔne] <> *vt* **1.** [gén] to give ;

[se débarrasser de] to give away ; **donner qqch à qqn** to give sth to sb, to give sthg to sb ; **donner qqch à faire à qqn** to give sb sthg to do, to give sth to sb to do ; **donner sa voiture à réparer** to leave one's car to be repaired ; **quel âge lui donnes-tu?** how old do you think he/she is? - **2.** [occasionner] to give, to cause. <> *vi* **1.** [s'ouvrir] : **donner sur** to look out onto - **2.** [produire] to produce, to yield.

donneur, euse [dɔnœr, øz] *nm, f* **1.** MÉD donor - **2.** [jeux de cartes] dealer.

dont [dɔ̃] *pron rel* **1.** [complément de verbe ou d'adjectif] : **la personne dont tu parles** the person you're speaking about, the person about whom you are speaking ; **l'accident dont il est responsable** the accident for which he is responsible ; **c'est quelqu'un dont on dit le plus grand bien** he's someone about whom people speak highly *(la traduction varie selon la préposition anglaise utilisée avec le verbe ou l'adjectif)* - **2.** [complément de nom ou de pronom - relatif à l'objet] of which, whose ; [- relatif à personne] whose ; **la boîte dont le couvercle est jaune** the box whose lid is yellow, the box with the yellow lid ; **c'est quelqu'un dont j'apprécie l'honnêteté** he's someone whose honesty I appreciate ; **celui dont les parents sont divorcés** the one whose parents are divorced - **3.** [indiquant la partie d'un tout] : **plusieurs personnes ont téléphoné, dont ton frère** several people phoned, one of which was your brother OU and among them was your brother.

dopage [dɔpaʒ] *nm* doping.

doper [3] [dɔpe] *vt* to dope. **se doper** *vp* to take stimulants.

dorade [dɔrad] = **daurade**.

doré, e [dɔre] *adj* **1.** [couvert de dorure] gilded, gilt - **2.** [couleur] golden.

dorénavant [dɔrenavɑ̃] *adv* from now on, in future.

dorer [3] [dɔre] *vt* **1.** [couvrir d'or] to gild - **2.** [peau] to tan - **3.** CULIN to glaze.

dorloter [3] [dɔrlɔte] *vt* to pamper, to cosset.

dormir [36] [dɔrmir] *vi* **1.** [sommeiller] to sleep - **2.** [rester inactif - personne] to slack, to stand around (doing nothing) ; [- capitaux] to lie idle.

dortoir [dɔrtwar] *nm* dormitory.

dos [do] *nm* back ; **de dos** from behind ; **'voir au dos'** 'see over' ; **dos crawlé** backstroke.

DOS, Dos [dɔs] (*abr de* **Disk Operating System**) *nm* DOS.

dosage [dozaʒ] *nm* [de médicament] dose ; [d'ingrédient] amount.

dos-d'âne [dodan] *nm inv* bump.

dose [doz] *nf* **1.** [quantité de médicament] dose - **2.** [quantité] share ; **forcer la dose** *fam fig* to overdo it ; **une (bonne) dose de bêtise** *fam fig* a lot of silliness.

doser [3] [doze] *vt* [médicament, ingrédient] to measure out ; *fig* to weigh up *UK*.

dossard [dosar] *nm* number (*on competitor's back*).

dossier [dosje] *nm* **1.** [de fauteuil] back - **2.** [documents] file, dossier - **3.** [classeur] file, folder - **4.** INFORM folder - **5.** UNIV : **dossier d'inscription** registration forms - **6.** *fig* [question] question.

dot [dɔt] *nf* dowry.

doter [3] [dɔte] *vt* [pourvoir] : **doter de** [talent] to endow with ; [machine] to equip with.

douane [dwan] *nf* **1.** [service, lieu] customs *pl* ; **passer la douane** to go through customs - **2.** [taxe] (import) duty.

douanier, ère [dwanje, ɛr] <> *adj* customs (*avant n*). <> *nm, f* customs officer.

doublage [dublaʒ] *nm* **1.** [renforcement] lining - **2.** [de film] dubbing - **3.** [d'acteur] understudying.

double [dubl] <> *adj* double. <> *adv* double. <> *nm* **1.** [quantité] : **le double** double - **2.** [copie] copy ; **en double** in duplicate - **3.** TENNIS doubles *pl*.

doublé [duble] *nm* [réussite double] double.

double-clic, doubles-clics [dublklik] *nm* INFORM double-click.

double-cliquer [3] [dublklike] *vt* INFORM to double-click on ; **double-cliquer sur l'image** to double-click on the picture.

doublement [dubləmã] *adv* doubly.

doubler [3] [duble] <> *vt* **1.** [multiplier] to double - **2.** [plier] to (fold) double - **3.** [renforcer] : **doubler (de)** to line (with) - **4.** [dépasser] to overtake *UK*, to pass *US* - **5.** [film, acteur] to dub - **6.** [augmenter] to double. <> *vi* **1.** [véhicule] to overtake *UK*, to pass *US* - **2.** [augmenter] to double.

doublure [dublyr] *nf* **1.** [renforcement] lining - **2.** CINÉ stand-in.

douce ⏵ **doux**.

doucement [dusmã] *adv* **1.** [descendre] carefully ; [frapper] gently - **2.** [traiter] gently ; [parler] softly.

douceur [dusœr] *nf* **1.** [de saveur, parfum] sweetness - **2.** [d'éclairage, de peau, de musique] softness - **3.** [de climat] mildness - **4.** [de caractère] gentleness. ⏵ **douceurs** *nfpl* [friandises] sweets *UK*, candy *US*.

douche [duʃ] *nf* **1.** [appareil, action] shower - **2.** *fam fig* [déception] letdown.

doucher [3] [duʃe] *vt* **1.** [donner une douche à] : **doucher qqn** to give sb a shower - **2.** *fam fig* [décevoir] to let down. ⏵ **se doucher** *vp* to take ou have a shower, to shower.

douchette [duʃɛt] *nf* bar-code reader ou scanner (*for bulky items*).

doué, e [dwe] *adj* talented ; **être doué pour** to have a gift for.

douillet, ette [duje, ɛt] <> *adj* **1.** [confortable] snug, cosy - **2.** [sensible] soft. <> *nm, f* wimp.

douleur [dulœr] *nf litt & fig* pain.

douloureux, euse [dulurø, øz] *adj* **1.** [physiquement] painful - **2.** [moralement] distressing - **3.** [regard, air] sorrowful.

doute [dut] *nm* doubt. ⏵ **sans doute** *loc adv* no doubt ; **sans aucun doute** without (a) doubt.

douter [3] [dute] <> *vt* [ne pas croire] : **douter que** (+ *subjonctif*) to doubt (that). <> *vi* [ne pas avoir confiance] : **douter de qqn/de qqch** to doubt sb/sthg, to have doubts about sb/sthg ; **j'en doute** I doubt it. ⏵ **se douter** *vp* : **se douter de qqch** to suspect sthg ; **je m'en doutais** I thought so.

douteux, euse [dutø, øz] *adj* **1.** [incertain] doubtful - **2.** [contestable] questionable - **3.** *péj* [mœurs] dubious ; [vêtements, personne] dubious-looking.

Douvres [duvr] *npr* Dover.

doux, douce [du, dus] *adj* **1.** [éclairage, peau, musique] soft - **2.** [saveur, parfum] sweet - **3.** [climat, condiment] mild - **4.** [pente, regard, caractère] gentle.

douzaine [duzen] *nf* **1.** [douze] dozen - **2.** [environ douze] : **une douzaine de** about twelve.

douze [duz] *adj num inv & nm* twelve ; *voir aussi* **six**.

douzième [duzjɛm] *adj num inv, nm & nmf* twelfth ; *voir aussi* **sixième**.

doyen, enne [dwajɛ̃, ɛn] *nm, f* [le plus ancien] most senior member.

Dr (*abr écrite de* **Docteur**) Dr.

draconien, enne [drakɔnjɛ̃, ɛn] *adj* draconian.

dragée [draʒe] *nf* **1.** [confiserie] sugared almond - **2.** [comprimé] pill.

dragon [dragɔ̃] *nm* **1.** [monstre, personne autoritaire] dragon - **2.** [soldat] dragoon.

draguer [3] [drage] *vt* **1.** [nettoyer] to dredge - **2.** *fam* [personne] to chat up *UK*, to get off with *UK*, to try to pick up *US*.

dragueur, euse [dragœr, øz] *nm, f fam* [homme] womanizer ; **quelle dragueuse!** she's always chasing after men!

drainage [drenaʒ] *nm* draining.

drainer [4] [drene] *vt* **1.** [terrain, plaie] to drain - **2.** *fig* [attirer] to drain off.

dramatique [dramatik] <> *nf* play.
<> *adj* **1.** THÉÂTRE dramatic - **2.** [grave]
tragic.

dramatiser [3] [dramatize] *vt* [exagérer] to
dramatize.

drame [dram] *nm* **1.** [catastrophe] tragedy ;
faire un drame de qqch *fig* to make a drama
of sthg - **2.** LITTÉR drama.

drap [dra] *nm* **1.** [de lit] sheet ; **drap housse**
fitted sheet - **2.** [tissu] woollen *UK* OU
woolen *US* cloth.

drapeau, x [drapo] *nm* flag ; **être sous les
drapeaux** *fig* to be doing military service.

draper [3] [drape] *vt* to drape.

draperie [drapri] *nf* [tenture] drapery.

dresser [4] [drese] *vt* **1.** [lever] to raise
- **2.** [faire tenir] to put up - **3.** *sout* [construire]
to erect - **4.** [acte, liste, carte] to draw up ;
[procès-verbal] to make out - **5.** [dompter] to
train - **6.** *fig* [opposer] : **dresser qqn contre
qqn** to set sb against sb. ➤ **se dresser** *vp*
1. [se lever] to stand up - **2.** [s'élever] to rise
(up) ; *fig* to stand ; **se dresser contre qqch** to
rise up against sthg.

dresseur, euse [drescer, øz] *nm, f* trainer.

dribbler [3] [drible] <> *vi* SPORT to dribble.
<> *vt* SPORT : **dribbler qqn** to dribble past
sb.

drogue [drog] *nf* [stupéfiant] drug ; **la
drogue** drugs *pl*.

drogué, e [droge] <> *adj* drugged.
<> *nm, f* drug addict.

droguer [3] [droge] *vt* [victime] to drug.
➤ **se droguer** *vp* [de stupéfiants] to take
drugs.

droguerie [drogri] *nf* hardware shop.

droguiste [drogist] *nmf* : **chez le droguiste**
at the hardware shop.

droit, e [drwa, drwat] *adj* **1.** [du côté droit]
right - **2.** [rectiligne, vertical, honnête]
straight. ➤ **droit** <> *adv* straight ; **tout
droit** straight ahead. <> *nm* **1.** DR law
- **2.** [prérogative] right ; **avoir droit à** to be
entitled to ; **avoir le droit de faire qqch** to be
allowed to do sthg ; **être en droit de faire
qqch** to have a right to do sthg ; **droit de
vote** right to vote ; **droits de l'homme**
human rights. ➤ **droite** *nf* **1.** [gén] right,
right-hand side ; **à droite** on the right ; **à
droite de** to the right of - **2.** POLIT : **la droite**
the right (wing) ; **de droite** right-wing.

droitier, ère [drwatje, ɛr] <> *adj* right-
handed. <> *nm, f* right-handed person,
right-hander.

drôle [drol] *adj* **1.** [amusant] funny - **2.** :
drôle de [bizarre] funny ; *fam* [remarquable]
amazing.

dromadaire [dromadɛr] *nm* dromedary.

dru, e [dry] *adj* thick.

ds *abr écrite de* **dans**.

du *art partitif* ➤ **de**.

dû, due [dy] <> *pp* ➤ **devoir**. <> *adj*
due, owing. ➤ **dû** *nm* due.

Dublin [dyblɛ̃] *npr* Dublin.

duc [dyk] *nm* duke.

duchesse [dyʃɛs] *nf* duchess.

duel [dɥɛl] *nm* duel.

dûment [dymɑ̃] *adv* duly.

dune [dyn] *nf* dune.

duo [dɥo] *nm* **1.** MUS duet - **2.** [couple] duo.

dupe [dyp] <> *nf* dupe. <> *adj* gullible.

duper [3] [dype] *vt sout* to dupe, to take sb
in.

duplex [dyplɛks] *nm* **1.** [appartement] split-
level flat, maisonette *UK*, duplex *US* - **2.** RA-
DIO & TV link-up.

duplicata [dyplikata] *nm inv* duplicate.

dupliquer [3] [dyplike] *vt* [document] to
duplicate.

duquel [dykɛl] ➤ **lequel**.

dur, e [dyr] <> *adj* **1.** [matière, personne,
travail] hard ; [carton] stiff - **2.** [viande] tough
- **3.** [climat, punition, loi] harsh. <> *nm, f*
fam **dur (à cuire)** tough nut. ➤ **dur** *adv*
hard.

durable [dyrabl] *adj* lasting.

durant [dyrɑ̃] *prép* **1.** [pendant] for - **2.** [au
cours de] during.

durcir [32] [dyrsir] <> *vt litt & fig* to
harden. <> *vi* to harden, to become hard.

durée [dyre] *nf* [période] length.

durement [dyrmɑ̃] *adv* **1.** [violemment]
hard, vigorously - **2.** [péniblement] severely
- **3.** [méchamment] harshly.

durer [3] [dyre] *vi* to last.

dureté [dyrte] *nf* **1.** [de matériau, de l'eau]
hardness - **2.** [d'époque, de climat, de
personne] harshness - **3.** [de punition] severity.

dus, dut *etc* ➤ **devoir**.

DUT (*abr de* **diplôme universitaire de technologie**) *nm university diploma in technology.*

duvet [dyvɛ] *nm* **1.** [plumes, poils fins]
down - **2.** [sac de couchage] sleeping bag.

DVD-ROM [dvdrom] (*abr de* **Digital Video
ou Versatile Disc Read Only Memory**) *nm*
DVD-ROM.

dynamique [dinamik] *adj* dynamic.

dynamisme [dinamism] *nm* dynamism.

dynamite [dinamit] *nf* dynamite.

dynastie [dinasti] *nf* dynasty.

dyslexique [dislɛksik] *adj* dyslexic.

écharde

E

e, E [ə] *nm inv* e, E. **E** (*abr écrite de* **est**) E.

eau, x [o] *nf* water ; **eau douce/salée/de mer** fresh/salt/sea water ; **eau gazeuse/plate** fizzy/still water ; **eau courante** running water ; **eau minérale** mineral water ; **eau oxygénée** hydrogen peroxide ; **eau du robinet** tap water ; **eau de toilette** toilet water ; **tomber à l'eau** *fig* to fall through.

eau-de-vie [odvi] (*pl* **eaux-de-vie**) *nf* brandy.

ébahi, e [ebai] *adj* staggered, astounded.

ébattre [83] [ebatr] **s'ébattre** *vp litt* to frolic.

ébauche [eboʃ] *nf* [esquisse] sketch ; *fig* outline ; **l'ébauche d'un sourire** the ghost of a smile.

ébaucher [3] [eboʃe] *vt* **1.** [esquisser] to rough out - **2.** *fig* [commencer] : **ébaucher un geste** to start to make a gesture.

ébène [ebɛn] *nf* ebony.

ébéniste [ebenist] *nm* cabinet-maker.

éberlué, e [ebɛrlɥe] *adj* flabbergasted.

éblouir [32] [ebluir] *vt* to dazzle.

éblouissement [ebluismɑ̃] *nm* **1.** [aveuglement] glare, dazzle - **2.** [vertige] dizziness - **3.** [émerveillement] amazement.

éborgner [3] [ebɔrɲe] *vt* : **éborgner qqn** to put sb's eye out.

éboueur [ebwœr] *nm* dustman *UK*, garbage collector *US*.

ébouillanter [3] [ebujɑ̃te] *vt* to scald.

éboulement [ebulmɑ̃] *nm* caving in, fall.

éboulis [ebuli] *nm* mass of fallen rocks.

ébouriffer [3] [eburife] *vt* [cheveux] to ruffle.

ébranler [3] [ebrɑ̃le] *vt* **1.** [bâtiment, opinion] to shake - **2.** [gouvernement, nerfs] to weaken. **s'ébranler** *vp* [train] to move off.

ébrécher [18] [ebreʃe] *vt* [assiette, verre] to chip ; *fam fig* to break into.

ébriété [ebrijete] *nf* drunkenness.

ébrouer [3] [ebrue] **s'ébrouer** *vp* [animal] to shake o.s.

ébruiter [3] [ebrɥite] *vt* to spread.

ébullition [ebylisjɔ̃] *nf* **1.** [de liquide] boiling point - **2.** [effervescence] : **en ébullition** *fig* in a state of agitation.

écaille [ekaj] *nf* **1.** [de poisson, reptile] scale ; [de tortue] shell - **2.** [de plâtre, peinture, vernis] flake - **3.** [matière] tortoiseshell ; **en écaille** [lunettes] horn-rimmed.

écailler [3] [ekaje] *vt* **1.** [poisson] to scale - **2.** [huîtres] to open. **s'écailler** *vp* to flake ou peel off.

écarlate [ekarlat] *adj & nf* scarlet.

écarquiller [3] [ekarkije] *vt* : **écarquiller les yeux** to stare wide-eyed.

écart [ekar] *nm* **1.** [espace] space - **2.** [temps] gap - **3.** [différence] difference - **4.** [déviation] : **faire un écart** [personne] to step aside ; [cheval] to shy ; **être à l'écart** to be in the background.

écarteler [25] [ekartəle] *vt fig* to tear apart.

écartement [ekartəmɑ̃] *nm* : **écartement entre** space between.

écarter [3] [ekarte] *vt* **1.** [bras, jambes] to open, to spread ; **écarter qqch de** to move sthg away from - **2.** [obstacle, danger] to brush aside - **3.** [foule, rideaux] to push aside ; [solution] to dismiss ; **écarter qqn de** to exclude sb from. **s'écarter** *vp* **1.** [se séparer] to part - **2.** [se détourner] : **s'écarter de** to deviate from.

ecchymose [ekimoz] *nf* bruise.

ecclésiastique [eklezjastik] <> *nm* clergyman. <> *adj* ecclesiastical.

écervelé, e [esɛrvəle] <> *adj* scatty, scatterbrained. <> *nm, f* scatterbrain.

échafaud [eʃafo] *nm* scaffold.

échafaudage [eʃafodaʒ] *nm* **1.** CONSTR scaffolding - **2.** [amas] pile.

échalote [eʃalɔt] *nf* shallot.

échancrure [eʃɑ̃kryr] *nf* **1.** [de robe] low neckline - **2.** [de côte] indentation.

échange [eʃɑ̃ʒ] *nm* [de choses] exchange ; **en échange (de)** in exchange (for).

échanger [17] [eʃɑ̃ʒe] *vt* **1.** [troquer] to swap, to exchange - **2.** [marchandise] : **échanger qqch (contre)** to change sthg (for) - **3.** [communiquer] to exchange.

échangisme [eʃɑ̃ʒism] *nm* [de partenaires sexuels] partner-swapping.

échantillon [eʃɑ̃tijɔ̃] *nm* [de produit, de population] sample.

échappatoire [eʃapatwar] *nf* way out.

échappement [eʃapmɑ̃] *nm* AUTO exhaust, **pot.**

échapper [3] [eʃape] *vi* **1.** : **échapper à** [personne, situation] to escape from ; [danger, mort] to escape ; [suj: détail, parole, sens] to escape - **2.** [glisser] : **laisser échapper** to let slip. **s'échapper** *vp* : **s'échapper (de)** to escape (from).

écharde [eʃard] *nf* splinter.

écharpe [eʃarp] *nf* scarf ; **en écharpe** in a sling.

écharper [3] [eʃarpe] *vt* to rip to pieces OU shreds.

échasse [eʃas] *nf* [de berger, oiseau] stilt.

échassier [eʃasje] *nm* wader.

échauffement [eʃofmɑ̃] *nm* SPORT warm-up.

échauffer [3] [eʃofe] *vt* **1.** [chauffer] to overheat - **2.** [exciter] to excite - **3.** [énerver] to irritate. ➡ **s'échauffer** *vp* **1.** SPORT to warm up - **2.** *fig* [s'animer] to become heated.

échéance [eʃeɑ̃s] *nf* **1.** [délai] expiry ; **à longue échéance** in the long term - **2.** [date] payment date ; **arriver à échéance** to fall due.

échéant [eʃeɑ̃] *adj* : **le cas échéant** if necessary, if need be.

échec [eʃɛk] *nm* **1.** [insuccès] failure ; **être en situation d'échec scolaire** to have learning difficulties - **2.** [jeux] **échec et mat** checkmate. ➡ **échecs** *nmpl* chess (U).

échelle [eʃɛl] *nf* **1.** [objet] ladder - **2.** [ordre de grandeur] scale.

échelon [eʃlɔ̃] *nm* **1.** [barreau] rung - **2.** *fig* [niveau] level.

échelonner [3] [eʃlone] *vt* [espacer] to spread out.

échevelé, e [eʃəvle] *adj* **1.** [ébouriffé] dishevelled UK, disheveled US - **2.** [frénétique] wild.

échine [eʃin] *nf* ANAT spine.

échiquier [eʃikje] *nm* [jeux] chessboard.

écho [eko] *nm* echo.

échographie [ekɔgrafi] *nf* [examen] ultrasound (scan).

échoir [70] [eʃwar] *vi* **1.** [être dévolu] : **échoir à** to fall to - **2.** [expirer] to fall due.

échoppe [eʃɔp] *nf* stall.

échouer [6] [eʃwe] *vi* [ne pas réussir] to fail ; **échouer à un examen** to fail an exam. ➡ **s'échouer** *vp* [navire] to run aground.

échu, e [eʃy] *pp* ➤ **échoir**.

éclabousser [3] [eklabuse] *vt* **1.** [suj: liquide] to spatter - **2.** *fig* [compromettre] to compromise.

éclair [eklɛr] ◇ *nm* **1.** [de lumière] flash of lightning - **2.** *fig* [instant] : **éclair de** flash of. ◇ *adj inv* : **visite éclair** flying visit ; **guerre éclair** blitzkrieg.

éclairage [eklɛraʒ] *nm* **1.** [lumière] lighting - **2.** *fig* [point de vue] light.

éclaircie [eklɛrsi] *nf* bright interval, sunny spell.

éclaircir [32] [eklɛrsir] *vt* **1.** [rendre plus clair] to lighten - **2.** [rendre moins épais] to

thin - **3.** *fig* [clarifier] to clarify. ➡ **s'éclaircir** *vp* **1.** [devenir plus clair] to clear - **2.** [devenir moins épais] to thin - **3.** [se clarifier] to become clearer.

éclaircissement [eklɛrsismɑ̃] *nm* [explication] explanation.

éclairer [4] [eklere] *vt* **1.** [de lumière] to light up - **2.** [expliquer] to clarify. ➡ **s'éclairer** *vp* **1.** [personne] to light one's way - **2.** [regard, visage] to light up - **3.** [rue, ville] to light up.

éclaireur [eklɛrœr] *nm* scout.

éclat [ekla] *nm* **1.** [de verre, d'os] splinter ; [de pierre] chip - **2.** [de lumière] brilliance - **3.** [de couleur] vividness - **4.** [beauté] radiance - **5.** [faste] splendour UK, splendor US - **6.** [bruit] burst ; **éclat de rire** burst of laughter ; **éclats de voix** shouts ; **faire un éclat** to cause a scandal ; **rire aux éclats** to roar OU shriek with laughter.

éclater [3] [eklate] *vi* **1.** [exploser - pneu] to burst ; [- verre] to shatter ; [- obus] to explode ; **faire éclater** [- ballon] to burst ; [- bombe] to explode ; [- pétard] to let off - **2.** [incendie, rires] to break out - **3.** [joie] to shine ; **laisser éclater** to give vent to - **4.** *fig* [nouvelles, scandale] to break. ➡ **s'éclater** *vp fam* to have a great time.

éclectique [eklɛktik] *adj* eclectic.

éclipse [eklips] *nf* ASTRON eclipse ; **éclipse de lune/soleil** eclipse of the moon/sun.

éclipser [3] [eklipse] *vt* to eclipse. ➡ **s'éclipser** *vp* **1.** ASTRON to go into eclipse - **2.** *fam* [s'esquiver] to slip away.

éclopé, e [eklope] ◇ *adj* lame. ◇ *nm, f* lame person.

éclore [113] [eklɔr] *vi* [s'ouvrir - fleur] to open out, to blossom ; [- œuf] to hatch.

éclos, e [eklo, oz] *pp* ➤ **éclore**.

écluse [eklyz] *nf* lock.

écœurant, e [ekœrɑ̃, ɑ̃t] *adj* **1.** [gén] disgusting - **2.** [démoralisant] sickening.

écœurer [5] [ekœre] *vt* **1.** [dégoûter] to sicken, to disgust - **2.** *fig* [indigner] to sicken - **3.** [décourager] to discourage.

école [ekɔl] *nf* **1.** [gén] school ; **école maternelle** nursery school ; **école normale** ≈ teacher training college UK, ≈ teachers college US ; **École normale supérieure** *grande école for secondary and university teachers* ; **école primaire/secondaire** primary/secondary school UK, grade/high school US ; **école publique** state school UK, public school US ; **grande école** *specialist school establishment, entered by competitive exam and highly prestigious* ; **faire l'école buissonnière** to play truant UK OU hooky US ; **faire école** to attract a following - **2.** [éducation] schooling ; **l'école privée** private education.

écolier, ère [ekɔlje, ɛr] *nm, f* [élève] pupil.

écolo [ekɔlɔ] *nmf fam* ecologist ; **les écolos** the Greens.

écologie [ekɔlɔʒi] *nf* ecology.

écologiste [ekɔlɔʒist] *nmf* ecologist.

écomusée [ekɔmyze] *nm* museum of the environment.

éconduire [98] [ekɔ̃dɥir] *vt* [repousser - demande] to dismiss ; [- visiteur, soupirant] to show to the door.

économe [ekɔnɔm] <> *nmf* bursar. <> *adj* careful, thrifty.

économie [ekɔnɔmi] *nf* **1.** [science] economics *(U)* - **2.** POLIT economy ; **économie de marché** market economy - **3.** [parcimonie] economy, thrift.

économique [ekɔnɔmik] *adj* **1.** ÉCON economic - **2.** [avantageux] economical.

économiser [3] [ekɔnɔmize] *vt litt & fig* to save.

économiste [ekɔnɔmist] *nmf* economist.

écoper [3] [ekɔpe] *vt* **1.** NAUT to bale out - **2.** *fam* [sanction] : **écoper (de) qqch** to get sthg.

écoproduit [ekɔprɔdɥi] *nm* green product.

écorce [ekɔrs] *nf* **1.** [d'arbre] bark - **2.** [d'agrume] peel - **3.** GÉOL crust.

écorcher [3] [ekɔrʃe] *vt* **1.** [lapin] to skin - **2.** [bras, jambe] to scratch - **3.** *fig* [langue, nom] to mispronounce.

écorchure [ekɔrʃyr] *nf* graze, scratch.

écorecharge [ekɔrəʃarʒ] *nf* ecorefill.

écossais, e [ekɔsɛ, ɛz] *adj* **1.** [de l'Écosse] Scottish ; [whisky] Scotch - **2.** [tissu] tartan. **écossais** *nm* [langue] Scots. **Écossais, e** *nm, f* Scot, Scotsman (*f* Scotswoman).

Écosse [ekɔs] *nf* : **l'Écosse** Scotland.

écosser [3] [ekɔse] *vt* to shell.

écosystème [ekɔsistɛm] *nm* ecosystem.

écotourisme [ekɔturism] *nm* ecotourism.

écouler [3] [ekule] *vt* to sell. **s'écouler** *vp* **1.** [eau] to flow - **2.** [personnes] to flow out - **3.** [temps] to pass.

écourter [3] [ekurte] *vt* to shorten.

écouter [3] [ekute] *vt* to listen to.

écouteur [ekutœr] *nm* [de téléphone] earpiece. **écouteurs** *nmpl* [de radio] headphones.

écoutille [ekutij] *nf* hatchway.

écran [ekrɑ̃] *nm* **1.** CINÉ & INFORM screen ; **écran tactile** tactile screen, touch screen - **2.** [de protection] shield.

écrasant, e [ekrazɑ̃, ɑ̃t] *adj fig* [accablant] overwhelming.

écraser [3] [ekraze] *vt* **1.** [comprimer - cigarette] to stub out ; [- pied] to tread on ; [- insecte, raisin] to crush - **2.** [accabler] :

écraser qqn (de) to burden sb (with) - **3.** [vaincre] to crush - **4.** [renverser] to run over. **s'écraser** *vp* [avion, automobile] : s'écraser (contre) to crash (into).

écrémer [18] [ekreme] *vt* [lait] to skim.

écrevisse [ekrəvis] *nf* crayfish.

écrier [10] [ekrije] **s'écrier** *vp* to cry out.

écrin [ekrɛ̃] *nm* case.

écrire [99] [ekrir] *vt* **1.** [phrase, livre] to write - **2.** [orthographier] to spell. **s'écrire** *vp* [s'épeler] to be spelled.

écrit, e [ekri, it] <> *pp* ► **écrire**. <> *adj* written. **écrit** *nm* **1.** [ouvrage] writing - **2.** [examen] written exam - **3.** [document] piece of writing. **par écrit** *loc adv* in writing.

écriteau, x [ekrito] *nm* notice.

écriture [ekrityr] *nf* [gén] writing.

écrivain [ekrivɛ̃] *nm* writer, author.

écrou [ekru] *nm* TECHNOL nut.

écrouer [3] [ekrue] *vt* to imprison.

écrouler [3] [ekrule] **s'écrouler** *vp litt & fig* to collapse.

écru, e [ekry] *adj* [naturel] unbleached.

ecsta [ɛksta] (*abr de* **ecstasy**) *nm* ecstasy, E.

écu [eky] *nm* **1.** [bouclier, armoiries] shield - **2.** [monnaie ancienne] crown.

écueil [ekœj] *nm* **1.** [rocher] reef - **2.** *fig* [obstacle] stumbling block.

écuelle [ekɥɛl] *nf* [objet] bowl.

éculé, e [ekyle] *adj* **1.** [chaussure] down-at-heel - **2.** *fig* [plaisanterie] hackneyed.

écume [ekym] *nf* [mousse, bave] foam.

écumoire [ekymwar] *nf* skimmer.

écureuil [ekyrœj] *nm* squirrel.

écurie [ekyri] *nf* **1.** [pour chevaux & SPORT] stable - **2.** *fig* [local sale] pigsty.

écusson [ekysɔ̃] *nm* **1.** [d'armoiries] coat-of-arms - **2.** MIL badge.

écuyer, ère [ekɥije, ɛr] *nm, f* [de cirque] rider. **écuyer** *nm* [de chevalier] squire.

eczéma [ɛgzema] *nm* eczema.

édenté, e [edɑ̃te] *adj* toothless.

EDF, Edf (*abr de* **Électricité de France**) *nf French national electricity company*.

édifice [edifis] *nm* **1.** [construction] building - **2.** *fig* [institution] : **l'édifice social** the fabric of society.

édifier [9] [edifje] *vt* **1.** [ville, église] to build - **2.** *fig* [théorie] to construct - **3.** [personne] to edify ; *iron* to enlighten.

Édimbourg [edɛ̃bur] *npr* Edinburgh.

éditer [3] [edite] *vt* to publish.

éditeur, trice [editœr, tris] *nm, f* publisher.

édition [edisjɔ̃] nf **1.** [profession] publishing - **2.** [de journal, livre] edition ; **édition électronique** electronic publishing.

éditorial, aux [editɔrjal, o] nm leader UK, editorial.

édredon [edrədɔ̃] nm eiderdown UK, comforter US.

éducateur, trice [edykatœr, tris] nm, f teacher ; **éducateur spécialisé** teacher of children with special educational needs.

éducatif, ive [edykatif, iv] adj educational.

éducation [edykasjɔ̃] nf **1.** [apprentissage] education ; **l'Éducation nationale** ≃ the Department for Education UK, ≃ the Department of Education US - **2.** [parentale] upbringing - **3.** [savoir-vivre] breeding.

édulcorant [edylkɔrɑ̃] nm : **édulcorant (de synthèse)** (artificial) sweetener.

édulcorer [3] [edylkɔre] vt **1.** sout [tisane] to sweeten - **2.** fig [propos] to tone down.

éduquer [3] [edyke] vt [enfant] to bring up ; [élève] to educate.

effacé, e [efase] adj **1.** [teinte] faded - **2.** [modeste - rôle] unobtrusive ; [- personne] self-effacing.

effacer [16] [efase] vt **1.** [mot] to erase, to rub out ; INFORM to delete - **2.** [souvenir] to erase - **3.** [réussite] to eclipse. ◆ **s'effacer** vp **1.** [s'estomper] to fade (away) - **2.** sout [s'écarter] to move aside - **3.** fig [s'incliner] to give way.

effarant, e [efarɑ̃, ɑ̃t] adj frightening.

effarer [3] [efare] vt to frighten, to scare.

effaroucher [3] [efaruʃe] vt **1.** [effrayer] to scare off - **2.** [intimider] to overawe.

effectif, ive [efɛktif, iv] adj **1.** [remède] effective - **2.** [aide] positive. ◆ **effectif** nm **1.** MIL strength - **2.** [de groupe] total number.

effectivement [efɛktivmɑ̃] adv **1.** [réellement] effectively - **2.** [confirmation] in fact.

effectuer [7] [efɛktɥe] vt [réaliser - manœuvre] to carry out ; [- trajet, paiement] to make.

efféminé, e [efemine] adj effeminate.

effervescent, e [efɛrvesɑ̃, ɑ̃t] adj [boisson] effervescent ; fig [pays] in turmoil.

effet [efɛ] nm **1.** [gén] effect ; **effet secondaire** MÉD side-effect ; **effets spéciaux** CINÉ special effects ; **sous l'effet de** under the effects of ; [alcool] under the influence of ; **effet de serre** greenhouse effect - **2.** [impression recherchée] impression - **3.** COMM [titre] bill. ◆ **en effet** loc adv in fact, indeed.

effeuiller [5] [efœje] vt [arbre] to remove the leaves from ; [fleur] to remove the petals from.

efficace [efikas] adj **1.** [remède, mesure] effective - **2.** [personne, machine] efficient.

effigie [efiʒi] nf effigy.

effiler [3] [efile] vt **1.** [tissu] to fray - **2.** [lame] to sharpen - **3.** [cheveux] to thin.

effilocher [3] [efilɔʃe] vt to fray. ◆ **s'effilocher** vp to fray.

efflanqué, e [eflɑ̃ke] adj emaciated.

effleurer [5] [eflœre] vt **1.** [visage, bras] to brush (against) - **2.** fig [problème, thème] to touch on - **3.** fig [suj: pensée, idée] : **effleurer qqn** to cross sb's mind.

effluve [eflyv] nm exhalation ; fig [d'enfance, du passé] breath.

effondrement [efɔ̃drəmɑ̃] nm collapse.

effondrer [3] [efɔ̃dre] ◆ **s'effondrer** vp litt & fig to collapse.

efforcer [16] [efɔrse] ◆ **s'efforcer** vp : **s'efforcer de faire qqch** to make an effort to do sthg.

effort [efɔr] nm **1.** [de personne] effort - **2.** TECHNOL stress.

effraction [efraksjɔ̃] nf breaking in ; **entrer par effraction dans** to break into.

effrayer [11] [efreje] vt to frighten, to scare.

effréné, e [efrene] adj [course] frantic.

effriter [3] [efrite] vt to cause to crumble. ◆ **s'effriter** vp [mur] to crumble.

effroi [efrwa] nm fear, dread.

effronté, e [efrɔ̃te] ◇ adj insolent. ◇ nm, f insolent person.

effronterie [efrɔ̃tri] nf insolence.

effroyable [efrwajabl] adj **1.** [catastrophe, misère] appalling - **2.** [laideur] hideous.

effusion [efyzjɔ̃] nf **1.** [de liquide] effusion - **2.** [de sentiments] effusiveness.

égal, e, aux [egal, o] ◇ adj **1.** [équivalent] equal - **2.** [régulier] even. ◇ nm, f equal.

également [egalmɑ̃] adv **1.** [avec égalité] equally - **2.** [aussi] as well, too.

égaler [3] [egale] vt **1.** MATH to equal - **2.** [beauté] to match, to compare with.

égaliser [3] [egalize] ◇ vt [haie, cheveux] to trim. ◇ vi SPORT to equalize UK, to tie US.

égalitaire [egaliter] adj egalitarian.

égalité [egalite] nf **1.** [gén] equality - **2.** [d'humeur] evenness - **3.** SPORT : **être à égalité** to be level UK, to be tied US ; [au tennis] at deuce.

égard [egar] nm consideration ; **à cet égard** in this respect. ◆ **à l'égard de** loc prép with regard to, towards, toward US.

égarement [egarmɑ̃] nm **1.** [de jeunesse] wildness - **2.** [de raisonnement] aberration.

égarer [3] [egare] *vt* **1.** [objet] to mislay, to lose - **2.** [personne] to mislead - **3.** *fig & sout* [suj: passion] to lead astray. ⟶ **s'égarer** *vp* **1.** [lettre] to get lost, to go astray ; [personne] to get lost, to lose one's way - **2.** *fig & sout* [personne] to stray from the point.

égayer [11] [egeje] *vt* **1.** [personne] to cheer up - **2.** [pièce] to brighten up.

égide [eʒid] *nf* protection ; **sous l'égide de** *litt* under the aegis of.

église [egliz] *nf* church. ⟶ **Église** *nf* : **l'Église** the Church.

égocentrique [egɔsɑ̃trik] *adj* self-centred *UK*, self-centered *US*, egocentric.

égoïsme [egɔism] *nm* selfishness, egoism.

égoïste [egɔist] ⟨⟩ *nmf* selfish person. ⟨⟩ *adj* selfish, egoistic.

égorger [17] [egɔrʒe] *vt* [animal, personne] to cut the throat of.

égosiller [3] [egɔzije] ⟶ **s'égosiller** *vp fam* **1.** [crier] to bawl, to shout - **2.** [chanter] to sing one's head off.

égout [egu] *nm* sewer.

égoutter [3] [egute] *vt* **1.** [vaisselle] to leave to drain - **2.** [légumes, fromage] to drain. ⟶ **s'égoutter** *vp* to drip, to drain.

égouttoir [egutwar] *nm* **1.** [à légumes] colander, strainer - **2.** [à vaisselle] rack *(for washing-up)*.

égratigner [3] [egratiɲe] *vt* to scratch ; *fig* to have a go ou dig at. ⟶ **s'égratigner** *vp* : **s'égratigner la main** to scratch one's hand.

égratignure [egratiɲyr] *nf* scratch, graze ; *fig* dig.

égrener [19] [egrəne] *vt* **1.** [détacher les grains de - épi, cosse] to shell ; [- grappe] to pick grapes from - **2.** [chapelet] to tell - **3.** *fig* [marquer] to mark.

égrillard, e [egrijar, ard] *adj* ribald, bawdy.

Égypte [eʒipt] *nf* : **l'Égypte** Egypt.

égyptien, enne [eʒipsjɛ̃, ɛn] *adj* Egyptian. ⟶ **égyptien** *nm* [langue] Egyptian. ⟶ **Égyptien, enne** *nm, f* Egyptian.

égyptologie [eʒiptɔlɔʒi] *nf* Egyptology.

eh [e] *interj* hey! ; **eh bien** well.

éhonté, e [eɔ̃te] *adj* shameless.

Eiffel [efɛl] *npr* : **la tour Eiffel** the Eiffel Tower.

éjaculation [eʒakylasjɔ̃] *nf* ejaculation.

éjectable [eʒɛktabl] *adj* : **siège éjectable** ejector seat.

éjecter [4] [eʒɛkte] *vt* **1.** [douille] to eject - **2.** *fam* [personne] to kick out.

élaboration [elabɔrasjɔ̃] *nf* [de plan, système] working out, development.

élaboré, e [elabɔre] *adj* elaborate.

élaborer [3] [elabɔre] *vt* [plan, système] to work out, to develop.

élaguer [3] [elage] *vt litt & fig* to prune.

élan [elɑ̃] *nm* **1.** ZOOL elk - **2.** SPORT run-up ; **prendre son élan** to take a run-up, to gather speed ; *Québec* [golf] swing - **3.** *fig* [de joie] outburst.

élancé, e [elɑ̃se] *adj* slender.

élancer [16] [elɑ̃se] *vi* MÉD to give shooting pains. ⟶ **s'élancer** *vp* **1.** [se précipiter] to rush, to dash - **2.** SPORT to take a run-up - **3.** *fig* [s'envoler] to soar.

élargir [32] [elarʒir] *vt* to widen ; [vêtement] to let out ; *fig* to expand. ⟶ **s'élargir** *vp* [s'agrandir] to widen ; [vêtement] to stretch ; *fig* to expand.

élasticité [elastisite] *nf* PHYS elasticity.

élastique [elastik] ⟨⟩ *nm* **1.** [pour attacher] elastic *UK* ou rubber *US* band - **2.** [matière] elastic. ⟨⟩ *adj* **1.** PHYS elastic - **2.** [corps] flexible - **3.** *fig* [conscience] accommodating.

électeur, trice [elɛktœr, tris] *nm, f* voter, elector.

élection [elɛksjɔ̃] *nf* [vote] election ; **élections municipales** local elections ; **élection présidentielle** presidential election.

électoral, e, aux [elɛktɔral, o] *adj* electoral ; [campagne, réunion] election *(avant n)*.

électricien, enne [elɛktrisjɛ̃, ɛn] *nm, f* electrician.

électricité [elɛktrisite] *nf* electricity.

électrifier [9] [elɛktrifje] *vt* to electrify.

électrique [elɛktrik] *adj litt & fig* electric.

électroaimant [elɛktrɔɛmɑ̃] *nm* electromagnet.

électrocardiogramme [elɛktrɔkardjɔgram] *nm* electrocardiogram.

électrochoc [elɛktrɔʃɔk] *nm* electroshock therapy.

électrocuter [3] [elɛktrɔkyte] *vt* to electrocute.

électrode [elɛktrɔd] *nf* electrode.

électroencéphalogramme [elɛktrɔɑ̃sefalɔgram] *nm* electroencephalogram.

électrogène [elɛktrɔʒɛn] *adj* : **groupe électrogène** generating unit.

électrolyse [elɛktrɔliz] *nf* electrolysis.

électromagnétique [elɛktrɔmaɲetik] *adj* electromagnetic.

électroménager [elɛktrɔmenaʒe] *nm* household electrical appliances *pl*.

électron [elɛktrɔ̃] *nm* electron.

électronicien, enne [elɛktrɔnisjɛ̃, ɛn] *nm, f* electronics specialist.

électronique [elɛktrɔnik] <> nf [sciences] electronics (U). <> adj electronic ; [microscope] electron (avant n).

électrophone [elɛktrɔfɔn] nm record player.

élégance [elegɑ̃s] nf [de personne, style] elegance.

élégant, e [elegɑ̃, ɑ̃t] adj 1. [personne, style] elegant - 2. [délicat - solution, procédé] elegant ; [- conduite] generous.

élément [elemɑ̃] nm 1. [gén] element ; **être dans son élément** to be in one's element - 2. [de machine] component.

élémentaire [elemɑ̃tɛr] adj 1. [gén] elementary - 2. [installation, besoin] basic.

éléphant [elefɑ̃] nm elephant.

élevage [ɛlvaʒ] nm breeding, rearing ; [installation] farm.

élévateur, trice [elevatœr, tris] adj elevator (avant n).

élevé, e [ɛlve] adj 1. [haut] high - 2. fig [sentiment, âme] noble - 3. [enfant] : **bien/mal élevé** well/badly brought up.

élève [elɛv] nmf [écolier, disciple] pupil.

élever [19] [ɛlve] vt 1. [gén] to raise - 2. [statue] to put up, to erect - 3. [à un rang supérieur] to elevate - 4. [esprit] to improve - 5. [enfant] to bring up - 6. [poulets] to rear, to breed. ➤ **s'élever** vp 1. [gén] to rise - 2. [montant] : **s'élever à** to add up to - 3. [protester] : **s'élever contre qqn/qqch** to protest against sb/sthg.

éleveur, euse [ɛlvœr, øz] nm, f breeder.

elfe [ɛlf] nm elf.

éligible [eliʒibl] adj eligible.

élimé, e [elime] adj threadbare.

élimination [eliminasjɔ̃] nf elimination.

éliminatoire [eliminatwar] <> nf (gén pl) SPORT qualifying heat ou round. <> adj qualifying (avant n).

éliminer [3] [elimine] vt to eliminate.

élire [106] [elir] vt to elect.

élite [elit] nf elite ; **d'élite** choice, select.

élitiste [elitist] nmf & adj elitist.

elle [ɛl] pron pers 1. [sujet - personne] she ; [- animal] it, she ; [- chose] it - 2. [complément - personne] her ; [- animal] it, her ; [- chose] it. ➤ **elles** pron pers pl 1. [sujet] they - 2. [complément] them. ➤ **elle-même** pron pers [personne] herself ; [animal] itself, herself ; [chose] itself. ➤ **elles-mêmes** pron pers pl themselves.

ellipse [elips] nf 1. GÉOM ellipse - 2. LING ellipsis.

élocution [elɔkysjɔ̃] nf delivery ; **défaut d'élocution** speech defect.

éloge [elɔʒ] nm [louange] praise ; **faire l'éloge de qqn/qqch** [louer] to speak highly of sb/sthg ; **couvrir qqn d'éloges** to shower sb with praise.

élogieux, euse [elɔʒjø, øz] adj laudatory.

éloignement [elwaɲmɑ̃] nm 1. [mise à l'écart] removal - 2. [séparation] absence - 3. [dans l'espace, le temps] distance.

éloigner [3] [elwaɲe] vt 1. [écarter] to move away ; **éloigner qqch de** to move sthg away from - 2. [détourner] to turn away - 3. [chasser] to dismiss. ➤ **s'éloigner** vp 1. [partir] to move ou go away - 2. fig : **s'éloigner du sujet** to stray from the point - 3. [se détacher] to distance o.s.

éloquence [elɔkɑ̃s] nf [d'orateur, d'expression] eloquence.

éloquent, e [elɔkɑ̃, ɑ̃t] adj 1. [avocat, silence] eloquent - 2. [données] significant.

élu, e [ely] <> pp ➤ **élire**. <> adj POLIT elected. <> nm, f 1. POLIT elected representative - 2. RELIG chosen one ; **l'élu de son cœur** hum & sout one's heart's desire.

élucider [3] [elyside] vt to clear up.

éluder [3] [elyde] vt to evade.

Élysée [elize] nm : **l'Élysée** the official residence of the French President and, by extension, the President himself.

émacié, e [emasje] adj litt emaciated.

émail, aux [emaj, emo] nm enamel ; **en émail** enamel, enamelled UK, enameled US.

e-mail [imɛl] (pl e-mails) nm e-mail, E-mail.

émanation [emanasjɔ̃] nf emanation ; **être l'émanation de** fig to emanate from.

émanciper [3] [emɑ̃sipe] vt to emancipate. ➤ **s'émanciper** vp 1. [se libérer] to become free ou liberated - 2. fam [se dévergonder] to become emancipated.

émaner [3] [emane] vi : **émaner de** to emanate from.

émarger [17] [emarʒe] vt [signer] to sign.

émasculer [3] [emaskyle] vt to emasculate.

emballage [ɑ̃balaʒ] nm packaging.

emballer [3] [ɑ̃bale] vt 1. [objet] to pack (up), to wrap (up) - 2. fam [plaire à] to thrill. ➤ **s'emballer** vp 1. [moteur] to race - 2. [cheval] to bolt - 3. fam [personne - s'enthousiasmer] to get carried away ; [- s'emporter] to lose one's temper.

embarcadère [ɑ̃barkadɛr] nm landing stage.

embarcation [ɑ̃barkasjɔ̃] nf small boat.

embardée [ɑ̃barde] nf swerve ; **faire une embardée** to swerve.

embargo [ɑ̃bargo] nm embargo.

embarquement [ɑ̃barkəmɑ̃] nm 1. [de marchandises] loading - 2. [de passagers] boarding.

embarquer [3] [ɑ̃barke] <> *vt* **1.** [marchandises] to load - **2.** [passagers] to (take on) board - **3.** *fam* [arrêter] to pick up - **4.** *fam fig* [engager] : **embarquer qqn dans** to involve sb in - **5.** *fam* [emmener] to cart off. <> *vi* : **embarquer (pour)** to sail (for). ◆ **s'embarquer** *vp* **1.** [sur un bateau] to (set) sail - **2.** *fam fig* [s'engager] : **s'embarquer dans** to get involved in.

embarras [ɑ̃bara] *nm* **1.** [incertitude] (state of) uncertainty ; **avoir l'embarras du choix** to be spoilt for choice - **2.** [situation difficile] predicament ; **être dans l'embarras** to be in a predicament ; **mettre qqn dans l'embarras** to place sb in an awkward position ; **tirer qqn d'embarras** to get sb out of a tight spot - **3.** [gêne] embarrassment - **4.** [souci] difficulty, worry.

embarrassé, e [ɑ̃barase] *adj* **1.** [encombré - pièce, bureau] cluttered ; **avoir les mains embarrassées** to have one's hands full - **2.** [gêné] embarrassed - **3.** [confus] confused.

embarrasser [3] [ɑ̃barase] *vt* **1.** [encombrer - pièce] to clutter up ; [- personne] to hamper - **2.** [gêner] to put in an awkward position. ◆ **s'embarrasser** *vp* [se charger] : **s'embarrasser de qqch** to burden o.s. with sthg ; *fig* to bother about sthg.

embauchage [ɑ̃boʃaʒ] *nm* = **embauche**.

embauche [ɑ̃boʃ] *nf* hiring, employment.

embaucher [3] [ɑ̃boʃe] *vt* **1.** [employer] to employ, to take on - **2.** *fam* [occuper] : **je t'embauche!** I need your help!

embaumer [3] [ɑ̃bome] <> *vt* **1.** [cadavre] to embalm - **2.** [parfumer] to scent. <> *vi* to be fragrant.

embellir [32] [ɑ̃belir] <> *vt* **1.** [agrémenter] to brighten up - **2.** *fig* [enjoliver] to embellish. <> *vi* [devenir plus beau] to become more attractive ; *fig & hum* to grow, to increase.

embêtant, e [ɑ̃betɑ̃, ɑ̃t] *adj fam* annoying.

embêtement [ɑ̃betmɑ̃] *nm fam* trouble.

embêter [4] [ɑ̃bete] *vt fam* [contrarier, importuner] to annoy. ◆ **s'embêter** *vp fam* [s'ennuyer] to be bored.

emblée [ɑ̃ble] ◆ **d'emblée** *loc adv* right away.

emblème [ɑ̃blɛm] *nm* emblem.

emboîter [3] [ɑ̃bwate] *vt* : **emboîter qqch dans qqch** to fit sthg into sthg. ◆ **s'emboîter** *vp* to fit together.

embonpoint [ɑ̃bɔ̃pwɛ̃] *nm* stoutness.

embouché, e [ɑ̃buʃe] *adj fam* **mal embouché** foul-mouthed.

embouchure [ɑ̃buʃyr] *nf* [de fleuve] mouth.

embourber [3] [ɑ̃burbe] ◆ **s'embourber** *vp* [s'enliser] to get stuck in the mud ; *fig* to get bogged down.

embourgeoiser [3] [ɑ̃burʒwaze] *vt* [personne] to instil *UK* ou instill *US* middle-class values in ; [quartier] to gentrify. ◆ **s'embourgeoiser** *vp* [personne] to adopt middle-class values ; [quartier] to become gentrified.

embout [ɑ̃bu] *nm* [protection] tip ; [extrémité d'un tube] nozzle.

embouteillage [ɑ̃buteja3] *nm* [circulation] traffic jam.

emboutir [32] [ɑ̃butir] *vt* **1.** *fam* [voiture] to crash into - **2.** TECHNOL to stamp.

embranchement [ɑ̃brɑ̃ʃmɑ̃] *nm* **1.** [carrefour] junction - **2.** [division] branching (out) ; *fig* branch.

embraser [3] [ɑ̃braze] *vt* [incendier, éclairer] to set ablaze ; *fig* [d'amour] to (set on) fire, to inflame. ◆ **s'embraser** *vp* [prendre feu, s'éclairer] to be ablaze ; *fig & litt* to be inflamed.

embrassade [ɑ̃brasad] *nf* embrace.

embrasser [3] [ɑ̃brase] *vt* **1.** [donner un baiser à] to kiss - **2.** [étreindre] to embrace - **3.** *fig* [du regard] to take in. ◆ **s'embrasser** *vp* to kiss (each other).

embrasure [ɑ̃brazyr] *nf* : **dans l'embrasure de la fenêtre** in the window.

embrayage [ɑ̃brɛja3] *nm* [mécanisme] clutch.

embrayer [11] [ɑ̃brɛje] *vi* AUTO to engage the clutch.

embrocher [3] [ɑ̃brɔʃe] *vt* to skewer.

embrouillamini [ɑ̃brujamini] *nm fam* muddle.

embrouiller [3] [ɑ̃bruje] *vt* **1.** [mélanger] to mix (up), to muddle (up) - **2.** *fig* [compliquer] to confuse.

embruns [ɑ̃brœ̃] *nmpl* spray *(U)*.

embryon [ɑ̃brijɔ̃] *nm litt & fig* embryo.

embûche [ɑ̃byʃ] *nf* pitfall.

embuer [7] [ɑ̃bɥe] *vt* **1.** [de vapeur] to steam up - **2.** [de larmes] to mist (over).

embuscade [ɑ̃byskad] *nf* ambush.

éméché, e [emeʃe] *adj fam* merry, tipsy.

émeraude [emrod] *nf* emerald.

émerger [17] [emerʒe] *vi* **1.** [gén] to emerge - **2.** *fig & NAUT* to surface.

émeri [ɛmri] *nm* : **papier** ou **toile émeri** emery paper.

émérite [emerit] *adj* distinguished, eminent.

émerveiller [4] [emerveje] *vt* to fill with wonder.

émetteur, trice [emetœr, tris] *adj* transmitting ; **poste émetteur** transmitter. ➤ **émetteur** *nm* [appareil] transmitter.

émettre [84] [emetr] *vt* **1.** [produire] to emit - **2.** [diffuser] to transmit, to broadcast - **3.** [mettre en circulation] to issue - **4.** [exprimer] to express.

émeute [emøt] *nf* riot.

émietter [4] [emjete] *vt* **1.** [du pain] to crumble - **2.** [morceler] to divide up.

émigrant, e [emigrã, ãt] *adj & nm, f* emigrant.

émigré, e [emigre] ◇ *adj* migrant. ◇ *nm, f* emigrant.

émigrer [3] [emigre] *vi* **1.** [personnes] to emigrate - **2.** [animaux] to migrate.

émincé, e [emɛ̃se] *adj* sliced thinly. ➤ **émincé** *nm thin slices of meat served in a sauce.*

éminemment [eminamã] *adv* eminently.

éminence [eminãs] *nf* hill.

éminent, e [eminã, ãt] *adj* eminent, distinguished.

émir [emir] *nm* emir.

émirat [emira] *nm* emirate. ➤ **Émirat** *nm* : **les Émirats arabes unis** the United Arab Emirates.

émis, e [emi, iz] *pp* ➤ **émettre**.

émissaire [emiser] ◇ *nm* [envoyé] emissary, envoy. ◇ *adj* ➤ **bouc**.

émission [emisjɔ̃] *nf* **1.** [de gaz, de son etc] emission - **2.** [RADIO & TV - transmission] transmission, broadcasting ; [- programme] programme *UK*, program *US* - **3.** [mise en circulation] issue.

emmagasiner [3] [ãmagazine] *vt* **1.** [stocker] to store - **2.** *fig* [accumuler] to store up.

emmailloter [3] [ãmajote] *vt* to wrap up.

emmanchure [ãmãʃyr] *nf* armhole.

emmêler [4] [ãmele] *vt* **1.** [fils] to tangle up - **2.** *fig* [idées] to muddle up, to confuse. ➤ **s'emmêler** *vp* **1.** [fils] to get into a tangle - **2.** *fig* [personne] to get mixed up.

emménagement [ãmenaʒmã] *nm* moving in.

emménager [17] [ãmenaʒe] *vi* to move in.

emmener [19] [ãmne] *vt* to take.

emmerder [3] [ãmerde] *vt tfam* to piss off. ➤ **s'emmerder** *vp tfam* [s'embêter] to be bored stiff.

emmitoufler [3] [ãmitufle] *vt* to wrap up. ➤ **s'emmitoufler** *vp* to wrap o.s. up.

émoi [emwa] *nm* **1.** *sout* [agitation] agitation, commotion ; **en émoi** in turmoil - **2.** [émotion] emotion.

emoticon [emɔtikɔ] *nm* INFORM emoticon.

émotif, ive [emɔtif, iv] *adj* emotional.

émotion [emosjɔ̃] *nf* **1.** [sentiment] emotion - **2.** [peur] fright, shock.

émotionnel, elle [emosjɔnel] *adj* emotional.

émousser [3] [emuse] *vt litt & fig* to blunt.

émouvant, e [emuvã, ãt] *adj* moving.

émouvoir [55] [emuvwar] *vt* **1.** [troubler] to disturb, to upset - **2.** [susciter la sympathie de] to move, to touch. ➤ **s'émouvoir** *vp* to show emotion, to be upset.

empailler [3] [ãpaje] *vt* **1.** [animal] to stuff - **2.** [chaise] to upholster (with straw).

empaler [3] [ãpale] *vt* to impale.

empaqueter [27] [ãpakte] *vt* to pack (up), to wrap (up).

empâter [3] [ãpate] *vt* **1.** [visage, traits] to fatten out - **2.** [bouche, langue] to coat, to fur up. ➤ **s'empâter** *vp* to put on weight.

empêchement [ãpɛʃmã] *nm* obstacle ; **j'ai un empêchement** something has come up.

empêcher [4] [ãpeʃe] *vt* to prevent ; **empêcher qqn/qqch de faire qqch** to prevent sb/sthg from doing sthg ; **empêcher que qqn (ne) fasse qqch** to prevent sb from doing sthg ; **(il) n'empêche que** nevertheless, all the same.

empereur [ãprœr] *nm* emperor.

empesé, e [ãpəze] *adj* **1.** [linge] starched - **2.** *fig* [style] stiff.

empester [3] [ãpeste] *vi* to stink.

empêtrer [4] [ãpetre] *vt* : **être empêtré dans** to be tangled up in. ➤ **s'empêtrer** *vp* : **s'empêtrer (dans)** to get tangled up in.

emphase [ãfaz] *nf péj* pomposity.

empiéter [18] [ãpjete] *vi* : **empiéter sur** to encroach on.

empiffrer [3] [ãpifre] ➤ **s'empiffrer** *vp fam* to stuff o.s.

empiler [3] [ãpile] *vt* [entasser] to pile up, to stack up.

empire [ãpir] *nm* **1.** HIST & *fig* empire - **2.** *sout* [contrôle] influence.

empirer [3] [ãpire] *vi & vt* to worsen.

empirique [ãpirik] *adj* empirical.

emplacement [ãplasmã] *nm* [gén] site, location ; [dans un camping] place.

emplette [ãplet] *nf* (*gén pl*) purchase.

emplir [32] [ãplir] *vt sout* : **emplir (de)** to fill (with). ➤ **s'emplir** *vp* : **s'emplir (de)** to fill (with).

emploi [ãplwa] *nm* **1.** [utilisation] use ; **emploi du temps** timetable *UK*, schedule *US* ; **mode d'emploi** instructions *pl* (for use) - **2.** [travail] job.

employé, e [ɑ̃plwaje] *nm, f* employeè ; **employé de bureau** office employee ou worker.

employer [13] [ɑ̃plwaje] *vt* **1.** [utiliser] to use - **2.** [salarier] to employ.

employeur, euse [ɑ̃plwajœr, øz] *nm, f* employer.

empocher [3] [ɑ̃pɔʃe] *vt fam* to pocket.

empoignade [ɑ̃pwaɲad] *nf* row.

empoigner [3] [ɑ̃pwaɲe] *vt* [saisir] to grasp. **s'empoigner** *vp fig* to come to blows.

empoisonnement [ɑ̃pwazɔnmɑ̃] *nm* [intoxication] poisoning.

empoisonner [3] [ɑ̃pwazɔne] *vt* **1.** [gén] to poison - **2.** *fam* [ennuyer] to annoy, to bug.

emporté, e [ɑ̃pɔrte] *adj* short-tempered.

emportement [ɑ̃pɔrtəmɑ̃] *nm* anger.

emporter [3] [ɑ̃pɔrte] *vt* **1.** [emmener] to take (away) ; **à emporter** [plats] to take away *UK*, to take out *US*, to go *US* - **2.** [entraîner] to carry along - **3.** [arracher] to tear off, to blow off - **4.** [faire mourir] to carry off - **5.** [surpasser] : **l'emporter sur** to get the better of. **s'emporter** *vp* to get angry, to lose one's temper.

empoté, e [ɑ̃pɔte] *fam* ◇ *adj* clumsy. ◇ *nm, f* clumsy person.

empreinte [ɑ̃prɛ̃t] *nf* [trace] print ; *fig* mark, trace ; **empreintes digitales** fingerprints.

empressement [ɑ̃presmɑ̃] *nm* **1.** [zèle] attentiveness - **2.** [enthousiasme] eagerness.

empresser [3] [ɑ̃prese] **s'empresser** *vp* : **s'empresser de faire qqch** to hurry to do sthg ; **s'empresser auprès de qqn** to be attentive to sb.

emprise [ɑ̃priz] *nf* [ascendant] influence.

emprisonnement [ɑ̃prizɔnmɑ̃] *nm* imprisonment.

emprisonner [3] [ɑ̃prizɔne] *vt* [voleur] to imprison.

emprunt [ɑ̃prœ̃] *nm* **1.** FIN loan - **2.** LING & *fig* borrowing.

emprunté, e [ɑ̃prœ̃te] *adj* awkward, self-conscious.

emprunter [3] [ɑ̃prœ̃te] *vt* **1.** [gén] to borrow ; **emprunter qqch à** to borrow sthg from - **2.** [route] to take.

ému, e [emy] ◇ *pp* émouvoir. ◇ *adj* [personne] moved, touched ; [regard, sourire] emotional.

émulation [emylasjɔ̃] *nf* **1.** [concurrence] rivalry - **2.** [imitation] emulation.

émule [emyl] *nmf* **1.** [imitateur] emulator - **2.** [concurrent] rival.

émulsion [emylsjɔ̃] *nf* emulsion.

en [ɑ̃] ◇ *prép* **1.** [temps] in ; **en 1994** in 1994 ; **en hiver/septembre** in winter/ September - **2.** [lieu] in ; [direction] to ; **habiter en Sicile/ville** to live in Sicily/town ; **aller en Sicile/ville** to go to Sicily/town - **3.** [matière] made of ; **c'est en métal** it's (made of) metal ; **une théière en argent** a silver teapot - **4.** [état, forme, manière] : **les arbres sont en fleurs** the trees are in blossom ; **du sucre en morceaux** sugar cubes ; **du lait en poudre** powdered milk ; **je la préfère en vert** I prefer it in green ; **agir en traître** to behave treacherously ; **je l'ai eu en cadeau** I was given it as a present ; **en re qqch en anglais** to say sthg in English ; **en vacances** on holiday - **5.** [moyen] : **en avion/bateau/train** by plane/boat/train - **6.** [mesure] in ; **vous l'avez en 38?** do you have it in a 38 ? ; **compter en dollars** to calculate in dollars - **7.** [devant un participe présent] : **en arrivant à Paris** on arriving in Paris, as he/she *etc* arrived in Paris ; **en faisant un effort** by making an effort ; **en mangeant** while eating ; **elle répondit en souriant** she replied with a smile. ◇ *pron pers* **1.** [complément de verbe, de nom, d'adjectif] : **il s'en est souvenu** he remembered it ; **nous en avons déjà parlé** we've already spoken about it ; **je m'en porte garant** I'll vouch for it - **2.** [avec un indéfini, exprimant une quantité] : **j'ai du chocolat, tu en veux?** I've got some chocolate, do you want some? ; **tu en as?** have you got any?, do you have any? ; **il y en a plusieurs** there are several (of them) - **3.** [provenance] from there.

ENA, Ena [ena] (*abr de* École nationale d'administration) *nf prestigious grande école training future government officials.*

encadrement [ɑ̃kadrəmɑ̃] *nm* **1.** [de tableau, porte] frame - **2.** [dans une entreprise] managerial staff ; [à l'armée] officers *pl* ; [à l'école] staff - **3.** [du crédit] restriction.

encadrer [3] [ɑ̃kadre] *vt* **1.** [photo, visage] to frame - **2.** [employés] to supervise ; [soldats] to be in command of ; [élèves] to teach.

encaissé, e [ɑ̃kese] *adj* [vallée] deep and narrow ; [rivière] steep-banked.

encaisser [4] [ɑ̃kese] *vt* **1.** [argent, coups, insultes] to take - **2.** [chèque] to cash.

encart [ɑ̃kar] *nm* insert.

encastrer [3] [ɑ̃kastre] *vt* to fit. **s'encastrer** *vp* to fit (exactly).

encaustique [ɑ̃kostik] *nf* [cire] polish.

enceinte [ɑ̃sɛ̃t] ◇ *adj f* pregnant ; **enceinte de 4 mois** 4 months pregnant. ◇ *nf* **1.** [muraille] wall - **2.** [espace] : **dans l'enceinte de** within (the confines of) - **3.** [baffle] : **enceinte (acoustique)** speaker.

encens [ɑ̃sɑ̃] *nm* incense.

encenser [3] [ɑ̃sɑ̃se] *vt* **1.** [brûler de l'encens dans] to burn incense in - **2.** *fig* [louer] to flatter.

encensoir [ãsãswar] *nm* censer.

encercler [3] [ãserkle] *vt* **1.** [cerner, environner] to surround - **2.** [entourer] to circle.

enchaînement [ãʃɛnmã] *nm* **1.** [succession] series - **2.** [liaison] link.

enchaîner [4] [ãʃene] <> *vt* **1.** [attacher] to chain up - **2.** *fig* [asservir] to enslave - **3.** [coordonner] to link. <> *vi* : enchaîner (sur) to move on (to). <> **s'enchaîner** *vp* [se suivre] to follow on from each other.

enchanté, e [ãʃãte] *adj* **1.** [ravi] delighted ; enchanté de faire votre connaissance pleased to meet you - **2.** [ensorcelé] enchanted.

enchantement [ãʃãtmã] *nm* **1.** [sortilège] magic spell ; comme par enchantement as if by magic - **2.** *sout* [ravissement] delight - **3.** [merveille] wonder.

enchanter [3] [ãʃãte] *vt* **1.** [ensorceler, charmer] to enchant - **2.** [ravir] to delight.

enchâsser [3] [ãʃase] *vt* **1.** [encastrer] to fit - **2.** [sertir] to set.

enchère [ãʃer] *nf* bid ; vendre qqch aux enchères to sell sthg at ou by auction.

enchevêtrer [4] [ãʃəvetre] *vt* [emmêler] to tangle up ; *fig* to muddle, to confuse.

enclave [ãklav] *nf* enclave.

enclencher [3] [ãklãʃe] *vt* [mécanisme] to engage. <> **s'enclencher** *vp* **1.** TECHNOL to engage - **2.** *fig* [commencer] to begin.

enclin, e [ãklɛ̃, in] *adj* : enclin à qqch/à faire qqch inclined to sthg/to do sthg.

enclore [113] [ãklɔr] *vt* to fence in, to enclose.

enclos, e [ãklo, oz] *pp* ▶ **enclore**. <> **enclos** *nm* enclosure.

enclume [ãklym] *nf* anvil.

encoche [ãkɔʃ] *nf* notch.

encoignure [ãkwaɲyr, ãkɔɲyr] *nf* [coin] corner.

encolure [ãkɔlyr] *nf* neck.

encombrant, e [ãkɔ̃brã, ãt] *adj* cumbersome ; *fig* [personne] undesirable.

encombre [ãkɔ̃br] <> **sans encombre** *loc adv* without a hitch.

encombré, e [ãkɔ̃bre] *adj* [lieu] busy, congested ; *fig* saturated.

encombrement [ãkɔ̃brəmã] *nm* **1.** [d'une pièce] clutter - **2.** [d'un objet] overall dimensions *pl* - **3.** [embouteillage] traffic jam - **4.** INFORM footprint.

encombrer [3] [ãkɔ̃bre] *vt* to clutter (up).

encontre [ãkɔ̃tr] <> **à l'encontre de** *loc prép* : aller à l'encontre de to go against, to oppose.

encore [ãkɔr] *adv* **1.** [toujours] still ; encore un mois one more month ; pas encore not yet ; elle ne travaille pas encore she's not working yet - **2.** [de nouveau] again ; il m'a

encore menti he's lied to me again ; quoi encore? what now? ; l'ascenseur est en panne - encore! the lift's out of order - not again! ; encore de la glace? some more ice cream? ; encore une fois once more, once again - **3.** [marque le renforcement] even ; encore mieux/pire even better/worse. <> **et encore** *loc adv* : j'ai eu le temps de prendre un sandwich, et encore! I had time to prepare a sandwich, but only just! <> **si encore** *loc adv* if only. <> **encore que** *loc conj* (+ *subjonctif*) although.

encouragement [ãkuraʒmã] *nm* [parole] (word of) encouragement.

encourager [17] [ãkuraʒe] *vt* to encourage ; encourager qqn à faire qqch to encourage sb to do sthg.

encourir [45] [ãkurir] *vt sout* to incur.

encouru, e [ãkury] *pp* ▶ **encourir**.

encrasser [3] [ãkrase] *vt* **1.** TECHNOL to clog up - **2.** *fam* [salir] to make dirty ou filthy. <> **s'encrasser** *vp* **1.** TECHNOL to clog up - **2.** *fam* [se salir] to get dirty ou filthy.

encre [ãkr] *nf* ink.

encrer [3] [ãkre] *vt* to ink.

encrier [ãkrije] *nm* inkwell.

encroûter [3] [ãkrute] <> **s'encroûter** *vp fam* to get into a rut ; s'encroûter dans ses habitudes to become set in one's ways.

encyclopédie [ãsiklɔpedi] *nf* encyclopaedia *UK*, encyclopedia *US*.

encyclopédique [ãsiklɔpedik] *adj* encyclopaedic *UK*, encyclopedic *US*.

endémique [ãdemik] *adj* endemic.

endetter [4] [ãdete] <> **s'endetter** *vp* to get into debt.

endeuiller [5] [ãdœje] *vt* to plunge into mourning.

endiablé, e [ãdjable] *adj* [frénétique] frantic, frenzied.

endiguer [3] [ãdige] *vt* **1.** [fleuve] to dam - **2.** *fig* [réprimer] to stem.

endimanché, e [ãdimãʃe] *adj* in one's Sunday best.

endive [ãdiv] *nf* chicory (U) *UK*, endive *US*.

endoctriner [3] [ãdɔktrine] *vt* to indoctrinate.

endommager [17] [ãdɔmaʒe] *vt* to damage.

endormi, e [ãdɔrmi] *adj* **1.** [personne] sleeping, asleep - **2.** *fig* [village] sleepy ; [jambe] numb ; [passion] dormant ; *fam* [apathique] sluggish.

endormir [36] [ãdɔrmir] *vt* **1.** [assoupir, ennuyer] to send to sleep - **2.** [anesthésier - patient] to anaesthetize *UK*, anesthetize *US* ;

127

[- douleur] to ease - **3.** *fig* [tromper] to allay.
s'endormir *vp* [s'assoupir] to fall asleep.

endosser [3] [ādose] *vt* **1.** [vêtement] to put on - **2.** FIN & DR to endorse ; **endosser un chèque** to endorse a cheque *UK* ou check *US* - **3.** *fig* [responsabilité] to take on.

endroit [ādrwa] *nm* **1.** [lieu, point] place ; **à quel endroit?** where? - **2.** [passage] part - **3.** [côté] right side ; **à l'endroit** the right way round *UK* ou around *US*.

enduire [98] [āduir] *vt* : **enduire qqch (de)** to coat sthg (with).

enduit, e [ādui, it] *pp* ➤ **enduire**.
enduit *nm* coating.

endurance [ādyrãs] *nf* endurance.

endurcir [32] [ādyrsir] *vt* to harden.
s'endurcir *vp* : **s'endurcir à** to become hardened to.

endurer [3] [ādyre] *vt* to endure.

énergétique [enerʒetik] *adj* **1.** [ressource] energy *(avant n)* - **2.** [aliment] energy-giving.

énergie [enerʒi] *nf* energy ; **énergie renouvelable** renewable energy.

énergique [enerʒik] *adj* [gén] energetic ; [remède] powerful ; [mesure] drastic.

énergumène [energymen] *nmf* rowdy character.

énerver [3] [enerve] *vt* to irritate, to annoy.
s'énerver *vp* [être irrité] to get annoyed ; [être excité] to get worked up ou excited.

enfance [āfãs] *nf* **1.** [âge] childhood - **2.** [enfants] children *pl* - **3.** *fig* [débuts] infancy ; [de civilisation, de l'humanité] dawn.

enfant [āfã] *nmf* [gén] child ; **attendre un enfant** to be expecting a baby. **bon enfant** *loc adj* good-natured.

enfanter [3] [āfāte] *vt litt* to give birth to.

enfantillage [āfātijaʒ] *nm* childishness *(U)*.

enfantin, e [āfātē, in] *adj* **1.** [propre à l'enfance] childlike ; *péj* childish ; [jeu, chanson] children's *(avant n)* - **2.** [facile] childishly simple.

enfer [āfer] *nm* RELIG & *fig* hell. **Enfers** *nmpl* : **les Enfers** the Underworld *sg*.

enfermer [3] [āferme] *vt* [séquestrer, ranger] to shut away. **s'enfermer** *vp* to shut o.s. away ou up ; **s'enfermer dans** *fig* to retreat into.

enfilade [āfilad] *nf* row.

enfiler [3] [āfile] *vt* **1.** [aiguille, sur un fil] to thread - **2.** [vêtements] to slip on.

enfin [āfē] *adv* **1.** [en dernier lieu] finally, at last ; [dans une liste] lastly - **2.** [avant une récapitulation] in a word, in short - **3.** [intro-

duit une rectification] that is, well - **4.** [introduit une concession] anyway, still, however.

enflammer [3] [āflame] *vt* **1.** [bois] to set fire to - **2.** *fig* [exalter] to inflame. **s'enflammer** *vp* **1.** [bois] to catch fire - **2.** *fig* [s'exalter] to flare up.

enflé, e [āfle] *adj* [style] turgid.

enfler [3] [āfle] *vi* to swell (up).

enfoncer [16] [āfɔ̃se] *vt* **1.** [faire pénétrer] to drive in ; **enfoncer qqch dans qqch** to drive sthg into sthg - **2.** [enfouir] : **enfoncer ses mains dans ses poches** to thrust one's hands into one's pockets - **3.** [défoncer] to break down. **s'enfoncer** *vp* **1.** : **s'enfoncer dans** [eau, boue] to sink into ; [bois, ville] to disappear into - **2.** [s'affaisser] to give way - **3.** [aggraver son cas] to get into deep ou deeper waters, to make matters worse.

enfouir [32] [āfwir] *vt* **1.** [cacher] to hide - **2.** [ensevelir] to bury.

enfourcher [3] [āfurʃe] *vt* to get on, to mount.

enfourner [3] [āfurne] *vt* **1.** [pain] to put in the oven - **2.** *fam* [avaler] to gobble up.

enfreindre [81] [āfrēdr] *vt* to infringe.

enfreint, e [āfrē, ēt] *pp* ➤ **enfreindre**.

enfuir [35] [āfɥir] **s'enfuir** *vp* [fuir] to run away.

enfumer [3] [āfyme] *vt* to fill with smoke.

engagé, e [āgaʒe] *adj* committed.

engageant, e [āgaʒã, ãt] *adj* engaging.

engagement [āgaʒmã] *nm* **1.** [promesse] commitment - **2.** DR contract - **3.** [MIL - de soldats] enlistment ; [- combat] engagement - **4.** FOOTBALL [rugby] kickoff.

engager [17] [āgaʒe] *vt* **1.** [lier] to commit - **2.** [embaucher] to take on, to engage - **3.** [faire entrer] : **engager qqch dans** to insert sthg into - **4.** [commencer] to start - **5.** [impliquer] to involve - **6.** [encourager] : **engager qqn à faire qqch** to urge sb to do sthg. **s'engager** *vp* **1.** [promettre] : **s'engager à qqch/à faire qqch** to commit o.s. to sthg/to doing sthg - **2.** MIL : **s'engager (dans)** to enlist (in) - **3.** [pénétrer] : **s'engager dans** to enter.

engelure [āʒlyr] *nf* chilblain.

engendrer [3] [āʒādre] *vt* **1.** *litt* to father - **2.** *fig* [produire] to cause, to give rise to ; [sentiment] to engender.

engin [āʒē] *nm* **1.** [machine] machine - **2.** MIL missile - **3.** *fam péj* [objet] thing.

englober [3] [āglɔbe] *vt* to include.

engloutir [32] [āglutir] *vt* **1.** [dévorer] to gobble up - **2.** [faire disparaître] to engulf - **3.** *fig* [dilapider] to squander.

engorger [17] [ɑ̃ɡɔʀʒe] vt **1.** [obstruer] to block, to obstruct - **2.** MÉD to engorge. ➤ **s'engorger** vp to become blocked.

engouement [ɑ̃ɡumɑ̃] nm [enthousiasme] infatuation.

engouffrer [3] [ɑ̃ɡufʀe] vt fam [dévorer] to wolf down. ➤ **s'engouffrer** vp : s'engouffrer dans to rush into.

engourdi, e [ɑ̃ɡuʀdi] adj numb ; fig dull.

engourdir [32] [ɑ̃ɡuʀdiʀ] vt to numb ; fig to dull. ➤ **s'engourdir** vp to go numb.

engrais [ɑ̃ɡʀɛ] nm fertilizer.

engraisser [4] [ɑ̃ɡʀese] ◇ vt **1.** [animal] to fatten - **2.** [terre] to fertilize. ◇ vi to put on weight.

engrenage [ɑ̃ɡʀənaʒ] nm **1.** TECHNOL gears pl - **2.** fig [circonstances] : être pris dans l'engrenage to be caught up in the system.

engueulade [ɑ̃ɡœlad] nf fam bawling out.

engueuler [5] [ɑ̃ɡœle] vt fam engueuler qqn to bawl sb out. ➤ **s'engueuler** vp fam to have a row, to have a slanging match UK.

enhardir [32] [ɑ̃aʀdiʀ] vt to make bold. ➤ **s'enhardir** vp to pluck up one's courage.

énième [enjɛm] adj fam la énième fois the nth time.

énigmatique [enigmatik] adj enigmatic.

énigme [eniɡm] nf **1.** [mystère] enigma - **2.** [jeu] riddle.

enivrant, e [ɑ̃nivʀɑ̃, ɑ̃t] adj litt & fig intoxicating.

enivrer [3] [ɑ̃nivʀe] vt litt to get drunk ; fig to intoxicate. ➤ **s'enivrer** vp : s'enivrer (de) to get drunk (on) ; fig to become intoxicated (with).

enjambée [ɑ̃ʒɑ̃be] nf stride.

enjamber [3] [ɑ̃ʒɑ̃be] vt **1.** [obstacle] to step over - **2.** [cours d'eau] to straddle.

enjeu [ɑ̃ʒø] nm [mise] stake ; quel est l'enjeu ici? fig what's at stake here?

enjoindre [82] [ɑ̃ʒwɛ̃dʀ] vt litt : enjoindre à qqn de faire qqch to enjoin sb to do sthg.

enjoint [ɑ̃ʒwɛ̃] pp inv ➤ enjoindre.

enjôler [3] [ɑ̃ʒole] vt to coax.

enjoliver [3] [ɑ̃ʒolive] vt to embellish.

enjoliveur [ɑ̃ʒolivœʀ] nm [de roue] hubcap ; [de calandre] badge.

enjoué, e [ɑ̃ʒwe] adj cheerful.

enlacer [16] [ɑ̃lase] vt [prendre dans ses bras] to embrace, to hug. ➤ **s'enlacer** vp [s'embrasser] to embrace, to hug.

enlaidir [32] [ɑ̃lediʀ] ◇ vt to make ugly. ◇ vi to become ugly.

enlèvement [ɑ̃lɛvmɑ̃] nm **1.** [action d'enlever] removal - **2.** [rapt] abduction.

enlever [19] [ɑ̃lve] vt **1.** [gén] to remove ; [vêtement] to take off - **2.** [prendre] : enlever qqch à qqn to take sthg away from sb - **3.** [kidnapper] to abduct.

enliser [3] [ɑ̃lize] ➤ **s'enliser** vp **1.** [s'embourber] to sink, to get stuck - **2.** fig [piétiner] : s'enliser dans qqch to get bogged down in sthg.

enluminure [ɑ̃lyminyʀ] nf illumination.

enneigé, e [ɑ̃neʒe] adj snow-covered.

ennemi, e [ɛnmi] ◇ adj enemy (avant n). ◇ nm, f enemy.

ennui [ɑ̃nɥi] nm **1.** [lassitude] boredom - **2.** [contrariété] annoyance ; l'ennui, c'est que... the annoying thing is that... - **3.** [problème] trouble (U) ; avoir des ennuis to have problems.

ennuyer [14] [ɑ̃nɥije] vt **1.** [agacer, contrarier] to annoy ; cela t'ennuierait de venir me chercher? would you mind picking me up? - **2.** [lasser] to bore - **3.** [inquiéter] to bother. ➤ **s'ennuyer** vp **1.** [se morfondre] to be bored - **2.** [déplorer l'absence] : s'ennuyer de qqn/qqch to miss sb/sthg.

ennuyeux, euse [ɑ̃nɥijø, øz] adj **1.** [lassant] boring - **2.** [contrariant] annoying.

énoncé [enɔ̃se] nm [libellé] wording.

énoncer [16] [enɔ̃se] vt **1.** [libeller] to word - **2.** [exposer] to expound ; [théorème] to set forth.

énorme [enɔʀm] adj **1.** litt & fig [immense] enormous - **2.** fam fig [incroyable] farfetched.

énormément [enɔʀmemɑ̃] adv enormously ; énormément de a great deal of.

enquête [ɑ̃kɛt] nf **1.** [de police, recherches] investigation - **2.** [sondage] survey.

enquêter [4] [ɑ̃kete] vi **1.** [police, chercheur] to investigate - **2.** [sonder] to conduct a survey.

enragé, e [ɑ̃ʀaʒe] adj **1.** [chien] rabid, with rabies - **2.** fig [invétéré] keen.

enrager [17] [ɑ̃ʀaʒe] vi to be furious ; faire enrager qqn to infuriate sb.

enrayer [11] [ɑ̃ʀeje] vt **1.** [épidémie] to check, to stop - **2.** [mécanisme] to jam. ➤ **s'enrayer** vp [mécanisme] to jam.

enregistrement [ɑ̃ʀəʒistʀəmɑ̃] nm **1.** [de son, d'images, d'informations] recording - **2.** [inscription] registration - **3.** [à l'aéroport] check-in ; enregistrement des bagages baggage registration.

enregistrer [3] [ɑ̃ʀəʒistʀe] vt **1.** [son, images, informations] to record - **2.** INFORM to store - **3.** [inscrire] to register - **4.** [à l'aéroport] to check in - **5.** fam [mémoriser] to make a mental note of.

enrhumé, e [ɑ̃ʀyme] adj : je suis enrhumé I have a cold.

enrhumer [3] [ɑ̃ryme] ➤ **s'enrhumer** vp to catch (a) cold.

enrichir [32] [ɑ̃riʃir] vt **1.** [financièrement] to make rich - **2.** fig [terre] to enrich. ➤ **s'enrichir** vp **1.** [financièrement] to grow rich - **2.** fig [sol] to become enriched.

enrobé, e [ɑ̃rɔbe] adj **1.** [recouvert] : **enrobé de** coated with - **2.** fam [grassouillet] plump.

enrober [3] [ɑ̃rɔbe] vt [recouvrir] : **enrober qqch de** to coat sthg with. ➤ **s'enrober** vp to put on weight.

enrôler [3] [ɑ̃role] vt to enrol UK, to enroll US ; MIL to enlist. ➤ **s'enrôler** vp to enrol UK, to enroll US ; MIL to enlist.

enroué, e [ɑ̃rwe] adj hoarse.

enrouler [3] [ɑ̃rule] vt to roll up ; **enrouler qqch autour de qqch** to wind sthg round UK ou around US sthg. ➤ **s'enrouler** vp **1.** [entourer] : **s'enrouler sur** ou **autour de qqch** to wind around sthg - **2.** [se pelotonner] : **s'enrouler dans qqch** to wrap o.s. up in sthg.

ensabler [3] [ɑ̃sable] vt to silt up. ➤ **s'ensabler** vp to silt up.

enseignant, e [ɑ̃seɲɑ̃, ɑ̃t] ◇ adj teaching (avant n). ◇ nm, f teacher.

enseigne [ɑ̃seɲ] nf **1.** [de commerce] sign - **2.** [drapeau, soldat] ensign.

enseignement [ɑ̃seɲmɑ̃] nm **1.** [gén] teaching ; **enseignement primaire/secondaire** primary/secondary education ; **enseignement privé** private education - **2.** [leçon] lesson.

enseigner [4] [ɑ̃seɲe] vt litt & fig to teach ; **enseigner qqch à qqn** to teach sb sthg, to teach sthg to sb.

ensemble [ɑ̃sɑ̃bl] ◇ adv together ; **aller ensemble** to go together. ◇ nm **1.** [totalité] whole ; **idée d'ensemble** general idea ; **dans l'ensemble** on the whole - **2.** [harmonie] unity - **3.** [vêtement] outfit - **4.** [série] collection - **5.** MATH set - **6.** MUS ensemble.

ensemencer [16] [ɑ̃səmɑ̃se] vt **1.** [terre] to sow - **2.** [rivière] to stock.

enserrer [4] [ɑ̃sere] vt [entourer] to encircle ; fig to imprison.

ensevelir [32] [ɑ̃səvlir] vt litt & fig to bury.

ensoleillé, e [ɑ̃sɔleje] adj sunny.

ensoleillement [ɑ̃sɔlejmɑ̃] nm sunshine.

ensommeillé, e [ɑ̃sɔmeje] adj sleepy.

ensorceler [24] [ɑ̃sɔrsəle] vt to bewitch.

ensuite [ɑ̃sɥit] adv **1.** [après, plus tard] after, afterwards, later - **2.** [puis] then, next, after that ; **et ensuite?** what then?, what next?

ensuivre [89] [ɑ̃sɥivr] ➤ **s'ensuivre** vp to follow ; **il s'ensuit que** it follows that.

entaille [ɑ̃taj] nf cut.

entailler [3] [ɑ̃taje] vt to cut.

entamer [3] [ɑ̃tame] vt **1.** [gâteau, fromage] to start (on) ; [bouteille, conserve] to start, to open - **2.** [capital] to dip into - **3.** [cuir, réputation] to damage - **4.** [courage] to shake.

entartrer [3] [ɑ̃tartre] vt to fur up. ➤ **s'entartrer** vp to fur up.

entasser [3] [ɑ̃tase] vt **1.** [accumuler, multiplier] to pile up - **2.** [serrer] to squeeze. ➤ **s'entasser** vp **1.** [objets] to pile up - **2.** [personnes] : **s'entasser dans** to squeeze into.

entendement [ɑ̃tɑ̃dmɑ̃] nm understanding.

entendre [73] [ɑ̃tɑ̃dr] vt **1.** [percevoir, écouter] to hear ; **entendre parler de qqch** to hear of ou about sthg - **2.** sout [comprendre] to understand ; **laisser entendre que** to imply that - **3.** sout [vouloir] : **entendre faire qqch** to intend to do sthg - **4.** [vouloir dire] to mean. ➤ **s'entendre** vp **1.** [sympathiser] : **s'entendre avec qqn** to get on with sb - **2.** [s'accorder] to agree.

entendu, e [ɑ̃tɑ̃dy] ◇ pp ➤ entendre. ◇ adj **1.** [compris] agreed, understood - **2.** [complice] knowing.

entente [ɑ̃tɑ̃t] nf **1.** [harmonie] understanding - **2.** [accord] agreement.

entériner [3] [ɑ̃terine] vt to ratify.

enterrement [ɑ̃termɑ̃] nm burial.

enterrer [4] [ɑ̃tere] vt litt & fig to bury ; **enterrer sa vie de garçon** to have a stag party.

en-tête [ɑ̃tɛt] (pl **en-têtes**) nm heading.

entêté, e [ɑ̃tete] adj stubborn.

entêter [4] [ɑ̃tete] ➤ **s'entêter** vp to persist ; **s'entêter à faire qqch** to persist in doing sthg.

enthousiasme [ɑ̃tuzjasm] nm enthusiasm.

enthousiasmer [3] [ɑ̃tuzjasme] vt to fill with enthusiasm. ➤ **s'enthousiasmer** vp : **s'enthousiasmer pour** to be enthusiastic about.

enticher [3] [ɑ̃tiʃe] ➤ **s'enticher** vp : **s'enticher de qqn/qqch** to become obsessed with sb/sthg.

entier, ère [ɑ̃tje, ɛr] adj whole, entire. ➤ **en entier** loc adv in its/their entirety.

entièrement [ɑ̃tjɛrmɑ̃] adv **1.** [complètement] fully - **2.** [pleinement] wholly, entirely.

entité [ɑ̃tite] nf entity.

entonner [3] [ɑ̃tɔne] vt [chant] to strike up.

entonnoir [ɑ̃tɔnwar] nm **1.** [instrument] funnel - **2.** [cavité] crater.

entorse [ɑ̃tɔrs] *nf* MÉD sprain ; **se faire une entorse à la cheville/au poignet** to sprain one's ankle/wrist.

entortiller [3] [ɑ̃tɔrtije] *vt* **1.** [entrelacer] to twist - **2.** [envelopper] : **entortiller qqch autour de qqch** to wrap sthg round *UK* ou around *US* sthg - **3.** *fam fig* [personne] to sweet-talk.

entourage [ɑ̃turaʒ] *nm* [milieu] entourage.

entourer [3] [ɑ̃ture] *vt* **1.** [enclore, encercler] : **entourer (de)** to surround (with) - **2.** *fig* [soutenir] to rally round.

entourloupette [ɑ̃turlupɛt] *nf fam* dirty trick.

entournure [ɑ̃turnyr] *nf* : **être gêné aux entournures** [financièrement] to feel the pinch ; [être mal à l'aise] to feel awkward.

entracte [ɑ̃trakt] *nm* interval ; *fig* interlude *UK*, intermission *US*.

entraide [ɑ̃trɛd] *nf* mutual assistance.

entrailles [ɑ̃traj] *nfpl* **1.** [intestins] entrails - **2.** *sout* [profondeurs] depths.

entrain [ɑ̃trɛ̃] *nm* drive.

entraînement [ɑ̃trɛnmɑ̃] *nm* [préparation] practice ; SPORT training.

entraîner [4] [ɑ̃trene] *vt* **1.** TECHNOL to drive - **2.** [tirer] to pull - **3.** [susciter] to lead to - **4.** SPORT to coach - **5.** [emmener] to take along - **6.** [séduire] to influence ; **entraîner qqn à faire qqch** to talk sb into sthg. ➤ **s'entraîner** *vp* to practise *UK*, to pratice *US* ; SPORT to train ; **s'entraîner à faire qqch** to practise *UK* ou practice *US* doing sthg.

entraîneur, euse [ɑ̃trɛnœr, øz] *nm, f* trainer, coach.

entrave [ɑ̃trav] *nf* hobble ; *fig* obstruction.

entraver [3] [ɑ̃trave] *vt* to hobble ; *fig* to hinder.

entre [ɑ̃tr] *prép* **1.** [gén] between ; **entre nous** between you and me, between ourselves - **2.** [parmi] among ; **l'un d'entre nous ira** one of us will go ; **généralement ils restent entre eux** they tend to keep themselves to themselves ; **ils se battent entre eux** they're fighting among ou amongst themselves. ➤ **entre autres** *loc prép* : **entre autres (choses)** among other things.

entrebâiller [3] [ɑ̃trəbaje] *vt* to open slightly.

entrechoquer [3] [ɑ̃trəʃɔke] *vt* to bang together. ➤ **s'entrechoquer** *vp* to bang into each other.

entrecôte [ɑ̃trəkot] *nf* entrecôte.

entrecouper [3] [ɑ̃trəkupe] *vt* to intersperse.

entrecroiser [3] [ɑ̃trəkrwaze] *vt* to interlace. ➤ **s'entrecroiser** *vp* to intersect.

entrée [ɑ̃tre] *nf* **1.** [arrivée, accès] entry, entrance ; **'entrée interdite'** 'no admittance' ; **'entrée libre'** [dans un musée] 'admission free' ; [dans une boutique] 'browsers welcome' - **2.** [porte] entrance - **3.** [vestibule] (entrance) hall - **4.** [billet] ticket - **5.** [plat] starter, first course.

entrefaites [ɑ̃trəfɛt] *nfpl* : **sur ces entrefaites** just at that moment.

entrefilet [ɑ̃trəfilɛ] *nm* paragraph.

entrejambe, entre-jambes [ɑ̃trəʒɑ̃b] *nm* crotch.

entrelacer [16] [ɑ̃trəlase] *vt* to intertwine.

entrelarder [3] [ɑ̃trəlarde] *vt* **1.** CULIN to lard - **2.** *fam fig* [discours] : **entrelarder de** to lace with.

entremêler [4] [ɑ̃trəmele] *vt* to mix ; **entremêler de** to mix with.

entremets [ɑ̃trəmɛ] *nm* dessert.

entremettre [84] [ɑ̃trəmɛtr] ➤ **s'entremettre** *vp* : **s'entremettre (dans)** to mediate (in).

entremise [ɑ̃trəmiz] *nf* intervention ; **par l'entremise de** through.

entrepont [ɑ̃trəpɔ̃] *nm* steerage.

entreposer [3] [ɑ̃trəpoze] *vt* to store.

entrepôt [ɑ̃trəpo] *nm* warehouse.

entreprendre [79] [ɑ̃trəprɑ̃dr] *vt* to undertake ; [commencer] to start ; **entreprendre de faire qqch** to undertake to do sthg.

entrepreneur, euse [ɑ̃trəprənœr, øz] *nm, f* [de services & CONSTR] contractor.

entrepris, e [ɑ̃trəpri, iz] *pp* ➤ **entreprendre.**

entreprise [ɑ̃trəpriz] *nf* **1.** [travail, initiative] enterprise - **2.** [société] company.

entrer [3] [ɑ̃tre] ⟨⟩ *vi (v aux : être)* **1.** [pénétrer] to enter, to go/come in ; **entrer dans** [gén] to enter ; [pièce] to go/come into ; [bain, voiture] to get into ; *fig* [sujet] to go into ; **entrer par** to go in ou come in by ; **faire entrer qqn** to show sb in ; **faire entrer qqch** to bring sthg in - **2.** [faire partie] : **entrer dans** to go into, to be part of - **3.** [être admis, devenir membre] : **entrer à** [club, parti] to join ; **entrer dans** [les affaires, l'enseignement] to go into ; [la police, l'armée] to join ; **entrer à l'université** to enter university *UK*, to go to college *US* ; **entrer à l'hôpital** to go into hospital *UK*, to enter the hospital *US*. ⟨⟩ *vt (v aux : avoir)* **1.** [gén] to bring in - **2.** INFORM to enter, to input.

entresol [ɑ̃trəsɔl] *nm* mezzanine.

entre-temps [ɑ̃trətɑ̃] *adv* meanwhile.

entretenir [40] [ɑ̃trətnir] *vt* **1.** [faire durer] to keep alive - **2.** [cultiver] to maintain - **3.** [soigner] to look after - **4.** [personne, famille] to support - **5.** [parler à] : **entretenir**

qqn de qqch to speak to sb about sthg. ➡ **s'entretenir** *vp* [se parler] : **s'entretenir (de)** to talk (about).

entretien [ɑ̃trətjɛ̃] *nm* **1.** [de voiture, jardin] maintenance, upkeep - **2.** [conversation] discussion ; [colloque] debate.

entre-tuer [7] [ɑ̃trətɥe] ➡ **s'entre-tuer** *vp* to kill each other.

entrevoir [62] [ɑ̃trəvwar] *vt* **1.** [distinguer] to make out - **2.** [voir rapidement] to see briefly - **3.** *fig* [deviner] to glimpse.

entrevu, e [ɑ̃trəvy] *pp* ➤ entrevoir.

entrevue [ɑ̃trəvy] *nf* meeting.

entrouvert, e [ɑ̃truver, ɛrt] <> *pp* ➤ entrouvrir. <> *adj* half-open.

entrouvrir [34] [ɑ̃truvrir] *vt* to open partly. ➡ **s'entrouvrir** *vp* to open partly.

énumération [enymerasjɔ̃] *nf* enumeration.

énumérer [18] [enymere] *vt* to enumerate.

env. (*abr écrite de* environ) approx.

envahir [32] [ɑ̃vair] *vt* **1.** [gén & MIL] to invade - **2.** *fig* [suj: sommeil, doute] to overcome - **3.** *fig* [déranger] to intrude on.

envahissant, e [ɑ̃vaisɑ̃, ɑ̃t] *adj* **1.** [herbes] invasive - **2.** [personne] intrusive.

envahisseur [ɑ̃vaisœr] *nm* invader.

enveloppe [ɑ̃vlɔp] *nf* **1.** [de lettre] envelope - **2.** [d'emballage] covering - **3.** [membrane] membrane ; [de graine] husk.

envelopper [3] [ɑ̃vlɔpe] *vt* **1.** [emballer] to wrap (up) - **2.** [suj: brouillard] to envelop - **3.** [déguiser] to mask. ➡ **s'envelopper** *vp* : **s'envelopper dans** to wrap o.s. up in.

envenimer [3] [ɑ̃vnime] *vt* **1.** [blessure] to infect - **2.** *fig* [querelle] to poison. ➡ **s'envenimer** *vp* **1.** [s'infecter] to become infected - **2.** *fig* [se détériorer] to become poisoned.

envergure [ɑ̃vergyr] *nf* **1.** [largeur] span ; [d'oiseau, d'avion] wingspan - **2.** *fig* [qualité] calibre - **3.** *fig* [importance] scope ; **prendre de l'envergure** to expand.

envers¹ [ɑ̃ver] *prép* towards, toward *US*.

envers² [ɑ̃ver] *nm* **1.** [de tissu] wrong side ; [de feuillet etc] back ; [de médaille] reverse - **2.** [face cachée] other side. ➡ **à l'envers** *loc adv* [vêtement] inside out ; [portrait, feuille] upside down ; *fig* the wrong way.

envi [ɑ̃vi] ➡ **à l'envi** *loc adv litt* trying to outdo each other.

envie [ɑ̃vi] *nf* **1.** [désir] desire ; **avoir envie de qqch/de faire qqch** to feel like sthg/like doing sthg, to want sthg/to do sthg - **2.** [convoitise] envy ; **ce tailleur me fait envie** I'd love to buy that suit.

envier [9] [ɑ̃vje] *vt* to envy.

envieux, euse [ɑ̃vjø, øz] <> *adj* envious. <> *nm, f* envious person ; **faire des envieux** to make other people envious.

environ [ɑ̃virɔ̃] *adv* [à peu près] about.

environnement [ɑ̃virɔnmɑ̃] *nm* environment ; INFORM environment, platform.

environnemental, e, aux [ɑ̃virɔnmɑ̃tal, o] *adj* environmental.

environs [ɑ̃virɔ̃] *nmpl* (surrounding) area *sg* ; **aux environs de** [lieu] near ; [époque] round about *UK*, around.

envisager [17] [ɑ̃vizaʒe] *vt* to consider ; **envisager de faire qqch** to be considering doing sthg.

envoi [ɑ̃vwa] *nm* **1.** [action] sending, dispatch - **2.** [colis] parcel.

envol [ɑ̃vɔl] *nm* takeoff.

envolée [ɑ̃vɔle] *nf* **1.** [d'oiseaux] flight - **2.** [augmentation] : **l'envolée du dollar** the rapid rise in the value of the dollar.

envoler [3] [ɑ̃vɔle] ➡ **s'envoler** *vp* **1.** [oiseau] to fly away - **2.** [avion] to take off - **3.** [disparaître] to disappear into thin air.

envoûter [3] [ɑ̃vute] *vt* to bewitch.

envoyé, e [ɑ̃vwaje] <> *adj* : **bien envoyé** well-aimed. <> *nm, f* envoy.

envoyer [30] [ɑ̃vwaje] *vt* to send ; **envoyer qqch à qqn** [expédier] to send sb sthg, to send sthg to sb ; [jeter] to throw sb sthg, to throw sthg to sb ; **envoyer qqn faire qqch** to send sb to do sthg ; **envoyer chercher qqn/qqch** to send for sb/sthg.

épagneul [epaɲœl] *nm* spaniel.

épais, aisse [epɛ, ɛs] *adj* **1.** [large, dense] thick - **2.** [grossier] crude.

épaisseur [epesœr] *nf* **1.** [largeur, densité] thickness - **2.** *fig* [consistance] depth.

épaissir [32] [epesir] *vt & vi* to thicken. ➡ **s'épaissir** *vp* **1.** [liquide] to thicken - **2.** *fig* [mystère] to deepen.

épanchement [epɑ̃ʃmɑ̃] *nm* **1.** [effusion] outpouring - **2.** MÉD effusion.

épancher [3] [epɑ̃ʃe] *vt* to pour out. ➡ **s'épancher** *vp* [se confier] to pour one's heart out.

épanoui, e [epanwi] *adj* **1.** [fleur] in full bloom - **2.** [expression] radiant - **3.** [corps] fully formed ; **aux formes épanouies** well-rounded.

épanouir [32] [epanwir] *vt* [personne] to make happy. ➡ **s'épanouir** *vp* **1.** [fleur] to open - **2.** [visage] to light up - **3.** [corps] to fill out - **4.** [personnalité] to blossom.

épanouissement [epanwismɑ̃] *nm* **1.** [de fleur] blooming, opening - **2.** [de visage] brightening - **3.** [de corps] filling out - **4.** [de personnalité] flowering.

épargnant, e [eparɲɑ̃, ɑ̃t] *nm, f* saver.

épargne [eparɲ] *nf* **1.** [action, vertu] saving - **2.** [somme] savings *pl* ; **épargne logement** savings account *(to buy property)*.

épargner [3] [eparɲe] *vt* **1.** [gén] to spare ; **épargner qqch à qqn** to spare sb sthg - **2.** [économiser] to save.

éparpiller [3] [eparpije] *vt* **1.** [choses, personnes] to scatter - **2.** *fig* [forces] to dissipate. ➡ **s'éparpiller** *vp* **1.** [se disperser] to scatter - **2.** *fig* [perdre son temps] to lack focus.

épars, e [epar, ars] *adj sout* [objets] scattered ; [végétation, cheveux] sparse.

épatant, e [epatɑ̃, ɑ̃t] *adj fam* great.

épaté, e [epate] *adj* **1.** [nez] flat - **2.** *fam* [étonné] amazed.

épaule [epol] *nf* shoulder.

épauler [3] [epole] *vt* to support, to back up.

épaulette [epolɛt] *nf* **1.** MIL epaulet - **2.** [rembourrage] shoulder pad.

épave [epav] *nf* wreck.

épée [epe] *nf* sword.

épeler [24] [eple] *vt* to spell.

éperdu, e [eperdy] *adj* [sentiment] passionate ; **éperdu de** [personne] overcome with.

éperon [eprɔ̃] *nm* [de cavalier, de montagne] spur ; [de navire] ram.

éperonner [3] [eprɔne] *vt* to spur on.

épervier [epervje] *nm* sparrowhawk.

éphèbe [efɛb] *nm hum* Adonis.

éphémère [efemɛr] ⬥ *adj* [bref] ephemeral, fleeting. ⬥ *nm* ZOOL mayfly.

éphéméride [efemerid] *nf* tear-off calendar.

épi [epi] *nm* **1.** [de céréale] ear - **2.** [cheveux] tuft.

épice [epis] *nf* spice.

épicé, e [epise] *adj* spicy.

épicéa [episea] *nm* spruce.

épicer [16] [epise] *vt* [plat] to spice.

épicerie [episri] *nf* **1.** [magasin] grocer's (shop) - **2.** [denrées] groceries *pl*.

épicier, ère [episje, ɛr] *nm, f* grocer.

épidémie [epidemi] *nf* epidemic.

épiderme [epidɛrm] *nm* epidermis.

épier [9] [epje] *vt* **1.** [espionner] to spy on - **2.** [observer] to look for.

épilation [epilasjɔ̃] *nf* hair removal.

épilepsie [epilɛpsi] *nf* epilepsy.

épiler [3] [epile] *vt* [jambes] to remove hair from ; [sourcils] to pluck. ➡ **s'épiler** *vp* : **s'épiler les jambes** to remove the hair from one's legs ; [à la cire] to wax one's legs ; **s'épiler les sourcils** to pluck one's eyebrows.

épilogue [epilɔg] *nm* **1.** [de roman] epilogue, epilog *US* - **2.** [d'affaire] outcome.

épinards [epinar] *nmpl* spinach *(U)*.

épine [epin] *nf* [piquant - de rosier] thorn ; [- de hérisson] spine.

épineux, euse [epinø, øz] *adj* thorny.

épingle [epɛ̃gl] *nf* [instrument] pin.

épingler [3] [epɛ̃gle] *vt* **1.** [fixer] to pin (up) - **2.** *fam fig* [arrêter] to nab, to nick *UK*.

épinière [epinjɛr] ➡ **moelle**.

Épiphanie [epifani] *nf* Epiphany.

épique [epik] *adj* epic.

épiscopal, e, aux [episkɔpal, o] *adj* episcopal.

épisode [epizɔd] *nm* episode.

épisodique [epizɔdik] *adj* **1.** [occasionnel] occasional - **2.** [secondaire] minor.

épistolaire [epistɔlɛr] *adj* **1.** [échange] of letters ; **être en relations épistolaires avec qqn** to be in (regular) correspondence with sb - **2.** [roman] epistolary.

épitaphe [epitaf] *nf* epitaph.

épithète [epitɛt] ⬥ *nf* **1.** GRAMM attribute - **2.** [qualificatif] term. ⬥ *adj* attributive.

épître [epitr] *nf* epistle.

éploré, e [eplɔre] *adj* [personne] in tears ; [visage, air] tearful.

épluche-légumes [eplyʃlegym] *nm inv* potato peeler.

éplucher [3] [eplyʃe] *vt* **1.** [légumes] to peel - **2.** [textes] to dissect ; [comptes] to scrutinize.

épluchure [eplyʃyr] *nf* peelings *pl*.

éponge [epɔ̃ʒ] *nf* sponge.

éponger [17] [epɔ̃ʒe] *vt* **1.** [liquide, déficit] to mop up - **2.** [visage] to mop, to wipe.

épopée [epɔpe] *nf* epic.

époque [epɔk] *nf* **1.** [de l'année] time - **2.** [de l'histoire] period.

épouiller [3] [epuje] *vt* to delouse.

époumoner [3] [epumɔne] ➡ **s'époumoner** *vp* to shout o.s. hoarse.

épouse ➡ **époux**.

épouser [3] [epuze] *vt* **1.** [personne] to marry - **2.** [forme] to hug - **3.** *fig* [idée, principe] to espouse.

épousseter [27] [epuste] *vt* to dust.

époustouflant, e [epustuflɑ̃, ɑ̃t] *adj fam* amazing.

épouvantable [epuvɑ̃tabl] *adj* dreadful.

épouvantail [epuvɑ̃taj] *nm* [à moineaux] scarecrow ; *fig* bogeyman.

épouvanter [3] [epuvɑ̃te] *vt* to terrify.

époux, épouse [epu, epuz] *nm, f* spouse.

éprendre [79] [eprɑ̃dr] ➡ **s'éprendre** *vp sout* : **s'éprendre de** to fall in love with.

épreuve [eprœv] *nf* **1.** [essai, examen] test ; **à l'épreuve du feu** fireproof ; **à l'épreuve des balles** bullet-proof ; **épreuve de force** *fig* trial of strength - **2.** [malheur] ordeal - **3.** SPORT event - **4.** TYPO proof - **5.** PHOTO print.

épris, e [epri, iz] ⟨⟩ *pp* ▶ **éprendre**. ⟨⟩ *adj sout* : **épris de** in love with.

éprouver [3] [epruve] *vt* **1.** [tester] to test - **2.** [ressentir] to feel - **3.** [faire souffrir] to distress ; **être éprouvé par** to be afflicted by - **4.** [difficultés, problèmes] to experience.

éprouvette [epruvɛt] *nf* **1.** [tube à essai] test tube - **2.** [échantillon] sample.

EPS (*abr de* **éducation physique et sportive**) *nf* PE.

épuisé, e [epɥize] *adj* **1.** [personne, corps] exhausted - **2.** [marchandise] sold out, out of stock ; [livre] out of print.

épuisement [epɥizmɑ̃] *nm* exhaustion.

épuiser [3] [epɥize] *vt* to exhaust.

épuisette [epɥizɛt] *nf* landing net.

épurer [3] [epyre] *vt* **1.** [eau, huile] to purify - **2.** POLIT to purge.

équarrir [32] [ekarir] *vt* **1.** [animal] to cut up - **2.** [poutre] to square - **3.** *fig* [personne] : **mal équarri** rough, crude.

équateur [ekwatœr] *nm* equator.

Équateur [ekwatœr] *nm* : **l'Équateur** Ecuador.

équation [ekwasjɔ̃] *nf* equation.

équatorial, e, aux [ekwatɔrjal, o] *adj* equatorial.

équerre [ekɛr] *nf* [instrument] set square ; [en T] T-square.

équestre [ekɛstr] *adj* equestrian.

équilatéral, e, aux [ekɥilateral, o] *adj* equilateral.

équilibre [ekilibr] *nm* **1.** [gén] balance - **2.** [psychique] stability.

équilibré, e [ekilibre] *adj* **1.** [personne] well-balanced - **2.** [vie] stable - **3.** ARCHIT : **aux proportions équilibrées** well-proportioned.

équilibrer [3] [ekilibre] *vt* to balance. ▶ **s'équilibrer** *vp* to balance each other out.

équilibriste [ekilibrist] *nmf* tightrope walker.

équipage [ekipaʒ] *nm* crew.

équipe [ekip] *nf* team.

équipé, e [ekipe] *adj* : **cuisine équipée** fitted kitchen.

équipement [ekipmɑ̃] *nm* **1.** [matériel] equipment - **2.** [aménagement] facilities *pl* ; **équipements sportifs/scolaires** sports/educational facilities.

équiper [3] [ekipe] *vt* **1.** [navire, armée] to equip - **2.** [personne, local] to equip, to fit out ; **équiper qqn/qqch de** to equip sb/sthg with, to fit sb/sthg out with. ▶ **s'équiper** *vp* : **s'équiper (de)** to equip o.s. (with).

équipier, ère [ekipje, ɛr] *nm, f* team member.

équitable [ekitabl] *adj* fair.

équitation [ekitasjɔ̃] *nf* riding, horse-riding UK, horseback riding US.

équité [ekite] *nf* fairness.

équivalent, e [ekivalɑ̃, ɑ̃t] *adj* equivalent. ▶ **équivalent** *nm* equivalent.

équivaloir [60] [ekivalwar] ▶ **équivaloir à** *v + prép* [être égal à] to be equal ou equivalent to.

équivoque [ekivɔk] ⟨⟩ *adj* **1.** [ambigu] ambiguous - **2.** [mystérieux] dubious. ⟨⟩ *nf* ambiguity ; **sans équivoque** unequivocal (*adj*), unequivocally (*adv*).

érable [erabl] *nm* maple.

éradiquer [3] [eradike] *vt* to eradicate.

érafler [3] [erafle] *vt* **1.** [peau] to scratch - **2.** [mur, voiture] to scrape.

éraflure [eraflyr] *nf* **1.** [de peau] scratch - **2.** [de mur, voiture] scrape.

éraillé, e [eraje] *adj* [voix] hoarse.

ère [ɛr] *nf* era.

érection [erɛksjɔ̃] *nf* erection.

éreintant, e [erɛtɑ̃, ɑ̃t] *adj* exhausting.

éreinter [3] [erɛte] *vt* **1.** [fatiguer] to exhaust - **2.** [critiquer] to pull to pieces.

ergonomique [ɛrgɔnɔmik] *adj* ergonomic.

ériger [17] [eriʒe] *vt* **1.** [monument] to erect - **2.** [tribunal] to set up - **3.** *fig* [transformer] : **ériger qqn en** to set sb up as.

ermite [ɛrmit] *nm* hermit.

éroder [3] [erɔde] *vt* to erode.

érogène [erɔʒɛn] *adj* erogenous.

érosion [erozjɔ̃] *nf* erosion.

érotique [erɔtik] *adj* erotic.

érotisme [erɔtism] *nm* eroticism.

errance [ɛrɑ̃s] *nf* wandering.

erratum [eratɔm] (*pl* **errata** [erata]) *nm* erratum.

errer [4] [ɛre] *vi* to wander.

erreur [ɛrœr] *nf* mistake ; **par erreur** by mistake.

erroné, e [ɛrɔne] *adj sout* wrong.

ersatz [ɛrzats] *nm inv* ersatz.

éructer [3] [erykte] *vi* to belch.

érudit, e [erydi, it] ⟨⟩ *adj* erudite, learned. ⟨⟩ *nm, f* learned person, scholar.

éruption [erypsjɔ̃] *nf* **1.** MÉD rash - **2.** [de volcan] eruption.

es ➤ être.

ès [εs] *prép* of *(in certain titles)* ; **docteur ès lettres** ≃ PhD, doctor of philosophy.

escabeau, x [εskabo] *nm* **1.** [échelle] step-ladder - **2.** *vieilli* [tabouret] stool.

escadre [εskadr] *nf* **1.** [navires] fleet - **2.** [avions] wing.

escadrille [εskadrij] *nf* **1.** [navires] flotilla - **2.** [avions] flight.

escadron [εskadrɔ̃] *nm* squadron.

escalade [εskalad] *nf* **1.** [de montagne, grille] climbing - **2.** [des prix, de violence] escalation.

escalader [3] [εskalade] *vt* to climb.

escale [εskal] *nf* **1.** [lieu - pour navire] port of call ; [- pour avion] stopover - **2.** [arrêt - de navire] call ; [- d'avion] stopover, stop ; **faire escale à** [- navire] to put in at, to call at ; [- avion] to stop over at.

escalier [εskalje] *nm* stairs *pl* ; **descendre/ monter l'escalier** to go downstairs/upstairs ; **escalier roulant** ou **mécanique** escalator.

escalope [εskalɔp] *nf* escalope.

escamotable [εskamɔtabl] *adj* **1.** [train d'atterrissage] retractable ; [antenne] tele-scopic - **2.** [table] folding.

escamoter [3] [εskamɔte] *vt* **1.** [faire dispa-raître] to make disappear - **2.** [voler] to lift - **3.** [rentrer] to retract - **4.** [phrase, mot] to swallow - **5.** [éluder - question] to evade ; [- objection] to get round *UK* ou around *US*.

escapade [εskapad] *nf* **1.** [voyage] outing - **2.** [fugue] escapade.

escargot [εskargo] *nm* snail.

escarmouche [εskarmuʃ] *nf* skirmish.

escarpé, e [εskarpe] *adj* steep.

escarpement [εskarpəmɑ̃] *nm* **1.** [de pente] steep slope - **2.** GÉOGR escarpment.

escarpin [εskarpɛ̃] *nm* court shoe *UK*, pump *US*.

escarre [εskar] *nf* bedsore, pressure sore.

escient [εsjɑ̃] *nm* : **à bon escient** advisedly ; **à mauvais escient** ill-advisedly.

esclaffer [3] [εsklafe] ➤ **s'esclaffer** *vp* to burst out laughing.

esclandre [εsklɑ̃dr] *nm* sout scene.

esclavage [εsklavaʒ] *nm* slavery.

esclave [εsklav] ◇ *nmf* slave. ◇ *adj* : **être esclave de** to be a slave to.

escompte [εskɔ̃t] *nm* discount.

escompter [3] [εskɔ̃te] *vt* **1.** [prévoir] to count on - **2.** FIN to discount.

escorte [εskɔrt] *nf* escort.

escorter [3] [εskɔrte] *vt* to escort.

escouade [εskwad] *nf* squad.

escrime [εskrim] *nf* fencing.

escrimer [3] [εskrime] ➤ **s'escrimer** *vp* : **s'escrimer à faire qqch** to work (away) at doing sthg.

escroc [εskro] *nm* swindler.

escroquer [3] [εskrɔke] *vt* to swindle ; **escroquer qqch à qqn** to swindle sb out of sthg.

escroquerie [εskrɔkri] *nf* swindle, swind-ling *(U)*.

eskimo, Eskimo ➤ esquimau.

espace [εspas] *nm* space ; **espace vert** green space, green area.

espacer [16] [εspase] *vt* **1.** [dans l'espace] to space out - **2.** [dans le temps - visites] to space out ; [- paiements] to spread out.

espadon [εspadɔ̃] *nm* [poisson] swordfish.

espadrille [εspadrij] *nf* espadrille.

Espagne [εspaɲ] *nf* : **l'Espagne** Spain.

espagnol, e [εspaɲɔl] *adj* Spanish. ➤ **espagnol** *nm* [langue] Spanish. ➤ **Espagnol, e** *nm, f* Spaniard ; **les Espagnols** the Spanish.

espèce [εspεs] *nf* **1.** BIOL, BOT & ZOOL species ; **espèce en voie de disparition** endangered species - **2.** [sorte] kind, sort ; **espèce d'idiot!** you stupid fool! ➤ **espèces** *nfpl* cash ; **payer en espèces** to pay (in) cash.

espérance [εsperɑ̃s] *nf* hope ; **espérance de vie** life expectancy.

espérer [18] [εspere] ◇ *vt* to hope for ; **espérer que** to hope (that) ; **espérer faire qqch** to hope to do sthg. ◇ *vi* to hope ; **espérer en qqn/qqch** to trust in sb/sthg.

espiègle [εspjεgl] *adj* mischievous.

espion, onne [εspjɔ̃, ɔn] *nm, f* spy.

espionnage [εspjɔnaʒ] *nm* spying ; **espion-nage industriel** industrial espionage.

espionner [3] [εspjɔne] *vt* to spy on.

esplanade [εsplanad] *nf* esplanade.

espoir [εspwar] *nm* hope.

esprit [εspri] *nm* **1.** [entendement, personne, pensée] mind ; **reprendre ses esprits** to recover - **2.** [attitude] spirit ; **esprit de compétition** competitive spirit ; **esprit criti-que** critical acumen - **3.** [humour] wit - **4.** [fantôme] spirit, ghost.

esquif [εskif] *nm* litt skiff.

esquimau, aude, aux [εskimo, od] *adj* Eskimo. ➤ **Esquimau, aude, Eskimo** *nm, f* Eskimo *(beware: the term 'Esquimau', like its English equivalent, is often considered offensive in North America. The term 'Inuit' is preferred)*.

esquinter [3] [εskɛ̃te] *vt* fam **1.** [abîmer] to ruin - **2.** [critiquer] to slate *UK*, to pan. ➤ **s'esquinter** *vp* : **s'esquinter à faire qqch** to kill o.s. doing sthg.

esquiver [3] [εskive] *vt* to dodge. ➤ **s'esqui-ver** *vp* to slip away.

essai [esɛ] *nm* **1.** [vérification] test, testing (U) ; **à l'essai** on trial - **2.** [tentative] attempt - **3.** [rugby] try.

essaim [esɛ̃] *nm litt & fig* swarm.

essayage [esɛjaʒ] *nm* fitting.

essayer [11] [eseje] *vt* to try ; **essayer de faire qqch** to try to do sthg.

essence [esɑ̃s] *nf* **1.** [fondement, de plante] essence ; **par essence** *sout* in essence - **2.** [carburant] petrol *UK*, gas *US* - **3.** [d'arbre] species.

essentiel, elle [esɑ̃sjɛl] *adj* **1.** [indispensable] essential - **2.** [fondamental] basic. ⬛ **essentiel** *nm* **1.** [point] : **l'essentiel** [le principal] the essential ou main thing ; [objets] the essentials *pl* - **2.** [quantité] : **l'essentiel de** the main ou greater part of.

essentiellement [esɑ̃sjɛlmɑ̃] *adv* **1.** [avant tout] above all - **2.** [par essence] essentially.

esseulé, e [esœle] *adj litt* forsaken.

essieu [esjø] *nm* axle.

essor [esɔr] *nm* flight, expansion, boom ; **prendre son essor** to take flight ; *fig* to take off.

essorer [3] [esɔre] *vt* [à la main, à rouleaux] to wring out ; [à la machine] to spin-dry *UK*, to tumble-dry ; [salade] to spin, to dry.

essoreuse [esɔrøz] *nf* [à rouleaux] mangle ; [électrique] spin-dryer *UK*, tumble-dryer ; [à salade] salad spinner.

essouffler [3] [esufle] *vt* to make breathless. ⬛ **s'essouffler** *vp* to be breathless ou out of breath ; *fig* to run out of steam.

essuie-glace [esɥiglas] (*pl* essuie-glaces) *nm* windscreen wiper *UK*, windshield wiper *US*.

essuie-mains [esɥimɛ̃] *nm inv* hand towel.

essuie-tout [esɥitu] *nm inv* kitchen roll *UK*, paper towels *US*.

essuyer [14] [esɥije] *vt* **1.** [sécher] to dry - **2.** [nettoyer] to wipe - **3.** *fig* [subir] to suffer. ⬛ **s'essuyer** *vp* to dry o.s.

est[1] [ɛst] *nm* east ; **un vent d'est** an easterly wind ; **à l'est** in the east ; **à l'est (de)** to the east (of). ⬦ *adj inv* [gén] east ; [province, région] eastern.

est[2] [ɛ] ➤ **être**.

estafette [ɛstafɛt] *nf* dispatch rider ; MIL liaison officer.

estafilade [ɛstafilad] *nf* slash, gash.

est-allemand, e [ɛstalmɑ̃, ɑ̃d] *adj* East German.

estampe [ɛstɑ̃p] *nf* print.

estampille [ɛstɑ̃pij] *nf* stamp.

est-ce que [ɛskə] *adv interr* : **est-ce qu'il fait beau?** is the weather good? ; **est-ce que**

vous aimez l'accordéon? do you like the accordion? ; **où est-ce que tu es?** where are you?

esthète [ɛstɛt] *nmf* aesthete.

esthétique [ɛstetik] *adj* **1.** [relatif à la beauté] aesthetic - **2.** [harmonieux] attractive.

estimation [ɛstimasjɔ̃] *nf* estimate, estimation.

estime [ɛstim] *nf* respect, esteem.

estimer [3] [ɛstime] *vt* **1.** [expertiser] to value - **2.** [évaluer] to estimate ; **j'estime la durée du voyage à 2 heures** I reckon the journey time is 2 hours - **3.** [respecter] to respect - **4.** [penser] : **estimer que** to feel (that).

estival, e, aux [ɛstival, o] *adj* summer (avant n).

estivant, e [ɛstivɑ̃, ɑ̃t] *nm, f* (summer) holiday-maker *UK* ou vacationer *US*.

estomac [ɛstɔma] *nm* ANAT stomach.

estomper [3] [ɛstɔpe] *vt* to blur ; *fig* [douleur] to lessen. ⬛ **s'estomper** *vp* to become blurred ; *fig* [douleur] to lessen.

Estonie [ɛstɔni] *nf* : **l'Estonie** Estonia.

estrade [ɛstrad] *nf* dais.

estragon [ɛstragɔ̃] *nm* tarragon.

estropié, e [ɛstrɔpje] ⬦ *adj* crippled. ⬦ *nm, f* cripple.

estuaire [ɛstɥɛr] *nm* estuary.

esturgeon [ɛstyrʒɔ̃] *nm* sturgeon.

et [e] *conj* **1.** [gén] and ; **et moi?** what about me? - **2.** [dans les fractions et les nombres composés] : **vingt et un** twenty-one ; **il y a deux ans et demi** two and a half years ago ; **à deux heures et demie** at half past two.

ét. (*abr écrite de* étage) fl.

ETA (*abr de* Euskadi ta Askatasuna) *nf* ETA.

étable [etabl] *nf* cowshed.

établi [etabli] *nm* workbench.

établir [32] [etablir] *vt* **1.** [gén] to establish ; [record] to set - **2.** [dresser] to draw up. ⬛ **s'établir** *vp* **1.** [s'installer] to settle - **2.** [s'instaurer] to become established.

établissement [etablismɑ̃] *nm* [institution] establishment ; **établissement hospitalier** hospital ; **établissement scolaire** educational establishment.

étage [etaʒ] *nm* **1.** [de bâtiment] floor, storey *UK*, story *US* ; **à l'étage** upstairs ; **un immeuble à quatre étages** a four-storey block of flats *UK*, a four-story block of apartments *US* ; **au premier étage** on the first floor *UK*, on the second floor *US* - **2.** [de fusée] stage.

étagère [etaʒɛr] *nf* **1.** [rayon] shelf - **2.** [meuble] shelves *pl*, set of shelves.

étain [etɛ̃] *nm* [métal] tin ; [alliage] pewter.

étais, était *etc* ▶ être.

étal [etal] (*pl* -s ou **étaux** [eto]) *nm* **1.** [éventaire] stall - **2.** [de boucher] butcher's block.

étalage [etalaʒ] *nm* **1.** [action, ensemble d'objets] display ; **faire étalage de** *fig* to flaunt - **2.** [devanture] window display.

étalagiste [etalaʒist] *nmf* **1.** [décorateur] window dresser - **2.** [vendeur] stallholder US.

étaler [3] [etale] *vt* **1.** [exposer] to display - **2.** [étendre] to spread out - **3.** [dans le temps] to stagger - **4.** [mettre une couche de] to spread - **5.** [exhiber] to parade. ➜ **s'étaler** *vp* **1.** [s'étendre] to spread - **2.** [dans le temps] : **s'étaler (sur)** to be spread (over) - **3.** *fam* [tomber] to come a cropper *UK*, to fall flat on one's face.

étalon [etalɔ̃] *nm* **1.** [cheval] stallion - **2.** [mesure] standard.

étamine [etamin] *nf* [de fleur] stamen.

étanche [etɑ̃ʃ] *adj* watertight ; [montre] waterproof.

étancher [3] [etɑ̃ʃe] *vt* **1.** [sang, larmes] to stem (the flow of) - **2.** [assouvir] to quench.

étang [etɑ̃] *nm* pond.

étant *p prés* ▶ être.

étape [etap] *nf* **1.** [gén] stage - **2.** [halte] stop ; **faire étape à** to break one's journey at.

état [eta] *nm* **1.** [manière d'être] state ; **être en état/hors d'état de faire qqch** to be in a/in no fit state to do sthg ; **en bon/mauvais état** in good/poor condition ; **en état de marche** in working order ; **état d'âme** mood ; **état d'esprit** state of mind ; **état de santé** (state of) health ; **être dans tous ses états** *fig* to be in a state - **2.** [métier, statut] status ; **état civil** ADMIN ≃ marital status - **3.** [inventaire - gén] inventory ; [- de dépenses] statement ; **état des lieux** *inventory and inspection of rented property*. ➜ **État** [nation] state ; **l'État** the State ; **État membre** member state.

état-major [etamaʒɔr] *nm* **1.** ADMIN & MIL staff ; [de parti] leadership - **2.** [lieu] headquarters *pl*.

États-Unis [etazyni] *nmpl* : **les États-Unis (d'Amérique)** the United States (of America).

étau [eto] *nm* vice, vise *US*.

étayer [11] [eteje] *vt* to prop up ; *fig* to back up.

etc. (*abr écrite de* et cætera) etc.

été [ete] ◇ *pp inv* ▶ être. ◇ *nm* summer ; **en été** in (the) summer.

éteindre [81] [etɛ̃dr] *vt* **1.** [incendie, bougie, cigarette] to put out ; [radio, chauffage, lampe] to turn off, to switch off - **2.** INFORM

to shut down. ➜ **s'éteindre** *vp* **1.** [feu, lampe] to go out - **2.** [bruit, souvenir] to fade (away) - **3.** *fig & litt* [personne] to pass away - **4.** [race] to die out.

étendard [etɑ̃dar] *nm* standard.

étendre [73] [etɑ̃dr] *vt* **1.** [déployer] to stretch ; [journal, linge] to spread (out) - **2.** [coucher] to lay - **3.** [appliquer] to spread - **4.** [accroître] to extend - **5.** [diluer] to dilute ; [sauce] to thin. ➜ **s'étendre** *vp* **1.** [se coucher] to lie down - **2.** [s'étaler au loin] : **s'étendre (de/jusqu'à)** to stretch (from/as far as) - **3.** [croître] to spread - **4.** [s'attarder] : **s'étendre sur** to elaborate on.

étendu, e [etɑ̃dy] ◇ *pp* ▶ étendre. ◇ *adj* **1.** [bras, main] outstretched - **2.** [plaine, connaissances] extensive. ➜ **étendue** *nf* **1.** [surface] area, expanse - **2.** [durée] length - **3.** [importance] extent - **4.** MUS range.

éternel, elle [etɛrnɛl] *adj* eternal ; **ce ne sera pas éternel** this won't last for ever.

éterniser [3] [etɛrnize] *vt* [prolonger] to drag out. ➜ **s'éterniser** *vp* **1.** [se prolonger] to drag out - **2.** *fam* [rester] to stay for ever.

éternité [etɛrnite] *nf* eternity.

éternuer [7] [etɛrnɥe] *vi* to sneeze.

êtes ▶ être.

étêter [4] [etete] *vt* to cut the head off.

éther [etɛr] *nm* ether.

Éthiopie [etjɔpi] *nf* : **l'Éthiopie** Ethiopia.

éthique [etik] ◇ *nf* ethics *(U or pl)*. ◇ *adj* ethical.

ethnie [ɛtni] *nf* ethnic group.

ethnique [ɛtnik] *adj* ethnic.

ethnologie [ɛtnɔlɔʒi] *nf* ethnology.

éthylisme [etilism] *nm* alcoholism.

étiez, étions *etc* ▶ être.

étincelant, e [etɛ̃slɑ̃, ɑ̃t] *adj* sparkling.

étinceler [24] [etɛ̃sle] *vi* to sparkle.

étincelle [etɛ̃sɛl] *nf* spark.

étioler [3] [etjɔle] ➜ **s'étioler** *vp* [plante] to wilt ; [personne] to weaken ; [mémoire] to go.

étiqueter [27] [etikte] *vt litt & fig* to label.

étiquette [etikɛt] *nf* **1.** *fig* [marque] label - **2.** [protocole] etiquette.

étirer [3] [etire] *vt* to stretch. ➜ **s'étirer** *vp* to stretch.

étoffe [etɔf] *nf* fabric, material.

étoile [etwal] *nf* star ; **étoile filante** shooting star ; **à la belle étoile** *fig* under the stars. ➜ **étoile de mer** *nf* starfish.

étoilé, e [etwale] *adj* **1.** [ciel, nuit] starry ; **la bannière étoilée** the Star-Spangled Banner - **2.** [vitre, pare-brise] shattered.

étole [etɔl] *nf* stole.

étonnant, e [etɔnɑ̃, ɑ̃t] *adj* astonishing.

étonnement [etɔnmɑ̃] *nm* astonishment, surprise.

étonner [3] [etɔne] *vt* to surprise, to astonish. ⏩ **s'étonner** *vp* : **s'étonner (de)** to be surprised (by) ; **s'étonner que** (+ *subjonctif*) to be surprised (that).

étouffant, e [etufɑ̃, ɑ̃t] *adj* stifling.

étouffée [etufe] ⏩ **à l'étouffée** *loc adv* steamed ; [viande] braised.

étouffer [3] [etufe] ⏩ *vt* **1.** [gén] to stifle - **2.** [asphyxier] to suffocate - **3.** [feu] to smother - **4.** [scandale, révolte] to suppress. ⏩ *vi* to suffocate. ⏩ **s'étouffer** *vp* [s'étrangler] to choke.

étourderie [eturdəri] *nf* **1.** [distraction] thoughtlessness - **2.** [bévue] careless mistake ; [acte irréfléchi] thoughtless act.

étourdi, e [eturdi] ⏩ *adj* scatterbrained. ⏩ *nm, f* scatterbrain.

étourdir [32] [eturdir] *vt* [assommer] to daze.

étourdissement [eturdismɑ̃] *nm* dizzy spell.

étourneau, x [eturno] *nm* starling.

étrange [etrɑ̃ʒ] *adj* strange.

étranger, ère [etrɑ̃ʒe, ɛr] ⏩ *adj* **1.** [gén] foreign - **2.** [différent, isolé] unknown, unfamiliar ; **être étranger à qqn** to be unknown to sb ; **être étranger à qqch** to have no connection with sthg ; **se sentir étranger** to feel like an outsider. ⏩ *nm, f* **1.** [de nationalité différente] foreigner - **2.** [inconnu] stranger - **3.** [exclu] outsider. ⏩ **étranger** *nm* : **à l'étranger** abroad.

étrangeté [etrɑ̃ʒte] *nf* strangeness.

étranglement [etrɑ̃ɡləmɑ̃] *nm* **1.** [strangulation] strangulation - **2.** [rétrécissement] constriction.

étrangler [3] [etrɑ̃ɡle] *vt* **1.** [gén] to choke - **2.** [strangler] to strangle - **3.** [réprimer] to stifle - **4.** [serrer] to constrict. ⏩ **s'étrangler** *vp* [s'étouffer] to choke.

étrave [etrav] *nf* stem.

être [2] [ɛtr] ⏩ *nm* **1.** BIOL & PHILO being ; **les êtres vivants/humains** living/human beings. - **2.** [personne] person. ⏩ *v aux* **1.** [pour les temps composés] to have/to be ; **il est parti hier** he left yesterday ; **il est déjà arrivé** he has already arrived ; **il est né en 1952** he was born in 1952 - **2.** [pour le passif] to be ; **la maison a été vendue** the house has been OU was sold. ⏩ *v att* **1.** [état] to be ; **la maison est blanche** the house is white ; **il est médecin** he's a doctor ; **sois sage!** be good! - **2.** [possession] : **être à qqn** to be-

long to sb ; **c'est à vous, cette voiture?** is this your car?, is this car yours? ; **cette maison est à lui/eux** this house is his/theirs, this is his/their house. ⏩ *v impers* **1.** [exprimant le temps] : **quelle heure est-il?** what time is it?, what's the time? ; **il est dix heures dix** it's ten past ten UK, it's ten after ten US - **2.** [suivi d'un adjectif] : **il est... it is...** ; **il est inutile de** it's useless to ; **il serait bon de/que** it would be good to/if, it would be a good idea to/if. ⏩ *vi* **1.** [exister] to be ; **n'être plus** *sout* [être décédé] to be no more - **2.** [indique une situation, un état] to be ; **il est à Paris** he's in Paris ; **nous sommes au printemps/en été** it's spring/summer - **3.** [indiquant une origine] : **il est de Paris** he's from Paris. ⏩ **être à** *v + prép* **1.** [indiquant une obligation] : **c'est à vérifier** it needs to be checked ; **c'est à voir** that remains to be seen - **2.** [indiquant une continuité] : **il est toujours à ne rien faire** he never does a thing.

étreindre [81] [etrɛ̃dr] *vt* **1.** [embrasser] to hug, to embrace - **2.** *fig* [tenailler] to grip, to clutch. ⏩ **s'étreindre** *vp* to embrace each other.

étreinte [etrɛ̃t] *nf* **1.** [enlacement] embrace - **2.** [pression] stranglehold.

étrenner [4] [etrene] *vt* to use for the first time.

étrennes [etren] *nfpl* Christmas box (*sing*) UK.

étrier [etrije] *nm* stirrup.

étriller [3] [etrije] *vt* **1.** [cheval] to curry - **2.** [personne] to wipe the floor with ; [film] to tear to pieces.

étriper [3] [etripe] *vt* **1.** [animal] to disembowel - **2.** *fam fig* [tuer] to murder. ⏩ **s'étriper** *vp fam* to tear each other to pieces.

étriqué, e [etrike] *adj* **1.** [vêtement] tight ; [appartement] cramped - **2.** [esprit] narrow.

étroit, e [etrwa, at] *adj* **1.** [gén] narrow - **2.** [intime] close - **3.** [serré] tight. ⏩ **à l'étroit** *loc adj* : **être à l'étroit** to be cramped.

étroitesse [etrwates] *nf* narrowness.

étude [etyd] *nf* **1.** [gén] study ; **à l'étude** under consideration ; **étude de marché** market research (*U*) - **2.** [de notaire - local] office ; [- charge] practice - **3.** MUS étude. ⏩ **études** *nfpl* studies ; **faire des études** to study.

étudiant, e [etydjɑ̃, ɑ̃t] *nm, f* student.

étudié, e [etydje] *adj* studied.

étudier [9] [etydje] *vt* [apprendre - général] to study ; [- leçon] to learn ; [- piano] to learn (to play), to study ; [- auteur, période] to study.

étui [etɥi] *nm* case ; **étui à cigarettes/lunettes** cigarette/glasses case.

étuve [etyv] *nf* **1.** [local] steam room ; *fig* oven - **2.** [appareil] sterilizer.

étuvée [etyve] ➤ **à l'étuvée** *loc adv* braised.

étymologie [etimɔlɔʒi] *nf* etymology.

eu, e [y] *pp* ▶ avoir.

E-U, E-U A *(abr de* États-Unis (d'Amérique)) *nmpl* US, USA.

eucalyptus [økaliptys] *nm* eucalyptus.

euh [ø] *interj* er.

eunuque [ønyk] *nm* eunuch.

euphémisme [øfemism] *nm* euphemism.

euphorie [øfɔri] *nf* euphoria.

euphorisant, e [øfɔrizɑ̃, ɑ̃t] *adj* exhilarating. ➤ **euphorisant** *nm* antidepressant.

eurent ▶ avoir.

euro [øro] *nm* euro ; **zone euro** euro zone, euro area.

eurodéputé [ørodepyte] *nm* Euro MP.

eurodevise [ørodəviz] *nf* Eurocurrency.

Europe [ørɔp] *nf* : **l'Europe** Europe.

européen, enne [ørɔpeɛ̃, ɛn] *adj* European. ➤ **Européen, enne** *nm, f* European. ➤ **européennes** *nfpl* POLIT European elections, Euro-elections, elections to the European Parliament.

eus, eut *etc* ▶ avoir.

eût ▶ avoir.

euthanasie [øtanazi] *nf* euthanasia.

euthanasier [9] [øtanazje] *vt* [animal] to put down, to put to sleep ; [personne] to practise euthanasia on, to help to die.

eux [ø] *pron pers* **1.** [sujet] they ; **ce sont eux qui me l'ont dit** they're the ones who told me - **2.** [complément] them. ➤ **eux-mêmes** *pron pers* themselves.

évacuer [7] [evakɥe] *vt* **1.** [gén] to evacuate - **2.** [liquide] to drain.

évadé, e [evade] *nm, f* escaped prisoner.

évader [3] [evade] ➤ **s'évader** *vp* : **s'évader (de)** to escape (from).

évaluation [evalɥasjɔ̃] *nf* [action] valuation ; [résultat] estimate.

évaluer [7] [evalɥe] *vt* [distance] to estimate ; [tableau] to value ; [risque] to assess.

évangélique [evɑ̃ʒelik] *adj* evangelical.

évangéliser [3] [evɑ̃ʒelize] *vt* to evangelize.

évangile [evɑ̃ʒil] *nm* gospel.

évanouir [32] [evanwir] ➤ **s'évanouir** *vp* **1.** [défaillir] to faint - **2.** [disparaître] to fade.

évanouissement [evanwismɑ̃] *nm* [syncope] fainting fit.

évaporer [3] [evapɔre] ➤ **s'évaporer** *vp* to evaporate.

évasé, e [evaze] *adj* flared.

évasif, ive [evazif, iv] *adj* evasive.

évasion [evazjɔ̃] *nf* escape.

évêché [eveʃe] *nm* [territoire] diocese ; [résidence] bishop's palace.

éveil [evej] *nm* awakening ; **en éveil** on the alert.

éveillé, e [eveje] *adj* **1.** [qui ne dort pas] wide awake - **2.** [vif, alerte] alert.

éveiller [4] [eveje] *vt* to arouse ; [intelligence, dormeur] to awaken. ➤ **s'éveiller** *vp* **1.** [dormeur] to wake, to awaken - **2.** [curiosité] to be aroused - **3.** [esprit, intelligence] to be awakened - **4.** [s'ouvrir] : **s'éveiller à qqch** to discover sthg.

événement [evenmɑ̃] *nm* event.

événementiel, elle [evɛnmɑ̃sjɛl] *adj* [histoire] factual.

éventail [evɑ̃taj] *nm* **1.** [objet] fan ; **en éventail** fan-shaped - **2.** [choix] range.

éventaire [evɑ̃tɛr] *nm* **1.** [étalage] stall, stand - **2.** [corbeille] tray.

éventer [3] [evɑ̃te] *vt* **1.** [rafraîchir] to fan - **2.** [divulguer] to give away. ➤ **s'éventer** *vp* **1.** [se rafraîchir] to fan o.s. - **2.** [parfum, vin] to go stale.

éventrer [3] [evɑ̃tre] *vt* **1.** [étriper] to disembowel - **2.** [fendre] to rip open.

éventualité [evɑ̃tɥalite] *nf* **1.** [possibilité] possibility - **2.** [circonstance] eventuality ; **dans l'éventualité de** in the event of.

éventuel, elle [evɑ̃tɥel] *adj* possible.

éventuellement [evɑ̃tɥelmɑ̃] *adv* possibly.

évêque [evɛk] *nm* bishop.

évertuer [7] [evertɥe] ➤ **s'évertuer** *vp* : **s'évertuer à faire qqch** to strive to do sthg.

évidemment [evidamɑ̃] *adv* obviously.

évidence [evidɑ̃s] *nf* [caractère] evidence ; [fait] obvious fact ; **mettre en évidence** to emphasize, to highlight.

évident, e [evidɑ̃, ɑ̃t] *adj* obvious.

évider [3] [evide] *vt* to hollow out.

évier [evje] *nm* sink.

évincer [16] [evɛ̃se] *vt* : **évincer qqn (de)** to oust sb (from).

éviter [3] [evite] *vt* **1.** [esquiver] to avoid - **2.** [s'abstenir] : **éviter de faire qqch** to avoid doing sthg - **3.** [épargner] : **éviter qqch à qqn** to save sb sthg.

évocateur, trice [evɔkatœr, tris] *adj* [geste, regard] meaningful.

évocation [evɔkasjɔ̃] *nf* evocation.

évolué, e [evɔlɥe] *adj* **1.** [développé] developed - **2.** [libéral, progressiste] broadminded.

évoluer [7] [evɔlɥe] *vi* **1.** [changer] to evolve ; [personne] to change - **2.** [se mouvoir] to move about.

évolution [evɔlysjɔ̃] *nf* **1.** [transformation] development - **2.** BIOL evolution - **3.** MÉD progress.

évoquer [3] [evɔke] *vt* **1.** [souvenir] to evoke - **2.** [problème] to refer to - **3.** [esprits, démons] to call up.

exacerber [3] [ɛgzasɛrbe] *vt* to heighten.

exact, e [ɛgzakt] *adj* **1.** [calcul] correct - **2.** [récit, copie] exact - **3.** [ponctuel] punctual.

exactement [ɛgzaktəmɑ̃] *adv* exactly.

exaction [ɛgzaksjɔ̃] *nf* extortion.

exactitude [ɛgzaktityd] *nf* **1.** [de calcul, montre] accuracy - **2.** [ponctualité] punctuality.

ex æquo [ɛgzeko] <> *adj inv* & *nmf* equal. <> *adv* equal ; **troisième ex æquo** third equal, tied for third.

exagération [ɛgzaʒerasjɔ̃] *nf* exaggeration.

exagéré, e [ɛgzaʒere] *adj* exaggerated.

exagérer [18] [ɛgzaʒere] *vt* & *vi* to exaggerate.

exalté, e [ɛgzalte] <> *adj* [sentiment] elated ; [tempérament] over-excited ; [imagination] vivid. <> *nm, f* fanatic.

exalter [3] [ɛgzalte] *vt* to excite. ➡ **s'exalter** *vp* to get carried away.

examen [ɛgzamɛ̃] *nm* examination ; SCOL exam, examination ; **examen médical** medical (examination) *UK*, physical (examination) *US* ; **mise en examen** DR indictment.

examinateur, trice [ɛgzaminatœr, tris] *nm, f* examiner.

examiner [3] [ɛgzamine] *vt* to examine.

exaspération [ɛgzasperasjɔ̃] *nf* exasperation.

exaspérer [18] [ɛgzaspere] *vt* to exasperate.

exaucer [16] [ɛgzose] *vt* to grant ; **exaucer qqn** to answer sb's prayers.

excédent [ɛksedɑ̃] *nm* surplus ; **en excédent** surplus *(avant n)*.

excéder [18] [ɛksede] *vt* **1.** [gén] to exceed - **2.** [exaspérer] to exasperate.

excellence [ɛkselɑ̃s] *nf* excellence ; **par excellence** par excellence.

excellent, e [ɛkselɑ̃, ɑ̃t] *adj* excellent.

exceller [4] [ɛksele] *vi* : **exceller en** OU **dans qqch** to excel at OU in sthg ; **exceller à faire qqch** to excel at doing sthg.

excentré, e [ɛksɑ̃tre] *adj* : **c'est très excentré** it's quite a long way out.

excentrique [ɛksɑ̃trik] <> *nmf* eccentric. <> *adj* **1.** [gén] eccentric - **2.** [quartier] outlying.

excepté, e [ɛksɛpte] *adj* : **tous sont venus, lui excepté** everyone came except (for) him. ➡ **excepté** *prép* apart from, except.

exception [ɛksɛpsjɔ̃] *nf* [hors norme] exception ; **à l'exception de** except for.

exceptionnel, elle [ɛksɛpsjɔnɛl] *adj* exceptional.

excès [ɛksɛ] <> *nm* excess ; **excès de zèle** overzealousness. <> *nmpl* excesses.

excessif, ive [ɛksesif, iv] *adj* **1.** [démesuré] excessive - **2.** *fam* [extrême] extreme.

excitant, e [ɛksitɑ̃, ɑ̃t] *adj* [stimulant, passionnant] exciting. ➡ **excitant** *nm* stimulant.

excitation [ɛksitasjɔ̃] *nf* **1.** [énervement] excitement - **2.** [stimulation] encouragement - **3.** MÉD stimulation.

excité, e [ɛksite] <> *adj* [énervé] excited. <> *nm, f* hothead.

exciter [3] [ɛksite] *vt* **1.** [gén] to excite - **2.** [inciter] : **exciter qqn (à qqch/à faire qqch)** to incite sb (to sthg/to do sthg) - **3.** MÉD to stimulate.

exclamation [ɛksklamasjɔ̃] *nf* exclamation.

exclamer [3] [ɛksklame] ➡ **s'exclamer** *vp* : **s'exclamer (devant)** to exclaim (at OU over).

exclu, e [ɛkskly] <> *pp* ➡ **exclure**. <> *adj* excluded. <> *nm, f* outsider.

exclure [96] [ɛksklyr] *vt* to exclude ; [expulser] to expel.

exclusion [ɛksklyzjɔ̃] *nf* expulsion ; **à l'exclusion de** to the exclusion of.

exclusivement [ɛksklyzivmɑ̃] *adv* **1.** [uniquement] exclusively - **2.** [non inclus] exclusive.

exclusivité [ɛksklyzivite] *nf* **1.** COMM exclusive rights *pl* - **2.** CINÉ sole screening rights *pl* ; **en exclusivité** exclusively - **3.** [de sentiment] exclusiveness.

excommunier [9] [ɛkskɔmynje] *vt* to excommunicate.

excrément [ɛkskremɑ̃] *nm* (gén pl) excrement (U).

excroissance [ɛkskrwasɑ̃s] *nf* excrescence.

excursion [ɛkskyrsjɔ̃] *nf* excursion.

excursionniste [ɛkskyrsjɔnist] *nmf* daytripper.

excuse [ɛkskyz] *nf* excuse.

excuser [3] [ɛkskyze] *vt* to excuse ; **excusez-moi** [pour réparer] I'm sorry ; [pour demander] excuse me. ➡ **s'excuser** *vp* [demander pardon] to apologize ; **s'excuser de qqch/de faire qqch** to apologize for sthg/for doing sthg.

exécrable [ɛgzekrabl] *adj* atrocious.

exécrer [18] [ɛgzekre] *vt* to loathe.

exécutant, e [ɛgzekytɑ̃, ɑ̃t] *nm, f* **1.** [personne] underling - **2.** MUS performer.

exécuter [3] [ɛgzekyte] *vt* **1.** [réaliser] to carry out ; [tableau] to paint - **2.** MUS to play, to perform - **3.** [mettre à mort] to execute. ➤ **s'exécuter** *vp* to comply.

exécutif, ive [ɛgzekytif, iv] *adj* executive. ➤ **exécutif** *nm* : **l'exécutif** the executive.

exécution [ɛgzekysjɔ̃] *nf* **1.** [réalisation] carrying out ; [de tableau] painting - **2.** MUS performance - **3.** [mise à mort] execution.

exemplaire [ɛgzɑ̃plɛr] ◇ *adj* exemplary. ◇ *nm* copy.

exemple [ɛgzɑ̃pl] *nm* example ; **par exemple** for example, for instance.

exempté, e [ɛgzɑ̃te] *adj* : **exempté (de)** exempt (from).

exercer [16] [ɛgzɛrse] *vt* **1.** [entraîner, mettre en usage] to exercise ; [autorité, influence] to exert - **2.** [métier] to carry on ; [médecine] to practise *UK*, to practice *US*. ➤ **s'exercer** *vp* **1.** [s'entraîner] to practise *UK*, to practice *US* ; **s'exercer à qqch/à faire qqch** to practise *UK* ou to practice *US* sthg/doing sthg - **2.** [se manifester] : **s'exercer (sur** ou **contre)** to be exerted (on).

exercice [ɛgzɛrsis] *nm* **1.** [gén] exercise - **2.** [entraînement] practice - **3.** [de métier, fonction] carrying out ; **en exercice** in office.

exhaler [3] [ɛgzale] *vt litt* **1.** [odeur] to give off - **2.** [plainte, soupir] to utter. ➤ **s'exhaler** *vp* **1.** [odeur] to rise - **2.** [plainte, soupir] : **s'exhaler de** to rise from.

exhaustif, ive [ɛgzostif, iv] *adj* exhaustive.

exhiber [3] [ɛgzibe] *vt* [présenter] to show ; [faire étalage de] to show off. ➤ **s'exhiber** *vp* to make an exhibition of o.s.

exhibitionniste [ɛgzibisjɔnist] *nmf* exhibitionist.

exhorter [3] [ɛgzɔrte] *vt* : **exhorter qqn à qqch/à faire qqch** to urge sb to sthg/to do sthg.

exhumer [3] [ɛgzyme] *vt* to exhume ; *fig* to unearth, to dig up.

exigeant, e [ɛgziʒɑ̃, ɑ̃t] *adj* demanding.

exigence [ɛgziʒɑ̃s] *nf* [demande] demand.

exiger [17] [ɛgziʒe] *vt* **1.** [demander] to demand ; **exiger que** (+ *subjonctif*) to demand that ; **exiger qqch de qqn** to demand sthg from sb - **2.** [nécessiter] to require.

exigible [ɛgziʒibl] *adj* payable.

exigu, ë [ɛgzigy] *adj* cramped.

exil [ɛgzil] *nm* exile ; **en exil** exiled.

exilé, e [ɛgzile] *nm, f* exile.

exiler [3] [ɛgzile] *vt* to exile. ➤ **s'exiler** *vp* **1.** POLIT to go into exile - **2.** *fig* [partir] to go into seclusion.

existence [ɛgzistɑ̃s] *nf* existence.

exister [3] [ɛgziste] ◇ *vi* to exist. ◇ *v impers* : **il existe** [il y a] there is/are.

exode [ɛgzɔd] *nm* exodus.

exonération [ɛgzɔnerasjɔ̃] *nf* exemption ; **exonération d'impôts** tax exemption.

exorbitant, e [ɛgzɔrbitɑ̃, ɑ̃t] *adj* exorbitant.

exorbité, e [ɛgzɔrbite] ➤ **œil**.

exorciser [3] [ɛgzɔrsize] *vt* to exorcize.

exotique [ɛgzɔtik] *adj* exotic.

exotisme [ɛgzɔtism] *nm* exoticism.

expansif, ive [ɛkspɑ̃sif, iv] *adj* expansive.

expansion [ɛkspɑ̃sjɔ̃] *nf* expansion.

expansionniste [ɛkspɑ̃sjɔnist] *nmf & adj* expansionist.

expatrié, e [ɛkspatrije] *adj & nm, f* expatriate.

expatrier [10] [ɛkspatrije] *vt* to expatriate. ➤ **s'expatrier** *vp* to leave one's country.

expédier [9] [ɛkspedje] *vt* **1.** [lettre, marchandise] to send, to dispatch - **2.** [personne] to get rid of ; [question] to dispose of - **3.** [travail] to dash off.

expéditeur, trice [ɛkspeditœr, tris] *nm, f* sender.

expéditif, ive [ɛkspeditif, iv] *adj* quick, expeditious.

expédition [ɛkspedisjɔ̃] *nf* **1.** [envoi] sending - **2.** [voyage, campagne militaire] expedition.

expérience [ɛksperjɑ̃s] *nf* **1.** [pratique] experience ; **avoir de l'expérience** to have experience, to be experienced - **2.** [essai] experiment.

expérimental, e, aux [ɛksperimɑ̃tal, o] *adj* experimental.

expérimenté, e [ɛksperimɑ̃te] *adj* experienced.

expert, e [ɛkspɛr, ɛrt] *adj* expert. ➤ **expert** *nm* expert.

expert-comptable [ɛkspɛrkɔ̃tabl] *nm* chartered accountant *UK*, certified public accountant *US*.

expertise [ɛkspɛrtiz] *nf* **1.** [examen] expert appraisal ; [estimation] (expert) valuation - **2.** [compétence] expertise.

expertiser [3] [ɛkspɛrtize] *vt* to value ; [dégâts] to assess.

expier [9] [ɛkspje] *vt* to pay for.

expiration [ɛkspirasjɔ̃] *nf* **1.** [d'air] exhalation - **2.** [de contrat] expiry *UK*, expiration *US* ; **arriver à expiration** to expire by ; **date d'expiration** expiry date.

expirer [3] [ɛkspire] ◇ *vt* to breathe out. ◇ *vi* [contrat] to expire.

explicatif, ive [ɛksplikatif, iv] *adj* explanatory.

explication [ɛksplikasjɔ̃] *nf* explanation ; explication de texte (literary) criticism.

explicite [ɛksplisit] *adj* explicit.

expliciter [3] [ɛksplisite] *vt* to make explicit.

expliquer [3] [ɛksplike] *vt* 1. [gén] to explain - 2. [texte] to criticize. ➡ **s'expliquer** *vp* 1. [se justifier] to explain o.s. - 2. [comprendre] to understand - 3. [discuter] to have it out - 4. [devenir compréhensible] to be explained.

exploit [ɛksplwa] *nm* exploit, feat ; *iron* [maladresse] achievement.

exploitant, e [ɛksplwatɑ̃, ɑ̃t] *nm, f* farmer.

exploitation [ɛksplwatasjɔ̃] *nf* 1. [mise en valeur] running ; [de mine] working - 2. [entreprise] operation, concern ; **exploitation agricole** farm - 3. [d'une personne] exploitation.

exploiter [3] [ɛksplwate] *vt* 1. [gén] to exploit - 2. [entreprise] to operate, to run.

explorateur, trice [ɛksplɔratœr, tris] *nm, f* explorer.

explorer [3] [ɛksplɔre] *vt* to explore.

exploser [3] [ɛksploze] *vi* to explode.

explosif, ive [ɛksplozif, iv] *adj* explosive. ➡ **explosif** *nm* explosive.

explosion [ɛksplozjɔ̃] *nf* explosion ; [de colère, joie] outburst.

expo [ɛkspo] *nf fam* exhibition.

exportateur, trice [ɛkspɔrtatœr, tris] ◇ *adj* exporting. ◇ *nm, f* exporter.

exportation [ɛkspɔrtasjɔ̃] *nf* export.

exporter [3] [ɛkspɔrte] *vt* to export.

exposé, e [ɛkspoze] *adj* 1. [orienté] : **bien exposé** facing the sun - 2. [vulnérable] exposed. ➡ **exposé** *nm* account ; SCOL talk.

exposer [3] [ɛkspoze] *vt* 1. [orienter, mettre en danger] to expose - 2. [présenter] to display ; [tableaux] to show, to exhibit - 3. [expliquer] to explain, to set out. ➡ **s'exposer** *vp* : **s'exposer à qqch** to expose o.s. to sthg.

exposition [ɛkspozisjɔ̃] *nf* 1. [présentation] exhibition - 2. [orientation] aspect.

exprès¹, esse [ɛksprɛs] *adj* [formel] formal, express. ➡ **exprès** *adj inv* [urgent] express.

exprès² [ɛksprɛ] *adv* on purpose ; **faire exprès de faire qqch** to do sthg deliberately OU on purpose.

express [ɛksprɛs] ◇ *nm inv* 1. [train] express - 2. [café] espresso. ◇ *adj inv* express.

expressément [ɛkspresemɑ̃] *adv* expressly.

expressif, ive [ɛkspresif, iv] *adj* expressive.

expression [ɛkspresjɔ̃] *nf* expression.

expresso [ɛkspreso] *nm* espresso, = express.

exprimer [3] [ɛksprime] *vt* [pensées, sentiments] to express. ➡ **s'exprimer** *vp* to express o.s.

expropriation [ɛksprɔprijasjɔ̃] *nf* expropriation.

exproprier [10] [ɛksprɔprije] *vt* to expropriate.

expulser [3] [ɛkspylse] *vt* : **expulser (de)** to expel (from) ; [locataire] to evict (from).

expulsion [ɛkspylsjɔ̃] *nf* expulsion ; [de locataire] eviction.

expurger [17] [ɛkspyrʒe] *vt* to expurgate.

exquis, e [ɛkski, iz] *adj* 1. [délicieux] exquisite - 2. [distingué, agréable] delightful.

exsangue [ɛksɑ̃g] *adj* [blème] deathly pale.

extase [ɛkstaz] *nf* ecstasy.

extasier [9] [ɛkstazje] ➡ **s'extasier** *vp* : **s'extasier devant** to go into ecstasies over.

extensible [ɛkstɑ̃sibl] *adj* stretchable.

extension [ɛkstɑ̃sjɔ̃] *nf* 1. [étirement] stretching - 2. [élargissement] extension ; **par extension** by extension.

exténuer [7] [ɛkstenɥe] *vt* to exhaust.

extérieur, e [ɛksterjœr] *adj* 1. [au dehors] outside ; [étranger] external ; [apparent] outward - 2. ÉCON & POLIT foreign. ➡ **extérieur** *nm* [dehors] outside ; [de maison] exterior ; **à l'extérieur de qqch** outside sthg.

extérieurement [ɛksterjœrmɑ̃] *adv* 1. [à l'extérieur] on the outside, externally - 2. [en apparence] outwardly.

extérioriser [3] [ɛksterjɔrize] *vt* to show.

exterminer [3] [ɛkstermine] *vt* to exterminate.

externaliser [3] [ɛksternalize] *vt* to outsource.

externat [ɛksterna] *nm* 1. SCOL day school - 2. MÉD *non-resident medical studentship*.

externe [ɛkstern] ◇ *nmf* 1. SCOL day pupil - 2. MÉD *non-resident medical student*, ≃ extern US. ◇ *adj* outer, external.

extincteur [ɛkstɛ̃ktœr] *nm* (fire) extinguisher.

extinction [ɛkstɛ̃ksjɔ̃] *nf* 1. [action d'éteindre] putting out, extinguishing - 2. *fig* [disparition] extinction ; **extinction de voix** loss of one's voice.

extirper [3] [ɛkstirpe] *vt* : **extirper (de)** [épine, réponse, secret] to drag (out of) ; [plante] to uproot (from) ; [erreur, préjugé] to root out (of).

extorquer [3] [ɛkstɔrke] *vt* : **extorquer qqch à qqn** to extort sthg from sb.

extra [ɛkstra] ◇ *nm inv* 1. [employé] extra help (*U*) - 2. [chose inhabituelle] (special) treat. ◇ *adj inv* 1. [de qualité] top-quality - 2. *fam* [génial] great, fantastic.

extraction [ɛkstraksjɔ̃] *nf* extraction.

extrader [3] [ɛkstrade] *vt* to extradite.

extraire [112] [ɛkstrɛr] *vt* : **extraire (de)** to extract (from).

extrait, e [ɛkstrɛ, ɛt] *pp* ► extraire. ◆ **extrait** *nm* extract ; **extrait de naissance** birth certificate.

extraordinaire [ɛkstraɔrdinɛr] *adj* extraordinary.

extrapoler [3] [ɛkstrapɔle] *vt & vi* to extrapolate.

extraterrestre [ɛkstratɛrɛstr] *nmf & adj* extraterrestrial.

extravagance [ɛkstravagɑ̃s] *nf* extravagance.

extravagant, e [ɛkstravagɑ̃, ɑ̃t] *adj* extravagant ; [idée, propos] wild.

extraverti, e [ɛkstravɛrti] *nm, f & adj* extrovert.

extrême [ɛkstrɛm] ⋄ *nm* extreme ; **d'un extrême à l'autre** from one extreme to the other. ⋄ *adj* extreme ; [limite] furthest ; **les sports extrêmes** extreme sports.

extrêmement [ɛkstrɛmmɑ̃] *adv* extremely.

extrême-onction [ɛkstrɛmɔ̃ksjɔ̃] *nf* last rites *pl*, extreme unction.

Extrême-Orient [ɛkstrɛmɔrjɑ̃] *nm* : **l'Extrême-Orient** the Far East.

extrémiste [ɛkstremist] *nmf & adj* extremist.

extrémité [ɛkstremite] *nf* **1.** [bout] end - **2.** [situation critique] straits *pl*.

exubérant, e [ɛgzyberɑ̃, ɑ̃t] *adj* **1.** [personne] exuberant - **2.** [végétation] luxuriant.

exulter [3] [ɛgzylte] *vi* to exult.

F

f, F [ɛf] *nm inv* f, F ; **F3** three-room flat *UK* ou apartment *US*. ◆ **F 1.** (*abr écrite de* **Fahrenheit**) F - **2.** (*abr écrite de* **franc**) F, Fr.

fa [fa] *nm inv* F ; [chanté] fa.

fable [fabl] *nf* fable.

fabricant, e [fabrikɑ̃, ɑ̃t] *nm, f* manufacturer.

fabrication [fabrikasjɔ̃] *nf* manufacture, manufacturing.

fabrique [fabrik] *nf* [usine] factory.

fabriquer [3] [fabrike] *vt* **1.** [confectionner]

to manufacture, to make - **2.** *fam* [faire] : **qu'est-ce que tu fabriques?** what are you up to? - **3.** [inventer] to fabricate.

fabulation [fabylasjɔ̃] *nf* fabrication.

fabuleux, euse [fabylø, øz] *adj* fabulous.

fac [fak] *nf fam* college, uni *UK*.

façade [fasad] *nf litt & fig* facade.

face [fas] *nf* **1.** [visage] face - **2.** [côté] side ; **faire face à qqch** [maison] to face sthg, to be opposite sthg ; *fig* [affronter] to face up to sthg ; **de face** from the front ; **en face de qqn/qqch** opposite sb/sthg.

face-à-face [fasafas] *nm inv* debate.

facétie [fasesi] *nf* practical joke.

facette [fasɛt] *nf litt & fig* facet.

fâché, e [faʃe] *adj* **1.** [en colère] angry ; [contrarié] annoyed - **2.** [brouillé] on bad terms.

fâcher [3] [faʃe] *vt* [mettre en colère] to anger, to make angry ; [contrarier] to annoy, to make annoyed. ◆ **se fâcher** *vp* **1.** [se mettre en colère] : **se fâcher (contre qqn)** to get angry (with sb) - **2.** [se brouiller] : **se fâcher (avec qqn)** to fall out (with sb).

fâcheux, euse [faʃø, øz] *adj* unfortunate.

facile [fasil] *adj* **1.** [aisé] easy ; **facile à faire/prononcer** easy to do/pronounce - **2.** [peu subtil] facile - **3.** [conciliant] easy-going.

facilement [fasilmɑ̃] *adv* easily.

facilité [fasilite] *nf* **1.** [de tâche, problème] easiness - **2.** [capacité] ease - **3.** [dispositions] aptitude - **4.** COMM : **facilités de paiement** easy (payment) terms.

faciliter [3] [fasilite] *vt* to make easier.

façon [fasɔ̃] *nf* **1.** [manière] way - **2.** [travail] work ; COUT making-up - **3.** [imitation] : **façon cuir** imitation leather. ◆ **de façon à** *loc prép* so as to. ◆ **de façon que** (+ *subjonctif*) *loc conj* so that. ◆ **de toute façon** *loc adv* anyway, in any case.

fac-similé [faksimile] (*pl* **fac-similés**) *nm* facsimile.

facteur, trice [faktœr, tris] *nm, f* [des postes] postman (*f* postwoman) *UK*, mailman *US*, mail ou letter carrier *US*. ◆ **facteur** *nm* [élément & MATH] factor.

factice [faktis] *adj* artificial.

faction [faksjɔ̃] *nf* **1.** [groupe] faction - **2.** MIL : **être en** ou **de faction** to be on guard (duty) ou on sentry duty.

facture [faktyr] *nf* **1.** COMM invoice ; [de gaz, d'électricité] bill - **2.** ART technique.

facturer [3] [faktyre] *vt* COMM to invoice.

facultatif, ive [fakyltatif, iv] *adj* optional.

faculté [fakylte] *nf* **1.** [don & UNIV] faculty ; **faculté de lettres/de droit/de médecine** Faculty of Arts/Law/Medicine - **2.** [possibilité] freedom - **3.** [pouvoir] power. ◆ **facultés** *nfpl* (mental) faculties.

fadaises [fadɛz] *nfpl* drivel *(U)*.

fade [fad] *adj* **1.** [sans saveur] bland - **2.** [sans intérêt] insipid.

fagot [fago] *nm* bundle of sticks.

faible [fɛbl] ◇ *adj* **1.** [gén] weak ; **être faible en maths** to be not very good at maths - **2.** [petit - montant, proportion] small ; [- revenu] low - **3.** [lueur, bruit] faint. ◇ *nmf* weak person ; **faible d'esprit** feeble-minded person. ◇ *nm* weakness.

faiblement [fɛbləmɑ̃] *adv* **1.** [mollement] weakly, feebly - **2.** [imperceptiblement] faintly - **3.** [peu] slightly.

faiblesse [fɛblɛs] *nf* **1.** [gén] weakness - **2.** [petitesse] smallness.

faiblir [32] [feblir] *vi* **1.** [personne, monnaie] to weaken - **2.** [forces] to diminish, to fail - **3.** [tempête, vent] to die down.

faïence [fajɑ̃s] *nf* earthenware.

faignant, e = faînéant.

faille [faj] ▶ **falloir**. ◇ *nf* **1.** GÉOL fault - **2.** [défaut] flaw.

faillible [fajibl] *adj* fallible.

faillir [46] [fajir] *vi* **1.** [manquer] : **faillir à** [promesse] to keep ; [devoir] not to do - **2.** [être sur le point de] : **faillir faire qqch** to nearly ou almost do sthg.

faillite [fajit] *nf* FIN bankruptcy ; **faire faillite** to go bankrupt ; **en faillite** bankrupt.

faim [fɛ̃] *nf* hunger ; **avoir faim** to be hungry.

faînéant, e [feneɑ̃, ɑ̃t], **feignant, e, faignant, e** [fɛɲɑ̃, ɑ̃t] ◇ *adj* lazy, idle. ◇ *nm, f* lazybones.

faire [109] [fer] ◇ *vt* **1.** [fabriquer, préparer] to make ; **faire une tarte/du café/un film** to make a tart/coffee/a film ; **faire qqch de qqch** [transformer] to make sthg into sthg ; **faire qqch de qqn** *fig* to make sthg of sb ; **il veut en faire un avocat** he wants him to be a lawyer, he wants to make a lawyer of him - **2.** [s'occuper à, entreprendre] to do ; **qu'est-ce qu'il fait dans la vie?** what does he do (for a living)? ; **que fais-tu dimanche?** what are you doing on Sunday? - **3.** [étudier] to do ; **faire de l'anglais/des maths/du droit** to do English/maths/law - **4.** [sport, musique] to play ; **faire du football/de la clarinette** to play football/the clarinet - **5.** [effectuer] to do ; **faire le ménage** to do the housework ; **faire la cuisine** to cook, to do the cooking ; **faire la lessive** to do the washing - **6.** [occasionner] : **faire de la peine à qqn** to hurt sb ; **faire du mal à** to harm ; **faire du bruit** to make a noise ; **ça ne fait rien** it doesn't matter - **7.** [imiter] : **faire le sourd/l'innocent** to act deaf/(the) innocent - **8.** [calcul, mesure] : **un et un font deux** one and one are ou make two ; **ça fait combien (de kilomètres) jusqu'à la mer?** how far is it

to the sea? ; **la table fait 2 mètres de long** the table is 2 metres UK ou meters US long ; **faire du 38** to take a size 38 ; [en tant que verbe substitutif] to do ; **je lui ai dit de prendre une échelle mais il ne l'a pas fait** I told him to use a ladder but he didn't ; **faites!** please do! - **9.** [coûter] to be, to cost ; **ça vous fait 10 euros en tout** that'll be 10 euros altogether - **10.** [dire] : **«tiens», fit-elle** 'really', she said - **11.** : **ne faire que** [faire sans cesse] to do nothing but ; **elle ne fait que bavarder** she does nothing but gossip, she's always gossiping ; **je ne fais que passer** I've just popped in. ◇ *vi* [agir] to do, to act ; **fais vite!** hurry up! ; **que faire?** what is to be done? ; **tu ferais bien d'aller voir ce qui se passe** you ought to ou you'd better go and see what's happening ; **faire comme chez soi** to make o.s. at home. ◇ *v att* [avoir l'air] to look ; **faire démodé/joli** to look old-fashioned/pretty ; **ça fait jeune** it makes you look young. ◇ *v impers* **1.** [climat, temps] : **il fait beau/froid** it's fine/cold ; **il fait 20 degrés** it's 20 degrees ; **il fait jour/nuit** it's light/dark - **2.** [exprime la durée, la distance] : **ça fait six mois que je ne l'ai pas vu** it's six months since I last saw him ; **ça fait six mois que je fais du portugais** I've been going to Portuguese classes for six months ; **ça fait 30 kilomètres qu'on roule sans phares** we've been driving without lights for 30 kilometres. ◇ *v aux* **1.** [à l'actif] to make ; **faire démarrer une voiture** to start a car ; **faire tomber qqch** to make sthg fall ; **l'aspirine fait baisser la fièvre** aspirin brings down the temperature ; **faire travailler qqn** to make sb work ; **faire traverser la rue à un aveugle** to help a blind man cross the road - **2.** [au passif] : **faire faire qqch (par qqn)** to have sthg done (by sb) ; **faire réparer sa voiture/nettoyer ses vitres** to have one's car repaired/one's windows cleaned. ▶ **se faire** *vp* **1.** [avoir lieu] to take place - **2.** [être convenable] : **ça ne se fait pas (de faire qqch)** it's not done (to do sthg) - **3.** [devenir] : **se faire (+ adj)** to get, to become ; **il se fait tard** it's getting late ; **se faire beau** to make o.s. beautiful - **4.** (+ nom) [causer] : **se faire mal** to hurt o.s. ; **se faire des amis** to make friends ; **se faire une idée sur qqch** to get some idea about sthg - **5.** (+ infinitif) **se faire écraser** to get run over ; **se faire opérer** to have an operation ; **se faire aider (par qqn)** to get help (from sb) ; **se faire faire un costume** to have a suit made (for o.s.) ; **comment se fait-il que...?** how is it that...?, how come...? ; **s'en faire** to worry ; **ne vous en faites pas!** don't worry! ▶ **se faire à** *vp + prép* to get used to.

faire-part [fɛrpar] *nm inv* announcement.

fais, fait *etc* ▶ **faire**.

faisable [fəzabl] *adj* feasible.

faisan, e [fəzɑ̃, an] *nm, f* pheasant.

faisandé, e [fəzɑ̃de] *adj* CULIN high.

faisceau, x [fɛso] *nm* [rayon] beam.

faisons ➤ faire.

fait, e [fɛ, fɛt] ◇ *pp* ➤ faire. ◇ *adj* **1.** [fabriqué] made ; **il n'est pas fait pour mener cette vie** he's not cut out for this kind of life - **2.** [physique] : **bien fait** well-built - **3.** [fromage] ripe ; **c'est bien fait pour lui** (it) serves him right ; **c'en est fait de nous** we're done for. ➤ **fait** *nm* **1.** [acte] act ; **mettre qqn devant le fait accompli** to present sb with a fait accompli ; **prendre qqn sur le fait** to catch sb in the act ; **faits et gestes** doings, actions - **2.** [événement] event ; **faits divers news in brief - 3.** [réalité] fact. ➤ **au fait** *loc adv* by the way. ➤ **en fait** *loc adv* in (actual) fact. ➤ **en fait de** *loc prép* by way of. ➤ **du fait de** *loc prép* because of.

faîte [fɛt] *nm* **1.** [de toit] ridge - **2.** [d'arbre] top - **3.** *fig* [sommet] pinnacle.

faites ➤ faire.

fait-tout (*pl inv*), **faitout** (*pl* faitouts) [fɛtu] *nm* stewpan.

fakir [fakir] *nm* fakir.

falaise [falɛz] *nf* cliff.

fallacieux, euse [falasjø, øz] *adj* **1.** [promesse] false - **2.** [argument] fallacious.

falloir [69] [falwar] *v impers* : **il me faut du temps** I need (some) time ; **il faut que tu partes** you must go ou leave, you'll have to go ou leave ; **il faut toujours qu'elle intervienne!** she always has to interfere! ; **il faut faire attention** we/you *etc* must be careful, we'll/you'll *etc* have to be careful ; **s'il le faut** if necessary. ➤ **s'en falloir** *v impers* : **il s'en faut de peu pour qu'il puisse acheter cette maison** he can almost afford to buy the house ; **il s'en faut de 20 cm pour que l'armoire tienne dans le coin** the cupboard is 20 cm too big to fit into the corner ; **il s'en faut de beaucoup pour qu'il ait l'examen** it'll take a lot for him to pass the exam ; **peu s'en est fallu qu'il démissionne** he very nearly resigned, he came close to resigning.

fallu [faly] *pp inv* ➤ falloir.

falot, e [falo, ɔt] *adj* dull.

falsifier [9] [falsifje] *vt* [document, signature, faits] to falsify.

famé, e [fame] *adj* : **mal famé** with a (bad) reputation.

famélique [famelik] *adj* half-starved.

fameux, euse [famø, øz] *adj* **1.** [célèbre] famous - **2.** *fam* [remarquable] great.

familial, e, aux [familjal, o] *adj* family (*avant n*).

familiariser [3] [familjarize] *vt* : **familiariser qqn avec** to familiarize sb with.

familiarité [familjarite] *nf* familiarity. ➤ **familiarités** *nfpl* liberties.

familier, ère [familje, ɛr] *adj* [connu] familiar. ➤ **familier** *nm* regular (customer).

famille [famij] *nf* family ; [ensemble des parents] relatives, relations ; **famille d'accueil** [lors d'un séjour linguistique] host family ; [pour enfant en difficulté] foster home ; **famille monoparentale** single-parent ou lone-parent family ; **famille recomposée** blended family.

famine [famin] *nf* famine.

fan [fan] *nmf* fam fan.

fanal, aux [fanal, o] *nm* **1.** [de phare] beacon - **2.** [lanterne] lantern.

fanatique [fanatik] ◇ *nmf* fanatic. ◇ *adj* fanatical.

fanatisme [fanatism] *nm* fanaticism.

faner [3] [fane] ◇ *vt* [altérer] to fade. ◇ *vi* **1.** [fleur] to wither - **2.** [beauté, couleur] to fade. ➤ **se faner** *vp* **1.** [fleur] to wither - **2.** [beauté, couleur] to fade.

fanfare [fɑ̃far] *nf* **1.** [orchestre] brass band - **2.** [musique] fanfare.

fanfaron, onne [fɑ̃farɔ̃, ɔn] ◇ *adj* boastful. ◇ *nm, f* braggart.

fange [fɑ̃ʒ] *nf litt* mire.

fanion [fanjɔ̃] *nm* pennant.

fantaisie [fɑ̃tezi] ◇ *nf* **1.** [caprice] whim - **2.** (U) [goût] fancy - **3.** [imagination] imagination. ◇ *adj inv* : **chapeau fantaisie** fancy hat ; **bijoux fantaisie** fake/costume jewellery UK ou jewelry US.

fantaisiste [fɑ̃tezist] ◇ *nmf* entertainer. ◇ *adj* [bizarre] fanciful.

fantasme [fɑ̃tasm] *nm* fantasy.

fantasque [fɑ̃task] *adj* **1.** [personne] whimsical - **2.** [humeur] capricious.

fantassin [fɑ̃tasɛ̃] *nm* infantryman.

fantastique [fɑ̃tastik] ◇ *adj* fantastic. ◇ *nm* : **le fantastique** the fantastic.

fantoche [fɑ̃tɔʃ] ◇ *adj* puppet (*avant n*). ◇ *nm* puppet.

fantôme [fɑ̃tom] ◇ *nm* ghost. ◇ *adj* [inexistant] phantom.

faon [fɑ̃] *nm* fawn.

farandole [farɑ̃dɔl] *nf* farandole.

farce [fars] *nf* **1.** CULIN stuffing - **2.** [blague] (practical) joke ; **farces et attrapes** jokes and novelties.

farceur, euse [farsœr, øz] *nm, f* (practical) joker.

farcir [32] [farsir] *vt* **1.** CULIN to stuff - **2.** [remplir] : **farcir qqch de** to stuff ou cram sthg with.

fard [far] *nm* make-up.

fardeau, x [fardo] *nm* [poids] load ; *fig* burden.

farder [3] [farde] *vt* [maquiller] to make up. ➤ **se farder** *vp* to make o.s. up, to put on one's make-up.

farfelu, e [farfəly] *fam* ⟨⟩ *adj* weird. ⟨⟩ *nm, f* weirdo.

farfouiller [3] [farfuje] *vi fam* to rummage.

farine [farin] *nf* flour ; **farine animale** animal flour.

farouche [faruʃ] *adj* **1.** [animal] wild, not tame ; [personne] shy, withdrawn - **2.** [sentiment] fierce.

fart [far(t)] *nm* (ski) wax.

fascicule [fasikyl] *nm* part, instalment *UK*, installment *US*.

fascination [fasinasjɔ̃] *nf* fascination.

fasciner [3] [fasine] *vt* to fascinate.

fascisme [faʃism] *nm* fascism.

fasse, fassions *etc* ➤ **faire**.

faste [fast] ⟨⟩ *nm* splendour *UK*, splendor *US*. ⟨⟩ *adj* [favorable] lucky.

fastidieux, euse [fastidjø, øz] *adj* boring.

fastueux, euse [fastɥø, øz] *adj* luxurious.

fatal, e [fatal] *adj* **1.** [mortel, funeste] fatal - **2.** [inévitable] inevitable.

fataliste [fatalist] *adj* fatalistic.

fatalité [fatalite] *nf* **1.** [destin] fate - **2.** [iné-luctabilité] inevitability.

fatigant, e [fatigɑ̃, ɑ̃t] *adj* **1.** [épuisant] tiring - **2.** [ennuyeux] tiresome.

fatiguant [fatigɑ̃] *p prés* ➤ **fatiguer**.

fatigue [fatig] *nf* tiredness.

fatigué, e [fatige] *adj* tired ; [cœur, yeux] strained.

fatiguer [3] [fatige] ⟨⟩ *vt* **1.** [épuiser] to tire - **2.** [cœur, yeux] to strain - **3.** [ennuyer] to wear out. ⟨⟩ *vi* **1.** [personne] to grow tired - **2.** [moteur] to strain. ➤ **se fatiguer** *vp* to get tired ; **se fatiguer de qqch** to get tired of sthg ; **se fatiguer à faire qqch** to wear o.s. out doing sthg.

fatras [fatra] *nm* jumble.

faubourg [fobur] *nm* suburb.

fauché, e [foʃe] *adj fam* broke, hard-up.

faucher [3] [foʃe] *vt* **1.** [couper - herbe, blé] to cut - **2.** *fam* [voler] : **faucher qqch à qqn** to pinch sthg from sb *UK* - **3.** [piéton] to run over - **4.** *fig* [suj: mort, maladie] to cut down.

faucille [fosij] *nf* sickle.

faucon [fokɔ̃] *nm* hawk.

faudra ➤ **falloir**.

faufiler [3] [fofile] *vt* to tack, to baste. ➤ **se faufiler** *vp* : **se faufiler dans** to slip into ; **se faufiler entre** to thread one's way between.

faune [fon] ⟨⟩ *nf* **1.** [animaux] fauna - **2.** *péj* [personnes] : **la faune qui fréquente ce bar** the sort of people who hang round that bar. ⟨⟩ *nm* MYTHOL faun.

faussaire [foser] *nmf* forger.

faussement [fosmɑ̃] *adv* **1.** [à tort] wrongly - **2.** [prétendument] falsely.

fausser [3] [fose] *vt* **1.** [déformer] to bend - **2.** [rendre faux] to distort.

fausseté [foste] *nf* **1.** [hypocrisie] duplicity - **2.** [de jugement, d'idée] falsity.

faut ➤ **falloir**.

faute [fot] *nf* **1.** [erreur] mistake, error ; **faute de frappe** [à la machine à écrire] typing error ; [à l'ordinateur] keying error ; **faute d'orthographe** spelling mistake - **2.** [méfait, infraction] offence *UK*, offense *US* ; **prendre qqn en faute** to catch sb out ; **faute professionnelle** professional misdemeanour *UK* ou misdemeanor *US* - **3.** TENNIS fault ; FOOTBALL foul - **4.** [responsabilité] fault ; **de ma/ta** *etc* **faute** my/your *etc* fault ; **par la faute de qqn** because of sb. ➤ **faute de** *loc prép* for want ou lack of ; **faute de mieux** for want ou lack of anything better. ➤ **sans faute** *loc adv* without fail.

fauteuil [fotœj] *nm* **1.** [siège] armchair ; **fauteuil roulant** wheelchair - **2.** [de théâtre] seat - **3.** [de président] chair ; [d'académicien] seat.

fautif, ive [fotif, iv] ⟨⟩ *adj* **1.** [coupable] guilty - **2.** [défectueux] faulty. ⟨⟩ *nm, f* guilty party.

fauve [fov] ⟨⟩ *nm* **1.** [animal] big cat - **2.** [couleur] fawn - **3.** ART Fauve. ⟨⟩ *adj* **1.** [animal] wild - **2.** [cuir, cheveux] tawny - **3.** ART Fauvist.

fauvette [fovɛt] *nf* warbler.

faux, fausse [fo, fos] *adj* **1.** [incorrect] wrong - **2.** [postiche, mensonger, hypocrite] false ; **faux témoignage** DR perjury - **3.** [monnaie, papiers] forged, fake ; [bijou, marbre] imitation, fake - **4.** [injustifié] : **fausse alerte** false alarm ; **c'est un faux problème** that's not an issue (here). ➤ **faux** ⟨⟩ *nm* [document, tableau] forgery, fake. ⟨⟩ *nf* scythe. ⟨⟩ *adv* : **chanter/jouer faux** MUS to sing/play out of tune ; **sonner faux** *fig* not to ring true.

faux-filet, faux filet [fofile] *nm* sirloin.

faux-fuyant [fofɥijɑ̃] *nm* excuse.

faux-monnayeur [fomɔnɛjœr] *nm* counterfeiter.

faux-sens [fosɑ̃s] *nm inv* mistranslation.

faveur [favœr] *nf* favour *UK*, favor *US*.

à la faveur de *loc prép* thanks to.

en faveur de *loc prép* in favour UK ou favor US of.

favorable [favɔrabl] *adj* : **favorable (à)** favourable UK ou favorable US (to).

favori, ite [favɔri, it] *adj & nm, f* favourite UK, favorite US.

favoriser [3] [favɔrize] *vt* **1.** [avantager] to favour UK, to favor US - **2.** [contribuer à] to promote.

fax [faks] *nm* fax.

faxer [3] [fakse] *vt* to fax.

fayot [fajo] *nm fam* [personne] creep, crawler.

fébrile [febril] *adj* feverish.

fécond, e [fekɔ̃, ɔ̃d] *adj* **1.** [femelle, terre, esprit] fertile - **2.** [écrivain] prolific.

fécondation [fekɔ̃dasjɔ̃] *nf* fertilization ; **fécondation in vitro** in vitro fertilization.

féconder [3] [fekɔ̃de] *vt* **1.** [ovule] to fertilize - **2.** [femme, femelle] to impregnate.

fécondité [fekɔ̃dite] *nf* **1.** [gén] fertility - **2.** [d'écrivain] productiveness.

fécule [fekyl] *nf* starch.

féculent, e [fekylɑ̃, ɑ̃t] *adj* starchy.
féculent *nm* starchy food.

fédéral, e, aux [federal, o] *adj* federal.

fédération [federasjɔ̃] *nf* federation.

fée [fe] *nf* fairy.

féerique [fe(e)rik] *adj* [enchanteur] enchanting.

feignant, e = **fainéant.**

feindre [81] [fɛ̃dr] <> *vt* to feign ; **feindre de faire qqch** to pretend to do sthg. <> *vi* to pretend.

feint, e [fɛ̃, fɛ̃t] *pp* **feindre.**

feinte [fɛ̃t] *nf* **1.** [ruse] ruse - **2.** FOOTBALL dummy ; [boxe] feint.

fêlé, e [fele] *adj* **1.** [assiette] cracked - **2.** *fam* [personne] cracked, loony.

fêler [4] [fele] *vt* to crack.

félicitations [felisitasjɔ̃] *nfpl* congratulations.

féliciter [3] [felisite] *vt* to congratulate.
se féliciter *vp* : **se féliciter de** to congratulate o.s. on.

félin, e [felɛ̃, in] *adj* feline. **félin** *nm* big cat.

fêlure [felyr] *nf* crack.

femelle [fəmɛl] *nf & adj* female.

féminin, e [feminɛ̃, in] *adj* **1.** [gén] feminine - **2.** [revue, équipe] women's *(avant n)*.
féminin *nm* GRAMM feminine.

féminisme [feminism] *nm* feminism.

féminité [feminite] *nf* femininity.

femme [fam] *nf* **1.** [personne de sexe

féminin] woman ; **femme de chambre** chambermaid ; **femme de ménage** cleaning woman - **2.** [épouse] wife.

fémur [femyr] *nm* femur.

fendre [73] [fɑ̃dr] *vt* **1.** [bois] to split - **2.** [foule, flots] to cut through. **se fendre** *vp* [se crevasser] to crack.

fendu, e [fɑ̃dy] *pp* **fendre.**

fenêtre [fənɛtr] *nf* [gén & INFORM] window.

fenouil [fənuj] *nm* fennel.

fente [fɑ̃t] *nf* **1.** [fissure] crack - **2.** [interstice, de vêtement] slit.

féodal, e, aux [feɔdal, o] *adj* feudal.

féodalité [feɔdalite] *nf* feudalism.

fer [fɛr] *nm* iron ; **fer à cheval** horseshoe ; **fer forgé** wrought iron ; **fer à repasser** iron ; **fer à souder** soldering iron.

ferai, feras *etc* **faire.**

fer-blanc [fɛrblɑ̃] *nm* tinplate, tin.

ferblanterie [fɛrblɑ̃tri] *nf* **1.** [commerce] tin industry - **2.** [ustensiles] tinware.

férié, e [ferje] **jour.**

férir [ferir] *vt* : **sans coup férir** *sout* without meeting any resistance ou obstacle.

ferme¹ [fɛrm] *nf* farm.

ferme² [fɛrm] <> *adj* firm ; **être ferme sur ses jambes** to be steady on one's feet. <> *adv* **1.** [beaucoup] a lot - **2.** [définitivement] : **acheter/vendre ferme** to make a firm purchase/sale.

fermement [fɛrməmɑ̃] *adv* firmly.

ferment [fɛrmɑ̃] *nm* **1.** [levure] ferment - **2.** *fig* [germe] seed, seeds *pl.*

fermentation [fɛrmɑ̃tasjɔ̃] *nf* CHIM fermentation ; *fig* ferment.

fermer [3] [fɛrme] <> *vt* **1.** [porte, tiroir, yeux] to close, to shut ; [store] to pull down ; [enveloppe] to seal - **2.** [bloquer] to close ; **fermer son esprit à qqch** to close one's mind to sthg - **3.** [gaz, lumière] to turn off - **4.** [vêtement] to do up - **5.** [entreprise] to close down - **6.** [interdire] : **fermer qqch à qqn** to close sthg to sb. <> *vi* **1.** [gén] to shut, to close - **2.** [vêtement] to do up - **3.** [entreprise] to close down. **se fermer** *vp* **1.** [porte, partie du corps] to close, to shut - **2.** [plaie] to close up - **3.** [vêtement] to do up.

fermeté [fɛrməte] *nf* firmness.

fermeture [fɛrmətyr] *nf* **1.** [de porte] closing - **2.** [de vêtement, sac] fastening ; **fermeture Éclair®** zip UK, zipper US - **3.** [d'établissement - temporaire] closing ; [- définitive] closure ; **fermeture hebdomadaire/annuelle** weekly/annual closing.

fermier, ère [fɛrmje, ɛr] *nm, f* farmer.

fermoir [fɛrmwar] *nm* clasp.

féroce [feʀɔs] *adj* [animal, appétit] ferocious ; [personne, désir] fierce.

ferraille [feʀaj] *nf* **1.** [vieux fer] scrap iron (*U*) ; **bon à mettre à la ferraille** fit for the scrap heap - **2.** *fam* [monnaie] loose change.

ferronnerie [feʀɔnʀi] *nf* **1.** [objet, métier] ironwork (*U*) - **2.** [atelier] ironworks *sg*.

ferroviaire [feʀɔvjeʀ] *adj* rail (*avant n*).

ferry-boat [feʀibot] (*pl* ferry-boats) *nm* ferry.

fertile [feʀtil] *adj litt & fig* fertile ; **fertile en** *fig* filled with, full of.

fertiliser [3] [feʀtilize] *vt* to fertilize.

fertilité [feʀtilite] *nf* fertility.

féru, e [feʀy] *adj sout* [passionné] : **être féru de qqch** to have a passion for sthg.

fervent, e [feʀvɑ̃, ɑ̃t] *adj* [chrétien] fervent ; [amoureux, démocrate] ardent.

ferveur [feʀvœʀ] *nf* [dévotion] fervour *UK*, fervor *US*.

fesse [fes] *nf* buttock.

fessée [fese] *nf* spanking, smack (on the bottom).

festin [festɛ̃] *nm* banquet, feast.

festival, als [festival] *nm* festival.

festivités [festivite] *nfpl* festivities.

feston [festɔ̃] *nm* **1.** ARCHIT festoon - **2.** COUT scallop.

festoyer [13] [festwaje] *vi* to feast.

fêtard, e [fetaʀ, aʀd] *nm, f* fun-loving person.

fête [fɛt] *nf* **1.** [congé] holiday ; **les fêtes (de fin d'année)** the Christmas holidays ; **fête nationale** national holiday - **2.** [réunion, réception] celebration - **3.** [kermesse] fair ; **fête foraine** funfair *UK*, carnival *US* - **4.** [jour de célébration - de personne] saint's day ; [- de saint] feast (day) - **5.** [soirée] party ; **faire (la) fête à qqn** to make a fuss of sb ; **faire la fête** to have a good time.

fêter [4] [fete] *vt* [événement] to celebrate ; [personne] to have a party for.

fétiche [fetiʃ] *nm* **1.** [objet de culte] fetish - **2.** [mascotte] mascot.

fétichisme [fetiʃism] *nm* [culte, perversion] fetishism.

fétide [fetid] *adj* fetid.

fétu [fety] *nm* : **fétu (de paille)** wisp (of straw).

feu¹, e [fø] *adj* : **feu M. X** the late Mr X ; **feu mon mari** my late husband.

feu², x [fø] *nm* **1.** [flamme, incendie] fire ; **au feu!** fire! ; **en feu** *litt & fig* on fire ; **avez-vous du feu?** have you got a light? ; **faire feu** MIL to fire ; **mettre le feu à qqch** to set fire to sthg, to set sthg on fire ; **prendre feu** to catch fire ; **feu de camp** camp fire ;

feu de cheminée chimney fire ; **feu follet** will-o'-the-wisp - **2.** [signal] light ; **feu rouge/vert** red/green light ; **feux de croisement** dipped *UK* ou dimmed *US* headlights ; **feux de position** sidelights ; **feux de route** headlights on full beam - **3.** CULIN ring *UK*, burner *US* ; **à feu doux/vif** on a low/high flame ; **à petit feu** gently - **4.** CINÉ & THÉÂTRE light (*U*). ◆ **feu d'artifice** *nm* firework.

feuillage [fœjaʒ] *nm* foliage.

feuille [fœj] *nf* **1.** [d'arbre] leaf ; **feuille morte** dead leaf ; **feuille de vigne** BOT vine leaf - **2.** [page] sheet ; **feuille de papier** sheet of paper - **3.** [document] form ; **feuille de soins** *claim form for reimbursement of medical expenses.*

feuillet [fœjɛ] *nm* page.

feuilleté, e [fœjte] *adj* **1.** CULIN : **pâte feuilletée** puff pastry - **2.** GÉOL foliated.

feuilleter [27] [fœjte] *vt* to flick through.

feuilleton [fœjtɔ̃] *nm* serial.

feutre [føtʀ] *nm* **1.** [étoffe] felt - **2.** [chapeau] felt hat - **3.** [crayon] felt-tip pen.

feutré, e [føtʀe] *adj* **1.** [garni de feutre] trimmed with felt ; [qui a l'aspect du feutre] felted - **2.** [bruit, cri] muffled.

feutrine [føtʀin] *nf* lightweight felt.

fève [fɛv] *nf* broad bean.

février [fevʀije] *nm* February ; *voir aussi* septembre.

fg *abr écrite de* faubourg.

fi [fi] *interj* : **faire fi de** *litt* to scorn.

fiable [fjabl] *adj* reliable.

fiacre [fjakʀ] *nm* hackney carriage.

fiançailles [fjɑ̃saj] *nfpl* engagement *sg*.

fiancé, e [fjɑ̃se] *nm, f* fiancé (*f* fiancée).

fiancer [16] [fjɑ̃se] ◆ **se fiancer** *vp* : **se fiancer (avec)** to get engaged (to).

fibre [fibʀ] *nf* ANAT, BIOL & TECHNOL fibre *UK*, fiber *US* ; **fibre de verre** fibreglass *UK* ou fiberglass *US*, glass fibre *UK*.

ficelé, e [fisle] *adj fam* dressed.

ficeler [24] [fisle] *vt* [lier] to tie up.

ficelle [fisel] *nf* **1.** [fil] string - **2.** [pain] thin French stick - **3.** (*gén pl*) [truc] trick.

fiche [fiʃ] *nf* **1.** [document] card ; **fiche de paie** pay slip - **2.** ÉLECTR & TECHNOL pin.

ficher [3] [fiʃe] *vt* **1.** [enfoncer] : **ficher qqch dans** to stick sthg into - **2.** (*participe passé* fiché) [inscrire] to put on file - **3.** (*participe passé* fichu) *fam* : **qu'est-ce qu'il fiche?** what's he doing? - **4.** (*participe passé* fichu) *fam* [mettre] to put ; **ficher qqch par terre** *fig* to mess up, to muck up. ◆ **se ficher** *vp* **1.** [s'enfoncer - suj: clou, pique] : **se ficher dans** to go into - **2.** *fam* [se moquer] :

se ficher de to make fun of - **3.** *fam* [ne pas tenir compte] : **se ficher de** not to give a damn about.

fichier [fiʃje] *nm* file.

fichu, e [fiʃy] *adj* **1.** *fam* [cassé, fini] done for - **2.** *(avant n)* [désagréable] nasty ; **être mal fichu** *fam* [personne] to feel rotten ; [objet] to be badly made ; **il n'est même pas fichu de faire son lit** *fam* he can't even make his own bed. ◆ **fichu** *nm* scarf.

fictif, ive [fiktif, iv] *adj* **1.** [imaginaire] imaginary - **2.** [faux] false.

fiction [fiksjɔ̃] *nf* **1.** LITTÉR fiction - **2.** [monde imaginaire] dream world.

fidèle [fidɛl] ◇ *nmf* **1.** RELIG believer - **2.** [adepte] fan. ◇ *adj* **1.** [loyal, exact, semblable] : **fidèle (à)** faithful (to) ; **fidèle à la réalité** accurate - **2.** [habitué] regular.

fidéliser [3] [fidelize] *vt* to attract and keep.

fidélité [fidelite] *nf* faithfulness.

fief [fjɛf] *nm* fief ; *fig* stronghold.

fiel [fjɛl] *nm litt & fig* gall.

fier¹, fière [fjɛr] *adj* **1.** [gén] proud ; **fier de qqn/qqch** proud of sb/sth ; **fier de faire qqch** proud to be doing sth - **2.** [noble] noble.

fier² [9] [fje] ◆ **se fier** *vp* : **se fier à** to trust, to rely on.

fierté [fjɛrte] *nf* **1.** [satisfaction, dignité] pride - **2.** [arrogance] arrogance.

fièvre [fjɛvr] *nf* **1.** MÉD fever ; **avoir 40 de fièvre** to have a temperature of 105 (degrees) ; [vétérinaire] : **fièvre aphteuse** foot and mouth disease - **2.** *fig* [excitation] excitement.

fiévreux, euse [fjevrø, øz] *adj litt & fig* feverish.

fig. *abr écrite de* **figure**.

figer [17] [fiʒe] *vt* to paralyse *UK*, to paralyze *US*. ◆ **se figer** *vp* **1.** [s'immobiliser] to freeze - **2.** [se solidifier] to congeal.

fignoler [3] [fiɲɔle] *vt* to put the finishing touches to.

figue [fig] *nf* fig.

figuier [figje] *nm* fig tree.

figurant, e [figyrɑ̃, ɑ̃t] *nm, f* extra.

figuratif, ive [figyratif, iv] *adj* figurative.

figure [figyr] *nf* **1.** [gén] figure ; **faire figure de** to look like - **2.** [visage] face.

figuré, e [figyre] *adj* [sens] figurative. ◆ **figuré** *nm* : **au figuré** in the figurative sense.

figurer [3] [figyre] ◇ *vt* to represent. ◇ *vi* : **figurer dans/parmi** to figure in/among.

figurine [figyrin] *nf* figurine.

fil [fil] *nm* **1.** [brin] thread ; **fil à plomb** plumb line ; **perdre le fil (de qqch)** *fig* to lose the thread (of sth) - **2.** [câble] wire ; **fil de fer** wire - **3.** [cours] course ; **au fil de** in the course of - **4.** [tissu] linen - **5.** [tranchant] edge.

filament [filamɑ̃] *nm* **1.** ANAT & ÉLECTR filament - **2.** [végétal] fibre *UK*, fiber *US* - **3.** [de colle, bave] thread.

filandreux, euse [filɑ̃drø, øz] *adj* [viande] stringy.

filasse [filas] ◇ *nf* tow. ◇ *adj inv* flaxen.

filature [filatyr] *nf* **1.** [usine] mill ; [fabrication] spinning - **2.** [poursuite] tailing.

file [fil] *nf* line ; **à la file** in a line ; **se garer en double file** to double-park ; **file d'attente** queue *UK*, line *US*.

filer [3] [file] ◇ *vt* **1.** [soie, coton] to spin - **2.** [personne] to tail - **3.** *fam* [donner] : **filer qqch à qqn** to slip sth to sb, to slip sb sth. ◇ *vi* **1.** [bas] to ladder *UK*, to run *US* - **2.** [aller vite - temps, véhicule] to fly (by) - **3.** *fam* [partir] to dash off ; **filer doux** to behave nicely.

filet [filɛ] *nm* **1.** [à mailles] net ; **filet de pêche** fishing net ; **filet à provisions** string bag - **2.** CULIN fillet, filet *US* ; **filet de sole** fillet ou filet *US* of sole - **3.** [de liquide] drop, dash ; [de lumière] shaft.

filial, e, aux [filjal, o] *adj* filial. ◆ **filiale** *nf* ÉCON subsidiary.

filiation [filjasjɔ̃] *nf* [lien de parenté] line.

filière [filjɛr] *nf* **1.** [voie] : **suivre la filière [professionnelle]** to work one's way up ; **suivre la filière hiérarchique** to go through the right channels - **2.** [réseau] network.

filiforme [filiform] *adj* skinny.

filigrane [filigran] *nm* [dessin] watermark ; **en filigrane** *fig* between the lines.

filin [filɛ̃] *nm* rope.

fille [fij] *nf* **1.** [enfant] daughter - **2.** [femme] girl ; **jeune fille** girl ; **fille mère** *péj* single mother ; **vieille fille** *péj* spinster.

fillette [fijɛt] *nf* little girl.

filleul, e [fijœl] *nm, f* godchild.

film [film] *nm* **1.** [gén] film, movie *US* ; **film catastrophe** disaster movie ; **film d'épouvante** horror film ; **film policier** detective film - **2.** *fig* [déroulement] course.

filmer [3] [filme] *vt* to film.

filmographie [filmɔgrafi] *nf* filmography, films *pl*.

filon [filɔ̃] *nm* **1.** [de mine] vein - **2.** *fam fig* [possibilité] cushy number.

fils [fis] *nm* son ; **fils de famille** boy from a privileged background.

filtrant, e [filtrɑ̃, ɑ̃t] *adj* [verre] tinted.

filtre [filtr] *nm* **1.** filter ; **filtre à café** coffee filter - **2.** INFORM : **filtre parental** internet filter, parental control filter.

filtrer [3] [filtre] <> *vt* to filter ; *fig* to screen. <> *vi* to filter ; *fig* to filter through.

fin, fine [fɛ̃, fin] <> *adj* **1.** [gén] fine - **2.** [partie du corps] slender ; [couche, papier] thin - **3.** [subtil] shrewd - **4.** [ouïe, vue] keen. <> *adv* finely ; **fin prêt** quite ready. ➡ **fin** *nf* end ; **fin mars** at the end of March ; **mettre fin à** to put a stop ou an end to ; **prendre fin** to come to an end ; **tirer** ou **toucher à sa fin** to draw to a close ; **arriver** ou **parvenir à ses fins** to achieve one's ends ou aims. ➡ **fin de série** *nf* oddment. ➡ **à la fin** *loc adv* : **tu vas m'écouter, à la fin?** will you listen to me? ➡ **à la fin de** *loc prép* at the end of. ➡ **sans fin** *loc adj* endless.

final, e [final] (*pl* finals ou finaux [fino]) *adj* final. ➡ **finale** *nf* SPORT final.

finalement [finalmɑ̃] *adv* finally.

finaliste [finalist] *nmf & adj* finalist.

finalité [finalite] *nf sout* [fonction] purpose.

finance [finɑ̃s] *nf* finance. ➡ **finances** *nfpl* finances.

financer [16] [finɑ̃se] *vt* to finance, to fund.

financier, ère [finɑ̃sje, ɛr] *adj* financial. ➡ **financier** *nm* financier.

finaud, e [fino, od] *adj* wily, crafty.

finesse [fines] *nf* **1.** [gén] fineness - **2.** [minceur] slenderness - **3.** [perspicacité] shrewdness - **4.** [subtilité] subtlety.

fini, e [fini] *adj* **1.** *péj* [fieffé] : **un crétin fini** a complete idiot - **2.** *fam* [usé, diminué] finished - **3.** [limité] finite. ➡ **fini** *nm* [d'objet] finish.

finir [32] [finir] <> *vt* **1.** [gén] to finish, to end - **2.** [vider] to empty. <> *vi* **1.** [gén] to finish, to end ; **finir par faire qqch** to do sthg eventually ; **tu vas finir par tomber!** you're going to fall! ; **mal finir** to end badly - **2.** [arrêter] : **finir de faire qqch** to stop doing sthg ; **en finir (avec)** to finish (with).

finition [finisjɔ̃] *nf* [d'objet] finish.

finlandais, e [fɛ̃lɑ̃dɛ, ɛz] *adj* Finnish. ➡ **Finlandais, e** *nm, f* Finn.

Finlande [fɛ̃lɑ̃d] *nf* : **la Finlande** Finland.

finnois, e [finwa, az] *adj* Finnish. ➡ **finnois** *nm* [langue] Finnish. ➡ **Finnois, e** *nm, f* Finn.

fiole [fjɔl] *nf* flask.

fioriture [fjɔrityr] *nf* flourish.

fioul = **fuel**.

firmament [firmamɑ̃] *nm* firmament.

firme [firm] *nf* firm.

fis, fit *etc* ➡ **faire**.

fisc [fisk] *nm* ≃ Inland Revenue *UK*, ≃ Internal Revenue Service *US*.

fiscal, e, aux [fiskal, o] *adj* tax (*avant n*), fiscal.

fiscalité [fiskalite] *nf* tax system.

fissure [fisyr] *nf litt & fig* crack.

fissurer [3] [fisyre] *vt* [fendre] to crack ; *fig* to split. ➡ **se fissurer** *vp* to crack.

fiston [fistɔ̃] *nm fam* son.

FIV [fiv] (*abr de* **fécondation in vitro**) *nf* IVF.

fixation [fiksasjɔ̃] *nf* **1.** [action de fixer] fixing - **2.** [attache] fastening, fastener ; [de ski] binding - **3.** PSYCHO fixation.

fixe [fiks] *adj* fixed ; [encre] permanent. ➡ **fixe** *nm* fixed salary.

fixement [fiksəmɑ̃] *adv* fixedly.

fixer [3] [fikse] *vt* **1.** [gén] to fix ; [règle] to set ; **fixer son choix sur** to decide on - **2.** [monter] to hang - **3.** [regarder] to stare at - **4.** [renseigner] : **fixer qqn sur qqch** to put sb in the picture about sthg ; **être fixé sur qqch** to know all about sthg. ➡ **se fixer** *vp* to settle ; **se fixer sur** [suj: choix, personne] to settle on ; [suj: regard] to rest on.

fjord [fjɔrd] *nm* fjord.

flacon [flakɔ̃] *nm* small bottle ; **flacon à parfum** perfume bottle.

flageller [4] [flaʒele] *vt* [fouetter] to flagellate.

flageoler [3] [flaʒɔle] *vi* to tremble.

flageolet [flaʒɔlɛ] *nm* **1.** [haricot] flageolet bean - **2.** MUS flageolet.

flagrant, e [flagrɑ̃, ɑ̃t] *adj* flagrant, ➤ **délit**.

flair [flɛr] *nm* sense of smell.

flairer [4] [flɛre] *vt* to sniff, to smell ; *fig* to scent.

flamand, e [flamɑ̃, ɑ̃d] *adj* Flemish. ➡ **flamand** *nm* [langue] Flemish. ➡ **Flamand, e** *nm, f* Flemish person, Fleming.

flamant [flamɑ̃] *nm* flamingo ; **flamant rose** pink flamingo.

flambeau, x [flɑ̃bo] *nm* torch ; *fig* flame.

flamber [3] [flɑ̃be] <> *vi* **1.** [brûler] to blaze - **2.** *fam* [jeux] to play for high stakes. <> *vt* **1.** [crêpe] to flambé - **2.** [volaille] to singe.

flamboyant, e [flɑ̃bwajɑ̃, ɑ̃t] *adj* **1.** [ciel, regard] blazing ; [couleur] flaming - **2.** ARCHIT flamboyant.

flamboyer [13] [flɑ̃bwaje] *vi* to blaze.

flamme [flam] *nf* flame ; *fig* fervour *UK*, fervor *US*, fire.

flan [flɑ̃] *nm* baked custard.

flanc [flɑ̃] *nm* [de personne, navire, montagne] side ; [d'animal, d'armée] flank.

flancher [3] [flɑ̃ʃe] *vi fam* to give up.

flanelle [flanɛl] *nf* flannel.

flâner [3] [flɑne] *vi* [se promener] to stroll.

flanquer [3] [flɑ̃ke] *vt* **1.** *fam* [jeter] : flanquer qqch par terre to fling sthg to the ground ; flanquer qqn dehors to chuck OU fling sb out - **2.** *fam* [donner] : flanquer une gifle à qqn to clout sb round the ear ; flanquer la frousse à qqn to put the wind up sb *UK* - **3.** [accompagner] : être flanqué de to be flanked by.

flapi, e [flapi] *adj fam* dead beat.

flaque [flak] *nf* pool.

flash [flaʃ] *nm* **1.** PHOTO flash - **2.** RADIO & TV : flash (d'information) newsflash ; flash de publicité commercial.

flash-back [flaʃbak] (*pl inv* OU **flash-backs**) *nm* CINÉ flashback.

flasher [3] [flaʃe] *vi fam* flasher sur qqn/qqch to be turned on by sb/sthg.

flasque [flask] <> *nf* flask. <> *adj* flabby, limp.

flatter [3] [flate] *vt* **1.** [louer] to flatter - **2.** [caresser] to stroke. ◆ se flatter *vp* to flatter o.s. ; je me flatte de le convaincre I flatter myself that I can convince him ; se flatter de faire qqch to pride o.s. on doing sthg.

flatterie [flatri] *nf* flattery.

flatteur, euse [flatœr, øz] <> *adj* flattering. <> *nm, f* flatterer.

fléau, x [fleo] *nm* **1.** *litt & fig* [calamité] scourge - **2.** [instrument] flail.

flèche [flɛʃ] *nf* **1.** [gén] arrow - **2.** [d'église] spire - **3.** *fig* [critique] shaft.

fléchette [fleʃɛt] *nf* dart. ◆ fléchettes *nfpl* darts *sg*.

fléchir [32] [fleʃir] <> *vt* to bend, to flex ; *fig* to sway. <> *vi* to bend ; *fig* to weaken.

fléchissement [fleʃismɑ̃] *nm* flexing, bending ; *fig* weakening.

flegmatique [flɛgmatik] *adj* phlegmatic.

flegme [flɛgm] *nm* composure.

flemmard, e [flemar, ard] *fam* <> *adj* lazy. <> *nm, f* lazybones *sg*.

flemme [flɛm] *nf fam* laziness ; j'ai la flemme (de sortir) I can't be bothered (to go out).

flétrir [32] [fletrir] *vt* [fleur, visage] to wither. ◆ se flétrir *vp* to wither.

fleur [flœr] *nf* BOT & *fig* flower ; en fleur, en fleurs [arbre] in flower, in blossom ; à fleurs [motif] flowered.

fleuret [flœrɛ] *nm* foil.

fleuri, e [flœri] *adj* **1.** [jardin, pré] in flower ; [vase] of flowers ; [tissu] flowered ; [table, appartement] decorated with flowers - **2.** *fig* [style] flowery.

fleurir [32] [flœrir] <> *vi* to blossom ; *fig* to flourish. <> *vt* [maison] to decorate with flowers ; [tombe] to lay flowers on.

fleuriste [flœrist] *nmf* florist.

fleuron [flœrɔ̃] *nm fig* jewel.

fleuve [flœv] *nm* **1.** [cours d'eau] river - **2.** (*en apposition*) [interminable] lengthy, interminable.

flexible [flɛksibl] *adj* flexible.

flexion [flɛksjɔ̃] *nf* **1.** [de genou, de poutre] bending - **2.** LING inflexion.

flibustier [flibystje] *nm* buccaneer.

flic [flik] *nm fam* cop.

flinguer [3] [flɛ̃ge] *vt fam* to gun down. ◆ se flinguer *vp fam* to blow one's brains out.

flipper [flipœr] *nm* pinball machine.

flirter [3] [flœrte] *vi* : flirter (avec qqn) to flirt (with sb) ; flirter avec qqch *fig* to flirt with sthg.

flocon [flɔkɔ̃] *nm* flake ; flocon de neige snowflake.

flonflon [flɔ̃flɔ̃] *nm* (*gén pl*) blare.

flop [flɔp] *nm* [échec] flop, failure.

floraison [flɔrɛzɔ̃] *nf litt & fig* flowering, blossoming.

floral, e, aux [flɔral, o] *adj* floral.

flore [flɔr] *nf* flora.

Floride [flɔrid] *nf* : la Floride Florida.

florissant, e [flɔrisɑ̃, ɑ̃t] *adj* [santé] blooming ; [économie] flourishing.

flot [flo] *nm* flood, stream ; être à flot [navire] to be afloat ; *fig* to be back to normal. ◆ flots *nmpl litt* waves.

flottaison [flɔtɛzɔ̃] *nf* floating.

flottant, e [flɔtɑ̃, ɑ̃t] *adj* **1.** [gén] floating ; [esprit] irresolute - **2.** [robe] loose-fitting.

flotte [flɔt] *nf* **1.** AÉRON & NAUT fleet - **2.** *fam* [eau] water - **3.** *fam* [pluie] rain.

flottement [flɔtmɑ̃] *nm* **1.** [indécision] hesitation, wavering - **2.** [de monnaie] floating.

flotter [3] [flɔte] <> *vi* **1.** [sur l'eau] to float - **2.** [drapeau] to flap ; [brume, odeur] to drift - **3.** [dans un vêtement] : tu flottes dedans it's baggy on you. <> *v impers fam* il flotte it's raining.

flotteur [flɔtœr] *nm* [de ligne de pêche, d'hydravion] float ; [de chasse d'eau] ballcock.

flou, e [flu] *adj* **1.** [couleur, coiffure] soft - **2.** [photo] blurred, fuzzy - **3.** [pensée] vague, woolly. ◆ flou *nm* [de photo] fuzziness ; [de décision] vagueness.

flouer [3] [flue] *vt fam* to do *UK*, to swindle.

fluctuer [3] [flyktɥe] *vi* to fluctuate.

fluet, ette [flyɛ, ɛt] *adj* [personne] thin, slender ; [voix] thin.

fluide [flųid] <> *nm* **1.** [matière] fluid - **2.** *fig* [pouvoir] (occult) power. <> *adj* [matière] fluid ; [circulation] flowing freely.

fluidifier [9] [flųidifje] *vt* [trafic] to improve the flow of.

fluidité [flųidite] *nf* [gén] fluidity ; [de circulation] easy flow.

fluor [flyɔr] *nm* fluorine.

fluorescent, e [flyɔresɑ̃, ɑ̃t] *adj* fluorescent.

flûte [flyt] <> *nf* **1.** MUS flute - **2.** [verre] flute (glass). <> *interj fam* bother! *UK*

flûtiste [flytist] *nmf* flautist *UK*, flutist *US*.

fluvial, e, aux [flyvjal, o] *adj* [eaux, pêche] river (avant n) ; [alluvions] fluvial.

flux [fly] *nm* **1.** [écoulement] flow - **2.** [marée] flood tide - **3.** PHYS flux - **4.** [sociologie] : **flux migratoire** massive population movement.

fluxion [flyksjɔ̃] *nf* inflammation.

FM (abr de **frequency modulation**) *nf* FM.

FMI (abr de **Fonds monétaire international**) *nm* IMF.

FN (abr de **Front national**) *nm extreme right-wing French political party*.

foc [fɔk] *nm* jib.

focal, e, aux [fɔkal, o] *adj* focal.

fœtal, e, aux [fetal, o] *adj* foetal.

fœtus [fetys] *nm* foetus.

foi [fwa] *nf* **1.** RELIG faith - **2.** [confiance] trust ; **avoir foi en qqn/qqch** to trust sb/sthg, to have faith in sb/sthg ; **être de bonne/ mauvaise foi** to be in good/bad faith.

foie [fwa] *nm* ANAT & CULIN liver.

foin [fwɛ̃] *nm* hay.

foire [fwar] *nf* **1.** [fête] funfair *UK*, carnival *US* - **2.** [exposition, salon] trade fair.

fois [fwa] *nf* time ; **une fois** once ; **deux fois** twice ; **trois/quatre fois** three/four times ; **deux fois plus long** twice as long ; **neuf fois sur dix** nine times out of ten ; **deux fois trois** two times three ; **cette fois** this time ; **il était une fois...** once upon a time there was... ; **une (bonne) fois pour toutes** once and for all. **à la fois** *loc adv* at the same time, at once. **des fois** *loc adv* [parfois] sometimes ; **non, mais des fois!** *fam* look here! **si des fois** *loc conj fam* if ever. **une fois que** *loc conj* once.

foison [fwazɔ̃] **à foison** *loc adv* in abundance.

foisonner [3] [fwazɔne] *vi* to abound.

folâtre [fɔlatr] *adj* playful.

folâtrer [3] [fɔlatre] *vi* to romp (about).

folie [fɔli] *nf litt & fig* madness.

folklore [fɔlklɔr] *nm* [de pays] folklore.

folklorique [fɔlklɔrik] *adj* **1.** [danse] folk - **2.** *fig* [situation, personne] bizarre, quaint.

folle ► **fou**.

follement [fɔlmɑ̃] *adv* madly, wildly.

follet [fɔlɛ] ► **feu**.

fomenter [3] [fɔmɑ̃te] *vt* to foment.

foncé, e [fɔ̃se] *adj* dark.

foncer [16] [fɔ̃se] *vi* **1.** [teinte] to darken - **2.** [se ruer] : **foncer sur** to rush at - **3.** *fam* [se dépêcher] to get a move on.

foncier, ère [fɔ̃sje, ɛr] *adj* **1.** [impôt] land (avant n) ; **propriétaire foncier** landowner - **2.** [fondamental] basic, fundamental.

foncièrement [fɔ̃sjɛrmɑ̃] *adv* basically.

fonction [fɔ̃ksjɔ̃] *nf* **1.** [gén] function ; **faire fonction de** to act as - **2.** [profession] post ; **entrer en fonction** to take up one's post ou duties. **en fonction de** *loc prép* according to. **de fonction** *loc adj* : **appartement** ou **logement de fonction** tied accommodation *UK*, accommodation that goes with the job.

fonctionnaire [fɔ̃ksjɔner] *nmf* [de l'État] state employee ; [dans l'administration] civil servant ; **haut fonctionnaire** senior civil servant.

fonctionnel, elle [fɔ̃ksjɔnɛl] *adj* functional.

fonctionnement [fɔ̃ksjɔnmɑ̃] *nm* working, functioning.

fonctionner [3] [fɔ̃ksjɔne] *vi* to work, to function.

fond [fɔ̃] *nm* **1.** [de récipient, puits, mer] bottom ; [de pièce] back ; **sans fond** bottomless - **2.** [substance] heart, root ; **le fond de ma pensée** what I really think ; **le fond et la forme** content and form - **3.** [arrière-plan] background. **fond de teint** *nm* foundation. **à fond** *loc adv* **1.** [entièrement] thoroughly ; **se donner à fond** to give one's all - **2.** [très vite] at top speed. **au fond, dans le fond** *loc adv* basically. **au fond de** *loc prép* : **au fond de moi-même/lui-même** *etc* at heart, deep down.

fondamental, e, aux [fɔ̃damɑ̃tal, o] *adj* fundamental.

fondant, e [fɔ̃dɑ̃, ɑ̃t] *adj* [neige, glace] melting ; [aliment] which melts in the mouth.

fondateur, trice [fɔ̃datœr, tris] *nm, f* founder.

fondation [fɔ̃dasjɔ̃] *nf* foundation. **fondations** *nfpl* CONSTR foundations.

fondé, e [fɔ̃de] *adj* [craintes, reproches] justified, well-founded ; **non fondé** unfounded. **fondé de pouvoir** *nm* authorized representative.

fondement [fɔ̃dmɑ̃] *nm* [base, motif] foundation ; **sans fondement** groundless, without foundation.

fonder [3] [fɔ̃de] *vt* **1.** [créer] to found - **2.** [baser] : **fonder qqch sur** to base sthg on ; **fonder de grands espoirs sur qqn** to pin one's hopes on sb. ◆ **se fonder** *vp* : **se fonder sur** [suj: personne] to base o.s. on ; [suj: argument] to be based on.

fonderie [fɔ̃dri] *nf* [usine] foundry.

fondre [75] [fɔ̃dr] ◇ *vt* **1.** [beurre, neige] to melt ; [sucre, sel] to dissolve ; [métal] to melt down - **2.** [mouler] to cast - **3.** [mêler] to blend. ◇ *vi* **1.** [beurre, neige] to melt ; [sucre, sel] to dissolve ; *fig* to melt away - **2.** [maigrir] to lose weight - **3.** [se ruer] : **fondre sur** to swoop down on.

fonds [fɔ̃] ◇ *nm* **1.** [ressources] fund ; **fonds commun de placement** unit trust *UK*, mutual fund *US* ; **le Fonds monétaire international** the International Monetary Fund - **2.** [bien immobilier] : **fonds (de commerce)** business. ◇ *nmpl* **1.** [ressources] funds - **2.** FIN : **fonds de pension** (private) pension fund.

fondu, e [fɔ̃dy] *pp* ▶ **fondre**. ◆ **fondue** *nf* fondue.

font ▶ **faire**.

fontaine [fɔ̃tɛn] *nf* [naturelle] spring ; [publique] fountain.

fonte [fɔ̃t] *nf* **1.** [de glace, beurre] melting ; [de métal] melting down - **2.** [alliage] cast iron.

foot [fut] = **football**.

football [futbol] *nm* football *UK*, soccer.

footballeur, euse [futbolœr, øz] *nm, f* footballer *UK*, soccer player.

footing [futiŋ] *nm* jogging.

for [fɔr] *nm* : **dans son for intérieur** in his/her heart of hearts.

forage [fɔraʒ] *nm* drilling.

forain, e [fɔrɛ̃, ɛn] *adj* ▶ **fête**. ◆ **forain** *nm* stallholder *UK*.

forçat [fɔrsa] *nm* convict.

force [fɔrs] *nf* **1.** [vigueur] strength ; **c'est ce qui fait sa force** that's where his strength lies - **2.** [violence, puissance, MIL & PHYS] force ; **faire faire qqch à qqn de force** to force sb to do sthg ; **avoir force de loi** to have force of law ; **obtenir qqch par la force** to obtain sthg by force ; **force centrifuge** PHYS centrifugal force. ◆ **forces** *nfpl* [physique] strength *sg* ; **de toutes ses forces** with all his/her strength. ◆ **à force de** *loc prép* by dint of.

forcément [fɔrsemɑ̃] *adv* inevitably.

forcené, e [fɔrsəne] *nm, f* maniac.

forceps [fɔrsɛps] *nm* forceps *pl*.

forcer [16] [fɔrse] ◇ *vt* **1.** [gén] to force ; **forcer qqn à qqch/à faire qqch** to force sb into sthg/to do sthg - **2.** [admiration, respect] to compel, to command - **3.** [talent, voix] to strain. ◇ *vi* : **ça ne sert à rien de forcer, ça ne passe pas** there's no point in forcing it, it won't go through ; **forcer sur qqch** to overdo sthg. ◆ **se forcer** *vp* [s'obliger] : **se forcer à faire qqch** to force o.s. to do sthg.

forcir [32] [fɔrsir] *vi* to put on weight.

forer [3] [fɔre] *vt* to drill.

forestier, ère [fɔrɛstje, ɛr] *adj* forest (avant n).

forêt [fɔrɛ] *nf* forest.

forfait [fɔrfɛ] *nm* **1.** [prix fixe] fixed price - **2.** [séjour] package deal - **3.** SPORT : **déclarer forfait** [abandonner] to withdraw ; *fig* to give up - **4.** *litt* [crime] heinous crime.

forfaitaire [fɔrfɛtɛr] *adj* inclusive.

forge [fɔrʒ] *nf* forge.

forger [17] [fɔrʒe] *vt* **1.** [métal] to forge - **2.** *fig* [caractère] to form.

forgeron [fɔrʒərɔ̃] *nm* blacksmith.

formaliser [3] [fɔrmalize] *vt* to formalize. ◆ **se formaliser** *vp* : **se formaliser (de)** to take offence *UK* ou offense *US* (at).

formalisme [fɔrmalism] *nm* formality.

formaliste [fɔrmalist] ◇ *nmf* formalist. ◇ *adj* [milieu] conventional ; [personne] : **être formaliste** to be a stickler for the rules.

formalité [fɔrmalite] *nf* formality.

format [fɔrma] *nm* [dimension] size.

formatage [fɔrmataʒ] *nm* INFORM formatting.

formater [3] [fɔrmate] *vt* INFORM to format.

formateur, trice [fɔrmatœr, tris] ◇ *adj* formative. ◇ *nm, f* trainer.

formation [fɔrmasjɔ̃] *nf* **1.** [gén] formation - **2.** [apprentissage] training ; **formation en alternance** sandwich course.

forme [fɔrm] *nf* **1.** [aspect] shape, form ; **en forme de** in the shape of - **2.** [état] form ; **être en (pleine) forme** to be in (great) shape, to be on *UK* ou in *US* (top) form. ◆ **formes** *nfpl* figure *sg*.

formel, elle [fɔrmɛl] *adj* **1.** [définitif, ferme] positive, definite - **2.** [poli] formal.

former [3] [fɔrme] *vt* **1.** [gén] to form - **2.** [personnel, élèves] to train - **3.** [goût, sensibilité] to develop. ◆ **se former** *vp* **1.** [se constituer] to form - **2.** [s'instruire] to train o.s.

Formica® [fɔrmika] *nm inv* Formica®.

formidable [fɔrmidabl] *adj* **1.** [épatant] great, tremendous - **2.** [incroyable] incredible.

formol [fɔrmɔl] *nm* formalin.

formulaire [fɔrmylɛr] *nm* form ; **remplir un formulaire** to fill in a form.

formule [fɔrmyl] *nf* **1.** [expression] expression ; **formule de politesse** [orale] polite phrase ; [épistolaire] letter ending - **2.** CHIM & MATH formula - **3.** [méthode] way, method.

formuler [3] [fɔrmyle] *vt* to formulate, to express.

fort, e [fɔr, fɔrt] ⟨⟩ *adj* **1.** [gén] strong ; **et le plus fort, c'est que...** and the most amazing thing about it is... ; **c'est plus fort que moi** I can't help it - **2.** [corpulent] heavy, big - **3.** [doué] gifted ; **être fort en qqch** to be good at sthg - **4.** [puissant - voix] loud ; [- vent, lumière, accent] strong - **5.** [considérable] large ; **il y a de fortes chances qu'il gagne** there's a good chance he'll win. ⟨⟩ *adv* **1.** [frapper, battre] hard ; [sonner, parler] loud, loudly - **2.** *sout* [très] very. ⟨⟩ *nm* **1.** [château] fort - **2.** [spécialité] : **ce n'est pas mon fort** it's not my forte OU strong point.

forteresse [fɔrtərɛs] *nf* fortress.

fortifiant, e [fɔrtifjɑ̃, ɑ̃t] *adj* fortifying. ⟨⟩ **fortifiant** *nm* tonic.

fortification [fɔrtifikasjɔ̃] *nf* fortification.

fortifier [9] [fɔrtifje] *vt* [personne, ville] to fortify ; **fortifier qqn dans qqch** *fig* to strengthen sb in sthg.

fortuit, e [fɔrtɥi, it] *adj* chance (avant n), fortuitous.

fortune [fɔrtyn] *nf* **1.** [richesse] fortune - **2.** [hasard] luck, fortune.

fortuné, e [fɔrtyne] *adj* **1.** [riche] wealthy - **2.** [chanceux] fortunate, lucky.

forum [fɔrɔm] *nm* forum.

fosse [fos] *nf* **1.** [trou] pit - **2.** [tombe] grave.

fossé [fose] *nm* ditch ; *fig* gap.

fossette [fosɛt] *nf* dimple.

fossile [fosil] *nm* **1.** [de plante, d'animal] fossil - **2.** *fig & péj* [personne] fossil, fogy.

fossoyeur, euse [foswajœr, øz] *nm, f* gravedigger.

fou, folle [fu, fɔl] ⟨⟩ *adj* (**fol** devant voyelle ou 'h' muet) mad, insane ; [prodigieux] tremendous. ⟨⟩ *nm, f* madman (f madwoman).

foudre [fudr] *nf* lightning.

foudroyant, e [fudrwajɑ̃, ɑ̃t] *adj* **1.** [progrès, vitesse] lightning (avant n) ; [succès] stunning - **2.** [nouvelle] devastating ; [regard] withering.

foudroyer [13] [fudrwaje] *vt* **1.** [suj: foudre] to strike ; **l'arbre a été foudroyé** the tree was struck by lightning - **2.** *fig* [abattre] to strike down, to kill ; **foudroyer qqn du regard** to glare at sb.

fouet [fwɛ] *nm* **1.** [en cuir] whip - **2.** CULIN whisk.

fouetter [4] [fwete] *vt* **1.** [gén] to whip ; [suj: pluie] to lash (against) - **2.** [stimuler] to stimulate.

fougère [fuʒɛr] *nf* fern.

fougue [fug] *nf* ardour *UK*, ardor *US*.

fougueux, euse [fugø, øz] *adj* ardent, spirited.

fouille [fuj] *nf* **1.** [de personne, maison] search - **2.** [du sol] dig, excavation.

fouiller [3] [fuje] ⟨⟩ *vt* **1.** [gén] to search - **2.** *fig* [approfondir] to examine closely. ⟨⟩ *vi* : **fouiller dans** to go through.

fouillis [fuji] *nm* jumble, muddle.

fouine [fwin] *nf* stone-marten.

fouiner [3] [fwine] *vi* to ferret about.

foulard [fular] *nm* scarf.

foule [ful] *nf* [de gens] crowd.

foulée [fule] *nf* [de coureur] stride.

fouler [3] [fule] *vt* [raisin] to press ; [sol] to walk on. ⟨⟩ **se fouler** *vp* MÉD : **se fouler le poignet/la cheville** to sprain one's wrist/ankle.

foulure [fulyr] *nf* sprain.

four [fur] *nm* **1.** [de cuisson] oven ; **four électrique/à micro-ondes** electric/microwave oven ; **four crématoire** HIST oven - **2.** THÉÂTRE flop.

fourbe [furb] *adj* treacherous, deceitful.

fourbu, e [furby] *adj* tired out, exhausted.

fourche [furʃ] *nf* **1.** [outil] pitchfork - **2.** [de vélo, route] fork - **3.** *Belgique* SCOL free period.

fourchette [furʃɛt] *nf* **1.** [couvert] fork - **2.** [écart] range, bracket.

fourgon [furgɔ̃] *nm* **1.** [camionnette] van ; **fourgon cellulaire** police van *UK*, patrol wagon *US* - **2.** [ferroviaire] : **fourgon à bestiaux** cattle truck ; **fourgon postal** mail van *UK*, mail truck *US*.

fourgonnette [furgɔnɛt] *nf* small van.

fourmi [furmi] *nf* [insecte] ant ; *fig* hard worker.

fourmilière [furmiljɛr] *nf* anthill.

fourmiller [3] [furmije] *vi* [pulluler] to swarm ; **fourmiller de** *fig* to be swarming with.

fournaise [furnɛz] *nf* furnace.

fourneau, x [furno] *nm* **1.** [cuisinière, poêle] stove - **2.** [de fonderie] furnace.

fournée [furne] *nf* batch.

fourni, e [furni] *adj* [barbe, cheveux] thick.

fournil [furnil] *nm* bakery.

fournir [32] [furnir] *vt* **1.** [procurer] : **fournir qqch à qqn** to supply OU provide sb with sthg - **2.** [produire] : **fournir un effort to** make an effort - **3.** [approvisionner] : **fournir qqn (en)** to supply sb (with).

fournisseur, euse [furnisœr, øz] *nm, f* supplier.

fourniture [furnityr] *nf* supply, supplying *(U).* ➤ **fournitures** *nfpl* : **fournitures de bureau** office supplies ; **fournitures scolaires** school supplies.

fourrage [furaʒ] *nm* fodder.

fourré [fure] *nm* thicket.

fourreau, x [furo] *nm* **1.** [d'épée] sheath ; [de parapluie] cover - **2.** [robe] sheath dress.

fourrer [3] [fure] *vt* **1.** CULIN to stuff, to fill - **2.** *fam* [mettre] : **fourrer qqch (dans)** to stuff sthg (into). ➤ **se fourrer** *vp* : **se fourrer une idée dans la tête** to get an idea into one's head ; **je ne savais plus où me fourrer** I didn't know where to put myself.

fourre-tout [furtu] *nm inv* **1.** [pièce] lumber room *UK*, junk room *US* - **2.** [sac] holdall *UK*, carryall *US.*

fourreur [furœr] *nm* furrier.

fourrière [furjɛr] *nf* pound.

fourrure [furyr] *nf* fur.

fourvoyer [13] [furvwaje] ➤ **se fourvoyer** *vp sout* [s'égarer] to lose one's way ; [se tromper] to go off on the wrong track.

foutre [116] [futr] *vt tfam* **1.** [mettre] to shove, to stick ; **foutre qqn dehors** OU **à la porte** to chuck sb out - **2.** [donner] : **foutre la trouille à qqn** to put the wind up sb *UK* ; **il lui a foutu une baffe** he thumped him one - **3.** [faire] to do ; **ne rien foutre de la journée** to not do a damn thing all day ; **j'en ai rien à foutre** I don't give a toss *UK.* ➤ **se foutre** *vp tfam* **1.** [se mettre] : **se foutre dans** (situation) to get o.s. into - **2.** [se moquer] : **se foutre de (la gueule de) qqn** to laugh at sb, to take the mickey out of sb *UK* - **3.** [ne pas s'intéresser] : **je m'en fous** I don't give a damn about it.

foyer [fwaje] *nm* **1.** [maison] home - **2.** [résidence] home, hostel - **3.** [point central] centre *UK*, center *US* - **4.** [de lunettes] focus ; **verres à double foyer** bifocals.

fracas [fraka] *nm* roar.

fracasser [3] [frakase] *vt* to smash, to shatter.

fraction [fraksjɔ̃] *nf* fraction.

fractionner [3] [fraksjɔne] *vt* to divide (up), to split up.

fracture [fraktyr] *nf* MÉD fracture.

fracturer [3] [fraktyre] *vt* **1.** MÉD to fracture - **2.** [coffre, serrure] to break open.

fragile [fraʒil] *adj* [gén] fragile ; [peau, santé] delicate.

fragiliser [3] [fraʒilize] *vt* to weaken.

fragilité [fraʒilite] *nf* fragility.

fragment [fragmã] *nm* **1.** [morceau] fragment - **2.** [extrait - d'œuvre] extract ; [- de conversation] snatch.

fragmenter [3] [fragmãte] *vt* to fragment, to break up.

fraîche ➤ **frais.**

fraîcheur [freʃœr] *nf* **1.** [d'air, d'accueil] coolness - **2.** [de teint, d'aliment] freshness.

frais, fraîche [fre, freʃ] *adj* **1.** [air, accueil] cool ; **boisson fraîche** cold drink - **2.** [récent - trace] fresh ; [- encre] wet - **3.** [teint] fresh, clear. ➤ **frais** ◇ *nm* : **mettre qqch au frais** to put sthg in a cool place. ◇ *nmpl* [dépenses] expenses, costs ; **aux frais de la maison** at the company's expense ; **faire des frais** to spend a lot of money ; **rentrer dans ses frais** to cover one's expenses ; **frais fixes** fixed costs. ◇ *adv* : **il fait frais** it's cool.

fraise [frez] *nf* **1.** [fruit] strawberry - **2.** [de dentiste] drill ; [de menuisier] bit.

fraiser [4] [freze] *vt* to countersink.

fraiseuse [frezøz] *nf* milling machine.

fraisier [frezje] *nm* **1.** [plante] strawberry plant - **2.** [gâteau] strawberry sponge.

framboise [frãbwaz] *nf* **1.** [fruit] raspberry - **2.** [liqueur] raspberry liqueur.

franc, franche [frã, frãʃ] *adj* **1.** [sincère] frank - **2.** [net] clear, definite. ➤ **franc** *nm* franc.

français, e [frãse, ɛz] *adj* French. ➤ **français** *nm* [langue] French. ➤ **Français, e** *nm, f* Frenchman (*f* Frenchwoman) ; **les Français** the French.

France [frãs] *nf* : **la France** France ; **France 2, France 3** TV *French state-owned television channels.*

franche ➤ **franc.**

franchement [frãʃmã] *adv* **1.** [sincèrement] frankly - **2.** [nettement] clearly - **3.** [tout à fait] completely, downright.

franchir [32] [frãʃir] *vt* **1.** [obstacle] to get over - **2.** [porte] to go through ; [seuil] to cross - **3.** [distance] to cover.

franchise [frãʃiz] *nf* **1.** [sincérité] frankness - **2.** COMM franchise - **3.** [d'assurance] excess - **4.** [détaxe] exemption.

francilien, enne [frãsiljẽ, ɛn] *adj* of OU from the Île-de-France. ➤ **Francilien, enne** *nm, f* inhabitant of the Île-de-France.

franciscain, e [frãsiskẽ, ɛn] *adj & nm, f* Franciscan.

franciser [3] [frãsize] *vt* to frenchify.

franc-jeu [frãʒø] *nm* : **jouer franc-jeu** play fair.

franc-maçon, onne [frãmasɔ̃, ɔn] *(mpl* francs-maçons) *(fpl* franc-maçonnes) *adj* masonic. ➤ **franc-maçon** *nm* freemason.

franc-maçonnerie [frãmasɔnri] *nf* freemasonry *(U).*

franco [frãko] *adv* COMM : **franco de port** carriage paid.

francophone [frãkɔfɔn] <> *adj* French-speaking. <> *nmf* French speaker.

francophonie [frãkɔfɔni] *nf* : **la francophonie** French-speaking nations *pl.*

franc-parler [frãparle] *nm* : **avoir son franc-parler** to speak one's mind.

franc-tireur [frãtirœr] *nm* MIL irregular.

frange [frãʒ] *nf* fringe.

frangipane [frãʒipan] *nf* almond paste.

franglais [frãglɛ] *nm* Franglais.

franquette [frãkɛt] ➤ **à la bonne franquette** *loc adv* informally, without any ceremony.

frappant, e [frapã, ãt] *adj* striking.

frapper [3] [frape] <> *vt* 1. [gén] to strike - 2. [boisson] to chill. <> *vi* to knock.

frasques [frask] *nfpl* pranks, escapades.

fraternel, elle [fratɛrnɛl] *adj* fraternal, brotherly.

fraterniser [3] [fratɛrnize] *vi* to fraternize.

fraternité [fratɛrnite] *nf* brotherhood.

fratricide [fratrisid] *nmf* fratricide.

fraude [frod] *nf* fraud.

frauder [3] [frode] *vt & vi* to cheat.

frauduleux, euse [frodylø, øz] *adj* fraudulent.

frayer [11] [freje] ➤ **se frayer** *vp* : **se frayer un chemin (à travers une foule)** to force one's way through (a crowd).

frayeur [frejœr] *nf* fright, fear.

fredaines [frədɛn] *nfpl* pranks.

fredonner [3] [frədɔne] *vt & vi* to hum.

freezer [frizœr] *nm* freezer compartment.

frégate [fregat] *nf* [bateau] frigate.

frein [frɛ̃] *nm* 1. AUTO brake ; **frein à main** handbrake - 2. *fig* [obstacle] brake, check.

freinage [frɛnaʒ] *nm* braking.

freiner [4] [frene] <> *vt* 1. [mouvement, véhicule] to slow down ; [inflation, dépenses] to curb - 2. [personne] to restrain. <> *vi* to brake.

frelaté, e [frəlate] *adj* [vin] adulterated ; *fig* corrupt.

frêle [frɛl] *adj* [enfant, voix] frail.

frelon [frəlɔ̃] *nm* hornet.

frémir [32] [fremir] *vi* 1. [corps, personne] to tremble - 2. [eau] to simmer.

frémissement [fremismã] *nm* 1. [de corps, personne] shiver, trembling *(U)* - 2. [d'eau] simmering.

frêne [frɛn] *nm* ash.

frénésie [frenezi] *nf* frenzy.

frénétique [frenetik] *adj* frenzied.

fréquemment [frekamã] *adv* frequently.

fréquence [frekãs] *nf* frequency.

fréquent, e [frekã, ãt] *adj* frequent.

fréquentation [frekãtasjɔ̃] *nf* 1. [d'endroit] frequenting - 2. [de personne] association. ➤ **fréquentations** *nfpl* company *(U).*

fréquenté, e [frekãte] *adj* : **très fréquenté** busy ; **c'est très bien/mal fréquenté** the right/wrong sort of people go there.

fréquenter [3] [frekãte] *vt* 1. [endroit] to frequent - 2. [personne] to associate with ; [petit ami] to go out with, to see.

frère [frɛr] <> *nm* brother. <> *adj* [parti, pays] sister *(avant n).*

fresque [frɛsk] *nf* fresco.

fret [frɛ] *nm* freight.

frétiller [3] [fretije] *vi* [poisson, personne] to wriggle.

fretin [frətɛ̃] *nm* : **le menu fretin** the small fry.

friable [frijabl] *adj* crumbly.

friand, e [frijã, ãd] *adj* : **être friand de** to be partial to.

friandise [frijãdiz] *nf* delicacy.

fric [frik] *nm fam* cash.

friche [friʃ] *nf* fallow land ; **en friche** fallow.

friction [friksjɔ̃] *nf* 1. [massage] massage - 2. *fig* [désaccord] friction.

frictionner [3] [friksjɔne] *vt* to rub.

Frigidaire® [friʒidɛr] *nm* fridge UK, refrigerator.

frigide [friʒid] *adj* frigid.

frigo [frigo] *nm fam* fridge UK.

frigorifié, e [frigɔrifje] *adj fam* frozen.

frileux, euse [frilø, øz] *adj* 1. [craignant le froid] sensitive to the cold - 2. [prudent] unadventurous.

frimas [frima] *nm litt* foggy winter weather.

frimer [3] [frime] *vi fam* [bluffer] to pretend ; [se mettre en valeur] to show off.

frimousse [frimus] *nf fam* dear little face.

fringale [frɛ̃gal] *nf fam* : **avoir la fringale** to be starving.

fringant, e [frɛ̃gã, ãt] *adj* high-spirited.

fripe [frip] *nf* : **les fripes** secondhand clothes.

fripon, onne [fripɔ̃, ɔn] <> *nm, f fam vieilli* rogue, rascal. <> *adj* mischievous, cheeky.

fripouille [fripuj] *nf fam* scoundrel ; **petite fripouille** little devil.

frire [115] [frir] ◇ *vt* to fry. ◇ *vi* to fry.

frise [friz] *nf* ARCHIT frieze.

frisé, e [frize] *adj* [cheveux] curly ; [personne] curly-haired.

friser [3] [frize] ◇ *vt* **1.** [cheveux] to curl - **2.** *fig* [ressembler à] to border on. ◇ *vi* to curl.

frisquet, ette [friskɛ] *adj* : **il fait frisquet** it's chilly.

frisson [frisɔ̃] *nm* [gén] shiver ; [de dégoût] shudder.

frissonner [3] [frisɔne] *vi* **1.** [trembler] to shiver ; [de dégoût] to shudder - **2.** [s'agiter - eau] to ripple ; [- feuillage] to tremble.

frit, e [fri, frit] *pp* ➤ **frire.**

frite [frit] *nf* chip *UK*, (French) fry *US*.

friteuse [fritøz] *nf* deep-fat fryer.

friture [frityr] *nf* **1.** [poisson] fried fish - **2.** *fam* RADIO crackle.

frivole [frivɔl] *adj* frivolous.

frivolité [frivɔlite] *nf* frivolity.

froid, froide [frwa, frwad] *adj litt & fig* cold ; **rester froid** to be unmoved. ➤ **froid** ◇ *nm* **1.** [température] cold ; **prendre froid** to catch (a) cold - **2.** [tension] coolness. ◇ *adv* : **il fait froid** it's cold ; **avoir froid** to be cold.

froidement [frwadmɑ̃] *adv* **1.** [accueillir] coldly - **2.** [écouter, parler] coolly - **3.** [tuer] cold-bloodedly.

froisser [3] [frwase] *vt* **1.** [tissu, papier] to crumple, to crease - **2.** *fig* [offenser] to offend. ➤ **se froisser** *vp* **1.** [tissu] to crumple, to crease - **2.** MÉD : **se froisser un muscle** to strain a muscle - **3.** [se vexer] to take offence *UK* ou offense *US*.

frôler [3] [frole] *vt* to brush against ; *fig* to have a brush with, to come close to.

fromage [frɔmaʒ] *nm* cheese ; **fromage de brebis** sheep's milk ; **fromage de chèvre** goat's cheese.

fromager, ère [frɔmaʒe, ɛr] *nm, f* [fabricant] cheesemaker.

fromagerie [frɔmaʒri] *nf* cheese shop.

froment [frɔmɑ̃] *nm* wheat.

froncer [16] [frɔ̃se] *vt* **1.** COUT to gather - **2.** [plisser] : **froncer les sourcils** to frown.

frondaison [frɔ̃dɛzɔ̃] *nf* **1.** [phénomène] foliation - **2.** [feuillage] foliage.

fronde [frɔ̃d] *nf* **1.** [arme] sling ; [jouet] catapult *UK*, slingshot *US* - **2.** [révolte] rebellion.

front [frɔ̃] *nm* **1.** ANAT forehead - **2.** *fig* [audace] cheek - **3.** [avant] front ; [de bâtiment] front, façade ; **front de mer** (sea) front - **4.** MÉTÉOR, MIL & POLIT front.

frontal, e, aux [frɔ̃tal, o] *adj* **1.** ANAT frontal - **2.** [collision, attaque] head-on.

frontalier, ère [frɔ̃talje, ɛr] ◇ *adj* frontier *(avant n)* ; **travailleur frontalier** *person who lives on one side of the border and works on the other.* ◇ *nm, f* inhabitant of border area.

frontière [frɔ̃tjɛr] ◇ *adj* border *(avant n).* ◇ *nf* frontier, border ; *fig* frontier.

fronton [frɔ̃tɔ̃] *nm* ARCHIT pediment.

frottement [frɔtmɑ̃] *nm* **1.** [action] rubbing - **2.** [contact, difficulté] friction.

frotter [3] [frɔte] ◇ *vt* to rub ; [parquet] to scrub. ◇ *vi* to rub, to scrape.

frottis [frɔti] *nm* smear.

fructifier [9] [fryktifje] *vi* **1.** [investissement] to give ou yield a profit - **2.** [terre] to be productive - **3.** [arbre, idée] to bear fruit.

fructueux, euse [fryktɥø, øz] *adj* fruitful, profitable.

frugal, e, aux [frygal, o] *adj* frugal.

fruit [frɥi] *nm litt & fig* fruit *(U)* ; **fruits de mer** seafood *(U).*

fruité, e [frɥite] *adj* fruity.

fruitier, ère [frɥitje, ɛr] ◇ *adj* [arbre] fruit *(avant n).* ◇ *nm, f* fruiterer *UK*, fruit seller *US.*

fruste [fryst] *adj* uncouth.

frustration [frystrasjɔ̃] *nf* frustration.

frustrer [3] [frystre] *vt* **1.** [priver] : **frustrer qqn de** to deprive sb of - **2.** [décevoir] to frustrate.

fuchsia [fyʃja] *nm* fuchsia.

fuel, fioul [fjul] *nm* **1.** [de chauffage] fuel - **2.** [carburant] fuel oil.

fugace [fygas] *adj* fleeting.

fugitif, ive [fyʒitif, iv] ◇ *adj* fleeting. ◇ *nm, f* fugitive.

fugue [fyg] *nf* **1.** [de personne] flight ; **faire une fugue** to run away - **2.** MUS fugue.

fui [fɥi] *pp inv* ➤ **fuir.**

fuir [35] [fɥir] ◇ *vi* **1.** [détaler] to flee - **2.** [tuyau] to leak - **3.** *fig* [s'écouler] to fly by. ◇ *vt* [éviter] to avoid, to shun.

fuite [fɥit] *nf* **1.** [de personne] escape, flight - **2.** [écoulement, d'information] leak.

fulgurant, e [fylgyrɑ̃, ɑ̃t] *adj* **1.** [découverte] dazzling - **2.** [vitesse] lightning *(avant n)* - **3.** [douleur] searing.

fulminer [3] [fylmine] *vi* [personne] : **fulminer (contre)** to fulminate (against).

fumé, e [fyme] *adj* **1.** CULIN smoked - **2.** [verres] tinted.

fumée [fyme] *nf* [de combustion] smoke.

fumer [3] [fyme] <> vi **1.** [personne, cheminée] to smoke - **2.** [bouilloire, plat] to steam. <> vt **1.** [cigarette, aliment] to smoke - **2.** AGRIC to spread manure on.

fumette [fymɛt] nf fam smoking marijuana ; **se faire une fumette** to get stoned.

fumeur, euse [fymœr, øz] nm, f smoker.

fumier [fymje] nm AGRIC dung, manure.

fumiste [fymist] nmf péj skiver UK, shirker.

fumisterie [fymistəri] nf fam skiving UK, shirking.

fumoir [fymwar] nm **1.** [pour aliments] smokehouse - **2.** [pièce] smoking room.

funambule [fynãbyl] nmf tightrope walker.

funèbre [fynɛbr] adj **1.** [de funérailles] funeral (avant n) - **2.** [lugubre] funereal ; [sentiments] dismal.

funérailles [fyneraj] nfpl funeral sg.

funéraire [fynerɛr] adj funeral (avant n).

funeste [fynɛst] adj **1.** [accident] fatal - **2.** [initiative, erreur] disastrous - **3.** [présage] of doom.

funiculaire [fynikylɛr] nm funicular railway.

fur [fyr] ⏵ **au fur et à mesure** loc adv as I/you etc go along ; **au fur et à mesure des besoins** as (and when) needed. ⏵ **au fur et à mesure que** loc conj as (and when).

furet [fyrɛ] nm [animal] ferret.

fureter [28] [fyrte] vi [fouiller] to ferret around.

fureur [fyrœr] nf [colère] fury.

furibond, e [fyribɔ̃, ɔ̃d] adj furious.

furie [fyri] nf **1.** [colère, agitation] fury ; **en furie** [personne] infuriated ; [éléments] raging - **2.** fig [femme] shrew.

furieux, euse [fyrjø, øz] adj **1.** [personne] furious - **2.** [énorme] tremendous.

furoncle [fyrɔ̃kl] nm boil.

furtif, ive [fyrtif, iv] adj furtive.

fus, fut etc ⏵ être.

fusain [fyzɛ̃] nm **1.** [crayon] charcoal - **2.** [dessin] charcoal drawing.

fuseau, x [fyzo] nm **1.** [outil] spindle - **2.** [pantalon] ski pants pl. ⏵ **fuseau horaire** nm time zone.

fusée [fyze] nf [pièce d'artifice & AÉRON] rocket.

fuselage [fyzlaʒ] nm fuselage.

fuselé, e [fyzle] adj [doigts] tapering ; [jambes] slender.

fuser [3] [fyze] vi [cri, rire] to burst forth ou out.

fusible [fyzibl] nm fuse.

fusil [fyzi] nm [arme] gun.

fusillade [fyzijad] nf [combat] gunfire (U), fusillade.

fusiller [3] [fyzije] vt [exécuter] to shoot.

fusion [fyzjɔ̃] nf **1.** [gén] fusion - **2.** [fonte] smelting - **3.** ÉCON & POLIT merger.

fusionnel, elle [fyzjɔnɛl] adj [couple] inseparable, intense ; [relation] intense.

fusionner [3] [fyzjɔne] vt & vi to merge.

fustiger [17] [fystiʒe] vt to castigate.

fut ⏵ être.

fût [fy] nm **1.** [d'arbre] trunk - **2.** [tonneau] barrel, cask - **3.** [d'arme] stock - **4.** [de colonne] shaft.

futaie [fytɛ] nf wood.

futile [fytil] adj **1.** [insignifiant] futile - **2.** [frivole] frivolous.

futur, e [fytyr] <> adj future (avant n). <> nm, f [fiancé] intended. ⏵ **futur** nm future.

futuriste [fytyrist] adj futuristic.

fuyant, e [fɥijã, ãt] adj **1.** [perspective, front] receding (avant n) - **2.** [regard] evasive.

fuyard, e [fɥijar, ard] nm, f runaway.

G

g, G [ʒe] nm inv g, G.

gabardine [gabardin] nf gabardine.

gabarit [gabari] nm [dimension] size.

Gabon [gabɔ̃] nm : **le Gabon** Gabon.

gâcher [3] [gaʃe] vt **1.** [gaspiller] to waste - **2.** [gâter] to spoil - **3.** CONSTR to mix.

gâchette [gaʃɛt] nf trigger.

gâchis [gaʃi] nm [gaspillage] waste (U).

gadget [gadʒɛt] nm gadget.

gadoue [gadu] nf fam [boue] mud ; [engrais] sludge.

gaélique [gaelik] <> adj Gaelic. <> nm Gaelic.

gaffe [gaf] nf **1.** fam [maladresse] clanger UK - **2.** [outil] boat hook.

gaffer [3] [gafe] vi fam to put one's foot in it.

gag [gag] nm gag.

gage [gaʒ] nm **1.** [dépôt] pledge ; **mettre qqch en gage** to pawn sthg - **2.** [assurance, preuve] proof - **3.** [dans jeu] forfeit.

gager [17] [gaʒe] vt : **gager que** to bet (that).

gageure [gaʒyr] *nf* challenge.

gagnant, e [gaɲɑ̃, ɑ̃t] <> *adj* winning *(avant n).* <> *nm, f* winner.

gagne-pain [gaɲpɛ̃] *nm inv* livelihood.

gagner [3] [gaɲe] <> *vt* 1. [salaire, argent, repos] to earn - 2. [course, prix, affection] to win - 3. [obtenir, économiser] to gain ; **gagner du temps/de la place** to gain time/space - 4. [atteindre - généralement] to reach ; [- suj: feu, engourdissement] to spread to ; [- suj: sommeil, froid] to overcome. <> *vi* 1. [être vainqueur] to win - 2. [bénéficier] to gain ; **gagner à faire qqch** to be better off doing sthg ; **qu'est-ce que j'y gagne?** what do I get out of it? - 3. [s'améliorer] : **gagner en** to increase in.

gai, e [ge] *adj* 1. [joyeux] cheerful, happy - 2. [vif, plaisant] bright.

gaieté [gete] *nf* 1. [joie] cheerfulness - 2. [vivacité] brightness.

gaillard, e [gajar, ard] <> *adj* 1. [alerte] sprightly, spry - 2. [licencieux] ribald. <> *nm, f* strapping individual.

gain [gɛ̃] *nm* 1. [profit] gain, profit - 2. [succès] winning - 3. [économie] saving. **gains** *nmpl* earnings.

gaine [gɛn] *nf* 1. [étui, enveloppe] sheath - 2. [sous-vêtement] girdle, corset.

gainer [4] [gene] *vt* to sheathe.

gala [gala] *nm* gala, reception.

galant, e [galɑ̃, ɑ̃t] *adj* 1. [courtois] gallant - 2. [amoureux] flirtatious. **galant** *nm* admirer.

galanterie [galɑ̃tri] *nf* 1. [courtoisie] gallantry, politeness - 2. [flatterie] compliment.

galaxie [galaksi] *nf* galaxy.

galbe [galb] *nm* curve.

gale [gal] *nf* MÉD scabies *(U).*

galère [galɛr] *nf* NAUT galley ; **quelle galère!** *fig* what a hassle!, what a drag!

galérer [18] [galere] *vi fam* to have a hard time.

galerie [galri] *nf* 1. [gén] gallery ; **galerie marchande** OU **commerciale** shopping arcade - 2. THÉÂTRE circle - 3. [porte-bagages] roof rack *UK.*

galet [galɛ] *nm* 1. [caillou] pebble - 2. TECHNOL wheel, roller.

galette [galɛt] *nf* CULIN pancake *(made from buckwheat flour).*

galipette [galipɛt] *nf fam* somersault.

Galles [gal] ▶ **pays.**

gallicisme [galisism] *nm* [expression] French idiom ; [dans une langue étrangère] gallicism.

gallois, e [galwa, az] *adj* Welsh. **gallois** *nm* [langue] Welsh. **Gallois, e** *nm, f* Welshman *(f* Welshwoman) ; **les Gallois** the Welsh.

galon [galɔ̃] *nm* 1. COUT braid *(U)* - 2. MIL stripe.

galop [galo] *nm* [allure] gallop ; **au galop** [cheval] at a gallop ; *fig* at the double *UK*, on the double *US.*

galoper [3] [galope] *vi* 1. [cheval] to gallop - 2. [personne] to run about - 3. [imagination] to run riot.

galopin [galɔpɛ̃] *nm fam* brat.

galvaniser [3] [galvanize] *vt litt & fig* to galvanize.

galvauder [3] [galvode] *vt* [ternir] to tarnish.

gambader [3] [gɑ̃bade] *vi* [sautiller] to leap about ; [agneau] to gambol.

gamelle [gamɛl] *nf* [plat] mess tin *UK*, kit *US.*

gamin, e [gamɛ̃, in] <> *adj* [puéril] childish. <> *nm, f fam* [enfant] kid.

gamme [gam] *nf* 1. [série] range - 2. MUS scale.

ganglion [gɑ̃glijɔ̃] *nm* ganglion.

gangrène [gɑ̃grɛn] *nf* gangrene ; *fig* corruption, canker.

gangue [gɑ̃g] *nf* 1. [de minerai] gangue - 2. *fig* [carcan] straitjacket.

gant [gɑ̃] *nm* glove ; **gant de toilette** facecloth, flannel *UK.*

garage [garaʒ] *nm* garage.

garagiste [garaʒist] *nmf* [propriétaire] garage owner ; [réparateur] garage mechanic.

garant, e [garɑ̃, ɑ̃t] *nm, f* [responsable] guarantor ; **se porter garant de** to vouch for. **garant** *nm* [garantie] guarantee.

garantie [garɑ̃ti] *nf* [gén] guarantee. **sous garantie** *loc adj* under guarantee ; **un appareil sous garantie** an appliance under guarantee.

garantir [32] [garɑ̃tir] *vt* 1. [assurer, COMM & FIN] to guarantee *UK*, to collateralize *US* ; **garantir à qqn que** to assure OU guarantee sb that - 2. [protéger] : **garantir qqch (de)** to protect sthg (from).

garçon [garsɔ̃] *nm* 1. [enfant] boy - 2. [célibataire] : **vieux garçon** confirmed bachelor - 3. [serveur] : **garçon (de café)** waiter.

garçonnet [garsɔnɛ] *nm* little boy.

garçonnière [garsɔnjɛr] *nf* bachelor flat *UK* OU apartment *US.*

garde [gard] <> *nf* 1. [surveillance] protection - 2. [veille] : **pharmacie de garde** duty chemist *UK*, emergency drugstore *US* - 3. MIL guard ; **monter la garde** to go on guard ; **être/se tenir sur ses gardes** to be/stay on one's guard ; **mettre qqn en garde contre**

qqch to put sb on their guard about sthg ; **mise en garde** warning. <> *nmf* keeper ; **garde du corps** bodyguard ; **garde d'enfants** childminder *UK*, babysitter *US*.

garde-à-vous [gardavu] *nm inv* attention ; **se mettre au garde-à-vous** to stand to attention.

garde-boue [gardəbu] *nm inv* mudguard, fender *US*.

garde-chasse [gardəʃas] (*pl* **gardes-chasse** OU **gardes-chasses**) *nm* gamekeeper.

garde-fou [gardəfu] (*pl* **garde-fous**) *nm* railing, parapet.

garde-malade [gardəmalad] (*pl* **gardes-malades**) *nmf* nurse.

garde-manger [gardəmãʒe] *nm inv* [pièce] pantry, larder ; [armoire] meat safe *UK*, cooler *US*.

garde-pêche [gardəpεʃ] (*pl* **gardes-pêche**) *nm* [personne] water bailiff *UK*, fishwarden *US*.

garder [3] [garde] *vt* **1.** [gén] to keep ; [vêtement] to keep on - **2.** [surveiller] to mind, to look after ; [défendre] to guard - **3.** [protéger] : **garder qqn de qqch** to save sb from sthg. ◆ **se garder** *vp* **1.** [se conserver] to keep - **2.** [se méfier] : **se garder de qqn/qqch** to beware of sb/sthg - **3.** [s'abstenir] : **se garder de faire qqch** to take care not to do sthg.

garderie [gardəri] *nf* crèche *UK*, day nursery *UK*, day-care center *US*.

garde-robe [gardərɔb] (*pl* **garde-robes**) *nf* wardrobe.

gardien, enne [gardjɛ̃, εn] *nm, f* **1.** [surveillant] guard, keeper ; **gardien de but** goalkeeper ; **gardien de nuit** night watchman - **2.** *fig* [défenseur] protector, guardian - **3.** [agent] : **gardien de la paix** policeman.

gare¹ [gar] *nf* station ; **gare routière** [de marchandises] road haulage depot *UK* ; [pour passagers] bus station.

gare² [gar] *interj* [attention] watch out ! ; **gare aux voleurs** watch out for pickpockets.

garer [3] [gare] *vt* **1.** [ranger] to park - **2.** [mettre à l'abri] to put in a safe place. ◆ **se garer** *vp* **1.** [stationner] to park - **2.** [se ranger] to pull over.

gargariser [3] [gargarize] ◆ **se gargariser** *vp* **1.** [se rincer] to gargle - **2.** *péj* [se délecter] : **se gargariser de** to delight OU revel in.

gargouiller [3] [garguje] *vi* **1.** [eau] to gurgle - **2.** [intestins] to rumble.

garnement [garnəmã] *nm* rascal, pest.

garni [garni] *nm vieilli* furnished accommodation *(U)* *UK* OU accommodations *(pl)* *US*.

Garnier [garnje] *npr* : **le palais Garnier** the old Paris Opera House.

garnir [32] [garnir] *vt* **1.** [équiper] to fit out, to furnish - **2.** [remplir] to fill - **3.** [orner] : **garnir qqch de** to decorate sthg with ; **COUT** to trim sthg with.

garnison [garnizɔ̃] *nf* garrison.

garniture [garnityr] *nf* **1.** [ornement] trimming ; [de lit] bed linen - **2.** [CULIN - pour accompagner] garnish *UK*, fixings *pl US* ; [- pour remplir] filling.

garrigue [garig] *nf* scrub.

garrot [garo] *nm* **1.** [de cheval] withers *pl* - **2.** MÉD tourniquet.

gars [ga] *nm fam* **1.** [garçon, homme] lad - **2.** [type] guy, bloke *UK*.

gas-oil [gazɔjl, gazwal], **gazole** [gazɔl] *nm* diesel oil.

gaspillage [gaspijaʒ] *nm* waste.

gaspiller [3] [gaspije] *vt* to waste.

gastrique [gastrik] *adj* gastric.

gastro-entérite [gastrɔ̃ãterit] (*pl* **gastro-entérites**) *nf* gastroenteritis *(U)*.

gastronome [gastrɔnɔm] *nmf* gourmet.

gastronomie [gastrɔnɔmi] *nf* gastronomy.

gâteau, x [gato] *nm* cake ; **gâteau sec** biscuit *UK*, cookie *US*.

gâter [3] [gate] *vt* **1.** [gén] to spoil ; [vacances, affaires] to ruin, to spoil - **2.** *iron* [combler] to be too good to ; **on est gâté !** just marvellous ! ◆ **se gâter** *vp* **1.** [temps] to change for the worse - **2.** [situation] to take a turn for the worse.

gâteux, euse [gatø, øz] *adj* senile.

gauche [goʃ] <> *nf* **1.** [côté] left, left-hand side ; **à gauche (de)** on the left (of) - **2.** POLIT : **la gauche** the left (wing) ; **de gauche** left-wing. <> *adj* **1.** [côté] left - **2.** [personne] clumsy.

gaucher, ère [goʃe, εr] <> *adj* left-handed. <> *nm, f* left-handed person.

gauchiste [goʃist] *nmf* leftist.

gaufre [gofr] *nf* waffle.

gaufrer [3] [gofre] *vt* to emboss.

gaufrette [gofrεt] *nf* wafer.

gaule [gol] *nf* **1.** [perche] pole - **2.** [canne à pêche] fishing rod.

gauler [3] [gole] *vt* to bring OU shake down.

gaulliste [golist] *nmf & adj* Gaullist.

gaulois, e [golwa, az] *adj* [de Gaule] Gallic. ◆ **Gaulois, e** *nm, f* Gaul.

gaver [3] [gave] *vt* **1.** [animal] to force-feed - **2.** [personne] : **gaver qqn de** to feed sb full of.

gay [gε] *adj inv & nm* gay.

gaz [gaz] *nm inv* gas.

gaze [gaz] *nf* gauze.

gazelle [gazɛl] *nf* gazelle.

gazer [3] [gaze] *vt* to gas.

gazette [gazɛt] *nf* newspaper, gazette.

gazeux, euse [gazø, øz] *adj* **1.** CHIM gaseous - **2.** [boisson] fizzy.

gazoduc [gazɔdyk] *nm* gas pipeline.

gazole = gas-oil.

gazon [gazɔ̃] *nm* [herbe] grass ; [terrain] lawn.

gazouiller [3] [gazuje] *vi* **1.** [oiseau] to chirp, to twitter - **2.** [bébé] to gurgle.

GB, G-B (*abr écrite de* Grande-Bretagne) *nf* GB.

gd *abr écrite de* grand.

GDF, Gdf (*abr de* Gaz de France) *French national gas company.*

geai [ʒɛ] *nm* jay.

géant, e [ʒeɑ̃, ɑ̃t] ◇ *adj* gigantic, giant. ◇ *nm, f* giant.

geindre [81] [ʒɛ̃dr] *vi* **1.** [gémir] to moan - **2.** *fam* [pleurnicher] to whine.

gel [ʒɛl] *nm* **1.** MÉTÉOR frost - **2.** [d'eau] freezing - **3.** [cosmétique] gel.

gélatine [ʒelatin] *nf* gelatine.

gelée [ʒəle] *nf* **1.** MÉTÉOR frost - **2.** CULIN jelly.

geler [25] [ʒəle] *vt & vi* **1.** [gén] to freeze - **2.** [projet] to halt.

gélule [ʒelyl] *nf* capsule.

Gémeaux [ʒemo] *nmpl* ASTROL Gemini.

gémir [32] [ʒemir] *vi* **1.** [gén] to moan - **2.** [par déception] to groan.

gémissement [ʒemismɑ̃] *nm* **1.** [gén] moan ; [du vent] moaning *(U)* - **2.** [de déception] groan.

gemme [ʒɛm] *nf* gem, precious stone.

gênant, e [ʒɛnɑ̃, ɑ̃t] *adj* **1.** [encombrant] in the way - **2.** [embarrassant] awkward, embarrassing - **3.** [énervant] : **être gênant** to be a nuisance.

gencive [ʒɑ̃siv] *nf* gum.

gendarme [ʒɑ̃darm] *nm* policeman.

gendarmerie [ʒɑ̃darməri] *nf* **1.** [corps] police force - **2.** [lieu] police station.

gendre [ʒɑ̃dr] *nm* son-in-law.

gène [ʒɛn] *nm* gene.

gêne [ʒɛn] *nf* **1.** [physique] difficulty - **2.** [psychologique] embarrassment - **3.** [financière] difficulty.

généalogie [ʒenealɔʒi] *nf* genealogy.

généalogique [ʒenealɔʒik] *adj* genealogical ; **arbre généalogique** family tree.

gêner [4] [ʒene] *vt* **1.** [physiquement - gén] to be too tight for ; [- suj: chaussures] to pinch - **2.** [moralement] to embarrass - **3.** [incommoder] to bother - **4.** [encombrer] to hamper.

général, e, aux [ʒeneral, o] *adj* general ; **en général** generally, in general ; **répétition générale** dress rehearsal. ▪▪ **général** *nm* MIL general. ▪▪ **générale** *nf* THÉÂTRE dress rehearsal.

généralement [ʒeneralmɑ̃] *adv* generally.

généralisation [ʒeneralizasjɔ̃] *nf* generalization.

généraliser [3] [ʒeneralize] *vt & vi* to generalize. ▪▪ **se généraliser** *vp* to become general OU widespread.

généraliste [ʒeneralist] ◇ *nmf* GP *UK*, family doctor. ◇ *adj* general.

généralité [ʒeneralite] *nf* **1.** [idée] generality - **2.** [universalité] general nature. ▪▪ **généralités** *nfpl* generalities.

générateur, trice [ʒeneratœr, tris] *adj* generating. ▪▪ **générateur** *nm* TECHNOL generator.

génération [ʒenerasjɔ̃] *nf* generation.

générer [18] [ʒenere] *vt* to generate.

généreux, euse [ʒenerø, øz] *adj* generous ; [terre] fertile.

générique [ʒenerik] ◇ *adj* generic ; **médicament générique** MÉD generic drug. ◇ *nm* **1.** CINÉ & TV credits *pl* - **2.** MÉD generic drug.

générosité [ʒenerɔzite] *nf* generosity.

genèse [ʒənɛz] *nf* [création] genesis. ▪▪ **Genèse** *nf* [bible] Genesis.

genêt [ʒənɛ] *nm* broom.

génétique [ʒenetik] ◇ *adj* genetic. ◇ *nf* genetics *(U)*.

Genève [ʒənɛv] *npr* Geneva.

génial, e, aux [ʒenjal, o] *adj* **1.** [personne] of genius - **2.** [idée, invention] inspired - **3.** *fam* [formidable] : **c'est génial!** that's great!, that's terrific!

génie [ʒeni] *nm* **1.** [personne, aptitude] genius - **2.** MYTHOL spirit, genie - **3.** TECHNOL engineering ; **le génie** MIL ≃ the Royal Engineers *UK*, ≃ the (Army) Corps of Engineers *US*.

genièvre [ʒənjɛvr] *nm* juniper.

génisse [ʒenis] *nf* heifer.

génital, e, aux [ʒenital, o] *adj* genital.

génitif [ʒenitif] *nm* genitive (case).

génocide [ʒenɔsid] *nm* genocide.

génotype [ʒenɔtip] *nm* genotype.

genou, x [ʒənu] *nm* knee ; **à genoux** on one's knees, kneeling.

genouillère [ʒənujɛr] *nf* **1.** [bandage] knee bandage - **2.** SPORT kneepad.

genre [ʒɑ̃r] *nm* **1.** [type] type, kind - **2.** LITTÉR genre - **3.** [style de personne] style - **4.** GRAMM gender.

gens [ʒɑ̃] *nmpl* people.

gentiane [ʒɑ̃sjan] *nf* gentian.

gentil, ille [ʒɑ̃ti, ij] *adj* **1.** [agréable] nice - **2.** [aimable] kind, nice.

gentillesse [ʒɑ̃tijɛs] *nf* kindness.

gentiment [ʒɑ̃timɑ̃] *adv* **1.** [sagement] nicely - **2.** [aimablement] kindly, nicely - **3.** *Suisse* [tranquillement] calmly, quietly.

génuflexion [ʒenyfleksjɔ̃] *nf* genuflexion.

géographie [ʒeɔgrafi] *nf* geography.

geôlier, ère [ʒolje, ɛr] *nm, f* gaoler *UK*, jailer *US*.

géologie [ʒeɔlɔʒi] *nf* geology.

géologue [ʒeɔlɔg] *nmf* geologist.

géomètre [ʒeɔmɛtr] *nmf* **1.** [spécialiste] geometer, geometrician - **2.** [technicien] surveyor.

géométrie [ʒeɔmetri] *nf* geometry.

gérance [ʒerɑ̃s] *nf* management.

géranium [ʒeranjɔm] *nm* geranium.

gérant, e [ʒerɑ̃, ɑ̃t] *nm, f* manager.

gerbe [ʒɛrb] *nf* **1.** [de blé] sheaf ; [de fleurs] spray - **2.** [d'étincelles, d'eau] shower.

gercé, e [ʒerse] *adj* chapped.

gérer [18] [ʒere] *vt* to manage.

gériatrie [ʒerjatri] *nf* geriatrics (*U*).

germain, e [ʒermɛ̃, ɛn] ► cousin.

germanique [ʒermanik] *adj* Germanic.

germe [ʒerm] *nm* **1.** BOT & MÉD germ ; [de pomme de terre] eye - **2.** *fig* [origine] seed, cause.

germer [3] [ʒerme] *vi* to germinate.

gésier [ʒezje] *nm* gizzard.

gésir [49] [ʒezir] *vi litt* to lie.

gestation [ʒɛstasjɔ̃] *nf* gestation.

geste [ʒɛst] *nm* **1.** [mouvement] gesture - **2.** [acte] act, deed.

gesticuler [3] [ʒɛstikyle] *vi* to gesticulate.

gestion [ʒɛstjɔ̃] *nf* **1.** [activité] management - **2.** DR administration - **3.** INFORM : gestion de fichiers file management.

Ghana [gana] *nm* : le Ghana Ghana.

ghetto [gɛto] *nm litt & fig* ghetto.

gibet [ʒibɛ] *nm* gallows *sg*, gibbet.

gibier [ʒibje] *nm* game ; *fig* [personne] prey.

giboulée [ʒibule] *nf* sudden shower.

gicler [3] [ʒikle] *vi* to squirt, to spurt.

gifle [ʒifl] *nf* slap.

gifler [3] [ʒifle] *vt* to slap ; *fig* [suj: vent, pluie] to whip, to lash.

gigantesque [ʒigɑ̃tɛsk] *adj* gigantic.

gigolo [ʒigɔlo] *nm* gigolo.

gigot [ʒigo] *nm* CULIN leg.

gigoter [3] [ʒigɔte] *vi* to squirm, to wriggle.

gilet [ʒilɛ] *nm* **1.** [cardigan] cardigan - **2.** [sans manches] waistcoat *UK*, vest *US*.

gin [dʒin] *nm* gin.

gingembre [ʒɛ̃ʒɑ̃br] *nm* ginger.

girafe [ʒiraf] *nf* giraffe.

giratoire [ʒiratwar] *adj* gyrating ; sens giratoire roundabout *UK*, traffic circle *US*.

girofle [ʒirɔfl] ► clou.

girouette [ʒirwɛt] *nf* weathercock.

gisement [ʒizmɑ̃] *nm* deposit.

gît ► gésir.

gitan, e [ʒitɑ̃, an] *adj* Gipsy (*avant n*). ► Gitan, e *nm, f* Gipsy.

gîte [ʒit] *nm* **1.** [logement] : gîte (rural) gîte self-catering accommodation in the country - **2.** [du bœuf] shin *UK*, shank *US*.

givre [ʒivr] *nm* frost.

glabre [glabr] *adj* hairless.

glace [glas] *nf* **1.** [eau congelée] ice - **2.** [crème glacée] ice cream - **3.** [vitre] pane ; [de voiture] window - **4.** [miroir] mirror.

glacé, e [glase] *adj* **1.** [gelé] frozen - **2.** [très froid] freezing - **3.** *fig* [hostile] cold - **4.** [dessert] iced ; [viande] glazed ; [fruit] glacé.

glacer [16] [glase] *vt* **1.** [geler, paralyser] to chill - **2.** [étoffe, papier] to glaze - **3.** [gâteau] to ice *UK*, to frost *US*.

glacial, e, aux [glasjal, o] *adj litt & fig* icy.

glacier [glasje] *nm* **1.** GÉOGR glacier - **2.** [marchand] ice cream seller ou man.

glaçon [glasɔ̃] *nm* **1.** [dans boisson] ice cube - **2.** [sur toit] icicle - **3.** *fam fig* [personne] iceberg.

glaïeul [glajœl] *nm* gladiolus.

glaire [glɛr] *nf* MÉD phlegm.

glaise [glɛz] *nf* clay.

glaive [glɛv] *nm* sword.

gland [glɑ̃] *nm* **1.** [de chêne] acorn - **2.** [ornement] tassel - **3.** ANAT glans.

glande [glɑ̃d] *nf* gland.

glaner [3] [glane] *vt* to glean.

glapir [32] [glapir] *vi* to yelp, to yap.

glas [gla] *nm* knell.

glauque [glok] *adj* **1.** [couleur] bluey-green - **2.** *fam* [lugubre] gloomy - **3.** *fam* [sordide] sordid.

glissade [glisad] *nf* slip.

glissant, e [glisɑ̃, ɑ̃t] *adj* slippery.

glissement [glismɑ̃] *nm* **1.** [action de glisser] gliding, sliding - **2.** *fig* [électoral] swing, shift.

glisser [3] [glise] ◇ *vi* **1.** [se déplacer] : glisser (sur) to glide (over), to slide (over) - **2.** [déraper] : glisser (sur) to slip (on) - **3.** *fig* [passer rapidement] : glisser sur to skate over - **4.** [surface] to be slippery - **5.** [progresser] to slip ; **glisser dans** to slip into, to slide into ; **glisser vers** to slip towards ou toward US, to slide towards ou toward US - **6.** INFORM to drag. <> vt to slip ; **glisser un regard à qqn** fig to give sb a sidelong glance. ➤ **se glisser** vp to slip ; **se glisser dans** [lit] to slip ou slide into ; fig to slip ou creep into.

glissière [glisjɛr] nf runner.

global, e, aux [glɔbal, o] adj global.

globalement [glɔbalmɑ̃] adv on the whole.

globe [glɔb] nm **1.** [sphère, terre] globe - **2.** [de verre] glass cover.

globule [glɔbyl] nm corpuscle, blood cell ; **globule blanc/rouge** white/red corpuscle.

globuleux [glɔbylø] ➤ œil.

gloire [glwar] nf **1.** [renommée] glory ; [de vedette] fame, stardom - **2.** [mérite] credit.

glorieux, euse [glɔrjø, øz] adj [mort, combat] glorious ; [héros, soldat] renowned.

glossaire [glɔsɛr] nm glossary.

glousser [3] [gluse] vi **1.** [poule] to cluck - **2.** fam [personne] to chortle, to chuckle.

glouton, onne [glutɔ̃, ɔn] <> adj greedy. <> nm, f glutton.

glu [gly] nf [colle] glue.

gluant, e [glyɑ̃, ɑ̃t] adj sticky.

glucide [glysid] nm glucide.

glycémie [glisemi] nf glycaemia.

glycine [glisin] nf wisteria.

go [go] ➤ **tout de go** loc adv straight.

GO (abr de **grandes ondes**) nfpl LW.

goal [gol] nm goalkeeper.

gobelet [gɔblɛ] nm beaker, tumbler.

gober [3] [gɔbe] vt **1.** [avaler] to gulp down - **2.** fam [croire] to swallow.

godet [gɔdɛ] nm **1.** [récipient] jar, pot - **2.** COUT flare.

godiller [3] [gɔdije] vi **1.** [rameur] to scull - **2.** [skieur] to wedeln.

goéland [gɔelɑ̃] nm gull, seagull.

goélette [gɔelɛt] nf schooner.

goguenard, e [gɔgnar, ard] adj mocking.

goinfre [gwɛ̃fr] nmf fam pig.

goitre [gwatr] nm goitre.

golf [gɔlf] nm [sport] golf ; [terrain] golf course.

golfe [gɔlf] nm gulf, bay ; **le golfe de Gascogne** the Bay of Biscay ; **le golfe Persique** the (Persian) Gulf.

gomme [gɔm] nf **1.** [substance, bonbon] gum - **2.** [pour effacer] rubber UK, eraser.

gommer [3] [gɔme] vt to rub out, to erase ; fig to erase.

gond [gɔ̃] nm hinge.

gondole [gɔ̃dɔl] nf gondola.

gondoler [3] [gɔ̃dɔle] vi [bois] to warp ; [carton] to curl.

gonfler [3] [gɔ̃fle] <> vt **1.** [ballon, pneu] to blow up, to inflate ; [rivière, poitrine, yeux] to swell ; [joues] to blow out - **2.** fig [grossir] to exaggerate. <> vi to swell.

gonflette [gɔ̃flɛt] nf fam **faire de la gonflette** to pump iron.

gong [gɔ̃g] nm gong.

gorge [gɔrʒ] nf **1.** [gosier, cou] throat - **2.** (gén pl) [vallée] gorge.

gorgée [gɔrʒe] nf mouthful.

gorger [17] [gɔrʒe] vt : **gorger qqn de qqch** [gaver] to stuff sb with sthg ; [combler] to heap sthg on sb ; **gorger qqch de** to fill sthg with.

gorille [gɔrij] nm [animal] gorilla.

gosier [gozje] nm throat, gullet.

gosse [gɔs] nmf fam kid.

gothique [gɔtik] adj **1.** ARCHIT Gothic - **2.** TYPO : **écriture gothique** Gothic script.

gouache [gwaʃ] nf gouache.

goudron [gudrɔ̃] nm tar.

goudronner [3] [gudrɔne] vt to tar.

gouffre [gufr] nm abyss.

goujat [guʒa] nm boor.

goulet [gulɛ] nm narrows pl.

goulot [gulo] nm neck.

goulu, e [guly] adj greedy, gluttonous.

goupillon [gupijɔ̃] nm **1.** RELIG (holy water) sprinkler - **2.** [à bouteille] bottle brush.

gourd, e [gur, gurd] adj numb.

gourde [gurd] <> nf **1.** [récipient] flask, water bottle - **2.** fam [personne] clot UK. <> adj fam thick.

gourdin [gurdɛ̃] nm club.

gourmand, e [gurmɑ̃, ɑ̃d] <> adj greedy. <> nm, f glutton.

gourmandise [gurmɑ̃diz] nf **1.** [caractère] greed, greediness - **2.** [sucrerie] sweet thing.

gourmette [gurmɛt] nf chain bracelet.

gousse [gus] nf pod ; **gousse d'ail** clove of garlic.

goût [gu] nm taste ; **de mauvais goût** tasteless, in bad taste ; **chacun ses goûts, à chacun son goût** each to his own.

goûter [3] [gute] <> vt **1.** [déguster] to taste - **2.** [savourer] to enjoy. <> vi to have an afternoon snack ; **goûter à** to taste. <> nm afternoon snack for children, typically consisting of bread, butter, chocolate and a drink.

goutte [gut] nf **1.** [de pluie, d'eau] drop - **2.** MÉD [maladie] gout. ➤ **gouttes** nfpl MÉD drops.

goutte-à-goutte [gutagut] *nm inv* (intravenous) drip *UK*, IV *US*.

gouttelette [gutlɛt] *nf* droplet.

gouttière [gutjɛr] *nf* **1.** [CONSTR - horizontale] gutter ; [- verticale] drainpipe - **2.** MÉD splint.

gouvernail [guvɛrnaj] *nm* rudder.

gouvernante [guvɛrnãt] *nf* **1.** [d'enfants] governess - **2.** [de maison] housekeeper.

gouvernement [guvɛrnəmã] *nm* POLIT government.

gouverner [3] [guvɛrne] *vt* to govern.

gouverneur [guvɛrnœr] *nm* governor.

GPS (*abr de* **global positionning system**) *nm* GPS.

grâce [gras] *nf* **1.** [charme] grace ; **de bonne grâce** with good grace, willingly ; **de mauvaise grâce** with bad grace, reluctantly - **2.** [faveur] favour *UK*, favor *US* - **3.** [miséricorde] mercy. ⬤ **grâce à** *loc prép* thanks to.

gracier [9] [grasje] *vt* to pardon.

gracieusement [grasjøzmã] *adv* **1.** [avec grâce] graciously - **2.** [gratuitement] free (of charge).

gracieux, euse [grasjø, øz] *adj* **1.** [charmant] graceful - **2.** [gratuit] free.

gradation [gradasjɔ̃] *nf* gradation.

grade [grad] *nm* [échelon] rank ; [universitaire] qualification.

gradé, e [grade] ⬤ *adj* non-commissioned. ⬤ *nm, f* non-commissioned officer, NCO.

gradin [gradɛ̃] *nm* [de stade, de théâtre] tier ; [de terrain] terrace.

graduation [graduasjɔ̃] *nf* graduation.

graduel, elle [graduɛl] *adj* gradual ; [difficultés] increasing.

graduer [7] [gradue] *vt* **1.** [récipient, règle] to graduate - **2.** *fig* [effort, travail] to increase gradually.

graff [graf] (*abr de* **graffiti**) *nm* (piece of) graffiti.

graffiti [grafiti] *nm inv* graffiti *(U)*.

grain [grɛ̃] *nm* **1.** [gén] grain ; [de moutarde] seed ; [de café] bean ; **grain de raisin** grape - **2.** [point] : **grain de beauté** mole, beauty spot - **3.** [averse] squall.

graine [grɛn] *nf* BOT seed.

graisse [grɛs] *nf* **1.** ANAT & CULIN fat - **2.** [pour lubrifier] grease.

graisser [4] [grese] *vt* **1.** [machine] to grease, to lubricate - **2.** [vêtements] to get grease on.

grammaire [gramɛr] *nf* grammar.

grammatical, e, aux [gramatikal, o] *adj* grammatical.

gramme [gram] *nm* gram, gramme *UK*.

grand, e [grã, grãd] *adj* **1.** [en hauteur] tall ; [en dimensions] big, large ; [en quantité, nombre] large, great ; **un grand nombre de** a large ou great number of ; **en grand** [dimension] full-size - **2.** [âgé] grown-up ; **les grandes personnes** grown-ups ; **grand frère** big ou older brother - **3.** [important, remarquable] great ; **un grand homme** a great man - **4.** [intense] : **un grand blessé/brûlé** a person with serious wounds/burns ; **un grand buveur/fumeur** a heavy drinker/smoker. ⬤ *nm, f* (*gén pl*) **1.** [personnage] great man (*f* woman) ; **c'est l'un des grands de l'électroménager** he's one of the big names in electrical appliances - **2.** [enfant] older ou bigger boy (*f* girl).

grand-angle [grãtãgl] *nm* wide-angle lens.

grand-chose [grãʃoz] ⬤ **pas grand-chose** *pron indéf* not much.

Grande-Bretagne [grãdbrətaɲ] *nf* : **la Grande-Bretagne** Great Britain.

grandeur [grãdœr] *nf* **1.** [taille] size - **2.** *fig* [apogée] greatness ; **grandeur d'âme** *fig* magnanimity.

grandir [32] [grãdir] ⬤ *vt* : **grandir qqn** [suj: chaussures] to make sb look taller ; *fig* to increase sb's standing. ⬤ *vi* [personne, plante] to grow ; [obscurité, bruit] to increase, to grow.

grand-mère [grãmɛr] *nf* grandmother ; *fam fig* old biddy.

grand-père [grãpɛr] *nm* grandfather ; *fam fig* old geezer.

grands-parents [grãparã] *nmpl* grandparents.

grange [grãʒ] *nf* barn.

granit(e) [granit] *nm* granite.

granulé, e [granyle] *adj* [surface] granular. ⬤ **granulé** *nm* tablet.

granuleux, euse [granylø, øz] *adj* granular.

graphique [grafik] ⬤ *nm* diagram ; [courbe] graph. ⬤ *adj* graphic.

graphisme [grafism] *nm* **1.** [écriture] handwriting - **2.** ART style of drawing.

graphologie [grafɔlɔʒi] *nf* graphology.

grappe [grap] *nf* **1.** [de fruits] bunch ; [de fleurs] stem - **2.** [de gens] knot.

grappiller [3] [grapije] *vt litt & fig* to gather, to pick up.

grappin [grapɛ̃] *nm* [ancre] grapnel.

gras, grasse [grã, gras] *adj* **1.** [personne, animal] fat - **2.** [plat, aliment] fatty ; **matières grasses** fats - **3.** [cheveux, mains] greasy - **4.** [sol] clayey ; [crayon] soft - **5.** *fig* [rire] throaty ; [toux] phlegmy. **gras** <> nm **1.** [du jambon] fat - **2.** TYPO bold (type) - **3.** [substance] grease. <> adv : **manger gras** to eat fatty foods.

grassement [grasmɑ̃] adv **1.** [rire] coarsely - **2.** [payer] a lot.

gratifier [9] [gratifje] vt **1.** [accorder] : **gratifier qqn de qqch** to present sb with sthg, to present sthg to sb ; fig to reward sb with sthg - **2.** [stimuler] to gratify.

gratin [gratɛ̃] nm **1.** CULIN dish sprinkled with breadcrumbs or cheese and browned ; **gratin dauphinois** sliced potatoes baked with cream and browned on top - **2.** fam fig [haute société] upper crust.

gratiné, e [gratine] adj **1.** CULIN sprinkled with breadcrumbs or cheese and browned - **2.** fam fig [ardu] stiff.

gratis [gratis] adv free.

gratitude [gratityd] nf : **gratitude (envers)** gratitude (to ou towards).

gratte-ciel [gratsjɛl] nm inv skyscraper.

grattement [gratmɑ̃] nm scratching.

gratter [3] [grate] <> vt [gén] to scratch ; [pour enlever] to scrape off. <> vi **1.** [démanger] to itch, to be itchy - **2.** fam [écrire] to scribble - **3.** [frapper] : **gratter à la porte** to tap at the door - **4.** fam [travailler] to slave, to slog. **se gratter** vp to scratch.

gratuit, e [gratɥi, it] adj **1.** [entrée] free - **2.** [violence] gratuitous.

gratuitement [gratɥitmɑ̃] adv **1.** [sans payer] free, for nothing - **2.** [sans raison] gratuitously.

gravats [grava] nmpl rubble (U).

grave [grav] <> adj **1.** [attitude, faute, maladie] serious, grave ; **ce n'est pas grave** [ce n'est rien] don't worry about it - **2.** [voix] deep - **3.** LING : **accent grave** grave accent. <> nm (gén pl) MUS low register.

gravement [gravmɑ̃] adv gravely, seriously.

graver [3] [grave] vt **1.** [gén] to engrave - **2.** [bois] to carve - **3.** INFORM to burn.

gravier [gravje] nm gravel (U).

gravillon [gravijɔ̃] nm fine gravel (U).

gravir [32] [gravir] vt to climb.

gravité [gravite] nf **1.** [importance] seriousness, gravity - **2.** PHYS gravity.

graviter [3] [gravite] vi **1.** [astre] to revolve - **2.** fig [évoluer] to gravitate.

gravure [gravyr] nf **1.** [technique] : **gravure (sur)** engraving (on) - **2.** [reproduction] print ; [dans livre] plate.

gré [gre] nm **1.** [goût] : **à mon/son gré** for my/his taste, for my/his liking - **2.** [volonté] : **bon gré mal gré** willy nilly ; **de gré ou**

de force fig whether you/they etc like it or not ; **de mon/son plein gré** of my/his own free will.

grec, grecque [grɛk] adj Greek. **grec** nm [langue] Greek. **Grec, Grecque** nm, f Greek.

Grèce [grɛs] nf : **la Grèce** Greece.

gréement [gremɑ̃] nm rigging.

greffe [grɛf] nf **1.** MÉD transplant ; [de peau] graft - **2.** BOT graft.

greffer [4] [grɛfe] vt **1.** MÉD to transplant ; [peau] to graft ; **greffer un rein/un cœur à qqn** to give sb a kidney/heart transplant - **2.** BOT to graft. **se greffer** vp : **se greffer sur qqch** to be added to sthg.

greffier [grɛfje] nm clerk of the court.

grégaire [gregɛr] adj gregarious.

grêle [grɛl] <> nf hail. <> adj **1.** [jambes] spindly - **2.** [son] shrill.

grêler [4] [grele] v impers to hail ; **il grêle** it's hailing.

grêlon [grelɔ̃] nm hailstone.

grelot [grəlo] nm bell.

grelotter [3] [grəlɔte] vi : **grelotter (de)** to shiver (with).

grenade [grənad] nf **1.** [fruit] pomegranate - **2.** MIL grenade.

grenat [grəna] adj inv dark red.

grenier [grənje] nm **1.** [de maison] attic - **2.** [à foin] loft.

grenouille [grənuj] nf frog.

grès [grɛ] nm **1.** [roche] sandstone - **2.** [poterie] stoneware.

grésiller [3] [grezije] vi **1.** [friture] to sizzle ; [feu] to crackle - **2.** [radio] to crackle.

grève [grɛv] nf **1.** [arrêt du travail] strike ; **être en grève** to be on strike ; **faire grève** to strike, to go on strike - **2.** [rivage] shore.

grever [19] [grəve] vt to burden ; [budget] to put a strain on.

gréviste [grevist] nmf striker.

gribouiller [3] [gribuje] vt & vi **1.** [écrire] to scrawl - **2.** [dessiner] to doodle.

grief [grijɛf] nm grievance ; **faire grief de qqch à qqn** to hold sthg against sb.

grièvement [grijɛvmɑ̃] adv seriously.

griffe [grif] nf **1.** [d'animal] claw - **2.** Belgique [éraflure] scratch.

griffer [3] [grife] vt [suj: chat etc] to claw.

grignoter [3] [griɲɔte] <> vt **1.** [manger] to nibble - **2.** fam fig [réduire - capital] to eat away (at) - **3.** fam fig [gagner - avantage] to gain. <> vi **1.** [manger] to nibble - **2.** fam fig [prendre] : **grignoter sur** nibble away at.

gril [gril] nm grill.

grillade [grijad] nf CULIN grilled meat.

grillage [grijaʒ] *nm* **1.** [de porte, de fenêtre] wire netting - **2.** [clôture] wire fence.

grille [grij] *nf* **1.** [portail] gate - **2.** [d'orifice, de guichet] grille ; [de fenêtre] bars *pl* - **3.** [de mots croisés, de loto] grid - **4.** [tableau] table.

grille-pain [grijpɛ̃] *nm inv* toaster.

griller [3] [grije] <> *vt* **1.** [viande] to grill *UK*, to broil *US* ; [pain] to toast ; [café, marrons] to roast - **2.** *fig* [au soleil - personne] to burn ; [- végétation] to shrivel - **3.** *fam fig* [dépasser - concurrents] to outstrip ; **griller un feu rouge** to jump the lights - **4.** *fig* [compromettre] to ruin. <> *vi* **1.** [viande] to grill *UK*, to broil *US* - **2.** [ampoule] to blow.

grillon [grijɔ̃] *nm* [insecte] cricket.

grimace [grimas] *nf* grimace.

grimer [3] [grime] *vt* CINÉ & THÉÂTRE to make up.

grimper [3] [grɛ̃pe] <> *vt* to climb. <> *vi* to climb ; **grimper à un arbre/une échelle** to climb a tree/a ladder.

grincement [grɛ̃smɑ̃] *nm* [de charnière] squeaking ; [de porte, plancher] creaking.

grincer [16] [grɛ̃se] *vi* [charnière] to squeak ; [porte, plancher] to creak.

grincheux, euse [grɛ̃ʃø, øz] <> *adj* grumpy. <> *nm, f* moaner, grumbler.

grippe [grip] *nf* MÉD flu *(U)*.

grippé, e [gripe] *adj* [malade] : **être grippé** to have flu.

gripper [3] [gripe] *vi* **1.** [mécanisme] to jam - **2.** *fig* [processus] to stall.

gris, e [gri, griz] *adj* **1.** [couleur] grey *UK*, gray *US* - **2.** [morne] dismal - **3.** [saoul] tipsy. <> **gris** *nm* [couleur] grey *UK*, gray *US*.

grisaille [grizaj] *nf* **1.** [de ciel] greyness *UK*, grayness *US* - **2.** *fig* [de vie] dullness.

grisant, e [grizɑ̃, ɑ̃t] *adj* intoxicating.

griser [3] [grize] *vt* to intoxicate.

grisonner [3] [grizɔne] *vi* to turn grey *UK* OU gray *US*.

grisou [grizu] *nm* firedamp.

grive [griv] *nf* thrush.

grivois, e [grivwa, az] *adj* ribald.

Groenland [grɔɛnlɑ̃d] *nm* : **le Groenland** Greenland.

grog [grɔg] *nm* (hot) toddy.

grognement [grɔɲmɑ̃] *nm* **1.** [son] grunt ; [d'ours, de chien] growl - **2.** [protestation] grumble.

grogner [3] [grɔɲe] *vi* **1.** [émettre un son] to grunt ; [ours, chien] to growl - **2.** [protester] to grumble.

groin [grwɛ̃] *nm* snout.

grommeler [24] [grɔmle] *vt & vi* to mutter.

grondement [grɔ̃dmɑ̃] *nm* [d'animal] growl ; [de tonnerre, de train] rumble ; [torrent] roar.

gronder [3] [grɔ̃de] <> *vi* [animal] to growl ; [tonnerre] to rumble. <> *vt* to scold.

gros, grosse [gro, gros] *adj (gén avant n)* **1.** [gén] large, big ; *péj* big - **2.** *(avant ou après n)* [corpulent] fat - **3.** [grossier] coarse - **4.** [fort, sonore] loud - **5.** [important, grave - ennuis] serious ; [- dépense] major. <> **gros** <> *adv* [beaucoup] a lot. <> *nm* [partie] : **le (plus) gros (de qqch)** the main part (of sthg). <> **en gros** *loc adv & loc adj* **1.** COMM wholesale - **2.** [en grands caractères] in large letters - **3.** [grosso modo] roughly.

groseille [grozɛj] *nf* currant.

grosse [gros] *adj* ► **gros**.

grossesse [grosɛs] *nf* pregnancy.

grosseur [grosœr] *nf* **1.** [dimension, taille] size - **2.** MÉD lump.

grossier, ère [grosje, ɛr] *adj* **1.** [matière] coarse - **2.** [sommaire] rough - **3.** [insolent] rude - **4.** [vulgaire] crude - **5.** [erreur] crass.

grossièrement [grosjɛrmɑ̃] *adv* **1.** [sommairement] roughly - **2.** [vulgairement] crudely.

grossir [32] [grosir] <> *vi* **1.** [prendre du poids] to put on weight ; **faire grossir** to add pounds, to make you put on weight ; [être calorique] to be fattening ; **ça fait grossir** it's fattening - **2.** [augmenter] to grow - **3.** [s'intensifier] to increase. <> *vt* **1.** [suj: microscope, verre] to magnify - **2.** [suj: vêtement] : **grossir qqn** to make sb look fatter - **3.** [exagérer] to exaggerate.

grossiste [grosist] *nmf* wholesaler.

grosso modo [grosomɔdo] *adv* roughly.

grotte [grɔt] *nf* cave.

grouiller [3] [gruje] *vi* : **grouiller (de)** to swarm (with).

groupe [grup] *nm* group ; **groupe armé** armed group. ► **groupe sanguin** *nm* blood group.

groupement [grupmɑ̃] *nm* **1.** [action] grouping - **2.** [groupe] group.

grouper [3] [grupe] *vt* to group. ► **se grouper** *vp* to come together.

grue [gry] *nf* TECHNOL & ZOOL crane.

grumeau, x [grymo] *nm* lump.

grunge [grʌnʒ] *adj* grunge *(modif)*.

guacamole [gwakamol(e)] *nm* guacamole.

Guadeloupe [gwadlup] *nf* : **la Guadeloupe** Guadeloupe.

Guatemala [gwatemala] *nm* : **le Guatemala** Guatemala.

gué [ge] *nm* ford ; **traverser à gué** to ford.

guenilles [gənij] *nfpl* rags.

guenon [gənɔ̃] *nf* female monkey.

guépard [gepar] *nm* cheetah.

guêpe [gɛp] *nf* wasp.

guêpier [gepje] *nm* wasp's nest ; *fig* hornet's nest.

guère [gɛr] *adv* [peu] hardly ; **ne** (+ *verbe*) **guère** [peu] hardly ; **il l'aime guère** he doesn't like him/her very much.

guéridon [geridɔ̃] *nm* pedestal table.

guérilla [gerija] *nf* guerrilla warfare.

guérir [32] [gerir] <> *vt* to cure ; **guérir qqn de** *litt & fig* to cure sb of. <> *vi* to recover, to get better.

guérison [gerizɔ̃] *nf* 1. [de malade] recovery - 2. [de maladie] cure.

guerre [gɛr] *nf* 1. *fig &* MIL war ; **faire la guerre à un pays** to make ou wage war on a country ; **Première/Seconde Guerre mondiale** First/Second World War ; **guerre atomique/nucléaire** atomic/nuclear war ; **guerre de religion** war of religion - 2. [technique] warfare (*U*) ; **guerre biologique/chimique** biological/chemical warfare ; **guerre bactériologique** germ warfare.

guerrier, ère [gɛrje, ɛr] *adj* 1. [de guerre] war (*avant n*) - 2. [peuple] warlike.
◆ **guerrier** *nm* warrior.

guet-apens [gɛtapɑ̃] *nm* ambush ; *fig* trap.

guêtre [gɛtr] *nf* gaiter.

guetter [4] [gete] *vt* 1. [épier] to lie in wait for - 2. [attendre] to be on the look-out for, to watch for - 3. [menacer] to threaten.

gueule [gœl] *nf* 1. [d'animal, ouverture] mouth - 2. *tfam* [bouche de l'homme] gob *UK*, yap *US* - 3. *fam* [visage] face.

gueuleton [gœltɔ̃] *nm fam* blowout.

gui [gi] *nm* mistletoe.

guichet [giʃɛ] *nm* counter ; [de gare, de théâtre] ticket office.

guide [gid] *nm* 1. [gén] guide - 2. [livre] guidebook.

guider [3] [gide] *vt* to guide.

guidon [gidɔ̃] *nm* handlebars *pl*.

guignol [giɲɔl] *nm* 1. [marionnette] glove puppet - 2. [théâtre] ≃ Punch and Judy show.

guillemet [gijmɛ] *nm* inverted comma *UK*, quotation mark.

guilleret, ette [gijrɛ, ɛt] *adj* perky.

guillotine [gijɔtin] *nf* 1. [instrument] guillotine - 2. [de fenêtre] sash.

guindé, e [gɛ̃de] *adj* stiff.

Guinée [gine] *nf* : **la Guinée** Guinea.

guirlande [girlɑ̃d] *nf* 1. [de fleurs] garland - 2. [de papier] chain ; [de Noël] tinsel (*U*).

guise [giz] *nf* : **à ma guise** as I please ou like ; **en guise de** by way of.

guitare [gitar] *nf* guitar.

guitariste [gitarist] *nmf* guitarist.

guttural, e, aux [gytyral, o] *adj* guttural.

Guyane [gɥijan] *nf* : **la Guyane** French Guiana.

gymnastique [ʒimnastik] *nf* SPORT *& fig* gymnastics (*U*) ; **faire de la gymnastique** to do keep-fit exercises *UK*.

gynécologie [ʒinekɔlɔʒi] *nf* gynaecology *UK*, gynecology *US*.

gynécologue [ʒinekɔlɔg] *nmf* gynaecologist *UK*, gynecologist *US*.

h¹, H [aʃ] *nm inv* h, H.

h² (*abr écrite de* **heure**) hr.

H³ 1. *abr écrite de* **homme** - 2. (*abr écrite de* **hydrogène**) H.

ha (*abr écrite de* **hectare**) ha.

hab. *abr écrite de* **habitant**.

habile [abil] *adj* skilful ; [démarche] clever.

habileté [abilte] *nf* skill.

habiller [3] [abije] *vt* 1. [vêtir] : **habiller qqn (de)** to dress sb (in) - 2. [recouvrir] to cover.
◆ **s'habiller** *vp* 1. [se vêtir] to dress, to get dressed - 2. [se vêtir élégamment] to dress up.

habit [abi] *nm* 1. [costume] suit - 2. RELIG habit. ◆ **habits** *nmpl* [vêtements] clothes.

habitacle [abitakl] *nm* [d'avion] cockpit ; [de voiture] passenger compartment.

habitant, e [abitɑ̃, ɑ̃t] *nm, f* 1. [de pays] inhabitant - 2. [d'immeuble] occupant - 3. *Québec* [paysan] farmer.

habitation [abitasjɔ̃] *nf* 1. [fait d'habiter] housing - 2. [résidence] house, home.

habiter [3] [abite] <> *vt* [résider] to live in. <> *vi* to live ; **habiter à** to live in.

habitude [abityd] *nf* [façon de faire] habit ; **avoir l'habitude de faire qqch** to be in the habit of doing sthg ; **d'habitude** usually.

habituel, elle [abitɥɛl] *adj* [coutumier] usual, customary.

habituer [7] [abitɥe] *vt* : **habituer qqn à qqch/à faire qqch** to get sb used to sthg/to doing sthg. ◆ **s'habituer** *vp* : **s'habituer à qqch/à faire qqch** to get used to sthg/to doing sthg.

hache [ˈaʃ] *nf* axe, ax *US*.

hacher [3] ['aʃe] vt 1. [couper - gén] to chop finely ; [- viande] to mince UK, to grind US - 2. [entrecouper] to interrupt.

hachisch = haschisch.

hachoir ['aʃwar] nm 1. [couteau] chopper - 2. [appareil] mincer UK, grinder US - 3. [planche] chopping board, cutting board US.

hachure ['aʃyr] nf hatching.

hagard, e ['agar, ard] adj haggard.

haie ['ε] nf 1. [d'arbustes] hedge - 2. [de personnes] row ; [de soldats, d'agents de police] line - 3. SPORT hurdle.

haillons ['ajɔ̃] nmpl rags.

haine ['εn] nf hatred.

haïr [33] ['aïr] vt to hate.

Haïti [aiti] npr Haiti.

hâle ['al] nm tan.

hâlé, e ['ale] adj tanned.

haleine [alεn] nf breath.

haleter [28] ['alte] vi to pant.

hall ['ol] nm 1. [vestibule, entrée] foyer, lobby - 2. [salle publique] concourse.

halle ['al] nf covered market.

hallucination [alysinasjɔ̃] nf hallucination.

halo ['alo] nm [cercle lumineux] halo.

halogène [alɔʒɛn] nm & adj halogen.

halte ['alt] nf stop. ◇ interj stop!

haltère [altɛr] nm dumbbell.

haltérophilie [alterɔfili] nf weightlifting.

hamac ['amak] nm hammock.

hamburger ['ãburɡœr] nm hamburger.

hameau, x ['amo] nm hamlet.

hameçon [amsɔ̃] nm fishhook.

hamster ['amster] nm hamster.

hanche ['ãʃ] nf hip.

handball ['ãdbal] nm handball.

handicap ['ãdikap] nm handicap.

handicapé, e ['ãdikape] ◇ adj handicapped. ◇ nm, f handicapped person.

handicaper [3] ['ãdikape] vt to handicap.

hangar ['ãgar] nm shed ; AÉRON hangar.

hanneton ['antɔ̃] nm cockchafer.

hanter [3] ['ãte] vt to haunt.

hantise ['ãtiz] nf obsession.

happer [3] ['ape] vt [attraper] to snap up.

haranguer [3] ['arãge] vt to harangue.

haras ['ara] nm stud (farm).

harassant, e ['arasã, ãt] adj exhausting.

harceler [25] ['arsəle] vt 1. [relancer] to harass - 2. MIL to harry - 3. [importuner] : harceler qqn (de) to pester sb (with).

hardes ['ard] nfpl old clothes.

hardi, e ['ardi] adj bold, daring.

hareng ['arã] nm herring.

hargne ['arɲ] nf spite (U), bad temper.

haricot ['ariko] nm bean ; haricots verts/blancs/rouges green ou string/haricot/kidney beans.

harmonica [armɔnika] nm harmonica, mouth organ.

harmonie [armɔni] nf 1. [gén] harmony - 2. [de visage] symmetry.

harmonieux, euse [armɔnjø, øz] adj 1. [gén] harmonious - 2. [voix] melodious - 3. [traits, silhouette] regular.

harmoniser [3] [armɔnize] vt MUS & fig to harmonize ; [salaires] to bring into line.

harnacher [3] ['arnaʃe] vt [cheval] to harness.

harnais ['arnε] nm 1. [de cheval, de parachutiste] harness - 2. TECHNOL train.

harpe ['arp] nf harp.

harpon ['arpɔ̃] nm harpoon.

harponner [3] ['arpɔne] vt 1. [poisson] to harpoon - 2. fam [personne] to collar.

hasard ['azar] nm chance ; au hasard at random ; par hasard by accident, by chance.

hasarder [3] ['azarde] vt 1. [tenter] to venture - 2. [risquer] to hazard. ◆ se hasarder vp : se hasarder à faire qqch to risk doing sthg.

haschisch, haschich, hachisch ['aʃiʃ] nm hashish.

hâte ['at] nf haste.

hâter [3] ['ate] vt 1. [activer] to hasten - 2. [avancer] to bring forward. ◆ se hâter vp to hurry ; se hâter de faire qqch to hurry to do sthg.

hausse ['os] nf [augmentation] rise, increase.

hausser [3] ['ose] vt to raise.

haut, e [o, ot] adj 1. [gén] high ; haut de 20 m 20 m high - 2. [classe sociale, pays, région] upper - 3. [responsable] senior. ◆ haut ◇ adv 1. [gén] high ; [placé] highly - 2. [fort] loudly. ◇ nm 1. [hauteur] height ; faire 2 m de haut to be 2 m high ou in height - 2. [sommet, vêtement] top ; avoir ou connaître des hauts et des bas to have one's ups and downs. ◆ de haut loc adv [avec dédain] haughtily ; le prendre de haut to react haughtily. ◆ de haut en bas loc adv from top to bottom. ◆ du haut de loc prép from the top of. ◆ en haut de loc prép at the top of.

hautain, e ['otε̃, εn] adj haughty.

hautbois ['obwa] nm oboe.

haut de gamme [odgam] ◇ adj upmarket, top-of-the-line US ; une chaîne haut de

gamme a state-of-the-art hi-fi system. ◇ *nm* top of the range, top-of-the-line *US*.

haute-fidélité [otfidelite] *nf* high fidelity, hi-fi.

hautement ['otmɑ̃] *adv* highly.

hauteur ['otœr] *nf* height ; **à hauteur d'épaule** at shoulder level ou height.

haut-fourneau ['ofurno] *nm* blast furnace.

haut-parleur ['oparlœr] (*pl* haut-parleurs) *nm* loudspeaker.

havre ['avr] *nm* [refuge] haven.

Haye ['ɛ] *npr* : **La Haye** the Hague.

hayon ['ajɔ̃] *nm* hatchback.

hebdomadaire [ɛbdɔmadɛr] *nm & adj* weekly.

hébergement [ebɛrʒəmɑ̃] *nm* accommodation *UK*, accommodations (*pl*) *US*.

héberger [17] [ebɛrʒe] *vt* 1. [loger] to put up - 2. [suj: hôtel] to take in.

hébété, e [ebete] *adj* dazed.

hébraïque [ebraik] *adj* Hebrew.

hébreu, x [ebrø] *adj* Hebrew. ➡ **hébreu** *nm* [langue] Hebrew. ➡ **Hébreu, x** *nm* Hebrew.

hécatombe [ekatɔ̃b] *nf litt & fig* slaughter.

hectare [ɛktar] *nm* hectare.

hectolitre [ɛktɔlitr] *nm* hectolitre, hectoliter *US*.

hégémonie [eʒemɔni] *nf* hegemony.

hein ['ɛ̃] *interj fam* eh?, what? ; **tu m'en veux, hein?** you're cross with me, aren't you?

hélas [elas] *interj* unfortunately, alas.

héler [18] ['ele] *vt sout* to hail.

hélice [elis] *nf* 1. [d'avion, de bateau] propeller - 2. MATH helix.

hélicoptère [elikɔptɛr] *nm* helicopter.

héliport [elipɔr] *nm* heliport.

hélium [eljɔm] *nm* helium.

Helsinki ['ɛlsiŋki] *npr* Helsinki.

hématome [ematom] *nm* MÉD h(a)ematoma.

hémicycle [emisikl] *nm* POLIT : **l'hémicycle** the Assemblée Nationale.

hémisphère [emisfɛr] *nm* hemisphere.

hémophile [emɔfil] ◇ *nmf* h(a)emophiliac. ◇ *adj* h(a)emophilic.

hémorragie [emɔraʒi] *nf* 1. MÉD haemorrhage - 2. *fig* [perte, fuite] loss.

hémorroïdes [emɔrɔid] *nfpl* h(a)emorrhoids, piles.

hennir [32] ['enir] *vi* to neigh, to whinny.

hépatite [epatit] *nf* MÉD hepatitis ; **hépatite C** hepatitis C.

herbe [ɛrb] *nf* 1. BOT grass - 2. CULIN & MÉD herb - 3. *fam* [marijuana] grass.

herbicide [ɛrbisid] *nm* weedkiller, herbicide.

herboriste [ɛrbɔrist] *nmf* herbalist.

héréditaire [ereditɛr] *adj* hereditary.

hérédité [eredite] *nf* [génétique] heredity.

hérésie [erezi] *nf* heresy.

hérisson ['erisɔ̃] *nm* ZOOL hedgehog.

héritage [eritaʒ] *nm* 1. [de biens] inheritance - 2. [culturel] heritage.

hériter [3] [erite] ◇ *vi* to inherit ; **hériter de qqch** to inherit sthg. ◇ *vt* : **hériter qqch de qqn** *litt & fig* to inherit sthg from sb.

héritier, ère [eritje, ɛr] *nm, f* heir (*f* heiress).

hermétique [ɛrmetik] *adj* 1. [étanche] hermetic - 2. [incompréhensible] inaccessible, impossible to understand - 3. [impénétrable] impenetrable.

hermine [ɛrmin] *nf* 1. [animal] stoat - 2. [fourrure] ermine.

hernie ['ɛrni] *nf* hernia.

héroïne [erɔin] *nf* 1. [personne] heroine - 2. [drogue] heroin.

héroïque [erɔik] *adj* heroic.

héroïsme [erɔism] *nm* heroism.

héron ['erɔ̃] *nm* heron.

héros ['ero] *nm* hero.

hertz ['ɛrts] *nm inv* hertz.

hésitant, e [ezitɑ̃, ɑ̃t] *adj* hesitant.

hésitation [ezitasjɔ̃] *nf* hesitation.

hésiter [3] [ezite] *vi* to hesitate ; **hésiter entre/sur** to hesitate between/over ; **hésiter à faire qqch** to hesitate to do sthg.

hétéroclite [eterɔklit] *adj* motley.

hétérogène [eterɔʒɛn] *adj* heterogeneous.

hétérosexuel, elle [eterɔsɛksɥel] *adj & nm, f* heterosexual.

hêtre ['ɛtr] *nm* beech.

heure [œr] *nf* 1. [unité de temps] hour ; **250 km à l'heure** 250 km per ou an hour ; **faire des heures supplémentaires** to work overtime - 2. [moment du jour] time ; **il est deux heures** it's two o'clock ; **à quelle heure?** when? ; (at) what time? ; **heure de pointe** rush hour ; **heures de bureau** office hours - 3. [fuseau horaire] : **l'heure d'été** British Summer Time *UK*, daylight (saving) time *US* ; **passer à l'heure d'été/d'hiver** to put the clocks forward/back - 4. SCOL class, period ; **c'est l'heure (de faire qqch)** it's time (to do sthg) ; **de bonne heure** early.

heureusement [œrøzmɑ̃] *adv* [par chance] luckily, fortunately.

heureux, euse [œrø, øz] *adj* **1.** [gén] happy ; [favorable] fortunate ; **être heureux de faire qqch** to be happy to do sthg - **2.** [réussi] successful, happy.

heurt ['œr] *nm* **1.** [choc] collision, impact - **2.** [désaccord] clash.

heurter [3] ['œrte] *vt* **1.** [rentrer dans - gén] to hit ; [- suj: personne] to bump into - **2.** [offenser - personne, sensibilité] to offend - **3.** [bon sens, convenances] to go against. ➤ **se heurter** *vp* **1.** [gén] : **se heurter (contre)** to collide (with) - **2.** [rencontrer] : **se heurter à qqch** to come up against sthg.

hexagonal, e, aux [ɛgzagɔnal, o] *adj* **1.** GÉOM hexagonal - **2.** [français] French.

hexagone [ɛgzagɔn] *nm* GÉOM hexagon. ➤ **Hexagone** *nm* : **l'Hexagone** (metropolitan) France.

hiatus [jatys] *nm inv* hiatus.

hiberner [3] [ibɛrne] *vi* to hibernate.

hibou, x ['ibu] *nm* owl.

hideux, euse ['idø, øz] *adj* hideous.

hier [ijɛr] *adv* yesterday.

hiérarchie ['jerarʃi] *nf* hierarchy.

hiéroglyphe [jerɔglif] *nm* hieroglyph, hieroglyphic.

hilare [ilar] *adj* beaming.

hilarité [ilarite] *nf* hilarity.

Himalaya [imalaja] *nm* : **l'Himalaya** the Himalayas *pl.*

hindou, e [ɛ̃du] *adj* Hindu. ➤ **Hindou, e** *nm, f* Hindu.

hippie, hippy ['ipi] (*pl* **hippies**) *nmf & adj* hippy.

hippique [ipik] *adj* horse (*avant n*).

hippodrome [ipɔdrom] *nm* racecourse, racetrack.

hippopotame [ipɔpɔtam] *nm* hippopotamus.

hirondelle [irɔ̃dɛl] *nf* swallow.

hirsute [irsyt] *adj* [chevelure, barbe] shaggy.

hispanique [ispanik] *adj* [gén] Hispanic.

hisser [3] ['ise] *vt* **1.** [voile, drapeau] to hoist - **2.** [charge] to heave, to haul. ➤ **se hisser** *vp* **1.** [grimper] : **se hisser (sur)** to heave ou haul o.s. up (onto) - **2.** *fig* [s'élever] : **se hisser à** to pull o.s. up to.

histoire [istwar] *nf* **1.** [science] history ; **histoire naturelle** natural history - **2.** [récit, mensonge] story - **3.** [aventure] funny ou strange thing - **4.** (*gén pl*) [ennui] trouble (*U*).

historique [istɔrik] *adj* **1.** [roman, recherches] historical - **2.** [monument, événement] historic.

hit-parade ['itparad] (*pl* **hit-parades**) *nm* : **le hit-parade** the charts *pl.*

hiver [ivɛr] *nm* winter ; **en hiver** in (the) winter.

HLM (*abr de* habitation à loyer modéré) *nm & nf* low-rent, state-owned housing, ≃ council house/flat *UK*, ≃ public housing unit *US*.

hobby ['ɔbi] (*pl* **hobbies**) *nm* hobby.

hocher [3] ['ɔʃe] *vt* : **hocher la tête** [affirmativement] to nod (one's head) ; [négativement] to shake one's head.

hochet ['ɔʃɛ] *nm* rattle.

hockey ['ɔke] *nm* hockey ; **hockey sur glace** ice hockey *UK*, hockey *US*.

holding ['ɔldiŋ] *nm & nf* holding company.

hold-up ['ɔldœp] *nm inv* holdup.

hollandais, e [ˈɔlɑ̃dɛ, ɛz] *adj* Dutch. ➤ **hollandais** *nm* [langue] Dutch. ➤ **Hollandais, e** *nm, f* Dutchman (*f* Dutchwoman).

Hollande [ˈɔlɑ̃d] *nf* : **la Hollande** Holland.

holocauste [ɔlɔkost] *nm* holocaust.

homard [ˈɔmar] *nm* lobster.

homéopathie [ɔmeɔpati] *nf* homeopathy.

homicide [ɔmisid] *nm* [meurtre] murder.

hommage [ɔmaʒ] *nm* [témoignage d'estime] tribute ; **rendre hommage à qqn/qqch** to pay tribute to sb/sthg.

homme [ɔm] *nm* man ; **homme d'affaires** businessman ; **homme d'État** statesman ; **homme politique** politician ; **l'homme de la rue** the man in the street.

homme-grenouille [ɔmgrənuj] *nm* frogman.

homogène [ɔmɔʒɛn] *adj* homogeneous.

homologue [ɔmɔlɔg] *nm* counterpart, opposite number.

homonyme [ɔmɔnim] *nm* **1.** LING homonym - **2.** [personne, ville] namesake.

homophobe [ɔmɔfɔb] *adj* homophobe.

homosexualité [ɔmɔsɛksɥalite] *nf* homosexuality.

homosexuel, elle [ɔmɔsɛksɥɛl] *adj & nm, f* homosexual.

Honduras ['ɔ̃dyras] *nm* : **le Honduras** Honduras.

Hongrie ['ɔ̃gri] *nf* : **la Hongrie** Hungary.

hongrois, e ['ɔ̃grwa, az] *adj* Hungarian. ➤ **hongrois** *nm* [langue] Hungarian. ➤ **Hongrois, e** *nm, f* Hungarian.

honnête [ɔnɛt] *adj* **1.** [intègre] honest - **2.** [correct] honourable *UK*, honorable *US* - **3.** [convenable - travail, résultat] reasonable.

honnêtement [ɔnɛtmɑ̃] *adv* **1.** [de façon intègre, franchement] honestly - **2.** [correctement] honourably *UK*, honorably *US*.

honnêteté [ɔnɛtte] *nf* honesty.

honneur [ɔnœr] *nm* honour *UK*, honor *US* ;

faire honneur à qqn/à qqch to be a credit to sb/to sthg ; **faire honneur à un repas** *fig* to do justice to a meal.

honorable [ɔnɔrabl] *adj* **1.** [digne] honourable *UK*, honorable *US* - **2.** [convenable] respectable.

honoraire [ɔnɔrɛr] *adj* honorary. **honoraires** *nmpl* fee *sg*, fees.

honorer [3] [ɔnɔre] *vt* **1.** [faire honneur à] to be a credit to - **2.** [payer] to honour *UK*, to honor *US*.

honte ['ɔ̃t] *nf* [sentiment] shame ; **avoir honte de qqn/qqch** to be ashamed of sb/sthg ; **avoir honte de faire qqch** to be ashamed of doing sthg.

honteux, euse ['ɔ̃tø, øz] *adj* shameful ; [personne] ashamed.

hooligan, houligan ['uligan] *nm* hooligan.

hôpital, aux [ɔpital, o] *nm* hospital.

hoquet ['ɔkɛ] *nm* hiccup.

horaire [ɔrɛr] <> *nm* **1.** [de départ, d'arrivée] timetable *UK*, schedule *US* - **2.** [de travail] hours *pl* (of work). <> *adj* hourly.

horizon [ɔrizɔ̃] *nm* **1.** [ligne, perspective] horizon - **2.** [panorama] view.

horizontal, e, aux [ɔrizɔ̃tal, o] *adj* horizontal. **horizontale** *nf* MATH horizontal.

horloge [ɔrlɔʒ] *nf* clock.

hormis ['ɔrmi] *prép* save.

hormone [ɔrmɔn] *nf* hormone.

hormonothérapie [ɔrmɔnɔterapi] *nf* MÉD hormone therapy ; [pour femmes ménopausées] hormone replacement therapy.

horodateur [ɔrɔdatœr] *nm* [à l'usine] clock ; [au parking] ticket machine.

horoscope [ɔrɔskɔp] *nm* horoscope.

horreur [ɔrœr] *nf* horror ; **avoir horreur de qqn/qqch** to hate sb/sthg ; **avoir horreur de faire qqch** to hate doing sthg ; **quelle horreur!** how dreadful!, how awful!

horrible [ɔribl] *adj* **1.** [affreux] horrible - **2.** *fig* [terrible] terrible, dreadful.

horrifier [9] [ɔrifje] *vt* to horrify.

horripiler [3] [ɔripile] *vt* to exasperate.

hors ['ɔr] *prép* ▶ **pair, service.** **hors de** *loc prép* outside.

hors-bord ['ɔrbɔr] *nm inv* speedboat.

hors-d'œuvre ['ɔrdœvr] *nm inv* hors d'oeuvre, starter *UK*, appetizer.

hors-jeu ['ɔrʒø] *nm inv & adj inv* offside.

hors-la-loi ['ɔrlalwa] *nm inv* outlaw.

hors-piste ['ɔrpist] *nm inv* off-piste skiing.

hors-série ['ɔrseri] <> *adj inv* special. <> *nm* special issue *ou* edition.

hortensia [ɔrtɑ̃sja] *nm* hydrangea.

horticulture [ɔrtikyltyr] *nf* horticulture.

hospice [ɔspis] *nm* home.

hospitalier, ère [ɔspitalje, ɛr] *adj* **1.** [accueillant] hospitable - **2.** [relatif aux hôpitaux] hospital *(avant n)*.

hospitaliser [3] [ɔspitalize] *vt* to hospitalize.

hospitalité [ɔspitalite] *nf* hospitality.

hostie [ɔsti] *nf* host.

hostile [ɔstil] *adj* : **hostile (à)** hostile (to).

hostilité [ɔstilite] *nf* hostility. **hostilités** *nfpl* hostilities.

hôte, hôtesse [ot, otɛs] *nm, f* host (*f* hostess) ; **hôtesse de l'air** air hostess *UK*, stewardess *US*. **hôte** *nm* [invité] guest.

hôtel [otɛl] *nm* **1.** [d'hébergement] hotel - **2.** [établissement public] public building ; **hôtel de ville** town *UK*, city hall *US* - **3.** [demeure] : **hôtel (particulier)** (private) mansion.

hot line ['ɔtlain] *(pl* hot lines*) nf* hot line.

hotte ['ɔt] *nf* **1.** [panier] basket - **2.** [d'aération] hood.

houblon ['ublɔ̃] *nm* **1.** BOT hop - **2.** [de la bière] hops *pl*.

houille ['uj] *nf* coal.

houiller, ère ['uje, ɛr] *adj* coal *(avant n)*. **houillère** *nf* coalmine.

houle ['ul] *nf* swell.

houlette ['ulɛt] *nf sout* : **sous la houlette de qqn** under the guidance of sb.

houppe ['up] *nf* **1.** [à poudre] powder puff - **2.** [de cheveux] tuft.

hourra, hurrah ['ura] *interj* hurrah!, hurray!

house [aws], **house music** [awsmjuzik] *nf* house (music).

houspiller [3] ['uspije] *vt* to tell off.

housse ['us] *nf* cover.

houx ['u] *nm* holly.

HS *(abr de* hors service*) adj* out of order ; **je suis HS** *fam* I'm completely washed out.

hublot ['yblo] *nm* [de bateau] porthole.

huer [7] ['ɥe] *vt* [siffler] to boo.

huile [ɥil] *nf* **1.** [gén] oil ; **huile d'arachide/ d'olive** groundnut *UK ou* peanut/olive oil - **2.** [peinture] oil painting - **3.** *fam* [personnalité] bigwig.

huis [ɥi] *nm litt* door ; **à huis clos** DR in camera.

huissier [ɥisje] *nm* **1.** [appariteur] usher - **2.** DR bailiff.

huit ['ɥit] <> *adj num inv* eight. <> *nm* eight ; **lundi en huit** a week on Monday *UK*, Monday week *UK*, a week from Monday *US* ; *voir aussi* **six.**

huitième ['ɥitjɛm] <> *adj num inv & nmf* eighth. <> *nm* eighth ; **le huitième de finale**

round before the quarterfinal. ⬦ *nf* SCOL ≃ second year OU form *(at junior school)* UK, ≃ fourth grade US ; *voir aussi* **sixième**.

huître [ɥitr] *nf* oyster.

humain, e [ymɛ̃, ɛn] *adj* **1.** [gén] human - **2.** [sensible] humane. ➡ **humain** *nm* [être humain] human (being).

humanitaire [ymanitɛr] ⬦ *adj* humanitarian. ⬦ *nm* : **l'humanitaire** humanitarian OU relief work ; **travailler dans l'humanitaire** to work for a humanitarian organization.

humanité [ymanite] *nf* humanity. ➡ **humanités** *nfpl Belgique* humanities.

humble [œ̃bl] *adj* humble.

humecter [4] [ymɛkte] *vt* to moisten.

humer [3] ['yme] *vt* to smell.

humérus [ymerys] *nm* humerus.

humeur [ymœr] *nf* **1.** [disposition] mood ; **être de bonne/mauvaise humeur** to be in a good/bad mood - **2.** [caractère] nature - **3.** *sout* [irritation] temper.

humide [ymid] *adj* [air, climat] humid ; [terre, herbe, mur] wet, damp ; [saison] rainy ; [front, yeux] moist.

humidité [ymidite] *nf* [de climat, d'air] humidity ; [de terre, mur] dampness.

humiliation [ymiljasjɔ̃] *nf* humiliation.

humilier [9] [ymilje] *vt* to humiliate. ➡ **s'humilier** *vp* : **s'humilier devant qqn** to grovel to sb.

humilité [ymilite] *nf* humility.

humoristique [ymɔristik] *adj* humorous.

humour [ymur] *nm* humour UK, humor US.

humus [ymys] *nm* humus.

huppé, e ['ype] *adj* **1.** *fam* [société] uppercrust - **2.** [oiseau] crested.

hurlement ['yrləmɑ̃] *nm* howl.

hurler [3] ['yrle] *vi* [gén] to howl.

hurrah = **hourra**.

hutte ['yt] *nf* hut.

hybride [ibrid] *nm & adj* hybrid.

hydratant, e [idratɑ̃, ɑ̃t] *adj* moisturizing.

hydrater [3] [idrate] *vt* **1.** CHIM to hydrate - **2.** [peau] to moisturize.

hydraulique [idrolik] *adj* hydraulic.

hydravion [idravjɔ̃] *nm* seaplane, hydroplane.

hydrocarbure [idrɔkarbyr] *nm* hydrocarbon.

hydrocution [idrɔkysjɔ̃] *nf* immersion syncope.

hydroélectrique [idrɔelɛktrik] *adj* hydroelectric.

hydrogène [idrɔʒɛn] *nm* hydrogen.

hydroglisseur [idrɔglisœr] *nm* jetfoil, hydroplane.

hydrophile [idrɔfil] *adj* ➡ **coton**.

hyène [jɛn] *nf* hyena.

hygiène [iʒjɛn] *nf* hygiene.

hygiénique [iʒjenik] *adj* **1.** [sanitaire] hygienic - **2.** [bon pour la santé] healthy.

hymne [imn] *nm* hymn ; **hymne national** national anthem.

hypermarché [ipɛrmarʃe] *nm* hypermarket.

hypermétrope [ipɛrmetrɔp] ⬦ *nmf* longsighted UK OU farsighted US person. ⬦ *adj* longsighted UK, farsighted US.

hypertension [ipɛrtɑ̃sjɔ̃] *nf* high blood pressure, hypertension.

hypertrophié [ipɛrtrɔfje] *adj* hypertrophic ; *fig* exaggerated.

hypnotiser [3] [ipnɔtize] *vt* to hypnotize ; *fig* to mesmerize.

hypoallergénique [ipɔalɛrʒenik] *adj* hypoallergenic.

hypocondriaque [ipɔkɔ̃drijak] *nmf & adj* hypochondriac.

hypocrisie [ipɔkrizi] *nf* hypocrisy.

hypocrite [ipɔkrit] ⬦ *nmf* hypocrite. ⬦ *adj* hypocritical.

hypoglycémie [ipɔglisemi] *nf* hypoglycaemia.

hypotension [ipɔtɑ̃sjɔ̃] *nf* low blood pressure.

hypothèque [ipɔtɛk] *nf* mortgage.

hypothèse [ipɔtɛz] *nf* hypothesis.

hystérie [isteri] *nf* hysteria.

hystérique [isterik] *adj* hysterical.

i, I [i] *nm inv* i, I ; **mettre les points sur les i** to dot the i's and cross the t's.

ibérique [iberik] *adj* : **la péninsule ibérique** the Iberian Peninsula.

iceberg [ajsbɛrg] *nm* iceberg.

ici [isi] *adv* **1.** [lieu] here ; **par ici** [direction] this way ; [alentour] around here - **2.** [temps] now ; **d'ici (à) une semaine** in a week's time, a week from now ; **d'ici là** by then.

icône [ikon] *nf* INFORM & RELIG icon.

idéal, e [ideal] *(pl* idéals OU idéaux [ideo]*) adj* ideal. ➡ **idéal** *nm* ideal.

idéaliste [idealist] ⬦ *nmf* idealist. ⬦ *adj* idealistic.

idée [ide] *nf* idea ; **à l'idée de/que** at the idea of/that ; **se faire des idées** to imagine things ; **cela ne m'est jamais venu à l'idée** it never occurred to me.

identifiant [idɑ̃tifjɑ̃] *nm* INFORM user name, login name.

identification [idɑ̃tifikasjɔ̃] *nf* : **identification (à)** identification (with).

identifier [9] [idɑ̃tifje] *vt* to identify. ➤ **s'identifier** *vp* : **s'identifier à qqn/qqch** to identify with sb/sthg.

identique [idɑ̃tik] *adj* : **identique (à)** identical (to).

identité [idɑ̃tite] *nf* identity.

idéologie [ideɔlɔʒi] *nf* ideology.

idiomatique [idjɔmatik] *adj* idiomatic.

idiot, e [idjo, ɔt] ⬦ *adj* idiotic ; MÉD idiot *(avant n)*. ⬦ *nm, f* idiot.

idiotie [idjɔsi] *nf* **1.** [stupidité] idiocy - **2.** [action, parole] idiotic thing.

idolâtrer [3] [idɔlatre] *vt* to idolize.

idole [idɔl] *nf* idol.

idylle [idil] *nf* [amour] romance.

idyllique [idilik] *adj* [idéal] idyllic.

if [if] *nm* yew.

igloo, iglou [iglu] *nm* igloo.

ignare [iɲar] ⬦ *nmf* ignoramus. ⬦ *adj* ignorant.

ignoble [iɲɔbl] *adj* **1.** [abject] base - **2.** [hideux] vile.

ignominie [iɲɔmini] *nf* **1.** [état] disgrace - **2.** [action] disgraceful act.

ignorance [iɲɔrɑ̃s] *nf* ignorance.

ignorant, e [iɲɔrɑ̃, ɑ̃t] ⬦ *adj* ignorant. ⬦ *nm, f* ignoramus.

ignorer [3] [iɲɔre] *vt* **1.** [ne pas savoir] not to know, to be unaware of - **2.** [ne pas tenir compte de] to ignore - **3.** [ne pas connaître] to have no experience of.

il [il] *pron pers* **1.** [sujet - personne] he ; [- animal] it, he ; [- chose] it - **2.** [sujet d'un verbe impersonnel] it ; **il pleut** it's raining. ➤ **ils** *pron pers pl* they.

île [il] *nf* island ; **les îles Anglo-Normandes** the Channel Islands ; **les îles Baléares** the Balearic Islands ; **les îles Britanniques** the British Isles ; **les îles Canaries** the Canary Islands ; **les îles Malouines** the Falkland Islands ; **l'île Maurice** Mauritius.

illégal, e, aux [ilegal, o] *adj* illegal.

illégalité [ilegalite] *nf* [fait d'être illégal] illegality.

illégitime [ileʒitim] *adj* **1.** [enfant] illegitimate ; [union] unlawful - **2.** [non justifié] unwarranted.

illettré, e [iletre] *adj & nm, f* illiterate.

illicite [ilisit] *adj* illicit.

illimité, e [ilimite] *adj* **1.** [sans limites] unlimited - **2.** [indéterminé] indefinite.

illisible [ilizibl] *adj* **1.** [indéchiffrable] illegible - **2.** [incompréhensible & INFORM] unreadable.

illogique [ilɔʒik] *adj* illogical.

illumination [ilyminasjɔ̃] *nf* **1.** [éclairage] lighting - **2.** [idée soudaine] inspiration.

illuminer [3] [ilymine] *vt* to light up ; [bâtiment, rue] to illuminate. ➤ **s'illuminer** *vp* : **s'illuminer de joie** to light up with joy.

illusion [ilyzjɔ̃] *nf* illusion.

illusoire [ilyzwar] *adj* illusory.

illustration [ilystrasjɔ̃] *nf* illustration.

illustre [ilystr] *adj* illustrious.

illustré, e [ilystre] *adj* illustrated. ➤ **illustré** *nm* illustrated magazine.

illustrer [3] [ilystre] *vt* **1.** [gén] to illustrate - **2.** [rendre célèbre] to make famous. ➤ **s'illustrer** *vp* to distinguish o.s.

îlot [ilo] *nm* **1.** [île] small island, islet - **2.** *fig* [de résistance] pocket.

ils ➤ **il.**

image [imaʒ] *nf* **1.** [vision mentale, comparaison, ressemblance] image - **2.** [dessin] picture.

imagerie [imaʒri] *nf* MÉD : **imagerie médicale** medical imaging.

imaginaire [imaʒinɛr] *adj* imaginary.

imagination [imaʒinasjɔ̃] *nf* imagination ; **avoir de l'imagination** to be imaginative.

imaginer [3] [imaʒine] *vt* **1.** [supposer, croire] to imagine - **2.** [trouver] to think of. ➤ **s'imaginer** *vp* **1.** [se voir] to see o.s. - **2.** [croire] to imagine.

imam [imam] *nm* imam.

imbattable [ɛ̃batabl] *adj* unbeatable.

imbécile [ɛ̃besil] *nmf* imbecile.

imberbe [ɛ̃bɛrb] *adj* beardless.

imbiber [3] [ɛ̃bibe] *vt* : **imbiber qqch de qqch** to soak sthg with OU in sthg.

imbriqué, e [ɛ̃brike] *adj* overlapping.

imbroglio [ɛ̃brɔljo] *nm* imbroglio.

imbu, e [ɛ̃by] *adj* : **être imbu de** to be full of.

imbuvable [ɛ̃byvabl] *adj* **1.** [eau] undrinkable - **2.** *fam* [personne] unbearable.

imitateur, trice [imitatœr, tris] *nm, f* **1.** [comique] impersonator - **2.** *péj* [copieur] imitator.

imitation [imitasjɔ̃] *nf* imitation.

imiter [3] [imite] *vt* **1.** [s'inspirer de, contrefaire] to imitate - **2.** [reproduire l'aspect de] to look (just) like.

immaculé, e [imakyle] *adj* immaculate.

immangeable [ɛ̃mɑ̃ʒabl] *adj* inedible.

immanquable [ɛ̃mɑ̃kabl] *adj* impossible to miss ; [sort, échec] inevitable.

immatriculation [imatrikylasjɔ̃] *nf* registration.

immédiat, e [imedja, at] *adj* immediate.

immédiatement [imedjatmɑ̃] *adv* immediately.

immense [imɑ̃s] *adj* immense.

immerger [17] [imɛrʒe] *vt* to submerge. ◆ **s'immerger** *vp* to submerge o.s.

immérité, e [imerite] *adj* undeserved.

immeuble [imœbl] *nm* building.

immigration [imigrasjɔ̃] *nf* immigration ; **immigration clandestine** illegal immigration.

immigré, e [imigre] *adj & nm, f* immigrant.

immigrer [3] [imigre] *vi* to immigrate.

imminent, e [iminɑ̃, ɑ̃t] *adj* imminent.

immiscer [16] [imise] ◆ **s'immiscer** *vp* : **s'immiscer dans** to interfere in OU with.

immobile [imɔbil] *adj* **1.** [personne, visage] motionless - **2.** [mécanisme] fixed, stationary - **3.** *fig* [figé] immovable.

immobilier, ère [imɔbilje, ɛr] *adj* : **biens immobiliers** property *(U)* UK, real estate *(U)* US.

immobiliser [3] [imɔbilize] *vt* to immobilize. ◆ **s'immobiliser** *vp* to stop.

immobilité [imɔbilite] *nf* immobility ; [de paysage, de lac] stillness.

immodéré, e [imɔdere] *adj* inordinate.

immoler [3] [imɔle] *vt* to sacrifice ; RELIG to immolate. ◆ **s'immoler** *vp* to immolate o.s.

immonde [imɔ̃d] *adj* **1.** [sale] foul - **2.** [abject] vile.

immondices [imɔ̃dis] *nfpl* waste *(U)*, refuse *(U)*.

immoral, e, aux [imɔral, o] *adj* immoral.

immortaliser [3] [imɔrtalize] *vt* to immortalize.

immortel, elle [imɔrtɛl] *adj* immortal. ◆ **Immortel, elle** *nm, f fam* member of the *Académie française*.

immuable [imɥabl] *adj* **1.** [éternel - loi] immutable - **2.** [constant] unchanging.

immuniser [3] [imynize] *vt* **1.** [vacciner] to immunize - **2.** *fig* [garantir] : **immuniser qqn contre qqch** to make sb immune to sthg.

immunité [imynite] *nf* immunity.

impact [ɛ̃pakt] *nm* impact ; **avoir de l'impact sur** to have an impact on.

impair, e [ɛ̃pɛr] *adj* odd. ◆ **impair** *nm* [faux-pas] gaffe.

imparable [ɛ̃parabl] *adj* **1.** [coup] unstoppable - **2.** [argument] unanswerable.

impardonnable [ɛ̃pardɔnabl] *adj* unforgivable.

imparfait, e [ɛ̃parfɛ, ɛt] *adj* **1.** [défectueux] imperfect - **2.** [inachevé] incomplete. ◆ **imparfait** *nm* GRAMM imperfect (tense).

impartial, e, aux [ɛ̃parsjal, o] *adj* impartial.

impartir [32] [ɛ̃partir] *vt* : **impartir qqch à qqn** *litt* [délai, droit] to grant sthg to sb ; [don] to bestow sthg upon sb ; [tâche] to assign sthg to sb.

impasse [ɛ̃pas] *nf* **1.** [rue] dead end - **2.** *fig* [difficulté] impasse, deadlock.

impassible [ɛ̃pasibl] *adj* impassive.

impatience [ɛ̃pasjɑ̃s] *nf* impatience.

impatient, e [ɛ̃pasjɑ̃, ɑ̃t] *adj* impatient.

impatienter [3] [ɛ̃pasjɑ̃te] *vt* to annoy. ◆ **s'impatienter** *vp* : **s'impatienter (de/contre)** to get impatient (at/with).

impayé, e [ɛ̃peje] *adj* unpaid, outstanding. ◆ **impayé** *nm* outstanding payment.

impeccable [ɛ̃pekabl] *adj* **1.** [parfait] impeccable, faultless - **2.** [propre] spotless, immaculate.

impénétrable [ɛ̃penetrabl] *adj* impenetrable.

impénitent, e [ɛ̃penitɑ̃, ɑ̃t] *adj* unrepentant.

impensable [ɛ̃pɑ̃sabl] *adj* unthinkable.

impératif, ive [ɛ̃peratif, iv] *adj* **1.** [ton, air] imperious - **2.** [besoin] imperative, essential. ◆ **impératif** *nm* GRAMM imperative.

impératrice [ɛ̃peratris] *nf* empress.

imperceptible [ɛ̃pɛrsɛptibl] *adj* imperceptible.

imperfection [ɛ̃pɛrfɛksjɔ̃] *nf* imperfection.

impérialisme [ɛ̃perjalism] *nm* POLIT imperialism ; *fig* dominance.

impérieux, euse [ɛ̃perjø, øz] *adj* **1.** [ton, air] imperious - **2.** [nécessité] urgent.

impérissable [ɛ̃perisabl] *adj* undying.

imperméabiliser [3] [ɛ̃pɛrmeabilize] *vt* to waterproof.

imperméable [ɛ̃pɛrmeabl] <> *adj* waterproof ; **imperméable à** [étanche] impermeable to ; *fig* impervious OU immune to. <> *nm* raincoat.

impersonnel, elle [ɛ̃pɛrsɔnɛl] *adj* impersonal.

impertinence [ɛ̃pɛrtinɑ̃s] *nf* impertinence *(U)*.

impertinent, e [ɛ̃pɛrtinɑ̃, ɑ̃t] <> *adj* impertinent. <> *nm, f* impertinent person.

imperturbable [ɛ̃pɛrtyrbabl] *adj* imperturbable.

impétueux, euse [ɛ̃petɥø, øz] *adj* [personne, caractère] impetuous.

impie [ɛ̃pi] *litt & vieilli adj* impious.

impitoyable [ɛ̃pitwajabl] *adj* merciless, pitiless.

implacable [ɛ̃plakabl] *adj* implacable.

implanter [3] [ɛ̃plɑ̃te] *vt* **1.** [entreprise, système] to establish - **2.** *fig* [préjugé] to implant. ▪ **s'implanter** *vp* [entreprise] to set up ; [coutume] to become established.

implication [ɛ̃plikasjɔ̃] *nf* **1.** [participation] : **implication (dans)** involvement (in) - **2.** *(gén pl)* [conséquence] implication.

implicite [ɛ̃plisit] *adj* implicit.

impliquer [3] [ɛ̃plike] *vt* **1.** [compromettre] : **impliquer qqn dans** to implicate sb in - **2.** [requérir, entraîner] to imply. ▪ **s'impliquer** *vp* : **s'impliquer dans** *fam* to become involved in.

implorer [3] [ɛ̃plɔre] *vt* to beseech.

implosion [ɛ̃plozjɔ̃] *nf* implosion.

impoli, e [ɛ̃pɔli] *adj* rude, impolite.

impopulaire [ɛ̃pɔpylɛr] *adj* unpopular.

importance [ɛ̃pɔrtɑ̃s] *nf* **1.** [gén] importance ; [de problème, montant] magnitude - **2.** [de dommages] extent - **3.** [de ville] size.

important, e [ɛ̃pɔrtɑ̃, ɑ̃t] *adj* **1.** [personnage, découverte, rôle] important ; [événement, changement] important, significant - **2.** [quantité, collection, somme] considerable, sizeable ; [dommages] extensive.

importation [ɛ̃pɔrtasjɔ̃] *nf fig & COMM* import.

importer [3] [ɛ̃pɔrte] ◇ *vt* to import. ◇ *v impers* : **importer (à)** to matter (to) ; **il importe de/que** it is important to/that ; **qu'importe!, peu importe!** it doesn't matter! ; **n'importe qui** anyone (at all) ; **n'importe quoi** anything (at all) ; **n'importe où** anywhere (at all) ; **n'importe quand** at any time (at all).

import-export [ɛ̃pɔrɛkspɔr] *nm* import-export.

importuner [3] [ɛ̃pɔrtyne] *vt* to irk.

imposable [ɛ̃pozabl] *adj* taxable ; **non imposable** nontaxable.

imposant, e [ɛ̃pozɑ̃, ɑ̃t] *adj* imposing.

imposé, e [ɛ̃poze] *adj* **1.** [contribuable] taxed - **2.** SPORT [figure] compulsory.

imposer [3] [ɛ̃poze] *vt* **1.** [gén] : **imposer qqch/qqn à qqn** to impose sthg/sb on sb - **2.** [impressionner] : **en imposer à qqn** to impress sb - **3.** [taxer] to tax. ▪ **s'imposer** *vp* **1.** [être nécessaire] to be essential OU imperative - **2.** [forcer le respect] to stand out - **3.** [avoir pour règle] : **s'imposer de faire qqch** to make it a rule to do sthg.

impossibilité [ɛ̃pɔsibilite] *nf* impossibility ; **être dans l'impossibilité de faire qqch** to find it impossible to OU to be unable to do sthg.

impossible [ɛ̃pɔsibl] ◇ *adj* impossible. ◇ *nm* : **tenter l'impossible** to attempt the impossible.

imposteur [ɛ̃pɔstœr] *nm* impostor.

impôt [ɛ̃po] *nm* tax ; **impôts locaux** council tax *UK*, local tax *US* ; **impôt sur le revenu** income tax.

impotent, e [ɛ̃pɔtɑ̃, ɑ̃t] *adj* disabled.

impraticable [ɛ̃pratikabl] *adj* **1.** [inapplicable] impracticable - **2.** [inaccessible] impassable.

imprécis, e [ɛ̃presi, iz] *adj* imprecise.

imprégner [18] [ɛ̃preɲe] *vt* [imbiber] : **imprégner qqch de qqch** to soak sthg in sthg ; **imprégner qqn de qqch** *fig* to fill sb with sthg. ▪ **s'imprégner** *vp* : **s'imprégner de qqch** [s'imbiber] to soak sthg up ; *fig* to soak sthg up, to become o.s. in sthg.

imprenable [ɛ̃prənabl] *adj* **1.** [forteresse] impregnable - **2.** [vue] unimpeded.

imprésario, impresario [ɛ̃presarjo] *nm* impresario.

impression [ɛ̃presjɔ̃] *nf* **1.** [gén] impression ; **avoir l'impression que** to have the impression OU feeling that - **2.** [de livre, tissu] printing - **3.** PHOTO print.

impressionner [3] [ɛ̃presjɔne] *vt* **1.** [frapper] to impress - **2.** [choquer] to shock, to upset - **3.** [intimider] to frighten - **4.** PHOTO to expose.

impressionniste [ɛ̃presjɔnist] *nmf & adj* impressionist.

imprévisible [ɛ̃previzibl] *adj* unforeseeable.

imprévu, e [ɛ̃prevy] *adj* unforeseen. ▪ **imprévu** *nm* unforeseen situation.

imprimante [ɛ̃primɑ̃t] *nf* printer.

imprimé, e [ɛ̃prime] *adj* printed. ▪ **imprimé** *nm* **1.** [mention postale] printed matter *(U)* - **2.** [formulaire] printed form - **3.** [tissu] print.

imprimer [3] [ɛ̃prime] *vt* **1.** [texte, tissu] to print - **2.** [mouvement] to impart - **3.** [marque, empreinte] to leave.

imprimerie [ɛ̃primri] *nf* **1.** [technique] printing - **2.** [usine] printing works *sg*.

improbable [ɛ̃prɔbabl] *adj* improbable.

improductif, ive [ɛ̃prɔdyktif, iv] *adj* unproductive.

impromptu, e [ɛ̃prɔ̃pty] *adj* impromptu.

impropre [ɛ̃prɔpr] *adj* **1.** GRAMM incorrect - **2.** [inadapté] : **impropre à** unfit for.

improviser [3] [ɛ̃prɔvize] *vt* to improvise.

s'improviser *vp* **1.** [s'organiser] to be improvised - **2.** [devenir] : **s'improviser metteur en scène** to act as director.

improviste [ɛ̃prɔvist] ➭ **à l'improviste** *loc adv* unexpectedly, without warning.

imprudence [ɛ̃prydɑ̃s] *nf* **1.** [de personne, d'acte] rashness - **2.** [acte] rash act.

imprudent, e [ɛ̃prydɑ̃, ɑ̃t] ➭ *adj* rash. ➭ *nm, f* rash person.

impubère [ɛ̃pybɛr] *adj* [avant la puberté] pre-pubescent.

impudent, e [ɛ̃pydɑ̃, ɑ̃t] ➭ *adj* impudent. ➭ *nm, f* impudent person.

impudique [ɛ̃pydik] *adj* shameless.

impuissant, e [ɛ̃pɥisɑ̃, ɑ̃t] *adj* **1.** [incapable] : **impuissant (à faire qqch)** powerless (to do sthg) - **2.** [homme, fureur] impotent. ➭ **impuissant** *nm* impotent man.

impulsif, ive [ɛ̃pylsif, iv] ➭ *adj* impulsive. ➭ *nm, f* impulsive person.

impulsion [ɛ̃pylsjɔ̃] *nf* **1.** [poussée, essor] impetus - **2.** [instinct] impulse, instinct - **3.** *fig* : **sous l'impulsion de qqn** [influence] at the prompting *ou* instigation of sb ; **sous l'impulsion de qqch** [effet] impelled by sthg.

impunément [ɛ̃pynemɑ̃] *adv* with impunity.

impunité [ɛ̃pynite] *nf* impunity ; **en toute impunité** with impunity.

impur, e [ɛ̃pyr] *adj* impure.

impureté [ɛ̃pyrte] *nf* impurity.

imputer [3] [ɛ̃pyte] *vt* : **imputer qqch à qqn/à qqch** to attribute sthg to sb/to sthg ; **imputer qqch à qqch** FIN to charge sthg to sthg.

imputrescible [ɛ̃pytresibl] *adj* [bois] rotproof ; [déchets] non-degradable.

inabordable [inabɔrdabl] *adj* **1.** [prix] prohibitive - **2.** GÉOGR inaccessible *(by boat)* - **3.** [personne] unapproachable.

inacceptable [inaksɛptabl] *adj* unacceptable.

inaccessible [inaksesibl] *adj* [destination, domaine, personne] inaccessible ; [objectif, poste] unattainable ; **inaccessible à** [sentiment] impervious to.

inaccoutumé, e [inakutyme] *adj* unaccustomed.

inachevé, e [inaʃve] *adj* unfinished, uncompleted.

inactif, ive [inaktif, iv] *adj* **1.** [sans occupation, non utilisé] idle - **2.** [sans effet] ineffective - **3.** [sans emploi] non-working.

inaction [inaksjɔ̃] *nf* inaction.

inadapté, e [inadapte] *adj* **1.** [non adapté] : **inadapté (à)** unsuitable (for), unsuited (to) - **2.** [asocial] maladjusted.

inadmissible [inadmisibl] *adj* [conduite] unacceptable.

inadvertance [inadvɛrtɑ̃s] *nf littéraire* oversight ; **par inadvertance** inadvertently.

inaliénable [inaljenabl] *adj* inalienable.

inaltérable [inalterabl] *adj* **1.** [matériau] stable - **2.** [sentiment] unfailing.

inamovible [inamɔvibl] *adj* fixed.

inanimé, e [inanime] *adj* **1.** [sans vie] inanimate - **2.** [inerte, évanoui] senseless.

inanition [inanisjɔ̃] *nf* : **tomber/mourir d'inanition** to faint with/die of hunger.

inaperçu, e [inapɛrsy] *adj* unnoticed.

inappréciable [inapresjabl] *adj* [précieux] invaluable.

inapprochable [inaprɔʃabl] *adj* : **il est vraiment inapprochable en ce moment** you can't say anything to him at the moment.

inapte [inapt] *adj* **1.** [incapable] : **inapte à qqch/à faire qqch** incapable of sthg/of doing sthg - **2.** MIL unfit.

inattaquable [inatakabl] *adj* **1.** [imprenable] impregnable - **2.** [irréprochable] irreproachable, beyond reproach - **3.** [irréfutable] irrefutable.

inattendu, e [inatɑ̃dy] *adj* unexpected.

inattention [inatɑ̃sjɔ̃] *nf* inattention ; **faute d'inattention** careless mistake.

inaudible [inodibl] *adj* [impossible à entendre] inaudible.

inauguration [inogyrasjɔ̃] *nf* [cérémonie] inauguration, opening (ceremony).

inaugurer [3] [inogyre] *vt* **1.** [monument] to unveil ; [installation, route] to open ; [procédé, édifice] to inaugurate - **2.** [époque] to usher in.

inavouable [inavwabl] *adj* unmentionable.

incalculable [ɛ̃kalkylabl] *adj* incalculable.

incandescence [ɛ̃kɑ̃desɑ̃s] *nf* incandescence.

incantation [ɛ̃kɑ̃tasjɔ̃] *nf* incantation.

incapable [ɛ̃kapabl] ➭ *nmf* [raté] incompetent. ➭ *adj* : **incapable de faire qqch** [inapte à] incapable of doing sthg ; [dans l'impossibilité de] unable to do sthg.

incapacité [ɛ̃kapasite] *nf* **1.** [impossibilité] : **incapacité à** *ou* **de faire qqch** inability to do sthg - **2.** [invalidité] disability.

incarcération [ɛ̃karserasjɔ̃] *nf* incarceration.

incarner [3] [ɛ̃karne] *vt* **1.** [personnifier] to be the incarnation of - **2.** CINÉ & THÉÂTRE to play.

incartade [ɛ̃kartad] *nf* misdemeanour *UK*, misdemeanor *US*.

incassable [ɛ̃kasabl] *adj* unbreakable.

incendie [ɛ̃sɑ̃di] *nm* fire ; *fig* flames *pl*.

incendier [9] [ɛ̃sɑ̃dje] *vt* [mettre le feu à] to set alight, to set fire to.

incertain, e [ɛ̃sɛrtɛ̃, ɛn] *adj* **1.** [gén] uncertain ; [temps] unsettled - **2.** [vague - lumière] dim ; [- contour] blurred.

incertitude [ɛ̃sɛrtityd] *nf* uncertainty.

incessamment [ɛ̃sesamɑ̃] *adv* at any moment, any moment now.

incessant, e [ɛ̃sesɑ̃, ɑ̃t] *adj* incessant.

inceste [ɛ̃sɛst] *nm* incest.

inchangé, e [ɛ̃ʃɑ̃ʒe] *adj* unchanged.

incidence [ɛ̃sidɑ̃s] *nf* [conséquence] effect, impact (U).

incident, e [ɛ̃sidɑ̃, ɑ̃t] *adj* [accessoire] incidental. **incident** *nm* [gén] incident ; [ennui] hitch.

incinérer [18] [ɛ̃sinere] *vt* **1.** [corps] to cremate - **2.** [ordures] to incinerate.

inciser [3] [ɛ̃size] *vt* to incise, to make an incision in.

incisif, ive [ɛ̃sizif, iv] *adj* incisive. **incisive** *nf* incisor.

inciter [3] [ɛ̃site] *vt* **1.** [provoquer] : **inciter qqn à qqch/à faire qqch** to incite sb to sthg/to do sthg - **2.** [encourager] : **inciter qqn à faire qqch** to encourage sb to do sthg.

incivilité [ɛ̃sivilite] *nf* **1.** [manque de courtoisie] rudeness, disrespect - **2.** [fraude] petty crime ; [insultes, vandalismes] antisocial behaviour.

inclassable [ɛ̃klasabl] *adj* unclassifiable.

inclinable [ɛ̃klinabl] *adj* reclinable, reclining.

inclinaison [ɛ̃klinɛzɔ̃] *nf* **1.** [pente] incline - **2.** [de tête, chapeau] angle, tilt.

incliner [3] [ɛ̃kline] *vt* [pencher] to tilt, to lean. **s'incliner** *vp* **1.** [se pencher] to tilt, to lean - **2.** [céder] : **s'incliner (devant)** to give in (to), to yield (to).

inclure [96] [ɛ̃klyr] *vt* [mettre dedans] : **inclure qqch dans qqch** to include sthg in sthg ; [joindre] to enclose sthg with sthg.

inclus, e [ɛ̃kly, yz] ◇ *pp* ▶ **inclure**. ◇ *adj* **1.** [compris - taxe, frais] included ; [joint - lettre] enclosed ; : **jusqu'à la page 10 incluse** up to and including page 10 - **2.** MATH : **être inclus dans** to be a subset of.

incoercible [ɛ̃kɔɛrsibl] *adj sout* uncontrollable.

incognito [ɛ̃kɔɲito] *adv* incognito.

incohérent, e [ɛ̃kɔerɑ̃, ɑ̃t] *adj* [paroles] incoherent ; [actes] inconsistent.

incollable [ɛ̃kɔlabl] *adj* **1.** [riz] nonstick - **2.** *fam* [imbattable] unbeatable.

incolore [ɛ̃kɔlɔr] *adj* colourless *UK*, colorless *US*.

incomber [3] [ɛ̃kɔ̃be] *vi* **1.** [revenir à] : **incomber à qqn** to be sb's responsibility - **2.** *(emploi impersonnel)* **il incombe à qqn de faire qqch** it falls to sb ou it is incumbent on sb to do sthg.

incommensurable [ɛ̃kɔmɑ̃syrabl] *adj* [immense] immeasurable.

incommoder [3] [ɛ̃kɔmɔde] *vt sout* to trouble.

incomparable [ɛ̃kɔ̃parabl] *adj* **1.** [différent] not comparable - **2.** [sans pareil] incomparable.

incompatible [ɛ̃kɔ̃patibl] *adj* incompatible.

incompétent, e [ɛ̃kɔ̃petɑ̃, ɑ̃t] *adj* [incapable] incompetent.

incomplet, ète [ɛ̃kɔ̃plɛ, ɛt] *adj* incomplete.

incompréhensible [ɛ̃kɔ̃preɑ̃sibl] *adj* incomprehensible.

incompris, e [ɛ̃kɔ̃pri, iz] ◇ *adj* misunderstood, not appreciated. ◇ *nm, f* misunderstood person.

inconcevable [ɛ̃kɔ̃svabl] *adj* unimaginable.

inconciliable [ɛ̃kɔ̃siljabl] *adj* irreconcilable.

inconditionnel, elle [ɛ̃kɔ̃disjɔnɛl] ◇ *adj* **1.** [total] unconditional - **2.** [fervent] ardent. ◇ *nm, f* ardent supporter ou admirer.

inconfortable [ɛ̃kɔ̃fɔrtabl] *adj* uncomfortable.

incongru, e [ɛ̃kɔ̃gry] *adj* **1.** [malséant] unseemly, inappropriate - **2.** [bizarre] incongruous.

inconnu, e [ɛ̃kɔny] ◇ *adj* unknown. ◇ *nm, f* stranger. **inconnue** *nf* **1.** MATH unknown - **2.** [variable] unknown (factor).

inconsciemment [ɛ̃kɔ̃sjamɑ̃] *adv* **1.** [sans en avoir conscience] unconsciously, unwittingly - **2.** [à la légère] thoughtlessly.

inconscient, e [ɛ̃kɔ̃sjɑ̃, ɑ̃t] *adj* **1.** [évanoui, machinal] unconscious - **2.** [irresponsable] thoughtless. **inconscient** *nm* : **l'inconscient** the unconscious.

inconsidéré, e [ɛ̃kɔ̃sidere] *adj* ill-considered, thoughtless.

inconsistant, e [ɛ̃kɔ̃sistɑ̃, ɑ̃t] *adj* **1.** [aliment] thin, watery - **2.** [caractère] frivolous.

inconsolable [ɛ̃kɔ̃sɔlabl] *adj* inconsolable.

incontestable [ɛ̃kɔ̃tɛstabl] *adj* unquestionable, indisputable.

incontinent, e [ɛ̃kɔ̃tinɑ̃, ɑ̃t] *adj* MÉD incontinent.

incontournable [ɛ̃kɔ̃turnabl] *adj* unavoidable.

inconvenant, e [ɛ̃kɔ̃vnɑ̃, ɑ̃t] *adj* improper, unseemly.

inconvénient [ɛ̃kɔ̃venjɑ̃] *nm* **1.** [obstacle] problem - **2.** [désavantage] disadvantage, drawback - **3.** [risque] risk.

incorporé, e [ɛ̃kɔrpɔre] *adj* [intégré] built-in.

incorporer [3] [ɛ̃kɔrpɔre] *vt* **1.** [gén] to incorporate ; **incorporer qqch dans** to incorporate sthg into ; **incorporer qqch à** CULIN to mix ou blend sthg into - **2.** MIL to enlist.

incorrect, e [ɛ̃kɔrɛkt] *adj* **1.** [faux] incorrect - **2.** [inconvenant] inappropriate ; [impoli] rude - **3.** [déloyal] unfair ; **être incorrect avec qqn** to treat sb unfairly.

incorrection [ɛ̃kɔrɛksjɔ̃] *nf* **1.** [impolitesse] impropriety - **2.** [de langage] grammatical mistake - **3.** [malhonnêteté] dishonesty.

incorrigible [ɛ̃kɔriʒibl] *adj* incorrigible.

incorruptible [ɛ̃kɔryptibl] *adj* incorruptible.

incrédule [ɛ̃kredyl] *adj* **1.** [sceptique] incredulous, sceptical *UK*, skeptical *US* - **2.** RELIG unbelieving.

increvable [ɛ̃krəvabl] *adj* **1.** [ballon, pneu] puncture-proof - **2.** *fam fig* [personne] tireless ; [machine] that will withstand rough treatment.

incriminer [3] [ɛ̃krimine] *vt* **1.** [personne] to incriminate - **2.** [conduite] to condemn.

incroyable [ɛ̃krwajabl] *adj* incredible, unbelievable.

incroyant, e [ɛ̃krwajɑ̃, ɑ̃t] *nm, f* unbeliever.

incruster [3] [ɛ̃kryste] *vt* **1.** [insérer] : **incruster qqch dans qqch** to inlay sthg into sthg - **2.** [décorer] : **incruster qqch de qqch** to inlay sthg with sthg - **3.** [couvrir d'un dépôt] to fur up. ➡ **s'incruster** *vp* [s'insérer] : **s'incruster dans qqch** to become embedded in sthg.

incubation [ɛ̃kybasjɔ̃] *nf* [d'œuf, de maladie] incubation ; *fig* hatching.

inculpation [ɛ̃kylpasjɔ̃] *nf* charge.

inculper [3] [ɛ̃kylpe] *vt* to charge ; **inculper qqn de** to charge sb with.

inculquer [3] [ɛ̃kylke] *vt* : **inculquer qqch à qqn** to instil *UK* ou instill *US* sthg in sb.

inculte [ɛ̃kylt] *adj* **1.** [terre] uncultivated - **2.** *péj* [personne] uneducated.

incurable [ɛ̃kyrabl] *adj* incurable.

incursion [ɛ̃kyrsjɔ̃] *nf* incursion, foray.

Inde [ɛ̃d] *nf* : **l'Inde** India.

indécent, e [ɛ̃desɑ̃, ɑ̃t] *adj* **1.** [impudique] indecent - **2.** [immoral] scandalous.

indéchiffrable [ɛ̃deʃifrabl] *adj* **1.** [texte, écriture] indecipherable - **2.** *fig* [regard] inscrutable, impenetrable.

indécis, e [ɛ̃desi, iz] ◇ *adj* **1.** [personne - sur le moment] undecided ; [- de nature] indecisive - **2.** [sourire] vague. ◇ *nm, f* indecisive person.

indécision [ɛ̃desizjɔ̃] *nf* indecision ; [perpétuelle] indecisiveness.

indécrottable [ɛ̃dekrɔtabl] *adj fam* **1.** [borné] incredibly dumb - **2.** [incorrigible] hopeless.

indéfendable [ɛ̃defɑ̃dabl] *adj* indefensible.

indéfini, e [ɛ̃defini] *adj* [quantité, pronom] indefinite.

indéfinissable [ɛ̃definisabl] *adj* indefinable.

indéformable [ɛ̃defɔrmabl] *adj* that retains its shape.

indélébile [ɛ̃delebil] *adj* indelible.

indélicat, e [ɛ̃delika, at] *adj* **1.** [mufle] indelicate - **2.** [malhonnête] dishonest.

indemne [ɛ̃dɛmn] *adj* unscathed, unharmed.

indemniser [3] [ɛ̃dɛmnize] *vt* : **indemniser qqn de qqch** [perte, préjudice] to compensate sb for sthg ; [frais] to reimburse sb for sthg.

indemnité [ɛ̃dɛmnite] *nf* **1.** [de perte, préjudice] compensation - **2.** [de frais] allowance.

indémodable [ɛ̃demɔdabl] *adj* : **ce style est indémodable** this style doesn't date.

indéniable [ɛ̃denjabl] *adj* undeniable.

indépendance [ɛ̃depɑ̃dɑ̃s] *nf* independence.

indépendant, e [ɛ̃depɑ̃dɑ̃, ɑ̃t] *adj* **1.** [gén] independent ; [entrée] separate ; **indépendant de ma volonté** beyond my control - **2.** [travailleur] self-employed.

indéracinable [ɛ̃derasinabl] *adj* [arbre] impossible to uproot ; *fig* ineradicable.

indescriptible [ɛ̃dɛskriptibl] *adj* indescribable.

indestructible [ɛ̃dɛstryktibl] *adj* indestructible.

indéterminé, e [ɛ̃determine] *adj* **1.** [indéfini] indeterminate, indefinite - **2.** [vague] vague - **3.** [personne] undecided.

index [ɛ̃dɛks] *nm* **1.** [doigt] index finger - **2.** [aiguille] pointer, needle - **3.** [registre] index.

indexer [4] [ɛ̃dɛkse] *vt* **1.** ÉCON : **indexer qqch sur qqch** to index sthg to sthg - **2.** [livre] to index.

indicateur, trice [ɛ̃dikatœr, tris] *adj* : **poteau indicateur** signpost ; **panneau indicateur** road sign. ➡ **indicateur** *nm* **1.** [guide] directory, guide ; **indicateur des chemins de fer** railway timetable *UK*, train schedule *US* - **2.** TECHNOL gauge - **3.** ÉCON indicator - **4.** [de police] informer.

indicatif, ive [ɛ̃dikatif, iv] *adj* indicative.
◆ **indicatif** *nm* **1.** RADIO & TV signature tune - **2.** [code]: **indicatif (téléphonique)** dialling code *UK*, area code *US* - **3.** GRAMM : **l'indicatif** the indicative.

indication [ɛ̃dikasjɔ̃] *nf* **1.** [mention] indication - **2.** [renseignement] information *(U)* - **3.** [directive] instruction ; THÉÂTRE direction ; **sauf indication contraire** unless otherwise instructed.

indice [ɛ̃dis] *nm* **1.** [signe] sign - **2.** [dans une enquête] clue - **3.** [taux] rating ; **indice du coût de la vie** ÉCON cost-of-living index - **4.** MATH index.

indicible [ɛ̃disibl] *adj* inexpressible.

indien, enne [ɛ̃djɛ̃, ɛn] *adj* **1.** [d'Inde] Indian - **2.** [d'Amérique] American Indian, Native American. ◆ **Indien, enne** *nm, f* **1.** [d'Inde] Indian - **2.** [d'Amérique] American Indian, Native American.

indifféremment [ɛ̃diferamɑ̃] *adv* indifferently.

indifférent, e [ɛ̃diferɑ̃, ɑ̃t] <> *adj* [gén] : **indifférent à** indifferent to. <> *nm, f* unconcerned person.

indigence [ɛ̃diʒɑ̃s] *nf* poverty.

indigène [ɛ̃diʒɛn] <> *nmf* native. <> *adj* [peuple] native ; [faune, flore] indigenous.

indigent, e [ɛ̃diʒɑ̃, ɑ̃t] <> *adj* [pauvre] destitute, poverty-stricken ; *fig* [intellectuellement] impoverished. <> *nm, f* poor person ; **les indigents** the poor, the destitute.

indigeste [ɛ̃diʒɛst] *adj* indigestible.

indigestion [ɛ̃diʒɛstjɔ̃] *nf* **1.** [alimentaire] indigestion - **2.** *fig* [saturation] surfeit.

indignation [ɛ̃diɲasjɔ̃] *nf* indignation.

indigné, e [ɛ̃diɲe] *adj* indignant.

indigner [3] [ɛ̃diɲe] *vt* to make indignant. ◆ **s'indigner** *vp* : **s'indigner de** ou **contre qqch** to get indignant about sthg.

indigo [ɛ̃digo] <> *nm* indigo. <> *adj inv* indigo (blue).

indiquer [3] [ɛ̃dike] *vt* **1.** [désigner] to indicate, to point out - **2.** [afficher, montrer - suj : carte, pendule, aiguille] to show, to indicate - **3.** [recommander] : **indiquer qqn/qqch à qqn** to tell sb of sb/sthg, to suggest sb/sthg to sb - **4.** [dire, renseigner sur] to tell ; **pourriez-vous m'indiquer l'heure?** could you tell me the time? - **5.** [fixer - heure, date, lieu] to name, to indicate.

indirect, e [ɛ̃dirɛkt] *adj* [gén] indirect ; [itinéraire] roundabout.

indiscipliné, e [ɛ̃disipline] *adj* **1.** [écolier, esprit] undisciplined, unruly - **2.** *fig* [mèches de cheveux] unmanageable.

indiscret, ète [ɛ̃diskrɛ, ɛt] <> *adj* indiscreet ; [curieux] inquisitive. <> *nm, f* indiscreet person.

indiscrétion [ɛ̃diskresjɔ̃] *nf* indiscretion ; [curiosité] curiosity.

indiscutable [ɛ̃diskytabl] *adj* unquestionable, indisputable.

indispensable [ɛ̃dispɑ̃sabl] *adj* indispensable, essential ; **indispensable à** indispensable to, essential to ; **il est indispensable de faire qqch** it is essential ou vital to do sthg.

indisponible [ɛ̃disponibl] *adj* unavailable.

indisposer [3] [ɛ̃dispoze] *vt sout* [rendre malade] to indispose.

indistinct, e [ɛ̃distɛ̃(kt), ɛ̃kt] *adj* indistinct ; [souvenir] hazy.

individu [ɛ̃dividy] *nm* individual.

individuel, elle [ɛ̃dividɥɛl] *adj* individual.

indivisible [ɛ̃divizibl] *adj* indivisible.

Indochine [ɛ̃dɔʃin] *nf* : **l'Indochine** Indochina.

indolent, e [ɛ̃dɔlɑ̃, ɑ̃t] *adj* **1.** [personne] indolent, lethargic - **2.** [geste, regard] languid.

indolore [ɛ̃dɔlɔr] *adj* painless.

indomptable [ɛ̃dɔ̃tabl] *adj* **1.** [animal] untamable - **2.** [personne] indomitable.

Indonésie [ɛ̃dɔnezi] *nf* : **l'Indonésie** Indonesia.

indu, e [ɛ̃dy] *adj* [heure] ungodly, unearthly.

indubitable [ɛ̃dybitabl] *adj* indubitable, undoubted ; **il est indubitable que** it is indisputable ou beyond doubt that.

induire [98] [ɛ̃dɥir] *vt* to induce ; **induire qqn à faire qqch** to induce sb to do sthg ; **induire qqn en erreur** to mislead sb ; **en induire que** to infer ou gather that.

induit, e [ɛ̃dɥi, ɥit] <> *pp* ▶ **induire**. <> *adj* **1.** [consécutif] resulting - **2.** ÉLECTR induced.

indulgence [ɛ̃dylʒɑ̃s] *nf* [de juge] leniency ; [de parent] indulgence.

indulgent, e [ɛ̃dylʒɑ̃, ɑ̃t] *adj* [juge] lenient ; [parent] indulgent.

indûment [ɛ̃dymɑ̃] *adv* unduly.

industrialisé, e [ɛ̃dystrijalize] *adj* industrialized ; **pays industrialisé** industrialized country.

industrialiser [3] [ɛ̃dystrijalize] *vt* to industrialize. ◆ **s'industrialiser** *vp* to become industrialized.

industrie [ɛ̃dystri] *nf* industry.

industriel, elle [ɛ̃dystrijɛl] *adj* industrial. ◆ **industriel** *nm* industrialist.

inébranlable [inebrãlabl] adj 1. [roc] solid, immovable - 2. fig [conviction] unshakeable.

inédit, e [inedi, it] adj 1. [texte] unpublished - 2. [trouvaille] novel, original.

ineffable [inefabl] adj ineffable.

ineffaçable [inefasabl] adj indelible.

inefficace [inefikas] adj 1. [personne, machine] inefficient - 2. [solution, remède, mesure] ineffective.

inefficacité [inefikasite] nf 1. [de personne, machine] inefficiency - 2. [de solution, remède, mesure] ineffectiveness.

inégal, e, aux [inegal, o] adj 1. [différent, disproportionné] unequal - 2. [irrégulier] uneven - 3. [changeant] changeable ; [artiste, travail] erratic.

inégalé, e [inegale] adj unequalled *UK*, unequaled *US*.

inégalité [inegalite] nf 1. [injustice, disproportion] inequality - 2. [différence] difference, disparity - 3. [irrégularité] unevenness - 4. [d'humeur] changeability.

inélégant, e [inelegã, ãt] adj 1. [dans l'habillement] inelegant - 2. fig [indélicat] discourteous.

inéligible [inelizibl] adj ineligible.

inéluctable [inelyktabl] adj inescapable.

inénarrable [inenarabl] adj very funny.

inepte [inɛpt] adj inept.

ineptie [inɛpsi] nf 1. [bêtise] ineptitude - 2. [chose idiote] nonsense *(U)*.

inépuisable [inepɥizabl] adj inexhaustible.

inerte [inɛrt] adj 1. [corps, membre] lifeless - 2. [personne] passive, inert - 3. PHYS inert.

inertie [inɛrsi] nf 1. [manque de réaction] apathy, inertia - 2. PHYS inertia.

inespéré, e [inɛspere] adj unexpected, unhoped-for.

inesthétique [inɛstetik] adj unaesthetic.

inestimable [inɛstimabl] adj : d'une valeur inestimable priceless ; fig invaluable.

inévitable [inevitabl] adj [obstacle] unavoidable ; [conséquence] inevitable.

inexact, e [inɛgza(kt), akt] adj 1. [faux, incomplet] inaccurate, inexact - 2. [en retard] unpunctual.

inexactitude [inɛgzaktityd] nf [erreur, imprécision] inaccuracy.

inexcusable [inɛkskyzabl] adj unforgivable, inexcusable.

inexistant, e [inɛgzistã, ãt] adj nonexistent.

inexorable [inɛgzɔrabl] adj inexorable.

inexpérience [inɛksperjãs] nf lack of experience, inexperience.

inexplicable [inɛksplikabl] adj inexplicable, unexplainable.

inexpliqué, e [inɛksplike] adj unexplained.

inexpressif, ive [inɛkspresif, iv] adj inexpressive.

inexprimable [inɛksprimabl] adj inexpressible.

inextensible [inɛkstãsibl] adj 1. [matériau] unstretchable - 2. [étoffe] non-stretch.

in extremis [inɛkstremis] adv at the last minute.

inextricable [inɛkstrikabl] adj 1. [fouillis] inextricable - 2. fig [affaire, mystère] that cannot be unravelled.

infaillible [ɛ̃fajibl] adj [personne, méthode] infallible ; [instinct] unerring.

infâme [ɛ̃fam] adj 1. [ignoble] despicable - 2. hum & litt [dégoûtant] vile.

infanterie [ɛ̃fãtri] nf infantry.

infanticide [ɛ̃fãtisid] <> nmf infanticide, child-killer. <>

infantile [ɛ̃fãtil] adj 1. [maladie] childhood *(avant n)* - 2. [médecine] for children - 3. [comportement] infantile.

infarctus [ɛ̃farktys] nm infarction, infarct ; infarctus du myocarde coronary thrombosis, myocardial infarction.

infatigable [ɛ̃fatigabl] adj 1. [personne] tireless - 2. [attitude] untiring.

infect, e [ɛ̃fɛkt] adj [dégoûtant] vile.

infecter [4] [ɛ̃fɛkte] vt 1. [eau] to contaminate - 2. [plaie] to infect - 3. [empoisonner] to poison. <> **s'infecter** vp to become infected, to turn septic.

infectieux, euse [ɛ̃fɛksjø, øz] adj infectious.

infection [ɛ̃fɛksjɔ̃] nf 1. MÉD infection - 2. fig & péj [puanteur] stench.

inférer [18] [ɛ̃fere] vt litt : inférer qqch de qqch to infer sthg from sthg.

inférieur, e [ɛ̃ferjœr] <> adj 1. [qui est en bas] lower - 2. [dans une hiérarchie] inferior ; inférieur à [qualité] inferior to ; [quantité] less than. <> nm, f inferior.

infériorité [ɛ̃ferjɔrite] nf inferiority.

infernal, e, aux [ɛ̃fɛrnal, o] adj 1. [personne] fiendish - 2. fig [bruit, chaleur, rythme] infernal ; [vision] diabolical.

infester [3] [ɛ̃fɛste] vt to infest ; être infesté de [rats, moustiques] to be infested with ; [touristes] to be overrun by.

infidèle [ɛ̃fidɛl] adj 1. [mari, femme, ami] : infidèle (à) unfaithful (to) - 2. [traducteur, historien] inaccurate.

infidélité [ɛ̃fidelite] nf [trahison] infidelity.

infiltration [ɛ̃filtrasjɔ̃] nf infiltration.

infiltrer [3] [ɛ̃filtre] *vt* to infiltrate. ➤ **s'infiltrer** *vp* **1.** [pluie, lumière] : **s'infiltrer par/dans** to filter through/into - **2.** [hommes, idées] to infiltrate.

infime [ɛ̃fim] *adj* minute, infinitesimal.

infini, e [ɛ̃fini] *adj* **1.** [sans bornes] infinite, boundless - **2.** MATH, PHILO & RELIG infinite - **3.** *fig* [interminable] endless, interminable. ➤ **infini** *nm* infinity. ➤ **à l'infini** *loc adv* **1.** MATH to infinity - **2.** [discourir] ad infinitum, endlessly.

infiniment [ɛ̃finimɑ̃] *adv* extremely, immensely.

infinité [ɛ̃finite] *nf* infinity, infinite number.

infinitif, ive [ɛ̃finitif, iv] *adj* infinitive. ➤ **infinitif** *nm* infinitive.

infirme [ɛ̃firm] ◇ *adj* [handicapé] disabled ; [avec l'âge] infirm. ◇ *nmf* disabled person.

infirmer [3] [ɛ̃firme] *vt* **1.** [démentir] to invalidate - **2.** DR to annul.

infirmerie [ɛ̃firməri] *nf* infirmary.

infirmier, ère [ɛ̃firmje, ɛr] *nm, f* nurse.

infirmité [ɛ̃firmite] *nf* **1.** [handicap] disability ; [de vieillesse] infirmity.

inflammable [ɛ̃flamabl] *adj* inflammable, flammable.

inflammation [ɛ̃flamasjɔ̃] *nf* inflammation.

inflation [ɛ̃flasjɔ̃] *nf* ÉCON inflation ; *fig* increase.

inflationniste [ɛ̃flasjɔnist] *adj & nmf* inflationist.

infléchir [32] [ɛ̃fleʃir] *vt* *fig* [politique] to modify.

inflexible [ɛ̃flɛksibl] *adj* inflexible.

inflexion [ɛ̃flɛksjɔ̃] *nf* **1.** [de tête] nod - **2.** [de voix] inflection.

infliger [17] [ɛ̃fliʒe] *vt* : **infliger qqch à qqn** to inflict sthg on sb ; [amende] to impose sthg on sb.

influençable [ɛ̃flyɑ̃sabl] *adj* easily influenced.

influence [ɛ̃flyɑ̃s] *nf* influence ; [de médicament] effect.

influencer [16] [ɛ̃flyɑ̃se] *vt* to influence.

influer [3] [ɛ̃flye] *vi* : **influer sur qqch** to influence sthg, to have an effect on sthg.

Infographie® [ɛ̃fɔgrafi] *nf* computer graphics *(U)*.

informaticien, enne [ɛ̃fɔrmatisjɛ̃, ɛn] *nm, f* computer scientist.

information [ɛ̃fɔrmasjɔ̃] *nf* **1.** [renseignement] piece of information - **2.** [renseignements & INFORM] information *(U)* - **3.** [nouvelle] piece of news. ➤ **informations** *nfpl* [média] news *sg*.

informatique [ɛ̃fɔrmatik] ◇ *nf* **1.** [technique] computers - **2.** [science] computer science. ◇ *adj* data-processing *(avant n)*, computer *(avant n)*.

informatiser [3] [ɛ̃fɔrmatize] *vt* to computerize.

informe [ɛ̃fɔrm] *adj* [masse, vêtement, silhouette] shapeless.

informel, elle [ɛ̃fɔrmɛl] *adj* informal.

informer [3] [ɛ̃fɔrme] *vt* to inform ; **informer qqn sur** ou **de qqch** to inform sb about sthg. ➤ **s'informer** *vp* to inform o.s. ; **s'informer de qqch** to ask about sthg ; **s'informer sur qqch** to find out about sthg.

infortune [ɛ̃fɔrtyn] *nf* misfortune.

infos [ɛ̃fo] *(abr de* **informations**) *nfpl fam* **les infos** the news *sg*.

infraction [ɛ̃fraksjɔ̃] *nf* offence ; **être en infraction** to be in breach of the law.

infranchissable [ɛ̃frɑ̃ʃisabl] *adj* insurmountable.

infrarouge [ɛ̃fraruʒ] *nm & adj* infrared.

infrastructure [ɛ̃frastryktyr] *nf* infrastructure.

infroissable [ɛ̃frwasabl] *adj* crease-resistant.

infructueux, euse [ɛ̃fryktɥø, øz] *adj* fruitless.

infuser [3] [ɛ̃fyze] *vi* [tisane] to infuse ; [thé] to brew.

infusion [ɛ̃fyzjɔ̃] *nf* infusion.

ingénier [9] [ɛ̃ʒenje] ➤ **s'ingénier** *vp* : **s'ingénier à faire qqch** to try hard to do sthg.

ingénieur [ɛ̃ʒenjœr] *nm* engineer.

ingénieux, euse [ɛ̃ʒenjø, øz] *adj* ingenious.

ingéniosité [ɛ̃ʒenjozite] *nf* ingenuity.

ingénu, e [ɛ̃ʒeny] *adj litt* [candide] artless ; *hum & péj* [trop candide] naïve.

ingérable [ɛ̃ʒerabl] *adj* unmanageable.

ingérer [18] [ɛ̃ʒere] *vt* to ingest. ➤ **s'ingérer** *vp* : **s'ingérer dans** to interfere in.

ingrat, e [ɛ̃gra, at] ◇ *adj* **1.** [personne] ungrateful - **2.** [métier] thankless, unrewarding - **3.** [sol] barren - **4.** [physique] unattractive. ◇ *nm, f* ungrateful wretch.

ingratitude [ɛ̃gratityd] *nf* ingratitude.

ingrédient [ɛ̃gredjɑ̃] *nm* ingredient.

inguérissable [ɛ̃gerisabl] *adj* incurable.

ingurgiter [3] [ɛ̃gyrʒite] *vt* **1.** [avaler] to swallow - **2.** *fig* [connaissances] to absorb.

inhabitable [inabitabl] *adj* uninhabitable.

inhabité, e [inabite] *adj* uninhabited.

inhabituel, elle [inabitɥɛl] *adj* unusual.

inhalateur, trice [inalatœr, tris] *adj* : appareil inhalateur inhaler. ➤ **inhalateur** *nm* inhaler.

inhalation [inalasjɔ̃] *nf* inhalation.

inhérent, e [inerɑ̃, ɑ̃t] *adj* : **inhérent à** inherent in.

inhibition [inibisjɔ̃] *nf* inhibition.

inhospitalier, ère [inɔspitalje, ɛr] *adj* inhospitable.

inhumain, e [inymɛ̃, ɛn] *adj* inhuman.

inhumation [inymasjɔ̃] *nf* burial.

inhumer [3] [inyme] *vt* to bury.

inimaginable [inimaʒinabl] *adj* incredible, unimaginable.

inimitable [inimitabl] *adj* inimitable.

ininflammable [inɛ̃flamabl] *adj* non-flammable.

inintelligible [inɛ̃teliʒibl] *adj* unintelligible.

inintéressant, e [inɛ̃teresɑ̃, ɑ̃t] *adj* uninteresting.

ininterrompu, e [inɛ̃terɔ̃py] *adj* [file, vacarme] uninterrupted ; [ligne, suite] unbroken ; [travail, effort] continuous.

inique [inik] *adj* iniquitous.

initial, e, aux [inisjal, o] *adj* [lettre] initial. ➤ **initiale** *nf* initial.

initiateur, trice [inisjatœr, tris] *nm, f* **1.** [maître] initiator - **2.** [précurseur] innovator.

initiation [inisjasjɔ̃] *nf* : **initiation (à)** [discipline] introduction (to) ; [rituel] initiation (into).

initiative [inisjativ] *nf* initiative ; **prendre l'initiative de qqch/de faire qqch** to take the initiative for sthg/in doing sthg.

initié, e [inisje] <> *adj* initiated. <> *nm, f* initiate.

initier [9] [inisje] *vt* : **initier qqn à** to initiate sb into.

injecté, e [ɛ̃ʒɛkte] *adj* : **yeux injectés de sang** bloodshot eyes.

injecter [4] [ɛ̃ʒɛkte] *vt* to inject.

injection [ɛ̃ʒɛksjɔ̃] *nf* injection.

injoignable [ɛ̃jwaɲabl] *adj* : **j'ai essayé de lui téléphoner mais il est injoignable** I tried to phone him but I couldn't get through to him ou reach him ou get hold of him.

injonction [ɛ̃ʒɔ̃ksjɔ̃] *nf* injunction.

injure [ɛ̃ʒyr] *nf* insult.

injurier [9] [ɛ̃ʒyrje] *vt* to insult.

injurieux, euse [ɛ̃ʒyrjø, øz] *adj* abusive, insulting.

injuste [ɛ̃ʒyst] *adj* unjust, unfair.

injustice [ɛ̃ʒystis] *nf* injustice.

inlassable [ɛ̃lasabl] *adj* tireless.

inlassablement [ɛ̃lasabləmɑ̃] *adv* tirelessly.

inné, e [ine] *adj* innate.

innocence [inɔsɑ̃s] *nf* innocence.

innocent, e [inɔsɑ̃, ɑ̃t] <> *adj* innocent. <> *nm, f* **1.** DR innocent person - **2.** [inoffensif, candide] innocent - **3.** *vieilli* [idiot] simpleton.

innocenter [3] [inɔsɑ̃te] *vt* **1.** DR to clear - **2.** *fig* [excuser] to justify.

innombrable [inɔ̃brabl] *adj* innumerable ; [foule] vast.

innover [3] [inɔve] *vi* to innovate.

inobservation [inɔpsɛrvasjɔ̃] *nf* inobservance.

inoccupé, e [inɔkype] *adj* [lieu] empty, unoccupied.

inoculer [3] [inɔkyle] *vt* MÉD : **inoculer qqch à qqn** [volontairement] to inoculate sb with sthg ; [accidentellement] to infect sb with sthg.

inodore [inɔdɔr] *adj* odourless *UK*, odorless *US*.

inoffensif, ive [inɔfɑ̃sif, iv] *adj* harmless.

inondation [inɔ̃dasjɔ̃] *nf* **1.** [action] flooding - **2.** [résultat] flood.

inonder [3] [inɔ̃de] *vt* to flood ; **inonder de** *fig* to flood with.

inopérable [inɔperabl] *adj* inoperable.

inopérant, e [inɔperɑ̃, ɑ̃t] *adj* ineffective.

inopiné, e [inɔpine] *adj* unexpected.

inopportun, e [inɔpɔrtœ̃, yn] *adj* inopportune.

inoubliable [inublijabl] *adj* unforgettable.

inouï, e [inwi] *adj* incredible, extraordinary.

Inox® [inɔks] *nm inv & adj inv* stainless steel.

inoxydable [inɔksidabl] *adj* stainless ; [casserole] stainless steel *(avant n)*.

inqualifiable [ɛ̃kalifjabl] *adj* unspeakable.

inquiet, ète [ɛ̃kjɛ, ɛt] *adj* **1.** [gén] anxious - **2.** [tourmenté] feverish.

inquiéter [18] [ɛ̃kjete] *vt* **1.** [donner du souci à] to worry - **2.** [déranger] to disturb. ➤ **s'inquiéter** *vp* **1.** [s'alarmer] to be worried - **2.** [se préoccuper] : **s'inquiéter de** [s'enquérir de] to enquire about ; [se soucier de] to worry about.

inquiétude [ɛ̃kjetyd] *nf* anxiety, worry.

inquisiteur, trice [ɛ̃kizitœr, tris] *adj* prying.

insaisissable [ɛ̃sezisabl] *adj* **1.** [personne] elusive - **2.** *fig* [nuance] imperceptible.

insalubre [ɛ̃salybr] *adj* unhealthy.

insatiable [ɛ̃sasjabl] *adj* insatiable.

insatisfait, e [ɛ̃satisfɛ, ɛt] <> *adj* [personne] dissatisfied. <> *nm, f* malcontent.

insaturé, e [ɛ̃satyre] *adj* unsaturated.

inscription [ɛ̃skripsjɔ̃] *nf* **1.** [action, écrit] inscription - **2.** [enregistrement] enrolment *UK*, enrollment *US*, registration.

inscrire [99] [ɛ̃skrir] *vt* **1.** [écrire] to write down ; [graver] to inscribe - **2.** [personne] : **inscrire qqn à qqch** to enrol *UK* ou enroll *US* sb for sthg, to register sb for sthg ; **inscrire qqn sur qqch** to put sb's name down on sthg - **3.** [inclure] to list, to include. ➤ **s'inscrire** *vp* [personne] : **s'inscrire à qqch** to enrol *UK* ou enroll *US* for sthg, to register for sthg ; **s'inscrire sur qqch** to put one's name down on sthg.

inscrit, e [ɛ̃skri, it] <> *pp* ➤ **inscrire**. <> *adj* [sur liste] registered ; **être inscrit sur une liste** to have one's name on a list. <> *nm, f* registered person.

insecte [ɛ̃sɛkt] *nm* insect.

insecticide [ɛ̃sɛktisid] *nm & adj* insecticide.

insécurité [ɛ̃sekyrite] *nf* insecurity.

insémination [ɛ̃seminasjɔ̃] *nf* insemination ; **insémination artificielle** artificial insemination.

insensé, e [ɛ̃sɑ̃se] *adj* **1.** [déraisonnable] insane - **2.** [incroyable, excentrique] extraordinary.

insensibiliser [3] [ɛ̃sɑ̃sibilize] *vt* to anaesthetize *UK*, to anesthetize *US* ; **insensibiliser qqn (à)** *fig* to make sb insensitive (to).

insensible [ɛ̃sɑ̃sibl] *adj* **1.** [gén] : **insensible (à)** insensitive (to) - **2.** [imperceptible] imperceptible.

insensiblement [ɛ̃sɑ̃siblǝmɑ̃] *adv* imperceptibly.

inséparable [ɛ̃separabl] *adj* : **inséparable (de)** inseparable (from).

insérer [18] [ɛ̃sere] *vt* to insert ; **insérer une annonce dans un journal** to put an advertisement in a newspaper. ➤ **s'insérer** *vp* [s'intégrer] : **s'insérer dans** to fit into.

insidieux, euse [ɛ̃sidjø, øz] *adj* insidious.

insigne [ɛ̃siɲ] <> *nm* badge. <> *adj* **1.** *litt* [honneur] distinguished - **2.** *hum* [maladresse] remarkable.

insignifiant, e [ɛ̃siɲifjɑ̃, ɑ̃t] *adj* insignificant.

insinuation [ɛ̃sinɥasjɔ̃] *nf* insinuation, innuendo.

insinuer [7] [ɛ̃sinɥe] *vt* to insinuate, to imply. ➤ **s'insinuer** *vp* : **s'insinuer dans** [eau, humidité, odeur] to seep into ; *fig* [personne] to insinuate o.s. into.

insipide [ɛ̃sipid] *adj* [aliment] insipid, tasteless ; *fig* insipid.

insistance [ɛ̃sistɑ̃s] *nf* insistence.

insister [3] [ɛ̃siste] *vi* to insist ; **insister sur** to insist on ; **insister pour faire qqch** to insist on doing sthg.

insolation [ɛ̃sɔlasjɔ̃] *nf* [malaise] sunstroke (U).

insolence [ɛ̃sɔlɑ̃s] *nf* insolence (U).

insolent, e [ɛ̃sɔlɑ̃, ɑ̃t] <> *adj* **1.** [personne, acte] insolent - **2.** [joie, succès] unashamed, blatant. <> *nm, f* insolent person.

insolite [ɛ̃sɔlit] *adj* unusual.

insoluble [ɛ̃sɔlybl] *adj* insoluble *UK*, insolvable *US*.

insolvable [ɛ̃sɔlvabl] *adj* insolvent.

insomnie [ɛ̃sɔmni] *nf* insomnia (U).

insondable [ɛ̃sɔ̃dabl] *adj* [gouffre, mystère] unfathomable ; [bêtise] abysmal.

insonoriser [3] [ɛ̃sɔnɔrize] *vt* to soundproof.

insouciance [ɛ̃susjɑ̃s] *nf* [légèreté] carefree attitude.

insouciant, e [ɛ̃susjɑ̃, ɑ̃t] *adj* [sans-souci] carefree.

insoumis, e [ɛ̃sumi, iz] *adj* **1.** [caractère] rebellious - **2.** [peuple] unsubjugated - **3.** [soldat] deserting.

insoumission [ɛ̃sumisjɔ̃] *nf* **1.** [caractère rebelle] rebelliousness - **2.** MIL desertion.

insoupçonné, e [ɛ̃supsɔne] *adj* unsuspected.

insoutenable [ɛ̃sutnabl] *adj* **1.** [rythme] unsustainable - **2.** [scène, violence] unbearable - **3.** [théorie] untenable.

inspecter [4] [ɛ̃spɛkte] *vt* to inspect.

inspecteur, trice [ɛ̃spɛktœr, tris] *nm, f* inspector.

inspection [ɛ̃spɛksjɔ̃] *nf* **1.** [contrôle] inspection - **2.** [fonction] inspectorate.

inspiration [ɛ̃spirasjɔ̃] *nf* **1.** [gén] inspiration ; [idée] bright idea, brainwave ; **avoir de l'inspiration** to be inspired - **2.** [d'air] breathing in.

inspiré, e [ɛ̃spire] *adj* inspired.

inspirer [3] [ɛ̃spire] *vt* **1.** [gén] to inspire ; **inspirer qqch à qqn** to inspire sb with sthg - **2.** [air] to breathe in, to inhale. ➤ **s'inspirer** *vp* [prendre modèle sur] : **s'inspirer de qqn/qqch** to be inspired by sb/sthg.

instable [ɛ̃stabl] *adj* **1.** [gén] unstable - **2.** [vie, temps] unsettled.

installation [ɛ̃stalasjɔ̃] *nf* **1.** [de gaz, eau, électricité] installation - **2.** [de personne - comme médecin, artisan] setting up ; [- dans appartement] settling in - **3.** (*gén pl*) [équipement] **installations** *pl*, fittings *pl* ; [usine] plant (U) ; [de loisirs] facilities *pl* ; **installation électrique** wiring.

installer [3] [ɛstale] vt 1. [gaz, eau, électricité] to install UK, to instal US, to put in - 2. INFORM to install - 3. [appartement] to fit out - 4. [rideaux, étagères] to put up ; [meubles] to put in - 5. [personne] : **installer qqn** to get sb settled, to install UK ou instal US sb. ➤ **s'installer** vp 1. [comme médecin, artisan etc] to set (o.s.) up - 2. [emménager] to settle in ; **s'installer chez qqn** to move in with sb - 3. [dans fauteuil] to settle down - 4. fig [maladie, routine] to set in.

instamment [ɛstamɑ̃] adv insistently.

instance [ɛstɑ̃s] nf 1. [autorité] authority - 2. DR proceedings pl - 3. [insistance] entreaties pl. ➤ **en instance** loc adv pending. ➤ **en instance de** loc adv on the point of.

instant [ɛstɑ̃] nm instant ; **à l'instant** [il y a peu de temps] a moment ago ; [immédiatement] this minute ; **à tout instant** [en permanence] at all times ; [d'un moment à l'autre] at any moment ; **pour l'instant** for the moment.

instantané, e [ɛstɑ̃tane] adj 1. [immédiat] instantaneous - 2. [soluble] instant. ➤ **instantané** nm snapshot.

instar [ɛstar] ➤ **à l'instar de** loc prép following the example of.

instaurer [3] [ɛstɔre] vt [instituer] to establish ; fig [peur, confiance] to instil UK, to instill US.

instigateur, trice [ɛstigatœr, tris] nm, f instigator.

instigation [ɛstigasjɔ̃] nf instigation. ➤ **à l'instigation de, sur l'instigation de** loc prép at the instigation of.

instinct [ɛstɛ̃] nm instinct.

instinctif, ive [ɛstɛ̃ktif, iv] <> adj instinctive. <> nm, f instinctive person.

instituer [7] [ɛstitɥe] vt 1. [pratique] to institute - 2. DR [personne] to appoint.

institut [ɛstity] nm 1. [établissement] institute ; **l'institut Pasteur** important medical research centre - 2. [de soins] : **institut de beauté** beauty salon.

instituteur, trice [ɛstitytœr, tris] nm, f primary school teacher UK, grade school teacher US.

institution [ɛstitysjɔ̃] nf 1. [gén] institution - 2. [école privée] private school. ➤ **institutions** nfpl POLIT institutions.

instructif, ive [ɛstryktif, iv] adj instructive, educational.

instruction [ɛstryksjɔ̃] nf 1. [enseignement, savoir] education - 2. [formation] training - 3. [directive] order - 4. DR (pretrial) investigation. ➤ **instructions** nfpl instructions.

instruit, e [ɛstrɥi, it] adj educated.

instrument [ɛstrymɑ̃] nm instrument ; **instrument de musique** musical instrument.

instrumentaliser [3] [ɛstrymɑ̃talize] vt to use, to manipulate.

insu [ɛsy] ➤ **à l'insu de** loc prép : **à l'insu de qqn** without sb knowing ; **ils ont tout organisé à mon insu** they organized it all without my knowing.

insubmersible [ɛsybmɛrsibl] adj unsinkable.

insubordination [ɛsybɔrdinasjɔ̃] nf insubordination.

insuccès [ɛsyksɛ] nm failure.

insuffisance [ɛsyfizɑ̃s] nf 1. [manque] insufficiency - 2. MÉD deficiency. ➤ **insuffisances** nfpl [faiblesses] shortcomings.

insuffisant, e [ɛsyfizɑ̃, ɑ̃t] adj 1. [en quantité] insufficient - 2. [en qualité] inadequate, unsatisfactory.

insuffler [3] [ɛsyfle] vt 1. [air] to blow - 2. fig [sentiment] : **insuffler qqch à qqn** to inspire sb with sthg.

insulaire [ɛsylɛr] <> nmf islander. <> adj GÉOGR island (avant n).

insuline [ɛsylin] nf insulin.

insulte [ɛsylt] nf insult.

insulter [3] [ɛsylte] vt to insult.

insupportable [ɛsypɔrtabl] adj unbearable.

insurgé, e [ɛsyrʒe] adj & nm, f insurgent, rebel.

insurger [17] [ɛsyrʒe] ➤ **s'insurger** vp to rebel, to revolt ; **s'insurger contre qqch** to protest against sthg.

insurmontable [ɛsyrmɔ̃tabl] adj [difficulté] insurmountable ; [dégoût] uncontrollable.

insurrection [ɛsyrɛksjɔ̃] nf insurrection.

intact, e [ɛtakt] adj intact.

intangible [ɛtɑ̃ʒibl] adj 1. litt [impalpable] intangible - 2. [sacré] inviolable.

intarissable [ɛtarisabl] adj inexhaustible ; **il est intarissable** he could go on talking for ever.

intégral, e, aux [ɛtegral, o] adj 1. [paiement] in full ; [texte] unabridged, complete - 2. MATH : **calcul intégral** integral calculus.

intégralement [ɛtegralmɑ̃] adv fully, in full.

intégrant, e [ɛtegrɑ̃, ɑ̃t] ► parti.

intègre [ɛtegr] adj honest, of integrity.

intégré, e [ɛtegre] adj [élément] built-in.

intégrer [18] [ɛtegre] vt [assimiler] : **intégrer (à ou dans)** to integrate (into). ➤ **s'intégrer** vp 1. [s'incorporer] : **s'intégrer dans ou à** to fit into - 2. [s'adapter] to integrate.

intégrisme [ɛ̃tegrism] *nm* fundamentalism.

intégrité [ɛ̃tegrite] *nf* **1.** [totalité] entirety - **2.** [honnêteté] integrity.

intellectuel, elle [ɛ̃telɛktɥɛl] *adj & nm, f* intellectual.

intelligence [ɛ̃teliʒɑ̃s] *nf* **1.** [facultés mentales] intelligence ; **intelligence artificielle** artificial intelligence - **2.** [compréhension, complicité] understanding.

intelligent, e [ɛ̃teliʒɑ̃, ɑ̃t] *adj* intelligent.

intelligible [ɛ̃teliʒibl] *adj* **1.** [voix] clear - **2.** [concept, texte] intelligible.

intello [ɛ̃telo] *adj inv & nmf péj* highbrow.

intempéries [ɛ̃tɑ̃peri] *nfpl* bad weather (U).

intempestif, ive [ɛ̃tɑ̃pɛstif, iv] *adj* untimely.

intenable [ɛ̃tənabl] *adj* **1.** [chaleur, personne] unbearable - **2.** [position] untenable, indefensible.

intendance [ɛ̃tɑ̃dɑ̃s] *nf* **1.** MIL commissariat ; SCOL & UNIV bursar's office - **2.** *fig* [questions matérielles] housekeeping.

intendant, e [ɛ̃tɑ̃dɑ̃, ɑ̃t] *nm, f* **1.** SCOL & UNIV bursar - **2.** [de manoir] steward. **◆ intendant** *nm* MIL quartermaster.

intense [ɛ̃tɑ̃s] *adj* [gén] intense.

intensif, ive [ɛ̃tɑ̃sif, iv] *adj* intensive.

intensité [ɛ̃tɑ̃site] *nf* intensity.

intenter [3] [ɛ̃tɑ̃te] *vt* DR : **intenter qqch contre qqn** OU **à qqn** to bring sthg against sb.

intention [ɛ̃tɑ̃sjɔ̃] *nf* intention ; **avoir l'intention de faire qqch** to intend to do sthg ; **intention de vote** voting intention ; **les intentions de vote pour le président** those leaning toward the président. **◆ à l'intention de** *loc prép* for.

intentionné, e [ɛ̃tɑ̃sjɔne] *adj* : **bien intentionné** well-meaning ; **mal intentionné** ill-disposed.

intentionnel, elle [ɛ̃tɑ̃sjɔnɛl] *adj* intentional.

interactif, ive [ɛ̃tɛraktif, iv] *adj* interactive.

intercalaire [ɛ̃tɛrkalɛr] `<>` *nm* insert. `<>` *adj* : **feuillet intercalaire** insert.

intercaler [3] [ɛ̃tɛrkale] *vt* : **intercaler qqch dans qqch** [feuillet, citation] to insert sthg in sthg ; [dans le temps] to fit sthg into sthg.

intercéder [18] [ɛ̃tɛrsede] *vi* : **intercéder pour** OU **en faveur de qqn auprès de qqn** to intercede with sb on behalf of sb.

intercepter [4] [ɛ̃tɛrsɛpte] *vt* **1.** [lettre, ballon] to intercept - **2.** [chaleur] to block.

interchangeable [ɛ̃tɛrʃɑ̃ʒabl] *adj* interchangeable.

interclasse [ɛ̃tɛrklas] *nm* break.

interdiction [ɛ̃tɛrdiksjɔ̃] *nf* **1.** [défense] : **'interdiction de stationner'** 'strictly no parking' - **2.** [prohibition, suspension] : **interdiction (de)** ban (on), banning (of) ; **interdiction de séjour** *order banning released prisoner from living in certain areas.*

interdire [103] [ɛ̃tɛrdir] *vt* **1.** [prohiber] : **interdire qqch à qqn** to forbid sb sthg ; **interdire à qqn de faire qqch** to forbid sb to do sthg - **2.** [empêcher] to prevent ; **interdire à qqn de faire qqch** to prevent sb from doing sthg - **3.** [bloquer] to block.

interdit, e [ɛ̃tɛrdi, it] `<>` *pp* **►** **interdire.** `<>` *adj* **1.** [défendu] forbidden ; **'film interdit aux moins de 18 ans'** ≃ (18) ; **il est interdit de fumer** you're not allowed to smoke - **2.** [ébahi] : **rester interdit** to be stunned - **3.** [privé] : **être interdit de chéquier** to have had one's chequebook UK OU checkbook US facilities withdrawn, to be forbidden to write cheques UK OU checks US ; **interdit de séjour** banned from entering the country.

intéressant, e [ɛ̃teresɑ̃, ɑ̃t] *adj* **1.** [captivant] interesting - **2.** [avantageux] advantageous, good.

intéressé, e [ɛ̃terese] *adj* [concerné] concerned, involved ; *péj* [motivé] self-interested.

intéresser [4] [ɛ̃terese] *vt* **1.** [captiver] to interest ; **intéresser qqn à qqch** to interest sb in sthg - **2.** COMM [faire participer] : **intéresser les employés (aux bénéfices)** to give one's employees a share in the profits ; **intéresser qqn dans son commerce** to give sb a financial interest in one's business - **3.** [concerner] to concern. **◆ s'intéresser** *vp* : **s'intéresser à qqn/qqch** to take an interest in sb/sthg, to be interested in sb/sthg.

intérêt [ɛ̃terɛ] *nm* **1.** [gén] interest ; **intérêt pour** interest in ; **avoir intérêt à faire qqch** to be well advised to do sthg - **2.** [importance] significance. **◆ intérêts** *nmpl* **1.** FIN interest *sg* - **2.** COMM : **avoir des intérêts dans** to have a stake in.

interface [ɛ̃tɛrfas] *nf* INFORM interface ; **interface graphique** graphic interface.

interférer [18] [ɛ̃tɛrfere] *vi* **1.** PHYS to interfere - **2.** *fig* [s'immiscer] : **interférer dans qqch** to interfere in sthg.

intérieur, e [ɛ̃terjœr] *adj* **1.** [gén] inner - **2.** [de pays] domestic. **◆ intérieur** *nm* **1.** [gén] inside ; **de l'intérieur** from the inside ; **à l'intérieur (de qqch)** inside (sthg) - **2.** [de pays] interior.

intérim [ɛ̃terim] *nm* **1.** [période] interim period ; **par intérim** acting - **2.** [travail temporaire] temporary OU casual work ; [dans un bureau] temping.

intérimaire [ēterimɛr] <> adj **1.** [ministre, directeur] **acting** *(avant n)* - **2.** [employé, fonctions] **temporary.** <> nmf [employé] **temp.**

intérioriser [3] [ēterjɔrize] vt to internalize.

interjection [ēterʒɛksjɔ̃] nf LING interjection.

interligne [ēterliɲ] nm (line) spacing.

interlocuteur, trice [ēterlɔkytœr, tris] nm, f **1.** [dans conversation] speaker ; **mon interlocuteur** the person to whom I am/was speaking - **2.** [dans négociation] negotiator.

interloquer [3] [ēterlɔke] vt to disconcert.

interlude [ēterlyd] nm interlude.

intermède [ētermɛd] nm interlude.

intermédiaire [ētermedjɛr] <> nm intermediary, go-between ; **par l'intermédiaire de qqn/qqch** through sb/sthg. <> adj intermediate.

interminable [ēterminabl] adj never-ending, interminable.

intermittence [ētermitɑ̃s] nf [discontinuité] : **par intermittence** intermittently, off and on.

intermittent, e [ētermitɑ̃, ɑ̃t] adj intermittent ; **les intermittents du spectacle** *people working in the performing arts.*

internat [ēterna] nm [SCOL - établissement] boarding school ; [- système] boarding.

international, e, aux [ēternasjɔnal, o] adj international.

internaute [ēternot] nmf INFORM (net) surfer, cybersurfer, cybernaut, Internet user.

interne [ētern] <> nmf **1.** [élève] boarder - **2.** MÉD & UNIV houseman UK, intern US. <> adj **1.** ANAT internal ; [oreille] inner - **2.** [du pays] domestic.

interner [3] [ēterne] vt **1.** MÉD to commit *(to psychiatric hospital)* - **2.** POLIT to intern.

Internet, internet [ēternet] nm : **(l')** Internet the internet, the Internet.

interpeller [26] [ēterpəle] vt **1.** [apostropher] to call ou shout out to - **2.** [interroger] to take in for questioning.

Interphone® [ēterfɔn] nm intercom ; [d'un immeuble] entry phone.

interposer [3] [ēterpoze] vt to interpose. **s'interposer** vp : **s'interposer entre qqn et qqn** to intervene ou come between sb and sb.

interprète [ēterprɛt] nmf **1.** [gén] interpreter - **2.** CINÉ, MUS & THÉÂTRE performer.

interpréter [18] [ēterprete] vt to interpret.

interrogateur, trice [ēterɔgatœr, tris] adj inquiring *(avant n)*.

interrogatif, ive [ēterɔgatif, iv] adj GRAMM interrogative.

interrogation [ēterɔgasjɔ̃] nf **1.** [de prisonnier] interrogation ; [de témoin] questioning - **2.** [question] question - **3.** SCOL test, quiz US.

interrogatoire [ēterɔgatwar] nm **1.** [de police, juge] questioning - **2.** [procès-verbal] statement.

interrogeable [ēterɔʒabl] adj : **répondeur interrogeable à distance** answerphone with remote playback facility.

interroger [17] [ēterɔʒe] vt **1.** [questionner] to question ; [accusé, base de données] to interrogate ; **interroger qqn (sur qqch)** to question sb (about sthg) - **2.** [faits, conscience] to examine. **s'interroger** vp : **s'interroger sur** to wonder about.

interrompre [78] [ēterɔ̃pr] vt to interrupt. **s'interrompre** vp to stop.

interrompu, e [ēterɔ̃py] pp ➤ interrompre.

interrupteur [ēteryptœr] nm switch.

interruption [ēterypsjɔ̃] nf **1.** [arrêt] break - **2.** [action] interruption.

intersection [ētersɛksjɔ̃] nf intersection.

interstice [ēterstis] nm chink, crack.

interurbain, e [ēteryrbɛ̃, ɛn] adj long-distance. **interurbain** nm : **l'interurbain** the long-distance telephone service.

intervalle [ēterval] nm **1.** [spatial] space, gap - **2.** [temporel] interval, period (of time) ; **à 6 jours d'intervalle** after 6 days - **3.** MUS interval.

intervenant, e [ētervənɑ̃, ɑ̃t] nm, f [orateur] speaker.

intervenir [40] [ētervənir] vi **1.** [personne] to intervene ; **intervenir auprès de qqn** to intervene with sb ; **intervenir dans qqch** to intervene in sthg ; **faire intervenir qqn** to bring ou call in sb - **2.** [événement] to take place.

intervention [ētervɑ̃sjɔ̃] nf **1.** [gén] intervention - **2.** MÉD operation ; **subir une intervention chirurgicale** to have an operation, to have surgery - **3.** [discours] speech.

intervenu, e [ētervəny] pp ➤ intervenir.

intervertir [32] [ētervertir] vt to reverse, to invert.

interview [ētervju] nf interview.

interviewer [3] [ētervjuve] vt to interview.

intestin [ētɛstɛ̃] nm intestine.

intestinal, e, aux [ētɛstinal, o] adj intestinal.

intime [ētim] <> nmf close friend. <> adj [gén] intimate ; [vie, journal] private.

intimider [3] [ētimide] vt to intimidate.

intimité [ɛ̃timite] *nf* **1.** [secret] depths *pl* - **2.** [familiarité, confort] intimacy - **3.** [vie privée] privacy.

intitulé [ɛ̃tityle] *nm* [titre] title ; [de paragraphe] heading.

intituler [3] [ɛ̃tityle] *vt* to call, to entitle. **s'intituler** *vp* [ouvrage] to be called ou entitled.

intolérable [ɛ̃tɔlerabl] *adj* intolerable.

intolérance [ɛ̃tɔlerɑ̃s] *nf* [religieuse, politique] intolerance.

intolérant, e [ɛ̃tɔlerɑ̃, ɑ̃t] *adj* intolerant.

intonation [ɛ̃tɔnasjɔ̃] *nf* intonation.

intouchable [ɛ̃tuʃabl] *nmf & adj* untouchable.

intoxication [ɛ̃tɔksikasjɔ̃] *nf* **1.** [empoisonnement] poisoning - **2.** *fig* [propagande] brainwashing.

intoxiquer [3] [ɛ̃tɔksike] *vt* : **intoxiquer qqn par** [empoisonner] to poison sb with ; *fig* to indoctrinate sb with.

intraduisible [ɛ̃tradyizibl] *adj* [texte] untranslatable.

intraitable [ɛ̃tretabl] *adj* : **intraitable (sur)** inflexible (about).

intransigeant, e [ɛ̃trɑ̃ziʒɑ̃, ɑ̃t] *adj* intransigent.

intransitif, ive [ɛ̃trɑ̃zitif, iv] *adj* intransitive.

intransportable [ɛ̃trɑ̃spɔrtabl] *adj* : **il est intransportable** he/it cannot be moved.

intraveineux, euse [ɛ̃travɛnø, øz] *adj* intravenous.

intrépide [ɛ̃trepid] *adj* bold, intrepid.

intrigue [ɛ̃trig] *nf* **1.** [manœuvre] intrigue - **2.** CINÉ, LITTÉR & THÉÂTRE plot.

intriguer [3] [ɛ̃trige] *vt* to intrigue. *vi* to scheme, to intrigue.

introduction [ɛ̃trɔdyksjɔ̃] *nf* **1.** [gén] : **introduction (à)** introduction (to) - **2.** [insertion] insertion.

introduire [98] [ɛ̃trɔdyir] *vt* **1.** [gén] to introduce - **2.** [faire entrer] to show in - **3.** [insérer] to insert ; **s'introduire** *vp* **1.** [pénétrer] to enter ; **s'introduire dans une maison** [cambrioleur] to get into ou enter a house - **2.** [s'implanter] to be introduced.

introduit, e [ɛ̃trɔdyi, it] *pp* introduire.

introspection [ɛ̃trɔspɛksjɔ̃] *nf* introspection.

introuvable [ɛ̃truvabl] *adj* nowhere ou no place US to be found.

introverti, e [ɛ̃trɔvɛrti] *adj* introverted. *nm, f* introvert.

intrus, e [ɛ̃try, yz] *nm, f* intruder.

intrusion [ɛ̃tryzjɔ̃] *nf* **1.** [gén & GÉOL] intrusion - **2.** [ingérence] interference.

intuitif, ive [ɛ̃tyitif, iv] *adj* intuitive.

intuition [ɛ̃tyisjɔ̃] *nf* intuition.

inusable [inyzabl] *adj* hardwearing.

inusité, e [inyzite] *adj* unusual, uncommon.

in utero [inyterɔ] *loc adj* & *loc adv* in utero.

inutile [inytil] *adj* [objet, personne] useless ; [effort, démarche] pointless.

inutilisable [inytilizabl] *adj* unusable.

inutilité [inytilite] *nf* [de personne, d'objet] uselessness ; [de démarche, d'effort] pointlessness.

invaincu, e [ɛ̃vɛ̃ky] *adj* SPORT unbeaten.

invalide [ɛ̃valid] *nmf* disabled person ; **invalide du travail** industrially disabled person. *adj* disabled.

invalidité [ɛ̃validite] *nf* **1.** DR invalidity - **2.** MÉD disability.

invariable [ɛ̃varjabl] *adj* **1.** [immuable] unchanging - **2.** GRAMM invariable.

invasion [ɛ̃vazjɔ̃] *nf* invasion.

invendable [ɛ̃vɑ̃dabl] *adj* unsaleable, unsellable.

invendu, e [ɛ̃vɑ̃dy] *adj* unsold. **invendu** *(gén pl) nm* remainder.

inventaire [ɛ̃vɑ̃tɛr] *nm* **1.** [gén] inventory - **2.** [COMM - activité] stocktaking *UK*, inventory *US* ; [- liste] list.

inventer [3] [ɛ̃vɑ̃te] *vt* DR [trésor] to discover, to find.

inventeur [ɛ̃vɑ̃tœr] *nm* [de machine] inventor.

invention [ɛ̃vɑ̃sjɔ̃] *nf* **1.** [découverte, mensonge] invention - **2.** [imagination] inventiveness.

inventorier [9] [ɛ̃vɑ̃tɔrje] *vt* to make an inventory of.

inverse [ɛ̃vɛrs] *nm* opposite, reverse. *adj* **1.** [sens] opposite ; [ordre] reverse ; **en sens inverse (de)** in the opposite direction (to) - **2.** [rapport] inverse.

inversement [ɛ̃vɛrsəmɑ̃] *adv* **1.** MATH inversely - **2.** [au contraire] on the other hand - **3.** [vice versa] vice versa.

inverser [3] [ɛ̃vɛrse] *vt* to reverse.

invertébré, e [ɛ̃vɛrtebre] *adj* invertebrate. **invertébré** *nm* invertebrate.

investigation [ɛ̃vɛstigasjɔ̃] *nf* investigation.

investir [32] [ɛ̃vɛstir] *vt* to invest. **s'investir dans** *vp + prép* : **s'investir dans son métier** to be involved ou absorbed in one's job ; **une actrice qui s'investit entièrement dans ses rôles** an actress who throws herself heart and soul into every part she plays ; **je me suis énormément investie dans le projet** the project really meant a lot to me.

investissement [ɛ̃vɛstismɑ̃] *nm* investment.

investisseur, euse [ɛ̃vɛstisœr, øz] *nm, f* investor.

investiture [ɛ̃vɛstityr] *nf* investiture.

invétéré, e [ɛ̃vetere] *adj péj* inveterate.

invincible [ɛ̃vɛ̃sibl] *adj* [gén] invincible ; [difficulté] insurmountable ; [charme] irresistible.

inviolable [ɛ̃vjɔlabl] *adj* **1.** DR inviolable - **2.** [coffre] impregnable.

invisible [ɛ̃vizibl] *adj* invisible.

invitation [ɛ̃vitasjɔ̃] *nf* : **invitation (à)** invitation (to) ; **sur invitation** by invitation.

invité, e [ɛ̃vite] <> *adj* [hôte] invited ; [professeur, conférencier] guest *(avant n)*. <> *nm, f* guest.

inviter [3] [ɛ̃vite] *vt* to invite ; **inviter qqn à faire qqch** to invite sb to do sthg ; *fig* [suj: chose] to be an invitation to sb to do sthg ; **je vous invite!** it's my treat!

in vitro [invitro] ➤ **fécondation.**

invivable [ɛ̃vivabl] *adj* unbearable.

involontaire [ɛ̃vɔlɔ̃tɛr] *adj* [acte] involuntary.

invoquer [3] [ɛ̃vɔke] *vt* **1.** [alléguer] to put forward - **2.** [citer, appeler à l'aide] to invoke ; [paix] to call for.

invraisemblable [ɛ̃vrɛsɑ̃blabl] *adj* **1.** [incroyable] unlikely, improbable - **2.** [extravagant] incredible.

invulnérable [ɛ̃vylnerabl] *adj* invulnerable.

iode [jɔd] *nm* iodine.

ion [jɔ̃] *nm* ion.

IRA [ira] *(abr de Irish Republican Army) nf* IRA.

irai, iras *etc* ➤ **aller.**

Irak, Iraq [irak] *nm* : **l'Irak** Iraq.

irakien, enne, iraquien, enne [irakjɛ̃, ɛn] *adj* Iraqi. ➤ **Irakien, enne, Iraquien, enne** *nm, f* Iraqi.

Iran [irɑ̃] *nm* : **l'Iran** Iran.

iranien, enne [iranjɛ̃, ɛn] *adj* Iranian. ➤ **iranien** *nm* [langue] Iranian. ➤ **Iranien, enne** *nm, f* Iranian.

Iraq = **Irak.**

iraquien = **irakien.**

irascible [irasibl] *adj* irascible.

iris [iris] *nm* ANAT & BOT iris.

irisé, e [irize] *adj* iridescent.

irlandais, e [irlɑ̃dɛ, ɛz] *adj* Irish. ➤ **irlandais** *nm* [langue] Irish. ➤ **Irlandais, e** *nm, f* Irishman (*f* Irishwoman).

Irlande [irlɑ̃d] *nf* : **l'Irlande** Ireland ; **l'Irlande du Nord/Sud** Northern/Southern Ireland.

IRM [iɛrɛm] *(abr de Imagerie par résonance magnétique) nm* MÉD MRI.

ironie [irɔni] *nf* irony.

ironique [irɔnik] *adj* ironic.

ironiser [3] [irɔnize] *vi* to speak ironically.

irradier [9] [iradje] <> *vi* to radiate. <> *vt* to irradiate.

irraisonné, e [irezɔne] *adj* irrational.

irrationnel, elle [irasjɔnɛl] *adj* irrational.

irréalisable [irealizabl] *adj* unrealizable.

irrécupérable [irekyperabl] *adj* **1.** [irrécouvrable] irretrievable - **2.** [irréparable] beyond repair - **3.** *fam* [personne] beyond hope.

irrécusable [irekyzabl] *adj* unimpeachable.

irréductible [iredyktibl] <> *nmf* diehard. <> *adj* **1.** CHIM, MATH & MÉD irreducible - **2.** *fig* [volonté] indomitable ; [personne] implacable ; [communiste] diehard *(before n)*.

irréel, elle [ireɛl] *adj* unreal.

irréfléchi, e [irefleʃi] *adj* unthinking.

irréfutable [irefytabl] *adj* irrefutable.

irrégularité [iregylarite] *nf* **1.** [gén] irregularity - **2.** [de terrain, performance] unevenness.

irrégulier, ère [iregylje, ɛr] *adj* **1.** [gén] irregular - **2.** [terrain, surface] uneven, irregular - **3.** [employé, athlète] erratic.

irrémédiable [iremedjabl] *adj* [irréparable] irreparable.

irremplaçable [irɑ̃plasabl] *adj* irreplaceable.

irréparable [ireparabl] *adj* **1.** [objet] beyond repair - **2.** *fig* [perte, erreur] irreparable.

irrépressible [irepresibl] *adj* irrepressible.

irréprochable [ireprɔʃabl] *adj* irreproachable.

irrésistible [irezistibl] *adj* **1.** [tentation, femme] irresistible - **2.** [amusant] entertaining.

irrésolu, e [irezɔly] *adj* **1.** [indécis] irresolute - **2.** [sans solution] unresolved.

irrespirable [irɛspirabl] *adj* **1.** [air] unbreathable - **2.** *fig* [oppressant] oppressive.

irresponsable [irɛspɔ̃sabl] <> *nmf* irresponsible person. <> *adj* irresponsible.

irréversible [irevɛrsibl] *adj* irreversible.

irrévocable [irevɔkabl] *adj* irrevocable.

irrigation [irigasjɔ̃] *nf* irrigation.

irriguer [3] [irige] *vt* to irrigate.

irritable [iritabl] *adj* irritable.

irritation [iritasjɔ̃] *nf* irritation.

irriter [3] [irite] *vt* **1.** [exaspérer] to irritate, to annoy - **2.** MÉD to irritate. ◆ **s'irriter** *vp* to get irritated ; **s'irriter contre qqn/de qqch** to get irritated with sb/at sthg.

irruption [irypsjɔ̃] *nf* **1.** [invasion] invasion - **2.** [entrée brusque] irruption.

islam [islam] *nm* Islam.

islamique [islamik] *adj* Islamic.

islandais, e [islɑ̃dɛ, ɛz] *adj* Icelandic. ◆ **islandais** *nm* [langue] Icelandic. ◆ **Islandais, e** *nm, f* Icelander.

Islande [islɑ̃d] *nf* : l'Islande Iceland.

isocèle [izɔsɛl] *adj* isoceles.

isolant, e [izɔlɑ̃, ɑ̃t] *adj* insulating. ◆ **isolant** *nm* insulator, insulating material.

isolation [izɔlasjɔ̃] *nf* insulation.

isolé, e [izɔle] *adj* isolated.

isoler [3] [izɔle] *vt* **1.** [séparer] to isolate - **2.** CONSTR & ÉLECTR to insulate ; **isoler qqch du froid** to insulate sthg (against the cold) ; **isoler qqch du bruit** to soundproof sthg. ◆ **s'isoler** *vp* : **s'isoler (de)** to isolate o.s. (from).

isoloir [izɔlwar] *nm* polling booth.

isotherme [izɔtɛrm] *adj* isothermal.

Israël [israɛl] *npr* Israel.

israélien, enne [israeljɛ̃, ɛn] *adj* Israeli. ◆ **Israélien, enne** *nm, f* Israeli.

israélite [israelit] *adj* Jewish. ◆ **Israélite** *nmf* Jew.

issu, e [isy] *adj* : **être issu de** [résulter de] to emerge ou stem from ; [personne] to come from. ◆ **issue** *nf* **1.** [sortie] exit ; **issue de secours** emergency exit - **2.** *fig* [solution] way out, solution - **3.** [terme] outcome.

isthme [ism] *nm* isthmus.

Italie [itali] *nf* : l'Italie Italy.

italien, enne [italjɛ̃, ɛn] *adj* Italian. ◆ **italien** *nm* [langue] Italian. ◆ **Italien, enne** *nm, f* Italian.

italique [italik] *nm* TYPO italics *pl* ; **en italique** in italics.

itinéraire [itinerɛr] *nm* itinerary, route ; **itinéraire bis** diversion.

itinérant, e [itinerɑ̃, ɑ̃t] *adj* [spectacle, troupe] itinerant.

IUT (*abr de* institut universitaire de technologie) *nm* ≃ technical college.

IVG (*abr de* interruption volontaire de grossesse) *nf* abortion.

ivoire [ivwar] *nm* ivory.

ivre [ivr] *adj* drunk.

ivresse [ivrɛs] *nf* drunkenness ; [extase] rapture.

ivrogne [ivrɔɲ] *nmf* drunkard.

J

j, J [ʒi] *nm inv* j, J.

j' ▶ je.

jabot [ʒabo] *nm* **1.** [d'oiseau] crop - **2.** [de chemise] frill.

jacasser [3] [ʒakase] *vi péj* to chatter, to jabber.

jacinthe [ʒasɛ̃t] *nf* hyacinth.

Jacuzzi® [ʒakuzi] *nm* Jacuzzi®.

jade [ʒad] *nm* jade.

jadis [ʒadis] *adv* formerly, in former times.

jaguar [ʒagwar] *nm* jaguar.

jaillir [32] [ʒajir] *vi* **1.** [liquide] to gush ; [flammes] to leap - **2.** [cri] to ring out - **3.** [personne] to spring out.

jais [ʒɛ] *nm* jet.

jalon [ʒalɔ̃] *nm* marker pole.

jalonner [3] [ʒalɔne] *vt* to mark (out).

jalousie [ʒaluzi] *nf* **1.** [envie] jealousy - **2.** [store] blind.

jaloux, ouse [ʒalu, uz] *adj* : **jaloux (de)** jealous (of).

Jamaïque [ʒamaik] *nf* : la Jamaïque Jamaica.

jamais [ʒamɛ] *adv* **1.** [sens négatif] never ; **ne... jamais, jamais ne** never ; **je ne reviendrai jamais, jamais je ne reviendrai** I'll never come back ; **(ne)... jamais plus, plus jamais (ne)** never again ; **je ne viendrai jamais plus, plus jamais je ne viendrai** I'll never come here again - **2.** [sens positif] : **plus que jamais** more than ever ; **il est plus triste que jamais** he's sadder than ever ; **si jamais tu le vois** if you should happen to see him, should you happen to see him. ◆ **à jamais** *loc adv* for ever.

jambe [ʒɑ̃b] *nf* leg.

jambières [ʒɑ̃bjɛr] *nfpl* [de football] shin pads ; [de cricket] pads.

jambon [ʒɑ̃bɔ̃] *nm* ham ; **jambon blanc** ham ; **un jambon beurre** *fam* a ham sandwich.

jante [ʒɑ̃t] *nf* (wheel) rim.

janvier [ʒɑ̃vje] *nm* January ; *voir aussi* septembre.

Japon [ʒapɔ̃] *nm* : le Japon Japan.

japonais, e [ʒapɔnɛ, ɛz] *adj* Japanese. ◆ **japonais** *nm* [langue] Japanese. ◆ **Japonais, e** *nm, f* Japanese (person) ; **les Japonais** the Japanese.

japper [3] [ʒape] *vi* to yap.

jaquette [ʒakɛt] *nf* **1.** [vêtement] jacket - **2.** [de livre] (dust) jacket.

jardin [ʒardɛ̃] *nm* [espace clos] garden ; [attaché à une maison] yard ; **jardin public** park.

jardinage [ʒardinaʒ] *nm* gardening.

jardinier, ère [ʒardinje, ɛr] *nm, f* gardener.
jardinière *nf* [bac à fleurs] window box.

jargon [ʒargɔ̃] *nm* **1.** [langage spécialisé] jargon - **2.** *fam* [charabia] gibberish.

jarret [ʒarɛ] *nm* **1.** ANAT back of the knee - **2.** CULIN knuckle of veal.

jarretelle [ʒartɛl] *nf* suspender *UK*, garter *US*.

jarretière [ʒartjer] *nf* garter.

jars [ʒar] *nm* gander.

jaser [3] [ʒaze] *vi* [bavarder] to gossip.

jasmin [ʒasmɛ̃] *nm* jasmine.

jatte [ʒat] *nf* bowl.

jauge [ʒoʒ] *nf* [instrument] gauge.

jauger [17] [ʒoʒe] *vt* to gauge.

jaunâtre [ʒonatr] *adj* yellowish.

jaune [ʒon] <> *nm* [couleur] yellow.
<> *adj* yellow. **jaune d'œuf** *nm* (egg) yolk.

jaunir [32] [ʒonir] *vt & vi* to turn yellow.

jaunisse [ʒonis] *nf* MÉD jaundice.

java [ʒava] *nf type of popular dance.*

Javel [ʒavɛl] *nf* : **eau de Javel** bleach.

javelot [ʒavlo] *nm* javelin.

jazz [dʒaz] *nm* jazz.

J.-C. (*abr écrite de* Jésus-Christ) J.C.

je [ʒə], **j'** (*devant voyelle ou 'h' muet*) *pron pers* I.

jean [dʒin], **jeans** [dʒins] *nm* jeans *pl*, pair of jeans.

Jeep® [dʒip] *nf* Jeep®.

jérémiades [ʒeremjad] *nfpl* moaning (*U*), whining (*U*).

jerrycan, jerricane [ʒerikan] *nm* jerry can.

jersey [ʒerze] *nm* jersey.

jésuite [ʒezɥit] *nm* Jesuit.

Jésus-Christ [ʒezykri] *nm* Jesus Christ.

jet¹ [ʒɛ] *nm* **1.** [action de jeter] throw - **2.** [de liquide] jet.

jet² [dʒɛt] *nm* [avion] jet.

jetable [ʒətabl] *adj* disposable.

jeté, e [ʒəte] *pp* ► jeter.

jetée [ʒəte] *nf* jetty.

jeter [27] [ʒəte] *vt* **1.** [gén] to throw ; [se débarrasser de] to throw away ; **jeter qqch à qqn** [lancer] to throw sthg to sb, to throw sb sthg ; [pour faire mal] to throw sthg at sb - **2.** [émettre - étincelle] to throw *ou* to give out (*sep*) ; [- lumière] to cast, to shed. **se jeter** *vp* : **se jeter sur** to pounce on ; **se jeter dans** [suj: rivière] to flow into.

jeton [ʒətɔ̃] *nm* [de jeu] counter ; [de téléphone] token.

jet-set [dʒɛtsɛt], **jet-society** [dʒɛtsɔsajti] *nf* jet set ; **membre de la jet-set** jet-setter.

jeu, x [ʒø] *nm* **1.** [divertissement] play (*U*), playing (*U*) ; **jeu de mots** play on words, pun - **2.** [régi par des règles] game ; **mettre un joueur hors jeu** to put a player offside ; **jeu de société** parlour *UK ou* parlor *US* game - **3.** [d'argent] : **le jeu** gambling - **4.** [d'échecs, de clés] set ; **jeu de cartes** pack *ou* deck of cards - **5.** [manière de jouer] MUS playing ; THÉÂTRE acting ; SPORT game - **6.** TECHNOL play ; **cacher son jeu** to play one's cards close to one's chest. **jeux Olympiques** *nmpl* : **les jeux Olympiques** the Olympic Games.

jeudi [ʒødi] *nm* Thursday ; *voir aussi* **samedi**.

jeun [ʒœ̃] **à jeun** *loc adv* on an empty stomach.

jeune [ʒœn] <> *adj* young ; [style, apparence] youthful ; **jeune homme/femme** young man/woman ; **jeune pousse** ÉCON start up (company). <> *nm* young person ; **les jeunes** young people.

jeûne [ʒøn] *nm* fast.

jeunesse [ʒœnɛs] *nf* **1.** [âge] youth ; [de style, apparence] youthfulness - **2.** [jeunes gens] young people *pl*.

jingle [dʒingəl] *nm* jingle.

JO *nmpl* (*abr de* jeux Olympiques) Olympic Games.

joaillier, ère [ʒɔaje, ɛr] *nm, f* jeweller *UK*, jeweler *US*.

job [dʒɔb] *nm fam* job.

jockey [ʒɔke] *nm* jockey.

jogging [dʒɔgin] *nm* **1.** [activité] jogging - **2.** [vêtement] tracksuit, jogging suit.

joie [ʒwa] *nf* joy.

joindre [82] [ʒwɛ̃dr] *vt* **1.** [rapprocher] to join ; [mains] to put together - **2.** [mettre avec] : **joindre qqch (à)** to add sthg (to) ; [ajouter] **joindre un fichier à un message électronique** to attach a file to an email message ; [adjoindre] to enclose sthg (with) - **3.** [par téléphone] to contact, to reach. **se joindre** *vp* : **se joindre à qqn** to join sb ; **se joindre à qqch** to join in sthg.

joint, e [ʒwɛ̃, ɛ̃t] *pp* ► joindre. **joint** *nm* **1.** [d'étanchéité] seal - **2.** *fam* [drogue] joint.

joker [ʒɔker] *nm* joker.

joli, e [ʒɔli] *adj* **1.** [femme, chose] pretty, attractive - **2.** [somme, situation] nice.

joliment [ʒɔlimã] adv 1. [bien] prettily, attractively ; iron nicely - 2. fam [beaucoup] really.

jonc [ʒɔ̃] nm rush, bulrush.

joncher [3] [ʒɔ̃ʃe] vt to strew ; être jonché de to be strewn with.

jonction [ʒɔ̃ksjɔ̃] nf [de routes] junction.

jongler [3] [ʒɔ̃gle] vi to juggle.

jongleur, euse [ʒɔ̃glœr, øz] nm, f juggler.

jonquille [ʒɔ̃kij] nf daffodil.

Jordanie [ʒɔrdani] nf : la Jordanie Jordan.

joue [ʒu] nf cheek ; tenir ou mettre qqn en joue fig to take aim at sb.

jouer [6] [ʒwe] ◇ vi 1. [gén] to play ; jouer avec qqn/qqch to play with sb/sthg ; jouer à qqch [jeu, sport] to play sthg ; jouer de MUS to play ; à toi de jouer! (it's) your turn! ; fig your move! - 2. CINÉ & THÉÂTRE to act - 3. [parier] to gamble. ◇ vt 1. [carte, partie] to play - 2. [somme d'argent] to bet, to wager ; fig to gamble with - 3. [THÉÂTRE - personnage, rôle] to play ; [- pièce] to put on, to perform - 4. [avoir à l'affiche] to show - 5. MUS to perform, to play.

jouet [ʒwe] nm toy.

joueur, euse [ʒwœr, øz] nm, f 1. SPORT player ; joueur de football footballer, football player - 2. [au casino] gambler.

joufflu, e [ʒufly] adj [personne] chubby-cheeked.

joug [ʒu] nm yoke.

jouir [32] [ʒwir] vi 1. [profiter] : jouir de to enjoy - 2. [sexuellement] to have an orgasm.

jouissance [ʒwisãs] nf 1. DR [d'un bien] use - 2. [sexuelle] orgasm.

joujou, x [ʒuʒu] nm toy.

jour [ʒur] nm 1. [unité de temps] day ; huit jours a week ; quinze jours a fortnight UK, two weeks ; de jour en jour day by day ; jour après jour day after day ; au jour le jour from day to day ; jour et nuit night and day ; le jour de l'an New Year's Day ; jour chômé public holiday ; jour de congé day off ; jour férié public holiday ; jour ouvrable working day - 2. [lumière] daylight ; de jour in the daytime, by day - 3. COUT opening (made by drawing threads) ; mettre qqch à jour to update sthg, to bring sthg up to date ; de nos jours these days, nowadays.

journal, aux [ʒurnal, o] nm 1. [publication] newspaper, paper - 2. TV : journal télévisé television news - 3. [écrit] : journal (intime) diary, journal.

journalier, ère [ʒurnalje, ɛr] adj daily.

journalisme [ʒurnalism] nm journalism.

journaliste [ʒurnalist] nmf journalist, reporter.

journée [ʒurne] nf day.

joute [ʒut] nf joust ; fig duel.

jovial, e, aux [ʒɔvjal, o] adj jovial, jolly.

joyau, x [ʒwajo] nm jewel.

joyeux, euse [ʒwajø, øz] adj joyful, happy ; joyeux Noël! Merry Christmas!

jubilé [ʒybile] nm jubilee.

jubiler [3] [ʒybile] vi fam to be jubilant.

jucher [3] [ʒyʃe] vt : jucher qqn sur qqch to perch sb on sthg.

judaïque [ʒydaik] adj [loi] Judaic ; [tradition, religion] Jewish.

judaïsme [ʒydaism] nm Judaism.

judas [ʒyda] nm [ouverture] peephole.

judéo-chrétien, enne [ʒydeɔkretjɛ̃, ɛn] (mpl judéo-chrétiens, fpl judéo-chrétiennes) adj Judaeo-Christian.

judiciaire [ʒydisjɛr] adj judicial.

judicieux, euse [ʒydisjø, øz] adj judicious.

judo [ʒydo] nm judo.

juge [ʒyʒ] nm judge ; juge d'instruction examining magistrate ; juge d'enfants children's judge, juvenile magistrate UK.

jugé [ʒyʒe] ◈ au jugé loc adv by guesswork ; tirer au jugé to fire blind.

jugement [ʒyʒmã] nm judgment ; prononcer un jugement to pass sentence.

jugeote [ʒyʒɔt] nf fam common sense.

juger [17] [ʒyʒe] ◇ vt to judge ; [accusé] to try ; juger que to judge (that), to consider (that) ; juger qqn/qqch inutile to consider sb/sthg useless. ◇ vi to judge ; juger de qqch to judge sthg ; si j'en juge d'après mon expérience judging from my experience ; jugez de ma surprise! imagine my surprise!

juif, ive [ʒɥif, iv] adj Jewish. ◈ Juif, ive nm, f Jew.

juillet [ʒɥije] nm July ; la fête du 14 Juillet national holiday to mark the anniversary of the storming of the Bastille ; voir aussi septembre.

juin [ʒɥɛ̃] nm June ; voir aussi septembre.

juke-box [dʒukbɔks] nm inv jukebox.

jumeau, elle, x [ʒymo, ɛl, o] ◇ adj twin (avant n). ◇ nm, f twin. ◈ jumelles nfpl [en optique] binoculars.

jumelé, e [ʒymle] adj [villes] twinned UK ; [maisons] semidetached UK.

jumeler [24] [ʒymle] vt UK to twin.

jumelle ▶ jumeau.

jument [ʒymã] nf mare.

jungle [ʒœ̃gl] nf jungle.

junior [ʒynjɔr] adj & nmf SPORT junior.

junte [ʒœ̃t] nf junta.

jupe [ʒyp] nf skirt.

jupe-culotte [ʒypkylɔt] nf culottes pl.

jupon [ʒypɔ̃] nm petticoat, slip.

juré [ʒyre] *nm* DR juror.

jurer [3] [ʒyre] <> *vt* : jurer qqch à qqn to swear OU pledge sthg to sb ; jurer (à qqn) que... to swear (to sb) that... ; jurer de faire qqch to swear OU vow to do sthg ; je vous jure! *fam* honestly! <> *vi* **1.** [blasphémer] to swear, to curse - **2.** [ne pas aller ensemble] : jurer (avec) to clash (with). **se jurer** *vp* : se jurer de faire qqch to swear OU vow to do sthg.

juridiction [ʒyridiksjɔ̃] *nf* jurisdiction.

juridique [ʒyridik] *adj* legal.

jurisprudence [ʒyrisprydɑ̃s] *nf* jurisprudence.

juriste [ʒyrist] *nmf* lawyer.

juron [ʒyrɔ̃] *nm* swearword, oath.

jury [ʒyri] *nm* **1.** DR jury - **2.** [SCOL - d'examen] examining board ; [- de concours] admissions board.

jus [ʒy] *nm* **1.** [de fruits, légumes] juice - **2.** [de viande] gravy.

jusque, jusqu' [ʒysk(ə)] **jusqu'à** *loc prép* **1.** [sens temporel] until, till ; jusqu'à nouvel ordre until further notice ; jusqu'à présent up until now, so far - **2.** [sens spatial] as far as ; jusqu'au bout to the end - **3.** [même] even. **jusqu'à ce que** *loc conj* until, till. **jusqu'en** *loc prép* up until. **jusqu'ici** *loc adv* [lieu] up to here ; [temps] up until now, so far. **jusque-là** *loc adv* [lieu] up to there ; [temps] up until then.

justaucorps [ʒystokɔr] *nm* [maillot] leotard.

juste [ʒyst] <> *adj* **1.** [équitable] fair - **2.** [exact] right, correct - **3.** [trop petit, trop court] tight. <> *adv* **1.** [bien] correctly, right - **2.** [exactement, seulement] just.

justement [ʒystəmɑ̃] *adv* **1.** [avec raison] rightly - **2.** [précisément] exactly, precisely.

justesse [ʒystɛs] *nf* [de remarque] aptness ; [de raisonnement] soundness. **de justesse** *loc adv* only just.

justice [ʒystis] *nf* **1.** DR justice ; passer en justice to stand trial - **2.** [équité] fairness.

justicier, ère [ʒystisje, ɛr] *nm, f* righter of wrongs.

justifiable [ʒystifjabl] *adj* justifiable.

justificatif, ive [ʒystifikatif, iv] *adj* supporting. **justificatif** *nm* written proof (U).

justification [ʒystifikasjɔ̃] *nf* justification.

justifier [9] [ʒystifje] *vt* [gén] to justify. **se justifier** *vp* to justify o.s.

jute [ʒyt] *nm* jute.

juteux, euse [ʒytø, øz] *adj* juicy.

juvénile [ʒyvenil] *adj* youthful.

juxtaposer [3] [ʒykstapoze] *vt* to juxtapose, to place side by side.

K

k, K [ka] *nm inv* k, K.

K7 [kasɛt] (*abr de* **cassette**) *nf* cassette.

kaki [kaki] <> *nm* **1.** [couleur] khaki - **2.** [fruit] persimmon. <> *adj inv* khaki.

kaléidoscope [kaleidɔskɔp] *nm* kaléidoscope.

kamikaze [kamikaz] *nm* kamikaze pilot.

kanak = canaque.

kangourou [kɑ̃guru] *nm* kangaroo.

karaoké [karaɔke] *nm* karaoke.

karaté [karate] *nm* karate.

karting [kartiŋ] *nm* go-karting.

kas(c)her, cascher [kaʃɛr] *adj inv* kosher.

kayak [kajak] *nm* kayak.

Kenya [kenja] *nm* : le Kenya Kenya.

képi [kepi] *nm* kepi.

kératine [keratin] *nf* keratin.

kermesse [kɛrmɛs] *nf* **1.** [foire] fair - **2.** [fête de bienfaisance] fête.

kérosène [kerɔzɛn] *nm* kerosene.

ketchup [kɛtʃœp] *nm* ketchup.

keuf [kœf] *nm fam* cop.

keum [kœm] *nm fam* guy, bloke.

kg (*abr écrite de* **kilogramme**) kg.

kibboutz [kibuts] *nm inv* kibbutz.

kidnapper [3] [kidnape] *vt* to kidnap.

kidnappeur, euse [kidnapœr, øz] *nm, f* kidnapper.

kilo [kilo] *nm* kilo.

kilogramme [kilɔgram] *nm* kilogram.

kilométrage [kilɔmetraʒ] *nm* **1.** [de voiture] ≃ mileage - **2.** [distance] distance.

kilomètre [kilɔmɛtr] *nm* kilometre *UK*, kilometer *US*.

kilo-octet [kilɔɔktɛ] *nm* INFORM kilobyte.

kilowatt [kilɔwat] *nm* kilowatt.

kilt [kilt] *nm* kilt.

kimono [kimɔno] *nm* kimono.

kiné [kine] *fam* <> *nmf* (*abr de* **kinésithérapeute**) physio <> *nmf* (*abr de* **kinésithérapie**) physio ; 5 séances de kiné 5 sessions of physio.

kinésithérapeute [keneziterapøt] *nmf* physiotherapist.

kinésithérapie [keneziterapi] *nf* physiotherapy.

kiosque [kjɔsk] *nm* **1.** [de vente] kiosk - **2.** [pavillon] pavilion.

kir [kir] *nm apéritif made with white wine and blackcurrant liqueur.*

kirsch [kirʃ] *nm* cherry brandy.

kitchenette [kitʃənɛt] *nf* kitchenette.

kitsch [kitʃ] *adj inv* kitsch.

kiwi [kiwi] *nm* **1.** [oiseau] kiwi - **2.** [fruit] kiwi, kiwi fruit *(U).*

Klaxon® [klaksɔ̃] *nm* horn.

klaxonner [3] [klaksɔne] *vi* to hoot *UK*, to honk *US*.

kleptomane, cleptomane [kleptɔman] *nmf* kleptomaniac.

km *(abr écrite de kilomètre)* km.

km/h *(abr écrite de kilomètre par heure)* kph.

Ko *(abr écrite de kilo-octet)* K.

K.-O. [kao] *nm* : **mettre qqn K.-O.** to knock sb out.

Koweït [kɔwɛt] *nm* [pays, ville] Kuwait ; **le Koweït** Kuwait.

krach [krak] *nm* crash ; **krach boursier** stock market crash.

kung-fu [kuŋfu] *nm* kung fu.

kurde [kyrd] <> *adj* Kurdish. <> *nm* [langue] Kurdish. ◆ **Kurde** *nmf* Kurd.

kyrielle [kirjɛl] *nf fam* stream ; [d'enfants] horde.

kyste [kist] *nm* cyst.

l, L [ɛl] <> *nm inv* l, L. <> *(abr écrite de litre)* l.

l' ▶ **le.**

la[1] [la] *art déf & pron pers* ▶ **le.**

la[2] [la] *nm inv* MUS A ; [chanté] la.

là [la] <> *adv* **1.** [lieu] there ; **à 3 kilomètres de là** 3 kilometres from there ; **passe par là** go that way ; **c'est là que je travaille** that's where I work ; **je suis là** I'm here - **2.** [temps] then ; **à quelques jours de là** a few days later, a few days after that - **3.** [avec une proposition relative] : **là où** [lieu] where ; [temps] when. <> *voir aussi* **ce,** *voir aussi* **là-bas,** *voir aussi* **là-dedans** *etc.*

là-bas [laba] *adv* (over) there.

label [labɛl] *nm* **1.** [étiquette] : **label de qualité** label guaranteeing quality - **2.** [commerce] label, brand name.

labeur [labœr] *nm sout* labour *UK*, labor *US*.

labo [labo] *(abr de laboratoire) nm fam* lab.

laborantin, e [labɔrɑ̃tɛ̃, in] *nm, f* laboratory assistant.

laboratoire [labɔratwar] *nm* laboratory.

laborieux, euse [labɔrjø, øz] *adj* [difficile] laborious.

labourer [3] [labure] *vt* **1.** AGRIC to plough *UK*, to plow *US* - **2.** *fig* [creuser] to make a gash in.

laboureur [laburœr] *nm* ploughman *UK*, plowman *US*.

labyrinthe [labirɛ̃t] *nm* labyrinth.

lac [lak] *nm* lake ; **les Grands Lacs** the Great Lakes ; **le lac Léman** Lake Geneva.

lacer [16] [lase] *vt* to tie.

lacérer [18] [lasere] *vt* **1.** [déchirer] to shred - **2.** [blesser, griffer] to slash.

lacet [lase] *nm* **1.** [cordon] lace - **2.** [de route] bend - **3.** [piège] snare.

lâche [laʃ] <> *nmf* coward. <> *adj* **1.** [nœud] loose - **2.** [personne, comportement] cowardly.

lâcher [3] [laʃe] <> *vt* **1.** [libérer - bras, objet] to let go of ; [- animal] to let go, to release - **2.** [émettre - son, mot] to let out, to come out with - **3.** [desserrer] to loosen - **4.** [laisser tomber] : **lâcher qqch** to drop sthg. <> *vi* to give way.

lâcheté [laʃte] *nf* **1.** [couardise] cowardice - **2.** [acte] cowardly act.

lacis [lasi] *nm* [labyrinthe] maze.

laconique [lakɔnik] *adj* laconic.

lacrymogène [lakrimɔʒɛn] *adj* tear *(avant n).*

lacune [lakyn] *nf* [manque] gap.

lacustre [lakystr] *adj* [faune, plante] lake *(avant n)* ; [cité, village] on stilts.

lad [lad] *nm* stable lad.

là-dedans [ladədɑ̃] *adv* inside, in there ; **il y a quelque chose qui m'intrigue là-dedans** there's something in that which intrigues me.

là-dessous [ladsu] *adv* underneath, under there ; *fig* behind that.

là-dessus [ladsy] *adv* on that ; **là-dessus, il partit à ce point** ou **with that, he left** ; **je suis d'accord là-dessus** I agree about that.

ladite ▶ **ledit.**

lagon [lagɔ̃] *nm* lagoon.

lagune [lagyn] *nf* = **lagon.**

là-haut [lao] *adv* up there.

laïc, laïque [laik] <> *adj* lay *(avant n)* ; [juridiction] civil *(avant n)* ; [école] state *(avant n).* <> *nm, f* layman *(f* laywoman*).*

laid, e [lɛ, lɛd] *adj* **1.** [esthétiquement] ugly - **2.** [moralement] wicked.

laideron [lɛdrɔ̃] *nm* ugly woman.

laideur [lɛdœr] *nf* **1.** [physique] ugliness - **2.** [morale] wickedness.

lainage [lɛnaʒ] *nm* [étoffe] woollen *UK* ou woolen *US* material ; [vêtement] woolly, woollen *UK* ou woolen *US* garment.

laine [lɛn] *nf* wool ; **laine polaire** polar fleece.

laineux, euse [lɛnø, øz] *adj* woolly.

laïque = **laïc**.

laisse [lɛs] *nf* [corde] lead *UK*, leash ; **tenir en laisse** [chien] to keep on a lead *UK* ou leash.

laisser [4] [lese] <> *v aux (+ infinitif)* **laisser qqn faire qqch** to let sb do sthg ; **laisse-le faire** leave him alone, don't interfere ; **laisser tomber qqch** *litt & fig* to drop sthg ; **laisse tomber!** *fam* drop it! <> *vt* **1.** [gén] to leave ; **laisser qqn/qqch à qqn** [confier] to leave sb/sthg with sb - **2.** [céder] : **laisser qqch à qqn** to let sb have sthg. <> **se laisser** *vp* : **se laisser faire** to let o.s. be persuaded ; **se laisser aller** to relax ; [dans son apparence] to let o.s. go ; **se laisser aller à qqch** to indulge in sthg.

laisser-aller [leseale] *nm inv* carelessness.

laissez-passer [lesepase] *nm inv* pass.

lait [lɛ] *nm* **1.** [gén] milk ; **lait entier/écrémé** whole/skimmed milk ; **lait concentré** ou **condensé** [sucré] condensed milk ; [non sucré] evaporated milk - **2.** [cosmétique] : **lait démaquillant** cleansing milk ou lotion. ◆ **au lait** *loc adj* with milk.

laitage [lɛtaʒ] *nm* dairy product.

laiterie [lɛtri] *nf* dairy.

laitier, ère [lɛtje, ɛr] <> *adj* dairy *(avant n)*. <> *nm, f* milkman (f milkwoman).

laiton [lɛtɔ̃] *nm* brass.

laitue [lety] *nf* lettuce.

laïus [lajys] *nm fam* long speech.

lambeau, x [lɑ̃bo] *nm* [morceau] shred.

lambris [lɑ̃bri] *nm* panelling *UK*, paneling *US*.

lame [lam] *nf* **1.** [fer] blade ; **lame de rasoir** razor blade - **2.** [lamelle] strip - **3.** [vague] wave.

lamé, e [lame] *adj* lamé. ◆ **lamé** *nm* lamé.

lamelle [lamɛl] *nf* **1.** [de champignon] gill - **2.** [tranche] thin slice - **3.** [de verre] slide.

lamentable [lamɑ̃tabl] *adj* **1.** [résultats, sort] appalling - **2.** [ton] plaintive.

lamentation [lamɑ̃tasjɔ̃] *nf* **1.** [plainte] lamentation - **2.** *(gén pl)* [jérémiade] moaning *(U)*.

lamenter [3] [lamɑ̃te] ◆ **se lamenter** *vp* to complain.

laminer [3] [lamine] *vt* [dans l'industrie] to laminate ; *fig* [personne, revenus] to eat away at.

lampadaire [lɑ̃padɛr] *nm* [d'intérieur] standard lamp *UK*, floor lamp *US* ; [de rue] street lamp ou light.

lampe [lɑ̃p] *nf* lamp, light ; **lampe de chevet** bedside lamp ; **lampe halogène** halogen light ; **lampe de poche** torch *UK*, flashlight *US*.

lampion [lɑ̃pjɔ̃] *nm* Chinese lantern.

lance [lɑ̃s] *nf* **1.** [arme] spear - **2.** [de tuyau] nozzle ; **lance d'incendie** fire hose.

lance-flammes [lɑ̃sflam] *nm inv* flamethrower.

lancement [lɑ̃smɑ̃] *nm* [d'entreprise, produit, navire] launching.

lance-pierres [lɑ̃spjɛr] *nm inv* catapult.

lancer [16] [lɑ̃se] <> *vt* **1.** [pierre, javelot] to throw ; **lancer qqch sur qqn** to throw sthg at sb - **2.** [fusée, produit, style] to launch - **3.** [émettre] to give off ; [cri] to let out ; [injures] to hurl ; [ultimatum] to issue - **4.** [moteur] to start up - **5.** [INFORM - programme] to start ; [- système] to boot (up) - **6.** *fig* [sur un sujet] : **lancer qqn sur qqch** to get sb started on sthg - **7.** [faire connaître] to launch. <> *nm* **1.** [à la pêche] casting - **2.** SPORT throwing ; **lancer du poids** shotput. ◆ **se lancer** *vp* **1.** [débuter] to make a name for o.s - **2.** [s'engager] : **se lancer dans** [dépenses, explication, lecture] to embark on.

lancinant, e [lɑ̃sinɑ̃, ɑ̃t] *adj* **1.** [douleur] shooting - **2.** *fig* [obsédant] haunting - **3.** [monotone] insistent.

landau [lɑ̃do] *nm* [d'enfant] pram *UK*, baby carriage *US*.

lande [lɑ̃d] *nf* moor.

langage [lɑ̃gaʒ] *nm* [gén] language.

lange [lɑ̃ʒ] *nm* nappy *UK*, diaper *US*.

langer [17] [lɑ̃ʒe] *vt* to change.

langoureux, euse [lɑ̃gurø, øz] *adj* languorous.

langouste [lɑ̃gust] *nf* crayfish.

langoustine [lɑ̃gustin] *nf* langoustine.

langue [lɑ̃g] *nf* **1.** *fig &* ANAT tongue - **2.** LING language ; **langue maternelle** mother tongue ; **langue morte/vivante** dead/modern language ; **langue officielle** official language - **3.** [forme] tongue.

languette [lɑ̃gɛt] *nf* tongue.

langueur [lɑ̃gœr] *nf* **1.** [dépérissement, mélancolie] languor - **2.** [apathie] apathy.

languir [32] [lɑ̃gir] *vi* **1.** [dépérir] : **languir (de)** to languish (with) - **2.** *sout* [attendre] to wait ; **faire languir qqn** to keep sb waiting.

lanière [lanjɛr] *nf* strip.

lanterne [lɑ̃tɛrn] *nf* **1.** [éclairage] lantern - **2.** [phare] light.

Laos [laɔs] *nm* : **le Laos** Laos.

laper [3] [lape] *vt & vi* to lap.

lapider [3] [lapide] *vt* [tuer] to stone.

lapin, e [lapɛ̃, in] *nm, f* CULIN & ZOOL rabbit. **lapin** *nm* [fourrure] rabbit fur.

Laponie [lapɔni] *nf* : **la Laponie** Lapland.

laps [laps] *nm* : **(dans) un laps de temps** (in) a while.

lapsus [lapsys] *nm* slip (of the tongue/pen).

laquais [lakɛ] *nm* lackey.

laque [lak] *nf* **1.** [vernis, peinture] lacquer - **2.** [pour cheveux] hair spray, lacquer *UK*.

laqué, e [lake] *adj* lacquered.

laquelle lequel.

larbin [larbɛ̃] *nm* **1.** [domestique] servant - **2.** [personne servile] yes-man.

larcin [larsɛ̃] *nm* **1.** [vol] larceny, theft - **2.** [butin] spoils *pl*.

lard [lar] *nm* **1.** [graisse de porc] lard - **2.** [viande] bacon.

lardon [lardɔ̃] *nm* **1.** CULIN cube or strip of bacon - **2.** *fam* [enfant] kid.

large [larʒ] *adj* **1.** [étendu, grand] wide ; **large de 5 mètres** 5 metres wide - **2.** [important, considérable] large, big - **3.** [esprit, sourire] broad - **4.** [généreux - personne] generous. *nm* [largeur] : **5 mètres de large** 5 metres wide - **2.** [mer] : **le large** the open sea ; **au large de la côte française** off the French coast.

largement [larʒəmɑ̃] *adv* **1.** [diffuser, répandre] widely ; **la porte était largement ouverte** the door was wide open - **2.** [donner, payer] generously ; [dépasser] considerably ; [récompenser] amply ; **avoir largement le temps** to have plenty of time - **3.** [au moins] easily.

largeur [larʒœr] *nf* **1.** [d'avenue, de cercle] width - **2.** *fig* [d'idées, d'esprit] breadth.

larguer [3] [large] *vt* **1.** [voile] to unfurl - **2.** [bombe, parachutiste] to drop - **3.** *fam fig* [abandonner] to chuck.

larme [larm] *nf* [pleur] tear ; **être en larmes** to be in tears.

larmoyant, e [larmwajɑ̃, ɑ̃t] *adj* **1.** [yeux, personne] tearful - **2.** *péj* [histoire] tearjerking.

larron [larɔ̃] *nm vieilli* [voleur] thief.

larve [larv] *nf* **1.** ZOOL larva - **2.** *péj* [personne] wimp.

laryngite [larɛ̃ʒit] *nf* laryngitis (*U*).

larynx [larɛ̃ks] *nm* larynx.

las, lasse [la, las] *adj litt* [fatigué] weary.

lascif, ive [lasif, iv] *adj* lascivious.

laser [lazɛr] *nm* laser. *adj inv* laser (*avant n*).

lasser [3] [lase] *vt sout* [personne] to weary ; [patience] to try. **se lasser** *vp* to weary.

lassitude [lasityd] *nf* lassitude.

lasso [laso] *nm* lasso.

latent, e [latɑ̃, ɑ̃t] *adj* latent.

latéral, e, aux [lateral, o] *adj* lateral.

latex [latɛks] *nm inv* latex.

latin, e [latɛ̃, in] *adj* Latin. **latin** *nm* [langue] Latin.

latiniste [latinist] *nmf* [spécialiste] Latinist ; [étudiant] Latin student.

latino-américain, e [latinɔamerikɛ̃, ɛn] (*mpl* **latino-américains**, *fpl* **latino-américaines**) *adj* Latin-American, Hispanic.

latitude [latityd] *nf litt & fig* latitude.

latrines [latrin] *nfpl* latrines.

latte [lat] *nf* lath, slat.

lauréat, e [lɔrea, at] *nm, f* prizewinner, winner.

laurier [lɔrje] *nm* BOT laurel.

lavable [lavabl] *adj* washable.

lavabo [lavabo] *nm* **1.** [cuvette] basin *UK*, washbowl *US* - **2.** (*gén pl*) [local] toilet *UK*, washroom *US*.

lavage [lavaʒ] *nm* washing.

lavande [lavɑ̃d] *nf* BOT lavender.

lave [lav] *nf* lava.

lave-glace [lavglas] (*pl* **lave-glaces**) *nm* windscreen washer *UK*, windshield washer *US*.

lave-linge [lavlɛ̃ʒ] *nm inv* washing machine.

laver [3] [lave] *vt* **1.** [nettoyer] to wash - **2.** *fig* [disculper] : **laver qqn de qqch** to clear sb of sthg. **se laver** *vp* [se nettoyer] to wash o.s., to have a wash *UK*, to wash up *US* ; **se laver les mains/les cheveux** to wash one's hands/hair.

laverie [lavri] *nf* [commerce] laundry ; **laverie automatique** launderette.

lavette [lavɛt] *nf* **1.** [brosse] washing-up brush *UK* ; [en tissu] dishcloth - **2.** *fam* [homme] drip.

laveur, euse [lavœr, øz] *nm, f* washer ; **laveur de carreaux** window cleaner (*person*).

lave-vaisselle [lavvesɛl] *nm inv* dishwasher.

lavoir [lavwar] *nm* [lieu] laundry.

laxatif, ive [laksatif, iv] *adj* laxative. **laxatif** *nm* laxative.

laxisme [laksism] *nm* laxity.

laxiste [laksist] *adj* lax.

layette [lɛjɛt] *nf* layette.

le, la [lə, la] (*pl* **les** [le]) (*l'* *devant une voyelle ou un 'h' muet*) ⬦ *art déf* **1.** [gén] the ; **le lac** the lake ; **la fenêtre** the window ; **l'homme** the man ; **les enfants** the children - **2.** [devant les noms abstraits] : **l'amour** love ; **la liberté** freedom ; **la vieillesse** old age - **3.** [temps] : **le 15 janvier 1953** 15th January 1953 UK, January 15th, 1953 US ; **je suis arrivé le 15 janvier 1953** I arrived on the 15th of January 1953 OU on January 15th, 1953 US ; **le lundi** [habituellement] on Mondays ; [jour précis] on (the) Monday - **4.** [possession] : **se laver les mains** to wash one's hands ; **avoir les cheveux blonds** to have fair hair - **5.** [distributif] per, a ; **2 euros le mètre** 2 euros per metre UK OU meter US, 2 euros a metre UK OU meter US - **6.** [dans les fractions] a, an - **7.** [avec un nom propre] the. ⬦ *pron pers* **1.** [personne] him (*f* her), them *pl* ; [chose] it, them *pl* ; [animal] it, him (*f* her), them *pl* ; **je le/la/les connais bien** I know him/her/them well ; **tu dois avoir la clé, donne-la moi** you must have the key, give it to me - **2.** [représente une proposition] : **je le sais bien** I know, I'm well aware (of it) ; **je te l'avais bien dit!** I told you so!

LEA (*abr de* **langues étrangères appliquées**) *nfpl* applied modern languages.

leader [lidœr] *nm* [de parti, course] leader.

leadership [lidœrʃip] *nm* leadership.

lécher [18] [leʃe] *vt* **1.** [passer la langue sur, effleurer] to lick ; [suj: vague] to wash against - **2.** *fam* [fignoler] to polish (up).

lèche-vitrines [lɛʃvitrin] *nm inv* window-shopping ; **faire du lèche-vitrines** to go window-shopping.

leçon [ləsɔ̃] *nf* **1.** [gén] lesson ; **leçons de conduite** driving lessons ; **leçons particulières** private lessons OU classes - **2.** [conseil] advice (*U*) ; **faire la leçon à qqn** to lecture sb.

lecteur, trice [lɛktœr, tris] *nm, f* **1.** [de livres] reader - **2.** UNIV foreign language assistant. ⬥ **lecteur** *nm* **1.** [gén] head ; **lecteur de cassettes/CD** cassette/CD player - **2.** INFORM reader.

lecture [lɛktyr] *nf* reading.

ledit, ladite [lədi, ladit] (*mpl* **lesdits** [ledi]) (*fpl* **lesdites** [ledit]) *adj* the said, the aforementioned.

légal, e, aux [legal, o] *adj* legal.

légalement [legalmɑ̃] *adv* legally.

légaliser [3] [legalize] *vt* [rendre légal] to legalize.

légalité [legalite] *nf* **1.** [de contrat, d'acte] legality, lawfulness - **2.** [loi] law.

légataire [legatɛr] *nmf* legatee.

légendaire [leʒɑ̃dɛr] *adj* legendary.

légende [leʒɑ̃d] *nf* **1.** [fable] legend - **2.** [de carte, de schéma] key.

léger, ère [leʒe, ɛr] *adj* **1.** [objet, étoffe, repas] light - **2.** [bruit, différence, odeur] slight - **3.** [alcool, tabac] low-strength - **4.** [femme] flighty - **5.** [insouciant - ton] light-hearted ; [- conduite] thoughtless. ⬥ **à la légère** *loc adv* lightly, thoughtlessly.

légèrement [leʒɛrmɑ̃] *adv* **1.** [s'habiller, poser] lightly - **2.** [agir] thoughtlessly - **3.** [blesser, remuer] slightly.

légèreté [leʒɛrte] *nf* **1.** [d'objet, de repas, de punition] lightness - **2.** [de style] gracefulness - **3.** [de conduite] thoughtlessness - **4.** [de personne] flightiness.

légiférer [18] [leʒifere] *vi* to legislate.

légion [leʒjɔ̃] *nf* MIL legion.

légionnaire [leʒjɔnɛr] *nm* legionary.

légion(n)ellose [leʒjɔnɛloz] *nf* MÉD legionnaires' disease.

législatif, ive [leʒislatif, iv] *adj* legislative. ⬥ **législatives** *nfpl* : **les législatives** the legislative elections, ≃ the general election (*sing*) UK.

législation [leʒislasjɔ̃] *nf* legislation.

légiste [leʒist] *adj* **1.** [juriste] jurist - **2.** ➤ **médecin**.

légitime [leʒitim] *adj* legitimate.

légitimer [3] [leʒitime] *vt* **1.** [reconnaître] to recognize ; [enfant] to legitimize - **2.** [justifier] to justify.

legs [lɛg] *nm* legacy.

léguer [18] [lege] *vt* : **léguer qqch à qqn** DR to bequeath sthg to sb ; *fig* to pass sthg on to sb.

légume [legym] *nm* vegetable.

leitmotiv [lajtmɔtif, lɛtmɔtiv] *nm* leitmotif.

Léman [lemɑ̃] ➤ **lac**.

lendemain [lɑ̃dmɛ̃] *nm* [jour] day after ; **le lendemain matin** the next morning ; **au lendemain de** after, in the days following.

lénifiant, e [lenifjɑ̃, ɑ̃t] *adj litt & fig* soothing.

lent, e [lɑ̃, lɑ̃t] *adj* slow.

lente [lɑ̃t] *nf* nit.

lentement [lɑ̃tmɑ̃] *adv* slowly.

lenteur [lɑ̃tœr] *nf* slowness (*U*).

lentille [lɑ̃tij] *nf* **1.** BOT & CULIN lentil - **2.** [d'optique] lens ; **lentilles de contact** contact lenses.

léopard [leɔpar] *nm* leopard.

lèpre [lɛpr] *nf* MÉD leprosy.

lequel, laquelle [ləkɛl, lakɛl] (*mpl* **lesquels** [lekɛl], *fpl* **lesquelles** [lekɛl]) (*contraction de* : "à + lequel" = **auquel** ; "de + lequel" = **duquel** ; "à + lesquels/lesquelles" = **auxquels/**

auxquelles *"de + lesquels/lesquelles"* = **desquels/desquelles)** ⬦ *pron rel* **1.** [complément - personne] whom ; [- chose] which - **2.** [sujet - personne] who ; [- chose] which. ⬦ *pron interr* : **lequel? which (one)?**

les ▶ le.

lesbienne [lɛsbjɛn] *nf* lesbian.

lesdits, lesdites ▶ ledit.

léser [18] [leze] *vt* [frustrer] to wrong.

lésiner [3] [lezine] *vi* to skimp ; **ne pas lésiner sur** not to skimp on.

lésion [lezjɔ̃] *nf* lesion.

lesquels, lesquelles ▶ lequel.

lessive [lesiv] *nf* **1.** [nettoyage, linge] washing UK, laundry US - **2.** [produit] washing powder UK, detergent US.

lest [lɛst] *nm* ballast.

leste [lɛst] *adj* **1.** [agile] nimble, agile - **2.** [licencieux] crude.

lester [3] [lɛste] *vt* [garnir de lest] to ballast.

léthargie [letarʒi] *nf litt & fig* lethargy.

Lettonie [lɛtɔni] *nf* : **la Lettonie** Latvia.

lettre [lɛtr] *nf* **1.** [gén] letter ; **en toutes lettres** in words, in full ; **lettre de motivation** covering UK ou cover US letter *(in support of one's application)* - **2.** [sens des mots] : **à la lettre** to the letter. ⬦ **lettres** *nfpl* **1.** [culture littéraire] letters - **2.** UNIV arts UK, humanities US ; **lettres classiques** classics ; **lettres modernes** French language and literature.

leucémie [løsemi] *nf* leukemia.

leucocyte [løkɔsit] *nm* leucocyte.

leur [lœr] *pron pers inv* (to) them ; **je voudrais leur parler** I'd like to speak to them ; **je leur ai donné la lettre** I gave them the letter, I gave the letter to them. ⬦ **leur** *(pl* leurs) *adj poss* their ; **c'est leur tour** it's their turn ; **leurs enfants** their children. ⬦ **le leur, la leur** *(pl* les leurs) *pron poss* theirs ; **il faudra qu'ils y mettent du leur** they've got to pull their weight.

leurrer [5] [lœre] *vt* to deceive. ⬦ **se leurrer** *vp* to deceive o.s.

levain [ləvɛ̃] *nm* CULIN : **pain au levain/sans levain** leavened/unleavened bread.

levant [ləvɑ̃] ⬦ *nm* east. ⬦ *adj* ▶ soleil.

lever [19] [ləve] ⬦ *vt* **1.** [objet, blocus, interdiction] to lift - **2.** [main, tête, armée] to raise - **3.** [scellés, difficulté] to remove - **4.** [séance] to close, to end - **5.** [impôts, courrier] to collect - **6.** [enfant, malade] : **lever qqn** to get sb up. ⬦ *vi* **1.** [plante] to come up - **2.** [pâte] to rise. ⬦ *nm* **1.** [d'astre] rising, rise ; **lever du jour** daybreak ; **lever du soleil** sunrise - **2.** [de personne] : **il est toujours de mauvaise humeur au lever** he's always in a bad mood

when he gets up. ⬦ **se lever** *vp* **1.** [personne] to get up, to rise ; [vent] to get up - **2.** [soleil, lune] to rise ; [jour] to break - **3.** [temps] to clear.

lève-tard [lɛvtar] *nmf* late riser.

lève-tôt [lɛvto] *nmf* early riser.

levier [ləvje] *nm litt & fig* lever ; **levier de vitesses** gear lever UK, gearshift US.

lévitation [levitasjɔ̃] *nf* levitation.

lèvre [lɛvr] *nf* ANAT lip ; [de vulve] labium.

lévrier, levrette [levrije, ləvrɛt] *nm, f* greyhound.

levure [ləvyr] *nf* yeast ; **levure chimique** baking powder.

lexicographie [lɛksikɔgrafi] *nf* lexicography.

lexique [lɛksik] *nm* **1.** [dictionnaire] glossary - **2.** [vocabulaire] vocabulary.

lézard [lezar] *nm* [animal] lizard.

lézarder [3] [lezarde] ⬦ *vt* to crack. ⬦ *vi fam* [paresser] to bask. ⬦ **se lézarder** *vp* to crack.

liaison [ljɛzɔ̃] *nf* **1.** [jonction, enchaînement] connection - **2.** CULIN & LING liaison - **3.** [contact, relation] contact ; **avoir une liaison** to have an affair - **4.** [transports] link.

liane [ljan] *nf* creeper.

liant, e [ljɑ̃, ɑ̃t] *adj* sociable. ⬦ **liant** *nm* [substance] binder.

liasse [ljas] *nf* bundle ; [de billets de banque] wad.

Liban [libɑ̃] *nm* : **le Liban** Lebanon.

libanais, e [libanɛ, ɛz] *adj* Lebanese. ⬦ **Libanais, e** *nm, f* Lebanese (person) ; **les Libanais** the Lebanese.

libeller [4] [libele] *vt* **1.** [chèque] to make out - **2.** [lettre] to word.

libellule [libelyl] *nf* dragonfly.

libéral, e, aux [liberal, o] ⬦ *adj* [attitude, idée, parti] liberal. ⬦ *nm, f* POLIT liberal.

libéraliser [3] [liberalize] *vt* to liberalize.

libéralisme [liberalism] *nm* liberalism.

libération [liberasjɔ̃] *nf* **1.** [de prisonnier] release, freeing - **2.** [de pays, de la femme] liberation - **3.** [d'énergie] release.

libérer [18] [libere] *vt* **1.** [prisonnier, fonds] to release, to free - **2.** [pays, la femme] to liberate ; **libérer qqn de qqch** to free sb from sthg - **3.** [passage] to clear - **4.** [énergie] to release - **5.** [instincts, passions] to give free rein to. ⬦ **se libérer** *vp* **1.** [se rendre disponible] to get away - **2.** [se dégager] : **se libérer de** [lien] to free o.s. from ; [engagement] to get out of.

liberté [libɛrte] *nf* **1.** [gén] freedom ; **en liberté** free ; **parler en toute liberté** to speak freely ; **vivre en liberté** to live in freedom ;

liberté d'expression freedom of expression ; **liberté d'opinion** freedom of thought - **2.** DR release - **3.** [loisir] free time.

libertin, e [libɛrtɛ̃, in] *nm, f* libertine.

libidineux, euse [libidinø, øz] *adj* lecherous.

libido [libido] *nf* libido.

libraire [librɛr] *nmf* bookseller.

librairie [librɛri] *nf* [magasin] bookshop *UK*, bookstore *US*.

libre [libr] *adj* **1.** [gén] free ; **libre de qqch** free from sthg ; **être libre de faire qqch** to be free to do sthg - **2.** [école, secteur] private - **3.** [passage] clear.

libre-échange [librɛʃãʒ] *nm* free trade (U).

librement [librəmã] *adv* freely.

libre-service [librəsɛrvis] *nm* [magasin] self-service store ou shop ; [restaurant] self-service restaurant.

Libye [libi] *nf* : **la Libye** Libya.

libyen, enne [libjɛ̃, ɛn] *adj* Libyan. ➡ **Libyen, enne** *nm, f* Libyan.

licence [lisãs] *nf* **1.** [permis] permit ; COMM licence *UK*, license *US* - **2.** UNIV (first) degree ; **licence ès lettres/en droit** ≃ Bachelor of Arts/Law degree - **3.** *litt* [liberté] licence *UK*, license *US*.

licencié, e [lisãsje] ◇ *adj* UNIV graduate (*avant n*). ◇ *nm, f* **1.** UNIV graduate - **2.** [titulaire d'un permis] permit holder ; COMM licence holder.

licenciement [lisãsimã] *nm* dismissal ; [économique] layoff, redundancy *UK*.

licencier [9] [lisãsje] *vt* [pour faute] to dismiss, to fire ; [pour raison économique] to lay off, to make redundant *UK* ; **se faire licencier** to be made redundant *UK*, to be laid off.

lichen [likɛn] *nm* lichen.

licite [lisit] *adj* lawful, legal.

licorne [likɔrn] *nf* unicorn.

lie [li] *nf* [dépôt] dregs *pl*, sediment.

lié, e [lje] *adj* **1.** [mains] bound - **2.** [amis] : **être très lié avec** to be great friends with.

lie-de-vin [lidəvɛ̃] *adj inv* burgundy, wine-coloured *UK*, wine-colored *US*.

liège [ljɛʒ] *nm* cork.

lien [ljɛ̃] *nm* **1.** [sangle] bond - **2.** [relation, affinité] bond, tie ; **avoir des liens de parenté avec** to be related to - **3.** *fig* [enchaînement] connection, link.

lier [9] [lje] *vt* **1.** [attacher] to tie (up) ; **lier qqn/qqch à** to tie sb/sthg to - **2.** [suj: contrat, promesse] to bind ; **lier qqn/qqch par** to bind sb/sthg by - **3.** [relier par la logique] to link, to connect ; **lier qqch à** to link sthg to, to connect sthg with - **4.** [commencer] : **lier connaissance/conversation avec** to strike up

an acquaintance/a conversation with - **5.** [suj: sentiment, intérêt] to unite - **6.** CULIN to thicken. ➡ **se lier** *vp* [s'attacher] : **se lier (d'amitié) avec qqn** to make friends with sb.

lierre [ljɛr] *nm* ivy.

liesse [ljɛs] *nf* jubilation.

lieu, x [ljø] *nm* [endroit] place ; **en lieu sûr** in a safe place ; **lieu de naissance** birthplace ; **avoir lieu** to take place. ➡ **lieux** *nmpl* **1.** [scène] scene *sg*, spot *sg* ; **sur les lieux (d'un crime/d'un accident)** at the scene (of a crime/an accident) - **2.** [domicile] premises. ➡ **lieu commun** *nm* commonplace. ➡ **au lieu de** *loc prép* : **au lieu de qqch/de faire qqch** instead of sthg/of doing sthg. ➡ **en dernier lieu** *loc adv* lastly. ➡ **en premier lieu** *loc adv* in the first place.

lieu-dit [ljødi] (*pl* lieux-dits) *nm* locality, place.

lieue [ljø] *nf* league.

lieutenant [ljøtnã] *nm* lieutenant.

lièvre [ljɛvr] *nm* hare.

lifter [3] [lifte] *vt* TENNIS to put topspin on.

lifting [liftiŋ] *nm* face-lift.

ligament [ligamã] *nm* ligament.

ligaturer [3] [ligatyre] *vt* MÉD to ligature, to ligate.

ligne [liɲ] *nf* **1.** [gén] line ; **à la ligne** new line ou paragraph ; **en ligne** [personnes] in a line ; INFORM on line ; **restez en ligne!** TÉLÉCOM who's speaking ou calling? ; **ligne de départ/d'arrivée** starting/finishing *UK* ou finish *US* line ; **ligne aérienne** airline ; **ligne de commande** INFORM command line ; **ligne de conduite line** of conduct ; **ligne directrice** guideline ; **lignes de la main** lines of the hand ; **les grandes lignes** [transports] the main lines - **2.** [forme - de voiture, meuble] lines *pl* - **3.** [silhouette] : **garder la ligne** to keep one's figure ; **surveiller sa ligne** to watch one's waistline - **4.** [de pêche] fishing line ; **pêcher à la ligne** to go angling ; **dans les grandes lignes** in outline ; **entrer en ligne de compte** to be taken into account.

lignée [liɲe] *nf* [famille] descendants *pl* ; **dans la lignée de** *fig* [d'écrivains, d'artistes] in the tradition of.

ligoter [3] [ligɔte] *vt* **1.** [attacher] to tie up ; **ligoter qqn à qqch** to tie sb to sthg - **2.** *fig* [entraver] to bind.

ligue [lig] *nf* league.

liguer [3] [lige] ➡ **se liguer** *vp* to form a league ; **se liguer contre** to conspire against.

lilas [lila] *nm & adj inv* lilac.

limace [limas] *nf* ZOOL slug.

limaille [limaj] *nf* filings *pl*.

limande [limãd] *nf* dab.

lime [lim] *nf* **1.** [outil] file ; **lime à ongles** nail file - **2.** BOT lime.

limer [3] [lime] *vt* [ongles] to file ; [aspérités] to file down ; [barreau] to file through.

limier [limje] *nm* **1.** [chien] bloodhound - **2.** [détective] sleuth.

liminaire [liminεr] *adj* introductory.

limitation [limitasjɔ̃] *nf* limitation ; [de naissances] control ; **limitation de vitesse** speed limit.

limite [limit] <> *nf* **1.** [gén] limit ; **à la limite** [au pire] at worst ; **à la limite, j'accepterais de le voir** if pushed, I'd agree to see him - **2.** [terme, échéance] deadline ; **limite d'âge** age limit. <> *adj* [extrême] maximum *(avant n)* ; **cas limite** borderline case ; **date limite** deadline ; **date limite de vente/consommation** sell-by/use-by date.

limiter [3] [limite] *vt* **1.** [borner] to border, to bound - **2.** [restreindre] to limit. ◆ **se limiter** *vp* **1.** [se restreindre] : **se limiter à qqch/à faire qqch** to limit o.s. to sthg/to doing sthg - **2.** [se borner] : **se limiter à** to be limited to.

limitrophe [limitrɔf] *adj* **1.** [frontalier] border *(avant n)* ; **être limitrophe de** to border on - **2.** [voisin] adjacent.

limoger [17] [limɔʒe] *vt* to dismiss.

limon [limɔ̃] *nm* GÉOL alluvium, silt.

limonade [limɔnad] *nf* lemonade.

limpide [lɛ̃pid] *adj* **1.** [eau] limpid - **2.** [ciel, regard] clear - **3.** [explication, style] clear, lucid.

lin [lɛ̃] *nm* **1.** BOT flax - **2.** [tissu] linen.

linceul [lɛ̃sœl] *nm* shroud.

linéaire [lineεr] *adj* [mesure, perspective] linear.

linge [lɛ̃ʒ] *nm* **1.** [lessive] washing - **2.** [de lit, de table] linen - **3.** [sous-vêtements] underwear - **4.** [morceau de tissu] cloth.

lingerie [lɛ̃ʒri] *nf* **1.** [local] linen room - **2.** [sous-vêtements] lingerie.

lingot [lɛ̃go] *nm* ingot.

linguistique [lɛ̃gɥistik] <> *nf* linguistics *(U)*. <> *adj* linguistic.

linoléum [linɔleɔm] *nm* lino, linoleum.

lion, lionne [ljɔ̃, ljɔn] *nm, f* lion *(f* lioness). ◆ **Lion** *nm* ASTROL Leo.

lionceau, x [ljɔ̃so] *nm* lion cub.

lipide [lipid] *nm* lipid.

liquéfier [9] [likefje] *vt* to liquefy. ◆ **se liquéfier** *vp* **1.** [matière] to liquefy - **2.** *fig* [personne] to turn to jelly.

liqueur [likœr] *nf* liqueur.

liquidation [likidasjɔ̃] *nf* **1.** [de compte & FIN] settlement - **2.** [de société, stock] liquidation.

liquide [likid] <> *nm* **1.** [substance] liquid ; **liquide vaisselle** washing-up liquid, dish soap *US* - **2.** [argent] cash ; **en liquide** in cash. <> *adj* [corps & LING] liquid.

liquider [3] [likide] *vt* **1.** [compte & FIN] to settle - **2.** [société, stock] to liquidate - **3.** *arg crime* [témoin] to liquidate, to eliminate ; *fig* [problème] to eliminate, to get rid of.

liquidité [likidite] *nf* liquidity. ◆ **liquidités** *nfpl* liquid assets.

liquoreux, euse [likɔrø, øz] *adj* syrupy.

lire[1] [106] [lir] *vt* to read ; **lu et approuvé** read and approved.

lire[2] [lir] *nf* lira.

lis, lys [lis] *nm* lily.

Lisbonne [lizbɔn] *npr* Lisbon.

liseré [lizre], **liséré** [lizere] *nm* **1.** [ruban] binding - **2.** [bande] border, edging.

liseron [lizrɔ̃] *nm* bindweed.

liseuse [lizøz] *nf* **1.** [vêtement] bedjacket - **2.** [lampe] reading light.

lisible [lizibl] *adj* [écriture] legible.

lisière [lizjεr] *nf* [limite] edge.

lisse [lis] *adj* [surface, peau] smooth.

lisser [3] [lise] *vt* **1.** [papier, vêtements] to smooth (out) - **2.** [moustache, cheveux] to smooth (down) - **3.** [plumes] to preen.

liste [list] *nf* list ; **liste d'attente** waiting list ; **liste électorale** electoral roll ; **liste de mariage** wedding present list ; **être sur la liste rouge** to be ex-directory *UK*, to have an unlisted number *US*.

lister [3] [liste] *vt* to list.

listeriose, listériose [listerjoz] *nf* MÉD listeriosis.

listing [listiŋ] *nm* listing.

lit [li] *nm* [gén] bed ; **faire son lit** to make one's bed ; **garder le lit** to stay in bed ; **se mettre au lit** to go to bed ; **lit à baldaquin** four-poster bed ; **lit de camp** camp bed *UK*, cot *US*.

litanie [litani] *nf* litany.

literie [litri] *nf* bedding.

lithographie [litɔgrafi] *nf* **1.** [procédé] lithography - **2.** [image] lithograph.

litière [litjεr] *nf* litter.

litige [litiʒ] *nm* **1.** DR lawsuit - **2.** [désaccord] dispute.

litigieux, euse [litiʒjø, øz] *adj* **1.** DR litigious - **2.** [douteux] disputed.

litre [litr] *nm* **1.** [mesure, quantité] litre *UK*, liter *US* - **2.** [récipient] litre *UK* ou liter *US* bottle.

littéraire [literεr] *adj* literary.

littéral, e, aux [literal, o] *adj* **1.** [gén] literal - **2.** [écrit] written.

littérature [literatyr] *nf* [gén] literature.

littoral, e, aux [litɔral, o] *adj* coastal.
➤ **littoral** *nm* coast, coastline.

Lituanie [lityani] *nf* : **la Lituanie** Lithuania.

liturgie [lityrʒi] *nf* liturgy.

livide [livid] *adj* [blême] pallid.

livraison [livrɛzɔ̃] *nf* [de marchandise] delivery ; **livraison à domicile** home delivery.

livre [livr] ◇ *nm* [gén] book ; **livre de cuisine** cookery book *UK*, cookbook *US* ; **livre électronique** e-book ; **livre d'images** picture book ; **livre d'or** visitors' book *UK* ; **livre de poche** paperback. ◇ *nf* pound ; **livre sterling** pound sterling.

livrée [livre] *nf* [uniforme] livery.

livrer [3] [livre] *vt* **1.** COMM to deliver ; **livrer qqch à qqn** [achat] to deliver sthg to sb ; *fig* [secret] to reveal *ou* give away sthg to sb - **2.** [coupable, complice] : **livrer qqn à qqn** to hand sb over to sb - **3.** [abandonner] : **livrer qqch à qqch** to give sthg over to sthg ; **livrer qqn à lui-même** to leave sb to his own devices. ➤ **se livrer** *vp* **1.** [se rendre] : **se livrer à** [police, ennemi] to give o.s. up to ; [amant] to give o.s. to - **2.** [se confier] : **se livrer à** [ami] to open up to, to confide in - **3.** [se consacrer] : **se livrer à** [occupation] to devote o.s. to ; [excès] to indulge in.

livret [livrɛ] *nm* **1.** [carnet] booklet ; **livret de caisse d'épargne** passbook, bankbook ; **livret de famille** *official family record book, given by registrar to newlyweds* ; **livret scolaire** ≃ school report *UK*, ≃ report card *US* - **2.** [catalogue] catalogue, catalog *US* - **3.** MUS book, libretto.

livreur, euse [livrœr, øz] *nm, f* delivery man (*f* woman).

lobby [lɔbi] (*pl* **lobbies**) *nm* lobby.

lobe [lɔb] *nm* ANAT & BOT lobe.

lober [3] [lɔbe] *vt* to lob.

local, e, aux [lɔkal, o] *adj* local ; [douleur] localized. ➤ **local** *nm* room, premises *pl*.
➤ **locaux** *nmpl* premises, offices.

localiser [3] [lɔkalize] *vt* **1.** [avion, bruit] to locate - **2.** [épidémie, conflit, produit multimédia] to localize.

localité [lɔkalite] *nf* (small) town.

locataire [lɔkatɛr] *nmf* tenant.

location [lɔkasjɔ̃] *nf* **1.** [de propriété - par propriétaire] letting *UK*, renting *US* ; [- par locataire] renting ; [de machine] leasing ; **location de voitures/vélos** car/bicycle hire *UK*, car/bicycle rental *US* - **2.** [bail] lease - **3.** [maison, appartement] rented property, rental *US* - **4.** [réservation] booking.

location-vente [lɔkasjɔ̃vɑ̃t] *nf* ≃ hire purchase *UK*, ≃ installment plan *US*.

locomotion [lɔkɔmɔsjɔ̃] *nf* locomotion.

locomotive [lɔkɔmɔtiv] *nf* **1.** [machine] locomotive - **2.** *fig* [leader] moving force.

locution [lɔkysjɔ̃] *nf* expression, phrase.

loft [lɔft] *nm* (converted) loft.

logarithme [lɔgaritm] *nm* logarithm.

loge [lɔʒ] *nf* **1.** [de concierge, de francs-maçons] lodge - **2.** [d'acteur] dressing room.

logement [lɔʒmɑ̃] *nm* **1.** [hébergement] accommodation *UK*, accommodations (*pl*) *US* - **2.** [appartement] flat *UK*, apartment *US* ; **logement de fonction** company flat *UK ou* apartment *US*.

loger [17] [lɔʒe] ◇ *vi* [habiter] to live. ◇ *vt* **1.** [amis, invités] to put up - **2.** [suj: hôtel, maison] to accommodate, to take. ➤ **se loger** *vp* **1.** [trouver un logement] to find accommodation *UK ou* accommodations *US* - **2.** [se placer - ballon, balle] : **se loger dans** to lodge in, to stick in.

logeur, euse [lɔʒœr, øz] *nm, f* landlord (*f* landlady).

logiciel [lɔʒisjɛl] *nm* software (*U*) ; **logiciel intégré** integrated software.

logique [lɔʒik] ◇ *nf* logic. ◇ *adj* logical.

logiquement [lɔʒikmɑ̃] *adv* logically.

logis [lɔʒi] *nm* abode.

logistique [lɔʒistik] *nf* logistics *pl*.

logo [logo] *nm* logo.

loi [lwa] *nf* [gén] law.

loin [lwɛ̃] *adv* **1.** [dans l'espace] far ; **plus loin** further - **2.** [dans le temps - passé] a long time ago ; [- futur] a long way off. ➤ **au loin** *loc adv* in the distance, far off. ➤ **de loin** *loc adv* [depuis une grande distance] from a distance ; **de plus loin** from further away. ➤ **loin de** *loc prép* **1.** [gén] far from ; **loin de là !** *fig* far from it! - **2.** [dans le temps] : **il n'est pas loin de 9 h** it's nearly 9 o'clock, it's not far off 9 o'clock.

lointain, e [lwɛ̃tɛ̃, ɛn] *adj* [pays, avenir, parent] distant.

loir [lwar] *nm* dormouse.

loisir [lwazir] *nm* **1.** [temps libre] leisure - **2.** (*gén pl*) [distractions] leisure activities *pl*.

londonien, enne [lɔ̃dɔnjɛ̃, ɛn] *adj* London (*avant n*). ➤ **Londonien, enne** *nm, f* Londoner.

Londres [lɔ̃dr] *npr* London.

long, longue [lɔ̃, lɔ̃g] *adj* **1.** [gén] long - **2.** [lent] slow ; **être long à faire qqch** to take a long time doing sthg - **3.** [qui existe depuis longtemps] long, long-standing. ➤ **long** ◇ *nm* [longueur] : **4 mètres de long** 4 metres long *ou* in length ; **de long en large** up and down, to and fro ; **en long et en large** in great detail ; **(tout) le long de** [espace] all along ; **tout au long de** [année,

carrière) throughout. <> *adv* [beaucoup] :
en savoir long sur qqch to know a lot about
sthg. ⟶ **à la longue** *loc adv* in the end.

longe [lɔ̃ʒ] *nf* [courroie] halter.

longer [17] [lɔ̃ʒe] *vt* **1.** [border] to go along
ou alongside - **2.** [marcher le long de] to
walk along ; [raser] to stay close to, to hug.

longévité [lɔ̃ʒevite] *nf* longevity.

longiligne [lɔ̃ʒiliɲ] *adj* long-limbed.

longitude [lɔ̃ʒityd] *nf* longitude.

longtemps [lɔ̃tɑ̃] *adv* (for) a long time ;
depuis longtemps (for) a long time ; **il y a
longtemps que...** it's been a long time
since... ; **il y a longtemps qu'il est là** he's
been here a long time ; **mettre longtemps à
faire qqch** to take a long time to do sthg.

longue ▶ **long.**

longuement [lɔ̃gmɑ̃] *adv* **1.** [longtemps]
for a long time - **2.** [en détail] at length.

longueur [lɔ̃gœr] *nf* length ; **faire 5 mètres
de longueur** to be 5 metres long ; **disposer
qqch en longueur** to put sthg lengthways ;
à longueur de journée/temps the entire
day/time ; **à longueur d'année** all year long ;
longueur d'onde wavelength ; **saut en
longueur** long jump. ⟶ **longueurs** *nfpl*
[de film, de livre] boring parts.

longue-vue [lɔ̃gvy] *nf* telescope.

look [luk] *nm* look ; **avoir un look** to have a
style.

looping [lupiŋ] *nm* loop the loop.

lopin [lɔpɛ̃] *nm* : **lopin (de terre)** patch ou
plot of land.

loquace [lɔkas] *adj* loquacious.

loque [lɔk] *nf* **1.** [lambeau] rag - **2.** *fig*
[personne] wreck.

loquet [lɔkɛ] *nm* latch.

lorgner [3] [lɔrɲe] *vt fam* **1.** [observer] to
eye - **2.** [guigner] to have one's eye on.

lors [lɔr] *adv* : **depuis lors** since that time ;
lors de at the time of.

lorsque [lɔrsk(ə)] *conj* when.

losange [lɔzɑ̃ʒ] *nm* lozenge.

lot [lo] *nm* **1.** [part] share ; [de terre] plot
- **2.** [stock] batch - **3.** [prix] prize - **4.** *fig*
[destin] fate, lot.

loterie [lɔtri] *nf* lottery.

loti, e [lɔti] *adj* : **être bien/mal loti** to be
well/badly off.

lotion [lɔsjɔ̃] *nf* lotion.

lotir [32] [lɔtir] *vt* to divide up.

lotissement [lɔtismɑ̃] *nm* [terrain] plot.

loto [lɔto] *nm* **1.** [jeu de société] lotto
- **2.** [loterie] *popular national lottery.*

lotte [lɔt] *nf* monkfish.

lotus [lɔtys] *nm* lotus.

louange [lwɑ̃ʒ] *nf* praise.

louche¹ [luʃ] *nf* ladle.

louche² [luʃ] *adj fam* [personne, histoire]
suspicious.

loucher [3] [luʃe] *vi* **1.** [être atteint de
strabisme] to squint - **2.** *fam fig* [lorgner] :
loucher sur to have one's eye on.

louer [6] [lwe] *vt* **1.** [glorifier] to praise
- **2.** [donner en location] to rent (out) ; **à
louer** for rent - **3.** [prendre en location] to
rent - **4.** [réserver] to book. ⟶ **se louer** *vp
sout* [se féliciter] : **se louer de qqch/de faire
qqch** to be very pleased about sthg/about
doing sthg.

loufoque [lufɔk] *fam adj* nuts, crazy.

loup [lu] *nm* **1.** [carnassier] wolf - **2.** [pois-
son] bass - **3.** [masque] mask.

loupe [lup] *nf* [optique] magnifying glass.

louper [3] [lupe] *vt fam* [travail] to make a
mess of ; [train] to miss.

loup-garou [lugaru] (*pl* **loups-garous**) *nm*
werewolf.

lourd, e [lur, lurd] *adj* **1.** [gén] heavy ; **lourd
de** *fig* full of - **2.** [tâche] difficult ; [faute]
serious - **3.** [maladroit] clumsy, heavy-
handed - **4.** MÉTÉOR close *UK.* ⟶ **lourd**
adv : **peser lourd** to be heavy, to weigh a
lot ; **il n'en fait pas lourd** *fam* he doesn't do
much.

loutre [lutr] *nf* otter.

louve [luv] *nf* she-wolf.

louveteau, x [luvto] *nm* **1.** ZOOL wolf cub
- **2.** [scout] cub.

louvoyer [13] [luvwaje] *vi* **1.** NAUT to tack
- **2.** *fig* [tergiverser] to beat about the bush.

Louvre [luvr] *npr* : **le Louvre** the Louvre
(museum).

lover [3] [lɔve] ⟶ **se lover** *vp* [serpent] to
coil up.

loyal, e, aux [lwajal, o] *adj* **1.** [fidèle] loyal
- **2.** [honnête] fair.

loyauté [lwajote] *nf* **1.** [fidélité] loyalty
- **2.** [honnêteté] fairness.

loyer [lwaje] *nm* rent.

LP (*abr de* **lycée professionnel**) *nm secondary
school for vocational training.*

lu, e [ly] *pp* ▶ **lire¹.**

lubie [lybi] *nf fam* whim.

lubrifier [9] [lybrifje] *vt* to lubricate.

lubrique [lybrik] *adj* lewd.

lucarne [lykarn] *nf* **1.** [fenêtre] skylight
- **2.** FOOTBALL top corner of the net.

lucide [lysid] *adj* lucid.

lucidité [lysidite] *nf* lucidity.

lucratif, ive [lykratif, iv] *adj* lucrative.

ludique [lydik] *adj* play *(avant n).*

ludothèque [lydɔtɛk] *nf* toy library.

lueur [lɥœr] *nf* **1.** [de bougie, d'étoile] light ;

à la lueur de by the light of - **2.** *fig* [de colère] gleam ; [de raison] spark ; **lueur d'espoir** glimmer of hope.

luge [lyʒ] *nf* toboggan.

lugubre [lygybr] *adj* lugubrious.

lui[1] [lɥi] *pp inv* ▶ **luire.**

lui[2] [lɥi] *pron pers* **1.** [complément d'objet indirect - homme] (to) him ; [- femme] (to) her ; [- animal, chose] (to) it ; **je lui ai parlé** I've spoken to him/to her ; **il lui a serré la main** he shook his/her hand - **2.** [sujet, en renforcement de "il"] he - **3.** [objet, après préposition, comparatif - personne] him ; [- animal, chose] it ; **sans lui** without him ; **je vais chez lui** I'm going to his place ; **elle est plus jeune que lui** she's younger than him OU than he is - **4.** [remplaçant 'soi' en fonction de pronom réfléchi - personne] himself ; [- animal, chose] itself ; **il est content de lui** he's pleased with himself. ▪▪▪ **lui-même** *pron pers* [personne] himself ; [animal, chose] itself.

luire [97] [lɥir] *vi* [soleil, métal] to shine ; *fig* [espoir] to glow, to glimmer.

luisant, e [lɥizɑ̃, ɑ̃t] *adj* gleaming.

lumière [lymjɛr] *nf fig* [éclairage] light.

lumineux, euse [lyminø, øz] *adj* **1.** [couleur, cadran] luminous - **2.** *fig* [visage] radiant ; [idée] brilliant - **3.** [explication] clear.

luminosité [lyminozite] *nf* **1.** [du regard, ciel] radiance - **2.** [sciences] luminosity.

lump [lœp] *nm* : **œufs de lump** lumpfish roe.

lunaire [lynɛr] *adj* **1.** ASTRON lunar - **2.** *fig* [visage] moon *(avant n)* ; [paysage] lunar.

lunatique [lynatik] *adj* temperamental.

lunch [lœ̃ʃ] *nm* buffet lunch.

lundi [lœ̃di] *nm* Monday ; *voir aussi* **samedi.**

lune [lyn] *nf* ASTRON moon ; **pleine lune** full moon.

lunette [lynɛt] *nf* ASTRON telescope. ▪▪▪ **lunettes** *nfpl* glasses ; **lunettes de soleil** sunglasses.

lurette [lyrɛt] *nf* : **il y a belle lurette que...** *fam* it's been ages since...

luron, onne [lyrɔ̃, ɔn] *nm, f fam* **un joyeux luron** a bit of a lad.

lustre [lystr] *nm* **1.** [luminaire] chandelier - **2.** [éclat] sheen, shine ; *fig* reputation.

lustrer [3] [lystre] *vt* **1.** [faire briller] to make shine - **2.** [user] to wear.

luth [lyt] *nm* lute.

lutin, e [lytɛ̃, in] *adj* mischievous. ▪▪▪ **lutin** *nm* imp.

lutte [lyt] *nf* **1.** [combat] fight, struggle ; **la lutte des classes** the class struggle - **2.** SPORT wrestling.

lutter [3] [lyte] *vi* to fight, to struggle ; **lutter contre** to fight (against).

lutteur, euse [lytœr, øz] *nm, f* SPORT wrestler ; *fig* fighter.

luxation [lyksasjɔ̃] *nf* dislocation.

luxe [lyks] *nm* luxury ; **de luxe** luxury.

Luxembourg [lyksãbur] *nm* [pays]: **le Luxembourg** Luxembourg.

luxueux, euse [lyksɥø, øz] *adj* luxurious.

luxure [lyksyr] *nf* lust.

luzerne [lyzɛrn] *nf* lucerne, alfalfa.

lycée [lise] *nm* ≃ secondary school UK, ≃ high school US ; **lycée technique/ professionnel** ≃ technical/training college.

lycéen, enne [liseɛ̃, ɛn] *nm, f* secondary school pupil UK, high school pupil US.

lymphatique [lɛ̃fatik] *adj* **1.** MÉD lymphatic - **2.** *fig* [apathique] sluggish.

lyncher [3] [lɛ̃ʃe] *vt* to lynch.

lynx [lɛ̃ks] *nm* lynx.

Lyon [ljɔ̃] *npr* Lyons.

lyre [lir] *nf* lyre.

lyrique [lirik] *adj fig* [poésie] lyrical ; [drame, chanteur, poète] lyric.

lys = **lis.**

m, M [ɛm] ⬦ *nm inv* m, M. ⬦ *(abr écrite de* mètre*)* m. ▪▪▪ **M 1.** *(abr écrite de* Monsieur*)* Mr - **2.** *(abr écrite de* million*)* M.

m' ▶ **me.**

ma ▶ **mon.**

macabre [makabr] *adj* macabre.

macadam [makadam] *nm* [revêtement] macadam ; [route] road.

macaron [makarɔ̃] *nm* **1.** [pâtisserie] macaroon - **2.** [autocollant] sticker.

macaronis [makarɔni] *nmpl* CULIN macaroni *(U)*.

macédoine [masedwan] *nf* CULIN : **macédoine de fruits** fruit salad.

macérer [18] [masere] ⬦ *vt* to steep. ⬦ *vi* **1.** [mariner] to steep ; **faire macérer** to steep - **2.** *fig & péj* [personne] to wallow.

mâche [maʃ] *nf* lamb's lettuce.

mâcher [3] [maʃe] *vt* [mastiquer] to chew.

machiavélique [makjavelik] *adj* Machiavellian.

machin [maʃɛ̃] *nm fam* [chose] thing, thingamajig.

Machin, e [maʃɛ̃, in] *nm, f fam* what's his name (*f* what's her name).

machinal, e, aux [maʃinal, o] *adj* mechanical.

machination [maʃinasjɔ̃] *nf* machination.

machine [maʃin] *nf* **1.** TECHNOL machine ; **machine à coudre** sewing machine ; **machine à écrire** typewriter ; **machine à laver** washing machine - **2.** [organisation] machinery *(U)* - **3.** NAUT engine.

machine-outil [maʃinuti] *nf* machine tool.

machiniste [maʃinist] *nm* **1.** CINÉ & THÉÂTRE scene shifter - **2.** [transports] driver.

macho [matʃo] *péj nm* macho man.

mâchoire [maʃwar] *nf* jaw.

mâchonner [3] [maʃɔne] *vt* [mâcher, mordiller] to chew.

maçon [masɔ̃] *nm* mason.

maçonnerie [masɔnri] *nf* [travaux] building ; [construction] masonry ; [franc-maçonnerie] freemasonry.

macramé [makrame] *nm* macramé.

macro [makro] *nf* INFORM macro.

macrobiotique [makrɔbjɔtik] *nf* macrobiotics *(U)*.

maculer [3] [makyle] *vt* to stain.

madame [madam] *(pl* **mesdames** [medam]) *nf* [titre] : **madame X** Mrs X ; **bonjour madame!** good morning! ; [dans hôtel, restaurant] good morning, madam! ; **bonjour mesdames!** good morning (ladies)! ; **Madame la Ministre n'est pas là** the Minister is out.

mademoiselle [madmwazɛl] *(pl* **mesdemoiselles** [medmwazɛl]) *nf* [titre] : **mademoiselle X** Miss X ; **bonjour mademoiselle!** good morning! ; [à l'école, dans hôtel] good morning, miss! ; **bonjour mesdemoiselles!** good morning (ladies)!

madone [madɔn] *nf* ART & RELIG Madonna.

Madrid [madrid] *npr* Madrid.

madrier [madrije] *nm* beam.

maf(f)ia [mafja] *nf* Mafia.

magasin [magazɛ̃] *nm* **1.** [boutique] shop *UK*, store *US* ; **grand magasin** department store ; **faire les magasins** *fig* to go round *UK* ou around *US* the shops *UK* ou stores *US* - **2.** [d'arme, d'appareil photo] magazine.

magazine [magazin] *nm* magazine.

mage [maʒ] *nm* : **les Rois mages** the Three Wise Men.

Maghreb [magrɛb] *nm* : **le Maghreb** the Maghreb.

maghrébin, e [magrebɛ̃, in] *adj* North African. ◆ **Maghrébin, e** *nm, f* North African.

magicien, enne [maʒisjɛ̃, ɛn] *nm, f* magician.

magie [maʒi] *nf* magic.

magique [maʒik] *adj* **1.** [occulte] magic - **2.** [merveilleux] magical.

magistral, e, aux [maʒistral, o] *adj* **1.** [œuvre, habileté] masterly - **2.** [dispute, fessée] enormous - **3.** [attitude, ton] authoritative.

magistrat [maʒistra] *nm* magistrate.

magistrature [maʒistratyr] *nf* magistracy, magistrature.

magma [magma] *nm* **1.** GÉOL magma - **2.** *fig* [mélange] muddle.

magnanime [maɲanim] *adj* magnanimous.

magnat [maɲa] *nm* magnate, tycoon.

magnésium [maɲezjɔm] *nm* magnesium.

magnétique [maɲetik] *adj* magnetic.

magnétisme [maɲetism] *nm* PHYS [fascination] magnetism.

magnéto(phone) [maɲeto(fɔn)] *nm* tape recorder.

magnétoscope [maɲetɔskɔp] *nm* videorecorder.

magnificence [maɲifisɑ̃s] *nf* magnificence.

magnifique [maɲifik] *adj* magnificent.

magnum [magnɔm] *nm* magnum.

magot [mago] *nm fam* tidy sum, packet.

mai [mɛ] *nm* May ; **le premier mai** May Day ; *voir aussi* **septembre**.

maigre [mɛgr] *adj* **1.** [très mince] thin - **2.** [aliment] low-fat ; [viande] lean - **3.** [peu important] meagre *UK*, meager *US* ; [végétation] sparse.

maigreur [mɛgrœr] *nf* thinness.

maigrir [32] [mɛgrir] *vi* to lose weight.

mail [mɛl] *nm* INFORM e-mail (message), mail.

mailing [mɛliŋ] *nm* mailing, mailshot *UK*.

maille [maj] *nf* **1.** [de tricot] stitch - **2.** [de filet] mesh.

maillet [majɛ] *nm* mallet.

maillon [majɔ̃] *nm* link.

maillot [majo] *nm* [de sport] shirt, jersey ; **maillot de bain** swimsuit ; **maillot (de bain) une pièce/deux pièces** one-piece/two-piece swimsuit ; **maillot de corps** vest *UK*, undershirt *US* ; **le maillot jaune** *the yellow shirt worn by the leading cyclist in the Tour de France or the cyclist himself.*

main [mɛ̃] <> *nf* hand ; **attaque à main armée** armed attack ; **main libres** [téléphone, kit] hands-free ; **donner la main à qqn** to take sb's hand ; **haut les mains!** hands up! ◇ *adv* [fabriqué, imprimé] by hand ; **fait/tricoté/trié main** hand-made/-knitted/-picked. ◆ **à main droite** *loc adv* on the right-hand side. ◆ **à main gauche** *loc adv* on the left-hand side. ◆ **de la main** *loc adv* with one's hand ; **saluer qqn de la main** [pour dire bonjour] to wave (hello) to sb ; [pour dire au revoir] to wave (goodbye) to sb, to wave sb goodbye ; **de la main, elle me fit signe d'approcher** she waved me over. ◆ **de la main à la main** *loc adv* directly, without any middleman ; **j'ai payé le plombier de la main à la main** I paid the plumber cash in hand. ◆ **de la main de** *loc prép* **1.** [fait par] by ; **la lettre est de la main même de Proust/de ma main** the letter is in Proust's own hand/in my handwriting - **2.** [donné par] from (the hand of) ; **elle a reçu son prix de la main du président** she received her award from the President himself. ◆ **de main en main** *loc adv* from hand to hand, from one person to the next. ◆ **d'une main** *loc adv* [ouvrir, faire] with one hand ; [prendre] with ou in one hand ; **donner qqch d'une main et le reprendre de l'autre** to give sthg with one hand and take it back with the other. ◆ **en main** ◇ *loc adj* : **l'affaire est en main** the question is in hand ou is being dealt with ; **le livre est actuellement en main** [il est consulté] the book is out on loan ou is being consulted at the moment. ◇ *loc adv* : **avoir qqch en main** to be holding sthg ; **avoir** ou **tenir qqch (bien) en main** *fig* to have sthg well in hand ou under control ; **quand tu auras la voiture bien en main** when you've got the feel of the car ; **prendre qqch en main** to take control of ou over sthg ; **prendre qqn en main** to take sb in hand ; **la société a été reprise en main** the company was taken over. ◆ **la main dans la main** *loc adv* [en se tenant par la main] hand in hand ; *fig* together ; *péj* hand in glove.

main-d'œuvre [mɛ̃dœvr] *nf* labour *UK*, labor *US*, workforce.

mainmise [mɛ̃miz] *nf* seizure.

maint, e [mɛ̃, mɛ̃t] *adj litt* many a ; **maints** many ; **maintes fois** time and time again.

maintenance [mɛ̃tnɑ̃s] *nf* maintenance.

maintenant [mɛ̃tnɑ̃] *adv* now. ◆ **maintenant que** *loc prép* now that.

maintenir [40] [mɛ̃tnir] *vt* **1.** [soutenir] to support ; **maintenir qqn à distance** to keep sb away - **2.** [garder, conserver] to maintain - **3.** [affirmer] : **maintenir que** to maintain (that). ◆ **se maintenir** *vp* **1.** [durer] to last - **2.** [rester] to remain.

maintenu, e [mɛ̃tny] *pp* ▶ maintenir.

maintien [mɛ̃tjɛ̃] *nm* **1.** [conservation] maintenance ; [de tradition] upholding - **2.** [tenue] posture.

maire [mɛr] *nm* mayor.

mairie [meri] *nf* **1.** [bâtiment] town hall *UK*, city hall *US* - **2.** [administration] town council *UK*, city hall *US*.

mais [mɛ] ◇ *conj* but ; **mais non!** of course not! ; **mais alors, tu l'as vu ou non?** so did you see him or not? ; **il a pleuré, mais pleuré!** he cried, and how! ; **non mais ça ne va pas!** that's just not on! ◇ *adv* but ; **vous êtes prêts? - mais bien sûr!** are you ready? - but of course! ◇ *nm* : **il y a un mais** there's a hitch ou a snag ; **il n'y a pas de mais** (there are) no buts.

maïs [mais] *nm* maize *UK*, corn *US*.

maison [mɛzɔ̃] *nf* **1.** [habitation, lignée & ASTROL] house ; **maison individuelle** detached house - **2.** [foyer] home ; [famille] family ; **à la maison** [au domicile] at home ; [dans la famille] in my/your etc family - **3.** COMM company - **4.** [institut] : **maison d'arrêt** prison ; **maison de la culture** arts centre *UK* ou center *US* ; **maison de retraite** old people's home - **5.** (en apposition) [artisanal] homemade ; [dans restaurant - vin] house (avant n).

Maison-Blanche [mɛzɔ̃blɑ̃ʃ] *nf* : **la Maison-Blanche** the White House.

maisonnée [mɛzɔne] *nf* household.

maisonnette [mɛzɔnɛt] *nf* small house.

maître, esse [mɛtr, mɛtrɛs] *nm, f* **1.** [professeur] teacher ; **maître chanteur** blackmailer ; **maître de conférences** UNIV ≃ senior lecturer ; **maître d'école** schoolteacher ; **maître nageur** swimming instructor - **2.** *fig* [modèle, artiste] master - **3.** [dirigeant] ruler ; [d'animal] master (f mistress) ; **maître d'hôtel** head waiter ; **être maître de soi** to be in control of oneself, to have self-control - **4.** (en apposition) [principal] main, principal. ◆ **Maître** *nm* form of address for lawyers. ◆ **maîtresse** *nf* [amie] mistress.

maître-assistant, e [mɛtrasistɑ̃, ɑ̃t] *nm, f* ≃ lecturer *UK*, ≃ assistant professor *US*.

maîtresse ▶ maître.

maîtrise [mɛtriz] *nf* **1.** [sang-froid, domination] control - **2.** [connaissance] mastery, command ; [habileté] skill - **3.** UNIV ≃ master's degree.

maîtriser [3] [mɛtrize] *vt* **1.** [animal, forcené] to subdue - **2.** [émotion, réaction] to control, to master - **3.** [incendie] to bring under control. ◆ **se maîtriser** *vp* to control o.s.

majesté [maʒɛste] *nf* majesty. ◆ **Majesté** *nf* : **Sa Majesté** His/Her Majesty.

majestueux, euse [maʒɛstɥø, øz] *adj* majestic.

majeur, e [maʒœr] *adj* **1.** [gén] major
- **2.** [personne] of age. **majeur** *nm*
middle finger.

major [maʒɔr] *nm* **1.** MIL ≃ adjutant
- **2.** SCOL : **major (de promotion)** first in OU
top of one's year group.

majordome [maʒɔrdɔm] *nm* majordomo.

majorer [3] [maʒɔre] *vt* to increase.

majorette [maʒɔrɛt] *nf* majorette.

majoritaire [maʒɔritɛr] *adj* majority *(avant
n)* ; **être majoritaire** to be in the majority.

majorité [maʒɔrite] *nf* majority ; **en
(grande) majorité** in the majority ; **majorité
absolue/relative** POLIT absolute/relative majority.

majuscule [maʒyskyl] ⟨⟩ *nf* capital (letter). ⟨⟩ *adj* capital *(avant n)*.

mal, maux [mal, mo] *nm* **1.** [ce qui est
contraire à la morale] evil - **2.** [souffrance
physique] pain ; **avoir mal au bras** to have a
sore arm ; **avoir mal au cœur** to feel sick ;
avoir mal au dos to have backache UK OU a
backache US ; **avoir mal à la gorge** to have a
sore throat ; **avoir le mal de mer** to be
seasick ; **avoir mal aux dents** to have
toothache UK OU a toothache US ; **avoir mal
à la tête** to have a headache ; **avoir mal au
ventre** to have (a) stomachache ; **faire mal à
qqn** to hurt sb ; **ça fait mal** it hurts ; **se faire
mal** to hurt o.s. - **3.** [difficulté] difficulty
- **4.** [douleur morale] pain, suffering *(U)* ;
être en mal de qqch to long for sthg ; **prendre
du mal (à qqn)** to hurt (sb). **mal** *adv*
1. [malade] ill ; **aller mal** not to be well ; **se
sentir mal** to feel ill ; **être au plus mal** to be
extremely ill - **2.** [respirer] with difficulty
- **3.** [informé, se conduire] badly ; **mal
prendre qqch** to take sthg badly ; **mal
tourner** to go wrong ; **pas mal** not bad *(adj)*,
not badly *(adv)* ; **pas mal de** quite a lot of.
mal à l'aise *loc adj* uncomfortable, ill
at ease ; **être/se sentir mal à l'aise** to be/feel
uncomfortable OU ill at ease ; **je suis mal à
l'aise devant elle** I feel ill at ease with her.

malade [malad] ⟨⟩ *nmf* invalid, sick
person ; **malade mental** mentally ill person.
⟨⟩ *adj* **1.** [souffrant - personne] ill, sick ;
[- organe] bad ; **tomber malade** to fall ill OU
sick - **2.** *fam* [fou] crazy.

maladie [maladi] *nf* **1.** MÉD illness ; **maladie
d'Alzheimer** Alzheimer's disease ; **maladie
contagieuse/héréditaire** contagious/hered-
itary disease ; **maladie de Creutzfeldt-Jakob**
Creutzfeldt-Jakob disease ; **maladie de
Parkinson** Parkinson's disease ; **maladie
sexuellement transmissible** sexually transmissible OU transmitted disease ; **maladie
de la vache folle** mad cow disease - **2.** [pas-
sion, manie] mania.

maladresse [maladrɛs] *nf* **1.** [inhabileté]
clumsiness - **2.** [bévue] blunder.

maladroit, e [maladrwa, at] *adj* clumsy.

malaise [malɛz] *nm* **1.** [indisposition] discomfort - **2.** [trouble] unease *(U)*.

malaisé, e [maleze] *adj* difficult.

Malaisie [malɛzi] *nf* : **la Malaisie** Malaya.

malappris, e [malapri, iz] *nm, f* lout.

malaria [malarja] *nf* malaria.

malaudition [malodisjɔ̃] *nf* MÉD hearing
loss, hardness of hearing ; **souffrir de
malaudition** to be hearing-impaired OU hard
of hearing.

malaxer [3] [malakse] *vt* to knead.

malbouffe [malbuf] *nf* junk food, bad
food.

malchance [malʃɑ̃s] *nf* bad luck *(U)*.

malchanceux, euse [malʃɑ̃sø, øz] ⟨⟩ *adj*
unlucky. ⟨⟩ *nm, f* unlucky person.

malcommode [malkɔmɔd] *adj* inconvenient ; [meuble] impractical.

mâle [mal] ⟨⟩ *adj* **1.** [enfant, animal,
hormone] male - **2.** [voix, assurance] manly
- **3.** ÉLECTR male. ⟨⟩ *nm* male.

malédiction [malediksjɔ̃] *nf* curse.

maléfique [malefik] *adj sout* evil.

malencontreux, euse [malɑ̃kɔ̃trø, øz] *adj*
[hasard, rencontre] unfortunate.

malentendant, e [malɑ̃tɑ̃dɑ̃, ɑ̃t] *nm, f*
person who is hard of hearing.

malentendu [malɑ̃tɑ̃dy] *nm* misunderstanding.

malfaçon [malfasɔ̃] *nf* defect.

malfaiteur [malfɛtœr] *nm* criminal.

malfamé, e, mal famé, e [malfame] *adj*
disreputable.

malformation [malfɔrmasjɔ̃] *nf* malformation.

malfrat [malfra] *nm fam* crook.

malgré [malgre] *prép* in spite of ; **malgré
tout** [quoi qu'il arrive] in spite of everything ;
[pourtant] even so, yet. **malgré que**
loc conj (+ subjonctif) fam although, in spite of
the fact that.

malhabile [malabil] *adj* clumsy.

malheur [malœr] *nm* misfortune ; **par
malheur** unfortunately ; **porter malheur à
qqn** to bring sb bad luck.

malheureusement [malœrøzmɑ̃] *adv* unfortunately.

malheureux, euse [malœrø, øz] ⟨⟩ *adj*
1. [triste] unhappy - **2.** [désastreux, regret-
table] unfortunate - **3.** [malchanceux] unlucky - **4.** *(avant n)* [sans valeur] pathetic,
miserable. ⟨⟩ *nm, f* **1.** [infortuné] poor soul
- **2.** [indigent] poor person.

malhonnête [malɔnɛt] ⟨⟩ *nmf* dishonest
person. ⟨⟩ *adj* **1.** [personne, affaire] dishonest - **2.** *hum* [proposition, propos] indecent.

malhonnêteté [malɔnɛtte] *nf* **1.** [de personne] dishonesty - **2.** [action] dishonest action.

Mali [mali] *nm* : **le Mali** Mali.

malice [malis] *nf* mischief.

malicieux, euse [malisjø, øz] *adj* mischievous.

malin, igne [malɛ̃, iɲ] ◇ *adj* **1.** [rusé] crafty, cunning ; [regard, sourire] knowing - **2.** [méchant] malicious, spiteful - **3.** MÉD malignant. ◇ *nm, f* cunning ou crafty person.

malingre [malɛ̃gr] *adj* sickly.

malle [mal] *nf* [coffre] trunk ; [de voiture] boot *UK*, trunk *US*.

malléable [maleabl] *adj* malleable.

mallette [malɛt] *nf* briefcase.

mal-logé, e [malloʒe] (*mpl* **mal-logés**) (*fpl* **mal-logées**) *nm, f* person living in poor accommodation.

malmener [19] [malmɔne] *vt* [brutaliser] to handle roughly, to ill-treat.

malnutrition [malnytrisjɔ̃] *nf* malnutrition.

malodorant, e [malodɔrɑ̃, ɑ̃t] *adj* smelly.

malotru, e [malɔtry] *nm, f* lout.

malpoli, e [malpɔli] *nm, f* rude person.

malpropre [malprɔpr] *adj* [sale] dirty.

malsain, e [malsɛ̃, ɛn] *adj* unhealthy.

malt [malt] *nm* **1.** [céréale] malt - **2.** [whisky] malt (whisky).

Malte [malt] *npr* Malta.

maltraiter [4] [maltrete] *vt* to ill-treat ; [en paroles] to attack, to run down.

malus [malys] *nm* increase in car insurance charges, due to loss of no-claims bonus.

malveillant, e [malvɛjɑ̃, ɑ̃t] *adj* spiteful.

malversation [malvɛrsasjɔ̃] *nf* embezzlement.

malvoyant, e [malvwajɑ̃, ɑ̃t] *nm, f* person who is partially sighted.

maman [mamɑ̃] *nf* mummy *UK*, mommy *US*.

mamelle [mamɛl] *nf* teat ; [de vache] udder.

mamelon [mamlɔ̃] *nm* [du sein] nipple.

mamie, mamy [mami] *nf* granny, grandma.

mammifère [mamifɛr] *nm* mammal.

mammouth [mamut] *nm* mammoth.

mamy = **mamie**.

management [manadʒmɛnt] *nm* management.

manager [manadʒɛr] *nm* manager.

manche [mɑ̃ʃ] ◇ *nf* **1.** [de vêtement] sleeve ; **manches courtes/longues** short/long

sleeves - **2.** [de jeu] round, game ; TENNIS set. ◇ *nm* **1.** [d'outil] handle ; **manche à balai** broomstick ; [d'avion] joystick - **2.** MUS neck.

Manche [mɑ̃ʃ] *nf* [mer] : **la Manche** the English Channel.

manchette [mɑ̃ʃɛt] *nf* **1.** [de chemise] cuff - **2.** [de journal] headline - **3.** [coup] forearm blow.

manchon [mɑ̃ʃɔ̃] *nm* **1.** [en fourrure] muff - **2.** TECHNOL casing, sleeve.

manchot, ote [mɑ̃ʃo, ɔt] ◇ *adj* one-armed. ◇ *nm, f* one-armed person. ➡ **manchot** *nm* penguin.

mandarine [mɑ̃darin] *nf* mandarin (orange).

mandat [mɑ̃da] *nm* **1.** [pouvoir, fonction] mandate - **2.** DR warrant ; **mandat de perquisition** search warrant - **3.** [titre postal] money order ; **mandat postal** postal order *UK*, money order *US*.

mandataire [mɑ̃datɛr] *nmf* proxy, representative.

mandibule [mɑ̃dibyl] *nf* mandible.

mandoline [mɑ̃dɔlin] *nf* mandolin.

manège [manɛʒ] *nm* **1.** [attraction] merry-go-round, roundabout *UK*, carousel *US* - **2.** [de chevaux - lieu] riding school - **3.** [manœuvre] scheme, game.

manette [manɛt] *nf* lever.

manga [mɑ̃ga] *nf* manga (comic).

manganèse [mɑ̃ganɛz] *nm* manganese.

mangeable [mɑ̃ʒabl] *adj* edible.

mangeoire [mɑ̃ʒwar] *nf* manger.

manger [17] [mɑ̃ʒe] ◇ *vt* **1.** [nourriture] to eat - **2.** [fortune] to get through, to squander. ◇ *vi* to eat.

mangue [mɑ̃g] *nf* mango.

maniable [manjabl] *adj* [instrument] manageable.

maniaque [manjak] ◇ *nmf* **1.** [méticuleux] fusspot - **2.** [fou] maniac. ◇ *adj* **1.** [méticuleux] fussy - **2.** [fou] maniacal.

manie [mani] *nf* **1.** [habitude] funny habit ; **avoir la manie de qqch/de faire qqch** to have a mania for sthg/for doing sthg - **2.** [obsession] mania.

maniement [manimɑ̃] *nm* handling.

manier [9] [manje] *vt* [manipuler, utiliser] to handle ; *fig* [ironie, mots] to handle skilfully.

manière [manjɛr] *nf* [méthode] manner, way ; **de toute manière** at any rate ; **d'une manière générale** generally speaking. ➡ **manières** *nfpl* manners. ➡ **de manière à** *loc conj* (in order) to ; **de manière à ce que** (+ *subjonctif*) so that. ➡ **de manière que** *loc conj* (+ *subjonctif*) in such a way that.

maniéré, e [manjere] *adj* affected.

manif [manif] *nf fam* demo *UK*.

manifestant, e [manifɛstã, ãt] *nm, f* demonstrator.

manifestation [manifɛstasjɔ̃] *nf* **1.** [témoignage] expression - **2.** [mouvement collectif] demonstration - **3.** [apparition - de maladie] appearance.

manifester [3] [manifɛste] <> *vt* to show, to express. <> *vi* to demonstrate. <> se **manifester** *vp* **1.** [apparaître] to show ou manifest itself - **2.** [se montrer] to turn up, to appear.

manigancer [16] [manigãse] *vt fam* to plot.

manioc [manjɔk] *nm* manioc.

manipuler [3] [manipyle] *vt* **1.** [colis, appareil] to handle - **2.** [statistiques, résultats] to falsify, to rig - **3.** *péj* [personne] to manipulate.

manivelle [manivɛl] *nf* crank.

manne [man] *nf* RELIG manna ; *fig & litt* godsend.

mannequin [man/kɛ̃] *nm* **1.** [forme humaine] model, dummy - **2.** [personne] model, mannequin.

manœuvre [manœvr] <> *nf* **1.** [d'appareil, de véhicule] driving, handling - **2.** MIL manoeuvre *UK*, maneuver *US*, exercise - **3.** [machination] ploy, scheme. <> *nm* labourer *UK*, laborer *US*.

manœuvrer [5] [manœvre] <> *vi* to manoeuvre *UK*, to maneuver *US*. <> *vt* **1.** [faire fonctionner] to operate, to work ; [voiture] to manoeuvre *UK*, to maneuver *US* - **2.** [influencer] to manipulate.

manoir [manwar] *nm* manor, country house.

manquant, e [mãkã, ãt] *adj* missing.

manque [mãk] *nm* **1.** [pénurie] lack, shortage ; **par manque de** for want of - **2.** [de toxicomane] withdrawal symptoms *pl* - **3.** [lacune] gap.

manqué, e [mãke] *adj* [raté] failed ; [rendez-vous] missed.

manquer [3] [mãke] <> *vi* **1.** [faire défaut] to be lacking, to be missing ; **l'argent/le temps me manque** I don't have enough money/time ; **tu me manques** I miss you - **2.** [être absent] : **manquer (à)** to be absent (from), to be missing (from) - **3.** [ne pas avoir assez] : **manquer de qqch** to lack sthg, to be short of sthg - **4.** [faillir] : **il a manqué de se noyer** he nearly ou almost drowned ; **ne manquez pas de lui dire** don't forget to tell him ; **je n'y manquerai pas** I certainly will, I'll definitely do it - **5.** [ne pas respecter] : **manquer à** [devoir] to fail in ; **manquer à sa parole** to break one's word. <> *vt* **1.** [gén] to miss - **2.** [échouer à] to bungle, to botch. <> *v impers* : **il manque quelqu'un** somebody is missing ; **il me manque 3 euros** I'm 3 euros short.

mansarde [mãsard] *nf* attic.

mansardé, e [mãsarde] *adj* attic *(avant n)*.

mansuétude [mãsɥetyd] *nf litt* indulgence.

mante [mãt] *nf* HIST mantle. <> **mante religieuse** *nf* praying mantis.

manteau, x [mãto] *nm* [vêtement] coat.

manucure [manykyr] *nmf* manicurist.

manuel, elle [manɥɛl] *adj* manual. <> **manuel** *nm* manual.

manufacture [manyfaktyr] *nf* [fabrique] factory.

manuscrit, e [manyskri, it] *adj* handwritten. <> **manuscrit** *nm* manuscript.

manutention [manytãsjɔ̃] *nf* handling.

manutentionnaire [manytãsjɔnɛr] *nmf* warehouseman.

mappemonde [mapmɔ̃d] *nf* **1.** [carte] map of the world - **2.** [sphère] globe.

maquereau, elle, x [makro, ɛl, o] *nm, f fam* pimp (*f* madam). <> **maquereau** *nm* mackerel.

maquette [makɛt] *nf* **1.** [ébauche] paste-up - **2.** [modèle réduit] model.

maquillage [makijaʒ] *nm* [action, produits] make-up.

maquiller [3] [makije] *vt* **1.** [farder] to make up - **2.** [fausser - gén] to disguise ; [- passeport] to falsify ; [- chiffres] to doctor. <> se **maquiller** *vp* to make up, to put on one's make-up.

maquis [maki] *nm* **1.** [végétation] scrub, brush - **2.** HIST Maquis.

marabout [marabu] *nm* **1.** ZOOL marabou - **2.** [guérisseur] marabout.

maraîcher, ère [mareʃe, ɛr] <> *adj* market garden *(avant n) UK*, truck farming *(avant n) US*. <> *nm, f* market gardener *UK*, truck farmer *US*.

marais [marɛ] *nm* [marécage] marsh, swamp ; **marais salant** saltpan.

marasme [marasm] *nm* [récession] stagnation.

marathon [maratɔ̃] *nm* marathon.

marâtre [maratr] *nf vieilli* **1.** [mauvaise mère] bad mother - **2.** [belle-mère] stepmother.

maraudage [marodaʒ] *nm* = **maraude**.

maraude [marod] *nf* pilfering.

marbre [marbr] *nm* [roche, objet] marble.

marc [mar] *nm* **1.** [eau-de-vie] *spirit distilled from grape residue* - **2.** [de fruits] residue ; [de thé] leaves ; **marc de café** grounds *pl*.

marcassin [markasɛ̃] *nm* young wild boar.

marchand, e [maʁʃɑ̃, ɑ̃d] <> adj [valeur] market (avant n) ; [prix] trade (avant n). <> nm, f [commerçant] merchant ; [détaillant] shopkeeper UK, storekeeper US ; **marchand de journaux** newsagent UK, newsdealer US.

marchander [3] [maʁʃɑ̃de] <> vt 1. [prix] to haggle over - 2. [appui] to begrudge. <> vi to bargain, to haggle.

marchandise [maʁʃɑ̃diz] nf merchandise (U), goods pl.

marche [maʁʃ] nf 1. [d'escalier] step - 2. [activité, sport] walking ; **marche à pied** walking ; **marche à suivre** fig correct procedure - 3. [promenade] walk ; **nous avons fait une marche de 8 km** we did an 8 km walk - 4. [défilé] : **marche silencieuse/ de protestation** silent/protest march - 5. MUS march - 6. [déplacement - du temps, d'astre] course ; **assis dans le sens de la marche** [en train] sitting facing the engine ; **en marche arrière** in reverse ; **faire marche arrière** to reverse ; fig to backpedal, to backtrack - 7. [fonctionnement] running, working ; **en marche** running ; **se mettre en marche** to start (up).

marché [maʁʃe] nm 1. [gén] market ; **faire son marché** to go shopping, to do one's shopping ; **le marché du travail** the labour UK ou labor US market ; **marché noir** black market ; **marché aux puces** flea market - 2. [contrat] bargain, deal ; **(à) bon marché** cheap. <> **Marché unique européen** nm the Single European Market.

marchepied [maʁʃəpje] nm [de train] step ; [escabeau] steps pl UK, stepladder ; fig stepping-stone.

marcher [3] [maʁʃe] vi 1. [aller à pied] to walk - 2. [poser le pied] to step - 3. [fonctionner, tourner] to work ; **son affaire marche bien** his business is doing well - 4. fam [accepter] to agree ; **faire marcher qqn** fam to take sb for a ride.

mardi [maʁdi] nm Tuesday ; **mardi gras** Shrove Tuesday ; voir aussi **samedi**.

mare [maʁ] nf pool.

marécage [maʁekaʒ] nm marsh, bog.

marécageux, euse [maʁekaʒø, øz] adj [terrain] marshy, boggy.

maréchal, aux [maʁeʃal, o] nm marshal.

marée [maʁe] nf 1. [de la mer] tide ; **(à) marée haute/basse** at high/low tide - 2. fig [de personnes] wave, surge. <> **marée noire** nf oil slick.

marelle [maʁɛl] nf hopscotch.

margarine [maʁgaʁin] nf margarine.

marge [maʁʒ] nf 1. [espace] margin ; **vivre en marge de la société** fig to live on the fringes of society - 2. [latitude] leeway ; **marge d'erreur** margin of error - 3. COMM margin ; **marge commerciale** gross margin.

margelle [maʁʒɛl] nf coping.

marginal, e, aux [maʁʒinal, o] <> adj 1. [gén] marginal - 2. [groupe] dropout (avant n). <> nm, f dropout.

marguerite [maʁgəʁit] nf 1. BOT daisy - 2. [d'imprimante] daisy wheel.

mari [maʁi] nm husband.

mariage [maʁjaʒ] nm 1. [union, institution] marriage - 2. [cérémonie] wedding ; **mariage civil/religieux** civil/church wedding - 3. fig [de choses] blend.

Marianne [maʁjan] npr personification of the French Republic.

marié, e [maʁje] <> adj married. <> nm, f groom, bridegroom (f bride).

marier [9] [maʁje] vt 1. [personne] to marry - 2. fig [couleurs] to blend. <> **se marier** vp 1. [personnes] to get married ; **se marier avec qqn** to marry sb - 2. fig [couleurs] to blend.

marihuana [maʁiʁwana], **marijuana** [maʁiʒwana] nf marijuana.

marin, e [maʁɛ̃, in] adj 1. [de la mer] sea (avant n) ; [faune, biologie] marine - 2. NAUT [carte, mille] nautical. <> **marin** nm 1. [navigateur] seafarer - 2. [matelot] sailor ; **marin pêcheur** deep-sea fisherman. <> **marine** <> nf 1. [navigation] seamanship, navigation - 2. [navires] navy ; **marine marchande** merchant navy UK ou marine US ; **marine nationale** navy. <> nm 1. MIL marine - 2. [couleur] navy (blue). <> adj inv navy.

mariner [3] [maʁine] <> vt to marinate. <> vi 1. [aliment] to marinate ; **faire mariner qqch** to marinate sthg - 2. fam fig [attendre] to hang around ; **faire mariner qqn** to let sb stew.

marinier [maʁinje] nm bargee UK, bargeman US.

marionnette [maʁjɔnɛt] nf puppet.

marital, e, aux [maʁital, o] adj : **autorisation maritale** husband's permission.

maritime [maʁitim] adj [navigation] maritime ; [ville] coastal.

mark [maʁk] nm [monnaie] mark.

marketing [maʁkɛtiŋ] nm marketing ; **marketing téléphonique** telemarketing.

marmaille [maʁmaj] nf fam brood (of kids).

marmelade [maʁməlad] nf stewed fruit.

marmite [maʁmit] nf [casserole] pot.

marmonner [3] [maʁmɔne] vt & vi to mutter, to mumble.

marmot [maʁmo] nm fam kid.

marmotte [maʁmɔt] nf marmot.

Maroc [maʁɔk] nm : **le Maroc** Morocco.

marocain, e [marɔkɛ̃, ɛn] *adj* Moroccan. ➡ **Marocain, e** *nm, f* Moroccan.

maroquinerie [marɔkinri] *nf* [magasin] leather-goods shop *UK* OU store *US*.

marotte [marɔt] *nf* [dada] craze.

marquant, e [markɑ̃, ɑ̃t] *adj* outstanding.

marque [mark] *nf* **1.** [signe, trace] mark ; *fig* stamp, mark - **2.** [label, fabricant] make, brand ; **de marque** designer *(avant n)* ; *fig* important ; **marque déposée** registered trademark - **3.** SPORT score ; **à vos marques, prêts, partez!** on your marks, get set, go!, ready, steady, go! *UK* - **4.** [témoignage] sign, token.

marqué, e [marke] *adj* **1.** [net] marked, pronounced - **2.** [personne, visage] marked.

marquer [3] [marke] ◇ *vt* **1.** [gén] to mark - **2.** *fam* [écrire] to write down, to note down - **3.** [indiquer, manifester] to show - **4.** [SPORT - but, point] to score ; [- joueur] to mark - **5.** [impressionner] to mark, to affect, to make an impression on. ◇ *vi* **1.** [événement, expérience] to leave its mark - **2.** SPORT to score.

marqueur [markœr] *nm* [crayon] marker (pen).

marquis, e [marki, iz] *nm, f* marquis (*f* marchioness).

marraine [marɛn] *nf* **1.** [de filleul] god-mother - **2.** [de navire] christener.

marrant, e [marɑ̃, ɑ̃t] *adj fam* funny.

marre [mar] *adv* : **en avoir marre (de)** *fam* to be fed up (with).

marrer [3] [mare] ➡ **se marrer** *vp fam* to split one's sides.

marron, onne [marɔ̃, ɔn] *adj péj* [médecin] quack *(avant n)* ; [avocat] crooked. ➡ **marron** ◇ *nm* **1.** [fruit] chestnut - **2.** [couleur] brown. ◇ *adj inv* brown.

marronnier [marɔnje] *nm* chestnut tree.

mars [mars] *nm* March ; *voir aussi* **septembre**.

Marseille [marsɛj] *npr* Marseilles.

marsouin [marswɛ̃] *nm* porpoise.

marteau, x [marto] ◇ *nm* **1.** [gén] hammer ; **marteau piqueur** OU **pneumatique** pneumatic drill *UK*, jackhammer *US* - **2.** [heurtoir] knocker. ◇ *adj fam* barmy *UK*.

marteler [25] [martəle] *vt* **1.** [pieu] to hammer ; [table, porte] to hammer on, to pound - **2.** [phrase] to rap out.

martial, e, aux [marsjal, o] *adj* martial.

martien, enne [marsjɛ̃, ɛn] *adj & nm, f* Martian.

martinet [martinɛ] *nm* **1.** ZOOL swift - **2.** [fouet] whip.

martingale [martɛ̃gal] *nf* **1.** [de vêtement] half-belt - **2.** [jeux] winning system.

Martini® [martini] *nm* Martini®.

Martinique [martinik] *nf* : **la Martinique** Martinique.

martyr, e [martir] ◇ *adj* martyred. ◇ *nm, f* martyr. ➡ **martyre** *nm* martyr-dom.

martyriser [3] [martirize] *vt* to torment.

marxisme [marksism] *nm* Marxism.

mascarade [maskarad] *nf* [mise en scène] masquerade.

mascotte [maskɔt] *nf* mascot.

masculin, e [maskylɛ̃, in] *adj* [apparence & GRAMM] masculine ; [métier, population, sexe] male. ➡ **masculin** *nm* GRAMM masculine.

maso [mazo] *fam* ◇ *nm* masochist. ◇ *adj* masochistic.

masochisme [mazɔʃism] *nm* masochism.

masque [mask] *nm* **1.** [gén] mask ; **masque à gaz** gas mask - **2.** *fig* [façade] front, façade.

masquer [3] [maske] *vt* **1.** [vérité, crime, problème] to conceal - **2.** [maison, visage] to conceal, to hide.

massacre [masakr] *nm litt & fig* massacre.

massacrer [3] [masakre] *vt* to massacre ; [voiture] to smash up.

massage [masaʒ] *nm* massage.

masse [mas] *nf* **1.** [de pierre] block ; [d'eau] volume - **2.** [grande quantité] : **une masse de** masses *pl* OU loads *pl* of - **3.** PHYS mass - **4.** ÉLECTR earth *UK*, ground *US* - **5.** [maillet] sledgehammer. ➡ **en masse** *loc adv* [venir] en masse, all together ; *fam* [acheter] in bulk.

masser [3] [mase] *vt* **1.** [assembler] to assemble - **2.** [frotter] to massage. ➡ **se masser** *vp* **1.** [s'assembler] to assemble, to gather - **2.** [se frotter] : **se masser le bras** to massage one's arm.

masseur, euse [masœr, øz] *nm, f* [personne] masseur (*f* masseuse).

massicot [masiko] *nm* guillotine.

massif, ive [masif, iv] *adj* **1.** [monument, personne, dose] massive - **2.** [or, chêne] solid. ➡ **massif** *nm* **1.** [de plantes] clump - **2.** [de montagnes] massif.

massue [masy] *nf* club.

mastic [mastik] *nm* mastic, putty.

mastiquer [3] [mastike] *vt* [mâcher] to chew.

masturber [3] [mastyrbe] ➡ **se masturber** *vp* to masturbate.

masure [mazyr] *nf* hovel.

mat, e [mat] *adj* **1.** [peinture, surface] matt

UK, matte US - 2. [peau, personne] dusky - 3. [bruit, son] dull - 4. [aux échecs] checkmated. ➤ **mat** *nm* checkmate.

mât [ma] *nm* 1. NAUT mast - 2. [poteau] pole, post.

match [matʃ] (*pl* matches ou matchs) *nm* match ; **(faire) match nul** (to) draw ; **match aller/retour** first/second leg.

matelas [matla] *nm inv* [de lit] mattress ; **matelas pneumatique** airbed *UK*.

matelot [matlo] *nm* sailor.

mater [3] [mate] *vt* 1. [soumettre, neutraliser] to subdue - 2. *fam* [regarder] to eye up.

matérialiser [3] [materjalize] ➤ **se matérialiser** *vp* [aspirations] to be realized.

matérialiste [materjalist] ◇ *nmf* materialist. ◇ *adj* materialistic.

matériau, x [materjo] *nm* material. ➤ **matériaux** *nmpl* CONSTR material *(U)*, materials.

matériel, elle [materjɛl] *adj* 1. [être, substance] material, physical ; [confort, avantage, aide] material - 2. [considération] practical. ➤ **matériel** *nm* 1. [gén] equipment *(U)* - 2. INFORM hardware *(U)*.

maternel, elle [matɛrnɛl] *adj* maternal ; [langue] mother *(avant n)*. ➤ **maternelle** *nf* nursery school.

maternité [matɛrnite] *nf* 1. [qualité] maternity, motherhood - 2. [hôpital] maternity hospital.

mathématicien, enne [matematisjɛ̃, ɛn] *nm, f* mathematician.

mathématique [matematik] *adj* mathematical. ➤ **mathématiques** *nfpl* mathematics *(U)*.

maths [mat] *nfpl fam* maths *UK*, math *US*.

matière [matjɛr] *nf* 1. [substance] matter ; **matières grasses** fats ; **matière grise** grey *UK* ou gray *US* matter - 2. [matériau] material ; **matières premières** raw materials - 3. [discipline, sujet] subject ; **en matière de sport/littérature** as far as sport/literature is concerned.

matin [matɛ̃] *nm* morning ; **le matin** in the morning ; **ce matin** this morning ; **à trois heures du matin** at 3 o'clock in the morning ; **du matin au soir** *fig* from dawn to dusk.

matinal, e, aux [matinal, o] *adj* 1. [gymnastique, émission] morning *(avant n)* - 2. [personne] : **être matinal** to be an early riser.

matinée [matine] *nf* 1. [matin] morning ; **faire la grasse matinée** to have a lie in *UK*, to sleep late - 2. [spectacle] matinée, afternoon performance.

matou [matu] *nm* tom, tomcat.

matraque [matrak] *nf* truncheon *UK*, billy club *US*, nightstick *US*.

matraquer [3] [matrake] *vt* 1. [frapper] to beat, to club - 2. *fig* [intoxiquer] to bombard.

matriarcat [matrijarka] *nm* matriarchy.

matrice [matris] *nf* 1. [moule] mould - 2. MATH matrix - 3. ANAT womb.

matricule [matrikyl] *nm* : **(numéro) matricule** number.

matrimonial, e, aux [matrimɔnjal, o] *adj* matrimonial.

matrone [matron] *nf péj* old bag.

mature [matyr] *adj* mature.

mâture [matyr] *nf* masts *pl*.

maturité [matyrite] *nf* maturity ; [de fruit] ripeness.

maudire [104] [modir] *vt* to curse.

maudit, e [modi, it] ◇ *pp* ➤ **maudire**. ◇ *adj* 1. [réprouvé] accursed - 2. *(avant n)* [exécrable] damned.

maugréer [15] [mogree] ◇ *vt* to mutter. ◇ *vi* : **maugréer (contre)** to grumble (about).

Maurice [moris] ➤ **île**.

mausolée [mozɔle] *nm* mausoleum.

maussade [mosad] *adj* 1. [personne, air] sullen - 2. [temps] gloomy.

mauvais, e [movɛ, ɛz] *adj* 1. [gén] bad - 2. [moment, numéro, réponse] wrong - 3. [mer] rough - 4. [personne, regard] nasty. ➤ **mauvais** *adv* : **il fait mauvais** the weather is bad ; **sentir mauvais** to smell bad.

mauve [mov] *nm & adj* mauve.

mauviette [movjɛt] *nf fam* 1. [physiquement] weakling - 2. [moralement] coward, wimp.

maux ➤ **mal**.

max [maks] (*abr de* maximum) *nm fam* **un max de fric** loads of money.

max. (*abr écrite de* maximum) max.

maxillaire [maksilɛr] *nm* jawbone.

maxime [maksim] *nf* maxim.

maximum [maksimɔm] (*pl* maxima [maksima]) ◇ *nm* maximum ; **le maximum de personnes** the greatest (possible) number of people ; **au maximum** at the most. ◇ *adj* maximum.

maya [maja] *adj* Mayan. ➤ **Maya** *nmf* : **les Mayas** the Maya.

mayonnaise [majɔnɛz] *nf* mayonnaise.

mazout [mazut] *nm* fuel oil.

me [mə], **m'** *(devant voyelle ou 'h' muet)* *pron pers* 1. [complément d'objet direct] me - 2. [complément d'objet indirect] (to) me - 3. [réfléchi] myself - 4. [avec un présentatif] : **me voici** here I am.

méandre [meɑ̃dr] nm [de rivière] meander, bend. **méandres** nmpl [détours sinueux] meanderings pl.

mec [mɛk] nm fam guy, bloke UK.

mécanicien, enne [mekanisjɛ̃, ɛn] nm, f **1.** [de garage] mechanic - **2.** [conducteur de train] train driver UK, engineer US.

mécanique [mekanik] <> nf **1.** TECHNOL mechanical engineering - **2.** MATH & PHYS mechanics (U) - **3.** [mécanisme] mechanism. <> adj mechanical.

mécanisme [mekanism] nm mechanism.

mécène [mesɛn] nm patron.

méchamment [meʃamɑ̃] adv [cruellement] nastily.

méchanceté [meʃɑ̃ste] nf **1.** [attitude] nastiness - **2.** fam [rosserie] nasty thing.

méchant, e [meʃɑ̃, ɑ̃t] <> adj **1.** [malveillant, cruel] nasty, wicked ; [animal] vicious - **2.** [désobéissant] naughty. <> nm, f [en langage enfantin] baddy.

mèche [mɛʃ] nf **1.** [de bougie] wick - **2.** [de cheveux] lock - **3.** [de bombe] fuse.

méchoui [meʃwi] nm whole roast sheep.

méconnaissable [mekɔnɛsabl] adj unrecognizable.

méconnu, e [mekɔny] adj unrecognized.

mécontent, e [mekɔ̃tɑ̃, ɑ̃t] <> adj unhappy. <> nm, f malcontent.

mécontenter [3] [mekɔ̃tɑ̃te] vt to displease.

Mecque [mɛk] npr : La Mecque Mecca.

mécréant, e [mekreɑ̃, ɑ̃t] nm, f nonbeliever.

médaille [medaj] nf **1.** [pièce, décoration] medal - **2.** [bijou] medallion - **3.** [de chien] identification disc UK ou disk US, tag.

médaillon [medajɔ̃] nm **1.** [bijou] locket - **2.** ART & CULIN medallion.

médecin [medsɛ̃] nm doctor ; **médecin conventionné** ≃ National Health doctor UK ; **médecin de famille** family doctor, GP UK ; **médecin de garde** doctor on duty, duty doctor ; **médecin généraliste** general practitioner, GP UK ; **médecin légiste** forensic scientist UK, medical examiner US ; **votre médecin traitant** your (usual) doctor ; **Médecins du monde, Médecins sans frontières** organizations providing medical aid to victims of war and disasters, especially in the Third World Doctors Without Borders US.

médecine [medsin] nf medicine.

Medef [medef] (abr de Mouvement des entreprises de France) nm national council of French employers, ≃ CBI UK.

média [medja] nm : **les médias** the (mass) media.

médian, e [medjɑ̃, an] adj median. **médiane** nf median.

médiateur, trice [medjatœr, tris] <> adj mediating (avant n). <> nm, f mediator ; [dans un conflit de travail] arbitrator. **médiateur** nm ADMIN ombudsman. **médiatrice** nf median.

médiathèque [medjatɛk] nf media library.

médiatique [medjatik] adj media (avant n).

médiatiser [3] [medjatize] vt péj to turn into a media event.

médical, e, aux [medikal, o] adj medical.

médicament [medikamɑ̃] nm medicine, drug.

médicinal, e, aux [medisinal, o] adj medicinal.

médico-légal, e, aux [medikɔlegal, o] adj forensic.

médiéval, e, aux [medjeval, o] adj medieval.

médiocre [medjɔkr] adj mediocre.

médiocrité [medjɔkrite] nf mediocrity.

médire [103] [medir] vi to gossip ; **médire de qqn** to speak ill of sb.

médisant, e [medizɑ̃, ɑ̃t] adj slanderous.

méditation [meditasjɔ̃] nf meditation.

méditer [3] [medite] <> vt [projeter] to plan ; **méditer de faire qqch** to plan to do sthg. <> vi : **méditer (sur)** to meditate (on).

Méditerranée [mediterane] nf : **la Méditerranée** the Mediterranean (Sea).

méditerranéen, enne [mediteraneɛ̃, ɛn] adj Mediterranean. **Méditerranéen, enne** nm, f person from the Mediterranean.

médium [medjɔm] nm [personne] medium.

médius [medjys] nm middle finger.

méduse [medyz] nf jellyfish.

méduser [3] [medyze] vt to dumbfound.

meeting [mitiŋ] nm meeting.

méfait [mefɛ] nm misdemeanour UK, misdemeanor US, misdeed. **méfaits** nmpl [du temps] ravages.

méfiance [mefjɑ̃s] nf suspicion, distrust.

méfiant, e [mefjɑ̃, ɑ̃t] adj suspicious, distrustful.

méfier [9] [mefje] **se méfier** vp to be wary ou careful ; **se méfier de qqn/qqch** to distrust sb/sthg.

mégalo [megalo] nmf & adj fam megalomaniac.

mégalomane [megalɔman] nmf & adj megalomaniac.

mégalomanie [megalɔmani] nf megalomania.

méga-octet [megaɔktə] *nm* megabyte.

mégapole [megapɔl] *nf* megalopolis, megacity.

mégarde [megard] ➤ **par mégarde** *loc adv* by mistake.

mégère [meʒɛr] *nf péj* shrew.

mégot [mego] *nm fam* fag-end *UK*, butt *US*.

meilleur, e [mejœr] ⟷ *adj (compar)* better ; *(superl)* best. ⟷ *nm, f* best. ➤ **meilleur** ⟷ *nm* : **le meilleur** the best. ⟷ *adv* better.

mél [mel] *nm* INFORM email.

mélancolie [melãkɔli] *nf* melancholy.

mélancolique [melãkɔlik] *adj* melancholy.

mélange [melãʒ] *nm* **1.** [action] mixing - **2.** [mixture] mixture.

mélanger [17] [melãʒe] *vt* **1.** [mettre ensemble] to mix - **2.** [déranger] to mix up, to muddle up. ➤ **se mélanger** *vp* **1.** [se mêler] to mix - **2.** [se brouiller] to get mixed up.

mêlée [mele] *nf* **1.** [combat] fray - **2.** [rugby] scrum.

mêler [4] [mele] *vt* **1.** [mélanger] to mix - **2.** [déranger] to muddle up, to mix up - **3.** [impliquer] : **mêler qqn à qqch** to involve sb in sthg. ➤ **se mêler** *vp* **1.** [se joindre] : **se mêler à** [groupe] to join - **2.** [s'ingérer] : **se mêler de qqch** to get mixed up in sthg ; **mêlez-vous de ce qui vous regarde!** mind your own business!

mélèze [melɛz] *nm* larch.

mélo [melo] *nm fam* melodrama.

mélodie [melɔdi] *nf* melody.

mélodieux, euse [melɔdjø, øz] *adj* melodious, tuneful.

mélodrame [melɔdram] *nm* melodrama.

mélomane [melɔman] ⟷ *nmf* music lover. ⟷ *adj* music-loving.

melon [məlɔ̃] *nm* **1.** [fruit] melon - **2.** [chapeau] bowler (hat) *UK*, derby (hat) *US*.

membrane [mãbran] *nf* membrane.

membre [mãbr] ⟷ *nm* **1.** [du corps] limb - **2.** [personne, pays, partie] member. ⟷ *adj* member *(avant n)*.

mémé = **mémère**.

même [mɛm] ⟷ *adj indéf* **1.** [indique une identité ou une ressemblance] same ; **il a le même âge que moi** he's the same age as me - **2.** [sert à souligner] : **ce sont ses paroles mêmes** those are his very words ; **elle est la bonté même** she's kindness itself. ⟷ *pron indéf* : **le/la même** the same one ; **ce sont toujours les mêmes qui gagnent** it's always the same people who win. ⟷ *adv* even ; **il n'est même pas diplômé** he isn't even qualified. ➤ **de même** *loc adv*

similarly, likewise ; **il en va de même pour lui** the same goes for him. ➤ **de même que** *loc conj* just as. ➤ **tout de même** *loc adv* all the same. ➤ **à même** *loc prép* : **s'asseoir à même le sol** to sit on the bare ground. ➤ **à même de** *loc prép* : **être à même de faire qqch** to be able to do sthg, to be in a position to do sthg. ➤ **même si** *loc conj* even if.

mémento [memɛ̃to] *nm* **1.** [agenda] pocket diary - **2.** [ouvrage] notes *(title of school textbook)*.

mémoire [memwar] ⟷ *nf* [gén & INFORM] memory ; **de mémoire** from memory ; **avoir bonne/mauvaise mémoire** to have a good/bad memory ; **mettre en mémoire** INFORM to store ; **mémoire tampon** INFORM buffer ; **mémoire vive** INFORM random access memory ; **à la mémoire de** in memory of. ⟷ *nm* UNIV dissertation, paper. ➤ **mémoires** *nmpl* memoirs.

mémorable [memɔrabl] *adj* memorable.

mémorial, aux [memɔrjal, o] *nm* [monument] memorial.

mémorisable [memɔrizabl] *adj* INFORM storable.

menaçant, e [mənasɑ̃, ɑ̃t] *adj* threatening.

menace [mənas] *nf* : **menace (pour)** threat (to).

menacer [16] [mənase] ⟷ *vt* to threaten ; **menacer de faire qqch** to threaten to do sthg ; **menacer qqn de qqch** to threaten sb with sthg. ⟷ *vi* : **la pluie menace** it looks like rain.

ménage [menaʒ] *nm* **1.** [nettoyage] housework *(U)* ; **faire le ménage** to do the housework - **2.** [couple] couple - **3.** ÉCON household.

ménagement [menaʒmã] *nm* [égards] consideration ; **sans ménagement** brutally.

ménager¹, ère [menaʒe, ɛr] *adj* household *(avant n)*, domestic. ➤ **ménagère** *nf* **1.** [femme] housewife - **2.** [de couverts] canteen *UK*.

ménager² [17] [menaʒe] *vt* **1.** [bien traiter] to treat gently - **2.** [économiser - réserves] to use sparingly ; [- argent, temps] to use carefully ; **ménager ses forces** to conserve one's strength ; **ménager sa santé** to take care of one's health - **3.** [préparer - surprise] to prepare. ➤ **se ménager** *vp* to take care of o.s., to look after o.s.

ménagerie [menaʒri] *nf* menagerie.

mendiant, e [mãdjã, ãt] *nm, f* beggar.

mendier [9] [mãdje] ⟷ *vt* [argent] to beg for. ⟷ *vi* to beg.

mener [19] [məne] <> vt **1.** [emmener] to take - **2.** [suj: escalier, route] to take, to lead - **3.** [diriger - débat, enquête] to conduct ; [- affaires] to manage, to run ; **mener qqch à bonne fin** OU **à bien** to see sthg through, to bring sthg to a successful conclusion - **4.** [être en tête de] to lead. <> vi to lead.

meneur, euse [mənœr, øz] nm, f [chef] ringleader ; **meneur d'hommes** born leader.

menhir [menir] nm standing stone.

méningite [menēʒit] nf meningitis (U).

ménisque [menisk] nm meniscus.

ménopause [menopoz] nf menopause.

menotte [mənɔt] nf [main] little hand. ➡ **menottes** nfpl handcuffs ; **passer les menottes à qqn** to handcuff sb.

mensonge [mãsɔ̃ʒ] nm [propos] lie.

mensonger, ère [mãsɔ̃ʒe, ɛr] adj false.

menstruel, elle [mãstryɛl] adj menstrual.

mensualiser [3] [mãsɥalize] vt to pay monthly.

mensualité [mãsɥalite] nf **1.** [traite] monthly instalment UK OU installment US - **2.** [salaire] (monthly) salary.

mensuel, elle [mãsɥɛl] adj monthly. ➡ **mensuel** nm monthly (magazine).

mensuration [mãsyrasjɔ̃] nf measuring. ➡ **mensurations** nfpl measurements.

mental, e, aux [mãtal, o] adj mental.

mentalité [mãtalite] nf mentality.

menteur, euse [mãtœr, øz] nm, f liar.

menthe [mãt] nf mint.

menti [mãti] pp inv ➤ **mentir**.

mention [mãsjɔ̃] nf **1.** [citation] mention - **2.** [note] note ; **'rayer la mention inutile'** 'delete as appropriate' - **3.** UNIV : **avec mention** with distinction.

mentionner [3] [mãsjɔne] vt to mention.

mentir [37] [mãtir] vi : **mentir (à)** to lie (to).

menton [mãtɔ̃] nm chin.

menu, e [məny] adj [très petit] tiny ; [mince] thin. ➡ **menu** nm [gén & INFORM] menu ; [repas à prix fixe] set menu ; **menu déroulant** INFORM pull-down menu ; **menu gastronomique/touristique** gourmet/tourist menu.

menuiserie [mənɥizri] nf **1.** [métier] joinery UK, carpentry - **2.** [atelier] joinery (workshop) UK.

menuisier [mənɥizje] nm joiner UK, carpenter.

méprendre [79] [meprãdr] ➡ **se méprendre** vp litt : **se méprendre sur** to be mistaken about.

mépris, e [mepri, iz] pp ➤ **méprendre**. ➡ **mépris** nm **1.** [dédain] : **mépris (pour)**

contempt (for), scorn (for) - **2.** [indifférence] : **mépris de** disregard for. ➡ **au mépris de** loc prép regardless of.

méprisable [meprizabl] adj contemptible, despicable.

méprisant, e [meprizã, ãt] adj contemptuous, scornful.

mépriser [3] [meprize] vt to despise ; [danger, offre] to scorn.

mer [mɛr] nf sea ; **en mer** at sea ; **prendre la mer** to put to sea ; **haute** OU **pleine mer** open sea ; **la mer d'Irlande** the Irish Sea ; **la mer Morte** the Dead Sea ; **la mer Noire** the Black Sea ; **la mer du Nord** the North Sea.

mercantile [mɛrkãtil] adj péj mercenary.

mercenaire [mɛrsənɛr] nm & adj mercenary.

mercerie [mɛrsəri] nf **1.** [articles] haberdashery UK, notions (pl) US - **2.** [boutique] haberdasher's shop UK, notions store US.

merci [mɛrsi] <> interj thank you!, thanks! ; **merci beaucoup!** thank you very much! <> nm : **merci (de** OU **pour)** thank you (for) ; **dire merci à qqn** to thank sb, to say thank you to sb. <> nf mercy ; **être à la merci de** to be at the mercy of.

mercier, ère [mɛrsje, ɛr] nm, f haberdasher UK, notions dealer US.

mercredi [mɛrkrədi] nm Wednesday ; voir aussi **samedi**.

mercure [mɛrkyr] nm mercury.

merde [mɛrd] tfam nf shit.

mère [mɛr] nf **1.** [génitrice] mother ; **mère biologique** MÉD & BIOL biological OU natural mother ; **mère de famille** mother - **2.** RELIG Mother.

merguez [mɛrgɛz] nf North African spiced sausage.

méridien, enne [meridjɛ̃, ɛn] adj [ligne] meridian. ➡ **méridien** nm meridian.

méridional, e, aux [meridjɔnal, o] adj southern ; [du sud de la France] Southern (French).

meringue [mərɛ̃g] nf meringue.

merisier [mərizje] nm **1.** [arbre] wild cherry (tree) - **2.** [bois] cherry.

mérite [merit] nm merit.

mériter [3] [merite] vt **1.** [être digne de, encourir] to deserve - **2.** [valoir] to be worth, to merit.

merlan [mɛrlã] nm whiting.

merle [mɛrl] nm blackbird.

merveille [mɛrvɛj] nf marvel, wonder ; **à merveille** marvellously UK, marvelously US, wonderfully.

merveilleux, euse [mɛrvɛjø, øz] adj **1.** [remarquable, prodigieux] marvellous UK, marvelous *US*, wonderful - **2.** [magique] magic, magical. **merveilleux** *nm* : le merveilleux the supernatural.

mes ▶ mon.

mésalliance [mezaljɑ̃s] *nf* unsuitable marriage, misalliance.

mésange [mezɑ̃ʒ] *nf* ZOOL tit.

mésaventure [mezavɑ̃tyr] *nf* misfortune.

mesdames ▶ madame.

mesdemoiselles ▶ mademoiselle.

mésentente [mezɑ̃tɑ̃t] *nf* disagreement.

mesquin, e [mɛskɛ̃, in] *adj* mean, petty.

mesquinerie [mɛskinri] *nf* [étroitesse d'esprit] meanness, pettiness.

mess [mɛs] *nm* mess.

message [mesaʒ] *nm* message ; **laisser un message à qqn** to leave a message for sb ; **message publicitaire** COMM commercial, spot.

messager, ère [mesaʒe, ɛr] *nm, f* messenger.

messagerie [mesaʒri] *nf* **1.** *(gén pl)* [transport de marchandises] freight *(U)* - **2.** INFORM : **messagerie électronique** electronic mail.

messe [mɛs] *nf* mass ; **aller à la messe** to go to mass.

messie [mesi] *nm* Messiah ; *fig* saviour *UK*, savior *US*.

messieurs ▶ monsieur.

mesure [məzyr] *nf* **1.** [disposition, acte] measure, step ; **prendre des mesures** to take measures OU steps ; **mesure de sécurité** safety measure - **2.** [évaluation, dimension] measurement ; **prendre les mesures de qqn/qqch** to measure sb/sthg - **3.** [étalon, récipient] measure - **4.** MUS time, tempo - **5.** [modération] moderation ; **dans la mesure du possible** as far as possible ; **être en mesure de** to be in a position to. **à la mesure de** *loc prép* worthy of. **à mesure que** *loc conj* as. **outre mesure** *loc adv* excessively. **sur mesure** *loc adj* custom-made ; [costume] made-to-measure.

mesurer [3] [məzyre] *vt* **1.** [gén] to measure ; **elle mesure 1,50 m** she's 5 feet tall ; **la table mesure 1,50 m** the table is 5 feet long - **2.** [risques, portée, ampleur] to weigh up *UK* ; **mesurer ses paroles** to weigh one's words. **se mesurer** *vp* : **se mesurer avec** OU **à qqn** to pit o.s. against sb.

métabolisme [metabɔlism] *nm* metabolism.

métal, aux [metal, o] *nm* metal.

métallique [metalik] *adj* **1.** [en métal] metal *(avant n)* - **2.** [éclat, son] metallic.

métallurgie [metalyrʒi] *nf* **1.** [industrie] metallurgical industry - **2.** [technique] metallurgy.

métamorphose [metamɔrfoz] *nf* metamorphosis.

métaphore [metafɔr] *nf* metaphor.

métaphysique [metafizik] <> *nf* metaphysics *(U).* <> *adj* metaphysical.

météore [meteɔr] *nm* meteor.

météorite [meteɔrit] *nm & nf* meteorite.

météorologie [meteɔrɔlɔʒi] *nf* [sciences] meteorology.

météorologique [meteɔrɔlɔʒik] *adj* meteorological, weather *(avant n).*

méthane [metan] *nm* methane.

méthode [metɔd] *nf* **1.** [gén] method - **2.** [ouvrage - gén] manual ; [- de lecture, de langue] primer.

méthodologie [metɔdɔlɔʒi] *nf* methodology.

méticuleux, euse [metikylø, øz] *adj* meticulous.

métier [metje] *nm* [profession - manuelle] occupation, trade ; [- intellectuelle] occupation, profession ; **il est du métier** he's in the same trade OU same line of work ; **avoir du métier** to have experience.

métis, isse [metis] *nm, f* half-caste. **métis** *nm* [tissu] cotton-linen mix.

métrage [metraʒ] *nm* **1.** [mesure] measurement, measuring - **2.** [COUT - coupon] length - **3.** CINÉ footage ; **long métrage** feature film ; **court métrage** short (film).

mètre [mɛtr] *nm* **1.** LITTÉR & MATH metre *UK*, meter *US* ; **mètre carré** square metre *UK* OU meter *US* ; **mètre cube** cubic metre *UK* OU meter *US* - **2.** [instrument] rule.

métro [metro] *nm* underground *UK*, subway *US*.

métronome [metrɔnɔm] *nm* metronome.

métropole [metrɔpɔl] *nf* **1.** [ville] metropolis - **2.** [pays] home country.

métropolitain, e [metrɔpɔlitɛ̃, ɛn] *adj* metropolitan ; **la France métropolitaine** metropolitan OU mainland France.

mets [mɛ] *nm* CULIN dish.

metteur [metœr] *nm* : **metteur en scène** THÉÂTRE producer *UK* ; CINÉ director.

mettre [84] [mɛtr] *vt* **1.** [placer] to put ; **mettre de l'eau à bouillir** to put some water on to boil - **2.** [revêtir] to put on ; **mets ta robe noire** put your black dress on ; **je ne**

mets plus ma robe noire I don't wear my black dress any more - **3.** [consacrer - temps] to take ; [- argent] to spend ; **mettre longtemps à faire qqch** to take a long time to do sthg - **4.** [allumer - radio, chauffage] to put on, to switch on - **5.** [installer] to put in ; **faire mettre l'électricité** to have electricity put in ; **faire mettre de la moquette** to have a carpet put down ou fitted - **6.** [inscrire] to put (down). ➡ **se mettre** vp **1.** [se placer] : **où est-ce que ça se met?** where does this go? ; **se mettre au lit** to get into bed ; **se mettre à côté de qqn** to sit/stand near to sb - **2.** [devenir] : **se mettre en colère** to get angry - **3.** [commencer] : **se mettre à qqch/à faire qqch** to start sthg/doing sthg - **4.** [revêtir] to put on ; **je n'ai rien à me mettre** I haven't got a thing to wear.

meuble [mœbl] <> nm piece of furniture ; **meubles** furniture (U). <> adj **1.** [terre, sol] easily worked - **2.** DR movable.

meublé, e [mœble] adj furnished. ➡ **meublé** nm furnished room/flat UK, furnished apartment US.

meubler [5] [mœble] vt **1.** [pièce, maison] to furnish - **2.** fig [occuper] : **meubler qqch (de)** to fill sthg (with). ➡ **se meubler** vp to furnish one's home.

meuf [mœf] nf fam woman.

meugler [5] [møgle] vi to moo.

meule [møl] nf **1.** [à moudre] millstone - **2.** [à aiguiser] grindstone - **3.** [de fromage] round - **4.** AGRIC stack ; **meule de foin** haystack.

meunier, ère [mønje, ɛr] nm, f miller (f miller's wife).

meurtre [mœrtr] nm murder.

meurtrier, ère [mœrtrije, ɛr] <> adj [épidémie, arme] deadly ; [fureur] murderous ; [combat] bloody. <> nm, f murderer.

meurtrir [32] [mœrtrir] vt **1.** [contusionner] to bruise - **2.** fig [blesser] to wound.

meurtrissure [mœrtrisyr] nf [marque] bruise.

meute [møt] nf pack.

mexicain, e [mɛksikɛ̃, ɛn] adj Mexican. ➡ **Mexicain, e** nm, f Mexican.

Mexique [mɛksik] nm : **le Mexique** Mexico.

mezzanine [mɛdzanin] nf mezzanine.

mezzo-soprano [mɛdzosoprano] (pl mezzo-sopranos) nm mezzo-soprano.

mi [mi] nm inv E ; [chanté] mi.

mi- [mi] <> adj inv half ; **à la mi-juin** in mid-June. <> adv half-.

miasme [mjasm] nm (gén pl) putrid ou foul smell.

miaulement [mjolmɑ̃] nm miaowing UK, meowing US.

miauler [3] [mjole] vi to miaow UK, to meow US.

mi-bas [miba] nm inv knee-sock.

mi-carême [mikarɛm] nf feast day on third Thursday in Lent.

mi-chemin [miʃmɛ̃] ➡ **à mi-chemin** loc adv halfway (there).

mi-clos, e [miklo, oz] adj half-closed.

micro [mikro] <> nm **1.** [microphone] mike - **2.** [micro-ordinateur] micro. <> nf microcomputing.

microbe [mikrɔb] nm **1.** MÉD microbe, germ - **2.** péj [avorton] (little) runt.

microclimat [mikroklima] nm microclimate.

microcosme [mikrɔkɔsm] nm microcosm.

microfiche [mikrɔfiʃ] nf microfiche.

microfilm [mikrɔfilm] nm microfilm.

micro-ondes [mikrɔ̃d] nfpl microwaves ; **four à micro-ondes** microwave (oven).

micro-ordinateur [mikroordinatœr] (pl micro-ordinateurs) nm micro, microcomputer.

microphone [mikrɔfɔn] nm microphone.

microprocesseur [mikroprosesœr] nm microprocessor.

microscope [mikrɔskɔp] nm microscope.

midi [midi] nm **1.** [période du déjeuner] lunchtime - **2.** [heure] midday, noon - **3.** [sud] south. ➡ **Midi** nm : **le Midi** the South of France.

mie [mi] nf [de pain] soft part, inside.

miel [mjɛl] nm honey.

mielleux, euse [mjɛlø, øz] adj [personne] unctuous ; [paroles, air] honeyed.

mien, mienne [mjɛ̃] ➡ **le mien, la mienne** [ləmjɛ̃, lamjɛn] (mpl **les miens** [lemjɛ̃], fpl **les miennes** [lemjɛn]) pron poss mine.

miette [mjɛt] nf **1.** [de pain] crumb, breadcrumb - **2.** (gén pl) [débris] shreds pl.

mieux [mjø] <> adv **1.** [comparatif] : **mieux (que)** better (than) ; **il pourrait mieux faire** he could do better ; **il va mieux** he's better ; **faire mieux de faire qqch** to do better to do sthg ; **vous feriez mieux de vous taire** you would do better to keep quiet, you would be well-advised to keep quiet - **2.** [superlatif] best ; **il est le mieux payé du service** he's the best ou highest paid member of the department ; **le mieux qu'il peut** as best he can. <> adj better. <> nm **1.** (sans déterminant) **j'espérais mieux** I was hoping for something better - **2.** (avec déterminant) best ; **il y a un** ou **du mieux** there's been an improvement ; **faire de son mieux** to do one's best. ➡ **au mieux** loc adv at best.

pour le mieux *loc adv* for the best.
de mieux en mieux *loc adv* better and better.

mièvre [mjɛvr] *adj* insipid.

mignon, onne [miɲɔ̃, ɔn] <> *adj* **1.** [charmant] sweet, cute - **2.** [gentil] nice. <> *nm, f* darling, sweetheart.

migraine [migrɛn] *nf* headache ; MÉD migraine.

migrant, e [migrɑ̃, ɑ̃t] *nm, f* migrant.

migrateur, trice [migratœr, tris] *adj* migratory.

migration [migrasjɔ̃] *nf* migration.

mijoter [3] [miʒɔte] <> *vt fam* [tramer] to cook up. <> *vi* CULIN to simmer.

mi-journée [miʒurne] *nf* : **les informations de la mi-journée** the lunchtime news.

mil [mij] *nm* millet.

milan [milɑ̃] *nm* kite *(bird)*.

milice [milis] *nf* militia.

milicien, enne [milisjɛ̃, ɛn] *nm, f* militiaman *(f* militiawoman).

milieu, x [miljø] *nm* **1.** [centre] middle ; **au milieu de** [au centre de] in the middle of ; [parmi] among, surrounded by - **2.** [stade intermédiaire] middle course - **3.** [sociologie] & BIOL. environment ; **milieu familial** family background - **4.** [pègre] : **le milieu** the underworld - **5.** FOOTBALL : **milieu de terrain** midfielder, midfield player.

militaire [militɛr] <> *nm* soldier ; **militaire de carrière** professional soldier. <> *adj* military.

militant, e [militɑ̃, ɑ̃t] *adj & nm, f* militant.

militer [3] [milite] *vi* to be active ; **militer pour** to militate in favour *UK* ou favor *US* of ; **militer contre** to militate against.

mille <> *nm inv* **1.** [unité] a ou one thousand - **2.** [de cible] : **dans le mille** on target - **3.** NAUT : **mille marin** nautical mile - **4.** *Québec* [distance] mile. <> *adj inv* thousand ; **c'est mille fois trop** it's far too much ; **je lui ai dit mille fois** I've told him/her a thousand times ; *voir aussi* **six.**

mille-feuille *(pl* mille-feuilles) [milfœj] *nm* ≃ vanilla slice *UK*, ≃ napoleon *US*.

millénaire [milenɛr] <> *nm* millennium, thousand years *pl.* <> *adj* thousand-year-old *(avant n).*

mille-pattes [milpat] *nm inv* centipede, millipede.

millésime [milezim] *nm* **1.** [de pièce] date - **2.** [de vin] vintage, year.

millésimé, e [milezime] *adj* [vin] vintage *(avant n).*

millet [mijɛ] *nm* millet.

milliard [miljar] *nm* thousand million *UK*, billion *US* ; **par milliards** *fig* in (their) millions.

milliardaire [miljardɛr] *nmf* multimillionaire *UK*, billionaire *US.*

millier [milje] *nm* thousand ; **un millier d'euros** about a thousand euros ; **un millier de personnes** about a thousand people ; **par milliers** in (their) thousands.

milligramme [miligram] *nm* milligram, milligramme.

millilitre [mililitr] *nm* millilitre *UK*, milliliter *US.*

millimètre [milimɛtr] *nm* millimetre *UK*, millimeter *US.*

million [miljɔ̃] *nm* million ; **un million d'euros** a million euros.

millionnaire [miljɔnɛr] *nmf* millionaire.

mime [mim] *nm* mime.

mimer [3] [mime] *vt* **1.** [exprimer sans parler] to mime - **2.** [imiter] to mimic.

mimétisme [mimetism] *nm* mimicry.

mimique [mimik] *nf* **1.** [grimace] face - **2.** [geste] sign language *(U).*

mimosa [mimoza] *nm* mimosa.

min. *(abr écrite de* minimum) min.

minable [minabl] *adj fam* **1.** [misérable] seedy, shabby - **2.** [médiocre] pathetic.

minaret [minarɛ] *nm* minaret.

minauder [3] [minode] *vi* to simper.

mince [mɛ̃s] *adj* **1.** [maigre - gén] thin ; [- personne, taille] slender, slim - **2.** *fig* [faible] small, meagre *UK*, meager *US.*

minceur [mɛ̃sœr] *nf* **1.** [gén] thinness ; [de personne] slenderness, slimness - **2.** *fig* [insuffisance] meagreness *UK*, meagerness *US.*

mincir [32] [mɛ̃sir] *vi* to get thinner ou slimmer.

mine [min] *nf* **1.** [expression] look ; **avoir bonne/mauvaise mine** to look well/ill - **2.** [apparence] appearance - **3.** *fig* [gisement] mine ; [exploitation] mining ; **mine de charbon** coalmine - **4.** [explosif] mine - **5.** [de crayon] lead.

miner [3] [mine] *vt* **1.** MIL to mine - **2.** [ronger] to undermine, to wear away ; *fig* to wear down.

minerai [minrɛ] *nm* ore.

minéral, e, aux [mineral, o] *adj* **1.** CHIM inorganic - **2.** [eau, source] mineral *(avant n).*
minéral *nm* mineral.

minéralogie [mineralɔʒi] *nf* mineralogy.

minéralogique [mineralɔʒik] *adj* **1.** AUTO : **plaque minéralogique** numberplate *UK*, license plate *US* - **2.** GÉOL mineralogical.

minet, ette [minɛ, ɛt] *nm, f fam* **1.** [chat] pussy cat, pussy - **2.** [personne] trendy.

mineur, e [minœr] ◇ *adj* minor. ◇ *nm, f* DR minor. ◈ **mineur** *nm* [ouvrier] miner ; **mineur de fond** face worker.

miniature [minjatyr] ◇ *nf* miniature. ◇ *adj* miniature.

miniaturiser [3] [minjatyrize] *vt* to miniaturize.

minibar [minibar] *nm* minibar.

minibus [minibys] *nm* minibus.

minichaîne [miniʃɛn] *nf* portable hi-fi.

minier, ère [minje, ɛr] *adj* mining *(avant n)*.

minijupe [miniʒyp] *nf* miniskirt.

minimal, e, aux [minimal, o] *adj* minimum.

minimalisme [minimalism] *nm* minimalism.

minime [minim] ◇ *nmf* SPORT ≃ junior. ◇ *adj* minimal.

minimiser [3] [minimize] *vt* to minimize.

minimum [minimɔm] *(pl* **minimums** OU **minima** [minima]) ◇ *nm* [gén & MATH] minimum ; **au minimum** at least ; **le strict minimum** the bare minimum. ◇ *adj* minimum.

ministère [ministɛr] *nm* **1.** [département] ministry *UK*, department - **2.** [cabinet] government - **3.** RELIG ministry.

ministériel, elle [ministerjɛl] *adj* [du ministère] departmental, ministerial *UK*.

ministre [ministr] *nm* secretary, minister *UK* ; **ministre d'État** secretary of state, cabinet minister *UK* ; **premier ministre** prime minister.

Minitel® [minitɛl] *nm teletext system run by the French national telephone company, providing an information and communication network.*

minitéliste [minitelist] *nmf* Minitel® user.

minois [minwa] *nm* sweet (little) face.

minoritaire [minɔritɛr] *adj* minority *(avant n)* ; **être minoritaire** to be in the minority.

minorité [minɔrite] *nf* minority ; **en minorité** in the minority.

minuit [minɥi] *nm* midnight.

minuscule [minyskyl] ◇ *nf* [lettre] small letter. ◇ *adj* **1.** [lettre] small - **2.** [très petit] tiny, minuscule.

minute [minyt] ◇ *nf* minute ; **dans une minute** in a minute ; **d'une minute à l'autre** in next to no time. ◇ *interj fam* hang on (a minute)!

minuter [3] [minyte] *vt* [chronométrer] to time (precisely).

minuterie [minytri] *nf* [d'éclairage] time switch, timer.

minuteur [minytœr] *nm* timer.

minutie [minysi] *nf* [soin] meticulousness ; [précision] attention to detail ; **avec minutie** [avec soin] meticulously ; [dans le détail] in minute detail.

minutieux, euse [minysjø, øz] *adj* [méticuleux] meticulous ; [détaillé] minutely detailed ; **un travail minutieux** a job requiring great attention to detail.

mioche [mjɔʃ] *nmf fam* kiddy.

mirabelle [mirabɛl] *nf* **1.** [fruit] mirabelle (plum) - **2.** [alcool] plum brandy.

miracle [mirakl] *nm* miracle ; **par miracle** by some OU a miracle, miraculously.

miraculeux, euse [mirakylø, øz] *adj* miraculous.

mirador [miradɔr] *nm* MIL watchtower.

mirage [miraʒ] *nm* mirage.

mire [mir] *nf* **1.** TV test card *UK*, test pattern *US* - **2.** [visée] : **ligne de mire** line of sight.

mirifique [mirifik] *adj* fabulous.

mirobolant, e [mirɔbɔlɑ̃, ɑ̃t] *adj* fabulous, fantastic.

miroir [mirwar] *nm* mirror.

miroiter [3] [mirwate] *vi* to sparkle, to gleam ; **faire miroiter qqch à qqn** to hold out the prospect of sthg to sb.

mis, e [mi, miz] *pp* ▶ **mettre**.

misanthrope [mizɑ̃trɔp] ◇ *nmf* misanthropist, misanthrope. ◇ *adj* misanthropic.

mise [miz] *nf* **1.** [action] putting ; **mise à jour** updating ; **mise en page** making up, composing ; **mise au point** PHOTO focusing ; TECHNOL adjustment ; *fig* clarification ; **mise en scène** production - **2.** [d'argent] stake.

miser [3] [mize] ◇ *vt* to bet. ◇ *vi* : **miser sur** to bet on ; *fig* to count on.

misérable [mizerabl] *adj* **1.** [pauvre] poor, wretched - **2.** [sans valeur] paltry, miserable.

misère [mizɛr] *nf* **1.** [indigence] poverty - **2.** [infortune] misery - **3.** *fig* [bagatelle] trifle.

miséricorde [mizerikɔrd] *nf* [clémence] mercy.

misogyne [mizɔʒin] *adj* misogynous.

misogynie [mizɔʒini] *nf* misogyny.

missel [misɛl] *nm* missal.

missile [misil] *nm* missile.

mission [misjɔ̃] *nf* mission ; **en mission** on a mission.

missionnaire [misjɔnɛr] *nmf* missionary.

missive [misiv] *nf* letter.

mistral [mistral] *nm strong cold wind that blows down the Rhône Valley and through Southern France.*

mitaine [mitɛn] *nf* fingerless glove.

mite [mit] *nf* (clothes) moth.

mité, e [mite] *adj* moth-eaten.

mi-temps [mitɑ̃] <> *nf inv* [SPORT - période] half ; [- pause] half-time. <> *nm* part-time work. ◆ **à mi-temps** *loc adj & loc adv* part-time.

miteux, euse [mitø, øz] *fam adj* seedy, dingy.

mitigé, e [mitiʒe] *adj* **1.** [tempéré] lukewarm - **2.** *fam* [mélangé] mixed.

mitonner [3] [mitɔne] <> *vt* **1.** [faire cuire] to simmer - **2.** [préparer avec soin] to prepare lovingly. <> *vi* CULIN to simmer.

mitoyen, enne [mitwajɛ̃, ɛn] *adj* [commun] common ; [attenant] adjoining ; **mur mitoyen** party wall.

mitrailler [3] [mitraje] *vt* **1.** MIL to machinegun - **2.** *fam* [photographier] to click away at - **3.** *fig* [assaillir] : **mitrailler qqn (de)** to bombard sb (with).

mitraillette [mitrajɛt] *nf* submachine gun.

mitrailleuse [mitrajøz] *nf* machinegun.

mitre [mitr] *nf* [d'évêque] mitre *UK*, miter *US*.

mi-voix [mivwa] ◆ **à mi-voix** *loc adv* in a low voice.

mixage [miksaʒ] *nm* CINÉ & RADIO (sound) mixing.

mixer¹, mixeur [miksœr] *nm* (food) mixer.

mixer² [3] [mikse] *vt* to mix.

mixte [mikst] *adj* mixed.

mixture [mikstyr] *nf* **1.** CHIM & CULIN mixture - **2.** *péj* [mélange] concoction.

MJC (*abr de* **maison des jeunes et de la culture**) *nf youth and cultural centre.*

ml (*abr écrite de* **millilitre**) ml.

Mlle (*abr écrite de* **Mademoiselle**) Miss.

mm (*abr écrite de* **millimètre**) mm.

MM (*abr écrite de* **Messieurs**) Messrs.

Mme (*abr écrite de* **Madame**) Mrs.

mnémotechnique [mnemɔtɛknik] *adj* mnemonic.

Mo (*abr de* **méga-octet**) MB.

mobile [mɔbil] <> *nm* **1.** [objet] mobile - **2.** [motivation] motive. <> *adj* **1.** [gén] movable, mobile ; [partie, pièce] moving - **2.** [population, main-d'œuvre] mobile.

mobilier, ère [mɔbilje, ɛr] *adj* DR movable. ◆ **mobilier** *nm* furniture.

mobilisation [mɔbilizasjɔ̃] *nf* mobilization.

mobiliser [3] [mɔbilize] *vt* **1.** [gén] to mobilize - **2.** [moralement] to rally. ◆ **se mobiliser** *vp* to mobilize, to rally.

mobilité [mɔbilite] *nf* mobility.

Mobylette® [mɔbilɛt] *nf* moped.

mocassin [mɔkasɛ̃] *nm* moccasin.

moche [mɔʃ] *adj fam* **1.** [laid] ugly - **2.** [triste, méprisable] lousy, rotten.

modalité [mɔdalite] *nf* [convention] form ; **modalités de paiement** methods of payment.

mode [mɔd] <> *nf* **1.** [gén] fashion ; **à la mode** in fashion, fashionable - **2.** [coutume] custom, style ; **à la mode de** in the style of. <> *nm* **1.** [manière] mode, form ; **mode de vie** way of life - **2.** [méthode] method ; **mode d'emploi** instructions (for use) - **3.** GRAMM mood - **4.** MUS mode - **5.** INFORM mode.

modèle [mɔdɛl] <> *nm* **1.** [gén] model ; **sur le modèle de** on the model of ; **modèle déposé** patented design - **2.** *(en apposition)* [exemplaire] model *(avant n)*. <> *adj* [parfait] model *(modif)*.

modeler [25] [mɔdle] *vt* to shape ; **modeler qqch sur qqch** *fig* to model sthg on sthg.

modélisme [mɔdelism] *nm* modelling *UK* OU modeling *US* (of scale models).

modération [mɔderasjɔ̃] *nf* moderation.

modéré, e [mɔdere] *adj & nm, f* moderate.

modérer [18] [mɔdere] *vt* to moderate. ◆ **se modérer** *vp* to restrain o.s., to control o.s.

moderne [mɔdɛrn] *adj* modern ; [mathématiques] new.

moderniser [3] [mɔdɛrnize] *vt* to modernize. ◆ **se moderniser** *vp* to become (more) modern.

modeste [mɔdɛst] *adj* modest ; [origine] humble.

modestie [mɔdɛsti] *nf* modesty ; **fausse modestie** false modesty.

modification [mɔdifikasjɔ̃] *nf* alteration, modification.

modifier [9] [mɔdifje] *vt* to alter, to modify. ◆ **se modifier** *vp* to alter.

modique [mɔdik] *adj* modest.

modiste [mɔdist] *nf* milliner.

modulation [mɔdylasjɔ̃] *nf* modulation.

module [mɔdyl] *nm* module.

moduler [3] [mɔdyle] *vt* **1.** [air] to warble - **2.** [structure] to adjust.

moelle [mwal] *nf* ANAT marrow. ◆ **moelle épinière** *nf* spinal cord.

moelleux, euse [mwalø, øz] *adj* **1.** [canapé, tapis] soft - **2.** [fromage, vin] mellow.

moellon [mwalɔ̃] *nm* rubble stone.

mœurs [mœr(s)] *nfpl* **1.** [morale] morals - **2.** [coutumes] customs, habits - **3.** ZOOL behaviour *(U) UK*, behavior *(U) US*.

mohair [mɔɛr] *nm* mohair.

moi [mwa] *pron pers* **1.** [objet, après préposition, comparatif] me ; **aide-moi** help me ; **il me l'a dit, à moi** he told ME ; **c'est pour moi** it's for me ; **plus âgé que moi** older than me ou than I (am) - **2.** [sujet] I ; **moi non plus, je n'en sais rien** I don't know anything about it either ; **qui est là? - (c'est) moi** who's there? - it's me ; **je l'ai vu hier - moi aussi** I saw him yesterday - me too ; **c'est moi qui lui ai dit de venir** I was the one who told him to come. **moi-même** *pron pers* myself.

moignon [mwaɲɔ̃] *nm* stump.

moindre [mwɛ̃dr] ⋄ *adj (superlatif)* : **le/la moindre** the least ; *(avec négation)* the least ou slightest ; **les moindres détails** the smallest details ; **sans la moindre difficulté** without the slightest problem ; **c'est la moindre des choses** it's the least I/you *etc* could do. ⋄ *adj compar* less ; [prix] lower ; **à un moindre degré** to a lesser extent.

moine [mwan] *nm* monk.

moineau, x [mwano] *nm* sparrow.

moins [mwɛ̃] ⋄ *adv* **1.** [quantité] less ; **moins de** less (than) ; **moins de lait** less milk ; **moins de gens** fewer people ; **moins de dix** less than ten ; **il est un peu moins de 10 heures** it's nearly 10 o'clock - **2.** [comparatif] : **moins (que)** less (than) ; **il est moins vieux que ton frère** he's not as old as your brother, he's younger than your brother ; **bien moins grand que** much smaller than ; **moins il mange, moins il travaille** the less he eats, the less he works - **3.** [superlatif] : **le moins** (the) least ; **le moins riche des hommes** the poorest man ; **c'est lui qui travaille le moins** he works (the) least ; **le moins possible** as little as possible. ⋄ *prép* **1.** [gén] minus ; **dix moins huit font deux** ten minus eight is two, ten take away eight is two ; **il fait moins vingt** it's twenty below, it's minus twenty - **2.** [servant à indiquer l'heure] : **il est 3 heures moins le quart** it's quarter to 3 ; **il est moins dix** it's ten to, it's ten of *US*. ⋄ *nm* [signe] minus (sign) ; **le moins qu'on puisse dire, c'est que...** it's an understatement to say... **à moins de** *loc prép* : **à moins de battre le record** unless I/you *etc* beat the record. **à moins que** *loc conj* (+ *subjonctif*) unless. **au moins** *loc adv* at least. **de moins en moins** *loc adv* less and less. **du moins** *loc adv* at least. **en moins** *loc adv* : **il a une dent en moins** he's missing ou minus a tooth ; **c'était le paradis, les anges en moins** it was heaven, minus the angels. **pour le moins** *loc adv* at (the very) least. **tout au moins** *loc adv* at (the very) least.

moiré, e [mware] *adj* **1.** [tissu] watered - **2.** *litt* [reflet] shimmering.

mois [mwa] *nm* [laps de temps] month.

moisi, e [mwazi] *adj* mouldy *UK*, moldy *US*. **moisi** *nm* mould *UK*, mold *US*.

moisir [32] [mwazir] *vi* **1.** [pourrir] to go mouldy *UK* ou moldy *US* - **2.** *fig* [personne] to rot.

moisissure [mwazisyr] *nf* mould *UK*, mold *US*.

moisson [mwasɔ̃] *nf* **1.** [récolte] harvest ; **faire la moisson** ou **les moissons** to harvest, to bring in the harvest - **2.** *fig* [d'idées, de projets] wealth.

moissonner [3] [mwasɔne] *vt* to harvest, to gather (in) ; *fig* to collect, to gather.

moissonneuse-batteuse [mwasɔnøzbatøz] *nf* combine (harvester).

moite [mwat] *adj* [peau, mains] moist, sweaty ; [atmosphère] muggy.

moiteur [mwatœr] *nf* [de peau, mains] moistness ; [d'atmosphère] mugginess.

moitié [mwatje] *nf* [gén] half ; **à moitié vide** half-empty ; **faire qqch à moitié** to half-do sthg ; **la moitié du temps** half the time ; **à la moitié de qqch** halfway through sthg.

moka [mɔka] *nm* **1.** [café] mocha (coffee) - **2.** [gâteau] coffee cake.

mol ► **mou**.

molaire [mɔlɛr] *nf* molar.

molécule [mɔlekyl] *nf* molecule.

molester [3] [mɔlɛste] *vt* to manhandle.

molle ► **mou**.

mollement [mɔlmɑ̃] *adv* **1.** [faiblement] weakly, feebly - **2.** *litt* [paresseusement] sluggishly, lethargically.

mollesse [mɔlɛs] *nf* **1.** [de chose] softness - **2.** [de personne] lethargy.

mollet [mɔlɛ] ⋄ *nm* calf. ⋄ *adj* ► **œuf**.

mollir [32] [mɔlir] *vi* **1.** [physiquement, moralement] to give way - **2.** [vent] to drop, to die down.

mollusque [mɔlysk] *nm* ZOOL mollusc.

molosse [mɔlɔs] *nm* **1.** [chien] large ferocious dog - **2.** *fig & péj* [personne] hulking great brute ou fellow.

môme [mom] *fam nmf* [enfant] kid, youngster.

moment [mɔmɑ̃] *nm* **1.** [gén] moment ; **au moment de l'accident** at the time of the accident, when the accident happened ; **au moment de partir** just as we/you *etc* were leaving ; **au moment où** just as ; **dans un moment** in a moment ; **d'un moment à l'autre, à tout moment** (at) any moment, any moment now ; **à un moment donné** at a given moment ; **par moments** at times, now and then ; **en ce moment** at the moment ; **pour le moment** for the moment - **2.** [durée] (short) time ; **passer un mauvais**

moment to have a bad time - **3.** [occasion] time ; **ce n'est pas le moment (de faire qqch)** this is not the time (to do sthg). **du moment que** *loc prép* since, as.

momentané, e [mɔmɑ̃tane] *adj* temporary.

momie [mɔmi] *nf* mummy.

mon, ma [mɔ̃, ma] (*pl* **mes** [me]) *adj poss* my.

monacal, e, aux [mɔnakal, o] *adj* monastic.

Monaco [mɔnako] *npr* : **(la principauté de) Monaco** (the principality of) Monaco.

monarchie [mɔnaʁʃi] *nf* monarchy ; **monarchie absolue/constitutionnelle** absolute/constitutional monarchy.

monarque [mɔnaʁk] *nm* monarch.

monastère [mɔnastɛʁ] *nm* monastery.

monceau, x [mɔ̃so] *nm* [tas] heap.

mondain, e [mɔ̃dɛ̃, ɛn] *adj* **1.** [chronique, journaliste] society *(avant n)* - **2.** *péj* [futile] frivolous, superficial.

mondanités [mɔ̃danite] *nfpl* **1.** [événements] society life *(U)* - **2.** [paroles] small talk *(U)* ; [comportements] formalities.

monde [mɔ̃d] *nm* **1.** [gén] world ; **le/la plus... au monde, le/la plus... du monde** the most... in the world ; **pour rien au monde** not for the world, not for all the tea in China ; **mettre un enfant au monde** to bring a child into the world ; **venir au monde** to come into the world - **2.** [gens] people *pl* ; **beaucoup/peu de monde** a lot of/not many people ; **tout le monde** everyone, everybody ; **c'est un monde!** that's really the limit! ; **se faire un monde de qqch** to make too much of sthg ; **noir de monde** packed with people.

mondial, e, aux [mɔ̃djal, o] *adj* world *(avant n)*.

mondialement [mɔ̃djalmɑ̃] *adv* throughout ou all over the world.

mondialisation *nf* globalization.

mondialiste [mɔ̃djalist] *adj* pro-globalization.

monétaire [mɔnetɛʁ] *adj* monetary.

Mongolie [mɔ̃gɔli] *nf* : **la Mongolie** Mongolia.

mongolien, enne [mɔ̃gɔljɛ̃, ɛn] *nm, f* Mongol.

moniteur, trice [mɔnitœʁ, tʁis] *nm, f* **1.** [enseignant] instructor, coach ; **moniteur d'auto-école** driving instructor - **2.** [de colonie de vacances] supervisor, leader. **moniteur** *nm* [appareil & INFORM] monitor.

monnaie [mɔnɛ] *nf* **1.** [moyen de paiement] money - **2.** [de pays] currency ; **monnaie unique** single currency - **3.** [pièces] change ; **avoir de la monnaie** to have change ; **avoir la monnaie** to have the change ; **faire (de) la monnaie** to get (some) change.

monnayer [11] [mɔnɛje] *vt* **1.** [biens] to convert into cash - **2.** *fig* [silence] to buy.

monochrome [mɔnɔkʁom] *adj* monochrome, monochromatic.

monocle [mɔnɔkl] *nm* monocle.

monocoque [mɔnɔkɔk] *nm & adj* [bateau] monohull.

monocorde [mɔnɔkɔʁd] *adj* [monotone] monotonous.

monogramme [mɔnɔgʁam] *nm* monogram.

monolingue [mɔnɔlɛ̃g] *adj* monolingual.

monologue [mɔnɔlɔg] *nm* **1.** THÉÂTRE soliloquy - **2.** [discours individuel] monologue.

monologuer [3] [mɔnɔlɔge] *vi* **1.** THÉÂTRE to soliloquize - **2.** *fig & péj* [parler] to talk away.

monoparental, e, aux [mɔnɔpaʁɑ̃tal, o] *adj* single-parent *(avant n)*.

monoplace [mɔnɔplas] *adj* single-seater *(avant n)*.

monopole [mɔnɔpɔl] *nm* monopoly ; **avoir le monopole de qqch** *litt & fig* to have a monopoly of ou on sthg ; **monopole d'État** state monopoly.

monopoliser [3] [mɔnɔpɔlize] *vt* to monopolize.

monoski [mɔnɔski] *nm* **1.** [objet] monoski - **2.** SPORT monoskiing.

monospace [mɔnɔspas] *nm* people carrier UK, minivan US.

monosyllabe [mɔnɔsilab] ⟨⟩ *nm* monosyllable. ⟨⟩ *adj* monosyllabic.

monotone [mɔnɔtɔn] *adj* monotonous.

monotonie [mɔnɔtɔni] *nf* monotony.

monseigneur [mɔ̃sɛɲœʁ] (*pl* **messeigneurs** [mesɛɲœʁ]) *nm* [titre - d'évêque, de duc] His Grace ; [- de cardinal] His Eminence ; [- de prince] His (Royal) Highness.

monsieur [məsjø] (*pl* **messieurs** [mesjø]) *nm* **1.** [titre] : **monsieur X** Mr X ; **bonjour monsieur** good morning ; [dans hôtel, restaurant] good morning, sir ; **bonjour messieurs** good morning (gentlemen) ; **messieurs dames** ladies and gentlemen ; **Monsieur le Ministre n'est pas là** the Minister is out - **2.** [homme quelconque] gentleman.

monstre [mɔ̃stʁ] *nm* **1.** [gén] monster - **2.** *(en apposition)* *fam* [énorme] colossal.

monstrueux, euse [mɔ̃stʁyø, øz] *adj* **1.** [gén] monstrous - **2.** *fig* [erreur] terrible.

monstruosité [mɔ̃stryozite] *nf* monstrosity.

mont [mɔ̃] *nm* GÉOGR Mount ; **le mont Blanc** Mont Blanc ; **le mont Cervin** the Matterhorn.

montage [mɔ̃taʒ] *nm* **1.** [assemblage] assembly ; [de bijou] setting - **2.** PHOTO photomontage - **3.** CINÉ editing.

montagnard, e [mɔ̃taɲar, ard] *nm, f* mountain dweller.

montagne [mɔ̃taɲ] *nf* **1.** [gén] mountain ; **les montagnes Rocheuses** the Rocky Mountains - **2.** [région] : **la montagne** the mountains *pl* ; **à la montagne** in the mountains ; **en haute montagne** at high altitudes. ➡ **montagnes russes** *nfpl* big dipper *(sing)* UK, roller coaster *sg*.

montagneux, euse [mɔ̃taɲø, øz] *adj* mountainous.

montant, e [mɔ̃tɑ̃, ɑ̃t] *adj* [mouvement] rising. ➡ **montant** *nm* **1.** [pièce verticale] upright - **2.** [somme] total (amount).

mont-de-piété [mɔ̃dpjete] *(pl* **monts-de-piété)** *nm* pawnshop.

monte-charge [mɔ̃tʃarʒ] *nm inv* goods lift UK, service elevator US.

montée [mɔ̃te] *nf* **1.** [de montagne] climb, ascent - **2.** [de prix] rise - **3.** [relief] slope, gradient.

monte-plats [mɔ̃tpla] *nm inv* dumbwaiter.

monter [3] [mɔ̃te] ◇ *vi (v aux : être)* **1.** [personne] to come/go up ; [température, niveau] to rise ; [route, avion] to climb ; **monter sur qqch** to climb onto sthg - **2.** [passager] to get on ; **monter dans un bus** to get on a bus ; **monter dans une voiture** to get into a car - **3.** [cavalier] to ride ; **monter à cheval** to ride - **4.** [marée] to go/come in. ◇ *vt (v aux : être)* **1.** [escalier, côte] to climb, to come/go up ; **monter la rue en courant** to run up the street - **2.** [chauffage, son] to turn up - **3.** [valise] to take/bring up - **4.** [meuble] to assemble ; COUT to assemble, to put ou sew together ; [tente] to put up - **5.** [cheval] to mount - **6.** THÉÂTRE to put on - **7.** [société, club] to set up - **8.** CULIN to beat, to whisk (up). ➡ **se monter** *vp* **1.** [s'assembler] : **se monter facilement** to be easy to assemble - **2.** [atteindre] : **se monter à** to amount to, to add up to.

monteur, euse [mɔ̃tœr, øz] *nm, f* **1.** TECHNOL fitter - **2.** CINÉ editor.

monticule [mɔ̃tikyl] *nm* mound.

montre [mɔ̃tr] *nf* watch ; **montre à quartz** quartz watch ; **montre en main** to the minute, exactly ; **contre la montre** [sport] time-trialling UK, time-trialing US ; [épreuve] time trial ; **une course contre la montre** *fig* a race against time.

montre-bracelet [mɔ̃trəbraslɛ] *nf* wristwatch.

montrer [3] [mɔ̃tre] *vt* **1.** [gén] to show ; **montrer qqch à qqn** to show sb sthg, to show sthg to sb - **2.** [désigner] to show, to point out ; **montrer qqch du doigt** to point at ou to sthg. ➡ **se montrer** *vp* **1.** [se faire voir] to appear - **2.** *fig* [se présenter] to show o.s. - **3.** *fig* [se révéler] to prove (to be).

monture [mɔ̃tyr] *nf* **1.** [animal] mount - **2.** [de lunettes] frame.

monument [mɔnymɑ̃] *nm* [gén] : **monument (à)** monument (to) ; **monument aux morts** war memorial.

monumental, e, aux [mɔnymɑ̃tal, o] *adj* monumental.

moquer [3] [mɔke] ➡ **se moquer** *vp* : **se moquer de** [plaisanter sur] to make fun of, to laugh at ; [ne pas se soucier de] not to give a damn about.

moquerie [mɔkri] *nf* mockery (U), jibe.

moquette [mɔkɛt] *nf* (fitted) carpet UK, wall-to-wall carpet US.

moqueur, euse [mɔkœr, øz] *adj* mocking.

moral, e, aux [mɔral, o] *adj* **1.** [éthique - conscience, jugement] moral ; **il n'a aucun sens moral** he has no sense of morality ; **se sentir dans l'obligation morale de faire qqch** to feel morally obliged ou a moral obligation to do sthg ; **prendre l'engagement moral de faire qqch** to be morally committed to do sthg ; [édifiant - auteur, conte, réflexion] moral ; **la fin de la pièce n'est pas très morale!** the end of the play is rather immoral! - **2.** [spirituel - douleur] mental ; [- soutien, victoire, résistance] moral. ➡ **moral** *nm* **1.** [mental] : **au moral comme au physique** mentally as well as physically - **2.** [état d'esprit] morale, spirits *pl* ; **avoir/ne pas avoir le moral** to be in good/bad spirits ; **j'ai le moral à zéro** *fam* I feel down in the dumps ou really low ; **remonter le moral à qqn** to cheer sb up. ➡ **morale** *nf* **1.** [science] moral philosophy, morals *pl* - **2.** [règle] morality - **3.** [mœurs] morals *pl* - **4.** [leçon] moral ; **faire la morale à qqn** to preach at ou lecture sb.

moralisateur, trice [mɔralizatœr, tris] ◇ *adj* moralizing. ◇ *nm, f* moralizer.

moraliste [mɔralist] *nmf* moralist.

moralité [mɔralite] *nf* **1.** [gén] morality - **2.** [enseignement] morals.

moratoire [mɔratwar] *nm* moratorium.

morbide [mɔrbid] *adj* morbid.

morceau, x [mɔrso] *nm* **1.** [gén] piece - **2.** [de poème, de film] passage.

morceler [24] [mɔrsəle] *vt* to break up, to split up.

mordant, e [mɔrdɑ̃, ɑ̃t] *adj* biting. ➡ **mordant** *nm* [vivacité] keenness, bite.

mordiller [3] [mɔrdije] *vt* to nibble.

mordoré, e [mɔrdɔre] *adj* bronze.

mordre [76] [mɔrdr] <> vt [blesser] to bite. <> vi **1.** [saisir avec les dents] : **mordre à** to bite - **2.** [croquer] : **mordre dans qqch** to bite into sthg - **3.** SPORT : **mordre sur la ligne** to step over the line.

mordu, e [mɔrdy] <> pp ▶ mordre. <> adj [amoureux] hooked. <> nm, f: **mordu de foot/ski** etc football/ski etc addict.

morfondre [75] [mɔrfɔ̃dr] ▶ **se morfondre** vp to mope.

morgue [mɔrg] nf **1.** [attitude] pride - **2.** [lieu] morgue.

moribond, e [mɔribɔ̃, ɔ̃d] <> adj dying. <> nm, f dying person.

morille [mɔrij] nf morel.

morne [mɔrn] adj [personne, visage] gloomy ; [paysage, temps, ville] dismal, dreary.

morose [mɔroz] adj gloomy.

morphine [mɔrfin] nf morphine.

morphologie [mɔrfɔlɔʒi] nf morphology.

mors [mɔr] nm bit.

morse [mɔrs] nm **1.** ZOOL walrus - **2.** [code] Morse (code).

morsure [mɔrsyr] nf bite.

mort, e [mɔr, mɔrt] <> pp ▶ mourir. <> adj dead ; **mort de fatigue** fig dead tired ; **mort de peur** fig frightened to death. <> nm, f **1.** [cadavre] corpse, dead body - **2.** [défunt] dead person. ▶ **mort** <> nm **1.** [victime] fatality - **2.** [partie de cartes] dummy. <> nf litt & fig death ; **de mort** [silence] deathly ; **être en danger de mort** to be in mortal danger ; **condamner qqn à mort** DR to sentence sb to death ; **se donner la mort** to take one's own life, to commit suicide.

mortadelle [mɔrtadɛl] nf mortadella.

mortalité [mɔrtalite] nf mortality, death rate.

mort-aux-rats [mɔrora] nf inv rat poison.

Morte ▶ mer.

mortel, elle [mɔrtɛl] <> adj **1.** [humain] mortal - **2.** [accident, maladie] fatal - **3.** fig [ennuyeux] deadly (dull). <> nm, f mortal.

morte-saison [mɔrtsɛzɔ̃] nf, slack season, off-season.

mortier [mɔrtje] nm mortar.

mortification [mɔrtifikasjɔ̃] nf mortification.

mort-né, e [mɔrne] (mpl **mort-nés**, fpl **mort-nées**) adj [enfant] still-born.

mortuaire [mɔrtɥɛr] adj funeral (avant n).

morue [mɔry] nf ZOOL cod.

mosaïque [mɔzaik] nf litt & fig mosaic.

Moscou [mɔsku] npr Moscow.

mosquée [mɔske] nf mosque.

mot [mo] nm **1.** [gén] word ; **gros mot** swearword ; **mot de passe** password ; **mots croisés** crossword (puzzle) sg - **2.** [message] note, message.

motard [mɔtar] nm **1.** [motocycliste] motor-cyclist - **2.** [policier] motorcycle policeman.

motel [mɔtɛl] nm motel.

moteur, trice [mɔtœr, tris] adj [force, énergie] driving (avant n) ; **à quatre roues motrices** AUTO with four-wheel drive. ▶ **moteur** nm TECHNOL motor, engine ; fig driving force ; **moteur à réaction** jet engine ; **moteur de recherche** INFORM search engine.

motif [mɔtif] nm **1.** [raison] motive, grounds pl - **2.** [dessin, impression] motif.

motion [mɔsjɔ̃] nf POLIT motion ; **motion de censure** motion of censure.

motiver [3] [mɔtive] vt **1.** [stimuler] to motivate - **2.** [justifier] to justify.

moto [mɔto] nf motorbike UK, motorcycle US.

motocross [mɔtɔkrɔs] nm motocross.

motoculteur [mɔtɔkyltœr] nm ≃ Rotavator®.

motocyclette [mɔtɔsiklɛt] nf motorcycle, motorbike UK.

motocycliste [mɔtɔsiklist] nmf motorcyclist.

motrice ▶ moteur.

motricité [mɔtrisite] nf motor functions pl.

motte [mɔt] nf : **motte (de terre)** clod, lump of earth ; **motte de beurre** slab of butter.

mou, molle [mu, mɔl] adj (**mol** devant voyelle ou 'h' muet) **1.** [gén] soft - **2.** [faible] weak - **3.** [résistance, protestation] half-hearted - **4.** fam [de caractère] wet, wimpy. ▶ **mou** nm **1.** [de corde] : **avoir du mou** to be slack - **2.** [abats] lungs pl, lights pl.

mouchard, e [muʃar, ard] nm, f fam [personne] sneak. ▶ **mouchard** nm fam [dans camion, train] spy in the cab.

mouche [muʃ] nf **1.** ZOOL fly - **2.** [accessoire féminin] beauty spot.

moucher [3] [muʃe] vt **1.** [nez] to wipe ; **moucher un enfant** to wipe a child's nose - **2.** [chandelle] to snuff out - **3.** fam fig [personne] : **moucher qqn** to put sb in his/her place. ▶ **se moucher** vp to blow ou wipe one's nose.

moucheron [muʃrɔ̃] nm [insecte] gnat.

moucheté, e [muʃte] adj **1.** [laine] flecked - **2.** [animal] spotted, speckled.

mouchoir [muʃwar] nm handkerchief.

moudre [85] [mudr] vt to grind.

moue [mu] nf pout ; **faire la moue** to pull a face.

mouette [mwɛt] nf seagull.

moufle [mufl] *nf* mitten.

mouflon [muflɔ̃] *nm* wild sheep.

mouillage [mujaʒ] *nm* [NAUT - emplacement] anchorage, moorings *pl*.

mouillé, e [muje] *adj* wet.

mouiller [3] [muje] *vt* 1. [personne, objet] to wet ; **se faire mouiller** to get wet OU soaked - 2. NAUT : **mouiller l'ancre** to drop anchor - 3. *fam fig* [compromettre] to involve. ◆ **se mouiller** *vp* 1. [se tremper] to get wet - 2. *fam fig* [prendre des risques] to stick one's neck out.

moulage [mulaʒ] *nm* 1. [action] moulding UK, molding US, casting - 2. [objet] cast.

moule [mul] <> *nm* mould UK, mold US ; **moule à gâteau** cake tin UK OU pan US ; **moule à tarte** flan dish. <> *nf* ZOOL mussel.

mouler [3] [mule] *vt* 1. [objet] to mould UK, to mold US - 2. [forme] to make a cast of.

moulin [mulɛ̃] *nm* mill ; **moulin à café** coffee mill ; **moulin à paroles** *fig* chatterbox.

moulinet [mulinɛ] *nm* 1. [à la pêche] reel - 2. [mouvement] : **faire des moulinets** to whirl one's arms around.

Moulinette® [mulinɛt] *nf* food mill.

moulu, e [muly] *adj* [en poudre] ground.

moulure [mulyr] *nf* moulding.

mourant, e [murɑ̃, ɑ̃t] <> *adj* 1. [moribond] dying - 2. *fig* [voix] faint. <> *nm, f* dying person.

mourir [42] [murir] *vi* 1. [personne] to die ; **s'ennuyer à mourir** to be bored to death - 2. [feu] to die down.

mousquetaire [muskətɛr] *nm* musketeer.

moussant, e [musɑ̃, ɑ̃t] *adj* foaming.

mousse [mus] <> *nf* 1. BOT moss - 2. [substance] foam ; **mousse à raser** shaving foam - 3. CULIN mousse - 4. [matière plastique] foam rubber. <> *nm* NAUT cabin boy.

mousseline [muslin] *nf* muslin.

mousser [3] [muse] *vi* to foam, to lather.

mousseux, euse [musø, øz] *adj* 1. [shampooing] foaming, frothy - 2. [vin, cidre] sparkling. ◆ **mousseux** *nm* sparkling wine.

mousson [musɔ̃] *nf* monsoon.

moussu, e [musy] *adj* mossy, moss-covered.

moustache [mustaʃ] *nf* moustache, mustache US. ◆ **moustaches** *nfpl* [d'animal] whiskers.

moustachu, e [mustaʃy] *adj* with a moustache UK OU mustache US.

moustiquaire [mustikɛr] *nf* mosquito net.

moustique [mustik] *nm* mosquito.

moutarde [mutard] *nf* mustard.

mouton [mutɔ̃] *nm* 1. ZOOL & *fig* sheep - 2. [viande] mutton - 3. *fam* [poussière] piece of fluff, fluff (U).

mouture [mutyr] *nf* 1. [de céréales, de café] grinding - 2. [de thème, d'œuvre] rehash.

mouvance [muvɑ̃s] *nf* [domaine] sphere of influence.

mouvant, e [muvɑ̃, ɑ̃t] *adj* 1. [terrain] unstable - 2. [situation] uncertain.

mouvement [muvmɑ̃] *nm* 1. [gén] movement ; **en mouvement** on the move - 2. [de colère, d'indignation] burst, fit.

mouvementé, e [muvmɑ̃te] *adj* 1. [terrain] rough - 2. [réunion, soirée] eventful.

mouvoir [54] [muvwar] *vt* to move. ◆ **se mouvoir** *vp* to move.

moyen, enne [mwajɛ̃, ɛn] *adj* 1. [intermédiaire] medium - 2. [médiocre, courant] average. ◆ **moyen** *nm* means *sg*, way ; **moyen de communication** means of communication ; **moyen de locomotion** OU **transport** means of transport. ◆ **moyenne** *nf* average ; **en moyenne** on average ; **la moyenne d'âge** the average age. ◆ **moyens** *nmpl* 1. [ressources] means ; **avoir les moyens** to be comfortably off - 2. [capacités] powers, ability ; **faire qqch par ses propres moyens** to do sthg on one's own. ◆ **au moyen de** *loc prép* by means of.

Moyen Âge [mwajɛnaʒ] *nm* : **le Moyen Âge** the Middle Ages *pl*.

Moyen-Orient [mwajɛnɔrjɑ̃] *nm* : **le Moyen-Orient** the Middle East.

MST *nf* 1. (abr de **maladie sexuellement transmissible**) STD - 2. (abr de **maîtrise de sciences et techniques**) masters degree in science and technology.

mû, mue [my] *pp* ▶ **mouvoir**.

mue [my] *nf* 1. [de pelage] moulting - 2. [de serpent] skin, slough - 3. [de voix] breaking.

muer [7] [mɥe] *vi* 1. [mammifère] to moult - 2. [serpent] to slough its skin - 3. [voix] to break ; [jeune homme] : **il mue** his voice is breaking.

muet, muette [mɥe, ɛt] <> *adj* 1. MÉD dumb - 2. [silencieux] silent ; **muet d'admiration/d'étonnement** speechless with admiration/surprise - 3. LING silent, mute. <> *nm, f* mute, dumb person. ◆ **muet** *nm* : **le muet** CINÉ silent films *pl*.

muezzin [mɥedzin] *nm* muezzin.

mufle [myfl] *nm* 1. [d'animal] muzzle, snout - 2. *fig* [goujat] lout.

muflerie [myfləri] *nf* loutishness.

mugir [32] [myʒir] *vi* 1. [vache] to moo - 2. [vent, sirène] to howl.

muguet [mygɛ] *nm* 1. [fleur] lily of the valley - 2. MÉD thrush.

mule [myl] *nf* mule.

mulet [mylɛ] *nm* **1.** [âne] mule - **2.** [poisson] mullet.

mulot [mylo] *nm* field mouse.

multicolore [myltikɔlɔr] *adj* multicoloured *UK*; multicolored *US*.

multicoque [myltikɔk] <> *adj* : **(bateau) multicoque** multihull ou multihulled boat. <> *nm* multihull.

multifonction [myltifɔ̃ksjɔ̃] *adj inv* multifunction.

multilatéral, e, aux [myltilateral, o] *adj* multilateral.

multinational, e, aux [myltinasjɔnal, o] *adj* multinational. ➡ **multinationale** *nf* multinational (company).

multiple [myltipl] <> *nm* multiple. <> *adj* **1.** [nombreux] multiple, numerous - **2.** [divers] many, various.

multiplication [myltiplikasjɔ̃] *nf* multiplication.

multiplier [10] [myltiplije] *vt* **1.** [accroître] to increase - **2.** MATH to multiply ; **X multiplié par Y égale Z** X multiplied by ou times Y equals Z. ➡ **se multiplier** *vp* to multiply.

multiracial, e, aux [myltirasjal, o] *adj* multiracial.

multirisque [myltirisk] *adj* comprehensive.

multitude [myltityd] *nf* : **multitude (de)** multitude (of).

municipal, e, aux [mynisipal, o] *adj* municipal. ➡ **municipales** *nfpl* : **les municipales** the local government elections.

municipalité [mynisipalite] *nf* **1.** [commune] municipality - **2.** [conseil] town council *UK*, city council *US*.

munir [32] [mynir] *vt* : **munir qqn/qqch de** to equip sb/sthg with. ➡ **se munir** *vp* : **se munir de** to equip o.s. with.

munitions [mynisjɔ̃] *nfpl* ammunition (U), munitions.

muqueuse [mykøz] *nf* mucous membrane.

mur [myr] *nm* **1.** [gén] wall - **2.** *fig* [obstacle] barrier, brick wall ; **mur du son** AÉRON sound barrier.

mûr, mûre [myr] *adj* ripe ; [personne] mature. ➡ **mûre** *nf* **1.** [de mûrier] mulberry - **2.** [de ronce] blackberry, bramble.

muraille [myraj] *nf* wall.

murène [myrɛn] *nf* moray eel.

murer [3] [myre] *vt* **1.** [boucher] to wall up, to block up - **2.** [enfermer] to wall in. ➡ **se murer** *vp* to shut o.s. up ou away ; **se murer dans** *fig* to retreat into.

muret [myrɛ] *nm* low wall.

mûrier [myrje] *nm* **1.** [arbre] mulberry tree - **2.** [ronce] blackberry bush, bramble bush.

mûrir [32] [myrir] *vi* **1.** [fruits, légumes] to ripen - **2.** *fig* [idée, projet] to develop - **3.** [personne] to mature.

murmure [myrmyr] *nm* murmur.

murmurer [3] [myrmyre] *vt & vi* to murmur.

musaraigne [myzarɛɲ] *nf* shrew.

musarder [3] [myzarde] *vi fam* to dawdle.

muscade [myskad] *nf* nutmeg.

muscat [myska] *nm* **1.** [raisin] muscat grape - **2.** [vin] *sweet wine*.

muscle [myskl] *nm* muscle.

musclé, e [myskle] *adj* **1.** [personne] muscular - **2.** *fig* [mesure, décision] forceful.

muscler [3] [myskle] *vt* : **muscler son corps** to build up one's muscles. ➡ **se muscler** *vp* to build up one's muscles.

musculation [myskylasjɔ̃] *nf* : **faire de la musculation** to do muscle-building exercises.

muse [myz] *nf* muse.

museau [myzo] *nm* **1.** [d'animal] muzzle, snout - **2.** *fam* [de personne] face.

musée [myze] *nm* museum ; [d'art] art gallery.

museler [24] [myzle] *vt litt & fig* to muzzle.

muselière [myzəljɛr] *nf* muzzle.

musette [myzɛt] *nf* haversack ; [d'écolier] satchel.

musical, e, aux [myzikal, o] *adj* **1.** [son] musical - **2.** [émission, critique] music *(avant n)*.

music-hall [myzikol] *(pl* music-halls*) nm* music hall *UK*, vaudeville *US*.

musicien, enne [myzisjɛ̃, ɛn] <> *adj* musical. <> *nm, f* musician.

musique [myzik] *nf* music ; **musique de chambre** chamber music ; **musique de film** *UK* ou movie *US* score.

musulman, e [myzylmɑ̃, an] *adj & nm, f* Muslim.

mutant, e [mytɑ̃, ɑ̃t] *adj & nm, f* mutant.

mutation [mytasjɔ̃] *nf* **1.** BIOL mutation - **2.** *fig* [changement] transformation - **3.** [de fonctionnaire] transfer.

muter [3] [myte] *vt* to transfer.

mutilation [mytilasjɔ̃] *nf* mutilation.

mutilé, e [mytile] *nm, f* disabled person.

mutiler [3] [mytile] *vt* to mutilate ; **il a été mutilé du bras droit** he lost his right arm.

mutin, e [mytɛ̃, in] *adj litt* impish. ➡ **mutin** *nm* rebel ; MIL & NAUT mutineer.

mutinerie [mytinri] *nf* rebellion ; MIL & NAUT mutiny.

mutisme [mytism] *nm* silence.

mutualité [mytɥalite] *nf* [assurance] mutual insurance.

mutuel, elle [mytɥɛl] *adj* mutual. ➡ **mutuelle** *nf* mutual insurance company.

mycose [mikoz] *nf* mycosis, fungal infection.

myocarde [mjɔkard] *nm* myocardium.

myopathie [mjɔpati] *nf* myopathy.

myope [mjɔp] <> *nmf* shortsighted UK ou nearsighted US person. <> *adj* shortsighted UK ou nearsighted US, myopic.

myopie [mjɔpi] *nf* shortsightedness UK, nearsightedness US, myopia.

myosotis [mjozɔtis] *nm* forget-me-not.

myrtille [mirtij] *nf* bilberry UK, blueberry US.

mystère [mistɛr] *nm* [gén] mystery.

mystérieux, euse [misterjø, øz] *adj* mysterious.

mysticisme [mistisism] *nm* mysticism.

mystification [mistifikasjɔ̃] *nf* [tromperie] hoax, practical joke.

mystifier [9] [mistifje] *vt* [duper] to take in.

mystique [mistik] <> *nmf* mystic. <> *adj* mystic, mystical.

mythe [mit] *nm* myth.

mythique [mitik] *adj* mythical.

mythologie [mitɔlɔʒi] *nf* mythology.

mythomane [mitɔman] *nmf* pathological liar.

N

n, N [ɛn] *nm inv* [lettre] n, N. ➡ **N** (*abr écrite de* nord) N.

n' ➤ ne.

nacelle [nasɛl] *nf* [de montgolfière] basket.

nacre [nakr] *nf* mother-of-pearl.

nage [naʒ] *nf* [natation] swimming ; **traverser à la nage** to swim across ; **en nage** bathed in sweat.

nageoire [naʒwar] *nf* fin.

nager [17] [naʒe] *vi* **1.** [se baigner] to swim - **2.** [flotter] to float - **3.** *fig* [dans vêtement] : **nager dans** to be lost in ; **nager dans la joie** to be incredibly happy.

nageur, euse [naʒœr, øz] *nm, f* swimmer.

naguère [nagɛr] *adv litt* a short time ago.

naïf, naïve [naif, iv] *adj* **1.** [ingénu, art] naive - **2.** *péj* [crédule] gullible.

nain, e [nɛ̃, nɛn] <> *adj* dwarf (*avant n*). <> *nm, f* dwarf ; **nain de jardin** garden gnome.

naissance [nɛsɑ̃s] *nf* **1.** [de personne] birth ; **donner naissance à** to give birth to ; **le contrôle des naissances** birth control - **2.** [endroit] source ; [du cou] nape - **3.** *fig* [de science, nation] birth ; **donner naissance à** to give rise to.

naissant, e [nɛsɑ̃, ɑ̃t] *adj* **1.** [brise] rising ; [jour] dawning - **2.** [barbe] incipient.

naître [92] [nɛtr] *vi* **1.** [enfant] to be born ; **elle est née en 1965** she was born in 1965 - **2.** [espoir] to spring up ; **naître de** to arise from ; **faire naître qqch** to give rise to sthg.

naïveté [naivte] *nf* **1.** [candeur] innocence - **2.** *péj* [crédulité] gullibility.

nana [nana] *nf fam* [jeune fille] girl.

nanti, e [nɑ̃ti] *nm, f* wealthy person.

nantir [32] [nɑ̃tir] *vt litt* : **nantir qqn de** to provide sb with.

nappe [nap] *nf* **1.** [de table] tablecloth, cloth - **2.** *fig* [étendue - gén] sheet ; [- de brouillard] blanket - **3.** [couche] layer.

napper [3] [nape] *vt* CULIN to coat.

napperon [naprɔ̃] *nm* tablemat.

narcisse [narsis] *nm* BOT narcissus.

narcissisme [narsisism] *nm* narcissism.

narcotique [narkɔtik] *nm & adj* narcotic.

narguer [3] [narge] *vt* [danger] to flout ; [personne] to scorn, to scoff at.

narine [narin] *nf* nostril.

narquois, e [narkwa, az] *adj* sardonic.

narrateur, trice [naratœr, tris] *nm, f* narrator.

narrer [3] [nare] *vt litt* to narrate.

nasal, e, aux [nazal, o] *adj* nasal.

naseau, x [nazo] *nm* nostril.

nasillard, e [nazijar, ard] *adj* nasal.

nasse [nas] *nf* keep net.

natal, e, als [natal] *adj* [d'origine] native.

natalité [natalite] *nf* birth rate.

natation [natasjɔ̃] *nf* swimming ; **faire de la natation** to swim.

natif, ive [natif, iv] <> *adj* [originaire] : **natif de** native of. <> *nm, f* native.

nation [nasjɔ̃] *nf* nation. ➡ **Nations unies** *nfpl* : **les Nations unies** the United Nations.

national, e, aux [nasjɔnal, o] *adj* national. **nationale** *nf* : **(route) nationale** ≃ A road *UK*, ≃ state highway *US*.

nationaliser [3] [nasjɔnalize] *vt* to nationalize.

nationalisme [nasjɔnalism] *nm* nationalism.

nationalité [nasjɔnalite] *nf* nationality ; **de nationalité française** of French nationality.

nativité [nativite] *nf* nativity.

natte [nat] *nf* **1.** [tresse] plait - **2.** [tapis] mat.

naturaliser [3] [natyralize] *vt* **1.** [personne, plante] to naturalize - **2.** [empailler] to stuff.

naturaliste [natyralist] ◇ *nmf* **1.** LITTÉR & ZOOL naturalist - **2.** [empailleur] taxidermist. ◇ *adj* naturalistic.

nature [natyr] ◇ *nf* nature. ◇ *adj inv* **1.** [simple] plain - **2.** *fam* [spontané] natural.

naturel, elle [natyrɛl] *adj* natural. **naturel** *nm* **1.** [tempérament] nature ; **être d'un naturel affable/sensible** *etc* to be affable/ sensitive *etc* by nature - **2.** [aisance, spontanéité] naturalness.

naturellement [natyrɛlmɑ̃] *adv* **1.** [gén] naturally - **2.** [logiquement] rationally.

naturiste [natyrist] *nmf* naturist.

naufrage [nofraʒ] *nm* **1.** [navire] shipwreck ; **faire naufrage** to be wrecked - **2.** *fig* [effondrement] collapse.

naufragé, e [nofraʒe] ◇ *adj* shipwrecked. ◇ *nm, f* shipwrecked person.

nauséabond, e [nozeabɔ̃, ɔ̃d] *adj* nauseating.

nausée [noze] *nf* **1.** MÉD nausea ; **avoir la nausée** to feel nauseous *ou* sick *UK* - **2.** [dégoût] disgust.

nautique [notik] *adj* nautical ; [ski, sport] water *(avant n)*.

naval, e, als [naval] *adj* naval.

navet [navɛ] *nm* **1.** BOT turnip - **2.** *fam péj* [œuvre] load of rubbish.

navette [navɛt] *nf* shuttle ; **navette spatiale** AÉRON space shuttle ; **faire la navette** to shuttle.

navigable [navigabl] *adj* navigable.

navigateur, trice [navigatœr, tris] *nm, f* navigator. **navigateur** *nm* INFORM browser.

navigation [navigasjɔ̃] *nf* navigation ; COMM shipping ; INFORM browsing.

naviguer [3] [navige] *vi* **1.** [voguer] to sail - **2.** [piloter] to navigate - **3.** INFORM to browse.

navire [navir] *nm* ship.

navrant, e [navrɑ̃, ɑ̃t] *adj* **1.** [triste] upsetting, distressing - **2.** [regrettable, mauvais] unfortunate.

navrer [3] [navre] *vt* to upset ; **être navré de qqch/de faire qqch** to be sorry about sthg/to do sthg.

nazi, e [nazi] *nm, f* Nazi.

nazisme [nazism] *nm* Nazism.

NB *(abr de Nota Bene)* NB.

NDLR *(abr écrite de note de la rédaction)* editor's note.

NDT *(abr écrite de note du traducteur)* translator's note.

ne [nə], **n'** *(devant voyelle ou 'h' muet) adv* **1.** [négation] **pas², plus, rien** *etc* - **2.** [négation implicite] : **il se porte mieux que je ne (le) croyais** he's in better health than I thought (he would be) - **3.** [avec verbes ou expressions marquant le doute, la crainte etc] : **je crains qu'il n'oublie** I'm afraid he'll forget ; **j'ai peur qu'il n'en parle** I'm frightened he'll talk about it.

né, e [ne] *adj* born ; **né en 1965** born in 1965 ; **né le 17 juin** born on the 17th June *UK*, born on June 17th *US* ; **Mme X, née Y** Mrs X née Y.

néanmoins [neɑ̃mwɛ̃] *adv* nevertheless.

néant [neɑ̃] *nm* **1.** [absence de valeur] worthlessness - **2.** [absence d'existence] nothingness ; **réduire à néant** to reduce to nothing.

nébuleux, euse [nebylø, øz] *adj* **1.** [ciel] cloudy - **2.** [idée, projet] nebulous. **nébuleuse** *nf* ASTRON nebula.

nécessaire [neseser] ◇ *adj* necessary ; **nécessaire à** necessary for ; **il est nécessaire de faire qqch** it is necessary to do sthg ; **il est nécessaire que** (+ *subjonctif*) : **il est nécessaire qu'elle vienne** she must come. ◇ *nm* **1.** [biens] necessities *pl* ; **le strict nécessaire** the bare essentials *pl* - **2.** [mesures] : **faire le nécessaire** to do the necessary - **3.** [trousse] bag.

nécessité [nesesite] *nf* [obligation, situation] necessity ; **être dans la nécessité de faire qqch** to have no choice *ou* alternative but to do sthg.

nécessiter [3] [nesesite] *vt* to necessitate.

nécrologique [nekrɔlɔʒik] *adj* obituary *(avant n)*.

nectar [nɛktar] *nm* nectar.

nectarine [nɛktarin] *nf* nectarine.

néerlandais, e [neerlɑ̃de, ɛz] *adj* Dutch. **néerlandais** *nm* [langue] Dutch. **Néerlandais, e** *nm, f* Dutchman (f Dutchwoman) ; **les Néerlandais** the Dutch.

nef [nɛf] *nf* **1.** [d'église] nave - **2.** *litt* [bateau] vessel.

néfaste [nefast] *adj* **1.** [jour, événement] fateful - **2.** [influence] harmful.

négatif, ive [negatif, iv] *adj* negative. ◆ **négatif** *nm* PHOTO negative. ◆ **négative** *nf* : **répondre par la négative** to reply in the negative.

négation [negasjɔ̃] *nf* **1.** [rejet] denial - **2.** GRAMM negative.

négligé, e [negliʒe] *adj* **1.** [travail, tenue] untidy - **2.** [ami, jardin] neglected.

négligeable [negliʒabl] *adj* negligible.

négligemment [negliʒamɑ̃] *adv* **1.** [sans soin] carelessly - **2.** [avec indifférence] casually.

négligence [negliʒɑ̃s] *nf* **1.** [laisser-aller] carelessness - **2.** [omission] negligence ; **par négligence** out of negligence.

négligent, e [negliʒɑ̃, ɑ̃t] *adj* **1.** [sans soin] careless - **2.** [indifférent] casual.

négliger [17] [negliʒe] *vt* **1.** [ami, jardin] to neglect ; **négliger de faire qqch** to fail to do sthg - **2.** [avertissement] to ignore. ◆ **se négliger** *vp* to neglect o.s.

négoce [negɔs] *nm* business.

négociant, e [negɔsjɑ̃, ɑ̃t] *nm, f* dealer.

négociateur, trice [negɔsjatœr, tris] *nm, f* negotiator.

négociation [negɔsjasjɔ̃] *nf* negotiation ; **négociations de paix** peace negotiations.

négocier [9] [negɔsje] *vt* to negotiate.

nègre, négresse [nɛgr, negrɛs] *nm, f* Negro (f negress) *(beware: the terms 'nègre' and 'négresse' are considered racist)*. ◆ **nègre** ⬦ *nm fam* ghost writer. ⬦ *adj* negro *(avant n) (beware: the term 'nègre' is considered racist)*.

neige [nɛʒ] *nf* [flocons] snow.

neiger [23] [neʒe] *v impers* : **il neige** it is snowing.

neigeux, euse [nɛʒø, øz] *adj* snowy.

nénuphar [nenyfar] *nm* water lily.

néologisme [neɔlɔʒism] *nm* neologism.

néon [neɔ̃] *nm* **1.** [gaz] neon - **2.** [enseigne] neon light.

néophyte [neɔfit] *nmf* novice.

néo-zélandais, e [neɔzelɑ̃dɛ, ɛz] (*mpl inv*) (*fpl* **néo-zélandaises**) *adj* New Zealand *(avant n)*. ◆ **Néo-Zélandais, e** *nm, f* New Zealander.

Népal [nepal] *nm* : **le Népal** Nepal.

nerf [nɛr] *nm* **1.** ANAT nerve - **2.** *fig* [vigueur] spirit.

nerveux, euse [nɛrvø, øz] *adj* **1.** [gén] nervous - **2.** [viande] stringy - **3.** [style] vigorous ; [voiture] nippy *UK*.

nervosité [nɛrvozite] *nf* nervousness.

nervure [nɛrvyr] *nf* [de feuille, d'aile] vein.

n'est-ce pas [nɛspa] *adv* : **vous me croyez, n'est-ce pas?** you believe me, don't you? ;

c'est délicieux, n'est-ce pas? it's delicious, isn't it? ; **n'est-ce pas que vous vous êtes bien amusés?** you enjoyed yourselves, didn't you?

net, nette [nɛt] *adj* **1.** [écriture, image, idée] clear - **2.** [propre, rangé] clean, neat - **3.** COMM & FIN net ; **net d'impôt** tax-free, tax-exempt *US* - **4.** [visible, manifeste] definite, distinct. ◆ **net** *adv* **1.** [sur le coup] on the spot ; **s'arrêter net** to stop dead ; **se casser net** to break clean off - **2.** COMM & FIN net.

Net [nɛt] *nm fam* **le Net** the Net, the net ; **surfer sur le Net** to surf the Net.

netéconomie [nɛtekɔnɔmi] *nf* (inter)net economy.

nettement [nɛtmɑ̃] *adv* **1.** [clairement] clearly - **2.** [incontestablement] definitely ; **nettement plus/moins** much more/less.

netteté [nɛtte] *nf* clearness.

nettoyage [netwajaʒ] *nm* [de vêtement] cleaning ; **nettoyage à sec** dry cleaning.

nettoyer [13] [netwaje] *vt* **1.** [gén] to clean - **2.** [vider] to clear out.

neuf¹, neuve [nœf, nœv] *adj* new. ◆ **neuf** *nm* : **vêtu de neuf** wearing new clothes ; **quoi de neuf?** what's new? ; **rien de neuf** nothing new.

neuf² [nœf] *adj num inv* & *nm* nine ; *voir aussi* **six**.

neurasthénique [nørastenik] *nmf* & *adj* depressive.

neurodégénératif, ive [nørɔdeʒeneratif, iv] *adj* MÉD neurodegenerative.

neurologie [nørɔlɔʒi] *nf* neurology.

neutraliser [3] [nøtralize] *vt* to neutralize.

neutralité [nøtralite] *nf* neutrality.

neutre [nøtr] ⬦ *nm* LING neuter. ⬦ *adj* **1.** [gén] neutral - **2.** LING neuter.

neutron [nøtrɔ̃] *nm* neutron.

neuve ➤ **neuf¹**.

neuvième [nœvjɛm] *adj num inv, nm & nmf* ninth ; *voir aussi* **sixième**.

névé [neve] *nm* snowbank.

neveu [nəvø] *nm* nephew.

névralgie [nevralʒi] *nf* MÉD neuralgia.

névrose [nevroz] *nf* neurosis.

névrosé, e [nevroze] *adj* & *nm, f* neurotic.

nez [ne] *nm* nose ; **saigner du nez** to have a nosebleed ; **nez aquilin** aquiline nose ; **nez busqué** hooked nose ; **nez à nez** face to face.

ni [ni] *conj* : **sans pull ni écharpe** without a sweater or a scarf ; **je ne peux ni ne veux venir** I neither can nor want to come. ◆ **ni... ni** *loc correlative* neither... nor ; **ni**

lui ni moi neither of us ; **ni l'un ni l'autre n'a parlé** neither of them spoke ; **je ne les aime ni l'un ni l'autre** I don't like either of them.

niais, e [nje, njɛz] ◇ *adj* silly, foolish. ◇ *nm, f* fool.

Nicaragua [nikaragwa] *nm* : **le Nicaragua** Nicaragua.

niche [niʃ] *nf* **1.** [de chien] kennel *UK*, doghouse *US* - **2.** [de statue] niche.

nicher [3] [niʃe] *vi* [oiseaux] to nest.

nickel [nikɛl] ◇ *nm* nickel. ◇ *adj inv fam* spotless, spick and span.

nicotine [nikɔtin] *nf* nicotine.

nid [ni] *nm* nest.

nièce [njɛs] *nf* niece.

nier [9] [nje] *vt* to deny.

nigaud, e [nigo, od] *nm, f* simpleton.

Niger [niʒɛr] *nm* **1.** [fleuve] : **le Niger** the River Niger - **2.** [État] : **le Niger** Niger.

Nigeria [niʒerja] *nm* : **le Nigeria** Nigeria.

Nil [nil] *nm* : **le Nil** the Nile.

n'importe ▶ importer.

nippon, one [nipɔ̃, ɔn] *adj* Japanese. **▶ Nippon, one** *nm, f* Japanese (person) ; **les Nippons** the Japanese.

nirvana [nirvana] *nm* nirvana.

nitrate [nitrat] *nm* nitrate.

nitroglycérine [nitrɔgliserin] *nf* nitroglycerine.

niveau, x [nivo] *nm* [gén] level ; **de même niveau** *fig* of the same standard ; **au-dessus du niveau de la mer** above sea level ; **niveau de vie** standard of living ; **au niveau de** at the level of ; *fig* [en ce qui concerne] as regards.

niveler [24] [nivle] *vt* to level ; *fig* to level out.

noble [nɔbl] ◇ *nmf* nobleman (*f* noblewoman). ◇ *adj* noble.

noblesse [nɔblɛs] *nf* nobility.

noce [nɔs] *nf* **1.** [mariage] wedding - **2.** [invités] wedding party. **▶ noces** *nfpl* wedding *sg* ; **noces d'or/d'argent** golden/silver wedding (anniversary).

nocif, ive [nɔsif, iv] *adj* [produit, gaz] noxious.

noctambule [nɔktɑ̃byl] *nmf* night bird.

nocturne [nɔktyrn] ◇ *nm & nf* [d'un magasin] late opening. ◇ *adj* **1.** [émission, attaque] night (*avant n*) - **2.** [animal] nocturnal.

Noël [nɔɛl] *nm* Christmas ; **joyeux Noël!** happy ou merry Christmas!

nœud [nø] *nm* **1.** [de fil, de bois] knot ; **double nœud** double knot - **2.** NAUT knot ; **filer à X nœuds** NAUT to do X knots - **3.** [de l'action, du problème] crux - **4.** [ornement] bow ; **nœud de cravate** knot (*in one's tie*) ; **nœud papillon** bow tie - **5.** ANAT, ASTRON, ÉLECTR & RAIL node.

noir, e [nwar] *adj* **1.** [gén] black ; **noir de** [poussière, suie] black with - **2.** [pièce, couloir] dark. **▶ Noir, e** *nm, f* black. **▶ noir** *nm* **1.** [couleur] black ; **noir sur blanc** *fig* in black and white - **2.** [obscurité] dark ; **acheter qqch au noir** to buy sthg on the black market ; **travail au noir** moonlighting. **▶ noire** *nf* crotchet *UK*, quarter note *US*.

noirâtre [nwaratr] *adj* blackish.

noirceur [nwarsœr] *nf fig* [méchanceté] wickedness.

noircir [32] [nwarsir] ◇ *vi* to darken. ◇ *vt litt & fig* to blacken.

Noire ▶ mer.

noisetier [nwaztje] *nm* hazel tree.

noisette [nwazɛt] *nf* [fruit] hazelnut.

noix [nwa] *nf* [fruit] walnut ; **noix de cajou** cashew (nut) ; **noix de coco** coconut ; **noix de muscade** nutmeg ; **à la noix** *fam* dreadful.

nom [nɔ̃] *nm* **1.** [gén] name ; **au nom de** in the name of ; **nom déposé** trade name ; **nom de famille** surname ; **nom de jeune fille** maiden name - **2.** [prénom] (first) name - **3.** GRAMM noun ; **nom propre/commun** proper/common noun.

nomade [nɔmad] ◇ *nmf* nomad. ◇ *adj* nomadic.

nombre [nɔ̃br] *nm* number ; **nombre pair/impair** even/odd number.

nombreux, euse [nɔ̃brø, øz] *adj* **1.** [famille, foule] large - **2.** [erreurs, occasions] numerous ; **peu nombreux** few.

nombril [nɔ̃bril] *nm* navel ; **il se prend pour le nombril du monde** he thinks the world revolves around him.

nominal, e, aux [nɔminal, o] *adj* **1.** [liste] of names - **2.** [valeur, autorité] nominal - **3.** GRAMM noun (*avant n*).

nomination [nɔminasjɔ̃] *nf* nomination, appointment.

nommé, e [nɔme] *adj* **1.** [désigné] named - **2.** [choisi] appointed.

nommément [nɔmemɑ̃] *adv* [citer] by name.

nommer [3] [nɔme] *vt* **1.** [appeler] to name, to call - **2.** [qualifier] to call - **3.** [promouvoir] to appoint, to nominate - **4.** [dénoncer, mentionner] to name. **▶ se nommer** *vp* **1.** [s'appeler] to be called - **2.** [se désigner] to give one's name.

non [nɔ̃] ◇ *adv* **1.** [réponse négative] no - **2.** [se rapportant à une phrase précédente] not ; **moi non** not me ; **moi non plus** (and) neither am/do etc I - **3.** [sert à demander une confirmation] : **c'est une bonne idée, non?**

it's a good idea, isn't it? - **4.** [modifie un adjectif ou un adverbe] not ; **non loin d'ici** not far from here ; **une difficulté non négligeable** a not inconsiderable problem. ◇ *nm inv* no. ◆ **non (pas) que... mais** *loc correlative* not that... but.

nonagénaire [nɔnaʒenɛr] *nmf & adj* nonagenarian.

non-agression [nɔnagresjɔ̃] *nf* non-aggression.

nonante [nɔnɑ̃t] *adj num inv Belgique & Suisse* ninety.

nonchalance [nɔ̃ʃalɑ̃s] *nf* nonchalance, casualness.

non-fumeur, euse [nɔ̃fymœr, øz] *nm, f* non-smoker.

non-lieu [nɔ̃ljø] (*pl* **non-lieux**) *nm* DR dismissal through lack of evidence ; **rendre un non-lieu** to dismiss a case for lack of evidence.

nonne [nɔn] *nf* nun.

non-sens [nɔ̃sɑ̃s] *nm inv* **1.** [absurdité] nonsense - **2.** [contresens] meaningless word.

non-violence [nɔ̃vjɔlɑ̃s] *nf* non-violence.

non-voyant, e [nɔ̃vwajɑ̃, ɑ̃t] *nm, f* visually handicapped *UK*, visually impaired *US*.

nord [nɔr] ◇ *nm* north ; **un vent du nord** a northerly wind ; **au nord** in the north ; **au nord (de)** to the north (of) ; **le grand Nord** the frozen North. ◇ *adj inv* north ; [province, région] northern.

nord-africain, e [nɔrafrikɛ̃, ɛn] (*mpl* **nord-africains**) (*fpl* **nord-africaines**) *adj* North African. ◆ **Nord-Africain, e** *nm, f* North African.

nord-américain, e [nɔramerikɛ̃, ɛn] (*mpl* **nord-américains**) (*fpl* **nord-américaines**) *adj* North American. ◆ **Nord-Américain, e** *nm, f* North American.

nord-est [nɔrest] *nm & adj inv* northeast.

nordique [nɔrdik] *adj* Nordic, Scandinavian. ◆ **Nordique** *nmf* **1.** [Scandinave] Scandinavian - **2.** *Québec* North Canadian.

nord-ouest [nɔrwest] *nm & adj inv* northwest.

normal, e, aux [nɔrmal, o] *adj* normal. ◆ **normale** *nf* [moyenne] : **la normale** the norm.

normalement [nɔrmalmɑ̃] *adv* normally, usually ; **normalement il devrait déjà être arrivé** he should have arrived by now.

normalien, enne [nɔrmaljɛ̃, ɛn] *nm, f* **1.** [élève d'une école normale] student at teacher training college *UK* OU teachers college *US* - **2.** [ancien élève de l'École normale supérieure] graduate of the École normale supérieure.

normaliser [3] [nɔrmalize] *vt* **1.** [situation] to normalize - **2.** [produit] to standardize.

normand, e [nɔrmɑ̃, ɑ̃d] *adj* Norman. ◆ **Normand, e** *nm, f* Norman.

Normandie [nɔrmɑ̃di] *nf* : **la Normandie** Normandy.

norme [nɔrm] *nf* **1.** [gén] standard, norm - **2.** [critère] criterion.

Norvège [nɔrvɛʒ] *nf* : **la Norvège** Norway.

norvégien, enne [nɔrveʒjɛ̃, ɛn] *adj* Norwegian. ◆ **norvégien** *nm* [langue] Norwegian. ◆ **Norvégien, enne** *nm, f* Norwegian.

nos ▶ notre.

nosocomial, e, aux [nɔzɔkɔmjal, o] *adj* nosocomial, contracted in hospital.

nostalgie [nɔstalʒi] *nf* nostalgia.

nostalgique [nɔstalʒik] *adj* nostalgic.

notable [nɔtabl] ◇ *adj* noteworthy, notable. ◇ *nm* notable.

notaire [nɔtɛr] *nm* ≃ solicitor *UK*, ≃ lawyer.

notamment [nɔtamɑ̃] *adv* in particular.

note [nɔt] *nf* **1.** [gén & MUS] note ; **prendre des notes** to take notes - **2.** SCOL & UNIV mark, grade *US* ; **avoir une bonne/mauvaise note** to have a good/bad mark - **3.** [facture] bill ; **note de frais** [à remplir] expense OU expenses claim (form) ; **présenter sa note de frais** to put in for expenses.

noter [3] [nɔte] *vt* **1.** [écrire] to note down - **2.** [constater] to note, to notice - **3.** SCOL & UNIV to mark, to grade *US*.

notice [nɔtis] *nf* instructions *pl*.

notifier [9] [nɔtifje] *vt* : **notifier qqch à qqn** to notify sb of sthg.

notion [nɔsjɔ̃] *nf* **1.** [conscience, concept] notion, concept - **2.** (*gén pl*) [rudiment] smattering (*U*).

notoire [nɔtwar] *adj* [fait] well-known ; [criminel] notorious.

notre [nɔtr] (*pl* **nos** [no]) *adj poss* our.

nôtre [nɔtr] ◆ **le nôtre, la nôtre** (*pl* **les nôtres**) *pron poss* ours ; **les nôtres** our family *sg* ; **serez-vous des nôtres demain?** will you be joining us tomorrow?

nouer [6] [nwe] *vt* **1.** [corde, lacet] to tie ; [bouquet] to tie up - **2.** *fig* [gorge, estomac] to knot. ◆ **se nouer** *vp* **1.** [gorge] to tighten up - **2.** [intrigue] to start.

noueux, euse [nwø, øz] *adj* [bois] knotty ; [mains] gnarled.

nougat [nuga] *nm* nougat.

nouille [nuj] *nf fam péj* idiot. ◆ **nouilles** *nfpl* [pâtes] pasta (*U*), noodles *pl*.

nourrice [nuris] *nf* [garde d'enfants] nanny *UK*, childminder *UK*, nursemaid *US* ; [qui allaite] wet nurse.

nourrir [32] [nurir] *vt* **1.** [gén] to feed

- **2.** [sentiment, projet] to nurture. **se nourrir** *vp* to eat ; **se nourrir de qqch** *litt & fig* to live on sthg.

nourrissant, e [nurisɑ̃, ɑ̃t] *adj* nutritious, nourishing.

nourrisson [nurisɔ̃] *nm* infant.

nourriture [nurityr] *nf* food.

nous [nu] *pron pers* **1.** [sujet] we - **2.** [objet] us. **nous-mêmes** *pron pers* ourselves.

nouveau, elle, x [nuvo, ɛl, o] *(nouvel devant une voyelle ou un 'h' muet)* <> *adj* new ; **nouveaux mariés** newlyweds. <> *nm, f* new boy (*f* new girl). **nouveau** *nm* : **il y a du nouveau** there's something new. **nouvelle** *nf* **1.** [information] (piece of) news (U) - **2.** [court récit] short story. **nouvelles** *nfpl* news ; **les nouvelles** [média] the news *sg* ; **il a donné de ses nouvelles** I/we *etc* have heard from him. **à nouveau** *loc adv* **1.** [encore] again - **2.** [de manière différente] afresh, anew. **de nouveau** *loc adv* again.

nouveau-né, e [nuvone] *(mpl* nouveau-nés, *fpl* nouveau-nées) *nm, f* newborn baby.

nouveauté [nuvote] *nf* **1.** [actualité] novelty - **2.** [innovation] something new - **3.** [ouvrage] new book/film *etc.*

nouvel, nouvelle ► nouveau.

Nouvelle-Calédonie [nuvɛlkaledɔni] *nf* : **la Nouvelle-Calédonie** New Caledonia.

Nouvelle-Guinée [nuvɛlgine] *nf* : **la Nouvelle-Guinée** New Guinea.

Nouvelle-Zélande [nuvɛlzelɑ̃d] *nf* : **la Nouvelle-Zélande** New Zealand.

novateur, trice [nɔvatœr, tris] <> *adj* innovative. <> *nm, f* innovator.

novembre [nɔvɑ̃br] *nm* November ; *voir aussi* septembre.

novice [nɔvis] <> *nmf* novice. <> *adj* inexperienced.

noyade [nwajad] *nf* drowning.

noyau, x [nwajo] *nm* **1.** [de fruit] stone *UK*, pit - **2.** ASTRON, BIOL & PHYS nucleus - **3.** *fig* [d'amis] group, circle ; [d'opposants, de résistants] cell ; **noyau dur** hard core - **4.** *fig* [centre] core.

noyauter [3] [nwajote] *vt* to infiltrate.

noyé, e [nwaje] <> *adj* **1.** [personne] drowned - **2.** [inondé] flooded ; **yeux noyés de larmes** eyes swimming with tears. <> *nm, f* drowned person.

noyer [13] [nwaje] *vt* **1.** [animal, personne] to drown - **2.** [terre, moteur] to flood - **3.** [estomper, diluer] to swamp ; [contours] to blur. **se noyer** *vp* **1.** [personne] to drown - **2.** *fig* [se perdre] : **se noyer dans** to become bogged down in.

NPI *(abr de* nouveaux pays industrialisés) *nmpl* NICs.

N/Réf *(abr écrite de* Notre référence) O/Ref.

nu, e [ny] *adj* **1.** [personne] naked - **2.** [paysage, fil électrique] bare - **3.** [style, vérité] plain. **nu** *nm* nude ; **à nu** stripped, bare ; **mettre à nu** to strip bare.

nuage [nɥaʒ] *nm* **1.** [gén] cloud - **2.** [petite quantité] : **un nuage de lait** a drop of milk.

nuageux, euse [nɥaʒø, øz] *adj* **1.** [temps, ciel] cloudy - **2.** *fig* [esprit] hazy.

nuance [nɥɑ̃s] *nf* [de couleur] shade ; [de son, de sens] nuance.

nubile [nybil] *adj* nubile.

nucléaire [nykleɛr] <> *nm* nuclear energy. <> *adj* nuclear.

nudisme [nydism] *nm* nudism, naturism.

nudité [nydite] *nf* **1.** [de personne] nudity, nakedness - **2.** [de lieu, style] bareness.

nuée [nɥe] *nf* **1.** [multitude] : **une nuée de** a horde of - **2.** *litt* [nuage] cloud.

nues [ny] *nfpl* : **tomber des nues** to be completely taken aback.

nui [nɥi] *pp inv* ► nuire.

nuire [97] [nɥir] *vi* : **nuire à** to harm, to injure.

nuisance [nɥizɑ̃s] *nf* nuisance (U), harm (U).

nuisette [nɥizɛt] *nf* short nightgown, babydoll nightgown.

nuisible [nɥizibl] *adj* harmful.

nuit [nɥi] *nf* **1.** [laps de temps] night ; **cette nuit** [la nuit dernière] last night ; [la nuit prochaine] tonight ; **de nuit** at night ; **bateau/vol de nuit** night ferry/flight ; **nuit blanche** sleepless night - **2.** [obscurité] darkness, night ; **il fait nuit** it's dark.

nuitée [nɥite] *nf* overnight stay.

nul, nulle [nyl] <> *adj indéf (avant n)* little no. <> *adj (après n)* **1.** [égal à zéro] nil - **2.** [sans valeur] useless, hopeless ; **être nul en maths** to be hopeless *ou* useless at maths - **3.** [sans résultat] : **match nul** draw *UK*, tie *US.* <> *nm, f péj* nonentity. <> *pron indéf sout* no one, nobody. **nulle part** *loc adv* nowhere, no place *US.*

nullement [nylmɑ̃] *adv* by no means.

nullité [nylite] *nf* **1.** [médiocrité] incompetence - **2.** DR invalidity, nullity.

numéraire [nymerɛr] *nm* cash.

numération [nymerasjɔ̃] *nf* MÉD : **numération globulaire** blood count.

numérique [nymerik] *adj* **1.** [gén] numerical - **2.** INFORM digital.

numéro [nymero] *nm* **1.** [gén] number ; **composer** *ou* **faire un numéro** to dial a number ; **faire un faux numéro** to dial a wrong number ; **numéro minéralogique** *ou* **d'immatriculation** registration *UK ou* license

US number ; **numéro de poste** extension number ; **numéro de téléphone** telephone number ; **numéro vert** ≃ freefone number *UK*, ≃ 800 *ou* tollfree number *US* - **2.** [de spectacle] act, turn - **3.** *fam* [personne] : **quel numéro!** what a character!

numéroter [3] [nymεrɔte] *vt* to number.

nu-pieds [nypje] *nm inv* [sandale] sandal.

nuptial, e, aux [nypsjal, o] *adj* nuptial.

nuque [nyk] *nf* nape.

nurse [nœrs] *nf* children's nurse, nanny *UK*.

nursery [nœrsəri] (*pl* **nurseries**) *nf* **1.** [dans un hôpital] nursery - **2.** [dans un lieu public] parent-and-baby clinic.

nutritif, ive [nytritif, iv] *adj* nutritious.

nutritionniste [nytrisjɔnist] *nmf* nutritionist, dietician.

Nylon® [nilɔ̃] *nm* nylon.

nymphe [nɛ̃f] *nf* nymph.

nymphomane [nɛ̃fɔman] *nf & adj* nymphomaniac.

o, O [o] *nm inv* [lettre] o, O. ◆ **O** (*abr écrite de* **Ouest**) W.

ô [o] *interj* oh!, O!

oasis [ɔazis] *nf* **1.** [dans désert] oasis - **2.** *fig* [de calme] haven, oasis.

obéir [32] [ɔbeir] *vi* **1.** [personne] : **obéir à qqn/qqch** to obey sb/sthg - **2.** [freins] to respond.

obéissant, e [ɔbeisɑ̃, ɑ̃t] *adj* obedient.

obélisque [ɔbelisk] *nm* obelisk.

obèse [ɔbεz] *adj* obese.

obésité [ɔbezite] *nf* obesity.

objecteur [ɔbʒεktœr] *nm* objector ; **objecteur de conscience** conscientious objector.

objectif, ive [ɔbʒεktif, iv] *adj* objective. ◆ **objectif** *nm* **1.** PHOTO lens - **2.** [but, cible] objective, target.

objection [ɔbʒεksjɔ̃] *nf* objection ; **faire objection à** to object to.

objectivité [ɔbʒεktivite] *nf* objectivity.

objet [ɔbʒε] *nm* **1.** [chose] object ; **objet d'art** objet d'art ; **objet de valeur** valuable ; **objets trouvés** lost property office *UK*, lost-and-found (office) *US* - **2.** [sujet] subject - **3.** DR matter.

obligation [ɔbligasjɔ̃] *nf* **1.** [gén] obligation ; **être dans l'obligation de faire qqch** to be obliged to do sthg - **2.** FIN bond, debenture.

obligatoire [ɔbligatwar] *adj* **1.** [imposé] compulsory, obligatory - **2.** *fam* [inéluctable] inevitable.

obligeance [ɔbliʒɑ̃s] *nf sout* obligingness ; **avoir l'obligeance de faire qqch** to be good *ou* kind enough to do sthg.

obliger [17] [ɔbliʒe] *vt* **1.** [forcer] : **obliger qqn à qqch** to impose sthg on sb ; **obliger qqn à faire qqch** to force sb to do sthg ; **être obligé de faire qqch** to be obliged to do sthg - **2.** [rendre service à] to oblige. ◆ **s'obliger** *vp* : **s'obliger à qqch** to impose sthg on o.s. ; **s'obliger à faire qqch** to force o.s. to do sthg.

oblique [ɔblik] *adj* oblique.

obliquer [3] [ɔblike] *vi* to turn off.

oblitérer [18] [ɔblitere] *vt* **1.** [tamponner] to cancel - **2.** MÉD [obstruer] to obstruct - **3.** [effacer] to obliterate.

obnubiler [3] [ɔbnybile] *vt* to obsess ; **être obnubilé par** to be obsessed with *ou* by.

obole [ɔbɔl] *nf* small contribution.

obscène [ɔpsεn] *adj* obscene.

obscénité [ɔpsenite] *nf* obscenity.

obscur, e [ɔpskyr] *adj* **1.** [sombre] dark - **2.** [confus] vague - **3.** [inconnu, douteux] obscure.

obscurantisme [ɔpskyrɑ̃tism] *nm* obscurantism.

obscurcir [32] [ɔpskyrsir] *vt* **1.** [assombrir] to darken - **2.** [embrouiller] to confuse. ◆ **s'obscurcir** *vp* **1.** [s'assombrir] to grow dark - **2.** [s'embrouiller] to become confused.

obscurité [ɔpskyrite] *nf* [nuit] darkness.

obsédé, e [ɔpsede] ◇ *adj* obsessed. ◇ *nm, f* obsessive.

obséder [18] [ɔpsede] *vt* to obsess, to haunt.

obsèques [ɔpsεk] *nfpl* funeral *sg*.

obséquieux, euse [ɔpsekjø, øz] *adj* obsequious.

observateur, trice [ɔpsεrvatœr, tris] ◇ *adj* observant. ◇ *nm, f* observer.

observation [ɔpsεrvasjɔ̃] *nf* **1.** [gén] observation ; **être en observation** MÉD to be under observation - **2.** [critique] remark.

observatoire [ɔpsεrvatwar] *nm* **1.** ASTRON observatory - **2.** [lieu de surveillance] observation post.

observer [3] [ɔpsεrve] *vt* **1.** [regarder, remarquer, respecter] to observe - **2.** [épier] to watch - **3.** [constater] **: observer que** to note that ; **faire observer qqch à qqn** to point sthg out to sb.

obsession [ɔpsesjɔ̃] *nf* obsession.

obsolète [ɔpsɔlɛt] *adj* obsolete.

obstacle [ɔpstakl] *nm* **1.** [entrave] obstacle - **2.** *fig* [difficulté] hindrance ; **faire obstacle à qqch/qqn** to hinder sthg/sb.

obstétrique [ɔpstetrik] *nf* obstetrics (*U*).

obstination [ɔpstinasjɔ̃] *nf* stubbornness, obstinacy.

obstiné, e [ɔpstine] *adj* **1.** [entêté] stubborn, obstinate - **2.** [acharné] dogged.

obstiner [3] [ɔpstine] ➤ **s'obstiner** *vp* to insist ; **s'obstiner à faire qqch** to persist stubbornly in doing sthg ; **s'obstiner dans qqch** to cling stubbornly to sthg.

obstruction [ɔpstryksjɔ̃] *nf* **1.** MÉD obstruction, blockage - **2.** POLIT & SPORT obstruction.

obstruer [3] [ɔpstrye] *vt* to block, to obstruct. ➤ **s'obstruer** *vp* to become blocked.

obtempérer [18] [ɔptɑ̃pere] *vi* **: obtempérer à** to comply with.

obtenir [40] [ɔptənir] *vt* to get, to obtain ; **obtenir qqch de qqn** to get sthg from sb ; **obtenir qqch à** OU **pour qqn** to obtain sthg for sb.

obtention [ɔptɑ̃sjɔ̃] *nf* obtaining.

obtenu, e [ɔptəny] *pp* ➤ **obtenir.**

obturer [3] [ɔptyre] *vt* to close, to seal ; [dent] to fill.

obtus, e [ɔpty, yz] *adj* obtuse.

obus [ɔby] *nm* shell.

OC (*abr écrite de* **ondes courtes**) SW.

occasion [ɔkazjɔ̃] *nf* **1.** [possibilité, chance] opportunity, chance ; **saisir l'occasion (de faire qqch)** to seize OU grab the chance (to do sthg) ; **rater une occasion (de faire qqch)** to miss a chance (to do sthg) ; **à l'occasion** some time ; [de temps en temps] sometimes, on occasion ; **à la première occasion** at the first opportunity - **2.** [circonstance] occasion ; **à l'occasion de** on the occasion of - **3.** [bonne affaire] bargain. ➤ **d'occasion** *loc adv* & *loc adj* second-hand.

occasionnel, elle [ɔkazjɔnɛl] *adj* [irrégulier - visite, problème] occasional ; [- travail] casual.

occasionner [3] [ɔkazjɔne] *vt* to cause.

occident [ɔksidɑ̃] *nm* west. ➤ **Occident** *nm* **: l'Occident** the West.

occidental, e, aux [ɔksidɑ̃tal, o] *adj* western. ➤ **Occidental, e** (*pl* -aux) *nm, f* Westerner.

occlusion [ɔklyzjɔ̃] *nf* **1.** MÉD blockage, obstruction - **2.** LING & CHIM occlusion.

occulte [ɔkylt] *adj* occult.

occulter [3] [ɔkylte] *vt* [sentiments] to conceal.

occupation [ɔkypasjɔ̃] *nf* **1.** [activité] occupation, job - **2.** MIL occupation.

occupé, e [ɔkype] *adj* **1.** [personne] busy ; **être occupé à qqch** to be busy with sthg - **2.** [appartement, zone] occupied - **3.** [place] taken ; [toilettes] engaged UK ; **c'est occupé** [téléphone] it's engaged UK OU busy US.

occuper [3] [ɔkype] *vt* **1.** [gén] to occupy - **2.** [espace] to take up - **3.** [place, poste] to hold - **4.** [main-d'œuvre] to employ. ➤ **s'occuper** *vp* **1.** [s'activer] to keep o.s. busy ; **s'occuper à qqch/à faire qqch** to be busy with sthg/doing sthg - **2. : s'occuper de qqch** [se charger de] to take care of sthg, to deal with sthg ; [s'intéresser à] to take an interest in, to be interested in ; **occupez-vous de vos affaires!** mind your own business! - **3.** [prendre soin] **: s'occuper de qqn** to take care of sb, to look after sb.

occurrence [ɔkyrɑ̃s] *nf* **1.** [circonstance] **: en l'occurrence** in this case - **2.** LING occurrence.

OCDE (*abr de* **Organisation de coopération et de développement économique**) *nf* OECD.

océan [ɔseɑ̃] *nm* ocean ; **l'océan Antarctique** the Antarctic Ocean ; **l'océan Arctique** the Arctic Ocean ; **l'océan Atlantique** the Atlantic Ocean ; **l'océan Indien** the Indian Ocean ; **l'océan Pacifique** the Pacific Ocean.

Océanie [ɔseani] *nf* **: l'Océanie** Oceania.

océanique [ɔseanik] *adj* ocean (*avant n*).

océanographie [ɔseanɔgrafi] *nf* oceanography.

ocre [ɔkr] *adj inv* & *nf* ochre UK, ocher US.

octante [ɔktɑ̃t] *adj num inv Belgique* & *Suisse* eighty.

octave [ɔktav] *nf* octave.

octet [ɔktɛ] *nm* INFORM byte.

octobre [ɔktɔbr] *nm* October ; *voir aussi* **septembre.**

octogénaire [ɔktɔʒenɛr] *nmf* & *adj* octogenarian.

octroyer [13] [ɔktrwaje] *vt* **: octroyer qqch à qqn** to grant sb sthg, to grant sthg to sb. ➤ **s'octroyer** *vp* to grant o.s., to treat o.s. to.

oculaire [ɔkylɛr] <> *nm* eyepiece. <> *adj* ocular, eye (*avant n*) ; **témoin oculaire** eyewitness.

oculiste [ɔkylist] *nmf* ophthalmologist.

ode [ɔd] *nf* ode.

odeur [ɔdœr] *nf* smell.

odieux, euse [ɔdjø, øz] *adj* **1.** [crime] odious, abominable - **2.** [personne, attitude] unbearable, obnoxious.

odorant, e [ɔdɔrɑ̃, ɑ̃t] *adj* sweet-smelling, fragrant.

odorat [ɔdɔra] *nm* (sense of) smell.

œdème [edɛm] *nm* oedema *UK*, edema *US*.

œil [œj] (*pl* **yeux** [jø]) *nm* [gén] eye ; **yeux bridés/exorbités/globuleux** slanting/bulging/protruding eyes ; **avoir les yeux cernés** to have bags under one's eyes ; **baisser/lever les yeux** to look down/up, to lower/raise one's eyes ; **à l'œil nu** to the naked eye ; **à vue d'œil** visibly ; **avoir qqch/qqn à l'œil** to have one's eye on sthg/sb ; **n'avoir pas froid aux yeux** not to be afraid of anything, to have plenty of nerve ; **mon œil !** *fam* like hell! ; **cela saute aux yeux** it's obvious.

œillade [œjad] *nf* wink ; **lancer une œillade à qqn** to wink at sb.

œillère [œjɛr] *nf* eyebath. ◆ **œillères** *nfpl* blinkers *UK*, blinders *US*.

œillet [œjɛ] *nm* **1.** [fleur] carnation - **2.** [de chaussure] eyelet.

œnologue [enɔlɔg] *nmf* wine expert.

œsophage [ezɔfaʒ] *nm* oesophagus *UK*, esophagus *US*.

œstrogène [ɛstrɔʒɛn] *nm* oestrogen *UK*, estrogen *US*.

œuf [œf] *nm* egg ; **œuf à la coque/au plat/poché** boiled/fried/poached egg ; **œuf mollet/dur** soft-boiled/hard-boiled egg ; **œufs brouillés** scrambled eggs.

œuvre [œvr] *nf* **1.** [travail] work ; **être à l'œuvre** to be working ou at work ; **se mettre à l'œuvre** to get down to work ; **mettre qqch en œuvre** to make use of sthg ; [loi, accord, projet] to implement sthg - **2.** [artistique] work ; [ensemble de la production d'un artiste] works *pl* ; **œuvre d'art** work of art ; **œuvre de bienfaisance** charity, charitable organization ; [organisation] charity.

off [ɔf] *adj inv* CINÉ [voix, son] off.

offense [ɔfɑ̃s] *nf* **1.** [insulte] insult - **2.** RELIG trespass.

offenser [3] [ɔfɑ̃se] *vt* **1.** [personne] to offend - **2.** [bon goût] to offend against. ◆ **s'offenser** *vp* : **s'offenser de** to take offence *UK* ou offense *US* at, to be offended by.

offensif, ive [ɔfɑ̃sif, iv] *adj* offensive. ◆ **offensive** *nf* **1.** MIL offensive ; **passer à l'offensive** to go on the offensive ; **prendre l'offensive** to take the offensive - **2.** *fig* [du froid] (sudden) onset.

offert, e [ɔfɛr, ɛrt] *pp* ▶ **offrir.**

office [ɔfis] *nm* **1.** [bureau] office, agency ; **office du tourisme** tourist office - **2.** [fonction] : **faire office de** to act as ; **remplir son office** to do its job, to fulfil its function

- **3.** RELIG service. ◆ **d'office** *loc adv* automatically, as a matter of course ; **commis d'office** officially appointed.

officialiser [3] [ɔfisjalize] *vt* to make official.

officiel, elle [ɔfisjɛl] *adj & nm, f* official.

officier[1] [9] [ɔfisje] *vi* to officiate.

officier[2] [ɔfisje] *nm* officer.

officieux, euse [ɔfisjø, øz] *adj* unofficial.

offrande [ɔfrɑ̃d] *nf* **1.** [don] offering - **2.** RELIG offertory.

offre [ɔfr] *nf* **1.** [proposition] offer ; [aux enchères] bid ; [pour contrat] tender ; **'offres d'emploi'** 'situations vacant *UK*', 'help wanted *US*', 'vacancies' ; **offre d'essai** trial offer ; **offre de lancement** introductory offer ; **offre publique d'achat** takeover bid - **2.** ÉCON supply ; **la loi de l'offre et de la demande** the law of supply and demand.

offrir [34] [ɔfrir] *vt* **1.** [faire cadeau] : **offrir qqch à qqn** to give sb sthg, to give sthg to sb - **2.** [proposer] : **offrir qqch à qqn** to offer sb sthg ou sthg to sb - **3.** [présenter] to offer, to present ; **son visage n'offrait rien d'accueillant** his/her face showed no sign of welcome. ◆ **s'offrir** *vp* **1.** [croisière, livre] to treat o.s. - **2.** [se présenter] to present itself - **3.** [se proposer] to offer one's services, to offer o.s.

offusquer [3] [ɔfyske] *vt* to offend. ◆ **s'offusquer** *vp* : **s'offusquer (de)** to take offence *UK* ou offense *US*(at).

ogive [ɔʒiv] *nf* **1.** ARCHIT ogive - **2.** MIL [d'obus] head ; [de fusée] nosecone ; **ogive nucléaire** nuclear warhead.

OGM (*abr de* **organisme génétiquement modifié**) *nm* GMO.

ogre, ogresse [ɔgr, ɔgrɛs] *nm, f* ogre (*f* ogress).

oh [o] *interj* oh! ; **oh là là!** dear oh dear!

ohé [ɔe] *interj* hey!

oie [wa] *nf* goose.

oignon [ɔɲɔ̃] *nm* **1.** [plante] onion - **2.** [bulbe] bulb - **3.** MÉD bunion.

oiseau, x [wazo] *nm* **1.** ZOOL bird ; **oiseau de proie** bird of prey - **2.** *fam péj* [individu] character.

oisif, ive [wazif, iv] ⋄ *adj* idle. ⋄ *nm, f* man of leisure (*f* woman of leisure).

oisillon [wazijɔ̃] *nm* fledgling.

oisiveté [wazivte] *nf* idleness.

O.K. [ɔke] *interj fam* okay.

ola [ɔla] *nf* Mexican wave *UK*, wave *US*.

oléoduc [ɔleɔdyk] *nm* (oil) pipeline.

olfactif, ive [ɔlfaktif, iv] *adj* olfactory.

olive [ɔliv] *nf* olive.

olivier [ɔlivje] *nm* [arbre] olive tree ; [bois] olive wood.

OLP (abr de **Organisation de libération de la Palestine**) nf PLO.

olympique [ɔlɛ̃pik] adj Olympic (avant n).

ombilical, e, aux [ɔ̃bilikal, o] adj umbilical.

ombrage [ɔ̃braʒ] nm shade.

ombragé, e [ɔ̃braʒe] adj shady.

ombrageux, euse [ɔ̃braʒø, øz] adj **1.** [personne] touchy, prickly - **2.** [cheval] nervous, skittish.

ombre [ɔ̃br] nf **1.** [zone sombre] shade ; **à l'ombre de** [arbre] in the shade of ; [personne] in the shadow of ; **laisser qqch dans l'ombre** fig to deliberately ignore sthg ; **vivre dans l'ombre** fig to live in obscurity - **2.** [forme, fantôme] shadow - **3.** [trace] hint.

ombrelle [ɔ̃brɛl] nf parasol.

OMC (abr de **Organisation mondiale du commerce**) nf WTO.

omelette [ɔmlɛt] nf omelette.

omettre [84] [ɔmɛtr] vt to omit ; **omettre de faire qqch** to omit to do sthg.

omis, e [ɔmi, iz] pp ▶ **omettre**.

omission [ɔmisjɔ̃] nf omission ; **par omission** by omission.

omnibus [ɔmnibys] nm stopping UK ou local US train.

omniprésent, e [ɔmniprezɑ̃, ɑ̃t] adj omnipresent.

omnisports [ɔmnispɔr] adj inv sports (avant n).

omnivore [ɔmnivɔr] ◇ nm omnivore. ◇ adj omnivorous.

omoplate [ɔmɔplat] nf [os] shoulder blade ; [épaule] shoulder.

OMS (abr de **Organisation mondiale de la santé**) nf WHO.

on [ɔ̃] pron indéf **1.** [indéterminé] you, one ; **on n'a pas le droit de fumer ici** you're not allowed ou one isn't allowed to smoke here, smoking isn't allowed here - **2.** [les gens, l'espèce humaine] they, people ; **on vit de plus en plus vieux en Europe** people in Europe are living longer and longer - **3.** [quelqu'un] someone ; **on vous a appelé au téléphone ce matin** there was a telephone call for you this morning - **4.** fam [nous] we ; **on s'en va** we're off, we're going.

oncle [ɔ̃kl] nm uncle.

onctueux, euse [ɔ̃ktɥø, øz] adj smooth.

onde [ɔ̃d] nf PHYS wave. ▶ **ondes** nfpl [radio] air sg.

ondée [ɔ̃de] nf shower (of rain).

ondoyer [13] [ɔ̃dwaje] vi to ripple.

ondulation [ɔ̃dylasjɔ̃] nf **1.** [mouvement] rippling ; [de sol, terrain] undulation - **2.** [de coiffure] wave.

onduler [3] [ɔ̃dyle] vi [drapeau] to ripple, to wave ; [cheveux] to be wavy ; [route] to undulate.

onéreux, euse [ɔnerø, øz] adj costly.

ongle [ɔ̃gl] nm **1.** [de personne] fingernail, nail ; **se ronger les ongles** to bite one's nails - **2.** [d'animal] claw.

onglet [ɔ̃glɛ] nm **1.** [de reliure] tab - **2.** [de lame] thumbnail groove - **3.** CULIN top skirt.

onguent [ɔ̃gɑ̃] nm ointment.

onomatopée [ɔnɔmatɔpe] nf onomatopoeia.

ont ▶ avoir.

ONU, Onu [ɔny] (abr de **Organisation des Nations unies**) nf UN, UNO.

onyx [ɔniks] nm onyx.

onze [ɔ̃z] ◇ adj num inv eleven. ◇ nm [chiffre & SPORT] eleven ; voir aussi **six**.

onzième [ɔ̃zjɛm] adj num inv, nm & nmf eleventh.

OPA (abr de **offre publique d'achat**) nf takeover bid.

opacité [ɔpasite] nf opacity.

opale [ɔpal] nf & adj inv opal.

opaline [ɔpalin] nf opaline.

opaque [ɔpak] adj : **opaque (à)** opaque (to).

OPEP, Opep [ɔpɛp] (abr de **Organisation des pays exportateurs de pétrole**) nf OPEC.

opéra [ɔpera] nm **1.** MUS opera - **2.** [théâtre] opera house.

opéra-comique [ɔperakɔmik] nm light opera.

opérateur, trice [ɔperatœr, tris] nm, f operator.

opération [ɔperasjɔ̃] nf **1.** [gén] operation - **2.** COMM deal, transaction.

opérationnel, elle [ɔperasjɔnɛl] adj operational.

opérer [18] [ɔpere] ◇ vt **1.** MÉD to operate on - **2.** [exécuter] to carry out, to implement ; [choix, tri] to make. ◇ vi [agir] to take effect ; [personne] to operate, to proceed. ▶ **s'opérer** vp to come about, to take place.

opérette [ɔperet] nf operetta.

ophtalmologiste [ɔftalmɔlɔʒist] nmf ophthalmologist.

Opinel® [ɔpinɛl] nm folding knife used especially for outdoor activities, scouting etc.

opiniâtre [ɔpinjatr] adj **1.** [caractère, personne] stubborn, obstinate - **2.** [effort] dogged ; [travail] unrelenting ; [fièvre, toux] persistent.

opinion [ɔpinjɔ̃] nf opinion ; **avoir (une) bonne/mauvaise opinion de** to have a good/bad opinion of ; **l'opinion publique** public opinion.

opium [ɔpjɔm] nm opium.

opportun, e [ɔpɔrtœ̃, yn] *adj* opportune, timely.

opportuniste [ɔpɔrtynist] <> *nmf* opportunist. <> *adj* opportunistic.

opportunité [ɔpɔrtynite] *nf* **1.** [à-propos] opportuneness, timeliness - **2.** [occasion] opportunity.

opposant, e [ɔpozɑ̃, ɑ̃t] <> *adj* opposing. <> *nm, f* : opposant (à) opponent (of).

opposé, e [ɔpoze] *adj* **1.** [direction, côté, angle] opposite - **2.** [intérêts, opinions] conflicting ; [forces] opposing - **3.** [hostile] : **opposé à** opposed to. ⬛ **opposé** *nm* : **l'opposé** the opposite ; **à l'opposé de** in the opposite direction from ; *fig* unlike, contrary to.

opposer [3] [ɔpoze] *vt* **1.** [mettre en opposition - choses, notions] : **opposer qqch (à)** to contrast sthg (with) - **2.** [mettre en présence - personnes, armées] to oppose ; **opposer deux équipes** to bring two teams together ; **opposer qqn à qqn** to pit ou set sb against sb - **3.** [refus, protestation, objection] to put forward - **4.** [diviser] to divide. ⬛ **s'opposer** *vp* **1.** [contraster] to contrast - **2.** [entrer en conflit] to clash - **3.** : **s'opposer à** [se dresser contre] to oppose, to be opposed to ; **s'opposer à ce que qqn fasse qqch** to be opposed to sb's doing sthg.

opposition [ɔpozisjɔ̃] *nf* **1.** [gén] opposition ; **faire opposition à** [décision, mariage] to oppose ; [chèque] to stop *UK* ; **entrer en opposition avec** to come into conflict with - **2.** DR : **opposition (à)** objection (to) - **3.** [contraste] contrast ; **par opposition à** in contrast with, as opposed to.

oppresser [4] [ɔprese] *vt* **1.** [étouffer] to suffocate, to stifle - **2.** *fig* [tourmenter] to oppress.

oppresseur [ɔprescœr] *nm* oppressor.

oppressif, ive [ɔpresif, iv] *adj* oppressive.

oppression [ɔpresjɔ̃] *nf* **1.** [asservissement] oppression - **2.** [malaise] tightness of the chest.

opprimé, e [ɔprime] <> *adj* oppressed. <> *nm, f* oppressed person.

opprimer [3] [ɔprime] *vt* **1.** [asservir] to oppress - **2.** [étouffer] to stifle.

opter [3] [ɔpte] *vi* : **opter pour** to opt for.

opticien, enne [ɔptisjɛ̃, ɛn] *nm, f* optician.

optimal, e, aux [ɔptimal, o] *adj* optimal.

optimiste [ɔptimist] <> *nmf* optimist. <> *adj* optimistic.

option [ɔpsjɔ̃] *nf* **1.** [gén] option ; **prendre une option sur** FIN to take (out) an option on - **2.** [accessoire] optional extra.

optionnel, elle [ɔpsjɔnɛl] *adj* optional.

optique [ɔptik] <> *nf* **1.** [science, technique] optics (U) - **2.** [perspective] viewpoint. <> *adj* [nerf] optic ; [verre] optical.

opulence [ɔpylɑ̃s] *nf* **1.** [richesse] opulence - **2.** [ampleur] fullness, ampleness.

opulent, e [ɔpylɑ̃, ɑ̃t] *adj* **1.** [riche] rich - **2.** [gros] ample.

or¹ [ɔr] *nm* **1.** [métal, couleur] gold ; **en or** [objet] gold *(avant n)* ; **une occasion en or** a golden opportunity ; **une affaire en or** [achat] an excellent bargain ; [commerce] a lucrative line of business ; **j'ai une femme en or** I've a wonderful wife ; **or massif** solid gold - **2.** [dorure] gilding.

or² [ɔr] *conj* [au début d'une phrase] now ; [pour introduire un contraste] well, but.

oracle [ɔrakl] *nm* oracle.

orage [ɔraʒ] *nm* [tempête] storm.

orageux, euse [ɔraʒø, øz] *adj* stormy.

oraison [ɔrɛzɔ̃] *nf* prayer ; **oraison funèbre** funeral oration.

oral, e, aux [ɔral, o] *adj* oral. ⬛ **oral** *nm* oral (examination) ; **oral de rattrapage** *oral examination taken after failing written exams.*

oralement [ɔralmɑ̃] *adv* orally.

orange [ɔrɑ̃ʒ] <> *nf* orange. <> *nm & adj inv* [couleur] orange.

orangé, e [ɔrɑ̃ʒe] *adj* orangey.

orangeade [ɔrɑ̃ʒad] *nf* orange squash *UK*, orangeade *US*.

oranger [ɔrɑ̃ʒe] *nm* orange tree.

orang-outan, orang-outang [ɔrɑ̃utɑ̃] *nm* orang-utang.

orateur, trice [ɔratœr, tris] *nm, f* **1.** [conférencier] speaker - **2.** [personne éloquente] orator.

orbital, e, aux [ɔrbital, o] *adj* [mouvement] orbital ; [station] orbiting.

orbite [ɔrbit] *nf* **1.** ANAT (eye) socket - **2.** *fig* & ASTRON orbit ; **mettre sur orbite** AÉRON to put into orbit ; *fig* to launch.

orchestre [ɔrkɛstr] *nm* **1.** MUS orchestra - **2.** CINÉ & THÉÂTRE stalls *pl UK*, orchestra *US* ; **fauteuil d'orchestre** seat in the stalls *UK*, orchestra seat *US*.

orchestrer [3] [ɔrkɛstre] *vt* *litt* & *fig* to orchestrate.

orchidée [ɔrkide] *nf* orchid.

ordinaire [ɔrdinɛr] <> *adj* **1.** [usuel, standard] ordinary, normal - **2.** *péj* [commun] ordinary, common. <> *nm* **1.** [moyenne] : **l'ordinaire** the ordinary - **2.** [alimentation] usual diet. ⬛ **d'ordinaire** *loc adv* normally, usually.

ordinal, e, aux [ɔrdinal, o] *adj* ordinal. ⬛ **ordinal, aux** *nm* ordinal (number).

ordinateur [ɔrdinatœr] *nm* computer ; **ordinateur individuel** personal computer, PC ; **ordinateur de bureau** desktop (computer) ; **ordinateur portable** laptop (computer) ; **ordinateur de poche** palmtop.

ordonnance [ɔrdɔnɑ̃s] <> nf **1.** MÉD prescription - **2.** [de gouvernement, juge] order. <> nm & nf MIL orderly.

ordonné, e [ɔrdɔne] adj [maison, élève] tidy.

ordonner [3] [ɔrdɔne] vt **1.** [ranger] to organize, to put in order - **2.** [enjoindre] to order, to tell ; **ordonner à qqn de faire qqch** to order sb to do sthg - **3.** RELIG to ordain - **4.** MATH to arrange in order. ◆ **s'ordonner** vp to be arranged OU put in order.

ordre [ɔrdr] nm **1.** [gén, MIL & RELIG] order ; **par ordre alphabétique/chronologique/décroissant** in alphabetical/chronological/descending order ; **donner un ordre à qqn** to give sb an order ; **être aux ordres de qqn** to be at sb's disposal ; **jusqu'à nouvel ordre** until further notice ; **l'ordre public** law and order - **2.** [bonne organisation] tidiness, orderliness ; **en ordre** orderly, tidy ; **mettre en ordre** to put in order, to tidy (up) - **3.** [catégorie] : **de premier ordre** first-rate ; **de second ordre** second-rate ; **d'ordre privé/pratique** of a private/practical nature ; **pouvez-vous me donner un ordre de grandeur?** can you give me some idea of the size/amount etc? - **4.** [corporation] professional association ; **l'Ordre des médecins** ≃ the British Medical Association UK, ≃ the American Medical Association US - **5.** FIN : **à l'ordre de** payable to. ◆ **ordre du jour** nm **1.** [de réunion] agenda ; **à l'ordre du jour** [de réunion] on the agenda ; fig topical - **2.** MIL order of the day.

ordure [ɔrdyr] nf **1.** fig [grossièreté] filth (U) - **2.** péj [personne] scum (U), bastard. ◆ **ordures** nfpl [déchets] rubbish (U) UK, garbage (U) US.

ordurier, ère [ɔrdyrje, ɛr] adj filthy, obscene.

orée [ɔre] nf edge.

oreille [ɔrɛj] nf **1.** ANAT ear - **2.** [ouïe] hearing - **3.** [de fauteuil, écrou] wing ; [de marmite, tasse] handle.

oreiller [ɔreje] nm pillow.

oreillette [ɔrɛjɛt] nf **1.** [du cœur] auricle - **2.** [de casquette] earflap.

oreillons [ɔrɛjɔ̃] nmpl mumps sg.

ores [ɔr] ◆ **d'ores et déjà** loc adv from now on.

orfèvre [ɔrfɛvr] nm goldsmith ; [d'argent] silversmith.

orfèvrerie [ɔrfɛvrəri] nf **1.** [art] goldsmith's art ; [d'argent] silversmith's art - **2.** [commerce] goldsmith's trade ; [d'argent] silversmith's trade.

organe [ɔrgan] nm **1.** ANAT organ - **2.** [institution] organ, body - **3.** fig [porte-parole] representative.

organigramme [ɔrganigram] nm **1.** [hiérarchique] organization chart - **2.** INFORM flow chart.

organique [ɔrganik] adj organic.

organisateur, trice [ɔrganizatœr, tris] <> adj organizing (avant n). <> nm, f organizer.

organisation [ɔrganizasjɔ̃] nf organization ; **Organisation mondiale du commerce** World Trade Organization.

organisé, e [ɔrganize] adj organized.

organiser [3] [ɔrganize] vt to organize. ◆ **s'organiser** vp **1.** [personne] to be OU get organized - **2.** [prendre forme] to take shape.

organisme [ɔrganism] nm **1.** BIOL & ZOOL organism ; **organisme génétiquement modifié** genetically modified organism - **2.** [institution] body, organization.

organiste [ɔrganist] nmf organist.

orgasme [ɔrgasm] nm orgasm.

orge [ɔrʒ] nf barley.

orgie [ɔrʒi] nf orgy.

orgue [ɔrg] nm organ.

orgueil [ɔrgœj] nm pride.

orgueilleux, euse [ɔrgœjø, øz] <> adj proud. <> nm, f proud person.

orient [ɔrjɑ̃] nm east. ◆ **Orient** nm : **l'Orient** the Orient, the East.

oriental, e, aux [ɔrjɑ̃tal, o] adj [région, frontière] eastern ; [d'Extrême-Orient] oriental.

orientation [ɔrjɑ̃tasjɔ̃] nf **1.** [direction] orientation ; **avoir le sens de l'orientation** to have a good sense of direction - **2.** SCOL career - **3.** [de maison] aspect - **4.** fig [de politique, recherche] direction, trend.

orienté, e [ɔrjɑ̃te] adj [tendancieux] biased.

orienter [3] [ɔrjɑ̃te] vt **1.** [disposer] to position - **2.** [voyageur, élève, recherches] to guide, to direct. ◆ **s'orienter** vp **1.** [se repérer] to find OU get one's bearings - **2.** fig [se diriger] : **s'orienter vers** to move towards OU toward US.

orifice [ɔrifis] nm orifice.

originaire [ɔriʒinɛr] adj **1.** [natif] : **être originaire de** to originate from ; [personne] to be a native of - **2.** [premier] original.

original, e, aux [ɔriʒinal, o] <> adj **1.** [premier, inédit] original - **2.** [singulier] eccentric. <> nm, f [personne] (outlandish) character. ◆ **original, aux** nm [œuvre, document] original.

originalité [ɔriʒinalite] nf **1.** [nouveauté] originality ; [caractéristique] original feature - **2.** [excentricité] eccentricity.

origine [ɔriʒin] nf **1.** [gén] origin ; **d'origine** [originel] original ; [de départ] of origin ; **pays d'origine** country of origin ; **d'origine**

anglaise of English origin ; **à l'origine** originally - 2. [souche] origins pl - 3. [provenance] source.

ORL nmf (abr de oto-rhino-laryngologiste) ENT specialist.

orme [ɔrm] nm elm.

ornement [ɔrnəmɑ̃] nm 1. [gén & MUS] ornament ; **d'ornement** [plante, arbre] ornamental - 2. ARCHIT embellishment.

orner [3] [ɔrne] vt 1. [décorer] : **orner (de)** to decorate (with) - 2. [agrémenter] to adorn.

ornière [ɔrnjɛr] nf rut.

ornithologie [ɔrnitɔlɔʒi] nf ornithology.

orphelin, e [ɔrfəlɛ̃, in] <> adj orphan (avant n), orphaned. <> nm, f orphan.

orphelinat [ɔrfəlina] nm orphanage.

orteil [ɔrtɛj] nm toe.

orthodontiste [ɔrtɔdɔ̃tist] nmf orthodontist.

orthodoxe [ɔrtɔdɔks] <> adj 1. RELIG Orthodox - 2. [conformiste] orthodox. <> nmf RELIG Orthodox Christian.

orthographe [ɔrtɔɡraf] nf spelling.

orthopédiste [ɔrtɔpedist] nmf orthop(a)edist.

orthophoniste [ɔrtɔfɔnist] nmf speech therapist.

ortie [ɔrti] nf nettle.

os [ɔs] (pl os [o]) nm 1. [gén] bone ; **os à moelle** marrowbone - 2. fam fig [difficulté] snag, hitch.

oscar [ɔskar] nm CINÉ Oscar.

oscariser [3] [ɔskarize] vt to award an oscar to.

oscillation [ɔsilasjɔ̃] nf oscillation ; [de navire] rocking.

osciller [3] [ɔsile] vi 1. [se balancer] to swing ; [navire] to rock - 2. [vaciller, hésiter] to waver.

osé, e [oze] adj daring, audacious.

oseille [ozɛj] nf BOT sorrel.

oser [3] [oze] vt to dare ; **oser faire qqch** to dare (to) do sthg.

osier [ozje] nm 1. BOT osier - 2. [fibre] wicker.

Oslo [ɔslo] npr Oslo.

ossature [ɔsatyr] nf 1. ANAT skeleton - 2. fig [structure] framework.

ossements [ɔsmɑ̃] nmpl bones.

osseux, euse [ɔsø, øz] adj 1. ANAT & MÉD bone (avant n) - 2. [maigre] bony.

ossuaire [ɔsɥɛr] nm ossuary.

ostensible [ɔstɑ̃sibl] adj conspicuous.

ostentation [ɔstɑ̃tasjɔ̃] nf ostentation.

ostéopathe [ɔsteopat] nmf osteopath.

otage [ɔtaʒ] nm hostage ; **prendre qqn en otage** to take sb hostage.

OTAN, Otan [ɔtɑ̃] (abr de Organisation du traité de l'Atlantique Nord) nf NATO.

otarie [ɔtari] nf sea lion.

ôter [3] [ote] vt 1. [enlever] to take off - 2. [soustraire] to take away - 3. [retirer, prendre] : **ôter qqch à qqn** to take sthg away from sb.

otite [ɔtit] nf ear infection.

oto-rhino-laryngologie [ɔtɔrinɔlarɛ̃ɡɔlɔ-ʒi] nf ear, nose and throat medicine, ENT.

ou [u] conj 1. [indique une alternative, une approximation] or - 2. [sinon] : **ou (bien)** or (else). ← **ou (bien)... ou (bien)** loc correlative either... or ; **ou c'est elle, ou c'est moi!** it's either her or me!

où [u] <> pron rel 1. [spatial] where ; **le village où j'habite** the village where I live, the village I live in ; **pose-le là où tu l'as trouvé** put it back where you found it ; **partout où vous irez** wherever you go - 2. [temporel] that ; **le jour où je suis venu** the day (that) I came. <> adv where ; **je vais où je veux** I go where I please ; **où que vous alliez** wherever you go. <> adv interr where? ; **où vas-tu?** where are you going? ; **dites-moi où il est allé** tell me where he's gone. ← **d'où** loc adv [conséquence] hence.

ouaté, e [wate] adj 1. [garni d'ouate] cotton wool UK (avant n), cotton US (avant n) ; [vêtement] quilted - 2. fig [feutré] muffled.

oubli [ubli] nm 1. [acte d'oublier] forgetting - 2. [négligence] omission ; [étourderie] oversight - 3. [général] oblivion ; **tomber dans l'oubli** to sink into oblivion.

oublier [10] [ublije] vt to forget ; [laisser quelque part] to leave behind ; **oublier de faire qqch** to forget to do sthg.

oubliettes [ublijɛt] nfpl dungeon sg.

ouest [wɛst] <> nm west ; **un vent d'ouest** a westerly wind ; **à l'ouest** in the west ; **à l'ouest (de)** to the west (of). <> adj inv [gén] west ; [province, région] western.

ouest-allemand, e [wɛstalmɑ̃, ɑ̃d] adj West German.

ouf [uf] interj phew!

Ouganda [uɡɑ̃da] nm : **l'Ouganda** Uganda.

oui [wi] <> adv yes ; **tu viens? - oui** are you coming? - yes (I am) ; **tu viens, oui ou non?** are you coming or not?, are you coming or aren't you? ; **je crois que oui** I think so ; **faire signe que oui** to nod ; **mais oui, bien sûr que oui** yes, of course. <> nm inv yes ; **pour un oui pour un non** for no apparent reason.

ouï-dire [widir] nm inv : **par ouï-dire** by ou from hearsay.

ouïe [wi] nf hearing ; **avoir l'ouïe fine** to have excellent hearing. ← **ouïes** nfpl [de poisson] gills.

ouragan [uraɡɑ̃] nm MÉTÉOR hurricane.

ourlet [urlɛ] nm COUT hem.

ours [urs] *nm* bear ; **ours (en peluche)** teddy (bear) ; **ours polaire** polar bear.

ourse [urs] *nf* she-bear.

oursin [ursɛ̃] *nm* sea urchin.

ourson [ursɔ̃] *nm* bear cub.

outil [uti] *nm* tool ; **boîte** OU **caisse à outils** toolbox.

outillage [utijaʒ] *nm* [équipement] tools *pl*, equipment.

outrage [utraʒ] *nm* **1.** *sout* [insulte] insult - **2.** DR : **outrage à la pudeur** indecent behaviour *(U) UK* OU behavior *(U) US*.

outrager [17] [utraʒe] *vt* [offenser] to insult.

outrance [utrãs] *nf* excess ; **à outrance** excessively.

outrancier, ère [utrãsje, ɛr] *adj* extravagant.

outre[1] [utr] *nf* wineskin.

outre[2] [utr] <> *prép* besides, as well as. <> *adv* : **passer outre** to go on, to proceed further. **en outre** *loc adv* moreover, besides.

outre-Atlantique [utratlãtik] *loc adv* across the Atlantic.

outre-Manche [utrəmãʃ] *loc adv* across the Channel.

outremer [utrəmɛr] <> *nm* [pierre] lapis lazuli ; [couleur] ultramarine. <> *adj inv* ultramarine.

outre-mer [utrəmɛr] *loc adv* overseas.

outrepasser [3] [utrəpase] *vt* to exceed.

outrer [3] [utre] *vt* [personne] to outrage.

outre-Rhin [utrərɛ̃] *loc adv* across the Rhine.

outsider [awtsajdœr] *nm* outsider.

ouvert, e [uvɛr, ɛrt] <> *pp* ➤ **ouvrir**. <> *adj* **1.** [gén] open ; **grand ouvert** wide open - **2.** [robinet] on, running.

ouvertement [uvɛrtəmã] *adv* openly.

ouverture [uvɛrtyr] *nf* **1.** [gén] opening ; [d'hostilités] outbreak ; **ouverture d'esprit** open-mindedness - **2.** MUS overture - **3.** PHOTO aperture. **ouvertures** *nfpl* [propositions] overtures.

ouvrable [uvrabl] *adj* working ; **heures ouvrables** hours of business.

ouvrage [uvraʒ] *nm* **1.** [travail] work *(U)*, task ; **se mettre à l'ouvrage** to start work - **2.** [objet produit] (piece of) work ; COUT work *(U)* - **3.** [livre, écrit] work ; **ouvrage de référence** reference work.

ouvré, e [uvre] *adj* : **jour ouvré** working day.

ouvre-boîtes [uvrəbwat] *nm inv* tin opener *UK*, can opener.

ouvre-bouteilles [uvrəbutɛj] *nm inv* bottle opener.

ouvreuse [uvrøz] *nf* usherette.

ouvrier, ère [uvrije, ɛr] <> *adj* [quartier, enfance] working-class ; [conflit] industrial ; [questions, statut] labour *(avant n) UK*, labor *(avant n) US* ; **classe ouvrière** working class. <> *nm, f* worker ; **ouvrier agricole** farm worker ; **ouvrier qualifié** skilled worker ; **ouvrier spécialisé** semiskilled worker.

ouvrir [34] [uvrir] <> *vt* **1.** [gén] to open - **2.** [chemin, voie] to open up - **3.** [gaz] to turn on. <> *vi* to open ; **ouvrir sur qqch** to open onto sthg. **s'ouvrir** *vp* **1.** [porte, fleur] to open - **2.** [route, perspectives] to open up - **3.** [personne] : **s'ouvrir (à qqn)** to confide (in sb), to open up (to sb) - **4.** [se blesser] : **s'ouvrir le genou** to cut one's knee open ; **s'ouvrir les veines** to slash OU cut one's wrists.

ovaire [ovɛr] *nm* ovary.

ovale [oval] *adj & nm* oval.

ovation [ovasjɔ̃] *nf* ovation ; **faire une ovation à qqn** to give sb an ovation.

overbooking [ovœrbukiŋ] *nm* overbooking.

overdose [ovœrdoz] *nf* overdose.

ovin, e [ovɛ̃, in] *adj* ovine. **ovin** *nm* sheep.

OVNI, Ovni [ovni] *(abr de objet volant non identifié) nm* UFO.

oxydation [ɔksidasjɔ̃] *nf* oxidation, oxidization.

oxyde [ɔksid] *nm* oxide.

oxyder [3] [ɔkside] *vt* to oxidize.

oxygène [ɔksiʒɛn] *nm* oxygen.

oxygéné, e [ɔksiʒene] *adj* CHIM oxygenated, ➤ **eau**.

ozone [ozon] *nm* ozone.

p[1]**, P** [pe] *nm inv* p, P.

p[2]**1.** *(abr écrite de page)* p - **2.** *abr écrite de pièce.*

pachyderme [paʃidɛrm] *nm* elephant ; **les pachydermes** (the) pachyderms.

pacifier [9] [pasifje] *vt* to pacify.

pacifique [pasifik] *adj* peaceful.

Pacifique [pasifik] *nm* : **le Pacifique** the Pacific (Ocean).

pacifiste [pasifist] *nmf & adj* pacifist.

pack [pak] *nm* pack.

pacotille [pakɔtij] *nf* shoddy goods *pl*, rubbish ; **de pacotille** cheap.

PACS [paks] (*abr de* **Pacte civil de solidarité**) *nm* Civil Solidarity Pact *civil contract conferring marital rights on the contracting parties.*

pacsé, e [pakse] *nm, f fam person who has signed a PACS agreement,* ≃ (life) partner.

pacser [3] [pakse] ➤ **se pacser** [pakse] *vpi* : **to sign a PACS agreement to have one's relationship legally recognized.**

pacte [pakt] *nm* pact.

pactiser [3] [paktize] *vi* : **pactiser avec** [faire un pacte avec] to make a pact with ; [transiger avec] to come to terms with.

pactole [paktɔl] *nm* gold mine *fig.*

pagaie [pagɛ] *nf* paddle.

pagaille, pagaye, pagaïe [pagaj] *nf fam* mess.

pagayer [11] [pageje] *vi* to paddle.

page [paʒ] <> *nf* **1.** [feuillet] page ; **page blanche** blank page ; **mettre en pages** TYPO to make up (into pages) - **2.** [INFORM page ; **page d'accueil** home page ; **page précédente** page up ; **page suivante** page down ; **être à la page** to be up-to-date. <> *nm* page (boy).

pagne [paɲ] *nm* loincloth.

pagode [pagɔd] *nf* pagoda.

paie, paye [pɛ] *nf* pay (U), wages *pl.*

paiement, payement [pɛmɑ̃] *nm* payment.

païen, ïenne [pajɛ̃, ɛn] *adj & nm, f* pagan, heathen.

paillard, e [pajar, ard] *adj* bawdy.

paillasse [pajas] *nf* **1.** [matelas] straw mattress - **2.** [d'évier] draining board UK, drainboard US.

paillasson [pajasɔ̃] *nm* [tapis] doormat.

paille [paj] *nf* **1.** BOT straw - **2.** [pour boire] straw. ➤ **paille de fer** *nf* steel wool.

pailleté, e [pajte] *adj* sequined.

paillette [pajɛt] *nf* (*gén pl*) **1.** [sur vêtements] sequin, spangle - **2.** [d'or] grain of gold dust - **3.** [de lessive, savon] flake ; **savon en paillettes** soap flakes *pl.*

pain [pɛ̃] *nm* **1.** [aliment] bread ; **un pain** a loaf ; **petit pain** (bread) roll ; **pain de campagne** ≃ farmhouse loaf ; **pain complet** wholemeal UK OU whole wheat US bread ; **pain d'épice** ≃ gingerbread ; **pain de mie** sandwich loaf - **2.** [de savon, cire] bar.

pair, e [pɛr] *adj* even. ➤ **pair** *nm* peer. ➤ **paire** *nf* pair ; **une paire de** [lunettes, ciseaux, chaussures] a pair of. ➤ **au pair** *loc adv* for board and lodging, for one's keep ; **jeune fille au pair** au pair (girl). ➤ **de pair** *loc adv* : **aller de pair avec** to go hand in hand with.

paisible [pɛzibl] *adj* peaceful.

paître [91] [pɛtr] *vi* to graze.

paix [pɛ] *nf* peace ; **en paix** [en harmonie] at peace ; [tranquillement] in peace ; **avoir la paix** to have peace and quiet ; **faire la paix avec qqn** to make peace with sb.

Pakistan [pakistɑ̃] *nm* : **le Pakistan** Pakistan.

palace [palas] *nm* luxury hotel.

palais [palɛ] *nm* **1.** [château] palace - **2.** [grand édifice] centre UK, center US ; **palais de justice** DR law courts *pl* ; **le Grand Palais** the Grand Palais ; **le Petit Palais** the Petit Palais - **3.** ANAT palate.

palan [palɑ̃] *nm* block and tackle, hoist.

pale [pal] *nf* [de rame, d'hélice] blade.

pâle [pal] *adj* pale.

paléontologie [paleɔ̃tɔlɔʒi] *nf* paleontology.

Palestine [palɛstin] *nf* : **la Palestine** Palestine.

palet [palɛ] *nm* [hockey] puck.

palette [palɛt] *nf* [de peintre] palette.

pâleur [palœr] *nf* [de visage] pallor.

palier [palje] *nm* **1.** [d'escalier] landing - **2.** [étape] level - **3.** TECHNOL bearing.

pâlir [32] [palir] *vi* [couleur, lumière] to fade ; [personne] to turn OU go pale.

palissade [palisad] *nf* [clôture] fence ; [de verdure] hedge.

palliatif, ive [paljatif, iv] *adj* palliative. ➤ **palliatif** *nm* **1.** MÉD palliative - **2.** *fig* stopgap measure.

pallier [9] [palje] *vt* to make up for.

palmarès [palmarɛs] *nm* **1.** [de lauréats] list of (medal) winners ; SCOL list of prizewinners - **2.** [de succès] record (of achievements).

palme [palm] *nf* **1.** [de palmier] palm leaf - **2.** [de nageur] flipper - **3.** [décoration, distinction] : **avec palme** MIL ≃ with bar.

palmé, e [palme] *adj* **1.** BOT palmate - **2.** ZOOL web-footed ; [patte] webbed.

palmeraie [palmərɛ] *nf* palm grove.

palmier [palmje] *nm* BOT palm tree.

palmipède [palmipɛd] *nm* web-footed bird.

palombe [palɔ̃b] *nf* woodpigeon.

pâlot, otte [palo, ɔt] *adj* pale, sickly-looking.

palourde [palurd] *nf* clam.

palper [3] [palpe] *vt* [toucher] to feel, to finger ; MÉD to palpate.

palpitant, e [palpitɑ̃, ɑ̃t] *adj* exciting, thrilling.

palpitation [palpitasjɔ̃] *nf* palpitation.

palpiter [3] [palpite] *vi* [paupières] to flutter ; [cœur] to pound.

paludisme [palydism] *nm* malaria.

pâmer [3] [pame] ➤ **se pâmer** *vp litt* [s'évanouir] to swoon (away).

pamphlet [pɑ̃flɛ] *nm* satirical tract.

pamplemousse [pɑ̃pləmus] *nm* grapefruit.

pan [pɑ̃] ◇ *nm* 1. [de vêtement] tail - 2. [d'affiche] piece, bit ; **pan de mur** section of wall. ◇ *interj* bang!

panache [panaʃ] *nm* 1. [de plumes, fumée] plume - 2. [éclat] panache.

panaché, e [panaʃe] *adj* 1. [de plusieurs couleurs] multicoloured *UK*, multicolored *US* - 2. [mélangé] mixed. ➤ **panaché** *nm* shandy *UK*.

Panama [panama] *nm* [pays] : **le Panama** Panama.

panaris [panari] *nm* whitlow.

pancarte [pɑ̃kart] *nf* 1. [de manifestant] placard - 2. [de signalisation] sign.

pancréas [pɑ̃kreas] *nm* pancreas.

pané, e [pane] *adj* breaded, in bread-crumbs.

panier [panje] *nm* basket ; **panier à provisions** shopping basket ; **mettre au panier** *fig* to throw out.

panini [panini] (*pl* **paninis**) *nm* panini.

panique [panik] ◇ *nf* panic. ◇ *adj* panicky ; **être pris d'une peur panique** to be panic-stricken.

paniquer [3] [panike] *vt & vi* to panic.

panne [pan] *nf* [arrêt] breakdown ; **tomber en panne** to break down ; **panne de courant** OU **d'électricité** power failure ; **tomber en panne d'essence** OU **en panne sèche** to run out of petrol *UK* OU gas *US*.

panneau, x [pano] *nm* 1. [pancarte] sign ; **panneau indicateur** signpost ; **panneau publicitaire** (advertising) hoarding *UK*, billboard *US* ; **panneau de signalisation** road sign - 2. [élément] panel.

panoplie [panɔpli] *nf* 1. [jouet] outfit - 2. *fig* [de mesures] package.

panorama [panɔrama] *nm* [vue] view, panorama ; *fig* overview.

panse [pɑ̃s] *nf* 1. [d'estomac] first stomach, rumen - 2. *fam* [gros ventre] belly, paunch - 3. [partie arrondie] bulge.

pansement [pɑ̃smɑ̃] *nm* dressing, bandage ; **pansement (adhésif)** (sticking) plaster *UK*, Band-Aid® *US*.

panser [3] [pɑ̃se] *vt* 1. [plaie] to dress, to bandage ; [jambe] to put a dressing on, to bandage ; [avec pansement adhésif] to put a plaster *UK* OU Band-Aid® *US* on - 2. [cheval] to groom.

pantacourt [pɑ̃takur] *nm* capri pants, capris, clamdiggers.

pantalon [pɑ̃talɔ̃] *nm* trousers *pl UK*, pants *pl US*, pair of trousers *UK* OU pants *US*.

pantelant, e [pɑ̃tlɑ̃, ɑ̃t] *adj* panting, gasping.

panthère [pɑ̃tɛr] *nf* panther.

pantin [pɑ̃tɛ̃] *nm* 1. [jouet] jumping jack - 2. *péj* [personne] puppet.

pantomime [pɑ̃tɔmim] *nf* [art, pièce] mime.

pantoufle [pɑ̃tufl] *nf* slipper.

PAO (*abr de* **publication assistée par ordinateur**) *nf* DTP.

paon [pɑ̃] *nm* peacock.

papa [papa] *nm* dad, daddy.

papauté [papote] *nf* papacy.

pape [pap] *nm* RELIG pope.

paperasse [papras] *nf péj* 1. [papier sans importance] bumf (*U*) *UK*, papers *pl* - 2. [papiers administratifs] paperwork (*U*).

papeterie [papɛtri] *nf* [magasin] stationer's ; [fabrique] paper mill.

papetier, ère [papɔtje, ɛr] *nm, f* [commerçant] stationer ; [fabricant] paper manufacturer.

papier [papje] *nm* [matière, écrit] paper ; **papier alu** OU **aluminium** aluminium *UK* OU aluminum *US* foil, tinfoil ; **papier carbone** carbon paper ; **papier crépon** crêpe paper ; **papier d'emballage** wrapping paper ; **papier à en-tête** headed notepaper ; **papier hygiénique** OU **toilette** toilet paper ; **papier à lettres** writing paper, notepaper ; **papier peint** wallpaper ; **papier de verre** glasspaper *UK*, sandpaper. ➤ **papiers** *nmpl* : **papiers (d'identité)** (identity) papers.

papier-calque [papjekalk] (*pl* **papiers-calque**) *nm* tracing paper.

papille [papij] *nf* : **papilles gustatives** taste buds.

papillon [papijɔ̃] *nm* 1. ZOOL butterfly - 2. [écrou] wing nut - 3. [nage] butterfly (stroke).

papillonner [3] [papijɔne] *vi* to flit about OU around.

papillote [papijɔt] *nf* 1. [de bonbon] sweet paper OU wrapper *UK*, candy paper *US* - 2. [de cheveux] curl paper.

papilloter [3] [papijɔte] *vi* [lumière] to twinkle ; [yeux] to blink.

papoter [3] [papɔte] *vi fam* to chatter.

paprika [paprika] *nm* paprika.

paquebot [pakbo] *nm* liner.

pâquerette [pakrɛt] *nf* daisy.

Pâques [pak] *nfpl* Easter *sg* ; **joyeuses Pâques** Happy Easter.

paquet [pakɛ] *nm* **1.** [colis] parcel UK, package US - **2.** [emballage] packet UK, package US ; **paquet-cadeau** gift-wrapped parcel UK ou package US.

paquetage [pakta3] *nm* MIL kit.

par [par] *prép* **1.** [spatial] through, by (way of) ; **passer par la Suède et le Danemark** to go via Sweden and Denmark ; **regarder par la fenêtre** to look out of the window ; **par endroits** in places ; **par ici/là** this/that way ; **mon cousin habite par ici** my cousin lives round here - **2.** [temporel] on ; **par un beau jour d'été** on a lovely summer's day ; **par le passé** in the past - **3.** [moyen, manière, cause] by ; **par bateau/train/avion** by boat/train/plane ; **par pitié** out of ou from pity ; **par accident** by accident, by chance - **4.** [introduit le complément d'agent] by ; **faire faire qqch par qqn** to have sthg done by sb - **5.** [sens distributif] per, a ; **une heure par jour** one hour a ou per day ; **deux par deux** two at a time ; **marcher deux par deux** to walk in twos. ● **par-ci par-là** *loc adv* here and there.

para [para] (*abr de* **parachutiste**) *nm fam* para UK.

parabole [parabɔl] *nf* **1.** [récit] parable - **2.** MATH parabola.

parabolique [parabɔlik] *adj* parabolic.

paracétamol [19] [parasetamɔl] *nm* paracetamol.

parachever [19] [paraʃve] *vt* to put the finishing touches to.

parachute [paraʃyt] *nm* parachute ; **parachute ascensionnel** parachute *(for parascending)*.

parachutiste [paraʃytist] *nmf* parachutist ; MIL paratrooper.

parade [parad] *nf* **1.** [spectacle] parade - **2.** [défense] parry ; *fig* riposte.

paradis [paradi] *nm* paradise.

paradoxal, e, aux [paradɔksal, o] *adj* paradoxical.

paradoxe [paradɔks] *nm* paradox.

parafe, paraphe [paraf] *nm* initials *pl*.

parafer, parapher [3] [parafe] *vt* to initial.

paraffine [parafin] *nf* paraffin UK, kerosene US ; [solide] paraffin wax.

parages [para3] *nmpl* : **être** ou **se trouver dans les parages** *fig* to be in the area ou vicinity.

paragraphe [paragraf] *nm* paragraph.

Paraguay [paragwɛ] *nm* : **le Paraguay** Paraguay.

paraître [91] [parɛtr] ⋄ *v att* to look, to seem, to appear. ⋄ *vi* **1.** [se montrer] to appear - **2.** [être publié] to come out, to be published. ⋄ *v impers* : **il paraît/paraîtrait que** it appears/would appear that.

parallèle [paralɛl] ⋄ *nm* parallel ; **établir un parallèle entre** *fig* to draw a parallel between. ⋄ *nf* parallel (line). ⋄ *adj* **1.** [action, en maths] parallel - **2.** [marché] unofficial ; [médecine, énergie] alternative.

parallélisme [paralelism] *nm* parallelism ; [de roues] alignment.

paralyser [3] [paralize] *vt* to paralyse UK, to paralyze US.

paralysie [paralizi] *nf* paralysis.

paramédical, e, aux [paramedikal, o] *adj* paramedical.

paramètre [parametr] *nm* parameter.

paranoïa [paranɔja] *nf* paranoia.

paranoïaque [paranɔjak] ⋄ *adj* paranoid. ⋄ *nmf* paranoiac.

parapente [parapɑ̃t] *nm* paragliding ; **faire du parapente** to go paragliding.

parapet [parapɛ] *nm* parapet.

paraphe = **parafe**.

parapher = **parafer**.

paraphrase [parafraz] *nf* paraphrase.

paraplégique [paraple3ik] *nmf & adj* paraplegic.

parapluie [paraplɥi] *nm* umbrella.

parasite [parazit] ⋄ *nm* parasite. ⋄ *adj* parasitic. ● **parasites** *nmpl* RADIO & TV interference (*U*).

parasol [parasɔl] *nm* parasol, sunshade.

paratonnerre [paratɔner] *nm* lightning conductor UK ou rod US.

paravent [paravɑ̃] *nm* screen.

parc [park] *nm* **1.** [jardin] park ; [de château] grounds *pl* ; **parc d'attractions** amusement park ; **parc de loisirs** ≃ leisure park ; **parc national** national park ; **parc à thème** ≃ theme park - **2.** [pour l'élevage] pen - **3.** [de bébé] playpen - **4.** [de voitures] fleet ; **le parc automobile** the number of cars on the roads. ● **parc des Princes** *npr m* Paris sports stadium, home to football team Paris Saint-Germain.

parcelle [parsel] *nf* **1.** [petite partie] fragment, particle - **2.** [terrain] parcel of land.

parce que [parsk(ə)] *loc conj* because.

parchemin [parʃəmɛ̃] *nm* parchment.

parcimonie [parsimɔni] *nf* parsimoniousness ; **avec parcimonie** sparingly, parsimoniously.

parcimonieux, euse [parsimɔnjø, øz] *adj* parsimonious.

parcmètre [parkmetr] *nm* parking meter.

parcourir [45] [parkurir] *vt* **1.** [région, route] to cover - **2.** [journal, dossier] to skim ou glance through, to scan.

parcours [parkur] *nm* **1.** [trajet, voyage] journey ; [itinéraire] route ; **parcours santé**

trail in the countryside where signs encourage people to do exercises for their health - **2.** [golf] [terrain] course ; [trajet] round.

parcouru, e [parkury] *pp* ▬ **parcourir**.

par-delà [pardəla] *prép* beyond.

par-derrière [pardɛrjer] *adv* **1.** [par le côté arrière] round *UK* ou around *US* the back - **2.** [en cachette] behind one's back.

par-dessous [pardəsu] *prép & adv* under, underneath.

pardessus [pardəsy] *nm inv* overcoat.

par-dessus [pardəsy] ◇ *prép* over, over the top of ; **par-dessus tout** above all. ◇ *adv* over, over the top.

par-devant [pardəvɑ̃] ◇ *prép* in front of. ◇ *adv* in front.

pardi [pardi] *interj fam* of course!

pardon [pardɔ̃] ◇ *nm* forgiveness ; **demander pardon** to say (one is) sorry. ◇ *interj* [excuses] (I'm) sorry! ; [pour attirer l'attention] excuse me! ; **pardon?** (I beg your) pardon? *UK*, pardon me? *US*

pardonner [3] [pardɔne] ◇ *vt* to forgive ; **pardonner qqch à qqn** to forgive sb for sthg ; **pardonner à qqn d'avoir fait qqch** to forgive sb for doing sthg. ◇ *vi* : **ce genre d'erreur ne pardonne pas** this kind of mistake is fatal.

paré, e [pare] *adj* [prêt] ready.

pare-balles [parbal] *adj inv* bullet-proof.

pare-brise [parbriz] *nm inv* windscreen *UK*, windshield *US*.

pare-chocs [parʃɔk] *nm inv* bumper.

pareil, eille [parɛj] *adj* **1.** [semblable] : **pareil (à)** similar (to) - **2.** [tel] such ; **un pareil film** such a film, a film like this ; **de pareils films** such films, films like these. ▬ **pareil** *adv fam* the same (way).

parent, e [parɑ̃, ɑ̃t] ◇ *adj* : **parent (de)** related (to). ◇ *nm, f* relative, relation. ▬ **parents** *nmpl* [père et mère] parents, mother and father.

parenté [parɑ̃te] *nf* [lien, affinité] relationship.

parenthèse [parɑ̃tɛz] *nf* **1.** [digression] digression, parenthesis - **2.** TYPO bracket *UK*, parenthesis ; **entre parenthèses** in brackets *UK* ; *fig* incidentally, by the way ; **ouvrir/ fermer la parenthèse** to open/close brackets *UK* ou parentheses *US*.

parer [3] [pare] ◇ *vt* **1.** *sout* [orner] to adorn - **2.** [vêtir] : **parer qqn de qqch** to dress sb up in sthg, to deck sb out in sthg ; *fig* to attribute sthg to sb - **3.** [contrer] to ward off, to parry. ◇ *vi* : **parer à** [faire face à] to deal with ; [pourvoir à] to prepare for ; **parer au plus pressé** to see to what is most urgent. ▬ **se parer** *vp* to dress up, to put on all one's finery.

pare-soleil [parsɔlɛj] *nm inv* sun visor.

paresse [parɛs] *nf* **1.** [fainéantise] laziness, idleness - **2.** MÉD sluggishness.

paresser [4] [parɛse] *vi* to laze about ou around.

paresseux, euse [parɛsø, øz] ◇ *adj* **1.** [fainéant] lazy - **2.** MÉD sluggish. ◇ *nm, f* [personne] lazy ou idle person. ▬ **paresseux** *nm* [animal] sloth.

parfaire [109] [parfɛr] *vt* to complete, to perfect.

parfait, e [parfɛ, ɛt] *adj* perfect. ▬ **parfait** *nm* GRAMM perfect (tense).

parfaitement [parfɛtmɑ̃] *adv* **1.** [admirablement, très] perfectly - **2.** [marque l'assentiment] absolutely.

parfois [parfwa] *adv* sometimes.

parfum [parfœ̃] *nm* **1.** [de fleur] scent, fragrance - **2.** [à base d'essences] perfume, scent - **3.** [de glace] flavour *UK*, flavor *US*.

parfumé, e [parfyme] *adj* **1.** [fleur] fragrant - **2.** [mouchoir] perfumed - **3.** [femme] : **elle est trop parfumée** she's wearing too much perfume.

parfumer [3] [parfyme] *vt* **1.** [suj: fleurs] to perfume - **2.** [mouchoir] to perfume, to scent - **3.** CULIN to flavour. ▬ **se parfumer** *vp* to put perfume on.

parfumerie [parfymri] *nf* perfumery.

pari [pari] *nm* **1.** [entre personnes] bet - **2.** [jeu] betting *(U)*.

paria [parja] *nm* pariah.

parier [9] [parje] *vt* : **parier (sur)** to bet (on).

parieur [parjœr] *nm* punter.

Paris [pari] *npr* Paris.

parisien, enne [parizjɛ̃, ɛn] *adj* [vie, société] Parisian ; [métro, banlieue, région] Paris *(avant n)*. ▬ **Parisien, enne** *nm, f* Parisian.

paritaire [pariter] *adj* : **commission paritaire** joint commission *(with both sides equally represented)*.

parité [parite] *nf* parity.

parjure [parʒyr] ◇ *nmf* [personne] perjurer. ◇ *nm* [faux serment] perjury.

parjurer [3] [parʒyre] ▬ **se parjurer** *vp* to perjure o.s.

parka [parka] *nm & nf* parka.

parking [parkiŋ] *nm* [parc] car park *UK*, parking lot *US*.

parlant, e [parlɑ̃, ɑ̃t] *adj* **1.** [qui parle] : **le cinéma parlant** talking pictures ; **l'horloge parlante** TÉLÉCOM the speaking clock - **2.** *fig* [chiffres, données] eloquent ; [portrait] vivid.

parlement [parləmɑ̃] *nm* parliament ; **le**

Parlement européen the European Parliament.

parlementaire [parləmãtɛr] ◇ *nmf* [député] member of parliament ; [négociateur] negotiator. ◇ *adj* parliamentary.

parlementer [3] [parləmãte] *vi* **1.** [négocier] to negotiate, to parley - **2.** [parler longtemps] to talk at length.

parler [3] [parle] ◇ *vi* **1.** [gén] to talk, to speak ; **parler à/avec qqn** to speak to/with sb, to talk to/with sb ; **parler de qqch à qqn** to speak ou talk to sb about sth ; **parler de qqn/qqch** to talk about sb/sth ; **parler de faire qqch** to talk about doing sth ; **parler en français** to speak in French ; **sans parler de** apart from, not to mention ; **à proprement parler** strictly speaking ; **tu parles!** *fam* you can say that again! ; **n'en parlons plus** we'll say no more about it - **2.** [avouer] to talk. ◇ *vt* [langue] to speak ; **parler (le) français** to speak French.

parloir [parlwar] *nm* parlour *UK*, parlor *US*.

parmi [parmi] *prép* among.

parodie [parɔdi] *nf* parody.

parodier [9] [parɔdje] *vt* to parody.

paroi [parwa] *nf* **1.** [mur] wall ; [cloison] partition ; **paroi rocheuse** rock face - **2.** [de récipient] inner side.

paroisse [parwas] *nf* parish.

paroissial, e, aux [parwasjal, o] *adj* parish *(avant n)*.

paroissien, enne [parwasjɛ̃, ɛn] *nm, f* parishioner.

parole [parɔl] *nf* **1.** [faculté de parler] : **la parole** speech - **2.** [propos, discours] : **adresser la parole à qqn** to speak to sb ; **couper la parole à qqn** to cut sb off ; **prendre la parole** to speak - **3.** [promesse, mot] word ; **tenir parole** to keep one's word ; **donner sa parole d'honneur** to give one's word of honour *UK* ou honor *US*. ◆ **paroles** *nfpl* MUS words, lyrics.

paroxysme [parɔksism] *nm* height.

parquer [3] [parke] *vt* **1.** [animaux] to pen in ou up - **2.** [prisonniers] to shut up ou in - **3.** [voiture] to park.

parquet [parke] *nm* **1.** [plancher] parquet floor - **2.** DR ≃ Crown Prosecution Service *UK*, ≃ District Attorney's office *US*.

parqueter [27] [parkəte] *vt* to lay a parquet floor in.

parrain [parɛ̃] *nm* **1.** [d'enfant] godfather - **2.** [de festival, sportif] sponsor.

parrainer [4] [parɛne] *vt* to sponsor, to back.

parricide [parisid] *nm* [crime] parricide.

parsemer [19] [parsəme] *vt* : **parsemer (de)** to strew (with).

part [par] *nf* **1.** [de gâteau] portion ; [de bonheur, d'héritage] share ; [partie] part - **2.** [participation] : **prendre part à qqch** to take part in sth ; **de la part de** from ; [appeler, remercier] on behalf of *UK*, in behalf of *US* ; **c'est de la part de qui?** [au téléphone] who's speaking ou calling? ; **dites-lui de ma part que...** tell him from me that... ; **ce serait bien aimable de votre part** it would be very kind of you ; **pour ma part** as far as I'm concerned ; **faire part à qqn de qqch** to inform sb of sth. ◆ **à part** ◇ *loc adv* aside, separately. ◇ *loc adj* exceptional. ◇ *loc prép* apart from. ◆ **autre part** *loc adv* somewhere ou someplace *US* else. ◆ **d'autre part** *loc adv* besides, moreover. ◆ **de part et d'autre** *loc adv* on both sides. ◆ **d'une part..., d'autre part** *loc correlative* on the one hand..., on the other hand. ◆ **quelque part** *loc adv* somewhere, someplace *US*.

part. *abr écrite de* particulier.

partage [partaʒ] *nm* [action] sharing (out).

partager [17] [partaʒe] *vt* **1.** [morceler] to divide (up) ; **être partagé** *fig* to be divided - **2.** [mettre en commun] : **partager qqch avec qqn** to share sth with sb. ◆ **se partager** *vp* **1.** [se diviser] to be divided - **2.** [partager son temps] to divide one's time - **3.** [se répartir] : **se partager qqch** to share sth between themselves/ourselves *etc.*

partance [partãs] *nf* : **en partance** outward bound ; **en partance pour** bound for.

partant, e [partã, ãt] *adj* : **être partant pour** to be ready for. ◆ **partant** *nm* starter.

partenaire [partənɛr] *nmf* partner.

partenariat [partənarja] *nm* partnership.

parterre [partɛr] *nm* **1.** [de fleurs] (flower) bed - **2.** THÉÂTRE stalls *pl UK*, orchestra *US*.

parti, e [parti] ◇ *pp* ► partir. ◇ *adj fam* [ivre] tipsy. ◆ **parti** *nm* **1.** POLIT party - **2.** [choix, décision] course of action ; **prendre parti** to make up one's mind ; **prendre le parti de faire qqch** to make up one's mind to do sth ; **en prendre son parti** to be resigned ; **être de parti pris** to be prejudiced ou biased ; **tirer parti de** to make (good) use of - **3.** [personne à marier] match. ◆ **partie** *nf* **1.** [élément, portion] part ; **en grande partie** largely ; **en majeure partie** for the most part ; **faire partie (intégrante) de qqch** to be (an integral) part of sth - **2.** [domaine d'activité] field, subject - **3.** SPORT [jeux] game - **4.** DR party ; **la partie adverse** the opposing party ; **prendre qqn à partie** to attack sb ; **ce n'est que partie remise** there'll be other opportunities, I'll reschedule it, I'll take a rain check *US*. ◆ **en partie** *loc adv* partly, in part.

partial, e, aux [parsjal, o] *adj* biased.

partialité [parsjalite] *nf* partiality, bias.

participant, e [partisipɑ̃, ɑ̃t] <> *adj* participating. <> *nm, f* **1.** [à réunion] participant - **2.** SPORT competitor - **3.** [à concours] entrant.

participation [partisipasjɔ̃] *nf* **1.** [collaboration] participation - **2.** ÉCON interest ; **participation aux bénéfices** profit sharing.

participe [partisip] *nm* participle ; **participe passé/présent** past/present participle.

participer [3] [partisipe] *vi* : **participer à** [réunion, concours] to take part in ; [frais] [payer pour] to contribute to ; [bénéfices] to share in.

particularité [partikylarite] *nf* distinctive feature.

particule [partikyl] *nf* **1.** [gén & LING] particle - **2.** [nobiliaire] nobiliary particle.

particulier, ère [partikylje, ɛr] *adj* **1.** [personnel, privé] private - **2.** [spécial] particular, special ; [propre] peculiar, characteristic ; **particulier à** peculiar to, characteristic of - **3.** [remarquable] unusual, exceptional ; **cas particulier** special case - **4.** [assez bizarre] peculiar. ◆ **particulier** *nm* [personne] private individual.

particulièrement [partikyljermɑ̃] *adv* particularly ; **tout particulièrement** especially.

partie ▶ **parti**.

partiel, elle [parsjɛl] *adj* partial. ◆ **partiel** *nm* UNIV ≃ end-of-term exam *UK*.

partir [43] [partir] *vi* **1.** [personne] to go, to leave ; **partir à** to go to ; **partir pour** to leave for ; **partir de** [bureau] to leave ; [aéroport, gare] to leave from ; [date] to run from ; [hypothèse, route] to start from ; **la rue part de la mairie** the street starts at the town hall - **2.** [voiture] to start - **3.** [coup de feu] to go off ; [bouchon] to pop - **4.** [tache] to come out, to go. ◆ **à partir de** *loc prép* from.

partisan, e [partizɑ̃, an] *adj* [partial] partisan ; **être partisan de** to be in favour *UK* ou favor *US* of. ◆ **partisan** *nm* [adepte] supporter, advocate.

partition [partisjɔ̃] *nf* **1.** [séparation] partition - **2.** MUS score.

partout [partu] *adv* everywhere ; **un peu partout** all over, everywhere.

paru, e [pary] *pp* ▶ **paraître**.

parure [paryr] *nf* (matching) set.

parution [parysjɔ̃] *nf* publication.

parvenir [40] [parvənir] *vi* : **parvenir à faire qqch** to manage to do sthg ; **faire parvenir qqch à qqn** to send sthg to sb.

parvenu, e [parvəny] <> *pp* ▶ **parvenir**. <> *nm, f péj* parvenu, upstart.

pas¹ [pa] *nm* **1.** [gén] step ; **allonger le pas** to quicken one's pace ; **revenir sur ses pas** to retrace one's steps ; **pas à pas** step by step ; **à pas de loup** *fig* stealthily ; **à pas feutrés** *fig* with muffled footsteps - **2.** TECHNOL thread ; **c'est à deux pas (d'ici)** it's very near (here) ; **faire les cent pas** to pace up and down ; **faire un faux pas** to slip ; *fig* to make a faux pas ; **faire le premier pas** to make the first move ; **franchir** ou **sauter le pas** to take the plunge ; **(rouler) au pas** (to move) at a snail's pace ; **sur le pas de la porte** on the doorstep ; **tirer qqn d'un mauvais pas** to get sb out of a tight spot.

pas² [pa] *adv* **1.** [avec ne] not ; **elle ne vient pas** she's not ou she isn't coming ; **elle n'a pas mangé** she hasn't eaten ; **je ne le connais pas** I don't know him ; **il n'y a pas de vin** there's no wine, there isn't any wine ; **je préférerais ne pas le rencontrer** I would rather not prefer not to meet him, I would rather not meet him - **2.** [sans ne] not ; **l'as-tu vu ou pas?** have you seen him or not? ; **il est très satisfait, moi pas** he's very pleased, but I'm not ; **pas encore** not yet ; **pas du tout** not at all - **3.** [avec pron indéf] : **pas un** [aucun] none, not one ; **pas un d'eux n'est venu** none of them ou not one of them came.

pascal, e [paskal] (*pl* **pascals** ou **pascaux** [pasko]) *adj* Easter (*avant n*). ◆ **pascal** *nm* **1.** INFORM Pascal - **2.** PHYS pascal.

pashmina [paʃmina] *nm* pashmina.

passable [pasabl] *adj* passable, fair.

passage [pasaʒ] *nm* **1.** [action - de passer] going past ; [- de traverser] crossing ; **être de passage** to be passing through - **2.** [endroit] passage, way ; **'passage interdit'** 'no entry' ; **passage clouté** ou **pour piétons** pedestrian crossing *UK*, crosswalk *US* ; **passage à niveau** level crossing *UK*, grade crossing *US* ; **passage protégé** priority given to traffic on the main road ; **passage souterrain** underpass, subway *UK* - **3.** [extrait] passage.

passager, ère [pasaʒe, ɛr] <> *adj* [bonheur] fleeting, short-lived. <> *nm, f* passenger.

passant, e [pasɑ̃, ɑ̃t] <> *adj* busy. <> *nm, f* passerby. ◆ **passant** *nm* [de ceinture] (belt) loop.

passe [pas] <> *nm* passkey. <> *nf* **1.** [au sport] pass - **2.** NAUT channel.

passé, e [pase] *adj* **1.** [qui n'est plus] past ; [précédent] : **la semaine passée** last week ; **au cours de la semaine passée** in the last week ; **il est trois heures passées** it's gone three *UK*, it's after three - **2.** [fané] faded. ◆ **passé** <> *nm* past ; **passé composé** perfect tense ; **passé simple** past historic. <> *prép* after.

passe-droit [pasdrwa] (*pl* **passe-droits**) *nm* privilege.

passe-montagne [pasmɔ̃taɲ] (*pl* **passe-montagnes**) *nm* balaclava (helmet).

passe-partout [paspartu] *nm inv* **1.** [clé] passkey - **2.** *(en apposition)* [tenue] all-purpose ; [phrase] stock *(avant n)*.

passeport [paspɔr] *nm* passport.

passer [3] [pase] <> *vi (v aux : être)* **1.** [se frayer un chemin] to pass, to get past - **2.** [défiler] to go by ou past - **3.** [aller] to go ; **passer à** ou **au travers** ou **par** to come ou pass through ; **passer chez qqn** to call on sb, to drop in on sb ; **passer devant** [bâtiment] to pass ; [juge] to come before ; **en passant** in passing - **4.** [venir - facteur] to come, to call - **5.** SCOL to pass, to be admitted ; **passer dans la classe supérieure** to move up UK, to be moved up (a class) UK - **6.** [être accepté] to be accepted - **7.** [fermer les yeux] : **passer sur qqch** to pass over sthg - **8.** [temps] to pass, to go by - **9.** [disparaître - souvenir, couleur] to fade ; [- douleur] to pass, to go away - **10.** CINÉ, TV & THÉÂTRE to be on ; **passer à la radio/télévision** to be on the radio/television - **11.** [aux cartes] to pass - **12.** [devenir] : **passer président/directeur** to become president/director, to be appointed president/director ; **passer inaperçu** to pass ou go unnoticed ; **passons...** let's move on... ; **passer pour** to be regarded as ; **se faire passer pour qqn** to pass o.s. off as sb ; **il y est passé** *fam* [mort] he kicked the bucket. <> *vt (v aux : être)* **1.** [franchir - frontière, rivière] to cross ; [- douane] to go through - **2.** [soirée, vacances] to spend - **3.** [sauter - ligne, tour] to miss - **4.** [défauts] : **passer qqch à qqn** to overlook sthg in sb - **5.** [faire aller - bras] to pass, to put - **6.** [filtrer - huile] to strain ; [- café] to filter - **7.** [film, disque] to put on - **8.** [vêtement] to slip on - **9.** [vitesses] to change ; **passer la** ou **en troisième** to change into third (gear) - **10.** [donner] : **passer qqch à qqn** to pass sb sthg ; **passe-moi le sel** pass me the salt - **11.** MÉD : **passer qqch à qqn** to give sb sthg - **12.** [accord] : **passer un contrat avec qqn** to have an agreement with sb - **13.** SCOL & UNIV [examen] to sit UK, to take - **14.** [au téléphone] : **je vous passe Mme Ledoux** [transmettre] I'll put you through to Mme Ledoux ; [donner l'écouteur à] I'll hand you Mme Ledoux. **se passer** *vp* **1.** [événement] to happen, to take place ; **comment ça s'est passé?** how did it go? ; **ça ne se passera pas comme ça!** I'm not putting up with that! - **2.** [s'enduire - crème] to put on - **3.** [s'abstenir] : **se passer de qqch/de faire qqch** to do without sthg/doing sthg.

passerelle [pasrɛl] *nf* **1.** [pont] footbridge - **2.** [passage mobile] gangway.

passe-temps [pastã] *nm inv* pastime.

passif, ive [pasif, iv] *adj* passive. **passif** *nm* **1.** GRAMM passive - **2.** FIN liabilities *pl*.

passion [pasjɔ̃] *nf* passion ; **avoir la passion de qqch** to have a passion for sthg.

passionnant, e [pasjɔnɑ̃, ɑ̃t] *adj* exciting, fascinating.

passionné, e [pasjɔne] <> *adj* **1.** [personne] passionate - **2.** [récit, débat] impassioned. <> *nm, f* passionate person ; **passionné de ski/d'échecs** *etc* skiing/chess *etc* fanatic.

passionnel, elle [pasjɔnɛl] *adj* [crime] of passion.

passionner [3] [pasjɔne] *vt* [personne] to grip, to fascinate. **se passionner** *vp* : **se passionner pour** to have a passion for.

passivité [pasivite] *nf* passivity.

passoire [paswar] *nf* [à liquide] sieve ; [à légumes] colander.

pastel [pastɛl] <> *nm* pastel. <> *adj inv* [couleur] pastel *(avant n)*.

pastèque [pastɛk] *nf* watermelon.

pasteur [pastœr] *nm* **1.** *litt* [berger] shepherd - **2.** RELIG pastor, minister. **Pasteur** [pastœr] *npr m* : **l'Institut pasteur** *important medical research centre*.

pasteuriser [3] [pastœrize] *vt* to pasteurize.

pastille [pastij] *nf* [bonbon] pastille, lozenge.

pastis [pastis] *nm* aniseed-flavoured aperitif.

patate [patat] *nf* **1.** [pomme de terre] spud - **2.** *fam* [imbécile] fathead.

patauger [17] [patoʒe] *vi* [barboter] to splash about.

patch [patʃ] *nm* MÉD patch.

pâte [pat] *nf* **1.** [à tarte] pastry ; [à pain] dough ; **pâte brisée** shortcrust pastry ; **pâte feuilletée** puff pastry ; **pâte à frire** batter ; **pâte à pain** bread dough - **2.** [mélange] paste ; **pâte d'amandes** almond paste ; **pâte de fruits** *jelly made from fruit paste* ; **pâte à modeler** modelling UK ou modeling US clay. **pâtes** *nfpl* pasta *sg*.

pâté [pate] *nm* **1.** CULIN pâté ; **pâté de campagne** farmhouse pâté ; **pâté en croûte** *pâté baked in a pastry case* ; **pâté de foie** liver pâté - **2.** [tache] ink blot - **3.** [bloc] : **pâté de maisons** block (of houses).

patelin [patlɛ̃] *nm fam* village, place.

patente [patɑ̃t] *nf* licence UK ou license US fee *(for traders and professionals)*.

patère [patɛr] *nf* [portemanteau] coat hook.

paternalisme [paternalism] *nm* paternalism.

paternel, elle [patɛrnɛl] *adj* [devoir, autorité] paternal ; [amour, ton] fatherly.

paternité [paternite] *nf* paternity, fatherhood ; *fig* authorship, paternity.

pâteux, euse [patø, øz] *adj* [aliment] doughy ; [encre] thick.

pathétique [patetik] *adj* moving, pathetic.

pathologie [patɔlɔʒi] *nf* pathology.

patibulaire [patibylɛr] *adj péj* sinister.

patience [pasjɑ̃s] *nf* **1.** [gén] patience ; **prendre son mal en patience** to put up with it - **2.** [jeu de cartes] patience *UK*, solitaire *US*.

patient, e [pasjɑ̃, ɑ̃t] <> *adj* patient. <> *nm, f* MÉD patient.

patienter [3] [pasjɑ̃te] *vi* to wait.

patin [patɛ̃] *nm* SPORT skate ; **patin à glace/à roulettes** ice/roller skate ; **faire du patin à glace/à roulettes** to go ice-/roller-skating.

patinage [patinaʒ] *nm* SPORT skating ; **patinage artistique/de vitesse** figure/speed skating.

patiner [3] [patine] <> *vi* **1.** SPORT to skate - **2.** [véhicule] to skid. <> *vt* [objet] to give a patina to ; [avec vernis] to varnish. **se patiner** *vp* to take on a patina.

patineur, euse [patinœr, øz] *nm, f* skater.

patinoire [patinwar] *nf* ice ou skating rink.

pâtisserie [patisri] *nf* **1.** [gâteau] pastry - **2.** [art, métier] pastry-making - **3.** [commerce] ≃ cake shop *UK*, bakery *US*, ≃ bakery *US*.

pâtissier, ère [patisje, ɛr] <> *adj* : **crème pâtissière** confectioner's custard. <> *nm, f* pastrycook.

patois [patwa] *nm* patois.

patriarche [patrijarʃ] *nm* patriarch.

patrie [patri] *nf* country, homeland.

patrimoine [patrimwan] *nm* [familial] inheritance ; [collectif] heritage.

patriote [patrijɔt] *nmf* patriot.

patriotique [patrijɔtik] *adj* patriotic.

patron, onne [patrɔ̃, ɔn] *nm, f* **1.** [d'entreprise] head - **2.** [chef] boss - **3.** RELIG patron saint. **patron** *nm* [modèle] pattern.

patronage [patrɔnaʒ] *nm* **1.** [protection] patronage ; [de saint] protection - **2.** [organisation] youth club.

patronal, e, aux [patrɔnal, o] *adj* [organisation, intérêts] employers' (avant n).

patronat [patrɔna] *nm* employers.

patronyme [patrɔnim] *nm* patronymic.

patrouille [patruj] *nf* patrol.

patte [pat] *nf* **1.** [d'animal] paw ; [d'oiseau] foot - **2.** *fam* [jambe] leg ; [pied] foot ; [main] hand, paw - **3.** [favori] sideburn.

pâturage [patyraʒ] *nm* [lieu] pasture land.

pâture [patyr] *nf* [nourriture] food, fodder ; *fig* intellectual nourishment.

paume [pom] *nf* **1.** [de main] palm - **2.** SPORT real tennis.

paumé, e [pome] *fam* <> *adj* lost. <> *nm, f* down and out.

paumer [3] [pome] *fam vt* to lose. **se paumer** *vp* to get lost.

paupière [popjɛr] *nf* eyelid.

pause [poz] *nf* **1.** [arrêt] break ; **pause-café** coffee-break - **2.** MUS pause.

pauvre [povr] <> *nmf* poor person. <> *adj* poor ; **pauvre en** low in.

pauvreté [povrəte] *nf* poverty.

pavaner [3] [pavane] **se pavaner** *vp* to strut.

pavé, e [pave] *adj* cobbled. **pavé** *nm* **1.** [chaussée] : **être sur le pavé** *fig* to be out on the streets ; **battre le pavé** *fig* to walk the streets - **2.** [de pierre] cobblestone, paving stone - **3.** *fam* [livre] tome - **4.** INFORM : **pavé numérique** numeric keypad.

pavillon [pavijɔ̃] *nm* **1.** [bâtiment] detached house *UK* - **2.** [de trompette] bell - **3.** [d'oreille] pinna, auricle - **4.** [drapeau] flag.

pavot [pavo] *nm* poppy.

payant, e [pɛjɑ̃, ɑ̃t] *adj* **1.** [hôte] paying (avant n) - **2.** [spectacle] with an admission charge - **3.** *fam* [affaire] profitable.

paye = **paie².**

payement = **paiement.**

payer [11] [peje] <> *vt* **1.** [gén] to pay ; [achat] to pay for ; **payer qqch à qqn** to buy sthg for sb, to buy sb sthg, to treat sb to sthg - **2.** [expier - crime, faute] to pay for. <> *vi* : **payer (pour)** to pay (for).

pays [pei] *nm* **1.** [gén] country - **2.** [région, province] region. **pays de Galles** *nm* : **le pays de Galles** Wales.

paysage [peizaʒ] *nm* **1.** [site, vue] landscape, scenery - **2.** [tableau] landscape.

paysagiste [peizaʒist] *nmf* **1.** [peintre] landscape artist - **2.** [concepteur de parcs] landscape gardener.

paysan, anne [peizɑ̃, an] <> *adj* [vie, coutume] country (avant n), rural ; [organisation, revendication] farmers' (avant n) ; *péj* peasant (avant n). <> *nm, f* **1.** [agriculteur] (small) farmer - **2.** *péj* [rustre] peasant.

Pays-Bas [peiba] *nmpl* : **les Pays-Bas** the Netherlands.

PC *nm* **1.** (abr de **Parti communiste**) Communist Party - **2.** (abr de **personal computer**) PC - **3.** (abr de **Petite Ceinture**) bus following the inner ring road in Paris.

PCV (abr de **à percevoir**) *nm* reverse-charge call *UK*, collect call *US*.

P-DG (abr de **président-directeur général**) *nm* Chairman and Managing Director *UK*, President and Chief Executive Officer *US*.

péage [peaʒ] *nm* toll.

peau [po] *nf* **1.** [gén] skin ; **peau d'orange** orange peel ; MÉD ≃ cellulite - **2.** [cuir] hide, leather (U).

peaufiner [3] [pofine] *vt fig* [travail] to polish up.

péché [pefe] *nm* sin.

pêche [pɛʃ] *nf* **1.** [fruit] peach - **2.** [activité] fishing ; [poissons] catch ; **aller à la pêche** to go fishing.

pécher [18] [pefe] *vi* to sin.

pêcher[1] [4] [pefe] *vt* **1.** [poisson] to catch - **2.** *fam* [trouver] to dig up.

pêcher[2] [pefe] *nm* peach tree.

pécheur, eresse [pefœr, pefrɛs] <> *adj* sinful. <> *nm, f* sinner.

pêcheur, euse [pefœr, øz] *nm, f* fisherman (f fisherwoman).

pectoral, e, aux [pɛktɔral, o] *adj* [sirop] cough *(avant n).* ➤ **pectoraux** *nmpl* pectorals.

pécuniaire [pekynjɛr] *adj* financial.

pédagogie [pedagɔʒi] *nf* **1.** [science] education, pedagogy - **2.** [qualité] teaching ability.

pédagogue [pedagɔg] <> *nmf* teacher. <> *adj* : **être pédagogue** to be a good teacher.

pédale [pedal] *nf* [gén] pedal.

pédaler [3] [pedale] *vi* [à bicyclette] to pedal.

Pédalo® [pedalo] *nm* pedal boat.

pédant, e [pedã, ãt] *adj* pedantic.

pédéraste [pederast] *nm* homosexual, pederast.

pédiatre [pedjatr] *nmf* pediatrician.

pédiatrie [pedjatri] *nf* pediatrics *(U).*

pédicure [pedikyr] *nmf* chiropodist, podiatrist *US.*

pédopsychiatre [pedɔpsikjatr] *nmf* child psychiatrist.

peigne [pɛɲ] *nm* **1.** [démêloir, barrette] comb - **2.** [de tissage] card.

peigner [4] [peɲe] *vt* **1.** [cheveux] to comb - **2.** [fibres] to card. ➤ **se peigner** *vp* to comb one's hair.

peignoir [peɲwar] *nm* dressing gown *UK*, robe *US*, bathrobe *US.*

peindre [81] [pɛ̃dr] *vt* to paint ; *fig* [décrire] to depict.

peine [pɛn] *nf* **1.** [châtiment] punishment, penalty ; DR sentence ; **sous peine de qqch** on pain of sthg ; **peine capitale** OU **de mort** capital punishment, death sentence - **2.** [chagrin] sorrow, sadness *(U)* ; **faire de la peine à qqn** to upset sb ; **ça ne vaut pas** OU **ce n'est pas la peine** it's not worth it - **4.** [difficulté] difficulty ; **avoir de la peine à faire qqch** to have difficulty OU trouble doing sthg ; **à grand-peine** with great difficulty ; **sans peine** without difficulty, easily.

➤ **à peine** *loc adv* scarcely, hardly ; **à peine... que** hardly... than ; **c'est à peine si on se parle** we hardly speak (to each other).

peint, e [pɛ̃, pɛ̃t] *pp* ➤ **peindre**.

peintre [pɛ̃tr] *nm* painter.

peinture [pɛ̃tyr] *nf* **1.** [gén] painting - **2.** [produit] paint ; **'peinture fraîche'** 'wet paint'.

péjoratif, ive [peʒɔratif, iv] *adj* pejorative.

Pékin [pekɛ̃] *npr* Peking, Beijing.

pékinois, e [pekinwa, az] *adj* of/from Peking. ➤ **pékinois** *nm* **1.** [langue] Mandarin - **2.** [chien] pekinese. ➤ **Pékinois, e** *nm, f* native OU inhabitant of Peking.

pelage [pəlaʒ] *nm* coat, fur.

pêle-mêle [pɛlmɛl] *adv* pell-mell.

peler [25] [pəle] *vt & vi* to peel.

pèlerin [pɛlrɛ̃] *nm* pilgrim.

pèlerinage [pɛlrinaʒ] *nm* **1.** [voyage] pilgrimage - **2.** [lieu] place of pilgrimage.

pélican [pelikã] *nm* pelican.

pelle [pɛl] *nf* **1.** [instrument] shovel - **2.** [machine] digger.

pelleter [27] [pɛlte] *vt* to shovel.

pellicule [pelikyl] *nf* film. ➤ **pellicules** *nfpl* dandruff *(U).*

pelote [pəlɔt] *nf* [de laine, ficelle] ball.

peloter [3] [pləte] *vt fam* to paw.

peloton [plɔtõ] *nm* **1.** [de soldats] squad ; **peloton d'exécution** firing squad - **2.** [de concurrents] pack.

pelotonner [3] [plɔtɔne] ➤ **se pelotonner** *vp* to curl up.

pelouse [pəluz] *nf* **1.** [de jardin] lawn - **2.** [de champ de courses] public enclosure - **3.** FOOTBALL [rugby] field.

peluche [pəlyʃ] *nf* **1.** [jouet] soft toy, stuffed animal - **2.** [d'étoffe] piece of fluff.

pelure [pəlyr] *nf* [fruit] peel.

pénal, e, aux [penal, o] *adj* penal.

pénaliser [3] [penalize] *vt* to penalize.

penalty [penalti] *(pl* penaltys OU penalties*)* *nm* penalty.

penaud, e [pəno, od] *adj* sheepish.

penchant [pãʃã] *nm* **1.** [inclination] tendency - **2.** [sympathie] : **penchant pour** liking OU fondness for.

pencher [3] [pãʃe] <> *vi* to lean ; **pencher vers** *fig* to incline towards OU toward *US* ; **pencher pour** to incline in favour *UK* OU favor *US* of. <> *vt* to bend. ➤ **se pencher** *vp* [s'incliner] to lean over ; [se baisser] to bend down ; **se pencher sur qqn/qqch** to lean over sb/sthg.

pendaison [pãdɛzõ] *nf* hanging.

pendant[1]**, e** [pãdã, ãt] *adj* [bras] hanging,

dangling. **pendant** *nm* **1.** [bijou] : **pendant d'oreilles** (drop) earring - **2.** [de paire] counterpart.

pendant² [pãdã] *prép* during. **pendant que** *loc conj* while, whilst *UK* ; **pendant que j'y suis,...** while I'm at it,...

pendentif [pãdãtif] *nm* pendant.

penderie [pãdri] *nf* wardrobe *UK*, walk-in closet *US*.

pendre [73] [pãdr] <> *vi* **1.** [être fixé en haut] : **pendre (à)** to hang (from) - **2.** [descendre trop bas] to hang down. <> *vt* **1.** [rideaux, tableau] to hang (up), to put up - **2.** [personne] to hang. **se pendre** *vp* [se suicider] to hang o.s.

pendule [pãdyl] <> *nm* pendulum. <> *nf* clock.

pénétrer [18] [penetre] <> *vi* to enter. <> *vt* [mur, vêtement] to penetrate.

pénible [penibl] *adj* **1.** [travail] laborious - **2.** [nouvelle, maladie] painful - **3.** *fam* [personne] tiresome.

péniche [peniʃ] *nf* barge.

pénicilline [penisilin] *nf* penicillin.

péninsule [penẽsyl] *nf* peninsula.

pénis [penis] *nm* penis.

pénitence [penitãs] *nf* **1.** [repentir] penitence - **2.** [peine, punition] penance.

pénitencier [penitãsje] *nm* prison, penitentiary *US*.

pénombre [penõbr] *nf* half-light.

pense-bête [pãsbɛt] (*pl* pense-bêtes) *nm* reminder.

pensée [pãse] *nf* **1.** [idée, faculté] thought - **2.** [esprit] mind, thoughts *pl* - **3.** [doctrine] thought, thinking - **4.** BOT pansy.

penser [3] [pãse] <> *vi* to think ; **penser à qqn/qqch** [avoir à l'esprit] to think of sb/sthg, to think about sb/sthg ; [se rappeler] to remember sb/sthg ; **penser à faire qqch** [avoir à l'esprit] to think of doing sthg ; [se rappeler] to remember to do sthg ; **qu'est-ce que tu en penses?** what do you think (of it)? ; **faire penser à qqn/qqch** to make one think of sb/sthg ; **faire penser à qqn à faire qqch** to remind sb to do sthg. <> *vt* to think ; **je pense que oui** I think so ; **je pense que non** I don't think so ; **penser faire qqch** to be planning to do sthg.

pensif, ive [pãsif, iv] *adj* pensive, thoughtful.

pension [pãsjõ] *nf* **1.** [allocation] pension ; **pension alimentaire** [dans un divorce] alimony - **2.** [hébergement] board and lodgings ; **pension complète** full board ; **demi-pension** half board - **3.** [hôtel] guesthouse ; **pension de famille** guesthouse, boarding house - **4.** [prix de l'hébergement]

≃ rent, keep - **5.** [internat] boarding school ; **être en pension** to be a boarder ou at boarding school.

pensionnaire [pãsjɔnɛr] *nmf* **1.** [élève] boarder - **2.** [hôte payant] lodger.

pensionnat [pãsjɔna] *nm* [internat] boarding school.

pentagone [pẽtagɔn] *nm* pentagon.

pente [pãt] *nf* slope ; **en pente** sloping, inclined.

pentecôte [pãtkot] *nf* [juive] Pentecost ; [chrétienne] Whitsun.

pénurie [penyri] *nf* shortage.

people [pipɔl] *adj* : **la presse people** celebrity (gossip) magazins.

pépier [9] [pepje] *vi* to chirp.

pépin [pepẽ] *nm* **1.** [graine] pip - **2.** *fam* [ennui] hitch - **3.** *fam* [parapluie] umbrella, brolly *UK*.

pépinière [pepinjɛr] *nf* tree nursery ; *fig* [école, établissement] nursery.

pépite [pepit] *nf* nugget.

perçant, e [pɛrsã, ãt] *adj* **1.** [regard, son] piercing - **2.** [froid] bitter, biting.

percepteur [pɛrsɛptœr] *nm* tax collector.

perception [pɛrsɛpsjõ] *nf* **1.** [d'impôts] collection - **2.** [bureau] tax office - **3.** [sensation] perception.

percer [16] [pɛrse] <> *vt* **1.** [mur, roche] to make a hole in ; [coffre-fort] to crack - **2.** [trou] to make ; [avec perceuse] to drill - **3.** [silence, oreille] to pierce - **4.** [foule] to make one's way through - **5.** *fig* [mystère] to penetrate. <> *vi* **1.** [soleil] to break through - **2.** [abcès] to burst ; **avoir une dent qui perce** to be cutting a tooth - **3.** [réussir] to make a name for o.s., to break through.

perceuse [pɛrsøz] *nf* drill.

percevoir [52] [pɛrsəvwar] *vt* **1.** [intention, nuance] to perceive - **2.** [retraite, indemnité] to receive - **3.** [impôts] to collect.

perche [pɛrʃ] *nf* **1.** [poisson] perch - **2.** [de bois, métal] pole.

percher [3] [pɛrʃe] <> *vi* [oiseau] to perch. <> *vt* to perch. **se percher** *vp* to perch.

perchoir [pɛrʃwar] *nm* perch.

percolateur [pɛrkɔlatœr] *nm* percolator.

perçu, e [pɛrsy] *pp* percevoir.

percussion [pɛrkysjõ] *nf* percussion.

percutant, e [pɛrkytã, ãt] *adj* **1.** [obus] explosive - **2.** *fig* [argument] forceful.

percuter [3] [pɛrkyte] <> *vt* to strike, to smash into. <> *vi* to explode.

perdant, e [pɛrdɑ̃, ɑ̃t] <> *adj* losing. <> *nm, f* loser.

perdre [77] [pɛrdr] <> *vt* **1.** [gén] to lose - **2.** [temps] to waste ; [occasion] to miss, to waste - **3.** [suj: bonté, propos] to be the ruin of. <> *vi* to lose. ◆ **se perdre** *vpi* **1.** [coutume] to die out, to become lost - **2.** [personne] to get lost, to lose one's way.

perdrix [pɛrdri] *nf* partridge.

perdu, e [pɛrdy] <> *pp* ► **perdre**. <> *adj* **1.** [égaré] lost - **2.** [endroit] out-of-the-way - **3.** [balle] stray - **4.** [emballage] non-returnable - **5.** [temps, occasion] wasted - **6.** [malade] dying - **7.** [récolte, robe] spoilt, ruined.

père [pɛr] *nm* [gén] father ; **père de famille** father. ◆ **père Noël** *nm* : **le père Noël** Father Christmas *UK*, Santa Claus.

péremptoire [perɑ̃ptwar] *adj* peremptory.

perfection [pɛrfɛksjɔ̃] *nf* [qualité] perfection.

perfectionner [3] [pɛrfɛksjɔne] *vt* to perfect. ◆ **se perfectionner** *vp* to improve.

perfide [pɛrfid] *adj* perfidious.

perforer [3] [pɛrfɔre] *vt* to perforate.

performance [pɛrfɔrmɑ̃s] *nf* performance.

performant, e [pɛrfɔrmɑ̃, ɑ̃t] *adj* **1.** [personne] efficient - **2.** [machine] high-performance *(avant n)*.

perfusion [pɛrfyzjɔ̃] *nf* perfusion.

péridurale [peridyral] *nf* epidural.

péril [peril] *nm* peril.

périlleux, euse [perijø, øz] *adj* perilous, dangerous.

périmé, e [perime] *adj* out-of-date ; *fig* [idées] outdated.

périmètre [perimɛtr] *nm* **1.** [contour] perimeter - **2.** [contenu] area.

période [perjɔd] *nf* period.

périodique [perjɔdik] <> *nm* periodical. <> *adj* periodic.

péripétie [peripesi] *nf* event.

périphérie [periferi] *nf* **1.** [de ville] outskirts *pl* - **2.** [bord] periphery ; [de cercle] circumference.

périph [perif] *nm fam abr de* **périphérique**.

périphérique [periferik] <> *nm* **1.** [route] ring road *UK*, beltway *US* - **2.** INFORM peripheral device. <> *adj* peripheral.

périphrase [perifraz] *nf* periphrasis.

périple [peripl] *nm* **1.** NAUT voyage - **2.** [voyage] trip.

périr [32] [perir] *vi* to perish.

périssable [perisabl] *adj* **1.** [denrée] perishable - **2.** *litt* [sentiment] transient.

perle [pɛrl] *nf* **1.** [de nacre] pearl - **2.** [de bois, verre] bead - **3.** [personne] gem.

permanence [pɛrmanɑ̃s] *nf* **1.** [continuité] permanence ; **en permanence** constantly - **2.** [service] : **être de permanence** to be on duty - **3.** SCOL : **(salle de) permanence** study room *UK*, study hall *US*.

permanent, e [pɛrmanɑ̃, ɑ̃t] *adj* permanent ; [cinéma] with continuous showings ; [comité] standing *(avant n)*. ◆ **permanente** *nf* perm.

permettre [84] [pɛrmɛtr] *vt* to permit, to allow ; **permettre à qqn de faire qqch** to permit ou allow sb to do sthg. ◆ **se permettre** *vp* : **se permettre qqch** to allow o.s sthg ; [avoir les moyens de] to be able to afford sthg ; **se permettre de faire qqch** to take the liberty of doing sthg.

permis, e [pɛrmi, iz] *pp* ► **permettre**. ◆ **permis** *nm* licence *UK*, license *US*, permit ; **permis de conduire** driving licence *UK*, driver's license *US* ; **permis de construire** planning permission *UK*, building permit *US* ; **permis à points** *driving licence with a penalty points system, introduced in France in 1992* ; **permis de travail** work permit.

permission [pɛrmisjɔ̃] *nf* **1.** [autorisation] permission - **2.** MIL leave.

permuter [3] [pɛrmyte] <> *vt* to change round ; [mots, figures] to transpose. <> *vi* to change, to switch.

pérorer [3] [perɔre] *vi péj* to hold forth.

Pérou [peru] *nm* : **le Pérou** Peru.

perpendiculaire [pɛrpɑ̃dikyler] <> *nf* perpendicular. <> *adj* : **perpendiculaire (à)** perpendicular (to).

perpétrer [18] [pɛrpetre] *vt* to perpetrate.

perpétuel, elle [pɛrpetɥɛl] *adj* **1.** [fréquent, continu] perpetual - **2.** [rente] life *(avant n)* ; [secrétaire] permanent.

perpétuer [7] [pɛrpetɥe] *vt* to perpetuate. ◆ **se perpétuer** *vp* to continue ; [espèce] to perpetuate itself.

perpétuité [pɛrpetɥite] *nf* perpetuity ; **à perpétuité** for life ; **être condamné à perpétuité** to be sentenced to life imprisonment.

perplexe [pɛrplɛks] *adj* perplexed.

perquisition [pɛrkizisjɔ̃] *nf* search.

perron [pɛrɔ̃] *nm* steps *pl (at entrance to building)*.

perroquet [pɛrɔkɛ] *nm* [animal] parrot.

perruche [pɛryʃ] *nf* budgerigar *UK*, parakeet *US*.

perruque [pɛryk] *nf* wig.

persan, e [pɛrsɑ̃, an] *adj* Persian. ◆ **persan** *nm* [chat] Persian (cat).

persécuter [3] [pɛrsekyte] vt **1.** [martyriser] to persecute - **2.** [harceler] to harass.

persécution [pɛrsekysjɔ̃] nf persecution.

persévérant, e [pɛrseverɑ̃, ɑ̃t] adj persevering.

persévérer [18] [pɛrsevere] vi : **persévérer (dans)** to persevere (in).

persienne [pɛrsjɛn] nf shutter.

persifler [3] [pɛrsifle] vt litt to mock.

persil [pɛrsi] nm parsley.

Persique [pɛrsik] ▶ golfe.

persistant, e [pɛrsistɑ̃, ɑ̃t] adj persistent ; **arbre à feuillage persistant** evergreen (tree).

persister [3] [pɛrsiste] vi to persist ; **persister à faire qqch** to persist in doing sthg.

perso [pɛrso] (abr de **personnel**) adj fam personal, private.

personnage [pɛrsonaʒ] nm **1.** THÉÂTRE character ; **personnage principal** main ou leading character ; ART figure - **2.** [personnalité] image.

personnalité [pɛrsonalite] nf **1.** [gén] personality - **2.** DR status.

personne [pɛrsɔn] ◇ nf person ; **personnes** people ; **en personne** in person, personally ; **personne âgée** elderly person. ◇ pron indéf **1.** [quelqu'un] anybody, anyone - **2.** [aucune personne] nobody, no one ; **personne ne viendra** nobody will come ; **il n'y a jamais personne** there's never anybody there, nobody is ever there.

personnel, elle [pɛrsɔnɛl] adj **1.** [gén] personal - **2.** [égoïste] self-centred UK, self-centered US. ▶ **personnel** nm staff, personnel.

personnellement [pɛrsonɛlmɑ̃] adv personally.

personnifier [9] [pɛrsɔnifje] vt to personify.

perspective [pɛrspɛktiv] nf **1.** ART [point de vue] perspective - **2.** [panorama] view - **3.** [éventualité] prospect.

perspicace [pɛrspikas] adj perspicacious.

persuader [3] [pɛrsɥade] vt : **persuader qqn de qqch/de faire qqch** to persuade sb of sthg/to do sthg, to convince sb of sthg/to do sthg.

persuasif, ive [pɛrsɥazif, iv] adj persuasive.

persuasion [pɛrsɥazjɔ̃] nf persuasion.

perte [pɛrt] nf **1.** [gén] loss - **2.** [gaspillage - de temps] waste - **3.** [ruine, déchéance] ruin. ▶ **pertes** nfpl [morts] losses. ▶ **à perte de vue** loc adv as far as the eye can see.

pertinent, e [pɛrtinɑ̃, ɑ̃t] adj pertinent, relevant.

perturber [3] [pɛrtyrbe] vt **1.** [gén] to disrupt ; **perturber l'ordre public** to disturb the peace - **2.** PSYCHO to disturb.

pervenche [pɛrvɑ̃ʃ] nf **1.** BOT periwinkle - **2.** fam [contractuelle] traffic warden UK, meter maid US.

pervers, e [pɛrvɛr, ɛrs] ◇ adj **1.** [vicieux] perverted - **2.** [effet] unwanted. ◇ nm, f pervert.

perversion [pɛrvɛrsjɔ̃] nf perversion.

perversité [pɛrvɛrsite] nf perversity.

pervertir [32] [pɛrvɛrtir] vt to pervert.

pesamment [pəzamɑ̃] adv heavily.

pesant, e [pəzɑ̃, ɑ̃t] adj **1.** [lourd] heavy - **2.** [style, architecture] ponderous.

pesanteur [pəzɑ̃tœr] nf **1.** PHYS gravity - **2.** [lourdeur] heaviness.

pesée [pəze] nf [opération] weighing.

pèse-personne [pɛzpɛrsɔn] (pl inv ou **pèse-personnes**) nm scales pl.

peser [19] [pəze] ◇ vt to weigh. ◇ vi **1.** [avoir un certain poids] to weigh - **2.** [être lourd] to be heavy - **3.** [appuyer] : **peser sur qqch** to press (down) on sthg.

peseta [pezeta] nf peseta.

pessimisme [pesimism] nm pessimism.

pessimiste [pesimist] ◇ nmf pessimist. ◇ adj pessimistic.

peste [pɛst] nf **1.** MÉD plague - **2.** [personne] pest.

pestiféré, e [pɛstifere] ◇ adj plague-stricken. ◇ nm, f plague victim.

pestilentiel, elle [pɛstilɑ̃sjɛl] adj pestilential.

pet [pɛ] nm fam fart.

pétale [petal] nm petal.

pétanque [petɑ̃k] nf ≈ bowls (U).

pétarader [3] [petarade] vi to backfire.

pétard [petar] nm **1.** [petit explosif] banger UK, firecracker - **2.** fam [revolver] gun - **3.** fam [haschich] joint.

péter [18] [pete] ◇ vi **1.** tfam [personne] to fart - **2.** fam [câble, élastique] to snap - **3.** tfam **péter plus haut que son cul** tfam to be full of oneself. ◇ vt fam to bust.

pétiller [3] [petije] vi **1.** [vin, eau] to sparkle, to bubble - **2.** [feu] to crackle - **3.** fig [yeux] to sparkle.

petit, e [pəti, it] ◇ adj **1.** [de taille, jeune] small, little ; **petit frère** little ou younger brother ; **petite sœur** little ou younger sister - **2.** [voyage, visite] short, little - **3.** [faible, infime - somme d'argent] small ; [- bruit] faint, slight ; **c'est une petite nature** he/she is slightly built - **4.** [de peu d'importance, de peu de valeur] minor - **5.** [médiocre, mesquin] petty -a **6.** [de rang modeste - commerçant, propriétaire, pays] small

[- fonctionnaire] minor. <> nm, f [enfant] little one, child ; **bonjour, mon petit/ma petite** good morning, my dear ; **pauvre petit!** poor little thing! ; **la classe des petits** SCOL the infant class. <> nm [jeune animal] young (U) ; **faire des petits** to have puppies/kittens etc. **petit à petit** loc adv little by little, gradually.

petit déjeuner [p(ə)tidezœne] nm breakfast.

petite-fille [p(ə)titfij] nf granddaughter.

petitement [p(ə)titmɑ̃] adv 1. [chichement - vivre] poorly - 2. [mesquinement] pettily.

petitesse [p(ə)titɛs] nf 1. [de personne, de revenu] smallness - 2. [d'esprit] pettiness.

petit-fils [p(ə)tifis] nm grandson.

petit-four [p(ə)tifur] nm petit four.

pétition [petisjɔ̃] nf petition.

petit-lait [p(ə)tilɛ] nm whey.

petit-nègre [p(ə)tinɛgr] nm inv fam pidgin French.

petits-enfants [p(ə)tizɑ̃fɑ̃] nmpl grandchildren.

petit-suisse [p(ə)tisɥis] nm fresh soft cheese, eaten with sugar.

pétrifier [9] [petrifje] vt litt & fig to petrify.

pétrin [petrɛ̃] nm 1. [de boulanger] kneading machine - 2. fam [embarras] pickle ; **se fourrer/être dans le pétrin** to get into/to be in a pickle.

pétrir [32] [petrir] vt [pâte, muscle] to knead.

pétrole [petrɔl] nm oil, petroleum.

pétrolier, ère [petrɔlje, ɛr] adj oil (avant n), petroleum (avant n). **pétrolier** nm [navire] oil tanker.

pétrolifère [petrɔlifɛr] adj oil-bearing.

pétulant, e [petylɑ̃, ɑ̃t] adj exuberant.

peu [pø] <> adv 1. (avec verbe, adjectif, adverbe) **il a peu dormi** he didn't sleep much, he slept little ; **peu souvent** not very often, rarely ; **très peu** very little - 2. : **peu de** (+ n sing) little, not much ; (+ n pl) few, not many ; **il a peu de travail** he hasn't got much work, he has little work ; **il reste peu de jours** there aren't many days left ; **peu de gens le connaissent** few OU not many know him. <> nm 1. [petite quantité] : **le peu de** (+ n sing) the little ; (+ n pl) the few - 2. (précédé de un) a little, a bit ; **je le connais un peu** I know him slightly OU a little ; **un (tout) petit peu** a little bit ; **elle est un peu sotte** she's a bit stupid ; **un peu de** a little ; **un peu de vin/patience** a little wine/patience. **avant peu** loc adv soon, before long. **depuis peu** loc adv ... ly. **peu à peu** loc adv gradually,

little by little. **pour peu que** (+ subjonctif) loc conj if ever, if only. **pour un peu** loc adv nearly, almost. **si peu que** (+ subjonctif) loc conj however little. **sous peu** loc adv soon, shortly.

peuplade [pœplad] nf tribe.

peuple [pœpl] nm 1. [gén] people ; **le peuple** the (common) people - 2. fam [multitude] : **quel peuple!** what a crowd!

peuplement [pœpləmɑ̃] nm 1. [action] populating - 2. [population] population.

peupler [5] [pœple] vt 1. [pourvoir d'habitants - région] to populate ; [- bois, étang] to stock - 2. [habiter, occuper] to inhabit - 3. fig [remplir] to fill. **se peupler** vp 1. [région] to become populated - 2. [rue, salle] to be filled.

peuplier [pøplije] nm poplar.

peur [pœr] nf fear ; **avoir peur de qqn/qqch** to be afraid of sb/sthg ; **avoir peur de faire qqch** to be afraid of doing sthg ; **avoir peur que** (+ subjonctif) to be afraid that ; **j'ai peur qu'il ne vienne pas** I'm afraid he won't come ; **faire peur à qqn** to frighten sb ; **par** OU **de peur de qqch** for fear of sthg ; **par** OU **de peur de faire qqch** for fear of doing sthg.

peureux, euse [pœrø, øz] <> adj fearful, timid. <> nm, f fearful OU timid person.

peut pouvoir.

peut-être [pøtɛtr] adv perhaps, maybe ; **peut-être qu'ils ne viendront pas, ils ne viendront peut-être pas** perhaps OU maybe they won't come.

peux pouvoir.

phalange [falɑ̃ʒ] nf ANAT phalanx.

phallocrate [falɔkrat] nm male chauvinist.

phallus [falys] nm phallus.

pharaon [faraɔ̃] nm pharaoh.

phare [far] <> nm 1. [tour] lighthouse - 2. AUTO headlight ; **phare antibrouillard** fog lamp UK, fog light US. <> adj landmark (avant n) ; **une industrie phare** a flagship OU pioneering industry.

pharmaceutique [farmasøtik] adj pharmaceutical.

pharmacie [farmasi] nf 1. [science] pharmacology - 2. [magasin] chemist's UK, drugstore US - 3. [meuble] (armoire à) **pharmacie** medicine cupboard UK OU chest US.

pharmacien, enne [farmasjɛ̃, ɛn] nm, f chemist UK, druggist US.

pharynx [farɛ̃ks] nm pharynx.

phase [faz] nf phase ; **être en phase avec qqn** to be on the same wavelength as sb. ; **phase terminale** final phase.

phénoménal, e, aux [fenɔmenal, o] adj phenomenal.

phénomène [fenɔmɛn] *nm* **1.** [fait] phenomenon - **2.** [être anormal] freak - **3.** *fam* [excentrique] character.

philanthropie [filɑ̃trɔpi] *nf* philanthropy.

philatélie [filateli] *nf* philately, stamp collecting.

philharmonique [filarmɔnik] *adj* philharmonic.

Philippines [filipin] *nfpl* : **les Philippines** the Philippines.

philologie [filɔlɔʒi] *nf* philology.

philosophe [filɔzɔf] <> *nmf* philosopher. <> *adj* philosophical.

philosophie [filɔzɔfi] *nf* philosophy.

phobie [fɔbi] *nf* phobia.

phonétique [fɔnetik] <> *nf* phonetics (U). <> *adj* phonetic.

phonographe [fɔnɔɡraf] *nm vieilli* gramophone *UK*, phonograph *US*.

phoque [fɔk] *nm* seal.

phosphate [fɔsfat] *nm* phosphate.

phosphore [fɔsfɔr] *nm* phosphorus.

phosphorescent, e [fɔsfɔresɑ̃, ɑ̃t] *adj* phosphorescent.

photo [fɔto] <> *nf* **1.** [technique] photography - **2.** [image] photo, picture ; **prendre qqn en photo** to take a photo of sb ; **photo d'identité** passport photo ; **photo couleur** colour *UK* ou color *US* photo ; **y'a pas photo** *fam* there's no comparison. <> *adj inv* : **appareil photo** camera.

photocomposition [fɔtokɔ̃pozisjɔ̃] *nf* filmsetting *UK*, photocomposition *US*.

photocopie [fɔtokɔpi] *nf* **1.** [procédé] photocopying - **2.** [document] photocopy.

photocopier [9] [fɔtokɔpje] *vt* to photocopy.

photocopieur [fɔtokɔpjœr] *nm* photocopier.

photocopieuse [fɔtokɔpjøz] *nf* = photocopieur.

photoélectrique [fɔtoelɛktrik] *adj* photoelectric.

photogénique [fɔtoʒenik] *adj* photogenic.

photographe [fɔtɔɡraf] *nmf* **1.** [artiste, technicien] photographer - **2.** [commerçant] camera dealer.

photographie [fɔtɔɡrafi] *nf* **1.** [technique] photography - **2.** [cliché] photograph.

photographier [9] [fɔtɔɡrafje] *vt* to photograph.

Photomaton® [fɔtɔmatɔ̃] *nm* photo booth.

photoreportage [fɔtɔrəpɔrtaʒ] *nm* PRESSE report (*consisting mainly of photographs*).

phrase [fraz] *nf* **1.** LING sentence ; **phrase toute faite** stock phrase - **2.** MUS phrase.

physicien, enne [fizisjɛ̃, ɛn] *nm, f* physicist.

physiologie [fizjɔlɔʒi] *nf* physiology.

physiologique [fizjɔlɔʒik] *adj* physiological.

physionomie [fizjɔnɔmi] *nf* **1.** [faciès] face - **2.** [apparence] physiognomy.

physionomiste [fizjɔnɔmist] *adj* : **être physionomiste** to have a good memory for faces.

physique [fizik] <> *adj* physical. <> *nf* [sciences] physics (U). <> *nm* **1.** [constitution] physical well-being - **2.** [apparence] physique.

physiquement [fizikmɑ̃] *adv* physically.

piaffer [3] [pjafe] *vi* **1.** [cheval] to paw the ground - **2.** [personne] to fidget.

piailler [3] [pjaje] *vi* **1.** [oiseaux] to cheep - **2.** [enfant] to squawk.

pianiste [pjanist] *nmf* pianist.

piano [pjano] <> *nm* piano. <> *adv* **1.** MUS piano - **2.** [doucement] gently.

pianoter [3] [pjanɔte] *vi* **1.** [jouer du piano] to plunk away (on the piano) - **2.** [sur table] to drum one's fingers.

piaule [pjol] *nf fam* [hébergement] place ; [chambre] room.

PIB (*abr de* **produit intérieur brut**) *nm* GDP.

pic [pik] *nm* **1.** [outil] pick, pickaxe *UK*, pickax *US* - **2.** [montagne] peak - **3.** [oiseau] woodpecker - **4.** *fig* [maximum] : **pic d'audience** top (audience) ratings ; **on a observé des pics de pollution** pollution levels reached a peak, pollution levels peaked. ⏵ **à pic** *loc adv* **1.** [verticalement] vertically ; **couler à pic** to sink like a stone - **2.** *fam fig* [à point nommé] just at the right moment.

pichenette [piʃnɛt] *nf* flick (of the finger).

pichet [piʃɛ] *nm* jug *UK*, pitcher *US*.

pickpocket [pikpɔkɛt] *nm* pickpocket.

picorer [3] [pikɔre] *vi & vt* to peck.

picotement [pikɔtmɑ̃] *nm* prickling (U), prickle.

pie [pi] <> *nf* **1.** [oiseau] magpie - **2.** *fig & péj* [bavard] chatterbox. <> *adj inv* [cheval] piebald.

pièce [pjɛs] *nf* **1.** [élément] piece ; [de moteur] part ; **pièce de collection** collector's item ; **pièce détachée** spare part - **2.** [unité] : **deux euros pièce** deux euros each ou apiece ; **acheter/vendre qqch à la pièce** to buy/sell sthg singly, to buy/sell sthg separately ; **travailler à la pièce** to do piecework - **3.** [document] document, paper ; **pièce d'identité** identification papers *pl* ; **pièce jointe** [e-mail] attachement ; **pièce jointe**

[document] enclosures ; **pièce justificative** written proof *(U)*, supporting document - **4.** [œuvre littéraire ou musicale] piece ; **pièce (de théâtre)** play - **5.** [argent] : **pièce (de monnaie)** coin - **6.** [de maison] room - **7.** COUT patch.

pied [pje] *nm* **1.** [gén] foot ; **à pied** on foot ; **avoir pied** to be able to touch the bottom ; **perdre pied** *litt & fig* to be out of one's depth ; **être/marcher pieds nus** OU **nu-pieds** to be/to go barefoot ; **pied bot** [handicap] clubfoot - **2.** [base - de montagne, table] foot ; [- de verre] stem ; [- de lampe] base - **3.** [plant - de tomate] stalk ; [- de vigne] stock ; **être sur pied** to be (back) on one's feet, to be up and about ; **faire du pied à** to play footsie with ; **mettre qqch sur pied** to get sthg on its feet, to get sthg off the ground ; **je n'ai jamais mis les pieds chez lui** I've never set foot in his house ; **au pied de la lettre** literally, to the letter. ● **en pied** *loc adj* [portrait] full-length.

pied-de-biche [pjedbiʃ] *(pl* **pieds-de-biche)** *nm* [outil] nail claw.

piédestal, aux [pjedɛstal, o] *nm* pedestal.

pied-noir [pjenwar] *nmf French settler in Algeria.*

piège [pjɛʒ] *nm litt & fig* trap.

piéger [22] [pjeʒe] *vt* **1.** [animal, personne] to trap - **2.** [colis, véhicule] to boobytrap.

piercing [pi:rsiŋ] *nm* body piercing.

pierraille [pjeraj] *nf* loose stones *pl*.

pierre [pjɛr] *nf* stone ; **pierre d'achoppement** *fig* stumbling block ; **pierre précieuse** precious stone.

pierreries [pjerri] *nfpl* precious stones, jewels.

piété [pjete] *nf* piety.

piétiner [3] [pjetine] ◇ *vi* **1.** [trépigner] to stamp (one's feet) - **2.** *fig* [ne pas avancer] to make no progress, to be at a standstill. ◇ *vt* [personne, parterre] to trample.

piéton, onne [pjetɔ̃, ɔn] ◇ *nm, f* pedestrian. ◇ *adj* pedestrian *(avant n)*.

piétonnier, ère [pjetɔnje, ɛr] *adj* pedestrian *(avant n)*.

piètre [pjɛtr] *adj* poor.

pieu, x [pjø] *nm* **1.** [poteau] post, stake - **2.** *fam* [lit] pit *UK*, sack *US*.

pieuvre [pjœvr] *nf* octopus ; *fig & péj* leech.

pieux, pieuse [pjø, pjøz] *adj* [personne, livre] pious.

pif [pif] *nm fam* conk *UK*, hooter *UK*, schnoz(zle) *US* ; **au pif** *fig* by guesswork.

pigeon [piʒɔ̃] *nm* **1.** [oiseau] pigeon - **2.** *fam* [personne] sucker.

pigeonnier [piʒɔnje] *nm* [pour pigeons] loft, dovecote.

pigment [pigmɑ̃] *nm* pigment.

pignon [piɲɔ̃] *nm* **1.** [de mur] gable - **2.** [d'engrenage] gearwheel - **3.** [de pomme de pin] pine kernel.

pile [pil] ◇ *nf* **1.** [de livres, journaux] pile - **2.** ÉLECTR battery - **3.** [de pièce] : **pile ou face** heads or tails. ◇ *adv fam* on the dot ; **tomber/arriver pile** to come/to arrive at just the right time.

piler [3] [pile] ◇ *vt* [amandes] to crush, to grind. ◇ *vi fam* AUTO to jam on the brakes.

pileux, euse [pilø, øz] *adj* hairy *(avant n)* ; **système pileux** hair.

pilier [pilje] *nm* **1.** [de construction] pillar - **2.** *fig* [soutien] mainstay, pillar - **3.** [rugby] prop *(forward)*.

pillard, e [pijar, ard] *nm, f* looter.

piller [3] [pije] *vt* **1.** [ville, biens] to loot - **2.** *fig* [ouvrage, auteur] to plagiarize.

pilon [pilɔ̃] *nm* **1.** [instrument] pestle - **2.** [de poulet] drumstick - **3.** [jambe de bois] wooden leg.

pilonner [3] [pilɔne] *vt* to pound.

pilori [pilɔri] *nm* pillory ; **mettre** OU **clouer qqn au pilori** *fig* to pillory sb.

pilotage [pilɔtaʒ] *nm* piloting ; **pilotage automatique** automatic piloting.

pilote [pilɔt] ◇ *nm* **1.** [d'avion] pilot ; [de voiture] driver ; **pilote automatique** autopilot ; **pilote de chasse** fighter pilot ; **pilote de course** racing *UK* OU race *US* driver ; **pilote d'essai** test pilot ; **pilote de ligne** airline pilot. ◇ *adj* pilot *(avant n)*, experimental.

piloter [3] [pilɔte] *vt* **1.** [avion] to pilot ; [voiture] to drive - **2.** [personne] to show around.

pilotis [pilɔti] *nm* pile.

pilule [pilyl] *nf* pill ; **prendre la pilule** to be on the pill.

piment [pimɑ̃] *nm* **1.** [plante] pepper, capsicum ; **piment rouge** chilli pepper, hot red pepper - **2.** *fig* [piquant] spice, pizzazz *US*.

pimpant, e [pɛ̃pɑ̃, ɑ̃t] *adj* smart.

pin [pɛ̃] *nm* pine ; **pin parasol** umbrella pine ; **pin sylvestre** Scots pine.

pin's [pinz] *nm inv* badge.

pince [pɛ̃s] *nf* **1.** [grande] pliers *pl* - **2.** [petite] : **pince (à épiler)** tweezers *pl* ; **pince à linge** clothes peg *UK*, clothespin *US* - **3.** [de crabe] pincer - **4.** COUT dart.

pinceau, x [pɛ̃so] *nm* [pour peindre] brush.

pincée [pɛ̃se] *nf* pinch.

pincer [16] [pɛ̃se] ◇ *vt* **1.** [serrer] to pinch ; MUS to pluck ; [lèvres] to purse - **2.** *fam fig* [arrêter] to nick *UK*, to catch - **3.** [suj: froid] to nip. ◇ *vi fam* [faire froid] : **ça pince!** it's a bit nippy!

pincettes [pɛ̃sɛt] *nfpl* [ustensile] tongs.

pingouin [pɛ̃gwɛ̃] *nm* penguin.

ping-pong [piŋpɔ̃g] *nm* ping pong, table tennis.

pinson [pɛ̃sɔ̃] *nm* chaffinch.

pintade [pɛ̃tad] *nf* guinea fowl.

pin-up [pinœp] *nf inv* pinup (girl).

pioche [pjɔʃ] *nf* **1.** [outil] pick - **2.** [jeux] pile.

piocher [3] [pjɔʃe] <> *vt* **1.** [terre] to dig - **2.** [jeux] to take - **3.** *fig* [choisir] to pick at random. <> *vi* **1.** [creuser] to dig - **2.** [jeux] to pick up ; **piocher dans** [tas] to delve into ; [économies] to dip into.

pion, pionne [pjɔ̃, pjɔn] *nm, f fam* SCOL *supervisor (often a student who does this as a part-time job).* **pion** *nm* [aux échecs] pawn ; [aux dames] piece ; **n'être qu'un pion** *fig* to be just a pawn in the game.

pionnier, ère [pjɔnje, ɛr] *nm, f* pioneer.

pipe [pip] *nf* pipe.

pipeline, pipe-line [pajplajn, piplin] (*pl* pipe-lines) *nm* pipeline.

pipi [pipi] *nm fam* wee UK, weewee ; **faire pipi** to have a wee.

piquant, e [pikɑ̃, ɑ̃t] *adj* **1.** [barbe, feuille] prickly - **2.** [sauce] spicy, hot. **piquant** *nm* **1.** [d'animal] spine ; [de végétal] thorn, prickle - **2.** *fig* [d'histoire] spice.

pique [pik] <> *nf* **1.** [arme] pike - **2.** *fig* [mot blessant] barbed comment. <> *nm* [aux cartes] spade.

pique-assiette [pikasjɛt] (*pl inv* OU **pique-assiettes**) *nmf péj* sponger.

pique-nique [piknik] (*pl* pique-niques) *nm* picnic.

piquer [3] [pike] <> *vt* **1.** [suj: guêpe, méduse] to sting ; [suj: serpent, moustique] to bite - **2.** [avec pointe] to prick - **3.** MED to give an injection to - **4.** [animal] to put down - **5.** [fleur] : **piquer qqch dans** to stick sthg into - **6.** [suj: tissu, barbe] to prickle - **7.** [suj: fumée, froid] to sting - **8.** COUT to sew, to machine - **9.** *fam* [voler] to pinch UK - **10.** *fig* [curiosité] to excite, to arouse - **11.** *fam* [voleur, escroc] to nick UK, to catch. <> *vi* **1.** [ronce] to prick ; [ortie] to sting - **2.** [guêpe, méduse] to sting ; [serpent, moustique] to bite - **3.** [épice] to burn - **4.** *fam* [voler] : **piquer (dans)** to pinch (from) - **5.** [avion] to dive.

piquet [pikɛ] *nm* [pieu] peg, stake. **piquet de grève** *nm* picket.

piqûre [pikyr] *nf* **1.** [de guêpe, de méduse] sting ; [de serpent, de moustique] bite - **2.** [d'ortie] sting - **3.** [injection] jab UK, shot.

piratage [pirataʒ] *nm* piracy ; INFORM hacking.

pirate [pirat] <> *nm* [corsaire] pirate ;

pirate de l'air hijacker, skyjacker. <> *adj* pirate *(avant n).*

pire [pir] <> *adj* **1.** [comparatif relatif] worse - **2.** [superlatif] : **le/la pire** the worst. <> *nm* : **le pire (de)** the worst (of).

pirogue [pirɔg] *nf* dugout canoe.

pirouette [pirwɛt] *nf* **1.** [saut] pirouette - **2.** *fig* [faux-fuyant] prevarication, evasive answer.

pis [pi] <> *adj litt* [pire] worse. <> *adv* worse ; **de mal en pis** from bad to worse. <> *nm* udder.

pis-aller [pizale] *nm inv* last resort.

pisciculture [pisikyltyr] *nf* fish farming.

piscine [pisin] *nf* swimming pool ; **piscine couverte/découverte** indoor/open-air swimming pool.

pissenlit [pisɑ̃li] *nm* dandelion.

pisser [3] [pise] *fam* <> *vt* **1.** [suj: personne] : **pisser du sang** to pass blood - **2.** [suj: plaie] : **son genou pissait le sang** blood was gushing from his knee. <> *vi* to pee, to piss.

pissotière [pisɔtjɛr] *nf fam* public urinal.

pistache [pistaʃ] *nf* [fruit] pistachio (nut).

piste [pist] *nf* **1.** [trace] trail - **2.** [zone aménagée] : **piste d'atterrissage** runway ; **piste cyclable** (bi)cycle path ; **piste de danse** dance floor ; **piste de ski** ski run - **3.** [chemin] path, track - **4.** [d'enregistrement] track - **5.** [divertissement] : **jeu de piste** treasure hunt.

pistil [pistil] *nm* pistil.

pistolet [pistɔlɛ] *nm* **1.** [arme] pistol, gun - **2.** [à peinture] spray gun.

piston [pistɔ̃] *nm* **1.** [de moteur] piston - **2.** MUS [d'instrument] valve - **3.** *fig* [appui] string-pulling.

pistonner [3] [pistɔne] *vt* to pull strings for ; **se faire pistonner** to have strings pulled for one.

pitance [pitɑ̃s] *nf péj & vieilli* sustenance.

pitbull, pit-bull [pitbul] (*pl* pit-bulls) *nm* pitbull (terrier).

piteux, euse [pitø, øz] *adj* piteous.

pitié [pitje] *nf* pity ; **avoir pitié de qqn** to have pity on sb, to pity sb.

piton [pitɔ̃] *nm* **1.** [clou] piton - **2.** [pic] peak.

pitoyable [pitwajabl] *adj* pitiful.

pitre [pitr] *nm* clown.

pitrerie [pitrəri] *nf* tomfoolery.

pittoresque [pitɔrɛsk] *adj* **1.** [région] picturesque - **2.** [détail] colourful UK, colorful US, vivid.

pivot [pivo] *nm* **1.** [de machine, au basket] pivot - **2.** [de dent] post - **3.** *fig* [centre] mainspring.

pivoter [3] [pivɔte] *vi* to pivot ; [porte] to revolve.

pizza [pidza] *nf* pizza.

Pl., pl. *abr écrite de* place.

placage [plakaʒ] *nm* [de bois] veneer.

placard [plakar] *nm* **1.** [armoire] cupboard - **2.** [affiche] poster, notice.

placarder [3] [plakarde] *vt* [affiche] to put up, to stick up ; [mur] to placard, to stick a notice on.

place [plas] *nf* **1.** [espace] space, room ; **prendre de la place** to take up (a lot of) space ; **faire place à** [amour, haine] to give way to - **2.** [emplacement, position] position ; **changer qqch de place** to put sthg in a different place, to move sthg ; **prendre la place de qqn** to take sb's place ; **à la place de qqn** instead of sb, in sb's place ; **à ta place** if I were you, in your place - **3.** [siège] seat ; **place assise** seat - **4.** [rang] place - **5.** [de ville] square - **6.** [emploi] position, job - **7.** MIL [de garnison] garrison (town) ; **place forte** fortified town. ▶ **sur place** *loc adv* there, on the spot ; **je serai déjà sur place** I'll already be there.

placement [plasmɑ̃] *nm* **1.** [d'argent] investment - **2.** [d'employé] placing.

placenta [plasɛ̃ta] *nm* ANAT placenta.

placer [16] [plase] *vt* **1.** [gén] to put, to place ; [invités, spectateurs] to seat - **2.** [mot, anecdote] to put in, to get in - **3.** [argent] to invest. ▶ **se placer** *vp* **1.** [prendre place - debout] to stand ; [- assis] to sit (down) - **2.** *fig* [dans une situation] to put o.s. - **3.** [se classer] to come, to be.

placide [plasid] *adj* placid.

plafond [plafɔ̃] *nm litt & fig* ceiling ; **faux plafond** false ceiling.

plafonner [3] [plafɔne] *vi* [prix, élève] to peak ; [avion] to reach its ceiling.

plage [plaʒ] *nf* **1.** [de sable] beach - **2.** [d'ombre, de prix] band ; *fig* [de temps] slot - **3.** [de disque] track - **4.** [dans une voiture] : **plage arrière** back shelf.

plagiat [plaʒja] *nm* plagiarism.

plagier [9] [plaʒje] *vt* to plagiarize.

plaider [4] [plede] ⟨⟩ *vt* DR to plead. ⟨⟩ *vi* DR to plead ; **plaider contre qqn** to plead against sb ; **plaider pour qqn** DR to plead for sb ; [justifier] to plead sb's cause.

plaidoirie [pledwari] *nf* DR speech for the defence UK ou defense US ; *fig* plea.

plaidoyer [pledwaje] *nm* = plaidoirie.

plaie [plɛ] *nf* **1.** *litt & fig* wound - **2.** *fam* [personne] pest.

plaindre [80] [plɛ̃dr] *vt* to pity. ▶ **se plaindre** *vp* to complain.

plaine [plɛn] *nf* plain.

plain-pied [plɛ̃pje] ▶ **de plain-pied** *loc adv* **1.** [pièce] on one floor ; **de plain-pied avec** *litt & fig* on a level with - **2.** *fig* [directement] straight.

plaint, e [plɛ̃, plɛ̃t] *pp* ▶ plaindre.

plainte [plɛ̃t] *nf* **1.** [gémissement] moan, groan ; *litt & fig* [du vent] moan - **2.** [doléance & DR] complaint ; **porter plainte** to lodge a complaint ; **plainte contre X** ≃ complaint against person or persons unknown.

plaintif, ive [plɛ̃tif, iv] *adj* plaintive.

plaire [110] [plɛr] *vi* to be liked ; **il me plaît** I like him ; **ça te plairait d'aller au cinéma?** would you like to go to the cinema? ; **s'il vous/te plaît** please.

plaisance [plɛzɑ̃s] ▶ **de plaisance** *loc adj* pleasure (*avant n*) ; **navigation de plaisance** sailing ; **port de plaisance** marina.

plaisancier, ère [plɛzɑ̃sje, ɛr] *nm, f* (amateur) sailor.

plaisant, e [plɛzɑ̃, ɑ̃t] *adj* pleasant.

plaisanter [3] [plɛzɑ̃te] *vi* to joke ; **tu plaisantes?** you must be joking!

plaisanterie [plɛzɑ̃tri] *nf* joke ; **c'est une plaisanterie?** *iron* you must be joking!

plaisantin [plɛzɑ̃tɛ̃] *nm* joker.

plaisir [plɛzir] *nm* pleasure ; **les plaisirs de la vie** life's pleasures ; **avoir du/prendre plaisir à faire qqch** to have/to take pleasure in doing sthg ; **faire plaisir à qqn** to please sb ; **avec plaisir** with pleasure ; **j'ai le plaisir de vous annoncer que...** I have the (great) pleasure of announcing that...

plan¹, e [plɑ̃, plan] *adj* level, flat.

plan² [plɑ̃] *nm* **1.** [dessin - de ville] map ; [- de maison] plan - **2.** [projet] plan ; **faire des plans** to make plans ; **avoir son plan** to have something in mind - **3.** [domaine] : **sur tous les plans** in all respects ; **sur le plan affectif** emotionally ; **sur le plan familial** as far as the family is concerned - **4.** [surface] : **plan d'eau** lake ; **plan de travail** work surface, worktop UK - **5.** GÉOM plane - **6.** CINÉ take ; **gros plan** close-up - **7.** BANQUE : **plan d'épargne** savings plan - **8.** [sécurité] : **plan vigipirate** security measures to protect against terrorist attacks - **9.** ÉCON : **plan social** redundancy scheme ou plan UK. ▶ **à l'arrière-plan** *loc adv* in the background. ▶ **au premier plan** *loc adv* [dans l'espace] in the foreground. ▶ **en plan** *loc adv* : **laisser qqn en plan** to leave sb stranded, to abandon sb ; **il a tout laissé en plan** he dropped everything. ▶ **sur le même plan** *loc adj* on the same level.

planche [plɑ̃ʃ] *nf* **1.** [en bois] plank ; **planche à dessin** drawing board ; **planche à repasser** ironing board ; **planche à voile** [planche] sailboard ; [sport] windsurfing ; **faire la planche** *fig* to float - **2.** [d'illustration] plate.

plancher [plɑ̃ʃe] *nm* **1.** [de maison, de voiture] floor - **2.** *fig* [limite] floor, lower limit.

plancton [plɑ̃ktɔ̃] *nm* plankton.

planer [3] [plane] *vi* **1.** [avion, oiseau] to glide - **2.** [nuage, fumée, brouillard] to float - **3.** *fig* [danger] : **planer sur qqn** to hang over sb - **4.** *fam fig* [personne] to be out of touch with reality.

planétaire [planeter] *adj* **1.** ASTRON planetary - **2.** [mondial] world *(avant n)*.

planétarium [planetarjɔm] *nm* planetarium.

planète [planɛt] *nf* planet.

planeur [planœr] *nm* glider.

planification [planifikasjɔ̃] *nf* ÉCON planning.

planisphère [planisfɛr] *nm* map of the world, planisphere.

planning [planiŋ] *nm* **1.** [de fabrication] workflow schedule - **2.** [agenda personnel] schedule ; **planning familial** [contrôle] family planning ; [organisme] family planning clinic.

planque [plɑ̃k] *nf fam* **1.** [cachette] hideout - **2.** *fig* [situation, travail] cushy number.

plant [plɑ̃] *nm* [plante] seedling.

plantaire [plɑ̃tɛr] *adj* plantar.

plantation [plɑ̃tasjɔ̃] *nf* **1.** [exploitation - d'arbres, de coton, de café] plantation ; [- de légumes] patch - **2.** [action] planting.

plante [plɑ̃t] *nf* **1.** BOT [plante] **plante verte** OU **d'appartement** OU **d'intérieur** house OU pot *UK* plant - **2.** ANAT sole.

planter [3] [plɑ̃te] ⋄ *vt* **1.** [arbre, terrain] to plant - **2.** [clou] to hammer in, to drive in ; [pieu] to drive in ; [couteau, griffes] to stick in - **3.** [tente] to pitch - **4.** *fam fig* [laisser tomber] to dump - **5.** *fig* [chapeau] to stick ; [baiser] to plant ; **planter son regard dans celui de qqn** to look sb right in the eyes. ⋄ *vi fam* INFORM to crash.

plantureux, euse [plɑ̃tyrø, øz] *adj* **1.** [repas] lavish - **2.** [femme] buxom.

plaque [plak] *nf* **1.** [de métal, de verre, de verglas] sheet ; [de marbre] slab ; **plaque chauffante** OU **de cuisson** hotplate ; **plaque de chocolat** bar of chocolate - **2.** [gravée] plaque ; **plaque d'immatriculation** OU **minéralogique** numberplate *UK*, license plate *US* - **3.** [insigne] badge - **4.** [sur la peau] patch - **5.** [dentaire] plaque.

plaqué, e [plake] *adj* [métal] plated ; **plaqué**

or/argent gold-/silver-plated. ➡ **plaqué** *nm* [métal] : **du plaqué or/argent** gold/silver plate.

plaquer [3] [plake] *vt* **1.** [métal] to plate - **2.** [bois] to veneer - **3.** [aplatir] to flatten ; **plaquer qqn contre qqch** to pin sb against sthg ; **plaquer qqch contre qqch** to stick sthg onto sthg - **4.** [rugby] to tackle - **5.** MUS [accord] to play - **6.** *fam* [travail, personne] to chuck.

plaquette [plakɛt] *nf* **1.** [de métal] plaque ; [de marbre] tablet - **2.** [de chocolat] bar ; [de beurre] pat - **3.** [de comprimés] packet, strip - **4.** *(gén pl)* BIOL platelet - **5.** AUTO : **plaquette de frein** brake pad.

plasma [plasma] *nm* plasma.

plastique [plastik] *adj & nm* plastic.

plastiquer [3] [plastike] *vt* to blow up *(with plastic explosives)*.

plat, e [pla, plat] *adj* **1.** [gén] flat - **2.** [eau] still. ➡ **plat** *nm* **1.** [partie plate] flat - **2.** [récipient] dish - **3.** [mets] course ; **plat cuisiné** ready-cooked meal OU dish ; **plat du jour** today's special ; **plat préparé** ready meal ; **plat de résistance** main course - **4.** [plongeon] belly-flop. ➡ **à plat** *loc adv* **1.** [horizontalement, dégonflé] flat - **2.** *fam* [épuisé] exhausted.

platane [platan] *nm* plane tree.

plateau [plato] *nm* **1.** [de cuisine] tray ; **plateau de/à fromages** cheeseboard - **2.** [de balance] pan - **3.** GÉOGR & *fig* plateau - **4.** THÉÂTRE stage ; CINÉ & TV set - **5.** [de vélo] chain wheel.

plateau-repas [platorəpa] *nm* tray (of food).

plate-bande [platbɑ̃d] *nf* flowerbed.

plate-forme [platfɔrm] *nf* [gén] platform ; **plate-forme de forage** drilling platform.

platine [platin] ⋄ *adj inv* platinum. ⋄ *nm* [métal] platinum. ⋄ *nf* [de tourne-disque] deck ; **platine laser** compact disc player.

platonique [platɔnik] *adj* [amour, amitié] platonic.

plâtras [platra] *nm* [gravats] rubble.

plâtre [platr] *nm* **1.** CONSTR & MÉD plaster - **2.** [sculpture] plaster cast - **3.** *péj* [fromage] : **c'est du vrai plâtre** it's like sawdust.

plâtrer [3] [platre] *vt* **1.** [mur] to plaster - **2.** MÉD to put in plaster.

plausible [plozibl] *adj* plausible.

play-back [plɛbak] *nm inv* miming ; **chanter en play-back** to mime.

play-boy [plɛbɔj] *(pl* play-boys) *nm* playboy.

plébiscite [plebisit] *nm* plebiscite.

plein, e [plɛ̃, plɛn] *adj* **1.** [rempli, complet] full ; **c'est la pleine forme** I am/they are etc in top form ; **en pleine nuit** in the middle of the night ; **en plein air** outdoor, open-air - **2.** [non creux] solid - **3.** [femelle] pregnant. ➤ **plein** ◇ *adv fam* **il a de l'encre plein les doigts** he has ink all over his fingers ; **en plein dans/sur qqch** right in/on sthg. ◇ *nm* [de réservoir] full tank ; **le plein, s'il vous plaît** fill her up, please ; **faire le plein** to fill up.

plein-air [plɛnɛr] *nm inv* SCOL games. ➤ **de plein-air, en plein-air** *loc adj* open-air, outdoor.

plein-temps [plɛ̃tã] *nm* full-time job.

plénitude [plenityd] *nf* fullness.

pléonasme [pleɔnasm] *nm* pleonasm.

pleurer [5] [plœre] ◇ *vi* **1.** [larmoyer] to cry ; **pleurer de joie** to weep for joy, to cry with joy - **2.** *péj* [se plaindre] to whinge *UK* - **3.** [se lamenter] : **pleurer sur** to lament. ◇ *vt* to mourn.

pleurnicher [3] [plœrniʃe] *vi* to whine, to whinge *UK*.

pleurs [plœr] *nmpl* : **être en pleurs** to be in tears.

pleuvoir [68] [pløvwar] *v impers litt & fig* to rain ; **il pleut** it is raining.

Plexiglas® [plɛksiglas] *nm* Plexiglass®.

plexus [plɛksys] *nm* plexus ; **plexus solaire** solar plexus.

pli [pli] *nm* **1.** [de tissu] pleat ; [de pantalon] crease ; **faux pli** crease - **2.** [du front] line ; [du cou] fold - **3.** [lettre] letter ; [enveloppe] envelope ; **sous pli séparé** under separate cover - **4.** [aux cartes] trick - **5.** GÉOL fold.

pliant, e [plijã, ãt] *adj* folding (*avant n*).

plier [10] [plije] ◇ *vt* **1.** [papier, tissu] to fold - **2.** [vêtement, vélo] to fold (up) - **3.** [branche, bras] to bend. ◇ *vi* **1.** [se courber] to bend - **2.** *fig* [céder] to bow. ➤ **se plier** *vp* **1.** [être pliable] to fold (up) - **2.** *fig* [se soumettre] : **se plier à qqch** to bow to sthg.

plinthe [plɛ̃t] *nf* plinth.

plissé, e [plise] *adj* **1.** [jupe] pleated - **2.** [peau] wrinkled.

plissement [plismã] *nm* **1.** [de front] creasing ; [d'yeux] screwing up - **2.** GÉOL fold.

plisser [3] [plise] ◇ *vt* **1.** COUT to pleat - **2.** [front] to crease ; [lèvres] to pucker ; [yeux] to screw up - ◇ *vi* [étoffe] to crease.

plomb [plɔ̃] *nm* **1.** [métal, de vitrail] lead - **2.** [de chasse] shot - **3.** ÉLECTR fuse ; **les plombs ont sauté** a fuse has blown ou gone - **4.** [de pêche] sinker.

plombage [plɔ̃baʒ] *nm* [de dent] filling.

plomber [3] [plɔ̃be] *vt* **1.** [ligne] to weight (with lead) - **2.** [dent] to fill.

plombier [plɔ̃bje] *nm* plumber.

plonge [plɔ̃ʒ] *nf fam* dishwashing ; **faire la plonge** to wash dishes.

plongeant, e [plɔ̃ʒã, ãt] *adj* **1.** [vue] from above - **2.** [décolleté] plunging.

plongée [plɔ̃ʒe] *nf* [immersion] diving ; **plongée sous-marine** scuba diving.

plongeoir [plɔ̃ʒwar] *nm* diving board.

plongeon [plɔ̃ʒɔ̃] *nm* [dans l'eau, au football] dive.

plonger [17] [plɔ̃ʒe] ◇ *vt* **1.** [immerger, enfoncer] to plunge ; **plonger la tête sous l'eau** to put one's head under the water - **2.** *fig* [précipiter] : **plonger qqn dans qqch** to throw sb into sthg ; **plonger une pièce dans l'obscurité** to plunge a room into darkness. ◇ *vi* **1.** [dans l'eau, gardien de but] to dive - **2.** *fam* [échouer] to decline, to fall off. ➤ **se plonger** *vp* **1.** [s'immerger] to submerge - **2.** *fig* [s'absorber] : **se plonger dans qqch** to immerse o.s. in sthg.

plongeur, euse [plɔ̃ʒœr, øz] *nm, f* **1.** [dans l'eau] diver - **2.** [dans restaurant] dishwasher.

ployer [13] [plwaje] *vt & vi litt & fig* to bend.

plu [ply] ◇ *pp inv* ➤ **plaire**. ◇ *pp inv* ➤ **pleuvoir**.

pluie [plɥi] *nf* **1.** [averse] rain (*U*) ; **sous la pluie** in the rain ; **une pluie battante** driving rain ; **une pluie fine** drizzle - **2.** *fig* [grande quantité] : **une pluie de** a shower of.

plume [plym] *nf* **1.** [d'oiseau] feather - **2.** [pour écrire - d'oiseau] quill pen ; [- de stylo] nib.

plumeau, x [plymo] *nm* feather duster.

plumer [3] [plyme] *vt* **1.** [volaille] to pluck - **2.** *fam fig & péj* [personne] to fleece.

plumier [plymje] *nm* pencil box.

plupart [plypar] *nf* : **la plupart de** most of, the majority of ; **la plupart du temps** most of the time, mostly ; **pour la plupart** mostly, for the most part.

pluriel, elle [plyrjɛl] *adj* **1.** GRAMM plural - **2.** [société] pluralist. ➤ **pluriel** *nm* plural ; **au pluriel** in the plural.

plus [ply(s)] ◇ *adv* **1.** [quantité] more ; **je ne peux vous en dire plus** I can't tell you anything more ; **beaucoup plus de** (*suivi d'un nom au singulier*) a lot more, much more ; (*suivi d'un nom au pluriel*) a lot more, many more ; **un peu plus de** (*suivi d'un nom au singulier*) a little more ; (*suivi d'un nom au pluriel*) a few more ; **il y a (un peu) plus de 15 ans** (a little) more than 15 years ago ; **plus j'y pense, plus je me dis que...** the more I think about it, the more I'm sure... - **2.** [comparaison] more ; **c'est plus court par là** it's shorter that way ; **viens plus souvent**

come more often ; **c'est un peu plus loin** it's a (little) bit further ; **plus jeune (que)** younger (than) ; **c'est plus simple qu'on ne le croit** it's simpler than you think - **3.** (superlatif) : **le plus** the most ; **c'est lui qui travaille le plus** he's the hardest worker, he's the one who works (the) hardest ; **un de ses tableaux les plus connus** one of his best-known paintings ; **le plus souvent** the most often ; **le plus loin the furthest** ; **le plus vite possible** as quickly as possible - **4.** (négation) no more ; **plus un mot!** not another word! ; **ne… plus** no longer, no more ; **il ne vient plus me voir** he doesn't come to see me any more, he no longer comes to see me ; **je n'y vais plus du tout** I don't go there any more. ◇ *nm* **1.** (signe) plus (sign) - **2.** *fig* (atout) plus. ◇ *prép* plus ; **trois plus trois font six** three plus three is six, three and three are six. ◆ **au plus** *loc adv* at the most ; **tout au plus** at the very most. ◆ **de plus** *loc adv* **1.** (en supplément, en trop) more ; **elle a cinq ans de plus que moi** she's five years older than me - **2.** (en outre) moreover, what's more. ◆ **de plus en plus** *loc adv* more and more. ◆ **de plus en plus de** *loc prép* more and more. ◆ **en plus** *loc adv* **1.** (en supplément) extra - **2.** (d'ailleurs) moreover, what's more. ◆ **en plus de** *loc prép* in addition to. ◆ **ni plus ni moins** *loc adv* no more no less. ◆ **plus ou moins** *loc adv* more or less. ◆ **sans plus** *loc adv* : **elle est gentille, sans plus** she's nice, but no more than that.

plusieurs [plyzjœr] *adj indéf pl & pron indéf pl* several.

plus-que-parfait [plyskəparfɛ] *nm* GRAMM pluperfect.

plus-value [plyvaly] *nf* **1.** (d'investissement) appreciation - **2.** (excédent) surplus - **3.** (bénéfice) profit ; (à la revente) capital gain.

plutôt [plyto] *adv* rather ; **plutôt que de faire qqch** instead of doing sthg, rather than doing ou do sthg.

pluvieux, euse [plyvjø, øz] *adj* rainy.

PME (*abr de* **petite et moyenne entreprise**) *nf* SME.

PMI *nf* (*abr de* **petite et moyenne industrie**) small industrial firm.

PMU (*abr de* **Pari mutuel urbain**) *nm* system for betting on horses.

PNB (*abr de* **produit national brut**) *nm* GNP.

pneu [pnø] *nm* (de véhicule) tyre *UK*, tire *US* ; **pneu arrière** rear tyre *UK* ou tire *US* ; **pneu-neige** winter tyre *UK* ou tire *US*.

pneumatique [pnømatik] ◇ *nf* PHYS pneumatics *(U)*. ◇ *adj* **1.** (fonctionnant à l'air) pneumatic - **2.** (gonflé à l'air) inflatable.

pneumonie [pnømɔni] *nf* pneumonia.

PO (*abr écrite de* **petites ondes**) MW.

poche [pɔʃ] *nf* **1.** (vêtement, de sac, d'air) pocket ; **de poche** pocket *(avant n)* - **2.** (sac, sous les yeux) bag ; **faire des poches** (vêtement) to bag - **3.** MÉD sac.

pocher [3] [pɔʃe] *vt* **1.** CULIN to poach - **2.** (blesser) : **pocher l'œil à qqn** to give sb a black eye.

pochette [pɔʃɛt] *nf* **1.** (enveloppe) envelope ; (d'allumettes) book ; (de photos) packet - **2.** (de disque) sleeve, jacket *US* - **3.** (mouchoir) (pocket) handkerchief.

pochoir [pɔʃwar] *nm* stencil.

podium [pɔdjɔm] *nm* podium.

poêle [pwal] ◇ *nf* pan ; **poêle à frire** frying pan. ◇ *nm* stove.

poème [pɔɛm] *nm* poem.

poésie [pɔezi] *nf* **1.** (genre, émotion) poetry - **2.** (pièce écrite) poem.

poète [pɔɛt] *nm* **1.** (écrivain) poet - **2.** *fig & hum* (rêveur) dreamer.

pogrom(e) [pɔgrɔm] *nm* pogrom.

poids [pwa] *nm* **1.** (gén) weight ; **quel poids fait-il?** how heavy is it/he? ; **perdre/prendre du poids** to lose/gain weight ; **vendre au poids** to sell by weight ; **poids lourd** (boxe) heavyweight ; (camion) heavy goods vehicle *UK* ; **de poids** (argument) weighty - **2.** SPORT (lancer) shot.

poignant, e [pwaɲɑ̃, ɑ̃t] *adj* poignant.

poignard [pwaɲar] *nm* dagger.

poignée [pwaɲe] *nf* **1.** (quantité, petit nombre) handful - **2.** (manche) handle. ◆ **poignée de main** *nf* handshake.

poignet [pwaɲɛ] *nm* **1.** ANAT wrist - **2.** (de vêtement) cuff.

poil [pwal] *nm* **1.** (du corps) hair - **2.** (d'animal) hair, coat - **3.** (de pinceau) bristle ; (de tapis) strand - **4.** *fam* (peu) : **il s'en est fallu d'un poil que je réussisse** I came within a hair's breadth of succeeding.

poilu, e [pwaly] *adj* hairy.

poinçon [pwɛ̃sɔ̃] *nm* **1.** (outil) awl - **2.** (marque) hallmark.

poinçonner [3] [pwɛ̃sɔne] *vt* **1.** (bijou) to hallmark - **2.** (billet, tôle) to punch.

poing [pwɛ̃] *nm* fist.

point [pwɛ̃] ◇ *nm* **1.** COUT (tricot) stitch ; **points de suture** MÉD stitches - **2.** (de ponctuation) : **point (final)** full stop *UK*, period *US* ; **point d'interrogation/d'exclamation** question/exclamation mark ; **points de suspension** suspension points - **3.** (petite tache) dot ; **point noir** (sur la peau) blackhead ; *fig* (problème) problem - **4.** (endroit) spot, point ; *fig* point ; **point d'appui** (support) something to lean on ; **point culminant** (en montagne) summit ;

fig climax ; **point de repère** [temporel] reference point ; [spatial] landmark ; **point de vente** point of sale, sale outlet ; **point de vue** [panorama] viewpoint ; *fig* [opinion, aspect] point of view ; **avoir un point commun avec qqn** to have something in common with sb - **5.** [degré] point ; **au point que, à tel point que** to such an extent that ; **je ne pensais pas que cela le vexerait à ce point** I didn't think it would make him so cross ; **être... au point de faire qqch** to be so... as to do sthg - **6.** *fig* [position] position - **7.** [réglage] : **mettre au point** [machine] to adjust ; [idée, projet] to finalize ; **à point** [cuisson] just right ; **à point (nommé)** just in time - **8.** [question, détail] point, detail ; **point faible** weak point - **9.** [score] point - **10.** [douleur] pain ; **point de côté** stitch - **11.** [début] : **être sur le point de faire qqch** to be on the point of doing sthg, to be about to do sthg - **12.** AUTO : **au point mort** in neutral - **13.** GÉOGR : **points cardinaux** points of the compass. <> *adv vieilli* : **ne point** not (at all).

pointe [pwɛ̃t] *nf* **1.** [extrémité] point ; [de nez] tip ; **se hausser sur la pointe des pieds** to stand on tiptoe ; **en pointe** pointed ; **tailler en pointe** to taper ; **se terminer en pointe** to taper ; **pointe d'asperge** asparagus tip - **2.** [clou] tack - **3.** [sommet] peak, summit ; **à la pointe de** *fig* at the peak of ; **à la pointe de la technique** at the forefront ou cutting edge of technology - **4.** *fig* [trait d'esprit] witticism - **5.** *fig* [petite quantité] : **une pointe de** a touch of. ➤ **pointes** *nfpl* [danse] points ; **faire des** ou **les pointes** to dance on one's points. ➤ **de pointe** *loc adj* **1.** [vitesse] maximum, top - **2.** [industrie, secteur] leading ; [technique] latest.

pointer [3] [pwɛ̃te] <> *vt* **1.** [cocher] to tick (off) - **2.** [employés - à l'entrée] to check in ; [- à la sortie] to check out - **3.** [diriger] : **pointer qqch vers** to point sthg towards ou toward US ; **pointer qqch sur** to point sthg at. <> *vi* **1.** [à l'usine - à l'entrée] to clock in ; [- à la sortie] to clock out - **2.** [à la pétanque] to get as close to the jack as possible - **3.** [jour] to break.

pointillé [pwɛ̃tije] *nm* **1.** [ligne] dotted line ; **en pointillé** [ligne] dotted ; *fig* [par sous-entendus] obliquely - **2.** [perforations] perforations *pl*.

pointilleux, euse [pwɛ̃tijø, øz] *adj* : **pointilleux (sur)** particular (about).

pointu, e [pwɛ̃ty] *adj* **1.** [objet] pointed - **2.** [voix, ton] sharp - **3.** [étude, formation] specialized.

pointure [pwɛ̃tyr] *nf* (shoe) size.

point-virgule [pwɛ̃virgyl] *nm* semi-colon.

poire [pwar] *nf* **1.** [fruit] pear - **2.** MÉD : **poire à injections** syringe - **3.** *fam* [visage] face - **4.** *fam* [naïf] dope.

poireau, x [pwaro] *nm* leek.

poirier [pwarje] *nm* pear tree.

pois [pwa] *nm* **1.** BOT pea ; **pois chiche** chickpea ; **petits pois** garden peas, petits pois ; **pois de senteur** sweet pea - **2.** *fig* [motif] dot, spot ; **à pois** spotted, polka-dot.

poison [pwazɔ̃] <> *nm* [substance] poison. <> *nmf fam fig* [personne] drag, pain ; [enfant] brat.

poisse [pwas] *nf fam* bad luck ; **porter la poisse** to be bad luck.

poisseux, euse [pwasø, øz] *adj* sticky.

poisson [pwasɔ̃] *nm* fish ; **poisson d'avril** [farce] April fool ; [en papier] *paper fish pinned to someone's back as a prank on April Fools' Day* ; **poisson rouge** goldfish. ➤ **Poissons** *nmpl* ASTROL Pisces *sg*.

poissonnerie [pwasɔnri] *nf* [boutique] fish shop, fishmonger's (shop) UK.

poissonnier, ère [pwasɔnje, ɛr] *nm, f* fishmonger UK.

poitrine [pwatrin] *nf* [thorax] chest ; [de femme] chest, bust.

poivre [pwavr] *nm* pepper ; **poivre blanc** white pepper ; **poivre gris, poivre noir** black pepper.

poivrier [pwavrije] *nm* pepper pot UK, pepperbox US.

poivrière [pwavrijɛr] *nf* = **poivrier**.

poivron [pwavrɔ̃] *nm* pepper, capsicum ; **poivron rouge/vert** red/green pepper.

poker [pɔkɛr] *nm* poker.

polaire [pɔlɛr] <> *adj* polar. <> *nf* [textile] (polar) fleece.

polar [pɔlar] *nm fam* thriller, whodunnit.

Polaroid® [pɔlarɔid] *nm* Polaroid®.

polder [pɔldɛr] *nm* polder.

pôle [pol] *nm* pole ; **pôle Nord/Sud** North/South Pole.

polémique [pɔlemik] <> *nf* controversy. <> *adj* [style, ton] polemical.

poli, e [pɔli] *adj* **1.** [personne] polite - **2.** [surface] polished.

police [pɔlis] *nf* **1.** [force de l'ordre] police ; **être de** ou **dans la police** to be in the police ; **police secours** *emergency service provided by the police* - **2.** [contrat] policy ; **police d'assurance** insurance policy.

polichinelle [pɔliʃinɛl] *nm* [personnage] Punch ; **secret de polichinelle** *fig* open secret.

policier, ère [pɔlisje, ɛr] *adj* **1.** [de la police] police *(avant n)* - **2.** [film, roman] detective *(avant n)*. ➤ **policier** *nm* police officer.

poliomyélite [pɔljɔmjelit] *nf* poliomyelitis.

polir [32] [pɔlir] *vt* to polish.

polisson, onne [pɔlisɔ̃, ɔn] ◇ *adj*
1. [chanson, propos] lewd, suggestive
- **2.** [enfant] naughty. ◇ *nm, f* [enfant]
naughty child.

politesse [pɔlitɛs] *nf* **1.** [courtoisie] politeness - **2.** [action] polite action.

politicien, enne [pɔlitisjɛ̃, ɛn] ◇ *adj péj*
politicking, politically unscrupulous.
◇ *nm, f* politician, politico.

politique [pɔlitik] ◇ *nf* **1.** [de gouvernement, de personne] policy - **2.** [affaires
publiques] politics (U). ◇ *adj* **1.** [pouvoir,
théorie] political ; **homme/femme politique**
politician, political figure - **2.** *litt* [choix,
réponse] politic.

politiser [3] [pɔlitize] *vt* to politicize.

pollen [pɔlɛn] *nm* pollen.

polluer [7] [pɔlɥe] *vt* to pollute.

pollution [pɔlysjɔ̃] *nf* pollution.

polo [pɔlo] *nm* **1.** [sport] polo - **2.** [chemise]
polo shirt.

Pologne [pɔlɔɲ] *nf*: **la Pologne** Poland.

polonais, e [pɔlɔnɛ, ɛz] *adj* Polish.
polonais *nm* [langue] Polish. **Polonais, e** *nm, f* Pole.

poltron, onne [pɔltrɔ̃, ɔn] ◇ *nm, f*
coward. ◇ *adj* cowardly.

polychrome [pɔlikrom] *adj* polychrome,
polychromatic.

polyclinique [pɔliklinik] *nf* general hospital.

polycopié, e [pɔlikɔpje] *adj* duplicate
(*avant n*). **polycopié** *nm* duplicated
lecture notes *pl*.

polyester [pɔliɛstɛr] *nm* polyester.

polygame [pɔligam] *adj* polygamous.

polyglotte [pɔliglɔt] *nmf & adj* polyglot.

polygone [pɔligon] *nm* MATH polygon.

Polynésie [pɔlinezi] *nf*: **la Polynésie** Polynesia.

polystyrène [pɔlistirɛn] *nm* polystyrene.

polytechnicien, enne [pɔlitɛknisjɛ̃, ɛn]
nm, f student or ex-student of the École
Polytechnique.

Polytechnique [pɔlitɛknik] *npr*: **l'École
Polytechnique** *prestigious engineering college*
= **grande école.**

polyvalent, e [pɔlivalɑ̃, ɑ̃t] *adj* **1.** [salle]
multi-purpose - **2.** [personne] versatile.

pommade [pɔmad] *nf* [médicament] ointment.

pomme [pɔm] *nf* **1.** [fruit] apple ; **pomme
de pin** pine ou fir cone - **2.** [pomme de terre] :
pommes allumettes *very thin chips* ; **pommes
frites** chips UK, (French) fries US ; **pommes
vapeur** steamed potatoes. **pomme
d'Adam** *nf* Adam's apple.

pomme de terre [pɔmdətɛr] *nf* potato.

pommette [pɔmɛt] *nf* cheekbone.

pommier [pɔmje] *nm* apple tree.

pompe [pɔ̃p] *nf* **1.** [appareil] pump ; **pompe
à essence** petrol pump UK, gas pump US
- **2.** [magnificence] pomp, ceremony - **3.** *fam*
[chaussure] shoe. **pompes funèbres**
nfpl undertaker's *sg*, funeral director's *(sing)*
UK, mortician's *(sing)* US.

pomper [3] [pɔ̃pe] *vt* [eau, air] to pump.

pompeux, euse [pɔ̃pø, øz] *adj* pompous.

pompier [pɔ̃pje] *nm* fireman, firefighter.

pompiste [pɔ̃pist] *nmf* petrol UK ou gas US
pump attendant.

pompon [pɔ̃pɔ̃] *nm* pompom.

pomponner [3] [pɔ̃pɔne] **se pomponner** *vp* to get dressed up.

ponce [pɔ̃s] *adj* : **pierre ponce** pumice
(stone).

poncer [16] [pɔ̃se] *vt* [bois] to sand (down).

ponceuse [pɔ̃søz] *nf* sander, sanding
machine.

ponction [pɔ̃ksjɔ̃] *nf* **1.** [MÉD - lombaire]
puncture ; [- pulmonaire] tapping - **2.** *fig*
[prélèvement] withdrawal.

ponctualité [pɔ̃ktɥalite] *nf* punctuality.

ponctuation [pɔ̃ktɥasjɔ̃] *nf* punctuation.

ponctuel, elle [pɔ̃ktɥɛl] *adj* **1.** [action]
specific, selective - **2.** [personne] punctual.

ponctuer [7] [pɔ̃ktɥe] *vt* to punctuate ;
ponctuer qqch de qqch *fig* to punctuate sthg
with sthg.

pondéré, e [pɔ̃dere] *adj* **1.** [personne] level-
headed - **2.** ÉCON weighted.

pondre [75] [pɔ̃dr] *vt* **1.** [œufs] to lay
- **2.** *fam fig* [projet, texte] to produce.

pondu, e [pɔ̃dy] *pp* **pondre.**

poney [pɔne] *nm* pony.

pont [pɔ̃] *nm* **1.** CONSTR bridge ; **ponts et
chaussées** ADMIN ≃ highways department
- **2.** [lien] link, connection ; **pont aérien**
airlift - **3.** [congé] *day off granted by an
employer to fill the gap between a national
holiday and a weekend* - **4.** [de navire] deck.

ponte [pɔ̃t] ◇ *nf* [action] laying ; [œufs]
clutch. ◇ *nm fam* [autorité] big shot.

pont-levis [pɔ̃ləvi] *nm* drawbridge.

ponton [pɔ̃tɔ̃] *nm* [plate-forme] pontoon.

pop [pɔp] ◇ *nm* pop. ◇ *adj* pop (*avant
n*).

pop-corn [pɔpkɔrn] *nm inv* popcorn (U).

populace [pɔpylas] *nf péj* mob.

populaire [pɔpylɛr] *adj* **1.** [du peuple -
volonté] popular, of the people ; [- quar-
tier] working-class ; [- art, chanson] folk
- **2.** [personne] popular.

populariser [3] [popylarize] *vt* to popularize.

popularité [popylarite] *nf* popularity.

population [popylasjɔ̃] *nf* population ; **population active** working population.

porc [pɔr] *nm* **1.** [animal] pig, hog *US* - **2.** *fig & péj* [personne] pig, swine - **3.** [viande] pork - **4.** [peau] pigskin.

porcelaine [pɔrsəlɛn] *nf* **1.** [matière] china, porcelain - **2.** [objet] piece of china ou porcelain.

porc-épic [pɔrkepik] *nm* porcupine.

porche [pɔrʃ] *nm* porch.

porcherie [pɔrʃəri] *nf litt & fig* pigsty.

porcin, e [pɔrsɛ̃, in] *adj* **1.** [élevage] pig *(avant n)* - **2.** *fig & péj* [yeux] piggy.

pore [pɔr] *nm* pore.

poreux, euse [pɔrø, øz] *adj* porous.

pornographie [pɔrnɔgrafi] *nf* pornography.

port [pɔr] *nm* **1.** [lieu] port ; **port de commerce/pêche** commercial/fishing port - **2.** [fait de porter sur soi - d'objet] carrying ; [- de vêtement, décoration] wearing ; **port d'armes** carrying of weapons - **3.** [transport] carriage ; **franco de port** carriage paid.

portable [pɔrtabl] <> *nm* TV portable ; INFORM laptop, portable ; [téléphone] mobile. <> *adj* **1.** [vêtement] wearable - **2.** [ordinateur, machine à écrire] portable, laptop.

portail [pɔrtaj] *nm* [gén & INFORM] portal.

portant, e [pɔrtɑ̃, ɑ̃t] *adj* : **être bien/mal portant** to be in good/poor health.

portatif, ive [pɔrtatif, iv] *adj* portable.

porte [pɔrt] *nf* **1.** [de maison, voiture] door ; **mettre qqn à la porte** to throw sb out ; **porte d'entrée** front door - **2.** AÉRON & SKI [d'une ville] gate - **3.** *fig* [de région] gateway.

porte-à-faux [pɔrtafo] *nm inv* [roche] overhang ; CONSTR cantilever ; **en porte-à-faux** overhanging ; CONSTR cantilevered ; *fig* in a delicate situation.

porte-à-porte [pɔrtapɔrt] *nm inv* : **faire du porte-à-porte** to sell from door to door.

porte-avions [pɔrtavjɔ̃] *nm inv* aircraft carrier.

porte-bagages [pɔrtbagaʒ] *nm inv* luggage rack *UK* ; [de voiture] roof rack *UK*.

porte-bonheur [pɔrtbɔnœr] *nm inv* lucky charm.

porte-clefs, porte-clés [pɔrtəkle] *nm inv* keyring.

porte-documents [pɔrtdɔkymɑ̃] *nm inv* attaché ou document case.

portée [pɔrte] *nf* **1.** [de missile] range ; **à portée de** within range of ; **à portée de main** within reach ; **à portée de voix** within earshot ; **à portée de vue** in sight ; **à la**

portée de qqn *fig* within sb's reach - **2.** [d'événement] impact, significance - **3.** MUS stave, staff - **4.** [de femelle] litter.

porte-fenêtre [pɔrtfənɛtr] *nf* French window ou door *US*.

portefeuille [pɔrtəfœj] *nm* **1.** [pour billets] wallet - **2.** FIN & POLIT portfolio.

porte-jarretelles [pɔrtʒartɛl] *nm inv* suspender belt *UK*, garter belt *US*.

portemanteau, x [pɔrtmɑ̃to] *nm* [au mur] coat-rack ; [sur pied] coat stand.

porte-monnaie [pɔrtmɔnɛ] *nm inv* purse.

porte-parole [pɔrtparɔl] *nm inv* spokesman *(f* spokeswoman).

porter [3] [pɔrte] <> *vt* **1.** [gén] to carry - **2.** [vêtement, lunettes, montre] to wear ; [barbe] to have - **3.** [nom, date, inscription] to bear - **4.** [inscrire] to put down, to write down ; **porté disparu** reported missing. <> *vi* **1.** [remarque] to strike home - **2.** [voix, tir] to carry. ➤ **se porter** <> *vp* [se sentir] : **se porter bien/mal** to be well/unwell. <> *v att* : **se porter garant de qqch** to guarantee sthg, to vouch for sthg ; **se porter candidat à** to stand for election to *UK*, to run for *US*.

porte-savon [pɔrtsavɔ̃] *(pl inv* ou **porte-savons)** *nm* soap dish.

porte-serviettes [pɔrtsɛrvjɛt] *nm inv* towel rail.

porteur, euse [pɔrtœr, øz] <> *adj* : **marché porteur** COMM growth market ; **mère porteuse** surrogate mother ; **mur porteur** load-bearing wall. <> *nm, f* **1.** [de message, nouvelle] bringer, bearer - **2.** [de bagages] porter - **3.** [détenteur - de papiers, d'actions] holder ; [- de chèque] bearer - **4.** [de maladie] carrier.

portier [pɔrtje] *nm* commissionaire *UK*, doorman *US*.

portière [pɔrtjɛr] *nf* [de voiture, train] door.

portillon [pɔrtijɔ̃] *nm* barrier, gate.

portion [pɔrsjɔ̃] *nf* [de gâteau] portion, helping.

portique [pɔrtik] *nm* **1.** ARCHIT portico - **2.** SPORT crossbeam *(for hanging apparatus)*.

porto [pɔrto] *nm* port.

Porto Rico [pɔrtoriko], **Puerto Rico** [pwɛrtoriko] *npr* Puerto Rico.

portrait [pɔrtrɛ] *nm* portrait ; PHOTO photograph ; **faire le portrait de qqn** *fig* to describe sb.

portraitiste [pɔrtrɛtist] *nmf* portrait painter.

portrait-robot [pɔrtrɛrobo] *nm* Photofit® picture, Identikit® picture.

portuaire [pɔrtɥɛr] *adj* port *(avant n)*, harbour *(avant n) UK*, harbor *(avant n) US*.

portugais, e [pɔrtygɛ, ɛz] *adj* Portuguese.
◆ **portugais** *nm* [langue] Portuguese.
◆ **Portugais, e** *nm, f* Portuguese (person) ; **les Portugais** the Portuguese.

Portugal [pɔrtygal] *nm* : **le Portugal** Portugal.

pose [poz] *nf* **1.** [de pierre, moquette] laying ; [de papier peint, rideaux] hanging - **2.** [position] pose - **3.** PHOTO exposure.

posé, e [poze] *adj* sober, steady.

poser [3] [poze] ◇ *vt* **1.** [mettre] to put down ; **poser qqch sur qqch** to put sthg on sthg - **2.** [installer - rideaux, papier peint] to hang ; [- étagère] to put up ; [- moquette, carrelage] to lay - **3.** [donner à résoudre - problème, difficulté] to pose ; **poser une question** to ask a question ; **poser sa candidature** to apply ; POLIT to stand *UK* ou run *US* for election. ◇ *vi* to pose. ◆ **se poser** *vp* **1.** [oiseau, avion] to land ; *fig* [choix, regard] : **se poser sur** to fall on - **2.** [question, problème] to arise, to come up.

positif, ive [pozitif, iv] *adj* positive.

position [pozisjɔ̃] *nf* position ; **prendre position** *fig* to take up a position, to take a stand.

posologie [pozɔlɔʒi] *nf* dosage.

posséder [18] [posede] *vt* **1.** [détenir - voiture, maison] to possess, to own ; [- diplôme] to have ; [- capacités, connaissances] to possess, to have - **2.** [langue, art] to have mastered - **3.** *fam* [personne] to have.

possesseur [posesœr] *nm* **1.** [de bien] possessor, owner - **2.** [de secret, diplôme] holder.

possessif, ive [posesif, iv] *adj* possessive.
◆ **possessif** *nm* GRAMM possessive.

possession [posesjɔ̃] *nf* [gén] possession ; **être en ma/ta etc possession** to be in my/your *etc* possession.

possibilité [posibilite] *nf* **1.** [gén] possibility - **2.** [moyen] chance, opportunity.

possible [posibl] ◇ *adj* possible ; **c'est/ce n'est pas possible** that's possible/impossible ; **dès que** ou **aussitôt que possible** as soon as possible. ◇ *nm* : **faire tout son possible** to do one's utmost, to do everything possible ; **dans la mesure du possible** as far as possible.

postal, e, aux [pɔstal, o] *adj* postal.

poste [pɔst] ◇ *nf* **1.** [service] post *UK*, mail *US* ; **envoyer/recevoir qqch par la poste** to send/receive sthg by post - **2.** [bureau] post office ; **poste restante** poste restante *UK*, general delivery *US*. ◇ *nm* **1.** [emplacement] post ; **poste de police** police station

- **2.** [emploi] position, post - **3.** [appareil] : **poste de radio** radio ; **poste de télévision** television (set) - **4.** TÉLÉCOM extension.

poster[1] [pɔstɛr] *nm* poster.

poster[2] [3] [pɔste] *vt* **1.** [lettre] to post *UK*, to mail *US* - **2.** [sentinelle] to post. ◆ **se poster** *vp* to position o.s., to station o.s.

postérieur, e [pɔsterjœr] *adj* **1.** [date] later, subsequent - **2.** [membre] hind *(avant n)*, back *(avant n)*. ◆ **postérieur** *nm hum* posterior.

posteriori [pɔsterjɔri] ◆ **a posteriori** *loc adv* a posteriori.

postérité [pɔsterite] *nf* [générations à venir] posterity.

posthume [pɔstym] *adj* posthumous.

postiche [pɔstiʃ] *adj* false.

postier, ère [pɔstje, ɛr] *nm, f* post-office worker.

postillonner [3] [pɔstijɔne] *vi* to splutter.

Post-it® [pɔstit] *nm inv* Post-it®, Post-it® note.

post-scriptum [pɔstskriptɔm] *nm inv* postscript.

postulant, e [pɔstylɑ̃, ɑ̃t] *nm, f* [pour emploi] applicant.

postuler [3] [pɔstyle] *vt* **1.** [emploi] to apply for - **2.** PHILO to postulate.

posture [pɔstyr] *nf* posture ; **être** ou **se trouver en mauvaise posture** *fig* to be in a difficult position.

pot [po] *nm* **1.** [récipient] pot, jar ; [à eau, à lait] jug *UK*, pitcher *US* ; **pot de chambre** chamber pot ; **pot de fleurs** flowerpot - **2.** AUTO : **pot catalytique** catalytic convertor ou converter ; **pot d'échappement** exhaust (pipe) ; [silencieux] silencer *UK*, muffler *US* - **3.** *fam* [boisson] drink ; **faire un pot** to have a drinks party *UK*.

potable [pɔtabl] *adj* **1.** [liquide] drinkable ; **eau potable** drinking water - **2.** *fam* [travail] acceptable.

potage [pɔtaʒ] *nm* soup.

potager, ère [pɔtaʒe, ɛr] *adj* : **jardin potager** vegetable garden ; **plante potagère** vegetable. ◆ **potager** *nm* kitchen ou vegetable garden.

potasser [3] [pɔtase] *vt fam* [cours] to swot up *UK*, to bone up on *US* ; [examen] to swot up for *UK*, to bone up for *US*.

potassium [pɔtasjɔm] *nm* potassium.

pot-au-feu [pɔtofø] *nm inv* ≃ beef-and-vegetable stew.

pot-de-vin [podvɛ̃] *(pl* pots-de-vin*)* *nm* bribe.

pote [pɔt] *nm fam* mate *UK*, buddy *US*.

poteau, x [pɔto] *nm* post ; **poteau de but**

goalpost ; **poteau indicateur** signpost ; **poteau télégraphique** telegraph pole *UK*, telephone pole *US*.

potelé, e [pɔtle] *adj* plump, chubby.

potence [pɔtɑ̃s] *nf* **1.** CONSTR bracket - **2.** [de pendaison] gallows *sg*.

potentiel, elle [pɔtɑ̃sjɛl] *adj* potential. ➤ **potentiel** *nm* potential.

poterie [pɔtri] *nf* **1.** [art] pottery - **2.** [objet] piece of pottery.

potiche [pɔtiʃ] *nf* [vase] vase.

potier, ère [pɔtje, ɛr] *nm, f* potter.

potin [pɔtɛ̃] *nm fam* [bruit] din. ➤ **potins** *nmpl fam* [ragots] gossip *(U)*.

potion [posjɔ̃] *nf* potion.

potiron [pɔtirɔ̃] *nm* pumpkin.

pot-pourri [popuri] *nm* potpourri.

pou, x [pu] *nm* louse.

poubelle [pubɛl] *nf* dustbin *UK*, trashcan *US* ; INFORM recycle bin.

pouce [pus] *nm* **1.** [de main] thumb ; [de pied] big toe - **2.** [mesure] inch.

poudre [pudr] *nf* powder ; **prendre la poudre d'escampette** to make off.

poudreux, euse [pudrø, øz] *adj* powdery. ➤ **poudreuse** *nf* powder (snow).

poudrier [pudrije] *nm* [boîte] powder compact.

poudrière [pudrijɛr] *nf* powder magazine ; *fig* powder keg.

pouf [puf] ◇ *nm* pouffe. ◇ *interj* thud!

pouffer [3] [pufe] *vi* : **pouffer (de rire)** to snigger.

pouilleux, euse [pujø, øz] *adj* **1.** [personne, animal] flea-ridden - **2.** [endroit] squalid.

poulailler [pulaje] *nm* **1.** [de ferme] henhouse - **2.** *fam* THÉÂTRE gods *sg*.

poulain [pulɛ̃] *nm* foal ; *fig* protégé.

poule [pul] *nf* **1.** ZOOL hen - **2.** *fam péj* [femme] bird *UK*, broad *US* - **3.** SPORT [compétition] round robin ; [rugby] pool.

poulet [pulɛ] *nm* **1.** ZOOL chicken ; **poulet fermier** free-range chicken - **2.** *fam* [policier] cop.

pouliche [puliʃ] *nf* filly.

poulie [puli] *nf* pulley.

poulpe [pulp] *nm* octopus.

pouls [pu] *nm* pulse.

poumon [pumɔ̃] *nm* lung.

poupe [pup] *nf* stern.

poupée [pupe] *nf* [jouet] doll.

poupon [pupɔ̃] *nm* **1.** [bébé] little baby - **2.** [jouet] baby doll.

pouponnière [pupɔnjɛr] *nf* nursery.

pour [pur] ◇ *prép* **1.** [gén] for - **2.** *(+ infinitif)* **pour faire** in order to do, (so as) to do ; **je suis venu pour vous voir** I've come to see you ; **pour m'avoir aidé** for having helped me, for helping me - **3.** [indique un rapport] for ; **avancé pour son âge** advanced for his/her age ; **pour moi** for my part, as far as I'm concerned ; **pour ce qui est de** as regards, with regard to. ◇ *adv* : **je suis pour** I'm (all) for it. ◇ *nm* : **le pour et le contre** the pros and cons *pl*. ➤ **pour que** *loc conj (+ subjonctif)* so that, in order that.

pourboire [purbwar] *nm* tip.

pourcentage [pursɑ̃taʒ] *nm* percentage.

pourparlers [purparle] *nmpl* talks.

pourpre [purpr] *nm & adj* crimson.

pourquoi [purkwa] ◇ *adv* why ; **pourquoi pas?** why not? ; **c'est pourquoi...** that's why... ◇ *nm inv* : **le pourquoi (de)** the reason (for).

pourri, e [puri] *adj* **1.** [fruit] rotten - **2.** [personne, milieu] corrupt - **3.** [enfant] spoiled rotten, ruined.

pourrir [32] [purir] ◇ *vt* **1.** [matière, aliment] to rot, to spoil - **2.** [enfant] to ruin, to spoil rotten. ◇ *vi* [matière] to rot ; [fruit, aliment] to go rotten ou bad.

pourriture [purityr] *nf* **1.** [d'aliment] rot - **2.** *fig* [de personne, de milieu] corruption - **3.** *injur* [personne] bastard.

poursuite [pursɥit] *nf* **1.** [de personne] chase - **2.** [d'argent, de vérité] pursuit - **3.** [de négociations] continuation. ➤ **poursuites** *nfpl* DR (legal) proceedings.

poursuivi, e [pursɥivi] *pp* ➤ **poursuivre.**

poursuivre [89] [pursɥivr] ◇ *vt* **1.** [voleur] to pursue, to chase ; [gibier] to hunt - **2.** [rêve, vengeance] to pursue - **3.** [enquête, travail] to carry on with, to continue - **4.** DR [criminel] to prosecute ; [voisin] to sue. ◇ *vi* to go on, to carry on.

pourtant [purtɑ̃] *adv* nevertheless, even so.

pourtour [purtur] *nm* perimeter.

pourvoi [purvwa] *nm* DR appeal.

pourvoir [64] [purvwar] ◇ *vt* : **pourvoir qqn de** to provide sb with ; **pourvoir qqch de** to equip ou fit sthg with. ◇ *vi* : **pourvoir à** to provide for.

pourvu, e [purvy] *pp* ➤ **pourvoir.** ➤ **pourvu que** *(+ subjonctif)* *loc conj* **1.** [condition] providing, provided (that) - **2.** [souhait] let's hope (that).

pousse [pus] *nf* **1.** [croissance] growth - **2.** [bourgeon] shoot - **3.** ÉCON : **jeune pousse** start-up.

poussé, e [puse] *adj* **1.** [travail] meticulous - **2.** [moteur] souped-up.

pousse-café [puskafe] *nm inv* fam liqueur.

poussée [puse] *nf* **1.** [pression] pressure - **2.** [coup] push - **3.** [de fièvre, inflation] rise.

pousse-pousse [puspus] *nm inv* **1.** [voiture] rickshaw - **2.** *Suisse* [poussette] pushchair.

pousser [3] [puse] <> *vt* **1.** [personne, objet] to push - **2.** [moteur, voiture] to drive hard - **3.** [recherches, études] to carry on, to continue - **4.** [cri, soupir] to give - **5.** [inciter] **: pousser qqn à faire qqch** to urge sb to do sthg - **6.** [au crime, au suicide] **: pousser qqn à** to drive sb to. <> *vi* **1.** [exercer une pression] to push - **2.** [croître] to grow - **3.** *fam* [exagérer] to overdo it. <> **se pousser** *vp* to move up.

poussette [puset] *nf* pushchair *UK*, stroller *US*.

poussière [pusjɛr] *nf* [gén] dust.

poussiéreux, euse [pusjerø, øz] *adj* **1.** [meuble] dusty - **2.** *fig* [organisation] old-fashioned.

poussif, ive [pusif, iv] *adj fam* wheezy.

poussin [pusɛ̃] *nm* **1.** ZOOL chick - **2.** SPORT under-11.

poutre [putr] *nf* beam.

poutrelle [putrɛl] *nf* girder.

pouvoir [58] [puvwar] <> *nm* **1.** [gén] power ; **pouvoir d'achat** purchasing power ; **les pouvoirs publics** the authorities - **2.** DR proxy, power of attorney. <> *vt* **1.** [avoir la possibilité de, parvenir à] **: pouvoir faire qqch** to be able to do sthg ; **je ne peux pas venir ce soir** I can't come tonight ; **pouvez-vous...?** can you...?, could you...? ; **je n'en peux plus** [exaspéré] I'm at the end of my tether ; [fatigué] I'm exhausted ; **je/tu n'y peux rien** there's nothing I/you can do about it ; **tu aurais pu me le dire!** you might have OU could have told me! - **2.** [avoir la permission de] **: je peux prendre la voiture?** can I borrow the car? ; **aucun élève ne peut partir** no pupil may leave - **3.** [indiquant l'éventualité] **: il peut pleuvoir** it may rain ; **vous pourriez rater votre train** you could OU might miss your train. <> **se pouvoir** *v impers* **: il se peut que je me trompe** I may be mistaken ; **cela se peut/pourrait bien** that's quite possible.

pragmatique [pragmatik] *adj* pragmatic.

Prague [prag] *npr* Prague.

prairie [preri] *nf* meadow ; [aux États-Unis] prairie.

praline [pralin] *nf* **1.** [amande] sugared almond - **2.** *Belgique* [chocolat] chocolate.

praticable [pratikabl] *adj* **1.** [route] passable - **2.** [plan] feasible, practicable.

praticien, enne [pratisjɛ̃, ɛn] *nm, f* practitioner ; MÉD medical practitioner.

pratiquant, e [pratikɑ̃, ɑ̃t] *adj* practising *UK*, practicing *US*.

pratique [pratik] <> *nf* **1.** [expérience] practical experience - **2.** [usage] practice ; **mettre qqch en pratique** to put sthg into practice. <> *adj* practical ; [gadget, outil] handy.

pratiquement [pratikmɑ̃] *adv* **1.** [en fait] in practice - **2.** [quasiment] practically.

pratiquer [3] [pratike] <> *vt* [métier] to practise *UK*, to practice *US* ; [sport] to do ; [jeu de ballon] to play ; [méthode] to apply - **2.** [ouverture] to make. <> *vi* RELIG to be a practising *UK* OU practicing *US* Christian/Jew/Muslim *etc*.

pré [pre] *nm* meadow.

préalable [prealabl] <> *adj* prior, previous. <> *nm* precondition. <> **au préalable** *loc adv* first, beforehand.

préambule [preɑ̃byl] *nm* **1.** [introduction, propos] preamble ; **sans préambule** immediately - **2.** [prélude] **: préambule de** prelude to.

préau, x [preo] *nm* [d'école] (covered) play area.

préavis [preavi] *nm inv* advance notice OU warning.

précaire [prekɛr] *adj* [incertain] precarious.

précariser [prekarize] *vt* to make (sthg) less secure OU stable ; **précariser l'emploi** to threaten job security ; **la crise a précarisé leur situation** the recession has made them more vulnerable.

précaution [prekosjɔ̃] *nf* **1.** [prévoyance] precaution ; **par précaution** as a precaution ; **prendre des précautions** to take precautions - **2.** [prudence] caution.

précédent, e [presedɑ̃, ɑ̃t] *adj* previous. <> **précédent** *nm* precedent ; **sans précédent** unprecedented.

précéder [18] [presede] *vt* **1.** [dans le temps - gén] to precede ; [- suj: personne] to arrive before - **2.** [marcher devant] to go in front of - **3.** *fig* [devancer] to get ahead of.

précepte [presɛpt] *nm* precept.

précepteur, trice [preseptœr, tris] *nm, f* (private) tutor.

prêcher [4] [preʃe] *vt & vi* to preach.

précieux, euse [presjø, øz] *adj* **1.** [pierre, métal] precious ; [objet] valuable ; [collaborateur] invaluable, valued - **2.** *péj* [style] precious, affected.

précipice [presipis] *nm* precipice.

précipitation [presipitasjɔ̃] *nf* **1.** [hâte] haste - **2.** CHIM precipitation. <> **précipitations** *nfpl* MÉTÉOR precipitation *(U)*.

précipiter [3] [presipite] *vt* **1.** [objet, personne] to throw, to hurl ; **précipiter qqn/qqch du haut de** to throw sb/sthg off, to hurl sb/sthg off - **2.** [départ] to hasten. <> **se précipiter** *vp* **1.** [se jeter] to throw o.s., to hurl o.s. - **2.** [s'élancer] : **se précipiter (vers qqn)** to rush ou hurry (towards sb) - **3.** [s'accélérer - gén] to speed up ; [- choses, événements] to move faster.

précis, e [presi, iz] *adj* **1.** [exact] precise, accurate - **2.** [fixé] definite, precise. ➭ **précis** *nm* handbook.

précisément [presizemɑ̃] *adv* precisely, exactly.

préciser [3] [presize] *vt* **1.** [heure, lieu] to specify - **2.** [pensée] to clarify. ➭ **se préciser** *vp* to become clear.

précision [presizjɔ̃] *nf* **1.** [de style, d'explication] precision - **2.** [détail] detail.

précoce [prekɔs] *adj* **1.** [plante, fruit] early - **2.** [enfant] precocious.

préconçu, e [prekɔ̃sy] *adj* preconceived.

préconiser [3] [prekɔnize] *vt* to recommend ; **préconiser de faire qqch** to recommend doing sthg.

précurseur [prekyrsœr] <> *nm* precursor, forerunner. <> *adj* precursory.

prédateur, trice [predatœr, tris] *adj* predatory. ➭ **prédateur** *nm* predator.

prédécesseur [predesesœr] *nm* predecessor.

prédestiner [3] [predɛstine] *vt* to predestine ; **être prédestiné à qqch/à faire qqch** to be predestined for sthg/to do sthg.

prédicateur, trice [predikatœr, tris] *nm, f* preacher.

prédiction [prediksjɔ̃] *nf* prediction.

prédilection [predilɛksjɔ̃] *nf* partiality ; **avoir une prédilection pour** to have a partiality ou liking for.

prédire [103] [predir] *vt* to predict.

prédit, e [predi, it] *pp* ➭ **prédire**.

prédominer [3] [predɔmine] *vt* to predominate.

préfabriqué, e [prefabrike] *adj* **1.** [maison] prefabricated - **2.** [accusation, sourire] false. ➭ **préfabriqué** *nm* prefabricated material.

préface [prefas] *nf* preface.

préfecture [prefɛktyr] *nf* prefecture.

préférable [preferabl] *adj* preferable.

préféré, e [prefere] *adj & nm, f* favourite *UK*, favorite *US*.

préférence [preferɑ̃s] *nf* preference ; **de préférence** preferably.

préférentiel, elle [preferɑ̃sjɛl] *adj* preferential.

préférer [18] [prefere] *vt* : **préférer qqn/qqch (à)** to prefer sb/sthg (to) ; **je préfère rentrer** I would rather go home, I would prefer to go home ; **je préfère ça!** I like that better!, I prefer that!

préfet [prefɛ] *nm* prefect.

préfixe [prefiks] *nm* prefix.

préhistoire [preistwar] *nf* prehistory.

préinscription [preɛ̃skripsjɔ̃] *nf* preregistration.

préjudice [preʒydis] *nm* harm (U), detriment (U) ; **porter préjudice à qqn** to harm sb.

préjugé [preʒyʒe] *nm* : **préjugé (contre)** prejudice (against).

prélasser [3] [prelase] ➭ **se prélasser** *vp* to lounge.

prélat [prela] *nm* prelate.

prélavage [prelavaʒ] *nm* pre-wash.

prélèvement [prelevmɑ̃] *nm* **1.** MÉD removal ; [de sang] sample - **2.** FIN deduction ; **prélèvement automatique** direct debit *UK* ; **prélèvement mensuel** monthly standing order *UK* ; **prélèvements obligatoires** tax and social security contributions.

prélever [19] [prelve] *vt* **1.** FIN : **prélever de l'argent (sur)** to deduct money (from) - **2.** MÉD to remove ; **prélever du sang** to take a blood sample.

préliminaire [preliminɛr] *adj* preliminary. ➭ **préliminaires** *nmpl* **1.** [de paix] preliminary talks - **2.** [de discours] preliminaries.

prématuré, e [prematyre] <> *adj* premature. <> *nm, f* premature baby.

préméditation [premeditasjɔ̃] *nf* premeditation ; **avec préméditation** [meurtre] premeditated ; [agir] with premeditation.

premier, ère [prəmje, ɛr] <> *adj* **1.** [gén] first ; [étage] first *UK*, second *US* - **2.** [qualité] top - **3.** [état] original. <> *nm, f* first ; **jeune premier** CINÉ leading man. ➭ **première** *nf* **1.** CINÉ première ; THÉÂTRE première, first night - **2.** [exploit] first - **3.** [première classe] first class - **4.** SCOL ≃ lower sixth year ou form *UK*, ≃ eleventh grade *US* - **5.** AUTO first (gear). ➭ **premier de l'an** *nm* : **le premier de l'an** New Year's Day. ➭ **en premier** *loc adv* first, firstly.

premièrement [prəmjɛrmɑ̃] *adv* first, firstly.

prémonition [premɔnisjɔ̃] *nf* premonition.

prémunir [32] [premynir] *vt* : **prémunir qqn (contre)** to protect sb (against). ➭ **se prémunir** *vp* to protect o.s. ; **se prémunir contre qqch** to guard against sthg.

prénatal, e [prenatal] (*pl* **prénatals** ou **prénataux** [prenato]) *adj* antenatal, prenatal *US* ; [allocation] maternity (*avant n*).

prendre [79] [prɑ̃dr] <> *vt* **1.** [gén] to take - **2.** [enlever] to take (away) ; **prendre qqch à qqn** to take sthg from sb - **3.** [aller chercher - objet] to get, to fetch ; [- personne] to pick up - **4.** [repas, boisson] to have ; **vous prendrez quelque chose?** would you like something to eat/drink? - **5.** [voleur] to catch ; **se faire prendre** to get caught - **6.** [responsabilité] to take (on) - **7.** [aborder - personne] to handle ; [- problème] to tackle - **8.** [réserver] to book ; [louer] to rent, to take ; [acheter] to buy - **9.** [poids] to gain, to put on. ⬥ *vi* **1.** [ciment, sauce] to set - **2.** [plante, greffe] to take ; [mode] to catch on - **3.** [feu] to catch - **4.** [se diriger] : **prendre à droite** to turn right. ⬥ **se prendre** *vp* [se considérer] : **pour qui se prend-il?** who does he think he is? ; **s'en prendre à qqn** [physiquement] to set about sb *UK* ; [verbalement] to take it out on sb ; **je sais comment m'y prendre** I know how to do it OU go about it.

prénom [prenõ] *nm* first name.

prénommer [3] [prenɔme] *vt* to name, to call. ⬥ **se prénommer** *vp* to be called.

prénuptial, e, aux [prenypsjal, o] *adj* pre-marital.

préoccupation [preɔkypasjõ] *nf* pre-occupation.

préoccuper [3] [preɔkype] *vt* to preoccupy. ⬥ **se préoccuper** *vp* : **se préoccuper de qqch** to be worried about sthg.

préparatifs [preparatif] *nmpl* preparations.

préparation [preparasjõ] *nf* preparation.

préparer [3] [prepare] *vt* **1.** [gén] to prepare ; [plat, repas] to cook, to prepare ; **préparer qqn à qqch** to prepare sb for sthg - **2.** [réserver] : **préparer qqch à qqn** to have sthg in store for sb - **3.** [congrès] to organize. ⬥ **se préparer** *vp* **1.** [personne] : **se préparer à qqch/à faire qqch** to prepare for sthg/to do sthg - **2.** [tempête] to be brewing.

prépondérant, e [prepõderã, ãt] *adj* dominating.

préposé, e [prepoze] *nm, f* (minor) official ; [de vestiaire] attendant ; [facteur] postman (*f* postwoman) *UK*, mailman *US*, mail OU letter carrier *US* ; **préposé à qqch** person in charge of sthg.

préposition [prepozisjõ] *nf* preposition.

préretraite [preretret] *nf* early retire-ment ; [allocation] early retirement pension.

prérogative [prerɔgativ] *nf* prerogative.

près [pre] *adv* near, close. ⬥ **de près** *loc adv* closely ; **regarder qqch de près** to watch sthg closely. ⬥ **près de** *loc prép* **1.** [dans l'espace] near, close to - **2.** [dans le temps] close to - **3.** [presque] nearly, almost. ⬥ **à peu près** *loc adv* more or less, just about ; **il est à peu près cinq heures** it's about five o'clock. ⬥ **à ceci près que, cela près que** *loc conj* except that, apart from the fact that. ⬥ **à... près** *loc adv* : **à dix centimètres près** to within ten centi-

metres ; **il n'en est pas à un ou deux jours près** a day or two more or less won't make any difference.

présage [preza3] *nm* omen.

présager [17] [preza3e] *vt* **1.** [annoncer] to portend - **2.** [prévoir] to predict.

presbytère [presbiter] *nm* presbytery.

presbytie [presbisi] *nf* longsightedness *UK*, farsightedness *US*.

prescription [preskripsjõ] *nf* **1.** MÉD pre-scription - **2.** DR limitation.

prescrire [99] [preskrir] *vt* **1.** [mesures, conditions] to lay down, to stipulate - **2.** MÉD to prescribe.

prescrit, e [preskri, it] *pp* ⬤ **prescrire**.

préséance [preseãs] *nf* precedence.

présélection [preseleksjõ] *nf* preselec-tion ; [pour concours] making a list of finalists, short-listing *UK*.

présence [prezãs] *nf* **1.** [gén] presence ; **en présence** face to face ; **en présence de** in the presence of - **2.** [compagnie] company (*U*) - **3.** [assiduité] attendance ; **feuille de présen-ce** attendance sheet. ⬥ **présence d'es-prit** *nf* presence of mind.

présent, e [prezã, ãt] *adj* [gén] present ; **le présent ouvrage** this work ; **la présente loi** this law ; **avoir qqch présent à l'esprit** to remember sthg. ⬥ **présent** *nm* **1.** [gén] present ; **à présent** at present ; **à présent que** now that ; **jusqu'à présent** up to now, so far ; **dès à présent** right away - **2.** GRAMM : **le présent** the present tense.

présentable [prezãtabl] *adj* [d'aspect] pre-sentable.

présentateur, trice [prezãtatœr, tris] *nm, f* presenter *UK*, anchorman (*f* anchor-woman).

présentation [prezãtasjõ] *nf* **1.** [de person-ne] : **faire les présentations** to make the introductions - **2.** [aspect extérieur] appear-ance - **3.** [de papiers, de produit, de film] presentation - **4.** [de magazine] layout.

présenter [3] [prezãte] *vt* **1.** [gén] to present ; [projet] to present, to submit - **2.** [invité] to introduce - **3.** [condoléances, félicitations, avantages] to offer ; [hommages] to pay ; **présenter qqch à qqn** to offer sb sthg. ⬥ **se présenter** *vp* **1.** [se faire connaître] : **se présenter (à)** to introduce o.s. (to) - **2.** [être candidat] : **se présenter à** to stand in *UK*, to run in *US* ; **se présenter aux présidentielles** to run for president - **3.** [exa-men] to sit *UK*, to take ; **se présenter pour un poste** to apply for a job - **4.** [paraître] to appear - **5.** [occasion, situation] to arise, to present itself - **6.** [affaire, contrat] : **se présen-ter bien/mal** to look good/bad.

présentoir [prezãtwar] *nm* display stand.

préservatif [prezεrvatif] *nm* condom.

préserver [3] [prezεrve] *vt* to preserve.
◆ **se préserver** *vp* : **se préserver de** to protect o.s. from.

présidence [prezidᾶs] *nf* **1.** [de groupe] chairmanship - **2.** [d'État] presidency.

président, e [prezidᾶt, ᾶt] *nm, f* **1.** [d'assemblée] chairman (*f* chairwoman) - **2.** [d'État] president ; **président de la République** President (of the Republic) of France - **3.** DR [de tribunal] presiding judge ; [de jury] foreman (*f* forewoman).

présider [3] [prezide] ◇ *vt* **1.** [réunion] to chair - **2.** [banquet, dîner] to preside over. ◇ *vi* : **présider à** to be in charge of ; *fig* to govern, to preside in.

présomption [prezɔpsjɔ̃] *nf* **1.** [hypothèse] presumption - **2.** DR presumption ; **présomption d'innocence** presumption of innocence.

présomptueux, euse [prezɔptɥø, øz] *adj* presumptuous.

presque [prεsk] *adv* almost, nearly ; **presque rien** next to nothing, scarcely anything ; **presque jamais** hardly ever.

presqu'île [prεskil] *nf* peninsula.

pressant, e [prεsᾶ, ᾶt] *adj* pressing.

presse [prεs] *nf* **1.** [journaux] press - **2.** [d'imprimerie] press.

pressé, e [prese] *adj* **1.** [travail] urgent - **2.** [personne] : **être pressé** to be in a hurry - **3.** [citron, orange] freshly squeezed.

pressentiment [presᾶtimᾶ] *nm* premonition.

pressentir [37] [presᾶtir] *vt* [événement] to have a premonition of.

presse-papiers [prεspapje] *nm inv* paperweight.

presser [4] [prese] *vt* **1.** [écraser - olives] to press ; [- citron, orange] to squeeze - **2.** [bouton] to press, to push - **3.** *sout* [harceler] : **presser qqn de faire qqch** to press sb to do sthg - **4.** [faire se hâter] : **presser le pas** to speed up, to walk faster. ◆ **se presser** *vp* **1.** [se dépêcher] to hurry (up) - **2.** [s'agglutiner] : **se presser (autour de)** to crowd (around) - **3.** [se serrer] to huddle.

pressing [presiŋ] *nm* [établissement] dry cleaner's.

pression [presjɔ̃] *nf* **1.** [gén] pressure ; **exercer une pression sur qqch** to exert pressure on sthg ; **sous pression** *fig* [liquide] under pressure ; [cabine] pressurized - **2.** [sur vêtement] press stud *UK*, popper *UK*, snap fastener *US* - **3.** [bière] draught *UK* ou draft *US* beer.

pressoir [preswar] *nm* **1.** [machine] press - **2.** [lieu] press house.

pressurer [3] [presyre] *vt* **1.** [objet] to press, to squeeze - **2.** *fig* [contribuable] to squeeze.

prestance [prεstᾶs] *nf* bearing ; **avoir de la prestance** to have presence.

prestataire [prεstatεr] *nmf* **1.** [bénéficiaire] person in receipt of benefit, claimant - **2.** [fournisseur] provider ; **prestataire de service** service provider.

prestation [prεstasjɔ̃] *nf* **1.** [allocation] benefit *UK* ; **prestation en nature** payment in kind - **2.** [de comédien] performance.

preste [prεst] *adj litt* nimble.

prestidigitateur, trice [prεstidiʒitatœr, tris] *nm, f* conjurer.

prestige [prεstiʒ] *nm* prestige.

prestigieux, euse [prεstiʒjø, øz] *adj* [réputé] prestigious.

présumer [3] [prezyme] ◇ *vt* to presume, to assume ; **être présumé coupable/ innocent** to be presumed guilty/innocent. ◇ *vi* : **présumer de qqch** to overestimate sthg.

prêt, e [prε, prεt] *adj* ready ; **prêt à qqch/à faire qqch** ready for sthg/to do sthg ; **prêts? partez!** SPORT get set, go!, ready, steady, go! *UK* ◆ **prêt** *nm* [action] lending (*U*) ; [somme] loan ; **prêt bancaire** bank loan.

prêt-à-porter [prεtaporte] (*pl* **prêts-à-porter**) *nm* ready-to-wear clothing (*U*).

prétendant [pretᾶdᾶ] *nm* **1.** [au trône] pretender - **2.** [amoureux] suitor.

prétendre [73] [pretᾶdr] *vt* **1.** [affecter] : **prétendre faire qqch** to claim to do sthg - **2.** [affirmer] : **prétendre que** to claim (that), to maintain (that).

prétendu, e [pretᾶdy] ◇ *pp* ▶ **prétendre**. ◇ *adj (avant n)* so-called.

prête-nom [prεtnɔ̃] (*pl* **prête-noms**) *nm* front man.

prétentieux, euse [pretᾶsjø, øz] *adj* pretentious.

prétention [pretᾶsjɔ̃] *nf* **1.** [suffisance] pretentiousness - **2.** [ambition] pretension, ambition ; **avoir la prétention de faire qqch** to claim ou pretend to do sthg.

prêter [4] [prete] *vt* **1.** [fournir] : **prêter qqch (à qqn)** [objet, argent] to lend (sb) sthg ; *fig* [concours, appui] to lend (sb) sthg, to give (sb) sthg - **2.** [attribuer] : **prêter qqch à qqn** to attribute sthg to sb. ◆ **se prêter** *vp* : **se prêter à** [participer à] to go along with ; [convenir à] to fit, to suit.

prétérit [preterit] *nm* preterite.

prêteur, euse [pretœr, øz] *nm, f* : **prêteur sur gages** pawnbroker.

prétexte [pretεkst] *nm* pretext, excuse ; **sous prétexte de faire qqch/que** on the pretext of doing sthg/that, under the pretext of doing sthg/that ; **sous aucun prétexte** on no account.

prétexter [4] [pretɛkste] *vt* to give as an excuse.

prétimbré, e [pretɛ̃bre] *adj* prepaid.

prêtre [prɛtr] *nm* priest.

preuve [prœv] *nf* **1.** [gén] proof - **2.** DR evidence - **3.** [témoignage] sign, token ; **faire preuve de qqch** to show sthg ; **faire ses preuves** to prove o.s./itself.

prévaloir [61] [prevalwar] *vi* [dominer] : **prévaloir (sur)** to prevail (over). ◆ **se prévaloir** *vp* : **se prévaloir de** to boast about.

prévalu [prevaly] *pp inv* ▶ **prévaloir.**

prévenance [prevnɑ̃s] *nf* [attitude] thoughtfulness, consideration.

prévenant, e [prevnɑ̃, ɑ̃t] *adj* considerate, attentive.

prévenir [40] [prevnir] *vt* **1.** [employé, élève] : **prévenir qqn (de)** to warn sb (about) - **2.** [police] to inform - **3.** [désirs] to anticipate - **4.** [maladie] to prevent.

préventif, ive [prevɑ̃tif, iv] *adj* **1.** [mesure, médecine] preventive - **2.** DR : **être en détention préventive** to be on remand.

prévention [prevɑ̃sjɔ̃] *nf* **1.** [protection] : **prévention (contre)** prevention (of) ; **prévention routière** road safety (measures) - **2.** DR remand.

prévenu, e [prevny] ◇ *pp* ▶ **prévenir.** ◇ *nm, f* accused, defendant.

prévision [previzjɔ̃] *nf* forecast, prediction ; **les prévisions météorologiques** the weather forecast ; [de coûts] estimate ; ÉCON forecast. ◆ **en prévision de** *loc prép* in anticipation of.

prévoir [63] [prevwar] *vt* **1.** [s'attendre à] to expect - **2.** [prédire] to predict - **3.** [anticiper] to foresee, to anticipate - **4.** [programmer] to plan ; **comme prévu** as planned, according to plan.

prévoyant, e [prevwajɑ̃, ɑ̃t] *adj* provident.

prévu, e [prevy] *pp* ▶ **prévoir.**

prier [10] [prije] ◇ *vt* **1.** RELIG to pray to - **2.** [implorer] to beg ; **(ne pas) se faire prier (pour faire qqch)** (not) to need to be persuaded (to do sthg) ; **je vous en prie** [de grâce] please, I beg you ; [de rien] don't mention it, not at all - **3.** *sout* [demander] : **prier qqn de faire qqch** to request sb to do sthg. ◇ *vi* RELIG to pray.

prière [prijɛr] *nf* **1.** [RELIG - recueillement] prayer (U), praying (U) ; [- formule] prayer - **2.** *litt* [demande] entreaty ; **prière de frapper avant d'entrer** please knock before entering.

prion [prijɔ̃] *nm* BIOL & MÉD prion.

primaire [primɛr] *adj* **1.** [premier] : **études primaires** primary education (U) - **2.** *péj* [primitif] limited.

prime [prim] ◇ *nf* **1.** [d'employé] bonus ; **prime d'intéressement** profit-related bonus - **2.** [allocation - de déménagement, de transport] allowance UK ; [- à l'exportation] incentive - **3.** [d'assurance] premium. ◇ *adj* **1.** [premier] : **de prime abord** at first glance ; **de prime jeunesse** in the first flush of youth - **2.** MATH prime.

primer [3] [prime] ◇ *vi* to take precedence, to come first. ◇ *vt* **1.** [être supérieur à] to take precedence over - **2.** [récompenser] to award a prize to ; **le film a été primé au festival** the film won an award at the festival.

primeur [primœr] *nf* immediacy ; **avoir la primeur de qqch** to be the first to hear sthg. ◆ **primeurs** *nfpl* early produce (U).

primevère [primvɛr] *nf* primrose.

primitif, ive [primitif, iv] ◇ *adj* **1.** [gén] primitive - **2.** [aspect] original. ◇ *nm, f* primitive.

primordial, e, aux [primɔrdjal, o] *adj* essential.

prince [prɛ̃s] *nm* prince.

princesse [prɛ̃sɛs] *nf* princess.

princier, ère [prɛ̃sje, ɛr] *adj* princely.

principal, e, aux [prɛ̃sipal, o] ◇ *adj* [gén] main, principal. ◇ *nm, f* **1.** [important] : **le principal** the main thing - **2.** SCOL headmaster (f headmistress) UK, principal US.

principalement [prɛ̃sipalmɑ̃] *adv* mainly, principally.

principauté [prɛ̃sipote] *nf* principality.

principe [prɛ̃sip] *nm* principle ; **par principe** on principle. ◆ **en principe** *loc adv* theoretically, in principle.

printanier, ère [prɛ̃tanje, ɛr] *adj* [temps] spring-like.

printemps [prɛ̃tɑ̃] *nm* **1.** [saison] spring - **2.** *fam* [année] : **avoir 20 printemps** to be 20.

priori [prijɔri] ◆ **a priori** ◇ *loc adv* in principle. ◇ *nm inv* initial reaction.

prioritaire [prijɔritɛr] *adj* **1.** [industrie, mesure] priority (avant n) - **2.** AUTO with right of way.

priorité [prijɔrite] *nf* **1.** [importance primordiale] priority ; **en priorité** first - **2.** AUTO right of way ; **priorité à droite** give way to the right.

pris, e [pri, priz] ◇ *pp* ▶ **prendre.** ◇ *adj* **1.** [place] taken ; [personne] busy ; [mains] full - **2.** [nez] blocked ; [gorge] sore. ◆ **prise** *nf* **1.** [sur barre, sur branche] grip, hold ; **lâcher prise** to let go ; *fig* to give up

- **2.** [action de prendre - de ville] seizure, capture ; **prise en charge** [par Sécurité sociale] (guaranteed) reimbursement ; **prise d'otages** hostage taking ; **prise de sang** blood test ; **prise de vue** shot ; **prise de vue** OU **vues** [action] filming, shooting - **3.** [à la pêche] haul - **4.** ÉLECTR : **prise (de courant)** [mâle] plug ; [femelle] socket - **5.** [de judo] hold.

prisme [prism] *nm* prism.

prison [prizõ] *nf* **1.** [établissement] prison - **2.** [réclusion] imprisonment.

prisonnier, ère [prizɔnje, ɛr] <> *nm, f* prisoner ; **faire qqn prisonnier** to take sb prisoner, to capture sb. <> *adj* imprisoned ; *fig* trapped.

privation [privasjõ] *nf* deprivation. ▸ **privations** *nfpl* privations, hardships.

privatisation [privatizasjõ] *nf* privatization.

privatiser [3] [privatize] *vt* to privatize.

privé, e [prive] *adj* private. ▸ **privé** *nm* **1.** ÉCON private sector - **2.** [détective] private eye - **3.** [intimité] : **en privé** in private ; **dans le privé** in private life.

priver [3] [prive] *vt* : **priver qqn (de)** to deprive sb (of).

privilège [privilɛʒ] *nm* privilege.

privilégié, e [privileʒje] <> *adj* **1.** [personne] privileged - **2.** [climat, site] favoured UK, favored US. <> *nm, f* privileged person.

prix [pri] *nm* **1.** [coût] price ; **à aucun prix** on no account ; **hors de prix** too expensive ; **à moitié prix** at half price ; **à tout prix** at all costs ; **y mettre le prix** to pay a lot - **2.** [importance] value - **3.** [récompense] prize ; **prix Goncourt** *the most prestigious French annual literary prize.*

probabilité [prɔbabilite] *nf* **1.** [chance] probability - **2.** [vraisemblance] probability, likelihood ; **selon toute probabilité** in all probability.

probable [prɔbabl] *adj* probable, likely.

probablement [prɔbabləmã] *adv* probably.

probant, e [prɔbã, ãt] *adj* convincing, conclusive.

probité [prɔbite] *nf* integrity.

problème [prɔblɛm] *nm* problem ; **sans problème!, (il n'y a) pas de problème!** *fam* no problem! ; **ça ne lui pose aucun problème** *hum* that doesn't worry him/her.

procédé [prɔsede] *nm* **1.** [méthode] process - **2.** [conduite] behaviour *(U)* UK, behavior *(U)* US.

procéder [18] [prɔsede] *vi* **1.** [agir] to proceed - **2.** [exécuter] : **procéder à qqch** to set about sth.

procédure [prɔsedyr] *nf* procedure ; [démarche] proceedings *pl*.

procès [prɔsɛ] *nm* DR trial ; **intenter un procès à qqn** to sue sb.

processeur [prɔsesœr] *nm* processor.

procession [prɔsesjõ] *nf* procession.

processus [prɔsesys] *nm* process.

procès-verbal [prɔsɛverbal] *nm* **1.** [contravention - gén] ticket ; [- pour stationnement interdit] parking ticket - **2.** [compte-rendu] minutes.

prochain, e [prɔʃɛ̃, ɛn] *adj* **1.** [suivant] next ; **à la prochaine!** *fam* see you! - **2.** [imminent] impending. ▸ **prochain** *nm litt* [semblable] fellow man.

prochainement [prɔʃɛnmã] *adv* soon, shortly.

proche [prɔʃ] *adj* **1.** [dans l'espace] near ; **proche de** near, close to ; [semblable à] very similar to, closely related to - **2.** [dans le temps] imminent, near ; **dans un proche avenir** in the immediate future - **3.** [ami, parent] close. ▸ **proches** *nmpl* : **les proches** close friends and relatives *sg*. ▸ **de proche en proche** *loc adv sout* gradually.

Proche-Orient [prɔʃɔrjã] *nm* : **le Proche-Orient** the Near East.

proclamation [prɔklamasjõ] *nf* proclamation.

proclamer [3] [prɔklame] *vt* to proclaim, to declare.

procréer [15] [prɔkree] *vt litt* to procreate.

procuration [prɔkyrasjõ] *nf* proxy ; **par procuration** by proxy.

procurer [3] [prɔkyre] *vt* : **procurer qqch à qqn** [suj: personne] to obtain sth for sb ; [suj: chose] to give OU bring sb sth. ▸ **se procurer** *vp* : **se procurer qqch** to obtain sth.

procureur [prɔkyrœr] *nm* : **Procureur de la République** *public prosecutor at a 'tribunal de grande instance'*, ≃ Attorney General.

prodige [prɔdiʒ] *nm* **1.** [miracle] miracle - **2.** [tour de force] marvel, wonder - **3.** [génie] prodigy.

prodigieux, euse [prɔdiʒjø, øz] *adj* fantastic, incredible.

prodigue [prɔdig] *adj* [dépensier] extravagant.

prodiguer [3] [prɔdige] *vt litt* [soins, amitié] : **prodiguer qqch (à)** to lavish sth (on).

producteur, trice [prɔdyktœr, tris] <> *nm, f* [gén] producer - **2.** AGRIC producer, grower. <> *adj* : **producteur de pétrole** oil-producing *(avant n).*

productif, ive [prɔdyktif, iv] *adj* productive.

production [prɔdyksjɔ̃] *nf* **1.** [gén] production ; **la production littéraire d'un pays** the literature of a country - **2.** [producteurs] producers *pl*.

productivité [prɔdyktivite] *nf* productivity.

produire [98] [prɔdɥir] *vt* **1.** [gén] to produce - **2.** [provoquer] to cause. ◆ **se produire** *vp* **1.** [arriver] to occur, to take place - **2.** [acteur, chanteur] to appear.

produit, e [prɔdɥi, it] *pp* ► **produire**. ◆ **produit** *nm* [gén] product ; **produits alimentaires** foodstuffs, foods ; **produit de beauté** cosmetic, beauty product ; **produits chimiques** chemicals ; **produits d'entretien** cleaning products ; **produit financier** financial product ; **produit de grande consommation** mass consumption product.

proéminent, e [prɔeminã, ãt] *adj* prominent.

profane [prɔfan] ◇ *nmf* **1.** [non religieux] non-believer - **2.** [novice] layman. ◇ *adj* **1.** [laïc] secular - **2.** [ignorant] ignorant.

profaner [3] [prɔfane] *vt* **1.** [église] to desecrate - **2.** *fig* [mémoire] to defile.

proférer [18] [prɔfere] *vt* to utter.

professeur [prɔfesœr] *nm* [gén] teacher ; [dans l'enseignement supérieur] lecturer ; [titulaire] professor.

profession [prɔfesjɔ̃] *nf* **1.** [métier] occupation ; **sans profession** unemployed - **2.** [corps de métier - libéral] profession ; **profession libérale** (liberal) profession ; **être en profession libérale** to work in a liberal profession ; [- manuel] trade.

professionnel, elle [prɔfesjɔnɛl] ◇ *adj* **1.** [gén] professional - **2.** [école] technical ; [enseignement] vocational. ◇ *nm, f* professional.

professorat [prɔfesɔra] *nm* teaching.

profil [prɔfil] *nm* **1.** [de personne, d'emploi] profile ; [de bâtiment] outline ; **de profil** [visage, corps] in profile ; [objet] from the side - **2.** [coupe] section - **3.** INFORM : **profil (utilisateur)** (user) profil.

profiler [3] [prɔfile] *vt* to shape. ◆ **se profiler** *vp* **1.** [bâtiment, arbre] to stand out - **2.** [solution] to emerge.

profit [prɔfi] *nm* **1.** [avantage] benefit ; **au profit de** in aid of ; **tirer profit de** to profit from, to benefit from - **2.** [gain] profit.

profitable [prɔfitabl] *adj* profitable ; **être profitable à qqn** to benefit sb, to be beneficial to sb.

profiter [3] [prɔfite] *vi* [tirer avantage] : **profiter de** [vacances] to benefit from ; [personne] to take advantage of ; **profiter de**

qqch pour faire qqch to take advantage of sth to do sth ; **en profiter** to make the most of it.

profond, e [prɔfɔ̃, ɔ̃d] *adj* **1.** [gén] deep - **2.** [pensée] deep, profound.

profondément [prɔfɔ̃demã] *adv* **1.** [enfoui] deep - **2.** [intensément - aimer, intéresser] deeply ; [- dormir] soundly ; **être profondément endormi** to be fast asleep - **3.** [extrêmement - convaincu, ému] deeply, profoundly ; [- différent] profoundly.

profondeur [prɔfɔ̃dœr] *nf* depth ; **en profondeur** in depth.

profusion [prɔfyzjɔ̃] *nf* : **une profusion de** a profusion of ; **à profusion** in abundance, in profusion.

progéniture [prɔʒenityr] *nf* offspring.

programmable [prɔgramabl] *adj* programmable.

programmateur, trice [prɔgramatœr, tris] *nm, f* programme UK ou program US planner. ◆ **programmateur** *nm* automatic control unit.

programmation [prɔgramasjɔ̃] *nf* **1.** INFORM programming - **2.** RADIO & TV programme UK ou program US planning.

programme [prɔgram] *nm* **1.** [gén] programme UK, program US - **2.** INFORM program - **3.** [planning] schedule - **4.** SCOL syllabus.

programmer [3] [prɔgrame] *vt* **1.** [organiser] to plan - **2.** RADIO & TV to schedule - **3.** INFORM to program.

programmeur, euse {prɔgramœr, øz] *nm, f* INFORM (computer) programmer.

progrès [prɔgrɛ] *nm* progress *(U)* ; **faire des progrès** to make progress.

progresser [4] [prɔgrese] *vi* **1.** [avancer] to progress, to advance - **2.** [maladie] to spread - **3.** [élève] to make progress.

progressif, ive [prɔgresif, iv] *adj* progressive ; [difficulté] increasing.

progression [prɔgresjɔ̃] *nf* **1.** [avancée] advance - **2.** [de maladie, du nationalisme] spread.

prohiber [3] [prɔibe] *vt* to ban, to prohibit.

proie [prwa] *nf* prey ; **être la proie de qqch** *fig* to be the victim of sth ; **être en proie à** [sentiment] to be prey to.

projecteur [prɔʒɛktœr] *nm* **1.** [de lumière] floodlight ; THÉÂTRE spotlight - **2.** [d'images] projector.

projectile [prɔʒɛktil] *nm* missile.

projection [prɔʒɛksjɔ̃] *nf* **1.** [gén] projection - **2.** [jet] throwing.

projectionniste [prɔʒɛksjɔnist] *nmf* projectionist.

projet [prɔʒɛ] *nm* **1.** [perspective] plan - **2.** [étude, ébauche] draft ; **projet de loi** bill.

projeter [27] [prɔʃte] *vt* **1.** [envisager] to

plan ; **projeter de faire qqch** to plan to do sthg - **2.** [missile, pierre] to throw - **3.** [film, diapositives] to show.

prolétaire [prɔletɛr] *nmf & adj* proletarian.

prolétariat [prɔletarja] *nm* proletariat.

proliférer [18] [prɔlifere] *vi* to proliferate.

prolifique [prɔlifik] *adj* prolific.

prologue [prɔlɔg] *nm* prologue.

prolongation [prɔlɔ̃gasjɔ̃] *nf* [extension] extension, prolongation. ➤ **prolongations** *nfpl* SPORT extra time *(U) UK*, overtime *US*.

prolongement [prɔlɔ̃ʒmɑ̃] *nm* [de mur, quai] extension ; **être dans le prolongement de** to be a continuation of. ➤ **prolongements** *nmpl* [conséquences] repercussions.

prolonger [17] [prɔlɔ̃ʒe] *vt* **1.** [dans le temps] : **prolonger qqch (de)** to prolong sthg (by) - **2.** [dans l'espace] : **prolonger qqch (de)** to extend sthg (by).

promenade [prɔmnad] *nf* **1.** [balade] walk, stroll ; *fig* trip, excursion ; **promenade en voiture** drive ; **promenade à vélo** ride ; **faire une promenade** to go for a walk - **2.** [lieu] promenade.

promener [19] [prɔmne] *vt* **1.** [personne] to take out (for a walk) ; [en voiture] to take for a drive - **2.** *fig* [regard, doigts] : **promener qqch sur** to run sthg over. ➤ **se promener** *vp* to go for a walk.

promesse [prɔmɛs] *nf* **1.** [serment] promise ; **tenir sa promesse** to keep one's promise - **2.** [engagement] undertaking ; **promesse d'achat/de vente** DR agreement to purchase/to sell - **3.** *fig* [espérance] : **être plein de promesses** to be very promising.

prometteur, euse [prɔmɛtœr, øz] *adj* promising.

promettre [84] [prɔmɛtr] ⟨⟩ *vt* to promise ; **promettre qqch à qqn** to promise sb sthg ; **promettre de faire qqch** to promise to do sthg ; **promettre à qqn que** to promise sb that. ⟨⟩ *vi* to be promising ; **ça promet!** *iron* that bodes well!

promis, e [prɔmi, iz] ⟨⟩ *pp* ➤ promettre. ⟨⟩ *adj* promised. ⟨⟩ *nm, f hum* intended.

promiscuité [prɔmiskɥite] *nf* overcrowding ; **promiscuité sexuelle** (sexual) promiscuity.

promontoire [prɔmɔ̃twar] *nm* promontory.

promoteur, trice [prɔmɔtœr, tris] *nm, f* **1.** [novateur] instigator - **2.** [constructeur] property developer.

promotion [prɔmɔsjɔ̃] *nf* **1.** [gén] promotion ; **en promotion** [produit] on special offer - **2.** MIL & SCOL year.

promouvoir [56] [prɔmuvwar] *vt* to promote.

prompt, e [prɔ̃, prɔ̃t] *adj sout* : **prompt (à faire qqch)** swift (to do sthg).

promu, e [prɔmy] *pp* ➤ promouvoir.

promulguer [3] [prɔmylge] *vt* to promulgate.

prôner [3] [prone] *vt sout* to advocate.

pronom [prɔnɔ̃] *nm* pronoun.

pronominal, e, aux [prɔnɔminal, o] *adj* pronominal.

prononcé, e [prɔnɔ̃se] *adj* marked.

prononcer [16] [prɔnɔ̃se] *vt* **1.** DR & LING to pronounce - **2.** [dire] to utter. ➤ **se prononcer** *vp* **1.** [se dire] to be pronounced - **2.** [trancher - assemblée] to decide, to reach a decision ; [- magistrat] to deliver a verdict ; **se prononcer sur** to give one's opinion of.

prononciation [prɔnɔ̃sjasjɔ̃] *nf* **1.** LING pronunciation - **2.** DR pronouncement.

pronostic [prɔnɔstik] *nm* **1.** *(gén pl)* [prévision] forecast - **2.** MÉD prognosis.

propagande [prɔpagɑ̃d] *nf* **1.** [endoctrinement] propaganda - **2.** *fig & hum* [publicité] : **faire de la propagande pour qqch** to plug sthg.

propager [17] [prɔpaʒe] *vt* to spread. ➤ **se propager** *vp* to spread ; BIOL to be propagated ; PHYS to propagate.

propane [prɔpan] *nm* propane.

prophète, prophétesse [prɔfɛt, prɔfetɛs] *nm, f* prophet *(f* prophetess).

prophétie [prɔfesi] *nf* prophecy.

prophétiser [3] [prɔfetize] *vt* to prophesy.

propice [prɔpis] *adj* favourable *UK*, favorable *US*.

proportion [prɔpɔrsjɔ̃] *nf* proportion ; **toutes proportions gardées** relatively speaking.

proportionné, e [prɔpɔrsjɔne] *adj* : **bien/mal proportionné** well-/badly-proportioned.

proportionnel, elle [prɔpɔrsjɔnɛl] *adj* : **proportionnel (à)** proportional (to). ➤ **proportionnelle** *nf* : **la proportionnelle** proportional representation.

propos [prɔpo] ⟨⟩ *nm* **1.** [discours] talk - **2.** [but] intention ; **c'est à quel propos?** what is it about? ; **hors de propos** at the wrong time. ⟨⟩ *nmpl* [paroles] talk *(U)*, words. ➤ **à propos** *loc adv* **1.** [opportunément] at (just) the right time - **2.** [au fait] by the way. ➤ **à propos de** *loc prép* about.

proposer [3] [prɔpoze] *vt* **1.** [offrir] to offer, to propose ; **proposer qqch à qqn** to offer sb sthg, to offer sthg to sb ; **proposer à qqn de faire qqch** to offer to do sthg for sb

- **2.** [suggérer] to suggest, to propose ; **proposer de faire qqch** to suggest OU propose doing sthg - **3.** [loi, candidat] to propose.

proposition [prɔpozisjɔ̃] *nf* **1.** [offre] offer, proposal - **2.** [suggestion] suggestion, proposal - **3.** GRAMM clause.

propre [prɔpr] <> *adj* **1.** [nettoyé] clean - **2.** [soigné] neat, tidy - **3.** [éduqué - enfant] toilet-trained ; [- animal] house-trained *UK*, housebroken *US* - **4.** [personnel] own - **5.** [particulier] : **propre à** peculiar to - **6.** [de nature] : **propre à faire qqch** capable of doing sthg. <> *nm* [propreté] cleanness, cleanliness ; **recopier qqch au propre** to make a fair copy of sthg, to copy sthg up. **au propre** *loc adv* LING literally.

proprement [prɔprəmɑ̃] *adv* **1.** [convenablement - habillé] neatly, tidily ; [- se tenir] correctly - **2.** [véritablement] completely ; **à proprement parler** strictly OU properly speaking ; **l'événement proprement dit** the event itself, the actual event.

propreté [prɔprəte] *nf* cleanness, cleanliness.

propriétaire [prɔprijetɛr] *nmf* **1.** [possesseur] owner ; **propriétaire terrien** landowner - **2.** [dans l'immobilier] landlord.

propriété [prɔprijete] *nf* **1.** [gén] property ; **propriété privée** private property - **2.** [droit] ownership - **3.** [terres] property (*U*) - **4.** [convenance] suitability - **5.** [qualité] property, characteristic, feature.

propulser [3] [prɔpylse] *vt litt & fig* to propel. **se propulser** *vp* to move forward, to propel o.s. forward OU along ; *fig* to shoot.

prorata [prɔrata] **au prorata de** *loc prép* in proportion to.

prosaïque [prɔzaik] *adj* prosaic, mundane.

proscrit, e [prɔskri, it] *adj* [interdit] banned, prohibited.

prose [proz] *nf* prose ; **en prose** in prose.

prospecter [4] [prɔspɛkte] *vt* **1.** [pays, région] to prospect - **2.** COMM to canvass.

prospection [prɔspɛksjɔ̃] *nf* **1.** [de ressources] prospecting - **2.** COMM canvassing.

prospectus [prɔspɛktys] *nm* (advertising) leaflet.

prospérer [18] [prɔspere] *vi* to prosper, to thrive ; [plante, insecte] to thrive.

prospérité [prɔsperite] *nf* **1.** [richesse] prosperity - **2.** [bien-être] well-being.

prostate [prɔstat] *nf* prostate (gland).

prosterner [3] [prɔstɛrne] **se prosterner** *vp* to bow down ; **se prosterner devant** to bow down before ; *fig* to kowtow to.

prostituée [prɔstitɥe] *nf* prostitute.

prostituer [7] [prɔstitɥe] **se prostituer** *vp* to prostitute o.s.

prostitution [prɔstitysjɔ̃] *nf* prostitution.

prostré, e [prɔstre] *adj* prostrate.

protagoniste [prɔtagɔnist] *nmf* protagonist, hero (*f* heroine).

protecteur, trice [prɔtɛktœr, tris] <> *adj* protective. <> *nm, f* **1.** [défenseur] protector - **2.** [des arts] patron - **3.** [souteneur] pimp.

protection [prɔtɛksjɔ̃] *nf* **1.** [défense] protection ; **prendre qqn sous sa protection** to take sb under one's wing - **2.** [des arts] patronage.

protectionnisme [prɔtɛksjɔnism] *nm* protectionism.

protégé, e [prɔteʒe] <> *adj* protected. <> *nm, f* protégé.

protège-cahier [prɔtɛʒkaje] (*pl* **protège-cahiers**) *nm* exercise book cover *US*, notebook cover *US*.

protège-poignets [prɔtɛʒpwanje] *nm inv* wrist guard, wrist protector.

protéger [22] [prɔteʒe] *vt* [gén] to protect.

protéine [prɔtein] *nf* protein.

protestant, e [prɔtɛstɑ̃, ɑ̃t] *adj & nm, f* Protestant.

protestation [prɔtɛstasjɔ̃] *nf* [contestation] protest.

protester [3] [prɔteste] *vi* to protest ; **protester contre qqch** to protest against sthg, to protest sthg *US*.

prothèse [prɔtɛz] *nf* prosthesis ; **prothèse dentaire** dentures (*pl*), false teeth *pl*.

protide [prɔtid] *nm* protein.

protocolaire [prɔtɔkɔlɛr] *adj* [poli] conforming to etiquette.

protocole [prɔtɔkɔl] *nm* protocol.

proton [prɔtɔ̃] *nm* proton.

prototype [prɔtɔtip] *nm* prototype.

protubérance [prɔtyberɑ̃s] *nf* bulge, protuberance.

proue [pru] *nf* bows *pl*, prow.

prouesse [prues] *nf* feat.

prouver [3] [pruve] *vt* **1.** [établir] to prove - **2.** [montrer] to demonstrate, to show.

provenance [prɔvnɑ̃s] *nf* origin ; **en provenance de** from.

provençal, e, aux [prɔvɑ̃sal, o] *adj* **1.** [de Provence] of/from Provence - **2.** CULIN *with tomatoes, garlic and onions*. **provençal** *nm* [langue] Provençal.

Provence [prɔvɑ̃s] *nf* : **la Provence** Provence ; **herbes de Provence** ≃ mixed herbs.

provenir [40] [prɔvnir] *vi* : **provenir de** to come from ; *fig* to be due to, to be caused by.

proverbe [prɔvɛrb] *nm* proverb.

proverbial, e, aux [prɔvɛrbjal, o] *adj* proverbial.

providence [prɔvidɑ̃s] *nf* providence.

providentiel, elle [prɔvidɑ̃sjɛl] *adj* providential.

province [prɔvɛ̃s] *nf* **1.** [gén] province - **2.** [campagne] provinces *pl.*

provincial, e, aux [prɔvɛ̃sjal, o] *adj &* *nm, f* provincial.

proviseur [prɔvizœr] *nm* ≃ head UK, ≃ headteacher UK, ≃ headmaster headmistress *f* UK, ≃ principal US.

provision [prɔvizjɔ̃] *nf* **1.** [réserve] stock, supply - **2.** FIN retainer, ▶ **chèque.** ➤ **provisions** *nfpl* provisions.

provisoire [prɔvizwar] <> *adj* temporary ; DR provisional. <> *nm* : **ce n'est que du provisoire** it's only a temporary arrangement.

provocant, e [prɔvɔkɑ̃, ɑ̃t] *adj* provocative.

provocation [prɔvɔkasjɔ̃] *nf* provocation.

provoquer [3] [prɔvɔke] *vt* **1.** [entraîner] to cause - **2.** [personne] to provoke.

proxénète [prɔksenɛt] *nm* pimp.

proximité [prɔksimite] *nf* [de lieu] proximity, nearness ; **à proximité de** near. ➤ **de proximité** *loc adj* **1.** TECHNOL proximity *(modif)* - **2.** [de quartier] : **commerces de proximité** local shops ; **police de proximité** community policing ; **élu de proximité** [de la communauté] local councillor, local representative ; [faisant valoir ses liens avec la communauté] local man OU woman ; **médias de proximité** locals OU community media.

prude [pryd] *adj* prudish.

prudence [prydɑ̃s] *nf* care, caution.

prudent, e [prydɑ̃, ɑ̃t] *adj* careful, cautious.

prune [pryn] *nf* plum.

pruneau, x [pryno] *nm* [fruit] prune.

prunelle [prynɛl] *nf* ANAT pupil.

prunier [prynje] *nm* plum tree.

PS¹ *(abr de Parti socialiste)* *nm* French socialist party.

PS², P-S *(abr de post-scriptum)* *nm* PS.

psalmodier [9] [psalmɔdje] <> *vt* to chant ; *fig & péj* to drone. <> *vi* to drone.

psaume [psom] *nm* psalm.

pseudonyme [psødɔnim] *nm* pseudonym.

psy [psi] *fam nmf (abr de psychiatre)* shrink.

psychanalyse [psikanaliz] *nf* psychoanalysis.

psychanalyste [psikanalist] *nmf* psychoanalyst, analyst.

psychédélique [psikedelik] *adj* psychedelic.

psychiatre [psikjatr] *nmf* psychiatrist.

psychiatrie [psikjatri] *nf* psychiatry.

psychique [psiʃik] *adj* psychic ; [maladie] psychosomatic.

psychologie [psikɔlɔʒi] *nf* psychology.

psychologique [psikɔlɔʒik] *adj* psychological.

psychologue [psikɔlɔg] <> *nmf* psychologist. <> *adj* psychological.

psychose [psikoz] *nf* **1.** MÉD psychosis - **2.** [crainte] obsessive fear.

psychosomatique [psikɔsɔmatik] *adj* psychosomatic.

psychothérapie [psikɔterapi] *nf* psychotherapy.

Pte *abr écrite de porte. ou de pointe.*

PTT *(abr de Postes, télécommunications et télédiffusion) nfpl former French post office and telecommunications network.*

pu [py] *pp* ▶ **pouvoir.**

puant, e [pɥɑ̃, ɑ̃t] *adj* **1.** [fétide] smelly, stinking - **2.** *fam fig* [personne] bumptious, full of oneself.

puanteur [pɥɑ̃tœr] *nf* stink, stench.

pub¹ [pyb] *nf fam* ad, advert UK ; [métier] advertising.

pub² [pœb] *nm* pub.

pubère [pybɛr] *adj* pubescent.

puberté [pybɛrte] *nf* puberty.

pubis [pybis] *nm* [zone] pubis.

public, ique [pyblik] *adj* public. ➤ **public** *nm* **1.** [auditoire] audience ; **en public** in public - **2.** [population] public.

publication [pyblikasjɔ̃] *nf* publication.

publicitaire [pyblisiter] *adj* [campagne] advertising *(avant n)* ; [vente, film] promotional.

publicité [pyblisite] *nf* **1.** [domaine] advertising ; **publicité comparative** comparative advertising ; **publicité mensongère** misleading advertising, deceptive advertising - **2.** [réclame] advertisement, advert UK - **3.** [autour d'une affaire] publicity *(U).*

publier [10] [pyblije] *vt* [livre] to publish ; [communiqué] to issue, to release.

publireportage [pyblirǝpɔrtaʒ] *nm* free write-up UK, special advertising section US.

puce [pys] *nf* **1.** [insecte] flea - **2.** INFORM (silicon) chip - **3.** *fig* [terme affectueux] pet, love.

puceau, elle, x [pyso, ɛl, o] *nm, f & adj fam* virgin.

pudeur [pydœr] *nf* **1.** [physique] modesty, decency - **2.** [morale] restraint.

pudibond, e [pydibɔ̃, ɔ̃d] *adj* prudish, prim and proper.

pudique [pydik] *adj* **1.** [physiquement] modest, decent - **2.** [moralement] restrained.

puer [7] [pɥe] <> *vi* to stink ; **ça pue ici!** it stinks in here! <> *vt* to reek of, to stink of.

puéricultrice [pɥerikyltris] *nf* nursery nurse.

puériculture [pɥerikyltyr] *nf* childcare.

puéril, e [pɥeril] *adj* childish.

Puerto Rico = Porto Rico.

pugilat [pyʒila] *nm* fight.

puis [pɥi] *adv* then ; **et puis** [d'ailleurs] and moreover ou besides.

puiser [3] [pɥize] *vt* [liquide] to draw ; **puiser qqch dans qqch** *fig* to draw ou take sthg from sthg.

puisque [pɥiskə] *conj* [gén] since.

puissance [pɥisɑ̃s] *nf* power. **en puissance** *loc adj* potential.

puissant, e [pɥisɑ̃, ɑ̃t] *adj* powerful. **puissant** *nm* : **les puissants** the powerful.

puisse, puisses *etc* **pouvoir**.

puits [pɥi] *nm* **1.** [d'eau] well - **2.** [de gisement] shaft ; **puits de pétrole** oil well.

pull [pyl], **pull-over** [pylɔver] (*pl* pullovers) *nm* jumper UK, sweater.

pulluler [3] [pylyle] *vi* to swarm.

pulmonaire [pylmɔner] *adj* lung (*avant n*), pulmonary.

pulpe [pylp] *nf* pulp.

pulsation [pylsasjɔ̃] *nf* beat, beating (*U*).

pulsion [pylsjɔ̃] *nf* impulse.

pulvérisation [pylverizasjɔ̃] *nf* **1.** [d'insecticide] spraying - **2.** MÉD spray ; [traitement] spraying.

pulvériser [3] [pylverize] *vt* **1.** [projeter] to spray - **2.** [détruire] to pulverize ; *fig* to smash.

puma [pyma] *nm* puma.

punaise [pynɛz] *nf* **1.** [insecte] bug - **2.** [clou] drawing pin UK, thumbtack US.

punch [pɔ̃ʃ] *nm* punch.

puni, e [pyni] *adj* punished.

punir [32] [pynir] *vt* : **punir qqn (de)** to punish sb (with).

punition [pynisjɔ̃] *nf* punishment.

pupille [pypij] <> *nf* ANAT pupil. <> *nmf* [orphelin] ward ; **pupille de l'État** ≃ child in care UK ; **pupille de la Nation** war orphan (*in care*).

pupitre [pypitr] *nm* **1.** [d'orateur] lectern ; MUS stand - **2.** TECHNOL console - **3.** [d'écolier] desk.

pur, e [pyr] *adj* **1.** [gén] pure - **2.** *fig* [absolu] pure, sheer ; **pur et simple** pure and simple - **3.** *fig & litt* [intention] honourable UK, honorable US - **4.** [lignes] pure, clean.

purée [pyre] *nf* purée ; **purée de pommes de terre** mashed potatoes *pl*.

purement [pyrmɑ̃] *adv* purely ; **purement et simplement** purely and simply.

pureté [pyrte] *nf* **1.** [gén] purity - **2.** [de sculpture, de diamant] perfection - **3.** [d'intention] honourableness UK, honorableness US.

purgatoire [pyrgatwar] *nm* purgatory.

purge [pyrʒ] *nf* **1.** MÉD & POLIT purge - **2.** [de radiateur] bleeding.

purger [17] [pyrʒe] *vt* **1.** MÉD & POLIT to purge - **2.** [radiateur] to bleed - **3.** [peine] to serve.

purifier [9] [pyrifje] *vt* to purify.

purin [pyrɛ̃] *nm* slurry.

puritain, e [pyritɛ̃, ɛn] <> *adj* [pudibond] puritanical. <> *nm, f* **1.** [prude] puritan - **2.** RELIG Puritan.

puritanisme [pyritanism] *nm* puritanism ; RELIG Puritanism.

pur-sang [pyrsɑ̃] *nm inv* thoroughbred.

purulent, e [pyrylɑ̃, ɑ̃t] *adj* purulent.

pus [py] *nm* pus.

pusillanime [pyzilanim] *adj* pusillanimous.

putain [pytɛ̃] *nf vulg* **1.** *péj* [prostituée] whore - **2.** *fig* [pour exprimer le mécontentement] : **(ce) putain de...** this/that sodding... UK, this/that goddam... US

putréfier [9] [pytrefje] **se putréfier** *vp* to putrefy, to rot.

putsch [putʃ] *nm* uprising, coup.

puzzle [pœzl] *nm* jigsaw (puzzle).

P-V *nm abr de* procès-verbal.

pyjama [piʒama] *nm* pyjamas *pl* UK, pajamas *pl* US.

pylône [pilon] *nm* pylon.

pyramide [piramid] *nf* pyramid ; **la Pyramide du Louvre** glass *pyramid in the courtyard of the Louvre which serves as its main entrance.*

Pyrénées [pirene] *nfpl* : **les Pyrénées** the Pyrenees.

Pyrex® [pirɛks] *nm* Pyrex®.

pyromane [pirɔman] *nmf* arsonist ; MÉD pyromaniac.

python [pitɔ̃] *nm* python.

Q

q, Q [ky] *nm inv* [lettre] q, Q.

QCM (*abr de* **questionnaire à choix multiple**) *nm* multiple choice questionnaire.

QG (*abr de* **quartier général**) *nm* HQ.

QI (*abr de* **quotient intellectuel**) *nm* IQ.

qqch (*abr écrite de* **quelque chose**) sthg.

qqn (*abr écrite de* **quelqu'un**) s.o., sb.

qu' ▶ que.

quad [kwad] *nm* [moto] four-wheel motorbike, quad bike ; [rollers] roller skate.

quadra [k(w)adra] *nm* fortysomething, babyboomer.

quadragénaire [kwadraʒenɛr] *nmf* forty year old.

quadrilatère [kwadrilatɛr] *nm* quadrilateral.

quadrillage [kadrijaʒ] *nm* **1.** [de papier, de tissu] criss-cross pattern - **2.** [policier] combing.

quadriller [3] [kadrije] *vt* **1.** [papier] to mark with squares - **2.** [ville - suj: rues] to criss-cross ; [- suj: police] to comb.

quadrimoteur [kwadrimɔtœr] *nm* four-engined plane.

quadrupède [k(w)adryped] *nm & adj* quadruped.

quadruplés, ées [k(w)adryple] *nmf pl* quadruplets, quads.

quai [ke] *nm* **1.** [de gare] platform - **2.** [de port] quay, wharf - **3.** [de rivière] embankment.

qualificatif, ive [kalifikatif, iv] *adj* qualifying. ▶ **qualificatif** *nm* term.

qualification [kalifikasjɔ̃] *nf* [gén] qualification.

qualifier [9] [kalifje] *vt* **1.** [gén] to qualify ; **être qualifié pour qqch/pour faire qqch** to be qualified for sthg/to do sthg - **2.** [caractériser] : **qualifier qqn/qqch de qqch** to describe sb/sthg as sthg, to call sb/sthg sthg. ▶ **se qualifier** *vp* to qualify.

qualitatif, ive [kalitatif, iv] *adj* qualitative.

qualité [kalite] *nf* **1.** [gén] quality ; **de bonne/mauvaise qualité** of good/poor quality - **2.** [condition] position, capacity.

quand [kã] ◇ *conj* [lorsque, alors que] when ; **quand tu le verras, demande-lui de me téléphoner** when you see him, ask him

to phone me. ◇ *adv interr* when ; **quand arriveras-tu?** when will you arrive? ; **jusqu'à quand restez-vous?** how long are you staying for? ▶ **quand même** ◇ *loc adv* all the same ; **je pense qu'il ne viendra pas, mais je l'inviterai quand même** I don't think he'll come but I'll invite him all the same ; **tu pourrais faire attention quand même!** you might at least be careful! ◇ *interj* : **quand même, à son âge!** really, at his/her age! ▶ **quand bien même** *loc conj sout* even though, even if.

quant [kã] ▶ **quant à** *loc prép* as for.

quantifier [9] [kãtifje] *vt* to quantify.

quantitatif, ive [kãtitatif, iv] *adj* quantitative.

quantité [kãtite] *nf* **1.** [mesure] quantity, amount - **2.** [abondance] : **(une) quantité de** a great many, a lot of ; **en quantité** in large numbers ; **des exemplaires en quantité** a large number of copies.

quarantaine [karãten] *nf* **1.** [nombre] : **une quarantaine de** about forty - **2.** [âge] : **avoir la quarantaine** to be in one's forties - **3.** [isolement] quarantine.

quarante [karãt] *adj num inv & nm* forty ; *voir aussi* **six**.

quarantième [karãtjem] *adj num inv, nm & nmf* fortieth ; *voir aussi* **sixième**.

quart [kar] *nm* **1.** [fraction] quarter ; **deux heures moins le quart** (a) quarter to two, (a) quarter of two *US* ; **deux heures et quart** (a) quarter past two, (a) quarter after two *US* ; **il est moins le quart** it's (a) quarter to, it's a quarter of *US* ; **un quart de** a quarter of - **2.** NAUT watch - **3.** SPORT : **quart de finale** quarterfinal.

quartier [kartje] *nm* **1.** [de ville] area, district ; **le quartier latin** the Latin quarter - **2.** [de fruit] piece ; [de viande] quarter - **3.** [héraldique, de lune] quarter - **4.** (*gén pl*) MIL quarters *pl* ; **quartier général** headquarters *pl* - **5.** [partie d'une prison] wing.

quart-monde [karmɔ̃d] (*pl* **quarts-mondes**) *nm* : **le quart-monde** the Fourth World.

quartz [kwarts] *nm* quartz ; **montre à quartz** quartz watch.

quasi [kazi] *adv* almost, nearly.

quasi- [kazi] *préf* near ; **quasi-collision** near collision.

quasiment [kazimã] *adv fam* almost, nearly.

quatorze [katɔrz] *adj num inv & nm* fourteen ; *voir aussi* **six**.

quatorzième [katɔrzjem] *adj num inv, nm & nmf* fourteenth ; *voir aussi* **sixième**.

quatrain [katrɛ̃] *nm* quatrain.

quatre [katr] ◇ *adj num inv* four ; **monter**

l'escalier quatre à quatre to take the stairs four at a time ; se mettre en quatre pour qqn to bend over backwards for sb. <> nm four ; voir aussi six.

quatre-vingt = quatre-vingts.

quatre-vingt-dix [katrəvɛ̃dis] adj num inv & nm ninety ; voir aussi six.

quatre-vingt-dixième [katrəvɛ̃dizjɛm] adj num inv, nm & nmf ninetieth ; voir aussi sixième.

quatre-vingtième [katrəvɛ̃tjɛm] adj num inv, nm & nmf eightieth ; voir aussi sixième.

quatre-vingts, quatre-vingt [katrəvɛ̃] adj num inv & nm eighty ; voir aussi six.

quatrième [katrijɛm] <> adj num inv, nm & nmf fourth. <> nf SCOL ≃ third year ou form UK, ≃ eighth grade US ; voir aussi sixième.

quatuor [kwatɥɔr] nm quartet.

que [k(ə)] <> conj **1.** [introduit une subordonnée] that ; il a dit qu'il viendrait he said (that) he'd come ; il veut que tu viennes he wants you to come - **2.** [introduit une hypothèse] whether ; que vous le vouliez ou non whether you like it or not - **3.** [reprend une autre conjonction] : s'il fait beau et que nous avons le temps... if the weather is good and we have time... - **4.** [indique un ordre, un souhait] : qu'il entre! let him come in! ; que tout le monde sorte! everybody out! - **5.** [après un présentatif] : voilà/voici que ça recommence! here we go again! - **6.** [comparatif - après moins, plus] than ; [- après autant, aussi, même] as ; plus jeune que moi younger than I (am) ou than me ; elle a la même robe que moi she has the same dress as I do ou as me - **7.** [seulement] : ne... que only ; je n'ai qu'une sœur I've only got one sister. <> pron rel [chose, animal] which, that ; le livre qu'il m'a prêté the book (which ou that) he lent me ; [personne] whom, that ; la femme que j'aime the woman (whom ou that) I love. <> pron interr what ; que savez-vous au juste? what exactly do you know? ; que faire? what can I/we/one do? ; je me demande que faire I wonder what I should do. <> adv excl : qu'elle est belle! how beautiful she is! ; que de monde! what a lot of people! ⏹ c'est que loc conj it's because ; si je vais me coucher, c'est que j'ai sommeil if I'm going to bed, it's because I'm tired. ⏹ qu'est-ce que pron interr what ; qu'est-ce que tu veux encore? what else do you want? ⏹ qu'est-ce qui pron interr what ; qu'est-ce qui se passe? what's going on?

Québec [kebɛk] nm [province] : le Québec Quebec.

québécois, e [kebekwa, az] adj Quebec

(avant n). ⏹ québécois nm [langue] Quebec French. ⏹ **Québécois, e** nm, f Quebecker, Québécois.

quel, quelle (mpl quels, fpl quelles) [kɛl] <> adj interr [personne] which ; [chose] what, which ; quel homme? which man? ; quel livre voulez-vous? what ou which book do you want? ; de quel côté es-tu? what ou which side are you on? ; je ne sais quels sont ses projets I don't know what his plans are ; quelle heure est-il? what time is it?, what's the time? <> adj excl : quel idiot! what an idiot! ; quelle honte! the shame of it! <> adj indéf : quel que (+ subjonctif) [chose, animal] whatever ; [personne] whoever ; il se baigne, quel que soit le temps he goes swimming whatever the weather ; il refuse de voir les nouveaux arrivants, quels qu'ils soient he refuses to see new arrivals, whoever they may be. <> pron interr which (one) ; de vous trois, quel est le plus jeune? which (one) of you three is the youngest?

quelconque [kɛlkɔ̃k] adj **1.** [n'importe lequel] any ; donner un prétexte quelconque to give any old excuse ; si pour une raison quelconque... if for any reason... ; une quelconque observation some remark or other - **2.** (après n) péj [banal] ordinary, mediocre.

quelque [kɛlk(ə)] <> adj indéf some ; à quelque distance de là some way away (from there) ; j'ai quelques lettres à écrire I have some ou a few letters to write ; vous n'avez pas quelques livres à me montrer? don't you have any books to show me? ; les quelques fois où j'étais absent the few times I wasn't there ; les quelque 30 euros qu'il m'a prêtés the 30 euros or so (that) he lent me ; quelque route que je prenne whatever route I take ; quelque peu somewhat, rather. <> adv [environ] about ; 30 euros et quelque some ou about 30 euros ; il est midi et quelque fam it's just after midday.

quelque chose [kɛlkəʃoz] pron indéf something ; quelque chose de différent something different ; quelque chose d'autre something else ; tu veux boire quelque chose? do you want something ou anything to drink? ; apporter un petit quelque chose à qqn to give sb a little something ; c'est quelque chose! [ton admiratif] it's really something! ; cela m'a fait quelque chose I really felt it.

quelquefois [kɛlkəfwa] adv sometimes, occasionally.

quelque part [kɛlkəpar] adv somewhere, someplace US ; l'as-tu vu quelque part? did you see him anywhere ou anyplace US?, have you seen him anywhere ou anyplace US?

quelques-uns, quelques-unes [kɛlkəzœ̃, yn] *pron indéf* some, a few.

quelqu'un [kɛlkœ̃] *pron indéf m* someone, somebody ; **c'est quelqu'un d'ouvert/d'intelligent** he's/she's a frank/an intelligent person.

quémander [3] [kemɑ̃de] *vt* to beg for ; **quémander qqch à qqn** to beg sb for sthg.

qu'en-dira-t-on [kɑ̃diratɔ̃] *nm inv fam* tittle-tattle.

quenelle [kənɛl] *nf very finely chopped mixture of fish or chicken cooked in stock.*

querelle [kərɛl] *nf* quarrel.

quereller [4] [kərele] ➡ **se quereller** *vp* : **se quereller (avec)** to quarrel (with).

querelleur, euse [kərɛlœr, øz] *adj* quarrelsome.

qu'est-ce que [kɛskə] ➤ **que.**

qu'est-ce qui [kɛski] ➤ **que.**

question [kɛstjɔ̃] *nf* question ; **poser une question à qqn** to ask sb a question ; **il est question de faire qqch** it's a question ou matter of doing sthg ; **il n'en est pas question** there is no question of it ; **remettre qqn/qqch en question** to question sb/sthg, to challenge sb/sthg ; **question subsidiaire** tiebreaker.

questionnaire [kɛstjɔnɛr] *nm* questionnaire.

questionner [3] [kɛstjɔne] *vt* to question.

quête [kɛt] *nf* **1.** *sout* [d'objet, de personne] quest ; **se mettre en quête de** to go in search of - **2.** [d'aumône] : **faire la quête** to take a collection.

quêter [4] [kete] ➡ *vi* to collect. ➡ *vt fig* to seek, to look for.

queue [kø] *nf* **1.** [d'animal] tail ; **faire une queue de poisson à qqn** AUTO to cut in front of sb - **2.** [de fruit] stalk - **3.** [de poêle] handle - **4.** [de liste, de classe] bottom ; [de file, peloton] rear - **5.** [file] queue *UK*, line *US* ; **faire la queue** to queue *UK*, to stand in line *US* ; **à la queue leu leu** in single file.

queue-de-cheval [kødʃəval] *(pl* **queues-de-cheval)** *nf* ponytail.

queue-de-pie [kødpi] *(pl* **queues-de-pie)** *nf fam* tails *pl.*

qui [ki] ➡ *pron rel* **1.** *(sujet)* [personne] who ; [chose] which, that ; **l'homme qui parle** the man who's talking ; **je l'ai vu qui passait** I saw him pass ; **le chien qui aboie** the barking dog, the dog which ou that is barking ; **qui plus est** (and) what's more ; **qui mieux est** even better, better still - **2.** *(complément d'objet direct)* who ; **tu vois qui je veux dire** you see who I mean ; **invite qui tu veux** invite whoever ou anyone you

like - **3.** *(après une prép)* who, whom ; **la personne à qui je parle** the person I'm talking to, the person to whom I'm talking - **4.** *(indéfini)* **qui que tu sois** whoever you are ; **qui que ce soit** whoever it may be. ➡ *pron interr* **1.** *(sujet)* who ; **qui es-tu?** who are you? ; **je voudrais savoir qui est là** I would like to know who's there - **2.** *(complément d'objet, après une prép)* who, whom ; **qui demandez-vous?** who do you want to see? ; **dites-moi qui vous demandez** tell me who you want to see ; **à qui vas-tu le donner?** who are you going to give it to?, to whom are you going to give it? ➡ **qui est-ce qui** *pron interr* who. ➡ **qui est-ce que** *pron interr* who, whom.

quiche [kiʃ] *nf* quiche.

quiconque [kikɔ̃k] ➡ *pron indéf* anyone, anybody. ➡ *pron indéf sout* anyone who, whoever.

quidam [kidam] *nm fam* chap *UK*, guy *US*.

quiétude [kjetyd] *nf* tranquillity *UK*, tranquility *US*.

quignon [kiɲɔ̃] *nm fam* hunk.

quille [kij] *nf* [de bateau] keel. ➡ **quilles** *nfpl* [jeu] : (jeu de) quilles skittles *(U)*.

quincaillerie [kɛ̃kajri] *nf* **1.** [magasin] ironmonger's (shop) *UK*, hardware shop - **2.** *fam fig* [bijoux] jewellery *UK*, jewelry *US*.

quinconce [kɛ̃kɔ̃s] *nm* : **en quinconce** in a staggered arrangement.

quinine [kinin] *nf* quinine.

quinqua [kɛ̃ka] *nmf* fiftysomething.

quinquagénaire [kɛ̃kaʒenɛr] *nmf* fifty year old.

quinquennal, e, aux [kɛ̃kenal, o] *adj* [plan] five-year *(avant n)* ; [élection] five-yearly.

quinquennat [kɛ̃kena] *nm* five-year period of office, quinquennium, lustrum.

quintal, aux [kɛ̃tal, o] *nm* quintal.

quinte [kɛ̃t] *nf* MUS fifth. ➡ **quinte de toux** *nf* coughing fit.

quintuple [kɛ̃typl] *nm & adj* quintuple.

quinzaine [kɛ̃zɛn] *nf* **1.** [nombre] fifteen (or so) ; **une quinzaine de** about fifteen - **2.** [deux semaines] fortnight *UK*, two weeks *pl.*

quinze [kɛ̃z] ➡ *adj num inv* fifteen ; **dans quinze jours** in a fortnight *UK*, in two weeks. ➡ *nm* [chiffre] fifteen ; *voir aussi* **six.**

quinzième [kɛ̃zjɛm] *adj num inv, nm & nmf* fifteenth ; *voir aussi* **sixième.**

quiproquo [kiprɔko] *nm* misunderstanding.

quittance [kitɑ̃s] *nf* receipt.

quitte [kit] *adj* quits ; **en être quitte pour**

qqch/pour faire qqch to get off with sthg/doing sthg ; **quitte à faire qqch** even if it means doing sthg.

quitter [3] [kite] *vt* **1.** [gén] to leave ; **ne quittez pas!** [au téléphone] hold the line, please! - **2.** [fonctions] to give up - **3.** INFORM to exit. ➡ **se quitter** *vp* to part.

qui-vive [kiviv] *nm inv* : **être sur le qui-vive** to be on the alert.

quoi [kwa] ◇ *pron rel (après prép)* **ce à quoi je me suis intéressé** what I was interested in ; **c'est en quoi vous avez tort** that's where you're wrong ; **après quoi** after which ; **avoir de quoi vivre** to have enough to live on ; **avez-vous de quoi écrire?** have you got something to write with? ; **merci il n'y a pas de quoi** thank you don't mention it. ◇ *pron interr* **what** ; **à quoi penses-tu?** what are you thinking about? ; **je ne sais pas quoi dire** I don't know what to say ; **à quoi bon?** what's the point ou use? ; **quoi de neuf?** what's new? ; **décide-toi, quoi!** *fam* make your mind up, will you? ; **tu viens ou quoi?** *fam* are you coming or what? ➡ **quoi que** *loc conj (+ subjonctif)* whatever ; **quoi qu'il arrive** whatever happens ; **quoi qu'il dise** whatever he says ; **quoi qu'il en soit** be that as it may.

quoique [kwakə] *conj* although, though.

quolibet [kɔlibɛ] *nm sout* jeer, taunt.

quota [k(w)ɔta] *nm* quota.

quotidien, enne [kɔtidjɛ̃, ɛn] *adj* daily. ➡ **quotidien** *nm* **1.** [routine] daily life ; **au quotidien** on a day-to-day basis - **2.** [journal] daily (newspaper).

quotient [kɔsjɑ̃] *nm* quotient ; **quotient intellectuel** intelligence quotient.

R

r¹, R [ɛr] *nm inv* [lettre] r, R.

r² *abr écrite de* **rue.**

rabâcher [3] [rabɑʃe] ◇ *vi fam* to harp on. ◇ *vt* to go over (and over).

rabais [rabɛ] *nm* reduction, discount ; **au rabais** *péj* [artiste] third-rate ; [travailler] for a pittance.

rabaisser [4] [rabese] *vt* **1.** [réduire] to reduce ; [orgueil] to humble - **2.** [personne] to belittle. ➡ **se rabaisser** *vp* **1.** [se

déprécier] to belittle o.s. - **2.** [s'humilier] : **se rabaisser à faire qqch** to demean o.s. by doing sthg.

rabat [raba] *nm* [partie rabattue] flap.

rabat-joie [rabaʒwa] ◇ *nm inv* killjoy. ◇ *adj inv* : **être rabat-joie** to be a killjoy.

rabattre [83] [rabatr] *vt* **1.** [col] to turn down - **2.** [siège] to tilt back ; [couvercle] to shut - **3.** [gibier] to drive. ➡ **se rabattre** *vp* **1.** [siège] to tilt back ; [couvercle] to shut - **2.** [voiture, coureur] to cut in - **3.** [se contenter] : **se rabattre sur** to fall back on.

rabattu, e [rabaty] *pp* ➡ **rabattre**.

rabbin [rabɛ̃] *nm* rabbi.

râble [rabl] *nm* [de lapin] back ; CULIN saddle.

râblé, e [rable] *adj* stocky.

rabot [rabo] *nm* plane.

raboter [3] [rabɔte] *vt* to plane.

rabougri, e [rabugri] *adj* **1.** [plante] stunted - **2.** [personne] shrivelled, wizened.

rabrouer [3] [rabrue] *vt* to snub.

raccommodage [rakɔmɔdaʒ] *nm* mending.

raccommoder [3] [rakɔmɔde] *vt* **1.** [vêtement] to mend - **2.** *fam fig* [personnes] to reconcile, to get back together.

raccompagner [3] [rakɔ̃paɲe] *vt* to see home, to take home.

raccord [rakɔr] *nm* **1.** [liaison] join - **2.** [pièce] connector, coupling - **3.** CINÉ link.

raccordement [rakɔrdəmɑ̃] *nm* connection, linking.

raccorder [3] [rakɔrde] *vt* : **raccorder qqch (à)** to connect sthg (to), to join sthg (to). ➡ **se raccorder** *vp* : **se raccorder à** to be connected to ; *fig* [faits] to tie in with.

raccourci [rakursi] *nm* shortcut ; **raccourci clavier** keyboard shortcut.

raccourcir [32] [rakursir] ◇ *vt* to shorten. ◇ *vi* to grow shorter.

raccrocher [3] [rakrɔʃe] ◇ *vt* to hang back up. ◇ *vi* [au téléphone] : **raccrocher (au nez de qqn)** to hang up (on sb), to put the phone down (on sb). ➡ **se raccrocher** *vp* : **se raccrocher à** to cling to, to hang on to.

race [ras] *nf* [humaine] race ; [animale] breed ; **de race** pedigree ; [cheval] thoroughbred.

racé, e [rase] *adj* **1.** [animal] purebred - **2.** [voiture] of distinction.

rachat [raʃa] *nm* **1.** [transaction] repurchase - **2.** *fig* [de péchés] atonement.

racheter [28] [raʃte] *vt* **1.** [acheter en plus - gén] to buy another ; [- pain, lait] to buy some more - **2.** [acheter d'occasion] to buy - **3.** [acheter après avoir vendu] to buy back - **4.** *fig* [péché, faute] to atone for ; [défaut, lapsus] to make up for - **5.** [prisonnier] to ransom - **6.** [honneur] to redeem - **7.** COMM [société] to buy out. ➤ **se racheter** *vp fig* to redeem o.s.

rachitique [raʃitik] *adj* suffering from rickets.

racial, e, aux [rasjal, o] *adj* racial.

racine [rasin] *nf* root ; [de nez] base ; **racine carrée/cubique** MATH square/cube root.

racisme [rasism] *nm* racism.

raciste [rasist] *nmf & adj* racist.

racketter [4] [rakete] *vt* : **racketter qqn** to subject sb to a protection racket.

raclée [rakle] *nf fam* hiding, thrashing.

racler [3] [rakle] *vt* to scrape. ➤ **se racler** *vp* : **se racler la gorge** to clear one's throat.

raclette [raklɛt] *nf* CULIN *melted Swiss cheese served with jacket potatoes.*

racoler [3] [rakɔle] *vt fam péj* [suj: commerçant] to tout for ; [suj: prostituée] to solicit.

racoleur, euse [rakɔlœr, øz] *adj fam péj* [air, sourire] come-hither ; [publicité] strident.

racontar [rakɔ̃tar] *nm fam péj* piece of gossip. ➤ **racontars** *nmpl fam péj* tittle-tattle *(U)*.

raconter [3] [rakɔ̃te] *vt* **1.** [histoire] to tell, to relate ; [événement] to relate, to tell about ; **raconter qqch à qqn** to tell sb sthg, to relate sthg to sb - **2.** [ragot, mensonge] to tell ; **qu'est-ce que tu racontes?** what are you on about?

radar [radar] *nm* radar.

rade [rad] *nf* (natural) harbour *UK* ou harbor *US*.

radeau, x [rado] *nm* [embarcation] raft.

radiateur [radjatœr] *nm* radiator.

radiation [radjasjɔ̃] *nf* **1.** PHYS radiation - **2.** [de liste, du barreau] striking off.

radical, e, aux [radikal, o] *adj* radical. ➤ **radical** *nm* **1.** [gén] radical - **2.** LING stem.

radier [9] [radje] *vt* to strike off.

radieux, euse [radjø, øz] *adj* radiant ; [soleil] dazzling.

radin, e [radɛ̃, in] *fam péj* ◇ *adj* stingy. ◇ *nm, f* skinflint.

radio [radjo] ◇ *nf* **1.** [station, poste] radio ; **à la radio** on the radio ; **radio locale** ou **privée** ou **libre** independent local radio station - **2.** MÉD : **passer une radio** to have an X-ray, to be X-rayed. ◇ *nm* radio operator.

radioactif, ive [radjɔaktif, iv] *adj* radioactive.

radioactivité [radjɔaktivite] *nf* radioactivity.

radiodiffuser [3] [radjɔdifyze] *vt* to broadcast.

radiographie [radjɔɡrafi] *nf* **1.** [technique] radiography - **2.** [image] X-ray.

radiologue [radjɔlɔɡ], **radiologiste** [radjɔlɔʒist] *nmf* radiologist.

radioréveil, radio-réveil [radjɔrevɛj] *nm* radio alarm, clock radio.

radiotélévisé, e [radjɔtelevize] *adj* broadcast on both radio and television.

radis [radi] *nm* radish.

radium [radjɔm] *nm* radium.

radoter [3] [radɔte] *vi* to ramble.

radoucir [32] [radusir] *vt* to soften. ➤ **se radoucir** *vp* [temps] to become milder ; [personne] to calm down.

radoucissement [radusismɑ̃] *nm* **1.** [d'attitude] softening - **2.** [de température] rise ; **un radoucissement du temps** a spell of milder weather.

rafale [rafal] *nf* **1.** [de vent] gust ; **en rafales** in gusts ou bursts - **2.** [de coups de feu, d'applaudissements] burst.

raffermir [32] [rafermir] *vt* **1.** [muscle] to firm up - **2.** *fig* [pouvoir] to strengthen.

raffinage [rafinaʒ] *nm* refining.

raffiné, e [rafine] *adj* refined.

raffinement [rafinmɑ̃] *nm* refinement.

raffiner [3] [rafine] *vt* to refine.

raffinerie [rafinri] *nf* refinery.

raffoler [3] [rafɔle] *vi* : **raffoler de qqn/qqch** to adore sb/sthg.

raffut [rafy] *nm fam* row, racket.

rafistoler [3] [rafistɔle] *vt fam* to patch up.

rafle [rafl] *nf* raid.

rafler [3] [rafle] *vt* to swipe.

rafraîchir [32] [rafreʃir] *vt* **1.** [nourriture, vin] to chill, to cool ; [air] to cool - **2.** [vêtement, appartement] to smarten up ; *fig* [mémoire, idées] to refresh ; [connaissances] to brush up - **3.** INFORM to refresh ; [navigateur] to reload. ➤ **se rafraîchir** *vp* **1.** [se refroidir] to cool (down) - **2.** [en buvant] to have a drink.

rafraîchissant, e [rafreʃisɑ̃, ɑ̃t] *adj* refreshing.

rafraîchissement [rafreʃismɑ̃] *nm* **1.** [de climat] cooling - **2.** [boisson] cold drink.

raft(ing) [raft(iŋ)] *nm* whitewater rafting.

ragaillardir [32] [ragajardir] *vt fam* to buck up, to perk up.

rage [raʒ] *nf* **1.** [fureur] rage ; **faire rage** [tempête] to rage - **2.** [maladie] rabies *(U)*. ➤ **rage de dents** *nf* (raging) toothache.

rager [17] [raʒe] *vi fam* to fume.

rageur, euse [raʒœr, øz] *adj* bad-tempered.

raglan [raglɑ̃] *adj inv* raglan *(avant n)*.

ragot [rago] *nm (gén pl) fam* (malicious) rumour *UK* ou rumor *US*, tittle-tattle *(U)*.

ragoût [ragu] *nm* stew.

rai [rɛ] *nm litt* [de soleil] ray.

raid [rɛd] *nm* AÉRON, FIN & MIL raid ; **raid aérien** air raid.

raide [rɛd] ⬦ *adj* **1.** [cheveux] straight - **2.** [tendu - corde] taut ; [- membre, cou] stiff - **3.** [pente] steep - **4.** [personne - attitude physique] stiff, starchy ; [- caractère] inflexible - **5.** *fam* [histoire] hard to swallow, farfetched - **6.** *fam* [chanson] rude, blue - **7.** *fam* [sans le sou] broke. ⬦ *adv* [abruptement] steeply ; **tomber raide mort** to fall down dead.

raideur [rɛdœr] *nf* **1.** [de membre] stiffness - **2.** [de personne - attitude physique] stiffness, starchiness ; [- caractère] inflexibility.

raidir [32] [rɛdir] *vt* [muscle] to tense ; [corde] to tighten, to tauten. ⬤ **se raidir** *vp* **1.** [se contracter] to grow stiff, to stiffen - **2.** *fig* [résister] : **se raidir contre** to steel o.s. against.

raie [rɛ] *nf* **1.** [rayure] stripe - **2.** [dans les cheveux] parting *UK*, part *US* - **3.** [des fesses] crack - **4.** [poisson] skate.

rail [raj] *nm* rail.

raillerie [rajri] *nf sout* mockery *(U)*.

railleur, euse [rajœr, øz] *sout* ⬦ *adj* mocking. ⬦ *nm, f* scoffer.

rainure [rɛnyr] *nf* [longue] groove, channel ; [courte] slot.

raisin [rɛzɛ̃] *nm* [fruit] grapes *pl*.

raison [rɛzɔ̃] *nf* **1.** [gén] reason ; **à plus forte raison** all the more (so) ; **se faire une raison** to resign o.s. ; **raison de plus pour faire qqch** all the more reason to do sthg - **2.** [justesse, équité] : **avoir raison** to be right ; **avoir raison de faire qqch** to be right to do sthg ; **donner raison à qqn** to prove sb right. ⬤ **à raison de** *loc prép* at (the rate of). ⬤ **en raison de** *loc prép* owing to, because of.

raisonnable [rɛzɔnabl] *adj* reasonable.

raisonnement [rɛzɔnmɑ̃] *nm* **1.** [faculté] reason, power of reasoning - **2.** [argumentation] reasoning, argument.

raisonner [3] [rɛzɔne] ⬦ *vt* [personne] to reason with. ⬦ *vi* **1.** [penser] to reason - **2.** [discuter] : **raisonner avec** to reason with.

rajeunir [32] [raʒœnir] ⬦ *vt* **1.** [suj: couleur, vêtement] : **rajeunir qqn** to make sb look younger - **2.** [suj: personne] : **rajeunir qqn de trois ans** to take three years off sb's age - **3.** [vêtement, canapé] to renovate, to do up ; [meubles] to modernize - **4.** *fig* [parti]

to rejuvenate. ⬦ *vi* [personne] to look younger ; [se sentir plus jeune] to feel younger ou rejuvenated.

rajouter [3] [raʒute] *vt* to add ; **en rajouter** *fam* to exaggerate.

rajuster [raʒyste], **réajuster** [3] [reaʒyste] *vt* to adjust ; [cravate] to straighten. ⬤ **se rajuster** *vp* to straighten one's clothes.

râle [rɑl] *nm* moan ; [de mort] death rattle.

ralenti, e [ralɑ̃ti] *adj* slow. ⬤ **ralenti** *nm* **1.** AUTO idling speed ; **tourner au ralenti** AUTO to idle ; *fig* to tick over *UK* - **2.** CINÉ slow motion.

ralentir [32] [ralɑ̃tir] ⬦ *vt* **1.** [allure, expansion] to slow (down) - **2.** [rythme] to slacken. ⬦ *vi* to slow down ou up.

ralentissement [ralɑ̃tismɑ̃] *nm* **1.** [d'allure, d'expansion] slowing (down) - **2.** [de rythme] slackening - **3.** [embouteillage] holdup - **4.** PHYS deceleration.

râler [3] [rɑle] *vi* **1.** [malade] to breathe with difficulty - **2.** *fam* [grogner] to moan.

ralliement [ralimɑ̃] *nm* rallying.

rallier [9] [ralje] *vt* **1.** [poste, parti] to join - **2.** [suffrages] to win - **3.** [troupes] to rally. ⬤ **se rallier** *vp* to rally ; **se rallier à** [parti] to join ; [cause] to rally to ; [avis] to come round *UK* ou around *US* to.

rallonge [ralɔ̃ʒ] *nf* **1.** [de table] leaf, extension - **2.** [électrique] extension (lead).

rallonger [17] [ralɔ̃ʒe] ⬦ *vt* to lengthen. ⬦ *vi* to lengthen, to get longer.

rallumer [3] [ralyme] *vt* **1.** [feu, cigarette] to relight ; *fig* [querelle] to revive - **2.** [appareil, lumière électrique] to switch (back) on again.

rallye [rali] *nm* rally.

ramadan [ramadɑ̃] *nm* Ramadan.

ramassage [ramasaʒ] *nm* collection ; **ramassage scolaire** [action] pick-up (of school children), busing *US* ; [service] school bus.

ramasser [3] [ramase] *vt* **1.** [récolter, réunir] to gather, to collect ; *fig* [forces] to gather - **2.** [prendre] to pick up - **3.** *fam* [claque, rhume] to get. ⬤ **se ramasser** *vp* **1.** [se replier] to crouch - **2.** *fam* [tomber, échouer] to come a cropper.

rambarde [rɑ̃bard] *nf* (guard) rail.

rame [ram] *nf* **1.** [aviron] oar - **2.** RAIL train - **3.** [de papier] ream.

rameau, x [ramo] *nm* branch.

ramener [19] [ramne] *vt* **1.** [remmener] to take back - **2.** [rapporter, restaurer] to bring back - **3.** [réduire] : **ramener qqch à qqch** to reduce sthg to sthg, to bring sthg down to sthg.

ramer [3] [rame] *vi* [rameur] to row.

rameur, euse [ramœr, øz] *nm, f* rower.

ramification [ramifikasjɔ̃] *nf* [division] branch.

ramolli, e [ramɔli] *adj* soft ; *fig* soft (in the head).

ramollir [32] [ramɔlir] *vt* **1.** [beurre] to soften - **2.** *fam fig* [ardeurs] to cool. ➡ **se ramollir** *vp* **1.** [beurre] to go soft, to soften - **2.** *fam fig* [courage] to weaken.

ramoner [3] [ramɔne] *vt* to sweep.

ramoneur [ramɔnœr] *nm* (chimney) sweep.

rampant, e [rɑ̃pɑ̃, ɑ̃t] *adj* **1.** [animal] crawling - **2.** [plante] creeping.

rampe [rɑ̃p] *nf* **1.** [d'escalier] banister, handrail - **2.** [d'accès] ramp ; **rampe de lancement** launch pad - **3.** THÉÂTRE : **la rampe** the footlights *pl*.

ramper [3] [rɑ̃pe] *vi* **1.** [animal, soldat, enfant] to crawl - **2.** [plante] to creep.

rance [rɑ̃s] *adj* [beurre] rancid.

rancir [32] [rɑ̃sir] *vi* to go rancid.

rancœur [rɑ̃kœr] *nf* rancour *UK*, rancor *US*, resentment.

rançon [rɑ̃sɔ̃] *nf* ransom ; *fig* price.

rancune [rɑ̃kyn] *nf* rancour *UK*, rancor *US*, spite ; **garder** OU **tenir rancune à qqn de qqch** to hold a grudge against sb for sthg ; **sans rancune!** no hard feelings!

rancunier, ère [rɑ̃kynje, ɛr] *adj* vindictive, spiteful.

randonnée [rɑ̃dɔne] *nf* **1.** [promenade - à pied] walk ; [- à cheval, à bicyclette] ride ; [- en voiture] drive - **2.** [activité] : **la randonnée** [à pied] walking ; [à cheval] riding ; **faire de la randonnée** to go trekking.

randonneur, euse [rɑ̃dɔnœr, øz] *nm, f* walker, rambler.

rang [rɑ̃] *nm* **1.** [d'objets, de personnes] row ; **se mettre en rang par deux** to line up in twos - **2.** MIL rank - **3.** [position sociale] station - **4.** *Québec* [peuplement rural] rural district - **5.** *Québec* [chemin] country road.

rangé, e [rɑ̃ʒe] *adj* [sérieux] well-ordered, well-behaved.

rangée [rɑ̃ʒe] *nf* row.

rangement [rɑ̃ʒmɑ̃] *nm* tidying up.

ranger [17] [rɑ̃ʒe] *vt* **1.** [chambre] to tidy - **2.** [objets] to arrange - **3.** [voiture] to park - **4.** *fig* [livre, auteur] : **ranger parmi** to rank among. ➡ **se ranger** *vp* **1.** [élèves, soldats] to line up - **2.** [voiture] to pull in - **3.** [piéton] to step aside - **4.** [s'assagir] to settle down - **5.** *fig* [se rallier] : **se ranger à** to go along with.

ranimer [3] [ranime] *vt* **1.** [personne] to revive, to bring round - **2.** [feu] to rekindle - **3.** *fig* [sentiment] to reawaken.

rap [rap] *nm* rap (music).

rapace [rapas] ◇ *nm* bird of prey. ◇ *adj* [cupide] rapacious, grasping.

rapatrier [10] [rapatrije] *vt* to repatriate.

râpe [rɑp] *nf* **1.** [de cuisine] grater - **2.** *Suisse fam* [avare] miser, skinflint.

râpé, e [rɑpe] *adj* **1.** CULIN grated - **2.** [manteau] threadbare - **3.** *fam* [raté] : **c'est râpé!** we've had it!

râper [3] [rɑpe] *vt* CULIN to grate.

râpeux, euse [rɑpø, øz] *adj* **1.** [tissu] rough - **2.** [vin] harsh.

rapide [rapid] ◇ *adj* **1.** [gén] rapid - **2.** [train, coureur] fast - **3.** [musique, intelligence] lively, quick. ◇ *nm* **1.** [train] express (train) - **2.** [de fleuve] rapid.

rapidement [rapidmɑ̃] *adv* rapidly.

rapidité [rapidite] *nf* rapidity.

rapiécer [20] [rapjese] *vt* to patch.

rappel [rapɛl] *nm* **1.** [de réservistes, d'ambassadeur] recall - **2.** [souvenir] reminder ; **rappel à l'ordre** call to order - **3.** TÉLÉCOM : **rappel automatique** recall - **4.** [de paiement] back pay - **5.** [de vaccination] booster - **6.** [au spectacle] curtain call, encore - **7.** SPORT abseiling *UK*, rapelling *US* ; **descendre en rappel** to abseil *UK* OU rappel *US* (down).

rappeler [24] [raple] *vt* **1.** [gén] to call back ; **rappeler qqn à qqch** *fig* to bring sb back to sthg - **2.** [faire penser à] : **rappeler qqch à qqn** to remind sb of sthg ; **ça me rappelle les vacances** it reminds me of my holidays. ➡ **se rappeler** *vp* to remember.

rapport [rapɔr] *nm* **1.** [corrélation] link, connection - **2.** [compte-rendu] report - **3.** [profit] return, yield - **4.** MATH ratio. ➡ **rapports** *nmpl* **1.** [relations] relations - **2.** [sexuels] : **rapports (sexuels)** intercourse *sg*. ➡ **par rapport à** *loc prép* in comparison to, compared with.

rapporter [3] [rapɔrte] *vt* to bring back. ➡ **se rapporter** *vp* : **se rapporter à** to refer OU relate to.

rapporteur, euse [rapɔrtœr, øz] ◇ *adj* sneaky, telltale *(avant n)*. ◇ *nm, f* sneak, telltale. ➡ **rapporteur** *nm* **1.** [de commission] rapporteur - **2.** GÉOM protractor.

rapprochement [raprɔʃmɑ̃] *nm* **1.** [d'objets, de personnes] bringing together - **2.** *fig* [entre événements] link, connection - **3.** *fig* [de pays, de parti] rapprochement, coming together.

rapprocher [3] [raprɔʃe] *vt* **1.** [mettre plus près] : **rapprocher qqn/qqch de qqch** to bring sb/sthg nearer to sthg, to bring sb/sthg closer to sthg - **2.** *fig* [personnes] to bring together - **3.** *fig* [idée, texte] : **rapprocher qqch (de)** to compare sthg (with). ➡ **se rapprocher** *vp* **1.** [approcher] : **se rapprocher (de qqn/qqch)** to approach (sb/sthg) - **2.** [se ressembler] : **se rapprocher de qqch** to be similar to sthg - **3.** [se réconcilier] : **se rapprocher de qqn** to become closer to sb.

rapt [rapt] *nm* abduction.

raquette [raket] *nf* **1.** [de tennis, de squash] racket ; [de ping-pong] bat *UK*, paddle - **2.** [à neige] snowshoe.

rare [rar] *adj* **1.** [peu commun, peu fréquent] rare ; **ses rares amis** his few friends - **2.** [peu dense] sparse - **3.** [surprenant] unusual, surprising.

raréfier [9] [rarefje] *vt* to rarefy. ➤ **se raréfier** *vp* to become rarefied.

rarement [rarmɑ̃] *adv* rarely.

rareté [rarte] *nf* **1.** [de denrées, de nouvelles] scarcity - **2.** [de visites, de lettres] infrequency - **3.** [objet précieux] rarity.

ras, e [ra, raz] *adj* **1.** [herbe, poil] short - **2.** [mesure] full. ➤ **ras** *adv* short ; **à ras de** level with ; **en avoir ras le bol** *fam* to be fed up.

rasade [razad] *nf* glassful.

rasage [razaʒ] *nm* shaving.

rasant, e [razɑ̃, ɑ̃t] *adj* **1.** [lumière] low-angled - **2.** *fam* [film, discours] boring.

raser [3] [raze] *vt* **1.** [barbe, cheveux] to shave off - **2.** [mur, sol] to hug - **3.** [village] to raze - **4.** *fam* [personne] to bore. ➤ **se raser** *vp* [avec rasoir] to shave.

ras-le-bol [ralbɔl] *nm inv fam* discontent.

rasoir [razwar] ◇ *nm* razor ; **rasoir électrique** electric shaver ; **rasoir mécanique** safety razor. ◇ *adj inv fam* boring.

rassasier [9] [rasazje] *vt* to satisfy.

rassemblement [rasɑ̃bləmɑ̃] *nm* **1.** [d'objets] collecting, gathering - **2.** [foule] crowd, gathering - **3.** [union, parti] union - **4.** MIL parade ; **rassemblement!** fall in!

rassembler [3] [rasɑ̃ble] *vt* **1.** [personnes, documents] to collect, to gather - **2.** [courage] to summon up ; [idées] to collect. ➤ **se rassembler** *vp* **1.** [manifestants] to assemble - **2.** [famille] to get together.

rasseoir [65] [raswar] ➤ **se rasseoir** *vp* to sit down again.

rasséréner [18] [raserene] *vt sout* to calm down.

rassis, e [rasi, iz] *adj* [pain] stale.

rassurant, e [rasyrɑ̃, ɑ̃t] *adj* reassuring.

rassuré, e [rasyre] *adj* confident, at ease.

rassurer [3] [rasyre] *vt* to reassure.

rat [ra] ◇ *nm* rat ; **petit rat** *fig* young ballet pupil. ◇ *adj fam* [avare] mean, stingy.

ratatiné, e [ratatine] *adj* [fruit, personne] shrivelled *UK* ou shriveled *US*.

rate [rat] *nf* **1.** [animal] female rat - **2.** [organe] spleen.

raté, e [rate] *nm, f* [personne] failure. ➤ **raté** *nm* **1.** [gén pl] AUTO misfiring *(U)* ; **faire des ratés** to misfire - **2.** *fig* [difficulté] problem.

râteau, x [rato] *nm* rake.

rater [3] [rate] ◇ *vt* **1.** [train, occasion] to miss - **2.** [plat, affaire] to make a mess of ; [examen] to fail. ◇ *vi* to go wrong.

ratification [ratifikasjɔ̃] *nf* ratification.

ratifier [9] [ratifje] *vt* to ratify.

ration [rasjɔ̃] *nf fig* share ; **ration alimentaire** food intake.

rationaliser [3] [rasjɔnalize] *vt* to rationalize.

rationnel, elle [rasjɔnɛl] *adj* rational.

rationnement [rasjɔnmɑ̃] *nm* rationing.

rationner [3] [rasjɔne] *vt* to ration.

ratissage [ratisaʒ] *nm* **1.** [de jardin] raking - **2.** [de quartier] search.

ratisser [3] [ratise] *vt* **1.** [jardin] to rake - **2.** [quartier] to search, to comb.

raton [ratɔ̃] *nm* ZOOL young rat. ➤ **raton laveur** *nm* racoon.

RATP (*abr de* Régie autonome des transports parisiens) *nf Paris transport authority.*

rattacher [3] [rataʃe] *vt* **1.** [attacher de nouveau] to do up, to fasten again - **2.** [relier] : **rattacher qqch à** to join sthg to ; *fig* to link sthg with - **3.** [unir] : **rattacher qqn à** to bind sb to. ➤ **se rattacher** *vp* : **se rattacher à** to be linked to.

ratte [rat] *nf* BOT & CULIN fingerling potato, (La) Ratte potato.

rattrapage [ratrapaʒ] *nm* **1.** SCOL : **cours de rattrapage** remedial class - **2.** [de salaires, prix] adjustment.

rattraper [3] [ratrape] *vt* **1.** [animal, prisonnier] to recapture - **2.** [temps] : **rattraper le temps perdu** to make up for lost time - **3.** [rejoindre] to catch up with - **4.** [erreur] to correct - **5.** [personne qui tombe] to catch. ➤ **se rattraper** *vp* **1.** [se retenir] : **se rattraper à qqn/qqch** to catch hold of sb/sthg - **2.** [se faire pardonner] to make amends.

rature [ratyr] *nf* alteration.

rauque [rok] *adj* hoarse, husky.

ravager [17] [ravaʒe] *vt* [gén] to devastate, to ravage.

ravages [ravaʒ] *nmpl* [de troupes] ravages, devastation *sg* ; [d'inondation] devastation *sg* ; [du temps] ravages.

ravaler [3] [ravale] *vt* **1.** [façade] to clean, to restore - **2.** [personne] : **ravaler qqn au rang de** to lower sb to the level of - **3.** *fig* [larmes, colère] to stifle, to hold back.

ravauder [3] [ravode] *vt* to mend, to repair.

ravi, e [ravi] *adj* : **ravi (de)** delighted (with) ;

je suis ravi de l'avoir trouvé I'm delighted that I found it, I'm delighted to have found it ; **ravi de vous connaître** pleased to meet you.

ravin [ravɛ̃] *nm* ravine, gully.

ravir [32] [ravir] *vt* **1.** [charmer] to delight ; **à ravir** beautifully - **2.** *litt* [arracher] : **ravir qqch à qqn** to rob sb of sthg.

raviser [3] [ravize] ◆ **se raviser** *vp* to change one's mind.

ravissant, e [ravisɑ̃, ɑ̃t] *adj* delightful, beautiful.

ravisseur, euse [ravisœr, øz] *nm, f* abductor.

ravitaillement [ravitajmɑ̃] *nm* [en denrées] resupplying ; [en carburant] refuelling UK, refueling US.

ravitailler [3] [ravitaje] *vt* [en denrées] to resupply ; [en carburant] to refuel.

raviver [3] [ravive] *vt* **1.** [feu] to rekindle - **2.** [couleurs] to brighten up - **3.** *fig* [douleur] to revive - **4.** [plaie] to reopen.

rayé, e [rɛje] *adj* **1.** [tissu] striped - **2.** [disque, vitre] scratched.

rayer [11] [rɛje] *vt* **1.** [disque, vitre] to scratch - **2.** [nom, mot] to cross out.

rayon [rɛjɔ̃] *nm* **1.** [de lumière] beam, ray ; *fig* [d'espoir] ray - **2.** *(gén pl)* [radiation] radiation (U) ; **rayon laser** laser beam ; **rayons X** X-rays - **3.** [de roue] spoke - **4.** GÉOM radius ; **dans un rayon de** *fig* within a radius of - **5.** [étagère] shelf - **6.** [dans un magasin] department.

rayonnant, e [rɛjɔnɑ̃, ɑ̃t] *adj litt & fig* radiant.

rayonnement [rɛjɔnmɑ̃] *nm* **1.** [gén] radiance ; [des arts] influence - **2.** PHYS radiation.

rayonner [3] [rɛjɔne] *vi* **1.** [soleil] to shine ; **rayonner de joie** *fig* to radiate happiness - **2.** [culture] to be influential - **3.** [avenues, lignes, chaleur] to radiate - **4.** [touriste] to tour around *(from a base)*.

rayure [rɛjyr] *nf* **1.** [sur étoffe] stripe - **2.** [sur disque, sur meuble] scratch.

raz [ra] ◆ **raz de marée** *nm* tidal wave ; *fig & POLIT* landslide.

razzia [razja] *nf fam* raid.

RDA *(abr de République démocratique allemande)* *nf* GDR.

RdC *abr écrite de* **rez-de-chaussée**.

ré [re] *nm inv* MUS D ; [chanté] re.

réacheminer [3] [reaʃmine] *vt* to forward.

réacteur [reaktœr] *nm* [d'avion] jet engine ; **réacteur nucléaire** nuclear reactor.

réaction [reaksjɔ̃] *nf* : **réaction (à/contre)** reaction (to/against).

réactionnaire [reaksjɔnɛr] *nmf & adj péj* reactionary.

réactiver [3] [reaktive] *vt* to reactivate.

réactualiser [3] [reaktɥalize] *vt* [moderniser] to update, to bring up to date.

réadapter [3] [readapte] *vt* to readapt ; [accidenté] to rehabilitate.

réagir [32] [reaʒir] *vi* : **réagir (à/contre)** to react (to/against) ; **réagir sur** to affect.

réajuster = **rajuster**.

réalisable [realizabl] *adj* **1.** [projet] feasible - **2.** FIN realizable.

réalisateur, trice [realizatœr, tris] *nm, f* CINÉ & TV director.

réaliser [3] [realize] *vt* **1.** [projet] to carry out ; [ambitions, rêves] to achieve, to realize - **2.** CINÉ & TV to produce - **3.** [s'apercevoir de] to realize. ◆ **se réaliser** *vp* **1.** [ambition] to be realized ; [rêve] to come true - **2.** [personne] to fulfil UK ou fulfill US o.s.

réaliste [realist] ◇ *nmf* realist. ◇ *adj* **1.** [personne, objectif] realistic - **2.** ART & LITTÉR realist.

réalité [realite] *nf* reality ; **en réalité** in reality ; **réalité virtuelle** INFORM virtual reality, VR.

reality-show, reality show [realitiʃo] *(pl reality(-)shows)* *nm* talk show focussing on real-life drama.

réaménagement [reamenaʒmɑ̃] *nm* **1.** [de projet] restructuring - **2.** [de taux d'intérêt] readjustment.

réamorcer [16] [reamɔrse] *vt* to start up again.

réanimation [reanimasjɔ̃] *nf* resuscitation ; **en réanimation** in intensive care.

réanimer [3] [reanime] *vt* to resuscitate.

réapparaître [91] [reaparɛtr] *vi* to reappear.

rébarbatif, ive [rebarbatif, iv] *adj* **1.** [personne, visage] forbidding - **2.** [travail] daunting.

rebâtir [32] [rəbatir] *vt* to rebuild.

rebattu, e [rəbaty] *adj* overworked, hackneyed.

rebelle [rəbɛl] *adj* **1.** [personne] rebellious ; [troupes] rebel *(avant n)* - **2.** [mèche, boucle] unruly.

rebeller [4] [rəbɛle] ◆ **se rebeller** *vp* : **se rebeller (contre)** to rebel (against).

rébellion [rebɛljɔ̃] *nf* rebellion.

rebiffer [3] [rəbife] ◆ **se rebiffer** *vp fam* : **se rebiffer (contre)** to rebel (against).

reboiser [3] [rəbwaze] *vt* to reafforest UK, to reforest US.

rebond [rəbɔ̃] *nm* bounce.

rebondir [32] [rəbɔ̃dir] *vi* **1.** [objet] to bounce ; [contre mur] to rebound - **2.** *fig* [affaire] to come to life (again).

rebondissement [rəbɔ̃dismɑ̃] *nm* [d'affaire] new development.

rebord [rəbɔr] *nm* [de table] edge ; [de fenêtre] sill, ledge.

reboucher [3] [rəbuʃe] *vt* [bouteille] to put the cork back in, to recork ; [trou] to fill in.

rebours [rəbur] ➤ **à rebours** *loc adv* the wrong way ; *fig* the wrong way round *UK* ou around *US*, back to front.

reboutonner [3] [rəbutɔne] *vt* to rebutton.

rebrousse-poil [rəbruspwal] ➤ **à rebrousse-poil** *loc adv* the wrong way ; **prendre qqn à rebrousse-poil** *fig* to rub sb up the wrong way.

rebrousser [3] [rəbruse] *vt* to brush back ; **rebrousser chemin** *fig* to retrace one's steps.

rébus [rebys] *nm* rebus.

rebut [rəby] *nm* scrap ; **mettre qqch au rebut** to get rid of sthg, to scrap sthg.

rebuter [3] [rəbyte] *vt* [suj: travail] to dishearten.

récalcitrant, e [rekalsitrɑ̃, ɑ̃t] *adj* recalcitrant, stubborn.

recaler [3] [rəkale] *vt fam* to fail.

récapitulatif, ive [rekapitylatif, iv] *adj* summary *(avant n)*. ➤ **récapitulatif** *nm* summary.

récapituler [3] [rekapityle] *vt* to recapitulate, to recap.

recel [rəsɛl] *nm* [action] receiving ou handling stolen goods ; [délit] possession of stolen goods.

receleur, euse [rəsəlœr, øz] *nm, f* receiver *(of stolen goods)*.

récemment [resamɑ̃] *adv* recently.

recensement [rəsɑ̃smɑ̃] *nm* **1.** [de population] census - **2.** [d'objets] inventory.

recenser [3] [rəsɑ̃se] *vt* **1.** [population] to take a census of - **2.** [objets] to take an inventory of.

récent, e [resɑ̃, ɑ̃t] *adj* recent.

recentrer [3] [rəsɑ̃tre] *vt* to refocus.

récépissé [resepise] *nm* receipt.

récepteur, trice [reseptœr, tris] *adj* receiving. ➤ **récepteur** *nm* receiver.

réception [resepsjɔ̃] *nf* **1.** [gén] reception ; **donner une réception** to hold a reception - **2.** [de marchandises] receipt - **3.** [bureau] reception (desk), front desk *US* - **4.** SPORT [de sauteur, skieur] landing ; [du ballon, avec la main] catch ; **bonne réception de X** [avec le pied] X traps the ball.

réceptionner [3] [resepsjɔne] *vt* **1.** [marchandises] to take delivery of - **2.** SPORT [avec la main] to catch ; [- avec le pied] to control.

réceptionniste [resepsjɔnist] *nmf* receptionist, desk clerk *US*.

récession [resesjɔ̃] *nf* recession.

recette [rəsɛt] *nf* **1.** COMM takings *pl* - **2.** CULIN recipe ; *fig* [méthode] recipe, formula.

recevable [rəsəvabl] *adj* **1.** [excuse, offre] acceptable - **2.** DR admissible.

receveur, euse [rəsəvœr, øz] *nm, f* **1.** ADMIN : **receveur des impôts** tax collector ; **receveur des postes** postmaster (*f* postmistress) - **2.** [de bus] conductor (*f* conductress) - **3.** [de greffe] recipient.

recevoir [52] [rəsəvwar] ◇ *vt* **1.** [gén] to receive - **2.** [coup] to get, to receive - **3.** [invités] to entertain ; [client] to see - **4.** SCOL & UNIV : **être reçu à un examen** to pass an exam. ◇ *vi* **1.** [donner une réception] to entertain - **2.** [avocat, médecin] to be available (to see clients). ➤ **se recevoir** *vp* SPORT to land.

rechange [rəʃɑ̃ʒ] ➤ **de rechange** *loc adj* spare ; *fig* alternative.

réchapper [3] [reʃape] *vi* : **réchapper de** to survive.

recharge [rəʃarʒ] *nf* [cartouche] refill.

rechargeable [rəʃarʒabl] *adj* [batterie] rechargeable ; [briquet] refillable.

réchaud [reʃo] *nm* (portable) stove.

réchauffé, e [reʃofe] *adj* [plat] reheated ; *fig* rehashed.

réchauffement [reʃofmɑ̃] *nm* warming (up).

réchauffer [3] [reʃofe] *vt* **1.** [nourriture] to reheat - **2.** [personne] to warm up. ➤ **se réchauffer** *vp* to warm up.

rêche [rɛʃ] *adj* rough.

recherche [rəʃɛrʃ] *nf* **1.** [quête & INFORM] search ; **être à la recherche de** to be in search of ; **faire** ou **effectuer des recherches** to make inquiries - **2.** [sciences] research ; **faire de la recherche** to do research - **3.** [raffinement] elegance.

recherché, e [rəʃɛrʃe] *adj* **1.** [ouvrage] sought-after - **2.** [raffiné - vocabulaire] refined ; [- mets] exquisite.

rechercher [3] [rəʃɛrʃe] *vt* **1.** [objet, personne] to search for, to hunt for - **2.** [compagnie] to seek out.

rechigner [3] [rəʃiɲe] *vi* : **rechigner à** to balk at.

rechute [rəʃyt] *nf* relapse.

récidive [residiv] *nf* **1.** DR repeat offence *UK* ou offense *US* - **2.** MÉD recurrence.

récidiver [3] [residive] *vi* **1.** DR to commit another offence *UK* ou offense *US* - **2.** MÉD to recur.

récidiviste [residivist] *nmf* repeat ou persistent offender.

récif [resif] *nm* reef.

récipient [resipjã] *nm* container.

réciproque [resiprɔk] <> *adj* reciprocal. <> *nf* : **la réciproque** the reverse.

réciproquement [resiprɔkmã] *adv* mutually ; **et réciproquement** and vice versa.

récit [resi] *nm* story.

récital, als [resital] *nm* recital.

récitation [resitasjɔ̃] *nf* recitation.

réciter [3] [resite] *vt* to recite.

réclamation [reklamasjɔ̃] *nf* complaint ; **faire/déposer une réclamation** to make/lodge a complaint.

réclame [reklam] *nf* 1. [annonce] advert *UK*, advertisement - 2. [publicité] : **la réclame** advertising - 3. [promotion] : **en réclame** on special offer.

réclamer [3] [reklame] *vt* 1. [demander] to ask for, to request ; [avec insistance] to demand - 2. [nécessiter] to require, to demand.

reclasser [3] [rəklase] *vt* 1. [dossiers] to refile - 2. ADMIN to regrade.

réclusion [reklyzjɔ̃] *nf* imprisonment ; **réclusion à perpétuité** life imprisonment.

recoiffer [3] [rəkwafe] ◆ **se recoiffer** *vp* to do one's hair again.

recoin [rəkwɛ̃] *nm* nook.

recoller [3] [rəkɔle] *vt* [objet brisé] to stick back together.

récolte [rekɔlt] *nf* 1. [AGRIC - action] harvesting *(U)*, gathering *(U)* ; [- produit] harvest, crop - 2. *fig* collection.

récolter [3] [rekɔlte] *vt* to harvest ; *fig* to collect.

recommandable [rəkɔmɑ̃dabl] *adj* commendable ; **peu recommandable** undesirable.

recommandation [rəkɔmɑ̃dasjɔ̃] *nf* recommendation.

recommandé, e [rəkɔmɑ̃de] *adj* 1. [envoi] registered ; **envoyer qqch en recommandé** to send sthg by registered post *UK* ou mail *US* - 2. [conseillé] advisable.

recommander [3] [rəkɔmɑ̃de] *vt* to recommend ; **recommander à qqn de faire qqch** to advise sb to do sthg ; **recommander qqn à qqn** to recommend sb to sb.

recommencer [16] [rəkɔmɑ̃se] <> *vt* [travail] to start ou begin again ; [erreur] to make again ; **recommencer à faire qqch** to start ou begin doing sthg again. <> *vi* to start ou begin again ; **ne recommence pas!** don't do that again!

récompense [rekɔ̃pɑ̃s] *nf* reward.

récompenser [3] [rekɔ̃pɑ̃se] *vt* to reward.

recompter [3] [rəkɔ̃te] *vt* to recount.

réconciliation [rekɔ̃siljasjɔ̃] *nf* reconciliation.

réconcilier [9] [rekɔ̃silje] *vt* to reconcile.

reconduire [98] [rəkɔ̃dɥir] *vt* 1. [personne] to accompany, to take - 2. [politique, bail] to renew.

reconduit, e [rəkɔ̃dɥi, it] *pp* ▶ reconduire.

réconfort [rekɔ̃fɔr] *nm* comfort.

réconfortant, e [rekɔ̃fɔrtɑ̃, ɑ̃t] *adj* comforting.

réconforter [3] [rekɔ̃fɔrte] *vt* to comfort.

reconnaissable [rəkɔnɛsabl] *adj* recognizable.

reconnaissance [rəkɔnɛsɑ̃s] *nf* 1. [gén] recognition - 2. MIL reconnaissance ; **aller/partir en reconnaissance** to go out on reconnaissance - 3. [gratitude] gratitude ; **exprimer sa reconnaissance à qqn** to show ou express one's gratitude to sb.

reconnaissant, e [rəkɔnɛsɑ̃, ɑ̃t] *adj* grateful ; **je vous serais reconnaissant de m'aider** I would be grateful if you would help me.

reconnaître [91] [rəkɔnɛtr] *vt* 1. [gén] to recognize - 2. [erreur] to admit, to acknowledge - 3. MIL to reconnoitre.

reconnu, e [rəkɔny] <> *pp* ▶ reconnaître. <> *adj* well-known.

reconquérir [39] [rəkɔ̃kerir] *vt* to reconquer.

reconquis, e [rəkɔ̃ki, iz] *pp* ▶ reconquérir.

reconsidérer [18] [rəkɔ̃sidere] *vt* to reconsider.

reconstituant, e [rəkɔ̃stitɥɑ̃, ɑ̃t] *adj* invigorating. ◆ **reconstituant** *nm* tonic.

reconstituer [7] [rəkɔ̃stitɥe] *vt* 1. [puzzle] to put together - 2. [crime, délit] to reconstruct.

reconstitution [rəkɔ̃stitysjɔ̃] *nf* 1. [de puzzle] putting together - 2. [de crime, délit] reconstruction.

reconstruction [rəkɔ̃stryksjɔ̃] *nf* reconstruction, rebuilding.

reconstruire [98] [rəkɔ̃strɥir] *vt* to reconstruct, to rebuild.

reconstruit, e [rəkɔ̃strɥi, it] *pp* ▶ reconstruire.

reconversion [rəkɔ̃vɛrsjɔ̃] *nf* 1. [d'employé] redeployment - 2. [d'usine, de société] conversion ; **reconversion économique/technique** economic/technical restructuring.

reconvertir [32] [rəkɔ̃vɛrtir] *vt* 1. [employé] to redeploy - 2. [économie] to restructure. ◆ **se reconvertir** *vp* : **se reconvertir dans** to move into.

recopier [9] [rəkɔpje] *vt* to copy out.

record [rəkɔr] <> nm record ; **détenir/améliorer/battre un record** to hold/improve/beat a record. <> adj inv record *(avant n)*.

recoucher [3] [rəkuʃe] vt to put back to bed. ◆ **se recoucher** vp to go back to bed.

recoudre [86] [rəkudr] vt to sew (up) again.

recoupement [rəkupmɑ̃] nm cross-check ; **par recoupement** by cross-checking.

recouper [3] [rəkupe] vt 1. [pain] to cut again - 2. COUT to recut - 3. *fig* [témoignages] to compare, to cross-check. ◆ **se recouper** vp 1. [lignes] to intersect - 2. [témoignages] to match up.

recourir [45] [rəkurir] vi : **recourir à** [médecin, agence] to turn to ; [force, mensonge] to resort to.

recours [rəkur] nm 1. [emploi] : **avoir recours à** [médecin, agence] to turn to ; [force, mensonge] to resort to, to have recourse to - 2. [solution] solution, way out ; **en dernier recours** as a last resort - 3. DR action ; **recours en cassation** appeal.

recouvert, e [rəkuvɛr, ɛrt] pp ▶ recouvrir.

recouvrir [34] [rəkuvrir] vt 1. [gén] to cover ; [fauteuil] to re-cover - 2. [personne] to cover (up). ◆ **se recouvrir** vp 1. [tuiles] to overlap - 2. [surface] : **se recouvrir (de)** to be covered (with).

recracher [3] [rəkraʃe] vt to spit out.

récréatif, ive [rekreatif, iv] adj entertaining.

récréation [rekreasjɔ̃] nf 1. [détente] relaxation, recreation - 2. SCOL break *UK*, recess *US*.

recréer [15] [rəkree] vt to recreate.

récrimination [rekriminasjɔ̃] nf complaint.

récrire [rekrir], **réécrire** [99] [reekrir] vt to rewrite.

recroqueviller [3] [rəkrɔkvije] ◆ **se recroqueviller** vp to curl up.

recru, e [rəkry] adj : **recru de fatigue** *litt* exhausted. ◆ **recrue** nf recruit.

recrudescence [rəkrydesɑ̃s] nf renewed outbreak.

recrutement [rəkrytmɑ̃] nm recruitment.

recruter [3] [rəkryte] vt to recruit.

rectal, e, aux [rɛktal, o] adj rectal.

rectangle [rɛktɑ̃gl] nm rectangle.

rectangulaire [rɛktɑ̃gylɛr] adj rectangular.

recteur [rɛktœr] nm SCOL *chief administrative officer of an education authority*, ≃ (Chief) Education Officer *UK*.

rectificatif, ive [rɛktifikatif, iv] adj correcting. ◆ **rectificatif** nm correction.

rectification [rɛktifikasjɔ̃] nf 1. [correction] correction - 2. [de tir] adjustment.

rectifier [9] [rɛktifje] vt 1. [tir] to adjust - 2. [erreur] to rectify, to correct ; [calcul] to correct.

rectiligne [rɛktiliɲ] adj rectilinear.

recto [rɛkto] nm right side ; **recto verso** on both sides.

rectorat [rɛktɔra] nm SCOL *offices of the education authority*, ≃ Education Offices *UK*.

reçu, e [rəsy] pp ▶ recevoir. ◆ **reçu** nm receipt.

recueil [rəkœj] nm collection.

recueillement [rəkœjmɑ̃] nm meditation.

recueillir [41] [rəkœjir] vt 1. [fonds] to collect - 2. [suffrages] to win - 3. [enfant] to take in. ◆ **se recueillir** vp to meditate.

recul [rəkyl] nm 1. [mouvement arrière] step backwards - 2. MIL retreat - 3. [d'arme à feu] recoil - 3. [de civilisation] decline ; [d'inflation, de chômage] : **recul (de)** downturn (in) - 4. *fig* [retrait] : **avec du recul** with hindsight.

reculé, e [rəkyle] adj distant.

reculer [3] [rəkyle] <> vt 1. [voiture] to back up - 2. [date] to put back, to postpone. <> vi 1. [aller en arrière] to move backwards ; [voiture] to reverse ; **ne reculer devant rien** *fig* to stop at nothing - 2. [maladie, pauvreté] to be brought under control - 3. [faiblir - cours, valeur] to fall, to weaken.

reculons [rəkylɔ̃] ◆ **à reculons** adv backwards.

récupération [rekyperasjɔ̃] nf [de déchets] salvage.

récupérer [18] [rekypere] <> vt 1. [objet] to get back - 2. [déchets] to salvage - 3. [idée] to pick up - 4. [journée] to make up. <> vi to recover, to recuperate.

récurer [3] [rekyre] vt to scour.

récuser [3] [rekyze] vt 1. DR to challenge - 2. *sout* [refuser] to reject.

recyclage [rəsiklaʒ] nm 1. [d'employé] retraining - 2. [de déchets] recycling.

recycler [3] [rəsikle] vt 1. [employé] to retrain - 2. [déchets] to recycle. ◆ **se recycler** vp [employé] to retrain.

rédacteur, trice [redaktœr, tris] nm, f [de journal] subeditor ; [d'ouvrage de référence] editor ; **rédacteur en chef** editor-in-chief.

rédaction [redaksjɔ̃] nf 1. [de texte] editing - 2. SCOL essay - 3. [personnel] editorial staff.

redécouvrir [34] [rədekuvrir] vt to rediscover.

redéfinir [32] [rədefinir] vt to redefine.

redéfinition [rədefinisjɔ̃] nf redefinition.

redemander [3] [rədəmɑ̃de] vt to ask again for.

rédemption [redɑ̃psjɔ̃] nf redemption.

redescendre [73] [rədesãdr] <> vt (v aux : être) **1.** [escalier] to go/come down again - **2.** [objet - d'une étagère] to take down again. <> vi (v aux : être) to go/come down again.

redevable [rədəvabl] adj : être redevable de 20 euros à qqn to owe sb 20 euros ; être redevable à qqn de qqch [service] to be indebted to sb for sthg.

redevance [rədəvãs] nf [de radio, télévision] licence UK ou license US fee ; [téléphonique] rental (fee).

rédhibitoire [redibitwar] adj [défaut] crippling ; [prix] prohibitive.

rediffusion [rədifyzjɔ̃] nf repeat.

rédiger [17] [rediʒe] vt to write.

redimensionner [3] [radimãsjɔne] vt IN-FORM to resize.

redire [102] [rədir] vt to repeat ; avoir ou trouver à redire à qqch fig to find fault with sthg.

redistribuer [7] [rədistribɥe] vt to redistribute.

redit, e [rədi, it] pp ▶ redire.

redite [rədit] nf repetition.

redondance [rədɔ̃dãs] nf redundancy.

redonner [3] [rədɔne] vt to give back ; [confiance, forces] to restore.

redoublant, e [rədublã, ãt] nm, f pupil who is repeating a year.

redoubler [3] [rəduble] <> vt **1.** [syllabe] to reduplicate - **2.** [efforts] to intensify - **3.** SCOL to repeat. <> vi to intensify.

redoutable [rədutabl] adj formidable.

redouter [3] [rədute] vt to fear.

redoux [rədu] nm thaw.

redressement [rədrɛsmã] nm **1.** [de pays, d'économie] recovery - **2.** DR : redressement fiscal payment of back taxes.

redresser [4] [rədrɛse] <> vt **1.** [poteau, arbre] to put ou set upright ; redresser la tête to raise one's head ; fig to hold up one's head - **2.** [situation] to set right. <> vi AUTO to straighten up. ▬ se redresser vp **1.** [personne] to stand ou sit straight - **2.** [pays] to recover.

réducteur, trice [redyktœr, tris] adj [limitatif] simplistic.

réduction [redyksjɔ̃] nf **1.** [gén] reduction - **2.** MÉD setting.

réduire [98] [redɥir] <> vt **1.** [gén] to reduce - **2.** INFORM to reduce en to reduce to - **2.** INFORM to minimize - **3.** MÉD to set - **4.** Suisse [ranger] to put away. <> vi CULIN to reduce ; faire réduire to reduce.

réduit, e [redɥi, it] <> pp ▶ réduire. <> adj reduced. ▬ **réduit** nm [local] small room.

rééchelonner [3] [reeʃlɔne] vt to reschedule.

réécrire = récrire.

réédition [reedisjɔ̃] nf new edition.

rééducation [reedykasjɔ̃] nf **1.** [de membre] re-education - **2.** [de délinquant, malade] rehabilitation, rehab US.

réel, elle [reɛl] adj real.

réélection [reelɛksjɔ̃] nf reelection.

réellement [reelmã] adv really.

rééquilibrer [3] [reekilibre] vt to balance (again).

réessayer [reeseje] vt to try again.

réévaluer [7] [reevalɥe] vt to revalue.

réexaminer [3] [reɛgzamine] vt to re-examine.

réexpédier [9] [reɛkspedje] vt to send back.

réf. (abr écrite de référence) ref.

refaire [109] [rəfɛr] vt **1.** [faire de nouveau - travail, devoir] to do again ; [- voyage] to make again - **2.** [mur, toit] to repair.

refait, e [rəfɛ, ɛt] pp ▶ refaire.

réfection [refɛksjɔ̃] nf repair.

réfectoire [refɛktwar] nm refectory.

référence [referãs] nf reference ; faire référence à to refer to.

référendum [referɛ̃dɔm] nm referendum.

référer [18] [refere] vi : en référer à qqn to refer the matter to sb.

refermer [3] [rəfɛrme] vt to close ou shut again.

réfléchi, e [refleʃi] adj **1.** [action] considered ; c'est tout réfléchi I've made up my mind, I've decided - **2.** [personne] thoughtful - **3.** GRAMM reflexive.

réfléchir [32] [refleʃir] <> vt **1.** [refléter] to reflect - **2.** [penser] : réfléchir que to think ou reflect that. <> vi to think, to reflect ; réfléchir à ou sur qqch to think about sthg.

reflet [rəflɛ] nm **1.** [image] reflection - **2.** [de lumière] glint.

refléter [18] [rəflete] vt to reflect. ▬ se refléter vp **1.** [se réfléchir] to be reflected - **2.** [transparaître] to be mirrored.

refleurir [32] [rəflœrir] vi [fleurir à nouveau] to flower again.

réflexe [reflɛks] <> nm reflex. <> adj reflex (avant n).

réflexion [reflɛksjɔ̃] nf **1.** [de lumière, d'ondes] reflection - **2.** [pensée] reflection, thought - **3.** [remarque] remark.

refluer [3] [rəflɥe] vi **1.** [liquide] to flow back - **2.** [foule] to flow back ; [avec violence] to surge back.

reflux [rəfly] nm **1.** [d'eau] ebb - **2.** [de personnes] backward surge.

refonte [rəfɔ̃t] *nf* **1.** [de métal] remelting - **2.** [d'ouvrage] recasting - **3.** [d'institution, de système] overhaul, reshaping.

reforestation [rəfɔrɛstasjɔ̃] *nf* reforestation.

réformateur, trice [reformatœr, tris] ◇ *adj* reforming. ◇ *nm, f* **1.** [personne] reformer - **2.** RELIG Reformer.

réforme [reform] *nf* reform.

réformé, e [reforme] *adj & nm, f* Protestant. ◆ **réformé** *nm* MIL *soldier who has been invalided out*.

reformer [3] [rəforme] *vt* to re-form.

réformer [3] [reforme] *vt* **1.** [améliorer] to reform, to improve - **2.** MIL to invalid out UK - **3.** [matériel] to scrap.

réformiste [reformist] *adj & nmf* reformist.

refoulé, e [rəfule] ◇ *adj* repressed, frustrated. ◇ *nm, f* repressed person.

refouler [3] [rəfule] *vt* **1.** [personnes] to repel, to repulse - **2.** PSYCHO to repress.

réfractaire [refraktɛr] ◇ *adj* **1.** [rebelle] insubordinate - **2.** [matière] refractory. ◇ *nmf* insubordinate.

refrain [rəfrɛ̃] *nm* MUS refrain, chorus ; **c'est toujours le même refrain** *fam fig* it's always the same old story.

refréner [18] [rəfrene] *vt* to check, to hold back.

réfrigérant, e [refriʒerɑ̃, ɑ̃t] *adj* **1.** [liquide] refrigerating, refrigerant - **2.** *fam* [accueil] icy.

réfrigérateur [refriʒeratœr] *nm* refrigerator.

refroidir [32] [rəfrwadir] ◇ *vt* **1.** [plat] to cool - **2.** [décourager] to discourage - **3.** *fam* [tuer] to rub out, to do in. ◇ *vi* to cool.

refroidissement [rəfrwadismɑ̃] *nm* **1.** [de température] drop, cooling - **2.** [grippe] chill.

refuge [rəfyʒ] *nm* **1.** [abri] refuge - **2.** [de montagne] hut.

réfugié, e [refyʒje] *nm, f* refugee.

réfugier [9] [refyʒje] ◆ **se réfugier** *vp* to take refuge.

refus [rəfy] *nm inv* refusal ; **ce n'est pas de refus** *fam* I wouldn't say no.

refuser [3] [rəfyze] *vt* **1.** [repousser] to refuse ; **refuser de faire qqch** to refuse to do sthg - **2.** [contester] : **refuser qqch à qqn** to deny sb sthg - **3.** [clients, spectateurs] to turn away - **4.** [candidat] : **être refusé** to fail. ◆ **se refuser** *vp* : **se refuser à faire qqch** to refuse to do sthg.

réfuter [3] [refyte] *vt* to refute.

regagner [3] [rəɡaɲe] *vt* **1.** [reprendre] to regain, to win back - **2.** [revenir à] to get back to.

regain [rəɡɛ̃] *nm* [retour] : **un regain de** a revival of, a renewal of ; **un regain de vie** a new lease of life.

régal, als [reɡal] *nm* treat, delight.

régaler [3] [reɡale] *vt* to treat ; **c'est moi qui régale!** it's my treat! ◆ **se régaler** *vp* : **je me régale** [nourriture] I'm thoroughly enjoying it ; [activité] I'm having the time of my life.

regard [rəɡar] *nm* look.

regardant, e [rəɡardɑ̃, ɑ̃t] *adj* **1.** *fam* [économe] mean - **2.** [minutieux] : **être très/peu regardant sur qqch** to be very/not very particular about sthg.

regarder [3] [rəɡarde] ◇ *vt* **1.** [observer, examiner, consulter] to look at ; [télévision, spectacle] to watch ; **regarder qqn faire qqch** to watch sb doing sthg ; **regarder les trains passer** to watch the trains go by - **2.** [considérer] to consider, to regard ; **regarder qqn/qqch comme** to regard sb/sthg as, to consider sb/sthg as - **3.** [concerner] to concern ; **cela ne te regarde pas** it's none of your business. ◇ *vi* **1.** [observer, examiner] to look - **2.** [faire attention] : **sans regarder à la dépense** regardless of the expense ; **y regarder à deux fois** to think twice about it.

régate [reɡat] *nf* (*gén pl*) regatta.

régénérer [18] [reʒenere] *vt* to regenerate. ◆ **se régénérer** *vp* to regenerate.

régent, e [reʒɑ̃, ɑ̃t] *nm, f* regent.

régenter [3] [reʒɑ̃te] *vt* : **vouloir tout régenter** *péj* to want to be the boss.

reggae [reɡe] *nm & adj inv* reggae.

régie [reʒi] *nf* **1.** [entreprise] state-controlled company - **2.** RADIO & TV [pièce] control room ; CINÉ, THÉÂTRE & TV [équipe] production team.

regimber [3] [rəʒɛ̃be] *vi* to balk.

régime [reʒim] *nm* **1.** [politique] regime - **2.** [administratif] system ; **régime carcéral** prison regime - **3.** [alimentaire] diet ; **se mettre au/suivre un régime** to go on/to be on a diet - **4.** [de moteur] speed - **5.** [de fleuve, des pluies] cycle - **6.** [de bananes, dattes] bunch.

régiment [reʒimɑ̃] *nm* **1.** MIL regiment - **2.** *fam* [grande quantité] : **un régiment de** masses of, loads of.

région [reʒjɔ̃] *nf* region.

régional, e, aux [reʒjonal, o] *adj* regional.

régir [32] [reʒir] *vt* to govern.

régisseur [reʒisœr] *nm* **1.** [intendant] steward - **2.** [de théâtre] stage manager.

registre [rəʒistr] *nm* [gén] register ; **registre de comptabilité** ledger.

réglable [reɡlabl] *adj* **1.** [adaptable] adjustable - **2.** [payable] payable.

réglage [regla3] *nm* adjustment, setting.

règle [rɛgl] *nf* **1.** [instrument] ruler - **2.** [principe, loi] rule ; **je suis en règle** my papers are in order. ◆ **en règle générale** *loc adv* as a general rule. ◆ **règles** *nfpl* [menstruation] period *sg*.

réglé, e [regle] *adj* [organisé] regular, well-ordered.

règlement [rɛgləmɑ̃] *nm* **1.** [résolution] settling ; **règlement de comptes** *fig* settling of scores - **2.** [règle] regulation - **3.** [paiement] settlement.

réglementaire [rɛgləmɑ̃tɛr] *adj* **1.** [régulier] statutory - **2.** [imposé] regulation *(avant n)*.

réglementation [rɛgləmɑ̃tasjɔ̃] *nf* **1.** [action] regulation - **2.** [ensemble de règles] regulations *pl*, rules *pl*.

régler [18] [regle] *vt* **1.** [affaire, conflit] to settle, to sort out - **2.** [appareil] to adjust - **3.** [payer - note] to settle, to pay ; [- commerçant] to pay.

réglisse [reglis] *nf* liquorice *UK*, licorice *US*.

règne [rɛɲ] *nm* **1.** [de souverain] reign ; **sous le règne de** in the reign of - **2.** [pouvoir] rule - **3.** BIOL kingdom.

régner [18] [reɲe] *vi* **1.** [souverain] to rule, to reign - **2.** [silence] to reign.

regonfler [3] [rəgɔ̃fle] *vt* **1.** [pneu, ballon] to blow up again, to reinflate - **2.** *fam* [personne] to cheer up.

regorger [17] [rəgɔrʒe] *vi* : **regorger de** to be abundant in.

régresser [4] [regrese] *vi* **1.** [sentiment, douleur] to diminish - **2.** [personne] to regress.

régression [regresjɔ̃] *nf* **1.** [recul] decline - **2.** PSYCHO regression.

regret [rəgrɛ] *nm* : **regret (de)** regret (for) ; **à regret** with regret ; **sans regret** with no regrets.

regrettable [rəgrɛtabl] *adj* regrettable.

regretter [4] [rəgrɛte] ◇ *vt* **1.** [époque] to miss, to regret ; [personne] to miss - **2.** [faute] to regret ; **regretter d'avoir fait qqch** to regret having done sthg - **3.** [déplorer] : **regretter que** (+ *subjonctif*) to be sorry ou to regret that. ◇ *vi* to be sorry.

regrouper [3] [rəgrupe] *vt* **1.** [grouper à nouveau] to regroup, to reassemble - **2.** [réunir] to group together. ◆ **se regrouper** *vp* to gather, to assemble.

régulariser [3] [regylarize] *vt* **1.** [documents] to sort out, to put in order ; [situation] to straighten out - **2.** [circulation, fonctionnement] to regulate.

régularité [regylarite] *nf* **1.** [gén] regularity - **2.** [de travail, résultats] consistency.

régulateur, trice [regylatœr, tris] *adj* regulating.

régulation [regylasjɔ̃] *nf* [contrôle] control, regulation.

régulier, ère [regylje, ɛr] *adj* **1.** [gén] regular - **2.** [uniforme, constant] steady, regular - **3.** [travail, résultats] consistent - **4.** [légal] legal ; **être en situation régulière** to have all the legally required documents.

régulièrement [regyljɛrmɑ̃] *adv* **1.** [gén] regularly - **2.** [uniformément] steadily, regularly ; [étalé, façonné] evenly.

réhabilitation [reabilitasjɔ̃] *nf* rehabilitation.

réhabiliter [3] [reabilite] *vt* **1.** [accusé] to rehabilitate, to clear ; *fig* [racheter] to restore to favour *UK* ou favor *US* - **2.** [rénover] to restore.

rehausser [3] [rəose] *vt* **1.** [surélever] to heighten - **2.** *fig* [mettre en valeur] to enhance.

rehausseur [rəosœr] *nm* booster seat.

rein [rɛ̃] *nm* kidney. ◆ **reins** *nmpl* small of the back *sg* ; **avoir mal aux reins** to have backache *UK* ou a backache *US*.

réincarnation [reɛ̃karnasjɔ̃] *nf* reincarnation.

réincarner [3] [reɛ̃karne] ◆ **se réincarner** *vpi* to be reincarnated ; **il voulait se réincarner en oiseau** he wanted to be reincarnated as a bird.

reine [rɛn] *nf* queen.

réinsertion [reɛ̃sɛrsjɔ̃] *nf* [de délinquant] rehabilitation ; [dans la vie professionnelle] reintegration.

réintégrer [18] [reɛ̃tegre] *vt* **1.** [rejoindre] to return to - **2.** DR to reinstate.

rejaillir [32] [rəʒajir] *vi* to splash up ; **rejaillir sur qqn** *fig* to rebound on sb.

rejet [rəʒɛ] *nm* **1.** [gén] rejection - **2.** [pousse] shoot.

rejeter [27] [rəʒte] *vt* **1.** [relancer] to throw back - **2.** [offre, personne] to reject - **3.** [partie du corps] : **rejeter la tête/les bras en arrière** to throw back one's head/one's arms - **4.** [imputer] : **rejeter la responsabilité de qqch sur qqn** to lay the responsibility for sthg at sb's door.

rejeton [rəʒtɔ̃] *nm* offspring *(U)*.

rejoindre [82] [rəʒwɛ̃dr] *vt* **1.** [retrouver] to join - **2.** [regagner] to return to - **3.** [concorder avec] to agree with - **4.** [rattraper] to catch up with. ◆ **se rejoindre** *vp* **1.** [personnes, routes] to meet - **2.** [opinions] to agree.

rejoint, e [rəʒwɛ̃, ɛ̃t] *pp* ► **rejoindre**.

réjoui, e [reʒwi] *adj* joyful.

réjouir [32] [reʒwir] vt to delight. ⬅ se **réjouir** vp to be delighted ; se réjouir de qqch to be delighted at ou about sthg.

réjouissance [reʒwisãs] nf rejoicing. ⬅ **réjouissances** nfpl festivities.

relâche [rəlɑʃ] nf 1. [pause] : sans relâche without respite ou a break - 2. THÉÂTRE : faire relâche to be closed.

relâchement [rəlɑʃmã] nm relaxation.

relâcher [3] [rəlɑʃe] vt 1. [étreinte, cordes] to loosen - 2. [discipline, effort] to relax, to slacken - 3. [prisonnier] to release. ⬅ se **relâcher** vp 1. [se desserrer] to loosen - 2. [faiblir - discipline] to become lax ; [- attention] to flag - 3. [se laisser aller] to slacken off.

relais [rəlɛ] nm 1. [auberge] post house ; relais routier transport café UK, truck stop US - 2. SPORT & TV : prendre/passer le relais to take/hand over ; (course de) relais relay.

relance [rəlãs] nf [économique] revival, boost ; [de projet] relaunch.

relancer [16] [rəlãse] vt 1. [renvoyer] to throw back - 2. [faire reprendre - économie] to boost ; [- projet] to relaunch ; [- moteur, machine] to restart ; INFORM to restart.

relater [3] [rəlate] vt litt to relate.

relatif, ive [rəlatif, iv] adj relative ; relatif à relating to ; tout est relatif it's all relative. ⬅ **relative** nf GRAMM relative clause.

relation [rəlasjɔ̃] nf relationship ; mettre qqn en relation avec qqn to put sb in touch with sb. ⬅ **relations** nfpl 1. [rapport] relationship sg ; relations sexuelles sexual relations, intercourse (U) - 2. [connaissance] acquaintance ; avoir des relations to have connections.

relationnel, elle [rəlasjɔnɛl] adj [problèmes] relationship (avant n).

relative ⬅ relatif.

relativement [rəlativmã] adv relatively.

relativiser [3] [rəlativize] vt to relativize.

relativité [rəlativite] nf relativity.

relax, relaxe [rəlaks] adj fam relaxed.

relaxation [rəlaksasjɔ̃] nf relaxation.

relaxe = relax.

relaxer [3] [rəlakse] vt 1. [reposer] to relax - 2. DR to discharge. ⬅ se **relaxer** vp to relax.

relayer [11] [rəleje] vt to relieve. ⬅ se **relayer** vp to take over from one another.

relecture [rəlɛktyr] nf second reading, rereading.

reléguer [18] [rəlege] vt to relegate.

relent [rəlã] nm 1. [odeur] stink, stench - 2. fig [trace] whiff.

relevé, e [rəlve] adj CULIN spicy. ⬅ **relevé** nm reading ; faire le relevé de qqch to read

sthg ; relevé de compte bank statement ; relevé d'identité bancaire bank account number.

relève [rəlɛv] nf relief ; prendre la relève to take over.

relever [19] [rəlve] ⬥ vt 1. [redresser - personne] to help up ; [- pays, économie] to rebuild ; [- moral, niveau] to raise - 2. [ramasser] to collect - 3. [tête, col, store] to raise ; [manches] to push up - 4. [CULIN - mettre en valeur] to bring out ; [- pimenter] to season - 5. fig [récit] to liven up, to spice up - 6. [noter] to note down ; [compteur] to read - 7. [relayer] to take over from, to relieve - 8. [erreur] to note. ⬥ vi 1. [se rétablir] : relever de to recover from - 2. [être du domaine] : relever de to come under. ⬅ se **relever** vp [se mettre debout] to stand up ; [sortir du lit] to get up.

relief [rəljɛf] nm relief ; en relief in relief, raised ; une carte en relief relief map ; mettre en relief fig to enhance, to bring out.

relier [9] [rəlje] vt 1. [livre] to bind - 2. [joindre] to connect - 3. fig [associer] to link up.

religieux, euse [rəliʒjø, øz] adj 1. [vie, chant] religious ; [mariage] religious, church (avant n) - 2. [respectueux] reverent. ⬅ **religieux** nm monk. ⬅ **religieuse** nf RELIG nun.

religion [rəliʒjɔ̃] nf 1. [culte] religion - 2. [croyance] religion, faith.

relique [rəlik] nf relic.

relire [106] [rəlir] vt 1. [lire] to reread - 2. [vérifier] to read over. ⬅ se **relire** vp to read what one has written.

reliure [rəljyr] nf binding.

reloger [17] [rələʒe] vt to rehouse.

relu, e [rəly] pp ▶ relire.

reluire [97] [rəlɥir] vi to shine, to gleam.

reluisant, e [rəlɥizã, ãt] adj shining, gleaming ; peu ou très reluisant fig [avenir, situation] not all that brilliant ; [personne] shady.

remaniement [rəmanimã] nm restructuring ; remaniement ministériel cabinet reshuffle.

remarier [9] [rəmarje] ⬅ se **remarier** vp to remarry.

remarquable [rəmarkabl] adj remarkable.

remarque [rəmark] nf 1. [observation] remark ; [critique] critical remark - 2. [annotation] note.

remarquer [3] [rəmarke] ⬥ vt 1. [apercevoir] to notice ; faire remarquer qqch (à qqn) to point sthg out (to sb) ; se faire remarquer péj to draw attention to o.s. - 2. [noter] to remark, to comment. ⬥ vi : ce n'est pas l'idéal, remarquez! it's not ideal, mind you! ⬅ se **remarquer** vp to be noticeable.

rembarrer [3] [rɑ̃bare] *vt fam* to snub.

remblai [rɑ̃blɛ] *nm* embankment.

rembobiner [3] [rɑ̃bɔbine] *vt* to rewind.

rembourrer [3] [rɑ̃bure] *vt* to stuff, to pad.

remboursement [rɑ̃bursəmɑ̃] *nm* refund, repayment.

rembourser [3] [rɑ̃burse] *vt* **1.** [dette] to pay back, to repay - **2.** [personne] to pay back ; **rembourser qqn de qqch** to reimburse sb for sthg ; **tu t'es fait rembourser ton trajet en taxi?** did they reimburse you for your taxi journey? - **3.** [dépense, achat] : **se faire rembourser** to get a refund.

rembrunir [32] [rɑ̃brynir] ➤ **se rembrunir** *vp* to cloud over, to become gloomy.

remède [rəmɛd] *nm litt & fig* remedy, cure.

remédier [9] [rəmedje] *vi* : **remédier à qqch** to put sthg right, to remedy sthg.

remembrement [rəmɑ̃brəmɑ̃] *nm* land regrouping.

remerciement [rəmɛrsimɑ̃] *nm* thanks *pl* ; **une lettre de remerciement** a thank-you letter.

remercier [9] [rəmɛrsje] *vt* **1.** [dire merci à] to thank ; **remercier qqn de** OU **pour qqch** to thank sb for sthg ; **non, je vous remercie** no, thank you - **2.** [congédier] to dismiss.

remettre [84] [rəmɛtr] *vt* **1.** [replacer] to put back ; **remettre en question** to call into question ; **remettre qqn à sa place** to put sb in his place - **2.** [enfiler de nouveau] to put back on - **3.** [rétablir - lumière, son] to put back on ; **remettre qqch en marche** to restart sthg ; **remettre de l'ordre dans qqch** to tidy sthg up ; **remettre une montre à l'heure** to put a watch right ; **remettre qqch en état de marche** to put sthg back in working order - **4.** [donner] : **remettre qqch à qqn** to hand sthg over to sb ; [médaille, prix] to present sthg to sb - **5.** [ajourner] : **remettre qqch (à)** to put sthg off (until). ➤ **se remettre** *vp* **1.** [recommencer] : **se remettre à qqch** to take up sthg again ; **se remettre à fumer** to start smoking again - **2.** [se rétablir] to get better ; **se remettre de qqch** to get over sthg - **3.** [redevenir] : **se remettre debout** to stand up again ; **le temps s'est remis au beau** the weather has cleared up.

réminiscence [reminisɑ̃s] *nf* reminiscence.

remis, e [rəmi, iz] *pp* ➤ **remettre**.

remise [rəmiz] *nf* **1.** [action] : **remise en jeu** throw-in ; **remise en marche** restarting ; **remise en question** OU **cause** calling into question - **2.** [de message, colis] handing over ; [de médaille, prix] presentation - **3.** [réduction] discount ; **remise de peine** DR remission - **4.** [hangar] shed.

rémission [remisjɔ̃] *nf* remission ; **sans rémission** [punir, juger] without mercy ; [pleuvoir] unremittingly.

remix [rəmiks] *nm* MUS [enregistrement, disque] remix ; [technique] remixing.

remodeler [25] [rəmɔdle] *vt* **1.** [forme] to remodel - **2.** [remanier] to restructure.

remontant, e [rəmɔ̃tɑ̃, ɑ̃t] *adj* [tonique] invigorating. ➤ **remontant** *nm* tonic.

remonte-pente [rəmɔ̃tpɑ̃t] (*pl* **remonte-pentes**) *nm* ski tow.

remonter [3] [rəmɔ̃te] ➤ *vt* (*v aux : être*) **1.** [escalier, pente] to go/come back up - **2.** [assembler] to put together again - **3.** [manches] to turn up - **4.** [horloge, montre] to wind up - **5.** [ragaillardir] to put new life into, to cheer up. ➤ *vi* (*v aux : être*) **1.** [monter à nouveau - personne] to go/come back up ; [- baromètre] to rise again ; [- prix, température] to go up again, to rise ; [- sur vélo] to get back on ; **remonter dans une voiture** to get back into a car - **2.** [dater] : **remonter à date** OU **go back to**.

remontoir [rəmɔ̃twar] *nm* winder.

remontrer [3] [rəmɔ̃tre] *vt* to show again ; **vouloir en remontrer à qqn** to try to show sb up.

remords [rəmɔr] *nm* remorse.

remorque [rəmɔrk] *nf* trailer ; **être en remorque** to be on tow.

remorquer [3] [rəmɔrke] *vt* [voiture, bateau] to tow.

remorqueur [rəmɔrkœr] *nm* tug, tugboat.

remous [rəmu] ➤ *nm* [de bateau] wash, backwash ; [de rivière] eddy. ➤ *nmpl fig* stir, upheaval.

rempailler [3] [rɑ̃paje] *vt* to re-cane.

rempart [rɑ̃par] *nm* (*gén pl*) rampart.

rempiler [3] [rɑ̃pile] ➤ *vt* to pile up again. ➤ *vi fam* MIL to sign on again.

remplaçable [rɑ̃plasabl] *adj* replaceable.

remplaçant, e [rɑ̃plasɑ̃, ɑ̃t] *nm, f* [suppléant] stand-in ; SPORT substitute.

remplacement [rɑ̃plasmɑ̃] *nm* **1.** [changement] replacing, replacement - **2.** [intérim] substitution ; **faire des remplacements** to stand in ; [docteur] to act as a locum *UK*.

remplacer [16] [rɑ̃plase] *vt* **1.** [gén] to replace - **2.** [prendre la place de] to stand in for ; SPORT to substitute.

remplir [32] [rɑ̃plir] *vt* **1.** [gén] to fill ; **remplir de** to fill with ; **remplir qqn de joie/d'orgueil** to fill sb with happiness/pride - **2.** [questionnaire] to fill in OU out - **3.** [mission, fonction] to complete, to fulfil.

remplissage [rɑ̃plisaʒ] *nm* **1.** [de récipient] filling up - **2.** *fig & péj* [de texte] padding out.

remporter [3] [rɑ̃pɔrte] *vt* **1.** [repartir avec] to take away again - **2.** [gagner] to win.

remuant, e [rəmɥɑ̃, ɑ̃t] *adj* restless, over-active.

remue-ménage [rəmymenaʒ] *nm inv* commotion, confusion.

remuer [7] [rəmɥe] ◇ *vt* **1.** [bouger, émouvoir] to move - **2.** [café, thé] to stir ; [salade] to toss. ◇ *vi* to move, to stir ; **arrête de remuer comme ça** stop being so restless. ◈ **se remuer** *vp* **1.** [se mouvoir] to move - **2.** *fig* [réagir] to make an effort.

rémunération [remynerasjɔ̃] *nf* remuneration.

rémunérer [18] [remynere] *vt* **1.** [personne] to remunerate, to pay - **2.** [activité] to pay for.

renâcler [3] [rənakle] *vi fam* to make a fuss ; **renâcler devant** OU **à qqch** to balk at sthg.

renaissance [rənɛsɑ̃s] *nf* rebirth.

renaître [92] [rənɛtr] *vi* **1.** [ressusciter] to come back to life, to come to life again ; **faire renaître** [passé, tradition] to revive - **2.** [revenir - sentiment, printemps] to return ; [- économie] to revive, to recover.

renard [rənar] *nm* fox.

renchérir [32] [rɑ̃ʃerir] *vi* **1.** [augmenter] to become more expensive ; [prix] to go up - **2.** [surenchérir] : **renchérir sur** to add to.

rencontre [rɑ̃kɔ̃tr] *nf* [gén] meeting ; **faire une bonne rencontre** to meet somebody interesting ; **faire une mauvaise rencontre** to meet an unpleasant person ; **aller/venir à la rencontre de qqn** to go/come to meet sb.

rencontrer [3] [rɑ̃kɔ̃tre] *vt* **1.** [gén] to meet - **2.** [heurter] to strike. ◈ **se rencontrer** *vp* **1.** [gén] to meet - **2.** [opinions] to agree.

rendement [rɑ̃dmɑ̃] *nm* [de machine, travailleur] output ; [de terre, placement] yield.

rendez-vous [rɑ̃devu] *nm inv* **1.** [rencontre] appointment ; [amoureux] date ; **on a tous rendez-vous au café** we're all meeting at the café ; **lors de notre dernier rendez-vous** at our last meeting ; **prendre rendez-vous avec qqn** to make an appointment with sb ; **donner rendez-vous à qqn** to arrange to meet sb ; **se donner rendez-vous** to arrange to meet - **2.** [lieu] meeting place.

rendormir [36] [rɑ̃dɔrmir] ◈ **se rendormir** *vp* to go back to sleep.

rendre [73] [rɑ̃dr] ◇ *vt* **1.** [restituer] : **rendre qqch à qqn** to give sthg back to sb, to return sthg to sb - **2.** [invitation, coup] to return - **3.** DR to pronounce - **4.** [produire un effet] to produce - **5.** [vomir] to vomit, to cough up - **6.** MIL [céder] to surrender ; **rendre les armes** to lay down one's arms - **7.** (+ adj) [faire devenir] to make ; **rendre**

qqn fou to drive sb mad - **8.** [exprimer] to render. ◇ *vi* **1.** [produire - champ] to yield - **2.** [vomir] to vomit, to be sick UK. ◈ **se rendre** *vp* **1.** [céder, capituler] to give in ; **j'ai dû me rendre à l'évidence** I had to face facts - **2.** [aller] : **se rendre à** to go to - **3.** (+ adj) [se faire tel] : **se rendre utile/malade** to make o.s. useful/ill.

rêne [rɛn] *nf* rein.

renégat, e [rənega, at] *nm, f sout* renegade.

renégocier [9] [rənegɔsje] *vt* to renegotiate.

renfermé, e [rɑ̃fɛrme] *adj* introverted, withdrawn. ◈ **renfermé** *nm* : **ça sent le renfermé** it smells stuffy in here.

renfermer [3] [rɑ̃fɛrme] *vt* [contenir] to contain. ◈ **se renfermer** *vp* to withdraw.

renflé, e [rɑ̃fle] *adj* bulging.

renflouer [3] [rɑ̃flue] *vt* **1.** [bateau] to refloat - **2.** *fig* [entreprise, personne] to bail out.

renfoncement [rɑ̃fɔ̃smɑ̃] *nm* recess.

renforcer [16] [rɑ̃fɔrse] *vt* to reinforce, to strengthen ; **cela me renforce dans mon opinion** that confirms my opinion.

renfort [rɑ̃fɔr] *nm* reinforcement ; **venir en renfort** to come as reinforcements.

renfrogné, e [rɑ̃frɔɲe] *adj* scowling.

renfrogner [3] [rɑ̃frɔɲe] ◈ **se renfrogner** *vp* to scowl, to pull a face.

rengaine [rɑ̃gɛn] *nf* **1.** [formule répétée] (old) story - **2.** [chanson] (old) song.

rengorger [17] [rɑ̃gɔrʒe] ◈ **se rengorger** *vp fig* to puff o.s. up.

renier [9] [rənje] *vt* **1.** [famille, ami] to disown - **2.** [foi, opinion] to renounce, to repudiate.

renifler [3] [rənifle] ◇ *vi* to sniff. ◇ *vt* to sniff ; **renifler quelque chose de louche** to smell a rat.

renne [rɛn] *nm* reindeer (inv).

renom [rənɔ̃] *nm* renown, fame.

renommé, e [rənɔme] *adj* renowned, famous. ◈ **renommée** *nf* renown, fame ; **de renommée internationale** world-famous, internationally renowned.

renoncement [rənɔ̃smɑ̃] *nm* : **renoncement (à)** renunciation (of).

renouer [6] [rənwe] ◇ *vt* **1.** [lacet, corde] to re-tie, to tie up again - **2.** [contact, conversation] to resume. ◇ *vi* : **renouer avec qqn** to take up with sb again ; **renouer avec sa famille** to make it up with one's family again.

renouveau, **x** [rənuvo] *nm* [transformation] revival.

renouvelable [rənuvlabl] *adj* renewable ; [expérience] repeatable.

renouveler [24] [rənuvle] *vt* [gén] to renew. ◆ **se renouveler** *vp* **1.** [être remplacé] to be renewed - **2.** [changer, innover] to have new ideas - **3.** [se répéter] to be repeated, to recur.

renouvellement [rənuvɛlmɑ̃] *nm* renewal.

rénovation [renɔvasjɔ̃] *nf* renovation, restoration.

rénover [3] [renɔve] *vt* **1.** [immeuble] to renovate, to restore - **2.** [système, méthodes] to reform.

renseignement [rɑ̃sɛɲəmɑ̃] *nm* information *(U)* ; **un renseignement** a piece of information ; **prendre des renseignements (sur)** to make enquiries (about). ◆ **renseignements** *nmpl* [service d'information] enquiries *UK*, information.

renseigner [4] [rɑ̃sɛɲe] *vt* : **renseigner qqn (sur)** to give sb information (about), to inform sb (about). ◆ **se renseigner** *vp* **1.** [s'enquérir] to make enquiries, to ask for information - **2.** [s'informer] to find out.

rentabiliser [3] [rɑ̃tabilize] *vt* to make profitable.

rentabilité [rɑ̃tabilite] *nf* profitability.

rentable [rɑ̃tabl] *adj* **1.** COMM profitable - **2.** *fam* [qui en vaut la peine] worthwhile.

rente [rɑ̃t] *nf* **1.** [d'un capital] revenue, income - **2.** [pension] pension, annuity.

rentier, **ère** [rɑ̃tje, ɛr] *nm, f* person of independent means.

rentrée [rɑ̃tre] *nf* **1.** [fait de rentrer] return - **2.** [reprise des activités] : **la rentrée parlementaire** the reopening of parliament ; **la rentrée des classes** the start of the new school year - **3.** CINÉ & THÉÂTRE comeback - **4.** [recette] income ; **avoir une rentrée d'argent** to come into some money.

rentrer [3] [rɑ̃tre] <> *vi (v aux : être)* **1.** [entrer de nouveau] to go/comeback in ; **tout a fini par rentrer dans l'ordre** everything returned to normal - **2.** [entrer] to go/come in - **3.** [revenir chez soi] to go/come back, to go/come home - **4.** [recouvrer, récupérer] : **rentrer dans** to recover, to get back ; **rentrer dans ses frais** to cover one's costs, to break even - **5.** [se jeter avec violence] : **rentrer dans** to crash into - **6.** [s'emboîter] to go in, to fit ; **rentrer les uns dans les autres** to fit together - **7.** [être perçu - fonds] to come in. <> *vt (v aux : être)* **1.** [mettre ou remettre à l'intérieur] to bring in ; [chemise] to tuck in - **2.** [ventre] to pull in ; [griffes] to retract, to draw in - **3.** *fig* [rage, larmes] to hold back.

renversant, **e** [rɑ̃vɛrsɑ̃, ɑ̃t] *adj* staggering, astounding.

renverse [rɑ̃vɛrs] *nf* : **tomber à la renverse** to fall over backwards.

renversement [rɑ̃vɛrsəmɑ̃] *nm* **1.** [inversion] turning upside down - **2.** [de situation] reversal.

renverser [3] [rɑ̃vɛrse] *vt* **1.** [mettre à l'envers] to turn upside down - **2.** [faire tomber - objet] to knock over ; [- piéton] to run over ; [- liquide] to spill - **3.** *fig* [obstacle] to overcome ; [régime] to overthrow ; [ministre] to throw out of office - **4.** [tête, buste] to tilt back - **5.** [accident] : **se faire renverser par une voiture** to get ou be knocked over by a car. ◆ **se renverser** *vp* **1.** [incliner le corps en arrière] to lean back - **2.** [tomber] to overturn.

renvoi [rɑ̃vwa] *nm* **1.** [licenciement] dismissal - **2.** [de colis, lettre] return, sending back - **3.** [ajournement] postponement - **4.** [référence] cross-reference - **5.** DR referral - **6.** [éructation] belch.

renvoyer [30] [rɑ̃vwaje] *vt* **1.** [faire retourner] to send back - **2.** [congédier] to dismiss - **3.** [colis, lettre] to send back, to return - **4.** [balle] to throw back - **5.** [réfléchir - lumière] to reflect ; [- son] to echo - **6.** [référer] : **renvoyer qqn à** to refer sb to - **7.** [différer] to postpone, to put off.

réorganisation [reɔrganizasjɔ̃] *nf* reorganization.

réorganiser [3] [reɔrganize] *vt* to reorganize.

réorienter [3] [reɔrjɑ̃te] *vt* to reorient, to reorientate.

réouverture [reuvɛrtyr] *nf* reopening.

repaire [rəpɛr] *nm* den.

répandre [74] [repɑ̃dr] *vt* **1.** [verser, renverser] to spill ; [larmes] to shed - **2.** [diffuser, dégager] to give off - **3.** *fig* [bienfaits] to pour out ; [effroi, terreur, nouvelle] to spread.

répandu, **e** [repɑ̃dy] <> *pp* ▶ **répandre**. <> *adj* [opinion, maladie] widespread.

réparable [reparabl] *adj* **1.** [objet] repairable - **2.** [erreur] that can be put right.

réparateur, **trice** [reparatœr, tris] <> *adj* [sommeil] refreshing. <> *nm, f* repairer.

réparation [reparasjɔ̃] *nf* **1.** [d'objet - action] repairing ; [- résultat] repair ; **en réparation** under repair - **2.** [de faute] : **réparation (de)** atonement (for) - **3.** [indemnité] reparation, compensation.

réparer [3] [repare] *vt* **1.** [objet] to repair - **2.** [faute, oubli] to make up for ; **réparer ses torts** to make amends.

reparler [3] [rəparle] *vi* : **reparler de qqn/qqch** to talk about sb/sthg again.

repartie [rəparti] *nf* retort ; **avoir de la repartie** to be good at repartee.

repartir [43] [rəpartir] ⟨⟩ *vt litt* to reply. ⟨⟩ *vi* **1.** [retourner] to go back, to return - **2.** [partir de nouveau] to set off again - **3.** [recommencer] to start again.

répartir [32] [repartir] *vt* **1.** [partager] to share out, to divide up - **2.** [dans l'espace] to spread out, to distribute - **3.** [classer] to divide ou split up. ▓ **se répartir** *vp* to divide up.

répartition [repartisjɔ̃] *nf* **1.** [partage] sharing out ; [de tâches] allocation - **2.** [dans l'espace] distribution.

repas [rəpa] *nm* meal ; **prendre son repas** to eat.

repassage [rəpasaʒ] *nm* ironing.

repasser [3] [rəpase] ⟨⟩ *vi (v aux : être)* [passer à nouveau] to go/come back ; [film] to be on again. ⟨⟩ *vt (v aux : être)* **1.** [frontière, montagne] to cross again, to recross - **2.** [examen] to resit *UK* - **3.** [film] to show again - **4.** [linge] to iron.

repêchage [rəpeʃaʒ] *nm* [de noyé, voiture] recovery.

repêcher [4] [rəpeʃe] *vt* **1.** [noyé, voiture] to fish out - **2.** *fam* [candidat] to let through.

repeindre [81] [rəpɛ̃dr] *vt* to repaint.

repeint, e [rəpɛ̃, ɛ̃t] *pp* ▶ repeindre.

repenser [3] [rəpɑ̃se] *vt* to rethink.

repentir [37] [rəpɑ̃tir] *nm* repentance. ▓ **se repentir** *vp* to repent ; **se repentir de qqch/d'avoir fait qqch** to be sorry for sthg/for having done sthg.

répercussion [reperkysjɔ̃] *nf* repercussion.

répercuter [3] [reperkyte] *vt* **1.** [lumière] to reflect ; [son] to throw back - **2.** [ordre, augmentation] to pass on. ▓ **se répercuter** *vp* **1.** [lumière] to be reflected ; [son] to echo - **2.** [influer] : **se répercuter sur** to have repercussions on.

repère [rəper] *nm* [marque] mark ; [objet concret] landmark ; **point de repère** point of reference.

repérer [18] [rəpere] *vt* **1.** [situer] to locate, to pinpoint - **2.** *fam* [remarquer] to spot ; **se faire repérer** to be spotted.

répertoire [repertwar] *nm* **1.** [agenda] thumb-indexed notebook - **2.** [de théâtre, d'artiste] repertoire - **3.** INFORM directory.

répertorier [9] [repertɔrje] *vt* to make a list of.

répéter [18] [repete] ⟨⟩ *vt* **1.** [gén] to repeat - **2.** [leçon] to go over, to learn ; [rôle] to rehearse. ⟨⟩ *vi* to rehearse. ▓ **se répéter** *vp* **1.** [radoter] to repeat o.s. - **2.** [se reproduire] to be repeated ; **que cela ne se répète pas!** don't let it happen again!

répétitif, ive [repetitif, iv] *adj* repetitive.

répétition [repetisjɔ̃] *nf* **1.** [réitération] repetition - **2.** MUS & THÉÂTRE rehearsal.

repeupler [5] [rəpœple] *vt* **1.** [région, ville] to repopulate - **2.** [forêt] to replant ; [étang] to restock.

repiquer [3] [rəpike] *vt* **1.** [replanter] to plant out - **2.** [disque, cassette] to tape.

répit [repi] *nm* respite ; **sans répit** without respite.

replacer [16] [rəplase] *vt* **1.** [remettre] to replace, to put back - **2.** [situer] to place, to put. ▓ **se replacer** *vp* to find new employment.

replanter [3] [rəplɑ̃te] *vt* to replant.

replet, ète [rəplɛ, ɛt] *adj* chubby.

repli [rəpli] *nm* **1.** [de tissu] fold ; [de rivière] bend - **2.** [de troupes] withdrawal.

replier [10] [rəplije] *vt* **1.** [plier de nouveau] to fold up again - **2.** [ramener en pliant] to fold back - **3.** [armée] to withdraw. ▓ **se replier** *vp* **1.** [armée] to withdraw - **2.** [personne] : **se replier sur soi-même** to withdraw into o.s. - **3.** [journal, carte] to fold.

réplique [replik] *nf* **1.** [riposte] reply ; **sans réplique** [argument] irrefutable ; [d'acteur] line ; **donner la réplique à qqn** to play opposite sb - **3.** [copie] replica ; [sosie] double.

répliquer [3] [replike] ⟨⟩ *vt* : **répliquer à qqn que** to reply to sb that. ⟨⟩ *vi* **1.** [répondre] to reply ; [avec impertinence] to answer back - **2.** *fig* [riposter] to retaliate.

replonger [17] [rəplɔ̃ʒe] ⟨⟩ *vt* to plunge back. ⟨⟩ *vi* to dive back. ▓ **se replonger** *vp* : **se replonger dans qqch** to immerse o.s. in sthg again.

répondeur [repɔ̃dœr] *nm* : **répondeur (téléphonique** ou **automatique** ou **-enregistreur)** answering machine.

répondre [75] [repɔ̃dr] ⟨⟩ *vi* : **répondre à qqn** [faire connaître sa pensée] to answer sb, to reply to sb ; [riposter] to answer sb back ; **répondre à qqch** [faire une réponse] to reply to sthg, to answer sthg ; [en se défendant] to respond to sthg ; **répondre au téléphone** to answer the telephone. ⟨⟩ *vt* to answer, to reply. ▓ **répondre à** *vt* **1.** [correspondre à - besoin] to answer ; [- conditions] to meet - **2.** [ressembler à - description] to match. ▓ **répondre de** *vt* to answer for.

répondu, e [repɔ̃dy] *pp* ▶ répondre.

réponse [repɔ̃s] *nf* **1.** [action de répondre] answer, reply ; **en réponse à votre lettre...** in reply ou in answer ou in response to your letter... - **2.** [solution] answer - **3.** [réaction] response - **4.** TECHNOL response.

report [rəpɔr] *nm* **1.** [de réunion, rendez-vous] postponement - **2.** COMM [d'écritures] carrying forward.

reportage [rəpɔrtaʒ] *nm* [article, enquête] report.

reporter¹ [rapɔrtɛr] *nm* reporter ; **grand reporter** international reporter.

reporter² [3] [rapɔrte] *vt* 1. [rapporter] to take back - 2. [différer] : **reporter qqch à** to postpone sthg till, to put sthg off till - 3. [somme] : **reporter (sur)** to carry forward (to) - 4. [transférer] : **reporter sur** to transfer to. ⏵ **se reporter** *vp* : **se reporter à** [se référer à] to refer to ; [se transporter en pensée à] to cast one's mind back to.

repos [rəpo] *nm* 1. [gén] rest ; **prendre un jour de repos** to take a day off - 2. [tranquillité] peace and quiet.

reposé, e [rəpoze] *adj* rested ; **à tête reposée** with a clear head.

reposer [3] [rəpoze] ◇ *vt* 1. [poser à nouveau] to put down again, to put back down - 2. [remettre] to put back - 3. [poser de nouveau - question] to ask again - 4. [appuyer] to rest - 5. [délasser] to rest, to relax. ◇ *vi* 1. [pâte] to sit, to stand ; [vin] to stand - 2. [théorie] : **reposer sur** to rest on. ⏵ **se reposer** *vp* 1. [se délasser] to rest - 2. [faire confiance] : **se reposer sur qqn** to rely on sb.

repositionnable [rapozisjɔnabl] *adj* repositionable, removable.

repoussant, e [rəpusɑ̃, ɑ̃t] *adj* repulsive.

repousser [3] [rapuse] ◇ *vi* to grow again, to grow back. ◇ *vt* 1. [écarter] to push away, to push back ; [l'ennemi] to repel, to drive back - 2. [éconduire] to reject - 3. [proposition] to reject, to turn down - 4. [différer] to put back, to postpone.

répréhensible [repreɑ̃sibl] *adj* reprehensible.

reprendre [79] [rəprɑ̃dr] ◇ *vt* 1. [prendre de nouveau] to take again ; **je passe te reprendre dans une heure** I'll come by and pick you up again in an hour ; **reprendre la route** to take to the road again ; **reprendre haleine** to get one's breath back - 2. [récupérer - objet prêté] to take back ; [- prisonnier, ville] to recapture - 3. COMM [entreprise, affaire] to take over - 4. [se resservir] : **reprendre un gâteau/de la viande** to take another cake/some more meat - 5. [recommencer] to resume ; **'et ainsi' reprit-il...** ' and so', he continued... - 6. [retoucher] to repair ; [jupe] to alter - 7. [corriger] to correct. ◇ *vi* 1. [affaires, plante] to pick up - 2. [recommencer] to start again.

représailles [rəprezaj] *nfpl* reprisals.

représentant, e [rəprezɑ̃tɑ̃, ɑ̃t] *nm, f* representative.

représentatif, ive [rəprezɑ̃tatif, iv] *adj* representative.

représentation [rəprezɑ̃tasjɔ̃] *nf* 1. [gén] representation - 2. [spectacle] performance.

représentativité [rəprezɑ̃tativite] *nf* representativeness.

représenter [3] [rəprezɑ̃te] *vt* to represent. ⏵ **se représenter** *vp* 1. [s'imaginer] : **se représenter qqch** to visualize sthg - 2. [se présenter à nouveau] : **se représenter à** [aux élections] to stand UK ou run US again at ; [à un examen] to resit UK, to represent.

répression [represjɔ̃] *nf* 1. [de révolte] repression - 2. [de criminalité, d'injustices] suppression.

réprimande [reprimɑ̃d] *nf* reprimand.

réprimander [3] [reprimɑ̃de] *vt* to reprimand.

réprimer [3] [reprime] *vt* 1. [émotion, rire] to repress, to check - 2. [révolte, crimes] to put down, to suppress.

repris, e [rəpri, iz] *pp* ▶ **reprendre.** ⏵ **repris** *nm* : **repris de justice** habitual criminal.

reprise [rapriz] *nf* 1. [recommencement - des hostilités] resumption, renewal ; [- des affaires] revival, recovery ; [- de pièce] revival ; **à plusieurs reprises** on several occasions, several times - 2. [boxe] round - 3. [raccommodage] mending.

repriser [3] [rəprize] *vt* to mend.

réprobateur, trice [reprɔbatœr, tris] *adj* reproachful.

réprobation [reprɔbasjɔ̃] *nf* disapproval.

reproche [rəprɔʃ] *nm* reproach ; **faire des reproches à qqn** to reproach sb ; **avec reproche** reproachfully ; **sans reproche** blameless.

reprocher [3] [rəprɔʃe] *vt* : **reprocher qqch à qqn** to reproach sb for sthg. ⏵ **se reprocher** *vp* : **se reprocher (qqch)** to blame o.s. (for sthg).

reproducteur, trice [rəprɔdyktœr, tris] *adj* reproductive.

reproduction [rəprɔdyksjɔ̃] *nf* reproduction ; **reproduction interdite** all rights (of reproduction) reserved.

reproduire [98] [rəprɔdɥir] *vt* to reproduce. ⏵ **se reproduire** *vp* 1. BIOL to reproduce, to breed - 2. [se répéter] to recur.

reproduit, e [rəprɔdɥi, it] *pp* ▶ **reproduire.**

réprouver [3] [repruve] *vt* [blâmer] to reprove.

reptile [rɛptil] *nm* reptile.

repu, e [rəpy] *adj* full, sated.

républicain, e [repyblikɛ̃, ɛn] *adj & nm, f* republican.

république [repyblik] *nf* republic ; **la République française** the French Republic ;

résister

la **République populaire de Chine** the People's Republic of China ; **la République tchèque** the Czech Republic.

répudier [9] [repydje] *vt* [femme] to repudiate.

répugnance [repynɑ̃s] *nf* **1.** [horreur] repugnance - **2.** [réticence] reluctance ; **avoir** ou **éprouver de la répugnance à faire qqch** to be reluctant to do sthg.

répugnant, e [repynɑ̃, ɑ̃t] *adj* repugnant.

répugner [3] [repyne] *vi* : **répugner à qqn** to disgust sb, to fill sb with repugnance ; **répugner à faire qqch** to be reluctant to do sthg, to be loath to do sthg.

répulsion [repylsjɔ̃] *nf* repulsion.

réputation [repytasjɔ̃] *nf* reputation ; **avoir une réputation de** to have a reputation for ; **avoir bonne/mauvaise réputation** to have a good/bad reputation.

réputé, e [repyte] *adj* famous, well-known.

requérir [39] [rəkerir] *vt* **1.** [nécessiter] to require, to call for - **2.** [solliciter] to solicit - **3.** DR [réclamer au nom de la loi] to demand.

requête [rəkɛt] *nf* **1.** [prière] petition - **2.** DR appeal.

requiem [rekɥijɛm] *nm inv* requiem.

requin [rəkɛ̃] *nm* shark.

requis, e [rəki, iz] <> *pp* ▶ **requérir**. <> *adj* required, requisite.

réquisition [rekizisjɔ̃] *nf* **1.** MIL requisition - **2.** DR closing speech for the prosecution.

réquisitionner [3] [rekizisjɔne] *vt* to requisition.

réquisitoire [rekizitwar] *nm* DR closing speech for the prosecution ; **réquisitoire (contre)** *fig* indictment (of).

RER (*abr de* réseau express régional) *nm* train service linking central Paris with its suburbs and airports.

rescapé, e [rɛskape] *nm, f* survivor.

rescousse [rɛskus] ▶ **à la rescousse** *loc adv* : **venir à la rescousse de qqn** to come to sb's rescue ; **appeler qqn à la rescousse** to call on sb for help.

réseau [rezo] *nm* network ; **réseau ferroviaire/routier** rail/roadnetwork.

réservation [rezɛrvasjɔ̃] *nf* reservation.

réserve [rezɛrv] *nf* **1.** [gén] reserve ; **en réserve** in reserve ; **officier de réserve** MIL reserve officer - **2.** [restriction] reservation ; **faire des réserves (sur)** to have reservations (about) ; **sous réserve de** subject to ; **sans réserve** unreservedly - **3.** [d'animaux, de plantes] reserve ; [d'Indiens] reservation ; **réserve faunique** *Québec* wildlife reserve ; **réserve naturelle** nature reserve - **4.** [local] storeroom.

réservé, e [rezɛrve] *adj* reserved.

réserver [3] [rezɛrve] *vt* **1.** [destiner] : **réserver qqch (à qqn)** [chambre, place] to reserve ou book sthg (for sb) ; *fig* [surprise, désagrément] to have sthg in store (for sb) - **2.** [mettre de côté, garder] : **réserver qqch (pour)** to put sthg on one side (for), to keep sthg (for). ▶ **se réserver** *vp* **1.** [s'accorder] : **se réserver qqch** to keep sthg for o.s. ; **se réserver le droit de faire qqch** to reserve the right to do sthg - **2.** [se ménager] to save o.s.

réservoir [rezɛrvwar] *nm* **1.** [cuve] tank - **2.** [bassin] reservoir.

résidence [rezidɑ̃s] *nf* **1.** [habitation] residence ; **résidence principale** main residence ou home ; **résidence secondaire** second home ; **résidence universitaire** hall of residence *UK*, dormitory *US* - **2.** [immeuble] block of luxury flats *UK*, luxury apartment block *US*. ▶ **résidence surveillée** *nf* : **en résidence surveillée** under house arrest.

résident, e [rezidɑ̃, ɑ̃t] *nm, f* **1.** [de pays] : **les résidents français en Écosse** French nationals resident in Scotland - **2.** [habitant d'une résidence] resident.

résidentiel, elle [rezidɑ̃sjɛl] *adj* residential.

résider [3] [rezide] *vi* **1.** [habiter] : **résider à/dans/en** to reside in - **2.** [consister] : **résider dans** to lie in.

résidu [rezidy] *nm* [reste] residue ; [déchet] waste.

résignation [reziɲasjɔ̃] *nf* resignation.

résigné, e [reziɲe] *adj* resigned.

résigner [3] [reziɲe] ▶ **se résigner** *vp* : **se résigner (à)** to resign o.s. (to).

résilier [9] [rezilje] *vt* to cancel, to terminate.

résille [rezij] *nf* **1.** [pour cheveux] hairnet - **2.** [pour les jambes] : **bas résille** fishnet stockings.

résine [rezin] *nf* resin.

résineux, euse [rezinø, øz] *adj* resinous. ▶ **résineux** *nm* conifer.

résistance [rezistɑ̃s] *nf* **1.** [gén, ÉLECTR & PHYS] resistance ; **manquer de résistance** to lack stamina ; **opposer une résistance** to put up resistance - **2.** [de radiateur, chaudière] element. ▶ **Résistance** *nf* : **la Résistance** HIST the Resistance.

résistant, e [rezistɑ̃, ɑ̃t] <> *adj* [personne] tough ; [tissu] hard-wearing, tough ; **être résistant au froid/aux infections** to be resistant to the cold/to infection. <> *nm, f* [gén] resistance fighter ; [de la Résistance] member of the Resistance.

résister [3] [reziste] *vi* to resist ; **résister à**

[attaque, désir] to resist ; [tempête, fatigue] to withstand ; [personne] to stand up to, to oppose.

résolu, e [rezɔly] <> pp ▶ **résoudre**. <> adj resolute ; **être bien résolu à faire qqch** to be determined to do sthg.

résolument [rezɔlymɑ̃] adv resolutely.

résolution [rezɔlysjɔ̃] nf 1. [décision] resolution ; **prendre la résolution de faire qqch** to make a resolution to do sthg - 2. [détermination] resolve, determination - 3. [solution] solving.

résonance [rezɔnɑ̃s] nf 1. ÉLECTR & PHYS resonance - 2. fig [écho] echo.

résonner [3] [rezɔne] vi [retentir] to resound ; [renvoyer le son] to echo.

résorber [3] [rezɔrbe] vt 1. [déficit] to absorb - 2. MÉD to resorb. ▪ **se résorber** vp 1. [déficit] to be absorbed - 2. MÉD to be resorbed.

résoudre [88] [rezudr] vt [problème] to solve, to resolve. ▪ **se résoudre** vp : **se résoudre à faire qqch** to make up one's mind to do sthg, to decide OU resolve to do sthg.

respect [rɛspɛ] nm respect.

respectable [rɛspɛktabl] adj respectable.

respecter [4] [rɛspɛkte] vt to respect ; **faire respecter la loi** to enforce the law.

respectif, ive [rɛspɛktif, iv] adj respective.

respectivement [rɛspɛktivmɑ̃] adv respectively.

respectueux, euse [rɛspɛktɥø, øz] adj respectful ; **être respectueux de** to have respect for.

respiration [rɛspirasjɔ̃] nf breathing (U) ; **retenir sa respiration** to hold one's breath.

respiratoire [rɛspiratwar] adj respiratory.

respirer [3] [rɛspire] <> vi 1. [inspirer-expirer] to breathe - 2. fig [se reposer] to get one's breath ; [être soulagé] to be able to breathe again. <> vt 1. [aspirer] to breathe in - 2. fig [exprimer] to exude.

resplendissant, e [rɛsplɑ̃disɑ̃, ɑ̃t] adj radiant.

responsabiliser [3] [rɛspɔ̃sabilize] vt : **responsabiliser qqn** to make sb aware of his/her responsibilities.

responsabilité [rɛspɔ̃sabilite] nf 1. [morale] responsibility ; **avoir la responsabilité de** to be responsible for, to have the responsibility of - 2. DR liability.

responsable [rɛspɔ̃sabl] <> adj 1. [gén] : **responsable (de)** responsible (for) ; [légalement] liable (for) ; [chargé de] in charge (of), responsible (for) - 2. [sérieux] responsible. <> nmf 1. [auteur, coupable] person responsible - 2. [dirigeant] official - 3. [personne compétente] person in charge.

resquiller [3] [rɛskije] vi 1. [au théâtre etc] to sneak in without paying - 2. [dans autobus etc] to dodge paying the fare.

resquilleur, euse [rɛskijœr, øz] nm, f 1. [au théâtre etc] person who sneaks in without paying - 2. [dans autobus etc] fare-dodger.

ressac [rəsak] nm undertow.

ressaisir [32] [rəsezir] ▪ **se ressaisir** vp to pull o.s. together.

ressasser [3] [rəsase] vt 1. [répéter] to keep churning out - 2. fig [mécontentement] to dwell on.

ressemblance [rəsɑ̃blɑ̃s] nf [gén] resemblance, likeness ; [trait] resemblance.

ressemblant, e [rəsɑ̃blɑ̃, ɑ̃t] adj lifelike.

ressembler [3] [rəsɑ̃ble] vi : **ressembler à** [physiquement] to resemble, to look like ; [moralement] to be like, to resemble ; **cela ne lui ressemble pas** that's not like him. ▪ **se ressembler** vp to look alike, to resemble each other.

ressemeler [24] [rəsəmle] vt to resole.

ressentiment [rəsɑ̃timɑ̃] nm resentment.

ressentir [37] [rəsɑ̃tir] vt to feel.

resserrer [4] [rəsere] vt 1. [ceinture, boulon] to tighten - 2. fig [lien] to strengthen. ▪ **se resserrer** vp 1. [route] to (become) narrow - 2. [nœud, étreinte] to tighten - 3. fig [relations] to grow stronger, to strengthen.

resservir [38] [rəservir] <> vt 1. [plat] to serve again ; fig [histoire] to trot out - 2. [personne] to give another helping to. <> vi to be used again. ▪ **se resservir** vp : **se resservir de qqch** [ustensile] to use sthg again ; [plat] to take another helping of sthg.

ressort [rəsɔr] nm 1. [mécanisme] spring - 2. fig [énergie] spirit - 3. fig [compétence] : **être du ressort de qqn** to be sb's area of responsibility, to come under sb's jurisdiction. ▪ **en dernier ressort** loc adv in the last resort, as a last resort.

ressortir [43] [rəsɔrtir] <> vi (v aux : être) 1. [personne] to go out again - 2. fig [couleur] : **ressortir (sur)** to stand out (against) ; **faire ressortir** to highlight - 3. fig [résulter de] : **ressortir de** to emerge from. <> vt (v aux : être) to take OU get OU bring out again.

ressortissant, e [rəsɔrtisɑ̃, ɑ̃t] nm, f national.

ressource [rəsurs] nf resort ; **votre seule ressource est de...** the only course open to you is to... **ressources** *nfpl* **1.** [financières] means - **2.** [énergétiques, de langue] resources ; **ressources naturelles** natural resources - **3.** [de personne] resourcefulness *(U)*.

ressurgir [32] [rəsyrʒir] *vi* to reappear.

ressusciter [3] [resysite] *vi* to rise (from the dead) ; *fig* to revive.

restant, e [restã, ãt] *adj* remaining, left. **restant** *nm* rest, remainder.

restaurant [restorã] *nm* restaurant ; **manger au restaurant** to eat out ; **restaurant d'entreprise** staff canteen *UK* ou cafeteria *US* ; **restaurant universitaire** ≃ university cafeteria ou refectory.

restaurateur, trice [restoratœr, tris] *nm, f* **1.** CULIN restaurant owner - **2.** ART restorer.

restauration [restorasjõ] *nf* **1.** CULIN restaurant business ; **restauration rapide** fast food - **2.** ART & POLIT restoration.

restaurer [3] [restore] *vt* to restore. **se restaurer** *vp* to have something to eat.

reste [rest] *nm* **1.** [de lait, temps] : **le reste (de)** the rest (of) - **2.** MATH remainder. **restes** *nmpl* **1.** [de repas] leftovers - **2.** [de mort] remains. **au reste, du reste** *loc adv* besides.

rester [3] [reste] *vi* **1.** [dans lieu, état] to stay, to remain ; **restez calme!** stay ou keep calm! - **2.** [subsister] to remain, to be left ; **le seul bien qui me reste** the only thing I have left - **3.** [s'arrêter] : **en rester à qqch** to stop at sthg ; **en rester là** to finish there ; **y rester** *fam* [mourir] to pop one's clogs *UK*. *v impers* : **il en reste un peu** there's still a little left ; **il te reste de l'argent?** do you still have some money left?

restituer [7] [restitɥe] *vt* **1.** [objet volé] to return, to restore ; [argent] to refund, to return - **2.** [énergie] to release - **3.** [son] to reproduce.

resto [resto] *nm fam* restaurant ; **les restos du cœur** *charity food distribution centres* ; **resto-U** UNIV university refectory, cafeteria.

Restoroute® [restorut] *nm* motorway cafe *UK*, highway restaurant *US*.

restreindre [81] [restrẽdr] *vt* to restrict. **se restreindre** *vp* **1.** [domaine, champ] to narrow - **2.** [personne] to cut back ; **se restreindre dans qqch** to restrict sthg.

restreint, e [restrẽ, ẽt] *pp* ► **restreindre**.

restrictif, ive [restriktif, iv] *adj* restrictive.

restriction [restriksjõ] *nf* **1.** [condition] condition ; **sans restriction** unconditionally - **2.** [limitation] restriction. **restrictions** *nfpl* [alimentaires] rationing *(U)*.

restructurer [3] [rəstryktyre] *vt* to restructure.

résultat [rezylta] *nm* result ; [d'action] outcome.

résulter [3] [rezylte] *vi* : **résulter de** to be the result of, to result from. *v impers* : **il en résulte que...** as a result,...

résumé [rezyme] *nm* summary, résumé ; **en résumé** [pour conclure] to sum up ; [en bref] in brief, summarized.

résumer [3] [rezyme] *vt* to summarize. **se résumer** *vp* [se réduire] : **se résumer à qqch/à faire qqch** to come down to sthg/to doing sthg.

résurgence [rezyrʒãs] *nf* resurgence.

résurrection [rezyrɛksjõ] *nf* resurrection.

rétablir [32] [retablir] *vt* **1.** [gén] to restore ; [malade] to restore (to health) - **2.** [communications, contact] to re-establish. **se rétablir** *vp* **1.** [silence] to return, to be restored - **2.** [malade] to recover - **3.** [gymnastique] to pull o.s. up.

rétablissement [retablismã] *nm* **1.** [d'ordre] restoration - **2.** [de communications] re-establishment - **3.** [de malade] recovery - **4.** [gymnastique] pull-up.

retard [rətar] *nm* **1.** [délai] delay ; **être en retard** [sur heure] to be late ; [sur échéance] to be behind ; **avoir du retard** to be late ou delayed - **2.** [de pays, peuple, personne] backwardness.

retardataire [rətardatɛr] *nmf* [en retard] latecomer.

retardement [rətardəmã] *nm* : **à retardement** belatedly ; *voir aussi* **bombe**.

retarder [3] [rətarde] *vt* **1.** [personne, train] to delay ; [sur échéance] to put back - **2.** [ajourner - rendez-vous] to put back ou off ; [- départ] to put back ou off, to delay - **3.** [montre] to put back. *vi* **1.** [horloge] to be slow - **2.** *fam* [ne pas être au courant] to be behind the times - **3.** [être en décalage] : **retarder sur** to be out of step ou tune with.

retenir [40] [rətnir] *vt* **1.** [physiquement - objet, personne, cri] to hold back ; [- souffle] to hold ; **retenir qqn de faire qqch** to stop ou restrain sb from doing sthg - **2.** [retarder] to keep, to detain - **3.** [montant, impôt] to keep back, to withhold - **4.** [chambre] to reserve - **5.** [leçon, cours] to remember - **6.** [projet] to accept, to adopt - **7.** [eau, chaleur] to retain - **8.** MATH to carry - **9.** [intérêt, attention] to hold. **se retenir** *vp* **1.** [s'accrocher] : **se retenir à** to hold onto - **2.** [se contenir] to hold on ; **se retenir de faire qqch** to refrain from doing sthg.

rétention [retãsjõ] *nf* MÉD retention.

retentir [32] [rətãtir] *vi* **1.** [son] to ring (out) - **2.** [pièce, rue] : **retentir de** to resound with - **3.** *fig* [fatigue, blessure] : **retentir sur** to have an effect on.

retentissant, e [rətɑ̃tisɑ̃, ɑ̃t] *adj* resounding.

retentissement [rətɑ̃tismɑ̃] *nm* [de mesure] repercussions *pl.*

retenu, e [rətny] *pp* ► retenir.

retenue [rətny] *nf* 1. [prélèvement] deduction - 2. MATH amount carried - 3. SCOL detention - 4. *fig* [de personne - dans relations] reticence ; [- dans comportement] restraint ; **sans retenue** without restraint.

réticence [retisɑ̃s] *nf* [hésitation] hesitation, reluctance ; **avec réticence** hesitantly.

réticent, e [retisɑ̃, ɑ̃t] *adj* hesitant, reluctant.

rétine [retin] *nf* retina.

retiré, e [rətire] *adj* [lieu] remote, isolated ; [vie] quiet.

retirer [3] [rətire] *vt* 1. [vêtement, emballage] to take off, to remove ; [permis, jouet] to take away ; **retirer qqch à qqn** to take sthg away from sb - 2. [plainte] to withdraw, to take back - 3. [avantages, bénéfices] : **retirer qqch de qqch** to get ou derive sthg from sthg - 4. [bagages, billet] to collect ; [argent] to withdraw. ◆ **se retirer** *vp* 1. [s'isoler] to withdraw, to retreat - 2. [des affaires] : **se retirer (de)** to retire (from) - 3. [refluer] to recede.

retombées [rətɔ̃be] *nfpl* repercussions, fallout *sg.*

retomber [3] [rətɔ̃be] *vi* 1. [gymnaste, chat] to land - 2. [redevenir] : **retomber malade** to relapse - 3. *fig* [colère] to die away - 4. [cheveux] to hang down - 5. *fig* [responsabilité] : **retomber sur** to fall on - 6. [dans un état] to fall back, to lapse *sout.*

rétorquer [3] [rətɔrke] *vt* to retort ; **rétorquer à qqn que...** to retort to sb that...

retors, e [rətɔr, ɔrs] *adj* wily.

rétorsion [retɔrsjɔ̃] *nf* retaliation ; **mesures de rétorsion** reprisals.

retouche [rətuʃ] *nf* 1. [de texte, vêtement] alteration - 2. ART & PHOTO touching up.

retoucher [3] [rətuʃe] *vt* 1. [texte, vêtement] to alter - 2. ART & PHOTO to touch up.

retour [rətur] *nm* 1. [gén] return ; **à mon/ton retour** when I/you get back, on my/your return ; **être de retour (de)** to be back (from) ; **retour en arrière** flashback ; **en retour** in return - 2. [trajet] journey back, return journey.

retourner [3] [rəturne] ◇ *vt (v aux : être)* 1. [carte, matelas] to turn over - 2. [terre] to turn (over) - 3. [compliment, objet prêté] : **retourner qqch (à qqn)** to return sthg (to sb) - 3. [lettre, colis] to send back, to return - 4. *fam fig* [personne] to shake up. ◇ *vi (v aux : être)* to come/go back ; **retourner en arrière** ou **sur ses pas** to retrace one's steps.

◆ **se retourner** *vp* 1. [basculer] to turn over - 2. [pivoter] to turn round UK ou around US - 3. *fam fig* [s'adapter] to sort o.s. out UK - 4. [rentrer] : **s'en retourner** to go back (home) - 5. *fig* [s'opposer] : **se retourner contre** to turn against.

retracer [16] [rətrase] *vt* 1. [ligne] to redraw - 2. [événement] to relate.

rétracter [3] [retrakte] *vt* to retract. ◆ **se rétracter** *vp* 1. [se contracter] to retract - 2. [se dédire] to back down.

retrait [rətrɛ] *nm* 1. [gén] withdrawal ; **retrait du permis** disqualification from driving - 2. BANQUE : **faire un retrait** to withdraw money - 3. [de bagages] collection - 4. [des eaux] ebbing. ◆ **en retrait** *loc adj & loc adv* 1. [maison] set back from the road ; **rester en retrait** *fig* to hang back - 2. [texte] indented.

retraite [rətrɛt] *nf* 1. [gén] retreat - 2. [cessation d'activité] retirement ; **être à la retraite** to be retired ; **retraite complémentaire** supplementary pension - 3. [revenu] (retirement) pension.

retraité, e [rətrete] ◇ *adj* 1. [personne] retired - 2. TECHNOL reprocessed. ◇ *nm, f* retired person, pensioner UK.

retrancher [3] [rətrɑ̃ʃe] *vt* 1. [passage] : **retrancher qqch (de)** to cut sthg out (from), to remove sthg (from) - 2. [montant] : **retrancher qqch (de)** to take sthg away (from), to deduct sthg (from). ◆ **se retrancher** *vp* to entrench o.s. ; **se retrancher derrière/dans** *fig* to take refuge behind/in.

retransmettre [84] [rətrɑ̃smɛtr] *vt* to broadcast.

retransmis, e [rətrɑ̃smi, iz] *pp* ► retransmettre.

retransmission [rətrɑ̃smisjɔ̃] *nf* broadcast.

retravailler [3] [rətravaje] ◇ *vt* : **retravailler qqch** to work on sthg again. ◇ *vi* to start work again.

rétrécir [32] [retresir] *vi* [tissu] to shrink.

rétrécissement [retresismɑ̃] *nm* 1. [de vêtement] shrinkage - 2. MÉD stricture.

rétribution [retribysjɔ̃] *nf* remuneration.

rétro [retro] ◇ *nm* 1. [style] old style ou fashion - 2. *fam* [rétroviseur] rearview mirror. ◇ *adj inv* old-style.

rétroactif, ive [retroaktif, iv] *adj* retrospective.

rétrograde [retrograd] *adj péj* reactionary.

rétrograder [3] [retrograde] ◇ *vt* to demote. ◇ *vi* AUTO to change down UK, to downshift US.

rétroprojecteur [retroprɔʒɛktœr] *nm* overhead projector.

rétrospectif, ive [retrɔspɛktif, iv] *adj* retrospective. ➤ **rétrospective** *nf* retrospective.

rétrospectivement [retrɔspɛktivmɑ̃] *adv* retrospectively.

retrousser [3] [rətruse] *vt* **1.** [manches, pantalon] to roll up - **2.** [lèvres] to curl.

retrouvailles [rətruvaj] *nfpl* reunion *sg.*

retrouver [3] [rətruve] *vt* **1.** [gén] to find ; [appétit] to recover, to regain - **2.** [reconnaître] to recognize - **3.** [ami] to meet, to see. ➤ **se retrouver** *vp* **1.** [entre amis] to meet (up) again ; **on se retrouve au café?** shall we meet up ou see each other at the café? - **2.** [être de nouveau] to find o.s. again - **3.** [par hasard] to end up - **4.** [s'orienter] to find one's way ; **ne pas s'y retrouver** [dans ses papiers] to be completely lost - **5.** [erreur, style] to be found, to crop up - **6.** [financièrement] : **s'y retrouver** *fam* to break even.

rétroviseur [retrɔvizœr] *nm* rearview mirror.

réunification [reynifikasjɔ̃] *nf* reunification.

réunifier [9] [reynifje] *vt* to reunify.

réunion [reynjɔ̃] *nf* **1.** [séance] meeting - **2.** [jonction] union, merging - **3.** [d'amis, de famille] reunion - **4.** SPORT meeting.

Réunion [reynjɔ̃] *nf* : **(l'île de) la Réunion** Réunion.

réunir [32] [reynir] *vt* **1.** [fonds] to collect - **2.** [extrémités] to put together, to bring together - **3.** [qualités] to combine - **4.** [personnes] to bring together ; [après séparation] to reunite. ➤ **se réunir** *vp* **1.** [personnes] to meet - **2.** [entreprises] to combine ; [états] to unite - **3.** [fleuves, rues] to converge.

réussi, e [reysi] *adj* successful ; **c'est réussi!** *fig & iron* congratulations!, well done!

réussir [32] [reysir] ◇ *vi* **1.** [personne, affaire] to succeed, to be a success ; **réussir à faire qqch** to succeed in doing sthg - **2.** [convenir] : **réussir à** to agree with. ◇ *vt* **1.** [portrait, plat] to make a success of - **2.** [examen] to pass.

réussite [reysit] *nf* **1.** [succès] success - **2.** [jeu de cartes] patience *UK*, solitaire *US*.

réutiliser [3] [reytilize] *vt* to reuse.

revaloriser [3] [rəvalɔrize] *vt* [monnaie] to revalue ; [salaires] to raise ; *fig* [idée, doctrine] to rehabilitate.

revanche [rəvɑ̃ʃ] *nf* **1.** [vengeance] revenge ; **prendre sa revanche** to take one's revenge - **2.** SPORT return (match). ➤ **en revanche** *loc adv* [par contre] on the other hand.

rêvasser [3] [rɛvase] *vi* to daydream.

rêve [rɛv] *nm* dream.

rêvé, e [rɛve] *adj* ideal.

revêche [rəvɛʃ] *adj* surly.

réveil [revɛj] *nm* **1.** [de personne] waking (up) ; *fig* awakening - **2.** [pendule] alarm clock.

réveiller [4] [reveje] *vt* **1.** [personne] to wake up - **2.** [courage] to revive. ➤ **se réveiller** *vp* **1.** [personne] to wake (up) - **2.** [ambitions] to reawaken.

réveillon [revɛjɔ̃] *nm* [jour - de Noël] Christmas Eve ; [- de nouvel an] New Year's Eve.

réveillonner [3] [revɛjɔne] *vi* to have a Christmas Eve/New Year's Eve meal.

révélateur, trice [revelatœr, tris] *adj* revealing. ➤ **révélateur** *nm* PHOTO developer ; *fig* [ce qui révèle] indication.

révélation [revelasjɔ̃] *nf* **1.** [gén] revelation - **2.** [artiste] discovery.

révéler [18] [revele] *vt* **1.** [gén] to reveal - **2.** [artiste] to discover. ➤ **se révéler** *vp* **1.** [apparaître] to be revealed - **2.** [s'avérer] to prove to be.

revenant [rəvnɑ̃] *nm* **1.** [fantôme] spirit, ghost - **2.** *fam* [personne] stranger.

revendeur, euse [rəvɑ̃dœr, øz] *nm, f* retailer.

revendication [rəvɑ̃dikasjɔ̃] *nf* claim, demand.

revendiquer [3] [rəvɑ̃dike] *vt* [dû, responsabilité] to claim ; [avec force] to demand.

revendre [73] [rəvɑ̃dr] *vt* **1.** [après utilisation] to resell - **2.** [vendre plus de] to sell more of.

revendu, e [rəvɑ̃dy] *pp* ➤ **revendre**.

revenir [40] [rəvnir] *vi* **1.** [gén] to come back, to return ; **revenir de** to come back from, to return from ; **revenir à** to come back to, to return to ; **revenir sur** [sujet] to go over again ; [décision] to go back on ; **revenir à soi** to come to - **2.** [mot, sujet] to crop up - **3.** [à l'esprit] : **revenir à** to come back to - **4.** [impliquer] : **cela revient au même/à dire que...** it amounts to the same thing/to saying (that)... - **5.** [coûter] : **revenir à** to come to, to amount to ; **revenir cher** to be expensive - **6.** [honneur, tâche] : **revenir à** to fall to ; **c'est à lui qu'il revient de...** it is up to him to... - **7.** CULIN : **faire revenir** to brown ; **sa tête ne me revient pas** I don't like the look of him/her ; **il n'en revenait pas** he couldn't get over it.

revente [rəvɑ̃t] *nf* resale.

revenu, e [rəvny] *pp* ➤ **revenir**. ➤ **revenu** *nm* [de pays] revenue ; [de personne] income.

rêver [4] [rɛve] ◇ *vi* to dream ; [rêvasser] to daydream ; **rêver de/à** to dream of/about. ◇ *vt* to dream ; **rêver que** to dream (that).

réverbération [reverberasjɔ̃] *nf* reverberation.

réverbère [reverber] *nm* street lamp OU light.

révérence [reverɑ̃s] *nf* 1. [salut] bow - 2. *litt* [déférence] reverence.

révérend, e [reverɑ̃, ɑ̃d] *adj* reverend.
◆ **révérend** *nm* reverend.

révérer [18] [revere] *vt* to revere.

rêverie [revri] *nf* reverie.

revers [rəver] *nm* 1. [de main] back ; [de pièce] reverse - 2. [de veste] lapel ; [de pantalon] turn-up UK, cuff US - 3. TENNIS backhand - 4. *fig* [de fortune] reversal.

reverser [3] [rəverse] *vt* 1. [liquide] to pour out more of - 2. FIN : reverser qqch sur to pay sthg into.

réversible [reversibl] *adj* reversible.

revêtement [rəvɛtmɑ̃] *nm* surface.

revêtir [44] [rəvetir] *vt* 1. [mur, surface] : revêtir (de) to cover (with) - 2. [aspect] to take on, to assume - 3. [vêtement] to put on ; [personne] to dress.

revêtu, e [rəvety] *pp* ▶ revêtir.

rêveur, euse [revœr, øz] ◇ *adj* dreamy. ◇ *nm, f* dreamer.

revient [rəvjɛ̃] ▶ prix.

revigorer [3] [rəvigɔre] *vt* to invigorate.

revirement [rəvirmɑ̃] *nm* [gén] change.

réviser [3] [revize] *vt* 1. [réexaminer, modifier] to revise, to review - 2. SCOL to revise UK, to review US - 3. [machine] to check.

révision [revizjɔ̃] *nf* 1. [réexamen, modification] revision, review - 2. [de machine] checkup.

revisser [3] [rəvise] *vt* to screw back again.

revivre [90] [rəvivr] ◇ *vi* [personne] to come back to life, to revive ; *fig* [espoir] to be revived, to revive ; faire revivre to revive. ◇ *vt* to relive ; faire revivre qqch à qqn to bring sthg back to sb.

revoici [rəvwasi] *prép* : me revoici! it's me again!, I'm back!

revoir [62] [rəvwar] *vt* 1. [renouer avec] to see again - 2. [corriger, étudier] to revise UK, to review US. ◆ **se revoir** *vp* [amis] to see each other again ; [professionnellement] to meet again. ◆ **au revoir** *interj & nm* goodbye.

révoltant, e [revɔltɑ̃, ɑ̃t] *adj* revolting.

révolte [revɔlt] *nf* revolt.

révolter [3] [revɔlte] *vt* to disgust. ◆ **se révolter** *vp* : se révolter (contre) to revolt (against).

révolu, e [revɔly] *adj* past ; avoir 15 ans révolus ADMIN to be over 15.

révolution [revɔlysjɔ̃] *nf* 1. [gén] revolution ; la Révolution française the French Revolution - 2. *fam* [effervescence] uproar.

révolutionnaire [revɔlysjɔner] *nmf & adj* revolutionary.

révolutionner [3] [revɔlysjɔne] *vt* 1. [transformer] to revolutionize - 2. [mettre en émoi] to stir up.

revolver [revɔlver] *nm* revolver.

révoquer [3] [revɔke] *vt* 1. [fonctionnaire] to dismiss - 2. [loi] to revoke.

revue [rəvy] *nf* 1. [gén] review ; revue de presse press review ; passer en revue *fig* to review - 2. [défilé] march-past - 3. [magazine] magazine - 4. [spectacle] revue.

rez-de-chaussée [redʃose] *nm inv* ground floor UK, first floor US.

RFA (*abr de* République fédérale d'Allemagne) *nf* FRG.

rhabiller [3] [rabije] *vt* to dress again. ◆ **se rhabiller** *vp* to get dressed again.

rhésus [rezys] *nm* rhesus (factor) ; rhésus positif/négatif rhesus positive/negative.

rhétorique [retɔrik] *nf* rhetoric.

Rhin [rɛ̃] *nm* : le Rhin the Rhine.

rhinocéros [rinɔserɔs] *nm* rhinoceros.

rhino-pharyngite [rinɔfarɛ̃ʒit] (*pl* rhino-pharyngites) *nf* throat infection.

rhododendron [rɔdɔdɛ̃drɔ̃] *nm* rhododendron.

Rhône [ron] *nm* : le Rhône the (River) Rhône.

rhubarbe [rybarb] *nf* rhubarb.

rhum [rɔm] *nm* rum.

rhumatisme [rymatism] *nm* rheumatism.

rhume [rym] *nm* cold ; attraper un rhume to catch a cold ; rhume des foins hay fever.

ri [ri] *pp inv* ▶ rire.

riant, e [rijɑ̃, ɑ̃t] *adj* smiling ; *fig* cheerful.

RIB, Rib [rib] (*abr de* relevé d'identité bancaire) *nm bank account identification slip.*

ribambelle [ribɑ̃bɛl] *nf* : ribambelle de string of.

ricaner [3] [rikane] *vi* to snigger.

riche [riʃ] ◇ *adj* 1. [gén] rich ; [personne, pays] rich, wealthy ; riche en OU de rich in - 2. [idée] great. ◇ *nmf* rich person ; les riches the rich.

richesse [riʃes] *nf* 1. [de personne, pays] wealth (U) - 2. [de faune, flore] abundance. ◆ **richesses** *nfpl* [gén] wealth (U).

ricochet [rikɔʃe] *nm litt & fig* rebound ; [de balle d'arme] ricochet ; par ricochet in an indirect way.

rictus [riktys] *nm* rictus.

ride [rid] *nf* wrinkle ; [de surface d'eau] ripple.

rideau, x [rido] *nm* curtain, drape *US* ;
rideau de fer [frontière] Iron Curtain.

rider [3] [ride] *vt* **1.** [peau] to wrinkle
- **2.** [surface] to ruffle. ◆ **se rider** *vp* to
become wrinkled.

ridicule [ridikyl] ◇ *adj* ridiculous.
◇ *nm* : **se couvrir de ridicule** to make o.s.
look ridiculous ; **tourner qqn/qqch en ridicule** to ridicule sb/sthg.

ridiculiser [3] [ridikylize] *vt* to ridicule.
◆ **se ridiculiser** *vp* to make o.s. look
ridiculous.

rien [rjɛ̃] ◇ *pron indéf* **1.** [en contexte
négatif] : **ne... rien** nothing, not... anything ;
je n'ai rien fait I've done nothing, I haven't
done anything ; **je n'en sais rien** I don't
know (anything about it), I know nothing
about it ; **rien ne m'intéresse** nothing
interests me ; **il n'y a plus rien dans le
réfrigérateur** there's nothing left in the
fridge - **2.** [aucune chose] nothing ; **que
fais-tu?** rien what are you doing? nothing ;
rien de nouveau nothing new ; **rien d'autre**
nothing else ; **rien du tout** nothing at all ;
rien à faire it's no good ; **rien! don't
mention it!, not at all!** ; **pour rien** for
nothing - **3.** [quelque chose] anything ; **sans
rien dire** without saying anything. ◇ *nm* :
pour un rien [se fâcher, pleurer] for nothing,
at the slightest thing ; **perdre son temps à
des riens** to waste one's time with trivia ;
en un rien de temps in no time at all.
◆ **rien que** *loc adv* only, just ; **la vérité,
rien que la vérité** the truth and nothing but
the truth ; **rien que l'idée des vacances la
comblait** just thinking about the holiday
filled her with joy.

rieur, rieuse [rijœr, rijøz] *adj* cheerful.

rigide [riʒid] *adj* rigid ; [muscle] tense.

rigidité [riʒidite] *nf* rigidity ; [de muscle]
tenseness ; [de principes, mœurs] strictness.

rigole [rigɔl] *nf* channel.

rigoler [3] [rigɔle] *vi fam* **1.** [rire] to laugh
- **2.** [plaisanter] : **rigoler (de)** to joke (about).

rigolo, ote [rigɔlo, ɔt] *fam* ◇ *adj* funny.
◇ *nm, f péj* phoney *UK*, phony *US*.

rigoureux, euse [rigurø, øz] *adj* **1.** [disci-
pline, hiver] harsh - **2.** [analyse] rigorous.

rigueur [rigœr] *nf* **1.** [de punition] severity,
harshness - **2.** [de climat] harshness
- **3.** [d'analyse] rigour *UK*, rigor *US*, exact-
ness. ◆ **à la rigueur** *loc adv* if necessary,
if need be.

rime [rim] *nf* rhyme.

rimer [3] [rime] *vi* : **rimer (avec)** to rhyme
(with).

rinçage [rɛ̃saʒ] *nm* rinsing.

rincer [16] [rɛ̃se] *vt* [bouteille] to rinse out ;
[cheveux, linge] to rinse.

ring [riŋ] *nm* **1.** [boxe] ring - **2.** *Belgique*
[route] bypass.

riposte [ripɔst] *nf* **1.** [réponse] retort, riposte - **2.** [contre-attaque] counterattack.

riposter [3] [ripɔste] ◇ *vt* : **riposter que**
to retort ou riposte that. ◇ *vi* **1.** [répondre]
to riposte - **2.** [contre-attaquer] to counter,
to retaliate.

rire [95] [rir] ◇ *nm* laugh ; **éclater de rire**
to burst out laughing. ◇ *vi* **1.** [gén] to
laugh - **2.** [plaisanter] : **pour rire** *fam* as a
joke, for a laugh.

risée [rize] *nf* ridicule ; **être la risée de** to be
the laughingstock of.

risible [rizibl] *adj* [ridicule] ridiculous.

risque [risk] *nm* risk ; **prendre des risques**
to take risks ; **à tes/vos risques et périls** at
your own risk.

risqué, e [riske] *adj* **1.** [entreprise] risky,
dangerous - **2.** [plaisanterie] risqué, daring.

risquer [3] [riske] *vt* **1.** [vie, prison] to risk ;
risquer de faire qqch to be likely to do sthg ;
je risque de perdre tout ce que j'ai I'm
running the risk of losing everything I
have ; **cela ne risque rien** it will be all right
- **2.** [tenter] to venture. ◆ **se risquer** *vp*
to venture ; **se risquer à faire qqch** to dare
to do sthg.

rissoler [3] [risɔle] *vi* to brown.

rite [rit] *nm* **1.** RELIG rite - **2.** *fig* [cérémonial]
ritual.

rituel, elle [rituɛl] *adj* ritual. ◆ **rituel**
nm ritual.

rivage [rivaʒ] *nm* shore.

rival, e, aux [rival, o] ◇ *adj* rival (avant
n). ◇ *nm, f* rival.

rivaliser [3] [rivalize] *vi* : **rivaliser avec** to
compete with.

rivalité [rivalite] *nf* rivalry.

rive [riv] *nf* [de rivière] bank ; **la rive droite**
[à Paris] the north bank of the Seine
(*generally considered more affluent than the south
bank*) ; **la rive gauche** [à Paris] the south
bank of the Seine (*generally associated with
students and artists*).

river [3] [rive] *vt* **1.** [fixer] : **river qqch à qqch**
to rivet sthg to sthg - **2.** [clou] to clinch ;
être rivé à *fig* to be riveted ou glued to.

riverain, e [rivrɛ̃, ɛn] *nm, f* resident.

rivet [rivɛ] *nm* rivet.

rivière [rivjɛr] *nf* river.

rixe [riks] *nf* fight, brawl.

riz [ri] *nm* rice.

rizière [rizjɛr] *nf* paddy (field).

RMI (*abr de* revenu minimum d'insertion)
*nm minimum guaranteed income (for people with
no other source of income).*

robe [rɔb] *nf* **1.** [de femme] dress ; robe de

mariée wedding dress - **2.** [peignoir] : **robe de chambre** dressing gown *UK*, (bath)robe *US* - **3.** [de cheval] coat - **4.** [de vin] colour *UK*, color *US*.

robinet [rɔbinɛ] *nm* tap *UK*, faucet *US*.

robinetterie [rɔbinɛtri] *nf* [installations] taps *(pl) UK*, faucets *(pl) US*.

robot [rɔbo] *nm* **1.** [gén] robot - **2.** [ménager] food processor.

robotique [rɔbɔtik] *nf* robotics *(U)*.

robotisation [rɔbɔtizasjɔ̃] *nf* automation, robotization *US*.

robuste [rɔbyst] *adj* **1.** [personne, santé] robust - **2.** [plante] hardy - **3.** [voiture] sturdy.

roc [rɔk] *nm* rock.

rocade [rɔkad] *nf* bypass.

rocaille [rɔkaj] *nf* **1.** [cailloux] loose stones *pl* - **2.** [dans un jardin] rockery.

rocailleux, euse [rɔkajø, øz] *adj* **1.** [terrain] rocky - **2.** *fig* [voix] harsh.

rocambolesque [rɔkɑ̃bɔlɛsk] *adj* fantastic.

roche [rɔʃ] *nf* rock.

rocher [rɔʃe] *nm* rock.

rocheux, euse [rɔʃø, øz] *adj* rocky. **➤ Rocheuses** *nfpl* : **les Rocheuses** the Rockies.

rock [rɔk] *nm* rock ('n' roll).

rodage [rɔdaʒ] *nm* **1.** [de véhicule] running in *UK*, break in *US* ; **en rodage** running in *UK* - **2.** *fig* [de méthode] running-in *UK* ou breaking-in *US* ou debugging period.

rodéo [rɔdeo] *nm* rodeo ; *fig & iron* free-for-all.

roder [3] [rɔde] *vt* **1.** [véhicule] to run in *UK*, to break in *US* - **2.** *fam* [méthode] to run in *UK*, to break in *US*, to debug ; [personne] to break in.

rôdeur, euse [rɔdœr, øz] *nm, f* prowler.

rogne [rɔɲ] *nf fam* bad temper ; **être/se mettre en rogne** to be in/to get into a bad mood, to be in/to get into a temper.

rogner [3] [rɔɲe] <> *vt* **1.** [ongles] to trim - **2.** [revenus] to eat into. <> *vi* : **rogner sur qqch** to cut down on sthg.

roi [rwa] *nm* king ; **tirer les rois** to celebrate Epiphany.

rôle [rol] *nm* role, part ; **jeu de rôle** role play.

roller [rɔlœr, rɔlɛr] *nm* [sport] rollerblading ; **les rollers** [patins] Rollerblades® ; **faire du roller** to go rollerblading, to rollerblade.

romain, e [rɔmɛ̃, ɛn] *adj* Roman. **➤ Romain, e** *nm, f* Roman.

roman, e [rɔmɑ̃, an] *adj* **1.** [langue] Romance - **2.** ARCHIT Romanesque. **➤ roman** *nm* LITTÉR novel.

romance [rɔmɑ̃s] *nf* [chanson] love song.

romancier, ère [rɔmɑ̃sje, ɛr] *nm, f* novelist.

romanesque [rɔmanɛsk] *adj* **1.** LITTÉR novelistic - **2.** [aventure] fabulous, storybook *(avant n)*.

roman-feuilleton [rɔmɑ̃fœjtɔ̃] *nm* serial ; *fig* soap opera.

roman-photo [rɔmɑ̃fɔto] *nm* story told in photographs.

romantique [rɔmɑ̃tik] *nmf & adj* romantic.

romantisme [rɔmɑ̃tism] *nm* **1.** ART Romantic movement - **2.** [sensibilité] romanticism.

romarin [rɔmarɛ̃] *nm* rosemary.

rompre [78] [rɔ̃pr] <> *vt* **1.** *sout* [objet] to break - **2.** [charme, marché] to break ; [fiançailles, relations] to break off. <> *vi* to break ; **rompre avec qqn** *fig* to break up with sb. **➤ se rompre** *vp* to break ; **se rompre le cou/les reins** to break one's neck/back.

ronce [rɔ̃s] *nf* [arbuste] bramble.

ronchonner [3] [rɔ̃ʃɔne] *vi fam* **ronchonner (après)** to grumble (at).

rond, e [rɔ̃, rɔ̃d] *adj* **1.** [forme, chiffre] round - **2.** [joue, ventre] chubby, plump - **3.** *fam* [ivre] tight. **➤ rond** *nm* **1.** [cercle] circle ; **en rond** in a circle ou ring ; **tourner en rond** *fig* to go round in circles - **2.** [anneau] ring - **3.** *fam* [argent] : **je n'ai pas un rond** I haven't got a penny ou bean.

ronde [rɔ̃d] *nf* **1.** [de surveillance] rounds *pl* ; [de policier] beat - **2.** [danse] round - **3.** MUS semibreve *UK*, whole note *US*. **➤ à la ronde** *loc adv* : **à des kilomètres à la ronde** for miles around.

rondelle [rɔ̃dɛl] *nf* **1.** [de saucisson] slice - **2.** [de métal] washer.

rondement [rɔ̃dmɑ̃] *adv* [efficacement] efficiently, briskly.

rondeur [rɔ̃dœr] *nf* **1.** [forme] roundness - **2.** [partie charnue] curve.

rond-point [rɔ̃pwɛ̃] *nm* roundabout *UK*, traffic circle *US*.

ronflant, e [rɔ̃flɑ̃, ɑ̃t] *adj péj* grandiose.

ronflement [rɔ̃fləmɑ̃] *nm* **1.** [de dormeur] snore - **2.** [de poêle, moteur] hum, purr.

ronfler [3] [rɔ̃fle] *vi* **1.** [dormeur] to snore - **2.** [poêle, moteur] to hum, to purr.

ronger [17] [rɔ̃ʒe] *vt* [bois, os] to gnaw ; [métal, falaise] to eat away at ; *fig* to gnaw at, to eat away at. **➤ se ronger** *vp* **1.** [grignoter] : **se ronger les ongles** to bite one's nails - **2.** *fig* [se tourmenter] to worry, to torture o.s.

rongeur, euse [rɔ̃ʒœr, øz] *adj* gnawing, rodent *(avant n)*. **rongeur** *nm* rodent.

ronronner [3] [rɔ̃rɔne] *vi* [chat] to purr ; [moteur] to purr, to hum.

ROR [ɛroɛr ou rɔr] *(abr de rougeole oreillons rubéole) nm* MMR (vaccine).

rosace [rozas] *nf* **1.** [ornement] rose - **2.** [vitrail] rose window - **3.** [figure géométrique] rosette.

rosbif [rɔsbif] *nm* [viande] roast beef.

rose [roz] *nf* rose. *nm* pink. *adj* pink.

rosé, e [roze] *adj* [teinte] rosy. **rosé** *nm* rosé. **rosée** *nf* dew.

roseau, x [rozo] *nm* reed.

rosier [rozje] *nm* rose bush.

rosir [32] [rozir] *vt & vi* to turn pink.

rosser [3] [rɔse] *vt* to thrash.

rossignol [rɔsiɲɔl] *nm* [oiseau] nightingale.

rot [ro] *nm* burp.

rotatif, ive [rɔtatif, iv] *adj* rotary.

rotation [rɔtasjɔ̃] *nf* rotation.

roter [3] [rɔte] *vi fam* to burp.

rôti, e [roti] *adj* roast. **rôti** *nm* roast, joint *UK*.

rotin [rɔtɛ̃] *nm* rattan.

rôtir [32] [rotir] *vt* to roast. *vi* CULIN to roast.

rôtisserie [rotisri] *nf* **1.** [restaurant] ≃ steakhouse - **2.** [magasin] *shop selling roast meat.*

rotonde [rɔtɔ̃d] *nf* [bâtiment] rotunda.

rotule [rɔtyl] *nf* kneecap.

rouage [rwaʒ] *nm* cog, gearwheel ; **les rouages de l'État** *fig* the wheels of State.

rouble [rubl] *nm* rouble.

roucouler [3] [rukule] *vt* to warble ; *fig* to coo. *vi* to coo ; *fig* to bill and coo.

roue [ru] *nf* **1.** [gén] wheel ; **la grande roue** the big wheel *UK*, the Ferris wheel *US* ; **roue de secours** spare wheel ; **un deux roues** a two-wheeled vehicle - **2.** [de paon] : **faire la roue** to display - **3.** [gymnastique] cartwheel.

rouer [6] [rwe] *vt* : **rouer qqn de coups** to thrash sb, to beat sb.

rouge [ruʒ] *nm* **1.** [couleur] red - **2.** *fam* [vin] red (wine) - **3.** [fard] rouge, blusher ; **rouge à lèvres** lipstick - **4.** AUTO : **passer au rouge** to turn red ; [conducteur] to go through a red light. *nmf péj &* POLIT Red. *adj* **1.** [gén] red - **2.** [fer, tison] red-hot - **3.** *péj &* POLIT Red.

rouge-gorge [ruʒgɔrʒ] *nm* robin.

rougeole [ruʒɔl] *nf* measles *sg.*

rougeoyer [13] [ruʒwaje] *vi* to turn red.

rougeur [ruʒœr] *nf* **1.** [de visage, de chaleur, d'effort] flush ; [de gêne] blush - **2.** [sur peau] red spot ou blotch.

rougir [32] [ruʒir] *vt* **1.** [colorer] to turn red - **2.** [chauffer] to make red-hot. *vi* **1.** [devenir rouge] to turn red - **2.** [d'émotion] : **rougir (de)** [de plaisir, colère] to flush (with) ; [de gêne] to blush (with) - **3.** *fig* [avoir honte] : **rougir de qqch** to be ashamed of sthg.

rougissant, e [ruʒisɑ̃, ɑ̃t] *adj* [ciel] reddening ; [jeune fille] blushing.

rouille [ruj] *nf* **1.** [oxyde] rust - **2.** CULIN *spicy garlic sauce for fish soup.* *adj inv* rust.

rouiller [3] [ruje] *vt* to rust, to make rusty. *vi* to rust.

roulade [rulad] *nf* [galipette] roll.

rouleau, x [rulo] *nm* **1.** [gén & TECHNOL] roller ; **rouleau compresseur** steamroller - **2.** [de papier] roll - **3.** [à pâtisserie] rolling pin - **4.** CULIN : **rouleau de printemps** spring roll, egg roll *US*.

roulement [rulmɑ̃] *nm* **1.** [gén] rolling - **2.** [de personnel] rotation ; **travailler par roulement** to work to a rota *UK* - **3.** [de tambour, tonnerre] roll - **4.** TECHNOL· rolling bearing - **5.** FIN circulation.

rouler [3] [rule] *vt* **1.** [déplacer] to wheel - **2.** [enrouler - tapis] to roll up ; [- cigarette] to roll - **3.** *fam* [balancer] to sway - **4.** LING to roll - **5.** *fam fig* [duper] to swindle, to do *UK*. *vi* **1.** [ballon, bateau] to roll - **2.** [véhicule] to go, to run ; [suj: personne] to drive. **se rouler** *vp* to roll about ; **se rouler par terre** to roll on the ground ; **se rouler en boule** to roll o.s. into a ball.

roulette [rulɛt] *nf* **1.** [petite roue] castor - **2.** [de dentiste] drill - **3.** [jeux] roulette.

roulis [ruli] *nm* roll.

roulotte [rulɔt] *nf* [de gitan] caravan ; [de tourisme] caravan *UK*, trailer *US* ; *fig* : **vol à la roulotte** theft of goods in car.

roumain, e [rumɛ̃, ɛn] *adj* Romanian. **roumain** *nm* [langue] Romanian. **Roumain, e** *nm, f* Romanian.

Roumanie [rumani] *nf* : **la Roumanie** Romania.

rouquin, e [rukɛ̃, in] *fam* *adj* redheaded. *nm, f* redhead.

rouspéter [18] [ruspete] *vi fam* to grumble, to moan.

rousse ► **roux**.

rousseur [rusœr] *nf* redness. **taches de rousseur** *nfpl* freckles.

roussir [32] [rusir] *vt* **1.** [rendre roux] to turn brown ; CULIN to brown - **2.** [brûler légèrement] to singe. *vi* to turn brown ; CULIN to brown.

route [rut] *nf* **1.** [gén] road ; **en route** on the way ; **en route!** let's go! ; **mettre en route** [démarrer] to start up ; *fig* to get under way ; **route départementale** secondary road **- 2.** [itinéraire] route.

routier, ère [rutje, ɛr] *adj* road *(avant n)*. ➤ **routier** *nm* **1.** [chauffeur] long-distance lorry driver *UK* ou trucker *US* **- 2.** [restaurant] ≃ transport cafe *UK*, ≃ truck stop *US*.

routine [rutin] *nf* routine.

routinier, ère [rutinje, ɛr] *adj* routine.

rouvert, e [ruver, ɛrt] *pp* ➤ **rouvrir**.

rouvrir [34] [ruvrir] *vt* to reopen, to open again. ➤ **se rouvrir** *vp* to reopen, to open again.

roux, rousse [ru, rus] ◇ *adj* **1.** [cheveux] red **- 2.** [sucre] brown. ◇ *nm, f* [personne] redhead. ➤ **roux** *nm* [couleur] red, russet.

royal, e, aux [rwajal, o] *adj* **1.** [de roi] royal **- 2.** [magnifique] princely.

royaliste [rwajalist] *nmf & adj* royalist.

royaume [rwajom] *nm* kingdom.

Royaume-Uni [rwajomyni] *nm* : **le Royaume-Uni** the United Kingdom.

royauté [rwajote] *nf* **1.** [fonction] kingship **- 2.** [régime] monarchy.

RPR *(abr de* **Rassemblement pour la République)** *nm* French political party to the right of the political spectrum.

rte *abr écrite de* **route.**

RTT [ɛrtete] *(abr de* **réduction du temps de travail)** ◇ *nf* (statutory) reduction in working hours. ◇ *nm* (extra) day off *(as a result of shorter working hours)* ; **poser/prendre un RTT** to book ou claim a day's holiday, to take a day off *US*.

ruade [ryad] *nf* kick.

ruban [rybã] *nm* ribbon ; **ruban adhésif** adhesive tape.

rubéole [rybeɔl] *nf* German measles *sg*, rubella.

rubis [rybi] *nm* [pierre précieuse] ruby.

rubrique [rybrik] *nf* **1.** [chronique] column **- 2.** [dans classement] heading.

ruche [ryʃ] *nf* [abri] hive, beehive ; *fig* hive of activity.

rude [ryd] *adj* **1.** [surface] rough **- 2.** [voix] harsh **- 3.** [personne, manières] rough, uncouth **- 4.** [hiver, épreuve] harsh, severe ; [tâche, adversaire] tough.

rudement [rydmã] *adv* **1.** [brutalement - tomber] hard ; [- répondre] harshly **- 2.** *fam* [très] damn.

rudesse [rydɛs] *nf* harshness, severity.

rudimentaire [rydimãtɛr] *adj* rudimentary.

rudoyer [13] [rydwaje] *vt* to treat harshly.

rue [ry] *nf* street ; **rue piétonne** ou **piétonnière** pedestrian area ou street.

ruée [rɥe] *nf* rush.

ruelle [rɥɛl] *nf* [rue] alley, lane.

ruer [7] [rɥe] *vi* to kick. ➤ **se ruer** *vp* : **se ruer sur** to pounce on.

rugby [rygbi] *nm* rugby.

rugir [32] [ryʒir] *vi* to roar ; [vent] to howl.

rugissement [ryʒismã] *nm* roar, roaring *(U)* ; [de vent] howling.

rugosité [rygozite] *nf* **1.** [de surface] roughness **- 2.** [aspérité] rough patch.

rugueux, euse [rygø, øz] *adj* rough.

ruine [rɥin] *nf* **1.** [gén] [financière] ruin **- 2.** [effondrement] ruin, downfall **- 3.** [humaine] wreck.

ruiner [3] [rɥine] *vt* to ruin. ➤ **se ruiner** *vp* to ruin o.s., to bankrupt o.s.

ruineux, euse [rɥinø, øz] *adj* ruinous.

ruisseau, x [rɥiso] *nm* **1.** [cours d'eau] stream **- 2.** *fig & péj* [caniveau] gutter.

ruisseler [24] [rɥisle] *vi* : **ruisseler (de)** to stream (with).

rumeur [rymœr] *nf* **1.** [bruit] murmur **- 2.** [nouvelle] rumour *UK*, rumor *US*.

ruminer [3] [rymine] *vt* to ruminate ; *fig* to mull over.

rupture [ryptyr] *nf* **1.** [cassure] breaking **- 2.** *fig* [changement] abrupt change **- 3.** [de négociations, fiançailles] breaking off ; [de contrat] breach **- 4.** [amoureuse] breakup, split.

rural, e, aux [ryral, o] *adj* country *(avant n)*, rural.

ruse [ryz] *nf* **1.** [habileté] cunning, craftiness **- 2.** [subterfuge] ruse.

rusé, e [ryze] *adj* cunning, crafty.

russe [rys] ◇ *adj* Russian. ◇ *nm* [langue] Russian. ➤ **Russe** *nmf* Russian.

Russie [rysi] *nf* : **la Russie** Russia.

rustine [rystin] *nf* small rubber patch for repairing bicycle tyres.

rustique [rystik] *adj* rustic.

rustre [rystr] *péj* ◇ *nmf* lout. ◇ *adj* loutish.

rutilant, e [rytilã, ãt] *adj* [brillant] gleaming.

rythme [ritm] *nm* **1.** MUS rhythm ; **en rythme** in rhythm **- 2.** [de travail, production] pace, rate.

rythmique [ritmik] *adj* rhythmical.

S

s, S [ɛs] *nm inv* **1.** [lettre] s, S - **2.** [forme] zigzag. ⏵ **S** (*abr écrite de* **Sud**) S.

s' ⏵ se, si.

s/ *abr écrite de* **sur**.

sa ⏵ son².

SA (*abr de* **société anonyme**) *nf* ≃ Ltd *UK*, ≃ Inc. *US*

sabbatique [sabatik] *adj* **1.** RELIG Sabbath (*avant n*) - **2.** [congé] sabbatical.

sable [sabl] *nm* sand ; **sables mouvants** quicksand (*sing*), quicksands.

sablé, e [sable] *adj* [route] sandy. ⏵ **sablé** ≃ shortbread (*U*).

sabler [3] [sable] *vt* **1.** [route] to sand - **2.** [boire] : **sabler le champagne** to crack a bottle of champagne.

sablier [sablije] *nm* hourglass.

sablonneux, euse [sablɔnø, øz] *adj* sandy.

saborder [3] [sabɔrde] *vt* [navire] to scuttle ; *fig* [entreprise] to wind up ; *fig* [projet] to scupper *UK*.

sabot [sabo] *nm* **1.** [chaussure] clog - **2.** [de cheval] hoof - **3.** AUTO : **sabot de Denver** wheel clamp, Denver boot.

sabotage [sabotaʒ] *nm* **1.** [volontaire] sabotage - **2.** [bâclage] bungling.

saboter [3] [sabɔte] *vt* **1.** [volontairement] to sabotage - **2.** [bâcler] to bungle.

saboteur, euse [sabɔtœr, øz] *nm, f* MIL & POLIT saboteur.

sabre [sabr] *nm* sabre *UK*, saber *US*.

sac [sak] *nm* **1.** [gén] bag ; [pour grains] sack ; [contenu] bag, bagful, sack, sackful ; **sac de couchage** sleeping bag ; **sac à dos** rucksack ; **sac à main** handbag ; **sac (en) plastique** [petit] plastic bag ; [solide et grand] plastic carrier (bag) *UK*, large plastic bag *US* ; **sac poubelle** bin liner *UK*, garbage can liner *US* ; [noir] black bag - **2.** *fam* [10 francs] 10 francs - **3.** *litt* [pillage] sack.

saccade [sakad] *nf* jerk.

saccadé, e [sakade] *adj* jerky.

saccage [sakaʒ] *nm* havoc.

saccager [17] [sakaʒe] *vt* **1.** [piller] to sack - **2.** [dévaster] to destroy.

sacerdoce [saserdɔs] *nm* priesthood ; *fig* vocation.

sachant *p prés* ⏵ savoir.

sache, saches *etc* ⏵ savoir.

sachet [saʃɛ] *nm* [de bonbons] bag ; [de shampooing] sachet ; **sachet de thé** teabag ; **soupe en sachet** packet soup *UK*, package soup *US*.

sacoche [sakɔʃ] *nf* **1.** [de médecin, d'écolier] bag - **2.** [de cycliste] pannier.

sac-poubelle [sakpubel] (*pl* **sacs-poubelle**) *nm* [petit] dustbin *UK* OU garbage can *US* liner ; [grand] rubbish bag *UK*, garbage bag *US*.

sacre [sakr] *nm* [de roi] coronation ; [d'évêque] consecration.

sacré, e [sakre] *adj* **1.** [gén] sacred - **2.** RELIG [ordres, écritures] holy - **3.** (*avant n*) *fam* [maudit] bloody *UK* (*avant n*), goddam *US* (*avant n*).

sacrement [sakrəmɑ̃] *nm* sacrament.

sacrément [sakremɑ̃] *adv fam vieilli* dashed.

sacrer [3] [sakre] *vt* **1.** [roi] to crown ; [évêque] to consecrate - **2.** *fig* [déclarer] to hail.

sacrifice [sakrifis] *nm* sacrifice.

sacrifié, e [sakrifje] *adj* **1.** [personne] sacrificed - **2.** [prix] giveaway (*avant n*).

sacrifier [9] [sakrifje] *vt* [gén] to sacrifice ; **sacrifier qqn/qqch à** to sacrifice sb/sthg to. ⏵ **se sacrifier** *vp* : **se sacrifier à/pour** to sacrifice o.s. to/for.

sacrilège [sakrilɛʒ] ◇ *nm* sacrilege. ◇ *adj* sacrilegious.

sacristain [sakristɛ̃] *nm* sacristan.

sacristie [sakristi] *nf* sacristy.

sadique [sadik] ◇ *nmf* sadist. ◇ *adj* sadistic.

sadisme [sadism] *nm* sadism.

safari [safari] *nm* safari.

safran [safrɑ̃] *nm* [épice] saffron.

saga [saga] *nf* saga.

sage [saʒ] ◇ *adj* **1.** [personne, conseil] wise, sensible - **2.** [enfant, chien] good - **3.** [goûts] modest ; [propos, vêtement] sober. ◇ *nm* wise man, sage.

sage-femme [saʒfam] *nf* midwife.

sagement [saʒmɑ̃] *adv* **1.** [avec bon sens] wisely, sensibly - **2.** [docilement] like a good girl/boy.

sagesse [saʒɛs] *nf* **1.** [bon sens] wisdom, good sense - **2.** [docilité] good behaviour *UK* OU behavior *US*.

Sagittaire [saʒitɛr] *nm* ASTROL Sagittarius.

Sahara [saara] *nm* : **le Sahara** the Sahara.

saignant, e [sɛɲɑ̃, ɑ̃t] *adj* **1.** [blessure] bleeding - **2.** [viande] rare, underdone.

saignement [sɛɲmɑ̃] *nm* bleeding.

saigner [4] [seɲe] <> vt **1.** [malade, animal] to bleed - **2.** [financièrement] **: saigner qqn (à blanc)** to bleed sb (white). <> vi to bleed ; **je saigne du nez** my nose is bleeding, I've got a nosebleed.

saillant, e [sajɑ̃, ɑ̃t] adj [proéminent] projecting, protruding ; [muscles] bulging ; [pommettes] prominent.

saillie [saji] nf [avancée] projection ; **en saillie** projecting.

saillir [50] [sajir] vi [balcon] to project, to protrude ; [muscles] to bulge.

sain, e [sɛ̃, sɛn] adj **1.** [gén] healthy ; **sain et sauf** safe and sound - **2.** [lecture] wholesome - **3.** [fruit] fit to eat ; [mur, gestion] sound.

saint, e [sɛ̃, sɛ̃t] <> adj **1.** [sacré] holy - **2.** [pieux] saintly - **3.** [extrême] **: avoir une sainte horreur de qqch** to detest sthg. <> nm, f saint.

saint-bernard [sɛ̃bɛrnar] nm inv **1.** [chien] St Bernard - **2.** fig [personne] good Samaritan.

saintement [sɛ̃tmɑ̃] adv **: vivre saintement** to lead a saintly life.

sainte-nitouche [sɛ̃tnituʃ] nf péj **: c'est une sainte-nitouche** butter wouldn't melt in her mouth.

sainteté [sɛ̃te] nf holiness.

saint-glinglin [sɛ̃glɛ̃glɛ̃] loc adv fam **: à la saint-glinglin** till Doomsday.

Saint-Père [sɛ̃pɛr] nm Holy Father.

sais, sait etc ➤ savoir.

saisie [sezi] nf **1.** [fiscalité & DR] distraint, seizure - **2.** INFORM input ; **saisie de données** data capture.

saisir [32] [sezir] vt **1.** [empoigner] to take hold of ; [avec force] to seize - **2.** FIN & DR to seize, to distrain - **3.** INFORM to capture - **4.** [comprendre] to grasp - **5.** [suj: sensation, émotion] to grip, to seize - **6.** [surprendre] **: être saisi par** to be struck by - **7.** CULIN to seal. ➤ **se saisir** vp **: se saisir de qqn/qqch** to seize sb/sthg, to grab sb/sthg.

saisissant, e [sezisɑ̃, ɑ̃t] adj **1.** [spectacle] gripping ; [ressemblance] striking - **2.** [froid] biting.

saison [sɛzɔ̃] nf season ; **en/hors saison** in/out of season ; **la haute/basse/morte saison** the high/low/off season.

saisonnier, ère [sɛzɔnje, ɛr] <> adj seasonal. <> nm, f seasonal worker.

salace [salas] adj salacious.

salade [salad] nf **1.** [plante] lettuce - **2.** [plat] (green) salad ; **salade composée** mixed salad ; **salade de fruits** fruit salad.

saladier [saladje] nm salad bowl.

salaire [salɛr] nm **1.** [rémunération] salary, wage ; **salaire brut/net/de base** gross/net/basic salary, gross/net/basic wage - **2.** fig [récompense] reward.

salant [salɑ̃] ➤ marais.

salarial, e, aux [salarjal, o] adj wage (avant n).

salarié, e [salarje] <> adj **1.** [personne] wage-earning - **2.** [travail] paid. <> nm, f salaried employee.

salaud [salo] vulg <> nm bastard. <> adj m shitty.

sale [sal] adj **1.** [linge, mains] dirty ; [couleur] dirty, dingy - **2.** (avant n) [type, gueule, coup] nasty ; [tour, histoire] dirty - **3.** [bête, temps] filthy.

salé, e [sale] adj **1.** [eau, saveur] salty ; [beurre] salted ; [viande, poisson] salt (avant n), salted - **2.** fig [histoire] spicy - **3.** fam fig [addition, facture] steep.

saler [3] [sale] vt **1.** [gén] to salt - **2.** fam fig [note] to bump up.

saleté [salte] nf **1.** [malpropreté] dirtiness, filthiness - **2.** [crasse] dirt (U), filth (U) ; **faire des saletés** to make a mess - **3.** fam [maladie] bug - **4.** [obscénité] dirty thing, obscenity ; **il m'a dit des saletés** he used obscenities to me - **5.** [action] disgusting thing ; **faire une saleté à qqn** to play a dirty trick on sb - **6.** [calomnie] (piece of) dirt - **7.** fam péj [personne] nasty piece of work UK.

salière [saljɛr] nf saltcellar, saltshaker US.

salir [32] [salir] vt **1.** [linge, mains] to (make) dirty, to soil - **2.** fig [réputation, personne] to sully.

salissant, e [salisɑ̃, ɑ̃t] adj **1.** [tissu] easily soiled - **2.** [travail] dirty, messy.

salive [saliv] nf saliva.

saliver [3] [salive] vi to salivate.

salle [sal] nf **1.** [pièce] room ; **en salle** [dans un café] inside ; **salle d'attente** waiting room ; **salle de bains** bathroom ; **salle de cinéma** cinema ; **salle de classe** classroom ; **salle d'eau, salle de douches** shower room ; **salle d'embarquement** departure lounge ; **salle à manger** dining room ; **salle d'opération** operating theatre UK ou room US ; **salle de séjour** living room ; **salle de spectacle** theatre UK, theater US ; **salle des ventes** saleroom UK, salesroom US - **2.** [de spectacle] auditorium - **3.** [public] audience, house ; **faire salle comble** to have a full house.

salon [salɔ̃] nm **1.** [de maison] lounge UK, living room - **2.** [commerce] **: salon de coiffure** hairdressing salon, hairdresser's ; **salon de thé** tearoom - **3.** [foire-exposition] show.

salope [salɔp] nf vulg bitch.

saloperie [salɔpri] nf fam **1.** [pacotille] rubbish (U) - **2.** [maladie] bug - **3.** [saleté] junk *(U)*, rubbish *(U)* ; **faire des saloperies** to make a mess - **4.** [action] dirty trick ; **faire des saloperies à qqn** to play dirty tricks on sb - **5.** [propos] dirty comment.

salopette [salɔpɛt] *nf* [d'ouvrier] overalls *pl* ; [à bretelles] dungarees *(pl)* UK, overalls US.

saltimbanque [saltēbāk] *nmf* acrobat.

salubrité [salybrite] *nf* healthiness.

saluer [7] [salɥe] *vt* **1.** [accueillir] to greet - **2.** [dire au revoir à] to take one's leave of - **3.** *fig* & MIL to salute. ◆ **se saluer** *vp* to say hello/goodbye (to one another).

salut [saly] ◇ *nm* **1.** [de la main] wave ; [de la tête] nod ; [propos] greeting - **2.** MIL salute - **3.** [sauvegarde] safety - **4.** RELIG salvation. ◇ *interj fam* [bonjour] hi! ; [au revoir] bye!, see you!

salutaire [salyter] *adj* **1.** [conseil, expérience] salutary - **2.** [remède, repos] beneficial.

salutation [salytasjɔ̃] *nf litt* salutation, greeting. ◆ **salutations** *nfpl* : **veuillez agréer, Monsieur, mes salutations distinguées** ou **mes sincères salutations** *sout* yours faithfully UK, yours sincerely.

salve [salv] *nf* salvo.

samedi [samdi] *nm* Saturday ; **nous sommes partis samedi** we left on Saturday ; **samedi 13 septembre** Saturday 13th September UK, Saturday September 13th US ; **samedi dernier/prochain** last/next Saturday ; **le samedi** on Saturdays.

SAMU, Samu [samy] *(abr de Service d'aide médicale d'urgence)* *nm* **1.** MÉD *French ambulance and emergency service,* ≃ *Ambulance Brigade UK,* ≃ *Paramedics US* - **2.** [aide sociale] : **le SAMU social** *a municipal service that deals with the homeless and assists persons in need.*

sanatorium [sanatɔrjɔm] *nm* sanatorium.

sanctifier [9] [sāktifje] *vt* **1.** [rendre saint] to sanctify - **2.** [révérer] to hallow.

sanction [sāksjɔ̃] *nf* sanction ; *fig* [conséquence] penalty, price ; **prendre des sanctions contre** to impose sanctions on.

sanctionner [3] [sāksjɔne] *vt* to sanction.

sanctuaire [sāktɥer] *nm* **1.** [d'église] sanctuary - **2.** [lieu saint] shrine.

sandale [sādal] *nf* sandal.

sandalette [sādalɛt] *nf* sandal.

sandwich [sādwitʃ] *(pl* **sandwiches** ou **sandwichs)** *nm* sandwich.

sandwicherie [sādwitʃri] *nf* sandwich shop ; [avec possibilité de manger sur place] sandwich bar.

sang [sā] *nm* blood.

sang-froid [sāfrwa] *nm inv* calm ; **de sang-froid** in cold blood ; **perdre/garder son sang-froid** to lose/to keep one's head.

sanglant, e [sāglā, āt] *adj* bloody ; *fig* cruel.

sangle [sāgl] *nf* strap ; [de selle] girth.

sangler [3] [sāgle] *vt* [attacher] to strap ; [cheval] to girth.

sanglier [sāglije] *nm* boar.

sanglot [sāglo] *nm* sob ; **éclater en sanglots** to burst into sobs.

sangloter [3] [sāglɔte] *vi* to sob.

sangsue [sāsy] *nf* leech ; *fig* [personne] bloodsucker.

sanguin, e [sāgɛ̃, in] *adj* **1.** ANAT blood *(avant n)* - **2.** [rouge - visage] ruddy ; [- orange] blood *(avant n)* - **3.** [emporté] quick-tempered.

sanguinaire [sāginer] *adj* **1.** [tyran] bloodthirsty - **2.** [lutte] bloody.

Sanisette® [sanizet] *nf automatic public toilet.*

sanitaire [saniter] *adj* **1.** [service, mesure] health *(avant n)* - **2.** [installation, appareil] bathroom *(avant n)*. ◆ **sanitaires** *nmpl* toilets and showers.

sans [sā] ◇ *prép* without ; **sans argent** without any money ; **sans faire un effort** without making an effort. ◇ *adv* : **passe-moi mon manteau, je ne veux pas sortir sans** pass me my coat, I don't want to go out without it. ◆ **sans que** *loc conj* (+ *subjonctif*) : **sans que vous le sachiez** without your knowing.

sans-abri [sāzabri] *nmf* homeless person.

sans-emploi [sāzāplwa] *nmf* unemployed person.

sans-gêne [sāʒɛn] ◇ *nm inv* [qualité] rudeness, lack of consideration. ◇ *nmf* [personne] rude ou inconsiderate person. ◇ *adj inv* rude, inconsiderate.

sans-plomb [sāplɔ̃] *nm inv* unleaded, unleaded petrol UK ou gas US, lead-free petrol UK ou gas US.

santé [sāte] *nf* health ; **à ta/votre santé!** cheers!, good health!

santon [sātɔ̃] *nm figure placed in Christmas crib.*

saoul = soûl.

saouler = soûler.

sapeur-pompier [sapœrpɔ̃pje] *nm* fireman, firefighter.

saphir [safir] *nm* sapphire.

sapin [sapɛ̃] *nm* **1.** [arbre] fir, firtree ; **sapin de Noël** Christmas tree - **2.** [bois] fir, deal UK.

sarcasme [sarkasm] *nm* sarcasm.

sarcastique [sarkastik] *adj* sarcastic.

sarcler [3] [sarkle] *vt* to weed.

sarcophage [sarkɔfaʒ] *nm* sarcophagus.

Sardaigne [sardɛɲ] *nf* : **la Sardaigne** Sardinia.

sardine [sardin] *nf* sardine.

SARL, Sarl (*abr de* **société à responsabilité limitée**) *nf* limited liability company *UK* ; **Leduc, SARL** ≃ Leduc Ltd *UK*, ≃ Leduc Inc *US*.

sarment [sarmɑ̃] *nm* [de vigne] shoot.

sas [sas] *nm* **1.** AÉRON & NAUT airlock - **2.** [d'écluse] lock - **3.** [tamis] sieve.

satanique [satanik] *adj* satanic.

satelliser [3] [satelize] *vt* **1.** [fusée] to put into orbit - **2.** [pays] to make a satellite.

satellite [satelit] *nm* satellite ; **satellite artificiel/météorologique/de télécommunications** artificial/meteorological/communications satellite.

satiété [sasjete] *nf* : **à satiété** [boire, manger] one's fill ; [répéter] ad nauseam.

satin [satɛ̃] *nm* satin.

satiné, e [satine] *adj* satin (*avant n*) ; [peau] satiny-smooth. ➡ **satiné** *nm* satin-like quality.

satire [satir] *nf* satire.

satirique [satirik] *adj* satirical.

satisfaction [satisfaksjɔ̃] *nf* satisfaction.

satisfaire [109] [satisfɛr] *vt* to satisfy. ➡ **se satisfaire** *vp* : **se satisfaire de** to be satisfied with.

satisfaisant, e [satisfəzɑ̃, ɑ̃t] *adj* **1.** [travail] satisfactory - **2.** [expérience] satisfying.

satisfait, e [satisfɛ, ɛt] <> *pp* ➤ **satisfaire.** <> *adj* satisfied ; **être satisfait de** to be satisfied with.

saturation [satyrasjɔ̃] *nf* saturation.

saturé, e [satyre] *adj* : **saturé (de)** saturated (with).

saturne [satyrn] *nm vieilli* lead. ➡ **Saturne** *nf* ASTRON Saturn.

satyre [satir] *nm* satyr ; *fig* sex maniac.

sauce [sos] *nf* CULIN sauce.

saucière [sosjer] *nf* sauceboat.

saucisse [sosis] *nf* CULIN sausage.

saucisson [sosisɔ̃] *nm* slicing sausage.

sauf[1] , **sauve** [sof, sov] *adj* [personne] safe, unharmed ; *fig* [honneur] saved, intact.

sauf[2] [sof] *prép* : [à l'exclusion de] except, apart from - **2.** [sous réserve de] barring ; **sauf que** except (that).

sauf-conduit [sofkɔ̃dɥi] (*pl* **sauf-conduits**) *nm* safe-conduct.

sauge [soʒ] *nf* CULIN sage.

saugrenu, e [sogrəny] *adj* ridiculous, nonsensical.

saule [sol] *nm* willow ; **saule pleureur** weeping willow.

saumon [somɔ̃] *nm* salmon ; **saumon fumé** CULIN smoked salmon *UK*, lox *US*.

saumoné, e [somɔne] *adj* salmon (*avant n*).

saumure [somyr] *nf* brine.

sauna [sona] *nm* sauna.

saupoudrer [3] [sopudre] *vt* : **saupoudrer qqch de** to sprinkle sthg with.

saurai, sauras *etc* ➤ **savoir.**

saut [so] *nm* **1.** [bond] leap, jump - **2.** SPORT : **saut en hauteur** high jump ; **saut en longueur** long jump, broad jump *US* ; **saut à l'élastique** bungee-jumping ; **faire du saut à l'élastique** to go bungee-jumping - **3.** [visite] : **faire un saut chez qqn** *fig* to pop in and see sb - **4.** INFORM : **(insérer un) saut de page** (insert) page break.

sauté, e [sote] *adj* sautéed.

saute-mouton [sotmutɔ̃] *nm inv* : **jouer à saute-mouton** to play leapfrog.

sauter [3] [sote] <> *vi* **1.** [bondir] to jump, to leap ; **sauter à la corde** to skip *UK*, to skip *ou* jump rope *US* ; **sauter d'un sujet à l'autre** *fig* to jump from one subject to another ; **sauter de joie** *fig* to jump for joy ; **sauter au cou de qqn** *fig* to throw one's arms around sb - **2.** [exploser] to blow up ; [fusible] to blow - **3.** [être projeté - bouchon] to fly out ; [- serrure] to burst off ; [- bouton] to fly off ; [- chaîne de vélo] to come off - **4.** *fam* [personne] to get the sack *UK*. <> *vt* **1.** [fossé, obstacle] to jump *ou* leap over - **2.** *fig* [page, repas] to skip.

sauterelle [sotrel] *nf* ZOOL grasshopper.

sauteur, euse [sotœr, øz] <> *adj* [insecte] jumping (*avant n*). <> *nm, f* [athlète] jumper.

sautiller [3] [sotije] *vi* to hop.

sautoir [sotwar] *nm* [bijou] chain.

sauvage [sovaʒ] <> *adj* **1.** [plante, animal] wild - **2.** [farouche - animal familier] shy, timid ; [- personne] unsociable - **3.** [conduite, haine] savage. <> *nmf* **1.** [solitaire] recluse - **2.** *péj* [brute, indigène] savage.

sauvagerie [sovaʒri] *nf* **1.** [férocité] brutality, savagery - **2.** [insociabilité] unsociableness.

sauve ➤ **sauf**[1] .

sauvegarde [sovgard] *nf* **1.** [protection] safeguard - **2.** INFORM saving ; [copie] backup.

sauvegarder [3] [sovgarde] *vt* **1.** [protéger] to safeguard - **2.** INFORM to save ; [copier] to back up.

sauve-qui-peut [sovkipø] <> *nm inv* [débandade] stampede. <> *interj* every man for himself!

sauver [3] [sove] *vt* **1.** [gén] to save ; **sauver qqn/qqch de** to save sb/sthg from, to rescue

sb/sthg from - **2.** [navire, biens] to salvage.
se sauver *vp* : **se sauver (de)** to run away (from) ; [prisonnier] to escape (from).

sauvetage [sovtaʒ] *nm* **1.** [de personne] rescue - **2.** [de navire, biens] salvage.

sauveteur [sovtœr] *nm* rescuer.

sauvette [sovɛt] **à la sauvette** *loc adv* hurriedly, at great speed.

savamment [savamɑ̃] *adv* **1.** [avec érudition] learnedly - **2.** [avec habileté] skilfully *UK*, skillfully *US*, cleverly.

savane [savan] *nf* savanna.

savant, e [savɑ̃, ɑ̃t] *adj* **1.** [érudit] scholarly - **2.** [habile] skilful, clever - **3.** [animal] performing *(avant n)*. **savant** *nm* scientist.

saveur [savœr] *nf* flavour *UK*, flavor *US* ; *fig* savour *UK*, savor *US*.

savoir [59] [savwar] *vt* **1.** [gén] to know ; **faire savoir qqch à qqn** to tell sb sthg, to inform sb of sthg ; **si j'avais su...** had I but known..., if I had only known... ; **sans le savoir** unconsciously, without being aware of it ; **tu (ne) peux pas savoir** *fam* you have no idea ; **pas que je sache** not as far as I know - **2.** [être capable de] to know how to ; **sais-tu conduire?** can you drive? ; **savoir s'y prendre avec les enfants** to know how to handle children, to be good with children. *nm* learning. **à savoir** *loc conj* namely, that is.

savoir-faire [savwarfɛr] *nm inv* know-how, expertise.

savoir-vivre [savwarvivr] *nm inv* good manners *pl*.

savon [savɔ̃] *nm* **1.** [matière] soap ; [pain] cake ou bar of soap ; **savon de Marseille** ≃ household soap - **2.** *fam* [réprimande] telling-off.

savonner [3] [savone] *vt* [linge] to soap. **se savonner** *vp* to soap o.s.

savonnette [savonɛt] *nf* guest soap.

savourer [3] [savure] *vt* to savour *UK*, to savor *US*.

savoureux, euse [savurø, øz] *adj* **1.** [mets] tasty - **2.** *fig* [anecdote] juicy.

saxophone [saksofon] *nm* saxophone.

s/c *(abr écrite de* **sous couvert de)** c/o.

scabreux, euse [skabrø, øz] *adj* **1.** [propos] shocking, indecent - **2.** [entreprise] risky.

scalpel [skalpɛl] *nm* scalpel.

scalper [3] [skalpe] *vt* to scalp.

scandale [skɑ̃dal] *nm* **1.** [fait choquant] scandal - **2.** [indignation] uproar - **3.** [tapage] scene ; **faire du** ou **un scandale** to make a scene.

scandaleux, euse [skɑ̃dalø, øz] *adj* scandalous, outrageous.

scandaliser [3] [skɑ̃dalize] *vt* to shock, to scandalize.

scander [3] [skɑ̃de] *vt* **1.** [vers] to scan - **2.** [slogan] to chant.

scandinave [skɑ̃dinav] *adj* Scandinavian. **Scandinave** *nmf* Scandinavian.

Scandinavie [skɑ̃dinavi] *nf* : **la Scandinavie** Scandinavia.

scanner [4] [skane] *vt* to scan.

scanner [skanɛr] *nm* scanner.

scaphandre [skafɑ̃dr] *nm* **1.** [de plongeur] diving suit - **2.** [d'astronaute] spacesuit.

scarabée [skarabe] *nm* beetle, scarab.

scatologique [skatɔlɔʒik] *adj* scatological.

sceau, x [so] *nm* seal ; *fig* stamp, hallmark.

scélérat, e [selera, at] *litt adj* wicked. *nm, f* villain ; *péj* rogue, rascal.

sceller [4] [sele] *vt* **1.** [gén] to seal - **2.** CONSTR [fixer] to embed.

scénario [senarjo] *nm* **1.** CINÉ, LITTÉR & THÉÂTRE [canevas] scenario - **2.** CINÉ & TV [découpage, synopsis] screenplay, script - **3.** *fig* [rituel] pattern.

scénariste [senarist] *nmf* scriptwriter.

scène [sɛn] *nf* **1.** [gén] scene - **2.** [estrade] stage ; **entrée en scène** THÉÂTRE entrance ; *fig* appearance ; **mettre en scène** THÉÂTRE to stage ; CINÉ to direct.

scepticisme [sɛptisism] *nm* scepticism *UK*, skepticism *US*.

sceptique [sɛptik] *nmf* sceptic *UK*, skeptic *US*. *adj* **1.** [incrédule] sceptical *UK*, skeptical *US* - **2.** PHILO sceptic *UK*, skeptic *US*.

sceptre [sɛptr] *nm* sceptre *UK*, scepter *US*.

schéma [ʃema] *nm* [diagramme] diagram.

schématique [ʃematik] *adj* **1.** [dessin] diagrammatic - **2.** [interprétation, exposé] simplified.

schématiser [3] [ʃematize] *vt péj* [généraliser] to oversimplify.

schisme [ʃism] *nm* **1.** RELIG schism - **2.** [d'opinion] split.

schizophrène [skizɔfrɛn] *nmf & adj* schizophrenic.

schizophrénie [skizɔfreni] *nf* schizophrenia.

sciatique [sjatik] *nf* sciatica. *adj* sciatic.

scie [si] *nf* [outil] saw.

sciemment [sjamɑ̃] *adv* knowingly.

science [sjɑ̃s] *nf* **1.** [connaissances scientifiques] science ; **sciences humaines** ou **sociales** UNIV social sciences - **2.** [érudition] knowledge - **3.** [art] art.

science-fiction [sjɑ̃sfiksjɔ̃] *nf* science fiction.

sciences-po [sjɑ̃spo] *nfpl* UNIV political science *sg*. ➤ **Sciences-Po** *npr* grande école for political science.

scientifique [sjɑ̃tifik] ◇ *nmf* scientist. ◇ *adj* scientific.

scier [9] [sje] *vt* [branche] to saw.

scierie [siri] *nf* sawmill.

scinder [3] [sɛ̃de] *vt* : **scinder (en)** to split (into), to divide (into). ➤ **se scinder** *vp* : **se scinder (en)** to split (into), to divide (into).

scintiller [3] [sɛ̃tije] *vi* to sparkle.

scission [sisjɔ̃] *nf* split.

sciure [sjyr] *nf* sawdust.

sclérose [skleroz] *nf* sclerosis ; *fig* ossification ; **sclérose en plaques** multiple sclerosis.

sclérosé, e [skleroze] *adj* sclerotic ; *fig* ossified.

scolaire [skɔlɛr] *adj* school *(avant n)* ; *péj* bookish.

scolarisable [skɔlarizabl] *adj* of school age.

scolarité [skɔlarite] *nf* schooling ; **frais de scolarité** SCOL school fees ; UNIV tuition fees.

scooter [skutœr] *nm* scooter.

scorbut [skɔrbyt] *nm* scurvy.

score [skɔr] *nm* SPORT score.

scorpion [skɔrpjɔ̃] *nm* scorpion. ➤ **Scorpion** *nm* ASTROL Scorpio.

scotch [skɔtʃ] *nm* [alcool] whisky, Scotch.

Scotch® [skɔtʃ] *nm* [adhésif] ≃ Sellotape® *UK*, ≃ Scotch tape® *US*.

scotché, e [skɔtʃe] *adj* : **être scotché devant la télévision** to be glued to the television.

scotcher [3] [skɔtʃe] *vt* to sellotape *UK*, to scotch-tape *US*.

scout, e [skut] *adj* scout *(avant n)*. ➤ **scout** *nm* scout.

scribe [skrib] *nm* HIST scribe.

script [skript] *nm* CINÉ & TV script.

scripte [skript] *nmf* CINÉ & TV continuity person.

scrupule [skrypyl] *nm* scruple ; **avec scrupule** scrupulously ; **sans scrupules** [être] unscrupulous ; [agir] unscrupulously.

scrupuleux, euse [skrypylø, øz] *adj* scrupulous.

scrutateur, trice [skrytatœr, tris] *adj* searching.

scruter [3] [skryte] *vt* to scrutinize.

scrutin [skrytɛ̃] *nm* 1. [vote] ballot - 2. [système] voting system ; **scrutin majoritaire** first-past-the-post system *UK* ; **scrutin proportionnel** proportional representation system.

sculpter [3] [skylte] *vt* to sculpt.

sculpteur [skyltœr] *nm* sculptor.

sculpture [skyltyr] *nf* sculpture.

SDF *(abr de* sans domicile fixe*) nmf* : **les SDF** the homeless.

se [sə], **s'** *(devant voyelle ou 'h' muet) pron pers* 1. *(réfléchi)* [personne] oneself, himself (*f* herself *pl* themselves) ; [chose, animal] itself (*pl* themselves) ; **elle se regarde dans le miroir** she looks at herself in the mirror - 2. *(réciproque)* each other, one another ; **ils se sont rencontrés hier** they met yesterday - 3. *(passif)* **ce produit se vend bien/partout** this product is selling well/is sold everywhere - 4. *[remplace l'adjectif possessif]* : **se laver les mains** to wash one's hands ; **se couper le doigt** to cut one's finger.

séance [seɑ̃s] *nf* 1. [réunion] meeting, sitting, session - 2. [période] session ; [de pose] sitting - 3. CINÉ & THÉÂTRE performance ; **séance tenante** right away, forthwith.

seau, x [so] *nm* 1. [récipient] bucket - 2. [contenu] bucketful.

sec, sèche [sɛk, sɛʃ] *adj* 1. [gén] dry - 2. [fruits] dried - 3. [personne - maigre] lean ; [- austère] austere - 4. *fig* [cœur] hard ; [voix, ton] sharp - 5. [sans autre prestation] : **vol sec** flight only. ➤ **sec** ◇ *adv* 1. [beaucoup] : **boire sec** to drink heavily - 2. [démarrer] sharply. ◇ *nm* : **tenir au sec** to keep in a dry place.

sécable [sekabl] *adj* divisible.

sécateur [sekatœr] *nm* secateurs *pl*.

sécession [sesesjɔ̃] *nf* secession ; **faire sécession (de)** to secede (from).

sèche-cheveux [sɛʃʃəvø] *nm inv* hairdryer.

sèche-linge [sɛʃlɛ̃ʒ] *nm inv* tumble-dryer.

sécher [18] [seʃe] ◇ *vt* 1. [linge] to dry - 2. *arg scol* [cours] to skip, to skive off *UK*. ◇ *vi* 1. [linge] to dry - 2. [peau] to dry out ; [rivière] to dry up - 3. *arg scol* [ne pas savoir répondre] to dry up.

sécheresse [seʃrɛs] *nf* 1. [de terre, climat, style] dryness - 2. [absence de pluie] drought - 3. [de réponse] curtness.

séchoir [seʃwar] *nm* 1. [tringle] airer, clotheshorse - 2. [électrique] dryer ; **séchoir à cheveux** hairdryer.

second, e [səgɔ̃, ɔ̃d] ◇ *adj num inv* second ; **dans un état second** dazed. ◇ *nm, f* second ; *voir aussi* **sixième**. ➤ **seconde** *nf* 1. [unité de temps & MUS] second - 2. SCOL ≃ fifth year *ou* form *UK*, ≃ tenth grade *US* - 3. [transports] second class - 4. AUTO second gear.

secondaire [səgɔ̃dɛr] ◇ *nm* : **le secondaire** GÉOL the Mesozoic ; SCOL secondary education ; ÉCON the secondary sector.

◇ *adj* **1.** [gén & SCOL] secondary ; **effets secondaires** MÉD side effects - **2.** GÉOL Mesozoic.

seconder [3] [səgɔ̃de] *vt* to assist.

secouer [6] [səkwe] *vt* [gén] to shake. ➡ **se secouer** *vp fam* to snap out of it.

secourable [səkurabl] *adj* helpful ; **main secourable** helping hand.

secourir [45] [səkurir] *vt* [blessé, miséreux] to help ; [personne en danger] to rescue.

secouriste [səkurist] *nmf* first-aid worker.

secours [səkur] *nm* **1.** [aide] help ; **appeler au secours** to call for help ; **les secours** emergency services ; **au secours!** help! - **2.** [dons] aid, relief - **3.** [renfort] relief, reinforcements *pl* - **4.** [soins] aid ; **les premiers secours** first aid (U). ➡ **de secours** *loc adj* **1.** [trousse, poste] first-aid *(avant n)* - **2.** [éclairage, issue] emergency *(avant n)* - **3.** [roue] spare.

secouru, e [səkury] *pp* ➤ **secourir.**

secousse [səkus] *nf* **1.** [mouvement] jerk, jolt - **2.** *fig* [bouleversement] upheaval ; [psychologique] shock - **3.** [tremblement de terre] tremor.

secret, ète [səkrɛ, ɛt] *adj* **1.** [gén] secret - **2.** [personne] reticent. ➡ **secret** *nm* **1.** [gén] secret - **2.** [discrétion] secrecy ; **dans le plus grand secret** in the utmost secrecy.

secrétaire [səkretɛr] ◇ *nmf* [personne] secretary ; **secrétaire de direction** executive secretary. ◇ *nm* [meuble] writing desk, secretaire.

secrétariat [səkretarja] *nm* **1.** [bureau] secretary's office - **2.** [d'organisation internationale] secretariat - **3.** [personnel] secretarial staff - **3.** [métier] secretarial work.

sécréter [18] [sekrete] *vt* to secrete ; *fig* to exude.

sécrétion [sekresjɔ̃] *nf* secretion.

sectaire [sɛktɛr] *nmf & adj* sectarian.

secte [sɛkt] *nf* sect.

secteur [sɛktœr] *nm* **1.** [zone] area ; **se trouver dans le secteur** *fam* to be somewhere OU someplace *US* around - **2.** ADMIN district - **3.** ÉCON, GÉOM & MIL sector ; **secteur primaire/secondaire/tertiaire** primary/secondary/tertiary sector ; **secteur privé/public** private/public sector - **4.** ÉLECTR mains ; **sur secteur** off OU from the mains.

section [sɛksjɔ̃] *nf* **1.** [gén] section ; [de parti] branch - **2.** MIL platoon.

sectionner [3] [sɛksjɔne] *vt* **1.** *fig* [diviser] to divide into sections - **2.** [trancher] to sever.

Sécu [seky] *fam abr de* **Sécurité Sociale.**

séculaire [sekylɛr] *adj* [ancien] age-old.

sécurisant, e [sekyrizɑ̃, ɑ̃t] *adj* [milieu] secure ; [attitude] reassuring.

sécurité [sekyrite] *nf* **1.** [d'esprit] security - **2.** [absence de danger] safety ; **la sécurité routière** road safety ; **en toute sécurité** safe and sound - **3.** [dispositif] safety catch - **4.** [organisme] : **la Sécurité sociale** ≃ the DSS *UK*, ≃ Social Security *US*.

sédatif, ive [sedatif, iv] *adj* sedative. ➡ **sédatif** *nm* sedative.

sédentaire [sedɑ̃tɛr] *adj* [personne, métier] sedentary ; [casanier] stay-at-home.

sédentariser [3] [sedɑ̃tarize] ➡ **se sédentariser** *vp* [tribu] to settle, to become settled.

sédiment [sedimɑ̃] *nm* sediment.

sédition [sedisjɔ̃] *nf* sedition.

séducteur, trice [sedyktœr, tris] ◇ *adj* seductive. ◇ *nm, f* seducer (f seductress).

séduire [98] [sedɥir] *vt* **1.** [plaire à] to attract, to appeal to - **2.** [abuser de] to seduce.

séduisant, e [sedɥizɑ̃, ɑ̃t] *adj* attractive.

séduit, e [sedɥi, it] *pp* ➤ **séduire.**

segment [sɛgmɑ̃] *nm* GÉOM segment.

segmenter [3] [sɛgmɑ̃te] *vt* to segment.

ségrégation [segregasjɔ̃] *nf* segregation.

seigle [sɛgl] *nm* rye.

seigneur [sɛɲœr] *nm* lord. ➡ **Seigneur** *nm* : **le Seigneur** the Lord.

sein [sɛ̃] *nm* breast ; *fig* bosom ; **donner le sein (à un bébé)** to breast-feed (a baby). ➡ **au sein de** *loc prép* within.

Seine [sɛn] *nf* : **la Seine** the (River) Seine.

séisme [seism] *nm* earthquake.

seize [sɛz] *adj num inv & nm* sixteen ; *voir aussi* **six.**

seizième [sɛzjɛm] *adj num inv, nm & nmf* sixteenth ; *voir aussi* **sixième.**

séjour [seʒur] *nm* **1.** [durée] stay ; **interdit de séjour** ≃ banned ; **séjour linguistique** stay abroad *(to develop language skills)* - **2.** [pièce] living room.

séjourner [3] [seʒurne] *vi* to stay.

sel [sɛl] *nm* salt ; *fig* piquancy.

sélection [selɛksjɔ̃] *nf* selection.

sélectionner [3] [selɛksjɔne] *vt* to select, to pick ; INFORM to select.

self-service [selfsɛrvis] *(pl* **self-services)** *nm* self-service cafeteria.

selle [sɛl] *nf* [gén] saddle.

seller [4] [sele] *vt* to saddle.

selon [səlɔ̃] *prép* **1.** [conformément à] in accordance with - **2.** [d'après] according to. ➡ **selon que** *loc conj* depending on whether.

semaine [səmɛn] *nf* [période] week ; **à la semaine** [être payé] by the week.

sémantique [semãtik] *adj* semantic.

semblable [sãblabl] <> *nm* [prochain] fellow man ; **il n'a pas son semblable** there's nobody like him. <> *adj* **1.** [analogue] similar ; **semblable à** like, similar to - **2.** *(avant n)* [tel] such.

semblant [sãblã] *nm* : **un semblant de** semblance of ; **faire semblant (de faire qqch)** to pretend (to do sthg).

sembler [3] [sãble] <> *vi* to seem. <> *v impers* : **il (me/te) semble que** it seems (to me/you) that.

semelle [səmɛl] *nf* [de chaussure - dessous] sole ; [- à l'intérieur] insole.

semence [səmãs] *nf* **1.** [graine] seed - **2.** [sperme] semen *(U).*

semer [19] [səme] *vt* **1.** *fig* [planter] to sow - **2.** [répandre] to scatter ; **semer qqch de** to scatter sthg with, to strew sthg with - **3.** *fam* [se débarrasser de] to shake off - **4.** *fam* [perdre] to lose - **5.** [propager] to bring.

semestre [səmɛstr] *nm* half year, six-month period ; SCOL semester.

semestriel, elle [səmɛstrijɛl] *adj* **1.** [qui a lieu tous les six mois] half-yearly, six-monthly - **2.** [qui dure six mois] six months', six-month.

séminaire [seminɛr] *nm* **1.** RELIG seminary - **2.** UNIV [colloque] seminar.

séminariste [seminarist] *nm* seminarist.

semi-remorque [səmirəmɔrk] *(pl* semi-remorques) *nm* articulated lorry *UK*, semitrailer *US*, rig *US*.

semis [səmi] *nm* **1.** [méthode] sowing broadcast - **2.** [plant] seedling.

semoule [səmul] *nf* semolina.

sempiternel, elle [sãpitɛrnɛl] *adj* eternal.

sénat [sena] *nm* senate ; **le Sénat** *upper house of the French parliament.*

sénateur, trice [senatœr, tris] *nm* senator.

Sénégal [senegal] *nm* : **le Sénégal** Senegal.

sénile [senil] *adj* senile.

sénilité [senilite] *nf* senility.

senior [senjɔr] *adj & nmf* **1.** SPORT senior - **2.** [tourisme] for the over-50s, for the young at heart ; [menu] over 50s' ; **notre clientèle senior** our over-50s customers - **3.** [personnes de plus de 50 ans] over-50 *(gén pl).*

sens [sãs] *nm* **1.** [fonction, instinct, raison] sense ; **le sens du toucher** the sense of touch ; **avoir le sens de la nuance** to be subtle ; **avoir le sens de l'humour** to have a sense of humour *UK* ou humor *US* ; **ne pas avoir le sens des réalités** to have no grasp of reality ; **bon sens** good sense - **2.** [direction] direction ; **dans le sens de la longueur** lengthways ; **dans le sens des aiguilles d'une montre** clockwise ; **dans le sens contraire des aiguilles d'une montre** anticlockwise *UK*, counterclockwise *US* ; **sens dessus dessous** upside down ; **sens interdit** ou **unique** one-way street ; **(rue à) sens unique** one-way street - **3.** [signification] meaning ; **cela n'a pas de sens!** it's nonsensical! ; **ce que tu dis n'a pas de sens** [c'est inintelligible, déraisonnable] what you're saying doesn't make sense ; **dans** ou **en un sens** in one sense ; **porteur de sens** meaningful ; **lourd** ou **chargé de sens** meaningful ; **au sens propre/figuré** in the literal/figurative sense - **4.** *fig* [orientation] line.

sensation [sãsasjõ] *nf* **1.** [perception] sensation, feeling - **2.** [impression] feeling.

sensationnel, elle [sãsasjɔnɛl] *adj* sensational.

sensé, e [sãse] *adj* sensible.

sensibiliser [3] [sãsibilize] *vt* **1.** MÉD & PHOTO to sensitize - **2.** *fig* [public] : **sensibiliser (à)** to make aware (of).

sensibilité [sãsibilite] *nf* : **sensibilité (à)** sensitivity (to).

sensible [sãsibl] *adj* **1.** [gén] : **sensible (à)** sensitive (to) - **2.** [notable] considerable, appreciable.

sensiblement [sãsibləmã] *adv* **1.** [à peu près] more or less - **2.** [notablement] appreciably, considerably.

sensoriel, elle [sãsɔrjɛl] *adj* sensory.

sensualité [sãsɥalite] *nf* [lascivité] sensuousness ; [charnelle] sensuality.

sensuel, elle [sãsɥɛl] *adj* **1.** [charnel] sensual - **2.** [lascif] sensuous.

sentence [sãtãs] *nf* **1.** [jugement] sentence - **2.** [maxime] adage.

sentencieux, euse [sãtãsjø, øz] *adj péj* sententious.

senteur [sãtœr] *nf litt* perfume.

senti, e [sãti] <> *pp* ▶ **sentir**. <> *adj* : **bien senti** [mots] well-chosen.

sentier [sãtje] *nm* path.

sentiment [sãtimã] *nm* feeling ; **veuillez agréer, Monsieur, l'expression de mes sentiments distingués / cordiaux / les meilleurs** yours faithfully *UK* / sincerely / truly.

sentimental, e, aux [sãtimãtal, o] <> *adj* **1.** [amoureux] love *(avant n)* - **2.** [sensible, romanesque] sentimental. <> *nm, f* sentimentalist.

sentinelle [sãtinɛl] *nf* sentry.

sentir [37] [sãtir] <> *vt* **1.** [percevoir - par l'odorat] to smell ; [- par le goût] to taste ; [- par le toucher] to feel - **2.** [exhaler - odeur] to smell of - **3.** [colère, tendresse] to feel - **4.** [affectation, plagiat] to smack of - **5.** [danger] to sense, to be aware of ; **sentir que** to feel (that) - **6.** [beauté] to feel, to appreciate. ◇ *vi* : **sentir bon/mauvais** to smell good/bad. ➤ **se sentir** ◇ *v att* : **se sentir bien/fatigué** to feel well/tired. ◇ *vp* [être perceptible] : **ça se sent!** you can really tell!

séparation [separasjɔ̃] *nf* separation.

séparatiste [separatist] *nmf* separatist.

séparé, e [separe] *adj* **1.** [intérêts] separate - **2.** [couple] separated.

séparer [3] [separe] *vt* **1.** [gén] : **séparer (de)** to separate (from) - **2.** [suj: divergence] to divide. ➤ **se séparer** *vp* **1.** [se défaire] : **se séparer de** to part with - **2.** [conjoints] to separate, to split up ; **se séparer de** to separate from, to split up with - **3.** [participants] to disperse - **4.** [route] : **se séparer (en)** to split (into), to divide (into).

sept [sɛt] *adj num inv & nm* seven ; *voir aussi* **six.**

septembre [sɛptɑ̃br] *nm* September ; **en septembre, au mois de septembre** in September ; **début septembre, au début du mois de septembre** at the beginning of September ; **fin septembre, à la fin du mois de septembre** at the end of September ; **d'ici septembre** by September ; **(à la) mi-septembre** (in) mid-September ; **le premier/deux/dix septembre** the first/second/tenth of September.

septennat [sɛptena] *nm* seven-year term (of office).

septicémie [sɛptisemi] *nf* septicaemia UK, septicemia US, blood poisoning.

septième [sɛtjɛm] *adj num inv, nm & nmf* seventh ; *voir aussi* **sixième.**

sépulcre [sepylkr] *nm* sepulchre UK, sepulcher US.

sépulture [sepyltyr] *nf* **1.** [lieu] burial place - **2.** [inhumation] burial.

séquelle [sekɛl] *nf (gén pl)* aftermath ; MÉD aftereffect.

séquence [sekɑ̃s] *nf* sequence ; [cartes à jouer] run, sequence.

séquestrer [3] [sekɛstre] *vt* **1.** [personne] to confine - **2.** [biens] to impound.

serai, seras *etc* ➤ **être.**

serbe [sɛrb] *adj* Serbian. ➤ **Serbe** *nmf* Serb.

Serbie [sɛrbi] *nf* : **la Serbie** Serbia.

serein, e [sərɛ̃, ɛn] *adj* **1.** [calme] serene - **2.** [impartial] calm, dispassionate.

sérénade [serenad] *nf* MUS serenade.

sérénité [serenite] *nf* serenity.

serf, serve [sɛrf, sɛrv] *nm, f* serf.

sergent [sɛrʒɑ̃] *nm* sergeant.

série [seri] *nf* **1.** [gén] series *sg* - **2.** SPORT rank ; [au tennis] seeding - **3.** COMM [dans l'industrie] : **produire qqch en série** to mass-produce sthg ; **hors série** custom-made ; *fig* outstanding, extraordinary.

sérieusement [serjøzmɑ̃] *adv* seriously.

sérieux, euse [serjø, øz] *adj* **1.** [grave] serious - **2.** [digne de confiance] reliable ; [client, offre] genuine - **3.** [consciencieux] responsible ; **ce n'est pas sérieux** it's irresponsible - **4.** [considérable] considerable. ➤ **sérieux** *nm* **1.** [application] sense of responsibility - **2.** [gravité] seriousness ; **garder son sérieux** to keep a straight face ; **prendre qqn/qqch au sérieux** to take sb/sthg seriously.

serin, e [sərɛ̃, in] *nm, f* [oiseau] canary.

seringue [sərɛ̃g] *nf* syringe.

serment [sɛrmɑ̃] *nm* **1.** [affirmation solennelle] oath ; **sous serment** on OU under oath - **2.** [promesse] vow, pledge.

sermon [sɛrmɔ̃] *nm litt & fig* sermon.

séronégatif, ive [seronegatif, iv] *adj* HIV-negative.

séropositif, ive [seropozitif, iv] *adj* HIV-positive.

séropositivité [seropozitivite] *nf* HIV infection.

serpe [sɛrp] *nf* billhook.

serpent [sɛrpɑ̃] *nm* ZOOL snake.

serpenter [3] [sɛrpɑ̃te] *vi* to wind.

serpillière [sɛrpijɛr] *nf* floor cloth UK, mop US.

serre [sɛr] *nf* [bâtiment] greenhouse, glasshouse UK. ➤ **serres** *nfpl* ZOOL talons, claws.

serré, e [sere] *adj* **1.** [écriture] cramped ; [tissu] closely-woven ; [rangs] serried - **2.** [vêtement, chaussure] tight - **3.** [discussion] closely argued ; [match] close-fought - **4.** [poing, dents] clenched ; **la gorge serrée** with a lump in one's throat ; **j'en avais le cœur serré** *fig* it was heartbreaking - **5.** [café] strong.

serrer [4] [sere] ◇ *vt* **1.** [saisir] to grip, to hold tight ; **serrer la main à qqn** to shake sb's hand ; **serrer qqn dans ses bras** to hug sb - **2.** *fig* [rapprocher] to bring together ; **serrer les rangs** to close ranks - **3.** [poing, dents] to clench ; [lèvres] to purse ; *fig* [cœur] to wring - **4.** [suj: vêtement, chaussure] to be too tight for - **5.** [vis, ceinture] to tighten - **6.** [trottoir, bordure] to hug. ◇ *vi* AUTO : **serrer à droite/gauche** to keep right/left. ➤ **se serrer** *vp* **1.** [se blottir] : **se serrer contre** to huddle up to OU against - **2.** [se rapprocher] to squeeze up.

serre-tête [sɛrtɛt] *nm inv* headband.

serrure [seryr] *nf* lock.

serrurier [seryrje] *nm* locksmith.

sertir [32] [sertir] *vt* **1.** [pierre précieuse] to set - **2.** TECHNOL [assujettir] to crimp.

sérum [serɔm] *nm* serum ; **sérum physiologique** saline.

servage [servaʒ] *nm* serfdom ; *fig* bondage.

servante [servɑ̃t] *nf* [domestique] maidservant.

serveur, euse [servœr, øz] *nm, f* [de restaurant] waiter (*f* waitress) ; [de bar] barman (*f* barmaid) *UK*, bartender *US*. ◆ **serveur** *nm* INFORM server.

servi, e [servi] *pp* ► **servir**.

serviable [servjabl] *adj* helpful, obliging.

service [servis] *nm* **1.** [gén] service ; **être en service** to be in use, to be set up ; **hors service** out of order - **2.** [travail] duty ; **pendant le service** while on duty - **3.** [département] department ; **service d'ordre** police and stewards *UK* (*at a demonstration*) - **4.** MIL : **service (militaire)** military ou national service - **5.** [aide, assistance] favour *UK*, favor *US* ; **rendre un service à qqn** to do sb a favour *UK* ou favor *US* ; **rendre service** to be helpful ; **service après-vente** after-sales service - **6.** [à table] : **premier/deuxième service** first/second sitting - **7.** [pourboire] service (charge) ; **service compris/non compris** service included/not included - **8.** [assortiment - de porcelaine] service, set ; [- de linge] set - **9.** SPORT service, serve.

serviette [servjεt] *nf* **1.** [de table] serviette, napkin - **2.** [de toilette] towel - **3.** [portedocuments] briefcase. ◆ **serviette hygiénique** *nf* sanitary towel *UK* ou napkin *US*.

serviette-éponge [servjεtepɔ̃ʒ] *nf* terry towel.

servile [servil] *adj* **1.** [gén] servile - **2.** [traduction, imitation] slavish.

servir [38] [servir] ◇ *vt* **1.** [gén] to serve ; **servir qqch à qqn** to serve sb sthg, to help sb to sthg - **2.** [avantager] to serve (well), to help. ◇ *vi* **1.** [avoir un usage] to be useful ou of use ; **ça peut toujours/encore servir** it may/may still come in useful - **2.** [être utile] : **servir à qqch/à faire qqch** to be used for sthg/for doing sthg ; **ça ne sert à rien** it's pointless - **3.** [tenir lieu] : **servir de** [personne] to act as ; [chose] to serve as - **4.** [domestique] to be in service - **5.** MIL & SPORT to serve - **6.** [jeu de cartes] to deal. ◆ **se servir** *vp* **1.** [prendre] : **se servir (de)** to help o.s. (to) ; **servez-vous!** help yourself! - **2.** [utiliser] : **se servir de qqn/qqch** to use sb/sthg.

serviteur [servitœr] *nm* servant.

servitude [servityd] *nf* **1.** [esclavage] servitude - **2.** (*gén pl*) [contrainte] constraint.

ses ► **son²**.

session [sesjɔ̃] *nf* **1.** [d'assemblée] session, sitting - **2.** UNIV exam session - **3.** INFORM : **ouvrir une session** to log in ou on ; **fermer** ou **clore une session** to log out ou off.

set [sεt] *nm* **1.** TENNIS set - **2.** [napperon] : **set (de table)** set of table ou place mats.

seuil [sœj] *nm litt* & *fig* threshold.

seul, e [sœl] ◇ *adj* **1.** [isolé] alone ; **seul à seul** alone (together), privately - **2.** [sans compagnie] alone, by o.s. ; **parler tout seul** to talk to o.s. - **3.** [sans aide] on one's own, by o.s. - **4.** [unique] : **le seul...** the only... ; **un seul...** a single... ; **pas un seul...** not one..., not a single... - **5.** [esseulé] lonely - **6.** [sans partenaire, non marié] alone, on one's own. ◇ *nm, f* : **le seul** the only one ; **un seul** a single one, only one.

seulement [sœlmɑ̃] *adv* **1.** [gén] only ; [exclusivement] only, solely - **2.** [même] even. ◆ **non seulement... mais (encore)** *loc correlative* not only... but (also).

sève [sεv] *nf* BOT sap.

sévère [sever] *adj* severe.

sévérité [severite] *nf* severity.

sévices [sevis] *nmpl sout* ill treatment (*U*).

sévir [32] [sevir] *vi* **1.** [épidémie, guerre] to rage - **2.** [punir] to give out a punishment.

sevrer [19] [səvre] *vt* to wean.

sexe [sεks] *nm* **1.** [gén] sex - **2.** [organe] genitals *pl*.

sexiste [sεksist] *nmf & adj* sexist.

sexologue [sεksɔlɔg] *nmf* sexologist.

sex-shop [sεksʃɔp] (*pl* sex-shops) *nm* sex shop.

sextant [sεkstɑ̃] *nm* sextant.

sexualité [sεksɥalite] *nf* sexuality.

sexuel, elle [sεksɥεl] *adj* sexual.

sexy [sεksi] *adj inv fam* sexy.

seyant, e [sεjɑ̃, ɑ̃t] *adj* becoming.

shampooing [ʃɑ̃pwɛ̃] *nm* shampoo.

shérif [ʃerif] *nm* sheriff.

shit [ʃit] *fam nm* hash.

shopping [ʃɔpiŋ] *nm* shopping ; **faire du shopping** to go (out) shopping.

short [ʃɔrt] *nm* shorts *pl*, pair of shorts.

show-business [ʃobiznεs] *nm inv* show business.

si¹ [si] *nm inv* MUS B ; [chanté] ti.

si² [si] ◇ *adv* **1.** [tellement] so ; **elle est si belle** she is so beautiful ; **il roulait si vite qu'il a eu un accident** he was driving so fast (that) he had an accident ; **ce n'est pas si facile que ça** it's not as easy as that ; **si vieux qu'il soit** however old he may be, old as he is - **2.** [oui] yes ; **tu n'aimes pas le café? si** don't you like coffee? yes, I do. ◇ *conj* **1.** [gén] if ; **si tu veux, on y va** we'll go if you want ; **si tu faisais cela, je te détesterais** I would hate you if you did that ; **si seulement** if only - **2.** [dans une question indirecte] if, whether ; **dites-moi si vous venez** tell me if OU whether you're coming. ➤ **si bien que** *loc conj* so that, with the result that.

SI *nm* (*abr de* **syndicat d'initiative**) tourist office.

siamois, e [sjamwa, az] *adj* : **frères siamois, sœurs siamoises** MÉD Siamese twins ; *fig* inseparable companions.

Sibérie [siberi] *nf* : **la Sibérie** Siberia.

sibyllin, e [sibilɛ̃, in] *adj* enigmatic.

SICAV, Sicav [sikav] (*abr de* **société d'investissement à capital variable**) *nf* **1.** [société] unit trust *UK*, mutual fund *US* - **2.** [action] share in a unit trust *UK* OU mutual fund *US*.

Sicile [sisil] *nf* : **la Sicile** Sicily.

SIDA, Sida [sida] (*abr de* **syndrome immunodéficitaire acquis**) *nm* AIDS.

side-car [sidkar] (*pl* **side-cars**) *nm* sidecar.

sidéen, enne [sideɛ̃, ɛn] *nm, f* person with AIDS.

sidérer [18] [sidere] *vt fam* to stagger.

sidérurgie [sideryrʒi] *nf* [industrie] iron and steel industry.

siècle [sjɛkl] *nm* **1.** [cent ans] century - **2.** [époque, âge] age - **3.** (*gén pl*) *fam* [longue durée] ages *pl*.

siège [sjɛʒ] *nm* **1.** [meuble & POLIT] seat - **2.** MIL siege - **3.** [d'organisme] headquarters, head office ; **siège social** registered office - **4.** MÉD : **se présenter par le siège** to be in the breech position.

siéger [22] [sjeʒe] *vi* **1.** [juge, assemblée] to sit - **2.** *litt* [mal] to have its seat ; [maladie] to be located.

sien [sjɛ̃] ➤ **le sien, la sienne** [ləsjɛ̃, lasjɛn] (*mpl* **les siens** [lesjɛ̃], *fpl* **les siennes** [lesjɛn]) *pron poss* [d'homme] his ; [de femme] hers ; [de chose, d'animal] its ; **les siens** his/her family ; **faire des siennes** to be up to one's usual tricks.

sieste [sjɛst] *nf* siesta.

sifflement [sifləmɑ̃] *nm* [son] whistling ; [de serpent] hissing.

siffler [3] [sifle] ⬦ *vi* to whistle ; [serpent] to hiss. ⬦ *vt* **1.** [air de musique] to whistle - **2.** [femme] to whistle at - **3.** [chien] to whistle (for) - **4.** [acteur] to boo, to hiss - **5.** *fam* [verre] to knock back.

sifflet [siflɛ] *nm* whistle. ➤ **sifflets** *nmpl* hissing (*U*), boos.

siffloter [3] [siflɔte] *vi* & *vt* to whistle.

sigle [sigl] *nm* acronym, (set of) initials.

signal, aux [siɲal, o] *nm* **1.** [geste, son] signal ; **signal d'alarme** alarm (signal) ; **donner le signal (de)** to give the signal (for) - **2.** [panneau] sign.

signalement [siɲalmɑ̃] *nm* description.

signaler [3] [siɲale] *vt* **1.** [fait] to point out ; **rien à signaler** nothing to report - **2.** [à la police] to denounce.

signalétique [siɲaletik] *adj* identifying.

signalisation [siɲalizasjɔ̃] *nf* [panneaux] signs *pl* ; [au sol] (road) markings *pl* ; NAUT signals *pl*.

signataire [siɲatɛr] *nmf* signatory.

signature [siɲatyr] *nf* **1.** [nom, marque] signature - **2.** [acte] signing.

signe [siɲ] *nm* **1.** [gén] sign ; **être signe de** to be a sign of ; **être né sous le signe de** ASTROL to be born under the sign of ; **signe avant-coureur** advance indication - **2.** [trait] mark ; **signe particulier** distinguishing mark.

signer [3] [siɲe] *vt* to sign. ➤ **se signer** *vp* to cross o.s.

signet [siɲɛ] *nm* bookmark (*attached to spine of book*).

significatif, ive [siɲifikatif, iv] *adj* significant.

signification [siɲifikasjɔ̃] *nf* [sens] meaning.

signifier [9] [siɲifje] *vt* **1.** [vouloir dire] to mean - **2.** [faire connaître] to make known - **3.** DR to serve notice of.

silence [silɑ̃s] *nm* **1.** [gén] silence ; **garder le silence (sur)** to remain silent (about) ; **silence radio** radio silence - **2.** MUS rest.

silencieux, euse [silɑ̃sjø, øz] *adj* **1.** [lieu, appareil] quiet - **2.** [personne - taciturne] quiet ; [- muet] silent. ➤ **silencieux** *nm* AUTO silencer *UK*, muffler *US*.

silex [silɛks] *nm* flint.

silhouette [silwɛt] *nf* **1.** [de personne] silhouette ; [de femme] figure ; [d'objet] outline - **2.** ART silhouette.

silicium [silisjɔm] *nm* silicon.

silicone [silikon] *nf* silicone.

sillage [sijaʒ] *nm* wake.

sillon [sijɔ̃] *nm* **1.** [tranchée, ride] furrow - **2.** [de disque] groove.

sillonner [3] [sijɔne] *vt* **1.** [champ] to furrow - **2.** [ciel] to crisscross.

silo [silo] *nm* silo.

simagrées [simagre] *nfpl péj* : **faire des simagrées** to make a fuss.

similaire [similɛr] *adj* similar.

similicuir [similikɥir] *nm* imitation leather.

similitude [similityd] *nf* similarity.

simple [sɛ̃pl] ⬦ *adj* **1.** [gén] simple

- **2.** [ordinaire] ordinary - **3.** [billet] : **un aller simple** a single ticket. ◇ nm TENNIS singles sg.

simplicité [sɛ̃plisite] nf simplicity.

simplifier [9] [sɛ̃plifje] vt to simplify.

simpliste [sɛ̃plist] adj péj simplistic.

simulacre [simylakr] nm **1.** [semblant] : **un simulacre de** a pretence of, a sham - **2.** [action simulée] enactment.

simulateur, trice [simylatœr, tris] nm, f pretender ; [de maladie] malingerer. ➡ **simulateur** nm TECHNOL simulator.

simulation [simylasjɔ̃] nf **1.** [gén] simulation - **2.** [comédie] shamming, feigning ; [de maladie] malingering.

simuler [3] [simyle] vt **1.** [gén] to simulate - **2.** [feindre] to feign, to sham.

simultané, e [simyltane] adj simultaneous.

sincère [sɛ̃sɛr] adj sincere.

sincèrement [sɛ̃sɛrmɑ̃] adv **1.** [franchement] honestly, sincerely - **2.** [vraiment] really, truly.

sincérité [sɛ̃serite] nf sincerity.

sine qua non [sinekwanɔn] adj : **condition sine qua non** prerequisite.

Singapour [sɛ̃gapur] npr Singapore.

singe [sɛ̃ʒ] nm ZOOL monkey ; [de grande taille] ape.

singer [17] [sɛ̃ʒe] vt **1.** [personne] to mimic, to ape - **2.** [sentiment] to feign.

singerie [sɛ̃ʒri] nf **1.** [grimace] face - **2.** [manières] fuss (U).

singulariser [3] [sɛ̃gylarize] vt to draw ou call attention to. ➡ **se singulariser** vp to draw ou call attention to o.s.

singularité [sɛ̃gylarite] nf **1.** litt [bizarrerie] strangeness - **2.** [particularité] peculiarity.

singulier, ère [sɛ̃gylje, ɛr] adj **1.** sout [bizarre] strange ; [spécial] uncommon - **2.** GRAMM singular - **3.** [d'homme à homme] : **combat singulier** single combat. ➡ **singulier** nm GRAMM singular.

singulièrement [sɛ̃gyljɛrmɑ̃] adv **1.** litt [bizarrement] strangely - **2.** [beaucoup, très] particularly.

sinistre [sinistr] ◇ nm **1.** [catastrophe] disaster - **2.** DR damage (U). ◇ adj **1.** [personne, regard] sinister ; [maison, ambiance] gloomy - **2.** (avant n) péj [crétin, imbécile] dreadful, terrible.

sinistré, e [sinistre] ◇ adj [région] disaster (avant n), disaster-stricken ; [famille] disaster-stricken. ◇ nm, f disaster victim.

sinon [sinɔ̃] conj **1.** [autrement] or else, otherwise - **2.** [sauf] except, apart from - **3.** [si ce n'est] if not.

sinueux, euse [sinɥø, øz] adj winding ; fig tortuous.

sinuosité [sinɥozite] nf bend, twist.

sinus [sinys] nm **1.** ANAT sinus - **2.** MATH sine.

sinusite [sinyzit] nf sinusitis (U).

sionisme [sjɔnism] nm Zionism.

siphon [sifɔ̃] nm **1.** [tube] siphon - **2.** [bouteille] soda siphon.

siphonner [3] [sifɔne] vt to siphon.

sirène [sirɛn] nf siren.

sirop [siro] nm syrup ; **sirop d'érable** maple syrup ; **sirop de grenadine** (syrup of) grenadine ; **sirop de menthe** mint cordial.

siroter [3] [sirɔte] vt fam to sip.

sis, e [si, siz] adj DR located.

sismique [sismik] adj seismic.

site [sit] nm **1.** [emplacement] site ; **site archéologique/historique** archaeological/historic site - **2.** [paysage] beauty spot - **3.** INFORM : **site Web** web site, Web site.

sitôt [sito] adv : **sitôt après** immediately after ; **pas de sitôt** not for some time, not for a while ; **sitôt arrivé,...** as soon as I/he etc arrived,... ; **sitôt dit, sitôt fait** no sooner said than done. ➡ **sitôt que** loc conj as soon as.

situation [sitɥasjɔ̃] nf **1.** [position, emplacement] position, location - **2.** [contexte, circonstance] situation ; **situation de famille** marital status - **3.** [emploi] job, position - **4.** FIN financial statement.

situer [7] [sitɥe] vt **1.** [maison] to site, to situate - **2.** [sur carte] to locate. ➡ **se situer** vp [scène] to be set ; [dans classement] to be.

six (en fin de phrase [sis], devant consonne ou 'h' aspiré [si], devant voyelle ou 'h' muet [siz]) ◇ adj num inv six ; **il a six ans** he is six (years old) ; **il est six heures** it's six (o'clock) ; **le six janvier** (on) the sixth of January UK, (on) January sixth US ; **daté du six septembre** dated the sixth of September UK ou September sixth US ; **Charles Six** Charles the Sixth ; **page six** page six. ◇ nm inv **1.** [gén] six ; **six de pique** six of spades - **2.** [adresse] (number) six. ◇ pron six ; **ils étaient six** there were six of them ; **six par six** six at a time.

sixième [sizjɛm] ◇ adj num inv sixth. ◇ nmf sixth ; **arriver/se classer sixième** to come (in)/to be placed sixth. ◇ nf SCOL ≃ first year ou form UK, ≃ sixth grade US ; **être en sixième** to be in the first year ou form UK, to be in sixth grade US ; **entrer en sixième** to go to secondary school. ◇ nm **1.** [part] : **le/un sixième de** one/a sixth of ;

cinq sixièmes five sixths - **2.** [arrondissement] sixth arrondissement - **3.** [étage] sixth floor *UK*, seventh floor *US*.

skateboard [skɛtbɔrd] *nm* skateboard.

sketch [skɛtʃ] (*pl* **sketches**) *nm* sketch (*in a revue etc*).

ski [ski] *nm* **1.** [objet] ski - **2.** [sport] skiing ; **faire du ski** to ski ; **ski acrobatique/alpin/de fond** freestyle/alpine/cross-country skiing ; **ski nautique** water skiing.

skier [10] [skje] *vi* to ski.

skieur, euse [skjœr, øz] *nm, f* skier.

skipper [skipœr] *nm* **1.** [capitaine] skipper - **2.** [barreur] helmsman.

slalom [slalɔm] *nm* **1.** SKI slalom - **2.** [zigzags] : **faire du slalom** to zigzag.

slave [slav] *adj* Slavonic. ◆ **Slave** *nmf* Slav.

slip [slip] *nm* briefs *pl*, underpants *pl* ; **slip de bain** [d'homme] swimming trunks *pl* ; [de femme] bikini bottoms *pl*.

slogan [slɔgã] *nm* slogan.

Slovaquie [slɔvaki] *nf* : **la Slovaquie** Slovakia.

Slovénie [slɔveni] *nf* : **la Slovénie** Slovenia.

slow [slo] *nm* slow dance.

smasher [3] [sma(t)ʃe] *vi* TENNIS to smash (the ball).

SME (*abr de* **Système monétaire européen**) *nm* EMS.

SMIC, Smic [smik] (*abr de* **salaire minimum interprofessionnel de croissance**) *nm* index-linked guaranteed minimum wage.

smiley [smajlɛ] *nm* smiley.

smoking [smɔkiŋ] *nm* dinner jacket, tuxedo *US*.

SNCF (*abr de* **Société nationale des chemins de fer français**) *nf* French railways board, ≃ BR *UK*.

snob [snɔb] ◇ *nmf* snob. ◇ *adj* snobbish.

snober [3] [snɔbe] *vt* to snub, to cold-shoulder.

snobisme [snɔbism] *nm* snobbery, snobbishness.

soap opera [sopɔpera] (*pl* **soap operas**), **soap** [sop] (*pl* **soaps**) *nm* soap (opera).

sobre [sɔbr] *adj* **1.** [personne] temperate - **2.** [style] sober ; [décor, repas] simple.

sobriété [sɔbrijete] *nf* sobriety.

sobriquet [sɔbrikɛ] *nm* nickname.

soc [sɔk] *nm* ploughshare *UK*, plowshare *US*.

sociable [sɔsjabl] *adj* sociable.

social, e, aux [sɔsjal, o] *adj* **1.** [rapports, classe, service] social - **2.** COMM : **capital social** share capital ; **raison sociale** company name. ◆ **social** *nm* : **le social** social affairs *pl*.

socialisme [sɔsjalism] *nm* socialism.

socialiste [sɔsjalist] *nmf & adj* socialist.

sociétaire [sɔsjetɛr] *nmf* member.

société [sɔsjete] *nf* **1.** [communauté, classe sociale, groupe] society ; **en société** in society - **2.** [présence] company, society - **3.** COMM company, firm.

sociologie [sɔsjɔlɔʒi] *nf* sociology.

sociologue [sɔsjɔlɔg] *nmf* sociologist.

socioprofessionnel, elle [sɔsjɔprɔfɛsjɔnɛl] *adj* socioprofessional.

socle [sɔkl] *nm* **1.** [de statue] plinth, pedestal - **2.** [de lampe] base.

socquette [sɔkɛt] *nf* ankle ou short sock.

soda [sɔda] *nm* fizzy drink.

sodium [sɔdjɔm] *nm* sodium.

sodomiser [3] [sɔdɔmize] *vt* to sodomize.

sœur [sœr] *nf* **1.** [gén] sister ; **grande/petite sœur** big/little sister - **2.** RELIG nun, sister.

sofa [sɔfa] *nm* sofa.

Sofia [sɔfja] *npr* Sofia.

software [sɔftwɛr] *nm* software.

soi [swa] *pron pers* oneself ; **chacun pour soi** every man for himself ; **cela va de soi** that goes without saying. ◆ **soi-même** *pron pers* oneself.

soi-disant [swadizã] ◇ *adj inv* (*avant n*) so-called. ◇ *adv fam* supposedly.

soie [swa] *nf* **1.** [textile] silk - **2.** [poil] bristle.

soierie [swari] *nf* (*gén pl*) [textile] silk.

soif [swaf] *nf* thirst ; **soif (de)** *fig* thirst (for), craving (for) ; **avoir soif** to be thirsty.

soigné, e [swaɲe] *adj* **1.** [travail] meticulous - **2.** [personne] well-groomed ; [jardin, mains] well-cared-for.

soigner [3] [swaɲe] *vt* **1.** [suj: médecin] to treat ; [suj: infirmière, parent] to nurse - **2.** [invités, jardin, mains] to look after - **3.** [travail, présentation] to take care over. ◆ **se soigner** *vp* to take care of o.s., to look after o.s.

soigneusement [swaɲøzmã] *adv* carefully.

soigneux, euse [swaɲø, øz] *adj* **1.** [personne] tidy, neat - **2.** [travail] careful.

soin [swẽ] *nm* **1.** [attention] care ; **avoir** ou **prendre soin de faire qqch** to be sure to do sthg ; **avec soin** carefully ; **sans soin** [procéder] carelessly ; [travail] careless ; **être aux petits soins pour qqn** *fig* to wait on sb hand and foot - **2.** [souci] concern. ◆ **soins** *nmpl* care (U) ; **les premiers soins** first aid *sg*.

soir [swar] *nm* evening ; **demain soir** tomorrow evening ou night ; **le soir** in the evening ; **à ce soir!** see you tonight!

soirée [sware] *nf* **1.** [soir] evening - **2.** [réception] party.

sois ▶ être.

soit[1] [swat] *adv* so be it.

soit[2] [swa] ◇ *v* ▶ être. ◇ *conj* **1.** [c'est-à-dire] in other words, that is to say - **2.** MATH [étant donné] : **soit une droite AB** given a straight line AB. ⧫ **soit... soit** *loc correlative* either... or. ⧫ **soit que... soit que** *loc correlative* whether... or (whether).

soixante [swasɑ̃t] ◇ *adj num inv* sixty ; **les années soixante** the Sixties. ◇ *nm* sixty ; *voir aussi* **six**.

soixante-dix [swasɑ̃tdis] ◇ *adj num inv* seventy ; **les années soixante-dix** the Seventies. ◇ *nm* seventy ; *voir aussi* **six**.

soixante-dixième [swasɑ̃tdizjɛm] *adj num inv, nm & nmf* seventieth ; *voir aussi* **sixième**.

soixantième [swasɑ̃tjɛm] *adj num inv, nm & nmf* sixtieth ; *voir aussi* **sixième**.

soja [sɔʒa] *nm* soya.

sol [sɔl] *nm* **1.** [terre] ground - **2.** [de maison] floor - **3.** [territoire] soil - **4.** MUS G ; [chanté] so.

solaire [sɔlɛr] *adj* **1.** [énergie, four] solar - **2.** [crème] sun *(avant n)*.

solarium [sɔlarjɔm] *nm* solarium.

soldat [sɔlda] *nm* **1.** MIL soldier ; [grade] private ; **le soldat inconnu** the Unknown Soldier - **2.** [jouet] (toy) soldier.

solde [sɔld] ◇ *nm* **1.** [de compte, facture] balance ; **solde créditeur/débiteur** credit/ debit balance - **2.** [rabais] : **en solde** [acheter] in a sale. ◇ *nf* MIL pay. ⧫ **soldes** *nmpl* sales.

solder [3] [sɔlde] *vt* **1.** [compte] to close - **2.** [marchandises] to sell off. ⧫ **se solder** *vp* : **se solder par** FIN to show ; *fig* [aboutir] to end in.

sole [sɔl] *nf* sole.

soleil [sɔlɛj] *nm* **1.** [astre, motif] sun ; **soleil couchant/levant** setting/rising sun - **2.** [lumière, chaleur] sun, sunlight ; **au soleil** in the sun ; **en plein soleil** right in the sun ; **il fait (du) soleil** it's sunny ; **prendre le soleil** to sunbathe.

solennel, elle [sɔlanɛl] *adj* **1.** [cérémonieux] ceremonial - **2.** [grave] solemn - **3.** *péj* [pompeux] pompous.

solennité [sɔlanite] *nf* **1.** [gravité] solemnity - **2.** [raideur] stiffness, formality - **3.** [fête] special occasion.

solfège [sɔlfɛʒ] *nm* : **apprendre le solfège** to learn the rudiments of music.

solidaire [sɔlidɛr] *adj* **1.** [lié] : **être solidaire de qqn** to be behind sb, to show solidarity with sb - **2.** [relié] interdependent, integral.

solidarité [sɔlidarite] *nf* [entraide] solidarity ; **par solidarité** [se mettre en grève] in sympathy.

solide [sɔlid] ◇ *adj* **1.** [état, corps] solid - **2.** [construction] solid, sturdy - **3.** [personne] sturdy, robust - **4.** [argument] solid, sound - **5.** [relation] stable, strong. ◇ *nm* solid ; **il nous faut du solide** *fig* we need something solid ou concrete.

solidifier [9] [sɔlidifje] *vt* **1.** [ciment, eau] to solidify - **2.** [structure] to reinforce. ⧫ **se solidifier** *vp* to solidify.

solidité [sɔlidite] *nf* **1.** [de matière, construction] solidity - **2.** [de mariage] stability, strength - **3.** [de raisonnement, d'argument] soundness.

soliloque [sɔlilɔk] *nm sout* soliloquy.

soliste [sɔlist] *nmf* soloist.

solitaire [sɔlitɛr] ◇ *adj* **1.** [de caractère] solitary - **2.** [esseulé, retiré] lonely. ◇ *nmf* [personne] loner, recluse. ◇ *nm* [jeu, diamant] solitaire.

solitude [sɔlityd] *nf* **1.** [isolement] loneliness - **2.** [retraite] solitude.

sollicitation [sɔlisitasjɔ̃] *nf (gén pl)* entreaty.

solliciter [3] [sɔlisite] *vt* **1.** [demander - entretien, audience] to request ; [- attention, intérêt] to seek - **2.** [s'intéresser à] : **être sollicité** to be in demand - **3.** [faire appel à] : **solliciter qqn pour faire qqch** to appeal to sb to do sthg.

sollicitude [sɔlisityd] *nf* solicitude, concern.

solo [sɔlo] *nm* solo ; **en solo** solo.

solstice [sɔlstis] *nm* : **solstice d'été/d'hiver** summer/winter solstice.

soluble [sɔlybl] *adj* **1.** [matière] soluble ; [café] instant - **2.** *fig* [problème] solvable.

solution [sɔlysjɔ̃] *nf* **1.** [résolution] solution, answer - **2.** [liquide] solution.

solvable [sɔlvabl] *adj* solvent, creditworthy.

solvant [sɔlvɑ̃] *nm* solvent.

Somalie [sɔmali] *nf* : **la Somalie** Somalia.

sombre [sɔ̃br] *adj* **1.** [couleur, costume, pièce] dark - **2.** *fig* [pensées, avenir] dark, gloomy - **3.** *(avant n) fam* [profond] : **c'est un sombre crétin** he's a prize idiot.

sombrer [3] [sɔ̃bre] *vi* to sink ; **sombrer dans** *fig* to sink into.

sommaire [sɔmɛr] ◇ *adj* **1.** [explication] brief - **2.** [exécution] summary - **3.** [installation] basic. ◇ *nm* summary.

sommation [sɔmasjɔ̃] *nf* **1.** [assignation] summons *sg* - **2.** [ordre - de payer] demand ; [- de se rendre] warning.

somme [sɔm] <> *nf* **1.** [addition] total, sum - **2.** [d'argent] sum, amount - **3.** [ouvrage] overview. <> *nm* nap. **➡ en somme** *loc adv* in short. **➡ somme toute** *loc adv* when all's said and done.

sommeil [sɔmɛj] *nm* sleep ; **avoir sommeil** to be sleepy.

sommeiller [4] [sɔmeje] *vi* **1.** [personne] to doze - **2.** *fig* [qualité] to be dormant.

sommelier, ère [sɔməlje, ɛr] *nm, f* wine waiter (*f* wine waitress).

sommes ➡ être.

sommet [sɔmɛ] *nm* **1.** [de montagne] summit, top - **2.** *fig* [de hiérarchie] top ; [de perfection] height - **3.** GÉOM apex.

sommier [sɔmje] *nm* base, bed base.

sommité [sɔmite] *nf* [personne] leading light.

somnambule [sɔmnɑ̃byl] <> *nmf* sleepwalker. <> *adj* : **être somnambule** to be a sleepwalker.

somnifère [sɔmnifɛr] *nm* sleeping pill.

somnolent, e [sɔmnɔlɑ̃, ɑ̃t] *adj* [personne] sleepy, drowsy ; *fig* [vie] dull ; *fig* [économie] sluggish.

somnoler [3] [sɔmnɔle] *vi* to doze.

somptueux, euse [sɔ̃ptɥø, øz] *adj* sumptuous, lavish.

somptuosité [sɔ̃ptɥozite] *nf* lavishness (*U*).

son¹ [sɔ̃] *nm* **1.** [bruit] sound ; **au son de** to the sound of ; **son et lumière** son et lumière - **2.** [céréale] bran.

son², sa, ses [sɔ̃, sa, se] *adj poss* **1.** [possesseur défini - homme] his ; [- femme] her ; [- chose, animal] its ; **il aime son père** he loves his father ; **elle aime ses parents** she loves her parents ; **la ville a perdu son charme** the town has lost its charm - **2.** [possesseur indéfini] one's ; [après «chacun», «tout le monde» etc] his/her, their.

sonate [sɔnat] *nf* sonata.

sondage [sɔ̃daʒ] *nm* **1.** [enquête] poll, survey ; **sondage d'opinion** opinion poll - **2.** TECHNOL drilling - **3.** MÉD probing.

sonde [sɔ̃d] *nf* **1.** MÉTÉOR sonde ; [spatiale] probe - **2.** MÉD probe - **3.** NAUT sounding line - **4.** TECHNOL drill.

sonder [3] [sɔ̃de] *vt* **1.** MÉD & NAUT to sound - **2.** [terrain] to drill - **3.** *fig* [opinion, personne] to sound out.

songe [sɔ̃ʒ] *nm litt* dream.

songer [17] [sɔ̃ʒe] <> *vt* : **songer que** to consider that. <> *vi* : **songer à** to think about.

songeur, euse [sɔ̃ʒœr, øz] *adj* pensive, thoughtful.

sonnant, e [sɔnɑ̃, ɑ̃t] *adj* : **à six heures sonnantes** at six o'clock sharp.

sonné, e [sɔne] *adj* **1.** [passé] : **il est trois heures sonnées** it's gone three o'clock ; **il a quarante ans bien sonnés** *fam fig* he's the wrong side of forty - **2.** *fig* [étourdi] groggy.

sonner [3] [sɔne] <> *vt* **1.** [cloche] to ring - **2.** [retraite, alarme] to sound - **3.** [domestique] to ring for - **4.** *fam fig* [siffler] : **je ne t'ai pas sonné!** who asked you! - **5.** *fam* [assommer] to knock out (*sep*), to stun ; [abasourdir] to stun, to stagger, to knock (out). <> *vi* [gén] to ring ; **sonner chez qqn** to ring sb's bell.

sonnerie [sɔnri] *nf* **1.** [bruit] ringing - **2.** [mécanisme] striking mechanism - **3.** [signal] call.

sonnet [sɔnɛ] *nm* sonnet.

sonnette [sɔnɛt] *nf* bell.

sono [sɔno] *nf fam* [de salle] P.A. (system) ; [de discothèque] sound system.

sonore [sɔnɔr] *adj* **1.** CINÉ & PHYS sound (*avant n*) - **2.** [voix, rire] ringing, resonant - **3.** [salle] resonant.

sonorisation [sɔnɔrizasjɔ̃] *nf* **1.** [action - de film] addition of the soundtrack ; [- de salle] wiring for sound - **2.** [matériel - de salle] public address system, P.A. (system) ; [- de discothèque] sound system.

sonoriser [3] [sɔnɔrize] *vt* **1.** [film] to add the soundtrack to - **2.** [salle] to wire for sound.

sonorité [sɔnɔrite] *nf* **1.** [de piano, voix] tone - **2.** [de salle] acoustics *pl*.

sont ➡ être.

Sopalin® [sɔpalɛ̃] *nm* kitchen roll *UK*, paper towels *US*.

sophistiqué, e [sɔfistike] *adj* sophisticated.

soporifique [sɔpɔrifik] <> *adj* soporific. <> *nm* sleeping drug, soporific.

soprano [sɔprano] (*pl* **sopranos** OU **soprani** [sɔprani]) *nm & nmf* soprano.

sorbet [sɔrbɛ] *nm* sorbet *UK*, sherbet *US*.

Sorbonne [sɔrbɔn] *nf* : **la Sorbonne** the Sorbonne (*highly respected Paris university*).

sorcellerie [sɔrsɛlri] *nf* witchcraft, sorcery.

sorcier, ère [sɔrsje, ɛr] *nm, f* sorcerer (*f* witch).

sordide [sɔrdid] *adj* squalid ; *fig* sordid.

sornettes [sɔrnɛt] *nfpl* nonsense (*U*).

sort [sɔr] *nm* **1.** [maléfice] spell ; **jeter un sort (à qqn)** to cast a spell (on sb) - **2.** [destinée] fate - **3.** [condition] lot - **4.** [hasard] : **le sort** fate ; **tirer au sort** to draw lots.

sortant, e [sɔrtɑ̃, ɑ̃t] *adj* **1.** [numéro] winning - **2.** [président, directeur] outgoing *(avant n)*.

sorte [sɔrt] *nf* sort, kind ; **une sorte de** a sort of, a kind of ; **toutes sortes de** all kinds of, all sorts of.

sortie [sɔrti] *nf* **1.** [issue] exit, way out ; [d'eau, d'air] outlet ; **sortie d'autoroute** motorway junction *ou* exit *UK*, freeway exit *US* ; **sortie de secours** emergency exit - **2.** [départ] : **c'est la sortie de l'école** it's home-time *UK* ; **à la sortie du travail** when work finishes, after work - **3.** [de produit] launch, launching ; [de disque] release ; [de livre] publication - **4.** *(gén pl)* [dépense] outgoings *pl UK*, expenditure *(U)* - **5.** [excursion] outing ; [au cinéma, au restaurant] evening *ou* night out ; **faire une sortie** to go out - **6.** MIL sortie - **7.** INFORM : **sortie imprimante** printout.

sortilège [sɔrtileʒ] *nm* spell.

sortir [43] [sɔrtir] ◇ *vi (v aux : être)* **1.** [de la maison, du bureau etc] to leave, to go/come out ; **sortir de** to go/come out of, to leave - **2.** [pour se distraire] to go out - **3.** *fig* [quitter] : **sortir de** [réserve, préjugés] to shed - **4.** *fig* : **sortir de** [coma] to come out of ; [de maladie] to get over, to recover from ; **je sors d'une grippe** I'm just recovering from a bout of flu - **5.** [film, livre, produit] to come out ; [disque] to be released - **6.** [au jeu - carte, numéro] to come up - **7.** [s'écarter de] : **sortir de** [sujet] to get away from ; [légalité, compétence] to be outside ; **sortir de l'ordinaire** to be out of the ordinary ; **d'où il sort, celui-là?** where did HE spring from? ◇ *vt (v aux : être)* **1.** [gén] : **sortir qqch (de)** to take sthg out (of) - **2.** [de situation difficile] to get out, to extract - **3.** [produit] to launch ; [disque] to bring out, to release ; [livre] to bring out, to publish. ◈ **se sortir** *vp fig* [de pétrin] to get out ; **s'en sortir** [en réchapper] to come out of it ; [y arriver] to get through it.

SOS *nm* SOS ; **SOS médecins/dépannage** emergency medical/repair service ; **SOS-Racisme** *voluntary organization set up to combat racism in French society* ; **lancer un SOS** to send out an SOS.

sosie [sɔzi] *nm* double.

sot, sotte [so, sɔt] ◇ *adj* silly, foolish. ◇ *nm, f* fool.

sottise [sɔtiz] *nf* stupidity *(U)*, foolishness *(U)* ; **dire/faire une sottise** to say/do something stupid.

sou [su] *nm* : **être sans le sou** to be penniless. ◈ **sous** *nmpl fam* money *(U)*.

soubassement [subasmɑ̃] *nm* base.

soubresaut [subrəso] *nm* **1.** [de voiture] jolt - **2.** [de personne] start.

souche [suʃ] *nf* **1.** [d'arbre] stump - **2.** [de carnet] counterfoil, stub.

souci [susi] *nm* **1.** [tracas] worry ; **se faire du souci** to worry - **2.** [préoccupation] concern - **3.** [fleur] marigold.

soucier [9] [susje] ◈ **se soucier** *vp* : **se soucier de** to care about.

soucieux, euse [susjø, øz] *adj* **1.** [préoccupé] worried, concerned - **2.** [concerné] : **être soucieux de qqch/de faire qqch** to be concerned about sthg/about doing sthg.

soucoupe [sukup] *nf* **1.** [assiette] saucer - **2.** [vaisseau] : **soucoupe volante** flying saucer.

soudain, e [sudɛ̃, ɛn] *adj* sudden. ◈ **soudain** *adv* suddenly, all of a sudden.

Soudan [sudɑ̃] *nm* : **le Soudan** the Sudan.

soude [sud] *nf* soda.

souder [3] [sude] *vt* **1.** TECHNOL to weld, to solder - **2.** MÉD to knit - **3.** *fig* [unir] to bind together.

soudoyer [13] [sudwaje] *vt* to bribe.

soudure [sudyr] *nf* TECHNOL welding ; [résultat] weld.

souffert, e [sufer, ɛrt] *pp* ▶ souffrir.

souffle [sufl] *nm* **1.** [respiration] breathing ; [expiration] puff, breath ; **un souffle d'air** *fig* a breath of air, a puff of wind - **2.** *fig* [inspiration] inspiration - **3.** [d'explosion] blast - **4.** MÉD : **souffle au cœur** heart murmur ; **avoir le souffle coupé** to have one's breath taken away.

souffler [3] [sufle] ◇ *vt* **1.** [bougie] to blow out - **2.** [vitre] to blow out, to shatter - **3.** [chuchoter] : **souffler qqch à qqn** to whisper sthg to sb - **4.** *fam* [prendre] : **souffler qqch à qqn** to pinch sthg from sb *UK* - **5.** *fam* [époustoufler - suj: événement, personne] to take aback, to stagger, to knock out *(sep)*. ◇ *vi* **1.** [gén] to blow - **2.** [respirer] to puff, to pant - **3.** [se reposer] to have a break.

soufflet [sufle] *nm* **1.** [instrument] bellows *sg* - **2.** [de train] connecting corridor, concertina vestibule - **3.** COUT gusset.

souffleur, euse [suflœr, øz] *nm, f* THÉÂTRE prompt. ◈ **souffleur** *nm* [de verre] blower.

souffrance [sufrɑ̃s] *nf* suffering.

souffrant, e [sufrɑ̃, ɑ̃t] *adj* poorly.

souffre-douleur [sufrədulœr] *nm inv* whipping boy.

souffrir [34] [sufrir] ◇ *vi* to suffer ; **souffrir de** to suffer from ; **souffrir du dos/cœur** to have back/heart problems. ◇ *vt* **1.** [ressentir] to suffer - **2.** *litt* [supporter] to stand, to bear.

soufre [sufr] *nm* sulphur *UK*, sulfur *US*.

souhait [swɛ] *nm* wish ; **à tes/vos souhaits!** bless you!

souhaiter [4] [swete] *vt* : **souhaiter qqch** to wish for sthg ; **souhaiter faire qqch** to hope to do sthg ; **souhaiter qqch à qqn** to wish sb sthg ; **souhaiter à qqn de faire qqch** to hope that sb does sthg ; **souhaiter que...** (+ *subjonctif*) to hope that...

souiller [3] [suje] *vt litt* [salir] to soil ; *fig & sout* to sully.

souillon [sujɔ̃] *nf péj* slut.

soûl, e, saoul, e [su, sul] *adj* drunk.

soulagement [sulaʒmɑ̃] *nm* relief.

soulager [17] [sulaʒe] *vt* [gén] to relieve.

soûler, saouler [3] [sule] *vt* **1.** *fam* [enivrer] : **soûler qqn** to get sb drunk ; *fig* to intoxicate sb - **2.** *fig & péj* [de plaintes] : **soûler qqn** to bore sb silly. ➤ **se soûler** *vp fam* to get drunk.

soulèvement [sulɛvmɑ̃] *nm* uprising.

soulever [19] [sulve] *vt* **1.** [fardeau, poids] to lift ; [rideau] to raise - **2.** *fig* [question] to raise, to bring up - **3.** *fig* [enthousiasme] to generate, to arouse ; [tollé] to stir up ; **soulever qqn contre** to stir sb up against. ➤ **se soulever** *vp* **1.** [s'élever] to raise o.s., to lift o.s. - **2.** [se révolter] to rise up.

soulier [sulje] *nm* shoe.

souligner [3] [suliɲe] *vt* **1.** [par un trait] to underline - **2.** *fig* [insister sur] to underline, to emphasize - **3.** [mettre en valeur] to emphasize.

soumettre [84] [sumɛtr] *vt* **1.** [astreindre] : **soumettre qqn à** to subject sb to - **2.** [ennemi, peuple] to subjugate - **3.** [projet, problème] : **soumettre qqch (à)** to submit sthg (to). ➤ **se soumettre** *vp* : **se soumettre (à)** to submit (to).

soumis, e [sumi, iz] ◇ *pp* ➤ **soumettre**. ◇ *adj* submissive.

soumission [sumisjɔ̃] *nf* submission.

soupape [supap] *nf* valve.

soupçon [supsɔ̃] *nm* [suspicion, intuition] suspicion.

soupçonner [3] [supsɔne] *vt* [suspecter] to suspect ; **soupçonner qqn de qqch/de faire qqch** to suspect sb of sthg/of doing sthg.

soupçonneux, euse [supsɔnø, øz] *adj* suspicious.

soupe [sup] *nf* CULIN soup ; **soupe populaire** soup kitchen.

souper [3] [supe] ◇ *nm* supper. ◇ *vi* to have supper.

soupeser [19] [supəze] *vt* **1.** [poids] to feel the weight of - **2.** *fig* [évaluer] to weigh up.

soupière [supjɛr] *nf* tureen.

soupir [supir] *nm* **1.** [souffle] sigh ; **pousser un soupir** to let out ou give a sigh - **2.** MUS crotchet rest *UK*, quarter-note rest *US*.

soupirail, aux [supiraj, o] *nm* barred basement window *(for ventilation purposes)*.

soupirant [supirɑ̃] *nm* suitor.

soupirer [3] [supire] *vi* [souffler] to sigh.

souple [supl] *adj* **1.** [gymnaste] supple - **2.** [pas] lithe - **3.** [paquet, col] soft - **4.** [tissu, cheveux] flowing - **5.** [tuyau, horaire, caractère] flexible.

souplesse [suplɛs] *nf* **1.** [de gymnaste] suppleness - **2.** [flexibilité - de tuyau] pliability, flexibility ; [- de matière] suppleness - **3.** [de personne] flexibility.

source [surs] *nf* **1.** [gén] source - **2.** [d'eau] spring ; **prendre sa source à** to rise in - **3.** [cause] source.

sourcil [sursi] *nm* eyebrow ; **froncer les sourcils** to frown.

sourcilière [sursiljɛr] ➤ **arcade**.

sourciller [3] [sursije] *vi* : **sans sourciller** without batting an eyelid.

sourcilleux, euse [sursijø, øz] *adj* fussy, finicky.

sourd, e [sur, surd] ◇ *adj* **1.** [personne] deaf - **2.** [bruit, voix] muffled - **3.** [douleur] dull - **4.** [lutte, hostilité] silent. ◇ *nm, f* deaf person.

sourdement [surdəmɑ̃] *adv* **1.** [avec un bruit sourd] dully - **2.** *fig* [secrètement] silently.

sourdine [surdin] *nf* mute ; **en sourdine** [sans bruit] softly ; [secrètement] in secret.

sourd-muet, sourde-muette [surmɥɛ, surdmɥɛt] *nm, f* deaf-mute, deaf-and-dumb person.

sourdre [73] [surdr] *vi* to well up.

souriant, e [surjɑ̃, ɑ̃t] *adj* smiling, cheerful.

souricière [surisjɛr] *nf* mousetrap ; *fig* trap.

sourire [95] [surir] ◇ *vi* to smile ; **sourire à qqn** to smile at sb ; *fig* [campagne] to appeal to sb ; [destin, chance] to smile on sb. ◇ *nm* smile.

souris [suri] *nf* INFORM & ZOOL mouse.

sournois, e [surnwa, az] *adj* **1.** [personne] underhand - **2.** *fig* [maladie, phénomène] unpredictable.

sous [su] *prép* **1.** [gén] under ; **nager sous l'eau** to swim underwater ; **sous la pluie** in the rain ; **sous cet aspect** ou **angle** from that point of view - **2.** [dans un délai de] within ; **sous huit jours** within a week.

sous-alimenté, e [suzalimɑ̃te] *adj* malnourished, underfed.

sous-bois [subwa] *nm inv* undergrowth.

souscription [suskripsjɔ̃] nf subscription.

souscrire [99] [suskrir] vi : **souscrire à** to subscribe to.

sous-développé, e [sudevlɔpe] adj ÉCON underdeveloped ; fig & péj backward.

sous-directeur, trice [sudirɛktœr, tris] nm, f assistant manager (f assistant manageress).

sous-ensemble [suzɑ̃sɑ̃bl] nm subset.

sous-entendu [suzɑ̃tɑ̃dy] nm insinuation.

sous-estimer [3] [suzɛstime] vt to underestimate, to underrate.

sous-évaluer [7] [suzevalɥe] vt to underestimate.

sous-jacent, e [suʒasɑ̃, ɑ̃t] adj underlying.

sous-louer [6] [sulwe] vt to sublet.

sous-marin, e [sumarɛ̃, in] adj underwater (avant n). ▪ **sous-marin** nm submarine.

sous-officier [suzɔfisje] nm non-commissioned officer.

sous-préfecture [suprefɛktyr] nf sub-prefecture.

sous-préfet [suprefɛ] nm sub-prefect.

sous-produit [suprɔdɥi] nm 1. [objet] by-product - 2. fig [imitation] pale imitation.

sous-répertoire [supertwar] (pl sous-répertoires) nm INFORM sub-directory.

soussigné, e [susine] <> adj : je soussigné I the undersigned. <> nm, f undersigned.

sous-sol [susɔl] nm 1. [de bâtiment] basement - 2. [naturel] subsoil.

sous-tasse [sutas] nf saucer.

sous-titre [sutitr] nm subtitle.

soustraction [sustraksjɔ̃] nf MATH subtraction.

soustraire [112] [sustrer] vt 1. [retrancher] : soustraire qqch de to subtract sthg from - 2. sout [voler] : soustraire qqch à qqn to take sthg away from sb. ▪ **se soustraire** vp : se soustraire à to escape from.

sous-traitant, e [sutrɛtɑ̃, ɑ̃t] adj subcontracting. ▪ **sous-traitant** nm subcontractor.

sous-verre [suvɛr] nm inv picture or document framed between a sheet of glass and a rigid backing.

sous-vêtement [suvɛtmɑ̃] nm undergarment ; sous-vêtements underwear (U), underclothes.

soutane [sutan] nf cassock.

soute [sut] nf hold.

soutenance [sutnɑ̃s] nf viva UK.

souteneur [sutnœr] nm procurer.

soutenir [40] [sutnir] vt 1. [immeuble, personne] to support, to hold up - 2. [effort, intérêt] to sustain - 3. [encourager] to support ; POLIT to back, to support - 4. [affirmer] :

soutenir que to maintain (that) - 5. [résister à] to withstand ; [regard, comparaison] to bear.

soutenu, e [sutny] adj 1. [style, langage] elevated - 2. [attention, rythme] sustained - 3. [couleur] vivid.

souterrain, e [sutɛrɛ̃, ɛn] adj underground. ▪ **souterrain** nm underground passage.

soutien [sutjɛ̃] nm support ; apporter son soutien à to give one's support to.

soutien-gorge [sutjɛ̃gɔrʒ] (pl soutiens-gorge) nm bra.

soutirer [3] [sutire] vt fig [tirer] : soutirer qqch à qqn to extract sthg from sb.

souvenir [40] [suvnir] nm 1. [réminiscence, mémoire] memory - 2. [objet] souvenir. ▪ **se souvenir** vp [ne pas oublier] : se souvenir de qqch/de qqn to remember sthg/sb ; se souvenir que to remember (that).

souvent [suvɑ̃] adv often.

souvenu, e [suvny] pp ▶ souvenir.

souverain, e [suvrɛ̃, ɛn] <> adj 1. [remède, état] sovereign - 2. [indifférence] supreme. <> nm, f [monarque] sovereign, monarch.

souveraineté [suvrɛnte] nf sovereignty.

soviétique [sɔvjetik] adj Soviet. ▪ **Soviétique** nmf Soviet (citizen).

soyeux, euse [swajø, øz] adj silky.

soyez ▶ être.

SPA (abr de Société protectrice des animaux) nf French society for the protection of animals, ≃ RSPCA UK, ≃ SPCA US.

spacieux, euse [spasjø, øz] adj spacious.

spaghettis [spageti] nmpl spaghetti (U).

sparadrap [sparadra] nm sticking plaster UK, Band-Aid® US.

spartiate [sparsjat] adj [austère] Spartan.

spasme [spasm] nm spasm.

spasmodique [spasmɔdik] adj spasmodic.

spatial, e, aux [spasjal, o] adj space (avant n).

spatule [spatyl] nf 1. [ustensile] spatula - 2. [de ski] tip.

speaker, speakerine [spikœr, spikrin] nm, f announcer.

spécial, e, aux [spesjal, o] adj 1. [particulier] special - 2. fam [bizarre] peculiar.

spécialiser [3] [spesjalize] vt to specialize. ▪ **se spécialiser** vp : se spécialiser (dans) to specialize (in).

spécialiste [spesjalist] nmf specialist.

spécialité [spesjalite] nf speciality UK, specialty US.

spécifier [9] [spesifje] vt to specify.

spécifique [spesifik] *adj* specific.

spécimen [spesimɛn] *nm* **1.** [représentant] specimen - **2.** [exemplaire] sample.

spectacle [spɛktakl] *nm* **1.** [représentation] show - **2.** [domaine] show business, entertainment - **3.** [tableau] spectacle, sight.

spectaculaire [spɛktakylɛr] *adj* spectacular.

spectateur, trice [spɛktatœr, tris] *nm, f* **1.** [témoin] witness - **2.** [de spectacle] spectator.

spectre [spɛktr] *nm* **1.** [fantôme] spectre UK, specter US - **2.** PHYS spectrum.

spéculateur, trice [spekylatœr, tris] *nm, f* speculator.

spéculation [spekylasjɔ̃] *nf* speculation.

spéculer [3] [spekyle] *vi* : **spéculer sur** FIN to speculate in ; *fig* [miser] to count on.

speech [spitʃ] (*pl* speeches) *nm* speech.

speed [spid] *adj fam* hyper ; **il est très speed** he's really hyper.

speeder [spide] *vi fam* to hurry.

spéléologie [speleɔlɔʒi] *nf* [exploration] potholing UK, spelunking US ; [science] speleology.

spermatozoïde [spɛrmatɔzɔid] *nm* sperm, spermatozoon.

sperme [spɛrm] *nm* sperm, semen.

sphère [sfɛr] *nf* sphere.

sphérique [sferik] *adj* spherical.

spirale [spiral] *nf* spiral.

spirituel, elle [spirityɛl] *adj* **1.** [de l'âme, moral] spiritual - **2.** [vivant, drôle] witty.

spiritueux [spirityø] *nm* spirit.

splendeur [splɑ̃dœr] *nf* **1.** [beauté, prospérité] splendour UK, splendor US - **2.** [merveille] : **c'est une splendeur!** it's magnificent!

splendide [splɑ̃did] *adj* magnificent, splendid.

spongieux, euse [spɔ̃ʒjø, øz] *adj* spongy.

sponsor [spɔ̃sɔr] *nm* sponsor.

sponsoriser [3] [spɔ̃sɔrize] *vt* to sponsor.

spontané, e [spɔ̃tane] *adj* spontaneous.

spontanéité [spɔ̃taneite] *nf* spontaneity.

sporadique [spɔradik] *adj* sporadic.

sport [spɔr] <> *nm* sport ; **sports d'hiver** winter sports. <> *adj inv* **1.** [vêtement] sports (*avant n*) - **2.** [fair play] sporting.

sportif, ive [spɔrtif, iv] <> *adj* **1.** [association, résultats] sports (*avant n*) - **2.** [personne, physique] sporty, athletic - **3.** [fair play] sportsmanlike, sporting. <> *nm, f* sportsman (*f* sportswoman).

spot [spɔt] *nm* **1.** [lampe] spot, spotlight - **2.** [publicité] : **spot (publicitaire)** commercial, advert UK.

sprint [sprint] *nm* [SPORT - accélération] spurt ; [- course] sprint.

square [skwar] *nm* small public garden.

squash [skwaʃ] *nm* squash.

squelette [skəlɛt] *nm* skeleton.

squelettique [skəletik] *adj* [corps] emaciated.

St (*abr écrite de* saint) St.

stabiliser [3] [stabilize] *vt* **1.** [gén] to stabilize ; [meuble] to steady - **2.** [terrain] to make firm. ⟶ **se stabiliser** *vp* **1.** [véhicule, prix, situation] to stabilize - **2.** [personne] to settle down.

stabilité [stabilite] *nf* stability.

stable [stabl] *adj* **1.** [gén] stable - **2.** [meuble] steady, stable.

stade [stad] *nm* **1.** [terrain] stadium - **2.** [étape & MÉD] stage ; **en être au stade de/où** to reach the stage of/at which.

Stade de France *nm* Stade de France *stadium built for the 1998 World Cup in the north of Paris.*

stage [staʒ] *nm* SCOL work placement UK, internship US ; [sur le temps de travail] in-service training ; **faire un stage** [cours] to go on a training course ; [expérience professionnelle] to go on a work placement UK, to undergo an internship US.

stagiaire [staʒjɛr] <> *nmf* trainee, intern US. <> *adj* trainee (*avant n*).

stagnant, e [stagnɑ̃, ɑ̃t] *adj* stagnant.

stagner [3] [stagne] *vi* to stagnate.

stalactite [stalaktit] *nf* stalactite.

stalagmite [stalagmit] *nf* stalagmite.

stand [stɑ̃d] *nm* **1.** [d'exposition] stand - **2.** [de fête] stall.

standard [stɑ̃dar] <> *adj inv* standard. <> *nm* **1.** [norme] standard - **2.** [téléphonique] switchboard.

standardiste [stɑ̃dardist] *nmf* switchboard operator.

standing [stɑ̃diŋ] *nm* standing ; **quartier de grand standing** select district.

star [star] *nf* CINÉ star.

starter [starter] *nm* AUTO choke ; **mettre le starter** to pull the choke out.

starting-block [startiŋblɔk] (*pl* starting-blocks) *nm* starting block.

start up [startɔp] *nf* start-up.

station [stasjɔ̃] *nf* **1.** [arrêt - de bus] stop ; [- de métro] station ; **à quelle station dois-je descendre?** which stop do I get off at? ; **station de taxis** taxi stand - **2.** [installations] station ; **station d'épuration** sewage treatment plant - **3.** [ville] resort ; **station balnéaire** seaside resort ; **station de ski/de sports d'hiver** ski/winter sports resort ;

station thermale spa (town) - **4.** [position] position - **5.** INFORM : **station de travail** work station.

stationnaire [stasjɔnɛr] *adj* stationary.

stationnement [stasjɔnmã] *nm* parking ; **'stationnement interdit'** 'no parking'.

stationner [3] [stasjɔne] *vi* to park.

station-service [stasjɔ̃sɛrvis] (*pl* **stations-service**) *nf* service station, petrol station *UK*, gas station *US*.

statique [statik] *adj* static.

statisticien, enne [statistisjɛ̃, ɛn] *nm, f* statistician.

statistique [statistik] <> *adj* statistical. <> *nf* [donnée] statistic.

statue [staty] *nf* statue.

statuer [7] [statɥe] *vi* : **statuer sur** to give a decision on.

statuette [statɥɛt] *nf* statuette.

statu quo [statykwo] *nm inv* status quo.

stature [statyr] *nf* stature.

statut [staty] *nm* status. ➤ **statuts** *nmpl* statutes, by laws *US*.

statutaire [statytɛr] *adj* statutory.

Ste (*abr écrite de* **sainte**) St.

Sté (*abr écrite de* **société**) Co.

steak [stɛk] *nm* steak ; **steak haché** mince *UK*, ground beef *US*.

stèle [stɛl] *nf* stele.

sténo [steno] <> *nmf* stenographer. <> *nf* shorthand.

sténodactylo [stenɔdaktilo] *nmf* short-hand typist *UK*, stenographer *US*.

sténodactylographie [stenɔdaktilɔgrafi] *nf* shorthand typing.

stentor [stɑ̃tɔr] ➤ **voix**.

steppe [stɛp] *nf* steppe.

stéréo [stereo] <> *adj inv* stereo. <> *nf* stereo ; **en stéréo** in stereo.

stéréotype [stereɔtip] *nm* stereotype.

stérile [steril] *adj* **1.** [personne] sterile, infertile ; [terre] barren - **2.** *fig* [inutile - discussion] sterile ; [- efforts] futile - **3.** MÉD sterile.

stérilet [sterilɛ] *nm* IUD, intrauterine device.

stériliser [3] [sterilize] *vt* to sterilize.

stérilité [sterilite] *nf litt & fig* sterility ; [d'efforts] futility.

sterling [stɛrliŋ] *adj inv & nm inv* sterling.

sternum [stɛrnɔm] *nm* breastbone, sternum.

stéthoscope [stetɔskɔp] *nm* stethoscope.

steward [stiwart] *nm* steward.

stigmate [stigmat] *nm* (*gén pl*) mark, scar.

stimulant, e [stimylɑ̃, ɑ̃t] *adj* stimulating. ➤ **stimulant** *nm* **1.** [remontant] stimulant - **2.** [motivation] incentive, stimulus.

stimulation [stimylasjɔ̃] *nf* stimulation.

stimuler [3] [stimyle] *vt* to stimulate.

stipuler [3] [stipyle] *vt* : **stipuler que** to stipulate (that).

stock [stɔk] *nm* stock ; **en stock** in stock.

stocker [3] [stɔke] *vt* **1.** [marchandises] to stock - **2.** INFORM to store.

Stockholm [stɔkɔlm] *npr* Stockholm.

stoïque [stɔik] *adj* stoical.

stop [stɔp] <> *interj* stop! <> *nm* **1.** [panneau] stop sign - **2.** [auto-stop] hitchhiking, hitching.

stopper [3] [stɔpe] <> *vt* [arrêter] to stop, to halt. <> *vi* to stop.

STP *abr de* **s'il te plaît**.

store [stɔr] *nm* **1.** [de fenêtre] blind - **2.** [de magasin] awning.

strabisme [strabism] *nm* squint.

strangulation [strɑ̃gylasjɔ̃] *nf* strangulation.

strapontin [strapɔ̃tɛ̃] *nm* [siège] pull-down seat.

strass [stras] *nm* paste.

stratagème [strataʒɛm] *nm* stratagem.

stratégie [strateʒi] *nf* strategy.

stratégique [strateʒik] *adj* strategic.

stress [strɛs] *nm* stress.

stressant, e [strɛsɑ̃, ɑ̃t] *adj* stressful.

strict, e [strikt] *adj* **1.** [personne, règlement] strict - **2.** [sobre] plain - **3.** [absolu - minimum] bare, absolute ; [- vérité] absolute ; **dans la plus stricte intimité** strictly in private ; **au sens strict du terme** in the strict sense of the word.

strident, e [stridɑ̃, ɑ̃t] *adj* strident, shrill.

strié, e [strije] *adj* [rayé] striped.

strier [10] [strije] *vt* to streak.

strip-tease [striptiz] (*pl* **strip-teases**) *nm* striptease.

strophe [strɔf] *nf* verse.

structure [stryktyr] *nf* structure.

structurer [3] [stryktyre] *vt* to structure.

studieux, euse [stydjø, øz] *adj* **1.** [personne] studious - **2.** [vacances] study *(avant n)*.

studio [stydjo] *nm* **1.** CINÉ, PHOTO & TV studio - **2.** [appartement] studio flat *UK*, studio apartment *US*.

stupéfaction [stypefaksjɔ̃] *nf* astonishment, stupefaction.

stupéfait, e [stypefɛ, ɛt] *adj* astounded, stupefied.

stupéfiant, e [stypefjɑ̃, ɑ̃t] *adj* astounding, stunning. ➤ **stupéfiant** *nm* narcotic, drug.

stupeur [stypœr] *nf* **1.** [stupéfaction] astonishment - **2.** MÉD stupor.

stupide [stypid] *adj* **1.** *péj* [abruti] stupid - **2.** [insensé - mort] senseless ; [- accident] stupid.

stupidité [stypidite] *nf* stupidity.

style [stil] *nm* **1.** [gén] style - **2.** GRAMM : style direct/indirect direct/indirect speech.

styliste [stilist] *nmf* COUT designer.

stylo [stilo] *nm* pen ; **stylo plume** fountain pen.

stylo-feutre [stilofœtr] *nm* felt-tip pen.

su, e [sy] *pp* ➤ savoir.

suave [sɥav] *adj* [voix] smooth ; [parfum] sweet.

subalterne [sybaltern] ◇ *nmf* subordinate, junior. ◇ *adj* [rôle] subordinate ; [employé] junior.

subconscient, e [sybkɔ̃sjɑ̃, ɑ̃t] *adj* subconscious. ➡ **subconscient** *nm* subconscious.

subdiviser [3] [sybdivize] *vt* to subdivide.

subir [32] [sybir] *vt* **1.** [conséquences, colère] to suffer ; [personne] to put up with - **2.** [opération, épreuve, examen] to undergo - **3.** [dommages, pertes] to sustain, to suffer ; subir une hausse to be increased.

subit, e [sybi, it] *adj* sudden.

subitement [sybitmɑ̃] *adv* suddenly.

subjectif, ive [sybʒɛktif, iv] *adj* [personnel, partial] subjective.

subjonctif [sybʒɔ̃ktif] *nm* subjunctive.

subjuguer [3] [sybʒyge] *vt* to captivate.

sublime [syblim] *adj* sublime.

submerger [17] [sybmɛrʒe] *vt* **1.** [inonder] to flood - **2.** [envahir] to overcome, to overwhelm - **3.** [déborder] to overwhelm ; être submergé de travail to be swamped with work.

subordination [sybɔrdinasjɔ̃] *nf* subordination.

subordonné, e [sybɔrdɔne] ◇ *adj* GRAMM subordinate, dependent. ◇ *nm, f* subordinate.

subornation [sybɔrnasjɔ̃] *nf* bribing, subornation.

subrepticement [sybrɛptismɑ̃] *adv* surreptitiously.

subsidiaire [sybzidjɛr] *adj* subsidiary.

subsistance [sybzistɑ̃s] *nf* subsistence.

subsister [3] [sybziste] *vi* **1.** [chose] to remain - **2.** [personne] to live, to subsist.

substance [sypstɑ̃s] *nf* **1.** [matière] substance - **2.** [essence] gist.

substantiel, elle [sypstɑ̃sjɛl] *adj* substantial.

substantif [sypstɑ̃tif] *nm* noun.

substituer [7] [sypstitɥe] *vt* : substituer qqch à qqch to substitute sthg for sthg. ➡ **se substituer** *vp* : se substituer à [personne] to stand in for, to substitute for ; [chose] to take the place of.

substitut [sypstity] *nm* **1.** [remplacement] substitute - **2.** DR deputy public prosecutor.

substitution [sypstitysjɔ̃] *nf* substitution.

subterfuge [sypterfyʒ] *nm* subterfuge.

subtil, e [syptil] *adj* subtle.

subtiliser [3] [syptilize] *vt* to steal.

subtilité [syptilite] *nf* subtlety.

subvenir [40] [sybvǝnir] *vi* : subvenir à to meet, to cover.

subvention [sybvɑ̃sjɔ̃] *nf* grant, subsidy.

subventionner [3] [sybvɑ̃sjɔne] *vt* to give a grant to, to subsidize.

subversif, ive [sybvɛrsif, iv] *adj* subversive.

succédané [syksedane] *nm* substitute.

succéder [18] [syksede] *vt* : succéder à [suivre] to follow ; [remplacer] to succeed, to take over from. ➡ **se succéder** *vp* to follow one another.

succès [syksɛ] *nm* **1.** [gén] success ; avoir du succès to be very successful ; sans succès [essai] unsuccessful ; [essayer] unsuccessfully - **2.** [chanson, pièce] hit.

successeur [syksesœr] *nm* **1.** [gén] successor - **2.** DR successor, heir.

successif, ive [syksesif, iv] *adj* successive.

succession [syksesjɔ̃] *nf* **1.** [gén] succession ; une succession de a succession of ; prendre la succession de qqn to take over from sb, to succeed sb - **2.** DR succession, inheritance ; droits de succession death duties UK, inheritance tax US.

succinct, e [syksɛ̃, ɛ̃t] *adj* **1.** [résumé] succinct - **2.** [repas] frugal.

succion [syksjɔ̃, sysjɔ̃] *nf* suction, sucking.

succomber [3] [sykɔ̃be] *vi* : succomber (à) to succumb (to).

succulent, e [sykylɑ̃, ɑ̃t] *adj* delicious.

succursale [sykyrsal] *nf* branch.

sucer [16] [syse] *vt* to suck.

sucette [sysɛt] *nf* [friandise] lolly UK, lollipop.

sucre [sykr] *nm* sugar ; sucre en morceaux lump sugar ; sucre en poudre, sucre semoule caster sugar UK, finely granulated sugar US ; sucre roux OU brun brown sugar.

sucré, e [sykre] *adj* [goût] sweet.

sucrer [3] [sykre] *vt* **1.** [café, thé] to sweeten, to sugar - **2.** *fam* [permission] to withdraw ; [passage, réplique] to cut ; sucrer qqch à qqn to take sthg away from sb.

sucrerie [sykrǝri] *nf* **1.** [usine] sugar refinery - **2.** [friandise] sweet UK, candy US.

sucrette [sykrɛt] *nf* sweetener.

sucrier [sykrije] *nm* sugar bowl.

sud [syd] <> *nm* south ; **un vent du sud** a southerly wind ; **au sud** in the south ; **au sud (de)** to the south (of). <> *adj inv* [gén] south ; [province, région] southern.

sud-africain, e [sydafrikɛ̃, ɛn] (*mpl* sud-africains, *fpl* sud-africaines) *adj* South African. ◆ **Sud-Africain, e** *nm, f* South African.

sud-américain, e [sydamerikɛ̃, ɛn] (*mpl* sud-américains, *fpl* sud-américaines) *adj* South American. ◆ **Sud-Américain, e** *nm, f* South American.

sudation [sydasjɔ̃] *nf* sweating.

sud-est [sydɛst] *nm & adj inv* southeast.

sud-ouest [sydwɛst] *nm & adj inv* southwest.

Suède [sɥɛd] *nf* : **la Suède** Sweden.

suédois, e [sɥedwa, az] *adj* Swedish. ◆ **suédois** *nm* [langue] Swedish. ◆ **Suédois, e** *nm, f* Swede.

suer [7] [sɥe] <> *vi* [personne] to sweat. <> *vt* to exude.

sueur [sɥœr] *nf* sweat ; **avoir des sueurs froides** *fig* to be in a cold sweat.

Suez [sɥɛz] *npr* : **le canal de Suez** the Suez Canal.

suffi [syfi] *pp inv* ▶ suffire.

suffire [100] [syfir] <> *vi* **1.** [être assez] : **suffire pour qqch/pour faire qqch** to be enough for sthg/to do sthg, to be sufficient for sthg/to do sthg ; **ça suffit!** that's enough! - **2.** [satisfaire] : **suffire à** to be enough for. <> *v impers* : **il suffit de...** all that is necessary is..., all that you have to do is... ; **il suffit d'un moment d'inattention pour que...** it only takes a moment of carelessness for... ; **il suffit que** (+ *subjonctif*) : **il suffit que vous lui écriviez** all (that) you need do is write to him. ◆ **se suffire** *vp* : **se suffire à soi-même** to be self-sufficient.

suffisamment [syfizamɑ̃] *adv* sufficiently.

suffisant, e [syfizɑ̃, ɑ̃t] *adj* **1.** [satisfaisant] sufficient - **2.** [vaniteux] self-important.

suffixe [syfiks] *nm* suffix.

suffocation [syfɔkasjɔ̃] *nf* suffocation.

suffoquer [3] [syfɔke] <> *vt* **1.** [suj: chaleur, fumée] to suffocate - **2.** *fig* [suj: colère] to choke ; [suj: nouvelle, révélation] to astonish, to stun. <> *vi* to choke.

suffrage [syfraʒ] *nm* vote.

suggérer [18] [sygʒere] *vt* **1.** [proposer] to suggest ; **suggérer qqch à qqn** to suggest sthg to sb ; **suggérer à qqn de faire qqch** to suggest that sb (should) do sthg - **2.** [faire penser à] to evoke.

suggestif, ive [sygʒestif, iv] *adj* **1.** [musique] evocative - **2.** [pose, photo] suggestive.

suggestion [sygʒestjɔ̃] *nf* suggestion.

suicidaire [sɥisidɛr] *adj* suicidal.

suicide [sɥisid] *nm* suicide.

suicider [3] [sɥiside] ◆ **se suicider** *vp* to commit suicide, to kill o.s.

suie [sɥi] *nf* soot.

suinter [3] [sɥɛ̃te] *vi* **1.** [eau, sang] to ooze, to seep - **2.** [surface, mur] to sweat ; [plaie] to weep.

suis ▶ être.

suisse [sɥis] <> *adj* Swiss. <> *nm* RELIG verger. ◆ **Suisse** <> *nf* [pays] : **la Suisse** Switzerland ; **la Suisse allemande/italienne/romande** German-/Italian-/French-speaking Switzerland. <> *nmf* [personne] Swiss (person) ; **les Suisses** the Swiss.

suite [sɥit] *nf* **1.** [de liste, feuilleton] continuation - **2.** [série de maisons, de succès] series ; [- d'événements] sequence - **3.** [succession] : **prendre la suite de** [personne] to succeed, to take over from ; [affaire] to take over ; **à la suite** one after the other ; **à la suite de** *fig* following - **4.** [escorte] retinue - **5.** MUS suite - **6.** [appartement] suite. ◆ **suites** *nfpl* consequences. ◆ **par la suite** *loc adv* afterwards. ◆ **par suite de** *loc prép* owing to, because of.

suivant, e [sɥivɑ̃, ɑ̃t] <> *adj* next, following. <> *nm, f* next ou following one ; **au suivant!** next!

suivi, e [sɥivi] <> *pp* ▶ suivre. <> *adj* [visites] regular ; [travail] sustained ; [qualité] consistent. ◆ **suivi** *nm* follow-up.

suivre [89] [sɥivr] <> *vt* **1.** [gén] to follow ; **'faire suivre'** 'please forward' ; **à suivre** to be continued - **2.** [suj: médecin] to treat. <> *vi* **1.** SCOL to keep up - **2.** [venir après] to follow. ◆ **se suivre** *vp* to follow one another.

sujet, ette [syʒɛ, ɛt] <> *adj* : **être sujet à qqch** to be subject ou prone to sthg. <> *nm, f* [de souverain] subject. ◆ **sujet** *nm* [gén] subject ; **c'est à quel sujet?** what is it about? ; **sujet de conversation** topic of conversation ; **au sujet de** about, concerning.

sulfate [sylfat] *nm* sulphate *UK*, sulfate *US*.

sulfurique [sylfyrik] *adj* sulphuric *UK*, sulfuric *US*.

Sup de Co [sypdəko] *fam abr de* École Supérieure de Commerce.

super [syper] *fam* <> *adj inv* super, great. <> *nm* four star (petrol) *UK*, premium *US*.

superbe [syperb] *adj* superb ; [enfant, femme] beautiful.

supercherie [syperʃəri] *nf* deception, trickery.

superficie [syperfisi] *nf* **1.** [surface] area - **2.** *fig* [aspect superficiel] surface.

superficiel, elle [syperfisjɛl] *adj* superficial.

superflu, e [syperfly] *adj* superfluous.
◆ **superflu** *nm* superfluity.

supérieur, e [syperjœr] ◇ *adj* **1.** [étage] upper - **2.** [intelligence, qualité] superior ; **intelligence supérieure à la moyenne** above-average intelligence ; **supérieur à** [température] higher than, above ; [notation] superior to ; **une note supérieure à 10** a mark above 10 - **3.** [dominant - équipe] superior ; [- cadre] senior - **4.** [SCOL - classe] upper, senior ; [- enseignement] higher - **5.** *péj* [air] superior. ◇ *nm, f* superior.

supériorité [syperjɔrite] *nf* superiority.

superlatif [syperlatif] *nm* superlative.

supermarché [sypermarʃe] *nm* supermarket.

superposer [3] [syperpoze] *vt* to stack.
◆ **se superposer** *vp* to be stacked.

superproduction [syperprɔdyksjɔ̃] *nf* spectacular.

superpuissance [syperpɥisɑ̃s] *nf* superpower.

supersonique [sypersɔnik] *adj* supersonic.

superstitieux, euse [syperstisjø, øz] *adj* superstitious.

superstition [syperstisjɔ̃] *nf* [croyance] superstition.

superviser [3] [sypervize] *vt* to supervise.

supplanter [3] [syplɑ̃te] *vt* to supplant.

suppléant, e [sypleɑ̃, ɑ̃t] ◇ *adj* acting *(avant n)*, temporary. ◇ *nm, f* substitute, deputy.

suppléer [15] [syplee] *vt* **1.** *litt* [carence] to compensate for - **2.** [personne] to stand in for.

supplément [syplemɑ̃] *nm* **1.** [surplus] : **un supplément de détails** additional details, extra details - **2.** PRESSE supplement - **3.** [de billet] extra charge.

supplémentaire [syplemɑ̃tɛr] *adj* extra, additional.

supplication [syplikasjɔ̃] *nf* plea.

supplice [syplis] *nm* torture ; *fig* [souffrance] torture, agony.

supplier [10] [syplije] *vt* : **supplier qqn de faire qqch** to beg *ou* implore sb to do sthg ; **je t'en** *ou* **vous en supplie** I beg *ou* implore you.

support [sypɔr] *nm* **1.** [socle] support, base - **2.** *fig* [de communication] medium ; **support pédagogique** teaching aid ; **support publicitaire** advertising medium.

supportable [sypɔrtabl] *adj* **1.** [douleur] bearable - **2.** [conduite] tolerable, acceptable.

supporter[1] [3] [sypɔrte] *vt* **1.** [soutenir, encourager] to support - **2.** [endurer] to bear, to stand ; **supporter que** (+ *subjonctif*) : **il ne supporte pas qu'on le contredise** he cannot bear being contradicted - **3.** [résister à] to withstand. ◆ **se supporter** *vp* [se tolérer] to bear *ou* stand each other.

supporter[2] [sypɔrter] *nm* supporter.

supposer [3] [sypoze] *vt* **1.** [imaginer] to suppose, to assure ; **en supposant que** (+ *subjonctif*), **à supposer que** (+ *subjonctif*) supposing (that) - **2.** [impliquer] to imply, to presuppose.

supposition [sypozisjɔ̃] *nf* supposition, assumption.

suppositoire [sypozitwar] *nm* suppository.

suppression [sypresjɔ̃] *nf* **1.** [de permis de conduire] withdrawal ; [de document] suppression - **2.** [de mot, passage] deletion - **3.** [de loi, poste] abolition.

supprimer [3] [syprime] *vt* **1.** [document] to suppress ; [obstacle, difficulté] to remove - **2.** [mot, passage] to delete - **3.** [loi, poste] to abolish - **4.** [témoin] to do away with, to eliminate - **5.** [permis de conduire, revenus] : **supprimer qqch à qqn** to take sthg away from sb - **6.** [douleur] to take away, to suppress - **7.** INFORM to delete.

suprématie [sypremasi] *nf* supremacy.

suprême [syprɛm] *adj* [gén] supreme.

sur [syr] *prép* **1.** [position - dessus] on ; [- au-dessus de] above, over ; **sur la table** on the table - **2.** [direction] towards, toward *US* ; **sur la droite/gauche** on the right/left, to the right/left - **3.** [distance] : **travaux sur 10 kilomètres** roadworks for 10 kilometres *UK ou* kilometers *US* - **4.** [d'après] by ; **juger qqn sur sa mine** to judge sb by his/her appearance - **5.** [grâce à] on ; **il vit sur les revenus de ses parents** he lives on *ou* off his parents' income - **6.** [au sujet de] on, about - **7.** [proportion] out of ; [mesure] by ; **9 sur 10** 9 out of 10 ; **un mètre sur deux** one metre *UK ou* meter *US* by two ; **un jour sur deux** every other day ; **une fois sur deux** every other time - **8.** [indiquant une relation de supériorité] over. ◆ **sur ce** *loc adv* whereupon.

sûr, e [syr] *adj* **1.** [sans danger] safe - **2.** [digne de confiance - personne] reliable, trustworthy ; [- goût] reliable, sound ; [- investissement] sound - **3.** [certain] sure, certain ; **sûr de** sure of ; **sûr et certain** absolutely certain ; **sûr de soi** self-confident.

surabondance [syrabɔ̃dɑ̃s] *nf* overabundance.

suraigu, ë [syregy] *adj* high-pitched, shrill.

suranné, e [syrane] *adj litt* old-fashioned, outdated.

surcharge [syrʃarʒ] *nf* **1.** [de poids] excess load ; [de bagages] excess weight - **2.** *fig* [surcroît]: **une surcharge de travail** extra work - **3.** [surabondance] surfeit - **4.** [de document] alteration.

surcharger [17] [syrʃarʒe] vt **1.** [véhicule, personne]: **surcharger (de)** to overload (with) - **2.** [texte] to alter extensively.

surchauffer [3] [syrʃofe] vt to overheat.

surchemise [syrʃəmiz] nf overshirt.

surcroît [syrkrwa] nm: **un surcroît de travail/d'inquiétude** additional work/anxiety.

surdimensionné, e [syrdimãsjɔne] adj oversize(d).

surdité [syrdite] nf deafness.

surdoué, e [syrdwe] adj exceptionally ou highly gifted.

sureffectif [syrefɛktif] nm overmanning, overstaffing.

surélever [19] [syrelve] vt to raise, to heighten.

sûrement [syrmã] adv **1.** [certainement] certainly ; **sûrement pas!** fam no way!, definitely not! - **2.** [sans doute] certainly, surely - **3.** [sans risque] surely, safely.

surenchère [syrãʃer] nf higher bid ; fig overstatement, exaggeration.

surenchérir [32] [syrãʃerir] vi to bid higher ; fig to try to go one better.

surendetté, e [syrãdete] adj overindebted.

surendettement [syrãdetmã] nm overindebtedness.

surestimer [3] [syrestime] vt **1.** [exagérer] to overestimate - **2.** [survaleur] to overvalue. ◆ **se surestimer** vp to overestimate o.s.

sûreté [syrte] nf **1.** [sécurité] safety ; **en sûreté** safe ; **de sûreté** safety (avant n) - **2.** [fiabilité] reliability - **3.** DR surety.

surexposer [3] [syrɛkspoze] vt to overexpose.

surf [sœrf] nm surfing ; **surf des neiges** snowboarding.

surface [syrfas] nf **1.** [extérieur, apparence] surface - **2.** [superficie] surface area. ◆ **grande surface** nf hypermarket UK, supermarket US.

surfait, e [syrfɛ, ɛt] adj overrated.

surfer [3] [sœrfe] vi **1.** SPORT to go surfing - **2.** INFORM to surf.

surgelé, e [syrʒəle] adj frozen. ◆ **surgelé** nm frozen food.

surgir [32] [syrʒir] vi to appear suddenly ; fig [difficulté] to arise, to come up.

surhumain, e [syrymɛ̃, ɛn] adj superhuman.

surimi [syrimi] nm surimi.

surimpression [syrɛ̃presjɔ̃] nf double exposure.

sur-le-champ [syrləʃã] loc adv immediately, straightaway.

surlendemain [syrlãdmɛ̃] nm: **le surlendemain** two days later ; **le surlendemain de mon départ** two days after I left.

surligner [3] [syrliɲe] vt to highlight.

surligneur [syrliɲœr] nm highlighter (pen).

surmenage [syrmənaʒ] nm overwork.

surmener [19] [syrməne] vt to overwork. ◆ **se surmener** vp to overwork.

surmonter [3] [syrmɔ̃te] vt **1.** [obstacle, peur] to overcome, to surmount - **2.** [suj: statue, croix] to surmount, to top.

surnager [17] [syrnaʒe] vi **1.** [flotter] to float (on the surface) - **2.** fig [subsister] to remain, to survive.

surnaturel, elle [syrnatyrɛl] adj supernatural. ◆ **surnaturel** nm: **le surnaturel** the supernatural.

surnom [syrnɔ̃] nm nickname.

surpasser [3] [syrpase] vt to surpass, to outdo. ◆ **se surpasser** vp to surpass ou excel o.s.

surpeuplé, e [syrpœple] adj overpopulated.

surplomb [syrplɔ̃] ◆ **en surplomb** loc adj overhanging.

surplomber [3] [syrplɔ̃be] <> vt to overhang. <> vi to be out of plumb.

surplus [syrply] nm [excédent] surplus.

surprenant, e [syrprənã, ãt] adj surprising, amazing.

surprendre [79] [syrprãdr] vt **1.** [voleur] to catch (in the act) - **2.** [secret] to overhear - **3.** [prendre à l'improviste] to surprise, to catch unawares - **4.** [étonner] to surprise, to amaze.

surpris, e [syrpri, iz] pp ▶ surprendre.

surprise [syrpriz] <> nf surprise ; **par surprise** by surprise ; **faire une surprise à qqn** to give sb a surprise. <> adj [inattendu] surprise (avant n) ; **grève surprise** lightning strike.

surproduction [syrprɔdyksjɔ̃] nf overproduction.

surréalisme [syrrealism] nm surrealism.

surréservation [syrlrezɛrvasjɔ̃] nm = overbooking.

sursaut [syrso] nm **1.** [de personne] jump, start ; **en sursaut** with a start - **2.** [d'énergie] burst, surge.

sursauter [3] [syrsote] vi to start, to give a start.

sursis [syrsi] nm fig & DR reprieve ; **six mois**

avec sursis six months' suspended sentence.

sursitaire [syrsiter] *nmf* MIL *person whose call-up has been deferred.*

surtaxe [syrtaks] *nf* surcharge.

surtout [syrtu] *adv* **1.** [avant tout] above all - **2.** [spécialement] especially, particularly ; **surtout pas** certainly not. ➡ **surtout que** *loc conj fam* especially as.

survécu [syrveky] *pp* ➡ **survivre**.

surveillance [syrvɛjɑ̃s] *nf* supervision ; [de la police, de militaire] surveillance.

surveillant, e [syrvɛjɑ̃, ɑ̃t] *nm, f* supervisor ; [de prison] guard, warder UK.

surveiller [4] [syrveje] *vt* **1.** [enfant] to watch, to keep an eye on ; [suspect] to keep a watch on - **2.** [travaux] to supervise ; [examen] to invigilate UK - **3.** [ligne, langage] to watch. ➡ **se surveiller** *vp* to watch o.s.

survenir [40] [syrvənir] *vi* [incident] to occur.

survenu, e [syrvəny] *pp* ➡ **survenir**.

survêtement [syrvɛtmɑ̃] *nm* tracksuit.

survie [syrvi] *nf* [de personne] survival.

survivant, e [syrvivɑ̃, ɑ̃t] ⬦ *nm, f* survivor. ⬦ *adj* surviving.

survivre [90] [syrvivr] *vi* to survive ; **survivre à** [personne] to outlive, to survive ; [accident, malheur] to survive.

survoler [3] [syrvɔle] *vt* **1.** [territoire] to fly over - **2.** [texte] to skim (through).

sus [sy(s)] *interj* : **sus à l'ennemi!** at the enemy! ➡ **en sus** *loc adv* moreover, in addition ; **en sus de** over and above, in addition to.

susceptibilité [syseptibilite] *nf* touchiness, sensitivity.

susceptible [syseptibl] *adj* **1.** [ombrageux] touchy, sensitive - **2.** [en mesure de] : **susceptible de faire qqch** liable ou likely to do sthg ; **susceptible d'amélioration, susceptible d'être amélioré** open to improvement.

susciter [3] [sysite] *vt* **1.** [admiration, curiosité] to arouse - **2.** [ennuis, problèmes] to create.

sushi [suʃi] *nm* sushi.

suspect, e [syspe, ɛkt] ⬦ *adj* **1.** [personne] suspicious - **2.** [douteux] suspect. ⬦ *nm, f* suspect.

suspecter [4] [syspɛkte] *vt* to suspect, to have one's suspicions about ; **suspecter qqn de qqch/de faire qqch** to suspect sb of sthg/of doing sthg.

suspendre [73] [syspɑ̃dr] *vt* **1.** [lustre, tableau] to hang (up) - **2.** [pourparlers] to suspend ; [séance] to adjourn ; [journal] to suspend publication of - **3.** [fonctionnaire, constitution] to suspend - **4.** [jugement] to postpone, to defer.

suspendu, e [syspɑ̃dy] ⬦ *pp* ➡ **suspendre**. ⬦ *adj* **1.** [fonctionnaire] suspended - **2.** [séance] adjourned - **3.** [lustre, tableau] : **suspendu au plafond/au mur** hanging from the ceiling/on the wall.

suspens [syspɑ̃] ➡ **en suspens** *loc adv* in abeyance.

suspense [syspɑ̃s, syspɛns] *nm* suspense.

suspension [syspɑ̃sjɔ̃] *nf* **1.** [gén] suspension ; **en suspension** in suspension, suspended - **2.** [de combat] halt ; [d'audience] adjournment - **3.** [lustre] light fitting.

suspicion [syspisjɔ̃] *nf* suspicion.

susurrer [3] [sysyre] *vt & vi* to murmur.

suture [sytyr] *nf* suture.

svelte [zvɛlt] *adj* slender.

SVP (*abr écrite de* s'il vous plaît), ➡ **plaire**.

sweat-shirt [switʃœrt] (*pl* **sweat-shirts**) *nm* sweatshirt.

syllabe [silab] *nf* syllable.

symbole [sɛ̃bɔl] *nm* symbol.

symbolique [sɛ̃bɔlik] *adj* **1.** [figure] symbolic - **2.** [geste, contribution] token (*avant n*) - **3.** [rémunération] nominal.

symboliser [3] [sɛ̃bɔlize] *vt* to symbolize.

symétrie [simetri] *nf* symmetry.

symétrique [simetrik] *adj* symmetrical.

sympa [sɛ̃pa] *adj fam* [personne] likeable, nice ; [soirée, maison] pleasant, nice ; [ambiance] friendly.

sympathie [sɛ̃pati] *nf* **1.** [pour personne, projet] liking ; **accueillir un projet avec sympathie** to look sympathetically ou favourably on a project - **2.** [condoléances] sympathy.

sympathique [sɛ̃patik] *adj* **1.** [personne] likeable, nice ; [soirée, maison] pleasant, nice ; [ambiance] friendly - **2.** ANAT & MÉD sympathetic.

sympathiser [3] [sɛ̃patize] *vi* to get on well ; **sympathiser avec qqn** to get on well with sb.

symphonie [sɛ̃fɔni] *nf* symphony.

symphonique [sɛ̃fɔnik] *adj* [musique] symphonic ; [concert, orchestre] symphony (*avant n*).

symptomatique [sɛ̃ptɔmatik] *adj* symptomatic.

symptôme [sɛ̃ptom] *nm* symptom.

synagogue [sinagɔg] *nf* synagogue.

synchroniser [3] [sɛ̃krɔnize] *vt* to synchronize.

syncope [sɛ̃kɔp] *nf* **1.** [évanouissement] blackout - **2.** MUS syncopation.

syndic [sɛ̃dik] *nm* [de copropriété] managing agent.

syndicaliste [sɛ̃dikalist] <> *nmf* trade unionist *UK*, union activist *US*. <> *adj* (trade) union *(avant n) UK*, labor union *(avant n) US*.

syndicat [sɛ̃dika] *nm* [d'employés, d'agriculteurs] (trade) union *UK*, labor union *US* ; [d'employeurs, de propriétaires] association. ➤ **syndicat d'initiative** *nm* tourist office.

syndiqué, e [sɛ̃dike] *adj* unionized.

syndrome [sɛ̃drom] *nm* syndrome ; **syndrome immunodéficitaire acquis** acquired immunodeficiency syndrome.

synergie [sinɛrʒi] *nf* synergy, synergism.

synonyme [sinɔnim] <> *nm* synonym. <> *adj* synonymous.

syntaxe [sɛ̃taks] *nf* syntax.

synthé [sɛ̃te] *nm fam* synth.

synthèse [sɛ̃tɛz] *nf* 1. [opération & CHIM] synthesis - 2. [exposé] overview.

synthétique [sɛ̃tetik] *adj* 1. [vue] overall - 2. [produit] synthetic.

synthétiseur [sɛ̃tetizœr] *nm* synthesizer.

syphilis [sifilis] *nf* syphilis.

Syrie [siri] *nf* : **la Syrie** Syria.

syrien, enne [sirjɛ̃, ɛn] *adj* Syrian. ➤ **Syrien, enne** *nm, f* Syrian.

systématique [sistematik] *adj* systematic.

systématiser [3] [sistematize] *vt* to systematize.

système [sistɛm] *nm* 1. [gén] system ; **système nerveux** nervous system ; **système solaire** solar system - 2. POLIT & ÉCON : **système monétaire européen** European Monetary System - 3. INFORM : **système expert** expert system ; **système d'exploitation** operating system.

T

t, T [te] *nm inv* t, T.

t' ► te.

ta ► ton².

tabac [taba] *nm* 1. [plante, produit] tobacco ; **tabac blond** mild ou Virginia tobacco ; **tabac brun** dark tobacco ; **tabac à priser** snuff - 2. [magasin] tobacconist's *UK*.

tabagisme [tabaʒism] *nm* 1. [intoxication] nicotine addiction - 2. [habitude] smoking.

tabernacle [tabɛrnakl] *nm* tabernacle.

table [tabl] *nf* [meuble] table ; **à table!** lunch/dinner *etc* is ready! ; **être à table** to be at table, to be having a meal ; **se mettre à table** to sit down to eat ; *fig* to come clean ; **dresser** ou **mettre la table** to lay the table ; **table de chevet** ou **de nuit** bedside table ; **table de cuisson** hob. ➤ **table des matières** *nf* contents *pl*, table of contents. ➤ **table de multiplication** *nf* (multiplication) table.

tableau, x [tablo] *nm* 1. [peinture] painting, picture ; *fig* [description] picture - 2. THÉÂTRE scene - 3. [panneau] board ; **tableau d'affichage** notice board *UK*, bulletin board *US* ; **tableau de bord** AÉRON instrument panel ; AUTO dashboard ; **tableau noir** blackboard - 4. [de données] table.

tabler [3] [table] *vi* : **tabler sur** to count ou bank on.

tablette [tablɛt] *nf* 1. [planchette] shelf - 2. [de chewing-gum] stick ; [de chocolat] bar.

tableur [tablœr] *nm* INFORM spreadsheet.

tablier [tablije] *nm* 1. [de cuisinière] apron ; [d'écolier] smock - 2. [de pont] roadway, deck.

tabloïd(e) [tablɔid] *nm* tabloid.

tabou, e [tabu] *adj* taboo. ➤ **tabou** *nm* taboo.

tabouret [taburɛ] *nm* stool.

tabulateur [tabylatœr] *nm* tabulator, tab.

tac [tak] *nm* : **du tac au tac** tit for tat.

tache [taʃ] *nf* 1. [de pelage] marking ; [de peau] mark ; **tache de rousseur** ou **de son** freckle - 2. [de couleur, lumière] spot, patch - 3. [sur nappe, vêtement] stain.

tâche [taʃ] *nf* task.

tacher [3] [taʃe] *vt* 1. [nappe, vêtement] to stain, to mark - 2. *fig* [réputation] to tarnish.

tâcher [3] [taʃe] *vi* : **tâcher de faire qqch** to try to do sthg.

tacheter [27] [taʃte] *vt* to spot, to speckle.

tacite [tasit] *adj* tacit.

taciturne [tasityrn] *adj* taciturn.

tact [takt] *nm* [délicatesse] tact ; **avoir du tact** to be tactful ; **manquer de tact** to be tactless.

tactique [taktik] <> *adj* tactical. <> *nf* tactics *pl*.

taffe [taf] *nf fam* drag, puff.

tag [tag] *nm identifying name written with a spray can on walls, the sides of trains etc.*

tagueur, euse [tagœr, øz] *nm, f person who sprays their 'tag' on walls, the sides of trains etc.*

taie [tɛ] *nf* [enveloppe] : **taie (d'oreiller)** pillowcase, pillowslip.

taille [taj] *nf* 1. [action - de pierre, diamant] cutting ; [- d'arbre, de haie] **pruning** - 2. [stature] height - 3. [mesure, dimensions] size ; **vous faites quelle taille?** what size are you?, what size do you take? ; **ce n'est pas à ma taille** it doesn't fit me ; **de taille** sizeable, considerable - **4.** [milieu du corps] waist - **5.** [partie d'un vêtement] waist.

taille-crayon [tajkrɛjɔ̃] (pl taille-crayons) nm pencil sharpener.

tailler [3] [taje] vt **1.** [couper - chair, pierre, diamant] to cut ; [- arbre, haie] to prune ; [- crayon] to sharpen ; [- bois] to carve - **2.** [vêtement] to cut out.

tailleur [tajœr] nm **1.** [couturier] tailor - **2.** [vêtement] (lady's) suit - **3.** [de diamants, pierre] cutter.

taillis [taji] nm coppice, copse.

tain [tɛ̃] nm silvering ; **miroir sans tain** two-way mirror.

taire [111] [tɛr] vt to conceal. ➤ **se taire** vp **1.** [rester silencieux] to be silent ou quiet - **2.** [cesser de s'exprimer] to fall silent ; **tais-toi!** shut up!

Taiwan [tajwan] npr Taiwan.

talc [talk] nm talcum powder.

talent [talɑ̃] nm talent ; **avoir du talent** to be talented, to have talent ; **les jeunes talents** young talent (U).

talentueux, euse [talɑ̃tɥø, øz] adj talented.

talisman [talismɑ̃] nm talisman.

talkie-walkie [tɔkiwɔki] nm walkie-talkie.

talon [talɔ̃] nm **1.** [gén] heel ; **talons aiguilles/hauts** stiletto/high heels ; **talons plats** low ou flat heels - **2.** [de chèque] counterfoil UK, stub - **3.** [jeux de cartes] stock.

talonner [3] [talɔne] vt **1.** [suj: poursuivant] to be hard on the heels of - **2.** [suj: créancier] to harry, to hound.

talonnette [talɔnɛt] nf [de chaussure] heel cushion, heel-pad.

talquer [3] [talke] vt to put talcum powder on.

talus [taly] nm embankment.

tambour [tɑ̃bur] nm **1.** [instrument, cylindre] drum - **2.** [musicien] drummer - **3.** [porte à tourniquet] revolving door.

tambourin [tɑ̃burɛ̃] nm **1.** [à grelots] tambourine - **2.** [tambour] tambourin.

tambouriner [3] [tɑ̃burine] vi : **tambouriner sur** ou **à** to drum on ; **tambouriner contre** to drum against.

tamis [tami] nm [crible] sieve.

Tamise [tamiz] nf : **la Tamise** the Thames.

tamisé, e [tamize] adj [éclairage] subdued.

tamiser [3] [tamize] vt **1.** [farine] to sieve - **2.** [lumière] to filter.

tampon [tɑ̃pɔ̃] nm **1.** [bouchon] stopper, plug - **2.** [éponge] pad ; **tampon à récurer** scourer - **3.** [de coton, d'ouate] pad ; **tampon hygiénique** ou **périodique** tampon - **4.** [cachet] stamp - **5.** litt & fig [amortisseur] buffer.

tamponner [3] [tɑ̃pɔne] vt **1.** [document] to stamp - **2.** [plaie] to dab.

tam-tam [tamtam] (pl tam-tams) nm tomtom.

tandem [tɑ̃dɛm] nm **1.** [vélo] tandem - **2.** [duo] pair ; **en tandem** together, in tandem.

tandis [tɑ̃di] ➤ **tandis que** loc conj **1.** [pendant que] while - **2.** [alors que] while, whereas.

tangage [tɑ̃gaʒ] nm pitching, pitch.

tangent, e [tɑ̃ʒɑ̃, ɑ̃t] adj : **c'était tangent** fig it was close, it was touch and go. ➤ **tangente** nf tangent.

tangible [tɑ̃ʒibl] adj tangible.

tango [tɑ̃go] nm tango.

tanguer [3] [tɑ̃ge] vi to pitch.

tanière [tanjɛr] nf den, lair.

tank [tɑ̃k] nm tank.

tanner [3] [tane] vt **1.** [peau] to tan - **2.** fam [personne] to pester, to annoy.

tant [tɑ̃] adv **1.** [quantité] : **tant de** so much ; **tant de travail** so much work - **2.** [nombre] : **tant de** so many ; **tant de livres/d'élèves** so many books/pupils - **3.** [tellement] such a lot, so much ; **il l'aime tant** he loves her so much - **4.** [quantité indéfinie] so much ; **ça coûte tant** it costs so much - **5.** [un jour indéfini] : **votre lettre du tant** your letter of such-and-such a date - **6.** [comparatif] : **tant que** as much as - **7.** [valeur temporelle] : **tant que** [aussi longtemps que] as long as ; [pendant que] while. ➤ **en tant que** loc conj as. ➤ **tant bien que mal** loc adv after a fashion, somehow or other. ➤ **tant mieux** loc adv so much the better ; **tant mieux pour lui** good for him. ➤ **tant pis** loc adv too bad ; **tant pis pour lui** too bad for him.

tante [tɑ̃t] nf [parente] aunt.

tantinet [tɑ̃tinɛ] nm : **un tantinet exagéré/trop long** a bit exaggerated/too long.

tantôt [tɑ̃to] adv **1.** [parfois] sometimes - **2.** vieilli [après-midi] this afternoon.

tapage [tapaʒ] nm **1.** [bruit] row - **2.** fig [battage] fuss (U).

tapageur, euse [tapaʒœr, øz] adj **1.** [hôte, enfant] rowdy - **2.** [style] flashy - **3.** [liaison, publicité] blatant.

tape [tap] nf slap.

tape-à-l'œil [tapalœj] adj inv flashy.

taper [3] [tape] <> vt **1.** [personne, cuisse] to slap ; **taper (un coup) à la porte** to knock at the door - **2.** [à la machine] to type. <> *vi* **1.** [frapper] to hit ; **taper du poing sur to** bang one's fist on ; **taper dans ses mains to** clap - **2.** [à la machine] to type - **3.** *fam* [soleil] to beat down - **4.** *fig* [critiquer] : **taper sur qqn** to run sb down.

tapis [tapi] *nm* [gén] carpet ; [de gymnase] mat ; **tapis roulant** [pour bagages] conveyor belt ; [pour personnes] travolator ; **dérouler le tapis rouge** *fig* to roll out the red carpet.

tapisser [3] [tapise] *vt* : **tapisser (de)** to cover (with).

tapisserie [tapisri] *nf* [de laine] tapestry ; [papier peint] wallpaper.

tapissier, ère [tapisje, ɛr] *nm, f* **1.** [artisan] tapestry maker - **2.** [décorateur] (interior) decorator - **3.** [commerçant] upholsterer.

tapoter [3] [tapɔte] <> *vt* to tap ; [joue] to pat. <> *vi* : **tapoter sur** to tap on.

taquin, e [takɛ̃, in] *adj* teasing.

taquiner [3] [takine] *vt* **1.** [suj: personne] to tease - **2.** [suj: douleur] to worry.

tarabuster [3] [tarabyste] *vt* **1.** [suj: personne] to badger - **2.** [suj: idée] to niggle at *UK*.

tard [tar] *adv* late ; **plus tard** later ; **au plus tard** at the latest.

tarder [3] [tarde] <> *vi* : **tarder à faire qqch** [attendre pour] to delay *ou* put off doing sthg ; [être lent à] to take a long time to do sthg ; **le feu ne va pas tarder à s'éteindre** it won't be long before the fire goes out ; **elle ne devrait plus tarder maintenant** she should be here any time now. <> *v impers* : **il me tarde de te revoir/qu'il vienne** I am longing to see you again/for him to come.

tardif, ive [tardif, iv] *adj* [heure] late.

tare [tar] *nf* **1.** [défaut] defect - **2.** [de balance] tare.

tarif [tarif] *nm* **1.** [prix - de restaurant, café] price ; [- de service] rate, price ; [douanier] tariff ; **demi-tarif** half rate *ou* price ; **tarif réduit** reduced price ; [au cinéma, théâtre] concession *UK* ; **à tarif réduit** [loisirs] reduced-price ; [transport] reduced-fare - **2.** [tableau] price list.

tarir [32] [tarir] *vi* to dry up ; **elle ne tarit pas d'éloges sur son professeur** she never stops praising her teacher. **se tarir** *vp* to dry up.

tarot [taro] *nm* tarot. **tarots** *nmpl* tarot cards.

tartare [tartar] *adj* Tartar ; **steak tartare** steak tartare.

tarte [tart] <> *nf* **1.** [gâteau] tart, pie *US* - **2.** *fam fig* [gifle] slap - **3.** [sujet, propos] hackneyed. <> *adj* (avec ou sans accord) *fam* [idiot] stupid.

tartiflette [tartiflɛt] *nf* cheese and potato gratin from the Savoy region.

tartine [tartin] *nf* [de pain] piece of bread and butter.

tartiner [3] [tartine] *vt* **1.** [pain] to spread ; **chocolat/fromage à tartiner** chocolate/cheese spread - **2.** *fam fig* [pages] to cover.

tartre [tartr] *nm* **1.** [de dents, vin] tartar - **2.** [de chaudière] fur, scale.

tas [ta] *nm* heap ; **un tas de** a lot of.

tasse [tas] *nf* cup ; **tasse à café/à thé** coffee/tea cup ; **tasse de café/de thé** cup of coffee/tea.

tasser [3] [tase] *vt* **1.** [neige] to compress, to pack down - **2.** [vêtements, personnes] : **tasser qqn/qqch dans** to stuff sb/sthg into. **se tasser** *vp* **1.** [fondations] to settle - **2.** *fig* [vieillard] to shrink - **3.** [personnes] to squeeze up - **4.** *fam fig* [situation] to settle down.

tâter [3] [tate] *vt* to feel ; *fig* to sound out. **se tâter** *vp fam* [hésiter] to be in *UK* *ou* of *US* two minds.

tatillon, onne [tatijɔ̃, ɔn] *adj* finicky.

tâtonnement [tatɔnmɑ̃] *nm (gén pl)* [tentative] trial and error *(U)*.

tâtonner [3] [tatɔne] *vi* to grope around.

tâtons [tatɔ̃] **à tâtons** *loc adv* : **marcher/procéder à tâtons** to feel one's way.

tatouage [tatwaʒ] *nm* [dessin] tattoo.

tatouer [6] [tatwe] *vt* to tattoo.

taudis [todi] *nm* slum.

taupe [top] *nf litt & fig* mole.

taureau, x [tɔro] *nm* [animal] bull. **Taureau** *nm* ASTROL Taurus.

tauromachie [tɔrɔmaʃi] *nf* bullfighting.

taux [to] *nm* rate ; [de cholestérol, d'alcool] level ; **taux de change** exchange rate ; **taux d'intérêt** interest rate ; **taux de natalité/mortalité** birth/death rate.

taverne [tavern] *nf* tavern.

taxe [taks] *nf* tax ; **hors taxe** COMM exclusive of tax, before tax ; [boutique, achat] duty-free ; **taxe sur la valeur ajoutée** value-added tax ; **taxe d'habitation** *tax paid on residence*, ≃ council tax *UK* /local tax *US* ; **toutes taxes comprises** inclusive of tax.

taxer [3] [takse] *vt* [imposer] to tax.

taxi [taksi] *nm* **1.** [voiture] taxi, cab *US* - **2.** [chauffeur] taxi driver.

TB, tb *(abr écrite de* **très bien)** VG.

Tchad [tʃad] *nm* : **le Tchad** Chad.

tchatche [tʃatʃ] *nf fam* : **avoir la tchatche** to have the gift of the gab.

tchatcher [tʃatʃe] *vi fam* to chat (away).

tchécoslovaque [tʃekɔslɔvak] *adj* Czechoslovakian. **Tchécoslovaque** *nmf* Czechoslovak.

Tchécoslovaquie [tʃekɔslɔvaki] *nf* : la Tchécoslovaquie Czechoslovakia.

tchèque [tʃɛk] <> *adj* Czech. <> *nm* [langue] Czech. **Tchèque** *nmf* Czech.

TD (*abr de* **travaux dirigés**) *nmpl* supervised practical work.

te [tə], **t'** *pron pers* **1.** [complément d'objet direct] you - **2.** [complément d'objet indirect] (to) you - **3.** [réfléchi] yourself - **4.** [avec un présentatif] : **te voici!** here you are!

technicien, enne [tɛknisjɛ̃, ɛn] *nm, f* **1.** [professionnel] technician - **2.** [spécialiste] : **technicien (de)** expert (in).

technico-commercial, e [tɛknikokɔmersjal] (*mpl* **technico-commerciaux**, *fpl* **technico-commerciales**) *nm, f* sales engineer.

technique [tɛknik] <> *adj* technical. <> *nf* technique.

techno [tɛkno] *adj & nf* techno.

technocrate [tɛknɔkrat] *nmf* technocrat.

technologie [tɛknɔlɔʒi] *nf* technology.

technologique [tɛknɔlɔʒik] *adj* technological.

teckel [tekɛl] *nm* dachshund.

tee-shirt (*pl* tee-shirts), **T-shirt** (*pl* T-shirts) [tiʃœrt] *nm* T-shirt.

teigne [tɛɲ] *nf* **1.** [mite] moth - **2.** MÉD ringworm - **3.** *fam fig & péj* [femme] cow *UK* ; [homme] bastard.

teindre [81] [tɛ̃dr] *vt* to dye.

teint, e [tɛ̃, tɛ̃t] <> *pp* ▶ teindre. <> *adj* dyed. **teint** *nm* [carnation] complexion. **teinte** *nf* colour *UK*, color *US*.

teinté, e [tɛ̃te] *adj* tinted ; **teinté de** *fig* tinged with.

teinter [3] [tɛ̃te] *vt* to stain.

teinture [tɛ̃tyr] *nf* **1.** [action] dyeing - **2.** [produit] dye. **teinture d'iode** *nf* tincture of iodine.

teinturerie [tɛ̃tyrri] *nf* **1.** [pressing] dry cleaner's - **2.** [métier] dyeing.

teinturier, ère [tɛ̃tyrje, ɛr] *nm, f* [de pressing] dry cleaner.

tel, telle (*mpl* tels, *fpl* telles) [tɛl] *adj* **1.** [valeur indéterminée] such-and-such a ; tel et tel such-and-such a - **2.** [semblable] such ; **un tel homme** such a man ; **de telles gens** such people ; **je n'ai rien dit de tel** I never said anything of the sort - **3.** [valeur emphatique ou intensive] such ; **un tel génie** such a genius ; **un tel bonheur** such happiness - **4.** [introduit un exemple ou une énumération] : **tel (que)** such as, like - **5.** [introduit une comparaison] like ; **il est tel que je l'avais toujours rêvé** he's just like I always

dreamt he would be ; **tel quel** as it is/was etc. **à tel point que** *loc conj* to such an extent that. **de telle manière que** *loc conj* in such a way that. **de telle sorte que** *loc conj* with the result that, so that.

tél. (*abr écrite de* **téléphone**) tel.

télé [tele] *nf fam* TV, telly *UK*.

téléachat [teleaʃa] *nm* TV teleshopping.

téléacteur, trice [teleaktœr, tris] *nm, f* telesalesperson.

télébenne [teleben], **télécabine** [telekabin] *nf* cable car.

télécharger [17] [teleʃarge] *vt* to download.

télécommande [telekɔmɑ̃d] *nf* remote control.

télécommunication [telekɔmynikasjɔ̃] *nf* telecommunications *pl*.

télécopie [telekɔpi] *nf* fax.

télécopieur [telekɔpjœr] *nm* fax (machine).

téléfilm [telefilm] *nm* film made for television.

télégramme [telegram] *nm* telegram, wire *US*, cable *US*.

télégraphe [telegraf] *nm* telegraph.

télégraphier [9] [telegrafje] *vt* to telegraph, to wire *US*, to cable *US*.

téléguider [3] [telegide] *vt* to operate by remote control ; *fig* to mastermind.

télématique [telematik] *nf* telematics (*U*).

téléobjectif [teleɔbʒɛktif] *nm* telephoto lens *sg*.

télépathie [telepati] *nf* telepathy.

téléphérique [teleferik] *nm* cableway.

téléphone [telefɔn] *nm* telephone ; **téléphone à carte** cardphone ; **téléphone sans fil** cordless telephone.

téléphoner [3] [telefɔne] *vi* to telephone, to phone ; **téléphoner à qqn** to telephone sb, to phone sb (up) *UK*. **se téléphoner** *vp (emploi réciproque)* to call each other ; **on se téléphone, d'accord?** we'll talk on the phone later, OK?

téléphonique [telefɔnik] *adj* telephone (*avant n*), phone (*avant n*).

téléprospection [teleprɔspɛksjɔ̃] *nf* telemarketing.

téléréalité [telerealite] *nf* TV reality TV, fly-on-the-wall television ; **une émission de téléréalité** fly-on-the-wall documentary ; [de style feuilleton] docusoap.

télescope [teleskɔp] *nm* telescope.

télescoper [3] [teleskɔpe] *vt* [véhicule] to crash into. **se télescoper** *vp* [véhicules] to concertina *UK*.

télescopique [teleskɔpik] *adj* [antenne] telescopic.

téléscripteur [teleskriptœr] *nm* teleprinter *UK*, teletypewriter *US*.

télésiège [telesjɛʒ] *nm* chairlift.

téléski [teleski] *nm* ski tow.

téléspectateur, trice [telespɛktatœr, tris] *nm, f* (television) viewer.

télétravail, aux [teletravaj, o] *nm* teleworking.

télétravailleur, euse [teletravajœr,øz] *nm, f* teleworker.

télévente [televãt] *nf* [à la télévision] television selling ; [via Internet] online selling ou commerce, e-commerce.

téléviseur [televizœr] *nm* television (set).

télévision [televizjɔ̃] *nf* television ; **à la télévision** on television ; **télévision numérique** digital television ; **télévision par satellite** satellite television.

télex [telɛks] *nm inv* telex.

tellement [tɛlmã] *adv* **1.** [si, à ce point] so ; *(+ comparatif)* so much ; **tellement plus jeune que** so much younger than ; **pas tellement** not especially, not particularly - **2.** [autant] : **tellement de** [personnes, objets] so many ; [gentillesse, travail] so much - **3.** [tant] so much ; **elle a tellement changé** she's changed so much ; **je ne comprends rien tellement il parle vite** he talks so quickly that I can't understand a word.

téméraire [temerer] <> *adj* **1.** [audacieux] bold - **2.** [imprudent] rash. <> *nmf* hothead.

témérité [temerite] *nf* **1.** [audace] boldness - **2.** [imprudence] rashness.

témoignage [temwaɲaʒ] *nm* **1.** DR testimony, evidence *(U)* ; **faux témoignage** perjury - **2.** [gage] token, expression ; **en témoignage de** as a token of - **3.** [récit] account.

témoigner [3] [temwaɲe] <> *vt* **1.** [manifester] to show, to display - **2.** DR : **témoigner que** to testify that. <> *vi* DR to testify ; **témoigner contre** to testify against.

témoin [temwɛ̃] <> *nm* **1.** [spectateur] witness ; **être témoin de qqch** to be a witness to sthg, to witness sthg - **2.** DR : **témoin oculaire** eyewitness - **3.** *litt* [marque] : **témoin de** evidence *(U)* of - **4.** SPORT baton. <> *adj* [appartement] show *(avant n)*.

tempe [tãp] *nf* temple.

tempérament [tãperamã] *nm* temperament ; **avoir du tempérament** to be hot-blooded.

température [tãperatyr] *nf* temperature ; **avoir de la température** to have a temperature.

tempéré, e [tãpere] *adj* [climat] temperate.

tempérer [18] [tãpere] *vt* [adoucir] to temper ; *fig* [enthousiasme, ardeur] to moderate.

tempête [tãpɛt] *nf* storm.

tempêter [4] [tãpete] *vi* to rage.

temple [tãpl] *nm* **1.** HIST temple - **2.** [protestant] church.

tempo [tempo] *nm* tempo.

temporaire [tãporɛr] *adj* temporary.

temporairement [tãporɛrmã] *adv* temporarily.

temporel, elle [tãporel] *adj* **1.** [défini dans le temps] time *(avant n)* - **2.** [terrestre] temporal.

temps [tã] *nm* **1.** [gén] time ; **à plein temps** full-time ; **à mi-temps** half-time ; **à temps partiel** part-time ; **un temps partiel** a part-time job ; **en un temps record** in record time ; **au** ou **du temps où** (in the days) when ; **de mon temps** in my day ; **ça prend un certain temps** it takes some time ; **ces temps-ci, ces derniers temps** these days ; **pendant ce temps** meanwhile ; **en temps utile** in due course ; **en temps de guerre/paix** in wartime/peacetime ; **il était temps!** *iron* and about time too! ; **avoir le temps de faire qqch** to have time to do sthg ; **temps libre** free time ; **à temps** in time ; **de temps à autre** now and then ou again ; **de temps en temps** from time to time ; **en même temps** at the same time ; **tout le temps** all the time, the whole time ; **avoir tout son temps** to have all the time in the world - **2.** MUS beat - **3.** GRAMM tense - **4.** MÉTÉOR weather.

tenable [tənabl] *adj* bearable.

tenace [tənas] *adj* **1.** [gén] stubborn - **2.** *fig* [odeur, rhume] lingering.

ténacité [tenasite] *nf* **1.** [d'odeur] lingering nature - **2.** [de préjugé, personne] stubbornness.

tenailler [3] [tənaje] *vt* to torment.

tenailles [tənaj] *nfpl* pincers.

tenancier, ère [tənãsje, ɛr] *nm, f* manager *(f* manageress).

tendance [tãdãs] *nf* **1.** [disposition] tendency ; **avoir tendance à qqch/à faire qqch** to have a tendency to sthg/to do sthg, to be inclined to sthg/to do sthg - **2.** [économique, de mode] trend - **3.** ÉCON trend.

tendancieux, euse [tãdãsjø, øz] *adj* tendentious.

tendeur [tãdœr] *nm* [sangle] elastic strap *(for fastening luggage etc)*.

tendinite [tãdinit] *nf* tendinitis.

tendon [tãdɔ̃] *nm* tendon.

tendre¹ [tãdr] <> *adj* **1.** [gén] tender - **2.** [matériau] soft - **3.** [couleur] delicate. <> *nmf* tender-hearted person.

tendre² [73] [tãdʀ] *vt* **1.** [corde] to tighten - **2.** [muscle] to tense - **3.** [objet, main] : **tendre qqch à qqn** to hold out sthg to sb - **4.** [bâche] to hang - **5.** [piège] to set (up). ➤ **se tendre** *vp* to tighten ; *fig* [relations] to become strained.

tendresse [tãdʀɛs] *nf* **1.** [affection] tenderness - **2.** [indulgence] sympathy.

tendu, e [tãdy] ◇ *pp* ▶ **tendre².** ◇ *adj* **1.** [fil, corde] taut - **2.** [personne] tense - **3.** [atmosphère, rapports] strained - **4.** [main] outstretched.

ténèbres [tenɛbʀ] *nfpl* darkness *sg*, shadows ; *fig* depths.

ténébreux, euse [tenebʀø, øz] *adj* **1.** *fig* [dessein, affaire] mysterious - **2.** [personne] serious, solemn.

teneur [tənœʀ] *nf* content ; [de traité] terms *pl* ; **teneur en alcool/cuivre** alcohol/copper content.

tenir [40] [təniʀ] ◇ *vt* **1.** [objet, personne, solution] to hold - **2.** [garder, conserver, respecter] to keep - **3.** [gérer - boutique] to keep, to run - **4.** [apprendre] : **tenir qqch de qqn** to have sthg from sb - **5.** [considérer] : **tenir qqn pour** to regard sb as. ◇ *vi* **1.** [être solide] to stay up, to hold together - **2.** [durer] to last - **3.** [pouvoir être contenu] to fit - **4.** [être attaché] : **tenir à** [personne] to care about ; [privilèges] to value - **5.** [vouloir absolument] : **tenir à faire qqch** to insist on doing sthg - **6.** [ressembler] : **tenir de** to take after - **7.** [relever de] : **tenir de** to have something of - **8.** [dépendre de] : **il ne tient qu'à toi de...** it's entirely up to you to... ; **tenir bon** to stand firm ; **tiens!** [en donnant] here! ; [surprise] well, well! ; [pour attirer attention] look! ➤ **se tenir** *vp* **1.** [réunion] to be held - **2.** [personnes] to hold one another ; **se tenir par la main** to hold hands - **3.** [être présent] to be - **4.** [être cohérent] to make sense - **5.** [se conduire] to behave (o.s.) - **6.** [se retenir] : **se tenir (à)** to hold on (to) - **7.** [se borner] : **s'en tenir à** to stick to.

tennis [tenis] ◇ *nm* [sport] tennis. ◇ *nmpl* tennis shoes, sneakers *US*.

ténor [tenɔʀ] *nm* **1.** [chanteur] tenor - **2.** *fig* [vedette] : **un ténor de la politique** a political star performer.

tension [tãsjɔ̃] *nf* **1.** [contraction, désaccord] tension - **2.** MÉD pressure ; **avoir de la tension** to have high blood pressure - **3.** ÉLECTR voltage ; **haute/basse tension** high/low voltage.

tentaculaire [tãtakylɛʀ] *adj fig* sprawling.

tentant, e [tãtã, ãt] *adj* tempting.

tentation [tãtasjɔ̃] *nf* temptation.

tentative [tãtativ] *nf* attempt ; **tentative de suicide** suicide attempt.

tente [tãt] *nf* tent.

tenter [3] [tãte] *vt* **1.** [entreprendre] : **tenter qqch/de faire qqch** to attempt sthg/to do sthg - **2.** [plaire] to tempt ; **être tenté par qqch/de faire qqch** to be tempted by sthg/to do sthg.

tenture [tãtyʀ] *nf* hanging.

tenu, e [təny] ◇ *pp* ▶ **tenir.** ◇ *adj* **1.** [obligé] : **être tenu de faire qqch** to be required OU obliged to do sthg - **2.** [en ordre] : **bien/mal tenu** [maison] well/badly kept.

ténu, e [teny] *adj* **1.** [fil] fine ; *fig* [distinction] tenuous - **2.** [voix] thin.

tenue [təny] *nf* **1.** [entretien] running - **2.** [manières] good manners *pl* - **3.** [maintien du corps] posture - **4.** [costume] dress ; **être en petite tenue** to be scantily dressed. ➤ **tenue de route** *nf* roadholding.

ter [tɛʀ] ◇ *adv* MUS three times. ◇ *adj* : **12 ter 12B.**

TER (*abr de* Train Express Régional) *nm* fast intercity train.

Tergal® [tɛʀgal] *nm* ≃ Terylene®.

tergiverser [3] [tɛʀʒivɛʀse] *vi* to shilly-shally.

terme [tɛʀm] *nm* **1.** [fin] end ; **mettre un terme à** to put an end OU a stop to - **2.** [de grossesse] term ; **avant terme** prematurely - **3.** [échéance] time limit ; [de loyer] rent day ; **à court/moyen/long terme** [calculer] in the short/medium/long term ; [projet] short-/medium-/long-term - **4.** [mot, élément] term. ➤ **termes** *nmpl* **1.** [expressions] words - **2.** [de contrat] terms.

terminaison [tɛʀminɛzɔ̃] *nf* GRAMM ending.

terminal, e, aux [tɛʀminal, o] *adj* **1.** [au bout] final - **2.** MÉD [phase] terminal. ➤ **terminal, aux** *nm* terminal. ➤ **terminale** *nf* SCOL ≃ upper sixth year OU form *UK*, ≃ twelfth grade *US*.

terminer [3] [tɛʀmine] *vt* to end, to finish ; [travail, repas] to finish. ➤ **se terminer** *vp* to end, to finish.

terminologie [tɛʀminɔlɔʒi] *nf* terminology.

terminus [tɛʀminys] *nm* terminus.

termite [tɛʀmit] *nm* termite.

terne [tɛʀn] *adj* dull.

ternir [32] [tɛʀniʀ] *vt* to dirty ; [métal, réputation] to tarnish.

terrain [teʀɛ̃] *nm* **1.** [sol] soil ; **vélo tout terrain** mountain bike - **2.** [surface] piece of land - **3.** [emplacement - de football, rugby] pitch *UK* ; [- de golf] course ; **terrain d'aviation** airfield ; **terrain de camping** campsite - **4.** *fig* [domaine] ground.

terrasse [teʀas] *nf* terrace.

terrassement [tɛrasmɑ̃] *nm* [action] excavation.

terrasser [3] [tɛrase] *vt* [suj: personne] to bring down ; [suj: émotion] to overwhelm ; [suj: maladie] to conquer.

terre [tɛr] *nf* 1. [monde] world - 2. [sol] ground ; **par terre** on the ground ; **terre à terre** *fig* down-to-earth - 3. [matière] earth, soil - 4. [propriété] land *(U)* - 5. [territoire, continent] land - 6. ÉLECTR earth *UK*, ground *US*. ◆ **Terre** *nf* : **la Terre** Earth.

terreau [tɛro] *nm* compost.

terre-plein [tɛrplɛ̃] (*pl* **terre-pleins**) *nm* platform.

terrer [4] [tɛre] ◆ **se terrer** *vp* to go to earth.

terrestre [tɛrɛstr] *adj* 1. [croûte, atmosphère] of the earth - 2. [animal, transport] land *(avant n)* - 3. [plaisir, paradis] earthly - 4. [considérations] worldly.

terreur [tɛrœr] *nf* terror.

terrible [tɛribl] *adj* 1. [gén] terrible - 2. [appétit, soif] terrific, enormous - 3. *fam* [excellent] brilliant.

terriblement [tɛribləmɑ̃] *adv* terribly.

terrien, enne [tɛrjɛ̃, ɛn] ◇ *adj* [foncier] : **propriétaire terrien** landowner. ◇ *nm, f* [habitant de la Terre] earthling.

terrier [tɛrje] *nm* 1. [tanière] burrow - 2. [chien] terrier.

terrifier [9] [tɛrifje] *vt* to terrify.

terrine [tɛrin] *nf* terrine.

territoire [tɛritwar] *nm* 1. [pays, zone] territory - 2. ADMIN area. ◆ **territoire d'outre-mer** *nm* (French) overseas territory.

territorial, e, aux [tɛritɔrjal, o] *adj* territorial.

terroir [tɛrwar] *nm* 1. [sol] soil - 2. [région rurale] country.

terroriser [3] [tɛrɔrize] *vt* to terrorize.

terrorisme [tɛrɔrism] *nm* terrorism.

terroriste [tɛrɔrist] *nmf* terrorist.

tertiaire [tɛrsjɛr] ◇ *nm* tertiary sector. ◇ *adj* tertiary.

tes ▶ **ton²**.

tesson [tɛsɔ̃] *nm* piece of broken glass.

test [tɛst] *nm* test ; **test de dépistage** screening test ; **test de grossesse** pregnancy test.

testament [tɛstamɑ̃] *nm* will ; *fig* legacy.

tester [3] [tɛste] *vt* to test.

testicule [tɛstikyl] *nm* testicle.

tétaniser [3] [tetanize] *vt* to cause to go into spasm ; *fig* to paralyse *UK*, to paralyze *US*.

tétanos [tetanos] *nm* tetanus.

têtard [tɛtar] *nm* tadpole.

tête [tɛt] *nf* 1. [gén] head ; **de la tête aux pieds** from head to foot ou toe ; **la tête en bas** head down ; **la tête la première** head first ; **calculer qqch de tête** to calculate sthg in one's head ; **tête chercheuse** homing head ; **tête de lecture** INFORM read head ; **tête de liste** POLIT main candidate ; **être tête en l'air** to have one's head in the clouds ; **faire la tête** to sulk ; **tenir tête à qqn** to stand up to sb - 2. [visage] face - 3. [devant - de cortège, peloton] head, front ; **en tête** SPORT in the lead ; **tête de série** SPORT seeded player.

tête-à-queue [tɛtakø] *nm inv* spin.

tête-à-tête [tɛtatɛt] *nm inv* tête-à-tête.

tête-bêche [tɛtbɛʃ] *loc adv* head to tail.

tétée [tete] *nf* feed.

tétine [tetin] *nf* 1. [de biberon, mamelle] nipple, teat - 2. [sucette] dummy *UK*, pacifier *US*.

Tétrabrick® [tetrabrik] *nm* carton.

têtu, e [tety] *adj* stubborn.

teuf [tœf] *nf fam* party, rave.

tex mex [tɛksmɛks] ◇ *adj* Tex Mex. ◇ *nm* Tex Mex food.

texte [tɛkst] *nm* 1. [écrit] wording - 2. [imprimé] text - 3. [extrait] passage.

textile [tɛkstil] ◇ *adj* textile *(avant n)*. ◇ *nm* 1. [matière] textile - 2. [industrie] : **le textile** textiles *pl*, the textile industry.

textuel, elle [tɛkstɥɛl] *adj* 1. [analyse] textual ; [citation] exact ; **il a dit ça, textuel** those were his very ou exact words - 2. [traduction] literal.

texture [tɛkstyr] *nf* texture.

TF1 (*abr de* **Télévision Française 1**) *nf French independent television company.*

TGV (*abr de* **train à grande vitesse**) *nm French high-speed train.*

thaïlandais, e [tajlɑ̃dɛ, ɛz] *adj* Thai. ◆ **Thaïlandais, e** *nm, f* Thai.

Thaïlande [tajlɑ̃d] *nf* : **la Thaïlande** Thailand.

thalasso(thérapie) [talasɔ(terapi)] *nf* seawater therapy.

thé [te] *nm* tea.

théâtral, e, aux [teatral, o] *adj* [ton] theatrical.

théâtre [teatr] *nm* 1. [bâtiment, représentation] theatre *UK*, theater *US* - 2. [art] : **faire du théâtre** to be on the stage ; **adapté pour le théâtre** adapted for the stage - 3. [œuvre] plays *pl* - 4. [lieu] scene ; **théâtre d'opérations** MIL theatre *UK* ou theater *US* of operations.

théière [tejɛr] *nf* teapot.

thématique [tematik] ◇ *adj* thematic. ◇ *nf* themes *pl*.

thème [tɛm] *nm* **1.** [sujet & MUS] theme - **2.** SCOL prose.

théologie [teɔlɔʒi] *nf* theology.

théorème [teɔrɛm] *nm* theorem.

théoricien, enne [teɔrisjɛ̃, ɛn] *nm, f* theoretician.

théorie [teɔri] *nf* theory ; **en théorie** in theory.

théorique [teɔrik] *adj* theoretical.

thérapeute [terapøt] *nmf* therapist.

thérapie [terapi] *nf* therapy ; **thérapie génique** gene therapy.

thermal, e, aux [tɛrmal, o] *adj* thermal.

thermes [tɛrm] *nmpl* thermal baths.

thermique [tɛrmik] *adj* thermal.

thermomètre [tɛrmɔmɛtr] *nm* [instrument] thermometer.

Thermos® [tɛrmos] *nm & nf* Thermos®(flask).

thermostat [tɛrmɔsta] *nm* thermostat.

thèse [tɛz] *nf* **1.** [opinion] argument - **2.** PHILO & UNIV thesis ; **thèse de doctorat** doctorate - **3.** [théorie] theory.

thon [tɔ̃] *nm* tuna.

thorax [tɔraks] *nm* thorax.

thym [tɛ̃] *nm* thyme.

thyroïde [tiroid] *nf* thyroid (gland).

Tibet [tibɛ] *nm* : **le Tibet** Tibet.

tibia [tibja] *nm* tibia.

tic [tik] *nm* tic.

ticket [tikɛ] *nm* ticket ; **ticket de caisse** (till) receipt *UK*, sales slip *US* ; **ticket-repas** ≃ luncheon voucher *UK*, ≃ meal ticket *US*.

tic-tac [tiktak] *nm inv* tick-tock.

tiède [tjɛd] *adj* **1.** [boisson, eau] tepid, lukewarm - **2.** [vent] mild - **3.** *fig* [accueil] lukewarm.

tiédir [32] [tjedir] ⬦ *vt* to warm. ⬦ *vi* to become warm ; **faire tiédir qqch** to warm sthg.

tien [tjɛ̃] ⬦ **le tien, la tienne** [lətjɛ̃, latjɛn] (*mpl* **les tiens** [letjɛ̃] , *fpl* **les tiennes** [letjɛn]) *pron poss* yours ; **à la tienne!** cheers!

tierce [tjɛrs] ⬦ *nf* **1.** MUS third - **2.** [cartes à jouer] [escrime] tierce. ⬦ *adj* ▶ **tiers.**

tiercé [tjɛrse] *nm* system of betting involving the first three horses in a race.

tiers, tierce [tjɛr, tjɛrs] *adj* : **une tierce personne** a third party. ⬦ **tiers** *nm* **1.** [étranger] outsider, stranger - **2.** [tierce personne] third party - **3.** [de fraction] : **le tiers de** one-third of.

tiers-monde [tjɛrmɔ̃d] *nm* : **le tiers-monde** the Third World.

tiers-mondisation [tjɛrmɔ̃dizasjɔ̃] *nf* : **la tiers-mondisation de ce pays** this country's economic degeneration to Third World levels.

tige [tiʒ] *nf* **1.** [de plante] stem, stalk - **2.** [de bois, métal] rod.

tignasse [tiɲas] *nf fam* mop (of hair).

tigre [tigr] *nm* tiger.

tigresse [tigrɛs] *nf* tigress.

tilleul [tijœl] *nm* lime (tree).

timbale [tɛ̃bal] *nf* **1.** [gobelet] (metal) cup - **2.** MUS kettledrum.

timbre [tɛ̃br] *nm* **1.** [gén] stamp - **2.** [de voix] timbre - **3.** [de bicyclette] bell.

timbrer [3] [tɛ̃bre] *vt* to stamp.

timide [timid] ⬦ *adj* **1.** [personne] shy - **2.** [protestation, essai] timid - **3.** [soleil] uncertain. ⬦ *nmf* shy person.

timing [tajmiŋ] *nm* **1.** [emploi du temps] schedule - **2.** [organisation] timing.

timoré, e [timɔre] *adj* fearful, timorous.

tintamarre [tɛ̃tamar] *nm fam* racket.

tintement [tɛ̃tmɑ̃] *nm* [de cloche, d'horloge] chiming ; [de pièces] jingling.

tinter [3] [tɛ̃te] *vi* **1.** [cloche, horloge] to chime - **2.** [pièces] to jingle.

tir [tir] *nm* **1.** [SPORT - activité] shooting ; [- lieu] : **(centre de) tir** shooting range ; **tir au but** penalty shoot-out - **2.** [trajectoire] shot - **3.** [salve] fire (*U*) ; **tir de roquette** rocket attack - **4.** [manière, action de tirer] firing.

tirage [tiraʒ] *nm* **1.** [de journal] circulation ; [de livre] : **à grand tirage** mass circulation - **2.** [du loto] draw ; **tirage au sort** drawing lots - **3.** [de cheminée] draught *UK*, draft *US*.

tiraillement [tirajmɑ̃] *nm* (*gén pl*) **1.** [crampe] cramp - **2.** *fig* [conflit] conflict.

tirailler [3] [tiraje] ⬦ *vt* **1.** [tirer sur] to tug (at) - **2.** *fig* [écarteler] : **être tiraillé par/entre qqch** to be torn by/between sthg. ⬦ *vi* to fire wildly.

tiré, e [tire] *adj* [fatigué] : **avoir les traits tirés** ou **le visage tiré** to look drawn.

tire-bouchon [tirbuʃɔ̃] (*pl* tire-bouchons) *nm* corkscrew. ➡ **en tire-bouchon** *loc adv* corkscrew (avant n).

tirelire [tirlir] *nf* moneybox *UK*, piggy bank *US*.

tirer [3] [tire] ⬦ *vt* **1.** [gén] to pull ; [rideaux] to draw ; [tiroir] to pull open - **2.** [tracer - trait] to draw - **3.** [revue, livre] to print - **4.** [avec arme] to fire - **5.** [faire sortir - vin] to draw off ; **tirer qqn de** *litt & fig* to help ou get sb out of ; **tirer un revolver/un mouchoir de sa poche** to pull a gun/a handkerchief out of one's pocket ; **tirer la langue** to stick out one's tongue - **6.** [aux cartes, au loto] to draw - **7.** [plaisir, profit] to derive - **8.** [déduire - conclusion] to draw ; [- leçon] to learn. ◇ *vi* **1.** [tendre] : **tirer sur** to pull on OU at - **2.** [aspirer] **tirer sur** [pipe] to draw OU pull on - **3.** [couleur] : **bleu tirant sur le vert** greenish blue - **4.** [cheminée] to draw - **5.** [avec arme] to fire, to shoot - **6.** SPORT to shoot. ◆ **se tirer** *vp* **1.** *fam* [s'en aller] to push off - **2.** [se sortir] : **se tirer de** to get o.s. out of ; **s'en tirer** *fam* to escape.

tiret [tirɛ] *nm* dash.

tireur, euse [tirœr, øz] *nm, f* [avec arme] gunman ; **tireur d'élite** marksman (*f* markswoman).

tiroir [tirwar] *nm* drawer.

tiroir-caisse [tirwarkɛs] *nm* till.

tisane [tizan] *nf* herb(al) tea.

tisonnier [tizɔnje] *nm* poker.

tissage [tisaʒ] *nm* weaving.

tisser [3] [tise] *vt litt & fig* to weave ; [suj: araignée] to spin.

tissu [tisy] *nm* **1.** [étoffe] cloth, material - **2.** BIOL tissue.

titiller [3] [titije] *vt* to titillate.

titre [titr] *nm* **1.** [gén] title - **2.** [de presse] headline ; **gros titre** headline - **3.** [universitaire] diploma, qualification - **4.** DR title ; **titre de propriété** title deed - **5.** FIN security. ◆ **titre de transport** *nm* ticket. ◆ **à titre de** *loc prép* : **à titre d'exemple** by way of example ; **à titre d'information** for information.

tituber [3] [titybe] *vi* to totter.

titulaire [titylɛr] ◇ *adj* [employé] permanent ; UNIV with tenure. ◇ *nmf* [de passeport, permis] **holder** ; [de poste, chaire] occupant.

titulariser [3] [titylarize] *vt* to give tenure to.

TNP (*abr de* **traité de non-prolifération**) *nm* NPT.

toast [tost] *nm* **1.** [pain grillé] toast (*U*) - **2.** [discours] toast ; **porter un toast à** to drink a toast to.

toboggan [tɔbɔgɑ̃] *nm* **1.** [traîneau] toboggan - **2.** [de terrain de jeu] slide ; [de piscine] chute.

toc [tɔk] ◇ *interj* : **et toc!** so there! ◇ *nm* *fam* **c'est du toc** it's fake ; **en toc** fake (*avant n*).

TOC [tɔk] (*abr de* **troubles obsessionnels compulsifs**) *nmpl* MÉD OCD.

Togo [tɔgo] *nm* : **le Togo** Togo.

toi [twa] *pron pers* you. ◆ **toi-même** *pron pers* yourself.

toile [twal] *nf* **1.** [étoffe] cloth ; [de lin] linen ; **toile cirée** oilcloth - **2.** [tableau]

canvas, picture. ◆ **toile d'araignée** *nf* spider's web. ◆ **Toile** *nf* : **la Toile** INFORM the Web, the web.

toilette [twalɛt] *nf* **1.** [de personne, d'animal] washing ; **faire sa toilette** to (have a) wash *UK*, to wash up *US* - **2.** [parure, vêtements] outfit, clothes *pl*. ◆ **toilettes** *nfpl* toilet(s) *UK*, bath room *US*, rest room *US*.

toise [twaz] *nf* height gauge.

toison [twazɔ̃] *nf* **1.** [pelage] fleece - **2.** [chevelure] mop (of hair).

toit [twa] *nm* roof ; **toit ouvrant** sunroof.

toiture [twatyr] *nf* roof, roofing.

tôle [tol] *nf* [de métal] sheet metal ; **tôle ondulée** corrugated iron.

tolérance [tɔlerɑ̃s] *nf* **1.** [gén] tolerance - **2.** [liberté] concession.

tolérant, e [tɔlerɑ̃, ɑ̃t] *adj* **1.** [large d'esprit] tolerant - **2.** [indulgent] liberal.

tolérer [18] [tɔlere] *vt* to tolerate. ◆ **se tolérer** *vp* to put up with OU tolerate each other.

tollé [tɔle] *nm* protest.

tomate [tɔmat] *nf* tomato.

tombal, e, aux [tɔ̃bal, o] *adj* : **pierre tombale** gravestone.

tombant, e [tɔ̃bɑ̃, ɑ̃t] *adj* [moustaches] drooping ; [épaules] sloping.

tombe [tɔ̃b] *nf* [fosse] grave, tomb.

tombeau, x [tɔ̃bo] *nm* tomb.

tombée [tɔ̃be] *nf* fall ; **à la tombée du jour** OU **de la nuit** at nightfall.

tomber [3] [tɔ̃be] *vi (v aux : être)* **1.** [gén] to fall ; **faire tomber qqn** to knock sb over OU down ; **tomber raide mort** to drop down dead ; **tomber bien** [robe] to hang well ; *fig* [visite, personne] to come at a good time - **2.** [cheveux] to fall out - **3.** [nouvelle] to break - **4.** [diminuer - prix] to drop, to fall ; [- fièvre, vent] to drop ; [- jour] to come to an end ; [- colère] to die down - **5.** [devenir brusquement] : **tomber malade** to fall ill ; **tomber amoureux** to fall in love ; **être bien/mal tombé** to be lucky/unlucky - **6.** [trouver] : **tomber sur** to come across - **7.** [attaquer] : **tomber sur** to set about - **8.** [date, événement] to fall on.

tombola [tɔ̃bɔla] *nf* raffle.

tome [tɔm] *nm* volume.

ton¹ [tɔ̃] *nm* **1.** [de voix] tone ; **hausser/baisser le ton** to raise/lower one's voice - **2.** MUS key ; **donner le ton** to give the chord ; *fig* to set the tone - **3.** [couleur] tone, shade.

ton², ta, tes [tɔ̃, ta, te] *adj poss* your.

tonalité [tɔnalite] *nf* **1.** MUS tonality - **2.** [au téléphone] dialling tone *UK*, dial tone *US*.

tondeuse [tɔ̃døz] *nf* [à cheveux] clippers *pl* ; **tondeuse (à gazon)** mower, lawnmower.

tondre [75] [tɔ̃dr] *vt* [gazon] to mow ; [mouton] to shear ; [caniche, cheveux] to clip.

tondu, e [tɔ̃dy] *adj* [caniche, cheveux] clipped ; [pelouse] mown.

tonicité [tɔnisite] *nf* [des muscles] tone.

tonifier [9] [tɔnifje] *vt* [peau] to tone ; [esprit] to stimulate.

tonique [tɔnik] *adj* **1.** [boisson] tonic *(avant n)* ; [froid] bracing ; [lotion] toning - **2.** LING & MUS tonic.

tonitruant, e [tɔnitryɑ̃, ɑ̃t] *adj* booming.

tonnage [tɔnaʒ] *nm* tonnage.

tonnant, e [tɔnɑ̃, ɑ̃t] *adj* thundering, thunderous.

tonne [tɔn] *nf* [1000 kg] tonne.

tonneau, x [tɔno] *nm* **1.** [baril] barrel, cask - **2.** [de voiture] roll - **3.** NAUT ton.

tonnelle [tɔnɛl] *nf* bower, arbour.

tonner [3] [tɔne] *vi* to thunder.

tonnerre [tɔnɛr] *nm* thunder ; **coup de tonnerre** thunderclap ; *fig* bombshell.

tonte [tɔ̃t] *nf* [de mouton] shearing ; [de gazon] mowing ; [de caniche, cheveux] clipping.

tonus [tɔnys] *nm* **1.** [dynamisme] energy - **2.** [de muscle] tone.

top [tɔp] *nm* [signal] beep.

toper [3] [tɔpe] *vi* : **tope-là!** right, you're on!

topographie [tɔpɔgrafi] *nf* topography.

toque [tɔk] *nf* [de juge, de jockey] cap ; [de cuisinier] hat.

torche [tɔrʃ] *nf* torch.

torcher [3] [tɔrʃe] *vt fam* **1.** [assiette, fesses] to wipe - **2.** [travail] to dash off.

torchon [tɔrʃɔ̃] *nm* **1.** [serviette] cloth - **2.** *fam* [travail] mess.

tordre [76] [tɔrdr] *vt* [gén] to twist. ◆ **se tordre** *vp* : **se tordre la cheville** to twist one's ankle ; **se tordre de rire** *fam fig* to double up with laughter.

tordu, e [tɔrdy] ◇ *pp* ► **tordre**. ◇ *adj fam* [bizarre, fou] **crazy** ; [esprit] warped.

tornade [tɔrnad] *nf* tornado.

torpeur [tɔrpœr] *nf* torpor.

torpille [tɔrpij] *nf* MIL torpedo.

torpiller [3] [tɔrpije] *vt* to torpedo.

torréfaction [tɔrefaksjɔ̃] *nf* roasting.

torrent [tɔrɑ̃] *nm* torrent ; **un torrent de** *fig* [injures] a stream of ; [lumière, larmes] a flood of.

torrentiel, elle [tɔrɑ̃sjɛl] *adj* torrential.

torride [tɔrid] *adj* torrid.

torse [tɔrs] *nm* chest.

torsade [tɔrsad] *nf* **1.** [de cheveux] twist, coil - **2.** [de pull] cable.

torsader [3] [tɔrsade] *vt* to twist.

torsion [tɔrsjɔ̃] *nf* twisting ; PHYS torsion.

tort [tɔr] *nm* **1.** [erreur] fault ; **avoir tort** to be wrong ; **être dans son** OU **en tort** to be in the wrong ; **à tort** wrongly - **2.** [préjudice] wrong.

torticolis [tɔrtikɔli] *nm* stiff neck.

tortiller [3] [tɔrtije] *vt* [enrouler] to twist ; [moustache] to twirl. ◆ **se tortiller** *vp* to writhe, to wriggle.

tortionnaire [tɔrsjɔnɛr] *nmf* torturer.

tortue [tɔrty] *nf* tortoise ; *fig* slowcoach *UK*, slowpoke *US*.

tortueux, euse [tɔrtɥø, øz] *adj* winding, twisting ; *fig* tortuous.

torture [tɔrtyr] *nf* torture.

torturer [3] [tɔrtyre] *vt* to torture.

tôt [to] *adv* **1.** [de bonne heure] early - **2.** [avant le moment prévu] soon - **3.** [vite] soon, early. ◆ **au plus tôt** *loc adv* at the earliest.

total, e, aux [tɔtal, o] *adj* total. ◆ **total** *nm* total.

totalement [tɔtalmɑ̃] *adv* totally.

totaliser [3] [tɔtalize] *vt* **1.** [additionner] to add up, to total - **2.** [réunir] to have a total of.

totalitaire [tɔtalitɛr] *adj* totalitarian.

totalitarisme [tɔtalitarism] *nm* totalitarianism.

totalité [tɔtalite] *nf* whole ; **en totalité** entirely.

totem [tɔtɛm] *nm* totem.

toubib [tubib] *nmf fam* doc.

touchant, e [tuʃɑ̃, ɑ̃t] *adj* touching.

touche [tuʃ] *nf* **1.** [de clavier] key ; **touche de fonction** function key - **2.** [de peinture] stroke - **3.** *fig* [note] : **une touche de** a touch of - **4.** [à la pêche] bite - **5.** [FOOTBALL - ligne] touch line ; [- remise en jeu] throw-in ; [rugby - ligne] touch (line) ; [- remise en jeu] line-out - **6.** [escrime] hit.

toucher [3] [tuʃe] ◇ *nm* : **le toucher** the (sense of) touch ; **au toucher** to the touch. ◇ *vt* **1.** [palper, émouvoir] to touch - **2.** [rivage, correspondant] to reach ; [cible] to hit - **3.** [salaire] to get, to be paid ; [chèque] to cash ; [gros lot] to win - **4.** [concerner] to affect, to concern. ◇ *vi* : **toucher à** to touch ; [problème] to touch on ; [inconscience, folie] to border OU verge on ; [maison] to adjoin ; **toucher à sa fin** to draw to a close. ◆ **se toucher** *vp* [maisons] to be adjacent (to each other), to adjoin (each other).

touffe [tuf] *nf* tuft.

touffu, e [tufy] *adj* [forêt] dense ; [barbe] bushy.

toujours [tuʒur] *adv* **1.** [continuité, répétition] always ; **ils s'aimeront toujours** they will always love one another, they will love one another forever ; **toujours plus** more and more ; **toujours moins** less and less - **2.** [encore] still - **3.** [de toute façon] anyway, anyhow. ◆ **de toujours** *loc adj* : **ce sont des amis de toujours** they are lifelong friends. ◆ **pour toujours** *loc adv* forever, for good. ◆ **toujours est-il que** *loc conj* the fact remains that.

toupet [tupɛ] *nm* **1.** [de cheveux] quiff *UK*, tuft of hair - **2.** *fam fig* [aplomb] cheek ; **avoir du toupet, ne pas manquer de toupet** *fam* to have a cheek.

toupie [tupi] *nf* (spinning) top.

tour [tur] ◇ *nm* **1.** [périmètre] circumference ; **faire le tour de** to go round ; **faire un tour** to go for a walk/drive *etc* ; **tour d'horizon** survey ; **tour de piste** SPORT lap ; **tour de taille** waist measurement - **2.** [rotation] turn ; **fermer à double tour** to double-lock - **3.** [plaisanterie] trick - **4.** [succession] turn ; **c'est à mon tour** it's my turn ; **à tour de rôle** in turn ; **tour à tour** alternately, in turn - **5.** [d'événements] turn - **6.** [de potier] wheel. ◇ *nf* **1.** [monument, de château] tower ; [immeuble] tower-block *UK*, high rise *US* - **2.** [échecs] rook, castle. ◆ **tour de contrôle** *nf* control tower. ◆ **Tour de France** *npr m* : **le Tour de France** the Tour de France cycle race.

tourbe [turb] *nf* peat.

tourbillon [turbijõ] *nm* **1.** [de vent] whirlwind - **2.** [de poussière, fumée] swirl - **3.** [d'eau] whirlpool - **4.** *fig* [agitation] hurly-burly.

tourbillonner [3] [turbijɔne] *vi* to whirl, to swirl ; *fig* to whirl (round).

tourelle [turɛl] *nf* turret.

tourisme [turism] *nm* tourism.

touriste [turist] *nmf* tourist.

touristique [turistik] *adj* tourist (*avant n*).

tourment [turmã] *nm sout* torment.

tourmente [turmãt] *nf* **1.** *litt* [tempête] storm, tempest - **2.** *fig* turmoil.

tourmenter [3] [turmãte] *vt* to torment. ◆ **se tourmenter** *vp* to worry o.s., to fret.

tournage [turnaʒ] *nm* CINÉ shooting.

tournant, e [turnã, ãt] *adj* [porte] revolving ; [fauteuil] swivel (*avant n*) ; [pont] swing (*avant n*). ◆ **tournant** *nm* bend ; *fig* turning point.

tourné, e [turne] *adj* [lait] sour, off.

tourne-disque [turnədisk] (*pl* **tourne-disques**) *nm* record player.

tournée [turne] *nf* **1.** [voyage] tour - **2.** *fam* [consommations] round.

tourner [3] [turne] ◇ *vt* **1.** [gén] to turn - **2.** [pas, pensées] to turn, to direct - **3.** [obstacle, loi] to get round *UK* ou around *US* - **4.** CINÉ to shoot. ◇ *vi* **1.** [gén] to turn ; [moteur] to turn over ; [planète] to revolve ; **tourner autour de qqn** *fig* to hang around sb ; **tourner autour du pot** ou **du sujet** *fig* to beat about the bush - **2.** *fam* [entreprise] to tick over *UK* - **3.** [lait] to go off *UK*, to go bad *US*. ◆ **se tourner** *vp* to turn (right) round *UK* ou around *US* ; **se tourner vers** to turn towards ou toward *US*.

tournesol [turnəsɔl] *nm* [plante] sunflower.

tournevis [turnəvis] *nm* screwdriver.

tourniquet [turnikɛ] *nm* **1.** [entrée] turnstile - **2.** MÉD tourniquet.

tournis [turni] *nm fam* **avoir le tournis** to feel dizzy ou giddy.

tournoi [turnwa] *nm* tournament.

tournoyer [13] [turnwaje] *vi* to wheel, to whirl.

tournure [turnyr] *nf* **1.** [apparence] turn - **2.** [formulation] form ; **tournure de phrase** turn of phrase.

tourteau, x [turto] *nm* [crabe] crab.

tourterelle [turtərɛl] *nf* turtledove.

tous ➡ tout.

Toussaint [tusɛ̃] *nf* : **la Toussaint** All Saints' Day.

tousser [3] [tuse] *vi* to cough.

toussotement [tusɔtmã] *nm* coughing.

toussoter [3] [tusɔte] *vi* to cough.

tout, toute [tu, tut] (*mpl* **tous** [tus], *fpl* **toutes** [tut]) ◇ *adj* **1.** (*avec substantif singulier déterminé*) all ; **tout le vin** all the wine ; **tout un gâteau** a whole cake ; **toute la journée/la nuit** all day/night, the whole day/night ; **toute sa famille** all his family, his whole family - **2.** (*avec pronom démonstratif*) **tout ceci/cela** all this/that ; **tout ce que je sais** all I know. ◇ *adj indéf* **1.** [exprime la totalité] all ; **tous les gâteaux** all the cakes ; **tous les deux** both of us/them/etc ; **tous les trois** all three of us/them *etc* - **2.** [chaque] every ; **tous les jours** every day ; **tous les deux ans** every two years ; **tous les combien?** how often? - **3.** [n'importe quel] any ; **à toute heure** at any time. ◇ *pron indéf* everything, all ; **je t'ai tout dit** I've told you everything ; **ils voulaient tous la voir** they all wanted to see her ; **ce sera tout?** will that be all ; **c'est tout** that's all. **tout** ◇ *adv* **1.** [entièrement, tout à fait] very, quite ; **tout jeune/près** very young/near ; **ils étaient tout seuls** they were all alone ; **tout en haut** right at the top - **2.** [avec un gérondif] : **tout en marchant** while walking. ◇ *nm* : **un tout** a whole ; **le tout est de...** the main thing is to... **du tout au tout** *loc adv* completely, entirely. **pas du tout** *loc adv* not at all. **tout à fait** *loc adv* **1.** [complètement] quite, entirely - **2.** [exactement] exactly. **tout à l'heure** *loc adv* **1.** [futur] in a little while, shortly ; **à tout à l'heure!** see you later! - **2.** [passé] a little while ago. **tout de suite** *loc adv* immediately, at once.

tout-à-l'égout [tutalegu] *nm inv* mains drainage.

toutefois [tutfwa] *adv* however.

tout-petit [tup(ə)ti] (*pl* **tout-petits**) *nm* toddler, tot.

tout-puissant, toute-puissante [tupɥisɑ̃, tutpɥisɑ̃t] (*mpl* **tout-puissants**) (*fpl* **toutes-puissantes**) *adj* omnipotent, all-powerful.

toux [tu] *nf* cough.

toxicomane [tɔksikɔman] *nmf* drug addict.

toxine [tɔksin] *nf* toxin.

toxique [tɔksik] *adj* toxic.

trac [trak] *nm* nerves *pl* ; THÉÂTRE stage fright ; **avoir le trac** to get nervous ; THÉÂTRE to get stage fright.

traçabilité [trasabilite] *nf* traceability.

tracas [traka] *nm* worry.

tracasser [3] [trakase] *vt* to worry, to bother. **se tracasser** *vp* to worry.

tracasserie [trakasri] *nf* annoyance.

trace [tras] *nf* **1.** [d'animal, de fugitif] track - **2.** [de brûlure, fatigue] mark - **3.** (*gén pl*) [vestige] trace - **4.** [très petite quantité] : **une trace de** a trace of.

tracé [trase] *nm* [lignes] plan, drawing ; [de parcours] line.

tracer [16] [trase] *vt* **1.** [dessiner, dépeindre] to draw - **2.** [route, piste] to mark out.

trachéite [trakeit] *nf* throat infection.

tract [trakt] *nm* leaflet.

tractations [traktasjɔ̃] *nfpl* negotiations, dealings.

tracter [3] [trakte] *vt* to tow.

tracteur [traktœr] *nm* tractor.

traction [traksjɔ̃] *nf* **1.** [action de tirer] towing, pulling ; **traction avant/arrière** front-/rear-wheel drive - **2.** TECHNOL tensile stress - **3.** [SPORT - au sol] press-up *UK*, push-up *US* ; [- à la barre] pull-up.

tradition [tradisjɔ̃] *nf* tradition.

traditionnel, elle [tradisjɔnɛl] *adj* **1.** [de tradition] traditional - **2.** [habituel] usual.

traducteur, trice [tradyktœr, tris] *nm, f* translator.

traduction [tradyksjɔ̃] *nf* [gén] translation.

traduire [98] [tradɥir] *vt* **1.** [texte] to translate ; **traduire qqch en français/anglais** to translate sthg into French/English - **2.** [révéler - crise] to reveal, to betray ; [- sentiments, pensée] to render, to express - **3.** DR : **traduire qqn en justice** to bring sb before the courts.

trafic [trafik] *nm* **1.** [de marchandises] traffic, trafficking - **2.** [circulation] traffic.

trafiquant, e [trafikɑ̃, ɑ̃t] *nm, f* trafficker, dealer.

trafiquer [3] [trafike] ◇ *vt* **1.** [falsifier] to tamper with - **2.** *fam* [manigancer] : **qu'est-ce que tu trafiques?** what are you up to? ◇ *vi* to be involved in trafficking.

tragédie [traʒedi] *nf* tragedy.

tragi-comédie [traʒikɔmedi] (*pl* **tragi-comédies**) *nf* tragicomedy.

tragique [traʒik] *adj* tragic.

tragiquement [traʒikmɑ̃] *adv* tragically.

trahir [32] [trair] *vt* **1.** [gén] to betray - **2.** [suj: moteur] to let down ; [suj: forces] to fail - **3.** [révéler, démasquer] to betray, to give away (*sep*). **se trahir** *vp* to give o.s. away.

trahison [traizɔ̃] *nf* **1.** [gén] betrayal - **2.** DR treason.

train [trɛ̃] *nm* **1.** [transports] train - **2.** [allure] pace ; **être en train** *fig* to be on form. **train de vie** lifestyle. **en train de** *loc prép* : **être en train de lire/travailler** to be reading/working.

traînant, e [trɛnɑ̃, ɑ̃t] *adj* [voix] drawling ; [démarche] dragging.

traîne [trɛn] *nf* [de robe] train ; **être à la traîne** to lag behind.

traîneau, x [trɛno] *nm* sleigh, sledge.

traînée [trɛne] *nf* **1.** [trace] trail - **2.** *tfam péj* [prostituée] tart, whore.

traîner [4] [trɛne] ◇ *vt* **1.** [tirer, emmener] to drag - **2.** [trimbaler] to lug around, to cart around - **3.** [maladie] to be unable to shake off. ◇ *vi* **1.** [personne, animal] to dawdle - **2.** [maladie, affaire] to drag on ; **traîner en longueur** to drag - **3.** [vêtements, livres] to lie around ou about. **se traîner** *vp* **1.** [personne] to drag o.s. along - **2.** [jour, semaine] to drag.

train-train [trɛ̃trɛ̃] *nm fam* routine, daily grind.

traire [112] [trɛr] *vt* [vache] to milk.

trait [trɛ] *nm* **1.** [ligne] line, stroke ; **trait d'union** hyphen - **2.** (*gén pl*) [de visage]

feature - **3.** [caractéristique] trait, feature ;
avoir trait à to be to do with, to concern.
d'un trait *loc adv* [boire, lire] in one go.

traitant, e [trɛtɑ̃, ɑ̃t] *adj* [shampooing,
crème] medicated, **médecin.**

traite [trɛt] *nf* **1.** [de vache] milking
- **2.** COMM bill, draft - **3.** [d'esclaves] : **la traite
des noirs** the slave trade ; **la traite des
blanches** the white slave trade. **d'une
seule traite** *loc adv* without stopping, in
one go.

traité [trete] *nm* **1.** [ouvrage] treatise - **2.** PO-
LIT treaty ; **traité de non-prolifération** non-
proliferation treaty.

traitement [trɛtmɑ̃] *nm* **1.** [gén & MÉD]
treatment - **2.** [rémunération] wage - **3.** [dans
l'industrie & INFORM] processing ; **traitement
de texte** word processing - **4.** [de problème]
handling.

traiter [4] [trete] *vt* **1.** [gén & MÉD] to
treat ; **bien/mal traiter qqn** to treat sb
well/badly - **2.** [qualifier] : **traiter qqn d'im-
bécile/de lâche** *etc* to call sb an imbecile/a
coward *etc* - **3.** [question, thème] to deal
with - **4.** [dans l'industrie & INFORM] to
process. *vi* **1.** [négocier] to negotiate
- **2.** [livre] : **traiter de** to deal with.

traiteur [trɛtœr] *nm* caterer.

traître, esse [trɛtr, ɛs] *adj* treacherous. *nm, f* traitor.

traîtrise [tretriz] *nf* **1.** [déloyauté] treachery - **2.** [acte] act of treachery.

trajectoire [traʒɛktwar] *nf* trajectory,
path ; *fig* path.

trajet [traʒɛ] *nm* **1.** [distance] distance
- **2.** [itinéraire] route - **3.** [voyage] journey.

trame [tram] *nf* weft ; *fig* framework.

tramer [3] [trame] *vt sout* to plot. **se
tramer** *vp* to be plotted. *v impers* :
il se trame quelque chose there's something
afoot.

tramontane [tramɔ̃tan] *nf strong cold wind
that blows through Languedoc-Roussillon in
southwest France.*

trampoline [trɑ̃pɔlin] *nm* trampoline.

tram(way) [tram(wɛ)] *nm* tram UK, streetcar US.

tranchant, e [trɑ̃ʃɑ̃, ɑ̃t] *adj* **1.** [instrument]
sharp - **2.** [personne] assertive - **3.** [ton] curt.
tranchant *nm* edge.

tranche [trɑ̃ʃ] *nf* **1.** [de gâteau, jambon]
slice ; **tranche d'âge** *fig* age bracket - **2.** [de
livre, pièce] edge - **3.** [période] part, section
- **4.** ÉCON & FIN [de revenus] portion ; [de
paiement] instalment UK, installment US ;
[fiscale] bracket.

trancher [3] [trɑ̃ʃe] *vt* [couper] to cut ;

[pain, jambon] to slice ; **trancher la question**
fig to settle the question. *vi* **1.** *fig*
[décider] to decide - **2.** [contraster] : **trancher
avec** OU **sur** to contrast with.

tranquille [trɑ̃kil] *adj* **1.** [endroit, vie]
quiet ; **laisser qqn/qqch tranquille** to leave
sb/sthg alone ; **se tenir/rester tranquille** to
keep/remain quiet - **2.** [rassuré] at ease,
easy ; **soyez tranquille** don't worry.

tranquillement [trɑ̃kilmɑ̃] *adv* **1.** [sans
s'agiter] quietly - **2.** [sans s'inquiéter] calmly.

tranquillisant, e [trɑ̃kilizɑ̃, ɑ̃t] *adj*
1. [nouvelle] reassuring - **2.** [médicament]
tranquillizing. **tranquillisant** *nm* tranquilizer UK, tranquilizer US.

tranquilliser [3] [trɑ̃kilize] *vt* to reassure.
se tranquilliser *vp* to set one's mind
at rest.

tranquillité [trɑ̃kilite] *nf* **1.** [calme] peace-
fulness, quietness - **2.** [sérénité] peace,
tranquillity UK, tranquility US.

transaction [trɑ̃zaksjɔ̃] *nf* transaction.

transat [trɑ̃zat] *nm* deckchair. *nf*
transatlantic race.

transatlantique [trɑ̃zatlɑ̃tik] *adj*
transatlantic. *nm* transatlantic liner.
nf transatlantic race.

transcription [trɑ̃skripsjɔ̃] *nf* [de document & MUS] transcription ; [dans un autre
alphabet] transliteration ; **transcription phonétique** phonetic transcription.

transcrire [99] [trɑ̃skrir] *vt* [document &
MUS] to transcribe ; [dans un autre alphabet]
to transliterate.

transcrit, e [trɑ̃skri, it] *pp* **transcrire.**

transe [trɑ̃s] *nf* : **être en transe** *fig* to be
beside o.s.

transférer [18] [trɑ̃sfere] *vt* to transfer.

transfert [trɑ̃sfɛr] *nm* transfer.

transfigurer [3] [trɑ̃sfigyre] *vt* to transfig-
ure.

transformateur, trice [trɑ̃sfɔrmatœr,
tris] *adj* [dans l'industrie] processing *(avant
n)*. **transformateur** *nm* transformer.

transformation [trɑ̃sfɔrmasjɔ̃] *nf* **1.** [de
pays, personne] transformation - **2.** [dans
l'industrie] processing - **3.** [rugby] conversion.

transformer [3] [trɑ̃sfɔrme] *vt* **1.** [gén] to
transform ; [magasin] to convert ; **transformer qqch en** to turn sthg into - **2.** [dans
l'industrie] [rugby] to convert. **se
transformer** *vp* : **se transformer en mons-
tre/papillon** to turn into a monster/butter-
fly.

transfuge [trɑ̃sfyʒ] *nmf* renegade.

transfuser [3] [trɑ̃sfyze] *vt* [sang] to
transfuse.

transfusion [trɑ̃sfyziʒ] *nf*: transfusion (sanguine) (blood) transfusion.

transgénique [trɑ̃sʒenik] *adj* transgenic.

transgresser [4] [trɑ̃sgrese] *vt* [loi] to infringe ; [ordre] to disobey.

transhumance [trɑ̃zymɑ̃s] *nf* transhumance.

transi, e [trɑ̃zi] *adj* : **être transi de** to be paralysed *UK* ou paralyzed *US*, to be transfixed with ; **être transi de froid** to be chilled to the bone.

transiger [17] [trɑ̃ziʒe] *vi* : **transiger (sur)** to compromise (on).

transistor [3] [trɑ̃zistɔr] *nm* transistor.

transit [trɑ̃zit] *nm* transit.

transiter [3] [trɑ̃zite] *vi* to pass in transit.

transitif, ive [trɑ̃zitif, iv] *adj* transitive.

transition [trɑ̃ziziʒ] *nf* transition ; **sans transition** with no transition, abruptly.

transitivité [trɑ̃zitivite] *nf* transitivity.

transitoire [trɑ̃zitwar] *adj* [passager] transitory.

translucide [trɑ̃slysid] *adj* translucent.

transmettre [84] [trɑ̃smɛtr] *vt* **1.** [message, salutations] : **transmettre qqch (à)** to pass sthg on (to) - **2.** [tradition, propriété] : **transmettre qqch (à)** to hand sthg down (to) - **3.** [fonction, pouvoir] : **transmettre qqch (à)** to hand sthg over (to) - **4.** [maladie] : **transmettre qqch (à)** to transmit sthg (to), to pass sthg on (to) - **5.** [concert, émission] to broadcast. ◆ **se transmettre** *vp* **1.** [maladie] to be passed on, to be transmitted - **2.** [nouvelle] to be passed on - **3.** [courant, onde] to be transmitted - **4.** [tradition] to be handed down.

transmis, e [trɑ̃smi, iz] *pp* ▶ **transmettre**.

transmissible [trɑ̃smisibl] *adj* **1.** [patrimoine] transferable - **2.** [maladie] transmissible.

transmission [trɑ̃smisiʒ] *nf* **1.** [de biens] transfer - **2.** [de maladie] transmission - **3.** [de message] passing on - **4.** [de tradition] handing down.

transparaître [91] [trɑ̃sparetr] *vi* to show.

transparence [trɑ̃sparɑ̃s] *nf* transparency.

transparent, e [trɑ̃sparɑ̃, ɑ̃t] *adj* transparent. ◆ **transparent** *nm* transparency.

transpercer [16] [trɑ̃sperse] *vt* to pierce ; *fig* [suj: froid, pluie] to go right through.

transpiration [trɑ̃spirasiʒ] *nf* [sueur] perspiration.

transpirer [3] [trɑ̃spire] *vi* [suer] to perspire.

transplanter [3] [trɑ̃splɑ̃te] *vt* to transplant.

transport [trɑ̃spɔr] *nm* transport (U), transportation (U) *US* ; **transports en commun** public transport *sg*.

transportable [trɑ̃spɔrtabl] *adj* [marchandise] transportable ; [blessé] fit to be moved.

transporter [3] [trɑ̃spɔrte] *vt* [marchandises, personnes] to transport.

transporteur [trɑ̃spɔrtœr] *nm* [personne] carrier ; **transporteur routier** road haulier *UK* ou hauler *US*.

transposer [3] [trɑ̃spoze] *vt* **1.** [déplacer] to transpose - **2.** [adapter] : **transposer qqch (à)** to adapt sthg (for).

transposition [trɑ̃spoziziʒ] *nf* **1.** [déplacement] transposition - **2.** [adaptation] : **transposition (à)** adaptation (for).

transsexuel, elle [trɑ̃sseksɥel] *adj & nm, f* transsexual.

transvaser [3] [trɑ̃svaze] *vt* to decant.

transversal, e, aux [trɑ̃sversal, o] *adj* **1.** [coupe] cross *(avant n)* - **2.** [chemin] running at right angles, cross *(avant n) US* - **3.** [vallée] transverse.

trapèze [trapɛz] *nm* **1.** GÉOM trapezium - **2.** [gymnastique] trapeze.

trapéziste [trapezist] *nmf* trapeze artist.

trappe [trap] *nf* **1.** [ouverture] trapdoor - **2.** [piège] trap.

trapu, e [trapy] *adj* **1.** [personne] stocky, solidly built - **2.** [édifice] squat.

traquenard [traknar] *nm* trap ; *fig* trap, pitfall.

traquer [3] [trake] *vt* [animal] to track ; [personne, faute] to track ou hunt down.

traumatiser [3] [tromatize] *vt* to traumatize.

traumatisme [tromatism] *nm* traumatism.

travail [travaj] *nm* **1.** [gén] work (U) ; **se mettre au travail** to get down to work ; **demander du travail** [projet] to require some work - **2.** [tâche, emploi] job ; **travail intérimaire** temporary work - **3.** [du métal, du bois] working - **4.** [phénomène - du bois] warping ; [- du temps, fermentation] action - **5.** MÉD : **être en travail** to be in labour *UK* ou labor *US* ; **entrer en travail** to go into labour *UK* ou labor *US*. ◆ **travaux** *nmpl* **1.** [d'aménagement] work (U) ; [routiers] roadworks *UK*, roadwork *US* ; **travaux publics** civil engineering *sg* - **2.** SCOL : **travaux dirigés** class work ; **travaux manuels** arts and crafts ; **travaux pratiques** practical work (U).

travaillé, e [travaje] *adj* **1.** [matériau] wrought, worked - **2.** [style] laboured *UK*, labored *US* - **3.** [tourmenté] : **être travaillé par** to be tormented by.

travailler [3] [travaje] ⟨⟩ *vi* **1.** [gén] to work ; **travailler chez/dans** to work at/in ;

travailler à qqch to work on sthg ; **travailler à temps partiel** to work part-time - **2.** [métal, bois] to warp. ◇ *vt* **1.** [étudier] to work at ou on ; [piano] to practise *UK*, to practice *US* - **2.** [essayer de convaincre] to work on - **3.** [suj: idée, remords] to torment - **4.** [matière] to work, to fashion.

travailleur, euse [travajœr, øz] ◇ *adj* hard-working. ◇ *nm, f* worker.

travelling [travliŋ] *nm* [mouvement] travelling *UK* ou traveling *US* shot.

travers [traver] *nm* failing, fault. ◆ **à travers** *loc adv & loc prép* through. ◆ **au travers** *loc adv* through. ◆ **au travers de** *loc prép* through. ◆ **de travers** *loc adv* **1.** [irrégulièrement - écrire] unevenly ; **marcher de travers** to stagger - **2.** [nez, escalier] crooked - **3.** [obliquement] sideways - **4.** [mal] wrong ; **aller de travers** to go wrong ; **comprendre qqch de travers** to misunderstand sthg. ◆ **en travers** *loc adv* crosswise. ◆ **en travers de** *loc prép* across.

traverse [travers] *nf* **1.** [de chemin de fer] sleeper *UK*, tie *US* - **2.** [chemin] short cut.

traversée [traverse] *nf* crossing.

traverser [3] [traverse] *vt* **1.** [rue, mer, montagne] to cross ; [ville] to go through - **2.** [peau, mur] to go through, to pierce - **3.** [crise, période] to go through.

traversin [traversɛ̃] *nm* bolster.

travesti, e [travesti] *adj* **1.** [pour s'amuser] dressed up (in fancy dress) - **2.** THÉÂTRE [comédien] playing a female part. ◆ **travesti** *nm* [homosexuel] transvestite.

travestir [32] [travestir] *vt* **1.** [déguiser] to dress up - **2.** *fig* [vérité, idée] to distort. ◆ **se travestir** *vp* **1.** [pour bal] to wear fancy dress - **2.** [en femme] to put on drag.

trébucher [3] [trebyʃe] *vi* : **trébucher (sur/contre)** to stumble (over/against).

trèfle [trefl] *nm* **1.** [plante] clover - **2.** [carte] club ; [famille] clubs *pl*.

treille [trej] *nf* **1.** [vigne] climbing vine - **2.** [tonnelle] trellised vines *pl*, vine arbour.

treillis [treji] *nm* **1.** [clôture] trellis (fencing) - **2.** [toile] canvas - **3.** MIL combat uniform.

treize [trez] *adj num inv & nm* thirteen ; *voir aussi* **six**.

treizième [trezjɛm] *adj num inv, nm & nmf* thirteenth ; **treizième mois** bonus corresponding to an extra month's salary which is paid annually ; *voir aussi* **sixième**.

trekking [trekiŋ] *nm* trek.

tréma [trema] *nm* diaeresis *UK*, dieresis *US*.

tremblant, e [trɑ̃blɑ̃, ɑ̃t] *adj* **1.** [personne - de froid] shivering ; [- d'émotion] trembling, shaking - **2.** [voix] quavering - **3.** [lumière] flickering.

tremblement [trɑ̃bləmɑ̃] *nm* **1.** [de corps] trembling - **2.** [de voix] quavering - **3.** [de feuilles] fluttering. ◆ **tremblement de terre** earthquake.

trembler [3] [trɑ̃ble] *vi* **1.** [personne - de froid] to shiver ; [- d'émotion] to tremble, to shake - **2.** [voix] to quaver - **3.** [lumière] to flicker - **4.** [terre] to shake.

trembloter [3] [trɑ̃blɔte] *vi* **1.** [personne] to tremble - **2.** [voix] to quaver - **3.** [lumière] to flicker.

trémousser [3] [tremuse] ◆ **se trémousser** *vp* to jig up and down.

trempe [trɑ̃p] *nf* **1.** [envergure] calibre ; **de sa trempe** of his/her calibre - **2.** *fam* [coups] thrashing.

tremper [3] [trɑ̃pe] ◇ *vt* **1.** [mouiller] to soak - **2.** [plonger] : **tremper qqch dans** to dip sthg into - **3.** [métal] to harden, to quench. ◇ *vi* [linge] to soak.

tremplin [trɑ̃plɛ̃] *nm litt & fig* springboard ; SKI ski jump.

trentaine [trɑ̃tɛn] *nf* **1.** [nombre] : **une trentaine de** about thirty - **2.** [âge] : **avoir la trentaine** to be in one's thirties.

trente [trɑ̃t] ◇ *adj num inv* thirty. ◇ *nm* thirty ; *voir aussi* **six**.

trentième [trɑ̃tjɛm] *adj num inv, nm & nmf* thirtieth ; *voir aussi* **sixième**.

trépasser [3] [trepase] *vi litt* to pass away.

trépidant, e [trepidɑ̃, ɑ̃t] *adj* [vie] hectic.

trépied [trepje] *nm* [support] tripod.

trépigner [3] [trepiɲe] *vi* to stamp one's feet.

très [trɛ] *adv* very ; **très bien** very well ; **être très aimé** to be much ou greatly liked ; **j'ai très envie de...** I'd very much like to...

trésor [trezɔr] *nm* treasure. ◆ **Trésor** *nm* : **le Trésor public** the public revenue department.

trésorerie [trezɔrri] *nf* **1.** [service] accounts department - **2.** [gestion] accounts *pl* - **3.** [fonds] finances *pl*, funds *pl*.

trésorier, ère [trezɔrje, ɛr] *nm, f* treasurer.

tressaillement [tresajmɑ̃] *nm* [de joie] thrill ; [de douleur] wince.

tressaillir [47] [tresajir] *vi* **1.** [de joie] to thrill ; [de douleur] to wince - **2.** [sursauter] to start, to jump.

tressauter [3] [tresote] *vi* [sursauter] to jump, to start ; [dans véhicule] to be tossed about.

tresse [tres] *nf* **1.** [de cheveux] plait - **2.** [de rubans] braid.

tresser [4] [trese] *vt* **1.** [cheveux] to plait - **2.** [osier] to braid - **3.** [panier, guirlande] to weave.

tréteau, x [treto] nm trestle.

treuil [trœj] nm winch, windlass.

trêve [trɛv] nf **1.** [cessez-le-feu] truce - **2.** fig [répit] rest, respite ; **trêve de plaisanteries/de sottises** that's enough joking/nonsense. ➤ **sans trêve** loc adv relentlessly, unceasingly.

tri [tri] nm [de lettres] sorting ; [de candidats] selection ; **faire le tri dans qqch** fig to sort sthg out ; [déchets] : **tri sélectif (des ordures)** sorting of rubbish into different types for recycling.

triage [trijaʒ] nm [de lettres] sorting ; [de candidats] selection.

triangle [trijɑ̃gl] nm triangle.

triangulaire [trijɑ̃gylɛr] adj triangular.

triathlon [trijatlɔ̃] nm triathlon.

tribal, e, aux [tribal, o] adj tribal.

tribord [tribɔr] nm starboard ; **à tribord** on the starboard side, to starboard.

tribu [triby] nf tribe.

tribulations [tribylasjɔ̃] nfpl tribulations, trials.

tribunal, aux [tribynal, o] nm DR court ; **tribunal correctionnel** ≃ magistrates' court UK, ≃ county court US ; **tribunal de grande instance** ≃ crown court UK, ≃ circuit court US.

tribune [tribyn] nf **1.** [d'orateur] platform - **2.** (gén pl) [de stade] stand.

tribut [triby] nm litt tribute.

tributaire [tribytɛr] adj : **être tributaire de** to depend ou be dependent on.

tricher [3] [triʃe] vi **1.** [au jeu, à un examen] to cheat - **2.** [mentir] : **tricher sur** to lie about.

tricherie [triʃri] nf cheating.

tricheur, euse [triʃœr, øz] nm, f cheat.

tricolore [trikɔlɔr] adj **1.** [à trois couleurs] three-coloured UK, three-colored US - **2.** [français] French.

tricot [triko] nm **1.** [vêtement] jumper UK, sweater - **2.** [ouvrage] knitting ; **faire du tricot** to knit - **3.** [étoffe] knitted fabric, jersey.

tricoter [3] [trikɔte] vi & vt to knit.

tricycle [trisikl] nm tricycle.

trier [10] [trije] vt **1.** [classer] to sort out - **2.** [sélectionner] to select.

trilingue [trilɛ̃g] adj trilingual.

trimestre [trimɛstr] nm SCOL term UK, trimester US, quarter US.

trimestriel, elle [trimɛstrijɛl] adj [loyer, magazine] quarterly ; SCOL end-of-term (avant n) UK.

tringle [trɛ̃gl] nf rod ; **tringle à rideaux** curtain rod.

trinité [trinite] nf litt trinity. ➤ **Trinité** nf : **la Trinité** the Trinity.

trinquer [3] [trɛ̃ke] vi [boire] to toast, to clink glasses ; **trinquer à** to drink to.

trio [trijo] nm trio.

triomphal, e, aux [trijɔ̃fal, o] adj [succès] triumphal ; [accueil] triumphant.

triomphant, e [trijɔ̃fɑ̃, ɑ̃t] adj [équipe] winning ; [air] triumphant.

triomphe [trijɔ̃f] nm triumph.

triompher [3] [trijɔ̃fe] vi [gén] to triumph ; **triompher de** to triumph over.

tripes [trip] nfpl **1.** [d'animal, de personne] guts - **2.** CULIN tripe sg.

triple [tripl] ◇ adj triple. ◇ nm : **le triple (de)** three times as much (as).

triplé, ées [triple] nm **1.** [au turf] bet on three horses winning in three different races - **2.** SPORT [trois victoires] hat-trick of victories. ➤ **triplés, ées** nmf pl triplets.

triste [trist] adj **1.** [personne, nouvelle] sad ; **être triste de qqch/de faire qqch** to be sad about sthg/about doing sthg - **2.** [paysage, temps] gloomy ; [couleur] dull - **3.** (avant n) [lamentable] sorry.

tristesse [tristɛs] nf **1.** [de personne, nouvelle] sadness - **2.** [de paysage, temps] gloominess.

triturer [3] [trityre] vt fam [mouchoir] to knead. ➤ **se triturer** vp fam **se triturer l'esprit** ou **les méninges** to rack one's brains.

trivial, e, aux [trivjal, o] adj **1.** [banal] trivial - **2.** péj [vulgaire] crude, coarse.

troc [trɔk] nm **1.** [échange] exchange - **2.** [système économique] barter.

trois [trwa] ◇ nm three. ◇ adj num inv three ; voir aussi **six**.

troisième [trwazjɛm] ◇ adj num inv & nmf third. ◇ nm **1.** [étage] third floor UK, fourth floor US. ◇ nf **1.** SCOL ≃ fourth year ou form UK, ≃ ninth grade US - **2.** [vitesse] third (gear) ; voir aussi **sixième**.

trombe [trɔ̃b] nf water spout.

trombone [trɔ̃bɔn] nm **1.** [agrafe] paper clip - **2.** [instrument] trombone.

trompe [trɔ̃p] nf **1.** [instrument] trumpet - **2.** [d'éléphant] trunk - **3.** [d'insecte] proboscis - **4.** ANAT tube.

trompe-l'œil [trɔ̃plœj] nm inv **1.** [peinture] trompe-l'œil ; **en trompe-l'œil** done in trompe-l'œil - **2.** [apparence] deception.

tromper [3] [trɔ̃pe] vt **1.** [personne] to deceive ; [époux] to be unfaithful to, to deceive - **2.** [vigilance] to elude. ➤ **se tromper** vp to make a mistake, to be mistaken ; **se tromper de jour/maison** to get the wrong day/house.

tromperie [trɔ̃pri] nf deception.

trompette [trɔ̃pɛt] *nf* trumpet.

trompettiste [trɔ̃petist] *nmf* trumpeter.

trompeur, euse [trɔ̃pœr, øz] *adj* **1.** [personne] deceitful - **2.** [calme, apparence] deceptive.

tronc [trɔ̃] *nm* **1.** [d'arbre, de personne] trunk - **2.** [d'église] collection box. ➤ **tronc commun** *nm* [de programmes] common element ou feature ; SCOL core syllabus.

tronçon [trɔ̃sɔ̃] *nm* **1.** [morceau] piece, length - **2.** [de route, de chemin de fer] section.

tronçonneuse [trɔ̃sɔnøz] *nf* chain saw.

trône [tron] *nm* throne.

trôner [3] [trone] *vi* **1.** [personne] to sit enthroned ; [objet] to have pride of place - **2.** *hum* [faire l'important] to lord it.

trop [tro] *adv* **1.** *(devant adj, adv)* too ; **trop vieux/loin** too old/far ; **nous étions trop nombreux** there were too many of us ; **avoir trop chaud/froid/peur** to be too hot/cold/frightened - **2.** *(avec verbe)* too much ; **nous étions trop** there were too many of us ; **je n'aime pas trop le chocolat** I don't like chocolate very much ; **sans trop savoir pourquoi** without really knowing why - **3.** *(avec complément)* **trop de** [quantité] too much ; [nombre] too many. ➤ **en trop, de trop** *loc adv* too much/many ; **2 euros de** ou **en trop** 2 euros too much ; **une personne de** ou **en trop** one person too many ; **être de trop** [personne] to be in the way, to be unwelcome.

trophée [trɔfe] *nm* trophy.

tropical, e, aux [trɔpikal, o] *adj* tropical.

tropique [trɔpik] *nm* tropic. ➤ **tropiques** *nmpl* tropics.

trop-plein [trɔplɛ̃] *(pl* **trop-pleins)** *nm* [excès] excess ; *fig* excess, surplus.

troquer [3] [trɔke] *vt* : **troquer qqch (contre)** to barter sthg (for) ; *fig* to swap sthg (for).

trot [tro] *nm* trot ; **au trot** at a trot.

trotter [3] [trɔte] *vi* **1.** [cheval] to trot - **2.** [personne] to run around.

trotteur, euse [trɔtœr, øz] *nm, f* trotter. ➤ **trotteuse** *nf* second hand.

trottiner [3] [trɔtine] *vi* to trot.

trottoir [trɔtwar] *nm* pavement *UK*, sidewalk *US*.

trou [tru] *nm* **1.** [gén] hole ; **trou d'air** air pocket - **2.** [manque, espace vide] gap ; **trou de mémoire** memory lapse - **3.** *fam* [endroit reculé] (little) place, hole *péj*, one-horse-town *hum*.

troublant, e [trublɑ̃, ɑ̃t] *adj* disturbing.

trouble [trubl] ◇ *adj* **1.** [eau] cloudy - **2.** [image, vue] blurred - **3.** [affaire] shady. ◇ *nm* **1.** [désordre] trouble, discord - **2.** [gêne] confusion ; [émoi] agitation - **3.** *(gén pl)* [dérèglement] disorder. ➤ **troubles** *nmpl* [sociaux] unrest *(U)*.

trouble-fête [trubləfɛt] *nmf* spoilsport.

troubler [3] [truble] *vt* **1.** [eau] to cloud, to make cloudy - **2.** [image, vue] to blur - **3.** [sommeil, événement] to disrupt, to disturb - **4.** [esprit, raison] to cloud - **5.** [inquiéter, émouvoir] to disturb - **6.** [rendre perplexe] to trouble. ➤ **se troubler** *vp* **1.** [eau] to become cloudy - **2.** [personne] to become flustered.

trouée [true] *nf* gap ; MIL breach.

trouer [3] [true] *vt* **1.** [chaussette] to make a hole in - **2.** *fig* [silence] to disturb.

trouille [truj] *nf fam* fear, terror.

troupe [trup] *nf* **1.** MIL troop - **2.** [d'amis] group, band ; [de singes] troop - **3.** THÉÂTRE theatre *UK* ou theater *US* group.

troupeau, x [trupo] *nm* [de vaches, d'éléphants] herd ; [de moutons, d'oies] flock ; *péj* [de personnes] herd.

trousse [trus] *nf* case, bag ; **trousse de secours** first-aid kit ; **trousse de toilette** toilet bag.

trousseau, x [truso] *nm* **1.** [de mariée] trousseau - **2.** [de clefs] bunch.

trouvaille [truvaj] *nf* **1.** [découverte] find, discovery - **2.** [invention] new idea.

trouver [3] [truve] ◇ *vt* to find ; **trouver que** to feel (that) ; **trouver bon/mauvais que...** to think (that) it is right/wrong that... ; **trouver qqch à faire/à dire** *etc* to find sthg to do/say *etc*. ◇ *v impers* : **il se trouve que...** the fact is that... ➤ **se trouver** *vp* **1.** [dans un endroit] to be - **2.** [dans un état] to find o.s. - **3.** [se sentir] to feel ; **se trouver mal** [s'évanouir] to faint.

truand [tryɑ̃] *nm* crook.

truc [tryk] *nm* **1.** [combine] trick - **2.** *fam* [chose] thing, thingamajig ; **ce n'est pas son truc** it's not his thing.

trucage = **truquage**.

truculent, e [trykylɑ̃, ɑ̃t] *adj* colourful *UK*, colorful *US*.

truelle [tryɛl] *nf* trowel.

truffe [tryf] *nf* **1.** [champignon] truffle - **2.** [museau] muzzle.

truffer [3] [tryfe] *vt* **1.** [volaille] to garnish with truffles - **2.** *fig* [discours] : **truffer de** to stuff with.

truie [trɥi] *nf* sow.

truite [trɥit] *nf* trout.

truquage, trucage [trykaʒ] *nm* CINÉ (special) effect.

truquer [3] [tryke] *vt* **1.** [élections] to rig - **2.** CINÉ to use special effects in.

trust [trœst] *nm* **1.** [groupement] trust - **2.** [entreprise] corporation.

ts *abr écrite de* **tous**.

tsar [tsar], **tzar** [dzar] *nm* tsar.

tsigane = **tzigane**.

TSVP (*abr de* **tournez s'il vous plaît**) PTO.

tt *abr écrite de* **tout**.

tt conf. *abr écrite de* **tout confort**.

ttes (*abr écrite de* **toutes**), ➤ **tout**.

TTX (*abr écrite de* **traitement de texte**) WP.

tu¹, e [ty] *pp* ➤ **taire**.

tu² [ty] *pron pers* you.

tuba [tyba] *nm* **1.** MUS tuba - **2.** [de plongée] snorkel.

tube [tyb] *nm* **1.** [gén] tube ; tube cathodique cathode ray tube - **2.** *fam* [chanson] hit. ➤ **tube digestif** *nm* digestive tract.

tubercule [tybɛrkyl] *nm* BOT tuber.

tuberculose [tybɛrkyloz] *nf* tuberculosis.

tuer [7] [tɥe] *vt* to kill. ➤ **se tuer** *vp* **1.** [se suicider] to kill o.s. - **2.** [par accident] to die.

tuerie [tyri] *nf* slaughter.

tue-tête [tytɛt] ➤ **à tue-tête** *loc adv* at the top of one's voice.

tueur, euse [tɥœr, øz] *nm, f* [meurtrier] killer ; **tueur en série** serial killer.

tuile [tɥil] *nf* **1.** [de toit] tile - **2.** *fam* [désagrément] blow.

tulipe [tylip] *nf* tulip.

tulle [tyl] *nm* tulle.

tuméfié, e [tymefje] *adj* swollen.

tumeur [tymœr] *nf* tumour *UK*, tumor *US*.

tumulte [tymylt] *nm* **1.** [désordre] hubbub - **2.** *litt* [trouble] tumult.

tunique [tynik] *nf* tunic.

Tunisie [tynizi] *nf* : **la Tunisie** Tunisia.

tunisien, enne [tynizjɛ̃, ɛn] *adj* Tunisian. ➤ **Tunisien, enne** *nm, f* Tunisian.

tunnel [tynɛl] *nm* tunnel.

turban [tyrbɑ̃] *nm* turban.

turbine [tyrbin] *nf* turbine.

turbo [tyrbo] *nm & nf* turbo.

turbulence [tyrbylɑ̃s] *nf* MÉTÉOR turbulence.

turbulent, e [tyrbylɑ̃, ɑ̃t] *adj* boisterous.

turc, turque [tyrk] *adj* Turkish. ➤ **turc** *nm* [langue] Turkish. ➤ **Turc, Turque** *nm, f* Turk.

turf [tœrf] *nm* [activité] : **le turf** racing.

turnover [tœrnɔvœr] *nm* turnover.

turque ➤ **turc**.

Turquie [tyrki] *nf* : **la Turquie** Turkey.

turquoise [tyrkwaz] *nf & adj inv* turquoise.

tutelle [tytɛl] *nf* **1.** DR guardianship - **2.** [dépendance] supervision.

tuteur, trice [tytœr, tris] *nm, f* guardian. ➤ **tuteur** *nm* [pour plante] stake.

tutoyer [13] [tytwaje] *vt* : **tutoyer qqn** to use the familiar "tu" form to sb ; **elle tutoie son professeur** ≃ she's on first-name terms with her teacher. ➤ **se tutoyer** *vp* to use the familiar "tu" form with each other.

tuyau, x [tɥijo] *nm* **1.** [conduit] pipe ; **tuyau d'arrosage** hosepipe - **2.** *fam* [renseignement] tip.

tuyauterie [tɥijotri] *nf* piping (U), pipes *pl*.

TV (*abr de* **télévision**) *nf* TV.

TVA (*abr de* **taxe à la valeur ajoutée**) *nf* ≃ VAT.

tweed [twid] *nm* tweed.

tympan [tɛ̃pɑ̃] *nm* ANAT eardrum.

type [tip] ◇ *nm* **1.** [exemple caractéristique] perfect example - **2.** [genre] type - **3.** *fam* [individu] guy, bloke *UK*. ◇ *adj inv* [caractéristique] typical.

typhoïde [tifɔid] *nf* typhoid.

typhon [tifɔ̃] *nm* typhoon.

typhus [tifys] *nm* typhus.

typique [tipik] *adj* typical.

typographie [tipɔgrafi] *nf* typography.

tyran [tirɑ̃] *nm* tyrant.

tyrannique [tiranik] *adj* tyrannical.

tyranniser [3] [tiranize] *vt* to tyrannize.

tzar = **tsar**.

tzigane [dzigan], **tsigane** [tsigan] *nmf* gipsy.

U

u, U [y] *nm inv* u, U.

UDF (*abr de* **Union pour la démocratie française**) *nf French political party to the right of the political spectrum*.

UE (*abr de* **Union européenne**) *nf* EU.

UFR (*abr de* **unité de formation et de recherche**) *nf university department*.

Ukraine [ykrɛn] *nf* : **l'Ukraine** the Ukraine.

ulcère [ylsɛr] *nm* ulcer.

ulcérer [18] [ylsere] *vt* **1.** MÉD to ulcerate - **2.** *sout* [mettre en colère] to enrage.

ULM (*abr de* **ultra léger motorisé**) *nm* microlight.

ultérieur, e [ylterjœr] *adj* later, subsequent.

ultimatum [yltimatɔm] *nm* ultimatum.

ultime [yltim] *adj* ultimate, final.

ultramoderne [yltramɔdɛrn] *adj* ultramodern.

ultrasensible [yltrasãsibl] *adj* [personne] ultra-sensitive ; [pellicule] high-speed.

ultrason [yltrasɔ̃] *nm* ultrasound (U).

ultraviolet, ette [yltravjɔle, ɛt] *adj* ultraviolet. ➡ **ultraviolet** *nm* ultraviolet.

UMP [yɛmpe] (*abr de* **Union pour un mouvement populaire**) *nf* POLIT French rightwing political party.

un, une [œ̃, yn] ◇ *art indéf* a, an (*devant voyelle*) ; **un homme** a man ; **un livre** a book ; **une femme** a woman ; **une pomme** an apple. ◇ *pron indéf* one ; **l'un de mes amis** one of my friends ; **l'un l'autre** each other ; **les uns les autres** one another ; **l'une..., l'autre one...,** the other ; **les uns..., les autres** some..., others ; **l'un et l'autre** both (of them) ; **l'un ou l'autre** either (of them) ; **ni l'un ni l'autre** neither one nor the other, neither (of them). ◇ *adj num inv* one ; **une personne à la fois** one person at a time. ◇ *nm* one ; *voir aussi* **six**. ➡ **une** *nf* : **faire la/être à la une** PRESSE to make the/to be on the front page.

unanime [ynanim] *adj* unanimous.

unanimité [ynanimite] *nf* unanimity ; **faire l'unanimité** to be unanimously approved ; **à l'unanimité** unanimously.

une [yn] ➤ **un**.

UNESCO, Unesco [ynɛsko] (*abr de* **United Nations Educational, Scientific and Cultural Organization**) *nf* UNESCO.

uni, e [yni] *adj* **1.** [joint, réuni] united - **2.** [famille, couple] close - **3.** [surface, mer] smooth ; [route] even - **4.** [étoffe, robe] plain, self-coloured *UK*, self-colored *US*.

UNICEF, Unicef [ynisɛf] (*abr de* **United Nations International Children's Emergency Fund**) *nm* UNICEF.

unifier [9] [ynifje] *vt* **1.** [régions, parti] to unify - **2.** [programmes] to standardize.

uniforme [ynifɔrm] ◇ *adj* uniform ; [régulier] regular. ◇ *nm* uniform.

uniformiser [3] [ynifɔrmize] *vt* **1.** [couleur] to make uniform - **2.** [programmes, lois] to standardize.

unijambiste [yniʒãbist] ◇ *adj* one-legged. ◇ *nmf* one-legged person.

unilatéral, e, aux [ynilateral, o] *adj* unilateral ; **stationnement unilatéral** parking on only one side of the street.

union [ynjɔ̃] *nf* **1.** [de couleurs] blending - **2.** [mariage] union ; **union libre** cohabitation - **3.** [de pays] union ; [de syndicats] confederation - **4.** [entente] unity. ➡ **Union européenne** *nf* European Union. ➡ **Union soviétique** *nf* : **l'(ex-)Union soviétique** the (former) Soviet Union.

unique [ynik] *adj* **1.** [seul - enfant, veston] only ; [- préoccupation] sole - **2.** [principe, prix] single - **3.** [exceptionnel] unique.

uniquement [ynikmã] *adv* **1.** [exclusivement] only, solely - **2.** [seulement] only, just.

unir [32] [ynir] *vt* **1.** [assembler - mots, qualités] to put together, to combine ; [- pays] to unite ; **unir qqch à** [- pays] to unite sthg with ; [- mot, qualité] to combine sthg with - **2.** [réunir - partis, familles] to unite - **3.** [marier] to unite, to join in marriage. ➡ **s'unir** *vp* **1.** [s'associer] to unite, to join together - **2.** [se marier] to be joined in marriage.

unitaire [yniter] *adj* [à l'unité] : **prix unitaire** unit price.

unité [ynite] *nf* **1.** [cohésion] unity - **2.** COMM, MATH & MIL unit. ➡ **unité centrale** *nf* INFORM central processing unit.

univers [yniver] *nm* universe ; *fig* world.

universel, elle [yniversel] *adj* universal.

universitaire [yniversiter] ◇ *adj* university (*avant n*). ◇ *nmf* academic.

université [yniversite] *nf* university.

uranium [yranjɔm] *nm* uranium.

urbain, e [yrbɛ̃, ɛn] *adj* **1.** [de la ville] urban - **2.** *litt* [affable] urbane.

urbaniser [3] [yrbanize] *vt* to urbanize.

urbanisme [yrbanism] *nm* town planning *UK*, city planning *US*.

urgence [yrʒãs] *nf* **1.** [de mission] urgency - **2.** MÉD emergency ; **les urgences** the casualty department (*sing*) *UK*. ➡ **d'urgence** *loc adv* immediately.

urgent, e [yrʒã, ãt] *adj* urgent.

urgentiste [yrʒãtist] *nmf* MÉD A&E doctor.

urine [yrin] *nf* urine.

uriner [3] [yrine] *vi* to urinate.

urinoir [yrinwar] *nm* urinal.

urne [yrn] *nf* **1.** [vase] urn - **2.** [de vote] ballot box.

URSS (*abr de* **Union des républiques socialistes soviétiques**) *nf* : **l'(ex-)URSS** the (former) USSR.

urticaire [yrtiker] *nf* urticaria, hives *pl*.

Uruguay [yrygwɛ] *nm* : **l'Uruguay** Uruguay.

USA (*abr de* **United States of America**) *nmpl* USA.

usage [yzaʒ] *nm* **1.** [gén] use ; **à usage**

externe/interne for external/internal use ;
hors d'usage out of action - 2. [coutume]
custom - 3. LING usage.

usagé, e [yzaʒe] *adj* worn, old.

usager [yzaʒe] *nm* user.

usé, e [yze] *adj* **1.** [détérioré] worn ; eaux
usées waste water *sg* - **2.** [personne] worn-
out - **3.** [plaisanterie] hackneyed, well-
worn.

user [3] [yze] <> *vt* **1.** [consommer] to use
- **2.** [vêtement] to wear out - **3.** [forces] to
use up ; [santé] to ruin ; [personne] to wear
out. <> *vi* [se servir] : **user de** [charme] to
use ; [droit, privilège] to exercise. ➡ **s'user**
vp **1.** [chaussure] to wear out - **2.** [amour] to
burn itself out.

usine [yzin] *nf* factory.

usiner [3] [yzine] *vt* **1.** [façonner] to machine - **2.** [fabriquer] to manufacture.

usité, e [yzite] *adj* in common use ;
très/peu usité commonly/rarely used.

USP [yɛspe] (*abr de* **unité de soins palliatifs**) *nf* MÉD palliative care unit.

ustensile [ystãsil] *nm* implement, tool.

usuel, elle [yzɥɛl] *adj* common, usual.

usufruit [yzyfrɥi] *nm* usufruct.

usure [yzyr] *nf* **1.** [de vêtement, meuble]
wear ; [de forces] wearing down ; **avoir qqn
à l'usure** *fam* to wear sb down - **2.** [intérêt]
usury.

usurier, ère [yzyrje, ɛr] *nm, f* usurer.

usurpateur, trice [yzyrpatœr, tris] *nm, f*
usurper.

usurper [3] [yzyrpe] *vt* to usurp.

ut [yt] *nm inv* C.

utérus [yterys] *nm* uterus, womb.

utile [ytil] *adj* useful ; **être utile à qqn** to be
useful ou of help to sb, to help sb.

utilisateur, trice [ytilizatœr, tris] *nm, f*
user.

utiliser [3] [ytilize] *vt* to use.

utilitaire [ytilitɛr] <> *adj* [pratique] utili-
tarian ; [véhicule] commercial. <> *nm*
INFORM utility (program).

utilité [ytilite] *nf* **1.** [usage] usefulness
- **2.** DR : **entreprise d'utilité publique** public
utility ; **organisme d'utilité publique** registered charity.

utopie [ytɔpi] *nf* **1.** [idéal] utopia - **2.** [projet
irréalisable] unrealistic idea.

utopiste [ytɔpist] *nmf* utopian.

UV <> *nf* (*abr de* **unité de valeur**) *university
course unit,* ≃ *credit.* <> (*abr de* **ultraviolet**)
UV.

v, V [ve] *nm inv* v, V.

v. 1. LITTÉR (*abr écrite de* **vers**) v. - **2.** (*abr écrite
de* **verset**) v. - **3.** [environ] (*abr écrite de* **vers**)
approx.

va [va] <> ► **aller.** <> *interj* : **courage,
va!** come on, cheer up! ; **va donc!** come
on! ; **va pour 10 euros/demain** OK, let's say
10 euros/tomorrow.

vacance [vakãs] *nf* vacancy. ➡ **vacances**
nfpl holiday (*sing*) *UK,* vacation (*sing*) *US* ;
être/partir en vacances to be/go on holiday ;
les grandes vacances the summer holidays.

vacancier, ère [vakãsje, ɛr] *nm, f* holiday-
maker *UK,* vacationer *US.*

vacant, e [vakã, ãt] *adj* [poste] vacant ;
[logement] vacant, unoccupied.

vacarme [vakarm] *nm* racket, din.

vacataire [vakater] <> *adj* [employé]
temporary. <> *nmf* temporary worker.

vacation [vakasjɔ̃] *nf* [d'expert] session.

vaccin [vaksɛ̃] *nm* vaccine.

vaccination [vaksinasjɔ̃] *nf* vaccination.

vacciner [3] [vaksine] *vt* : **vacciner qqn
(contre)** MÉD to vaccinate sb (against) ; *fam
fig* to make sb immune (to).

vache [vaʃ] <> *nf* **1.** ZOOL cow - **2.** [cuir]
cowhide - **3.** *fam péj* [femme] cow *UK* ;
[homme] pig. <> *adj fam* rotten.

vachement [vaʃmã] *adv fam* bloody *UK,*
dead *UK,* real *US.*

vaciller [3] [vasije] *vi* **1.** [jambes, fonda-
tions] to shake ; [lumière] to flicker ; **vaciller
sur ses jambes** to be unsteady on one's legs
- **2.** [mémoire, santé] to fail.

va-et-vient [vaevjɛ̃] *nm inv* **1.** [de person-
nes] comings and goings *pl,* toing and
froing - **2.** [de balancier] to-and-fro movement - **3.** ÉLECTR two-way switch.

vagabond, e [vagabɔ̃, ɔ̃d] <> *adj*
1. [chien] stray ; [vie] vagabond (*avant n*)
- **2.** [humeur] restless. <> *nm, f* [rôdeur]
vagrant, tramp ; *litt* [voyageur] wanderer.

vagabondage [vagabɔ̃daʒ] *nm* [délit] va-
grancy ; [errance] wandering, roaming.

vagin [vaʒɛ̃] *nm* vagina.

vagissement [vaʒismã] *nm* cry, wail.

vague [vag] <> *adj* **1.** [idée, promesse]
vague - **2.** [vêtement] loose-fitting - **3.** (*avant
n*) [quelconque] : **il a un vague travail dans**

un bureau he has some job or other in an office - **4.** *(avant n)* [cousin] distant. <> *nf* wave ; **une vague de froid** a cold spell ; **vague de chaleur** heatwave.

vaguement [vagmɑ̃] *adv* vaguely.

vaillant, e [vajɑ̃, ɑ̃t] *adj* **1.** [enfant, vieillard] hale and hearty - **2.** *litt* [héros] valiant.

vain, e [vɛ̃, vɛn] *adj* **1.** [inutile] vain, useless ; **en vain** in vain, to no avail - **2.** *litt* [vaniteux] vain.

vaincre [114] [vɛ̃kr] *vt* **1.** [ennemi] to defeat - **2.** [obstacle, peur] to overcome.

vaincu, e [vɛ̃ky] <> *pp* ► vaincre. <> *adj* defeated. <> *nm, f* defeated person.

vainement [vɛnmɑ̃] *adv* vainly.

vainqueur [vɛ̃kœr] <> *nm* **1.** [de combat] conqueror, victor - **2.** SPORT winner. <> *adj m* victorious, conquering.

vais ► aller.

vaisseau, x [vɛso] *nm* **1.** NAUT vessel, ship ; **vaisseau spatial** AÉRON spaceship - **2.** ANAT vessel - **3.** ARCHIT nave.

vaisselle [vɛsɛl] *nf* crockery ; **faire OU la vaisselle** to do the dishes, to wash up *UK*.

val [val] *(pl* **vals** OU **vaux** [vo]) *nm* valley.

valable [valabl] *adj* **1.** [passeport] valid - **2.** [raison, excuse] valid, legitimate - **3.** [œuvre] good, worthwhile.

valet [valɛ] *nm* **1.** [serviteur] servant - **2.** [cartes à jouer] jack, knave.

valeur [valœr] *nf* [gén & MUS] value ; **avoir de la valeur** to be valuable ; **mettre en valeur** [talents] to bring out ; [terre] to exploit ; **valeur ajoutée** ÉCON added value ; **de (grande) valeur** [chose] (very) valuable ; [personne] of (great) worth OU merit - **2.** *(gén pl)* FIN stocks and shares *pl,* securities *pl* - **3.** [mérite] worth, merit - **4.** *fig* [importance] value, importance - **5.** [équivalent] : **la valeur de** the equivalent of.

valide [valid] *adj* **1.** [personne] spry - **2.** [contrat] valid.

valider [3] [valide] *vt* to validate, to authenticate.

validité [validite] *nf* validity.

valise [valiz] *nf* case *UK,* suitcase ; **faire sa valise/ses valises** to pack one's case/cases ; *fam fig* [partir] to pack one's bags.

vallée [vale] *nf* valley.

vallon [valɔ̃] *nm* small valley.

vallonné, e [valɔne] *adj* undulating.

valoir [60] [valwar] <> *vi* **1.** [gén] to be worth ; **ça vaut combien?** how much is it? ; **que vaut ce film?** is this film any good? ; **ne rien valoir** not to be any good, to be worthless ; **ça vaut mieux** *fam* that's best ; **ça ne vaut pas la peine** it's not worth it ;

faire valoir [vues] to assert ; [talent] to show - **2.** [règle] : **valoir pour** to apply to, to hold good for. <> *vt* [médaille, gloire] to bring, to earn. <> *v impers* : **il vaudrait mieux que nous partions** it would be better if we left, we'd better leave. ◄► **se valoir** *vp* to be equally good/bad.

valoriser [3] [valɔrize] *vt* [immeuble, région] to develop ; [individu, société] to improve the image of.

valse [vals] *nf* waltz.

valser [3] [valse] *vi* to waltz ; **envoyer valser qqch** *fam fig* to send sthg flying.

valu [valy] *pp inv* ► valoir.

valve [valv] *nf* valve.

vampire [vɑ̃pir] *nm* **1.** [fantôme] vampire - **2.** ZOOL vampire bat.

vandalisme [vɑ̃dalism] *nm* vandalism.

vanille [vanij] *nf* vanilla.

vanité [vanite] *nf* vanity.

vaniteux, euse [vanitø, øz] *adj* vain, conceited.

vanne [van] *nf* **1.** [d'écluse] lockgate - **2.** *fam* [remarque] gibe.

vannerie [vanri] *nf* basketwork, wickerwork.

vantard, e [vɑ̃tar, ard] <> *adj* bragging, boastful. <> *nm, f* boaster.

vanter [3] [vɑ̃te] *vt* to vaunt. ◄► **se vanter** *vp* to boast, to brag ; **se vanter de faire qqch** to boast OU brag about doing sthg.

va-nu-pieds [vanypje] *nmf fam* beggar.

vapeur [vapœr] *nf* **1.** [d'eau] steam ; **à la vapeur** steamed ; **bateau à vapeur** steamboat, steamer ; **locomotive à vapeur** steam engine - **2.** [émanation] vapour *UK,* vapor *US.* ◄► **vapeurs** *nfpl* [émanations] fumes ; **avoir ses vapeurs** *vieilli* to have the vapours *UK* OU vapors *US.*

vapocuiseur [vapɔkɥizœr] *nm* pressure cooker.

vaporisateur [vapɔrizatœr] *nm* **1.** [atomiseur] spray, atomizer - **2.** [dans l'industrie] vaporizer.

vaporiser [3] [vapɔrize] *vt* **1.** [parfum, déodorant] to spray - **2.** PHYS to vaporize.

vaquer [3] [vake] *vi* : **vaquer à** to see to, to attend to.

varappe [varap] *nf* rock climbing.

variable [varjabl] <> *adj* **1.** [temps] changeable - **2.** [distance, résultats] varied, varying - **3.** [température] variable. <> *nf* variable.

variante [varjɑ̃t] *nf* variant.

variateur [varjatœr] *nm* ÉLECTR dimmer switch.

variation [varjasjɔ̃] *nf* variation.

varice [varis] *nf* varicose vein.

varicelle [varisɛl] *nf* chickenpox.

varié, e [varje] *adj* **1.** [divers] various - **2.** [non monotone] varied, varying.

varier [9] [varje] *vt & vi* to vary.

variété [varjete] *nf* variety. ➡ **variétés** *nfpl* variety show *sg.*

variole [varjɔl] *nf* smallpox.

Varsovie [varsɔvi] *npr* Warsaw ; **le pacte de Varsovie** the Warsaw Pact.

vas ➡ aller.

vase [vaz] ◇ *nm* vase. ◇ *nf* mud, silt.

vaseline [vazlin] *nf* Vaseline®, petroleum jelly *UK.*

vaste [vast] *adj* vast, immense.

Vatican [vatikã] *nm* : **le Vatican** the Vatican.

vaudrait ➡ valoir.

vaut ➡ valoir.

vautour [votur] *nm* vulture.

vd (*abr écrite de* vend), ➡ vendre.

veau, x [vo] *nm* **1.** [animal] calf - **2.** [viande] ➡ veal - **3.** [peau] calfskin.

vecteur [vɛktœr] *nm* **1.** GÉOM vector - **2.** [intermédiaire] vehicle ; MÉD carrier.

vécu, e [veky] ◇ *pp* ➡ vivre. ◇ *adj* real.

vedette [vədɛt] *nf* **1.** NAUT patrol boat - **2.** [star] star.

végétal, e, aux [veʒetal, o] *adj* [huile] vegetable (*avant n*) ; [cellule, fibre] plant (*avant n*).

végétalien, enne [veʒetaljɛ̃, ɛn] *adj & nm, f* vegan.

végétarien, enne [veʒetarjɛ̃, ɛn] *adj & nm, f* vegetarian.

végétation [veʒetasjɔ̃] *nf* vegetation. ➡ **végétations** *nfpl* adenoids.

végéter [18] [veʒete] *vi* to vegetate.

véhémence [veemãs] *nf* vehemence.

véhicule [veikyl] *nm* vehicle.

veille [vɛj] *nf* **1.** [jour précédent] day before, eve ; **la veille de mon anniversaire** the day before my birthday ; **la veille de Noël** Christmas Eve - **2.** [éveil] wakefulness ; [privation de sommeil] sleeplessness.

veillée [veje] *nf* **1.** [soirée] evening - **2.** [de mort] watch.

veiller [4] [veje] ◇ *vi* **1.** [rester éveillé] to stay up - **2.** [rester vigilant] : **veiller à qqch** to look after sthg ; **veiller à faire qqch** to see that sthg is done ; **veiller sur** to watch over. ◇ *vt* to sit up with.

veilleur [vejœr] *nm* : **veilleur de nuit** night watchman.

veilleuse [vejøz] *nf* **1.** [lampe] nightlight - **2.** AUTO sidelight - **3.** [de chauffe-eau] pilot light.

veinard, e [vɛnar, ard] *fam* ◇ *adj* lucky. ◇ *nm, f* lucky devil.

veine [vɛn] *nf* **1.** [gén] vein - **2.** [de marbre] vein ; [de bois] grain - **3.** [filon] seam, vein - **4.** *fam* [chance] luck.

veineux, euse [venø, øz] *adj* **1.** ANAT venous - **2.** [marbre] veined ; [bois] grainy.

véliplanchiste [veliplɑ̃ʃist] *nmf* windsurfer.

velléité [veleite] *nf* whim.

vélo [velo] *nm fam* bike ; **faire du vélo** to go cycling.

vélocité [velɔsite] *nf* swiftness, speed.

vélodrome [velɔdrom] *nm* velodrome.

vélomoteur [velɔmɔtœr] *nm* light motorcycle, moped.

velours [vəlur] *nm* velvet.

velouté, e [vəlute] *adj* velvety. ➡ **velouté** *nm* **1.** [de peau] velvetiness - **2.** [potage] cream soup.

velu, e [vəly] *adj* hairy.

vénal, e, aux [venal, o] *adj* venal.

vendange [vãdãʒ] *nf* **1.** [récolte] grape harvest, wine harvest - **2.** [période] : **les vendanges** (grape) harvest time *sg.*

vendanger [17] [vãdãʒe] *vi* to harvest the grapes.

vendeur, euse [vãdœr, øz] *nm, f* salesman (*f* saleswoman).

vendre [73] [vãdr] *vt* to sell ; **'à vendre'** 'for sale'.

vendredi [vãdrədi] *nm* Friday ; **Vendredi Saint** Good Friday ; *voir aussi* **samedi.**

vendu, e [vãdy] ◇ *pp* ➡ vendre. ◇ *adj* **1.** [cédé] sold - **2.** [corrompu] corrupt. ◇ *nm, f* traitor.

vénéneux, euse [venenø, øz] *adj* poisonous.

vénérable [venerabl] *adj* venerable.

vénération [venerasjɔ̃] *nf* veneration, reverence.

vénérer [18] [venere] *vt* to venerate, to revere.

vénérien, enne [venerjɛ̃, ɛn] *adj* venereal.

Venezuela [venezɥela] *nm* : **le Venezuela** Venezuela.

vengeance [vãʒãs] *nf* vengeance.

venger [17] [vãʒe] *vt* to avenge. ➡ **se venger** *vp* to get one's revenge ; **se venger de qqn** to take revenge on sb ; **se venger de qqch** to take revenge for sthg ; **se venger sur** to take it out on.

vengeur, vengeresse [vãʒœr, vãʒrɛs] ◇ *adj* vengeful. ◇ *nm, f* avenger.

venimeux, euse [vənimø, øz] *adj* venomous.

venin [vənɛ̃] *nm* venom.

venir [40] [vənir] *vi* to come ; [plante, arbre] to come on ; **venir de** [personne, mot] to come from ; [échec] to be due to ; **venir de faire qqch** to have just done sthg ; **je viens de la voir** I've just seen her ; **s'il venait à mourir...** if he was to die... ; **où veux-tu en venir?** what are you getting at?

vent [vã] *nm* wind ; **il fait** OU **il y a du vent** headwind.

vente [vãt] *nf* **1.** [cession, transaction] sale ; **en vente** on sale UK, for sale US ; **en vente libre** available over the counter ; **vente par correspondance** mail order ; **vente en ligne** e-commerce ; **vente par téléphone** telesales, telemarketing - **2.** [technique] selling.

venteux, euse [vãtø, øz] *adj* windy.

ventilateur [vãtilatœr] *nm* fan.

ventilation [vãtilasjɔ̃] *nf* **1.** [de pièce] ventilation - **2.** FIN breakdown.

ventouse [vãtuz] *nf* **1.** [de caoutchouc] suction pad ; [d'animal] sucker - **2.** MÉD cupping glass - **3.** TECHNOL air vent.

ventre [vãtr] *nm* [de personne] stomach ; **avoir/prendre du ventre** to have/be getting (a bit of) a paunch ; **à plat ventre** flat on one's stomach.

ventriloque [vãtrilɔk] *nmf* ventriloquist.

venu, e [vəny] <> *pp* ► **venir**. <> *adj* : **bien venu** welcome ; **mal venu** unwelcome ; **il serait mal venu de faire cela** it would be improper to do that. <> *nm, f* : **nouveau venu** newcomer. ► **venue** *nf* coming, arrival.

vépéciste [vepesist] *nm* mail-order company.

vêpres [vɛpr] *nfpl* vespers.

ver [vɛr] *nm* worm.

véracité [verasite] *nf* truthfulness.

véranda [verãda] *nf* veranda.

verbal, e, aux [vɛrbal, o] *adj* **1.** [promesse, violence] verbal - **2.** GRAMM verb *(avant n)*.

verbaliser [3] [vɛrbalize] <> *vt* to verbalize. <> *vi* to make out a report.

verbe [vɛrb] *nm* GRAMM verb.

verdeur [vɛrdœr] *nf* **1.** [de personne] vigour UK, vigor US, vitality - **2.** [de langage] crudeness.

verdict [vɛrdikt] *nm* verdict.

verdir [32] [vɛrdir] *vt & vi* to turn green.

verdoyant, e [vɛrdwajã, ãt] *adj* green.

verdure [vɛrdyr] *nf* [végétation] greenery.

véreux, euse [verø, øz] *adj* worm-eaten, maggoty ; *fig* shady.

verge [vɛrʒ] *nf* **1.** ANAT penis - **2.** *litt* [baguette] rod, stick.

verger [vɛrʒe] *nm* orchard.

vergeture [vɛrʒətyr] *nf* stretchmark.

verglas [vɛrgla] *nm* (black) ice.

véridique [veridik] *adj* truthful.

vérification [verifikasjɔ̃] *nf* [contrôle] check, checking.

vérifier [9] [verifje] *vt* **1.** [contrôler] to check - **2.** [confirmer] to prove, to confirm.

véritable [veritabl] *adj* real ; [ami] true.

vérité [verite] *nf* **1.** [chose vraie, réalité, principe] truth (U) - **2.** [sincérité] sincerity. ► **en vérité** *loc adv* actually, really.

vermeil, eille [vɛrmɛj] *adj* scarlet. ► **vermeil** *nm* silver-gilt.

vermicelle [vɛrmisɛl] *nm* vermicelli (U).

vermine [vɛrmin] *nf* [parasites] vermin.

vermoulu, e [vɛrmuly] *adj* riddled with woodworm ; *fig* moth-eaten.

verni, e [vɛrni] *adj* **1.** [bois] varnished - **2.** [souliers] : **chaussures vernies** patent-leather shoes - **3.** *fam* [chanceux] lucky.

vernir [32] [vɛrnir] *vt* to varnish.

vernis [vɛrni] *nm* varnish ; *fig* veneer ; **vernis à ongles** nail polish OU varnish.

vernissage [vɛrnisaʒ] *nm* **1.** [de meuble] varnishing - **2.** [d'exposition] private viewing.

verre [vɛr] *nm* **1.** [matière, récipient] glass ; [quantité] glassful, glass ; **verre dépoli** frosted glass - **2.** [optique] lens ; **verres de contact** contact lenses ; **verres progressifs** progressive lenses, progressives UK - **3.** [boisson] drink ; **boire un verre** to have a drink.

verrière [vɛrjɛr] *nf* [toit] glass roof.

verrou [vɛru] *nm* bolt.

verrouillage [vɛrujaʒ] *nm* AUTO : **verrouillage central** central locking.

verrouiller [3] [vɛruje] *vt* **1.** [porte] to bolt - **2.** [personne] to lock up.

verrue [vɛry] *nf* wart ; **verrue plantaire** verruca.

vers[1] [vɛr] <> *nm* line. <> *nmpl* : **en vers** in verse ; **faire des vers** to write poetry.

vers[2] [vɛr] *prép* **1.** [dans la direction de] towards, toward US - **2.** [aux environs de - temporel] around, about ; [- spatial] near ; **vers la fin du mois** towards OU toward US the end of the month.

versant [vɛrsã] *nm* side.

versatile [vɛrsatil] *adj* changeable, fickle.

verse [vɛrs] ► **à verse** *loc adv* : **pleuvoir à verse** to pour down.

Verseau [vɛrso] *nm* ASTROL Aquarius.

versement [vɛrsəmã] *nm* payment.

verser [3] [vɛrse] <> vt **1.** [eau] to pour ; [larmes, sang] to shed - **2.** [argent] to pay. <> vi to overturn, to tip over.

verset [vɛrsɛ] nm verse.

version [vɛrsjɔ̃] nf **1.** [gén] version ; **version française/originale** French/original version - **2.** [traduction] translation (into mother tongue).

verso [vɛrso] nm back.

vert, e [vɛr, vɛrt] adj **1.** [couleur, fruit, légume, bois] green - **2.** fig [vieillard] spry, sprightly - **3.** [réprimande] sharp - **4.** [à la campagne] : **le tourisme vert** country holidays pl UK. **vert** nm [couleur] green. **Verts** nmpl : **les Verts** POLIT the Greens.

vertébral, e, aux [vɛrtebral, o] adj vertebral.

vertèbre [vɛrtɛbr] nf vertebra.

vertébré, e [vɛrtebre] adj vertebrate. **vertébré** nm vertebrate.

vertement [vɛrtəmɑ̃] adv sharply.

vertical, e, aux [vɛrtikal, o] adj vertical. **verticale** nf vertical ; **à la verticale** [descente] vertical ; [descendre] vertically.

vertige [vɛrtiʒ] nm **1.** [peur du vide] vertigo - **2.** [étourdissement] dizziness ; fig intoxication ; **avoir des vertiges** to suffer from OU have dizzy spells.

vertigineux, euse [vɛrtiʒinø, øz] adj **1.** fig [vue, vitesse] breathtaking - **2.** [hauteur] dizzy.

vertu [vɛrty] nf **1.** [morale, chasteté] virtue - **2.** [pouvoir] properties pl, power.

vertueux, euse [vɛrtɥø, øz] adj virtuous.

verve [vɛrv] nf eloquence.

vésicule [vezikyl] nf vesicle.

vessie [vesi] nf bladder.

veste [vɛst] nf [vêtement] jacket ; **veste croisée/droite** double-/single-breasted jacket.

vestiaire [vɛstjɛr] nm **1.** [au théâtre] cloakroom - **2.** (gén pl) SPORT changing room UK, locker room US.

vestibule [vɛstibyl] nm [pièce] hall, vestibule.

vestige [vɛstiʒ] nm (gén pl) [de ville] remains pl ; fig [de civilisation, grandeur] vestiges pl, relic.

vestimentaire [vɛstimɑ̃tɛr] adj [industrie] clothing (avant n) ; [dépense] on clothes ; **détail vestimentaire** accessory.

veston [vɛstɔ̃] nm jacket.

vétéciste [vetesist] nmf hybrid bike rider.

vététiste [vetetist] nmf mountain biker.

vêtement [vɛtmɑ̃] nm garment, article of clothing ; **vêtements** clothing (U), clothes.

vétéran [veterɑ̃] nm veteran.

vétérinaire [veterinɛr] nmf vet UK, veterinary surgeon UK, veterinarian US.

vêtir [44] [vetir] vt to dress. **se vêtir** vp to dress, to get dressed.

veto [veto] nm inv veto ; **mettre son veto à qqch** to veto sthg.

véto [veto] nmf fam vet.

vêtu, e [vety] <> pp ▶ vêtir. <> adj : **vêtu (de)** dressed (in).

vétuste [vetyst] adj dilapidated.

veuf, veuve [vœf, vœv] nm, f widower (f widow).

veuille etc ▶ vouloir.

veut ▶ vouloir.

veuvage [vœvaʒ] nm [de femme] widowhood ; [d'homme] widowerhood.

veuve ▶ veuf.

veux ▶ vouloir.

vexation [vɛksasjɔ̃] nf [humiliation] insult.

vexer [4] [vɛkse] vt to offend. **se vexer** vp to take offence UK OU offense US.

VF (abr de **version française**) nf indicates that a film has been dubbed into French.

via [vja] prép via.

viabiliser [3] [vjabilize] vt to service.

viable [vjabl] adj viable.

viaduc [vjadyk] nm viaduct.

viager, ère [vjaʒe, ɛr] adj life (avant n). **viager** nm life annuity.

viande [vjɑ̃d] nf meat.

vibration [vibrasjɔ̃] nf vibration.

vibrer [3] [vibre] vi **1.** [trembler] to vibrate - **2.** fig [être ému] : **vibrer (de)** to be stirred (with).

vibreur [vibrœr] nm TÉLÉCOM VibraCall® (alert ou feature).

vice [vis] nm **1.** [de personne] vice - **2.** [d'objet] fault, defect.

vice-président, e [visprezidɑ̃, ɑ̃t] (mpl vice-présidents) (fpl vice-présidentes) nm, f POLIT vice-president ; [de société] vice-chairman (f vice-chairwoman).

vice versa [vis(e)vɛrsa] loc adv vice versa.

vicié, e [visje] adj [air] polluted, tainted.

vicieux, euse [visjø, øz] adj **1.** [personne, conduite] perverted, depraved - **2.** [animal] restive - **3.** [attaque] underhand.

victime [viktim] nf victim ; [blessé] casualty.

victoire [viktwar] nf MIL victory ; POLIT & SPORT win, victory.

victorieux, euse [viktɔrjø, øz] adj **1.** MIL victorious ; POLIT & SPORT winning (avant n), victorious - **2.** [air] triumphant.

victuailles [viktɥaj] nfpl provisions.

vidange [vidɑ̃ʒ] nf **1.** [action] emptying,

draining - **2.** AUTO oil change - **3.** [mécanisme] waste outlet. ➤ **vidanges** *nfpl* sewage *(U)*.

vidanger [17] [vidɑ̃ʒe] *vt* to empty, to drain.

vide [vid] ◇ *nm* **1.** [espace] void ; *fig* [néant, manque] emptiness - **2.** [absence d'air] vacuum ; **conditionné sous vide** vacuum-packed - **3.** [ouverture] gap, space - **4.** DR : **vide juridique** legal vacuum. ◇ *adj* empty.

vidéo [video] ◇ *adj inv* video *(avant n)*. ◇ *nf* video.

vidéocassette [videokasɛt] *nf* video cassette.

vidéoconférence [videokɔ̃ferɑ̃s] = **visioconférence**.

vidéodisque [videodisk] *nm* videodisc *UK*, videodisk *US*.

vide-ordures [vidɔrdyr] *nm inv* rubbish chute *UK*, garbage chute *US*.

vidéoprojecteur *nm* video projector.

vidéothèque [videotɛk] *nf* video library.

vidéotransmission [videotrɑ̃smisjɔ̃] *nf* video transmission.

vide-poches [vidpɔʃ] *nm inv* [de voiture] glove compartment.

vider [3] [vide] *vt* **1.** [rendre vide] to empty - **2.** [évacuer] : **vider les lieux** to vacate the premises - **3.** [poulet] to clean - **4.** *fam* [personne - épuiser] to drain ; [- expulser] to chuck out. ➤ **se vider** *vp* **1.** [eaux] : **se vider dans** to empty into, to drain into - **2.** [baignoire, salle] to empty.

videur [vidœr] *nm* bouncer.

vie [vi] *nf* **1.** [gén] life ; **sauver la vie à qqn** to save sb's life ; **être en vie** to be alive ; **à vie** for life - **2.** [subsistance] cost of living ; **gagner sa vie** to earn one's living.

vieil ➤ **vieux**.

vieillard [vjɛjar] *nm* old man.

vieille ➤ **vieux**.

vieillerie [vjɛjri] *nf* [objet] old thing.

vieillesse [vjɛjɛs] *nf* [fin de la vie] old age.

vieillir [32] [vjejir] ◇ *vi* **1.** [personne] to grow old, to age - **2.** CULIN to mature, to age - **3.** [tradition, idée] to become dated ou outdated. ◇ *vt* : **vieillir qqn** to make sb look older ; **c'est fou ce que les cheveux longs la vieillissent!** [coiffure, vêtement] long hair makes her look a lot older! ; **ils m'ont vieilli de cinq ans** [personne] they said I was five years older than I actually am.

vieillissement [vjejismɑ̃] *nm* [de personne] ageing.

Vienne [vjɛn] *npr* [en Autriche] Vienna.

vierge [vjɛrʒ] ◇ *nf* virgin ; **la (Sainte)**

Vierge the Virgin (Mary). ◇ *adj* **1.** [personne] virgin - **2.** [terre] virgin ; [page] blank ; [casier judiciaire] clean. ➤ **Vierge** *nf* ASTROL Virgo.

Viêt Nam [vjɛtnam] *nm* : **le Viêt Nam** Vietnam.

vieux, vieille [vjø, vjɛj] ◇ *adj (vieil* *devant voyelle ou 'h' muet)* old ; **vieux jeu** old-fashioned. ◇ *nm, f* **1.** [personne âgée] old man (*f* woman) ; **les vieux** the old - **2.** *fam* [ami] : **mon vieux** old chap ou boy *UK*, old buddy *US* ; **ma vieille** old girl.

vif, vive [vif, viv] *adj* **1.** [preste - enfant] lively ; [- imagination] vivid - **2.** [couleur, œil] bright ; **rouge/jaune vif** bright red/ yellow - **3.** [reproche] sharp ; [discussion] bitter - **4.** *sout* [vivant] alive - **5.** [douleur, déception] acute ; [intérêt] keen ; [amour, haine] intense, deep. ➤ **à vif** *loc adj* [plaie] open ; **j'ai les nerfs à vif** *fig* my nerves are frayed.

vigie [viʒi] *nf* [NAUT - personne] lookout ; [- poste] crow's nest.

vigilant, e [viʒilɑ̃, ɑ̃t] *adj* vigilant, watchful.

vigile [viʒil] *nm* watchman.

vigne [viɲ] *nf* **1.** [plante] vine, grapevine - **2.** [plantation] vineyard. ➤ **vigne vierge** *nf* Virginia creeper.

vigneron, onne [viɲrɔ̃, ɔn] *nm, f* wine grower.

vignette [viɲɛt] *nf* **1.** [timbre] label ; [de médicament] price sticker *(for reimbursement by the social security services)* ; AUTO tax disc *UK* - **2.** [motif] vignette.

vignoble [viɲɔbl] *nm* **1.** [plantation] vineyard - **2.** [vignes] vineyards *pl*.

vigoureux, euse [vigurø, øz] *adj* [corps, personne] vigorous ; [bras, sentiment] strong.

vigueur [vigœr] *nf* vigour *UK*, vigor *US*. ➤ **en vigueur** *loc adj* in force.

VIH, V.I.H. (*abr de* **virus d'immunodéficience humaine**) *nm* HIV.

vilain, e [vilɛ̃, ɛn] *adj* **1.** [gén] nasty - **2.** [laid] ugly.

vilebrequin [vilbrəkɛ̃] *nm* **1.** [outil] brace and bit - **2.** AUTO crankshaft.

villa [vila] *nf* villa.

village [vilaʒ] *nm* village.

villageois, e [vilaʒwa, az] *nm, f* villager.

ville [vil] *nf* [petite, moyenne] town ; [importante] city ; **aller en ville** to go into town ; **habiter en ville** to live in town ; **ville d'eau** spa (town).

villégiature [vileʒjatyr] *nf* holiday *UK*, vacation *US*.

vin [vɛ̃] *nm* wine ; **vin blanc/rosé/rouge** white/rosé/red wine. ◆ **vin d'honneur** *nm* reception.

vinaigre [vinɛgr] *nm* vinegar.

vinaigrette [vinɛgrɛt] *nf* oil and vinegar dressing.

vindicatif, ive [vɛ̃dikatif, iv] *adj* vindictive.

vingt [vɛ̃] *adj num inv & nm* twenty ; *voir aussi* **six.**

vingtaine [vɛ̃tɛn] *nf* : **une vingtaine de** about twenty.

vingtième [vɛ̃tjɛm] *adj num inv, nm & nmf* twentieth ; *voir aussi* **sixième.**

vinicole [vinikɔl] *adj* wine-growing, wine-producing.

viol [vjɔl] *nm* **1.** [de femme] rape - **2.** [de sépulture] desecration ; [de sanctuaire] violation.

violation [vjɔlasjɔ̃] *nf* violation, breach.

violence [vjɔlɑ̃s] *nf* violence ; **se faire violence** to force o.s.

violent, e [vjɔlɑ̃, ɑ̃t] *adj* **1.** [personne, tempête] violent - **2.** *fig* [douleur, angoisse, chagrin] acute ; [haine, passion] violent.

violer [3] [vjɔle] *vt* **1.** [femme] to rape - **2.** [loi, traité] to break - **3.** [sépulture] to desecrate ; [sanctuaire] to violate.

violet, ette [vjɔle, ɛt] *adj* purple ; [pâle] violet. ◆ **violet** *nm* purple ; [pâle] violet.

violette [vjɔlɛt] *nf* violet.

violeur [vjɔlœr] *nm* rapist.

violon [vjɔlɔ̃] *nm* [instrument] violin.

violoncelle [vjɔlɔ̃sɛl] *nm* [instrument] cello.

violoniste [vjɔlɔnist] *nmf* violinist.

vipère [vipɛr] *nf* viper.

virage [viraʒ] *nm* **1.** [sur route] bend - **2.** [changement] turn.

viral, e, aux [viral, o] *adj* viral.

virement [virmɑ̃] *nm* FIN transfer ; **virement bancaire/postal** bank/giro *UK* transfer ; **virement automatique** automatic transfer, standing order.

virer [3] [vire] ◇ *vi* **1.** [tourner] : **virer à droite/à gauche** to turn right/left - **2.** [étoffe] to change colour *UK* OU color *US* ; **virer au blanc/jaune** to go white/yellow - **3.** MÉD to react positively. ◇ *vt* **1.** FIN to transfer - **2.** *fam* [renvoyer] to kick out.

virevolter [3] [virvɔlte] *vi* [tourner] to twirl OU spin round *UK* ou around *US*.

virginité [virʒinite] *nf* **1.** [de personne] virginity - **2.** [de sentiment] purity.

virgule [virgyl] *nf* [entre mots] comma ; [entre chiffres] (decimal) point.

viril, e [viril] *adj* virile.

virilité [virilite] *nf* virility.

virtuel, elle [virtɥɛl] *adj* potential.

virtuose [virtɥoz] *nmf* virtuoso.

virulence [virylɑ̃s] *nf* virulence.

virulent, e [virylɑ̃, ɑ̃t] *adj* virulent.

virus [virys] *nm* INFORM & MÉD virus.

vis [vis] *nf* screw.

visa [viza] *nm* visa.

visage [vizaʒ] *nm* face.

vis-à-vis [vizavi] *nm* **1.** [personne] person sitting opposite - **2.** [immeuble] : **avoir un vis-à-vis** to have a building opposite. ◆ **vis-à-vis de** *loc prép* **1.** [en face de] opposite - **2.** [en comparaison de] beside, compared with - **3.** [à l'égard de] towards, toward *US*.

viscéral, e, aux [viseral, o] *adj* **1.** ANAT visceral - **2.** *fam* [réaction] gut *(avant n)* ; [haine, peur] deep-seated.

viscère [visɛr] *nm* *(gén pl)* innards *pl.*

viscose [viskoz] *nf* viscose.

visé, e [vize] *adj* **1.** [concerné] concerned - **2.** [vérifié] stamped.

visée [vize] *nf* **1.** [avec arme] aiming - **2.** *(gén pl) fig* [intention, dessein] aim.

viser [3] [vize] ◇ *vt* **1.** [cible] to aim at - **2.** *fig* [poste] to aspire to, to aim for ; [personne] to be directed OU aimed at - **3.** [document] to check, to stamp. ◇ *vi* to aim, to take aim ; **viser à** to aim at ; **viser à faire qqch** to aim to do sthg, to be intended to do sthg ; **viser haut** *fig* to aim high.

viseur [vizœr] *nm* **1.** [d'arme] sights *pl* - **2.** PHOTO viewfinder.

visibilité [vizibilite] *nf* visibility.

visible [vizibl] *adj* **1.** [gén] visible - **2.** [personne] : **il n'est pas visible** he's not seeing visitors.

visiblement [vizibləmɑ̃] *adv* visibly.

visière [vizjɛr] *nf* **1.** [de casque] visor - **2.** [de casquette] peak - **3.** [de protection] eyeshade.

visioconférence [vizjokɔ̃ferɑ̃s], **vidéoconférence** [videokɔ̃ferɑ̃s] *nf* videoconference.

vision [vizjɔ̃] *nf* **1.** [faculté] eyesight, vision - **2.** [représentation] view, vision - **3.** [mirage] vision.

visionnaire [vizjɔnɛr] *nmf & adj* visionary.

visionner [3] [vizjɔne] *vt* to view.

visite [vizit] *nf* **1.** [chez un ami, officielle] visit ; **rendre visite à qqn** to pay sb a visit - **2.** [MÉD - à l'extérieur] call, visit ; [- à l'hôpital] rounds *pl* ; **passer une visite médicale** to have a medical *UK* OU a physical *US* - **3.** [de monument] tour - **4.** [d'expert] inspection.

visiter [3] [vizite] *vt* **1.** [en touriste] to tour - **2.** [malade, prisonnier] to visit.

visiteur, euse [vizitœr, øz] *nm, f* visitor.

vison [vizɔ̃] *nm* mink.

visqueux, euse [viskø, øz] *adj* **1.** [liquide] viscous - **2.** [surface] sticky.

visser [3] [vise] *vt* **1.** [planches] to screw together - **2.** [couvercle] to screw down - **3.** [bouchon] to screw in ; [écrou] to screw on.

visualiser [3] [vizɥalize] *vt* **1.** [gén] to visualize - **2.** INFORM to display ; TECHNOL to make visible.

visuel, elle [vizɥɛl] *adj* visual. ◆ **visuel** *nm* INFORM visual display unit ; **visuel graphique** graphical display unit.

vital, e, aux [vital, o] *adj* vital.

vitalité [vitalite] *nf* vitality.

vitamine [vitamin] *nf* vitamin.

vitaminé, e [vitamine] *adj* with added vitamins, vitamin-enriched.

vite [vit] *adv* **1.** [rapidement] quickly, fast ; **fais vite!** hurry up! - **2.** [tôt] soon.

vitesse [vites] *nf* **1.** [gén] speed ; **à toute vitesse** at top speed - **2.** AUTO gear.

viticole [vitikɔl] *adj* wine-growing.

viticulteur, trice [vitikyltœr, tris] *nm, f* wine-grower.

vitrail, aux [vitraj, o] *nm* stained-glass window.

vitre [vitr] *nf* **1.** [de fenêtre] pane of glass, windowpane - **2.** [de voiture, train] window.

vitré, e [vitre] *adj* glass (avant n).

vitreux, euse [vitrø, øz] *adj* **1.** [roche] vitreous - **2.** [œil, regard] glassy, glazed.

vitrifier [9] [vitrifje] *vt* **1.** [parquet] to seal and varnish - **2.** [émail] to vitrify.

vitrine [vitrin] *nf* **1.** [de boutique] (shop) window ; *fig* showcase - **2.** [meuble] display cabinet.

vivable [vivabl] *adj* [appartement] liveable ; [situation] bearable, tolerable ; [personne] : **il n'est pas vivable** he's impossible to live with.

vivace [vivas] *adj* **1.** [plante] perennial ; [arbre] hardy - **2.** *fig* [haine, ressentiment] deep-rooted, entrenched ; [souvenir] enduring.

vivacité [vivasite] *nf* **1.** [promptitude - de personne] liveliness, vivacity ; **vivacité d'esprit** quick-wittedness - **2.** [de coloris, teint] intensity, brightness - **3.** [de propos] sharpness.

vivant, e [vivɑ̃, ɑ̃t] *adj* **1.** [en vie] alive, living - **2.** [enfant, quartier] lively - **3.** [souvenir] still fresh. ◆ **vivant** *nm* [personne] : **les vivants** the living.

vive[1] [viv] *nf* [poisson] weever.

vive[2] [viv] *interj* three cheers for ; **vive le roi!** long live the King!

vivement [vivmɑ̃] ⟨⟩ *adv* **1.** [agir] quickly - **2.** [répondre] sharply - **3.** [affecter] deeply. ⟨⟩ *interj* : **vivement les vacances!** roll on the holidays! ; **vivement que l'été arrive** I'll be glad when summer comes, summer can't come quick enough.

vivifiant, e [vivifjɑ̃, ɑ̃t] *adj* invigorating, bracing.

vivisection [vivisɛksjɔ̃] *nf* vivisection.

vivre [90] [vivr] ⟨⟩ *vi* to live ; [être en vie] to be alive ; **vivre de** to live on ; **faire vivre sa famille** to support one's family ; **être difficile/facile à vivre** to be hard/easy to get on with ; **avoir vécu** to have seen life. ⟨⟩ *vt* **1.** [passer] to spend - **2.** [éprouver] to experience. ◆ **vivres** *nmpl* provisions.

vizir [vizir] *nm* vizier.

VO (*abr de* **version originale**) *nf* indicates that a film has not been dubbed ; **en VO sous-titrée** in the original version with subtitles.

vocable [vɔkabl] *nm* term.

vocabulaire [vɔkabylɛr] *nm* **1.** [gén] vocabulary - **2.** [livre] lexicon, glossary.

vocal, e, aux [vɔkal, o] *adj* : **ensemble vocal** choir ; ▶ **corde**.

vocation [vɔkasjɔ̃] *nf* **1.** [gén] vocation - **2.** [d'organisation] mission.

vocifération [vɔsiferasjɔ̃] *nf* shout, scream.

vociférer [18] [vɔsifere] *vt* to shout, to scream.

vodka [vɔdka] *nf* vodka.

vœu, x [vø] *nm* **1.** RELIG [résolution] vow ; **faire vœu de silence** to take a vow of silence - **2.** [souhait, requête] wish. ◆ **vœux** *nmpl* greetings.

vogue [vɔg] *nf* vogue, fashion ; **en vogue** fashionable, in vogue.

voguer [3] [vɔge] *vi litt* to sail.

voici [vwasi] *prép* **1.** [pour désigner, introduire] here is/are ; **le voici** here he/it is ; **les voici** here they are ; **vous cherchiez des allumettes? en voici** were you looking for matches? there are some here ; **voici ce qui s'est passé** this is what happened - **2.** [il y a] : **voici trois mois** three months ago ; **voici quelques années que je ne l'ai pas vu** I haven't seen him for some years (now), it's been some years since I last saw him.

voie [vwa] *nf* **1.** [route] road ; **route à deux voies** two-lane road ; **la voie publique** the public highway ; **voie sans issue** no through road ; **voie privée** private road - **2.** [rails] track, line ; [quai] platform ; **voie ferrée** railway line *UK*, railroad line *US* ; **voie de garage** siding ; *fig* dead-end job - **3.** [mode de transport] route - **4.** ANAT passage, tract ; **par voie buccale** OU **orale** orally, by mouth ; **par voie rectale** by rectum ; **voie respiratoire** respiratory tract - **5.** *fig* [chemin] way - **6.** [filière, moyen] means *pl.* ➤ **Voie lactée** *nf*: **la Voie lactée** the Milky Way. ➤ **en voie de** *loc prép* on the way OU road to ; **en voie de développement** developing.

voilà [vwala] *prép* **1.** [pour désigner] there is/are ; **le voilà** there he/it is ; **les voilà** there they are ; **me voilà** that's me, there I am ; **vous cherchiez de l'encre? en voilà** you were looking for ink? there is some (over) there ; **nous voilà arrivés** we've arrived - **2.** [reprend ce dont on a parlé] that is ; [introduit ce dont on va parler] this is ; **voilà ce que j'en pense** this is/that is what I think ; **voilà tout** that's all ; **et voilà!** there we are! - **3.** [il y a] : **voilà dix jours** ten days ago ; **voilà dix ans que je le connais** I've known him for ten years (now).

voile [vwal] ⬦ *nf* **1.** [de bateau] sail - **2.** [activité] sailing. ⬦ *nm* **1.** [textile] voile - **2.** [coiffure] veil - **3.** [de brume] mist.

voilé, e [vwale] *adj* **1.** [visage, allusion] veiled - **2.** [ciel, regard] dull - **3.** [roue] buckled - **4.** [son, voix] muffled.

voiler [3] [vwale] *vt* **1.** [visage] to veil - **2.** [vérité, sentiment] to hide - **3.** [suj: brouillard, nuages] to cover. ➤ **se voiler** *vp* **1.** [femme] to wear a veil - **2.** [ciel] to cloud over ; [yeux] to mist over - **3.** [roue] to buckle.

voilier [vwalje] *nm* [bateau] sailing boat *UK*, sailboat *US*.

voilure [vwalyr] *nf* [de bateau] sails *pl*.

voir [62] [vwar] ⬦ *vt* [gén] to see ; **je l'ai vu tomber** I saw him fall ; **faire voir qqch à qqn** to show sb sthg ; **ne rien avoir à voir avec** *fig* to have nothing to do with ; **voyons,...** [en réfléchissant] let's see,... ⬦ *vi* to see. ➤ **se voir** *vp* **1.** [se regarder] to see o.s., to watch o.s. - **2.** [s'imaginer] to see OU to imagine OU to picture o.s. - **3.** [se rencontrer] to see one another OU each other - **4.** [se remarquer] to be obvious, to show ; **ça se voit!** you can tell!

voire [vwar] *adv* even.

voirie [vwari] *nf* ADMIN ≃ Department of Transport.

voisin, e [vwazɛ̃, in] ⬦ *adj* **1.** [pays, ville] neighbouring *UK*, neighboring *US* ; [maison] next-door - **2.** [idée] similar. ⬦ *nm, f* neighbour *UK*, neighbor *US* ; **voisin de palier** next-door neighbour *UK* OU neighbor *US* (*in a flat*).

voisinage [vwazinaʒ] *nm* **1.** [quartier] neighbourhood *UK*, neighborhood *US* - **2.** [environs] vicinity - **3.** [relations] : **rapports de bon voisinage** (good) neighbourliness *UK* OU neighborliness *US*.

voiture [vwatyr] *nf* **1.** [automobile] car ; **voiture de fonction** company car ; **voiture de location** hire *UK* OU rental *US* car ; **voiture d'occasion/de sport** second-hand/sports car - **2.** [de train] carriage *UK*, car *US*.

voix [vwa] *nf* **1.** [gén] voice ; **voix de stentor** stentorian voice ; **à mi-voix** in an undertone ; **à voix basse** in a low voice, quietly ; **à voix haute** [parler] in a loud voice ; [lire] aloud ; **de vive voix** in person - **2.** [suffrage] vote.

vol [vɔl] *nm* **1.** [d'oiseau, avion] flight ; **vol (en) charter** charter flight ; **à vol d'oiseau** as the crow flies ; **en plein vol** in flight - **2.** [groupe d'oiseaux] flight, flock - **3.** [délit] theft.

vol. (*abr écrite de* **volume**) vol.

volage [vɔlaʒ] *adj litt* fickle.

volaille [vɔlaj] *nf*: **la volaille** poultry, (domestic) fowl.

volant, e [vɔlɑ̃, ɑ̃t] *adj* **1.** [qui vole] flying - **2.** [mobile] : **feuille volante** loose sheet. ➤ **volant** *nm* **1.** [de voiture] steering wheel - **2.** [de robe] flounce - **3.** [de badminton] shuttlecock.

volatiliser [3] [vɔlatilize] ➤ **se volatiliser** *vp* to volatilize ; *fig* to vanish into thin air.

volcan [vɔlkɑ̃] *nm* volcano ; *fig* spitfire.

volcanique [vɔlkanik] *adj* volcanic ; *fig* [tempérament] fiery.

volée [vɔle] *nf* **1.** [de flèches] volley ; **une volée de coups** a hail of blows - **2.** FOOTBALL & TENNIS volley.

voler [3] [vɔle] ⬦ *vi* to fly. ⬦ *vt* [personne] to rob ; [chose] to steal.

volet [vɔlɛ] *nm* **1.** [de maison] shutter - **2.** [de dépliant] leaf ; [d'émission] part.

voleur, euse [vɔlœr, øz] *nm, f* thief.

volière [vɔljɛr] *nf* aviary.

volley-ball [vɔlebol] (*pl* **volley-balls**) *nm* volleyball.

volontaire [vɔlɔ̃tɛr] ⬦ *nmf* volunteer. ⬦ *adj* **1.** [omission] deliberate ; [activité] voluntary - **2.** [enfant] strong-willed.

volonté [vɔlɔ̃te] *nf* **1.** [vouloir] will ; **à volonté** unlimited, as much as you like - **2.** [disposition] : **bonne volonté** willingness, good will ; **mauvaise volonté** unwillingness - **3.** [détermination] willpower.

volontiers [vɔlɔ̃tje] *adv* **1.** [avec plaisir] with pleasure, gladly, willingly - **2.** [affable, bavard] naturally.

volt [vɔlt] *nm* volt.

voltage [vɔltaʒ] *nm* voltage.

volte-face [vɔltəfas] *nf inv* about-turn *UK*, about-face *US* ; *fig* U-turn, about-turn *UK*, about-face *US*.

voltige [vɔltiʒ] *nf* **1.** [au trapèze] trapeze work ; **haute voltige** flying trapeze act ; *fam fig* mental gymnastics *(U)* - **2.** [à cheval] circus riding - **3.** [en avion] aerobatics *(U)*.

voltiger [17] [vɔltiʒe] *vi* **1.** [insecte, oiseau] to flit *ou* flutter about - **2.** [feuilles] to flutter about.

volubile [vɔlybil] *adj* voluble.

volume [vɔlym] *nm* **1.** [tome] volume - **2.** [en acoustique] volume - **3.** [quantité globale] volume, amount - **4.** [poids, épaisseur] volume - **5.** INFORM [unité] volume.

volumineux, euse [vɔlyminø, øz] *adj* voluminous, bulky.

volupté [vɔlypte] *nf* [sensuelle] sensual *ou* voluptuous pleasure ; [morale, esthétique] delight.

voluptueux, euse [vɔlyptɥø, øz] *adj* voluptuous.

volute [vɔlyt] *nf* **1.** [de fumée] wreath - **2.** ARCHIT volute, helix.

vomi [vɔmi] *nm fam* vomit.

vomir [32] [vɔmir] *vt* **1.** [aliments] to bring up - **2.** [fumées] to belch, to spew (out) ; [injures] to spit out.

vont ▶ aller.

vorace [vɔras] *adj* voracious.

voracité [vɔrasite] *nf* voracity.

vos ▶ votre.

vote [vɔt] *nm* vote.

voter [3] [vɔte] ◇ *vi* to vote. ◇ *vt* POLIT to vote for ; [crédits] to vote ; [loi] to pass.

votre [vɔtr] (*pl* **vos** [vo]) *adj poss* your.

vôtre [votr] ◇ **le vôtre, la vôtre** (*pl* les **vôtres**) *pron poss* yours ; **les vôtres** your family ; **vous et les vôtres** people like you ; **à la vôtre!** your good health!

vouer [6] [vwe] *vt* **1.** [promettre, jurer] : **vouer qqch à qqn** to swear *ou* vow sthg to sb - **2.** [consacrer] to devote - **3.** [condamner] : **être voué à** to be doomed to.

vouloir [57] [vulwar] ◇ *vt* **1.** [gén] to want ; **voulez-vous boire quelque chose?** would you like something to drink? ; **veux-tu te taire!** will you be quiet! ; **je voudrais savoir** I would like to know ; **vouloir que** (+ *subjonctif*) : **je veux qu'il parte** I want him to leave ; **vouloir qqch de qqn/qqch** to want sthg from sb/sthg ; **combien voulez-vous de votre maison?** how much do you want for your house? ; **ne pas vouloir de qqn/qqch** not to want sb/sthg ; **je veux bien** I don't mind ; **si tu veux** if you like, if you want ; **veuillez vous asseoir** please take a seat ; **sans le vouloir** without meaning *ou* wishing to, unintentionally - **2.** [suj: coutume] to demand - **3.** [s'attendre à] to expect ; **que voulez-vous que j'y fasse?** what do you want me to do

about it? ; **vouloir dire** to mean ; **si on veut** more or less, if you like ; **en vouloir à qqn** to have a grudge against sb. ◇ *nm* : **le bon vouloir de qqn** sb's goodwill. ◈ **se vouloir** *vp* : **elle se veut différente** she thinks she's different ; **s'en vouloir de faire qqch** to be cross with o.s. for doing sthg.

voulu, e [vuly] ◇ *pp* ▶ vouloir. ◇ *adj* **1.** [requis] requisite - **2.** [délibéré] intentional.

vous [vu] *pron pers* **1.** [sujet, objet direct] you - **2.** [objet indirect] (to) you - **3.** [après préposition, comparatif] you - **4.** [réfléchi] yourself (, yourselves *Pl*). ◈ **vous-même** *pron pers* yourself. ◈ **vous-mêmes** *pron pers* yourselves.

voûte [vut] *nf* **1.** ARCHIT vault ; *fig* arch - **2.** ANAT : **voûte du palais** roof of the mouth ; **voûte plantaire** arch (of the foot).

voûter [3] [vute] *vt* to arch over, to vault. ◈ **se voûter** *vp* to be *ou* become stooped.

vouvoyer [13] [vuvwaje] *vt* : **vouvoyer qqn** to use the "vous" form to sb. ◈ **se vouvoyer** *vp* to use the formal "vous" form with each other.

voyage [vwajaʒ] *nm* journey, trip ; **les voyages** travel (*sing*), travelling *(U)* UK, traveling *(U)* US ; **partir en voyage** to go away, to go on a trip ; **voyage d'affaires** business trip ; **voyage organisé** package tour ; **voyage de noces** honeymoon.

voyager [17] [vwajaʒe] *vi* to travel.

voyageur, euse [vwajaʒœr, øz] *nm, f* traveller UK, traveler US.

voyance [vwajɑ̃s] *nf* clairvoyance.

voyant, e [vwajɑ̃, ɑ̃t] ◇ *adj* loud, gaudy. ◇ *nm, f* [devin] seer. ◈ **voyant** *nm* [lampe] light ; AUTO indicator (light) ; **voyant d'essence/d'huile** petrol/oil warning light.

voyelle [vwajɛl] *nf* vowel.

voyeur, euse [vwajœr, øz] *nm, f* voyeur, Peeping Tom.

voyou [vwaju] *nm* **1.** [garnement] urchin - **2.** [loubard] lout.

vrac [vrak] ◈ **en vrac** *loc adv* **1.** [sans emballage] loose - **2.** [en désordre] higgledy-piggledy - **3.** [au poids] in bulk.

vrai, e [vrɛ] *adj* **1.** [histoire] true ; **c'est** *ou* **il est vrai que...** it's true that... - **2.** [or, perle, nom] real - **3.** [personne] natural - **4.** [ami, raison] real, true. ◈ **vrai** *nm* : **à vrai dire, à dire vrai** to tell the truth.

vraiment [vrɛmɑ̃] *adv* really.

vraisemblable [vrɛsɑ̃blabl] *adj* likely, probable ; [excuse] plausible.

vraisemblance [vrɛsɑ̃blɑ̃s] *nf* likelihood, probability ; [d'excuse] plausibility.

V/Réf *(abr écrite de* **Votre référence)** your ref.

vrille [vrij] *nf* **1.** BOT tendril - **2.** [outil] gimlet - **3.** [spirale] spiral.

vrombir [32] [vrɔ̃bir] *vi* to hum.

vrombissement [vrɔ̃bismɑ̃] *nm* humming *(U)*.

VTC [vetese] *(abr de* **vélo tout chemin)** *nf* SPORT hybrid bike.

VTT *(abr de* **vélo tout terrain)** *nm* mountain bike.

vu, e [vy] ◇ *pp* ▶ **voir.** ◇ *adj* **1.** [perçu] : **être bien/mal vu** to be acceptable/unacceptable - **2.** [compris] clear. ▬ **vu** *prép* given, in view of. ▬ **vue** *nf* **1.** [sens, vision] sight, eyesight - **2.** [regard] gaze ; **à première vue** at first sight ; **de vue** by sight ; **en vue** [vedette] in the public eye ; **perdre qqn de vue** to lose touch with sb - **3.** [panorama, idée] view - **4.** CINÉ ▶ **prise.** ▬ **en vue de** *loc prép* with a view to. ▬ **vu que** *loc conj* given that, seeing that.

vulgaire [vylgɛr] *adj* **1.** [grossier] vulgar, coarse - **2.** *(avant n) péj* [quelconque] common.

vulgarisation [vylgarizasjɔ̃] *nf* popularization.

vulgariser [3] [vylgarize] *vt* to popularize.

vulgarité [vylgarite] *nf* vulgarity, coarseness.

vulnérable [vylnerabl] *adj* vulnerable.

vulve [vylv] *nf* vulva.

w, W [dublǝve] *nm inv* w, W.

wagon [vagɔ̃] *nm* carriage *UK*, car *US* ; **wagon de première/seconde classe** first-class/second-class carriage *UK* OU car *US*.

wagon-lit [vagɔ̃li] *nm* sleeping car, sleeper.

wagon-restaurant [vagɔ̃rɛstorɑ̃] *nm* restaurant *UK* OU dining *US* car.

Walkman® [wokman] *nm* personal stereo, Walkman®.

wallon, onne [walɔ̃, ɔn] *adj* Walloon. ▬ **wallon** *nm* [langue] Walloon. ▬ **Wallon, onne** *nm, f* Walloon.

Washington [waʃiŋtɔn] *npr* **1.** [ville] Washington DC - **2.** [État] Washington State.

water-polo [watɛrpɔlo] *nm* water polo.

waterproof [watɛrpru:f] *adj inv* waterproof.

watt [wat] *nm* watt.

W.-C. [vese] *(abr de* **water closet)** *nmpl* WC *sg*, toilets.

Web [wɛb] *nm* : **le Web** the Web, the web.

webcam [wɛbkam] *nf* webcam.

webmestre [wɛbmɛstr], **webmaster** [wɛbmastœr] *nm* webmaster.

week-end [wikɛnd] *(pl* **week-ends)** *nm* weekend.

western [wɛstɛrn] *nm* western.

whisky [wiski] *(pl* **whiskies)** *nm* [écossais] whisky, scotch ; [irlandais ou américain] whiskey.

white-spirit [wajtspirit] *(pl* **white-spirits)** *nm* white spirit *UK*.

WWW *(abr de* **World Wide Web)** *nf* WWW.

x, X [iks] *nm inv* x, X ; **l'X** *prestigious engineering college in Paris.*

xénophobie [gzenɔfɔbi] *nf* xenophobia.

xérès [gzerɛs, xerɛs] *nm* sherry.

xylophone [ksilɔfɔn] *nm* xylophone.

y¹, Y [igrɛk] *nm inv* y, Y.

y² [i] ◇ *adv* [lieu] there ; **j'y vais demain** I'm going there tomorrow ; **mets-y du sel** put some salt in it ; **va voir sur la table si les clefs y sont** go and see if the keys are on the table ; **ils ont ramené des vases anciens et y ont fait pousser des fleurs exotiques** they brought back some antique vases and grew exotic flowers in them. ◇ *pron pers (la traduction varie selon la préposition utilisée avec le verbe)* **pensez-y** think about it ; **n'y comptez pas** don't count on it ; **j'y suis!** I've got it! ; *voir aussi* **aller,** *voir aussi* **avoir** *etc.*

yacht [jot] *nm* yacht.

yaourt [jaurt], **yogourt, yoghourt** [jɔgurt] *nm* yoghurt.

Yémen [jemɛn] *nm* : **le Yémen** Yemen.

yen [jen] *nm* yen.

yeux ▶ **œil.**

yiddish [jidiʃ] *nm inv & adj inv* Yiddish.

yoga [jɔga] *nm* yoga.

yoghourt = **yaourt.**

yogourt = **yaourt.**

yougoslave [jugɔslav] *adj* Yugoslav, Yugoslavian. ➤ **Yougoslave** *nmf* Yugoslav, Yugoslavian.

Yougoslavie [jugɔslavi] *nf*: **la Yougoslavie** Yugoslavia ; **l'ex-Yougoslavie** the former Yugoslavia.

yoyo [jojo] *nm* MÉD grommet.

Z

z, Z [zɛd] *nm inv* z, Z.

Zaïre [zair] *nm*: **le Zaïre** Zaïre.

zapper [3] [zape] *vi* to zap.

zapping [zapiŋ] *nm* zapping, channel-hopping.

zèbre [zebr] *nm* zebra ; **un drôle de zèbre** *fam fig* an oddball.

zébrure [zebryr] *nf* **1.** [de pelage] stripe - **2.** [marque] weal.

zébu [zeby] *nm* zebu.

zèle [zɛl] *nm* zeal ; **faire du zèle** *péj* to be over-zealous.

zélé, e [zele] *adj* zealous.

zénith [zenit] *nm* zenith.

zéro [zero] <> *nm* **1.** [chiffre] zero, nought *UK* ; [énoncé dans un numéro de téléphone] O *UK*, zero *US* - **2.** [nombre] nought *UK*, nothing - **3.** [de graduation] freezing point, zero ; **au-dessus/au-dessous de zéro** above/below (zero) ; **avoir le moral à zéro** *fig* to be *ou* feel down. <> *adj* : **zéro faute** no mistakes.

zeste [zɛst] *nm* peel, zest.

zézayer [11] [zezeje] *vi* to lisp.

zigzag [zigzag] *nm* zigzag ; **en zigzag** winding.

zigzaguer [3] [zigzage] *vi* to zigzag (along).

zinc [zɛ̃g] *nm* **1.** [matière] zinc - **2.** *fam* [comptoir] bar - **3.** *fam* [avion] crate.

zizi [zizi] *nm fam* willy *UK*, peter *US*.

zodiaque [zɔdjak] *nm* zodiac.

zone [zon] *nf* **1.** [région] zone, area ; **zone bleue** restricted parking zone ; **zone industrielle** industrial estate *UK* ou park *US* ; **zone piétonne** ou **piétonnière** pedestrian precinct *UK* ou park *US* - **2.** *fam* [faubourg] : **la zone** the slum belt.

zoner [3] [zone] *vi fam* to hang about, to hang around.

zoo [zo(o)] *nm* zoo.

zoologie [zɔɔlɔʒi] *nf* zoology.

zoom [zum] *nm* **1.** [objectif] zoom (lens) - **2.** [gros plan] zoom.

zut [zyt] *interj fam* damn!

a¹ (*pl* as OR **a's**), **A** (*pl* As OR **A's**) [eɪ] *n* [letter] a *m inv*, A *m inv* ; **to get from A to B** aller d'un point à un autre. ◆ **A** *n* **1.** MUS la *m inv* - **2.** SCH [mark] A *m inv*.

a² (*weak form* [ə], *strong form* [eɪ], *before vowel or silent 'h'* an *weak form* [æn], *strong form* [ən]) *indef art* **1.** [gen] un (une) ; **a boy** un garçon ; **a table** une table ; **an orange** une orange - **2.** [referring to occupation] : **to be a doctor/lawyer/plumber** être médecin/avocat/plombier - **3.** [before numbers, quantities] un (une) ; **a hundred/thousand pounds** cent/mille livres - **4.** [to express prices, ratios etc] : **20p a kilo** 20p le kilo ; **£10 a person** 10 livres par personne ; **twice a week/month** deux fois par semaine/mois ; **50 km an hour** 50 km à l'heure.

AA *n* **1.** (*abbrev of* **Automobile Association**) *automobile club britannique*, ≃ ACF *m*, ≃ TCF *m* - **2.** (*abbrev of* **Alcoholics Anonymous**) Alcooliques Anonymes *mpl*.

AAA *n* (*abbrev of* **American Automobile Association**) *automobile club américain*, ≃ ACF *m*, ≃ TCF *m*.

AB *n* US *abbrev of* **Bachelor of Arts**.

aback [ə'bæk] *adv* : **to be taken aback** être décontenancé(e).

abandon [ə'bændən] ◇ *vt* abandonner. ◇ *n* : **with abandon** avec abandon.

abashed [ə'bæʃt] *adj* confus(e).

abate [ə'beɪt] *vi* [storm, fear] se calmer ; [noise] faiblir.

abattoir ['æbətwɑːr] *n* abattoir *m*.

abbey ['æbɪ] *n* abbaye *f*.

abbot ['æbət] *n* abbé *m*.

abbreviate [ə'briːvɪeɪt] *vt* abréger.

abbreviation [ə,briːvɪ'eɪʃn] *n* abréviation *f*.

ABC *n* **1.** [alphabet] alphabet *m* - **2.** *fig* [basics] B.A.-Ba *m*, abc *m*.

abdicate ['æbdɪkeɪt] *vt & vi* abdiquer.

abdomen ['æbdəmən] *n* abdomen *m*.

abduct [əb'dʌkt] *vt* enlever.

aberration [,æbə'reɪʃn] *n* aberration *f*.

abet [ə'bet] *vt* ➤ **aid**.

abeyance [ə'beɪəns] *n* : **in abeyance** en attente.

abhor [əb'hɔːr] *vt* exécrer, abhorrer.

abide [ə'baɪd] *vt* supporter, souffrir. ◆ **abide by** *vt insep* respecter, se soumettre à.

ability [ə'bɪlətɪ] *n* **1.** [capacity, capability] aptitude *f* - **2.** [skill] talent *m*.

abject ['æbdʒekt] *adj* **1.** [poverty] noir(e) - **2.** [person] pitoyable ; [apology] servile.

ablaze [ə'bleɪz] *adj* [on fire] en feu.

able ['eɪbl] *adj* **1.** [capable] : **to be able to do sthg** pouvoir faire qqch - **2.** [accomplished] compétent(e).

ably ['eɪblɪ] *adv* avec compétence, habilement.

abnormal [æb'nɔːml] *adj* anormal(e).

aboard [ə'bɔːd] ◇ *adv* à bord. ◇ *prep* [ship, plane] à bord ; [bus, train] dans.

abode [ə'bəʊd] *n fml* : **of no fixed abode** sans domicile fixe.

abolish [ə'bɒlɪʃ] *vt* abolir.

abolition [,æbə'lɪʃn] *n* abolition *f*.

abominable [ə'bɒmɪnəbl] *adj* abominable.

aborigine [,æbə'rɪdʒənɪ] *n* aborigène *mf* d'Australie.

abort [ə'bɔːt] *vt* **1.** [pregnancy] interrompre - **2.** *fig* [plan, project] abandonner, faire avorter - **3.** COMPUT abandonner.

abortion [ə'bɔːʃn] *n* avortement *m*, interruption *f* (volontaire) de grossesse ; **to have an abortion** se faire avorter.

abortive [ə'bɔːtɪv] *adj* manqué(e).

abound [ə'baʊnd] *vi* **1.** [be plentiful] abonder - **2.** [be full] : **to abound with** OR **in** abonder en.

about [ə'baʊt] ◇ *adv* **1.** [approximately] environ, à peu près ; **about fifty/a hundred/a**

thousand environ cinquante/cent/mille ; **at about five o'clock** vers cinq heures ; **I'm just about ready** je suis presque prêt - **2.** [referring to place] : **to run about** courir çà et là ; **to leave things lying about** laisser traîner des affaires ; **to walk about** aller et venir, se promener - **3.** [on the point of] : **to be about to do sthg** être sur le point de faire qqch. ◇ *prep* **1.** [relating to, concerning] au sujet de ; **a film about Paris** un film sur Paris ; **what is it about?** de quoi s'agit-il? ; **to talk about sthg** parler de qqch - **2.** [referring to place] : **his belongings were scattered about the room** ses affaires étaient éparpillées dans toute la pièce ; **to wander about the streets** errer de par les rues.

about-turn *UK*, **about-face** *US n* **1.** MIL demi-tour *m* ; *fig* volte-face *f inv* - **2.** POL revirement *m*.

above [ə'bʌv] ◇ *adv* **1.** [on top, higher up] au-dessus - **2.** [in text] ci-dessus, plus haut - **3.** [more, over] plus ; **children aged 5 and above** les enfants âgés de 5 ans et plus OR de plus de 5 ans. ◇ *prep* **1.** [on top of, higher up than] au-dessus de - **2.** [more than] plus de. ◈ **above all** *adv* avant tout.

aboveboard [ə,bʌv'bɔːd] *adj* honnête.

abrasive [ə'breɪsɪv] *adj* [substance] abrasif(ive) ; *fig* caustique, acerbe.

abreast [ə'brest] *adv* de front. ◈ **abreast of** *prep* : **to keep abreast of** se tenir au courant de.

abridged [ə'brɪdʒd] *adj* abrégé(e).

abroad [ə'brɔːd] *adv* à l'étranger.

abrupt [ə'brʌpt] *adj* **1.** [sudden] soudain(e), brusque - **2.** [brusque] abrupt(e).

abscess ['æbsɪs] *n* abcès *m*.

abscond [əb'skɒnd] *vi* s'enfuir.

abseil ['æbseɪl] *vi UK* descendre en rappel.

absence ['æbsəns] *n* absence *f*.

absent ['æbsənt] *adj* : **absent (from)** absent(e) (de).

absentee [,æbsən'tiː] *n* absent *m*, -e *f*.

absent-minded [-'maɪndɪd] *adj* distrait(e).

absolute ['æbsəluːt] *adj* **1.** [complete - fool, disgrace] complet(ète) - **2.** [totalitarian - ruler, power] absolu(e).

absolutely ['æbsə'luːtlɪ] *adv* absolument.

absolve [əb'zɒlv] *vt* : **to absolve sb (from)** absoudre qqn (de).

absorb [əb'zɔːb] *vt* absorber ; [information] retenir, assimiler ; **to be absorbed in sthg** être absorbé(e) dans qqch.

absorbent [əb'zɔːbənt] *adj* absorbant(e).

absorption [əb'zɔːpʃn] *n* absorption *f*.

abstain [əb'steɪn] *vi* : **to abstain (from)** s'abstenir (de).

abstemious [æb'stiːmjəs] *adj fml* frugal(e), sobre.

abstention [əb'stenʃn] *n* abstention *f*.

abstract ◇ *adj* ['æbstrækt] abstrait(e). ◇ *n* ['æbstrækt] [summary] résumé *m*, abrégé *m*.

absurd [əb'sɜːd] *adj* absurde.

ABTA ['æbtə] (*abbrev of* **Association of British Travel Agents**) *n association des agences de voyage britanniques.*

abundant [ə'bʌndənt] *adj* abondant(e).

abundantly [ə'bʌndəntlɪ] *adv* **1.** [clear, obvious] parfaitement, tout à fait - **2.** [exist, grow] en abondance.

abuse ◇ *n* [ə'bjuːs] (*U*) **1.** [offensive remarks] insultes *fpl*, injures *fpl* - **2.** [maltreatment] mauvais traitement *m* ; **child abuse** mauvais traitements infligés aux enfants - **3.** [of power, drugs etc] abus *m*. ◇ *vt* [ə'bjuːz] **1.** [insult] insulter, injurier - **2.** [maltreat] maltraiter - **3.** [power, drugs etc] abuser de.

abusive [ə'bjuːsɪv] *adj* grossier(ère), injurieux(euse).

abysmal [ə'bɪzml] *adj* épouvantable, abominable.

abyss [ə'bɪs] *n* abîme *m*, gouffre *m*.

a/c (*abbrev of* **account (current)**) cc.

AC *n* (*abbrev of* **alternating current**) courant *m* alternatif.

academic [,ækə'demɪk] ◇ *adj* **1.** [of college, university] universitaire - **2.** [person] intellectuel(elle) - **3.** [question, discussion] théorique. ◇ *n* universitaire *mf*.

academy [ə'kædəmɪ] *n* **1.** [school, college] école *f* ; **academy of music** conservatoire *m* - **2.** [institution, society] académie *f*.

ACAS ['eɪkæs] (*abbrev of* **Advisory Conciliation and Arbitration Service**) *n organisme britannique de conciliation des conflits du travail.*

accede [æk'siːd] *vi* **1.** [agree] : **to accede to** agréer, donner suite à - **2.** [monarch] : **to accede to the throne** monter sur le trône.

accelerate [ək'seləreɪt] *vi* **1.** [car, driver] accélérer - **2.** [inflation, growth] s'accélérer.

acceleration [ək,selə'reɪʃn] *n* accélération *f*.

accelerator [ək'seləreɪtər] *n* accélérateur *m*.

accent ['æksent] *n* accent *m*.

accept [ək'sept] *vt* **1.** [gen] accepter ; [for job, as member of club] recevoir, admettre - **2.** [agree] : **to accept that...** admettre que...

acceptable [ək'septəbl] *adj* acceptable.

acceptance [ək'septəns] *n* **1.** [gen] acceptation *f* - **2.** [for job, as member of club] admission *f*.

access ['ækses] *n* **1.** [entry, way in] accès *m*

- 2. [opportunity to use, see] **: to have access to sthg** avoir accès à qqch à sa disposition, disposer de qqch.

accessible [ək'sesəbl] *adj* **1.** [reachable - place] accessible **- 2.** [available] disponible.

accessory [ək'sesərɪ] *n* **1.** [of car, vacuum cleaner] accessoire *m* **- 2.** LAW complice *mf* **- 3.** COMPUT accessoire *m*.

accident ['æksɪdənt] *n* accident *m* **; accident and emergency department** *UK* (service *m* des) urgences *fpl* **; by accident** par hasard, par accident.

accidental [ˌæksɪ'dentl] *adj* accidentel(elle).

accidentally [ˌæksɪ'dentəlɪ] *adv* **1.** [drop, break] par mégarde **- 2.** [meet] par hasard.

accident-prone *adj* prédisposé(e) aux accidents.

acclaim [ə'kleɪm] ⬦ *n (U)* éloges *mpl*. ⬦ *vt* louer.

acclimatize, *UK* **-ise** [ə'klaɪmətaɪz], *US* **acclimate** ['ækləmeɪt] *vi* **: to acclimatize (to)** s'acclimater (à).

accommodate [ə'kɒmədeɪt] *vt* **1.** [provide room for] loger **- 2.** [oblige - person, wishes] satisfaire.

accommodating [ə'kɒmədeɪtɪŋ] *adj* obligeant(e).

accommodation *UK* [əˌkɒmə'deɪʃn] *n* logement *m*.

accommodations *US* [əˌkɒmə'deɪʃnz] *npl* = accommodation.

accompany [ə'kʌmpənɪ] *vt* [gen] accompagner.

accomplice [ə'kʌmplɪs] *n* complice *mf*.

accomplish [ə'kʌmplɪʃ] *vt* accomplir.

accomplishment [ə'kʌmplɪʃmənt] *n* **1.** [action] accomplissement *m* **- 2.** [achievement] réussite *f*. ⬦ **accomplishments** *npl* talents *mpl*.

accord [ə'kɔːd] *n* **: to do sthg of one's own accord** faire qqch de son propre chef OR de soi-même.

accordance [ə'kɔːdəns] *n* **: in accordance with** conformément à.

according [ə'kɔːdɪŋ] ⬦ **according to** *prep* **1.** [as stated or shown by] d'après **; to go according to plan** se passer comme prévu **- 2.** [with regard to] suivant, en fonction de.

accordingly [ə'kɔːdɪŋlɪ] *adv* **1.** [appropriately] en conséquence **- 2.** [consequently] par conséquent.

accordion [ə'kɔːdjən] *n* accordéon *m*.

accost [ə'kɒst] *vt* accoster.

account [ə'kaʊnt] *n* **1.** [with bank, shop, company] compte *m* **- 2.** [report] compte-rendu *m* **- 3.** [business, patronage] appui *m* **;** [in advertising] budget *m* **; to put sth to good**

account tirer parti de qqch **; to take account of sthg, to take sthg into account** prendre qqch en compte **; to be of no account** n'avoir aucune importance **; on no account** sous aucun prétexte, en aucun cas. ⬦ **accounts** *npl* [of business] comptabilité *f*, comptes *mpl*. ⬦ **by all accounts** *adv* d'après ce que l'on dit, au dire de tous. ⬦ **on account** *adv* à crédit **; I paid £100 on account** j'ai versé un acompte de 100 livres. ⬦ **on account of** *prep* à cause de. ⬦ **on no account** *adv* en aucun cas, sous aucun prétexte. ⬦ **account for** *vt insep* **1.** [explain] justifier, expliquer **- 2.** [represent] représenter.

accountable [ə'kaʊntəbl] *adj* [responsible] **: accountable (for)** responsable (de).

accountancy [ə'kaʊntənsɪ] *n* comptabilité *f*.

accountant [ə'kaʊntənt] *n* comptable *mf*.

accrue [ə'kruː] *vi* [money] fructifier **;** [interest] courir.

accumulate [ə'kjuːmjʊleɪt] ⬦ *vt* accumuler, amasser. ⬦ *vi* s'accumuler.

accuracy ['ækjʊrəsɪ] *n* **1.** [of description, report] exactitude *f* **- 2.** [of weapon, typist, figures] précision *f*.

accurate ['ækjʊrət] *adj* **1.** [description, report] exact(e) **- 2.** [weapon, typist, figures] précis(e).

accurately ['ækjʊrətlɪ] *adv* **1.** [truthfully - describe, report] fidèlement **- 2.** [precisely - aim] avec précision **;** [- type] sans faute.

accusation [ˌækju:'zeɪʃn] *n* accusation *f*.

accuse [ə'kjuːz] *vt* **: to accuse sb of sthg/of doing sthg** accuser qqn de qqch/de faire qqch.

accused [ə'kjuːzd] (*pl* accused) *n* LAW **: the accused** l'accusé *m*, -e *f*.

accustomed [ə'kʌstəmd] *adj* **: to be accustomed to sthg/to doing sthg** avoir l'habitude de qqch/de faire qqch.

ace [eɪs] *n* as *m*.

ache [eɪk] ⬦ *n* douleur *f*. ⬦ *vi* **1.** [back, limb] faire mal **; my head aches** j'ai mal à la tête **- 2.** *fig* [want] **: to be aching for sthg/to do sthg** mourir d'envie de qqch/de faire qqch.

achieve [ə'tʃiːv] *vt* [success, victory] obtenir, remporter **;** [goal] atteindre **;** [ambition] réaliser **;** [fame] parvenir à.

achievement [ə'tʃiːvmənt] *n* [success] réussite *f*.

Achilles' tendon *n* tendon *m* d'Achille.

acid ['æsɪd] ⬦ *adj* lit & fig acide. ⬦ *n* acide *m*.

acid house *n* MUS house *f* (music).

acid rain *(U)* *n* pluies *fpl* acides.

acknowledge [ək'nɒlɪdʒ] *vt* **1.** [fact, situation, person] reconnaître - **2.** [letter] : **to acknowledge (receipt of)** accuser réception de - **3.** [greet] saluer.

acne ['ækni] *n* acné *f*.

acorn ['eɪkɔːn] *n* gland *m*.

acoustic [ə'kuːstɪk] *adj* acoustique.
➡ **acoustics** *npl* [of room] acoustique *f*.

acquaint [ə'kweɪnt] *vt* : **to acquaint sb with sthg** mettre qqn au courant de qqch ; **to be acquainted with sb** connaître qqn.

acquaintance [ə'kweɪntəns] *n* [person] connaissance *f*.

acquire [ə'kwaɪəʳ] *vt* acquérir.

acquisitive [ə'kwɪzɪtɪv] *adj* avide de possessions.

acquit [ə'kwɪt] *vt* **1.** LAW acquitter - **2.** [perform] : **to acquit o.s. well/badly** bien/mal se comporter.

acquittal [ə'kwɪtl] *n* acquittement *m*.

acre ['eɪkəʳ] *n* ≃ demi-hectare *m* (= 4046,9 *m²*).

acrid ['ækrɪd] *adj* [taste, smell] âcre ; *fig* acerbe.

acrimonious [,ækrɪ'məʊnjəs] *adj* acrimonieux(euse).

acrobat ['ækrəbæt] *n* acrobate *mf*.

across [ə'krɒs] ⬦ *adv* **1.** [from one side to the other] en travers - **2.** [in measurements] : **the river is 2 km across** la rivière mesure 2 km de large - **3.** [in crossword] : **21 across** 21 horizontalement. ⬦ *prep* **1.** [from one side to the other] d'un côté à l'autre de, en travers de ; **to walk across the road** traverser la route ; **to run across the road** traverser la route en courant - **2.** [on the other side of] de l'autre côté de ; **the house across the road** la maison d'en face. ➡ **across from** *prep* en face de.

acrylic [ə'krɪlɪk] ⬦ *adj* acrylique. ⬦ *n* acrylique *m*.

act [ækt] ⬦ *n* **1.** [action, deed] acte *m* ; **to catch sb in the act of doing sthg** surprendre qqn en train de faire qqch - **2.** LAW loi *f* - **3.** [of play, opera] acte *m* ; [in cabaret etc] numéro *m* ; *fig* [pretence] : **to put on an act** jouer la comédie ; **to get one's act together** se reprendre en main. ⬦ *vi* **1.** [gen] agir - **2.** [behave] se comporter ; **to act as if** se conduire comme si, se comporter comme si ; **to act like** se conduire comme - **3.** [in play, film] jouer ; *fig* [pretend] jouer la comédie - **4.** [function] : **to act as** [person] être ; [object] servir de. ⬦ *vt* [part] jouer. ➡ **act on** *vt insep* **1.** [advice, suggestion] suivre ; [order] exécuter ; **acting on your instructions, we have**

cancelled your account selon vos instructions, nous avons fermé votre compte - **2.** [chemical, drug] agir sur.

ACT (*abbrev of* **American College Test**) *n* examen américain de fin d'études secondaires.

acting ['æktɪŋ] ⬦ *adj* par intérim, provisoire. ⬦ *n* [in play, film] interprétation *f*.

action ['ækʃn] *n* **1.** [gen] action *f* ; **to take action** agir, prendre des mesures ; **to put sthg into action** mettre qqch à exécution ; **in action** [person] en action ; [machine] en marche ; **out of action** [person] hors de combat ; [machine] hors service, hors d'usage - **2.** LAW procès *m*, action *f*.

action movie *n* film *m* d'action.

action replay *n UK* répétition *f* immédiate (au ralenti).

activate ['æktɪveɪt] *vt* mettre en marche.

active ['æktɪv] *adj* **1.** [gen] actif(ive) ; [encouragement] vif (vive) - **2.** [volcano] en activité.

active duty *US* = **active service**.

actively ['æktɪvlɪ] *adv* activement.

activity [æk'tɪvətɪ] *n* activité *f*.

actor ['æktəʳ] *n* acteur *m*.

actress ['æktrɪs] *n* actrice *f*.

actual ['æktʃʊəl] *adj* réel(elle).

actually ['æktʃʊəlɪ] *adv* **1.** [really, in truth] vraiment - **2.** [by the way] au fait.

acumen ['ækjʊmen] *n* flair *m*.

acupuncture ['ækjʊpʌŋktʃəʳ] *n* acupuncture *f*, acuponcture *f*.

acute [ə'kjuːt] *adj* **1.** [severe - pain, illness] aigu(ë) ; [- danger] sérieux(euse), grave - **2.** [perceptive - person, mind] perspicace - **3.** [keen - eyesight] perçant(e) ; [- hearing] fin(e) ; [- sense of smell] développé(e) - **4.** MATHS : **acute angle** angle *m* aigu - **5.** LING : **e acute** e accent aigu.

ad [æd] (*abbrev of* **advertisement**) *n inf* [in newspaper] annonce *f* ; [on TV] pub *f*.

AD (*abbrev of* **Anno Domini**) ap. J.-C.

adamant ['ædəmənt] *adj* : **to be adamant** être inflexible.

Adam's apple ['ædəmz-] *n* pomme *f* d'Adam.

adapt [ə'dæpt] ⬦ *vt* adapter. ⬦ *vi* : **to adapt (to)** s'adapter (à).

adaptability [ə,dæptə'bɪlətɪ] *n* souplesse *f*.

adaptable [ə'dæptəbl] *adj* [person] souple.

adapter, adaptor [ə'dæptəʳ] *n* [ELEC *UK* [- for several devices] prise *f* multiple ; [- for foreign plug] adaptateur *m*.

add [æd] *vt* **1.** [gen] : **to add sthg (to)** ajouter qqch (à) - **2.** [numbers] additionner. ➡ **add on** *vt sep* : **to add sthg on (to)**

ajouter qqch (à) ; [charge, tax] rajouter qqch (à). **add to** vt insep ajouter à, augmenter. **add up** vt sep additionner. **add up to** vt insep se monter à.

adder ['ædər] n vipère f.

addict ['ædɪkt] n drogué m, -e f ; **drug addict** drogué.

addicted [ə'dɪktɪd] adj : **addicted (to)** drogué(e) (à) ; fig passionné(e) (de).

addiction [ə'dɪkʃn] n : **addiction (to)** dépendance f (à) ; fig penchant m (pour).

addictive [ə'dɪktɪv] adj qui rend dépendant(e).

addition [ə'dɪʃn] n addition f ; **in addition (to)** en plus (de).

additional [ə'dɪʃənl] adj supplémentaire.

additive ['ædɪtɪv] n additif m.

address [ə'dres] ◇ n **1.** [place] adresse f - **2.** [speech] discours m. ◇ vt **1.** [gen] adresser - **2.** [meeting, conference] prendre la parole à - **3.** [problem, issue] aborder, examiner.

address book n carnet m d'adresses.

adenoids ['ædɪnɔɪdz] npl végétations fpl.

adept ['ædept] adj : **adept (at)** doué(e) (pour).

adequate ['ædɪkwət] adj adéquat(e).

adhere [əd'hɪər] vi **1.** [stick] : **to adhere (to)** adhérer (à) - **2.** [observe] : **to adhere to** obéir à - **3.** [keep] : **to adhere to** adhérer à.

adhesive [əd'hi:sɪv] ◇ adj adhésif(ive). ◇ n adhésif m.

adhesive tape n ruban m adhésif.

adjacent [ə'dʒeɪsənt] adj : **adjacent (to)** adjacent(e) (à), contigu(ë) (à).

adjective ['ædʒɪktɪv] n adjectif m.

adjoining [ə'dʒɔɪnɪŋ] ◇ adj voisin(e). ◇ prep attenant à.

adjourn [ə'dʒɜːn] ◇ vt ajourner. ◇ vi suspendre la séance.

adjudicate [ə'dʒuːdɪkeɪt] vi : **to adjudicate (on** OR **upon)** se prononcer (sur).

adjust [ə'dʒʌst] ◇ vt ajuster, régler. ◇ vi : **to adjust (to)** s'adapter (à).

adjustable [ə'dʒʌstəbl] adj réglable.

adjustment [ə'dʒʌstmənt] n **1.** [modification] ajustement m ; TECH réglage m - **2.** [change in attitude] : **adjustment (to)** adaptation f (à).

ad lib [,æd'lɪb] ◇ adj improvisé(e). ◇ adv à volonté. ◇ n improvisation f. **ad-lib** vi improviser.

administer [əd'mɪnɪstər] vt **1.** [company, business] administrer, gérer - **2.** [justice, punishment] dispenser - **3.** [drug, medication] administrer.

administration [əd,mɪnɪ'streɪʃn] n administration f.

administrative [əd'mɪnɪstrətɪv] adj administratif(ive).

admirable ['ædmərəbl] adj admirable.

admiral ['ædmərəl] n amiral m.

admiration [,ædmə'reɪʃn] n admiration f.

admire [əd'maɪər] vt admirer.

admirer [əd'maɪərər] n admirateur m, -trice f.

admission [əd'mɪʃn] n **1.** [permission to enter] admission f - **2.** [to museum etc] entrée f - **3.** [confession] confession f, aveu m.

admit [əd'mɪt] ◇ vt **1.** [confess] reconnaître ; **to admit (that)...** reconnaître que... ; **to admit doing sthg** reconnaître avoir fait qqch ; **to admit defeat** fig s'avouer vaincu(e) - **2.** [allow to enter, join] admettre ; **to be admitted to hospital** UK OR **to the hospital** US être admis(e) à l'hôpital. ◇ vi : **to admit to** admettre, reconnaître.

admittance [əd'mɪtəns] n admission f ; **'no admittance'** 'entrée interdite'.

admittedly [əd'mɪtɪdlɪ] adv de l'aveu général.

admonish [əd'mɒnɪʃ] vt réprimander.

ad nauseam [,æd'nɔːzɪæm] adv [talk] à n'en plus finir.

ado [ə'duː] n : **without further** OR **more ado** sans plus de cérémonie.

adolescence [,ædə'lesns] n adolescence f.

adolescent [,ædə'lesnt] ◇ adj adolescent(e) ; pej puéril(e). ◇ n adolescent m, -e f.

adopt [ə'dɒpt] vt adopter.

adoption [ə'dɒpʃn] n adoption f.

adore [ə'dɔːr] vt adorer.

adorn [ə'dɔːn] vt orner.

adrenalin [ə'drenəlɪn] n adrénaline f.

Adriatic [,eɪdrɪ'ætɪk] n : **the Adriatic (Sea)** l'Adriatique f, la mer Adriatique.

adrift [ə'drɪft] ◇ adj à la dérive. ◇ adv : **to go adrift** fig aller à la dérive.

ADSL [,eɪdɪes'el] (abbrev of **Asymmetric Digital Subscriber Line**) n ADSL m, RNA m offic.

adult ['ædʌlt] ◇ adj **1.** [gen] adulte - **2.** [films, literature] pour adultes. ◇ n adulte mf.

adultery [ə'dʌltərɪ] n adultère m.

advance [əd'vɑːns] ◇ n **1.** [gen] avance f - **2.** [progress] progrès m. ◇ comp à l'avance. ◇ vt **1.** [gen] avancer - **2.** [improve] faire progresser OR avancer. ◇ vi **1.** [gen] avancer - **2.** [improve] progresser.

advances *npl* : **to make advances to sb** [sexual] faire des avances à qqn ; [business] faire des propositions à qqn. **in advance** *adv* à l'avance.

advanced [əd'vɑːnst] *adj* avancé(e).

advantage [əd'vɑːntɪdʒ] *n* : **advantage (over)** avantage *m* (sur) ; **to be to one's advantage** être à son avantage ; **to take advantage of sthg** profiter de qqch ; **to take advantage of sb** exploiter qqn.

advent ['ædvənt] *n* avènement *m*. **Advent** *n* RELIG Avent *m*.

adventure [əd'ventʃər] *n* aventure *f*.

adventure playground *n* UK terrain *m* d'aventures.

adventurous [əd'ventʃərəs] *adj* aventureux(euse).

adverb ['ædvɜːb] *n* adverbe *m*.

adverse ['ædvɜːs] *adj* défavorable.

advert ['ædvɜːt] UK = **advertisement**.

advertise ['ædvətaɪz] *vt* COMM faire de la publicité pour ; [event] annoncer. *vi* faire de la publicité ; **to advertise for sb/sthg** chercher qqn/qqch par voie d'annonce.

advertisement [əd'vɜːtɪsmənt] *n* [in newspaper] annonce *f* ; *fig* & COMM publicité *f*.

advertiser ['ædvətaɪzər] *n* annonceur *m*, -euse *f*.

advertising ['ædvətaɪzɪŋ] *n* (U) publicité *f*.

advice [əd'vaɪs] *n* (U) conseils *mpl* ; **a piece of advice** un conseil ; **to give sb advice** donner des conseils à qqn ; **to take sb's advice** suivre les conseils de qqn.

advisable [əd'vaɪzəbl] *adj* conseillé(e), recommandé(e).

advise [əd'vaɪz] *vt* **1.** [give advice to] : **to advise sb to do sthg** conseiller à qqn de faire qqch ; **to advise sb against sthg** déconseiller qqch à qqn ; **to advise sb against doing sthg** déconseiller à qqn de faire qqch - **2.** [professionally] : **to advise sb on sthg** conseiller qqn sur qqch - **3.** [inform] : **to advise sb (of sthg)** aviser qqn (de qqch). *vi* **1.** [give advice] : **to advise against sthg/against doing sthg** déconseiller qqch/de faire qqch - **2.** [professionally] : **to advise on sthg** conseiller sur qqch.

advisedly [əd'vaɪzɪdlɪ] *adv* en connaissance de cause, délibérément.

adviser, US **advisor** [əd'vaɪzər] *n* conseiller *m*, -ère *f*.

advisory [əd'vaɪzərɪ] *adj* consultatif(ive).

advocate *n* ['ædvəkət] **1.** LAW avocat *m*, -e *f* - **2.** [supporter] partisan *m*. *vt* ['ædvəkeɪt] préconiser, recommander.

Aegean [iː'dʒiːən] *n* : **the Aegean (Sea)** la mer Égée.

aerial ['eərɪəl] *adj* aérien(enne). *n* UK antenne *f*.

aerobics [eə'rəubɪks] *n* (U) aérobic *m*.

aerodynamic [ˌeərəudaɪ'næmɪk] *adj* aérodynamique. **aerodynamics** *n* (U) aérodynamique *f*. *npl* [aerodynamic qualities] aérodynamisme *m*.

aeroplane ['eərəpleɪn] *n* UK avion *m*.

aerosol ['eərəsɒl] *n* aérosol *m*.

aesthetic, US **esthetic** [iːs'θetɪk] *adj* esthétique.

afar [ə'fɑː] *adv* : **from afar** de loin.

affable ['æfəbl] *adj* affable.

affair [ə'feə] *n* **1.** [gen] affaire *f* - **2.** [extramarital relationship] liaison *f*.

affect [ə'fekt] *vt* **1.** [influence] avoir un effet OR des conséquences sur - **2.** [emotionally] affecter, émouvoir - **3.** [put on] affecter.

affection [ə'fekʃn] *n* affection *f*.

affectionate [ə'fekʃnət] *adj* affectueux(euse).

affinity card [ə'fɪnɪtɪˌkɑːd] *n* carte *f* affinitaire.

affirm [ə'fɜːm] *vt* **1.** [declare] affirmer - **2.** [confirm] confirmer.

affix [ə'fɪks] *vt* [stamp] coller.

afflict [ə'flɪkt] *vt* affliger ; **to be afflicted with sthg** souffrir de.

affluence ['æfluəns] *n* prospérité *f*.

affluent ['æfluənt] *adj* riche.

afford [ə'fɔːd] *vt* **1.** [buy, pay for] : **to be able to afford sthg** avoir les moyens d'acheter qqch - **2.** [spare] : **to be able to afford the time (to do sthg)** avoir le temps (de faire qqch) - **3.** [harmful, embarrassing thing] : **to be able to afford sthg** pouvoir se permettre qqch - **4.** [provide, give] procurer.

affront [ə'frʌnt] *n* affront *m*, insulte *f*. *vt* insulter, faire un affront à.

Afghanistan [æf'gænɪstæn] *n* Afghanistan *m*.

afield [ə'fiːld] *adv* : **far afield** loin.

afloat [ə'fləut] *adj* lit & fig à flot.

afoot [ə'fut] *adj* en préparation.

afraid [ə'freɪd] *adj* **1.** [frightened] : **to be afraid (of)** avoir peur (de) ; **to be afraid of doing** OR **to do sthg** avoir peur de faire qqch - **2.** [reluctant, apprehensive] : **to be afraid of doing** craindre de faire qqch - **3.** [in apologies] : **to be afraid (that)...** regretter que... ; **I'm afraid so/not** j'ai bien peur que oui/non.

afresh [ə'freʃ] *adv* de nouveau.

Africa ['æfrɪkə] *n* Afrique *f*.

African ['æfrɪkən] *adj* africain(e). *n* Africain *m*, -e *f*.

aft [ɑːft] *adv* sur OR à l'arrière.

after ['ɑ:ftər] <> prep 1. [gen] après ; **to be after sb/sthg** inf [in search of] chercher qqn/qqch ; **after you!** après vous ! ; **to name sb after sb** donner à qqn le nom de qqn - 2. [in time] après ; **it's twenty after three** US il est trois heures vingt. <> adv après. <> conj après que. ▪ **afters** npl UK inf dessert m. ▪ **after all** après tout. ▪ **one after another, one after the other** adv l'un après l'autre.

afterlife ['ɑ:ftəlaɪf] (pl -lives [-laɪvz]) n vie f future.

aftermath ['ɑ:ftəmæθ] n conséquences fpl, suites fpl.

afternoon [,ɑ:ftə'nu:n] n après-midi m inv ; **in the afternoon** l'après-midi ; **good afternoon** bonjour.

aftershave ['ɑ:ftəʃeɪv] n après-rasage m.

aftertaste ['ɑ:ftəteɪst] n lit & fig arrière-goût m.

afterthought ['ɑ:ftəθɔ:t] n pensée f OR réflexion f après coup.

afterward(s) ['ɑ:ftəwəd(z)] adv après.

again [ə'gen] adv encore une fois, de nouveau ; **to do again** refaire ; **to say again** répéter ; **to start again** recommencer ; **again and again** à plusieurs reprises ; **all over again** une fois de plus ; **time and again** maintes et maintes fois ; **half as much again** à moitié autant ; **(twice) as much again** deux fois autant ; **come again?** inf comment ?, pardon ? ; **then** OR **there again** d'autre part.

against [ə'genst] prep & adv contre ; **(as) against** contre.

age [eɪdʒ] (cont ageing, cont aging) <> n 1. [gen] âge m ; **she's 20 years of age** elle a 20 ans ; **what age are you?** quel âge avez-vous ? ; **to be under age** être mineur(e) ; **to come of age** atteindre sa majorité - 2. [old age] vieillesse f - 3. [in history] époque f. <> vt & vi vieillir. ▪ **ages** npl : **ages ago** il y a une éternité ; **I haven't seen him for ages** je ne l'ai pas vu depuis une éternité.

aged <> adj 1. [eɪdʒd] [of stated age] : **aged 15** âgé(e) de 15 ans - 2. ['eɪdʒɪd] [very old] âgé(e), vieux (vieille). <> npl ['eɪdʒɪd] : **the aged** les personnes fpl âgées.

age group n tranche f d'âge.

agency ['eɪdʒənsɪ] n 1. [business] agence f - 2. [organization] organisme m.

agenda [ə'dʒendə] (pl -s) n ordre m du jour.

agent ['eɪdʒənt] n agent m, -e f.

aggravate ['ægrəveɪt] vt 1. [make worse] aggraver - 2. [annoy] agacer.

aggregate ['ægrɪgət] <> adj total(e). <> n [total] total m.

aggressive [ə'gresɪv] adj agressif(ive).

aggrieved [ə'gri:vd] adj blessé(e), froissé(e).

aghast [ə'gɑ:st] adj : **aghast (at sthg)** atterré(e) (par qqch).

agile [UK 'ædʒaɪl, US 'ædʒəl] adj agile.

agitate ['ædʒɪteɪt] <> vt 1. [disturb] inquiéter - 2. [shake] agiter. <> vi : **to agitate for/against** faire campagne pour/contre.

AGM (abbrev of annual general meeting) n UK AGA f.

agnostic [æg'nɒstɪk] <> adj agnostique. <> n agnostique mf.

ago [ə'gəʊ] adv : **a long time ago** il y a longtemps ; **three days ago** il y a trois jours.

agog [ə'gɒg] adj : **to be agog (with)** être en ébullition (à propos de).

agonizing ['ægənaɪzɪŋ] adj déchirant(e).

agony ['ægənɪ] n 1. [physical pain] douleur f atroce ; **to be in agony** souffrir le martyre - 2. [mental pain] angoisse f ; **to be in agony** être angoissé(e).

agony aunt n UK inf personne qui tient la rubrique du courrier du cœur.

agree [ə'gri:] <> vi 1. [concur] : **to agree (with/about)** être d'accord (avec/au sujet de) ; **to agree on** [price, terms] convenir de - 2. [consent] : **to agree to sthg** donner son consentement (à qqch) - 3. [be consistent] concorder - 4. [suit sb] : **to agree with** réussir à - 5. GRAM : **to agree (with)** s'accorder (avec). <> vt 1. [concur, concede] : **to agree (that)...** admettre que... - 2. [arrange] : **to agree to do sthg** se mettre d'accord pour faire qqch - 3. [price, conditions] accepter, convenir de.

agreeable [ə'griəbl] adj 1. [pleasant] agréable - 2. [willing] : **to be agreeable to** consentir à.

agreed [ə'gri:d] adj : **to be agreed (on sthg)** être d'accord (à propos de qqch).

agreement [ə'gri:mənt] n 1. [gen] accord m ; **to be in agreement (with)** être d'accord (avec) - 2. [consistency] concordance f.

agricultural [,ægrɪ'kʌltʃərəl] adj agricole.

agriculture ['ægrɪkʌltʃər] n agriculture f.

aground [ə'graʊnd] adv : **to run aground** s'échouer.

ahead [ə'hed] adv 1. [in front] devant, en avant ; **right ahead, straight ahead** droit devant - 2. [in better position] en avance ; **Scotland are ahead by two goals to one** l'Écosse mène par deux à un ; **to get ahead** [be successful] réussir - 3. [in time] à l'avance ; **the months ahead** les mois à venir. ▪ **ahead of** prep 1. [in front of] devant - 2. [in time] avant ; **ahead of schedule** [work] en avance sur le planning.

aid [eɪd] <> n aide f ; **with the aid of**

[person] avec l'aide de ; [thing] à l'aide de ;
in aid of au profit de. ⋄ *vt* **1.** [help] aider
- **2.** LAW : **to aid and abet** être complice de.

AIDS, Aids (*abbrev of* **acquired immune deficiency syndrome**) [eɪdz] ⋄ *n* SIDA *m*, sida *m*. ⋄ *comp* : **AIDS patient** sidéen *m*, -enne *f*.

ailing ['eɪlɪŋ] *adj* **1.** [ill] souffrant(e) - **2.** *fig* [economy, industry] dans une mauvaise passe.

ailment ['eɪlmənt] *n* maladie *f*.

aim [eɪm] ⋄ *n* **1.** [objective] but *m*, objectif *m* - **2.** [in firing gun, arrow] : **to take aim at** viser. ⋄ *vt* **1.** [gun, camera] : **to aim sthg at** braquer qqch sur - **2.** *fig* : **to be aimed at** [plan, campaign etc] être destiné(e) à, viser ; [criticism] être dirigé(e) contre. ⋄ *vi* : **to aim (at)** viser ; **to aim at** OR **for** *fig* viser ; **to aim to do sthg** viser à faire qqch.

aimless ['eɪmlɪs] *adj* [person] désœuvré(e) ; [life] sans but.

ain't [eɪnt] *inf* = **am not**, = **are not**, = **is not**, = **have not**, = **has not**.

air [eər] ⋄ *n* **1.** [gen] air *m* ; **to throw sthg into the air** jeter qqch en l'air ; **by air** [travel] par avion ; **to be (up) in the air** *fig* [plans] être vague - **2.** RADIO & TV : **on the air** être à l'antenne. ⋄ *comp* [transport] aérien(enne). ⋄ *vt* **1.** [room, linen] aérer - **2.** [make publicly known] faire connaître OR communiquer - **3.** [broadcast] diffuser. ⋄ *vi* sécher.

airbag ['eabæg] *n* AUT Airbag® *m*.

airbase ['eəbeɪs] *n* base *f* aérienne.

airbed ['eəbed] *n* UK matelas *m* pneumatique.

airborne ['eəbɔːn] *adj* **1.** [troops etc] aéroporté(e) ; [seeds] emporté(e) par le vent - **2.** [plane] qui a décollé.

air-conditioned [-kən'dɪʃnd] *adj* climatisé(e), à air conditionné.

air-conditioning [-kən'dɪʃnɪŋ] *n* climatisation *f*.

aircraft ['eəkrɑːft] (*pl* aircraft) *n* avion *m*.

aircraft carrier *n* porte-avions *m inv*.

airfield ['eəfiːld] *n* terrain *m* d'aviation.

airforce ['eəfɔːs] *n* armée *f* de l'air.

airgun ['eəgʌn] *n* carabine *f* OR fusil *m* à air comprimé.

air hostess ['eə,həʊstɪs] *n* UK dated hôtesse *f* de l'air.

airlift ['eəlɪft] ⋄ *n* pont *m* aérien. ⋄ *vt* transporter par pont aérien.

airline ['eəlaɪn] *n* compagnie *f* aérienne.

airliner ['eəlaɪnər] *n* [short-distance] (avion *m*) moyen-courrier *m* ; [long-distance] (avion *m*) long-courrier *m*.

airlock ['eəlɒk] *n* **1.** [in tube, pipe] poche *f* d'air - **2.** [airtight chamber] sas *m*.

airmail ['eəmeɪl] *n* poste *f* aérienne ; **by airmail** par avion.

airplane ['eəpleɪn] *n* US avion *m*.

airport ['eəpɔːt] *n* aéroport *m*.

air raid *n* raid *m* aérien, attaque *f* aérienne.

air rifle *n* carabine *f* à air comprimé.

airsick ['eəsɪk] *adj* : **to be airsick** avoir le mal de l'air.

airspace ['eəspeɪs] *n* espace *m* aérien.

air steward *n* steward *m*.

airstrip ['eəstrɪp] *n* piste *f* (d'atterrissage).

air terminal *n* aérogare *f*.

airtight ['eətaɪt] *adj* hermétique.

air-traffic controller *n* aiguilleur *m* (du ciel).

airy ['eəri] *adj* **1.** [room] aéré(e) - **2.** [notions, promises] chimérique, vain(e) - **3.** [nonchalant] nonchalant(e).

aisle [aɪl] *n* allée *f* ; [in plane] couloir *m*.

ajar [ə'dʒɑːr] *adj* entrouvert(e).

aka (*abbrev of* **also known as**) alias.

akin [ə'kɪn] *adj* : **to be akin to** être semblable à.

alacrity [ə'lækrətɪ] *n* empressement *m*.

alarm [ə'lɑːm] ⋄ *n* **1.** [fear] alarme *f*, inquiétude *f* - **2.** [device] alarme *f* ; **to raise** OR **sound the alarm** donner OR sonner l'alarme. ⋄ *vt* alarmer, alerter.

alarm clock *n* réveil *m*, réveille-matin *m inv*.

alarming [ə'lɑːmɪŋ] *adj* alarmant(e), inquiétant(e).

alas [ə'læs] *excl* hélas!

Albania [æl'beɪnjə] *n* Albanie *f*.

Albanian [æl'beɪnjən] ⋄ *adj* albanais(e). ⋄ *n* **1.** [person] Albanais *m*, -e *f* - **2.** [language] albanais *m*.

albeit [ɔːl'biːɪt] *conj* bien que (+ *subjunctive*).

albino [æl'biːnəʊ] *n* (*pl* -s) albinos *mf*.

album ['ælbəm] *n* album *m*.

alcohol ['ælkəhɒl] *n* alcool *m*.

alcoholic [,ælkə'hɒlɪk] ⋄ *adj* [person] alcoolique ; [drink] alcoolisé(e). ⋄ *n* alcoolique *mf*.

alcopop ['ælkəʊpɒp] *n* boisson gazeuse faiblement alcoolisée.

alcove ['ælkəʊv] *n* alcôve *f*.

alderman ['ɔːldəmən] (*pl* -men [-mən]) *n* conseiller *m* municipal.

ale [eɪl] *n* bière *f*.

alert [ə'lɜːt] ⋄ *adj* **1.** [vigilant] vigilant(e) - **2.** [perceptive] vif (vive), éveillé(e) - **3.** [aware] : **to be alert to** être conscient(e) de. ⋄ *n* [warning] alerte *f* ; **on the alert**

[watchful] sur le qui-vive ; MIL en état d'alerte. ◇ *vt* alerter ; **to alert sb to sthg** avertir qqn de qqch.

A level (*abbrev of* **Advanced level**) *n* ≃ baccalauréat *m*.

alfresco [æl'freskəʊ] *adj & adv* en plein air.

algae ['ældʒiː] *npl* algues *fpl*.

algebra ['ældʒɪbrə] *n* algèbre *f*.

Algeria [æl'dʒɪərɪə] *n* Algérie *f*.

alias ['eɪlɪəs] ◇ *adv* alias. ◇ *n* (*pl* -es [-iːz]) 1. faux nom *m*, nom *m* d'emprunt - 2. COMPUT [in e-mail, on desktop] alias *m*.

alibi ['ælɪbaɪ] *n* alibi *m*.

alien ['eɪljən] ◇ *adj* 1. [gen] étranger(ère) - 2. [from outer space] extraterrestre. ◇ *n* 1. [from outer space] extraterrestre *mf* - 2. LAW [foreigner] étranger *m*, -ère *f*.

alienate ['eɪljəneɪt] *vt* aliéner.

alight [ə'laɪt] ◇ *adj* allumé(e), en feu. ◇ *vi* 1. [bird etc] se poser - 2. [from bus, train] : **to alight from** descendre de.

align [ə'laɪn] *vt* [line up] aligner.

alike [ə'laɪk] ◇ *adj* semblable. ◇ *adv* de la même façon ; **to look alike** se ressembler.

alimony ['ælɪmənɪ] *n* pension *f* alimentaire.

alive [ə'laɪv] *adj* 1. [living] vivant(e), en vie - 2. [practice, tradition] vivace ; **to keep alive** préserver - 3. [lively] plein(e) de vitalité ; **to come alive** [story, description] prendre vie ; [person, place] s'animer.

alkali ['ælkəlaɪ] (*pl* -s *or* -es) *n* alcali *m*.

all [ɔːl] ◇ *adj* 1. (*with sg noun*) tout (toute) ; **all day/night/evening** toute la journée/la nuit/la soirée ; **all the drink** toute la boisson ; **all the time** tout le temps - 2. (*with pl noun*) tous (toutes) ; **all the boxes** toutes les boîtes ; **all men** tous les hommes ; **all three died** ils sont morts tous les trois, tous les trois sont morts. ◇ *pron* 1. (*sg*) [the whole amount] tout *m* ; **she drank it all, she drank all of it** elle a tout bu - 2. (*pl*) [everybody, everything] tous (toutes) ; **all of them came, they all came** ils sont tous venus - 3. (*with superl*)... **of all**... de tous (toutes) ; **I like this one best of all** je préfère celui-ci entre tous - 4. : **above all** ▶ **above** ; **after all** ▶ **after** ; **at all** ▶ **at**. ◇ *adv* 1. [entirely] complètement ; **I'd forgotten all about that** j'avais complètement oublié cela ; **all alone** tout seul (toute seule) - 2. [in sport, competitions] : **the score is five all** le score est cinq partout - 3. (*with compar*) **to run all the faster** courir d'autant plus vite ; **all the better** d'autant mieux. ◆ **all but** *adv* presque, pratiquement. ◆ **all in all** *adv* dans l'ensemble. ◆ **in all** *adv* en tout.

Allah ['ælə] *n* Allah *m*.

all-around *US* = **all-round**.

allay [ə'leɪ] *vt* [fears, anger] apaiser, calmer ; [doubts] dissiper.

all clear *n* signal *m* de fin d'alerte ; *fig* feu *m* vert.

allegation [ˌælɪ'geɪʃn] *n* allégation *f*.

allege [ə'ledʒ] *vt* prétendre, alléguer ; **she is alleged to have done it** on prétend qu'elle l'a fait.

allegedly [ə'ledʒɪdlɪ] *adv* prétendument.

allegiance [ə'liːdʒəns] *n* allégeance *f*.

allergic [ə'lɜːdʒɪk] *adj* : **allergic (to)** allergique (à).

allergy ['ælədʒɪ] *n* allergie *f* ; **to have an allergy to sthg** être allergique à qqch.

alleviate [ə'liːvɪeɪt] *vt* apaiser, soulager.

alley(way) ['ælɪ(weɪ)] *n* [street] ruelle *f* ; [in garden] allée *f*.

alliance [ə'laɪəns] *n* alliance *f*.

allied ['ælaɪd] *adj* 1. MIL allié(e) - 2. [related] connexe.

alligator ['ælɪgeɪtər] (*pl* **alligator** *OR* -s) *n* alligator *m*.

all-important *adj* capital(e), crucial(e).

all-in *adj* *UK* [price] global(e). ◆ **all in** *adv* [inclusive] tout compris.

all-night *adj* [party etc] qui dure toute la nuit ; [bar etc] ouvert(e) toute la nuit.

allocate ['æləkeɪt] *vt* [money, resources] : **to allocate sthg (to sb)** attribuer qqch (à qqn).

allot [ə'lɒt] *vt* [job] assigner ; [money, resources] attribuer ; [time] allouer.

allotment [ə'lɒtmənt] *n* 1. *UK* [garden] jardin *m* ouvrier (*loué par la commune*) - 2. [sharing out] attribution *f* - 3. [share] part *f*.

allow [ə'laʊ] *vt* 1. [permit - activity, behaviour] autoriser, permettre ; **to allow sb to do sthg** permettre à qqn de faire qqch, autoriser qqn à faire qqch - 2. [set aside - money, time] prévoir - 3. [concede] : **to allow that**... admettre que... ◆ **allow for** *vt insep* tenir compte de.

allowance [ə'laʊəns] *n* 1. *UK* [money received] indemnité *f* - 2. *US* [pocket money] argent *m* de poche - 3. [excuse] : **to make allowances for sb** faire preuve d'indulgence envers qqn ; **to make allowances for sthg** prendre qqch en considération.

alloy ['ælɔɪ] *n* alliage *m*.

all right ◇ *adv* bien ; [in answer - yes] d'accord. ◇ *adj* 1. [healthy] en bonne santé ; [unharmed] sain et sauf (saine et sauve) - 2. *inf* [acceptable, satisfactory] : **it was all right** c'était pas mal ; **that's all right** [never mind] ce n'est pas grave.

all-round UK, **all-around** US adj [multi-skilled] doué(e) dans tous les domaines.

all-terrain vehicle [ɔːltəˌreɪnˈviːɪkl] n véhicule m tout terrain, 4x4 m.

all-time adj [record] sans précédent.

allude [əˈluːd] vi : **to allude to** faire allusion à.

alluring [əˈljʊərɪŋ] adj séduisant(e).

allusion [əˈluːʒn] n allusion f.

ally <> n [ˈælaɪ] allié m, -e f. <> vt : **to ally o.s. with** s'allier à.

almighty [ɔːlˈmaɪtɪ] adj inf [noise] terrible.

almond [ˈɑːmənd] n [nut] amande f.

almost [ˈɔːlməʊst] adv presque ; **I almost missed the bus** j'ai failli rater le bus.

alms [ɑːmz] npl dated aumône f.

aloft [əˈlɒft] adv [in the air] en l'air.

alone [əˈləʊn] <> adj seul(e). <> adv seul ; **to leave sthg alone** ne pas toucher à qqch ; **leave me alone!** laisse-moi tranquille!

along [əˈlɒŋ] <> adv : **to walk along** se promener ; **to move along** avancer ; **can I come along (with you)?** est-ce que je peux venir (avec vous)? <> prep le long de ; **to run/walk along the street** courir/marcher le long de la rue. ● **all along** adv depuis le début. ● **along with** prep ainsi que.

alongside [əˌlɒŋˈsaɪd] <> prep le long de, à côté de ; [person] à côté de. <> adv bord à bord.

aloof [əˈluːf] <> adj distant(e). <> adv : **to remain aloof (from)** garder ses distances (vis-à-vis de).

aloud [əˈlaʊd] adv à voix haute, tout haut.

alphabet [ˈælfəbet] n alphabet m.

alphabetical [ˌælfəˈbetɪkl] adj alphabétique.

Alps [ælps] npl : **the Alps** les Alpes fpl.

already [ɔːlˈredɪ] adv déjà.

alright [ˌɔːlˈraɪt] = **all right**.

Alsace [ælˈsæs] n Alsace f.

Alsatian [ælˈseɪʃn] n UK [dog] berger m allemand.

also [ˈɔːlsəʊ] adv aussi.

altar [ˈɔːltər] n autel m.

alter [ˈɔːltər] <> vt changer, modifier. <> vi changer.

alteration [ˌɔːltəˈreɪʃn] n modification f, changement m.

alternate <> adj [UK ɔːlˈtɜːnət, US ˈɔːltərnət] alterné(e), alternatif(ive) ; **alternate days** tous les deux jours, un jour sur deux. <> vt [ˈɔːltərneɪt] faire alterner. <> vi [ˈɔːltərneɪt] : **to alternate (with)** alterner (avec) ; **to alternate between sthg and sthg** passer de qqch à qqch.

alternately [ɔːlˈtɜːnətlɪ] adv alternativement.

alternating current [ˈɔːltəneɪtɪŋ-] n courant m alternatif.

alternative [ɔːlˈtɜːnətɪv] <> adj 1. [different] autre - 2. [non-traditional - society] parallèle ; [- art, energy] alternatif(ive). <> n 1. [between two solutions] alternative f - 2. [other possibility] : **alternative (to)** solution f de remplacement (à) ; **to have no alternative but to do sthg** ne pas avoir d'autre choix que de faire qqch.

alternatively [ɔːlˈtɜːnətɪvlɪ] adv ou bien.

alternative medicine n médecine f parallèle OR douce.

alternator [ˈɔːltəneɪtər] n ELEC alternateur m.

although [ɔːlˈðəʊ] conj bien que (+ subjunctive).

altitude [ˈæltɪtjuːd] n altitude f.

alto [ˈæltəʊ] (pl -s) n 1. [male voice] haute-contre f - 2. [female voice] contralto m.

altogether [ˌɔːltəˈgeðər] adv 1. [completely] entièrement, tout à fait - 2. [considering all things] tout compte fait - 3. [in all] en tout.

aluminium UK [ˌæljʊˈmɪnɪəm], **aluminum** US [əˈluːmɪnəm] <> n aluminium m. <> comp en aluminium.

always [ˈɔːlweɪz] adv toujours.

always-on [ˌɔːlweɪzˈɒn] adj permanent(e).

Alzheimer's (disease) [ˈælts,haɪməz -] n maladie f d'Alzheimer.

am [æm] ► **be**.

a.m. (abbrev of ante meridiem) : **at 3 a.m.** à 3h (du matin).

AM (abbrev of amplitude modulation) n AM f.

amalgamate [əˈmælgəmeɪt] vt & vi [unite] fusionner.

amass [əˈmæs] vt amasser.

amateur [ˈæmətər] <> adj amateur (inv) ; pej d'amateur Québec. <> n amateur m.

amateurish [ˌæmətəˈrɪʃ] adj d'amateur.

amaze [əˈmeɪz] vt étonner, stupéfier.

amazed [əˈmeɪzd] adj stupéfait(e).

amazement [əˈmeɪzmənt] n stupéfaction f.

amazing [əˈmeɪzɪŋ] adj 1. [surprising] étonnant(e), ahurissant(e) - 2. [wonderful] excellent(e).

Amazon [ˈæməzn] n 1. [river] : **the Amazon** l'Amazone f - 2. [region] : **the Amazon (Basin)** l'Amazonie f ; **the Amazon rain forest** la forêt amazonienne.

ambassador [æm'bæsədəʳ] *n* ambassadeur *m*, -drice *f*.

amber ['æmbəʳ] *n* [substance] ambre *m*.

ambiguous [æm'bɪgjuəs] *adj* ambigu(ë).

ambition [æm'bɪʃn] *n* ambition *f*.

ambitious [æm'bɪʃəs] *adj* ambitieux(euse).

amble ['æmbl] *vi* déambuler.

ambulance ['æmbjʊləns] *n* ambulance *f*.

ambush ['æmbʊʃ] <> *n* embuscade *f*. <> *vt* tendre une embuscade à.

amenable [ə'mi:nəbl] *adj* : **amenable (to)** ouvert(e) (à).

amend [ə'mend] *vt* modifier ; [law] amender. ➡ **amends** *npl* : **to make amends (for)** se racheter (pour).

amendment [ə'mendmənt] *n* modification *f* ; [to law] amendement *m*.

amenities [ə'mi:nətɪz] *npl* [features] agréments *mpl* ; [facilities] équipements *mpl*.

America [ə'merɪkə] *n* Amérique *f* ; **in America** en Amérique.

American [ə'merɪkn] <> *adj* américain(e). <> *n* Américain *m*, -e *f*.

American Indian *n* Indien *m*, -enne *f* d'Amérique, Amérindien *m*, -enne *f*.

American Samoa *n* Samoa américaines *fpl*.

amiable ['eɪmjəbl] *adj* aimable.

amicable ['æmɪkəbl] *adj* amical(e).

amid(st) [ə'mɪd(st)] *prep* au milieu de, parmi.

amiss [ə'mɪs] <> *adj* : **is there anything amiss?** y a-t-il quelque chose qui ne va pas ? <> *adv* : **to take sthg amiss** prendre qqch de travers.

ammonia [ə'məʊnjə] *n* [liquid] ammoniaque *f*.

ammunition [ˌæmjʊ'nɪʃn] *(U) n* **1.** MIL munitions *fpl* - **2.** *fig* [argument] argument *m*.

amnesia [æm'ni:zjə] *n* amnésie *f*.

amnesty ['æmnəstɪ] *n* amnistie *f*.

amok [ə'mɒk] *adv* : **to run amok** être pris(e) d'une crise de folie furieuse.

among [ə'mʌŋ], *US* **amongst** [ə'mʌŋst] *UK prep* parmi, entre ; **among other things** entre autres (choses).

amoral [ˌeɪ'mɒrəl] *adj* amoral(e).

amorous ['æmərəs] *adj* amoureux(euse).

amount [ə'maʊnt] *n* **1.** [quantity] quantité *f* ; **a great amount of** beaucoup de - **2.** [sum of money] somme *f*, montant *m*. ➡ **amount to** *vt insep* **1.** [total] s'élever à - **2.** [be equivalent to] revenir à, équivaloir à.

amp [æmp] *n abbrev of* **ampere**.

ampere ['æmpeəʳ] *n* ampère *m*.

amphibious [æm'fɪbɪəs] *adj* amphibie.

ample ['æmpl] *adj* **1.** [enough] suffisamment de, assez de - **2.** [large] ample.

amplifier ['æmplɪfaɪəʳ] *n* amplificateur *m*.

amputate ['æmpjʊteɪt] *vt & vi* amputer.

Amsterdam [ˌæmstə'dæm] *n* Amsterdam.

Amtrak® ['æmtræk] *n société nationale de chemins de fer aux États-Unis.*

amuck [ə'mʌk] = **amok**.

amuse [ə'mju:z] *vt* **1.** [make laugh] amuser, faire rire - **2.** [entertain] divertir, distraire ; **to amuse o.s. (by doing sthg)** s'occuper (à faire qqch).

amused [ə'mju:zd] *adj* **1.** [laughing] amusé(e) ; **to be amused at** OR **by sthg** trouver qqch amusant - **2.** [entertained] : **to keep o.s. amused** s'occuper.

amusement [ə'mju:zmənt] *n* **1.** [laughter] amusement *m* - **2.** [diversion, game] distraction *f*.

amusement arcade *n UK* galerie *f* de jeux.

amusement park *n* parc *m* d'attractions.

amusing [ə'mju:zɪŋ] *adj* amusant(e).

an *(stressed* [æn]*, unstressed* [ən]*)* ➤ **a**.

anabolic steroid [ˌænə'bɒlɪk-] *n* (stéroïde *m*) anabolisant *m*.

anaemic *UK*, **anemic** *US* [ə'ni:mɪk] *adj* anémique ; *fig & pej* fade, plat(e).

anaesthetic *UK*, **anesthetic** *US* [ˌænɪs'θetɪk] *n* anesthésique *m* ; **under anaesthetic** sous anesthésie ; **local/general anaesthetic** anesthésie *f* locale/générale.

analogue, *US* **analog** ['ænəlɒg] *adj* [watch, clock] analogique.

analogy [ə'nælədʒɪ] *n* analogie *f* ; **by analogy** par analogie.

analyse *UK*, **-yze** *US* ['ænəlaɪz] *vt* analyser.

analysis [ə'næləsɪs] *(pl* **-ses** [-si:z]*) n* analyse *f*.

analyst ['ænəlɪst] *n* analyste *mf*.

analytic(al) [ˌænə'lɪtɪk(l)] *adj* analytique.

analyze *US* = **analyse**.

anarchist ['ænəkɪst] *n* anarchiste *mf*.

anarchy ['ænəkɪ] *n* anarchie *f*.

anathema [ə'næθəmə] *n* anathème *m*.

anatomy [ə'nætəmɪ] *n* anatomie *f*.

ANC *(abbrev of* **African National Congress**) *n* ANC *m*.

ancestor ['ænsestəʳ] *n lit & fig* ancêtre *m*.

anchor ['æŋkəʳ] <> *n* **1.** NAUT ancre *f* ; **to drop/weigh anchor** jeter/lever l'ancre - **2.** TV présentateur *m*, -trice *f*. <> *vt* **1.** [secure] ancrer - **2.** TV présenter. <> *vi* NAUT jeter l'ancre.

anchovy ['æntʃəvɪ] *(pl* **anchovy** OR **-ies**) *n* anchois *m*.

ancient ['eɪnʃənt] adj 1. [monument etc] historique ; [custom] ancien(enne) - 2. hum [car etc] antique ; [person] vieux (vieille).

ancillary [æn'sɪlərɪ] adj auxiliaire.

and (stressed [ænd], unstressed [ənd] OR [ən]) conj 1. [as well as, plus] et - 2. [in numbers] : one hundred and eighty cent quatre-vingts ; six and a half six et demi - 3. [to] : **come and look!** venez voir ! ; **try and come** essayez de venir ; **wait and see** vous verrez bien. ➤ **and so on, and so forth** adv et ainsi de suite.

Andes ['ændiːz] npl : **the Andes** les Andes fpl.

Andorra [æn'dɔːrə] n Andorre f.

anecdote ['ænɪkdəʊt] n anecdote f.

anemic US = **anaemic**.

anesthetic US = **anaesthetic**.

anew [ə'njuː] adv : **to start anew** recommencer (à zéro).

angel ['eɪndʒəl] n ange m.

anger ['æŋgər] <> n colère f. <> vt fâcher, irriter.

angina [æn'dʒaɪnə] n angine f de poitrine.

angle ['æŋgl] n 1. [gen] angle m ; **at an angle** de travers, en biais - 2. [point of view] point m de vue, angle m.

angler ['æŋglər] n pêcheur m (à la ligne).

Anglican ['æŋglɪkən] <> adj anglican(e). <> n anglican m, -e f.

angling ['æŋglɪŋ] n pêche f à la ligne.

angry ['æŋgrɪ] adj [person] en colère, fâché(e) ; [words, quarrel] violent(e) ; **to be angry with** OR **at sb** être en colère OR fâché contre qqn ; **to get angry** se mettre en colère, se fâcher.

anguish ['æŋgwɪʃ] n angoisse f.

angular ['æŋgjʊlər] adj anguleux(euse).

animal ['ænɪml] <> n animal m ; pej brute f. <> adj animal(e).

animate ['ænɪmət] adj animé(e), vivant(e).

animated ['ænɪmeɪtɪd] adj animé(e).

aniseed ['ænɪsiːd] n anis m.

ankle ['æŋkl] <> n cheville f. <> comp : **ankle socks** socquettes fpl ; **ankle boots** bottines fpl.

annex ['æneks], UK **annexe** n [building] annexe f.

annihilate [ə'naɪəleɪt] vt anéantir, annihiler.

anniversary [,ænɪ'vɜːsərɪ] n anniversaire m.

announce [ə'naʊns] vt annoncer.

announcement [ə'naʊnsmənt] n 1. [statement] déclaration f ; [in newspaper] avis m - 2. (U) [act of stating] annonce f.

announcer [ə'naʊnsər] n RADIO & TV speaker m, speakerine f.

annoy [ə'nɔɪ] vt agacer, contrarier.

annoyance [ə'nɔɪəns] n contrariété f.

annoyed [ə'nɔɪd] adj mécontent(e), agacé(e) ; **to get annoyed** se fâcher ; **to be annoyed at sthg** être contrarié(e) par qqch ; **to be annoyed with sb** être fâché(e) contre qqn.

annoying [ə'nɔɪɪŋ] adj agaçant(e).

annual ['ænjʊəl] <> adj annuel(elle). <> n 1. [plant] plante f annuelle - 2. [book - gen] publication f annuelle ; [- for children] album m.

annual general meeting n UK assemblée f générale annuelle.

annul [ə'nʌl] vt annuler ; [law] abroger.

annum ['ænəm] n : **per annum** par an.

anomaly [ə'nɒməlɪ] n anomalie f.

anonymous [ə'nɒnɪməs] adj anonyme.

anorak ['ænəræk] n anorak m.

anorexia (nervosa) [,ænə'reksɪə (nɜː'vəʊsə)] n anorexie f mentale.

anorexic [,ænə'reksɪk] <> adj anorexique. <> n anorexique mf.

another [ə'nʌðər] <> adj 1. [additional] : **another apple** encore une pomme, une pomme de plus, une autre pomme ; **in another few minutes** dans quelques minutes ; **(would you like) another drink?** (voulez-vous) encore un verre ? - 2. [different] : **another job** un autre travail. <> pron 1. [additional one] un autre (une autre), encore un (encore une) ; **one after another** l'un après l'autre (l'une après l'autre) - 2. [different one] un autre (une autre) ; **one another** l'un l'autre (l'une l'autre).

answer ['ɑːnsər] <> n 1. [gen] réponse f ; **in answer to** en réponse à - 2. [to problem] solution f. <> vt répondre à ; **to answer the door** aller ouvrir la porte ; **to answer the phone** répondre au téléphone. <> vi [reply] répondre. ➤ **answer back** <> vt sep répondre à. <> vi répondre. ➤ **answer for** vt insep être responsable de, répondre de.

answerable ['ɑːnsərəbl] adj : **answerable to sb/for sthg** responsable devant qqn/de qqch.

answering machine ['ɑːnsərɪŋ-] n répondeur m.

ant [ænt] n fourmi f.

antagonism [æn'tægənɪzm] n antagonisme m, hostilité f.

antagonize, UK **-ise** [æn'tægənaɪz] vt éveiller l'hostilité de.

Antarctic [æn'tɑːktɪk] <> n : **the Antarctic** l'Antarctique m. <> adj antarctique.

antelope ['æntɪləʊp] (*pl* antelope OR -s) *n* antilope *f*.

antenatal [ˌæntɪ'neɪtl] *adj* prénatal(e).

antenatal clinic *n* service *m* de consultation prénatale.

antenna [æn'tenə] *n* **1.** (*pl* antennae [-ni:]) [of insect] antenne *f* - **2.** (*pl* -s) *US* [for TV, radio] antenne *f*.

anthem ['ænθəm] *n* hymne *m*.

anthology [æn'θɒlədʒɪ] *n* anthologie *f*.

antibiotic [ˌæntɪbaɪ'ɒtɪk] *n* antibiotique *m*.

antibody ['æntɪˌbɒdɪ] *n* anticorps *m*.

anticipate [æn'tɪsɪpeɪt] *vt* **1.** [expect] s'attendre à, prévoir - **2.** [request, movement] anticiper ; [competitor] prendre de l'avance sur - **3.** [look forward to] savourer à l'avance.

anticipation [ænˌtɪsɪ'peɪʃn] *n* [expectation] attente *f* ; [eagerness] impatience *f* ; **in anticipation of** en prévision de.

anticlimax [ˌæntɪ'klaɪmæks] *n* déception *f*.

anticlockwise [ˌæntɪ'klɒkwaɪz] *adj & adv* UK dans le sens inverse des aiguilles d'une montre.

antics ['æntɪks] *npl* **1.** [of children, animals] gambades *fpl* - **2.** *pej* [of politicians etc] bouffonneries *fpl*.

anticyclone [ˌæntɪ'saɪkləʊn] *n* anticyclone *m*.

antidepressant [ˌæntɪdɪ'presnt] *n* antidépresseur *m*.

antidote ['æntɪdəʊt] *n lit & fig* : **antidote (to)** antidote *m* (contre).

antifreeze ['æntɪfriːz] *n* antigel *m*.

antihistamine [ˌæntɪ'hɪstəmɪn] *n* antihistaminique *m*.

antiperspirant [ˌæntɪ'pɜːspərənt] *n* déodorant *m*, antipreperspirant.

antiquated ['æntɪkweɪtɪd] *adj* dépassé(e).

antique [æn'tiːk] <> *adj* ancien(enne). <> *n* [object] objet *m* ancien ; [piece of furniture] meuble *m* ancien.

antique shop *n* magasin *m* d'antiquités.

anti-Semitism [-semɪtɪzəm] *n* antisémitisme *m*.

antiseptic [ˌæntɪ'septɪk] <> *adj* antiseptique. <> *n* désinfectant *m*.

antisocial [ˌæntɪ'səʊʃl] *adj* **1.** [against society] antisocial(e) - **2.** [unsociable] peu sociable, sauvage.

anus ['eɪnəs] *n* anus *m*.

anvil ['ænvɪl] *n* enclume *f*.

anxiety [æŋ'zaɪətɪ] *n* **1.** [worry] anxiété *f* - **2.** [cause of worry] souci *m* - **3.** [keenness] désir *m* farouche.

anxious ['æŋkʃəs] *adj* **1.** [worried]

anxieux(euse), très inquiet(ète) ; **to be anxious about** se faire du souci au sujet de - **2.** [keen] : **to be anxious to do sthg** tenir à faire qqch ; **to be anxious that** tenir à ce que (+ *subjunctive*).

any ['enɪ] <> *adj* **1.** *(with negative)* de, d' ; **I haven't got any money/tickets** je n'ai pas d'argent/de billets ; **he never does any work** il ne travaille jamais - **2.** [some - with sg noun] du, de l', de la ; [- with pl noun] des ; **have you got any money/milk/cousins?** est-ce que vous avez de l'argent/du lait/des cousins? - **3.** [no matter which] n'importe quel (n'importe quelle) ; **any box will do** n'importe quelle boîte fera l'affaire. <> *pron* **1.** *(with negative)* en ; **I didn't buy any (of them)** je n'en ai pas acheté ; **I didn't know any of the guests** je ne connaissais aucun des invités - **2.** [some] en ; **do you have any?** est-ce que vous en avez? - **3.** [no matter which one or ones] n'importe lequel (n'importe laquelle) ; **take any you like** prenez n'importe lequel/laquelle, prenez celui/celle que vous voulez. <> *adv* **1.** *(with negative)* **I can't see it any more** je ne le vois plus ; **I can't stand it any longer** je ne peux plus le supporter - **2.** [some, a little] un peu ; **do you want any more potatoes?** voulez-vous encore des pommes de terre? ; **is that any better/different?** est-ce que c'est mieux/différent comme ça? ; *see also* **case**, *see also* **day**, *see also* **moment**, *see also* **rate**.

anybody ['enɪˌbɒdɪ] = anyone.

anyhow ['enɪhaʊ] *adv* **1.** [in spite of that] quand même, néanmoins - **2.** [carelessly] n'importe comment - **3.** [in any case] de toute façon.

any more, *US* anymore *adv* : **they don't live here any more** ils n'habitent plus ici.

anyone ['enɪwʌn] *pron* **1.** *(in negative sentences)* **I didn't see anyone** je n'ai vu personne - **2.** *(in questions)* quelqu'un - **3.** [any person] n'importe qui.

anyplace ['enɪpleɪs] *US* = anywhere.

anything ['enɪθɪŋ] *pron* **1.** *(in negative sentences)* **I didn't see anything** je n'ai rien vu - **2.** *(in questions)* quelque chose ; **anything else?** [in shop] et avec ceci? - **3.** [any object, event] n'importe quoi ; **if anything happens...** s'il arrive quoi que ce soit...

anyway ['enɪweɪ] *adv* [in any case] de toute façon.

anywhere ['enɪweəʳ], *US* anyplace ['enɪpleɪs] *adv* **1.** *(in negative sentences)* **I haven't seen him anywhere** je ne l'ai vu nulle part - **2.** *(in questions)* quelque part - **3.** [any place] n'importe où.

apart [ə'pɑːt] *adv* **1.** [separated] séparé(e), éloigné(e) ; **we're living apart** nous sommes séparés - **2.** [to one side] à l'écart - **3.** [aside] :

joking apart sans plaisanter, plaisanterie à part. **apart from** *prep* **1.** [except for] à part, sauf - **2.** [as well as] en plus de, outre.

apartheid [ə'pɑːtheɪt] *n* apartheid *m*.

apartment [ə'pɑːtmənt] *n* appartement *m*.

apartment building *n* US immeuble *m* (d'habitation).

apathy ['æpəθɪ] *n* apathie *f*.

ape [eɪp] <> *n* singe *m*. <> *vt* singer.

aperitif [əperə'tiːf] *n* apéritif *m*.

aperture ['æpə,tjʊə'] *n* **1.** [hole, opening] orifice *m*, ouverture *f* - **2.** PHOT ouverture *f*.

apex ['eɪpeks] (*pl* **-es** [-iːz] OR **apices** ['eɪpɪsiːz]) *n* sommet *m*.

APEX ['eɪpeks] (*abbrev of* **advance purchase excursion**) *n* : APEX ticket billet *m* APEX.

apices ['eɪpɪsiːz] *npl* ▶ **apex**.

apiece [ə'piːs] *adv* [for each person] chacun(e), par personne ; [for each thing] chacun(e), pièce (*inv*).

apocalypse [ə'pɒkəlɪps] *n* apocalypse *f*.

apologetic [ə,pɒlə'dʒetɪk] *adj* [letter etc] d'excuse ; **to be apologetic about sthg** s'excuser de qqch.

apologize, UK **-ise** [ə'pɒlədʒaɪz] *vi* s'excuser ; **to apologize to sb (for sthg)** faire des excuses à qqn (pour qqch).

apology [ə'pɒlədʒɪ] *n* excuses *fpl*.

apostle [ə'pɒsl] *n* RELIG apôtre *m*.

apostrophe [ə'pɒstrəfɪ] *n* apostrophe *f*.

appal UK, **appall** US [ə'pɔːl] *vt* horrifier.

appalling [ə'pɔːlɪŋ] *adj* épouvantable.

apparatus [,æpə'reɪtəs] (*pl* **apparatus** OR **-es** [-iːz]) *n* **1.** [device] appareil *m*, dispositif *m* - **2.** (*U*) [in gym] agrès *mpl* - **3.** [system, organization] appareil *m*.

apparel [ə'pærəl] *n* US habillement *m*.

apparent [ə'pærənt] *adj* **1.** [evident] évident(e) - **2.** [seeming] apparent(e).

apparently [ə'pærəntlɪ] *adv* **1.** [it seems] à ce qu'il paraît - **2.** [seemingly] apparemment, en apparence.

appeal [ə'piːl] <> *vi* **1.** [request] : **to appeal (to sb for sthg)** lancer un appel (à qqn pour obtenir qqch) - **2.** [make a plea] : **to appeal to** faire appel à - **3.** LAW : **to appeal (against)** faire appel (de) - **4.** [attract, interest] : **to appeal to sb** plaire à qqn ; **it appeals to me** ça me plaît. <> *n* **1.** [request] appel *m* - **2.** LAW appel *m* - **3.** [charm, interest] intérêt *m*, attrait *m*.

appealing [ə'piːlɪŋ] *adj* [attractive] attirant(e), sympathique.

appear [ə'pɪə'] *vi* **1.** [gen] apparaître ; [book] sortir, paraître - **2.** [seem] sembler, paraître ; **to appear to be/do** sembler être/faire ; **it would appear (that)...** il semblerait que... - **3.** [in play, film etc] jouer - **4.** LAW comparaître.

appearance [ə'pɪərəns] *n* **1.** [gen] apparition *f* ; **to make an appearance** se montrer - **2.** [look] apparence *f*, aspect *m*.

appease [ə'piːz] *vt* apaiser.

append [ə'pend] *vt* ajouter ; [signature] apposer.

appendices [ə'pendɪsiːz] *npl* ▶ **appendix**.

appendicitis [ə,pendɪ'saɪtɪs] *n* (*U*) appendicite *f*.

appendix [ə'pendɪks] (*pl* **-dixes** [-dɪksiːz] OR **-dices** [-dɪsiːz]) *n* appendice *m* ; **to have one's appendix out** OR **removed** OR **taken out** US se faire opérer de l'appendicite.

appetite ['æpɪtaɪt] *n* **1.** [for food] : **appetite (for)** appétit *m* (pour) - **2.** *fig* [enthusiasm] : **appetite (for)** goût *m* (de OR pour).

appetizer, UK **-iser** ['æpɪtaɪzə'] *n* [food] amuse-gueule *m inv* ; [drink] apéritif *m*.

appetizing, US **-ising** ['æpɪtaɪzɪŋ] *adj* [food] appétissant(e).

applaud [ə'plɔːd] <> *vt* **1.** [clap] applaudir - **2.** [approve] approuver, applaudir à. <> *vi* applaudir.

applause [ə'plɔːz] *n* (*U*) applaudissements *mpl*.

apple ['æpl] *n* pomme *f*.

apple tree *n* pommier *m*.

appliance [ə'plaɪəns] *n* [device] appareil *m*.

applicable [ə'plɪkəbl] *adj* : **applicable (to)** applicable (à).

applicant ['æplɪkənt] *n* : **applicant (for)** [job] candidat *m*, -e *f* (à) ; [state benefit] demandeur *m*, -euse *f* (de) ; UNIV : **college** US OR **university applicant** candidat à l'inscription à l'université.

application [,æplɪ'keɪʃn] *n* **1.** [gen] application *f* - **2.** [for job etc] : **application (for)** demande *f* (de).

application form *n* [for post] dossier *m* de candidature ; UNIV dossier *m* d'inscription.

applications program [,æplɪ'keɪʃns -] *n* COMPUT programme *m* d'application.

applied [ə'plaɪd] *adj* [science] appliqué(e).

apply [ə'plaɪ] <> *vt* appliquer ; **to apply the brakes** freiner. <> *vi* **1.** [for work, grant] : **to apply (for)** faire une demande (de) ; **to apply to sb (for sthg)** s'adresser à qqn (pour obtenir qqch) ; **to apply for a job** faire une demande d'emploi - **2.** [be relevant] : **to apply (to)** s'appliquer (à), concerner.

appoint [ə'pɔɪnt] *vt* **1.** [to job, position] : **to appoint sb (as sthg)** nommer qqn (qqch) ; **to appoint sb to sthg** nommer qqn à qqch - **2.** [time, place] fixer.

appointment [ə'pɔɪntmənt] *n* **1.** [to job, position] nomination *f*, désignation *f* - **2.** [job, position] poste *m*, emploi *m* - **3.** [arrangement to meet] rendez-vous *m* ; **to make an appointment** prendre un rendez-vous.

apportion [ə'pɔ:ʃn] *vt* répartir.

appraisal [ə'preɪzl] *n* évaluation *f*.

appreciable [ə'pri:ʃəbl] *adj* [difference] sensible ; [amount] appréciable.

appreciate [ə'pri:ʃieɪt] <> *vt* **1.** [value, like] apprécier, aimer - **2.** [recognize, understand] comprendre, se rendre compte de - **3.** [be grateful for] être reconnaissant(e) de. <> *vi* FIN prendre de la valeur.

appreciation [ə,pri:ʃi'eɪʃn] *n* **1.** [liking] contentement *m* - **2.** [understanding] compréhension *f* - **3.** [gratitude] reconnaissance *f*.

appreciative [ə'pri:ʃjətɪv] *adj* [person] reconnaissant(e) ; [remark] élogieux(euse).

apprehensive [,æprɪ'hensɪv] *adj* inquiet(ète) ; **to be apprehensive about sthg** appréhender OR craindre qqch.

apprentice [ə'prentɪs] *n* apprenti *m*, -e *f*.

apprenticeship [ə'prentɪsʃɪp] *n* apprentissage *m*.

approach [ə'prəʊtʃ] <> *n* **1.** [gen] approche *f* - **2.** [method] démarche *f*, approche *f* - **3.** [to person] : **to make an approach to sb** faire une proposition à qqn. <> *vt* **1.** [come near to - place, person, thing] s'approcher de - **2.** [speak to] parler à - **3.** [tackle - problem] aborder. <> *vi* s'approcher.

approachable [ə'prəʊtʃəbl] *adj* accessible.

appropriate <> *adj* [ə'prəʊprɪət] [clothing] convenable ; [action] approprié(e) ; [moment] opportun(e). <> *vt* [ə'prəʊprɪeɪt] **1.** LAW s'approprier - **2.** [allocate] affecter.

approval [ə'pru:vl] *n* approbation *f* ; **on approval** COMM à condition, à l'essai.

approve [ə'pru:v] <> *vi* : **to approve (of sthg)** approuver (qqch). <> *vt* [ratify] approuver, ratifier.

approx. [ə'prɒks] (*abbrev of* **approximately**) approx., env.

approximate *adj* [ə'prɒksɪmət] approximatif(ive).

approximately [ə'prɒksɪmətlɪ] *adv* à peu près, environ.

apricot ['eɪprɪkɒt] *n* abricot *m*.

April ['eɪprəl] *n* avril *m* ; *see also* **September**.

April Fools' Day *n* le 1er avril.

apron ['eɪprən] *n* [clothing] tablier *m*.

apt [æpt] *adj* **1.** [pertinent] pertinent(e), approprié(e) - **2.** [likely] : **to be apt to do sthg** avoir tendance à faire qqch.

aptitude ['æptɪtju:d] *n* aptitude *f*, disposition *f* ; **to have an aptitude for** avoir des dispositions pour.

aptly ['æptlɪ] *adv* avec justesse, à propos.

aqualung ['ækwəlʌŋ] *n* scaphandre *m* autonome.

aquarium [ə'kweərɪəm] (*pl* **-riums** OR **-ria** [-rɪə]) *n* aquarium *m*.

Aquarius [ə'kweərɪəs] *n* Verseau *m*.

aquarobics [,ækwə'rəʊbɪks] *n* aquagym *f*.

aquatic [ə'kwætɪk] *adj* **1.** [animal, plant] aquatique - **2.** [sport] nautique.

aqueduct ['ækwɪdʌkt] *n* aqueduc *m*.

Arab ['ærəb] <> *adj* arabe. <> *n* [person] Arabe *mf*.

Arabian [ə'reɪbjən] *adj* d'Arabie, arabe.

Arabic ['ærəbɪk] <> *adj* arabe. <> *n* arabe *m*.

Arabic numeral *n* chiffre *m* arabe.

arable ['ærəbl] *adj* arable.

arbitrary ['ɑ:bɪtrərɪ] *adj* arbitraire.

arbitration [,ɑ:bɪ'treɪʃn] *n* arbitrage *m* ; **to go to arbitration** recourir à l'arbitrage.

arcade [ɑ:'keɪd] *n* **1.** [for shopping] galerie *f* marchande - **2.** [covered passage] arcades *fpl* - **3.** US galerie *f* de jeux.

arch [ɑ:tʃ] <> *adj* malicieux(euse), espiègle. <> *n* **1.** ARCHIT arc *m*, voûte *f* - **2.** [of foot] voûte *f* plantaire, cambrure *f*. <> *vt* cambrer, arquer. <> *vi* former une voûte.

archaeologist [,ɑ:kɪ'ɒlədʒɪst] *n* archéologue *mf*.

archaeology [,ɑ:kɪ'ɒlədʒɪ] *n* archéologie *f*.

archaic [ɑ:'keɪɪk] *adj* archaïque.

archbishop [,ɑ:tʃ'bɪʃəp] *n* archevêque *m*.

archenemy [,ɑ:tʃ'enɪmɪ] *n* ennemi *m* numéro un.

archeology [,ɑ:kɪ'ɒlədʒɪ] = **archaeology**.

archer ['ɑ:tʃər] *n* archer *m*.

archery ['ɑ:tʃərɪ] *n* tir *m* à l'arc.

archetypal [,ɑ:kɪ'taɪpl] *adj* typique.

architect ['ɑ:kɪtekt] *n* lit & fig architecte *mf*.

architecture ['ɑ:kɪtektʃər] *n* [gen & COMPUT] architecture *f*.

archway ['ɑ:tʃweɪ] *n* passage *m* voûté.

ardent ['ɑ:dənt] *adj* fervent(e), passionné(e).

arduous ['ɑ:djʊəs] *adj* ardu(e).

are (*weak form* [ər], *strong form* [ɑ:r]) ➤ **be**.

area ['eərɪə] *n* **1.** [region] région *f* ; **parking area** aire *f* de stationnement ; **in the area of** [approximately] environ, à peu près - **2.** [surface size] aire *f*, superficie *f* - **3.** [of knowledge, interest etc] domaine *m*.

area code *n* US indicatif *m* de zone.

arena [əˈriːnə] *n lit & fig* arène *f*.

aren't [ɑːnt] = are not.

Argentina [ˌɑːdʒənˈtiːnə] *n* Argentine *f*.

Argentine [ˈɑːdʒəntaɪn], **Argentinian** [ˌɑːdʒənˈtɪnɪən] <> *adj* argentin(e). <> *n* Argentin *m*, -e *f*.

arguably [ˈɑːgjuəblɪ] *adv* : she's arguably the best on peut soutenir qu'elle est la meilleure.

argue [ˈɑːgjuː] <> *vi* 1. [quarrel] : to argue (with sb about sthg) se disputer (avec qqn à propos de qqch) - 2. [reason] : to argue (for/against) argumenter (pour/contre). <> *vt* débattre de, discuter de ; to argue that soutenir OR maintenir que.

argument [ˈɑːgjəmənt] *n* 1. [quarrel] dispute *f* - 2. [reason] argument *m* - 3. *(U)* [reasoning] discussion *f*, débat *m*.

argumentative [ˌɑːgjʊˈmentətɪv] *adj* querelleur(euse), batailleur(euse).

arid [ˈærɪd] *adj lit & fig* aride.

Aries [ˈeəriːz] *n* Bélier *m*.

arise [əˈraɪz] (*pt* arose, *pp* arisen [əˈrɪzn]) *vi* [appear] surgir, survenir ; to arise from résulter de, provenir de ; if the need arises si le besoin se fait sentir.

aristocrat [*UK* ˈærɪstəkræt, *US* əˈrɪstəkræt] *n* aristocrate *mf*.

arithmetic [əˈrɪθmətɪk] *n* arithmétique *f*.

ark [ɑːk] *n* arche *f*.

arm [ɑːm] <> *n* 1. [of person, chair] bras *m* ; arm in arm bras dessus bras dessous ; to keep sb at arm's length *UK fig* tenir qqn à distance ; to twist sb's arm *fig* forcer la main à qqn - 2. [of garment] manche *f*. <> *vt* armer. **arms** *npl* armes *fpl* ; to take up arms prendre les armes ; to be up in arms about sthg s'élever contre qqch.

armaments [ˈɑːməmənts] *npl* [weapons] matériel *m* de guerre, armements *mpl*.

arm candy [ˈɑːmkændɪ] *n inf pej* jeune et jolie compagne *f*.

armchair [ˈɑːmtʃeəʳ] *n* fauteuil *m*.

armed [ɑːmd] *adj lit & fig* : armed (with) armé(e) (de).

armed forces *npl* forces *fpl* armées.

armhole [ˈɑːmhəʊl] *n* emmanchure *f*.

armour *UK*, **armor** *US* [ˈɑːməʳ] *n* 1. [for person] armure *f* - 2. [for military vehicle] blindage *m*.

armoured car *UK*, **armored car** *US* [ˌɑːməd-] *n* voiture *f* blindée.

armoury *UK*, **armory** *US* [ˈɑːmərɪ] *n* arsenal *m*.

armpit [ˈɑːmpɪt] *n* aisselle *f*.

armrest [ˈɑːmrest] *n* accoudoir *m*.

arms control [ˈɑːmz-] *n* contrôle *m* des armements.

army [ˈɑːmɪ] *n lit & fig* armée *f*.

aroma [əˈrəʊmə] *n* arôme *m*.

arose [əˈrəʊz] *pt* ➤ arise.

around [əˈraʊnd] <> *adv* 1. [about, round] : to walk around se promener ; to lie around [clothes etc] traîner - 2. [on all sides] (tout) autour - 3. [near] dans les parages - 4. [in circular movement] : to turn around se retourner ; he has been around *inf* il n'est pas né d'hier, il a de l'expérience. <> *prep* 1. [gen] autour de ; to walk around a garden/town faire le tour d'un jardin/d'une ville ; all around the country dans tout le pays - 2. [near] : around here par ici - 3. [approximately] environ, à peu près.

arouse [əˈraʊz] *vt* 1. [excite - feeling] éveiller, susciter ; [- person] exciter - 2. [wake] réveiller.

arrange [əˈreɪndʒ] *vt* 1. [flowers, books, furniture] arranger, disposer - 2. [event, meeting etc] organiser, fixer ; to arrange to do sthg convenir de faire qqch - 3. MUS arranger.

arrangement [əˈreɪndʒmənt] *n* 1. [agreement] accord *m*, arrangement *m* ; to come to an arrangement s'entendre, s'arranger - 2. [of furniture, books] arrangement *m* - 3. MUS arrangement *m*. **arrangements** *npl* dispositions *fpl*, préparatifs *mpl*.

array [əˈreɪ] <> *n* [of objects] étalage *m*. <> *vt* [ornaments etc] disposer.

arrears [əˈrɪəz] *npl* [money owed] arriéré *m* ; to be in arrears [late] être en retard ; [owing money] avoir des arriérés.

arrest [əˈrest] <> *n* [by police] arrestation *f* ; under arrest en état d'arrestation. <> *vt* 1. [gen] arrêter - 2. *fml* [sb's attention] attirer, retenir.

arrival [əˈraɪvl] *n* 1. [gen] arrivée *f* ; late arrival [of train etc] retard *m* - 2. [person - at airport, hotel] arrivant *m*, -e *f* ; new arrival [- person] nouveau venu *m*, nouvelle venue *f* ; [- baby] nouveau-né *m*, nouveau-née *f*.

arrive [əˈraɪv] *vi* arriver ; [baby] être né(e) ; to arrive at [conclusion, decision] arriver à.

arrogant [ˈærəgənt] *adj* arrogant(e).

arrow [ˈærəʊ] *n* flèche *f*.

arse *UK* [ɑːs], **ass** *US* [æs] *n v inf* cul *m*.

arsenal [ˈɑːsənl] *n* arsenal *m*.

arsenic [ˈɑːsnɪk] *n* arsenic *m*.

arson [ˈɑːsn] *n* incendie *m* criminel OR volontaire.

art [ɑːt] <> *n* art *m*. <> *comp* [exhibition] d'art ; [college] des beaux-arts ; art student étudiant *m*, -e *f* d'une école des beaux-arts. **arts** *npl* **1.** UK SCH & UNIV lettres *fpl* - **2.** [fine arts] : **the arts** les arts *mpl*.

artefact ['ɑːtɪfækt] = artifact.

artery ['ɑːtərɪ] *n* artère *f*.

art gallery *n* [public] musée *m* d'art ; [for selling paintings] galerie *f* d'art.

art house *n* cinéma *m* d'art et d'essai.

art-house *adj* [cinema, film] d'art et d'essai.

arthritis [ɑː'θraɪtɪs] *n* arthrite *f*.

artichoke ['ɑːtɪtʃəʊk] *n* artichaut *m*.

article ['ɑːtɪkl] *n* article *m* ; **article of clothing** vêtement *m*.

articulate <> *adj* [ɑː'tɪkjʊlət] [person] qui sait s'exprimer ; [speech] net (nette), distinct(e). <> *vt* [ɑː'tɪkjʊleɪt] [thought, wish] formuler.

articulated lorry [ɑː'tɪkjʊleɪtɪd-] *n* UK semi-remorque *m*.

artifact ['ɑːtɪfækt] *n* objet *m* fabriqué.

artificial [ˌɑːtɪ'fɪʃl] *adj* **1.** [not natural] artificiel(elle) - **2.** [insincere] affecté(e).

artillery [ɑː'tɪlərɪ] *n* artillerie *f*.

artist ['ɑːtɪst] *n* artiste *m*.

artiste [ɑː'tiːst] *n* artiste *mf*.

artistic [ɑː'tɪstɪk] *adj* [person] artiste ; [style etc] artistique.

artistry ['ɑːtɪstrɪ] *n* art *m*, talent *m* artistique.

artless ['ɑːtlɪs] *adj* naturel(elle), ingénu(e).

as (stressed [æz], unstressed [əz]) <> *conj* **1.** [referring to time] comme, alors que ; **I'm speaking as your friend** je te parle en ami ; **she works as a nurse** elle est infirmière - **2.** [referring to attitude, reaction] : **it came as a shock** cela nous a fait un choc. <> *adv* (in comparisons) **as rich as** aussi riche que ; **as red as a tomato** rouge comme une tomate ; **he's as tall as I am** il est aussi grand que moi ; **twice as big as** deux fois plus gros que ; **as much/many as** autant que ; **as much wine/many chocolates as** autant de vin/de chocolats que. **as for** *prep* quant à. **as from**, **as of** *prep* dès, à partir de. **as if**, **as though** *conj* comme si ; **it looks as if** OR **as though it will rain** on dirait qu'il va pleuvoir. **as to** *prep* **1.** [concerning] en ce qui concerne, au sujet de - **2.** = **as for**.

asafoetida, **asafetida** US [ˌæsəfəʊ'etɪdə] *n* ase *f* fétide.

asbestos [æs'bestəs] *n* asbeste *m*, amiante *m*.

ascend [ə'send] *vt* & *vi* monter.

ascendant [ə'sendənt] *n* : **to be in the ascendant** avoir le dessus.

ascent [ə'sent] *n lit* & *fig* ascension *f*.

ascertain [ˌæsə'teɪn] *vt* établir.

ascribe [ə'skraɪb] *vt* : **to ascribe sthg to** attribuer qqch à ; [blame] imputer qqch à.

ash [æʃ] *n* **1.** [from cigarette, fire] cendre *f* - **2.** [tree] frêne *m*.

ashamed [ə'ʃeɪmd] *adj* honteux(euse), confus(e) ; **to be ashamed of** avoir honte de ; **to be ashamed to do sthg** avoir honte de faire qqch.

ashen-faced ['æʃn,feɪst] *adj* blême.

ashore [ə'ʃɔːr] *adv* à terre.

ashtray ['æʃtreɪ] *n* cendrier *m*.

Ash Wednesday *n* le mercredi des Cendres.

Asia [UK 'eɪʃə, US 'eɪʒə] *n* Asie *f*.

Asian [UK 'eɪʃn, US 'eɪʒn] <> *adj* asiatique. <> *n* [person] Asiatique *mf*.

aside [ə'saɪd] <> *adv* **1.** [to one side] de côté ; **to move aside** s'écarter ; **to take sb aside** prendre qqn à part - **2.** [apart] à part ; **aside from** à l'exception de. <> *n* **1.** [in play] aparté *m* - **2.** [remark] réflexion *f*, commentaire *m*.

ask [ɑːsk] <> *vt* **1.** [gen] demander ; **to ask sb sthg** demander qqch à qqn ; **he asked me my name** il m'a demandé mon nom ; **to ask sb for sthg** demander qqch à qqn ; **to ask sb to do sthg** demander à qqn de faire qqch - **2.** [put - question] poser - **3.** [invite] inviter. <> *vi* demander. **ask after** *vt insep* demander des nouvelles de. **ask for** *vt insep* **1.** [person] demander à voir - **2.** [thing] demander.

askance [ə'skæns] *adv* : **to look askance at sb** regarder qqn d'un air désapprobateur.

askew [ə'skjuː] *adj* [not straight] de travers.

asking price ['ɑːskɪŋ-] *n* prix *m* demandé.

asleep [ə'sliːp] *adj* endormi(e) ; **to fall asleep** s'endormir.

asparagus [ə'spærəgəs] *n* (U) asperges *fpl*.

aspect ['æspekt] *n* **1.** [gen] aspect *m* - **2.** [of building] orientation *f*.

aspersions [ə'spɜːʃnz] *npl* : **to cast aspersions on** jeter le discrédit sur.

asphalt ['æsfælt] *n* asphalte *m*.

asphyxiate [əs'fɪksɪeɪt] *vt* asphyxier.

aspiration [ˌæspə'reɪʃn] *n* aspiration *f*.

aspire [ə'spaɪər] *vi* : **to aspire to sthg/to do sthg** aspirer à qqch/à faire qqch.

aspirin ['æsprɪn] *n* aspirine *f*.

ass [æs] *n* **1.** [donkey] âne *m* - **2.** *inf* [idiot] imbécile *mf*, idiot *m*, -e *f* - **3.** *US vulg* = **arse**.

assailant [ə'seɪlənt] *n* assaillant *m*, -e *f*.

assassin [ə'sæsɪn] *n* assassin *m*.

assassinate [ə'sæsɪneɪt] *vt* assassiner.

assassination [ə,sæsɪ'neɪʃn] *n* assassinat *m*.

assault [ə'sɔːlt] ⬥ *n* **1.** MIL : **assault (on)** assaut *m* (de), attaque *f* (de) - **2.** [physical attack] : **assault (on sb)** agression *f* (contre qqn). ⬥ *vt* [attack - physically] agresser ; [- sexually] violenter.

assemble [ə'sembl] ⬥ *vt* **1.** [gather] réunir - **2.** [fit together] assembler, monter. ⬥ *vi* se réunir, s'assembler.

assembly [ə'semblɪ] *n* **1.** [gen] assemblée *f* - **2.** [fitting together] assemblage *m*.

assembly line *n* chaîne *f* de montage.

assent [ə'sent] ⬥ *n* consentement *m*, assentiment *m*. ⬥ *vi* : **to assent (to)** donner son consentement OR assentiment (à).

assert [ə'sɜːt] *vt* **1.** [fact, belief] affirmer, soutenir - **2.** [authority] imposer.

assertive [ə'sɜːtɪv] *adj* assuré(e).

assess [ə'ses] *vt* évaluer, estimer.

assessment [ə'sesmənt] *n* **1.** [opinion] opinion *f* - **2.** [calculation] évaluation *f*, estimation *f*.

assessor [ə'sesər] *n* [of tax] contrôleur *m*, -euse *f* (des impôts).

asset ['æset] *n* avantage *m*, atout *m*. ➤ **assets** *npl* COMM actif *m*.

assign [ə'saɪn] *vt* **1.** [allot] : **to assign sthg (to)** assigner qqch (à) - **2.** [give task to] : **to assign sb (to sthg/to do sthg)** nommer qqn (à qqch/pour faire qqch).

assignment [ə'saɪnmənt] *n* **1.** [task] mission *f* ; SCH devoir *m* - **2.** [act of assigning] attribution *f*.

assimilate [ə'sɪmɪleɪt] *vt* assimiler.

assist [ə'sɪst] *vt* : **to assist sb (with sthg/in doing sthg)** aider qqn (dans qqch/à faire qqch) ; [professionally] assister qqn (dans qqch/pour faire qqch).

assistance [ə'sɪstəns] *n* aide *f* ; **to be of assistance (to)** être utile (à).

assistant [ə'sɪstənt] ⬥ *n* assistant *m*, -e *f* ; **(shop) assistant** *UK* vendeur *m*, -euse *f*. ⬥ *comp* : **assistant editor** rédacteur en chef adjoint *m*, rédactrice en chef adjointe *f* ; **assistant manager** sous-directeur *m*, -trice *f*.

assistant referee *n* SPORT assistant-arbitre *m*.

associate ⬥ *adj* [ə'səʊʃɪət] associé(e). ⬥ *n* [ə'səʊʃɪət] associé *m*, -e *f*. ⬥ *vt* [ə'səʊʃɪeɪt] : **to associate sb/sthg (with)**

associer qqn/qqch (à) ; **to be associated with** être associé(e) à. ⬥ *vi* [ə'səʊʃɪeɪt] : **to associate with sb** fréquenter qqn.

association [ə,səʊsɪ'eɪʃn] *n* association *f* ; **in association with** avec la collaboration de.

assorted [ə'sɔːtɪd] *adj* varié(e).

assortment [ə'sɔːtmənt] *n* mélange *m*.

assume [ə'sjuːm] *vt* **1.** [suppose] supposer, présumer - **2.** [power, responsibility] assumer - **3.** [appearance, attitude] adopter.

assumed name [ə'sjuːmd-] *n* nom *m* d'emprunt.

assuming [ə'sjuːmɪŋ] *conj* en supposant que.

assumption [ə'sʌmpʃn] *n* [supposition] supposition *f*.

assurance [ə'ʃʊərəns] *n* **1.** [gen] assurance *f* - **2.** [promise] garantie *f*, promesse *f*.

assure [ə'ʃʊər] *vt* : **to assure sb (of)** assurer qqn (de).

assured [ə'ʃʊəd] *adj* assuré(e).

asterisk ['æstərɪsk] *n* astérisque *m*.

astern [ə'stɜːn] *adv* NAUT en poupe.

asthma ['æsmə] *n* asthme *m*.

astonish [ə'stɒnɪʃ] *vt* étonner.

astonishment [ə'stɒnɪʃmənt] *n* étonnement *m*.

astound [ə'staʊnd] *vt* stupéfier.

astray [ə'streɪ] *adv* : **to go astray** [become lost] s'égarer ; **to lead sb astray** détourner qqn du droit chemin.

astride [ə'straɪd] ⬥ *adv* à cheval, à califourchon. ⬥ *prep* à cheval OR califourchon sur.

astrology [ə'strɒlədʒɪ] *n* astrologie *f*.

astronaut ['æstrənɔːt] *n* astronaute *mf*.

astronomical [,æstrə'nɒmɪkl] *adj* astronomique.

astronomy [ə'strɒnəmɪ] *n* astronomie *f*.

astute [ə'stjuːt] *adj* malin(igne).

asylum [ə'saɪləm] *n* asile *m*.

at (*stressed* [æt], *unstressed* [ət] OR [ət]) *prep* **1.** [indicating place, position] à ; **at my father's** chez mon père ; **at home** à la maison, chez soi ; **at school** à l'école ; **at work** au travail - **2.** [indicating direction] vers ; **to look at sb** regarder qqn ; **to smile at sb** sourire à qqn ; **to shoot at sb** tirer sur qqn - **3.** [indicating a particular time] à ; **at midnight/noon/eleven o'clock** à minuit/midi/onze heures ; **at night** la nuit ; **at Christmas/Easter** à Noël/Pâques - **4.** [indicating age, speed, rate] à ; **at 52 (years of age)** à 52 ans ; **at 100 mph** à 160 km/h - **5.** [indicating price] : **at £50 a pair** 50 livres la paire - **6.** [indicating particular state, condition] en ; **at peace/war** en paix/guerre ; **to be at lunch/dinner** être en train de déjeuner/dîner

- **7.** *(after adjectives)* amused/appalled/puzzled at sthg diverti(e)/effaré(e)/intrigué(e) par qqch ; **delighted at sthg** ravi(e) de qqch ; **to be glad/good at sthg** être mauvais(e)/bon (bonne) en qqch - **8.** [in electronic address] ar(r)obas *f*. **at all** *adv* **1.** *(with negative)* **not at all** [when thanked] je vous en prie ; [when answering a question] pas du tout ; **she's not at all happy** elle n'est pas du tout contente - **2.** [in the slightest] : **anything at all will do** n'importe quoi fera l'affaire ; **do you know her at all?** est-ce que vous la connaissez?

ate [*UK* et, *US* eɪt] *pt* **eat**.

atheist ['eɪθɪɪst] *n* athée *mf*.

Athens ['æθɪnz] *n* Athènes.

athlete ['æθliːt] *n* athlète *mf*.

athletic [æθ'letɪk] *adj* athlétique. **athletics** *npl UK* athlétisme *m* ; *US* sports *mpl*.

Atlantic [ət'læntɪk] *adj* atlantique. *n* : **the Atlantic (Ocean)** l'océan *m* Atlantique, l'Atlantique *m*.

atlas ['ætləs] *n* atlas *m*.

atmosphere ['ætmə,sfɪər] *n* atmosphère *f*.

atmospheric [,ætməs'ferɪk] *adj* **1.** [pressure, pollution] atmosphérique - **2.** [film, music] d'ambiance.

atom ['ætəm] *n* **1.** TECH atome *m* - **2.** *fig* [tiny amount] grain *m*, parcelle *f*.

atom bomb *n* bombe *f* atomique.

atomic [ə'tɒmɪk] *adj* atomique.

atomic bomb = **atom bomb**.

atomizer, *UK* **-iser** ['ætəmaɪzər] *n* atomiseur *m*, vaporisateur *m*.

atone [ə'təʊn] *vi* : **to atone for** racheter.

A to Z *n* plan *m* de ville.

atrocious [ə'trəʊʃəs] *adj* [very bad] atroce, affreux(euse).

atrocity [ə'trɒsətɪ] *n* [terrible act] atrocité *f*.

attach [ə'tætʃ] *vt* **1.** [gen] : **to attach sthg (to)** attacher qqch (à) - **2.** [letter etc] joindre.

attaché case *n* attaché-case *m*.

attached [ə'tætʃt] *adj* [fond] : **attached to** attaché(e) à.

attachment [ə'tætʃmənt] *n* **1.** [device] accessoire *m* - **2.** [fondness] : **attachment (to)** attachement *m* (à) - **3.** COMPUT pièce *f* jointe.

attack [ə'tæk] *n* **1.** [physical, verbal] : **attack (on)** attaque *f* (contre) - **2.** [of illness] crise *f*. *vt* **1.** [gen] attaquer - **2.** [job, problem] s'attaquer à. *vi* attaquer.

attacker [ə'tækər] *n* **1.** [assailant] agresseur *m* - **2.** SPORT attaquant *m*, -e *f*.

attain [ə'teɪn] *vt* atteindre, parvenir à.

attainment [ə'teɪnmənt] *n* **1.** [of success, aims etc] réalisation *f* - **2.** [skill] talent *m*.

attempt [ə'tempt] *n* : **attempt (at)**

tentative *f* (de) ; **attempt on sb's life** tentative d'assassinat. *vt* tenter, essayer ; **to attempt to do sthg** essayer OR tenter de faire qqch.

attend [ə'tend] *vt* **1.** [meeting, party] assister à - **2.** [school, church] aller à. *vi* **1.** [be present] être présent(e) - **2.** [pay attention] : **to attend (to)** prêter attention (à). **attend to** *vt insep* **1.** [deal with] s'occuper de, régler - **2.** [look after - customer] s'occuper de ; [- patient] soigner.

attendance [ə'tendəns] *n* **1.** [number present] assistance *f*, public *m* - **2.** [presence] présence *f*.

attendant [ə'tendənt] *adj* [problems] qui en découle. *n* [at museum, car park] gardien *m*, -enne *f* ; [at petrol station] pompiste *mf*.

attention [ə'tenʃn] *n* (*U*) **1.** [gen] attention *f* ; **to bring sthg to sb's attention, to draw sb's attention to sthg** attirer l'attention de qqn sur qqch ; **to attract** OR **catch sb's attention** attirer l'attention de qqn ; **to pay attention to** prêter attention à ; **for the attention of** COMM à l'attention de - **2.** [care] soins *mpl*, attentions *fpl*. *excl* MIL garde-à-vous!

attentive [ə'tentɪv] *adj* attentif(ive).

attic ['ætɪk] *n* grenier *m*.

attitude ['ætɪtjuːd] *n* **1.** [gen] : **attitude (to** OR **towards)** attitude *f* (envers) - **2.** [posture] pose *f*.

attn. *(abbrev of* **for the attention of***)* à l'attention de.

attorney [ə'tɜːnɪ] *n US* avocat *m*, -e *f*.

attorney general (*pl* **attorneys general**) *n* ministre *m* de la Justice.

attract [ə'trækt] *vt* attirer.

attraction [ə'trækʃn] *n* **1.** [gen] attraction *f* ; **attraction to sb** attirance *f* envers qqn - **2.** [of thing] attrait *m*.

attractive [ə'træktɪv] *adj* [person] attirant(e), séduisant(e) ; [thing, idea] attrayant(e), séduisant(e) ; [investment] intéressant(e).

attribute *vt* [ə'trɪbjuːt] : **to attribute sthg to** attribuer qqch à. *n* ['ætrɪbjuːt] attribut *m*.

attrition [ə'trɪʃn] *n* usure *f*.

aubergine ['əʊbəʒiːn] *n UK* aubergine *f*.

auburn ['ɔːbən] *adj* auburn *(inv)*.

auction ['ɔːkʃn] *n* vente *f* aux enchères ; **at** OR **by auction** aux enchères ; **to put sthg up for auction** mettre qqch (dans une vente) aux enchères. *vt* vendre aux enchères. **auction off** *vt sep* vendre aux enchères.

auctioneer [,ɔːkʃə'nɪər] *n* commissaire-priseur *m*.

audacious [ɔːˈdeɪʃəs] *adj* audacieux(euse).

audible [ˈɔːdəbl] *adj* audible.

audience [ˈɔːdjəns] *n* **1.** [of play, film] public *m*, spectateurs *mpl* ; [of TV programme] téléspectateurs *mpl* - **2.** [formal meeting] audience *f*.

audiovisual [,ɔːdɪəʊvɪzjʊəl] *adj* audiovisuel(elle).

audit [ˈɔːdɪt] <> *n* audit *m*, vérification *f* des comptes. <> *vt* **1.** vérifier, apurer - **2.** *US* UNIV : **he audits several courses** il assiste à plusieurs cours en tant qu'auditeur libre.

audition [ɔːˈdɪʃn] *n* THEAT audition *f* ; CIN bout *m* d'essai.

auditor [ˈɔːdɪtər] *n* auditeur *m*, -trice *f*.

auditorium [,ɔːdɪˈtɔːrɪəm] (*pl* **-riums** OR **-ria** [-rɪə]) *n* salle *f*.

augur [ˈɔːgər] *vi* : **to augur well/badly** être de bon/mauvais augure.

August [ˈɔːgəst] *n* août *m* ; *see also* September.

Auld Alliance [,ɔːld-] *n* l'ancienne alliance unissant l'Ecosse et la France contre l'Angleterre.

Auld Lang Syne [,ɔːldlæŋˈsaɪn] *n* chant traditionnel britannique correspondant à "ce n'est qu'un au revoir, mes frères".

aunt [ɑːnt] *n* tante *f*.

auntie, aunty [ˈɑːntɪ] *n inf* tata *f*, tantine *f*.

au pair [,əʊˈpeər] *n* jeune fille *f* au pair.

aura [ˈɔːrə] *n* atmosphère *f*.

aural [ˈɔːrəl] *adj* auditif(ive).

auspices [ˈɔːspɪsɪz] *npl* : **under the auspices of** sous les auspices de.

auspicious [ɔːˈspɪʃəs] *adj* prometteur(euse).

Aussie [ˈɒzɪ] *inf* <> *adj* australien(enne). <> *n* Australien *m*, -enne *f*.

austere [ɒˈstɪər] *adj* austère.

austerity [ɒˈsterətɪ] *n* austérité *f*.

Australia [ɒˈstreɪljə] *n* Australie *f*.

Australian [ɒˈstreɪljən] <> *adj* australien(enne). <> *n* Australien *m*, -enne *f*.

Austria [ˈɒstrɪə] *n* Autriche *f*.

Austrian [ˈɒstrɪən] <> *adj* autrichien(enne). <> *n* Autrichien *m*, -enne *f*.

authentic [ɔːˈθentɪk] *adj* authentique.

author [ˈɔːθər] *n* auteur *m*.

authoritarian [ɔː,θɒrɪˈteərɪən] *adj* autoritaire.

authoritative [ɔːˈθɒrɪtətɪv] *adj* **1.** [person, voice] autoritaire - **2.** [study] qui fait autorité.

authority [ɔːˈθɒrətɪ] *n* **1.** [organization, power] autorité *f* ; **to be in authority** être le/la responsable - **2.** [permission] autorisation *f* - **3.** [expert] : **authority (on sthg)** expert *m*, -e *f* (en qqch). ◆ **authorities** *npl* : **the authorities** les autorités *fpl*.

authorize, *UK* **-ise** [ˈɔːθəraɪz] *vt* : **to authorize sb (to do sthg)** autoriser qqn (à faire qqch).

autistic [ɔːˈtɪstɪk] *adj* [child] autiste ; [behaviour] autistique.

auto [ˈɔːtəʊ] (*pl* **-s**) *n US* auto *f*, voiture *f*.

autobiography [,ɔːtəbaɪˈɒgrəfɪ] *n* autobiographie *f*.

autocratic [,ɔːtəˈkrætɪk] *adj* autocratique.

autograph [ˈɔːtəgrɑːf] <> *n* autographe *m*. <> *vt* signer.

automate [ˈɔːtəmeɪt] *vt* automatiser.

automatic [,ɔːtəˈmætɪk] <> *adj* [gen] automatique. <> *n* **1.** [car] voiture *f* à transmission automatique - **2.** [gun] automatique *m* - **3.** [washing machine] lave-linge *m* automatique.

automatically [,ɔːtəˈmætɪklɪ] *adv* [gen] automatiquement.

automation [,ɔːtəˈmeɪʃn] *n* automatisation *f*, automation *f*.

automobile [ˈɔːtəməbiːl] *n US* automobile *f*.

autonomy [ɔːˈtɒnəmɪ] *n* autonomie *f*.

autopsy [ˈɔːtɒpsɪ] *n* autopsie *f*.

autumn [ˈɔːtəm] *n* automne *m*.

auxiliary [ɔːgˈzɪljərɪ] <> *adj* auxiliaire. <> *n* auxiliaire *mf*.

av. (*abbrev of* **average**) *adj* moyen(ne).

Av. (*abbrev of* **avenue**) av.

avail [əˈveɪl] <> *n* : **to no avail** en vain, sans résultat. <> *vt* : **to avail o.s. of** profiter de.

available [əˈveɪləbl] *adj* disponible.

avalanche [ˈævəlɑːnʃ] *n lit & fig* avalanche *f*.

avarice [ˈævərɪs] *n* avarice *f*.

Ave. (*abbrev of* **avenue**) av.

avenge [əˈvendʒ] *vt* venger.

avenue [ˈævənjuː] *n* avenue *f*.

average [ˈævərɪdʒ] <> *adj* moyen(enne). <> *n* moyenne *f* ; **on average** en moyenne. <> *vt* : **the cars were averaging 90 mph** les voitures roulaient en moyenne à 150 km/h. ◆ **average out** *vi* : **to average out at** donner la moyenne de.

aversion [əˈvɜːʃn] *n* : **aversion (to)** aversion *f* (pour).

avert [əˈvɜːt] *vt* **1.** [avoid] écarter ; [accident] empêcher - **2.** [eyes, glance] détourner.

aviary [ˈeɪvjərɪ] *n* volière *f*.

avid [ˈævɪd] *adj* : **avid (for)** avide (de).

avocado [,ævəˈkɑːdəʊ] (*pl* **-s** OR **-es**) *n* : **avocado (pear)** avocat *m*.

avoid [ə'vɔɪd] *vt* éviter ; **to avoid doing sthg** éviter de faire qqch.

avoidance [ə'vɔɪdəns] *n* ► **tax avoidance.**

await [ə'weɪt] *vt* attendre.

awake [ə'weɪk] <> *adj* [not sleeping] réveillé(e) ; **are you awake?** tu dors ? <> *vt* (*pt* awoke OR awaked, *pp* awoken) 1. [wake up] réveiller - 2. *fig* [feeling] éveiller. <> *vi* (*pt* awoke OR awaked, *pp* awoken) 1. [wake up] se réveiller - 2. *fig* [feeling] s'éveiller.

awakening [ə'weɪknɪŋ] *n* 1. [from sleep] réveil *m* - 2. *fig* [of feeling] éveil *m*.

award [ə'wɔːd] <> *n* [prize] prix *m*. <> *vt* : **to award sb sthg, to award sthg to sb** [prize] décerner qqch à qqn ; [compensation, free kick] accorder qqch à qqn.

aware [ə'weər] *adj* : **to be aware of sthg** se rendre compte de qqch, être conscient(e) de qqch ; **to be aware that** se rendre compte que, être conscient que.

awareness [ə'weənɪs] *n* (U) conscience *f.*

awash [ə'wɒʃ] *adj* lit & fig : **awash (with)** inondé(e) (de).

away [ə'weɪ] <> *adv* 1. [in opposite direction] : **to move** OR **walk away (from)** s'éloigner (de) ; **to look away** détourner le regard ; **to turn away** se détourner - 2. [in distance] : **we live 4 miles away (from here)** nous habitons à 6 kilomètres (d'ici) - 3. [in time] : **the elections are a month away** les élections se dérouleront dans un mois - 4. [absent] absent(e) ; **she's away on holiday** elle est partie en vacances - 5. [in safe place] : **to put sthg away** ranger qqch - 6. [so as to be gone or used up] : **to fade away** disparaître ; **to give sthg away** donner qqch, faire don de qqch ; **to take sthg away** emporter qqch - 7. [continuously] : **to be working away** travailler sans arrêt. <> *adj* SPORT [team, fans] de l'équipe des visiteurs ; **away game** match *m* à l'extérieur.

awe [ɔː] *n* respect *m* mêlé de crainte ; **to be in awe of sb** être impressionné(e) par qqn.

awesome ['ɔːsəm] *adj* impressionnant(e).

awful ['ɔːful] *adj* 1. [terrible] affreux(euse) - 2. *inf* [very great] : **an awful lot (of)** énormément (de).

awfully ['ɔːflɪ] *adv inf* [bad, difficult] affreusement ; [nice, good] extrêmement.

awhile [ə'waɪl] *adv* un moment.

awkward ['ɔːkwəd] *adj* 1. [clumsy] gauche, maladroit(e) - 2. [embarrassed] mal à l'aise, gêné(e) - 3. [difficult - person, problem, task] difficile - 4. [inconvenient] incommode - 5. [embarrassing] embarrassant(e), gênant(e).

awning ['ɔːnɪŋ] *n* 1. [of tent] auvent *m* - 2. [of shop] banne *f.*

awoke [ə'wəuk] *pt* ► **awake.**

awoken [ə'wəukn] *pp* ► **awake.**

awry [ə'raɪ] <> *adj* de travers. <> *adv* : **to go awry** aller de travers, mal tourner.

axe, *US* **ax** [æks] <> *n* hache *f.* <> *vt* [project] abandonner ; [jobs] supprimer.

axes ['æksiːz] *npl* ► **axis.**

axis ['æksɪs] (*pl* **axes** ['æksiːz]) *n* axe *m.*

axle ['æksl] *n* essieu *m.*

aye [aɪ] <> *adv* oui. <> *n* oui *m* ; [in voting] voix *f* pour.

azalea [ə'zeɪljə] *n* azalée *f.*

Azores [ə'zɔːz] *npl* : **the Azores** les Açores *fpl.*

B

b (*pl* **b's** OR **bs**), **B** (*pl* **B's** OR **Bs** [biː]) *n* [letter] b *m inv*, B *m inv*. ◆ **B** *n* 1. MUS si *m* - 2. SCH [mark] B *m inv.*

B &B *n abbrev of* **bed and breakfast.**

BA *n abbrev of* **Bachelor of Arts.**

babble ['bæbl] <> *n* [of voices] murmure *m*, rumeur *f.* <> *vi* [person] babiller.

baboon [bə'buːn] *n* babouin *m.*

baby ['beɪbɪ] *n* 1. [child] bébé *m* - 2. *inf* [darling] chéri *m*, -e *f.*

baby buggy *n* 1. *UK* [foldable pushchair] poussette *f* - 2. *US* = **baby carriage.**

baby carriage *n US* landau *m.*

baby-sit *vi* faire du baby-sitting.

baby-sitter [-,sɪtər] *n* baby-sitter *mf.*

baby tooth *n US* = **milk tooth.**

bachelor ['bætʃələr] *n* célibataire *m.*

bachelorette party *US* = **hen party.**

Bachelor of Arts *n* [degree] ≃ licence *f* en OR ès lettres ; [person] ≃ licencié *m*, -e *f* en OR ès lettres.

Bachelor of Science *n* [degree] ≃ licence *f* en OR ès sciences ; [person] ≃ licencié *m*, -e *f* en OR ès science.

back [bæk] <> *adv* 1. [backwards] en arrière ; **to step/move back** reculer ; **to push back** repousser - 2. [to former position or state] : **I'll be back at five** je rentrerai OR serai de retour à dix-sept heures ; **I'd like my money back** [in shop] je voudrais me faire rembourser ; **to go back** retourner ; **to come back** revenir, rentrer ; **to drive back** rentrer en voiture ; **to go back and forth** [person]

faire des allées et venues ; **to go back to sleep** se rendormir ; **to be back (in fashion)** revenir à la mode - **3.** [earlier] : **to think back (to)** se souvenir (de) - **4.** [in return] : **to phone** OR **call back** rappeler. ◇ *n* **1.** [of person, animal] dos *m* ; **behind sb's back** *fig* derrière le dos de qqn - **2.** [of door, book, hand] dos *m* ; [of head] derrière *m* ; [of envelope, cheque] revers *m* ; [of page] verso *m* ; [of chair] dossier *m* - **3.** [of room, fridge] fond *m* ; [of car] arrière *m* - **4.** SPORT arrière *m*. ◇ *adj (in compounds)* **1.** [at the back] de derrière ; [seat, wheel] arrière *(inv)* ; [page] dernier(ère) - **2.** [overdue] : **back rent** arriéré *m* de loyer. ◇ *vt* **1.** [reverse] reculer - **2.** [support] appuyer, soutenir - **3.** [bet on] parier sur, miser sur. ◇ *vi* reculer.
● **back to back** *adv* **1.** [stand] dos à dos - **2.** [happen] l'un après l'autre. ● **back to front** *adv* à l'envers. ● **back down** *vi* céder. ● **back out** *vi* [of promise etc] se dédire. ● **back up** ◇ *vt sep* **1.** [support - claim] appuyer, soutenir ; [- person] épauler, soutenir - **2.** [reverse] reculer - **3.** COMPUT. sauvegarder, faire une copie de sauvegarde de. ◇ *vi* [reverse] reculer.

backache ['bækeɪk] *n* : **to have backache** *UK*, **to have a backache** *US* avoir mal aux reins OR au dos.

backbencher [,bæk'bentʃər] *n UK* POL *député qui n'a aucune position officielle au gouvernement ni dans aucun parti.*

backbone ['bækbəʊn] *n* épine *f* dorsale, colonne *f* vertébrale ; *fig* [main support] pivot *m*.

backcloth ['bækklɒθ] *UK* = **backdrop**.

backdate [,bæk'deɪt] *vt* antidater.

back door *n* porte *f* de derrière.

backdrop ['bækdrɒp] *n lit & fig* toile *f* de fond.

backfill ['bækfɪl] ◇ *vt* remplir. ◇ *n* matériau de construction.

backfire [,bæk'faɪər] *vi* **1.** AUT pétarader - **2.** [plan] : **to backfire (on sb)** se retourner (contre qqn).

backgammon ['bæk,gæmən] *n* backgammon *m*, ≃ jacquet *m*.

background ['bækgraʊnd] *n* **1.** [in picture, view] arrière-plan *m* ; **in the background** dans le fond, à l'arrière-plan ; *fig* au second plan - **2.** [of event, situation] contexte *m* - **3.** [upbringing] milieu *m*.

backhand ['bækhænd] *n* revers *m*.

backhanded ['bækhændɪd] *adj fig* ambigu(ë), équivoque.

backhander ['bækhændər] *n UK inf* pot-de-vin *m*.

backing ['bækɪŋ] *n* **1.** [support] soutien *m* - **2.** [lining] doublage *m*.

backlash ['bæklæʃ] *n* contrecoup *m*, choc *m* en retour.

backlog ['bæklɒg] *n* : **backlog (of work)** arriéré *m* de travail, travail *m* en retard.

back number *n* vieux numéro *m*.

backpack ['bækpæk] *n* sac *m* à dos.

back pay *n* rappel *m* de salaire.

back seat *n* [in car] siège *m* OR banquette *f* arrière ; **to take a back seat** *fig* jouer un rôle secondaire.

backside [,bæk'saɪd] *n inf* postérieur *m*, derrière *m*.

backstage [,bæk'steɪdʒ] *adv* dans les coulisses.

back street *n* petite rue *f*.

backstroke ['bækstrəʊk] *n* dos *m* crawlé.

backup ['bækʌp] ◇ *adj* [plan, team] de secours, de remplacement. ◇ *n* **1.** [gen] aide *f*, soutien *m* - **2.** COMPUT (copie *f* de) sauvegarde *f*.

backward ['bækwəd] ◇ *adj* **1.** [movement, look] en arrière - **2.** [country] arriéré(e) ; [person] arriéré(e), attardé(e). ◇ *adv US* = **backwards**.

backwards ['bækwədz], *US* **backward** ['bækwərd] *adv* [move, go] en arrière, à reculons ; [read list] à rebours, à l'envers ; **backwards and forwards** [movement] de va-et-vient, d'avant en arrière et d'arrière en avant ; **to walk backwards and forwards** aller et venir.

backwater ['bæk,wɔːtər] *n fig* désert *m*.

backyard [,bæk'jɑːd] *n* **1.** *UK* [yard] arrière-cour *f* - **2.** *US* [garden] jardin *m* de derrière.

bacon ['beɪkən] *n* bacon *m*.

bacteria [bæk'tɪərɪə] *npl* bactéries *fpl*.

bad [bæd] ◇ *adj* (comp **worse**, superl **worst**) **1.** [not good] mauvais(e) ; **to be bad at sthg** être mauvais en qqch ; **too bad!** dommage! ; **not bad** pas mal - **2.** [unhealthy] malade ; **smoking is bad for you** fumer est mauvais pour la santé ; **I'm feeling bad** je ne suis pas dans mon assiette ; **he's in a bad way** il va mal, il est en piteux état - **3.** [serious] : **a bad cold** un gros rhume - **4.** [rotten] pourri(e), gâté(e) ; **to go bad** se gâter, s'avarier - **5.** [guilty] : **to feel bad about sthg** se sentir coupable de qqch - **6.** [naughty] méchant(e). ◇ *adv US* = **badly**.

badge [bædʒ] *n* **1.** [metal, plastic] badge *m* - **2.** [sewn-on] écusson *m*.

badger ['bædʒər] ◇ *n* blaireau *m*. ◇ *vt* : **to badger sb (to do sthg)** harceler qqn (pour qu'il fasse qqch).

badly ['bædlɪ] (comp **worse**, superl **worst**) *adv* **1.** [not well] mal ; **badly made/organized** mal fait/organisé - **2.** [seriously - wounded] grièvement ; [- affected] gravement, sérieusement ; **to be badly in need of sthg** avoir vraiment OR absolument besoin de qqch.

badly-off *adj* [poor] pauvre, dans le besoin.

bad-mannered [-'mænəd] *adj* [child] mal élevé(e) ; [shop assistant] impoli(e).

badminton ['bædmɪntən] *n* badminton *m*.

bad-tempered [-'tempəd] *adj* **1.** [by nature] qui a mauvais caractère - **2.** [in a bad mood] de mauvaise humeur.

baffle ['bæfl] *vt* déconcerter, confondre.

bag [bæg] <> *n* **1.** [gen] sac *m* ; **to pack one's bags** *fig* plier bagage - **2.** [handbag] sac *m* à main. <> *vt UK inf* [reserve] garder. ● **bags** *npl* **1.** [under eyes] poches *fpl* - **2.** *UK inf* [lots] : **bags of** plein OR beaucoup de.

bagel ['beɪgəl] *n petit pain en couronne.*

baggage ['bægɪdʒ] *n* (U) bagages *mpl*.

baggage reclaim *n* retrait *m* des bagages.

baggy ['bægɪ] *adj* ample.

bagpipes ['bægpaɪps] *npl* cornemuse *f*.

Bahamas [bə'hɑːməz] *npl* : **the Bahamas** les Bahamas *fpl*.

bail [beɪl] *n* (U) caution *f* ; **on bail** sous caution. ● **bail out** <> *vt sep* **1.** [pay bail for] se porter garant(e) de - **2.** *fig* [rescue] tirer d'affaire. <> *vi* [from plane] sauter (en parachute).

bailiff ['beɪlɪf] *n* huissier *m*.

bait [beɪt] <> *n* appât *m*. <> *vt* **1.** [put bait on] appâter - **2.** [tease] tourmenter.

bake [beɪk] <> *vt* **1.** CULIN faire cuire au four - **2.** [clay, bricks] cuire. <> *vi* [food] cuire au four.

baked beans [beɪkt-] *npl* haricots *mpl* blancs à la tomate.

baked potato [beɪkt-] *n* pomme *f* de terre en robe des champs OR de chambre.

baker ['beɪkə] *n* boulanger *m*, -ère *f* ; **baker's (shop)** boulangerie *f*.

bakery ['beɪkərɪ] *n* boulangerie *f*.

baking ['beɪkɪŋ] *n* cuisson *f*.

balaclava (helmet) [,bælə'klɑːvə-] *n UK* passe-montagne *m*.

balance ['bæləns] <> *n* **1.** [equilibrium] équilibre *m* ; **to keep/lose one's balance** garder/perdre l'équilibre ; **off balance** déséquilibré(e) ; **to strike a balance between the practical and the idealistic** trouver un juste milieu entre la réalité et l'idéal - **2.** *fig* [counterweight] contrepoids *m* ; [of evidence] poids *m*, force *f* - **3.** [scales] balance *f* - **4.** FIN solde *m*. <> *vt* **1.** [keep in balance] maintenir en équilibre - **2.** [compare] : **to balance sthg against sthg** mettre qqch et qqch en balance - **3.** [in accounting] : **to balance a**

budget équilibrer un budget ; **to balance the books** clôturer les comptes, dresser le bilan. <> *vi* **1.** [maintain equilibrium] se tenir en équilibre - **2.** [budget, accounts] s'équilibrer. ● **on balance** *adv* tout bien considéré. ● **balance out** *vi insep* : **the advantages and disadvantages balance out** les avantages contrebalancent OR compensent les inconvénients.

balanced diet [,bælənst-] *n* alimentation *f* équilibrée.

balance of payments *n* balance *f* des paiements.

balance of trade *n* balance *f* commerciale.

balance sheet *n* bilan *m*.

balcony ['bælkənɪ] *n* balcon *m*.

bald [bɔːld] *adj* **1.** [head, man] chauve - **2.** [tyre] lisse - **3.** *fig* [blunt] direct(e).

bale [beɪl] *n* balle *f*. ● **bale out** *UK* <> *vt sep* [boat] écoper, vider. <> *vi* [from plane] sauter en parachute.

Balearic Islands [,bælɪ'ærɪk-], **Balearics** [,bælɪ'ærɪks] *npl* : **the Balearic Islands** les Baléares *fpl*.

baleful ['beɪlful] *adj* sinistre.

balk [bɔːk] *vi* : **to balk (at)** hésiter OR reculer (devant).

Balkans ['bɔːlkənz], **Balkan States** ['bɔːlkən-] *npl* : **the Balkans** les Balkans *mpl*, les États *mpl* balkaniques.

ball [bɔːl] *n* **1.** [round shape] boule *f* ; [in game] balle *f* ; [football] ballon *m* ; **to be on the ball** *fig* connaître son affaire, s'y connaître - **2.** [of food] plante *f* - **3.** [dance] bal *m*. ● **balls** *vulg* <> *npl* [testicles] couilles *fpl*. <> *n* (U) [nonsense] conneries *fpl*.

ballad ['bæləd] *n* ballade *f*.

ballast ['bæləst] *n* lest *m*.

ball bearing *n* roulement *m* à billes.

ball boy *n* ramasseur *m* de balles.

ballerina [,bælə'riːnə] *n* ballerine *f*.

ballet ['bæleɪ] *n* **1.** (U) [art of dance] danse *f* - **2.** [work] ballet *m*.

ballet dancer *n* danseur *m*, -euse *f* de ballet.

ball game *n* **1.** *US* [baseball match] match *m* de base-ball - **2.** *inf* [situation] : **it's a whole new ball game** c'est une autre paire de manches.

balloon [bə'luːn] *n* **1.** [gen] ballon *m* - **2.** [in cartoon] bulle *f*.

ballot ['bælət] <> *n* **1.** [voting paper] bulletin *m* de vote - **2.** [voting process] scrutin *m*. <> *vt* appeler à voter.

ballot box *n* **1.** [container] urne *f* - **2.** [voting process] scrutin *m*.

ballot paper *n* bulletin *m* de vote.

ballroom ['bɔːlrʊm] *n* salle *f* de bal.

ballroom dancing *n* (U) danse *f* de salon.

balm [bɑːm] *n* baume *m*.

balmy ['bɑːmɪ] *adj* doux (douce).

balsa(wood) ['bɒlsə(wʊd)] *n* balsa *m*.

balti ['bɔːltɪ] *n* [pan] *récipient métallique utilisé dans la cuisine indienne* ; [food] *plat épicé préparé dans un 'balti'.*

Baltic ['bɔːltɪk] <> *adj* [port, coast] de la Baltique. <> *n* : **the Baltic (Sea)** la Baltique.

Baltic Republic *n* : **the Baltic Republics** les républiques *fpl* baltes.

bamboo [bæm'buː] *n* bambou *m*.

bamboozle [bæm'buːzl] *vt inf* embobiner.

ban [bæn] <> *n* interdiction *f* ; **there is a ban on smoking** il est interdit de fumer. <> *vt* interdire ; **to ban sb from doing sthg** interdire à qqn de faire qqch.

banal [bə'nɑːl] *adj pej* banal(e), ordinaire.

banana [bə'nɑːnə] *n* banane *f*.

band [bænd] *n* **1.** [MUS - rock] groupe *m* ; [- military] fanfare *f* ; [- jazz] orchestre *m* - **2.** [group, strip] bande *f* - **3.** [stripe] rayure *f* - **4.** [range] tranche *f*. ◆ **band together** *vi* s'unir.

bandage ['bændɪdʒ] <> *n* bandage *m*, bande *f*. <> *vt* mettre un pansement OR un bandage sur.

Band-Aid® *n* pansement *m* adhésif.

b and b, B and B *n abbrev of* **bed and breakfast.**

bandit ['bændɪt] *n* bandit *m*.

bandstand ['bændstænd] *n* kiosque *m* à musique.

bandwagon ['bændwægən] *n* : **to jump on the bandwagon** suivre le mouvement.

bandy ['bændɪ] *adj* qui a les jambes arquées ; **to have bandy legs** avoir les jambes arquées. ◆ **bandy about, bandy around** *vt sep* répandre, faire circuler.

bandy-legged [-,legd] *adj* = **bandy.**

bang [bæŋ] <> *adv* [exactly] : **bang in the middle** en plein milieu ; **to be bang on time** être pile à l'heure. <> *n* **1.** [blow] coup *m* violent - **2.** [of gun etc] détonation *f* ; [of door] claquement *m*. <> *vt* frapper violemment ; [door] claquer ; **to bang one's head/knee** se cogner la tête/le genou. <> *vi* **1.** [knock] : **to bang on** frapper à - **2.** [make a loud noise - gun etc] détoner ; [- door] claquer - **3.** [crash] : **to bang into** se cogner contre. <> *excl* boum! ◆ **bangs** *npl US* frange *f*.

banger ['bæŋər] *n UK* **1.** *inf* [sausage] saucisse *f* - **2.** *inf* [old car] vieille guimbarde *f* - **3.** [firework] pétard *m*.

bangle ['bæŋgl] *n* bracelet *m*.

banish ['bænɪʃ] *vt* bannir.

banister ['bænɪstər] *n* rampe *f*.

bank [bæŋk] <> *n* **1.** *fig & FIN* banque *f* - **2.** [of river, lake] rive *f*, bord *m* - **3.** [of earth] talus *m* - **4.** [of clouds] masse *f* ; [of fog] nappe *f*. <> *vt FIN* mettre or déposer à la banque. <> *vi* **1.** *FIN* : **to bank with** avoir un compte à - **2.** [plane] tourner. ◆ **bank on** *vt insep* compter sur.

bank account *n* compte *m* en banque.

bank balance *n* solde *m* bancaire.

bank card = **banker's card.**

bank charges *npl* frais *mpl* bancaires.

bank draft *n* traite *f* bancaire.

banker ['bæŋkər] *n* banquier *m*.

banker's card *n UK* carte *f* d'identité bancaire.

bank holiday *n UK* jour *m* férié.

banking ['bæŋkɪŋ] *n* : **to go into banking** travailler dans la banque.

bank manager *n* directeur *m*, -trice *f* de banque.

bank note *n* billet *m* de banque.

bank rate *n* taux *m* d'escompte.

bankrupt ['bæŋkrʌpt] *adj* failli(e) ; **to go bankrupt** faire faillite.

bankruptcy ['bæŋkrəptsɪ] *n* [gen] faillite *f*.

bank statement *n* relevé *m* de compte.

banner ['bænər] *n* **1.** [flag] banderole *f* - **2.** COMPUT bandeau *m*.

banoffee [bə'nɒfiː] *n* (U) banoffee *m*, caramel *m* banane.

banquet ['bæŋkwɪt] *n* banquet *m*.

banter ['bæntər] *n* (U) plaisanterie *f*, badinage *m*.

bap [bæp] *n UK* petit pain (rond) *m*.

baptism ['bæptɪzm] *n* baptême *m*.

Baptist ['bæptɪst] *n* baptiste *mf*.

baptize, UK -ise [UK bæp'taɪz, US 'bæptaɪz] *vt* baptiser.

bar [bɑːr] <> *n* **1.** [piece of gold] lingot *m* ; [- of chocolate] tablette *f* ; **a bar of soap** une savonnette - **2.** [length of wood, metal] barre *f* ; **to be behind bars** être derrière les barreaux OR sous les verrous - **3.** *fig* [obstacle] obstacle *m* - **4.** [pub] bar *m* - **5.** [counter of pub] comptoir *m*, zinc *m* - **6.** MUS mesure *f*. <> *vt* **1.** [door, road] barrer ; [window] mettre des barreaux à ; **to bar sb's way** barrer la route OR le passage à qqn - **2.** [ban] interdire, défendre ; **to bar sb (from)** interdire à qqn (de). <> *prep* sauf, excepté ; **bar none** sans exception. ◆ **Bar** *n LAW* : **the Bar** *UK* le barreau ; *US* les avocats *mpl*.

Barbadian [bɑː'beɪdɪən] <> *adj* barbadien(ne). <> *n* Barbadien *m*, -ne *f*.

barbaric [bɑː'bærɪk] *adj* barbare.

barbecue ['bɑːbɪkjuː] n barbecue m.

barbed wire [bɑːbd-], US **barbwire** ['bɑːbwaɪər] n (U) fil m de fer barbelé.

barber ['bɑːbər] n coiffeur m (pour hommes) ; **barber's (shop)** salon m de coiffure (pour hommes) ; **to go to the barber's** aller chez le coiffeur.

barbiturate [bɑːˈbɪtjʊrət] n barbiturique m.

bar code n code m à barres, code-barres m.

bard margin n Ir = **hard shoulder**.

bare [beər] <> adj **1.** [feet, arms etc] nu(e) ; [trees, hills etc] dénudé(e) - **2.** [absolute, minimum] : **the bare facts** les simples faits ; **the bare minimum** le strict minimum - **3.** [empty] vide. <> vt découvrir ; **to bare one's teeth** montrer les dents.

bareback ['beəbæk] adv à cru, à nu.

barefaced ['beəfeɪst] adj éhonté(e).

barefoot(ed) [ˌbeəˈfʊt(ɪd)] <> adj aux pieds nus. <> adv nu-pieds, pieds nus.

barely ['beəlɪ] adv [scarcely] à peine, tout juste.

bargain ['bɑːgɪn] <> n **1.** [agreement] marché m ; **into the bargain** en plus, par-dessus le marché - **2.** [good buy] affaire f, occasion f. <> vi négocier ; **to bargain with sb for sthg** négocier qqch avec qqn. ➤ **bargain for, bargain on** vt insep compter sur, prévoir.

barge [bɑːdʒ] <> n péniche f. <> vi inf : **to barge past sb** bousculer qqn. ➤ **barge in** vi inf : **to barge in (on)** interrompre.

barista [bəˈriːstə] n barman m, barmaid f.

baritone ['bærɪtəʊn] n baryton m.

bark [bɑːk] <> n **1.** [of dog] aboiement m - **2.** [on tree] écorce f. <> vi [dog] : **to bark (at)** aboyer (après).

barley ['bɑːlɪ] n orge f.

barley sugar n UK sucre m d'orge.

barley water n UK orgeat m.

barmaid ['bɑːmeɪd] n barmaid f, serveuse f de bar.

barman ['bɑːmən] (pl -men [-mən]) n UK barman m, serveur m de bar.

barn [bɑːn] n grange f.

barometer [bəˈrɒmɪtər] n lit & fig baromètre m.

baron ['bærən] n baron m.

baroness ['bærənɪs] n baronne f.

barrack ['bærək] vt UK huer, conspuer. ➤ **barracks** npl caserne f.

barrage ['bærɑːʒ] n **1.** [of firing] barrage m - **2.** [of questions etc] avalanche f, déluge m - **3.** UK [dam] barrage m.

barrel ['bærəl] n **1.** [for beer, wine] tonneau m, fût m - **2.** [for oil] baril m - **3.** [of gun] canon m.

barren ['bærən] adj stérile.

barricade [ˌbærɪˈkeɪd] n barricade f.

barrier ['bærɪər] n lit & fig barrière f.

barring ['bɑːrɪŋ] prep sauf.

barrister ['bærɪstər] n UK avocat m, -e f.

barrow ['bærəʊ] n brouette f.

bartender ['bɑːtendər] n US barman m.

barter ['bɑːtər] <> n troc m. <> vt : **to barter sthg (for)** troquer OR échanger qqch (contre). <> vi faire du troc.

base [beɪs] <> n base f. <> vt baser ; **to base sthg on** OR **upon** baser OR fonder qqch sur. <> adj indigne, ignoble.

baseball ['beɪsbɔːl] n base-ball m.

baseball cap n casquette f de base-ball.

Basel ['bɑːzl] n Bâle.

basement ['beɪsmənt] n sous-sol m.

base rate n taux m de base.

bases ['beɪsiːz] npl ➤ **basis**.

bash [bæʃ] inf <> n **1.** [painful blow] coup m - **2.** [attempt] : **to have a bash** tenter le coup. <> vt [hit - gen] frapper, cogner ; [- car] percuter.

bashful ['bæʃfʊl] adj timide.

basic ['beɪsɪk] adj fondamental(e) ; [vocabulary, salary] de base. ➤ **basics** npl [rudiments] éléments mpl, bases fpl.

BASIC ['beɪsɪk] (abbrev of Beginner's All-purpose Symbolic Instruction Code) n basic m.

basically ['beɪsɪklɪ] adv **1.** [essentially] au fond, fondamentalement - **2.** [really] en fait.

basil ['bæzl] n basilic m.

basin ['beɪsn] n **1.** UK [bowl - for cooking] terrine f ; [- for washing] cuvette f - **2.** UK [in bathroom] lavabo m - **3.** GEOG bassin m.

basis ['beɪsɪs] (pl -ses [-siːz]) n base f ; **on the basis of** sur la base de ; **on a regular basis** de façon régulière ; **to be paid on a weekly/monthly basis** toucher un salaire hebdomadaire/mensuel.

bask [bɑːsk] vi : **to bask in the sun** se chauffer au soleil.

basket ['bɑːskɪt] n corbeille f ; [with handle] panier m.

basketball ['bɑːskɪtbɔːl] n basket-ball m, basket m.

bass [beɪs] <> adj bas (basse). <> n **1.** [singer] basse f - **2.** [double bass] contre-basse f - **3.** = **bass guitar**.

bass drum [beɪs-] n grosse caisse f.

bass guitar [beɪs-] n basse f.

bassoon [bəˈsuːn] n basson m.

bastard ['bɑːstəd] n **1.** [illegitimate child] bâtard m, -e f, enfant naturel m, enfant naturelle f - **2.** v inf [unpleasant person] salaud m, saligaud m.

bastion ['bæstɪən] n bastion m.

bat [bæt] n **1.** [animal] chauve-souris f - **2.** [for cricket, baseball] batte f ; UK [for table-tennis] raquette f ; **to do sthg off one's own bat** UK faire qqch de son propre chef.

batch [bætʃ] n **1.** [of papers] tas m, liasse f ; [of letters, applicants] série f - **2.** [of products] lot m.

bated ['beɪtɪd] adj : **with bated breath** en retenant son souffle.

bath [bɑːθ] n **1.** UK [bathtub] baignoire f - **2.** [act of washing] bain m ; **to have** UK OR **take a bath** prendre un bain. ◇ vt UK baigner, donner un bain à. ◈ **baths** npl UK piscine f.

bathe [beɪð] ◇ vt **1.** [wound] laver - **2.** [subj: light, sunshine] : **to be bathed in** OR **with** être baigné(e) de. ◇ vi **1.** UK [swim] se baigner - **2.** US [take a bath] prendre un bain.

bathing ['beɪðɪŋ] n (U) baignade f.

bathing cap n bonnet m de bain.

bathing costume UK, **bathing suit** n maillot m de bain.

bathrobe ['bɑːθrəʊb] n [made of towelling] sortie f de bain ; [dressing gown] peignoir m.

bathroom ['bɑːθrʊm] n **1.** [room with bath] salle f de bains - **2.** US [toilet] toilettes fpl.

bath towel n serviette f de bain.

bathtub ['bɑːθtʌb] n baignoire f.

baton ['bætən] n **1.** [of conductor] baguette f - **2.** [in relay race] témoin m - **3.** UK [of policeman] bâton m, matraque f.

batsman ['bætsmən] (pl -men [-mən]) n batteur m.

battalion [bə'tæljən] n bataillon m.

batten ['bætn] n planche f, latte f.

batter ['bætər] ◇ n (U) pâte f. ◇ vt battre.

battered ['bætəd] adj **1.** [child, woman] battu(e) - **2.** [car, hat] cabossé(e).

battery ['bætərɪ] n batterie f ; [of calculator, toy] pile f.

battle ['bætl] ◇ n **1.** [in war] bataille f - **2.** [struggle] : **battle (for/against/with)** lutte f (pour/contre/avec), combat m (pour/contre/avec). ◇ vi : **to battle (for/against/with)** se battre (pour/contre/avec), lutter (pour/contre/avec).

battlefield ['bætlfiːld], **battleground** ['bætlɡraʊnd] n MIL champ m de bataille.

battlements ['bætlmənts] npl remparts mpl.

battleship ['bætlʃɪp] n cuirassé m.

bauble ['bɔːbl] n babiole f, colifichet m.

baulk [bɔːk] UK = **balk**.

bawdy ['bɔːdɪ] adj grivois(e), salé(e).

bawl [bɔːl] vt & vi brailler.

bay [beɪ] n **1.** GEOG baie f - **2.** [for loading] aire f (de chargement) - **3.** [for parking] place f (de stationnement) ; **to keep sb/sthg at bay** tenir qqn/qqch à distance, tenir qqn/qqch en échec.

bay leaf n feuille f de laurier.

bay window n fenêtre f en saillie.

bazaar [bə'zɑːr] n **1.** [market] bazar m - **2.** [charity sale] vente f de charité.

B2B [,biːtə'biː] (abbrev of **business to business**) n COMM B to B.

BBC (abbrev of **British Broadcasting Corporation**) n office national britannique de radiodiffusion.

B2C [,biːtə'siː] (abbrev of **business to customer**) n COMM B to C.

BC (abbrev of **before Christ**) av. J.-C.

Bcc [,biːsiː'siː] (abbrev of **blind carbon copy**) n Cci m.

BCE adv (abbrev of **before the Common Era**) av. J.-C.

be [biː] (pt **was** OR **were**, pp **been**) ◇ aux vb **1.** (in combination with ppr: to form cont tense) **what is he doing?** qu'est-ce qu'il fait? ; **it's snowing** il neige ; **they've been promising reform for years** ça fait des années qu'ils nous promettent des réformes - **2.** (in combination with pp: to form passive) être ; **to be loved** être aimé(e) ; **there was no one to be seen** il n'y avait personne - **3.** (in tag questions and answers) **the meal was delicious, wasn't it?** le repas était délicieux, non? OR vous n'avez pas trouvé? - **4.** (followed by 'to' + infin) **I'm to be promoted** je vais avoir de l'avancement ; **you're not to tell anyone** ne le dis à personne. ◇ cop vb **1.** (with adj, n) être ; **to be a doctor/lawyer/plumber** être médecin/avocat/plombier ; **she's intelligent/attractive** elle est intelligente/jolie ; **I'm hot/cold** j'ai chaud/froid ; **1 and 1 are 2** 1 et 1 font 2 - **2.** [referring to health] aller, se porter ; **to be seriously ill** être gravement malade ; **she's better now** elle va mieux maintenant ; **how are you?** comment allez-vous? - **3.** [referring to age] : **how old are you?** quel âge avez-vous? ; **I'm 20 (years old)** j'ai 20 ans - **4.** [cost] coûter, faire ; **how much was it?** combien cela a-t-il coûté? ; combien ça faisais? ; **that will be £10, please** cela fait 10 livres, s'il vous plaît. ◇ vi **1.** [exist] être, exister ; **be that as it may** qu'il en soit - **2.** [referring to place] être ; **Toulouse is in France** Toulouse se trouve OR est en France ; **he will be here tomorrow** il sera là demain - **3.** [referring to movement] aller, être ; **I've been to the cinema** j'ai été OR je suis allé au cinéma. <> *impers vb* **1.** [referring to time, dates, distance] être ; **it's two o'clock** il est deux heures ; **it's 3 km to the next town** la ville voisine est à 3 km - **2.** [referring to the weather] faire ; **it's hot/cold** il fait chaud/froid ; **it's windy** il y a du vent - **3.** [for emphasis] : **it's me/Paul/the milkman** c'est moi/Paul/le laitier.

beach [biːtʃ] <> *n* plage *f*. <> *vt* échouer.

beacon ['biːkən] *n* **1.** [warning fire] feu *m*, fanal *m* - **2.** [lighthouse] phare *m* - **3.** [radio beacon] radiophare *m*.

bead [biːd] *n* **1.** [of wood, glass] perle *f* - **2.** [of sweat] goutte *f*.

beagle ['biːgl] *n* beagle *m*.

beak [biːk] *n* bec *m*.

beaker ['biːkə'] *n* gobelet *m*.

beam [biːm] <> *n* **1.** [of wood, concrete] poutre *f* - **2.** [of light] rayon *m*. <> *vt* [signal, news] transmettre. <> *vi* [smile] faire un sourire radieux.

bean [biːn] *n* [gen] haricot *m* ; [of coffee] grain *m* ; **to be full of beans** *UK inf* péter le feu ; **to spill the beans** *inf* manger le morceau.

beanbag ['biːnbæg] *n* [chair] sacco *m*.

beanshoot ['biːnʃuːt], **beansprout** ['biːnspraut] *n* germe *m* OR pousse *f* de soja.

bear [beə'] <> *n* [animal] ours *m*. <> *vt* (*pt* **bore**, *pp* **borne**) **1.** [carry, have] porter - **2.** [endure, tolerate] supporter - **3.** [feeling] : **to bear sb a grudge** garder rancune à qqn. <> *vi* (*pt* **bore**, *pp* **borne**) : **to bear left/right** se diriger vers la gauche/la droite ; **to bring pressure/influence to bear on sb** exercer une pression/une influence sur qqn. **bear out** *vt sep* confirmer, corroborer. **bear up** *vi* tenir le coup. **bear with** *vt insep* être patient(e) avec.

beard [biəd] *n* barbe *f*.

bearer ['beərə'] *n* **1.** [gen] porteur *m*, -euse *f* - **2.** [of passport] titulaire *mf*.

bearing ['beərɪŋ] *n* **1.** [connection] : **bearing (on)** rapport *m* (avec) - **2.** [deportment] allure *f*, maintien *m* - **3.** TECH [for shaft] palier *m* - **4.** [on compass] orientation *f* ; **to get one's bearings** s'orienter, se repérer.

beast [biːst] *n* **1.** [animal] bête *f* - **2.** *inf pej* [person] brute *f*.

beastly ['biːstlɪ] *adj UK dated* [person] malveillant(e), cruel(elle) ; [headache, weather] épouvantable.

beat [biːt] <> *n* **1.** [of heart, drum, wings] battement *m* - **2.** MUS [rhythm] mesure *f*, temps *m* - **3.** [of policeman] ronde *f*. <> *vt* (*pt* **beat**, *pp* **beaten**) **1.** [gen] battre - **2.** [be better than] être bien mieux que, valoir mieux que ; **beat it!** *inf* décampe!, fiche le camp! <> *vi* (*pt* **beat**, *pp* **beaten**) battre.

beat off *vt sep* [resist] repousser. **beat up** *vt sep inf* tabasser ; **to beat o.s. up (about sthg)** culpabiliser (à propos de qqch).

beating ['biːtɪŋ] *n* **1.** [blows] raclée *f*, rossée *f* - **2.** [defeat] défaite *f*.

beautiful ['bjuːtɪfʊl] *adj* **1.** [gen] beau (belle) - **2.** *inf* [very good] joli(e).

beautifully ['bjuːtəflɪ] *adv* **1.** [attractively - dressed] élégamment ; [- decorated] avec goût - **2.** *inf* [very well] parfaitement, à la perfection.

beauty ['bjuːtɪ] *n* [gen] beauté *f*.

beauty parade *n* défilé *m* d'un concours de beauté.

beauty parlour *UK*, **beauty parlor** *US n* institut *m* de beauté.

beauty salon = **beauty parlour**.

beauty spot *n* **1.** [picturesque place] site *m* pittoresque - **2.** [on skin] grain *m* de beauté.

beaver ['biːvə'] *n* castor *m*.

became [bɪ'keɪm] *pt* ▸ **become**.

because [bɪ'kɒz] *conj* parce que. **because of** *prep* à cause de.

beck [bek] *n* : **to be at sb's beck and call** être aux ordres OR à la disposition de qqn.

beckon ['bekən] <> *vt* [signal to] faire signe à. <> *vi* [signal] : **to beckon to sb** faire signe à qqn.

become [bɪ'kʌm] (*pt* **became**, *pp* **become**) *vi* devenir ; **to become quieter** se calmer ; **to become irritated** s'énerver.

becoming [bɪ'kʌmɪŋ] *adj* **1.** [attractive] seyant(e), qui va bien - **2.** [appropriate] convenable.

bed [bed] *n* **1.** [to sleep on] lit *m* ; **to go to bed** se coucher ; **to go to bed with sb** *euph* coucher avec qqn - **2.** [flowerbed] parterre *m* - **3.** [of sea, river] lit *m*, fond *m*.

bed and breakfast *n* ≃ chambre *f* d'hôte.

bedclothes ['bedkləʊðz] *npl* draps *mpl* et couvertures *fpl*.

bedlam ['bedləm] *n* pagaille *f*.

bed linen *n* (*U*) draps *mpl* et taies *fpl*.

bedraggled [bɪ'drægld] *adj* [person] débraillé(e) ; [hair] embroussaillé(e).

bedridden ['bed,rɪdn] *adj* grabataire.

bedroom ['bedrʊm] *n* chambre *f* (à coucher).

bedside ['bedsaɪd] *n* chevet *m*.

bedsore ['bedsɔː'] *n* escarre *f*.

bedspread ['bedspred] *n* couvre-lit *m*, dessus-de-lit *m inv*.

bedtime ['bedtaɪm] *n* heure *f* du coucher.

bee [biː] *n* abeille *f*.

beeline ['biːlaɪn] *n* : **to make a beeline for** *inf* aller tout droit OR directement vers.

been [bi:n] *pp* ► be.

beeper *n US* = bleeper.

beer [bɪəʳ] *n* bière *f*.

beet [bi:t] *n UK* betterave *f*.

beetle ['bi:tl] *n* scarabée *m*.

beetroot ['bi:tru:t] *n* betterave *f*.

before [bɪ'fɔːʳ] <> *adv* auparavant, avant ; **I've never been there before** je n'y suis jamais allé(e) ; **I've seen it before** je l'ai déjà vu ; **the year before** l'année d'avant OR précédente. <> *prep* **1.** [in time] avant - **2.** [in space] devant. <> *conj* avant de (+ *infin*), avant que (+ *subjunctive*) ; **before leaving** avant de partir ; **before you leave** avant que vous ne partiez.

beforehand [bɪ'fɔːhænd] *adv* à l'avance.

befriend [bɪ'frend] *vt* prendre en amitié.

beg [beg] <> *vt* **1.** [money, food] mendier - **2.** [favour] solliciter, quémander ; [forgiveness] demander ; **to beg sb to do sthg** prier OR supplier qqn de faire qqch. <> *vi* **1.** [for money, food] : **to beg (for sthg)** mendier (qqch) - **2.** [plead] supplier ; **to beg for** [forgiveness etc] demander.

began [bɪ'gæn] *pt* ► begin.

beggar ['begəʳ] *n* mendiant *m*, -e *f*.

begin [bɪ'gɪn] (*pt* began, *pp* begun) <> *vt* [start] commencer ; **to begin doing** OR **to do sthg** commencer OR se mettre à faire qqch. <> *vi* commencer ; **to begin with** pour commencer, premièrement.

beginner [bɪ'gɪnəʳ] *n* débutant *m*, -e *f*.

beginning [bɪ'gɪnɪŋ] *n* début *m*, commencement *m*.

begrudge [bɪ'grʌdʒ] *vt* **1.** [envy] : **to begrudge sb sthg** envier qqch à qqn - **2.** [do unwillingly] : **to begrudge doing sthg** rechigner à faire qqch.

begun [bɪ'gʌn] *pp* ► begin.

behalf [bɪ'hɑːf] *n* : **on behalf of** *UK*, **in behalf of** *US* de la part de, au nom de.

behave [bɪ'heɪv] <> *vt* : **to behave o.s.** bien se conduire OR se comporter. <> *vi* **1.** [in a particular way] se conduire, se comporter ; **to well/badly** bien/mal se comporter - **2.** [acceptably] bien se tenir - **3.** [to function] fonctionner, marcher.

behaviour *UK*, **behavior** *US* [bɪ'heɪvjəʳ] *n* conduite *f*, comportement *m*.

behead [bɪ'hed] *vt* décapiter.

beheld [bɪ'held] *pt & pp* ► behold.

behind [bɪ'haɪnd] <> *prep* **1.** [gen] derrière - **2.** [in time] en retard sur. <> *adv* **1.** [gen] derrière - **2.** [in time] en retard ; **to leave sthg behind** oublier qqch ; **to stay behind** rester ; **to be behind with sthg** être en retard dans qqch. <> *n inf* derrière *m*, postérieur *m*.

behold [bɪ'həʊld] (*pt & pp* **beheld**) *vt lit* voir, regarder.

beige [beɪʒ] <> *adj* beige. <> *n* beige *m*.

being ['biːɪŋ] *n* **1.** [creature] être *m* - **2.** [existence] : **in being** existant(e) ; **to come into being** voir le jour, prendre naissance.

Beirut [ˌbeɪ'ruːt] *n* Beyrouth.

belated [bɪ'leɪtɪd] *adj* tardif(ive).

belch [beltʃ] <> *n* renvoi *m*, rot *m*. <> *vt* [smoke, fire] vomir, cracher. <> *vi* [person] éructer, roter.

beleaguered [bɪ'liːgəd] *adj* assiégé(e) ; *fig* harcelé(e), tracassé(e).

Belgian ['beldʒən] <> *adj* belge. <> *n* Belge *mf*.

Belgium ['beldʒəm] *n* Belgique *f* ; **in Belgium** en Belgique.

Belgrade [ˌbel'greɪd] *n* Belgrade.

belie [bɪ'laɪ] (*cont* belying) *vt* **1.** [disprove] démentir - **2.** [give false idea of] donner une fausse idée de.

belief [bɪ'liːf] *n* **1.** [faith, certainty] : **belief (in)** croyance *f* (en) - **2.** [principle, opinion] opinion *f*, conviction *f*.

believe [bɪ'liːv] <> *vt* croire ; **believe it or not** tu ne me croiras peut-être pas. <> *vi* croire ; **to believe in sb** croire en qqn ; **to believe in sthg** croire à qqch.

believer [bɪ'liːvəʳ] *n* **1.** RELIG croyant *m*, -e *f* - **2.** [in idea, action] : **believer in** partisan *m*, -e *f* de.

belittle [bɪ'lɪtl] *vt* dénigrer, rabaisser.

bell [bel] *n* [of church] cloche *f* ; [handbell] clochette *f* ; [on door] sonnette *f* ; [on bike] timbre *m*.

belligerent [bɪ'lɪdʒərənt] *adj* **1.** [at war] belligérant(e) - **2.** [aggressive] belliqueux(euse).

bellow ['beləʊ] *vi* **1.** [person] brailler, beugler - **2.** [bull] beugler.

bellows ['beləʊz] *npl* soufflet *m*.

belly ['belɪ] *n* [of person] ventre *m* ; [of animal] panse *f*.

bellyache ['belɪeɪk] *n* mal *m* de ventre.

belly button *n inf* nombril *m*.

belong [bɪ'lɒŋ] *vi* **1.** [be property] : **to belong to sb** appartenir OR être à qqn - **2.** [be member] : **to belong to sthg** être membre de qqch - **3.** [be in right place] être à sa place ; **that chair belongs here** ce fauteuil va là.

belongings [bɪ'lɒŋɪŋz] *npl* affaires *fpl*.

beloved [bɪ'lʌvd] *adj* bien-aimé(e).

below [bɪ'ləʊ] <> *adv* **1.** [lower] en dessous, en bas - **2.** [in text] ci-dessous - **3.** NAUT en bas. <> *prep* sous, au-dessous de ; **to be below sb in rank** occuper un rang inférieur à qqn.

belt [belt] <> n 1. [for clothing] ceinture f - 2. TECH courroie f. <> vt inf flanquer une raclée à.

beltway ['belt,weɪ] n US route f périphérique.

bemused [bɪ'mju:zd] adj perplexe.

bench [bentʃ] n 1. [gen & POL] banc m - 2. [in lab, workshop] établi m.

bend [bend] <> n 1. [in road] courbe f, virage m - 2. [in pipe, river] coude m ; **round UK OR around US the bend** inf dingue, fou (folle). <> vt (pt & pp **bent**) 1. [arm, leg] plier - 2. [wire, fork etc] tordre, courber. <> vi (pt & pp **bent**) [person] se baisser, se courber ; [tree, rod] plier ; **to bend over backwards for sb** se mettre en quatre pour qqn.

beneath [bɪ'ni:θ] <> adv dessous, en bas. <> prep 1. [under] sous - 2. [unworthy of] indigne de.

benefactor ['benɪfæktər] n bienfaiteur m.

beneficial [,benɪ'fɪʃl] adj : **beneficial (to sb)** salutaire (à qqn) ; **beneficial (to sthg)** utile (à qqch).

beneficiary [,benɪ'fɪʃərɪ] n bénéficiaire mf.

benefit ['benɪfɪt] <> n 1. [advantage] avantage m ; **for the benefit of** dans l'intérêt de ; **to be to sb's benefit, to be of benefit to sb** être dans l'intérêt de qqn - 2. ADMIN [allowance of money] allocation f, prestation f. <> vt profiter à. <> vi : **to benefit from** tirer avantage de, profiter de.

Benelux ['benɪlʌks] n Bénélux m.

benevolent [bɪ'nevələnt] adj bienveillant(e).

benign [bɪ'naɪn] adj 1. [person] gentil(ille), bienveillant(e) - 2. MED bénin(igne).

bent [bent] <> pt & pp ▶ **bend**. <> adj 1. [wire, bar] tordu(e) - 2. [person, body] courbé(e), voûté(e) - 3. UK inf [dishonest] véreux(euse) - 4. [determined] : **to be bent on doing sthg** vouloir absolument faire qqch, être décidé(e) à faire qqch. <> n : **bent (for)** penchant m (pour).

bento ['bentəʊ] n (U) bento m.

bento box n boîte f à bento.

bequeath [bɪ'kwi:ð] vt lit & fig léguer.

bequest [bɪ'kwest] n legs m.

berate [bɪ'reɪt] vt réprimander.

bereaved [bɪ'ri:vd] <> adj endeuillé(e), affligé(e). <> n (pl **bereaved**) : **the bereaved** la famille du défunt.

beret ['bereɪ] n béret m.

berk [bɜ:k] n UK inf idiot m, -e f, andouille f.

Berlin [bɜ:'lɪn] n Berlin.

berm [bɜ:m] n US bas-côté m.

Bermuda [bə'mju:də] n Bermudes fpl.

Bern [bɜ:n] n Berne.

berry ['berɪ] n baie f.

berserk [bə'zɜ:k] adj : **to go berserk** devenir fou furieux (folle furieuse).

berth [bɜ:θ] <> n 1. [in harbour] poste m d'amarrage, mouillage m - 2. [in ship, train] couchette f. <> vi [ship] accoster, se ranger à quai.

beseech [bɪ'si:tʃ] (pt & pp **besought** OR **beseeched**) vt lit : **to beseech sb (to do sthg)** implorer OR supplier qqn (de faire qqch).

beset [bɪ'set] <> adj : **beset with** OR **by** [doubts etc] assailli(e) de. <> vt (pt & pp **beset**) assaillir.

beside [bɪ'saɪd] prep 1. [next to] à côté de, auprès de - 2. [compared with] comparé(e) à, à côté de ; **to be beside o.s. with anger** être hors de soi ; **to be beside o.s. with joy** être fou (folle) de joie.

besides [bɪ'saɪdz] <> adv en outre, en plus. <> prep en plus de.

besiege [bɪ'si:dʒ] vt 1. [town, fortress] assiéger - 2. fig [trouble, annoy] assaillir, harceler.

besotted [bɪ'sɒtɪd] adj : **besotted (with sb)** entiché(e) (de qqn).

besought [bɪ'sɔ:t] pt & pp ▶ **beseech**.

best [best] <> adj le meilleur (la meilleure). <> adv le mieux. <> n le mieux ; **to do one's best** faire de son mieux ; **all the best!** meilleurs souhaits! ; **to be for the best** être pour le mieux ; **to make the best of sthg** s'accommoder de qqch, prendre son parti de qqch. ▶ **at best** adv au mieux.

best man n garçon m d'honneur.

bestow [bɪ'stəʊ] vt fml : **to bestow sthg on sb** conférer qqch à qqn.

best-seller n [book] best-seller m.

bet [bet] <> n pari m. <> vt (pt & pp **bet** OR **-ted**) parier. <> vi (pt & pp **bet** OR **-ted**) parier ; **I wouldn't bet on it** fig je n'en suis pas si sûr(e).

betray [bɪ'treɪ] vt trahir.

betrayal [bɪ'treɪəl] n [of person] trahison f.

better ['betər] <> adj (compar of good) meilleur(e) ; **to get better** s'améliorer ; [after illness] se remettre, se rétablir. <> adv (compar of well) mieux ; **I'd better leave** il faut que je parte, je dois partir. <> n meilleur m, -e f ; **to get the better of sb** avoir raison de qqn. <> vt améliorer ; **to better o.s.** s'élever.

better off adj 1. [financially] plus à l'aise - 2. [in better situation] mieux.

betting ['betɪŋ] n (U) paris mpl.

betting shop n UK ≃ bureau m de P.M.U.

between [bɪ'twi:n] <> prep entre ; **to**

choose between sth and sth choisir entre qch et qch. <> *adv* : **(in) between** [in space] au milieu ; [in time] dans l'intervalle.

beverage ['bevərıdʒ] *n fml* boisson *f*.

bevvy ['bevɪ] *n inf* breuvage, boisson alcoolisée.

beware [bɪ'weəʳ] *vi* : **to beware (of)** prendre garde (à), se méfier (de) ; **beware of...** attention à...

bewildered [bɪ'wɪldəd] *adj* déconcerté(e), perplexe.

bewitching [bɪ'wɪtʃɪŋ] *adj* charmeur(euse), ensorcelant(e).

beyond [bɪ'jɒnd] *prep* **1.** [in space] au-delà de - **2.** [in time] après, plus tard que - **3.** [exceeding] au-dessus de ; **it's beyond my control** je n'y peux rien ; **it's beyond my responsibility** cela n'entre pas dans le cadre de mes responsabilités. <> *adv* au-delà.

bias ['baɪəs] *n* **1.** [prejudice] préjugé *m*, parti *m* pris - **2.** [tendency] tendance *f*.

biased ['baɪəst] *adj* partial(e) ; **to be biased towards sb/sthg** favoriser qqn/qqch ; **to be biased against sb/sthg** défavoriser qqn/qqch.

bib [bɪb] *n* [for baby] bavoir *m*, bavette *f*.

Bible ['baɪbl] *n* : **the Bible** la Bible.

bicarbonate of soda [baɪ'kɑːbənət-] *n* bicarbonate *m* de soude.

biceps ['baɪseps] (*pl* **biceps**) *n* biceps *m*.

bicker ['bɪkəʳ] *vi* se chamailler.

bicycle ['baɪsɪkl] <> *n* bicyclette *f*, vélo *m*. <> *vi* aller à bicyclette OR vélo.

bicycle path *n* piste *f* cyclable.

bicycle pump *n* pompe *f* à vélo.

bid [bɪd] <> *n* (*pt & pp* **bid**, *cont* **bidding**) [attempt] tentative *f*. <> *vt* (*pt & pp* **bid**, *cont* **bidding**) [at auction] faire une enchère de. <> *vi* **1.** [at auction] : **to bid (for)** faire une enchère (pour) - **2.** [attempt] : **to bid for sthg** briguer qqch - **3.** COMM faire une soumission, répondre à un appel d'offres.

bidder ['bɪdəʳ] *n* enchérisseur *m*, -euse *f*.

bidding ['bɪdɪŋ] *n* (U) enchères *fpl*.

bide [baɪd] *vt* : **to bide one's time** attendre son heure OR le bon moment.

bifocals [baɪ'fəʊklz] *npl* lunettes *fpl* bifocales.

big [bɪg] *adj* **1.** [gen] grand(e) - **2.** [in amount, bulk - box, crowd, book] gros (grosse).

bigamy ['bɪgəmɪ] *n* bigamie *f*.

big deal *inf* <> *n* : **it's no big deal** ce n'est pas dramatique ; **what's the big deal?** où est le problème? <> *excl* tu parles!, et alors?

big dipper [-'dɪpəʳ] *n* **1.** UK [rollercoaster] montagnes *fpl* russes - **2.** US ASTRON : **the Big Dipper** la Grande Ourse.

bigheaded [ˌbɪg'hedɪd] *adj inf* crâneur(euse).

bigot ['bɪgət] *n* sectaire *mf*.

bigoted ['bɪgətɪd] *adj* sectaire.

bigotry ['bɪgətrɪ] *n* sectarisme *m*.

big time *n inf* **to make** OR **to hit** OR **to reach the big time** réussir, arriver en haut de l'échelle.

big toe *n* gros orteil *m*.

big top *n* chapiteau *m*.

big wheel *n* UK [at fairground] grande roue *f*.

bike [baɪk] *n inf* **1.** [bicycle] vélo *m* - **2.** [motorcycle] bécane *f*, moto *f*.

bikeway ['baɪkweɪ] *n* US piste *f* cyclable.

bikini [bɪ'kiːnɪ] *n* Bikini® *m*.

bile [baɪl] *n* **1.** [fluid] bile *f* - **2.** [anger] mauvaise humeur *f*.

bilingual [baɪ'lɪŋgwəl] *adj* bilingue.

bill [bɪl] <> *n* **1.** [statement of cost] : **bill (for)** note *f* OR facture *f* (de) ; [in restaurant] addition *f* (de) - **2.** [in parliament] projet *m* de loi - **3.** [of show, concert] programme *m* - **4.** US [banknote] billet *m* de banque - **5.** [poster] : **'post** OR **stick** UK **no bills'** 'défense d'afficher' - **6.** [beak] bec *m*. <> *vt* **1.** [invoice] : **to bill sb (for)** envoyer une facture à qqn (pour) - **2.** [advertise] annoncer ; **they're billed as the best band in the world** on les présente comme le meilleur groupe du monde.

billboard ['bɪlbɔːd] *n* panneau *m* d'affichage.

billet ['bɪlɪt] *n* logement *m* (chez l'habitant).

billfold ['bɪlfəʊld] *n* US portefeuille *m*.

billiards ['bɪljədz] *n* billard *m*.

billion ['bɪljən] *num* **1.** US [thousand million] milliard *m* - **2.** UK [million million] billion *m*.

Bill of Rights *n* : **the Bill of Rights** les dix premiers amendements à la Constitution américaine.

billy club *n* matraque *f*.

bimbo ['bɪmbəʊ] (*pl* **-s** OR **-es**) *n inf pej* : **she's a bit of a bimbo** c'est le genre 'pin-up'.

bin [bɪn] *n* **1.** UK [for rubbish] poubelle *f* - **2.** [for grain, coal] coffre *m*.

bind [baɪnd] *vt* (*pt & pp* **bound**) **1.** [tie up] attacher, lier - **2.** [unite] lier - **3.** [bandage] panser - **4.** [book] relier - **5.** [constrain] contraindre, forcer.

binder ['baɪndəʳ] *n* [cover] classeur *m*.

binding ['baɪndɪŋ] <> *adj* qui lie OR engage ; [agreement] irrévocable. <> *n* [on book] reliure *f*.

binge [bɪndʒ] *inf* <> *n* : **to go on a binge** prendre une cuite. <> *vi* : **to binge on sthg** se gaver OR se bourrer de qqch.

bingo ['bɪŋɡəʊ] *n* bingo *m*, ≃ loto *m*.

binoculars [bɪ'nɒkjʊləz] *npl* jumelles *fpl*.

biochemistry [ˌbaɪəʊ'kemɪstrɪ] *n* biochimie *f*.

biodegradable [ˌbaɪəʊdɪ'ɡreɪdəbl] *adj* biodégradable.

bioethics [ˌbaɪəʊ'eθɪks] *n (sg)* bioéthique *f*.

biography [baɪ'ɒɡrəfɪ] *n* biographie *f*.

biological [ˌbaɪə'lɒdʒɪkl] *adj* biologique ; [washing powder] aux enzymes.

biological mother *n* mère *f* biologique.

biology [baɪ'ɒlədʒɪ] *n* biologie *f*.

biome ['baɪəʊm] *n* biome *m*.

biotechnology [ˌbaɪəʊtek'nɒlədʒɪ] *n* biotechnologie *f*.

bioterrorism [ˌbaɪəʊ'terərɪzm] *n* bioterrorisme *m*.

biowarfare [ˌbaɪəʊ'wɔːfeə] *n* guerre *f* biologique.

bipolar disorder [baɪ'pəʊlə'-] *n* MED trouble *m* bipolaire.

birch [bɜːtʃ] *n* [tree] bouleau *m*.

bird [bɜːd] *n* **1.** [creature] oiseau *m* - **2.** UK *inf* [woman] gonzesse *f*.

birdie ['bɜːdɪ] *n* **1.** [childrens' vocabulary] petit oiseau *m* - **2.** GOLF birdie *m*.

bird's-eye view *n lit* vue *f* aérienne ; *fig* vue *f* d'ensemble.

bird-watcher [-ˌwɒtʃə] *n* observateur *m*, -trice *f* d'oiseaux.

Biro® ['baɪərəʊ] *n* UK stylo *m* à bille.

birth [bɜːθ] *n lit & fig* naissance *f* ; **to give birth (to)** donner naissance (à).

birth certificate *n* acte *m* OR extrait *m* de naissance.

birth control *n (U)* régulation *f* OR contrôle *m* des naissances.

birthday ['bɜːθdeɪ] *n* anniversaire *m*.

birthmark ['bɜːθmɑːk] *n* tache *f* de vin.

birth mother *n* mère *f* gestationnelle.

birthrate ['bɜːθreɪt] *n* (taux *m* de) natalité *f*.

Biscay ['bɪskeɪ] *n* : **the Bay of Biscay** le golfe de Gascogne.

biscuit ['bɪskɪt] *n* UK gâteau *m* sec, biscuit *m* ; US scone *m*.

bisect [baɪ'sekt] *vt* couper OR diviser en deux.

bishop ['bɪʃəp] *n* **1.** RELIG évêque *mf* - **2.** [in chess] fou *m*.

bison ['baɪsn] *(pl* bison OR **-s)** *n* bison *m*.

bit [bɪt] <> *pt* ▶ **bite**. <> *n* **1.** [small piece - of paper, cheese etc] morceau *m*, bout *m* ; [- of book, film] passage *m* ; **bits and pieces** UK petites affaires *fpl* OR choses *fpl* ; **to take sthg to bits** démonter qqch - **2.** [amount] : **a bit of shopping** quelques courses ; **it's a bit of a nuisance** c'est un peu embêtant ; **a bit of trouble** un petit problème ; **quite a bit of** pas mal de, beaucoup de - **3.** [short time] : **for a bit** pendant quelque temps - **4.** [of drill] mèche *f* - **5.** [of bridle] mors *m* - **6.** COMPUT bit *m*. ▶ **a bit** *adv* un peu ; **I'm a bit tired** je suis un peu fatigué(e). ▶ **bit by bit** *adv* petit à petit.

bitch [bɪtʃ] *n* **1.** [female dog] chienne *f* - **2.** *v inf pej* [woman] salope *f*, garce *f*.

bitchy ['bɪtʃɪ] *adj inf* vache, rosse.

bite [baɪt] <> *n* **1.** [act of biting] morsure *f*, coup *m* de dent - **2.** *inf* [food] : **to have a bite (to eat)** manger un morceau - **3.** [wound] piqûre *f*. <> *vt (pt* bit, *pp* bitten) **1.** [subj: person, animal] mordre - **2.** [subj: insect, snake] piquer, mordre. <> *vi (pt* bit, *pp* bitten) **1.** [animal, person] : **to bite (into)** mordre (dans) ; **to bite off sthg** arracher qqch d'un coup de dents - **2.** [insect, snake] mordre, piquer - **3.** [grip] adhérer, mordre - **4.** *fig* [take effect] se faire sentir.

biting ['baɪtɪŋ] *adj* **1.** [very cold] cinglant(e), piquant(e) - **2.** [humour, comment] mordant(e), caustique.

bitten ['bɪtn] *pp* ▶ **bite**.

bitter ['bɪtə] <> *adj* **1.** [gen] amer(ère) - **2.** [icy] glacial(e) - **3.** [argument] violent(e). <> *n* UK bière relativement amère, à forte teneur en houblon.

bitter lemon *n* Schweppes® *m* au citron.

bitterness ['bɪtənɪs] *n* **1.** [gen] amertume *f* - **2.** [of wind, weather] âpreté *f*.

bizarre [bɪ'zɑː] *adj* bizarre.

blab [blæb] *vi inf* lâcher le morceau.

black [blæk] <> *adj* **1.** noir(e) - **2.** [coffee] noir(e) ; [tea] nature *(inv)*. <> *n* **1.** [colour] noir *m* - **2.** [person] noir *m*, -e *f* ; **in the black** [financially solvent] solvable, sans dettes. <> *vt* UK [boycott] boycotter. ▶ **black out** *vi* [faint] s'évanouir.

blackberry ['blækbərɪ] *n* mûre *f*.

blackbird ['blækbɜːd] *n* merle *m*.

blackboard ['blækbɔːd] *n* tableau *m* (noir).

blackcurrant [ˌblæk'kʌrənt] *n* cassis *m*.

blacken ['blækn] <> *vt* [make dark] noircir. <> *vi* s'assombrir.

black eye *n* œil *m* poché OR au beurre noir.

blackhead ['blækhed] *n* [acne] point *m* noir.

black ice *n* verglas *m*.

blackleg ['blækleg] *n* UK *pej* jaune *m*.

blacklist ['blæklɪst] <> *n* liste *f* noire. <> *vt* mettre sur la liste noire.

blackmail ['blækmeɪl] <> *n lit & fig* chantage *m*. <> *vt* **1.** [for money] faire chanter - **2.** *fig* [emotionally] faire du chantage à.

black market *n* marché *m* noir.

blackout ['blækaʊt] *n* **1.** MIL & PRESS blackout *m* - **2.** [power cut] panne *f* d'électricité - **3.** [fainting fit] évanouissement *m*.

black pudding *n* UK boudin *m*.

Black Sea *n* : the Black Sea la mer Noire.

black sheep *n* brebis *f* galeuse.

blacksmith ['blæksmɪθ] *n* forgeron *m* ; [for horses] maréchal-ferrant *m*.

black spot *n* UK AUT point *m* noir.

bladder ['blædər] *n* vessie *f*.

blade [bleɪd] *n* **1.** [of knife, saw] lame *f* - **2.** [of propeller] pale *f* - **3.** [of grass] brin *m*.

blame [bleɪm] <> *n* responsabilité *f*, faute *f* ; to take the blame for sthg endosser la responsabilité de qqch. <> *vt* blâmer, condamner ; to blame sthg on rejeter la responsabilité de qqch sur, imputer qqch à ; to blame sb/sthg for sthg reprocher qqch à qqn/qqch ; to be to blame for sthg être responsable de qqch.

bland [blænd] *adj* **1.** [person] terne - **2.** [food] fade, insipide - **3.** [music, style] insipide.

blank [blæŋk] <> *adj* **1.** [sheet of paper] blanc (blanche) ; [wall] nu(e) - **2.** *fig* [look] vide, sans expression. <> *n* **1.** [empty space] blanc *m* - **2.** [cartridge] cartouche *f* à blanc.

blank cheque UK, **blank check** US *n* chèque *m* en blanc ; *fig* carte *f* blanche.

blanket ['blæŋkɪt] *n* **1.** [for bed] couverture *f* - **2.** [of snow] couche *f*, manteau *m* ; [of fog] nappe *f*.

blare [bleər] *vi* hurler ; [radio] beugler.

blasphemy ['blæsfəmɪ] *n* blasphème *m*.

blast [blɑ:st] <> *n* **1.** [explosion] explosion *f* - **2.** [of air, from bomb] souffle *m*. <> *vt* [hole, tunnel] creuser à la dynamite. <> *excl* UK *inf* zut!, mince! ◆ **(at) full blast** *adv* [play music etc] à pleins gaz OR tubes ; [work] d'arrache-pied.

blasted ['blɑ:stɪd] *adj inf* fichu(e), maudit(e).

blast-off *n* [of space shuttle] lancement *m*.

blatant ['bleɪtənt] *adj* criant(e), flagrant(e).

blaze [bleɪz] <> *n* **1.** [fire] incendie *m* - **2.** *fig* [of colour, light] éclat *m*, flamboiement *m*. <> *vi* **1.** [fire] flamber - **2.** *fig* [with colour] flamboyer.

blazer ['bleɪzər] *n* blazer *m*.

bleach [bli:tʃ] <> *n* eau *f* de Javel. <> *vt* [hair] décolorer ; [clothes] blanchir.

bleached [bli:tʃt] *adj* décoloré(e).

bleachers ['bli:tʃəz] *npl* US SPORT gradins *mpl*.

bleak [bli:k] *adj* **1.** [future] sombre - **2.** [place, weather, face] lugubre, triste.

bleary-eyed [,blɪərɪ'aɪd] *adj* aux yeux troubles.

bleat [bli:t] <> *n* bêlement *m*. <> *vi* bêler ; *fig* [person] se plaindre, geindre.

bleed [bli:d] (*pt & pp* bled [bled]) <> *vi* saigner. <> *vt* [radiator etc] purger.

bleeper ['bli:pər] UK *n* bip *m*, biper *m*.

blemish ['blemɪʃ] *n lit & fig* défaut *m*.

blend [blend] <> *n* mélange *m*. <> *vt* : to blend sthg (with) mélanger qqch (avec OR à). <> *vi* : to blend (with) se mêler (à avec).

blender ['blendər] *n* mixer *m*.

bless [bles] (*pt & pp* -ed OR blest) *vt* bénir ; bless you! [after sneezing] à vos souhaits! ; [thank you] merci mille fois!

blessing ['blesɪŋ] *n lit & fig* bénédiction *f*.

blest [blest] *pt & pp* ▶ bless.

blew [blu:] *pt* ▶ blow.

blight [blaɪt] *vt* gâcher, briser.

blimey ['blaɪmɪ] *excl* UK *inf* zut alors!, mince alors!

blind [blaɪnd] <> *adj lit & fig* aveugle ; to be blind to sthg ne pas voir qqch. <> *n* **1.** [for window] store *m* - **2.** US [for watching birds, animals] cachette *f*. <> *npl* : the blind les aveugles *mpl*. <> *vt* aveugler ; to blind sb to sthg *fig* cacher qqch à qqn.

blind alley *n lit & fig* impasse *f*.

blind corner *n* UK AUT virage *m* sans visibilité.

blind date *n* rendez-vous avec quelqu'un qu'on ne connaît pas.

blinders ['blaɪndəz] *npl* US œillères *fpl*.

blindfold ['blaɪndfəʊld] <> *adv* les yeux bandés. <> *n* bandeau *m*. <> *vt* bander les yeux à.

blindly ['blaɪndlɪ] *adv* [unseeingly] à l'aveuglette ; [without thinking] aveuglément.

blindness ['blaɪndnɪs] *n* cécité *f* ; blindness (to sthg) *fig* aveuglement *m* (devant qqch).

blind spot *n* **1.** AUT angle *m* mort - **2.** *fig* [inability to understand] blocage *m*.

blink [blɪŋk] <> *n* ; on the blink [machine]

détraqué(-e). <> vt [eyes] cligner. <> vi
1. [person] cligner des yeux - 2. [light]
clignoter.

blinkered ['bliŋkəd] adj : to be blinkered lit
& fig avoir des œillères.

blinkers ['bliŋkəz] npl UK œillères fpl.

bliss [blis] n bonheur m suprême, félicité f.

blissful ['blisful] adj [day, silence] merveil-
leux(euse) ; [ignorance] total(e).

blister ['blistər] <> n [on skin] ampoule f,
cloque f. <> vi 1. [skin] se couvrir d'am-
poules - 2. [paint] cloquer, se boursoufler.

blithely ['blaiðli] adv gaiement, joyeuse-
ment.

blitz [blits] n MIL bombardement m aérien.

blizzard ['blizəd] n tempête f de neige.

bloated ['bləʊtid] adj 1. [face] bouffi(e)
- 2. [with food] ballonné(e).

blob [blɒb] n 1. [drop] goutte f - 2. [indis-
tinct shape] forme f ; a blob of colour une
tache de couleur.

block [blɒk] <> n 1. [building] : office block
UK immeuble m de bureaux ; block of flats
UK immeuble m - 2. US [of buildings] pâté m
de maisons - 3. [of stone, ice] bloc m
- 4. [obstruction] blocage m. <> vt 1. [road,
pipe, view] boucher - 2. [prevent] bloquer,
empêcher.

blockade [blɒ'keid] <> n blocus m. <> vt
faire le blocus de.

blockage ['blɒkidʒ] n obstruction f.

blockbuster ['blɒkbʌstər] n inf [book]
best-seller m ; [film] film m à succès.

block capitals npl majuscules fpl d'imprimerie.

block letters npl majuscules fpl d'imprimerie.

blog [blɒg] (abbrev of **weblog**) n COMPUT
blog m.

bloke [bləʊk] n UK inf type m.

blond [blɒnd] adj blond(e).

blonde [blɒnd] <> adj blond(e). <> n
[woman] blonde f.

blood [blʌd] n sang m ; in cold blood de
sang-froid.

bloodbath ['blʌdbɑːθ] (pl [-bɑːðz]) n bain
m de sang, massacre m.

blood cell n globule m.

blood donor n donneur m, -euse f de sang.

blood group n UK groupe m sanguin.

bloodhound ['blʌdhaʊnd] n limier m.

blood poisoning n septicémie f.

blood pressure n tension f artérielle ; to
have high blood pressure faire de l'hypertension.

bloodshed ['blʌdʃed] n carnage m.

bloodshot ['blʌdʃɒt] adj [eyes] injecté(e)
de sang.

bloodstream ['blʌdstriːm] n sang m.

blood test n prise f de sang.

bloodthirsty ['blʌd,θɜːsti] adj sanguinaire.

blood transfusion n transfusion f sanguine.

bloody ['blʌdi] <> adj 1. [gen] sanglant(e)
- 2. UK v inf foutu(e) ; you bloody idiot!
espèce de con! <> adv UK v inf vachement.

bloody-minded [-'maindid] adj UK inf
contrariant(e).

bloom [bluːm] <> n fleur f. <> vi fleurir.

blooming ['bluːmiŋ] <> adj UK inf [to
show annoyance] sacré(e), fichu(e). <> adv
UK inf sacrément.

blossom ['blɒsəm] <> n [of tree] fleurs
fpl ; in blossom en fleur(s). <> vi 1. [tree]
fleurir - 2. fig [person] s'épanouir.

blot [blɒt] <> n lit & fig tache f. <> vt
1. [paper] faire des pâtés sur - 2. [ink] sécher.
◆ **blot out** vt sep voiler, cacher ;
[memories] effacer.

blotchy ['blɒtʃi] adj couvert(e) de marbru-
res OR taches.

blotting paper ['blɒtiŋ-] n (U) (papier m)
buvard m.

blouse [blaʊz] n chemisier m.

blow [bləʊ] <> vi (pt blew, pp blown)
1. [gen] souffler - 2. [in wind] : to blow off
s'envoler - 3. [fuse] sauter. <> vt (pt blew,
pp blown) 1. [subj: wind] faire voler, chasser
- 2. [with mouth, nose] : to blow one's nose
se moucher - 3. [trumpet] jouer de, souffler
dans ; to blow a whistle donner un coup de
sifflet, siffler - 4. [spoil - chance] gâcher ;
blew it! j'ai tout gâché! <> n [hit] coup m.
◆ **blow out** vt sep souffler. <> vi
1. [candle] s'éteindre - 2. [tyre] éclater.
◆ **blow over** vi se calmer. ◆ **blow up**
<> vt sep 1. [inflate] gonfler - 2. [with bomb]
faire sauter - 3. [photograph] agrandir.
<> vi exploser.

blow-dry <> n Brushing® m. <> vt faire
un Brushing® à.

blowlamp UK ['bləʊlæmp], **blowtorch**
['bləʊtɔːtʃ] n chalumeau m, lampe f à
souder.

blown [bləʊn] pp ▶ blow.

blowout ['bləʊaʊt] n 1. esp US [of tyre]
éclatement m - 2. [of gas] éruption f.

blowtorch = blowlamp.

blubber ['blʌbər] <> n graisse f de
baleine. <> vi pej chialer.

bludgeon ['blʌdʒən] vt matraquer.

blue [bluː] <> adj 1. [colour] bleu(e) - 2. inf

[sad] triste, cafardeux(euse) - **3.** [pornographic] porno *(inv)*. ◇ *n* bleu *m* ; **out of the blue** [happen] subitement ; [arrive] à l'improviste. **blues** *npl* [sad feeling] le blues, le cafard.

bluebell ['blu:bel] *n* jacinthe *f* des bois.

blueberry ['blu:bərɪ] *n* myrtille *f*.

bluebottle ['blu:,bɒtl] *n* mouche *f* bleue, mouche de la viande.

blue cheese *n* (fromage *m*) bleu *m*.

blue-collar *adj* manuel(elle).

blue jeans *npl US* blue-jean *m*, jean *m*.

blueprint ['blu:prɪnt] *n* photocalque *m* ; *fig* plan *m*, projet *m*.

bluff [blʌf] ◇ *adj* franc (franche). ◇ *n* **1.** [deception] bluff *m* ; **to call sb's bluff** prendre qqn au mot - **2.** [cliff] falaise *f* à pic. ◇ *vt* bluffer, donner le change à. ◇ *vi* faire du bluff, bluffer.

blunder ['blʌndər] ◇ *n* gaffe *f*, bévue *f*. ◇ *vi* [make mistake] faire une gaffe, commettre une bévue.

blunt [blʌnt] ◇ *adj* **1.** [knife] émoussé(e) ; [pencil] épointé(e) ; [object, instrument] contondant(e) - **2.** [person, manner] direct(e), carré(e). ◇ *vt lit & fig* émousser.

blur [blɜːr] ◇ *n* forme *f* confuse, tache *f* floue. ◇ *vt* [vision] troubler, brouiller.

blurb [blɜːb] *n* texte *m* publicitaire.

blurt [blɜːt] ◆ **blurt out** *vt sep* laisser échapper.

blush [blʌʃ] ◇ *n* rougeur *f*. ◇ *vi* rougir.

blusher ['blʌʃər] *n* fard *m* à joues, blush *m*.

blustery ['blʌstərɪ] *adj* venteux(euse).

BMX *(abbrev of* **bicycle motocross)** *n* bicross *m*.

BO *abbrev of* **body odour.**

boar [bɔːr] *n* **1.** [male pig] verrat *m* - **2.** [wild pig] sanglier *m*.

board [bɔːd] ◇ *n* **1.** [plank] planche *f* - **2.** [for notices] panneau *m* d'affichage - **3.** [for games - gen] tableau *m* ; [- for chess] échiquier *m* - **4.** [blackboard] tableau *m* (noir) - **5.** [of company] : **board (of directors)** conseil *m* d'administration - **6.** [committee] comité *m*, conseil *m* - **7.** *UK* [at hotel, guesthouse] pension *f* ; **board and lodging** pension ; **full board** pension complète ; **half board** demi-pension *f* - **8.** : **on board** [on ship, plane, bus, train] à bord ; **above board** régulier(-ère), dans les règles. ◇ *vt* [ship, aeroplane] monter à bord de ; [train, bus] monter dans.

boarder ['bɔːdər] *n* **1.** [lodger] pensionnaire *mf* - **2.** [at school] interne *mf*, pensionnaire *mf*.

boarding card ['bɔːdɪŋ-] *n esp UK* carte *f* d'embarquement.

boarding house ['bɔːdɪŋhaʊs] *(pl* [-haʊzɪz]) *n* pension *f* de famille.

boarding pass ['bɔːdɪŋ-] *n esp US* carte *f* d'embarquement.

boarding school ['bɔːdɪŋ-] *n* pensionnat *m*, internat *m*.

Board of Trade *n UK* : **the Board of Trade** ≃ le ministère *m* du Commerce.

boardroom ['bɔːdrʊm] *n* salle *f* du conseil (d'administration).

boast [bəʊst] ◇ *n* vantardise *f*, fanfaronnade *f*. ◇ *vi* : **to boast (about)** se vanter (de).

boastful ['bəʊstfʊl] *adj* vantard(e), fanfaron(onne).

boat [bəʊt] *n* [large] bateau *m* ; [small] canot *m*, embarcation *f* ; **by boat** en bateau.

boater ['bəʊtər] *n* [hat] canotier *m*.

boatswain ['bəʊsn] *n* maître *m* d'équipage.

bob [bɒb] ◇ *n* **1.** [hairstyle] coupe *f* au carré - **2.** *UK inf dated* [shilling] shilling *m* - **3.** = **bobsleigh.** ◇ *vi* [boat, ship] tanguer.

bobbin ['bɒbɪn] *n* bobine *f*.

bobby ['bɒbɪ] *n UK inf* agent *m* de police.

bobsleigh ['bɒbsleɪ] *UK*, **bobsled** ['bɒbsled] *US n* bobsleigh *m*.

bode [bəʊd] *vi lit* : **to bode ill/well (for)** être de mauvais/bon augure (pour).

bodily ['bɒdɪlɪ] ◇ *adj* [needs] matériel(elle) ; [pain] physique. ◇ *adv* [lift, move] à bras-le-corps.

body ['bɒdɪ] *n* **1.** [of person] corps *m* - **2.** [corpse] corps *m*, cadavre *m* - **3.** [organization] organisme *m*, organisation *f* - **4.** [of car] carrosserie *f* ; [of plane] fuselage *m* - **5.** *(U)* [of wine] corps *m* - **6.** *(U)* [of hair] volume *m* - **7.** [garment] body *m*.

body building *n* culturisme *m*.

bodyguard ['bɒdɪgɑːd] *n* garde *m* du corps.

body odour *UK*, **body odor** *US n* odeur *f* corporelle.

body piercing *n* piercing *m*.

bodywork ['bɒdɪwɜːk] *n* carrosserie *f*.

bog [bɒg] *n* **1.** [marsh] marécage *m* - **2.** *UK v inf* [toilet] chiottes *fpl*.

bogged down [,bɒgd-] *adj* **1.** *fig* [in work] : **bogged down (in)** submergé(e) (de) - **2.** [car etc] : **bogged down (in)** enlisé(e) (dans).

boggle ['bɒgl] *vi* : **the mind boggles!** ce n'est pas croyable!, on croit rêver!

bogus ['bəʊgəs] *adj* faux (fausse), bidon *(inv)*.

boil [bɔɪl] ◇ *n* **1.** MED furoncle *m* - **2.** [boiling point] : **to bring sthg to the boil** porter qqch à ébullition ; **to come to the boil** venir à ébullition. ◇ *vt* **1.** [water, food] faire

bouillir - 2. [kettle] mettre sur le feu. <> *vi* [water] bouillir. ➤ **boil down to** *vt insep* fig revenir à, se résumer à. ➤ **boil over** *vi* **1.** [liquid] déborder - **2.** fig [feelings] exploser.

boiled ['bɔɪld] *adj* : **boiled egg** œuf *m* à la coque ; **boiled sweet** UK bonbon *m* (à sucer).

boiler ['bɔɪlər] *n* chaudière *f*.

boiler room *n* chaufferie *f*.

boiler suit *n* UK bleu *m* de travail.

boiling ['bɔɪlɪŋ] *adj* **1.** [liquid] bouillant(e) - **2.** inf [weather] très chaud(e), torride ; [person] : **I'm boiling (hot)!** je crève de chaleur!

boiling point *n* point *m* d'ébullition.

boisterous ['bɔɪstərəs] *adj* turbulent(e), remuant(e).

bold [bəʊld] *adj* **1.** [confident] hardi(e), audacieux(euse) - **2.** [lines, design] hardi(e) ; [colour] vif (vive), éclatant(e) - **3.** TYPO : **bold type** OR **print** caractères *mpl* gras.

bollard ['bɒlɑːd] *n* UK [on road] borne *f*.

bollocks ['bɒləks] UK v inf <> *npl* couilles *fpl*. <> *excl* quelles conneries!

bolster ['bəʊlstər] <> *n* [pillow] traversin *m*. <> *vt* renforcer, affirmer. ➤ **bolster up** *vt sep* soutenir, appuyer.

bolt [bəʊlt] <> *n* **1.** [on door, window] verrou *m* - **2.** [type of screw] boulon *m*. <> *adv* : **bolt upright** droit(e) comme un piquet. <> *vt* **1.** [fasten together] boulonner - **2.** [close, window] verrouiller - **3.** [food] engouffrer, engloutir. <> *vi* [run] détaler.

bomb [bɒm] <> *n* bombe *f*. <> *vt* bombarder.

bombard [bɒm'bɑːd] *vt* fig & MIL : **to bombard (with)** bombarder (de).

bombastic [bɒm'bæstɪk] *adj* pompeux(euse).

bomb disposal squad *n* équipe *f* de déminage.

bomber ['bɒmər] *n* **1.** [plane] bombardier *m* - **2.** [person] plastiqueur *m*.

bombing ['bɒmɪŋ] *n* bombardement *m*.

bombshell ['bɒmʃel] *n* fig bombe *f*.

bona fide [,bəʊnə'faɪdɪ] *adj* véritable, authentique ; [offer] sérieux(euse).

bond [bɒnd] <> *n* **1.** [between people] lien *m* - **2.** [promise] engagement *m* - **3.** FIN bon *m*, titre *m*. <> *vt* **1.** [glue] : **to bond sthg to sthg** coller qqch sur qqch - **2.** fig [people] unir.

bondage ['bɒndɪdʒ] *n* servitude *f*, esclavage *m*.

bone [bəʊn] <> *n* os *m* ; [of fish] arête *f*. <> *vt* [meat] désosser ; [fish] enlever les arêtes de.

bone-dry *adj* tout à fait sec (sèche).

bone-idle *adj* paresseux(euse) comme une couleuvre OR un lézard.

bonfire ['bɒn,faɪər] *n* [for fun] feu *m* de joie ; [to burn rubbish] feu.

Bonn [bɒn] *n* Bonn.

bonnet ['bɒnɪt] *n* **1.** UK [of car] capot *m* - **2.** [hat] bonnet *m*.

bonny ['bɒnɪ] *adj* Scot beau (belle), joli(e).

bonus ['bəʊnəs] (*pl* **-es** [-iːz]) *n* **1.** [extra money] prime *f*, gratification *f* - **2.** fig [added advantage] plus *m*.

bony ['bəʊnɪ] *adj* **1.** [person, hand, face] maigre, osseux(euse) - **2.** [meat] plein(e) d'os ; [fish] plein(e) d'arêtes.

boo [buː] <> *excl* hou! <> *n* (*pl* **-s**) huée *f*. <> *vt* & *vi* huer.

boob [buːb] UK, **boo-boo** [buːbuː] US *n* inf [mistake] gaffe *f*, bourde *f*. ➤ **boobs** *npl* v inf nichons *mpl*.

booby trap *n* **1.** [bomb] objet *m* piégé - **2.** [practical joke] farce *f*.

book [bʊk] <> *n* **1.** [for reading] livre *m* - **2.** [of stamps, tickets, cheques] carnet *m* ; [of matches] pochette *f*. <> *vt* **1.** [reserve-gen] réserver ; [- performer] engager ; **to be fully booked** être complet(ète) - **2.** inf [subj: police] coller un PV à - **3.** UK FOOTBALL prendre le nom de. <> *vi* réserver. ➤ **books** *npl* COMM livres *mpl* de comptes. ➤ **book up** *vt sep* réserver, retenir.

bookcase ['bʊkkeɪs] *n* bibliothèque *f*.

Booker Prize [bʊkə-] *n* : **the Booker Prize** prix littéraire britannique.

bookie ['bʊkɪ] *n* inf bookmaker *m*.

booking ['bʊkɪŋ] *n* UK **1.** [reservation] réservation *f* - **2.** FOOTBALL : **to get a booking** recevoir un carton jaune.

booking office *n* UK bureau *m* de réservation OR location.

bookkeeping ['bʊk,kiːpɪŋ] *n* comptabilité *f*.

booklet ['bʊklɪt] *n* brochure *f*.

bookmaker ['bʊk,meɪkər] *n* bookmaker *m*.

bookmark ['bʊkmɑːk] *n* signet *m*.

bookseller ['bʊk,selər] *n* libraire *mf*.

bookshelf ['bʊkʃelf] (*pl* **-shelves** [-ʃelvz]) *n* rayon *m* OR étagère *f* à livres.

bookshop UK ['bʊkʃɒp], **bookstore** US ['bʊkstɔːr] *n* librairie *f*.

book token *n* UK chèque-livre *m*.

boom [buːm] <> *n* **1.** [loud noise] grondement *m* - **2.** [in business, trade] boom *m* - **3.** NAUT bôme *f* - **4.** [for TV camera, microphone] girafe *f*, perche *f*. <> *vi* **1.** [make noise] gronder - **2.** [business, trade] être en plein essor OR en hausse.

boom box *n US* grand radiocassette *m* portatif.

boon [buːn] *n* avantage *m*, bénédiction *f*.

boost [buːst] <> *n* [to production, sales] augmentation *f* ; [to economy] croissance *f*. <> *vt* **1.** [production, sales] stimuler - **2.** [popularity] accroître, renforcer.

booster ['buːstər] *n MED* rappel *m* ; **booster shot** piqûre *f* de rappel.

boot [buːt] <> *n* **1.** [for walking, sport] chaussure *f* - **2.** [fashion item] botte *f* - **3.** *UK* [of car] coffre *m*. <> *vt inf* flanquer des coups de pied à. **to boot** *adv* par-dessus le marché, en plus.

booth [buːð] *n* **1.** [at fair] baraque *f* foraine - **2.** [telephone booth] cabine *f* - **3.** [voting booth] isoloir *m*.

booty ['buːtɪ] *n* butin *m*.

booze [buːz] *inf* <> *n (U)* alcool *m*, boisson *f* alcoolisée. <> *vi* picoler.

bop [bɒp] *inf* <> *n* **1.** [hit] coup *m* - **2.** [disco, dance] boum *f*. <> *vi* [dance] danser.

border ['bɔːdər] <> *n* **1.** [between countries] frontière *f* - **2.** [edge] bord *m* - **3.** [in garden] bordure *f*. <> *vt* **1.** [country] être limitrophe de - **2.** [edge] border. **border on** *vt insep* friser, être voisin(e) de.

borderline ['bɔːdəlaɪn] <> *adj* : **borderline case** cas *m* limite. <> *n fig* limite *f*, ligne *f* de démarcation.

bore [bɔːr] <> *pt* ▶ **bear**. <> *n* **1.** [person] raseur *m*, -euse *f* ; [situation, event] corvée *f* - **2.** [of gun] calibre *m*. <> *vt* **1.** [not interest] ennuyer, raser ; **to bore sb stiff** OR **to tears** OR **to death** ennuyer qqn à mourir - **2.** [drill] forer, percer.

bored [bɔːd] *adj* [person] qui s'ennuie ; [look] d'ennui ; **to be bored with** en avoir assez de.

boredom ['bɔːdəm] *n (U)* ennui *m*.

boring ['bɔːrɪŋ] *adj* ennuyeux(euse).

born [bɔːn] *adj* né(e) ; **to be born** naître ; **I was born in 1965** je suis né(e) en 1965 ; **when were you born?** quelle est ta date de naissance?

borne [bɔːn] *pp* ▶ **bear**.

borough ['bʌrə] *n* municipalité *f*.

borrow ['bɒrəu] *vt* emprunter ; **to borrow sthg (from sb)** emprunter qqch (à qqn).

Bosnia ['bɒznɪə] *n* Bosnie *f*.

Bosnia-Herzegovina [-,hɜːtsəgə'viːnə] *n* Bosnie-Herzégovine *f*.

Bosnian ['bɒznɪən] <> *adj* bosniaque. <> *n* Bosniaque *mf*.

bosom ['buzəm] *n* poitrine *f*, seins *mpl* ; *fig* sein *m* ; **bosom friend** ami *m*, -e *f* intime.

boss [bɒs] <> *n* patron *m*, -onne *f*, chef *m*.

<> *vt pej* donner des ordres à, régenter. **boss about**, **boss around** *vt sep pej* donner des ordres à, régenter.

bossy ['bɒsɪ] *adj* autoritaire.

bosun ['bəusn] = **boatswain**.

botany ['bɒtənɪ] *n* botanique *f*.

botch [bɒtʃ] **botch up** *vt sep inf* bousiller, saboter.

both [bəuθ] <> *adj* les deux. <> *pron* : **both (of them)** (tous) les deux ((toutes) les deux) ; **both of us are coming** on vient tous les deux. <> *adv* : **she is both intelligent and amusing** elle est à la fois intelligente et drôle.

bother ['bɒðər] <> *vt* **1.** [worry] ennuyer, inquiéter ; **to bother o.s. (about)** se tracasser (au sujet de) ; **I can't be bothered to do it** *esp UK* je n'ai vraiment pas envie de le faire - **2.** [pester, annoy] embêter ; **I'm sorry to bother you** excusez-moi de vous déranger. <> *vi* : **to bother about sthg** s'inquiéter de qqch ; **don't bother (to do it)** ce n'est pas la peine (de le faire). <> *n (U)* embêtement *m* ; **it's no bother at all** cela ne me dérange OR m'ennuie pas du tout.

bothered ['bɒðəd] *adj* inquiet(ète) ; **I am really bothered that so many people are unemployed** cela m'inquiète que tant de personnes soient au chômage ; **I am bothered about it** OR **I am bothered by it** *UK* cela me dérange.

bottle ['bɒtl] <> *n* **1.** [gen] bouteille *f* ; [medicine, perfume] flacon *m* ; [for baby] biberon *m* - **2.** *(U) UK inf* [courage] cran *m*, culot *m*. <> *vt* [wine etc] mettre en bouteilles ; [fruit] mettre en bocal. **bottle up** *vt sep* [feelings] refouler, contenir.

bottle bank *n UK* container *m* pour verre usagé.

bottleneck ['bɒtlnek] *n* **1.** [in traffic] bouchon *m*, embouteillage *m* - **2.** [in production] goulet *m* d'étranglement.

bottle-opener *n* ouvre-bouteilles *m inv*, décapsuleur *m*.

bottom ['bɒtəm] <> *adj* **1.** [lowest] du bas - **2.** [in class] dernier(ère). <> *n* **1.** [of bottle, lake, garden] fond *m* ; [of page, ladder, street] bas *m* ; [of hill] pied *m* - **2.** [of scale] bas *m* ; [of class] dernier *m*, -ère *f* - **3.** [buttocks] derrière *m* - **4.** [cause] : **to get to the bottom of sthg** aller au fond de qqch, découvrir la cause de qqch - **5.** [of two-piece garment] bas *m* ; **pyjama bottoms** bas de pyjama. **bottom out** *vi* atteindre son niveau le plus bas.

bottom line *n fig* : **the bottom line** l'essentiel *m*.

bough [bau] *n* branche *f*.

bought [bɔːt] *pt & pp* ▶ **buy**.

boulder ['bəʊldər] *n* rocher *m*.

bounce [baʊns] <> *vi* **1.** [ball] rebondir ; [person] sauter - **2.** *inf* [cheque] être sans provision. <> *vt* **1.** [ball] faire rebondir - **2.** *inf* [cheque] être sans provision. <> *n* rebond *m*.

bouncer ['baʊnsər] *n inf* videur *m*.

bound [baʊnd] <> *pt & pp* ► **bind**. <> *adj* **1.** [certain] : **he's bound to win il va sûrement gagner** ; **she's bound to see it elle ne peut pas manquer de le voir** - **2.** [obliged] : **to be bound to do sthg** être obligé(e) OR tenu(e) de faire qqch ; **I'm bound to say/admit** je dois dire/reconnaître - **3.** [for place] : **to be bound for** [subj: person] être en route pour ; [subj: plane, train] être à destination de. <> *n* [leap] bond *m*, saut *m*. <> *vt* : **to be bounded by** [subj: field] être limité(e) OR délimité(e) par ; [subj: country] être limitrophe de. ► **bounds** *npl* limites *fpl* ; **out of bounds** interdit, défendu.

boundary ['baʊndəri] *n* [gen] frontière *f* ; [of property] limite *f*, borne *f*.

bourbon ['bɜːbən] *n* bourbon *m*.

bout [baʊt] *n* **1.** [of illness] accès *m* ; **a bout of flu** une grippe - **2.** [session] période *f* - **3.** [boxing match] combat *m*.

bow¹ [baʊ] <> *n* **1.** [in greeting] révérence *f* - **2.** [of ship] proue *f*, avant *m*. <> *vt* [head] baisser, incliner. <> *vi* **1.** [make a bow] saluer - **2.** [defer] : **to bow to** s'incliner devant.

bow² [bəʊ] *n* **1.** [weapon] arc *m* - **2.** MUS archet *m* - **3.** [knot] nœud *m*.

bowl [bəʊl] <> *n* **1.** [container - gen] jatte *f*, saladier *m* ; [- small] bol *m* ; [- for washing up] cuvette *f* - **2.** [of toilet, sink] cuvette *f* ; [of pipe] fourneau *m*. <> *vi* CRICKET lancer la balle. ► **bowls** *n* (U) boules *fpl* (sur herbe). ► **bowl over** *vt sep lit & fig* renverser.

bow-legged [ˌbəʊ'legɪd] *adj* aux jambes arquées.

bowler ['bəʊlər] *n* **1.** CRICKET lanceur *m* - **2.** UK **bowler (hat)** chapeau *m* melon.

bowling ['bəʊlɪŋ] *n* (U) bowling *m*.

bowling alley *n* [building] bowling *m* ; [alley] piste *f* de bowling.

bowling green *n* terrain *m* de boules (sur herbe).

bow tie [bəʊ-] *n* nœud *m* papillon.

box [bɒks] <> *n* **1.** [gen] boîte *f* - **2.** THEAT loge *f* - **3.** UK *inf* [television] : **the box** la télé. <> *vi* boxer, faire de la boxe.

boxer ['bɒksər] *n* **1.** [fighter] boxeur *m*, -euse *f* - **2.** [dog] boxer *m*.

boxer shorts *npl* boxer-short *m*.

boxing ['bɒksɪŋ] *n* boxe *f*.

Boxing Day *n* le 26 décembre.

boxing glove *n* gant *m* de boxe.

box office *n* bureau *m* de location.

boxroom ['bɒksrʊm] *n* UK débarras *m*.

boy [bɔɪ] <> *n* [male child] garçon *m*. <> *excl inf* **(oh) boy!** ben, mon vieux!, ben, dis-donc!

boycott ['bɔɪkɒt] <> *n* boycott *m*, boycottage *m*. <> *vt* boycotter.

boyfriend ['bɔɪfrend] *n* copain *m*, petit ami *m*.

boyish ['bɔɪɪʃ] *adj* **1.** [appearance - of man] gamin(e) ; [- of woman] de garçon - **2.** [behaviour] garçonnier(ère).

BR *(abbrev of British Rail)* *n* ≃ SNCF *f*.

bra [brɑː] *n* soutien-gorge *m*.

brace [breɪs] <> *n* **1.** [on teeth] appareil *m* (dentaire) - **2.** [on leg] appareil *m* orthopédique. <> *vt* **1.** [steady] soutenir, consolider ; **to brace o.s.** s'accrocher, se cramponner - **2.** *fig* [prepare] : **to brace o.s. (for sthg)** se préparer (à qqch). ► **braces** *npl* **1.** UK [for trousers] bretelles *fpl* - **2.** [for teeth] appareil *m* dentaire OR orthodontique.

bracelet ['breɪslɪt] *n* bracelet *m*.

bracing ['breɪsɪŋ] *adj* vivifiant(e).

bracken ['brækn] *n* fougère *f*.

bracket ['brækɪt] *n* **1.** [support] support *m* - **2.** [parenthesis - round] parenthèse *f* ; [- square] crochet *m* ; **in brackets** entre parenthèses/crochets - **3.** [group] : **income/age bracket** tranche *f* d'âge/de revenus. <> *vt* [enclose in brackets] mettre entre parenthèses/crochets.

brag [bræg] *vi* se vanter.

braid [breɪd] <> *n* **1.** [on uniform] galon *m* - **2.** [of hair] tresse *f*, natte *f*. <> *vt* [hair] tresser, natter.

brain [breɪn] *n* cerveau *m*. ► **brains** *npl* [intelligence] intelligence *f*.

brainchild ['breɪntʃaɪld] *n inf* idée *f* personnelle, invention *f* personnelle.

brainwash ['breɪnwɒʃ] *vt* faire un lavage de cerveau à.

brainwave ['breɪnweɪv] *n* idée *f* géniale OR de génie.

brainy ['breɪnɪ] *adj inf* intelligent(e).

brake [breɪk] <> *n lit & fig* frein *m*. <> *vi* freiner.

brake light *n* stop *m*, feu *m* arrière.

bramble ['bræmbl] *n* [bush] ronce *f* ; UK [fruit] mûre *f*.

bran [bræn] *n* son *m*.

branch [brɑːntʃ] <> *n* **1.** [of tree, subject] branche *f* - **2.** [of railway] bifurcation *f*, embranchement *m* - **3.** [of company] filiale *f*, succursale *f* ; [of bank] agence *f*. <> *vi*

38

bifurquer. **branch out** vi [person, company] étendre ses activités, se diversifier.

brand [brænd] <> n 1. COMM marque f - 2. fig [type, style] type m, genre m. <> vt 1. [cattle] marquer au fer rouge - 2. fig [classify] : **to brand sb (as) sthg** étiqueter qqn comme qqch, coller à qqn l'étiquette de qqch.

brandish ['brændɪʃ] vt brandir.

brand name n marque f.

brand-new adj flambant neuf (flambant neuve), tout neuf (toute neuve).

brandy ['brændɪ] n cognac m.

brash [bræʃ] adj effronté(e).

brass [brɑːs] n 1. [metal] laiton m, cuivre m jaune - 2. MUS : **the brass** les cuivres mpl.

brass band n fanfare f.

brassiere [UK 'bræsɪər, US brə'zɪr] n soutien-gorge m.

brat [bræt] n inf pej sale gosse m.

bravado [brə'vɑːdəʊ] n bravade f.

brave [breɪv] <> adj courageux(euse), brave. <> n guerrier m indien, brave m. <> vt braver, affronter.

bravery ['breɪvərɪ] n courage m, bravoure f.

brawl [brɔːl] n bagarre f, rixe f.

brawn [brɔːn] n (U) 1. [muscle] muscle m - 2. UK [meat] fromage m de tête.

bray [breɪ] vi [donkey] braire.

brazen ['breɪzn] adj [person] effronté(e), impudent(e) ; [lie] éhonté(e). **brazen out** vt sep : **to brazen it out** crâner.

brazier ['breɪzjər] n brasero m.

Brazil [brə'zɪl] n Brésil m.

Brazilian [brə'zɪljən] <> adj brésilien(enne). <> n Brésilien m, -enne f.

brazil nut n noix f du Brésil.

breach [briːtʃ] <> n 1. [of law, agreement] infraction f, violation f ; [of promise] rupture f ; **breach of contract** rupture f de contrat - 2. [opening, gap] trou m, brèche f. <> vt 1. [agreement, contract] rompre - 2. [make hole in] faire une brèche dans.

breach of the peace n atteinte f à l'ordre public.

bread [bred] n pain m ; **bread and butter** tartine f beurrée, pain m beurré ; fig gagne-pain m.

bread bin UK, **bread box** US n boîte f à pain.

breadcrumbs ['bredkrʌmz] npl chapelure f.

breadline ['bredlaɪn] n : **to be on the breadline** être sans ressources OR sans le sou.

breadth [bretθ] n 1. [width] largeur f - 2. fig [scope] ampleur f, étendue f.

breadwinner ['bred,wɪnər] n soutien m de famille.

break [breɪk] <> n 1. [gap] : **break (in)** trouée f (dans) - 2. [fracture] fracture f - 3. [pause - gen] pause f ; UK [- at school] récréation f ; **to take a break** [- short] faire une pause ; [- longer] prendre des jours de congé ; **without a break** sans interruption ; **to have a break from doing sthg** arrêter de faire qqch - 4. inf [luck] : **(lucky) break** chance f, veine f. <> vt (pt broke, pp broken) 1. [gen] casser, briser ; **to break one's arm/leg** se casser le bras/la jambe ; **to break sb's heart** briser le cœur à qqn ; **to break a record** battre un record - 2. [interrupt - journey] interrompre ; [- contact, silence] rompre - 3. [not keep - law, rule] enfreindre, violer ; [- promise] manquer à - 4. [tell] : **to break the news (of sthg to sb)** annoncer la nouvelle (de qqch à qqn). <> vi (pt broke, pp broken) 1. [gen] se casser, se briser ; **to break loose** OR **free** se dégager, s'échapper - 2. [pause] s'arrêter, faire une pause - 3. [weather] se gâter - 4. [voice - with emotion] se briser ; [- at puberty] muer - 5. [news] se répandre, éclater ; **to break even** rentrer dans ses frais. **break away** vi [escape] s'échapper. **break down** <> vt sep 1. [destroy - barrier] démolir ; [- door] enfoncer - 2. [analyse] analyser. <> vi 1. [car, machine] tomber en panne ; [resistance] céder ; [negotiations] échouer - 2. [emotionally] fondre en larmes, éclater en sanglots. **break in** <> vi 1. [burglar] entrer par effraction - 2. [interrupt] : **to break in (on sb/sthg)** interrompre (qqn/qqch). <> vt sep [horse] dresser ; [person] rompre, accoutumer. **break into** vt insep 1. [subj: burglar] entrer par effraction dans - 2. [begin] : **to break into song/applause** se mettre à chanter/applaudir. **break off** <> vt sep 1. [detach] détacher - 2. [talks, relationship] rompre ; [holiday] interrompre. <> vi 1. [become detached] se casser, se détacher - 2. [stop talking] s'interrompre, se taire. **break out** vi 1. [begin - fire] se déclarer ; [- fighting] éclater - 2. [escape] : **to break out (of)** s'échapper (de), s'évader (de). **break up** <> vt sep 1. [into smaller pieces] mettre en morceaux - 2. [end - marriage, relationship] détruire ; [- fight, party] mettre fin à. <> vi 1. [into smaller pieces - gen] se casser en morceaux ; [- ship] se briser - 2. [end - marriage, relationship] se briser ; [- talks, party] prendre fin ; [- school] finir, fermer ; **to break up (with sb)** rompre (avec qqn) - 3. [crowd] se disperser.

breakage ['breɪkɪdʒ] n bris m.

breakdown ['breɪkdaʊn] n 1. [of vehicle,

machine] panne *f* ; [of negotiations] échec *m* ; [in communications] rupture *f* - **2.** [analysis] détail *m*.

breakfast ['brekfəst] *n* petit déjeuner *m*.

breakfast television *n* UK télévision *f* du matin.

break-in *n* cambriolage *m*.

breaking ['breɪkɪŋ] *n* : **breaking and entering** LAW entrée *f* par effraction.

breakneck ['breɪknek] *adj* : **at breakneck speed** à fond de train.

breakthrough ['breɪkθru:] *n* percée *f*.

breakup ['breɪkʌp] *n* [of marriage, relationship] rupture *f*.

breast [brest] *n* **1.** [of woman] sein *m* ; [of man] poitrine *f* - **2.** [meat of bird] blanc *m*.

breast-feed *vt & vi* allaiter.

breast milk *n* (U) lait *m* maternel.

breaststroke ['breststrəʊk] *n* brasse *f*.

breath [breθ] *n* souffle *m*, haleine *f* ; **to take a deep breath** inspirer profondément ; **out of breath** hors d'haleine, à bout de souffle ; **to get one's breath back** reprendre haleine OR son souffle.

breathalyse UK, **-yze** US ['breθəlaɪz] *vt* ≃ faire subir l'Alcootest® à.

breathe [bri:ð] *vi* respirer. *vt* **1.** [inhale] respirer - **2.** [give out - smell] souffler des relents de. **breathe in** *vi* inspirer. *vt sep* aspirer. **breathe out** *vi* expirer.

breather ['bri:ðər] *n inf* moment *m* de repos OR répit.

breathing ['bri:ðɪŋ] *n* respiration *f*.

breathless ['breθlɪs] *adj* **1.** [out of breath] hors d'haleine, essoufflé(e) - **2.** [with excitement] fébrile, fiévreux(euse).

breathtaking ['breθˌteɪkɪŋ] *adj* à vous couper le souffle.

breed [bri:d] (*pt & pp* **bred** [bred]) *n lit & fig* race *f*, espèce *f*. *vt* **1.** [animals, plants] élever - **2.** *fig* [suspicion, contempt] faire naître, engendrer. *vi* se reproduire.

breeding ['bri:dɪŋ] *n* (U) **1.** [of animals, plants] élevage *m* - **2.** [manners] bonnes manières *fpl*, savoir-vivre *m*.

breeze [bri:z] *n* brise *f*.

breezy ['bri:zɪ] *adj* **1.** [windy] venteux(euse) - **2.** [cheerful] jovial(e), enjoué(e).

brevity ['brevɪtɪ] *n* brièveté *f*.

brew [bru:] *vt* [beer] brasser ; [tea] faire infuser ; [coffee] préparer. *vi* **1.** [tea] infuser ; [coffee] se faire - **2.** *fig* [trouble, storm] se préparer, couver.

brewer ['bru:ər] *n* brasseur *m*.

brewery ['bruərɪ] *n* brasserie *f*.

bribe [braɪb] *n* pot-de-vin *m*. *vt* : **to bribe sb (to do sthg)** soudoyer qqn (pour qu'il fasse qqch).

bribery ['braɪbərɪ] *n* corruption *f*.

brick [brɪk] *n* brique *f*.

bricklayer ['brɪkˌleɪər] *n* maçon *m*.

bridal ['braɪdl] *adj* [dress] de mariée ; [suite etc] nuptial(e).

bride [braɪd] *n* mariée *f*.

bridegroom ['braɪdgrʊm] *n* marié *m*.

bridesmaid ['braɪdzmeɪd] *n* demoiselle *f* d'honneur.

bridge [brɪdʒ] *n* **1.** [gen] pont *m* - **2.** [on ship] passerelle *f* - **3.** [of nose] arête *f* - **4.** [card game, for teeth] bridge *m*. *vt fig* [gap] réduire.

bridle ['braɪdl] *n* bride *f*.

bridle path *n* piste *f* cavalière.

brief [bri:f] *adj* **1.** [short] bref (brève), court(e) ; **in brief** en bref, en deux mots - **2.** [revealing] très court(e). *n* **1.** LAW affaire *f*, dossier *m* - **2.** UK [instructions] instructions *fpl*. *vt* : **to brief sb (on)** [bring up to date] mettre qqn au courant (de) ; [instruct] briefer qqn (sur). **briefs** *npl* slip *m*.

briefcase ['bri:fkeɪs] *n* serviette *f*.

briefing ['bri:fɪŋ] *n* instructions *fpl*, briefing *m*.

briefly ['bri:flɪ] *adv* **1.** [for a short time] un instant - **2.** [concisely] brièvement.

brigade [brɪ'geɪd] *n* brigade *f*.

brigadier [ˌbrɪgə'dɪər] *n* général *m* de brigade.

bright [braɪt] *adj* **1.** [room] clair(e) ; [light, colour] vif (vive) ; [sunlight] éclatant(e) ; [eyes, future] brillant(e) - **2.** [intelligent] intelligent(e).

brighten ['braɪtn] *vi* **1.** [become lighter] s'éclaircir - **2.** [face, mood] s'éclairer. **brighten up** *vt sep* égayer. *vi* **1.** [person] s'égayer, s'animer - **2.** [weather] se dégager, s'éclaircir.

brilliance ['brɪljəns] *n* **1.** [cleverness] intelligence *f* - **2.** [of colour, light] éclat *m*.

brilliant ['brɪljənt] *adj* **1.** [gen] brillant(e) - **2.** [colour] éclatant(e) - **3.** *inf* [wonderful] super (*inv*), génial(e).

Brillo pad® ['brɪləʊ-] *n* ≃ tampon *m* Jex®.

brim [brɪm] *n* bord *m*. *vi* : **to brim with** *lit & fig* être plein(e) de.

brine [braɪn] *n* saumure *f*.

bring [brɪŋ] (*pt & pp* **brought**) *vt* **1.** [person] amener ; [object] apporter - **2.** [cause - happiness, shame] entraîner, causer ; **to bring sthg to an end** mettre fin à qqch. **bring about** *vt sep* causer, provoquer. **bring around** *vt sep* [make conscious] ranimer. **bring back** vt sep **1.** [object] rapporter ; [person] ramener - **2.** [memories] rappeler - **3.** [reinstate] rétablir. **bring down** vt sep **1.** [plane] abattre ; [government] renverser - **2.** [prices] faire baisser. **bring forward** vt sep **1.** [gen] avancer - **2.** [in bookkeeping] reporter. **bring in** vt sep **1.** [law] introduire - **2.** [money - subj: person] gagner ; [- subj: deal] rapporter. **bring off** vt sep [plan] réaliser, réussir ; [deal] conclure, mener à bien. **bring out** vt sep **1.** [product] lancer ; [book] publier, faire paraître - **2.** [cause to appear] faire ressortir. **bring round** UK, **bring to** vt sep = **bring around**. **bring up** vt sep **1.** [raise - children] élever - **2.** [mention] mentionner - **3.** [vomit] rendre, vomir.

brink [brɪŋk] n : **on the brink of** au bord de, à la veille de.

brisk [brɪsk] adj **1.** [quick] vif (vive), rapide - **2.** [manner, tone] déterminé(e).

bristle ['brɪsl] <> n poil m. <> vi lit & fig se hérisser.

Britain ['brɪtn] n Grande-Bretagne f ; **in Britain** en Grande-Bretagne.

British ['brɪtɪʃ] adj britannique.

British Isles npl : **the British Isles** les îles fpl Britanniques.

British Library n la bibliothèque nationale britannique.

British Rail n société des chemins de fer britanniques, ≃ SNCF f.

British Telecom [-'telɪkɒm] n société britannique de télécommunications.

Briton ['brɪtn] n Britannique mf.

Brittany ['brɪtənɪ] n Bretagne f.

brittle ['brɪtl] adj fragile.

broach [brəʊtʃ] vt [subject] aborder.

broad [brɔːd] adj **1.** [wide - gen] large ; [- range, interests] divers(e), varié(e) - **2.** [description] général(e) - **3.** [hint] transparent(e) ; [accent] prononcé(e). **in broad daylight** adv en plein jour.

broadband ['brɔːdbænd] n COMPUT à large bande.

broad bean n fève f.

broadcast ['brɔːdkɑːst] (pt & pp broadcast) <> n RADIO & TV émission f. <> vt RADIO radiodiffuser ; TV téléviser.

broaden ['brɔːdn] <> vt élargir. <> vi s'élargir.

broad jump US n = **long jump**.

broadly ['brɔːdlɪ] adv [generally] généralement.

broccoli ['brɒkəlɪ] n brocoli m.

brochure ['brəʊʃə'] n brochure f, prospectus m.

broil [brɔɪl] vt US griller.

broke [brəʊk] <> pt ▶ **break**. <> adj inf fauché(e).

broken ['brəʊkn] <> pp ▶ **break**. <> adj **1.** [gen] cassé(e) ; **to have a broken leg** avoir la jambe cassée - **2.** [interrupted - journey, sleep] interrompu(e) ; [- line] brisé(e) - **3.** [marriage] brisé(e), détruit(e) ; [home] désuni(e) - **4.** [hesitant] : **to speak in broken English** parler un anglais hésitant.

broker ['brəʊkə'] n courtier m, -ière f ; **(insurance) broker** assureur m, courtier, -ière f d'assurances.

brolly ['brɒlɪ] n UK inf pépin m.

bronchitis [brɒŋ'kaɪtɪs] n (U) bronchite f.

bronze [brɒnz] <> adj [colour] (couleur) bronze (inv). <> n [gen] bronze m.

brooch [brəʊtʃ] n broche f.

brood [bruːd] <> n [of animals] couvée f. <> vi : **to brood (over** OR **about sthg)** ressasser (qqch), remâcher (qqch).

brook [brʊk] n ruisseau m.

broom [bruːm] n balai m.

broomstick ['bruːmstɪk] n manche m à balai.

Bros, bros (abbr of brothers) Frères.

broth [brɒθ] n bouillon m.

brothel ['brɒθl] n bordel m.

brother ['brʌðə'] n frère m.

brother-in-law (pl **brothers-in-law**) n beau-frère m.

brought [brɔːt] pt & pp ▶ **bring**.

brow [braʊ] n **1.** [forehead] front m - **2.** [eyebrow] sourcil m - **3.** [of hill] sommet m.

brown [braʊn] <> adj **1.** [colour] brun(e), marron (inv) ; **brown bread** pain m bis - **2.** [tanned] bronzé(e), hâlé(e). <> n [colour] marron m, brun m. <> vt [food] faire dorer.

Brownie point ['braʊnɪ-] n bon point m.

brown paper n papier m d'emballage, papier kraft.

brown rice n riz m complet.

brown sugar n sucre m roux.

browse [braʊz] <> vi **1.** [look] : **I'm just browsing** [in shop] je ne fais que regarder ; **to browse through** [magazines etc] feuilleter - **2.** [animal] brouter - **3.** COMPUT naviguer. <> vt [file, document] parcourir ; **to browse a site** COMPUT naviguer sur un site.

browser ['braʊzə'] n navigateur m, browser m.

bruise [bruːz] <> n bleu m. <> vt **1.** [skin, arm] se faire un bleu à ; [fruit] taler - **2.** fig [pride] meurtrir, blesser.

brunch [brʌntʃ] n brunch m.

brunette [bruː'net] n brunette f.

brunt [brʌnt] *n* : **to bear** OR **take the brunt of** subir le plus gros de.

brush [brʌʃ] ◇ *n* **1.** [gen] brosse *f* ; [of painter] pinceau *m* - **2.** [encounter] : **to have a brush with the police** avoir des ennuis avec la police. ◇ *vt* **1.** [clean with brush] brosser - **2.** [touch lightly] effleurer. ◆ **brush aside** *vt sep fig* écarter, repousser. ◆ **brush off** *vt sep* [dismiss] envoyer promener. ◆ **brush up** ◇ *vt sep* [revise] réviser. ◇ *vi* : **to brush up on sthg** réviser qqch.

brush-off *n inf* **to give sb the brush-off** envoyer promener qqn.

brushwood ['brʌʃwʊd] *n (U)* brindilles *fpl*.

brusque, *US* **brusk** [bruːsk] *adj* brusque.

Brussels ['brʌslz] *n* Bruxelles.

brussels sprout *n* chou *m* de Bruxelles.

brutal ['bruːtl] *adj* brutal(e).

brute [bruːt] ◇ *adj* [force] brutal(e). ◇ *n* brute *f*.

BSc *(abbrev of* **Bachelor of Science)** *n UK* (titulaire d'une) licence de sciences.

BT *(abbrev of* **British Telecom)** *n* société britannique de télécommunications.

BTW *(abbr of* **by the way)** *adv inf* à propos.

bubble ['bʌbl] ◇ *n* bulle *f*. ◇ *vi* **1.** [liquid] faire des bulles, bouillonner - **2.** *fig* [person] : **to bubble with** déborder de.

bubble bath *n* bain *m* moussant.

bubble gum *n* bubble-gum *m*.

bubblejet printer ['bʌbldʒet-] *n* imprimante *f* à jet d'encre.

Bucharest [ˌbjuːkəˈrest] *n* Bucarest.

buck [bʌk] ◇ *n* **1.** [male animal] mâle *m* - **2.** *inf* [dollar] dollar *m* - **3.** *inf* [responsibility] : **to pass the buck** refiler la responsabilité. ◇ *vi* [horse] ruer. ◆ **buck up** *inf* **1.** [hurry up] se remuer, se dépêcher - **2.** [cheer up] ne pas se laisser abattre.

bucket ['bʌkɪt] *n* [gen] seau *m*.

Buckingham Palace ['bʌkɪŋəm-] *n* le palais de Buckingham *(résidence officielle du souverain britannique)*.

buckle ['bʌkl] ◇ *n* boucle *f*. ◇ *vt* **1.** [fasten] boucler - **2.** [bend] boucler. ◇ *vi* [wheel] se voiler ; [knees, legs] se plier.

bud [bʌd] ◇ *n* bourgeon *m*. ◇ *vi* bourgeonner.

Budapest [ˌbjuːdəˈpest] *n* Budapest.

Buddha ['bʊdə] *n* Bouddha *m*.

Buddhism ['bʊdɪzm] *n* bouddhisme *m*.

budding ['bʌdɪŋ] *adj* [writer, artist] en herbe.

buddy ['bʌdɪ] *n inf* pote *m*.

budge [bʌdʒ] ◇ *vt* faire bouger. ◇ *vi* bouger.

budgerigar ['bʌdʒərɪgɑːr] *n UK* perruche *f*.

budget ['bʌdʒɪt] ◇ *adj* [holiday, price] pour petits budgets. ◇ *n* budget *m*. ◆ **budget for** *vt insep* prévoir.

budgie ['bʌdʒɪ] *n UK inf* perruche *f*.

buff [bʌf] ◇ *adj* [brown] chamois *(inv)*. ◇ *n inf* [expert] mordu *m*, -e *f*.

buffalo ['bʌfələʊ] *(pl* **buffalo**, **-es** OR **-s)** *n* buffle *m* ; *US* bison *m*.

buffer ['bʌfər] *n* **1.** [gen] tampon *m* - **2.** COMPUT mémoire *f* tampon.

buffet[1] [*UK* 'bʊfeɪ, *US* bəˈfeɪ] *n* [food, cafeteria] buffet *m*.

buffet[2] ['bʌfɪt] *vt* [physically] frapper.

buffet car ['bʊfeɪ-] *n* wagon-restaurant *m*.

bug [bʌg] ◇ *n* **1.** [insect] punaise *f* - **2.** *inf* [germ] microbe *m* - **3.** *inf* [listening device] micro *m* - **4.** COMPUT bogue *m*, bug *m*. ◇ *vt* **1.** *inf* [telephone] mettre sur table d'écoute ; [room] cacher des micros dans - **2.** *inf* [annoy] embêter.

bugger ['bʌgər] *UK v inf* ◇ *n* [person] con *m*, conne *f*. ◇ *excl* merde! ◆ **bugger off** *vi* : **bugger off!** fous le camp!

buggy ['bʌgɪ] *n* **1.** [carriage] boghei *m* - **2.** [pushchair] poussette *f* ; *US* [pram] landau *m*.

bugle ['bjuːgl] *n* clairon *m*.

build [bɪld] ◇ *vt (pt & pp* **built)** *lit & fig* construire, bâtir. ◇ *n* carrure *f*. ◆ **build on**, **build upon** ◇ *vt insep* [success] tirer avantage de. ◇ *vt sep* [base on] baser sur. ◆ **build up** ◇ *vt sep* [business] développer ; [reputation] bâtir. ◇ *vi* [clouds] s'amonceler ; [traffic] augmenter.

builder ['bɪldər] *n* entrepreneur *m*, -euse *f*.

building ['bɪldɪŋ] *n* bâtiment *m*.

building and loan association *n US* société d'épargne et de financement immobilier.

building site *n* chantier *m*.

building society *n UK* ≃ société *f* d'épargne et de financement immobilier.

buildup ['bɪldʌp] *n* [increase] accroissement *m*.

built [bɪlt] *pt & pp* ➤ **build**.

built-in *adj* **1.** CONSTR encastré(e) - **2.** [inherent] inné(e).

built-up *adj* : **built-up area** agglomération *f*.

bulb [bʌlb] *n* **1.** ELEC ampoule *f* - **2.** BOT oignon *m*.

Bulgaria [bʌlˈgeərɪə] *n* Bulgarie *f*.

Bulgarian [bʌlˈgeərɪən] ◇ *adj* bulgare. ◇ *n* **1.** [person] Bulgare *mf* - **2.** [language] bulgare *m*.

bulge [bʌldʒ] ◇ n [lump] bosse f. ◇ vi : **to bulge (with)** être gonflé (de).

bulk [bʌlk] ◇ n 1. [mass] volume m - 2. [of person] corpulence f - 3. COMM : **in bulk** en gros - 4. [majority] : **the bulk of** le plus gros de. ◇ adj en gros.

bulky ['bʌlkɪ] adj volumineux(euse).

bull [bʊl] n [male cow] taureau m ; [male elephant, seal] mâle m.

bulldog ['bʊldɒg] n bouledogue m.

bulldozer ['bʊldəʊzər] n bulldozer m.

bullet ['bʊlɪt] n [for gun] balle f.

bulletin ['bʊlətɪn] n bulletin m.

bullfight ['bʊlfaɪt] n corrida f.

bullfighter ['bʊl,faɪtər] n toréador mf.

bullfighting ['bʊl,faɪtɪŋ] n (U) courses fpl de taureaux ; [art] tauromachie f.

bullhorn US = loudhailer.

bullion ['bʊljən] n (U) **gold bullion** or m en barres.

bullock ['bʊlək] n bœuf m.

bullring ['bʊlrɪŋ] n arène f.

bull's-eye n centre m.

bully ['bʊlɪ] ◇ n tyran m. ◇ vt tyranniser, brutaliser.

bum [bʌm] n 1. UK inf [bottom] derrière m - 2. inf pej [tramp] clochard m.

bumblebee ['bʌmblbiː] n bourdon m.

bump [bʌmp] ◇ n 1. [lump] bosse f - 2. [knock, blow] choc m - 3. [noise] bruit m sourd. ◇ vt [head etc] cogner ; [car] heurter. **bump into** vt insep [meet by chance] rencontrer par hasard.

bumper ['bʌmpər] ◇ adj [harvest, edition] exceptionnel(elle). ◇ n 1. AUT pare-chocs m inv - 2. US RAIL tampon m.

bumper cars npl auto fpl tamponneuses.

bumptious ['bʌmpʃəs] adj suffisant(e).

bumpy ['bʌmpɪ] adj 1. [surface] défoncé(e) - 2. [ride] cahoteux(euse) ; [sea crossing] agité(e).

bun [bʌn] n 1. [cake] petit pain m aux raisins ; [bread roll] petit pain au lait - 2. [hairstyle] chignon m.

bunch [bʌntʃ] ◇ n [of people] groupe m ; [of flowers] bouquet m ; [of grapes] grappe f ; [of bananas] régime m ; [of keys] trousseau m. ◇ vi se grouper. **bunches** npl UK [hairstyle] couettes fpl.

bundle ['bʌndl] ◇ n [of clothes] paquet m ; [of notes, newspapers] liasse f ; [of wood] fagot m. ◇ vt [put roughly - person] entasser ; [- clothes] fourrer, entasser.

bung [bʌŋ] ◇ n bonde f. ◇ vt UK inf envoyer.

bungalow ['bʌŋgələʊ] n bungalow m.

bungle ['bʌŋgl] vt gâcher, bâcler.

bunion ['bʌnjən] n oignon m.

bunk [bʌŋk] n [bed] couchette f.

bunk bed n lit m superposé.

bunker ['bʌŋkər] n 1. GOLF & MIL bunker m - 2. [for coal] coffre m.

bunny ['bʌnɪ] n : **bunny (rabbit)** lapin m.

bunting ['bʌntɪŋ] n (U) guirlandes fpl (de drapeaux).

buoy [UK bɔɪ, US 'buːɪ] n bouée f. **buoy up** vt sep [encourage] soutenir.

buoyant ['bɔɪənt] adj 1. [able to float] qui flotte - 2. fig [person] enjoué(e) ; [economy] florissant(e) ; [market] ferme.

burden ['bɜːdn] ◇ n lit & fig : **burden (on)** charge f (pour), fardeau m (pour). ◇ vt : **to burden sb with** [responsibilities, worries] accabler qqn de.

bureau ['bjʊərəʊ] (pl -x [-z]) n 1. UK [desk] bureau m ; US [chest of drawers] commode f - 2. [office] bureau m.

bureaucracy [bjʊə'rɒkrəsɪ] n bureaucratie f.

bureaux ['bjʊərəʊz] npl ► bureau.

burger ['bɜːgər] n hamburger m.

burglar ['bɜːglər] n cambrioleur m, -euse f.

burglar alarm n système m d'alarme.

burglarize US = burgle.

burglary ['bɜːglərɪ] n cambriolage m.

burgle ['bɜːgl], US **burglarize** ['bɜːgləraɪz] vt cambrioler.

Burgundy ['bɜːgəndɪ] n Bourgogne f.

burial ['berɪəl] n enterrement m.

burlap ['bɜːlæp] n US jute f.

burly ['bɜːlɪ] adj bien charpenté(e).

Burma ['bɜːmə] n Birmanie f.

burn [bɜːn] ◇ vt (pt & pp burnt OR -ed) [heat] brûler ; **I've burned my hand** je me suis brûlé la main. ◇ vi (pt & pp burnt OR -ed) 1. brûler - 2. COMPUT graver ; **to burn a CD** graver un CD. ◇ n brûlure f. **burn down** ◇ vt sep [building, town] incendier. ◇ vi [building] brûler complètement.

burner ['bɜːnər] n brûleur m.

Burns' Night [bɜːnz-] n fête célébrée en l'honneur du poète écossais Robert Burns, le 25 janvier.

burnt [bɜːnt] pt & pp ► burn.

burp [bɜːp] inf ◇ n rot m. ◇ vi roter.

burqa ['bɜːkə] n burqa f.

burrow ['bʌrəʊ] ◇ n terrier m. ◇ vi 1. [dig] creuser un terrier - 2. fig [search] fouiller.

bursar ['bɜːsər] n 1. [treasure] intendant m, -e f - 2. Scot [student] boursier m, -ère f.

bursary ['bɜːsərɪ] n UK [scholarship, grant] bourse f.

burst [bɜːst] <> vi (pt & pp burst) [break, explode] éclater. <> vt (pt & pp burst) faire éclater. <> n [of gunfire] rafale f ; [of enthusiasm] élan m ; a burst of applause un tonnerre d'applaudissements. **burst into** vt insep 1. [room] faire irruption dans - 2. [begin suddenly] : to burst into tears fondre en larmes ; to burst into flames prendre feu. **burst out** vt insep [say suddenly] s'exclamer ; to burst out laughing éclater de rire.

bursting ['bɜːstɪŋ] adj 1. [full] plein(e), bourré(e) - 2. [with emotion] : bursting with débordé(e) de - 3. [eager] : to be bursting to do sthg mourir d'envie de faire qqch.

bury ['berɪ] vt 1. [in ground] enterrer - 2. [hide] cacher, enfouir.

bus [bʌs] n autobus m, bus m ; [long-distance] car m ; by bus en autobus OR car.

bush [bʊʃ] n 1. [plant] buisson m - 2. [open country] : the bush la brousse ; she doesn't beat about the bush elle n'y va pas par quatre chemins.

bushy ['bʊʃɪ] adj touffu(e).

business ['bɪznɪs] n 1. (U) [commerce] affaires fpl ; we do a lot of business with them nous travaillons beaucoup avec eux ; on business pour affaires ; to mean business inf ne pas plaisanter ; to go out of business fermer, faire faillite - 2. [company, duty] affaire f ; mind your own business! inf occupe-toi de tes oignons! - 3. [affair, matter] histoire f, affaire f.

business class n classe f affaires.

businesslike ['bɪznɪslaɪk] adj efficace.

businessman ['bɪznɪsmæn] (pl -men [-men]) n homme m d'affaires.

business trip n voyage m d'affaires.

businesswoman ['bɪznɪs,wʊmən] (pl -women [-,wɪmɪn]) n femme f d'affaires.

busing ['bʌsɪŋ] US n système de ramassage scolaire aux États-Unis, qui organise la répartition des enfants noirs et des enfants blancs dans les écoles afin de lutter contre la ségrégation raciale.

busker ['bʌskər] n UK chanteur m, -euse f des rues.

bus shelter n Abribus® m.

bus station n gare f routière.

bus stop n arrêt m de bus.

bust [bʌst] <> adj inf 1. [broken] foutu(e) - 2. [bankrupt] : to go bust faire faillite. <> n 1. [bosom] poitrine f - 2. [statue] buste m. <> vt (pt & pp bust OR -ed) inf [break] péter.

bustle ['bʌsl] <> n (U) [activity] remue-ménage m inv. <> vi s'affairer.

busy ['bɪzɪ] <> adj 1. [gen] occupé(e) ; to be busy doing sthg être occupé à faire qqch - 2. [life, week] chargé(e) ; [town, office] animé(e). <> vt : to busy o.s. (doing sthg) s'occuper (à faire qqch).

busybody ['bɪzɪ,bɒdɪ] n pej mouche f du coche.

busy signal n US TELEC tonalité f "occupé".

but [bʌt] <> conj mais ; I'm sorry, but I don't agree je suis désolé, mais je ne suis pas d'accord. <> prep sauf, excepté ; everyone was at the party but Jane tout le monde était à la soirée sauf Jane ; he has no one but himself to blame il ne peut s'en prendre qu'à lui-même. <> adv fml seulement, ne... que ; had I but known! si j'avais su! ; we can but try on peut toujours essayer. **but for** prep sans.

butcher ['bʊtʃər] <> n boucher m, -ère f ; butcher's (shop) boucherie f. <> vt 1. [animal] abattre - 2. fig [massacre] massacrer.

butler ['bʌtlər] n maître m d'hôtel (chez un particulier).

butt [bʌt] <> n 1. [of cigarette, cigar] mégot m - 2. [of rifle] crosse f - 3. [for water] tonneau m - 4. [of joke, criticism] cible f. <> vt donner un coup de tête à. **butt in** vi [interrupt] : to butt in on sb interrompre qqn ; to butt in on sthg s'immiscer OR s'imposer dans qqch.

butter ['bʌtər] <> n beurre m. <> vt beurrer.

buttercup ['bʌtəkʌp] n bouton m d'or.

butter dish n beurrier m.

butterfly ['bʌtəflaɪ] n [swimming stroke, insect] papillon m.

buttocks ['bʌtəks] npl fesses fpl.

button ['bʌtn] <> n 1. [gen] bouton m - 2. US [badge] badge m. <> vt = button up. **button up** vt sep boutonner.

button mushroom n champignon m de Paris.

buttress ['bʌtrɪs] n contrefort m.

buxom ['bʌksəm] adj bien en chair.

buy [baɪ] <> vt (pt & pp bought) acheter ; to buy sthg from sb acheter qqch à qqn. <> n : a good buy une bonne affaire. **buy up** vt sep acheter en masse.

buyer ['baɪər] n acheteur m, -euse f.

buyout ['baɪaʊt] n rachat m.

buzz [bʌz] <> n 1. [of insect] bourdonnement m - 2. inf [telephone call] : to give sb a buzz passer un coup de fil à qqn. <> vi : to buzz (with) bourdonner (de). <> vt [on intercom] appeler.

buzzer ['bʌzər] n sonnerie f.

buzzword ['bʌzwɜːd] n inf mot m à la mode.

by [baɪ] *prep* **1.** [indicating cause, agent] par ; **caused/written/killed by** causé/écrit/tué par - **2.** [indicating means, method, manner] : **to pay by cheque** payer par chèque ; **to travel by bus/train/plane/ship** voyager en bus/par le train/en avion/en bateau ; **he's a lawyer by profession** il est avocat de son métier ; **by doing sthg** en faisant qqch ; **by nature** de nature, de tempérament - **3.** [beside, close to] près de ; **by the sea** au bord de la mer ; **I sat by her bed** j'étais assis à son chevet - **4.** [past] : **to pass by sb/sthg** passer devant qqn/qqch ; **to drive by sb/sthg** passer en voiture devant qqn/qqch - **5.** [via, through] par ; **come in by the back door** entrez par la porte de derrière - **6.** [at or before a particular time] avant, pas plus tard que ; **I'll be there by eight** j'y serai avant huit heures - **7.** [during] : **by day** le OR de jour ; **by night** la OR de nuit - **8.** [according to] selon, suivant ; **by law** conformément à la loi - **9.** [in quantities, amounts] à ; **she won by five points** elle a gagné de cinq points ; **by the yard** au mètre ; **by the thousands** par milliers ; **paid by the day/week/month** payé à la journée/à la semaine/au mois ; **to cut prices by 50%** réduire les prix de 50% - **10.** [in arithmetic] par ; **divide/multiply 20 by 2** divisez/multipliez 20 par 2 - **11.** [in measurements] : **2 metres by 4** 2 mètres sur 4 - **12.** [indicating gradual change] : **day by day** jour après jour, de jour en jour ; **one by one** un à un, un par un ; **(all) by oneself** (tout) seul ((toute) seule) ; **I'm all by myself today** je suis tout seul aujourd'hui. ◆ **by and by** *adv lit* bientôt. ◆ **by the by** *adj* : **that's by the by** ça n'a pas d'importance.

bye(-bye) [baɪ(baɪ)] *excl inf* au revoir!, salut!

bye-election *UK* = by-election.

byelaw ['baɪlɔː] = bylaw.

by-election *UK* n élection f partielle.

bygone ['baɪɡɒn] *adj* d'autrefois. ◆ **bygones** *npl* : **to let bygones be bygones** oublier le passé.

bylaw ['baɪlɔː] n arrêté m.

bypass ['baɪpɑːs] ◇ n **1.** [road] route f de contournement - **2.** MED : **bypass (operation)** pontage m. ◇ vt [town, difficulty] contourner ; [subject] éviter.

by-product, byproduct *US* n **1.** [product] dérivé m - **2.** *fig* [consequence] conséquence f.

bystander ['baɪˌstændər] n spectateur m, -trice f.

byte [baɪt] n COMPUT octet m.

byword ['baɪwɜːd] n [symbol] : **to be a byword for** être synonyme de.

C

c [siː] (*pl* **c's** OR **cs**), **C** (*pl* **C's** OR **Cs**) n [letter] c m inv, C m inv. ◆ **C** n **1.** MUS do m - **2.** SCH [mark] C m inv - **3.** (*abbrev of* **Celsius, centigrade**) C.

c., ca. *abbrev of* **circa**.

cab [kæb] n **1.** [taxi] taxi m - **2.** [of lorry] cabine f.

cabaret ['kæbəreɪ] n cabaret m.

cabbage ['kæbɪdʒ] n [vegetable] chou m.

cabin ['kæbɪn] n **1.** [on ship, plane] cabine f - **2.** [house] cabane f.

cabin class n seconde classe f.

cabinet ['kæbɪnɪt] n **1.** [cupboard] meuble m - **2.** POL cabinet m.

cable ['keɪbl] ◇ n cable m. ◇ vt [news] câbler ; [person] câbler à.

cable car n téléphérique m.

cable television, cable TV n câble m, télévision f par câble.

cache [kæʃ] n **1.** [store] cache f - **2.** COMPUT mémoire-cache f, antémémoire f.

cache memory ['kæʃˌmemərɪ] n COMPUT antémémoire f, mémoire f cache.

cackle ['kækl] vi **1.** [hen] caqueter - **2.** [person] jacasser.

cactus ['kæktəs] (*pl* **-tuses** [-təsiːz] OR **-ti** [-taɪ]) n cactus m.

cadet [kə'det] n élève m officier.

cadge [kædʒ] *inf* ◇ vt : **to cadge sthg off** OR **from sb** taper qqn de qqch. ◇ vi : **to cadge off** OR **from sb** taper qqn.

caesarean (section), *US* **cesarean (section)** [sɪ'zeəriən-] n césarienne f.

cafe, café ['kæfeɪ] n café m.

cafeteria [ˌkæfɪ'tɪəriə] n cafétéria f, cantine f.

caffeine ['kæfiːn] n caféine f.

caftan, kaftan ['kæftæn] n cafetan m.

cage [keɪdʒ] n [for animal] cage f.

cagey ['keɪdʒɪ] (*comp* **-ier**, *superl* **-iest**) *adj inf* discret(ète).

cagoule [kə'ɡuːl] n *UK* K-way® m inv.

cajole [kə'dʒəʊl] vt : **to cajole sb (into doing sthg)** enjôler qqn (pour qu'il fasse qqch).

cake [keɪk] n **1.** CULIN gâteau m ; [of fish, potato] croquette f ; **it's a piece of cake** *inf fig* c'est du gâteau - **2.** [of soap] pain m.

caked [keɪkt] *adj* : **caked with mud** recouvert(e) de boue séchée.

CAL (*abbrev of* **computer assisted (OR aided) learning**) *n* enseignement *m* assisté par ordinateur.

calcium ['kælsɪəm] *n* calcium *m*.

calculate ['kælkjʊleɪt] *vt* **1.** [result, number] calculer ; [consequences] évaluer - **2.** [plan] : **to be calculated to do sthg** être calculé(e) pour faire qqch.

calculating ['kælkjʊleɪtɪŋ] *adj pej* calculateur(trice).

calculation [,kælkjʊ'leɪʃn] *n* calcul *m*.

calculator ['kælkjʊleɪtər] *n* calculatrice *f*.

calendar ['kælɪndər] *n* calendrier *m*.

calendar year *n* année *f* civile.

calf [kɑːf] (*pl* **calves** [kɑːvz]) *n* **1.** [of cow, leather] veau *m* ; [of elephant] éléphanteau *m* ; [of seal] bébé *m* phoque - **2.** ANAT mollet *m*.

calibre, *US* **caliber** ['kælɪbər] *n* calibre *m*.

California [,kælɪ'fɔːnjə] *n* Californie *f*.

calipers *US* = **callipers**.

call [kɔːl] ⋄ *n* **1.** [cry] appel *m*, cri *m* - **2.** TELEC appel *m* (téléphonique) - **3.** [summons, invitation] appel *m* ; **to be on call** [doctor etc] être de garde - **4.** [visit] visite *f* ; **to pay a call on sb** rendre visite à qqn - **5.** [demand] : **call (for)** demande *f* (de). ⋄ *vt* **1.** [name, describe] : **what's this thing called?** comment ça s'appelle ce truc? ; **she's called Joan** elle s'appelle Joan ; **let's call it £10** disons 10 livres ; **he called me a liar** il m'a traité de menteur - **2.** [shout, summon] appeler - **3.** [announce - meeting] convoquer ; [- strike] lancer ; [- flight] appeler ; [- election] annoncer. ⋄ *vi* **1.** [shout - person] crier ; [- animal, bird] pousser un cri/des cris - **2.** TELEC appeler ; **who's calling?** qui est à l'appareil? - **3.** [visit] passer. ◆ **call away** *vt sep* : **she's often called away on business** elle doit souvent partir en déplacement OR s'absenter pour affaires. ◆ **call back** ⋄ *vt sep* rappeler. ⋄ *vi* **1.** TELEC rappeler - **2.** [visit again] repasser. ◆ **call for** *vt insep* **1.** [collect - person] passer prendre ; [- package, goods] passer chercher - **2.** [demand] demander. ◆ **call in** ⋄ *vt sep* **1.** [expert, police etc] faire venir - **2.** COMM [goods] rappeler ; FIN [loan] exiger le remboursement de. ⋄ *vi* passer. ◆ **call off** *vt sep* **1.** [cancel] annuler - **2.** [dog] rappeler. ◆ **call on** *vt insep* **1.** [visit] passer voir - **2.** [ask] : **to call on sb to do sthg** demander à qqn de faire qqch. ◆ **call out** ⋄ *vt sep* **1.** [police, doctor] appeler - **2.** [cry out] crier. ⋄ *vi* [cry out] crier. ◆ **call round** *vi* passer. ◆ **call up** *vt sep* **1.** MIL & TELEC appeler - **2.** COMPUT rappeler - **3.** appeler à.

CALL (*abbrev of* **computer assisted (OR aided) language learning**) *n* enseignement *m* des langues assisté par ordinateur.

call box *n UK* cabine *f* (téléphonique).

caller ['kɔːlər] *n* **1.** [visitor] visiteur *m*, -euse *f* - **2.** TELEC demandeur *m*.

caller ID display, **caller display** *n* TELEC présentation *f* du numéro.

call-in *n US* RADIO & TV programme *m* à ligne ouverte.

calling ['kɔːlɪŋ] *n* **1.** [profession] métier *m* - **2.** [vocation] vocation *f*.

calling card *n US* carte *f* de visite.

callipers *UK*, **calipers** *US* ['kælɪpəz] *npl* **1.** MATHS compas *m* - **2.** MED appareil *m* orthopédique.

callous ['kæləs] *adj* dur(e).

callus ['kæləs] (*pl* **-es** [-iːz]) *n* cal *m*, durillon *m*.

calm [kɑːm] ⋄ *adj* calme. ⋄ *n* calme *m* ; **calm before the storm** le calme avant la tempête. ⋄ *vt* calmer. ◆ **calm down** ⋄ *vt sep* calmer. ⋄ *vi* se calmer.

Calor gas® ['kælər-] *n UK* butane *m*.

calorie ['kælərɪ] *n* calorie *f*.

calves [kɑːvz] *npl* ▶ **calf**.

camber ['kæmbər] *n* [of road] bombement *m*.

Cambodia [kæm'bəʊdjə] *n* Cambodge *m*.

camcorder ['kæm,kɔːdər] *n* Caméscope® *m*.

came [keɪm] *pt* ▶ **come**.

camel ['kæml] *n* chameau *m*.

cameo ['kæmɪəʊ] (*pl* **-s**) *n* **1.** [jewellery] camée *m* - **2.** CIN & THEAT courte apparition *f* (*d'une grande vedette*).

camera ['kæmərə] *n* PHOT appareil photo *m* ; CIN & TV caméra *f*. ◆ **in camera** *adv* à huis clos.

cameraman ['kæmərəmæn] (*pl* **-men** [-men]) *n* cameraman *m*, cadreur *m*.

Cameroon [,kæmə'ruːn] *n* Cameroun *m*.

camouflage ['kæməflɑːʒ] ⋄ *n* camouflage *m*. ⋄ *vt* camoufler.

camp [kæmp] ⋄ *n* camp *m*. ⋄ *vi* camper. ◆ **camp out** *vi* camper.

campaign [kæm'peɪn] ⋄ *n* campagne *f*. ⋄ *vi* : **to campaign (for/against)** mener une campagne (pour/contre).

camp bed *n UK* lit *m* de camp.

camper ['kæmpər] *n* **1.** [person] campeur *m*, -euse *f* - **2.** [vehicle] : **camper (van)** camping-car *m*.

campground ['kæmpɡraʊnd] *n US* terrain *m* de camping.

camping ['kæmpɪŋ] *n* camping *m* ; **to go camping** faire du camping.

camping site, **campsite** ['kæmpsaɪt] *n* (terrain *m* de) camping *m*.

campus ['kæmpəs] (*pl* -es [-i:z]) *n* campus *m*.

can¹ [kæn] <> *n* [of drink, food] boîte *f* ; [of oil] bidon *m* ; [of paint] pot *m*. <> *vt* (*pt & pp* -ned, *cont* -ning) mettre en boîte.

can² (*weak form* [kən], *strong form* [kæn], *conditional and preterit form* **could**; *negative form* **cannot** *and* **can't**) *modal vb* **1.** [be able to] pouvoir ; **can you come to lunch?** tu peux venir déjeuner? ; **can you see/hear/smell something?** tu vois/entends/sens quelque chose? - **2.** [know how to] savoir ; **can you drive/cook?** tu sais conduire/cuisiner? ; **I can speak French** je parle le français - **3.** [indicating permission, in polite requests] pouvoir ; **you can use my car if you like** tu peux prendre ma voiture si tu veux ; **can I speak to John, please?** est-ce que je pourrais parler à John, s'il vous plaît? - **4.** [indicating disbelief, puzzlement] pouvoir ; **what can she have done with it?** qu'est-ce qu'elle a bien pu en faire? ; **you can't be serious!** tu ne parles pas sérieusement! - **5.** [indicating possibility] : **I could see you tomorrow** je pourrais vous voir demain ; **the train could have been cancelled** peut-être que le train a été annulé.

Canada ['kænədə] *n* Canada *m* ; **in Canada** au Canada.

Canadian [kə'neɪdjən] <> *adj* canadien(enne). <> *n* Canadien *m*, -enne *f*.

canal [kə'næl] *n* canal *m*.

Canaries [kə'neərɪz] *npl* : **the Canaries** les Canaries *fpl*.

canary [kə'neərɪ] *n* canari *m*.

cancel ['kænsl] (*UK & US*) *vt* **1.** [gen] annuler ; [appointment, delivery] décommander - **2.** [stamp] oblitérer ; [cheque] faire opposition à. ◆ **cancel out** *vt sep* annuler ; **to cancel each other out** s'annuler.

cancellation [,kænsə'leɪʃn] *n* annulation *f*.

cancer ['kænsər] *n* cancer *m*. ◆ **Cancer** *n* Cancer *m*.

candelabra [,kændɪ'lɑ:brə] *n* candélabre *m*.

candid ['kændɪd] *adj* franc (franche).

candidate ['kændɪdət] *n* : **candidate (for)** candidat *m*, -e *f* (pour).

candle ['kændl] *n* bougie *f*, chandelle *f*.

candlelight ['kændllaɪt] *n* lueur *f* d'une bougie OR d'une chandelle.

candlelit ['kændllɪt] *adj* aux chandelles.

candlestick ['kændlstɪk] *n* bougeoir *m*.

candour *UK*, **candor** *US* ['kændər] *n* franchise *f*.

candy ['kændɪ] *n* **1.** (*U*) [confectionery] confiserie *f* - **2.** [sweet] bonbon *m*.

candyfloss ['kændɪflɒs] *n UK* barbe *f* à papa.

cane [keɪn] <> *n* **1.** (*U*) [for furniture] rotin *m* - **2.** [walking stick] canne *f* - **3.** [for punishment] : **the cane** la verge - **4.** [for supporting plant] tuteur *m*. <> *vt* fouetter.

canine ['keɪnaɪn] <> *adj* canin(e). <> *n* : **canine (tooth)** canine *f*.

canister ['kænɪstər] *n* [for film, tea] boîte *f* ; [for gas, smoke] bombe *f*.

cannabis ['kænəbɪs] *n* cannabis *m*.

canned [kænd] *adj* [food, drink] en boîte.

cannibal ['kænɪbl] *n* cannibale *mf*.

cannon ['kænən] (*pl* **cannon** OR **-s**) *n* canon *m*.

cannonball ['kænənbɔːl] *n* boulet *m* de canon.

cannot ['kænɒt] *fml* = **can²**.

canny ['kænɪ] *adj* [shrewd] adroit(e).

canoe [kə'nuː] *n* canoë *m*, kayak *m*.

canoeing [kə'nuːɪŋ] *n* (*U*) canoë-kayak *m*.

canon ['kænən] *n* canon *m*.

can opener *n* ouvre-boîtes *m inv*.

canopy ['kænəpɪ] *n* **1.** [over bed] baldaquin *m* ; [over seat] dais *m* - **2.** [of trees, branches] voûte *f*.

can't [kɑːnt] = **cannot**.

cantankerous [kæn'tæŋkərəs] *adj* hargneux(euse).

canteen [kæn'tiːn] *UK n* **1.** [restaurant] cantine *f* - **2.** [box of cutlery] ménagère *f*.

canter ['kæntər] <> *n* petit galop *m*. <> *vi* aller au petit galop.

cantilever ['kæntɪliːvər] *n* cantilever *m*.

canvas ['kænvəs] *n* toile *f*.

canvass ['kænvəs] *vt* **1.** POL [person] solliciter la voix de - **2.** [opinion] sonder.

canyon ['kænjən] *n* canyon *m*.

cap [kæp] <> *n* **1.** [hat - gen] casquette *f* - **2.** [of pen] capuchon *m* ; [of bottle] capsule *f* ; [of lipstick] bouchon *m*. <> *vt* **1.** [top] : **to be capped with** être coiffé(e) de - **2.** [outdo] : **to cap it all** pour couronner le tout.

capability [,keɪpə'bɪlətɪ] *n* capacité *f*.

capable ['keɪpəbl] *adj* : **capable (of)** capable (de).

capacity [kə'pæsɪtɪ] *n* **1.** (*U*) [limit] capacité *f*, contenance *f* - **2.** [ability] : **capacity (for)** aptitude *f* (à) - **3.** [role] qualité *f* ; **in an advisory capacity** en tant que conseiller.

cape [keɪp] *n* **1.** GEOG cap *m* - **2.** [cloak] cape *f*.

caper ['keɪpər] *n* **1.** CULIN câpre *f* - **2.** *inf* [dishonest activity] coup *m*, combine *f*.

capita ▶ **per capita**.

capital ['kæpɪtl] <> *adj* **1.** [letter] majuscule - **2.** [offence] capital(e). <> *n* **1.** [of country] : **capital (city)** capitale *f* - **2.** TYPO :

capital (letter) majuscule *f* - **3.** *(U)* [money] capital *m* ; **to make capital (out) of** *fig* tirer profit de.

capital expenditure *n (U)* dépenses *fpl* d'investissement.

capital gains tax *n* impôt *m* sur les plus-values.

capital goods *npl* biens *mpl* d'équipement.

capitalism ['kæpɪtəlɪzm] *n* capitalisme *m*.

capitalist ['kæpɪtəlɪst] <> *adj* capitaliste. <> *n* capitaliste *mf*.

capitalize, *UK* **-ise** ['kæpɪtəlaɪz] *vi* : **to capitalize on** tirer parti de.

capital punishment *n* peine *f* capitale OR de mort.

Capitol Hill ['kæpɪtl-] *n* siège du Congrès à Washington.

capitulate [kə'pɪtjʊleɪt] *vi* capituler.

Capricorn ['kæprɪkɔːn] *n* Capricorne *m*.

capsize [kæp'saɪz] <> *vt* faire chavirer. <> *vi* chavirer.

capsule ['kæpsjuːl] *n* **1.** [gen] capsule *f* - **2.** MED gélule *f*.

captain ['kæptɪn] *n* capitaine *mf*.

caption ['kæpʃn] *n* légende *f*.

captivate ['kæptɪveɪt] *vt* captiver.

captive ['kæptɪv] <> *adj* captif(ive). <> *n* captif *m*, -ive *f*.

captor ['kæptə'] *n* ravisseur *m*, -euse *f*.

capture ['kæptʃə'] <> *vt* **1.** [person, animal] capturer ; [city] prendre ; [market] conquérir - **2.** [attention, imagination] captiver - **3.** COMPUT saisir. <> *n* [of person, animal] capture *f* ; [of city] prise *f*.

car [kɑː'] <> *n* **1.** AUT voiture *f* - **2.** RAIL wagon *m*, voiture *f*. <> *comp* [door, accident] de voiture ; [industry] automobile.

carafe [kə'ræf] *n* carafe *f*.

car alarm *n* AUT alarme *f* de voiture.

carambola [ˌkærəm'bəʊlə] *n* carambole *f*.

caramel ['kærəmel] *n* caramel *m*.

carat ['kærət] *n UK* carat *m* ; **24-carat gold** or à 24 carats.

caravan ['kærəvæn] *n* [people travelling] caravane *f* ; *UK* [vehicle] caravane *f* ; [towed by horse] roulotte *f*.

caravan site *n UK* camping *m* pour caravanes.

carbohydrate [ˌkɑːbəʊ'haɪdreɪt] *n* CHEM hydrate *m* de carbone. **carbohydrates** *npl* [in food] glucides *mpl*.

carbon ['kɑːbən] *n* [element] carbone *m*.

carbonated ['kɑːbəneɪtɪd] *adj* [mineral water] gazeux(euse).

carbon copy *n* **1.** [document] carbone *m* - **2.** *fig* [exact copy] réplique *f*.

carbon dioxide [-daɪ'ɒksaɪd] *n* gaz *m* carbonique.

carbon monoxide *n* oxyde *m* de carbone.

carbon paper *n (U)* (papier *m*) carbone *m*.

car-boot sale *n UK* brocante en plein air où les coffres des voitures servent d'étal.

carburettor *UK*, **carburetor** *US* [ˌkɑːbə'retə'] *n* carburateur *m*.

carcass ['kɑːkəs] *n* [of animal] carcasse *f*.

card [kɑːd] *n* **1.** [gen] carte *f* - **2.** *(U)* [cardboard] carton *m* - **3.** COMPUT carte *f*. **cards** *npl* : **to play cards** jouer aux cartes. **on the cards** *US* **in the cards** *US adv inf* it's on the cards that... il y a de grandes chances pour que...

cardboard ['kɑːdbɔːd] <> *n (U)* carton *m*. <> *comp* en carton.

cardboard box *n* boîte *f* en carton.

cardiac ['kɑːdɪæk] *adj* cardiaque.

cardigan ['kɑːdɪgən] *n* cardigan *m*.

cardinal ['kɑːdɪnl] <> *adj* cardinal(e). <> *n* RELIG cardinal *m*.

card index *n UK* fichier *m*.

cardphone ['kɑːdfəʊn] *n UK* téléphone *m* à carte.

card table *n* table *f* de jeu.

care [keə'] <> *n* **1.** *(U)* [protection, supervision] soin *m*, attention *f* ; **to take care of** [look after] s'occuper de ; **take care!** faites bien attention à vous! - **2.** [cause of worry] souci *m* - **3.** *UK* ADMIN : **the baby was put in care** OR **taken into care** on a retiré aux parents la garde de leur bébé. <> *vi* **1.** [be concerned] : **to care about** se soucier de - **2.** [mind] : **I don't care** ça m'est égal ; **who cares?** qu'est-ce que ça peut faire? **care of** *prep* chez. **care for** *vt insep dated* [like] aimer.

career [kə'rɪə'] <> *n* carrière *f*. <> *vi* aller à toute vitesse.

careers adviser *n UK* conseiller *m*, -ère *f* d'orientation.

carefree ['keəfriː] *adj* insouciant(e).

careful ['keəfʊl] *adj* **1.** [cautious] prudent(e) ; **to be careful to do sthg** prendre soin de faire qqch, faire attention à faire qqch ; **be careful!** fais attention! ; **to be careful with one's money** regarder à la dépense - **2.** [work] soigné(e) ; [worker] consciencieux(euse).

carefully ['keəflɪ] *adv* **1.** [cautiously] prudemment - **2.** [thoroughly] soigneusement.

careless ['keəlɪs] *adj* **1.** [work] peu soigné(e) ; [driver] négligent(e) - **2.** [unconcerned] insouciant(e).

caress [kə'res] <> *n* caresse *f*. <> *vt* caresser.

caretaker ['keəˌteɪkə'] *n UK* concierge *mf*.

car ferry *n* ferry *m*.

cargo ['ka:gəʊ] *n* (*pl* -es *or* -s) cargaison *f*.

car hire *n* UK location *f* de voitures.

Caribbean [UK kærɪ'bi:ən, US kə'rɪbɪən] *n* : **the Caribbean (Sea)** la mer des Caraïbes *or* des Antilles.

caring ['keərɪŋ] *adj* bienveillant(e).

carnage ['ka:nɪdʒ] *n* carnage *m*.

carnal ['ka:nl] *adj lit* charnel(elle).

carnation [ka:'neɪʃn] *n* œillet *m*.

carnival ['ka:nɪvl] *n* **1.** [festival] carnaval *m* - **2.** US [fun fair] fête *f* foraine.

carnivorous [ka:'nɪvərəs] *adj* carnivore.

carol ['kærəl] *n* : **(Christmas) carol** chant *m* de Noël.

carousel [,kærə'sel] *n* **1.** [at fair] manège *m* - **2.** [at airport] carrousel *m*.

carp [ka:p] ⋄ *n* (*pl* carp *or* -s) carpe *f*. ⋄ *vi* : **to carp (about sthg)** critiquer (qqch).

car park *n* UK parking *m*.

carpenter ['ka:pəntər] *n* [on building site, in shipyard] charpentier *m* ; [furniture-maker] menuisier *m*..

carpentry ['ka:pəntrɪ] *n* [on building site, in shipyard] charpenterie *f* ; [furniture-making] menuiserie *f*.

carpet ['ka:pɪt] ⋄ *n lit* & *fig* tapis *m* ; **(fitted) carpet** moquette *f*. ⋄ *vt* [floor] recouvrir d'un tapis ; [with fitted carpet] recouvrir de moquette, moquetter.

carpet slipper *n* pantoufle *f*.

carpet sweeper [-,swi:pər] *n* balai *m* mécanique.

car rental *n* US location *f* de voitures.

carriage ['kærɪdʒ] *n* **1.** [of train, horse-drawn] voiture *f* - **2.** (U) UK [transport of goods] transport *m* ; **carriage paid** *or* **free** franco de port.

carriage return *n* retour *m* chariot.

carriageway ['kærɪdʒweɪ] *n* UK chaussée *f*.

carrier ['kærɪər] *n* **1.** COMM transporteur *m* - **2.** [of disease] porteur *m*, -euse *f* - **3.** = **carrier bag**.

carrier bag *n* sac *m* (en plastique).

carrot ['kærət] *n* carotte *f*.

carry ['kærɪ] ⋄ *vt* **1.** [subj: person, wind, water] porter ; [subj: vehicle] transporter - **2.** [disease] transmettre - **3.** [responsibility] impliquer ; [consequences] entraîner - **4.** [motion, proposal] voter - **5.** [baby] attendre - **6.** MATHS retenir. ⋄ *vi* [sound] porter. ◆ **carry away** *vt insep* : **to get carried away** s'enthousiasmer. ◆ **carry forward** *vt sep* FIN reporter. ◆ **carry off** *vt sep* **1.** [plan] mener à bien - **2.** [prize] remporter. ◆ **carry on** ⋄ *vt insep* continuer ; **to carry on doing sthg** continuer à *or* de faire qqch. ⋄ *vi* **1.** [continue] continuer ; **to carry on with sthg** continuer qqch - **2.** *inf* [make a fuss] faire des histoires. ◆ **carry out** *vt insep* [task] remplir ; [plan, order] exécuter ; [experiment] effectuer ; [investigation] mener. ◆ **carry through** *vt sep* [accomplish] réaliser.

carryall ['kærɔ:l] *n* US fourre-tout *m inv*.

carrycot ['kærɪkɒt] *n* UK couffin *m*.

carry-out, US **carryout** *n* plat *m* à emporter.

carsick ['ka:,sɪk] *adj* : **to be carsick** être malade en voiture.

cart [ka:t] ⋄ *n* charrette *f*. ⋄ *vt inf* traîner.

carton ['ka:tn] *n* **1.** [box] boîte *f* en carton - **2.** [of cream, yoghurt] pot *m* ; [of milk] carton *m*.

cartoon [ka:'tu:n] *n* **1.** [satirical drawing] dessin *m* humoristique - **2.** [comic strip] bande *f* dessinée - **3.** [film] dessin *m* animé.

cartridge ['ka:trɪdʒ] *n* **1.** [for gun, pen] cartouche *f* - **2.** [for camera] chargeur *m*.

cartwheel ['ka:twi:l] *n* [movement] roue *f*.

carve [ka:v] ⋄ *vt* **1.** [wood, stone] sculpter ; [design, name] graver - **2.** [slice - meat] découper. ⋄ *vi* découper. ◆ **carve out** *vt sep fig* se tailler. ◆ **carve up** *vt sep fig* diviser.

carving ['ka:vɪŋ] *n* [of wood] sculpture *f* ; [of stone] ciselure *f*.

carving knife *n* couteau *m* à découper.

car wash *n* [process] lavage *m* de voitures ; [place] station *f* de lavage de voitures.

case [keɪs] *n* **1.** [gen] cas *m* ; **to be the case** être le cas ; **in case of** en cas de ; **in that case** dans ce cas ; **in which case** auquel cas ; **as *or* whatever the case may be** selon le cas - **2.** [argument] : **case (for/against)** arguments *mpl* (pour/contre) - **3.** LAW affaire *f*, procès *m* - **4.** [container - gen] caisse *f* ; [- for glasses etc] étui *m* - **5.** UK [suitcase] valise *f*. ◆ **in any case** *adv* quoi qu'il en soit, de toute façon. ◆ **in case** ⋄ *conj* au cas où. ⋄ *adv* : **(just) in case** à tout hasard.

cash [kæʃ] ⋄ *n* (U) **1.** [notes and coins] liquide *m* ; **to pay (in) cash** payer comptant *or* en espèces - **2.** *inf* [money] sous *mpl*, fric *m* - **3.** [payment] : **cash in advance** paiement *m* à l'avance ; **cash on delivery** paiement à la livraison. ⋄ *vt* encaisser.

cash and carry *n* UK libre-service *m* de gros, cash-and-carry *m*.

cashbook ['kæʃbʊk] *n* livre *m* de caisse.

cash box *n* caisse *f*.

cash card *n* carte *f* de retrait.

cash desk *n* UK caisse *f*.

cash dispenser [-dɪˌspensəʳ] *n* distributeur *m* automatique de billets.

cashew (nut) ['kæʃuː-] *n* noix *f* de cajou.

cashier [kæ'ʃɪəʳ] *n* caissier *m*, -ère *f*.

cash machine *n* distributeur *m* de billets.

cashmere [kæʃ'mɪəʳ] *n* cachemire *m*.

cash register *n* caisse *f* enregistreuse.

casing ['keɪsɪŋ] *n* revêtement *m* ; TECH boîtier *m*.

casino [kə'siːnəʊ] (*pl* -s) *n* casino *m*.

cask [kɑːsk] *n* tonneau *m*.

casket ['kɑːskɪt] *n* 1. [for jewels] coffret *m* - 2. US [coffin] cercueil *m*.

casserole ['kæsərəʊl] *n* 1. [stew] ragoût *m* - 2. [pot] cocotte *f*.

cassette [kæ'set] *n* [of magnetic tape] cassette *f* ; PHOT recharge *f*.

cassette player *n* lecteur *m* de cassettes.

cassette recorder *n* magnétophone *m* à cassettes.

cast [kɑːst] <> *n* 1. CIN & THEAT [actors] acteurs *mpl* ; [list of actors] distribution *f* - 2. MED [for broken limb] plâtre *m* ; **her arm was in a cast** elle avait un bras dans le plâtre. <> *vt* (*pt & pp* **cast**) 1. [throw] jeter ; **to cast doubt on sthg** jeter le doute sur qqch ; **to cast lots** UK tirer au sort - 2. CIN & THEAT donner un rôle à - 3. [vote] : **to cast one's vote** voter - 4. [metal] couler ; [statue] mouler. ◆ **cast aside** *vt sep fig* écarter, rejeter. ◆ **cast off** *vi* NAUT larguer les amarres.

castaway ['kɑːstəweɪ] *n* naufragé *m*, -e *f*.

caster ['kɑːstəʳ] *n* [wheel] roulette *f*.

caster sugar *n* UK sucre *m* en poudre.

casting vote *n* voix *f* prépondérante.

cast iron *n* fonte *f*.

castle ['kɑːsl] *n* 1. [building] château *m* - 2. CHESS tour *f*.

castor ['kɑːstəʳ] = caster.

castor oil *n* huile *f* de ricin.

castor sugar = caster sugar.

castrate [kæ'streɪt] *vt* châtrer.

casual ['kæʒʊəl] *adj* 1. [relaxed, indifferent] désinvolte - 2. [offhand] sans-gêne - 3. [chance] fortuit(e) - 4. [clothes] décontracté(e), sport (*inv*) - 5. [work, worker] temporaire.

casually ['kæʒʊəlɪ] *adv* [in a relaxed manner] avec désinvolture ; **casually dressed** habillé simplement.

casualty ['kæʒjʊəltɪ] *n* 1. [dead person] mort *m*, -e *f*, victime *f* ; [injured person] blessé *m*, -e *f* ; [of road accident] accidenté *m*, -e *f* - 2. UK = casualty department.

casualty department *n* UK service *m* des urgences.

cat [kæt] *n* 1. [domestic] chat *m* - 2. [wild] fauve *m*.

catalogue, US **catalog** ['kætəlɒg] <> *n* [gen] catalogue *m* ; [in library] fichier *m*. <> *vt* cataloguer.

catalyst ['kætəlɪst] *n lit & fig* catalyseur *m*.

catalytic convertor, **catalytic converter** [ˌkætə'lɪtɪkkən'vɜːtəʳ] *n* pot *m* catalytique.

catapult ['kætəpʌlt] <> *n* UK [hand-held] lance-pierres *m inv*. <> *vt lit & fig* catapulter.

cataract ['kætərækt] *n* cataracte *f*.

catarrh [kə'tɑːʳ] *n* catarrhe *m*.

catastrophe [kə'tæstrəfɪ] *n* catastrophe *f*.

catch [kætʃ] <> *vt* (*pt & pp* **caught**) 1. [gen] attraper ; **to catch sight** OR **a glimpse of** apercevoir ; **to catch sb's attention** attirer l'attention de qqn ; **to catch the post** UK arriver à temps pour la levée - 2. [discover, surprise] prendre, surprendre ; **to catch sb doing sthg** surprendre qqn à faire qqch - 3. [hear clearly] saisir, comprendre - 4. [trap] : **I caught my finger in the door** je me suis pris le doigt dans la porte - 5. [strike] frapper. <> *vi* (*pt & pp* **caught**) 1. [become hooked, get stuck] se prendre - 2. [fire] prendre, partir. <> *n* 1. [of ball, thing caught] prise *f* ; **he's a good catch** c'est une belle prise - 2. [fastener - of box] fermoir *m* ; [- of window] loqueteau *m* ; [- of door] loquet *m* - 3. [snag] hic *m*, entourloupette *f*. ◆ **catch on** *vi* 1. [become popular] prendre - 2. *inf* [understand] : **to catch on (to sthg)** piger (qqch). ◆ **catch out** *vt sep* UK [trick] prendre en défaut, coincer. ◆ **catch up** <> *vt sep* rattraper. <> *vi* : **to catch up on sthg** rattraper qqch. ◆ **catch up with** *vt insep* rattraper.

catching ['kætʃɪŋ] *adj* contagieux(euse).

catchment area ['kætʃmənt-] *n* UK [of school] secteur *m* de recrutement scolaire ; [of hospital] circonscription *f* hospitalière.

catchphrase ['kætʃfreɪz] *n* rengaine *f*.

catchy ['kætʃɪ] *adj* facile à retenir, entraînant(e).

categorically [ˌkætɪ'gɒrɪklɪ] *adv* catégoriquement.

category ['kætəgərɪ] *n* catégorie *f*.

cater ['keɪtəʳ] *vi* [provide food] s'occuper de la nourriture, prévoir les repas. ◆ **cater for** *vt insep* UK 1. [tastes, needs] pourvoir à, satisfaire ; [customers] s'adresser à - 2. [anticipate] prévoir. ◆ **cater to** *vt insep* satisfaire.

caterer ['keɪtərəʳ] *n* traiteur *m*.

catering ['keɪtərɪŋ] *n* [trade] restauration *f*.

caterpillar ['kætəpɪlə'] *n* chenille *f*.

caterpillar tracks *npl* chenille *f*.

cathedral [kə'θi:drəl] *n* cathédrale *f*.

Catholic ['kæθlɪk] <> *adj* catholique. <> *n* catholique *mf*. **catholic** *adj* [tastes] éclectique.

Catseyes® ['kætsaɪz] *npl* UK catadioptres *mpl*.

cattle ['kætl] *npl* bétail *m*.

catty ['kætɪ] *adj inf pej* [spiteful] rosse, vache.

catwalk ['kætwɔ:k] *n* passerelle *f*.

caucus ['kɔ:kəs] *n* **1.** US POL comité *m* électoral (*d'un parti*) - **2.** UK POL comité *m* (*d'un parti*).

caught [kɔ:t] *pt & pp* ➤ catch.

cauliflower ['kɒlɪ,flauə'] *n* chou-fleur *m*.

cause [kɔ:z] <> *n* cause *f*; **I have no cause for complaint** je n'ai pas à me plaindre, je n'ai pas lieu de me plaindre ; **to have cause to do sthg** avoir lieu OR des raisons de faire qqch. <> *vt* causer ; **to cause sb to do sthg** faire faire qqch à qqn ; **to cause sthg to be done** faire faire qqch.

caustic ['kɔ:stɪk] *adj* caustique.

caution ['kɔ:ʃn] <> *n* **1.** (U) [care] précaution *f*, prudence *f* - **2.** [warning] avertissement *m* - **3.** UK LAW réprimande *f*. <> *vt* **1.** [warn] : **to caution sb against doing sthg** déconseiller à qqn de faire qqch - **2.** UK [subj: police officer] : **to caution sb for sthg** réprimander qqn pour qqch.

cautious ['kɔ:ʃəs] *adj* prudent(e).

cavalry ['kævlrɪ] *n* cavalerie *f*.

cave [keɪv] *n* caverne *f*, grotte *f*. ➤ **cave in** *vi* [roof, ceiling] s'affaisser.

caveman ['keɪvmæn] (*pl* -men [-men]) *n* homme *m* des cavernes.

cavernous ['kævənəs] *adj* [room, building] immense.

caviar(e) ['kævɪɑ:'] *n* caviar *m*.

cavity ['kævətɪ] *n* cavité *f*.

cavort [kə'vɔ:t] *vi* gambader.

CB *n* (*abbrev of* citizens' band) CB *f*.

CBI *n abbrev of* Confederation of British Industry.

cc *n* **1.** (*abbrev of* cubic centimetre) cm³ - **2.** (*abbrev of* carbon copy) pcc.

CD *n* (*abbrev of* compact disc) CD *m*.

CD burner *n* COMPUT graveur *m* de CD.

CD player *n* lecteur *m* de CD.

CD-R [,si:di:'ɑ:'] (*abbrev of* compact disc recordable) *n* CD(-R) *m*.

CD-R drive [,si:di:'ɑ:,draɪv] *n* lecteur-graveur *m* de CD.

CD-ROM [,si:di:'rɒm] (*abbrev of* compact disc read only memory) *n* CD-ROM *m*, CD-Rom *m*.

CD-RW [,si:di:ɑ:'dʌblju:] (*abbrev of* compact disc rewriteable) *n* CD-RW *m*.

CD tower *n* colonne *f* (de rangement) pour CD.

cease [si:s] *fml* <> *vt* cesser ; **to cease doing** OR **to do sthg** cesser de faire qqch. <> *vi* cesser.

cease-fire *n* cessez-le-feu *m inv*.

ceaseless ['si:slɪs] *adj fml* incessant(e), continuel(elle).

cedar (tree) ['si:də'-] *n* cèdre *m*.

cedilla [sɪ'dɪlə] *n* cédille *f*.

ceiling ['si:lɪŋ] *n lit & fig* plafond *m*.

celebrate ['selɪbreɪt] <> *vt* [gen] célébrer, fêter. <> *vi* faire la fête.

celebrated ['selɪbreɪtɪd] *adj* célèbre.

celebration [,selɪ'breɪʃn] *n* **1.** (U) [activity, feeling] fête *f*, festivités *fpl* - **2.** [event] festivités *fpl*.

celebrity [sɪ'lebrətɪ] *n* célébrité *f*.

celery ['selərɪ] *n* céleri *m* (en branches).

celibate ['selɪbət] *adj* célibataire.

cell [sel] *n* [gen & COMPUT] cellule *f*.

cellar ['selə'] *n* cave *f*.

cello ['tʃeləu] (*pl* -s) *n* violoncelle *m*.

Cellophane® ['seləfeɪn] *n* Cellophane® *f*.

Celsius ['selsɪəs] *adj* Celsius (*inv*).

Celt [kelt] *n* Celte *mf*.

Celtic ['keltɪk] <> *adj* celte. <> *n* [language] celte *m*.

cement [sɪ'ment] <> *n* ciment *m*. <> *vt lit & fig* cimenter.

cement mixer *n* bétonnière *f*.

cemetery ['semɪtrɪ] *n* cimetière *m*.

censor ['sensə'] <> *n* censeur *m*. <> *vt* censurer.

censorship ['sensəʃɪp] *n* censure *f*.

censure ['senʃə'] <> *n* blâme *m*, critique *f*. <> *vt* blâmer, critiquer.

census ['sensəs] (*pl* -es [-i:z]) *n* recensement *m*.

cent [sent] *n* **1.** [pour le dollar] cent *m* - **2.** [pour l'euro] centime *m*, (euro) cent *m offic*.

centenary UK [sen'ti:nərɪ], **centennial** US [sen'tenjəl] *n* centenaire *m*.

center *etc* US = centre *etc*.

centigrade ['sentɪgreɪd] *adj* centigrade.

centilitre UK, **centiliter** US ['sentɪ,li:tə'] *n* centilitre *m*.

centimetre UK, **centimeter** US ['sentɪ,mi:tə'] *n* centimètre *m*.

centipede ['sentɪpi:d] *n* mille-pattes *m inv*.

central ['sentrəl] *adj* central(e).

Central America *n* Amérique *f* centrale.

central heating *n* chauffage *m* central.

centralize, UK **-ise** ['sentrəlaɪz] *vt* centraliser.

central locking [-'lɒkɪŋ] *n* AUT verrouillage *m* centralisé.

central reservation *n* UK AUT terre-plein *m* central.

centre UK, **center** US ['sentər] ⟨⟩ *n* centre *m* ; **centre of attention** centre d'attraction, point *m* de mire ; **centre of gravity** centre de gravité. ⟨⟩ *adj* **1.** [middle] central(e) ; **a centre parting** une raie au milieu - **2.** POL du centre, centriste. ⟨⟩ *vt* centrer.

centre back UK, **center back** US *n* FOOTBALL arrière *m* central.

centre forward UK, **center forward** US *n* FOOTBALL avant-centre *m inv*.

centre half UK, **center half** US *n* FOOTBALL arrière *m* central.

century ['sentʃʊrɪ] *n* siècle *m*.

ceramic [sɪ'ræmɪk] *adj* en céramique. ➤ **ceramics** *npl* [objects] objets *mpl* en céramique.

cereal ['sɪərɪəl] *n* céréale *f*.

ceremonial [,serɪ'məʊnjəl] ⟨⟩ *adj* [dress] de cérémonie ; [duties] honorifique. ⟨⟩ *n* cérémonial *m*.

ceremony ['serɪmənɪ] *n* **1.** [event] cérémonie *f* - **2.** (U) [pomp, formality] cérémonies *fpl* ; **to stand on ceremony** faire des cérémonies.

certain ['sɜːtn] *adj* [gen] certain(e) ; **he is certain to be late** il est certain qu'il sera en retard, il sera certainement en retard ; **to be certain of sthg/of doing sthg** être assuré de qqch/de faire qqch, être sûr de qqch/de faire qqch ; **to make certain** vérifier ; **to make certain of** s'assurer de ; **I know for certain that...** je suis sûr OR certain que... ; **to a certain extent** jusqu'à un certain point, dans une certaine mesure.

certainly ['sɜːtnlɪ] *adv* certainement.

certainty ['sɜːtntɪ] *n* certitude *f*.

certificate [sə'tɪfɪkət] *n* certificat *m*.

certified ['sɜːtɪfaɪd] *adj* [teacher] diplômé(e) ; [document] certifié(e).

certified mail *n* US envoi *m* recommandé.

certified public accountant *n* US expert-comptable *m*.

certify ['sɜːtɪfaɪ] *vt* **1.** [declare true] : **to certify (that)** certifier OR attester que - **2.** [declare insane] déclarer mentalement aliéné(e).

cervical [sə'vaɪkl] *adj* [cancer] du col de l'utérus.

cervical smear *n* UK frottis *m* vaginal.

cervix ['sɜːvɪks] (*pl* **-ices** [-ɪsiːz]) *n* col *m* de l'utérus.

cesarean (section) [sɪ'zeərɪən-] US = **caesarean (section)**.

cesspit ['sespɪt], **cesspool** ['sespuːl] *n* fosse *f* d'aisance.

cf. (*abbrev of* **confer**) cf.

CFC (*abbrev of* **chlorofluorocarbon**) *n* CFC *m*.

ch. (*abbrev of* **chapter**) chap.

chafe [tʃeɪf] *vt* [rub] irriter.

chaffinch ['tʃæfɪntʃ] *n* pinson *m*.

chain [tʃeɪn] ⟨⟩ *n* chaîne *f* ; **chain of events** suite *f* OR série *f* d'événements. ⟨⟩ *vt* [person, animal] enchaîner ; [object] attacher avec une chaîne.

chain reaction *n* réaction *f* en chaîne.

chain saw *n* tronçonneuse *f*.

chain-smoke *vi* fumer cigarette sur cigarette.

chain store *n* grand magasin *m* (*à succursales multiples*).

chair [tʃeər] ⟨⟩ *n* **1.** [gen] chaise *f* ; [armchair] fauteuil *m* - **2.** [university post] chaire *f* - **3.** [of meeting] présidence *f* - **4.** *inf* US **the chair** la chaise électrique. ⟨⟩ *vt* [meeting] présider ; [discussion] diriger.

chairlift *n* télésiège *m*.

chairman ['tʃeəmən] (*pl* **-men** [-mən]) *n* président *m*, -e *f*.

chairperson ['tʃeə,pɜːsn] (*pl* **-s**) *n* président *m*, -e *f*.

chalet ['ʃæleɪ] *n* chalet *m*.

chalk [tʃɔːk] *n* craie *f*.

chalkboard ['tʃɔːkbɔːd] *n* US tableau *m* (noir).

challenge ['tʃælɪndʒ] ⟨⟩ *n* défi *m*. ⟨⟩ *vt* **1.** [to fight, competition] : **she challenged me to a race/a game of chess** elle m'a défié à la course/aux échecs ; **to challenge sb to do sthg** défier qqn de faire qqch - **2.** [question] mettre en question OR en doute.

challenging ['tʃælɪndʒɪŋ] *adj* **1.** [task, job] stimulant(e) - **2.** [look, tone of voice] provocateur(trice).

chamber ['tʃeɪmbər] *n* [gen] chambre *f*.

chambermaid ['tʃeɪmbəmeɪd] *n* femme *f* de chambre.

chamber music *n* musique *f* de chambre.

chamber of commerce *n* chambre *f* de commerce.

chameleon [kə'miːljən] *n* caméléon *m*.

champagne [,ʃæm'peɪn] *n* champagne *m*.

champion ['tʃæmpjən] *n* champion *m*, -onne *f*.

championship ['tʃæmpjənʃɪp] *n* championnat *m*.

chance [tʃɑːns] ⬦ n **1.** (U) [luck] hasard m ; **by chance** par hasard ; **if by any chance** si par hasard - **2.** [likelihood] chance f ; **she didn't stand a chance (of doing sthg)** elle n'avait aucune chance (de faire qqch) ; **on the off chance** à tout hasard - **3.** [opportunity] occasion f - **4.** [risk] risque m ; **to take a chance** risquer le coup ; **to take a chance on doing sthg** se risquer à faire qqch. ⬦ adj fortuit(e), accidentel(elle). ⬦ vt [risk] risquer ; **to chance it** tenter sa chance. ➡ **chances** npl chances fpl ; **(the) chances are (that)** he'll never find out il y a de fortes OR grandes chances qu'il ne l'apprenne jamais ; **what are her chances of making a full recovery?** quelles sont ses chances de se rétablir complètement?

chancellor [ˈtʃɑːnsələr] n **1.** [chief minister] chancelier m, -ière f - **2.** UNIV président m, -e f honoraire.

Chancellor of the Exchequer n UK Chancelier m de l'Échiquier, ≃ ministre m des Finances.

chandelier [ˌʃændəˈlɪər] n lustre m.

change [tʃeɪndʒ] ⬦ n **1.** [gen] : **change (in sb/in sthg)** changement m (en qqn/de qqch) ; **change of clothes** vêtements mpl de rechange ; **for a change** pour changer (un peu) - **2.** [money] monnaie f. ⬦ vt **1.** [gen] changer ; **to change sthg into sthg** changer OR transformer qqch en qqch ; **to change one's mind** changer d'avis - **2.** [jobs, trains, sides] changer de - **3.** [money] changer. ⬦ vi **1.** [gen] changer - **2.** [change clothes] se changer - **3.** [be transformed] : **to change into** se changer en. ➡ **change over** vi [convert] : **to change over from/to** passer de/à.

changeable [ˈtʃeɪndʒəbl] adj [mood] changeable ; [weather] variable.

change machine n distributeur m de monnaie.

changeover [ˈtʃeɪndʒ,əʊvər] n : **changeover (to)** passage m (à), changement m (pour).

changing [ˈtʃeɪndʒɪŋ] adj changeant(e).

changing room n UK SPORT vestiaire m ; [in shop] cabine f d'essayage.

channel [ˈtʃænl] ⬦ n **1.** TV chaîne f ; RADIO station f - **2.** [for irrigation] canal m ; [duct] conduit m - **3.** [on river, sea] chenal m. ⬦ vt (UK & US) lit & fig canaliser. ➡ **Channel** n : **the (English) Channel** la Manche. ➡ **channels** npl : **to go through the proper channels** suivre OR passer la filière.

Channel Islands npl : **the Channel Islands** les îles fpl Anglo-Normandes.

Channel tunnel n : **the Channel tunnel** le tunnel sous la Manche.

chant [tʃɑːnt] ⬦ n chant m. ⬦ vt **1.** RELIG chanter - **2.** [words, slogan] scander.

chaos [ˈkeɪɒs] n chaos m.

chaotic [keɪˈɒtɪk] adj chaotique.

chap [tʃæp] n UK inf [man] type m.

chapel [ˈtʃæpl] n chapelle f.

chaplain [ˈtʃæplɪn] n aumônier m.

chapped [tʃæpt] adj [skin, lips] gercé(e).

chapter [ˈtʃæptər] n chapitre m.

char [tʃɑːr] vt [burn] calciner.

character [ˈkærəktər] n **1.** [gen] caractère m - **2.** [in film, book, play] personnage m - **3.** inf [eccentric] phénomène m, original m.

characteristic [ˌkærəktəˈrɪstɪk] ⬦ adj caractéristique. ⬦ n caractéristique f.

characterize, UK **-ise** [ˈkærəktəraɪz] vt caractériser.

charade [ʃəˈrɑːd] n farce f. ➡ **charades** n (U) charades fpl.

charcoal [ˈtʃɑːkəʊl] n [for drawing] charbon m ; [for burning] charbon de bois.

charge [tʃɑːdʒ] ⬦ n **1.** [cost] prix m ; **free of charge** gratuit - **2.** LAW accusation f, inculpation f - **3.** [responsibility] : **to take charge of** se charger de ; **to be in charge of, to have charge of** être responsable de, s'occuper de ; **in charge** responsable - **4.** ELEC & MIL charge f. ⬦ vt **1.** [customer, sum] faire payer ; **how much do you charge?** vous prenez combien? ; **to charge sthg to sb** mettre qqch sur le compte de qqn - **2.** [suspect, criminal] : **to charge sb (with)** accuser qqn (de) - **3.** ELEC & MIL charger. ⬦ vi [rush] se précipiter, foncer.

charge card n carte f de compte crédit (auprès d'un magasin).

charger [ˈtʃɑːdʒər] n [for batteries] chargeur m, -euse f.

chariot [ˈtʃærɪət] n char m.

charisma [kəˈrɪzmə] n charisme m.

charity [ˈtʃærətɪ] n charité f.

charm [tʃɑːm] ⬦ n charme m. ⬦ vt charmer.

charming [ˈtʃɑːmɪŋ] adj charmant(e).

chart [tʃɑːt] ⬦ n **1.** [diagram] graphique m, diagramme m - **2.** [map] carte f. ⬦ vt **1.** [plot, map] porter sur une carte - **2.** fig [record] retracer - **3.** être au hit-parade. ➡ **charts** npl : **the charts** le hit-parade.

charter [ˈtʃɑːtər] ⬦ n [document] charte f. ⬦ vt [plane, boat] affréter.

chartered accountant [ˌtʃɑːtəd-] n UK expert-comptable m.

charter flight n vol m charter.

charter member *n US* [founder] membre *m* fondateur.

chase [tʃeɪs] ◇ *n* [pursuit] poursuite *f*, chasse *f*. ◇ *vt* **1.** [pursue] poursuivre - **2.** [drive away] chasser. ◇ *vi* : **to chase after sb/sthg** courir après qqn/qqch.

chasm ['kæzm] *n lit & fig* abîme *m*.

chassis ['ʃæsɪ] (*pl* **chassis**) *n* châssis *m*.

chat [tʃæt] ◇ *n* causerie *f*, bavardage *m* ; **to have a chat** causer, bavarder. ◇ *vi* causer, bavarder. **chat up** *vt sep UK inf* baratiner.

chatline ['tʃætlaɪn] *n* [gen] réseau *m* téléphonique (payant) ; [for sexual encounters] téléphone *m* rose.

chatroom ['tʃætrʊm] *n* salle *f* de chat.

chat show *n UK* talk-show *m*.

chatter ['tʃætə] ◇ *n* **1.** [of person] bavardage *m* - **2.** [of animal, bird] caquetage *m*. ◇ *vi* **1.** [person] bavarder - **2.** [animal, bird] jacasser, caqueter - **3.** [teeth] : **his teeth were chattering** il claquait des dents.

chatterbox ['tʃætəbɒks] *n inf* moulin à paroles.

chatty ['tʃætɪ] *adj* [person] bavard(e) ; [letter] plein(e) de bavardages.

chauffeur ['ʃəʊfə] *n* chauffeur *m*.

chauvinist ['ʃəʊvɪnɪst] *n* **1.** [sexist] macho *m* - **2.** [nationalist] chauvin *m*, -e *f*.

cheap [tʃi:p] ◇ *adj* **1.** [inexpensive] pas cher (chère), bon marché (*inv*) - **2.** [at a reduced price - fare, rate] réduit(e) ; [- ticket] à prix réduit - **3.** [low-quality] de mauvaise qualité - **4.** [joke, comment] facile. ◇ *adv* (à) bon marché.

cheapen ['tʃi:pn] *vt* [degrade] rabaisser.

cheaply ['tʃi:plɪ] *adv* à bon marché, pour pas cher.

cheat [tʃi:t] ◇ *n* tricheur *m*, -euse *f*. ◇ *vt* tromper ; **to cheat sb out of sthg** escroquer qqch à qqn. ◇ *vi* **1.** [in game, exam] tricher - **2.** *inf* [be unfaithful] : **to cheat on sb** tromper qqn.

check [tʃek] ◇ *n* **1.** [inspection, test] : **check (on)** contrôle *m* (de) - **2.** [restraint] : **check (on)** frein *m* (à), restriction *f* (sur) ; **to put a check on sthg** freiner qqch - **3.** *US* [bill] note *f* - **4.** [pattern] carreaux *mpl* - **5.** *US* [mark, tick] coche *f* - **6.** *US* = **cheque**. ◇ *vt* **1.** [test, verify] vérifier ; [passport, ticket] contrôler - **2.** [restrain, stop] enrayer, arrêter. ◇ *vi* : **to check (for sthg)** vérifier (qqch) ; **to check on sthg** vérifier OR contrôler qqch. **check in** ◇ *vt sep* [luggage, coat] enregistrer. ◇ *vi* **1.** [at hotel] signer le registre - **2.** [at airport] se présenter à l'enregistrement. **check into** *vt insep* : **to check into a hotel** descendre dans un hôtel. **check out** ◇ *vt sep* **1.** [luggage,

coat] retirer - **2.** [investigate] vérifier - **3.** *inf* **check this out** [look] vise un peu ça ; [listen] écoute-moi ça. ◇ *vi* [from hotel] régler sa note. **check up** *vi* : **to check up on sb** prendre des renseignements sur qqn ; **to check up (on sthg)** vérifier (qqch).

checkbook *US* = **chequebook**.

checked [tʃekt] *adj* à carreaux.

checkerboard ['tʃekəbɔ:d] *n US* damier.

checkered *US* = **chequered**.

checkers ['tʃekəz] *n* (*U*) *US* jeu *m* de dames.

check-in *n* enregistrement *m*.

checking account ['tʃekɪŋ-] *n US* compte *m* courant.

checkmate ['tʃekmeɪt] *n* échec et mat *m*.

checkout ['tʃekaʊt] *n* [in supermarket] caisse *f*.

checkpoint ['tʃekpɔɪnt] *n* [place] (poste *m* de) contrôle *m*.

checkup ['tʃekʌp] *n* MED bilan *m* de santé, check-up *m*.

Cheddar (cheese) ['tʃedə-] *n* (fromage *m* de) cheddar *m*.

cheek [tʃi:k] *n* **1.** [of face] joue *f* - **2.** *inf* [impudence] culot *m*.

cheekbone ['tʃi:kbəʊn] *n* pommette *f*.

cheeky ['tʃi:kɪ] *adj* insolent(e), effronté(e).

cheer [tʃɪə] ◇ *n* [shout] acclamation *f*. ◇ *vt* **1.** [shout for] acclamer - **2.** [gladden] réjouir. ◇ *vi* applaudir. **cheers** *excl* **1.** [said before drinking] santé! - **2.** *UK inf* [goodbye] salut!, ciao!, tchao! - **3.** *UK inf* [thank you] merci. **cheer up** ◇ *vt sep* remonter le moral à. ◇ *vi* s'égayer.

cheerful ['tʃɪəfʊl] *adj* joyeux(euse), gai(e).

cheerio [,tʃɪərɪ'əʊ] *excl UK inf* au revoir!, salut!

cheese [tʃi:z] *n* fromage *m*.

cheeseboard ['tʃi:zbɔ:d] *n* plateau *m* à fromage.

cheeseburger ['tʃi:z,bɜ:gə] *n* cheeseburger *m*, hamburger *m* au fromage.

cheesecake ['tʃi:zkeɪk] *n* CULIN gâteau *m* au fromage blanc, cheesecake *m*.

cheetah ['tʃi:tə] *n* guépard *m*.

chef [ʃef] *n* chef *mf*.

chemical ['kemɪkl] ◇ *adj* chimique. ◇ *n* produit *m* chimique.

chemist ['kemɪst] *n* **1.** *UK* [pharmacist] pharmacien *m*, -enne *f* ; **chemist's (shop)** pharmacie *f* - **2.** [scientist] chimiste *mf*.

chemistry ['kemɪstrɪ] *n* chimie *f*.

cheque *UK*, **check** *US* [tʃek] *n* chèque *m*.

chequebook *UK*, **checkbook** *US* ['tʃekbʊk] *n* chéquier *m*, carnet *m* de chèques.

cheque card *n UK* carte *f* bancaire.

chequered UK, **checkered** US ['tʃekerd] ['tʃekəd] adj fig [career, life] mouvementé(e).

cherish ['tʃerıʃ] vt chérir ; [hope] nourrir, caresser.

cherry ['tʃerı] n [fruit] cerise f ; **cherry (tree)** cerisier m.

chess [tʃes] n (U) échecs mpl.

chessboard ['tʃesbɔːd] n échiquier m.

chessman ['tʃesmæn] (pl -men [-men]) n pièce f.

chest [tʃest] n 1. ANAT poitrine f - 2. [box] coffre m.

chestnut ['tʃesnʌt] <> adj [colour] châtain (inv). <> n [nut] châtaigne f ; **chestnut (tree)** châtaignier m.

chest of drawers (pl chests of drawers) n commode f.

chew [tʃuː] <> n UK [sweet] bonbon m (à mâcher). <> vt mâcher. **chew up** vt sep mâchouiller.

chewing gum ['tʃuːɪŋ-] n chewing-gum m.

chic [ʃiːk] adj chic (inv).

chick [tʃık] n [bird] oisillon m ; [chicken] poussin m.

chicken ['tʃıkın] n 1. [bird, food] poulet m - 2. inf [coward] froussard m, -e f. **chicken out** vi inf se dégonfler.

chickenpox ['tʃıkınpɒks] n (U) varicelle f.

chickpea ['tʃıkpiː] n pois m chiche.

chicory ['tʃıkərı] n UK [vegetable] endive f.

chief [tʃiːf] <> adj 1. [main - aim, problem] principal(e) - 2. [head] en chef. <> n chef m.

chief executive n directeur général m, directrice générale f.

chiefly ['tʃiːflı] adv 1. [mainly] principalement - 2. [above all] surtout.

chiffon ['ʃıfɒn] n mousseline f.

chilblain ['tʃılbleın] n engelure f.

child [tʃaıld] (pl children ['tʃıldrən]) n enfant mf.

child benefit n (U) UK ≃ allocations fpl familiales.

childbirth ['tʃaıldbɜːθ] n (U) accouchement m.

childhood ['tʃaıldhʊd] n enfance f.

childish ['tʃaıldıʃ] adj pej puéril(e), enfantin(e).

childlike ['tʃaıldlaık] adj enfantin(e), d'enfant.

childminder ['tʃaıld,maındə] n UK gardienne f d'enfants, nourrice f.

childproof ['tʃaıldpruːf] adj [container] qui ne peut pas être ouvert par les enfants ; **childproof lock** verrouillage m de sécurité pour enfants.

children ['tʃıldrən] npl ▶ child.

children's home n maison f d'enfants.

child support n US LAW pension f alimentaire.

Chile ['tʃılı] n Chili m.

Chilean ['tʃılıən] <> adj chilien(enne). <> n Chilien m, -enne f.

chili ['tʃılı] = chilli.

chill [tʃıl] <> adj frais (fraîche). <> n 1. [illness] coup m de froid - 2. [in temperature] : **there's a chill in the air** le fond de l'air est frais - 3. [feeling of fear] frisson m. <> vt 1. [drink, food] mettre au frais - 2. [person] faire frissonner. <> vi [drink, food] rafraîchir.

chilli ['tʃılı] (pl -es) n [vegetable] piment m.

chilling ['tʃılıŋ] adj 1. [very cold] glacial(e) - 2. [frightening] qui glace le sang.

chilly ['tʃılı] adj froid(e) ; **to feel chilly** avoir froid ; **it's chilly** il fait froid.

chime [tʃaım] <> n [of bell, clock] carillon m. <> vt [time] sonner. <> vi [bell, clock] carillonner.

chimney ['tʃımnı] n cheminée f.

chimneypot ['tʃımnıpɒt] n mitre f de cheminée.

chimneysweep ['tʃımnıswiːp] n ramoneur m.

chimp(anzee) [tʃımp(ən'ziː)] n chimpanzé m.

chin [tʃın] n menton m.

china ['tʃaınə] n porcelaine f.

China ['tʃaınə] n Chine f.

Chinese [,tʃaı'niːz] <> adj chinois(e). <> n [language] chinois m. <> npl : **the Chinese** les Chinois mpl.

Chinese cabbage n chou m chinois.

Chinese leaves npl UK = Chinese cabbage.

chink [tʃıŋk] n 1. [narrow opening] fente f - 2. [sound] tintement m.

chip [tʃıp] <> n 1. UK [fried potato] frite f ; US [potato crisp] chip m - 2. [of glass, metal] éclat m ; [of wood] copeau m - 3. [flaw] ébréchure f - 4. [microchip] puce f - 5. [for gambling] jeton m. <> vt [cup, glass] ébrécher. **chip in** inf vi 1. [contribute] contribuer - 2. [interrupt] mettre son grain de sel. **chip off** vt sep enlever petit morceau par petit morceau.

chipboard ['tʃıpbɔːd] n aggloméré m.

chip shop n UK friterie f.

chiropodist [kı'rɒpədıst] n pédicure mf.

chirp [tʃɜːp] vi [bird] pépier ; [cricket] chanter.

chirpy ['tʃɜːpı] adj gai(e).

chisel ['tʃɪzl] <> n [for wood] ciseau m ; [for metal, rock] burin m. <> vt (UK & US) ciseler.

chit [tʃɪt] n [note] note f, reçu m.

chitchat ['tʃɪtʃæt] n (U) inf bavardage m.

chivalry ['ʃɪvlrɪ] n (U) **1.** lit [of knights] chevalerie f - **2.** [good manners] galanterie f.

chives [tʃaɪvz] npl ciboulette f.

chlorine ['klɔːriːn] n chlore m.

choc-ice ['tʃɒkaɪs] n UK Esquimau® m.

chock [tʃɒk] n cale f.

chock-a-block, chock-full adj inf chock-a-block (with) plein(e) à craquer (de).

chocolate ['tʃɒkələt] <> n chocolat m. <> comp au chocolat.

choice [tʃɔɪs] <> n choix m. <> adj de choix.

choir ['kwaɪər] n chœur m.

choirboy ['kwaɪəbɔɪ] n jeune choriste m.

choke [tʃəʊk] <> n AUT starter m. <> vt **1.** [strangle] étrangler, étouffer - **2.** [block] obstruer, boucher. <> vi s'étrangler.

cholera ['kɒlərə] n choléra m.

choose [tʃuːz] (pt chose, pp chosen) <> vt **1.** [select] choisir - **2.** [decide] : **to choose to do sthg** décider OR choisir de faire qqch. <> vi [select] : **to choose (from)** choisir (parmi OR entre).

choos(e)y ['tʃuːzɪ] (comp -ier, superl -iest) adj difficile.

chop [tʃɒp] <> n CULIN côtelette f. <> vt **1.** [wood] couper - **2.** [vegetables] hacher - **3.** inf fig [funding, budget] réduire ; **to chop and change** changer sans cesse d'avis. ⏵ **chops** npl inf babines fpl. ⏵ **chop down** vt sep [tree] abattre. ⏵ **chop up** vt sep couper en morceaux.

chopper ['tʃɒpər] n **1.** [axe] couperet m - **2.** inf [helicopter] hélico m.

choppy ['tʃɒpɪ] adj [sea] agité(e).

chord [kɔːd] n MUS accord m.

chore [tʃɔːr] n corvée f ; **household chores** travaux mpl ménagers.

chortle ['tʃɔːtl] vi glousser.

chorus ['kɔːrəs] n **1.** [part of song] refrain m - **2.** [singers] chœur m - **3.** fig [of praise, complaints] concert m.

chose [tʃəʊz] pt ▶ choose.

chosen ['tʃəʊzn] pp ▶ choose.

Christ [kraɪst] <> n Christ m. <> excl Seigneur!, bon Dieu!

christen ['krɪsn] vt **1.** [baby] baptiser - **2.** [name] nommer.

christening ['krɪsnɪŋ] n baptême m.

Christian ['krɪstʃən] <> adj RELIG chrétien(enne). <> n chrétien m, -enne f.

Christianity [ˌkrɪstɪˈænətɪ] n christianisme m.

Christian name n prénom m.

Christmas ['krɪsməs] n Noël m ; **happy** OR **merry Christmas!** joyeux Noël!

Christmas card n carte f de Noël.

Christmas Day n jour m de Noël.

Christmas Eve n veille f de Noël.

Christmas pudding n UK pudding m (de Noël).

Christmas tree n arbre m de Noël.

chrome [krəʊm], **chromium** ['krəʊmɪəm] <> n chrome m. <> comp chromé(e).

chronic ['krɒnɪk] adj [illness, unemployment] chronique ; [liar, alcoholic] invétéré(e).

chronicle ['krɒnɪkl] n chronique f.

chronological [ˌkrɒnəˈlɒdʒɪkl] adj chronologique.

chrysanthemum [krɪˈsænθəməm] (pl -s) n chrysanthème m.

chubby ['tʃʌbɪ] adj [cheeks, face] joufflu(e) ; [person, hands] potelé(e).

chuck [tʃʌk] vt inf **1.** [throw] lancer, envoyer - **2.** [job, boyfriend] laisser tomber. ⏵ **chuck away, chuck out** vt sep inf jeter, balancer.

chuckle ['tʃʌkl] vi glousser.

chug [tʃʌg] vi [train] faire teuf-teuf.

chum [tʃʌm] n inf copain m, copine f.

chunk [tʃʌŋk] n gros morceau m.

church [tʃɜːtʃ] n [building] église f ; **to go to church** aller à l'église ; [Catholics] aller à la messe.

Church of England n : **the Church of England** l'Église d'Angleterre.

churchyard ['tʃɜːtʃjɑːd] n cimetière m.

churlish ['tʃɜːlɪʃ] adj grossier(ère).

churn [tʃɜːn] <> n **1.** [for making butter] baratte f - **2.** [for milk] bidon m. <> vt [stir up] battre. ⏵ **churn out** vt sep inf produire en série.

chute [ʃuːt] n glissière f ; **rubbish** UK OR **garbage** US **chute** vide-ordures m inv.

chutney ['tʃʌtnɪ] n chutney m.

CIA (abbrev of **Central Intelligence Agency**) n CIA f.

CID (abbrev of **Criminal Investigation Department**) n la police judiciaire britannique.

cider ['saɪdər] n UK cidre m ; **hard cider** US cidre m.

cigar [sɪˈɡɑːr] n cigare m.

cigarette [ˌsɪɡəˈret] n cigarette f.

cinder ['sɪndər] n cendre f.

Cinderella [ˌsɪndəˈrelə] n Cendrillon f.

cine-camera ['sɪnɪ-] n caméra f.

cine-film ['sɪnɪ-] n UK film m.

cinema ['sɪnəmə] n UK cinéma m.

cinnamon ['sɪnəmən] n cannelle f.

cipher ['saɪfər] n [secret writing] code m.

circa ['sɜːkə] prep environ.

circle ['sɜːkl] ⬦ n 1. [gen] cercle m ; to go round in circles fig tourner en rond - 2. [in theatre, cinema] balcon m. ⬦ vt 1. [draw a circle round] entourer (d'un cercle) - 2. [move round] faire le tour de. ⬦ vi [plane] tourner en rond.

circuit ['sɜːkɪt] n 1. [gen & ELEC] circuit m - 2. [lap] tour m ; [movement round] révolution f.

circuitous [sə'kjuːɪtəs] adj indirect(e).

circular ['sɜːkjʊlər] ⬦ adj [gen] circulaire. ⬦ n [letter] circulaire f ; [advertisement] prospectus m.

circulate ['sɜːkjʊleɪt] ⬦ vi 1. [gen] circuler - 2. [socialize] se mêler aux invités. ⬦ vt [rumour] propager ; [document] faire circuler.

circulation [,sɜːkjʊ'leɪʃn] n 1. [gen] circulation f - 2. PRESS tirage m.

circumcision [,sɜːkəm'sɪʒn] n circoncision f.

circumference [sə'kʌmfərəns] n circonférence f.

circumflex ['sɜːkəmfleks] n : circumflex (accent) accent m circonflexe.

circumspect ['sɜːkəmspekt] adj circonspect(e).

circumstances ['sɜːkəmstənsɪz] npl circonstances fpl ; under OR in no circumstances en aucun cas ; under OR in the circumstances en de telles circonstances.

circumvent [,sɜːkəm'vent] vt fml [law, rule] tourner, contourner.

circus ['sɜːkəs] n cirque m.

CIS (abbrev of Commonwealth of Independent States) n CEI f.

cistern ['sɪstən] n 1. UK [inside roof] réservoir m d'eau - 2. [in toilet] réservoir m de chasse d'eau.

cite [saɪt] vt citer.

citizen ['sɪtɪzn] n 1. [of country] citoyen m, -enne f - 2. [of town] habitant m, -e f.

Citizens' Advice Bureau n service britannique d'information et d'aide au consommateur.

Citizens' Band n citizen band f (fréquence radio réservée au public).

citizenship ['sɪtɪznʃɪp] n citoyenneté f.

citrus fruit ['sɪtrəs-] n agrume m.

city ['sɪtɪ] n ville f, cité f. ⬥ City n UK : the City la City (quartier financier de Londres).

city centre UK n centre-ville m.

city hall n US ≃ mairie f, ≃ hôtel m de ville.

city technology college n UK établissement d'enseignement technique du secondaire subventionné par les entreprises.

civic ['sɪvɪk] adj [leader, event] municipal(e) ; [duty, pride] civique.

civic centre UK, **civic center** US n centre m administratif municipal.

civil ['sɪvl] adj 1. [public] civil(e) - 2. [polite] courtois(e), poli(e).

civil engineering n génie m civil.

civilian [sɪ'vɪljən] ⬦ n civil m, -e f. ⬦ comp civil(e).

civilization [,sɪvəlaɪ'zeɪʃn] n civilisation f.

civilized ['sɪvəlaɪzd] adj civilisé(e).

civil law n droit m civil.

civil liberties npl libertés fpl civiques.

civil rights npl droits mpl civils.

civil servant n fonctionnaire mf.

civil service n fonction f publique.

civil war n guerre f civile.

cl (abbrev of **centilitre**) cl.

clad [klæd] adj lit [dressed] : clad in vêtu(e) de.

claim [kleɪm] ⬦ n 1. [demand] demande f - 2. [right] droit m ; to lay claim to sthg revendiquer qqch - 3. [assertion] affirmation f. ⬦ vt 1. [ask for] réclamer - 2. [responsibility, credit] revendiquer - 3. [maintain] prétendre. ⬦ vi : to claim for sthg faire une demande d'indemnité pour qqch ; to claim (on one's insurance) faire une déclaration de sinistre.

claimant ['kleɪmənt] n [to throne] prétendant m, -e f ; [of state benefit] demandeur m, -eresse f, requérant m, -e f.

clairvoyant [kleə'vɔɪənt] n voyant m, -e f.

clam [klæm] n palourde f.

clamber ['klæmbər] vi grimper.

clammy ['klæmɪ] adj [skin] moite ; [weather] lourd et humide.

clamour UK, **clamor** US ['klæmər] ⬦ n (U) [noise] cris mpl. ⬦ vi : to clamour for sthg demander qqch à cor et à cri.

clamp [klæmp] ⬦ n 1. [gen] pince f, agrafe f - 2. [for carpentry] serre-joint m - 3. MED clamp m - 4. AUT sabot m de Denver. ⬦ vt 1. [gen] serrer - 2. AUT poser un sabot de Denver à. ⬥ **clamp down** vi : to clamp down (on) sévir (contre).

clan [klæn] n clan m.

clandestine [klæn'destɪn] adj clandestin(e).

clang [klæŋ] n bruit m métallique.

clap [klæp] <> vt [hands] : **to clap one's hands** applaudir, taper des mains. <> vi applaudir, taper des mains.

clapping ['klæpɪŋ] n (U) applaudissements mpl.

claret ['klærət] n 1. [wine] bordeaux m rouge - 2. [colour] bordeaux m inv.

clarify ['klærɪfaɪ] vt [explain] éclaircir, clarifier.

clarinet [,klærə'net] n clarinette f.

clarity ['klærətɪ] n clarté f.

clash [klæʃ] <> n 1. [of interests, personalities] conflit m - 2. [fight, disagreement] heurt m, affrontement m - 3. [noise] fracas m. <> vi 1. [fight, disagree] se heurter - 2. [differ, conflict] entrer en conflit - 3. [coincide] : **to clash (with sthg)** tomber en même temps (que qqch) - 4. [colours] jurer.

clasp [klɑːsp] <> n [on necklace etc] fermoir m ; [on belt] boucle f. <> vt [hold tight] serrer.

class [klɑːs] <> n 1. [gen] classe f - 2. [lesson] cours m, classe f - 3. [category] catégorie f. <> vt classer.

classic ['klæsɪk] <> adj classique. <> n classique m.

classical ['klæsɪkl] adj classique.

classified ['klæsɪfaɪd] adj [information, document] classé secret (classée secrète).

classified ad n petite annonce f.

classify ['klæsɪfaɪ] vt classifier, classer.

classmate ['klɑːsmeɪt] n camarade mf de classe.

classroom ['klɑːsrʊm] n (salle f de) classe f.

classroom assistant n SCH aide-éducateur m, -trice f.

classy ['klɑːsɪ] adj inf chic (inv).

clatter ['klætər] n cliquetis m ; [louder] fracas m.

clause [klɔːz] n 1. [in document] clause f - 2. GRAM proposition f.

claw [klɔː] <> n 1. [of cat, bird] griffe f - 2. [of crab, lobster] pince f. <> vt griffer. <> vi [person] : **to claw at** s'agripper à.

clay [kleɪ] n argile f.

clean [kliːn] <> adj 1. [not dirty] propre - 2. [sheet of paper, driving licence] vierge ; [reputation] sans tache - 3. [joke] de bon goût - 4. [smooth] net (nette). <> vt nettoyer ; **to clean one's teeth** se brosser OR laver les dents. <> vi [person] faire le ménage. ◆ **clean out** vt sep [room, drawer] nettoyer à fond. ◆ **clean up** vt sep [clear up] nettoyer.

cleaner ['kliːnər] n 1. [person] personne f qui fait le ménage - 2. [substance] produit m d'entretien.

cleaning ['kliːnɪŋ] n nettoyage m.

cleanliness ['klenlɪnɪs] n propreté f.

cleanse [klenz] vt 1. [skin, wound] nettoyer - 2. fig [make pure] purifier.

cleanser ['klenzər] n [detergent] détergent m ; [for skin] démaquillant m.

clean-shaven [-'ʃeɪvn] adj rasé(e) de près.

clear [klɪər] <> adj 1. [gen] clair(e) ; [glass, plastic] transparent(e) - 2. [road, space] libre, dégagé(e). <> adv : **to stand clear** s'écarter ; **to steer clear of sb/sthg, to steer clear of sb/sthg** éviter qqn/qqch. <> vt 1. [road, path] dégager ; [table] débarrasser ; [obstacle, fallen tree] enlever ; **I went for a walk to clear my head** j'ai fait un tour pour m'éclaircir les idées - 2. LAW innocenter - 3. [jump] sauter, franchir - 4. [authorize] donner le feu vert à. <> vi [fog, smoke] se dissiper ; [weather, sky] s'éclaircir. ◆ **clear away** vt sep [plates] débarrasser ; [books] enlever. ◆ **clear off** vi UK inf dégager. ◆ **clear out** <> vt sep [cupboard] vider ; [room] ranger. <> vi inf [leave] dégager. ◆ **clear up** <> vt sep 1. [tidy] ranger ; [mystery, misunderstanding] éclaircir. <> vi 1. [weather] s'éclaircir - 2. [tidy up] tout ranger.

clearance ['klɪərəns] n 1. [of rubbish] enlèvement m ; [of land] déblaiement m - 2. [permission] autorisation f.

clear-cut adj net (nette).

clearing ['klɪərɪŋ] n [in wood] clairière f.

clearing bank n UK banque f de dépôt.

clearly ['klɪəlɪ] adv 1. [distinctly, lucidly] clairement - 2. [obviously] manifestement.

clearway ['klɪəweɪ] n UK route où le stationnement n'est autorisé qu'en cas d'urgence.

cleavage ['kliːvɪdʒ] n [between breasts] décolleté m.

cleaver ['kliːvər] n couperet m.

clef [klef] n clef f.

cleft [kleft] n fente f.

clench [klentʃ] vt serrer.

clergy ['klɜːdʒɪ] npl : **the clergy** le clergé.

clergyman ['klɜːdʒɪmən] (pl -men [-mən]) n membre m du clergé.

clerical ['klerɪkl] adj 1. ADMIN de bureau - 2. RELIG clérical(e).

clerk [UK klɑːk, US klɜːrk] n 1. [in office] employé m, -e f de bureau - 2. LAW clerc mf - 3. US [shop assistant] vendeur m, -euse f.

clever ['klevər] adj 1. [intelligent - person] intelligent(e) ; [- idea] ingénieux(euse) - 2. [skilful] habile, adroit(e).

click [klɪk] <> n [of lock] déclic m ; [of tongue, heels] claquement m. <> vt 1. faire claquer - 2. COMPUT cliquer ; **to click on** cliquer sur. <> vi 1. [heels] claquer ; [camera] faire un déclic.

client ['klaɪənt] *n* client *m*, -e *f*.

cliff [klɪf] *n* falaise *f*.

climate ['klaɪmɪt] *n* climat *m*.

climax ['klaɪmæks] *n* [culmination] apogée *m*.

climb [klaɪm] ◇ *n* ascension *f*, montée *f*. ◇ *vt* [tree, rope] monter à ; [stairs] monter ; [wall, hill] escalader. ◇ *vi* **1.** [person] monter, grimper - **2.** [plant] grimper ; [road] monter ; [plane] prendre de l'altitude - **3.** [increase] augmenter.

climb-down *n* UK reculade *f*.

climber ['klaɪmə'] *n* [person] alpiniste *mf*, grimpeur *m*, -euse *f*.

climbing ['klaɪmɪŋ] *n* [rock climbing] escalade *f* ; [mountain climbing] alpinisme *m*.

clinch [klɪntʃ] *vt* [deal] conclure.

cling [klɪŋ] (*pt & pp* clung) *vi* **1.** [hold tightly] : **to cling (to)** s'accrocher (à), se cramponner (à) - **2.** [clothes] : **to cling (to)** coller (à).

clingfilm ['klɪŋfɪlm] *n* UK film *m* alimentaire transparent.

clinic ['klɪnɪk] *n* [building] centre *m* médical, clinique *f*.

clinical ['klɪnɪkl] *adj* **1.** MED clinique - **2.** *fig* [attitude] froid(e).

clink [klɪŋk] *vi* tinter.

clip [klɪp] ◇ *n* **1.** [for paper] trombone *m* ; [for hair] pince *f* ; [of earring] clip *m* - **2.** [excerpt] extrait *m*. ◇ *vt* **1.** [fasten] attacher - **2.** [nails] couper ; [hedge] tailler ; [newspaper cutting] découper.

clipboard ['klɪpbɔːd] *n* écritoire *f* à pince.

clippers ['klɪpəz] *npl* [for hair] tondeuse *f* ; [for nails] pince *f* à ongles ; [for hedge] cisaille *f* à haie ; [for pruning] sécateur *m*.

clipping ['klɪpɪŋ] *n* US [from newspaper] coupure *f*.

cloak [kləʊk] *n* [garment] cape *f*.

cloakroom ['kləʊkrʊm] *n* **1.** [for clothes] vestiaire *m* - **2.** UK [toilets] toilettes *fpl*.

clock [klɒk] *n* **1.** [large] horloge *f* ; [small] pendule *f* ; **(a)round the clock** [work, be open] 24 heures sur 24 - **2.** AUT [mileometer] compteur *m*. ◆ **clock in**, **clock on** *vi* [at work] pointer *(à l'arrivée)*. ◆ **clock off**, **clock out** *vi* [at work] pointer *(à la sortie)*.

clockwise ['klɒkwaɪz] *adj & adv* dans le sens des aiguilles d'une montre.

clockwork ['klɒkwɜːk] ◇ *n* : **to go like clockwork** *fig* aller OR marcher comme sur des roulettes. ◇ *comp* [toy] mécanique.

clog [klɒg] *vt* boucher. ◆ **clogs** *npl* sabots *mpl*. ◆ **clog up** ◇ *vt sep* boucher. ◇ *vi* se boucher.

close¹ [kləʊs] ◇ *adj* **1.** [near] : **close (to)** proche (de), près (de) ; **a close friend** un ami intime (une amie intime) ; **close up, close to** de près ; **close by, close at hand** tout près ; **that was a close shave** OR **thing** OR **call** on l'a échappé belle - **2.** [link, resemblance] fort(e) ; [cooperation, connection] étroit(e) - **3.** [questioning] serré(e) ; [examination] minutieux(euse) ; **to keep a close watch on sb/sthg** surveiller qqn/qqch de près ; **to pay close attention** faire très attention - **4.** UK [weather] lourd(e) ; [air in room] renfermé(e) - **5.** [result, contest, race] serré(e). ◇ *adv* : **close (to)** près (de) ; **to come closer (together)** se rapprocher. ◆ **close on**, **close to** *prep* [almost] près de.

close² [kləʊz] ◇ *vt* **1.** [gen] fermer - **2.** [end] clore - **3.** CÔMPUT fermer ; **to close (a window)** fermer (une fenêtre) ; **to close (an application)** quitter (une application). ◇ *vi* **1.** [shop, bank] fermer ; [door, lid] (se) fermer - **2.** [end] se terminer, finir. ◇ *n* fin *f*. ◆ **close down** *vt sep & vi* fermer.

closed [kləʊzd] *adj* fermé(e).

close-knit [,kləʊs-] *adj* (très) uni(e).

closely ['kləʊslɪ] *adv* [listen, examine, watch] de près ; [resemble] beaucoup ; **to be closely related to** OR **with** être proche parent de.

closet ['klɒzɪt] ◇ *n* US [cupboard] placard *m*. ◇ *adj inf* non avoué(e).

close-up ['kləʊs-] *n* gros plan *m*.

closing time ['kləʊzɪŋ-] *n* heure *f* de fermeture.

closure ['kləʊʒə'] *n* fermeture *f*.

clot [klɒt] ◇ *n* **1.** [of blood, milk] caillot *m* - **2.** UK *inf* [fool] empoté *m*, -e *f*. ◇ *vi* [blood] coaguler.

cloth [klɒθ] *n* **1.** (U) [fabric] tissu *m* - **2.** [duster] chiffon *m* ; [for drying] torchon *m*.

clothe [kləʊð] *vt fml* [dress] habiller.

clothes [kləʊðz] *npl* vêtements *mpl*, habits *mpl* ; **to put one's clothes on** s'habiller ; **to take one's clothes off** se déshabiller.

clothes brush *n* brosse *f* à habits.

clothesline ['kləʊðzlaɪn] *n* corde *f* à linge.

clothes peg UK, **clothespin** US ['kləʊðzpɪn] *n* pince *f* à linge.

clothing ['kləʊðɪŋ] *n* (U) vêtements *mpl*, habits *mpl*.

cloud [klaʊd] *n* nuage *m*. ◆ **cloud over** *vi* [sky] se couvrir.

cloudy ['klaʊdɪ] *adj* **1.** [sky, day] nuageux(euse) - **2.** [liquid] trouble.

clout [klaʊt] *inf* ◇ *n* (U) [influence] poids *m*, influence *f*. ◇ *vt* donner un coup à.

clove [kləʊv] *n* : **a clove of garlic** une gousse d'ail. ◆ **cloves** *npl* [spice] clous *mpl* de girofle.

clover ['kləʊvə^r] *n* trèfle *m*.

clown [klaʊn] <> *n* **1.** [performer] clown *mf* - **2.** [fool] pitre *m*. <> *vi* faire le pitre.

cloying ['klɔɪɪŋ] *adj* **1.** [smell] écœurant(e) - **2.** [sentimentality] à l'eau de rose.

club [klʌb] <> *n* **1.** [organization, place] club *m* - **2.** [weapon] massue *f* - **3. :** (golf) club club *m*. <> *vt* matraquer. ⬥ **clubs** *npl* [playing cards] trèfle *m*. ⬥ **club together** *vi* se cotiser.

club car *n US* RAIL wagon-restaurant *m*.

club class *n* classe *f* club.

clubhouse ['klʌbhaʊs] (*pl* [-haʊzɪz]) *n* club *m*, pavillon *m*.

cluck [klʌk] *vi* glousser.

clue [klu:] *n* **1.** [in crime] indice *m* ; **I haven't (got) a clue (about)** je n'ai aucune idée (sur) - **2.** [in crossword] définition *f*.

clued-up [klu:d-] *adj UK inf* calé(e).

clump [klʌmp] *n* [of trees, bushes] massif *m*, bouquet *m*.

clumsy ['klʌmzɪ] *adj* **1.** [ungraceful] maladroit(e), gauche - **2.** [tactless] gauche, sans tact.

clung [klʌŋ] *pt & pp* ➤ **cling**.

cluster ['klʌstə^r] <> *n* [group] groupe *m*. <> *vi* [people] se rassembler ; [buildings etc] être regroupé(e).

clutch [klʌtʃ] <> *n* AUT embrayage *m*. <> *vt* agripper. <> *vi* : **to clutch at** s'agripper à.

clutter ['klʌtə^r] <> *n* désordre *m*. <> *vt* mettre en désordre.

cm (*abbrev of* **centimetre**) *n* cm.

CND (*abbrev of* **Campaign for Nuclear Disarmament**) *n* mouvement pour le désarmement nucléaire.

CNG [si:en'dʒi:] (*abbrev of* **compressed natural gas**) *n* GNC.

c/o (*abbrev of* **care of**) a/s.

Co. 1. (*abbrev of* **Company**) Cie - **2.** *abbrev of* **County**.

coach [kəʊtʃ] <> *n* **1.** *UK* [bus] car *m*, autocar *m* - **2.** *UK* RAIL voiture *f* - **3.** [horse-drawn] carrosse *m* - **4.** SPORT entraîneur *m* - **5.** [tutor] répétiteur *m*, -trice *f*. <> *vt* **1.** SPORT entraîner - **2.** [tutor] donner des leçons (particulières) à.

coal [kəʊl] *n* charbon *m*.

coalfield ['kəʊlfi:ld] *n* bassin *m* houiller.

coalition [ˌkəʊə'lɪʃn] *n* coalition *f*.

coalman ['kəʊlmæn] (*pl* -men [-men]) *n UK* charbonnier *m*.

coalmine ['kəʊlmaɪn] *n* mine *f* de charbon.

coarse [kɔ:s] *adj* **1.** [rough - cloth] grossier(ère) ; [- hair] épais(aisse) ; [- skin] granuleux(euse) - **2.** [vulgar] grossier(ère).

coast [kəʊst] <> *n* côte *f*. <> *vi* [in car, on bike] avancer en roue libre.

coastal ['kəʊstl] *adj* côtier(ère).

coaster ['kəʊstə^r] *n* [small mat] dessous *m* de verre.

coastguard ['kəʊstgɑ:d] *n* **1.** [person] garde-côte *m* - **2.** [organization] : **the coastguard** la gendarmerie maritime.

coastline ['kəʊstlaɪn] *n* côte *f*.

coat [kəʊt] <> *n* **1.** [garment] manteau *m* - **2.** [of animal] pelage *m* - **3.** [layer] couche *f*. <> *vt* : **to coat sthg (with)** recouvrir qqch (de) ; [with paint etc] enduire qqch (de).

coat hanger *n* cintre *m*.

coating ['kəʊtɪŋ] *n* couche *f* ; CULIN glaçage *m*.

coat of arms (*pl* **coats of arms**) *n* blason *m*.

coax [kəʊks] *vt* : **to coax sb (to do** OR **into doing sthg)** persuader qqn (de faire qqch) à force de cajoleries.

cob [kɒb] *n* ➤ **corn**.

cobbled ['kɒbld] *adj* pavé(e).

cobbler ['kɒblə^r] *n* cordonnier *m*, -ière *f*.

cobbles ['kɒblz], **cobblestones** ['kɒblstəʊnz] *npl* pavés *mpl*.

cobweb ['kɒbweb] *n* toile *f* d'araignée.

Coca-Cola® [ˌkəʊkə'kəʊlə] *n* Coca-Cola® *m inv*.

cocaine [kəʊ'keɪn] *n* cocaïne *f*.

cock [kɒk] <> *n* **1.** [male chicken] coq *m* - **2.** [male bird] mâle *m*- **3.** [gun] armer - **2.** [head] incliner. ⬥ **cock up** *vt sep UK v inf* faire merder.

cockerel ['kɒkrəl] *n* jeune coq *m*.

cockeyed ['kɒkaɪd] *adj inf* **1.** [lopsided] de travers - **2.** [foolish] complètement fou (folle).

cockle ['kɒkl] *n* [shellfish] coque *f*.

Cockney ['kɒknɪ] *n* (*pl* **Cockneys**) [person] Cockney *mf* (*personne issue des quartiers populaires de l'est de Londres*).

cockpit ['kɒkpɪt] *n* [in plane] cockpit *m*.

cockroach ['kɒkrəʊtʃ] *n* cafard *m*.

cocksure [ˌkɒk'ʃɔ:r] *adj* trop sûr(e) de soi.

cocktail ['kɒkteɪl] *n* cocktail *m*.

cock-up *n UK v inf* **to make a cock-up** se planter.

cocky ['kɒkɪ] *adj inf* suffisant(e).

cocoa ['kəʊkəʊ] *n* cacao *m*.

coconut ['kəʊkənʌt] *n* noix *f* de coco.

cod [kɒd] (*pl* **cod**) *n* morue *f*.

COD *abbrev of* **cash on delivery**.

code [kəʊd] <> *n* code *m*. <> *vt* coder.

cod-liver oil *n* huile *f* de foie de morue.

coerce [kəʊ'ɜːs] *vt* : **to coerce sb (into doing sthg)** contraindre qqn (à faire qqch).

C of E *abbrev of* **Church of England**.

coffee ['kɒfɪ] *n* café *m*.

coffee bar *n UK* café *m*.

coffee break *n* pause-café *f*.

coffee grinder *n* moulin *m* à café.

coffee morning *n UK réunion matinale pour prendre le café.*

coffeepot ['kɒfɪpɒt] *n* cafetière *f*.

coffee shop *n* **1.** *UK* [shop] café *m* - **2.** *US* [restaurant] ≃ café-restaurant *m*.

coffee table *n* table *f* basse.

coffin ['kɒfɪn] *n* cercueil *m*.

cog [kɒg] *n* [tooth on wheel] dent *f* ; [wheel] roue *f* dentée.

coherent [kəʊ'hɪərənt] *adj* cohérent(e).

cohesive [kəʊ'hiːsɪv] *adj* cohésif(ive).

coil [kɔɪl] <> *n* **1.** [of rope etc] rouleau *m* ; [one loop] boucle *f* - **2.** ELEC bobine *f* - **3.** *UK* [contraceptive device] stérilet *m*. <> *vt* enrouler. <> *vi* s'enrouler. ➡ **coil up** *vt sep* enrouler.

coin [kɔɪn] <> *n* pièce *f* (de monnaie). <> *vt* [word] inventer.

coinage ['kɔɪnɪdʒ] *n* (U) [currency] monnaie *f*.

coin-box *n UK* cabine *f* (publique) à pièces.

coincide [,kəʊɪn'saɪd] *vi* coïncider.

coincidence [kəʊ'ɪnsɪdəns] *n* coïncidence *f*.

coincidental [kəʊ,ɪnsɪ'dentl] *adj* de coïncidence.

coke [kəʊk] *n* **1.** [fuel] coke *m* - **2.** *drug sl* coco *f*, coke *f*.

Coke® [kəʊk] *n* Coca® *m*.

cola ['kəʊlə] *n* cola *m*.

colander ['kʌləndər] *n* passoire *f*.

cold [kəʊld] <> *adj* froid(e) ; **it's cold** il fait froid ; **to be cold** avoir froid ; **to get cold** [person] avoir froid ; [hot food] refroidir. <> *n* **1.** [illness] rhume *m* ; **to catch (a) cold** attraper un rhume, s'enrhumer - **2.** [low temperature] froid *m*.

cold-blooded [-'blʌdɪd] *adj fig* [killer] sans pitié ; [murder] de sang-froid.

cold sore *n* bouton *m* de fièvre.

cold war *n* : **the cold war** la guerre froide.

coleslaw ['kəʊlslɔː] *n* chou *m* cru mayonnaise.

colic ['kɒlɪk] *n* colique *f*.

collaborate [kə'læbəreɪt] *vi* collaborer.

collapse [kə'læps] <> *n* [gen] écroulement *m*, effondrement *m* ; [of marriage] échec *m*.

<> *vi* **1.** [building, person] s'effondrer, s'écrouler ; [marriage] échouer - **2.** [fold up] être pliant(e).

collapsible [kə'læpsəbl] *adj* pliant(e).

collar ['kɒlər] <> *n* **1.** [on clothes] col *m* - **2.** [for dog] collier *m* - **3.** TECH collier *m*, bague *f*. <> *vt inf* [detain] coincer.

collarbone ['kɒləbəʊn] *n* clavicule *f*.

collate [kə'leɪt] *vt* collationner.

collateral [kɒ'lætərəl] *n* (U) nantissement *m*.

colleague ['kɒliːg] *n* collègue *mf*.

collect [kə'lekt] <> *vt* **1.** [gather together - gen] rassembler, recueillir ; [- wood etc] ramasser ; **to collect o.s.** se reprendre - **2.** [as a hobby] collectionner - **3.** [go to get] aller chercher, passer prendre - **4.** [money] recueillir ; [taxes] percevoir. <> *vi* **1.** [crowd, people] se rassembler - **2.** [dust, leaves, dirt] s'amasser, s'accumuler - **3.** [for charity, gift] faire la quête. <> *adv US* TELEC : **to call (sb) collect** téléphoner (à qqn) en PCV.

collection [kə'lekʃn] *n* **1.** [of objects] collection *f* - **2.** LIT recueil *m* - **3.** [of money] quête *f* - **4.** [of mail] levée *f*.

collective [kə'lektɪv] <> *adj* collectif(ive). <> *n* coopérative *f*.

collector [kə'lektər] *n* **1.** [as a hobby] collectionneur *m*, -euse *f* - **2.** [of debts, rent] encaisseur *m* ; **collector of taxes** percepteur *m*.

college ['kɒlɪdʒ] *n* **1.** [gen] ≃ école *f* d'enseignement (technique) supérieur - **2.** [of university] *maison communautaire d'étudiants sur un campus universitaire.*

college of education *n* ≃ institut *m* de formation de maîtres.

collide [kə'laɪd] *vi* : **to collide (with)** entrer en collision (avec).

collie ['kɒlɪ] *n* colley *m*.

colliery ['kɒljərɪ] *n esp UK* mine *f*.

collision [kə'lɪʒn] *n* [crash] : **collision (with/ between)** collision *f* (avec/entre) ; **to be on a collision course (with)** *fig* aller au-devant de l'affrontement (avec).

colloquial [kə'ləʊkwɪəl] *adj* familier(ère).

collude [kə'luːd] *vi* : **to collude with sb** comploter avec qqn.

Colombia [kə'lɒmbɪə] *n* Colombie *f*.

colon ['kəʊlən] *n* **1.** ANAT côlon *m* - **2.** [punctuation mark] deux-points *m inv*.

colonel ['kɜːnl] *n* colonel *m*.

colonial [kə'ləʊnjəl] *adj* colonial(e).

colonize, *UK* -**ise** ['kɒlənaɪz] *vt* coloniser.

colony ['kɒlənɪ] *n* colonie *f*.

color etc *US* = **colour** etc.

colossal [kə'lɒsl] *adj* colossal(e).

colour UK, **color** US ['kʌlər] <> n couleur f ; **in colour** en couleur. <> adj en couleur. <> vt **1.** [food, liquid etc] colorer ; [with pen, crayon] colorier - **2.** [dye] teindre - **3.** fig [judgment] fausser. <> vi rougir.

colour bar UK, **color bar** US n discrimination f raciale.

colour barrier UK, **color barrier** US n discrimination f raciale.

colour-blind UK, **color-blind** US adj lit daltonien(enne) ; fig qui ne fait pas de discrimination raciale.

coloured UK, **colored** US ['kʌləd] adj de couleur ; **brightly coloured** de couleur vive.

colourful UK, **colorful** US ['kʌləful] adj **1.** [gen] coloré(e) - **2.** [person, area] haut(e) en couleur.

colouring UK, **coloring** US ['kʌlərɪŋ] n **1.** [dye] colorant m - **2.** (U) [complexion] teint m.

colour scheme UK, **color scheme** US n combinaison f de couleurs.

colt [kəʊlt] n [young horse] poulain m.

column ['kɒləm] n **1.** [gen] colonne f - **2.** PRESS [article] rubrique f.

columnist ['kɒləmnɪst] n chroniqueur m.

coma ['kəʊmə] n coma m.

comb [kəʊm] <> n [for hair] peigne m. <> vt **1.** [hair] peigner - **2.** [search] ratisser.

combat ['kɒmbæt] <> n combat m. <> vt combattre.

combination [ˌkɒmbɪ'neɪʃn] n combinaison f.

combine <> vt [kəm'baɪn] [gen] rassembler ; [pieces] combiner ; **to combine sthg with sthg** [two substances] mélanger qqch avec OR à qqch ; fig allier qqch à qqch. <> vi [kəm'baɪn] COMM & POL : **to combine (with)** fusionner (avec). <> n ['kɒmbaɪn] **1.** [group] cartel m - **2.** = combine harvester.

combine harvester [-'hɑːvɪstər] n moissonneuse-batteuse f.

come [kʌm] (pt **came**, pp **come**) vi **1.** [move] venir ; [arrive] arriver, venir ; **coming!** j'arrive! ; **I've got people coming** [short stay] j'ai des invités ; [long stay] il y a des gens qui viennent ; **the news came as a shock** la nouvelle m'a/lui a etc fait un choc - **2.** [reach] : **to come up to** arriver à, monter jusqu'à ; **to come down to** descendre OR tomber jusqu'à - **3.** [happen] arriver, se produire ; **come what may** quoi qu'il arrive - **4.** [become] : **to come true** se réaliser ; **to come undone** se défaire ; **to come unstuck** se décoller - **5.** [begin gradually] : **to come to do sthg** en arriver à OR en venir à faire qqch - **6.** [be placed in order] venir, être place(e) ; **P comes before Q** P vient avant Q, P précède Q ; **she came second in the exam** elle était deuxième

à l'examen. **to come** adv à venir ; **in (the) days/years to come** dans les jours/ années à venir. **come about** vi [happen] arriver, se produire. **come across** vt insep tomber sur, trouver par hasard. **come along** vi **1.** [arrive by chance] arriver - **2.** [improve - work] avancer ; [- student] faire des progrès. **come apart** vi **1.** [fall to pieces] tomber en morceaux - **2.** [come off] se détacher. **come around**, **come round** UK vi [regain consciousness] reprendre connaissance, revenir à soi. **come at** vt insep [attack] attaquer. **come back** vi **1.** [in talk, writing] : **to come back to sthg** revenir à qqch - **2.** [memory] : **to come back to sb** revenir (à qqn). **come by** vt insep [get, obtain] trouver, dénicher. **come down** vi **1.** [decrease] baisser - **2.** [descend] descendre. **come down to** vt insep se résumer à, se réduire à. **come down with** vt insep [cold, flu] attraper. **come forward** vi se présenter. **come from** vt insep venir de. **come in** vi [enter] entrer. **come in for** vt insep [criticism] être l'objet de. **come into** vt insep **1.** [inherit] hériter de - **2.** [begin to be] : **to come into being** prendre naissance, voir le jour. **come off** vi **1.** [button, label] se détacher ; [stain] s'enlever - **2.** [joke, attempt] réussir ; **come off it!** inf et puis quoi encore!, non mais sans blague! **come on** vi **1.** [start] commencer, apparaître - **2.** [start working - light, heating] s'allumer - **3.** [progress, improve] avancer, faire des progrès ; **come on!** [expressing encouragement] allez! ; [hurry up] allez, dépêche-toi! ; [expressing disbelief] allons donc! **come out** vi **1.** [become known] être découvert(e) - **2.** [appear - product, book, film] sortir, paraître ; [- sun, moon, stars] paraître - **3.** [go on strike] faire grève - **4.** [declare publicly] : **to come out for/ against sthg** se déclarer pour/contre qqch. **come round** UK vi = come around. **come through** vt insep survivre à. **come to** <> vt insep **1.** [reach] : **to come to an end** se terminer, prendre fin ; **to come to a decision** arriver à OR prendre une décision - **2.** [amount to] s'élever à. <> vi [regain consciousness] revenir à soi, reprendre connaissance. **come under** vt insep [be subjected to - authority, control] dépendre de ; [- influence] tomber sous, être soumis à ; **the government is coming under pressure to lower taxes** le gouvernement subit des pressions visant à réduire les impôts ; **to come under attack (from)** être en butte aux attaques (de). **come up** vi **1.** [be mentioned] survenir - **2.** [be imminent] approcher - **3.** [happen unexpectedly] se présenter - **4.** [sun] se lever. **come up against** vt insep se heurter à. **come up**

to vt insep **1.** [approach - in space] s'approcher de - **2.** [equal] répondre à. ◆ **come up with** vt insep [answer, idea] proposer.

comeback ['kʌmbæk] n come-back m ; **to make a comeback** [fashion] revenir à la mode ; [actor etc] revenir à la scène.

comedian [kə'mi:djən] n [comic] comique m ; THEAT comédien m.

comedown ['kʌmdaʊn] n inf **it was a comedown for her** elle est tombée bien bas pour faire ça.

comedy ['kɒmədɪ] n comédie f.

comet ['kɒmɪt] n comète f.

come-uppance [,kʌm'ʌpəns] n : **to get one's come-uppance** inf recevoir ce qu'on mérite.

comfort ['kʌmfət] <> n **1.** (U) [ease] confort m - **2.** [luxury] commodité f - **3.** [solace] réconfort m, consolation f. <> vt réconforter, consoler.

comfortable ['kʌmftəbl] adj **1.** [gen] confortable - **2.** fig [person - at ease, financially] à l'aise - **3.** [after operation, accident] : **he's comfortable** son état est stationnaire.

comfortably ['kʌmftəblɪ] adv **1.** [sit, sleep] confortablement - **2.** [without financial difficulty] à l'aise - **3.** [win] aisément.

comfort station n US dated toilettes fpl publiques.

comic ['kɒmɪk] <> adj comique, amusant(e). <> n **1.** [comedian] comique m, actrice f comique - **2.** [magazine] bande f dessinée.

comical ['kɒmɪkl] adj comique, drôle.

comic strip n bande f dessinée.

coming ['kʌmɪŋ] <> adj [future] à venir, futur(e). <> n : **comings and goings** allées et venues fpl.

comma ['kɒmə] n virgule f.

command [kə'mɑ:nd] <> n **1.** [order] ordre m - **2.** (U) [control] commandement m - **3.** [of language, subject] maîtrise f ; **to have at one's command** [language] maîtriser ; [resources] avoir à sa disposition - **4.** COMPUT commande f. <> vt **1.** [order] : **to command sb to do sthg** ordonner OR commander à qqn de faire qqch - **2.** MIL [control] commander - **3.** [deserve - respect] inspirer ; [- attention, high price] mériter.

commandeer [,kɒmən'dɪər] vt réquisitionner.

commander [kə'mɑ:ndər] n **1.** [in army] commandant m - **2.** [in navy] capitaine m de frégate.

commando [kə'mɑ:ndəʊ] (pl -s OR -es) n commando m.

commemorate [kə'meməreɪt] vt commémorer.

commemoration [kə,memə'reɪʃn] n commémoration f.

commence [kə'mens] fml <> vt commencer, entamer ; **to commence doing sthg** commencer à faire qqch. <> vi commencer.

commend [kə'mend] vt **1.** [praise] : **to commend sb (on OR for)** féliciter qqn (de) - **2.** [recommend] : **to commend sthg (to sb)** recommander qqch (à qqn).

commensurate [kə'menʃərət] adj fml : **commensurate with** correspondant(e) à.

comment ['kɒment] <> n commentaire m, remarque f ; **no comment!** sans commentaire! <> vt : **to comment that** remarquer que. <> vi : **to comment (on)** faire des commentaires OR remarques (sur).

commentary ['kɒməntrɪ] n commentaire m.

commentator ['kɒmənteɪtər] n commentateur m, -trice f.

commerce ['kɒmɜ:s] n (U) commerce m, affaires fpl.

commercial [kə'mɜ:ʃl] <> adj commercial(e). <> n publicité f, spot m publicitaire.

commercial break n publicités fpl.

commiserate [kə'mɪzəreɪt] vi : **to commiserate with sb** témoigner de la compassion pour qqn.

commission [kə'mɪʃn] <> n **1.** [money, investigative body] commission f - **2.** [order for work] commande f. <> vt [work] commander ; **to commission sb to do sthg** charger qqn de faire qqch.

commissionaire [kə,mɪʃə'neər] n UK portier m (d'un hôtel, etc).

commissioner [kə'mɪʃnər] n [in police] commissaire mf.

commit [kə'mɪt] vt **1.** [crime, sin etc] commettre ; **to commit suicide** se suicider - **2.** [promise - money, resources] allouer ; **to commit o.s. (to sthg/to doing sthg)** s'engager (à qqch/à faire qqch) - **3.** [consign] : **to commit sb to prison** faire incarcérer qqn ; **to commit sthg to memory** apprendre qqch par cœur.

commitment [kə'mɪtmənt] n **1.** (U) [dedication] engagement m - **2.** [responsibility] obligation f.

committee [kə'mɪtɪ] n commission f, comité m.

commodity [kə'mɒdətɪ] n marchandise f.

common ['kɒmən] <> adj **1.** [frequent] courant(e) - **2.** [shared] : **common (to)** commun(e) (à) - **3.** [ordinary] banal(e) - **4.** UK pej [vulgar] vulgaire. <> n [land] terrain m communal. ◆ **in common** adv en commun.

common law *n* droit *m* coutumier.
common-law *adj* : **common-law wife** concubine *f*.

commonly ['kɒmənlɪ] *adv* [generally] d'une manière générale, généralement.

Common Market *n dated* : **the Common Market** le Marché commun.

commonplace ['kɒmənpleɪs] *adj* banal(e), ordinaire.

common room *n* [staffroom] salle *f* des professeurs ; [for students] salle commune.

Commons ['kɒmənz] *npl UK* **the Commons** les Communes *fpl*, la Chambre des Communes.

common sense *n (U)* bon sens *m*.

Commonwealth ['kɒmənwelθ] *n* : **the Commonwealth** le Commonwealth.

Commonwealth of Independent States *n* : **the Commonwealth of Independent States** la Communauté des États Indépendants.

commotion [kə'məʊʃn] *n* remue-ménage *m*.

communal ['kɒmjunl] *adj* [kitchen, garden] commun(e) ; [life etc] communautaire, collectif(ive).

commune ⬦ *n* ['kɒmju:n] communauté *f*. ⬦ *vi* [kə'mju:n] : **to commune with** communier avec.

communicate [kə'mju:nɪkeɪt] *vt & vi* communiquer.

communication [kə,mju:nɪ'keɪʃn] *n* contact *m* ; TELEC communication *f*.

communication cord *n UK* sonnette *f* d'alarme.

communion [kə'mju:njən] *n* communion *f*.
Communion *n (U)* RELIG communion *f*.

Communism ['kɒmjunɪzm] *n* communisme *m*.

Communist ['kɒmjunɪst] ⬦ *adj* communiste. ⬦ *n* communiste *mf*.

community [kə'mju:nətɪ] *n* communauté *f*.

community centre *UK*, **community center** *US n* foyer *m* municipal.

community charge *n UK* ≃ impôts *mpl* locaux.

commutation ticket [,kɒmju:'teɪʃn] *n US* carte *f* de transport.

commute [kə'mju:t] ⬦ *vt* LAW commuer. ⬦ *vi* [to work] faire la navette pour se rendre à son travail.

commuter [kə'mju:tər] *n* personne qui fait tous les jours la navette de banlieue en ville pour se rendre à son travail.

compact ⬦ *adj* [kəm'pækt] compact(e).

⬦ *n* ['kɒmpækt] **1.** [for face powder] poudrier *m* - **2.** *US* AUT : **compact (car)** petite voiture *f*.

compact disc *n* compact *m* (disc *m*), disque *m* compact.

compact disc player *n* lecteur *m* de disques compacts.

companion [kəm'pænjən] *n* [person] camarade *mf*.

companionship [kəm'pænjənʃɪp] *n* compagnie *f*.

company ['kʌmpənɪ] *n* **1.** [COMM - gen] société *f* ; [- insurance, airline, shipping company] compagnie *f* - **2.** [companionship] compagnie *f* ; **to keep sb company** tenir compagnie à qqn - **3.** [of actors] troupe *f*.

company secretary *n* secrétaire général *m*, secrétaire générale *f*.

comparable ['kɒmprəbl] *adj* : **comparable (to** OR **with)** comparable (à).

comparative [kəm'pærətɪv] *adj* **1.** [relative] relatif(ive) - **2.** [study, in grammar] comparatif(ive).

comparatively [kəm'pærətɪvlɪ] *adv* [relatively] relativement.

compare [kəm'peər] ⬦ *vt* : **to compare sb/sthg (with), to compare sb/sthg (to)** comparer qqn/qqch (avec), comparer qqn/qqch (à) ; **compared with** OR **to** par rapport à. ⬦ *vi* : **to compare (with)** être comparable (à).

comparison [kəm'pærɪsn] *n* comparaison *f* ; **in comparison with** OR **to** en comparaison de, par rapport à.

compartment [kəm'pɑ:tmənt] *n* compartiment *m*.

compass ['kʌmpəs] *n* [magnetic] boussole *f*. **compasses** *npl* : **(a pair of) compasses** un compas.

compassion [kəm'pæʃn] *n* compassion *f*.

compassionate [kəm'pæʃənət] *adj* compatissant(e).

compatible [kəm'pætəbl] *adj* [gen & COMPUT] : **compatible (with)** compatible (avec).

compel [kəm'pel] *vt* [force] : **to compel sb (to do sthg)** contraindre OR obliger qqn (à faire qqch).

compelling [kəm'pelɪŋ] *adj* [forceful] irrésistible.

compensate ['kɒmpenseɪt] ⬦ *vt* : **to compensate sb for sthg** [financially] dédommager OR indemniser qqn de qqch. ⬦ *vi* : **to compensate for sthg** compenser qqch.

compensation [,kɒmpen'seɪʃn] *n* **1.** [money] : **compensation (for)** dédommagement *m* (pour) - **2.** [way of compensating] : **compensation (for)** compensation *f* (pour).

compete [kəm'pi:t] *vi* **1.** [vie - people] : **to**

compete with sb for sthg disputer qqch à qqn ; **to compete for sthg** se disputer qqch **- 2.** COMM : **to compete (with)** être en concurrence (avec) ; **to compete for sthg** se faire concurrence pour qqch **- 3.** [take part] être en compétition.

competence ['kɒmpɪtəns] n (U) [proficiency] compétence f, capacité f.

competent ['kɒmpɪtənt] adj compétent(e).

competition [,kɒmpɪ'tɪʃn] n **1.** (U) [rivalry] rivalité f, concurrence f **- 2.** (U) COMM concurrence f **- 3.** [race, contest] concours m, compétition f.

competitive [kəm'petətɪv] adj **1.** [person] qui a l'esprit de compétition ; [match, sport] de compétition **- 2.** [COMM - goods] compétitif(ive) ; [- manufacturer] concurrentiel(elle).

competitor [kəm'petɪtər] n concurrent m, -e f.

compile [kəm'paɪl] vt rédiger.

complacency [kəm'pleɪsnsɪ] n autosatisfaction f.

complain [kəm'pleɪn] vi **1.** [make complaint] : **to complain (about)** se plaindre (de) **- 2.** MED : **to complain of** se plaindre de.

complaint [kəm'pleɪnt] n **1.** [gen] plainte f ; [in shop] réclamation f **- 2.** MED affection f, maladie f.

complement ⃟ n ['kɒmplɪmənt] **1.** [accompaniment] accompagnement m **- 2.** [number] effectif m **- 3.** GRAM complément m. ⃟ vt ['kɒmplɪ,ment] aller bien avec.

complementary [,kɒmplɪ'mentərɪ] adj complémentaire.

complete [kəm'pliːt] ⃟ adj **1.** [gen] complet(ète) ; **complete with** doté(e) de, muni(e) de **- 2.** [finished] achevé(e). ⃟ vt **1.** [make whole] compléter **- 2.** [finish] achever, terminer **- 3.** [questionnaire, form] remplir.

completely [kəm'pliːtlɪ] adv complètement.

completion [kəm'pliːʃn] n achèvement m.

complex ['kɒmpleks] ⃟ adj complexe. ⃟ n [mental, of buildings] complexe m.

complexion [kəm'plekʃn] n teint m.

compliance [kəm'plaɪəns] n : **compliance (with)** conformité f (à).

complicate ['kɒmplɪkeɪt] vt compliquer.

complicated ['kɒmplɪkeɪtɪd] adj compliqué(e).

complication [,kɒmplɪ'keɪʃn] n complication f.

compliment ⃟ n ['kɒmplɪmənt] compliment m. ⃟ vt ['kɒmplɪ,ment] : **to compliment sb (on)** féliciter qqn (de). ⇐ **compliments** npl fml compliments mpl.

complimentary [,kɒmplɪ'mentərɪ] adj **1.** [admiring] flatteur(euse) **- 2.** [free] gratuit(e).

complimentary ticket n billet m de faveur.

comply [kəm'plaɪ] vi : **to comply with** se conformer à.

component [kəm'pəʊnənt] n composant m.

compose [kəm'pəʊz] vt **1.** [gen] composer ; **to be composed of** se composer de, être composé de **- 2.** [calm] : **to compose o.s.** se calmer.

composed [kəm'pəʊzd] adj [calm] calme.

composer [kəm'pəʊzər] n compositeur m, -trice f.

composition [,kɒmpə'zɪʃn] n composition f.

compost [UK 'kɒmpɒst, US 'kɒmpəʊst] n compost m.

composure [kəm'pəʊzər] n sang-froid m, calme m.

compound n ['kɒmpaʊnd] **1.** CHEM & LING composé m **- 2.** [enclosed area] enceinte f.

compound fracture n fracture f multiple.

comprehend [,kɒmprɪ'hend] vt [understand] comprendre.

comprehension [,kɒmprɪ'henʃn] n compréhension f.

comprehensive [,kɒmprɪ'hensɪv] ⃟ adj **1.** [account, report] exhaustif(ive), détaillé(e) **- 2.** [insurance] tous-risques (inv). ⃟ n UK = **comprehensive school**.

comprehensive school n établissement secondaire britannique d'enseignement général.

compress [kəm'pres] vt **1.** [squeeze, press] comprimer **- 2.** [shorten - text] condenser.

comprise [kəm'praɪz] vt comprendre ; **to be comprised of** consister en, comprendre.

compromise ['kɒmprəmaɪz] ⃟ n compromis m. ⃟ vt compromettre. ⃟ vi transiger.

compulsion [kəm'pʌlʃn] n **1.** [strong desire] : **to have a compulsion to do sthg** ne pas pouvoir s'empêcher de faire qqch **- 2.** (U) [obligation] obligation f.

compulsive [kəm'pʌlsɪv] adj **1.** [smoker, liar etc] invétéré(e) **- 2.** [book, TV programme] captivant(e).

compulsory [kəm'pʌlsərɪ] adj obligatoire.

computer [kəm'pjuːtər] n ordinateur m.

computer game n jeu m électronique.

computerized, UK **-ised** [kəm'pjuːtəraɪzd] adj informatisé(e).

computer science *n* informatique *f.*

computer scientist *n* informaticien *m*, -enne *f.*

computing [kəm'pjuːtɪŋ] *n* informatique *f.*

comrade ['kɒmreɪd] *n* camarade *mf.*

con [kɒn] *inf* ⬦ *n* [trick] escroquerie *f.* ⬦ *vt* [trick]: **to con sb (out of)** escroquer qqn (de) ; **to con sb into doing sthg** persuader qqn de faire qqch (en lui mentant).

concave [,kɒn'keɪv] *adj* concave.

conceal [kən'siːl] *vt* cacher, dissimuler ; **to conceal sthg from sb** cacher qqch à qqn.

concede [kən'siːd] ⬦ *vt* concéder. ⬦ *vi* céder.

conceit [kən'siːt] *n* [arrogance] vanité *f.*

conceited [kən'siːtɪd] *adj* vaniteux(euse).

conceive [kən'siːv] ⬦ *vt* concevoir. ⬦ *vi* **1.** MED concevoir - **2.** [imagine]: **to conceive of** concevoir.

concentrate ['kɒnsəntreɪt] ⬦ *vt* concentrer. ⬦ *vi*: **to concentrate (on)** se concentrer (sur).

concentration [,kɒnsən'treɪʃn] *n* concentration *f.*

concentration camp *n* camp *m* de concentration.

concept ['kɒnsept] *n* concept *m.*

concern [kən'sɜːn] ⬦ *n* **1.** [worry, anxiety] souci *m*, inquiétude *f* - **2.** COMM [company] affaire *f.* ⬦ *vt* **1.** [worry] inquiéter ; **to be concerned (about)** s'inquiéter (de) - **2.** [involve] concerner, intéresser ; **as far as I'm concerned** en ce qui me concerne ; **to be concerned with** [subj: person] s'intéresser à ; **to concern o.s. with sthg** s'intéresser à, s'occuper de - **3.** [subj: book, film] traiter de.

concerning [kən'sɜːnɪŋ] *prep* en ce qui concerne.

concert ['kɒnsət] *n* concert *m.*

concerted [kən'sɜːtɪd] *adj* [effort] concerté(e).

concert hall *n* salle *f* de concert.

concertina [,kɒnsə'tiːnə] *n* concertina *m.*

concerto [kən'tʃɜːtəʊ] (*pl* -s) *n* concerto *m.*

concession [kən'seʃn] *n* **1.** [gen] concession *f* - **2.** UK [special price] réduction *f.*

conciliatory [kən'sɪlɪətrɪ] *adj* conciliant(e).

concise [kən'saɪs] *adj* concis(e).

conclude [kən'kluːd] ⬦ *vt* conclure. ⬦ *vi* [meeting] prendre fin ; [speaker] conclure.

conclusion [kən'kluːʒn] *n* conclusion *f.*

conclusive [kən'kluːsɪv] *adj* concluant(e).

concoct [kən'kɒkt] *vt* préparer ; *fig* concocter.

concoction [kən'kɒkʃn] *n* préparation *f.*

concourse ['kɒŋkɔːs] *n* [hall] hall *m.*

concrete ['kɒŋkriːt] ⬦ *adj* [definite] concret(ète). ⬦ *n* (U) béton *m.* ⬦ *comp* [made of concrete] en béton.

concubine ['kɒŋkjʊbaɪn] *n* concubine *f.*

concur [kən'kɜːr] *vi* [agree]: **to concur (with)** être d'accord (avec).

concurrently [kən'kʌrəntlɪ] *adv* simultanément.

concussion [kən'kʌʃn] *n* commotion *f.*

condemn [kən'dem] *vt* condamner.

condensation [,kɒnden'seɪʃn] *n* condensation *f.*

condense [kən'dens] ⬦ *vt* condenser. ⬦ *vi* se condenser.

condensed milk [kən'denst-] *n* lait *m* concentré ; **sweetened condensed milk** lait *m* concentré sucré.

condescending [,kɒndɪ'sendɪŋ] *adj* condescendant(e).

condition [kən'dɪʃn] ⬦ *n* **1.** [gen] condition *f* ; **in (a) good/bad condition** en bon/mauvais état ; **out of condition** pas en forme - **2.** MED maladie *f.* ⬦ *vt* [gen] conditionner.

conditional [kən'dɪʃənl] *adj* conditionnel(elle).

conditionality [kən,dɪʃə'nælətɪ] *n* conditionnalité *f.*

conditioner [kən'dɪʃnər] *n* **1.** [for hair] après-shampooing *m* - **2.** [for clothes] assouplissant *m.*

condolences [kən'dəʊlənsɪz] *npl* condoléances *fpl.*

condom ['kɒndəm] *n* préservatif *m.*

condominium [,kɒndə'mɪnɪəm] *n* US **1.** [apartment] appartement *m* dans un immeuble en copropriété - **2.** [apartment block] immeuble *m* en copropriété.

condone [kən'dəʊn] *vt* excuser.

conducive [kən'djuːsɪv] *adj*: **to be conducive to sthg/to doing sthg** inciter à qqch/à faire qqch.

conduct ⬦ *n* ['kɒndʌkt] conduite *f.* ⬦ *vt* [kən'dʌkt] **1.** [carry out, transmit] conduire - **2.** [behave]: **to conduct o.s. well/badly** se conduire bien/mal - **3.** MUS diriger.

conducted tour [kən'dʌktɪd-] *n* UK visite *f* guidée.

conductor [kən'dʌktər] *n* **1.** MUS chef *m* d'orchestre - **2.** [on bus] receveur *m* - **3.** US [on train] chef *m* de train.

conductress [kən'dʌktrɪs] *n* [on bus] receveuse *f.*

cone [kəʊn] n **1.** [shape] cône m - **2.** [for ice cream] cornet m - **3.** [from tree] pomme f de pin.

confectioner [kən'fekʃnər] n confiseur m ; **confectioner's (shop)** confiserie f.

confectionery [kən'fekʃnərɪ] n confiserie f.

confederation [kən,fedə'reɪʃn] n confédération f.

Confederation of British Industry n: **the Confederation of British Industry** ≃ le conseil du patronat.

confer [kən'fɜːr] ⟨⟩ vt: **to confer sthg (on sb)** conférer qqch (à qqn). ⟨⟩ vi: **to confer (with sb on** OR **about sthg)** s'entretenir (avec qqn de qqch).

conference ['kɒnfərəns] n conférence f.

confess [kən'fes] ⟨⟩ vt **1.** [admit] avouer, confesser - **2.** RELIG confesser. ⟨⟩ vi: **to confess to sthg** avouer qqch.

confession [kən'feʃn] n confession f.

confetti [kən'fetɪ] n (U) confettis mpl.

confide [kən'faɪd] vi: **to confide in sb** se confier à qqn.

confidence ['kɒnfɪdəns] n **1.** [self-assurance] confiance f en soi, assurance f - **2.** [trust] confiance f; **to have confidence in** avoir confiance en - **3.** [secrecy]: **in confidence** en confidence - **4.** [secret] confidence f.

confidence trick n abus m de confiance.

confident ['kɒnfɪdənt] adj **1.** [self-assured] : **to be confident** avoir confiance en soi - **2.** [sure] sûr(e).

confidential [,kɒnfɪ'denʃl] adj confidentiel(elle).

confine [kən'faɪn] vt **1.** [limit] limiter ; **to confine o.s. to** se limiter à - **2.** [shut up] enfermer, confiner.

confined [kən'faɪnd] adj [space, area] restreint(e).

confinement [kən'faɪnmənt] n [imprisonment] emprisonnement m.

confines ['kɒnfaɪnz] npl confins mpl.

confirm [kən'fɜːm] vt confirmer.

confirmation [,kɒnfə'meɪʃn] n confirmation f.

confirmed [kən'fɜːmd] adj [habitual] invétéré(e) ; [bachelor, spinster] endurci(e).

confiscate ['kɒnfɪskeɪt] vt confisquer.

conflict ⟨⟩ n ['kɒnflɪkt] conflit m. ⟨⟩ vi [kən'flɪkt]: **to conflict (with)** s'opposer (à), être en conflit (avec).

conflicting [kən'flɪktɪŋ] adj contradictoire.

conform [kən'fɔːm] vi: **to conform (to** OR **with)** se conformer (à).

confound [kən'faʊnd] vt [confuse, defeat] déconcerter.

confront [kən'frʌnt] vt **1.** [problem, enemy] affronter - **2.** [challenge]: **to confront sb (with)** confronter qqn (avec).

confrontation [,kɒnfrʌn'teɪʃn] n affrontement m.

confuse [kən'fjuːz] vt **1.** [disconcert] troubler ; **to confuse the issue** brouiller les cartes - **2.** [mix up] confondre.

confused [kən'fjuːzd] adj **1.** [not clear] compliqué(e) - **2.** [disconcerted] troublé(e), désorienté(e) ; **I'm confused** je n'y comprends rien.

confusing [kən'fjuːzɪŋ] adj pas clair(e).

confusion [kən'fjuːʒn] n confusion f.

congeal [kən'dʒiːl] vi [blood] se coaguler.

congenial [kən'dʒiːnjəl] adj sympathique, agréable.

congested [kən'dʒestɪd] adj **1.** [street, area] encombré(e) - **2.** MED congestionné(e).

congestion [kən'dʒestʃn] n **1.** [of traffic] encombrement m - **2.** MED congestion f.

conglomerate [,kən'glɒmərət] n COMM conglomérat m.

congratulate [kən'grætʃʊleɪt] vt: **to congratulate sb (on sthg/on doing sthg)** féliciter qqn (de qqch/d'avoir fait qqch).

congratulations [kən,grætʃʊ'leɪʃənz] npl félicitations fpl.

congregate ['kɒngrɪgeɪt] vi se rassembler.

congregation [,kɒŋgrɪ'geɪʃn] n assemblée f des fidèles.

congress ['kɒŋgres] n [meeting] congrès m. ➤ **Congress** n US POL le Congrès.

congressman ['kɒŋgresmən] (pl -men [-mən]) n US POL membre m du Congrès.

conifer ['kɒnɪfər] n conifère m.

conjugation [,kɒndʒʊ'geɪʃn] n GRAM conjugaison f.

conjunction [kən'dʒʌŋkʃn] n GRAM conjonction f.

conjunctivitis [kən,dʒʌŋktɪ'vaɪtɪs] n conjonctivite f.

conjure vi ['kʌndʒər] [by magic] faire des tours de prestidigitation. ➤ **conjure up** vt sep évoquer.

conjurer ['kʌndʒərər] n prestidigitateur m, -trice f.

conjuror ['kʌndʒərər] = conjurer.

conk [kɒŋk] n inf UK pif m. ➤ **conk out** vi inf tomber en panne.

conker ['kɒŋkər] n UK marron m.

conman ['kɒnmæn] (pl -men [-mən]) n escroc m.

connect [kə'nekt] ⟨⟩ vt **1.** [join]: **to connect sthg (to)** relier qqch (à) - **2.** [on telephone] mettre en communication - **3.** [associate] associer ; **to connect sb/sthg to, to connect sb/sthg with** associer qqn/ qqch à - **4.** ELEC [to power supply] : **to connect sthg to** brancher qqch à. <> vi [train, plane, bus] : **to connect (with)** assurer la correspondance (avec).

connected [kə'nektɪd] adj [related] : **to be connected with** avoir un rapport avec.

connection [kə'nekʃn] n **1.** [relationship] : **connection (between/with)** rapport m (entre/avec) ; **in connection with** à propos de - **2.** ELEC branchement m, connexion f - **3.** [on telephone] communication f - **4.** [plane, train, bus] correspondance f - **5.** [professional acquaintance] relation f.

connive [kə'naɪv] vi **1.** [plot] comploter - **2.** [allow to happen] : **to connive at sthg** fermer les yeux sur qqch.

connoisseur [ˌkɒnə'sɜːʳ] n connaisseur m, -euse f.

conquer ['kɒŋkəʳ] vt **1.** [country etc] conquérir - **2.** [fears, inflation etc] vaincre.

conqueror ['kɒŋkərəʳ] n conquérant m, -e f.

conquest ['kɒŋkwest] n conquête f.

cons [kɒnz] npl **1.** UK inf **all mod cons** tout confort - **2.** ► **pro.**

conscience ['kɒnʃəns] n conscience f.

conscientious [ˌkɒnʃɪ'enʃəs] adj consciencieux(euse).

conscious ['kɒnʃəs] adj **1.** [not unconscious] conscient(e) - **2.** [aware] : **conscious of sthg** conscient(e) de qqch - **3.** [intentional - insult] délibéré(e), intentionnel(elle) ; [- effort] conscient(e).

consciousness ['kɒnʃəsnɪs] n conscience f.

conscript n ['kɒnskrɪpt] MIL conscrit m.

conscription [kən'skrɪpʃn] n conscription f.

consecutive [kən'sekjʊtɪv] adj consécutif(ive).

consent [kən'sent] <> n (U) **1.** [permission] consentement m - **2.** [agreement] accord m. <> vi : **to consent (to)** consentir (à).

consequence ['kɒnsɪkwəns] n **1.** [result] conséquence f ; **in consequence** par conséquent - **2.** [importance] importance f.

consequently ['kɒnsɪkwəntlɪ] adv par conséquent.

conservation [ˌkɒnsə'veɪʃn] n [of nature] protection f ; [of buildings] conservation f ; [of energy, water] conservation f.

conservative [kən'sɜːvətɪv] <> adj **1.** [traditionalist] traditionaliste - **2.** [cautious] prudent(e). <> n traditionaliste mf.

► **Conservative** <> adj POL conservateur(trice). <> n POL conservateur m, -trice f.

Conservative Party n : **the Conservative Party** le parti conservateur.

conservatory [kən'sɜːvətrɪ] n [of house] jardin m d'hiver.

conserve <> n ['kɒnsɜːv] confiture f. <> vt [kən'sɜːv] [energy, supplies] économiser ; [nature, wildlife] protéger.

consider [kən'sɪdəʳ] vt **1.** [think about] examiner - **2.** [take into account] prendre en compte ; **all things considered** tout compte fait - **3.** [judge] considérer.

considerable [kən'sɪdrəbl] adj considérable.

considerably [kən'sɪdrəblɪ] adv considérablement.

considerate [kən'sɪdərət] adj prévenant(e).

consideration [kənˌsɪdə'reɪʃn] n **1.** (U) [careful thought] réflexion f ; **to take sthg into consideration** tenir compte de qqch, prendre qqch en considération ; **under consideration** à l'étude - **2.** (U) [care] attention f - **3.** [factor] facteur m.

considering [kən'sɪdərɪŋ] <> prep étant donné. <> conj étant donné que.

consign [kən'saɪn] vt : **to consign sb/sthg to** reléguer qqn/qqch à.

consigner US = **consignor.**

consignment [kən'saɪnmənt] n [load] expédition f.

consist [kən'sɪst] ► **consist in** vt insep : **to consist in sthg** consister dans qqch ; **to consist in doing sthg** consister à faire qqch. ► **consist of** vt insep consister en.

consistency [kən'sɪstənsɪ] n **1.** [coherence] cohérence f - **2.** [texture] consistance f.

consistent [kən'sɪstənt] adj **1.** [regular - behaviour] conséquent(e) ; [- improvement] régulier(ère) ; [- supporter] constant(e) - **2.** [coherent] cohérent(e) ; **to be consistent with** [with one's position] être compatible avec ; [with the facts] correspondre avec.

consolation [ˌkɒnsə'leɪʃn] n réconfort m.

console <> n ['kɒnsəʊl] tableau m de commande ; COMPUT & MUS console f. <> vt [kən'səʊl] consoler.

consonant ['kɒnsənənt] n consonne f.

consortium [kən'sɔːtjəm] (pl -tiums OR -tia [-tjə]) n consortium m.

conspicuous [kən'spɪkjʊəs] adj voyant(e), qui se remarque.

conspiracy [kən'spɪrəsɪ] n conspiration f, complot m.

conspire [kən'spaɪər] *vt* : to conspire to do sthg comploter de faire qqch ; [subj: events] contribuer à faire qqch.

constable ['kʌnstəbl] *n UK* [policeman] agent *m* de police.

constabulary [kən'stæbjʊlərɪ] *n UK* police *f*.

constant ['kɒnstənt] *adj* **1.** [unvarying] constant(e) - **2.** [recurring] continuel(elle).

constantly ['kɒnstəntlɪ] *adv* constamment.

consternation [,kɒnstə'neɪʃn] *n* consternation *f*.

constipated ['kɒnstɪpeɪtɪd] *adj* constipé(e).

constipation [,kɒnstɪ'peɪʃn] *n* constipation *f*.

constituency [kən'stɪtjʊənsɪ] *n* [area] circonscription *f* électorale.

constituent [kən'stɪtjʊənt] *n* **1.** [voter] électeur *m*, -trice *f* - **2.** [element] composant *m*.

constitute ['kɒnstɪtjuːt] *vt* **1.** [form, represent] représenter, constituer - **2.** [establish, set up] constituer.

constitution [,kɒnstɪ'tjuːʃn] *n* constitution *f*.

constraint [kən'streɪnt] *n* **1.** [restriction] : constraint (on) limitation *f* (à) - **2.** *(U)* [self-control] retenue *f*, réserve *f* - **3.** [coercion] contrainte *f*.

construct *vt* [kən'strʌkt] construire.

construction [kən'strʌkʃn] *n* construction *f*.

constructive [kən'strʌktɪv] *adj* constructif(ive).

construe [kən'struː] *vt fml* [interpret] : to construe sthg as interpréter qqch comme.

consul ['kɒnsəl] *n* consul *m*, -e *f*.

consulate ['kɒnsjʊlət] *n* consulat *m*.

consult [kən'sʌlt] <> *vt* consulter. <> *vi* : to consult with sb s'entretenir avec qqn.

consultant [kən'sʌltənt] *n* **1.** [expert] expert-conseil *m* - **2.** *UK* [hospital doctor] spécialiste *mf*.

consultation [,kɒnsəl'teɪʃn] *n* [meeting, discussion] entretien *m*.

consulting [kən'sʌltɪŋ] *n* cabinet *m* d'expert.

consulting fee *n* honoraires *mpl* d'expert.

consulting room *n* MÉD cabinet *m* de consultation.

consume [kən'sjuːm] *vt* [food, fuel etc] consommer.

consumer [kən'sjuːmər] *n* consommateur *m*, -trice *f*.

consumer goods *npl* biens *mpl* de consommation.

consumer society *n* société *f* de consommation.

consummate *vt* ['kɒnsəmeɪt] consommer.

consumption [kən'sʌmpʃn] *n* [use] consommation *f*.

cont. *abbrev of* continued.

contact ['kɒntækt] <> *n* **1.** *(U)* [touch, communication] contact *m* ; in contact (with sb) en rapport OR contact (avec qqn) ; to lose contact with sb perdre le contact avec qqn - **2.** [person] relation *f*, contact *m*. <> *vt* contacter, prendre contact avec ; [by phone] joindre, contacter.

contact lens *n* verre *m* OR lentille *f* de contact.

contacts ['kɒntækts] *npl* lentilles *fpl* (de contact).

contagious [kən'teɪdʒəs] *adj* contagieux(euse).

contain [kən'teɪn] *vt* **1.** [hold, include] contenir, renfermer - **2.** *fml* [control] contenir ; [epidemic] circonscrire.

container [kən'teɪnər] *n* **1.** [box, bottle etc] récipient *m* - **2.** [for transporting goods] conteneur *m*, container *m*.

contaminate [kən'tæmɪneɪt] *vt* contaminer.

cont'd *abbr of* continued.

contemplate ['kɒntempleɪt] <> *vt* **1.** [consider] envisager - **2.** *fml* [look at] contempler. <> *vi* [consider] méditer.

contemporary [kən'tempərərɪ] <> *adj* contemporain(e). <> *n* contemporain *m*, -e *f*.

contempt [kən'tempt] *n* **1.** [scorn] : contempt (for) mépris *m* (pour) - **2.** LAW : contempt (of court) outrage *m* à la cour.

contemptuous [kən'temptʃʊəs] *adj* méprisant(e) ; contemptuous of sthg dédaigneux(euse) de qqch.

contend [kən'tend] <> *vi* **1.** [deal] : to contend with sthg faire face à qqch - **2.** [compete] : to contend for [subj: several people] se disputer ; [subj: one person] se battre pour ; to contend against lutter contre. <> *vt fml* [claim] : to contend that... soutenir OR prétendre que...

contender [kən'tendər] *n* [in election] candidat *m*, -e *f* ; [in competition] concurrent *m*, -e *f* ; [in boxing etc] prétendant *m*, -e *f*.

content <> *adj* [kən'tent] : content (with) satisfait(e) (de), content(e) (de) ; to be content to do sthg ne pas demander mieux que de faire qqch. <> *n* ['kɒntent] **1.** [amount] teneur *f* - **2.** [subject matter] contenu *m*. <> *vt* [kən'tent] : to content o.s. with sthg/with doing sthg se contenter

de qqch/de faire qqch. **contents** *npl*
1. [of container, document] contenu *m* - **2.** [at
front of book] table *f* des matières.

contented [kən'tentɪd] *adj* satisfait(e).

contention [kən'tenʃn] *n fml* **1.** [argument,
assertion] assertion *f*, affirmation *f* - **2.** *(U)*
[disagreement] dispute *f*, contestation *f*.

contest ⟨⟩ *n* ['kɒntest] **1.** [competition]
concours *m* - **2.** [for power, control] combat
m, lutte *f*. ⟨⟩ *vt* [kən'test] **1.** [compete for]
disputer - **2.** [dispute] contester.

contestant [kən'testənt] *n* concurrent *m*,
-e *f*.

context ['kɒntekst] *n* contexte *m*.

context-sensitive *adj* COMPUT contex-
tuel(le).

continent ['kɒntɪnənt] *n* continent *m*.
Continent *n* UK **: the Continent** l'Europe *f* continentale.

continental [,kɒntɪ'nentl] *adj* GEOG conti-
nental(e).

continental breakfast *n* petit déjeuner *m*
(par opposition à 'English breakfast').

continental quilt *n* UK couette *f*.

contingency [kən'tɪndʒənsɪ] *n* éventualité
f.

contingency plan *n* plan *m* d'urgence.

continual [kən'tɪnjʊəl] *adj* continuel(elle).

continually [kən'tɪnjʊəlɪ] *adv* continuellement.

continuation [kən,tɪnjʊ'eɪʃn] *n* **1.** *(U)* [act]
continuation *f* - **2.** [sequel] suite *f*.

continue [kən'tɪnjuː] ⟨⟩ *vt* **1.** [carry on]
continuer, poursuivre **; to continue doing** OR
to do sthg continuer à OR de faire qqch
- **2.** [after an interruption] reprendre. ⟨⟩ *vi*
1. [carry on] continuer **; to continue with**
sthg poursuivre qqch, continuer qqch
- **2.** [after an interruption] reprendre, se
poursuivre.

continuous [kən'tɪnjʊəs] *adj* continu(e).

continuously [kən'tɪnjʊəslɪ] *adv* sans arrêt, continuellement.

contort [kən'tɔːt] *vt* tordre.

contortion [kən'tɔːʃn] *n* **1.** *(U)* [twisting]
torsion *f* - **2.** [position] contorsion *f*.

contour ['kɒn,tʊər] *n* **1.** [outline] contour *m*
- **2.** [on map] courbe *f* de niveau.

contraband ['kɒntrəbænd] ⟨⟩ *adj* de
contrebande. ⟨⟩ *n* contrebande *f*.

contraception [,kɒntrə'sepʃn] *n* contraception *f*.

contraceptive [,kɒntrə'septɪv] ⟨⟩ *adj*
[method, device] anticonceptionnel(elle),
contraceptif(ive) ; [advice] sur la contraception. ⟨⟩ *n* contraceptif *m*.

contract ⟨⟩ *n* ['kɒntrækt] contrat *m*.
⟨⟩ *vt* [kən'trækt] **1.** [gen] contracter

- **2.** COMM **: to contract sb (to do sthg)** passer
un contrat avec qqn (pour faire qqch) **; to**
contract to do sthg s'engager par contrat à
faire qqch. ⟨⟩ *vi* [decrease in size, length]
se contracter.

contraction [kən'trækʃn] *n* contraction *f*.

contractor [kən'træktər] *n* entrepreneur
m.

contradict [,kɒntrə'dɪkt] *vt* contredire.

contradiction [,kɒntrə'dɪkʃn] *n* contradiction *f*.

contraflow ['kɒntrəfləʊ] *n* UK circulation
f à contre-sens.

contraption [kən'træpʃn] *n* machin *m*,
truc *m*.

contrary ['kɒntrərɪ] ⟨⟩ *adj* **1.** [opposite] :
contrary (to) contraire (à), opposé(e) (à)
- **2.** [kən'treərɪ] [awkward] contrariant(e).
⟨⟩ *n* contraire *m* **; on the contrary** au
contraire. **contrary to** *prep* contrairement à.

contrast [kən'trɑːst] ⟨⟩ *n* ['kɒntrɑːst]
contraste *m* **; by** OR **in contrast** par contraste ;
in contrast with OR **to sthg** par contraste
avec qqch. ⟨⟩ *vt* contraster. ⟨⟩ *vi* **: to**
contrast (with) faire contraste (avec).

contravene [,kɒntrə'viːn] *vt* enfreindre,
transgresser.

contribute [kən'trɪbjuːt] ⟨⟩ *vt* [money]
apporter ; [help, advice, ideas] donner,
apporter. ⟨⟩ *vi* **1.** [gen] **: to contribute (to)**
contribuer (à) - **2.** [write material] **: to con-**
tribute to collaborer à.

contribution [,kɒntrɪ'bjuːʃn] *n* **1.** [of mon-
ey] **: contribution (to)** cotisation *f* (à), contribution *f* (à) - **2.** [article] article *m*.

contributor [kən'trɪbjʊtər] *n* **1.** [of money]
donateur *m*, -trice *f* - **2.** [to magazine,
newspaper] collaborateur *m*, -trice *f*.

contributory pension plan US & Can
= **contributory pension scheme**

contrive [kən'traɪv] *vt fml* **1.** [engineer]
combiner - **2.** [manage] **: to contrive to do**
sthg se débrouiller pour faire qqch, trouver
moyen de faire qqch.

contrived [kən'traɪvd] *adj* tiré(e) par les
cheveux.

control [kən'trəʊl] ⟨⟩ *n* [gen] contrôle *m* ;
[of traffic] régulation *f* **; to get sb/sthg under**
control maîtriser qqn/qqch **; to be in control**
of sthg [subj: boss, government] diriger
qqch ; [subj: army] avoir le contrôle de
qqch ; [of emotions, situation] maîtriser
qqch **; to lose control** [of emotions] perdre le
contrôle. ⟨⟩ *vt* **1.** [company, country] être
à la tête de, diriger - **2.** [operate] commander, faire fonctionner - **3.** [restrict, restrain -
disease] enrayer, juguler ; [- inflation]
mettre un frein à, contenir ; [- children]

tenir ; [- crowd] contenir ; [- emotions] maîtriser, contenir ; **to control o.s.** se maîtriser, se contrôler. ➤ **controls** *npl* [of machine, vehicle] commandes *fpl*.

controller [kən'trəʊləʳ] *n* [person] contrôleur *m*.

control panel *n* tableau *m* de bord.

control tower *n* tour *f* de contrôle.

controversial [ˌkɒntrə'vɜ:ʃl] *adj* [writer, theory etc] controversé(e) ; **to be controversial** donner matière à controverse.

controversy ['kɒntrəvɜ:sɪ, UK kən'trɒvəsɪ] *n* controverse *f*, polémique *f*.

convalesce [ˌkɒnvə'les] *vi* se remettre d'une maladie, relever de maladie.

convene [kən'vi:n] ➤ *vt* convoquer, réunir. ➤ *vi* se réunir, s'assembler.

convenience [kən'vi:njəns] *n* **1.** [usefulness] commodité *f* - **2.** [personal comfort, advantage] agrément *m*, confort *m* ; **at your earliest convenience** *fml* dès que possible.

convenience store *n* US petit supermarché de quartier.

convenient [kən'vi:njənt] *adj* **1.** [suitable] qui convient - **2.** [handy] pratique, commode.

convent ['kɒnvənt] *n* couvent *m*.

convention [kən'venʃn] *n* **1.** [agreement, assembly] convention *f* - **2.** [practice] usage *m*, convention *f*.

conventional [kən'venʃənl] *adj* conventionnel(elle).

converge [kən'vɜ:dʒ] *vi* : **to converge (on)** converger (sur).

convergence criteria *npl* critères *mpl* de convergence.

conversant [kən'vɜ:sənt] *adj fml* : **conversant with sthg** familiarisé(e) avec qqch, qui connaît bien qqch.

conversation [ˌkɒnvə'seɪʃn] *n* conversation *f*.

converse ➤ *n* ['kɒnvɜ:s] [opposite] : **the converse** le contraire, l'inverse *m*. ➤ *vi* [kən'vɜ:s] *fml* converser.

conversely [kən'vɜ:slɪ] *adv fml* inversement.

conversion [kən'vɜ:ʃn] *n* **1.** [changing, in religious beliefs] conversion *f* - **2.** [in building] aménagement *m*, transformation *f* - **3.** RUGBY transformation *f*.

convert ➤ *vt* [kən'vɜ:t] **1.** [change] : **to convert sthg to** OR **into** convertir qqch en ; **to convert sb (to)** RELIG convertir qqn (à) - **2.** [building, ship] : **to convert sthg to** OR **into** transformer qqch en, aménager qqch en. ➤ *vi* [kən'vɜ:t] : **to convert from sthg to sthg** passer de qqch à qqch. ➤ *n* ['kɒnvɜ:t] converti *m*, -e *f*.

convertible [kən'vɜ:təbl] *n* (voiture *f*) décapotable *f*.

convex [kɒn'veks] *adj* convexe.

convey [kən'veɪ] *vt* **1.** *fml* [transport] transporter - **2.** [express] : **to convey sthg (to sb)** communiquer qqch (à qqn).

conveyor belt [kən'veɪəʳ-] *n* tapis *m* roulant.

convict ➤ *n* ['kɒnvɪkt] détenu *m*. ➤ *vt* [kən'vɪkt] : **to convict sb of sthg** reconnaître qqn coupable de qqch.

conviction [kən'vɪkʃn] *n* **1.** [belief, fervour] conviction *f* - **2.** LAW [of criminal] condamnation *f*.

convince [kən'vɪns] *vt* convaincre, persuader ; **to convince sb of sthg/to do sthg** convaincre qqn de qqch/de faire qqch, persuader qqn de qqch/de faire qqch.

convincing [kən'vɪnsɪŋ] *adj* **1.** [persuasive] convaincant(e) - **2.** [resounding - victory] retentissant(e), éclatant(e).

convoluted [ˈkɒnvəluːtɪd] *adj* [tortuous] compliqué(e).

convoy ['kɒnvɔɪ] *n* convoi *m*.

convulse [kən'vʌls] *vt* [person] : **to be convulsed with** se tordre de.

convulsion [kən'vʌlʃn] *n* MED convulsion *f*.

coo [ku:] *vi* [for a baby] roucouler.

cook [kʊk] ➤ *n* cuisinier *m*, -ère *f*. ➤ *vt* [food] faire cuire ; [meal] préparer. ➤ *vi* [person] cuisiner, faire la cuisine ; [food] cuire.

cookbook ['kʊk,bʊk] = **cookery book**.

cooker ['kʊkəʳ] *n* UK [stove] cuisinière *f*.

cookery ['kʊkərɪ] *n* cuisine *f*.

cookery book *n* UK livre *m* de cuisine.

cookie ['kʊkɪ] *n* **1.** *esp* US [biscuit] biscuit *m*, gâteau *m* sec - **2.** COMPUT cookie *m*, mouchard *m* offic.

cooking ['kʊkɪŋ] *n* cuisine *f*.

cool [ku:l] ➤ *adj* **1.** [not warm] frais (fraîche) ; [dress] léger(ère) - **2.** [calm] calme - **3.** [unfriendly] froid(e) - **4.** *inf* [excellent] génial(e) ; [trendy] branché(e). ➤ *vt* faire refroidir. ➤ *vi* [become less warm] refroidir. ➤ *n* [calm] : **to keep/lose one's cool** garder/perdre son sang-froid, garder/perdre son calme. ➤ **cool down** *vi* [become less warm - food, engine] refroidir ; [- person] se rafraîchir.

cool box *n* UK glacière *f*.

cooler *n* US glacière *f*.

coop [ku:p] *n* poulailler *m*. ➤ **coop up** *vt sep inf* confiner.

Co-op ['kəʊ,ɒp] (*abbrev of* **Co-operative society**) *n* Coop *f*.

cooperate [kəʊˈɒpəreɪt] *vi* : to cooperate (with sb/sthg) coopérer (avec qqn/à qqch), collaborer (avec qqn/à qqch).

cooperation [kəʊˌɒpəˈreɪʃn] *n (U)* **1.** [collaboration] coopération *f*, collaboration *f* - **2.** [assistance] aide *f*, concours *m*.

cooperative [kəʊˈɒpərətɪv] <> *adj* coopératif(ive). <> *n* coopérative *f*.

coordinate <> *n* [kəʊˈɔːdɪnət] [on map, graph] coordonnée *f*. <> *vt* [kəʊˈɔːdɪneɪt] coordonner. ➡ **coordinates** *npl* [clothes] coordonnés *mpl*.

coordination [kəʊˌɔːdɪˈneɪʃn] *n* coordination *f*.

cop [kɒp] *n inf* flic *m*.

cope [kəʊp] *vi* se débrouiller ; to cope with faire face à.

Copenhagen [ˌkəʊpənˈheɪgən] *n* Copenhague.

copier [ˈkɒpɪəʳ] *n* copieur *m*, photocopieur *m*.

cop-out *n inf* dérobade *f*, échappatoire *f*.

copper [ˈkɒpəʳ] *n* **1.** [metal] cuivre *m* - **2.** UK *inf* [police officer] flic *m*.

coppice [ˈkɒpɪs], **copse** [kɒps] *n* taillis *m*.

copy [ˈkɒpɪ] <> *n* **1.** [imitation] copie *f*, reproduction *f* - **2.** [duplicate] copie *f* - **3.** [of book] exemplaire *m* ; [of magazine] numéro *m*. <> *vt* **1.** [imitate] copier, imiter - **2.** [photocopy] photocopier.

copyright [ˈkɒpɪraɪt] *n* copyright *m*, droit *m* d'auteur.

coral [ˈkɒrəl] *n* corail *m*.

cord [kɔːd] *n* **1.** [string] ficelle *f* ; [rope] corde *f* - **2.** [electric] fil *m*, cordon *m* - **3.** [fabric] velours *m* côtelé. ➡ **cords** *npl* pantalon *m* en velours côtelé.

cordial [ˈkɔːdjəl] <> *adj* cordial(e), chaleureux(euse). <> *n* cordial *m*.

cordon [ˈkɔːdn] *n* cordon *m*. ➡ **cordon off** *vt sep* barrer (par un cordon de police).

corduroy [ˈkɔːdərɔɪ] *n* velours *m* côtelé.

core [kɔːʳ] <> *n* **1.** [of apple etc] trognon *m*, cœur *m* - **2.** [of cable, Earth] noyau *m* ; [of nuclear reactor] cœur *m* - **3.** *fig* [of people] noyau *m* ; [of problem, policy] essentiel *m*. <> *vt* enlever le cœur de.

Corfu [kɔːˈfuː] *n* Corfou.

corgi [ˈkɔːgɪ] (*pl* -s) *n* corgi *m*.

coriander [ˌkɒrɪˈændəʳ] *n* coriandre *f*.

cork [kɔːk] *n* **1.** [material] liège *m* - **2.** [stopper] bouchon *m*.

corkscrew [ˈkɔːkskruː] *n* tire-bouchon *m*.

corn [kɔːn] *n* **1.** UK [wheat] grain *m* ; US [maize] maïs *m* ; **corn on the cob** épi *m* de maïs cuit - **2.** [on foot] cor *m*.

cornea [ˈkɔːnɪə] (*pl* -s) *n* cornée *f*.

corned beef [kɔːnd-] *n* UK corned-beef *m inv*.

corner [ˈkɔːnəʳ] <> *n* **1.** [angle] coin *m*, angle *m* ; to cut corners *fig* brûler les étapes - **2.** [bend in road] virage *m*, tournant *m* - **3.** FOOTBALL corner *m*. <> *vt* **1.** [person, animal] acculer - **2.** [market] accaparer.

corner shop *n* magasin *m* du coin OR du quartier.

cornerstone [ˈkɔːnəstəʊn] *n fig* pierre *f* angulaire.

cornet [ˈkɔːnɪt] *n* **1.** [instrument] cornet *m* à pistons - **2.** UK [ice-cream cone] cornet *m* de glace.

cornflakes [ˈkɔːnfleɪks] *npl* corn-flakes *mpl*.

cornflour UK [ˈkɔːnflaʊəʳ], **cornstarch** US [ˈkɔːnstɑːtʃ] *n* ≃ Maïzena® *f*, fécule *f* de maïs.

Cornwall [ˈkɔːnwɔːl] *n* Cornouailles *f*.

corny [ˈkɔːnɪ] *adj inf* [joke] peu original(e) ; [story, film] à l'eau de rose.

coronary [ˈkɒrənrɪ], **coronary thrombosis** [-θrɒmˈbəʊsɪs] (*pl* -ses [-siːz]) *n* infarctus *m* du myocarde.

coronation [ˌkɒrəˈneɪʃn] *n* couronnement *m*.

coroner [ˈkɒrənəʳ] *n* coroner *m*.

corporal [ˈkɔːpərəl] *n* [gen] caporal *m* ; [in artillery] brigadier *m*.

corporal punishment *n* châtiment *m* corporel.

corporate [ˈkɔːpərət] *adj* **1.** [business] corporatif(ive), de société - **2.** [collective] collectif(ive).

corporation [ˌkɔːpəˈreɪʃn] *n* **1.** UK [town council] conseil *m* municipal - **2.** [large company] compagnie *f*, société *f* enregistrée.

corps [kɔːʳ] (*pl* corps) *n* corps *m*.

corpse [kɔːps] *n* cadavre *m*.

correct [kəˈrekt] <> *adj* **1.** [accurate] correct(e), exact(e) ; you're quite correct tu as parfaitement raison - **2.** [proper, socially acceptable] correct(e), convenable. <> *vt* corriger.

correction [kəˈrekʃn] *n* correction *f*.

correlation [ˌkɒrəˈleɪʃn] *n* corrélation *f*.

correspond [ˌkɒrɪˈspɒnd] *vi* **1.** [gen] : to correspond (with OR to) correspondre (à) - **2.** [write letters] : to correspond (with sb) correspondre (avec qqn).

correspondence [ˌkɒrɪˈspɒndəns] *n* : correspondence (with) correspondance *f* (avec).

correspondence course *n* cours *m* par correspondance.

correspondent [ˌkɒrɪˈspɒndənt] *n* correspondant *m*, -e *f*.

corridor ['kɒrɪdɔːr] *n* [in building] couloir *m*, corridor *m*.

corroborate [kə'rɒbəreɪt] *vt* corroborer.

corrode [kə'rəʊd] <> *vt* corroder, attaquer. <> *vi* se corroder.

corrosion [kə'rəʊʒn] *n* corrosion *f*.

corrugated ['kɒrəgeɪtɪd] *adj* ondulé(e).

corrugated iron *n* tôle *f* ondulée.

corrupt [kə'rʌpt] <> *adj* [gen & COMPUT] corrompu(e). <> *vt* corrompre, dépraver.

corruption [kə'rʌpʃn] *n* corruption *f*.

corset ['kɔːsɪt] *n* corset *m*.

Corsica ['kɔːsɪkə] *n* Corse *f*.

cosh [kɒʃ] UK <> *n* matraque *f*, gourdin *m*. <> *vt* frapper, matraquer.

cosmetic [kɒz'metɪk] <> *n* cosmétique *m*, produit *m* de beauté. <> *adj fig* superficiel(elle).

cosmopolitan [kɒzmə'pɒlɪtn] *adj* cosmopolite.

cosset ['kɒsɪt] *vt* dorloter, choyer.

cost [kɒst] <> *n lit & fig* coût *m* ; **at all costs** à tout prix, coûte que coûte. <> *vt* **1.** *(pt & pp* cost) *lit & fig* coûter ; **how much does it cost?** combien ça coûte?, combien cela coûte-t-il? ; **it cost me £10** ça m'a coûté 10 livres - **2.** *(pt & pp -ed)* COMM [estimate] évaluer le coût de. ⏺ **costs** *npl* LAW dépens *mpl*.

co-star ['kəʊ-] *n* partenaire *mf*.

Costa Rica [ˌkɒstə'riːkə] *n* Costa Rica *m*.

cost-effective *adj* rentable.

costing ['kɒstɪŋ] *n* évaluation *f* du coût.

costly ['kɒstlɪ] *adj lit & fig* coûteux(euse).

cost of living *n* coût *m* de la vie.

costume ['kɒstjuːm] *n* **1.** [gen] costume *m* - **2.** UK [swimming costume] maillot *m* (de bain).

costume jewellery UK, **costume jewelry** US *n* (U) bijoux *mpl* fantaisie.

cosy UK, **cozy** US ['kəʊzɪ] *adj* [house, room] douillet(ette) ; [atmosphere] chaleureux(euse) ; **to feel cosy** se sentir bien au chaud.

cot [kɒt] *n* **1.** UK [for child] lit *m* d'enfant, petit lit - **2.** US [folding bed] lit *m* de camp.

cottage ['kɒtɪdʒ] *n* cottage *m*, petite maison *f* (de campagne).

cottage cheese *n* fromage *m* blanc.

cottage pie *n* UK ≃ hachis *m* Parmentier.

cotton ['kɒtn] <> *n* [gen] coton *m*. <> *comp* de coton. ⏺ **cotton on** *vi inf* to cotton on (to sthg) piger (qqch), comprendre (qqch).

cotton candy *n* US barbe *f* à papa.

cotton wool *n* UK ouate *f*, coton *m* hydrophile.

couch [kaʊtʃ] *n* **1.** [sofa] canapé *m*, divan *m* - **2.** [in doctor's surgery] lit *m*.

cough [kɒf] <> *n* toux *f*. <> *vi* tousser.

cough drop US, **cough sweet** UK *n* pastille *f* pour la toux.

cough mixture *n* UK sirop *m* pour la toux.

cough syrup US = cough mixture.

could [kʊd] *modal vb* ▶ can².

couldn't ['kʊdnt] = could not.

could've ['kʊdəv] = could have.

council ['kaʊnsl] *n* conseil *m*.

council estate *n* UK quartier *m* de logements sociaux.

council house *n* UK maison *f* qui appartient à la municipalité, ≃ H.L.M. *m* ou *f*

councillor UK, **councilor** US ['kaʊnsələr] *n* UK conseiller *m*, -ère *f*.

councilman US = councillor.

councilor US = councillor.

council tax *n* UK ≃ impôts *mpl* locaux.

councilwoman US = councilor.

counsel ['kaʊnsəl] *n* **1.** *(U) fml* [advice] conseil *m* - **2.** [lawyer] avocat *m*, -e *f*.

counsellor UK, **counselor** US ['kaʊnsələr] *n* **1.** [gen] conseiller *m*, -ère *f* - **2.** US [lawyer] avocat *m*.

count [kaʊnt] <> *n* **1.** [total] total *m* ; **to keep count of** tenir le compte de ; **to lose count of sthg** ne plus savoir qqch, ne pas se rappeler qqch - **2.** [aristocrat] comte *m*. <> *vt* **1.** [gen] compter - **2.** [consider] : **to count sb as sthg** considérer qqn comme qqch. <> *vi* [gen] compter ; **to count (up) to** compter jusqu'à. ⏺ **count against** *vt insep* jouer contre. ⏺ **count (up)on** *vt insep* **1.** [rely on] compter sur - **2.** [expect] s'attendre à, prévoir. ⏺ **count up** *vt insep* compter.

countdown ['kaʊntdaʊn] *n* compte *m* à rebours.

counter ['kaʊntər] <> *n* **1.** [in shop, bank] comptoir *m* - **2.** [in board game] pion *m*. <> *vt* : **to counter sthg (with)** [criticism etc] riposter à qqch (par). <> *vi* : **to counter with sthg/by doing sthg** riposter par qqch/en faisant qqch. ⏺ **counter to** *adv* contrairement à ; **to run counter to** aller à l'encontre de.

counteract [ˌkaʊntə'rækt] *vt* contrebalancer, compenser.

counterattack ['kaʊntərə,tæk] *vt & vi* contre-attaquer.

counterclockwise [ˌkaʊntə'klɒkwaɪz] *adj & adv* US dans le sens inverse des aiguilles d'une montre.

counterfeit ['kaʊntəfɪt] <> *adj* faux (fausse). <> *vt* contrefaire.

counterfoil ['kaʊntəfɔɪl] *n UK* talon *m*, souche *f*.

countermand [ˌkaʊntə'mɑːnd] *vt* annuler.

counterpart ['kaʊntəpɑːt] *n* [person] homologue *mf* ; [thing] équivalent *m*, -e *f*.

counterproductive [ˌkaʊntəprə'dʌktɪv] *adj* qui a l'effet inverse.

countess ['kaʊntɪs] *n* comtesse *f*.

countless ['kaʊntlɪs] *adj* innombrable.

country ['kʌntrɪ] *n* **1.** [nation] pays *m* - **2.** [countryside] : **the country** la campagne ; **in the country** à la campagne - **3.** [region] région *f* ; [terrain] terrain *m* - **4.** MUS = **country and western.**

country dancing *n UK* (*U*) danse *f* folklorique.

country house *n* manoir *m*.

countryman ['kʌntrɪmən] (*pl* -**men** [-mən]) *n* [from same country] compatriote *m*.

country park *n UK* parc *m* naturel.

countryside ['kʌntrɪsaɪd] *n* campagne *f*.

county ['kaʊntɪ] *n* comté *m*.

county council *n UK* conseil *m* général.

coup [kuː] *n* **1.** [rebellion] : **coup (d'état)** coup *m* d'État - **2.** [success] coup *m* (de maître), beau coup *m*.

couple ['kʌpl] ◇ *n* **1.** [in relationship] couple *m* - **2.** [small number] : **a couple (of)** [two] deux ; [a few] quelques, deux ou trois. ◇ *vt* [join] : **to couple sthg (to)** atteler qqch (à).

coupon ['kuːpɒn] *n* **1.** [voucher] bon *m* - **2.** [form] coupon *m*.

courage ['kʌrɪdʒ] *n* courage *m* ; **to take courage (from sthg)** être encouragé (par qqch).

courgette [kɔː'ʒet] *n UK* courgette *f*.

courier ['kʊrɪə] *n* **1.** *UK* [on holiday] guide *m*, accompagnateur *m*, -trice *f* - **2.** [to deliver letters, packages] courrier *m*, messager *m*.

course [kɔːs] *n* **1.** [gen] cours *m* ; **course of action** ligne *f* de conduite ; **in the course of** au cours de - **2.** SCH & UNIV enseignement *m*, cours *mpl* ; **it's a five-year course** c'est un enseignement sur cinq ans ; **I'm taking** OR **doing a computer course** je suis des cours OR un stage d'informatique - **3.** MED [of injections] série *f* ; **course of treatment** traitement *m* - **4.** [of ship, plane] route *f* ; **to be on course** suivre le cap fixé ; *fig* [on target] être dans la bonne voie ; **to be off course** faire fausse route - **5.** [of meal] plat *m* - **6.** SPORT terrain *m*. ⟶ **of course** *adv* **1.** [inevitably, not surprisingly] évidemment, naturellement - **2.** [certainly] bien sûr ; **of course not** bien sûr que non.

coursebook ['kɔːsbʊk] *n UK* livre *m* de cours.

coursework ['kɔːswɜːk] *n* (*U*) travail *m* personnel.

court [kɔːt] ◇ *n* **1.** [LAW - building, room] cour *f*, tribunal *m* ; [- judge, jury etc] : **the court** la justice ; **to take sb to court** faire un procès à qqn - **2.** [SPORT - gen] court *m* ; [- for basketball, volleyball] terrain *m* - **3.** [courtyard, of monarch] cour *f*. ◇ *vi dated* sortir ensemble, se fréquenter.

courteous ['kɜːtjəs] *adj* courtois(e), poli(e).

courtesy ['kɜːtɪsɪ] *n* courtoisie *f*, politesse *f*. ⟶ **(by) courtesy of** *prep* avec la permission de.

courthouse ['kɔːthaʊs] (*pl* [-haʊzɪz]) *n US* palais *m* de justice, tribunal *m*.

courtier ['kɔːtjə] *n* courtisan *m*.

court-martial *n* (*pl* **court-martials** OR **courts-martial**) cour *f* martiale.

courtroom ['kɔːtrʊm] *n* salle *f* de tribunal.

courtyard ['kɔːtjɑːd] *n* cour *f*.

cousin ['kʌzn] *n* cousin *m*, -e *f*.

cove [kəʊv] *n* [bay] crique *f*.

covenant ['kʌvənənt] *n* [of money] engagement *m* contractuel.

Covent Garden [ˌkɒvnt-] *n ancien marché de Londres, aujourd'hui importante galerie marchande.*

cover ['kʌvə] ◇ *n* **1.** [covering - of furniture] housse *f* ; [- of pan] couvercle *m* ; [- of book, magazine] couverture *f* - **2.** [blanket] couverture *f* - **3.** [protection, shelter] abri *m* ; **to take cover** s'abriter, se mettre à l'abri ; **under cover** à l'abri, à couvert ; **under cover of darkness** à la faveur de la nuit - **4.** [concealment] couverture *f* - **5.** *UK* [insurance] couverture *f*, garantie *f* ; **to have cover against sthg** être couvert OR assuré contre qqch - **6.** MUS = **cover version.** ◇ *vt* **1.** [gen] : **to cover sthg (with)** couvrir qqch (de) - **2.** [include, deal with] englober, comprendre - **3.** [insure] : **to cover sb against** couvrir qqn en cas de - **4.** PRESS, RADIO & TV [report on] couvrir, faire la couverture de. ◇ *vi* : **to cover for sb** [replace] remplacer qqn. ⟶ **cover up** *vt sep fig* [scandal etc] dissimuler, cacher.

coverage ['kʌvərɪdʒ] *n* [of news] reportage *m*.

cover charge *n* couvert *m*.

covering ['kʌvərɪŋ] *n* [of floor etc] revêtement *m* ; [of snow, dust] couche *f*.

covering letter *UK*, **cover letter** *US n* lettre *f* explicative OR d'accompagnement.

cover note *n UK* lettre *f* de couverture, attestation *f* provisoire d'assurance.

covert ['kʌvət] *adj* [activity] clandestin(e) ; [look, glance] furtif(ive).

cover-up *n* étouffement *m*.

covet ['kʌvɪt] *vt* convoiter.

cow [kaʊ] ◇ *n* **1.** [farm animal] vache *f* - **2.** [female elephant etc] femelle *f*. ◇ *vt* intimider, effrayer.

coward ['kaʊəd] *n* lâche *mf*.

cowardly ['kaʊədlɪ] *adj* lâche.

cowboy ['kaʊbɔɪ] *n* [cattlehand] cow-boy *m*.

cower ['kaʊər] *vi* se recroqueviller.

cox [kɒks], **coxswain** ['kɒksən] *n* barreur *m*.

coy [kɔɪ] *adj* qui fait le/la timide.

cozy *US* = cosy.

CPA *n abbrev of* **certified public accountant**.

CPS (*abbrev of* **Crown Prosecution Service**) *n* ≃ ministère *m* public.

crab [kræb] *n* crabe *m*.

crab apple *n* pomme *f* sauvage.

crack [kræk] ◇ *n* **1.** [in glass, pottery] fêlure *f* ; [in wall, wood, ground] fissure *f* ; [in skin] gerçure *f* - **2.** [gap - in door] entrebâillement *m* ; [- in curtains] interstice *m* - **3.** [noise - of whip] claquement *m* ; [- of twigs] craquement *m* - **4.** *inf* [attempt] : **to have a crack at sthg** tenter qqch, essayer de faire qqch - **5.** *drug sl* crack *m*. ◇ *adj* [troops etc] de première classe. ◇ *vt* **1.** [glass, plate] fêler ; [wood, wall] fissurer - **2.** [egg, nut] casser - **3.** [whip] faire claquer - **4.** [bang, hit sharply] : **to crack one's head** se cogner la tête - **5.** [solve - problem] résoudre ; [- code] déchiffrer - **6.** *inf* [make - joke] faire. ◇ *vi* **1.** [glass, pottery] se fêler ; [ground, wood, wall] se fissurer ; [skin] se crevasser, se gercer - **2.** [break down - person] craquer, s'effondrer ; [- resistance] se briser. ➡ **crack down** *vi* : **to crack down (on)** sévir (contre). ➡ **crack up** *vi* **1.** [ice] se fissurer ; [paint] se craqueler ; [ground] se crevasser - **2.** *inf* [person] craquer, s'effondrer ; **I must be cracking up** je débloque - **3.** *inf* [with laughter] se tordre de rire.

cracker ['krækər] *n* **1.** [biscuit] cracker *m*, craquelin *m* - **2.** *UK* [for Christmas] diablotin *m*.

crackers ['krækəz] *adj UK inf* dingue, cinglé(e).

crackle ['krækl] *vi* [fire] crépiter ; [frying food, radio] grésiller.

cradle ['kreɪdl] ◇ *n* berceau *m* ; TECH nacelle *f*. ◇ *vt* [baby] bercer ; [object] tenir délicatement.

craft [krɑːft] (*pl* craft) *n* **1.** [trade, skill] métier *m* - **2.** [boat] embarcation *f*.

craftsman ['krɑːftsmən] (*pl* -men [-mən]) *n* artisan *m*, homme *m* de métier.

craftsmanship ['krɑːftsmənʃɪp] *n* (*U*) **1.** [skill] dextérité *f*, art *m* - **2.** [skilled work] travail *m*, exécution *f*.

craftsmen *npl* ➤ craftsman.

crafty ['krɑːftɪ] *adj* [person, idea, scheme] malin(igne), astucieux(ieuse) ; *pej* [person] rusé(e), roublard(e) ; [idea, scheme] rusé(e).

crag [kræg] *n* rocher *m* escarpé.

cram [kræm] ◇ *vt* **1.** [stuff] fourrer - **2.** [overfill] : **to cram sthg with** bourrer qqch de. ◇ *vi* bachoter.

cramp [kræmp] ◇ *n* crampe *f*. ◇ *vt* gêner, entraver.

cranberry ['krænbərɪ] *n* canneberge *f*, airelle *f*.

crane [kreɪn] *n* grue *f*.

crank [kræŋk] ◇ *n* **1.** TECH manivelle *f* - **2.** *inf* [person] excentrique *mf*. ◇ *vt* [wind - handle] tourner ; [- mechanism] remonter (à la manivelle).

crankshaft ['kræŋkʃɑːft] *n* vilebrequin *m*.

cranny ['krænɪ] *n* ➤ nook.

crap [kræp] *n* (*U*) *v inf* merde *f* ; **it's a load of crap** tout ça, c'est des conneries.

crash [kræʃ] ◇ *n* **1.** [accident] accident *m* - **2.** [noise] fracas *m*. ◇ *vt* **1.** : **I crashed the car** j'ai eu un accident avec la voiture - **2.** COMPUT planter. ◇ *vi* **1.** [cars, trains] se percuter, se rentrer dedans ; [car, train] avoir un accident ; [plane] s'écraser ; **to crash into** [wall] rentrer dans, emboutir - **2.** [fall, hit loudly or violently] : **the tree came crashing down** l'arbre est tombé avec fracas ; **the vase crashed to the ground** le vase s'est écrasé au sol - **3.** [FIN - business, company] faire faillite ; [- stock market] s'effondrer - **4.** *inf* [sleep] dormir ; [fall asleep] s'endormir.

crash course *n* cours *m* intensif.

crash helmet *n* casque *m* de protection.

crash-land *vi* atterrir en catastrophe.

crass [kræs] *adj* [comment, person] lourd(e) ; [behaviour, stupidity] grossier(ère).

crate [kreɪt] *n* cageot *m*, caisse *f*.

crater ['kreɪtər] *n* cratère *m*.

cravat [krə'væt] *n* cravate *f*.

crave [kreɪv] ◇ *vt* [affection, luxury] avoir soif de ; [cigarette, chocolate] avoir un besoin fou OR maladif de. ◇ *vi* : **to crave for** [affection, luxury] avoir soif de ; [cigarette, chocolate] avoir un besoin fou OR maladif de.

crawdad, **crawfish** = crayfish.

crawl [krɔːl] ◇ *vi* **1.** [baby] marcher à quatre pattes ; [person] se traîner - **2.** [insect] ramper - **3.** [vehicle, traffic] avancer au pas

- 4. *inf* [place, floor] **: to be crawling with** grouiller de. ◇ *n* [swimming stroke] **: the crawl** le crawl.

crayfish ['kreɪfɪʃ] (*pl* **crayfish** OR **-es**) *n* écrevisse *f*.

crayon ['kreɪɒn] *n* crayon *m* de couleur.

craze [kreɪz] *n* engouement *m*.

crazy ['kreɪzɪ] *adj inf* **1.** [mad] fou (folle) - **2.** [enthusiastic] **: to be crazy about sb/sthg** être fou (folle) de qqn/qqch.

CRB [ˌsiːɑːˈbiː] (*abbrev of* **Criminal Records Bureau**) *n Organisme chargé de vérifier le casier judiciaire de personnels sensibles.*

creak [kriːk] *vi* [door, handle] craquer ; [floorboard, bed] grincer.

cream [kriːm] ◇ *adj* [in colour] crème *(inv).* ◇ *n* [gen] crème *f*.

cream cake *n* UK gâteau *m* à la crème.

cream cheese *n* fromage *m* frais.

cream cracker *n* UK biscuit *m* salé *(souvent mangé avec du fromage).*

cream tea *n* UK *goûter de scones servis avec de la crème de la et confiture.*

crease [kriːs] ◇ *n* [in fabric - deliberate] pli *m* ; [- accidental] (faux) pli. ◇ *vt* froisser. ◇ *vi* [fabric] se froisser.

create [kriːˈeɪt] *vt* créer.

creation [kriːˈeɪʃn] *n* création *f*.

creative [kriːˈeɪtɪv] *adj* créatif(ive).

creature ['kriːtʃər] *n* créature *f*.

crèche [kreʃ] *n* UK crèche *f*.

credence ['kriːdns] *n* **: to give** OR **lend credence to sthg** ajouter foi à qqch.

credentials [krɪˈdenʃlz] *npl* **1.** [papers] papiers *mpl* d'identité ; *fig* [qualifications] capacités *fpl* - **2.** [references] références *fpl*.

credibility [ˌkredəˈbɪlətɪ] *n* crédibilité *f*.

credit ['kredɪt] ◇ *n* **1.** FIN crédit *m* ; **to be in credit** [person] avoir un compte approvisionné ; [account] être approvisionné ; **on credit** à crédit - **2.** *(U)* [praise] honneur *m*, mérite *m* ; **to give sb credit for sthg** reconnaître que qqn a fait qqch - **3.** UNIV unité *f* de valeur. ◇ *comp* [boom] du crédit ; [sales] à crédit ; **credit entry** écriture *f* au crédit ; **credit side** crédit *m*, avoir *m* ; **to run a credit check on sb** [to ensure enough money in account] vérifier la solvabilité de qqn, vérifier que le compte de qqn est approvisionné ; [to ensure no record of bad debts] vérifier le passé bancaire de qqn. ◇ *vt* **1.** FIN **: to credit £10 to an account, to credit an account with £10** créditer un compte de 10 livres - **2.** *inf* [believe] croire - **3.** [give the credit to] **: to credit sb with sthg** accorder OR attribuer qqch à qqn. ➤ **credits** *npl* CIN générique *m*.

credit card *n* carte *f* de crédit.

credit note *n* avoir *m* ; FIN note *f* de crédit.

creditor ['kredɪtər] *n* créancier *m*, -ère *f*.

creed [kriːd] *n* **1.** [belief] principes *mpl* - **2.** RELIG croyance *f*.

creek [kriːk] *n* **1.** [inlet] crique *f* - **2.** US [stream] ruisseau *m*.

creep [kriːp] ◇ *vi* (*pt & pp* **crept**) **1.** [insect] ramper ; [traffic] avancer au pas - **2.** [move stealthily] se glisser. ◇ *n inf* [nasty person] sale type *m*. ➤ **creeps** *npl* **: to give sb the creeps** *inf* donner la chair de poule à qqn.

creeper ['kriːpər] *n* [plant] plante *f* grimpante.

creepy ['kriːpɪ] *adj inf* qui donne la chair de poule.

creepy-crawly [-'krɔːlɪ] (*pl* **creepy-crawlies**) *n inf* bestiole *f* qui rampe.

cremate [krɪˈmeɪt] *vt* incinérer.

cremation [krɪˈmeɪʃn] *n* incinération *f*.

crematorium UK [ˌkreməˈtɔːrɪəm] (*pl* **-riums** OR **-ria** [-rɪə]), **crematory** US ['kremətrɪ] *n* crématorium *m*.

crepe [kreɪp] *n* **1.** [cloth, rubber] crêpe *m* - **2.** [pancake] crêpe *f*.

crepe bandage *n* UK bande *f* Velpeau®.

crepe paper *n (U)* papier *m* crépon.

crept [krept] *pt & pp* ➤ **creep**.

crescent ['kresnt] *n* **1.** [shape] croissant - **2.** UK [street] rue *f* en demi-cercle.

cress [kres] *n* cresson *m*.

crest [krest] *n* **1.** [of bird, hill] crête *f* - **2.** [on coat of arms] timbre *m*.

crestfallen ['krest,fɔːln] *adj* découragé(e).

Crete [kriːt] *n* Crète *f*.

cretin ['kretɪn] *n inf* [idiot] crétin *m*, -e *f*.

Creutzfeldt-Jakob disease [ˌkrɔɪtsfelt'jækɒb-] *n* maladie *f* de Creutzfeldt-Jakob.

crevice ['krevɪs] *n* fissure *f*.

crew [kruː] *n* **1.** [of ship, plane] équipage *m* - **2.** [team] équipe *f*.

crew cut *n* coupe *f* en brosse.

crib [krɪb] ◇ *n* [cot] lit *m* d'enfant. ◇ *vt inf* [copy] **: to crib sthg off** OR **from sb** copier qqch sur qqn.

crib death *n* US = **cot death**.

crick [krɪk] *n* [in neck] torticolis *m*.

cricket ['krɪkɪt] *n* **1.** [game] cricket *m* - **2.** [insect] grillon *m*.

crime [kraɪm] *n* crime *m* ; **crimes against humanity** crimes *mpl* contre l'humanité.

criminal ['krɪmɪnl] ◇ *adj* criminel(elle). ◇ *n* criminel *m*, -elle *f*.

Criminal Records Bureau *n* Organisme chargé de vérifier le casier judiciaire de personnels sensibles.

crimson ['krɪmzn] ◇ *adj* [in colour] rouge foncé *(inv)* ; [with embarrassment] cramoisi(e). ◇ *n* cramoisi *m*.

cringe [krɪndʒ] *vi* **1.** [in fear] avoir un mouvement de recul (par peur) - **2.** *inf* [with embarrassment] : **to cringe (at sthg)** ne plus savoir où se mettre (devant qqch).

crinkle ['krɪŋkl] *vt* [clothes] froisser.

cripple ['krɪpl] ◇ *n* dated & offens infirme *mf*. ◇ *vt* **1.** MED [disable] estropier - **2.** [country] paralyser ; [ship, plane] endommager.

crisis ['kraɪsɪs] (*pl* **crises** ['kraɪsiːz]) *n* crise *f*.

crisp [krɪsp] *adj* **1.** [pastry] croustillant(e) ; [apple, vegetables] croquant(e) ; [snow] craquant(e) - **2.** [weather, manner] vif (vive). ➡ **crisps** *npl UK* chips *fpl*.

crisscross ['krɪskrɒs] ◇ *adj* entrecroisé(e). ◇ *vt* entrecroiser.

criterion [kraɪ'tɪərɪən] (*pl* **-rions** OR **-ria** [-rɪə]) *n* critère *m*.

critic ['krɪtɪk] *n* **1.** [reviewer] critique *mf* - **2.** [detractor] détracteur *m*, -trice *f*.

critical ['krɪtɪkl] *adj* critique ; **to be critical of sb/sthg** critiquer qqn/qqch.

critically ['krɪtɪklɪ] *adv* **1.** [ill] gravement ; critically important d'une importance capitale - **2.** [analytically] de façon critique.

criticism ['krɪtɪsɪzm] *n* critique *f*.

criticize, *UK* **-ise** ['krɪtɪsaɪz] *vt & vi* critiquer.

croak [krəʊk] *vi* **1.** [frog] coasser ; [raven] croasser - **2.** [person] parler d'une voix rauque.

Croat ['krəʊæt], **Croatian** [krəʊ'eɪʃn] ◇ *adj* croate. ◇ *n* **1.** [person] Croate *mf* - **2.** [language] croate *m*.

Croatia [krəʊ'eɪʃə] *n* Croatie *f*.

Croatian = Croat.

crochet ['krəʊʃeɪ] *n* crochet *m*.

crockery ['krɒkərɪ] *n* dated vaisselle *f*.

crocodile ['krɒkədaɪl] (*pl* **crocodile** OR **-s**) *n* crocodile *m*.

crocus ['krəʊkəs] (*pl* **-es** [-iːz]) *n* crocus *m*.

croft [krɒft] *n UK* petite ferme *f* (particulièrement en Écosse).

crony ['krəʊnɪ] *n inf* copain *m*, copine *f*.

crook [krʊk] *n* **1.** [criminal] escroc *m* - **2.** [of arm, elbow] pliure *f* - **3.** [shepherd's staff] houlette *f*.

crooked ['krʊkɪd] *adj* **1.** [bent] courbé(e) - **2.** [teeth, tie] de travers - **3.** *inf* [dishonest] malhonnête.

crop [krɒp] *n* **1.** [kind of plant] culture *f* - **2.** [harvested produce] récolte *f* - **3.** [whip] cravache *f*. ➡ **crop up** *vi* survenir.

croquette [krɒ'ket] *n* croquette *f*.

cross [krɒs] ◇ *adj* [person] fâché(e) ; [look] méchant(e) ; **to get cross (with sb)** se fâcher (contre qqn). ◇ *n* **1.** [gen] croix *f* - **2.** [hybrid] croisement *m*. ◇ *vt* **1.** [gen] traverser ; **the bridge crosses the river at Orléans** le pont franchit OR enjambe le fleuve à Orléans - **2.** [arms, legs] croiser - **3.** *UK* [cheque] barrer. ◇ *vi* **1.** [go across] traverser ; **she crossed (over) to the other side of the road** elle a traversé la route ; **they crossed from Dover to Boulogne** ils ont fait la traversée de Douvres à Boulogne - **2.** [intersect] se croiser. ➡ **cross off**, **cross out** *vt sep* rayer.

crossbar ['krɒsbɑːr] *n* **1.** SPORT barre *f* transversale - **2.** [on bicycle] barre *f*.

cross-Channel *adj* transManche.

cross-country ◇ *adj* : **cross-country running** cross *m* ; **cross-country skiing** ski *m* de fond. ◇ *n* cross-country *m*, cross *m*.

cross-examine *vt* LAW faire subir un contre-interrogatoire à ; *fig* questionner de près.

cross-eyed [-aɪd] *adj* qui louche.

crossfire ['krɒs,faɪər] *n* (U) feu *m* croisé.

crossing ['krɒsɪŋ] *n* **1.** [on road] passage *m* clouté ; [on railway line] passage à niveau - **2.** [sea journey] traversée *f*.

cross-legged [-legd] *adv* en tailleur.

cross-purposes *npl* : **to talk at cross-purposes** ne pas parler de la même chose ; **to be at cross-purposes** ne pas être sur la même longueur d'ondes.

cross-reference *n* renvoi *m*.

crossroads ['krɒsrəʊdz] (*pl* **crossroads**) *n* croisement *m*.

cross-section *n* **1.** [drawing] coupe *f* transversale - **2.** [sample] échantillon *m*.

crosswalk ['krɒswɔːk] *n US* passage *m* clouté, passage pour piétons.

crossways ['krɒsweɪz] = **crosswise.**

crosswind ['krɒswɪnd] *n* vent *m* de travers.

crosswise ['krɒswaɪz] *adv* en travers.

crossword (puzzle) ['krɒswɜːd-] *n* mots croisés *mpl*.

crotch [krɒtʃ] *n* entrejambe *m*.

crotchety ['krɒtʃɪtɪ] *adj UK inf* grognon(onne).

crouch [kraʊtʃ] *vi* s'accroupir.

crow [krəʊ] ◇ *n* corbeau *m* ; **as the crow flies** à vol d'oiseau. ◇ *vi* **1.** [cock] chanter - **2.** *inf* [person] frimer.

crowbar ['krəʊbɑːr] *n* pied-de-biche *m*.

crowd [kraʊd] <> n [mass of people] foule f. <> vi s'amasser. <> vt 1. [streets, town] remplir - 2. [force into small space] entasser.

crowded ['kraʊdɪd] adj : crowded (with) bondé(e) (de), plein(e) (de).

crown [kraʊn] <> n 1. [of king, on tooth] couronne f - 2. [of head, hill] sommet m ; [of hat] fond m. <> vt couronner. ➤ **Crown** n : the Crown [monarchy] la Couronne.

crown jewels npl joyaux mpl de la Couronne.

crown prince n prince m héritier.

crow's feet npl pattes fpl d'oie.

CRT [si:ɑ:'ti:] (abbrev of cathode ray tube) n tube m cathodique.

crucial ['kru:ʃl] adj crucial(e).

crucifix ['kru:sɪfɪks] n crucifix m.

Crucifixion [,kru:sɪ'fɪkʃn] n : the Crucifixion la Crucifixion.

crude [kru:d] adj 1. [material] brut(e) - 2. [joke, drawing] grossier(ère).

crude oil n (U) brut m.

cruel [krʊəl] adj cruel(elle).

cruelty ['krʊəltɪ] n (U) cruauté f.

cruet ['kru:ɪt] n service m à condiments.

cruise [kru:z] <> n croisière f. <> vi 1. [sail] croiser - 2. [car] rouler ; [plane] voler.

cruiser ['kru:zər] n 1. [warship] croiseur m - 2. [cabin cruiser] yacht m de croisière.

crumb [krʌm] n [of food] miette f.

crumble ['krʌmbl] <> n crumble m (aux fruits). <> vt émietter. <> vi 1. [bread, cheese] s'émietter ; [building, wall] s'écrouler ; [cliff] s'ébouler ; [plaster] s'effriter - 2. fig [society, relationship] s'effondrer.

crumbly ['krʌmblɪ] adj friable.

crumpet ['krʌmpɪt] n CULIN petite crêpe f épaisse.

crumple ['krʌmpl] vt [crease] froisser.

crunch [krʌntʃ] <> n crissement m ; when it comes to the crunch inf au moment crucial OR décisif ; if it comes to the crunch inf s'il le faut. <> vt 1. [with teeth] croquer - 2. [underfoot] crisser.

crunchy ['krʌntʃɪ] adj [food] croquant(e).

crusade [kru:'seɪd] n lit & fig croisade f.

crush [krʌʃ] <> n 1. [crowd] foule f - 2. inf [infatuation] : to have a crush on sb avoir le béguin pour qqn. <> vt 1. [gen] écraser ; [seeds, grain] broyer ; [ice] piler - 2. fig [hopes] anéantir.

crust [krʌst] n croûte f.

crutch [krʌtʃ] n [stick] béquille f ; fig soutien m.

crux [krʌks] n nœud m.

cry [kraɪ] <> n [of person, bird] cri m. <> vi 1. [weep] pleurer - 2. [shout] crier.

➤ **cry off** vi UK se dédire. ➤ **cry out** <> vt crier. <> vi crier ; [in pain, dismay] pousser un cri.

cryptic ['krɪptɪk] adj mystérieux(euse), énigmatique.

crystal ['krɪstl] n cristal m.

crystal clear adj [obvious] clair(e) comme de l'eau de roche.

CSE (abbrev of Certificate of Secondary Education) n ancien brevet de l'enseignement secondaire en Grande-Bretagne.

CTC abbrev of city technology college.

cub [kʌb] n 1. [young animal] petit m - 2. [boy scout] louveteau m.

Cuba ['kju:bə] n Cuba.

Cuban ['kju:bən] <> adj cubain(e). <> n Cubain m, -e f.

cubbyhole ['kʌbɪhəʊl] n cagibi m.

cube [kju:b] <> n cube m. <> vt MATHS élever au cube.

cubic ['kju:bɪk] adj cubique.

cubicle ['kju:bɪkl] n cabine f.

Cub Scout n louveteau m.

cuckoo ['kʊku:] n coucou m.

cuckoo clock n coucou m.

cucumber ['kju:kʌmbər] n concombre m.

cuddle ['kʌdl] <> n caresse f, câlin m. <> vt caresser, câliner. <> vi se faire un câlin, se câliner.

cuddly toy n jouet m en peluche.

cue [kju:] n 1. RADIO, THEAT & TV signal m ; on cue au bon moment - 2. [in snooker, pool] queue f (de billard).

cuff [kʌf] n 1. [of sleeve] poignet m ; off the cuff au pied levé - 2. US [of trouser] revers m inv - 3. [blow] gifle f.

cuff link n bouton m de manchette.

cul-de-sac ['kʌldəsæk] n cul-de-sac m.

cull [kʌl] <> n massacre m. <> vt 1. [kill] massacrer - 2. [gather] recueillir.

culminate ['kʌlmɪneɪt] vi : to culminate in sthg se terminer par qqch, aboutir à qqch.

culmination [,kʌlmɪ'neɪʃn] n apogée m.

culottes [kju:'lɒts] npl jupe-culotte f.

culpable ['kʌlpəbl] adj coupable.

culprit ['kʌlprɪt] n coupable mf.

cult [kʌlt] <> n culte m. <> comp culte.

cultivate ['kʌltɪveɪt] vt cultiver.

cultivation [,kʌltɪ'veɪʃn] n (U) [farming] culture f.

cultural ['kʌltʃərəl] adj culturel(elle).

culture ['kʌltʃər] n culture f.

cultured ['kʌltʃəd] adj [educated] cultivé(e).

cumbersome ['kʌmbəsəm] adj [object] encombrant(e).

cunning ['kʌnɪŋ] ⬦ *adj* **1.** [shrewd] astucieux(euse), malin(igne) ; *pej* rusé(e), fourbe - **2.** [skilful] habile, astucieux(euse). ⬦ *n* (U) **1.** [guile] finesse *f*, astuce *f* ; *pej* ruse *f*, fourberie *f* - **2.** [skill] habileté *f*, adresse *f*.

cup [kʌp] *n* **1.** [container, unit of measurement] tasse *f* - **2.** [prize, competition] coupe *f* - **3.** [of bra] bonnet *m*.

cupboard ['kʌbəd] *n* placard *m*.

cup tie *n* UK match *m* de coupe.

curate ['kjuərət] *n* UK vicaire *m*.

curator [,kjuə'reɪtər] *n* conservateur *m*, -trice *f*.

curb [kɜːb] ⬦ *n* **1.** [control] : **curb (on)** frein *m* (à) - **2.** US [of road] bord *m* du trottoir. ⬦ *vt* mettre un frein à.

curdle ['kɜːdl] *vi* cailler.

cure [kjuər] ⬦ *n* : **cure (for)** MED remède *m* (contre) ; *fig* remède (à). ⬦ *vt* **1.** MED guérir - **2.** [solve - problem] éliminer - **3.** [rid] : **to cure sb of sthg** guérir qqn de qqch, faire perdre l'habitude de qqch à qqn - **4.** [preserve - by smoking] fumer ; [- by salting] saler ; [- tobacco, hide] sécher.

cure-all *n* panacée *f*.

curfew ['kɜːfjuː] *n* couvre-feu *m*.

curio ['kjuərɪəu] (*pl* -s) *n* bibelot *m*.

curiosity [,kjuərɪ'ɒsətɪ] *n* curiosité *f*.

curious ['kjuərɪəs] *adj* : **curious (about)** curieux(euse) (à propos de).

curl [kɜːl] ⬦ *n* [of hair] boucle *f*. ⬦ *vt* **1.** [hair] boucler - **2.** [roll up] enrouler. ⬦ *vi* **1.** [hair] boucler - **2.** [roll up] s'enrouler. ➤ **curl up** *vi* [person, animal] se mettre en boule, se pelotonner.

curler ['kɜːlər] *n* bigoudi *m*.

curling iron *n* US fer *m* à friser.

curling tongs *npl* UK fer *m* à friser.

curly ['kɜːlɪ] *adj* [hair] bouclé(e).

currant ['kʌrənt] *n* [dried grape] raisin *m* de Corinthe, raisin sec.

currency ['kʌrənsɪ] *n* **1.** [type of money] monnaie *f* - **2.** (U) [money] devise *f* - **3.** *fml* [acceptability] : **to gain currency** s'accréditer.

current ['kʌrənt] ⬦ *adj* [price, method] actuel(elle) ; [year, week] en cours ; [boyfriend, girlfriend] du moment ; **current issue** dernier numéro. ⬦ *n* [of water, air, electricity] courant *m*.

current account *n* UK compte *m* courant.

current affairs *npl* actualité *f*, questions *fpl* d'actualité.

currently ['kʌrəntlɪ] *adv* actuellement.

curriculum [kə'rɪkjələm] (*pl* -lums OR -la [-lə]) *n* programme *m* d'études.

curriculum vitae [-'viːtaɪ] (*pl* curricula vitae) *n* curriculum vitae *m*.

curry ['kʌrɪ] *n* curry *m*.

curse [kɜːs] ⬦ *n* **1.** [evil spell] malédiction *f* ; *fig* fléau *m* - **2.** [swearword] juron *m*. ⬦ *vt* maudire. ⬦ *vi* jurer.

cursor ['kɜːsər] *n* COMPUT curseur *m*.

cursory ['kɜːsərɪ] *adj* superficiel(elle).

curt [kɜːt] *adj* brusque.

curtail [kɜː'teɪl] *vt* [visit] écourter.

curtain ['kɜːtn] *n* rideau *m*.

curts(e)y ['kɜːtsɪ] (*pt & pp* curtsied) ⬦ *n* révérence *f*. ⬦ *vi* faire une révérence.

curve [kɜːv] ⬦ *n* courbe *f*. ⬦ *vi* faire une courbe.

cushion ['kuʃn] ⬦ *n* coussin *m*. ⬦ *vt* [fall, blow, effects] amortir.

cushy ['kuʃɪ] *adj inf* pépère, peinard(e).

custard ['kʌstəd] *n* UK crème *f* anglaise.

custodian [kʌ'stəudjən] *n* [of building] gardien *m*, -enne *f* ; [of museum] conservateur *m*.

custody ['kʌstədɪ] *n* **1.** [of child] garde *f* - **2.** LAW : **in custody** en garde à vue.

custom ['kʌstəm] *n* **1.** [tradition, habit] coutume *f* - **2.** COMM clientèle *f*. ➤ **customs** *n* [place] douane *f*.

customary ['kʌstəmrɪ] *adj* [behaviour] coutumier(ère) ; [way, time] habituel(elle).

customer ['kʌstəmər] *n* **1.** [client] client *m*, -e *f* - **2.** *inf* [person] type *m*.

customize, UK -**ise** ['kʌstəmaɪz] *vt* [make] fabriquer OR assembler sur commande ; [modify] modifier sur commande.

Customs and Excise *n* UK ≃ service *m* des contributions indirectes.

customs duty *n* droit *m* de douane.

customs officer *n* douanier *m*, -ère *f*.

cut [kʌt] ⬦ *n* **1.** [in wood etc] entaille *f* ; [in skin] coupure *f* - **2.** [of meat] morceau *m* - **3.** [reduction] : **cut (in)** [taxes, salary, personnel] réduction *f* (de) ; [film, article] coupure *f* (dans) ; **budget cuts** FIN compressions *fpl* budgétaires - **4.** [of suit, hair] coupe *f*. ⬦ *vt* (*pt & pp* cut) **1.** [gen] couper ; **to cut one's finger** se couper le doigt - **2.** *inf* [lecture, class] sécher. ⬦ *vi* (*pt & pp* cut) **1.** [gen] couper - **2.** [intersect] se couper. ➤ **cut back** ⬦ *vt sep* **1.** [prune] tailler - **2.** [reduce] réduire. ⬦ *vi* : **to cut back on** réduire, diminuer. ➤ **cut down** ⬦ *vt sep* **1.** [chop down] couper - **2.** [reduce] réduire, diminuer. ⬦ *vi* : **to cut down on smoking/ eating/spending** fumer/manger/dépenser moins. ➤ **cut in** *vi* **1.** [interrupt] : **to cut in (on sb)** interrompre (qqn) - **2.** AUT & SPORT se rabattre. ➤ **cut off** *vt sep* **1.** [piece, crust] couper ; [finger, leg - subj: surgeon] amputer - **3.** [power, telephone, funding] couper - **4.** [separate] : **to be cut off (from)**

[person] être coupé(e) (de) ; [village] être isolé(e) (de). ➤ **cut out** *vt sep* **1.** [photo, article] découper ; [sewing pattern] couper ; [dress] tailler - **2.** [stop] : **to cut out smoking/chocolates** arrêter de fumer/de manger des chocolats ; **cut it out!** *inf* ça suffit ! - **3.** [exclude] exclure. ➤ **cut up** *vt sep* [chop up] couper, hacher.

cutback ['kʌtbæk] *n* : **cutback (in)** réduction *f* (de).

cute [kjuːt] *adj* [appealing] mignon(onne).

cuticle ['kjuːtɪkl] *n* envie *f*.

cutlery ['kʌtlərɪ] *n* (U) couverts *mpl*.

cutlet ['kʌtlɪt] *n* côtelette *f*.

cutout ['kʌtaʊt] *n* **1.** [on machine] disjoncteur *m* - **2.** [shape] découpage *m*.

cut-price UK, **cut-rate** US *adj* à prix réduit.

cutthroat ['kʌtθrəʊt] *adj* [ruthless] acharné(e).

cutting ['kʌtɪŋ] ◇ *adj* [sarcastic - remark] cinglant(e) ; [- wit] acerbe. ◇ *n* **1.** [of plant] bouture *f* - **2.** UK [from newspaper] coupure *f* - **3.** UK [for road, railway] tranchée *f*.

cutting board *n* US planche *f* à découper.

CV (*abbrev of* **curriculum vitae**) *n* CV *m*.

cwt. *abbrev of* **hundredweight**.

cyanide ['saɪənaɪd] *n* cyanure *m*.

cybercafé ['saɪbə,kæfeɪ] *n* cybercafé *m*.

cybernaut ['saɪbə,nɔːt] *n* cybernaute *mf*.

cyberpet ['saɪbə,pet] *n* animal *m* virtuel.

cyberspace ['saɪbəspeɪs] *n* cyberespace *m*.

cybersurfer ['saɪbə,sɜːfə'] *n* cybernaute *mf*.

cycle ['saɪkl] ◇ *n* **1.** [of events, songs] cycle *m* - **2.** [bicycle] bicyclette *f*. ◇ *comp* [path, track] cyclable ; [race] cycliste ; [shop] de cycles. ◇ *vi* faire de la bicyclette.

cycling ['saɪklɪŋ] *n* cyclisme *m*.

cyclist ['saɪklɪst] *n* cycliste *mf*.

cygnet ['sɪgnɪt] *n* jeune cygne *m*.

cylinder ['sɪlɪndə'] *n* cylindre *m*.

cymbal ['sɪmbl] *n* cymbale *f*.

cynic ['sɪnɪk] *n* cynique *mf*.

cynical ['sɪnɪkl] *adj* cynique.

cynicism ['sɪnɪsɪzm] *n* cynisme *m*.

cypress ['saɪprəs] *n* cyprès *m*.

Cypriot ['sɪprɪət] ◇ *adj* chypriote. ◇ *n* Chypriote *mf*.

Cyprus ['saɪprəs] *n* Chypre *f*.

cyst [sɪst] *n* kyste *m*.

cystitis [sɪs'taɪtɪs] *n* cystite *f*.

czar [zɑː'] *n* [sovereign] tsar *m* ; [top person] éminence *f* grise, ponte *m*.

Czech [tʃek] ◇ *adj* tchèque. ◇ *n* **1.** [person] Tchèque *mf* - **2.** [language] tchèque *m*.

Czechoslovak [,tʃekə'sləʊvæk] = **Czechoslovakian**.

Czechoslovakia [,tʃekəslə'vækɪə] *n* Tchécoslovaquie *f*.

Czechoslovakian [,tʃekəslə'vækɪən] ◇ *adj* tchécoslovaque. ◇ *n* Tchécoslovaque *mf*.

Czech Republic *n* République *f* tchèque.

D

d [diː] (*pl* **d's** OR **ds**), **D** (*pl* **D's** OR **Ds**) *n* [letter] d *m inv*, D *m inv*. ➤ **D** *n* **1.** MUS ré *m* - **2.** SCH [mark] D *m inv*.

DA *abbrev of* **district attorney**.

dab [dæb] ◇ *n* [of cream, powder, ointment] petit peu *m* ; [of paint] touche *f*. ◇ *vt* **1.** [skin, wound] tamponner - **2.** [apply - cream, ointment] : **to dab sthg on** OR **onto** appliquer qqch sur.

dabble ['dæbl] *vi* : **to dabble in** toucher un peu à.

dachshund ['dækshʊnd] *n* teckel *m*.

dad [dæd], **daddy** ['dædɪ] *n inf* papa *m*.

daddy longlegs [-'lɒŋlegz] (*pl* **daddy longlegs**) *n* faucheur *m*.

daffodil ['dæfədɪl] *n* jonquille *f*.

daft [dɑːft] *adj* UK *inf* stupide, idiot(e).

dagger ['dægə'] *n* poignard *m*.

daily ['deɪlɪ] ◇ *adj* **1.** [occurrence] quotidien(enne) - **2.** [rate, output] journalier(ère). ◇ *adv* [happen, write] quotidiennement ; **twice daily** deux fois par jour. ◇ *n* [newspaper] quotidien *m*.

dainty ['deɪntɪ] *adj* délicat(e).

dairy ['deərɪ] *n* **1.** [on farm] laiterie *f* - **2.** [shop] crémerie *f*.

dairy products *npl* produits *mpl* laitiers.

dais ['deɪɪs] *n* estrade *f*.

daisy ['deɪzɪ] *n* [weed] pâquerette *f* ; [cultivated] marguerite *f*.

daisy-wheel printer *n* imprimante *f* à marguerite.

dale [deɪl] *n* vallée *f*.

dam [dæm] ◇ *n* [across river] barrage *m*. ◇ *vt* construire un barrage sur.

damage ['dæmɪdʒ] ◇ *n* **1.** [physical harm]

dommage m, dégât m - 2. [harmful effect] tort m. ⋄ vt 1. [harm physically] endommager, abîmer - 2. [have harmful effect on] nuire à. ◆ **damages** npl LAW dommages et intérêts mpl.

damn [dæm] ⋄ adj inf fichu(e), sacré(e). ⋄ adv inf sacrément. ⋄ n inf **not to give OR care a damn (about sthg)** se ficher pas mal (de qqch). ⋄ vt RELIG [condemn] damner. ⋄ excl inf zut!

damned [dæmd] inf ⋄ adj fichu(e), sacré(e) ; **well I'll be** US OR **I'm damned!** UK c'est trop fort!, elle est bien bonne celle-là! ⋄ adv sacrément.

damning ['dæmɪŋ] adj accablant(e).

damp [dæmp] ⋄ adj humide. ⋄ n humidité f. ⋄ vt [make wet] humecter.

dampen ['dæmpən] vt 1. [make wet] humecter - 2. fig [emotion] abattre.

damson ['dæmzn] n prune f de Damas.

dance [dɑːns] ⋄ n 1. [gen] danse f - 2. [social event] bal m. ⋄ vi danser.

dancer ['dɑːnsər] n danseur m, -euse f.

dancing ['dɑːnsɪŋ] n (U) danse f.

dandelion ['dændɪlaɪən] n pissenlit m.

dandruff ['dændrʌf] n (U) pellicules fpl.

Dane [deɪn] n Danois m, -e f.

danger ['deɪndʒər] n 1. (U) [possibility of harm] danger m ; **in danger** en danger ; **out of danger** hors de danger - 2. [hazard ; risk] : **danger (to)** risque m (pour) ; **to be in danger of doing sthg** risquer de faire qqch.

dangerous ['deɪndʒərəs] adj dangereux(euse).

dangle ['dæŋgl] ⋄ vt laisser pendre. ⋄ vi pendre.

Danish ['deɪnɪʃ] ⋄ adj danois(e). ⋄ n 1. [language] danois m - 2. US = **Danish pastry**. ⋄ npl : **the Danish** les Danois mpl.

Danish pastry n gâteau feuilleté fourré aux fruits.

dank [dæŋk] adj humide et froid(e).

dapper ['dæpər] adj pimpant(e).

dappled ['dæpld] adj 1. [light] tacheté(e) - 2. [horse] pommelé(e).

dare [deər] ⋄ vt 1. [be brave enough] : **to dare to do sthg** oser faire qqch - 2. [challenge] : **to dare sb to do sthg** défier qqn de faire qqch ; **I dare say** je suppose, sans doute. ⋄ vi oser ; **how dare you!** comment osez-vous! ⋄ n défi m.

daredevil ['deə,devl] n casse-cou m inv.

daring ['deərɪŋ] ⋄ adj audacieux(euse). ⋄ n audace f.

dark [dɑːk] ⋄ adj 1. [room, night] sombre ; **it's getting dark** il commence à faire nuit - 2. [in colour] foncé(e) - 3. [dark-haired] brun(e) ; [dark-skinned] basané(e). ⋄ n

1. [darkness] : **the dark** l'obscurité f ; **to be in the dark about sthg** ignorer qqch à propos de qqch - 2. [night] : **before/after dark** avant/après la tombée de la nuit.

darken ['dɑːkn] ⋄ vt assombrir. ⋄ vi s'assombrir.

dark glasses npl lunettes fpl noires.

darkness ['dɑːknɪs] n obscurité f.

darkroom ['dɑːkrʊm] n chambre f noire.

darling ['dɑːlɪŋ] ⋄ adj [dear] chéri(e). ⋄ n 1. [loved person, term of address] chéri m, -e f - 2. [idol] chouchou m, idole f.

darn [dɑːn] ⋄ vt repriser. ⋄ adj inf sacré(e), satané(e). ⋄ adv inf sacrément.

dart [dɑːt] ⋄ n [arrow] fléchette f. ⋄ vi se précipiter. ◆ **darts** n [game] jeu m de fléchettes.

dartboard ['dɑːtbɔːd] n cible f de jeu de fléchettes.

dash [dæʃ] ⋄ n 1. [of milk, wine] goutte f ; [of cream] soupçon m ; [of salt] pincée f ; [of colour, paint] touche f - 2. [in punctuation] tiret m - 3. [rush] : **to make a dash for** se ruer vers. ⋄ vt [throw] jeter avec violence. ⋄ vi se précipiter.

dashboard ['dæʃbɔːd] n tableau m de bord.

dashing ['dæʃɪŋ] adj fringant(e).

data ['deɪtə] n (U) données fpl.

database ['deɪtəbeɪs] n base f de données.

data processing n traitement m de données.

date [deɪt] ⋄ n 1. [in time] date f ; **to date** à ce jour - 2. [appointment] rendez-vous m inv - 3. [person] petit ami m, petite amie f - 4. [fruit] datte f. ⋄ vt 1. [gen] dater - 2. [go out with] sortir avec. ⋄ vi 1. [go out of fashion] dater - 2. [go out on dates] sortir avec des garçons/filles ; **how long have you two been dating?** ça fait combien de temps que vous sortez ensemble OR que vous vous voyez?

dated ['deɪtɪd] adj qui date.

date of birth n date f de naissance.

daub [dɔːb] vt : **to daub sthg with sthg** barbouiller qqch de qqch.

daughter ['dɔːtər] n fille f.

daughter-in-law (pl daughters-in-law) n belle-fille f.

daunting ['dɔːntɪŋ] adj intimidant(e).

dawdle ['dɔːdl] vi flâner.

dawn [dɔːn] ⋄ n lit & fig aube f. ⋄ vi 1. [day] poindre - 2. [era, period] naître. ◆ **dawn (up)on** vt insep venir à l'esprit de.

day [deɪ] n jour m ; [duration] journée f ; **the day before** la veille ; **the day after** le lendemain ; **the day before yesterday**

avant-hier ; **the day after tomorrow** après-demain ; **any day now** d'un jour à l'autre ; **one day, some day, one of these days** un jour (ou l'autre), un de ces jours ; **to make sb's day** réchauffer le cœur de qqn. ➡ **days** *adv* le jour.

daybreak ['deɪbreɪk] *n* aube *f* ; **at daybreak** à l'aube.

daydream ['deɪdriːm] *vi* rêvasser.

daylight ['deɪlaɪt] *n* **1.** [light] lumière *f* du jour - **2.** [dawn] aube *f*.

day off (*pl* days off) *n* jour *m* de congé.

day return *n* UK billet aller et retour valable pour une journée.

daytime ['deɪtaɪm] ⟨⟩ *n* jour *m*, journée *f*. ⟨⟩ *comp* [job, flight] de jour.

day-to-day *adj* [routine, life] journalier(ère) ; **on a day-to-day basis** au jour le jour.

day trip *n* excursion *f* d'une journée.

daze [deɪz] ⟨⟩ *n* : **in a daze** hébété(e), ahuri(e). ⟨⟩ *vt* **1.** [subj: blow] étourdir - **2.** *fig* [subj: shock, event] abasourdir, sidérer.

dazzle ['dæzl] *vt* éblouir.

DC *n* (*abbrev of* **direct current**) courant *m* continu.

D-day, D-Day ['diːdeɪ] *n fig & HIST* le jour J.

DEA (*abbrev of* **Drug Enforcement Administration**) *n* agence américaine de lutte contre la drogue.

deacon ['diːkn] *n* diacre *m*.

deactivate [,diː'æktɪveɪt] *vt* désamorcer.

dead [ded] ⟨⟩ *adj* **1.** [not alive, not lively] mort(e) ; **to shoot sb dead** abattre qqn - **2.** [numb] engourdi(e) - **3.** [not operating - battery] à plat - **4.** [complete - silence] de mort. ⟨⟩ *adv* **1.** [directly, precisely] : **dead ahead** droit devant soi ; **dead on time** pile à l'heure - **2.** *inf* [completely] tout à fait - **3.** [suddenly] : **to stop dead** s'arrêter net. ⟨⟩ *npl* : **the dead** les morts *mpl*.

deaden ['dedn] *vt* [sound] assourdir ; [pain] calmer.

dead end *n* impasse *f*.

dead heat *n* arrivée *f* ex-aequo.

deadline ['dedlaɪn] *n* dernière limite *f*.

deadlock ['dedlɒk] *n* impasse *f*.

dead loss *n* UK *inf* : **to be a dead loss** [person, thing] être complètement nul (nulle) à rien.

deadly ['dedlɪ] ⟨⟩ *adj* **1.** [poison, enemy] mortel(elle) - **2.** [accuracy] imparable. ⟨⟩ *adv* [boring, serious] tout à fait.

deadpan ['dedpæn] ⟨⟩ *adj* pince-sans-rire (*inv*). ⟨⟩ *adv* impassiblement.

deaf [def] ⟨⟩ *adj* sourd(e) ; **to be deaf to sthg** être sourd à qqch. ⟨⟩ *npl* : **the deaf** les sourds *mpl*.

deaf-and-dumb *adj* sourd-muet (sourde-muette).

deafen ['defn] *vt* assourdir.

deaf-mute ⟨⟩ *adj* sourd-muet (sourde-muette). ⟨⟩ *n* sourd-muet *m*, sourde-muette *f*.

deafness ['defnɪs] *n* surdité *f*.

deal [diːl] ⟨⟩ *n* **1.** [quantity] : **a good** OR **great deal** beaucoup ; **a good** OR **great deal of** beaucoup de, bien de/des - **2.** [business agreement] marché *m*, affaire *f* ; **to do** OR **strike a deal with sb** conclure un marché avec qqn - **3.** *inf* [treatment] : **to get a bad deal** ne pas faire une affaire. ⟨⟩ *vt* (*pt & pp* dealt) **1.** [strike] : **to deal sb/sthg a blow, to deal a blow to sb/sthg** porter un coup à qqn/qqch - **2.** [cards] donner, distribuer. ⟨⟩ *vi* (*pt & pp* dealt) **1.** [at cards] donner, distribuer - **2.** [in drugs] faire le trafic (de drogues). ➡ **deal in** *vt insep* COMM faire le commerce de. ➡ **deal out** *vt sep* distribuer. ➡ **deal with** *vt insep* **1.** [handle] s'occuper de - **2.** [be about] traiter de - **3.** [do business with] traiter OR négocier avec.

dealer ['diːlər] *n* **1.** [trader] négociant *m* ; [in drugs] trafiquant *m* - **2.** [cards] donneur *m*.

dealing ['diːlɪŋ] *n* commerce *m*. ➡ **dealings** *npl* relations *fpl*, rapports *mpl*.

dealt [delt] *pt & pp* ➤ **deal**.

dean [diːn] *n* doyen *m*.

dear [dɪər] ⟨⟩ *adj* : **dear (to)** cher (chère) (à) ; **Dear Sir** [in letter] Cher Monsieur ; **Dear Madam** Chère Madame. ⟨⟩ *n* chéri *m*, -e *f*. ⟨⟩ *excl* : **oh dear!** mon Dieu!

dearly ['dɪəlɪ] *adv* [love, wish] de tout son cœur.

death [deθ] *n* mort *f* ; **to frighten sb to death** faire une peur bleue à qqn ; **to be sick to death of sthg/of doing sthg** en avoir marre de qqch/de faire qqch.

death certificate *n* acte *m* de décès.

death duty UK, **death tax** US *n* droits *mpl* de succession.

deathly ['deθlɪ] *adj* de mort.

death penalty *n* peine *f* de mort.

death rate *n* taux *m* de mortalité.

death tax US = death duty.

death trap *n inf* véhicule *m* /bâtiment *m* dangereux.

debar [diː'bɑːr] *vt* : **to debar sb (from)** [place] exclure qqn (de) ; **to debar sb from doing sthg** interdire à qqn de faire qqch.

debase [dɪ'beɪs] *vt* dégrader ; **to debase o.s.** s'avilir.

debate [dɪ'beɪt] <> n débat m ; **open to debate** discutable. <> vt débattre, discuter ; **to debate whether** s'interroger pour savoir si. <> vi débattre.

debating society [dɪ'beɪtɪŋ-] n UK club m de débats.

debauchery [dɪ'bɔːtʃərɪ] n débauche f.

debit ['debɪt] <> n débit m. <> vt débiter.

debit card n carte f de paiement à débit immédiat.

debit note n note f de débit.

debris ['deɪbriː] n (U) débris mpl.

debt [det] n dette f ; **to be in debt** avoir des dettes, être endetté(e) ; **to be in sb's debt** être redevable à qqn.

debt collector n agent m de recouvrements.

debtor ['detər] n débiteur m, -trice f.

debug [ˌdiː'bʌg] vt COMPUT [program] mettre au point, déboguer.

debunk [ˌdiː'bʌŋk] vt démentir.

debut ['deɪbjuː] n débuts mpl.

decade ['dekeɪd] n décennie f.

decadence ['dekədəns] n décadence f.

decadent ['dekədənt] adj décadent(e).

decaffeinated [dɪ'kæfɪneɪtɪd] adj décaféiné(e).

decanter [dɪ'kæntər] n carafe f.

decathlon [dɪ'kæθlɒn] n décathlon m.

decay [dɪ'keɪ] <> n 1. [of body, plant] pourriture f, putréfaction f ; [of tooth] carie f - 2. fig [of building] délabrement m ; [of society] décadence f. <> vi 1. [rot] pourrir ; [tooth] se carier - 2. fig [building] se délabrer, tomber en ruines ; [society] tomber en décadence.

deceased [dɪ'siːst] <> adj décédé(e). <> n (pl **deceased**) : **the deceased** le défunt, la défunte.

deceit [dɪ'siːt] n tromperie f, supercherie f.

deceitful [dɪ'siːtfʊl] adj trompeur(euse).

deceive [dɪ'siːv] vt [person] tromper, duper ; [subj: memory, eyes] jouer des tours à ; **to deceive o.s.** se leurrer, s'abuser.

December [dɪ'sembər] n décembre m ; see also **September**.

decency ['diːsnsɪ] n décence f, bienséance f ; **to have the decency to do sthg** avoir la décence de faire qqch.

decent ['diːsnt] adj 1. [behaviour, dress] décent(e) - 2. [wage, meal] correct(e), décent(e) - 3. [person] gentil(ille), brave.

deception [dɪ'sepʃn] n 1. [lie, pretence] tromperie f, duperie f - 2. (U) [lying] supercherie f.

deceptive [dɪ'septɪv] adj trompeur(euse).

decide [dɪ'saɪd] <> vt décider ; **to decide to do sthg** décider de faire qqch. <> vi se décider. ■ **decide (up)on** vt insep se décider pour, choisir.

decided [dɪ'saɪdɪd] adj 1. [definite] certain(e), incontestable - 2. [resolute] décidé(e), résolu(e).

decidedly [dɪ'saɪdɪdlɪ] adv 1. [clearly] manifestement, incontestablement - 2. [resolutely] résolument.

deciduous [dɪ'sɪdjʊəs] adj à feuilles caduques.

decimal ['desɪml] <> adj décimal(e). <> n décimale f.

decimal point n virgule f.

decimate ['desɪmeɪt] vt décimer.

decipher [dɪ'saɪfər] vt déchiffrer.

decision [dɪ'sɪʒn] n décision f.

decisive [dɪ'saɪsɪv] adj 1. [person] déterminé(e), résolu(e) - 2. [factor, event] décisif(ive).

deck [dek] n 1. [of ship] pont m - 2. [of bus] étage m ; **top** OR **upper deck** impériale f - 3. [of cards] jeu m - 4. US [of house] véranda f.

deckchair ['dektʃeər] n chaise longue f, transat m.

declaration [ˌdeklə'reɪʃn] n déclaration f.

Declaration of Independence n : **the Declaration of Independence** la Déclaration d'Indépendance des États-Unis d'Amérique (1776).

declare [dɪ'kleər] vt déclarer.

decline [dɪ'klaɪn] <> n déclin m ; **to be in decline** être en déclin ; **on the decline** en baisse. <> vt décliner ; **to decline to do sthg** refuser de faire qqch. <> vi 1. [deteriorate] décliner - 2. [refuse] refuser.

decode [ˌdiː'kəʊd] vt décoder.

decompose [ˌdiːkəm'pəʊz] vi se décomposer.

decongestant [ˌdiːkən'dʒestənt] n décongestionnant m.

decorate ['dekəreɪt] vt décorer.

decoration [ˌdekə'reɪʃn] n décoration f.

decorator ['dekəreɪtər] n décorateur m, -trice f.

decoy <> n ['diːkɔɪ] [for hunting] appât m, leurre m ; [person] compère m. <> vt [dɪ'kɔɪ] attirer dans un piège.

decrease <> n ['diːkriːs] : **decrease (in)** diminution f (de), baisse f (de). <> vt [dɪ'kriːs] diminuer, réduire. <> vi [dɪ'kriːs] diminuer, décroître.

decree [dɪ'kriː] <> n 1. [order, decision] décret m - 2. US LAW arrêt m, jugement m. <> vt décréter, ordonner.

decree nisi [-'naɪsaɪ] (pl **decrees nisi**) n UK jugement m provisoire.

decrepit [dɪ'krepɪt] *adj* [person] décrépit(e) ; [house] délabré(e).

dedicate ['dedɪkeɪt] *vt* **1.** [book etc] dédier - **2.** [life, career] consacrer.

dedication [ˌdedɪ'keɪʃn] *n* **1.** [commitment] dévouement *m* - **2.** [in book] dédicace *f*.

deduce [dɪ'dju:s] *vt* déduire, conclure.

deduct [dɪ'dʌkt] *vt* déduire, retrancher.

deduction [dɪ'dʌkʃn] *n* déduction *f*.

deed [di:d] *n* **1.** [action] action *f*, acte *m* - **2.** LAW acte *m* notarié.

deem [di:m] *vt* juger, considérer ; **to deem it wise to do sthg** juger prudent de faire qqch.

deep [di:p] ◇ *adj* profond(e). ◇ *adv* profondément ; **deep down** [fundamentally] au fond.

deepen ['di:pn] *vi* **1.** [river, sea] devenir profond(e) - **2.** [crisis, recession, feeling] s'aggraver.

deep freeze *n* congélateur *m*.

deeply ['di:plɪ] *adv* profondément.

deep-sea *adj* : **deep-sea diving** plongée *f* sous-marine ; **deep-sea fishing** pêche *f* hauturière.

deer [dɪər] (*pl* deer) *n* cerf *m*.

deface [dɪ'feɪs] *vt* barbouiller.

defamatory [dɪ'fæmətrɪ] *adj* diffamatoire, diffamant(e).

default [dɪ'fɔːlt] ◇ *n* **1.** [failure] défaillance *f* ; **by default** par défaut - **2.** COMPUT valeur *f* par défaut. ◇ *vi* manquer à ses engagements.

defeat [dɪ'fiːt] ◇ *n* défaite *f* ; **to admit defeat** s'avouer battu(e) OR vaincu(e). ◇ *vt* **1.** [team, opponent] vaincre, battre - **2.** [motion, proposal] rejeter.

defeatist [dɪ'fiːtɪst] ◇ *adj* défaitiste. ◇ *n* défaitiste *mf*.

defect ◇ *n* ['diːfekt] défaut *m*. ◇ *vi* [dɪ'fekt] : **to defect to** passer à.

defective [dɪ'fektɪv] *adj* défectueux(euse).

defence UK, **defense** US [dɪ'fens] *n* **1.** [gen] défense *f* - **2.** [protective device, system] protection *f* - **3.** LAW : **the defence** la défense.

defenceless UK, **defenseless** US [dɪ'fenslɪs] *adj* sans défense.

defend [dɪ'fend] *vt* défendre.

defendant [dɪ'fendənt] *n* défendeur *m*, -eresse *f* ; [in trial] accusé *m*, -e *f*.

defender [dɪ'fendər] *n* défenseur *m*.

defense US = defence.

defenseless US = defenceless.

defensive [dɪ'fensɪv] ◇ *adj* défensif(ive). ◇ *n* : **on the defensive** sur la défensive.

defer [dɪ'fɜːr] ◇ *vt* différer. ◇ *vi* : **to defer to sb** s'en remettre à (l'opinion de) qqn.

deferential [ˌdefə'renʃl] *adj* respectueux(euse).

defiance [dɪ'faɪəns] *n* défi *m* ; **in defiance of** au mépris de.

defiant [dɪ'faɪənt] *adj* [person] intraitable, intransigeant(e) ; [action] de défi.

defibrillator [diː'fɪbrɪleɪtər] *n* MED défibrillateur *m*.

deficiency [dɪ'fɪʃnsɪ] *n* **1.** [lack] manque *m* ; [of vitamins etc] carence *f* - **2.** [inadequacy] imperfection *f*.

deficient [dɪ'fɪʃnt] *adj* **1.** [lacking] : **to be deficient in** manquer de - **2.** [inadequate] insuffisant(e), médiocre.

deficit ['defɪsɪt] *n* déficit *m*.

defile [dɪ'faɪl] *vt* souiller, salir.

define [dɪ'faɪn] *vt* définir.

definite ['defɪnɪt] *adj* **1.** [plan] bien déterminé(e) ; [date] certain(e) - **2.** [improvement, difference] net (nette), marqué(e) - **3.** [answer] précis(e), catégorique - **4.** [confident - person] assuré(e).

definitely ['defɪnɪtlɪ] *adv* **1.** [without doubt] sans aucun doute, certainement - **2.** [for emphasis] catégoriquement.

definition [ˌdefɪ'nɪʃn] *n* **1.** [gen] définition *f* - **2.** [clarity] clarté *f*, précision *f*.

deflate [dɪ'fleɪt] ◇ *vt* [balloon, tyre] dégonfler. ◇ *vi* [balloon, tyre] se dégonfler.

deflation [dɪ'fleɪʃn] *n* ECON déflation *f*.

deflect [dɪ'flekt] *vt* [ball, bullet] dévier ; [stream] détourner, dériver ; [criticism] détourner.

defogger [ˌdiː'fɒgər] *n* US AUT dispositif *m* antibuée.

deformed [dɪ'fɔːmd] *adj* difforme.

Defra ['defrə] (*abbrev of* Department for Environment, Food & Rural Affairs) *n* UK ADMIN ministère *m* de l'Agriculture britannique *m*.

defragment [ˌdiː'fræg'ment] *vt* COMPUT défragmenter.

defraud [dɪ'frɔːd] *vt* [person] escroquer ; [Inland Revenue etc] frauder.

defrost [ˌdiː'frɒst] ◇ *vt* **1.** [fridge] dégivrer ; [frozen food] décongeler - **2.** US [AUT - de-ice] dégivrer ; [- demist] désembuer. ◇ *vi* [fridge] dégivrer ; [frozen food] se décongeler.

deft [deft] *adj* adroit(e).

defunct [dɪ'fʌŋkt] *adj* qui n'existe plus ; [person] défunt(e).

defuse [ˌdiː'fjuːz] *vt* désamorcer.

defy [dɪ'faɪ] vt **1.** [gen] défier ; **to defy sb to do sthg** mettre qqn au défi de faire qqch - **2.** [efforts] résister à, faire échouer.

degenerate <> adj [dɪ'dʒenərət] dégénéré(e). <> vi [dɪ'dʒenəreɪt] : **to degenerate (into)** dégénérer (en).

degrading [dɪ'greɪdɪŋ] adj dégradant(e), avilissant(e).

degree [dɪ'griː] n **1.** [measurement] degré m - **2.** UNIV diplôme m universitaire - **3.** [amount] : **to a certain degree** jusqu'à un certain point, dans une certaine mesure ; **a degree of risk** un certain risque ; **a degree of truth** une certaine part de vérité ; **by degrees** progressivement, petit à petit.

dehydrated [ˌdiːhaɪ'dreɪtɪd] adj déshydraté(e).

de-ice [diː'aɪs] vt dégivrer.

deign [deɪn] vt : **to deign to do sthg** daigner faire qqch.

deity ['diːɪtɪ] n dieu m, déesse f, divinité f.

dejected [dɪ'dʒektɪd] adj abattu(e), découragé(e).

delay [dɪ'leɪ] <> n retard m, délai m. <> vt **1.** [cause to be late] retarder - **2.** [defer] différer ; **to delay doing sthg** tarder à faire qqch. <> vi : **to delay (in doing sthg)** tarder (à faire qqch).

delayed [dɪ'leɪd] adj : **to be delayed** [person, train] être retardé(e).

delectable [dɪ'lektəbl] adj délicieux(euse).

delegate <> n ['delɪgət] délégué m, -e f. <> vt ['delɪgeɪt] déléguer ; **to delegate sb to do sthg** déléguer qqn pour faire qqch ; **to delegate sthg to sb** déléguer qqch à qqn.

delegation [ˌdelɪ'geɪʃn] n délégation f.

delete [dɪ'liːt] vt supprimer, effacer.

delete key n COMPUT touche f effacer.

deli ['delɪ] n inf abbrev of **delicatessen**.

deliberate <> adj [dɪ'lɪbərət] **1.** [intentional] voulu(e), délibéré(e) - **2.** [slow] lent(e), sans hâte. <> vi [dɪ'lɪbəreɪt] délibérer.

deliberately [dɪ'lɪbərətlɪ] adv [on purpose] exprès, à dessein.

delicacy ['delɪkəsɪ] n **1.** [gen] délicatesse f - **2.** [food] mets m délicat.

delicate ['delɪkət] adj délicat(e) ; [movement] gracieux(euse).

delicatessen [ˌdelɪkə'tesn] n épicerie f fine.

delicious [dɪ'lɪʃəs] adj délicieux(euse).

delight [dɪ'laɪt] <> n [great pleasure] délice m ; **to take delight in doing sthg** prendre grand plaisir à faire qqch. <> vt enchanter, charmer. <> vi : **to delight in sthg/in doing sthg** prendre grand plaisir à qqch/à faire qqch.

delighted [dɪ'laɪtɪd] adj : **delighted (by** OR **with)** enchanté(e) (de), ravi(e) (de) ; **to be delighted to do sthg** être enchanté OR ravi de faire qqch.

delightful [dɪ'laɪtfʊl] adj ravissant(e), charmant(e) ; [meal] délicieux(euse).

delinquent [dɪ'lɪŋkwənt] <> adj délinquant(e). <> n délinquant m, -e f.

delirious [dɪ'lɪrɪəs] adj lit & fig délirant(e).

deliver [dɪ'lɪvər] vt **1.** [distribute] : **to deliver sthg (to sb)** [mail, newspaper] distribuer qqch (à qqn) ; COMM livrer qqch (à qqn) - **2.** [speech] faire ; [warning] donner ; [message] remettre ; [blow, kick] donner, porter - **3.** [baby] mettre au monde - **4.** [free] délivrer - **5.** US POL [votes] obtenir.

delivery [dɪ'lɪvərɪ] n **1.** COMM livraison f - **2.** [way of speaking] élocution f - **3.** [birth] accouchement m.

delude [dɪ'luːd] vt tromper, induire en erreur ; **to delude o.s.** se faire des illusions.

delusion [dɪ'luːʒn] n illusion f.

delve [delv] vi : **to delve into** [past] fouiller ; [bag etc] fouiller dans.

demand [dɪ'mɑːnd] <> n **1.** [claim, firm request] revendication f, exigence f ; **on demand** sur demande - **2.** ECON & COMM : **demand (for)** demande f (de) ; **in demand** demandé(e), recherché(e). <> vt **1.** [ask for - justice, money] réclamer ; [- explanation, apology] exiger ; **to demand to do sthg** exiger de faire qqch - **2.** [require] demander, exiger.

demanding [dɪ'mɑːndɪŋ] adj **1.** [exhausting] astreignant(e) - **2.** [not easily satisfied] exigeant(e).

demean [dɪ'miːn] vt : **to demean o.s.** s'abaisser.

demeaning [dɪ'miːnɪŋ] adj avilissant(e), dégradant(e).

demeanour UK, **demeanor** US [dɪ'miːnər] n (U) fml comportement m.

demented [dɪ'mentɪd] adj fou (folle), dément(e).

demise [dɪ'maɪz] n (U) décès m ; fig mort f, fin f.

demister [ˌdiː'mɪstər] n UK dispositif m antibuée.

demo ['deməʊ] (abbrev of **demonstration**) n UK inf manif f.

democracy [dɪ'mɒkrəsɪ] n démocratie f.

democrat ['deməkræt] n démocrate mf.
 ➤ **Democrat** n US démocrate mf.

democratic [ˌdemə'krætɪk] adj démocratique. ➤ **Democratic** adj US démocrate.

Democratic Party n US : **the Democratic Party** le Parti démocrate.

demolish [dɪ'mɒlɪʃ] vt [destroy] démolir.

demonstrate ['demənstreɪt] <> vt

1. [prove] démontrer, prouver - **2.** [machine, computer] faire une démonstration de. ◇ *vi* : **to demonstrate (for/against)** manifester (pour/contre).

demonstration [demən'streɪʃn] *n* **1.** [of machine, emotions] démonstration *f* - **2.** [public meeting] manifestation *f*.

demonstrator ['demənstreɪtər] *n* **1.** [in march] manifestant *m*, -e *f* - **2.** [of machine, product] démonstrateur *m*, -trice *f*.

demoralized [dɪ'mɒrəlaɪzd] *adj* démoralisé(e).

demote [ˌdiː'məʊt] *vt* rétrograder.

demure [dɪ'mjʊər] *adj* modeste, réservé(e).

den [den] *n* [of animal] antre *m*, tanière *f*.

denial [dɪ'naɪəl] *n* [of rights, facts, truth] dénégation *f* ; [of accusation] démenti *m* ; **in denial** en déni.

denier ['deniər] *n* denier *m*.

denigrate ['denigreit] *vt* dénigrer.

denim ['denim] *n* jean *m*. ◆ **denims** *npl* : **a pair of denims** un jean.

denim jacket *n* veste *f* en jean.

Denmark ['denmɑːk] *n* Danemark *m*.

denomination [dɪˌnɒmɪ'neɪʃn] *n* **1.** RELIG confession *f* - **2.** [money] valeur *f*.

denounce [dɪ'naʊns] *vt* dénoncer.

dense [dens] *adj* **1.** [crowd, forest] dense ; [fog] dense, épais(aisse) - **2.** *inf* [stupid] bouché(e).

density ['densətɪ] *n* densité *f*.

dent [dent] ◇ *n* bosse *f*. ◇ *vt* cabosser.

dental ['dentl] *adj* dentaire ; **dental appointment** rendez-vous *m* chez le dentiste.

dental floss *n* fil *m* dentaire.

dental hygienist *n* = **hygienist**.

dental surgeon *n* chirurgien-dentiste *m*.

dentist ['dentist] *n* dentiste *mf*.

dentures ['dentʃəz] *npl* dentier *m*.

deny [dɪ'naɪ] *vt* **1.** [refute] nier - **2.** *fml* [refuse] nier, refuser ; **to deny sb sthg** refuser qqch à qqn.

deodorant [diː'əʊdərənt] *n* déodorant *m*.

depart [dɪ'pɑːt] *vi fml* **1.** [leave] : **to depart (from)** partir (de) - **2.** [differ] : **to depart from sthg** s'écarter de qqch.

department [dɪ'pɑːtmənt] *n* **1.** [in organization] service *m* - **2.** [in shop] rayon *m* - **3.** SCH & UNIV département *m* - **4.** [in government] département *m*, ministère *m*.

department store *n* grand magasin *m*.

departure [dɪ'pɑːtʃər] *n* **1.** [leaving] départ *m* - **2.** [change] nouveau départ *m* ; **a departure from tradition** un écart par rapport à la tradition.

departure lounge *n* salle *f* d'embarquement.

depend [dɪ'pend] *vi* : **to depend on** [be dependent on] dépendre de ; [rely on] compter sur ; [emotionally] se reposer sur ; **it depends** cela dépend ; **depending on** selon.

dependable [dɪ'pendəbl] *adj* [person] sur qui on peut compter ; [source of income] sûr(e) ; [car] fiable.

dependant [dɪ'pendənt] *n* personne *f* à charge.

dependent [dɪ'pendənt] *adj* **1.** [reliant] : **dependent (on)** dépendant(e) (de) ; **to be dependent on sb/sthg** dépendre de qqn/qqch - **2.** [addicted] dépendant(e), accro - **3.** [contingent] : **to be dependent on** dépendre de.

depict [dɪ'pɪkt] *vt* **1.** [show in picture] représenter - **2.** [describe] : **to depict sb/sthg as** dépeindre qqn/qqch comme.

deplete [dɪ'pliːt] *vt* épuiser.

deplorable [dɪ'plɔːrəbl] *adj* déplorable.

deplore [dɪ'plɔːr] *vt* déplorer.

deploy [dɪ'plɔɪ] *vt* déployer.

depopulation [diːˌpɒpjʊ'leɪʃn] *n* dépeuplement *m*.

deport [dɪ'pɔːt] *vt* expulser.

depose [dɪ'pəʊz] *vt* déposer.

deposit [dɪ'pɒzɪt] ◇ *n* **1.** [gen] dépôt *m* ; **to make a deposit** [into bank account] déposer de l'argent - **2.** [payment - as guarantee] caution *f* ; [- as instalment] acompte *m* ; [- on bottle] consigne *f*. ◇ *vt* déposer.

deposit account *n* UK compte *m* sur livret.

depot ['depəʊ] *n* **1.** [gen] dépôt *m* - **2.** US [station] gare *f*.

depreciate [dɪ'priːʃɪeɪt] *vi* se déprécier.

depress [dɪ'pres] *vt* **1.** [sadden, discourage] déprimer - **2.** [weaken - economy] affaiblir ; [- prices] faire baisser.

depressed [dɪ'prest] *adj* **1.** [sad] déprimé(e) - **2.** [run-down - area] en déclin.

depressing [dɪ'presɪŋ] *adj* déprimant(e).

depression [dɪ'preʃn] *n* **1.** [gen] dépression *f* - **2.** [sadness] tristesse *f*.

deprivation [ˌdeprɪ'veɪʃn] *n* privation *f*.

deprive [dɪ'praɪv] *vt* : **to deprive sb of sthg** priver qqn de qqch.

depth [depθ] *n* profondeur *f* ; **in depth** [study, analyse] en profondeur ; **to be out of one's depth** [in water] ne pas avoir pied ; *fig* avoir perdu pied, être dépassé. ◆ **depths** *npl* : **the depths** [of seas] les profondeurs *fpl* ; [of memory, archives] le fin fond ; **in the depths of winter** au cœur de l'hiver ; **to be in the depths of despair** toucher le fond du désespoir.

deputation [ˌdepjʊ'teɪʃn] *n* délégation *f*.

deputize

deputize, *UK* **-ise** ['depjʊtaɪz] *vi* : **to deputize for sb** assurer les fonctions de qqn, remplacer qqn.

deputy ['depjʊtɪ] <> *adj* adjoint(e) ; **deputy chairman** vice-président *m* ; **deputy head** SCH directeur *m* adjoint ; **deputy leader** POL vice-président *m*. <> *n* **1.** [second-in-command] adjoint *m*, -e *f* - **2.** *US* [deputy sheriff] shérif *m* adjoint.

derail [dɪ'reɪl] *vt* [train] faire dérailler.

deranged [dɪ'reɪndʒd] *adj* dérangé(e).

derby [*UK* 'dɑːbɪ, *US* 'dɜːbɪ] *n* **1.** SPORT derby *m* - **2.** *US* [hat] chapeau *m* melon.

derelict ['derɪlɪkt] *adj* en ruines.

deride [dɪ'raɪd] *vt* railler.

derisory [də'raɪzərɪ] *adj* **1.** [puny, trivial] dérisoire - **2.** [derisive] moqueur(euse).

derivative [dɪ'rɪvətɪv] <> *adj pej* pas original(e). <> *n* dérivé *m*.

derive [dɪ'raɪv] <> *vt* **1.** [draw, gain] : **to derive sthg from sthg** tirer qqch de qqch - **2.** [originate] : **to be derived from** venir de. <> *vi* : **to derive from** venir de.

derogatory [dɪ'rɒgətrɪ] *adj* [comment, remark] désobligeant(e) ; [word] péjoratif(ive).

derv [dɜːv] *n UK* gas-oil *m*.

descend [dɪ'send] <> *vt fml* [go down] descendre. <> *vi* **1.** *fml* [go down] descendre - **2.** [fall] : **to descend (on)** [enemy] s'abattre (sur) ; [subj: silence, gloom] tomber (sur) - **3.** [stoop] : **to descend to sthg/to doing sthg** s'abaisser à qqch/à faire qqch.

descendant [dɪ'sendənt] *n* descendant *m*, -e *f*.

descended [dɪ'sendɪd] *adj* : **to be descended from sb** descendre de qqn.

descent [dɪ'sent] *n* **1.** [downwards movement] descente *f* - **2.** [origin] origine *f*.

describe [dɪ'skraɪb] *vt* décrire.

description [dɪ'skrɪpʃn] *n* **1.** [account] description *f* - **2.** [type] sorte *f*, genre *m*.

desecrate ['desɪkreɪt] *vt* profaner.

desert <> *n* ['dezət] désert *m*. <> *vt* [dɪ'zɜːt] **1.** [place] déserter - **2.** [person, group] déserter, abandonner. <> *vi* [dɪ'zɜːt] MIL déserter. **deserts** *npl* [dɪ'zɜːts] : **to get one's just deserts** recevoir ce que l'on mérite.

deserted [dɪ'zɜːtɪd] *adj* désert(e).

deserter [dɪ'zɜːtər] *n* déserteur *m*.

desert island ['dezət-] *n* île *f* déserte.

deserve [dɪ'zɜːv] *vt* mériter ; **to deserve to do sthg** mériter de faire qqch.

deserving [dɪ'zɜːvɪŋ] *adj* [person] méritant(e) ; [cause, charity] méritoire.

design [dɪ'zaɪn] <> *n* **1.** [plan, drawing] plan *m*, étude *f* - **2.** (U) [art] design *m*

- **3.** [pattern] motif *m*, dessin *m* - **4.** [shape] ligne *f* ; [of dress] style *m* - **5.** *fml* [intention] dessein *m* ; **by design** à dessein ; **to have designs on sb/sthg** avoir des desseins sur qqn/qqch. <> *vt* **1.** [draw plans for - building, car] faire les plans de, dessiner ; [- dress] créer - **2.** [plan] concevoir, mettre au point ; **to be designed for sthg/to do sthg** être conçu pour qqch/pour faire qqch.

designate <> *adj* ['dezɪgnət] désigné(e). <> *vt* ['dezɪgneɪt] désigner.

designer [dɪ'zaɪnər] <> *adj* de marque. <> *n* INDUST concepteur *m*, -trice *f* ; ARCHIT dessinateur *m*, -trice *f* ; [of dresses etc] styliste *mf* ; THEAT décorateur *m*, -trice *f*.

desirable [dɪ'zaɪərəbl] *adj* **1.** [enviable, attractive] désirable - **2.** *fml* [appropriate] désirable, souhaitable.

desire [dɪ'zaɪər] <> *n* désir *m* ; **desire for sthg/to do sthg** désir de qqch/de faire qqch. <> *vt* désirer.

desist [dɪ'zɪst] *vi fml* : **to desist (from doing sthg)** cesser (de faire qqch).

desk [desk] *n* bureau *m* ; **reception desk** réception *f* ; **information desk** bureau *m* de renseignements.

desktop publishing *n* publication *f* assistée par ordinateur.

desolate ['desələt] *adj* **1.** [place] abandonné(e) - **2.** [person] désespéré(e), désolé(e).

despair [dɪ'speər] <> *n* (U) désespoir *m*. <> *vi* désespérer ; **to despair of** désespérer de ; **to despair of doing sthg** désespérer de faire qqch.

despairing [dɪ'speərɪŋ] *adj* de désespoir.

despatch [dɪ'spætʃ] *UK* = **dispatch**.

desperate ['desprət] *adj* désespéré(e) ; **to be desperate for sthg** avoir absolument besoin de qqch.

desperately ['desprətlɪ] *adv* désespérément ; **desperately ill** gravement malade.

desperation [,despə'reɪʃn] *n* désespoir *m* ; **he agreed in desperation** en désespoir de cause, il a accepté.

despicable [dɪ'spɪkəbl] *adj* ignoble.

despise [dɪ'spaɪz] *vt* [person] mépriser ; [racism] exécrer.

despite [dɪ'spaɪt] *prep* malgré.

despondent [dɪ'spɒndənt] *adj* abattu(e), consterné(e).

dessert [dɪ'zɜːt] *n* dessert *m*.

dessertspoon [dɪ'zɜːtspuːn] *n* [spoon] cuillère *f* à dessert.

destination [,destɪ'neɪʃn] *n* destination *f*.

destined [dɪ'stɪnd] *adj* **1.** [intended] : **destined for** destiné(e) à ; **destined to do sthg** destiné à faire qqch - **2.** [bound] : **destined for** à destination de.

destiny ['destɪnɪ] n destinée f.

destitute ['destɪtjuːt] adj indigent(e).

de-stress [diː'stres] n dé-stresser inf.

destroy [dɪ'strɔɪ] vt [ruin] détruire.

destruction [dɪ'strʌkʃn] n destruction f.

detach [dɪ'tætʃ] vt 1. [pull off] détacher ; to detach sthg from sthg détacher qqch de qqch - 2. [dissociate] : to detach o.s. from sthg [from reality] se détacher de qqch ; [from proceedings, discussions] s'écarter de qqch.

detached [dɪ'tætʃt] adj [unemotional] détaché(e).

detached house n UK maison f individuelle.

detachment [dɪ'tætʃmənt] n détachement m.

detail ['diːteɪl] <> n 1. [small point] détail m ; to go into detail entrer dans les détails ; in detail en détail - 2. MIL détachement m. <> vt [list] détailler. **details** npl [personal information] coordonnées fpl.

detailed ['diːteɪld] adj détaillé(e).

detain [dɪ'teɪn] vt 1. [in police station] détenir ; [in hospital] garder - 2. [delay] retenir.

detect [dɪ'tekt] vt 1. [subj: person] déceler - 2. [subj: machine] détecter.

detection [dɪ'tekʃn] n (U) 1. [of crime] dépistage m - 2. [of aircraft, submarine] détection f.

detective [dɪ'tektɪv] n détective mf.

detective novel n roman m policier.

detention [dɪ'tenʃn] n 1. [of suspect, criminal] détention f - 2. SCH retenue f.

deter [dɪ'tɜːr] vt dissuader ; to deter sb from doing sthg dissuader qqn de faire qqch.

detergent [dɪ'tɜːdʒənt] n détergent m.

deteriorate [dɪ'tɪərɪəreɪt] vi se détériorer.

determination [dɪˌtɜːmɪ'neɪʃn] n détermination f.

determine [dɪ'tɜːmɪn] vt 1. [establish, control] déterminer - 2. fml [decide] : to determine to do sthg décider de faire qqch.

determined [dɪ'tɜːmɪnd] adj 1. [person] déterminé(e) ; determined to do sthg déterminé à faire qqch - 2. [effort] obstiné(e).

deterrent [dɪ'terənt] n moyen m de dissuasion.

detest [dɪ'test] vt détester.

detonate ['detəneɪt] <> vt faire détoner. <> vi détoner.

detour ['diːˌtuər] <> n détour m. <> vi faire un détour. <> vt (faire) dévier.

detract [dɪ'trækt] vi : to detract from diminuer.

detriment ['detrɪmənt] n : to the detriment of au détriment de.

detrimental [ˌdetrɪ'mentl] adj préjudiciable.

deuce [djuːs] n TENNIS égalité f.

devaluation [ˌdiːvæljʊ'eɪʃn] n dévaluation f.

devastated ['devəsteɪtɪd] adj 1. [area, city] dévasté(e) - 2. fig [person] accablé(e).

devastating ['devəsteɪtɪŋ] adj 1. [hurricane, remark] dévastateur(trice) - 2. [upsetting] accablant(e) - 3. [attractive] irrésistible.

develop [dɪ'veləp] <> vt 1. [gen] développer - 2. [land, area] aménager, développer - 3. [illness, fault, habit] contracter - 4. [resources] développer, exploiter. <> vi 1. [grow, advance] se développer - 2. [appear - problem, trouble] se déclarer.

developing country [dɪ'veləpɪŋ-] n pays m en voie de développement.

development [dɪ'veləpmənt] n 1. [gen] développement m - 2. (U) [of land, area] exploitation f - 3. [land being developed] zone f d'aménagement ; [developed area] zone aménagée - 4. [group of buildings] lotissement m - 5. (U) [of illness, fault] évolution f.

deviate ['diːvɪeɪt] vi : to deviate (from) dévier (de), s'écarter (de).

device [dɪ'vaɪs] n 1. [apparatus] appareil m, dispositif m - 2. [plan, method] moyen m.

devil ['devl] n 1. [evil spirit] diable m - 2. inf [person] type m ; poor devil! pauvre diable! - 3. [for emphasis] : who/where/why the devil...? qui/où/pourquoi diable...? **Devil** n [Satan] : the Devil le Diable.

devious ['diːvjəs] adj 1. [dishonest - person] retors(e), sournois(e) ; [- scheme, means] détourné(e) - 2. [tortuous] tortueux(euse).

devise [dɪ'vaɪz] vt concevoir.

devoid [dɪ'vɔɪd] adj fml : devoid of dépourvu(e) de, dénué(e) de.

devolution [ˌdiːvə'luːʃn] n POL décentralisation f.

devote [dɪ'vəʊt] vt : to devote sthg to sthg consacrer qqch à qqch.

devoted [dɪ'vəʊtɪd] adj dévoué(e) ; a devoted mother une mère dévouée à ses enfants.

devotee [ˌdevə'tiː] n [fan] passionné m, -e f.

devotion [dɪ'vəʊʃn] n 1. [commitment] : devotion (to) dévouement m (à) - 2. RELIG dévotion f.

devour [dɪ'vaʊər] vt lit & fig dévorer.

devout [dɪ'vaʊt] adj dévot(e).

dew [djuː] n rosée f.

diabetes [ˌdaɪə'biːtiːz] n diabète m.

diabetic [ˌdaɪəˈbetɪk] <> *adj* [person] diabétique. <> *n* diabétique *mf*.

diabolic(al) [ˌdaɪəˈbɒlɪk(l)] *adj* **1.** [evil] diabolique - **2.** *inf* [very bad] atroce.

diagnose [ˈdaɪəgnəʊz] *vt* diagnostiquer.

diagnosis [ˌdaɪəgˈnəʊsɪs] (*pl* -**ses** [-siːz]) *n* diagnostic *m*.

diagonal [daɪˈægənl] <> *adj* [line] diagonal(e). <> *n* diagonale *f*.

diagram [ˈdaɪəgræm] *n* diagramme *m*.

dial [ˈdaɪəl] <> *n* cadran *m* ; [of radio] cadran de fréquences. <> *vt* (*UK & US*) [number] composer.

dialect [ˈdaɪəlekt] *n* dialecte *m*.

dialling code [ˈdaɪəlɪŋ-] *n UK* indicatif *m*.

dialling tone *UK* [ˈdaɪəlɪŋ-], **dial tone** *US* *n* tonalité *f*.

dialogue *UK*, **dialog** *US* [ˈdaɪəlɒg] *n* dialogue *m*.

dial tone *US* = **dialling tone**.

dialysis [daɪˈælɪsɪs] *n* dialyse *f*.

diameter [daɪˈæmɪtər] *n* diamètre *m*.

diamond [ˈdaɪəmənd] *n* **1.** [gem] diamant *m* - **2.** [shape] losange *m*. ◆ **diamonds** *npl* carreau *m*.

diaper [ˈdaɪəpər] *n US* couche *f*.

diaphragm [ˈdaɪəfræm] *n* diaphragme *m*.

diarrhoea *UK*, **diarrhea** *US* [ˌdaɪəˈrɪə] *n* diarrhée *f*.

diary [ˈdaɪərɪ] *n* **1.** [appointment book] agenda *m* - **2.** [journal] journal *m*.

dice [daɪs] <> *n* (*pl* **dice**) [for games] dé *m*. <> *vt* couper en dés.

dictate [dɪkˈteɪt OR ˈdɪkteɪt] <> *vt* [dɪkˈteɪt] dicter. <> *n* [ˈdɪkteɪt] ordre *m*.

dictation [dɪkˈteɪʃn] *n* dictée *f*.

dictator [dɪkˈteɪtər] *n* dictateur *m*.

dictatorship [dɪkˈteɪtəʃɪp] *n* dictature *f*.

dictionary [ˈdɪkʃənrɪ] *n* dictionnaire *m*.

did [dɪd] *pt* ➤ **do**.

diddle [ˈdɪdl] *vt inf* escroquer, rouler.

didn't [ˈdɪdnt] *abbrev of* **did not**.

die [daɪ] <> *vi* (*pt & pp* **died**, *cont* **dying**) mourir ; **to be dying** se mourir ; **to be dying to do sthg** mourir d'envie de faire qqch ; **to be dying for a drink/cigarette** mourir d'envie de boire un verre/de fumer une cigarette. <> *n* (*pl* **dice** [daɪs]) [dice] dé *m*. ◆ **die away** *vi* [sound] s'éteindre ; [wind] tomber. ◆ **die down** *vi* [sound] s'affaiblir ; [wind] tomber ; [fire] baisser. ◆ **die out** *vi* s'éteindre, disparaître.

diehard [ˈdaɪhɑːd] *n* : **to be a diehard** être coriace ; [reactionary] être réactionnaire.

diesel [ˈdiːzl] *n* diesel *m*.

diesel engine *n* AUT moteur *m* diesel ; RAIL locomotive *f* diesel.

diesel fuel, **diesel oil** *n* diesel *m*.

diet [ˈdaɪət] <> *n* **1.** [eating pattern] alimentation *f* - **2.** [to lose weight] régime *m* ; **to be on a diet** être au régime ; **to go on a diet** faire OR suivre un régime. <> *comp* [low-calorie] de régime. <> *vi* faire OR suivre un régime.

differ [ˈdɪfər] *vi* **1.** [be different] être différent(e), différer ; [people] être différent ; **to differ from** être différent de - **2.** [disagree] : **to differ with sb (about sthg)** ne pas être d'accord avec qqn (à propos de qqch).

difference [ˈdɪfrəns] *n* différence *f* ; **it doesn't make any difference** cela ne change rien.

different [ˈdɪfrənt] *adj* : **different (from)** différent(e) (de).

differentiate [ˌdɪfəˈrenʃɪeɪt] <> *vt* : **to differentiate sthg from sthg** différencier qqch de qqch, faire la différence entre qqch et qqch. <> *vi* : **to differentiate (between)** faire la différence (entre).

difficult [ˈdɪfɪkəlt] *adj* difficile.

difficulty [ˈdɪfɪkəltɪ] *n* difficulté *f* ; **to have difficulty in doing sthg** avoir de la difficulté OR du mal à faire qqch.

diffident [ˈdɪfɪdənt] *adj* [person] qui manque d'assurance ; [manner, voice, approach] hésitant(e).

diffuse *vt* [dɪˈfjuːz] diffuser, répandre.

dig [dɪg] <> *vi* (*pt & pp* **dug**) **1.** [in ground] creuser - **2.** [subj: belt, strap] : **to dig into sb** couper qqn. <> *vt* (*pt & pp* **dug**) **1.** [hole] creuser - **2.** [garden] bêcher. <> *n* **1.** *fig* [unkind remark] pique *f* - **2.** ARCHEOL fouilles *fpl*. ◆ **dig out** *vt sep inf* [find] dénicher. ◆ **dig up** *vt sep* **1.** [from ground] déterrer ; [potatoes] arracher - **2.** *inf* [information] dénicher.

digest <> *n* [ˈdaɪdʒest] résumé *m*, digest *m*. <> *vt* [dɪˈdʒest] *lit & fig* digérer.

digestion [dɪˈdʒestʃn] *n* digestion *f*.

digestive biscuit [daɪˈdʒestɪv-] *n UK* ≃ sablé *m* (à la farine complète).

digit [ˈdɪdʒɪt] *n* **1.** [figure] chiffre *m* - **2.** [finger] doigt *m* ; [toe] orteil *m*.

digital [ˈdɪdʒɪtl] *adj* numérique.

digital camera *n* appareil *m* photo numérique.

digital radio *n* radio *f* numérique.

digital television *n* [technique] télévision *f* numérique.

dignified [ˈdɪgnɪfaɪd] *adj* digne, plein(e) de dignité.

dignity [ˈdɪgnətɪ] *n* dignité *f*.

digress [daɪ'gres] *vi* : to digress (from) s'écarter (de).

digs [dɪgz] *npl* UK *inf* piaule *f*.

dike [daɪk] *n* 1. [wall, bank] digue *f* - 2. *inf offens* [lesbian] gouine *f*.

dilapidated [dɪ'læpɪdeɪtɪd] *adj* délabré(e).

dilate [daɪ'leɪt] <> *vt* dilater. <> *vi* se dilater.

dilemma [dɪ'lemə] *n* dilemme *m*.

diligent ['dɪlɪdʒənt] *adj* appliqué(e).

dilute [daɪ'luːt] <> *adj* dilué(e). <> *vt* : to dilute sthg (with) diluer qqch (avec).

dim [dɪm] <> *adj* 1. [dark - light] faible ; [- room] sombre - 2. [indistinct - memory, outline] vague - 3. [weak - eyesight] faible - 4. *inf* [stupid] borné(e). <> *vt & vi* baisser.

dime [daɪm] *n* US (pièce *f* de) dix cents *mpl*.

dimension [dɪ'menʃn] *n* dimension *f*.

diminish [dɪ'mɪnɪʃ] *vt & vi* diminuer.

diminutive [dɪ'mɪnjʊtɪv] *fml* <> *adj* minuscule. <> *n* GRAM diminutif *m*.

dimmers ['dɪmərz] *npl* US [dipped headlights] phares *mpl* code (*inv*) ; [parking lights] feux *mpl* de position.

dimmer (switch) ['dɪmər-] *n* 1. variateur *m* de lumière - 2. US = dipswitch.

dimple ['dɪmpl] *n* fossette *f*.

din [dɪn] *n inf* barouf *m*.

dine [daɪn] *vi fml* dîner. ◆ **dine out** *vi* dîner dehors.

diner ['daɪnər] *n* 1. [person] dîneur *m*, -euse *f* - 2. US [café] petit restaurant *m* sans façon.

dinghy ['dɪŋgɪ] *n* [for sailing] dériveur *m* ; [for rowing] (petit) canot *m*.

dingy ['dɪndʒɪ] *adj* [shabby] miteux(euse) ; [dirty] douteux(euse) ; [colour] terne.

dining car ['daɪnɪŋ-] *n* wagon-restaurant *m*.

dining room ['daɪnɪŋ-] *n* 1. [in house] salle *f* à manger - 2. [in hotel] restaurant *m*.

dinner ['dɪnər] *n* dîner *m*.

dinner jacket *n* smoking *m*.

dinner party *n* dîner *m* (sur invitation).

dinnertime ['dɪnətaɪm] *n* heure *f* du dîner.

dinosaur ['daɪnəsɔːr] *n* dinosaure *m*.

dint [dɪnt] *n fml* : by dint of à force de.

dip [dɪp] *n* 1. [in road, ground] déclivité *f* - 2. [sauce] sauce *f*, dip *m* - 3. [swim] baignade *f* (rapide) ; to go for a dip aller se baigner en vitesse, aller faire trempette. <> *vt* 1. [into liquid] : to dip sthg in OR into tremper OR plonger qqch dans - 2. UK AUT : to dip one's headlights se mettre en code. <> *vi* 1. [sun] baisser, descendre à l'horizon ; [wing] plonger - 2. [road, ground] descendre.

diploma [dɪ'pləʊmə] (*pl* -s) *n* diplôme *m*.

diplomacy [dɪ'pləʊməsɪ] *n* diplomatie *f*.

diplomat ['dɪpləmæt] *n* diplomate *m*.

diplomatic [,dɪplə'mætɪk] *adj* 1. [service] diplomatique - 2. [tactful] diplomate.

dipstick ['dɪpstɪk] *n* AUT jauge *f* (de niveau d'huile).

dire ['daɪər] *adj* [need, consequences] extrême ; [warning] funeste ; in dire straits dans une situation désespérée.

direct [dɪ'rekt] <> *adj* direct(e) ; [challenge] manifeste. <> *vt* 1. [gen] diriger - 2. [aim] : to direct sthg at sb [question, remark] adresser qqch à qqn ; the campaign is directed at teenagers cette campagne vise les adolescents - 3. CIN, RADIO & TV [film, programme] réaliser ; [actors] diriger ; THEAT [play] mettre en scène - 4. [order] : to direct sb to do sthg ordonner à qqn de faire qqch. <> *adv* directement.

direct current *n* courant *m* continu.

direct debit *n* UK prélèvement *m* automatique.

direction [dɪ'rekʃn] *n* direction *f*. ◆ **directions** *npl* 1. [to find a place] indications *fpl* - 2. [for use] instructions *fpl*.

directly [dɪ'rektlɪ] *adv* 1. [in straight line] directement - 2. [honestly, clearly] sans détours - 3. [exactly - behind, above] exactement - 4. [immediately] immédiatement - 5. [very soon] tout de suite.

director [dɪ'rektər] *n* 1. [of company] directeur *m*, -trice *f* - 2. THEAT metteur *m* en scène ; CIN & TV réalisateur *m*, -trice *f*.

directory [dɪ'rektərɪ] *n* 1. [annual publication] annuaire *m* - 2. COMPUT répertoire *m*.

directory enquiries UK, **directory assistance** US *n* (service *m* des) renseignements *mpl* téléphoniques.

dirt [dɜːt] *n* (U) 1. [mud, dust] saleté *f* - 2. [earth] terre *f*.

dirty ['dɜːtɪ] <> *adj* 1. [not clean, not fair] sale - 2. [smutty - language, person] grossier(ère) ; [- book, joke] cochon(onne). <> *vt* salir.

disability [,dɪsə'bɪlətɪ] *n* infirmité *f* ; people with disabilities les handicapés.

disabled [dɪs'eɪbld] <> *adj* [person] handicapé(e), infirme. <> *npl* : the disabled les handicapés, les infirmes.

disadvantage [,dɪsəd'vɑːntɪdʒ] *n* désavantage *m*, inconvénient *m* ; to be at a disadvantage être désavantagé.

disadvantaged [,dɪsəd'vɑːntɪdʒd] *adj* défavorisé(e).

disagree [,dɪsə'griː] *vi* 1. [have different opinions] : to disagree (with) ne pas être d'accord (avec) - **2.** [differ] ne pas concorder - **3.** [subj: food, drink] : **to disagree with sb** ne pas réussir à qqn.

disagreeable [ˌdɪsəˈgriːəbl] *adj* désagréable.

disagreement [ˌdɪsəˈgriːmənt] *n* **1.** [in opinion] désaccord *m* - **2.** [argument] différend *m*.

disallow [ˌdɪsəˈlaʊ] *vt* **1.** *fml* [appeal, claim] rejeter - **2.** [goal] refuser.

disappear [ˌdɪsəˈpɪər] *vi* disparaître.

disappearance [ˌdɪsəˈpɪərəns] *n* disparition *f*.

disappoint [ˌdɪsəˈpɔɪnt] *vt* décevoir.

disappointed [ˌdɪsəˈpɔɪntɪd] *adj* : **disappointed (in OR with)** déçu(e) (par).

disappointing [ˌdɪsəˈpɔɪntɪŋ] *adj* décevant(e).

disappointment [ˌdɪsəˈpɔɪntmənt] *n* déception *f*.

disapproval [ˌdɪsəˈpruːvl] *n* désapprobation *f*.

disapprove [ˌdɪsəˈpruːv] *vi* : **to disapprove of sb/sthg** désapprouver qqn/qqch.

disarm [dɪsˈɑːm] *vt & vi lit & fig* désarmer.

disarmament [dɪsˈɑːməmənt] *n* désarmement *m*.

disarray [ˌdɪsəˈreɪ] *n* : **in disarray** en désordre ; [government] en pleine confusion.

disaster [dɪˈzɑːstər] *n* **1.** [damaging event] catastrophe *f* - **2.** *(U)* [misfortune] échec *m*, désastre *m* - **3.** *inf* [failure] désastre *m*.

disastrous [dɪˈzɑːstrəs] *adj* désastreux(euse).

disband [dɪsˈbænd] <> *vt* [organization] dissoudre. <> *vi* [organization] se dissoudre.

disbelief [ˌdɪsbɪˈliːf] *n* : **in OR with disbelief** avec incrédulité.

disc *UK*, **disk** *US* [dɪsk] *n* disque *m*.

discard [dɪsˈkɑːd] *vt* mettre au rebut.

discern [dɪˈsɜːn] *vt* discerner, distinguer.

discerning [dɪˈsɜːnɪŋ] *adj* judicieux(euse).

discharge <> *n* [ˈdɪstʃɑːdʒ] **1.** [of patient] autorisation *f* de sortie, décharge *f* ; LAW relaxe *f* ; **to get one's discharge** MIL être rendu à la vie civile - **2.** [emission - of smoke] émission *f* ; [- of sewage] déversement *m* ; MED écoulement *m*. <> *vt* [dɪsˈtʃɑːdʒ] **1.** [allow to leave - patient] signer la décharge de ; [- prisoner, defendant] relaxer ; [- soldier] rendre à la vie civile - **2.** *fml* [fulfil] assumer - **3.** [emit - smoke] émettre ; [- sewage, chemicals] déverser.

disciple [dɪˈsaɪpl] *n* disciple *m*.

discipline [ˈdɪsɪplɪn] <> *n* discipline *f*. <> *vt* **1.** [control] discipliner - **2.** [punish] punir.

disc jockey *n* disc-jockey *m*.

disclaim [dɪsˈkleɪm] *vt fml* nier.

disclose [dɪsˈkləʊz] *vt* révéler, divulguer.

disclosure [dɪsˈkləʊʒər] *n* révélation *f*, divulgation *f*.

disco [ˈdɪskəʊ] *(pl -s)* *(abbrev of* **discotheque)** *n* discothèque *f*.

discomfort [dɪsˈkʌmfət] *n* **1.** *(U)* [physical pain] douleur *f* - **2.** *(U)* [anxiety, embarrassment] malaise *m*.

disconcert [ˌdɪskənˈsɜːt] *vt* déconcerter.

disconnect [ˌdɪskəˈnekt] *vt* **1.** [detach] détacher - **2.** [from gas, electricity - appliance] débrancher ; [- house] couper - **3.** TELEC couper.

disconsolate [dɪsˈkɒnsələt] *adj* triste, inconsolable.

discontent [ˌdɪskənˈtent] *n* : **discontent (with)** mécontentement *m* (à propos de).

discontented [ˌdɪskənˈtentɪd] *adj* mécontent(e).

discontinue [ˌdɪskənˈtɪnjuː] *vt* cesser, interrompre.

discord [ˈdɪskɔːd] *n* **1.** *(U)* [disagreement] discorde *f*, désaccord *m* - **2.** MUS dissonance *f*.

discotheque [ˈdɪskəʊtek] *n* discothèque *f*.

discount <> *n* [ˈdɪskaʊnt] remise *f*. <> *vt* [*UK* dɪsˈkaʊnt, *US* ˈdɪskaʊnt] [report, claim] ne pas tenir compte de.

discourage [dɪsˈkʌrɪdʒ] *vt* décourager ; **to discourage sb from doing sthg** dissuader qqn de faire qqch.

discover [dɪsˈkʌvər] *vt* découvrir.

discovery [dɪsˈkʌvəri] *n* découverte *f*.

discredit [dɪsˈkredɪt] <> *n* discrédit *m*. <> *vt* discréditer.

discreet [dɪˈskriːt] *adj* discret(ète).

discrepancy [dɪˈskrepənsɪ] *n* : **discrepancy (in/between)** divergence *f* (entre).

discretion [dɪˈskreʃn] *n* *(U)* **1.** [tact] discrétion *f* - **2.** [judgment] jugement *m*, discernement *m* ; **at the discretion of** à la discrétion de.

discriminate [dɪˈskrɪmɪneɪt] *vi* **1.** [distinguish] différencier, distinguer ; **to discriminate between** faire la distinction entre - **2.** [be prejudiced] : **to discriminate against sb** faire de la discrimination envers qqn.

discriminating [dɪˈskrɪmɪneɪtɪŋ] *adj* judicieux(ieuse).

discrimination [dɪˌskrɪmɪˈneɪʃn] *n* **1.** [prejudice] discrimination *f* - **2.** [judgment] discernement *m*, jugement *m*.

discus [ˈdɪskəs] *(pl -es* [-iːz]*)* *n* disque *m*.

discuss [dɪsˈkʌs] *vt* discuter (de) ; **to discuss sthg with sb** discuter de qqch avec qqn.

discussion [dɪ'skʌʃn] *n* discussion *f*; **under discussion** en discussion.

disdain [dɪs'deɪn] *n* : **disdain (for)** dédain *m* (pour).

disease [dɪ'ziːz] *n* [illness] maladie *f*.

disembark [ˌdɪsɪm'bɑːk] *vi* débarquer.

disenchanted [ˌdɪsɪn'tʃɑːntɪd] *adj* : **disenchanted (with)** désenchanté(e) (de).

disengage [ˌdɪsɪn'geɪdʒ] *vt* **1.** [release] : **to disengage sthg (from)** libérer OR dégager qqch (de) - **2.** TECH déclencher ; **to disengage the gears** débrayer.

disfavour UK, **disfavor** US [dɪs'feɪvər] *n* [dislike, disapproval] désapprobation *f*.

disfigure [dɪs'fɪɡər] *vt* défigurer.

disgrace [dɪs'ɡreɪs] ◇ *n* **1.** [shame] honte *f* ; **to bring disgrace on sb** jeter la honte sur qqn ; **in disgrace** en défaveur - **2.** [cause of shame - thing] honte *f*, scandale *m* ; [- person] honte *f*. ◇ *vt* faire honte à ; **to disgrace o.s.** se couvrir de honte.

disgraceful [dɪs'ɡreɪsful] *adj* honteux(euse), scandaleux(euse).

disgruntled [dɪs'ɡrʌntld] *adj* mécontent(e).

disguise [dɪs'ɡaɪz] ◇ *n* déguisement *m* ; **in disguise** déguisé(e). ◇ *vt* **1.** [person, voice] déguiser - **2.** [hide - fact, feelings] dissimuler.

disgust [dɪs'ɡʌst] ◇ *n* : **disgust (at)** [behaviour, violence etc] dégoût *m* (pour) ; [decision] dégoût (devant). ◇ *vt* dégoûter, écœurer.

disgusting [dɪs'ɡʌstɪŋ] *adj* dégoûtant(e).

dish [dɪʃ] *n* plat *m* ; US [plate] assiette *f*. **dishes** *npl* vaisselle *f* ; **to do** OR **wash the dishes** faire la vaisselle. **dish out** *vt sep inf* distribuer. **dish up** *vt sep inf* servir.

dish aerial UK, **dish antenna** US *n* antenne *f* parabolique.

dishcloth ['dɪʃklɒθ] *n* lavette *f*.

disheartened [dɪs'hɑːtnd] *adj* découragé(e).

dishevelled UK, **disheveled** US [dɪ'ʃevəld] *adj* [person] échevelé(e) ; [hair] en désordre.

dishonest [dɪs'ɒnɪst] *adj* malhonnête.

dishonour UK, **dishonor** US [dɪs'ɒnər] ◇ *n* déshonneur *m*. ◇ *vt* déshonorer.

dishonourable UK, **dishonorable** US [dɪs'ɒnərəbl] *adj* [person] peu honorable ; [behaviour] déshonorant(e).

dishtowel ['dɪʃtaʊəl] *n* torchon *m*.

dishwasher ['dɪʃˌwɒʃər] *n* [machine] lave-vaisselle *m inv*.

dish(washing) soap *n* US liquide *m* pour la vaisselle.

disillusioned [ˌdɪsɪ'luːʒnd] *adj* désillusionné(e), désenchanté(e) ; **to be disillusioned with** ne plus avoir d'illusions sur.

disincentive [ˌdɪsɪn'sentɪv] *n* : **to be a disincentive** avoir un effet dissuasif ; [in work context] être démotivant(e).

disinclined [ˌdɪsɪn'klaɪnd] *adj* : **to be disinclined to do sthg** être peu disposé(e) à faire qqch.

disinfect [ˌdɪsɪn'fekt] *vt* désinfecter.

disinfectant [ˌdɪsɪn'fektənt] *n* désinfectant *m*.

disintegrate [dɪs'ɪntɪɡreɪt] *vi* [object] se désintégrer, se désagréger.

disinterested [ˌdɪs'ɪntrəstɪd] *adj* **1.** [objective] désintéressé(e) - **2.** [uninterested] : **disinterested (in)** indifférent(e) (à).

disjointed [dɪs'dʒɔɪntɪd] *adj* décousu(e).

disk [dɪsk] *n* **1.** COMPUT disque *m*, disquette *f* - **2.** US = **disc**.

disk drive *n* COMPUT lecteur *m* de disques OR de disquettes.

diskette [dɪs'ket] *n* COMPUT disquette *f*.

dislike [dɪs'laɪk] ◇ *n* : **dislike (of)** aversion *f* (pour) ; **to take a dislike to sb/sthg** prendre qqn/qqch en grippe. ◇ *vt* ne pas aimer.

dislocate ['dɪsləkeɪt] *vt* **1.** MED se démettre - **2.** [disrupt - plans] désorganiser, perturber.

dislodge [dɪs'lɒdʒ] *vt* : **to dislodge sthg (from)** déplacer qqch (de) ; [free] décoincer qqch (de).

disloyal [ˌdɪs'lɔɪəl] *adj* : **disloyal (to)** déloyal(e) (envers).

dismal ['dɪzml] *adj* **1.** [gloomy, depressing] lugubre - **2.** [unsuccessful - attempt] infructueux(euse) ; [- failure] lamentable.

dismantle [dɪs'mæntl] *vt* démanteler.

dismay [dɪs'meɪ] ◇ *n* consternation *f*. ◇ *vt* consterner.

dismiss [dɪs'mɪs] *vt* **1.** [from job] : **to dismiss sb (from)** congédier qqn (de) - **2.** [refuse to take seriously - idea, person] écarter ; [- plan, challenge] rejeter - **3.** [allow to leave - class] laisser sortir ; [- troops] faire rompre les rangs à - **4.** LAW [hung jury] dissoudre ; **to dismiss a charge** [judge] rendre une ordonnance de non-lieu ; **case dismissed!** affaire classée!

dismissal [dɪs'mɪsl] *n* **1.** [from job] licenciement *m*, renvoi *m* - **2.** [refusal to take seriously] rejet *m*.

dismount [ˌdɪs'maʊnt] *vi* : **to dismount (from)** descendre (de).

disobedience [ˌdɪsə'biːdjəns] *n* désobéissance *f*.

disobedient [ˌdɪsə'biːdjənt] *adj* désobéissant(e).

disobey [,dısə'beı] *vt* désobéir à.

disorder [dıs'ɔːdər] *n* **1.** [disarray] : **in disorder** en désordre - **2.** (U) [rioting] troubles *mpl* - **3.** MED trouble *m*.

disorderly [dıs'ɔːdəlı] *adj* **1.** [untidy - room] en désordre ; [- appearance] désordonné(e) - **2.** [unruly] indiscipliné(e).

disorganized, UK **-ised** [dıs'ɔːgənaızd] *adj* [person] désordonné(e), brouillon(onne) ; [system] mal conçu(e).

disoriented [dıs'ɔːrıəntıd], **disorientated** UK [dıs'ɔːrıənteıtıd] *adj* désorienté(e).

disown [dıs'əun] *vt* désavouer.

disparaging [dı'spærıdʒıŋ] *adj* désobligeant(e).

dispassionate [dı'spæʃnət] *adj* impartial(e).

dispatch [dı'spætʃ] <> *n* [message] dépêche *f*. <> *vt* [send] envoyer, expédier.

dispel [dı'spel] *vt* [feeling] dissiper, chasser.

dispensary [dı'spensərı] *n* officine *f*.

dispense [dı'spens] *vt* [justice, medicine] administrer. ◆ **dispense with** *vt insep* **1.** [do without] se passer de - **2.** [make unnecessary] rendre superflu(e) ; **to dispense with the need for sthg** rendre qqch superflu.

dispensing chemist [dı'spensıŋ-] *n* UK pharmacien *m*, -enne *f*.

disperse [dı'spɜːs] <> *vt* **1.** [crowd] disperser - **2.** [knowledge, news] répandre, propager. <> *vi* se disperser.

dispirited [dı'spırıtıd] *adj* découragé(e), abattu(e).

displace [dıs'pleıs] *vt* **1.** [cause to move] déplacer - **2.** [supplant] supplanter.

display [dı'spleı] <> *n* **1.** [arrangement] exposition *f* ; [of goods, merchandise] étalage *m*, exposition *f* - **2.** [demonstration] manifestation *f* - **3.** [public event] spectacle *m* - **4.** [COMPUT - device] écran *m* ; [- information displayed] affichage *m*, visualisation *f*. <> *vt* **1.** [arrange] exposer - **2.** [show] faire preuve de, montrer.

displease [dıs'pliːz] *vt* déplaire à, mécontenter.

displeasure [dıs'pleʒər] *n* mécontentement *m*.

disposable [dı'spəuzəbl] *adj* [throw away] jetable.

disposal [dı'spəuzl] *n* **1.** [removal] enlèvement *m* - **2.** [availability] : **at sb's disposal** à la disposition de qqn.

dispose [dı'spəuz] ◆ **dispose of** *vt insep* [get rid of] se débarrasser de ; [problem] résoudre.

disposed [dı'spəuzd] *adj* **1.** [willing] : **to be disposed to do sthg** être disposé(e) à faire

qqch - **2.** [friendly] : **to be well disposed to** OR **towards sb** être bien disposé(e) envers qqn.

disposition [,dıspə'zıʃn] *n* **1.** [temperament] caractère *m*, tempérament *m* - **2.** [tendency] : **disposition to do sthg** tendance *f* à faire qqch.

disprove [,dıs'pruːv] *vt* réfuter.

dispute [dı'spjuːt] <> *n* **1.** [quarrel] dispute *f* - **2.** (U) [disagreement] désaccord *m* - **3.** INDUST conflit *m*. <> *vt* contester.

disqualify [,dıs'kwɒlıfaı] *vt* **1.** [subj: authority] : **to disqualify sb (from doing sthg)** interdire à qqn (de faire qqch) ; **to disqualify sb from driving** UK retirer le permis de conduire à qqn - **2.** SPORT disqualifier.

disquiet [dıs'kwaıət] *n* inquiétude *f*.

disregard [,dısrı'gɑːd] <> *n* (U) **disregard (for)** [money, danger] mépris *m* (pour) ; [feelings] indifférence *f* (à). <> *vt* [fact] ignorer ; [danger] mépriser ; [warning] ne pas tenir compte de.

disrepair [,dısrı'peər] *n* délabrement *m* ; **to fall into disrepair** se délabrer.

disreputable [dıs'repjutəbl] *adj* peu respectable.

disrepute [,dısrı'pjuːt] *n* : **to bring sthg into disrepute** discréditer qqch ; **to fall into disrepute** acquérir une mauvaise réputation.

disrupt [dıs'rʌpt] *vt* perturber.

dissatisfaction ['dıs,sætıs'fækʃn] *n* mécontentement *m*.

dissatisfied [,dıs'sætısfaıd] *adj* : **dissatisfied (with)** mécontent(e) (de), pas satisfait(e) (de).

dissect [dı'sekt] *vt* lit & fig disséquer.

dissent [dı'sent] <> *n* dissentiment *m*. <> *vi* : **to dissent (from)** être en désaccord (avec).

dissertation [,dısə'teıʃn] *n* dissertation *f*.

disservice [,dıs'sɜːvıs] *n* : **to do sb a disservice** rendre un mauvais service à qqn.

dissimilar [,dı'sımılər] *adj* : **dissimilar (to)** différent(e) (de).

dissipate ['dısıpeıt] *vt* **1.** PHYS [heat, energy] dissiper - **2.** [fortune] dilapider, gaspiller.

dissociate [dı'səuʃıeıt] *vt* dissocier ; **to dissociate o.s. from** se dissocier de.

dissolute ['dısəluːt] *adj* dissolu(e).

dissolve [dı'zɒlv] <> *vt* dissoudre. <> *vi* **1.** [substance] se dissoudre - **2.** *fig* [disappear] disparaître.

dissuade [dı'sweıd] *vt* : **to dissuade sb (from)** dissuader qqn (de).

distance ['dıstəns] *n* distance *f* ; **from a distance** de loin ; **in the distance** au loin.

distant ['dɪstənt] *adj* **1.** [gen] : **distant (from)** éloigné(e) (de) - **2.** [reserved - person, manner] distant(e).

distaste [dɪs'teɪst] *n* : **distaste (for)** dégoût *m* (pour).

distasteful [dɪs'teɪstfʊl] *adj* répugnant(e), déplaisant(e).

distended [dɪ'stendɪd] *adj* [stomach] ballonné(e) gonflé(e).

distil *UK*, **distill** *US* [dɪ'stɪl] *vt* **1.** [liquid] distiller - **2.** *fig* [information] tirer.

distillery [dɪ'stɪlərɪ] *n* distillerie *f*.

distinct [dɪ'stɪŋkt] *adj* **1.** [different] : **distinct (from)** distinct(e) (de), différent(e) (de) ; **as distinct from** par opposition à - **2.** [definite - improvement] net(nette).

distinction [dɪ'stɪŋkʃn] *n* **1.** [difference] distinction *f*, différence *f* ; **to draw** OR **make a distinction between** faire une distinction entre - **2.** *(U)* [excellence] distinction *f* - **3.** [exam result] mention *f* très bien.

distinctive [dɪ'stɪŋktɪv] *adj* distinctif(ive).

distinguish [dɪ'stɪŋgwɪʃ] *vt* **1.** [tell apart] : **to distinguish sthg from sthg** distinguer qqch de qqch, faire la différence entre qqch et qqch - **2.** [perceive] distinguer - **3.** [characterize] caractériser.

distinguished [dɪ'stɪŋgwɪʃt] *adj* distingué(e).

distinguishing [dɪ'stɪŋgwɪʃɪŋ] *adj* [feature, mark] distinctif(ive).

distort [dɪ'stɔːt] *vt* déformer.

distract [dɪ'strækt] *vt* : **to distract sb (from)** distraire qqn (de).

distracted [dɪ'stræktɪd] *adj* [preoccupied] distrait(e).

distraction [dɪ'strækʃn] *n* [interruption, diversion] distraction *f*.

distraught [dɪ'strɔːt] *adj* éperdu(e).

distress [dɪ'stres] <> *n* [anxiety] détresse *f* ; [pain] douleur *f*, souffrance *f*. <> *vt* affliger.

distressing [dɪ'stresɪŋ] *adj* [news, image] pénible.

distribute [dɪ'strɪbjuːt] *vt* **1.** [gen] distribuer - **2.** [spread out] répartir.

distribution [ˌdɪstrɪ'bjuːʃn] *n* **1.** [gen] distribution *f* - **2.** [spreading out] répartition *f*.

distributor [dɪ'strɪbjutər] *n* AUT & COMM distributeur *m*.

district ['dɪstrɪkt] *n* **1.** [area - of country] région *f* ; [- of town] quartier *m* - **2.** ADMIN district *m*.

district attorney *n* US ≃ procureur *m* de la République.

district council *n* UK ≃ conseil *m* général.

district nurse *n* UK infirmière *f* visiteuse OR à domicile.

distrust [dɪs'trʌst] <> *n* méfiance *f*. <> *vt* se méfier de.

disturb [dɪ'stɜːb] *vt* **1.** [interrupt] déranger - **2.** [upset, worry] inquiéter - **3.** [sleep, surface] troubler.

disturbance [dɪ'stɜːbəns] *n* **1.** POL troubles *mpl* ; [fight] tapage *m* - **2.** [interruption] dérangement *m* - **3.** [of mind, emotions] trouble *m*.

disturbed [dɪ'stɜːbd] *adj* **1.** [emotionally, mentally] perturbé(e) - **2.** [worried] inquiet(ète).

disturbing [dɪ'stɜːbɪŋ] *adj* [image] bouleversant(e) ; [news] inquiétant(e).

disuse [ˌdɪs'juːs] *n* : **to fall into disuse** [word, custom, law] tomber en désuétude.

disused [ˌdɪs'juːzd] *adj* désaffecté(e).

ditch [dɪtʃ] <> *n* fossé *m*. <> *vt inf* [boyfriend, girlfriend] plaquer ; [old car, clothes] se débarrasser de ; [plan] abandonner.

dither ['dɪðər] *vi* hésiter.

ditto ['dɪtəʊ] *adv* idem.

dive [daɪv] <> *vi* (*UK*, *pt* & *pp* **-d** *US*, *pt* & *pp* **-d** OR **dove**) plonger ; [bird, plane] piquer. <> *n* **1.** [gen] plongeon *m* - **2.** [of plane] piqué *m* - **3.** *inf pej* [bar, restaurant] bouge *m*.

diver ['daɪvər] *n* plongeur *m*, -euse *f*.

diverge [daɪ'vɜːdʒ] *vi* : **to diverge (from)** diverger (de).

diversify [daɪ'vɜːsɪfaɪ] <> *vt* diversifier. <> *vi* se diversifier.

diversion [daɪ'vɜːʃn] *n* **1.** [amusement] distraction *f* ; [tactical] diversion *f* - **2.** *UK* [of traffic] déviation *f* - **3.** [of river, funds] détournement *m*.

diversity [daɪ'vɜːsətɪ] *n* diversité *f*.

divert [daɪ'vɜːt] *vt* **1.** *UK* [traffic] dévier - **2.** [river, funds] détourner - **3.** [person - amuse] distraire ; [- tactically] détourner.

divide [dɪ'vaɪd] <> *vt* **1.** [separate] séparer - **2.** [share out] diviser, partager - **3.** [split up] : **to divide sthg (into)** diviser qqch (en) - **4.** MATHS : **89 divided by 3** 89 divisé par 3 - **5.** [people - in disagreement] diviser. <> *vi* se diviser.

dividend ['dɪvɪdend] *n* dividende *m*.

divine [dɪ'vaɪn] *adj* divin(e).

diving ['daɪvɪŋ] *n* *(U)* plongeon *m* ; [with breathing apparatus] plongée *f* (sous-marine).

diving board *n* plongeoir *m*.

divinity [dɪ'vɪnətɪ] *n* **1.** [godliness, god] divinité *f* - **2.** [study] théologie *f*.

division [dɪ'vɪʒn] *n* **1.** [gen] division *f* - **2.** [separation] séparation *f*.

divorce [dɪ'vɔːs] ◇ n divorce m. ◇ vt [husband, wife] divorcer.

divorcé [dɪ'vɔːseɪ] n divorcé m.

divorced [dɪ'vɔːst] adj divorcé(e).

divorcée [dɪvɔː'siː] n divorcée f.

divulge [daɪ'vʌldʒ] vt divulguer.

DIY (abbrev of do-it-yourself) n UK bricolage m.

dizzy ['dɪzɪ] adj [giddy] : **to feel dizzy** avoir la tête qui tourne.

DJ, deejay n (abbrev of disc jockey) disc-jockey m.

DNA (abbrev of deoxyribonucleic acid) n ADN m.

DNS [ˌdiːenˈes] (abbrev of Domain Name System) n COMPUT DNS m, système m de nom de domaine.

do [duː] ◇ aux vb (pt did, pp done) 1. (in negatives) **don't leave it there** ne le laisse pas là - 2. (in questions) **what did he want?** qu'est-ce qu'il voulait? ; **do you think she'll come?** tu crois qu'elle viendra? - 3. (referring back to previous verb) **she reads more than I do** elle lit plus que moi ; **I like reading - so do I** j'aime lire – moi aussi - 4. (in question tags) **so you think you can dance, do you?** alors tu t'imagines que tu sais danser, c'est ça? - 5. [for emphasis] : **I did tell you but you've forgotten** je te l'avais bien dit, mais tu l'as oublié ; **do come in** entrez donc. ◇ vt (pt did, pp done) 1. [perform an activity, a service] faire ; **to do aerobics/gymnastics** faire de l'aérobic/de la gymnastique ; **shall we do lunch?** on allait déjeuner ensemble? ; **to do the cooking/housework** faire la cuisine/le ménage ; **to do one's hair** se coiffer ; **to do one's teeth** se laver OR se brosser les dents - 2. [take action] faire ; **to do something about sthg** trouver une solution pour qqch - 3. [referring to job] : **what do you do?** qu'est-ce que vous faites dans la vie? - 4. [study] faire ; **I did physics at school** j'ai fait de la physique à l'école - 5. [travel at a particular speed] faire, rouler ; **the car can do 110 mph** ≃ la voiture peut faire du 180 à l'heure. ◇ vi (pt did, pp done) 1. [act] faire ; **do as I tell you** fais comme je te dis - 2. [perform in a particular way] : **they're doing really well** leurs affaires marchent bien ; **he could do better** il pourrait mieux faire ; **how did you do in the exam?** comment ça a marché à l'examen? - 3. [be good enough, be sufficient] suffire, aller ; **will £6 do?** est-ce que 6 livres suffiront? ◇ n (pl dos OR do's) [party] fête f, soirée f. ◆ **dos** npl : **dos and don'ts** ce qu'il faut faire et ne pas faire. ◆ **do away with** vt insep supprimer. ◆ **do out of** vt sep inf **to do sb out of sthg** escroquer OR carotter qqch à qqn. ◆ **do up** vt sep 1. [fasten - shoelaces, shoes] attacher ; [- buttons, coat] boutonner - 2. [decorate - room, house] refaire - 3. [wrap up] emballer. ◆ **do with** vt insep 1. [need] avoir besoin de - 2. [have connection with] : **that has nothing to do with it** ça n'a rien à voir, ça n'a aucun rapport ; **I had nothing to do with it** je n'y étais pour rien. ◆ **do without** ◇ vt insep se passer de. ◇ vi s'en passer.

Doberman ['dəʊbəmən] (pl -s) n doberman m.

docile [UK 'dəʊsaɪl, US 'dɒsəl] adj docile.

dock [dɒk] ◇ n 1. [in harbour] docks mpl - 2. LAW banc m des accusés. ◇ vi [ship] arriver à quai.

docker ['dɒkə] n docker mf.

docklands ['dɒkləndz] npl UK docks mpl.

dockworker ['dɒkwɜːkə] = docker.

dockyard ['dɒkjɑːd] n chantier m naval.

doctor ['dɒktə] ◇ n 1. MED docteur m, médecin m ; **to go to the doctor('s)** aller chez le docteur - 2. UNIV docteur m. ◇ vt [results, report] falsifier ; [text, food] altérer.

doctorate ['dɒktərət], **doctor's degree** n doctorat m.

doctrine ['dɒktrɪn] n doctrine f.

document n ['dɒkjʊmənt] document m.

documentary [ˌdɒkjʊ'mentərɪ] ◇ adj documentaire. ◇ n documentaire m.

dodge [dɒdʒ] ◇ n inf combine f. ◇ vt éviter, esquiver. ◇ vi s'esquiver.

dodgy ['dɒdʒɪ] adj UK inf [plan, deal] douteux(euse).

doe [dəʊ] n 1. [deer] biche f - 2. [rabbit] lapine f.

does (weak form [dəz], strong form [dʌz]) ▶ do.

doesn't ['dʌznt] = does not.

dog [dɒg] ◇ n [animal] chien m, chienne f. ◇ vt 1. [subj: person - follow] suivre de près - 2. [subj: problems, bad luck] poursuivre.

dog collar n 1. [of dog] collier m de chien - 2. [of priest] col m d'ecclésiastique.

dog-eared [-ɪəd] adj écorné(e).

dog food n nourriture f pour chiens.

dogged ['dɒgɪd] adj tenace.

dogsbody ['dɒgzˌbɒdɪ] n UK inf [woman] bonne f à tout faire ; [man] factotum m.

doing ['duːɪŋ] n : **is this your doing?** c'est toi qui es cause de tout cela? ◆ **doings** npl actions fpl.

do-it-yourself n (U) bricolage m.

doldrums ['dɒldrəmz] npl : **to be in the doldrums** fig être dans le marasme.

dole [dəʊl] n UK [unemployment benefit]

allocation f de chômage ; **to be on the dole** être au chômage. **dole out** vt sep [food, money] distribuer au compte-gouttes.

doleful ['dəʊlfʊl] adj morne.

doll [dɒl] n poupée f.

dollar ['dɒlə'] n dollar m.

dollarization [dɒləraɪ'zeɪʃn] n dollarisation f.

dollop ['dɒləp] n inf bonne cuillerée f.

dolphin ['dɒlfɪn] n dauphin m.

domain [də'meɪn] n lit & fig & COMPUT domaine m.

dome [dəʊm] n dôme m.

domestic [də'mestɪk] <> adj 1. [policy, flight, market] intérieur(e) - 2. [chores, animal] domestique - 3. [home-loving] casanier(ère). <> n domestique mf.

domestic appliance n appareil m ménager.

dominant ['dɒmɪnənt] adj dominant(e) ; [personality, group] dominateur(trice).

dominate ['dɒmɪneɪt] vt dominer.

domineering [,dɒmɪ'nɪərɪŋ] adj autoritaire.

dominion [də'mɪnjən] n 1. (U) [power] domination f - 2. [land] territoire m.

domino ['dɒmɪnəʊ] (pl -es) n domino m. **dominoes** npl dominos mpl.

don [dɒn] n UK UNIV professeur m d'université.

donate [də'neɪt] vt faire don de.

done [dʌn] <> pp **do**. <> adj 1. [job, work] achevé(e) ; **I'm nearly done** j'ai presque fini - 2. [cooked] cuit(e). <> excl [to conclude deal] tope!

donkey ['dɒŋkɪ] (pl -s) n âne m, ânesse f.

donor ['dəʊnə'] n 1. MED donneur m, -euse f - 2. [to charity] donateur m, -trice f.

donor card n carte f de donneur.

don't [dəʊnt] = do not.

doodle ['du:dl] <> n griffonnage m. <> vi griffonner.

doom [du:m] n [fate] destin m.

doomed [du:md] adj condamné(e) ; **the plan was doomed to failure** le plan était voué à l'échec.

door [dɔː'] n porte f ; [of vehicle] portière f.

doorbell ['dɔːbel] n sonnette f.

doorknob ['dɔːnɒb] n bouton m de porte.

doorman ['dɔːmən] (pl -men [-mən]) n portier m.

doormat ['dɔːmæt] n lit & fig paillasson m.

doorstep ['dɔːstep] n pas m de la porte.

doorway ['dɔːweɪ] n embrasure f de la porte.

dope [dəʊp] <> n inf 1. drug sl dope f - 2. [for athlete, horse] dopant m - 3. inf [fool] imbécile mf. <> vt [horse] doper.

dopey, **dopy** ['dəʊpɪ] (comp -ier, super -iest) adj inf [silly] idiot(e), abruti(e).

dorm inf n US = dormitory.

dormant ['dɔːmənt] adj 1. [volcano] endormi(e) - 2. [law] inappliqué(e).

dormitory ['dɔːmɪtrɪ] n 1. [gen] dortoir m - 2. US [in university] ≃ cité f universitaire.

Dormobile® ['dɔːmə,biːl] n UK camping-car m.

DOS [dɒs] (abbrev of **disk operating system**) n DOS m.

dose [dəʊs] n 1. MED dose f - 2. fig [amount] : **a dose of the measles** la rougeole.

dosser ['dɒsə'] n UK inf clochard m, -e f.

dosshouse ['dɒshaʊs] (pl [-haʊzɪz]) n UK inf asile m de nuit.

dot [dɒt] <> n point m ; **on the dot** à l'heure pile. <> vt : **dotted with** parsemé(e) de.

dote [dəʊt] **dote (up)on** vt insep adorer.

dot-matrix printer n imprimante f matricielle.

dotted line ['dɒtɪd-] n ligne f pointillée.

double ['dʌbl] <> adj double ; **double doors** porte f à deux battants. <> adv 1. [twice] : **double the amount** deux fois plus ; **to see double** voir double - 2. [in two] en deux ; **to bend double** se plier en deux. <> n 1. [twice as much] : **I earn double what I used to** je gagne le double de ce que je gagnais auparavant ; **at** OR **on the double** au pas de course - 2. [drink, look-alike] double m - 3. CIN doublure f. <> vt doubler. <> vi [increase twofold] doubler. **doubles** npl TENNIS double m. **double back** vi insep [animal, person, road] tourner brusquement ; **the path doubles back on itself** le sentier te ramène sur tes pas.

double-barrelled UK, **double-barreled** US [-'bærəld] adj 1. [shotgun] à deux coups - 2. UK [name] à rallonge.

double bass [-beɪs] n contrebasse f.

double bed n lit m pour deux personnes, grand lit.

double-breasted [-'brestɪd] adj [jacket] croisé(e).

double-check vt & vi revérifier.

double chin n double menton m.

double cream n UK crème f fraîche épaisse.

double-cross vt trahir.

double-decker [-'dekə'] n UK [bus] autobus m à impériale.

double digits US = double figures.

double Dutch *n* UK charabia *m*.

double-glazing [-'gleɪzɪŋ] *n* double vitrage *m*.

double room *n* chambre *f* pour deux personnes.

double vision *n* vue *f* double.

doubly ['dʌblɪ] *adv* doublement.

doubt [daʊt] ◇ *n* doute *m* ; **there is no doubt that** il n'y a aucun doute que ; **without (a) doubt** sans aucun doute ; **to be in doubt** [person] ne pas être sûr(e) ; [outcome] être incertain(e) ; **to cast doubt on sthg** mettre qqch en doute ; **no doubt** sans aucun doute. ◇ *vt* douter ; **to doubt whether** OR **if** douter que.

doubtful ['daʊtful] *adj* **1.** [decision, future] incertain(e) - **2.** [person, value] douteux(euse).

doubtless ['daʊtlɪs] *adv* sans aucun doute.

dough [dəʊ] *n (U)* **1.** CULIN pâte *f* - **2.** *v inf* [money] fric *m*.

doughnut ['dəʊnʌt] *n* beignet *m*.

douse [daʊs] *vt* **1.** [fire, flames] éteindre - **2.** [drench] tremper.

dove[1] [dʌv] *n* [bird] colombe *f*.

dove[2] [dəʊv] US *pt* ► dive.

Dover ['dəʊvər] *n* Douvres.

dovetail ['dʌvteɪl] *fig vi* coïncider.

dowdy ['daʊdɪ] *adj* sans chic.

down [daʊn] ◇ *adv* **1.** [downwards] en bas, vers le bas ; **to bend down** se pencher ; **to climb down** descendre ; **to fall down** tomber (par terre) ; **to pull down** tirer vers le bas - **2.** [along] : **we went down to have a look** on est allé jeter un coup d'œil ; **I'm going down to the shop** je vais au magasin - **3.** [southwards] : **we travelled down to London** on est descendu à Londres - **4.** [lower in amount] : **prices are coming down** les prix baissent ; **down to the last detail** jusqu'au moindre détail. ◇ *prep* **1.** [downwards] : **they ran down the hill/stairs** ils ont descendu la colline/l'escalier en courant - **2.** [along] : **to walk down the street** descendre la rue. ◇ *adj* **1.** *inf* [depressed] : **to feel down** avoir le cafard - **2.** [computer, telephones] en panne. ◇ *n (U)* duvet *m*. ◇ *vt* **1.** [knock over] abattre - **2.** [drink] avaler d'un trait. ◆ **downs** *npl* UK collines *fpl*.

down-and-out ◇ *adj* indigent(e). ◇ *n* personne *f* dans le besoin.

down-at-heel, US **down-at-the-heels** *adj* déguenillé(e).

downbeat ['daʊnbiːt] *adj inf* pessimiste.

downcast ['daʊnkɑːst] *adj* [sad] démoralisé(e).

downfall ['daʊnfɔːl] *n (U)* ruine *f*.

downhearted [,daʊn'hɑːtɪd] *adj* découragé(e).

downhill [,daʊn'hɪl] ◇ *adj* [downward] en pente. ◇ *n* [race in skiing] descente *f*. ◇ *adv* : **to walk downhill** descendre la côte ; **her career is going downhill** *fig* sa carrière est sur le déclin.

Downing Street ['daʊnɪŋ-] *n* rue du centre de Londres où réside le Premier ministre.

down payment *n* acompte *m*.

downpour ['daʊnpɔːr] *n* pluie *f* torrentielle.

downright ['daʊnraɪt] ◇ *adj* [lie] effronté(e). ◇ *adv* franchement.

downscale [,daʊn'skeɪl] *adj* US = downmarket.

downstairs [,daʊn'steəz] ◇ *adj* du bas ; [on floor below] à l'étage en-dessous. ◇ *adv* en bas ; [on floor below] à l'étage en-dessous ; **to come** OR **go downstairs** descendre.

downstream [,daʊn'striːm] *adv* en aval.

down-to-earth *adj* terre-à-terre *(inv)*.

downtown [,daʊn'taʊn] *esp US* ◇ *adj* : **downtown Paris** le centre de Paris. ◇ *adv* en ville.

downturn ['daʊntɜːn] *n* : **downturn (in)** baisse *f* (de).

down under *adv* en Australie/Nouvelle-Zélande.

downward ['daʊnwəd] ◇ *adj* **1.** [towards ground] vers le bas - **2.** [trend] à la baisse. ◇ *adv* = downwards.

downwards ['daʊnwədz] *adv* [look, move] vers le bas.

dowry ['daʊərɪ] *n* dot *f*.

doz. *(abbrev of* dozen*)* douz.

doze [dəʊz] ◇ *n* somme *m*. ◇ *vi* sommeiller. ◆ **doze off** *vi* s'assoupir.

dozen ['dʌzn] ◇ *num adj* : **a dozen eggs** une douzaine d'œufs. ◇ *n* douzaine *f* ; **50p a dozen** 50p la douzaine ; **dozens of** *inf* des centaines de.

dozy ['dəʊzɪ] *adj* **1.** [sleepy] somnolent(e) - **2.** UK *inf* [stupid] lent(e).

Dr. 1. *(abbr of* Drive*)* av - **2.** *(abbrev of* Doctor*)* Dr.

drab [dræb] *adj* [colour] terne, fade.

draft [drɑːft] ◇ *n* **1.** [early version] premier jet *m*, ébauche *f* ; [of letter] brouillon *m* - **2.** [money order] traite *f* - **3.** US MIL : **the draft** la conscription *f* - **4.** US = draught. ◇ *vt* **1.** [speech] ébaucher, faire le plan de ; [letter] faire le brouillon de - **2.** US MIL appeler - **3.** [staff] muter.

draftsman US = draughtsman.

drafty US = draughty.

drag [dræg] ◇ *vt* **1.** [gen] traîner - **2.** [lake,

river] draguer - **3.** COMPUT faire glisser ; **to drag and drop** glisser-lâcher. ◇ *vi* **1.** [dress, coat] traîner - **2.** *fig* [time, action] traîner en longueur. ◇ *n* **1.** *inf* [bore] plaie *f* - **2.** *inf* [on cigarette] bouffée *f* - **3.** [cross-dressing] : **in drag** en travesti. ◆ **drag on** *vi* [meeting, time] s'éterniser, traîner en longueur.

dragon ['drægən] *n* *lit* & *fig* dragon *m*.

dragonfly ['drægnflaɪ] *n* libellule *f*.

drain [dreɪn] ◇ *n* **1.** [pipe] égout *m* - **2.** [depletion - of resources, funds] : **drain on** épuisement *m* de. ◇ *vt* **1.** [vegetables] égoutter ; [land] assécher, drainer - **2.** [strength, resources] épuiser - **3.** [drink, glass] boire. ◇ *vi* [dishes] égoutter.

drainage ['dreɪnɪdʒ] *n* **1.** [pipes, ditches] (système *m* du) tout-à-l'égout *m* - **2.** [draining - of land] drainage *m*.

draining board UK ['dreɪnɪŋ-], **drainboard** US ['dreɪnbɔːd] *n* égouttoir *m*.

drainpipe ['dreɪnpaɪp] *n* tuyau *m* d'écoulement.

dram [dræm] *n* Scot goutte *f* (de whisky).

drama ['drɑːmə] *n* **1.** [play, excitement] drame *m* - **2.** (U) [art] théâtre *m*.

dramatic [drə'mætɪk] *adj* **1.** [gen] dramatique - **2.** [sudden, noticeable] spectaculaire.

dramatist ['dræmətɪst] *n* dramaturge *mf*.

dramatize, UK **-ise** ['dræmətaɪz] *vt* **1.** [rewrite as play, film] adapter pour la télévision/la scène/l'écran - **2.** *pej* [make exciting] dramatiser.

drank [dræŋk] *pt* ► drink.

drape [dreɪp] *vt* draper ; **to be draped with** OR **in** être drapé(e) de. ◆ **drapes** *npl* US rideaux *mpl*.

drapery ['dreɪpərɪ] *n* UK mercerie *f*.

drastic ['dræstɪk] *adj* **1.** [measures] drastique, radical(e) - **2.** [improvement, decline] spectaculaire.

draught UK, **draft** US [drɑːft] *n* **1.** [air current] courant *m* d'air - **2.** [from barrel] : **on draught** [beer] à la pression. ◆ **draughts** *n* UK jeu *m* de dames.

draught beer UK, **draft beer** US *n* bière *f* à la pression.

draughtboard ['drɑːftbɔːd] *n* UK damier *m*.

draughtsman UK (*pl* **-men** [-mən]), **draftsman** US (*pl* **-men** [-mən] ['drɑːftsmən]) *n* dessinateur *m*, -trice *f*.

draughty UK (*comp* **-ier**, *superl* **-iest**), **drafty** US ['drɑːftɪ] *adj* plein(e) de courants d'air.

draw [drɔː] ◇ *vt* (*pt* **drew**, *pp* **drawn**) **1.** [pull, take] tirer - **2.** [sketch] dessiner - **3.** [comparison, distinction] établir, faire - **4.** [attract, lead] attirer, entraîner ; **to draw**

sb's attention to attirer l'attention de qqn sur. ◇ *vi* (*pt* **drew**, *pp* **drawn**) **1.** [sketch] dessiner - **2.** [move] : **to draw near** [person] s'approcher ; [time] approcher ; **to draw away** reculer - **3.** SPORT faire match nul ; **to be drawing** être à égalité. ◇ *n* **1.** SPORT [result] match *m* nul - **2.** [lottery] tirage *m* - **3.** [attraction] attraction *f*. ◆ **draw out** *vt sep* **1.** [encourage - person] faire sortir de sa coquille - **2.** [prolong] prolonger - **3.** [money] faire un retrait de, retirer. ◆ **draw up** ◇ *vt sep* [contract, plan] établir, dresser. ◇ *vi* [vehicle] s'arrêter.

drawback ['drɔːbæk] *n* inconvénient *m*, désavantage *m*.

drawbridge ['drɔːbrɪdʒ] *n* pont-levis *m*.

drawer [drɔːr] *n* [in desk, chest] tiroir *m*.

drawing ['drɔːɪŋ] *n* dessin *m*.

drawing board *n* planche *f* à dessin.

drawing pin *n* UK punaise *f*.

drawing room *n* salon *m*.

drawl [drɔːl] *n* voix *f* traînante.

drawn [drɔːn] *pp* ► draw.

dread [dred] ◇ *n* (U) épouvante *f*. ◇ *vt* appréhender ; **to dread doing sthg** appréhender de faire qqch.

dreadful ['dredfʊl] *adj* affreux(euse), épouvantable.

dreadfully ['dredfʊlɪ] *adv* **1.** [badly] terriblement - **2.** [extremely] extrêmement ; **I'm dreadfully sorry** je regrette infiniment.

dream [driːm] ◇ *n* **1.** rêve *m* - **2.** [wish, fantasy] rêve *m*, désir *m*. ◇ *adj* de rêve. ◇ *vt* (*pt* & *pp* **-ed** OR **dreamt**) rêver ; **to dream (that)...** rêver que... ◇ *vi* (*pt* & *pp* **-ed** OR **dreamt**) : **to dream (of** OR **about)** rêver (de) ; **I wouldn't dream of it** cela ne me viendrait même pas à l'idée. ◆ **dream up** *vt sep* inventer.

dreamt [dremt] *pt* & *pp* ► dream.

dreamy ['driːmɪ] *adj* **1.** [distracted] rêveur(euse) - **2.** [dreamlike] de rêve.

dreary ['drɪərɪ] *adj* **1.** [weather] morne - **2.** [person] ennuyeux(euse).

dredge [dredʒ] ◇ *n* = dredger. ◇ *vt* draguer. ◆ **dredge up** *vt sep* **1.** [with dredger] draguer - **2.** *fig* [from past] déterrer.

dregs [dregz] *npl* *lit* & *fig* lie *f*.

drench [drentʃ] *vt* tremper ; **to be drenched in** OR **with** être inondé(e) de.

dress [dres] ◇ *n* **1.** [woman's garment] robe *f* - **2.** (U) [clothing] costume *m*, tenue *f*. ◇ *vt* **1.** [clothe] habiller ; **to be dressed** être habillé(e) ; **to be dressed in** être vêtu(e) de ; **to get dressed** s'habiller - **2.** [bandage] panser - **3.** CULIN [salad] assaisonner. ◇ *vi* s'habiller. ◆ **dress up** *vi* **1.** [in costume] se déguiser - **2.** [in best clothes] s'habiller (élégamment).

dress circle *n* UK premier balcon *m*.

dresser ['dresə'] *n* 1. [for dishes] vaisselier *m* - 2. US [chest of drawers] commode *f*.

dressing ['dresɪŋ] *n* 1. [bandage] pansement *m* - 2. [for salad] assaisonnement *m* - 3. US [for turkey etc] farce *f*.

dressing gown UK *n* robe *f* de chambre.

dressing room *n* 1. THEAT loge *f* - 2. SPORT vestiaire *m*.

dressing table *n* coiffeuse *f*.

dressmaker ['dres,meɪkə'] *n* couturier *m*, -ère *f*.

dressmaking ['dres,meɪkɪŋ] *n* couture *f*.

dress rehearsal *n* générale *f*.

dressy ['dresɪ] *adj* habillé(e).

drew [dru:] *pt* ► draw.

dribble ['drɪbl] ◇ *n* 1. [saliva] bave *f* - 2. [trickle] traînée *f*. ◇ *vt* SPORT dribbler. ◇ *vi* 1. [drool] baver - 2. [liquid] tomber goutte à goutte, couler.

dried [draɪd] *adj* [milk, eggs] en poudre ; [fruit] sec (sèche) ; [flowers] séché(e).

drier ['draɪə'] = dryer.

drift [drɪft] ◇ *n* 1. [movement] mouvement *m* ; [direction] direction *f*, sens *m* - 2. [meaning] sens *m* général - 3. [of snow] congère *f* ; [of sand, leaves] amoncellement *m*, entassement *m*. ◇ *vi* 1. [boat] dériver - 2. [snow, sand, leaves] s'amasser, s'amonceler.

driftwood ['drɪftwʊd] *n* bois *m* flottant.

drill [drɪl] ◇ *n* 1. [tool] perceuse *f* ; [dentist's] fraise *f* ; [in mine etc] perforatrice *f* - 2. [exercise, training] exercice *m*. ◇ *vt* 1. [wood, hole] percer ; [tooth] fraiser ; [well] forer - 2. [soldiers] entraîner. ◇ *vi* [excavate] : **to drill for oil** forer à la recherche de pétrole.

drink [drɪŋk] ◇ *n* 1. [gen] boisson *f* ; [alcoholic] verre *m* ; **we invited them in for a drink** nous les avons invités à prendre un verre - 2. (U) [alcohol] alcool *m*. ◇ *vt* (*pt* drank, *pp* drunk) boire. ◇ *vi* (*pt* drank, *pp* drunk) boire.

drink-driving UK, **drunk driving** US, **drunken driving** US *n* conduite *f* en état d'ivresse.

drinker ['drɪŋkə'] *n* buveur *m*, -euse *f*.

drinking water *n* eau *f* potable.

drip [drɪp] ◇ *n* 1. [drop] goutte *f* - 2. MED goutte-à-goutte *m inv*. ◇ *vi* [gen] goutter, tomber goutte à goutte.

drip-dry *adj* qui ne se repasse pas.

drive [draɪv] ◇ *n* 1. [in car] trajet *m* (en voiture) ; **to go for a drive** faire une promenade (en voiture) - 2. [urge] désir *m*, besoin *m* - 3. [campaign] campagne *f* - 4. (U) [energy] dynamisme *m*, énergie *f* - 5. [road

to house] allée *f* - 6. SPORT drive *m*. ◇ *vt* (*pt* drove, *pp* driven) 1. [vehicle, passenger] conduire - 2. TECH entraîner, actionner - 3. [animals, people] pousser - 4. [motivate, push] pousser ; **he drives himself too hard** il exige trop de lui-même - 5. [force] : **to drive sb to sthg/to do sthg** pousser qqn à qqch/à faire qqch, conduire qqn à qqch/à faire qqch ; **to drive sb mad** OR **crazy** rendre qqn fou - 6. [nail, stake] enfoncer. ◇ *vi* (*pt* drove, *pp* driven) [driver] conduire ; [travel by car] aller en voiture.

drive-by (*pl* drive-bys) *n inf* : **drive-by shooting** fusillade *f* en voiture.

drivel ['drɪvl] *n* (U) *inf* foutaises *fpl*, idioties *fpl*.

driven ['drɪvn] *pp* ► drive.

driver ['draɪvə'] *n* [of vehicle - gen] conducteur *m*, -trice *f* ; [- of taxi] chauffeur *m*.

driver's license US = driving licence.

drive shaft *n* arbre *m* de transmission.

driveway ['draɪvweɪ] *n* allée *f*.

driving ['draɪvɪŋ] ◇ *adj* [rain] battant(e) ; [wind] cinglant(e). ◇ *n* (U) conduite *f*.

driving instructor *n* moniteur *m*, -trice *f* d'auto-école.

driving lesson *n* leçon *f* de conduite.

driving licence UK, **driver's license** US *n* permis *m* de conduire.

driving mirror *n* rétroviseur *m*.

driving school *n* auto-école *f*.

driving test *n* (examen *m* du) permis *m* de conduire.

drizzle ['drɪzl] ◇ *n* bruine *f*. ◇ *impers vb* bruiner.

droll [drəʊl] *adj* drôle.

drone [drəʊn] *n* 1. [of traffic, voices] ronronnement *m* ; [of insect] bourdonnement *m* - 2. [male bee] abeille *f* mâle, fauxbourdon *m*.

drool [dru:l] *vi* baver ; **to drool over** *fig* baver (d'admiration) devant.

droop [dru:p] *vi* [head] pencher ; [shoulders, eyelids] tomber.

drop [drɒp] ◇ *n* 1. [of liquid] goutte *f* - 2. [decrease] baisse *f*, chute *f* - 3. [distance down] dénivellation *f* ; **sheer drop** à-pic *m inv* - 4. [delivery] livraison *f* ; [from plane] parachutage *m*, droppage *m* ; **to make a drop** déposer un colis - 5. [sweet] pastille *f*. ◇ *vt* 1. [let fall] laisser tomber - 2. [voice, speed, price] baisser - 3. [abandon] abandonner ; [player] exclure - 4. [let out of car] déposer - 5. [utter] : **to drop a hint that** laisser entendre que - 6. [send] : **to drop sb a note** OR **line** écrire un petit mot à qqn. ◇ *vi* 1. [fall] tomber - 2. [temperature, demand] baisser ; [voice, wind] tomber. ◆ **drops** *npl* MED gouttes *fpl*. ◆ **drop in**

vi inf **to drop in (on sb)** passer (chez qqn).
◆ **drop off** ◇ *vt sep* déposer. ◇ *vi*
1. [fall asleep] s'endormir - **2.** [interest, sales]
baisser. ◆ **drop out** *vi* : **to drop out of
society** vivre en marge de la société.

dropout ['drɒpaʊt] *n* [from society] marginal *m*, -e *f* ; [from college] étudiant *m*, -e *f*
qui abandonne ses études.

droppings ['drɒpɪŋz] *npl* [of bird] fiente *f* ;
[of animal] crottes *fpl*.

drought [draʊt] *n* sécheresse *f*.

drove [drəʊv] *pt* ➤ **drive**.

drown [draʊn] ◇ *vt* [in water] noyer.
◇ *vi* se noyer.

drowsy ['draʊzɪ] *adj* assoupi(e), somno-
lent(e).

drudgery ['drʌdʒərɪ] *n (U)* corvée *f*.

drug [drʌg] ◇ *n* **1.** [medicine] médicament *m* - **2.** [narcotic] drogue *f*. ◇ *vt*
droguer.

drug abuse *n* usage *m* de stupéfiants.

drug addict *n* drogué *m*, -e *f*, toxicomane
mf.

druggist ['drʌgɪst] *n US* pharmacien *m*,
-enne *f*.

drug peddler, **drug pusher** *n* revendeur
m, -euse *f* de drogue.

drug test *n* [of athlete, horse] contrôle *m*
antidopage.

drum [drʌm] ◇ *n* **1.** MUS tambour *m*
- **2.** [container] bidon *m*. ◇ *vt & vi*
tambouriner. ◆ **drums** *npl* batterie *f*.
◆ **drum up** *vt sep* [support, business]
rechercher, solliciter.

drummer ['drʌmə^r] *n* [gen] (joueur *m*,
-euse *f* de) tambour *m* ; [in pop group]
batteur *m*, -euse *f*.

drumstick ['drʌmstɪk] *n* **1.** [for drum]
baguette *f* de tambour - **2.** [of chicken] pilon
m.

drunk [drʌŋk] ◇ *pp* ➤ **drink**. ◇ *adj*
[on alcohol] ivre, soûl(e) ; **to get drunk** se
soûler, s'enivrer. ◇ *n* soûlard *m*, -e *f*.

drunkard ['drʌŋkəd] *n* alcoolique *mf*.

drunk driving *US* = **drink-driving**.

drunken ['drʌŋkn] *adj* [person] ivre ;
[quarrel] d'ivrognes.

drunken driving *US* = **drink-driving**.

dry [draɪ] ◇ *adj* **1.** [gen] sec (sèche) ; [day]
sans pluie - **2.** [river, earth] asséché(e)
- **3.** [wry] pince-sans-rire *(inv)*. ◇ *vt* [gen]
sécher ; [with cloth] essuyer. ◇ *vi* sécher.
◆ **dry up** ◇ *vt sep* [dishes] essuyer.
◇ *vi* **1.** [river, lake] s'assécher - **2.** [supply]
se tarir - **3.** [actor, speaker] avoir un trou,
sécher - **4.** *UK* [dry dishes] essuyer.

dry cleaner *n* : **dry cleaner's** pressing *m*.

dryer ['draɪə^r] *n* [for clothes] séchoir *m*.

dry land *n* terre *f* ferme.

dry rot *n* pourriture *f* sèche.

dry ski slope *n esp UK* piste *f* de ski
artificielle.

drysuit ['draɪsuːt] *n* combinaison de plongée (étanche) *f*.

DSS *(abbrev of* **Department of Social Security**) *n* ministère britannique de la sécurité sociale.

DTI *(abbrev of* **Department of Trade and
Industry**) *n* ministère britannique du commerce
et de l'industrie.

DTP *(abbrev of* **desktop publishing**) *n* PAO *f*.

dual ['djuːəl] *adj* double.

dual carriageway *n UK* route *f* à quatre
voies.

dubbed [dʌbd] *adj* **1.** CIN doublé(e)
- **2.** [nicknamed] surnommé(e).

dubious ['djuːbjəs] *adj* **1.** [suspect] dou-
teux(euse) - **2.** [uncertain] hésitant(e), incer-
tain(e) ; **to be dubious about doing sthg**
hésiter à faire qqch.

Dublin ['dʌblɪn] *n* Dublin.

duchess ['dʌtʃɪs] *n* duchesse *f*.

duck [dʌk] ◇ *n* canard *m*. ◇ *vt* **1.** [head]
baisser - **2.** [responsibility] esquiver, se
dérober à. ◇ *vi* [lower head] se baisser.

duckling ['dʌklɪŋ] *n* caneton *m*.

duct [dʌkt] *n* **1.** [pipe] canalisation *f*
- **2.** ANAT canal *m*.

dud [dʌd] ◇ *adj* [bomb] non éclaté(e) ;
[cheque] sans provision, en bois. ◇ *n*
obus *m* non éclaté.

dude [djuːd] *n US inf* [man] gars *m*, type *m*.

due [djuː] ◇ *adj* **1.** [expected] : **the book is
due out in May** le livre doit sortir en mai ;
she's due back shortly elle devrait rentrer
sous peu ; **when is the train due?** à quelle
heure le train doit-il arriver? - **2.** [appropri-
ate] dû (due), qui convient ; **in due course**
[at the appropriate time] en temps voulu ;
[eventually] à la longue - **3.** [owed, owing]
dû (due). ◇ *adv* : **due west** droit vers
l'ouest. ◇ *n* dû *m*. ◆ **dues** *npl* cotisation
f. ◆ **due to** *prep* [owing to] dû à ; [because
of] provoqué par, à cause de.

duel ['djuːəl] ◇ *n* duel *m*. ◇ *vi* (*UK &
US*) se battre en duel.

duet [djuː'et] *n* duo *m*.

duffel bag ['dʌfl-] *n* sac *m* marin.

duffel coat ['dʌfl-] *n* duffel-coat *m*.

duffle bag ['dʌfl-] = **duffel bag**.

duffle coat ['dʌfl-] = **duffel coat**.

dug [dʌg] *pt & pp* ➤ **dig**.

duke [djuːk] *n* duc *m*.

dull [dʌl] ◇ *adj* **1.** [boring - book, conver-
sation] ennuyeux(euse) ; [- person] terne

- **2.** [colour, light] **terne** - **3.** [weather] **maussade** - **4.** [sound, ache] **sourd(e).** <> vt **1.** [pain] **atténuer** ; [senses] **émousser** - **2.** [make less bright] **ternir.**

duly ['dju:lɪ] adv **1.** [properly] **dûment** - **2.** [as expected] **comme prévu.**

dumb [dʌm] adj **1.** [unable to speak] **muet(ette)** - **2.** inf [stupid] **idiot(e).**

dumbfounded [dʌm'faʊndɪd] adj [person] **abasourdi(e), interloqué(e).**

dummy ['dʌmɪ] <> adj **faux (fausse).** <> n **1.** [of tailor] **mannequin** m - **2.** [mockup] **maquette** f - **3.** UK [for baby] **sucette** f, **tétine** f - **4.** SPORT **feinte** f.

dump [dʌmp] <> n **1.** [for rubbish] **décharge** f - **2.** MIL **dépôt** m. <> vt **1.** [put down] **déposer** - **2.** [dispose of] **jeter** - **3.** inf [boyfriend, girlfriend] **laisser tomber, plaquer.** <> vi inf ; **to dump on sb mettre qn dans la merde** vulg.

dumper (truck) UK ['dʌmpə-], **dump truck** US n **tombereau** m, **dumper** m.

dumping ['dʌmpɪŋ] n **décharge** f ; **'no dumping'** '**décharge interdite'.**

dumpling ['dʌmplɪŋ] n **boulette** f **de pâte.**

dump truck US = **dumper (truck).**

dumpy ['dʌmpɪ] adj inf **boulot(otte).**

dunce [dʌns] n **cancre** m.

dune [dju:n] n **dune** f.

dung [dʌŋ] n **fumier** m.

dungarees [,dʌŋgə'ri:z] npl UK [for work] **bleu** m **de travail** ; [fashion garment] **salopette** f.

dungeon ['dʌndʒən] n **cachot** m.

Dunkirk [dʌn'kɜːk] n **Dunkerque** f.

duo ['dju:əʊ] n **duo** m.

duplex ['dju:pleks] n US **1.** [apartment] **duplex** m - **2.** [house] **maison** f **jumelée.**

duplicate <> adj ['dju:plɪkət] [key, document] **en double.** <> n ['dju:plɪkət] **double** m ; **in duplicate en double.** <> vt ['dju:plɪkeɪt] [copy - gen] **faire un double de** ; [- on photocopier] **photocopier.**

durable ['djʊərəbl] adj **solide, résistant(e).**

duration [dju'reɪʃn] n **durée** f ; **for the duration of jusqu'à la fin de.**

duress [dju'res] n : **under duress sous la contrainte.**

Durex® ['djʊəreks] n **préservatif** m.

during ['djʊərɪŋ] prep **pendant, au cours de.**

dusk [dʌsk] n **crépuscule** m.

dust [dʌst] <> n (U) **poussière** f. <> vt **1.** [clean] **épousseter** - **2.** [cover with powder] : **to dust sthg (with) saupoudrer qqch (de).**

dustbin ['dʌstbɪn] n UK **poubelle** f.

dustcart ['dʌstkɑːt] n UK **camion** m **des boueux.**

duster ['dʌstər] n [cloth] **chiffon** m (à poussière).

dust jacket n [on book] **jaquette** f.

dustman ['dʌstmən] (pl -men [-mən]) n UK **éboueur** m, -se f.

dustpan ['dʌstpæn] n **pelle** f **à poussière.**

dusty ['dʌstɪ] adj **poussiéreux(euse).**

Dutch [dʌtʃ] <> adj **néerlandais(e), hollandais(e).** <> n [language] **néerlandais** m, **hollandais** m. <> npl : **the Dutch les Néerlandais, les Hollandais.** <> adv : **to go Dutch partager les frais.**

dutiful ['dju:tɪfʊl] adj **obéissant(e).**

duty ['dju:tɪ] n **1.** (U) [responsibility] **devoir** m ; **to do one's duty faire son devoir** - **2.** [work] : **to be on/off duty être/ne pas être de service** - **3.** [tax] **droit** m. **duties** npl **fonctions** fpl.

duty-free adj **hors taxe.**

duvet ['du:veɪ] n UK **couette** f.

duvet cover n UK **housse** f **de couette.**

DVD (abbrev of Digital Video or Versatile Disc) n **DVD** m.

DVD player n **lecteur** m **de DVD.**

DVD-ROM (abbrev of Digital Video or Versatile Disc read only memory) n **DVD-ROM** m.

dwarf [dwɔːf] <> n (pl -s OR dwarves [dwɔːvz]) **nain** m, -e f. <> vt [tower over] **écraser.**

dwell [dwel] (pt & pp dwelt OR -ed) vi lit **habiter.** **dwell on** vt insep **s'étendre sur.**

dwelling ['dwelɪŋ] n lit **habitation** f.

dwelt [dwelt] pt & pp **dwell.**

dwindle ['dwɪndl] vi **diminuer.**

dye [daɪ] <> n **teinture** f. <> vt **teindre.**

dying ['daɪɪŋ] <> cont **die.** <> adj [person] **mourant(e), moribond(e)** ; [plant, language, industry] **moribond.**

dyke [daɪk] = **dike.**

dynamic [daɪ'næmɪk] adj **dynamique.**

dynamite ['daɪnəmaɪt] n (U) lit & fig **dynamite** f.

dynamo ['daɪnəməʊ] (pl -s) n **dynamo** f.

dynasty [UK 'dɪnəstɪ, US 'daɪnəstɪ] n **dynastie** f.

dysfunctional [dɪs'fʌŋkʃənəl] adj **dysfonctionnel(elle)** ; **dysfunctional family famille** f **disfonctionnelle.**

dyslexia [dɪs'leksɪə] n **dyslexie** f.

dyslexic [dɪs'leksɪk] adj **dyslexique.**

E

e [i:] (pl **e's** OR **es**), **E** (pl **E's** OR **Es**) n (letter) e m inv, E m inv. ➤ **E** n **1.** MUS mi m - **2.** (abbrev of **east**) E.

each [i:tʃ] ◇ adj chaque. ◇ pron chacun(e) ; **the books cost £10.99 each** les livres coûtent 10,99 livres (la) pièce ; **each other** l'un l'autre (l'une l'autre), les uns les autres (les unes les autres) ; **they love each other** ils s'aiment ; **we've known each other for years** nous nous connaissons depuis des années.

eager ['i:gər] adj passionné(e), avide ; **to be eager for** être avide de ; **to be eager to do sthg** être impatient de faire qqch.

eagle ['i:gl] n (bird) aigle m.

ear [ɪər] n **1.** (gen) oreille f - **2.** (of corn) épi m.

earache ['ɪəreɪk] n : **to have earache, to have an earache** US avoir mal à l'oreille.

earbuds npl oreillettes fpl.

eardrum ['ɪədrʌm] n tympan m.

earl [ɜːl] n comte m.

earlier ['ɜːlɪər] ◇ adj (previous) précédent(e) ; (more early) plus tôt. ◇ adv plus tôt ; **earlier on** plus tôt.

earliest ['ɜːlɪəst] ◇ adj (first) premier(ère) ; (most early) le plus tôt. ◇ n : **at the earliest** au plus tôt.

earlobe ['ɪələʊb] n lobe m de l'oreille.

early ['ɜːlɪ] ◇ adj **1.** (before expected time) en avance - **2.** (in day) de bonne heure ; **the early train** le premier train ; **to make an early start** partir de bonne heure - **3.** (at beginning) : **in the early sixties** au début des années soixante. ◇ adv **1.** (before expected time) en avance ; **I was ten minutes early** j'étais en avance de dix minutes - **2.** (in day) tôt, de bonne heure ; **as early as** dès ; **early on** tôt - **3.** (at beginning) : **early in her life** dans sa jeunesse.

early retirement n retraite f anticipée.

earmark ['ɪəmɑːk] vt : **to be earmarked for** être réservé(e) à.

earn [ɜːn] vt **1.** (as salary) gagner - **2.** COMM rapporter - **3.** fig (respect, praise) gagner, mériter.

earnest ['ɜːnɪst] adj sérieux(euse). ➤ **in earnest** ◇ adj sérieux(euse). ◇ adv pour de bon, sérieusement.

earnings ['ɜːnɪŋz] npl (of person) salaire m, gains mpl ; (of company) bénéfices mpl.

earphones ['ɪəfəʊnz] npl casque m.

earplugs ['ɪəplʌgz] npl boules fpl Quiès®.

earring ['ɪərɪŋ] n boucle f d'oreille.

earshot ['ɪəʃɒt] n : **within earshot** à portée de voix ; **out of earshot** hors de portée de voix.

earth [ɜːθ] ◇ n (gen & ELEC) terre f ; **how/what/where/why on earth...?** mais comment/que/où/pourquoi donc...? ; **to cost the earth** UK coûter les yeux de la tête. ◇ vt UK ELEC : **to be earthed** être à la masse.

earthenware ['ɜːθnweər] n (U) poteries fpl.

earthquake ['ɜːθkweɪk] n tremblement m de terre.

earthworm ['ɜːθwɜːm] n ver m de terre.

earthy ['ɜːθɪ] adj **1.** fig (humour, person) truculent(e) - **2.** (taste, smell) de terre, terreux(euse).

earwig ['ɪəwɪg] n perce-oreille m.

ease [i:z] ◇ n (U) **1.** (lack of difficulty) facilité f ; **to do sthg with ease** faire qqch sans difficulté OR facilement - **2.** (comfort) : **at ease** à l'aise ; **ill at ease** mal à l'aise. ◇ vt **1.** (pain) calmer ; (restrictions) modérer - **2.** (move carefully) : **to ease sthg in/out** faire entrer/sortir qqch délicatement. ◇ vi (problem) s'arranger ; (pain) s'atténuer ; (rain) diminuer. ➤ **ease off** vi (pain) s'atténuer ; (rain) diminuer. ➤ **ease up** vi **1.** (rain) diminuer - **2.** (relax) se détendre.

easel ['i:zl] n chevalet m.

easily ['i:zɪlɪ] adv **1.** (without difficulty) facilement - **2.** (without doubt) de loin - **3.** (in a relaxed manner) tranquillement.

east [i:st] ◇ n **1.** (direction) est m - **2.** (region) : **the east** l'est m. ◇ adj (inv) (side) est ; (wind) d'est. ◇ adv à l'est, vers l'est ; **east of** à l'est de. ➤ **East** n : **the East** (gen & POL) l'Est m ; (Asia) l'Orient m.

East End n : **the East End** les quartiers est de Londres.

Easter ['i:stər] n Pâques m.

Easter egg n œuf m de Pâques.

easterly ['i:stəlɪ] adj à l'est, de l'est ; (wind) de l'est.

eastern ['i:stən] adj de l'est. ➤ **Eastern** adj (gen & POL) de l'Est ; (from Asia) oriental(e).

East German ◇ adj d'Allemagne de l'Est. ◇ n Allemand m, -e f de l'Est.

East Germany n : (former) **East Germany** (l'ex-) Allemagne f de l'Est.

eastward ['iːstwəd] <> adj à l'est, vers l'est. <> adv = **eastwards**.

eastwards ['iːstwədz] adv vers l'est.

easy ['iːzɪ] <> adj **1.** [not difficult, comfortable] facile - **2.** [relaxed - manner] naturel(elle). <> adv : **to take it** OR **things easy** inf ne pas se fatiguer.

easy chair n fauteuil m.

easygoing [,iːzɪ'gəʊɪŋ] adj [person] facile à vivre ; [manner] complaisant(e).

easy-peasy n fastoche inf hum, facile.

eat [iːt] (pt ate, pp eaten) vt & vi manger.
➤ **eat away, eat into** vt insep **1.** [subj: acid, rust] ronger - **2.** [deplete] grignoter.

eaten ['iːtn] pp ➤ **eat**.

eaves ['iːvz] npl avant-toit m.

eavesdrop ['iːvzdrɒp] vi : **to eavesdrop (on sb)** écouter (qqn) de façon indiscrète.

ebb [eb] <> n reflux m. <> vi [tide, sea] se retirer, refluer.

ebony ['ebənɪ] <> adj [colour] noir(e) d'ébène. <> n ébène f.

e-business n **1.** [company] cyberentreprise f - **2.** (U) [trade] cybercommerce m, commerce m électronique.

EC (abbrev of **European Community**) n CE f.

e-cash n argent m virtuel OR électronique.

ECB (abbrev of **European Central bank**) n BCE f.

eccentric [ɪk'sentrɪk] <> adj [odd] excentrique, bizarre. <> n [person] excentrique mf.

echo ['ekəʊ] <> n (pl -es) lit & fig écho m. <> vt [words] répéter ; [opinion] faire écho à. <> vi retentir, résonner.

éclair [eɪ'kleə'] n éclair m.

eclipse [ɪ'klɪps] <> n lit & fig éclipse f. <> vt fig éclipser.

eco-friendly adj qui respecte l'environnement.

ecological [,iːkə'lɒdʒɪkl] adj écologique.

ecology [ɪ'kɒlədʒɪ] n écologie f.

e-commerce n (U) commerce m électronique, cybercommerce m.

economic [,iːkə'nɒmɪk] adj **1.** ECON économique - **2.** [profitable] rentable.

economical [,iːkə'nɒmɪkl] adj **1.** [cheap] économique - **2.** [person] économe.

Economic and Monetary Union n Union f économique et monétaire.

economics [,iːkə'nɒmɪks] <> n (U) économie f (politique), sciences fpl économiques. <> npl [of plan, business] aspect m financier.

economize, UK -**ise** [ɪ'kɒnəmaɪz] vi économiser.

economy [ɪ'kɒnəmɪ] n économie f ; **economies of scale** économies d'échelle.

economy class n classe f touriste.

economy-class syndrome n syndrome m de la classe économique.

ecotax ['iːkəʊtæks] n écotaxe f.

ecotourism ['iːkəʊ,tʊərɪzm] n écotourisme m, tourisme m vert.

ecstasy ['ekstəsɪ] n **1.** [pleasure] extase f, ravissement m - **2.** [drug] ecstasy m ou f.

ecstatic [ek'stætɪk] adj [person] en extase ; [feeling] extatique.

ECU, Ecu ['ekjuː] (abbrev of **European Currency Unit**) n ECU m, écu m.

eczema ['eksɪmə] n eczéma m.

Eden ['iːdn] n : **(the Garden of) Eden** le jardin m d'Éden, l'Éden m.

edge [edʒ] <> n **1.** [gen] bord m ; [of coin, book] tranche f ; [of knife] tranchant m ; **to be on the edge of** fig être à deux doigts de - **2.** [advantage] : **to have an edge over** OR **the edge on** avoir un léger avantage sur. <> vi : **to edge forward** avancer tout doucement.
➤ **on edge** adj contracté(e), tendu(e).

edgeways UK ['edʒweɪz], **edgewise** US ['edʒwaɪz] adv latéralement, de côté.

edgy ['edʒɪ] adj contracté(e), tendu(e).

edible ['edɪbl] adj [safe to eat] comestible.

edict ['iːdɪkt] n décret m.

Edinburgh ['edɪnbrə] n Édimbourg.

edit ['edɪt] vt **1.** [correct - text] corriger - **2.** CIN monter ; RADIO & TV réaliser - **3.** [magazine] diriger ; [newspaper] être le rédacteur en chef de.

edition [ɪ'dɪʃn] n édition f.

editor ['edɪtə'] n **1.** [of magazine] directeur m, -trice f ; [of newspaper] rédacteur m, -trice f en chef - **2.** [of text] correcteur m, -trice f - **3.** CIN monteur m, -euse f ; RADIO & TV réalisateur m, -trice f.

editorial [,edɪ'tɔːrɪəl] <> adj [department, staff] de la rédaction ; [style, policy] éditorial(e). <> n éditorial m.

educate ['edʒʊkeɪt] vt **1.** SCH & UNIV instruire - **2.** [inform] informer, éduquer.

education [,edʒʊ'keɪʃn] n **1.** [gen] éducation f ; **standards of education** niveau m scolaire - **2.** [teaching] enseignement m, instruction f.

educational [,edʒʊ'keɪʃənl] adj **1.** [establishment, policy] pédagogique - **2.** [toy, experience] éducatif(ive).

eel [iːl] n anguille f.

eery ['ɪərɪ] (comp -**ier**, superl -**iest**) adj inquiétant(e), sinistre.

eery ['ɪərɪ] (comp -**ier**, superl -**iest**) adj inquiétant(e), sinistre.

efface [ɪ'feɪs] vt effacer.

effect [ɪ'fekt] <> n [gen] effet m ; **to have an effect on** avoir OR produire un effet sur ; **for effect** pour attirer l'attention, pour se faire remarquer ; **to take effect** [law] prendre effet, entrer en vigueur ; **to put sthg into effect** [policy, law] mettre qqch en application. <> vt [repairs, change] effectuer ; [reconciliation] amener. ➤ **effects** npl : **(special) effects** effets mpl spéciaux.

effective [ɪ'fektɪv] adj **1.** [successful] efficace - **2.** [actual, real] effectif(ive).

effectively [ɪ'fektɪvlɪ] adv **1.** [successfully] efficacement - **2.** [in fact] effectivement.

effectiveness [ɪ'fektɪvnɪs] n efficacité f.

effeminate [ɪ'femɪnət] adj efféminé(e).

effervescent [,efə'vesənt] adj [liquid] effervescent(e) ; [drink] gazeux(euse).

efficiency [ɪ'fɪʃənsɪ] n [of person, method] efficacité f ; [of factory, system] rendement m.

efficient [ɪ'fɪʃənt] adj efficace.

effluent ['efluənt] n effluent m.

effort ['efət] n effort m ; **to be worth the effort** valoir la peine ; **with effort** avec peine ; **to make the effort to do sthg** s'efforcer de faire qqch ; **to make an/no effort to do sthg** faire un effort/ne faire aucun effort pour faire qqch.

effortless ['efətlɪs] adj [easy] facile ; [natural] aisé(e).

effusive [ɪ'fju:sɪv] adj [person] démonstratif(ive) ; [welcome] plein(e) d'effusions.

e.g. (abbrev of exempli gratia) adv par exemple.

egg [eg] n œuf m. ➤ **egg on** vt sep pousser, inciter.

eggcup ['egkʌp] n coquetier m.

eggplant ['egplɑ:nt] n US aubergine f.

eggshell ['egʃel] n coquille f d'œuf.

egg white n blanc m d'œuf.

egg yolk n jaune m d'œuf.

egis n US = aegis.

ego ['i:gəʊ] (pl -s) n moi m.

egoism ['i:gəʊɪzm] n égoïsme m.

egoistic [,i:gəʊ'ɪstɪk] adj égoïste.

egotistic(al) [,i:gə'tɪstɪk(l)] adj égotiste.

Egypt ['i:dʒɪpt] n Égypte f.

Egyptian [ɪ'dʒɪpʃn] <> adj égyptien(enne). <> n Égyptien m, -enne f.

eiderdown ['aɪdədaʊn] n esp UK [bed cover] édredon m.

eight [eɪt] num huit ; see also **six**.

eighteen [,eɪ'ti:n] num dix-huit ; see also **six**.

eighth [eɪtθ] num huitième ; see also **sixth**.

eighty ['eɪtɪ] num quatre-vingts ; see also **sixty**.

Eire ['eərə] n République f d'Irlande.

either ['aɪðər OR 'i:ðər] <> adj **1.** [one or the other] l'un ou l'autre (l'une ou l'autre) (des deux) ; **she couldn't find either jumper** elle ne trouva ni l'un ni l'autre des pulls ; **either way** de toute façon - **2.** [each] chaque ; **on either side** de chaque côté. <> pron : **either (of them)** l'un ou l'autre m, l'une ou l'autre f ; **I don't like either (of them)** je n'aime aucun des deux, je n'aime ni l'un ni l'autre. <> adv (in negatives) non plus ; **I don't either** moi non plus. <> conj : **either... or** soit... ou... ou ; **I'm not fond of either him or his wife** je ne les aime ni lui ni sa femme.

eject [ɪ'dʒekt] vt **1.** [troublemaker] expulser - **2.** [cartridge, pilot] éjecter.

eke [i:k] ➤ **eke out** vt sep [make last] faire durer.

elaborate <> adj [ɪ'læbrət] [ceremony, procedure] complexe ; [explanation, plan] détaillé(e), minutieux(euse). <> vi [ɪ'læbəreɪt] : **to elaborate (on)** donner des précisions (sur).

elapse [ɪ'læps] vi s'écouler.

elastic [ɪ'læstɪk] <> adj lit & fig élastique. <> n (U) élastique m.

elasticated UK [ɪ'læstɪkeɪtɪd], **elasticized** US [ɪ'læstɪsaɪzd] adj élastique.

elastic band n UK élastique m, caoutchouc m.

elated [ɪ'leɪtɪd] adj transporté(e) (de joie).

elbow ['elbəʊ] n coude m.

elder ['eldər] <> adj aîné(e). <> n **1.** [older person] aîné m, -e f - **2.** [of tribe, church] ancien m - **3.** : **elder (tree)** sureau m.

elderly ['eldəlɪ] <> adj âgé(e). <> npl : **the elderly** les personnes fpl âgées.

eldest ['eldɪst] adj aîné(e).

elect [ɪ'lekt] <> adj élu(e). <> vt **1.** [by voting] élire - **2.** fml [choose] : **to elect to do sthg** choisir de faire qqch.

election [ɪ'lekʃn] n élection f ; **to have** OR **hold an election** procéder à une élection.

electioneering [ɪ,lekʃə'nɪərɪŋ] n (U) pej propagande f électorale.

elector [ɪ'lektər] n électeur m, -trice f.

electorate [ɪ'lektərət] n : **the electorate** l'électorat m.

electric [ɪ'lektrɪk] adj lit & fig électrique. ➤ **electrics** npl UK inf [in car, machine] installation f électrique.

electrical [ɪ'lektrɪkl] adj électrique.

electrical shock = electric shock.

electric blanket n couverture f chauffante.

electric cooker *n* cuisinière *f* électrique.

electric fire *n* radiateur *m* électrique.

electrician [,ɪlek'trɪʃn] *n* électricien *m*, -enne *f*.

electricity [,ɪlek'trɪsətɪ] *n* électricité *f*.

electric shock *n* décharge *f* électrique.

electrify [ɪ'lektrɪfaɪ] *vt* **1.** TECH électrifier - **2.** *fig* [excite] galvaniser, électriser.

electrocute [ɪ'lektrəkju:t] *vt* électrocuter.

electrolysis [,ɪlek'trɒləsɪs] *n* électrolyse *f*.

electron [ɪ'lektrɒn] *n* électron *m*.

electronic [,ɪlek'trɒnɪk] *adj* électronique. **➡ electronics** ◇ *n* (U) [technology, science] électronique *f*. ◇ *npl* [equipment] (équipement *m*) électronique *f*.

electronic data processing *n* traitement *m* électronique de données.

electronic mail *n* courrier *m* électronique.

electronic tag *n* bracelet *m* électronique.

electronic tagging *n* (U) étiquetage *m* électronique.

elegant ['elɪgənt] *adj* élégant(e).

element ['elɪmənt] *n* **1.** [gen] élément *m* ; **an element of truth** une part de vérité - **2.** [in heater, kettle] résistance *f*. **➡ elements** *npl* **1.** [basics] rudiments *mpl* - **2.** [weather] : **the elements** les éléments *mpl*.

elementary [,elɪ'mentərɪ] *adj* élémentaire.

elementary school *n* US école *f* primaire.

elephant ['elɪfənt] (*pl* **elephant** OR **-s**) *n* éléphant *m*.

elevate ['elɪveɪt] *vt* **1.** [give importance to] : **to elevate sb/sthg (to)** élever qqn/qqch (à) - **2.** [raise] soulever.

elevator ['elɪveɪtər] *n* US ascenseur *m*.

eleven [ɪ'levn] *num* onze ; *see also* **six**.

elevenses [ɪ'levnzɪz] *n* (U) UK ≃ pause-café *f*.

eleventh [ɪ'levnθ] *num* onzième ; *see also* **sixth**.

elicit [ɪ'lɪsɪt] *vt fml* : **to elicit sthg (from sb)** arracher qqch (à qqn).

eligible ['elɪdʒəbl] *adj* [suitable, qualified] admissible ; **to be eligible for sthg** avoir droit à qqch ; **to be eligible to do sthg** avoir le droit de faire qqch.

eliminate [ɪ'lɪmɪneɪt] *vt* : **to eliminate sb/ sthg (from)** éliminer qqn/qqch (de).

elite [ɪ'li:t] ◇ *adj* d'élite. ◇ *n* élite *f*.

elitist [ɪ'li:tɪst] ◇ *adj* élitiste. ◇ *n* élitiste *mf*.

elk [elk] (*pl* **elk** OR **-s**) *n* élan *m*.

elm [elm] *n* : **elm (tree)** orme *m*.

elocution [,elə'kju:ʃn] *n* élocution *f*, diction *f*.

elongated ['i:lɒŋgeɪtɪd] *adj* allongé(e) ; [fingers] long (longue).

elope [ɪ'ləʊp] *vi* : **to elope (with)** s'enfuir (avec).

eloquent ['eləkwənt] *adj* éloquent(e).

El Salvador [,el'sælvədɔːr] *n* Salvador *m*.

else [els] *adv* : **anything else** n'importe quoi d'autre ; **anything else?** [in shop] et avec ça?, ce sera tout? ; **he doesn't need anything else** il n'a besoin de rien d'autre ; **everyone else** tous les autres ; **nothing else** rien d'autre ; **someone else** quelqu'un d'autre ; **something else** quelque chose d'autre ; **somewhere else** autre part ; **who/what else?** qui/quoi d'autre? ; **where else?** (à) quel autre endroit? **➡ or else** *conj* [or if not] sinon, sans quoi.

elsewhere [els'weər] *adv* ailleurs, autre part.

elude [ɪ'lu:d] *vt* échapper à.

elusive [ɪ'lu:sɪv] *adj* insaisissable ; [success] qui échappe.

emaciated [ɪ'meɪʃɪeɪtɪd] *adj* [face] émacié(e) ; [person, limb] décharné(e).

e-mail, email (*abbrev of* **electronic mail**) *n* [message] (e-)mail *m*, courrier *m* électronique ; **to send an e-mail** envoyer un mail ; [address] e-mail *m*, adresse *f* électronique, courriel *m* *Québec*.

emanate ['emǝneɪt] *fml vi* : **to emanate from** émaner de.

emancipate [ɪ'mænsɪpeɪt] *vt* : **to emancipate sb (from)** affranchir OR émanciper qqn (de).

embankment [ɪm'bæŋkmǝnt] *n* [of river] berge *f* ; [of railway] remblai *m* ; [of road] banquette *f*.

embark [ɪm'bɑːk] *vi* **1.** [board ship] : **to embark (on)** embarquer (sur) - **2.** [start] : **to embark on** OR **upon sthg** s'embarquer dans qqch.

embarkation [,embɑː'keɪʃn] *n* embarquement *m*.

embarrass [ɪm'bærǝs] *vt* embarrasser.

embarrassed [ɪm'bærǝst] *adj* embarrassé(e).

embarrassing [ɪm'bærǝsɪŋ] *adj* embarrassant(e).

embarrassment [ɪm'bærǝsmǝnt] *n* embarras *m* ; **to be an embarrassment** [person] causer de l'embarras ; [thing] être embarrassant.

embassy ['embǝsɪ] *n* ambassade *f*.

embedded [ɪm'bedɪd] *adj* [in wood] enfoncé(e) ; [in rock] scellé(e) ; [in cement] scellé(e), noyé(e) ; [jewels] enchâssé(e), incrusté(e).

embellish [ɪm'belɪʃ] *vt* **1.** [decorate] : **to**

embellish sthg (with) [room, house] décorer qqch (de) ; [dress] orner qqch (de) - **2.** [story] enjoliver.

embers ['embəz] *npl* braises *fpl*.

embezzle [ɪm'bezl] *vt* détourner.

embittered [ɪm'bɪtəd] *adj* aigri(e).

emblem ['embləm] *n* emblème *m*.

embody [ɪm'bɒdɪ] *vt* incarner ; **to be embodied in sthg** être exprimé dans qqch.

embossed [ɪm'bɒst] *adj* **1.** [heading, design] : **embossed (on)** inscrit(e) (sur), gravé(e) en relief (sur) - **2.** [wallpaper, leather] gaufré(e).

embrace [ɪm'breɪs] <> *n* étreinte *f*. <> *vt* embrasser. <> *vi* s'embrasser, s'étreindre.

embroider [ɪm'brɔɪdə'] <> *vt* **1.** SEW broder - **2.** *pej* [embellish] enjoliver. <> *vi* SEW broder.

embroidery [ɪm'brɔɪdərɪ] *n* (U) broderie *f*.

embroil [ɪm'brɔɪl] *vt* : **to be embroiled (in)** être mêlé(e) (à).

embryo ['embrɪəʊ] (*pl* -s) *n* embryon *m*.

emerald ['emərəld] <> *adj* [colour] émeraude (*inv*). <> *n* [stone] émeraude *f*.

emerge [ɪ'mɜːdʒ] <> *vi* **1.** [come out] : **to emerge (from)** émerger (de) - **2.** [from experience, situation] : **to emerge from** sortir de - **3.** [become known] apparaître - **4.** [come into existence - poet, artist] percer ; [- movement, organization] émerger. <> *vt* : **it emerges that...** il ressort OR il apparaît que...

emergence [ɪ'mɜːdʒəns] *n* émergence *f*.

emergency [ɪ'mɜːdʒənsɪ] <> *adj* d'urgence. <> *n* urgence *f* ; **in an emergency, in emergencies** en cas d'urgence.

emergency exit *n* sortie *f* de secours.

emergency landing *n* atterrissage *m* forcé.

emergency services *npl* ≈ police-secours *f*.

emery board ['emərɪ-] *n* lime *f* à ongles.

emigrant ['emɪɡrənt] *n* émigré *m*, -e *f*.

emigrate ['emɪɡreɪt] *vi* : **to emigrate (to)** émigrer (en/à).

eminent ['emɪnənt] *adj* éminent(e).

emission [ɪ'mɪʃn] *n* émission *f*.

emit [ɪ'mɪt] *vt* émettre.

emotion [ɪ'məʊʃn] *n* **1.** (U) [strength of feeling] émotion *f* - **2.** [particular feeling] sentiment *m*.

emotional [ɪ'məʊʃənl] *adj* **1.** [sensitive, demonstrative] émotif(ive) - **2.** [moving] émouvant(e) - **3.** [psychological] émotionnel(elle).

emotional intelligence *n* intelligence *f* émotionnelle.

empathize, *UK* **-ise** ['empəθaɪz] *vt* : **to empathize with** s'identifier à.

emperor ['empərə'] *n* empereur *m*.

emphasis ['emfəsɪs] (*pl* -ses [-siːz]) *n* : **emphasis (on)** accent *m* (sur) ; **to lay** OR **place emphasis on sthg** insister sur OR souligner qqch.

emphasize, *UK* **-ise** ['emfəsaɪz] *vt* insister sur.

emphatic [ɪm'fætɪk] *adj* [forceful] catégorique.

emphatically [ɪm'fætɪklɪ] *adv* **1.** [with emphasis] catégoriquement - **2.** [certainly] absolument.

empire ['empaɪə'] *n* empire *m*.

employ [ɪm'plɔɪ] *vt* employer ; **to be employed as** être employé comme ; **to employ sthg as sthg/to do sthg** employer qqch comme qqch/pour faire qqch.

employee [ɪm'plɔiː] *n* employé *m*, -e *f*.

employer [ɪm'plɔɪə'] *n* employeur *m*, -euse *f*.

employment [ɪm'plɔɪmənt] *n* emploi *m*, travail *m*.

employment agency *n* bureau *m* OR agence *f* de placement.

empower [ɪm'paʊə'] *vt fml* : **to be empowered to do sthg** être habilité(e) à faire qqch.

empress ['emprɪs] *n* impératrice *f*.

empty ['emptɪ] <> *adj* **1.** [containing nothing] vide - **2.** *pej* [meaningless] vain(e). <> *vt* vider ; **to empty sthg into/out of** vider qqch dans/de. <> *vi* se vider. <> *n inf* bouteille *f* vide.

empty-handed [-'hændɪd] *adj* les mains vides.

EMS (*abbrev of* **European Monetary System**) *n* SME *m*.

EMU (*abbrev of* **Economic and Monetary Union**) *n* UEM *f*.

emulate ['emjʊleɪt] *vt* imiter.

emulsion [ɪ'mʌlʃn] *n UK* : **emulsion (paint)** peinture *f* mate OR à émulsion.

enable [ɪ'neɪbl] *vt* : **to enable sb to do sthg** permettre à qqn de faire qqch.

enact [ɪ'nækt] *vt* **1.** LAW promulguer - **2.** THEAT jouer.

enamel [ɪ'næml] *n* **1.** [material] émail *m* - **2.** [paint] peinture *f* laquée.

encampment [ɪn'kæmpmənt] *n* campement *m*.

encapsulate [ɪn'kæpsjʊleɪt] *vt* : **to encapsulate sthg (in)** résumer qqch (en).

encase [ɪn'keɪs] *vt* : **to be encased in** [armour] être enfermé(e) dans ; [leather] être bardé(e) de.

enchanted [ɪn'tʃɑːntɪd] *adj* : enchanted (by/with) enchanté(e) (par/de).

enchanting [ɪn'tʃɑːntɪŋ] *adj* enchanteur(eresse).

encircle [ɪn'sɜːkl] *vt* entourer ; [subj: troops] encercler.

enclose [ɪn'kləʊz] *vt* **1.** [surround, contain] entourer - **2.** [put in envelope] joindre ; **please find enclosed...** veuillez trouver ci-joint...

enclosure [ɪn'kləʊʒər] *n* **1.** [place] enceinte *f* - **2.** [in letter] pièce *f* jointe.

encompass [ɪn'kʌmpəs] *vt fml* **1.** [include] contenir - **2.** [surround] entourer ; [subj: troops] encercler.

encore ['ɒŋkɔːr] <> *n* rappel *m*. <> *excl* bis!

encounter [ɪn'kaʊntər] <> *n* rencontre *f*. <> *vt fml* rencontrer.

encourage [ɪn'kʌrɪdʒ] *vt* **1.** [give confidence to] : **to encourage sb (to do sthg)** encourager qqn (à faire qqch) - **2.** [promote] encourager, favoriser.

encouragement [ɪn'kʌrɪdʒmənt] *n* encouragement *m*.

encroach [ɪn'krəʊtʃ] *vi* : **to encroach on** OR **upon** empiéter sur.

encryption [en'krɪpʃn] *n* (U) **1.** COMPUT cryptage *m* - **2.** TV codage *m*, encodage *m*.

encyclop(a)edia [ɪn,saɪklə'piːdjə] *n* encyclopédie *f*.

end [end] <> *n* **1.** [gen] fin *f* ; **at an end** terminé, fini ; **to come to an end** se terminer, s'arrêter ; **to put an end to sthg** mettre fin à qqch ; **at the end of the day** *fig* en fin de compte ; **in the end** [finally] finalement - **2.** [of rope, path, garden, table etc] bout *m*, extrémité *f* ; [of box] côté *m* - **3.** [leftover part - of cigarette] mégot *m* ; [- of pencil] bout *m*. <> *vt* mettre fin à ; [day] finir ; **to end sthg with** terminer OR finir qqch par. <> *vi* se terminer ; **to end in** se terminer par ; **to end with** se terminer par OR avec. ◆ **on end** *adv* **1.** [upright] debout - **2.** [continuously] d'affilée. ◆ **end up** *vi* finir ; **to end up doing sthg** finir par faire qqch.

endanger [ɪn'deɪndʒər] *vt* mettre en danger.

endearing [ɪn'dɪərɪŋ] *adj* [smile] engageant(e).

endeavour UK, **endeavor** US *fml* [ɪn'devər] <> *n* effort *m*, tentative *f*. <> *vt* : **to endeavour to do sthg** s'efforcer OR tenter de faire qqch.

ending ['endɪŋ] *n* fin *f*, dénouement *m*.

endive ['endaɪv] *n* **1.** US [salad vegetable] endive *f* - **2.** UK [chicory] chicorée *f*.

endless ['endlɪs] *adj* **1.** [unending] interminable ; [patience, possibilities] infini(e) ; [resources] inépuisable - **2.** [vast] infini(e).

endorse [ɪn'dɔːs] *vt* **1.** [approve] approuver - **2.** [cheque] endosser.

endorsement [ɪn'dɔːsmənt] *n* **1.** [approval] approbation *f* - **2.** UK [on driving licence] *contravention portée au permis de conduire.*

endoscope ['endəskəʊp] *n* MED endoscope *m*.

endow [ɪn'daʊ] *vt* **1.** [equip] : **to be endowed with sthg** être doté(e) de qqch - **2.** [donate money] faire des dons à.

endurance [ɪn'djʊərəns] *n* endurance *f*.

endure [ɪn'djʊər] <> *vt* supporter, endurer. <> *vi* perdurer.

endways UK ['endweɪz], **endwise** US ['endwaɪz] *adv* **1.** [not sideways] en long - **2.** [with ends touching] bout à bout.

enemy ['enɪmɪ] <> *n* ennemi *m*, -e *f*. <> *comp* ennemi(e).

energetic [,enə'dʒetɪk] *adj* énergique ; [person] plein(e) d'entrain.

energy ['enədʒɪ] *n* énergie *f*.

enforce [ɪn'fɔːs] *vt* appliquer, faire respecter.

enforced [ɪn'fɔːst] *adj* forcé(e).

engage [ɪn'geɪdʒ] <> *vt* **1.** [attention, interest] susciter, éveiller - **2.** TECH engager - **3.** *fml* [employ] engager ; **to be engaged in** OR **on sthg** prendre part à qqch. <> *vi* [be involved] : **to engage in** s'occuper de.

engaged [ɪn'geɪdʒd] *adj* **1.** UK [to be married] : **engaged (to sb)** fiancé(e) (à qqn) ; **to get engaged** se fiancer - **2.** [busy] occupé(e) ; **engaged in sthg** engagé dans qqch - **3.** UK [telephone, toilet] occupé(e).

engaged tone *n* UK tonalité *f* 'occupé'.

engagement [ɪn'geɪdʒmənt] *n* **1.** [to be married] fiançailles *fpl* - **2.** [appointment] rendez-vous *m inv*.

engagement ring *n* bague *f* de fiançailles.

engaging [ɪn'geɪdʒɪŋ] *adj* engageant(e) ; [personality] attirant(e).

engender [ɪn'dʒendər] *vt fml* engendrer, susciter.

engine ['endʒɪn] *n* **1.** [of vehicle] moteur *m* - **2.** RAIL locomotive *f*.

engine driver *n* UK mécanicien *m*.

engineer [,endʒɪ'nɪər] *n* **1.** [of roads] ingénieur *m*, -(e) *f* ; [of machinery, on ship] mécanicien *m*, -ienne *f* ; [of electrical equipment] technicien *m*, -ienne *f* - **2.** US [train driver] mécanicien *m*, -ienne *f*.

engineering [,endʒɪ'nɪərɪŋ] *n* ingénierie *f*.

England ['ɪŋglənd] *n* Angleterre *f* ; **in England** en Angleterre.

English ['ɪŋglɪʃ] <> *adj* anglais(e). <> *n* [language] anglais *m*. <> *npl* : **the English** les Anglais.

English breakfast *n* petit déjeuner *m* anglais traditionnel.

English Channel *n* : **the English Channel** la Manche.

Englishman ['ɪŋglɪʃmən] (*pl* -**men** [-mən]) *n* Anglais *m*.

Englishwoman ['ɪŋglɪʃ,wʊmən] (*pl* -**women** [-wɪmɪn]) *n* Anglaise *f*.

engrave [ɪn'greɪv] *vt* : **to engrave sthg (on** stone/in one's memory) graver qqch (sur la pierre/dans sa mémoire).

engraving [ɪn'greɪvɪŋ] *n* gravure *f*.

engrossed [ɪn'grəʊst] *adj* : **to be engrossed (in sthg)** être absorbé(e) (par qqch).

engulf [ɪn'gʌlf] *vt* engloutir.

enhance [ɪn'hɑːns] *vt* améliorer.

enjoy [ɪn'dʒɔɪ] *vt* **1.** [like] aimer ; **to enjoy doing sthg** avoir plaisir à OR aimer faire qqch ; **to enjoy o.s.** s'amuser - **2.** *fml* [possess] jouir de.

enjoyable [ɪn'dʒɔɪəbl] *adj* agréable.

enjoyment [ɪn'dʒɔɪmənt] *n* [gen] plaisir *m*.

enlarge [ɪn'lɑːdʒ] *vt* agrandir. ✒ **enlarge (up)on** *vt insep* développer.

enlargement [ɪn'lɑːdʒmənt] *n* **1.** [expansion] extension *f* - **2.** PHOT agrandissement *m*.

enlighten [ɪn'laɪtn] *vt* éclairer.

enlightened [ɪn'laɪtnd] *adj* éclairé(e).

enlightenment [ɪn'laɪtnmənt] *n (U)* éclaircissement *m*.

enlist [ɪn'lɪst] <> *vt* **1.** MIL enrôler - **2.** [recruit] recruter - **3.** [obtain] s'assurer. <> *vi* MIL : **to enlist (in)** s'enrôler (dans).

enmity ['enmətɪ] *n* hostilité *f*.

enormity [ɪ'nɔːmətɪ] *n* [extent] étendue *f*.

enormous [ɪ'nɔːməs] *adj* énorme ; [patience, success] immense.

enough [ɪ'nʌf] <> *adj* assez de ; **enough money/time** assez d'argent/de temps. <> *pron* assez ; **more than enough** largement, bien assez ; **to have had enough (of sthg)** en avoir assez (de qqch). <> *adv* **1.** [sufficiently] assez ; **big enough for sthg/to do sthg** assez grand pour qqch/pour faire qqch ; **to be good enough to do sthg** *fml* être assez gentil pour OR de faire qqch, être assez aimable pour OR de faire qqch - **2.** [rather] plutôt ; **strangely enough** bizarrement, c'est bizarre.

enquire [ɪn'kwaɪər] <> *vt UK* **to enquire when/whether/how...** demander quand/si/comment... <> *vi* : **to enquire (about)** se renseigner (sur).

enquiry [ɪn'kwaɪərɪ] *n* **1.** [question] demande *f* de renseignements ; **'Enquiries'** 'renseignements' - **2.** [investigation] enquête *f*.

enraged [ɪn'reɪdʒd] *adj* [person] furieux(ieuse) ; [animal] enragé(e).

enrol *UK*, **enroll** *US* [ɪn'rəʊl] <> *vt* inscrire. <> *vi* : **to enrol (in)** s'inscrire (à).

ensign ['ensaɪn] *n* [flag] pavillon *m*.

ensue [ɪn'sjuː] *vi* s'ensuivre.

ensure [ɪn'ʃʊər] *vt* assurer ; **to ensure (that)...** s'assurer que...

ENT (*abbrev of* Ear, Nose &Throat) *n* ORL *f*.

entail [ɪn'teɪl] *vt* entraîner ; **what does the work entail?** en quoi consiste le travail?

enter ['entər] <> *vt* **1.** [room, vehicle] entrer dans - **2.** [university, army] entrer à ; [school] s'inscrire à, s'inscrire dans - **3.** [competition, race] s'inscrire à ; [politics] se lancer dans - **4.** [register] : **to enter sb/sthg for sthg** inscrire qqn/qqch à qqch - **5.** [write down] inscrire - **6.** COMPUT entrer. <> *vi* **1.** [come or go in] entrer - **2.** [register] : **to enter (for)** s'inscrire (à). ✒ **enter into** *vt insep* [negotiations, correspondence] entamer.

enter key *n* COMPUT (touche *f*) entrée *f*.

enterprise ['entəpraɪz] *n* entreprise *f*.

enterprise zone *n UK* zone dans une région défavorisée qui bénéficie de subsides de l'État.

enterprising ['entəpraɪzɪŋ] *adj* qui fait preuve d'initiative.

entertain [,entə'teɪn] *vt* **1.** [amuse] divertir - **2.** [invite - guests] recevoir - **3.** *fml* [thought, proposal] considérer.

entertainer [,entə'teɪnər] *n* fantaisiste *mf*.

entertaining [,entə'teɪnɪŋ] *adj* divertissant(e).

entertainment [,entə'teɪnmənt] *n* **1.** *(U)* [amusement] divertissement *m* - **2.** [show] spectacle *m*.

enthral *UK*, **enthrall** *US* [ɪn'θrɔːl] *vt* captiver.

enthrone [ɪn'θrəʊn] *vt* introniser.

enthusiasm [ɪn'θjuːzɪæzm] *n* **1.** [passion, eagerness] : **enthusiasm (for)** enthousiasme *m* (pour) - **2.** [interest] passion *f*.

enthusiast [ɪn'θjuːzɪæst] *n* enthousiaste *mf*.

enthusiastic [ɪn,θjuːzɪ'æstɪk] *adj* enthousiaste.

entice [ɪn'taɪs] *vt* séduire.

entire [ɪn'taɪər] *adj* entier(ère).

entirely [ɪn'taɪəlɪ] *adv* entièrement, totalement.

entirety [ɪn'taɪrətɪ] *n* : **in its entirety** en entier.

entitle [ɪn'taɪtl] *vt* [allow] : **to entitle sb to sthg** donner droit à qqch à qqn ; **to entitle sb to do sthg** autoriser qqn à faire qqch.

entitled [ɪn'taɪtld] *adj* **1.** [allowed] autorisé(e) ; **to be entitled to sthg** avoir droit à qqch ; **to be entitled to do sthg** avoir le droit de faire qqch - **2.** [called] intitulé(e).

entitlement [ɪn'taɪtlmənt] *n* droit *m*.

entrance ⋄ *n* ['entrəns] **1.** [way in] : **entrance (to)** entrée *f* (de) - **2.** [arrival] entrée *f* - **3.** [entry] : **to gain entrance to** [building] obtenir l'accès à ; [society, university] être admis(e) dans. ⋄ *vt* [ɪn'trɑːns] ravir, enivrer.

entrance examination *n* examen *m* d'entrée.

entrance fee *n* **1.** [to cinema, museum] droit *m* d'entrée - **2.** [for club] droit *m* d'inscription.

entrant ['entrənt] *n* [in race, competition] concurrent *m*, -e *f*.

entreat [ɪn'triːt] *vt* : **to entreat sb (to do sthg)** supplier qqn (de faire qqch).

entrenched [ɪn'trentʃt] *adj* ancré(e).

entrepreneur [ˌɒntrəprə'nɜːr] *n* entrepreneur *m*.

entrust [ɪn'trʌst] *vt* : **to entrust sthg to sb, to entrust sb with sthg** confier qqch à qqn.

entry ['entrɪ] *n* **1.** [gen] entrée *f* ; **to gain entry to** avoir accès à ; **'no entry'** 'défense d'entrer' ; AUT 'sens interdit' - **2.** [in competition] inscription *f* - **3.** [in dictionary] entrée *f* ; [in diary, ledger] inscription *f*.

entry form *n* formulaire *m* OR feuille *f* d'inscription.

envelop [ɪn'veləp] *vt* envelopper.

envelope ['envələʊp] *n* enveloppe *f*.

envious ['envɪəs] *adj* envieux(euse).

environment [ɪn'vaɪərənmənt] *n* **1.** [surroundings] milieu *m*, cadre *m* - **2.** [natural world] : **the environment** l'environnement *m*.

environmental [ɪnˌvaɪərən'mentl] *adj* [pollution, awareness] de l'environnement ; [impact] sur l'environnement.

environmentally [ɪnˌvaɪərən'mentəlɪ] *adv* [damaging] pour l'environnement ; **to be environmentally aware** être sensible aux problèmes de l'environnement.

environment-friendly *adj* [policy] respectueux(euse) de l'environnement ; [product] non polluant(e).

envisage [ɪn'vɪzɪdʒ], **envision** US [ɪn'vɪʒn] *vt* envisager.

envoy ['envɔɪ] *n* émissaire *m*.

envy ['envɪ] ⋄ *n* envie *f*, jalousie *f*. ⋄ *vt* envier ; **to envy sb sthg** envier qqch à qqn.

epic ['epɪk] ⋄ *adj* épique. ⋄ *n* épopée *f*.

epidemic [ˌepɪ'demɪk] *n* épidémie *f*.

epileptic [ˌepɪ'leptɪk] ⋄ *adj* épileptique. ⋄ *n* épileptique *mf*.

episode ['epɪsəʊd] *n* épisode *m*.

epistle [ɪ'pɪsl] *n* épître *f*.

epitaph ['epɪtɑːf] *n* épitaphe *f*.

epitome [ɪ'pɪtəmɪ] *n* : **the epitome of** le modèle de.

epitomize, UK **-ise** [ɪ'pɪtəmaɪz] *vt* incarner.

epoch ['iːpɒk] *n* époque *f*.

EQ [iː'kjuː] (*abbrev of* **emotional intelligence quotient**) *n* QE *m*, quotient *m* émotionnel.

equable ['ekwəbl] *adj* [character, person] égal(e), placide.

equal ['iːkwəl] ⋄ *adj* **1.** [gen] : **equal (to)** égal(e) (à) ; **on equal terms** d'égal à égal - **2.** [capable] : **equal to sthg** à la hauteur de qqch. ⋄ *n* égal *m*, -e *f*. ⋄ *vt* (*UK & US*) égaler.

equality [iː'kwɒlətɪ] *n* égalité *f*.

equalize, UK **-ise** ['iːkwəlaɪz] ⋄ *vt* niveler. ⋄ *vi* UK SPORT égaliser.

equalizer ['iːkwəlaɪzər] *n* UK SPORT but *m* égalisateur.

equally ['iːkwəlɪ] *adv* **1.** [important, stupid etc] tout aussi - **2.** [in amount] en parts égales - **3.** [also] en même temps.

equal opportunities *npl* égalité *f* des chances.

equanimity [ˌekwə'nɪmətɪ] *n* sérénité *f*, égalité *f* d'âme.

equate [ɪ'kweɪt] *vt* : **to equate sthg with** assimiler qqch à.

equation [ɪ'kweɪʒn] *n* équation *f*.

equator [ɪ'kweɪtər] *n* : **the equator** l'équateur *m*.

equilibrium [ˌiːkwɪ'lɪbrɪəm] *n* équilibre *m*.

equip [ɪ'kwɪp] *vt* équiper ; **to equip sb/sthg with** équiper qqn/qqch de, munir qqn/qqch de ; **he's well equipped for the job** il est bien préparé pour ce travail.

equipment [ɪ'kwɪpmənt] *n* (U) équipement *m*, matériel *m*.

equities ['ekwətɪz] *npl* FIN actions *fpl* ordinaires.

equivalent [ɪ'kwɪvələnt] ⋄ *adj* équivalent(e) ; **to be equivalent to** être équivalent à, équivaloir à. ⋄ *n* équivalent *m*.

equivocal [ɪ'kwɪvəkl] *adj* équivoque.

er [ɜːr] *excl* euh!

era ['ɪərə] (*pl* **-s**) *n* ère *f*, période *f*.

eradicate [ɪ'rædɪkeɪt] *vt* éradiquer.

erase [ɪ'reɪz] *vt* **1.** [rub out] gommer - **2.** *fig* [memory] effacer ; [hunger, poverty] éliminer.

eraser [ɪ'reɪzər] *n* gomme *f*.

erect [ɪ'rekt] <> adj **1.** [person, posture] droit(e) - **2.** [penis] en érection. <> vt **1.** [statue] ériger ; [building] construire - **2.** [tent] dresser.

erection [ɪ'rekʃn] n **1.** (U) [of statue] érection f ; [of building] construction f - **2.** [erect penis] érection f.

ERM (abbrev of **Exchange Rate Mechanism**) n mécanisme m des changes (du SME).

ermine ['ɜːmɪn] n [fur] hermine f.

erode [ɪ'rəʊd] <> vt **1.** [rock, soil] éroder - **2.** fig [confidence, rights] réduire. <> vi **1.** [rock, soil] s'éroder - **2.** fig [confidence] diminuer ; [rights] se réduire.

erosion [ɪ'rəʊʒn] n **1.** [of rock, soil] érosion f - **2.** fig [of confidence] baisse f ; [of rights] diminution f.

erotic [ɪ'rɒtɪk] adj érotique.

err [ɜːr] vi se tromper.

errand ['erənd] n course f, commission f ; **to go on** OR **run an errand** faire une course.

erratic [ɪ'rætɪk] adj irrégulier(ère).

error ['erər] n erreur f ; **a spelling/typing error** une faute d'orthographe/de frappe ; **an error of judgment** une erreur de jugement ; **in error** par erreur.

erupt [ɪ'rʌpt] vi **1.** [volcano] entrer en éruption - **2.** fig [violence, war] éclater.

eruption [ɪ'rʌpʃn] n **1.** [of volcano] éruption f - **2.** [of violence] explosion f ; [of war] déclenchement m.

escalate ['eskəleɪt] vi **1.** [conflict] s'intensifier - **2.** [costs] monter en flèche.

escalator ['eskəleɪtər] n escalier m roulant.

escapade [,eskə'peɪd] n aventure f, exploit m.

escape [ɪ'skeɪp] <> n **1.** [gen] fuite f, évasion f ; **to make one's escape** s'échapper ; **to have a lucky escape** l'échapper belle - **2.** [leakage - of gas, water] fuite f. <> vt échapper à. <> vi **1.** [gen] s'échapper, fuir ; [from prison] s'évader ; **to escape from** [place] s'échapper de ; [danger, person] échapper à - **2.** [survive] s'en tirer.

escape artist US = **escapologist**.

escapism [ɪ'skeɪpɪzm] n (U) évasion f (de la réalité).

escort <> n ['eskɔːt] **1.** [guard] escorte f ; **under escort** sous escorte - **2.** [companion - male] cavalier m ; [- female] hôtesse f. <> vt [ɪ'skɔːt] escorter, accompagner.

ESF [iːes'ef] (abbrev of **European Social Fund**) n FSE m.

Eskimo ['eskɪməʊ] n (pl -s) [person] Esquimau m, -aude f (attention: le terme 'Eskimo',

comme son équivalent français, est souvent considéré comme injurieux en Amérique du Nord. On préférera le terme 'Inuit').

espadrille [,espə'drɪl] n espadrille f.

especially [ɪ'speʃəlɪ] adv **1.** [in particular] surtout - **2.** [more than usually] particulièrement - **3.** [specifically] spécialement.

espionage ['espɪə,nɑːʒ] n espionnage m.

esplanade [,esplə'neɪd] n esplanade f.

Esquire [ɪ'skwaɪər] n : **G. Curry Esquire** Monsieur G. Curry.

essay ['eseɪ] n **1.** SCH & UNIV dissertation f - **2.** LIT essai m.

essence ['esns] n **1.** [nature] essence f, nature f ; **in essence** par essence - **2.** CULIN extrait m.

essential [ɪ'senʃl] adj **1.** [absolutely necessary] : **essential (to** OR **for)** indispensable (à) - **2.** [basic] essentiel(elle), de base. ⚫ **essentials** npl **1.** [basic commodities] produits mpl de première nécessité - **2.** [most important elements] essentiel m.

essentially [ɪ'senʃəlɪ] adv essentiellement, fondamentalement.

establish [ɪ'stæblɪʃ] vt **1.** [gen] établir ; **to establish contact with** établir le contact avec - **2.** [organization, business] fonder, créer.

establishment [ɪ'stæblɪʃmənt] n **1.** [gen] établissement m - **2.** [of organization, business] fondation f, création f. ⚫ **Establishment** n [status quo] : **the Establishment** l'ordre m établi, l'Establishment m.

estate [ɪ'steɪt] n **1.** [land, property] propriété f, domaine m - **2.** UK **(housing) estate** lotissement m - **3.** US **(industrial) estate** zone f industrielle - **4.** LAW [inheritance] biens mpl.

estate agency n UK agence f immobilière.

estate agent n UK agent m immobilier.

estate car n UK break m.

esteem [ɪ'stiːm] <> n estime f. <> vt estimer.

esthetic etc US = **aesthetic** etc.

estimate <> n ['estɪmət] **1.** [calculation, judgment] estimation f, évaluation f - **2.** COMM devis m. <> vt ['estɪmeɪt] estimer, évaluer.

estimation [,estɪ'meɪʃn] n **1.** [opinion] opinion f - **2.** [calculation] estimation f, évaluation f.

Estonia [e'stəʊnɪə] n Estonie f.

estranged [ɪ'streɪndʒd] adj [couple] séparé(e) ; [husband, wife] dont on s'est séparé.

estuary ['estjʊərɪ] n estuaire m.

e-tailer n détaillant m en ligne.

etc. (abbrev of **et cetera**) etc.

etching ['etʃɪŋ] n gravure f à l'eau forte.

eternal [ɪ'tɜ:nl] *adj* **1.** [life] éternel(elle) - **2.** *fig* [complaints, whining] sempiternel(elle) - **3.** [truth, value] immuable.

eternity [ɪ'tɜ:nətɪ] *n* éternité *f*.

ethic ['eθɪk] *n* éthique *f*, morale *f*. ➡ **ethics** ⟨⟩ *n (U)* [study] éthique *f*, morale *f*. ⟨⟩ *npl* [morals] morale *f*.

ethical ['eθɪkl] *adj* moral(e).

Ethiopia [,i:θɪ'əʊpɪə] *n* Éthiopie *f*.

ethnic ['eθnɪk] *adj* **1.** [traditions, groups] ethnique - **2.** [clothes] folklorique.

ethos ['i:θɒs] *n* éthos *m*.

etiquette ['etɪket] *n* convenances *fpl*, étiquette *f*.

e-trade *n (U)* cybercommerce *m*, commerce *m* électronique.

EU *(abbrev of* **European Union)** *n* UE *f* ; **EU policy** la politique de l'Union Européenne, la politique communautaire.

eulogy ['ju:lədʒɪ] *n* panégyrique *m*.

euphemism ['ju:fəmɪzm] *n* euphémisme *m*.

euphoria [ju:'fɔ:rɪə] *n* euphorie *f*.

euro ['jʊərəʊ] *n* euro *m*.

Eurocheque ['jʊərəʊ,tʃek] *n* UK eurochèque *m*.

Europe ['jʊərəp] *n* Europe *f*.

European [,jʊərə'pi:ən] ⟨⟩ *adj* européen(enne). ⟨⟩ *n* Européen *m*, -enne *f*.

European Central Bank *n* Banque *f* centrale européenne.

European Commission *n* Commission *f* des communautés européennes.

European Community *n* Communauté *f* européenne.

European Monetary System *n* Système *m* monétaire européen.

European Union *n* Union *f* européenne.

Eurostar® ['jʊərəʊstɑ:r] *n* Eurostar® *m*.

euro zone *n* zone *f* euro.

euthanasia [,ju:θə'neɪzjə] *n* euthanasie *f*.

evacuate [ɪ'vækjʊeɪt] *vt* évacuer.

evade [ɪ'veɪd] *vt* **1.** [gen] échapper à - **2.** [issue, question] esquiver, éluder.

evaluate [ɪ'væljʊeɪt] *vt* évaluer.

evaporate [ɪ'væpəreɪt] *vi* **1.** [liquid] s'évaporer - **2.** *fig* [hopes, fears] s'envoler ; [confidence] disparaître.

evaporated milk [ɪ'væpəreɪtɪd-] *n* lait *m* condensé (non sucré).

evasion [ɪ'veɪʒn] *n* **1.** [of responsibility] dérobade *f* - **2.** [lie] faux-fuyant *m*.

evasive [ɪ'veɪsɪv] *adj* évasif(ive).

eve [i:v] *n* veille *f*.

even ['i:vn] ⟨⟩ *adj* **1.** [speed, rate] régulier(ère) ; [temperature, temperament] égal(e)

- **2.** [flat, level] plat(e), régulier(ère) - **3.** [equal - contest] équilibré(e) ; [- teams, players] de la même force ; [- scores] à égalité ; **to get even with sb** se venger de qqn - **4.** [not odd - number] pair(e). ⟨⟩ *adv* **1.** [gen] même ; **even now** encore maintenant ; **even then** même alors - **2.** [in comparisons] : **even bigger/better/more stupid** encore plus grand/mieux/plus bête. ➡ **even if** *conj* même si. ➡ **even so** *adv* quand même. ➡ **even though** *conj* bien que *(+ subjunctive)*. ➡ **even out** ⟨⟩ *vt sep* égaliser. ⟨⟩ *vi* s'égaliser.

evening ['i:vnɪŋ] *n* soir *m* ; [duration, entertainment] soirée *f* ; **in the evening** le soir. ➡ **evenings** *adv US* le soir.

evening class *n* cours *m* du soir.

evening dress *n* [worn by man] habit *m* de soirée ; [worn by woman] robe *f* du soir.

event [ɪ'vent] *n* **1.** [happening] événement *m* - **2.** SPORT épreuve *f* - **3.** [case] : **in the event of** en cas de ; **in the event that** au cas où. ➡ **in any event** *adv* en tout cas, de toute façon. ➡ **in the event** *adv UK* en l'occurrence, en réalité.

eventful [ɪ'ventfʊl] *adj* mouvementé(e).

eventual [ɪ'ventʃʊəl] *adj* final(e).

eventuality [ɪ,ventʃʊ'ælətɪ] *n* éventualité *f*.

eventually [ɪ'ventʃʊəlɪ] *adv* finalement, en fin de compte.

ever ['evər] *adv* **1.** [at any time] jamais ; **have you ever been to Paris?** êtes-vous déjà allé à Paris? ; **I hardly ever see him** je ne le vois presque jamais - **2.** [all the time] toujours ; **as ever** comme toujours ; **for ever** pour toujours - **3.** [for emphasis] : **ever so** *UK* tellement ; **ever such** *UK* vraiment ; **why/how ever?** pourquoi/comment donc? ➡ **ever since** ⟨⟩ *adv* depuis (ce moment-là). ⟨⟩ *conj* depuis que. ⟨⟩ *prep* depuis.

evergreen ['evəgri:n] ⟨⟩ *adj* à feuilles persistantes. ⟨⟩ *n* arbre *m* à feuilles persistantes.

everlasting [,evə'lɑ:stɪŋ] *adj* éternel(elle).

every ['evrɪ] *adj* chaque ; **every morning** chaque matin, tous les matins. ➡ **every now and then**, **every so often** *adv* de temps en temps, de temps à autre. ➡ **every other** *adj* : **every other day** tous les deux jours, un jour sur deux ; **every other street** une rue sur deux. ➡ **every which way** *adv US* partout, de tous côtés.

everybody ['evrɪ,bɒdɪ] = **everyone**.

everyday ['evrɪdeɪ] *adj* quotidien(enne).

everyone ['evrɪwʌn] *pron* chacun, tout le monde.

everyplace *inf US* = **everywhere**.

everything ['evrɪθɪŋ] *pron* tout.

everywhere ['evrɪweə'] *adv* partout.

evict [ɪ'vɪkt] *vt* expulser.

evidence ['evɪdəns] *n* (U) **1.** [proof] preuve *f* - **2.** LAW [of witness] témoignage *m* ; **to give evidence** témoigner.

evident ['evɪdənt] *adj* évident(e), manifeste.

evidently ['evɪdəntlɪ] *adv* **1.** [seemingly] apparemment - **2.** [obviously] de toute évidence, manifestement.

evil ['iːvl] <> *adj* [person] mauvais(e), malveillant(e). <> *n* mal *m*.

evoke [ɪ'vəʊk] *vt* [memory] évoquer ; [emotion, response] susciter.

evolution [ˌiːvə'luːʃn] *n* évolution *f*.

evolve [ɪ'vɒlv] <> *vt* développer. <> *vi* : **to evolve (into/from)** se développer (en/à partir de).

ewe [juː] *n* brebis *f*.

ex- [eks] *prefix* ex-.

exacerbate [ɪg'zæsəbeɪt] *vt* [feeling] exacerber ; [problems] aggraver.

exact [ɪg'zækt] <> *adj* exact(e), précis(e) ; **to be exact** pour être exact OR précis, exactement. <> *vt* : **to exact sthg (from)** exiger qqch (de).

exacting [ɪg'zæktɪŋ] *adj* [job, standards] astreignant(e) ; [person] exigeant(e).

exactly [ɪg'zæktlɪ] <> *adv* exactement. <> *excl* exactement!, parfaitement!

exaggerate [ɪg'zædʒəreɪt] *vt & vi* exagérer.

exaggeration [ɪg,zædʒə'reɪʃn] *n* exagération *f*.

exalted [ɪg'zɔːltɪd] *adj* haut placé(e).

exam [ɪg'zæm] *n* examen *m* ; **to take** OR **sit** UK **an exam** passer un examen.

examination [ɪg,zæmɪ'neɪʃn] *n* examen *m*.

examine [ɪg'zæmɪn] *vt* **1.** [gen] examiner ; [passport] contrôler - **2.** LAW, SCH & UNIV interroger.

examiner [ɪg'zæmɪnə'] *n* UK examinateur *m*, -trice *f*.

example [ɪg'zɑːmpl] *n* exemple *m* ; **for example** par exemple.

exam room US = **consulting room**.

exasperate [ɪg'zæspəreɪt] *vt* exaspérer.

exasperation [ɪg,zæspə'reɪʃn] *n* exaspération *f*.

excavate ['ekskəveɪt] *vt* **1.** [land] creuser - **2.** [object] déterrer.

exceed [ɪk'siːd] *vt* **1.** [amount, number] excéder - **2.** [limit, expectations] dépasser.

exceedingly [ɪk'siːdɪŋlɪ] *adv* extrêmement.

excel [ɪk'sel] *vi* : **to excel (in** OR **at)** exceller (dans) ; **to excel o.s.** UK se surpasser.

excellence ['eksələns] *n* excellence *f*, supériorité *f*.

excellent ['eksələnt] *adj* excellent(e).

except [ɪk'sept] <> *prep & conj* : **except (for)** à part, sauf. <> *vt* : **to except sb (from)** exclure qqn (de).

excepting [ɪk'septɪŋ] *fml prep & conj* = **except**.

exception [ɪk'sepʃn] *n* **1.** [exclusion] : **exception (to)** exception *f* (à) ; **with the exception of** à l'exception de - **2.** [offence] : **to take exception to** s'offenser de, se froisser de.

exceptional [ɪk'sepʃənl] *adj* exceptionnel(elle).

excerpt ['eksɜːpt] *n* : **excerpt (from)** extrait *m* (de), passage *m* (de).

excess [ɪk'ses] *(before nouns* ['ekses]*)* <> *adj* excédentaire. <> *n* excès *m*.

excess baggage *n* excédent *m* de bagages.

excess fare *n* UK supplément *m*.

excessive [ɪk'sesɪv] *adj* excessif(ive).

exchange [ɪks'tʃeɪndʒ] <> *n* **1.** [gen] échange *m* ; **in exchange (for)** en échange (de) - **2.** TELEC : **(telephone) exchange** central *m* (téléphonique). <> *vt* [swap] échanger ; **to exchange sthg for sthg** échanger qqch contre qqch ; **to exchange sthg with sb** échanger qqch avec qqn.

exchange rate *n* FIN taux *m* de change.

Exchequer [ɪks'tʃekə'] *n* UK : **the Exchequer** ≃ le ministère des Finances.

excise ['eksaɪz] *n* (U) contributions *fpl* indirectes.

excite [ɪk'saɪt] *vt* exciter.

excited [ɪk'saɪtɪd] *adj* excité(e).

excitement [ɪk'saɪtmənt] *n* [state] excitation *f*.

exciting [ɪk'saɪtɪŋ] *adj* passionnant(e) ; [prospect] excitant(e).

exclaim [ɪk'skleɪm] <> *vt* s'écrier. <> *vi* s'exclamer.

exclamation [,eksklə'meɪʃn] *n* exclamation *f*.

exclamation mark UK, **exclamation point** US *n* point *m* d'exclamation.

exclude [ɪk'skluːd] *vt* : **to exclude sb/sthg (from)** exclure qqn/qqch (de).

excluding [ɪk'skluːdɪŋ] *prep* sans compter, à l'exclusion de.

exclusive [ɪk'skluːsɪv] <> *adj* **1.** [high-class] fermé(e) - **2.** [unique - use, news story] exclusif(ive). <> *n* PRESS exclusivité *f*.
➦ **exclusive of** *prep* : **exclusive of interest** intérêts non compris.

excrement ['ekskrɪmənt] *n* excrément *m*.

excruciating [ɪk'skruːʃɪeɪtɪŋ] *adj* atroce.

excursion [ɪk'skɜːʃn] *n* [trip] excursion *f*.

excuse ⬥ *n* [ɪk'skjuːs] excuse *f*. ⬥ *vt* [ɪk'skjuːz] **1.** [gen] excuser ; **to excuse sb for sthg/for doing sthg** excuser qqn de qqch/de faire qqch ; **excuse me** [to attract attention] excusez-moi ; [forgive me] pardon, excusez-moi ; *US* [sorry] pardon **- 2.** [let off] : **to excuse sb (from)** dispenser qqn (de).

ex-directory *adj UK* sur la liste rouge.

execute ['eksɪkjuːt] *vt* exécuter.

execution [ˌeksɪ'kjuːʃn] *n* exécution *f*.

executioner [ˌeksɪ'kjuːʃnər] *n* bourreau *m*.

executive [ɪg'zekjʊtɪv] ⬥ *adj* [power, board] exécutif(ive). ⬥ *n* **1.** COMM cadre *m* **- 2.** [of government] exécutif *m* ; [of political party] comité *m* central, bureau *m*.

executive director *n* cadre *m* supérieur.

executor [ɪg'zekjʊtər] *n* exécuteur *m* testamentaire.

exemplify [ɪg'zemplɪfaɪ] *vt* **1.** [typify] exemplifier **- 2.** [give example of] exemplifier, illustrer.

exempt [ɪg'zempt] ⬥ *adj* : **exempt (from)** exempt(e) (de). ⬥ *vt* : **to exempt sb (from)** exempter qqn (de).

exercise ['eksəsaɪz] ⬥ *n* exercice *m*. ⬥ *vt* [gen] exercer. ⬥ *vi* prendre de l'exercice.

exercise book *n UK* [notebook] cahier *m* d'exercices ; [published book] livre *m* d'exercices.

exert [ɪg'zɜːt] *vt* exercer ; [strength] employer ; **to exert o.s.** se donner du mal.

exertion [ɪg'zɜːʃn] *n* effort *m*.

exhale [eks'heɪl] ⬥ *vt* exhaler. ⬥ *vi* expirer.

exhaust [ɪg'zɔːst] ⬥ *n* **1.** *(U)* [fumes] gaz *mpl* d'échappement **- 2.** : **exhaust (pipe)** pot *m* OR tuyau *m* d'échappement. ⬥ *vt* épuiser.

exhausted [ɪg'zɔːstɪd] *adj* épuisé(e).

exhausting [ɪg'zɔːstɪŋ] *adj* épuisant(e).

exhaustion [ɪg'zɔːstʃn] *n* épuisement *m*.

exhaustive [ɪg'zɔːstɪv] *adj* complet(ète), exhaustif(ive).

exhibit [ɪg'zɪbɪt] ⬥ *n* **1.** ART objet *m* exposé **- 2.** LAW pièce *f* à conviction. ⬥ *vt* **1.** [demonstrate - feeling] montrer ; [- skill] faire preuve de **- 2.** ART exposer.

exhibition [ˌeksɪ'bɪʃn] *n* **1.** ART exposition *f* **- 2.** [of feeling] démonstration *f* ; **to make an exhibition of o.s.** *UK* se donner en spectacle.

exhilarating [ɪg'zɪləreɪtɪŋ] *adj* [experience] grisant(e) ; [walk] vivifiant(e).

exile ['eksaɪl] ⬥ *n* **1.** [condition] exil *m* ; **in exile** en exil **- 2.** [person] exilé *m*, -e *f*. ⬥ *vt* : **to exile sb (from/to)** exiler qqn (de/vers).

exist [ɪg'zɪst] *vi* exister.

existence [ɪg'zɪstəns] *n* existence *f* ; **in existence** qui existe, existant(e) ; **to come into existence** naître.

existing [ɪg'zɪstɪŋ] *adj* existant(e).

exit ['eksɪt] ⬥ *n* sortie *f*. ⬥ *vi* sortir.

exodus ['eksədəs] *n* exode *m*.

exonerate [ɪg'zɒnəreɪt] *vt* : **to exonerate sb (from)** disculper qqn (de).

exorbitant [ɪg'zɔːbɪtənt] *adj* exorbitant(e).

exotic [ɪg'zɒtɪk] *adj* exotique.

expand [ɪk'spænd] ⬥ *vt* [production, influence] accroître ; [business, department, area] développer. ⬥ *vi* [population, influence] s'accroître ; [business, department, market] se développer ; [metal] se dilater. ⬅ **expand (up)on** *vt insep* développer.

expanse [ɪk'spæns] *n* étendue *f*.

expansion [ɪk'spænʃn] *n* [of production, population] accroissement *m* ; [of business, department, area] développement *m* ; [of metal] dilatation *f*.

expect [ɪk'spekt] ⬥ *vt* **1.** [anticipate] s'attendre à ; [event, letter, baby] attendre ; **when do you expect it to be ready?** quand pensez-vous que cela sera prêt? ; **to expect sb to do sthg** s'attendre à ce que qqn fasse qqch **- 2.** [count on] compter sur **- 3.** [demand] exiger, demander ; **to expect sb to do sthg** attendre de qqn qu'il fasse qqch ; **to expect sthg from sb** exiger qqch de qqn **- 4.** *UK* [suppose] supposer ; **I expect so** je crois que oui. ⬥ *vi* **1.** [anticipate] : **to expect to do sthg** compter faire qqch **- 2.** [be pregnant] : **to be expecting** être enceinte, attendre un bébé.

expectancy ➤ life expectancy.

expectant [ɪk'spektənt] *adj* qui est dans l'expectative.

expectant mother *n* femme *f* enceinte.

expectation [ˌekspek'teɪʃn] *n* **1.** [hope] espoir *m*, attente *f* **- 2.** [belief] : **it's my expectation that...** à mon avis,... ; **against all expectation** OR **expectations, contrary to all expectation** OR **expectations** contre toute attente.

expedient [ɪk'spiːdjənt] *fml* ⬥ *adj* indiqué(e). ⬥ *n* expédient *m*.

expedition [ˌekspɪ'dɪʃn] *n* expédition *f*.

expel [ɪk'spel] *vt* **1.** [gen] expulser **- 2.** SCH renvoyer.

expend [ɪk'spend] *vt* : **to expend time/money (on)** consacrer du temps/de l'argent (à).

expendable [ɪk'spendəbl] *adj* [person, workforce, equipment] superflu(e) ; [troops, spies] qui peut être sacrifié(e).

expenditure [ɪk'spendɪtʃər] *n (U)* dépense *f*.

expense [ɪk'spens] *n* **1.** [amount spent] dépense *f* - **2.** *(U)* [cost] frais *mpl* ; **at the expense of** au prix de ; **at sb's expense** [financial] aux frais de qqn ; *fig* aux dépens de qqn. ➡ **expenses** *npl* COMM frais *mpl*.

expense account *n* frais *mpl* de représentation.

expensive [ɪk'spensɪv] *adj* **1.** [financially - gen] cher (chère), coûteux(euse) ; [- tastes] dispendieux(euse) - **2.** [mistake] qui coûte cher.

experience [ɪk'spɪərɪəns] <> *n* expérience *f*. <> *vt* [difficulty] connaître ; [disappointment] éprouver, ressentir ; [loss, change] subir.

experienced [ɪk'spɪərɪənst] *adj* expérimenté(e) ; **to be experienced at** OR **in sthg** avoir de l'expérience en OR en matière de qqch.

experiment [ɪk'sperɪmənt] <> *n* expérience *f* ; **to carry out an experiment** faire une expérience. <> *vi* : **to experiment (with sthg)** expérimenter (qqch).

expert ['ekspɜːt] <> *adj* expert(e) ; [advice] d'expert. <> *n* expert *m*, -e *f*.

expertise [ˌekspɜː'tiːz] *n (U)* compétence *f*.

expiration US = expiry.

expiration date US = expiry date.

expire [ɪk'spaɪər] *vi* expirer.

expiry [ɪk'spaɪərɪ] *n* UK expiration *f*.

explain [ɪk'spleɪn] <> *vt* expliquer ; **to explain sthg to sb** expliquer qqch à qqn. <> *vi* s'expliquer ; **to explain to sb (about sthg)** expliquer (qqch) à qqn.

explanation [ˌekspləˈneɪʃn] *n* : **explanation (for)** explication *f* (de).

explicit [ɪk'splɪsɪt] *adj* explicite.

explode [ɪk'spləʊd] <> *vt* [bomb] faire exploser. <> *vi lit & fig* exploser.

exploit <> *n* ['eksplɔɪt] exploit *m*. <> *vt* [ɪk'splɔɪt] exploiter.

exploitation [ˌeksplɔɪˈteɪʃn] *n (U)* exploitation *f*.

exploration [ˌekspləˈreɪʃn] *n* exploration *f*.

explore [ɪk'splɔːr] *vt & vi* explorer.

explorer [ɪk'splɔːrər] *n* explorateur *m*, -trice *f*.

explosion [ɪk'spləʊʒn] *n* explosion *f* ; [of interest, emotion] débordement *m*.

explosive [ɪk'spləʊsɪv] <> *adj lit & fig* explosif(ive). <> *n* explosif *m*.

exponent [ɪk'spəʊnənt] *n* [of theory] défenseur *m*.

export <> *n* ['ekspɔːt] exportation *f*. <> *comp* ['ekspɔːt] d'exportation. <> *vt* [ɪk'spɔːt] exporter.

exporter [ek'spɔːtər] *n* exportateur *m*, -trice *f*.

expose [ɪk'spəʊz] *vt* **1.** [uncover] exposer, découvrir ; **to be exposed to sthg** être exposé à qqch - **2.** [unmask - corruption] révéler ; [- person] démasquer.

exposed [ɪk'spəʊzd] *adj* [land, house, position] exposé(e).

exposure [ɪk'spəʊʒər] *n* **1.** [to light, radiation] exposition *f* - **2.** MED : **to die of exposure** mourir de froid - **3.** [PHOT - time] temps *m* de pose ; [- photograph] pose *f* - **4.** *(U)* [publicity] publicité *f* ; [coverage] couverture *f*.

exposure meter *n* posemètre *m*.

expound [ɪk'spaʊnd] *fml* <> *vt* exposer. <> *vi* : **to expound on** faire un exposé sur.

express [ɪk'spres] <> *adj* **1.** UK [letter, delivery] exprès *(inv)* - **2.** [train, coach] express *(inv)* - **3.** *fml* [specific] exprès(esse). <> *adv* exprès. <> *n* [train] rapide *m*, express *m*. <> *vt* exprimer.

expression [ɪk'spreʃn] *n* expression *f*.

expressive [ɪk'spresɪv] *adj* expressif(ive).

expressly [ɪk'spreslɪ] *adv* expressément.

expressway [ɪk'spreswer] *n* US voie *f* express.

exquisite [ɪk'skwɪzɪt] *adj* exquis(e).

ext., extn. *(abbrev of* extension) : ext. 4174 p. 4174.

extend [ɪk'stend] <> *vt* **1.** [enlarge - building] agrandir - **2.** [make longer - gen] prolonger ; [- visa] proroger ; [- deadline] repousser - **3.** [expand - rules, law] étendre (la portée de) ; [- power] accroître - **4.** [stretch out - arm, hand] étendre - **5.** [offer - help] apporter, offrir ; [- credit] accorder. <> *vi* [stretch - in space] s'étendre ; [- in time] continuer.

extension [ɪk'stenʃn] *n* **1.** [to building] agrandissement *m* - **2.** [lengthening - gen] prolongement *m* ; [- of visit] prolongation *f* ; [- of visa] prorogation *f* ; [- of deadline] report *m* - **3.** [of power] accroissement *m* ; [of law] élargissement *m* - **4.** TELEC poste *m* - **5.** ELEC prolongateur *m*.

extension cable *n* rallonge *f*.

extensive [ɪk'stensɪv] *adj* **1.** [in amount] considérable - **2.** [in area] vaste - **3.** [in range - discussions] approfondi(e) ; [- changes, use] considérable.

extensively [ɪk'stensɪvlɪ] *adv* **1.** [in amount] considérablement - **2.** [in range] abondamment, largement.

extent [ɪk'stent] *n* **1.** [of land, area] étendue *f*, superficie *f* ; [of problem, damage] étendue - **2.** [degree] : **to what extent...?** dans quelle mesure...? ; **to the extent that** [in so far as] dans la mesure où ; [to the point where] au point que ; **to a certain extent** jusqu'à un certain point ; **to a large** OR **great extent** en grande partie ; **to some extent** en partie.

extenuating circumstances [ɪk'stenjʊeɪtɪŋ-] *npl* circonstances *fpl* atténuantes.

exterior [ɪk'stɪərɪər] <> *adj* extérieur(e). <> *n* **1.** [of house, car] extérieur *m* - **2.** [of person] dehors *m*, extérieur *m*.

exterminate [ɪk'stɜːmɪneɪt] *vt* exterminer.

external [ɪk'stɜːnl] *adj* externe.

extinct [ɪk'stɪŋkt] *adj* **1.** [species] disparu(e) - **2.** [volcano] éteint(e).

extinguish [ɪk'stɪŋgwɪʃ] *vt* [fire, cigarette] éteindre.

extinguisher [ɪk'stɪŋgwɪʃər] *n* = **fire extinguisher**.

extn. = **ext.**

extol, *US* **extoll** [ɪk'stəʊl] *vt* louer.

extort [ɪk'stɔːt] *vt* : **to extort sthg from sb** extorquer qqch à qqn.

extortionate [ɪk'stɔːʃnət] *adj pej* exorbitant(e).

extra ['ekstrə] <> *adj* supplémentaire. <> *n* **1.** [addition] supplément *m* ; optional **extra option** *f* - **2.** CIN & THEAT figurant *m*, -e *f*. <> *adv* [hard, big etc] extra ; [pay, charge etc] en plus.

extra- ['ekstrə] *prefix* extra-.

extract <> *n* ['ekstrækt] extrait *m*. <> *vt* [ɪk'strækt] **1.** [take out - tooth] arracher ; **to extract sthg from sb** tirer qqch de - **2.** [confession, information] : **to extract sthg (from sb)** arracher qqch (à qqn), tirer qqch (de qqn) - **3.** [coal, oil] extraire.

extradite ['ekstrədaɪt] *vt* : **to extradite sb (from/to)** extrader qqn (de/vers).

extramarital [ˌekstrə'mærɪtl] *adj* extra-conjugal(e).

extramural [ˌekstrə'mjʊərəl] *adj* UNIV hors faculté.

extraordinary [ɪk'strɔːdnrɪ] *adj* UK extraordinaire.

extraordinary general meeting *n* UK assemblée *f* générale extraordinaire.

extravagance [ɪk'strævəgəns] *n* **1.** *(U)* [excessive spending] gaspillage *m*, prodigalités *fpl* - **2.** [luxury] extravagance *f*, folie *f*.

extravagant [ɪk'strævəgənt] *adj* **1.** [wasteful - person] dépensier(ère) ; [- use, tastes] dispendieux(euse) - **2.** [elaborate, exaggerated] extravagant(e).

extreme [ɪk'striːm] <> *adj* extrême. <> *n* extrême *m*.

extremely [ɪk'striːmlɪ] *adv* extrêmement.

extremist [ɪk'striːmɪst] <> *adj* extrémiste. <> *n* extrémiste *mf*.

extricate ['ekstrɪkeɪt] *vt* : **to extricate sthg**

(from) dégager qqch (de) ; **to extricate o.s. (from)** [from seat belt etc] s'extirper (de) ; [from difficult situation] se tirer (de).

extrovert ['ekstrəvɜːt] <> *adj* extraverti(e). <> *n* extraverti *m*, -e *f*.

exuberance [ɪg'zjuːbərəns] *n* exubérance *f*.

exultant [ɪg'zʌltənt] *adj* triomphant(e).

eye [aɪ] <> *n* **1.** [gen] œil *m* ; **to cast** OR **run one's eye over sthg** jeter un coup d'œil sur qqch ; **to catch sb's eye** attirer l'attention de qqn ; **to have one's eye on sb** avoir qqn à l'œil ; **to have one's eye on sthg** avoir repéré qqch ; **to keep one's eyes open for sthg** [try to find] essayer de repérer qqch ; **to keep an eye on sthg** surveiller qqch, garder l'œil sur qqch - **2.** [of needle] chas *m*. <> *vt* (*cont* eyeing, *cont* eying) regarder, reluquer.

eyeball ['aɪbɔːl] *n* globe *m* oculaire.

eyebath ['aɪbɑːθ] *n* œillère *f* (*pour bains d'œil*).

eyebrow ['aɪbraʊ] *n* sourcil *m*.

eyebrow pencil *n* crayon *m* à sourcils.

eye candy *n* (U) *inf* tape *m* à l'oeil *hum* & *pej*.

eyelash ['aɪlæʃ] *n* cil *m*.

eyelid ['aɪlɪd] *n* paupière *f*.

eyeliner ['aɪˌlaɪnər] *n* eye-liner *m*.

eye-opener *n inf* révélation *f*.

eye shadow *n* fard *m* à paupières.

eyesight ['aɪsaɪt] *n* vue *f*.

eyesore ['aɪsɔːr] *n pej* horreur *f*.

eyestrain ['aɪstreɪn] *n* fatigue *f* des yeux.

eyewitness [ˌaɪ'wɪtnɪs] *n* témoin *mf* oculaire.

F

f [ef] (*pl* **f's** OR **fs**), **F** (*pl* **F's** OR **Fs**) *n* [letter] f *m* inv, F *m* inv. ➡ **F** *n* **1.** MUS fa *m* - **2.** (*abbrev of* **Fahrenheit**) F.

fab [fæb] *adj inf* super.

fable ['feɪbl] *n* fable *f*.

fabric ['fæbrɪk] *n* **1.** [cloth] tissu *m* - **2.** [of building, society] structure *f*.

fabrication [ˌfæbrɪ'keɪʃn] *n* **1.** [lie, lying] fabrication *f*, invention *f* - **2.** [manufacture] fabrication *f*.

fabulous ['fæbjʊləs] *adj* **1.** [gen] fabuleux(euse) - **2.** *inf* [excellent] sensationnel(elle), fabuleux(euse).

facade, façade [fə'sɑːd] *n* façade *f*.

face [feɪs] ◇ *n* **1.** [of person] visage *m*, figure *f* ; **face to face** face à face ; **to say sthg to sb's face** dire qqch à qqn en face - **2.** [expression] visage *m*, mine *f* ; **to make** OR **pull a face** faire la grimace - **3.** [of cliff, mountain] face *f*, paroi *f* ; [of building] façade *f* ; [of clock, watch] cadran *m* ; [of coin, shape] face - **4.** [surface - of planet] surface *f* - **5.** [respect] : **to save/lose face** sauver/ perdre la face. ◇ *vt* **1.** [look towards - subj: person, building] faire face à ; **the house faces the sea/south** la maison donne sur la mer/est orientée vers le sud - **2.** [decision, crisis] être confronté(e) à ; [problem, danger] faire face à - **3.** [truth] faire face à, admettre ; **we must face facts** il faut voir les choses comme elles sont - **4.** *inf* [cope with] affronter. **face down** *adv* [person] face contre terre ; [object] à l'envers ; [card] face en dessous. **face up** *adv* [person] sur le dos ; [object] à l'endroit ; [card] face en dessus. **in the face of** *prep* devant. **face up to** *vt insep* faire face à.

facecloth ['feɪsklɒθ] *n* UK gant *m* de toilette.

face cream *n* crème *f* pour le visage.

facelift ['feɪslɪft] *n* lifting *m* ; *fig* restauration *f*, rénovation *f*.

face powder *n* poudre *f* de riz, poudre pour le visage.

face-saving [-ˌseɪvɪŋ] *adj* qui sauve la face.

facet ['fæsɪt] *n* facette *f*.

facetious [fə'siːʃəs] *adj* facétieux(euse).

face value *n* [of coin, stamp] valeur *f* nominale ; **to take sthg at face value** prendre qqch au pied de la lettre.

facial mask, facial masque US = face mask.

facility [fə'sɪlətɪ] *n* [feature] fonction *f*. **facilities** *npl* [amenities] équipement *m*, aménagement *m*.

facing ['feɪsɪŋ] *adj* d'en face ; [sides] opposé(e).

facsimile [fæk'sɪmɪlɪ] *n* **1.** [fax] télécopie *f*, fax *m* - **2.** [copy] fac-similé *m*.

fact [fækt] *n* **1.** [true piece of information] fait *m* ; **to know sthg for a fact** savoir pertinemment qqch - **2.** *(U)* [truth] faits *mpl*, réalité *f*. **in fact** *adv* en fait.

fact of life *n* fait *m*, réalité *f* ; **the facts of life** *euph* les choses *fpl* de la vie.

factor ['fæktər] *n* facteur *m*, -trice *f*.

factory ['fæktərɪ] *n* fabrique *f*, usine *f*.

fact sheet *n* résumé *m*, brochure *f*.

factual ['fæktʃʊəl] *adj* factuel(elle), basé(e) sur les faits.

faculty ['fæklti] *n* **1.** [gen] faculté *f* - **2.** US [of college] : **the faculty** le corps enseignant.

FA Cup *n* en Angleterre, championnat de football dont la finale se joue à Wembley.

fad [fæd] *n* engouement *m*, mode *f* ; [personal] marotte *f*.

fade [feɪd] ◇ *vt* [jeans, curtains, paint] décolorer. ◇ *vi* **1.** [jeans, curtains, paint] se décolorer ; [colour] passer ; [flower] se flétrir - **2.** [light] baisser, diminuer - **3.** [sound] diminuer, s'affaiblir - **4.** [memory] s'effacer ; [feeling, interest] diminuer.

faeces UK, **feces** US ['fiːsiːz] *npl* fèces *fpl*.

fag [fæg] *n inf* **1.** UK [cigarette] clope *m* - **2.** US *offens* [homosexual] pédé *m*.

Fahrenheit ['færənhaɪt] *adj* Fahrenheit *(inv)*.

fail [feɪl] ◇ *vt* **1.** [exam, test] rater, échouer à - **2.** [not succeed] : **to fail to do sthg** ne pas arriver à faire qqch - **3.** [neglect] : **to fail to do sthg** manquer OR omettre de faire qqch - **4.** [candidate] refuser. ◇ *vi* **1.** [not succeed] ne pas réussir OR y arriver - **2.** [not pass exam] échouer - **3.** [stop functioning] lâcher - **4.** [weaken - health, daylight] décliner ; [- eyesight] baisser.

failing ['feɪlɪŋ] ◇ *n* [weakness] défaut *m*, point *m* faible. ◇ *prep* à moins de ; **failing that** à défaut.

failure ['feɪljər] *n* **1.** [lack of success, unsuccessful thing] échec *m* - **2.** [person] raté *m*, -e *f* - **3.** [of engine, brake etc] défaillance *f* ; [of crop] perte *f*.

faint [feɪnt] ◇ *adj* **1.** [smell] léger(ère) ; [memory] vague ; [sound, hope] faible - **2.** [slight - chance] petit(e), faible - **3.** [dizzy] : **I'm feeling a bit faint** je ne me sens pas bien. ◇ *vi* s'évanouir.

fair [feər] ◇ *adj* **1.** [just - person] juste, équitable - **2.** [quite large] grand(e), important(e) - **3.** [quite good] assez bon (assez bonne) - **4.** [hair] blond(e) - **5.** [skin, complexion] clair(e) - **6.** [weather] beau (belle). ◇ *n* **1.** UK [funfair] fête *f* foraine - **2.** [trade fair] foire *f*. ◇ *adv* [fairly] loyalement. **fair enough** *adv inf* OK, d'accord.

fair-haired [-'heəd] *adj* [person] blond(e).

fairly ['feəlɪ] *adv* **1.** [rather] assez ; **fairly certain** presque sûr - **2.** [justly] équitablement ; [describe] avec impartialité ; [fight, play] loyalement.

fairness ['feənɪs] *n* [justness] équité *f*.

fairy ['feərɪ] *n* [imaginary creature] fée *f* ; *inf offens* pédé *m*.

fairy tale *n* conte *m* de fées.

faith [feɪθ] *n* **1.** [belief] foi *f*, confiance *f* - **2.** RELIG foi *f*.

faithful ['feɪθfʊl] *adj* [person] fidèle.

faithfully ['feɪθfʊlɪ] *adv* [loyally] fidèlement ; **Yours faithfully** UK [in letter] je vous prie d'agréer mes salutations distinguées.

fake [feɪk] <> adj faux (fausse). <> n
1. [object, painting] faux m - **2.** [person]
imposteur m. <> vt **1.** [results] falsifier ;
[signature] imiter - **2.** [illness, emotions]
simuler. <> vi [pretend] simuler, faire
semblant.

falcon ['fɔːlkən] n faucon m.

Falkland Islands ['fɔːklənd-], **Falklands**
['fɔːkləndz] npl : **the Falkland Islands** les îles
fpl Falkland, les Malouines fpl.

fall [fɔːl] <> vi (pt fell, pp fallen) **1.** [gen]
tomber ; **to fall flat** [joke] tomber à plat
- **2.** [decrease] baisser - **3.** [become] : **to fall
asleep** s'endormir ; **to fall ill** tomber
malade ; **to fall in love** tomber amou-
reux(euse). <> n **1.** [gen] : **fall (in)** chute
(de) - **2.** US [autumn] automne m. ◆ **falls**
npl chutes fpl. ◆ **fall apart** vi **1.** [disinte-
grate - book, chair] tomber en morceaux
- **2.** fig [country] tomber en ruine ; [person]
s'effondrer. ◆ **fall back** vi [person, crowd]
reculer. ◆ **fall back on** vt insep [resort to]
se rabattre sur. ◆ **fall behind** vi **1.** [in
race] se faire distancer - **2.** [with rent] être
en retard ; **to fall behind with** UK **or in** US
one's work avoir du retard dans son travail.
◆ **fall for** vt insep **1.** inf [fall in love with]
tomber amoureux(euse) de - **2.** [trick, lie] se
laisser prendre à. ◆ **fall in** vi **1.** [roof,
ceiling] s'écrouler, s'affaisser - **2.** MIL former
les rangs. ◆ **fall off** vi **1.** [branch, handle]
se détacher, tomber - **2.** [demand, numbers]
baisser, diminuer. ◆ **fall out** vi **1.** [hair,
tooth] tomber - **2.** [friends] se brouiller
- **3.** MIL rompre les rangs. ◆ **fall over**
<> vt insep : **to fall over sthg** trébucher sur
qqch et tomber. <> vi [person, chair etc]
tomber. ◆ **fall through** vi [plan, deal]
échouer.

fallacy ['fæləsɪ] n erreur f, idée f fausse.

fallen ['fɔːln] pp ► **fall**.

fallible ['fæləbl] adj faillible.

fallout ['fɔːlaʊt] n (U) [radiation] retombées fpl.

fallout shelter n abri m antiatomique.

fallow ['fæləʊ] adj : **to lie fallow** être en
jachère.

false [fɔːls] adj [generally] faux (fausse).

false alarm n fausse alerte f.

falsely ['fɔːlslɪ] adv à tort ; [smile, laugh]
faussement.

false teeth npl dentier m.

falsify ['fɔːlsɪfaɪ] vt falsifier.

falter ['fɔːltər] vi **1.** [move unsteadily] chanceler - **2.** [steps, voice] devenir hésitant(e)
- **3.** [hesitate, lose confidence] hésiter.

fame [feɪm] n gloire f, renommée f.

familiar [fə'mɪljər] adj familier(ère) ; familiar with sthg familiarisé(e) avec qqch.

familiarity [fə,mɪlɪ'ærətɪ] n (U) [knowled-
ge] : **familiarity with sthg** connaissance f de
qqch, familiarité f avec qqch.

familiarize, UK **-ise** [fə'mɪljəraɪz] vt : **to
familiarize o.s. with sthg** se familiariser avec
qqch ; **to familiarize sb with sthg** familiariser
qqn avec qqch.

family ['fæmlɪ] n famille f.

family credit n (U) UK ≃ complément m
familial.

family doctor n médecin m de famille.

family planning n planning m familial ;
family planning clinic centre m de planning
familial.

famine ['fæmɪn] n famine f.

famished ['fæmɪʃt] adj inf [very hungry]
affamé(e) ; **I'm famished!** je meurs de faim!

famous ['feɪməs] adj : **famous (for)** célèbre
(pour).

famously ['feɪməslɪ] adv dated : **to get on**
OR along famously s'entendre comme lar-
rons en foire.

fan [fæn] <> n **1.** [of paper, silk] éventail m
- **2.** [electric or mechanical] ventilateur m
- **3.** [enthusiast] fan mf. <> vt **1.** [face]
éventer - **2.** [fire, feelings] attiser. ◆ **fan
out** vi se déployer.

fanatic [fə'nætɪk] n fanatique mf.

fan belt n courroie f de ventilateur.

fanciful ['fænsɪfʊl] adj **1.** [odd] bizarre,
fantasque - **2.** [elaborate] extravagant(e).

fancy ['fænsɪ] <> adj **1.** [elaborate - hat,
clothes] extravagant(e) ; [- food, cakes]
raffiné(e) - **2.** [expensive - restaurant, hotel]
de luxe ; [- prices] fantaisiste. <> n UK
[desire, liking] envie f, lubie f ; **to take a
fancy to sb** se prendre d'affection pour
qqn ; **to take a fancy to sthg** se mettre à
aimer qqch ; **to take sb's fancy** faire envie à
qqn, plaire à qqn. <> vt **1.** UK inf [want]
avoir envie de ; **to fancy doing sthg** avoir
envie de faire qqch - **2.** UK inf [like] : **I fancy
her** elle me plaît - **3.** [imagine] : **fancy that!**
ça alors!

fancy dress n (U) déguisement m.

fancy-dress party n fête f déguisée.

fanfare ['fænfeər] n fanfare f.

fang [fæŋ] n [of wolf] croc m ; [of snake]
crochet m.

fan heater n radiateur m soufflant.

fanny ['fænɪ] n US inf [buttocks] fesses fpl.

fantasize, UK **-ise** ['fæntəsaɪz] vi : **to
fantasize (about sthg/about doing sthg)**
fantasmer (sur qqch/sur le fait de faire
qqch).

fantastic [fæn'tæstɪk] adj **1.** inf [wonderful]
fantastique, formidable - **2.** [incredible] extraordinaire, incroyable.

fantasy ['fæntəsɪ] n **1.** [dream, imaginary event] rêve m, fantasme m - **2.** (U) [fiction] fiction f - **3.** [imagination] fantaisie f.

fantasy football n jeu où chaque participant se constitue une équipe virtuelle avec les noms de footballeurs réels, chaque but marqué par ceux-ci dans la réalité valant un point dans le jeu.

fao (abbrev of **for the attention of**) à l'attention de.

FAQ [fak or ɛfeɪ'kjuː] <> n COMPUT (abbrev of **frequently asked questions**) foire f aux questions, FAQ f. <> adj & adv (abbrev of **free alongside quay**) FLQ.

far [fɑːr] <> adv **1.** [in distance] loin ; **how far is it?** c'est à quelle distance?, (est-ce que) c'est loin? ; **have you come far?** vous venez de loin? ; **far away** OR **off** loin ; **far and wide** partout ; **as far as** jusqu'à - **2.** [in time] : **far away** OR **off** loin ; **so far** jusqu'à maintenant, jusqu'ici - **3.** [in degree or extent] bien ; **I wouldn't trust him very far** je ne lui ferais pas tellement confiance ; **as far as** autant que ; **as far as I'm concerned** en ce qui me concerne ; **as far as possible** autant que possible, dans la mesure du possible ; **far and away, by far** de loin ; **far from it** loin de là, au contraire ; **so far so good** jusqu'ici tout va bien ; **to go so far as to do sthg** aller jusqu'à faire qqch ; **to go too far** aller trop loin. <> adj (comp **farther** OR **further**, superl **farthest** OR **furthest**) [extreme] : **the far end of the street** l'autre bout de la rue ; **the far right of the party** l'extrême droite du parti ; **the door on the far left** la porte la plus à gauche.

faraway ['fɑːrəweɪ] adj lointain(e).

farce [fɑːs] n **1.** THEAT farce f - **2.** fig [disaster] pagaille f, vaste rigolade f.

farcical ['fɑːsɪkl] adj grotesque.

fare [feər] n **1.** [payment] prix m, tarif m - **2.** dated [food] nourriture f.

Far East n : **the Far East** l'Extrême-Orient m.

farewell [,feə'wel] <> n adieu m. <> excl lit adieu!

farm [fɑːm] <> n ferme f. <> vt cultiver.

farmer ['fɑːmər] n fermier m, -ière f.

farmhand ['fɑːmhænd] n ouvrier m, -ère f agricole.

farmhouse ['fɑːmhaʊs] (pl [-haʊzɪz]) n ferme f.

farming ['fɑːmɪŋ] n (U) agriculture f ; [of animals] élevage m.

farm labourer UK, **farm laborer** US = farmhand.

farmland ['fɑːmlænd] n (U) terres fpl cultivées OR arables.

farmstead ['fɑːmsted] n US ferme f.

farm worker = farmhand.

farmyard ['fɑːmjɑːd] n cour f de ferme.

Faroese <> adj féroïen(ne). <> n **1.** GEOG Féroïen m, -ne f - **2.** LING féroïen m.

far-reaching [-'riːtʃɪŋ] adj d'une grande portée.

farsighted [,fɑː'saɪtɪd] adj **1.** [person] prévoyant(e) ; [plan] élaboré(e) avec clairvoyance - **2.** US [longsighted] hypermétrope.

fart [fɑːt] v inf <> n [air] pet m. <> vi péter.

farther ['fɑːðər] compar ► far.

farthest ['fɑːðəst] superl ► far.

fascinate ['fæsɪneɪt] vt fasciner.

fascinating ['fæsɪneɪtɪŋ] adj [person, country] fascinant(e) ; [job] passionnant(e) ; [idea, thought] très intéressant(e).

fascination [,fæsɪ'neɪʃn] n fascination f.

fascism ['fæʃɪzm] n fascisme m.

fashion ['fæʃn] <> n **1.** [clothing, style] mode f ; **to be in/out of fashion** être/ne plus être à la mode - **2.** [manner] manière f. <> vt fml façonner, fabriquer.

fashionable ['fæʃnəbl] adj à la mode.

fashion show n défilé m de mode.

fast [fɑːst] <> adj **1.** [rapid] rapide - **2.** [clock, watch] en avance. <> adv **1.** [rapidly] vite - **2.** [firmly] solidement ; **to hold fast to sthg** lit & fig s'accrocher à qqch ; **fast asleep** profondément endormi. <> n jeûne m. <> vi jeûner.

fasten ['fɑːsn] <> vt [jacket, bag] fermer ; [seat belt] attacher ; **to fasten sthg to sthg** attacher qqch à qqch. <> vi : **to fasten on to sb/sthg** se cramponner à qqn/qqch.

fastener ['fɑːsnər] n [of bag, necklace] fermoir m ; [of dress] fermeture f.

fastening ['fɑːsnɪŋ] n fermeture f.

fast food n fast-food m, restauration f rapide.

fastidious [fə'stɪdɪəs] adj [fussy] méticuleux(euse).

fat [fæt] <> adj **1.** [overweight] gros (grosse), gras (grasse) ; **to get fat** grossir - **2.** [not lean - meat] gras (grasse) - **3.** [thick - file, wallet] gros (grosse), épais(aisse). <> n **1.** [flesh, on meat, in food] graisse f - **2.** (U) [for cooking] matière f grasse.

fatal ['feɪtl] adj **1.** [serious - mistake] fatal(e) ; [- decision, words] fatidique - **2.** [accident, illness] mortel(elle).

fatality [fə'tælətɪ] n [accident victim] mort m.

fate [feɪt] n **1.** [destiny] destin m ; **to tempt fate** tenter le diable - **2.** [result, end] sort m.

fateful ['feɪtfʊl] adj fatidique.

fat-free adj sans matières grasses.

father ['fɑːðər] n père m.

Father Christmas n UK le Père Noël.

father-in-law (pl **fathers-in-law**) n beau-père m.

fatherly ['fɑːðəlɪ] adj paternel(elle).

fathom ['fæðəm] ⟨⟩ n brasse f. ⟨⟩ vt : **to fathom sb/sthg (out)** comprendre qqn/qqch.

fatigue [fəˈtiːg] n **1.** [exhaustion] épuisement m - **2.** [in metal] fatigue f.

fatten ['fætn] vt engraisser.

fattening ['fætnɪŋ] adj qui fait grossir.

fatty ['fætɪ] ⟨⟩ adj gras (grasse). ⟨⟩ n inf pej gros m, grosse f.

fatuous ['fætjʊəs] adj fml stupide, niais(e).

faucet ['fɔːsɪt] n US robinet m.

fault ['fɔːlt] ⟨⟩ n **1.** [responsibility, in tennis] faute f ; **it's my fault** c'est de ma faute - **2.** [mistake, imperfection] défaut m ; **to find fault with sb/sthg** critiquer qqn/qqch ; **at fault** fautif(ive) - **3.** GEOL faille f. ⟨⟩ vt : **to fault sb (on sthg)** prendre qqn en défaut (sur qqch).

faultless ['fɔːltlɪs] adj impeccable.

faulty ['fɔːltɪ] adj défectueux(euse).

fauna ['fɔːnə] n faune f.

favour UK, **favor** US ['feɪvər] ⟨⟩ n **1.** [approval] faveur f, approbation f ; **in sb's favour** en faveur de qqn ; **to be in/out of favour with sb** avoir/ne pas avoir les faveurs de qqn, avoir/ne pas avoir la cote avec qqn ; **to curry favour with sb** chercher à gagner la faveur de qqn - **2.** [kind act] service m ; **to do sb a favour** rendre (un) service à qqn - **3.** [favouritism] favoritisme m. ⟨⟩ vt **1.** [prefer] préférer, privilégier - **2.** [treat better, help] favoriser. ⟨⟩ **in favour** adv [in agreement] pour, d'accord. ⟨⟩ **in favour of** prep **1.** [in preference to] au profit de - **2.** [in agreement with] : **to be in favour of sthg/of doing sthg** être partisan(e) de qqch/de faire qqch.

favourable UK, **favorable** US ['feɪvrəbl] adj [positive] favorable.

favourite UK, **favorite** US ['feɪvrɪt] ⟨⟩ adj favori(ite). ⟨⟩ n [person] favori m, -ite f. ⟨⟩ **favorites** npl COMPUT favoris mpl, signets mpl.

favouritism UK, **favoritism** US ['feɪvrɪtɪzm] n favoritisme m.

fawn [fɔːn] ⟨⟩ adj fauve (inv). ⟨⟩ n [animal] faon m. ⟨⟩ vi : **to fawn on sb** flatter qqn servilement.

fax [fæks] ⟨⟩ n fax m, télécopie f. ⟨⟩ vt **1.** [person] envoyer un fax à - **2.** [document] envoyer en fax.

fax machine n fax m, télécopieur m.

fax modem n modem m fax.

FBI (abbrev of **Federal Bureau of Investigation**) n US FBI m.

FDD [,efdiːˈdiː] (abbrev of **floppy disk drive**) n COMPUT lecteur m de disquettes.

fear [fɪər] ⟨⟩ n **1.** (U) [feeling] peur f - **2.** [object of fear] crainte f - **3.** [risk] risque m ; **for fear of** de peur de (+ infin), de peur que (+ subjunctive). ⟨⟩ vt **1.** [be afraid of] craindre, avoir peur de - **2.** [anticipate] craindre ; **to fear (that)...** craindre que..., avoir peur que...

fearful ['fɪəfʊl] adj **1.** fml [frightened] peureux(euse) ; **to be fearful of sthg** avoir peur de qqch - **2.** [frightening] effrayant(e).

fearless ['fɪəlɪs] adj intrépide.

feasible ['fiːzəbl] adj faisable, possible.

feast [fiːst] ⟨⟩ n [meal] festin m, banquet m. ⟨⟩ vi : **to feast on** OR **off sthg** se régaler de qqch.

feat [fiːt] n exploit m, prouesse f.

feather ['feðər] n plume f.

feature ['fiːtʃər] ⟨⟩ n **1.** [characteristic] caractéristique f - **2.** GEOG particularité f - **3.** [article] article m de fond - **4.** RADIO & TV émission f spéciale, spécial m - **5.** CIN long métrage m. ⟨⟩ vt **1.** [subj: film, exhibition] mettre en vedette - **2.** [comprise] présenter, comporter. ⟨⟩ vi : **to feature (in)** figurer en vedette (dans). ⟨⟩ **features** npl [of face] traits mpl.

feature film n long métrage m.

February ['februərɪ] n février m ; see also **September**.

feces US = **faeces**.

fed [fed] ⟨⟩ pt & pp ▶ **feed**. ⟨⟩ n US inf agent m, -e f du FBI.

fed. abbr of **federal**, abbr of **federation**, abbr of **federated**.

federal ['fedrəl] adj fédéral(e).

federation [,fedəˈreɪʃn] n fédération f.

fed up adj : **to be fed up (with)** en avoir marre (de).

fee [fiː] n [of school] frais mpl ; [of doctor] honoraires mpl ; [for membership] cotisation f ; [for entrance] tarif m, prix m.

feeble ['fiːbəl] adj faible.

feed [fiːd] ⟨⟩ vt (pt & pp **fed**) **1.** [give food to] nourrir - **2.** [fire, fears etc] alimenter - **3.** [put, insert] : **to feed sthg into sthg** mettre OR insérer qqch dans qqch. ⟨⟩ vi (pt & pp **fed**) [take food] : **to feed (on** OR **off)** se nourrir (de). ⟨⟩ n **1.** [for baby] repas m - **2.** [animal food] nourriture f.

feedback ['fiːdbæk] n (U) **1.** [reaction] réactions fpl - **2.** ELEC réaction f, rétroaction f.

feeding bottle ['fiːdɪŋ-] n UK biberon m.

feeding frenzy *n* frénésie *f* alimentaire ; **to have a feeding frenzy** *fig* avoir un comportement agressif.

feel [fi:l] ◇ *vt* (*pt & pp* felt) **1.** [touch] toucher - **2.** [sense, experience, notice] sentir ; [emotion] ressentir ; **to feel o.s. doing sthg** se sentir faire qqch - **3.** [believe] : **to feel (that)...** croire que..., penser que... ; **I'm not feeling myself today** je ne suis pas dans mon assiette aujourd'hui. ◇ *vi* (*pt & pp* felt) **1.** [have sensation] : **to feel cold/hot/sleepy** avoir froid/chaud/sommeil ; **to feel like sthg/like doing sthg** [be in mood for] avoir envie de qqch/de faire qqch - **2.** [have emotion] se sentir ; **to feel angry** être en colère - **3.** [seem] sembler ; **it feels strange** ça fait drôle - **4.** [by touch] : **to feel for sthg** chercher qqch. ◇ *n* **1.** [sensation, touch] toucher *m*, sensation *f* - **2.** [atmosphere] atmosphère *f*.

feeler ['fi:lər] *n* antenne *f*.

feeling ['fi:lɪŋ] *n* **1.** [emotion] sentiment *m* - **2.** [physical sensation] sensation *f* - **3.** [intuition, sense] sentiment *m*, impression *f* - **4.** [understanding] sensibilité *f* ; **to have a feeling for sthg** comprendre OR apprécier qqch. ◆ **feelings** *npl* sentiments *mpl* ; **to hurt sb's feelings** blesser (la sensibilité de) qqn ; **no hard feelings!** sans rancune !

feet [fi:t] *npl* ▶ foot.

feign [feɪn] *vt fml* feindre.

fell [fel] ◇ *pt* ▶ fall. ◇ *vt* [tree, person] abattre. ◆ **fells** *npl* GEOG lande *f*.

fellow ['feləʊ] ◇ *n* **1.** *dated* [man] homme *m* - **2.** [comrade, peer] camarade *m*, compagnon *m* - **3.** [of society, college] membre *m*, associé *m*. ◇ *adj* : **one's fellow men** ses semblables ; **fellow passenger** compagnon *m*, compagne *f* (de voyage) ; **fellow student** camarade *mf* (d'études).

fellowship ['feləʊʃɪp] *n* **1.** [comradeship] amitié *f*, camaraderie *f* - **2.** [society] association *f*, corporation *f* - **3.** [of society, college] titre *m* de membre OR d'associé - **4.** UNIV [scholarship] bourse *f* d'études dans l'enseignement supérieur ; [status] poste *m* de chercheur(euse).

felony ['felənɪ] *n* LAW crime *m*, forfait *m*.

felt [felt] ◇ *pt & pp* ▶ feel. ◇ *n* (*U*) feutre *m*.

felt-tip pen *n* stylo-feutre *m*.

female ['fi:meɪl] ◇ *adj* [person] de sexe féminin ; [animal, plant] femelle ; [sex, figure] féminin(e) ; **female student** étudiante *f*. ◇ *n* femelle *f*.

feminine ['femɪnɪn] ◇ *adj* féminin(e). ◇ *n* GRAM féminin *m*.

feminist ['femɪnɪst] *n* féministe *mf*.

fence [fens] ◇ *n* [barrier] clôture *f* ; **to sit**

on the fence *fig* ménager la chèvre et le chou. ◇ *vt* clôturer, entourer d'une clôture.

fencing ['fensɪŋ] *n* SPORT escrime *f*.

fend [fend] *vi* : **to fend for o.s.** se débrouiller tout seul. ◆ **fend off** *vt sep* [blows] parer ; [questions, reporters] écarter.

fender ['fendər] *n* **1.** [around fireplace] pare-feu *m inv* - **2.** [on boat] défense *f* - **3.** US [on car] aile *f*.

ferment ◇ *n* ['fɜːment] (*U*) [unrest] agitation *f*, effervescence *f*. ◇ *vi* [fə'ment] [wine, beer] fermenter.

fern [fɜːn] *n* fougère *f*.

ferocious [fə'rəʊʃəs] *adj* [animal, criticism] féroce.

ferret ['ferɪt] *n* furet *m*. ◆ **ferret about, ferret around** *vi inf* fureter un peu partout.

Ferris wheel ['ferɪs-] *n esp US* grande roue *f*.

ferry ['ferɪ] ◇ *n* ferry *m*, ferry-boat *m* ; [smaller] bac *m*. ◇ *vt* transporter.

ferryboat ['ferɪbəʊt] *n* = ferry.

fertile ['fɜːtaɪl] *adj* **1.** [land, imagination] fertile, fécond(e) - **2.** [person] fécond(e).

fertilizer, UK **-iser** ['fɜːtɪlaɪzər] *n* engrais *m*.

fervent ['fɜːvənt] *adj* fervent(e).

fester ['festər] *vi* [wound, sore] suppurer.

festival ['festəvl] *n* **1.** [event, celebration] festival *m* - **2.** [holiday] fête *f*.

festive ['festɪv] *adj* de fête.

festive season *n* UK **the festive season** la période des fêtes.

festivity [fes'tɪvətɪ] (*pl* -ies) *n* [merriness] fête *f*. ◆ **festivities** *npl* festivités *fpl*.

festoon [fe'stuːn] *vt* décorer de guirlandes ; **to be festooned with** être décoré de.

fetch [fetʃ] *vt* **1.** [go and get] aller chercher - **2.** [raise - money] rapporter. ◆ **fetch up** *inf vi insep* [end up] se retrouver ; **to fetch up in hospital/in a ditch** se retrouver à l'hôpital/dans un fossé.

fetching ['fetʃɪŋ] *adj* séduisant(e).

fete, fête [feɪt] *n* fête *f*, kermesse *f*.

fetish ['fetɪʃ] *n* **1.** [sexual obsession] objet *m* de fétichisme - **2.** [mania] manie *f*, obsession *f*.

fetus ['fi:təs] US = foetus.

feud [fjuːd] ◇ *n* querelle *f*. ◇ *vi* se quereller.

feudal ['fjuːdl] *adj* féodal(e).

fever ['fiːvər] *n* fièvre *f*.

feverish ['fiːvərɪʃ] *adj* fiévreux(euse).

few [fjuː] ◇ *adj* peu de ; **the first few pages** les toutes premières pages ; **quite a few, a good few** pas mal de, un bon nombre de ; **few and far between** rares. <> *pron* peu ; **a few** quelques-uns *mpl*, quelques-unes *f*.

fewer ['fju:ə^r] <> *adj* moins (de). <> *pron* moins.

fewest ['fju:əst] *adj* le moins (de).

fiancé [fɪ'ɒnseɪ] *n* fiancé *m*.

fiancée [fɪ'ɒnseɪ] *n* fiancée *f*.

fiasco [fɪ'æskəʊ] (*UK, pl* -s *esp US, pl* -es) *n* fiasco *m*.

fib [fɪb] *inf* <> *n* bobard *m*, blague *f*. <> *vi* raconter des bobards OR des blagues.

fibre *UK*, **fiber** *US* ['faɪbə^r] *n* fibre *f*.

fibreglass *UK*, **fiberglass** *US* ['faɪbəglɑːs] *n* (U) fibre *f* de verre.

fibre-tip (pen) *UK* = felt-tip pen.

fickle ['fɪkl] *adj* versatile.

fiction ['fɪkʃn] *n* fiction *f*.

fictional ['fɪkʃənl] *adj* fictif(ive).

fictitious [fɪk'tɪʃəs] *adj* [false] fictif(ive).

fiddle ['fɪdl] <> *vi* [play around] : **to fiddle with sthg** tripoter qqch. <> *vt UK inf* truquer. <> *n* **1.** [violin] violon *m* - **2.** *UK inf* [fraud] combine *f*, escroquerie *f*.

fiddly ['fɪdlɪ] *adj UK inf* délicat(e).

fidget ['fɪdʒɪt] *vi* remuer.

field [fiːld] *n* **1.** [gen & COMPUT] champ *m* - **2.** [for sports] terrain *m* - **3.** [of knowledge] domaine *m*.

field day *n* : **to have a field day** s'en donner à cœur joie.

field glasses *npl* jumelles *fpl*.

field marshal *n* ≃ maréchal *m* (de France).

field trip *n* SCH voyage *m* d'étude.

fieldwork ['fiːldwɜːk] *n* (U) recherches *fpl* sur le terrain.

fiend [fiːnd] *n* **1.** [cruel person] monstre *m* - **2.** *inf* [fanatic] fou *m*, folle *f*, mordu *m*, -e *f*.

fiendish ['fiːndɪʃ] *adj* **1.** [evil] diabolique - **2.** *inf* [very difficult, complex] abominable, atroce.

fierce [fɪəs] *adj* féroce ; [heat] torride ; [storm, temper] violent(e).

fiery ['faɪərɪ] *adj* **1.** [burning] ardent(e) - **2.** [volatile - speech] enflammé(e) ; [- temper, person] fougueux(euse).

fifteen [fɪf'tiːn] *num* quinze ; *see also* **six**.

fifth [fɪfθ] *num* cinquième ; *see also* **sixth**.

fifty ['fɪftɪ] *num* cinquante ; *see also* **sixty**.

fifty-fifty <> *adj* moitié-moitié, fifty-fifty ; **to have a fifty-fifty chance** avoir cinquante pour cent de chances. <> *adv* moitié-moitié, fifty-fifty.

fig [fɪg] *n* figue *f*.

fight [faɪt] <> *n* **1.** [physical] bagarre *f* ; **to have a fight (with sb)** se battre (avec qqn),

se bagarrer (avec qqn) ; **to put up a fight** se battre, se défendre - **2.** *fig* [battle, struggle] lutte *f*, combat *m* - **3.** [argument] dispute *f* ; **to have a fight (with sb)** se disputer (avec qqn). <> *vt* (*pt & pp* fought) **1.** [physically] se battre contre OR avec - **2.** [conduct - war] mener - **3.** [enemy, racism] combattre. <> *vi* (*pt & pp* fought) **1.** [in war, punch-up] se battre - **2.** *fig* [struggle] : **to fight for/against sthg** lutter pour/contre qqch - **3.** [argue] : **to fight (about OR over)** se battre OR se disputer (à propos de). **fight back** <> *vt insep* refouler. <> *vi* riposter.

fighter ['faɪtə^r] *n* **1.** [plane] avion *m* de chasse, chasseur *m* - **2.** [soldier] combattant *m* - **3.** [combative person] battant *m*, -e *f*.

fighting ['faɪtɪŋ] *n* (U) [punch-up] bagarres *fpl* ; [in war] conflits *mpl*.

figment ['fɪgmənt] *n* : **a figment of sb's imagination** le fruit de l'imagination de qqn.

figurative ['fɪgərətɪv] *adj* [meaning] figuré(e).

figure [*UK* 'fɪgə^r, *US* 'fɪgjər] <> *n* **1.** [statistic, number] chiffre *m* - **2.** [human shape, outline] silhouette *f*, forme *f* - **3.** [personality, diagram] figure *f* - **4.** [shape of body] ligne *f*. <> *vt esp US* [suppose] penser, supposer. <> *vi* [feature] figurer, apparaître. **figure out** *vt sep* **1.** [understand] comprendre ; [find] trouver.

figurehead ['fɪgəhed] *n* **1.** [on ship] figure *f* de proue - **2.** *fig & pej* [leader] homme *m* de paille.

figure of speech *n* figure *f* de rhétorique.

Fiji ['fiːdʒiː] *n* Fidji *fpl*.

file [faɪl] <> *n* **1.** [folder, report] dossier *m* ; **on file, on the files** répertorié dans les dossiers - **2.** COMPUT fichier *m* - **3.** [tool] lime *f* - **4.** [line] : **in single file** en file indienne. <> *vt* **1.** [document] classer - **2.** [LAW - accusation, complaint] porter, déposer ; [- lawsuit] intenter ; **to file an appeal** *US* interjeter OR faire appel - **3.** [fingernails, wood] limer. <> *vi* **1.** [walk in single file] marcher en file indienne - **2.** LAW : **to file for divorce** demander le divorce.

filet *US* = fillet.

filing cabinet ['faɪlɪŋ-] *n* classeur *m*, fichier *m*.

Filipino [,fɪlɪ'piːnəʊ] <> *adj* philippin(e). <> *n* (*pl* -s) Philippin *m*, -e *f*.

fill [fɪl] <> *vt* **1.** [gen] remplir ; **to fill sthg with sthg** remplir qqch de qqch - **2.** [gap, hole] boucher - **3.** [vacancy - subj: employer] pourvoir à ; [- subj: employee] prendre. <> *n* : **to eat one's fill** manger à sa faim. **fill in** <> *vt sep* **1.** [form] remplir - **2.** [inform] : **to fill sb in (on)** mettre qqn au courant (de). <> *vi* [substitute] : **to fill in for**

sb remplacer qqn. **fill out** vt sep [form] remplir. **fill up** ◇ vt sep remplir. ◇ vi se remplir.

fillet UK, **filet** US ['fɪlɪt] n filet m.

fillet steak n filet m de bœuf.

filling ['fɪlɪŋ] ◇ adj très nourrissant(e). ◇ n 1. [in tooth] plombage m - 2. [in cake, sandwich] garniture f.

filling station n station-service f.

film [fɪlm] ◇ n 1. [movie] film m - 2. [layer, for camera] pellicule f - 3. [footage] images fpl. ◇ vt & vi filmer.

film noir n CIN film m noir.

film star n vedette f de cinéma.

Filofax® ['faɪləʊfæks] n Filofax® m.

filter ['fɪltər] ◇ n filtre m. ◇ vt [coffee] passer ; [water, oil, air] filtrer.

filter coffee n café m filtre.

filter lane n UK ≃ voie f de droite.

filter-tipped [-'tɪpt] adj à bout filtre.

filth [fɪlθ] n (U) 1. [dirt] saleté f, crasse f - 2. [obscenity] obscénités fpl.

filthy ['fɪlθɪ] adj 1. [very dirty] dégoûtant(e), répugnant(e) - 2. [obscene] obscène.

fin [fɪn] n [of fish] nageoire f.

final ['faɪnl] ◇ adj 1. [last] dernier(ère) - 2. [at end] final(e) - 3. [definitive] définitif(ive). ◇ n finale f. **finals** npl UNIV examens mpl de dernière année.

finale [fɪ'nɑːlɪ] n finale m.

finalize, UK **-ise** ['faɪnəlaɪz] vt [details, plans] mettre au point.

finally ['faɪnəlɪ] adv enfin.

finance ◇ n ['faɪnæns] (U) finance f. ◇ vt [faɪ'næns] financer. **finances** npl finances fpl.

financial [fɪ'nænʃl] adj financier(ère).

find [faɪnd] ◇ vt (pt & pp found) 1. [gen] trouver - 2. [realize] : to find (that)... s'apercevoir que... - 3. LAW : to be found guilty/not guilty (of) être déclaré(e) coupable/non coupable (de). ◇ n trouvaille f. **find out** ◇ vi se renseigner ◇ vt insep 1. [information] se renseigner sur - 2. [truth] découvrir, apprendre. ◇ vt sep démasquer.

findings ['faɪndɪŋz] npl conclusions fpl.

fine [faɪn] ◇ adj 1. [good - work] excellent(e) ; [- building, weather] beau (belle) - 2. [perfectly satisfactory] très bien ; I'm fine ça va bien - 3. [thin, smooth] fin(e) - 4. [minute - detail, distinction] subtil(e) ; [- adjustment, tuning] délicat(e). ◇ adv [very well] très bien. ◇ n amende f. ◇ vt condamner à une amende.

fine arts npl beaux-arts mpl.

finely ['faɪnlɪ] adv 1. [chopped, ground] fin - 2. [tuned, balanced] délicatement.

finery ['faɪnərɪ] n (U) parure f.

fine-tune vt [mechanism] régler avec précision ; fig [plan] peaufiner.

finger ['fɪŋgər] ◇ n doigt m. ◇ vt [feel] palper.

fingernail ['fɪŋgəneɪl] n ongle m (de la main).

fingerprint ['fɪŋgəprɪnt] n empreinte f (digitale).

fingertip ['fɪŋgətɪp] n bout m du doigt ; at one's fingertips sur le bout des doigts.

finicky ['fɪnɪkɪ] adj pej [eater, task] difficile ; [person] tatillon(onne).

finish ['fɪnɪʃ] ◇ n 1. [end] fin f ; [of race] arrivée f - 2. [texture] finition f. ◇ vt finir, terminer ; [exhaust] achever, tuer ; to finish doing sthg finir OR terminer de faire qqch. ◇ vi finir, terminer ; [school, film] se terminer. **finish off** vt sep finir, terminer. **finish up** vi finir.

finishing line ['fɪnɪʃɪŋ-] UK, **finish line** US n ligne f d'arrivée.

finishing school ['fɪnɪʃɪŋ-] n école privée pour jeunes filles surtout axée sur l'enseignement des bonnes manières.

finite ['faɪnaɪt] adj fini(e).

Finland ['fɪnlənd] n Finlande f.

Finn [fɪn] n Finlandais m, -e f.

Finnish ['fɪnɪʃ] ◇ adj finlandais(e), finnois(e). ◇ n [language] finnois m.

fir [fɜːr] n sapin m.

fire ['faɪər] ◇ n 1. [gen] feu m ; on fire en feu ; to catch fire prendre feu ; to set fire to sthg mettre le feu à qqch - 2. [out of control] incendie m - 3. UK [heater] appareil m de chauffage - 4. (U) [shooting] coups mpl de feu ; to open fire (on) ouvrir le feu (sur). ◇ vt 1. [shoot] tirer - 2. esp US [dismiss] renvoyer. ◇ vi : to fire (on OR at) faire feu (sur), tirer (sur).

fire alarm n avertisseur m d'incendie.

firearm ['faɪərɑːm] n arme f à feu.

firebomb ['faɪəbɒm] ◇ n bombe f incendiaire. ◇ vt lancer des bombes incendiaires à.

fire brigade UK, **fire department** US n sapeurs-pompiers mpl.

fire door n porte f coupe-feu.

fire engine n voiture f de pompiers.

fire escape n escalier m de secours.

fire extinguisher n extincteur m d'incendie.

firefight ['faɪəfaɪt] n bataille f armée.

fireguard ['faɪəgɑːd] n garde-feu m inv.

firehouse US = fire station.

firelighter ['faɪəlaɪtər] n allume-feu m inv.

fireman ['faɪəmən] (pl -men [-mən]) n pompier m, -ière f.

fireplace ['faɪəpleɪs] n cheminée f.

fireproof ['faɪəpruːf] adj ignifugé(e).

fireside ['faɪəsaɪd] n : **by the fireside** au coin du feu.

fire station n caserne f des pompiers.

fire truck US = fire engine.

firewall ['faɪəwɔːl] n COMPUT pare-feu m.

firewood ['faɪəwʊd] n bois m de chauffage.

firework ['faɪəwɜːk] n pièce f d'artifice. ➡ **fireworks** npl [outburst of anger] étincelles fpl ; [display] feu m d'artifice.

firing ['faɪərɪŋ] n (U) MIL tir m, fusillade f.

firing squad n peloton m d'exécution.

firm [fɜːm] ◇ adj 1. [gen] ferme ; **to stand firm** tenir bon - 2. [support, structure] solide - 3. [evidence, news] certain(e). ◇ n firme f, société f.

first [fɜːst] ◇ adj premier(ère) ; **for the first time** pour la première fois ; **first thing in the morning** tôt le matin. ◇ adv 1. [before anyone else] en premier - 2. [before anything else] d'abord ; **first of all** tout d'abord - 3. [for the first time] (pour) la première fois. ◇ n 1. [person] premier m, -ère f - 2. [unprecedented event] première f - 3. UK UNIV diplôme universitaire avec mention très bien. ➡ **at first** adv d'abord. ➡ **at first hand** adv de première main.

first aid n (U) premiers secours mpl.

first-aid kit n trousse f de premiers secours.

first-class adj 1. [excellent] excellent(e) - 2. [ticket, compartment] de première classe ; [stamp, letter] tarif normal.

first floor n UK premier étage m ; US rez-de-chaussée m inv.

firsthand [fɜːst'hænd] adj & adv de première main.

first lady n première dame f du pays.

firstly ['fɜːstlɪ] adv premièrement.

First Minister n [in Scottish Parliament] président m du Parlement écossais.

first name n prénom m.

first-rate adj excellent(e).

First Secretary n [in Welsh Assembly] président m de l'Assemblée galloise.

firtree ['fɜːtriː] = fir.

fish [fɪʃ] ◇ n (pl fish) poisson m. ◇ vt [river, sea] pêcher dans. ◇ vi [fisherman] : **to fish (for sthg)** pêcher (qqch).

fish and chips npl UK poisson m frit avec frites.

fish-and-chip shop n UK magasin vendant du poisson frit et des frites.

fishbowl ['fɪʃbəʊl] n bocal m (à poissons).

fishcake ['fɪʃkeɪk] n croquette f de poisson.

fisherman ['fɪʃəmən] (pl -men [-mən]) n pêcheur m, -se f.

fish farm n centre m de pisciculture.

fish finger UK, **fish stick** US n CULIN bâtonnet m de poisson pané.

fishing ['fɪʃɪŋ] n pêche f ; **to go fishing** aller à la pêche.

fishing boat n bateau m de pêche.

fishing line n ligne f de pêche.

fishing rod n canne f à pêche.

fishmonger ['fɪʃˌmʌŋgər] n UK poissonnier m, -ère f ; **fishmonger's (shop)** poissonnerie f.

fish stick US = fish finger.

fishy ['fɪʃɪ] adj 1. [smell, taste] de poisson - 2. [suspicious] louche.

fist [fɪst] n poing m.

fit [fɪt] ◇ adj 1. [suitable] convenable ; **to be fit for sthg** être bon (bonne) à qqch ; **to be fit to do sthg** être apte à faire qqch - 2. [healthy] en forme ; **to keep fit** se maintenir en forme. ◇ n 1. [of clothes, shoes etc] ajustement m ; **it's a tight fit** c'est un peu juste ; **it's a good fit** c'est la bonne taille - 2. [epileptic seizure] crise f ; **to have a fit** avoir une crise ; fig piquer une crise - 3. [bout - of crying] crise f ; [- of rage] accès m ; [- of sneezing] suite f ; **in fits and starts** par à-coups. ◇ vt 1. [be correct size for] aller à - 2. [place] : **to fit sthg into sthg** insérer qqch dans qqch - 3. [provide] : **to fit sthg with sthg** équiper OR munir qqch de qqch - 4. [be suitable for] correspondre à. ◇ vi [be correct size, go] aller ; [into container] entrer. ➡ **fit in** ◇ vt sep [find time for - patient] prendre. ◇ vi s'intégrer ; **to fit in with sthg** correspondre à qqch ; **to fit in with sb** s'accorder à qqn.

fitful ['fɪtfʊl] adj [sleep] agité(e) ; [wind, showers] intermittent(e).

fitment ['fɪtmənt] n UK meuble m encastré.

fitness ['fɪtnɪs] n (U) 1. [health] forme f - 2. [suitability] : **fitness (for)** aptitude f (pour).

fitted carpet [ˌfɪtəd-] n UK moquette f.

fitted kitchen [ˌfɪtəd-] n UK cuisine f intégrée OR équipée.

fitter ['fɪtər] n [mechanic] monteur m.

fitting ['fɪtɪŋ] ◇ adj fml approprié(e). ◇ n 1. [part] appareil m - 2. [for clothing] essayage m. ➡ **fittings** npl UK installations fpl.

fitting room n cabine f d'essayage.

five [faɪv] *num* cinq ; *see also* **six.**

fiver ['faɪvər] *n inf* **1.** *UK* [amount] cinq livres *fpl* ; [note] billet *m* de cinq livres - **2.** *US* [amount] cinq dollars *mpl* ; [note] billet *m* de cinq dollars.

fix [fɪks] <> *vt* **1.** [gen] fixer ; **to fix sthg to sthg** fixer qqch à qqch - **2.** [in memory] graver - **3.** [repair] réparer - **4.** *inf* [rig] truquer - **5.** [food, drink] préparer. <> *n* **1.** *inf* [difficult situation] : **to be in a fix** être dans le pétrin - **2.** *drug sl* piqûre *f*. **fix up** *vt sep* **1.** [provide] : **to fix sb up with sthg** obtenir qqch pour qqn - **2.** [arrange] arranger.

fixation [fɪk'seɪʃn] *n* : **fixation (on** OR **about)** obsession *f* (de).

fixed [fɪkst] *adj* **1.** [attached] fixé(e) - **2.** [set, unchanging] fixe ; [smile] figé(e).

fixture ['fɪkstʃər] *n* **1.** [furniture] installation *f* - **2.** [permanent feature] tradition *f* bien établie - **3.** *UK* SPORT rencontre *f* (sportive).

fizz [fɪz] *vi* [lemonade, champagne] pétiller ; [fireworks] crépiter.

fizzle ['fɪzl] **fizzle out** *vi* [fire] s'éteindre ; [firework] se terminer ; [interest, enthusiasm] se dissiper.

fizzy ['fɪzɪ] *adj* pétillant(e).

flabbergasted ['flæbəgɑːstɪd] *adj* sidéré(e).

flabby ['flæbɪ] *adj* mou (molle).

flag [flæg] <> *n* drapeau *m*. <> *vi* [person, enthusiasm, energy] faiblir ; [conversation] traîner. **flag down** *vt sep* [taxi] héler ; **to flag sb down** faire signe à qqn de s'arrêter.

flagpole ['flæɡpəʊl] *n* mât *m*.

flagrant ['fleɪɡrənt] *adj* flagrant(e).

flagstaff = **flagpole.**

flagstone ['flæɡstəʊn] *n* dalle *f*.

flair [fleər] *n* **1.** [talent] don *m* - **2.** (U) [stylishness] style *m*.

flak [flæk] *n* (U) **1.** [gunfire] tir *m* antiaérien - **2.** *inf* [criticism] critiques *fpl* sévères.

flake [fleɪk] <> *n* [of paint, plaster] écaille *f* ; [of snow] flocon *m* ; [of skin] petit lambeau *m*. <> *vi* [paint, plaster] s'écailler ; [skin] peler.

flamboyant [flæm'bɔɪənt] *adj* **1.** [showy, confident] extravagant(e) - **2.** [brightly coloured] flamboyant(e).

flame [fleɪm] *n* flamme *f* ; **in flames** en flammes ; **to burst into flames** s'enflammer.

flamingo [flə'mɪŋɡəʊ] (*pl* **-s** OR **-es**) *n* flamant *m* rose.

flammable ['flæməbl] *adj* inflammable.

flan [flæn] *n* *UK* tarte *f* ; *US* flan *m*.

flank [flæŋk] <> *n* flanc *m*. <> *vt* : **to be flanked by** être flanqué(e) de.

flannel ['flænl] *n* **1.** [fabric] flanelle *f* - **2.** *UK* [facecloth] gant *m* de toilette.

flap [flæp] <> *n* **1.** [of envelope, pocket] rabat *m* - **2.** *UK inf* [panic] : **in a flap** paniqué(e). <> *vt & vi* battre.

flapjack ['flæpdʒæk] *n* **1.** *UK* [biscuit] biscuit *m* à l'avoine - **2.** *US* [pancake] crêpe *f* épaisse.

flare [fleər] <> *n* [distress signal] fusée *f* éclairante. <> *vi* **1.** [burn brightly] : **to flare (up)** s'embraser - **2.** [intensify] : **to flare up** [war, revolution] s'intensifier soudainement ; [person] s'emporter - **3.** [widen - trousers, skirt] s'évaser ; [- nostrils] se dilater. **flares** *npl* *UK* pantalon *m* à pattes d'éléphant.

flash [flæʃ] <> *n* **1.** [of light, colour] éclat *m* ; **flash of lightning** éclair *m* - **2.** PHOT flash *m* - **3.** [sudden moment] éclair *m* ; **in a flash** en un rien de temps. <> *vt* **1.** [shine] projeter ; **to flash one's headlights** faire un appel de phares - **2.** [send out - signal, smile] envoyer ; [- look] jeter - **3.** [show] montrer. <> *vi* **1.** [torch] briller - **2.** [light - on and off] clignoter ; [eyes] jeter des éclairs - **3.** [rush] : **to flash by** OR **past** passer comme un éclair.

flashback ['flæʃbæk] *n* flash-back *m*, retour *m* en arrière.

flashbulb ['flæʃbʌlb] *n* ampoule *f* de flash.

flashgun ['flæʃɡʌn] *n* flash *m*.

flashlight ['flæʃlaɪt] *n* *esp US* [torch] lampe *f* électrique.

flashy ['flæʃɪ] *adj inf* tape-à-l'œil (*inv*).

flask [flɑːsk] *n* **1.** [thermos flask] Thermos® *m ou f* - **2.** CHEM ballon *m* - **3.** [hip flask] flasque *f*.

flat [flæt] <> *adj* **1.** [gen] plat(e) - **2.** [tyre] crevé(e) - **3.** [refusal, denial] catégorique - **4.** [business, trade] calme - **5.** [dull - voice, tone] monotone ; [- performance, writing] terne - **6.** [MUS - person] qui chante trop grave ; [- note] bémol - **7.** [fare, price] fixe - **8.** [beer, lemonade] éventé(e) - **9.** [battery] à plat. <> *adv* **1.** [level] à plat - **2.** [exactly] : **two hours flat** deux heures pile. <> *n* **1.** *UK* [apartment] appartement *m* - **2.** MUS bémol *m*. **flat out** *adv* [work] d'arrache-pied ; [travel - subj: vehicle] le plus vite possible.

flatly ['flætlɪ] *adv* **1.** [absolutely] catégoriquement - **2.** [dully - say] avec monotonie ; [- perform] de façon terne.

flatmate ['flætmeɪt] *n* *UK personne avec laquelle on partage un appartement.*

flat rate *n* tarif *m* forfaitaire.

flatten ['flætn] *vt* **1.** [make flat - steel, paper]

aplatir ; [- wrinkles, bumps] aplanir - 2. [destroy] raser. ➤ **flatten out** ⟨⟩ vi s'aplanir. ⟨⟩ vt sep aplanir.

flatter ['flætər] vt flatter.

flattering ['flætərɪŋ] adj 1. [complimentary] flatteur(euse) - 2. [clothes] seyant(e).

flattery ['flætərɪ] n flatterie f.

flaunt [flɔːnt] vt faire étalage de.

flavour UK, **flavor** US ['fleɪvər] ⟨⟩ n 1. [of food] goût m ; [of ice cream, yoghurt] parfum m - 2. fig [atmosphere] atmosphère f. ⟨⟩ vt parfumer.

flavouring UK, **flavoring** US ['fleɪvərɪŋ] n (U) parfum m.

flaw [flɔː] n [in material, character] défaut m ; [in plan, argument] faille f.

flawless ['flɔːlɪs] adj parfait(e).

flax [flæks] n lin m.

flea [fliː] n puce f.

flea market n marché m aux puces.

fleck [flek] ⟨⟩ n moucheture f, petite tache f. ⟨⟩ vt : **flecked with** moucheté(e) de.

fled [fled] pt & pp ➤ flee.

flee [fliː] (pt & pp fled) vt & vi fuir.

fleece [fliːs] ⟨⟩ n [animal] toison f ; [fabric] polaire f. ⟨⟩ vt inf escroquer.

fleet [fliːt] n 1. [of ships] flotte f - 2. [of cars, buses] parc m.

fleeting ['fliːtɪŋ] adj [moment] bref (brève) ; [look] fugitif(ive) ; [visit] éclair (inv).

Fleet Street n rue de Londres dont le nom est utilisé pour désigner la presse britannique.

Flemish ['flemɪʃ] ⟨⟩ adj flamand(e). ⟨⟩ n [language] flamand m. ⟨⟩ npl : **the Flemish** les Flamands mpl.

flesh [fleʃ] n chair f ; **his/her flesh and blood** [family] les siens.

flesh wound n blessure f superficielle.

flew [fluː] pt ➤ fly.

flex [fleks] ⟨⟩ n ELEC fil m. ⟨⟩ vt [bend] fléchir.

flexible ['fleksəbl] adj flexible.

flexitime ['fleksɪtaɪm], US **flextime** ['flekstaɪm] n (U) horaire m à la carte OR flexible.

flick [flɪk] ⟨⟩ n 1. [of whip, towel] petit coup m - 2. [with finger] chiquenaude f - 3. inf [cinema] film m. ⟨⟩ vt [switch] appuyer sur. ➤ **flick through** vt insep feuilleter.

flicker ['flɪkər] vi 1. [candle, light] vaciller - 2. [shadow] trembler ; [eyelids] ciller.

flick knife n UK couteau m à cran d'arrêt.

flight [flaɪt] n 1. [gen] vol m - 2. [of steps, stairs] volée f - 3. [escape] fuite f.

flight attendant n steward m, hôtesse f de l'air.

flight crew n équipage m.

flight deck n 1. [of aircraft carrier] pont m d'envol - 2. [of plane] cabine f de pilotage.

flight recorder n enregistreur m de vol.

flimsy ['flɪmzɪ] adj [dress, material] léger(ère) ; [building, bookcase] peu solide ; [excuse] piètre.

flinch [flɪntʃ] vi tressaillir ; **to flinch from sthg/from doing sthg** reculer devant qqch/à l'idée de faire qqch.

fling [flɪŋ] ⟨⟩ n inf [affair] aventure f, affaire f. ⟨⟩ vt (pt & pp flung) lancer.

flint [flɪnt] n 1. [rock] silex m - 2. [in lighter] pierre f.

flip [flɪp] ⟨⟩ vt 1. [turn - pancake] faire sauter ; [- record] tourner - 2. [switch] appuyer sur. ⟨⟩ n 1. [flick] chiquenaude f - 2. [somersault] saut m périlleux. ➤ **flip through** vt insep feuilleter.

flip-flop n [shoe] tong f.

flippant ['flɪpənt] adj désinvolte.

flipper ['flɪpər] n 1. [of animal] nageoire f - 2. [for swimmer, diver] palme f.

flirt [flɜːt] ⟨⟩ n flirt m. ⟨⟩ vi [with person] : **to flirt (with sb)** flirter (avec qqn).

flirtatious [flɜːˈteɪʃəs] adj flirteur(euse).

flit [flɪt] vi [bird] voleter.

float [fləʊt] ⟨⟩ n 1. [for buoyancy] flotteur m - 2. [in procession] char m - 3. [money] petite caisse f. ⟨⟩ vt [on water] faire flotter. ⟨⟩ vi [on water] flotter ; [through air] glisser.

flock [flɒk] n 1. [of birds] vol m ; [of sheep] troupeau m - 2. fig [of people] foule f.

flog [flɒg] vt 1. [whip] flageller - 2. UK inf [sell] refiler.

flood [flʌd] ⟨⟩ n 1. [of water] inondation f - 2. [great amount] déluge m, avalanche f. ⟨⟩ vt 1. [with water, light] inonder - 2. [overwhelm] : **to flood sthg (with)** inonder qqch (de).

flooding ['flʌdɪŋ] n (U) inondations fpl.

floodlight ['flʌdlaɪt] n projecteur m.

floor [flɔːr] ⟨⟩ n 1. [of room - gen] sol m ; [of club, disco] piste f - 2. [of valley, sea, forest] fond m - 3. [storey] étage m - 4. [at meeting, debate] auditoire m. ⟨⟩ vt 1. [knock down] terrasser - 2. [baffle] dérouter.

floorboard ['flɔːbɔːd] n plancher m.

floor show n spectacle m de cabaret.

flop [flɒp] n inf [failure] fiasco m.

floppy ['flɒpɪ] adj [ears, flower] tombant(e) ; [collar] lâche.

floppy (disk) n disquette f, disque m souple.

flora ['flɔːrə] *n* flore *f*.

florid ['flɒrɪd] *adj* **1.** [red] rougeaud(e) - **2.** [extravagant] fleuri(e).

florist ['flɒrɪst] *n* fleuriste *mf* ; **florist's (shop)** magasin *m* de fleuriste.

flotsam ['flɒtsəm] *n (U)* **flotsam and jetsam** débris *mpl* ; *fig* épaves *fpl*.

flounder ['flaʊndər] *vi* **1.** [in water, mud, snow] patauger - **2.** [in conversation] bredouiller.

flour ['flaʊər] *n* farine *f*.

flourish ['flʌrɪʃ] ◇ *vi* [plant, flower] bien pousser ; [children] être en pleine santé ; [company, business] prospérer ; [arts] s'épanouir. ◇ *n* brandir. ◇ *n* grand geste *m*.

flout [flaʊt] *vt* bafouer.

flow [fləʊ] ◇ *n* **1.** [movement - of water, information] circulation *f* ; [- of funds] mouvement *m* ; [- of words] flot *m* - **2.** [of tide] flux *m*. ◇ *vi* **1.** [gen] couler - **2.** [traffic, information] s'écouler - **3.** [hair, clothes] flotter - **4.** [days, weeks] : **to flow by** s'écouler.

flow chart, **flow diagram** *n* organigramme *m*.

flower ['flaʊər] ◇ *n* fleur *f*. ◇ *vi* [bloom] fleurir.

flowerbed ['flaʊəbed] *n* parterre *m*.

flowerpot ['flaʊəpɒt] *n* pot *m* de fleurs.

flowery ['flaʊərɪ] *adj* **1.** [dress, material] à fleurs - **2.** *pej* [style] fleuri(e).

flown [fləʊn] *pp* ► **fly**.

flu [fluː] *n (U)* grippe *f*.

fluctuate ['flʌktjʊeɪt] *vi* [rate, temperature, results] fluctuer.

fluency ['fluːənsɪ] *n* aisance *f*.

fluent ['fluːənt] *adj* **1.** [in foreign language] : **to speak fluent French** parler couramment le français - **2.** [writing, style] coulant(e), aisé(e).

fluff [flʌf] *n (U)* **1.** [down] duvet *m* - **2.** [dust] moutons *mpl*.

fluffy ['flʌfɪ] *adj* duveteux(euse) ; [toy] en peluche.

fluid ['fluːɪd] ◇ *n* fluide *m* ; [in diet, for cleaning] liquide *m*. ◇ *adj* **1.** [flowing] fluide - **2.** [unfixed] changeant(e).

fluid ounce *n* = 0,03 litre.

fluke [fluːk] *n inf* [chance] coup *m* de bol.

flummox ['flʌməks] *vt* désarçonner.

flung [flʌŋ] *pt & pp* ► **fling**.

flunk [flʌŋk] *esp US inf vt* **1.** [exam, test] rater - **2.** [student] recaler.

fluorescent [flʊə'resənt] *adj* fluorescent(e).

fluoride ['flʊəraɪd] *n* fluorure *m*.

flurry ['flʌrɪ] *n* **1.** [of snow] rafale *f* - **2.** *fig* [of objections] concert *m* ; [of activity, excitement] débordement *m*.

flush [flʌʃ] ◇ *adj* [level] : **flush with** de niveau avec. ◇ *n* **1.** [in lavatory] chasse *f* d'eau - **2.** [blush] rougeur *f* - **3.** [sudden feeling] accès *m*. ◇ *vt* [toilet] : **to flush the toilet** tirer la chasse d'eau. ◇ *vi* [blush] rougir.

flushed [flʌʃt] *adj* **1.** [red-faced] rouge - **2.** [excited] : **flushed with** exalté(e) par.

flustered ['flʌstəd] *adj* troublé(e).

flute [fluːt] *n* MUS flûte *f*.

flutter ['flʌtər] ◇ *n* **1.** [of wings] battement *m* - **2.** *inf* [of excitement] émoi *m*. ◇ *vi* **1.** [bird, insect] voleter ; [wings] battre - **2.** [flag, dress] flotter.

flux [flʌks] *n* [change] : **to be in a state of flux** être en proie à des changements permanents.

fly [flaɪ] ◇ *n* **1.** [insect] mouche *f* - **2.** [of trousers] braguette *f*. ◇ *vt (pt* **flew**, *pp* **flown) 1.** [kite, plane] faire voler - **2.** [passengers, supplies] transporter par avion - **3.** [flag] faire flotter. ◇ *vi (pt* **flew**, *pp* **flown) 1.** [bird, insect, plane] voler - **2.** [pilot] faire voler un avion - **3.** [passenger] voyager en avion - **4.** [move fast, pass quickly] filer - **5.** [flag] flotter. ◆ **fly away** *vi* s'envoler.

fly-fishing *n* pêche *f* à la mouche.

flying ['flaɪɪŋ] ◇ *adj* volant(e). ◇ *n* aviation *f* ; **to like flying** aimer prendre l'avion.

flying colours *UK*, **flying colors** *US npl* : **to pass (sthg) with flying colours** réussir (qqch) haut la main.

flying picket *n* piquet *m* de grève volant.

flying saucer *n* soucoupe *f* volante.

flying squad *n UK* force d'intervention rapide de la police.

flying start *n* : **to get off to a flying start** prendre un départ sur les chapeaux de roue.

flying visit *n* visite *f* éclair.

flyover ['flaɪ,əʊvər] *n UK* saut-de-mouton *m*.

flysheet ['flaɪʃiːt] *n UK* auvent *m*.

fly spray *n* insecticide *m*.

FM *n (abbrev of* **frequency modulation)** FM *f*.

FMD [,efem'diː] *(abbrev of* **foot and mouth disease)** *n* fièvre *f* aphteuse.

foal [fəʊl] *n* poulain *m*.

foam [fəʊm] ◇ *n (U)* **1.** [bubbles] mousse *f* - **2.** : **foam (rubber)** caoutchouc *m* Mousse®. ◇ *vi* [water, champagne] mousser.

fob [fɒb] ◆ **fob off** *vt sep* repousser ; **to**

fob sthg **off on** sb refiler qqch à qqn ; **to fob sb off with** sthg se débarrasser de qqn à l'aide de qqch.

focal point n foyer m ; fig point m central.

focus ['fəʊkəs] <> n (pl -cuses [-kəsi:z] OR -ci [-sai]) **1.** PHOT mise f au point ; **in focus** net ; **out of focus** flou - **2.** [centre - of rays] foyer m ; [- of earthquake] centre m. <> vt [lens, camera] mettre au point. <> vi **1.** [with camera, lens] se fixer ; [eyes] accommoder ; **to focus on** sthg [with camera, lens] se fixer sur qqch ; [with eyes] fixer qqch - **2.** [attention] : **to focus on** sthg se concentrer sur qqch.

fodder ['fɒdər] n (U) fourrage m.

foe [fəʊ] n lit ennemi m.

foetus UK, **fetus** US ['fi:təs] n fœtus m.

fog [fɒg] n (U) brouillard m.

foggy ['fɒgɪ] adj [misty] brumeux(euse).

foghorn ['fɒghɔːn] n sirène f de brume.

fog lamp UK, **fog light** US n feu m de brouillard.

foible ['fɔɪbl] n marotte f.

foil [fɔɪl] <> n (U) [metal sheet - of tin, silver] feuille f ; CULIN papier m d'aluminium. <> vt déjouer.

fold [fəʊld] <> vt **1.** [bend, close up] plier ; **to fold one's arms** croiser les bras - **2.** [wrap] envelopper. <> vi **1.** [close up - table, chair] se plier ; [- petals, leaves] se refermer - **2.** inf [company, project] échouer ; THEAT quitter l'affiche. <> n **1.** [in material, paper] pli m - **2.** [for animals] parc m - **3.** fig [spiritual home] : **the fold** le bercail. **fold up** <> vt sep plier. <> vi **1.** [close up - table, map] se plier ; [- petals, leaves] se refermer - **2.** [company, project] échouer.

folder ['fəʊldər] n [for papers - wallet] chemise f ; [- binder] classeur m.

folding ['fəʊldɪŋ] adj [table, umbrella] pliant(e) ; [doors] en accordéon.

foliage ['fəʊlɪɪdʒ] n feuillage m.

folk [fəʊk] <> adj [art, dancing] folklorique ; [medicine] populaire. <> npl [people] gens mpl. **folks** npl inf [relatives] famille f.

folklore ['fəʊklɔːr] n folklore m.

folk music n musique f folk.

folk song n chanson f folk.

follow ['fɒləʊ] <> vt suivre. <> vi **1.** [gen] suivre - **2.** [be logical] tenir debout ; **it follows that...** il s'ensuit que... **follow up** vt sep **1.** [pursue - idea, suggestion] prendre en considération ; [- advertisement] donner suite à - **2.** [complete] : **to follow** sthg **up with** faire suivre qqch de.

follower ['fɒləʊər] n [believer] disciple mf.

following ['fɒləʊɪŋ] <> adj suivant(e). <> n groupe m d'admirateurs. <> prep après.

folly ['fɒlɪ] n (U) [foolishness] folie f.

fond [fɒnd] adj [affectionate] affectueux(euse) ; **to be fond of** aimer beaucoup.

fondle ['fɒndl] vt caresser.

font [fɒnt] n **1.** [in church] fonts mpl baptismaux - **2.** COMPUT & TYPO police f (de caractères).

food [fu:d] n nourriture f.

food mixer n mixer m.

food poisoning [-,pɔɪznɪŋ] n intoxication f alimentaire.

food processor [-,prəʊsesər] n robot m ménager.

foodstuffs ['fu:dstʌfs] npl denrées fpl alimentaires.

fool [fu:l] <> n **1.** [idiot] idiot m, -e f - **2.** UK [dessert] ≃ mousse f. <> vt duper ; **to fool sb into doing** sthg amener qqn à faire qqch en le dupant. <> vi faire l'imbécile. **fool about, fool around** vi **1.** [behave foolishly] faire l'imbécile - **2.** inf [be unfaithful] être infidèle.

foolhardy ['fu:l,hɑ:dɪ] adj téméraire.

foolish ['fu:lɪʃ] adj idiot(e), stupide.

foolproof ['fu:lpru:f] adj infaillible.

foot [fʊt] <> n **1.** (pl feet [fi:t]) [gen] pied m ; [of animal] patte f ; [of page, stairs] bas m ; **to be on one's feet** être debout ; **to get to one's feet** se mettre debout, se lever ; **on foot** à pied ; **to put one's foot in it** mettre les pieds dans le plat ; **to put one's feet up** se reposer - **2.** (pl foot OR feet) [unit of measurement] = 30,48 cm, ≃ pied m. <> vt inf **to foot the bill** payer la note.

footage ['fʊtɪdʒ] n (U) séquences fpl.

football ['fʊtbɔːl] n **1.** [game - soccer] football m, foot m ; [- American football] football américain - **2.** [ball] ballon m de football OR foot.

footballer ['fʊtbɔːlər] n UK joueur m, -euse f de football, footballeur m, -euse f.

football ground n UK terrain m de football.

football player = **footballer**.

footbrake ['fʊtbreɪk] n frein m (à pied).

footbridge ['fʊtbrɪdʒ] n passerelle f.

foothills ['fʊthɪlz] npl contreforts mpl.

foothold ['fʊthəʊld] n prise f (de pied).

footing ['fʊtɪŋ] n **1.** [foothold] prise f ; **to lose one's footing** trébucher - **2.** fig [basis] position f.

footlights ['fʊtlaɪts] npl THEAT rampe f.

footnote ['fʊtnəʊt] n note f en bas de page.

footpath ['fʊtpɑːθ] (*pl* [-pɑːðz]) *n* sentier *m*.

footprint ['fʊtprɪnt] *n* empreinte *f* (de pied), trace *f* (de pas).

footstep ['fʊtstep] *n* 1. [sound] bruit *m* de pas - 2. [footprint] empreinte *f* (de pied).

footwear ['fʊtweə'] *n* (U) chaussures *fpl*.

for [fɔː'] ⋄ *prep* 1. [referring to intention, destination, purpose] pour ; **this is for you** c'est pour vous ; **the plane for Paris** l'avion à destination de Paris ; **let's meet for a drink** retrouvons-nous pour prendre un verre ; **we did it for a laugh** OR **for fun** on l'a fait pour rire ; **what's it for?** ça sert à quoi? - 2. [representing, on behalf of] pour ; **the MP for Barnsley** le député de Barnsley ; **let me do that for you** laissez-moi faire, je vais vous le faire - 3. [because of] pour, en raison de ; **for various reasons** pour plusieurs raisons ; **a prize for swimming** un prix de natation ; **for fear of being ridiculed** de OR par peur d'être ridiculisé - 4. [with regard to] pour ; **to be ready for sthg** être prêt à OR pour qqch ; **it's not for me to say** ce n'est pas à moi à le dire ; **to be young for one's age** être jeune pour son âge ; **to feel sorry for sb** plaindre qqn - 5. [indicating amount of time, space] : **there's no time for that now** on n'a pas le temps de faire cela OR de s'occuper de cela maintenant ; **there's room for another person** il y a de la place pour encore une personne - 6. [indicating period of time] : **she'll be away for a month** elle sera absente (pendant) un mois ; **we talked for hours** on a parlé pendant des heures ; **I've lived here for 3 years** j'habite ici depuis 3 ans, cela fait 3 ans que j'habite ici ; **I can do it for you for tomorrow** je peux vous le faire pour demain - 7. [indicating distance] pendant, pour ; **for 50 kilometres** pendant OR sur 50 kilomètres ; **I walked for miles** j'ai marché (pendant) des kilomètres - 8. [indicating particular occasion] pour ; **for Christmas** pour Noël - 9. [indicating amount of money, price] : **they're 50p for ten** cela coûte 50p les dix ; **I bought/sold it for £10** je l'ai acheté/vendu 10 livres - 10. [in favour of, in support of] pour ; **to vote for sthg** voter pour qqch ; **to be all for sthg** être tout à fait pour en faveur de qqch - 11. [in ratios] pour - 12. [indicating meaning, exchange] : **P for Peter** P comme Peter ; **what's the Greek for 'mother'?** comment dit-on 'mère' en grec? ⋄ *conj fml* [as, since] car. ⬛ **for all** ⋄ *prep* malgré ; **for all his money...** malgré tout son argent... ⋄ *conj* : **for all I know** pour autant que je sache. ⬛ **for ever** *adv* = forever.

forage ['fɒrɪdʒ] *vi* : **to forage (for)** fouiller (pour trouver).

foray ['fɒreɪ] *n* : **foray (into)** *lit* incursion *f* (dans).

forbad [fə'bæd], **forbade** [fə'beɪd] *pt* ⬛ **forbid**.

forbid [fə'bɪd] (*pt* -**bade** OR -**bad**, *pp* **forbid** OR -**bidden**) *vt* interdire, défendre ; **to forbid sb to do sthg** interdire OR défendre à qqn de faire qqch.

forbidden [fə'bɪdn] ⋄ *pp* ⬛ **forbid**. ⋄ *adj* interdit(e), défendu(e).

forbidding [fə'bɪdɪŋ] *adj* [severe, unfriendly] austère ; [threatening] sinistre.

force [fɔːs] ⋄ *n* 1. [gen] force *f* ; **by force** de force ; **the force of gravity** la pesanteur - 2. [effect] : **to be in/to come into force** être/entrer en vigueur. ⋄ *vt* 1. [gen] forcer ; **to force sb to do sthg** forcer qqn à faire qqch - 2. [press] : **to force sthg on sb** imposer qqch à qqn. ⬛ **forces** *npl* : **the forces** les forces *fpl* armées ; **to join forces** joindre ses efforts.

force-feed *vt* nourrir de force.

forceful ['fɔːsfʊl] *adj* [person] énergique ; [speech] vigoureux(euse).

forceps ['fɔːseps] *npl* forceps *m*.

forcibly ['fɔːsəblɪ] *adv* 1. [using physical force] de force - 2. [powerfully] avec vigueur.

ford [fɔːd] *n* gué *m*.

fore [fɔː'] ⋄ *adj* NAUT à l'avant. ⋄ *n* : **to come to the fore** s'imposer.

forearm ['fɔːrɑːm] *n* avant-bras *m inv*.

foreboding [fɔː'bəʊdɪŋ] *n* pressentiment *m*.

forecast ['fɔːkɑːst] ⋄ *n* prévision *f* ; **(weather) forecast** prévisions météorologiques. ⋄ *vt* (*pt* & *pp* **forecast** OR -**ed**) prévoir.

foreclose [fɔː'kləʊz] ⋄ *vt* saisir. ⋄ *vi* : **to foreclose on sb** saisir les biens de qqn.

forecourt ['fɔːkɔːt] *n* [of petrol station] devant *m* ; [of building] avant-cour *f*.

forefinger ['fɔːˌfɪŋgə'] *n* index *m*.

forefront ['fɔːfrʌnt] *n* : **in** OR **at the forefront of** au premier plan de.

forego [fɔː'gəʊ] = **forgo**.

foregone conclusion ['fɔːgɒn-] *n* : **it's a foregone conclusion** c'est couru.

foreground ['fɔːgraʊnd] *n* premier plan *m*.

forehand ['fɔːhænd] *n* TENNIS coup *m* droit.

forehead ['fɔːhed] *n* front *m*.

foreign ['fɒrən] *adj* 1. [gen] étranger(ère) ; [correspondent] à l'étranger - 2. [policy, trade] extérieur(e).

foreign affairs *npl* affaires *fpl* étrangères.

foreign currency *n* (U) devises *fpl* étrangères.

foreigner ['fɒrənə'] *n* étranger *m*, -ère *f*.

foreign minister *n* ministre *m* des Affaires étrangères.

Foreign Office *n UK* **the Foreign Office** ≃ le ministère des Affaires étrangères.

Foreign Secretary *n UK* ≃ ministre *m* des Affaires étrangères.

foreleg ['fɔːleg] *n* [of horse] membre *m* antérieur ; [of other animals] patte *f* de devant.

foreman ['fɔːmən] (*pl* -men [-mən]) *n* **1.** [of workers] contremaître *m*, -esse *f* - **2.** LAW président *m* du jury.

foremost ['fɔːməʊst] <> *adj* principal(e). <> *adv* : **first and foremost** tout d'abord.

forensic [fə'rensɪk] *adj* [department, investigation] médico-légal(e).

forensic medicine, forensic science *n* médecine *f* légale.

forerunner ['fɔː,rʌnəʳ] *n* précurseur *m*.

foresee [fɔː'siː] (*pt* -saw [-'sɔː] , *pp* -seen) *vt* prévoir.

foreseeable [fɔː'siːəbl] *adj* prévisible ; **for the foreseeable future** pour tous les jours/mois *(etc)* à venir.

foreseen [fɔː'siːn] *pp* ► foresee.

foreshadow [fɔː'ʃædəʊ] *vt* présager.

foresight ['fɔːsaɪt] *n (U)* prévoyance *f*.

forest ['fɒrɪst] *n* forêt *f*.

forestall [fɔː'stɔːl] *vt* [attempt, discussion] prévenir ; [person] devancer.

forestry ['fɒrɪstrɪ] *n* sylviculture *f*.

foretaste ['fɔːteɪst] *n* avant-goût *m*.

foretell [fɔː'tel] (*pt & pp* -told) *vt* prédire.

foretold [fɔː'təʊld] *pt & pp* ► foretell.

forever [fə'revəʳ] *adv* [eternally] (pour) toujours.

forewarn [fɔː'wɔːn] *vt* avertir.

foreword ['fɔːwɜːd] *n* avant-propos *m inv*.

forfeit ['fɔːfɪt] <> *n* amende *f* ; [in game] gage *m*. <> *vt* perdre.

forgave [fə'geɪv] *pt* ► forgive.

forge [fɔːdʒ] <> *n* forge *f*. <> *vt* **1.** fig & INDUST forger - **2.** [signature, money] contrefaire ; [passport] falsifier. ◆ **forge ahead** *vi* prendre de l'avance.

forger ['fɔːdʒəʳ] *n* faussaire *mf*.

forgery ['fɔːdʒərɪ] *n* **1.** (*U*) [crime] contrefaçon *f* - **2.** [forged article] faux *m*.

forget [fə'get] (*pt* -got, *pp* -gotten) <> *vt* oublier ; **to forget to do sthg** oublier de faire qqch ; **forget it!** laisse tomber! <> *vi* : **to forget (about sthg)** oublier (qqch).

forgetful [fə'getfʊl] *adj* distrait(e), étourdi(e).

forget-me-not *n* myosotis *m*.

forgive [fə'gɪv] (*pt* -gave, *pp* -given [-'gɪvn]) *vt* pardonner ; **to forgive sb for sthg/for doing sthg** pardonner qqch à qqn/à qqn d'avoir fait qqch.

forgiveness [fə'gɪvnɪs] *n (U)* pardon *m*.

forgo [fɔː'gəʊ] (*pt* -went, *pp* -gone [-'gɒn]) *vt fml* renoncer à.

forgot [fə'gɒt] *pt* ► forget.

forgotten [fə'gɒtn] *pp* ► forget.

fork [fɔːk] <> *n* **1.** [for eating] fourchette *f* - **2.** [for gardening] fourche *f* - **3.** [in road] bifurcation *f* ; [of river] embranchement *m*. <> *vi* bifurquer. ◆ **fork out** *inf* <> *vt insep* allonger, débourser. <> *vi* : **to fork out (for)** casquer (pour).

forklift truck ['fɔːklɪft-] *n* chariot *m* élévateur.

forlorn [fə'lɔːn] *adj* **1.** [person, face] malheureux(euse), triste - **2.** [place, landscape] désolé(e) - **3.** [hope, attempt] désespéré(e).

form [fɔːm] <> *n* **1.** [shape, fitness, type] forme *f* ; **on form** *UK*, **in form** *US* en pleine forme ; **off form** *esp UK* pas en forme ; **in the form of** sous forme de - **2.** [questionnaire] formulaire *m* - **3.** *UK* SCH classe *f*. <> *vt* former. <> *vi* se former.

formal ['fɔːml] *adj* **1.** [official, conventional] officiel(elle) - **2.** [person] formaliste ; [language] soutenu(e).

formality [fɔː'mælətɪ] *n* formalité *f*.

format ['fɔːmæt] <> *n* [gen & COMPUT] format *m*. <> *vt* COMPUT formater.

formation [fɔː'meɪʃn] *n* **1.** [gen] formation *f* - **2.** [of idea, plan] élaboration *f*.

formative ['fɔːmətɪv] *adj* formateur(trice).

former ['fɔːməʳ] <> *adj* **1.** [previous] ancien(enne) ; **former husband** ex-mari *m* ; **former pupil** ancien élève *m*, ancienne élève *f* - **2.** [first of two] premier(ère). <> *n* : **the former** le premier (la première), celui-là (celle-là).

formerly ['fɔːməlɪ] *adv* autrefois.

formidable ['fɔːmɪdəbl] *adj* redoutable, terrible.

formula ['fɔːmjʊlə] (*pl* -as OR -ae [-iː]) *n* formule *f*.

formulate ['fɔːmjʊleɪt] *vt* formuler.

forsake [fə'seɪk] (*pt* forsook, *pp* forsaken) *vt lit* [person] abandonner ; [habit] renoncer à.

forsaken [fə'seɪkn] *adj* abandonné(e).

forsook [fə'sʊk] *pt* ► forsake.

fort [fɔːt] *n* fort *m*.

forte ['fɔːtɪ] *n* point *m* fort.

forth [fɔːθ] *adv lit* en avant.

forthcoming [fɔːθ'kʌmɪŋ] *adj* **1.** [imminent] à venir - **2.** [helpful] communicatif(ive).

forthright ['fɔːθraɪt] *adj* franc (franche), direct(e).

forthwith [ˌfɔːθ'wɪθ] *adv fml* aussitôt.

fortified wine ['fɔːtɪfaɪd-] *n* vin *m* de liqueur.

fortify ['fɔːtɪfaɪ] *vt* **1.** MIL fortifier - **2.** *fig* [resolve etc] renforcer.

fortnight ['fɔːtnaɪt] *n UK* quinze jours *mpl*, quinzaine *f*.

fortnightly ['fɔːtˌnaɪtlɪ] <> *adj UK* bimensuel(elle). <> *adv* tous les quinze jours.

fortress ['fɔːtrɪs] *n* forteresse *f*.

fortunate ['fɔːtʃnət] *adj* heureux(euse) ; **to be fortunate** avoir de la chance.

fortunately ['fɔːtʃnətlɪ] *adv* heureusement.

fortune ['fɔːtʃuːn] *n* **1.** [wealth] fortune *f* - **2.** [luck] fortune *f*, chance *f* - **3.** [future] : **to tell sb's fortune** dire la bonne aventure à qqn.

fortune-teller [-ˌtelər] *n* diseuse *f* de bonne aventure.

forty ['fɔːtɪ] *num* quarante ; *see also* **sixty**.

forward ['fɔːwəd] <> *adj* **1.** [movement] en avant - **2.** [planning] à long terme - **3.** [impudent] effronté(e). <> *adv* **1.** [ahead] en avant ; **to go** OR **move forward** avancer - **2.** [in time] : **to bring a meeting forward** avancer la date d'une réunion. <> *n* SPORT avant *m*. <> *vt* [letter] faire suivre ; [goods] expédier.

forwarding address ['fɔːwədɪŋ-] *n* adresse *f* où faire suivre le courrier.

forwards ['fɔːwədz] *adv* = **forward**.

forward slash *n* COMPUT barre *f* oblique.

forwent [fɔː'went] *pt* ► **forgo**.

fossil ['fɒsl] *n* fossile *m*.

foster ['fɒstər] <> *adj* [family] d'accueil. <> *vt* **1.** [child] accueillir - **2.** *fig* [nurture] nourrir, entretenir.

foster child *n* enfant *m* placé en famille d'accueil.

foster parent *n* parent *m* nourricier.

fought [fɔːt] *pt & pp* ► **fight**.

foul [faul] <> *adj* **1.** [gen] infect(e) ; [water] croupi(e) - **2.** [language] grossier(ère), ordurier(ère). <> *n* SPORT faute *f*. <> *vt fml* **1.** [make dirty] souiller, salir - **2.** SPORT commettre une faute contre.

found [faund] <> *pt & pp* ► **find**. <> *vt* **1.** [hospital, town] fonder - **2.** [base] : **to found sthg on** fonder OR baser qqch sur.

foundation [faun'deɪʃn] *n* **1.** [creation, organization] fondation *f* - **2.** [basis] fondement *m*, base *f* - **3.** : **foundation (cream)** fond *m* de teint. ◆ **foundations** *npl* CONSTR fondations *fpl*.

founder ['faundər] <> *n* fondateur *m*, -trice *f*. <> *vi* [ship] sombrer.

foundry ['faundrɪ] *n* fonderie *f*.

fountain ['fauntɪn] *n* fontaine *f*.

fountain pen *n* stylo *m* à encre.

four [fɔːr] *num* quatre ; **on all fours** à quatre pattes ; *see also* **six**.

four-letter word *n* mot *m* grossier.

four-poster (bed) *n* lit *m* à baldaquin.

foursome ['fɔːsəm] *n* groupe *m* de quatre.

fourteen [ˌfɔː'tiːn] *num* quatorze ; *see also* **six**.

fourth [fɔːθ] *num* quatrième ; *see also* **sixth**.

Fourth of July *n* : **the Fourth of July** Fête de l'Indépendance américaine, célébrée le 4 juillet.

four-wheel drive *n* : **with four-wheel drive** à quatre roues motrices.

fowl [faul] (*pl* **fowl** OR **-s**) *n* volaille *f*.

fox [fɒks] <> *n* renard *m*. <> *vt* laisser perplexe.

foxglove ['fɒksglʌv] *n* digitale *f*.

foyer ['fɔɪeɪ] *n* **1.** [of hotel, theatre] foyer *m* - **2.** *US* [of house] hall *m* d'entrée.

fracas ['frækɑː, *US* 'freɪkəs] (*UK*, *pl* **fracas** *US*, *pl* **-ses** [-siːz]) *n* bagarre *f*.

fraction ['frækʃn] *n* fraction *f* ; **a fraction too big** légèrement OR un petit peu trop grand.

fractionally ['frækʃnəlɪ] *adv* un tout petit peu.

fracture ['fræktʃər] <> *n* fracture *f*. <> *vt* fracturer.

fragile ['frædʒaɪl] *adj* fragile.

fragment *n* ['frægmənt] fragment *m*.

fragrance ['freɪgrəns] *n* parfum *m*.

fragrant ['freɪgrənt] *adj* parfumé(e).

frail [freɪl] *adj* fragile.

frame [freɪm] <> *n* **1.** [gen] cadre *m* ; [of glasses] monture *f* ; [of door, window] encadrement *m* ; [of boat] carcasse *f* - **2.** [physique] charpente *f*. <> *vt* **1.** [gen] encadrer - **2.** [express] formuler - **3.** [set up] *inf* monter un coup contre.

frame of mind *n* état *m* d'esprit.

framework ['freɪmwɜːk] *n* **1.** [structure] armature *f*, carcasse *f* - **2.** *fig* [basis] structure *f*, cadre *m*.

France [frɑːns] *n* France *f* ; **in France** en France.

franchise ['fræntʃaɪz] *n* **1.** POL droit *m* de vote - **2.** COMM franchise *f*.

frank [fræŋk] <> *adj* franc (franche). <> *vt UK* affranchir.

frankly ['fræŋklɪ] *adv* franchement.

frantic ['fræntɪk] *adj* frénétique.

fraternity [frə'tɜːnətɪ] *n* **1.** [community]

confrérie f - 2. (U) [friendship] fraternité f
- 3. US [of students] club m d'étudiants (de
sexe masculin).

fraternize, UK **-ise** ['frætənaɪz] vi fraterniser.

fraud [frɔːd] n 1. (U) [crime] fraude f - 2. pej
[impostor] imposteur m.

fraught [frɔːt] adj 1. [full]: **fraught with**
plein(e) de - 2. UK [person] tendu(e) ; [time,
situation] difficile.

fray [freɪ] <> vt fig : my nerves were frayed
j'étais extrêmement tendu(e), j'étais à bout
de nerfs. <> vi [material, sleeves] s'user ;
tempers frayed fig l'atmosphère était ten-
due or électrique. <> n lit bagarre f.

frayed [freɪd] adj [jeans, collar] élimé(e).

freak [friːk] <> adj bizarre, insolite. <> n
1. [strange creature] monstre m, phénomène
m - 2. [unusual event] accident m bizarre
- 3. inf [fanatic] fana mf. ◆ **freak out** inf vi
[get angry] exploser (de colère) ; [panic]
paniquer.

freckle ['frekl] n tache f de rousseur.

free [friː] <> adj (comp **freer**, superl **freest**)
1. [gen] libre ; **to be free to do sthg** être libre
de faire qqch ; **feel free!** je t'en prie! ; **to set
free** libérer - 2. [not paid for] gratuit(e).
<> adv 1. [without payment] gratuitement ;
free of charge gratuitement ; **for free**
gratuitement - 2. [run, live] librement.
<> vt (pt & pp **freed**) 1. [gen] libérer
- 2. [trapped person, object] dégager.

freedom ['friːdəm] n 1. [gen] liberté f ;
freedom of speech liberté d'expression
- 2. [exception] : **freedom (from)** exemption
f (de).

Freefone® ['friːfəʊn] n (U) UK ≃ numéro
m vert.

free-for-all n mêlée f générale.

free gift n prime f.

freehand ['friːhænd] adj & adv à main
levée.

freehold ['friːhəʊld] n propriété f foncière
inaliénable.

free house n UK pub m en gérance libre.

free kick n coup m franc.

freelance ['friːlɑːns] <> adj indépen-
dant(e), free-lance (inv). <> n indépendant
m, -e f, free-lance mf inv.

freely ['friːlɪ] adv 1. [gen] librement
- 2. [generously] sans compter.

Freemason ['friː,meɪsn] n franc-maçon m.

Freepost® ['friːpəʊst] n UK port m payé.

free-range adj de ferme.

freestyle ['friːstaɪl] n [in swimming] nage f
libre.

free trade n (U) libre-échange m.

freeway ['friːweɪ] n US autoroute f.

freewheel [,friː'wiːl] vi [on bicycle] rouler
en roue libre ; [in car] rouler au point mort.

free will n (U) libre arbitre m ; **to do sthg
of one's own free will** faire qqch de son
propre gré.

freeze [friːz] <> vt (pt **froze**, pp **frozen**)
1. [gen] geler ; [food] congeler - 2. [wages,
prices] bloquer. <> vi (pt **froze**, pp **frozen**)
1. [gen] geler - 2. [stop moving] s'arrêter.
<> n 1. [cold weather] gel m - 2. [of wages,
prices] blocage m.

freeze-dried [-'draɪd] adj lyophilisé(e).

freezer ['friːzər] n congélateur m.

freezing ['friːzɪŋ] <> adj glacé(e) ; **I'm
freezing** je gèle. <> n = **freezing point**.

freezing point n point m de congélation.

freight [freɪt] n [goods] fret m.

freight train n US train m de marchandises.

French [frentʃ] <> adj français(e). <> n
[language] français m. <> npl : **the French**
les Français mpl.

French bean n UK haricot m vert.

French bread n (U) baguette f.

French Canadian <> adj canadien français (canadienne française). <> n Canadien français m, Canadienne française f.

French doors = **French windows**.

French dressing n [in UK] vinaigrette f ;
[in US] sauce-salade à base de mayonnaise et de
ketchup.

French fries npl esp US frites fpl.

Frenchman ['frentʃmən] (pl **-men** [-mən])
n Français m.

French stick n UK baguette f.

French windows npl porte-fenêtre f.

Frenchwoman ['frentʃ,wʊmən] (pl
-women [-,wɪmɪn]) n Française f.

frenetic [frə'netɪk] adj frénétique.

frenzy ['frenzɪ] n frénésie f.

frequency ['friːkwənsɪ] n fréquence f.

frequent <> adj ['friːkwənt] fréquent(e).
<> vt [frɪ'kwent] fréquenter.

frequently ['friːkwəntlɪ] adv fréquemment.

fresh [freʃ] adj 1. [gen] frais (fraîche)
- 2. [not salty] doux (douce) - 3. [new - drink,
piece of paper] autre ; [- look, approach]
nouveau(elle) - 4. inf dated [cheeky] fami-
lier(ère).

freshen ['freʃn] <> vt rafraîchir. <> vi
[wind] devenir plus fort. ◆ **freshen up** vi
faire un brin de toilette.

fresher ['freʃər] n UK UNIV bizut m, étudiant
m, -e f de première année.

freshly ['freʃlɪ] adv [squeezed, ironed]
fraîchement.

freshman ['freʃmən] (*pl* -men [-mən]) *n US* UNIV bizut *m*, étudiant *m*, -e *f* de première année.

freshness ['freʃnɪs] *n* (*U*) **1.** [gen] fraîcheur *f* - **2.** [originality] nouveauté *f*.

freshwater ['freʃ,wɔːtə'] *adj* d'eau douce.

fret [fret] *vi* [worry] s'inquiéter.

friar ['fraɪə'] *n* frère *m*.

friction ['frɪkʃn] *n* (*U*) friction *f*.

friction tape *n US & Can* chatterton *m*.

Friday ['fraɪdɪ] *n* vendredi *m* ; *see also* Saturday.

fridge [frɪdʒ] *n* frigo *m*.

fridge-freezer *n UK* réfrigérateur-congélateur *m*.

fried [fraɪd] *adj* frit(e) ; **fried egg** œuf *m* au plat.

friend [frend] *n* ami *m*, -e *f* ; **to be friends with sb** être ami avec qqn ; **to make friends (with sb)** se lier d'amitié (avec qqn).

friendly ['frendlɪ] *adj* [person, manner, match] amical(e) ; [nation] ami(e) ; [argument] sans conséquence ; **to be friendly with sb** être ami avec qqn.

friendship ['frendʃɪp] *n* amitié *f*.

fries [fraɪz] = French fries.

frieze [friːz] *n* frise *f*.

fright [fraɪt] *n* peur *f* ; **to give sb a fright** faire peur à qqn ; **to take fright** prendre peur.

frighten ['fraɪtn] *vt* faire peur à, effrayer.

frightened ['fraɪtnd] *adj* apeuré(e) ; **to be frightened of sthg/of doing sthg** avoir peur de qqch/de faire qqch.

frightening ['fraɪtnɪŋ] *adj* effrayant(e).

frightful ['fraɪtful] *adj* dated effroyable.

frigid ['frɪdʒɪd] *adj* [sexually] frigide.

frill [frɪl] *n* **1.** [decoration] volant *m* - **2.** *inf* [extra] supplément *m*.

fringe [frɪndʒ] *n* **1.** [gen] frange *f* - **2.** [edge - of village] bordure *f* ; [- of wood, forest] lisière *f*.

fringe benefit *n* avantage *m* extrasalarial.

frisk [frɪsk] *vt* fouiller.

frisky ['frɪskɪ] *adj inf* vif (vive).

fritter ['frɪtə'] *n* beignet *m*. ◆ **fritter away** *vt sep* gaspiller.

frivolous ['frɪvələs] *adj* frivole.

frizzy ['frɪzɪ] *adj* crépu(e).

fro [frəʊ] ▶ to.

frock [frɒk] *n* dated robe *f*.

frog [frɒg] *n* [animal] grenouille *f* ; **to have a frog in one's throat** avoir un chat dans la gorge.

frogman ['frɒgmən] (*pl* -men [-mən]) *n* homme-grenouille *m*.

frogmen ['frɒgmən] *npl* ▶ frogman.

frolic ['frɒlɪk] *vi* (*pt & pp* -ked, *cont* -king) folâtrer.

from (*weak form* [frəm], *strong form* [frɒm]) *prep* **1.** [indicating source, origin, removal] de ; **where are you from?** d'où venez-vous?, d'où êtes-vous? ; **I got a letter from her today** j'ai reçu une lettre d'elle aujourd'hui ; **a flight from Paris** un vol en provenance de Paris ; **to translate from Spanish into English** traduire d'espagnol en anglais ; **to drink from a glass** boire dans un verre ; **to take sthg (away) from sb** prendre qqch à qqn - **2.** [indicating a deduction] de ; **to deduct sthg from sthg** retrancher qqch de qqch - **3.** [indicating escape, separation] de ; **he ran away from home** il a fait une fugue, il s'est sauvé de chez lui - **4.** [indicating position] de ; **seen from above/below** vu d'en haut/d'en bas - **5.** [indicating distance] de ; **it's 60 km from here** c'est à 60 km d'ici - **6.** [indicating material object is made out of] en ; **it's made from wood/plastic** c'est en bois/plastique - **7.** [starting at a particular time] de ; **from 2 pm** OR **till 6 pm** de 14 h à 18 h ; **from the moment I saw him** dès que OR dès l'instant où je l'ai vu - **8.** [indicating difference] de ; **to be different from sb/sthg** être différent de qqn/qqch - **9.** [indicating change : **from... to...**] de... à ; **the price went up from £100 to £150** le prix est passé OR monté de 100 livres à 150 livres - **10.** [because of, as a result of] : **to suffer from cold/hunger** souffrir du froid/de la faim - **11.** [on the evidence of] d'après, à - **12.** [indicating lowest amount] depuis, à partir de ; **prices start from £50** le premier prix est de 50 livres.

front [frʌnt] ⬦ *n* **1.** [most forward part - gen] avant *m* ; [- of dress, envelope, house] devant *m* ; [- of class] premier rang *m* - **2.** METEOR & MIL front *m* - **3.** : **(sea)front** front *m* de mer - **4.** [outward appearance - of person] contenance *f* ; *pej* [- of business] façade *f*. ⬦ *adj* [tooth, garden] de devant ; [row, wheel] premier(ère). ◆ **in front** *adv* **1.** [further forward - walk, push] devant ; [- people] à l'avant - **2.** [winning] : **to be in front** gagner. ◆ **in front of** *prep* devant.

frontbench [,frʌnt'bentʃ] *n UK à la chambre des Communes, bancs occupés respectivement par les ministres du gouvernement en exercice et ceux du gouvernement fantôme.*

front door *n* porte *f* d'entrée.

frontier ['frʌn,tɪə', *US* frʌn'tɪər] *n* [border] frontière *f* ; *fig* limite *f*.

front man *n* **1.** [of company, organization] porte-parole *m inv* - **2.** TV présentateur *m*.

front room *n* salon *m*.

front-runner *n* favori *m*, -ite *f*.

front-wheel drive *n* traction *f* avant.

frost [frɒst] n gel m.

frostbite ['frɒstbaɪt] n (U) gelure f.

frosted ['frɒstɪd] adj 1. [glass] dépoli(e) - 2. US CULIN glacé(e).

frosty ['frɒstɪ] adj 1. [weather, welcome] glacial(e) - 2. [field, window] gelé(e).

froth [frɒθ] n [on beer] mousse f ; [on sea] écume f.

frown [fraʊn] vi froncer les sourcils.
◆ **frown (up)on** vt insep désapprouver.

froze [frəʊz] pt ▶ freeze.

frozen [frəʊzn] ◇ pp ▶ freeze. ◇ adj gelé(e) ; [food] congelé(e).

frugal ['fru:gl] adj 1. [meal] frugal(e) - 2. [person, life] économe.

fruit [fru:t] n (pl fruit OR -s) fruit m.

fruitcake ['fru:tkeɪk] n cake m.

fruiterer ['fru:tərər] n UK dated fruitier m.

fruitful ['fru:tfʊl] adj [successful] fructueux(euse).

fruition [fru:'ɪʃn] n : to come to fruition se réaliser.

fruit juice n jus m de fruits.

fruitless ['fru:tlɪs] adj vain(e).

fruit machine n UK machine f à sous.

fruit salad n salade f de fruits, macédoine f.

frumpish ['frʌmpɪʃ] = frumpy.

frumpy ['frʌmpɪ] adj mal habillé(e).

frustrate [frʌ'streɪt] vt 1. [annoy, disappoint] frustrer - 2. [prevent] faire échouer.

frustrated [frʌ'streɪtɪd] adj 1. [person, artist] frustré(e) - 2. [effort, love] vain(e).

frustration [frʌ'streɪʃn] n frustration f.

fry [fraɪ] (pt & pp fried) vt & vi frire.

frying pan ['fraɪɪŋ-] n poêle f à frire.

FSA [,efes'eɪ] (abbrev of Food Standards Agency) UK agence pour la sécurité alimentaire.

ft. abbrev of foot, abbrev of feet.

FTP [,efti:'pi:] (abbrev of file transfer protocol) n FTP m.

fuck [fʌk] vulg vt & vi baiser. ◆ **fuck off** vi vulg fuck off! fous le camp!

fudge [fʌdʒ] n (U) [sweet] caramel m (mou).

fuel [fjʊəl] ◇ n combustible m ; [for engine] carburant m. ◇ vt (UK & US) 1. [supply with fuel] alimenter (en combustible/carburant) - 2. fig [speculation] nourrir.

fuel pump n pompe f d'alimentation.

fuel tank n réservoir m à carburant.

fugitive ['fju:dʒətɪv] n fugitif m, -ive f.

fulfil UK, **fulfill** US [fʊl'fɪl] vt 1. [duty, role] remplir ; [hope] répondre à ; [ambition, prophecy] réaliser - 2. [satisfy - need] satisfaire.

fulfilment UK, **fulfillment** US [fʊl'fɪlmənt] n (U) 1. [satisfaction] grande satisfaction f - 2. [of ambition, dream] réalisation f ; [of role, promise] exécution f ; [of need] satisfaction f.

full [fʊl] ◇ adj 1. [gen] plein(e) ; [bus, car park] complet(ète) ; [with food] gavé(e), repu(e) - 2. [complete - recovery, control] total(e) ; [- explanation, day] entier(ère) ; [- volume] maximum - 3. [busy - life] rempli(e) ; [- timetable, day] chargé(e) - 4. [flavour] riche - 5. [plump - figure] rondelet(ette) ; [- mouth] charnu(e) - 6. [skirt, sleeve] ample. ◇ adv [very] : you know full well that... tu sais très bien que... ◇ n : in full complètement, entièrement.

full-blown [-'bləʊn] adj général(e) ; to have full-blown AIDS avoir le Sida avéré.

full board n pension f complète.

full-fledged US = fully-fledged.

full moon n pleine lune f.

full-scale adj 1. [life-size] grandeur nature (inv) - 2. [complete] de grande envergure.

full stop UK n point m.

full time n UK SPORT fin f de match.
◆ **full-time** adj & adv [work, worker] à temps plein.

full up adj [bus, train] complet(ète) ; [with food] gavé(e), repu(e).

fully ['fʊlɪ] adv [understand, satisfy] tout à fait ; [trained, describe] entièrement.

fully-fledged UK, **full-fledged** US [-'fledʒd] adj diplômé(e).

fulsome ['fʊlsəm] adj excessif(ive).

fumble ['fʌmbl] vi fouiller, tâtonner ; to fumble for fouiller pour trouver.

fume [fju:m] vi [with anger] rager.
◆ **fumes** npl [from paint] émanations fpl ; [from smoke] fumées fpl ; [from car] gaz mpl d'échappement.

fumigate ['fju:mɪgeɪt] vt fumiger.

fun [fʌn] n (U) 1. [pleasure, amusement] : to have fun s'amuser ; for fun, for the fun of it pour s'amuser - 2. [playfulness] : to be full of fun être plein(e) d'entrain - 3. [ridicule] : to make fun of OR poke fun at sb se moquer de qqn.

function ['fʌŋkʃn] ◇ n 1. [gen] fonction f - 2. [formal social event] réception f officielle - 3. [software] fonctionnalité f. ◇ vi fonctionner ; to function as servir de.

functional ['fʌŋkʃnəl] adj 1. [practical] fonctionnel(elle) - 2. [operational] en état de marche.

functionality [fʌŋkʃ'nælətɪ] n fonctionnalité f.

fund [fʌnd] ◇ n fonds m ; fig [of knowledge] puits m. ◇ vt financer. ◆ **funds** npl fonds mpl.

fundamental [ˌfʌndə'mentl] *adj* : **fundamental (to)** fondamental(e) (à).

funding ['fʌndɪŋ] *n* (U) financement *m*.

funeral ['fjuːnərəl] *n* obsèques *fpl*.

funeral director *n* entrepreneur *m* de pompes funèbres.

funeral home *US* = **funeral parlour**.

funeral parlour *UK*, **funeral home** *US n* entreprise *f* de pompes funèbres.

funfair ['fʌnfeəʳ] *n UK* fête *f* foraine.

fungus ['fʌŋgəs] (*pl* -**gi** [-gaɪ] OR -**guses** [-gəsiːz]) *n* champignon *m*.

funnel ['fʌnl] *n* **1.** [tube] entonnoir *m* - **2.** [of ship] cheminée *f*.

funny ['fʌnɪ] *adj* [amusing, odd] drôle.

fur [fɜːʳ] *n* fourrure *f*.

fur coat *n* (manteau *m* de) fourrure *f*.

furious ['fjʊərɪəs] *adj* **1.** [very angry] furieux(euse) - **2.** [wild - effort, battle] acharné(e) ; [- temper] déchaîné(e).

furlong ['fɜːlɒŋ] *n* = 201,17 mètres.

furnace ['fɜːnɪs] *n* [fire] fournaise *f*.

furnish ['fɜːnɪʃ] *vt* **1.** [fit out] meubler - **2.** *fml* [provide] fournir ; **to furnish sb with sthg** fournir qqch à qqn.

furnished ['fɜːnɪʃt] *adj* meublé(e).

furnishings ['fɜːnɪʃɪŋz] *npl* mobilier *m*.

furniture ['fɜːnɪtʃəʳ] *n* (U) meubles *mpl* ; **a piece of furniture** un meuble.

furrow ['fʌrəʊ] *n* **1.** [in field] sillon *m* - **2.** [on forehead] ride *f*.

furry ['fɜːrɪ] *adj* **1.** [animal] à fourrure - **2.** [material] recouvert(e) de fourrure.

further ['fɜːðəʳ] <> *compar* ► **far**. <> *adv* **1.** [gen] plus loin ; **how much further is it?** combien de kilomètres y a-t-il? ; **further on** plus loin - **2.** [more - complicate, develop] davantage ; [- enquire] plus avant - **3.** [in addition] de plus. <> *adj* nouveau(elle), supplémentaire ; **until further notice** jusqu'à nouvel ordre. <> *vt* [career, aims] faire avancer ; [cause] encourager.

further education *n UK & Aus* éducation *f* post-scolaire.

furthermore [ˌfɜːðə'mɔːʳ] *adv* de plus.

furthest ['fɜːðɪst] <> *superl* ► **far**. <> *adj* le plus éloigné (la plus éloignée). <> *adv* le plus loin.

furtive ['fɜːtɪv] *adj* [person] sournois(e) ; [glance] furtif(ive).

fury ['fjʊərɪ] *n* fureur *f*.

fuse [fjuːz] <> *n* **1.** ELEC fusible *m*, plomb *m* - **2.** [of bomb] détonateur *m* ; [of firework] amorce *f*. <> *vt* **1.** [join by heat] réunir par la fusion - **2.** [combine] fusionner. <> *vi*

1. ELEC : **the lights have fused** les plombs ont sauté - **2.** [join by heat] fondre - **3.** [combine] fusionner.

fuse-box *n* boîte *f* à fusibles.

fused [fjuːzd] *adj* [plug] avec fusible incorporé.

fuselage ['fjuːzəlɑːʒ] *n* fuselage *m*.

fuss [fʌs] <> *n* **1.** [excitement, anxiety] agitation *f* ; **to make a fuss** faire des histoires - **2.** (U) [complaints] protestations *fpl*. <> *vi* faire des histoires.

fussy ['fʌsɪ] *adj* **1.** [fastidious - person] tatillon(onne) ; [- eater] difficile - **2.** [overdecorated] tarabiscoté(e).

futile ['fjuːtaɪl] *adj* vain(e).

futon ['fuːtɒn] *n* futon *m*.

future ['fjuːtʃəʳ] <> *n* **1.** [gen] avenir *m* ; **in future** à l'avenir ; **in the future** dans le futur, à l'avenir - **2.** GRAM futur *m*. <> *adj* futur(e).

fuze *US* = **fuse** (*n sense 2*).

fuzzy ['fʌzɪ] *adj* **1.** [hair] crépu(e) - **2.** [photo, image] flou(e) - **3.** [thoughts, mind] confus(e).

G

g¹ [dʒiː] (*pl* **g's** OR **gs**), **G** (*pl* **G's** OR **Gs**) *n* [letter] g *m inv*, G *m inv*. ◆ **G** <> *n* MUS sol *m*. <> (*abbrev of* **good**) B.

g² (*abbrev of* **gram**) g.

gab [gæb] ► **gift**.

gabble ['gæbl] <> *vt & vi* baragouiner. <> *n* charabia *m*.

gable ['geɪbl] *n* pignon *m*.

gadget ['gædʒɪt] *n* gadget *m*.

Gaelic ['geɪlɪk] <> *adj* gaélique. <> *n* gaélique *m*.

gag [gæg] <> *n* **1.** [for mouth] bâillon *m* - **2.** *inf* [joke] blague *f*, gag *m*. <> *vt* [put gag on] bâillonner.

gage *US* = **gauge**.

gaiety ['geɪətɪ] *n* gaieté *f*.

gaily ['geɪlɪ] *adv* **1.** [cheerfully] gaiement - **2.** [thoughtlessly] allègrement.

gain [geɪn] <> *n* **1.** [gen] profit *m* - **2.** [improvement] augmentation *f*. <> *vt* **1.** [acquire] gagner - **2.** [increase in - speed, weight] prendre ; [- confidence] gagner en ; [- quantity, time] gagner. <> *vi* **1.** [advance] : **to gain in sthg** gagner en qqch

- **2.** [benefit] : **to gain from** OR **by sthg** tirer un avantage de qqch - **3.** [watch, clock] avancer. ◆ **gain on** vt insep rattraper.

gait [geɪt] n démarche f.

gal., **gall.** abbrev of **gallon**.

gala ['gɑːlə] n [celebration] gala m.

galaxy ['gæləksɪ] n galaxie f.

gale [geɪl] n [wind] grand vent m.

gall [gɔːl] n [nerve] : **to have the gall to do sthg** avoir le toupet de faire qqch.

gallant ['gælənt OR gə'lænt OR 'gælənt] adj **1.** ['gælənt] [courageous] courageux(euse) - **2.** [gə'lænt OR 'gælənt] [polite to women] galant.

gall bladder n vésicule f biliaire.

gallery ['gælərɪ] n **1.** [gen] galerie f - **2.** [for displaying art] musée m - **3.** [in theatre] paradis m.

galley ['gælɪ] (pl -s) n **1.** [ship] galère f - **2.** [kitchen] coquerie f.

Gallic ['gælɪk] adj français(e).

galling ['gɔːlɪŋ] adj humiliant(e).

gallivant [,gælɪ'vænt] vi inf mener une vie de patachon.

gallon ['gælən] n = 4,546 litres gallon m.

gallop ['gæləp] <> n galop m. <> vi galoper.

gallows ['gæləʊz] (pl **gallows**) n gibet m.

gallstone ['gɔːlstəʊn] n calcul m biliaire.

galore [gə'lɔːr] adj en abondance.

galvanize, UK **-ise** ['gælvənaɪz] vt **1.** TECH galvaniser - **2.** [impel] : **to galvanize sb into action** pousser qqn à agir.

gambit ['gæmbɪt] n entrée f en matière.

gamble ['gæmbl] <> n [calculated risk] risque m. <> vi **1.** [bet] jouer ; **to gamble on** jouer de l'argent sur - **2.** [take risk] : **to gamble on** miser sur.

gambler ['gæmblər] n joueur m, -euse f.

gambling ['gæmblɪŋ] n (U) jeu m.

game [geɪm] <> n **1.** [gen] jeu m - **2.** [match] match m - **3.** (U) [hunted animals] gibier m. <> adj **1.** [brave] courageux(euse) - **2.** [willing] : **game (for sthg/to do sthg)** partant(e) (pour qqch/pour faire qqch). ◆ **games** <> n UK SCH éducation f physique. <> npl [sporting contest] jeux mpl.

gamekeeper ['geɪm,kiːpər] n garde-chasse m.

game reserve n réserve f (de chasse).

games console [geɪmz -] n COMPUT console f de jeux.

game show n jeu m télévisé.

gaming ['geɪmɪŋ] n (U) jeux mpl informatiques.

gammon ['gæmən] n esp UK jambon m fumé.

gamut ['gæmət] n gamme f.

gang [gæŋ] n **1.** [of criminals] gang m - **2.** [of young people] bande f. ◆ **gang up** vi inf **to gang up (on)** se liguer (contre).

gangland ['gæŋlænd] n (U) milieu m.

gangrene ['gæŋgriːn] n gangrène f.

gangster ['gæŋstər] n gangster m.

gangway ['gæŋweɪ] n **1.** UK [aisle] allée f - **2.** [gangplank] passerelle f.

gantry ['gæntrɪ] n portique m.

gaol [dʒeɪl] UK dated = **jail**.

gap [gæp] n **1.** [empty space] trou m ; [in text] blanc m ; fig [in knowledge, report] lacune f - **2.** fig [great difference] fossé m.

gape [geɪp] vi **1.** [person] rester bouche bée - **2.** [hole, shirt] bâiller.

gaping ['geɪpɪŋ] adj **1.** [open-mouthed] bouche bée (inv) - **2.** [wide-open] béant(e) ; [shirt] grand ouvert (grande ouverte).

garage [UK 'gærɑːʒ OR 'gærɪdʒ, US gə'rɑːʒ] n **1.** [gen] garage m - **2.** UK [for fuel] station-service f.

garbage ['gɑːbɪdʒ] n (U) **1.** esp US [refuse] détritus mpl - **2.** inf [nonsense] idioties fpl.

garbage bag n US sac-poubelle m.

garbage can n US poubelle f.

garbage truck n US camion-poubelle m.

garbled ['gɑːbld] adj [story, message, explanation - involuntarily] embrouillé(e), confus(e) ; [- deliberately] déformé(e), dénaturé(e).

garden ['gɑːdn] <> n jardin m. <> vi jardiner.

garden centre UK, **garden center** US n jardinerie f.

gardener ['gɑːdnər] n [professional] jardinier m, -ère f ; [amateur] personne f qui aime jardiner, amateur m, -rice f de jardinage.

gardening ['gɑːdnɪŋ] n jardinage m.

garden shed n abri m de jardin.

gargle ['gɑːgl] vi se gargariser.

gargoyle ['gɑːgɔɪl] n gargouille f.

garish ['geərɪʃ] adj [colour] criard(e).

garland ['gɑːlənd] n guirlande f de fleurs.

garlic ['gɑːlɪk] n ail m.

garlic bread n pain m à l'ail.

garment ['gɑːmənt] n vêtement m.

garnish ['gɑːnɪʃ] <> n garniture f. <> vt garnir.

garrison ['gærɪsn] n [soldiers] garnison f.

garrulous ['gærələs] adj volubile.

garter ['gɑːtəʳ] n **1.** [for socks] support-chaussette m ; [for stockings] jarretière f - **2.** US [suspender] jarretelle f.

gas [gæs] ◇ n (pl **gases** OR **gasses** [gæsi:z]) **1.** [gen] gaz m inv - **2.** US [for vehicle] essence f. ◇ vt gazer.

gas cooker n UK cuisinière f à gaz.

gas cylinder n bouteille f de gaz.

gas fire n UK appareil m de chauffage à gaz.

gas gauge n US jauge f d'essence.

gas guzzler n US **to be a gas guzzler** consommer beaucoup (d'essence).

gash [gæʃ] ◇ n entaille f. ◇ vt entailler.

gasket ['gæskɪt] n joint m d'étanchéité.

gasman ['gæsmæn] (pl -men [-men]) n [who reads meter] employé m du gaz ; [for repairs] installateur m de gaz.

gas mask n masque m à gaz.

gas meter n compteur m à gaz.

gasoline ['gæsəli:n] n US essence f.

gasp [gɑːsp] ◇ n halètement m. ◇ vi **1.** [breathe quickly] haleter - **2.** [in shock, surprise] avoir le souffle coupé.

gas pedal n US accélérateur m.

gas station n US station-service f.

gas stove = **gas cooker**.

gas tank n US réservoir m.

gas tap n [for mains supply] robinet m de gaz ; [on gas fire] prise f de gaz.

gastroenteritis ['gæstrəʊˌentə'raɪtɪs] n gastro-entérite f.

gastronomy [gæs'trɒnəmɪ] n gastronomie f.

gasworks ['gæswɜːks] (pl **gasworks**) n usine f à gaz.

gate [geɪt] n [of garden, farm] barrière f ; [of town, at airport] porte f ; [of park] grille f.

gatecrash ['geɪtkræʃ] inf ◇ vi [at party] s'inviter, jouer les pique-assiette ; [at paying event] resquiller. ◇ vt : **to gatecrash a party** aller à une fête sans invitation.

gateway ['geɪtweɪ] n **1.** [entrance] entrée f - **2.** [means of access] : **gateway to** porte f de ; fig clé f de.

gather ['gæðəʳ] ◇ vt **1.** [collect] ramasser ; [flowers] cueillir ; [information] recueillir ; [courage, strength] rassembler ; **to gather together** rassembler - **2.** [increase - speed, force] prendre - **3.** [understand] : **to gather (that)...** croire comprendre que... - **4.** [cloth - into folds] plisser. ◇ vi [come together] se rassembler ; [clouds] s'amonceler.

gathering ['gæðərɪŋ] n [meeting] rassemblement m.

gaudy ['gɔːdɪ] adj voyant(e).

gauge ['gɔːdʒ], US **gage** [geɪdʒ] ◇ n **1.** [for rain] pluviomètre m ; [for fuel] jauge f (d'essence) ; [for tyre pressure] manomètre m - **2.** [of gun, wire] calibre m - **3.** RAIL écartement m. ◇ vt **1.** [measure] mesurer - **2.** [evaluate] jauger.

Gaul [gɔːl] n **1.** [country] Gaule f - **2.** [person] Gaulois m, -e f.

gaunt [gɔːnt] adj **1.** [thin] hâve - **2.** [bare, grim] désolé(e).

gauntlet ['gɔːntlɪt] n gant m (de protection) ; **to run the gauntlet of sthg** endurer qqch ; **to throw down the gauntlet (to sb)** jeter le gant (à qqn).

gauze [gɔːz] n gaze f.

gave [geɪv] pt ► **give**.

gawk [gɔːk], **gawp** UK [gɔːp] vi inf **to gawk (at)** rester bouche bée (devant).

gawky ['gɔːkɪ] adj inf [person] dégingandé(e) ; [movement] désordonné(e).

gawp UK = **gawk**.

gay [geɪ] ◇ adj **1.** [gen] gai(e) - **2.** [homosexual] homo (inv), gay (inv). ◇ n homo mf, gay mf.

gaze [geɪz] ◇ n regard m (fixe). ◇ vi : **to gaze at sb/sthg** regarder qqn/qqch (fixement).

gazelle [gə'zel] (pl **gazelle** OR -s) n gazelle f.

gazetteer [ˌgæzɪ'tɪəʳ] n index m géographique.

gazump [gə'zʌmp] vt UK inf **to be gazumped** être victime d'une suroffre.

GB[1] (abbrev of **Great Britain**) n G-B f.

GB[2] [dʒiː'biː] (abbrev of **gigabyte**), **Gb** n gigabyte m.

GCSE (abbrev of **General Certificate of Secondary Education**) n examen de fin d'études secondaires en Grande-Bretagne.

GDP (abbrev of **gross domestic product**) n PIB m.

gear [gɪəʳ] ◇ n **1.** TECH [mechanism] embrayage m - **2.** [speed - of car, bicycle] vitesse f ; **to be in/out of gear** être en prise/au point mort - **3.** (U) [equipment, clothes] équipement m. ◇ vt : **to gear sthg to sb/sthg** destiner qqch à qqn/qqch.
◆ **gear up** vi : **to gear up for sthg/to do sthg** se préparer pour qqch/à faire qqch.

gearbox ['gɪəbɒks] n UK boîte f de vitesses.

gearknob ['gɪənɒb] n AUT boule f du levier de vitesse.

gear lever UK, **gear stick** UK, **gear shift** US n levier m de vitesse.

gearwheel n pignon m, roue f d'engrenage.

geek ['giːk] n inf débile mf ; **a movie / computer geek** un dingue de cinéma / d'informatique.

geese [gi:s] *npl* ▶ **goose**.

gel [dʒel] ⇔ *n* [for hair] gel *m*. ⇔ *vi*
1. [thicken] prendre - **2.** *fig* [take shape]
prendre tournure.

gelatin ['dʒelətɪn], **gelatine** [,dʒelə'ti:n] *n*
gélatine *f*.

gelignite ['dʒelɪgnaɪt] *n* gélignite *f*.

gem [dʒem] *n* **1.** [jewel] pierre *f* précieuse,
gemme *f* - **2.** *fig* [person, thing] perle *f*.

Gemini ['dʒemɪnaɪ] *n* Gémeaux *mpl*.

gender ['dʒendər] *n* **1.** [sex] sexe *m* - **2.** GRAM
genre *m*.

gene [dʒi:n] *n* gène *m*.

general ['dʒenərəl] ⇔ *adj* général(e).
⇔ *n* général *m*. ▶ **in general** *adv* en
général.

general anaesthetic *UK*, **general anesthetic** *US* *n* anesthésie *f* générale.

general delivery *n* *US* poste *f* restante.

general election *n* élections *fpl* législatives.

generalization, *UK* **-isation** [,dʒenərəlaɪ'zeɪʃn] *n* généralisation *f*.

general knowledge *n* culture *f* générale.

generally ['dʒenərəlɪ] *adv* **1.** [usually, in
most cases] généralement - **2.** [unspecifically] en général ; [describe] en gros.

general practitioner *n* (médecin *m*) généraliste *m*.

general public *n* : **the general public** le
grand public.

general strike *n* grève *f* générale.

generate ['dʒenəreɪt] *vt* [energy, jobs]
générer ; [electricity, heat] produire ; [interest, excitement] susciter.

generation [,dʒenə'reɪʃn] *n* **1.** [gen] génération *f* - **2.** [creation - of jobs] création *f* ;
[- of electricity] production *f* ; [- of interest,
excitement] induction *f*.

generator ['dʒenəreɪtər] *n* ELEC génératrice
f, générateur *m*.

generosity [,dʒenə'rɒsətɪ] *n* générosité *f*.

generous ['dʒenərəs] *adj* généreux(euse).

genetic [dʒɪ'netɪk] *adj* génétique. ▶ **genetics** *n* (U) génétique *f*.

genetically [dʒɪ'netɪklɪ] *adv* génétiquement ; **genetically modified** génétiquement
modifié(e) ; **genetically modified organism**
organisme *m* génétiquement modifié.

genetic code *n* code *m* génétique.

Geneva [dʒɪ'ni:və] *n* Genève.

genial ['dʒi:njəl] *adj* [person] aimable,
affable ; [expression] cordial(e), chaleureux(euse).

genitals ['dʒenɪtlz] *npl* organes *mpl* génitaux.

genius ['dʒi:njəs] (*pl* **-es** [-i:z]) *n* génie *m*.

gent [dʒent] *n* *UK* *inf* *dated* gentleman *m*.
▶ **gents** *n* *UK* [toilets] toilettes *fpl* pour
hommes ; [sign on door] messieurs.

genteel [dʒen'ti:l] *adj* [refined] distingué(e).

gentle ['dʒentl] *adj* doux (douce) ; [hint]
discret(ète) ; [tap, telling-off] léger(ère).

gentleman ['dʒentlmən] (*pl* **-men** [-mən])
n **1.** [well-behaved man] gentleman *m*
- **2.** [man] monsieur *m*.

gently ['dʒentlɪ] *adv* [gen] doucement ;
[speak, smile] avec douceur.

gentry ['dʒentrɪ] *n* petite noblesse *f*.

genuine ['dʒenjuɪn] *adj* authentique ;
[interest, customer] sérieux(euse) ; [person,
concern] sincère.

geography [dʒɪ'ɒgrəfɪ] *n* géographie *f*.

geology [dʒɪ'ɒlədʒɪ] *n* géologie *f*.

geometric(al) [,dʒɪə'metrɪk(l)] *adj* géométrique.

geometry [dʒɪ'ɒmətrɪ] *n* géométrie *f*.

geranium [dʒɪ'reɪnjəm] (*pl* **-s**) *n* géranium
m.

gerbil ['dʒɜ:bɪl] *n* gerbille *f*.

geriatric [,dʒerɪ'ætrɪk] *adj* **1.** MED gériatrique - **2.** *pej* [person] décrépit(e) ; [object]
vétuste.

germ [dʒɜ:m] *n* **1.** [bacterium] germe *m*,
microbe *m* - **2.** *fig* [of idea, plan] embryon *m*.

German ['dʒɜ:mən] ⇔ *adj* allemand(e).
⇔ *n* **1.** [person] Allemand *m*, -e *f* - **2.** [language] allemand *m*.

German measles *n* (U) rubéole *f*.

Germany ['dʒɜ:mənɪ] *n* Allemagne *f*.

germinate ['dʒɜ:mɪneɪt] *vi* *lit* & *fig*
germer.

gerund ['dʒerənd] *n* gérondif *m*.

gesticulate [dʒes'tɪkjuleɪt] *vi* *fml* gesticuler.

gesture ['dʒestʃər] ⇔ *n* geste *m*. ⇔ *vi* :
to gesture to OR **towards sb** faire signe à
qqn.

get [get] (*UK*, *pt* & *pp* **got** *US*, *pt* **got**,
pp **gotten**) ⇔ *vt* **1.** [cause to do] : **to get sb
to do sthg** faire faire qqch à qqn ; **I'll get my
sister to help** je vais demander à ma sœur
de nous aider - **2.** [cause to be done] : **to get
sthg done** faire faire qqch ; **I got the car
fixed** j'ai fait réparer la voiture - **3.** [cause to
become] : **to get sb pregnant** rendre qqn
enceinte ; **I can't get the car started** je
n'arrive pas à mettre la voiture en marche
- **4.** [cause to move] : **to get sb/sthg through
sthg** faire passer qqn/qqch par qqch ; **to
get sb/sthg out of sthg** faire sortir qqn/qqch
de qqch - **5.** [bring, fetch] aller chercher ;
can I get you something to eat/drink? est-ce
que je peux vous offrir quelque chose à

manger/boire ? - **6.** [obtain - gen] obtenir ; [- job, house] trouver - **7.** [receive] recevoir, avoir ; **what did you get for your birthday?** qu'est-ce que tu as eu pour ton anniversaire? ; **she gets a good salary** elle touche un bon traitement - **8.** [experience a sensation] avoir ; **do you get the feeling he doesn't like us?** tu n'as pas l'impression qu'il ne nous aime pas? - **9.** [be infected with, suffer from] avoir, attraper ; **to get a cold** attraper un rhume - **10.** [understand] comprendre, saisir ; **I don't get it** *inf* je ne comprends pas, je ne saisis pas - **11.** [catch - bus, train, plane] prendre - **12.** [capture] prendre, attraper - **13.** [find] : **you get a lot of artists here** on trouve OR il y a beaucoup d'artistes ici. ◇ *vi* **1.** [become] devenir ; **to get suspicious** devenir méfiant ; **I'm getting cold/bored** je commence à avoir froid/à m'ennuyer ; **it's getting late** ça se fait tard ; **2.** [arrive] arriver ; **I only got back yesterday** je suis rentré hier seulement - **3.** [eventually succeed in] : **to get to do sthg** parvenir à OR finir par faire qqch ; **did you get to see him?** est-ce que tu as réussi à le voir? - **4.** [progress] : **how far have you got?** où en es-tu? ; **we're getting nowhere** on n'arrive à rien. ◇ *aux vb* : **to get excited** s'exciter ; **to get hurt** se faire mal ; **to get beaten up, to get beat up** *esp US* se faire tabasser ; **let's get going** OR **moving** allons-y ; *see also* **have.** ◆ **get about** *UK*, **get around** *vi* [move from place to place] se déplacer ; *see also* **get around**, *see also* **round.** ◆ **get along** *vi* **1.** [manage] se débrouiller - **2.** [progress] avancer, faire des progrès - **3.** [have a good relationship] s'entendre ; **she's easy to get along with** elle est facile à vivre. ◆ **get around, get round** *UK* ◇ *vt insep* [overcome] venir à bout de, surmonter. ◇ *vi* **1.** [circulate - news, rumour] circuler, se répandre - **2.** [eventually do] : **to get around to (doing) sthg** trouver le temps de faire qqch ; *see also* **get about**, *see also* **get round.** ◆ **get at** *vt insep* **1.** [reach] parvenir à - **2.** [imply] vouloir dire ; **what are you getting at?** où veux-tu en venir? - **3.** *UK inf* [criticize] critiquer, dénigrer. ◆ **get away** *vi* **1.** [leave] partir, s'en aller - **2.** [go on holiday] partir en vacances - **3.** [escape] s'échapper, s'évader. ◆ **get away with** *vt insep* : **to let sb get away with sthg** passer qqch à qqn. ◆ **get back** ◇ *vt sep* [recover, regain] retrouver, récupérer. ◇ *vi* [move away] s'écarter. ◆ **get back to** *vt insep* **1.** [return to previous state, activity] revenir à ; **to get back to sleep** se rendormir ; **to get back to work** [after pause] se remettre au travail ; [after illness] reprendre son travail - **2.** *inf* [phone back] rappeler ; **I'll get back to you on that** je te reparlerai de ça plus tard. ◆ **get by** *vi* se débrouiller, s'en sortir. ◆ **get down** *vt sep* **1.** [depress] déprimer

- **2.** [fetch from higher level] descendre. ◆ **get down to** *vt insep* : **to get down to doing sthg** se mettre à faire qqch. ◆ **get in** *vi* **1.** [enter - gen] entrer ; [- to vehicle] monter - **2.** [arrive] arriver ; [arrive home] rentrer. ◆ **get into** *vt insep* **1.** [car] monter dans - **2.** [become involved in] se lancer dans ; **to get into an argument with sb** se disputer avec qqn - **3.** [enter into a particular situation, state] : **to get into a panic** s'affoler ; **to get into trouble** s'attirer des ennuis ; **to get into the habit of doing sthg** prendre l'habitude de faire qqch. ◆ **get off** ◇ *vt sep* [remove] enlever. ◇ *vt insep* **1.** [go away from] partir de - **2.** [train, bus etc] descendre de. ◇ *vi* **1.** [leave bus, train] descendre - **2.** [escape punishment] s'en tirer - **3.** [depart] partir. ◆ **get on** ◇ *vt insep* **1.** [bus, train, plane] monter dans - **2.** [horse] monter sur. ◇ *vi* **1.** [enter bus, train] monter - **2.** [have good relationship] s'entendre, s'accorder - **3.** [progress] avancer, progresser ; **how are you getting on?** comment ça va? - **4.** [proceed] : **to get on (with sthg)** continuer (qqch), poursuivre (qqch) - **5.** [be successful professionally] réussir. ◆ **get out** ◇ *vt sep* **1.** [take out] sortir - **2.** [remove] enlever. ◇ *vi* **1.** [leave - of car, train] descendre - **2.** [news] s'ébruiter. ◆ **get out of** *vt insep* **1.** [car etc] descendre de - **2.** [escape from] s'évader de, s'échapper de - **3.** [avoid] éviter, se dérober à ; **to get out of doing sthg** se dispenser de faire qqch. ◆ **get over** *vt insep* **1.** [recover from] se remettre de - **2.** [overcome] surmonter, venir à bout de. ◆ **get round** *vt insep & vi* *UK* = **get around.** ◆ **get through** ◇ *vt insep* **1.** [job, task] arriver au bout de - **2.** [exam] réussir à - **3.** [food, drink] consommer - **4.** [unpleasant situation] endurer, supporter. ◇ *vi* **1.** [make o.s. understood] : **to get through (to sb)** se faire comprendre (de qqn) - **2.** TELEC obtenir la communication. ◆ **get to** *vt insep* *inf* [annoy] taper sur les nerfs à. ◆ **get together** ◇ *vt sep* [organize - team, belongings] rassembler ; [- project, report] préparer. ◇ *vi* se réunir. ◆ **get up** ◇ *vi* se lever. ◇ *vt insep* [petition, demonstration] organiser. ◆ **get up to** *vt insep* *inf* faire.

getaway ['getəweɪ] *n* fuite *f*.

get-together *n inf* réunion *f*.

geyser ['giːzər] *n* **1.** [hot spring] geyser *m* - **2.** *UK* [water heater] chauffe-eau *m inv*.

Ghana ['gɑːnə] *n* Ghana *m*.

ghastly ['gɑːstlɪ] *adj* **1.** *inf* [very bad, unpleasant] épouvantable - **2.** [horrifying, macabre] effroyable.

gherkin ['gɜːkɪn] *n* cornichon *m*.

ghetto ['getəʊ] (*pl* **-s** OR **-es**) *n* ghetto *m*.

ghetto blaster [-ˌblɑːstəʳ] *n inf* grand radiocassette *m* portatif.

ghost [gəʊst] *n* [spirit] spectre *m*.

giant ['dʒaɪənt] <> *adj* géant(e). <> *n* géant *m*.

gibberish ['dʒɪbərɪʃ] *n (U)* charabia *m*, inepties *fpl*.

gibe [dʒaɪb] *n* insulte *f*.

giblets ['dʒɪblɪts] *npl* abats *mpl*.

Gibraltar [dʒɪ'brɔːltəʳ] *n* Gibraltar *m*.

Gibraltarian [ˌdʒɪbrɔːl'teərɪən] *n* Gibraltarien *m*, -ne *f*.

giddy ['gɪdɪ] *adj* [dizzy] : **to feel giddy** avoir la tête qui tourne.

gift [gɪft] *n* **1.** [present] cadeau *m* - **2.** [talent] don *m* ; **to have a gift for sthg/for doing sthg** avoir un don pour qqch/pour faire qqch ; **the gift of the gab** le bagou.

gift certificate *US* = **gift token**.

gifted ['gɪftɪd] *adj* doué(e).

gift token, **gift voucher** *n UK* chèque-cadeau *m*.

gig [gɪg] *n inf* [concert] concert *m*.

gigabyte ['gaɪgəbaɪt] *n* COMPUT giga-octet *m*.

gigantic [dʒaɪ'gæntɪk] *adj* énorme, gigantesque.

giggle ['gɪgl] <> *n* **1.** [laugh] fou rire *m* - **2.** *UK inf* [fun] : **to be a giggle** être marrant(e) OR tordant(e) ; **to have a giggle** bien s'amuser. <> *vi* [laugh] rire bêtement.

gilded ['gɪldɪd] *adj* = **gilt**.

gill [dʒɪl] *n* [unit of measurement] quart *m* de pinte (= 0,142 litre).

gills [gɪlz] *npl* [of fish] branchies *fpl*.

gilt [gɪlt] <> *adj* [covered in gold] doré(e). <> *n (U)* [gold layer] dorure *f*.

gimmick ['gɪmɪk] *n* astuce *f*.

gin [dʒɪn] *n* gin *m* ; **gin and tonic** gin tonic.

ginger ['dʒɪndʒəʳ] <> *n* **1.** [root] gingembre *m* - **2.** [powder] gingembre *m* en poudre. <> *adj UK* [colour] roux (rousse).

ginger ale *n* boisson gazeuse au gingembre.

ginger beer *n* boisson britannique non-alcoolisée au gingembre.

gingerbread ['dʒɪndʒəbred] *n* pain *m* d'épice.

ginger-haired [-'heəd] *adj UK* roux (rousse).

gingerly ['dʒɪndʒəlɪ] *adv* avec précaution.

gipsy *UK*, **gypsy** ['dʒɪpsɪ] <> *adj* gitan(e). <> *n* gitan *m*, -e *f* ; *pej* bohémien *m*, -enne *f*.

giraffe [dʒɪ'rɑːf] (*pl* **giraffe** OR **-s**) *n* girafe *f*.

girder ['gɜːdəʳ] *n* poutrelle *f*.

girdle ['gɜːdl] *n* [corset] gaine *f*.

girl [gɜːl] *n* **1.** [gen] fille *f* - **2.** [girlfriend] petite amie *f*.

girlfriend ['gɜːlfrend] *n* **1.** [female lover] petite amie *f* - **2.** [female friend] amie *f*.

girl guide *UK*, **girl scout** *US n dated* éclaireuse *f*, guide *f*.

giro ['dʒaɪrəʊ] (*pl* **-s**) *n UK* **1.** *(U)* [system] virement *m* postal - **2.** : **giro (cheque)** chèque *m* d'indemnisation *f* (chômage OR maladie).

girth [gɜːθ] *n* **1.** [circumference - of tree] circonférence *f* ; [- of person] tour *m* de taille - **2.** [of horse] sangle *f*.

gist [dʒɪst] *n* substance *f* ; **to get the gist of sthg** comprendre OR saisir l'essentiel de qqch.

give [gɪv] <> *vt* (*pt* **gave**, *pp* **given**) **1.** [gen] donner ; [message] transmettre ; [attention, time] consacrer ; **to give sb/sthg sthg** donner qqch à qqn/qqch ; **to give sb pleasure/a fright/a smile** faire plaisir/peur/un sourire à qqn ; **to give a sigh** pousser un soupir ; **to give a speech** faire un discours - **2.** [as present] : **to give sb sthg, to give sthg to sb** donner qqch à qqn, offrir qqch à qqn. <> *vi* (*pt* **gave**, *pp* **given**) [collapse, break] céder, s'affaisser. <> *n* [elasticity] élasticité *f*, souplesse *f*. ◆ **give or take** *prep* : **give or take a day/£10** à un jour/10 livres près. ◆ **give away** *vt sep* **1.** [get rid of] donner - **2.** [reveal] révéler. ◆ **give back** *vt sep* [return] rendre. ◆ **give in** *vi* **1.** [admit defeat] abandonner, se rendre - **2.** [agree unwillingly] : **to give in to sthg** céder à qqch. ◆ **give off** *vt insep* [smell] exhaler ; [smoke] faire ; [heat] produire. ◆ **give out** <> *vt sep* [distribute] distribuer. <> *vi* [supplies] s'épuiser ; [car] lâcher. ◆ **give up** <> *vt sep* **1.** [stop] renoncer à ; **to give up drinking/smoking** arrêter de boire/de fumer - **2.** [surrender] : **to give o.s. up (to sb)** se rendre (à qqn). <> *vi* abandonner, se rendre.

given ['gɪvn] <> *adj* **1.** [set, fixed] convenu(e), fixé(e) - **2.** [prone] : **to be given to sthg/to doing sthg** être enclin(e) à qqch/à faire qqch. <> *prep* étant donné ; **given that** étant donné que.

given name *n esp US* prénom *m*.

glacier ['glæsjəʳ] *n* glacier *m*.

glad [glæd] *adj* **1.** [happy, pleased] content(e) ; **to be glad about sthg** être content de qqch - **2.** [willing] : **to be glad to do sthg** faire qqch volontiers OR avec plaisir - **3.** [grateful] : **to be glad of sthg** être content(e) de qqch.

glad-hand ['glædhænd] *vt inf pej* accueillir avec de grandes démonstrations d'amitié.

gladly ['glædlɪ] *adv* **1.** [happily, eagerly] avec joie - **2.** [willingly] avec plaisir.

glamor *US* = **glamour**.

glamorous ['glæmərəs] *adj* [person] séduisant(e) ; [appearance] élégant(e) ; [job, place] prestigieux(euse).

glamour *UK*, **glamor** *US* ['glæmə'] *n* [of person] charme *m* ; [of appearance] élégance *f*, chic *m* ; [of job, place] prestige *m*.

glance [glɑːns] ◇ *n* [quick look] regard *m*, coup d'œil *m* ; **at a glance** d'un coup d'œil ; **at first glance** au premier coup d'œil. ◇ *vi* [look quickly] : **to glance at sb/sthg** jeter un coup d'œil à qqn/qqch. ◆ **glance off** *vt insep* [subj: ball, bullet] ricocher sur.

glancing ['glɑːnsɪŋ] *adj* de côté, oblique.

gland [glænd] *n* glande *f*.

glandular fever [ˌglændjulə'-] *n UK* mononucléose *f* infectieuse.

glare [gleə'] ◇ *n* 1. [scowl] regard *m* mauvais - 2. *(U)* [of headlights, publicity] lumière *f* aveuglante. ◇ *vi* 1. [scowl] : **to glare at sb/sthg** regarder qqn/qqch d'un œil mauvais - 2. [sun, lamp] briller d'une lumière éblouissante.

glaring ['gleərɪŋ] *adj* 1. [very obvious] flagrant(e) - 2. [blazing, dazzling] aveuglant(e).

glasnost ['glæznɒst] *n* glasnost *f*, transparence *f*.

glass [glɑːs] ◇ *n* 1. [gen] verre *m* - 2. *(U)* [glassware] verrerie *f*. ◇ *comp* [bottle, jar] en OR de verre ; [door, partition] vitré(e). ◆ **glasses** *npl* [spectacles] lunettes *fpl*.

glassware ['glɑːsweə'] *n (U)* verrerie *f*.

glassy ['glɑːsɪ] *adj* 1. [smooth, shiny] lisse comme un miroir - 2. [blank, lifeless] vitreux(euse).

glaze [gleɪz] ◇ *n* [on pottery] vernis *m* ; [on pastry, flan] glaçage *m*. ◇ *vt* [pottery, tiles, bricks] vernisser ; [pastry, flan] glacer.

glazier ['gleɪzjə'] *n* vitrier *m*, -ière *f*.

gleam [gliːm] ◇ *n* [of gold] reflet *m* ; [of fire, sunset, disapproval] lueur *f*. ◇ *vi* 1. [surface, object] luire - 2. [light, eyes] briller.

gleaming ['gliːmɪŋ] *adj* brillant(e).

glean [gliːn] *vt* [gather] glaner.

glee [gliː] *n (U)* [joy] joie *f*, jubilation *f*.

glen [glen] *n Scot* vallée *f*.

glib [glɪb] *adj pej* [salesman, politician] qui a du bagout ; [promise, excuse] facile.

glide [glaɪd] *vi* 1. [move smoothly - dancer, boat] glisser sans effort ; [- person] se mouvoir sans effort - 2. [to fly] planer.

glider ['glaɪdə'] *n* [plane] planeur *m*.

gliding ['glaɪdɪŋ] *n* [sport] vol *m* à voile.

glimmer ['glɪmə'] *n* [faint light] faible lueur *f* ; *fig* signe *m*, lueur.

glimpse [glɪmps] ◇ *n* 1. [look, sight] aperçu *m* - 2. [idea, perception] idée *f*. ◇ *vt* 1. [catch sight of] apercevoir, entrevoir - 2. [perceive] pressentir.

glint [glɪnt] ◇ *n* 1. [flash] reflet *m* - 2. [in eyes] éclair *m*. ◇ *vi* étinceler.

glisten ['glɪsn] *vi* luire.

glitter ['glɪtə'] ◇ *n (U)* scintillement *m*. ◇ *vi* 1. [object, light] scintiller - 2. [eyes] briller.

gloat [gləʊt] *vi* : **to gloat (over sthg)** se réjouir (de qqch).

global ['gləʊbl] *adj* [worldwide] mondial(e).

globalization, -isation *UK* [ˌgləʊbəlaɪ'zeɪʃn] *n* mondialisation *f*.

global warming [-'wɔːmɪŋ] *n* réchauffement *m* de la planète.

globe [gləʊb] *n* 1. [Earth] : **the globe** la terre - 2. [spherical map] globe *m* terrestre - 3. [spherical object] globe *m*.

gloom [gluːm] *n (U)* 1. [darkness] obscurité *f* - 2. [unhappiness] tristesse *f*.

gloomy ['gluːmɪ] *adj* 1. [room, sky, prospects] sombre - 2. [person, atmosphere, mood] triste, lugubre.

glorious ['glɔːrɪəs] *adj* 1. [beautiful, splendid] splendide - 2. [very enjoyable] formidable - 3. [successful, impressive] magnifique.

glory ['glɔːrɪ] *n* 1. *(U)* [fame, admiration] gloire *f* - 2. *(U)* [beauty] splendeur *f*. ◆ **glory in** *vt insep* [relish] savourer.

gloss [glɒs] *n* 1. *(U)* [shine] brillant *m*, lustre *m* - 2. [paint] peinture *f* brillante. ◆ **gloss over** *vt insep* passer sur.

glossary ['glɒsərɪ] *n* glossaire *m*.

glossy ['glɒsɪ] *adj* 1. [hair, surface] brillant(e) - 2. [book, photo] sur papier glacé.

glove [glʌv] *n* gant *m*.

glove box, glove compartment *n* boîte *f* à gants.

glow [gləʊ] ◇ *n (U)* [of fire, light, sunset] lueur *f*. ◇ *vi* 1. [shine out - fire] rougeoyer ; [light, stars, eyes] flamboyer - 2. [shine in light] briller.

glower ['glaʊə'] *vi* : **to glower (at)** lancer des regards noirs (à).

glucose ['gluːkəʊs] *n* glucose *m*.

glue [gluː] ◇ *n (U)* colle *f*. ◇ *vt* (*cont* glueing, *cont* gluing) [stick with glue] coller ; **to glue sthg to sthg** coller qqch à OR avec qqch.

glum [glʌm] *adj* [unhappy] triste, morose.

glut [glʌt] *n* surplus *m*.

glutton ['glʌtn] *n* [greedy person] glouton *m*, -onne *f* ; **to be a glutton for punishment** être maso, être masochiste.

GM (*abbrev of* **genetically modified**) *adj* génétiquement modifié(e).

gnarled [nɑ:ld] *adj* [tree, hands] noueux(euse).

gnash [næʃ] *vt* : **to gnash one's teeth** grincer des dents.

gnat [næt] *n* moucheron *m*.

gnaw [nɔ:] <> *vt* [chew] ronger. <> *vi* [worry] : **to gnaw (away) at sb** ronger qqn.

gnome [nəʊm] *n* gnome *m*, lutin *m*.

GNP (*abbrev of* **gross national product**) *n* PNB *m*.

GNVQ *UK* (*abbrev of* **general national vocational qualification**) *n* diplôme sanctionnant deux années d'études professionnelles à la fin du secondaire, ≃ baccalauréat *m* professionnel.

go [gəʊ] <> *vi* (*pt* went, *pp* gone) 1. [move, travel] aller ; **where are you going?** où vas-tu? ; **he's gone to Portugal** il est allé au Portugal ; **we went by bus/train** nous sommes allés en bus/par le train ; **where does this path go?** où mène ce chemin? ; **to go and do sthg** aller faire qqch ; **to go swimming/shopping/jogging** aller nager/faire les courses/faire du jogging ; **to go for a walk** aller se promener, faire une promenade ; **to go to work** aller travailler OR à son travail - 2. [depart] partir, s'en aller ; **I must go** *esp UK*, **I have to go** il faut que je m'en aille ; **what time does the bus go?** *UK* à quelle heure part le bus? ; **let's go!** allons-y! - 3. [become] devenir ; **to go grey** *UK* OR **gray** *US* grisonner, devenir gris ; **to go mad** OR **crazy** devenir fou - 4. [pass - time] passer - 5. [progress] marcher, se dérouler ; **the conference went very smoothly** la conférence s'est déroulée sans problème OR s'est très bien passée ; **to go well/badly** aller bien/mal ; **how's it going?** *inf* comment ça va? - 6. [function, work] marcher ; **the car won't go** *esp UK* la voiture ne veut pas démarrer - 7. [indicating intention, expectation] : **to be going to do sthg** aller faire qqch ; **he said he was going to be late** il a prévenu qu'il allait arriver en retard ; **we're going (to go) to America in June** on va (aller) en Amérique en juin ; **she's going to have a baby** elle va attendre un bébé - 8. [bell, alarm] sonner - 9. [stop working, break - light bulb, fuse] sauter - 10. [deteriorate - hearing, sight etc] baisser - 11. [match, be compatible] : **to go (with)** aller (avec) ; **those colours don't really go (well together)** ces couleurs ne vont pas bien ensemble - 12. [fit] aller - 13. [belong] aller, se mettre ; **the plates go in the cupboard** les assiettes vont OR se mettent dans le placard - 14. [in division] : **three into two won't go, three won't go into two** deux divisé par trois n'y va pas - 15. *inf* [expressing irritation, surprise] : **now what's**

he gone and done? qu'est-ce qu'il a fait encore? <> *n* (*pl* goes) 1. *UK* [turn] tour *m* ; **it's my go** c'est à moi (de jouer) - 2. *inf* [attempt] : **to have a go (at sthg)** essayer (de faire qqch) ; **to have a go at sb** *UK inf* s'en prendre à qqn, engueuler qqn ; **to be on the go** *inf* être sur la brèche. <> **to go** *adv* [remaining] : **there are only three days to go** il ne reste que trois jours. <> **go about** <> *vt insep* [perform] : **to go about one's business** vaquer à ses occupations. <> *vi* = **go around**. <> **go ahead** *vi* 1. [proceed] : **to go ahead with sthg** mettre qqch à exécution ; **go ahead!** allez-y! - 2. [take place] avoir lieu. <> **go along** *vi* [proceed] avancer ; **as you go along** au fur et à mesure. <> **go along with** *vt insep* [suggestion, idea] appuyer, soutenir ; [person] suivre. <> **go around** *vi* 1. [frequent] : **to go around with sb** fréquenter qqn - 2. [spread] circuler, courir. <> **go away** *vi insep* partir, s'en aller ; **go away!** va-t-en! ; **I'm going away for a few days** je pars pour quelques jours. <> **go back on** *vt insep* [one's word, promise] revenir sur. <> **go back to** *vt insep* 1. [return to activity] reprendre, se remettre à ; **to go back to sleep** se rendormir - 2. [date from] remonter à, dater de. <> **go by** <> *vi* [time] s'écouler, passer. <> *vt insep* 1. [be guided by] suivre - 2. [judge from] juger d'après. <> **go down** <> *vi* 1. [get lower - prices etc] baisser - 2. [be accepted] : **to go down well/badly** être bien/mal accueilli - 3. [sun] se coucher - 4. [tyre, balloon] se dégonfler. <> *vt insep* descendre. <> **go for** *vt insep* 1. [choose] choisir - 2. [be attracted to] être attiré(e) par - 3. [attack] tomber sur, attaquer - 4. [try to obtain - job, record] essayer d'obtenir. <> **go in** *vi* entrer. <> **go in for** *vt insep* 1. [competition] prendre part à ; [exam] se présenter à - 2. [activity - enjoy] aimer ; [- participate in] faire, s'adonner à. <> **go into** *vt insep* 1. [investigate] étudier, examiner - 2. [take up as a profession] entrer dans. <> **go off** <> *vi* 1. [explode] exploser - 2. [alarm] sonner - 3. *UK* [go bad - food] se gâter - 4. [lights, heating] s'éteindre - 5. *US inf* [person] s'emporter. <> *vt insep* [lose interest in] ne plus aimer. <> **go on** <> *vi* 1. [take place, happen] se passer - 2. [heating etc] se mettre en marche - 3. [continue] : **to go on (doing)** continuer (à faire) - 4. [proceed to further activity] : **to go on to sthg** passer à qqch ; **to go on to do sthg** faire qqch après - 5. [talk for too long] parler à n'en plus finir ; **to go on about sthg** ne pas arrêter de parler de qqch. <> *vt insep* [be guided by] se fonder sur. <> **go on at** *vt insep* *UK* [nag] harceler. <> **go out** *vi* 1. [leave] sortir - 2. [for amusement] : **to go out (with sb)** sortir (avec qqn) - 3. [light, fire, cigarette] s'éteindre. <> **go over** *vt insep*

1. [examine] examiner, vérifier - **2.** [repeat, review] repasser. ◆ **go round** vi UK [revolve] tourner ; see also **go around**. ◆ **go through** vt insep **1.** [experience] subir, souffrir - **2.** [study, search through] examiner ; **she went through his pockets** elle lui a fait les poches, elle a fouillé dans ses poches. ◆ **go through with** vt insep [action, threat] aller jusqu'au bout de. ◆ **go toward(s)** vt insep contribuer à. ◆ **go under** vi lit & fig couler. ◆ **go up** ⬦ vi **1.** [gen] monter - **2.** [prices] augmenter. ⬦ vt insep monter. ◆ **go without** ⬦ vt insep se passer de. ⬦ vi s'en passer.

goad [gəʊd] vt [provoke] talonner.

go-ahead ⬦ adj [dynamic] dynamique. ⬦ n (U) [permission] feu m vert.

goal [gəʊl] n but m.

goalkeeper ['gəʊl,kiːpə^r] n gardien m de but.

goalmouth ['gəʊlmaʊθ] (pl [-maʊðz]) n but m.

goalpost ['gəʊlpəʊst] n poteau m de but.

goat [gəʊt] n chèvre f.

gob [gɒb] v inf ⬦ n UK [mouth] gueule f. ⬦ vi [spit] mollarder.

gobble ['gɒbl] vt engloutir. ◆ **gobble down**, **gobble up** vt sep engloutir.

go-between n intermédiaire mf.

gobsmacked ['gɒbsmækt] adj UK inf bouche bée (inv).

go-cart = **go-kart**.

god [gɒd] n dieu m, divinité f. ◆ **God** ⬦ n Dieu m ; **God knows** Dieu seul le sait ; **for God's sake** pour l'amour de Dieu ; **thank God** Dieu merci. ⬦ excl : **(my) God!** mon Dieu!

godchild ['gɒdtʃaɪld] (pl **-children** [-,tʃɪldrən]) n filleul m, -e f.

goddaughter ['gɒd,dɔːtə^r] n filleule f.

goddess ['gɒdɪs] n déesse f.

godfather ['gɒd,fɑːðə^r] n parrain m.

godforsaken ['gɒdfə,seɪkn] adj morne, désolé(e).

godmother ['gɒd,mʌðə^r] n marraine f.

godsend ['gɒdsend] n aubaine f.

godson ['gɒdsʌn] n filleul m.

goes [gəʊz] ➤ **go**.

goggles ['gɒglz] npl lunettes fpl.

going ['gəʊɪŋ] ⬦ n (U) **1.** [rate of advance] allure f - **2.** [travel conditions] conditions fpl. ⬦ adj **1.** UK [available] disponible - **2.** [rate, salary] en vigueur.

go-kart [-kɑːt] n kart m.

gold [gəʊld] ⬦ n (U) [metal, jewellery] or m. ⬦ comp [made of gold] en or. ⬦ adj [gold-coloured] doré(e).

golden ['gəʊldən] adj **1.** [made of gold] en or - **2.** [gold-coloured] doré(e).

goldfish ['gəʊldfɪʃ] (pl **goldfish**) n poisson m rouge.

gold leaf n (U) feuille f d'or.

gold medal n médaille f d'or.

goldmine ['gəʊldmaɪn] n lit & fig mine f d'or.

gold-plated [-'pleɪtɪd] adj plaqué(e) or.

goldsmith ['gəʊldsmɪθ] n orfèvre mf.

golf [gɒlf] n golf m.

golf ball n **1.** [for golf] balle f de golf - **2.** [for typewriter] boule f.

golf club n [stick, place] club m de golf.

golf course n terrain m de golf.

golfer ['gɒlfə^r] n golfeur m, -euse f.

gone [gɒn] ⬦ pp ➤ **go**. ⬦ adj [no longer here] parti(e). ⬦ prep UK **it's gone ten (o'clock)** il est dix heures passées.

gong [gɒŋ] n gong m.

good [gʊd] ⬦ adj (comp **better**, superl **best**). **1.** [gen] bon (bonne). **it's good to see you again** ça fait plaisir de te revoir ; **to be good at sthg** être bon en qqch ; **to be good with** [animals, children] savoir y faire avec ; [one's hands] être habile de ; **it's good for you** c'est bon pour toi OR pour la santé ; **to feel good** [person] se sentir bien ; **it's good that...** c'est bien que... ; **good!** très bien! - **2.** [kind - person] gentil(ille) ; **to be good to sb** être très attentionné envers qqn ; **to be good enough to do sthg** avoir l'amabilité de faire qqch - **3.** [well-behaved - child] sage ; [- behaviour] correct(e) ; **be good!** sois sage!, tiens-toi tranquille! ⬦ n **1.** (U) [benefit] bien m ; **it will do him good** ça lui fera du bien - **2.** [use] utilité f ; **what's the good of** OR **in** esp US **doing that?** à quoi bon faire ça? ; **it's no good** ça ne sert à rien ; **it's no good crying/worrying** ça ne sert à rien de pleurer/de s'en faire - **3.** (U) [morally correct behaviour] bien m ; **to be up to no good** préparer un sale coup. ◆ **goods** npl [merchandise] marchandises fpl, articles mpl. ◆ **as good as** adv pratiquement, pour ainsi dire. ◆ **for good** adv [forever] pour de bon, définitivement. ◆ **good afternoon** excl bonjour! ◆ **good evening** excl bonsoir! ◆ **good morning** excl bonjour! ◆ **good night** excl bonsoir! ; [at bedtime] bonne nuit!

goodbye [,gʊd'baɪ] ⬦ excl au revoir! ⬦ n au revoir m.

Good Friday n Vendredi m saint.

good-humoured *UK*, **good-humored** *US* [-'hju:məd] *adj* [person] de bonne humeur ; [smile, remark, rivalry] bon enfant.

good-looking [-'lʊkɪŋ] *adj* [person] beau (belle).

good-natured [-'neɪtʃəd] *adj* [person] d'un naturel aimable ; [rivalry, argument] bon enfant.

goodness ['gʊdnɪs] <> *n (U)* **1.** [kindness] bonté *f* - **2.** [nutritive quality] valeur *f* nutritive. <> *excl* : **(my) goodness!** mon Dieu!, Seigneur! ; **for goodness' sake!** par pitié!, pour l'amour de Dieu! ; **thank goodness!** grâce à Dieu!

goods train *n UK* train *m* de marchandises.

goodwill [,gʊd'wɪl] *n* bienveillance *f*.

goody ['gʊdɪ] *inf* <> *n UK* [person] bon *m*. <> *excl* chouette! ◆ **goodies** *npl inf* **1.** [delicious food] friandises *fpl* - **2.** [desirable objects] merveilles *fpl*, trésors *mpl*.

goose [gu:s] (*pl* **geese** [gi:z]) *n* [bird] oie *f*.

gooseberry ['gʊzbərɪ] *n* **1.** [fruit] groseille *f* à maquereau - **2.** *UK inf* [third person] : **to play gooseberry** tenir la chandelle.

gooseflesh ['gu:sfleʃ] *n* chair *f* de poule. *UK* **goose pimples** *npl* = **gooseflesh**.

gore [gɔ:r] <> *n (U)* *lit* [blood] sang *m*. <> *vt* encorner.

gorge [gɔ:dʒ] <> *n* gorge *f*, défilé *m*. <> *vt* : **to gorge o.s. on** OR **with sthg** se bourrer OR se goinfrer de qqch.

gorgeous ['gɔ:dʒəs] *adj* divin(e) ; *inf* [good-looking] magnifique, splendide.

gorilla [gə'rɪlə] *n* gorille *m*.

gormless ['gɔ:mlɪs] *adj UK inf* bêta (bêtasse).

gorse [gɔ:s] *n (U)* ajonc *m*.

gory ['gɔ:rɪ] *adj* sanglant(e).

gosh [gɒʃ] *excl inf* ça alors!

go-slow *n UK* grève *f* du zèle.

gospel ['gɒspl] *n* [doctrine] évangile *m*. ◆ **Gospel** *n* Évangile *m*.

gossip ['gɒsɪp] <> *n* **1.** [conversation] bavardage *m* ; *pej* commérage *m* - **2.** [person] commère *f*. <> *vi* [talk] bavarder, papoter ; *pej* cancaner.

gossip column *n* échos *mpl*.

got [gɒt] *pt & pp* ▶ **get**.

gotten ['gɒtn] *US pp* ▶ **get**.

goulash ['gu:læʃ] *n* goulache *m*.

gourmet ['gʊəmeɪ] <> *n* gourmet *m*. <> *comp* [food, restaurant] gastronomique ; [cook] gastronome.

gout [gaʊt] *n (U)* MED goutte *f*.

govern ['gʌvən] <> *vt* **1.** [gen] gouverner - **2.** [control] régir. <> *vi* POL gouverner.

governess ['gʌvənɪs] *n* gouvernante *f*.

government ['gʌvnmənt] *n* gouvernement *m*.

governor ['gʌvənər] *n* **1.** POL gouverneur *m* - **2.** *UK* [of school] ≃ membre *m* du conseil d'établissement ; [of bank] gouverneur *m* - **3.** *UK* [of prison] directeur *m*.

gown [gaʊn] *n* **1.** [for woman] robe *f* - **2.** [for surgeon] blouse *f* ; [for judge, academic, graduate] robe *f*, toge *f*.

GP *n UK abbrev of* **general practitioner**.

GPS [,dʒi:pi:'es] (*abbrev of* **Global Positioning System**) *n* GPS *m*.

grab [græb] <> *vt* **1.** [seize] saisir - **2.** *inf* [sandwich] avaler en vitesse ; **to grab a few hours' sleep** dormir quelques heures - **3.** *inf* [appeal to] emballer. <> *vi* : **to grab at sthg** faire un geste pour attraper qqch.

grace [greɪs] <> *n* **1.** [elegance] grâce *f* - **2.** *(U)* [extra time] répit *m* - **3.** [prayer] grâces *fpl*. <> *vt fml* **1.** [honour] honorer de sa présence - **2.** [decorate] orner, décorer.

graceful ['greɪsfʊl] *adj* gracieux(euse), élégant(e).

gracious ['greɪʃəs] <> *adj* [polite] courtois(e). <> *excl* : **(good)gracious!** juste ciel!

grade [greɪd] <> *n* **1.** [quality - of worker] catégorie *f* ; [- of wool, paper] qualité *f* ; [- of petrol] type *m* ; [- of eggs] calibre *m* - **2.** *US* [class] classe *f* - **3.** *US* [mark] note *f*. <> *vt* **1.** [classify] classer - **2.** [mark, assess] noter.

grade crossing *n US* passage *m* à niveau.

grade school *n US* école *f* primaire.

gradient ['greɪdjənt] *n* pente *f*, inclinaison *f*.

gradual ['grædjʊəl] *adj* graduel(elle), progressif(ive).

gradually ['grædjʊəlɪ] *adv* graduellement, petit à petit.

graduate <> *n* ['grædjʊət] **1.** [from university] diplômé *m*, -e *f* - **2.** *US* [of high school] ≃ titulaire *mf* du baccalauréat. <> *vi* ['grædjʊeɪt] **1.** [from university] : **to graduate (from)** ≃ obtenir son diplôme (à) - **2.** *US* [from high school] : **to graduate (from)** ≃ obtenir son baccalauréat (à).

graduation [,grædjʊ'eɪʃn] *n (U)* [ceremony] remise *f* des diplômes.

graffiti [grə'fi:tɪ] *n (U)* graffiti *mpl*.

graft [grɑ:ft] <> *n* **1.** [from plant] greffe *f*, greffon *m* - **2.** MED greffe *f* - **3.** *UK* [hard work] boulot *m* - **4.** *US inf* [corruption] graissage *m* de patte. <> *vt* [plant, skin] greffer ; **to graft sthg onto sthg** greffer qqch sur qqch.

grain [greɪn] *n* **1.** [gen] grain *m* - **2.** *(U)* [crops] céréales *fpl* - **3.** *(U)* [pattern - in wood] fil *m* ; [- in material] grain *m* ; [- in stone, marble] veines *fpl*.

gram [græm] *n* gramme *m*.

grammar ['græmə'] *n* grammaire *f*.

grammar checker *n* COMPUT vérificateur *m* grammatical.

grammar school *n* [in UK] ≃ lycée *m* ; [in US] école *f* primaire.

grammatical [grə'mætɪkl] *adj* grammatical(e).

gramme [græm] *UK* = **gram**.

gramophone ['græməfəun] *n dated* gramophone *m*, phonographe *m*.

gran [græn] *n UK inf* mamie *f*, mémé *f*.

grand [grænd] ◇ *adj* **1.** [impressive] grandiose, imposant(e) - **2.** [ambitious] grand(e) - **3.** [important] important(e) ; [socially] distingué(e) - **4.** *inf dated* [excellent] sensationnel(elle), formidable. ◇ *n* (*pl* **grand**) *inf* [thousand pounds] mille livres *fpl* ; [thousand dollars] mille dollars *mpl*.

grandchild ['græntʃaɪld] (*pl* **-children** [-,tʃɪldrən]) *n* [boy] petit-fils *m* ; [girl] petite-fille *f*. ◆ **grandchildren** *npl* petits-enfants *mpl*.

grand(d)ad ['grændæd] *n inf* papi *m*, pépé *m*.

granddaughter ['græn,dɔːtə'] *n* petite-fille *f*.

grandeur ['grændʒə'] *n* [splendour] splendeur *f*, magnificence *f*.

grandfather ['grænd,fɑːðə'] *n* grand-père *m*.

grandma ['grænmɑː] *n inf* mamie *f*, mémé *f*.

grandmother ['græn,mʌðə'] *n* grand-mère *f*.

grandpa ['grænpɑː] *n inf* papi *m*, pépé *m*.

grandparents ['græn,peərənts] *npl* grands-parents *mpl*.

grand piano *n* piano *m* à queue.

grand slam *n* SPORT grand chelem *m*.

grandson ['grænsʌn] *n* petit-fils *m*.

grandstand ['grændstænd] *n* tribune *f*.

grand total *n* somme *f* globale, total *m* général.

granite ['grænɪt] *n* granit *m*.

granny ['grænɪ] *n inf* mamie *f*, mémé *f*.

grant [grɑːnt] ◇ *n* subvention *f* ; [for study] bourse *f*. ◇ *vt* **1.** [wish, appeal] accorder ; [request] accéder à - **2.** [admit] admettre, reconnaître - **3.** [give] accorder ; **to take sb for granted** [not appreciate sb's help] penser que tout ce que qqn fait va de soi ; [not value sb's presence] penser que qqn fait partie des meubles ; **to take sthg for granted** [result, sb's agreement] considérer qqch comme acquis.

granulated sugar ['grænjuleɪtɪd-] *n* sucre *m* cristallisé.

granule ['grænjuːl] *n* granule *m* ; [of sugar] grain *m*.

grape [greɪp] *n* (grain *m* de) raisin *m* ; **a bunch of grapes** une grappe de raisin.

grapefruit ['greɪpfruːt] (*pl* **grapefruit** OR **-s**) *n* pamplemousse *m*.

grapevine ['greɪpvaɪn] *n* vigne *f* ; **on the grapevine** *fig* par le téléphone arabe.

graph [grɑːf] *n* graphique *m*.

graphic ['græfɪk] *adj* **1.** [vivid] vivant(e) - **2.** ART graphique. ◆ **graphics** *npl* graphique *f*.

graphite ['græfaɪt] *n (U)* graphite *m*, mine *f* de plomb.

graph paper *n (U)* papier *m* millimétré.

grapple ['græpl] ◆ **grapple with** *vt insep* **1.** [person, animal] lutter avec - **2.** [problem] se débattre avec, se colleter avec.

grasp [grɑːsp] ◇ *n* **1.** [grip] prise *f* - **2.** [understanding] compréhension *f* ; **to have a good grasp of sthg** avoir une bonne connaissance de qqch. ◇ *vt* **1.** [grip, seize] saisir, empoigner - **2.** [understand] saisir, comprendre - **3.** [opportunity] saisir.

grasping ['grɑːspɪŋ] *adj pej* avide, cupide.

grass [grɑːs] ◇ *n drug sl & BOT* herbe *f*. ◇ *vi UK crime sl* moucharder ; **to grass on sb** dénoncer qqn.

grasshopper ['grɑːs,hɒpə'] *n* sauterelle *f*.

grass roots ◇ *npl fig* base *f*. ◇ *comp* du peuple.

grass snake *n* couleuvre *f*.

grate [greɪt] ◇ *n* grille *f* de foyer. ◇ *vt* râper. ◇ *vi* grincer, crisser.

grateful ['greɪtful] *adj* : **to be grateful to sb (for sthg)** être reconnaissant(e) à qqn (de qqch).

grater ['greɪtə'] *n* râpe *f*.

gratify ['grætɪfaɪ] *vt* **1.** [please - person] : **to be gratified** être content(e), être satisfait(e) - **2.** [satisfy - wish] satisfaire, assouvir.

grating ['greɪtɪŋ] ◇ *adj* grinçant(e) ; [voix] de crécelle. ◇ *n* [grille] grille *f*.

gratitude ['grætɪtjuːd] *n (U)* **gratitude (to sb for sthg)** gratitude *f* OR reconnaissance *f* (envers qqn de qqch).

gratuitous [grə'tjuːɪtəs] *adj fml* gratuit(e).

grave¹ [greɪv] ◇ *adj* grave ; [concern] sérieux(euse). ◇ *n* tombe *f*.

grave² [grɑːv] *adj* LING : **e grave** *m* accent grave.

gravel ['grævl] *n (U)* gravier *m*.

gravestone ['greɪvstəun] *n* pierre *f* tombale.

graveyard ['greɪvjɑːd] *n* cimetière *m*.

gravity ['grævətɪ] *n* **1.** [force] gravité *f*, pesanteur *f* - **2.** [seriousness] gravité *f*.

gravy ['greɪvɪ] *n (U)* [meat juice] jus *m* de viande.

gray *US* = **grey**.

graze [greɪz] ◇ *vt* **1.** [subj: cows, sheep] brouter, paître - **2.** [subj: farmer] faire paître - **3.** [skin] écorcher, égratigner - **4.** [touch lightly] frôler, effleurer. ◇ *vi* brouter, paître. ◇ *n* écorchure *f*, égratignure *f*.

grease [griːs] ◇ *n* graisse *f*. ◇ *vt* graisser.

greaseproof paper [ˌgriːspruːf-] *n (U) UK* papier *m* sulfurisé.

greasy ['griːzɪ] *adj* **1.** [covered in grease] graisseux(euse) ; [clothes] taché(e) de graisse - **2.** [food, skin, hair] gras (grasse).

great [greɪt] *adj* **1.** [gen] grand(e) ; **great big** énorme - **2.** *inf* [splendid] génial(e), formidable ; **to feel great** se sentir en pleine forme ; **great!** super!, génial!

Great Britain *n* Grande-Bretagne *f* ; **in Great Britain** en Grande-Bretagne.

greatcoat ['greɪtkəʊt] *n* pardessus *m*.

Great Dane *n* danois *m*.

great-grandchild *n* [boy] arrière-petit-fils *m* ; [girl] arrière-petite-fille *f*. ▶ **great-grandchildren** *npl* arrière-petits-enfants *mpl*.

great-grandfather *n* arrière-grand-père *m*.

great-grandmother *n* arrière-grand-mère *f*.

greatly ['greɪtlɪ] *adv* beaucoup ; [different] très.

greatness ['greɪtnɪs] *n* grandeur *f*.

Greece [griːs] *n* Grèce *f*.

greed [griːd] *n (U)* **1.** [for food] gloutonnerie *f* - **2.** *fig* [for money, power] : **greed (for)** avidité *f* (de).

greedy ['griːdɪ] *adj* **1.** [for food] glouton(onne) - **2.** [for money, power] : **greedy for sthg** avide de qqch.

Greek [griːk] ◇ *adj* grec (grecque). ◇ *n* **1.** [person] Grec *m*, Grecque *f* - **2.** [language] grec *m*.

green [griːn] ◇ *adj* **1.** [in colour, unripe] vert(e) - **2.** [ecological - issue, politics] écologique ; [- person] vert(e) - **3.** *inf* [inexperienced] inexpérimenté(e), jeune. ◇ *n* **1.** [colour] vert *m* - **2.** GOLF green *m* - **3.** : **village green** pelouse *f* communale. ▶ **Green** *n* POL vert *m*, -e *f*, écologiste *mf* ; **the Greens** les Verts, les Écologistes. ▶ **greens** *npl* [vegetables] légumes *mpl* verts.

greenback ['griːnbæk] *n US inf* billet *m* vert.

green belt *n UK* ceinture *f* verte.

green card *n* **1.** *UK* [for vehicle] carte *f* verte - **2.** *US* [residence permit] carte *f* de séjour.

greenery ['griːnərɪ] *n* verdure *f*.

greenfly ['griːnflaɪ] (*pl* **greenfly** OR **-ies**) *n* puceron *m*.

greengage ['griːngeɪdʒ] *n* reine-claude *f*.

greengrocer ['griːnˌgrəʊsər] *n esp UK* marchand *m*, -e *f* de légumes ; **greengrocer's (shop)** magasin *m* de fruits et légumes.

greenhouse ['griːnhaʊs] (*pl* [-haʊzɪz]) *n* serre *f*.

greenhouse effect *n* : **the greenhouse effect** l'effet *m* de serre.

Greenland ['griːnlənd] *n* Groenland *m*.

green salad *n* salade *f* verte.

greet [griːt] *vt* **1.** [say hello to] saluer - **2.** [receive] accueillir.

greeting ['griːtɪŋ] *n* salutation *f*, salut *m*. ▶ **greetings** *npl* : **Christmas/birthday greetings** vœux *mpl* de Noël/d'anniversaire.

greetings card *UK*, **greeting card** *US* *n* carte *f* de vœux.

grenade [grə'neɪd] *n* : **(hand)grenade** grenade *f* (à main).

grew [gruː] *pt* ▶ **grow**.

grey *UK*, **gray** *US* [greɪ] ◇ *adj* **1.** [in colour] gris(e) - **2.** [grey-haired] : **to go grey** grisonner - **3.** [dull, gloomy] morne, triste. ◇ *n* gris *m*.

grey-haired *UK*, **gray-haired** *US* [-'heəd] *adj* aux cheveux gris.

greyhound ['greɪhaʊnd] *n* lévrier *m*.

grid [grɪd] *n* **1.** [grating] grille *f* - **2.** [system of squares] quadrillage *m*.

griddle ['grɪdl] *n* plaque *f* à cuire.

gridlock ['grɪdlɒk] *n US* embouteillage *m*.

grief [griːf] *n (U)* **1.** [sorrow] chagrin *m*, peine *f* - **2.** *inf* [trouble] ennuis *mpl* ; **to come to grief** [person] avoir de gros problèmes ; [project] échouer, tomber à l'eau ; **good grief!** Dieu du ciel!, mon Dieu!

grievance ['griːvns] *n* grief *m*, doléance *f*.

grieve [griːv] *vi* [at death] être en deuil ; **to grieve for sb/sthg** pleurer qqn/qqch.

grievous ['griːvəs] *adj fml* grave ; [shock] cruel(elle).

grievous bodily harm *n (U)* coups *mpl* et blessures *fpl*.

grill [grɪl] ◇ *n* [on cooker, fire] gril *m*. ◇ *vt* **1.** [cook on grill] griller, faire griller - **2.** *inf* [interrogate] cuisiner.

grille [grɪl] *n* grille *f*.

grim [grɪm] *adj* **1.** [stern - face, expression] sévère ; [- determination] inflexible - **2.** [cheerless - truth, news] sinistre ; [- room, walls] lugubre ; [- day] morne, triste.

grimace [grɪ'meɪs] <> n grimace f. <> vi grimacer, faire la grimace.

grime [graɪm] n (U) crasse f, saleté f.

grimy ['graɪmɪ] adj sale, encrassé(e).

grin [grɪn] <> n (large) sourire m. <> vi : **to grin (at sb/sthg)** adresser un large sourire (à qqn/qqch).

grind [graɪnd] <> vt (pt & pp ground) [crush] moudre. <> vi (pt & pp ground) [scrape] grincer. <> n [hard, boring work] corvée f. **grind down** vt sep [oppress] opprimer. **grind up** vt sep pulvériser.

grinder ['graɪndə] n moulin m.

grip [grɪp] <> n 1. [grasp, hold] prise f - 2. [control] contrôle m ; **he's got a good grip on the situation** il a la situation bien en main ; **to get to grips with sthg** s'attaquer à qqch ; **to get a grip on o.s.** se ressaisir - 3. [adhesion] adhérence f - 4. [handle] poignée f - 5. [bag] sac m (de voyage). <> vt 1. [grasp] saisir ; [subj: tyres] adhérer à - 2. fig [imagination, country] captiver.

gripe [graɪp] inf <> n [complaint] plainte f. <> vi : **to gripe (about sthg)** râler OR rouspéter (contre qqch).

gripping ['grɪpɪŋ] adj passionnant(e).

grisly ['grɪzlɪ] adj [horrible, macabre] macabre.

gristle ['grɪsl] n (U) nerfs mpl.

grit [grɪt] <> n 1. [stones] gravillon m ; [in eye] poussière f - 2. inf [courage] cran m. <> vt sabler.

gritty ['grɪtɪ] adj 1. [stony] couvert(e) de gravillon - 2. inf [brave - person] qui a du cran ; [- performance, determination] courageux(euse).

groan [grəʊn] <> n gémissement m. <> vi 1. [moan] gémir - 2. [creak] grincer, gémir.

grocer ['grəʊsə] n épicier m, -ère f ; **grocer's (shop)** épicerie f.

groceries ['grəʊsərɪz] npl [foods] provisions fpl.

grocery ['grəʊsərɪ] n [shop] épicerie f.

groggy ['grɒgɪ] adj groggy (inv).

groin [grɔɪn] n aine f.

groom [gruːm] <> n 1. [of horses] palefrenier m, -ière f, garçon m d'écurie - 2. [bridegroom] marié m. <> vt 1. [brush] panser - 2. fig [prepare] : **to groom sb (for sthg)** préparer OR former qqn (pour qqch).

groove [gruːv] n [in metal, wood] rainure f ; [in record] sillon m.

groovy ['gruːvɪ] adj inf 1. [excellent] super, génial(e) - 2. [fashionable] branché(e).

grope [grəʊp] vi : **to grope (about OR around US) for sthg** chercher qqch à tâtons.

gross [grəʊs] <> adj 1. [total] brut(e) - 2. fml [serious - negligence] coupable ; [- misconduct] choquant(e) ; [- inequality] flagrant(e) - 3. [coarse, vulgar] grossier(ère) - 4. inf [obese] obèse, énorme. <> n (pl gross OR -es [-iːz]) grosse f, douze douzaines fpl.

grossly ['grəʊslɪ] adv [seriously] extrêmement, énormément.

grotesque [grəʊ'tesk] adj grotesque.

grotto ['grɒtəʊ] (pl -es OR -s) n grotte f.

grotty ['grɒtɪ] adj UK inf minable.

ground [graʊnd] <> pt & pp ► **grind**. <> n 1. (U) [surface of earth] sol m, terre f ; **above ground** en surface ; **below ground** sous terre ; **on the ground** par terre, au sol - 2. (U) [area of land] terrain m - 3. [for sport etc] terrain m - 4. [advantage] : **to gain/lose ground** gagner/perdre du terrain - 5. : **to drive/to work o.s. into the ground** se tuer au travail. <> vt 1. [base] : **to be grounded on** OR **in sthg** être fondé(e) sur qqch - 2. [aircraft, pilot] interdire de vol - 3. inf [child] priver de sortie - 4. US ELEC : **to be grounded** être à la masse. **grounds** npl 1. [reason] motif m, raison f ; **grounds for sthg** motifs de qqch ; **grounds for doing sthg** raisons de faire qqch - 2. [land round house] parc m - 3. [of coffee] marc m.

ground crew n personnel m au sol.

ground floor n rez-de-chaussée m inv.

grounding ['graʊndɪŋ] n : **grounding (in)** connaissances fpl de base (en).

groundless ['graʊndlɪs] adj sans fondement.

groundsheet ['graʊndʃiːt] n tapis m de sol.

ground staff n 1. [at sports ground] personnel m d'entretien (d'un terrain de sport) - 2. UK = **ground crew**.

groundswell ['graʊndswel] n vague f de fond.

groundwork ['graʊndwɜːk] n (U) travail m préparatoire.

ground zero n revenir au début.

group [gruːp] <> n groupe m. <> vt grouper, réunir. <> vi : **to group (together)** se grouper.

groupie ['gruːpɪ] n inf groupie f.

grouse [graʊs] <> n (pl grouse OR -s) [bird] grouse f, coq m de bruyère. <> vi inf râler, rouspéter.

grove [grəʊv] n [group of trees] bosquet m.

grovel ['grɒvl] (UK & US) vi : **to grovel (to sb)** ramper (devant qqn).

grow [grəʊ] (pt grew, pp grown) <> vi 1. [gen] pousser ; [person, animal] grandir ; [company, city] s'agrandir ; [fears, influence, traffic] augmenter, s'accroître ; [problem, idea, plan] prendre de l'ampleur ; [economy]

se développer - **2.** [become] devenir ; **to grow old** vieillir ; **to grow tired of sthg** se fatiguer de qqch. ◇ *vt* **1.** [plants] faire pousser - **2.** [hair, beard] laisser pousser. ➤ **grow on** *vt insep inf* plaire de plus en plus à ; **it'll grow on you** cela finira par te plaire. ➤ **grow out of** *vt insep* **1.** [clothes, shoes] devenir trop grand pour - **2.** [habit] perdre. ➤ **grow up** *vi* **1.** [become adult] grandir, devenir adulte ; **grow up!** ne fais pas l'enfant! - **2.** [develop] se développer.

grower ['grəʊə'] *n* cultivateur *m*, -trice *f*.

growl [graʊl] *vi* [animal] grogner, gronder ; [engine] vrombir, gronder ; [person] grogner.

grown [grəʊn] ◇ *pp* ➤ **grow**. ◇ *adj* adulte.

grown-up ◇ *adj* **1.** [fully grown] adulte, grand(e) - **2.** [mature] mûr(e). ◇ *n* adulte *mf*, grande personne *f*.

growth [grəʊθ] *n* **1.** [increase - gen] croissance *f* ; [- of opposition, company] développement *m* ; [- of population] augmentation *f*, accroissement *m* - **2.** MED [lump] tumeur *f*, excroissance *f*.

grub [grʌb] *n* **1.** [insect] larve *f* - **2.** *inf* [food] bouffe *f*.

grubby ['grʌbɪ] *adj* sale, malpropre.

grudge [grʌdʒ] ◇ *n* rancune *f* ; **to bear sb a grudge, to bear a grudge against sb** garder rancune à qqn. ◇ *vt* : **to grudge sb sthg** donner qqch à qqn à contrecœur ; [success] en vouloir à qqn à cause de qqch.

gruelling *UK*, **grueling** *US* ['grʊəlɪŋ] *adj* épuisant(e), exténuant(e).

gruesome ['gru:səm] *adj* horrible.

gruff [grʌf] *adj* **1.** [hoarse] gros (grosse) - **2.** [rough, unfriendly] brusque, bourru(e).

grumble ['grʌmbl] *vi* **1.** [complain] : **to grumble about sthg** rouspéter OR grommeler contre qqch - **2.** [rumble - thunder, train] gronder ; [- stomach] gargouiller.

grumpy ['grʌmpɪ] *adj inf* renfrogné(e).

grunge [grʌndʒ] *n* **1.** *inf* [dirt] crasse *f* - **2.** [music, fashion] grunge *m*.

grunt [grʌnt] ◇ *n* grognement *m*. ◇ *vi* grogner.

G-string *n* cache-sexe *m inv*.

guarantee [,gærən'ti:] ◇ *n* garantie *f*. ◇ *vt* garantir.

guard [gɑ:d] ◇ *n* **1.** [person] garde *m* ; [in prison] gardien *m* - **2.** [group of guards] garde *f* - **3.** [defensive operation] garde *f* ; **to be on guard** être de garde OR de faction ; **to catch sb off guard** prendre qqn au dépourvu - **4.** *UK* RAIL chef *m* de train - **5.** [protective device - for body] protection *f* ; [- for fire] garde-feu *m inv*. ◇ *vt* **1.** [protect - building]

protéger, garder ; [- person] protéger - **2.** [prisoner] garder, surveiller - **3.** [hide - secret] garder.

guard dog *n* chien *m* de garde.

guarded ['gɑ:dɪd] *adj* prudent(e).

guardian ['gɑ:djən] *n* **1.** [of child] tuteur *m*, -trice *f* - **2.** [protector] gardien *m*, -enne *f*, protecteur *m*, -trice *f*.

guardrail ['gɑ:dreɪl] *n US* [on road] barrière *f* de sécurité.

guard's van *n UK* wagon *m* du chef de train.

guerilla [gə'rɪlə] = **guerrilla**.

Guernsey ['gɜ:nzɪ] *n* [place] Guernesey *f*.

guerrilla [gə'rɪlə] *n* guérillero *m* ; **urban guerrilla** guérillero *m* des villes.

guerrilla warfare *n* (U) guérilla *f*.

guess [ges] ◇ *n* conjecture *f*. ◇ *vt* deviner ; **guess what?** tu sais quoi? ◇ *vi* **1.** [conjecture] deviner ; **to guess at sthg** deviner qqch - **2.** [suppose] : **I guess (so)** je suppose (que oui).

guesswork ['geswɜ:k] *n* (U) conjectures *fpl*, hypothèses *fpl*.

guest [gest] *n* **1.** [gen] invité *m*, -e *f* - **2.** [at hotel] client *m*, -e *f*.

guesthouse ['gesthaʊs] (*pl* [-haʊzɪz]) *n* pension *f* de famille.

guestroom ['gestrʊm] *n* chambre *f* d'amis.

guffaw [gʌ'fɔ:] ◇ *n* gros rire *m*. ◇ *vi* rire bruyamment.

guidance ['gaɪdəns] *n* (U) **1.** [help] conseils *mpl* - **2.** [leadership] direction *f*.

guide [gaɪd] ◇ *n* **1.** [person, book] guide *m* - **2.** [indication] indication *f*. ◇ *vt* **1.** [show by leading] guider - **2.** [control] diriger - **3.** [influence] : **to be guided by sb/sthg** se laisser guider par qqn/qqch. ➤ **Guide** *n* éclaireuse *f*, guide *f*.

guide book, guidebook *n* guide *m*.

guide dog *n* chien *m* d'aveugle.

guidelines ['gaɪdlaɪnz] *npl* directives *fpl*, lignes *fpl* directrices.

guild [gɪld] *n* **1.** HIST corporation *f*, guilde *f* - **2.** [association] association *f*.

guile [gaɪl] *n* (U) *lit* ruse *f*, astuce *f*.

guillotine ['gɪlə,ti:n] ◇ *n* **1.** [for executions] guillotine *f* - **2.** [for paper] massicot *m*. ◇ *vt* [execute] guillotiner.

guilt [gɪlt] *n* culpabilité *f*.

guilty ['gɪltɪ] *adj* coupable ; **to be guilty of sthg** être coupable de qqch ; **to be found guilty/not guilty** LAW être reconnu coupable/non coupable.

guinea pig ['gɪnɪ-] *n* cobaye *m*.

guise [gaɪz] *n fml* apparence *f*.

guitar [gɪ'tɑ:'] *n* guitare *f*.

guitarist [gɪ'tɑːrɪst] *n* guitariste *mf*.

gulf [gʌlf] *n* **1.** [sea] golfe *m* - **2.** [breach, chasm]: **gulf (between)** abîme *m* (entre).
◆ **Gulf** *n* : **the Gulf** le Golfe.

gull [gʌl] *n* mouette *f*.

gullet ['gʌlɪt] *n* œsophage *m* ; [of bird] gosier *m*.

gullible ['gʌləbl] *adj* crédule.

gully ['gʌlɪ] *n* **1.** [valley] ravine *f* - **2.** [ditch] rigole *f*.

gulp [gʌlp] ◇ *n* [of drink] grande gorgée *f* ; [of food] grosse bouchée *f*. ◇ *vt* avaler.
◇ *vi* avoir la gorge nouée. ◆ **gulp down** *vt sep* avaler.

gum [gʌm] ◇ *n* **1.** [chewing gum] chewing-gum *m* - **2.** [adhesive] colle *f*, gomme *f* - **3.** ANAT gencive *f*. ◇ *vt* coller.

gumboots ['gʌmbuːts] *npl* UK dated bottes *fpl* de caoutchouc.

gun [gʌn] *n* **1.** [weapon - small] revolver *m* ; [- rifle] fusil *m* ; [- large] canon *m* - **2.** [starting pistol] pistolet *m* - **3.** [tool] pistolet *m* ; [for staples] agrafeuse *f*. ◆ **gun down** *vt sep* abattre.

gunboat ['gʌnbəʊt] *n* canonnière *f*.

gunfire ['gʌnfaɪər] *n (U)* coups *mpl* de feu.

gunman ['gʌnmən] (*pl* **-men** [-mən]) *n* personne *f* armée.

gunpoint ['gʌnpɔɪnt] *n* : **at gunpoint** sous la menace d'un fusil OR pistolet.

gunpowder ['gʌn,paʊdər] *n* poudre *f* à canon.

gunshot ['gʌnʃɒt] *n* [firing of gun] coup *m* de feu.

gunsmith ['gʌnsmɪθ] *n* armurier *m*, -ière *f*.

gurgle ['gɜːgl] *vi* **1.** [water] glouglouter - **2.** [baby] gazouiller.

guru ['gʊruː] *n* gourou *mf*, guru *mf*.

gush [gʌʃ] ◇ *n* jaillissement *m*. ◇ *vi* **1.** [flow out] jaillir - **2.** *pej* [enthuse] s'exprimer de façon exubérante.

gusset ['gʌsɪt] *n* gousset *m*.

gust [gʌst] *n* rafale *f*, coup *m* de vent.

gusto ['gʌstəʊ] *n* : **with gusto** avec enthousiasme.

gut [gʌt] ◇ *n* MED intestin *m*. ◇ *vt* **1.** [remove organs from] vider - **2.** [destroy] éventrer. ◆ **guts** *npl inf* **1.** [intestines] intestins *mpl* ; **to hate sb's guts** ne pas pouvoir piffer qqn, ne pas pouvoir voir qqn en peinture - **2.** [courage] cran *m*.

gutter ['gʌtər] *n* **1.** [ditch] rigole *f* - **2.** [on roof] gouttière *f*.

gutter press *n* UK *pej* presse *f* à sensation.

guy [gaɪ] *n* **1.** *inf* [man] type *m* - **2.** [person] copain *m*, copine *f* - **3.** UK [dummy] *effigie de Guy Fawkes*.

Guy Fawkes' Night [-'fɔːks-] *n fête célébrée le 5 novembre en Grande-Bretagne*.

guyline US, **guy rope** *n* corde *f* de tente.

guzzle ['gʌzl] ◇ *vt* bâfrer ; [drink] lamper.
◇ *vi* s'empiffrer.

gym [dʒɪm] *n inf* **1.** [gymnasium] gymnase *m* - **2.** [exercises] gym *f*.

gymnasium [dʒɪm'neɪzjəm] (*pl* **-iums** OR **-ia** [-jə]) *n* gymnase *m*.

gymnast ['dʒɪmnæst] *n* gymnaste *mf*.

gymnastics [dʒɪm'næstɪks] *n (U)* gymnastique *f*.

gym shoes *npl* (chaussures *fpl* de) tennis *mpl*.

gymslip ['dʒɪm,slɪp] *n* UK tunique *f*.

gynaecologist UK, **gynecologist** US [,gaɪnə'kɒlədʒɪst] *n* gynécologue *mf*.

gynaecology UK, **gynecology** US [,gaɪnə'kɒlədʒɪ] *n* gynécologie *f*.

gypsy ['dʒɪpsɪ] UK = **gipsy**.

Gypsy ['dʒɪpsɪ] (*pl* **-ies**) *n* gitan *m*, -ne *f*.

gyrate [dʒaɪ'reɪt] *vi* tournoyer.

h [eɪtʃ] (*pl* **h's** OR **hs**), **H** (*pl* **H's** OR **Hs**) *n* [letter] h *m inv*, H *m inv*.

haberdashery ['hæbədæʃərɪ] *n* UK mercerie *f*.

habit ['hæbɪt] *n* **1.** [customary practice] habitude *f* ; **out of habit** par habitude ; **to make a habit of doing sthg** avoir l'habitude de faire qqch - **2.** [garment] habit *m*.

habitat ['hæbɪtæt] *n* habitat *m*.

habitual [hə'bɪtjʊəl] *adj* **1.** [usual, characteristic] habituel(elle) - **2.** [regular] invétéré(e).

hack [hæk] ◇ *n* [writer] écrivailleur *m*, -euse *f*. ◇ *vt* [cut] tailler. ◆ **hack into** *vt insep* COMPUT pirater.

hacker ['hækər] *n* : **(computer) hacker** pirate *m* informatique.

hackneyed ['hæknɪd] *adj* rebattu(e).

hacksaw ['hæksɔː] *n* scie *f* à métaux.

had (*weak form* [həd], *strong form* [hæd]) *pt & pp* ▶ **have**.

haddock ['hædək] (*pl* **haddock**) *n* églefin *m*, aiglefin *m*.

hadn't ['hædnt] = **had not**.

haemophiliac [,hiːmə'fɪlɪæk] UK = **hemophiliac**.

haemorrhage ['hemərɪdʒ] *UK* = **hemor-rhage.**

haemorrhoids ['hemərɔɪdz] *UK* = **hemor-rhoids.**

haggard ['hægəd] *adj* [face] défait(e) ; [person] abattu(e).

haggis ['hægɪs] *n* plat typique écossais fait d'une panse de brebis farcie, le plus souvent servie avec des navets et des pommes de terre.

haggle ['hægl] *vi* marchander ; **to haggle over** OR **about sthg** marchander qqch.

Hague [heɪg] *n* : **The Hague** La Haye.

hail [heɪl] <> *n* grêle *f* ; *fig* pluie *f*. <> *vt* **1.** [call] héler - **2.** [acclaim] : **to hail sb/sthg as sthg** acclamer qqn/qqch comme qqch. <> *impers vb* grêler.

hailstone ['heɪlstəʊn] *n* grêlon *m*.

hair [heəʳ] *n* **1.** *(U)* [on human head] cheveux *mpl* ; **to do one's hair** se coiffer - **2.** *(U)* [on animal, human skin] poils *mpl* - **3.** [individual hair - on head] cheveu *m* ; [- on skin] poil *m*.

hairbrush ['heəbrʌʃ] *n* brosse *f* à cheveux.

haircut ['heəkʌt] *n* coupe *f* de cheveux.

hairdo ['heədu:] *(pl -s)* *n inf dated* coiffure *f*.

hairdresser ['heə,dresəʳ] *n* coiffeur *m*, -euse *f* ; **hairdresser's (salon)** salon *m* de coiffure.

hairdryer ['heə,draɪəʳ] *n* [handheld] sèche-cheveux *m inv* ; [over the head] casque *m*.

hair gel *n* gel *m* coiffant.

hairgrip ['heəgrɪp] *n UK* pince *f* à cheveux.

hairpin ['heəpɪn] *n* épingle *f* à cheveux.

hairpin bend *UK*, **hairpin turn** *US n* virage *m* en épingle à cheveux.

hair-raising [-,reɪzɪŋ] *adj* à faire dresser les cheveux sur la tête ; [journey] effrayant(e).

hair remover [-rɪ,mu:vəʳ] *n* (crème *f*) dépilatoire *m*.

hair slide *n UK* barrette *f*.

hairspray ['heəspreɪ] *n* laque *f*.

hairstyle ['heəstaɪl] *n* coiffure *f*.

hairy ['heərɪ] *adj* **1.** [covered in hair] velu(e), poilu(e) - **2.** *inf* [frightening] à faire dresser les cheveux sur la tête.

Haiti ['heɪtɪ] *n* Haïti *m*.

hake [heɪk] *(pl hake* OR *-s) n* colin *m*, merluche *f*.

half [*UK* hɑ:f, *US* hæf] <> *adj* demi(e) ; **half a dozen** une demi-douzaine ; **half an hour** une demi-heure ; **half a pound** une demi-livre ; **half English** à moitié anglais. <> *adv* **1.** [gen] à moitié ; **half-and-half** moitié-moitié - **2.** [by half] demie ; **half** [in telling the time] : **half past ten** *UK*, **half after ten** *US* dix heures et demie ; **it's half past** il est la demie. <> *n (pl* **halves** *(senses 1 and 2)* [*UK* hɑ:vz] [*US* hævz], **halves** *(pl senses 3, 4 and 5))* **1.** [gen] moitié *f* ; **in half** en deux ; **to go halves (with sb)** partager (avec qqn) - **2.** SPORT [of match] mi-temps *f* - **3.** SPORT [halfback] demi *m* - **4.** *UK* [of beer] demi *m* - **5.** *UK* [child's ticket] demi-tarif *m*, tarif *m* enfant. <> *pron* la moitié ; **half of them** la moitié d'entre eux.

halfback ['hɑ:fbæk] *n* SPORT demi *m*.

half board *n esp UK* demi-pension *f*.

half-breed <> *adj* métis(isse). <> *n* métis *m*, -isse *f* (attention: le terme 'half-breed' est considéré comme raciste).

half-caste [-kɑ:st] <> *adj* métis(isse). <> *n* métis *m*, -isse *f* (attention: le terme 'half-caste' est considéré comme raciste).

half-hearted [-'hɑ:tɪd] *adj* sans enthousiasme.

half hour *n* demi-heure *f*.

half-mast *n* : **at half-mast** [flag] en berne.

half moon *n* demi-lune *f*.

half note *n US* MUS blanche *f*.

halfpenny ['heɪpnɪ] *(pl* **-pennies** *or* **-pence** [-pens]) *n UK* demi-penny *m*.

half-price *adj* à moitié prix.

half term *n UK* congé *m* de mi-trimestre.

half-time *n (U)* mi-temps *f*.

halfway [hɑ:f'weɪ] <> *adj* à mi-chemin. <> *adv* **1.** [in space] à mi-chemin - **2.** [in time] à la moitié.

halibut ['hælɪbət] *(pl halibut* OR *-s) n* flétan *m*.

hall [hɔ:l] *n* **1.** [in house] vestibule *m*, entrée *f* - **2.** [meeting room, building] salle *f* - **3.** [country house] manoir *m*.

hallmark ['hɔ:lmɑ:k] *n* **1.** [typical feature] marque *f* - **2.** [on metal] poinçon *m*.

hallo [hə'ləʊ] *UK* = **hello.**

hall of residence *(pl* **halls of residence)** *n UK* UNIV résidence *f* universitaire.

Hallowe'en, Halloween [,hæləʊ'i:n] *n* Halloween *f* (fête des sorcières et des fantômes).

hallucinate [hə'lu:sɪneɪt] *vi* avoir des hallucinations.

hallway ['hɔ:lweɪ] *n* vestibule *m*.

halo ['heɪləʊ] *(pl* **-es** OR **-s)** *n* nimbe *m* ; ASTRON halo *m*.

halt [hɔ:lt] <> *n* [stop] : **to come to a halt** [vehicle] s'arrêter, s'immobiliser ; [activity] s'interrompre ; **to call a halt to sthg** mettre fin à qqch. <> *vt* arrêter. <> *vi* s'arrêter.

halterneck ['hɔ:ltənek], *US* **halter top** *adj* dos nu (*inv*).

halve [*UK* hɑ:v, *US* hæv] *vt* **1.** [reduce by half] réduire de moitié - **2.** [divide] couper en deux.

halves [*UK* hɑːvz, *US* hævz] *npl* ► **half.**

ham [hæm] ◇ *n* [meat] jambon *m*. ◇ *comp* au jambon.

hamburger ['hæmbɜːgər] *n* **1.** [burger] hamburger *m* - **2.** *(U) US* [mince] viande *f* hachée.

hamlet ['hæmlɪt] *n* hameau *m*.

hammer ['hæmər] ◇ *n* marteau *m*. ◇ *vt* **1.** [with tool] marteler ; [nail] enfoncer à coups de marteau - **2.** *fig* [with fist] marteler du poing - **3.** *inf* [defeat] battre à plates coutures. ◇ *vi* [with fist] : **to hammer (on)** cogner du poing (à). ◆ **hammer out** *vt insep* [agreement, solution] parvenir finalement à.

hammock ['hæmək] *n* hamac *m*.

hamper ['hæmpər] ◇ *n* **1.** *UK* [for food] panier *m* d'osier - **2.** *US* [for laundry] panier *m* à linge sale. ◇ *vt* gêner.

hamster ['hæmstər] *n* hamster *m*.

hamstring ['hæmstrɪŋ] *n* tendon *m* du jarret.

hand [hænd] ◇ *n* **1.** [part of body] main *f* ; **to hold hands** se tenir la main ; **by hand** à la main ; **to get** OR **lay one's hands on** mettre la main sur ; **to get out of hand** échapper à tout contrôle ; **to have a situation in hand** avoir une situation en main ; **to have one's hands full** avoir du pain sur la planche ; **to try one's hand at sthg** s'essayer à qqch - **2.** [help] coup *m* de main ; **to give** OR **lend sb a hand (with sthg)** donner un coup de main à qqn (pour faire qqch) - **3.** [worker] ouvrier *m*, -ère *f* - **4.** [of clock, watch] aiguille *f* - **5.** [handwriting] écriture *f* - **6.** [of cards] jeu *m*, main *f*. ◇ *vt* : **to hand sthg to sb, to hand sb sthg** passer qqch à qqn. ◆ **(close) at hand** *adv* proche. ◆ **on hand** *adv* disponible. ◆ **on the other hand** *conj* d'autre part. ◆ **out of hand** *adv* [completely] d'emblée. ◆ **to hand** *adv* à portée de la main, sous la main. ◆ **hand down** *vt sep* transmettre. ◆ **hand in** *vt sep* remettre. ◆ **hand out** *vt sep* distribuer. ◆ **hand over** ◇ *vt sep* **1.** [baton, money] remettre - **2.** [responsibility, power] transmettre. ◇ *vi* : **to hand over (to)** passer le relais (à).

handbag ['hændbæg] *n* sac *m* à main.

handball ['hændbɔːl] *n* [game] handball *m*.

handbook ['hændbʊk] *n* manuel *m* ; *UK* [for tourist] guide *m*.

handbrake ['hændbreɪk] *n* frein *m* à main.

handcuffs ['hændkʌfs] *npl* menottes *fpl*.

handful ['hændfʊl] *n* [of sand, grass, people] poignée *f*.

handgun ['hændgʌn] *n* revolver *m*, pistolet *m*.

handheld PC *n* (ordinateur) portable *m*.

handicap ['hændɪkæp] ◇ *n* handicap *m*. ◇ *vt* handicaper ; [progress, work] entraver.

handicapped ['hændɪkæpt] ◇ *adj* handicapé(e). ◇ *npl* : **the handicapped** les handicapés *mpl*.

handicraft ['hændɪkrɑːft] *n* activité *f* artisanale.

handiwork ['hændɪwɜːk] *n (U)* ouvrage *m*.

handkerchief ['hæŋkətʃɪf] *(pl* **-chiefs** OR **-chieves** [-tʃiːvz]) *n* mouchoir *m*.

handle ['hændl] ◇ *n* poignée *f* ; [of jug, cup] anse *f* ; [of knife, pan] manche *m*. ◇ *vt* **1.** [with hands] manipuler ; [without permission] toucher à - **2.** [deal with, be responsible for] s'occuper de ; [difficult situation] faire face à - **3.** [treat] traiter, s'y prendre avec.

handlebars ['hændlbɑːz] *npl* guidon *m*.

handler ['hændlər] *n* **1.** [of dog] maître-chien *m* - **2.** [at airport] : **(baggage) handler** bagagiste *m*.

hand luggage *n (U) UK* bagages *mpl* à main.

handmade [ˌhænd'meɪd] *adj* fait(e) (à la) main.

handout ['hændaʊt] *n* **1.** [gift] don *m* - **2.** [leaflet] prospectus *m*.

hand puppet *n US* marionnette *f* (à gaine).

handrail ['hændreɪl] *n* rampe *f*.

handset ['hændset] *n* combiné *m*.

handshake ['hændʃeɪk] *n* serrement *m* OR poignée *f* de main.

handsome ['hænsəm] *adj* **1.** [good-looking] beau (belle) - **2.** [reward, profit] beau (belle) ; [gift] généreux(euse).

handstand ['hændstænd] *n* équilibre *m* (sur les mains).

handwriting ['hænd,raɪtɪŋ] *n* écriture *f*.

handy ['hændɪ] *adj inf* **1.** [useful] pratique ; **to come in handy** être utile - **2.** [skilful] adroit(e) - **3.** [near] tout près, à deux pas.

handyman ['hændɪmæn] *(pl* **-men** [-men]) *n* bricoleur *m*.

hang [hæŋ] ◇ *vt* **1.** *(pp* hung) [suspend] suspendre - **2.** *(pp* hung OR hanged) [execute] pendre. ◇ *vi* **1.** *(pp* hung) [be suspended] pendre, être accroché(e) - **2.** *(pp* hung OR hanged) [be executed] être pendu(e) - **3.** *(pp* hung) COMPUT planter. ◇ *n* : **to get the hang of sthg** *inf* saisir le truc OR attraper le coup pour faire qqch. ◆ **hang about, hang around** *vi* [be idle, waste time] traîner ; **she doesn't hang about** OR **around** [soon gets what she wants] elle ne perd pas de temps. ◆ **hang on** *vi* **1.** [keep hold] : **to hang on (to)** s'accrocher OR se cramponner (à) - **2.** *inf* [continue waiting] attendre - **3.** [persevere] tenir bon. ◆ **hang out** *vi inf* [spend time] traîner. ◆ **hang**

round *vt insep UK* = hang about. ➤ **hang up** ◇ *vt sep* pendre. ◇ *vi* [on telephone] raccrocher. ➤ **hang up on** *vt insep* TELEC raccrocher au nez de.

hangar ['hæŋər] *n* hangar *m*.

hanger ['hæŋər] *n* cintre *m*.

hanger-on (*pl* hangers-on) *n pej* parasite *m*.

hang gliding *n* deltaplane *m*, vol *m* libre.

hangover ['hæŋ‚əʊvər] *n* [from drinking] gueule *f* de bois.

hang-up *n inf* complexe *m*.

hanker ['hæŋkər] ➤ **hanker after**, **hanker for** *vt insep* convoiter.

hankie, hanky ['hæŋkɪ] (*abbrev of* handkerchief) *n inf* mouchoir *m*.

haphazard [‚hæp'hæzəd] *adj* fait(e) au hasard.

hapless ['hæplɪs] *adj lit* infortuné(e).

happen ['hæpən] *vi* **1.** [occur] arriver, se passer ; **to happen to sb** arriver à qqn - **2.** [chance] : **I just happened to meet him** je l'ai rencontré par hasard ; **as it happens** en fait.

happening ['hæpənɪŋ] *n* événement *m*.

happily ['hæpɪlɪ] *adv* **1.** [with pleasure] de bon cœur - **2.** [contentedly] : **to be happily doing sthg** être bien tranquillement en train de faire qqch - **3.** [fortunately] heureusement.

happiness ['hæpɪnɪs] *n* bonheur *m*.

happy ['hæpɪ] *adj* **1.** [gen] heureux(euse) ; **to be happy to do sthg** être heureux de faire qqch ; **happy birthday!** joyeux anniversaire! ; **happy Christmas** *UK* ; **happy New Year!** bonne année! - **2.** [satisfied] heureux(euse), content(e) ; **to be happy with** OR **about sthg** être heureux de qqch.

happy-go-lucky *adj* décontracté(e).

happy medium *n* juste milieu *m*.

harangue [hə'ræŋ] ◇ *n* harangue *f*. ◇ *vt* haranguer.

harass ['hærəs] *vt* harceler.

harbour *UK*, **harbor** *US* ['hɑːbər] ◇ *n* port *m*. ◇ *vt* **1.** [feeling] entretenir ; [doubt, grudge] garder - **2.** [person] héberger.

hard [hɑːd] ◇ *adj* **1.** [gen] dur(e) ; **to be hard on sb/sthg** être dur avec qqn/pour qqch - **2.** [winter, frost] rude - **3.** [water] calcaire - **4.** [fact] concret(ète) ; [news] sûr(e), vérifié(e) - **5.** *UK* POL : **hard left/right** extrême gauche/droite. ◇ *adv* **1.** [strenuously - work] dur ; [- listen, concentrate] avec effort ; **to try hard (to do sthg)** faire de son mieux (pour faire qqch) - **2.** [forcefully] fort - **3.** [heavily - rain] à verse ; [- snow] dru ; **to be hard pushed** OR **put** OR **pressed to do sthg** avoir bien de la peine à faire qqch ; **to feel hard done by** avoir l'impression d'avoir été traité injustement.

hardback ['hɑːdbæk] ◇ *adj* relié(e). ◇ *n* livre *m* relié.

hardball ['hɑːdbɔːl] *n* : **to play hardball** *inf fig* employer les grands moyens.

hardboard ['hɑːdbɔːd] *n* panneau *m* de fibres.

hard-boiled *adj* CULIN : **hard-boiled egg** œuf *m* dur.

hard cash *n* (U) espèces *fpl*.

hard copy *n* COMPUT sortie *f* papier.

hard disk *n* COMPUT disque *m* dur.

harden ['hɑːdn] ◇ *vt* durcir ; [steel] tremper. ◇ *vi* **1.** [glue, concrete] durcir - **2.** [attitude, opposition] se durcir.

hard-headed [-'hedɪd] *adj* [decision] pragmatique ; **to be hard-headed** [person] avoir la tête froide.

hard-hearted [-'hɑːtɪd] *adj* insensible, impitoyable.

hard labour *UK*, **hard labor** *US* *n* (U) travaux *mpl* forcés.

hard-liner *n* partisan *m* de la manière forte.

hardly ['hɑːdlɪ] *adv* **1.** [scarcely] à peine, ne... guère ; **hardly ever/anything** presque jamais/rien ; **I can hardly move/wait** je peux à peine bouger/attendre - **2.** [only just] à peine.

hard margin *n Ir* = hard shoulder.

hardness ['hɑːdnɪs] *n* **1.** [firmness] dureté *f* - **2.** [difficulty] difficulté *f*.

hardship ['hɑːdʃɪp] *n* **1.** (U) [difficult conditions] épreuves *fpl* - **2.** [difficult circumstance] épreuve *f*.

hard shoulder *n UK* AUT bande *f* d'arrêt d'urgence.

hard up *adj inf* fauché(e) ; **hard up for sthg** à court de qqch.

hardware ['hɑːdweər] *n* (U) **1.** [tools, equipment] quincaillerie *f* - **2.** COMPUT hardware *m*, matériel *m*.

hardware shop, **hardware store** *n* quincaillerie *f*.

hardwearing [‚hɑːd'weərɪŋ] *adj UK* résistant(e).

hardworking [‚hɑːd'wɜːkɪŋ] *adj* travailleur(euse).

hardy ['hɑːdɪ] *adj* **1.** [person, animal] vigoureux(euse), robuste - **2.** [plant] résistant(e), vivace.

hare [heər] *n* lièvre *m*.

harebrained ['heə‚breɪnd] *adj inf* [person] écervelé(e) ; [scheme, idea] insensé(e).

harelip [‚heə'lɪp] *n* bec-de-lièvre *m*.

haricot (bean) ['hærɪkəʊ-] *n* haricot *m* blanc.

harm [hɑːm] <> *n* **1.** [injury] mal *m* - **2.** [damage - to clothes, plant] dommage *m* ; [- to reputation] tort *m* ; **to do harm to sb, to do sb harm** faire du tort à qqn ; **to do harm to sthg, to do sthg harm** endommager qqch ; **to be out of harm's way** [- person] être en sûreté OR lieu sûr ; [- thing] être en lieu sûr. <> *vt* **1.** [injure] faire du mal à - **2.** [damage - clothes, plant] endommager ; [- reputation] faire du tort à.

harmful ['hɑːmfʊl] *adj* nuisible, nocif(ive).

harmless ['hɑːmlɪs] *adj* **1.** [not dangerous] inoffensif(ive) - **2.** [inoffensive] innocent(e).

harmonica [hɑːˈmɒnɪkə] *n* harmonica *m*.

harmonize, UK **-ise** ['hɑːmənaɪz] <> *vt* harmoniser. <> *vi* s'harmoniser.

harmony ['hɑːmənɪ] *n* harmonie *f*.

harness ['hɑːnɪs] <> *n* [for horse, child] harnais *m*. <> *vt* **1.** [horse] harnacher - **2.** [energy, resources] exploiter.

harp [hɑːp] *n* harpe *f*. ➤ **harp on** *vi* : to **harp on (about sthg)** rabâcher (qqch).

harpoon [hɑːˈpuːn] <> *n* harpon *m*. <> *vt* harponner.

harpsichord ['hɑːpsɪkɔːd] *n* clavecin *m*.

harrowing ['hærəʊɪŋ] *adj* [experience] éprouvant(e) ; [report, film] déchirant(e).

harsh [hɑːʃ] *adj* **1.** [life, conditions] rude ; [criticism, treatment] sévère - **2.** [to senses - sound] discordant(e) ; [- light, voice] criard(e) ; [- surface] rugueux(euse), rêche ; [- taste] âpre.

harvest ['hɑːvɪst] <> *n* [of cereal crops] moisson *f* ; [of fruit] récolte *f* ; [of grapes] vendange *f*, vendanges *fpl*. <> *vt* [cereals] moissonner ; [fruit] récolter ; [grapes] vendanger.

has *(weak form* [həz], *strong form* [hæz]) ➤ **have**.

has-been *n inf pej* ringard *m*, -e *f*.

hash [hæʃ] *n* **1.** [food] hachis *m* - **2.** UK inf [mess] : **to make a hash of sthg** faire un beau gâchis de qqch.

hashish ['hæʃiːʃ] *n* haschich *m*.

hasn't ['hæznt] = has not.

hassle ['hæsl] *inf* <> *n* [annoyance] tracas *m*, embêtement *m*. <> *vt* tracasser.

haste [heɪst] *n* hâte *f* ; **to do sthg in haste** faire qqch à la hâte ; **to make haste** *dated* se hâter.

hasten ['heɪsn] *fml* <> *vt* hâter, accélérer. <> *vi* se hâter, se dépêcher ; **to hasten to do sthg** s'empresser de faire qqch.

hastily ['heɪstɪlɪ] *adv* **1.** [quickly] à la hâte - **2.** [rashly] sans réfléchir.

hasty ['heɪstɪ] *adj* **1.** [quick] hâtif(ive) - **2.** [rash] irréfléchi(e).

hat [hæt] *n* chapeau *m*.

hatch [hætʃ] <> *vt* **1.** [chick] faire éclore ; [egg] couver - **2.** *fig* [scheme, plot] tramer. <> *vi* [chick, egg] éclore. <> *n* : (serving) **hatch** passe-plats *m inv*.

hatchback ['hætʃˌbæk] *n* voiture *f* avec hayon.

hatchet ['hætʃɪt] *n* hachette *f*.

hatchway ['hætʃˌweɪ] *n* passe-plats *m inv*, guichet *m*.

hate [heɪt] <> *n* (U) haine *f*. <> *vt* **1.** [detest] haïr - **2.** [dislike] détester ; **to hate doing sthg** avoir horreur de faire qqch.

hateful ['heɪtfʊl] *adj* odieux(euse).

hatred ['heɪtrɪd] *n* (U) haine *f*.

hat trick *n* SPORT : **to score a hat trick** marquer trois buts.

haughty ['hɔːtɪ] *adj* hautain(e).

haul [hɔːl] <> *n* **1.** [of drugs, stolen goods] prise *f*, butin *m* - **2.** [distance] : **long haul** long voyage OR trajet *m* ; [period of time] : **on the long haul** à long terme. <> *vt* [pull] traîner, tirer.

haulage ['hɔːlɪdʒ] *n* UK transport *m* routier OR ferroviaire, camionnage *m*.

haulier UK ['hɔːlɪər], **hauler** US ['hɔːlər] *n* entrepreneur *m* de transports routiers.

haunch [hɔːntʃ] *n* [of person] hanche *f* ; [of animal] derrière *m*, arrière-train *m*.

haunt [hɔːnt] <> *n* repaire *m*. <> *vt* hanter.

have [hæv] (*pt & pp* had) <> *aux vb* [to form perfect tenses - gen] avoir ; [- with many intransitive verbs] être ; **to have eaten** avoir mangé ; **to have left** être parti(e) ; **she hasn't gone yet, has she?** elle n'est pas encore partie, si? ; **I was out of breath, having run all the way** j'étais essoufflé d'avoir couru tout le long du chemin. <> *vt* **1.** [possess, receive] : **to have (got)** avoir ; **I don't have any money** US, **I have no money, I haven't got any money** je n'ai pas d'argent ; **I've got things to do** j'ai (des choses) à faire - **2.** [experience illness] avoir ; **to have flu** UK OR **the flu** US avoir la grippe - **3.** *(referring to an action, instead of another verb)* **to have a read** UK lire ; **to have a swim** nager ; **to have a bath/shower** prendre un bain/une douche ; **to have a cigarette** fumer une cigarette ; **to have a meeting** tenir une réunion - **4.** [give birth to] : **to have a baby** avoir un bébé - **5.** [cause to be done] : **to have sb do sthg** faire faire qqch à qqn ; **to have sthg done** faire faire qqch ; **to have one's hair cut** se faire couper les cheveux - **6.** [be treated in a certain way] : **I had my car stolen** je me suis fait voler ma voiture, on m'a volé ma voiture - **7.** *inf* [cheat] : **to be had** se faire avoir ; **to have it in for sb** en avoir après qqn, en vouloir à qqn ; **to have had it** [car, machine, clothes] avoir fait son temps. ◇ *modal vb* [be obliged] : **to have (got) to do sthg** devoir faire qqch, être obligé(e) de faire qqch ; **do you have to go?, have you got to go?** *esp UK* est-ce que tu dois partir?, est-ce que tu es obligé de partir? ; **I've got to go to work** il faut que j'aille travailler ; **you've got to be joking!** vous plaisantez!, c'est une plaisanterie! ◆ **have on** *vt sep* **1.** [be wearing] porter - **2.** *UK* [tease] faire marcher. ◆ **have out** *vt sep* **1.** [have removed] : **to have one's appendix/tonsils out** se faire opérer de l'appendicite/des amygdales - **2.** [discuss frankly] : **to have it out with sb** s'expliquer avec qqn.

haven ['heɪvn] *n* havre *m*.

haven't ['hævnt] = **have not**.

haversack ['hævəsæk] *n dated* sac *m* à dos.

havoc ['hævək] *n* (U) dégâts *mpl* ; **to play havoc with** [gen] abîmer ; [with health] détraquer ; [with plans] ruiner.

Hawaii [hə'waɪɪ] *n* Hawaii *m*.

hawk [hɔːk] *n* faucon *m*.

hawker ['hɔːkər] *n* colporteur *m*, -euse *f*.

hay [heɪ] *n* foin *m*.

hay fever *n* (U) rhume *m* des foins.

haystack ['heɪ,stæk] *n* meule *f* de foin.

haywire ['heɪ,waɪər] *adj inf* **to go haywire** [person] perdre la tête ; [machine] se détraquer.

hazard ['hæzəd] ◇ *n* hasard *m*. ◇ *vt* hasarder.

hazardous ['hæzədəs] *adj* hasardeux(euse).

hazard (warning) lights *npl UK* AUT feux *mpl* de détresse.

haze [heɪz] *n* brume *f*.

hazel ['heɪzl] *adj* noisette *(inv)*.

hazelnut ['heɪzl,nʌt] *n* noisette *f*.

hazy ['heɪzɪ] *adj* **1.** [misty] brumeux(euse) - **2.** [memory, ideas] flou(e), vague.

HDD *(abbrev of* **hard disk drive)** *n* COMPUT disque *m* dur.

he [hiː] *pers pron* **1.** *(unstressed)* il ; **he's tall** il est grand ; **there he is** le voilà - **2.** *(stressed)* lui ; **HE can't do it** lui ne peut pas le faire.

head [hed] ◇ *n* **1.** [of person, animal] tête *f* ; **a** OR **per head** par tête, par personne ; **to laugh one's head off** rire à gorge déployée ; **to be off one's head** *UK*, **to be out of one's head** *US* être dingue ; **to be soft in the head** *UK inf* être débile ; **to go to one's head** [alcohol, praise] monter à la tête ; **to keep one's head** garder son sang-froid ; **to lose one's head** perdre la tête - **2.** [of table, bed, hammer] tête *f* ; [of stairs, page] haut *m* - **3.** [of flower] tête *f* ; [of cabbage] pomme *f* - **4.** [leader] chef *m* ; **head of state** chef *m* d'État - **5.** *esp UK* [head teacher] directeur *m*, -trice *f*. ◇ *vt* **1.** [procession, list] être en tête de - **2.** [be in charge of] être à la tête de - **3.** FOOTBALL : **to head the ball** faire une tête. ◇ *vi* : **where are you heading?** où allez-vous? ◆ **heads** *npl* [on coin] face *f* ; **heads or tails?** pile ou face? ◆ **head for** *vt insep* **1.** [place] se diriger vers - **2.** *fig* [trouble, disaster] aller au devant de.

headache ['hedeɪk] *n* mal *m* de tête ; **to have a headache** avoir mal à la tête.

headband ['hedbænd] *n* bandeau *m*.

head boy *n UK* élève chargé de la discipline et qui siège aux conseils de son école.

headdress ['hed,dres] *n* coiffe *f*.

header ['hedər] *n* FOOTBALL tête *f*.

headfirst [,hed'fɜːst] *adv* (la) tête la première.

head girl *n UK* élève chargée de la discipline et qui siège aux conseils de son école.

heading ['hedɪŋ] *n* titre *m*, intitulé *m*.

headlamp ['hedlæmp] *n UK* phare *m*.

headland ['hedlənd] *n* cap *m*.

headlight ['hedlaɪt] *n* phare *m*.

headline ['hedlaɪn] *n* [in newspaper] gros titre *m* ; TV & RADIO grand titre *m*.

headlong ['hedlɒŋ] *adv* **1.** [quickly] à toute allure - **2.** [unthinkingly] tête baissée - **3.** [headfirst] (la) tête la première.

headmaster [,hed'mɑːstər] *n esp UK* directeur *m* (d'une école).

headmistress [,hed'mɪstrɪs] *n esp UK* directrice *f* (d'une école).

head office *n* siège *m* social.

head-on ◇ *adj* [collision] de plein fouet ; [confrontation] de front. ◇ *adv* de plein fouet.

headphones ['hedfəʊnz] *npl* casque *m*.

headquarter [hed'kwɔːtər] *vt* : **to be headquartered in** avoir son siège à.

headquarters [,hed'kwɔːtəz] *npl* [of business, organization] siège *m* ; [of armed forces] quartier *m* général.

headrest ['hedrest] *n* appui-tête *m*.

headroom ['hedrum] *n* (U) hauteur *f*.

headscarf ['hedskɑːf] *(pl* **-scarves** [-skɑːvz] OR **-scarfs)** *n* foulard *m*.

headset ['hedset] *n* casque *m*.

head start *n* avantage *m* au départ ; **head start on** OR **over** avantage sur.

headstrong ['hedstrɒŋ] *adj* volontaire, têtu(e).

head waiter *n* maître *m* d'hôtel.

headway ['hedwei] *n* : **to make headway** faire des progrès.

headwind ['hedwind] *n* vent *m* contraire.

heady ['hedi] *adj* **1.** [exciting] grisant(e) - **2.** [causing giddiness] capiteux(euse).

heal [hi:l] ◇ *vt* **1.** [cure] guérir - **2.** *fig* [troubles, discord] apaiser. ◇ *vi* se guérir.

healing ['hi:lɪŋ] ◇ *adj* curatif(ive). ◇ *n* (U) guérison *f*.

health [helθ] *n* santé *f*.

health centre *n* UK ≃ centre *m* médico-social.

health food *n* (U) produits *mpl* diététiques OR naturels OR biologiques.

health-food shop *n* magasin *m* de produits diététiques.

health service *n* UK ≃ sécurité *f* sociale.

healthy ['helθi] *adj* **1.** [gen] sain(e) - **2.** [well] en bonne santé, bien portant(e) - **3.** *fig* [economy, company] qui se porte bien - **4.** [profit] bon (bonne).

heap [hi:p] ◇ *n* tas *m*. ◇ *vt* [pile up] entasser. ➡ **heaps** *npl inf* **heaps of** [people, objects] des tas de ; [time, money] énormément de.

hear [hɪər] (*pt & pp* heard [hɜ:d]) ◇ *vt* **1.** [gen & LAW] entendre - **2.** [learn of] apprendre ; **to hear (that)...** apprendre que... ◇ *vi* **1.** [perceive sound] entendre - **2.** [know] : **to hear about** entendre parler de - **3.** [receive news] : **to hear about** avoir des nouvelles de ; **to hear from sb** recevoir des nouvelles de qqn ; **to have heard of** avoir entendu parler de ; **I won't hear of it!** je ne veux pas en entendre parler!

hearing ['hɪərɪŋ] ◇ *n* **1.** [sense] ouïe *f* ; **hard of hearing** dur(e) d'oreille - **2.** [trial] audience *f*. ◇ *adj* entendant(e).

hearing aid *n* audiophone *m*.

hearsay ['hɪəseɪ] *n* ouï-dire *m*.

hearse [hɜ:s] *n* corbillard *m*.

heart [hɑ:t] *n lit & fig* cœur *m* ; **from the heart** du fond du cœur ; **to lose heart** perdre courage ; **to break sb's heart** briser le cœur à qqn. ➡ **hearts** *npl* [cards] cœur *m*. ➡ **at heart** *adv* au fond (de soi). ➡ **by heart** *adv* par cœur.

heartache ['hɑ:teɪk] *n fig* peine *f* de cœur.

heart attack *n* crise *f* cardiaque.

heartbeat ['hɑ:tbi:t] *n* battement *m* de cœur ; MED pulsation *f* cardiaque.

heartbroken ['hɑ:t,brəʊkn] *adj* qui a le cœur brisé.

heartburn ['hɑ:tbɜ:n] *n* (U) brûlures *fpl* d'estomac.

heart failure *n* [end of heart beat] arrêt *m* cardiaque ; [condition] défaillance *f* cardiaque.

heartfelt ['hɑ:tfelt] *adj* sincère.

hearth [hɑ:θ] *n* foyer *m*.

heartless ['hɑ:tlɪs] *adj* sans cœur.

heartwarming ['hɑ:t,wɔ:mɪŋ] *adj* réconfortant(e).

hearty ['hɑ:tɪ] *adj* **1.** [greeting, person] cordial(e) - **2.** [substantial - meal] copieux(euse) ; [- appetite] gros (grosse).

heat [hi:t] ◇ *n* **1.** (U) [warmth] chaleur *f* - **2.** (U) *fig* [pressure] pression *f* - **3.** [eliminating round] éliminatoire *f* - **4.** ZOOL : **on** UK OR **in** US **heat** en chaleur. ◇ *vt* chauffer. ➡ **heat up** ◇ *vt sep* réchauffer. ◇ *vi* chauffer.

heated ['hi:tɪd] *adj* [argument, discussion, person] animé(e) ; [issue] chaud(e).

heater ['hi:tər] *n* appareil *m* de chauffage.

heath [hi:θ] *n* lande *f*.

heathen ['hi:ðn] ◇ *adj* païen(enne). ◇ *n* païen *m*, -enne *f*.

heather ['heðər] *n* bruyère *f*.

heating ['hi:tɪŋ] *n* chauffage *m*.

heatstroke ['hi:tstrəʊk] *n* (U) coup *m* de chaleur.

heat wave *n* canicule *f*, vague *f* de chaleur.

heave [hi:v] ◇ *vt* **1.** [pull] tirer (avec effort) ; [push] pousser (avec effort) - **2.** *inf* [throw] lancer. ◇ *vi* **1.** [pull] tirer - **2.** [rise and fall] se soulever - **3.** [retch] avoir des haut-le-cœur.

heaven ['hevn] *n* paradis *m*. ➡ **heavens** ◇ *npl* : **the heavens** *lit* les cieux *mpl*. ◇ *excl* : **(good) heavens!** juste ciel!

heavenly ['hevnlɪ] *adj inf* [delightful] délicieux(euse), merveilleux(euse).

heavily ['hevɪlɪ] *adv* **1.** [booked, in debt] lourdement ; [rain, smoke, drink] énormément - **2.** [solidly - built] solidement - **3.** [breathe, sigh] péniblement, bruyamment - **4.** [fall, sit down] lourdement.

heavy ['hevɪ] *adj* **1.** [gen] lourd(e) ; **how heavy is it?** ça pèse combien? - **2.** [traffic] dense ; [rain] battant(e) ; [fighting] acharné(e) ; [casualties, corrections] nombreux(euses) ; [smoker, drinker] gros (grosse) - **3.** [noisy - breathing] bruyant(e) - **4.** [schedule] chargé(e) - **5.** [physically exacting - work, job] pénible.

heavy cream *n* US crème *f* fraîche épaisse.

heavy goods vehicle *n* UK poids lourd *m*.

heavyweight ['hevɪweɪt] ◇ *adj* SPORT poids lourd. ◇ *n* SPORT poids lourd *m*.

Hebrew ['hi:bru:] ◇ *adj* hébreu, hébraïque. ◇ *n* **1.** [person] Hébreu *m*, Israélite *mf* - **2.** [language] hébreu *m*.

Hebrides ['hebrɪdi:z] *npl* : **the Hebrides** les (îles *fpl*) Hébrides.

heck [hek] *excl inf* **what/where/why the**

heck...? que/où/pourquoi diable...? ; **a heck of a nice guy** un type vachement sympa ; **a heck of a lot of people** un tas de gens.

heckle ['hekl] ⋄ vt interpeller. ⋄ vi interrompre bruyamment.

hectic ['hektɪk] adj [meeting, day] agité(e), mouvementé(e).

he'd [hi:d] = he had, = he would.

hedge [hedʒ] ⋄ n haie f. ⋄ vi [prevaricate] répondre de façon détournée.

hedgehog ['hedʒhɒg] n hérisson m.

heed [hi:d] ⋄ n : **to take heed of sthg** tenir compte de qqch. ⋄ vt fml tenir compte de.

heedless ['hi:dlɪs] adj : **heedless of sthg** qui ne tient pas compte de qqch.

heel [hi:l] n talon m.

hefty ['heftɪ] adj **1.** [well-built] costaud(e) - **2.** [large] gros (grosse).

heifer ['hefər] n génisse f.

height [haɪt] n **1.** [of building, mountain] hauteur f ; [of person] taille f ; **5 metres in height** 5 mètres de haut ; **what height is it?** ça fait quelle hauteur? ; **what height are you?** combien mesurez-vous? - **2.** [above ground - of aircraft] altitude f - **3.** [zenith] : **at the height of the summer/season** au cœur de l'été/de la saison ; **at the height of his fame** au sommet de sa gloire.

heighten ['haɪtn] vt & vi augmenter.

heir [eər] n héritier m.

heiress ['eərɪs] n héritière f.

heirloom ['eəlu:m] n meuble m /bijou m de famille.

heist [haɪst] n inf casse m.

held [held] pt & pp ➤ hold.

helicopter ['helɪkɒptər] n hélicoptère m.

helium ['hi:lɪəm] n hélium m.

hell [hel] ⋄ n **1.** lit & fig enfer m - **2.** inf [for emphasis] : **he's a hell of a nice guy** c'est un type vachement sympa ; **what/where/why the hell...?** que/où/pourquoi..., pour sang? ; **to do sthg for the hell of it** faire qqch pour le plaisir, faire qqch juste comme ça ; **to give sb hell** inf [verbally] engueuler qqn ; **go to hell!** v inf va te faire foutre! ⋄ excl inf merde!, zut!

he'll [hi:l] = he will.

hellish ['helɪʃ] adj infernal(e).

hello [hə'ləʊ] excl **1.** [as greeting] bonjour! ; [on phone] allô! - **2.** [to attract attention] hé!

helm [helm] n lit & fig barre f.

helmet ['helmɪt] n casque m.

help [help] ⋄ n **1.** (U) [assistance] aide f ; **he gave me a lot of help** il m'a beaucoup aidé ; **with the help of sthg** à l'aide de qqch ; **with sb's help** avec l'aide de qqn ; **to be of** help rendre service - **2.** (U) [emergency aid] secours m - **3.** [useful person or object] : **to be a help** aider, rendre service. ⋄ vi aider. ⋄ vt **1.** [assist] aider ; **to help sb (to) do sthg** aider qqn à faire qqch ; **to help sb with sthg** aider qqn à faire qqch ; **may I help you?** que désirez-vous? - **2.** [avoid] : **I can't help it** je n'y peux rien ; **I couldn't help laughing** je ne pouvais pas m'empêcher de rire ; **to help o.s. (to sthg)** se servir (de qqch). ⋄ excl au secours!, à l'aide! ➤ **help out** vt sep & vi aider.

help desk n service m d'assistance technique.

helper ['helpər] n **1.** [gen] aide mf - **2.** US [to do housework] femme f de ménage.

helpful ['helpfʊl] adj **1.** [person] serviable - **2.** [advice, suggestion] utile.

helping ['helpɪŋ] n portion f ; [of cake, tart] part f.

helpless ['helplɪs] adj impuissant(e) ; [look, gesture] d'impuissance.

helpline ['helplaɪn] n ligne f d'assistance téléphonique.

Helsinki [hel'sɪŋkɪ] n Helsinki.

hem [hem] ⋄ n ourlet m. ⋄ vt ourler. ➤ **hem in** vt sep encercler.

hemisphere ['hemɪ,sfɪər] n hémisphère m.

hemline ['hemlaɪn] n ourlet m.

hemophiliac [,hi:mə'fɪlɪæk] n hémophile mf.

hemorrhage ['hemərɪdʒ] n hémorragie f.

hemorrhoids ['hemərɔɪdz] npl hémorroïdes fpl.

hen [hen] n **1.** [female chicken] poule f - **2.** [female bird] femelle f.

hence [hens] adv fml **1.** [therefore] d'où - **2.** [from now] d'ici.

henchman ['hentʃmən] (pl -men [-mən]) n pej acolyte m.

henna ['henə] ⋄ n henné m. ⋄ vt [hair] appliquer du henné sur.

henpecked ['henpekt] adj pej dominé par sa femme.

her [hɜːr] ⋄ pers pron **1.** [direct - unstressed] la, l' (+ vowel or silent 'h') ; [- stressed] elle ; **I know/like her** je la connais/l'aime (bien) ; **it's her** c'est elle - **2.** [referring to animal, car, ship etc] follow the gender of your translation - **3.** (indirect) lui ; **we spoke to her** nous lui avons parlé ; **he sent her a letter** il lui a envoyé une lettre - **4.** (after prep, in comparisons etc) elle ; **I'm shorter than her** je suis plus petit qu'elle. ⋄ poss adj son (sa), ses (pl) ; **her coat** son manteau ; **her bedroom** sa chambre ; **her children** ses enfants ; **it was her fault** c'était de sa faute à elle.

herald ['herəld] ⋄ vt fml annoncer. ⋄ n [messenger] héraut m.

herb [hɜːb] *n* herbe *f*.

herd [hɜːd] <> *n* troupeau *m*. <> *vt* **1.** [cattle, sheep] **mener - 2.** *fig* [people] conduire, mener ; [into confined space] parquer.

here [hɪər] *adv* **1.** [in this place] ici ; **here he is/they are** le/les voici ; **here it is** le/la voici ; **here is/are** voici ; **here and there** çà et là **- 2.** [present] là.

hereabouts *UK* [ˌhɪərə'baʊts], **hereabout** *US* [ˌhɪərə'baʊt] *adv* par ici.

hereafter [ˌhɪər'ɑːftər] <> *adv fml* ci-après. <> *n* : **the hereafter** l'au-delà *m*.

hereby [ˌhɪə'baɪ] *adv fml* par la présente.

hereditary [hɪ'redɪtrɪ] *adj* héréditaire.

heresy ['herəsɪ] *n* hérésie *f*.

herewith [ˌhɪə'wɪð] *adv fml* [with letter] ci-joint, ci-inclus.

heritage ['herɪtɪdʒ] *n* héritage *m*, patrimoine *m*.

hermetically [hɜː'metɪklɪ] *adv* : **hermetically sealed** fermé(e) hermétiquement.

hermit ['hɜːmɪt] *n* ermite *m*.

hernia ['hɜːnjə] *n* hernie *f*.

hero ['hɪərəʊ] (*pl* -es) *n* héros *m*.

heroic [hɪ'rəʊɪk] *adj* héroïque.

heroin ['herəʊɪn] *n* héroïne *f*.

heroine ['herəʊɪn] *n* héroïne *f*.

heron ['herən] (*pl* heron OR -s) *n* héron *m*.

herring ['herɪŋ] (*pl* herring OR -s) *n* hareng *m*.

hers [hɜːz] *poss pron* le sien (la sienne), les siens (les siennes) (*pl*) ; **that money is hers** cet argent est à elle OR est le sien ; **a friend of hers** un ami à elle, un de ses amis.

herself [hɜː'self] *pron* **1.** *(reflexive)* se ; *(after prep)* elle **- 2.** *(for emphasis)* elle-même.

he's [hiːz] = **he is**, = **he has**.

hesitant ['hezɪtənt] *adj* hésitant(e).

hesitate ['hezɪteɪt] *vi* hésiter ; **to hesitate to do sthg** hésiter à faire qqch.

hesitation [ˌhezɪ'teɪʃn] *n* hésitation *f*.

heterogeneous [ˌhetərə'dʒiːnjəs] *adj fml* hétérogène.

heterosexual [ˌhetərəʊ'sekʃʊəl] <> *adj* hétérosexuel(elle). <> *n* hétérosexuel *m*, -elle *f*.

het up [het-] *adj UK inf dated* excité(e), énervé(e).

hexagon ['heksəgən] *n* hexagone *m*.

hey [heɪ] *excl* hé !

heyday ['heɪdeɪ] *n* âge *m* d'or.

HGV (*abbrev of* **heavy goods vehicle**) *n* PL *m*.

hi [haɪ] *excl inf* salut !

hiatal hernia = **hiatus hernia**.

hiatus [haɪ'eɪtəs] (*pl* -es [-iːz]) *n fml* pause *f*.

hibernate ['haɪbəneɪt] *vi* hiberner.

hiccup ['hɪkʌp], **hiccough** <> *n* hoquet *m* ; *fig* [difficulty] accroc *m* ; **to have (the) hiccups** avoir le hoquet. <> *vi* hoqueter.

hickey [hɪkɪ] *n US* suçon *m*.

hid [hɪd] *pt* ▶ hide.

hidden ['hɪdn] <> *pp* ▶ hide. <> *adj* caché(e).

hide [haɪd] <> *vt* (*pt* hid, *pp* hidden) : **to hide sthg (from sb)** cacher qqch (à qqn) ; [information] taire qqch (à qqn). <> *vi* (*pt* hid, *pp* hidden) se cacher. <> *n* **1.** [animal skin] peau *f* **- 2.** *UK* [for watching birds, animals] cachette *f*.

hide-and-seek *n* cache-cache *m*.

hideaway ['haɪdəweɪ] *n* cachette *f*.

hideous ['hɪdɪəs] *adj* hideux(euse) ; [error, conditions] abominable.

hiding ['haɪdɪŋ] *n* **1.** [concealment] : **to be in hiding** se tenir caché(e) **- 2.** *inf* [beating] : **to give sb a (good) hiding** donner une (bonne) raclée OR correction à qqn.

hiding place *n* cachette *f*.

hierarchy ['haɪərɑːkɪ] *n* hiérarchie *f*.

hi-fi ['haɪfaɪ] *n* hi-fi *f inv*.

high [haɪ] <> *adj* **1.** [gen] haut(e) ; **it's 3 feet/6 metres high** cela fait 3 pieds/6 mètres de haut ; **how high is it?** cela fait combien de haut? **- 2.** [speed, figure, altitude, office] élevé(e) **- 3.** [high-pitched] aigu(uë) **- 4.** *drug sl* qui plane, défoncé(e) **- 5.** *inf* [drunk] bourré(e). <> *adv* haut. <> *n* [highest point] maximum *m*.

highbrow ['haɪbraʊ] *adj* intellectuel(elle).

high chair *n* chaise *f* haute *(d'enfant)*.

high-class *adj* de premier ordre ; [hotel, restaurant] de grande classe.

high court *n US* LAW Cour *f* suprême.

High Court *n UK & Scot* LAW Cour *f* d'appel.

higher ['haɪər] *adj* [exam, qualification] supérieur(e). ▶ **Higher** *n* : **Higher (Grade)** SCH *examen de fin d'études secondaires en Écosse.*

higher education *n* (*U*) études *fpl* supérieures.

high gear *n US* quatrième/cinquième vitesse *f* ; *fig* : **to move into high gear** passer la surmultipliée.

high-handed [-'hændɪd] *adj* despotique.

high heels *npl* talons *mpl* aiguilles.

high jump *n* saut *m* en hauteur.

Highland Games ['haɪlənd-] *npl* jeux *mpl* écossais.

Highlands ['haɪləndz] *npl* : **the Highlands** les Highlands *fpl* (*région montagneuse du nord de l'Écosse*).

highlight ['haɪlaɪt] <> n [of event, occasion] moment m OR point m fort. <> vt souligner ; [with highlighter & COMPUT] surligner. ◆ **highlights** npl [in hair] reflets mpl, mèches fpl.

highlighter (pen) ['haɪlaɪtə-] n surligneur m ; Stabilo® m.

highly ['haɪlɪ] adv 1. [very] extrêmement, très - 2. [in important position]: **highly placed** haut placé(e) - 3. [favourably]: **to think highly of sb/sthg** penser du bien de qqn/qqch.

highly-strung adj UK nerveux(euse).

Highness ['haɪnɪs] n : **His/Her/Your (Royal) Highness** Son/Votre Altesse (Royale) ; **their (Royal) Highnesses** leurs Altesses (Royales).

high-pitched [-'pɪtʃt] adj aigu(uë).

high point n [of occasion] point m fort.

high-powered [-'pauəd] adj 1. [powerful] de forte puissance - 2. [prestigious - activity, place] de haut niveau ; [- job, person] très important(e).

high-ranking [-'ræŋkɪŋ] adj de haut rang.

high rise n tour f (immeuble). ◆ **high-rise** adj : **high-rise block of flats** UK tour f.

high school n UK établissement d'enseignement secondaire ; US ≃ lycée m.

high season n haute saison f.

high spot n point m fort.

high street n UK rue f principale.

high-tech [-'tek] adj [method, industry] de pointe.

high tide n marée f haute.

highway ['haɪweɪ] n 1. US [motorway] autoroute f - 2. [main road] grande route f.

Highway Code n UK **the Highway Code** le code de la route.

hijack ['haɪdʒæk] <> n détournement m. <> vt détourner.

hijacker ['haɪdʒækə'] n [of aircraft] pirate m de l'air ; [of vehicle] pirate m de la route.

hike [haɪk] <> n [long walk] randonnée f. <> vi faire une randonnée.

hiker ['haɪkə'] n randonneur m, -euse f.

hiking ['haɪkɪŋ] n marche f.

hilarious [hɪ'leərɪəs] adj hilarant(e).

hill [hɪl] n 1. [mound] colline f - 2. [slope] côte f.

hillside ['hɪlsaɪd] n coteau m.

hilly ['hɪlɪ] adj vallonné(e).

hilt [hɪlt] n garde f ; **to support/defend sb to the hilt** soutenir/défendre qqn à fond.

him [hɪm] pers pron 1. [direct - unstressed] le, l' (+ vowel or silent 'h') ; [- stressed] lui ; **I know/like him** je le connais/l'aime (bien) ; **it's him** c'est lui - 2. (indirect) lui ; **we spoke to him** nous lui avons parlé ; **she sent him a**

letter elle lui a envoyé une lettre - 3. (after prep, in comparisons etc) lui ; **I'm shorter than him** je suis plus petit que lui.

Himalayas [,hɪmə'leɪəz] npl : **the Himalayas** l'Himalaya m.

himself [hɪm'self] pron 1. (reflexive) se ; (after prep) lui - 2. (for emphasis) lui-même.

hind [haɪnd] <> adj de derrière. <> n (pl hind OR -s) esp UK biche f.

hinder ['hɪndə'] vt gêner, entraver.

Hindi ['hɪndɪ] n hindi m.

hindrance ['hɪndrəns] n obstacle m.

hindsight ['haɪndsaɪt] n : **with the benefit of hindsight** avec du recul.

Hindu ['hɪndu:] <> adj hindou(e). <> n (pl -s) Hindou m, -e f.

hinge [hɪndʒ] n [whole fitting] charnière f ; [pin] gond m. ◆ **hinge (up)on** vt insep [depend on] dépendre de.

hint [hɪnt] <> n 1. [indication] allusion f ; **to drop a hint** faire une allusion - 2. [piece of advice] conseil m, indication f - 3. [small amount] soupçon m. <> vi : **to hint at sthg** faire allusion à qqch. <> vt : **to hint that...** insinuer que...

hip [hɪp] <> n hanche f. <> adj inf [fashionable] branché.

hippie ['hɪpɪ] = hippy.

hippo ['hɪpəu] (pl -s) n hippopotame m.

hippopotamus [,hɪpə'pɒtəməs] (pl -muses [-məsi:z] OR -mi [-maɪ]) n hippopotame m.

hippy ['hɪpɪ] n hippie mf.

hire ['haɪə'] <> n (U) UK [of car, equipment] location f ; **for hire** [bicycles etc] à louer ; [taxi] libre. <> vt 1. UK [rent] louer - 2. [employ] employer les services de ; **a hired killer** un tueur à gages. ◆ **hire out** vt sep UK louer.

hire car n UK voiture f de location.

hire purchase n (U) UK achat m à crédit OR à tempérament.

his [hɪz] <> poss adj son (sa), ses (pl) ; **his house** sa maison ; **his money** son argent ; **his children** ses enfants ; **his name is Joe** il s'appelle Joe. <> poss pron le sien (la sienne), les siens (les siennes) (pl) ; **that money is his** cet argent est à lui OR est le sien ; **it wasn't her fault, it was HIS** ce n'était pas de sa faute à elle, c'était de sa faute à lui ; **a friend of his** un ami à lui, un de ses amis.

hiss [hɪs] <> n [of animal, gas etc] sifflement m ; [of crowd] sifflet m. <> vi [animal, gas etc] siffler.

historic [hɪ'stɒrɪk] adj historique.

historical [hɪ'stɒrɪkəl] adj historique.

history ['hɪstərɪ] n 1. [gen] histoire f

- **2.** [past record] antécédents *mpl* ; **medical history** passé *m* médical - **3.** COMPUT historique *m*.

hit [hɪt] <> *n* **1.** [blow] coup *m* - **2.** [successful strike] coup *m* OR tir *m* réussi ; [in fencing] touche *f* - **3.** [success] succès *m* ; **to be a hit with** plaire à - **4.** COMPUT visite *f* (d'un site Internet). <> *comp* à succès. <> *vt* (*pt & pp* **hit**) **1.** [strike] frapper ; [nail] taper sur - **2.** [crash into] heurter, percuter - **3.** [reach] atteindre - **4.** [affect badly] toucher, affecter ; **to hit it off (with sb)** bien s'entendre (avec qqn).

hit-and-miss = hit-or-miss.

hit-and-run *adj* [accident] avec délit de fuite ; **hit-and-run driver** chauffard *m* (*qui a commis un délit de fuite*).

hitch [hɪtʃ] <> *n* [problem, snag] ennui *m*. <> *vt* **1.** [catch] : **to hitch a lift** OR **a ride** *US* faire du stop - **2.** [fasten] : **to hitch sthg on** OR **onto** accrocher OR attacher qqch à. <> *vi* [hitchhike] faire du stop. **hitch up** *vt sep* [pull up] remonter.

hitchhike ['hɪtʃhaɪk] *vi* faire de l'auto-stop.

hitchhiker ['hɪtʃhaɪkə'] *n* auto-stoppeur *m*, -euse *f*.

hi-tech [ˌhaɪ'tek] = high-tech.

hitherto [ˌhɪðə'tuː] *adv fml* jusqu'ici.

hit-or-miss *adj* aléatoire.

HIV (*abbrev of* **human immunodeficiency virus**) *n* VIH *m*, HIV *m* ; **to be HIV-positive** être séropositif(ive).

hive [haɪv] *n* ruche *f* ; **a hive of activity** une véritable ruche. **hive off** *vt sep UK* [assets] séparer.

HNC (*abbrev of* **Higher National Certificate**) *n brevet de technicien en Grande-Bretagne.*

HND (*abbrev of* **Higher National Diploma**) *n brevet de technicien supérieur en Grande-Bretagne.*

hoard [hɔːd] <> *n* [store] réserves *fpl* ; [of useless items] tas *m*. <> *vt* amasser ; [food, petrol] faire des provisions de.

hoarding ['hɔːdɪŋ] *n UK* [for advertisements] panneau *m* d'affichage publicitaire.

hoarfrost ['hɔːfrɒst] *n* gelée *f* blanche.

hoarse [hɔːs] *adj* [person, voice] enroué(e) ; [shout, whisper] rauque.

hoax [həʊks] *n* canular *m*.

hob [hɒb] *n UK* [on cooker] rond *m*, plaque *f*.

hobble ['hɒbl] *vi* [limp] boitiller.

hobby ['hɒbɪ] *n* passe-temps *m inv*, hobby *m*, violon *m* d'Ingres.

hobbyhorse ['hɒbɪhɔːs] *n* **1.** [toy] cheval *m* à bascule - **2.** *fig* [favourite topic] dada *m*.

hobo ['həʊbəʊ] (*pl* **-es** OR **-s**) *n US dated* clochard *m*, -e *f*.

hockey ['hɒkɪ] *n* **1.** *esp UK* [on grass] hockey *m* - **2.** *US* [ice hockey] hockey *m* sur glace.

hoe [həʊ] <> *n* houe *f*. <> *vt* biner.

hog [hɒg] <> *n* **1.** *US* [pig] cochon *m* - **2.** *inf* [greedy person] goinfre *m* ; **to go the whole hog** aller jusqu'au bout. <> *vt inf* [monopolize] accaparer, monopoliser.

Hogmanay ['hɒgməneɪ] *n la Saint-Sylvestre en Écosse.*

hoist [hɔɪst] <> *n* [device] treuil *m*. <> *vt* hisser.

hold [həʊld] <> *vt* (*pt & pp* **held**) **1.** [gen] tenir - **2.** [keep in position] maintenir - **3.** [as prisoner] détenir ; **to hold sb prisoner/ hostage** détenir qqn prisonnier/comme otage - **4.** [have, possess] avoir - **5.** *fml* [consider] considérer, estimer ; **to hold sb responsible for sthg** rendre qqn responsable de qqch, tenir qqn pour responsable de qqch - **6.** [on telephone] : **please hold the line, please hold** *US* ne quittez pas, je vous prie - **7.** [keep, maintain] tenir - **8.** [sustain, support] supporter - **9.** [contain] contenir ; **hold it!, hold everything!** attendez!, arrêtez! ; **to hold one's own** se défendre. <> *vi* (*pt & pp* **held**) **1.** [remain unchanged - gen] tenir ; [- luck] persister ; [- weather] se maintenir ; **to hold still** OR **steady** ne pas bouger, rester tranquille - **2.** [on phone] patienter. <> *n* **1.** [grasp, grip] prise *f*, étreinte *f* ; **to get** OR **lay hold of sthg** saisir qqch ; **to get hold of sthg** [obtain] se procurer qqch ; **to get hold of sb** [find] joindre - **2.** [control, influence] prise *f* - **3.** [of ship, aircraft] cale *f*. **hold back** *vt sep* **1.** [restrain, prevent] retenir ; [anger] réprimer ; **to hold sb back from doing sthg** retenir qqn de faire qqch - **2.** [keep secret] cacher. **hold down** *vt sep* [job] garder. **hold off** *vt sep* [fend off] tenir à distance ; [wait] reporter. **hold on** *vi* **1.** [wait] attendre ; [on phone] ne pas quitter - **2.** [grip] : **to hold on (to sthg)** se tenir (à qqch). **hold out** <> *vt sep* [hand, arms] tendre. <> *vi* **1.** [last] durer - **2.** [resist] : **to hold out (against sb/sthg)** résister (à qqn/ qqch). **hold up** *vt sep* **1.** [raise] lever - **2.** [delay] retarder.

holdall ['həʊldɔːl] *n UK* fourre-tout *m inv*.

holder ['həʊldə'] *n* **1.** [for cigarette] porte-cigarettes *m inv* - **2.** [owner] détenteur *m*, -trice *f* ; [of position, title] titulaire *mf*.

holding ['həʊldɪŋ] *n* **1.** [investment] effets *mpl* en portefeuille - **2.** [farm] ferme *f*.

hold-up ['həʊldʌp] *n* **1.** [robbery] hold-up *m* - **2.** [delay] retard *m*.

hole [həʊl] *n* **1.** [gen] trou *m* - **2.** *UK inf* [predicament] pétrin *m*.

holiday ['hɒlɪdeɪ] *n* **1.** *UK* [vacation] vacances *fpl* ; **to be/go on holiday** être/partir en vacances - **2.** [public holiday] jour *m* férié.

holiday camp *n* UK camp *m* de vacances.

holidaymaker ['hɒlɪdɪ,meɪkəʳ] *n* UK vacancier *m*, -ère *f*.

holiday pay *n* UK *salaire payé pendant les vacances.*

holiday resort *n* UK lieu *m* de vacances.

holistic [həʊ'lɪstɪk] *adj* holistique.

Holland ['hɒlənd] *n* Hollande *f*.

holler ['hɒləʳ] *vi & vt inf* gueuler, brailler.

hollow ['hɒləʊ] ◇ *adj* creux (creuse) ; [eyes] cave ; [promise, victory] faux (fausse) ; [laugh] qui sonne faux. ◇ *n* creux *m*.
◈ **hollow out** *vt sep* creuser, évider.

holly ['hɒlɪ] *n* houx *m*.

holocaust ['hɒləkɔːst] *n* [destruction] destruction *f*, holocauste *m*. ◈ **Holocaust** *n* : the Holocaust l'holocauste *m*.

Holstein ['hɒlstaɪn] *esp* US = Friesian.

Holstein-Friesian [hɒlstaɪn'friːzən] *esp* UK = Friesian.

holster ['həʊlstəʳ] *n* étui *m*.

holy ['həʊlɪ] *adj* saint(e) ; [ground] sacré(e).

Holy Ghost *n* : the Holy Ghost le Saint-Esprit.

Holy Land *n* : the Holy Land la Terre sainte.

Holy Spirit *n* : the Holy Spirit le Saint-Esprit.

home [həʊm] ◇ *n* 1. [house, institution] maison *f* ; **to make one's home** s'établir, s'installer - 2. [own country] patrie *f* ; [city] ville *f* natale - 3. [one's family] foyer *m* ; **to leave home** quitter la maison - 4. *fig* [place of origin] berceau *m*. ◇ *adj* 1. [not foreign - gen] intérieur(e) ; [- product] national(e) - 2. [in one's own home - cooking] familial(e) ; [- life] de famille ; [- improvements] domestique - 3. [SPORT - game] sur son propre terrain ; [- team] qui reçoit. ◇ *adv* [to or at one's house] chez soi, à la maison.
◈ **at home** *adv* 1. [in one's house, flat] chez soi, à la maison - 2. [comfortable] à l'aise ; **at home with sthg** à l'aise dans qqch ; **to make o.s. at home** faire comme chez soi - 3. [in one's own country] chez nous.

home address *n* adresse *f* du domicile.

home brew *n (U)* [beer] bière *f* faite à la maison.

home computer *n* ordinateur *m* domestique.

Home Counties *npl* : the Home Counties *les comtés entourant Londres.*

home economics *n (U)* économie *f* domestique.

home help *n* UK aide *f* ménagère.

homeland ['həʊmlænd] *n* 1. [country of birth] patrie *f* - 2. [formerly in South Africa] homeland *m*, bantoustan *m*.

homeless ['həʊmlɪs] ◇ *adj* sans abri.
◇ *npl* : the homeless les sans-abri *mpl*.

homely ['həʊmlɪ] *adj* 1. UK [simple] simple - 2. US [unattractive] ordinaire.

homemade [,həʊm'meɪd] *adj* fait(e) (à la) maison.

Home Office *n* UK : the Home Office ≃ le ministère de l'Intérieur.

homeopath [,həʊmɪ'ɒpæθ] *n* UK homéopathe *mf*.

homeopathy [,həʊmɪ'ɒpəθɪ] *n* homéopathie *f*.

home page *n* COMPUT page *f* d'accueil.

homer *inf n* US = home run.

Home Secretary *n* UK ≃ ministre *m* de l'Intérieur.

homesick ['həʊmsɪk] *adj* qui a le mal du pays.

homeward ['həʊmwəd] ◇ *adj* de retour. ◇ *adv* vers la maison.

homewards ['həʊmwədz] *adv* = homeward.

homework ['həʊmwɜːk] *n (U)* 1. SCH devoirs *mpl* - 2. *inf* [preparation] boulot *m*.

homey, homy ['həʊmɪ] *adj* US confortable, agréable.

homicide ['hɒmɪsaɪd] *n* homicide *m*.

homoeopathy *etc* [,həʊmɪ'ɒpəθɪ] UK = homeopathy *etc*.

homogeneous [,hɒmə'dʒiːnjəs] *adj* homogène.

homosexual [,hɒmə'sekʃʊəl] ◇ *adj* homosexuel(elle). ◇ *n* homosexuel *m*, -elle *f*.

homy = homey.

hon *abbrev* of **honourable** UK, **honorable** US. *abbrev* of **honorary**.

hone [həʊn] *vt* aiguiser.

honest ['ɒnɪst] ◇ *adj* 1. [trustworthy] honnête, probe - 2. [frank] franc (franche), sincère ; **to be honest...** pour dire la vérité..., à dire vrai... - 3. [legal] légitime. ◇ *adv inf* = honestly *(sense 2).*

honestly ['ɒnɪstlɪ] ◇ *adv* 1. [truthfully] honnêtement - 2. [expressing sincerity] je vous assure. ◇ *excl* [expressing impatience, disapproval] franchement !

honesty ['ɒnɪstɪ] *n* honnêteté *f*, probité *f*.

honey ['hʌnɪ] *n* 1. [food] miel *m* - 2. [dear] chéri *m*, -e *f*.

honeycomb ['hʌnɪkəʊm] *n* gâteau *m* de miel.

honeymoon ['hʌnɪmuːn] ◇ *n lit & fig* lune *f* de miel. ◇ *vi* aller en voyage de noces, passer sa lune de miel.

honeysuckle ['hʌnɪ,sʌkl] *n* chèvrefeuille *m*.

Hong Kong [,hɒŋ'kɒŋ] *n* Hong Kong, Hongkong.

honk [hɒŋk] ⟨⟩ *vi* **1.** [motorist] klaxonner - **2.** [goose] cacarder. ⟨⟩ *vt* : **to honk the horn** klaxonner.

honor *etc US* = **honour** *etc*.

honorary [*UK* 'ɒnərəri, *US* ɒnə'reəri] *adj* honoraire.

honors *npl US* = **honours** (*sense 1*).

honour *UK*, **honor** *US* ['ɒnər] ⟨⟩ *n* honneur *m* ; **in honour of sb/sthg** en l'honneur de qqn/qqch. ⟨⟩ *vt* honorer. **honours** *npl* **1.** [tokens of respect] honneurs *mpl* - **2.** *UK* [of university degree] ≃ licence *f*.

honourable *UK*, **honorable** *US* ['ɒnrəbl] *adj* honorable.

hood [hʊd] *n* **1.** [on cloak, jacket] capuchon *m* - **2.** [of cooker] hotte *f* - **3.** [of pram, convertible car] capote *f* - **4.** *US* [car bonnet] capot *m* - **5.** *US* [gangster] gangster *m*.

hoodlum ['hu:dləm] *n inf dated* gangster *m*, truand *m*.

hoof [hu:f OR hʊf] (*pl* -**s** OR **hooves** [hu:vz]) *n* sabot *m*.

hook [hʊk] ⟨⟩ *n* **1.** [for hanging things on] crochet *m* - **2.** [for catching fish] hameçon *m* - **3.** [fastener] agrafe *f* - **4.** [of telephone] : **off the hook** décroché. ⟨⟩ *vt* **1.** [attach with hook] accrocher - **2.** [catch with hook] prendre. **hook up** *vt sep* : **to hook sthg up to sthg** connecter qqch à qqch.

hooked [hʊkt] *adj* **1.** [shaped like a hook] crochu(e) - **2.** *inf* [addicted] : **to be hooked (on)** être accro (à) ; [music, art] être mordu(e) (de).

hook(e)y ['hʊkɪ] *n US inf* **to play hookey** faire l'école buissonnière.

hooligan ['hu:lɪgən] *n* hooligan *m*, vandale *m*.

hoop [hu:p] *n* **1.** [circular band] cercle *m* - **2.** [toy] cerceau *m*.

hooray [hʊ'reɪ] = **hurray**.

hoot [hu:t] ⟨⟩ *n* **1.** [of owl] hululement *m* - **2.** *UK* [of horn] coup *m* de Klaxon® - **3.** *UK inf* [something amusing] : **to be a hoot** être tordant(e). ⟨⟩ *vi* **1.** [owl] hululer - **2.** *UK* [horn] klaxonner. ⟨⟩ *vt UK* **to hoot the horn** klaxonner.

hootch = **hooch**.

hooter ['hu:tər] *n UK* [horn] Klaxon® *m*.

Hoover® *UK* ['hu:vər] *n* aspirateur *m*. **hoover** *vt* [room] passer l'aspirateur dans ; [carpet] passer à l'aspirateur.

hooves [hu:vz] *npl* ▶ **hoof**.

hop [hɒp] ⟨⟩ *n* saut *m* ; [on one leg] saut à cloche-pied. ⟨⟩ *vi* sauter ; [on one leg] sauter à cloche-pied ; [bird] sautiller. **hops** *npl* houblon *m*.

hope [həʊp] ⟨⟩ *vi* espérer ; **to hope for sthg** espérer qqch ; **I hope so** j'espère bien ; **I hope not** j'espère bien que non. ⟨⟩ *vt* : **to hope (that)** espérer que ; **to hope to do sthg** espérer faire qqch. ⟨⟩ *n* espoir *m* ; **in the hope of** dans l'espoir de.

hopeful ['həʊpfʊl] *adj* **1.** [optimistic] plein(e) d'espoir ; **to be hopeful of doing sthg** avoir bon espoir de faire qqch ; **to be hopeful of sthg** espérer qqch - **2.** [promising] encourageant(e), qui promet.

hopefully ['həʊpfəlɪ] *adv* **1.** [in a hopeful way] avec bon espoir, avec optimisme - **2.** [with luck] : **hopefully,...** espérons que...

hopeless ['həʊplɪs] *adj* **1.** [gen] désespéré(e) ; [tears] de désespoir - **2.** *inf* [useless] nul (nulle).

hopelessly ['həʊplɪslɪ] *adv* **1.** [despairingly] avec désespoir - **2.** [completely] complètement.

horizon [hə'raɪzn] *n* horizon *m* ; **on the horizon** *lit & fig* à l'horizon.

horizontal [,hɒrɪ'zɒntl] ⟨⟩ *adj* horizontal(e). ⟨⟩ *n* : **the horizontal** l'horizontale *f*.

hormone ['hɔ:məʊn] *n* hormone *f*.

horn [hɔ:n] *n* **1.** [of animal] corne *f* - **2.** MUS [instrument] cor *m* - **3.** [on car] Klaxon® *m* ; [on ship] sirène *f*.

hornet ['hɔ:nɪt] *n* frelon *m*.

horny ['hɔ:nɪ] *adj* **1.** [hard] corné(e) ; [hand] calleux(euse) - **2.** *v inf* [sexually excited] excité(e) (sexuellement).

horoscope ['hɒrəskəʊp] *n* horoscope *m*.

horrendous [hɒ'rendəs] *adj* horrible.

horrible ['hɒrəbl] *adj* horrible.

horrid ['hɒrɪd] *adj* [unpleasant] horrible.

horrific [hɒ'rɪfɪk] *adj* horrible.

horrify ['hɒrɪfaɪ] *vt* horrifier.

horror ['hɒrər] *n* horreur *f*.

horror film *esp UK*, **horror movie** *US n* film *m* d'épouvante.

horse [hɔ:s] *n* [animal] cheval *m*.

horseback ['hɔ:sbæk] ⟨⟩ *adj* à cheval ; **horseback riding** *US* équitation *f*. ⟨⟩ *n* : **on horseback** à cheval.

horse chestnut *n* [nut] marron *m* d'Inde ; **horse chestnut (tree)** marronnier *m* d'Inde.

horseman ['hɔ:smən] (*pl* -**men** [-mən]) *n* cavalier *m*.

horsepower ['hɔ:s,paʊər] *n* puissance *f* en chevaux.

horse racing *n* (U) courses *fpl* de chevaux.

horseradish ['hɔːsˌrædɪʃ] n [plant] raifort m.

horserider ['hɔːsraɪdə] n esp US cavalier m, -ère f.

horse riding n UK équitation f.

horseshoe ['hɔːsʃuː] n fer m à cheval.

horsetrailer US = horse box.

horsewoman ['hɔːsˌwʊmən] (pl -women [-ˌwɪmɪn]) n cavalière f.

horticulture ['hɔːtɪkʌltʃər] n horticulture f.

hose [həʊz] <> n [hosepipe] tuyau m. <> vt arroser au jet.

hosepipe ['həʊzpaɪp] n = hose.

hosiery ['həʊziəri] n bonneterie f.

hospitable [hɒ'spɪtəbl] adj hospitalier(ère), accueillant(e).

hospital ['hɒspɪtl] n hôpital m.

hospitality [ˌhɒspɪ'tælətɪ] n hospitalité f.

host [həʊst] <> n **1.** [gen] hôte m - **2.** [compere] animateur m, -trice f - **3.** [large number] : **a host of** une foule de. <> vt **1.** fig [meeting] présenter, animer - **2.** [website] héberger.

hostage ['hɒstɪdʒ] n otage m.

hostel ['hɒstl] n **1.** [basic accommodation] foyer m - **2.** [youth hostel] auberge f de jeunesse.

hostess ['həʊstes] n hôtesse f.

host family n famille f d'accueil.

hostile [UK 'hɒstaɪl, US 'hɒstl] adj : hostile (to) hostile (à).

hostility [hɒ'stɪlətɪ] n [antagonism, unfriendliness] hostilité f. ◆ **hostilities** npl hostilités fpl.

hot [hɒt] adj **1.** [gen] chaud(e) ; **I'm hot** j'ai chaud ; **it's hot** il fait chaud - **2.** [spicy] épicé(e) - **3.** inf [expert] fort(e), calé(e) ; **to be hot on** OR **at sthg** être fort OR calé en qqch - **4.** [recent] de dernière heure OR minute - **5.** [temper] colérique.

hot-air balloon n montgolfière f.

hotbed ['hɒtbed] n foyer m.

hot cross bun n petit pain sucré que l'on mange le vendredi saint.

hot-desking n bureau m tournant.

hot dog n hot dog m.

hotel [həʊ'tel] n hôtel m.

hot flush UK, **hot flash** US n bouffée f de chaleur.

hotfoot ['hɒtˌfʊt] adv à toute vitesse.

hotheaded [ˌhɒt'hedɪd] adj impulsif(ive).

hothouse ['hɒthaʊs] n (pl [-haʊzɪz]) [greenhouse] serre f.

hot line n **1.** [between government heads] téléphone m rouge - **2.** [special line] hot line f, assistance f téléphonique.

hotly ['hɒtlɪ] adv **1.** [passionately] avec véhémence - **2.** [closely] de près.

hotplate ['hɒtpleɪt] n plaque f chauffante.

hot-tempered [-'tempəd] adj colérique.

hot-water bottle n bouillotte f.

hound [haʊnd] <> n [dog] chien m. <> vt **1.** [persecute] poursuivre, pourchasser - **2.** [drive] : **to hound sb out (of)** chasser qqn (de).

hour ['aʊər] n heure f ; **half an hour** une demi-heure ; **70 miles per** OR **an hour** 110 km à l'heure ; **on the hour** à l'heure juste. ◆ **hours** npl [of business] heures fpl d'ouverture.

hourly ['aʊəlɪ] <> adj **1.** [happening every hour] toutes les heures - **2.** [per hour] à l'heure. <> adv **1.** [every hour] toutes les heures - **2.** [per hour] à l'heure.

house <> n [haʊs] (pl ['haʊzɪz]) **1.** [gen] maison f ; **on the house** aux frais de la maison - **2.** POL chambre f - **3.** [in debates] assistance f - **4.** THEAT [audience] auditoire m, salle f ; **to bring the house down, to bring down the house** inf faire crouler la salle sous les applaudissements - **5.** MUS = **house music**. <> vt [haʊz] [accommodate] loger, héberger ; [department, store] abriter. <> adj [haʊs] **1.** [within business] d'entreprise ; [style] de la maison - **2.** [wine] maison (inv).

house arrest n : **under house arrest** en résidence surveillée.

houseboat ['haʊsbəʊt] n péniche f aménagée.

housebreaking ['haʊsˌbreɪkɪŋ] n (U) cambriolage m.

housecoat ['haʊskəʊt] n peignoir m.

household ['haʊshəʊld] <> adj **1.** [domestic] ménager(ère) - **2.** [word, name] connu(e) de tous. <> n maison f, ménage m.

housekeeper ['haʊsˌkiːpər] n gouvernante f.

housekeeping ['haʊsˌkiːpɪŋ] n (U) **1.** [work] ménage m - **2.** : **housekeeping (money)** argent m du ménage.

house music, house n house music f.

House of Commons n UK : **the House of Commons** la Chambre des communes.

House of Lords n UK : **the House of Lords** la Chambre des lords.

House of Representatives n US : **the House of Representatives** la Chambre des représentants.

house plant, houseplant ['haʊsplɑːnt] n plante f d'appartement.

Houses of Parliament *npl* : the Houses of Parliament le Parlement britannique *(où se réunissent la Chambre des communes et la Chambre des lords).*

housewarming (party) ['haʊs,wɔːmɪŋ-] *n* pendaison *f* de crémaillère.

housewife ['haʊswaɪf] *(pl* -**wives** [-waɪvz]*) n* femme *f* au foyer.

housework ['haʊswɜːk] *n (U)* ménage *m*.

housing ['haʊzɪŋ] *n (U)* [accommodation] logement *m*.

housing association *n* UK association *f* d'aide au logement.

housing benefit *n (U)* UK allocation *f* logement.

housing estate UK, **housing project** US *n* cité *f*.

hovel ['hɒvl] *n* masure *f*, taudis *m*.

hover ['hɒvər] *vi* [fly] planer.

hovercraft ['hɒvəkrɑːft] *(pl* hovercraft OR -s*) n* aéroglisseur *m*, hovercraft *m*.

how [haʊ] *adv* **1.** [gen] comment ; **how do you do it?** comment fait-on ? ; **how are you?** comment allez-vous? ; **how do you do?** enchanté(e) (de faire votre connaissance) - **2.** [referring to degree, amount] : **how high is it?** combien cela fait-il de haut?, quelle en est la hauteur? ; **how long have you been waiting?** cela fait combien de temps que vous attendez? ; **how many people came?** combien de personnes sont venues? ; **how old are you?** quel âge as-tu? - **3.** [in exclamations] : **how nice!** que c'est bien! ; **how awful!** quelle horreur! ◆ **how about** *adv* : **how about a drink?** si on prenait un verre? ; **how about you?** et toi? ◆ **how much** ◇ *pron* combien ; **how much does it cost?** combien ça coûte? ◇ *adj* combien de ; **how much bread?** combien de pain?

however [haʊ'evər] ◇ *adv* **1.** [nevertheless] cependant, toutefois - **2.** [no matter how] quelque... que (+ *subjunctive)*, si... que (+ *subjunctive)* ; **however many/much** peu importe la quantité de - **3.** [how] comment. ◇ *conj* [in whatever way] de quelque manière que (+ *subjunctive)*.

howl [haʊl] ◇ *n* hurlement *m* ; [of laughter] éclat *m*. ◇ *vi* hurler ; [with laughter] rire aux éclats.

hp *(abbrev of* horsepower*) n* CV *m*.

HP *n* **1.** UK *(abbrev of* hire purchase*)* **to buy sthg on HP** acheter qqch à crédit - **2.** = **hp**.

HQ *(abbrev of* headquarters*) n* QG *m*.

hr *(abbrev of* hour*)* h.

hub [hʌb] *n* **1.** [of wheel] moyeu *m* - **2.** [of activity] centre *m*.

hubbub ['hʌbʌb] *n* vacarme *m*, brouhaha *m*.

hubcap ['hʌbkæp] *n* enjoliveur *m*.

huddle ['hʌdl] ◇ *vi* se blottir. ◇ *n* petit groupe *m*.

hue [hjuː] *n* [colour] teinte *f*, nuance *f*.

huff [hʌf] *n* : **in a huff** froissé(e).

hug [hʌg] ◇ *n* étreinte *f* ; **to give sb a hug** serrer qqn dans ses bras. ◇ *vt* **1.** [embrace] étreindre, serrer dans ses bras - **2.** [hold] tenir - **3.** [stay close to] serrer.

huge [hjuːdʒ] *adj* énorme ; [subject] vaste ; [success] fou (folle).

hulk [hʌlk] *n* **1.** [of ship] carcasse *f* - **2.** [person] malabar *m*, mastodonte *m*.

hull [hʌl] *n* coque *f*.

hullo [hə'ləʊ] *excl* UK = **hello**.

hum [hʌm] ◇ *vi* **1.** [buzz] bourdonner ; [machine] vrombir, ronfler - **2.** [sing] fredonner, chantonner - **3.** [be busy] être en pleine activité. ◇ *vt* fredonner, chantonner.

human ['hjuːmən] ◇ *adj* humain(e). ◇ *n* : **human (being)** être *m* humain.

humane [hjuː'meɪn] *adj* humain(e).

Human Genome Project *n* : the Human Genome Project le projet génome humain.

humanitarian [hjuː,mænɪ'teərɪən] *adj* humanitaire.

humanity [hjuː'mænɪtɪ] *n* humanité *f*. ◆ **humanities** *npl* : the humanities les humanités *fpl*, les sciences *fpl* humaines.

human race *n* : the human race la race humaine.

human rights *npl* droits *mpl* de l'homme.

humble ['hʌmbl] ◇ *adj* humble ; [origins, employee] modeste. ◇ *vt* humilier.

humbug ['hʌmbʌg] *n* **1.** *dated* [hypocrisy] hypocrisie *f* - **2.** UK [sweet] *type de bonbon dur.*

humdrum ['hʌmdrʌm] *adj* monotone.

humid ['hjuːmɪd] *adj* humide.

humidity [hjuː'mɪdɪtɪ] *n* humidité *f*.

humiliate [hjuː'mɪlɪeɪt] *vt* humilier.

humiliation [hjuː,mɪlɪ'eɪʃn] *n* humiliation *f*.

humility [hjuː'mɪlɪtɪ] *n* humilité *f*.

humor US = **humour**.

humorous ['hjuːmərəs] *adj* humoristique ; [person] plein(e) d'humour.

humour UK, **humor** US ['hjuːmə] ◇ *n* **1.** [sense of fun] humour *m* - **2.** [of situation, remark] côté *m* comique - **3.** *dated* [mood] humeur *f*. ◇ *vt* se montrer conciliant(e) envers.

hump [hʌmp] *n* bosse *f*.

humpbacked bridge UK, **humpback bridge** ['hʌmpbækt-] *n* pont *m* en dos d'âne.

hunch [hʌntʃ] *n inf* pressentiment *m*, intuition *f*.

hunchback ['hʌntʃbæk] n bossu m, -e f.

hunched [hʌntʃt] adj voûté(e).

hundred ['hʌndrəd] num cent ; **a** OR **one hundred** cent ; see also **six**. ➡ **hundreds** npl des centaines.

hundredth ['hʌndrətθ] num centième ; see also **sixth**.

hundredweight ['hʌndrədweɪt] n [in UK] poids m de 112 livres = 50,8 kg ; [in US] poids m de 100 livres = 45,3 kg.

hung [hʌŋ] pt & pp ➡ hang.

Hungarian [hʌŋ'geərɪən] ◇ adj hongrois(e). ◇ n 1. [person] Hongrois m, -e f - 2. [language] hongrois m.

Hungary ['hʌŋgərɪ] n Hongrie f.

hunger ['hʌŋgər] n 1. [gen] faim f - 2. [strong desire] soif f. ➡ **hunger after**, **hunger for** vt insep fig avoir faim de, avoir soif de.

hunger strike n grève f de la faim.

hung over adj inf **to be hung over** avoir la gueule de bois.

hungry ['hʌŋgrɪ] adj 1. [for food] : **to be hungry** avoir faim ; [starving] être affamé(e) ; avoir envie de - 2. [eager] : **to be hungry for sthg** être avide de.

hung up adj inf **to be hung up (on** OR **about)** être obsédé(e) (par).

hunk [hʌŋk] n 1. [large piece] gros morceau m - 2. inf [man] beau mec m.

hunt [hʌnt] ◇ n chasse f ; [for missing person] recherches fpl. ◇ vi 1. [chase animals, birds] chasser - 2. UK [chase foxes] chasser le renard - 3. [search] : **to hunt (for sthg)** chercher partout (qqch). ◇ vt 1. [animals, birds] chasser - 2. [person] poursuivre, pourchasser.

hunter ['hʌntər] n [of animals, birds] chasseur m, -euse f.

hunting ['hʌntɪŋ] n 1. [of animals] chasse f - 2. UK [of foxes] chasse f au renard.

hurdle ['hɜːdl] ◇ n 1. [in race] haie f - 2. [obstacle] obstacle m. ◇ vt [jump over] sauter.

hurl [hɜːl] vt 1. [throw] lancer avec violence - 2. [shout] lancer.

hurray [hʊ'reɪ] excl hourra !

hurricane ['hʌrɪkən] n ouragan m.

hurried ['hʌrɪd] adj [hasty] précipité(e).

hurriedly ['hʌrɪdlɪ] adv précipitamment ; [eat, write] vite, en toute hâte.

hurry ['hʌrɪ] ◇ vt [person] faire se dépêcher ; [process] hâter ; **to hurry to do sthg** se dépêcher OR se presser de faire qqch. ◇ vi se dépêcher, se presser. ◇ n hâte f, précipitation f ; **to be in a hurry** être pressé ; **to do sthg in a hurry** faire qqch à la hâte. ➡ **hurry up** vi se dépêcher.

hurt [hɜːt] ◇ vt (pt & pp hurt) 1. [physically, emotionally] blesser ; [one's leg, arm] se faire mal à ; **to hurt o.s.** se faire mal - 2. fig [harm] faire du mal à. ◇ vi (pt & pp hurt) 1. [gen] faire mal ; **my leg hurts** ma jambe me fait mal - 2. fig [do harm] faire du mal. ◇ adj blessé(e) ; [voice] offensé(e).

hurtful ['hɜːtfʊl] adj blessant(e).

hurtle ['hɜːtl] vi aller à toute allure.

husband ['hʌzbənd] n mari m.

hush [hʌʃ] ◇ n silence m. ◇ excl silence !, chut !

husk [hʌsk] n [of seed, grain] enveloppe f.

husky ['hʌskɪ] ◇ adj [hoarse] rauque. ◇ n husky m.

hustle ['hʌsl] ◇ vt [hurry] pousser, bousculer. ◇ n agitation f.

hut [hʌt] n 1. [rough house] hutte f - 2. [shed] cabane f.

hutch [hʌtʃ] n clapier m.

hyacinth ['haɪəsɪnθ] n jacinthe f.

hydrant ['haɪdrənt] n bouche f d'incendie.

hydraulic [haɪ'drɔːlɪk] adj hydraulique.

hydroelectric [ˌhaɪdrəʊɪ'lektrɪk] adj hydro-électrique.

hydrofoil ['haɪdrəfɔɪl] n hydroptère m.

hydrogen ['haɪdrədʒən] n hydrogène m.

hyena [haɪ'iːnə] n hyène f.

hygiene ['haɪdʒiːn] n hygiène f.

hygienic [haɪ'dʒiːnɪk] adj hygiénique.

hymn [hɪm] n hymne m, cantique m.

hype [haɪp] inf ◇ n (U) battage m publicitaire. ◇ vt faire un battage publicitaire autour de.

hyperactive [ˌhaɪpər'æktɪv] adj hyperactif(ive).

hypermarket ['haɪpə,mɑːkɪt] n esp UK hypermarché m.

hyphen ['haɪfn] n trait m d'union.

hypnosis [hɪp'nəʊsɪs] n hypnose f.

hypnotic [hɪp'nɒtɪk] adj hypnotique.

hypnotize, UK **-ise** ['hɪpnətaɪz] vt hypnotiser.

hypocrisy [hɪ'pɒkrəsɪ] n hypocrisie f.

hypocrite ['hɪpəkrɪt] n hypocrite mf.

hypocritical [ˌhɪpə'krɪtɪkl] adj hypocrite.

hypothesis [haɪ'pɒθɪsɪs] (pl -theses [-θɪsiːz]) n hypothèse f.

hypothetical [ˌhaɪpə'θetɪkl] adj hypothétique.

hysteria [hɪs'tɪərɪə] n hystérie f.

hysterical [hɪs'terɪkl] adj 1. [gen] hystérique - 2. inf [very funny] désopilant(e).

hysterics [hɪs'terɪks] npl 1. [panic, excitement] crise f de nerfs - 2. inf [laughter] fou rire m.

i [aɪ] (pl **i's** OR **is**), **I** (pl **I's** OR **Is**) n [letter] i m inv, I m inv.

I [aɪ] pers pron **1.** (unstressed) je, j' (before vowel or silent 'h') ; **he and I are leaving for Paris** lui et moi (nous) partons pour Paris - **2.** (stressed) moi ; **I can't do it** moi je ne peux pas le faire.

ice [aɪs] <> n **1.** [frozen water, ice cream] glace f - **2.** (U) [on road] verglas m - **3.** (U) [ice cubes] glaçons mpl. <> vt CULIN glacer.
◆ **ice over, ice up** vi [lake, pond] geler ; [window, windscreen] givrer ; [road] se couvrir de verglas.

iceberg ['aɪsbɜːg] n iceberg m.

iceberg lettuce n laitue f iceberg.

icebox ['aɪsbɒks] n **1.** UK [in refrigerator] freezer m - **2.** US dated [refrigerator] réfrigérateur m.

ice cream n glace f.

ice cube n glaçon m.

ice hockey n UK hockey m sur glace.

Iceland ['aɪslənd] n Islande f.

Icelandic [aɪs'lændɪk] <> adj islandais(e). <> n [language] islandais m.

ice lolly n UK sucette f glacée.

ice pick n pic m à glace.

ice rink n patinoire f.

ice skate n patin m à glace. ◆ **ice-skate**, **ice skate** vi faire du patin (à glace).

ice-skating, ice skating n patinage m (sur glace).

icicle ['aɪsɪkl] n glaçon m (naturel).

icing ['aɪsɪŋ] n (U) glaçage m, glace f.

icing sugar n UK sucre m glace.

icon ['aɪkɒn] n [gen & COMPUT] icône f.

icy ['aɪsɪ] adj **1.** [weather, manner] glacial(e) - **2.** [covered in ice] verglacé(e).

ID n (U) (abbrev of **identification**) papiers mpl.

I'd [aɪd] = I would, = I had.

idea [aɪ'dɪə] n idée f ; [intention] intention f ; **to have an idea (that)...** avoir idée que... ; **to have no idea** n'avoir aucune idée ; **to get the idea** inf piger.

ideal [aɪ'dɪəl] <> adj idéal(e). <> n idéal m.

ideally [aɪ'dɪəlɪ] adv idéalement ; [suited] parfaitement.

identical [aɪ'dentɪkl] adj identique.

identification [aɪ,dentɪfɪ'keɪʃn] n (U) **1.** [gen] : **identification (with)** identification f (à) - **2.** [documentation] pièce f d'identité.

identification parade n UK séance d'identification d'un suspect dans un échantillon de plusieurs personnes.

identify [aɪ'dentɪfaɪ] <> vt **1.** [recognize] identifier - **2.** [subj: document, card] permettre de reconnaître - **3.** [associate] : **to identify sb with sthg** associer qqn à qqch. <> vi [empathize] : **to identify with** s'identifier à.

Identikit® picture [aɪ'dentɪkɪt-] n portrait-robot m.

identity [aɪ'dentətɪ] n identité f.

identity card n carte f d'identité.

ideology [,aɪdɪ'ɒlədʒɪ] n idéologie f.

idiom ['ɪdɪəm] n **1.** [phrase] expression f idiomatique - **2.** fml [style] langue f.

idiomatic [,ɪdɪə'mætɪk] adj idiomatique.

idiosyncrasy [,ɪdɪə'sɪŋkrəsɪ] n particularité f, caractéristique f.

idiot ['ɪdɪət] n idiot m, -e f, imbécile mf.

idiotic [,ɪdɪ'ɒtɪk] adj idiot(e).

idle ['aɪdl] <> adj **1.** [lazy] oisif(ive), désœuvré(e) - **2.** [not working - machine, factory] arrêté(e) ; [- worker] qui chôme, en chômage - **3.** [threat] vain(e) - **4.** [curiosity] simple, pur(e). <> vi tourner au ralenti.
◆ **idle away** vt sep [time] perdre à ne rien faire.

idol ['aɪdl] n idole f.

idolize, UK **-ise** ['aɪdəlaɪz] vt idolâtrer, adorer.

idyllic [ɪ'dɪlɪk] adj idyllique.

i.e. (abbrev of **id est**) c-à-d.

if [ɪf] conj **1.** [gen] si ; **if I were you** à ta place, si j'étais toi - **2.** [though] bien que. ◆ **if anything** adv plutôt ; **he doesn't look any slimmer, if anything, he's put on weight** il n'a pas l'air plus mince, il a même plutôt grossi. ◆ **if not** conj sinon. ◆ **if only** <> conj **1.** [naming a reason] ne serait-ce que - **2.** [expressing regret] si seulement. <> excl si seulement!

igloo ['ɪgluː] (pl **-s**) n igloo m, iglou m.

ignite [ɪg'naɪt] <> vt mettre le feu à, enflammer ; [firework] tirer. <> vi prendre feu, s'enflammer.

ignition [ɪg'nɪʃn] n **1.** [act of igniting] ignition f - **2.** AUT allumage m ; **to switch on the ignition** mettre le contact.

ignition key n clef f de contact.

ignorance ['ɪgnərəns] n ignorance f.

ignorant ['ɪgnərənt] adj **1.** [uneducated, unaware] ignorant(e) ; **to be ignorant of sthg** être ignorant de qqch - **2.** [rude] mal élevé(e).

ignore [ɪg'nɔːr] *vt* [advice, facts] ne pas tenir compte de ; [person] faire semblant de ne pas voir.

ilk [ɪlk] *n* : **of that ilk** [of that sort] de cet acabit, de ce genre.

ill [ɪl] <> *adj* **1.** [unwell] malade ; **to feel ill** se sentir malade OR souffrant ; **to be taken ill** *esp UK*, **to fall ill** tomber malade - **2.** [bad] mauvais(e) ; **ill luck** malchance *f*. <> *adv* mal ; **to speak/think ill of sb** dire/penser du mal de qqn.

I'll [aɪl] = **I will**, = **I shall**.

ill-advised [-əd'vaɪzd] *adj fml* [remark, action] peu judicieux(euse) ; [person] mala-visé(e).

ill at ease *adj* mal à l'aise.

illegal [ɪ'liːgl] *adj* illégal(e) ; [immigrant] en situation irrégulière.

illegible [ɪ'ledʒəbl] *adj* illisible.

illegitimate [,ɪlɪ'dʒɪtɪmət] *adj* illégitime.

ill-equipped [-ɪ'kwɪpt] *adj* : **to be ill-equipped to do sthg** être mal placé(e) pour faire qqch.

ill-fated [-'feɪtɪd] *adj* fatal(e), funeste.

ill feeling *n* animosité *f*.

ill health *n* mauvaise santé *f*.

illicit [ɪ'lɪsɪt] *adj* illicite.

illiteracy [ɪ'lɪtərəsɪ] *n* analphabétisme *m*, illettrisme *m*.

illiterate [ɪ'lɪtərət] <> *adj* analphabète, illettré(e). <> *n* analphabète *mf*, illettré *m*, -e *f*.

illness ['ɪlnɪs] *n* maladie *f*.

illogical [ɪ'lɒdʒɪkl] *adj* illogique.

ill-suited *adj* mal assorti(e) ; **to be ill-suited for sthg** être inapte à qqch.

ill-timed [-'taɪmd] *adj* déplacé(e), mal à propos.

ill-treat *vt* maltraiter.

illuminate [ɪ'luːmɪneɪt] *vt* éclairer.

illumination [ɪ,luːmɪ'neɪʃn] *n fml* [lighting] éclairage *m*. ◆ **illuminations** *npl UK* illuminations *fpl*.

illusion [ɪ'luːʒn] *n* illusion *f* ; **to have no illusions about** ne se faire OR n'avoir aucune illusion sur ; **to be under the illusion that** croire OR s'imaginer que, avoir l'illusion que.

illustrate ['ɪləstreɪt] *vt* illustrer.

illustration [,ɪlə'streɪʃn] *n* illustration *f*.

illustrious [ɪ'lʌstrɪəs] *adj* illustre, célèbre.

ill will *n* animosité *f*.

I'm [aɪm] = **I am**.

image ['ɪmɪdʒ] *n* **1.** [gen] image *f* - **2.** [of company, politician] image *f* de marque.

imagery ['ɪmɪdʒrɪ] *n* (U) images *fpl*.

imaginary [ɪ'mædʒɪnrɪ] *adj* imaginaire.

imagination [ɪ,mædʒɪ'neɪʃn] *n* **1.** [ability] imagination *f* - **2.** [fantasy] invention *f*.

imaginative [ɪ'mædʒɪnətɪv] *adj* imagi-natif(ive) ; [solution] plein(e) d'imagination.

imagine [ɪ'mædʒɪn] *vt* imaginer ; **to imagine doing sthg** s'imaginer OR se voir faisant qqch ; **imagine (that)!** tu t'imagines!

imam [ɪ'mɑːm] *n* imam *m*.

imbalance [,ɪm'bæləns] *n* déséquilibre *m*.

imbecile ['ɪmbɪsiːl] *n* imbécile *mf*, idiot *m*, -e *f*.

IMF (*abbrev of* **International Monetary Fund**) *n* FMI *m*.

IMHO (*abbrev of* **in my humble opinion**) *adv inf* à mon humble avis.

imitate ['ɪmɪteɪt] *vt* imiter.

imitation [,ɪmɪ'teɪʃn] <> *n* imitation *f*. <> *adj* [leather] imitation (*before n*) ; [jewellery] en toc.

immaculate [ɪ'mækjʊlət] *adj* impeccable.

immaterial [,ɪmə'tɪərɪəl] *adj* [unimportant] sans importance.

immature [,ɪmə'tjʊər] *adj* **1.** [lacking judg-ment] qui manque de maturité - **2.** [not fully grown] jeune, immature.

immediate [ɪ'miːdjət] *adj* **1.** [urgent] immédiat(e) ; [problem, meeting] urgent(e) - **2.** [very near] immédiat(e) ; [family] le plus proche.

immediately [ɪ'miːdjətlɪ] <> *adv* **1.** [at once] immédiatement - **2.** [directly] direc-tement. <> *conj* dès que.

immense [ɪ'mens] *adj* immense ; [improve-ment, change] énorme.

immerse [ɪ'mɜːs] *vt* : **to immerse sthg in sthg** immerger OR plonger qqch dans qqch ; **to immerse o.s. in sthg** *fig* se plonger dans qqch.

immersion heater [ɪ'mɜːʃn-] *n UK* chauf-fe-eau *m* électrique.

immigrant ['ɪmɪgrənt] *n* immigré *m*, -e *f*.

immigration [,ɪmɪ'greɪʃn] *n* immigration *f*.

imminent ['ɪmɪnənt] *adj* imminent(e).

immobilize, *UK* **-ise** [ɪ'məʊbɪlaɪz] *vt* im-mobiliser.

immobilizer [ɪ'məʊbɪlaɪzər] *n AUT* système *m* antidémarrage.

immoral [ɪ'mɒrəl] *adj* immoral(e).

immortal [ɪ'mɔːtl] <> *adj* immortel(elle). <> *n* immortel *m*, -elle *f*.

immortalize, *UK* **-ise** [ɪ'mɔːtəlaɪz] *vt* im-mortaliser.

immune [ɪ'mjuːn] *adj* **1.** MED : **immune (to)** immunisé(e) (contre) - **2.** *fig* [protected] : **to be immune to** OR **from** être à l'abri de.

immunity [ɪˈmjuːnətɪ] *n* **1.** MED : **immunity (to)** immunité *f* (contre) - **2.** *fig* [protection] : **immunity to** OR **from** immunité *f* contre.

immunize, *UK* **-ise** [ˈɪmjuːnaɪz] *vt* : to **immunize sb (against)** immuniser qqn (contre).

imp [ɪmp] *n* **1.** [creature] lutin *m* - **2.** [naughty child] petit diable *m*, coquin *m*, -e *f*.

impact <> *n* [ˈɪmpækt] impact *m* ; to **make an impact on** OR **upon sb** faire une forte impression sur qqn ; to **make an impact on** OR **upon sthg** avoir un impact sur qqch. <> *vt* [ɪmˈpækt] **1.** [collide with] entrer en collision avec - **2.** [influence] avoir un impact sur.

impair [ɪmˈpeər] *vt* affaiblir, abîmer ; [efficiency] réduire.

impart [ɪmˈpɑːt] *vt fml* **1.** [information] : to **impart sthg (to sb)** communiquer OR transmettre qqch (à qqn) - **2.** [feeling, quality] : to **impart sthg (to)** donner qqch (à).

impartial [ɪmˈpɑːʃl] *adj* impartial(e).

impassable [ɪmˈpɑːsəbl] *adj* impraticable.

impassive [ɪmˈpæsɪv] *adj* impassible.

impatience [ɪmˈpeɪʃns] *n* **1.** [gen] impatience *f* - **2.** [irritability] irritation *f*.

impatient [ɪmˈpeɪʃnt] *adj* **1.** [gen] impatient(e) ; to **be impatient to do sthg** être impatient de faire qqch ; to **be impatient for sthg** attendre qqch avec impatience - **2.** [irritable] : to **become** OR **get impatient** s'impatienter.

impeccable [ɪmˈpekəbl] *adj* impeccable.

impede [ɪmˈpiːd] *vt* entraver, empêcher ; [person] gêner.

impediment [ɪmˈpedɪmənt] *n* **1.** [obstacle] obstacle *m* - **2.** [disability] défaut *m*.

impel [ɪmˈpel] *vt* : to **impel sb to do sthg** inciter qqn à faire qqch.

impending [ɪmˈpendɪŋ] *adj* imminent(e).

imperative [ɪmˈperətɪv] <> *adj* [essential] impératif(ive), essentiel(elle). <> *n* impératif *m*.

imperfect [ɪmˈpɜːfɪkt] <> *adj* imparfait(e). <> *n* GRAM : **imperfect (tense)** imparfait *m*.

imperial [ɪmˈpɪərɪəl] *adj* **1.** [of empire] impérial(e) - **2.** [system of measurement] *qui a cours légal dans le Royaume-Uni.*

imperil [ɪmˈperɪl] (*UK & US*) *vt* mettre en péril OR en danger ; [project] compromettre.

impersonal [ɪmˈpɜːsnl] *adj* impersonnel(elle).

impersonate [ɪmˈpɜːsəneɪt] *vt* se faire passer pour.

impersonation [ɪmˌpɜːsəˈneɪʃn] *n* usurpation *f* d'identité ; [by mimic] imitation *f*.

impertinent [ɪmˈpɜːtɪnənt] *adj* impertinent(e).

impervious [ɪmˈpɜːvjəs] *adj* [not influenced] : **impervious to** indifférent(e) à.

impetuous [ɪmˈpetʃʊəs] *adj* impétueux(euse).

impetus [ˈɪmpɪtəs] *n* (*U*) **1.** [momentum] élan *m* - **2.** [stimulus] impulsion *f*.

impinge [ɪmˈpɪndʒ] *vi* : to **impinge on sb/sthg** affecter qqn/qqch.

implant <> *n* [ˈɪmplɑːnt] implant *m*. <> *vt* [ɪmˈplɑːnt] : to **implant sthg in** OR **into sb** implanter qqch dans qqn.

implausible [ɪmˈplɔːzəbl] *adj* peu plausible.

implement <> *n* [ˈɪmplɪmənt] outil *m*, instrument *m*. <> *vt* [ˈɪmplɪment] exécuter, appliquer.

implication [ˌɪmplɪˈkeɪʃn] *n* implication *f* ; **by implication** par voie de conséquence.

implicit [ɪmˈplɪsɪt] *adj* **1.** [inferred] implicite - **2.** [belief, faith] absolu(e).

implore [ɪmˈplɔːʳ] *vt* : to **implore sb (to do sthg)** implorer qqn (de faire qqch).

imply [ɪmˈplaɪ] *vt* **1.** [suggest] sous-entendre, laisser supposer OR entendre - **2.** [involve] impliquer.

impolite [ˌɪmpəˈlaɪt] *adj* impoli(e).

import <> *n* [ˈɪmpɔːt] [product, action] importation *f*. <> *vt* [ɪmˈpɔːt] [gen & COMPUT] importer.

importance [ɪmˈpɔːtns] *n* importance *f*.

important [ɪmˈpɔːtnt] *adj* important(e) ; to **be important to sb** importer à qqn.

importer [ɪmˈpɔːtər] *n* importateur *m*, -trice *f*.

impose [ɪmˈpəʊz] <> *vt* [force] : to **impose sthg (on)** imposer qqch (à). <> *vi* [cause trouble] : to **impose (on sb)** abuser (de la gentillesse de qqn).

imposing [ɪmˈpəʊzɪŋ] *adj* imposant(e).

imposition [ˌɪmpəˈzɪʃn] *n* **1.** [of tax, limitations etc] imposition *f* - **2.** [cause of trouble] : **it's an imposition** c'est abuser de ma/notre gentillesse.

impossible [ɪmˈpɒsəbl] *adj* impossible.

impostor, **imposter** [ɪmˈpɒstəʳ] *n* imposteur *m*.

impotent [ˈɪmpətənt] *adj* impuissant(e).

impound [ɪmˈpaʊnd] *vt* confisquer.

impoverished [ɪmˈpɒvərɪʃt] *adj* appauvri(e).

impractical [ɪmˈpræktɪkl] *adj* pas pratique.

impregnable [ɪmˈpregnəbl] *adj* **1.** [fortress, defences] imprenable - **2.** *fig* [person] inattaquable.

impregnate [ˈɪmpregneɪt] *vt* **1.** [introduce

substance into] : **to impregnate sthg with** imprégner qqch de - **2.** *fml* [fertilize] féconder.

impress [ɪmˈpres] *vt* **1.** [person] impressionner - **2.** [stress] : **to impress sthg on sb** faire bien comprendre qqch à qqn.

impression [ɪmˈpreʃn] *n* **1.** [gen] impression *f* ; **to be under the impression (that)...** avoir l'impression que... ; **to make an impression** faire impression - **2.** [impersonation] imitation *f* - **3.** [of stamp, book] impression *f*, empreinte *f*.

impressive [ɪmˈpresɪv] *adj* impressionnant(e).

imprint [ˈɪmprɪnt] *n* **1.** [mark] empreinte *f* - **2.** [publisher's name] nom *m* de l'éditeur.

imprison [ɪmˈprɪzn] *vt* emprisonner.

improbable [ɪmˈprɒbəbl] *adj* [story, excuse] improbable.

impromptu [ɪmˈprɒmptjuː] *adj* impromptu(e).

improper [ɪmˈprɒpəʳ] *adj* **1.** [unsuitable] impropre - **2.** [incorrect, illegal] incorrect(e) - **3.** [rude] indécent(e).

improve [ɪmˈpruːv] ⋄ *vi* s'améliorer ; [patient] aller mieux ; **to improve on** OR **upon** sthg améliorer qqch. ⋄ *vt* améliorer.

improvement [ɪmˈpruːvmənt] *n* : improvement **(on/in)** amélioration *f* (par rapport à/de).

improvise [ˈɪmprəvaɪz] *vt & vi* improviser.

impudent [ˈɪmpjʊdənt] *adj* impudent(e).

impulse [ˈɪmpʌls] *n* impulsion *f* ; **on impulse** par impulsion.

impulsive [ɪmˈpʌlsɪv] *adj* impulsif(ive).

impunity [ɪmˈpjuːnətɪ] *n* : **with impunity** avec impunité.

impurity [ɪmˈpjʊərətɪ] *n* impureté *f*.

in [ɪn] ⋄ *prep* **1.** [indicating place, position] dans ; **in a box/bag/drawer** dans une boîte/un sac/un tiroir ; **in Paris** à Paris ; **in Belgium** en Belgique ; **in Canada** au Canada ; **in the United States** aux États-Unis ; **in the country** à la campagne ; **to be in hospital** *UK*, **to be in the hospital** *US* être à l'hôpital ; **in here** ici ; **in there** là - **2.** [wearing] en ; **dressed in a suit** vêtu d'un costume - **3.** [at a particular time, season] : **in 2004** en 2004 ; **in April** en avril ; **in (the) spring** au printemps ; **in (the) winter** en hiver ; **at two o'clock in the afternoon** à deux heures de l'après-midi - **4.** [period of time - within] en ; [- after] dans ; **he learned to type in two weeks** il a appris à taper à la machine en deux semaines ; **I'll be ready in five minutes** je serai prêt dans 5 minutes - **5.** [during] : **it's my first decent meal in weeks** c'est mon premier repas correct depuis des semaines - **6.** [indicating situation, circumstances] : **in the sun** au soleil ; **in the rain** sous la pluie ; **to live/die in poverty** vivre/mourir dans la misère ; **in danger/difficulty** en danger/difficulté - **7.** [indicating manner, condition] : **in a loud/soft voice** d'une voix forte/douce ; **to write in pencil/ink** écrire au crayon/à l'encre ; **to speak in English/French** parler (en) anglais/français - **8.** [indicating cause] : **in anger** sous le coup de la colère - **9.** [specifying area of activity] dans ; **he's in computers** il est dans l'informatique - **10.** [referring to quantity, numbers, age] : **in large/small quantities** en grande/petite quantité ; **in (their) thousands** par milliers ; **she's in her sixties** elle a la soixantaine - **11.** [describing arrangement] : **in twos** par deux ; **in a line/row/circle** en ligne/rang/cercle - **12.** [as regards] : **to be three metres in length/width** faire trois mètres de long/large ; **a change in direction** un changement de direction - **13.** [in ratios] : **5 pence in the pound** *UK* 5 pence par livre sterling ; **one in ten** un sur dix - **14.** *(after superl)* de ; **the longest river in the world** le fleuve le plus long du monde - **15.** *(+ present participle)* **in doing sthg** en faisant qqch. ⋄ *adv* **1.** [inside] dedans, à l'intérieur - **2.** [at home, work] à la maison ; **I'm staying in tonight** je reste à la maison OR chez moi ce soir ; **is Judith in?** est-ce que Judith est là? - **3.** [arrived] : **to be in** être arrivé - **4.** [of tide] : **the tide's in** c'est la marée haute ; **we're in for some bad weather** nous allons avoir du mauvais temps ; **you're in for a shock** tu vas avoir un choc. ⋄ *adj* **1.** SPORT [within area of court] : **the umpire said that the ball was in** l'arbitre a dit que la balle était bonne - **2.** *inf* à la mode. ◆ **ins** *npl* : **the ins and outs** les tenants et les aboutissants *mpl*. ◆ **in all** *adv* en tout ; **there are 30 in all** il y en a 30 en tout. ◆ **in between** ⋄ *adv* **1.** [in intermediate position] : **a row of bushes with little clumps of flowers in between** une rangée d'arbustes séparés par des petites touffes de fleurs ; **she either plays very well or very badly, never in between** elle joue très bien ou très mal, jamais entre les deux - **2.** [in time] entre-temps, dans l'intervalle. ⋄ *prep* entre.

in. *abbrev of* **inch**.

inability [ˌɪnəˈbɪlətɪ] *n* : **inability (to do sthg)** incapacité *f* (à faire qqch).

inaccessible [ˌɪnəkˈsesəbl] *adj* inaccessible.

inaccurate [ɪnˈækjʊrət] *adj* inexact(e).

inadequate [ɪnˈædɪkwət] *adj* insuffisant(e).

inadvertently [ˌɪnədˈvɜːtəntlɪ] *adv* par inadvertance.

inadvisable [ˌɪnədˈvaɪzəbl] *adj* déconseillé(e).

inane [ɪ'neɪn] *adj* inepte ; [person] stupide.

inanimate [ɪn'ænɪmət] *adj* inanimé(e).

inappropriate [ɪnə'prəʊprɪət] *adj* inopportun(e) ; [expression, word] impropre ; [clothing] peu approprié(e).

inarticulate [ˌɪnɑː'tɪkjʊlət] *adj* inarticulé(e), indistinct(e) ; [person] qui s'exprime avec difficulté ; [explanation] mal exprimé(e).

inasmuch [ˌɪnəz'mʌtʃ] ➡ **inasmuch as** *conj fml* attendu que.

inaudible [ɪ'nɔːdɪbl] *adj* inaudible.

inaugural [ɪ'nɔːgjʊrəl] *adj* inaugural(e).

inauguration [ɪˌnɔːgjʊ'reɪʃn] *n* [of leader, president] investiture *f* ; [of building, system] inauguration *f*.

in-basket, *US* **in-box** = in-tray.

in-between *adj* intermédiaire.

inborn [ˌɪn'bɔːn] *adj* inné(e).

inbound ['ɪnbaʊnd] *adj* qui arrive.

inbox ['ɪnbɒks] *n* COMPUT boîte *f* de réception.

inbred [ˌɪn'bred] *adj* **1.** [closely related] consanguin(e) ; [animal] croisé(e) - **2.** [inborn] inné(e).

inbuilt [ˌɪn'bɪlt] *adj* UK [inborn] inné(e).

inc. (*abbrev of* **inclusive**) : **12-15 April inc.** du 12 au 15 avril inclus.

Inc. [ɪŋk] (*abbrev of* **incorporated**) *US* ≃ SARL.

incapable [ɪn'keɪpəbl] *adj* incapable ; **to be incapable of sthg/of doing sthg** être incapable de qqch/de faire qqch.

incapacitated [ˌɪnkə'pæsɪteɪtɪd] *adj* inapte physiquement ; **incapacitated for work** mis(e) dans l'incapacité de travailler.

incarcerate [ɪn'kɑːsəreɪt] *vt* incarcérer.

incendiary device [ɪn'sendjərɪ-] *n* dispositif *m* incendiaire.

incense ⬥ *n* ['ɪnsens] encens *m*. ⬥ *vt* [ɪn'sens] [anger] mettre en colère.

incentive [ɪn'sentɪv] *n* **1.** [encouragement] motivation *f* - **2.** COMM récompense *f*, prime *f*.

incentive program *US*, **incentive scheme** *UK n* programme *m* d'encouragement.

incentivize [ɪn'sentɪvaɪz] *vt* motiver.

inception [ɪn'sepʃn] *n fml* commencement *m*.

incessant [ɪn'sesnt] *adj* incessant(e).

incessantly [ɪn'sesntlɪ] *adv* sans cesse.

incest ['ɪnsest] *n* inceste *m*.

inch [ɪntʃ] ⬥ *n* = 2,5 cm, ≃ pouce *m*. ⬥ *vi* : **to inch forward** avancer petit à petit.

incidence ['ɪnsɪdəns] *n fml* [of disease, theft] fréquence *f*.

incident ['ɪnsɪdənt] *n* incident *m*.

incidental [ˌɪnsɪ'dentl] *adj* accessoire.

incidentally [ˌɪnsɪ'dentəlɪ] *adv* à propos.

incinerate [ɪn'sɪnəreɪt] *vt* incinérer.

incipient [ɪn'sɪpɪənt] *adj fml* naissant(e).

incisive [ɪn'saɪsɪv] *adj* incisif(ive).

incite [ɪn'saɪt] *vt* inciter ; **to incite sb to do sthg** inciter qqn à faire qqch.

inclination [ˌɪnklɪ'neɪʃn] *n* **1.** (*U*) [liking, preference] inclination *f*, goût *m* - **2.** [tendency] : **inclination to do sthg** inclination *f* à faire qqch.

incline ⬥ *n* ['ɪnklaɪn] inclinaison *f*. ⬥ *vt* [ɪn'klaɪn] [head] incliner.

inclined [ɪn'klaɪnd] *adj* **1.** [tending] : **to be inclined to sthg/to do sthg** avoir tendance à qqch/à faire qqch - **2.** [wanting] : **to be inclined to do sthg** être enclin(e) à faire qqch - **3.** [sloping] incliné(e).

include [ɪn'kluːd] *vt* inclure.

included [ɪn'kluːdɪd] *adj* inclus(e).

including [ɪn'kluːdɪŋ] *prep* y compris.

inclusive [ɪn'kluːsɪv] *adj* inclus(e) ; [including all costs] tout compris ; **inclusive of VAT** TVA incluse OR comprise.

inclusivity [ˌɪnkluː'sɪvɪtɪ] *n* inclusion *f*, politique *f* d'inclusion.

incoherent [ˌɪnkəʊ'hɪərənt] *adj* incohérent(e).

income ['ɪŋkʌm] *n* revenu *m*.

income support *n* UK allocations supplémentaires accordées aux personnes ayant un faible revenu.

income tax *n* impôt *m* sur le revenu.

incompatible [ˌɪnkəm'pætɪbl] *adj* : **incompatible (with)** incompatible (avec).

incompetent [ɪn'kɒmpɪtənt] *adj* incompétent(e).

incomplete [ˌɪnkəm'pliːt] *adj* incomplet(ète).

incomprehensible [ɪnˌkɒmprɪ'hensəbl] *adj* incompréhensible.

inconceivable [ˌɪnkən'siːvəbl] *adj* inconcevable.

inconclusive [ˌɪnkən'kluːsɪv] *adj* peu concluant(e).

incongruous [ɪn'kɒŋgrʊəs] *adj* incongru(e).

inconsequential [ˌɪnkɒnsɪ'kwenʃl] *adj* sans importance.

inconsiderable [ˌɪnkən'sɪdərəbl] *adj* : **not inconsiderable** non négligeable.

inconsiderate [ˌɪnkən'sɪdərət] *adj* inconsidéré(e) ; [person] qui manque de considération.

inconsistency [ˌɪnkən'sɪstənsɪ] *n* inconsistance *f*.

inconsistent [ˌɪnkən'sɪstənt] *adj* **1.** [not agreeing, contradictory] contradictoire ; [person] inconséquent(e) ; **inconsistent with sthg** en contradiction avec qqch - **2.** [erratic] inconsistant(e).

inconspicuous [ˌɪnkən'spɪkjʊəs] *adj* qui passe inaperçu(e).

inconvenience [ˌɪnkən'viːnjəns] ◇ *n* désagrément *m*. ◇ *vt* déranger.

inconvenient [ˌɪnkən'viːnjənt] *adj* inopportun(e).

incorporate [ɪn'kɔːpəreɪt] ◇ *vt* **1.** [integrate] : **to incorporate sb/sthg (into)** incorporer qqn/qqch (dans) - **2.** [comprise] contenir, comprendre. ◇ *vi* COMM [to form a corporation] se constituer en société commerciale.

incorporated [ɪn'kɔːpəreɪtɪd] *adj* COMM constitué(e) en société commerciale.

incorrect [ˌɪnkə'rekt] *adj* incorrect(e).

incorrigible [ɪn'kɒrɪdʒəbl] *adj* incorrigible.

increase ◇ *n* ['ɪnkriːs] : **increase (in)** augmentation *f* (de) ; **to be on the increase** aller en augmentant. ◇ *vt & vi* [ɪn'kriːs] augmenter.

increasing [ɪn'kriːsɪŋ] *adj* croissant(e).

increasingly [ɪn'kriːsɪŋlɪ] *adv* de plus en plus.

incredible [ɪn'kredəbl] *adj* incroyable.

incredulous [ɪn'kredjʊləs] *adj* incrédule.

increment ['ɪnkrɪmənt] *n* augmentation *f*.

incriminating [ɪn'krɪmɪneɪtɪŋ] *adj* compromettant(e).

incubator ['ɪnkjʊbeɪtəʳ] *n* [for baby] incubateur *m*, couveuse *f*.

incumbent [ɪn'kʌmbənt] *fml* ◇ *adj* : **to be incumbent on** OR **upon sb to do sthg** incomber à qqn de faire qqch. ◇ *n* [of post] titulaire *m*.

incur [ɪn'kɜːʳ] *vt* encourir.

incurred expenses *npl* = **incurred expenditure**.

indebted [ɪn'detɪd] *adj* [grateful] : **indebted to sb** redevable à qqn.

indecent [ɪn'diːsnt] *adj* **1.** [improper] indécent(e) - **2.** [unreasonable] malséant(e).

indecent assault *n* attentat *m* à la pudeur.

indecent exposure *n* outrage *m* public à la pudeur.

indecisive [ˌɪndɪ'saɪsɪv] *adj* indécis(e).

indeed [ɪn'diːd] *adv* **1.** [certainly, to express surprise] vraiment ; **indeed I am, yes indeed** certainement - **2.** [in fact] en effet - **3.** [for

emphasis] : **very big/bad indeed** extrêmement grand/mauvais, vraiment grand/mauvais.

indefinite [ɪn'defɪnɪt] *adj* **1.** [not fixed] indéfini(e) - **2.** [imprecise] vague.

indefinitely [ɪn'defɪnətlɪ] *adv* **1.** [for unfixed period] indéfiniment - **2.** [imprecisely] vaguement.

indemnity [ɪn'demnətɪ] *n* indemnité *f*.

indent [ɪn'dent] *vt* **1.** [dent] entailler - **2.** [text] mettre en retrait.

independence [ˌɪndɪ'pendəns] *n* indépendance *f*.

Independence Day *n* fête de l'indépendance américaine, le 4 juillet.

independent [ˌɪndɪ'pendənt] *adj* : **independent (of)** indépendant(e) (de).

independent school *n* UK école *f* privée.

in-depth *adj* approfondi(e).

indescribable [ˌɪndɪ'skraɪbəbl] *adj* indescriptible.

indestructible [ˌɪndɪ'strʌktəbl] *adj* indestructible.

index ['ɪndeks] *n* **1.** (*pl* -**dexes** [-deksiːz]) [of book] index *m* - **2.** (*pl* -**dexes** [-deksiːz]) [in library] répertoire *m*, fichier *m* - **3.** (*pl* -**dexes** OR -**dices** [-dɪsiːz]) ECON indice *m*.

index card *n* fiche *f*.

index finger *n* index *m*.

index-linked UK [-ˌlɪŋkt], **indexed** US *adj* ECON indexé(e).

index page *n* index *m*, page *f* d'accueil.

India ['ɪndjə] *n* Inde *f*.

Indian ['ɪndjən] ◇ *adj* indien(enne). ◇ *n* Indien *m*, -enne *f*.

Indian Ocean *n* : **the Indian Ocean** l'océan *m* Indien.

indicate ['ɪndɪkeɪt] ◇ *vt* indiquer. ◇ *vi* UK AUT mettre son clignotant.

indication [ˌɪndɪ'keɪʃn] *n* **1.** [suggestion] indication *f* - **2.** [sign] signe *m*.

indicative [ɪn'dɪkətɪv] ◇ *adj* : **indicative of** indicatif(ive) de. ◇ *n* GRAM indicatif *m*.

indicator ['ɪndɪkeɪtəʳ] *n* **1.** [sign] indicateur *m* - **2.** UK AUT clignotant *m*.

indices ['ɪndɪsiːz] *npl* ▶ **index**.

indict [ɪn'daɪt] *vt* : **to indict sb (for)** accuser qqn (de), mettre qqn en examen (pour).

indictment [ɪn'daɪtmənt] *n* [LAW - bill] acte *m* d'accusation ; [- process] mise *f* en examen.

indifference [ɪn'dɪfrəns] *n* indifférence *f*.

indifferent [ɪn'dɪfrənt] *adj* **1.** [uninterested] : **indifferent (to)** indifférent(e) (à) - **2.** [mediocre] médiocre.

indigenous [ɪn'dɪdʒɪnəs] *adj* indigène.

indigestion [ˌɪndɪ'dʒestʃn] *n (U)* indigestion *f.*

indignant [ɪn'dɪgnənt] *adj* : indignant (at) indigné(e) (de).

indignity [ɪn'dɪgnətɪ] *n* indignité *f.*

indigo ['ɪndɪgəʊ] <> *adj* indigo *(inv).* <> *n* indigo *m.*

indirect [ˌɪndɪ'rekt] *adj* indirect(e).

indiscreet [ˌɪndɪ'skri:t] *adj* indiscret(ète).

indiscriminate [ˌɪndɪ'skrɪmɪnət] *adj* [person] qui manque de discernement ; [treatment] sans distinction ; [killing] commis au hasard.

indispensable [ˌɪndɪ'spensəbl] *adj* indispensable.

indisputable [ˌɪndɪ'spju:təbl] *adj* indiscutable.

indistinguishable [ˌɪndɪ'stɪŋgwɪʃəbl] *adj* : indistinguishable (from) que l'on ne peut distinguer (de).

individual [ˌɪndɪ'vɪdʒʊəl] <> *adj* **1.** [separate, for one person] individuel(elle) - **2.** [distinctive] personnel(elle). <> *n* individu *m.*

individually [ˌɪndɪ'vɪdʒʊəlɪ] *adv* individuellement.

indoctrination [ɪnˌdɒktrɪ'neɪʃn] *n* endoctrinement *m.*

Indonesia [ˌɪndə'ni:zjə] *n* Indonésie *f.*

indoor ['ɪndɔ:r] *adj* d'intérieur ; [swimming pool] couvert(e) ; [sports] en salle.

indoors [ɪn'dɔ:z] *adv* à l'intérieur.

induce [ɪn'dju:s] *vt* **1.** [persuade] : to induce sb to do sthg inciter OR pousser qqn à faire qqch - **2.** [bring about] provoquer.

inducement [ɪn'dju:smənt] *n* [incentive] incitation *f*, encouragement *m.*

induction [ɪn'dʌkʃn] *n* **1.** [into official position] : induction (into) installation *f* (à) - **2.** [introduction] introduction *f* - **3.** ELEC induction *f.*

induction course *n* UK stage *m* d'initiation.

indulge [ɪn'dʌldʒ] <> *vt* **1.** [whim, passion] céder à - **2.** [child, person] gâter. <> *vi* : to indulge in sthg se permettre qqch.

indulgence [ɪn'dʌldʒəns] *n* **1.** [act of indulging] indulgence *f* - **2.** [special treat] gâterie *f.*

indulgent [ɪn'dʌldʒənt] *adj* indulgent(e).

industrial [ɪn'dʌstrɪəl] *adj* [gen] industriel(elle).

industrial action *esp* UK, **job action** US *n* *esp* UK to take industrial action se mettre en grève.

industrial estate UK, **industrial park** US *n* zone *f* industrielle.

industrialist [ɪn'dʌstrɪəlɪst] *n* industriel *m*, -elle *f.*

industrial park US = industrial estate.

industrial relations *npl* relations *fpl* patronat-syndicats.

industrial revolution *n* révolution *f* industrielle.

industrious [ɪn'dʌstrɪəs] *adj* industrieux(euse).

industry ['ɪndəstrɪ] *n* **1.** [gen] industrie *f* - **2.** *(U)* [hard work] assiduité *f*, application *f.*

inebriated [ɪ'ni:brɪeɪtɪd] *adj fml* ivre.

inedible [ɪn'edɪbl] *adj* **1.** [meal, food] immangeable - **2.** [plant, mushroom] non comestible.

ineffective [ˌɪnɪ'fektɪv] *adj* inefficace.

ineffectual [ˌɪnɪ'fektʃʊəl] *adj fml* inefficace ; [person] incapable, incompétent(e).

inefficiency [ˌɪnɪ'fɪʃnsɪ] *n* inefficacité *f* ; [of person] incapacité *f*, incompétence *f.*

inefficient [ˌɪnɪ'fɪʃnt] *adj* inefficace ; [person] incapable, incompétent(e).

ineligible [ɪn'elɪdʒəbl] *adj* inéligible ; to be ineligible for sthg ne pas avoir droit à qqch.

inept [ɪ'nept] *adj* inepte ; [person] stupide.

inequality [ˌɪnɪ'kwɒlətɪ] *n* inégalité *f.*

inert [ɪ'nɜ:t] *adj* inerte.

inertia [ɪ'nɜ:ʃə] *n* inertie *f.*

inescapable [ˌɪnɪ'skeɪpəbl] *adj* inéluctable.

inevitable [ɪn'evɪtəbl] <> *adj* inévitable. <> *n* : the inevitable l'inévitable *m.*

inevitably [ɪn'evɪtəblɪ] *adv* inévitablement.

inexcusable [ˌɪnɪk'skju:zəbl] *adj* inexcusable, impardonnable.

inexhaustible [ˌɪnɪg'zɔ:stəbl] *adj* inépuisable.

inexpensive [ˌɪnɪk'spensɪv] *adj* bon marché *(inv)*, pas cher (chère).

inexperienced [ˌɪnɪk'spɪərɪənst] *adj* inexpérimenté(e), qui manque d'expérience.

inexplicable [ˌɪnɪk'splɪkəbl] *adj* inexplicable.

infallible [ɪn'fæləbl] *adj* infaillible.

infamous ['ɪnfəməs] *adj* infâme.

infancy ['ɪnfənsɪ] *n* petite enfance *f* ; in its infancy *fig* à ses débuts.

infant ['ɪnfənt] *n* **1.** [baby] nouveau-né *m*, nouveau-née *f*, nourrisson *m* - **2.** [young child] enfant *mf* en bas âge.

infantry ['ɪnfəntrɪ] *n* infanterie *f.*

infant school *n* UK école *f* maternelle (de 5 à 7 ans).

infatuated [ɪn'fætjʊeɪtɪd] *adj* : **infatuated (with)** entiché(e) (de).

infatuation [ɪn,fætjʊ'eɪʃn] *n* : **infatuation (with)** béguin *m* (pour).

infect [ɪn'fekt] *vt* **1.** MED infecter - **2.** *fig* [subj: enthusiasm etc] se propager à.

infection [ɪn'fekʃn] *n* infection *f*.

infectious [ɪn'fekʃəs] *adj* **1.** [disease] infectieux(euse) - **2.** *fig* [feeling, laugh] contagieux(euse).

infer [ɪn'fɜːr] *vt* [deduce] : **to infer sthg (from)** déduire qqch (de).

inferior [ɪn'fɪərɪər] <> *adj* **1.** [in status] inférieur(e) - **2.** [product] de qualité inférieure ; [work] médiocre. <> *n* [in status] subalterne *mf*.

inferiority [ɪn,fɪərɪ'ɒrətɪ] *n* infériorité *f*.

inferiority complex *n* complexe *m* d'infériorité.

inferno [ɪn'fɜːnəʊ] (*pl* -s) *n* brasier *m*.

infertile [ɪn'fɜːtaɪl] *adj* **1.** [woman] stérile - **2.** [soil] infertile.

infested [ɪn'festɪd] *adj* : **infested with** infesté(e) de.

infighting ['ɪn,faɪtɪŋ] *n* (U) querelles *fpl* intestines.

infiltrate ['ɪnfɪltreɪt] *vt* infiltrer.

infinite ['ɪnfɪnət] *adj* infini(e).

infinitive [ɪn'fɪnɪtɪv] *n* infinitif *m*.

infinity [ɪn'fɪnətɪ] *n* infini *m*.

infirm [ɪn'fɜːm] *fml* <> *adj* infirme. <> *npl* : **the infirm** les infirmes *mpl*.

infirmary [ɪn'fɜːmərɪ] *n* UK [in names] hôpital *m* ; US SCH & UNIV infirmerie *f*.

infirmity [ɪn'fɜːmətɪ] *n* fml infirmité *f*.

inflamed [ɪn'fleɪmd] *adj* MED enflammé(e).

inflammable [ɪn'flæməbl] *adj* inflammable.

inflammation [,ɪnflə'meɪʃn] *n* MED inflammation *f*.

inflatable [ɪn'fleɪtəbl] *adj* gonflable.

inflate [ɪn'fleɪt] *vt* **1.** [tyre, life jacket etc] gonfler - **2.** ECON [prices, salaries] hausser, gonfler.

inflation [ɪn'fleɪʃn] *n* ECON inflation *f*.

inflationary [ɪn'fleɪʃnrɪ] *adj* ECON inflationniste.

inflict [ɪn'flɪkt] *vt* : **to inflict sthg on sb** infliger qqch à qqn.

influence ['ɪnflʊəns] <> *n* influence *f* ; **under the influence of** [person, group] sous l'influence de ; [alcohol, drugs] sous l'effet OR l'empire de. <> *vt* influencer.

influential [,ɪnflʊ'enʃl] *adj* influent(e).

influenza [,ɪnflʊ'enzə] *n* (U) grippe *f*.

influx ['ɪnflʌks] *n* afflux *m*.

inform [ɪn'fɔːm] *vt* : **to inform sb (of)** informer qqn (de) ; **to inform sb about** renseigner qqn sur. ◆ **inform on** *vt insep* dénoncer.

informal [ɪn'fɔːml] *adj* **1.** [party, person] simple ; [clothes] de tous les jours - **2.** [negotiations, visit] officieux(euse) ; [meeting] informel(elle).

informant [ɪn'fɔːmənt] *n* informateur *m*, -trice *f*.

informatics [,ɪnfə'mætɪks] *n* (sg) sciences *fpl* de l'information.

information [,ɪnfə'meɪʃn] *n* (U) information (on OR about) renseignements *mpl* OR informations *fpl* (sur) ; **a piece of information** un renseignement ; **for your information** *fml* à titre d'information.

information desk *n* bureau *m* de renseignements.

information highway, information superhighway *n* autoroute *f* de l'information.

information superhighway = **information highway**.

information technology *n* informatique *f*.

informative [ɪn'fɔːmətɪv] *adj* informatif(ive).

informer [ɪn'fɔːmər] *n* indicateur *m*, -trice *f*.

infrared [,ɪnfrə'red] *adj* infrarouge.

infrastructure ['ɪnfrə,strʌktʃər] *n* infrastructure *f*.

infringe [ɪn'frɪndʒ] <> *vt* **1.** [right] empiéter sur - **2.** [law, agreement] enfreindre. <> *vi* **1.** [on right] : **to infringe on** empiéter sur - **2.** [on law, agreement] : **to infringe on** enfreindre.

infringement [ɪn'frɪndʒmənt] *n* **1.** [of right] : **infringement (of)** atteinte *f* (à) - **2.** [of law, agreement] transgression *f*.

infuriating [ɪn'fjʊərɪeɪtɪŋ] *adj* exaspérant(e).

ingenious [ɪn'dʒiːnjəs] *adj* ingénieux(euse).

ingenuity [,ɪndʒɪ'njuːətɪ] *n* ingéniosité *f*.

ingenuous [ɪn'dʒenjʊəs] *adj* ingénu(e), naïf(naïve).

ingot ['ɪŋgət] *n* lingot *m*.

ingrained [,ɪn'greɪnd] *adj* **1.** [dirt] incrusté(e) - **2.** *fig* [belief, hatred] enraciné(e).

ingratiating [ɪn'greɪʃɪeɪtɪŋ] *adj pej* doucereux(euse), mielleux(euse).

ingredient [ɪn'griːdjənt] *n* ingrédient *m* ; *fig* élément *m*.

inhabit [ɪn'hæbɪt] *vt* habiter.

inhabitant [ɪn'hæbɪtənt] *n* habitant *m*, -e *f*.

inhale [ɪn'heɪl] <> vt inhaler, respirer. <> vi [breathe in] respirer.

inhaler [ɪn'heɪlər] n MED inhalateur m.

inherent [ɪn'hɪərənt OR ɪn'herənt] adj : inherent (in) inhérent(e) (à).

inherently [ɪn'hɪərəntlɪ OR ɪn'herəntlɪ] adv fondamentalement, en soi.

inherit [ɪn'herɪt] vi hériter.

inheritance [ɪn'herɪtəns] n héritage m.

inhibit [ɪn'hɪbɪt] vt 1. [prevent] empêcher - 2. PSYCHOL inhiber.

inhibition [ˌɪnhɪ'bɪʃn] n inhibition f.

inhospitable [ˌɪnhɒ'spɪtəbl] adj inhospitalier(ère).

in-house <> adj interne ; [staff] de la maison. <> adv [produce, work] sur place.

inhuman [ɪn'hjuːmən] adj inhumain(e).

initial [ɪ'nɪʃl] <> adj initial(e), premier(ère) ; initial letter initiale f. <> vt (UK & US) parapher. ➡ **initials** npl initiales fpl.

initially [ɪ'nɪʃəlɪ] adv initialement, au début.

initiate [ɪ'nɪʃɪeɪt] vt 1. [talks] engager ; [scheme] ébaucher, inaugurer - 2. [teach] : to initiate sb into sthg initier qqn à qqch.

initiative [ɪ'nɪʃətɪv] n 1. [gen] initiative f - 2. [advantage] : to have the initiative avoir l'avantage m.

inject [ɪn'dʒekt] vt 1. MED : to inject sb with sthg, to inject sthg into sb injecter qqch à qqn - 2. fig [excitement] insuffler ; [money] injecter.

injection [ɪn'dʒekʃn] n lit & fig injection f.

injure ['ɪndʒər] vt 1. [limb, person] blesser ; to injure one's arm se blesser au bras - 2. fig [reputation, chances] compromettre.

injured ['ɪndʒəd] <> adj [limb, person] blessé(e). <> npl : the injured les blessés mpl.

injury ['ɪndʒərɪ] n 1. [to limb, person] blessure f ; to do o.s. an injury se blesser - 2. fig [to reputation] coup m, atteinte f.

injury time n (U) UK arrêts mpl de jeu.

injustice [ɪn'dʒʌstɪs] n injustice f ; to do sb an injustice se montrer injuste envers qqn.

ink [ɪŋk] n encre f.

ink-jet printer, inkjet printer n COMPUT imprimante f à jet d'encre.

inkling ['ɪŋklɪŋ] n : to have an inkling of avoir une petite idée de.

inlaid [ˌɪn'leɪd] adj : inlaid (with) incrusté(e) (de).

inland <> adj ['ɪnlənd] intérieur(e). <> adv [ɪn'lænd] à l'intérieur.

Inland Revenue n UK : the Inland Revenue ≃ le fisc.

in-laws npl inf [parents-in-law] beaux-parents mpl ; [others] belle-famille f.

inlet ['ɪnlet] n 1. [of lake, sea] avancée f - 2. TECH arrivée f.

in-line skating n SPORT roller m.

inmate ['ɪnmeɪt] n [of prison] détenu m, -e f ; [of mental hospital] interné m, -e f.

inn [ɪn] n auberge f.

innate [ɪ'neɪt] adj inné(e).

inner ['ɪnər] adj 1. [on inside] interne, intérieur(e) - 2. [feelings] intime.

inner city n : the inner city les quartiers mpl pauvres.

inner tube n chambre f à air.

innings ['ɪnɪŋz] (pl innings) n UK CRICKET tour m de batte.

innocence ['ɪnəsəns] n innocence f.

innocent ['ɪnəsənt] <> adj innocent(e) ; innocent of [crime] non coupable de. <> n innocent m, -e f.

innocuous [ɪ'nɒkjuəs] adj inoffensif(ive).

innovation [ˌɪnə'veɪʃn] n innovation f.

innovative ['ɪnəvətɪv] adj 1. [idea, design] innovateur(trice) - 2. [person, company] novateur(trice).

innuendo [ˌɪnjuː'endəʊ] (pl -es OR -s) n insinuation f.

innumerable [ɪ'njuːmərəbl] adj innombrable.

inoculate [ɪ'nɒkjʊleɪt] vt : to inoculate sb (with sthg) inoculer (qqch à) qqn.

inordinately [ɪ'nɔːdɪnətlɪ] adv fml excessivement.

in-patient n malade hospitalisé m, malade hospitalisée f.

input ['ɪnpʊt] <> n 1. [contribution] contribution f, concours m - 2. COMPUT & ELEC entrée f. <> vt (pt & pp input OR -ted) COMPUT entrer.

inquest ['ɪnkwest] n enquête f.

inquire [ɪn'kwaɪər] <> vt : to inquire when/whether/how... demander quand/si/comment... <> vi : to inquire (about) se renseigner (sur). ➡ **inquire after** vt insep s'enquérir de. ➡ **inquire into** vt insep enquêter sur.

inquiry [ɪn'kwaɪərɪ] n 1. [question] demande f de renseignements ; 'Inquiries' UK 'renseignements' - 2. [investigation] enquête f.

inquiry desk n UK bureau m de renseignements.

inquisitive [ɪn'kwɪzətɪv] adj inquisiteur(trice).

inroads ['ɪnrəʊdz] *npl* : **to make inroads into** [savings] entamer.

insane [ɪn'seɪn] *adj* fou(folle).

insanity [ɪn'sænətɪ] *n* folie *f*.

insatiable [ɪn'seɪʃəbl] *adj* insatiable.

inscription [ɪn'skrɪpʃn] *n* **1.** [engraved] inscription *f* - **2.** [written] dédicace *f*.

inscrutable [ɪn'skruːtəbl] *adj* impénétrable.

insect ['ɪnsekt] *n* insecte *m*.

insecticide [ɪn'sektɪsaɪd] *n* insecticide *m*.

insect repellent *n* lotion *f* anti-moustiques.

insecure [ˌɪnsɪ'kjʊər] *adj* **1.** [person] anxieux(euse) - **2.** [job, investment] incertain(e).

insensible [ɪn'sensəbl] *adj* **1.** [unconscious] inconscient(e) - **2.** [unaware, not feeling] : **insensible of/to** insensible à.

insensitive [ɪn'sensətɪv] *adj* : **insensitive (to)** insensible (à).

inseparable [ɪn'seprəbl] *adj* inséparable.

insert *vt* [ɪn'sɜːt] : **to insert sthg (in** OR **into)** insérer qqch (dans). ⟨⟩ *n* ['ɪnsɜːt] [in newspaper] encart *m*.

insertion [ɪn'sɜːʃn] *n* insertion *f*.

in-service training *n* formation *f* en cours d'emploi.

inshore ⟨⟩ *adj* ['ɪnʃɔːr] côtier(ère). ⟨⟩ *adv* [ɪn'ʃɔːr] [to be situated] près de la côte ; [move] vers la côte.

inside [ɪn'saɪd] ⟨⟩ *prep* **1.** [building, object] à l'intérieur de, dans ; [group, organization] au sein de - **2.** [time] : **inside (of) three weeks** en moins de trois semaines. ⟨⟩ *adv* **1.** [gen] dedans, à l'intérieur ; **to go inside** entrer ; **come inside!** entrez! - **2.** *prison sl* en taule. ⟨⟩ *adj* intérieur(e) - **2.** FOOTBALL : **inside left/right** inter *m* gauche/droit. ⟨⟩ *n* **1.** [interior] : **the inside** l'intérieur *m* ; **inside out** [clothes] à l'envers ; **to know sthg inside out** connaître qqch à fond - **2.** AUT : **the inside** [in UK] la gauche ; [in Europe, US etc] la droite. ⟨⟩ **insides** *npl inf* tripes *fpl*. ⟨⟩ **inside of** *prep US* [building, object] à l'intérieur de, dans.

insight ['ɪnsaɪt] *n* **1.** [wisdom] sagacité *f*, perspicacité *f* - **2.** [glimpse] : **insight (into)** aperçu *m* (de).

insignificant [ˌɪnsɪg'nɪfɪkənt] *adj* insignifiant(e).

insincere [ˌɪnsɪn'sɪər] *adj* pas sincère.

insinuate [ɪn'sɪnjʊeɪt] *vt* insinuer, laisser entendre.

insipid [ɪn'sɪpɪd] *adj* insipide.

insist [ɪn'sɪst] ⟨⟩ *vt* **1.** [claim] : **to insist (that)...** insister sur le fait que... - **2.** [demand] : **to insist (that)...** insister pour que

(+ *subjunctive*)... ⟨⟩ *vi* : **to insist (on sthg)** exiger (qqch) ; **to insist on doing sthg** tenir à faire qqch, vouloir absolument faire qqch.

insistent [ɪn'sɪstənt] *adj* **1.** [determined] insistant(e) ; **to be insistent on** insister sur - **2.** [continual] incessant(e).

insofar [ˌɪnsəʊ'fɑːr] ⟨⟩ **insofar as** *conj fml* dans la mesure où.

insole ['ɪnsəʊl] *n* semelle *f* intérieure.

insolent ['ɪnsələnt] *adj* insolent(e).

insolvent [ɪn'sɒlvənt] *adj* insolvable.

insomnia [ɪn'sɒmnɪə] *n* insomnie *f*.

inspect [ɪn'spekt] *vt* **1.** [letter, person] examiner - **2.** [factory, troops etc] inspecter.

inspection [ɪn'spekʃn] *n* **1.** [investigation] examen *m* - **2.** [official check] inspection *f*.

inspector [ɪn'spektər] *n* inspecteur *m*, -trice *f*.

inspiration [ˌɪnspə'reɪʃn] *n* inspiration *f*.

inspire [ɪn'spaɪər] *vt* : **to inspire sb to do sthg** pousser OR encourager qqn à faire qqch ; **to inspire sb with sthg, to inspire sthg in sb** inspirer qqch à qqn.

install, *UK* **instal** [ɪn'stɔːl] *vt* [fit & COMPUT] installer.

installation [ˌɪnstə'leɪʃn] *n* installation *f*.

instalment *UK*, **installment** *US* [ɪn'stɔːlmənt] *n* **1.** [payment] acompte *m* ; **in instalments** par acomptes - **2.** [episode] épisode *m*.

instance ['ɪnstəns] *n UK* exemple *m* ; **for instance** par exemple.

instant ['ɪnstənt] ⟨⟩ *adj* **1.** [immediate] instantané(e), immédiat(e) - **2.** [coffee] soluble ; [food] à préparation rapide. ⟨⟩ *n* instant *m* ; **the instant (that)...** dès OR aussitôt que... ; **this instant** tout de suite, immédiatement.

instantly ['ɪnstəntlɪ] *adv* immédiatement.

instant replay *n US* = **action replay**.

instead [ɪn'sted] *adv* au lieu de cela. ⟨⟩ **instead of** *prep* au lieu de ; **instead of him** à sa place.

instep ['ɪnstep] *n* cou-de-pied *m*.

instigate ['ɪnstɪgeɪt] *vt* être à l'origine de, entreprendre.

instil *UK*, **instill** *US* [ɪn'stɪl] *vt* : **to instil sthg in** OR **into sb** instiller qqch à qqn.

instinct ['ɪnstɪŋkt] *n* **1.** [intuition] instinct *m* - **2.** [impulse] réaction *f*, mouvement *m*.

instinctive [ɪn'stɪŋktɪv] *adj* instinctif(ive).

institute ['ɪnstɪtjuːt] ⟨⟩ *n* institut *m*. ⟨⟩ *vt* instituer.

institution [ˌɪnstɪ'tjuːʃn] *n* institution *f*.

institutional racism, institutionalized racism *n* racisme *m* institutionnel.

instruct [ɪn'strʌkt] *vt* **1.** [tell, order] : **to**

instruct sb to do sthg charger qqn de faire qqch - **2.** [teach] instruire ; **to instruct sb in sthg** enseigner qqch à qqn.

instruction [ɪn'strʌkʃn] *n* instruction *f*.
➡ **instructions** *npl* mode *m* d'emploi, instructions *fpl*.

instructor [ɪn'strʌktər] *n* **1.** [gen] instructeur *m*, -trice *f*, moniteur *m*, -trice *f* - **2.** *US* SCH enseignant *m*, -e *f*.

instrument ['ɪnstrʊmənt] *n lit & fig* instrument *m*.

instrumental [ˌɪnstrʊ'mentl] *adj* [important, helpful] : **to be instrumental in** contribuer à.

instrument panel *n* tableau *m* de bord.

insubordinate [ˌɪnsə'bɔːdɪnət] *adj* insubordonné(e).

insubstantial [ˌɪnsəb'stænʃl] *adj* [structure] peu solide ; [meal] peu substantiel(elle).

insufficient [ˌɪnsə'fɪʃnt] *adj fml* insuffisant(e).

insular ['ɪnsjʊlər] *adj pej* [outlook] borné(e) ; [person] à l'esprit étroit.

insulate ['ɪnsjʊleɪt] *vt* **1.** [loft, cable] isoler ; [hot water tank] calorifuger - **2.** [protect] : **to insulate sb against** OR **from sthg** protéger qqn de qqch.

insulating tape ['ɪnsjʊleɪtɪŋ-] *n UK* chatterton *m*.

insulation [ˌɪnsjʊ'leɪʃn] *n* isolation *f*.

insulin ['ɪnsjʊlɪn] *n* insuline *f*.

insult <> *vt* [ɪn'sʌlt] insulter, injurier. <> *n* ['ɪnsʌlt] insulte *f*, injure *f*.

insuperable [ɪn'suːprəbl] *adj fml* insurmontable.

insurance [ɪn'ʃʊərəns] *n* **1.** [against fire, accident, theft] assurance *f* - **2.** *fig* [safeguard, protection] protection *f*, garantie *f*.

insurance policy *n* police *f* d'assurance.

insure [ɪn'ʃʊər] <> *vt* **1.** [against fire, accident, theft] : **to insure sb/sthg against sthg** assurer qqn/qqch contre qqch - **2.** *US* [make certain] s'assurer. <> *vi* [prevent] : **to insure against** se protéger de.

insurer [ɪn'ʃʊərər] *n* assureur *m*.

insurmountable [ˌɪnsə'maʊntəbl] *adj fml* insurmontable.

intact [ɪn'tækt] *adj* intact(e).

intake ['ɪnteɪk] *n* **1.** [amount consumed] consommation *f* - **2.** *UK* [people recruited] admission *f* - **3.** [inlet] prise *f*, arrivée *f*.

integral ['ɪntɪɡrəl] *adj* intégral(e) ; **to be integral to sthg** faire partie intégrante de qqch.

integrate ['ɪntɪɡreɪt] <> *vi* s'intégrer. <> *vt* intégrer.

integrity [ɪn'teɡrətɪ] *n* **1.** [honour] intégrité *f*, honnêteté *f* - **2.** *fml* [wholeness] intégrité *f*, totalité *f*.

intellect ['ɪntəlekt] *n* **1.** [ability to think] intellect *m* - **2.** [cleverness] intelligence *f*.

intellectual [ˌɪntə'lektjʊəl] <> *adj* intellectuel(elle). <> *n* intellectuel *m*, -elle *f*.

intelligence [ɪn'telɪdʒəns] *n* (*U*) **1.** [ability to think] intelligence *f* - **2.** [information service] service *m* de renseignements - **3.** [information] informations *fpl*, renseignements *mpl*.

intelligent [ɪn'telɪdʒənt] *adj* intelligent(e).

intelligent card *n* carte *f* à puce OR à mémoire.

intend [ɪn'tend] *vt* [mean] avoir l'intention de ; **to be intended for** être destiné à ; **to be intended to do sthg** être destiné à faire qqch, viser à faire qqch ; **to intend doing** OR **to do sthg** avoir l'intention de faire qqch.

intended [ɪn'tendɪd] *adj* [result] voulu(e) ; [victim] visé(e).

intense [ɪn'tens] *adj* **1.** [gen] intense - **2.** [serious - person] sérieux(euse).

intensely [ɪn'tenslɪ] *adv* **1.** [irritating, boring] extrêmement ; [suffer] énormément - **2.** [look] intensément.

intensify [ɪn'tensɪfaɪ] <> *vt* intensifier, augmenter. <> *vi* s'intensifier.

intensity [ɪn'tensətɪ] *n* intensité *f*.

intensive [ɪn'tensɪv] *adj* intensif(ive).

intensive care *n* : **to be in intensive care** être en réanimation.

intent [ɪn'tent] <> *adj* **1.** [absorbed] absorbé(e) - **2.** [determined] : **to be intent on** OR **upon doing sthg** être résolu(e) OR décidé(e) à faire qqch. <> *n fml* intention *f*, dessein *m* ; **to** OR **for all intents and purposes** pratiquement, virtuellement.

intention [ɪn'tenʃn] *n* intention *f*.

intentional [ɪn'tenʃənl] *adj* intentionnel(elle), voulu(e).

intently [ɪn'tentlɪ] *adv* avec attention, attentivement.

interact [ˌɪntər'ækt] *vi* **1.** [communicate, work together] : **to interact (with sb)** communiquer (avec qqn) - **2.** [react] : **to interact (with sthg)** interagir (avec qqch).

interactivity [ˌɪntəræk'tɪvɪtɪ] *n* interactivité *f*.

intercede [ˌɪntə'siːd] *vi fml* : **to intercede (with sb)** intercéder (auprès de qqn).

intercept [ˌɪntə'sept] *vt* intercepter.

interchange <> *n* ['ɪntətʃeɪndʒ] **1.** [exchange] échange *m* - **2.** [road junction] échangeur *m*. ◇ *vt* [ˌɪntəˈtʃeɪndʒ] échanger.

interchangeable [ˌɪntəˈtʃeɪndʒəbl] *adj* : **interchangeable (with)** interchangeable (avec).

intercity [ˌɪntəˈsɪtɪ] *n* système de trains rapides reliant les grandes villes en Grande-Bretagne ; **Intercity 125®** train rapide pouvant rouler à 125 miles (200 km) à l'heure.

intercom [ˈɪntəkɒm] *n* Interphone® *m*.

intercourse [ˈɪntəkɔːs] *n* (U) UK [sexual] rapports *mpl* (sexuels).

interest [ˈɪntrəst] ◇ *n* **1.** [gen] intérêt *m* ; **to lose interest** se désintéresser - **2.** [hobby] centre *m* d'intérêt - **3.** (U) FIN intérêt *m*, intérêts *mpl*. ◇ *vt* intéresser.

interested [ˈɪntrəstɪd] *adj* intéressé(e) ; **to be interested in** s'intéresser à ; **I'm not interested in that** cela ne m'intéresse pas ; **to be interested in doing sthg** avoir envie de faire qqch.

interesting [ˈɪntrəstɪŋ] *adj* intéressant(e).

interest rate *n* taux *m* d'intérêt.

interface *n* [ˈɪntəfeɪs] **1.** COMPUT interface *f* - **2.** *fig* [junction] rapports *mpl*, relations *fpl*.

interfere [ˌɪntəˈfɪər] *vi* **1.** [meddle] : **to interfere in sthg** s'immiscer dans qqch, se mêler de qqch - **2.** [damage] : **to interfere with sthg** gêner OR contrarier qqch ; [routine] déranger qqch.

interference [ˌɪntəˈfɪərəns] *n* (U) **1.** [meddling] : **interference (with OR in)** ingérence *f* (dans), intrusion *f* (dans) - **2.** TELEC parasites *mpl*.

interim [ˈɪntərɪm] ◇ *adj* provisoire. ◇ *n* : **in the interim** dans l'intérim, entre-temps.

interior [ɪnˈtɪərɪər] ◇ *adj* **1.** [inner] intérieur(e) - **2.** POL de l'Intérieur. ◇ *n* intérieur *m*.

interlock [ˌɪntəˈlɒk] *vi* [gears] s'enclencher, s'engrener ; [fingers] s'entrelacer.

interloper [ˈɪntələʊpər] *n pej* intrus *m*, -e *f*.

interlude [ˈɪntəluːd] *n* **1.** [pause] intervalle *m* - **2.** [interval] interlude *m*.

intermediary [ˌɪntəˈmiːdjərɪ] *n* intermédiaire *mf*.

intermediate [ˌɪntəˈmiːdjət] *adj* **1.** [transitional] intermédiaire - **2.** [post-beginner-level] moyen(enne) ; [- student, group] de niveau moyen.

interminable [ɪnˈtɜːmɪnəbl] *adj* interminable, sans fin.

intermission [ˌɪntəˈmɪʃn] *n* US entracte *m*.

intermittent [ˌɪntəˈmɪtənt] *adj* intermittent(e).

intern ◇ *vt* [ɪnˈtɜːn] interner. ◇ *n* [ˈɪntɜːn] US [gen] stagiaire *mf* ; MED interne *mf*.

internal [ɪnˈtɜːnl] *adj* **1.** [gen] interne - **2.** [within country] intérieur(e).

internally [ɪnˈtɜːnəlɪ] *adv* **1.** [within the body] : **to bleed internally** faire une hémorragie interne - **2.** [within country] à l'intérieur - **3.** [within organization] intérieurement.

Internal Revenue Service *n* US *inf* **the Internal Revenue Service** ≃ le fisc.

international [ˌɪntəˈnæʃənl] ◇ *adj* international(e). ◇ *n* UK **1.** SPORT [match] match *m* international - **2.** SPORT [player] international *m*, -e *f*.

internet, Internet [ˈɪntənet] *n* : **the internet** l'Internet *m*.

Internet access *n* (U) accès à l'internet *m*.

Internet café *n* cybercafé *m*.

Internet connection *n* connexion *f* internet OR à l'Internet.

internet radio *n* radio *f* par internet.

Internet Service Provider *n* fournisseur *m* d'accès.

Internet start-up, Internet start-up company *n* start-up *f*, jeune *f* pousse d'entreprise *offic*.

Internet television, Internet TV *n* (U) télévision *f* internet.

interpret [ɪnˈtɜːprɪt] ◇ *vt* : **to interpret sthg (as)** interpréter qqch (comme). ◇ *vi* [translate] faire l'interprète.

interpreter [ɪnˈtɜːprɪtər] *n* interprète *mf*.

interracial [ˌɪntəˈreɪʃl] *adj* entre des races différentes, racial(e).

interrelate [ˌɪntərɪˈleɪt] ◇ *vt* mettre en corrélation. ◇ *vi* : **to interrelate (with)** être lié(e) (à), être en corrélation (avec).

interrogate [ɪnˈterəgeɪt] *vt* interroger.

interrogation [ɪnˌterəˈgeɪʃn] *n* interrogatoire *m*.

interrogation mark, interrogation point *n* US point *m* d'interrogation.

interrogative [ˌɪntəˈrɒgətɪv] ◇ *adj* GRAM interrogatif(ive). ◇ *n* GRAM interrogatif *m*.

interrupt [ˌɪntəˈrʌpt] ◇ *vt* interrompre ; [calm] rompre. ◇ *vi* interrompre.

interruption [ˌɪntəˈrʌpʃn] *n* interruption *f*.

intersect [ˌɪntəˈsekt] ◇ *vi* s'entrecroiser, s'entrecouper. ◇ *vt* croiser, couper.

intersection [ˌɪntəˈsekʃn] *n* [in road] croisement *m*, carrefour *m*.

intersperse [ˌɪntəˈspɜːs] *vt* : **to be interspersed with** être émaillé(e) de, être entremêlé(e) de.

interval [ˈɪntəvl] *n* **1.** [gen] intervalle *m* ; **at intervals** par intervalles ; **at monthly/yearly intervals** tous les mois/ans - **2.** UK [at play, concert] entracte *m*.

intervene [,ɪntə'viːn] *vi* 1. [person, police] : to intervene (in) intervenir (dans), s'interposer (dans) - 2. [event, war, strike] survenir - 3. [time] s'écouler.

intervention [,ɪntə'venʃn] *n* intervention *f*.

interview ['ɪntəvjuː] ⋄ *n* 1. [for job] entrevue *f*, entretien *m* - 2. PRESS interview *f*. ⋄ *vt* 1. [for job] faire passer une entrevue OR un entretien à ; [for opinion poll] interroger, sonder - 2. PRESS interviewer.

interviewer ['ɪntəvjuːə'] *n* 1. [for job] personne *f* qui fait passer une entrevue - 2. PRESS interviewer *m*.

intestine [ɪn'testɪn] *n* intestin *m*.

intimacy ['ɪntɪməsɪ] *n* 1. [closeness] : intimacy (between/with) intimité *f* (entre/avec) - 2. [intimate remark] familiarité *f*.

intimate ⋄ *adj* ['ɪntɪmət] 1. [gen] intime - 2. [detailed - knowledge] approfondi(e). ⋄ *vt* ['ɪntɪmeɪt] *fml* faire savoir, faire connaître.

intimately ['ɪntɪmətlɪ] *adv* 1. [very closely] étroitement - 2. [as close friends] intimement - 3. [in detail] à fond.

intimidate [ɪn'tɪmɪdeɪt] *vt* intimider.

into ['ɪntʊ] *prep* 1. [inside] dans - 2. [against] : to bump into sthg se cogner contre qqch ; to crash into rentrer dans - 3. [referring to change in state] en ; to translate sthg into Spanish traduire qqch en espagnol - 4. [concerning] : research/investigation into recherche/enquête sur - 5. MATHS : 3 into 2 2 divisé par 3 - 6. *inf* [interested in] : to be into sthg être passionné(e) par qqch.

intolerable [ɪn'tɒlrəbl] *adj* intolérable, insupportable.

intolerance [ɪn'tɒlərəns] *n* intolérance *f*.

intolerant [ɪn'tɒlərənt] *adj* intolérant(e).

intoxicated [ɪn'tɒksɪkeɪtɪd] *adj* 1. [drunk] ivre - 2. *fig* [excited] : to be intoxicated by OR with sthg être grisé(e) OR enivré(e) par qqch.

intractable [ɪn'træktəbl] *adj* 1. [stubborn] intraitable - 2. [insoluble] insoluble.

intranet, Intranet ['ɪntrənet] *n* intranet *m*.

intransitive [ɪn'trænzətɪv] *adj* intransitif(ive).

intravenous [,ɪntrə'viːnəs] *adj* intraveineux(euse).

in-tray, US in-basket, US in-box *n* casier *m* des affaires à traiter.

intricate ['ɪntrɪkət] *adj* compliqué(e).

intrigue [ɪn'triːg] ⋄ *n* intrigue *f*. ⋄ *vt* intriguer, exciter la curiosité de.

intriguing [ɪn'triːgɪŋ] *adj* fascinant(e).

intrinsic [ɪn'trɪnsɪk] *adj* intrinsèque.

introduce [,ɪntrə'djuːs] *vt* 1. [present] présenter ; to introduce sb to sb présenter qqn à qqn - 2. [bring in] : to introduce sthg (to OR into) introduire qqch (dans) - 3. [allow to experience] : to introduce sb to sthg initier qqn à qqch, faire découvrir qqch à qqn - 4. [signal beginning of] annoncer.

introduction [,ɪntrə'dʌkʃn] *n* 1. [in book, of new method etc] introduction *f* - 2. [of people] : introduction (to sb) présentation *f* (à qqn).

introductory [,ɪntrə'dʌktrɪ] *adj* d'introduction, préliminaire.

introvert ['ɪntrəvɜːt] *n* introverti *m*, -e *f*.

introverted ['ɪntrəvɜːtɪd] *adj* introverti(e).

intrude [ɪn'truːd] *vi* faire intrusion ; to intrude on sb déranger qqn.

intruder [ɪn'truːdə'] *n* intrus *m*, -e *f*.

intrusive [ɪn'truːsɪv] *adj* gênant(e), importun(e).

intuition [,ɪntjuː'ɪʃn] *n* intuition *f*.

inundate ['ɪnʌndeɪt] *vt* 1. *fml* [flood] inonder - 2. [overwhelm] : to be inundated with être submergé(e) de.

invade [ɪn'veɪd] *vt* 1. *fig* & MIL envahir - 2. [disturb - privacy etc] violer.

invalid ⋄ *adj* [ɪn'vælɪd] 1. [illegal, unacceptable] non valide, non valable - 2. [not reasonable] non valable. ⋄ *n* ['ɪnvəlɪd] invalide *mf*.

invaluable [ɪn'væljʊəbl] *adj* : invaluable (to) [help, advice, person] précieux(euse) (pour) ; [experience, information] inestimable (pour).

invariably [ɪn'veərɪəblɪ] *adv* invariablement, toujours.

invasion [ɪn'veɪʒn] *n lit* & *fig* invasion *f*.

invent [ɪn'vent] *vt* inventer.

invention [ɪn'venʃn] *n* invention *f*.

inventive [ɪn'ventɪv] *adj* inventif(ive).

inventor [ɪn'ventə'] *n* inventeur *m*, -trice *f*.

inventory ['ɪnvəntrɪ] *n* 1. [list] inventaire *m* - 2. *US* [goods] stock *m*.

invert [ɪn'vɜːt] *vt* retourner.

inverted commas [ɪn,vɜːtɪd-] *npl UK* guillemets *mpl*.

invest [ɪn'vest] ⋄ *vt* 1. [money] : to invest sthg (in) investir qqch (dans) - 2. [time, energy] : to invest sthg in sthg/in doing sthg consacrer qqch à qqch/à faire qqch, employer qqch à qqch/à faire qqch. ⋄ *vi* 1. FIN : to invest (in sthg) investir (dans qqch) - 2. *fig* [buy] : to invest in sthg se payer qqch, s'acheter qqch.

investigate [ɪn'vestɪgeɪt] *vt* enquêter sur, faire une enquête sur ; [subj: scientist] faire des recherches sur.

investigation [ɪn,vestɪ'geɪʃn] *n* **1.** [enquiry] : **investigation (into)** enquête *f* (sur) ; [scientific] recherches *fpl* (sur) - **2.** (*U*) [investigating] investigation *f*.

investment [ɪn'vestmənt] *n* **1.** FIN investissement *m*, placement *m* - **2.** [of energy] dépense *f*.

investor [ɪn'vestər] *n* investisseur *m*.

inveterate [ɪn'vetərət] *adj* invétéré(e).

invidious [ɪn'vɪdɪəs] *adj* [task] ingrat(e) ; [comparison] injuste.

invigilate [ɪn'vɪdʒɪleɪt] *UK* <> *vi* surveiller les candidats (à un examen). <> *vt* surveiller.

invigorating [ɪn'vɪgəreɪtɪŋ] *adj* tonifiant(e), vivifiant(e).

invincible [ɪn'vɪnsɪbl] *adj* [army, champion] invincible ; [record] imbattable.

invisible [ɪn'vɪzɪbl] *adj* invisible.

invitation [,ɪnvɪ'teɪʃn] *n* [request] invitation *f*.

invite [ɪn'vaɪt] *vt* **1.** [ask to come] : **to invite sb (to)** inviter qqn (à) - **2.** [ask politely] : **to invite sb to do sthg** inviter qqn à faire qqch - **3.** [encourage] : **to invite trouble** aller au devant des ennuis ; **to invite gossip** faire causer.

inviting [ɪn'vaɪtɪŋ] *adj* attrayant(e), agréable ; [food] appétissant(e).

invoice ['ɪnvɔɪs] <> *n* facture *f*. <> *vt* **1.** [client] envoyer la facture à - **2.** [goods] facturer.

invoke [ɪn'vəʊk] *vt* **1.** *fml* [law, act] invoquer - **2.** [feelings] susciter, faire naître ; [help] demander, implorer.

involuntary [ɪn'vɒləntrɪ] *adj* involontaire.

involve [ɪn'vɒlv] *vt* **1.** [entail] nécessiter ; **what's involved?** de quoi s'agit-il? ; **to involve doing sthg** nécessiter de faire qqch - **2.** [concern, affect] toucher - **3.** [person] : **to involve sb in sthg** impliquer qqn dans qqch.

involved [ɪn'vɒlvd] *adj* **1.** [complex] complexe, compliqué(e) - **2.** [participating, implicated] : **to be involved in sthg** participer OR prendre part à qqch - **3.** [in relationship] : **to be involved with sb** avoir des relations intimes avec qqn.

involvement [ɪn'vɒlvmənt] *n* **1.** [participation] : **involvement (in)** participation *f* (à) - **2.** [concern, enthusiasm] : **involvement (in)** engagement *m* (dans).

inward ['ɪnwəd] <> *adj* **1.** [inner] intérieur(e) - **2.** [towards the inside] vers l'intérieur. <> *adv US* = **inwards**.

inwards ['ɪnwədz] *adv* vers l'intérieur.

in-your-face *adj inf* provocant(e).

iodine [*UK* 'aɪədiːn, *US* 'aɪədaɪn] *n* iode *m*.

iota [aɪ'əʊtə] *n* brin *m*, grain *m*.

IOU (*abbrev of* **I owe you**) *n* reconnaissance *f* de dette.

IQ (*abbrev of* **intelligence quotient**) *n* QI *m*.

IRA *n* (*abbrev of* **Irish Republican Army**) IRA *f*.

Iran [ɪ'rɑːn] *n* Iran *m*.

Iranian [ɪ'reɪnjən] <> *adj* iranien(enne). <> *n* Iranien *m*, -enne *f*.

Iraq [ɪ'rɑːk] *n* Iraq *m*, Irak *m*.

Iraqi [ɪ'rɑːkɪ] <> *adj* iraquien(enne), irakien(enne). <> *n* Iraquien *m*, -enne *f*, Irakien *m*, -enne *f*.

irate [aɪ'reɪt] *adj* furieux(euse).

Ireland ['aɪələnd] *n* Irlande *f*.

iris ['aɪərɪs] (*pl* **-es** [-iːz]) *n* iris *m*.

Irish ['aɪrɪʃ] <> *adj* irlandais(e). <> *n* [language] irlandais *m*. <> *npl* : **the Irish** les Irlandais.

Irishman ['aɪrɪʃmən] (*pl* **-men** [-mən]) *n* Irlandais *m*.

Irish Sea *n* : **the Irish Sea** la mer d'Irlande.

Irishwoman ['aɪrɪʃ,wʊmən] (*pl* **-women** [-,wɪmɪn]) *n* Irlandaise *f*.

irksome ['ɜːksəm] *adj* ennuyeux(euse), assommant(e).

iron ['aɪən] <> *adj* **1.** [made of iron] de OR en fer - **2.** *fig* [very strict] de fer. <> *n* **1.** [metal, golf club] fer *m* - **2.** [for clothes] fer *m* à repasser. <> *vt* repasser. ◆ **iron out** *vt sep fig* [difficulties] aplanir ; [problems] résoudre.

Iron Curtain *n* : **the Iron Curtain** le rideau de fer.

ironic(al) [aɪ'rɒnɪk(l)] *adj* ironique.

ironing ['aɪənɪŋ] *n* repassage *m*.

ironing board *n* planche *f* OR table *f* à repasser.

ironmonger ['aɪən,mʌŋgər] *n UK dated* quincaillier *m* ; **ironmonger's (shop)** quincaillerie *f*.

irony ['aɪrənɪ] *n* ironie *f*.

irrational [ɪ'ræʃənl] *adj* irrationnel(elle), déraisonnable ; [person] non rationnel(elle).

irreconcilable [ɪ,rekən'saɪləbl] *adj* inconciliable.

irregular [ɪ'regjʊlər] *adj* irrégulier(ère).

irrelevant [ɪ'reləvənt] *adj* sans rapport.

irreparable [ɪ'repərəbl] *adj* irréparable.

irreplaceable [,ɪrɪ'pleɪsəbl] *adj* irremplaçable.

irrepressible [,ɪrɪ'presəbl] *adj* [enthusiasm] que rien ne peut entamer ; **he's irrepressible** il est d'une bonne humeur à toute épreuve.

irresistible [,ɪrɪ'zɪstəbl] *adj* irrésistible.

irrespective [,ɪrɪ'spektɪv] ◆ **irrespective of** *prep* sans tenir compte de.

irresponsible [,ɪrɪ'spɒnsəbl] *adj* irresponsable.

irrigate ['ɪrɪgeɪt] *vt* irriguer.

irrigation [,ɪrɪ'geɪʃn] ⬦ *n* irrigation *f*. ⬦ *comp* d'irrigation.

irritable ['ɪrɪtəbl] *adj* irritable.

irritate ['ɪrɪteɪt] *vt* irriter.

irritating ['ɪrɪteɪtɪŋ] *adj* irritant(e).

irritation [ɪrɪ'teɪʃn] *n* **1.** [anger, soreness] irritation *f* - **2.** [cause of anger] source *f* d'irritation.

IRS (*abbrev of* **Internal Revenue Service**) *n* US : **the IRS** ≃ le fisc.

is [ɪz] ▶ be.

Islam ['ɪzlɑːm] *n* islam *m*.

Islamic fundamentalist *n* fondamentaliste *mf* islamiste.

Islamist ['ɪzləmɪst] *adj & n* islamiste *mf*.

island ['aɪlənd] *n* **1.** [isle] île *f* - **2.** AUT refuge *m* pour piétons.

islander ['aɪləndər] *n* habitant *m*, -e *f* d'une île.

isle [aɪl] *n* île *f*.

Isle of Man *n* : **the Isle of Man** l'île *f* de Man.

Isle of Wight [-waɪt] *n* : **the Isle of Wight** l'île *f* de Wight.

isn't ['ɪznt] = is not.

isobar ['aɪsəbɑːr] *n* isobare *f*.

isolate ['aɪsəleɪt] *vt* : **to isolate sb/sthg (from)** isoler qqn/qqch (de).

isolated ['aɪsəleɪtɪd] *adj* isolé(e).

ISP *n abbrev of* **Internet Service Provider**.

Israel ['ɪzreɪəl] *n* Israël *m*.

Israeli [ɪz'reɪlɪ] ⬦ *adj* israélien(enne). ⬦ *n* Israélien *m*, -enne *f*.

issue ['ɪʃuː] ⬦ *n* **1.** [important subject] question *f*, problème *m* ; *pej* : **to make an issue of sthg** faire toute une affaire de qqch ; **at issue** en question, en cause - **2.** [edition] numéro *m* - **3.** [bringing out - of banknotes, shares] émission *f*. ⬦ *vt* **1.** [make public - decree, statement] faire ; [- warning] lancer - **2.** [bring out - banknotes, shares] émettre ; [- book] publier - **3.** [passport etc] délivrer.

isthmus ['ɪsməs] *n* isthme *m*.

it [ɪt] ⬦ *pron* **1.** [referring to specific person or thing - subj] il (elle) ; [- direct object] le (la), l' (+ *vowel or silent 'h'*) ; [- indirect object] lui ; **did you find it?** tu l'as trouvé(e) ? ; **give it to me at once** donne-moi ça tout de suite - **2.** [with prepositions] : **put the vegetables in it** mettez-y les légumes ; **on it** dessus ; **under it** dessous ; **beside it** à côté ; **from/of it** en ; **he's very proud of it** il en est très fier - **3.** [impersonal use] il, ce ; **it is today** il fait froid aujourd'hui ; **it's two o'clock** il est deux heures ; **who is it?** it's Mary/me qui est-ce ? c'est Mary/moi. ⬦ *n inf* **1.** [in games] : **you're it!** c'est toi le chat!, c'est toi qui y es! - **2.** [most important person] : **he thinks he's it** il s'y croit.

IT *n abbrev of* **information technology**.

Italian [ɪ'tæljən] ⬦ *adj* italien(enne). ⬦ *n* **1.** [person] Italien *m*, -enne *f* - **2.** [language] italien *m*.

italic [ɪ'tælɪk] *adj* italique. ▶ **italics** *npl* italiques *fpl*.

Italy ['ɪtəlɪ] *n* Italie *f*.

itch [ɪtʃ] ⬦ *n* démangeaison *f*. ⬦ *vi* **1.** [be itchy] : **my arm itches** mon bras me démange - **2.** *fig* [be impatient] : **to be itching to do sthg** mourir d'envie de faire qqch.

itchy ['ɪtʃɪ] *adj* qui démange.

it'd ['ɪtəd] = it would, = it had.

item ['aɪtəm] *n* **1.** [gen] chose *f*, article *m* ; [on agenda] question *f*, point *m* - **2.** PRESS article *m*.

itemize, UK **-ise** ['aɪtəmaɪz] *vt* détailler.

itinerary [aɪ'tɪnərərɪ] *n* itinéraire *m*.

it'll ['ɪtl] = it will.

its [ɪts] *poss adj* son (sa), ses (*pl*).

it's [ɪts] = it is, = it has.

itself [ɪt'self] *pron* **1.** [reflexive] se ; [after prep] soi - **2.** [for emphasis] lui-même(elle-même) ; **in itself** en soi.

ITV (*abbrev of* **Independent Television**) *n* sigle désignant les programmes diffusés par les chaînes relevant de l'IBA.

I've [aɪv] = I have.

ivory ['aɪvərɪ] *n* ivoire *m*.

ivy ['aɪvɪ] *n* lierre *m*.

Ivy League *n* US les huit grandes universités de l'est des États-Unis.

J

j [dʒeɪ] (*pl* **j's** OR **js**), **J** (*pl* **J's** OR **Js**) *n* [letter] j *m inv*, J *m inv*.

jab [dʒæb] ⬦ *n* **1.** UK *inf* [injection] piqûre *f* - **2.** [in boxing] direct *m*. ⬦ *vt* : **to jab sthg into** planter OR enfoncer qqch dans.

jabber ['dʒæbər] *vt & vi* baragouiner.

jack [dʒæk] *n* **1.** [device] cric *m* - **2.** [playing card] valet *m*. ▶ **jack up** *vt sep* **1.** [car] soulever avec un cric - **2.** *fig* [prices] faire grimper.

jackal ['dʒækəl] *n* chacal *m*.

jackdaw ['dʒækdɔː] *n* choucas *m*.

jacket ['dʒækɪt] *n* **1.** [garment] veste *f* - **2.** [of potato] peau *f*, pelure *f* - **3.** [of book] jaquette *f* - **4.** *US* [of record] pochette *f*.

jacket potato *n UK* pomme de terre *f* en robe de chambre.

jackhammer ['dʒæk,hæmər] *n US* marteau piqueur *m*.

jack plug *n UK* ELEC jack *m*.

jackpot ['dʒækpɒt] *n* gros lot *m*.

jaded ['dʒeɪdɪd] *adj* blasé(e).

jagged ['dʒægɪd] *adj* déchiqueté(e), dentelé(e).

jail [dʒeɪl] ⋄ *n* prison *f*. ⋄ *vt* emprisonner, mettre en prison.

jailer ['dʒeɪlər] *n* geôlier *m*, -ère *f*.

jam [dʒæm] ⋄ *n* **1.** [preserve] confiture *f* - **2.** [of traffic] embouteillage *m*, bouchon *m* - **3.** *inf* [difficult situation] : **to get into/be in a jam** être dans le pétrin. ⋄ *vt* **1.** [mechanism, door] bloquer, coincer - **2.** [push tightly] : **to jam sthg into** entasser OR tasser qqch dans ; **to jam sthg onto** enfoncer qqch sur - **3.** [block - streets] embouteiller ; [- switchboard] surcharger - **4.** RADIO brouiller. ⋄ *vi* [lever, door] se coincer ; [brakes] se bloquer.

Jamaica [dʒə'meɪkə] *n* la Jamaïque.

jam-packed [-'pækt] *adj inf* plein(e) à craquer.

jangle ['dʒæŋgl] ⋄ *vt* [keys] faire cliqueter ; [bells] faire retentir. ⋄ *vi* [keys] cliqueter ; [bells] retentir.

janitor ['dʒænɪtər] *n US & Scot* concierge *mf*.

January ['dʒænjʊərɪ] *n* janvier *m* ; *see also* **September**.

Japan [dʒə'pæn] *n* Japon *m*.

Japanese [,dʒæpə'ni:z] ⋄ *adj* japonais(e). ⋄ *n* (*pl* **Japanese**) [language] japonais *m*. ⋄ *npl* [people] : **the Japanese** les Japonais *mpl*.

jar [dʒɑ:r] ⋄ *n* pot *m*. ⋄ *vt* [shake] secouer. ⋄ *vi* **1.** [noise, voice] : **to jar (on sb)** irriter (qqn), agacer (qqn) - **2.** [colours] jurer.

jargon ['dʒɑ:gən] *n* jargon *m*.

jaundice ['dʒɔ:ndɪs] *n* jaunisse *f*.

jaundiced ['dʒɔ:ndɪst] *adj fig* [attitude, view] aigri(e).

jaunt [dʒɔ:nt] *n* balade *f*.

jaunty ['dʒɔ:ntɪ] *adj* désinvolte, insouciant(e).

javelin ['dʒævlɪn] *n* javelot *m*.

jaw [dʒɔ:] *n* mâchoire *f*.

jawbone ['dʒɔ:bəʊn] *n* (os *m*) maxillaire *m*.

jay [dʒeɪ] *n* geai *m*.

jaywalker ['dʒeɪwɔ:kər] *n* piéton *m* qui traverse en dehors des clous.

jazz [dʒæz] *n* MUS jazz *m*. ⬤ **jazz up** *vt sep inf* égayer.

jazzy ['dʒæzɪ] *adj* [bright] voyant(e).

jealous ['dʒeləs] *adj* jaloux(ouse).

jealousy ['dʒeləsɪ] *n* jalousie *f*.

jeans [dʒi:nz] *npl* jean *m*, blue-jean *m*.

Jeep® [dʒi:p] *n* Jeep® *f*.

jeer [dʒɪər] ⋄ *vt* huer, conspuer. ⋄ *vi* : **to jeer (at sb)** huer (qqn), conspuer (qqn).

Jehovah's Witness [dʒɪ,həʊvəz-] *n* témoin *m* de Jéhovah.

Jell-O® ['dʒeləʊ] *n US* gelée *f*.

jelly ['dʒelɪ] *n* (*pl* **jellies**) **1.** *UK* gelée *f* - **2.** *US* [jam] confiture *f*.

jellyfish ['dʒelɪfɪʃ] (*pl* **jellyfish** OR **-es** [-i:z]) *n* méduse *f*.

jeopardize, *UK* **-ise** ['dʒepədaɪz] *vt* compromettre, mettre en danger.

jerk [dʒɜ:k] ⋄ *n* **1.** [movement] secousse *f*, saccade *f* - **2.** *v inf* [fool] abruti *m*, -e *f*. ⋄ *vi* [person] sursauter ; [vehicle] cahoter.

jersey ['dʒɜ:zɪ] (*pl* **-s**) *n* **1.** [sweater] pull *m* - **2.** [cloth] jersey *m*.

Jersey ['dʒɜ:zɪ] *n* **1.** *UK* Jersey *f* - **2.** *US* New-Jersey *m*.

jest [dʒest] *n fml* plaisanterie *f* ; **in jest** pour rire.

Jesus (Christ) ['dʒi:zəs-] *n* Jésus *m*, Jésus-Christ *m*.

jet [dʒet] *n* **1.** [plane] jet *m*, avion *m* à réaction - **2.** [of fluid] jet *m* - **3.** [nozzle, outlet] ajutage *m*.

jet-black *adj* noir(e) comme (du) jais.

jet engine *n* moteur *m* à réaction.

jetfoil ['dʒetfɔɪl] *n* hydroglisseur *m*.

jet lag *n* fatigue *f* due au décalage horaire.

jetsam ['dʒetsəm] ➤ **flotsam**.

jettison ['dʒetɪsən] *vt* **1.** [cargo] jeter, larguer - **2.** *fig* [ideas] abandonner, renoncer à.

jetty ['dʒetɪ] *n* jetée *f*.

Jew [dʒu:] *n* Juif *m*, -ive *f*.

jewel ['dʒu:əl] *n* bijou *m* ; [in watch] rubis *m*.

jewel case *n* boîte *f* de CD.

jeweller *UK*, **jeweler** *US* ['dʒu:ələr] *n* bijoutier *m*, -ière *f* ; **jeweller's (shop)** *UK* bijouterie *f*.

jewellery *UK*, **jewelry** *US* ['dʒu:əlrɪ] *n* (*U*) bijoux *mpl*.

jewelry store *US n* bijouterie *f*.

Jewess ['dʒu:ɪs] *n* juive *f*.

Jewish ['dʒu:ɪʃ] *adj* juif(ive).

jib [dʒɪb] *n* **1.** [of crane] flèche *f* - **2.** [sail] foc *m*.

jibe [dʒaɪb] *n* sarcasme *m*, moquerie *f*.

jiffy ['dʒɪfɪ] *n inf* **in a jiffy** en un clin d'œil.

Jiffy bag® *n* enveloppe *f* matelassée.

jig [dʒɪg] *n* gigue *f*.

jigsaw (puzzle) ['dʒɪgsɔ:-] *n* puzzle *m*.

jilt [dʒɪlt] *vt* laisser tomber.

jingle ['dʒɪŋgl] ⋄ *n* **1.** [sound] cliquetis *m* - **2.** [song] jingle *m*, indicatif *m*. ⋄ *vi* [bell] tinter ; [coins, bracelets] cliqueter.

jinx [dʒɪŋks] *n* poisse *f*.

jitters ['dʒɪtəz] *npl inf* **the jitters** le trac.

job [dʒɒb] *n* **1.** [employment] emploi *m* - **2.** [task] travail *m*, tâche *f* - **3.** [difficult task] : **to have a job doing sthg** avoir du mal à faire qqch - **4.** [state of affairs] : **it's a good job they were home** heureusement qu'ils étaient à la maison ; **thanks for the map, it's just the job** merci pour la carte, c'est exactement ce qu'il me fallait ; **to give sb/sthg up as a bad job** laisser tomber qqn/qqch qui n'en vaut pas la peine ; **we decided to make the best of a bad job** nous avons décidé de faire avec ce que nous avions.

job action *n US* = industrial action.

job centre *n UK* agence *f* pour l'emploi.

jobless ['dʒɒblɪs] *adj* au chômage.

jobsharing ['dʒɒbʃeərɪŋ] *n* partage *m* de l'emploi.

jockey ['dʒɒkɪ] (*pl* -s) ⋄ *n* jockey *mf*. ⋄ *vi* : **to jockey for position** manœuvrer pour devancer ses concurrents.

jocular ['dʒɒkjʊlə] *adj fml* **1.** [cheerful] enjoué(e), jovial(e) - **2.** [funny] amusant(e).

jodhpurs ['dʒɒdpəz] *npl* jodhpurs *mpl*, culotte *f* de cheval.

jog [dʒɒg] ⋄ *n* : **to go for a jog** faire du jogging. ⋄ *vt* pousser ; **to jog sb's memory** rafraîchir la mémoire de qqn. ⋄ *vi* faire du jogging, jogger.

jogging ['dʒɒgɪŋ] *n* jogging *m*.

john [dʒɒn] *n US inf* petit coin *m*, cabinets *mpl*.

join [dʒɔɪn] ⋄ *n* raccord *m*, joint *m*. ⋄ *vt* **1.** [connect - gen] unir, joindre ; [- towns etc] relier - **2.** [get together with] rejoindre, retrouver - **3.** [political party] devenir membre de ; [club] s'inscrire à ; [army] s'engager dans ; **to join a queue** *UK*, **to join a line** *US* prendre la queue. ⋄ *vi* **1.** [connect] se joindre - **2.** [become a member - gen] devenir membre ; [- of club] s'inscrire. ◆ **join in** ⋄ *vt insep* prendre part à, participer à. ⋄ *vi* participer. ◆ **join up** *vi UK* MIL s'engager dans l'armée.

joiner ['dʒɔɪnə] *n UK* menuisier *m*, -ière *f*.

joinery ['dʒɔɪnərɪ] *n UK* menuiserie *f*.

joint [dʒɔɪnt] ⋄ *adj* [effort] conjugué(e) ; [responsibility] collectif(ive). ⋄ *n* **1.** [gen & TECH] joint *m* - **2.** ANAT articulation *f* - **3.** *UK* [of meat] rôti *m* - **4.** *inf* [place] bouge *m* - **5.** *drug sl* joint *m*.

joint account *n* compte *m* joint.

jointly ['dʒɔɪntlɪ] *adv* conjointement.

joke [dʒəʊk] ⋄ *n* blague *f*, plaisanterie *f* ; **to play a joke on sb** faire une blague à qqn, jouer un tour à qqn ; **it's no joke** *inf* [not easy] ce n'est pas de la tarte. ⋄ *vi* plaisanter, blaguer ; **to joke about sthg** plaisanter sur qqch, se moquer de qqch.

joker ['dʒəʊkə] *n* **1.** [person] blagueur *m*, -euse *f* - **2.** [playing card] joker *m*.

jolly ['dʒɒlɪ] ⋄ *adj* [person] jovial(e), enjoué(e) ; [time, party] agréable. ⋄ *adv UK inf* drôlement, rudement.

jolt [dʒəʊlt] ⋄ *n* **1.** [jerk] secousse *f*, soubresaut *m* - **2.** [shock] choc *m*. ⋄ *vt* secouer.

Jordan ['dʒɔ:dn] *n* Jordanie *f*.

jostle ['dʒɒsl] ⋄ *vt* bousculer. ⋄ *vi* se bousculer.

jot [dʒɒt] *n* [of truth] grain *m*, brin *m*. ◆ **jot down** *vt sep* noter, prendre note de.

journal ['dʒɜ:nl] *n* **1.** [magazine] revue *f* - **2.** [diary] journal *m*.

journalism ['dʒɜ:nəlɪzm] *n* journalisme *m*.

journalist ['dʒɜ:nəlɪst] *n* journaliste *mf*.

journey ['dʒɜ:nɪ] (*pl* -s) *n* voyage *m*.

jovial ['dʒəʊvjəl] *adj* jovial(e).

jowls [dʒaʊlz] *npl* bajoues *fpl*.

joy [dʒɔɪ] *n* joie *f*.

joyful ['dʒɔɪfʊl] *adj* joyeux(euse).

joyride ['dʒɔɪraɪd] *n* virée *f* (*dans une voiture volée*).

joystick ['dʒɔɪstɪk] *n* AERON manche *m* (à balai) ; COMPUT manette *f*.

JP *n abbrev of* Justice of the Peace.

Jr. (*abbrev of* Junior) Jr.

jubilant ['dʒu:bɪlənt] *adj* [person] débordant(e) de joie, qui jubile ; [shout] de joie.

jubilee ['dʒu:bɪli:] *n* jubilé *m*.

judge [dʒʌdʒ] ⋄ *n* juge *mf*. ⋄ *vt* **1.** [gen] juger - **2.** [estimate] évaluer, juger. ⋄ *vi* juger ; **to judge from** OR **by, judging from** OR **by** à en juger par.

judg(e)ment ['dʒʌdʒmənt] *n* jugement *m*.

judicial [dʒu:'dɪʃl] *adj* judiciaire.

judiciary [dʒu:'dɪʃərɪ] *n* : **the judiciary** la magistrature.

judicious [dʒu:'dɪʃəs] *adj* judicieux(euse).

judo ['dʒu:dəʊ] *n* judo *m*.

jug [dʒʌg] *n UK* pot *m*, pichet *m*.

juggernaut ['dʒʌgənɔːt] *n* UK poids *m* lourd.

juggle ['dʒʌgl] ◇ *vt* lit & fig jongler avec. ◇ *vi* jongler.

juggler ['dʒʌglə'] *n* jongleur *m*, -euse *f*.

jugular (vein) ['dʒʌgjulə'-] *n* (veine *f*) jugulaire *f*.

juice [dʒuːs] *n* jus *m*.

juicy ['dʒuːsɪ] *adj* [fruit] juteux(euse).

jukebox ['dʒuːkbɒks] *n* juke-box *m*.

July [dʒuː'laɪ] *n* juillet *m* ; see also **September**.

jumble ['dʒʌmbl] ◇ *n* [mixture] mélange *m*, fatras *m*. ◇ *vt* : **to jumble (up)** mélanger, embrouiller.

jumble sale *n* UK vente *f* de charité (où sont vendus des articles d'occasion).

jumbo jet ['dʒʌmbəʊ-] *n* jumbo-jet *m*.

jumbo-sized [-saɪzd] *adj* géant(e), énorme.

jump [dʒʌmp] ◇ *n* **1.** [leap] saut *m*, bond *m* - **2.** [fence] obstacle *m* - **3.** [rapid increase] flambée *f*, hausse *f* brutale. ◇ *vt* **1.** [fence, stream etc] sauter, franchir d'un bond - **2.** inf [attack] sauter sur, tomber sur. ◇ *vi* **1.** [gen] sauter, bondir ; [in surprise] sursauter - **2.** [increase rapidly] grimper en flèche, faire un bond. ◆ **jump at** *vt insep* fig sauter sur.

jumper ['dʒʌmpə'] *n* **1.** UK [pullover] pull *m*, sweat *m* inf - **2.** US [dress] robe *f* chasuble.

jumper cables *npl* US = jump leads.

jumper leads *npl* UK & Aus = jump leads.

jump leads *npl* câbles *mpl* de démarrage.

jump rope *n* US corde *f* à sauter.

jump-start *vt* : **to jump-start a car** faire démarrer une voiture en la poussant.

jumpsuit ['dʒʌmpsuːt] *n* combinaison-pantalon *f*.

jumpy ['dʒʌmpɪ] *adj* inf nerveux(euse).

Jun. abbrev of **Junr**.

junction ['dʒʌŋkʃn] *n* UK [of roads] carrefour *m* ; RAIL embranchement *m*.

June [dʒuːn] *n* juin *m* ; see also **September**.

jungle ['dʒʌŋgl] *n* lit & fig jungle *f*.

junior ['dʒuːnjə'] ◇ *adj* **1.** [gen] jeune - **2.** US [after name] junior. ◇ *n* **1.** [in rank] subalterne *mf* - **2.** [in age] cadet *m*, -ette *f* - **3.** US SCH ≃ élève *mf* de première - **4.** US UNIV ≃ étudiant *m*, -e *f* de troisième année ; ≃ étudiant *m*, -e *f* en licence.

junior high school *n* US ≃ collège *m* d'enseignement secondaire.

junior school *n* UK école *f* primaire.

junk [dʒʌŋk] *n* [unwanted objects] bric-à-brac *m*.

junk food *n* (U) pej : **to eat junk food** manger des cochonneries.

junkie ['dʒʌŋkɪ] *n* drug sl drogué *m*, -e *f*.

junk mail *n* (U) pej prospectus *mpl* publicitaires envoyés par la poste.

junk shop *n* boutique *f* de brocanteur.

Junr (abbrev of **Junior**) Jr.

Jupiter ['dʒuːpɪtə'] *n* [planet] Jupiter *f*.

jurisdiction [,dʒʊərɪs'dɪkʃn] *n* juridiction *f*.

juror ['dʒʊərə'] *n* juré *m*, -e *f*.

jury ['dʒʊərɪ] *n* jury *m*.

just [dʒʌst] ◇ *adv* **1.** [recently] : **he's just left** il vient de partir - **2.** [at that moment] : **I was just about to go** j'allais juste partir, j'étais sur le point de partir ; **I'm just going to do it now** je vais le faire tout de suite OR à l'instant ; **she arrived just as I was leaving** elle est arrivée au moment même où je partais OR juste comme je partais - **3.** [only, simply] : **just add water** vous n'avez plus qu'à ajouter de l'eau ; **just a minute** OR **moment** OR **second!** un (petit) instant! - **4.** [almost not] tout juste, à peine ; **I only just missed the train** j'ai manqué le train de peu ; **we have just enough time** on a juste assez de temps - **5.** [for emphasis] : **the coast is just marvellous** la côte est vraiment magnifique ; **just look at this mess!** non, mais regarde un peu ce désordre! - **6.** [exactly, precisely] tout à fait, exactement ; **it's just what I need** c'est tout à fait ce qu'il me faut - **7.** [in requests] : **could you just move over please?** pourriez-vous vous pousser un peu s'il vous plaît? ◇ *adj* juste, équitable. ◆ **just about** *adv* à peu près, plus ou moins. ◆ **just as** *adv* [in comparison] tout aussi ; **you're just as clever/as smart** US **as he is** tu es tout aussi intelligent que lui. ◆ **just in case** ◇ *conj* juste au cas où ; **just in case we don't see each other** juste au cas où nous ne nous verrions pas. ◇ *adv* au cas où ; **take a coat, just in case** prends un manteau, on ne sait jamais OR au cas où. ◆ **just now** *adv* **1.** [a short time ago] il y a un moment, tout à l'heure - **2.** [at this moment] en ce moment. ◆ **just then** *adv* à ce moment-là. ◆ **just the same** *adv* [nonetheless] quand même.

justice ['dʒʌstɪs] *n* **1.** [gen] justice *f* - **2.** [of claim, cause] bien-fondé *m*.

Justice of the Peace (pl **Justices of the Peace**) *n* juge *m* de paix.

justify ['dʒʌstɪfaɪ] *vt* [give reasons for] justifier.

jut [dʒʌt] *vi* : **to jut (out)** faire saillie, avancer.

juvenile ['dʒuːvənaɪl] ◇ *adj* **1.** LAW mineur(e), juvénile - **2.** [childish] puéril(e). ◇ *n* LAW mineur *m*, -e *f*.

juxtapose [,dʒʌkstə'pəʊz] *vt* juxtaposer.

K

k¹ (*pl* **k's** OR **ks**), **K** (*pl* **K's** OR **Ks**) [keɪ] *n* [letter] k *m inv*, K *m inv*.

K² **1.** (*abbrev of* **kilobyte**) Ko - **2.** (*abbrev of* **thousand**) K.

kaleidoscope [kə'laɪdəskəʊp] *n* kaléidoscope *m*.

kangaroo [,kæŋgə'ru:] *n* kangourou *m*.

kaput [kə'pʊt] *adj inf* fichu(e), foutu(e).

karat ['kærət] *n* US [for gold] carat *m*.

karate [kə'rɑːtɪ] *n* karaté *m*.

kayak ['kaɪæk] *n* kayak *m*.

kB, **KB** (*abbrev of* **kilobyte(s)**) *n* COMPUT Ko *m*.

kcal (*abbrev of* **kilocalorie**) Kcal.

kebab [kɪ'bæb] *n* brochette *f*.

keel [kiːl] *n* quille *f*; **on an even keel** stable. ◆ **keel over** *vi* [ship] chavirer ; [person] tomber dans les pommes.

keen [kiːn] *adj* UK **1.** [enthusiastic] enthousiaste, passionné(e) ; **to be keen on sthg** avoir la passion de qqch ; **he's keen on her** elle lui plaît ; **to be keen to do** OR **on doing sthg** tenir à faire qqch - **2.** [interest, desire, mind] vif(vive) ; [competition] âpre, acharné(e) - **3.** [sense of smell] fin(e) ; [eyesight] perçant(e).

keep [kiːp] ◇ *vt* (*pt & pp* **kept**) **1.** [retain, store] garder ; **keep the change!** gardez la monnaie! - **2.** [prevent] : **to keep sb/sthg from doing sthg** empêcher qqn/qqch de faire qqch ; **I couldn't keep myself from laughing** je n'ai pas pu m'empêcher de rire - **3.** [detain] retenir ; [prisoner] détenir ; **to keep sb waiting** faire attendre qqn - **4.** [promise] tenir ; [appointment] aller à ; [vow] être fidèle à - **5.** [not disclose] : **to keep sthg from sb** cacher qqch à qqn ; **to keep sthg to o.s.** garder qqch pour soi - **6.** [diary, record, notes] tenir - **7.** [own - sheep, pigs etc] élever ; [- shop] tenir ; [- car] avoir, posséder ; **they keep themselves to themselves** ils restent entre eux, ils se tiennent à l'écart. ◇ *vi* (*pt & pp* **kept**) **1.** [remain] : **to keep warm** se tenir au chaud ; **to keep quiet** garder le silence ; **keep quiet!** taisez-vous! - **2.** [continue] : **he keeps interrupting me** il n'arrête pas de m'interrompre ; **to keep talking/walking** continuer à parler/à marcher - **3.** [continue moving] : **to keep left/right** garder sa gauche/sa droite ; **to keep north/south** continuer vers le nord/le sud - **4.** [food] se conserver - **5.** UK [in health] : **how are you keeping?** *dated* comment allez-vous? ◇ *n* : **to earn one's keep** gagner sa vie. ◆ **keeps** *n* : **for keeps** pour toujours. ◆ **keep away** ◇ *vt sep* tenir éloigné, empêcher d'approcher ; **spectators were kept away by the fear of violence** la peur de la violence tenait les spectateurs à distance. ◇ *vi insep* ne pas s'approcher ; **keep away from those people** évitez ces gens-là. ◆ **keep back** *vt sep* **1.** [keep at a distance - crowd, spectators] tenir éloigné, empêcher de s'approcher - **2.** [information] cacher, ne pas divulguer. ◆ **keep from** *vt insep* s'empêcher de, se retenir de ; **I couldn't keep from laughing** je n'ai pas pu m'empêcher de rire. ◆ **keep in with** *vt insep* : **to keep in with sb** rester en bons termes avec qqn. ◆ **keep off** ◇ *vt sep* [dogs, birds, trespassers] éloigner ; [rain, sun] protéger de ; **this cream will keep the mosquitoes off** cette crème vous/le/te etc protégera contre les moustiques ; **keep your hands off!** pas touche!, bas les pattes! ◇ *vt insep* : **'keep off the grass'** '(il est) interdit de marcher sur la pelouse'. ◆ **keep on** *vi* **1.** [continue] : **to keep on (doing sthg)** [without stopping] continuer (de OR à faire qqch) ; [repeatedly] ne pas arrêter (de faire qqch) - **2.** [talk incessantly] : **to keep on (about sthg)** ne pas arrêter de parler (de qqch). ◆ **keep out** ◇ *vt sep* empêcher d'entrer. ◇ *vi* : **'keep out'** 'défense d'entrer'. ◆ **keep to** *vt insep* [rules, deadline] respecter, observer. ◆ **keep up** ◇ *vt sep* [continue to do] continuer ; [maintain] maintenir. ◇ *vi* [maintain pace, level etc] : **to keep up (with sb)** aller aussi vite (que qqn).

keeper ['kiːpə'] *n* gardien *m*, -enne *f*.

keep-fit *n* (*U*) UK gymnastique *f*.

keeping ['kiːpɪŋ] *n* **1.** [care] garde *f* - **2.** [conformity, harmony] : **to be in/out of keeping with** [rules etc] être/ne pas être conforme à ; [subj: furniture] aller/ne pas aller avec.

keepsake ['kiːpseɪk] *n* souvenir *m*.

keg [keg] *n* tonnelet *m*, baril *m*.

kennel ['kenl] *n* UK [shelter for dog] niche *f* ; US chenil *m*. ◆ **kennels** *npl* UK chenil *m*.

Kenya ['kenjə] *n* Kenya *m*.

Kenyan ['kenjən] ◇ *adj* kenyan(e). ◇ *n* Kenyan *m*, -e *f*.

kept [kept] *pt & pp* ▶ **keep**.

kerb [kɜːb] *n* UK bordure *f* du trottoir.

kernel ['kɜːnl] *n* amande *f*.

kerosene ['kerəsiːn] *n* kérosène *m* ; US [paraffin] paraffine *f*.

ketchup ['ketʃəp] *n* ketchup *m*.

kettle ['ketl] n bouilloire f.

key [ki:] <> n **1.** [gen & MUS] clef f, clé f ; **the key (to sthg)** fig la clé (de qqch) - **2.** [of typewriter, computer, piano] touche f - **3.** [of map] légende f. <> adj clé (after n). ◆ **key in** vt sep [text, data] saisir ; [code] composer.

keyboard ['ki:bɔːd] n [gen & COMPUT] clavier m.

keyboard shortcut n raccourci m clavier.

key card n badge m.

keyed up [,ki:d-] adj tendu(e), énervé(e).

keyhole ['ki:həʊl] n trou m de serrure.

keynote ['ki:nəʊt] <> n note f dominante. <> comp : **keynote speech** discours-programme m.

keypad ['ki:pæd] n COMPUT pavé m numérique.

key ring n porte-clés m inv.

kg (abbrev of **kilogram**) kg.

khaki ['kɑːkɪ] <> adj kaki (inv). <> n [colour] kaki m.

kick [kɪk] <> n **1.** [with foot] coup m de pied - **2.** inf [excitement] : **to get a kick from** OR **out of sthg** trouver qqch excitant ; **to do sthg for kicks** faire qqch pour le plaisir. <> vt **1.** [with foot] donner un coup de pied à ; **to kick o.s.** fig se donner des gifles OR des claques - **2.** inf [give up] : **to kick the habit** arrêter. <> vi **1.** [person - repeatedly] donner des coups de pied ; [- once] donner un coup de pied - **2.** [baby] gigoter - **3.** [animal] ruer. ◆ **kick about, kick around** <> vt sep **1.** : **to kick a ball around** jouer au ballon - **2.** inf [idea] débattre ; **we kicked a few ideas around** on a discuté à bâtons rompus. <> vi UK inf traîner. ◆ **kick in** <> vt sep défoncer à coups de pied ; **I'll kick his teeth in!** inf je vais lui casser la figure! <> vi insep inf entrer en action. ◆ **kick off** vi **1.** FOOTBALL donner le coup d'envoi - **2.** inf fig [start] démarrer. ◆ **kick out** vt sep inf vider, jeter dehors.

kid [kɪd] <> n **1.** inf [child] gosse mf, gamin m, -e f - **2.** inf [young person] petit jeune m, petite jeune f - **3.** [goat, leather] chevreau m. <> comp esp US inf [brother, sister] petit(e). <> vt inf **1.** [tease] faire marcher - **2.** [delude] : **to kid o.s.** se faire des illusions. <> vi inf : **to be kidding** plaisanter.

kidnap ['kɪdnæp] (esp US) vt kidnapper, enlever.

kidnapper UK, **kidnaper** esp US ['kɪdnæpə'] n kidnappeur m, -euse f, ravisseur m, -euse f.

kidnapping, esp US **kidnaping** ['kɪdnæpɪŋ] n enlèvement m.

kidney ['kɪdnɪ] (pl **-s**) n **1.** ANAT rein m - **2.** CULIN rognon m.

kidney bean n haricot m rouge.

kill [kɪl] <> vt **1.** [cause death of] tuer - **2.** fig [hope, chances] mettre fin à ; [pain] supprimer. <> vi tuer. <> n mise f à mort.

killer ['kɪlə'] n [person] meurtrier m, -ère f ; [animal] tueur m, -euse f.

killing ['kɪlɪŋ] n meurtre m.

killjoy ['kɪldʒɔɪ] n pej rabat-joie m inv.

kiln [kɪln] n four m.

kilo ['kiːləʊ] (pl **-s**) (abbrev of **kilogram**) n kilo m.

kilobyte ['kɪləbaɪt] n COMPUT kilo-octet m.

kilogram, esp UK **kilogramme** ['kɪləgræm] n kilogramme m.

kilohertz ['kɪləhɜːtz] (pl **kilohertz**) n kilohertz m.

kilometre UK ['kɪlə,miːtə'], **kilometer** US [kɪ'lɒmɪtə'] n kilomètre m.

kilowatt ['kɪləwɒt] n kilowatt m.

kilt [kɪlt] n kilt m.

kin [kɪn] ▶ **kith**.

kind [kaɪnd] <> adj gentil(ille), aimable. <> n [sort, type] genre m, sorte f ; **they're two of a kind** ils se ressemblent ; **a kind of** une sorte de, une espèce de ; **I had a kind of (a) feeling you'd come** j'avais comme l'impression que tu viendrais ; **kind of** inf plutôt ; **it's kind of big and round** c'est plutôt OR dans le genre grand et rond ; **I'm kind of sad about it** ça me rend un peu triste ; **did you hit him? – well, kind of** tu l'as frappé? – oui, si on veut. ◆ **in kind** adv [with goods, services] en nature ; **to pay sb in kind** payer qqn en nature.

kindergarten ['kɪndə,gɑːtn] n UK jardin m d'enfants ; US ≃ première classe de la maternelle.

kind-hearted [-'hɑːtɪd] adj qui a bon cœur, bon(bonne).

kindle ['kɪndl] vt **1.** [fire] allumer - **2.** fig [feeling] susciter.

kindly ['kaɪndlɪ] <> adj **1.** dated [person] plein(e) de bonté, bienveillant(e) - **2.** [gesture] plein(e) de gentillesse. <> adv **1.** [speak, smile etc] avec gentillesse - **2.** [please] : **kindly leave the room!** veuillez sortir, s'il vous plaît ! ; **will you kindly...?** veuillez..., je vous prie de...

kindness ['kaɪndnɪs] n gentillesse f.

kindred ['kɪndrɪd] adj [similar] semblable, similaire ; **kindred spirit** âme f sœur.

king [kɪŋ] n roi m.

kingdom ['kɪŋdəm] n **1.** [country] royaume m - **2.** [of animals, plants] règne m.

kingfisher ['kɪŋ,fɪʃə'] n martin-pêcheur m.

king-size(d) [-saɪz(d)] adj [cigarette] long(longue) ; [pack] géant(e) ; **a king-sized bed** un grand lit (de 195 cm).

kinky ['kɪŋkɪ] adj inf vicieux(euse).

kiosk ['ki:ɒsk] *n* **1.** [small shop] kiosque *m* - **2.** *UK* [telephone box] cabine *f* (téléphonique).

kip [kɪp] *UK inf* ◇ *n* somme *m*, roupillon *m*. ◇ *vi* faire OR piquer un petit somme.

kipper ['kɪpə'] *n* hareng *m* fumé OR saur.

kiss [kɪs] ◇ *n* baiser *m* ; **to give sb a kiss** embrasser qqn, donner un baiser à qqn. ◇ *vt* embrasser. ◇ *vi* s'embrasser.

kiss of life *n UK* **the kiss of life** le bouche-à-bouche.

kit [kɪt] *n* **1.** [set] trousse *f* - **2.** *(U)* SPORT affaires *fpl*, équipement *m* - **3.** [to be assembled] kit *m*.

kit bag *n* sac *m* de marin.

kitchen ['kɪtʃɪn] *n* cuisine *f*.

kitchen sink *n* évier *m*.

kitchen unit *n* élément *m* de cuisine.

kite [kaɪt] *n* [toy] cerf-volant *m*.

kith [kɪθ] *n dated* : **kith and kin** parents et amis *mpl*.

kitten ['kɪtn] *n* chaton *m*.

kitty ['kɪtɪ] *n* **1.** [shared fund] cagnotte *f* - **2.** *inf* [animal] chat(te).

kiwi ['ki:wi:] *n* **1.** [bird] kiwi *m*, aptéryx *m* - **2.** *inf* [New Zealander] Néo-Zélandais *m*, -e *f*.

km (*abbrev of* **kilometre**) km.

km/h (*abbrev of* **kilometres per hour**) km/h.

knack [næk] *n* : **to have a** OR **the knack (for doing sthg)** avoir le coup (pour faire qqch).

knackered ['nækəd] *adj UK v inf* crevé(e), claqué(e).

knapsack ['næpsæk] *n* sac *m* à dos.

knead [ni:d] *vt* pétrir.

knee [ni:] *n* genou *m*.

kneecap ['ni:kæp] *n* rotule *f*.

kneel [ni:l] (*UK*, *pt & pp* **knelt** *US*, *pt & pp* **knelt** OR **-ed**) *vi* se mettre à genoux, s'agenouiller. ◆ **kneel down** *vi* se mettre à genoux, s'agenouiller.

knelt [nelt] *pt & pp* ▶ **kneel**.

knew [nju:] *pt* ▶ **know**.

knickers ['nɪkəz] *npl* **1.** *UK* [underwear] culotte *f* - **2.** *US* [knickerbockers] pantalon *m* de golf.

knick-knack ['nɪknæk] *n* babiole *f*, bibelot *m*.

knife [naɪf] ◇ *n* (*pl* **knives** [naɪvz]) couteau *m*. ◇ *vt* donner un coup de couteau à, poignarder.

knight [naɪt] ◇ *n* **1.** [in history, member of nobility] chevalier *m* - **2.** [in chess] cavalier *m*. ◇ *vt* faire chevalier.

knighthood ['naɪthʊd] *n* titre *m* de chevalier.

knit [nɪt] ◇ *adj* : **closely** OR **tightly knit** *fig*

très uni(e). ◇ *vt* (*pt & pp* **knit** OR **-ted**) tricoter. ◇ *vi* (*pt & pp* **knit** OR **-ted**) **1.** [with wool] tricoter - **2.** [broken bones] se souder.

knitting ['nɪtɪŋ] *n* (*U*) tricot *m*.

knitting needle *n* aiguille *f* à tricoter.

knitwear ['nɪtweə'] *n* (*U*) tricots *mpl*.

knives [naɪvz] *npl* ▶ **knife**.

knob [nɒb] *n* **1.** [on door] poignée *f*, bouton *m* ; [on drawer] poignée ; [on bedstead] pomme *f* - **2.** [on TV, radio etc] bouton *m*.

knock [nɒk] ◇ *n* **1.** [hit] coup *m* - **2.** *fig* [setback] coup *m* dur. ◇ *vt* **1.** [hit] frapper, cogner ; **to knock sb/sthg over** renverser qqn/qqch - **2.** *inf* [criticize] critiquer, dire du mal de. ◇ *vi* **1.** [on door] : **to knock on** OR **at the door** frapper (à la porte) - **2.** [car engine] cogner, avoir des ratés. ◆ **knock down** *vt sep* **1.** [subj: car, driver] renverser - **2.** [building] démolir. ◆ **knock off** *vi inf* [stop working] finir son travail OR sa journée. ◆ **knock out** *vt sep* **1.** [make unconscious] assommer - **2.** [from competition] éliminer. ◆ **knock over** *vt sep* renverser, faire tomber.

knocker ['nɒkə'] *n* [on door] heurtoir *m*.

knock-kneed [-'ni:d] *adj* cagneux(euse), qui a les genoux cagneux.

knock-on effect *n UK* réaction *f* en chaîne.

knockout ['nɒkaʊt] *n* knock-out *m*, K.-O. *m*

knot [nɒt] ◇ *n* **1.** [gen] nœud *m* ; **to tie/untie a knot** faire/défaire un nœud - **2.** [of people] petit attroupement *m*. ◇ *vt* nouer, faire un nœud à.

knotty ['nɒtɪ] *adj fig* épineux(euse).

know [nəʊ] ◇ *vt* (*pt* **knew**, *pp* **known**) **1.** [gen] savoir ; [language] savoir parler ; **to know (that)...** savoir que... ; **to let sb know (about sthg)** faire savoir (qqch) à qqn, informer qqn (de qqch) ; **to get to know sthg** apprendre qqch - **2.** [person, place] connaître ; **to get to know sb** apprendre à mieux connaître qqn. ◇ *vi* (*pt* **knew**, *pp* **known**) savoir ; **to know of sthg** connaître qqch ; **to know about** [be aware of] être au courant de ; [be expert in] s'y connaître en. ◇ *n* : **to be in the know** être au courant.

know-all *UK*, **know-it-all** *US n* (monsieur) je-sais-tout *m*, (madame) je-sais-tout *f*.

know-how *n* savoir-faire *m*, technique *f*.

knowing ['nəʊɪŋ] *adj* [smile, look] entendu(e).

knowingly ['nəʊɪŋlɪ] *adv* **1.** [smile, look] d'un air entendu - **2.** [intentionally] sciemment.

know-it-all *US* = **know-all**.

knowledge ['nɒlɪdʒ] *n* (*U*) **1.** [gen]

connaissance f ; **without my knowledge** à mon insu ; **to the best of my knowledge** à ma connaissance, autant que je sache - **2.** [learning, understanding] savoir m, connaissances fpl.

knowledgeable ['nɒlɪdʒəbl] adj bien informé(e).

known [nəʊn] pp ► know.

knuckle ['nʌkl] n **1.** ANAT articulation f OR jointure f du doigt - **2.** [of meat] jarret m.

knuckle-duster n coup-de-poing m américain.

koala (bear) [kəʊ'ɑːlə-] n koala m.

Koran [kɒ'rɑːn] n : **the Koran** le Coran.

Korea [kə'rɪə] n Corée f.

Korean [kə'rɪən] <> adj coréen(enne). <> n **1.** [person] Coréen m, -enne f - **2.** [language] coréen m.

kosher ['kəʊʃər] adj **1.** [meat] kasher (inv) - **2.** inf [reputable] O.K. (inv), réglo (inv).

Kosovar [kɒsəvɑːr] n kosovar mf.

Kosovo [kɒsəvəʊ] n Kosovo m.

Koweit = **Kuwait**.

kung fu [ˌkʌŋ'fuː] n kung-fu m.

Kurd [kɜːd] n Kurde mf.

Kuwait [kʊ'weɪt], **Koweit** [kəʊ'weɪt] n **1.** [country] Koweït m - **2.** [city] Koweït City.

L

l¹[el] (pl **l's** OR **ls**), **L** (pl **L's** OR **Ls**) n [letter] l m inv, L m inv.

l² (abbrev of **litre**) l.

lab [læb] n inf labo m.

label ['leɪbl] <> n **1.** [identification] étiquette f - **2.** [of record] label m, maison f de disques. <> vt (UK & US) **1.** [fix label to] étiqueter - **2.** [describe] : **to label sb (as)** cataloguer OR étiqueter qqn (comme).

labor etc US = **labour** etc.

laboratory [UK lə'bɒrətrɪ, US 'læbrə,tɔːrɪ] n laboratoire m.

laborious [lə'bɔːrɪəs] adj laborieux(euse).

labor union n US syndicat m.

labour UK, **labor** US ['leɪbər] <> n **1.** [gen & MED] travail m - **2.** [workers, work carried out] main d'œuvre f. <> vi travailler dur ;

to labour at OR **over** peiner sur. ◆ **Labour** UK <> adj POL travailliste. <> n (U) POL les travaillistes mpl.

laboured UK, **labored** US ['leɪbəd] adj [breathing] pénible ; [style] lourd(e), laborieux(euse).

labourer UK, **laborer** US ['leɪbərər] n travailleur manuel m, travailleuse manuelle f ; [agricultural] ouvrier agricole m, ouvrière agricole f.

Labour Party n UK : **the Labour Party** le parti travailliste.

Labrador ['læbrədɔːr] n [dog] labrador m.

labyrinth ['læbərɪnθ] n labyrinthe m.

lace [leɪs] <> n **1.** [fabric] dentelle f - **2.** [of shoe etc] lacet m. <> vt **1.** [shoe etc] lacer - **2.** [drink, food] verser de l'alcool OR une drogue dans. ◆ **lace up** vt sep lacer.

lace-up n UK chaussure f à lacets.

lack [læk] <> n manque m ; **for** OR **through lack of** par manque de ; **no lack of** bien assez de. <> vt manquer de. <> vi : **to be lacking in sthg** manquer de qqch ; **to be lacking** manquer, faire défaut.

lackadaisical [ˌlækə'deɪzɪkl] adj pej nonchalant(e).

lacklustre UK, **lackluster** US ['læk,lʌstər] adj terne.

laconic [lə'kɒnɪk] adj fml laconique.

lacquer ['lækər] <> n [for wood] vernis m, laque f ; UK [for hair] laque f. <> vt laquer.

lacrosse [lə'krɒs] n crosse f.

lad [læd] n UK inf [boy] garçon m, gars m.

ladder ['lædər] <> n **1.** [for climbing] échelle f - **2.** UK [in tights] maille f filée, estafilade f. <> vt & vi UK [tights] filer.

laden ['leɪdn] adj : **laden (with)** chargé(e) (de).

ladies UK ['leɪdɪz], **ladies' room** US n toilettes fpl (pour dames).

ladle ['leɪdl] <> n louche f. <> vt servir (à la louche).

lady ['leɪdɪ] <> n [gen] dame f. <> comp : **a lady doctor** une femme docteur. ◆ **Lady** n Lady f.

ladybird UK ['leɪdɪbɜːd], **ladybug** US ['leɪdɪbʌg] n coccinelle f.

lady-in-waiting [-'weɪtɪŋ] (pl **ladies-in-waiting**) n dame f d'honneur.

ladylike ['leɪdɪlaɪk] adj distingué(e).

lag [læg] <> vi : **to lag (behind)** [person, runner] traîner ; [economy, development] être en retard, avoir du retard. <> vt [roof, pipe] calorifuger. <> n [timelag] décalage m.

lager ['lɑːgər] n (bière f) blonde f.

lagoon [lə'guːn] n lagune f.

laid [leɪd] *pt & pp* ► lay.

laid-back *adj inf* relaxe, décontracté(e).

lain [leɪn] *pp* ► lie.

lair [leər] *n* repaire *m*, antre *m*.

lairy ['leərɪ] *adj* tape à l'oeil (*inv*) *inf*, bruyant(e).

laity ['leɪətɪ] *n* RELIG : **the laity** les laïcs *mpl*.

lake [leɪk] *n* lac *m*.

Lake District *n* : **the Lake District** la région des lacs (*au nord-ouest de l'Angleterre*).

Lake Geneva *n* le lac Léman OR de Genève.

lamb [læm] *n* agneau *m*.

lambswool ['læmzwʊl] ◇ *n* lambswool *m*. ◇ *comp* en lambswool, en laine d'agneau.

lame [leɪm] *adj lit & fig* boiteux(euse).

lament [lə'ment] ◇ *n* lamentation *f*. ◇ *vt* se lamenter sur.

lamentable ['læməntəbl] *adj* lamentable.

laminated ['læmɪneɪtɪd] *adj* [wood] stratifié(e) ; [glass] feuilleté(e) ; [steel] laminé(e).

lamp [læmp] *n* lampe *f*.

lampoon [læm'pu:n] ◇ *n* satire *f*. ◇ *vt* faire la satire de.

lamppost ['læmppəʊst] *n* réverbère *m*.

lampshade ['læmpʃeɪd] *n* abat-jour *m*.

lance [lɑ:ns] ◇ *n* lance *f*. ◇ *vt* [for a boil] percer.

lance corporal *n* caporal *m*.

land [lænd] ◇ *n* **1.** [solid ground] terre *f* (ferme) ; [farming ground] terre, terrain *m* - **2.** [property] terres *fpl*, propriété *f* - **3.** [nation] pays *m*. ◇ *vt* **1.** [from ship, plane] débarquer - **2.** [catch - fish] prendre - **3.** [plane] atterrir - **4.** *inf* [obtain] décrocher - **5.** *inf* [place] : **to land sb in trouble** attirer des ennuis à qqn ; **to be landed with sthg** se coltiner qqch. ◇ *vi* **1.** [plane] atterrir - **2.** [fall] tomber. ► **land up** *vi inf* atterrir.

landing ['lændɪŋ] *n* **1.** [of stairs] palier *m* - **2.** AERON atterrissage *m* - **3.** [of goods from ship] débarquement *m*.

landing card *n* carte *f* de débarquement.

landing gear *n* (*U*) train *m* d'atterrissage.

landing stage *n* débarcadère *m*.

landing strip *n* piste *f* d'atterrissage.

landlady ['lænd,leɪdɪ] *n* [living in] logeuse *f* ; [owner] propriétaire *f*.

landlord ['lændlɔ:d] *n* **1.** [of rented property] propriétaire *m* - **2.** UK [of pub] patron *m*.

landmark ['lændmɑ:k] *n* point *m* de repère ; *fig* événement *m* marquant.

landowner ['lænd,əʊnər] *n* propriétaire foncier *m*, propriétaire foncière *f*.

landscape ['lændskeɪp] *n* paysage *m*.

landslide ['lændslaɪd] *n* **1.** [of earth] glissement *m* de terrain ; [of rocks] éboulement *m* - **2.** *fig* [election victory] victoire *f* écrasante.

lane [leɪn] *n* **1.** [in country] petite route *f*, chemin *m* - **2.** [in town] ruelle *f* - **3.** [for traffic] voie *f* ; **'keep in lane'** 'ne changez pas de file' - **4.** AERON & SPORT couloir *m*.

language ['læŋgwɪdʒ] *n* **1.** [of people, country] langue *f* - **2.** [terminology, ability to speak] langage *m*.

language lab(oratory) *n* labo(ratoire) *m* de langues.

languid ['læŋgwɪd] *adj lit* indolent(e).

languish ['læŋgwɪʃ] *vi* languir.

lank [læŋk] *adj* terne.

lanky ['læŋkɪ] *adj* dégingandé(e).

lantern ['læntən] *n* lanterne *f*.

Lao = **Laotian**.

lap [læp] ◇ *n* **1.** [of person] : **on sb's lap** sur les genoux de qqn - **2.** [of race] tour *m* de piste. ◇ *vt* **1.** [subj: animal] laper - **2.** [in race] prendre un tour d'avance sur. ◇ *vi* [water, waves] clapoter.

lapel [lə'pel] *n* revers *m*.

Lapland ['læplænd] *n* Laponie *f*.

lapse [læps] ◇ *n* **1.** [failing] défaillance *f* - **2.** [in behaviour] écart *m* de conduite - **3.** [of time] intervalle *m*, laps *m* de temps. ◇ *vi* **1.** [passport] être périmé(e) ; [membership] prendre fin ; [tradition] se perdre - **2.** [person] : **to lapse into bad habits** prendre de mauvaises habitudes.

laptop computer *n* (ordinateur *m*) portable *m*.

larceny ['lɑ:sənɪ] *n* (*U*) vol *m* (simple).

lard [lɑ:d] *n* saindoux *m*.

larder ['lɑ:dər] *n dated* garde-manger *m inv*.

large [lɑ:dʒ] *adj* grand(e) ; [person, animal, book] gros(grosse). ► **at large** *adv* **1.** [as a whole] dans son ensemble - **2.** [prisoner, animal] en liberté. ► **by and large** *adv* dans l'ensemble.

largely ['lɑ:dʒlɪ] *adv* en grande partie.

lark [lɑ:k] *n* **1.** [bird] alouette *f* - **2.** *inf* [joke] blague *f*. ► **lark about** *vi* s'amuser.

laryngitis [,lærɪn'dʒaɪtɪs] *n* (*U*) laryngite *f*.

larynx ['lærɪŋks] *n* larynx *m*.

lasagna, lasagne [lə'zænjə] *n* (*U*) lasagnes *fpl*.

laser ['leɪzər] *n* laser *m*.

laser printer *n* imprimante *f* (à) laser.

lash [læʃ] ◇ *n* **1.** [eyelash] cil *m* - **2.** [with whip] coup *m* de fouet. ◇ *vt* **1.** [gen] fouetter - **2.** [tie] attacher. ► **lash out** *vi* **1.** [physically] : **to lash out (at OR against)**

envoyer un coup (à) - **2.** UK inf [spend money] : **to lash out (on sthg)** faire une folie (en s'achetant qqch).

lass [læs] n esp Scot jeune fille f.

lasso [læ'su:] <> n (pl -s) lasso m. <> vt attraper au lasso.

last [lɑːst] <> adj dernier(ère) ; **last week/year** la semaine/l'année dernière, la semaine/l'année passée ; **last night** hier soir ; **down to the last detail/penny** jusqu'au moindre détail/dernier sou ; **last but one** avant-dernier(avant-dernière). <> adv **1.** [most recently] la dernière fois - **2.** [finally] en dernier, le dernier(la dernière). <> pron : **the Saturday before last** pas samedi dernier, mais le samedi d'avant ; **the year before last** il y a deux ans ; **the last but one** l'avant-dernier m, l'avant-dernière f ; **to leave sthg till last** faire qqch en dernier. <> n : **the last I saw of him** la dernière fois que je l'ai vu. <> vi durer ; [food] se garder, se conserver ; [feeling] persister. ⏪ **at last** adv enfin.

last-ditch adj ultime, désespéré(e).

lasting ['lɑːstɪŋ] adj durable.

lastly ['lɑːstlɪ] adv pour terminer, finalement.

last-minute adj de dernière minute.

last name n nom m de famille.

latch [lætʃ] n loquet m. ⏪ **latch onto** vt insep inf s'accrocher à.

latchkey kid n enfant qui rentre seul après l'école et qui a la clé du domicile familial.

late [leɪt] <> adj **1.** [not on time] : **to be late (for sthg)** être en retard (pour qqch) - **2.** [near end of] : **in late December, late in December** vers la fin décembre ; **at this late stage** à ce stade avancé - **3.** [later than normal] tardif(ive) - **4.** [former] ancien(enne) - **5.** [dead] : **her late husband** son défunt mari, feu son mari fml. <> adv **1.** [not on time] en retard ; **to arrive 20 minutes late** arriver avec 20 minutes de retard - **2.** [later than normal] tard ; **to work/go to bed late** travailler/se coucher tard ; **late in the afternoon** tard dans l'après-midi ; **late in the day** lit vers la fin de la journée ; **it's rather late in the day to be thinking about that** c'est un peu tard pour penser à ça. ⏪ **of late** adv récemment, dernièrement.

latecomer ['leɪt,kʌmər] n retardataire mf.

lately ['leɪtlɪ] adv ces derniers temps, dernièrement.

latent ['leɪtənt] adj latent(e).

later ['leɪtər] <> adj [date] ultérieur(e) ; [edition] postérieur(e). <> adv : **later (on)** plus tard.

lateral ['lætərəl] adj latéral(e).

latest ['leɪtɪst] <> adj dernier(ère). <> n : **at the latest** au plus tard.

lathe [leɪð] n tour m.

lather ['lɑːðər] <> n mousse f (de savon). <> vt savonner.

Latin ['lætɪn] <> adj latin(e). <> n [language] latin m.

Latin America n Amérique f latine.

Latin American n [person] Latino-Américain m, -e f.

Latin–American adj latino-américain(e).

latitude ['lætɪtjuːd] n latitude f.

latter ['lætər] <> adj **1.** [later] dernier(ère) - **2.** [second] deuxième. <> n : **the latter** celui-ci(celle-ci), ce dernier(cette dernière).

latterly ['lætəlɪ] adv fml récemment.

lattice ['lætɪs] n treillis m, treillage m.

Latvia ['lætvɪə] n Lettonie f.

laudable ['lɔːdəbl] adj louable.

laugh [lɑːf] <> n rire m ; **we had a good laugh** inf on a bien rigolé, on s'est bien amusé ; **to do sthg for laughs** OR **a laugh** inf faire qqch pour rire OR rigoler. <> vi rire. ⏪ **laugh at** vt insep [mock] se moquer de, rire de. ⏪ **laugh off** vt sep tourner en plaisanterie.

laughable ['lɑːfəbl] adj ridicule, risible.

laughingstock ['lɑːfɪŋstɒk] n risée f.

laughter ['lɑːftər] n (U) rire m, rires mpl.

launch [lɔːntʃ] <> n **1.** [gen] lancement m - **2.** [boat] chaloupe f. <> vt lancer.

launch(ing) pad, launchpad ['lɔːntʃ(ɪŋ)-] n pas m de tir.

launder ['lɔːndər] vt lit & fig blanchir.

launderette, UK **Launderette®** [lɔːn'dret], US **Laundromat®** ['lɔːndrəmæt] n laverie f automatique.

laundry ['lɔːndrɪ] n **1.** (U) [clothes] lessive f - **2.** [business] blanchisserie f.

laurel ['lɒrəl] n laurier m.

lava ['lɑːvə] n lave f.

lavatory ['lævətrɪ] n esp UK toilettes fpl.

lavender ['lævəndər] n [plant] lavande f.

lavish ['lævɪʃ] <> adj **1.** [generous] généreux(euse) ; **to be lavish with** être prodigue de - **2.** [sumptuous] somptueux(euse). <> vt : **to lavish sthg on sb** prodiguer qqch à qqn.

law [lɔː] n **1.** [gen] loi f ; **against the law** contraire à la loi, illégal(e) ; **to break the law** enfreindre OR transgresser la loi ; **law and order** ordre m public - **2.** LAW droit m - **3.** [scientific principle] loi f ; **the law of supply and demand** ECON la loi de l'offre et de la demande.

law-abiding [-ə,baɪdɪŋ] adj respectueux(euse) des lois.

law court n tribunal m, cour f de justice.

lawful ['lɔːfʊl] adj légal(e), licite.

lawn [lɔːn] n pelouse f, gazon m.

lawnmower ['lɔːn,məʊər] n tondeuse f à gazon.

lawn tennis n tennis m (sur gazon).

law school n faculté f de droit.

lawsuit ['lɔːsuːt] n procès m.

lawyer ['lɔːjər] n [in court] avocat m ; [of company] conseiller m, -ère f juridique ; [for wills, sales] notaire m.

lax [læks] adj relâché(e).

laxative ['læksətɪv] n laxatif m.

lay [leɪ] ⬦ pt ➤ lie. ⬦ vt (pt & pp laid) 1. [gen] poser, mettre ; fig : to lay the blame for sthg on sb rejeter la responsabilité de qqch sur qqn - 2. [trap, snare] tendre, dresser ; [plans] faire ; to lay the table UK mettre la table OR le couvert - 3. [egg] pondre. ⬦ adj 1. RELIG laïque - 2. [untrained] profane. ⬥ **lay aside** vt sep mettre de côté. ⬥ **lay down** vt sep 1. [guidelines, rules] imposer, stipuler - 2. [put down] déposer. ⬥ **lay off** ⬦ vt sep [make redundant] licencier. ⬦ vt insep inf 1. [leave alone] ficher la paix à - 2. [give up] arrêter. ⬥ **lay on** vt sep UK [provide, supply] organiser. ⬥ **lay out** vt sep 1. [arrange] arranger, disposer - 2. [design] concevoir.

layabout ['leɪəbaʊt] n UK inf fainéant m, -e f.

lay-by (pl lay-bys) n UK aire f de stationnement.

layer ['leɪər] n couche f ; fig [level] niveau m.

layman ['leɪmən] (pl -men [-mən]) n 1. [untrained person] profane m - 2. RELIG laïc m.

layout ['leɪaʊt] n [of office, building] agencement m ; [of garden] plan m ; [of page] mise f en page.

laze [leɪz] vi : to laze (about OR around) paresser.

lazy ['leɪzɪ] adj [person] paresseux(euse), fainéant(e) ; [action] nonchalant(e).

lazybones ['leɪzɪbəʊnz] (pl lazybones) n inf paresseux m, -euse f, fainéant m, -e f.

lb (abbrev of pound) livre (unité de poids).

LCD (abbrev of liquid crystal display) n affichage à cristaux liquides.

lead¹[liːd] ⬦ n 1. [winning position] : to be in OR have the lead mener, être en tête - 2. [initiative, example] initiative f, exemple m ; to take the lead montrer l'exemple - 3. THEAT : the lead le rôle principal - 4. [clue] indice m - 5. UK [for dog] laisse f - 6. [wire, cable] câble m, fil m. ⬦ adj [role etc] principal(e). ⬦ vt (pt & pp led) 1. [be at front of] mener, être à la tête de - 2. [guide]

guider, conduire - 3. [be in charge of] être à la tête de, diriger - 4. [life] mener - 5. [cause, bring] : to lead sb to do sthg inciter OR pousser qqn à faire qqch. ⬦ vi (pt & pp led) 1. [go] mener, conduire ; to lead to/into donner sur, donner accès à - 2. [be ahead] mener - 3. [result in] : to lead to sthg aboutir à qqch, causer qqch. ⬥ **lead up to** vt insep 1. [precede] conduire à, aboutir à - 2. [build up to] amener.

lead²[led] ⬦ n plomb m ; [in pencil] mine f. ⬦ comp en OR de plomb.

leaded ['ledɪd] adj [petrol] au plomb ; [window] à petits carreaux.

leader ['liːdər] n 1. [head, chief] chef mf ; POL leader mf - 2. [in race, competition] premier m, -ère f - 3. UK PRESS éditorial m.

leadership ['liːdəʃɪp] n 1. [people in charge] : the leadership les dirigeants mpl - 2. [position of leader] direction f - 3. [qualities of leader] qualités fpl de chef.

lead-free [led-] adj sans plomb.

lead guitar [liːd-] n première f guitare.

leading ['liːdɪŋ] adj 1. [most important] principal(e) - 2. [at front] de tête.

leading light n personnage m très important OR influent.

leaf [liːf] (pl leaves [liːvz]) n 1. [of tree, plant] feuille f - 2. [of table - hinged] abattant m ; [- pull-out] rallonge f - 3. [of book] feuille f, page f. ⬥ **leaf through** vt insep [magazine etc] parcourir, feuilleter.

leaflet ['liːflɪt] n prospectus m.

league [liːg] n ligue f ; SPORT championnat m ; to be in league with être de connivence avec.

leak [liːk] ⬦ n lit & fig fuite f. ⬦ vt [secret, information] divulguer. ⬦ vi fuir. ⬥ **leak out** vi 1. [liquid] fuir - 2. fig [secret, information] transpirer, être divulgué(e).

leakage ['liːkɪdʒ] n fuite f.

lean [liːn] ⬦ adj 1. [slim] mince - 2. [meat] maigre - 3. fig [month, time] mauvais(e). ⬦ vt (pt & pp leant OR -ed) [rest] : to lean sthg against appuyer qqch contre, adosser qqch à. ⬦ vi (pt & pp leant OR -ed) 1. [bend, slope] se pencher - 2. [rest] : to lean on/against s'appuyer sur/contre.

leaning ['liːnɪŋ] n : leaning (towards) penchant m (pour).

leant [lent] pt & pp ➤ lean.

lean-to (pl lean-tos) n appentis m.

leap [liːp] ⬦ n lit & fig bond m. ⬦ vi (pt & pp leapt OR -ed) 1. [gen] bondir - 2. fig [increase] faire un bond.

leapfrog ['liːpfrɒg] ⬦ n saute-mouton m inv. ⬦ vt dépasser (d'un bond). ⬦ vi : to leapfrog over sauter par-dessus.

leapt [lept] pt & pp ➤ leap.

leap year n année f bissextile.

learn [lɜːn] (pt & pp -ed OR learnt) <> vt : to learn (that)... apprendre que... ; to learn (how) to do sthg apprendre à faire qqch. <> vi : to learn (of OR about sthg) apprendre (qqch).

learned ['lɜːnɪd] adj savant(e).

learner ['lɜːnəʳ] n débutant m, -e f.

learner (driver) n UK conducteur débutant m, conductrice débutante f (qui n'a pas encore son permis).

learning ['lɜːnɪŋ] n savoir m, érudition f.

learning disability n difficultés fpl d'apprentissage.

learnt [lɜːnt] pt & pp ▶ learn.

lease [liːs] <> n bail m. <> vt louer ; to lease sthg from sb louer qqch à qqn ; to lease sthg to sb louer qqch à qqn.

leasehold ['liːshəʊld] <> adj loué(e) à bail, tenu(e) à bail. <> adv à bail.

leash [liːʃ] n US laisse f.

least [liːst] (superl of little) <> adj : the least le moindre(la moindre), le plus petit (la plus petite). <> pron [smallest amount] : the least le moins ; it's the least (that) he can do c'est la moindre des choses qu'il puisse faire ; not in the least pas du tout, pas le moins du monde ; to say the least c'est le moins qu'on puisse dire. <> adv : (the) least le moins (la moins). ▶ at least adv au moins ; [to correct] du moins. ▶ least of all adv surtout pas, encore moins. ▶ not least adv fml notamment.

leather ['leðəʳ] <> n cuir m. <> comp en cuir.

leave [liːv] <> vt (pt & pp left) 1. [gen] laisser ; to leave sb alone laisser qqn tranquille - 2. [go away from] quitter - 3. [bequeath] : to leave sb sthg, to leave sthg to sb léguer OR laisser qqch à qqn. <> vi (pt & pp left) partir. <> n 1. congé m ; to be on leave [from work] être en congé ; [from army] être en permission - 2. fml [permission] permission f, autorisation f ; by OR with your leave avec votre permission - 3. [farewell] congé m ; to take one's leave (of sb) prendre congé (de qqn) ; to take leave of one's senses fig perdre la tête OR la raison ; see also left. ▶ leave aside vt sep laisser de côté ; leaving aside the question of cost si on laisse de côté la question du coût. ▶ leave behind vt sep 1. [go away from] abandonner, laisser ; she soon left the other runners behind elle a vite distancé tous les autres coureurs - 2. [forget] oublier, laisser. ▶ leave out vt sep omettre, exclure ; leave it out! UK v inf lâche-moi! ▶ leave over vt sep [allow or cause to remain] laisser ; to be left over rester ; there are still one or two left over il en reste encore un ou deux.

leave of absence n congé m.

leaves [liːvz] npl ▶ leaf.

Lebanon ['lebənən] n Liban m.

lecherous ['letʃərəs] adj pej lubrique, libidineux(euse).

lecture ['lektʃəʳ] <> n 1. [talk - gen] conférence f ; UNIV cours m magistral - 2. [scolding] : to give sb a lecture réprimander qqn, sermonner qqn. <> vt [scold] réprimander, sermonner. <> vi : to lecture on sthg faire un cours sur qqch ; to lecture in sthg être professeur de qqch.

lecturer ['lektʃərəʳ] n [speaker] conférencier m, -ère f ; UK UNIV maître assistant m.

led [led] pt & pp ▶ lead¹.

ledge [ledʒ] n 1. [of window] rebord m - 2. [of mountain] corniche f.

ledger ['ledʒəʳ] n grand livre m.

leech [liːtʃ] n lit & fig sangsue f.

leek [liːk] n poireau m.

leer [lɪəʳ] <> n regard m libidineux. <> vi : to leer at reluquer.

leeway ['liːweɪ] n [room to manoeuvre] marge f de manœuvre.

left [left] <> pt & pp ▶ leave. <> adj 1. [remaining] : to be left rester ; have you OR do you have US any money left? il te reste de l'argent? - 2. [not right] gauche. <> adv à gauche. <> n : on OR to the left à gauche. ▶ Left n POL : the Left la Gauche.

left-hand adj de gauche ; left-hand side gauche f, côté m gauche.

left-hand drive adj [car] avec la conduite à gauche.

left-handed [-'hændɪd] adj 1. [person] gaucher(ère) - 2. [implement] pour gaucher.

left luggage (office) n UK consigne f.

leftover ['leftəʊvəʳ] adj qui reste, en surplus. ▶ leftovers npl restes mpl.

left wing n POL gauche f. ▶ left-wing adj POL de gauche.

leg [leg] n 1. [of person, trousers] jambe f ; [of animal] patte f ; to pull sb's leg faire marcher qqn - 2. CULIN [of lamb] gigot m ; [of pork, chicken] cuisse f - 3. [of furniture] pied m - 4. [of journey, match] étape f.

legacy ['legəsɪ] n lit & fig legs m, héritage m.

legal ['liːgl] adj 1. [concerning the law] juridique - 2. [lawful] légal(e).

legalize, UK -ise ['liːgəlaɪz] vt légaliser, rendre légal.

legal tender n monnaie f légale.

legend ['ledʒənd] n lit & fig légende f.

leggings ['legɪnz] npl jambières fpl, leggings mpl & fpl.

legible ['ledʒəbl] adj lisible.

legislation [,ledʒɪs'leɪʃn] *n* législation *f*.

legislature ['ledʒɪsleɪtʃər] *n* corps *m* législatif.

legitimate [lɪ'dʒɪtɪmət] *adj* légitime.

legless ['leglɪs] *adj UK inf* [drunk] bourré(e), rond(e).

legroom ['legrʊm] *n* (U) place *f* pour les jambes.

legwarmers [-,wɔːməz] *npl* jambières *fpl*.

leisure [UK 'leʒər, US 'liːʒər] *n* loisir *m*, temps *m* libre ; **at (one's) leisure** à loisir, tout à loisir.

leisure centre *n UK* centre *m* de loisirs.

leisurely [UK 'leʒəlɪ, US 'liːʒərlɪ] <> *adj* [pace] lent(e), tranquille. <> *adv* [walk] sans se presser.

leisure time *n* (U) temps *m* libre, loisirs *mpl*.

lemon ['lemən] *n* [fruit] citron *m*.

lemonade [,lemə'neɪd] *n* **1.** *UK* [fizzy] limonade *f* - **2.** *esp US* [flat] citronnade *f* - **3.** *US* [juice] citron *m* pressé.

lemongrass ['lemənɡrɑːs] *n* (U) citronnelle *f*.

lemon juice *n* jus *m* de citron.

lemon sole *n* limande-sole *f*.

lemon squash *n UK* citronnade *f*.

lemon squeezer [-'skwiːzər] *n* presse-citron *m inv*.

lemon tea *n* thé *m* (au) citron.

lend [lend] (*pt & pp* lent) *vt* **1.** [loan] prêter ; **to lend sb sthg, to lend sthg to sb** prêter qqch à qqn - **2.** [offer] : **to lend support (to sb)** offrir son soutien (à qqn) ; **to lend assistance (to sb)** prêter assistance (à qqn) - **3.** [add] : **to lend sthg to sthg** [quality etc] ajouter qqch à qqch.

lending rate ['lendɪŋ-] *n* taux *m* de crédit.

length [leŋθ] *n* **1.** [gen] longueur *f* ; **what length is it?** ça fait quelle longueur ? ; **it's five metres in length** cela fait cinq mètres de long - **2.** [piece : of string, wood] morceau *m*, bout *m* ; [- of cloth] coupon *m* - **3.** [duration] durée *f* ; **to go to great lengths to do sthg** tout faire pour faire qqch. ◆ **at length** *adv* **1.** [eventually] enfin - **2.** [in detail] à fond.

lengthen ['leŋθən] <> *vt* [dress etc] rallonger ; [life] prolonger. <> *vi* allonger.

lengthways ['leŋθweɪz], **lengthwise** ['leŋθwaɪz] *adv* dans le sens de la longueur.

lengthy ['leŋθɪ] *adj* très long (longue).

lenient ['liːnjənt] *adj* [person] indulgent(e) ; [laws] clément(e).

lens [lenz] *n* **1.** [of camera] objectif *m* ; [of glasses] verre *m* - **2.** [contact lens] verre *m* de contact, lentille *f* (cornéenne).

lent [lent] *pt & pp* ▶ lend.

Lent [lent] *n* Carême *m*.

lentil ['lentɪl] *n* lentille *f*.

Leo ['liːəʊ] *n* Lion *m*.

leopard ['lepəd] *n* léopard *m*.

leotard ['liːətɑːd] *n* collant *m*.

leper ['lepər] *n* lépreux *m*, -euse *f*.

leprosy ['leprəsɪ] *n* lèpre *f*.

lesbian ['lezbɪən] *n* lesbienne *f*.

less [les] (*compar of little*) <> *adj* moins de ; **less money/time than me** moins d'argent/de temps que moi. <> *pron* moins ; **it costs less than you think** ça coûte moins cher que tu ne le crois ; **no less than £50** pas moins de 50 livres ; **the less... the less...** moins... moins... <> *adv* moins ; **less than five** moins de cinq ; **less and less** de moins en moins. <> *prep* [minus] moins. ◆ **no less** *adv* rien de moins ; **he won the Booker prize, no less!** il a obtenu le Booker prize, rien de moins que ça! ; **taxes rose by no less than 15%** les impôts ont augmenté de 15 %, ni plus ni moins.

lessen ['lesn] <> *vt* [risk, chance] diminuer, réduire ; [pain] atténuer. <> *vi* [gen] diminuer ; [pain] s'atténuer.

lesser ['lesər] *adj* moindre ; **to a lesser extent** OR **degree** à un degré moindre.

lesson ['lesn] *n* leçon *f*, cours *m* ; **to teach sb a lesson** *fig* donner une (bonne) leçon à qqn.

let [let] (*pt & pp* let) *vt* **1.** [allow] : **to let sb do sthg** laisser qqn faire qqch ; **to let sb know sthg** dire qqch à qqn ; **to let go of sb/sthg** lâcher qqn/qqch ; **to let sb go** [gen] laisser (partir) qqn ; [prisoner] libérer qqn - **2.** [in verb forms] : **let's go!** allons-y! ; **let's see** voyons ; **let them wait** qu'ils attendent - **3.** *esp UK* [rent out] louer ; **'to let'** 'à louer'. ◆ **let alone** *conj* encore moins-, sans parler de. ◆ **let down** *vt sep* **1.** *UK* [deflate] dégonfler - **2.** [disappoint] décevoir. ◆ **let in** *vt sep* [admit] laisser OR faire entrer. ◆ **let off** *vt sep* **1.** *UK* [excuse] : **to let sb off sthg** dispenser qqn de qqch - **2.** [not punish] ne pas punir - **3.** [bomb] faire éclater ; [gun, firework] faire partir. ◆ **let on** *vi* : **don't let on!** *UK* ne dis rien (à personne)! ◆ **let out** <> *vt sep* **1.** [allow to go out] laisser sortir ; **to let air out of sthg** dégonfler qqch - **2.** [laugh, scream] laisser échapper. <> *vi US* SCH finir. ◆ **let up** *vi* **1.** [rain] diminuer - **2.** [person] s'arrêter.

letdown ['letdaʊn] *n inf* déception *f*.

lethal ['liːθl] *adj* mortel(elle), fatal(e).

lethargic [lə'θɑːdʒɪk] *adj* léthargique.

let's [lets] = let us.

letter ['letər] *n* lettre *f*.

letter bomb *n* lettre *f* piégée.

letterbox ['letəbɒks] *n UK* boîte *f* aux OR à lettres.

letter of credit *n* lettre *f* de crédit.

lettuce ['letɪs] *n* laitue *f*, salade *f*.

letup ['letʌp] *n* [in fighting] répit *m* ; [in work] relâchement *m*.

leukaemia, *esp US* **leukemia** [lu:'ki:mɪə] *n* leucémie *f*.

level ['levl] <> *adj* **1.** [equal in height] à la même hauteur ; [horizontal] horizontal(e) ; **to be level with** être au niveau de - **2.** [equal in standard] à égalité - **3.** [flat] plat(e), plan(e). <> *n* **1.** [gen] niveau *m* ; **to be on the level** *inf* être réglo - **2.** *US* [spirit level] niveau *m* à bulle. <> *vt* (*UK & US*) **1.** [make flat] niveler, aplanir - **2.** [demolish] raser. **level off, level out** *vi* **1.** [inflation etc] se stabiliser - **2.** [aeroplane] se mettre en palier. **level with** *vt insep inf* être franc (franche) OR honnête avec.

level crossing *n UK* passage *m* à niveau.

level-headed [-'hedɪd] *adj* raisonnable.

lever [*UK* 'li:vər, *US* 'levər] *n* levier *m*.

leverage [*UK* 'li:vərɪdʒ, *US* 'levərɪdʒ] *n* (*U*) **1.** [force] : **to get leverage on sthg** avoir une prise sur qqch - **2.** *fig* [influence] influence *f*.

levy ['levɪ] <> *n* prélèvement *m*, impôt *m*. <> *vt* prélever, percevoir.

lewd [lju:d] *adj* obscène.

liability [,laɪə'bɪlətɪ] *n* **1.** responsabilité *f* - **2.** *fig* [person, thing] danger *m* public. **liabilities** *npl* FIN dettes *fpl*, passif *m*.

liable ['laɪəbl] *adj* **1.** [likely] : **to be liable to do sthg** risquer de faire qqch, être susceptible de faire qqch - **2.** [prone] : **to be liable to sthg** être sujet(ette) à qqch - **3.** LAW : **to be liable (for)** être responsable (de) ; **to be liable to sthg** être passible de.

liaise [lɪ'eɪz] *vi UK* **to liaise with** assurer la liaison avec.

liar ['laɪər] *n* menteur *m*, -euse *f*.

libel ['laɪbl] <> *n* LAW diffamation *f*. <> *vt* (*UK & US*) diffamer.

liberal ['lɪbərəl] <> *adj* **1.** [tolerant] libéral(e) - **2.** [generous] généreux(euse). <> *n* libéral *m*, -e *f*. **Liberal** <> *adj* POL libéral(e). <> *n* POL libéral *m*, -e *f*.

Liberal Democrat *n* adhérent du principal parti centriste britannique.

liberate ['lɪbəreɪt] *vt* libérer.

liberation [,lɪbə'reɪʃn] *n* libération *f*.

liberty ['lɪbətɪ] *n* liberté *f* ; **at liberty** en liberté ; **to be at liberty to do sthg** être libre de faire qqch ; **to take liberties (with sb)** prendre des libertés (avec qqn).

Libra ['li:brə] *n* Balance *f*.

librarian [laɪ'breərɪən] *n* bibliothécaire *mf*.

library ['laɪbrərɪ] *n* bibliothèque *f*.

library book *n* livre *m* de bibliothèque.

libretto [lɪ'bretəʊ] (*pl* **-s**) *n* livret *m*.

Libya ['lɪbɪə] *n* Libye *f*.

lice [laɪs] *npl* > louse.

licence ['laɪsəns] <> *n* **1.** *UK* [gen] permis *m*, autorisation *f* ; **driving licence** *UK*, **driver's licence** *US* permis *m* de conduire ; **TV licence** redevance *f* télé - **2.** *UK* COMM licence *f*. <> *vt US* = **license.**

license ['laɪsəns] <> *vt* autoriser. <> *n US* = **licence.**

licensed ['laɪsənst] *adj* **1.** [person] : **to be licensed to do sthg** avoir un permis pour OR l'autorisation de faire qqch - **2.** *UK* [premises] qui détient une licence de débit de boissons.

license plate *n US* plaque *f* d'immatriculation.

lick [lɪk] *vt* **1.** [gen] lécher - **2.** *inf* [defeat] écraser.

licorice ['lɪkərɪs] *US* = **liquorice.**

lid [lɪd] *n* **1.** [cover] couvercle *m* - **2.** [eyelid] paupière *f*.

lie [laɪ] <> *n* mensonge *m* ; **to tell lies** mentir, dire des mensonges. <> *vi* (*pt* **lay**, *pp* **lain**, *cont* **lying**) **1.** (*pt & pp* **lied**) [tell lie] : **to lie (to sb)** mentir (à qqn) - **2.** [be horizontal] être allongé(e), être couché(e) - **3.** [lie down] s'allonger, se coucher - **4.** [be situated] se trouver, être - **5.** [difficulty, solution] résider ; **to lie low** *inf* se planquer, se tapir. **lie about, lie around** *vi UK* traîner. **lie down** *vi* s'allonger, se coucher. **lie in** *vi UK* rester au lit, faire la grasse matinée.

Liechtenstein ['lɪktənstaɪn] *n* Liechtenstein *m*.

lie-down *n UK* : **to have a lie-down** faire une sieste OR un (petit) somme.

lie-in *n UK* : **to have a lie-in** faire la grasse matinée.

lieutenant [*UK* lef'tenənt, *US* lu:'tenənt] *n* lieutenant *m*, -e *f*.

life [laɪf] *n* (*pl* **lives** [laɪvz]) **1.** [gen] vie *f* ; **for life** à vie ; **that's life!** c'est la vie! ; **to scare the life out of sb** faire une peur bleue à qqn - **2.** [liveliness] vie *f* ; **there's more life in Sydney than in Wellington** Sydney est plus animé que Wellington ; **to come to life** s'animer ; **she was the life and soul of the party** c'est elle qui a mis de l'ambiance dans la soirée - **3.** ART nature *f* ; **to draw from life** dessiner d'après nature ; LIT réalité *f* ; **his novels are very true to life** ses romans sont très réalistes - **4.** (*U*) *inf* [life imprisonment] emprisonnement *m* à perpétuité.

life assurance *esp UK* = **life insurance.**

lifebelt *n* bouée *f* de sauvetage.

lifeboat ['laɪfbəʊt] *n* canot *m* de sauvetage.

life buoy *n* bouée *f* de sauvetage.

life expectancy [-ɪk'spektənsɪ] *n* espérance *f* de vie.

lifeguard ['laɪfgɑːd] *n* [at swimming pool] maître-nageur sauveteur *m* ; [at beach] gardien *m* de plage.

life imprisonment [-ɪm'prɪznmənt] *n* emprisonnement *m* à perpétuité.

life insurance *n* assurance-vie *f*.

life jacket *n* gilet *m* de sauvetage.

lifeless ['laɪflɪs] *adj* 1. [dead] sans vie, inanimé(e) - 2. [listless - performance] qui manque de vie ; [- voice] monotone.

lifelike ['laɪflaɪk] *adj* 1. [statue, doll] qui semble vivant(e) - 2. [portrait] ressemblant(e).

lifeline ['laɪflaɪn] *n* corde *f* (de sauvetage) ; *fig* lien *m* vital (avec l'extérieur).

lifelong ['laɪflɒŋ] *adj* de toujours.

life preserver [-prɪˌzɜːvəʳ] *n US* [life belt] bouée *f* de sauvetage ; [life jacket] gilet *m* de sauvetage.

life raft *n* canot *m* pneumatique (de sauvetage).

lifesaver ['laɪfˌseɪvəʳ] *n* [person] maître-nageur sauveteur *m*.

life sentence *n* condamnation *f* à perpétuité.

life-size(d) [-saɪz(d)] *adj* grandeur nature *(inv)*.

lifespan ['laɪfspæn] *n* 1. [of person, animal] espérance *f* de vie - 2. [of product, machine] durée *f* de vie.

lifestyle ['laɪfstaɪl] *n* mode *m* OR style *m* de vie.

life-support system *n* respirateur *m* artificiel.

lifetime ['laɪftaɪm] *n* vie *f* ; **in my lifetime** de mon vivant.

lift [lɪft] <> *n* 1. [in car] : **to give sb a lift** emmener OR prendre qqn en voiture - 2. *UK* [elevator] ascenseur *m*. <> *vt* 1. [gen] lever ; [weight] soulever - 2. [plagiarize] plagier - 3. *inf* [steal] voler. <> *vi* 1. [lid etc] s'ouvrir - 2. [fog etc] se lever.

liftoff *n* décollage *m*.

light [laɪt] <> *adj* 1. [not dark] clair(e) - 2. [not heavy] léger(ère) - 3. [not much, not intense] [traffic] fluide ; [corrections] peu nombreux(euses) ; **I had a light lunch** j'ai mangé légèrement à midi, j'ai déjeuné léger - 4. [not difficult] facile. <> *n* 1. (U) [brightness] lumière *f* - 2. [device] lampe *f* - 3. [AUT - gen] feu *m* ; [- headlamp] phare *m* - 4. [for cigarette etc] feu *m* ; **have you got a light?** vous avez du feu ? ; **to set light to**

sthg mettre le feu à qqch - 5. [perspective] : **in the light of** *UK*, **in light of** *US* à la lumière de ; **in a good/bad light** sous un jour favorable/défavorable ; **to come to light** être découvert(-e) OR dévoilé(-e). <> *vt* (*vt & pp* **lit** OR **-ed**) 1. [lamp, cigarette] allumer - 2. [room, stage] éclairer. <> *adv* : **to travel light** voyager léger. ➡ **light up** <> *vt sep* 1. [illuminate] éclairer - 2. [cigarette etc] allumer. <> *vi* 1. [face] s'éclairer - 2. *inf* [start smoking] allumer une cigarette.

lightbulb *n* ampoule *f*.

lighten ['laɪtn] <> *vt* 1. [give light to] éclairer ; [make less dark] éclaircir - 2. [make less heavy] alléger. <> *vi* [brighten] s'éclaircir.

lighter ['laɪtəʳ] *n* [cigarette lighter] briquet *m*.

light-headed [-'hedɪd] *adj* : **to feel light-headed** avoir la tête qui tourne.

light-hearted [-'hɑːtɪd] *adj* 1. [cheerful] joyeux(euse), gai(e) - 2. [amusing] amusant(e).

lighthouse ['laɪthaʊs] (*pl* [-haʊzɪz]) *n* phare *m*.

lighting ['laɪtɪŋ] *n* éclairage *m*.

light meter *n* PHOT posemètre *m*, cellule *f* photoélectrique.

lightning ['laɪtnɪŋ] *n* (U) éclair *m*, foudre *f*.

lightweight ['laɪtweɪt] <> *adj* [object] léger(ère). <> *n* [boxer] poids *m* léger.

likable ['laɪkəbl] *adj* sympathique.

like [laɪk] <> *prep* 1. [gen] comme ; **to look like sb/sthg** ressembler à qqn/qqch ; **to taste like sthg** avoir un goût de qqch ; **like this/that** comme ci/ça - 2. [such as] tel que, comme. <> *vt* 1. [gen] aimer ; **I like her** elle me plaît ; **to like doing** OR **to do sthg** aimer faire qqch - 2. [in offers, requests] : **would you like some more cake?** vous prendrez encore du gâteau ? ; **I'd like to go** je voudrais bien OR j'aimerais y aller ; **I'd like you to come** je voudrais bien OR j'aimerais que vous veniez ; **if you like** si vous voulez. <> *n* : **the like** une chose pareille. ➡ **likes** *npl* : **likes and dislikes** goûts *mpl* ; **the likes of us/them** *etc inf* les gens comme nous/eux *etc*.

likeable ['laɪkəbl] = likable.

likelihood ['laɪklɪhʊd] *n* (U) chances *fpl*, probabilité *f*.

likely ['laɪklɪ] *adj* 1. [probable] probable ; **he's likely to get angry** il risque de se fâcher ; **a likely story!** *iro* à d'autres! - 2. [candidate] prometteur(euse).

liken ['laɪkn] *vt* : **to liken sb/sthg to** assimiler qqn/qqch à.

likeness ['laɪknɪs] *n* **1.** [resemblance] : likeness (to) ressemblance *f* (avec) - **2.** [portrait] portrait *m*.

likewise ['laɪkwaɪz] *adv* [similarly] de même ; **to do likewise** faire pareil OR de même.

liking ['laɪkɪŋ] *n* [for person] affection *f*, sympathie *f* ; [for food, music] goût *m*, penchant *m* ; **to have a liking for sthg** avoir le goût de qqch ; **to be to sb's liking** être du goût de qqn, plaire à qqn.

lilac ['laɪlək] *adj* [colour] lilas *(inv)*. *n* lilas *m*.

Lilo® ['laɪləʊ] *(pl* **-s)** *n* UK matelas *m* pneumatique.

lily ['lɪlɪ] *n* lis *m*.

lily of the valley *(pl* lilies of the valley) *n* muguet *m*.

limb [lɪm] *n* **1.** [of body] membre *m* - **2.** [of tree] branche *f*.

limber ['lɪmbər] ⇐ **limber up** *vi* s'échauffer.

limbo ['lɪmbəʊ] *(pl* **-s)** *n* (U) [uncertain state] : **to be in limbo** être dans les limbes.

lime [laɪm] *n* **1.** [fruit] citron *m* vert - **2.** [drink] : **lime (juice)** jus *m* de citron vert - **3.** [linden tree] tilleul *m* - **4.** [substance] chaux *f*.

limelight ['laɪmlaɪt] *n* : **to be in the limelight** être au premier plan.

limerick ['lɪmərɪk] *n* *poème humoristique en cinq vers.*

limestone ['laɪmstəʊn] *n* (U) pierre *f* à chaux, calcaire *m*.

limey ['laɪmɪ] *(pl* **-s)** *n* US inf *terme péjoratif désignant un Anglais.*

limit ['lɪmɪt] *n* limite *f* ; **off limits** esp US d'accès interdit ; **within limits** [to an extent] dans une certaine mesure. *vt* limiter, restreindre.

limitation [,lɪmɪ'teɪʃn] *n* limitation *f*, restriction *f*.

limited ['lɪmɪtɪd] *adj* limité(e), restreint(e).

limited (liability) company *n* UK société *f* anonyme.

limousine ['lɪməzi:n] *n* limousine *f*.

limp [lɪmp] *adj* mou (molle). *n* : **to have a limp** boiter. *vi* boiter ; **to go limp** s'affaisser.

limpet ['lɪmpɪt] *n* patelle *f*, bernique *f*.

line [laɪn] *n* **1.** [gen] ligne *f* - **2.** [row] rangée *f* - **3.** [queue] file *f*, queue *f* ; **to stand** OR **wait in line** faire la queue - **4.** [RAIL - track] voie *f* ; [- route] ligne *f* - **5.** [of writing, text] ligne *f* ; [of poem, song] vers *m* - **6.** TELEC ligne *f* ; **hold the line!** ne quittez pas! - **7.** [conformity] : **to step out of line** faire cavalier seul - **8.** *inf* [work] : **line of business**

branche *f* - **9.** [wrinkle] ride *f* - **10.** [string, wire etc] corde *f* ; **a fishing line** une ligne - **11.** [borderline, limit] frontière *f* ; **to draw the line at sthg** refuser de faire OR d'aller jusqu'à faire qqch - **12.** COMM gamme *f*. *vt* [drawer, box] tapisser ; [clothes] doubler. ⇐ **out of line** *adj* [remark, behaviour] déplacé(e). ⇐ **line up** *vt sep* **1.** [in rows] aligner - **2.** [organize] prévoir. *vi* [in row] s'aligner ; [in queue] faire la queue.

lined [laɪnd] *adj* **1.** [paper] réglé(e) - **2.** [wrinkled] ridé(e).

linen ['lɪnɪn] *n* (U) **1.** [cloth] lin *m* - **2.** [tablecloths, sheets] linge *m* (de maison).

liner ['laɪnər] *n* [ship] paquebot *m*.

linesman ['laɪnzmən] *(pl* **-men** [-mən]) *n* TENNIS juge *m* de ligne ; FOOTBALL juge *m* de touche.

lineup ['laɪnʌp] *n* **1.** SPORT équipe *f* - **2.** US [identity parade] rangée *f* de suspects *(pour identification par un témoin).*

linger ['lɪŋgər] *vi* **1.** [person] s'attarder - **2.** [doubt, pain] persister.

lingo ['lɪŋgəʊ] *(pl* **-es)** *n* inf jargon *m*.

linguist ['lɪŋgwɪst] *n* linguiste *mf*.

linguistics [lɪŋ'gwɪstɪks] *n* (U) linguistique *f*.

lining ['laɪnɪŋ] *n* **1.** [of coat, curtains, box] doublure *f* - **2.** [of stomach] muqueuse *f* - **3.** AUT [of brakes] garniture *f*.

link [lɪŋk] *n* **1.** [of chain] maillon *m* - **2.** [connection] : **link (between/with)** lien *m* (entre/avec) - **3.** COMPUT lien *m* ; **links to sthg** liens vers qqc. *vt* [cities, parts] relier ; **to link arms** se donner le bras. *vi* COMPUT avoir un lien vers ; **to link to sth** mettre un lien avec qch. ⇐ **link up** *vt sep* relier ; **to link sthg up with sthg** relier qqch avec OR à qqch.

links [lɪŋks] *(pl* links) *n* terrain *m* de golf *(au bord de la mer).*

lino UK ['laɪnəʊ], **linoleum** [lɪ'nəʊlɪəm] *n* lino *m*, linoléum *m*.

lintel ['lɪntl] *n* linteau *m*.

lion ['laɪən] *n* lion *m*.

lioness ['laɪənes] *n* lionne *f*.

lip [lɪp] *n* **1.** [of mouth] lèvre *f* - **2.** [of container] bord *m*.

lip balm US = **lip salve**.

lip-read *vi* lire sur les lèvres.

lip salve UK [-sælv], **lip balm** US *n* pommade *f* pour les lèvres.

lip service *n* : **to pay lip service to sthg** approuver qqch pour la forme.

lipstick ['lɪpstɪk] *n* rouge *m* à lèvres.

liqueur [lɪ'kjʊər] *n* liqueur *f*.

liquid ['lɪkwɪd] ⬦ *adj* liquide. ⬦ *n* liquide *m*.

liquidation [,lɪkwɪ'deɪʃn] *n* liquidation *f*.

liquid courage US = Dutch courage.

liquidize, UK -ise ['lɪkwɪdaɪz] *vt* UK CULIN passer au mixer.

liquidizer ['lɪkwɪdaɪzər] *n* UK mixer *m*.

liquor ['lɪkər] *n* (U) alcool *m*, spiritueux *mpl*.

liquorice UK, **licorice** US ['lɪkərɪs] *n* réglisse *f*.

liquor store *n* US magasin *m* de vins et d'alcools.

Lisbon ['lɪzbən] *n* Lisbonne.

lisp [lɪsp] ⬦ *n* zézaiement *m*. ⬦ *vi* zézayer.

list [lɪst] ⬦ *n* liste *f*. ⬦ *vt* [in writing] faire la liste de ; [in speech] énumérer.

listed building [,lɪstɪd-] *n* UK monument *m* classé.

listen ['lɪsn] *vi* : **to listen to (sb/sthg)** écouter (qqn/qqch) ; **to listen for sthg** guetter qqch.

listener ['lɪsnər] *n* auditeur *m*, -trice *f*.

listless ['lɪstlɪs] *adj* apathique, mou (molle).

lit [lɪt] *pt & pp* ► light.

liter US = litre.

literacy ['lɪtərəsɪ] *n* fait *m* de savoir lire et écrire.

literal ['lɪtərəl] *adj* littéral(e).

literally ['lɪtərəlɪ] *adv* littéralement ; **to take sthg literally** prendre qqch au pied de la lettre.

literary ['lɪtərərɪ] *adj* littéraire.

literate ['lɪtərət] *adj* **1.** [able to read and write] qui sait lire et écrire - **2.** [well-read] cultivé(e).

literature ['lɪtrətʃər] *n* littérature *f* ; [printed information] documentation *f*.

lithe [laɪð] *adj* souple, agile.

Lithuania [,lɪθjʊ'eɪnɪjə] *n* Lituanie *f*.

litigation [,lɪtɪ'ɡeɪʃn] *n* litige *m* ; **to go to litigation** aller en justice.

litre UK, **liter** US ['liːtər] *n* litre *m*.

litter ['lɪtər] ⬦ *n* **1.** (U) [rubbish] ordures *fpl*, détritus *mpl* - **2.** [of animals] portée *f*. ⬦ *vt* : **to be littered with** être couvert(e) de.

litterbin ['lɪtə,bɪn] *n* UK boîte *f* à ordures.

little ['lɪtl] ⬦ *adj* **1.** [not big] petit(e) ; **the shop is a little way along the street** le magasin se trouve un peu plus loin dans la rue ; **a little while** un petit moment - **2.** (*comp* less, *superl* least) [not much] peu de ; **little money** peu d'argent ; **a little money** un peu d'argent. ⬦ *pron* **1.** [small amount] : **little of the money was left** il ne restait pas beaucoup d'argent, il restait peu d'argent - **2.** [certain amount] : **a little of everything** un peu de tout ; **the little I saw looked excellent** le peu que j'en ai vu paraissait excellent. ⬦ *adv* peu, pas beaucoup ; **little by little** peu à peu. ➤ **a little** ⬦ *n* un peu de ; **I speak a little French** je parle quelques mots de français. ⬦ *pron* un peu. ⬦ *adv* un peu ; **I'm a little tired** je suis un peu fatigué ; **I walked on a little** j'ai marché encore un peu.

little finger *n* petit doigt *m*, auriculaire *m*.

live¹ [lɪv] ⬦ *vi* **1.** [gen] vivre - **2.** [have one's home] habiter, vivre ; **to live in Paris** habiter (à) Paris - **3.** [support o.s.] vivre ; **they don't earn enough to live** ils ne gagnent pas de quoi vivre ; **he lives by teaching** il gagne sa vie en enseignant ; **how does she live on that salary?** comment s'en sort-elle avec ce salaire? ⬦ *vt* : **to live a quiet life** mener une vie tranquille ; **she lived the life of a film star** elle a vécu comme une star de cinéma ; **to live it up** *inf* faire la noce. ➤ **live down** *vt sep* faire oublier. ➤ **live off** *vt insep* [savings, the land] vivre de ; [family] vivre aux dépens de. ➤ **live on** ⬦ *vt insep* vivre de. ⬦ *vi* [memory, feeling] rester, survivre. ➤ **live through** *vt insep* connaître ; **they've lived through war and famine** ils ont connu la guerre et la famine. ➤ **live together** *vi* vivre ensemble. ➤ **live up to** *vt insep* : **to live up to sb's expectations** répondre à l'attente de qqn ; **to live up to one's reputation** faire honneur à sa réputation. ➤ **live with** *vt insep* **1.** [cohabit with] vivre avec - **2.** *inf* [accept] se faire à, accepter.

live² [laɪv] *adj* **1.** [living] vivant(e) - **2.** [coal] ardent(e) - **3.** [bullet, bomb] non explosé(e) - **4.** ELEC sous tension - **5.** RADIO & TV en direct ; [performance] en public.

livelihood ['laɪvlɪhʊd] *n* gagne-pain *m inv*.

lively ['laɪvlɪ] *adj* **1.** [person] plein(e) d'entrain - **2.** [debate, meeting] animé(e) - **3.** [mind] vif (vive).

liven ['laɪvn] ➤ **liven up** ⬦ *vt sep* [person] égayer ; [place] animer. ⬦ *vi* s'animer.

liver ['lɪvər] *n* foie *m*.

livery ['lɪvərɪ] *n* livrée *f*.

lives [laɪvz] *npl* ► life.

livestock ['laɪvstɒk] *n* (U) bétail *m*.

livid ['lɪvɪd] *adj* **1.** *inf* [angry] furieux(euse) - **2.** [bruise] violacé(e).

living ['lɪvɪŋ] ⬦ *adj* vivant(e), en vie. ⬦ *n* : **to earn** OR **make a living** gagner sa vie ; **what do you do for a living?** qu'est-ce que vous faites dans la vie?

living conditions *npl* conditions *fpl* de vie.

living room *n* salle *f* de séjour, living *m*.

living standards *npl* niveau *m* de vie.

living wage *n* minimum *m* vital.

lizard ['lɪzəd] *n* lézard *m*.

llama ['lɑːmə] (*pl* llama OR **-s**) *n* lama *m*.

load [ləʊd] <> *n* **1.** [burden, thing carried] chargement *m*, charge *f* - **2.** [large amount] : **loads of, a load of** *inf* des tas de, plein de ; **a load of rubbish** OR **of bull** *US inf* de la foutaise. <> *vt* [gen & COMPUT] charger ; [video recorder] mettre une vidéo-cassette dans ; **to load sb/sthg with** charger qqn/qqch de ; **to load a gun/camera (with)** charger un fusil/un appareil (avec) ; **to load the dice** piper les dés. <> *vi* **1.** [receive freight] charger ; **the ship is loading** le navire est en cours de chargement - **2.** [computer program] se charger. ⬛ **load down** *vt sep* charger (lourdement) ; **he was loaded down with packages** il avait des paquets plein les bras ; **I'm loaded down with work** je suis surchargé de travail. ⬛ **load up** *vt sep* & *vi* charger.

loaded ['ləʊdɪd] *adj* **1.** [question] insidieux(euse) - **2.** *inf* [rich] plein(e) aux as - **3.** *esp US* [drunk] ivre.

loading bay ['ləʊdɪŋ-] *n* aire *f* de chargement.

loaf [ləʊf] (*pl* loaves [ləʊvz]) *n* : **a loaf (of bread)** un pain.

loafer ['ləʊfər] *n* [shoe] mocassin *m*.

loan [ləʊn] <> *n* prêt *m* ; **on loan** prêté(e). <> *vt* prêter ; **to loan sthg to sb, to loan sb sthg** prêter qqch à qqn.

loath [ləʊθ] *adj fml* : **to be loath to do sthg** ne pas vouloir faire qqch, hésiter à faire qqch.

loathe [ləʊð] *vt* détester ; **to loathe doing sthg** avoir horreur de OR détester faire qqch.

loathsome ['ləʊðsəm] *adj* dégoûtant(e), répugnant(e).

loaves [ləʊvz] *npl* ▶ loaf.

lob [lɒb] <> *n* TENNIS lob *m*. <> *vt* **1.** [throw] lancer - **2.** TENNIS : **to lob a ball** lober, faire un lob.

lobby ['lɒbɪ] <> *n* **1.** [of hotel] hall *m* - **2.** [pressure group] lobby *m*, groupe *m* de pression. <> *vt* faire pression sur.

lobe [ləʊb] *n* lobe *m*.

lobster ['lɒbstər] *n* homard *m*.

local ['ləʊkl] <> *adj* local(e). <> *n inf* **1.** [person] : **the locals** les gens *mpl* du coin OR du pays - **2.** *UK* [pub] café *m* OR bistro *m* du coin.

local authority *n UK* autorités *fpl* locales.

local call *n* communication *f* urbaine.

local government *n* administration *f* municipale.

locality [ləʊˈkælətɪ] *n* endroit *m*.

localization [ˌləʊkəlaɪˈzeɪʃn] *n* COMPUT localisation *f*.

localized, *UK* **-ised** ['ləʊkəlaɪzd] *adj* localisé(e).

locally ['ləʊkəlɪ] *adv* **1.** [on local basis] localement - **2.** [nearby] dans les environs, à proximité.

locate [*UK* ləʊˈkeɪt, *US* ˈləʊkeɪt] *vt* **1.** [find - position] trouver, repérer ; [- source, problem] localiser - **2.** [situate - business, factory] implanter, établir ; **to be located** être situé.

location [ləʊˈkeɪʃn] *n* **1.** [place] emplacement *m* - **2.** CIN : **on location** en extérieur.

loch [lɒk OR lɒx] *n Scot* loch *m*, lac *m*.

lock [lɒk] <> *n* **1.** [of door etc] serrure *f* - **2.** [on canal] écluse *f* - **3.** AUT [steering lock] angle *m* de braquage - **4.** [of hair] mèche *f* - **5.** TECH [device - gen] verrou *m* ; [- on gun] percuteur *m* ; [- on keyboard] : **shift** OR **caps lock** touche *f* de verrouillage majuscule. <> *vt* **1.** [door, car, drawer] fermer à clef ; [bicycle] cadenasser - **2.** [immobilize] bloquer. <> *vi* **1.** [door, suitcase] fermer à clef - **2.** [become immobilized] se bloquer. ⬛ **lock away** *vt sep* [valuables] mettre sous clef ; [criminal] incarcérer, mettre sous les verrous ; **we keep the alcohol locked away** nous gardons l'alcool sous clef. ⬛ **lock in** *vt sep* enfermer (à clef). ⬛ **lock out** *vt sep* **1.** [accidentally] enfermer dehors, laisser dehors ; **to lock o.s. out** s'enfermer dehors - **2.** [deliberately] empêcher d'entrer, mettre à la porte. ⬛ **lock up** *vt sep* **1.** [person - in prison] mettre en prison OR sous les verrous ; [- in asylum] enfermer - **2.** [house] fermer à clef - **3.** [valuables] enfermer, mettre sous clef.

locker ['lɒkər] *n* casier *m*.

locker room *n* vestiaire *m*.

locket ['lɒkɪt] *n* médaillon *m*.

locksmith ['lɒksmɪθ] *n* serrurier *m*, -ière *f*.

locomotive ['ləʊkə,məʊtɪv] *n* locomotive *f*.

locum ['ləʊkəm] (*pl* **-s**) *n esp UK* remplaçant *m*, -e *f*.

locust ['ləʊkəst] *n* sauterelle *f*, locuste *f*.

lodge [lɒdʒ] <> *n* **1.** [of caretaker, freemasons] loge *f* - **2.** [of manor house] pavillon *m* (de gardien) - **3.** [for hunting] pavillon *m* de chasse. <> *vi* **1.** *fml* [stay] : **to lodge with sb** loger chez qqn - **2.** [become stuck] se loger, se coincer - **3.** *fig* [in mind] s'enraciner, s'ancrer. <> *vt* [complaint] déposer ; **to lodge an appeal** interjeter OR faire appel.

lodger ['lɒdʒər] *n* locataire *mf*.

lodging ['lɒdʒɪŋ] *n* ▶ board. ⬛ **lodgings** *npl* chambre *f* meublée.

loft [lɒft] *n* grenier *m*.

lofty ['lɒftɪ] *adj* **1.** [noble] noble - **2.** *pej* [haughty] hautain(e), arrogant(e) - **3.** *lit* [high] haut(e), élevé(e).

log [lɒg] ⋄ *n* **1.** [of wood] bûche *f* - **2.** [of ship] journal *m* de bord ; [of plane] carnet *m* de vol. ⋄ *vt* consigner, enregistrer.
◆ **log in**, **log on** *vi* COMPUT ouvrir une session. ◆ **log off**, **log out** *vi* COMPUT fermer une session.

logbook ['lɒgbʊk] *n* **1.** [of ship] journal *m* de bord ; [of plane] carnet *m* de vol - **2.** *UK* [of car] ≃ carte *f* grise.

loggerheads ['lɒgəhedz] *n* : **at logger-heads** en désaccord.

logic ['lɒdʒɪk] *n* logique *f*.

logical ['lɒdʒɪkl] *adj* logique.

logistics [lə'dʒɪstɪks] ⋄ *n* (U) MIL logistique *f*. ⋄ *npl fig* organisation *f*.

logo ['ləʊgəʊ] (*pl* -s) *n* logo *m*.

loin [lɔɪn] *n* filet *m*.

loiter ['lɔɪtər] *vi* traîner.

loll [lɒl] *vi* **1.** [sit, lie about] se prélasser - **2.** [hang down - head, tongue] pendre.

lollipop ['lɒlɪpɒp] *n* sucette *f*.

lollipop lady *n UK* dame qui fait traverser la rue aux enfants à la sortie des écoles.

lollipop man *n UK* monsieur qui fait traverser la rue aux enfants à la sortie des écoles.

lolly ['lɒlɪ] *n UK inf* **1.** [lollipop] sucette *f* - **2.** [ice lolly] sucette *f* glacée.

London ['lʌndən] *n* Londres.

Londoner ['lʌndənər] *n* Londonien *m*, -enne *f*.

lone [ləʊn] *adj* solitaire.

loneliness ['ləʊnlɪnɪs] *n* [of person] solitude *f* ; [of place] isolement *m*.

lonely ['ləʊnlɪ] *adj* **1.** [person] solitaire, seul(e) - **2.** [childhood] solitaire - **3.** [place] isolé(e).

loner ['ləʊnər] *n* solitaire *mf*.

lonesome ['ləʊnsəm] *adj US inf* **1.** [person] solitaire, seul(e) - **2.** [place] isolé(e).

long [lɒŋ] ⋄ *adj* [in space] long (longue). ⋄ *adv* longtemps ; **how long will it take?** combien de temps cela va-t-il prendre? ; **how long will you be?** tu en as pour combien de temps? ; **how long is the book?** le livre fait combien de pages? ; **so long!** *inf* au revoir!, salut! ◆ **as long as**, **so long as** *conj* [during the time that] tant que.
◆ **long for** *vt insep* [want very much] désirer ardemment ; [look forward to] attendre avec impatience.

long-distance *adj* [runner, race] de fond ; **long-distance lorry** *UK* OR **truck** *UK* **driver** routier *m*.

long-distance call *n* communication *f* interurbaine.

longhand ['lɒŋhænd] *n* écriture *f* normale.

long-haul *adj* long-courrier.

longing ['lɒŋɪŋ] ⋄ *adj* plein(e) de convoitise. ⋄ *n* **1.** [desire] envie *f*, convoitise *f* ; **a longing for** un grand désir OR une grande envie de - **2.** [nostalgia] nostalgie *f*, regret *m*.

longitude ['lɒndʒɪtjuːd] *n* longitude *f*.

long jump *n* saut *m* en longueur.

long-life *adj* [milk] longue conservation (inv) ; [battery] longue durée (inv).

longlist ['lɒŋlɪst] *n* première *f* liste.

long-playing record [-'pleɪɪŋ-] *n* 33 tours *m*.

long-range *adj* **1.** [missile, bomber] à longue portée - **2.** [plan, forecast] à long terme.

long shot *n* [guess] coup *m* à tenter (sans grand espoir de succès).

longsighted [,lɒŋ'saɪtɪd] *adj UK* presbyte.

long-standing *adj* de longue date.

long-suffering *adj* [person] à la patience infinie.

long term *n* : **in the long term** à long terme.

long wave *n* (U) grandes ondes *fpl*.

longwinded [,lɒŋ'wɪndɪd] *adj* [person] prolixe, verbeux(euse) ; [speech] interminable, qui n'en finit pas.

loo [luː] (*pl* -s) *n UK inf* cabinets *mpl*, petit coin *m*.

look [lʊk] ⋄ *n* **1.** [with eyes] regard *m* ; **to take** OR **have a look (at sthg)** regarder (qqch), jeter un coup d'œil (à qqch) ; **to give sb a look** jeter un regard à qqn, regarder qqn de travers - **2.** [search] : **to have a look (for sthg)** *US* chercher (qqch) - **3.** [appearance] aspect *m*, air *m* ; **by the look** OR **looks of it**, **by the look** OR **looks of things** vraisemblablement, selon toute probabilité. ⋄ *vi* **1.** [with eyes] regarder - **2.** [search] chercher - **3.** [seem] avoir l'air, sembler ; **it looks like rain** OR **as if it will rain** on dirait qu'il va pleuvoir ; **she looks like her mother** elle ressemble à sa mère - **4.** [building, window] : **to look (out) onto** donner sur. ◆ **looks** *npl* [attractiveness] beauté *f*. ◆ **look after** *vt insep* s'occuper de. ◆ **look around** *vt insep US* = **look round**. ◆ **look at** *vt insep* **1.** [see, glance at] regarder ; [examine] examiner - **2.** [judge] considérer. ◆ **look down on** *vt insep* [condescend to] mépriser. ◆ **look for** *vt insep* chercher. ◆ **look forward to** *vt insep* attendre avec impatience. ◆ **look into** *vt insep* examiner, étudier. ◆ **look on** *vi* regarder. ◆ **look out** *vi* prendre garde, faire attention ; **look out!** attention! ◆ **look out for** *vt insep* [person] guetter ; [new book] être à l'affût de, essayer de repérer. ◆ **look round** *UK*, **look around** *US* ⋄ *vt insep* [house, shop, town] faire le

tour de. ◇ vi 1. [turn] se retourner
- 2. [browse] regarder. ➤ **look to** vt insep
1. [depend on] compter sur - 2. [future]
songer à. ➤ **look up** ◇ vt sep 1. [in
book] chercher - 2. [visit - person] aller OR
passer voir. ◇ vi [improve - business]
reprendre ; **things are looking up** ça va
mieux, la situation s'améliore. ➤ **look
up to** vt insep admirer.

lookout ['lʊkaʊt] n 1. [place] poste m de
guet - 2. [person] guetteur m - 3. [search] : **to
be on the lookout for** être à la recherche de.

loom [luːm] ◇ n métier m à tisser. ◇ vi
[building, person] se dresser ; fig [date, threat]
être imminent(e). ➤ **loom up** vi surgir.

loony ['luːnɪ] inf ◇ adj cinglé(e), tim-
bré(e). ◇ n cinglé m, -e f, fou m, folle f.

loop [luːp] n 1. [gen & COMPUT] boucle f
- 2. [contraceptive] stérilet m.

loophole ['luːphəʊl] n faille f, échappatoire
f.

loose [luːs] adj 1. [not firm - joint] desser-
ré(e) ; [- handle, peg] branlant(e) ; [- tooth]
qui bouge OR branle ; [- knot] défait(e)
- 2. [unpackaged - sweets, nails] en vrac, au
poids - 3. [clothes] ample, large - 4. [not
restrained, fixed - hair] dénoué(e) ; [- animal]
en liberté, détaché(e) - 5. [vague, imprecise
- translation] approximatif(ive) ; [- connection, link] vague ; **they have loose ties with
other political groups** ils sont vaguement
liés à d'autres groupes politiques - 6. pej &
dated [woman] facile ; [living] dissolu(e).

loose change n petite OR menue monnaie
f.

loose end n : **to be at a loose end** UK, **to be
at loose ends** US être désœuvré, n'avoir rien
à faire.

loosely ['luːslɪ] adv 1. [not firmly] sans
serrer - 2. [inexactly] approximativement.

loosen ['luːsn] vt desserrer, défaire.
➤ **loosen up** vi 1. [before game, race]
s'échauffer - 2. inf [relax] se détendre.

loot [luːt] ◇ n butin m. ◇ vt piller.

looting ['luːtɪŋ] n pillage m.

lop [lɒp] vt élaguer, émonder. ➤ **lop off**
vt sep couper.

lopsided [-'saɪdɪd] adj [table] bancal(e),
boiteux(euse) ; [picture] de travers.

lord [lɔːd] n UK seigneur m. ➤ **Lord** n
1. RELIG : **the Lord** [God] le Seigneur ; **good
Lord!** Seigneur!, mon Dieu! - 2. UK [in titles]
Lord m ; [as form of address] : **my Lord**
Monsieur le duc/comte etc. ➤ **Lords** npl
UK POL : **the (House of) Lords** la Chambre des
lords.

Lordship ['lɔːdʃɪp] n : **your/his Lordship**
Monsieur le duc/comte etc.

lore [lɔːʳ] n (U) traditions fpl.

lorry ['lɒrɪ] n UK camion m.

lorry driver n UK camionneur m, conducteur m de poids lourd.

lose [luːz] (pt & pp lost) ◇ vt 1. [gen]
perdre ; **he lost four games to Karpov** il a
perdu quatre parties contre Karpov ; **to lose
one's appetite** perdre l'appétit ; **to lose one's
balance** perdre l'équilibre ; **to lose consciousness** perdre connaissance ; **to lose one's
head** perdre la tête ; **to lose sight of** lit & fig
perdre de vue ; **to lose one's way** se perdre,
perdre son chemin ; fig être un peu perdu ;
to lose weight perdre du poids - 2. [subj:
clock, watch] retarder de ; **to lose time**
retarder - 3. [pursuers] semer. ◇ vi perdre.
➤ **lose out** vi être perdant(e).

loser ['luːzəʳ] n 1. [gen] perdant m, -e f
- 2. inf pej [unsuccessful person] raté m, -e f.

loss [lɒs] n [gen] perte f ; **to be at a loss** être
perplexe, être embarrassé(-e).

lost [lɒst] ◇ pt & pp ➤ lose. ◇ adj
[gen] perdu(e) ; **to get lost** se perdre ; **get
lost!** inf fous/foutez le camp!

lost-and-found office n US bureau m des
objets trouvés.

lost property office n UK bureau m des
objets trouvés.

lot [lɒt] n 1. [large amount] : **a lot (of), lots
(of)** beaucoup (de) ; UK inf [entire amount] :
the lot le tout - 2. [at auction] lot m
- 3. [destiny] sort m - 4. US [of land] terrain
m ; [car park] parking m ; **to draw lots** tirer
au sort. ➤ **a lot** adv beaucoup.

lotion ['ləʊʃn] n lotion f.

lottery ['lɒtərɪ] n lit & fig loterie f.

loud [laʊd] ◇ adj 1. [not quiet, noisy -
gen] fort(e) ; [- person] bruyant(e)
- 2. [colour, clothes] voyant(e). ◇ adv fort.

loudhailer [ˌlaʊd'heɪləʳ] n UK mégaphone
m, porte-voix m inv.

loudly ['laʊdlɪ] adv 1. [noisily] fort
- 2. [gaudily] de façon voyante.

loudspeaker [ˌlaʊd'spiːkəʳ] n haut-parleur
m.

lounge [laʊndʒ] ◇ n 1. UK [in house]
salon m - 2. [in airport] hall m, salle f - 3. UK
= lounge bar. ◇ vi se prélasser.

lounge bar n UK l'une des deux salles d'un
bar, la plus confortable.

louse [laʊs] n 1. (pl lice [laɪs]) [insect] pou
m - 2. (pl -s) inf pej [person] salaud m.

lousy ['laʊzɪ] adj inf minable, nul(le) ;
[weather] pourri(e).

lout [laʊt] n rustre m.

louvre UK, **louver** US ['luːvəʳ] n persienne
f.

lovable ['lʌvəbl] adj adorable.

love [lʌv] ◇ n 1. [gen] amour m ; **to be in**

love être amoureux(euse) ; **to fall in love** tomber amoureux(euse) ; **to make love** faire l'amour ; **give her my love** embrasse-la pour moi ; **love from** [at end of letter] affectueusement, grosses bises - **2.** *UK inf* [form of address] mon chéri (ma chérie) - **3.** TENNIS zéro *m*. ◇ *vt* aimer ; **to love to do sthg** OR **doing sthg** aimer OR adorer faire qqch.

love affair *n* liaison *f*.

love life *n* vie *f* amoureuse.

lovely ['lʌvlɪ] *adj* **1.** [beautiful] très joli(e) - **2.** [pleasant] très agréable, excellent(e).

lover ['lʌvə] *n* **1.** [sexual partner] amant *m*, -e *f* - **2.** [enthusiast] passionné *m*, -e *f*, amoureux *m*, -euse *f*.

loving ['lʌvɪŋ] *adj* [person, relationship] affectueux(euse) ; [care] tendre.

low [ləʊ] ◇ *adj* **1.** [not high - gen] bas (basse) ; [- wall, building] peu élevé(e) ; [- standard, quality] mauvais(e) ; [- intelligence] faible ; [- neckline] décolleté(e) - **2.** [little remaining] presque épuisé(e) - **3.** [not loud - voice] bas (basse) ; [- whisper, moan] faible - **4.** [depressed] déprimé(e) - **5.** [not respectable] bas (basse). ◇ *adv* **1.** [not high] bas - **2.** [not loudly - speak] à voix basse ; [- whisper] faiblement - **3.** [in intensity] bas ; **stocks are running low** les réserves baissent ; **the batteries are running low** les piles sont usées. ◇ *n* **1.** [low point] niveau *m* OR point *m* bas - **2.** METEOR dépression *f*.

low-calorie *adj* à basses calories.

low-cut *adj* décolleté(e).

lower ['ləʊə] ◇ *adj* inférieur(e). ◇ *vt* **1.** [gen] baisser ; [flag] abaisser - **2.** [reduce - price, level] baisser ; [- age of consent] abaisser ; [- resistance] diminuer.

low-fat *adj* [yogurt, crisps] allégé(e) ; [milk] demi-écrémé(e).

low-key *adj* discret(ète).

lowly ['ləʊlɪ] *adj* modeste, humble.

low-lying *adj* bas (basse).

loyal ['lɔɪəl] *adj* loyal(e).

loyalty ['lɔɪəltɪ] *n* loyauté *f*.

lozenge ['lɒzɪndʒ] *n* **1.** [tablet] pastille *f* - **2.** [shape] losange *m*.

LP (*abbrev of* **long-playing record**) *n* 33 tours *m*.

LPG [,elpiː'dʒiː] (*abbrev of* **liquified petroleum gas**) *n* GPL *m*.

L-plate *n UK plaque signalant que le conducteur du véhicule est en conduite accompagnée.*

Ltd, ltd (*abbrev of* **limited**) *esp UK* ≃ SARL ; **Smith and Sons, Ltd** ≃ Smith &Fils, SARL.

lubricant ['luːbrɪkənt] *n* lubrifiant *m*.

lubricate ['luːbrɪkeɪt] *vt* lubrifier.

lucid ['luːsɪd] *adj* lucide.

luck [lʌk] *n* chance *f* ; **good luck** chance *f* ; **good luck!** bonne chance! ; **bad luck** malchance *f* ; **bad** OR **hard luck!** pas de chance! ; **to be in luck** avoir de la chance ; **with (any) luck** avec un peu de chance.

luckily ['lʌkɪlɪ] *adv* heureusement.

lucky ['lʌkɪ] *adj* **1.** [fortunate - person] qui a de la chance ; [- event] heureux(euse) - **2.** [bringing good luck] porte-bonheur (*inv*).

lucrative ['luːkrətɪv] *adj* lucratif(ive).

ludicrous ['luːdɪkrəs] *adj* ridicule.

lug [lʌg] *vt inf* traîner.

luggage ['lʌgɪdʒ] *n* (U) bagages *mpl*.

luggage rack *n* porte-bagages *m inv*.

lukewarm ['luːkwɔːm] *adj lit & fig* tiède.

lull [lʌl] ◇ *n* : **lull (in)** [storm] accalmie *f* (de) ; [fighting, conversation] arrêt *m* (de). ◇ *vt* : **to lull sb to sleep** endormir qqn en le berçant ; **to lull sb into a false sense of security** endormir les soupçons de qqn.

lullaby ['lʌləbaɪ] *n* berceuse *f*.

lumber ['lʌmbər] *n* (U) **1.** *US* [timber] bois *m* de charpente - **2.** *UK* [bric-a-brac] bric-à-brac *m inv*. ◆ **lumber with** *vt sep UK inf* : **to lumber sb with sthg** coller qqch à qqn.

lumberjack ['lʌmbədʒæk] *n* bûcheron *m*, -onne *f*.

luminous ['luːmɪnəs] *adj* [dial] lumineux(euse) ; [paint, armband] phosphorescent(e).

lump [lʌmp] ◇ *n* **1.** [gen] morceau *m* ; [of earth, clay] motte *f* ; [in sauce] grumeau *m* - **2.** [on body] grosseur *f*. ◇ *vt* : **to lump sthg together** réunir qqch ; **to lump it** *inf* faire avec, s'en accommoder.

lump sum *n* somme *f* globale.

lunacy ['luːnəsɪ] *n* folie *f*.

lunar ['luːnər] *adj* lunaire.

lunatic ['luːnətɪk] ◇ *adj pej* dément(e), démentiel(elle). ◇ *n* **1.** *pej* [fool] fou *m*, folle *f* - **2.** *dated* [insane person] fou *m*, folle *f*, aliéné *m*, -e *f*.

lunch [lʌntʃ] ◇ *n* déjeuner *m*. ◇ *vi* déjeuner.

luncheon ['lʌntʃən] *n fml* déjeuner *m*.

luncheon meat, *US* **lunchmeat** *n* sorte de saucisson.

luncheon voucher *n UK* ticket-restaurant *m*.

lunch hour *n* pause *f* de midi.

lunchtime ['lʌntʃtaɪm] *n* heure *f* du déjeuner.

lung [lʌŋ] *n* poumon *m*.

lunge [lʌndʒ] *vi* faire un brusque mouvement (du bras) en avant ; **to lunge at sb** s'élancer sur qqn.

lurch [lɜːtʃ] ◇ *n* [of person] écart *m*

brusque ; [of car] embardée *f* ; **to leave sb in the lurch** laisser qqn dans le pétrin. ◇ *vi* [person] tituber ; [car] faire une embardée.

lure [ljʊə] ◇ *n* charme *m* trompeur. ◇ *vt* attirer OR persuader par la ruse.

lurid ['ljʊərɪd] *adj* 1. [outfit] aux couleurs criardes - 2. [story, details] affreux(euse).

lurk [lɜːk] *vi* 1. [person] se cacher, se dissimuler - 2. [memory, danger, fear] subsister.

luscious ['lʌʃəs] *adj* 1. [delicious] succulent(e) - 2. *inf fig* [woman] appétissant(e).

lush [lʌʃ] *adj* 1. [luxuriant] luxuriant(e) - 2. [rich] luxueux(euse).

lust [lʌst] *n* 1. [sexual desire] désir *m* - 2. *fig* : **lust for sth** soif de qqch. ◆ **lust after, lust for** *vt insep* 1. [wealth, power etc] être assoiffé(e) de - 2. [person] désirer.

lusty ['lʌstɪ] *adj* vigoureux(euse).

Luxembourg ['lʌksəmbɜːg] *n* 1. [country] Luxembourg *m* - 2. [city] Luxembourg.

luxurious [lʌg'ʒʊərɪəs] *adj* 1. [expensive] luxueux(euse) - 2. [pleasurable] voluptueux(euse).

luxury ['lʌkʃərɪ] ◇ *n* luxe *m*. ◇ *comp* de luxe.

LW (*abbrev of* **long wave**) GO.

Lycra® ['laɪkrə] ◇ *n* Lycra® *m*. ◇ *comp* en Lycra®.

lying ['laɪɪŋ] ◇ *adj* [person] menteur(euse). ◇ *n* (U) mensonges *mpl*.

lynch [lɪntʃ] *vt* lyncher.

lyric ['lɪrɪk] *adj* lyrique.

lyrical ['lɪrɪkl] *adj* lyrique.

lyrics ['lɪrɪks] *npl* paroles *fpl*.

M

m¹ [em] (*pl* **m's** OR **ms**), **M** (*pl* **M's** OR **Ms**) *n* [letter] m *m inv*, M *m inv*.

M² *UK abbrev of* **motorway**.

m³ 1. (*abbrev of* **metre**) m - 2. (*abbrev of* **million**) M - 3. *abbrev of* **mile**.

MA *n abbrev of* **Master of Arts**.

mac [mæk] (*abbrev of* **mackintosh**) *n UK inf* [coat] imper *m*.

macaroni [ˌmækə'rəʊnɪ] *n* (U) macaronis *mpl*.

Mace® [meɪs] ◇ *n* [spray] gaz *m* lacrymogène. ◇ *vt US inf* bombarder au gaz lacrymogène.

mace [meɪs] *n* 1. [ornamental rod] masse *f* - 2. [spice] macis *m*.

machine [mə'ʃiːn] ◇ *n lit & fig* machine *f*. ◇ *vt* 1. SEW coudre à la machine - 2. TECH usiner.

machinegun [mə'ʃiːngʌn] *n* mitrailleuse *f*.

machine language *n* COMPUT langage *m* machine.

machinery [mə'ʃiːnərɪ] *n* (U) machines *fpl* ; *fig* mécanisme *m*.

macho ['mætʃəʊ] *adj inf* macho *(inv)*.

mackerel ['mækrəl] (*pl* **mackerel** OR **-s**) *n* maquereau *m*.

mackintosh ['mækɪntɒʃ] *n UK dated* imperméable *m*.

mad [mæd] *adj* 1. [insane] fou (folle) ; **to go mad** devenir fou - 2. *esp UK inf* [foolish] insensé(e) - 3. [furious] furieux(euse) - 4. [hectic - rush, pace] fou (folle) - 5. [very enthusiastic] : **to be mad about sb/sthg** *inf* être fou (folle) de qqn/qqch.

Madagascar [ˌmædə'gæskər] *n* Madagascar *m*.

madam ['mædəm] *n* madame *f*.

madcap ['mædkæp] *adj* risqué(e), insensé(e).

mad cow disease *n inf* maladie *f* de la vache folle.

madden ['mædn] *vt* exaspérer.

made [meɪd] *pt & pp* ▶ **make**.

Madeira [mə'dɪərə] *n* 1. [wine] madère *m* - 2. GEOG Madère *f*.

made-to-measure *adj* fait(e) sur mesure.

made-up *adj* 1. [with make-up] maquillé(e) - 2. [invented] fabriqué(e).

madly ['mædlɪ] *adv* [frantically] comme un fou ; **madly in love** follement amoureux.

madman ['mædmən] (*pl* **-men** [-mən]) *n* fou *m*.

madness ['mædnɪs] *n lit & fig* folie *f*, démence *f*.

Madrid [mə'drɪd] *n* Madrid.

Mafia ['mæfɪə] *n* : **the Mafia** la Mafia.

magazine [ˌmægə'ziːn] *n* 1. PRESS revue *f*, magazine *m* ; RADIO & TV magazine - 2. [of gun] magasin *m*.

maggot ['mægət] *n* ver *m*, asticot *m*.

magic ['mædʒɪk] ◇ *adj* magique. ◇ *n* magie *f*.

magical ['mædʒɪkl] *adj* magique.

magician [mə'dʒɪʃn] *n* magicien *m*, -ienne *f*.

magistrate ['mædʒɪstreɪt] *n* magistrat *m*, -e *f*, juge *m*.

magistrates' court *n* UK ≃ tribunal *m* d'instance.

magnanimous [mæg'nænɪməs] *adj* magnanime.

magnate ['mægneɪt] *n* magnat *m*.

magnesium [mæg'niːzɪəm] *n* magnésium *m*.

magnet ['mægnɪt] *n* aimant *m*.

magnetic [mæg'netɪk] *adj* lit & fig magnétique.

magnetic tape *n* bande *f* magnétique.

magnificent [mæg'nɪfɪsənt] *adj* magnifique, superbe.

magnify ['mægnɪfaɪ] *vt* [in vision] grossir ; [sound] amplifier ; fig exagérer.

magnifying glass ['mægnɪfaɪɪŋ-] *n* loupe *f*.

magnitude ['mægnɪtjuːd] *n* envergure *f*, ampleur *f*.

magpie ['mægpaɪ] *n* pie *f*.

mahogany [mə'hɒgənɪ] *n* acajou *m*.

maid [meɪd] *n* [servant] domestique *f*.

maiden ['meɪdn] ⬦ *adj* [flight, voyage] premier(ère). ⬦ *n* lit jeune fille *f*.

maiden aunt *n* dated tante *f* célibataire.

maiden name *n* nom *m* de jeune fille.

mail [meɪl] ⬦ *n* **1.** [letters, parcels] courrier *m* - **2.** [system] poste *f*. ⬦ *vt* esp US poster.

mailbox ['meɪlbɒks] *n* US boîte *f* à OR aux lettres.

mail carrier = mailman.

mailing list ['meɪlɪŋ-] *n* liste *f* d'adresses.

mailman ['meɪlmæn] (*pl* -men [-mən]) *n* US facteur *m*, -rice *f*.

mail order *n* vente *f* par correspondance.

mailshot ['meɪlʃɒt] *n* UK publipostage *m*.

maim [meɪm] *vt* estropier.

main [meɪn] ⬦ *adj* principal(e). ⬦ *n* [pipe] conduite *f*. ➤ **mains** *npl* : **the mains** le secteur. ➤ **in the main** *adv* dans l'ensemble.

main course *n* plat *m* principal.

mainframe (computer) ['meɪnfreɪm-] *n* gros ordinateur *m*, processeur *m* central.

mainland ['meɪnlənd] ⬦ *adj* continental(e). ⬦ *n* : **the mainland** le continent.

main line *n* RAIL grande ligne *f*.

mainly ['meɪnlɪ] *adv* principalement.

main office *n* esp US siège *m* social.

main road *n* route *f* à grande circulation.

mainstay ['meɪnsteɪ] *n* pilier *m*, élément *m* principal.

mainstream ['meɪnstriːm] ⬦ *adj* dominant(e). ⬦ *n* : **the mainstream** la tendance générale.

maintain [meɪn'teɪn] *vt* **1.** [preserve, keep constant] maintenir - **2.** [provide for, look after] entretenir - **3.** [assert] : **to maintain (that)...** maintenir que..., soutenir que...

maintenance ['meɪntənəns] *n* **1.** [of public order] maintien *m* - **2.** [care] entretien *m*, maintenance *f* - **3.** UK LAW pension *f* alimentaire.

maize [meɪz] *n* UK maïs *m*.

majestic [mə'dʒestɪk] *adj* majestueux(euse).

majesty ['mædʒəstɪ] *n* [grandeur] majesté *f*. ➤ **Majesty** *n* : **His/Her Majesty** Sa Majesté le roi/la reine.

major ['meɪdʒər] ⬦ *adj* **1.** [important] majeur(e) - **2.** [main] principal(e) - **3.** MUS majeur(e). ⬦ *n* **1.** [in army] ≃ chef *m* de bataillon ; [in air force] commandant *m* - **2.** US UNIV [subject] matière *f*.

Majorca [mə'dʒɔːkə OR mə'jɔːkə] *n* Majorque *f*.

majority [mə'dʒɒrətɪ] *n* majorité *f* ; **in a** OR **the majority** dans la majorité.

make [meɪk] ⬦ *vt* (*pt & pp* **made**) **1.** [gen - produce] faire ; [- manufacture] faire, fabriquer ; **to make a meal** préparer un repas ; **to make a film** OR **movie** US tourner OR réaliser un film - **2.** [perform an action] faire ; **to make a mistake** faire une erreur, se tromper ; **to make a decision** prendre une décision - **3.** [cause to have] rendre ; **to make sb happy/sad** rendre qqn heureux/triste - **4.** [force, cause to do] : **to make sb do sthg** faire faire qqch à qqn, obliger qqn à faire qqch ; **to make sb laugh** faire rire qqn - **5.** [be constructed] : **to be made of** être en ; **what's it made of?** c'est en quoi ? - **6.** [add up to] faire ; **2 and 2 make 4** 2 et 2 font 4 - **7.** UK [calculate] : **I make it 50** UK d'après moi il y en a 50, j'en ai compté 50 ; **what time do you make it?** UK quelle heure as-tu? ; **I make it 6 o'clock** UK il est 6 heures (à ma montre) - **8.** [earn] gagner, se faire ; **to make a profit** faire des bénéfices ; **to make a loss** essuyer des pertes - **9.** [reach] arriver à - **10.** [gain - friend, enemy] se faire ; **to make friends (with sb)** se lier d'amitié (avec qqn) - **11.** [be a success] réussir, arriver ; [be able to attend] se libérer, pouvoir venir ; **to make do with** se contenter de. ⬦ *n* [brand] marque *f*. ➤ **make for** *vt insep* **1.** [move towards] se diriger vers - **2.** [contribute to, be conducive to] rendre probable, favoriser. ➤ **make of** ⬦ *vt sep* [understand] comprendre. ⬦ *vt insep* [think of] penser de ; **what do you make of the Smiths?** qu'est-ce que tu penses des Smith? ➤ **make off** *vi inf* filer. ➤ **make out** ⬦ *vt sep* **1.** [see, hear] discerner ; [understand] comprendre - **2.** [fill out - cheque] libeller ; [- bill, receipt] faire ; [- form] remplir. ⬦ *vt insep*

1. [pretend, claim]: **to make out (that)...** prétendre que... - **2.** [fill out - form, cheque] remplir ; **who shall I make the cheque out to?** je fais le chèque à quel ordre? ◇ *vi insep* **1.** *inf* [manage] se débrouiller ; **how did you make out at work today?** comment ça s'est passé au boulot aujourd'hui? - **2.** *v inf* [neck, pet] se peloter ; **to make out with sb** [have sex] s'envoyer qqn. **make over** *vt sep* **1.** [transfer] transférer, céder - **2.** [change appearance] transformer ; **the garage had been made over into a workshop** le garage a été transformé en atelier. **make up** ◇ *vt sep* **1.** [compose, constitute] composer, constituer - **2.** [story, excuse] inventer - **3.** [apply cosmetics to] maquiller - **4.** [prepare - gen] faire ; [- prescription] préparer, exécuter - **5.** [make complete] compléter. ◇ *vi* [become friends again] se réconcilier. **make up for** *vt insep* compenser. **make up to** *vt sep*: **to make it up to sb (for sthg)** se racheter auprès de qqn (pour qqch).

make-believe *n*: **it's all make-believe** c'est (de la) pure fantaisie.

maker ['meɪkəʳ] *n* [of product] fabricant *m*, -e *f* ; [of film] réalisateur *m*, -trice *f*.

makeshift ['meɪkʃɪft] *adj* de fortune.

make-up *n* **1.** [cosmetics] maquillage *m* ; **make-up remover** démaquillant *m* - **2.** [person's character] caractère *m* - **3.** [of team, group, object] constitution *f*.

making ['meɪkɪŋ] *n* fabrication *f* ; **his problems are of his own making** ses problèmes sont de sa faute ; **in the making** en formation ; **to have the makings of** avoir l'étoffe de.

malaise [mə'leɪz] *n fml* malaise *m*.

malaria [mə'leərɪə] *n* malaria *f*.

Malaya [mə'leɪə] *n* Malaisie *f*, Malaysia *f* occidentale.

Malaysia [mə'leɪzɪə] *n* Malaysia *f*.

male [meɪl] ◇ *adj* [gen] mâle ; [sex] masculin(e). ◇ *n* mâle *m*.

male nurse *n* infirmier *m*.

malevolent [mə'levələnt] *adj fml* malveillant(e).

malfunction [mæl'fʌŋkʃn] *vi* mal fonctionner.

malice ['mælɪs] *n* méchanceté *f*.

malicious [mə'lɪʃəs] *adj* malveillant(e).

malign [mə'laɪn] ◇ *adj fml* pernicieux(euse). ◇ *vt* calomnier.

malignant [mə'lɪɡnənt] *adj* MED malin(igne).

mall [mɔːl] *n esp US* **(shopping) mall** centre *m* commercial.

mallet ['mælɪt] *n* maillet *m*.

malnutrition [,mælnjuː'trɪʃn] *n* malnutrition *f*.

malpractice [,mæl'præktɪs] *n (U)* LAW faute *f* professionnelle.

malt [mɔːlt] *n* malt *m*.

Malta ['mɔːltə] *n* Malte *f*.

mammal ['mæml] *n* mammifère *m*.

mammoth ['mæməθ] ◇ *adj* gigantesque. ◇ *n* mammouth *m*.

man [mæn] ◇ *n* (*pl* **men** [men]) **1.** homme *m* ; **the man in the street** l'homme de la rue - **2.** *esp US inf* [as form of address] mon vieux. ◇ *vt* [ship, spaceship] fournir du personnel pour ; [telephone] répondre au ; [switchboard] assurer le service de. ◇ *excl inf* **man, was it big!** bon sang, qu'est-ce que c'était grand!

manage ['mænɪdʒ] ◇ *vi* **1.** [cope] se débrouiller, y arriver - **2.** [get by financially] s'en sortir. ◇ *vt* **1.** [succeed, cope with]: **to manage to do sthg** arriver à faire qqch - **2.** [be responsible for, control] gérer - **3.** [be available for]: **can you manage 9 o'clock/next Saturday?** pouvez-vous venir à 9 h/samedi prochain? ; **can you manage lunch tomorrow?** pouvez-vous déjeuner avec moi demain?

manageable ['mænɪdʒəbl] *adj* maniable.

management ['mænɪdʒmənt] *n* **1.** [control, running] gestion *f* - **2.** [people in control] direction *f*.

manager ['mænɪdʒəʳ] *n* [of organization] directeur *m*, -trice *f* ; [of shop, restaurant, hotel] gérant *m*, -e *f* ; [of football team, pop star] manager *m*.

manageress [,mænɪdʒə'res] *n UK* [of organization] directrice *f* ; [of shop, restaurant, hotel] gérante *f*.

managerial [,mænɪ'dʒɪərɪəl] *adj* directorial(e).

managing director ['mænɪdʒɪŋ-] *n* directeur général *m*, directrice générale *f*.

mandarin ['mændərɪn] *n* [fruit] mandarine *f*.

mandate ['mændeɪt] *n* mandat *m*.

mandatory ['mændətrɪ] *adj* obligatoire.

mane [meɪn] *n* crinière *f*.

maneuver *US* = **manoeuvre**.

manfully ['mænfʊlɪ] *adv* courageusement, vaillamment.

mangle ['mæŋɡl] *vt* mutiler, déchirer.

mango ['mæŋɡəʊ] (*pl* **-es** OR **-s**) *n* mangue *f*.

mangy ['meɪndʒɪ] *adj* galeux(euse).

manhandle ['mæn,hændl] *vt* malmener.

manhole ['mænhəʊl] *n* regard *m*, trou *m* d'homme.

manhood ['mænhʊd] *n*: **to reach manhood** devenir un homme.

man-hour *n* FIN heure-homme *f*.

mania ['meɪnjə] *n* : **mania (for)** manie *f* (de).

maniac ['meɪnɪæk] *n* fou *m*, folle *f* ; **a sex maniac** un obsédé sexuel (une obsédée sexuelle).

manic ['mænɪk] *adj* fig [person] surexcité(e) ; [behaviour] de fou.

manicure ['mænɪ,kjʊər] *n* manucure *f*.

manifest ['mænɪfest] *fml* <> *adj* manifeste, évident(e). <> *vt* manifester.

manifesto [,mænɪ'festəʊ] (*pl* -**s** OR -**es**) *n* manifeste *m*.

manipulate [mə'nɪpjʊleɪt] *vt* lit & fig manipuler.

manipulative [mə'nɪpjʊlətɪv] *adj* [person] rusé(e) ; [behaviour] habile, subtil(e).

mankind [mæn'kaɪnd] *n* humanité *f*, genre *m* humain.

manly ['mænlɪ] *adj* viril(e).

man-made *adj* [fabric, fibre] synthétique ; [environment] artificiel(elle) ; [problem] causé(e) par l'homme.

manner ['mænər] *n* **1.** [method] manière *f*, façon *f* - **2.** [attitude] attitude *f*, comportement *m*. <> **manners** *npl* manières *fpl*.

mannerism ['mænərɪzm] *n* tic *m*, manie *f*.

mannish ['mænɪʃ] *adj* masculin(e).

manoeuvre *UK*, **maneuver** *US* [mə'nu:vər] <> *n* manœuvre *f*. <> *vt & vi* manœuvrer.

manor ['mænər] *n* manoir *m*.

manpower ['mæn,paʊər] *n* main-d'œuvre *f*.

mansion ['mænʃn] *n* château *m*.

manslaughter ['mæn,slɔ:tər] *n* homicide *m* involontaire.

mantelpiece ['mæntlpi:s] *n* (dessus *m* de) cheminée *f*.

manual ['mænjʊəl] <> *adj* manuel(elle). <> *n* manuel *m*.

manual worker *n* travailleur manuel *m*, travailleuse manuelle *f*.

manufacture [,mænjʊ'fæktʃər] <> *n* fabrication *f* ; [of cars] construction *f*. <> *vt* fabriquer ; [cars] construire.

manufacturer [,mænjʊ'fæktʃərər] *n* fabricant *m* ; [of cars] constructeur *m*.

manure [mə'njʊər] *n* fumier *m*.

manuscript ['mænjʊskrɪpt] *n* manuscrit *m*.

many ['menɪ] <> *adj* (*comp* **more**, *superl* **most**) beaucoup de ; **how many...?** combien de...? ; **too many** trop de ; **as many... as** autant de... que ; **so many** autant de ; **a good** OR **great many** un grand nombre de. <> *pron* [a lot, plenty] beaucoup.

map [mæp] *n* carte *f*. <> **map out** *vt sep* [plan] élaborer ; [timetable] établir ; [task] définir.

maple ['meɪpl] *n* érable *m*.

mar [mɑ:r] *vt* gâter, gâcher.

marathon ['mærəθn] <> *adj* marathon *(inv)*. <> *n* marathon *m*.

marauder [mə'rɔ:dər] *n* maraudeur *m*, -euse *f*.

marble ['mɑ:bl] *n* **1.** [stone] marbre *m* - **2.** [for game] bille *f*.

march [mɑ:tʃ] <> *n* marche *f*. <> *vi* **1.** [soldiers etc] marcher au pas - **2.** [demonstrators] manifester, faire une marche de protestation - **3.** [quickly] : **to march up to sb** s'approcher de qqn d'un pas décidé.

March [mɑ:tʃ] *n* mars *m* ; *see also* **September**.

marcher ['mɑ:tʃər] *n* [protester] marcheur *m*, -euse *f*.

mare [meər] *n* jument *f*.

marg. [mɑ:dʒ] *n* = **margin**.

margarine [,mɑ:dʒə'ri:n OR ,mɑ:gə'ri:n] *n* margarine *f*.

marge [mɑ:dʒ] *n UK inf* margarine *f*.

margin ['mɑ:dʒɪn] *n* **1.** [gen] marge *f* ; **to win by a narrow margin** gagner de peu OR de justesse - **2.** [edge - of an area] bord *m*.

marginal ['mɑ:dʒɪnl] *adj* marginal(e), secondaire.

marginally ['mɑ:dʒɪnəlɪ] *adv* très peu.

marginal seat *n* POL en Grande-Bretagne, circonscription électorale où la majorité passe facilement d'un parti à un autre.

marigold ['mærɪgəʊld] *n* souci *m*.

marihuana, marijuana [,mærɪ'wɑ:nə] *n* marihuana *f*.

marine [mə'ri:n] *adj* marin(e).

Marine *n* marine *m*.

marital ['mærɪtl] *adj* [sex, happiness] conjugal(e) ; [problems] matrimonial(e).

marital status *n* situation *f* de famille.

maritime ['mærɪtaɪm] *adj* maritime.

mark [mɑ:k] <> *n* **1.** [sign, symbol] marque *f* - **2.** [trace, stain] tache *f*, marque *f* - **3.** *esp UK* [in exam] note *f*, point *m* - **4.** [stage, level] barre *f* - **5.** [currency] mark *m*. <> *vt* **1.** [gen] marquer - **2.** [stain] marquer, tacher - **3.** *esp UK* [exam, essay] noter, corriger. <> **mark off** *vt sep* **1.** [divide, isolate] délimiter ; **one corner of the field had been marked off by a fence** un coin du champ avait été isolé par une barrière - **2.** [cross off] cocher.

marked [mɑ:kt] *adj* [change, difference] marqué(e) ; [improvement, deterioration] sensible.

marker ['mɑːkər] n **1.** [sign] repère m - **2.** [pen] marqueur m.

marker pen n marqueur m.

market ['mɑːkɪt] <> n **1.** [generally] marché m - **2.** FIN marché m ; [index] indice m ; **the market has risen 10 points** l'indice est en hausse de 10 points. <> vt commercialiser.

market garden n UK jardin m maraîcher.

marketing ['mɑːkɪtɪŋ] n marketing m.

marketplace ['mɑːkɪtpleɪs] n **1.** [in a town] place f du marché - **2.** COMM marché m.

market research n étude f de marché.

market value n valeur f marchande.

marking ['mɑːkɪŋ] n SCH correction f. **markings** npl [on animal, flower] taches fpl, marques fpl ; [on road] signalisation f horizontale.

marksman ['mɑːksmən] (pl -men [-mən]) n tireur m d'élite.

markswoman ['mɑːkswəmən] (pl -men [-mən]) n tireuse f d'élite.

marmalade ['mɑːməleɪd] n confiture f d'oranges amères.

maroon [mə'ruːn] adj bordeaux (inv).

marooned [mə'ruːnd] adj abandonné(e).

marquee [mɑː'kiː] n UK grande tente f.

marriage ['mærɪdʒ] n mariage m.

marriage bureau n UK agence f matrimoniale.

marriage certificate n acte m de mariage.

marriage guidance UK Aus, **marriage counseling** US n conseil m conjugal.

married ['mærɪd] adj **1.** [person] marié(e) ; **to get married** se marier - **2.** [life] conjugal(e).

marrow ['mærəʊ] n **1.** UK [vegetable] courge f - **2.** [in bones] moelle f.

marry ['mærɪ] <> vt **1.** [become spouse of] épouser, se marier avec - **2.** [subj: priest, registrar] marier. <> vi se marier.

Mars [mɑːz] n [planet] Mars f.

marsh [mɑːʃ] n marais m, marécage m.

marshal ['mɑːʃl] <> n **1.** MIL maréchal m - **2.** [steward] membre m du service d'ordre - **3.** US [law officer] officier m de police fédérale. <> vt (UK & US) lit & fig rassembler.

martial arts npl arts mpl martiaux.

martial law n loi f martiale.

martyr ['mɑːtər] n martyr m, -e f.

martyrdom ['mɑːtədəm] n martyre m.

marvel ['mɑːvl] <> n merveille f. <> vi (UK & US) : **to marvel (at)** s'émerveiller (de), s'étonner (de).

marvellous UK, **marvelous** US ['mɑːvələs] adj merveilleux(euse).

Marxism ['mɑːksɪzm] n marxisme m.

Marxist ['mɑːksɪst] <> adj marxiste. <> n marxiste mf.

marzipan ['mɑːzɪpæn] n (U) pâte f d'amandes.

mascara [mæs'kɑːrə] n mascara m.

masculine ['mæskjʊlɪn] adj masculin(e).

mash [mæʃ] vt UK inf faire une purée de.

mashed potato UK [mæʃt-], **mashed potatoes** n purée f de pommes de terre.

mask [mɑːsk] lit & fig <> n masque m. <> vt masquer.

masochist ['mæsəkɪst] n masochiste mf.

mason ['meɪsn] n **1.** [stonemason] maçon m - **2.** [freemason] franc-maçon m.

masonry ['meɪsnrɪ] n [stones] maçonnerie f.

masquerade [,mæskə'reɪd] vi : **to masquerade as** se faire passer pour.

mass [mæs] <> n [gen & PHYS] masse f. <> adj [protest, meeting] en masse, en nombre ; [unemployment, support] massif(ive). <> vi se masser. **Mass** n RELIG messe f. **masses** npl **1.** esp UK inf [lots] : **masses (of)** des masses (de) ; [food] des tonnes (de) - **2.** [workers] : **the masses** les masses fpl.

massacre ['mæsəkər] <> n massacre m. <> vt massacrer.

massage [UK 'mæsɑːʒ, US mə'sɑːʒ] <> n massage m. <> vt masser.

massive ['mæsɪv] adj massif(ive), énorme.

mass media n & npl : **the mass media** les (mass) media mpl.

mass production n fabrication f OR production f en série.

mast [mɑːst] n **1.** [on boat] mât m - **2.** RADIO & TV pylône m.

master ['mɑːstər] <> n **1.** [gen] maître m - **2.** UK [SCH - in primary school] instituteur m, maître m ; [- in secondary school] professeur m. <> adj maître. <> vt maîtriser ; [difficulty] surmonter, vaincre ; [situation] se rendre maître de.

master key n passe m, passe-partout m inv.

masterly ['mɑːstəlɪ] adj magistral(e).

mastermind ['mɑːstəmaɪnd] <> n cerveau m. <> vt organiser, diriger.

Master of Arts (pl **Masters of Arts**) n **1.** [degree] maîtrise f ès lettres - **2.** [person] titulaire mf d'une maîtrise ès lettres.

Master of Science (pl **Masters of Science**) n **1.** [degree] maîtrise f ès sciences - **2.** [person] titulaire mf d'une maîtrise ès sciences.

masterpiece ['mɑːstəpiːs] n chef-d'œuvre m.

master's degree n ≃ maîtrise f.

mastery ['mɑːstərɪ] *n* maîtrise *f*.

mat [mæt] *n* **1.** [on floor] petit tapis *m* ; [at door] paillasson *m* - **2.** [on table] set *m* (de table) ; [coaster] dessous *m* de verre.

match [mætʃ] <> *n* **1.** [game] match *m* - **2.** [for lighting] allumette *f* - **3.** [equal] : **to be no match for sb** ne pas être de taille à lutter contre qqn. <> *vt* **1.** [be the same as, go with] correspondre à, s'accorder avec ; **the gloves match the scarf** les gants sont assortis à l'écharpe - **2.** [pair off] faire correspondre - **3.** [be equal with] égaler, rivaliser avec. <> *vi* **1.** [be the same] correspondre - **2.** [go together well] être assorti(e).

matchbox ['mætʃbɒks] *n* boîte *f* à allumettes.

matching ['mætʃɪŋ] *adj* assorti(e).

mate [meɪt] <> *n* **1.** *UK inf* [friend] copain *m*, copine *f*, pote *m* - **2.** *UK inf* [term of address] mon vieux - **3.** [of female animal] mâle *m* ; [of male animal] femelle *f* - **4.** NAUT : **(first) mate** second *m*. <> *vi* s'accoupler.

material [mə'tɪərɪəl] <> *adj* **1.** [goods, benefits, world] matériel(elle) - **2.** [important] important(e), essentiel(elle). <> *n* **1.** [substance] matière *f*, substance *f* ; [type of substance] matériau *m*, matière - **2.** [fabric] tissu *m*, étoffe *f* ; [type of fabric] tissu - **3.** (U) [information for book, article etc] matériaux *mpl*. **materials** *npl* matériaux *mpl*.

materialistic [mə,tɪərɪə'lɪstɪk] *adj* matérialiste.

materialize, *UK* **-ise** [mə'tɪərɪəlaɪz] *vi* **1.** [offer, threat] se concrétiser, se réaliser - **2.** [person, object] apparaître.

maternal [mə'tɜːnl] *adj* maternel(elle).

maternity [mə'tɜːnətɪ] *n* maternité *f*.

maternity dress *n* robe *f* de grossesse.

maternity hospital *n* maternité *f*.

math *US* = **maths**.

mathematical [,mæθə'mætɪkl] *adj* mathématique.

mathematics [,mæθə'mætɪks] *n* (U) mathématiques *fpl*.

maths *UK* [mæθs], **math** *US* (*abbrev of* **mathematics**) *inf* [mæθ] *n* (U) maths *fpl*.

matinée, matinee ['mætɪneɪ] *n* matinée *f*.

mating season ['meɪtɪŋ-] *n* saison *f* des amours.

matrices ['meɪtrɪsiːz] *npl* ► **matrix**.

matriculation [mə,trɪkjʊ'leɪʃn] *n* inscription *f*.

matrimonial [,mætrɪ'məʊnjəl] *adj fml* matrimonial(e), conjugal(e).

matrimony ['mætrɪmənɪ] *n* (U) *fml* mariage *m*.

matrix ['meɪtrɪks] (*pl* **matrices** ['meɪtrɪsiːz] OR **-es** [-iːz]) *n* **1.** [context, framework] contexte *m*, structure *f* - **2.** MATHS & TECH matrice *f*.

matron ['meɪtrən] *n* **1.** *UK* [in hospital] infirmière *f* en chef - **2.** *UK* [in school] infirmière *f*.

matronly ['meɪtrənlɪ] *adj euph* [woman] qui a l'allure d'une matrone ; [figure] de matrone.

matt *UK*, **matte** *US* [mæt] *adj* mat(e).

matted ['mætɪd] *adj* emmêlé(e).

matter ['mætər] <> *n* **1.** [question, situation] question *f*, affaire *f* ; **that's another** OR **a different matter** c'est tout autre chose, c'est une autre histoire ; **as a matter of course** automatiquement ; **to make matters worse** aggraver la situation ; **and to make matters worse...** pour tout arranger... ; **that's a matter of opinion** c'est (une) affaire OR question d'opinion - **2.** [trouble, cause of pain] : **there's something the matter with my radio** il y a quelque chose qui cloche OR ne va pas dans ma radio ; **what's the matter?** qu'est-ce qu'il y a? ; **what's the matter with him?** qu'est-ce qu'il a? - **3.** PHYS matière *f* - **4.** (U) [material] matière *f* ; **reading matter** choses *fpl* à lire. <> *vi* [be important] importer, avoir de l'importance ; **it doesn't matter** cela n'a pas d'importance. **as a matter of fact** *adv* en fait, à vrai dire. **for that matter** *adv* d'ailleurs. **no matter** *adv* : **no matter what** coûte que coûte, à tout prix ; **no matter how hard I try to explain...** j'ai beau essayer de lui expliquer...

Matterhorn ['mætə,hɔːn] *n* : **the Matterhorn** le mont Cervin.

matter-of-fact *adj* terre-à-terre, neutre.

mattress ['mætrɪs] *n* matelas *m*.

mature [mə'tjʊər] <> *adj* **1.** [person, attitude] mûr(e) - **2.** [cheese] fait(e) ; [wine] arrivé(e) à maturité. <> *vi* **1.** [person] mûrir - **2.** [cheese, wine] se faire.

mature student *n UK* UNIV *étudiant qui a commencé ses études sur le tard*.

maul [mɔːl] *vt* mutiler.

mauve [məʊv] <> *adj* mauve. <> *n* mauve *m*.

max. [mæks] (*abbrev of* **maximum**) max.

maxim ['mæksɪm] (*pl* **-s**) *n* maxime *f*.

maxima ['mæksɪmə] *npl* ► **maximum**.

maximum ['mæksɪməm] <> *adj* maximum (*inv*). <> *n* (*pl* **maxima** ['mæksɪmə] OR **-s**) maximum *m*.

may [meɪ] *modal vb* **1.** [expressing possibility] : **it may rain** il se peut qu'il pleuve, il va peut-être pleuvoir ; **be that as it may** quoi qu'il en soit - **2.** [expressing permission] : **may I come in?** puis-je entrer? - **3.** [as contrast] : **it may be expensive but...** c'est peut-être cher, mais... - **4.** *fml* [can] pouvoir ; **on a clear day the coast may be seen** on peut voir la côte par temps clair - **5.** *fml* [expressing wish, hope] : **may they be happy!** qu'ils soient heureux! ; **may as well : can I go home now? – you may as well** est-ce que je peux rentrer chez moi maintenant? – tu ferais aussi bien ; **we may as well have another drink** tant qu'à faire, autant prendre un autre verre ; *see also* **might**.

May [meɪ] *n* mai *m* ; *see also* **September**.

maybe ['meɪbi:] *adv* peut-être ; **maybe I'll come** je viendrai peut-être.

May Day *n* le Premier mai.

mayhem ['meɪhem] *n* pagaille *f*.

mayonnaise [,meɪə'neɪz] *n* mayonnaise *f*.

mayor [meəʳ] *n* maire *m*.

mayoress ['meərɪs] *n esp UK* **1.** [female mayor] femme *f* maire - **2.** [mayor's wife] femme *f* du maire.

maze [meɪz] *n lit & fig* labyrinthe *m*, dédale *m*.

MB (*abbrev of* megabyte) Mo.

MD *n UK abbrev of* **managing director**.

me [mi:] *pers pron* **1.** [direct, indirect] me, m' (+ vowel or silent 'h') ; **can you see/hear me?** tu me vois/m'entends? ; **it's me** c'est moi ; **they spoke to me** ils m'ont parlé ; **she gave it to me** elle me l'a donné - **2.** [stressed, after prep, in comparisons *etc*] moi ; **you can't expect ME to do it** tu ne peux pas exiger que ce soit moi qui le fasse ; **she's shorter than me** elle est plus petite que moi.

meadow ['medəʊ] *n* prairie *f*, pré *m*.

meagre *UK*, **meager** *US* ['mi:gəʳ] *adj* maigre.

meal [mi:l] *n* repas *m*.

mealtime ['mi:ltaɪm] *n* heure *f* du repas.

mean [mi:n] ◇ *vt* (*pt & pp* meant) **1.** [signify] signifier, vouloir dire - **2.** [intend] : **to mean to do sthg** vouloir faire qqch, avoir l'intention de faire qqch ; **I didn't mean to drop it** je n'ai pas fait exprès de le laisser tomber ; **to be meant for sb/sthg** être destiné(e) à qqn/qqch ; **to be meant to do sthg** être censé(e) faire qqch ; **to mean well** agir dans une bonne intention - **3.** [be serious about] : **I mean it** je suis sérieux(euse) - **4.** [entail] occasionner, entraîner ; **I mean** [as explanation] c'est vrai ; [as correction] je veux dire. ◇ *adj* **1.** *UK* [miserly] radin(e), chiche ; **to be mean with sthg** être avare de qqch - **2.** [unkind] mesquin(e), méchant(e) ;

to be mean to sb être mesquin envers qqn - **3.** [average] moyen(enne). ◇ *n* [average] moyenne *f* ; *see also* **means**.

meander [mɪ'ændəʳ] *vi* [river, road] serpenter ; [person] errer.

meaning ['mi:nɪŋ] *n* sens *m*, signification *f*.

meaningful ['mi:nɪŋfʊl] *adj* [look] significatif(ive) ; [relationship, discussion] important(e).

meaningless ['mi:nɪŋlɪs] *adj* [gesture, word] dénué(e) OR vide de sens ; [proposal, discussion] sans importance.

means [mi:nz] ◇ *n* [method, way] moyen *m* ; **by means of** au moyen de. ◇ *npl* [money] moyens *mpl*, ressources *fpl*. ◆ **by all means** *adv* mais certainement, bien sûr. ◆ **by no means** *adv* nullement, en aucune façon.

meant [ment] *pt & pp* ► **mean**.

meantime ['mi:n,taɪm] *n* : **in the meantime** en attendant.

meanwhile ['mi:n,waɪl] *adv* **1.** [at the same time] pendant ce temps - **2.** [between two events] en attendant.

measles ['mi:zlz] *n* : **(the) measles** la rougeole.

measly ['mi:zlɪ] *adj inf* misérable, minable.

measure ['meʒəʳ] ◇ *n* **1.** [gen] mesure *f* - **2.** [indication] : **it is a measure of her success that...** la preuve de son succès, c'est que... ◇ *vt & vi* mesurer.

measurement ['meʒəmənt] *n* mesure *f*.

meat [mi:t] *n* viande *f*.

meatball ['mi:tbɔ:l] *n* boulette *f* de viande.

meat pie *n UK* tourte *f* à la viande.

meaty ['mi:tɪ] *adj fig* important(e).

Mecca ['mekə] *n* La Mecque.

mechanic [mɪ'kænɪk] *n* mécanicien *m*, -enne *f*. ◆ **mechanics** ◇ *n* (*U*) [study] mécanique *f*. ◇ *npl fig* mécanisme *m*.

mechanical [mɪ'kænɪkl] *adj* **1.** [device] mécanique - **2.** [person, mind] fort(e) en mécanique - **3.** [routine, automatic] machinal(e).

mechanism ['mekənɪzm] *n lit & fig* mécanisme *m*.

medal ['medl] *n* médaille *f*.

medallion [mɪ'dæljən] *n* médaillon *m*.

meddle ['medl] *vi* : **to meddle in** se mêler de.

media ['mi:djə] ◇ *npl* ► **medium**. ◇ *n & npl* : **the media** les médias *mpl*.

mediaeval [,medɪ'i:vl] = **medieval**.

median ['mi:djən] *n US* [of road] bande *f* médiane (*qui sépare les deux côtés d'une grande route*).

mediate ['mi:dɪeɪt] <> vt négocier. <> vi : **to mediate (for/between)** servir de médiateur (pour/entre).

mediator ['mi:dɪeɪtər] n médiateur m, -trice f.

Medicaid ['medɪkeɪd] n US assistance médicale aux personnes sans ressources.

medical ['medɪkl] <> adj médical(e). <> n UK examen m médical.

medical officer n [in factory etc] médecin m du travail ; MIL médecin militaire.

Medicare ['medɪkeər] n US programme fédéral d'assistance médicale pour personnes âgées.

medicated ['medɪkeɪtɪd] adj traitant(e).

medicine ['medsɪn] n 1. [subject, treatment] médecine f ; **Doctor of Medicine** UNIV docteur m en médecine - 2. [substance] médicament m.

medieval [,medɪ'i:vl] adj médiéval(e).

mediocre [,mi:dɪ'əʊkər] adj médiocre.

meditate ['medɪteɪt] vi : **to meditate (on** OR **upon)** méditer (sur).

Mediterranean [,medɪtə'reɪnjən] <> n [sea] : **the Mediterranean (Sea)** la (mer) Méditerranée. <> adj méditerranéen(enne).

medium ['mi:djəm] <> adj moyen(enne). <> n 1. (pl **media** ['mi:djə]) [way of communicating] moyen m - 2. (pl **mediums**) [spiritualist] médium m.

medium-size(d) [-saɪz(d)] adj de taille moyenne.

medium wave n onde f moyenne.

medley ['medlɪ] (pl **-s**) n 1. [mixture] mélange m - 2. MUS pot-pourri m.

meek [mi:k] adj docile.

meet [mi:t] <> vt (pt & pp **met**) 1. [gen] rencontrer ; [by arrangement] retrouver ; **fancy meeting you here!** je ne m'attendais pas à vous trouver ici! - 2. [go to meet - person] aller/venir attendre, aller/venir chercher ; [- train, plane] aller attendre - 3. [need, requirement] satisfaire, répondre à - 4. [problem] résoudre ; [challenge] répondre à - 5. [costs] payer. <> vi (pt & pp **met**) 1. [gen] se rencontrer ; [by arrangement] se retrouver ; [for a purpose] se réunir - 2. [join] se joindre. <> n US [meeting] meeting m. ⬅ **meet up** vi se retrouver ; **to meet up with sb** rencontrer qqn, retrouver qqn. ⬅ **meet with** vt insep 1. [encounter - disapproval] être accueilli(e) par ; [- success] remporter ; [- failure] essuyer - 2. US [by arrangement] retrouver.

meeting ['mi:tɪŋ] n 1. [for discussions, business] réunion f - 2. [by chance] rencontre f ; [by arrangement] entrevue f.

megabyte ['megəbaɪt] n COMPUT mégaoctet m.

megaphone ['megəfəʊn] n mégaphone m, porte-voix m inv.

melancholy ['melənkəlɪ] <> adj [person] mélancolique ; [news, facts] triste. <> n mélancolie f.

mellow ['meləʊ] <> adj [light, voice] doux (douce) ; [taste, wine] moelleux(euse). <> vi s'adoucir.

melody ['melədɪ] n mélodie f.

melon ['melən] n melon m.

melt [melt] <> vt faire fondre. <> vi 1. [become liquid] fondre - 2. fig : **his heart melted at the sight** il fut tout attendri devant ce spectacle - 3. [disappear] : **to melt (away)** fondre. ⬅ **melt down** vt sep fondre.

meltdown ['meltdaʊn] n 1. PHYS fusion f du cœur (du réacteur) - 2. inf ECON effondrement m.

melting pot ['meltɪŋ-] n fig creuset m.

member ['membər] n membre m ; [of club] adhérent m, -e f.

Member of Congress (pl **Members of Congress**) n US membre m du Congrès.

Member of Parliament (pl **Members of Parliament**) n UK ≃ député m.

Member of the Scottish Parliament n membre m du Parlement écossais.

membership ['membəʃɪp] n 1. [of organization] adhésion f - 2. [number of members] nombre m d'adhérents - 3. [members] : **the membership** les membres mpl.

membership card n carte f d'adhésion.

memento [mɪ'mentəʊ] (pl **-s**) n souvenir m.

memo ['meməʊ] (pl **-s**) n note f de service.

memoirs ['memwɑ:z] npl mémoires mpl.

memorandum [,memə'rændəm] (pl **-da** [-də] OR **-dums**) n fml note f de service.

memorial [mɪ'mɔ:rɪəl] <> adj commémoratif(ive). <> n monument m.

memorize, UK **-ise** ['meməraɪz] vt [phone number, list] retenir ; [poem] apprendre par cœur.

memory ['memərɪ] n 1. [gen & COMPUT] mémoire f ; **from memory** de mémoire - 2. [event, experience] souvenir m.

men [men] npl ⬅ **man**.

menace ['menəs] <> n 1. [gen] menace f - 2. inf [nuisance] plaie f. <> vt menacer.

menacing ['menəsɪŋ] adj menaçant(e).

mend [mend] <> n inf **to be on the mend** aller mieux. <> vt réparer ; [clothes] raccommoder ; [sock, pullover] repriser.

menial ['mi:njəl] adj avilissant(e).

meningitis [,menɪn'dʒaɪtɪs] n (U) méningite f.

menopause ['menəpɔ:z] *n* : the menopause *UK*, menopause *US* la ménopause.

men's room *n US* : the men's room les toilettes *fpl* pour hommes.

menstruation [,menstrʊ'eɪʃn] *n* MED menstruation *f*.

menswear ['menzweər] *n (U)* vêtements *mpl* pour hommes.

mental ['mentl] *adj* mental(e) ; [image, picture] dans la tête.

mental hospital *n* hôpital *m* psychiatrique.

mentality [men'tælətɪ] *n* mentalité *f*.

mentally handicapped *npl* : the mentally handicapped les handicapés *mpl* mentaux.

mention ['menʃn] *vt* mentionner, signaler ; not to mention sans parler de ; don't mention it! je vous en prie! *n* mention *f*.

menu ['menju:] *n* [gen & COMPUT] menu *m*.

meow *US* = miaow.

MEP (*abbrev of* Member of the European Parliament) *n* parlementaire *m* européen.

mercenary ['mɜ:sɪnrɪ] *pej adj* mercenaire. *n* mercenaire *m*.

merchandise ['mɜ:tʃəndaɪz] *n (U)* marchandises *fpl*.

merchant ['mɜ:tʃənt] *n* marchand *m*, -e *f*, commerçant *m*, -e *f*.

merchant bank *n UK* banque *f* d'affaires.

merchant navy *UK*, **merchant marine** *US n* marine *f* marchande.

merciful ['mɜ:sɪfʊl] *adj* 1. [person] clément(e) - 2. [death, release] qui est une délivrance.

merciless ['mɜ:sɪlɪs] *adj* impitoyable.

mercury ['mɜ:kjʊrɪ] *n* mercure *m*.

Mercury ['mɜ:kjʊrɪ] *n* [planet] Mercure *f*.

mercy ['mɜ:sɪ] *n* 1. [kindness, pity] pitié *f* ; at the mercy of *fig* à la merci de - 2. [blessing] : what a mercy that... quelle chance que...

mere [mɪər] *adj* seul(e) ; she's a mere child ce n'est qu'une enfant ; it cost a mere £10 cela n'a coûté que 10 livres.

merely ['mɪəlɪ] *adv* seulement, simplement.

merge [mɜ:dʒ] *vt* COMM & COMPUT fusionner. *vi* 1. COMM : to merge (with) fusionner (avec) - 2. [roads, lines] : to merge (with) se joindre (à) - 3. [colours] se fondre. *n* COMPUT fusion *f*.

merger ['mɜ:dʒər] *n* fusion *f*.

meringue [mə'ræŋ] *n* meringue *f*.

merit ['merɪt] *n* [value] mérite *m*, valeur *f*. *vt fml* mériter. **merits** *npl* [advantages] qualités *fpl*.

mermaid ['mɜ:meɪd] *n* sirène *f*.

merry ['merɪ] *UK adj* 1. *lit* [happy] joyeux(euse) ; Merry Christmas! joyeux Noël! - 2. *inf* [tipsy] gai(e), éméché(e).

merry-go-round *n* manège *m*.

mesh [meʃ] *n* maille *f* (du filet) ; wire mesh grillage *m*. *vi* [gears] s'engrener.

mesmerize, *UK* **-ise** ['mezməraɪz] *vt* : to be mesmerized by être fasciné(e) par.

mess [mes] *n* 1. [untidy state] désordre *m* ; *fig* gâchis *m* - 2. MIL mess *m*. **mess about** *UK*, **mess around** *UK inf vt sep* : to mess sb about traiter qqn par-dessus OR par-dessous la jambe. *vi* 1. [fool around] perdre OR gaspiller son temps - 2. [interfere] : to mess about with sthg s'immiscer dans qqch. **mess up** *vt sep inf* 1. [room] mettre en désordre ; [clothes] salir - 2. *fig* [spoil] gâcher.

message ['mesɪdʒ] *n* message *m*.

messenger ['mesɪndʒər] *n* messager *m*, -ère *f*.

Messrs, Messrs. (*abbrev of* messieurs) ['mesəz] MM.

messy ['mesɪ] *adj* 1. [dirty] sale ; [untidy] désordonné(e) ; a messy job un travail salissant - 2. *inf* [divorce] difficile ; [situation] embrouillé(e).

met [met] *pt & pp* meet.

metal ['metl] *n* métal *m*. *comp* en OR de métal.

metallic [mɪ'tælɪk] *adj* 1. [sound, ore] métallique - 2. [paint, finish] métallisé(e).

metalwork ['metlwɜ:k] *n* [craft] ferronnerie *f*.

metaphor ['metəfər] *n* métaphore *f*.

mete [mi:t] **mete out** *vt sep fml* [punishment] infliger.

meteor ['mi:tɪər] *n* météore *m*.

meteorology [mi:tjə'rɒlədʒɪ] *n* météorologie *f*.

meter ['mi:tər] *n* 1. [device] compteur *m* - 2. *US* = metre. *vt* [gas, electricity] établir la consommation de.

metered ['mi:təd] *adj* décompté(e) à la minute.

method ['meθəd] *n* méthode *f*.

methodical [mɪ'θɒdɪkl] *adj* méthodique.

Methodist ['meθədɪst] *adj* méthodiste. *n* méthodiste *mf*.

meths [meθs] *n UK inf* alcool *m* à brûler.

methylated spirits ['meθɪleɪtɪd-] *n* alcool *m* à brûler.

meticulous [mɪ'tɪkjʊləs] *adj* méticuleux(euse).

metre *UK*, **meter** *US* ['mi:tər] *n* mètre *m*.

metric ['metrɪk] *adj* métrique.

metronome ['metrənəum] *n* métronome *m.*

metropolitan [,metrə'pɒlɪtn] *adj* métropolitain(e).

Metropolitan Police *npl* : the Metropolitan Police la police de Londres.

mettle ['metl] *n* : to be on one's mettle être d'attaque ; to show OR prove one's mettle montrer ce dont on est capable.

mew [mju:] = miaow.

mews [mju:z] (*pl* mews) *n* UK ruelle *f.*

Mexican ['meksɪkn] <> *adj* mexicain(e). <> *n* Mexicain *m*, -e *f.*

Mexico ['meksɪkəu] *n* Mexique *m.*

MI5 (*abbrev of* Military Intelligence 5) *n* service de contre-espionnage britannique.

MI6 (*abbrev of* Military Intelligence 6) *n* service de renseignements britannique.

miaow UK [mi:'au], **meow** US [mɪ'au] <> *n* miaulement *m*, miaou *m*. <> *vi* miauler.

mice [maɪs] *npl* ► mouse.

mickey ['mɪkɪ] *n* : to take the mickey out of sb UK *inf* se payer la tête de qqn, faire marcher qqn.

microchip ['maɪkrəutʃɪp] *n* COMPUT puce *f.*

microcomputer [,maɪkrəukəm'pju:tər] *n* micro-ordinateur *m.*

microfilm ['maɪkrəufɪlm] *n* microfilm *m.*

microphone ['maɪkrəfəun] *n* microphone *m*, micro *m.*

microscope ['maɪkrəskəup] *n* microscope *m.*

microscopic [,maɪkrə'skɒpɪk] *adj* microscopique.

microwave (oven) ['maɪkrəweɪv-] *n* (four *m* à) micro-ondes *m.*

mid- [mɪd] *prefix* : mid-height mi-hauteur ; mid-morning milieu de la matinée ; midwinter plein hiver.

midair [mɪd'eər] <> *adj* en plein ciel. <> *n* : in midair en plein ciel.

midday ['mɪddeɪ] *n* midi *m.*

middle ['mɪdl] <> *adj* [centre] du milieu, du centre. <> *n* **1.** [centre] milieu *m*, centre *m* ; in the middle (of) au milieu (de) - **2.** [in time] milieu *m* ; to be in the middle of doing sthg être en train de faire qqch ; to be in the middle of a meeting être en pleine réunion ; in the middle of the night au milieu de la nuit, en pleine nuit - **3.** [waist] taille *f.*

middle-aged *adj* d'une cinquantaine d'années.

Middle Ages *npl* : the Middle Ages le Moyen Âge.

middle-class *adj* bourgeois(e).

middle classes *npl* : the middle classes la bourgeoisie.

Middle East *n* : the Middle East le Moyen-Orient.

middleman ['mɪdlmæn] (*pl* -men [-men]) *n* intermédiaire *mf.*

middle name *n* second prénom *m.*

middleweight ['mɪdlweɪt] *n* poids *m* moyen.

middling ['mɪdlɪŋ] *adj* moyen(enne).

Mideast [,mɪd'i:st] *n* US : the Mideast le Moyen-Orient.

midfield [,mɪd'fi:ld] *n* FOOTBALL milieu *m* de terrain.

midge [mɪdʒ] *n* moucheron *m.*

midget ['mɪdʒɪt] *n* nain *m*, -e *f.*

midi system, MIDI system ['mɪdɪ-] *n* UK chaîne *f* midi.

Midlands ['mɪdləndz] *npl* : the Midlands les comtés du centre de l'Angleterre.

midnight ['mɪdnaɪt] *n* minuit *m.*

midriff ['mɪdrɪf] *n* diaphragme *m.*

midst [mɪdst] *n* *fml* **1.** [in space] : in the midst of au milieu de - **2.** [in time] : to be in the midst of doing sthg être en train de faire qqch.

midsummer ['mɪd,sʌmər] *n* cœur *m* de l'été.

Midsummer Day *n* UK 24 juin.

mid-term election *n* US élection *f* de mi-mandat.

midway [,mɪd'weɪ] *adv* **1.** [in space] : midway (between) à mi-chemin (entre) - **2.** [in time] : midway through the meeting en pleine réunion.

midweek <> *adj* ['mɪdwi:k] du milieu de la semaine. <> *adv* [mɪd'wi:k] en milieu de semaine.

midwife ['mɪdwaɪf] (*pl* -wives [-waɪvz]) *n* sage-femme *f.*

midwifery ['mɪd,wɪfərɪ] *n* obstétrique *f.*

might [maɪt] <> *modal vb* **1.** [expressing possibility] : the criminal might be armed il est possible que le criminel soit armé - **2.** [expressing suggestion] : it might be better to wait il vaut peut-être mieux attendre - **3.** *fml* [asking permission] : he asked if he might leave the room il demanda s'il pouvait sortir de la pièce. <> *n (U)* force *f.*

mighty ['maɪtɪ] *esp* UK <> *adj* [powerful] puissant(e). <> *adv* US *inf* drôlement, vachement.

migraine ['mi:greɪn OR 'maɪgreɪn] *n* migraine *f.*

migrant ['maɪgrənt] <> *adj* **1.** [bird, animal] migrateur(trice) - **2.** [workers] émigré(e). ◇ *n* **1.** [bird, animal] migrateur *m* - **2.** [person] émigré *m*, -e *f*.

migrate [*UK* maɪˈgreɪt, *US* ˈmaɪgreɪt] *vi* **1.** [bird, animal] migrer - **2.** [person] émigrer.

mike [maɪk] (*abbrev of* **microphone**) *n inf* micro *m*.

mild [maɪld] *adj* **1.** [disinfectant, reproach] léger(ère) - **2.** [tone, weather] doux (douce) - **3.** [illness] bénin(igne).

mildew [ˈmɪldjuː] *n* (U) moisissure *f*.

mildly [ˈmaɪldlɪ] *adv* **1.** [gently] doucement ; **that's putting it mildly** c'est le moins qu'on puisse dire - **2.** [not strongly] légèrement - **3.** [slightly] un peu.

mile [maɪl] *n* mile *m* ; NAUT mille *m* ; **to be miles away** *fig* être très loin.

mileage [ˈmaɪlɪdʒ] *n* distance *f* en miles, ≈ kilométrage *m*.

mil(e)ometer [maɪˈlɒmɪtər] *n UK* compteur *m* de miles, ≈ compteur kilométrique.

milestone [ˈmaɪlstəun] *n* [marker stone] borne *f* ; *fig* événement *m* marquant OR important.

militant [ˈmɪlɪtənt] ◇ *adj* militant(e). ◇ *n* militant *m*, -e *f*.

military [ˈmɪlɪtrɪ] ◇ *adj* militaire. ◇ *n* : **the military** les militaires *mpl*, l'armée *f*.

militia [mɪˈlɪʃə] *n* milice *f*.

milk [mɪlk] ◇ *n* lait *m*. ◇ *vt* **1.** [cow] traire - **2.** *fig* [use to own ends] exploiter.

milk chocolate *n* chocolat *m* au lait.

milkman [ˈmɪlkmən] (*pl* -men [-mən]) *n* laitier *m*, -ière *f*.

milk shake *n* milk-shake *m*.

milky [ˈmɪlkɪ] *adj* **1.** *UK* [coffee] avec beaucoup de lait - **2.** [pale white] laiteux(euse).

Milky Way *n* : **the Milky Way** la Voie lactée.

mill [mɪl] ◇ *n* **1.** [flour-mill, grinder] moulin *m* - **2.** [factory] usine *f*. ◇ *vt* moudre. ➤ **mill about**, **mill around** *vi* grouiller.

millennium [mɪˈlenɪəm] (*pl* millennia [mɪˈlenɪə]) *n* millénaire *m*.

miller [ˈmɪlər] *n* meunier *m*, -ière *f*.

millet [ˈmɪlɪt] *n* millet *m*.

milligram, *UK* **milligramme** [ˈmɪlɪgræm] *n* milligramme *m*.

millimetre *UK*, **millimeter** *US* [ˈmɪlɪˌmiːtər] *n* millimètre *m*.

millinery [ˈmɪlɪnrɪ] *n* chapellerie *f* féminine.

million [ˈmɪljən] *n* million *m* ; **a million, millions of** *fig* des milliers de, un million de.

millionaire [ˌmɪljəˈneər] *n* millionnaire *mf*.

millstone [ˈmɪlstəun] *n* meule *f*.

milometer *UK* [maɪˈlɒmɪtər] = **mileometer**.

mime [maɪm] ◇ *n* mime *m*. ◇ *vt & vi* mimer.

mimic [ˈmɪmɪk] ◇ *n* imitateur *m*, -trice *f*. ◇ *vt* (*pt & pp* -**ked**, *cont* -**king**) imiter.

mimicry [ˈmɪmɪkrɪ] *n* imitation *f*.

min. [mɪn] **1.** (*abbrev of* **minute**) mn, min - **2.** (*abbrev of* **minimum**) min.

mince [mɪns] ◇ *n UK* viande *f* hachée. ◇ *vt* [garlic] hacher. ◇ *vi* marcher à petits pas maniérés.

mincemeat [ˈmɪnsmiːt] *n* **1.** [fruit] *mélange de pommes, raisins secs et épices utilisé en pâtisserie* - **2.** *UK* [meat] viande *f* hachée.

mince pie *n* tartelette *f* de Noël.

mincer [ˈmɪnsər] *n UK* hachoir *m*.

mind [maɪnd] ◇ *n* **1.** [gen] esprit *m* ; **state of mind** état d'esprit ; **to bear sthg in mind** ne pas oublier qqch ; **to come into/cross sb's mind** venir à/traverser l'esprit de qqn ; **to have sthg on one's mind** avoir l'esprit préoccupé, être préoccupé par qqch ; **to keep an open mind** réserver son jugement ; **to have sthg in mind** avoir qqch dans l'idée ; **to have a mind to do sthg** avoir bien envie de faire qqch ; **to make one's mind up** se décider - **2.** [attention] : **to put one's mind to sthg** s'appliquer à qqch ; **to keep one's mind on sthg** se concentrer sur qqch - **3.** [opinion] : **to change one's mind** changer d'avis ; **to my mind** à mon avis ; **to speak one's mind** parler franchement ; **to be in** *UK* **or of** *US* **two minds (about sthg)** se tâter OR être indécis (à propos de qqch) - **4.** [person] cerveau *m*. ◇ *vi* [be bothered] : **I don't mind** ça m'est égal ; **I hope you don't mind** j'espère que vous n'y voyez pas d'inconvénient ; **do you mind!** *iro* [politely] vous permettez? ; [indignantly] non mais! ; **never mind** [don't worry] ne t'en fais pas ; [it's not important] ça ne fait rien. ◇ *vt* **1.** [be bothered about, dislike] : **I don't mind waiting** ça ne me gêne OR dérange pas d'attendre ; **I wouldn't mind a beer** je prendrais bien une bière - **2.** *esp UK* [pay attention to] faire attention à, prendre garde à - **3.** *esp UK* [take care of - luggage] garder, surveiller ; [- shop] tenir. ➤ **mind you** *adv* remarquez.

minder [ˈmaɪndər] *n UK inf* [bodyguard] ange *m* gardien.

mindful [ˈmaɪndful] *adj* : **mindful of** [risks] attentif(ive) à ; [responsibility] soucieux(euse) de.

mindless [ˈmaɪndlɪs] *adj* stupide, idiot(e).

mine[1] [maɪn] *poss pron* le mien (la mienne), les miens (les miennes) (*pl*) ; **that money is mine** cet argent est à moi ; **it wasn't your fault, it was MINE** ce n'était pas de votre faute, c'était de la mienne OR de ma faute à moi ; **a friend of mine** un ami à moi, un de mes amis.

mine²[maɪn] ◇ *n* mine *f*. ◇ *vt* **1.** [coal, gold] extraire - **2.** [road, beach, sea] miner.

minefield ['maɪnfiːld] *n* champ *m* de mines ; *fig* situation *f* explosive.

miner ['maɪnər] *n* mineur *m*, -euse *f*.

mineral ['mɪnərəl] ◇ *adj* minéral(e). ◇ *n* minéral *m*.

mineral water *n* eau *f* minérale.

minesweeper ['maɪn,swiːpər] *n* dragueur *m* de mines.

minging ['mɪŋɪŋ] *adj* UK *v inf* horrible.

mingle ['mɪŋgl] *vi* : **to mingle (with)** [sounds, fragrances] se mélanger (à) ; [people] se mêler (à).

miniature ['mɪnətʃər] ◇ *adj* miniature. ◇ *n* **1.** [painting] miniature - **2.** [of alcohol] bouteille *f* miniature - **3.** [small scale] : **in miniature** en miniature.

minibus ['mɪnɪbʌs] (*pl* **-es**) *n* minibus *m*.

minicab ['mɪnɪkæb] *n* UK radiotaxi *m*.

minidish ['mɪnɪdɪʃ] *n* mini-parabole *f*.

minima ['mɪnɪmə] *npl* ► minimum.

minimal ['mɪnɪml] *adj* [cost] insignifiant(e) ; [damage] minime.

minimum ['mɪnɪməm] ◇ *adj* minimum (*inv*). ◇ *n* (*pl* **minima** ['mɪnɪmə] OR **-s**) minimum *m*.

mining ['maɪnɪŋ] ◇ *n* exploitation *f* minière. ◇ *adj* minier(ère).

miniskirt ['mɪnɪskɜːt] *n* minijupe *f*.

minister ['mɪnɪstər] *n* **1.** POL ministre *m* - **2.** RELIG pasteur *m*. ◆ **minister to** *vt insep* [person] donner OR prodiguer ses soins à ; [needs] pourvoir à.

ministerial [,mɪnɪ'stɪərɪəl] *adj* ministériel(elle).

minister of state *n* UK secrétaire *mf* d'État.

ministry ['mɪnɪstrɪ] *n* **1.** POL ministère *m* - **2.** RELIG : **the ministry** le saint ministère.

mink [mɪŋk] (*pl* **mink**) *n* vison *m*.

minnow ['mɪnəʊ] *n* vairon *m*.

minor ['maɪnər] ◇ *adj* [gen & MUS] mineur(e) ; [detail] petit(e) ; [role] secondaire. ◇ *n* mineur *m*, -e *f*.

minority [maɪ'nɒrətɪ] *n* minorité *f*.

mint [mɪnt] ◇ *n* **1.** [herb] menthe *f* - **2.** [sweet] bonbon *m* à la menthe - **3.** [for coins] : **the Mint** l'hôtel de la Monnaie ; **in mint condition** en parfait état. ◇ *vt* [coins] battre.

minus ['maɪnəs] ◇ *prep* moins. ◇ *adj* [answer, quantity] négatif(ive). ◇ *n* (*pl* **-es** [-iːz]) **1.** MATHS signe *m* moins - **2.** [disadvantage] handicap *m*.

minus sign *n* signe *m* moins.

minute¹['mɪnɪt] ◇ *n* minute *f* ; **at any minute** à tout moment, d'une minute à l'autre ; **stop that this minute!** arrête tout de suite OR immédiatement ! ◇ *adj* [news] : **up-to-the-minute** de dernière heure. ◆ **minutes** *npl* procès-verbal *m*, compte rendu *m*.

minute²[maɪ'njuːt] *adj* minuscule.

miracle ['mɪrəkl] *n* miracle *m*.

miraculous [mɪ'rækjʊləs] *adj* miraculeux(euse).

mirage [mɪ'rɑːʒ] *n* *lit & fig* mirage *m*.

mire [maɪər] *n* fange *f*, boue *f*.

mirror ['mɪrər] ◇ *n* miroir *m*, glace *f*. ◇ *vt* [mirror, water] refléter ; COMPUT donner un site miroir à.

mirror site *n* COMPUT site *m* miroir.

mirth [mɜːθ] *n* *lit* hilarité *f*, gaieté *f*.

misadventure [,mɪsəd'ventʃər] *n* UK LAW : **death by misadventure** UK LAW mort *f* accidentelle.

misapprehension ['mɪs,æprɪ'henʃn] *n* idée *f* fausse.

misappropriation ['mɪsə,prəʊprɪ'eɪʃn] *n* détournement *m*.

miscalculate [,mɪs'kælkjʊleɪt] ◇ *vt* mal calculer. ◇ *vi* se tromper.

miscarriage [,mɪs'kærɪdʒ] *n* MED fausse couche *f* ; **to have a miscarriage** faire une fausse couche.

miscarriage of justice *n* erreur *f* judiciaire.

miscellaneous [,mɪsə'leɪnjəs] *adj* varié(e), divers(e).

mischief ['mɪstʃɪf] *n* (*U*) **1.** [playfulness] malice *f*, espièglerie *f* - **2.** [naughty behaviour] sottises *fpl*, bêtises *fpl* - **3.** [harm] dégât *m*.

mischievous ['mɪstʃɪvəs] *adj* **1.** [playful] malicieux(euse) - **2.** [naughty] espiègle, coquin(e).

misconception [,mɪskən'sepʃn] *n* idée *f* fausse.

misconduct [,mɪs'kɒndʌkt] *n* inconduite *f*.

misconstrue [,mɪskən'struː] *vt* *fml* mal interpréter.

miscount [,mɪs'kaʊnt] *vt & vi* mal compter.

misdeed [,mɪs'diːd] *n* *fml* méfait *m*.

misdemeanour UK, **misdemeanor** US [,mɪsdɪ'miːnər] *n* LAW délit *m*.

miser ['maɪzər] *n* avare *mf*.

miserable ['mɪzrəbl] *adj* **1.** [person] malheureux(euse), triste - **2.** [conditions, life]

misérable ; [pay] dérisoire ; [weather] maussade - **3.** [failure] pitoyable, lamentable.

miserly ['maɪzəlɪ] *adj* avare.

misery ['mɪzərɪ] *n* **1.** [of person] tristesse *f* - **2.** [of conditions, life] misère *f*.

misfire [,mɪs'faɪə] *vi* **1.** [gun, plan] rater - **2.** [car engine] avoir des ratés.

misfit ['mɪsfɪt] *n* inadapté *m*, -e *f*.

misfortune [mɪs'fɔːtʃuːn] *n* **1.** [bad luck] malchance *f* - **2.** [piece of bad luck] malheur *m*.

misgivings [mɪs'gɪvɪŋz] *npl* craintes *fpl*, doutes *mpl* ; **to have misgivings about** avoir des doutes quant à, douter de.

misguided [,mɪs'gaɪdɪd] *adj* [person] malavisé(e) ; [attempt] malencontreux(euse) ; [opinion] peu judicieux(euse).

mishandle [,mɪs'hændl] *vt* **1.** [person, animal] manier sans précaution - **2.** [negotiations] mal mener ; [business] mal gérer.

mishap ['mɪshæp] *n* mésaventure *f*.

misinterpret [,mɪsɪn'tɜːprɪt] *vt* mal interpréter.

misjudge [,mɪs'dʒʌdʒ] *vt* **1.** [distance, time] mal évaluer - **2.** [person, mood] méjuger, se méprendre sur.

mislay [,mɪs'leɪ] (*pt & pp* **-laid** [-'leɪd]) *vt* égarer.

mislead [,mɪs'liːd] (*pt & pp* **-led**) *vt* induire en erreur.

misleading [,mɪs'liːdɪŋ] *adj* trompeur(euse).

misled [,mɪs'led] *pt & pp* ➤ **mislead**.

misnomer [,mɪs'nəʊmə] *n* nom *m* mal approprié.

misplace [,mɪs'pleɪs] *vt* égarer.

misprint ['mɪsprɪnt] *n* faute *f* d'impression.

miss [mɪs] ◇ *vt* **1.** [gen] rater, manquer - **2.** [home, person] : **I miss my family/her** ma famille/elle me manque - **3.** [avoid, escape] échapper à ; **I just missed being run over** j'ai failli me faire écraser - **4.** [be short of, lack] manquer de ; **I'm missing two books from my collection** il me manque deux livres de ma collection, deux livres de ma collection ont disparu. ◇ *vi* rater. ◇ *n* : **to give sthg a miss** *UK inf* ne pas aller à qqch. ➤ **miss out** ◇ *vt sep UK* [omit - by accident] oublier ; [- deliberately] omettre. ◇ *vi* : **to miss out on sthg** ne pas pouvoir profiter de qqch.

Miss [mɪs] *n* Mademoiselle *f*.

misshapen [,mɪs'ʃeɪpn] *adj* difforme.

missile [*UK* 'mɪsaɪl, *US* 'mɪsəl] *n* **1.** [weapon] missile *m* - **2.** [thrown object] projectile *m*.

missing ['mɪsɪŋ] *adj* **1.** [lost] perdu(e), égaré(e) - **2.** [not present] manquant(e), qui manque.

mission ['mɪʃn] *n* mission *f*.

missionary ['mɪʃənrɪ] *n* missionnaire *mf*.

misspend [,mɪs'spend] (*pt & pp* **-spent** [-'spent]) *vt* gaspiller.

mist [mɪst] *n* brume *f*. ➤ **mist over**, **mist up** *vi* s'embuer.

mistake [mɪ'steɪk] ◇ *n* erreur *f* ; **by mistake** par erreur ; **to make a mistake** faire une erreur, se tromper. ◇ *vt* (*pt* **-took**, *pp* **-taken**) **1.** [misunderstand - meaning] mal comprendre ; [- intention] se méprendre sur - **2.** [fail to recognize] : **to mistake sb/sthg for** prendre qqn/qqch pour, confondre qqn/qqch avec.

mistaken [mɪ'steɪkn] ◇ *pp* ➤ **mistake**. ◇ *adj* **1.** [person] : **to be mistaken (about)** se tromper (en ce qui concerne OR sur) - **2.** [belief, idea] erroné(e), faux (fausse).

mister ['mɪstə] *n inf* monsieur *m*. ➤ **Mister** *n* Monsieur *m*.

mistletoe ['mɪsltəʊ] *n* gui *m*.

mistook [mɪ'stʊk] *pt* ➤ **mistake**.

mistreat [,mɪs'triːt] *vt* maltraiter.

mistress ['mɪstrɪs] *n* maîtresse *f*.

mistrust [,mɪs'trʌst] ◇ *n* méfiance *f*. ◇ *vt* se méfier de.

misty ['mɪstɪ] *adj* brumeux(euse).

misunderstand [,mɪsʌndə'stænd] (*pt & pp*-**stood**) *vt & vi* mal comprendre.

misunderstanding [,mɪsʌndə'stændɪŋ] *n* malentendu *m*.

misunderstood [,mɪsʌndə'stʊd] *pt & pp* ➤ **misunderstand**.

misuse ◇ *n* [,mɪs'juːs] **1.** [of one's time, resources] mauvais emploi *m* - **2.** [of power] abus *m* ; [of funds] détournement *m*. ◇ *vt* [,mɪs'juːz] **1.** [one's time, resources] mal employer - **2.** [power] abuser de ; [funds] détourner.

miter *esp US* = **mitre**.

mitigate ['mɪtɪgeɪt] *vt* atténuer, mitiger.

mitre *UK*, **miter** *esp US* ['maɪtə] *n* **1.** [hat] mitre *f* - **2.** [joint] onglet *m*.

mitt [mɪt] *n* **1.** *inf* = **mitten** - **2.** [in baseball] gant *m*.

mitten ['mɪtn] *n* moufle *f*.

mix [mɪks] ◇ *vt* **1.** [gen] mélanger - **2.** [activities] : **to mix sthg with sthg** combiner OR associer qqch et qqch - **3.** [drink] préparer ; [cement] malaxer. ◇ *vi* **1.** [gen] se mélanger - **2.** [socially] : **to mix with** fréquenter. ◇ *n* **1.** [gen] mélange *m* - **2.** MUS mixage *m*. ➤ **mix up** *vt sep* **1.** [confuse] confondre - **2.** [disorganize] mélanger.

mixed [mɪkst] *adj* **1.** [assorted] assortis(ies) - **2.** [sexually, racially] mixte.

mixed-ability *adj UK* [class] tous niveaux confondus.

mixed grill *n* assortiment *m* de grillades.

mixed up *adj* **1.** [confused - person] qui ne sait plus où il en est, paumé(e) ; [- mind] embrouillé(e) - **2.** [involved] : **to be mixed up in sthg** être mêlé(e) à qqch.

mixer ['mɪksər] *n* [for food] mixer *m*.

mixture ['mɪkstʃər] *n* **1.** [gen] mélange *m* - **2.** MED préparation *f*.

mix-up *n inf* confusion *f*.

mm (*abbrev of* **millimetre**) mm.

MMR [,emem'ɑːr] (*abbrev of* **measles, mumps &rubella**) *n* MED ROR *m*.

moan [məʊn] <> *n* [of pain, sadness] gémissement *m*. <> *vi* **1.** [in pain, sadness] gémir - **2.** *inf* [complain] : **to moan (about)** rouspéter OR râler (à propos de).

moat [məʊt] *n* douves *fpl*.

mob [mɒb] <> *n* foule *f*. <> *vt* assaillir.

mobile ['məʊbaɪl] <> *adj* **1.** [gen] mobile - **2.** [able to travel] motorisé(e). <> *n* mobile *m*.

mobile home *n* auto-caravane *f*.

mobile phone *n esp UK* téléphone *m* portable.

mobilize, *UK* **-ise** ['məʊbɪlaɪz] *vt & vi* mobiliser.

mock [mɒk] <> *adj* faux (fausse) ; **mock exam** *UK* examen blanc. <> *vt* se moquer de. <> *vi* se moquer.

mockery ['mɒkərɪ] *n* moquerie *f*.

mod cons [,mɒd-] (*abbrev of* **modern conveniences**) *npl UK inf* **all mod cons** tout confort, tt. conf.

mode [məʊd] *n* mode *m*.

model ['mɒdl] <> *n* **1.** [gen] modèle *m* - **2.** [fashion model] mannequin *m*. <> *adj* **1.** [perfect] modèle - **2.** [reduced-scale] (en) modèle réduit. <> *vt* (*UK & US*) **1.** [clay] modeler - **2.** [clothes] : **to model a dress** présenter un modèle de robe - **3.** [emulate] : **to model o.s. on sb** prendre modèle OR exemple sur qqn, se modeler sur qqn. <> *vi* (*UK & US*) être mannequin.

modem ['məʊdem] *n* COMPUT modem *m*.

moderate <> *adj* ['mɒdərət] modéré(e). <> *n* ['mɒdərət] POL modéré *m*, -e *f*. <> *vt* ['mɒdəreɪt] modérer. <> *vi* ['mɒdəreɪt] se modérer.

moderation [,mɒdə'reɪʃn] *n* modération *f* ; **in moderation** avec modération.

modern ['mɒdən] *adj* moderne.

modernize, *UK* **-ise** ['mɒdənaɪz] <> *vt* moderniser. <> *vi* se moderniser.

modern languages *npl* langues *fpl* vivantes.

modest ['mɒdɪst] *adj* modeste.

modesty ['mɒdɪstɪ] *n* modestie *f*.

modicum ['mɒdɪkəm] *n* minimum *m*.

modify ['mɒdɪfaɪ] *vt* modifier.

module ['mɒdjuːl] *n* module *m*.

mogul ['məʊgl] *n fig* magnat *m*.

mohair ['məʊheər] *n* mohair *m*.

moist [mɔɪst] *adj* [soil, climate] humide ; [cake] moelleux(euse).

moisten ['mɔɪsn] *vt* humecter.

moisture ['mɔɪstʃər] *n* humidité *f*.

moisturizer ['mɔɪstʃəraɪzər] *n* crème *f* hydratante, lait *m* hydratant.

molar ['məʊlər] *n* molaire *f*.

molasses [mə'læsɪz] *n (U)* mélasse *f*.

mold *etc US* = **mould**.

mole [məʊl] *n* **1.** [animal, spy] taupe *f* - **2.** [on skin] grain *m* de beauté.

molecule ['mɒlɪkjuːl] *n* molécule *f*.

molest [mə'lest] *vt* **1.** [attack sexually] attenter à la pudeur de - **2.** [attack] molester.

mollusc, *US* **mollusk** ['mɒləsk] *n* mollusque *m*.

mollycoddle ['mɒlɪ,kɒdl] *vt inf* chouchouter.

molt *US* = **moult**.

molten ['məʊltn] *adj* en fusion.

mom [mɒm] *n US inf* maman *f*.

moment ['məʊmənt] *n* moment *m*, instant *m* ; **at any moment** d'un moment à l'autre ; **at the moment** en ce moment ; **for the moment** pour le moment.

momentarily ['məʊməntərɪlɪ] *adv* **1.** [for a short time] momentanément - **2.** *US* [soon] très bientôt.

momentary ['məʊməntrɪ] *adj* momentané(e), passager(ère).

momentous [mə'mentəs] *adj* capital(e), très important(e).

momentum [mə'mentəm] *n (U)* **1.** PHYS moment *m* - **2.** *fig* [speed, force] vitesse *f* ; **to gather momentum** prendre de la vitesse.

momma ['mɒmə], **mommy** ['mɒmɪ] *n US inf* maman *f*.

Monaco ['mɒnəkəʊ] *n* Monaco.

monarch ['mɒnək] *n* monarque *m*.

monarchy ['mɒnəkɪ] *n* monarchie *f*.

monastery ['mɒnəstrɪ] *n* monastère *m*.

Monday ['mʌndɪ] *n* lundi *m* ; *see also* **Saturday**.

monetary ['mʌnɪtrɪ] *adj* monétaire.

money ['mʌnɪ] *n* argent *m* ; **to make money** gagner de l'argent ; **to get one's money's worth** en avoir pour son argent.

moneybox ['mʌnɪbɒks] *n UK* tirelire *f*.

moneylender ['mʌnɪ,lendər] *n* prêteur *m*, -euse *f* sur gages.

money order *n* mandat *m* postal.

money-spinner [-,spɪnər] *n esp UK inf* mine *f* d'or.

mongol ['mɒŋgəl] *dated & offens n* mongolien *m*, -ienne *f*.

Mongolia [mɒŋ'gəʊlɪə] *n* Mongolie *f*.

mongrel ['mʌŋgrəl] *n* [dog] bâtard *m*.

monitor ['mɒnɪtər] <> *n* COMPUT, MED & TV moniteur *m*. <> *vt* **1.** [check] contrôler, suivre de près - **2.** [broadcasts, messages] être à l'écoute de.

monk [mʌŋk] *n* moine *m*.

monkey ['mʌŋkɪ] (*pl* -s) *n* singe *m*.

monkey nut *n UK* cacahuète *f*.

monkey wrench *n* clef *f* à molette.

mono ['mɒnəʊ] <> *adj* mono (*inv*). <> *n* [sound] monophonie *f*.

monochrome ['mɒnəkrəʊm] *adj* monochrome.

monocle ['mɒnəkl] *n* monocle *m*.

monologue, *US* **monolog** ['mɒnəlɒg] *n* monologue *m*.

monopolize, *UK* **-ise** [mə'nɒpəlaɪz] *vt* monopoliser.

monopoly [mə'nɒpəlɪ] *n* : **monopoly (on** OR **of)** monopole *m* (de).

monotone ['mɒnətəʊn] *n* ton *m* monocorde.

monotonous [mə'nɒtənəs] *adj* monotone.

monotony [mə'nɒtənɪ] *n* monotonie *f*.

monsoon [mɒn'suːn] *n* mousson *f*.

monster ['mɒnstər] *n* **1.** [creature, cruel person] monstre *m* - **2.** [huge thing, person] colosse *m*.

monstrosity [mɒn'strɒsətɪ] *n* monstruosité *f*.

monstrous ['mɒnstrəs] *adj* monstrueux(euse).

Mont Blanc [,mɔ̃'blɑ̃] *n* le mont Blanc.

month [mʌnθ] *n* mois *m*.

monthly ['mʌnθlɪ] <> *adj* mensuel(elle). <> *adv* mensuellement. <> *n* [publication] mensuel *m*.

Montreal [,mɒntrɪ'ɔːl] *n* Montréal.

monument ['mɒnjʊmənt] *n* monument *m*.

monumental [,mɒnjʊ'mentl] *adj* monumental(e).

moo [muː] <> *n* (*pl* -s) meuglement *m*, beuglement *m*. <> *vi* meugler, beugler.

mood [muːd] *n* [generally] humeur *f* ; **in a (bad) mood** de mauvaise humeur ; **in a good mood** de bonne humeur.

moody ['muːdɪ] *adj pej* **1.** [changeable] lunatique - **2.** [bad-tempered] de mauvaise humeur, mal luné(e).

moon [muːn] *n UK* lune *f*.

moonlight ['muːnlaɪt] <> *n* clair *m* de lune. <> *vi* (*pt & pp* -ed) travailler au noir.

moonlighting ['muːnlaɪtɪŋ] *n* (U) travail *m* au noir.

moonlit ['muːnlɪt] *adj* [countryside] éclairé(e) par la lune ; [night] de lune.

moor [mɔːr] <> *n* lande *f*. <> *vt* amarrer. <> *vi* mouiller.

moorland ['mɔːlənd] *n esp UK* lande *f*.

moose [muːs] (*pl* moose) *n* [North American] original *m*.

mop [mɒp] <> *n* **1.** [for cleaning] balai *m* à laver - **2.** *inf* [hair] tignasse *f*. <> *vt* **1.** [floor] laver - **2.** [sweat] essuyer ; **to mop one's brow** s'essuyer le front. **mop up** *vt sep* [clean up] éponger.

mope [məʊp] *vi* broyer du noir.

moped ['məʊped] *n* vélomoteur *m*.

moral ['mɒrəl] <> *adj* moral(e). <> *n* [lesson] morale *f*. **morals** *npl* moralité *f*.

morale [mə'rɑːl] *n* (U) moral *m*.

morality [mə'rælətɪ] *n* moralité *f*.

morass [mə'ræs] *n fig* [of detail, paperwork] fatras *m*.

morbid ['mɔːbɪd] *adj* morbide.

more [mɔːr] <> *adv* **1.** (*with adj and adverbs*) plus ; **more important (than)** plus important (que) ; **more often/quickly (than)** plus souvent/rapidement (que) - **2.** [to a greater degree] plus, davantage - **3.** [another time] : **once/twice more** une fois/deux fois de plus, encore une fois/deux fois. <> *adj* **1.** [larger number, amount of] plus de, davantage de ; **there are more trains in the morning** il y a plus de trains le matin ; **more than 70 people** plus de 70 personnes ont péri - **2.** [additional, further] encore (de) ; **I finished two more chapters today** j'ai fini deux autres OR plus encore deux chapitres aujourd'hui ; **have some more tea** prends encore du thé ; **we need more money/time** il nous faut plus d'argent/de temps, il nous faut davantage d'argent/de temps. <> *pron* [greater amount, number] plus, davantage ; **more than five** plus de cinq ; **he's got more than I have** il en a plus que moi ; **no more** no less ni plus ni moins. **any more** *adv* : **not... any more** ne... plus. **more and more** <> *adv & pron* de plus en plus ; **more and more depressed** de plus en plus déprimé. <> *adj* de plus en plus de ; **there**

are more and more cars on the roads il y a de plus en plus de voitures sur les routes. **more or less** *adv* **1.** [almost] plus ou moins - **2.** [approximately] environ, à peu près. **not... any more** *adv* : we don't go there any more nous n'y allons plus ; he still works here, doesn't he? - not any more (he doesn't) il travaille encore ici, n'est-ce pas ? - non, plus maintenant.

moreover [mɔː'rəʊvər] *adv* de plus.

morgue [mɔːg] *n* morgue *f*.

Mormon ['mɔːmən] *n* mormon *m*, -e *f*.

morning ['mɔːnɪŋ] *n* matin *m* ; [duration] matinée *f* ; **I work in the morning** je travaille le matin ; **I'll do it tomorrow morning** OR **in the morning** je le ferai demain. **mornings** *adv US* le matin.

Moroccan [mə'rɒkən] <> *adj* marocain(e). <> *n* Marocain *m*, -e *f*.

Morocco [mə'rɒkəʊ] *n* Maroc *m*.

moron ['mɔːrɒn] *n inf* idiot *m*, -e *f*, crétin *m*, -e *f*.

morose [mə'rəʊs] *adj* morose.

morphine ['mɔːfiːn] *n* morphine *f*.

Morse (code) [mɔːs-] *n* morse *m*.

morsel ['mɔːsl] *n* bout *m*, morceau *m*.

mortal ['mɔːtl] <> *adj* mortel(elle). <> *n* mortel *m*, -elle *f*.

mortality [mɔː'tælətɪ] *n* mortalité *f*.

mortar ['mɔːtər] *n* mortier *m*.

mortgage ['mɔːgɪdʒ] <> *n* emprunt-logement *m*. <> *vt* hypothéquer.

mortified ['mɔːtɪfaɪd] *adj* mortifié(e).

mortuary ['mɔːtʃʊərɪ] *n* morgue *f*.

mosaic [mə'zeɪɪk] *n* mosaïque *f*.

Moscow ['mɒskəʊ] *n* Moscou.

Moslem ['mɒzləm] = **Muslim**.

mosque [mɒsk] *n* mosquée *f*.

mosquito [mə'skiːtəʊ] (*pl* -es OR -s) *n* moustique *m*.

moss [mɒs] *n* mousse *f*.

most [məʊst] (*superl of* **many**) <> *adj* **1.** [the majority of] la plupart de ; **most tourists here are German** la plupart des touristes ici sont allemands - **2.** [largest amount of] : (the) most le plus de ; **she's got (the) most money/sweets** c'est elle qui a le plus d'argent/de bonbons. <> *pron* **1.** [the majority] la plupart ; **most of the tourists here are German** la plupart des touristes ici sont allemands ; **most of them** la plupart d'entre eux - **2.** [largest amount] : (the) most le plus ; **at most** au maximum, tout au plus ; **to make the most of sthg** profiter de qqch au maximum. <> *adv* **1.** [to greatest extent] : (the) most le plus - **2.** *fml* [very] très, fort - **3.** *US* [almost] presque.

mostly ['məʊstlɪ] *adv* principalement, surtout.

MOT *n* UK (*abbrev of* **Ministry of Transport (test)**) *contrôle technique annuel obligatoire pour les véhicules de plus de trois ans.*

motel [məʊ'tel] *n* motel *m*.

moth [mɒθ] *n* papillon *m* de nuit ; [in clothes] mite *f*.

mothball ['mɒθbɔːl] *n* boule *f* de naphtaline.

mother ['mʌðər] <> *n* mère *f*. <> *vt* [child] materner, dorloter.

motherhood ['mʌðəhʊd] *n* maternité *f*.

mother-in-law (*pl* **mothers-in-law**) *n* belle-mère *f*.

motherly ['mʌðəlɪ] *adj* maternel(elle).

mother-of-pearl *n* nacre *f*.

mother-to-be (*pl* **mothers-to-be**) *n* future maman *f*.

mother tongue *n* langue *f* maternelle.

motif [məʊ'tiːf] *n* motif *m*.

motion ['məʊʃn] <> *n* **1.** [gen] mouvement *m* ; **to set sthg in motion** mettre qqch en branle - **2.** [in debate] motion *f*. <> *vt* : **to motion sb to do sthg** faire signe à qqn de faire qqch. <> *vi* : **to motion to sb** faire signe à qqn.

motionless ['məʊʃənlɪs] *adj* immobile.

motion picture *n US* film *m*.

motivated ['məʊtɪveɪtɪd] *adj* motivé(e).

motivation [,məʊtɪ'veɪʃn] *n* motivation *f*.

motive ['məʊtɪv] *n* motif *m*.

motley ['mɒtlɪ] *adj pej* hétéroclite.

motor ['məʊtər] <> *adj UK* automobile. <> *n* [engine] moteur *m*.

motorbike ['məʊtəbaɪk] *n UK inf* moto *f*.

motorboat ['məʊtəbəʊt] *n* canot *m* automobile.

motorcar ['məʊtəkɑːr] *n UK* automobile *f*, voiture *f*.

motorcycle ['məʊtə,saɪkl] *n* moto *f*.

motorcyclist ['məʊtə,saɪklɪst] *n* motocycliste *mf*.

motoring ['məʊtərɪŋ] *UK* <> *adj* [magazine, correspondent] automobile. <> *n* tourisme *m* automobile.

motorist ['məʊtərɪst] *n UK* automobiliste *mf*.

motor racing *n* (*U*) *UK* course *f* automobile.

motor scooter *n* scooter *m*.

motorsport ['məʊtəspɔːt] *n* sport *m* mécanique.

motor vehicle *n* véhicule *m* automobile.

motorway ['məʊtəweɪ] *UK n* autoroute *f*.

mottled ['mɒtld] *adj* [leaf] tacheté(e) ; [skin] marbré(e).

motto ['mɒtəʊ] (*pl* -s OR -es) *n* devise *f*.

mould UK, **mold** US [məʊld] ◇ *n* **1.** [growth] moisissure *f* - **2.** [shape] moule *m*. ◇ *vt* **1.** [shape] mouler, modeler - **2.** *fig* [influence] former, façonner.

moulding UK, **molding** US ['məʊldɪŋ] *n* [decoration] moulure *f*.

mouldy UK, **moldy** US ['məʊldɪ] *adj* moisi(e).

moult UK, **molt** US [məʊlt] *vi* muer.

mound [maʊnd] *n* **1.** [small hill] tertre *m*, butte *f* - **2.** [pile] tas *m*, monceau *m*.

mount [maʊnt] ◇ *n* **1.** [support - for jewel] monture *f* ; [- for photograph] carton *m* de montage ; [- for machine] support *m* - **2.** [horse] monture *f* - **3.** [mountain] mont *m*. ◇ *vt* monter ; **to mount a horse** monter sur un cheval ; **to mount a bike** monter sur OR enfourcher un vélo. ◇ *vi* **1.** [increase] monter, augmenter - **2.** [climb on horse] se mettre en selle.

mountain ['maʊntɪn] *n lit & fig* montagne *f*.

mountain bike *n* VTT *m*.

mountaineer [,maʊntɪ'nɪər] *n* alpiniste *mf*.

mountaineering [,maʊntɪ'nɪərɪŋ] *n* alpinisme *m*.

mountainous ['maʊntɪnəs] *adj* [region] montagneux(euse).

mounted police *n* : **the mounted police** la police montée.

mourn [mɔːn] ◇ *vt* pleurer. ◇ *vi* : **to mourn (for sb)** pleurer (qqn).

mourner ['mɔːnər] *n* [related] parent *m* du défunt ; [unrelated] ami *m*, -e *f* du défunt.

mournful ['mɔːnfʊl] *adj* [face] triste ; [sound] lugubre.

mourning ['mɔːnɪŋ] *n* deuil *m* ; **in mourning** en deuil.

mouse [maʊs] (*pl* **mice** [maɪs]) *n* COMPUT & ZOOL souris *f*.

mousetrap ['maʊstræp] *n* souricière *f*.

mousse [muːs] *n* mousse *f*.

moustache [mə'stɑːʃ], **mustache** US ['mʌstæʃ] *n* moustache *f*.

mouth *n* [maʊθ] **1.** [of person, animal] bouche *f* ; [of dog, cat, lion] gueule *f* - **2.** [of cave] entrée *f* ; [of river] embouchure *f*.

mouthful ['maʊθfʊl] *n* [of food] bouchée *f* ; [of drink] gorgée *f*.

mouth organ ['maʊθ,ɔːgən] *n* harmonica *m*.

mouthpiece ['maʊθpiːs] *n* **1.** [of telephone] microphone *m* ; [of musical instrument] bec *m* - **2.** [spokesperson] porte-parole *m inv*.

mouthwash ['maʊθwɒʃ] *n* eau *f* dentifrice.

mouth-watering [-,wɔːtərɪŋ] *adj* alléchant(e).

movable ['muːvəbl] *adj* mobile.

move [muːv] ◇ *n* **1.** [movement] mouvement *m* ; **to get a move on** *inf* se remuer, se grouiller - **2.** [change - of house] déménagement *m* ; [- of job] changement *m* d'emploi - **3.** [in game - action] coup *m* ; [- turn to play] tour *m*. ◇ *vt* **1.** [shift] déplacer, bouger - **2.** [change - job, office] changer de ; **to move house** UK déménager - **3.** [emotionally] émouvoir - **4.** [cause] : **to move sb to do sthg** inciter qqn à faire qqch - **5.** [propose] : **to move sthg/that...** proposer qqch/que... ◇ *vi* **1.** [shift] bouger - **2.** [travel] : **to move house** UK déménager ; [to new house] déménager ; [to new job] changer d'emploi - **3.** [act] agir. ◆ **move about** *vi* **1.** [fidget] remuer - **2.** [travel] voyager. ◆ **move along** ◇ *vt sep* faire avancer. ◇ *vi* se déplacer ; **the police asked him to move along** la police lui a demandé de circuler. ◆ **move around** *vi* = **move about**. ◆ **move away** *vi* [leave] partir. ◆ **move in** *vi* [to house] emménager. ◆ **move on** ◇ *vi* **1.** [after stopping] se remettre en route - **2.** [in discussion] changer de sujet. ◇ *vi* US [in life] se tourner vers l'avenir. ◆ **move out** *vi* [from house] déménager. ◆ **move over** *vi* s'écarter, se pousser. ◆ **move up** *vi* **1.** [on bench *etc*] se déplacer - **2.** *fig* : **you've moved up in the world!** tu en as fait du chemin!

moveable ['muːvəbl] = **movable**.

movement ['muːvmənt] *n* mouvement *m*.

movie ['muːvɪ] *n esp* US film *m*.

movie camera *n* caméra *f*.

moving ['muːvɪŋ] *adj* **1.** [emotionally] émouvant(e), touchant(e) - **2.** [not fixed] mobile.

mow [məʊ] (*pt* -ed, *pp* -ed OR mown) *vt* faucher ; [lawn] tondre. ◆ **mow down** *vt sep* faucher.

mower ['məʊər] *n* tondeuse *f* à gazon.

mown [məʊn] *pp* ► mow.

MP *n* **1.** (*abbrev of* **Military Police**) PM - **2.** UK (*abbrev of* **Member of Parliament**) ≃ député *m*.

mpg (*abbrev of* **miles per gallon**) *n* miles au gallon.

mph (*abbrev of* **miles per hour**) *n* miles à l'heure.

Mr ['mɪstər] *n* Monsieur *m* ; [on letter] M.

Mrs ['mɪsɪz] *n* Madame *f* ; [on letter] Mme.

MS *n* (*abbrev of* **multiple sclerosis**) SEP *f*.

Ms [mɪz] *n* titre que les femmes peuvent utiliser

au lieu de madame ou mademoiselle pour éviter la distinction entre les femmes mariées et les célibataires.

MSc *(abbrev of* **Master of Science)** *n (titulaire d'une)* maîtrise *f* de sciences.

msg [emes'dʒi:] *n* message *m*.

MSP *n abbr of* **Member of the Scottish Parliament.**

much [mʌtʃ] <> *adj (comp* **more,** *superl* **most)** beaucoup de ; **there isn't much rice left** il ne reste pas beaucoup de riz ; **as much money as...** autant d'argent que... ; **too much** trop de ; **how much...?** combien de...? ; **how much money do you earn?** tu gagnes combien? <> *pron* beaucoup ; **I don't think much of his new house** sa nouvelle maison ne me plaît pas trop ; **too much** trop ; **I'm not much of a cook** je suis un piètre cuisinier ; **so much for all my hard work** tout ce travail pour rien ; **I thought as much** c'est bien ce que je pensais. <> *adv* beaucoup ; **I don't go out much** je ne sors pas beaucoup OR souvent ; **thank you very much** merci beaucoup ; **without so much as...** sans même... <> **much as** *conj* bien que (+ subjunctive).

muck [mʌk] *inf n* (U) **1.** [dirt] saletés *fpl* - **2.** [manure] fumier *m*. <> **muck about,** UK **muck around** *inf* <> *vt sep* : **to muck sb about** traiter qqn par-dessus OR par-dessous la jambe. <> *vi* traîner. <> **muck up** *vt sep* UK *inf* gâcher.

mucky ['mʌki] *adj* **1.** [gen] sale - **2.** UK *inf* pornographique.

mucus ['mju:kəs] *n* mucus *m*.

mud [mʌd] *n* boue *f*.

muddle ['mʌdl] <> *n* désordre *m*, fouillis *m*. <> *vt* **1.** [papers] mélanger - **2.** [person] embrouiller. <> **muddle along** *vi* se débrouiller tant bien que mal. <> **muddle through** *vi* se tirer d'affaire, s'en sortir tant bien que mal. <> **muddle up** *vt sep* mélanger.

muddy ['mʌdi] <> *adj* boueux(euse). <> *vt fig* embrouiller.

mudguard ['mʌdgɑːd] *n* garde-boue *m inv*.

mudslinging ['mʌd,slɪŋɪŋ] *n* (U) *fig* attaques *fpl*.

muesli ['mju:zli] *n* muesli *m*.

muff [mʌf] <> *n* manchon *m*. <> *vt* UK *inf* louper.

muffin ['mʌfɪn] *n* muffin *m*.

muffle ['mʌfl] *vt* étouffer.

muffler ['mʌflər] *n* US [for car] silencieux *m*.

mug [mʌg] <> *n* **1.** [cup] (grande) tasse *f* - **2.** UK *inf* [fool] andouille *f*. <> *vt* [attack] agresser.

mugging ['mʌgɪŋ] *n* agression *f*.

muggy ['mʌgi] *adj* lourd(e), moite.

mule [mju:l] *n* mule *f*.

mull [mʌl] <> **mull over** *vt sep* ruminer, réfléchir à.

mulled [mʌld] *adj* : **mulled wine** vin *m* chaud.

multicoloured UK, **multicolored** US ['mʌlti,kʌləd] *adj* multicolore.

multifaith ['mʌltɪfeɪθ] *adj* multiconfessionnel(le) ; **multifaith organization** organisation multiconfessionnelle.

multigym ['mʌltɪdʒɪm] *n* UK appareil *m* de musculation.

multilateral [,mʌltɪ'lætərəl] *adj* multilatéral(e).

multinational [,mʌltɪ'næʃənl] *n* multinationale *f*.

multiple ['mʌltɪpl] <> *adj* multiple. <> *n* multiple *m*.

multiple sclerosis [-sklɪ'rəʊsɪs] *n* sclérose *f* en plaques.

multiplex cinema UK, **multiplex theater** US ['mʌltɪpleks-] *n* complexe *m* multi-salles.

multiplication [,mʌltɪplɪ'keɪʃn] *n* multiplication *f*.

multiply ['mʌltɪplaɪ] <> *vt* multiplier. <> *vi* se multiplier.

multistorey UK, **multistory** US [,mʌltɪ'stɔːrɪ] <> *adj* à étages. <> *n* [car park] parking *m* à étages.

multitude ['mʌltɪtju:d] *n* multitude *f*.

multivitamin [UK 'mʌltɪvɪtəmɪn, US 'mʌltɪvaɪtəmɪn] *n* multivitamine *f*.

mum [mʌm] *inf* <> *n* UK maman *f*. <> *adj* : **to keep mum** ne pas piper mot.

mumble ['mʌmbl] *vt & vi* marmotter.

mummy ['mʌmi] *n* **1.** UK [mother] maman *f* - **2.** [preserved body] momie *f*.

mumps [mʌmps] *n* (U) oreillons *mpl*.

munch [mʌntʃ] *vt & vi* croquer.

mundane [mʌn'deɪn] *adj* banal(e), ordinaire.

municipal [mju:'nɪsɪpl] *adj* municipal(e).

municipality [mju:,nɪsɪ'pælətɪ] *n* municipalité *f*.

mural ['mju:ərəl] *n* peinture *f* murale.

murder ['mɜːdər] <> *n* meurtre *m*. <> *vt* assassiner.

murderer ['mɜːdərər] *n* meurtrier *m*, assassin *m*.

murderous ['mɜːdərəs] *adj* meurtrier(ère).

murky ['mɜːki] *adj* **1.** [place] sombre - **2.** [water, past] trouble.

murmur ['mɜːmər] <> *n* murmure *m* ; MED souffle *m* au cœur. <> *vt & vi* murmurer.

muscle ['mʌsl] n muscle m ; fig [power] poids m, impact m. ◆ **muscle in** vi intervenir, s'immiscer.

muscular ['mʌskjʊlər] adj 1. [spasm, pain] musculaire - 2. [person] musclé(e).

muse [mju:z] ◇ n muse f. ◇ vi méditer, réfléchir.

museum [mju:'zi:əm] n musée m.

mushroom ['mʌʃrʊm] ◇ n champignon m. ◇ vi [organization, party] se développer, grandir ; [houses] proliférer.

music ['mju:zɪk] n musique f.

musical ['mju:zɪkl] ◇ adj 1. [event, voice] musical(e) - 2. [child] doué(e) pour la musique, musicien(enne). ◇ n comédie f musicale.

musical instrument n instrument m de musique.

music centre UK, **music center** US n chaîne f compacte.

music hall n UK music-hall m.

musician [mju:'zɪʃn] n musicien m, -enne f.

Muslim ['mʊzlɪm] ◇ adj musulman(e). ◇ n Musulman m, -e f.

muslin ['mʌzlɪn] n mousseline f.

mussel ['mʌsl] n moule f.

must [mʌst] ◇ modal vb 1. [expressing obligation] devoir ; **I must go** il faut que je m'en aille, je dois partir ; **you must come and visit** il faut absolument que tu viennes nous voir - 2. [expressing likelihood] : **they must have known** ils devaient le savoir. ◇ n inf : **a must** un must, un impératif.

mustache US = moustache.

mustard ['mʌstəd] n moutarde f.

muster ['mʌstər] ◇ vt rassembler. ◇ vi se réunir, se rassembler.

musn't [mʌsnt] = must not.

must've ['mʌstəv] = must have.

musty ['mʌstɪ] adj [smell] de moisi ; [room] qui sent le renfermé OR le moisi.

mute [mju:t] ◇ adj muet(ette). ◇ n muet m, -ette f.

muted ['mju:tɪd] adj 1. [colour] sourd(e) - 2. [reaction] peu marqué(e) ; [protest] voilé(e).

mutilate ['mju:tɪleɪt] vt mutiler.

mutiny ['mju:tɪnɪ] ◇ n mutinerie f. ◇ vi se mutiner.

mutter ['mʌtər] ◇ vt [threat, curse] marmonner. ◇ vi marmotter, marmonner.

mutton ['mʌtn] n mouton m.

mutual ['mju:tʃʊəl] adj 1. [feeling, help] réciproque, mutuel(elle) - 2. [friend, interest] commun(e).

mutually ['mju:tʃʊəlɪ] adv mutuellement, réciproquement.

muzzle ['mʌzl] ◇ n 1. [of dog - mouth] museau m ; [- guard] muselière f - 2. [of gun] gueule f. ◇ vt lit & fig museler.

MW (abbrev of medium wave) PO.

my [maɪ] poss adj 1. [referring to oneself] mon (ma), mes (pl) ; **my dog** mon chien ; **my house** ma maison ; **my children** mes enfants ; **my name is Joe/Sarah** je m'appelle Joe/Sarah ; **it wasn't MY fault** ce n'était pas de ma faute à moi - 2. [in titles] : **yes, my Lord** oui, monsieur le comte/duc etc.

myriad ['mɪrɪəd] lit ◇ adj innombrable. ◇ n myriade f.

myself [maɪ'self] pron 1. (reflexive) me ; (after prep) moi - 2. (for emphasis) moi-même ; **I did it myself** je l'ai fait tout seul.

mysterious [mɪ'stɪərɪəs] adj mystérieux(euse).

mystery ['mɪstərɪ] n mystère m.

mystical ['mɪstɪkl] adj mystique.

mystified ['mɪstɪfaɪd] adj perplexe.

mystifying ['mɪstɪfaɪɪŋ] adj inexplicable, déconcertant(e).

mystique [mɪ'sti:k] n mystique f.

myth [mɪθ] n mythe m.

mythical ['mɪθɪkl] adj mythique.

mythology [mɪ'θɒlədʒɪ] n mythologie f.

N

n [en] (pl n's OR ns), **N** (pl N's OR Ns) n [letter] n m inv, N m inv. ◆ **N** (abbr of north) N.

n/a, N/A (abbrev of not applicable) s.o.

nab [næb] vt inf 1. [arrest] pincer - 2. [get quickly] attraper, accaparer.

nag [næg] ◇ vt harceler. ◇ n inf [horse] canasson m.

nagging ['nægɪŋ] adj 1. [doubt] persistant(e), tenace - 2. [husband, wife] enquiquineur(euse).

nail [neɪl] ◇ n 1. [for fastening] clou m - 2. [of finger, toe] ongle m. ◇ vt clouer. ◆ **nail down** vt sep 1. [lid] clouer - 2. fig [person] : **to nail sb down to sthg** faire préciser qqch à qqn.

nailbrush ['neɪlbrʌʃ] n brosse f à ongles.

nail clippers npl = nail scissors.

nail file n lime f à ongles.

nail polish *n* vernis *m* à ongles.

nail scissors *npl* ciseaux *mpl* à ongles.

nail varnish *n UK* vernis *m* à ongles.

nail varnish remover [-rɪˈmuːvəʳ] *n* dissolvant *m*.

naive, naïve [naɪˈiːv] *adj* naïf(ïve).

naked [ˈneɪkɪd] *adj* **1.** [body, flame] nu(e) ; **with the naked eye** à l'œil nu - **2.** [emotions] manifeste, évident(e) ; [aggression] non déguisé(e).

name [neɪm] ◇ *n* **1.** [identification] nom *m* ; **what's your name?** comment vous appelez-vous? ; **to know sb by name** connaître qqn de nom ; **in my/his name** à mon/son nom ; **in the name of peace** au nom de la paix ; **to call sb names** traiter qqn de tous les noms, injurier qqn - **2.** [reputation] réputation *f* - **3.** [famous person] grand nom *m*, célébrité *f*. ◇ *vt* [give name to] nommer ; **to name sb/sthg after, to name sb/sthg for** *US* donner à qqn/à qqch le nom de.

nameless [ˈneɪmlɪs] *adj* inconnu(e), sans nom ; [author] anonyme.

namely [ˈneɪmlɪ] *adv* à savoir, c'est-à-dire.

namesake [ˈneɪmseɪk] *n* homonyme *m*.

nanny [ˈnænɪ] *n UK* nurse *f*, bonne *f* d'enfants.

nanometre [ˈnænəʊˌmiːtəʳ], **nanometer** *US* *n* nanomètre *m*.

nap [næp] ◇ *n* : **to have** OR **take a nap** faire un petit somme. ◇ *vi* faire un petit somme ; **to be caught napping** *inf* *fig* être pris au dépourvu.

nape [neɪp] *n* nuque *f*.

napkin [ˈnæpkɪn] *n* serviette *f*.

nappy [ˈnæpɪ] *n UK* couche *f*.

nappy liner *n UK* change *m* (jetable).

narcissi [nɑːˈsɪsaɪ] *npl* ▶ **narcissus**.

narcissus [nɑːˈsɪsəs] *(pl* **-cissuses** OR **-cissi** [-sɪsaɪ]*)* *n* narcisse *m*.

narcotic [nɑːˈkɒtɪk] *n* stupéfiant *m*.

narrative [ˈnærətɪv] ◇ *adj* narratif(ive). ◇ *n* **1.** [story] récit *m*, narration *f* - **2.** [skill] art *m* de la narration.

narrator [*UK* nəˈreɪtəʳ, *US* ˈnæreɪtəʳ] *n* narrateur *m*, -trice *f*.

narrow [ˈnærəʊ] ◇ *adj* **1.** [gen] étroit(e) ; **to have a narrow escape** l'échapper belle - **2.** [victory, majority] de justesse. ◇ *vt* **1.** [reduce] réduire, limiter - **2.** [eyes] fermer à demi, plisser. ◇ *vi* *lit & fig* se rétrécir.
▬ **narrow down** *vt sep* réduire, limiter.

narrowly [ˈnærəʊlɪ] *adv* **1.** [win, lose] de justesse - **2.** [miss] de peu.

narrow-minded [-ˈmaɪndɪd] *adj* [person] à l'esprit étroit, borné(e) ; [attitude] étroit(e), borné(e).

nasal [ˈneɪzl] *adj* nasal(e).

NASDAQ [ˈnæzdæk] *(abbrev of* **National Association of Securities Dealers Automated Quotation)** *n* [in US] NASDAQ *m*.

nasty [ˈnɑːstɪ] *adj* **1.** [unpleasant - smell, feeling] mauvais(e) ; [- weather] vilain(e), mauvais(e) - **2.** [unkind] méchant(e) - **3.** [problem] difficile, délicat(e) - **4.** [injury] vilain(e) ; [accident] grave ; [fall] mauvais(e).

nation [ˈneɪʃn] *n* nation *f*.

national [ˈnæʃənl] ◇ *adj* national(e) ; [campaign, strike] à l'échelon national ; [custom] du pays, de la nation. ◇ *n* ressortissant *m*, -e *f*.

national anthem *n* hymne *m* national.

national dress *n* costume *m* national.

National Health Service *n* : **the National Health Service** *le service national de santé britannique*.

National Insurance *UK n (U)* **1.** [system] *système de sécurité sociale (maladie, retraite) et d'assurance chômage* - **2.** [payment] ≃ contributions *fpl* à la Sécurité sociale.

nationalism [ˈnæʃnəlɪzm] *n* nationalisme *m*.

nationalist [ˈnæʃnəlɪst] ◇ *adj* nationaliste. ◇ *n* nationaliste *mf*.

nationality [ˌnæʃəˈnælətɪ] *n* nationalité *f*.

nationalize, *UK* -ise [ˈnæʃnəlaɪz] *vt* nationaliser.

national park *n* parc *m* national.

national service *n UK* MIL service *m* national OR militaire.

National Trust *n UK* : **the National Trust** *organisme non gouvernemental assurant la conservation de certains sites et monuments historiques*.

nationwide [ˈneɪʃənwaɪd] ◇ *adj* dans tout le pays ; [campaign, strike] à l'échelon national. ◇ *adv* à travers tout le pays.

native [ˈneɪtɪv] ◇ *adj* **1.** [country, area] natal(e) - **2.** [language] maternel(elle) ; **a native English speaker** une personne de langue maternelle anglaise - **3.** [plant, animal] indigène ; **native to** originaire de. ◇ *n* autochtone *mf* ; [of colony] indigène *mf*.

Native American *n* Indien *m*, -enne *f* d'Amérique, Amérindien *m*, -enne *f*.

NATO [ˈneɪtəʊ] *(abbrev of* **North Atlantic Treaty Organization)** *n* OTAN *f*.

natural [ˈnætʃrəl] *adj* **1.** [gen] naturel(elle) - **2.** [instinct, talent] inné(e) - **3.** [footballer, musician] né(e).

natural disaster *n* catastrophe *f* naturelle.

natural gas *n* gaz *m* naturel.

natural history *n* histoire *f* naturelle.

naturalize, *UK* -ise [ˈnætʃrəlaɪz] *vt* naturaliser ; **to be naturalized** se faire naturaliser.

naturally ['nætʃrəlɪ] *adv* **1.** [gen] naturellement - **2.** [unaffectedly] sans affectation, avec naturel.

natural wastage *n* (U) UK départs *mpl* volontaires.

nature ['neɪtʃər] *n* nature *f* ; **by nature** [basically] par essence ; [by disposition] de nature, naturellement.

nature reserve *n* réserve *f* naturelle.

naughty ['nɔːtɪ] *adj* **1.** [badly behaved] vilain(e), méchant(e) - **2.** [indecent] grivois(e).

nausea ['nɔːzjə] *n* nausée *f*.

nauseam ['nɔːzɪæm] ➤ **ad nauseam**.

nauseating ['nɔːsɪeɪtɪŋ] *adj lit & fig* écœurant(e).

nautical ['nɔːtɪkl] *adj* nautique.

naval ['neɪvl] *adj* naval(e).

nave [neɪv] *n* nef *f*.

navel ['neɪvl] *n* nombril *m*.

navigate ['nævɪgeɪt] <> *vt* **1.** [plane] piloter ; [ship] gouverner - **2.** [seas, river] naviguer sur. <> *vi* AERON & NAUT naviguer ; AUT lire la carte.

navigation [,nævɪ'geɪʃn] *n* navigation *f*.

navigator ['nævɪgeɪtər] *n* navigateur *m*.

navvy ['nævɪ] *n* UK inf dated terrassier *m*.

navy ['neɪvɪ] <> *n* marine *f*. <> *adj* [in colour] bleu marine (inv).

navy blue <> *adj* bleu marine (inv). <> *n* bleu *m* marine.

Nazareth ['næzərɪθ] *n* Nazareth.

Nazi ['nɑːtsɪ] <> *adj* nazi(e). <> *n* (pl **-s**) Nazi *m*, -e *f*.

NB, N.B. (abbrev of nota bene) NB.

near [nɪər] <> *adj* proche ; **a near disaster** une catastrophe évitée de justesse OR de peu ; **in the near future** dans un proche avenir, dans un avenir prochain ; **it was a near thing** UK il était moins cinq ; **your nearest and dearest** hum vos proches. <> *adv* **1.** [close] près - **2.** [almost] : **near impossible** presque impossible ; **nowhere near ready/enough** loin d'être prêt/assez. <> *prep* : **near (to)** [in space] près de ; [in time] près de, vers ; **near (to) tears** au bord des larmes ; **near (to) death** sur le point de mourir. <> *vt* approcher de. <> *vi* approcher.

nearby [nɪə'baɪ] <> *adj* proche. <> *adv* tout près, à proximité.

nearly ['nɪəlɪ] *adv* presque ; **I nearly fell** j'ai failli tomber ; **not nearly enough/as good** loin d'être suffisant/aussi bon.

near miss *n* **1.** SPORT coup *m* qui a raté de peu - **2.** [between planes, vehicles] quasi-collision *f*.

nearside ['nɪəsaɪd] UK *n* [right-hand drive] côté *m* gauche ; [left-hand drive] côté droit.

nearsighted [,nɪə'saɪtɪd] *adj* US myope.

neat [niːt] *adj* **1.** [room, house] bien tenu(e), en ordre ; [work] soigné(e) ; [handwriting] net (nette) ; [appearance] soigné(e), net (nette) - **2.** [solution, manoeuvre] habile, ingénieux(euse) - **3.** [alcohol] pur(e), sans eau - **4.** US inf [very good] chouette, super (inv).

neatly ['niːtlɪ] *adv* **1.** [arrange] avec ordre ; [write] soigneusement ; [dress] avec soin - **2.** [skilfully] habilement, adroitement.

nebulous ['nebjuləs] *adj* nébuleux(euse).

necessarily [UK 'nesəsrəlɪ OR ,nesə'serɪlɪ] *adv* forcément, nécessairement.

necessary ['nesəsrɪ] *adj* **1.** [required] nécessaire, indispensable ; **to make the necessary arrangements** faire le nécessaire - **2.** [inevitable] inévitable, inéluctable.

necessity [nɪ'sesətɪ] *n* nécessité *f* ; **of necessity** inévitablement, fatalement.

neck [nek] <> *n* **1.** ANAT cou *m* - **2.** [of shirt, dress] encolure *f* - **3.** [of bottle] col *m*, goulot *m*. <> *vi* inf se bécoter.

necklace ['neklɪs] *n* collier *m*.

neckline ['neklaɪn] *n* encolure *f*.

necktie ['nektaɪ] *n* US cravate *f*.

nectarine ['nektərɪn] *n* brugnon *m*, nectarine *f*.

need [niːd] <> *n* besoin *m* ; **there's no need to get up** ce n'est pas la peine de te lever ; **there's no need for such language** tu n'as pas besoin d'être grossier ; **need for sthg/to do sthg** besoin de qqch/de faire qqch ; **to be in** OR **have need of sthg** fml avoir besoin de qqch ; **if need be** si besoin est, si nécessaire ; **in need** dans le besoin. <> *vt* **1.** [require] : **to need sthg/to do sthg** avoir besoin de qqch/de faire qqch ; **I need to go to the doctor** il faut que j'aille chez le médecin - **2.** [be obliged] : **to need to do sthg** être obligé(e) de faire qqch. <> *modal vb* : **need we go?** faut-il qu'on y aille? ; **it need not happen** cela ne doit pas forcément se produire.

needle ['niːdl] <> *n* **1.** [gen] aiguille *f* - **2.** [stylus] saphir *m*. <> *vt* inf [annoy] asticoter, lancer des piques à.

needless ['niːdlɪs] *adj* [risk, waste] inutile ; [remark] déplacé(e) ; **needless to say...** bien entendu...

needlework ['niːdlwɜːk] *n* **1.** [embroidery] travail *m* d'aiguille - **2.** (U) [activity] couture *f*.

needn't ['niːdnt] = need not.

needy ['niːdɪ] *adj* nécessiteux(euse), indigent(e).

negative ['negətɪv] <> *adj* négatif(ive).

◇ *n* **1.** PHOT négatif *m* - **2.** LING négation *f* ; **to answer in the negative** répondre négativement OR par la négative.

neglect [nɪˈglekt] ◇ *n* [of garden] mauvais entretien *m* ; [of children] manque *m* de soins ; [of duty] manquement *m*. ◇ *vt* négliger ; [garden] laisser à l'abandon ; **to neglect to do sthg** négliger OR omettre de faire qqch.

neglectful [nɪˈglektfʊl] *adj* négligent(e).

negligee [ˈneglɪʒeɪ] *n* déshabillé *m*, négligé *m*.

negligence [ˈneglɪdʒəns] *n* négligence *f*.

negligible [ˈneglɪdʒəbl] *adj* négligeable.

negotiate [nɪˈgəʊʃɪeɪt] ◇ *vt* **1.** COMM & POL négocier - **2.** [obstacle] franchir ; [bend] prendre, négocier. ◇ *vi* négocier ; **to negotiate with sb (for sthg)** engager des négociations avec qqn (pour obtenir qqch).

negotiation [nɪ,gəʊʃɪˈeɪʃn] *n* négociation *f*.

Negress [ˈniːgrɪs] *n* négresse *f* (attention: le terme 'Negress' est considéré raciste).

Negro [ˈniːgrəʊ] ◇ *adj* noir(e). ◇ *n* (*pl* **-es**) Noir *m* (attention: le terme 'Negro' est considéré raciste).

neigh [neɪ] *vi* [horse] hennir.

neighbour UK, **neighbor** US [ˈneɪbər] *n* voisin *m*, -e *f*.

neighbourhood UK, **neighborhood** US [ˈneɪbəhʊd] *n* **1.** [of town] voisinage *m*, quartier *m* - **2.** [approximate figure]: **in the neighbourhood of £300** environ 300 livres, dans les 300 livres.

neighbouring UK, **neighboring** US [ˈneɪbərɪŋ] *adj* avoisinant(e).

neighbourly UK, **neighborly** US [ˈneɪbəlɪ] *adj* bon voisin (bonne voisine).

neither [ˈnaɪðər OR ˈniːðər] ◇ *adv* : **neither good nor bad** ni bon ni mauvais ; **that's neither here nor there** cela n'a rien à voir. ◇ *pron & adj* ni l'un ni l'autre (ni l'une ni l'autre). ◇ *conj* : **neither do I** moi non plus.

neon [ˈniːɒn] *n* néon *m*.

neon light *n* néon *m*, lumière *f* au néon.

nephew [ˈnefjuː] *n* neveu *m*.

Neptune [ˈneptjuːn] *n* [planet] Neptune *f*.

nerve [nɜːv] *n* **1.** ANAT nerf *m* - **2.** [courage] courage *m*, sang-froid *m* *inv* ; **to lose one's nerve** se dégonfler, flancher - **3.** [cheek] culot *m*, toupet *m*. ◆ **nerves** *npl* nerfs *mpl* ; **to get on sb's nerves** taper sur les nerfs OR le système de qqn.

nerve-racking [-ˌrækɪŋ] *adj* angoissant(e), éprouvant(e).

nervous [ˈnɜːvəs] *adj* **1.** [gen] nerveux(euse) - **2.** [apprehensive - smile, person etc] inquiet(ète) ; [- performer] qui a le trac ; **to be nervous about sthg** appréhender qqch.

nervous breakdown *n* dépression *f* nerveuse.

nest [nest] ◇ *n* nid *m* ; **nest of tables** table *f* gigogne. ◇ *vi* [bird] faire son nid, nicher.

nest egg *n* pécule *m*, bas *m* de laine.

nestle [ˈnesl] *vi* se blottir.

net[1][net] ◇ *adj* net (nette) ; **net result** résultat final. ◇ *n* **1.** [gen] filet *m* - **2.** [fabric] voile *m*, tulle *m*. ◇ *vt* **1.** [fish] prendre au filet - **2.** [money - subj: person] toucher net, gagner net ; [- subj: deal] rapporter net.

net[2], **Net** [net] *n* : **the net** le Net ; **to surf the net** surfer sur le Net.

netball [ˈnetbɔːl] *n* UK netball *m*.

net curtains *npl* UK voilage *m*.

Netherlands [ˈneðələndz] *npl* : **the Netherlands** les Pays-Bas *mpl*.

netiquette, **Netiquette** [ˈnetiket] *n* nétiquette *f*.

net profit *n* bénéfice *m* net.

net revenue *n* US chiffre *m* d'affaires.

net surfer, **Net surfer** *n* internaute *mf*.

nett [net] *adj* = **net**[1].

netting [ˈnetɪŋ] *n* **1.** [metal, plastic] grillage *m* - **2.** [fabric] voile *m*, tulle *m*.

nettle [ˈnetl] *n* ortie *f*.

network [ˈnetwɜːk] ◇ *n* réseau *m*. ◇ *vt* RADIO & TV diffuser.

neurosis [ˌnjʊəˈrəʊsɪs] (*pl* **-ses** [-siːz]) *n* névrose *f*.

neurotic [ˌnjʊəˈrɒtɪk] ◇ *adj* névrosé(e). ◇ *n* névrosé *m*, -e *f*.

neuter [ˈnjuːtər] ◇ *adj* neutre. ◇ *vt* [cat, dog] châtrer.

neutral [ˈnjuːtrəl] ◇ *adj* [gen] neutre. ◇ *n* AUT point *m* mort.

neutrality [njuːˈtrælətɪ] *n* neutralité *f*.

neutralize, UK **-ise** [ˈnjuːtrəlaɪz] *vt* neutraliser.

never [ˈnevər] *adv* jamais... ne, ne... jamais ; **never ever** jamais, au grand jamais ; **well I never!** ça par exemple!

never-ending *adj* interminable.

nevertheless [ˌnevəðəˈles] *adv* néanmoins, pourtant.

new *adj* [njuː] **1.** [gen] nouveau(elle) ; **there's nothing new under the sun** *prov* (il n'y a) rien de nouveau sous le soleil - **2.** [not used, fresh] neuf (neuve) ; **as good as new** comme neuf. ◆ **news** *n* [njuːz] (*U*) **1.** [information] nouvelle *f* ; **a piece of news**

une nouvelle ; **that's news to me** première nouvelle - **2.** TV journal *m* télévisé, actualités *fpl* - **3.** RADIO informations *fpl*.

New Age traveller *n* UK voyageur *m* New Age.

newborn ['nju:bɔ:n] *adj* nouveau-né(e).

newcomer ['nju:,kʌmər] *n* : **newcomer (to sthg)** nouveau-venu *m*, nouvelle-venue *f* (dans qqch).

newfangled [,nju:'fæŋɡld] *adj inf pej* ultra-moderne, trop moderne.

newfound *adj* récent(e), de fraîche date.

newly ['nju:lɪ] *adv* récemment, fraîchement.

newlyweds ['nju:lɪwedz] *npl* nouveaux OR jeunes mariés *mpl*.

new moon *n* nouvelle lune *f*.

news agency *n* agence *f* de presse.

newsagent UK ['nju:zeɪdʒənt], **news-dealer** US ['nju:zdi:lər] *n* marchand *m* de journaux.

newscaster ['nju:zkɑ:stər] *n* présentateur *m*, -trice *f*.

newsdealer US = **newsagent**.

newsflash ['nju:zflæʃ] *n* flash *m* d'information.

newsletter ['nju:z,letər] *n* bulletin *m*.

newspaper ['nju:z,peɪpər] *n* journal *m*.

newsprint ['nju:zprɪnt] *n* papier *m* journal.

newsreader ['nju:z,ri:dər] *n* UK présentateur *m*, -trice *f*.

newsreel ['nju:zri:l] *n* actualités *fpl* filmées.

newsstand ['nju:zstænd] *n* kiosque *m* à journaux.

newt [nju:t] *n* triton *m*.

new town *n* UK ville *f* nouvelle.

New Year *n* nouvel an *m*, nouvelle année *f* ; **Happy New Year!** bonne année!

New Year's Day *n* jour *m* de l'an, premier *m* de l'an.

New Year's Eve *n* la Saint-Sylvestre.

New York [-'jɔ:k] *n* **1.** [city] : **New York (City)** New York - **2.** [state] : **New York (State)** l'État *m* de New York.

New Zealand [-'zi:lənd] *n* Nouvelle-Zélande *f*.

New Zealander [-'zi:ləndər] *n* Néo-Zélandais *m*, -e *f*.

next [nekst] <> *adj* prochain(e) ; [room] d'à côté ; [page] suivant(e) ; **next Tuesday** mardi prochain ; **next time** la prochaine fois ; **next week** la semaine prochaine ; **the next week** la semaine suivante OR d'après ; **next year** l'année prochaine ; **next, please!** au suivant! ; **the day after next** le surlendemain ; **the week after next** dans deux

semaines. <> *adv* **1.** [afterwards] ensuite, après - **2.** [again] la prochaine fois - **3.** *(with superlatives)* **he's the next biggest after Dan** c'est le plus grand après OR à part Dan. <> *prep* US à côté de. ⏩ **next to** *prep* à côté de ; **it cost next to nothing** cela a coûté une bagatelle OR trois fois rien ; **I know next to nothing** je ne sais presque OR pratiquement rien.

next door *adv* à côté. ⏩ **next-door** *adj* : **next-door neighbour** voisin *m*, -e *f* d'à côté.

next of kin *n* plus proche parent *m*.

NF *n* (*abbrev of* **National Front**) ≃ FN *m*.

NHS (*abbrev of* **National Health Service**) *n* service national de santé en Grande-Bretagne, ≃ sécurité sociale *f*.

NI *n abbrev of* **National Insurance**.

nib [nɪb] *n* plume *f*.

nibble ['nɪbl] *vt* grignoter, mordiller.

Nicaragua [,nɪkə'ræɡjʊə] *n* Nicaragua *m*.

nice [naɪs] *adj* **1.** [holiday, food] bon (bonne) ; [day, picture] beau (belle) ; [dress] joli(e) - **2.** [person] gentil(ille), sympathique ; **to be nice to sb** être gentil OR aimable avec qqn.

nice-looking [-'lʊkɪŋ] *adj* joli(e), beau (belle).

nicely ['naɪslɪ] *adv* **1.** [made, manage etc] bien ; [dressed] joliment ; **that will do nicely** cela fera très bien l'affaire - **2.** [politely - ask] poliment, gentiment ; [- behave] bien.

niche [ni:ʃ] *n* [in wall] niche *f* ; *fig* bonne situation *f*, voie *f*.

nick [nɪk] <> *n* **1.** [cut] entaille *f*, coupure *f* - **2.** UK *inf* [condition] : **in good/bad nick** en bon/mauvais état ; **in the nick of time** juste à temps. <> *vt* **1.** [cut] couper, entailler - **2.** UK *inf* [steal] piquer, faucher - **3.** UK *inf* [arrest] arrêter, choper.

nickel ['nɪkl] *n* **1.** [metal] nickel *m* - **2.** US [coin] pièce *f* de cinq cents.

nickname ['nɪkneɪm] <> *n* sobriquet *m*, surnom *m*. <> *vt* surnommer.

nicotine ['nɪkəti:n] *n* nicotine *f*.

niece [ni:s] *n* nièce *f*.

Nigeria [naɪ'dʒɪərɪə] *n* Nigeria *m*.

Nigerian [naɪ'dʒɪərɪən] <> *adj* nigérian(e). <> *n* Nigérian *m*, -e *f*.

niggle ['nɪɡl] *vt* **1.** UK [worry] tracasser - **2.** [criticize] faire des réflexions à, critiquer.

night [naɪt] *n* **1.** [not day] nuit *f* ; **at night** la nuit - **2.** [evening] soir *m* ; **at night** le soir ; **to have an early night** se coucher de bonne heure ; **to have a late night** veiller, se coucher tard. ⏩ **nights** *adv* **1.** US [at night] la nuit - **2.** UK [nightshift] : **to work nights** travailler OR être de nuit.

nightcap ['naɪtkæp] n [drink] boisson alcoolisée prise avant de se coucher.

night class n US = **evening class**.

nightclub ['naɪtklʌb] n boîte f de nuit.

nightdress ['naɪtdres] n chemise f de nuit.

nightfall ['naɪtfɔːl] n tombée f de la nuit OR du jour.

nightgown ['naɪtɡaʊn] n chemise f de nuit.

nightie ['naɪtɪ] n inf chemise f de nuit.

nightingale ['naɪtɪŋɡeɪl] n rossignol m.

nightlife ['naɪtlaɪf] n vie f nocturne, activités fpl nocturnes.

nightly ['naɪtlɪ] <> adj (de) toutes les nuits OR tous les soirs. <> adv toutes les nuits, tous les soirs.

nightmare ['naɪtmeər] n lit & fig cauchemar m.

night porter n UK veilleur m de nuit.

night school n (U) cours mpl du soir.

night shift n [period] poste m de nuit.

nightshirt ['naɪtʃɜːt] n chemise f de nuit d'homme.

nighttime ['naɪttaɪm] n nuit f.

nil [nɪl] n néant m ; UK SPORT zéro m.

Nile [naɪl] n : **the Nile** le Nil.

nimble ['nɪmbl] adj agile, leste ; fig [mind] vif (vive).

NIMBY (abbrev of **not in my back yard**) pas près de chez moi.

nine [naɪn] num neuf ; see also **six**.

nineteen [,naɪn'tiːn] num dix-neuf ; see also **six**.

ninety ['naɪntɪ] num quatre-vingt-dix ; see also **sixty**.

ninth [naɪnθ] num neuvième ; see also **sixth**.

nip [nɪp] n **1.** [pinch] pinçon m - **2.** [bite] morsure f - [of drink] goutte m, doigt m. <> vt [pinch] pincer ; [bite] mordre.

nipple ['nɪpl] n **1.** ANAT bout m de sein, mamelon m - **2.** [of bottle] tétine f.

NIST (abbrev of **National Institute of Standards and Technology**) n service américain des poids et mesures.

nit [nɪt] n **1.** [in hair] lente f - **2.** UK inf [idiot] idiot m, -e f, crétin m, -e f.

nitpicking ['nɪtpɪkɪŋ] n inf ergotage m, pinaillage m.

nitrogen ['naɪtrədʒən] n azote m.

nitty-gritty [,nɪtɪ'ɡrɪtɪ] n inf **to get down to the nitty-gritty** en venir à l'essentiel OR aux choses sérieuses.

no [nəʊ] <> adv **1.** [gen] non ; [expressing disagreement] mais non - **2.** [not any] : **no bigger/smaller** pas plus grand/petit ; **no better** pas mieux. <> adj aucun(e), pas de ;

there's no telling what will happen impossible de dire ce qui va se passer ; **he's no friend of mine** je ne le compte pas parmi mes amis. <> n (pl **noes** [nəʊz]) non m ; **she won't take no for an answer** elle n'accepte pas de refus OR qu'on lui dise non.

No., no. (abbrev of **number**) No, no.

nobility [nə'bɪlətɪ] n noblesse f.

noble ['nəʊbl] <> adj noble. <> n noble m.

nobody ['nəʊbədɪ] <> pron personne, aucun(e). <> n pej rien-du-tout mf, moins que rien mf.

nocturnal [nɒk'tɜːnl] adj nocturne.

nod [nɒd] <> vt : **to nod one's head** incliner la tête, faire un signe de tête. <> vi **1.** [in agreement] faire un signe de tête affirmatif, faire signe que oui - **2.** [to indicate sthg] faire un signe de tête - **3.** [as greeting] : **to nod to sb** saluer qqn d'un signe de tête.
◆ **nod off** vi somnoler, s'assoupir.

noise [nɔɪz] n bruit m.

noisy ['nɔɪzɪ] adj bruyant(e).

no-man's-land n no man's land m.

nominal ['nɒmɪnl] adj **1.** [in name only] de nom seulement, nominal(e) - **2.** [very small] nominal(e), insignifiant(e).

nominate ['nɒmɪneɪt] vt **1.** [propose] : **to nominate sb (for/as sthg)** proposer qqn (pour/comme qqch) - **2.** [appoint] : **to nominate sb (as sthg)** nommer qqn (qqch) ; **to nominate sb (to sthg)** nommer qqn (à qqch).

nominee [,nɒmɪ'niː] n personne f nommée OR désignée.

non- [nɒn] prefix non-.

nonalcoholic [,nɒnælkə'hɒlɪk] adj non-alcoolisé(e).

nonaligned [,nɒnə'laɪnd] adj non-aligné(e).

nonchalant [UK 'nɒnʃələnt, US ,nɒnʃə'lɑːnt] adj nonchalant(e).

noncommittal [,nɒnkə'mɪtl] adj évasif(ive).

nonconformist [,nɒnkən'fɔːmɪst] <> adj non-conformiste. <> n non-conformiste mf.

nondescript [UK 'nɒndɪskrɪpt, US ,nɒndɪ'skrɪpt] adj quelconque, terne.

none [nʌn] <> pron **1.** [gen] aucun(e) ; there was none left il n'y en avait plus, il n'en restait plus ; **I'll have none of your nonsense** je ne tolérerai pas de bêtises de ta part - **2.** [nobody] personne, nul (nulle). <> adv : **none the worse/wiser** pas plus mal/avancé ; **none the better** pas mieux.
◆ **none too** adv pas tellement OR trop.

nonentity [nɒ'nentətɪ] n nullité f, zéro m.

nonetheless [ˌnʌnðə'les] *adv* néanmoins, pourtant.

non-event *n* événement *m* raté OR décevant.

nonexistent [ˌnɒnɪg'zɪstənt] *adj* inexistant(e).

nonfiction [ˌnɒn'fɪkʃn] *n* (U) ouvrages *mpl* généraux.

no-nonsense *adj* direct(e), sérieux(euse).

nonpayment [ˌnɒn'peɪmənt] *n* non-paiement *m*.

nonplussed, US **nonplused** [ˌnɒn'plʌst] *adj* déconcerté(e), perplexe.

nonreturnable [ˌnɒnrɪ'tɜ:nəbl] *adj* [bottle] non consigné(e).

nonsense ['nɒnsəns] ◇ *n* (U) **1.** [meaningless words] charabia *m* - **2.** [foolish idea] : **it was nonsense to suggest...** il était absurde de suggérer... - **3.** [foolish behaviour] bêtises *fpl*, idioties *fpl* ; **to make (a) nonsense of sthg** gâcher OR saboter qqch. ◇ *excl* quelles bêtises OR foutaises !

nonsensical [nɒn'sensɪkl] *adj* absurde, qui n'a pas de sens.

nonsmoker [ˌnɒn'sməʊkər] *n* non-fumeur *m*, -euse *f*, personne *f* qui ne fume pas.

nonstick [ˌnɒn'stɪk] *adj* qui n'attache pas, téflonisé(e).

nonstop [ˌnɒn'stɒp] ◇ *adj* [flight] direct(e), sans escale ; [activity] continu(e) ; [rain] continuel(elle). ◇ *adv* [talk, work] sans arrêt ; [rain] sans discontinuer.

noodles ['nu:dlz] *npl* nouilles *fpl*.

nook [nʊk] *n* [of room] coin *m*, recoin *m* ; **every nook and cranny** tous les coins, les coins et les recoins.

noon [nu:n] *n* midi *m*.

no one *pron* = nobody.

noose [nu:s] *n* nœud *m* coulant.

noplace US = nowhere.

nor [nɔːr] *conj* : **nor do I** moi non plus
► **neither**.

norm [nɔːm] *n* norme *f*.

normal ['nɔːml] *adj* normal(e).

normality [nɔː'mælɪtɪ], US **normalcy** ['nɔːmlsɪ] *n* normalité *f*.

normally ['nɔːməlɪ] *adv* normalement.

Normandy ['nɔːməndɪ] *n* Normandie *f*.

north [nɔːθ] ◇ *n* **1.** [direction] nord *m* - **2.** [region] : **the north** le nord. ◇ *adj* nord *(inv)* ; [wind] du nord. ◇ *adv* au nord, vers le nord ; **north of** au nord de.

North Africa *n* Afrique *f* du Nord.

North America *n* Amérique *f* du Nord.

North American ◇ *adj* nord-américain(e). ◇ *n* Nord-Américain *m*, -e *f*.

northeast [ˌnɔːθ'iːst] ◇ *n* **1.** [direction]

nord-est *m* - **2.** [region] : **the northeast** le nord-est. ◇ *adj* nord-est *(inv)* ; [wind] du nord-est. ◇ *adv* au nord-est, vers le nord-est ; **northeast of** au nord-est de.

northerly ['nɔːðəlɪ] *adj* du nord ; **in a northerly direction** vers le nord, en direction du nord.

northern ['nɔːðən] *adj* du nord, nord *(inv)*.

Northern Ireland *n* Irlande *f* du Nord.

northernmost ['nɔːðənməʊst] *adj* le plus au nord (la plus au nord), à l'extrême nord.

North Korea *n* Corée *f* du Nord.

North Pole *n* : **the North Pole** le pôle Nord.

North Sea *n* : **the North Sea** la mer du Nord.

northward ['nɔːθwəd] ◇ *adj* au nord. ◇ *adv* = **northwards**.

northwards ['nɔːθwədz] *adv* au nord, vers le nord.

northwest [ˌnɔːθ'west] ◇ *n* **1.** [direction] nord-ouest *m* - **2.** [region] : **the northwest** le nord-ouest. ◇ *adj* nord-ouest *(inv)* ; [wind] du nord-ouest. ◇ *adv* au nord-ouest, vers le nord-ouest ; **northwest of** au nord-ouest de.

Norway ['nɔːweɪ] *n* Norvège *f*.

Norwegian [nɔː'wiːdʒən] ◇ *adj* norvégien(enne). ◇ *n* **1.** [person] Norvégien *m*, -enne *f* - **2.** [language] norvégien *m*.

nose [nəʊz] *n* nez *m* ; **keep your nose out of my business** occupe-toi OR mêle-toi de tes affaires, occupe-toi OR mêle-toi de tes oignons ; **to look down one's nose at sb** *fig* traiter qqn de haut ; **to look down one's nose at sthg** *fig* considérer qqch avec mépris ; **on the nose** US *inf* dans le mille ; **to poke** OR **stick one's nose into sthg** mettre OR fourrer son nez dans qqch ; **to turn up one's nose at sthg** dédaigner qqch. ◆ **nose about, nose around** *vi* fouiner, fureter.

nosebleed ['nəʊzbliːd] *n* : **to have a nosebleed** saigner du nez.

nosedive ['nəʊzdaɪv] ◇ *n* [of plane] piqué *m*. ◇ *vi* **1.** [plane] descendre en piqué, piquer du nez - **2.** *fig* [prices] dégringoler ; [hopes] s'écrouler.

nosey ['nəʊzɪ] = nosy.

nostalgia [nɒ'stældʒə] *n* : **nostalgia (for sthg)** nostalgie *f* (de qqch).

nostril ['nɒstrəl] *n* narine *f*.

nosy ['nəʊzɪ] *adj* curieux(euse), fouinard(e).

not [nɒt] *adv* ne pas, pas ; **not that...** ce n'est pas que..., non pas que... ; **not at all** [no] pas du tout ; [to acknowledge thanks] de rien, je vous en prie.

notable ['nəʊtəbl] *adj* notable, remarquable ; **to be notable for sthg** être célèbre pour qqch.

notably ['nəʊtəbli] *adv* **1.** [in particular] notamment, particulièrement - **2.** [noticeably] sensiblement, nettement.

notary ['nəʊtəri] *n* : **notary (public)** notaire *m*.

notch [nɒtʃ] *n* **1.** [cut] entaille *f*, encoche *f* - **2.** *fig* [on scale] cran *m*.

note [nəʊt] <> *n* **1.** [gen] note *f* ; [short letter] mot *m* ; **to take note of sthg** prendre note de qqch - **2.** *UK* [money] billet *m* (de banque). <> *vt* **1.** [notice] remarquer, constater - **2.** [mention] mentionner, signaler. ◆ **notes** *npl* [in book] notes *fpl*. ◆ **note down** *vt sep* noter, inscrire.

notebook ['nəʊtbʊk] *n* **1.** [for notes] carnet *m*, calepin *m* - **2.** COMPUT ordinateur *m* portable compact.

noted ['nəʊtɪd] *adj* célèbre, éminent(e).

notepad ['nəʊtpæd] *n* [for notes] bloc-notes *m*.

notepaper ['nəʊtpeɪpər] *n* papier *m* à lettres.

noteworthy ['nəʊt,wɜːðɪ] *adj* remarquable, notable.

nothing ['nʌθɪŋ] <> *pron* rien ; **I've got nothing to do** je n'ai rien à faire ; **for nothing** pour rien ; **nothing if not** avant tout, surtout ; **nothing but** ne... que, rien que ; **there's nothing for it (but to do sthg)** *UK* il n'y a rien d'autre à faire (que de faire qqch). <> *adv* : **you're nothing like your brother** tu ne ressembles pas du tout OR en rien à ton frère ; **I'm nothing like finished** je suis loin d'avoir fini.

notice ['nəʊtɪs] <> *n* **1.** [written announcement] affiche *f*, placard *m* - **2.** [attention] : **to take notice (of sb/sthg)** faire OR prêter attention (à qqn/qqch) ; **to take no notice (of sb/sthg)** ne pas faire attention (à qqn/qqch) - **3.** [warning] avis *m*, avertissement *m* ; **at short notice** dans un bref délai ; **until further notice** jusqu'à nouvel ordre - **4.** [at work] : **to be given one's notice** recevoir son congé, être renvoyé(e) ; **to hand in one's notice** donner sa démission, demander son congé. <> *vt* remarquer, s'apercevoir de.

noticeable ['nəʊtɪsəbl] *adj* sensible, perceptible.

notice board *n UK* panneau *m* d'affichage.

notify ['nəʊtɪfaɪ] *vt* : **to notify sb (of sthg)** avertir OR aviser qqn (de qqch).

notion ['nəʊʃn] *n* idée *f*, notion *f*. ◆ **notions** *npl US* mercerie *f*.

notorious [nəʊ'tɔːrɪəs] *adj* [criminal] notoire ; [place] mal famé(e).

notwithstanding [,nɒtwɪð'stændɪŋ] *fml* <> *prep* malgré, en dépit de. <> *adv* néanmoins, malgré tout.

nought [nɔːt] *num* zéro *m* ; **noughts and crosses** *UK* morpion *m*.

noun [naʊn] *n* nom *m*.

nourish ['nʌrɪʃ] *vt* nourrir.

nourishing ['nʌrɪʃɪŋ] *adj* nourrissant(e).

nourishment ['nʌrɪʃmənt] *n (U)* nourriture *f*, aliments *mpl*.

novel ['nɒvl] <> *adj* nouveau (nouvelle), original(e). <> *n* roman *m*.

novelist ['nɒvəlɪst] *n* romancier *m*, -ère *f*.

novelty ['nɒvltɪ] *n* **1.** [gen] nouveauté *f* - **2.** [cheap object] gadget *m*.

November [nə'vembər] *n* novembre *m* ; *see also* **September**.

novice ['nɒvɪs] *n* novice *mf*.

now [naʊ] <> *adv* **1.** [at this time, at once] maintenant ; **any day/time now** d'un jour/moment à l'autre ; **now and then** OR **again** de temps en temps, de temps à autre - **2.** [in past] à ce moment-là, alors - **3.** [to introduce statement] : **now let's just calm down** bon, on se calme maintenant. <> *conj* : **now (that)** maintenant que. <> *n* : **for now** pour le présent ; **from now on** à partir de maintenant, désormais ; **up until now** jusqu'à présent ; **by now** déjà.

nowadays ['naʊədeɪz] *adv* actuellement, aujourd'hui.

nowhere ['nəʊweər], **noplace** *US adv* nulle part ; **nowhere near** loin de ; **we're getting nowhere** on n'avance pas, on n'arrive à rien.

nozzle ['nɒzl] *n* ajutage *m*, buse *f*.

NSF *abbrev of* **not sufficient funds**.

nuance ['njuːɒns] *n* nuance *f*.

nuclear ['njuːklɪər] *adj* nucléaire.

nuclear bomb *n* bombe *f* nucléaire.

nuclear disarmament *n* désarmement *m* nucléaire.

nuclear energy *n* énergie *f* nucléaire.

nuclear power *n* énergie *f* nucléaire.

nuclear reactor *n* réacteur *m* nucléaire.

nucleus ['njuːklɪəs] *(pl* **-lei** [-lɪaɪ]) *n lit & fig* noyau *m*.

nude [njuːd] <> *adj* nu(e). <> *n* nu *m* ; **in the nude** nu(e).

nudge [nʌdʒ] *vt* pousser du coude ; *fig* encourager, pousser.

nudist ['njuːdɪst] <> *adj* nudiste. <> *n* nudiste *mf*.

nugget ['nʌgɪt] *n* pépite *f*.

nuisance ['njuːsns] *n* ennui *m*, embêtement *m* ; **it's a nuisance having to attend all these meetings** c'est pénible de devoir assister à toutes ces réunions ; **to make a nuisance of o.s.** embêter le monde ; **what a nuisance!** quelle plaie!

nuke [njuːk] *inf* <> *n* bombe *f* nucléaire. <> *vt* atomiser.

null [nʌl] *adj* : **null and void** nul et non avenu.

numb [nʌm] <> *adj* engourdi(e) ; **to be numb with** [fear] être paralysé par ; [cold] être transi de. <> *vt* engourdir.

number ['nʌmbər] <> *n* **1.** [numeral] chiffre *m* - **2.** [of telephone, house, car] numéro *m* - **3.** [quantity] nombre *m* ; **a number of** un certain nombre de, plusieurs ; **any number of** un grand nombre de, bon nombre de - **4.** [song] chanson *f* ; **a dance number** un numéro de danse. <> *vt* **1.** [amount to, include] compter - **2.** [give number to] numéroter. <> *vi* : **she numbers among the great writers of the century** elle compte parmi les grands écrivains de ce siècle.

number one <> *adj* premier(ère), principal(e). <> *n inf* [oneself] soi, sa pomme.

numberplate ['nʌmbəpleɪt] *n UK* plaque *f* d'immatriculation.

Number Ten *n la résidence officielle du Premier ministre britannique.*

numeral ['njuːmərəl] *n* chiffre *m*.

numerate ['njuːmərət] *adj UK* [person] qui sait compter.

numerical [njuː'merɪkl] *adj* numérique.

numerous ['njuːmərəs] *adj* nombreux(euse).

nun [nʌn] *n* religieuse *f*, sœur *f*.

nurse [nɜːs] <> *n* infirmière *f* ; (male) **nurse** infirmier *m*. <> *vt* **1.** [patient, cold] soigner - **2.** *fig* [desires, hopes] nourrir - **3.** [subj: mother] allaiter.

nursery ['nɜːsəri] *n* **1.** [for children] garderie *f* - **2.** [for plants] pépinière *f*.

nursery rhyme *n* comptine *f*.

nursery school *n* (école *f*) maternelle *f*.

nursery slopes *npl UK* pistes *fpl* pour débutants.

nursing ['nɜːsɪŋ] *n* métier *m* d'infirmière.

nursing home *n* [for old people] maison *f* de retraite privée ; *UK* [for childbirth] maternité *f* privée.

nurture ['nɜːtʃər] *vt* **1.** [children] élever ; [plants] soigner - **2.** *fig* [hopes etc] nourrir.

nut [nʌt] *n* **1.** [to eat] *terme générique désignant les fruits tels que les noix, noisettes etc* - **2.** [of metal] écrou *m* - **3.** *inf* [mad person] cinglé *m*, -e *f*. ◆ **nuts** <> *adj inf* **to be nuts** être dingue. <> *excl US inf* zut!

nutcrackers ['nʌtˌkrækəz] *npl* casse-noix *m inv*, casse-noisettes *m inv*.

nutmeg ['nʌtmeg] *n* (noix *f* de) muscade *f*.

nutritious [njuː'trɪʃəs] *adj* nourrissant(e).

nutshell ['nʌtʃel] *n* : **in a nutshell** en un mot.

nuzzle ['nʌzl] <> *vt* frotter son nez contre. <> *vi* : **to nuzzle (up) against** se frotter contre, frotter son nez contre.

NVQ (*abbrev of* **National Vocational Qualification**) *n examen sanctionnant une formation professionnelle.*

nylon ['naɪlɒn] <> *n* Nylon® *m*. <> *comp* en Nylon®.

O

o [əʊ] (*pl* **o's** OR **os**), **O** (*pl* **O's** OR **Os**) *n* **1.** [letter] o *m inv*, O *m inv* - **2.** [zero] zéro *m*.

oak [əʊk] <> *n* chêne *m*. <> *comp* de OR en chêne.

OAP (*abbrev of* **old age pensioner**) *n UK* retraité *m*, -e *f*.

oar [ɔːr] *n* rame *f*, aviron *m*.

oasis [əʊ'eɪsɪs] (*pl* **oases** [əʊ'eɪsiːz]) *n* oasis *f*.

oatcake ['əʊtkeɪk] *n* galette *f* d'avoine.

oath [əʊθ] *n* **1.** [promise] serment *m* ; **on** OR **under oath** sous serment - **2.** [swearword] juron *m*.

oatmeal ['əʊtmiːl] *n* (U) flocons *mpl* d'avoine.

oats [əʊts] *npl* [grain] avoine *f* ; **is he getting his oats?** *inf* est-ce qu'il a ce qu'il lui faut au lit?

obedience [ə'biːdjəns] *n* obéissance *f*.

obedient [ə'biːdjənt] *adj* obéissant(e), docile.

obese [əʊ'biːs] *adj fml* obèse.

obey [ə'beɪ] <> *vt* obéir à. <> *vi* obéir.

obituary [ə'bɪtʃʊərɪ] *n* nécrologie *f*.

object <> *n* ['ɒbdʒɪkt] **1.** [gen] objet *m* - **2.** [aim] objectif *m*, but *m* - **3.** GRAM complément *m* d'objet. <> *vt* [ɒb'dʒekt] objecter. <> *vi* [ɒb'dʒekt] protester ; **to object to sthg** faire objection à qqch, s'opposer à qqch ; **to object to doing sthg** se refuser à faire qqch.

objection [əb'dʒekʃn] *n* objection *f* ; **to have no objection to sthg/to doing sthg** ne voir aucune objection à qqch/à faire qqch.

objectionable [əb'dʒekʃənəbl] *adj* [person, behaviour] désagréable ; [language] choquant(e).

objective [əb'dʒektɪv] <> adj objectif(ive). <> n objectif m.

obligation [ˌɒblɪ'geɪʃn] n obligation f.

obligatory [ə'blɪgətrɪ] adj obligatoire.

oblige [ə'blaɪdʒ] vt 1. [force] : **to oblige sb to do sthg** forcer OR obliger qqn à faire qqch - 2. fml [do a favour to] obliger.

obliging [ə'blaɪdʒɪŋ] adj obligeant(e).

oblique [ə'bli:k] <> adj oblique ; [reference, hint] indirect(e). <> n TYPO barre f oblique.

obliterate [ə'blɪtəreɪt] vt [destroy] détruire, raser.

oblivion [ə'blɪvɪən] n oubli m.

oblivious [ə'blɪvɪəs] adj : **to be oblivious to** OR **of** être inconscient(e) de.

oblong ['ɒblɒŋ] <> adj rectangulaire. <> n rectangle m.

obnoxious [əb'nɒkʃəs] adj [person] odieux(euse) ; [smell] infect(e), fétide ; [comment] désobligeant(e).

oboe ['əʊbəʊ] n hautbois m.

obscene [əb'si:n] adj obscène.

obscure [əb'skjʊər] <> adj obscur(e). <> vt 1. [gen] obscurcir - 2. [view] masquer.

observance [əb'zɜ:vəns] n observation f.

observant [əb'zɜ:vnt] adj observateur(trice).

observation [ˌɒbzə'veɪʃn] n observation f.

observatory [əb'zɜ:vətrɪ] n observatoire m.

observe [əb'zɜ:v] vt 1. [gen] observer - 2. [remark] remarquer, faire observer.

observer [əb'zɜ:vər] n observateur m, -trice f.

obsess [əb'ses] vt obséder ; **to be obsessed by** OR **with sb/sthg** être obsédé par qqn/qqch.

obsessive [əb'sesɪv] adj [person] obsessionnel(elle) ; [need etc] qui est une obsession.

obsolescent [ˌɒbsə'lesnt] adj [system] qui tombe en désuétude ; [machine] obsolescent(e).

obsolete ['ɒbsəli:t] adj obsolète.

obstacle ['ɒbstəkl] n obstacle m.

obstetrics [ɒb'stetrɪks] n obstétrique f.

obstinate ['ɒbstənət] adj 1. [stubborn] obstiné(e) - 2. [cough] persistant(e) ; [stain, resistance] tenace.

obstruct [əb'strʌkt] vt 1. [block] obstruer - 2. [hinder] entraver, gêner.

obstruction [əb'strʌkʃn] n 1. [in road] encombrement m ; [in pipe] engorgement m - 2. SPORT obstruction f.

obtain [əb'teɪn] vt obtenir.

obtainable [əb'teɪnəbl] adj que l'on peut obtenir.

obtrusive [əb'tru:sɪv] adj [behaviour] qui attire l'attention ; [smell] fort(e).

obtuse [əb'tju:s] adj obtus(e).

obvious ['ɒbvɪəs] adj évident(e).

obviously ['ɒbvɪəslɪ] adv 1. [of course] bien sûr - 2. [clearly] manifestement.

occasion [ə'keɪʒn] <> n 1. [gen] occasion f - 2. [important event] événement m ; **to rise to the occasion** se montrer à la hauteur de la situation. <> vt [cause] provoquer, occasionner.

occasional [ə'keɪʒənl] adj [showers] passager(ère) ; [visit] occasionnel(elle) ; **I have the occasional drink/cigarette** je bois un verre/je fume une cigarette de temps à autre.

occasionally [ə'keɪʒnəlɪ] adv de temps en temps, quelquefois.

occult [ɒ'kʌlt] adj occulte.

occupant ['ɒkjʊpənt] n occupant m, -e f ; [of vehicle] passager m.

occupation [ˌɒkjʊ'peɪʃn] n 1. [job] profession f - 2. [pastime, by army] occupation f.

occupational hazard n risque m du métier.

occupational therapy n thérapeutique f occupationnelle, ergothérapie f.

occupier ['ɒkjʊpaɪər] n occupant m, -e f.

occupy ['ɒkjʊpaɪ] vt occuper ; **to occupy o.s.** s'occuper.

occur [ə'kɜ:r] vi 1. [happen - gen] avoir lieu, se produire ; [- difficulty] se présenter - 2. [be present] se trouver, être présent(e) - 3. [thought, idea] : **to occur to sb** venir à l'esprit de qqn.

occurrence [ə'kʌrəns] n [event] événement m, circonstance f.

ocean ['əʊʃn] n océan m ; **oceans of** inf fig des tonnes de.

oceangoing ['əʊʃnˌgəʊɪŋ] adj au long cours.

ochre UK, **ocher** US ['əʊkər] adj ocre (inv).

o'clock [ə'klɒk] adv : **two o'clock** deux heures.

octave ['ɒktɪv] n octave f.

October [ɒk'təʊbər] n octobre m ; see also **September**.

octopus ['ɒktəpəs] (pl -puses OR -pi [-paɪ]) n pieuvre f.

OD abbrev of **overdose**. abbrev of **overdrawn**.

odd [ɒd] adj 1. [strange] bizarre, étrange - 2. [occasional] : **I play the odd game of tennis** je joue au tennis de temps en temps - 3. [not part of pair] dépareillé(e) - 4. [number] impair(e) ; **twenty odd years** une vingtaine d'années. ⬥ **odds** npl [probability] : **the odds** les chances fpl ; **the odds**

are that... il y a des chances pour que... (+ subjunctive), iil est probable que... ; **against the odds** envers et contre tout ; **odds and sods** inf UK, **odds and ends** [miscellaneous objects] objets mpl divers, bric-à-brac m inv ; [leftovers] restes mpl ; **to be at odds with sb** être en désaccord avec qqn.

oddity ['ɒdɪtɪ] n **1.** [person] personne f bizarre ; [thing] chose f bizarre - **2.** [strangeness] étrangeté f.

odd jobs npl petits travaux mpl.

oddly ['ɒdlɪ] adv curieusement ; **oddly enough** chose curieuse.

oddments ['ɒdmənts] npl fins fpl de série.

odds-on ['ɒdz-] adj inf **odds-on favourite** grand favori.

odometer [əʊ'dɒmɪtər] n odomètre m.

odor US = odour.

odour UK ['əʊdər] n odeur f.

of (stressed [ɒv], unstressed [əv]) prep **1.** [gen] de ; **the cover of a book** la couverture d'un livre ; **to die of cancer** mourir d'un cancer - **2.** [expressing quantity, amount, age etc] de ; **thousands of people** des milliers de gens ; **a piece of cake** un morceau de gâteau ; **a cup of coffee** une tasse de café ; **a pound of tomatoes** une livre de tomates ; **a child of five** un enfant de cinq ans - **3.** [made from] en - **4.** [with dates, periods of time]: **the 12th of February** le 12 février.

off [ɒf] <> adv **1.** [indicating movement or distance away]: **the ball hit the wall and bounced off** la balle a heurté le mur et a rebondi ; **10 miles off** à 16 kilomètres ; **two days off** dans deux jours ; **far off** au loin - **2.** [so as to remove]: **to take sthg off** enlever OR ôter qqch ; **to cut sthg off** couper qqch - **3.** [so as to complete]: **to finish off** terminer ; **to kill off** achever - **4.** [not at work etc]: **a day/week off** un jour/une semaine de congés - **5.** [discounted]: **£10 off** 10 livres de remise OR réduction. <> prep **1.** [at a distance from, away from] de ; **to get off a bus** descendre d'un bus ; **to take a book off a shelf** prendre un livre sur une étagère ; **off the coast** près de la côte - **2.** [not attending]: **to be off work** ne pas travailler ; **off school** absent de l'école - **3.** [no longer liking]: **she's off her food** elle n'a pas d'appétit - **4.** [deducted from] sur - **5.** inf [from]: **to buy sthg off sb** acheter qqch à qqn. <> adj **1.** UK [food] avarié(e), gâté(e) ; [milk] tourné(e) - **2.** [TV, light] éteint(e) ; [engine] coupé(e) - **3.** [cancelled] annulé(e) - **4.** [not at work etc] absent(e) - **5.** UK inf [offhand]: **he was a bit off with me** il n'a pas été sympa avec moi.

offal ['ɒfl] n (U) abats mpl.

off-chance n : **on the off-chance that...** au cas où...

off colour adj UK [ill] patraque.

off duty adj qui n'est pas de service ; [doctor, nurse] qui n'est pas de garde.

offence UK, **offense** US [ə'fens] n **1.** [crime] délit m - **2.** [upset]: **to cause sb offence** vexer qqn ; **to take offence** se vexer.

offend [ə'fend] vt offenser.

offender [ə'fendər] n **1.** [criminal] criminel m, -elle f - **2.** [culprit] coupable mf.

offense [ə'fens] US n **1.** = offence - **2.** SPORT attaque f.

offensive [ə'fensɪv] <> adj **1.** [behaviour, comment] blessant(e) - **2.** [weapon, action] offensif(ive). <> n offensive f.

offer ['ɒfər] <> n **1.** [gen] offre f, proposition f - **2.** [price, bid] offre f - **3.** [in shop] promotion f ; **on offer** [available] en vente ; [at a special price] en réclame, en promotion. <> vt **1.** [gen] offrir ; **to offer sthg to sb, to offer sb sthg** offrir qqch à qqn ; **to offer to do sthg** proposer OR offrir de faire qqch - **2.** [provide - services etc] proposer ; [- hope] donner. <> vi s'offrir.

offering ['ɒfərɪŋ] n RELIG offrande f.

off-guard adv au dépourvu.

offhand [,ɒf'hænd] <> adj cavalier(ère). <> adv tout de suite.

office ['ɒfɪs] n **1.** [place, staff] bureau m - **2.** [department] département m, service m - **3.** [position] fonction f, poste m ; **in office** en fonction ; **to take office** entrer en fonction.

office automation n bureautique f.

office block n UK immeuble m de bureaux.

office hours npl heures fpl de bureau.

officer ['ɒfɪsər] n **1.** [in armed forces] officier m - **2.** [in organization] agent mf, fonctionnaire mf - **3.** [in police force] officier m (de police).

office worker n employé m, -e f de bureau.

official [ə'fɪʃl] <> adj officiel(elle). <> n fonctionnaire mf.

officialdom [ə'fɪʃəldəm] n bureaucratie f.

offing ['ɒfɪŋ] n : **in the offing** en vue, en perspective.

off-licence n UK magasin autorisé à vendre des boissons alcoolisées à emporter.

off-line adj COMPUT non connecté(e).

off-peak adj [electricity] utilisé(e) aux heures creuses ; [fare] réduit(e) aux heures creuses.

off-putting [-,pʊtɪŋ] adj désagréable, rébarbatif(ive).

off season n : **the off season** la morte-saison.

offset [,ɒf'set] (pt & pp **offset**) vt [losses] compenser.

offshoot ['ɒfʃuːt] n : to be an offshoot of sthg être né(e) OR provenir de qqch.

offshore ['ɒfʃɔːr] ◇ adj [oil rig] en mer, offshore (inv) ; [island] proche de la côte ; [fishing] côtier(ère). ◇ adv au large.

offside ◇ adj [,ɒf'said] 1. [right-hand drive] de droite ; [left-hand drive] de gauche - 2. SPORT hors-jeu (inv). ◇ adv [,ɒf'said] SPORT hors-jeu. ◇ n ['ɒfsaid] [right-hand drive] côté m droit ; [left-hand drive] côté gauche.

offspring ['ɒfsprɪŋ] (pl **offspring**) n rejeton m.

offstage [,ɒf'steɪdʒ] adj & adv dans les coulisses.

off-the-peg UK, **off-the-rack** US adj de prêt-à-porter.

off-the-record ◇ adj officieux(euse). ◇ adv confidentiellement.

off-white adj blanc cassé (inv).

often ['ɒfn OR 'ɒftn] adv souvent, fréquemment ; how often do you visit her? vous la voyez tous les combien? ; as often as not assez souvent ; every so often de temps en temps ; more often than not le plus souvent, la plupart des temps.

ogle ['əʊgl] vt reluquer.

oh [əʊ] excl oh! ; [expressing hesitation] euh!

oil [ɔɪl] ◇ n 1. [gen] huile f - 2. [for heating] mazout m - 3. [petroleum] pétrole m. ◇ vt graisser, lubrifier.

oilcan ['ɔɪlkæn] n burette f d'huile.

oilfield ['ɔɪlfiːld] n gisement m pétrolifère.

oil filter n filtre m à huile.

oil-fired [-,faɪəd] adj au mazout.

oil painting n peinture f à l'huile.

oilrig ['ɔɪlrɪg] n [at sea] plate-forme f de forage OR pétrolière ; [on land] derrick m.

oilskins ['ɔɪlskɪnz] npl ciré m.

oil slick n marée f noire.

oil tanker n 1. [ship] pétrolier m, tanker m - 2. [lorry] camion-citerne m.

oil well n puits m de pétrole.

oily ['ɔɪlɪ] adj [rag etc] graisseux(euse) ; [food] gras (grasse).

ointment ['ɔɪntmənt] n pommade f.

OK, okay [,əʊ'keɪ] inf ◇ adj : is it OK with OR by you? ça vous va?, vous êtes d'accord? ; are you OK? ça va? ◇ excl 1. [expressing agreement] d'accord, O.K. - 2. [to introduce new topic] : OK, can we start now? bon, on commence? ◇ vt (pt & pp **-ed**, cont **-ing**) approuver, donner le feu vert à.

old [əʊld] ◇ adj 1. [gen] vieux (vieille), âgé(e) ; how old are you? quel âge as-tu? ;

I'm 20 years old j'ai 20 ans - 2. [former] ancien(enne) - 3. inf [as intensifier] : any old n'importe quel (n'importe quelle). ◇ npl : the old les personnes fpl âgées.

old age n vieillesse f.

old age pensioner n UK retraité m, -e f.

Old Bailey [-'beɪlɪ] n : the Old Bailey la Cour d'assises de Londres.

old-fashioned [-'fæʃnd] adj 1. [outmoded] démodé(e), passé(e) de mode - 2. [traditional] vieux jeu (inv).

old people's home n hospice m de vieillards.

O level n UK examen optionnel destiné, jusqu'en 1988, aux élèves de niveau seconde ayant obtenu de bons résultats.

olive ['ɒlɪv] ◇ adj olive (inv). ◇ n olive f.

olive green adj vert olive (inv).

olive oil n huile f d'olive.

Olympic [ə'lɪmpɪk] adj olympique. ➤ **Olympics** npl : the Olympics les Jeux mpl Olympiques.

Olympic Games npl : the Olympic Games les Jeux mpl Olympiques.

ombudsman ['ɒmbʊdzmən] (pl **-men** [-mən]) n ombudsman m.

omelet(te) ['ɒmlɪt] n omelette f ; mushroom omelette omelette aux champignons.

omen ['əʊmen] n augure m, présage m.

ominous ['ɒmɪnəs] adj [event, situation] de mauvais augure ; [sign] inquiétant(e) ; [look, silence] menaçant(e).

omission [ə'mɪʃn] n omission f.

omit [ə'mɪt] vt omettre ; to omit to do sthg oublier de faire qqch.

omnibus ['ɒmnɪbəs] n 1. [book] recueil m - 2. UK RADIO & TV diffusion groupée des épisodes de la semaine.

on [ɒn] ◇ prep 1. [indicating position, location] sur ; on a chair/the wall sur une chaise/le mur ; on the ceiling au plafond ; the information is on disk l'information est sur disquette ; on the left/right à gauche/droite - 2. [indicating means] : the car runs on petrol la voiture marche à l'essence ; to be shown on TV passer à la télé ; on the radio à la radio ; on the telephone au téléphone ; to live on fruit vivre OR se nourrir de fruits ; to hurt o.s. on sthg se faire mal avec qqch - 3. [indicating mode of transport] : to travel on a bus/train/ship voyager en bus/par le train/en bateau ; I was on the bus j'étais dans le bus ; on foot à pied - 4. [concerning] sur ; a book on astronomy un livre sur l'astronomie - 5. [indicating time] : on Thursday jeudi ; on the 10th of February le 10 février ; on my birthday le jour de mon anniversaire ; on my return à mon retour - **6.** [indicating what or who is affected] **sur ; the impact on the environment** l'impact sur l'environnement - **7.** [using, supported by] **: to be on social security** recevoir l'aide sociale ; **he's on tranquillizers** il prend des tranquillisants ; **to be on drugs** se droguer - **8.** [earning] **: to be on £25,000 a year** gagner 25 000 livres par an ; **to be on a low income** avoir un faible revenu - **9.** [in ratios] **: 25 cents on the dollar** 25 cents par dollar - **10.** [referring to musical instrument] **: to play sthg on the violin/flute/guitar** jouer qqch au violon/à la flûte/à la guitare - **11.** *inf* [paid by] **: the drinks are on me** c'est moi qui régale, c'est ma tournée. *<> adv* **1.** [indicating covering, clothing] **: put the lid on** mettez le couvercle ; **to put a sweater on** mettre un pull ; **what did she have on?** qu'est-ce qu'elle portait? ; **he had nothing on** il était tout nu - **2.** [working] **: turn on the power** mets le courant - **3.** [indicating continuing action] **: to work on** continuer à travailler ; **he kept on walking** il continua à marcher - **4.** [forward] **: send my mail on (to me)** faites suivre mon courrier ; **later on** plus tard ; **earlier on** plus tôt. *<> adj* **1.** [working - electricity, light, radio, TV] allumé(e) ; [- gas, tap] ouvert(e) ; [- engine, machine] en marche ; [- handbrake] serré(e) ; **the radio was on very loud** la radio hurlait ; **the "on" button** le bouton de mise en marche - **2.** [happening] **: there's a conference on next week** il y a une conférence la semaine prochaine ; **it's on at the local cinema** ça passe au cinéma du quartier ; **your favourite TV programme is on tonight** il y a ton émission préférée à la télé ce soir ; **is our deal still on?** est-ce que notre affaire tient toujours? - **3.** *inf* [feasible, possible] **: we'll never be ready by tomorrow, it just isn't on** nous ne serons jamais prêts pour demain, c'est tout bonnement impossible - **4.** *inf* [in agreement] **: are you still on for dinner tonight?** ça marche toujours pour le dîner de ce soir? ; **shall we say £10? – you're on!** disons 10 livres? – d'accord OR tope là! *<> from...* **on** *adv* **: from now on** dorénavant, désormais ; **from then on** à partir de ce moment-là. *<> and off* *adv* de temps en temps. *<> on to, onto* *prep* (written as *onto for senses 4 and 5 only)* **1.** [to a position on top of] **sur ; she jumped on to the chair** elle a sauté sur la chaise - **2.** [to a position on a vehicle] **dans ; she got on to the bus** elle est montée dans le bus ; **he jumped on to his bicycle** il a sauté sur sa bicyclette - **3.** [to a position attached to] **: stick the photo on to the page with glue** colle la photo sur la page - **4.** [aware of wrongdoing] **: to be onto sb** être sur la piste de qqn - **5.** *UK* [into contact with] **: get onto the factory** contactez l'usine.

once [wʌns] *<> adv* **1.** [on one occasion] une fois ; **once a day** une fois par jour ; **once again** OR **more** encore une fois ; **once and for all** une fois pour toutes ; **once in a while** de temps en temps ; **once or twice** une ou deux fois ; **for once** pour une fois - **2.** [previously] autrefois, jadis ; **once upon a time** il était une fois. *<> conj* dès que. *<> at once* *adv* **1.** [immediately] immédiatement - **2.** [at the same time] en même temps ; **all at once** tout d'un coup.

oncoming ['ɒn,kʌmɪŋ] *adj* [traffic] venant en sens inverse ; [danger] imminent(e).

one [wʌn] *<> num* [the number 1] un (une) ; **page one** page un ; **one of my friends** l'un de mes amis, un ami à moi ; **one fifth** un cinquième. *<> adj* **1.** [only, single] seul(e), unique ; **it's her one ambition/love** c'est son unique ambition/son seul amour - **2.** [indefinite] **: one of these days** un de ces jours. *<> pron* **1.** [referring to a particular thing or person] **: which one do you want?** lequel voulez-vous? ; **this one** celui-ci ; **that one** celui-là ; **she's the one I told you about** c'est celle dont je vous ai parlé - **2.** *fml* [you, anyone] on ; **to do one's duty** faire son devoir. *<> for one* *adv* **: I for one remain unconvinced** pour ma part je ne suis pas convaincu.

one-armed bandit *n* machine *f* à sous.

one-man *adj* [business] dirigé(e) par un seul homme.

one-man band *n* [musician] homme-orchestre *m*.

one-off *UK inf <> adj* [offer, event, product] unique. *<> n* **: a one-off** [product] un exemplaire unique ; [event] un événement unique.

one-on-one *US* = **one-to-one**.

one-parent family *n* famille *f* monoparentale.

oneself [wʌn'self] *pron* **1.** *(reflexive)* se ; *(after prep)* soi - **2.** *(emphatic)* soi-même.

one-sided [-'saɪdɪd] *adj* **1.** [unequal] inégal(e) - **2.** [biased] partial(e).

one-to-one *UK*, **one-on-one** *US adj* [discussion] en tête-à-tête ; **one-to-one tuition** cours *mpl* particuliers.

one-touch dialling *UK*, **one-touch dialing** *US n* numérotation *f* rapide.

one-upmanship [,wʌn'ʌpmənʃɪp] *n* art *m* de faire toujours mieux que les autres.

one-way *adj* **1.** [street] à sens unique - **2.** [ticket] simple.

ongoing ['ɒn,gəʊɪŋ] *adj* en cours, continu(e).

onion ['ʌnjən] *n* oignon *m*.

online ['ɒnlaɪn] *adj* & *adv* COMPUT en ligne, connecté(e).

online banking *n* gestion *f* de compte ligne.

onlooker ['ɒn,lʊkər] *n* spectateur *m*, -trice *f*.

only ['əʊnlı] ◇ *adj* seul(e), unique ; **an only child** un enfant unique. ◇ *adv* **1.** ne... que, seulement ; **he only reads science fiction** il ne lit que de la science fiction ; **it's only a scratch** c'est juste une égratignure ; **he left only a few minutes ago** il est parti il n'y a pas deux minutes - **2.** [for emphasis] : **I only wish I could** je voudrais bien ; **it's only natural (that)...** c'est tout à fait normal que... ; **I was only too willing to help** je ne demandais qu'à aider ; **not only... but also** non seulement... mais encore ; **I only just caught the train** j'ai eu le train de justesse. ◇ *conj* seulement, mais.

onset ['ɒnset] *n* début *m*, commencement *m*.

onshore ['ɒnʃɔːr] *adj & adv* [from sea] du large ; [on land] à terre.

onslaught ['ɒnslɔːt] *n* attaque *f*.

onto *(stressed* ['ɒntuː] *unstressed before consonant* ['ɒntə] *unstressed before vowel* ['ɒntʊ]) = **on to**.

onus ['əʊnəs] *n* responsabilité *f*, charge *f*.

onward ['ɒnwəd] *adj & adv* en avant.

onwards ['ɒnwədz] *adv* en avant ; **from now onwards** dorénavant, désormais ; **from then onwards** à partir de ce moment-là.

ooze [uːz] ◇ *vt fig* [charm, confidence] respirer. ◇ *vi* : **to ooze from** OR **out of sthg** suinter de qqch.

opaque [əʊ'peık] *adj* opaque ; *fig* obscur(e).

OPEC ['əʊpek] *(abbrev of* **Organization of Petroleum Exporting Countries)** *n* OPEP *f*.

open ['əʊpn] ◇ *adj* **1.** [gen] ouvert(e) - **2.** [view, road, space] dégagé(e) - **3.** [uncovered - car, wagon] découvert(e) - **4.** [meeting - public(ique) ; [competition] ouvert(e) à tous - **5.** [receptive] : **to be open (to)** être réceptif(ive) (à) - **6.** [disbelief, honesty] manifeste, évident(e) - **7.** [unresolved] non résolu(e). ◇ *n* : **in the open** [sleep] à la belle étoile ; [eat] au grand air ; **to bring sthg out into the open** divulguer qqch, exposer qqch au grand jour - **2.** SPORT : **the British Open** l'open *m* OR le tournoi open de Grande-Bretagne. ◇ *vt* **1.** [gen] ouvrir - **2.** [inaugurate] inaugurer - **3.** COMPUT ouvrir *(program-me)*, démarrer. ◇ *vi* **1.** [door, flower] s'ouvrir - **2.** [shop, library etc] ouvrir - **3.** [meeting, play etc] commencer. ◆ **open on to** *vt insep* [subj: room, door] donner sur. ◆ **open up** ◇ *vt sep* **1.** [for business] ouvrir - **2.** [develop] exploiter, développer. ◇ *vi* **1.** [possibilities etc] s'offrir, se présenter - **2.** [door, building etc] ouvrir.

opener ['əʊpnər] *n* [for cans] ouvre-boîtes *m inv* ; [for bottles] ouvre-bouteilles *m inv*, décapsuleur *m*.

opening ['əʊpnıŋ] ◇ *adj* [first] premier(ère) ; [remarks] préliminaire. ◇ *n* **1.** [beginning] commencement *m*, début *m* - **2.** [in fence] trou *m*, percée *f* ; [in clouds] trouée *f*, déchirure *f* - **3.** [opportunity - gen] occasion *f* ; COMM débouché *m* - **4.** [job vacancy] poste *m*.

opening hours *npl* heures *fpl* d'ouverture.

openly ['əʊpənlı] *adv* ouvertement, franchement.

open-minded [-'maındıd] *adj* [person] qui a l'esprit large ; [attitude] large.

open-plan *adj* non cloisonné(e).

Open University *n UK* : **the Open University** ≃ centre *m* national d'enseignement à distance.

opera ['ɒpərə] *n* opéra *m*.

opera house *n* opéra *m*.

operate ['ɒpəreıt] ◇ *vt* **1.** [machine] faire marcher, faire fonctionner - **2.** COMM diriger. ◇ *vi* **1.** [rule, law, system] jouer, être appliqué(e) ; [machine] fonctionner, marcher - **2.** COMM marcher, travailler - **3.** MED opérer ; **to operate on sb/sthg** opérer qqn/de qqch.

operating theatre *UK*, **operating room** *US* ['ɒpəreıtıŋ-] *n* salle *f* d'opération.

operation [,ɒpə'reıʃn] *n* **1.** [gen & MED] opération *f* ; **to have an operation (for)** se faire opérer (de) - **2.** [of machine] marche *f*, fonctionnement *m* ; **to be in operation** [machine] être en marche OR en service ; [law, system] être en vigueur - **3.** [COMM - company] exploitation *f* ; [- management] administration *f*, gestion *f*.

operational [,ɒpə'reıʃənl] *adj* [machine] en état de marche.

operative ['ɒprətıv] ◇ *adj* en vigueur. ◇ *n* ouvrier *m*, -ère *f*.

operator ['ɒpəreıtər] *n* **1.** TELEC standardiste *mf* - **2.** [of machine] opérateur *m*, -trice *f* - **3.** COMM directeur *m*, -trice *f*.

opinion [ə'pınjən] *n* opinion *f*, avis *m* ; **to be of the opinion that** être d'avis que, estimer que ; **in my opinion** à mon avis.

opinionated [ə'pınjəneıtıd] *adj pej* dogmatique.

opinion poll *n* sondage *m* d'opinion.

opponent [ə'pəʊnənt] *n* adversaire *mf*.

opportune ['ɒpətjuːn] *adj* opportun(e).

opportunist [,ɒpə'tjuːnıst] *n* opportuniste *mf*.

opportunity [,ɒpə'tjuːnətı] *n* occasion *f* ;

to take the opportunity to do OR of doing sthg profiter de l'occasion pour faire qqch.

oppose [ə'pəʊz] vt s'opposer à.

opposed [ə'pəʊzd] adj opposé(e) ; **to be opposed to** être contre, être opposé à ; **as opposed to** par opposition à.

opposing [ə'pəʊzɪŋ] adj opposé(e).

opposite ['ɒpəzɪt] ⧫ adj opposé(e) ; [house] d'en face. ⧫ adv en face. ⧫ prep en face de. ⧫ n contraire m.

opposite number n homologue mf.

opposition [,ɒpə'zɪʃn] n 1. [gen] opposition f - 2. [opposing team] adversaire mf.
➤ **Opposition** n UK POL : **the Opposition** l'opposition.

oppress [ə'pres] vt 1. [persecute] opprimer - 2. [depress] oppresser.

oppressive [ə'presɪv] adj 1. [unjust] oppressif(ive) - 2. [weather, heat] étouffant(e), lourd(e) - 3. [silence] oppressant(e).

opt [ɒpt] ⧫ vt : **to opt to do sthg** choisir de faire qqch. ⧫ vi : **to opt for** opter pour.
➤ **opt in** vi : **to opt in (to)** choisir de participer (à). ➤ **opt out** vi : **to opt out (of)** [gen] choisir de ne pas participer (à) ; [of responsibility] se dérober (à) ; [of NHS] ne plus faire partie (de).

optical ['ɒptɪkl] adj optique.

optician [ɒp'tɪʃn] n 1. [who sells glasses] opticien m, -enne f - 2. [ophthalmologist] ophtalmologiste m.

optimist ['ɒptɪmɪst] n optimiste mf.

optimistic [,ɒptɪ'mɪstɪk] adj optimiste.

optimum ['ɒptɪməm] adj optimum.

option ['ɒpʃn] n option f, choix m ; **to have the option to do** OR **of doing sthg** pouvoir faire qqch, avoir la possibilité de faire qqch.

optional ['ɒpʃənl] adj facultatif(ive) ; **an optional extra** un accessoire.

or [ɔːr] conj 1. [gen] ou - 2. [after negative] : **he can't read or write** il ne sait ni lire ni écrire - 3. [otherwise] sinon - 4. [as correction] ou plutôt.

oral ['ɔːrəl] ⧫ adj 1. [spoken] oral(e) - 2. [MED - medicine] par voie orale, par la bouche ; [- hygiene] buccal(e). ⧫ n oral m, épreuve f orale.

orally ['ɔːrəlɪ] adv 1. [in spoken form] oralement - 2. MED par voie orale.

orange ['ɒrɪndʒ] ⧫ adj orange (inv).
⧫ n 1. [fruit] orange f - 2. [colour] orange m.

orator ['ɒrətər] n orateur m, -trice f.

orbit ['ɔːbɪt] ⧫ n orbite f. ⧫ vt décrire une orbite autour de.

orchard ['ɔːtʃəd] n verger m ; **apple orchard** champ m de pommiers, pommeraie f.

orchestra ['ɔːkɪstrə] n orchestre m.

orchestral [ɔː'kestrəl] adj orchestral(e).

orchid ['ɔːkɪd] n orchidée f.

ordain [ɔː'deɪn] vt 1. [decree] ordonner, décréter - 2. RELIG : **to be ordained** être ordonné prêtre.

ordeal [ɔː'diːl] n épreuve f.

order ['ɔːdər] ⧫ n 1. [gen] ordre m ; **to be under orders to do sthg** avoir (reçu) l'ordre de faire qqch - 2. COMM commande f ; **to place an order with sb for sthg** passer une commande de qqch à qqn ; **to order sur commande** - 3. [sequence] ordre m ; **in order** dans l'ordre ; **in order of importance** par ordre d'importance - 4. [fitness for use] : **in working order** en état de marche ; **out of order** [machine] en panne ; [behaviour] déplacé(e) ; **in order** [correct] en ordre - 5. (U) [discipline - gen] ordre m ; [- in classroom] discipline f - 6. FIN : (money)order mandat m ; **pay to the order of A. Jones** payez à l'ordre de A. Jones - 7. US [portion] part f. ⧫ vt 1. [command] ordonner ; **to order sb to do sthg** ordonner à qqn de faire qqch ; **to order that** ordonner que - 2. COMM commander. ➤ **in the order of** UK, **on the order of** US adv environ, de l'ordre de. ➤ **in order that** conj pour que, afin que (+ subjunctive). ➤ **in order to** conj pour, afin de. ➤ **order about, order around** vt sep commander.

order form n bulletin m de commande.

orderly ['ɔːdəlɪ] ⧫ adj [person] ordonné(e) ; [crowd] discipliné(e) ; [office, room] en ordre. ⧫ n [in hospital] garçon m de salle.

ordinarily ['ɔːdənrəlɪ] adv d'habitude, d'ordinaire.

ordinary ['ɔːdənrɪ] ⧫ adj 1. [normal] ordinaire - 2. pej [unexceptional] ordinaire, quelconque. ⧫ n : **out of the ordinary** qui sort de l'ordinaire, exceptionnel(le).

ordnance ['ɔːdnəns] n (U) 1. [supplies] matériel m militaire - 2. [artillery] artillerie f.

ore [ɔːr] n minerai m.

oregano [,ɒrɪ'gɑːnəʊ] n origan m.

organ ['ɔːgən] n 1. [gen] organe m - 2. MUS orgue m.

organic [ɔː'gænɪk] adj 1. [of animals, plants] organique - 2. [farming, food] biologique, bio.

organization, UK **-isation** [,ɔːgənaɪ'zeɪʃn] n organisation f.

organize, UK **-ise** ['ɔːgənaɪz] vt organiser.

organizer, UK **-iser** ['ɔːgənaɪzər] n 1. [person] organisateur m, -trice f - 2. [diary] organiseur m.

orgasm ['ɔːgæzm] n orgasme m.

orgy ['ɔːdʒɪ] n lit & fig orgie f.

Orient ['ɔːrɪənt] *n* : **the Orient** l'Orient *m*.

oriental [,ɔːrɪ'entl] *adj* oriental(e).

orienteering [,ɔːrɪən'tɪərɪŋ] *n (U)* course *f* d'orientation.

origami [,ɒrɪ'ɡɑːmɪ] *n* origami *m*.

origin ['ɒrɪdʒɪn] *n* **1.** [of river] source *f* ; [of word, conflict] origine *f* - **2.** [birth] : **country of origin** pays *m* d'origine. ➤ **origins** *npl* origines *fpl*.

original [ə'rɪdʒənl] ◇ *adj* original(e) ; [owner] premier(ère). ◇ *n* original *m*.

originally [ə'rɪdʒənəlɪ] *adv* à l'origine, au départ.

originate [ə'rɪdʒəneɪt] ◇ *vt* être l'auteur de, être à l'origine de. ◇ *vi* [belief, custom] : **to originate (in)** prendre naissance (dans) ; **to originate from** provenir de.

Orkney Islands ['ɔːknɪ-], **Orkneys** ['ɔːknɪz] *npl* : **the Orkney Islands** les Orcades *fpl*.

ornament ['ɔːnəmənt] *n* **1.** [object] bibelot *m* - **2.** *(U)* [decoration] ornement *m*.

ornamental [,ɔːnə'mentl] *adj* [garden, pond] d'agrément ; [design] décoratif(ive).

ornate [ɔː'neɪt] *adj* orné(e).

ornithology [,ɔːnɪ'θɒlədʒɪ] *n* ornithologie *f*.

orphan ['ɔːfn] ◇ *n* orphelin *m*, -e *f*. ◇ *vt* : **to be orphaned** devenir orphelin(e).

orphanage ['ɔːfənɪdʒ] *n* orphelinat *m*.

orthodox ['ɔːθədɒks] *adj* **1.** [conventional] orthodoxe - **2.** RELIG [traditional] traditionaliste.

orthopa(e)dic [,ɔːθə'piːdɪk] *adj* orthopédique.

oscillate ['ɒsɪleɪt] *vi* lit & fig osciller.

Oslo ['ɒzləʊ] *n* Oslo.

ostensible [ɒ'stensəbl] *adj* prétendu(e).

ostentatious [,ɒsten'teɪʃəs] *adj* ostentatoire.

osteopath ['ɒstɪəpæθ] *n* ostéopathe *mf*.

ostracize, *UK* **-ise** ['ɒstrəsaɪz] *vt* frapper d'ostracisme, mettre au ban.

ostrich ['ɒstrɪtʃ] *n* autruche *f*.

other ['ʌðər] ◇ *adj* autre ; **the other one** l'autre ; **the other day/week** l'autre jour/ semaine. ◇ *adv* : **there was nothing to do other than confess** il ne pouvait faire autrement que d'avouer ; **other than John** John à part. ◇ *pron* : **others** d'autres ; **the other** l'autre ; **the others** les autres ; **one after the other** l'un après l'autre (l'une après l'autre) ; **one or other of you** l'un (l'une) de vous deux ; **none other than** nul (nulle) autre que. ➤ **something or other** *pron* quelque chose, je ne sais quoi. ➤ **somehow or other** *adv* d'une manière ou d'une autre.

otherwise ['ʌðəwaɪz] ◇ *adv* autrement ; **or otherwise** [or not] ou non. ◇ *conj* sinon.

otter ['ɒtər] *n* loutre *f*.

ouch [aʊtʃ] *excl* aïe!, ouïe!

ought [ɔːt] *aux vb* **1.** [sensibly] : **I really ought to go** il faut absolument que je m'en aille ; **you ought to see a doctor** tu devrais aller chez le docteur - **2.** [morally] : **you ought not to have done that** tu n'aurais pas dû faire cela ; **you ought to look after your children better** tu devrais t'occuper un peu mieux de tes enfants - **3.** [expressing probability] : **she ought to pass her exam** elle devrait réussir à son examen.

ounce [aʊns] *n* once *f* (= 28,35 g).

our ['aʊər] *poss adj* notre, nos *(pl)* ; **our money/house** notre argent/maison ; **our children** nos enfants ; **it wasn't OUR fault** ce n'était pas de notre faute à nous.

ours ['aʊəz] *poss pron* le nôtre (la nôtre), les nôtres *(pl)* ; **that money is ours** cet argent est à nous or est le nôtre ; **it wasn't their fault, it was OURS** ce n'était pas de leur faute, c'était de notre faute à nous or de la nôtre ; **a friend of ours** un ami à nous, un de nos amis.

ourselves [aʊə'selvz] *pron pl* **1.** *(reflexive)* nous - **2.** *(for emphasis)* nous-mêmes ; **we did it by ourselves** nous l'avons fait tout seuls.

oust [aʊst] *vt* : **to oust sb (from)** évincer qqn (de).

out [aʊt] *adv* **1.** [not inside, out of doors] dehors ; **I'm going out for a walk** je sors me promener ; **to run out** sortir en courant ; **out here** ici ; **out there** là-bas - **2.** [not at home, office] sorti(e) ; **John's out at the moment** John est sorti, John n'est pas là en ce moment ; **an afternoon out** une sortie l'après-midi - **3.** [extinguished] éteint(e) ; **the lights went out** les lumières se sont éteintes - **4.** [of tides] : **the tide is out** la marée est basse - **5.** [out of fashion] démodé(e), passé(e) de mode - **6.** [in flower] en fleur - **7.** [finished] : **before the year is out** avant la fin de l'année - **8.** *inf* [on strike] en grève - **9.** [determined] : **to be out to do sthg** être résolu(e) or décidé(e) à faire qqch. ➤ **out of** *prep* **1.** [outside] en dehors de ; **to go out of the room** sortir de la pièce ; **to be out of the country** être à l'étranger - **2.** [indicating cause] par ; **out of spite/love/ boredom** par dépit/amour/ennui - **3.** [indicating origin, source] de, dans ; **a page out of a book** une page d'un livre - **4.** [without] sans ; **out of petrol/money** à court d'essence/ d'argent - **5.** [sheltered from] à l'abri de ; **we're out of the wind here** nous sommes à l'abri du vent ici **- 6.** [to indicate proportion] sur ; **one out of ten people** une personne sur dix ; **ten out of ten** dix sur dix.

out-and-out *adj* [liar] fieffé(e) ; [disgrace] complet(ète).

outback ['aʊtbæk] *n* : **the outback** l'intérieur *m* du pays *(en Australie)*.

outboard (motor) ['aʊtbɔːd-] *n* (moteur *m*) hors-bord *m*.

outbreak ['aʊtbreɪk] *n* [of war, crime] début *m*, déclenchement *m* ; [of spots etc] éruption *f*.

outburst ['aʊtbɜːst] *n* explosion *f*.

outcast ['aʊtkɑːst] *n* paria *m*.

outcome ['aʊtkʌm] *n* issue *f*, résultat *m*.

outcrop ['aʊtkrɒp] *n* affleurement *m*.

outcry ['aʊtkraɪ] *n* tollé *m*.

outdated [ˌaʊt'deɪtɪd] *adj* démodé(e), vieilli(e).

outdid [ˌaʊt'dɪd] *pt* ➤ outdo.

outdo [ˌaʊt'duː] (*pt* -did, *pp* -done [-'dʌn]) *vt* surpasser.

outdoor ['aʊtdɔːr] *adj* [life, swimming pool] en plein air ; [activities] de plein air.

outdoors [aʊt'dɔːz] *adv* dehors.

outer ['aʊtər] *adj* extérieur(e).

outer space *n* cosmos *m*.

outfit ['aʊtfɪt] *n* **1.** [clothes] tenue *f* **- 2.** *inf* [organization] équipe *f*.

outfitters ['aʊtˌfɪtəz] *n* UK *dated* [for clothes] magasin *m* spécialisé de confection pour hommes.

outgoing ['aʊtˌgəʊɪŋ] *adj* **1.** [chairman etc] sortant(e) ; [mail] à expédier ; [train] en partance **- 2.** [friendly, sociable] ouvert(e). ➤ **outgoings** *npl* UK dépenses *fpl*.

outgrow [ˌaʊt'grəʊ] (*pt* -grew, *pp* -grown) *vt* **1.** [clothes] devenir trop grand(e) pour **- 2.** [habit] se défaire de.

outhouse ['aʊthaʊs] (*pl* [-haʊzɪz]) *n* **1.** UK [outbuilding] remise *f* **- 2.** US [toilet] toilettes *fpl* extérieures.

outing ['aʊtɪŋ] *n* [trip] sortie *f*.

outlandish [aʊt'lændɪʃ] *adj* bizarre.

outlaw ['aʊtlɔː] ⋄ *n* hors-la-loi *m inv*. ⋄ *vt* [practice] proscrire.

outlay ['aʊtleɪ] *n* dépenses *fpl*.

outlet ['aʊtlet] *n* **1.** [for emotion] exutoire *m* **- 2.** [hole, pipe] sortie *f* **- 3.** [shop] : **retail outlet** point *m* de vente **- 4.** US ELEC prise *f* (de courant).

outline ['aʊtlaɪn] ⋄ *n* **1.** [brief description] grandes lignes *fpl* ; **in outline** en gros **- 2.** [silhouette] silhouette *f*. ⋄ *vt* [describe briefly] exposer les grandes lignes de.

outlive [ˌaʊt'lɪv] *vt* [subj: person] survivre à.

outlook ['aʊtlʊk] *n* **1.** [disposition] attitude *f*, conception *f* **- 2.** [prospect] perspective *f*.

outlying ['aʊtˌlaɪɪŋ] *adj* [village] reculé(e) ; [suburbs] écarté(e).

outmoded [ˌaʊt'məʊdɪd] *adj* démodé(e).

outnumber [ˌaʊt'nʌmbər] *vt* surpasser en nombre.

out-of-date *adj* [passport] périmé(e) ; [clothes] démodé(e) ; [belief] dépassé(e).

out of doors *adv* dehors.

out-of-the-way *adj* [village] perdu(e) ; [pub] peu fréquenté(e).

outpatient ['aʊtˌpeɪʃnt] *n* malade *mf* en consultation externe.

outpost ['aʊtpəʊst] *n* avant-poste *m*.

output ['aʊtpʊt] *n* **1.** [production] production *f* **- 2.** COMPUT sortie *f*.

outrage ['aʊtreɪdʒ] ⋄ *n* **1.** [emotion] indignation *f* **- 2.** [act] atrocité *f*. ⋄ *vt* outrager.

outrageous [aʊt'reɪdʒəs] *adj* **1.** [offensive, shocking] scandaleux(euse), monstrueux(euse) **- 2.** [very unusual] choquant(e) **- 3.** US *inf* [extravagant] extravagant(e).

outright ⋄ *adj* ['aʊtraɪt] absolu(e), total(e). ⋄ *adv* [ˌaʊt'raɪt] **1.** [deny] carrément, franchement **- 2.** [win, fail] complètement, totalement.

outset ['aʊtset] *n* : **at the outset** au commencement, au début ; **from the outset** depuis le commencement OR début.

outside ⋄ *adj* ['aʊtsaɪd] **1.** [gen] extérieur(e) ; **an outside opinion** une opinion indépendante **- 2.** [unlikely - chance, possibility] faible. ⋄ *adv* [ˌaʊt'saɪd] à l'extérieur ; **to go/run/look outside** aller/courir/regarder dehors. ⋄ *prep* ['aʊtsaɪd] **1.** [not inside] à l'extérieur de, en dehors de **- 2.** [beyond] : **outside office hours** en dehors des heures de bureau. ⋄ *n* ['aʊtsaɪd] extérieur *m*. ➤ **outside of** *prep* US [apart from] à part.

outside lane *n* AUT [in UK] voie *f* de droite ; [in Europe, US] voie *f* de gauche.

outside line *n* TELEC ligne *f* extérieure.

outsider [ˌaʊt'saɪdər] *n* **1.** [in race] outsider *m* **- 2.** [from society] étranger *m*, -ère *f*.

outsize ['aʊtsaɪz] *adj* **1.** [bigger than usual] énorme, colossal(e) **- 2.** [clothes] grande taille *(inv)*.

outskirts ['aʊtskɜːts] *npl* : **the outskirts** la banlieue.

outsource ['aʊtsɔːs] *vt* COMM sous-traiter, externaliser.

outspoken [ˌaʊt'spəʊkn] *adj* franc (franche).

outstanding [ˌaʊt'stændɪŋ] *adj* **1.** [excellent] exceptionnel(elle), remarquable

- **2.** [example] marquant(e) - **3.** [not paid] impayé(e) - **4.** [unfinished - work, problem] en suspens.

outstay [ˌaʊtˈsteɪ] *vt* : **I don't want to outstay my welcome** je ne veux pas abuser de votre hospitalité.

outstretched [ˌaʊtˈstretʃt] *adj* [arms, hands] tendu(e) ; [wings] déployé(e).

outstrip [ˌaʊtˈstrɪp] *vt* devancer.

outward [ˈaʊtwəd] <> *adj* **1.** [going away] : **outward journey** aller *m* - **2.** [apparent, visible] extérieur(e). <> *adv* US = **outwards**.

outwardly [ˈaʊtwədlɪ] *adv* [apparently] en apparence.

outwards [ˈaʊtwədz], **outward** US *adv* vers l'extérieur.

outweigh [ˌaʊtˈweɪ] *vt fig* primer sur.

outwit [ˌaʊtˈwɪt] *vt* se montrer plus malin(igne) que.

oval [ˈəʊvl] <> *adj* ovale. <> *n* ovale *m*.

Oval Office *n* : **the Oval Office** *bureau du président des États-Unis à la Maison-Blanche.*

ovary [ˈəʊvərɪ] *n* ovaire *m*.

ovation [əʊˈveɪʃn] *n* ovation *f* ; **the audience gave her a standing ovation** le public l'a ovationnée.

oven [ˈʌvn] *n* [for cooking] four *m*.

ovenproof [ˈʌvnpruːf] *adj* qui va au four.

over [ˈəʊvər] <> *prep* **1.** [above] au-dessus de - **2.** [on top of] sur - **3.** [to or on the far side of] par-dessus ; **they live over the road** ils habitent en face ; **to go over the border** franchir la frontière - **4.** [more than] plus de ; **over and above** en plus de - **5.** [concerning] à propos de, au sujet de - **6.** [during] pendant - **7.** [senior to] : **he's over me at work** il occupe un poste plus élevé que le mien. <> *adv* **1.** [movement or location across] : **they flew over to America** ils se sont envolés pour les États-Unis ; **we invited them over** nous les avons invités chez nous ; **over here** ici ; **over there** là-bas - **2.** [more] plus - **3.** [remaining] : **there's nothing (left) over** il ne reste rien - **4.** RADIO : **over and out!** terminé! - **5.** [involving repetitions] : **(all) over again** (tout) au début ; **over and over again** à maintes reprises, maintes fois ; **to do sthg over** US recommencer qqch. <> *adj* [finished] fini(e), terminé(e). ◆ **all over** <> *prep* [throughout] partout, dans tout ; **all over the world** dans le monde entier. <> *adv* [everywhere] partout. <> *adj* [finished] fini(e).

overall <> *adj* [ˈəʊvərɔːl] [general] d'ensemble. <> *adv* [ˌəʊvərˈɔːl] en général. <> *n* [ˈəʊvərɔːl] **1.** UK [gen] tablier *m* - **2.** US

[for work] bleu *m* de travail. ◆ **overalls** *npl* **1.** [for work] bleu *m* de travail - **2.** US [dungarees] salopette *f*.

overawe [ˌəʊvərˈɔː] *vt* impressionner.

overbalance [ˌəʊvəˈbæləns] *vi* basculer.

overbearing [ˌəʊvəˈbeərɪŋ] *adj* autoritaire.

overboard [ˈəʊvəbɔːd] *adv* : **to fall overboard** tomber par-dessus bord.

overbook [ˌəʊvəˈbʊk] *vi* surréserver.

overcame [ˌəʊvəˈkeɪm] *pt* ▶ **overcome**.

overcast [ˌəʊvəˈkɑːst] *adj* couvert(e).

overcharge [ˌəʊvəˈtʃɑːdʒ] *vt* : **to overcharge sb (for sthg)** faire payer (qqch) trop cher à qqn.

overcoat [ˈəʊvəkəʊt] *n* pardessus *m*.

overcome [ˌəʊvəˈkʌm] (*pt* -**came**, *pp* -**come**) *vt* **1.** [fears, difficulties] surmonter - **2.** [overwhelm] : **to be overcome (by** OR **with)** [emotion] être submergé(e) (de) ; [grief] être accablé(e) (de).

overcrowded [ˌəʊvəˈkraʊdɪd] *adj* bondé(e).

overcrowding [ˌəʊvəˈkraʊdɪŋ] *n* surpeuplement *m*.

overdo [ˌəʊvəˈduː] (*pt* -**did** [-ˈdɪd], *pp* -**done**) *vt* **1.** [exaggerate] exagérer - **2.** [do too much] trop faire ; **to overdo it** se surmener - **3.** [overcook] trop cuire.

overdone [ˌəʊvəˈdʌn] <> *pp* ▶ **overdo**. <> *adj* [food] trop cuit(e).

overdose *n* [ˈəʊvədəʊs] overdose *f*.

overdraft [ˈəʊvədrɑːft] *n* découvert *m*.

overdrawn [ˌəʊvəˈdrɔːn] *adj* à découvert.

overdue [ˌəʊvəˈdjuː] *adj* **1.** [late] : **overdue (for)** en retard (pour) - **2.** [change, reform] : **(long) overdue** attendu(e) (depuis longtemps) - **3.** [unpaid] arriéré(e), impayé(e).

overestimate [ˌəʊvərˈestɪmeɪt] *vt* surestimer.

overflow <> *vi* [ˌəʊvəˈfləʊ] **1.** [gen] déborder - **2.** [streets, box] : **to be overflowing (with)** regorger (de). <> *n* [ˈəʊvəfləʊ] [pipe, hole] trop-plein *m*.

overgrown [ˌəʊvəˈɡrəʊn] *adj* [garden] envahi(e) par les mauvaises herbes.

overhaul <> *n* [ˈəʊvəhɔːl] **1.** [of car, machine] révision *f* - **2.** *fig* [of system] refonte *f*, remaniement *m*. <> *vt* [ˌəʊvəˈhɔːl] **1.** [car, machine] réviser - **2.** *fig* [system] refondre, remanier.

overhead <> *adj* [ˈəʊvəhed] aérien(enne). <> *adv* [ˌəʊvəˈhed] au-dessus. <> *n* [ˈəʊvəhed] *(U)* US frais *mpl* généraux. ◆ **overheads** *npl* UK frais *mpl* généraux.

overhead projector *n* rétroprojecteur *m*.

overhear [ˌəʊvəˈhɪər] (*pt & pp* -**heard** [-ˈhɜːd]) *vt* entendre par hasard.

overheat [,əʊvə'hi:t] ⟨⟩ *vt* surchauffer. ⟨⟩ *vi* [engine] chauffer.

overjoyed [,əʊvə'dʒɔɪd] *adj* : **overjoyed (at)** transporté(e) de joie (à).

overkill [,əʊvəkɪl] *n* [excess] : **that would be overkill** ce serait de trop.

overladen [,əʊvə'leɪdn] ⟨⟩ *pp* ➤ **overload.** ⟨⟩ *adj* surchargé(e).

overland [,əʊvəlænd] *adj & adv* par voie de terre.

overlap *vi lit & fig* se chevaucher.

overleaf [,əʊvə'li:f] *adv* au verso, au dos.

overload [,əʊvə'ləʊd] (*pp* -**loaded** OR -**laden**) *vt* surcharger.

overlook [,əʊvə'lʊk] *vt* 1. [subj: building, room] donner sur - 2. [disregard, miss] oublier, négliger - 3. [excuse] passer sur, fermer les yeux sur.

overnight ⟨⟩ *adj* ['əʊvənaɪt] 1. [journey, parking] de nuit ; [stay] d'une nuit - 2. *fig* [sudden] : **overnight success** succès *m* immédiat. ⟨⟩ *adv* [,əʊvə'naɪt] 1. [stay, leave] la nuit - 2. [suddenly] du jour au lendemain.

overpass ['əʊvəpɑːs] *n US* ≃ saut-de-mouton *m*.

overpower [,əʊvə'paʊər] *vt* 1. [in fight] vaincre - 2. *fig* [overwhelm] accabler, terrasser.

overpowering [,əʊvə'paʊərɪŋ] *adj* [desire] irrésistible ; [smell] entêtant(e).

overran [,əʊvə'ræn] *pt* ➤ **overrun.**

overrated [,əʊvə'reɪtɪd] *adj* surfait(e).

override [,əʊvə'raɪd] (*pt* -**rode**, *pp* -**ridden**) *vt* 1. [be more important than] l'emporter sur, prévaloir sur - 2. [overrule - decision] annuler.

overriding [,əʊvə'raɪdɪŋ] *adj* [need, importance] primordial(e).

overrode [,əʊvə'rəʊd] *pt* ➤ **override.**

overrule [,əʊvə'ruːl] *vt* [person] prévaloir contre ; [decision] annuler ; [objection] rejeter.

overrun [,əʊvə'rʌn] (*pt* -**ran**, *pp* -**run**) ⟨⟩ *vt* 1. MIL [occupy] occuper - 2. *fig* [cover, fill] : **to be overrun with** [weeds] être envahi(e) de ; [rats] être infesté(e) de. ⟨⟩ *vi* [programme, speech] dépasser (le temps alloué).

oversaw [,əʊvə'sɔː] *pt* ➤ **oversee.**

overseas ⟨⟩ *adj* ['əʊvəsiːz] [sales, company] à l'étranger ; [market] extérieur(e) ; [visitor, student] étranger(ère) ; **overseas aid** aide *f* aux pays étrangers. ⟨⟩ *adv* [,əʊvə'siːz] à l'étranger.

oversee [,əʊvə'siː] (*pt* -**saw**, *pp* -**seen** [-'siːn]) *vt* surveiller.

overseer ['əʊvə,siːər] *n* contremaître *m*.

overshadow [,əʊvə'ʃædəʊ] *vt* [subj: building, tree] dominer ; *fig* éclipser.

overshoot [,əʊvə'ʃuːt] (*pt & pp* -**shot**) *vt* dépasser, rater.

oversight ['əʊvəsaɪt] *n* oubli *m* ; **through oversight** par mégarde.

oversleep [,əʊvə'sliːp] (*pt & pp* -**slept** [-'slept]) *vi* ne pas se réveiller à temps.

overspill ['əʊvəspɪl] *n* [of population] excédent *m*.

overstep [,əʊvə'step] *vt* dépasser ; **to overstep the mark** dépasser la mesure.

overt ['əʊvɜːt] *adj* déclaré(e), non déguisé(e).

overtake [,əʊvə'teɪk] (*pt* -**took**, *pp* -**taken** [-'teɪkn]) ⟨⟩ *vt* 1. *UK* AUT doubler, dépasser - 2. [subj: misfortune, emotion] frapper. ⟨⟩ *vi UK* AUT doubler.

overthrow ⟨⟩ *n* ['əʊvəθrəʊ] [of government] coup *m* d'État. ⟨⟩ *vt* [,əʊvə'θrəʊ] (*pt* -**threw** [-'θruː] , *pp* -**thrown** [-'θrəʊn]) [government] renverser.

overtime ['əʊvətaɪm] ⟨⟩ *n* (U) 1. [extra work] heures *fpl* supplémentaires - 2. *US* SPORT prolongations *fpl*. ⟨⟩ *adv* : **to work overtime** faire des heures supplémentaires.

overtones ['əʊvətəʊnz] *npl* notes *fpl*, accents *mpl*.

overtook [,əʊvə'tʊk] *pt* ➤ **overtake.**

overture ['əʊvə,tjʊər] *n* MUS ouverture *f*.

overturn [,əʊvə'tɜːn] ⟨⟩ *vt* 1. [gen] renverser - 2. [decision] annuler. ⟨⟩ *vi* [vehicle] se renverser ; [boat] chavirer.

overweight [,əʊvə'weɪt] *adj* trop gros (grosse).

overwhelm [,əʊvə'welm] *vt* 1. [subj: grief, despair] accabler ; **to be overwhelmed with joy** être au comble de la joie - 2. MIL [gain control of] écraser.

overwhelming [,əʊvə'welmɪŋ] *adj* 1. [overpowering] irrésistible, irrépressible - 2. [defeat, majority] écrasant(e).

overwork [,əʊvə'wɜːk] ⟨⟩ *n* surmenage *m*. ⟨⟩ *vt* [person, staff] surmener.

overwrought [,əʊvə'rɔːt] *adj* excédé(e), à bout.

owe [əʊ] *vt* : **to owe sthg to sb, to owe sb sthg** devoir qqch à qqn.

owing ['əʊɪŋ] *adj* dû (due). ➤ **owing to** *prep* à cause de, en raison de.

owl [aʊl] *n* hibou *m*.

own [əʊn] ⟨⟩ *adj* propre ; **my own car** ma propre voiture ; **she has her own style** elle a son style à elle. ⟨⟩ *pron* : **I've got my own** j'ai le mien ; **he has a house of his own** il a une maison à lui, il a sa propre maison ; **on one's own** tout seul (toute seule) ; **to get one's own back** *inf* prendre sa revanche. ⟨⟩ *vt* posséder. ➤ **own up** *vi* : **to own up (to sthg)** avouer OR confesser (qqch).

owner ['əʊnəʳ] *n* propriétaire *mf*.

ownership ['əʊnəʃɪp] *n* propriété *f*.

ox [ɒks] (*pl* **oxen** ['ɒksn]) *n* bœuf *m*.

Oxbridge ['ɒksbrɪdʒ] *n* désignation collective des universités d'Oxford et de Cambridge.

oxen ['ɒksn] *npl* ➤ **ox**.

oxtail soup ['ɒksteɪl-] *n* soupe *f* à la queue de bœuf.

oxygen ['ɒksɪdʒən] *n* oxygène *m*.

oxygen mask *n* masque *m* à oxygène.

oxygen tent *n* tente *f* à oxygène.

oyster ['ɔɪstəʳ] *n* huître *f*.

oz. *abbrev of* **ounce**.

ozone ['əʊzəʊn] *n* ozone *m*.

ozone-friendly *adj* qui préserve la couche d'ozone.

ozone layer *n* couche *f* d'ozone.

P

p¹ (*pl* **p's** OR **ps**), **P** (*pl* **P's** OR **Ps**) [piː] *n* [letter] p *m inv*, P *m inv*.

p² 1. (*abbrev of* **page**) p - 2. *abbrev of* **penny**, *abbrev of* **pence**.

p &p *abbrev of* **postage and packing**.

pa [pɑː] *n esp US inf* papa *m*.

p.a. (*abbrev of* **per annum**) p.a.

PA *n* 1. *UK abbrev of* **personal assistant** - 2. (*abbrev of* **public address system**) sono *f*.

pace [peɪs] ◇ *n* 1. [speed, rate] vitesse *f*, allure *f*; **to keep pace (with sb)** marcher à la même allure (que qqn) ; **to keep pace (with sthg)** se maintenir au même niveau (que qqch) - 2. [step] pas *m*. ◇ *vi* : **to pace (up and down)** faire les cent pas.

pacemaker ['peɪsˌmeɪkəʳ] *n* 1. MED stimulateur *m* cardiaque - 2. SPORT meneur *m*, -euse *f*.

Pacific [pə'sɪfɪk] ◇ *adj* du Pacifique. ◇ *n* : **the Pacific (Ocean)** l'océan *m* Pacifique, le Pacifique.

pacifier ['pæsɪfaɪəʳ] *n US* [for child] tétine *f*, sucette *f*.

pacifist ['pæsɪfɪst] *n* pacifiste *mf*.

pacify ['pæsɪfaɪ] *vt* 1. [person, baby] apaiser - 2. [country] pacifier.

pack [pæk] ◇ *n* 1. [bag] sac *m* - 2. *esp US* [packet] paquet *m* - 3. [of cards] jeu *m* - 4. [of dogs] meute *f* ; [of wolves, thieves] bande *f*. ◇ *vt* 1. [clothes, belongings] emballer ; **to pack one's bags** faire ses bagages - 2. [fill] remplir ; **to be packed into** être entassé dans. ◇ *vi* [for journey] faire ses bagages OR sa valise. ➡ **pack in** *UK inf* ◇ *vt sep* [stop] plaquer ; **pack it in!** [stop annoying me] arrête!, ça suffit maintenant! ; [shut up] la ferme! ◇ *vi* tomber en panne. ➡ **pack off** *vt sep inf* [send away] expédier.

package ['pækɪdʒ] ◇ *n* 1. [of books, goods] paquet *m* - 2. *fig* [of proposals etc] ensemble *m*, série *f* - 3. COMPUT progiciel *m*. ◇ *vt* [wrap up] conditionner.

package deal *n* forfait *m* global.

package tour *n* vacances *fpl* organisées.

packaging ['pækɪdʒɪŋ] *n* conditionnement *m*.

packed [pækt] *adj* : **packed (with)** bourré(e) (de).

packed lunch *n UK* panier-repas *m*.

packet ['pækɪt] *n* [gen] paquet *m*.

packing ['pækɪŋ] *n* [material] emballage *m*.

packing case *n* caisse *f* d'emballage.

pact [pækt] *n* pacte *m*.

pad [pæd] ◇ *n* 1. [of cotton wool etc] morceau *m* - 2. [of paper] bloc *m* - 3. [for space shuttle] : **(launch) pad** pas *m* de tir - 4. [of cat, dog] coussinet *m* - 5. *inf* [home] pénates *mpl*. ◇ *vt* [furniture, jacket] rembourrer ; [wound] tamponner. ◇ *vi* [walk softly] marcher à pas feutrés.

padding ['pædɪŋ] *n* 1. [material] rembourrage *m* - 2. *fig* [in speech, letter] délayage *m*.

paddle ['pædl] ◇ *n* 1. [for canoe etc] pagaie *f* - 2. [in sea] : **to have a paddle** faire trempette. ◇ *vi* 1. [in canoe etc] avancer en pagayant - 2. *UK* [in sea] faire trempette.

paddle boat, **paddle steamer** *n* bateau *m* à aubes.

paddling pool ['pædlɪŋ-] *n UK* 1. [in park etc] pataugeoire *f* - 2. [inflatable] piscine *f* gonflable.

paddock ['pædək] *n* 1. [small field] enclos *m* - 2. [at racecourse] paddock *m*.

paddy field ['pædɪ-] *n* rizière *f*.

padlock ['pædlɒk] ◇ *n* cadenas *m*. ◇ *vt* cadenasser.

paediatrics [ˌpiːdɪ'ætrɪks] *UK* = **pediatrics**.

pagan ['peɪgən] ◇ *adj* païen(enne). ◇ *n* païen *m*, -enne *f*.

page [peɪdʒ] ◇ *n* 1. [of book] page *f* - 2. [sheet of paper] feuille *f*. ◇ *vt* [in airport] appeler au micro.

pageant ['pædʒənt] *n* [show] spectacle *m* historique.

pageantry ['pædʒəntrɪ] *n* apparat *m*.

paid [peɪd] ◇ *pt & pp* ➤ **pay**. ◇ *adj* [work, holiday, staff] rémunéré(e), payé(e).

pail [peɪl] *n* seau *m*.

pain [peɪn] *n* **1.** [hurt] douleur *f* ; to be in pain souffrir - **2.** *inf* [annoyance] : it's/he is such a pain c'est/il est vraiment assommant. ► **pains** *npl* [effort, care] : to be at pains to do sthg vouloir absolument faire qqch ; to take pains to do sthg se donner beaucoup de mal OR peine pour faire qqch.

pained [peɪnd] *adj* peiné(e).

painful ['peɪnfʊl] *adj* **1.** [physically] douloureux(euse) - **2.** [emotionally] pénible.

painfully ['peɪnfʊlɪ] *adv* **1.** [fall, hit] douloureusement - **2.** [remember, feel] péniblement.

painkiller ['peɪn,kɪlər] *n* calmant *m*, analgésique *m*.

painless ['peɪnlɪs] *adj* **1.** [without hurt] indolore, sans douleur - **2.** *fig* [changeover] sans heurt.

painstaking ['peɪnz,teɪkɪŋ] *adj* [worker] assidu(e) ; [detail, work] soigné(e).

paint [peɪnt] ◇ *n* peinture *f*. ◇ *vt* [gen] peindre.

paintbrush ['peɪntbrʌʃ] *n* pinceau *m*.

painter ['peɪntər] *n* peintre *mf*.

painting ['peɪntɪŋ] *n* **1.** *(U)* [gen] peinture *f* - **2.** [picture] toile *f*, tableau *m*.

paint stripper *n* décapant *m*.

paintwork ['peɪntwɜːk] *n (U)* surfaces *fpl* peintes.

pair [peər] *n* **1.** [of shoes, wings etc] paire *f* ; a pair of trousers un pantalon - **2.** [couple] couple *m*.

pajamas [pə'dʒɑːməz] *US* = pyjamas.

Pakistan [*UK* ,pɑːkɪ'stɑːn, *US* ,pækɪ'stæn] *n* Pakistan *m*.

Pakistani [*UK* ,pɑːkɪ'stɑːn, *US* 'pækɪstænɪ] ◇ *adj* pakistanais(e). ◇ *n* Pakistanais *m*, -e *f*.

pal [pæl] *n inf* **1.** [friend] copain *m*, copine *f* - **2.** [as term of address] mon vieux *m*.

palace ['pælɪs] *n* palais *m*.

palatable ['pælətəbl] *adj* **1.** [food] agréable au goût - **2.** *fig* [idea] acceptable, agréable.

palate ['pælət] *n* palais *m*.

palaver [pə'lɑːvər] *n (U) inf* **1.** [talk] palabres *fpl* - **2.** [fuss] histoire *f*, affaire *f*.

pale [peɪl] *adj* pâle.

paleontology *US* = palaeontology.

Palestine ['pælə,staɪn] *n* Palestine *f*.

Palestinian [,pælə'stɪnɪən] ◇ *adj* palestinien(enne). ◇ *n* Palestinien *m*, -enne *f*.

palette ['pælət] *n* palette *f*.

palings ['peɪlɪŋz] *npl* palissade *f*.

pall [pɔːl] ◇ *n* **1.** [of smoke] voile *m* - **2.** *US* [coffin] cercueil *m*. ◇ *vi* perdre de son charme.

pallet ['pælɪt] *n* palette *f*.

palliative care *n (U)* MED soins *mpl* palliatifs.

pallor ['pælər] *n lit* pâleur *f*.

palm [pɑːm] *n* **1.** [tree] palmier *m* - **2.** [of hand] paume *f*. ► **palm off** *vt sep inf* : to palm sthg off on sb refiler qqch à qqn ; to palm sb off with sthg se débarrasser de qqn avec qqch.

Palm Sunday *n* dimanche *m* des Rameaux.

palmtop *n* COMPUT ordinateur *m* de poche.

palm tree *n* palmier *m*.

palpable ['pælpəbl] *adj* évident(e), manifeste.

paltry ['pɔːltrɪ] *adj* dérisoire.

pamper ['pæmpər] *vt* choyer, dorloter.

pamphlet ['pæmflɪt] *n* brochure *f*.

pan [pæn] ◇ *n* **1.** [gen] casserole *f* - **2.** *US* [for bread, cakes etc] moule *m*. ◇ *vt inf* [criticize] démolir. ◇ *vi* CIN faire un panoramique.

panacea [,pænə'sɪə] *n* panacée *f*.

panama [,pænə'mɑː] *n* : panama (hat) panama *m*.

Panama ['pænəmɑː] *n* Panama *m*.

Panama Canal *n* : the Panama Canal le canal de Panama.

pancake ['pænkeɪk] *n* crêpe *f*.

Pancake Day *n UK* mardi gras *m*.

Pancake Tuesday *n UK* mardi gras *m*.

panda ['pændə] *(pl* panda OR **-s)** *n* panda *m*.

panda car *n UK* voiture *f* de patrouille.

pandemonium [,pændɪ'məʊnjəm] *n* tohubohu *m inv*.

pander ['pændər] *vi* : to pander to sb se prêter aux exigences de qqn ; to pander to sthg se plier à qqch.

pane [peɪn] *n* vitre *f*, carreau *m*.

panel ['pænl] *n* **1.** TV & RADIO invités *mpl* ; [of experts] comité *m* - **2.** [of wood] panneau *m* - **3.** [of machine] tableau *m* de bord.

panelling *UK*, **paneling** *US* ['pænəlɪŋ] *n (U)* lambris *m*.

pang [pæŋ] *n* tiraillement *m*.

panic ['pænɪk] ◇ *n* [alarm, fear] panique *f*. ◇ *vi (pt & pp* **-ked,** *cont* **-king)** paniquer.

panicky ['pænɪkɪ] *adj* [person] paniqué(e) ; [feeling] de panique.

panic-stricken *adj* affolé(e), pris(e) de panique.

panorama [,pænə'rɑːmə] *n* panorama *m*.

pansy ['pænzɪ] *n* [flower] pensée *f*.

pant [pænt] *vi* haleter.

panther ['pænθər] *(pl* panther OR **-s)** *n* panthère *f*.

panties ['pæntɪz] *npl inf* culotte *f*.

pantihose ['pæntɪhəʊz] = panty hose.

pantomime ['pæntəmaɪm] *n UK spectacle de Noël pour enfants, généralement inspiré de contes de fées.*

pantry ['pæntrɪ] *n* garde-manger *m inv.*

pants [pænts] *npl* **1.** *UK* [underpants - for men] slip *m* ; [- for women] culotte *f*, slip - **2.** *US* [trousers] pantalon *m.*

panty hose ['pæntɪhəʊz] *npl US* collant *m.*

papa [*UK* pə'pɑ:, *US* 'pɑ:pə] *n* papa *m.*

paper ['peɪpər] <> *n* **1.** *(U)* [for writing on] papier *m* ; **a piece of paper** [sheet] une feuille de papier ; [scrap] un bout de papier ; **on paper** [written down] par écrit ; [in theory] sur le papier - **2.** [newspaper] journal *m* - **3.** [in exam - test] épreuve *f* ; [- answers] copie *f* - **4.** [essay] : **paper (on)** essai *m* (sur). <> *adj* [hat, bag etc] en papier ; *fig* [profits] théorique. <> *vt* tapisser. **papers** *npl* [official documents] papiers *mpl.*

paperback ['peɪpəbæk] *n* : **paperback (book)** livre *m* de poche.

paper clip *n* trombone *m.*

paper handkerchief *n* mouchoir *m* en papier.

paper knife *n* coupe-papier *m inv.*

paper shop *n UK* marchand *m* de journaux.

paper tray *n* COMPUT bac *m* à papier.

paperweight ['peɪpəweɪt] *n* presse-papiers *m inv.*

paperwork ['peɪpəwɜːk] *n* paperasserie *f.*

paprika ['pæprɪkə] *n* paprika *m.*

Pap smear *US* = cervical smear.

par [pɑːr] *n* **1.** [parity] : **on a par with** à égalité avec - **2.** GOLF par *m*, normale *f Québec* - **3.** [good health] : **below** OR **under par** pas en forme.

parable ['pærəbl] *n* parabole *f.*

paracetamol [,pærə'siːtəmɒl] *n* paracétamol *m.*

parachute ['pærəʃuːt] <> *n* parachute *m.* <> *vi* sauter en parachute.

parade [pə'reɪd] <> *n* **1.** [celebratory] parade *f*, revue *f* - **2.** MIL défilé *m.* <> *vt* **1.** [people] faire défiler - **2.** [object] montrer - **3.** *fig* [flaunt] afficher. <> *vi* défiler.

paradise ['pærədaɪs] *n* paradis *m.*

paradox ['pærədɒks] *n* paradoxe *m.*

paradoxically [,pærə'dɒksɪklɪ] *adv* paradoxalement.

paraffin ['pærəfɪn] *n UK* paraffine *f.*

paragliding ['pærə,glaɪdɪŋ] *n* parapente *m.*

paragon ['pærəgən] *n* modèle *m*, parangon *m.*

paragraph ['pærəgrɑːf] *n* paragraphe *m.*

Paraguay ['pærəgwaɪ] *n* Paraguay *m.*

parallel ['pærəlel] <> *adj lit & fig* : **parallel (to** OR **with) parallèle (à).** <> *n* **1.** GEOM parallèle *f* - **2.** [similarity & GEOG] parallèle *m* - **3.** *fig* [similar person, object] équivalent *m.*

paralyse *UK*, **paralyze** *US* ['pærəlaɪz] *vt lit & fig* paralyser.

paralysis [pə'rælɪsɪs] (*pl* **-lyses** [-lɪsiːz]) *n* paralysie *f.*

paramedic [,pærə'medɪk] *n* auxiliaire médical *m*, auxiliaire médicale *f.*

parameter [pə'ræmɪtər] *n* paramètre *m.*

paramount ['pærəmaʊnt] *adj* primordial(e) ; **of paramount importance** d'une importance suprême.

paranoid ['pærənɔɪd] *adj* paranoïaque.

paraphernalia [,pærəfə'neɪljə] *n (U)* attirail *m*, bazar *m.*

parasite ['pærəsaɪt] *n lit & fig* parasite *m.*

parasol ['pærəsɒl] *n* [above table] parasol *m* ; [hand-held] ombrelle *f.*

paratrooper ['pærətruːpər] *n* parachutiste *mf.*

parcel ['pɑːsl] *UK n* paquet *m.* **parcel up** *vt sep* (*US*) empaqueter.

parched [pɑːtʃt] *adj* **1.** [gen] desséché(e) - **2.** *inf* [very thirsty] assoiffé(e), mort(e) de soif.

parchment ['pɑːtʃmənt] *n* parchemin *m.*

pardon ['pɑːdn] <> *n* **1.** LAW grâce *f* - **2.** *(U)* [forgiveness] pardon *m* ; **I beg your pardon?** [showing surprise, asking for repetition] comment?, pardon? ; **I beg your pardon!** [to apologize] je vous demande pardon! <> *vt* **1.** [forgive] pardonner ; **to pardon sb for sthg** pardonner qqch à qqn ; **pardon me!** pardon!, excusez-moi! - **2.** LAW gracier. <> *excl* comment?

parent ['peərənt] *n* père *m*, mère *f.* **parents** *npl* parents *mpl.*

parental [pə'rentl] *adj* parental(e).

parenthesis [pə'renθɪsɪs] (*pl* **-theses** [-θɪsiːz]) *n* parenthèse *f.*

Paris ['pærɪs] *n* Paris.

parish ['pærɪʃ] *n* **1.** RELIG paroisse *f* - **2.** *UK* [area of local government] commune *f.*

Parisian [pə'rɪzjən] <> *adj* parisien(enne). <> *n* Parisien *m*, -enne *f.*

parity ['pærətɪ] *n* égalité *f.*

park [pɑːk] <> *n* parc *m*, jardin *m* public ; **industrial park** = **industrial estate.** <> *vt* garer. <> *vi* se garer, stationner.

parking ['pɑːkɪŋ] *n* stationnement *m* ; **'no parking'** 'défense de stationner', 'stationnement interdit'.

parking lot *n US* parking *m.*

parking meter *n* parcmètre *m.*

parking ticket *n* contravention *f*, PV *m.*

parlance ['pɑ:ləns] n : in common/legal parlance etc en langage courant/juridique etc.

parliament ['pɑ:ləmənt] n parlement m.

parliamentary [,pɑ:lə'mentəri] adj parlementaire.

parlour UK, **parlor** US ['pɑ:lər] n dated salon m.

parochial [pə'rəʊkjəl] adj pej de clocher.

parody ['pærədi] <> n parodie f. <> vt parodier.

parole [pə'rəʊl] n (U) parole f ; on parole en liberté conditionnelle.

parrot ['pærət] n perroquet m.

parry ['pæri] vt 1. [blow] parer - 2. [question] éluder.

parsley ['pɑ:sli] n persil m.

parsnip ['pɑ:snip] n panais m.

parson ['pɑ:sn] n pasteur m.

part [pɑ:t] <> n 1. [gen] partie f ; for the most part dans l'ensemble - 2. [of TV serial etc] épisode m - 3. [component] pièce f - 4. [in proportions] mesure f - 5. THEAT rôle m - 6. [involvement] : part in participation f à ; to play an important part in jouer un rôle important dans ; to take part in participer à ; for my part en ce qui me concerne - 7. US [hair parting] raie f. <> adv en partie. <> vt to part one's hair se faire une raie. <> vi 1. [couple] se séparer - 2. [curtains] s'écarter, s'ouvrir. **parts** npl : in these parts dans cette région. **part with** vt insep [money] débourser ; [possession] se défaire de.

part exchange n UK reprise f ; to take sthg in part exchange reprendre qqch.

partial ['pɑ:ʃl] adj 1. [incomplete] partiel(elle) - 2. [biased] partial(e) - 3. [fond] : to be partial to avoir un penchant pour.

participant [pɑ:'tisipənt] n participant m, -e f.

participate [pɑ:'tisipeit] vi : to participate (in) participer (à).

participation [pɑ:,tisi'peiʃn] n participation f.

participle ['pɑ:tisipl] n participe m.

particle ['pɑ:tikl] n particule f.

parti-coloured UK, **parti-colored** US ['pɑ:ti-] adj bariolé(e).

particular [pə'tikjʊlər] adj 1. [gen] particulier(ère) - 2. [fussy] pointilleux(euse) ; particular about exigeant(e) à propos de. **particulars** npl renseignements mpl. **in particular** en particulier.

particularly [pə'tikjʊləli] adv particulièrement.

parting ['pɑ:tiŋ] n 1. [separation] séparation f - 2. UK [in hair] raie f.

partisan [,pɑ:ti'zæn] <> adj partisan(e). <> n partisan m, -e f.

partition [pɑ:'tiʃn] <> n [wall, screen] cloison f. <> vt 1. [room] cloisonner - 2. [country] partager.

partly ['pɑ:tli] adv partiellement, en partie.

partner ['pɑ:tnər] <> n 1. [in game dance] partenaire mf ; [spouse] conjoint m, -e f ; [not married] compagnon m, compagne f - 2. [in a business, crime] associé m, -e f. <> vt être le partenaire de.

partnership ['pɑ:tnəʃip] n association f.

partridge ['pɑ:tridʒ] n perdrix f.

part-time adj & adv à temps partiel.

party ['pɑ:ti] <> n 1. POL parti m - 2. [social gathering] fête f, réception f ; to have or throw a party donner une fête - 3. [group] groupe m - 4. LAW partie f. <> vi inf faire la fête.

party line n 1. POL ligne f du parti - 2. TELEC ligne f commune à deux abonnés.

pass [pɑ:s] <> n 1. SPORT passe f - 2. [document - for security] laissez-passer m inv ; [- for travel] carte f d'abonnement - 3. UK [in exam] mention f passable - 4. [between mountains] col m ; to make a pass at sb faire du plat à qqn. <> vt 1. [object, time] passer ; to pass sthg to sb, to pass sb sthg passer qqch à qqn - 2. [person in street etc] croiser - 3. [place] passer devant - 4. AUT dépasser, doubler - 5. [exceed] dépasser - 6. [exam] réussir (à) ; [driving test] passer - 7. [candidate] recevoir, admettre - 8. [law, motion] voter - 9. [opinion] émettre ; [judgment] rendre, prononcer. <> vi 1. [gen] passer - 2. AUT doubler, dépasser - 3. SPORT faire une passe - 4. [in exam] réussir, être reçu(e). **pass as** vt insep passer pour. **pass away** vi s'éteindre. **pass by** <> vt sep : the news passed him by la nouvelle ne l'a pas affecté. <> vi passer à côté. **pass for** vt insep = pass as. **pass on** <> vt sep : to pass sthg on (to) [object] faire passer qqch (à) ; [tradition, information] transmettre qqch (à). <> vi 1. [move on] continuer son chemin - 2. = pass away. **pass out** vi 1. [faint] s'évanouir - 2. UK MIL finir OR terminer les classes. **pass over** vt insep [problem, topic] passer sous silence. **pass up** vt sep [opportunity, invitation] laisser passer.

passable ['pɑ:səbl] adj 1. [satisfactory] passable - 2. [road] praticable ; [river] franchissable.

passage ['pæsidʒ] n 1. [gen] passage m - 2. [between rooms] couloir m - 3. [sea journey] traversée f.

passageway ['pæsidʒwei] n [between houses] passage m ; [between rooms] couloir m.

passbook ['pɑ:sbʊk] n livret m (d'épargne).

passenger ['pæsɪndʒər] *n* passager *m*, -ère *f*.

passerby [,pɑːsə'baɪ] (*pl* **passersby** [,pɑːsəz'baɪ]) *n* passant *m*, -e *f*.

passing ['pɑːsɪŋ] *adj* [remark] en passant ; [trend] passager(ère). ➡ **in passing** *adv* en passant.

passion ['pæʃn] *n* passion *f*.

passionate ['pæʃənət] *adj* passionné(e).

passive ['pæsɪv] *adj* passif(ive).

Passover ['pɑːs,əʊvər] *n* : **(the) Passover** la Pâque juive.

passport ['pɑːspɔːt] *n* [document] passeport *m*.

passport control *n* contrôle *m* des passeports.

password ['pɑːswɜːd] *n* mot *m* de passe.

past [pɑːst] ◇ *adj* **1.** [former] passé(e) ; **for the past five years** ces cinq dernières années ; **the past week** la semaine passée OR dernière - **2.** [finished] fini(e). ◇ *adv* **1.** [in times] : **it's ten past** il est dix - **2.** [in front] : **to drive past** passer (devant) en voiture ; **to run past** passer (devant) en courant. ◇ *n* passé *m* ; **in the past** dans le temps. ◇ *prep* **1.** [in times] : **it's half past eight** il est huit heures et demie ; **it's five past nine** il est neuf heures cinq - **2.** [in front of] devant ; **we drove past them** nous les avons dépassés en voiture - **3.** [beyond] après, au-delà de.

pasta ['pæstə] *n* (U) pâtes *fpl*.

paste [peɪst] ◇ *n* **1.** [gen] pâte *f* - **2.** CULIN pâté *m* - **3.** (U) [glue] colle *f*. ◇ *vt* coller.

pastel ['pæstl] ◇ *adj* pastel (*inv*). ◇ *n* pastel *m*.

pasteurize, UK **-ise** ['pɑːstʃəraɪz] *vt* pasteuriser.

pastille ['pæstɪl] *n* pastille *f*.

pastime ['pɑːstaɪm] *n* passe-temps *m inv*.

pastor ['pɑːstər] *n* pasteur *m*.

past participle *n* participe *m* passé.

pastry ['peɪstrɪ] *n* **1.** [mixture] pâte *f* - **2.** [cake] pâtisserie *f*.

past tense *n* passé *m*.

pasture ['pɑːstʃər] *n* pâturage *m*, pré *m*.

pasty[1]['peɪstɪ] *adj* blafard(e), terreux(euse).

pasty[2]['pæstɪ] *n* UK petit pâté *m*, friand *m*.

pat [pæt] ◇ *n* **1.** [light stroke] petite tape *f* ; [to animal] caresse *f* - **2.** [of butter] noix *f*, noisette *f*. ◇ *vt* [person] tapoter, donner une tape à ; [animal] caresser.

patch [pætʃ] ◇ *n* **1.** [piece of material] pièce *f* ; [to cover eye] bandeau *m* - **2.** [small area - of snow, ice] plaque *f* - **3.** [of land] parcelle *f*, lopin *m* ; **vegetable patch** carré *m* de légumes - **4.** MED patch *m* - **5.** [period of time] : **a difficult patch** une mauvaise passe. ◇ *vt* rapiécer. ➡ **patch up** *vt sep* **1.** [mend] rafistoler, bricoler - **2.** [quarrel] régler, arranger ; **to patch up a relationship** se raccommoder.

patchwork ['pætʃwɜːk] *n* patchwork *m*.

patchy ['pætʃɪ] *adj* [gen] inégal(e) ; [knowledge] insuffisant(e), imparfait(e).

pâté ['pæteɪ] *n* pâté *m*.

patent [UK 'peɪtənt, US 'pætənt] ◇ *adj* [obvious] évident(e), manifeste. ◇ *n* brevet *m* (d'invention). ◇ *vt* faire breveter.

patent leather *n* cuir *m* verni.

paternal [pə'tɜːnl] *adj* paternel(elle).

path [pɑːθ] (*pl* [pɑːðz]) *n* **1.** [track] chemin *m*, sentier *m* - **2.** [way ahead, course of action] voie *f*, chemin *m* - **3.** [trajectory] trajectoire *f* - **4.** COMPUT chemin *m* (d'accès).

pathetic [pə'θetɪk] *adj* **1.** [causing pity] pitoyable, attendrissant(e) - **2.** [useless - efforts, person] pitoyable, minable.

pathname ['pɑːθneɪm] *n* chemin *m* (d'accès).

pathological [,pæθə'lɒdʒɪkl] *adj* pathologique.

pathology [pə'θɒlədʒɪ] *n* pathologie *f*.

pathos ['peɪθɒs] *n* pathétique *m*.

pathway ['pɑːθweɪ] *n* chemin *m*, sentier *m*.

patience ['peɪʃns] *n* **1.** [of person] patience *f* - **2.** UK [card game] réussite *f*.

patient ['peɪʃnt] ◇ *adj* patient(e). ◇ *n* [in hospital] patient *m*, -e *f*, malade *mf* ; [of doctor] patient.

patio ['pætɪəʊ] (*pl* -s) *n* patio *m*.

patriotic [UK ,pætrɪ'ɒtɪk, US ,peɪtrɪ'ɒtɪk] *adj* [gen] patriotique ; [person] patriote.

patrol [pə'trəʊl] ◇ *n* patrouille *f*. ◇ *vt* patrouiller dans, faire une patrouille dans.

patrol car *n* voiture *f* de police.

patrolman [pə'trəʊlmən] (*pl* -men [-mən]) *n* US agent *m* de police.

patron ['peɪtrən] *n* **1.** [of arts] mécène *m*, protecteur *m*, -trice *f* - **2.** UK [of charity] patron *m*, -onne *f* - **3.** *fml* [customer] client *m*, -e *f*.

patronize, UK **-ise** ['pætrənaɪz] *vt* **1.** [talk down to] traiter avec condescendance - **2.** *fml* [back financially] patronner, protéger.

patronizing, UK **-ising** ['pætrənaɪzɪŋ] *adj* condescendant(e).

patter ['pætər] ◇ *n* **1.** [sound - of rain]

crépitement *m* - **2.** [talk] baratin *m*, bavardage *m*. ⬦ *vi* [feet, paws] trottiner ; [rain] frapper, fouetter.

pattern ['pætən] *n* **1.** [design] motif *m*, dessin *m* - **2.** [of distribution, population] schéma *m* ; [of life, behaviour] mode *m* - **3.** [diagram]: **(sewing) pattern** patron *m* - **4.** [model] modèle *m*.

paunch [pɔːntʃ] *n* bedaine *f*.

pauper ['pɔːpər] *n* indigent *m*, -e *f*, nécessiteux *m*, -euse *f*.

pause [pɔːz] ⬦ *n* **1.** [short silence] pause *f*, silence *m* - **2.** [break] pause *f*, arrêt *m*. ⬦ *vi* **1.** [stop speaking] marquer un temps - **2.** [stop moving, doing] faire une pause, s'arrêter.

pave [peɪv] *vt* paver ; **to pave the way for sb/sthg** ouvrir la voie à qqn/qqch.

pavement ['peɪvmənt] *n* **1.** *UK* [at side of road] trottoir *m* - **2.** *US* [roadway] chaussée *f*.

pavilion [pə'vɪljən] *n* pavillon *m*.

paving ['peɪvɪŋ] *n* (U) pavé *m*.

paving stone *n* pavé *m*.

paw [pɔː] *n* patte *f*.

pawn [pɔːn] ⬦ *n* lit & fig pion *m*. ⬦ *vt* mettre en gage.

pawnbroker ['pɔːn,brəʊkər] *n* prêteur *m*, -euse *f* sur gages.

pawnshop ['pɔːnʃɒp] *n* boutique *f* de prêteur sur gages.

pay [peɪ] ⬦ *vt* (pt & pp paid) **1.** [gen] payer ; **to pay sb for sthg** payer qqn pour qqch, payer qqch à qqn ; **I paid £20 for that shirt** j'ai payé cette chemise 20 livres ; **to pay money into an account** verser de l'argent sur un compte ; **to pay a cheque into an account** déposer un chèque sur un compte - **2.** [be profitable to] rapporter à - **3.** [give, make]: **to pay attention (to sb/sthg)** prêter attention (à qqn/qqch) ; **to pay sb a compliment** faire un compliment à qqn ; **to pay sb a visit** rendre visite à qqn. ⬦ *vi* (pt & pp paid) payer ; **to pay dearly for sthg** fig payer qqch cher. ⬦ *n* salaire *m*, traitement *m*. ⬤ **pay back** *vt sep* **1.** [return loan of money] rembourser - **2.** [revenge oneself on] revaloir ; **I'll pay you back for that** tu me le paieras, je te le revaudrai. ⬤ **pay off** ⬦ *vt sep* **1.** [repay - debt] s'acquitter de, régler ; [- loan] rembourser - **2.** [dismiss] licencier, congédier - **3.** [bribe] soudoyer, acheter. ⬦ *vi* [course of action] être payant(e). ⬤ **pay up** *vi* payer.

payable ['peɪəbl] *adj* **1.** [gen] payable - **2.** [on cheque]: **payable to** à l'ordre de.

pay-as-you-go [,peɪ.diː'ef] *n* système *m* sans forfait.

paycheck ['peɪtʃek] *n* US paie *f*.

payday ['peɪdeɪ] *n* jour *m* de paie.

payee [peɪ'iː] *n* bénéficiaire *mf*.

pay envelope *n* US salaire *m*.

payment ['peɪmənt] *n* paiement *m*.

pay packet *n UK* **1.** [envelope] enveloppe *f* de paie - **2.** [wages] paie *f*.

pay phone, *US* **pay station** *n* téléphone *m* public, cabine *f* téléphonique.

payroll ['peɪrəʊl] *n* registre *m* du personnel.

payslip ['peɪslɪp] *n UK* feuille *f* OR bulletin *m* de paie.

pay station *US* = **pay phone**.

pc (abbrev of **per cent**) p. cent.

PC *n* **1.** (abbrev of **personal computer**) PC *m*, micro *m* - **2.** abbrev of **police constable**.

PDF (abbrev of **portable document format**) *n* COMPUT PDF *m*.

PE (abbrev of **physical education**) *n UK* EPS *f*.

pea [piː] *n* pois *m*.

peace [piːs] *n (U)* paix *f* ; [quiet, calm] calme *m*, tranquillité *f* ; **to make (one's) peace with sb** faire la paix avec qqn.

peaceable ['piːsəbl] *adj* paisible, pacifique.

peaceful ['piːsful] *adj* **1.** [quiet, calm] paisible, calme - **2.** [not aggressive - person] pacifique ; [- demonstration] non-violent(e).

peacetime ['piːstaɪm] *n* temps *m* de paix.

peach [piːtʃ] ⬦ *adj* couleur pêche (inv). ⬦ *n* pêche *f*.

peacock ['piːkɒk] *n* paon *m*.

peak [piːk] ⬦ *n* **1.** [mountain top] sommet *m*, cime *f* - **2.** fig [of career, success] apogée *m*, sommet *m* - **3.** [of cap] visière *f*. ⬦ *adj* [condition] optimum. ⬦ *vi* atteindre un niveau maximum.

peaked [piːkt] *adj* [cap] à visière.

peak hours *npl* heures *fpl* d'affluence OR de pointe.

peak period *n* période *f* de pointe.

peak rate *n* tarif *m* normal.

peal [piːl] ⬦ *n* [of bells] carillonnement *m* ; [of laughter] éclat *m* ; [of thunder] coup *m*. ⬦ *vi* [bells] carillonner.

peanut ['piːnʌt] *n* cacahuète *f*.

peanut butter *n* beurre *m* de cacahuètes.

pear [peər] *n* poire *f*.

pearl [pɜːl] *n* perle *f*.

peasant ['peznt] *n* [in countryside] paysan *m*, -anne *f*.

peat [piːt] *n* tourbe *f*.

pebble ['pebl] *n* galet *m*, caillou *m*.

peck [pek] ⬦ *n* **1.** [with beak] coup *m* de

bec - 2. [kiss] bise f. <> vt 1. [with beak] picoter, becqueter - 2. [kiss] : **to peck sb on the cheek** faire une bise à qqn.

pecking order ['pekɪŋ-] n hiérarchie f.

peckish ['pekɪʃ] adj UK inf **to feel peckish** avoir un petit creux.

peculiar [pɪ'kjuːljər] adj 1. [odd] bizarre, curieux(euse) - 2. [slightly ill] : **to feel peculiar** se sentir tout drôle (toute drôle) OR tout chose (toute chose) - 3. [characteristic] : **peculiar to** propre à, particulier(ère) à.

peculiarity [pɪ,kjuːlɪ'ærətɪ] n 1. [oddness] bizarrerie f, singularité f - 2. [characteristic] particularité f, caractéristique f.

pedal ['pedl] <> n pédale f. <> vi (UK & US) pédaler.

pedal bin n UK poubelle f à pédale.

pedantic [pɪ'dæntɪk] adj pej pédant(e).

peddle ['pedl] vt 1. [drugs] faire le trafic de - 2. [gossip, rumour] colporter, répandre.

pedestal ['pedɪstl] n piédestal m.

pedestrian [pɪ'destrɪən] <> adj pej médiocre, dépourvu(e) d'intérêt. <> n piéton m.

pedestrian crossing n UK passage m pour piétons, passage clouté.

pedestrian precinct UK, **pedestrian zone** US n zone f piétonne.

pediatrics [,piːdɪ'ætrɪks] n pédiatrie f.

pedigree ['pedɪgriː] <> adj [animal] de race. <> n 1. [of animal] pedigree m - 2. [of person] ascendance f, généalogie f.

pedlar UK, **peddler** US ['pedlər] n colporteur m.

pee [piː] inf <> n pipi m, pisse f. <> vi faire pipi, pisser.

peek [piːk] inf <> n coup m d'œil furtif. <> vi jeter un coup d'œil furtif.

peel [piːl] <> n [of apple, potato] peau f ; [of orange, lemon] écorce f. <> vt éplucher, peler. <> vi 1. [paint] s'écailler - 2. [wallpaper] se décoller - 3. [skin] peler.

peelings ['piːlɪŋz] npl épluchures fpl.

peep [piːp] <> n 1. [look] coup m d'œil OR regard m furtif - 2. inf [sound] bruit m. <> vi jeter un coup d'œil furtif. ◆ **peep out** vi apparaître, se montrer.

peephole ['piːphəʊl] n judas m.

peer [pɪər] <> n pair m. <> vi scruter, regarder attentivement.

peerage ['pɪərɪdʒ] n [rank] pairie f ; **the peerage** les pairs mpl.

peer group n pairs mpl.

peeved [piːvd] adj inf fâché(e), irrité(e).

peevish ['piːvɪʃ] adj grincheux(euse).

peg [peg] <> n 1. [hook] cheville f - 2. UK [for clothes] pince f à linge - 3. [for tent] piquet m. <> vt fig [prices] bloquer.

pejorative [pɪ'dʒɒrətɪv] adj péjoratif(ive).

pekinese [,piːkə'niːz], **pekingese** [,piːkɪŋ'iːz] [dog] pékinois m.

Peking [piː'kɪŋ] n Pékin m.

pekingese = pekinese.

pelican ['pelɪkən] (pl pelican OR -s) n pélican m.

pelican crossing n UK passage pour piétons avec feux de circulation.

pellet ['pelɪt] n 1. [small ball] boulette f - 2. [for gun] plomb m.

pelmet ['pelmɪt] n UK lambrequin m.

pelt [pelt] <> n [animal skin] peau f, fourrure f. <> vt : **to pelt sb (with sthg)** bombarder qqn (de qqch). <> vi [run fast] : **to pelt along** courir ventre à terre ; **to pelt down the stairs** dévaler l'escalier. ◆ **pelt down** impers vb [rain] : **it's pelting down** il pleut à verse.

pelvis ['pelvɪs] (pl -vises OR -ves [-viːz]) n pelvis m, bassin m.

pen [pen] <> n 1. [for writing] stylo m - 2. [enclosure] parc m, enclos m - 3. US inf (abbr of penitentiary) taule f. <> vt [enclose] parquer.

penal ['piːnl] adj pénal(e).

penalize, UK **-ise** ['piːnəlaɪz] vt 1. [gen] pénaliser - 2. [put at a disadvantage] désavantager.

penalty ['penltɪ] n 1. [punishment] pénalité f ; **to pay the penalty (for sthg)** fig supporter OR subir les conséquences (de qqch) - 2. [fine] amende f - 3. [in hockey] pénalité f ; **penalty (kick)** FOOTBALL penalty m ; RUGBY (coup m de pied de) pénalité f.

penance ['penəns] n 1. RELIG pénitence f - 2. fig [punishment] corvée f, pensum m.

pence [pens] UK npl ➤ penny.

penchant [UK pãʃã, US 'pentʃənt] n : **to have a penchant for sthg** avoir un faible pour qqch ; **to have a penchant for doing sthg** avoir tendance à OR bien aimer faire qqch.

pencil ['pensl] <> n crayon m ; **in pencil** au crayon. <> vt (UK & US) griffonner au crayon, crayonner.

pencil case n trousse f (d'écolier).

pencil sharpener n taille-crayon m.

pendant ['pendənt] n [jewel on chain] pendentif m.

pending ['pendɪŋ] fml <> adj 1. [imminent] imminent(e) - 2. [court case] en instance. <> prep en attendant.

pendulum ['pendjʊləm] (*pl* **-s**) *n* balancier *m*.

penetrate ['penɪtreɪt] *vt* **1.** [gen] pénétrer dans ; [subj: light] percer ; [subj: rain] s'infiltrer dans - **2.** [subj: spy] infiltrer.

pen friend *n* UK correspondant *m*, -e *f*.

penguin ['peŋgwɪn] *n* manchot *m*.

penicillin [,penɪ'sɪlɪn] *n* pénicilline *f*.

peninsula [pə'nɪnsjʊlə] (*pl* **-s**) *n* péninsule *f*.

penis ['piːnɪs] (*pl* penises [-ɪz]) *n* pénis *m*.

penitentiary [,penɪ'tenʃərɪ] *n* US prison *f*.

penknife ['pennaɪf] (*pl* **-knives** [-naɪvz]) *n* canif *m*.

pen name *n* pseudonyme *m*.

pennant ['penənt] *n* fanion *m*, flamme *f*.

penniless ['penɪlɪs] *adj* sans le sou.

penny ['penɪ] *n* **1.** (*pl* **-ies**) UK [coin] penny *m* ; US cent *m* - **2.** (*pl* **pence** [pens]) UK [value] pence *m*.

pen pal *n inf* correspondant *m*, -e *f*.

pension ['penʃn] *n* **1.** UK [on retirement] retraite *f* - **2.** [from disability] pension *f*.

pensioner ['penʃənər] *n* UK : **(old-age) pensioner** retraité *m*, -e *f*.

pensive ['pensɪv] *adj* songeur(euse).

pentagon ['pentəgən] *n* pentagone *m*.
➭ **Pentagon** *n* US : **the Pentagon** le Pentagone (*siège du ministère américain de la Défense*).

Pentecost ['pentɪkɒst] *n* Pentecôte *f*.

penthouse ['penthaʊs] (*pl* **-hauziz**]) *n* appartement *m* de luxe (au dernier étage).

pent-up ['pent-] *adj* [emotions] refoulé(e) ; [energy] contenu(e).

penultimate [pe'nʌltɪmət] *adj* avant-dernier(ère).

people ['piːpl] <> *n* [nation, race] nation *f*, peuple *m*. <> *npl* **1.** [persons] personnes *fpl* ; few/a lot of people peu/beaucoup de monde, peu/beaucoup de gens ; there were a lot of people present il y avait beaucoup de monde - **2.** [in general] gens *mpl* ; people say that... on dit que... - **3.** [inhabitants] habitants *mpl* - **4.** POL : the people le peuple. <> *vt* : to be peopled by OR with être peuplé(e) de.

people carrier *n* UK monospace *m*.

pep [pep] *n* (*U*) (*U*) *inf* entrain *m*, pep *m*.
➭ **pep up** *vt sep inf* **1.** [person] remonter, requinquer - **2.** [party, event] animer.

pepper ['pepər] *n* **1.** [spice] poivre *m* - **2.** [vegetable] poivron *m*.

pepperbox *n* US = pepper pot.

peppermint ['pepəmɪnt] *n* **1.** [sweet] bonbon *m* à la menthe - **2.** [herb] menthe *f* poivrée.

pepper pot UK, **pepperbox** US ['pepəbɒks] *n* poivrier *m*.

pep talk *n inf* paroles *fpl* OR discours *m* d'encouragement.

per [pɜːr] *prep* : **per person** par personne ; to be paid £10 per hour être payé 10 livres de l'heure ; **per kilo** le kilo ; **as per instructions** conformément aux instructions.

per annum *adv* par an.

per capita [pə'kæpɪtə] *adj & adv* par habitant OR tête.

perceive [pə'siːv] *vt* **1.** [notice] percevoir - **2.** [understand, realize] remarquer, s'apercevoir de - **3.** [consider] : **to perceive sb/sthg as** considérer qqn/qqch comme.

percent *adv* pour cent.

percentage [pə'sentɪdʒ] *n* pourcentage *m*.

perception [pə'sepʃn] *n* **1.** [aural, visual] perception *f* - **2.** [insight] perspicacité *f*, intuition *f*.

perceptive [pə'septɪv] *adj* perspicace.

perch [pɜːtʃ] <> *n* **1.** *lit & fig* [position] perchoir *m* - **2.** (*pl* perch OR **-es**) [fish] perche *f*. <> *vi* se percher.

percolator ['pɜːkəleɪtər] *n* cafetière *f* à pression.

percussion [pə'kʌʃn] *n* MUS percussion *f*.

perennial [pə'renjəl] <> *adj* permanent(e), perpétuel(elle) ; BOT vivace. <> *n* BOT plante *f* vivace.

perfect <> *adj* ['pɜːfɪkt] parfait(e) ; **he's a perfect nuisance** il est absolument insupportable. <> *n* ['pɜːfɪkt] GRAM : **perfect (tense)** parfait *m*. <> *vt* [pə'fekt] parfaire, mettre au point.

perfection [pə'fekʃn] *n* perfection *f* ; **to perfection** parfaitement (bien).

perfectionist [pə'fekʃənɪst] *n* perfectionniste *mf*.

perfectly ['pɜːfɪktlɪ] *adv* parfaitement ; you know perfectly well tu sais très bien.

perforate ['pɜːfəreɪt] *vt* perforer.

perforations [,pɜːfə'reɪʃnz] *npl* [in paper] pointillés *mpl*.

perform [pə'fɔːm] <> *vt* **1.** [carry out - gen] exécuter ; [- function] remplir - **2.** [play, concert] jouer. <> *vi* **1.** [machine] marcher, fonctionner ; [team, person] : **to perform well/badly** avoir de bons/mauvais résultats - **2.** [actor] jouer ; [singer] chanter.

performance [pə'fɔːməns] *n* **1.** [carrying out] exécution *f* - **2.** [show] représentation *f* - **3.** [by actor, singer etc] interprétation *f* - **4.** [of car, engine] performance *f*.

performer [pə'fɔːmər] *n* artiste *mf*, interprète *mf*.

perfume ['pɜːfjuːm] *n* parfum *m*.

perfunctory [pə'fʌŋktərɪ] *adj* rapide, superficiel(elle).

perhaps [pə'hæps] *adv* peut-être ; **perhaps so/not** peut-être que oui/non.

peril ['peril] *n* danger *m*, péril *m*.

perimeter [pə'rimitə'] *n* périmètre *m* ; **perimeter fence** clôture *f* ; **perimeter wall** mur *m* d'enceinte.

period ['piəriəd] <> *n* **1.** [gen] période *f* - **2.** SCH ≃ heure *f* - **3.** [menstruation] règles *fpl* - **4.** US [full stop] point *m*. <> *comp* [dress, house] d'époque.

periodic [,piəri'ɒdik] *adj* périodique.

periodical [,piəri'ɒdikl] <> *adj* = **periodic**. <> *n* [magazine] périodique *m*.

peripheral [pə'rifərəl] <> *adj* **1.** [unimportant] secondaire - **2.** [at edge] périphérique. <> *n* COMPUT périphérique *m*.

perish ['perif] *vi* **1.** [die] périr, mourir - **2.** [food] pourrir, se gâter ; [rubber] se détériorer.

perishable ['perifəbl] *adj* périssable. **perishables** *npl* denrées *fpl* périssables.

perjury ['pɜːdʒəri] *n* (U) LAW parjure *m*, faux témoignage *m*.

perk [pɜːk] *n inf* à-côté *m*, avantage *m*. **perk up** *vi* se ragaillardir.

perky ['pɜːki] *adj inf* [cheerful] guilleret(ette) ; [lively] plein(e) d'entrain.

perm [pɜːm] *n* permanente *f*.

permanent ['pɜːmənənt] <> *adj* permanent(e). <> *n US* [perm] permanente *f*.

permeate ['pɜːmieit] *vt* **1.** [subj: liquid, smell] s'infiltrer dans, pénétrer - **2.** [subj: feeling, idea] se répandre dans.

permissible [pə'misəbl] *adj* acceptable, admissible.

permission [pə'miʃn] *n* permission *f*, autorisation *f*.

permissive [pə'misiv] *adj* permissif(ive).

permit <> *vt* permettre ; **to permit sb to do sthg** permettre à qqn de faire qqch, autoriser qqn à faire qqch ; **to permit sb sthg** permettre qqch à qqn. <> *n* ['pɜːmit] permis *m*.

pernicious [pə'niʃəs] *adj fml* [harmful] pernicieux(euse).

pernickety [pə'nikəti] *adj inf* [fussy] tatillon(onne), pointilleux(euse).

perpendicular [,pɜːpən'dikjulə'] <> *adj* perpendiculaire. <> *n* perpendiculaire *f*.

perpetrate ['pɜːpitreit] *vt* perpétrer, commettre.

perpetual [pə'petʃuəl] *adj* **1.** *pej* [continuous] continuel(elle), incessant(e) - **2.** [long-lasting] perpétuel(elle).

perplex [pə'pleks] *vt* rendre perplexe.

perplexing [pə'pleksiŋ] *adj* déroutant(e), déconcertant(e).

persecute ['pɜːsikjuːt] *vt* persécuter, tourmenter.

perseverance [,pɜːsi'viərəns] *n* persévérance *f*, ténacité *f*.

persevere [,pɜːsi'viə'] *vi* **1.** [with difficulty] persévérer, persister ; **to persevere with** persévérer OR persister dans - **2.** [with determination] : **to persevere in doing sthg** persister à faire qqch.

Persian ['pɜːʃn] *adj* persan(e) ; HIST perse.

persist [pə'sist] *vi* : **to persist (in doing sthg)** persister OR s'obstiner (à faire qqch).

persistence [pə'sistəns] *n* persistance *f*.

persistent [pə'sistənt] *adj* **1.** [noise, rain] continuel(elle) ; [problem] constant(e) - **2.** [determined] tenace, obstiné(e).

person ['pɜːsn] (*pl* **people** ['piːpl] OR **persons**) *fml n* **1.** [man or woman] personne *f* ; **in person** en personne - **2.** *fml* [body] : **about one's person** sur soi.

personable ['pɜːsnəbl] *adj* sympathique, agréable.

personal ['pɜːsənl] *adj* **1.** [gen] personnel(elle) - **2.** *pej* [rude] désobligeant(e).

personal assistant *n* secrétaire *mf* de direction.

personal column *n* petites annonces *fpl*.

personal computer *n* ordinateur *m* personnel OR individuel.

personality [,pɜːsə'næləti] *n* personnalité *f*.

personally ['pɜːsnəli] *adv* personnellement ; **to take sthg personally** se sentir visé par qqch.

personal organizer *n* organiseur *m*.

personal property *n* (U) LAW biens *mpl* personnels.

personal stereo *n* baladeur *m*, Walkman® *m*.

personify [pə'sɒnifai] *vt* personnifier.

personnel [,pɜːsə'nel] <> *n* (U) [department] service *m* du personnel. <> *npl* [staff] personnel *m*.

perspective [pə'spektiv] *n* **1.** ART perspective *f* - **2.** [view, judgment] point *m* de vue, optique *f*.

Perspex® ['pɜːspeks] *n UK* ≃ Plexiglas® *m*.

perspiration [,pɜːspə'reiʃn] *n* **1.** [sweat] sueur *f* - **2.** [act of perspiring] transpiration *f*.

persuade [pə'sweid] *vt* : **to persuade sb to do sthg** persuader OR convaincre qqn de faire qqch ; **to persuade sb that** convaincre qqn que ; **to persuade sb of** convaincre qqn de.

persuasion [pə'sweiʒn] *n* **1.** [act of persuading] **persuasion** f - **2.** [belief - religious] confession f ; [- political] opinion f, conviction f.

persuasive [pə'sweɪsɪv] adj [person] persuasif(ive) ; [argument] convaincant(e).

pert [pɜːt] adj mutin(e), coquin(e).

pertain [pə'teɪn] vi fml : **pertaining to** concernant, relatif(ive) à.

pertinent ['pɜːtɪnənt] adj pertinent(e), approprié(e).

perturb [pə'tɜːb] vt inquiéter, troubler.

Peru [pə'ruː] n Pérou m.

peruse [pə'ruːz] vt lire attentivement.

pervade [pə'veɪd] vt [subj: smell] se répandre dans ; [subj: feeling, influence] envahir.

perverse [pə'vɜːs] adj [contrary - person] contrariant(e) ; [- enjoyment] malin(igne).

perversion [UK pə'vɜːʃn, US pə'vɜːrʒn] n **1.** [sexual] perversion f - **2.** [of truth] travestissement m.

pervert ◇ n ['pɜːvɜːt] pervers m, -e f ◇ vt [pə'vɜːt] **1.** [truth, meaning] travestir, déformer ; [course of justice] entraver - **2.** [sexually] pervertir.

pessimist ['pesɪmɪst] n pessimiste mf.

pessimistic [ˌpesɪ'mɪstɪk] adj pessimiste.

pest [pest] n **1.** [insect] insecte m nuisible ; [animal] animal m nuisible - **2.** inf [nuisance] casse-pieds mf inv.

pester ['pestər] vt harceler, importuner.

pet [pet] ◇ adj [favourite] : **pet subject** dada m ; **pet hate** bête f noire. ◇ n **1.** [animal] animal m (familier) - **2.** [favourite person] chouchou m, -oute f. ◇ vt caresser, câliner. ◇ vi se peloter, se caresser.

petal ['petl] n pétale m.

peter ['piːtər] ⏵ **peter out** vi [path] s'arrêter, se perdre ; [interest] diminuer, décliner.

petite [pə'tiːt] adj menu(e).

petition [pɪ'tɪʃn] ◇ n pétition f. ◇ vt adresser une pétition à.

petrified ['petrɪfaɪd] adj [terrified] paralysé(e) OR pétrifié(e) de peur.

petrol ['petrəl] n UK essence f.

petrol bomb n UK cocktail m Molotov.

petrol can n UK bidon m à essence.

petroleum [pɪ'trəʊljəm] n pétrole m.

petrol pump n UK pompe f à essence.

petrol station n UK station-service f.

petrol tank n UK réservoir m d'essence.

pet shop n animalerie f.

petticoat ['petɪkəʊt] n jupon m.

petty ['petɪ] adj **1.** [small-minded] mesquin(e) - **2.** [trivial] insignifiant(e), sans importance.

petty cash n (U) caisse f des dépenses courantes.

petty officer n second maître m.

petulant ['petjʊlənt] adj irritable.

pew [pjuː] n banc m d'église.

pewter ['pjuːtər] n étain m.

phantom ['fæntəm] ◇ adj fantomatique, spectral(e). ◇ n [ghost] fantôme m.

pharmaceutical [ˌfɑːmə'sjuːtɪkl] adj pharmaceutique.

pharmacist ['fɑːməsɪst] n pharmacien m, -enne f.

pharmacy ['fɑːməsɪ] n pharmacie f.

phase [feɪz] n phase f. ⏵ **phase in** vt sep introduire progressivement. ⏵ **phase out** vt sep supprimer progressivement.

PhD (abbrev of Doctor of Philosophy) n (titulaire d'un) doctorat de 3ᵉ cycle.

pheasant ['feznt] (pl pheasant OR -s) n faisan m.

phenomena [fɪ'nɒmɪnə] npl ⏵ phenomenon.

phenomenal [fɪ'nɒmɪnl] adj phénoménal(e), extraordinaire.

phenomenon [fɪ'nɒmɪnən] (pl -mena [-mɪnə]) n phénomène m.

phial ['faɪəl] n fiole f.

philanthropist [fɪ'lænθrəpɪst] n philanthrope mf.

philately [fɪ'lætəlɪ] n philatélie f.

Philippine ['fɪlɪpiːn] adj philippin(e). ⏵ **Philippines** npl : **the Philippines** les Philippines fpl.

philosopher [fɪ'lɒsəfər] n philosophe mf.

philosophical [ˌfɪlə'sɒfɪkl] adj **1.** [gen] philosophique - **2.** [stoical] philosophe.

philosophy [fɪ'lɒsəfɪ] n philosophie f.

phlegm [flem] n flegme m.

phlegmatic [fleg'mætɪk] adj flegmatique.

phobia ['fəʊbjə] n phobie f.

phone [fəʊn] ◇ n téléphone m ; **to be on the phone** [speaking] être au téléphone ; UK [connected to network] avoir le téléphone. ◇ comp téléphonique. ◇ vt téléphoner à, appeler. ◇ vi téléphoner. ⏵ **phone up** vt sep & vi UK téléphoner.

phone book n annuaire m (du téléphone).

phone booth, **phone box** UK n cabine f téléphonique.

phone call n coup m de téléphone OR fil ; **to make a phone call** passer OR donner un coup de fil.

phonecard ['fəʊnkɑːd] n ≃ Télécarte® f.

phone-in *n* RADIO & TV programme *m* à ligne ouverte.

phone number *n* numéro *m* de téléphone.

phonetics [fə'netɪks] *n (U)* phonétique *f*.

phoney, phony *US inf* ['fəʊnɪ] ⬦ *adj*
1. [passport, address] bidon *(inv)* - **2.** [person] hypocrite, pas franc (pas franche). ⬦ *n* poseur *m*, -euse *f*.

phosphorus ['fɒsfərəs] *n* phosphore *m*.

photo ['fəʊtəʊ] *n* photo *f* ; **to take a photo of sb/sthg** photographier qqn/qqch, prendre qqn/qqch en photo.

photocopier ['fəʊtəʊ,kɒpɪə*r*] *n* photocopieur *m*, copieur *m*.

photocopy ['fəʊtəʊ,kɒpɪ] ⬦ *n* photocopie *f*. ⬦ *vt* photocopier.

photograph ['fəʊtəgrɑːf] ⬦ *n* photographie *f* ; **to take a photograph (of sb/sthg)** prendre (qqn/qqch) en photo, photographier (qqn/qqch). ⬦ *vt* photographier, prendre en photo.

photographer [fə'tɒgrəfə*r*] *n* photographe *mf*.

photography [fə'tɒgrəfɪ] *n* photographie *f*.

photoshoot ['fəʊtəʊʃuːt] *n* prise *f* de vue.

phrasal verb ['freɪzl-] *n* verbe *m* à postposition.

phrase [freɪz] ⬦ *n* expression *f*. ⬦ *vt* exprimer, tourner.

phrasebook ['freɪzbʊk] *n* guide *m* de conversation *(pour touristes)*.

physical ['fɪzɪkl] ⬦ *adj* **1.** [gen] physique - **2.** [world, objects] matériel(elle). ⬦ *n* [examination] visite *f* médicale.

physical education *n* éducation *f* physique.

physically ['fɪzɪklɪ] *adv* physiquement.

physically handicapped ⬦ *adj* : **to be physically handicapped** être handicapé(e) physique. ⬦ *npl* : **the physically handicapped** les handicapés *mpl* physiques.

physician [fɪ'zɪʃn] *n* médecin *m*.

physicist ['fɪzɪsɪst] *n* physicien *m*, -enne *f*.

physics ['fɪzɪks] *n (U)* physique *f*.

physiotherapy [,fɪzɪəʊ'θerəpɪ] *n* kinésithérapie *f*.

physique [fɪ'ziːk] *n* physique *m*.

pianist ['pɪənɪst] *n* pianiste *mf*.

piano [pɪ'ænəʊ] *(pl* **-s)** *n* piano *m*.

pick [pɪk] ⬦ *n* **1.** [tool] pioche *f*, pic *m* - **2.** [selection] : **to take one's pick** choisir, faire son choix - **3.** [best] : **the pick of** le meilleur (la meilleure) (de). ⬦ *vt* **1.** [select, choose] choisir, sélectionner - **2.** [gather] cueillir - **3.** [remove] enlever - **4.** [nose] : **to pick one's nose** se décrotter le nez ; **to pick**

one's teeth se curer les dents - **5.** [fight, quarrel] chercher ; **to pick a fight (with sb)** chercher la bagarre (à qqn) - **6.** [lock] crocheter. ⬥ **pick on** *vt insep* s'en prendre à, être sur le dos de. ⬥ **pick out** *vt sep* **1.** [recognize] repérer, reconnaître - **2.** [select, choose] choisir, désigner. ⬥ **pick up** ⬦ *vt sep* **1.** [lift up] ramasser - **2.** [collect] aller chercher, passer prendre - **3.** [collect in car] prendre, chercher - **4.** [skill, language] apprendre ; [habit] prendre ; [bargain] découvrir ; **to pick up speed** prendre de la vitesse - **5.** *inf* [sexually - woman, man] draguer - **6.** RADIO & TELEC [detect, receive] capter, recevoir - **7.** [conversation, work] reprendre, continuer. ⬦ *vi* [improve, start again] reprendre.

pickaxe *UK*, **pickax** *US* ['pɪkæks] *n* pioche *f*, pic *m*.

picket ['pɪkɪt] ⬦ *n* piquet *m* de grève. ⬦ *vt* mettre un piquet de grève devant.

picket line *n* piquet *m* de grève.

pickle ['pɪkl] ⬦ *n* [in the UK] pickles *mpl* ; [in the US] cornichon *m* ; **to be in a pickle** être dans le pétrin. ⬦ *vt* conserver dans du vinaigre, de la saumure *etc*.

pickpocket ['pɪk,pɒkɪt] *n* pickpocket *m*, voleur *m* à la tire.

pick-up *n* **1.** [of record player] pick-up *m* - **2.** [truck] camionnette *f*.

picnic ['pɪknɪk] ⬦ *n* pique-nique *m*. ⬦ *vi* *(pt & pp* **-ked**, *cont* **-king)** pique-niquer.

pictorial [pɪk'tɔːrɪəl] *adj* illustré(e).

picture ['pɪktʃə*r*] ⬦ *n* **1.** [painting] tableau *m*, peinture *f* ; [drawing] dessin *m* - **2.** [photograph] photo *f*, photographie *f* - **3.** TV image *f* - **4.** CIN film *m* - **5.** [in mind] tableau *m*, image *f* - **6.** *fig* [situation] tableau *m* ; **to get the picture** *inf* piger ; **to put sb in the picture** mettre qqn au courant. ⬦ *vt* **1.** [in mind] imaginer, s'imaginer, se représenter - **2.** [in photo] photographier - **3.** [in painting] représenter, peindre. ⬥ **pictures** *npl* *UK* : **the pictures** le cinéma.

picture book *n* livre *m* d'images.

picturesque [,pɪktʃə'resk] *adj* pittoresque.

pie [paɪ] *n* *UK* [savoury] tourte *f* ; [sweet] tarte *f*.

piece [piːs] *n* **1.** [gen] morceau *m* ; [of string] bout *m* ; **a piece of furniture** un meuble ; **a piece of clothing** un vêtement ; **a piece of advice** un conseil ; **a piece of information** un renseignement ; **to fall to pieces** tomber en morceaux ; **to take sthg to pieces** démonter qqch ; **in pieces** en morceaux ; **in one piece** [intact] intact(e) ; [unharmed] sain et sauf (saine et sauve) - **2.** [coin, item, in chess] pièce *f*; [in draughts] pion *m* - 3. PRESS article *m*. ➤ **piece together** *vt sep* [facts] coordonner.

piecemeal ['pi:smi:l] ◇ *adj* fait(e) petit à petit. ◇ *adv* petit à petit, peu à peu.

piecework ['pi:swɜːk] *n (U)* travail *m* à la pièce OR aux pièces.

pie chart *n* camembert *m*, graphique *m* rond.

pier [pɪə^r] *n* [at seaside] jetée *f*.

pierce [pɪəs] *vt* percer, transpercer; **to have one's ears pierced** se faire percer les oreilles.

piercing ['pɪəsɪŋ] *adj* **1.** [sound, look] perçant(e) - **2.** [wind] pénétrant(e).

pig [pɪg] *n* **1.** [animal] porc *m*, cochon *m* - **2.** *inf pej* [greedy eater] goinfre *m*, glouton *m* - **3.** *inf pej* [unkind person] sale type *m*.

pigeon ['pɪdʒɪn] *(pl* pigeon OR *-s) n* pigeon *m*.

pigeonhole ['pɪdʒɪnhəʊl] ◇ *n* [compartment] casier *m*. ◇ *vt* [classify] étiqueter, cataloguer.

piggy bank ['pɪgɪbæŋk] *n* tirelire *f*.

pigheaded [,pɪg'hedɪd] *adj* têtu(e).

pigment ['pɪgmənt] *n* pigment *m*.

pigpen *US =* pigsty.

pigskin ['pɪgskɪn] *n* (peau *f* de) porc *m*.

pigsty ['pɪgstaɪ], *US* **pigpen** ['pɪgpen] *n lit & fig* porcherie *f*.

pigtail ['pɪgteɪl] *n* natte *f*.

pike [paɪk] *(pl sense 1 only* pike) *n* **1.** *(pl* pike) [fish] brochet *m* - **2.** [spear] pique *f*.

pilchard ['pɪltʃəd] *n* pilchard *m*.

pile [paɪl] ◇ *n* **1.** [heap] tas *m*; **a pile of, piles of** un tas OR des tas de - **2.** [neat stack] pile *f* - **3.** [of carpet] poil *m*. ◇ *vt* empiler. ➤ **piles** *npl* MED hémorroïdes *fpl*. ➤ **pile into** *vt insep inf* s'entasser dans, s'empiler dans. ➤ **pile up** ◇ *vt sep* empiler, entasser. ◇ *vi* **1.** [form a heap] s'entasser - **2.** *fig* [work, debts] s'accumuler.

pileup ['paɪlʌp] *n* AUT carambolage *m*.

pilfer ['pɪlfə^r] ◇ *vt* chaparder. ◇ *vi* : **to pilfer (from)** faire du chapardage (dans).

pilgrim ['pɪlgrɪm] *n* pèlerin *m*.

pilgrimage ['pɪlgrɪmɪdʒ] *n* pèlerinage *m*.

pill [pɪl] *n* **1.** [gen] pilule *f* - **2.** [contraceptive] : **the pill** la pilule ; **to be on the pill** prendre la pilule.

pillage ['pɪlɪdʒ] *vt* piller.

pillar ['pɪlə^r] *n lit & fig* pilier *m*.

pillar box *n UK* boîte *f* aux lettres.

pillion ['pɪljən] *n* siège *m* arrière ; **to ride pillion** monter derrière.

pillow ['pɪləʊ] *n* **1.** [for bed] oreiller *m* - **2.** *US* [on sofa, chair] coussin *m*.

pillowcase ['pɪləʊkeɪs], **pillowslip** ['pɪləʊslɪp] *n* taie *f* d'oreiller.

pilot ['paɪlət] ◇ *n* **1.** AERON & NAUT pilote *mf* - **2.** TV émission *f* pilote. ◇ *comp* pilote. ◇ *vt* piloter.

pilot burner, pilot light *n* veilleuse *f*.

pilot study *n* étude *f* pilote OR expérimentale.

pimp [pɪmp] *n inf* maquereau *m*, souteneur *m*.

pimple ['pɪmpl] *n* bouton *m*.

pin [pɪn] ◇ *n* **1.** [for sewing] épingle *f*; **to have pins and needles** avoir des fourmis - **2.** *US* [brooch] broche *f* - **3.** *UK* [drawing pin] punaise *f* - **4.** [safety pin] épingle *f* de nourrice OR de sûreté - **5.** [of plug] fiche *f* - **6.** TECH goupille *f*, cheville *f*. ◇ *vt* : **to pin sthg to/on sthg** épingler qqch à/sur qqch ; **to pin sb against** OR **to clouer qqn contre** ; **to pin sthg on sb** [blame] mettre OR coller qqch sur le dos de qqn ; **to pin one's hopes on sb/sthg** mettre tous ses espoirs en qqn/dans qqch. ➤ **pin down** *vt sep* **1.** [identify] définir, identifier - **2.** [force to make a decision] : **to pin sb down** obliger qqn à prendre une décision.

pinafore ['pɪnəfɔː^r] *n* **1.** [apron] tablier *m* - **2.** *UK* [dress] chasuble *f*.

pinball ['pɪnbɔːl] *n* flipper *m*.

pincers ['pɪnsəz] *npl* **1.** [tool] tenailles *fpl* - **2.** [of crab] pinces *fpl*.

pinch [pɪntʃ] ◇ *n* **1.** [nip] pincement *m* - **2.** [of salt] pincée *f*. ◇ *vt* **1.** [nip] pincer - **2.** [subj: shoes] serrer - **3.** *UK inf* [steal] piquer, faucher. ➤ **at a pinch** *UK*, **in a pinch** *US adv* à la rigueur.

pincushion ['pɪn,kʊʃn] *n* pelote *f* à épingles.

pine [paɪn] ◇ *n* pin *m*. ◇ *vi* : **to pine for** désirer ardemment. ➤ **pine away** *vi* languir.

pineapple ['paɪnæpl] *n* ananas *m*.

pinetree ['paɪntriː] *n* pin *m*.

ping [pɪŋ] *n* [of bell] tintement *m* ; [of metal] bruit *m* métallique.

Ping-Pong® [-pɒŋ] *n* ping-pong *m*.

pink [pɪŋk] ◇ *adj* rose ; **to go** OR **turn pink** rosir, rougir. ◇ *n* [colour] rose *m*.

pinkeye *US =* conjunctivitis.

pinnacle ['pɪnəkl] *n* **1.** [mountain peak, spire] pic *m*, cime *f* - **2.** *fig* [high point] apogée *m*.

pinpoint ['pɪnpɔɪnt] *vt* **1.** [cause, problem] définir, mettre le doigt sur - **2.** [position] localiser.

pin-striped [-,straɪpt] *adj* à très fines rayures.

pint [paɪnt] *n* **1.** *UK* [unit of measurement] =

0,568 litre, ≃ demi-litre *m* - **2.** *US* [unit of measurement] = *0,473 litre,* ≃ demi-litre *m* - **3.** *UK* [beer] ≃ demi *m*.

pioneer [ˌpaɪə'nɪəʳ] ◇ *n lit & fig* pionnier *m*. ◇ *vt* : **to pioneer sthg** être un des premiers (une des premières) à faire qqch.

pious ['paɪəs] *adj* **1.** RELIG pieux (pieuse) - **2.** *pej* [sanctimonious] moralisateur(trice).

pip [pɪp] *n* **1.** [seed] pépin *m* - **2.** *UK* RADIO top *m*.

pipe [paɪp] ◇ *n* **1.** [for gas, water] tuyau *m* - **2.** [for smoking] pipe *f*. ◇ *vt* acheminer par tuyau. ◆ **pipes** *npl* MUS cornemuse *f*.
◆ **pipe down** *vi inf* se taire, la fermer.
◆ **pipe up** *vi inf* se faire entendre.

pipe cleaner *n* cure-pipe *m*.

pipe dream *n* projet *m* chimérique.

pipeline ['paɪplaɪn] *n* [for gas] gazoduc *m* ; [for oil] oléoduc *m*, pipeline *m*.

piper ['paɪpəʳ] *n* joueur *m*, -euse *f* de cornemuse.

piping hot ['paɪpɪŋ-] *adj* bouillant(e).

pique [pi:k] *n* dépit *m*.

pirate ['paɪrət] ◇ *adj* [video, program] pirate. ◇ *n* pirate *m*. ◇ *vt* [video, program] pirater.

pirate radio *n UK* radio *f* pirate.

pirouette [ˌpɪru'et] ◇ *n* pirouette *f*. ◇ *vi* pirouetter.

Pisces ['paɪsi:z] *n* Poissons *mpl*.

piss [pɪs] *vulg* ◇ *n* [urine] pisse *f*. ◇ *vi* pisser.

pissed [pɪst] *adj vulg* **1.** *UK* [drunk] bourré(e) - **2.** *US* [annoyed] en boule.

pissed off *adj vulg* qui en a plein le cul.

pistol ['pɪstl] *n* pistolet *m*.

piston ['pɪstən] *n* piston *m*.

pit [pɪt] ◇ *n* **1.** [hole] trou *m* ; [in road] petit trou ; [on face] marque *f* - **2.** [for orchestra] fosse *f* - **3.** [mine] mine *f* - **4.** *US* [of fruit] noyau *m*. ◇ *vt* : **to pit sb against sb** opposer qqn à qqn. ◆ **pits** *npl* [in motor racing] : **the pits** les stands *mpl*.

pitch [pɪtʃ] ◇ *n* **1.** *UK* SPORT terrain *m* - **2.** MUS ton *m* - **3.** [level, degree] degré *m* - **4.** *UK* [selling place] place *f* - **5.** *inf* [sales talk] baratin *m*. ◇ *vt* **1.** [throw] lancer - **2.** [set - price] fixer ; [- speech] adapter - **3.** [tent] dresser ; [camp] établir. ◇ *vi* **1.** [ball] rebondir - **2.** [fall] : **to pitch forward** être projeté(e) en avant - **3.** AERON & NAUT tanguer.

pitch-black *adj* : **it's pitch-black in here** il fait noir comme dans un four.

pitched battle [ˌpɪtʃt-] *n* bataille *f* rangée.

pitcher ['pɪtʃəʳ] *n US* **1.** [jug] cruche *f* - **2.** [in baseball] lanceur *m*.

pitchfork ['pɪtʃfɔːk] *n* fourche *f*.

piteous ['pɪtɪəs] *adj* pitoyable.

pitfall ['pɪtfɔːl] *n* piège *m*.

pith [pɪθ] *n* **1.** [in plant] moelle *f* - **2.** [of fruit] peau *f* blanche.

pithy ['pɪθɪ] *adj* [brief] concis(e) ; [terse] piquant(e).

pitiful ['pɪtɪfʊl] *adj* [condition] pitoyable ; [excuse, effort] lamentable.

pitiless ['pɪtɪlɪs] *adj* sans pitié, impitoyable.

pit stop *n* **1.** [in motor racing] arrêt *m* aux stands - **2.** *US hum* arrêt *m* pipi.

pittance ['pɪtəns] *n* [wage] salaire *m* de misère.

pity ['pɪtɪ] ◇ *n* pitié *f* ; **what a pity!** quel dommage! ; **it's a pity** c'est dommage ; **to take** OR **have pity on sb** prendre qqn en pitié, avoir pitié de qqn. ◇ *vt* plaindre.

pivot ['pɪvət] *n lit & fig* pivot *m*.

pizza ['pi:tsə] *n* pizza *f*.

placard ['plækɑːd] *n* placard *m*, affiche *f*.

placate [plə'keɪt] *vt* calmer, apaiser.

place [pleɪs] ◇ *n* **1.** [location] endroit *m*, lieu *m* ; **place of birth** lieu de naissance - **2.** [proper position, seat, vacancy, rank] place *f* - **3.** [home] : **at/to my place** chez moi - **4.** [in book] : **to lose one's place** perdre sa page - **5.** MATHS : **decimal place** décimale *f* - **6.** [instance] : **in the first place** tout de suite ; **in the first place... and in the second place...** premièrement... et deuxièmement... ; **to take place** avoir lieu ; **to take the place of** prendre la place de, remplacer. ◇ *vt* **1.** [position, put] placer, mettre - **2.** [apportion] : **to place the responsibility for sthg on sb** tenir qqn pour responsable de qqch - **3.** [identify] remettre - **4.** [an order] passer ; **to place a bet** parier - **5.** [in race] : **to be placed** être placé(e). ◆ **all over the place** *adv* partout. ◆ **in place** *adv* **1.** [in proper position] à sa place - **2.** [established] mis en place. ◆ **in place of** *prep* à la place de. ◆ **out of place** *adv* pas à sa place ; *fig* déplacé(e).

place mat *n* set *m* (de table).

placement ['pleɪsmənt] *n* placement *m*.

placid ['plæsɪd] *adj* **1.** [person] placide - **2.** [sea, place] calme.

plagiarize, *UK* **-ise** ['pleɪdʒəraɪz] *vt* plagier.

plague [pleɪg] ◇ *n* **1.** MED peste *f* - **2.** *fig* [nuisance] fléau *m*. ◇ *vt* : **to be plagued by** [bad luck] être poursuivi(e) par ; [doubt] être rongé(e) par ; **to plague sb with questions** harceler qqn de questions.

plaice [pleɪs] (*pl* **plaice**) *n* carrelet *m*.

plaid [plæd] *n* plaid *m*.

Plaid Cymru [ˌplaɪd'kʌmrɪ] *n* parti nationaliste gallois.

plain [pleɪn] <> adj **1.** [not patterned] uni(e) - **2.** [simple] simple - **3.** [clear] clair(e), évident(e) - **4.** [blunt] carré(e), franc (franche) - **5.** [absolute] pur(e) (et simple) - **6.** [not pretty] quelconque, ordinaire. <> adv inf complètement. <> n GEOG plaine f.

plain chocolate n UK chocolat m à croquer.

plain-clothes adj en civil.

plain flour n UK farine f (sans levure).

plainly ['pleɪnlɪ] adv **1.** [obviously] manifestement - **2.** [frankly] carrément, sans détours - **3.** [distinctly] clairement - **4.** [simply] simplement.

plaintiff ['pleɪntɪf] n demandeur m, -eresse f.

plait [plæt] <> n natte f. <> vt natter, tresser.

plan [plæn] <> n plan m, projet m ; **to go according to plan** se passer OR aller comme prévu. <> vt **1.** [organize] préparer - **2.** [intend] : **to plan to do sthg** projeter de faire qqch, avoir l'intention de faire qqch - **3.** [design] concevoir. <> vi : **to plan (for sthg)** faire des projets (pour qqch).
◆ **plans** npl plans mpl, projets mpl ; **have you any plans for tonight?** avez-vous prévu quelque chose pour ce soir ? ◆ **plan on** vt insep : **to plan on doing sthg** prévoir de faire qqch.

plane [pleɪn] <> adj plan(e). <> n **1.** [aircraft] avion m - **2.** GEOM plan m - **3.** fig [level] niveau m - **4.** [tool] rabot m - **5.** [tree] platane m.

planet ['plænɪt] n planète f.

plank [plæŋk] n **1.** [of wood] planche f - **2.** POL [policy] point m.

planning ['plænɪŋ] n **1.** [designing] planification f - **2.** [preparation] préparation f, organisation f.

planning permission n UK permis m de construire.

plant [plɑːnt] <> n **1.** BOT plante f - **2.** [factory] usine f - **3.** (U) [heavy machinery] matériel m. <> vt **1.** [gen] planter - **2.** [bomb] poser.

plantation [plæn'teɪʃn] n plantation f.

plaque [plɑːk] n **1.** [commemorative sign] plaque f - **2.** (U) [on teeth] plaque f dentaire.

plaster ['plɑːstər] <> n **1.** [material] plâtre m - **2.** UK [bandage] pansement m adhésif. <> vt **1.** [wall, ceiling] plâtrer - **2.** [cover] : **to plaster sthg (with)** couvrir qqch (de).

plaster cast n **1.** [for broken bones] plâtre m - **2.** [model, statue] moule m.

plastered ['plɑːstəd] adj inf [drunk] bourré(e).

plasterer ['plɑːstərər] n plâtrier m.

plaster of Paris n plâtre m de moulage.

plastic ['plæstɪk] <> adj plastique. <> n [material] plastique m.

Plasticine® UK ['plæstɪsiːn] n pâte f à modeler.

plastic surgery n chirurgie f esthétique OR plastique.

plastic wrap n US film m alimentaire.

plate [pleɪt] <> n **1.** [dish] assiette f - **2.** [sheet of metal, plaque] tôle f - **3.** (U) [metal covering] : **gold/silver plate** plaqué m or/argent - **4.** [in book] planche f - **5.** [in dentistry] dentier m. <> vt : **to be plated (with)** être plaqué(e) (de).

plateau ['plætəʊ] (pl **-s** OR **-x** [-z]) n plateau m ; fig phase f OR période f de stabilité.

plate-glass adj vitré(e).

platform ['plætfɔːm] n **1.** [stage] estrade f ; [for speaker] tribune f - **2.** [raised structure, of bus, of political party] plate-forme f - **3.** RAIL quai m.

platform ticket n UK ticket m de quai.

platinum ['plætɪnəm] n platine m.

platoon [plə'tuːn] n section f.

platter ['plætər] n [dish] plat m.

plausible ['plɔːzəbl] adj plausible.

play [pleɪ] <> n **1.** (U) [amusement] jeu m, amusement m - **2.** THEAT pièce f (de théâtre) ; **a radio play** une pièce radiophonique - **3.** [game] : **play on words** jeu m de mots - **4.** TECH jeu m. <> vt **1.** [gen] jouer ; **to play a part** OR **role in** fig jouer un rôle dans - **2.** [game, sport] jouer à - **3.** [team, opponent] jouer contre - **4.** MUS [instrument] jouer de ; **to play it safe** ne pas prendre de risques. <> vi jouer. ◆ **play along** vi : **to play along (with sb)** entrer dans le jeu (de qqn). ◆ **play down** vt sep minimiser. ◆ **play up** <> vt sep [emphasize] insister sur. <> vi UK **1.** [machine] faire des siennes - **2.** [child] ne pas être sage.

play-act vi jouer la comédie.

playboy ['pleɪbɔɪ] n playboy m.

play dough US pâte f à modeler.

player ['pleɪər] n **1.** [gen] joueur m, -euse f - **2.** THEAT acteur m, -trice f.

playful ['pleɪfʊl] adj **1.** [person, mood] taquin(e) - **2.** [kitten, puppy] joueur(euse).

playground ['pleɪgraʊnd] n **1.** UK cour f de récréation - **2.** [in park] aire f de jeu.

playgroup ['pleɪgruːp] n UK jardin m d'enfants.

playing card ['pleɪɪŋ-] n carte f à jouer.

playing field ['pleɪɪŋ-] n terrain m de sport.

playmate ['pleɪmeɪt] n camarade mf.

playoff n **1.** SPORT belle f - **2.** US finale f de championnat.

playpen ['pleɪpen] n parc m.

playschool ['pleɪskuːl] *n UK* jardin *m* d'enfants.

plaything ['pleɪθɪŋ] *n lit & fig* jouet *m*.

playtime ['pleɪtaɪm] *n UK* récréation *f*.

playwright ['pleɪraɪt] *n* dramaturge *m*.

plc *UK abbrev of* **public limited company.**

plea [pliː] *n* **1.** [for forgiveness, mercy] supplication *f* ; [for help, quiet] appel *m* - **2.** LAW : **to enter a plea of not guilty** plaider non coupable.

plead [pliːd] (*pt & pp* **-ed** OR **pled**) <> *vt* **1.** LAW plaider - **2.** [give as excuse] invoquer. <> *vi* **1.** [beg] : **to plead with sb (to do sthg)** supplier qqn (de faire qqch) ; **to plead for sthg** implorer qqch - **2.** LAW plaider.

pleasant ['pleznt] *adj* agréable.

pleasantry ['plezntrɪ] *n* : **to exchange pleasantries** échanger des propos aimables.

please [pliːz] <> *vt* plaire à, faire plaisir à ; **to please o.s.** faire comme on veut ; **please yourself!** comme vous voulez! <> *vi* plaire, faire plaisir ; **to do as one pleases** faire comme on veut. <> *adv* s'il vous plaît.

pleased [pliːzd] *adj* **1.** [satisfied] : **to be pleased (with)** être content(e) (de) - **2.** [happy] : **to be pleased (about)** être heureux(euse) (de) ; **pleased to meet you!** enchanté(e) !

pleasing ['pliːzɪŋ] *adj* plaisant(e).

pleasure ['pleʒər] *n* plaisir *m* ; **with pleasure** avec plaisir, volontiers ; **it's a pleasure, my pleasure** je vous en prie.

pleat [pliːt] <> *n* pli *m*. <> *vt* plisser.

pled [pled] *pt & pp* > **plead.**

pledge [pledʒ] <> *n* **1.** [promise] promesse *f* - **2.** [token] gage *m*. <> *vt* **1.** [promise] promettre - **2.** [make promise] : **to pledge o.s. to** s'engager à ; **to pledge sb to secrecy** faire promettre le secret à qqn - **3.** [pawn] mettre en gage.

plentiful ['plentɪfʊl] *adj* abondant(e).

plenty ['plentɪ] <> *n (U)* abondance *f*. <> *pron* : **plenty of** beaucoup de ; **we've got plenty of time** nous avons largement le temps. <> *adv US* [very] très.

pliable ['plaɪəbl], **pliant** ['plaɪənt] *adj* **1.** [material] pliable, souple - **2.** *fig* [person] docile.

pliers ['plaɪəz] *npl* tenailles *fpl*, pinces *fpl*.

plight [plaɪt] *n* condition *f* critique.

plimsoll ['plɪmsəl] *n UK* tennis *m*.

plinth [plɪnθ] *n* socle *m*.

PLO (*abbrev of* **Palestine Liberation Organization**) *n* OLP *f*.

plod [plɒd] *vi* **1.** [walk slowly] marcher lentement OR péniblement - **2.** [work slowly] peiner.

plodder ['plɒdər] *n pej* bûcheur *m*, -euse *f*.

plonk [plɒŋk] *n (U) UK inf* [wine] pinard *m*, vin *m* ordinaire. **plonk down** *vt sep inf* poser brutalement.

plot [plɒt] <> *n* **1.** [plan] complot *m*, conspiration *f* - **2.** [story] intrigue *f* - **3.** [of land] (parcelle *f* de) terrain *m*, lopin *m*. <> *vt* **1.** [plan] comploter ; **to plot to do sthg** comploter de faire qqch - **2.** [chart] déterminer, marquer - **3.** MATHS tracer, marquer. <> *vi* comploter.

plotter ['plɒtər] *n* [schemer] conspirateur *m*, -trice *f*.

plough *UK*, **plow** *US* [plaʊ] <> *n* charrue *f*. <> *vt* [field] labourer. **plough into** <> *vt sep* [money] investir. <> *vt insep* [subj: car] rentrer dans.

ploughman's ['plaʊmənz] (*pl* **ploughman's**) *n UK* : **ploughman's (lunch)** *repas de pain, fromage et pickles.*

plow *etc US* = **plough** *etc.*

ploy [plɔɪ] *n* stratagème *m*, ruse *f*.

pls (*abbrev of* **please**) *adv* [in an email] svp.

pluck [plʌk] <> *vt* **1.** [flower, fruit] cueillir - **2.** [pull sharply] arracher - **3.** [chicken, turkey] plumer - **4.** [eyebrows] épiler - **5.** MUS pincer. <> *n (U) dated* courage *m*, cran *m*. **pluck up** *vt insep* : **to pluck up the courage to do sthg** rassembler son courage pour faire qqch.

plucky ['plʌkɪ] *adj dated* qui a du cran, courageux(euse).

plug [plʌg] <> *n* **1.** ELEC prise *f* de courant - **2.** *US* TELEC jack *m* - **3.** [for bath, sink] bonde *f*. <> *vt* **1.** [hole] boucher, obturer - **2.** *inf* [new book, film etc] faire de la publicité pour. **plug away** *vi insep* travailler dur. **plug in** *vt sep* brancher.

plughole ['plʌghəʊl] *n* bonde *f*, trou *m* d'écoulement.

plum [plʌm] <> *adj* **1.** [colour] prune (*inv*) - **2.** [very good] : **a plum job** un poste en or. <> *n* [fruit] prune *f*.

plumb [plʌm] <> *adv* **1.** *UK* [exactly] exactement, en plein - **2.** *US* [completely] complètement. <> *vt* : **to plumb the depths of** toucher le fond de.

plumber ['plʌmər] *n* plombier *m*.

plumbing ['plʌmɪŋ] *n (U)* **1.** [fittings] plomberie *f*, tuyauterie *f* - **2.** [work] plomberie *f*.

plume [pluːm] *n* **1.** [feather] plume *f* - **2.** [on hat] panache *m* - **3.** [column] : **a plume of smoke** un panache de fumée.

plummet ['plʌmɪt] *vi* **1.** [bird, plane] plonger - **2.** *fig* [decrease] dégringoler.

plump [plʌmp] *adj* bien en chair, grassouillet(ette). **plump for** *vt insep* opter pour, choisir. **plump up** *vt sep* [cushion] secouer.

plum pudding *n* pudding *m* de Noël.

plunder ['plʌndər] ⟨⟩ n (U) **1.** [stealing, raiding] pillage m - **2.** [stolen goods] butin m. ⟨⟩ vt piller.

plunge [plʌndʒ] ⟨⟩ n **1.** [dive] plongeon m ; **to take the plunge** se jeter à l'eau - **2.** fig [decrease] dégringolade f, chute f. ⟨⟩ vt : **to plunge sthg into** plonger qqch dans. ⟨⟩ vi **1.** [dive] plonger, tomber - **2.** fig [decrease] dégringoler.

plunger ['plʌndʒər] n débouchoir m à ventouse.

pluperfect [ˌpluːˈpɜːfɪkt] n : **pluperfect (tense)** plus-que-parfait m.

plural ['plʊərəl] ⟨⟩ adj **1.** GRAM pluriel (elle) - **2.** [not individual] collectif(ive) - **3.** [multicultural] multiculturel(elle). ⟨⟩ n pluriel m.

plus [plʌs] ⟨⟩ adj : **30 plus** 30 ou plus. ⟨⟩ n (pl **pluses** OR **plusses** [plʌsiːz]) **1.** MATHS signe m plus - **2.** inf [bonus] plus m, atout m. ⟨⟩ prep et. ⟨⟩ conj [moreover] de plus.

plush [plʌʃ] adj luxueux(euse), somptueux(euse).

plus sign n signe m plus.

Pluto ['pluːtəʊ] n [planet] Pluton f.

plutonium [pluːˈtəʊniəm] n plutonium m.

ply [plaɪ] ⟨⟩ n [of wool] fil m ; [of wood] pli m. ⟨⟩ vt **1.** [trade] exercer - **2.** [supply] : **to ply sb with drink** ne pas arrêter de remplir le verre de qqn. ⟨⟩ vi [ship etc] faire la navette.

plywood ['plaɪwʊd] n contreplaqué m.

p.m., pm (abbrev of **post meridiem**): **at 3 p.m.** à 15 h.

PM abbrev of **prime minister**.

PMT abbrev of **premenstrual tension**.

pneumatic [njuːˈmætɪk] adj pneumatique.

pneumatic drill n UK marteau piqueur m.

pneumonia [njuːˈməʊnjə] n (U) pneumonie f.

poach [pəʊtʃ] ⟨⟩ vt **1.** [fish] pêcher sans permis ; [deer etc] chasser sans permis - **2.** fig [idea] voler - **3.** CULIN pocher. ⟨⟩ vi braconner.

poacher ['pəʊtʃər] n braconnier m.

poaching ['pəʊtʃɪŋ] n braconnage m.

PO Box (abbrev of **Post Office Box**) n BP f.

pocket ['pɒkɪt] ⟨⟩ n lit & fig poche f ; **to be out of pocket** UK en être de sa poche ; **to pick sb's pocket** faire les poches à qqn. ⟨⟩ adj de poche. ⟨⟩ vt empocher.

pocketbook ['pɒkɪtbʊk] n **1.** [notebook] carnet m - **2.** US [handbag] sac m à main.

pocketknife ['pɒkɪtnaɪf] (pl **-knives** [-naɪvz]) n canif m.

pocket money n UK argent m de poche.

pockmark ['pɒkmɑːk] n marque f de la petite vérole.

pod [pɒd] n **1.** [of plants] cosse f - **2.** [of spacecraft] nacelle f.

podgy ['pɒdʒɪ] adj UK inf boulot(otte), rondelet(ette).

podiatrist [pəˈdaɪətrɪst] n US pédicure mf.

podiatry [pəˈdaɪətrɪ] n US pédicure f.

podium ['pəʊdiəm] (pl **-diums** OR **-dia** [-dɪə]) n podium m.

poem ['pəʊɪm] n poème m.

poet ['pəʊɪt] n poète m.

poetic [pəʊˈetɪk] adj poétique.

poetry ['pəʊɪtrɪ] n poésie f.

poignant ['pɔɪnjənt] adj poignant(e).

point [pɔɪnt] ⟨⟩ n **1.** [tip] pointe f - **2.** [place] endroit m, point m - **3.** [time] stade m, moment m - **4.** [detail, argument] question f, détail m ; **you have a point** il y a du vrai dans ce que vous dites ; **to make a point** faire une remarque ; **to make one's point** dire ce qu'on a à dire, dire son mot - **5.** [main idea] point essentiel ; **to get** OR **come to the point** en venir au fait ; **to miss the point** ne pas comprendre ; **beside the point** à côté de la question - **6.** [feature] : **good point** qualité f ; **bad point** défaut m - **7.** [purpose] : **what's the point in buying a new car?** à quoi bon acheter une nouvelle voiture? ; **there's no point in having a meeting** cela ne sert à rien d'avoir une réunion - **8.** [on scale, in scores] point m - **9.** MATHS : **two point six** deux virgule six - **10.** [of compass] aire f du vent - **11.** UK ELEC prise f (de courant) - **12.** [punctuation mark] point m ; [in decimals] virgule f ; **to make a point of doing sthg** ne pas manquer de faire qqch. ⟨⟩ vt : **to point sthg (at)** [gun, camera] braquer qqch (sur) ; [finger, hose] pointer qqch (sur). ⟨⟩ vi **1.** [indicate with finger] : **to point (at sb/sthg), to point (to sb/sthg)** montrer (qqn/qqch) du doigt, indiquer (qqn/qqch) du doigt - **2.** fig [suggest] : **to point to sthg** suggérer qqch, laisser supposer qqch. ⟪⟫ **points** npl UK RAIL aiguillage m. ⟪⟫ **up to a point** adv jusqu'à un certain point, dans une certaine mesure. ⟪⟫ **on the point of** prep sur le point de. ⟪⟫ **point out** vt sep [person, place] montrer, indiquer ; [fact, mistake] signaler.

point-blank adv **1.** [refuse] catégoriquement ; [ask] de but en blanc - **2.** [shoot] à bout portant.

pointed ['pɔɪntɪd] adj **1.** [sharp] pointu(e) - **2.** fig [remark] mordant(e), incisif(ive).

pointer ['pɔɪntər] n **1.** [piece of advice] tuyau m, conseil m - **2.** [needle] aiguille f - **3.** [stick] baguette f - **4.** COMPUT pointeur m.

pointless ['pɔɪntlɪs] adj inutile, vain(e).

point of view (*pl* **points of view**) *n* point *m* de vue.

poise [pɔɪz] *n fig* calme *m*, sang-froid *m inv*.

poised [pɔɪzd] *adj* **1.** [ready] : **poised (for)** prêt(e) (pour) ; **to be poised to do sthg** se tenir prêt à faire qqch - **2.** *fig* [calm] calme, posé(e).

poison [ˈpɔɪzn] <> *n* poison *m*. <> *vt* **1.** [gen] empoisonner - **2.** [pollute] polluer.

poisoning [ˈpɔɪznɪŋ] *n* empoisonnement *m* ; **food poisoning** intoxication *f* alimentaire.

poisonous [ˈpɔɪznəs] *adj* **1.** [fumes] toxique ; [plant] vénéneux(euse) - **2.** [snake] venimeux(euse).

poke [pəʊk] <> *vt* **1.** [prod] pousser, donner un coup de coude à - **2.** [put] fourrer - **3.** [fire] attiser, tisonner. <> *vi* [protrude] sortir, dépasser. ⚫️ **poke about, poke around** *vi inf* fouiller, fourrager.

poker [ˈpəʊkə] *n* **1.** [game] poker *m* - **2.** [for fire] tisonnier *m*.

poker-faced [-ˌfeɪst] *adj* au visage impassible.

poky [ˈpəʊkɪ] *adj pej* [room] exigu(ë), minuscule.

Poland [ˈpəʊlənd] *n* Pologne *f*.

polar [ˈpəʊlə] *adj* polaire.

polar fleece *n* laine *f* polaire.

Polaroid® [ˈpəʊlərɔɪd] *n* **1.** [camera] Polaroïd® *m* - **2.** [photograph] photo *f* polaroïd.

pole [pəʊl] *n* **1.** [rod, post] perche *f*, mât *m* - **2.** ELEC & GEOG pôle *m*.

Pole [pəʊl] *n* Polonais *m*, -e *f*.

pole vault *n* : **the pole vault** le saut à la perche.

police [pəˈliːs] <> *npl* **1.** [police force] : **the police** la police - **2.** [policemen] agents *mpl* de police. <> *vt* maintenir l'ordre dans.

police car *n* voiture *f* de police.

police constable *n* UK agent *m* de police.

police force *n* police *f*.

policeman [pəˈliːsmən] (*pl* -men [-mən]) *n* agent *m* de police.

police officer *n* policier *m*.

police record *n* casier *m* judiciaire.

police station *n* commissariat *m* (de police).

policewoman [pəˈliːsˌwʊmən] (*pl* -women [-ˌwɪmɪn]) *n* femme *f* agent de police.

policy [ˈpɒləsɪ] *n* **1.** [plan] politique *f* - **2.** [document] police *f*.

polio [ˈpəʊlɪəʊ] *n* polio *f*.

polish [ˈpɒlɪʃ] <> *n* **1.** [for shoes] cirage *m* ; [for floor] cire *f*, encaustique *f* - **2.** [shine] brillant *m*, lustre *m* - **3.** *fig* [refinement] raffinement *m*. <> *vt* [shoes, floor] cirer ;

[car] astiquer ; [cutlery, glasses] faire briller. ⚫️ **polish off** *vt sep inf* expédier. ⚫️ **polish up** *vt sep* [maths, language] perfectionner ; [travail] peaufiner.

Polish [ˈpəʊlɪʃ] <> *adj* polonais(e). <> *n* [language] polonais *m*. <> *npl* : **the Polish** les Polonais *mpl*.

polished [ˈpɒlɪʃt] *adj* **1.** [refined] raffiné(e) - **2.** [accomplished] accompli(e), parfait(e).

polite [pəˈlaɪt] *adj* [courteous] poli(e).

politic [ˈpɒlɪtɪk] *adj* politique.

political [pəˈlɪtɪkl] *adj* politique.

politically correct [pəˌlɪtɪklɪ-] *adj* conforme au mouvement qui préconise de remplacer les termes jugés discriminants par d'autres 'politiquement corrects'.

politician [ˌpɒlɪˈtɪʃn] *n* homme *m* politique, femme *f* politique.

politics [ˈpɒlətɪks] <> *n* (U) politique *f*. <> *npl* **1.** [personal beliefs] : **what are his politics?** de quel bord est-il? - **2.** [of group, area] politique *f*.

polka [ˈpɒlkə] *n* polka *f*.

polka dot *n* pois *m*.

poll [pəʊl] <> *n* [vote] vote *m*, scrutin *m*. <> *vt* **1.** [people] interroger, sonder - **2.** [votes] obtenir. ⚫️ **polls** *npl* : **to go to the polls** aller aux urnes.

pollen [ˈpɒlən] *n* pollen *m*.

polling booth *n* isoloir *m*.

polling day *n* UK jour *m* du scrutin OR des élections.

polling station *n* UK bureau *m* de vote.

pollute [pəˈluːt] *vt* polluer.

pollution [pəˈluːʃn] *n* pollution *f*.

polo [ˈpəʊləʊ] *n* polo *m*.

polo neck *n* UK **1.** [neck] col *m* roulé - **2.** [jumper] pull *m* à col roulé.

polyethylene US = polythene.

Polynesia [ˌpɒlɪˈniːzjə] *n* Polynésie *f*.

polystyrene [ˌpɒlɪˈstaɪriːn] *n* polystyrène *m*.

polytechnic [ˌpɒlɪˈteknɪk] *n* UK établissement d'enseignement supérieur; en 1993, les 'polytechnics' ont été transformés en universités.

polythene UK [ˈpɒlɪθiːn], **polyethylene** US [ˌpɒlɪˈeθɪliːn] *n* polyéthylène *m*.

polythene bag *n* UK sac *m* en plastique.

pomegranate [ˈpɒmɪˌɡrænɪt] *n* grenade *f*.

pomp [pɒmp] *n* pompe *f*, faste *m*.

pompom [ˈpɒmpɒm] *n* pompon *m*.

pompous [ˈpɒmpəs] *adj* **1.** [person] fat(e), suffisant(e) - **2.** [style, speech] pompeux(euse).

pond [pɒnd] *n* étang *m*, mare *f*.

ponder [ˈpɒndə] *vt* considérer, peser.

ponderous ['pɒndərəs] *adj* **1.** [dull] lourd(e) - **2.** [large, heavy] pesant(e).

pong [pɒŋ] *UK inf n* f puanteur *f*.

pontoon [pɒn'tu:n] *n* **1.** [bridge] ponton *m* - **2.** *UK* [game] vingt-et-un *m*.

pony ['pəʊnɪ] *n* poney *m*.

ponytail ['pəʊnɪteɪl] *n* queue-de-cheval *f*.

pony-trekking [-,trekɪŋ] *n* randonnée *f* à cheval OR en poney.

poodle ['pu:dl] *n* caniche *m*.

pool [pu:l] ◇ *n* **1.** [pond, of blood] mare *f* ; [of rain, light] flaque *f* - **2.** [swimming pool] piscine *f* - **3.** SPORT billard *m* américain. ◇ *vt* [resources etc] mettre en commun. ⬥ **pools** *npl UK* : **the pools** ≃ le loto sportif.

poor [pɔ:r] ◇ *adj* **1.** [gen] pauvre - **2.** [not very good] médiocre, mauvais(e). ◇ *npl* : **the poor** les pauvres *mpl*.

poorly ['pɔ:lɪ] ◇ *adj UK* souffrant(e). ◇ *adv* mal, médiocrement.

pop [pɒp] ◇ *n* **1.** (U) [music] pop *m* - **2.** (U) *inf* [fizzy drink] boisson *f* gazeuse - **3.** *esp US inf* [father] papa *m* - **4.** [sound] pan *m*. ◇ *vt* **1.** [burst] faire éclater, crever - **2.** [put quickly] mettre, fourrer. ◇ *vi* **1.** [balloon] éclater, crever ; [cork, button] sauter - **2.** [eyes] : **his eyes popped** il a écarquillé les yeux. ⬥ **pop in** *vi* faire une petite visite. ⬥ **pop up** *vi* surgir.

pop concert *n* concert *m* pop.

popcorn ['pɒpkɔ:n] *n* pop-corn *m*.

pope [pəʊp] *n* pape *m*.

pop group *n* groupe *m* pop.

poplar ['pɒplər] *n* peuplier *m*.

poppy ['pɒpɪ] *n* coquelicot *m*, pavot *m*.

Popsicle® ['pɒpsɪkl] *n US* sucette *f* glacée.

populace ['pɒpjʊləs] *n* : **the populace** le peuple.

popular ['pɒpjʊlər] *adj* **1.** [gen] populaire - **2.** [name, holiday resort] à la mode.

popularize, *UK* **-ise** ['pɒpjʊləraɪz] *vt* **1.** [make popular] populariser - **2.** [simplify] vulgariser.

population [,pɒpjʊ'leɪʃn] *n* population *f*.

porcelain ['pɔ:səlɪn] *n* porcelaine *f*.

porch [pɔ:tʃ] *n* **1.** [entrance] porche *m* - **2.** *US* [verandah] véranda *f*.

porcupine ['pɔ:kjʊpaɪn] *n* porc-épic *m*.

pore [pɔ:r] *n* pore *m*. ⬥ **pore over** *vt insep* examiner de près.

pork [pɔ:k] *n* porc *m*.

pork pie *n* pâté *m* de porc en croûte.

pornography [pɔ:'nɒgrəfɪ] *n* pornographie *f*.

porous ['pɔ:rəs] *adj* poreux(euse).

porridge ['pɒrɪdʒ] *n* porridge *m*.

port [pɔ:t] *n* **1.** [town, harbour] port *m* - **2.** NAUT [left-hand side] bâbord *m* - **3.** [drink] porto *m* - **4.** COMPUT port *m*.

portable ['pɔ:təbl] *adj* portatif(ive).

portent ['pɔ:tənt] *n* présage *m*.

porter ['pɔ:tər] *n* **1.** *UK* [doorman] concierge *m*, portier *m* - **2.** [for luggage] porteur *m* - **3.** *US* [on train] employé *m*, -e *f* des wagons-lits.

portfolio [,pɔ:t'fəʊljəʊ] (*pl* **-s**) *n* **1.** [case] serviette *f* - **2.** [sample of work] portfolio *m* - **3.** FIN portefeuille *m*.

porthole ['pɔ:thəʊl] *n* hublot *m*.

portion ['pɔ:ʃn] *n* **1.** [section] portion *f*, part *f* - **2.** [of food] portion *f*.

portly ['pɔ:tlɪ] *adj* corpulent(e).

portrait ['pɔ:treɪt] *n* portrait *m*.

portray [pɔ:'treɪ] *vt* **1.** CIN & THEAT jouer, interpréter - **2.** [describe] dépeindre - **3.** [paint] faire le portrait de.

Portugal ['pɔ:tʃʊgl] *n* Portugal *m*.

Portuguese [,pɔ:tʃʊ'gi:z] ◇ *adj* portugais(e). ◇ *n* [language] portugais *m*. ◇ *npl* : **the Portuguese** les Portugais *mpl*.

pose [pəʊz] ◇ *n* **1.** [stance] pose *f* - **2.** *pej* [affectation] pose *f*, affectation *f*. ◇ *vt* **1.** [danger] présenter - **2.** [problem, question] poser. ◇ *vi* **1.** *pej* & ART poser - **2.** [pretend to be] : **to pose as** se faire passer pour.

posh [pɒʃ] *adj inf* **1.** [hotel, clothes etc] chic *(inv)* - **2.** *UK* [accent, person] de la haute.

position [pə'zɪʃn] ◇ *n* **1.** [gen] position *f* - **2.** [job] poste *m*, emploi *m* - **3.** [state] situation *f*. ◇ *vt* placer, mettre en position.

positive ['pɒzətɪv] *adj* **1.** [gen] positif(ive) - **2.** [sure] sûr(e), certain(e) ; **to be positive about sthg** être sûr de qqch - **3.** [optimistic] positif(ive), optimiste ; **to be positive about sthg** avoir une attitude positive au sujet de qqch - **4.** [definite] formel(elle), précis(e) - **5.** [evidence] irréfutable, indéniable - **6.** [downright] véritable.

posse ['pɒsɪ] *n US* détachement *m*, troupe *f*.

possess [pə'zes] *vt* posséder.

possession [pə'zeʃn] *n* possession *f*. ⬥ **possessions** *npl* possessions *fpl*, biens *mpl*.

possessive [pə'zesɪv] ◇ *adj* possessif(ive). ◇ *n* GRAM possessif *m*.

possibility [,pɒsə'bɪlətɪ] *n* **1.** [chance, likelihood] possibilité *f*, chances *fpl* ; **there is a possibility that...** il se peut que... (+ *subjunctive*) - **2.** [option] possibilité *f*, option *f*.

possible ['pɒsəbl] ◇ *adj* possible ; **as**

much as possible autant que possible ; **as soon as possible** dès que possible. ◇ *n* possible *m*.

possibly ['pɒsəblɪ] *adv* **1.** [perhaps] peut-être **- 2.** [expressing surprise] : **how could he possibly have known?** mais comment a-t-il pu le savoir? **- 3.** [for emphasis] : **I can't possibly accept your money** je ne peux vraiment pas accepter cet argent.

post [pəust] ◇ *n* **1.** UK [service] : **the post** la poste ; **by post** par la poste **- 2.** UK [letters, delivery] courrier *m* **- 3.** UK [collection] levée *f* **- 4.** [pole] poteau *m* **- 5.** [position, job] poste *m*, emploi *m* **- 6.** MIL poste *m*. ◇ *vt* **1.** UK [by mail] poster, mettre à la poste **- 2.** [employee] muter **- 3.** COMPUT [message, question, advertisement] envoyer sur Internet.

postage ['pəustɪdʒ] *n* affranchissement *m* ; **postage and packing** frais *mpl* de port et d'emballage.

postal ['pəustl] *adj* postal(e).

postal order *n* UK mandat *m* postal.

postbox ['pəustbɒks] *n* UK boîte *f* aux lettres.

postcard ['pəustkɑːd] *n* carte *f* postale.

postcode ['pəustkəud] *n* UK code *m* postal.

postdate [ˌpəust'deɪt] *vt* postdater.

poster ['pəustər] *n* [for advertising] affiche *f* ; [for decoration] poster *m*.

poste restante [ˌpəust'restɑːnt] *n* poste *f* restante.

posterior [pɒ'stɪərɪər] ◇ *adj* postérieur(e). ◇ *n hum* postérieur *m*, derrière *m*.

postgraduate [ˌpəust'grædʒuət] ◇ *adj* de troisième cycle. ◇ *n* étudiant *m*, -e *f* de troisième cycle.

posthumous ['pɒstjuməs] *adj* posthume.

Post-it (note)® *n* Post-it® *m*, becquet *m*.

postman ['pəustmən] (*pl* -men [-mən]) *n* UK facteur *m*, -rice *f*.

postmark ['pəustmɑːk] ◇ *n* cachet *m* de la poste. ◇ *vt* timbrer, tamponner.

postmaster ['pəustˌmɑːstər] *n* receveur *m* des postes.

postmortem [ˌpəust'mɔːtəm] *n lit & fig* autopsie *f*.

post office *n* **1.** [organization] : **the Post Office** les Postes et Télécommunications *fpl* **- 2.** [building] (bureau *m* de) poste *f*.

post-office box *n* boîte *f* postale.

postpone [ˌpəust'pəun] *vt* reporter, remettre.

postscript ['pəustskrɪpt] *n* post-scriptum *m inv* ; *fig* supplément *m*, addenda *m inv*.

posture ['pɒstʃər] *n* **1.** (U) [pose] position *f*, posture *f* **- 2.** *fig* [attitude] attitude *f*.

postwar [ˌpəust'wɔːr] *adj* d'après-guerre.

posy ['pəuzɪ] *n* petit bouquet *m* de fleurs.

pot [pɒt] ◇ *n* **1.** [for cooking] marmite *f*, casserole *f* **- 2.** [for tea] théière *f* ; [for coffee] cafetière *f* **- 3.** [for paint, jam, plant] pot *m* **- 4.** (U) *inf* [cannabis] herbe *f*. ◇ *vt* [plant] mettre en pot.

potassium [pə'tæsɪəm] *n* potassium *m*.

potato [pə'teɪtəu] (*pl* -es) *n* pomme *f* de terre.

potato peeler [-ˌpiːlər] *n* (couteau *m*) éplucheur *m*.

potent ['pəutənt] *adj* **1.** [powerful, influential] puissant(e) **- 2.** [drink] fort(e) **- 3.** [man] viril.

potential [pə'tenʃl] ◇ *adj* [energy, success] potentiel(elle) ; [uses, danger] possible ; [enemy] en puissance. ◇ *n* (U) [of person] capacités *fpl* latentes ; **to have potential** [person] promettre ; [company] avoir de l'avenir ; [scheme] offrir des possibilités.

potentially [pə'tenʃəlɪ] *adv* potentiellement.

pothole ['pɒthəul] *n* **1.** [in road] nid-de-poule *m* **- 2.** [underground] caverne *f*, grotte *f*.

potholing ['pɒtˌhəulɪŋ] *n* UK **to go potholing** faire de la spéléologie.

potion ['pəuʃn] *n* [magic] breuvage *m* ; **love potion** philtre *m*.

potluck [ˌpɒt'lʌk] *n* : **to take potluck** [gen] choisir au hasard ; [at meal] manger à la fortune du pot.

potshot ['pɒtˌʃɒt] *n* : **to take a potshot (at sthg)** tirer (sur qqch) sans viser.

potted ['pɒtɪd] *adj* **1.** [plant] : **potted plant** plante *f* d'appartement **- 2.** [food] conservé(e) en pot.

potter ['pɒtər] *n* potier *m*, -ière *f*. ◆ **potter about, potter around** *vi* UK bricoler.

pottery ['pɒtərɪ] *n* poterie *f* ; **a piece of pottery** une poterie.

potty ['pɒtɪ] UK *inf* ◇ *adj* : **potty (about)** toqué(e) (de). ◇ *n* pot *m* de chambre).

pouch [pautʃ] *n* **1.** [small bag] petit sac *m* ; **tobacco pouch** blague *f* à tabac **- 2.** [of kangaroo] poche *f* ventrale.

poultry ['pəultrɪ] ◇ *n* (U) [meat] volaille *f*. ◇ *npl* [birds] volailles *fpl*.

pounce [pauns] *vi* : **to pounce (on)** [bird] fondre (sur) ; [person] se jeter (sur).

pound [paund] ◇ *n* **1.** UK [money] livre *f* **- 2.** [weight] = 453,6 grammes, ≃ **livre** *f* **- 3.** [for cars, dogs] fourrière *f*. ◇ *vt* **1.** [strike loudly] marteler **- 2.** [crush] piler, broyer. ◇ *vi* **1.** [strike loudly] : **to pound**

on donner de grands coups à - 2. [heart] battre fort ; **my head is pounding** j'ai des élancements dans la tête.

pound sterling *n* livre *f* sterling.

pour [pɔːr] <> *vt* verser ; **shall I pour you a drink?** je te sers quelque chose à boire? <> *vi* 1. [liquid] couler à flots - 2. *fig* [rush] : **to pour in/out** entrer/sortir en foule. <> *impers vb* [rain hard] pleuvoir à verse.
pour in *vi* [letters, news] affluer.
pour out *vt sep* 1. [empty] vider - 2. [serve - drink] verser, servir.

pouring ['pɔːrɪŋ] *adj* [rain] torrentiel(elle).

pout [paʊt] *vi* faire la moue.

poverty ['pɒvətɪ] *n* pauvreté *f* ; *fig* [of ideas] indigence *f*, manque *m*.

poverty-stricken *adj* [person] dans la misère ; [area] misérable, très pauvre.

powder ['paʊdər] <> *n* poudre *f*. <> *vt* [face, body] poudrer.

powder compact *n* poudrier *m*.

powdered ['paʊdəd] *adj* 1. [milk, eggs] en poudre - 2. [face] poudré(e).

powdered sugar *n US* sucre *m* en poudre.

powder puff *n* houppette *f*.

powder room *n* toilettes *fpl* pour dames.

power ['paʊər] <> *n* 1. (U) [authority, ability] pouvoir *m* ; **to take power** prendre le pouvoir ; **to come to power** parvenir au pouvoir ; **to be in power** être au pouvoir ; **to be in** OR **within one's power to do sthg** être en son pouvoir de faire qqch - 2. [strength, powerful person] puissance *f*, force *f* - 3. (U) [energy] énergie *f* - 4. [electricity] courant *m*, électricité *f*. <> *vt* faire marcher, actionner.

powerboat ['paʊəbəʊt] *n* hors-bord *m inv*.

power cut *n* coupure *f* de courant.

power failure *n* panne *f* de courant.

powerful ['paʊəfʊl] *adj* 1. [gen] puissant(e) - 2. [smell, voice] fort(e) - 3. [speech, novel] émouvant(e).

powerless ['paʊəlɪs] *adj* impuissant(e) ; **to be powerless to do sthg** être dans l'impossibilité de faire qqch, ne pas pouvoir faire qqch.

power point *n UK* prise *f* de courant.

power station *n* centrale *f* électrique.

power steering *n* direction *f* assistée.

pp *(abbrev of per procurationem)* pp.

PR *n* 1. *abbrev of* **proportional representation** - 2. *abbrev of* **public relations**.

practicable ['præktɪkəbl] *adj* réalisable, faisable.

practical ['præktɪkl] <> *adj* 1. [gen] pratique - 2. [plan, solution] réalisable. <> *n* épreuve *f* pratique.

practicality [,præktɪ'kælətɪ] *n* (U) aspect *m* pratique.

practical joke *n* farce *f*.

practically ['præktɪklɪ] *adv* 1. [in a practical way] d'une manière pratique - 2. [almost] presque, pratiquement.

practice ['præktɪs] *n* 1. (U) [at sport] entraînement *m* ; [at music etc] répétition *f* ; **to be out of practice** être rouillé(e) - 2. [training session - at sport] séance *f* d'entraînement ; [- at music etc] répétition *f* - 3. [act of doing] : **to put sthg into practice** mettre qqch en pratique ; **in practice** [in fact] en réalité, en fait - 4. [habit] pratique *f*, coutume *f* - 5. (U) [of profession] exercice *m* - 6. [of doctor] cabinet *m* ; [of lawyer] étude *f*.

practicing US = **practising**.

practise UK, **practice** US ['præktɪs] <> *vt* 1. [sport] s'entraîner à ; [piano etc] s'exercer à - 2. [custom] suivre, pratiquer ; [religion] pratiquer - 3. [profession] exercer. <> *vi* 1. SPORT s'entraîner ; MUS s'exercer - 2. [doctor, lawyer] exercer.

practising UK, **practicing** US ['præktɪsɪŋ] *adj* [doctor, lawyer] en exercice ; [Christian etc] pratiquant(e) ; [homosexual] déclaré(e).

practitioner [præk'tɪʃnər] *n* praticien *m*, -enne *f*.

Prague [prɑːg] *n* Prague.

prairie ['preərɪ] *n* prairie *f*.

praise [preɪz] <> *n* (U) louange *f*, louanges *fpl*, éloge *m*, éloges *mpl*. <> *vt* louer, faire l'éloge de.

praiseworthy ['preɪz,wɜːðɪ] *adj* louable, méritoire.

pram [præm] *n UK* landau *m*.

prance [prɑːns] *vi* 1. [person] se pavaner - 2. [horse] caracoler.

prank [præŋk] *n* tour *m*, niche *f*.

prawn [prɔːn] *n* crevette *f* rose.

pray [preɪ] *vi* : **to pray (to sb)** prier (qqn).

prayer [preər] *n lit & fig* prière *f*.

prayer book *n* livre *m* de messe.

preach [priːtʃ] <> *vt* [gen] prêcher ; [sermon] prononcer. <> *vi* 1. RELIG : **to preach (to sb)** prêcher (qqn) - 2. *pej* [pontificate] : **to preach (at sb)** sermonner (qqn).

preacher ['priːtʃər] *n* prédicateur *m*, -trice *f*, pasteur *m*, -(e) *f*.

precarious [prɪ'keərɪəs] *adj* précaire.

precaution [prɪ'kɔːʃn] *n* précaution *f*.

precede [prɪ'siːd] *vt* précéder.

precedence ['presɪdəns] *n* : **to take precedence over sthg** avoir la priorité sur qqch ; **to have** OR **take precedence over sb** avoir la préséance sur qqn.

precedent ['presɪdənt] *n* précédent *m*.

precinct ['pri:sıŋkt] *n* **1.** *UK* [area] : **pedestrian precinct** zone *f* piétonne ; **shopping precinct** centre *m* commercial - **2.** *US* [district] circonscription *f* (administrative). ➡ **precincts** *npl* [of institution] enceinte *f*.

precious ['preʃəs] *adj* **1.** [gen] précieux(euse) - **2.** *inf iro* [damned] sacré(e) - **3.** [affected] affecté(e).

precipice ['presıpıs] *n* précipice *m*, paroi *f* à pic.

precipitate *fml* ⬦ *adj* [prı'sıpıtət] hâtif(ive). ⬦ *vt* [prı'sıpıteıt] [hasten] hâter, précipiter.

precise [prı'saıs] *adj* précis(e) ; [measurement, date] exact(e).

precisely [prı'saıslı] *adv* précisément, exactement.

precision [prı'sıʒn] *n* précision *f*, exactitude *f*.

preclude [prı'klu:d] *vt fml* empêcher ; [possibility] écarter ; **to preclude sb from doing sthg** empêcher qqn de faire qqch.

precocious [prı'kəuʃəs] *adj* précoce.

preconceived [ˌpri:kən'si:vd] *adj* préconçu(e).

precondition [ˌpri:kən'dıʃn] *n fml* condition *f* sine qua non.

predator ['predətə'] *n* **1.** [animal, bird] prédateur *m*, rapace *m* - **2.** *fig* [person] corbeau *m*.

predecessor ['pri:dısesə'] *n* **1.** [person] prédécesseur *m* - **2.** [thing] précédent *m*, -e *f*.

predicament [prı'dıkəmənt] *n* situation *f* difficile ; **to be in a predicament** être dans de beaux draps.

predict [prı'dıkt] *vt* prédire.

predictable [prı'dıktəbl] *adj* prévisible.

prediction [prı'dıkʃn] *n* prédiction *f*.

predispose [ˌpri:dıs'pəuz] *vt* : **to be predisposed to sthg/to do sthg** être prédisposé(e) à qqch/à faire qqch.

predominant [prı'dɒmınənt] *adj* prédominant(e).

predominantly [prı'dɒmınəntlı] *adv* principalement, surtout.

preempt [ˌpri:'empt] *vt* [action, decision] devancer, prévenir.

preemptive [ˌpri:'emptıv] *adj* préventif(ive).

preen [pri:n] *vt* **1.** [subj: bird] lisser, nettoyer - **2.** *fig* [subj: person] : **to preen o.s.** se faire beau (belle).

prefab ['pri:fæb] *n inf* maison *f* préfabriquée.

preface ['prefıs] *n* : **preface (to)** préface *f* (de), préambule *m* (de).

prefect ['pri:fekt] *n UK* [pupil] *élève de terminale qui aide les professeurs à maintenir la discipline.*

prefer [prı'fɜ:'] *vt* préférer ; **to prefer sthg to sthg** préférer qqch à qqch, aimer mieux qqch que qqch ; **to prefer to do sthg** préférer faire qqch, aimer mieux faire qqch.

preferable ['prefrəbl] *adj* : **preferable (to)** préférable (à).

preferably ['prefrəblı] *adv* de préférence.

preference ['prefərəns] *n* préférence *f*.

preferential [ˌprefə'renʃl] *adj* préférentiel(elle).

prefix ['pri:fıks] *n* préfixe *m*.

pregnancy ['pregnənsı] *n* grossesse *f*.

pregnant ['pregnənt] *adj* [woman] enceinte ; [animal] pleine, gravide.

prehistoric [ˌpri:hı'stɒrık] *adj* préhistorique.

prejudice ['predʒudıs] ⬦ *n* **1.** [biased view] : **prejudice (in favour of/against)** préjugé *m* (en faveur de/contre), préjugés *mpl* (en faveur de/contre) - **2.** (*U*) [harm] préjudice *m*, tort *m*. ⬦ *vt* **1.** [bias] : **to prejudice sb (in favour of/against)** prévenir qqn (en faveur de/contre), influencer qqn (en faveur de/contre) - **2.** [harm] porter préjudice à.

prejudiced ['predʒudıst] *adj* [person] qui a des préjugés ; [opinion] préconçu(e) ; **to be prejudiced in favour of/against** avoir des préjugés en faveur de/contre.

prejudicial [ˌpredʒu'dıʃl] *adj* : **prejudicial (to)** préjudiciable (à), nuisible (à).

preliminary [prı'lımınərı] *adj* préliminaire.

prelude ['prelju:d] *n* [event] : **prelude to sthg** prélude *m* de qqch.

premarital [ˌpri:'mærıtl] *adj* avant le mariage.

premature ['premə,tjuə'] *adj* prématuré(e).

premeditated [ˌpri:'medıteıtıd] *adj* prémédité(e).

premenstrual syndrome, premenstrual tension [pri:'menstruəl-] *n* syndrome *m* prémenstruel.

premier ['premjə'] ⬦ *adj* primordial(e), premier(ère). ⬦ *n* premier ministre *m*.

premiere ['premıeə'] *n* première *f*.

premise ['premıs] *n* prémisse *f*. ➡ **premises** *npl* local *m*, locaux *mpl* ; **on the premises** sur place, sur les lieux.

premium ['pri:mjəm] *n* prime *f* ; **at a premium** [above usual value] à prix d'or ; [in great demand] très recherché OR demandé.

premium bond *n UK* ≃ billet *m* de loterie.

premonition [ˌpreməˈnɪʃn] n prémonition f, pressentiment m.

prenatal clinic n service m de consultation prénatale.

pre-nup (abbrev of **pre-nuptial contract**) n inf contrat m de mariage.

preoccupied [priːˈɒkjupaɪd] adj : **preoccupied (with)** préoccupé(e) (de).

prep [prep] n (U) UK inf devoirs mpl.

prepaid [ˈpriːpeɪd] adj payé(e) d'avance ; [envelope] affranchi(e).

preparation [ˌprepəˈreɪʃn] n préparation f. ➤ **preparations** npl préparatifs mpl ; **to make preparations for** faire des préparatifs pour, prendre ses dispositions pour.

preparatory [prɪˈpærətrɪ] adj [work, classes] préparatoire ; [actions, measures] préliminaire.

preparatory school n [in UK] école f primaire privée ; [in US] école privée qui prépare à l'enseignement supérieur.

prepare [prɪˈpeər] ⬦ vt préparer. ⬦ vi : **to prepare for sthg/to do sthg** se préparer à qqch/à faire qqch.

prepared [prɪˈpeəd] adj **1.** [done beforehand] préparé(e) d'avance - **2.** [willing] : **to be prepared to do sthg** être prêt(e) OR disposé(e) à faire qqch - **3.** [ready] : **to be prepared for sthg** être prêt(e) pour qqch.

preposition [ˌprepəˈzɪʃn] n préposition f.

preposterous [prɪˈpɒstərəs] adj ridicule, absurde.

prep school abbrev of **preparatory school**.

prerequisite [ˌpriːˈrekwɪzɪt] n condition f préalable.

prerogative [prɪˈrɒgətɪv] n prérogative f, privilège m.

Presbyterian [ˌprezbɪˈtɪərɪən] ⬦ adj presbytérien(enne). ⬦ n presbytérien m, -enne f.

preschool [ˌpriːˈskuːl] ⬦ adj préscolaire. ⬦ n US école f maternelle.

prescribe [prɪˈskraɪb] vt **1.** MED prescrire - **2.** [order] ordonner, imposer.

prescription [prɪˈskrɪpʃn] n [MED - written form] ordonnance f ; [- medicine] médicament m.

prescriptive [prɪˈskrɪptɪv] adj normatif(ive).

presence [ˈprezns] n présence f ; **to be in sb's presence** OR **in the presence of sb** être en présence de qqn.

presence of mind n présence f d'esprit.

present ⬦ adj [ˈpreznt] **1.** [current] actuel(elle) - **2.** [in attendance] présent(e) ; **to be present at** assister à. ⬦ n [ˈpreznt] **1.** [current time] : **the present** le présent ; **at present** actuellement, en ce moment

- **2.** [gift] cadeau m - **3.** GRAM : **present (tense)** présent m. ⬦ vt [prɪˈzent] **1.** [gen] présenter ; [opportunity] donner - **2.** [give] donner, remettre ; **to present sb with sthg, to present sthg to sb** donner OR remettre qqch à qqn - **3.** [portray] représenter, décrire - **4.** [arrive] : **to present o.s.** se présenter.

presentable [prɪˈzentəbl] adj présentable.

presentation [ˌpreznˈteɪʃn] n **1.** [gen] présentation f - **2.** [ceremony] remise f (de récompense/prix) - **3.** [talk] exposé m - **4.** [of play] représentation f.

present day n : **the present day** aujourd'hui. ➤ **present-day** adj d'aujourd'hui, contemporain(e).

presenter [prɪˈzentər] n UK présentateur m, -trice f.

presently [ˈprezntlɪ] adv **1.** [soon] bientôt, tout à l'heure - **2.** [at present] actuellement, en ce moment.

preservation [ˌprezəˈveɪʃn] n (U) **1.** [maintenance] maintien m - **2.** [protection] protection f, conservation f.

preservative [prɪˈzɜːvətɪv] n conservateur m.

preserve [prɪˈzɜːv] ⬦ vt **1.** [maintain] maintenir - **2.** [protect] conserver - **3.** [food] conserver, mettre en conserve. ⬦ n [jam] confiture f. ➤ **preserves** npl [jam] confiture f ; [vegetables] pickles mpl, condiments mpl.

preset [ˌpriːˈset] (pt & pp **preset**) vt prérégler.

president [ˈprezɪdənt] n **1.** [gen] président m - **2.** US [company chairman] P-DG m.

presidential [ˌprezɪˈdenʃl] adj présidentiel(elle).

press [pres] ⬦ n **1.** [push] pression f - **2.** [journalism] : **the press** [newspapers] la presse, les journaux mpl ; [reporters] les journalistes mpl - **3.** [printing machine] presse f ; [for wine] pressoir m. ⬦ vt **1.** [push] appuyer sur ; **to press sthg against sthg** appuyer qqch sur qqch - **2.** [squeeze] serrer - **3.** [iron] repasser, donner un coup de fer à - **4.** [urge] : **to press sb (to do sthg** OR **into doing sthg)** presser qqn (de faire qqch) - **5.** [pursue - claim] insister sur. ⬦ vi **1.** [push] : **to press (on sthg)** appuyer (sur qqch) - **2.** [squeeze] : **to press (on sthg)** serrer (qqch) - **3.** [crowd] se presser. ➤ **press for** vt insep demander avec insistance. ➤ **press on** vi [continue] : **to press on (with sthg)** continuer (qqch), ne pas abandonner (qqch).

press agency n agence f de presse.

press clipping n US = **press cutting**.

press conference n conférence f de presse.

pressed [prest] *adj* : **to be pressed for time/money** être à court de temps/d'argent.

pressing ['presɪŋ] *adj* urgent(e).

press officer *n* attaché *m* de presse.

press release *n* communiqué *m* de presse.

press stud *n* UK pression *f*.

press-up *n* UK pompe *f*, traction *f*.

pressure ['preʃər] *n* (U) **1.** [gen] pression *f* ; **to put pressure on sb (to do sthg)** faire pression sur qqn (pour qu'il fasse qqch) - **2.** [stress] tension *f*.

pressure cooker *n* Cocotte-Minute® *f*, autocuiseur *m*.

pressure gauge *n* manomètre *m*.

pressure group *n* groupe *m* de pression.

pressurize, UK **-ise** ['preʃəraɪz] *vt* **1.** TECH pressuriser - **2.** UK [force] : **to pressurize sb to do or into doing sthg** forcer qqn à faire qqch.

prestige [pre'stiːʒ] *n* prestige *m*.

presumably [prɪ'zjuːməblɪ] *adv* vraisemblablement.

presume [prɪ'zjuːm] *vt* présumer ; **to presume (that)...** supposer que... ; **missing, presumed dead** MIL manque à l'appel or porté disparu, présumé mort.

presumption [prɪ'zʌmpʃn] *n* **1.** [assumption] supposition *f*, présomption *f* - **2.** (U) [audacity] présomption *f*.

presumptuous [prɪ'zʌmptʃʊəs] *adj* présomptueux(euse).

pretence UK, US **pretense** [prɪ'tens] *n* prétention *f* ; **to make a pretence of doing sthg** faire semblant de faire qqch ; **under false pretences** sous des prétextes fallacieux.

pretend [prɪ'tend] *vt* : **to pretend to do sthg** faire semblant de faire qqch. *vi* faire semblant.

pretense US = pretence.

pretension [prɪ'tenʃn] *n* prétention *f*.

pretentious [prɪ'tenʃəs] *adj* prétentieux(euse).

pretext ['priːtekst] *n* prétexte *m* ; **on or under the pretext that...** sous prétexte que... ; **on or under the pretext of doing sthg** sous prétexte de faire qqch.

pretty ['prɪtɪ] *adj* joli(e). *adv* [quite] plutôt ; **pretty much or well** pratiquement, presque.

prevail [prɪ'veɪl] *vi* **1.** [be widespread] avoir cours, régner - **2.** [triumph] : **to prevail (over)** prévaloir (sur), l'emporter (sur) - **3.** [persuade] : **to prevail on or upon sb to do sthg** persuader qqn de faire qqch.

prevailing [prɪ'veɪlɪŋ] *adj* **1.** [current] actuel(elle) - **2.** [wind] dominant(e).

prevalent ['prevələnt] *adj* courant(e), répandu(e).

prevent [prɪ'vent] *vt* : **to prevent sb/sthg (from doing sthg)** empêcher qqn/qqch (de faire qqch).

preventive [prɪ'ventɪv] *adj* préventif(ive).

preview ['priːvjuː] *n* avant-première *f*.

previous ['priːvjəs] *adj* **1.** [earlier] antérieur(e) - **2.** [preceding] précédent(e).

previously ['priːvjəslɪ] *adv* avant, auparavant.

prewar [ˌpriː'wɔːr] *adj* d'avant-guerre.

prey [preɪ] *n* proie *f*. **prey on** *vt insep* **1.** [live off] faire sa proie de - **2.** [trouble] : **to prey on sb's mind** ronger qqn, tracasser qqn.

price [praɪs] *n* [cost] prix *m* ; **at any price** à tout prix. *vt* fixer le prix de.

priceless ['praɪslɪs] *adj* sans prix, inestimable.

price list *n* tarif *m*.

price tag *n* [label] étiquette *f*.

pricey ['praɪsɪ] *adj inf* chérot.

prick [prɪk] *n* **1.** [scratch, wound] piqûre *f* - **2.** *vulg* [stupid person] con *m*, conne *f*. *vt* piquer. **prick up** *vt insep* : **to prick up one's ears** [animal] dresser les oreilles ; [person] dresser or tendre l'oreille.

prickle ['prɪkl] *n* **1.** [thorn] épine *f* - **2.** [sensation on skin] picotement *m*. *vi* picoter.

prickly ['prɪklɪ] *adj* **1.** [plant, bush] épineux(euse) - **2.** *fig* [person] irritable.

prickly heat *n* (U) boutons *mpl* de chaleur.

pride [praɪd] *n* (U) **1.** [satisfaction] fierté *f* ; **to take pride in sthg/in doing sthg** être fier de qqch/de faire qqch - **2.** [self-esteem] orgueil *m*, amour-propre *m* - **3.** *pej* [arrogance] orgueil *m*. *vt* : **to pride o.s. on sthg** être fier (fière) de qqch.

priest [priːst] *n* prêtre *m*.

priestess [ˈpriːstɪs] *n* prêtresse *f*.

priesthood ['priːsthʊd] *n* **1.** [position, office] : **the priesthood** le sacerdoce - **2.** [priests] : **the priesthood** le clergé.

prig [prɪg] *n* petit saint *m*, petite sainte *f*.

prim [prɪm] *adj* guindé(e).

primarily ['praɪmərɪlɪ] *adv* principalement.

primary ['praɪmərɪ] *adj* **1.** [main] premier(ère), principal(e) - **2.** SCH primaire. *n* US POL primaire *f*.

primary school *n* école *f* primaire.

primate ['praɪmeɪt] *n* **1.** ZOOL primate *m* - **2.** RELIG primat *m*.

prime [praɪm] *adj* **1.** [main] principal(e), primordial(e) - **2.** [excellent] excellent(e) ; **prime quality** première qualité. *n* : **to be in one's prime** être dans la fleur de l'âge. ◇ vt **1.** [gun, pump] amorcer - **2.** [paint] apprêter - **3.** [inform] : **to prime sb about sthg** mettre qqn au courant de qqch.

prime minister n premier ministre m.

primer ['praɪmər] n **1.** [paint] apprêt m - **2.** [textbook] introduction f.

primeval [praɪ'miːvl] adj [ancient] primitif(ive).

primitive ['prɪmɪtɪv] adj primitif(ive).

primrose ['prɪmrəuz] n primevère f.

Primus stove® ['praɪməs-] n réchaud m de camping.

prince [prɪns] n prince m.

princess [prɪn'ses] n princesse f.

principal ['prɪnsəpl] ◇ adj principal(e). ◇ n SCH directeur m, -trice f ; UNIV doyen m, -enne f.

principle ['prɪnsəpl] n principe m ; **on principle, as a matter of principle** par principe. ⬥ **in principle** adv en principe.

print [prɪnt] ◇ n **1.** (U) [type] caractères mpl ; **to be in print** être disponible ; **to be out of print** être épuisé - **2.** ART gravure f - **3.** [photograph] épreuve f - **4.** [fabric] imprimé m - **5.** [mark] empreinte f. ◇ vt **1.** [produce by printing] imprimer - **2.** [publish] publier - **3.** [write in block letters] écrire en caractères d'imprimerie. ◇ vi [printer] imprimer. ⬥ **print out** vt sep COMPUT imprimer.

printed matter ['prɪntɪd-] n (U) imprimés mpl.

printer ['prɪntər] n **1.** [person, firm] imprimeur mf - **2.** COMPUT imprimante f.

printing ['prɪntɪŋ] n (U) **1.** [act of printing] impression f - **2.** [trade] imprimerie f.

printout ['prɪntaʊt] n COMPUT sortie f d'imprimante, listing m.

prior ['praɪər] ◇ adj antérieur(e), précédent(e). ◇ n [monk] prieur m. ⬥ **prior to** prep avant ; **prior to doing sthg** avant de faire qqch.

priority [praɪ'ɒrətɪ] n priorité f ; **to have** OR **take priority (over)** avoir la priorité (sur).

prise [praɪz] vt : **to prise sthg away from sb** arracher qqch à qqn ; **to prise sthg open** forcer qqch.

prison ['prɪzn] n prison f.

prisoner ['prɪznər] n prisonnier m, -ère f.

prisoner of war (pl **prisoners of war**) n prisonnier m, -ère f de guerre.

privacy [UK 'prɪvəsɪ, US 'praɪvəsɪ] n intimité f.

private ['praɪvɪt] ◇ adj **1.** [not public] privé(e) - **2.** [confidential] confidentiel(elle) - **3.** [personal] personnel(elle) - **4.** [unsocia-

ble - person] secret(ète). ◇ n **1.** [soldier] (simple) soldat m - **2.** [secrecy] : **in private** en privé.

private enterprise n (U) entreprise f privée.

private eye n détective m privé.

privately ['praɪvɪtlɪ] adv **1.** [not by the state] : **privately owned** du secteur privé - **2.** [confidentially] en privé - **3.** [personally] intérieurement, dans son for intérieur.

private property n propriété f privée.

private school n école f privée.

privatize, UK -ise ['praɪvɪtaɪz] vt privatiser.

privet ['prɪvɪt] n troène m.

privilege ['prɪvɪlɪdʒ] n privilège m.

privy ['prɪvɪ] adj : **to be privy to sthg** être dans le secret de qqch.

Privy Council n UK : **the Privy Council** le Conseil privé.

prize [praɪz] ◇ adj [possession] très précieux(euse) ; [animal] primé(e) ; [idiot, example] parfait(e). ◇ n prix m. ◇ vt priser.

prize-giving [-,gɪvɪŋ] n UK distribution f des prix.

prizewinner ['praɪz,wɪnər] n gagnant m, -e f.

pro [prəu] (pl **-s**) n **1.** inf [professional] pro mf - **2.** [advantage] : **the pros and cons** le pour et le contre.

probability [,prɒbə'bɪlətɪ] n probabilité f.

probable ['prɒbəbl] adj probable.

probably ['prɒbəblɪ] adv probablement.

probation [prə'beɪʃn] n (U) **1.** LAW mise f à l'épreuve ; **to put sb on probation** mettre qqn en sursis avec mise à l'épreuve - **2.** [trial period] essai m ; **to be on probation** être à l'essai.

probe [prəub] ◇ n **1.** [investigation] : **probe (into)** enquête f (sur) - **2.** MED & TECH sonde f. ◇ vt sonder.

problem ['prɒbləm] ◇ n problème m ; **no problem!** inf pas de problème! ◇ comp difficile.

procedure [prə'siːdʒər] n procédure f.

proceed ◇ vt [prə'siːd] [do subsequently] : **to proceed to do sthg** se mettre à faire qqch. ◇ vi [prə'siːd] **1.** [continue] : **to proceed (with sthg)** continuer (qqch), poursuivre (qqch) - **2.** fml [advance] avancer. ⬥ **proceeds** npl ['prəusiːdz] recette f.

proceedings [prə'siːdɪŋz] npl **1.** [of meeting] débats mpl - **2.** LAW poursuites fpl.

process ['prəuses] ◇ n **1.** [series of actions] processus m ; **in the process** ce faisant ; **to be in the process of doing sthg** être en train de faire qqch - **2.** [method]

procédé *m.* <> *vt* [raw materials, food, data] traiter, transformer ; [application] s'occuper de.

processing ['prəʊsesɪŋ] *n* traitement *m*, transformation *f.*

procession [prə'seʃn] *n* cortège *m*, procession *f.*

proclaim [prə'kleɪm] *vt* [declare] proclamer.

procrastinate [prə'kræstɪneɪt] *vi* faire traîner les choses.

procure [prə'kjʊər] *vt* [for oneself] se procurer ; [for someone else] procurer ; [release] obtenir.

prod [prɒd] *vt* [push, poke] pousser doucement.

prodigal ['prɒdɪgl] *adj* prodigue.

prodigy ['prɒdɪdʒɪ] *n* prodige *m.*

produce <> *n* ['prɒdjuːs] (*U*) produits *mpl.* <> *vt* [prə'djuːs] 1. [gen] produire - 2. [cause] provoquer, causer - 3. [show] présenter - 4. UK THEAT mettre en scène.

producer [prə'djuːsər] *n* 1. [of film, manufacturer] producteur *m*, -trice *f* - 2. UK THEAT metteur *m* en scène.

product ['prɒdʌkt] *n* produit *m.*

production [prə'dʌkʃn] *n* 1. (*U*) [manufacture, of film] production *f* - 2. (*U*) [output] rendement *m* - 3. UK (*U*) THEAT [of play] mise *f* en scène - 4. [show - gen] production *f* ; THEAT pièce *f.*

production line *n* chaîne *f* de fabrication.

productive [prə'dʌktɪv] *adj* 1. [land, business, workers] productif(ive) - 2. [meeting, experience] fructueux(euse).

productivity [,prɒdʌk'tɪvətɪ] *n* productivité *f.*

profane [prə'feɪn] *adj* impie.

profession [prə'feʃn] *n* profession *f* ; **by profession** de son métier.

professional [prə'feʃənl] <> *adj* 1. [gen] professionnel(elle) - 2. [of high standard] de (haute) qualité. <> *n* professionnel *m*, -elle *f.*

professor [prə'fesər] *n* 1. UK UNIV professeur *m*, -(e) *f* (de faculté) - 2. US & Can [teacher] professeur *m.*

proficiency [prə'fɪʃənsɪ] *n* : **proficiency (in)** compétence *f* (en).

profile ['prəʊfaɪl] *n* profil *m.*

profit ['prɒfɪt] <> *n* 1. [financial] bénéfice *m*, profit *m* ; **to make a profit** faire un bénéfice - 2. [advantage] profit *m.* <> *vi* [financially] être le bénéficiaire ; [gain advantage] tirer avantage OR profit.

profitability [,prɒfɪtə'bɪlətɪ] *n* rentabilité *f.*

profitable ['prɒfɪtəbl] *adj* 1. [financially] rentable, lucratif(ive) - 2. [beneficial] fructueux(euse), profitable.

profiteering [,prɒfɪ'tɪərɪŋ] *n* affairisme *m*, mercantilisme *m.*

profound [prə'faʊnd] *adj* profond(e).

profusely [prə'fjuːslɪ] *adv* [sweat, bleed] abondamment ; **to apologize profusely** se confondre en excuses.

profusion [prə'fjuːʒn] *n* profusion *f.*

progeny ['prɒdʒənɪ] *n* progéniture *f.*

prognosis [prɒg'nəʊsɪs] (*pl* **-ses** [-siːz]) *n* pronostic *m.*

program ['prəʊgræm] <> *n* 1. COMPUT programme *m* - 2. US = programme UK. <> *vt* (*pt* & *pp* **-med** OR **-ed**, *cont* **-ming**, *cont* **-ing**) 1. COMPUT programmer - 2. US = programme UK.

programer US = **programmer.**

programme UK, **program** US ['prəʊgræm] <> *n* 1. [schedule, booklet] programme *m* - 2. RADIO & TV émission *f.* <> *vt* programmer ; **to programme sthg to do sthg** programmer qqch pour faire qqch.

programmer, **programer** US ['prəʊgræmər] *n* COMPUT programmeur *m*, -euse *f.*

programming ['prəʊgræmɪŋ] *n* programmation *f.*

progress <> *n* ['prəʊgres] progrès *m* ; **to make progress** [improve] faire des progrès ; **to make progress in sthg** avancer dans qqch ; **in progress** en cours. <> *vi* [prə'gres] 1. [improve - gen] progresser, avancer ; [- person] faire des progrès - 2. [continue] avancer.

progressive [prə'gresɪv] *adj* 1. [enlightened] progressiste - 2. [gradual] progressif(ive).

prohibit [prə'hɪbɪt] *vt* prohiber ; **to prohibit sb from doing sthg** interdire OR défendre à qqn de faire qqch.

project <> *n* ['prɒdʒekt] 1. [plan, idea] projet *m*, plan *m* - 2. SCH [study] : **project (on)** dossier *m* (sur), projet *m* (sur). <> *vt* [prə'dʒekt] 1. [gen] projeter - 2. [estimate] prévoir. <> *vi* [prə'dʒekt] [jut out] faire saillie.

projectile [prə'dʒektaɪl] *n* projectile *m.*

projection [prə'dʒekʃn] *n* 1. [estimate] prévision *f* - 2. [protrusion] saillie *f* - 3. (*U*) [display, showing] projection *f.*

projector [prə'dʒektər] *n* projecteur *m.*

proletariat [,prəʊlɪ'teərɪət] *n* prolétariat *m.*

prolific [prə'lɪfɪk] *adj* prolifique.

prologue, US **prolog** ['prəʊlɒg] *n* lit & fig prologue *m.*

prolong [prə'lɒŋ] *vt* prolonger.

prom [prɒm] *n* **1.** UK *inf* (*abbrev of* **promenade**) promenade *f*, front *m* de mer - **2.** US [ball] bal *m* d'étudiants - **3.** UK *inf* (*abbrev of* **promenade concert**) concert *m* promenade.

promenade [ˌprɒməˈnɑːd] *n* UK [road by sea] promenade *f*, front *m* de mer.

promenade concert *n* UK concert *m* promenade.

prominent [ˈprɒmɪnənt] *adj* **1.** [important] important(e) - **2.** [noticeable] proéminent(e).

promiscuous [prɒˈmɪskjʊəs] *adj* [person] aux mœurs légères ; [behaviour] immoral(e).

promise [ˈprɒmɪs] <> *n* promesse *f*. <> *vt* : **to promise (sb) to do sthg** promettre (à qqn) de faire qqch ; **to promise sb sthg** promettre qqch à qqn. <> *vi* promettre.

promising [ˈprɒmɪsɪŋ] *adj* prometteur(euse).

promontory [ˈprɒməntrɪ] *n* promontoire *m*.

promote [prəˈməʊt] *vt* **1.** [foster] promouvoir - **2.** [push, advertise] promouvoir, lancer - **3.** [in job] promouvoir.

promoter [prəˈməʊtər] *n* **1.** [organizer] organisateur *m*, -trice *f* - **2.** [supporter] promoteur *m*, -trice *f*.

promotion [prəˈməʊʃn] *n* promotion *f*, avancement *m*.

prompt [prɒmpt] <> *adj* rapide, prompt(e). <> *adv* : **at nine o'clock prompt** à neuf heures précises OR tapantes. <> *vt* **1.** [motivate, encourage] : **to prompt sb (to do sthg)** pousser OR inciter qqn (à faire qqch) - **2.** THEAT souffler sa réplique à. <> *n* THEAT réplique *f*.

promptly [ˈprɒmptlɪ] *adv* **1.** [immediately] rapidement, promptement - **2.** [punctually] ponctuellement.

prone [prəʊn] *adj* **1.** [susceptible] : **to be prone to sthg** être sujet(ette) à qqch ; **to be prone to do sthg** avoir tendance à faire qqch - **2.** [lying flat] étendu(e) face contre terre.

prong [prɒŋ] *n* [of fork] dent *f*.

pronoun [ˈprəʊnaʊn] *n* pronom *m*.

pronounce [prəˈnaʊns] <> *vt* prononcer. <> *vi* : **to pronounce on** se prononcer sur.

pronounced [prəˈnaʊnst] *adj* prononcé(e).

pronouncement [prəˈnaʊnsmənt] *n* déclaration *f*.

pronunciation [prəˌnʌnsɪˈeɪʃn] *n* prononciation *f*.

proof [pruːf] *n* **1.** [evidence] preuve *f* - **2.** [of book etc] épreuve *f* - **3.** [of alcohol] teneur *f* en alcool.

prop [prɒp] <> *n* **1.** [physical support] support *m*, étai *m* - **2.** *fig* [supporting thing, person] soutien *m*. <> *vt* : **to prop sthg against** appuyer qqch contre OR à. ➡ **props** *npl* accessoires *mpl*. ➡ **prop up** *vt sep* **1.** [physically support] soutenir, étayer - **2.** *fig* [sustain] soutenir.

propaganda [ˌprɒpəˈgændə] *n* propagande *f*.

propel [prəˈpel] *vt* propulser ; *fig* pousser.

propeller [prəˈpelər] *n* hélice *f*.

propelling pencil [prəˈpelɪŋ-] *n* UK porte-mine *m*.

propensity [prəˈpensətɪ] *n* : **propensity (for OR to)** propension *f* (à).

proper [ˈprɒpər] *adj* **1.** [real] vrai(e) - **2.** [correct] correct(e), bon (bonne) - **3.** [decent - behaviour etc] convenable.

properly [ˈprɒpəlɪ] *adv* **1.** [satisfactorily, correctly] correctement, comme il faut - **2.** [decently] convenablement, comme il faut.

proper name, **proper noun** *n* nom *m* propre.

property [ˈprɒpətɪ] *n* **1.** (U) [possessions] biens *mpl*, propriété *f* - **2.** [building] bien *m* immobilier ; [land] terres *fpl* - **3.** [quality] propriété *f*.

property owner *n* propriétaire *m* (foncier).

prophecy [ˈprɒfɪsɪ] *n* prophétie *f*.

prophesy [ˈprɒfɪsaɪ] *vt* prédire.

prophet [ˈprɒfɪt] *n* prophète *m*.

proportion [prəˈpɔːʃn] *n* **1.** [part] part *f*, partie *f* - **2.** [ratio] rapport *m*, proportion *f* - **3.** ART : **in proportion** proportionné(e) ; **out of proportion** mal proportionné ; **a sense of proportion** *fig* le sens de la mesure.

proportional [prəˈpɔːʃənl] *adj* proportionnel(elle).

proportional representation *n* représentation *f* proportionnelle.

proportionate [prəˈpɔːʃnət] *adj* proportionnel(elle).

proposal [prəˈpəʊzl] *n* **1.** [suggestion] proposition *f*, offre *f* - **2.** [offer of marriage] demande *f* en mariage.

propose [prəˈpəʊz] <> *vt* **1.** [suggest] proposer - **2.** [intend] : **to propose to do OR doing sthg** avoir l'intention de faire qqch, se proposer de faire qqch - **3.** [toast] porter. <> *vi* faire une demande en mariage ; **to propose to sb** demander qqn en mariage.

proposition [ˌprɒpəˈzɪʃn] *n* proposition *f*.

proprietor [prəˈpraɪətər] *n* propriétaire *mf*.

propriety [prəˈpraɪətɪ] *fml n* (U) [moral correctness] bienséance *f*.

pro rata [-ˈrɑːtə] <> *adj* proportionnel(elle). <> *adv* au prorata.

prose [prəʊz] *n* (U) prose *f*.

prosecute ['prɒsɪkjuːt] <> *vt* poursuivre (en justice). <> *vi* [police] engager des poursuites judiciaires ; [lawyer] représenter la partie plaignante.

prosecution [,prɒsɪ'kjuːʃn] *n* poursuites *fpl* judiciaires, accusation *f* ; **the prosecution** la partie plaignante ; [in Crown case] ≃ le ministère public.

prosecutor ['prɒsɪkjuːtə'] *n esp US* plaignant *m*, -e *f*.

prospect <> *n* ['prɒspekt] **1.** [hope] possibilité *f*, chances *fpl* - **2.** [probability] perspective *f*. <> *vi* [prə'spekt] : **to prospect (for sthg)** prospecter (pour chercher qqch). ● **prospects** *npl* : **prospects (for)** chances *fpl* (de), perspectives *fpl* (de) ; **the prospect(s) for the automobile industry** les perspectives d'avenir de l'industrie automobile.

prospecting [prə'spektɪŋ] *n* prospection *f*.

prospective [prə'spektɪv] *adj* éventuel(elle).

prospector [prə'spektə'] *n* prospecteur *m*, -trice *f*.

prospectus [prə'spektəs] (*pl* -es) *n* prospectus *m*.

prosper ['prɒspə'] *vi* prospérer.

prosperity [prɒ'sperətɪ] *n* prospérité *f*.

prosperous ['prɒspərəs] *adj* prospère.

prostitute ['prɒstɪtjuːt] *n* prostituée *f*.

prostrate *adj* ['prɒstreɪt] **1.** [lying down] à plat ventre - **2.** [with grief etc] prostré(e).

protagonist [prə'tægənɪst] *n* protagoniste *mf*.

protect [prə'tekt] *vt* : **to protect sb/sthg (against)**, **to protect sb/sthg (from)** protéger qqn/qqch (contre), protéger qqn/qqch (de).

protection [prə'tekʃn] *n* : **protection (from** OR **against)** protection *f* (contre), défense *f* (contre).

protective [prə'tektɪv] *adj* **1.** [layer, clothing] de protection - **2.** [person, feelings] protecteur(trice).

protein ['prəutiːn] *n* protéine *f*.

protest <> *n* ['prəutest] protestation *f*. <> *vt* [prə'test] **1.** [state] protester de - **2.** *US* [protest against] protester contre. <> *vi* [prə'test] : **to protest (about/against)** protester (à propos de/contre).

Protestant ['prɒtɪstənt] <> *adj* protestant(e). <> *n* protestant *m*, -e *f*.

protester [prə'testə'] *n* [on march, at demonstration] manifestant *m*, -e *f*.

protest march *n* manifestation *f*, marche *f* de protestation.

protocol ['prəutəkɒl] *n* protocole *m*.

prototype ['prəutətaɪp] *n* prototype *m*.

protracted [prə'træktɪd] *adj* prolongé(e).

protrude [prə'truːd] *vi* avancer, dépasser.

protuberance [prə'tjuːbərəns] *n* protubérance *f*.

proud [praud] *adj* **1.** [satisfied, dignified] fier (fière) - **2.** *pej* [arrogant] orgueilleux(euse), fier (fière).

prove [pruːv] (*pp* **-d** OR **proven**) <> *vt* [show] prouver ; **to prove o.s. to be sthg** se révéler être qqch. <> *vi* [turn out] : **to prove (to be) false/useful** s'avérer faux/utile.

proven ['pruːvn] OR ['prəuvn]) <> *pp* ▶ **prove.** <> *adj* [fact] avéré(e), établi(e) ; [liar] fieffé(e).

Provence [prɒ'vɑːns] *n* Provence *f*.

proverb ['prɒvɜːb] *n* proverbe *m*.

provide [prə'vaɪd] *vt* fournir ; **to provide sb with sthg** fournir qqch à qqn ; **to provide sthg for sb** fournir qqch à qqn. ● **provide for** *vt insep* **1.** [support] subvenir aux besoins de - **2.** *fml* [make arrangements for] prévoir.

provided [prə'vaɪdɪd] ● **provided (that)** *conj* à condition que (+ *subjunctive*), pourvu que (+ *subjunctive*).

providing [prə'vaɪdɪŋ] ● **providing (that)** *conj* à condition que (+ *subjunctive*), pourvu que (+ *subjunctive*).

province ['prɒvɪns] *n* **1.** [part of country] province *f* - **2.** [speciality] domaine *m*, compétence *f*.

provincial [prə'vɪnʃl] *adj* **1.** [town, newspaper] de province - **2.** *pej* [narrow-minded] provincial(e).

provision [prə'vɪʒn] *n* **1.** (U) [act of supplying] : **provision (of)** approvisionnement *m* (en), fourniture *f* (de) - **2.** [supply] provision *f*, réserve *f* - **3.** (U) [arrangements] : **to make provision for** [the future] prendre des mesures pour ; [one's family] pourvoir aux besoins de - **4.** [in agreement, law] clause *f*, disposition *f*. ● **provisions** *npl* [supplies] provisions *fpl*.

provisional [prə'vɪʒənl] *adj* provisoire.

proviso [prə'vaɪzəu] (*pl* -s) *n* condition *f*, stipulation *f* ; **with the proviso that** à (la) condition que (+ *subjunctive*).

provocative [prə'vɒkətɪv] *adj* provocant(e).

provoke [prə'vəuk] *vt* **1.** [annoy] agacer, contrarier - **2.** [cause - fight, argument] provoquer ; [- reaction] susciter.

prow [prau] *n* proue *f*.

prowess ['prauɪs] *n* prouesse *f*.

prowl [praul] <> *n* : **to be on the prowl** rôder. <> *vt* [streets etc] rôder dans. <> *vi* rôder.

prowler ['praulə'] *n* rôdeur *m*, -euse *f*.

proxy ['prɒksɪ] *n* : **by proxy** par procuration.

prudent ['pruːdnt] *adj* prudent(e).

prudish ['pruːdɪʃ] *adj* prude, pudibond(e).

prune [pruːn] <> *n* [fruit] pruneau *m*.
<> *vt* [tree, bush] tailler.

pry [praɪ] *vi* se mêler de ce qui ne vous regarde pas ; **to pry into sthg** chercher à découvrir qqch.

PS (*abbrev of* **postscript**) *n* PS *m*.

psalm [sɑːm] *n* psaume *m*.

pseudonym ['sjuːdənɪm] *n* pseudonyme *m*.

psyche ['saɪkɪ] *n* psyché *f*.

psychiatric [ˌsaɪkɪˈætrɪk] *adj* psychiatrique.

psychiatrist [saɪˈkaɪətrɪst] *n* psychiatre *mf*.

psychiatry [saɪˈkaɪətrɪ] *n* psychiatrie *f*.

psychic ['saɪkɪk] <> *adj* **1.** [clairvoyant - person] doué(e) de seconde vue ; [- powers] parapsychique - **2.** MED psychique. <> *n* médium *m*.

psychoanalysis [ˌsaɪkəʊəˈnæləsɪs] *n* psychanalyse *f*.

psychoanalyst [ˌsaɪkəʊˈænəlɪst] *n* psychanalyste *mf*.

psychological [ˌsaɪkəˈlɒdʒɪkl] *adj* psychologique.

psychologist [saɪˈkɒlədʒɪst] *n* psychologue *mf*.

psychology [saɪˈkɒlədʒɪ] *n* psychologie *f*.

psychopath ['saɪkəpæθ] *n* psychopathe *mf*.

psychotic [saɪˈkɒtɪk] <> *adj* psychotique. <> *n* psychotique *mf*.

pt *abbrev of* **pint**. *abbrev of* **point**.

PT (*abbrev of* **physical training**) *n* UK EPS *f*.

pub [pʌb] *n* pub *m*.

puberty ['pjuːbətɪ] *n* puberté *f*.

pubic ['pjuːbɪk] *adj* du pubis.

public ['pʌblɪk] <> *adj* public(ique) ; [library] municipal(e). <> *n* : **the public** le public ; **in public** en public.

public-address system *n* système *m* de sonorisation.

publican ['pʌblɪkən] *n* UK & Aus gérant *m*, -e *f* d'un pub.

publication [ˌpʌblɪˈkeɪʃn] *n* publication *f*.

public bar *n* UK bar *m*.

public company *n* société *f* anonyme (*cotée en Bourse*).

public convenience *n* UK toilettes *fpl* publiques.

public holiday *n* UK jour *m* férié.

public house *n* UK pub *m*.

publicity [pʌbˈlɪsɪtɪ] *n* (U) publicité *f*.

publicize, UK **-ise** ['pʌblɪsaɪz] *vt* faire connaître au public.

public limited company *n* UK société *f* anonyme (*cotée en Bourse*).

public opinion *n* (U) opinion *f* publique.

public prosecutor *n* ≃ procureur *m* de la République.

public relations <> *n* (U) relations *fpl* publiques. <> *npl* relations *fpl* publiques.

public school *n* **1.** UK [private school] école *f* privée - **2.** US [state school] école *f* publique.

public-spirited *adj* qui fait preuve de civisme.

public transport *n* (U) transports *mpl* en commun.

publish ['pʌblɪʃ] *vt* publier.

publisher ['pʌblɪʃər] *n* éditeur *m*, -trice *f*.

publishing ['pʌblɪʃɪŋ] *n* (U) [industry] édition *f*.

pub lunch *n* repas de midi servi dans un pub.

pucker ['pʌkər] *vt* plisser.

pudding ['pʊdɪŋ] *n* **1.** [food - sweet] entremets *m* ; [- savoury] pudding *m* - **2.** (U) UK [course] dessert *m*.

puddle ['pʌdl] *n* flaque *f*.

puff [pʌf] <> *n* **1.** [of cigarette, smoke] bouffée *f* - **2.** [gasp] souffle *m*. <> *vt* [cigarette etc] tirer sur. <> *vi* **1.** [smoke] : **to puff at** OR **on sthg** fumer qqch - **2.** [pant] haleter. ◆ **puff out** *vt sep* [cheeks, chest] gonfler.

puffed [pʌft] *adj* [swollen] : **puffed (up)** gonflé(e).

puffin ['pʌfɪn] *n* macareux *m*.

puff pastry, US **puff paste** *n* (U) pâte *f* feuilletée.

puffy ['pʌfɪ] *adj* gonflé(e), bouffi(e).

pugnacious [pʌgˈneɪʃəs] *adj* fml querelleur(euse), batailleur(euse).

Pulitzer Prize [pʊlɪtsə-] *n* [in US] prix *m* Pulitzer.

pull [pʊl] <> *vt* **1.** [gen] tirer - **2.** [strain - muscle, hamstring] se froisser - **3.** [tooth] arracher ; **to have a tooth pulled** US se faire arracher une dent - **4.** [attract] attirer - **5.** [gun] sortir. <> *vi* tirer. <> *n* **1.** [tug with hand] : **to give sthg a pull** tirer sur qqch - **2.** (U) [influence] influence *f*. ◆ **pull apart** *vt sep* [separate] séparer. ◆ **pull at** *vt insep* tirer sur. ◆ **pull away** *vi* **1.** AUT démarrer - **2.** [in race] prendre de l'avance. ◆ **pull down** *vt sep* [building] démolir. ◆ **pull in** *vi* AUT se ranger. ◆ **pull off** *vt sep* **1.** [take off] enlever, ôter - **2.** [succeed in] réussir. ◆ **pull out** <> *vt sep* [troops etc] retirer. <> *vi* **1.** RAIL partir, démarrer - **2.** AUT déboîter - **3.** [withdraw] se retirer. ◆ **pull over** *vi* AUT se ranger. ◆ **pull through** *vi* s'en sortir, s'en tirer. ◆ **pull together** *vt sep* : **to pull o.s. together** se

ressaisir, se reprendre. ◆ **pull up**
◇ vt sep **1.** [raise] remonter - **2.** [chair]
avancer. ◇ vi s'arrêter.

pulley ['pʊlɪ] (pl **-s**) n poulie f.

pullover ['pʊl,əʊvəʳ] n pull m.

pulp [pʌlp] ◇ adj [fiction, novel] de quatre
sous. ◇ n **1.** [for paper] pâte f à papier
- **2.** [of fruit] pulpe f.

pulpit ['pʊlpɪt] n chaire f.

pulsate [pʌl'seɪt] vi [heart] battre fort ; [air,
music] vibrer.

pulse [pʌls] ◇ n **1.** MED pouls m - **2.** TECH
impulsion f. ◇ vi battre, palpiter.
◆ **pulses** npl [food] légumes mpl secs.

puma ['pjuːmə] (pl **puma** OR **-s**) n puma m.

pumice (stone) ['pʌmɪs-] n pierre f ponce.

pummel ['pʌml] (UK & US) vt bourrer de
coups.

pump [pʌmp] ◇ n US pompe f. ◇ vt
1. [water, gas etc] pomper - **2.** inf [interrogate]
essayer de tirer les vers du nez à. ◇ vi
[heart] battre fort. ◆ **pumps** npl [shoes]
escarpins mpl.

pumpkin ['pʌmpkɪn] n potiron m.

pun [pʌn] n jeu m de mots, calembour m.

punch [pʌntʃ] ◇ n **1.** [blow] coup m de
poing - **2.** [tool] poinçonneuse f - **3.** [drink]
punch m. ◇ vt **1.** [hit - once] donner un
coup de poing à ; [- repeatedly] donner des
coups de poing à - **2.** [ticket] poinçonner ;
[paper] perforer.

Punch-and-Judy show [-'dʒuːdɪ-] n guignol m.

punch(ed) card [pʌntʃ(t)-] n carte f perfo-
rée.

punch line n chute f.

punch-up n UK inf bagarre f.

punchy ['pʌntʃɪ] adj inf [style] incisif(ive).

punctual ['pʌŋktʃʊəl] adj ponctuel(elle).

punctuation [,pʌŋktʃʊ'eɪʃn] n ponctuation f.

punctuation mark n signe m de ponctuation.

puncture ['pʌŋktʃəʳ] ◇ n crevaison f.
◇ vt [tyre, ball] crever ; [skin] piquer.

pundit ['pʌndɪt] n pontife m.

pungent ['pʌndʒənt] adj **1.** [smell] âcre ;
[taste] piquant(e) - **2.** fig [criticism] caustique, acerbe.

punish ['pʌnɪʃ] vt punir ; to punish sb for
sthg/for doing sthg punir qqn pour qqch/
pour avoir fait qqch.

punishing ['pʌnɪʃɪŋ] adj [schedule, work]
épuisant(e), éreintant(e) ; [defeat] cui-
sant(e).

punishment ['pʌnɪʃmənt] n punition f,
châtiment m.

punk [pʌŋk] ◇ adj punk (inv). ◇ n

1. (U) [music] : **punk (rock)** punk m - **2.** [per-
son] : **punk (rocker)** punk mf - **3.** US inf [lout]
loubard m.

punt [pʌnt] n [boat] bateau m à fond plat.

punter ['pʌntəʳ] n UK **1.** [gambler] parieur
m, -euse f - **2.** inf [customer] client m, -e f.

puny ['pjuːnɪ] adj chétif(ive).

pup [pʌp] n **1.** [young dog] chiot m
- **2.** [young seal] bébé phoque m.

pupil ['pjuːpl] n **1.** [student] élève mf - **2.** [of
eye] pupille f.

puppet ['pʌpɪt] n **1.** [toy] marionnette f
- **2.** pej [person, country] fantoche m, pantin
m.

puppy ['pʌpɪ] n chiot m.

purchase ['pɜːtʃəs] ◇ n achat m. ◇ vt
acheter.

purchaser ['pɜːtʃəsəʳ] n acheteur m, -euse f.

purchasing power ['pɜːtʃəsɪŋ-] n pouvoir
m d'achat.

pure [pjʊəʳ] adj pur(e).

puree ['pjʊəreɪ] n purée f.

purely ['pjʊəlɪ] adv purement.

purge [pɜːdʒ] ◇ n POL purge f. ◇ vt
1. POL purger - **2.** [rid] débarrasser, purger.

purify ['pjʊərɪfaɪ] vt purifier, épurer.

purist ['pjʊərɪst] n puriste mf.

puritan ['pjʊərɪtən] ◇ adj puritain(e).
◇ n puritain m, -e f.

purity ['pjʊərətɪ] n pureté f.

purl [pɜːl] ◇ n maille f à l'envers. ◇ vt
tricoter à l'envers.

purple ['pɜːpl] ◇ adj violet(ette). ◇ n
violet m.

purport [pə'pɔːt] vi fml : to purport to do/be
sthg prétendre faire/être qqch.

purpose ['pɜːpəs] n **1.** [reason] raison f,
motif m - **2.** [aim] but m, objet m ; to no
purpose en vain, pour rien - **3.** [determina-
tion] détermination f. ◆ **on purpose** adv
exprès.

purposeful ['pɜːpəsfʊl] adj résolu(e), dé-
terminé(e).

purr [pɜːʳ] vi ronronner.

purse [pɜːs] ◇ n **1.** [for money] porte-
monnaie m inv, bourse f - **2.** US [handbag]
sac m à main. ◇ vt [lips] pincer.

purser ['pɜːsəʳ] n commissaire m de bord.

pursue [pə'sjuː] vt **1.** [follow] poursuivre,
pourchasser - **2.** [policy, aim] poursuivre ;
[question] continuer à débattre ; [matter]
approfondir ; [project] donner suite à ; to
pursue an interest in sthg se livrer à qqch.

pursuer [pə'sjuːəʳ] n poursuivant m, -e f.

pursuit [pə'sjuːt] n **1.** (U) fml [attempt to
obtain] recherche f, poursuite f - **2.** [chase,
in sport] poursuite f - **3.** [occupation] occupation f, activité f.

pus [pʌs] *n* pus *m*.

push [puʃ] ⬡ *vt* **1.** [press, move - gen] pousser ; [- button] appuyer sur - **2.** [encourage] : **to push sb (to do sthg)** inciter OR pousser qqn (à faire qqch) - **3.** [force] : **to push sb (into doing sthg)** forcer OR obliger qqn (à faire qqch) - **4.** *inf* [promote] faire de la réclame pour. ⬡ *vi* **1.** [gen] pousser ; [on button] appuyer - **2.** [campaign] : **to push for sthg** faire pression pour obtenir qqch. ⬡ *n* **1.** [with hand] poussée *f* - **2.** [forceful effort] effort *m*. ⬤ **push around** *vt sep inf* *fig* marcher sur les pieds de. ⬤ **push in** *vi* [in queue] resquiller. ⬤ **push off** *vi inf* filer, se sauver. ⬤ **push on** *vi* continuer. ⬤ **push through** *vt sep* [law, reform] faire accepter.

pushchair ['puʃtʃeər] *n UK* poussette *f*.

pushed [puʃt] *adj inf* **to be pushed for sthg** être à court de qqch ; **to be hard pushed to do sthg** avoir du mal OR de la peine à faire qqch.

pusher ['puʃər] *n drug sl* dealer *m*.

pushover ['puʃ,əuvər] *n inf* **it's a pushover** c'est un jeu d'enfant.

push-up *n* pompe *f*, traction *f*.

pushy ['puʃi] *adj pej* qui se met toujours en avant.

puss [pus], **pussy (cat)** ['pusɪ-] *n inf* minet *m*, minou *m*.

put [put] (*pt & pp* **put**) *vt* **1.** [gen] mettre - **2.** [place] mettre, poser, placer ; **to put the children to bed** coucher les enfants - **3.** [express] dire, exprimer - **4.** [question] poser - **5.** [estimate] estimer, évaluer - **6.** [invest] : **to put money into** investir de l'argent dans. ⬤ **put across** *vt sep* [ideas] faire comprendre. ⬤ **put away** *vt sep* **1.** [tidy away] ranger - **2.** *inf* [lock up] enfermer. ⬤ **put back** *vt sep* **1.** [replace] remettre (à sa place OR en place) - **2.** [postpone] remettre - **3.** [clock, watch] retarder. ⬤ **put by** *vt sep* [money] mettre de côté. ⬤ **put down** *vt sep* **1.** [lay down] poser, déposer - **2.** [quell - rebellion] réprimer - **3.** [write down] inscrire, noter - **4.** *UK* [kill] : **to have a dog/cat put down** faire piquer un chien/chat. ⬤ **put down to** *vt sep* attribuer à. ⬤ **put forward** *vt sep* **1.** [propose] proposer, avancer - **2.** [meeting, clock, watch] avancer. ⬤ **put in** *vt sep* **1.** [time, effort] passer - **2.** [submit] présenter. ⬤ **put off** *vt sep* **1.** [postpone] remettre (à plus tard) - **2.** [cause to wait] décommander - **3.** [discourage] dissuader - **4.** [disturb] déconcerter, troubler - **5.** [cause to dislike] dégoûter - **6.** [switch off - radio, TV] éteindre. ⬤ **put on** *vt sep* **1.** [clothes] mettre, enfiler - **2.** [arrange - exhibition etc] organiser ; [- play] monter - **3.** [gain] : **to put on weight** prendre du poids, grossir - **4.** [switch on - radio, TV] allumer, mettre ; **to put the light on** allumer (la lumière) ; **to**

put the brake on freiner - **5.** [record, CD, tape] passer, mettre - **6.** [start cooking] mettre à cuire - **7.** [pretend - gen] feindre ; [- accent etc] prendre - **8.** [bet] parier, miser - **9.** [add] ajouter. ⬤ **put out** *vt sep* **1.** [place outside] mettre dehors - **2.** [book, statement] publier ; [record] sortir - **3.** [fire, cigarette] éteindre ; **to put the light out** éteindre (la lumière) - **4.** [extend - hand] tendre - **5.** [annoy, upset] : **to be put out** être contrarié(e) - **6.** [inconvenience] déranger. ⬤ **put through** *vt sep* TELEC passer. ⬤ **put up** ⬡ *vt sep* **1.** [build - gen] ériger ; [- tent] dresser - **2.** [umbrella] ouvrir ; [flag] hisser - **3.** [fix to wall] accrocher - **4.** [provide - money] fournir - **5.** [propose - candidate] proposer - **6.** *UK* [increase] augmenter - **7.** [provide accommodation for] loger, héberger. ⬡ *vt insep* : **to put up a fight** se défendre. ⬤ **put up with** *vt insep* supporter.

putrid ['pju:trɪd] *adj* putride.

putt [pʌt] ⬡ *n* putt *m*. ⬡ *vt & vi* putter.

putting green ['pʌtɪŋ-] *n* green *m*.

putty ['pʌtɪ] *n* mastic *m*.

puzzle ['pʌzl] ⬡ *n* **1.** [toy] puzzle *m* ; [mental] devinette *f* - **2.** [mystery] mystère *m*, énigme *f*. ⬡ *vt* rendre perplexe. ⬡ *vi* : **to puzzle over sthg** essayer de comprendre qqch. ⬤ **puzzle out** *vt sep* comprendre.

puzzling ['pʌzlɪŋ] *adj* curieux(euse).

pyjamas [pə'dʒɑːməz] *npl UK* pyjama *m* ; **a pair of pyjamas** un pyjama.

pylon ['paɪlən] *n* pylône *m*.

pyramid ['pɪrəmɪd] *n* pyramide *f*.

Pyrenees [,pɪrə'niːz] *npl* : **the Pyrenees** les Pyrénées *fpl*.

Pyrex® ['paɪreks] *n* Pyrex® *m*.

python ['paɪθn] (*pl* **python** OR **-s**) *n* python *m*.

Q

q [kju:] (*pl* **q's** OR **qs**), **Q** (*pl* **Q's** OR **Qs**) *n* [letter] q *m inv*, Q *m inv*.

quack [kwæk] *n* **1.** [noise] coin-coin *m inv* - **2.** *inf* [doctor] charlatan *m*.

quadrangle ['kwɒdræŋgl] *n* **1.** [figure] quadrilatère *m* - **2.** [courtyard] cour *f*.

quadruple [kwɒ'druːpl] ⬡ *adj* quadruple. ⬡ *vt & vi* quadrupler.

quadruplets ['kwɒdruplɪts] *npl* quadruplés *mpl*.

quads [kwɒdz] *npl inf* quadruplés *mpl*.

quagmire ['kwæɡmaɪə*r*] *n* bourbier *m*.

quail [kweɪl] <> *n* (*pl* quail OR -s) caille *f*. <> *vi lit* reculer.

quaint [kweɪnt] *adj* pittoresque.

quake [kweɪk] <> *n inf* (*abbrev of* **earthquake**) tremblement *m* de terre. <> *vi* trembler.

Quaker ['kweɪkə*r*] *n* quaker *m*, -eresse *f*.

qualification [,kwɒlɪfɪ'keɪʃn] *n* **1.** [certificate] diplôme *m* - **2.** [quality, skill] compétence *f* - **3.** [qualifying statement] réserve *f*.

qualified ['kwɒlɪfaɪd] *adj* **1.** [trained] diplômé(e) - **2.** [able] : **to be qualified to do sthg** avoir la compétence nécessaire pour faire qqch - **3.** [limited] restreint(e), modéré(e).

qualify ['kwɒlɪfaɪ] <> *vt* **1.** [modify] apporter des réserves à - **2.** [entitle] : **to qualify sb to do sthg** qualifier qqn pour faire qqch. <> *vi* **1.** [pass exams] obtenir un diplôme - **2.** [be entitled] : **to qualify (for sthg)** avoir droit (à qqch), remplir les conditions requises (pour qqch) - **3.** SPORT se qualifier.

quality ['kwɒlətɪ] <> *n* qualité *f*. <> *comp* de qualité.

qualms [kwɑːmz] *npl* doutes *mpl*.

quandary ['kwɒndərɪ] *n* embarras *m* ; **to be in a quandary about** OR **over sthg** être bien embarrassé à propos de qqch.

quantify ['kwɒntɪfaɪ] *vt* quantifier.

quantity ['kwɒntətɪ] *n* quantité *f*.

quantity surveyor *n* métreur *m*, -euse *f*.

quarantine ['kwɒrəntiːn] <> *n* quarantaine *f*. <> *vt* mettre en quarantaine.

quark [kwɑːk] *n* quark *m*.

quarrel ['kwɒrəl] <> *n* querelle *f*, dispute *f*. <> *vi* (UK & US) **to quarrel (with)** se quereller (avec), se disputer (avec).

quarrelsome ['kwɒrəlsəm] *adj* querelleur(euse).

quarry ['kwɒrɪ] *n* **1.** [place] carrière *f* - **2.** [prey] proie *f*.

quart [kwɔːt] *n* UK = 1,136 litre ; US = 0,946 litre, ≃ litre *m*.

quarter ['kwɔːtə*r*] *n* **1.** [fraction, weight] quart *m* ; **a quarter past two, a quarter after two** US deux heures et quart ; **a quarter to two, a quarter of two** US deux heures moins le quart - **2.** [of year] trimestre *m* - **3.** US [coin] pièce *f* de 25 cents - **4.** [area in town] quartier *m* - **5.** [direction] : **from all quarters** de tous côtés. ◆ **quarters** *npl* [rooms] quartiers *mpl*. ◆ **at close quarters** *adv* de près.

quarterfinal [,kwɔːtə'faɪnl] *n* quart *m* de finale.

quarterly ['kwɔːtəlɪ] <> *adj* trimestriel(elle). <> *adv* trimestriellement. <> *n* publication *f* trimestrielle.

quartermaster ['kwɔːtə,mɑːstə*r*] *n* MIL intendant *m*.

quartet [kwɔː'tet] *n* quatuor *m*.

quartz [kwɔːts] *n* quartz *m*.

quartz watch *n* montre *f* à quartz.

quash [kwɒʃ] *vt* **1.** [sentence] annuler, casser - **2.** [rebellion] réprimer.

quasi- ['kweɪzaɪ] *prefix* quasi-.

quaver ['kweɪvə*r*] <> *n* **1.** MUS croche *f* - **2.** [in voice] tremblement *m*, chevrotement *m*. <> *vi* trembler, chevroter.

quay [kiː] *n* quai *m*.

quayside ['kiːsaɪd] *n* bord *m* du quai.

queasy ['kwiːzɪ] *adj* : **to feel queasy** avoir mal au cœur.

Quebec [kwɪ'bek] *n* [province] Québec *m*.

queen [kwiːn] *n* **1.** [gen] reine *f* - **2.** [playing card] dame *f*.

Queen Mother *n* : **the Queen Mother** la reine mère.

queer [kwɪə*r*] <> *adj* [odd] étrange, bizarre. <> *n inf pej* pédé *m*, homosexuel *m*.

quell [kwel] *vt* réprimer, étouffer.

quench [kwentʃ] *vt* : **to quench one's thirst** se désaltérer.

querulous ['kwerʊləs] *adj* [child] ronchonneur(euse) ; [voice] plaintif(ive).

query ['kwɪərɪ] <> *n* question *f*. <> *vt* mettre en doute, douter de.

quest [kwest] *n lit* : **quest (for)** quête *f* (de).

question ['kwestʃn] <> *n* **1.** [gen] question *f* ; **to ask (sb) a question** poser une question (à qqn) - **2.** [doubt] doute *m* ; **to call** OR **bring sthg into question** mettre qqch en doute ; **without question** incontestablement, sans aucun doute ; **beyond question** [know] sans aucun doute ; **there's no question of...** il n'est pas question de... <> *vt* **1.** [interrogate] questionner - **2.** [express doubt about] mettre en question OR doute. ◆ **in question** *adv* : **the... in question** le/la/les... en question. ◆ **out of the question** *adv* hors de question.

questionable ['kwestʃənəbl] *adj* **1.** [uncertain] discutable - **2.** [not right, not honest] douteux(euse).

question mark *n* point *m* d'interrogation.

questionnaire [,kwestʃə'neə*r*] *n* questionnaire *m*.

queue [kjuː] UK <> *n* queue *f*, file *f*. <> *vi* faire la queue.

quibble ['kwɪbl] *pej* ◇ *n* chicane *f.*
◇ *vi* : **to quibble (over** OR **about)** chicaner
(à propos de). .

quiche [kiːʃ] *n* quiche *f.*

quick [kwɪk] ◇ *adj* **1.** [gen] rapide - **2.** [response, decision] prompt(e), rapide. ◇ *adv*
vite, rapidement.

quicken ['kwɪkn] ◇ *vt* accélérer, presser.
◇ *vi* s'accélérer.

quickly ['kwɪklɪ] *adv* **1.** [rapidly] vite, rapidement - **2.** [without delay] promptement,
immédiatement.

quicksand ['kwɪksænd] *n* sables *mpl* mouvants.

quick-witted [-'wɪtɪd] *adj* [person] à l'esprit vif.

quid [kwɪd] (*pl* quid) *n* UK *inf* livre *f.*

quiet ['kwaɪət] ◇ *adj* **1.** [not noisy]
tranquille ; [voice] bas (basse) ; [engine]
silencieux(euse) ; **be quiet!** taisez-vous!
- **2.** [not busy] calme - **3.** [silent] silencieux(euse) ; **to keep quiet about sthg** ne
rien dire à propos de qqch, garder qqch
secret - **4.** [intimate] intime - **5.** [colour]
discret(ète), sobre. ◇ *n* tranquillité *f* ; **on
the quiet** *inf* en douce. ◇ *vt* US calmer,
apaiser. ◆ **quiet down** ◇ *vt sep* calmer,
apaiser. ◇ *vi* se calmer.

quieten ['kwaɪətn] UK *vt* calmer, apaiser.
◆ **quieten down** ◇ *vt sep* calmer,
apaiser. ◇ *vi* se calmer.

quietly ['kwaɪətlɪ] *adv* **1.** [without noise]
sans faire de bruit, silencieusement ; [say]
doucement - **2.** [without excitement] tranquillement, calmement - **3.** [without fuss -
leave] discrètement.

quilt [kwɪlt] *n* [padded] édredon *m* ;
(continental) UK quilt couette *f.*

quinine [kwɪ'niːn] *n* quinine *f.*

quins UK [kwɪnz], **quints** US [kwɪnts] *npl*
inf quintuplés *mpl.*

quintet [kwɪn'tet] *n* quintette *m.*

quints US = quins.

quintuplets [kwɪn'tjuːplɪts] *npl* quintuplés *mpl.*

quip [kwɪp] ◇ *n* raillerie *f.* ◇ *vi* railler.

quirk [kwɜːk] *n* bizarrerie *f.*

quit [kwɪt] (UK, *pt & pp* quit OR -ted US,
pt & pp quit) ◇ *vt* **1.** [resign from] quitter
- **2.** [stop] : **to quit smoking** arrêter de fumer
- **3.** COMPUT quitter ; **to quit an application**
quitter une application. ◇ *vi* **1.** [resign]
démissionner - **2.** [give up] abandonner
- **3.** COMPUT quitter.

quite [kwaɪt] *adv* **1.** [completely] tout à fait,
complètement ; **I quite agree** je suis
entièrement d'accord ; **not quite** pas tout à
fait ; **I don't quite understand** je ne
comprends pas bien - **2.** [fairly, a little]

assez, plutôt - **3.** [for emphasis] : **she's quite
a singer** c'est une chanteuse formidable
- **4.** UK [to express agreement] : **quite (so)!**
exactement!

quits [kwɪts] *adj inf* **to be quits (with sb)**
être quitte (envers qqn) ; **to call it quits** en
rester là.

quiver ['kwɪvər] ◇ *n* **1.** [shiver] frisson *m*
- **2.** [for arrows] carquois *m.* ◇ *vi* frissonner.

quiz [kwɪz] ◇ *n* (*pl* quizzes) **1.** [gen] quiz
m, jeu-concours *m* - **2.** US SCH interrogation
f. ◇ *vt* : **to quiz sb (about sthg)** interroger
qqn (au sujet de qqch).

quizzical ['kwɪzɪkl] *adj* narquois(e), moqueur(euse).

quota ['kwəʊtə] *n* quota *m.*

quotation [kwəʊ'teɪʃn] *n* **1.** [citation] citation *f* - **2.** COMM devis *m.*

quotation marks *npl* guillemets *mpl* ; **in
quotation marks** entre guillemets.

quote [kwəʊt] ◇ *n* **1.** [citation] citation *f*
- **2.** COMM devis *m.* ◇ *vt* **1.** [cite] citer
- **2.** COMM indiquer, spécifier. ◇ *vi* **1.** [cite] :
to quote (from sthg) citer (qqch) - **2.** COMM :
to quote for sthg établir un devis pour
qqch.

quotient ['kwəʊʃnt] *n* quotient *m.*

R

r [ɑːr] (*pl* **r's** OR **rs**), **R** (*pl* **R's** OR **Rs**) *n* [letter] r
m inv, R *m inv.*

R [1. (*abbrev of* **right**) dr. - **2.** *abbrev of* **River**
- **3.** (*abbr of* **Réaumur**) R - **4.** (*abbrev of*
restricted) aux États-Unis, indique qu'un film
est interdit aux moins de 17 ans - **5.** US *abbrev
of* **Republican** - **6.** UK (*abbrev of* **Rex**) suit le
nom d'un roi - **7.** UK (*abbrev of* **Regina**) suit le
nom d'une reine.

R &D (*abbrev of* **research and development**)
n R-D *f.*

rabbi ['ræbaɪ] *n* rabbin *m.*

rabbit ['ræbɪt] *n* lapin *m.*

rabbit hutch *n* clapier *m.*

rabble ['ræbl] *n* cohue *f.*

rabies ['reɪbiːz] *n* rage *f.*

RAC (*abbrev of* **Royal Automobile Club**) *n*
club automobile britannique, ≃ TCF *m*, ≃ ACF
m.

race [reɪs] ◇ *n* **1.** [competition] course *f*

- 2. [people, ethnic background] race f. ⬦ vt **1.** [compete against] faire la course avec **- 2.** [horse] faire courir. ⬦ vi **1.** [compete] courir ; **to race against sb** faire la course avec qqn **- 2.** [rush] : **to race in/out** entrer/sortir à toute allure **- 3.** [pulse] être très rapide **- 4.** [engine] s'emballer.

race car US = **racing car**.

racecourse ['reɪskɔːs] n champ m de courses.

race driver US = **racing driver**.

racehorse ['reɪshɔːs] n cheval m de course.

racetrack ['reɪstræk] n piste f ; US [racecourse] champ m de course.

racewalking ['reɪswɔːkɪŋ] n marche f athlétique.

racial discrimination ['reɪʃl-] n discrimination f raciale.

racing ['reɪsɪŋ] n (U) **(horse) racing** les courses fpl.

racing car UK, **race car** US n voiture f de course.

racing driver UK, **race driver** US n coureur m automobile, pilote m de course.

racism ['reɪsɪzm] n racisme m.

racist ['reɪsɪst] ⬦ adj raciste. ⬦ n raciste mf.

rack [ræk] n **1.** [shelf - for bottles] casier m ; [- for luggage] **porte-bagages** m inv ; [- for plates] **égouttoir** m ; **toast rack** porte-toasts m inv **- 2.** CULIN : **rack of lamb** carré m d'agneau.

racket ['rækɪt] n **1.** inf [noise] **boucan** m **- 2.** [illegal activity] **racket** m **- 3.** SPORT **raquette** f.

racquet ['rækɪt] n raquette f.

racy ['reɪsɪ] adj [novel, style] osé(e).

radar ['reɪdɑːʳ] n radar m.

radiant ['reɪdjənt] adj [happy] radieux(euse).

radiate ['reɪdɪeɪt] ⬦ vt **1.** [heat, light] émettre, dégager **- 2.** fig [confidence, health] respirer. ⬦ vi **1.** [heat, light] irradier **- 2.** [roads, lines] rayonner.

radiation [,reɪdɪ'eɪʃn] n [radioactive] radiation f.

radiator ['reɪdɪeɪtəʳ] n radiateur m.

radical ['rædɪkl] ⬦ adj radical(e). ⬦ n POL radical m, -e f.

radically ['rædɪklɪ] adv radicalement.

radii ['reɪdɪaɪ] npl ➤ **radius**.

radio ['reɪdɪəʊ] ⬦ n (pl -s) radio f ; **on the radio** à la radio. ⬦ comp de radio. ⬦ vt [person] appeler par radio ; [information] envoyer par radio.

radioactive [,reɪdɪəʊ'æktɪv] adj radioactif(ive).

radio alarm n radio-réveil m.

radio-controlled [-kən'trəʊld] adj téléguidé(e).

radiography [,reɪdɪ'ɒgrəfɪ] n radiographie f.

radiology [,reɪdɪ'ɒlədʒɪ] n radiologie f.

radiotherapy [,reɪdɪəʊ'θerəpɪ] n radiothérapie f.

radish ['rædɪʃ] n radis m.

radius ['reɪdɪəs] (pl **radii** ['reɪdɪaɪ]) n **1.** MATHS rayon m **- 2.** ANAT radius m.

RAF [ɑːreɪ'ef OR ræf] n UK abbrev of **Royal Air Force**.

raffle ['ræfl] ⬦ n tombola f. ⬦ vt mettre en tombola.

raft [rɑːft] n [of wood] radeau m.

rafter ['rɑːftəʳ] n chevron m.

rag [ræg] n **1.** [piece of cloth] **chiffon** m **- 2.** pej [newspaper] **torchon** m. ➠ **rags** npl [clothes] guenilles fpl.

rag-and-bone man n UK chiffonnier m.

rag doll n poupée f de chiffon.

rage [reɪdʒ] ⬦ n **1.** [fury] rage f, fureur f **- 2.** inf [fashion] : **to be (all) the rage** faire fureur. ⬦ vi **1.** [person] être furieux(euse) **- 2.** [storm, argument] faire rage.

ragged ['rægɪd] adj **1.** [person] en haillons ; [clothes] en lambeaux **- 2.** [line, edge, performance] inégal(e).

rag week n UK semaine de carnaval organisée par des étudiants afin de collecter des fonds pour des œuvres charitables.

raid [reɪd] ⬦ n **1.** MIL raid m **- 2.** [by criminals] **hold-up** m inv ; [by police] **descente** f. ⬦ vt **1.** MIL faire un raid sur **- 2.** [subj: criminals] faire un hold-up dans ; [subj: police] faire une descente dans.

raider ['reɪdəʳ] n **1.** [attacker] agresseur m **- 2.** [thief] braqueur m.

rail [reɪl] ⬦ n **1.** [on ship] bastingage m ; [on staircase] rampe f ; [on walkway] garde-fou m **- 2.** [bar] barre f **- 3.** RAIL rail m ; **by rail** en train. ⬦ comp [transport, travel] par le train ; [strike] des cheminots.

railcard ['reɪlkɑːd] n UK carte donnant droit à des tarifs préférentiels sur les chemins de fer.

railing ['reɪlɪŋ] n [fence] grille f ; [on ship] bastingage m ; [on staircase] rampe f ; [on walkway] garde-fou m.

railway UK ['reɪlweɪ], **railroad** US ['reɪlrəʊd] n [system, company] chemin m de fer ; [track] voie f ferrée.

railway line UK, **railroad line** US n [route] ligne f de chemin de fer ; [track] voie f ferrée.

railwayman ['reɪlweɪmən] (pl **-men** [-mən]) n UK cheminot m.

railway station UK, **railroad station** US n gare f.

railway track UK, **railroad track** US n voie f ferrée.

rain [reɪn] <> n pluie f. <> impers vb METEOR pleuvoir ; **it's raining** il pleut. <> vi [fall like rain] pleuvoir.

rainbow ['reɪnbəʊ] n arc-en-ciel m.

rain check n US : **I'll take a rain check (on that)** une autre fois peut-être.

raincoat ['reɪnkəʊt] n imperméable m.

raindrop ['reɪndrɒp] n goutte f de pluie.

rainfall ['reɪnfɔːl] n [shower] chute f de pluie ; [amount] précipitations fpl.

rain forest n forêt f tropicale humide.

rainy ['reɪnɪ] adj pluvieux(euse).

raise [reɪz] <> vt **1.** [lift up] lever ; **to raise o.s.** se lever - **2.** [increase - gen] augmenter ; [- standards] élever ; **to raise one's voice** élever la voix - **3.** [subject, doubt] soulever ; [memories] évoquer - **4.** [children, cattle] élever - **5.** [crops] cultiver - **6.** [build] ériger, élever. <> n US augmentation f (de salaire).

raisin ['reɪzn] n raisin m sec.

rake [reɪk] <> n **1.** [implement] râteau m - **2.** dated & lit [immoral man] débauché m. <> vt [path, lawn] ratisser ; [leaves] râteler.

rally ['rælɪ] <> n **1.** [meeting] rassemblement m - **2.** [car race] rallye m - **3.** SPORT [exchange of shots] échange m. <> vt rallier. <> vi **1.** [supporters] se rallier - **2.** [patient] aller mieux ; [prices] remonter. ◆ **rally round** UK, **rally around** US <> vt insep apporter son soutien à. <> vi inf venir en aide.

ram [ræm] <> n bélier m. <> vt **1.** [crash into] percuter contre, emboutir - **2.** [force] tasser.

RAM [ræm] (abbrev of **random access memory**) n RAM f.

ramble ['ræmbl] <> n randonnée f, promenade f à pied. <> vi **1.** [walk] faire une promenade à pied - **2.** pej [talk] radoter. ◆ **ramble on** vi pej radoter.

rambler ['ræmblər] n [walker] randonneur m, -euse f.

rambling ['ræmblɪŋ] adj **1.** [house] plein(e) de coins et recoins - **2.** [speech] décousu(e).

ramp [ræmp] n **1.** [slope] rampe f - **2.** UK AUT [to slow traffic down] ralentisseur m - **3.** US AUT [to or from highway] bretelle f.

rampage [ræm'peɪdʒ] n : **to go on the rampage** tout saccager.

rampant ['ræmpənt] adj qui sévit.

ramparts ['ræmpɑːts] npl rempart m.

ramshackle ['ræm,ʃækl] adj branlant(e).

ran [ræn] pt ► run.

ranch [rɑːntʃ] n ranch m.

rancher ['rɑːntʃər] n propriétaire mf de ranch.

rancid ['rænsɪd] adj rance.

rancour UK, **rancor** US ['ræŋkər] n rancœur f.

random ['rændəm] <> adj fait(e) au hasard ; [number] aléatoire. <> n : **at random** au hasard.

random access memory n COMPUT mémoire f vive.

R and R (abbrev of **rest and recreation**) n US permission f.

randy ['rændɪ] adj inf excité(e).

rang [ræŋ] pt ► ring.

range [reɪndʒ] <> n **1.** [of plane, telescope etc] portée f ; **at close range** à bout portant - **2.** [of subjects, goods] gamme f ; **price range** éventail m des prix - **3.** [of mountains] chaîne f - **4.** [shooting area] champ m de tir - **5.** MUS [of voice] tessiture f. <> vt [place in row] mettre en rang. <> vi **1.** [vary] : **to range between... and...** varier entre... et... ; **to range from... to...** varier de... à... - **2.** [include] : **to range over sthg** couvrir qqch.

ranger ['reɪndʒər] n garde m forestier.

rank [ræŋk] <> adj **1.** [absolute - disgrace, stupidity] complet(ète) ; [- injustice] flagrant(e) ; **he's a rank outsider** il n'a aucune chance - **2.** [smell] fétide. <> n **1.** [in army, police etc] grade m - **2.** [social class] rang m - **3.** [row] rangée f ; **the rank and file** la masse ; [of union] la base. <> vt [classify] classer. <> vi : **to rank among** compter parmi ; **to rank as** être aux rangs de. ◆ **ranks** npl **1.** MIL : **the ranks** le rang - **2.** fig [members] rangs mpl.

rankle ['ræŋkl] vi : **it rankled with him** ça lui est resté sur l'estomac OR le cœur.

ransack ['rænsæk] vt [search through] mettre tout sens dessus dessous dans ; [damage] saccager.

ransom ['rænsəm] n rançon f ; **to hold sb to ransom** [keep prisoner] mettre qqn à rançon ; fig exercer un chantage sur qqn.

rant [rænt] vi déblatérer.

rap [ræp] <> n **1.** [knock] coup m sec - **2.** MUS rap m. <> vt [table] frapper sur ; [knuckles] taper sur.

rape [reɪp] <> n **1.** [crime, attack] viol m - **2.** fig [of countryside etc] destruction f - **3.** [plant] colza m. <> vt violer.

rapeseed ['reɪpsiːd] n graine f de colza.

rapid ['ræpɪd] adj rapide. ◆ **rapids** npl rapides mpl.

rapidly ['ræpɪdlɪ] adv rapidement.

rapist ['reɪpɪst] n violeur m.

rapport [ræ'pɔːr] n rapport m.

rapture ['ræptʃər] n ravissement m.

rapturous ['ræptʃərəs] *adj* [applause, welcome] enthousiaste.

rare [reəʳ] *adj* **1.** [gen] rare - **2.** [meat] saignant(e).

rarely ['reəlɪ] *adv* rarement.

raring ['reərɪŋ] *adj* : **to be raring to go** être impatient(e) de commencer.

rarity ['reərətɪ] *n* rareté *f*.

rascal ['rɑːskl] *n* polisson *m*, -onne *f*.

rash [ræʃ] <> *adj* irréfléchi(e), imprudent(e). <> *n* **1.** MED éruption *f* - **2.** [spate] succession *f*, série *f*.

rasher ['ræʃəʳ] *n* tranche *f*.

rasp [rɑːsp] *n* [harsh sound] grincement *m*.

raspberry ['rɑːzbərɪ] *n* **1.** [fruit] framboise *f* - **2.** [rude sound] : **to blow a raspberry** faire pfft.

rat [ræt] *n* **1.** [animal] rat *m* - **2.** *inf pej* [person] ordure *f*, salaud *m*.

rate [reɪt] <> *n* **1.** [speed] vitesse *f* ; [of pulse] fréquence *f* ; **at this rate** à ce train-là - **2.** [ratio, proportion] taux *m* - **3.** [price] tarif *m*. <> *vt* **1.** [consider] : **I rate her very highly** je la tiens en haute estime ; **to rate sb/sthg as** considérer qqn/qqch comme ; **to rate sb/sthg among** classer qqn/qqch parmi - **2.** [deserve] mériter. ⏵ **rates** *npl UK dated* impôts *mpl* locaux. ⏵ **at any rate** *adv* en tout cas.

ratepayer ['reɪt,peɪəʳ] *n UK* contribuable *mf*.

rather ['rɑːðəʳ] *adv* **1.** [somewhat, more exactly] plutôt - **2.** [to small extent] un peu - **3.** [preferably] : **I'd rather wait** je préférerais attendre ; **she'd rather not go** elle préférerait ne pas y aller - **4.** [on the contrary] : **(but) rather...** au contraire... ⏵ **rather than** *conj* plutôt que.

ratify ['rætɪfaɪ] *vt* ratifier, approuver.

rating ['reɪtɪŋ] *n* [of popularity etc] cote *f*.

ratio ['reɪʃɪəʊ] (*pl* **-s**) *n* rapport *m*.

ration ['ræʃn] <> *n* ration *f*. <> *vt* rationner. ⏵ **rations** *npl* vivres *mpl*.

rational ['ræʃənl] *adj* rationnel(elle).

rationale [,ræʃə'nɑːl] *n* logique *f*.

rationalize, *UK* **-ise** ['ræʃənəlaɪz] *vt* rationaliser.

rat race *n* jungle *f*.

rattle ['rætl] <> *n* **1.** [of bottles, typewriter keys] cliquetis *m* ; [of engine] bruit *m* de ferraille - **2.** [toy] hochet *m*. <> *vt* **1.** [bottles] faire s'entrechoquer ; [keys] faire cliqueter - **2.** [unsettle] secouer. <> *vi* [bottles] s'entrechoquer ; [keys, machine] cliqueter ; [engine] faire un bruit de ferraille.

rattlesnake ['rætlsneɪk], *US* **rattler** ['rætləʳ] *n* serpent *m* à sonnettes.

raucous ['rɔːkəs] *adj* [voice, laughter] rauque ; [behaviour] bruyant(e).

ravage ['rævɪdʒ] *vt* ravager. ⏵ **ravages** *npl* ravages *mpl*.

rave [reɪv] <> *adj* [review] élogieux(euse). <> *n UK inf* [party] rave *f*. <> *vi* **1.** [talk angrily] : **to rave at** OR **against** tempêter OR fulminer contre - **2.** [talk enthusiastically] : **to rave about** parler avec enthousiasme de.

raven ['reɪvn] *n* corbeau *m*.

ravenous ['rævənəs] *adj* [person] affamé(e) ; [animal, appetite] vorace.

ravine [rə'viːn] *n* ravin *m*.

raving ['reɪvɪŋ] *adj* : **raving lunatic** fou furieux (folle furieuse).

ravioli [,rævɪ'əʊlɪ] *n* (U) ravioli *mpl*.

ravishing ['rævɪʃɪŋ] *adj* ravissant(e), enchanteur(eresse).

raw [rɔː] *adj* **1.** [uncooked] cru(e) - **2.** [untreated] brut(e) - **3.** [painful] à vif - **4.** [inexperienced] novice ; **raw recruit** bleu *m* - **5.** [weather] froid(e) ; [wind] âpre.

raw deal *n* : **to get a raw deal** être défavorisé(e).

raw material *n* matière *f* première.

ray [reɪ] *n* [beam] rayon *m* ; *fig* [of hope] lueur *f*.

rayon ['reɪɒn] *n* rayonne *f*.

raze [reɪz] *vt* raser.

razor ['reɪzəʳ] *n* rasoir *m*.

razor blade *n* lame *f* de rasoir.

RC *abbrev of* **Roman Catholic**.

Rd *abbrev of* **Road**.

re [riː] *prep* concernant.

RE *n* (*abbrev of* **religious education**) instruction *f* religieuse.

reach [riːtʃ] <> *vt* [contact] joindre, contacter. <> *vi* **1.** [with hand] tendre la main ; **to reach out** tendre le bras ; **to reach down to pick sthg up** se pencher pour ramasser qqch - **2.** [land] s'étendre - **3.** [be long enough] : **it won't reach** ce n'est pas assez long. <> *n* [range] portée *f*, atteinte *f* ; **within reach** [object] à portée ; [place] à proximité ; **out of** OR **beyond sb's reach** [object] hors de portée ; [place] d'accès difficile, difficilement accessible.

react [rɪ'ækt] *vi* [gen] réagir.

reaction [rɪ'ækʃn] *n* réaction *f*.

reactionary [rɪ'ækʃənrɪ] <> *adj* réactionnaire. <> *n* réactionnaire *mf*.

reactor [rɪ'æktəʳ] *n* réacteur *m*.

read [riːd] <> *vt* (*pt & pp* **read** [red]) **1.** [gen] lire - **2.** [subj: sign, letter] dire - **3.** [interpret, judge] interpréter - **4.** [subj: meter, thermometer etc] indiquer - **5.** *UK* UNIV étudier. <> *vi* (*pt & pp* **read** [red]) lire ; **the**

book reads well le livre se lit bien. ◆ **read out** vt sep lire à haute voix. ◆ **read up on** vt insep étudier.

readable ['ri:dəbl] adj agréable à lire.

reader ['ri:dər] n [of book, newspaper] lecteur m, -trice f.

readership ['ri:dəʃɪp] n [of newspaper] nombre m de lecteurs.

readily ['redɪlɪ] adv 1. [willingly] volontiers - 2. [easily] facilement.

reading ['ri:dɪŋ] n 1. (U) [gen] lecture f - 2. [interpretation] interprétation f - 3. [on thermometer, meter etc] indications fpl.

readjust [,ri:ə'dʒʌst] ◇ vt [instrument] régler (de nouveau) ; [mirror] rajuster ; [policy] rectifier. ◇ vi [person] : **to readjust (to)** se réadapter (à).

readout ['ri:daʊt] n COMPUT affichage m.

ready ['redɪ] ◇ adj 1. [prepared] prêt(e) ; **to be ready to do sthg** être prêt à faire qqch ; **to get ready** se préparer ; **to get sthg ready** préparer qqch - 2. [willing] : **to be ready to do sthg** être prêt(e) OR disposé(e) à faire qqch. ◇ vt préparer.

ready cash n liquide m.

ready-made adj lit & fig tout fait (toute faite).

ready meal n plat m préparé.

ready money n liquide m.

ready-to-wear adj prêt-à-porter.

reafforestation ['ri:ə,fɒrɪ'steɪʃn] n UK reboisement m.

real ['rɪəl] ◇ adj 1. [gen] vrai(e), véritable ; **real life** réalité f ; **for real** pour de vrai ; **this is the real thing** [object] c'est de l'authentique ; [situation] c'est pour de vrai OR de bon - 2. [actual] réel(elle) ; **in real terms** dans la pratique. ◇ adv US très.

real estate n (U) biens mpl immobiliers.

realign [,ri:ə'laɪn] vt POL regrouper.

realism ['rɪəlɪzm] n réalisme m.

realistic [,rɪə'lɪstɪk] adj réaliste.

reality [rɪ'ælətɪ] n réalité f.

reality TV n (U) télévision/TV f réalité.

realization [,rɪəlaɪ'zeɪʃn] n réalisation f.

realize, UK **-ise** ['rɪəlaɪz] vt 1. [understand] se rendre compte de, réaliser - 2. [sum of money, idea, ambition] réaliser.

really ['rɪəlɪ] ◇ adv 1. [gen] vraiment - 2. [in fact] en réalité. ◇ excl 1. [expressing doubt] **vraiment?** - 2. [expressing surprise] **pas possible!** - 3. [expressing disapproval] **franchement!, ça alors!**

realm [relm] n 1. fig [subject area] domaine m - 2. [kingdom] royaume m.

realtor ['rɪəltər] n US agent m immobilier.

reap [ri:p] vt 1. [harvest] moissonner - 2. fig [obtain] récolter.

reappear [,ri:ə'pɪər] vi réapparaître, reparaître.

rear [rɪər] ◇ adj arrière (inv), de derrière. ◇ n 1. [back] arrière m ; **to bring up the rear** fermer la marche - 2. inf [bottom] derrière m. ◇ vt [children, animals] élever. ◇ vi [horse] : **to rear (up)** se cabrer.

rearm [ri:'ɑ:m] vt & vi réarmer.

rearmost ['rɪəməʊst] adj dernier(ère).

rearrange [,ri:ə'reɪndʒ] vt 1. [furniture, room] réarranger ; [plans] changer - 2. [meeting - to new time] changer l'heure de ; [- to new date] changer la date de.

rearview mirror ['rɪəvju:-] n rétroviseur m.

reason ['ri:zn] ◇ n 1. [cause] : **reason (for)** raison f (de) ; **for some reason** pour une raison ou pour une autre - 2. (U) [justification] : **to have reason to do sthg** avoir de bonnes raisons de faire qqch - 3. [common sense] bon sens m ; **he won't listen to reason** on ne peut pas lui faire entendre raison ; **it stands to reason** c'est logique. ◇ vt déduire. ◇ vi raisonner. ◆ **reason with** vt insep raisonner (avec).

reasonable ['ri:znəbl] adj raisonnable.

reasonably ['ri:znəblɪ] adv 1. [quite] assez - 2. [sensibly] raisonnablement.

reasoned ['ri:znd] adj raisonné(e).

reasoning ['ri:znɪŋ] n raisonnement m.

reassess [,ri:ə'ses] vt réexaminer.

reassurance [,ri:ə'ʃʊərəns] n 1. [comfort] réconfort m - 2. [promise] assurance f.

reassure [,ri:ə'ʃʊər] vt rassurer.

reassuring [,ri:ə'ʃʊərɪŋ] adj rassurant(e).

rebate ['ri:beɪt] n [on product] rabais m ; **tax rebate** ≃ dégrèvement m fiscal.

rebel ◇ n ['rebl] rebelle mf. ◇ vi [rɪ'bel] : **to rebel (against)** se rebeller (contre).

rebellion [rɪ'beljən] n rébellion f.

rebellious [rɪ'beljəs] adj rebelle.

reboot [,ri:'bu:t] vi redémarrer, réamorcer offic.

rebound ◇ n ['ri:baʊnd] [of ball] rebond m. ◇ vi [rɪ'baʊnd] [ball] rebondir.

rebrand [,ri:'brænd] vt changer la marque de.

rebuff [rɪ'bʌf] n rebuffade f.

rebuild [,ri:'bɪld] (pt & pp **rebuilt** [,ri:'bɪlt]) vt reconstruire.

rebuke [rɪ'bju:k] ◇ n réprimande f. ◇ vt réprimander.

rebuttal [ri:'bʌtl] n réfutation f.

recalcitrant [rɪ'kælsɪtrənt] *adj* récalcitrant(e).

recall [rɪ'kɔːl] ◇ *n* [memory] rappel *m*. ◇ *vt* **1.** [remember] se rappeler, se souvenir de - **2.** [summon back] rappeler.

recant [rɪ'kænt] *vi* se rétracter ; RELIG abjurer.

recap ['riːkæp] ◇ *n* récapitulation *f*. ◇ *vt* [summarize] récapituler. ◇ *vi* récapituler.

recapitulate [ˌriːkə'pɪtjʊleɪt] *vt & vi* récapituler.

recd, rec'd *abbrev of* **received.**

recede [riː'siːd] *vi* [person, car etc] s'éloigner ; [hopes] s'envoler.

receding [rɪ'siːdɪŋ] *adj* [hairline] dégarni(e) ; [chin, forehead] fuyant(e).

receipt [rɪ'siːt] *n* **1.** [piece of paper] reçu *m* - **2.** (U) [act of receiving] réception *f*. ➡ **receipts** *npl* recettes *fpl*.

receive [rɪ'siːv] *vt* **1.** [gen] recevoir ; [news] apprendre - **2.** [welcome] accueillir, recevoir.

receiver [rɪ'siːvə'] *n* **1.** [of telephone] récepteur *m*, combiné *m* - **2.** [radio, TV set] récepteur *m* - **3.** [criminal] receleur *m*, -euse *f* - **4.** FIN [official] administrateur *m*, -trice *f* judiciaire.

recent ['riːsnt] *adj* récent(e).

recently ['riːsntlɪ] *adv* récemment ; **until recently** jusqu'à ces derniers temps.

receptacle [rɪ'septəkl] *n* récipient *m*.

reception [rɪ'sepʃn] *n* **1.** [gen] réception *f* - **2.** [welcome] accueil *m*, réception *f*.

reception desk *n* réception *f*.

receptionist [rɪ'sepʃənɪst] *n* réceptionniste *mf*.

recess ['riːses OR rɪ'ses] *n* **1.** [alcove] niche *f* - **2.** [secret place] recoin *m* - **3.** POL : **to be in recess** être en vacances - **4.** US SCH récréation *f*.

recession [rɪ'seʃn] *n* récession *f*.

recharge [ˌriː'tʃɑːdʒ] *vt* recharger.

recipe ['resɪpɪ] *n lit & fig* recette *f*.

recipient [rɪ'sɪpɪənt] *n* [of letter] destinataire *mf* ; [of cheque] bénéficiaire *mf* ; [of award] récipiendaire *mf*.

reciprocal [rɪ'sɪprəkl] *adj* réciproque.

recital [rɪ'saɪtl] *n* récital *m*.

recite [rɪ'saɪt] *vt* **1.** [say aloud] réciter - **2.** [list] énumérer.

reckless ['reklɪs] *adj* imprudent(e).

reckon ['rekn] *vt* **1.** *inf* [think] penser - **2.** [consider, judge] considérer - **3.** [calculate] calculer. ➡ **reckon on** *vt insep* compter sur. ➡ **reckon with** *vt insep* [expect] s'attendre à.

reckoning ['rekənɪŋ] *n* (U) [calculation] calculs *mpl*.

reclaim [rɪ'kleɪm] *vt* **1.** [claim back] réclamer - **2.** [land] assécher.

recline [rɪ'klaɪn] *vi* [person] être allongé(e).

reclining [rɪ'klaɪnɪŋ] *adj* [chair] à dossier réglable.

recluse [rɪ'kluːs] *n* reclus *m*, -e *f*.

recognition [ˌrekəg'nɪʃn] *n* reconnaissance *f* ; **in recognition of** en reconnaissance de ; **the town has changed beyond** OR **out of all recognition** la ville est méconnaissable.

recognizable ['rekəgnaɪzəbl] *adj* reconnaissable.

recognize, UK -ise ['rekəgnaɪz] *vt* reconnaître.

recoil ◇ *vi* [rɪ'kɔɪl] : **to recoil (from)** reculer (devant). ◇ *n* ['riːkɔɪl] [of gun] recul *m*.

recollect [ˌrekə'lekt] *vt* se rappeler.

recollection [ˌrekə'lekʃn] *n* souvenir *m*.

recommend [ˌrekə'mend] *vt* **1.** [commend] : **to recommend sb/sthg (to sb)** recommander qqn/qqch (à qqn) - **2.** [advise] conseiller, recommander.

recompense ['rekəmpens] ◇ *n* dédommagement *m*. ◇ *vt* dédommager.

reconcile ['rekənsaɪl] *vt* **1.** [beliefs, ideas] concilier - **2.** [people] réconcilier - **3.** [accept] : **to reconcile o.s. to sthg** se faire à l'idée de qqch.

reconditioned [ˌriːkən'dɪʃnd] *adj* remis(e) en état.

reconnaissance [rɪ'kɒnɪsəns] *n* reconnaissance *f*.

reconnoitre UK, **reconnoiter** US [ˌrekə'nɔɪtə'] ◇ *vt* reconnaître. ◇ *vi* aller en reconnaissance.

reconsider [ˌriːkən'sɪdə'] ◇ *vt* reconsidérer. ◇ *vi* reconsidérer la question.

reconstruct [ˌriːkən'strʌkt] *vt* **1.** [gen] reconstruire - **2.** [crime, event] reconstituer.

record ◇ *n* ['rekɔːd] **1.** [written account] rapport *m* ; [file] dossier *m* ; **to keep sthg on record** archiver qqch ; **(police) record** casier *m* judiciaire ; **off the record** non officiel - **2.** [vinyl disc] disque *m* - **3.** [best achievement] record *m*. ◇ *adj* ['rekɔːd] record *(inv)*. ◇ *vt* [rɪ'kɔːd] **1.** [write down] noter - **2.** [put on tape] enregistrer.

recorded delivery [rɪ'kɔːdɪd-] *n* : **to send sthg by recorded delivery** envoyer qqch en recommandé.

recorder [rɪ'kɔːdə'] *n* [musical instrument] flûte *f* à bec.

record holder *n* détenteur *m*, -trice *f* du record.

recording [rɪ'kɔːdɪŋ] *n* enregistrement *m*.

record player *n* tourne-disque *m*.

recount <> *n* ['ri:kaʊnt] [of vote] deuxième dépouillement *m* du scrutin. <> *vt* **1.** [rɪ'kaʊnt] [narrate] raconter - **2.** [,ri:'kaʊnt] [count again] recompter.

recoup [rɪ'ku:p] *vt* récupérer.

recourse [rɪ'kɔ:s] *n* : **to have recourse to** avoir recours à.

recover [rɪ'kʌvər] <> *vt* **1.** [retrieve] récupérer ; **to recover sthg from sb** reprendre qqch à qqn - **2.** [one's balance] retrouver ; [consciousness] reprendre. <> *vi* **1.** [from illness] se rétablir ; [from shock, divorce] se remettre - **2.** *fig* [economy] se redresser ; [trade] reprendre.

recovery [rɪ'kʌvərɪ] *n* **1.** [from illness] guérison *f*, rétablissement *m* - **2.** *fig* [of economy] redressement *m*, reprise *f* - **3.** [retrieval] récupération *f*.

recreation [,rekrɪ'eɪʃn] *n* (U) [leisure] récréation *f*, loisirs *mpl*.

recrimination [rɪ,krɪmɪ'neɪʃn] *n* récrimination *f*.

recruit [rɪ'kru:t] <> *n* recrue *f*. <> *vt* recruter ; **to recruit sb to do sthg** *fig* embaucher qqn pour faire qqch. <> *vi* recruter.

recruitment [rɪ'kru:tmənt] *n* recrutement *m*.

rectangle ['rek,tæŋgl] *n* rectangle *m*.

rectangular [rek'tæŋgjʊlər] *adj* rectangulaire.

rectify ['rektɪfaɪ] *vt* [mistake] rectifier.

rector ['rektər] *n* **1.** [priest] pasteur *m* - **2.** *Scot* [head - of school] directeur *m* ; [- of college, university] *président élu par les étudiants*.

rectory ['rektərɪ] *n* presbytère *m*.

recuperate [rɪ'ku:pəreɪt] *vi* se rétablir.

recur [rɪ'kɜ:r] *vi* [error, problem] se reproduire ; [dream] revenir ; [pain] réapparaitre.

recurrence [rɪ'kʌrəns] *n* répétition *f*.

recurrent [rɪ'kʌrənt] *adj* [error, problem] qui se reproduit souvent ; [dream] qui revient souvent.

recycle [,ri:'saɪkl] *vt* recycler.

recycle bin *n* COMPUT poubelle *f*, corbeille *f*.

recycling [,ri:'saɪklɪŋ] *n* recyclage *m*.

red [red] <> *adj* rouge ; [hair] roux (rousse). <> *n* rouge *m* ; **to be in the red** *inf* être à découvert.

red card *n* FOOTBALL : **to be shown the red card**, **to get a red card** recevoir un carton rouge.

red carpet *n* : **to roll out the red carpet for sb** dérouler le tapis rouge pour qqn.

➤ **red-carpet** *adj* : **to give sb the red-carpet treatment** recevoir qqn en grande pompe.

Red Cross *n* : **the Red Cross** la Croix-Rouge.

redcurrant ['red,kʌrənt] *n* [fruit] groseille *f* ; [bush] groseillier *m*.

redden ['redn] *vt* & *vi* rougir.

redecorate [,ri:'dekəreɪt] <> *vt* repeindre et retapisser. <> *vi* refaire la peinture et les papiers peints.

redeem [rɪ'di:m] *vt* **1.** [save, rescue] racheter - **2.** [from pawnbroker] dégager.

redeeming [rɪ'di:mɪŋ] *adj* qui rachète (les défauts).

redeploy [,ri:dɪ'plɔɪ] *vt* MIL redéployer ; [staff] réorganiser, réaffecter.

red-faced [-'feɪst] *adj* rougeaud(e), rubicond(e) ; [with embarrassment] rouge de confusion.

red-haired [-'heəd] *adj* roux (rousse).

red-handed [-'hændɪd] *adj* : **to catch sb red-handed** prendre qqn en flagrant délit OR la main dans le sac.

redhead ['redhed] *n* roux *m*, rousse *f*.

red herring *n* *fig* fausse piste *f*.

red-hot *adj* **1.** [extremely hot] brûlant(e) ; [metal] chauffé(e) au rouge - **2.** [very enthusiastic] ardent(e).

redid [,ri:'dɪd] *pt* ➤ redo.

residence hall US = hall of residence.

redirect [,ri:dɪ'rekt] *vt* **1.** [energy, money] réorienter - **2.** [traffic] détourner - **3.** *UK* [letters] faire suivre.

rediscover [,ri:dɪ'skʌvər] *vt* redécouvrir.

red light *n* [traffic signal] feu *m* rouge.

red-light district *n* quartier *m* chaud.

redneck ['rednek] *US inf pej n* *Américain d'origine modeste qui a des idées réactionnaires et des préjugés racistes*.

redo [,ri:'du:] (*pt* -did, *pp* -done) *vt* refaire.

redolent ['redələnt] *adj lit* **1.** [reminiscent] : **redolent of** qui rappelle, évocateur(trice) de - **2.** [smelling] : **redolent of** qui sent.

redone [,ri:'dʌn] *pp* ➤ redo.

redouble [,ri:'dʌbl] *vt* : **to redouble one's efforts (to do sthg)** redoubler d'efforts (pour faire qqch).

redraft [,ri:'drɑ:ft] *vt* rédiger à nouveau.

redress [rɪ'dres] <> *n* (U) *fml* réparation *f*. <> *vt* : **to redress the balance** rétablir l'équilibre.

Red Sea *n* : **the Red Sea** la mer Rouge.

red tape *n* *fig* paperasserie *f* administrative.

reduce [rɪ'dju:s] <> *vt* réduire ; **to be reduced to doing sthg** en être réduit à faire qqch ; **to reduce sb to tears** faire pleurer qqn. ◇ *vi* US [diet] suivre un régime amaigrissant.

reduction [rɪ'dʌkʃn] *n* **1.** [decrease] : **reduction (in)** réduction *f* (de), baisse *f* (de) - **2.** [discount] rabais *m*, réduction *f*.

redundancy [rɪ'dʌndənsɪ] *n* UK [dismissal] licenciement *m* ; [unemployment] chômage *m*.

redundant [rɪ'dʌndənt] *adj* **1.** UK [jobless] : **to be made redundant** être licencié(e) - **2.** [not required] superflu(e).

reed [ri:d] *n* **1.** [plant] roseau *m* - **2.** MUS anche *f*.

reef [ri:f] *n* récif *m*, écueil *m*.

reek [ri:k] ◇ *n* relent *m*. ◇ *vi* : **to reek (of sthg)** puer (qqch), empester (qqch).

reel [ri:l] ◇ *n* **1.** [roll] bobine *f* - **2.** [on fishing rod] moulinet *m*. ◇ *vi* [stagger] chanceler. ◆ **reel in** *vt sep* remonter. ◆ **reel off** *vt sep* [list] débiter.

reenact [,ri:ɪ'nækt] *vt* [play] reproduire ; [event] reconstituer.

ref [ref] *n* **1.** *inf* (*abbrev of* **referee**) arbitre *m* - **2.** ADMIN (*abbrev of* **reference**) réf. *f*

refectory [rɪ'fektərɪ] *n* réfectoire *m*.

refer [rɪ'fɜ:r] *vt* **1.** [person] : **to refer sb to** [hospital] envoyer qqn à ; [specialist] adresser qqn à - **2.** ADMIN renvoyer qqn à - **2.** [report, case, decision] : **to refer sthg to** soumettre qqch à. ◆ **refer to** *vt insep* **1.** [speak about] parler de, faire allusion à OR mention de - **2.** [apply to] s'appliquer à, concerner - **3.** [consult] se référer à, se reporter à.

referee [,refə'ri:] ◇ *n* **1.** SPORT arbitre *mf* - **2.** UK [for job application] répondant *m*, -e *f*. ◇ *vt* SPORT arbitrer. ◇ *vi* SPORT être arbitre.

reference ['refrəns] *n* **1.** [mention] : **reference (to)** allusion *f* (à), mention *f* (de) ; **with reference to** comme suite à - **2.** *(U)* [for advice, information] : **reference (to)** consultation *f* (de), référence *f* (à) - **3.** COMM référence *f* - **4.** [in book] renvoi *m* ; **map reference** coordonnées *fpl* - **5.** [for job application - letter] référence *f* ; [- person] répondant *m*, -e *f*.

reference book *n* ouvrage *m* de référence.

reference number *n* numéro *m* de référence.

referendum [,refə'rendəm] (*pl* **-s** OR **-da** [-də]) *n* référendum *m*.

refill ◇ *n* ['ri:fɪl] **1.** [for pen] recharge *f* - **2.** *inf* [drink] : **would you like a refill?** vous voulez encore un verre? ◇ *vt* [,ri:'fɪl] remplir à nouveau.

refine [rɪ'faɪn] *vt* raffiner ; *fig* peaufiner.

refined [rɪ'faɪnd] *adj* raffiné(e) ; [system, theory] perfectionné(e).

refinement [rɪ'faɪnmənt] *n* **1.** [improvement] perfectionnement *m* - **2.** *(U)* [gentility] raffinement *m*.

reflect [rɪ'flekt] ◇ *vt* **1.** [be a sign of] refléter - **2.** [light, image] réfléchir, refléter ; [heat] réverbérer - **3.** [think] : **to reflect that...** se dire que... ◇ *vi* [think] : **to reflect (on** OR **upon)** réfléchir (sur), penser (à).

reflection [rɪ'flekʃn] *n* **1.** [sign] indication *f*, signe *m* - **2.** [criticism] : **reflection on** critique *f* de - **3.** [image] reflet *m* - **4.** *(U)* [of light, heat] réflexion *f* - **5.** [thought] réflexion *f* ; **on reflection** réflexion faite.

reflector [rɪ'flektər] *n* réflecteur *m*.

reflex ['ri:fleks] *n* : **reflex (action)** réflexe *m*.

reflexive [rɪ'fleksɪv] *adj* GRAM [pronoun] réfléchi(e).

reflexively [rɪ'fleksɪvlɪ] *adv* GRAM [in meaning] au sens réfléchi ; [in form] à la forme réfléchie.

reforestation [ri:,fɒrɪ'steɪʃn] US = **reafforestation**.

reform [rɪ'fɔ:m] ◇ *n* réforme *f*. ◇ *vt* [gen] réformer ; [person] corriger. ◇ *vi* [behave better] se corriger, s'amender.

Reformation [,refə'meɪʃn] *n* : **the Reformation** la Réforme.

reformatory [rɪ'fɔ:mətrɪ] *n* US centre *m* d'éducation surveillée (pour jeunes délinquants).

reformer [rɪ'fɔ:mər] *n* réformateur *m*, -trice *f*.

refrain [rɪ'freɪn] ◇ *n* refrain *m*. ◇ *vi* : **to refrain from doing sthg** s'abstenir de faire qqch.

refresh [rɪ'freʃ] *vt* rafraîchir, revigorer.

refreshed [rɪ'freʃt] *adj* reposé(e).

refresher course [rɪ'freʃər-] *n* cours *m* de recyclage OR remise à niveau.

refreshing [rɪ'freʃɪŋ] *adj* **1.** [pleasantly different] agréable, réconfortant(e) - **2.** [drink, swim] rafraîchissant(e).

refreshments [rɪ'freʃmənts] *npl* rafraîchissements *mpl*.

refrigerator [rɪ'frɪdʒəreɪtər] *n* réfrigérateur *m*, Frigidaire ® *m*.

refrigerator-freezer *esp* US = **fridge-freezer**.

refuel [,ri:'fjʊəl] (UK & US) ◇ *vt* ravitailler. ◇ *vi* se ravitailler en carburant.

refuge ['refju:dʒ] *n* *lit* & *fig* refuge *m*, abri *m* ; **to take refuge in** se réfugier dans.

refugee [,refjʊ'dʒi:] *n* réfugié *m*, -e *f*.

refund ◇ *n* ['ri:fʌnd] remboursement *m*. ◇ *vt* [rɪ'fʌnd] : **to refund sthg to sb, to refund sb sthg** rembourser qqch à qqn.

refurbish [,ri:'fɜ:bɪʃ] *vt* remettre à neuf, rénover.

refusal [rɪ'fjuːzl] *n* : refusal (to do sthg) refus *m* (de faire qqch).

refuse[1] [rɪ'fjuːz] <> *vt* refuser ; to refuse to do sthg refuser de faire qqch. <> *vi* refuser.

refuse[2] ['refjuːs] *n* (U) [rubbish] ordures *fpl*, détritus *mpl*.

refuse collection ['refjuːs-] *n* UK enlèvement *m* des ordures ménagères.

refute [rɪ'fjuːt] *vt* réfuter.

regain [rɪ'geɪn] *vt* [composure, health] retrouver ; [leadership] reprendre.

regal ['riːgl] *adj* majestueux(euse), royal(e).

regalia [rɪ'geɪljə] *n* (U) insignes *mpl*.

regard [rɪ'gɑːd] <> *n* 1. (U) [respect] estime *f*, respect *m* - 2. [aspect] : in this/that regard à cet égard. <> *vt* considérer ; to regard o.s. as se considérer comme ; to be highly regarded être tenu(e) en haute estime. **regards** *npl* : (with best) regards bien amicalement ; give her my regards faites-lui mes amitiés. **as regards** *prep* en ce qui concerne. **in regard to, with regard to** *prep* en ce qui concerne, relativement à.

regarding [rɪ'gɑːdɪŋ] *prep* concernant, en ce qui concerne.

regardless [rɪ'gɑːdlɪs] *adv* quand même. **regardless of** *prep* sans tenir compte de, sans se soucier de.

regime [reɪ'ʒiːm] *n* régime *m*.

regiment ['redʒɪmənt] *n* régiment *m*.

region ['riːdʒən] *n* région *f* ; in the region of environ.

regional ['riːdʒənl] *adj* régional(e).

register ['redʒɪstər] <> *n* [record] registre *m*. <> *vt* 1. [show, measure] indiquer, montrer - 2. [express] exprimer. <> *vi* 1. [on official list] s'inscrire, se faire inscrire - 2. [at hotel] signer le registre - 3. *inf* [advice, fact] : it didn't register je n'ai pas compris.

registered ['redʒɪstəd] *adj* 1. [person] inscrit(e) ; [car] immatriculé(e) ; [charity] agréé(e) par le gouvernement - 2. [letter, parcel] recommandé(e).

Registered Trademark *n* marque *f* déposée.

registrar [,redʒɪ'strɑːr] *n* 1. [keeper of records] officier *m* de l'état civil - 2. UNIV secrétaire *m* général - 3. UK [doctor] chef *m* de clinique.

registration [,redʒɪ'streɪʃn] *n* 1. [gen] enregistrement *m*, inscription *f* - 2. AUT = registration number.

registration number *n* UK AUT numéro *m* d'immatriculation.

registry ['redʒɪstrɪ] *n* UK bureau *m* de l'enregistrement.

registry office *n* UK bureau *m* de l'état civil.

regret [rɪ'gret] <> *n* regret *m*. <> *vt* [be sorry about] : to regret sthg/doing sthg regretter qqch/d'avoir fait qqch.

regretfully [rɪ'gretfʊlɪ] *adv* à regret.

regrettable [rɪ'gretəbl] *adj* regrettable, fâcheux(euse).

regroup [,riː'gruːp] *vi* se regrouper.

regular ['regjʊlər] <> *adj* 1. [gen] régulier(ère) ; [customer] fidèle - 2. [usual] habituel(elle) - 3. US [normal - size] standard (*inv*) - 4. US [pleasant] sympa (*inv*). <> *n* [at pub] habitué *m*, -e *f* ; [at shop] client *m*, -e *f* fidèle.

regularly ['regjʊləlɪ] *adv* régulièrement.

regulate ['regjʊleɪt] *vt* régler.

regulation [,regjʊ'leɪʃn] <> *adj* [standard] réglementaire. <> *n* 1. [rule] règlement *m* - 2. (U) [control] réglementation *f*.

rehabilitate [,riːə'bɪlɪteɪt] *vt* [criminal] réinsérer, réhabiliter ; [patient] rééduquer.

rehearsal [rɪ'hɜːsl] *n* répétition *f*.

rehearse [rɪ'hɜːs] *vt & vi* répéter.

reign [reɪn] <> *n* règne *m*. <> *vi* : to reign (over) *lit & fig* régner (sur).

reimburse [,riːɪm'bɜːs] *vt* : to reimburse sb (for) rembourser qqn (de).

rein [reɪn] *n fig* : to give (a) free rein to sb, to give sb free rein laisser la bride sur le cou à qqn. **reins** *npl* [for horse] rênes *fpl*.

reindeer ['reɪn,dɪər] (*pl* reindeer) *n* renne *m*.

reinforce [,riːɪn'fɔːs] *vt* 1. [strengthen] renforcer - 2. [back up, confirm] appuyer, étayer.

reinforced concrete [,riːɪn'fɔːst-] *n* béton *m* armé.

reinforcement [,riːɪn'fɔːsmənt] *n* 1. (U) [strengthening] renforcement *m* - 2. [strengthener] renfort *m*. **reinforcements** *npl* renforts *mpl*.

reinstall *vt* COMPUT réinstaller.

reinstate [,riːɪn'steɪt] *vt* [employee] rétablir dans ses fonctions, réintégrer ; [policy, method] rétablir.

reissue [riː'ɪʃuː] <> *n* [of book] réédition *f*. <> *vt* [book] rééditer ; [film, record] ressortir.

reiterate [riː'ɪtəreɪt] *vt* réitérer, répéter.

reject <> *n* ['riːdʒekt] [product] article *m* de rebut. <> *vt* [rɪ'dʒekt] 1. [not accept] rejeter - 2. [candidate, coin] refuser.

rejection [rɪ'dʒekʃn] *n* 1. [non-acceptance] rejet *m* - 2. [of candidate] refus *m*.

rejoice [rɪ'dʒɔɪs] *vi* : to rejoice (at OR in) réjouir (de).

rejuvenate [rɪ'dʒuːvəneɪt] *vt* rajeunir.

rekindle [,riː'kɪndl] *vt fig* ranimer, raviver.

relapse [rɪ'læps] ⋄ *n* rechute *f*. ⋄ *vi* : **to relapse into** retomber dans.

relate [rɪ'leɪt] ⋄ *vt* **1.** [connect] : **to relate sthg to sthg** établir un lien OR rapport entre qqch et qqch - **2.** [tell] raconter. ⋄ *vi* **1.** [be connected] : **to relate to** avoir un rapport avec - **2.** [concern] : **to relate to se** rapporter à - **3.** [empathize] : **to relate (to sb)** s'entendre (avec qqn). ▬ **relating to** *prep* concernant.

related [rɪ'leɪtɪd] *adj* **1.** [people] apparenté(e) - **2.** [issues, problems etc] lié(e).

relation [rɪ'leɪʃn] *n* **1.** [connection] : **relation (to/between)** rapport *m* (avec/entre) - **2.** [person] parent *m*, -e *f*. ▬ **relations** *npl* [relationship] relations *fpl*, rapports *mpl*.

relationship [rɪ'leɪʃnʃɪp] *n* **1.** [between people, countries] relations *fpl*, rapports *mpl* ; [romantic] liaison *f* - **2.** [connection] rapport *m*, lien *m*.

relative [ˈrelətɪv] ⋄ *adj* relatif(ive). ⋄ *n* parent *m*, -e *f*. ▬ **relative to** *prep* [compared with] relativement à ; [connected with] se rapportant à, relatif(ive) à.

relatively [ˈrelətɪvlɪ] *adv* relativement.

relax [rɪ'læks] ⋄ *vt* **1.** [person] détendre, relaxer - **2.** [muscle, body] décontracter, relâcher - **3.** [one's grip] desserrer - **3.** [rule] relâcher. ⋄ *vi* **1.** [person] se détendre, se décontracter - **2.** [muscle, body] se relâcher, se décontracter - **3.** [one's grip] se desserrer.

relaxation [,riːlækˈseɪʃn] *n* **1.** [of person] relaxation *f*, détente *f* - **2.** [of rule] relâchement *m*.

relaxed [rɪ'lækst] *adj* détendu(e), décontracté(e).

relaxing [rɪ'læksɪŋ] *adj* relaxant(e), qui détend.

relay [ˈriːleɪ] ⋄ *n* **1.** SPORT : **relay (race)** course *f* de relais - **2.** RADIO & TV [broadcast] retransmission *f*. ⋄ *vt* **1.** RADIO & TV [broadcast] relayer - **2.** [message, information] transmettre, communiquer.

release [rɪ'liːs] ⋄ *n* **1.** [from prison, cage] libération *f* - **2.** [from pain, misery] délivrance *f* - **3.** [statement] communiqué *m* - **4.** [of gas, heat] échappement *m* - **5.** (*U*) [of film, record] sortie *f* - **6.** [film] nouveau film *m* ; [record] nouveau disque *m*. ⋄ *vt* **1.** [set free] libérer - **2.** [lift restriction on] : **to release sb from** dégager qqn de - **3.** [make available - supplies] libérer ; [- funds] débloquer - **4.** [let go of] lâcher - **5.** [TECH - brake, handle] desserrer ; [- mechanism] déclencher - **6.** [gas, heat] faire : **to be released (from/into)** se dégager (de/dans), s'échapper (de/dans) - **7.** [film, record] sortir ; [statement, report] publier.

relegate [ˈrelɪɡeɪt] *vt* reléguer ; **to be relegated** UK SPORT être relégué à la division inférieure.

relent [rɪ'lent] *vi* [person] se laisser fléchir ; [wind, storm] se calmer.

relentless [rɪ'lentlɪs] *adj* implacable.

relevant [ˈreləvənt] *adj* **1.** [connected] : **relevant (to)** qui a un rapport (avec) - **2.** [significant] : **relevant (to)** important(e) (pour) - **3.** [appropriate - information] utile ; [- document] justificatif(ive).

reliable [rɪ'laɪəbl] *adj* [person] sur qui on peut compter, fiable ; [device] fiable ; [company, information] sérieux(euse).

reliably [rɪ'laɪəblɪ] *adv* de façon fiable ; **to be reliably informed (that)...** savoir de source sûre que...

reliant [rɪ'laɪənt] *adj* : **to be reliant on** être dépendant(e) de.

relic [ˈrelɪk] *n* relique *f* ; [of past] vestige *m*.

relief [rɪ'liːf] *n* **1.** [comfort] soulagement *m* - **2.** [for poor, refugees] aide *f*, assistance *f* - **3.** US [social security] aide *f* sociale.

relieve [rɪ'liːv] *vt* **1.** [pain, anxiety] soulager ; **to relieve sb of sthg** [take away from] délivrer qqn de qqch - **2.** [take over from] relayer - **3.** [give help to] secourir, venir en aide à.

religion [rɪ'lɪdʒn] *n* religion *f*.

religious [rɪ'lɪdʒəs] *adj* religieux(euse) ; [book] de piété.

relinquish [rɪ'lɪŋkwɪʃ] *vt* [power] abandonner ; [claim, plan] renoncer à ; [post] quitter.

relish [ˈrelɪʃ] ⋄ *n* **1.** [enjoyment] : **with (great) relish** avec délectation - **2.** [pickle] condiment *m*. ⋄ *vt* [enjoy] prendre plaisir à ; **I don't relish the thought** OR **idea** OR **prospect of seeing him** la perspective de le voir ne m'enchante OR ne me sourit guère.

relocate [,riːləʊˈkeɪt] ⋄ *vt* installer ailleurs, transférer. ⋄ *vi* s'installer ailleurs, déménager.

reluctance [rɪ'lʌktəns] *n* répugnance *f*.

reluctant [rɪ'lʌktənt] *adj* peu enthousiaste ; **to be reluctant to do sthg** rechigner à faire qqch, être peu disposé à faire qqch.

reluctantly [rɪ'lʌktəntlɪ] *adv* à contrecœur, avec répugnance.

rely [rɪ'laɪ] ▬ **rely on** *vt insep* **1.** [count on] compter sur ; **to rely on sb to do sthg** compter sur qqn OR faire confiance à qqn pour faire qqch - **2.** [be dependent on] dépendre de.

remain [rɪ'meɪn] ⋄ *vt* rester ; **to remain to be done** rester à faire. ⋄ *vi* rester. ▬ **remains** *npl* **1.** [remnants] restes *mpl* - **2.** [antiquities] ruines *fpl*, vestiges *mpl*.

remainder [rɪ'meɪndər] *n* reste *m*.

remaining [rɪ'meɪnɪŋ] *adj* qui reste.

remand [rɪ'mɑːnd] ◇ *n* LAW : **on remand** en détention préventive. ◇ *vt* LAW : **to remand sb (in custody)** placer qqn en détention préventive.

remark [rɪ'mɑːk] ◇ *n* [comment] remarque *f*, observation *f*. ◇ *vt* [comment] : **to remark that...** faire remarquer que...

remarkable [rɪ'mɑːkəbl] *adj* remarquable.

remarry [,rɪ:'mærɪ] *vi* se remarier.

remedial [rɪ'miːdjəl] *adj* **1.** [pupil, class] de rattrapage - **2.** [exercise] correctif(ive) ; [action] de rectification.

remedy ['remədɪ] ◇ *n* : **remedy (for)** MED remède *m* (pour OR contre) ; *fig* remède (à OR contre). ◇ *vt* remédier à.

remember [rɪ'membər] ◇ *vt* [gen] se souvenir de, se rappeler ; **to remember to do sthg** ne pas oublier de faire qqch, penser à faire qqch ; **to remember doing sthg** se souvenir d'avoir fait qqch, se rappeler avoir fait qqch. ◇ *vi* se souvenir, se rappeler.

remembrance [rɪ'membrəns] *n* : **in remembrance of** en souvenir OR mémoire de.

Remembrance Day *n* UK l'Armistice *m*.

remind [rɪ'maɪnd] *vt* [tell] : **to remind sb of** OR **about sthg** rappeler qqch à qqn ; **to remind sb to do sthg** rappeler à qqn de faire qqch, faire penser à qqn à faire qqch.

reminder [rɪ'maɪndər] *n* **1.** [to jog memory] : **to give sb a reminder (to do sthg)** faire penser à qqn (à faire qqch) - **2.** [letter, note] rappel *m*.

reminisce [,remɪ'nɪs] *vi* évoquer des souvenirs ; **to reminisce about sthg** évoquer qqch.

reminiscent [,remɪ'nɪsnt] *adj* : **reminiscent of** qui rappelle, qui fait penser à.

remiss [rɪ'mɪs] *adj* négligent(e).

remit[1] [rɪ'mɪt] *vt* [money] envoyer, verser.

remit[2] ['riːmɪt] *n* UK [responsibility] attributions *fpl*.

remittance [rɪ'mɪtns] *n* **1.** [amount of money] versement *m* - **2.** COMM règlement *m*, paiement *m*.

remnant ['remnənt] *n* **1.** [remaining part] reste *m*, restant *m* - **2.** [of cloth] coupon *m*.

remorse [rɪ'mɔːs] *n* (U) remords *m*.

remorseful [rɪ'mɔːsful] *adj* plein(e) de remords.

remorseless [rɪ'mɔːslɪs] *adj* implacable.

remote [rɪ'məʊt] *adj* **1.** [far-off - place] éloigné(e) ; [- time] lointain(e) - **2.** [person] distant(e) - **3.** [possibility, chance] vague.

remote control *n* télécommande *f*.

remotely [rɪ'məʊtlɪ] *adv* **1.** [in the slightest] : **not remotely** pas le moins du monde, absolument pas - **2.** [far off] au loin.

remould UK, **remold** US ['riːməʊld] *n* pneu *m* rechapé.

removable [rɪ'muːvəbl] *adj* [detachable] détachable, amovible.

removal [rɪ'muːvl] *n* **1.** (U) [act of removing] enlèvement *m* - **2.** UK [change of house] déménagement *m*.

removal van *n* UK camion *m* de déménagement.

remove [rɪ'muːv] *vt* **1.** [take away - gen] enlever ; [- stain] faire partir, enlever ; [- problem] résoudre ; [- suspicion] dissiper - **2.** [clothes] ôter, enlever - **3.** [employee] renvoyer.

remuneration [rɪ,mjuːnə'reɪʃn] *n* rémunération *f*.

render ['rendər] *vt* rendre ; [assistance] porter ; FIN [account] présenter.

rendering ['rendərɪŋ] *n* [of play, music etc] interprétation *f*.

rendezvous ['rɒndɪvuː] (*pl* **rendezvous**) *n* rendez-vous *m inv*.

renegade ['renɪgeɪd] *n* renégat *m*, -e *f*.

renew [rɪ'njuː] *vt* **1.** [gen] renouveler ; [negotiations, strength] reprendre ; [interest] faire renaître ; **to renew acquaintance with sb** renouer connaissance avec qqn - **2.** [replace] remplacer.

renewable [rɪ'njuːəbl] *adj* renouvelable.

renewal [rɪ'njuːəl] *n* **1.** [of activity] reprise *f* - **2.** [of contract, licence etc] renouvellement *m*.

renounce [rɪ'naʊns] *vt* [reject] renoncer à.

renovate ['renəveɪt] *vt* rénover.

renown [rɪ'naʊn] *n* renommée *f*, renom *m*.

renowned [rɪ'naʊnd] *adj* : **renowned (for)** renommé(e) (pour).

rent [rent] ◇ *n* [for house] loyer *m*. ◇ *vt* louer.

rental ['rentl] ◇ *adj* de location. ◇ *n* [for car, television, video] prix *m* de location ; [for house] loyer *m*.

rental car *n* US voiture *f* de location.

renunciation [rɪ,nʌnsɪ'eɪʃn] *n* renonciation *f*.

reorganize, UK **-ise** [,riː'ɔːgənaɪz] *vt* réorganiser.

rep [rep] *n inf* **1.** (*abbrev of* **representative**) VRP *m* - **2.** *abbrev of* **repertory**.

repaid [riː'peɪd] *pt & pp* ▶ **repay**.

repair [rɪ'peər] ◇ *n* réparation *f* ; **in good/ bad repair** en bon/mauvais état. ◇ *vt* réparer.

repair kit *n* trousse *f* à outils.

repartee [,repɑː'tiː] *n* repartie *f*.

repatriate [,riː'pætrɪeɪt] *vt* rapatrier.

repay [riː'peɪ] (*pt & pp* **repaid**) *vt* **1.** [money] : **to repay sb sthg, to repay sthg**

to sb rembourser qqch à qqn - **2.** [favour] payer de retour, récompenser.

repayment [rɪ'peɪmənt] *n* rembourse-ment *m*.

repeal [rɪ'piːl] *<> n* abrogation *f. <> vt* abroger.

repeat [rɪ'piːt] *<> vt* **1.** [gen] répéter - **2.** RADIO & TV rediffuser. *<> n* RADIO & TV reprise *f*, rediffusion *f*.

repeatedly [rɪ'piːtɪdlɪ] *adv* à maintes reprises, très souvent.

repel [rɪ'pel] *vt* repousser.

repellent [rɪ'pelənt] *<> adj* répugnant(e), repoussant(e). *<> n* : **insect repellent** crème *f* anti-insecte.

repent [rɪ'pent] *<> vt* se repentir de. *<> vi* : **to repent (of)** se repentir (de).

repentance [rɪ'pentəns] *n* (*U*) repentir *m*.

repercussions [ˌriːpə'kʌʃnz] *npl* réper-cussions *fpl*.

repertoire ['repətwɑːr] *n* répertoire *m*.

repertory ['repətrɪ] *n* répertoire *m*.

repetition [ˌrepɪ'tɪʃn] *n* répétition *f*.

repetitious [ˌrepɪ'tɪʃəs], **repetitive** [rɪ'petɪtɪv] *adj* [action, job] répétitif(ive) ; [article, speech] qui a des redites.

replace [rɪ'pleɪs] *vt* **1.** [gen] remplacer - **2.** [put back] remettre (à sa place).

replacement [rɪ'pleɪsmənt] *n* **1.** [substitut-ing] remplacement *n* ; [putting back] repla-cement *m* - **2.** [new person] : **replacement (for sb)** remplaçant *m*, -e *f* (de qqn).

replay *<> n* ['riːpleɪ] match *m* rejoué. *<> vt* [ˌriː'pleɪ] **1.** [match, game] rejouer - **2.** [film, tape] repasser.

replenish [rɪ'plenɪʃ] *vt* : **to replenish one's supply of sthg** se réapprovisionner en qqch.

replica ['replɪkə] *n* copie *f* exacte, réplique *f*.

reply [rɪ'plaɪ] *<> n* : **reply (to)** réponse *f* (à). *<> vt & vi* répondre.

reply coupon *n* coupon-réponse *m*.

report [rɪ'pɔːt] *<> n* **1.** [account] rapport *m*, compte *m* rendu - **2.** PRESS reportage *m* - **3.** UK SCH bulletin *m*. *<> vt* **1.** [news, crime] rapporter, signaler - **2.** [make known] : **to report that...** annoncer que... - **3.** [complain about] : **to report sb (to)** dénoncer qqn (à). *<> vi* **1.** [give account] : **to report (on)** faire un rapport (sur) ; PRESS faire un reportage (sur) - **2.** [present oneself] : **to report (to sb/for sthg)** se présenter (à qqn/pour qqch).

report card *n* US bulletin *m* scolaire.

reportedly [rɪ'pɔːtɪdlɪ] *adv* à ce qu'il paraît.

reporter [rɪ'pɔːtər] *n* reporter *m*.

repose [rɪ'pəʊz] *n lit* repos *m*.

repossess [ˌriːpə'zes] *vt* saisir.

reprehensible [ˌreprɪ'hensəbl] *adj* répré-hensible.

represent [ˌreprɪ'zent] *vt* [gen] repré-senter.

representation [ˌreprɪzen'teɪʃn] *n* [gen] représentation *f*. **representations** *npl* : **to make representations to sb** faire une démarche auprès de qqn.

representative [ˌreprɪ'zentətɪv] *<> adj* représentatif(ive). *<> n* représentant *m*, -e *f*.

repress [rɪ'pres] *vt* réprimer.

repression [rɪ'preʃn] *n* répression *f* ; [sexual] refoulement *m*.

reprieve [rɪ'priːv] *<> n* **1.** *fig* [delay] sursis *m*, répit *m* - **2.** LAW sursis *m*. *<> vt* accorder un sursis à.

reprimand ['reprɪmɑːnd] *<> n* répri-mande *f*. *<> vt* réprimander.

reprisal [rɪ'praɪzl] (*U*) *n* représailles *fpl*.

reproach [rɪ'prəʊtʃ] *<> n* reproche *m*. *<> vt* : **to reproach sb for** OR **with sthg** reprocher qqch à qqn.

reproachful [rɪ'prəʊtʃful] *adj* [look, words] de reproche.

reproduce [ˌriːprə'djuːs] *<> vt* repro-duire. *<> vi* se reproduire.

reproduction [ˌriːprə'dʌkʃn] *n* reproduc-tion *f*.

reproof [rɪ'pruːf] *n* reproche *m*, blâme *m*.

reprove [rɪ'pruːv] *vt* : **to reprove sb (for)** blâmer qqn (pour OR de), réprimander qqn (pour).

reptile ['reptaɪl] *n* reptile *m*.

republic [rɪ'pʌblɪk] *n* république *f*.

republican [rɪ'pʌblɪkən] *<> adj* répu-blicain(e). *<> n* républicain *m*, -e *f*. **Republican** *<> adj* républicain(e) ; **the Republican Party** US le parti républicain. *<> n* républicain *m*, -e *f*.

repudiate [rɪ'pjuːdɪeɪt] *vt fml* [offer, sugges-tion] rejeter ; [friend] renier.

repulse [rɪ'pʌls] *vt* repousser.

repulsive [rɪ'pʌlsɪv] *adj* repoussant(e).

reputable ['repjʊtəbl] *adj* de bonne répu-tation.

reputation [ˌrepjʊ'teɪʃn] *n* réputation *f*.

repute [rɪ'pjuːt] *n* : **of good repute** de bonne réputation.

reputed [rɪ'pjuːtɪd] *adj* réputé(e) ; **to be reputed to be sthg** être réputé pour être qqch, avoir la réputation d'être qqch.

reputedly [rɪ'pjuːtɪdlɪ] *adv* à OR d'après ce qu'on dit.

request [rɪ'kwest] *<> n* : **request (for)**

demande f (de) ; **on request** sur demande. <> *vt* demander ; **to request sb to do sthg** demander à qqn de faire qqch.

request stop *n* UK arrêt *m* facultatif.

require [rɪ'kwaɪər] *vt* **1.** [subj: person] avoir besoin de ; [subj: situation] nécessiter ; **to require sb to do sthg** exiger de qqn qu'il fasse qqch.

requirement [rɪ'kwaɪəmənt] *n* besoin *m*.

requisition [,rekwɪ'zɪʃn] *vt* réquisitionner.

reran [,riː'ræn] *pt* ▶ **rerun**.

rerun <> *n* ['riːrʌn] [of TV programme] rediffusion *f*, reprise *f* ; *fig* répétition *f*. <> *vt* [,riː'rʌn] (*pt* -**ran**, *pp* -**run**) **1.** [race] réorganiser - **2.** [TV programme] rediffuser ; [tape] passer à nouveau, repasser.

resat [,riː'sæt] *pt & pp* ▶ **resit**.

rescind [rɪ'sɪnd] *vt* [contract] annuler ; [law] abroger.

rescue ['reskjuː] <> *n* **1.** (U) [help] secours *mpl* - **2.** [successful attempt] sauvetage *m*. <> *vt* sauver, secourir.

rescuer ['reskjuər] *n* sauveteur *m*, -euse *f*.

research [,rɪ'sɜːtʃ] <> *n* (U) **research (on** OR **into)** recherche *f* (sur), recherches *fpl* (sur) ; **research and development** recherche et développement. <> *vt* faire des recherches sur.

researcher [rɪ'sɜːtʃər] *n* chercheur *m*, -euse *f*.

resemblance [rɪ'zembləns] *n* : **resemblance (to)** ressemblance *f* (avec).

resemble [rɪ'zembl] *vt* ressembler à.

resent [rɪ'zent] *vt* être indigné(e) par.

resentful [rɪ'zentfʊl] *adj* plein(e) de ressentiment.

resentment [rɪ'zentmənt] *n* ressentiment *m*.

reservation [,rezə'veɪʃn] *n* **1.** [booking] réservation *f* - **2.** [uncertainty] : **without reservation** sans réserve - **3.** US [for Native Americans] réserve *f* indienne. ➡ **reservations** *npl* [doubts] réserves *fpl*.

reserve [rɪ'zɜːv] <> *n* **1.** [gen] réserve *f* ; **in reserve** en réserve - **2.** SPORT remplaçant *m*, -e *f*. <> *vt* **1.** [save] garder, réserver - **2.** [book] réserver - **3.** [retain] : **to reserve the right to do sthg** se réserver le droit de faire qqch.

reserved [rɪ'zɜːvd] *adj* réservé(e).

reservoir ['rezəvwɑːr] *n* réservoir *m*.

reset [,riː'set] (*pt & pp* **reset**) *vt* **1.** [clock, watch] remettre à l'heure ; [meter, controls] remettre à zéro - **2.** COMPUT ré-initialiser.

reshape [,riː'ʃeɪp] *vt* [policy, thinking] réorganiser.

reshuffle [,riː'ʃʌfl] <> *n* remaniement *m* ; **cabinet reshuffle** remaniement ministériel. <> *vt* remanier.

reside [rɪ'zaɪd] *vi fml* résider.

residence ['rezɪdəns] *n* résidence *f*.

residence permit *n* permis *m* de séjour.

resident ['rezɪdənt] <> *adj* résidant(e) ; [chaplain, doctor] à demeure. <> *n* résident *m*, -e *f*.

residential [,rezɪ'denʃl] *adj* : **residential course** *stage ou formation avec logement sur place* ; **residential institution** internat *m*.

residential area *n* quartier *m* résidentiel.

residue ['rezɪdjuː] *n* reste *m* ; CHEM résidu *m*.

resign [rɪ'zaɪn] <> *vt* **1.** [job] démissionner de - **2.** [accept calmly] : **to resign o.s. to** se résigner à. <> *vi* : **to resign (from)** démissionner (de).

resignation [,rezɪg'neɪʃn] *n* **1.** [from job] démission *f* - **2.** [calm acceptance] résignation *f*.

resigned [rɪ'zaɪnd] *adj* : **resigned (to)** résigné(e) (à).

resilient [rɪ'zɪliənt] *adj* [material] élastique ; [person] qui a du ressort.

resin ['rezɪn] *n* résine *f*.

resist [rɪ'zɪst] *vt* résister à.

resistance [rɪ'zɪstəns] *n* résistance *f*.

resit UK <> *n* ['riːsɪt] deuxième session *f*. <> *vt* [,riː'sɪt] (*pt & pp* -**sat**) repasser, se représenter à.

resolute ['rezəluːt] *adj* résolu(e).

resolution [,rezə'luːʃn] *n* résolution *f*.

resolve [rɪ'zɒlv] <> *n* (U) [determination] résolution *f*. <> *vt* **1.** [decide] : **to resolve (that)...** décider que... ; **to resolve to do sthg** résoudre OR décider de faire qqch - **2.** [solve] résoudre.

resort [rɪ'zɔːt] *n* **1.** [for holidays] lieu *m* de vacances - **2.** [recourse] recours *m* ; **as a last resort, in the last resort** en dernier ressort OR recours. ➡ **resort to** *vt insep* recourir à, avoir recours à.

resound [rɪ'zaʊnd] *vi* **1.** [noise] résonner - **2.** [place] : **to resound with** retentir de.

resounding [rɪ'zaʊndɪŋ] *adj* retentissant(e).

resource [rɪ'sɔːs] *n* ressource *f*.

resourceful [rɪ'sɔːsfʊl] *adj* plein(e) de ressources, débrouillard(e).

respect [rɪ'spekt] <> *n* **1.** [gen] : **respect (for)** respect *m* (pour) ; **with respect** avec respect ; **with respect,...** sauf votre respect,... - **2.** [aspect] : **in this** OR **that respect** à cet égard ; **in some respects** à certains égards. <> *vt* respecter ; **to respect sb for**

sthg respecter qqn pour qqch. **respects** *npl* respects *mpl*, hommages *mpl*. **with respect to** *prep* en ce qui concerne, quant à.

respectable [rɪ'spektəbl] *adj* **1.** [morally correct] respectable - **2.** [adequate] raisonnable, honorable.

respectful [rɪ'spektful] *adj* respectueux(euse).

respective [rɪ'spektɪv] *adj* respectif(ive).

respectively [rɪ'spektɪvlɪ] *adv* respectivement.

respite ['respaɪt] *n* répit *m*.

resplendent [rɪ'splendənt] *adj* resplendissant(e).

respond [rɪ'spɒnd] *vi* : **to respond (to)** répondre (à).

response [rɪ'spɒns] *n* réponse *f*.

responsibility [rɪ,spɒnsə'bɪlətɪ] *n* : **responsibility (for)** responsabilité *f* (de).

responsible [rɪ'spɒnsəbl] *adj* **1.** [gen] : **responsible (for sthg)** responsable (de qqch) ; **to be responsible to sb** être responsable devant qqn - **2.** [job, position] qui comporte des responsabilités.

responsibly [rɪ'spɒnsəblɪ] *adv* de façon responsable.

responsive [rɪ'spɒnsɪv] *adj* **1.** [quick to react] qui réagit bien - **2.** [aware] : **responsive (to)** attentif(ive) (à).

rest [rest] ◇ *n* **1.** [remainder] : **the rest (of)** le reste (de) ; **the rest (of them)** les autres *mf pl* - **2.** [relaxation, break] repos *m* ; **to have a rest** se reposer - **3.** [support] support *m*, appui *m*. ◇ *vt* **1.** [relax] faire OR laisser reposer - **2.** [support] : **to rest sthg on/against** appuyer qqch sur/contre ; **rest assured** soyez certain(-e). ◇ *vi* **1.** [relax] se reposer - **2.** [be supported] : **to rest on/against** s'appuyer sur/contre - **3.** *fig* [argument, result] : **to rest on** reposer sur.

restaurant ['restərɒnt] *n* restaurant *m*.

restaurant car *n UK* wagon-restaurant *m*.

restful ['restful] *adj* reposant(e).

rest home *n* maison *f* de repos.

restive ['restɪv] *adj* agité(e).

restless ['restlɪs] *adj* agité(e).

restoration [,restə'reɪʃn] *n* **1.** [of law and order, monarchy] rétablissement *m* - **2.** [renovation] restauration *f*.

restore [rɪ'stɔːr] *vt* **1.** [law and order, monarchy] rétablir ; [confidence] redonner - **2.** [renovate] restaurer - **3.** [give back] rendre, restituer.

restrain [rɪ'streɪn] *vt* [person, crowd] contenir, retenir ; [emotions] maîtriser, contenir ; **to restrain o.s. from doing sthg** se retenir de faire qqch.

restrained [rɪ'streɪnd] *adj* [tone] mesuré(e) ; [person] qui se domine.

restraint [rɪ'streɪnt] *n* **1.** [restriction] restriction *f*, entrave *f* - **2.** (U) [self-control] mesure *f*, retenue *f*.

restrict [rɪ'strɪkt] *vt* restreindre, limiter.

restriction [rɪ'strɪkʃn] *n* restriction *f*, limitation *f*.

restrictive [rɪ'strɪktɪv] *adj* restrictif(ive).

rest room *n US* toilettes *fpl*.

result [rɪ'zʌlt] ◇ *n* résultat *m* ; **as a result** en conséquence ; **as a result of** [as a consequence of] à la suite de ; [because of] à cause de. ◇ *vi* **1.** [cause] : **to result in** aboutir à - **2.** [be caused] : **to result (from)** résulter (de).

resume [rɪ'zjuːm] *vt & vi* reprendre.

résumé ['rezjuːmeɪ] *n* **1.** [summary] résumé *m* - **2.** *US* [curriculum vitae] curriculum vitae *m inv*, CV *m*.

resumption [rɪ'zʌmpʃn] *n* reprise *f*.

resurgence [rɪ'sɜːdʒəns] *n* réapparition *f*.

resurrection [,rezə'rekʃn] *n fig* résurrection *f*.

resuscitation [rɪ,sʌsɪ'teɪʃn] *n* réanimation *f*.

retail ['riːteɪl] ◇ *n* (U) détail *m*. ◇ *adv* au détail.

retailer ['riːteɪlər] *n* détaillant *m*, -e *f*.

retail price *n* prix *m* de détail.

retain [rɪ'teɪn] *vt* conserver.

retainer [rɪ'teɪnər] *n* [fee] provision *f*.

retaliate [rɪ'tælɪeɪt] *vi* rendre la pareille, se venger.

retaliation [rɪ,tælɪ'eɪʃn] *n* (U) vengeance *f*, représailles *fpl*.

retarded [rɪ'tɑːdɪd] *adj* retardé(e).

retch [retʃ] *vi* avoir des haut-le-cœur.

retentive [rɪ'tentɪv] *adj* [memory] fidèle.

reticent ['retɪsənt] *adj* peu communicatif(ive) ; **to be reticent about sthg** ne pas beaucoup parler de qqch.

retina ['retɪnə] *(pl -nas OR -nae [-niː])* *n* rétine *f*.

retinue ['retɪnjuː] *n* suite *f*.

retire [rɪ'taɪər] *vi* **1.** [from work] prendre sa retraite - **2.** [withdraw] se retirer - **3.** [to bed] (aller) se coucher.

retired [rɪ'taɪəd] *adj* à la retraite, retraité(e).

retirement [rɪ'taɪəmənt] *n* retraite *f*.

retiring [rɪ'taɪərɪŋ] *adj* [shy] réservé(e).

retort [rɪ'tɔːt] ◇ *n* [sharp reply] riposte *f*. ◇ *vt* riposter.

retrace [rɪ'treɪs] *vt* : **to retrace one's steps** revenir sur ses pas.

retract [rɪ'trækt] <> vt **1.** [statement] rétracter - **2.** [undercarriage] rentrer, escamoter ; [claws] rentrer. <> vi [undercarriage] rentrer, s'escamoter.

retrain [,ri:'treɪn] vt recycler.

retraining [,ri:'treɪnɪŋ] n recyclage m.

retread n ['ri:tred] pneu m rechapé.

retreat [rɪ'tri:t] <> n retraite f. <> vi [move away] se retirer ; MIL battre en retraite.

retribution [,retrɪ'bju:ʃn] n châtiment m.

retrieval [rɪ'tri:vl] n (U) COMPUT recherche f et extraction f.

retrieve [rɪ'tri:v] vt **1.** [get back] récupérer - **2.** COMPUT rechercher et extraire - **3.** [situation] sauver.

retriever [rɪ'tri:vər] n [dog] retriever m.

retrograde ['retrəgreɪd] adj rétrograde.

retrospect ['retrəspekt] n : **in retrospect** après coup.

retrospective [,retrə'spektɪv] adj **1.** [mood, look] rétrospectif(ive) - **2.** LAW [law, pay rise] rétroactif(ive).

return [rɪ'tɜ:n] <> n **1.** (U) [arrival back, giving back] retour m - **2.** TENNIS renvoi m - **3.** UK [ticket] aller et retour m - **4.** [profit] rapport m, rendement m. <> vt **1.** [gen] rendre ; [a loan] rembourser ; [library book] rapporter - **2.** [send back] renvoyer - **3.** [replace] remettre - **4.** POL élire. <> vi [come back] revenir ; [go back] retourner. ◆ **returns** npl COMM recettes fpl ; **many happy returns (of the day!)** bon anniversaire ! ◆ **in return** adv en retour, en échange. ◆ **in return for** prep en échange de.

return ticket n UK aller et retour m.

reunification [,ri:ju:nɪfɪ'keɪʃn] n réunification f.

reunion [,ri:'ju:njən] n réunion f.

reunite [,ri:ju:'naɪt] vt : **to be reunited with sb** retrouver qqn.

rev [rev] inf <> n (abbrev of **revolution**) tour m. <> vt : **to rev the engine (up)** emballer le moteur. <> vi : **to rev (up)** s'emballer.

revamp [,ri:'væmp] vt inf [system, department] réorganiser ; [house] retaper.

reveal [rɪ'vi:l] vt révéler.

revealing [rɪ'vi:lɪŋ] adj **1.** [clothes - low-cut] décolleté(e) ; [- transparent] qui laisse deviner le corps - **2.** [comment] révélateur(trice).

reveille [rɪ'vælɪ, US 'revəlɪ] n réveil m.

revel ['revl] (UK & US) vi : **to revel in sthg** se délecter de qqch.

revelation [,revə'leɪʃn] n révélation f.

revenge [rɪ'vendʒ] <> n vengeance f ; **to**

---

take revenge (on sb) se venger (de qqn). <> vt venger ; **to revenge o.s. on sb** se venger de qqn.

revenue ['revənju:] n revenu m.

reverberate [rɪ'vɜ:bəreɪt] vi retentir, se répercuter ; fig avoir des répercussions.

reverberations [rɪ,vɜ:bə'reɪʃnz] npl réverbérations fpl ; fig répercussions fpl.

revere [rɪ'vɪər] vt révérer, vénérer.

reverence ['revərəns] n révérence f, vénération f.

Reverend ['revərənd] n révérend m.

reverie ['revərɪ] n rêverie f.

reversal [rɪ'vɜ:sl] n **1.** [of policy, decision] revirement m - **2.** [ill fortune] revers m de fortune.

reverse [rɪ'vɜ:s] <> adj [order, process] inverse. <> n **1.** AUT : **reverse (gear)** marche f arrière - **2.** [opposite] : **the reverse** le contraire - **3.** [back] : **the reverse** [of paper] le verso, le dos ; [of coin] le revers. <> vt **1.** [order, positions] inverser ; [decision, trend] renverser - **2.** [turn over] retourner - **3.** UK TELEC : **to reverse the charges** téléphoner en PCV. <> vi AUT faire marche arrière.

reverse-charge call n UK appel m en PCV.

reversing light [rɪ'vɜ:sɪŋ-] n UK feu m de marche arrière.

revert [rɪ'vɜ:t] vi : **to revert to** retourner à.

review [rɪ'vju:] <> n **1.** [of salary, spending] révision f ; [of situation] examen m - **2.** [of book, play etc] critique f, compte rendu m. <> vt **1.** [salary] réviser ; [situation] examiner - **2.** [book, play etc] faire la critique de - **3.** [troops] passer en revue - **4.** US [study again] réviser.

reviewer [rɪ'vju:ər] n critique mf.

revile [rɪ'vaɪl] vt injurier.

revise [rɪ'vaɪz] <> vt **1.** [reconsider] modifier - **2.** [rewrite] corriger - **3.** UK [study again] réviser. <> vi UK : **to revise (for)** réviser (pour).

revision [rɪ'vɪʒn] n révision f.

revitalize, UK **-ise** [,ri:'vaɪtəlaɪz] vt revitaliser.

revival [rɪ'vaɪvl] n [of economy, trade] reprise f ; [of interest] regain m.

revive [rɪ'vaɪv] <> vt **1.** [person] ranimer - **2.** fig [economy] relancer ; [interest] faire renaître ; [tradition] rétablir ; [musical, play] reprendre ; [memories] ranimer, raviver. <> vi **1.** [person] reprendre connaissance - **2.** fig [economy] repartir, reprendre ; [hopes] renaître.

revolt [rɪ'vəʊlt] <> n révolte f. <> vt révolter, dégoûter. <> vi se révolter.

revolting [rɪ'vəʊltɪŋ] adj dégoûtant(e) ; [smell] infect(e).

revolution [ˌrevəˈluːʃn] *n* **1.** [gen] révolution *f* - **2.** TECH tour *m*, révolution *f*.

revolutionary [ˌrevəˈluːʃnərɪ] ⬦ *adj* révolutionnaire. ⬦ *n* révolutionnaire *mf*.

revolve [rɪˈvɒlv] *vi* : **to revolve (around)** tourner (autour de).

revolver [rɪˈvɒlvər] *n* revolver *m*.

revolving [rɪˈvɒlvɪŋ] *adj* tournant(e) ; [chair] pivotant(e).

revolving door *n* tambour *m*.

revue [rɪˈvjuː] *n* revue *f*.

revulsion [rɪˈvʌlʃn] *n* répugnance *f*.

reward [rɪˈwɔːd] ⬦ *n* récompense *f*. ⬦ *vt* : **to reward sb (for/with sthg)** récompenser qqn (de/par qqch).

rewarding [rɪˈwɔːdɪŋ] *adj* [job] qui donne de grandes satisfactions ; [book] qui vaut la peine d'être lu(e).

rewind [ˌriːˈwaɪnd] (*pt & pp* **rewound**) *vt* [tape] rembobiner.

rewire [ˌriːˈwaɪər] *vt* [house] refaire l'installation électrique de.

reword [ˌriːˈwɜːd] *vt* reformuler.

rewound [ˌriːˈwaʊnd] *pt & pp* ▶ **rewind**.

rewrite [ˌriːˈraɪt] (*pt* **rewrote** [ˌriːˈrəʊt], *pp* **rewritten** [ˌriːˈrɪtn]) *vt* récrire.

Reykjavik [ˈrekjəvɪk] *n* Reykjavik.

rhapsody [ˈræpsədɪ] *n* rhapsodie *f* ; **to go into rhapsodies about sthg** s'extasier sur qqch.

rhetoric [ˈretərɪk] *n* rhétorique *f*.

rhetorical question [rɪˈtɒrɪkl-] *n* question *f* pour la forme.

rheumatism [ˈruːmətɪzm] *n (U)* rhumatisme *m*.

Rhine [raɪn] *n* : **the Rhine** le Rhin.

rhino [ˈraɪnəʊ] (*pl* **rhino** OR **-s**), **rhinoceros** [raɪˈnɒsərəs] (*pl* **rhinoceros** OR **-es**) *n* rhinocéros *m*.

rhododendron [ˌrəʊdəˈdendrən] *n* rhododendron *m*.

Rhône [rəʊn] *n* : **the (River) Rhône** le Rhône.

rhubarb [ˈruːbɑːb] *n* rhubarbe *f*.

rhyme [raɪm] ⬦ *n* **1.** [word, technique] rime *f* - **2.** [poem] poème *m*. ⬦ *vi* : **to rhyme (with)** rimer (avec).

rhythm [ˈrɪðm] *n* rythme *m*.

rib [rɪb] *n* **1.** ANAT côte *f* - **2.** [of umbrella] baleine *f* ; [of structure] membrure *f*.

ribbed [rɪbd] *adj* [jumper, fabric] à côtes.

ribbon [ˈrɪbən] *n* ruban *m*.

rice [raɪs] *n* riz *m*.

rice pudding *n* riz *m* au lait.

rich [rɪtʃ] ⬦ *adj* riche ; [clothes, fabrics] somptueux(euse) ; **to be rich in** être riche en. ⬦ *npl* : **the rich** les riches *mpl*. ⬥ **riches** *npl* richesses *fpl*, richesse *f*.

richly [ˈrɪtʃlɪ] *adv* **1.** [rewarded] largement ; [provided] très bien - **2.** [sumptuously] richement.

richness [ˈrɪtʃnɪs] *n (U)* richesse *f*.

rickets [ˈrɪkɪts] *n (U)* rachitisme *m*.

rickety [ˈrɪkətɪ] *adj* branlant(e).

rickshaw [ˈrɪkʃɔː] *n* pousse-pousse *m inv*.

ricochet [ˈrɪkəʃeɪ] ⬦ *n* ricochet *m*. ⬦ *vi* (*pt & pp* **-ed** OR **-ted**, *cont* **-ing**, *cont* **-ting**) : **to ricochet (off)** ricocher (sur).

rid [rɪd] *vt* (*pt* **rid** OR **-ded**, *pp* **rid**) : **to rid sb/sthg of** débarrasser qqn/qqch de ; **to get rid of** se débarrasser de.

ridden [ˈrɪdn] *pp* ▶ **ride**.

riddle [ˈrɪdl] *n* énigme *f*.

riddled [ˈrɪdld] *adj* : **to be riddled with** être criblé(e) de.

ride [raɪd] ⬦ *n* [trip] promenade *f*, tour *m* ; **to go for a ride** [on horse] faire une promenade à cheval ; [on bike] faire une promenade à vélo ; [in car] faire un tour en voiture ; **to take sb for a ride** *inf fig* faire marcher qqn. ⬦ *vt* (*pt* **rode**, *pp* **ridden**) **1.** [travel on] : **to ride a horse/a bicycle** monter à cheval/à bicyclette - **2.** US [travel in - bus, train, elevator] prendre - **3.** [distance] parcourir, faire. ⬦ *vi* (*pt* **rode**, *pp* **ridden**) [on horseback] monter à cheval, faire du cheval ; [on bicycle] faire de la bicyclette OR du vélo ; **to ride in a car/bus** aller en voiture/bus.

rider [ˈraɪdər] *n* [of horse] cavalier *m*, -ère *f* ; [of bicycle] cycliste *mf* ; [of motorbike] motocycliste *mf*.

ridge [rɪdʒ] *n* **1.** [of mountain, roof] crête *f*, arête *f* - **2.** [on surface] strie *f*.

ridicule [ˈrɪdɪkjuːl] ⬦ *n* ridicule *m*. ⬦ *vt* ridiculiser.

ridiculous [rɪˈdɪkjʊləs] *adj* ridicule.

riding [ˈraɪdɪŋ] *n* équitation *f*.

riding school *n* école *f* d'équitation.

rife [raɪf] *adj* répandu(e).

riffraff [ˈrɪfræf] *n* racaille *f*.

rifle [ˈraɪfl] ⬦ *n* fusil *m*. ⬦ *vt* [drawer, bag] vider.

rifle range *n* [indoor] stand *m* de tir ; [outdoor] champ *m* de tir.

rift [rɪft] *n* **1.** GEOL fissure *f* - **2.** [quarrel] désaccord *m*.

rig [rɪg] ⬦ *n* **1.** : **(oil) rig** [on land] derrick *m* ; [at sea] plate-forme *f* de forage - **2.** US [truck] semi-remorque *m*. ⬦ *vt* [match, election] truquer. ⬥ **rig up** *vt sep* installer avec les moyens du bord.

rigging [ˈrɪgɪŋ] *n* [of ship] gréement *m*.

right [raɪt] <> adj **1.** [correct - answer, time] juste, exact(e) ; [- decision, direction, idea] bon (bonne) ; **to be right (about)** avoir raison (au sujet de) - **2.** [morally correct] bien (inv) ; **to be right to do sthg** avoir raison de faire qqch - **3.** [appropriate] qui convient - **4.** [not left] droit(e) - **5.** UK inf [complete] véritable. <> n **1.** (U) [moral correctness] bien m ; **to be in the right** avoir raison - **2.** [entitlement, claim] droit m ; **by rights** en toute justice - **3.** [not left] droite f. <> adv **1.** [correctly] correctement - **2.** [not left] à droite - **3.** [emphatic use] : **right down/up** tout en bas/en haut ; **right here** ici (même) ; **right in the middle** en plein milieu ; **go right to the end of the street** allez tout au bout de la rue ; **right now** tout de suite ; **right away** immédiatement. <> vt **1.** [injustice, wrong] réparer - **2.** [ship] redresser. <> excl bon ! ◆ **Right** n POL : **the Right** la droite.

right angle n angle m droit ; **to be at right angles (to)** faire un angle droit (avec).

righteous ['raɪtʃəs] adj [person] droit(e) ; [indignation] justifié(e).

rightful ['raɪtfʊl] adj légitime.

right-hand adj de droite ; **right-hand side** droite f, côté m droit.

right-hand drive adj avec conduite à droite.

right-handed [-'hændɪd] adj [person] droitier(ère).

right-hand man n bras m droit.

rightly ['raɪtlɪ] adv **1.** [answer, believe] correctement - **2.** [behave] bien - **3.** [angry, worried etc] à juste titre.

right of way n **1.** AUT priorité f - **2.** [access] droit m de passage.

right-on adj inf branché(e).

right wing n : **the right wing** la droite. ◆ **right-wing** adj de droite.

rigid ['rɪdʒɪd] adj **1.** [gen] rigide - **2.** [harsh] strict(e).

rigmarole ['rɪgmərəʊl] n pej **1.** [process] comédie f - **2.** [story] galimatias m.

rigor US = rigour.

rigorous ['rɪgərəs] adj rigoureux(euse).

rigour UK, **rigor** US ['rɪgər] n rigueur f.

rile [raɪl] vt agacer.

rim [rɪm] n [of container] bord m ; [of wheel] jante f ; [of spectacles] monture f.

rind [raɪnd] n [of fruit] peau f ; [of cheese] croûte f ; [of bacon] couenne f.

ring [rɪŋ] <> n **1.** [telephone call] : **to give sb a ring** donner OR passer un coup de téléphone à qqn - **2.** [sound of bell] sonnerie f - **3.** [circular object] anneau m ; [on finger] bague f ; [for napkin] rond m - **4.** [of people, trees etc] cercle m - **5.** [for boxing] ring m - **6.** [of criminals, spies] réseau m. <> vt

(pt rang, pp rung) **1.** UK [make phone call to] téléphoner à, appeler - **2.** [bell] (faire) sonner ; **to ring the doorbell** sonner à la porte - **3.** (pt & pp ringed) [draw a circle round, surround] entourer. <> vi (pt rang, pp rung) **1.** UK [make phone call] téléphoner - **2.** [bell, telephone, person] sonner ; **to ring for sb** sonner qqn - **3.** [resound] : **to ring with** résonner de. ◆ **ring back** vt sep & vi UK rappeler. ◆ **ring off** vi UK raccrocher. ◆ **ring up** vt sep UK téléphoner à, appeler.

ring binder n classeur m à anneaux.

ringing ['rɪŋɪŋ] n [of bell] sonnerie f ; [in ears] tintement m.

ringing tone n sonnerie f.

ringleader ['rɪŋ,liːdər] n chef m.

ringlet ['rɪŋlɪt] n anglaise f.

ring road n UK (route f) périphérique m.

rink [rɪŋk] n [for ice skating] patinoire f ; [for roller-skating] skating m.

rinse [rɪns] vt rincer ; **to rinse one's mouth out** se rincer la bouche.

riot ['raɪət] <> n émeute f ; **to run riot** se déchaîner. <> vi participer à une émeute.

rioter ['raɪətər] n émeutier m, -ère f.

riotous ['raɪətəs] adj [crowd] tapageur(euse) ; [behaviour] séditieux(euse) ; [party] bruyant(e).

riot police npl ≃ CRS mpl.

rip [rɪp] <> n déchirure f, accroc m. <> vt **1.** [tear] déchirer - **2.** [remove violently] arracher. <> vi se déchirer.

RIP (abbrev of rest in peace) qu'il/elle repose en paix.

ripe [raɪp] adj mûr(e).

ripen ['raɪpn] vt & vi mûrir.

rip-off n inf that's a rip-off ! c'est de l'escroquerie OR de l'arnaque !

ripple ['rɪpl] <> n ondulation f, ride f ; **a ripple of applause** des applaudissements discrets. <> vt rider.

rise [raɪz] <> n **1.** [increase] augmentation f, hausse f ; [in temperature] élévation f, hausse - **2.** UK [increase in salary] augmentation f (de salaire) - **3.** [to power, fame] ascension f - **4.** [slope] côte f, pente f ; **to give rise to** donner lieu à. <> vi (pt rose, pp risen ['rɪzn]) **1.** [move upwards] s'élever, monter ; **to rise to power** arriver au pouvoir ; **to rise to fame** devenir célèbre ; **to rise to a challenge/to the occasion** se montrer à la hauteur d'un défi/de la situation - **2.** [from chair, bed] se lever - **3.** [increase - gen] monter, augmenter ; [- voice, level] s'élever - **4.** [rebel] se soulever.

rising ['raɪzɪŋ] <> adj **1.** [ground, tide] montant(e) - **2.** [prices, inflation, temperature] en hausse - **3.** [star, politician etc] à l'avenir prometteur. ◇ *n* [revolt] soulèvement *m*.

risk [rɪsk] ◇ *n* risque *m*, danger *m* ; **at one's own risk** à ses risques et périls ; **to run the risk of doing sthg** courir le risque de faire qqch ; **to take a risk** prendre un risque ; **at risk** en danger. ◇ *vt* [health, life etc] risquer ; **to risk doing sthg** courir le risque de faire qqch.

risky ['rɪskɪ] *adj* risqué(e).

risqué ['ri:skeɪ] *adj* risqué(e), osé(e).

rissole ['rɪsəʊl] *n* UK rissole *f*.

rite [raɪt] *n* rite *m*.

ritual ['rɪtʃʊəl] ◇ *adj* rituel(elle). ◇ *n* rituel *m*.

rival ['raɪvl] ◇ *adj* rival(e), concurrent(e). ◇ *n* rival *m*, -e *f*. ◇ *vt* (UK & US) rivaliser avec.

rivalry ['raɪvlrɪ] *n* rivalité *f*.

river ['rɪvər] *n* rivière *f*, fleuve *m*.

river bank *n* berge *f*, rive *f*.

riverbed ['rɪvəbed] *n* lit *m* (de rivière OR de fleuve).

riverside ['rɪvəsaɪd] *n* : **the riverside** le bord de la rivière OR du fleuve.

rivet ['rɪvɪt] ◇ *n* rivet *m*. ◇ *vt* **1.** [fasten with rivets] river, riveter - **2.** fig [fascinate] : **to be riveted by** être fasciné(e) par.

Riviera [,rɪvɪ'eərə] *n* : **the French Riviera** la Côte d'Azur ; **the Italian Riviera** la Riviera italienne.

road [rəʊd] *n* route *f* ; [small] chemin *m* ; [in town] rue *f* ; **by road** par la route ; **on the road to** fig sur le chemin de.

roadblock ['rəʊdblɒk] *n* barrage *m* routier.

road hog *n* inf pej chauffard *m*.

roadkill ['rəʊdkɪl] *n* animal *m* tué sur une route.

road map *n* carte *f* routière.

road rage *n* accès de colère de la part d'un automobiliste, se traduisant parfois par un acte de violence.

road safety *n* sécurité *f* routière.

roadside ['rəʊdsaɪd] *n* : **the roadside** le bord de la route.

road sign *n* panneau *m* routier OR de signalisation.

road tax *n* UK ≃ vignette *f*.

roadway ['rəʊdweɪ] *n* chaussée *f*.

roadworks UK, **roadwork** US [-wɜ:ks] *npl* travaux *mpl* (de réfection des routes).

roadworthy ['rəʊd,wɜ:ðɪ] *adj* en bon état de marche.

roam [rəʊm] ◇ *vt* errer dans. ◇ *vi* errer.

roar [rɔ:r] ◇ *vi* [person, lion] rugir ; [wind] hurler ; [car] gronder ; [plane] vrombir ; **to roar with laughter** se tordre de rire. ◇ *vt*

hurler. ◇ *n* [of person, lion] rugissement *m* ; [of traffic] grondement *m* ; [of plane, engine] vrombissement *m*.

roaring ['rɔ:rɪŋ] *adj* : **a roaring fire** une belle flambée ; **roaring drunk** complètement saoul(e) ; **to do a roaring trade** faire des affaires en or.

roast [rəʊst] ◇ *adj* rôti(e). ◇ *n* rôti *m*. ◇ *vt* **1.** [meat, potatoes] rôtir - **2.** [coffee, nuts etc] griller.

roast beef *n* rôti *m* de bœuf, rosbif *m*.

rob [rɒb] *vt* [person] voler ; [bank] dévaliser ; **to rob sb of sthg** [money, goods] voler OR dérober qqch à qqn ; [opportunity, glory] enlever qqch à qqn.

robber ['rɒbər] *n* voleur *m*, -euse *f*.

robbery ['rɒbərɪ] *n* vol *m*.

robe [rəʊb] *n* **1.** [gen] robe *f* - **2.** US [dressing gown] peignoir *m*.

robin ['rɒbɪn] *n* rouge-gorge *m*.

robot ['rəʊbɒt] *n* robot *m*.

robust [rəʊ'bʌst] *adj* robuste.

rock [rɒk] ◇ *n* **1.** (U) [substance] roche *f* - **2.** [boulder] rocher *m* - **3.** US [pebble] caillou *m* - **4.** [music] rock *m* - **5.** UK [sweet] sucre *m* d'orge. ◇ *comp* [music, band] de rock. ◇ *vt* **1.** [baby] bercer ; [cradle, boat] balancer - **2.** [shock] secouer. ◇ *vi* (se) balancer. ◆ **on the rocks** *adv* **1.** [drink] avec de la glace OR des glaçons - **2.** [marriage, relationship] près de la rupture.

rock and roll *n* rock *m*, rock and roll *m*.

rock bottom *n* : **at rock bottom** au plus bas ; **to hit rock bottom** toucher le fond. ◆ **rock-bottom** *adj* [price] sacrifié(e).

rockery ['rɒkərɪ] *n* rocaille *f*.

rocket ['rɒkɪt] ◇ *n* **1.** [gen] fusée *f* - **2.** MIL fusée *f*, roquette *f*. ◇ *vi* monter en flèche.

rocket launcher [-,lɔ:ntʃər] *n* lance-fusées *m* inv, lance-roquettes *m* inv.

rocking chair ['rɒkɪŋ-] *n* fauteuil *m* à bascule, rocking-chair *m*.

rocking horse ['rɒkɪŋ-] *n* cheval *m* à bascule.

rock'n'roll [,rɒkən'rəʊl] = **rock and roll**.

rocky ['rɒkɪ] *adj* **1.** [ground, road] rocailleux(euse), caillouteux(euse) - **2.** fig [economy, marriage] précaire.

Rocky Mountains *npl* : **the Rocky Mountains** les montagnes *fpl* Rocheuses.

rod [rɒd] *n* [metal] tige *f* ; [wooden] baguette *f* ; **(fishing) rod** canne *f* à pêche.

rode [rəʊd] *pt* ▶ **ride**.

rodent ['rəʊdənt] *n* rongeur *m*.

roe [rəʊ] *n* (U) œufs *mpl* de poisson.

roe deer *n* chevreuil *m*.

rogue [rəʊg] *n* **1.** [likeable rascal] coquin *m*, -e *f* - **2.** dated [dishonest person] filou *m*, crapule *f*.

role [rəʊl] *n* rôle *m*.

roll [rəʊl] <> *n* **1.** [of material, paper etc] rouleau *m* - **2.** [of bread] petit pain *m* - **3.** [list] liste *f* - **4.** [of drums, thunder] roulement *m*. <> *vt* rouler ; [log, ball etc] faire rouler. <> *vi* rouler. **► roll about** UK, **roll around** *vi* [person] se rouler ; [object] rouler çà et là. **► roll over** *vi* se retourner. **► roll up** <> *vt sep* **1.** [carpet, paper etc] rouler - **2.** [sleeves] retrousser. <> *vi inf* [arrive] s'amener, se pointer.

roll call *n* appel *m*.

roller ['rəʊlər] *n* rouleau *m*.

Rollerblades® ['rəʊləbleɪd] *n* rollers *mpl*, patins *mpl* en ligne.

rollerblading ['rəʊləbleɪdɪŋ] *n* roller *m*.

roller coaster *n* montagnes *fpl* russes.

roller skate *n* patin *m* à roulettes.

rolling ['rəʊlɪŋ] *adj* [hills] onduleux(euse) ; **to be rolling in it** *inf* rouler sur l'or.

rolling pin *n* rouleau *m* à pâtisserie.

rolling stock *n* matériel *m* roulant.

roll-on *adj* [deodorant] à bille.

ROM [rɒm] (*abbrev of* **read only memory**) *n* ROM *f*.

Roman ['rəʊmən] <> *adj* romain(e). <> *n* Romain *m*, -e *f*.

Roman Catholic <> *adj* catholique. <> *n* catholique *mf*.

romance [rəʊ'mæns] *n* **1.** (U) [romantic quality] charme *m* - **2.** [love affair] idylle *f* - **3.** [book] roman *m* (d'amour).

Romania [ru:'meɪnjə] *n* Roumanie *f*.

Romanian [ru:'meɪnjən] <> *adj* roumain(e). <> *n* **1.** [person] Roumain *m*, -e *f* - **2.** [language] roumain *m*.

Roman numerals *npl* chiffres *mpl* romains.

romantic [rəʊ'mæntɪk] *adj* romantique.

Rome [rəʊm] *n* Rome.

romp [rɒmp] <> *n* ébats *mpl*. <> *vi* s'ébattre.

rompers ['rɒmpəz] *npl* barboteuse *f*.

romper suit ['rɒmpər-] *n* = rompers.

roof [ru:f] *n* toit *m* ; [of cave, tunnel] plafond *m* ; **the roof of the mouth** la voûte du palais ; **to go through** OR **hit the roof** *fig* exploser.

roofing ['ru:fɪŋ] *n* toiture *f*.

roof rack *n* UK galerie *f*.

rooftop ['ru:ftɒp] *n* toit *m*.

rook [rʊk] *n* **1.** [bird] freux *m* - **2.** [chess piece] tour *f*.

rookie ['rʊkɪ] *n* US inf bleu *m*.

room [ru:m OR rʊm] *n* **1.** [in building] pièce *f* - **2.** [bedroom] chambre *f* - **3.** (U) [space] place *f*.

roomer ['ru:mər] *n* US locataire *mf* de rapport.

rooming house ['ru:mɪŋ-] *n* US maison *f* de rapport.

roommate ['ru:mmeɪt] *n* camarade *mf* de chambre.

room service *n* service *m* dans les chambres.

roomy ['ru:mɪ] *adj* spacieux(euse).

roost [ru:st] <> *n* perchoir *m*, juchoir *m*. <> *vi* se percher, se jucher.

rooster ['ru:stər] *n* coq *m*.

root [ru:t] <> *n* racine *f* ; *fig* [of problem] origine *f* ; **to take root** *lit & fig* prendre racine. <> *vi* : **to root through** fouiller dans. **► roots** *npl* racines *fpl*. **► root for** *vt insep* US *inf* encourager. **► root out** *vt sep* [eradicate] extirper.

rope [rəʊp] <> *n* corde *f* ; **to know the ropes** connaître son affaire, être au courant. <> *vt* corder ; [climbers] encorder. **► rope in** *vt sep inf fig* enrôler.

rosary ['rəʊzərɪ] *n* rosaire *m*.

rose [rəʊz] <> *pt* ► **rise**. <> *adj* [pink] rose. <> *n* [flower] rose *f*.

rosé ['rəʊzeɪ] *n* rosé *m*.

rosebud ['rəʊzbʌd] *n* bouton *m* de rose.

rose bush *n* rosier *m*.

rosemary ['rəʊzmərɪ] *n* romarin *m*.

rosette [rəʊ'zet] *n* rosette *f*.

roster ['rɒstər] *n* liste *f*, tableau *m*.

rostrum ['rɒstrəm] (*pl* -**trums** OR -**tra** [-trə]) *n* tribune *f*.

rosy ['rəʊzɪ] *adj* rose.

rot [rɒt] <> *n* (U) **1.** [decay] pourriture *f* - **2.** UK *dated* [nonsense] bêtises *fpl*, balivernes *fpl*. <> *vt & vi* pourrir.

rota ['rəʊtə] *n* UK liste *f*, tableau *m*.

rotary ['rəʊtərɪ] <> *adj* rotatif(ive). <> *n* US [roundabout] rond-point *m*.

rotate [rəʊ'teɪt] <> *vt* [turn] faire tourner. <> *vi* [turn] tourner.

rotation [rəʊ'teɪʃn] *n* [turning movement] rotation *f*.

rote [rəʊt] *n* : **by rote** de façon machinale, par cœur.

rotten ['rɒtn] *adj* **1.** [decayed] pourri(e) - **2.** *inf* [bad] moche - **3.** *inf* [unwell] : **to feel rotten** se sentir mal fichu(e).

rouge [ru:ʒ] *n* rouge *m* à joues.

rough [rʌf] <> *adj* **1.** [not smooth - surface] rugueux(euse), rêche ; [- road] accidenté(e) ; [- sea] agité(e), houleux(euse) ; [- crossing] mauvais(e) - **2.** [person, treatment] brutal(e) ; [manners, conditions] rude ; [area] mal fréquenté(e) - **3.** [guess] approximatif(ive) ; **rough copy, rough draft** brouillon *m* ; **rough sketch** ébauche *f* - **4.** [harsh - voice, wine] âpre ; [- life] dur(e) ; **to have a rough time** en baver. <> *adv* : **to sleep**

rough *UK* coucher à la dure. ◇ *n* **1.** GOLF rough *m* - **2.** [undetailed form] : **in rough** au brouillon. ◇ *vt* ; **to rough it** vivre à la dure. ◆ **rough up** *vt sep inf* [person] tabasser, passer à tabac.

roughage ['rʌfɪdʒ] *n* (U) fibres *fpl* alimentaires.

rough and ready *adj* rudimentaire.

roughcast ['rʌfkɑːst] *n* crépi *m*.

roughen ['rʌfn] *vt* rendre rugueux(euse) OR rêche.

roughly ['rʌflɪ] *adv* **1.** [approximately] approximativement - **2.** [handle, treat] brutalement - **3.** [built, made] grossièrement.

roulette [ru:'let] *n* roulette *f*.

round [raʊnd] ◇ *adj* rond(e). ◇ *prep UK* autour de ; **round here** par ici ; **all round the country** dans tout le pays ; **just round the corner** au coin de la rue ; *fig* tout près ; **to go round sthg** [obstacle] contourner qqch ; **to go round a museum** visiter un musée. ◇ *adv UK* **1.** [surrounding] : **all round** tout autour - **2.** [near] : **round about** dans le coin - **3.** [in measurements] : **10 metres round** 10 mètres de diamètre - **4.** [to other side] : **to go round** faire le tour ; **to turn round** se retourner ; **to look round** se retourner (pour regarder) - **5.** [at or to nearby place] : **come round and see us** venez OR passez nous voir ; **he's round at her house** il est chez elle - **6.** [approximately] : **round (about)** vers, environ. ◇ *n* **1.** [of talks etc] série *f* ; **a round of applause** une salve d'applaudissements - **2.** [of competition] manche *f* - **3.** [of doctor] visites *fpl* ; [of postman, milkman] tournée *f* - **4.** [of ammunition] cartouche *f* - **5.** [of drinks] tournée *f* - **6.** [in boxing] reprise *f*, round *m* - **7.** [in golf] partie *f*. ◇ *vt* [corner] tourner ; [bend] prendre. ◆ **rounds** *npl* [of doctor] visites *fpl* ; **to do** OR **go the rounds** [story, joke] circuler ; [illness] faire des ravages. ◆ **round down** *vt sep* arrondir au chiffre inférieur. ◆ **round off** *vt sep* terminer, conclure. ◆ **round up** *vt sep* **1.** [gather together] rassembler - **2.** MATHS arrondir au chiffre supérieur.

roundabout ['raʊndəbaʊt] ◇ *adj* détourné(e). ◇ *n UK* **1.** [on road] rond-point *m* - **2.** [at fairground] manège *m*.

rounders ['raʊndəz] *n UK* sorte de baseball.

roundly ['raʊndlɪ] *adv* [beaten] complètement ; [condemned etc] franchement, carrément.

round-shouldered [-'ʃəʊldəd] *adj* voûté(e).

round trip *n* aller et retour *m*.

roundup ['raʊndʌp] *n* [summary] résumé *m*.

rouse [raʊz] *vt* **1.** [wake up] réveiller - **2.** [impel] : **to rouse o.s. to do sthg** se forcer à faire qqch ; **to rouse sb to action** pousser OR inciter qqn à agir - **3.** [emotions] susciter, provoquer.

rousing ['raʊzɪŋ] *adj* [speech] vibrant(e), passionné(e) ; [welcome] enthousiaste.

rout [raʊt] ◇ *n* déroute *f*. ◇ *vt* mettre en déroute.

route [ru:t] ◇ *n* **1.** [gen] itinéraire *m* - **2.** *fig* [way] chemin *m*, voie *f*. ◇ *vt* [goods] acheminer.

route map *n* [for journey] croquis *m* d'itinéraire ; [for buses, trains] carte *f* du réseau.

routine [ru:'ti:n] ◇ *adj* **1.** [normal] habituel(elle), de routine - **2.** *pej* [uninteresting] de routine. ◇ *n* routine *f*.

roving ['rəʊvɪŋ] *adj* itinérant(e).

row[1] [rəʊ] ◇ *n* **1.** [line] rangée *f* ; [of seats] rang *m* - **2.** *fig* [of defeats, victories] série *f* ; **in a row** d'affilée, de suite. ◇ *vt* [boat] faire aller à la rame ; [person] transporter en canot OR bateau. ◇ *vi* ramer.

row[2] [raʊ] ◇ *n* **1.** [quarrel] dispute *f*, querelle *f* - **2.** *inf* [noise] vacarme *m*, raffut *m*. ◇ *vi* [quarrel] se disputer, se quereller.

rowboat ['rəʊbəʊt] *n US* canot *m*.

rowdy ['raʊdɪ] *adj* chahuteur(euse), tapageur(euse).

row house [rəʊ-] *n US* maison attenante aux maisons voisines.

rowing ['rəʊɪŋ] *n* SPORT aviron *m*.

rowing boat *n UK* canot *m*.

royal ['rɔɪəl] ◇ *adj* royal(e). ◇ *n inf* membre *m* de la famille royale.

Royal Air Force *n* : **the Royal Air Force** l'armée *f* de l'air britannique.

royal family *n* famille *f* royale.

Royal Mail *n* : **the Royal Mail** la Poste britannique.

Royal Navy *n* : **the Royal Navy** la marine de guerre (britannique).

royalty ['rɔɪəltɪ] *n* royauté *f*. ◆ **royalties** *npl* droits *mpl* d'auteur.

rpm *npl* (abbrev of **revolutions per minute**) tours *mpl* par minute, tr/min.

RSPCA (abbrev of **Royal Society for the Prevention of Cruelty to Animals**) *n* société britannique protectrice des animaux, ≃ SPA *f*.

RSVP (abbrev of **répondez s'il vous plaît**) RSVP.

Rt Hon (abbrev of **Right Honourable**) expression utilisée pour des titres nobiliaires.

rub [rʌb] ◇ *vt* frotter ; **to rub sthg in** [cream etc] faire pénétrer qqch (en frottant) ; **to rub one's eyes/hands** se frotter les yeux/les mains ; **to rub sb up the wrong way** *UK*, **to rub sb the wrong way** *US fig* prendre qqn à rebrousse-poil. ◇ *vi* frotter. **rub off on** *vt insep* [subj: quality] déteindre sur. **rub out** *vt sep* [erase] effacer.

rubber ['rʌbər] <> *adj* en caoutchouc. <> *n* **1.** [substance] caoutchouc *m* - **2.** UK [eraser] gomme *f* - **3.** US *inf* [condom] préservatif *m* - **4.** [in bridge] robre *m*, rob *m*.

rubber band *n* élastique *m*.

rubber plant *n* caoutchouc *m*.

rubber stamp *n* tampon *m*. **rubber-stamp** *vt fig* approuver sans discussion.

rubbish ['rʌbɪʃ] UK <> *n* (U) **1.** [refuse] détritus *mpl*, ordures *fpl* - **2.** *inf fig* [worthless objects] camelote *f* ; **the play was rubbish** la pièce était nulle - **3.** *inf* [nonsense] bêtises *fpl*, inepties *fpl*. <> *vt inf* débiner.

rubbish bin *n* UK poubelle *f*.

rubbish dump *n* UK dépotoir *m*.

rubble ['rʌbl] *n* (U) décombres *mpl*.

ruby ['ru:bɪ] *n* rubis *m*.

rucksack ['rʌksæk] *n* sac *m* à dos.

ructions ['rʌkʃnz] *npl inf* grabuge *m*.

rudder ['rʌdər] *n* gouvernail *m*.

ruddy ['rʌdɪ] *adj* **1.** [complexion, face] coloré(e) - **2.** UK *inf dated* [damned] sacré(e).

rude [ru:d] *adj* **1.** [impolite - gen] impoli(e) ; [- word] grossier(ère) ; [- noise] incongru(e) - **2.** [sudden] : **it was a rude awakening** le réveil fut pénible.

rudimentary [,ru:dɪ'mentərɪ] *adj* rudimentaire.

rueful ['ru:fʊl] *adj* triste.

ruffian ['rʌfjən] *n* voyou *m*.

ruffle ['rʌfl] *vt* **1.** [hair] ébouriffer ; [water] troubler - **2.** [person] froisser ; [composure] faire perdre.

rug [rʌg] *n* **1.** [carpet] tapis *m* - **2.** [blanket] couverture *f*.

rugby ['rʌgbɪ] *n* rugby *m*.

rugged ['rʌgɪd] *adj* **1.** [landscape] accidenté(e) ; [features] rude - **2.** [vehicle etc] robuste.

rugger ['rʌgər] *n* UK *inf* rugby *m*.

ruin ['ru:ɪn] <> *n* ruine *f*. <> *vt* ruiner ; [clothes, shoes] abîmer. **in ruin(s)** *adv lit & fig* en ruine.

rule [ru:l] <> *n* **1.** [gen] règle *f* ; **as a rule** en règle générale - **2.** [regulation] règlement *m* - **3.** (U) [control] autorité *f*. <> *vt* **1.** [control] dominer - **2.** [govern] gouverner - **3.** [decide] : **to rule (that)...** décider que... <> *vi* **1.** [give decision - gen] décider ; LAW statuer - **2.** *fml* [be paramount] prévaloir - **3.** [king, queen] régner ; POL gouverner. **rule out** *vt sep* exclure, écarter.

ruled [ru:ld] *adj* [paper] réglé(e).

ruler ['ru:lər] *n* **1.** [for measurement] règle *f* - **2.** [leader] chef *m* d'État.

ruling ['ru:lɪŋ] <> *adj* au pouvoir. <> *n* décision *f*.

rum [rʌm] *n* rhum *m*.

Rumania [ru:'meɪnjə] = **Romania**.

Rumanian [ru:'meɪnjən] = **Romanian**.

rumble ['rʌmbl] <> *n* [of thunder, traffic] grondement *m* ; [in stomach] gargouillement *m*. <> *vi* [thunder, traffic] gronder ; [stomach] gargouiller.

rummage ['rʌmɪdʒ] *vi* fouiller.

rumour UK, **rumor** US ['ru:mər] *n* rumeur *f*.

rumoured UK, **rumored** US ['ru:məd] *adj* : **he is rumoured to be very wealthy** le bruit court OR on dit qu'il est très riche.

rump [rʌmp] *n* **1.** [of animal] croupe *f* - **2.** *inf* [of person] derrière *m*.

rump steak *n* romsteck *m*.

rumpus ['rʌmpəs] *n inf* chahut *m*.

run [rʌn] <> *n* **1.** [on foot] course *f* ; **to go for a run** faire un petit peu de course à pied ; **on the run** en fuite, en cavale - **2.** [in car - for pleasure] tour *m* ; [- journey] trajet *m* - **3.** [series] suite *f*, série *f* ; **a run of bad luck** une période de déveine ; **in the short/long run** à court/long terme - **4.** THEAT : **to have a long run** tenir longtemps l'affiche - **5.** [great demand] : **run on** ruée *f* sur - **6.** [in tights] échelle *f* - **7.** [in cricket, baseball] point *m* - **8.** [track - for skiing, bobsleigh] piste *f*. <> *vt* (*pt* ran, *pp* run) **1.** [race, distance] courir - **2.** [manage - business] diriger ; [- shop, hotel] tenir ; [- course] organiser - **3.** [operate] faire marcher - **4.** [car] avoir, entretenir - **5.** [water, bath] faire couler - **6.** [publish] publier - **7.** *inf* [drive] : **can you run me to the station?** tu peux m'amener OR me conduire à la gare? - **8.** [move] : **to run sthg along/over sthg** passer qqch le long de/sur qqch. <> *vi* (*pt* ran, *pp* run) **1.** [on foot] courir - **2.** [pass - road, river, pipe] passer ; **to run through sthg** traverser qqch - **3.** US [in election] : **to run (for)** être candidat (à) - **4.** [operate - machine, factory] marcher ; [- engine] tourner ; **everything is running smoothly** tout va comme sur des roulettes, tout va bien ; **to run on sthg** marcher à qqch ; **to run off sthg** marcher sur qqch - **5.** [bus, train] faire le service ; **trains run every hour** il y a un train toutes les heures - **6.** [flow] couler ; **my nose is running** j'ai le nez qui coule - **7.** [colour] déteindre ; [ink] baver - **8.** [continue - contract, insurance policy] être valide ; THEAT se jouer. **run across** *vt insep* [meet] tomber sur. **run away** *vi* [flee] : **to run away (from)** s'enfuir (de) ; **to run away from home** faire une fugue. **run down** <> *vt sep* **1.** [in vehicle] renverser - **2.** [criticize] dénigrer - **3.** [production] restreindre ; [industry] réduire l'activité de. <> *vi* [clock] s'arrêter ;

[battery] se décharger. **run into** vt insep **1.** [encounter - problem] se heurter à ; [- person] tomber sur - **2.** [in vehicle] rentrer dans. **run off** vt sep [a copy] tirer. ◇ vi : **to run off (with)** s'enfuir (avec). **run out** vi **1.** [food, supplies] s'épuiser ; **time is running out** il ne reste plus beaucoup de temps - **2.** [licence, contract] expirer. **run out of** vt insep manquer de ; **to run out of petrol** tomber en panne d'essence, tomber en panne sèche. **run over** vt sep renverser. **run through** vt insep **1.** [practise] répéter - **2.** [read through] parcourir. **run to** vt insep [amount to] monter à, s'élever à. **run up** vt insep [bill, debt] laisser accumuler. **run up against** vt insep se heurter à.

runaway ['rʌnəweɪ] ◇ adj [train, lorry] fou (folle) ; [horse] emballé(e) ; [victory] haut la main ; [inflation] galopant(e). ◇ n fuyard m, fugitif m, -ive f.

rundown ['rʌndaʊn] n **1.** [report] bref résumé m - **2.** [of industry] réduction f délibérée. **run-down** adj **1.** [building] délabré(e) - **2.** [person] épuisé(e).

rung [rʌŋ] ◇ pp ► **ring**. ◇ n échelon m, barreau m.

runner ['rʌnə'] n **1.** [athlete] coureur m, -euse f - **2.** [of guns, drugs] contrebandier m, -ière f - **3.** [of sledge] patin m ; [for car seat] glissière f ; [for drawer] coulisseau m.

runner bean n UK haricot m à rames.

runner-up (pl runners-up) n second m, -e f.

running ['rʌnɪŋ] ◇ adj **1.** [argument, battle] continu(e) - **2.** [consecutive] : **three weeks running** trois semaines de suite - **3.** [water] courant(e) ; **to be up and running** être opérationnel. ◇ n **1.** (U) SPORT course f ; **to go running** faire de la course - **2.** [management] direction f, administration f - **3.** [of machine] marche f, fonctionnement m ; **to be in the running (for)** avoir des chances de réussir (dans) ; **to be out of the running (for)** n'avoir aucune chance de réussir (dans).

runny ['rʌnɪ] adj **1.** [food] liquide - **2.** [nose] qui coule.

run-of-the-mill adj banal(e), ordinaire.

runt [rʌnt] n avorton m.

run-up n **1.** [preceding time] : **in the run-up to sthg** dans la période qui précède qqch - **2.** SPORT course f d'élan.

runway ['rʌnweɪ] n piste f.

rupture ['rʌptʃə'] n rupture f.

rural ['rʊərəl] adj rural(e).

ruse [ru:z] n ruse f.

rush [rʌʃ] ◇ n **1.** [hurry] hâte f - **2.** [surge] ruée f, bousculade f ; **to make a rush for sthg** se ruer OR se précipiter vers qqch ; **a rush of**

air une bouffée d'air - **3.** [demand] : **rush (on** OR **for)** ruée f (sur). ◇ vt **1.** [hurry - work] faire à la hâte ; [- person] bousculer ; [- meal] expédier ; [send quickly] transporter OR envoyer d'urgence - **3.** [attack suddenly] prendre d'assaut. ◇ vi **1.** [hurry] se dépêcher ; **to rush into sthg** faire qqch sans réfléchir - **2.** [move quickly, suddenly] se précipiter, se ruer ; **the blood rushed to her head** le sang lui monta à la tête. **rushes** npl BOT joncs mpl.

rush hour n heures fpl de pointe OR d'affluence.

rusk [rʌsk] n biscotte f.

Russia ['rʌʃə] n Russie f.

Russian ['rʌʃn] ◇ adj russe. ◇ n **1.** [person] Russe mf - **2.** [language] russe m.

Russian Federation n : **the Russian Federation** la Fédération de Russie.

rust [rʌst] ◇ n rouille f. ◇ vi se rouiller.

rustic ['rʌstɪk] adj rustique.

rustle ['rʌsl] ◇ vt **1.** [paper] froisser - **2.** US [cattle] voler. ◇ vi [leaves] bruire ; [papers] produire un froissement.

rusty ['rʌstɪ] adj lit & fig rouillé(e).

rut [rʌt] n ornière f ; **to get into a rut** s'encroûter ; **to be in a rut** être prisonnier de la routine.

ruthless ['ru:θlɪs] adj impitoyable.

RV n US (abbrev of **recreational vehicle**) camping-car m.

rye [raɪ] n [grain] seigle m.

rye bread n pain m de seigle.

s [1] (pl **ss** OR **s's**), **S** (pl **Ss** OR **S's**) [es] n [letter] s m inv, S m inv.

S

S [2] (abbrev of **south**) S.

Sabbath ['sæbəθ] n : **the Sabbath** le sabbat.

sabbatical [sə'bætɪkl] n année f sabbatique ; **to be on sabbatical** faire une année sabbatique.

sabotage ['sæbətɑ:ʒ] ◇ n sabotage m. ◇ vt saboter.

saccharin(e) ['sækərɪn] n saccharine f.

sachet ['sæʃeɪ] n sachet m.

sack [sæk] ◇ n **1.** [bag] sac m - **2.** UK inf

[dismissal] : **to get** OR **be given the sack** être renvoyé(e), se faire virer. <> vt UK inf [dismiss] renvoyer, virer.

sacking ['sækɪŋ] n [fabric] toile f à sac.

sacred ['seɪkrɪd] adj sacré(e).

sacrifice ['sækrɪfaɪs] lit & fig <> n sacrifice m. <> vt sacrifier.

sacrilege ['sækrɪlɪdʒ] n lit & fig sacrilège m.

sacrosanct ['sækrəʊsæŋkt] adj sacrosaint(e).

sad [sæd] adj triste.

sadden ['sædn] vt attrister, affliger.

saddle ['sædl] <> n selle f. <> vt 1. [horse] seller - 2. fig [burden] : **to saddle sb with sthg** coller qqch à qqn.

saddlebag ['sædlbæg] n sacoche f (de selle ou de bicyclette).

sadistic [sə'dɪstɪk] adj sadique.

sadly ['sædlɪ] adv 1. [unhappily] tristement - 2. [unfortunately] malheureusement.

sadness ['sædnɪs] n tristesse f.

s.a.e., **sae** abbrev of **stamped addressed envelope**.

safari [sə'fɑːrɪ] n safari m.

safe [seɪf] <> adj 1. [not dangerous - gen] sans danger ; [- driver, play, guess] prudent(e) ; **it's safe to say (that)...** on peut dire à coup sûr que... - 2. [not in danger] hors de danger, en sécurité ; **safe and sound** sain et sauf (saine et sauve) - 3. [not risky - bet, method] sans risque ; [- investment] sûr(e) ; **to be on the safe side** par précaution. <> n coffre-fort m.

safe-conduct n sauf-conduit m.

safe-deposit box n coffre-fort m.

safeguard ['seɪfɡɑːd] <> n : **safeguard (against)** sauvegarde f (contre). <> vt : **to safeguard sb/sthg (against)** sauvegarder qqn/qqch (contre), protéger qqn/qqch (contre).

safekeeping [,seɪf'kiːpɪŋ] n bonne garde f.

safely ['seɪflɪ] adv 1. [not dangerously] sans danger - 2. [not in danger] en toute sécurité, à l'abri du danger - 3. [arrive - person] à bon port, sain et sauf (saine et sauve) ; [- parcel] à bon port - 4. [for certain] : **I can safely say (that)...** je peux dire à coup sûr que...

safe sex n sexe m sans risques, S.S.R. m

safety ['seɪftɪ] n sécurité f.

safety belt n ceinture f de sécurité.

safety pin n épingle f de sûreté OR de nourrice.

saffron ['sæfrən] n safran m.

sag [sæɡ] vi [sink downwards] s'affaisser, fléchir.

sage [seɪdʒ] <> adj sage. <> n 1. (U) [herb] sauge f - 2. [wise man] sage m.

Sagittarius [,sædʒɪ'teərɪəs] n Sagittaire m.

Sahara [sə'hɑːrə] n : **the Sahara (Desert)** le (désert m du) Sahara.

said [sed] pt & pp ➤ **say**.

sail [seɪl] <> n 1. [of boat] voile f ; **to set sail** faire voile, prendre la mer - 2. [journey] tour m en bateau. <> vt 1. [boat] piloter, manœuvrer - 2. [sea] parcourir. <> vi 1. [person - gen] aller en bateau ; SPORT faire de la voile - 2. [boat - move] naviguer ; [- leave] partir, prendre la mer - 3. fig [through air] voler. ➤ **sail through** vt insep fig réussir les doigts dans le nez.

sailboat US = **sailing boat**.

sailing ['seɪlɪŋ] n 1. (U) SPORT voile f ; **to go sailing** faire de la voile - 2. [departure] départ m.

sailing boat UK, **sailboat** US ['seɪlbəʊt] n bateau m à voiles, voilier m.

sailing ship n voilier m.

sailor ['seɪlər] n marin m, matelot m.

saint [seɪnt] n saint m, -e f.

saintly ['seɪntlɪ] adj [person] saint(e) ; [life] de saint.

Saint Patrick's Day [-'pætrɪks-] n la Saint-Patrick.

sake [seɪk] n : **for the sake of sb** par égard pour qqn, pour (l'amour de) qqn ; **for the children's sake** pour les enfants ; **for the sake of argument** à titre d'exemple ; **for God's** OR **heaven's sake** pour l'amour de Dieu OR du ciel.

salad ['sæləd] n salade f.

salad bowl n saladier m.

salad cream n UK sorte de mayonnaise douce.

salad dressing n vinaigrette f.

salami [sə'lɑːmɪ] n salami m.

salary ['sælərɪ] n salaire m, traitement m.

sale [seɪl] n 1. [gen] vente f ; **on sale** UK, **for sale** US en vente ; **(up) for sale** à vendre - 2. [at reduced prices] soldes mpl. ➤ **sales** npl 1. [quantity sold] ventes fpl - 2. [at reduced prices] : **the sales** les soldes mpl.

saleroom UK ['seɪlrʊm], **salesroom** US ['seɪlzrʊm] n salle f des ventes.

sales assistant ['seɪlz-] UK, **salesclerk** ['seɪlzklɜːrk] US n vendeur m, -euse f.

salesman ['seɪlzmən] (pl -men [-mən]) n [in shop] vendeur m ; [travelling] représentant m de commerce.

sales rep n inf représentant m de commerce.

salesroom US = **saleroom**.

saleswoman ['seɪlz,wʊmən] (*pl* **-women** [-,wɪmɪn]) *n* [in shop] vendeuse *f* ; [travelling] représentante *f* de commerce.

salient ['seɪljənt] *adj fml* qui ressort.

saliva [sə'laɪvə] *n* salive *f*.

sallow ['sæləʊ] *adj* cireux(euse).

salmon ['sæmən] (*pl* **salmon** OR **-s**) *n* saumon *m*.

salmonella [,sælmə'nelə] *n* salmonelle *f*.

salon ['sælɒn] *n* salon *m*.

saloon [sə'lu:n] *n* **1.** UK [car] berline *f* - **2.** US [bar] saloon *m* - **3.** UK [in pub] : **saloon (bar)** bar *m* - **4.** [in ship] salon *m*.

salt [sɔːlt OR sɒlt] <> *n* sel *m*. <> *vt* [food] saler ; [roads] mettre du sel sur. ◆ **salt away** *vt sep* mettre de côté.

saltcellar, US **saltshaker** [-,ʃeɪkər] *n* salière *f*.

saltwater ['sɔːlt,wɔːtər] <> *n* eau *f* de mer. <> *adj* de mer.

salty ['sɔːltɪ] *adj* [food] salé(e) ; [water] saumâtre.

salutary ['sæljʊtrɪ] *adj* salutaire.

salute [sə'luːt] <> *n* salut *m*. <> *vt* saluer. <> *vi* faire un salut.

salvage ['sælvɪdʒ] <> *n* (U) **1.** [rescue of ship] sauvetage *m* - **2.** [property rescued] biens *mpl* sauvés. <> *vt* sauver.

salvation [sæl'veɪʃn] *n* salut *m*.

Salvation Army *n* : **the Salvation Army** l'Armée *f* du Salut.

same [seɪm] <> *adj* même ; **she was wearing the same jumper as I was** elle portait le même pull que moi ; **at the same time** en même temps ; **one and the same** un seul et même (une seule et même). <> *pron* : **the same** le même (la même), les mêmes (*pl*) ; **I'll have the same as you** je prendrai la même chose que toi ; **she earns the same as I do** elle gagne autant que moi ; **to do the same** faire de même, en faire autant ; **all** OR **just the same** [anyway] quand même, tout de même ; **it's all the same to me** ça m'est égal ; **it's not the same** ce n'est pas pareil. <> *adv* : **the same** [treat, spelled] de la même manière.

sample ['sɑːmpl] <> *n* échantillon *m*. <> *vt* [taste] goûter.

sanatorium, US **sanitorium** (*pl* **-riums** OR **-ria** [-rɪə]) [,sænə'tɔːrɪəm] *n* sanatorium *m*.

sanctimonious [,sæŋktɪ'məʊnjəs] *adj* moralisateur(trice).

sanction ['sæŋkʃn] <> *n* sanction *f*. <> *vt* sanctionner.

sanctity ['sæŋktətɪ] *n* sainteté *f*.

sanctuary ['sæŋktʃʊərɪ] *n* **1.** [for birds, wildlife] réserve *f* - **2.** [refuge] asile *m*.

sand [sænd] <> *n* sable *m*. <> *vt* [wood] poncer.

sandal ['sændl] *n* sandale *f*.

sandalwood ['sændlwʊd] *n* (bois *m* de) santal *m*.

sandbox US = **sandpit**.

sandcastle ['sænd,kɑːsl] *n* château *m* de sable.

sand dune *n* dune *f*.

sandpaper ['sænd,peɪpər] <> *n* (U) papier *m* de verre. <> *vt* poncer (au papier de verre).

sandpit UK ['sændpɪt], **sandbox** US ['sændbɒks] *n* bac *m* à sable.

sandstone ['sændstəʊn] *n* grès *m*.

sandwich ['sænwɪdʒ] <> *n* sandwich *m*. <> *vt fig* : **to be sandwiched between** être (pris(e)) en sandwich entre.

sandwich board *n* panneau *m* publicitaire (*d'homme sandwich ou posé comme un tréteau*).

sandwich course *n* UK stage *m* de formation professionnelle.

sandy ['sændɪ] *adj* **1.** [beach] de sable ; [earth] sableux(euse) - **2.** [sand-coloured] sable (*inv*).

sane [seɪn] *adj* **1.** [not mad] sain(e) d'esprit - **2.** [sensible] raisonnable, sensé(e).

sang [sæŋ] *pt* ▶ **sing**.

sanitary ['sænɪtrɪ] *adj* **1.** [method, system] sanitaire - **2.** [clean] hygiénique, salubre.

sanitary towel UK, **sanitary napkin** US *n* serviette *f* hygiénique.

sanitation [,sænɪ'teɪʃn] *n* (U) [in house] installations *fpl* sanitaires.

sanitorium US = **sanatorium**.

sanity ['sænətɪ] *n* (U) **1.** [saneness] santé *f* mentale, raison *f* - **2.** [good sense] bon sens *m*.

sank [sæŋk] *pt* ▶ **sink**.

Santa (Claus) ['sæntə,klɔːz,] *n* le père Noël.

sap [sæp] <> *n* [of plant] sève *f*. <> *vt* [weaken] saper.

sapling ['sæplɪŋ] *n* jeune arbre *m*.

sapphire ['sæfaɪər] *n* saphir *m*.

sarcastic [sɑː'kæstɪk] *adj* sarcastique.

sardine [sɑː'diːn] *n* sardine *f*.

Sardinia [sɑː'dɪnjə] *n* Sardaigne *f*.

sardonic [sɑː'dɒnɪk] *adj* sardonique.

SAS (*abbrev of* **Special Air Service**) *n* commando d'intervention spéciale de l'armée britannique.

SASE *abbrev of* **self-addressed stamped envelope**.

sash [sæʃ] *n* [of cloth] écharpe *f*.

sat [sæt] *pt & pp* ▶ **sit**.

SAT [sæt] n **1.** (*abbrev of* **Standard Assessment Test**) *examen national en Grande-Bretagne pour les élèves de 7 ans, 11 ans et 14 ans* - **2.** (*abbrev of* **Scholastic Aptitude Test**) *examen d'entrée à l'université aux États-Unis.*

Satan ['seɪtn] n Satan m.

satchel ['sætʃəl] n cartable m.

satellite ['sætəlaɪt] <> n satellite m. <> comp [country, company] satellite.

satellite TV n télévision f par satellite.

satin ['sætɪn] <> n satin m. <> comp [sheets, pyjamas] de OR en satin ; [wallpaper, finish] satiné(e).

satire ['sætaɪə'] n satire f.

satisfaction [,sætɪs'fækʃn] n satisfaction f.

satisfactory [,sætɪs'fæktərɪ] adj satisfaisant(e).

satisfied ['sætɪsfaɪd] adj [happy] : **satisfied (with)** satisfait(e) (de).

satisfy ['sætɪsfaɪ] vt **1.** [gen] satisfaire - **2.** [convince] convaincre, persuader ; **to satisfy sb that** convaincre qqn que.

satisfying ['sætɪsfaɪɪŋ] adj satisfaisant(e).

satsuma [,sæt'suːmə] n satsuma f.

saturate ['sætʃəreɪt] vt : **to saturate sthg (with)** saturer qqch (de).

Saturday ['sætədɪ] <> n samedi m ; **it's Saturday** on est samedi ; **on Saturday** samedi ; **on Saturdays** le samedi ; **last Saturday** samedi dernier ; **this Saturday** ce samedi ; **next Saturday** samedi prochain ; **every Saturday** tous les samedis ; **every other Saturday** un samedi sur deux ; **the Saturday before** l'autre samedi ; **the Saturday before last** pas samedi dernier, mais le samedi d'avant ; **the Saturday after next**, **Saturday week** UK, **a week on Saturday** UK samedi en huit. <> comp [paper] du OR de samedi ; **Saturday morning/afternoon/evening** samedi matin/après-midi/soir.

sauce [sɔːs] n CULIN sauce f.

saucepan ['sɔːspən] n casserole f.

saucer ['sɔːsə'] n sous-tasse f, soucoupe f.

saucy ['sɔːsɪ] adj inf coquin(e).

Saudi Arabia ['saʊdɪ-] n Arabie f Saoudite.

Saudi (Arabian) ['saʊdɪ-] <> adj saoudien(enne). <> n [person] Saoudien m, -enne f.

sauna ['sɔːnə] n sauna m.

saunter ['sɔːntə'] vi flâner.

sausage ['sɒsɪdʒ] n saucisse f.

sausage roll n UK feuilleté m à la saucisse.

sauté [UK 'səʊteɪ, US səʊ'teɪ] <> adj sauté(e). <> vt (pt & pp **sautéed** OR **sautéd**) [potatoes] faire sauter ; [onions] faire revenir.

savage ['sævɪdʒ] <> adj [fierce] féroce.

<> n sauvage mf. <> vt attaquer avec férocité.

save [seɪv] <> vt **1.** [rescue] sauver ; **to save sb's life** sauver la vie à OR de qqn - **2.** [money - set aside] mettre de côté ; [- spend less] économiser - **3.** [time] gagner ; [strength] économiser ; [food] garder - **4.** [avoid] éviter, épargner ; **to save sb sthg** épargner qqch à qqn ; **to save sb from doing sthg** éviter à qqn de faire qqch - **5.** SPORT arrêter - **6.** COMPUT sauvegarder. <> vi [save money] mettre de l'argent de côté. <> n SPORT arrêt m. <> prep fml : **save (for)** sauf, à l'exception de. **save up** vi mettre de l'argent de côté.

saving grace ['seɪvɪŋ-] n : **its saving grace was...** ce qui le rachetait, c'était...

savings ['seɪvɪŋz] npl économies fpl.

savings account n US compte m d'épargne.

savings and loan association n US société f de crédit immobilier.

savings bank n caisse f d'épargne.

saviour UK, **savior** US ['seɪvjə'] n sauveur m.

savour UK, **savor** US ['seɪvə'] vt lit & fig savourer.

savoury UK, **savory** US <> adj **1.** [food] salé(e) - **2.** [respectable] recommandable. <> n UK petit plat m salé.

saw [sɔː] <> pt ⯈ see. <> n scie f. <> vt (UK, pt **-ed**, pp **sawn** US, pt & pp **-ed**) scier.

sawdust ['sɔːdʌst] n sciure f (de bois).

sawed-off shotgun US = sawn-off shotgun.

sawmill ['sɔːmɪl] n scierie f, moulin m à scie Québec.

sawn [sɔːn] UK pp ⯈ saw.

sawn-off shotgun UK, **sawed-off shotgun** ['sɔːd-] US n carabine f à canon scié.

saxophone ['sæksəfəʊn] n saxophone m.

say [seɪ] <> vt (pt & pp **said**) **1.** [gen] dire ; **could you say that again?** vous pouvez répéter ce que vous venez de dire? ; **(let's) say you won a lottery...** supposons que tu gagnes le gros lot... ; **it says a lot about him** cela en dit long sur lui ; **she's said to be...** on dit qu'elle est... ; **that goes without saying** cela va sans dire ; **it has a lot to be said for it** cela a beaucoup d'avantages - **2.** [subj: clock, label] indiquer. <> n : **to have a/no say** avoir/ne pas avoir voix au chapitre ; **to have a say in sthg** avoir son mot à dire sur qqch ; **to have one's say** dire ce que l'on a à dire, dire son mot. **that is to say** adv c'est-à-dire.

saying ['seɪɪŋ] n dicton m.

scab [skæb] *n* **1.** [of wound] croûte *f* - **2.** *inf pej* [non-striker] jaune *m*.

scaffold ['skæfəʊld] *n* échafaud *m*.

scaffolding ['skæfəldɪŋ] *n* échafaudage *m*.

scald [skɔːld] <> *n* brûlure *f*. <> *vt* ébouillanter ; **to scald one's arm** s'ébouillanter le bras.

scale [skeɪl] <> *n* **1.** [gen] échelle *f* ; **to scale** [map, drawing] à l'échelle - **2.** [of ruler, thermometer] graduation *f* - **3.** MUS gamme *f* - **4.** [of fish, snake] écaille *f* - **5.** US = **scales**. <> *vt* **1.** [cliff, mountain, fence] escalader - **2.** [fish] écailler. **scales** *npl* balance *f*. **scale down** *vt insep* réduire.

scale model *n* modèle *m* réduit.

scallop ['skɒləp] <> *n* [shellfish] coquille *f* Saint-Jacques. <> *vt* [edge, garment] festonner.

scalp [skælp] <> *n* **1.** ANAT cuir *m* chevelu - **2.** [trophy] scalp *m*. <> *vt* scalper.

scalpel ['skælpəl] *n* scalpel *m*.

scamper ['skæmpər] *vi* trottiner.

scampi ['skæmpɪ] *n* (U) scampi *mpl*.

scan [skæn] <> *n* MED scanographie *f* ; [during pregnancy] échographie *f*. <> *vt* **1.** [examine carefully] scruter - **2.** [glance at] parcourir - **3.** TECH balayer - **4.** COMPUT faire un scannage de.

scandal ['skændl] *n* **1.** [gen] scandale *m* - **2.** [gossip] médisance *f*.

scandalize, *UK* **-ise** ['skændəlaɪz] *vt* scandaliser.

Scandinavia [ˌskændɪ'neɪvjə] *n* Scandinavie *f*.

Scandinavian [ˌskændɪ'neɪvjən] <> *adj* scandinave. <> *n* [person] Scandinave *mf*.

scant [skænt] *adj* insuffisant(e).

scanty ['skæntɪ] *adj* [amount, resources] insuffisant(e) ; [income] maigre ; [dress] minuscule.

scapegoat ['skeɪpgəʊt] *n* bouc *m* émissaire.

scar [skɑːr] *n* cicatrice *f*.

scarce ['skeəs] *adj* rare, peu abondant(e).

scarcely ['skeəslɪ] *adv* à peine ; **scarcely anyone** presque personne ; **I scarcely ever go there now** je n'y vais presque OR pratiquement plus jamais.

scare [skeər] <> *n* **1.** [sudden fear] : **to give sb a scare** faire peur à qqn - **2.** [public fear] panique *f* ; **bomb scare** alerte *f* à la bombe. <> *vt* faire peur à, effrayer. **scare away, scare off** *vt sep* faire fuir.

scarecrow ['skeəkrəʊ] *n* épouvantail *m*.

scared ['skeəd] *adj* apeuré(e) ; **to be scared** avoir peur ; **to be scared stiff** OR **to death** être mort de peur.

scarf [skɑːf] (*pl* **-s** OR **scarves** [skɑːvz]) *n* [wool] écharpe *f* ; [silk etc] foulard *m*.

scarlet ['skɑːlət] <> *adj* écarlate. <> *n* écarlate *f*.

scarlet fever *n* scarlatine *f*.

scarves [skɑːvz] *npl* scarf.

scathing ['skeɪðɪŋ] *adj* [criticism] acerbe ; [reply] cinglant(e).

scatter ['skætər] <> *vt* [clothes, paper etc] éparpiller ; [seeds] semer à la volée. <> *vi* se disperser.

scatterbrained ['skætəbreɪnd] *adj inf* écervelé(e).

scavenger ['skævɪndʒər] *n* **1.** [animal] animal *m* nécrophage - **2.** [person] personne *f* qui fait les poubelles.

scenario [sɪ'nɑːrɪəʊ] (*pl* **-s**) *n* **1.** [possible situation] hypothèse *f*, scénario *m* - **2.** [of film, play] scénario *m*.

scene [siːn] *n* **1.** [in play, film, book] scène *f* ; **behind the scenes** dans les coulisses - **2.** [sight] spectacle *m*, vue *f* ; [picture] tableau *m* - **3.** [location] lieu *m*, endroit *m* - **4.** [area of activity] : **the political scene** la scène politique ; **the music scene** le monde de la musique ; **to set the scene for sb** mettre qqn au courant de la situation ; **to set the scene for sthg** préparer la voie à qqch.

scenery ['siːnərɪ] *n* (U) **1.** [of countryside] paysage *m* - **2.** THEAT décor *m*, décors *mpl*.

scenic ['siːnɪk] *adj* [tour] touristique ; **a scenic view** un beau panorama.

scent [sent] *n* **1.** [smell - of flowers] senteur *f*, parfum *m* ; [- of animal] odeur *f*, fumet *m* - **2.** (U) [perfume] parfum *m*.

scepter *US* = **sceptre**.

sceptic *UK*, **skeptic** *US* ['skeptɪk] *n* sceptique *mf*.

sceptical *UK*, **skeptical** *US* ['skeptɪkl] *adj* : **sceptical (about)** sceptique (sur).

sceptre *UK*, **scepter** *US* ['septər] *n* sceptre *m*.

schedule [*UK* 'ʃedjuːl, *US* 'skedʒʊl] <> *n* **1.** [plan] programme *m*, plan *m* ; **on schedule** [at expected time] à l'heure (prévue) ; [on expected day] à la date prévue ; **ahead of/behind schedule** en avance/en retard (sur le programme) - **2.** [list - of times] horaire *m* ; [- of prices] tarif *m* - **3.** *US* [calendar] calendrier *m* ; [timetable] emploi *m* du temps. <> *vt* : **to schedule sthg (for)** prévoir qqch (pour).

scheduled flight [*UK* 'ʃedjuːld-, *US* 'skedʒʊld-] *n* vol *m* régulier.

scheme [skiːm] <> *n* **1.** [plan] plan *m*, projet *m* - **2.** *pej* [dishonest plan] combine *f*

- 3. [arrangement] arrangement *m* ; **colour scheme** combinaison *f* de couleurs. <> *vi pej* conspirer.

scheming ['ski:mɪŋ] *adj* intrigant(e).

schism ['sɪzm OR 'skɪzm] *n* schisme *m*.

schizophrenic [,skɪtsə'frenɪk] <> *adj* schizophrène. <> *n* schizophrène *mf*.

scholar ['skɒlər] *n* **1.** [expert] érudit *m*, -e *f*, savant *m*, -e *f* - **2.** *dated* [student] écolier *m*, -ère *f*, élève *mf* - **3.** [holder of scholarship] boursier *m*, -ère *f*.

scholarship ['skɒləʃɪp] *n* **1.** [grant] bourse *f* (d'études) - **2.** [learning] érudition *f*.

school [sku:l] *n* **1.** [gen] école *f* ; [secondary school] lycée *m*, collège *m* - **2.** [university department] faculté *f* - **3.** *US* [university] université *f*.

school age *n* âge *m* scolaire.

schoolbook ['sku:lbʊk] *n* livre *m* scolaire OR de classe.

schoolboy ['sku:lbɔɪ] *n* écolier *m*, élève *m*.

schoolchild ['sku:ltʃaɪld] (*pl* **-children** [-tʃɪldrən]) *n* écolier *m*, -ère *f*, élève *mf*.

schooldays ['sku:ldeɪz] *npl* années *fpl* d'école.

schoolgirl ['sku:lgɜ:l] *n* écolière *f*, élève *f*.

schooling ['sku:lɪŋ] *n* instruction *f*.

school-leaver [-,li:vər] *n UK* élève qui a fini ses études secondaires.

schoolmaster ['sku:l,mɑ:stər] *n* [primary] instituteur *m*, maître *m* d'école ; [secondary] professeur *m*.

schoolmistress ['sku:l,mɪstrɪs] *n* [primary] institutrice *f*, maîtresse *f* d'école ; [secondary] professeur *m*.

school of thought *n* école *f* (de pensée).

schoolteacher ['sku:l,ti:tʃər] *n* [primary] instituteur *m*, -trice *f* ; [secondary] professeur *m*.

schoolyard *n US* cour *f* de récréation.

school year *n* année *f* scolaire.

schooner ['sku:nər] *n* **1.** [ship] schooner *m*, goélette *f* - **2.** *UK* [sherry glass] grand verre *m* à xérès.

sciatica [saɪ'ætɪkə] *n* sciatique *f*.

science ['saɪəns] *n* science *f*.

science fiction *n* science-fiction *f*.

scientific [,saɪən'tɪfɪk] *adj* scientifique.

scientist ['saɪəntɪst] *n* scientifique *mf*.

scintillating ['sɪntɪleɪtɪŋ] *adj* brillant(e).

scissors ['sɪzəz] *npl* ciseaux *mpl* ; **a pair of scissors** une paire de ciseaux.

sclerosis [sklɪ'rəʊsɪs] ► **multiple sclerosis**.

scoff [skɒf] <> *vt UK inf* bouffer, boulotter. <> *vi* : **to scoff (at)** se moquer (de).

scold [skəʊld] *vt* gronder, réprimander.

scone [skɒn] *n* scone *m*.

scoop [sku:p] <> *n* **1.** [for sugar] pelle *f* à main ; [for ice cream] cuiller *f* à glace - **2.** [of ice cream] boule *f* - **3.** [news report] exclusivité *f*, scoop *m*. <> *vt* [with hands] prendre avec les mains ; [with scoop] prendre avec une pelle à main. **scoop out** *vt sep* évider.

scooter ['sku:tər] *n* **1.** [toy] trottinette *f* - **2.** [motorcycle] scooter *m*.

scope [skəʊp] *n* (*U*) **1.** [opportunity] occasion *f*, possibilité *f* - **2.** [of report, inquiry] étendue *f*, portée *f*.

scorch [skɔ:tʃ] *vt* [clothes] brûler légèrement, roussir ; [skin] brûler ; [land, grass] dessécher.

scorching ['skɔ:tʃɪŋ] *adj inf* [day] torride ; [sun] brûlant(e).

score [skɔ:r] <> *n* **1.** SPORT score *m* - **2.** [in test] note *f* - **3.** *dated* [twenty] vingt - **4.** MUS partition *f* - **5.** [subject] : **on that score** à ce sujet, sur ce point. <> *vt* **1.** [goal, point etc] marquer ; **to score 100%** avoir 100 sur 100 - **2.** [success, victory] remporter - **3.** [cut] entailler. <> *vi* SPORT marquer (un but/point *etc*). **score out** *vt sep UK* barrer, rayer.

scoreboard ['skɔ:bɔ:d] *n* tableau *m*.

scorer ['skɔ:rər] *n* marqueur *m*.

scorn [skɔ:n] <> *n* (*U*) mépris *m*, dédain *m*. <> *vt* **1.** [person, attitude] mépriser - **2.** [help, offer] rejeter, dédaigner.

scornful ['skɔ:nfʊl] *adj* méprisant(e) ; **to be scornful of sthg** mépriser qqch, dédaigner qqch.

Scorpio ['skɔ:pɪəʊ] (*pl* -s) *n* Scorpion *m*.

scorpion ['skɔ:pjən] *n* scorpion *m*.

Scot [skɒt] *n* Écossais *m*, -e *f*.

scotch [skɒtʃ] *vt* [rumour] étouffer ; [plan] faire échouer.

Scotch [skɒtʃ] <> *adj* écossais(e). <> *n* scotch *m*, whisky *m*.

Scotch (tape)® *n US* Scotch® *m*.

scot-free *adj inf* **to get off scot-free** s'en tirer sans être puni(e).

Scotland ['skɒtlənd] *n* Écosse *f*.

Scots [skɒts] <> *adj* écossais(e). <> *n* [dialect] écossais *m*.

Scotsman ['skɒtsmən] (*pl* -men [-mən]) *n* Écossais *m*.

Scotswoman ['skɒtswʊmən] (*pl* -women [-,wɪmɪn]) *n* Écossaise *f*.

Scottish ['skɒtɪʃ] *adj* écossais(e).

Scottish Parliament *n* Parlement *m* écossais.

scoundrel ['skaʊndrəl] *n dated* gredin *m*.

scour [skaʊər] vt 1. [clean] récurer - 2. [search - town etc] parcourir ; [- countryside] battre.

scourge [skɜːdʒ] n fléau m.

scout [skaʊt] n MIL éclaireur m. ◆ **Scout** n [boy scout] Scout m. ◆ **scout around** vi : **to scout around (for)** aller à la recherche (de).

scowl [skaʊl] ⬦ n regard m noir. ⬦ vi se renfrogner, froncer les sourcils ; **to scowl at sb** jeter des regards noirs à qqn.

scrabble ['skræbl] vi 1. [scrape] : **to scrabble at sthg** gratter qqch - 2. [feel around] : **to scrabble around for sthg** tâtonner pour trouver qqch.

scraggy ['skrægi] adj décharné(e), maigre.

scramble ['skræmbl] ⬦ n [rush] bousculade f, ruée f. ⬦ vi 1. [climb] : **to scramble up a hill** grimper une colline en grattant des mains OR à quatre pattes - 2. [compete] : **to scramble for sthg** se disputer qqch.

scrambled eggs ['skræmbld-] npl œufs mpl brouillés.

scrap [skræp] ⬦ n 1. [of paper, material] bout m ; [of information] fragment m ; [of conversation] bribe f - 2. [metal] ferraille f - 3. inf [fight, quarrel] bagarre f. ⬦ vt [car] mettre à la ferraille ; [plan, system] abandonner, laisser tomber. ◆ **scraps** npl [food] restes mpl.

scrapbook ['skræpbʊk] n album m (de coupures de journaux etc).

scrap dealer n ferrailleur m, marchand m de ferraille.

scrape [skreɪp] ⬦ n 1. [scraping noise] raclement m, grattement m - 2. inf dated [difficult situation] : **to get into a scrape** se fourrer dans le pétrin. ⬦ vt 1. [clean, rub] gratter, racler ; **to scrape sthg off sthg** enlever qqch de qqch en grattant OR raclant - 2. [surface, car, skin] érafler. ⬦ vi gratter. ◆ **scrape through** vt insep réussir de justesse.

scraper ['skreɪpər] n grattoir m, racloir m.

scrap merchant n UK ferrailleur m, marchand m de ferraille.

scrap paper UK, **scratch paper** US n (papier m) brouillon m.

scrapyard ['skræpjɑːd] n parc m à ferraille.

scratch [skrætʃ] ⬦ n 1. [wound] égratignure f, éraflure f - 2. [on glass, paint etc] éraflure f ; to be up to scratch être à la hauteur ; **to do sthg from scratch** faire qqch à partir de rien. ⬦ vt 1. [wound] écorcher, égratigner - 2. [mark - paint, glass etc] rayer, érafler - 3. [rub] gratter - 4. SPORT [cancel] annuler. ⬦ vi gratter ; [person] se gratter.

scratch card n carte f à gratter.

scratch paper US = scrap paper.

scrawl [skrɔːl] ⬦ n griffonnage m, gribouillage m. ⬦ vt griffonner, gribouiller.

scrawny ['skrɔːnɪ] adj [person] efflanqué(e) ; [body, animal] décharné(e).

scream [skriːm] ⬦ n [cry] cri m perçant, hurlement m ; [of laughter] éclat m. ⬦ vt hurler. ⬦ vi [cry out] crier, hurler.

scree [skriː] n éboulis m.

screech [skriːtʃ] ⬦ n 1. [cry] cri m perçant - 2. [of tyres] crissement m. ⬦ vt hurler. ⬦ vi 1. [cry out] pousser des cris perçants - 2. [tyres] crisser.

screen [skriːn] ⬦ n 1. [gen] écran m - 2. [panel] paravent m. ⬦ vt 1. CIN projeter, passer ; TV téléviser, passer - 2. [hide] cacher, masquer - 3. [shield] protéger - 4. [candidate, employee] passer au crible, filtrer.

screen break n COMPUT pause f.

screening ['skriːnɪŋ] n 1. CIN projection f ; TV passage m à la télévision - 2. [for security] sélection f, tri m - 3. MED dépistage m.

screenplay ['skriːnpleɪ] n scénario m.

screenshot ['skriːnʃɒt] n copie f d'écran, capture f d'écran.

screw [skruː] ⬦ n [for fastening] vis f. ⬦ vt 1. [fix with screws] : **to screw sthg to sthg** visser qqch à OR sur qqch - 2. [twist] visser - 3. vulg [woman] baiser. ⬦ vi [bolt, lid] se visser. ◆ **screw up** vt sep 1. [crumple up] froisser, chiffonner - 2. [eyes] plisser ; [face] tordre - 3. v inf [ruin] gâcher, bousiller.

screwdriver ['skruː,draɪvər] n [tool] tournevis m.

scribble ['skrɪbl] ⬦ n gribouillage m, griffonnage m. ⬦ vt & vi gribouiller, griffonner.

script [skrɪpt] n 1. [of play, film etc] scénario m, script m - 2. [writing system] écriture f - 3. [handwriting] (écriture f) script m.

Scriptures ['skrɪptʃəz] npl : **the Scriptures** les (saintes) Écritures fpl.

scriptwriter ['skrɪpt,raɪtər] n scénariste mf.

scroll [skrəʊl] ⬦ n rouleau m. ⬦ vt COMPUT faire défiler.

scrounge [skraʊndʒ] inf vt : **to scrounge money off sb** taper qqn ; **can I scrounge a cigarette off you?** je peux te piquer une cigarette ?

scrounger ['skraʊndʒər] n inf parasite m.

scrub [skrʌb] ⬦ n 1. [rub] : **to give sthg a scrub** nettoyer qqch à la brosse - 2. (U) [undergrowth] broussailles fpl. ⬦ vt [floor, clothes etc] laver OR nettoyer à la brosse ; [hands, back] frotter ; [saucepan] récurer.

scruff [skrʌf] *n* : **by the scruff of the neck** par la peau du cou.

scruffy ['skrʌfɪ] *adj* mal soigné(e), débraillé(e).

scrum(mage) ['skrʌm(ɪdʒ)] *n* RUGBY mêlée *f*.

scruples ['skru:plz] *npl* scrupules *mpl*.

scrutinize, *UK* **-ise** ['skru:tɪnaɪz] *vt* scruter, examiner attentivement.

scrutiny ['skru:tɪnɪ] *n* (U) examen *m* attentif.

scuba diving ['sku:bə-] *n* plongée *f* sous-marine (*avec bouteilles*).

scuff [skʌf] *vt* **1.** [damage] érafler - **2.** [drag] : **to scuff one's feet** traîner les pieds.

scuffle ['skʌfl] *n* bagarre *f*, échauffourée *f*.

scullery ['skʌlərɪ] *n* arrière-cuisine *f*.

sculptor ['skʌlptər] *n* sculpteur *m*, -eur(e) *f* OR -trice *f*.

sculpture ['skʌlptʃər] <> *n* sculpture *f*. <> *vt* sculpter.

scum [skʌm] *n* **1.** (U) [froth] écume *f*, mousse *f* - **2.** *v inf pej* [person] salaud *m* - **3.** (U) *v inf pej* [people] déchets *mpl*.

scupper ['skʌpər] *vt* **1.** NAUT couler - **2.** *UK fig* [plan] saboter, faire tomber à l'eau.

scurrilous ['skʌrələs] *adj* calomnieux(euse).

scurry ['skʌrɪ] *vi* se précipiter ; **to scurry away** OR **off** se sauver, détaler.

scuttle ['skʌtl] <> *n* seau *m* à charbon. <> *vi* courir précipitamment OR à pas précipités.

scythe [saɪð] *n* faux *f*.

SDLP (*abbrev of* Social Democratic and Labour Party) *n* parti travailliste d'Irlande du Nord.

sea [si:] <> *n* [gen] mer *f* ; **at sea** en mer ; **by sea** par mer ; **by the sea** au bord de la mer ; **out to sea** au large ; **to be all at sea** nager complètement. <> *comp* [voyage] en mer ; [animal] marin(e), de mer.

seabed ['si:bed] *n* : **the seabed** le fond de la mer.

seaboard ['si:bɔ:d] *n* littoral *m*, côte *f*.

sea breeze *n* brise *f* de mer.

seafood ['si:fu:d] *n* (U) fruits *mpl* de mer.

seafront ['si:frʌnt] *n* front *m* de mer.

seagull ['si:gʌl] *n* mouette *f*.

seal [si:l] <> *n* (*pl* **seal** OR **-s**) **1.** [animal] phoque *m* - **2.** [official mark] cachet *m*, sceau *m* - **3.** [official fastening] cachet *m*. <> *vt* **1.** [envelope] coller, fermer - **2.** [document, letter] sceller, cacheter - **3.** [block off] obturer, boucher. ◆ **seal off** *vt sep* [area, entrance] interdire l'accès de.

sea level *n* niveau *m* de la mer.

sea lion (*pl* **sea lion** OR **-s**) *n* otarie *f*.

seam [si:m] *n* **1.** SEW couture *f* - **2.** [of coal] couche *f*, veine *f*.

seaman ['si:mən] (*pl* **-men** [-mən]) *n* marin *m*.

seamy ['si:mɪ] *adj* sordide.

séance ['seɪɒns] *n* séance *f* de spiritisme.

seaplane ['si:pleɪn] *n* hydravion *m*.

seaport ['si:pɔ:t] *n* port *m* de mer.

search [sɜ:tʃ] <> *n* [of person, luggage, house] fouille *f* ; [for lost person, thing] recherche *f*, recherches *fpl* ; **search for** recherche de ; **in search of** à la recherche de. <> *vt* [house, area, person] fouiller ; [memory, mind, drawer] fouiller dans. <> *vi* : **to search (for sb/sthg)** chercher (qqn/qqch).

search engine *n* COMPUT moteur *m* de recherche.

searching ['sɜ:tʃɪŋ] *adj* [question] poussé(e), approfondi(e) ; [look] pénétrant(e) ; [review, examination] minutieux(euse).

searchlight ['sɜ:tʃlaɪt] *n* projecteur *m*.

search party *n* équipe *f* de secours.

search warrant *n* mandat *m* de perquisition.

seashell ['si:ʃel] *n* coquillage *m*.

seashore ['si:ʃɔ:r] *n* : **the seashore** le rivage, la plage.

seasick ['si:sɪk] *adj* : **to be** OR **feel seasick** avoir le mal de mer.

seaside ['si:saɪd] *n* : **the seaside** le bord de la mer.

seaside resort *n* station *f* balnéaire.

season ['si:zn] <> *n* **1.** [gen] saison *f* ; **in season** [food] de saison ; **out of season** [holiday] hors saison ; [food] hors de saison - **2.** [of films, programmes] cycle *m*. <> *vt* assaisonner, relever.

seasonal ['si:zənl] *adj* saisonnier(ère).

seasoned ['si:znd] *adj* [traveller, campaigner] chevronné(e), expérimenté(e) ; [soldier] aguerri(e).

seasoning ['si:znɪŋ] *n* assaisonnement *m*.

season ticket *n* carte *f* d'abonnement.

seat [si:t] <> *n* **1.** [gen] siège *m* ; [in theatre] fauteuil *m* ; **take a seat!** asseyez-vous! - **2.** [place to sit - in bus, train] place *f* - **3.** [of trousers] fond *m*. <> *vt* [sit down] faire asseoir, placer ; **please be seated** veuillez vous asseoir.

seat belt *n* ceinture *f* de sécurité.

seating ['si:tɪŋ] *n* (U) [capacity] sièges *mpl*, places *fpl* (assises).

seawater ['si:,wɔ:tər] *n* eau *f* de mer.

seaweed ['si:wi:d] *n* (U) algue *f*.

seaworthy ['si:,wɜ:ðɪ] *adj* en bon état de navigabilité.

sec. *abbrev of* **second**.

secede [sɪ'siːd] *vi fml* : **to secede (from)** se séparer (de), faire sécession (de).

secluded [sɪ'kluːdɪd] *adj* retiré(e), écarté(e).

seclusion [sɪ'kluːʒn] *n* solitude *f*, retraite *f*.

second ['sekənd] <> *n* **1.** [gen] seconde *f* ; **wait a second!** une seconde!, (attendez) un instant! ; **second (gear)** seconde - **2.** *UK UNIV* ≃ licence *f* avec mention assez bien. <> *num* deuxième, second(e) ; **his score was second only to hers** il n'y a qu'elle qui ait fait mieux que lui OR qui l'ait surpassé. <> *vt* [proposal, motion] appuyer ; *see also* **sixth.** **seconds** *npl* **1.** COMM articles *mpl* de second choix - **2.** [of food] rabiot *m*.

secondary ['sekəndrɪ] *adj* secondaire ; **to be secondary to** être moins important(e) que.

secondary school *n UK* école *f* secondaire, lycée *m*.

second-class ['sekənd-] *adj* **1.** *pej* [citizen] de deuxième zone ; [product] de second choix - **2.** [ticket] de seconde OR deuxième classe - **3.** [stamp] à tarif réduit - **4.** *UK UNIV* [degree] ≃ avec mention assez bien.

second hand ['sekənd-] *n* [of clock] trotteuse *f*.

second-hand ['sekənd-] <> *adj* **1.** [goods, shop] d'occasion - **2.** *fig* [information] de seconde main. <> *adv* [not new] d'occasion.

secondly ['sekəndlɪ] *adv* deuxièmement, en second lieu.

secondment [sɪ'kɒndmənt] *n UK* affectation *f* temporaire.

second-rate ['sekənd-] *adj pej* de deuxième ordre, médiocre.

second thought ['sekənd-] *n* : **to have second thoughts about sthg** avoir des doutes sur qqch ; **on second thoughts** *UK*, **on second thought** *US* réflexion faite, tout bien réfléchi.

secrecy ['siːkrəsɪ] *n* (U) secret *m*.

secret ['siːkrɪt] <> *adj* secret(ète). <> *n* secret *m* ; **in secret** en secret.

secretarial [,sekrə'teərɪəl] *adj* [course, training] de secrétariat, de secrétaire ; **secretarial staff** secrétaires *mpl*.

secretary [*UK* 'sekrətrɪ, *US* 'sekrə,terɪ] *n* **1.** [gen] secrétaire *mf* - **2.** POL [minister] ministre *mf*.

Secretary of State *n* **1.** *UK* **Secretary of State (for)** ministre *m* (de) - **2.** *US* ≃ ministre *m* des Affaires étrangères.

secretive ['siːkrətɪv] *adj* secret(ète), dissimulé(e).

secretly ['siːkrɪtlɪ] *adv* secrètement.

sect [sekt] *n* secte *f*.

sectarian [sek'teərɪən] *adj* [killing, violence] d'ordre religieux.

section ['sekʃn] <> *n* **1.** [portion - gen] section *f*, partie *f* ; [- of road, pipe] tronçon *m* ; [- of document, law] article *m*. GEOM coupe *f*, section *f*. <> *vt* sectionner.

sector ['sektər] *n* secteur *m*.

secular ['sekjʊlər] *adj* [life] séculier(ère) ; [education] laïque ; [music] profane.

secure [sɪ'kjʊər] <> *adj* **1.** [fixed - gen] fixe ; [- windows, building] bien fermé(e) - **2.** [safe - job, future] sûr(e) ; [- valuable object] en sécurité, en lieu sûr - **3.** [free of anxiety - childhood] sécurisant(e) ; [- marriage] solide. <> *vt* **1.** [obtain] obtenir - **2.** [fasten - gen] attacher ; [- door, window] bien fermer - **3.** [make safe] assurer la sécurité de.

security [sɪ'kjʊərətɪ] *n* sécurité *f*. **securities** *npl* FIN titres *mpl*, valeurs *fpl*.

security gate *n* [at airport] portique *m*.

security guard *n* garde *m* de sécurité.

sedan [sɪ'dæn] *n US* berline *f*.

sedate [sɪ'deɪt] <> *adj* posé(e), calme. <> *vt* donner un sédatif à.

sedation [sɪ'deɪʃn] *n* (U) sédation *f* ; **under sedation** sous calmants.

sedative ['sedətɪv] *n* sédatif *m*, calmant *m*.

sediment ['sedɪmənt] *n* sédiment *m*, dépôt *m*.

seduce [sɪ'djuːs] *vt* séduire ; **to seduce sb into doing sthg** amener OR entraîner qqn à faire qqch.

seductive [sɪ'dʌktɪv] *adj* séduisant(e).

see [siː] (*pt* **saw**, *pp* **seen**) <> *vt* **1.** [gen] voir ; **see you!** au revoir! ; **see you soon/later/tomorrow!** *etc* à bientôt/tout à l'heure/demain! *etc* - **2.** [accompany] : **I saw her to the door** je l'ai accompagnée OR reconduite jusqu'à la porte ; **I saw her onto the train** je l'ai accompagnée au train - **3.** [make sure] : **to see (that)...** s'assurer que... <> *vi* voir ; **you see,...** voyez-vous,... ; **I see** je vois, je comprends ; **let's see, let me see** voyons, voyons voir. **seeing as**, **seeing that** *conj inf* vu que, étant donné que. **see about** *vt insep* [arrange] s'occuper de. **see off** *vt sep* **1.** [say goodbye to] accompagner (pour dire au revoir) - **2.** *UK* [chase away] faire partir OR fuir. **see out** *vt sep* [accompany to the door] reconduire OR raccompagner à la porte ; **can you see yourself out?** pouvez-vous trouver la sortie tout seul? **see through** <> *vt insep* [scheme] voir clair dans ; **to see through sb** voir dans le jeu de qqn. ⬦ *vt sep* [deal, project] mener à terme, mener à bien. ⬥ **see to** *vt insep* s'occuper de, se charger de.

seed [si:d] *n* **1.** [of plant] graine *f* - **2.** SPORT : **fifth seed** joueur classé cinquième *m*, joueuse classée cinquième *f*. ⬥ **seeds** *npl fig* germes *mpl*, semences *fpl*.

seedling ['si:dlɪŋ] *n* jeune plant *m*, semis *m*.

seedy ['si:dɪ] *adj* miteux(euse).

seek [si:k] (*pt & pp* sought) *vt* **1.** [gen] chercher ; [peace, happiness] rechercher ; **to seek to do sthg** chercher à faire qqch - **2.** [advice, help] demander.

seem [si:m] ⬦ *vi* sembler, paraître ; **to seem bored** avoir l'air de s'ennuyer ; **to seem sad/tired** avoir l'air triste/fatigué. ⬦ *impers vb* : **it seems (that)...** il semble OR paraît que...

seemingly ['si:mɪŋlɪ] *adv* apparemment.

seen [si:n] *pp* ▶ **see**.

seep [si:p] *vi* suinter.

seesaw ['si:sɔ:] *n* bascule *f*.

seethe [si:ð] *vi* **1.** [person] bouillir, être furieux(euse) - **2.** [place] : **to be seething with** grouiller de.

see-through *adj* transparent(e).

segment ['segmənt] *n* **1.** [section] partie *f*, section *f* - **2.** [of fruit] quartier *m*.

segregate ['segrɪgeɪt] *vt* séparer.

Seine [seɪn] *n* : **the (River) Seine** la Seine.

seize [si:z] *vt* **1.** [grab] saisir, attraper - **2.** [capture] s'emparer de, prendre - **3.** [arrest] arrêter - **4.** *fig* [opportunity, chance] saisir, sauter sur. ⬥ **seize (up)on** *vt insep* saisir, sauter sur. ⬥ **seize up** *vi* **1.** [body] s'ankyloser - **2.** [engine, part] se gripper.

seizure ['si:ʒə'] *n* **1.** MED crise *f*, attaque *f* - **2.** (*U*) [of town] capture *f* ; [of power] prise *f*.

seldom ['seldəm] *adv* peu souvent, rarement.

select [sɪ'lekt] ⬦ *adj* **1.** [carefully chosen] choisi(e) - **2.** [exclusive] de premier ordre, d'élite. ⬦ *vt* sélectionner, choisir.

selection [sɪ'lekʃn] *n* sélection *f*, choix *m*.

selective [sɪ'lektɪv] *adj* sélectif(ive) ; [person] difficile.

self [self] (*pl* selves [selvz]) *n* moi *m* ; **she's her old self again** elle est redevenue elle-même.

self-addressed stamped envelope [-ə'drest-] *n* US enveloppe *f* affranchie pour la réponse.

self-assured *adj* sûr(e) de soi, plein(e) d'assurance.

self-catering *adj* UK [holiday - in house] en maison louée ; [- in flat] en appartement loué.

self-centred UK, **self-centered** US [-'sentəd] *adj* égocentrique.

self-confessed [-kən'fest] *adj* de son propre aveu.

self-confident *adj* sûr(e) de soi, plein(e) d'assurance.

self-conscious *adj* timide.

self-contained [-kən'teɪnd] *adj* [flat] indépendant(e), avec entrée particulière ; [person] qui se suffit à soi-même.

self-control *n* maîtrise *f* de soi.

self-defence UK, **self-defense** US *n* auto-défense *f*.

self-discipline *n* autodiscipline *f*.

self-employed [-ɪm'plɔɪd] *adj* qui travaille à son propre compte.

self-esteem *n* respect *m* de soi, estime *f* de soi.

self-evident *adj* qui va de soi, évident(e).

self-explanatory *adj* évident(e), qui ne nécessite pas d'explication.

self-government *n* autonomie *f*.

self-important *adj* suffisant(e).

self-indulgent *adj pej* [person] qui ne se refuse rien ; [film, book, writer] nombriliste.

self-interest *n* (*U*) *pej* intérêt *m* personnel.

selfish ['selfɪʃ] *adj* égoïste.

selfishness ['selfɪʃnɪs] *n* égoïsme *m*.

selfless ['selflɪs] *adj* désintéressé(e).

self-made *adj* : **self-made man** self-made-man *m*.

self-medication *n* automédication *f*.

self-opinionated *adj* opiniâtre.

self-pity *n* apitoiement *m* sur soi-même.

self-portrait *n* autoportrait *m*.

self-possessed *adj* maître (maîtresse) de soi.

self-raising flour UK [-,reɪzɪŋ-], **self-rising flour** US *n* farine *f* avec levure incorporée.

self-reliant *adj* indépendant(e), qui ne compte que sur soi.

self-respect *n* respect *m* de soi.

self-respecting [-rɪs'pektɪŋ] *adj* qui se respecte.

self-restraint *n* (*U*) retenue *f*, mesure *f*.

self-righteous *adj* satisfait(e) de soi.

self-rising flour US = **self-raising flour**.

self-sacrifice *n* abnégation *f*.

self-satisfied *adj* suffisant(e), content(e) de soi.

self-service *n* libre-service *m*, self-service *m*.

self-study ◇ *n* autoformation *f*. ◇ *adj* d'autoformation.

self-sufficient *adj* autosuffisant(e) ; **to be self-sufficient in** satisfaire à ses besoins en.

self-taught *adj* autodidacte.

sell [sel] (*pt & pp* **sold**) ◇ *vt* **1.** [gen] vendre ; **to sell sthg for £100** vendre qqch 100 livres ; **to sell sthg to sb, to sell sb sthg** vendre qqch à qqn - **2.** *fig* [make acceptable] : **to sell sthg to sb, to sell sb sthg** faire accepter qqch à qqn. ◇ *vi* **1.** [person] vendre - **2.** [product] se vendre ; **it sells for** OR **at £10** il se vend 10 livres. ◆ **sell off** *vt sep* vendre, liquider. ◆ **sell out** ◇ *vt sep* : **the performance is sold out** il ne reste plus de places, tous les billets ont été vendus. ◇ *vi* **1.** [shop] : **we've sold out** on n'en a plus - **2.** [betray one's principles] être infidèle à ses principes.

sell-by date *n* UK date *f* limite de vente.

seller ['selər] *n* vendeur *m*, -euse *f*.

selling price *n* prix *m* de vente.

Sellotape® ['seləteɪp] *n* UK ≃ Scotch® *m*, ruban *m* adhésif.

sell-out *n* : **the match was a sell-out** on a joué à guichets fermés.

selves [selvz] *npl* ➤ **self**.

semaphore ['seməfɔːr] *n (U)* signaux *mpl* à bras.

semblance ['sembləns] *n* semblant *m*.

semen ['siːmen] *n (U)* sperme *m*, semence *f*.

semester [sɪ'mestər] *n* semestre *m*.

semiannual US = **half-yearly**.

semicircle ['semɪ,sɜːkl] *n* demi-cercle *m*.

semicolon [,semɪ'kəʊlən] *n* point-virgule *m*.

semidetached [,semɪdɪ'tætʃt] UK ◇ *adj* jumelé(e). ◇ *n* maison *f* jumelée.

semifinal [,semɪ'faɪnl] *n* demi-finale *f*.

seminar ['semɪnɑːr] *n* séminaire *m*.

seminary ['semɪnərɪ] *n* RELIG séminaire *m*.

semiskilled [,semɪ'skɪld] *adj* spécialisé(e).

semolina [,semə'liːnə] *n* semoule *f*.

Senate ['senɪt] *n* POL : **the Senate** le sénat ; **the United States Senate** le Sénat américain.

senator ['senətər] *n* sénateur *m*, -trice *f*.

send [send] (*pt & pp* **sent**) *vt* [gen] envoyer ; [letter] expédier, envoyer ; **to send sthg to sb** envoyer qqch à qqn ; **send her my love** embrasse-la pour moi ; **to send sb for sthg** envoyer qqn chercher qqch. ◆ **send for** *vt insep* **1.** [person] appeler, faire venir - **2.** [by post] commander par correspondance. ◆ **send in** *vt sep*

[report, application] envoyer, soumettre. ◆ **send off** *vt sep* **1.** [by post] expédier - **2.** *UK* SPORT expulser. ◆ **send off for** *vt insep* commander par correspondance. ◆ **send up** *vt sep UK inf* [imitate] parodier, ridiculiser.

sender ['sendər] *n* expéditeur *m*, -trice *f*.

send-off *n* fête *f* d'adieu.

senile ['siːnaɪl] *adj* sénile.

senior ['siːnjər] ◇ *adj* **1.** [highest-ranking] plus haut placé(e) - **2.** [higher-ranking] : **senior to sb** d'un rang plus élevé que qqn - **3.** SCH [pupils, classes] grand(e). ◇ *n* **1.** [older person] aîné *m*, -e *f* - **2.** SCH grand *m*, -e *f*.

senior citizen *n* personne *f* âgée OR du troisième âge.

sensation [sen'seɪʃn] *n* sensation *f*.

sensational [sen'seɪʃənl] *adj* [gen] sensationnel(elle).

sensationalist [sen'seɪʃnəlɪst] *adj pej* à sensation.

sense [sens] ◇ *n* **1.** [ability, meaning] sens *m* ; **to make sense** [have meaning] avoir un sens ; **sense of humour** sens de l'humour ; **sense of smell** odorat *m* - **2.** [feeling] sentiment *m* - **3.** [wisdom] bon sens *m*, intelligence *f* ; **to make sense** [be sensible] être logique ; **to come to one's senses** [be sensible again] revenir à la raison ; [regain consciousness] reprendre connaissance. ◇ *vt* [feel] sentir. ◆ **in a sense** *adv* dans un sens.

senseless ['senslɪs] *adj* **1.** [stupid] stupide - **2.** [unconscious] sans connaissance.

sensibilities [,sensɪ'bɪlətɪz] *npl* susceptibilité *f*.

sensible ['sensəbl] *adj* [reasonable] raisonnable, judicieux(euse).

sensitive ['sensɪtɪv] *adj* **1.** [gen] : **sensitive (to)** sensible (à) - **2.** [subject] délicat(e) - **3.** [easily offended] : **sensitive (about)** susceptible (en ce qui concerne).

sensual ['sensjʊəl] *adj* sensuel(elle).

sensuous ['sensjʊəs] *adj* qui affecte les sens.

sent [sent] *pt & pp* ➤ **send**.

sentence ['sentəns] ◇ *n* **1.** GRAM phrase *f* - **2.** LAW condamnation *f*, sentence *f*. ◇ *vt* : **to sentence sb (to)** condamner qqn (à).

sentiment ['sentɪmənt] *n* **1.** [feeling] sentiment *m* - **2.** [opinion] opinion *f*, avis *m*.

sentimental [,sentɪ'mentl] *adj* sentimental(e).

sentry ['sentrɪ] *n* sentinelle *f*.

separate ◇ *adj* ['seprət] **1.** [not joined] : **separate (from)** séparé(e) (de) - **2.** [individual, distinct] distinct(e). ◇ *vt* ['sepəreɪt] **1.** [gen] : **to separate sb/sthg (from)** séparer qqn/qqch (de) ; **to separate sthg into** diviser OR séparer qqch en - **2.** [distinguish] : **to separate sb/sthg (from)** distinguer qqn/qqch (de). ⬦ *vi* ['sepəreɪt] se séparer ; **to separate into** se diviser OR se séparer en. ➤ **separates** ['seprəts] *npl* UK coordonnés *mpl*.

separately ['seprətlɪ] *adv* séparément.

separation [,sepə'reɪʃn] *n* séparation *f*.

September [sep'tembər] *n* septembre *m* ; **in September** en septembre ; **last September** en septembre dernier ; **this September** en septembre de cette année ; **next September** en septembre prochain ; **by September** en septembre, d'ici septembre ; **every September** tous les ans en septembre ; **during September** pendant le mois de septembre ; **at the beginning of September** au début du mois de septembre, début septembre ; **at the end of September** à la fin du mois de septembre, fin septembre ; **in the middle of September** au milieu du mois de septembre, à la mi-septembre.

septic ['septɪk] *adj* infecté(e).

septic tank *n* fosse *f* septique.

sequel ['si:kwəl] *n* **1.** [book, film] : **sequel (to)** suite *f* (de) - **2.** [consequence] : **sequel (to)** conséquence *f* (de).

sequence ['si:kwəns] *n* **1.** [series] suite *f*, succession *f* - **2.** [order] ordre *m* - **3.** [of film] séquence *f*.

Serb = Serbian.

Serbia ['sɜːbjə] *n* Serbie *f*.

Serbian ['sɜːbjən], **Serb** [sɜːb] ⬦ *adj* serbe. ⬦ *n* **1.** [person] Serbe *mf* - **2.** [dialect] serbe *m*.

serene [sɪ'ri:n] *adj* [calm] serein(e), tranquille.

sergeant ['sɑːdʒənt] *n* **1.** MIL sergent *m*, -e *f* - **2.** [in police] brigadier *m*, -ière *f*.

sergeant major *n* sergent-major *m*.

serial ['sɪərɪəl] *n* feuilleton *m*.

serial cable *n* câble *f* série.

serial number *n* numéro *m* de série.

series ['sɪəriːz] (*pl* series) *n* série *f*.

serious ['sɪərɪəs] *adj* **1.** [causing concern] [situation, problem, threat] sérieux(euse) ; [illness, accident, trouble] grave - **2.** [not joking] sérieux(euse) ; **to be serious about doing sthg** songer sérieusement à faire qqch - **3.** [careful, thoughtful] sérieux(euse), sincère.

seriously ['sɪərɪəslɪ] *adv* sérieusement ; [ill] gravement ; [wounded] grièvement, gravement ; **to take sb/sthg seriously** prendre qqn/qqch au sérieux.

seriousness ['sɪərɪəsnɪs] *n* **1.** [of mistake, illness] gravité *f* - **2.** [of person, speech] sérieux *m*.

sermon ['sɜːmən] *n* sermon *m*.

serrated [sɪ'reɪtɪd] *adj* en dents de scie.

servant ['sɜːvənt] *n* domestique *mf*.

serve [sɜːv] ⬦ *vt* **1.** [work for] servir - **2.** [have effect] : **to serve to do sthg** servir à faire qqch ; **to serve a purpose** [subj: device etc] servir à un usage - **3.** [provide for] desservir - **4.** [meal, drink, customer] servir ; **to serve sthg to sb, to serve sb sthg** servir qqch à qqn - **5.** LAW : **to serve sb with a summons/writ, to serve a summons/writ on sb** signifier une assignation/une citation à qqn - **6.** [prison sentence] purger, faire ; [apprenticeship, term] faire - **7.** SPORT servir ; **it serves him/you right** c'est bien fait pour lui/toi. ⬦ *vi* servir ; **to serve as** servir de. ⬦ *n* SPORT service *m*. ➤ **serve out, serve up** *vt sep* [food] servir.

service ['sɜːvɪs] ⬦ *n* **1.** [gen] service *m* ; **in/out of service** en/hors service ; **to be of service (to sb)** être utile (à qqn), rendre service (à qqn) - **2.** [of car] révision *f* ; [of machine] entretien *m* - **3.** MIL service *m*. ⬦ *vt* [car] réviser ; [machine] assurer l'entretien de. ➤ **services** *npl* **1.** UK [on motorway] aire *f* de services - **2.** [armed forces] : **the services** les forces *fpl* armées - **3.** [help] service *m*.

serviceable ['sɜːvɪsəbl] *adj* pratique.

service area *n* aire *f* de services.

service charge *n* service *m*.

serviceman ['sɜːvɪsmən] (*pl* -men [-mən]) *n* soldat *m*, militaire *m*.

service provider *n* COMPUT fournisseur *m* d'accès.

service station *n* station-service *f*.

serviette [,sɜːvɪ'et] *n* serviette *f* (de table).

sesame ['sesəmɪ] *n* sésame *m*.

session ['seʃn] *n* **1.** [gen] séance *f* - **2.** US [school term] trimestre *m*.

set [set] ⬦ *adj* **1.** [fixed - gen] fixe ; [- phrase] figé(e) - **2.** UK SCH [ready] : **set (for sthg/to do sthg)** prêt(e) (à qqch/à faire qqch) - **4.** [determined] : **to be set on sthg** vouloir absolument qqch ; **to be set on doing sthg** être résolu(e) à faire qqch ; **to be dead set against sthg** s'opposer formellement à qqch. ⬦ *n* **1.** [group] [of facts, conditions, characteristics] ensemble *m* ; [of keys, tools, golf clubs etc] jeu *m* ; [of stamps, books] collection *f* ; [of saucepans] série *f* ; **a set of teeth** [natural] une dentition, une denture ; [false] un dentier - **2.** [television, radio] poste *m* - **3.** CIN plateau *m* ; THEAT scène *f* - **4.** TENNIS manche *f*, set *m*. ⬦ *vt* (*pt & pp* set) **1.** [place] placer, poser, mettre ; [jewel] sertir, monter - **2.** [cause to be or do] : **to set sb free** libérer qqn, mettre qqn en liberté ; **to set sthg in motion** mettre qqch en branle OR en route ;

to set sthg on fire mettre le feu à qqch - **3.** [prepare - trap] tendre ; [- table] mettre - **4.** [adjust] régler - **5.** [fix - date, deadline, target] fixer - **6.** [establish - example] donner ; [- trend] lancer ; [- record] établir - **7.** [homework, task] donner ; [problem] poser - **8.** MED [bone, leg] remettre - **9.** [story] : **to be set in** se passer à, se dérouler à. ◇ *vi* (*pt & pp* **set**) **1.** [sun] se coucher - **2.** [jelly] prendre ; [glue, cement] durcir. ◆ **set about** *vt insep* [start] entreprendre, se mettre à ; **to set about doing sthg** se mettre à faire qqch. ◆ **set aside** *vt sep* **1.** [save] mettre de côté - **2.** [not consider] rejeter, écarter. ◆ **set back** *vt sep* [delay] retarder. ◆ **set off** *vt sep* **1.** [cause] déclencher, provoquer - **2.** [bomb] faire exploser ; [firework] faire partir. ◇ *vi* se mettre en route, partir. ◆ **set out** ◇ *vt sep* **1.** [arrange] disposer - **2.** [explain] présenter, exposer. ◇ *vt insep* [intend] : **to set out to do sthg** entreprendre OR tenter de faire qqch. ◇ *vi* [on journey] se mettre en route, partir. ◆ **set up** *vt sep* **1.** [organization] créer, fonder ; [committee, procedure] constituer, mettre en place ; [meeting] arranger, organiser - **2.** [statue, monument] dresser, ériger ; [roadblock] placer, installer - **3.** [equipment] préparer, installer - **4.** *inf* [make appear guilty] monter un coup contre. ◆ **set upon** *vt insep* [physically or verbally] attaquer, s'en prendre à.

setback ['setbæk] *n* contretemps *m*, revers *m*.

set menu *n* menu *m* fixe.

settee [se'ti:] *n* canapé *m*.

setting ['setɪŋ] *n* **1.** [surroundings] décor *m*, cadre *m* - **2.** [of dial, machine] réglage *m*.

settle ['setl] ◇ *vt* **1.** [argument] régler ; **that's settled then** (c'est) entendu - **2.** [bill, account] régler, payer - **3.** [calm - nerves] calmer ; **to settle one's stomach** calmer les douleurs d'estomac - **4.** [make comfortable] installer. ◇ *vi* **1.** [make one's home] s'installer, se fixer - **2.** [make oneself comfortable] s'installer - **3.** [dust] retomber ; [sediment] se déposer - **4.** [bird, insect] se poser. ◆ **settle down** *vi* **1.** [give one's attention] : **to settle down to sthg/to doing sthg** se mettre à qqch/à faire qqch - **2.** [make oneself comfortable] s'installer - **3.** [become respectable] se ranger - **4.** [become calm] se calmer. ◆ **settle for** *vt insep* accepter, se contenter de. ◆ **settle in** *vi* s'adapter. ◆ **settle on** *vt insep* [choose] fixer son choix sur, se décider pour. ◆ **settle up** *vi* : **to settle up (with sb)** régler (qqn).

settlement ['setlmənt] *n* **1.** [agreement] accord *m* - **2.** [colony] colonie *f* - **3.** [payment] règlement *m*.

settler ['setlər] *n* colon *m*.

set-up *n inf* **1.** [system] : **what's the set-up?** comment est-ce que c'est organisé? - **2.** [trick to incriminate] coup *m* monté.

seven ['sevn] *num* sept ; *see also* **six**.

seventeen [,sevn'ti:n] *num* dix-sept ; *see also* **six**.

seventeenth [,sevn'ti:nθ] *num* dix-septième ; *see also* **sixth**.

seventh ['sevnθ] *num* septième ; *see also* **sixth**.

seventy ['sevntɪ] *num* soixante-dix ; *see also* **sixty**.

sever ['sevər] *vt* **1.** [cut through] couper - **2.** *fig* [relationship, ties] rompre.

several ['sevrəl] ◇ *adj* plusieurs. ◇ *pron* plusieurs *mf pl*.

severance ['sevrəns] *n* [of relations] rupture *f*.

severance pay *n* indemnité *f* de licenciement.

severe [sɪ'vɪər] *adj* **1.** [weather] rude, rigoureux(euse) ; [shock] gros (grosse), dur(e) ; [pain] violent(e) ; [illness, injury] grave - **2.** [person, criticism] sévère.

severity [sɪ'verətɪ] *n* **1.** [of storm] violence *f* ; [of problem, illness] gravité *f* - **2.** [sternness] sévérité *f*.

sew [səʊ] (*UK*, *pp* sewn, *pt & pp* -ied *US*, *pp* sewed OR sewn) *vt & vi* coudre. ◆ **sew up** *vt sep* [join] recoudre.

sewage ['su:ɪdʒ] *n* (*U*) eaux *fpl* d'égout, eaux usées.

sewer ['suər] *n* égout *m*.

sewing ['səʊɪŋ] *n* (*U*) **1.** [activity] couture *f* - **2.** [work] ouvrage *m*.

sewing machine *n* machine *f* à coudre.

sewn [səʊn] *pp* ► sew.

sex [seks] *n* **1.** [gender] sexe *m* - **2.** (*U*) [sexual intercourse] rapports *mpl* (sexuels) ; **to have sex with** avoir des rapports (sexuels) avec.

sexist ['seksɪst] ◇ *adj* sexiste. ◇ *n* sexiste *mf*.

sexual ['sekʃʊəl] *adj* sexuel(elle).

sexual harassment *n* harcèlement *m* sexuel.

sexual intercourse *n* (*U*) rapports *mpl* (sexuels).

sexy ['seksɪ] *adj inf* sexy (*inv*).

shabby ['ʃæbɪ] *adj* **1.** [clothes] élimé(e), râpé(e) ; [furniture] minable ; [person, street] miteux(euse) - **2.** [behaviour] moche, méprisable.

shack [ʃæk] *n* cabane *f*, hutte *f*.

shackle ['ʃækl] *vt* enchaîner ; *fig* entraver. ◆ **shackles** *npl* fers *mpl* ; *fig* entraves *fpl*.

shade [ʃeɪd] ◇ *n* **1.** (*U*) [shadow] ombre *f*

- **2.** [lampshade] abat-jour *m inv* - **3.** [colour] nuance *f*, ton *m* - **4.** [of meaning, opinion] nuance *f*. ⬦ *vt* [from light] abriter.
➤ **shades** *npl inf* [sunglasses] lunettes *fpl* de soleil.

shadow ['ʃædəʊ] *n* ombre *f* ; **there's not a** OR **the shadow of a doubt** il n'y a pas l'ombre d'un doute.

shadow cabinet *n* UK cabinet *m* fantôme.

shadowy ['ʃædəʊ] *adj* **1.** [dark] ombreux(euse) - **2.** [sinister] mystérieux(euse).

shady ['ʃeɪdɪ] *adj* **1.** [garden, street etc] ombragé(e) ; [tree] qui donne de l'ombre - **2.** *inf* [dishonest] louche.

shaft [ʃɑːft] *n* **1.** [vertical passage] puits *m* ; [of lift] cage *f* - **2.** TECH arbre *m* - **3.** [of light] rayon *m* - **4.** [of tool, golf club] manche *m*.

shaggy ['ʃægɪ] *adj* hirsute.

shake [ʃeɪk] ⬦ *vt* (*pt* **shook**, *pp* **shaken**) **1.** [move vigorously - gen] secouer ; [- bottle] agiter ; **to shake sb's hand** serrer la main de OR à qqn ; **to shake hands** se serrer la main ; **to shake one's head** secouer la tête ; [- to say no] faire non de la tête - **2.** [shock] ébranler, secouer. ⬦ *vi* (*pt* **shook**, *pp* **shaken**) trembler. ⬦ *n* [tremble] tremblement *m* ; **to give sthg a shake** secouer qqch. ➤ **shake off** *vt sep* [police, pursuers] semer ; [illness] se débarrasser de.

shaken ['ʃeɪkn] *pp* ➤ **shake**.

shaky ['ʃeɪkɪ] *adj* [building, table] branlant(e) ; [hand] tremblant(e) ; [person] faible ; [argument, start] incertain(e).

shall (*weak form* [ʃəl], *strong form* [ʃæl]) *aux vb* **1.** (*1st person sg & 1st person pl*) (*to express future tense*) **I shall be...** je serai... - **2.** (*esp 1st person sg & 1st person pl*) (*in questions*) **shall we have lunch now?** tu veux qu'on déjeune maintenant? ; **where shall I put this?** où est-ce qu'il faut mettre ça? - **3.** *(in orders)* **you shall tell me!** tu vas OR dois me le dire!

shallow ['ʃæləʊ] *adj* **1.** [water, dish, hole] peu profond(e) - **2.** *pej* [superficial] superficiel(elle).

sham [ʃæm] ⬦ *adj* feint(e), simulé(e). ⬦ *n* comédie *f*.

shambles ['ʃæmblz] *n* désordre *m*, pagaille *f*.

shame [ʃeɪm] ⬦ *n* **1.** (*U*) [remorse, humiliation] honte *f* ; **to bring shame on** OR **upon sb** faire la honte de qqn - **2.** [pity] **it's a shame (that...)** c'est dommage (que... (+ *subjunctive*)) ; **what a shame!** quel dommage! ⬦ *vt* faire honte à, mortifier ; **to shame sb into doing sthg** obliger qqn à faire qqch en lui faisant honte.

shamefaced [,ʃeɪm'feɪst] *adj* honteux(euse), penaud(e).

shameful ['ʃeɪmfʊl] *adj* honteux(euse), scandaleux(euse).

shameless ['ʃeɪmlɪs] *adj* effronté(e), éhonté(e).

shampoo [ʃæm'puː] ⬦ *n* (*pl* -s) shampooing *m*. ⬦ *vt* (*pt & pp* -ed, *cont* -ing) : **to shampoo sb** OR **sb's hair** faire un shampooing à qqn.

shamrock ['ʃæmrɒk] *n* trèfle *m*.

shandy ['ʃændɪ] *n* panaché *m*.

shan't [ʃɑːnt] = shall not.

shantytown ['ʃæntɪtaʊn] *n* bidonville *m*.

shape [ʃeɪp] ⬦ *n* **1.** [gen] forme *f* ; **to take shape** prendre forme OR tournure - **2.** [health] : **to be in good/bad shape** être en bonne/mauvaise forme. ⬦ *vt* **1.** [pastry, clay etc] : **to shape sthg (into)** façonner OR modeler qqch (en) - **2.** [ideas, project, character] former. ➤ **shape up** *vi* [person, plans] se développer, progresser ; [job, events] prendre tournure OR forme.

-shaped ['ʃeɪpt] *suffix* : **egg-shaped** en forme d'œuf ; **L-shaped** en forme de L.

shapeless ['ʃeɪplɪs] *adj* informe.

shapely ['ʃeɪplɪ] *adj* bien fait(e).

share [ʃeəʳ] ⬦ *n* [portion, contribution] part *f*. ⬦ *vt* partager. ⬦ *vi* : **to share (in sthg)** partager (qqch). ➤ **shares** *npl* actions *fpl*. ➤ **share out** *vt sep* partager, répartir.

shareholder ['ʃeə,həʊldəʳ] *n* actionnaire *mf*.

shark [ʃɑːk] *n* (*pl* **shark** OR -s) *n* [fish] requin *m*.

sharp [ʃɑːp] ⬦ *adj* **1.** [knife, razor] tranchant(e), affilé(e) ; [needle, pencil, teeth] pointu(e) - **2.** [image, outline, contrast] net (nette) - **3.** [person, mind] vif (vive) - **4.** [sudden - change, rise] brusque, soudain(e) ; [- hit, tap] sec (sèche) - **5.** [words, order, voice] cinglant(e) - **6.** [cry, sound] perçant(e) ; [pain, cold] vif (vive) ; [taste] piquant(e) - **7.** MUS : **C/D sharp** do/ré dièse. ⬦ *adv* **1.** [punctually] : **at 8 o'clock sharp** à 8 heures pile OR tapantes - **2.** [immediately] : **sharp left/right** tout à fait à gauche/droite. ⬦ *n* MUS dièse *m*.

sharpen ['ʃɑːpn] *vt* [knife, tool] aiguiser ; [pencil] tailler.

sharpener ['ʃɑːpnəʳ] *n* [for pencil] taille-crayon *m* ; [for knife] aiguisoir *m* (pour couteaux).

sharp-eyed [-'aɪd] *adj* : **she's very sharp-eyed** elle remarque tout, rien ne lui échappe.

sharply ['ʃɑːplɪ] *adv* **1.** [distinctly] nettement - **2.** [suddenly] brusquement - **3.** [harshly] sévèrement, durement.

shat [ʃæt] *pt & pp* ➤ **shit**.

shatter ['ʃætər] ⬦ *vt* 1. [window, glass] briser, fracasser - 2. *fig* [hopes, dreams] détruire. ⬦ *vi* se fracasser, voler en éclats.

shattered ['ʃætəd] *adj* 1. [upset] bouleversé(e) - 2. *UK inf* [very tired] flapi(e).

shave [ʃeɪv] ⬦ *n* : **to have a shave** se raser. ⬦ *vt* 1. [remove hair from] raser - 2. [wood] planer, raboter. ⬦ *vi* se raser.

shaver ['ʃeɪvər] *n* rasoir *m* électrique.

shaving brush ['ʃeɪvɪŋ-] *n* blaireau *m*.

shaving cream ['ʃeɪvɪŋ-] *n* crème *f* à raser.

shaving foam ['ʃeɪvɪŋ-] *n* mousse *f* à raser.

shavings ['ʃeɪvɪŋz] *npl* [of wood, metal] copeaux *mpl*.

shawl [ʃɔːl] *n* châle *m*.

she [ʃiː] ⬦ *pers pron* 1. [referring to woman, girl, animal] elle ; **she's tall** elle est grande ; **SHE can't do it** elle, elle ne peut pas le faire ; **there she is** la voilà ; **if I were** OR **was she** *fml* si j'étais elle, à sa place - 2. [referring to boat, car, country] **she's a fine ship** c'est un bateau magnifique ; **she can do over 120 mph** elle fait plus de 150 km à l'heure. ⬦ *comp* : **she-elephant** éléphant *m* femelle ; **she-wolf** louve *f*.

sheaf [ʃiːf] (*pl* **sheaves** [ʃiːvz]) *n* 1. [of papers, letters] liasse *f* - 2. [of corn, grain] gerbe *f*.

shear [ʃɪər] (*pt* **-ed**, *pp* **-ed** OR **shorn**) *vt* [sheep] tondre. ⬦ **shears** *npl* 1. [for garden] sécateur *m* - 2. [for dressmaking] ciseaux *mpl*. ⬦ **shear off** ⬦ *vt sep* [branch] couper ; [piece of metal] cisailler. ⬦ *vi* se détacher.

sheath [ʃiːθ] (*pl* **sheaths** [ʃiːðz]) *n* 1. [for knife, cable] gaine *f* - 2. *UK* [condom] préservatif *m*.

sheaves [ʃiːvz] *npl* ▶ sheaf.

shed [ʃed] ⬦ *n* [small] remise *f*, cabane *f* ; [larger] hangar *m*. ⬦ *vt* (*pt & pp* **shed**) 1. [hair, skin, leaves] perdre - 2. [tears] verser, répandre - 3. [employees] se défaire de, congédier.

she'd (*weak form* [ʃɪd], *strong form* [ʃiːd]) = she had, = she would.

sheen [ʃiːn] *n* lustre *m*, éclat *m*.

sheep [ʃiːp] (*pl* **sheep**) *n* mouton *m*.

sheepdog ['ʃiːpdɒg] *n* chien *m* de berger.

sheepish ['ʃiːpɪʃ] *adj* penaud(e).

sheepskin ['ʃiːpskɪn] *n* peau *f* de mouton.

sheer [ʃɪər] *adj* 1. [absolute] pur(e) - 2. [very steep] à pic, abrupt(e) - 3. [material] fin(e).

sheet [ʃiːt] *n* 1. [for bed] drap *m* - 2. [of paper, glass, wood] feuille *f* ; [of metal] plaque *f*.

sheik(h) [ʃeɪk] *n* cheik *m*.

shelf [ʃelf] (*pl* **shelves** [ʃelvz]) *n* [for storage] rayon *m*, étagère *f*.

shell [ʃel] ⬦ *n* 1. [of egg, nut, snail] coquille *f* - 2. [of tortoise, crab] carapace *f* - 3. [on beach] coquillage *m* - 4. [of building, car] carcasse *f* - 5. MIL obus *m*. ⬦ *vt* 1. [peas] écosser ; [nuts, prawns] décortiquer ; [eggs] enlever la coquille de, écaler - 2. MIL bombarder.

she'll [ʃiːl] = she will, = she shall.

shellfish ['ʃelfɪʃ] (*pl* **shellfish**) *n* 1. [creature] crustacé *m*, coquillage *m* - 2. *(U)* [food] fruits *mpl* de mer.

shell suit *n UK* survêtement en Nylon® imperméabilisé.

shelter ['ʃeltər] ⬦ *n* abri *m*. ⬦ *vt* 1. [protect] abriter, protéger - 2. [refugee, homeless person] offrir un asile à ; [criminal, fugitive] cacher. ⬦ *vi* s'abriter, se mettre à l'abri.

sheltered ['ʃeltəd] *adj* 1. [from weather] abrité(e) - 2. [life, childhood] protégé(e), sans soucis.

shelve [ʃelv] *vt fig* mettre au Frigidaire®, mettre en sommeil.

shelves [ʃelvz] *npl* ▶ shelf.

shepherd ['ʃepəd] ⬦ *n* berger *m*. ⬦ *vt fig* conduire.

shepherd's pie ['ʃepədz-] *n* ≃ hachis *m* Parmentier.·

sheriff ['ʃerɪf] *n US* shérif *m*.

sherry ['ʃerɪ] *n* xérès *m*, sherry *m*.

she's [ʃiːz] = she is, = she has.

Shetland ['ʃetlənd] *n* : **(the)Shetland (Islands)** les (îles) Shetland *fpl*.

sh(h) [ʃ] *excl* chut !

shield [ʃiːld] ⬦ *n* 1. [armour] bouclier *m* - 2. *UK* [sports trophy] plaque *f*. ⬦ *vt* : **to shield sb (from)** protéger qqn (de OR contre).

shift [ʃɪft] ⬦ *n* 1. [change] changement *m*, modification *f* - 2. [period of work] poste *m* ; [workers] équipe *f*. ⬦ *vt* 1. [move] déplacer, changer de place - 2. [change] changer, modifier. ⬦ *vi* 1. [move - gen] changer de place ; [- wind] tourner, changer - 2. [change] changer, se modifier - 3. *US* AUT changer de vitesse.

shiftless ['ʃɪftlɪs] *adj* fainéant(e), paresseux(euse).

shifty ['ʃɪftɪ] *adj inf* sournois(e), louche.

shilling ['ʃɪlɪŋ] *n* shilling *m*.

shilly-shally ['ʃɪlɪˌʃælɪ] *vi* hésiter, être indécis(e).

shimmer ['ʃɪmər] ⬦ *n* reflet *m*, miroitement *m*. ⬦ *vi* miroiter.

shin [ʃɪn] *n* tibia *m*.

shinbone ['ʃɪnbəʊn] *n* tibia *m*.

shine [ʃaɪn] ⬦ *n* brillant *m*. ⬦ *vt*

(*pt & pp* **shone**) **1.** [direct] : **to shine a torch on sthg** éclairer qqch - **2.** [polish] faire briller, astiquer. ⬦ *vi* (*pt & pp* **shone**) briller.

shingle ['ʃɪŋgl] *n* (U) [on beach] galets *mpl*.
➡ **shingles** *n* (U) zona *m*.

shiny ['ʃaɪnɪ] *adj* brillant(e).

ship [ʃɪp] ⬦ *n* bateau *m* ; [larger] navire *m*. ⬦ *vt* [goods] expédier ; [troops, passengers] transporter.

shipbuilding ['ʃɪp,bɪldɪŋ] *n* construction *f* navale.

shipment ['ʃɪpmənt] *n* [cargo] cargaison *f*, chargement *m*.

shipper ['ʃɪpəʳ] *n* affréteur *m*, chargeur *m*.

shipping ['ʃɪpɪŋ] *n* (U) **1.** [transport] transport *m* maritime - **2.** [ships] navires *mpl*.

shipshape ['ʃɪpʃeɪp] *adj* bien rangé(e), en ordre.

shipwreck ['ʃɪprek] ⬦ *n* **1.** [destruction of ship] naufrage *m* - **2.** [wrecked ship] épave *f*. ⬦ *vt* : **to be shipwrecked** faire naufrage.

shipyard ['ʃɪpjɑːd] *n* chantier *m* naval.

shire [ʃaɪəʳ] *n* [county] comté *m*.

shirk [ʃɜːk] *vt* se dérober à.

shirt [ʃɜːt] *n* chemise *f*.

shirtsleeves ['ʃɜːtsliːvz] *npl* : **to be in (one's) shirtsleeves** être en manches OR en bras de chemise.

shit [ʃɪt] *vulg* ⬦ *n* **1.** [excrement] merde *f* - **2.** (U) [nonsense] conneries *fpl*. ⬦ *vi* (*pt & pp* **-ted** OR **shat**) chier. ⬦ *excl* merde !

shiver ['ʃɪvəʳ] ⬦ *n* frisson *m*. ⬦ *vi* : **to shiver (with)** trembler (de), frissonner (de).

shoal [ʃəʊl] *n* [of fish] banc *m*.

shock [ʃɒk] ⬦ *n* **1.** [surprise] choc *m*, coup *m* - **2.** (U) MED : **to be suffering from shock, to be in (a state of) shock** être en état de choc - **3.** [impact] choc *m*, heurt *m* - **4.** ELEC décharge *f* électrique. ⬦ *vt* **1.** [upset] bouleverser - **2.** [offend] choquer, scandaliser.

shock absorber [-əb,zɔːbəʳ] *n* amortisseur *m*.

shocking ['ʃɒkɪŋ] *adj* **1.** UK [very bad] épouvantable, terrible - **2.** [outrageous] scandaleux(euse).

shod [ʃɒd] ⬦ *pt & pp* ➡ **shoe**. ⬦ *adj* chaussé(e).

shoddy ['ʃɒdɪ] *adj* [goods, work] de mauvaise qualité ; [treatment] indigne, méprisable.

shoe [ʃuː] ⬦ *n* chaussure *f*, soulier *m*. ⬦ *vt* (*pt & pp* **-ed** OR **shod**) [horse] ferrer.

shoebrush ['ʃuːbrʌʃ] *n* brosse *f* à chaussures.

shoehorn ['ʃuːhɔːn] *n* chausse-pied *m*.

shoelace ['ʃuːleɪs] *n* lacet *m* de soulier.

shoe polish *n* cirage *m*.

shoe shop *n* magasin *m* de chaussures.

shoestring ['ʃuːstrɪŋ] *n* fig : **on a shoestring** à peu de frais.

shone [ʃɒn] *pt & pp* ➡ **shine**.

shoo [ʃuː] ⬦ *vt* chasser. ⬦ *excl* ouste !

shook [ʃʊk] *pt* ➡ **shake**.

shoot [ʃuːt] ⬦ *vt* (*pt & pp* **shot**) **1.** [kill with gun] tuer d'un coup de feu ; [wound with gun] blesser d'un coup de feu ; **to shoot o.s.** [kill o.s.] se tuer avec une arme à feu - **2.** UK [hunt] chasser - **3.** [fire - gun] tirer un coup de ; [- bullet] tirer ; [- arrow] tirer, décocher - **4.** CIN tourner. ⬦ *vi* (*pt & pp* **shot**) **1.** [fire gun] : **to shoot (at)** tirer (sur) - **2.** UK [hunt] chasser - **3.** [move quickly] : **to shoot in/out/past** entrer/sortir/passer en trombe, entrer/sortir/passer comme un bolide - **4.** CIN tourner - **5.** SPORT tirer, shooter. ⬦ *n* **1.** UK [hunting expedition] partie *f* de chasse - **2.** [of plant] pousse *f*.
➡ **shoot down** *vt sep* **1.** [aeroplane] descendre, abattre - **2.** [person] abattre.
➡ **shoot up** *vi* **1.** [child, plant] pousser vite - **2.** [price, inflation] monter en flèche.

shooting ['ʃuːtɪŋ] *n* **1.** [killing] meurtre *m* - **2.** (U) UK [hunting] chasse *f*.

shooting star *n* étoile *f* filante.

shop [ʃɒp] ⬦ *n* **1.** [store] magasin *m*, boutique *f* - **2.** [workshop] atelier *m*. ⬦ *vi* faire ses courses ; **to go shopping** aller faire les courses OR commissions.

shop assistant *n* UK vendeur *m*, -euse *f*.

shop floor *n* : **the shop floor** fig les ouvriers *mpl*.

shopkeeper ['ʃɒp,kiːpəʳ] *n* commerçant *m*, -e *f*.

shoplifting ['ʃɒp,lɪftɪŋ] *n* (U) vol *m* à l'étalage.

shopper ['ʃɒpəʳ] *n* personne *f* qui fait ses courses.

shopping ['ʃɒpɪŋ] *n* (U) [purchases] achats *mpl*.

shopping bag *n* sac *m* à provisions.

shopping basket *n* panier *m* de course.

shopping cart *n* US caddie® *m*.

shopping centre UK, **shopping mall** US, **shopping plaza** US [-,plɑːzə] *n* centre *m* commercial.

shopsoiled UK ['ʃɒpsɔɪld], **shopworn** US ['ʃɒpwɔːn] *adj* qui a fait l'étalage, abîmé(e) (en magasin).

shop steward *n* délégué syndical *m*, déléguée syndicale *f*.

shopwindow [,ʃɒp'wɪndəʊ] *n* vitrine *f*.

shopworn US = shopsoiled.

shore [ʃɔːr] n rivage m, bord m ; **on shore** à terre. ◆ **shore up** vt sep étayer, étançonner ; fig consolider.

shorn [ʃɔːn] ◇ pp ► shear. ◇ adj tondu(e).

short [ʃɔːt] ◇ adj 1. [not long - in time] court(e), bref (brève) ; [- in space] court - 2. [not tall] petit(e) - 3. [curt] brusque, sec (sèche) - 4. [lacking] : **time/money is short** nous manquons de temps/d'argent ; **to be short of** manquer de - 5. [abbreviated] : **to be short for** être le diminutif de. ◇ adv : **to be running short of** [running out of] commencer à manquer de, commencer à être à court de ; **to cut sthg short** [visit, speech] écourter qqch ; [discussion] couper court à qqch ; **to stop short** s'arrêter net. ◇ n 1. UK [alcoholic drink] alcool m fort - 2. [film] court métrage m. ◆ **shorts** npl 1. [gen] short m - 2. US [underwear] caleçon m. ◆ **for short** adv : **he's called Bob for short** Bob est son diminutif. ◆ **in short** adv (enfin) bref. ◆ **nothing short of** prep rien moins que, pratiquement. ◆ **short of** prep [unless, without] : **short of doing sthg** à moins de faire qqch, à part faire qqch.

shortage ['ʃɔːtɪdʒ] n manque m, insuffisance f.

shortbread ['ʃɔːtbred] n sablé m.

short-change vt 1. [subj: shopkeeper] : **to short-change sb** ne pas rendre assez à qqn - 2. fig [cheat] tromper, rouler.

short circuit n court-circuit m.

shortcomings ['ʃɔːt,kʌmɪŋz] npl défauts mpl.

shortcrust pastry ['ʃɔːtkrʌst-] n pâte f brisée.

shortcut n 1. [quick route] raccourci m - 2. [quick method] solution f miracle.

shorten ['ʃɔːtn] ◇ vt 1. [holiday, time] écourter - 2. [skirt, rope etc] raccourcir. ◇ vi [days] raccourcir.

shortfall ['ʃɔːtfɔːl] n déficit m.

shorthand ['ʃɔːthænd] n (U) [writing system] sténographie f.

shorthand typist n UK dated sténodactylo f.

short list n UK liste f des candidats sélectionnés.

shortly ['ʃɔːtlɪ] adv [soon] bientôt.

shortsighted [,ʃɔːt'saɪtɪd] adj UK myope ; fig imprévoyant(e).

short-staffed [-'stɑːft] adj : **to be short-staffed** manquer de personnel.

short story n nouvelle f.

short-tempered [-'tempəd] adj emporté(e), irascible.

short-term adj [effects, solution] à court terme ; [problem] de courte durée.

short wave n (U) ondes fpl courtes.

shot [ʃɒt] ◇ pt & pp ► shoot. ◇ n 1. [gunshot] coup m de feu ; **like a shot** sans tarder, sans hésiter - 2. [marksman] tireur m - 3. SPORT coup m - 4. [photograph] photo f ; CIN plan m - 5. inf [attempt] : **to have a shot at sthg** essayer de faire qqch - 6. [injection] piqûre f.

shotgun ['ʃɒtgʌn] n fusil m de chasse.

should [ʃʊd] aux vb 1. [indicating duty] : **we should leave now** il faudrait partir maintenant ; **you should go if you're invited** tu devrais y aller si tu es invité - 2. [seeking advice, permission] : **should I go too?** est-ce que je devrais y aller aussi? - 3. [as suggestion] : **I should deny everything** moi, je nierais tout - 4. [indicating probability] : **she should be home soon** elle devrait être de retour bientôt, elle va bientôt rentrer - 5. [was or were expected] : **they should have won the match** ils auraient dû gagner le match - 6. [indicating intention, wish] : **I should like to come with you** j'aimerais bien venir avec vous - 7. (as conditional) **you should go if you're invited** tu devrais y aller si tu es invité - 8. (in subordinate clauses) **we decided that you should meet him** nous avons décidé que ce serait toi qui irais le chercher - 9. [expressing uncertain opinion] : **I should think he's about 50 (years old)** je pense qu'il doit avoir dans les 50 ans.

shoulder ['ʃəʊldər] ◇ n 1. [body] épaule f - 2. [road] accotement m, bas côté m ; US bande f d'arrêt d'urgence. ◇ vt 1. [carry] porter - 2. [responsibility] endosser.

shoulder blade n omoplate f.

shoulder strap n 1. [on dress] bretelle f - 2. [on bag] bandoulière f.

shouldn't ['ʃʊdnt] = should not.

should've ['ʃʊdəv] = should have.

shout [ʃaʊt] ◇ n [cry] cri m. ◇ vt & vi crier. ◆ **shout down** vt sep huer, conspuer.

shouting ['ʃaʊtɪŋ] n (U) cris mpl.

shove [ʃʌv] ◇ n : **to give sb/sthg a shove** pousser qqn/qqch. ◇ vt pousser ; **to shove clothes into a bag** fourrer des vêtements dans un sac. ◆ **shove off** vi 1. [in boat] pousser au large - 2. inf [go away] ficher le camp, filer.

shovel ['ʃʌvl] ◇ n [tool] pelle f. ◇ vt (UK & US) enlever à la pelle, pelleter.

show [ʃəʊ] ◇ n 1. [display] démonstration f, manifestation f - 2. [at theatre] spectacle m ; [on radio, TV] émission f - 3. CIN séance f - 4. [exhibition] exposition f. ◇ vt (pt -ed, pp shown OR -ed) 1. [gen] montrer ; [profit, loss] indiquer ; [respect] témoigner ; [courage, mercy] faire preuve de ; **to show sb sthg, to show sthg to sb**

montrer qqch à qqn - **2.** [escort] : **to show sb to his seat/table** conduire qqn à sa place/sa table - **3.** [film] projeter, passer ; [TV programme] donner, passer. ⬦ *vi* (*pt* -**ed**, *pp* **shown** OR -**ed**) **1.** [indicate] indiquer, montrer - **2.** [be visible] se voir, être visible - **3.** CIN : **what's showing tonight?** qu'est-ce qu'on joue comme film ce soir? ▸ **show off** ⬦ *vt sep* exhiber. ⬦ *vi* faire l'intéressant(e). ▸ **show up** ⬦ *vt sep* [embarrass] embarrasser, faire honte à. ⬦ *vi* **1.** [stand out] se voir, ressortir - **2.** [arrive] s'amener, rappliquer.

show business *n* (*U*) monde *m* du spectacle, show-business *m*.

showdown ['ʃəʊdaʊn] *n* : **to have a show-down with sb** s'expliquer avec qqn, mettre les choses au point avec qqn.

shower ['ʃaʊər] ⬦ *n* **1.** [device, act] douche *f* ; **to have** OR **take a shower** prendre une douche, se doucher - **2.** [of rain] averse *f* - **3.** *fig* [of questions, confetti] avalanche *f*, déluge *m*. ⬦ *vt* : **to shower sb with** couvrir qqn de. ⬦ *vi* [wash] prendre une douche, se doucher.

shower cap *n* bonnet *m* de douche.

shower room *n* salle *f* d'eau.

showing ['ʃəʊɪŋ] *n* CIN projection *f*.

show jumping [-ˌdʒʌmpɪŋ] *n* jumping *m*.

shown [ʃəʊn] *pp* ▸ **show**.

show-off *n inf* m'as-tu-vu *m*, -e *f*.

showpiece ['ʃəʊpiːs] *n* [main attraction] joyau *m*, trésor *m*.

showroom ['ʃəʊrʊm] *n* salle *f* OR magasin *m* d'exposition ; [for cars] salle de démonstration.

shrank [ʃræŋk] *pt* ▸ **shrink**.

shrapnel ['ʃræpnl] *n* (*U*) éclats *mpl* d'obus.

shred [ʃred] ⬦ *n* **1.** [of material, paper] lambeau *m*, brin *m* - **2.** *fig* [of evidence] parcelle *f* ; [of truth] once *f*, grain *m*. ⬦ *vt* [food] râper ; [paper] déchirer en lambeaux.

shredder ['ʃredər] *n* [machine] destructeur *m* de documents.

shrewd [ʃruːd] *adj* fin(e), astucieux(euse).

shriek [ʃriːk] ⬦ *n* cri *m* perçant, hurlement *m* ; [of laughter] éclat *m*. ⬦ *vi* pousser un cri perçant.

shrill [ʃrɪl] *adj* [sound, voice] aigu(ë) ; [whistle] strident(e).

shrimp [ʃrɪmp] *n* crevette *f*.

shrine [ʃraɪn] *n* [place of worship] lieu *m* saint.

shrink [ʃrɪŋk] ⬦ *n inf hum* psy *mf*. ⬦ *vt* (*pt* **shrank**, *pp* **shrunk**) rétrécir. ⬦ *vi* (*pt* **shrank**, *pp* **shrunk**) **1.** [cloth, garment] rétrécir ; [person] rapetisser ; *fig* [income, popularity *etc*] baisser, diminuer - **2.** [recoil] :

to shrink away from sthg reculer devant qqch ; **to shrink from doing sthg** rechigner OR répugner à faire qqch.

shrinkage ['ʃrɪŋkɪdʒ] *n* rétrécissement *m* ; *fig* diminution *f*, baisse *f*.

shrink-wrap *vt* emballer sous film plastique.

shrivel ['ʃrɪvl] (*UK & US*) ⬦ *vt* : **to shrivel (up)** rider, flétrir. ⬦ *vi* : **to shrivel (up)** se rider, se flétrir.

shroud [ʃraʊd] ⬦ *n* [cloth] linceul *m*. ⬦ *vt* : **to be shrouded in** [darkness, fog] être enseveli(e) sous ; [mystery] être enveloppé(e) de.

Shrove Tuesday ['ʃrəʊv-] *n* Mardi *m* gras.

shrub [ʃrʌb] *n* arbuste *m*.

shrubbery ['ʃrʌbəri] *n* massif *m* d'arbustes.

shrug [ʃrʌg] ⬦ *vt* : **to shrug one's shoulders** hausser les épaules. ⬦ *vi* hausser les épaules. ▸ **shrug off** *vt sep* ignorer.

shrunk [ʃrʌŋk] *pp* ▸ **shrink**.

shudder ['ʃʌdər] *US vi* **1.** [tremble] : **to shudder (with)** frémir (de), frissonner (de) - **2.** [shake] vibrer, trembler.

shuffle ['ʃʌfl] *vt* **1.** [drag] : **to shuffle one's feet** traîner les pieds - **2.** [cards] mélanger, battre.

shun [ʃʌn] *vt* fuir, éviter.

shunt [ʃʌnt] *vt* RAIL aiguiller.

shut [ʃʌt] ⬦ *adj* [closed] fermé(e). ⬦ *vt* (*pt & pp* **shut**) fermer. ⬦ *vi* (*pt & pp* **shut**) **1.** [door, window] se fermer - **2.** [shop] fermer. ▸ **shut away** *vt sep* [valuables, papers] mettre sous clef. ▸ **shut down** ⬦ *vt sep & vi* [close] fermer. ⬦ *vt sep* [computer] éteindre. ▸ **shut out** *vt sep* [noise] supprimer ; [light] ne pas laisser entrer ; **to shut sb out** laisser qqn à la porte. ▸ **shut up** *inf* ⬦ *vt sep* [silence] faire taire. ⬦ *vi* se taire.

shutter ['ʃʌtər] *n* **1.** [on window] volet *m* - **2.** [in camera] obturateur *m*.

shuttle ['ʃʌtl] ⬦ *adj* : **shuttle service** (service *m* de) navette *f*. ⬦ *n* [train, bus, plane] navette *f*.

shuttlecock ['ʃʌtlkɒk] *n* volant *m*.

shy [ʃaɪ] ⬦ *adj* [timid] timide. ⬦ *vi* [horse] s'effaroucher.

Siberia [saɪ'bɪərɪə] *n* Sibérie *f*.

sibling ['sɪblɪŋ] *n* [brother] frère *m* ; [sister] sœur *f*.

Sicily ['sɪsɪlɪ] *n* Sicile *f*.

sick [sɪk] *adj* **1.** [ill] malade - **2.** [nauseous] : **to feel sick** *UK* avoir envie de vomir, avoir mal au cœur ; **to be sick** *UK* [vomit] vomir - **3.** [fed up] : **to be sick of** en avoir assez OR marre de - **4.** [joke, humour] macabre.

sickbay ['sɪkbeɪ] *n* infirmerie *f*.

sicken ['sɪkn] <> *vt* écœurer, dégoûter. <> *vi UK* : **to be sickening for sthg** couver qqch.

sickening ['sɪknɪŋ] *adj* [disgusting] écœurant(e), dégoûtant(e).

sickle ['sɪkl] *n* faucille *f*.

sick leave *n (U)* congé *m* de maladie.

sickly ['sɪklɪ] *adj* 1. [unhealthy] maladif(ive), souffreteux(euse) - 2. [smell, taste] écœurant(e).

sickness ['sɪknɪs] *n UK* 1. [illness] maladie *f* - 2. *(U) UK* [nausea] nausée *f*, nausées *fpl* ; [vomiting] vomissement *m*, vomissements *mpl*.

sick pay *n (U)* indemnité *f* OR allocation *f* de maladie.

side [saɪd] <> *n* 1. [gen] côté *m* ; **at** OR **by my/her** *etc* **side** à mes/ses *etc* côtés ; **on every side, on all sides** de tous côtés ; **from side to side** d'un côté à l'autre ; **side by side** côte à côte - 2. [of table, river] bord *m* - 3. [of hill, valley] versant *m*, flanc *m* - 4. [in war, debate] camp *m*, côté *m* ; SPORT équipe *f*, camp ; [of argument] point *m* de vue ; **to take sb's side** prendre le parti de qqn - 5. [aspect - gen] aspect *m* ; [- of character] facette *f* ; **to be on the safe side** pour plus de sûreté, par précaution. <> *adj* [situated on side] latéral(e). **side with** *vt insep* prendre le parti de, se ranger du côté de.

sideboard ['saɪdbɔːd] *n* [cupboard] buffet *m*.

sideboards *UK* ['saɪdbɔːdz], **sideburns** *US* ['saɪdbɜːnz] *npl* favoris *mpl*, rouflaquettes *fpl*.

side effect *n* 1. MED effet *m* secondaire OR indésirable - 2. [unplanned result] effet *m* secondaire, répercussion *f*.

sidelight ['saɪdlaɪt] *n* AUT feu *m* de position.

sideline ['saɪdlaɪn] *n* 1. [extra business] activité *f* secondaire - 2. SPORT ligne *f* de touche.

sidelong ['saɪdlɒŋ] *adj & adv* de côté.

sidesaddle ['saɪd,sædl] *adv* : **to ride side-saddle** monter en amazone.

sideshow ['saɪdʃəʊ] *n* spectacle *m* forain.

sidestep ['saɪdstep] *vt* faire un pas de côté pour éviter OR esquiver ; *fig* éviter.

side street *n* [not main street] petite rue *f* ; [off main street] rue transversale.

sidetrack ['saɪdtræk] *vt* : **to be sidetracked** se laisser distraire.

sidewalk ['saɪdwɔːk] *n US* trottoir *m*.

sideways ['saɪdweɪz] *adj & adv* de côté.

siding ['saɪdɪŋ] *n* voie *f* de garage.

sidle ['saɪdl] **sidle up** *vi* : **to sidle up to sb** se glisser vers qqn.

siege [siːdʒ] *n* siège *m*.

sieve [sɪv] <> *n* [for flour, sand etc] tamis *m* ; [for liquids] passoire *f*. <> *vt* [flour etc] tamiser ; [liquid] passer.

sift [sɪft] <> *vt* 1. [flour, sand] tamiser - 2. *fig* [evidence] passer au crible. <> *vi* : **to sift through** examiner, éplucher.

sigh [saɪ] <> *n* soupir *m*. <> *vi* [person] soupirer, pousser un soupir.

sight [saɪt] <> *n* 1. [seeing] vue *f* ; **in sight** en vue ; **in/out of sight** en/hors de vue ; **at first sight** à première vue, au premier abord - 2. [spectacle] spectacle *m* - 3. [on gun] mire *f*. <> *vt* apercevoir. **sights** *npl* [of city] attractions *fpl* touristiques.

sightseeing ['saɪt,siːɪŋ] *n* tourisme *m* ; **to go sightseeing** faire du tourisme.

sightseer ['saɪt,siːər] *n* touriste *mf*.

sign [saɪn] <> *n* 1. [gen] signe *m* ; **no sign of** aucune trace de - 2. [notice] enseigne *f* ; AUT panneau *m*. <> *vt* signer. <> *vi* [use sign language] communiquer par signes. **sign on** *vi* 1. [enrol - MIL] s'engager ; [- for course] s'inscrire - 2. *UK* [register as unemployed] s'inscrire au chômage. **sign up** <> *vt sep* [worker] embaucher ; [soldier] engager. <> *vi* MIL s'engager ; [for course] s'inscrire.

signal ['sɪgnl] <> *n* signal *m*. <> *vt (UK & US)* 1. [indicate] indiquer - 2. [gesture to] : **to signal sb (to do sthg)** faire signe à qqn (de faire qqch). <> *vi (UK & US)* 1. AUT clignoter, mettre son clignotant - 2. [gesture] : **to signal to sb (to do sthg)** faire signe à qqn (de faire qqch).

signalman ['sɪgnlmən] *(pl* **-men** [-mən]*)* RAIL aiguilleur *m*.

signature ['sɪgnətʃər] *n* [name] signature *f*.

signature tune *n* indicatif *m*.

signet ring ['sɪgnɪt-] *n* chevalière *f*.

significance [sɪg'nɪfɪkəns] *n* 1. [importance] importance *f*, portée *f* - 2. [meaning] signification *f*.

significant [sɪg'nɪfɪkənt] *adj* 1. [considerable] considérable - 2. [important] important(e) - 3. [meaningful] significatif(ive).

signify ['sɪgnɪfaɪ] *vt* signifier, indiquer.

signpost ['saɪnpəʊst] *n* poteau *m* indicateur.

Sikh [siːk] <> *adj* sikh *(inv)*. <> *n* [person] Sikh *mf*.

silence ['saɪləns] <> *n* silence *m*. <> *vt* réduire au silence, faire taire.

silencer ['saɪlənsər] *n* silencieux *m*.

silent ['saɪlənt] *adj* 1. [person, place] silencieux(euse) - 2. CIN & LING muet(ette).

silhouette [ˌsɪluː'et] *n* silhouette *f*.

silicon chip [ˌsɪlɪkən-] *n* puce *f*, pastille *f* de silicium.

silk [sɪlk] <> *n* soie *f*. <> *comp* en OR de soie.

silky ['sɪlkɪ] *adj* soyeux(euse).

sill [sɪl] *n* [of window] rebord *m*.

silly ['sɪlɪ] *adj* stupide, bête.

silo ['saɪləʊ] (*pl* -s) *n* silo *m*.

silt [sɪlt] *n* vase *f*, limon *m*.

silver ['sɪlvər] <> *adj* [colour] argenté(e). <> *n* (*U*) **1.** [metal] argent *m* - **2.** [coins] pièces *fpl* d'argent - **3.** [silverware] argenterie *f*. <> *comp* en argent, d'argent.

silver foil, silver paper *n* (*U*) papier *m* d'argent OR d'étain.

silver-plated [-'pleɪtɪd] *adj* plaqué(e) argent.

silversmith ['sɪlvəsmɪθ] *n* orfèvre *mf*.

silverware ['sɪlvəweər] *n* (*U*) **1.** [dishes, spoons, etc] argenterie *f* - **2.** US [cutlery] couverts *mpl*.

similar ['sɪmɪlər] *adj* : **similar (to)** semblable (à), similaire (à).

similarly ['sɪmɪləlɪ] *adv* de la même manière, pareillement.

simmer ['sɪmər] *vt* faire cuire à feu doux, mijoter.

simpering ['sɪmpərɪŋ] *adj* affecté(e).

simple ['sɪmpl] *adj* **1.** [gen] simple - **2.** *dated* [mentally retarded] simplet(ette), simple d'esprit.

simple-minded [-'maɪndɪd] *adj* simplet(ette), simple d'esprit.

simplicity [sɪm'plɪsətɪ] *n* simplicité *f*.

simplify ['sɪmplɪfaɪ] *vt* simplifier.

simply ['sɪmplɪ] *adv* **1.** [gen] simplement - **2.** [for emphasis] absolument ; **quite simply** tout simplement.

simulate ['sɪmjʊleɪt] *vt* simuler.

simultaneous [UK ˌsɪmʊl'teɪnjəs, US ˌsaɪməl'teɪnjəs] *adj* simultané(e).

sin [sɪn] <> *n* péché *m*. <> *vi* : **to sin (against)** pécher (contre).

since [sɪns] <> *adv* depuis. <> *prep* depuis. <> *conj* **1.** [in time] depuis que - **2.** [because] comme, puisque.

sincere [sɪn'sɪər] *adj* sincère.

sincerely [sɪn'sɪəlɪ] *adv* sincèrement ; **Yours sincerely** [at end of letter] veuillez agréer, Monsieur/Madame, l'expression de mes sentiments les meilleurs.

sincerity [sɪn'serətɪ] *n* sincérité *f*.

sinew ['sɪnjuː] *n* tendon *m*.

sinful ['sɪnfʊl] *adj* [thought] mauvais(e) ; [desire, act] coupable ; **sinful person** pécheur *m*, -eresse *f*.

sing [sɪŋ] (*pt* sang, *pp* sung) *vt* & *vi* chanter.

Singapore [ˌsɪŋə'pɔːr] *n* Singapour *m*.

singe [sɪndʒ] *vt* brûler légèrement ; [cloth] roussir.

singer ['sɪŋər] *n* chanteur *m*, -euse *f*.

singing ['sɪŋɪŋ] *n* (*U*) chant *m*.

single ['sɪŋgl] <> *adj* **1.** [only one] seul(e), unique ; **every single** chaque - **2.** [unmarried] célibataire - **3.** UK [ticket] simple. <> *n* **1.** UK [one-way ticket] billet *m* simple, aller *m* (simple) - **2.** MUS (disque *m*) 45 tours *m*. ◆ **singles** *npl* TENNIS simples *mpl*. ◆ **single out** *vt sep* : **to single sb out (for)** choisir qqn (pour).

single bed *n* lit *m* à une place.

single-breasted [-'brestɪd] *adj* [jacket] droit(e).

single-click <> *n* clic *m*. <> *vi* : **to single-click on smthg** cliquer une fois sur qqch. <> *vi* cliquer une fois.

single cream *n* UK crème *f* liquide.

single currency *n* monnaie *f* unique.

single file *n* : **in single file** en file indienne, à la file.

single-handed [-'hændɪd] *adv* tout seul (toute seule).

single-minded [-'maɪndɪd] *adj* résolu(e).

single parent *n* père *m* OR mère *f* célibataire.

single-parent family *n* famille *f* monoparentale.

single room *n* chambre *f* pour une personne OR à un lit.

singlet ['sɪŋglɪt] *n* UK tricot *m* de peau ; SPORT maillot *m*.

singular ['sɪŋgjʊlər] <> *adj* singulier(ère). <> *n* singulier *m*.

sinister ['sɪnɪstər] *adj* sinistre.

sink [sɪŋk] <> *n* [in kitchen] évier *m* ; [in bathroom] lavabo *m*. <> *vt* (*pt* sank, *pp* sunk) **1.** [ship] couler - **2.** [teeth, claws] : **to sink sthg into** enfoncer qqch dans. <> *vi* (*pt* sank, *pp* sunk) **1.** [in water - ship] couler, sombrer ; [- person, object] couler - **2.** [ground] s'affaisser ; [sun] baisser ; **to sink into poverty/despair** sombrer dans la misère/le désespoir - **3.** [value, amount] baisser, diminuer ; [voice] faiblir. ◆ **sink in** *vi* : **it hasn't sunk in yet** je n'ai pas encore réalisé.

sink school *n* dépotoir *m*.

sink unit *n* bloc-évier *m*.

sinner ['sɪnər] *n* pécheur *m*, -eresse *f*.

sinus ['saɪnəs] (*pl* -es [-iːz]) *n* sinus *m inv*.

sip [sɪp] <> *n* petite gorgée *f*. <> *vt* siroter, boire à petits coups.

siphon ['saɪfn] <> *n* siphon *m*. <> *vt*

1. [liquid] siphonner - **2.** fig [money] canaliser. ➤ **siphon off** vt sep **1.** [liquid] siphonner - **2.** fig [money] canaliser.

sir [sɜːr] n **1.** [form of address] monsieur m - **2.** [in titles] : **Sir Phillip Holden** sir Phillip Holden.

siren ['saɪərən] n sirène f.

sirloin (steak) ['sɜːlɔɪn-] n bifteck m dans l'aloyau OR d'aloyau.

sissy ['sɪsɪ] n inf poule f mouillée, dégonflé m, -e f.

sister ['sɪstər] n **1.** [sibling] sœur f - **2.** [nun] sœur f, religieuse f - **3.** UK [senior nurse] infirmière f chef.

sister-in-law (pl **sisters-in-law**) n belle-sœur f.

sit [sɪt] (pt & pp **sat**) ➤ vt UK [exam] passer. ➤ vi **1.** [person] s'asseoir ; **to be sitting** être assis(e) ; **to sit on a committee** faire partie OR être membre d'un comité - **2.** [court, parliament] siéger, être en séance. ➤ **sit about, sit around** vi rester assis(e) à ne rien faire. ➤ **sit down** vi s'asseoir. ➤ **sit in on** vt insep assister à. ➤ **sit through** vt insep rester jusqu'à la fin de. ➤ **sit up** vi **1.** [sit upright] se redresser, s'asseoir - **2.** [stay up] veiller.

sitcom ['sɪtkɒm] n inf sitcom f.

site [saɪt] ➤ n **1.** COMPUT site m - **2.** [of town, building] emplacement m ; CONSTR chantier m. ➤ vt situer, placer.

sit-in n sit-in m, occupation f des locaux.

sitting ['sɪtɪŋ] n **1.** [of meal] service m - **2.** [of court, parliament] séance f.

sitting room n salon m.

situated ['sɪtjʊeɪtɪd] adj : **to be situated** être situé(e), se trouver.

situation [,sɪtjʊ'eɪʃn] n **1.** [gen] situation f - **2.** [job] situation f, emploi m ; **'situations vacant'** UK 'offres d'emploi'.

six [sɪks] ➤ num adj six (inv) ; **she's six (years old)** elle a six ans. ➤ num pron six mf & pl ; **I want six** j'en veux six ; **there were six of us** nous étions six. ➤ num n **1.** [gen] six m inv ; **two hundred and six** deux cent six - **2.** [six o'clock] : **it's six** il est six heures ; **we arrived at six** nous sommes arrivés à six heures.

sixteen [sɪks'tiːn] num seize ; see also **six**.

sixteenth [sɪks'tiːnθ] num seizième ; see also **sixth**.

sixth [sɪksθ] ➤ num adj sixième. ➤ num adv **1.** [in race, competition] sixième, en sixième place - **2.** [in list] sixièmement. ➤ num pron sixième mf. ➤ n **1.** [fraction] sixième m - **2.** [in dates] : **the sixth (of September)** le six (septembre).

sixth form n UK SCH ≃ (classe f) terminale f.

sixth form college n UK établissement préparant aux A-levels.

sixty ['sɪkstɪ] num soixante ; see also **six**. ➤ **sixties** npl **1.** [decade] : **the sixties** les années fpl soixante - **2.** [in ages] : **to be in one's sixties** être sexagénaire.

size [saɪz] n [of person, clothes, company] taille f ; [of building] grandeur f, dimensions fpl ; [of problem] ampleur f, taille ; [of shoes] pointure f. ➤ **size up** vt sep [person] jauger ; [situation] apprécier, peser.

sizeable ['saɪzəbl] adj assez important(e).

sizzle ['sɪzl] vi grésiller.

skate [skeɪt] ➤ n **1.** [ice skate, roller skate] patin m - **2.** (pl **skate** OR **-s**) [fish] raie f. ➤ vi [on ice skates] faire du patin à glace, patiner ; [on roller skates] faire du patin à roulettes.

skateboard ['skeɪtbɔːd] n planche f à roulettes, skateboard m, skate m.

skater ['skeɪtər] n [on ice] patineur m, -euse f ; [on roller skates] patineur m, -euse f ; [on roller skates] patineur m, -euse f à roulettes.

skating ['skeɪtɪŋ] n [on ice] patinage m ; [on roller skates] patinage à roulettes.

skating rink n patinoire f.

skeleton ['skelɪtn] n squelette m.

skeleton key n passe m, passe-partout m inv.

skeleton staff n personnel m réduit.

skeptic etc US = **sceptic** etc.

sketch [sketʃ] ➤ n **1.** [drawing] croquis m, esquisse f - **2.** [description] aperçu m, résumé m - **3.** [by comedian] sketch m. ➤ vt **1.** [draw] dessiner, faire un croquis de - **2.** [describe] donner un aperçu de, décrire à grands traits.

sketchbook ['sketʃbʊk] n carnet m à dessins.

sketchpad ['sketʃpæd] n bloc m à dessins.

sketchy ['sketʃɪ] adj incomplet(ète).

skewer ['skjʊər] ➤ n brochette f, broche f. ➤ vt embrocher.

ski [skiː] ➤ n ski m. ➤ vi (pt & pp **skied**, cont **skiing**) skier, faire du ski.

ski boots npl chaussures fpl de ski.

skid [skɪd] ➤ n dérapage m ; **to go into a skid** déraper. ➤ vi déraper.

skier ['skiːər] n skieur m, -euse f.

skies [skaɪz] npl ➤ **sky**.

skiing ['skiːɪŋ] n (U) ski m ; **to go skiing** faire du ski.

ski jump n [slope] tremplin m ; [event] saut m à OR en skis.

skilful UK, **skillful** US ['skɪlfʊl] adj habile, adroit(e).

ski lift n remonte-pente m.

skill [skıl] n **1.** (U) [ability] habileté f, adresse f - **2.** [technique] technique f, art m.

skilled [skıld] adj **1.** [skilful] : **skilled (in OR at doing sthg)** habile OR adroit(e) (pour faire qqch) - **2.** [trained] qualifié(e).

skillful etc US = **skilful** etc.

skim [skım] ◇ vt **1.** [cream] écrémer ; [soup] écumer - **2.** [move above] effleurer, raser. ◇ vi : **to skim through sthg** [newspaper, book] parcourir qqch.

skim(med) milk [skım(d)-] n lait m écrémé.

skimp [skımp] ◇ vt lésiner sur. ◇ vi : **to skimp on** lésiner sur.

skimpy ['skımpı] adj [meal] maigre ; [clothes] étriqué(e) ; [facts] insuffisant(e).

skin [skın] ◇ n peau f. ◇ vt **1.** [dead animal] écorcher, dépouiller ; [fruit] éplucher, peler - **2.** [graze] : **to skin one's knee** s'érafler OR s'écorcher le genou.

skin-deep adj superficiel(elle).

skin diving n plongée f sous-marine.

skinny ['skını] adj maigre.

skin-tight adj moulant(e), collant(e).

skip [skıp] ◇ n **1.** [jump] petit saut m - **2.** UK [container] benne f. ◇ vt [page, class, meal] sauter. ◇ vi **1.** [gen] sauter, sautiller - **2.** UK [over rope] sauter à la corde.

ski pants npl fuseau m.

ski pole n bâton m de ski.

skipper ['skıpər] n NAUT & SPORT capitaine m.

skipping rope n UK corde f à sauter.

skirmish ['skɜːmıʃ] n escarmouche f.

skirt [skɜːt] ◇ n [garment] jupe f. ◇ vt **1.** [town, obstacle] contourner - **2.** [problem] éviter. ◆ **skirt round** UK vt insep **1.** [town, obstacle] contourner - **2.** [problem] éviter.

skit [skıt] n sketch m.

skittle ['skıtl] n UK quille f. ◆ **skittles** n (U) [game] quilles fpl.

skive [skaıv] vi UK inf **to skive (off)** s'esquiver, tirer au flanc.

skulk [skʌlk] vi [hide] se cacher ; [prowl] rôder.

skull [skʌl] n crâne m.

skunk [skʌŋk] n [animal] mouffette f.

sky [skaı] n ciel m.

skylight ['skaılaıt] n lucarne f.

sky marshal n garde m de sécurité (à bord d'un avion).

skyscraper ['skaı,skreıpər] n gratte-ciel m inv.

slab [slæb] n [of concrete] dalle f ; [of stone] bloc m ; [of cake] pavé m.

slack [slæk] ◇ adj **1.** [not tight] lâche

- **2.** [not busy] calme - **3.** [person] négligent(e), pas sérieux(euse). ◇ n [in rope] mou m.

slacken ['slækn] ◇ vt [speed, pace] ralentir ; [rope] relâcher. ◇ vi [speed, pace] ralentir.

slag [slæg] n (U) [waste material] scories fpl.

slagheap ['slæghiːp] n terril m.

slain [sleın] pp ▶ **slay**.

slam [slæm] ◇ vt **1.** [shut] claquer - **2.** [place with force] : **to slam sthg on OR onto** jeter qqch brutalement sur, flanquer qqch sur. ◇ vi claquer.

slander ['slɑːndər] ◇ n calomnie f ; LAW diffamation f. ◇ vt calomnier ; LAW diffamer.

slang [slæŋ] n (U) argot m.

slant [slɑːnt] ◇ n **1.** [angle] inclinaison f - **2.** [perspective] point m de vue, perspective f. ◇ vt [bias] présenter d'une manière tendancieuse. ◇ vi [slope] être incliné(e), pencher.

slanting ['slɑːntıŋ] adj [roof] en pente.

slap [slæp] ◇ n [slap] claque f, tape f ; [on face] gifle f. ◇ vt **1.** [person, face] gifler ; [back] donner une claque OR une tape à - **2.** [place with force] : **to slap sthg on OR onto** jeter qqch brutalement sur, flanquer qqch sur. ◇ adv inf [directly] en plein.

slapdash ['slæpdæʃ] adj inf [work] bâclé(e) ; [person, attitude] négligent(e).

slapstick ['slæpstık] n (U) grosse farce f.

slap-up adj UK inf [meal] fameux(euse).

slash [slæʃ] ◇ n **1.** [long cut] entaille f - **2.** esp US [oblique stroke] barre f oblique. ◇ vt **1.** [cut] entailler - **2.** inf [prices] casser ; [budget, unemployment] réduire considérablement.

slasher movie n film m d'horreur inf.

slat [slæt] n lame f ; [wooden] latte f.

slate [sleıt] ◇ n ardoise f. ◇ vt inf [criticize] descendre en flammes.

slaughter ['slɔːtər] ◇ n **1.** [of animals] abattage m - **2.** [of people] massacre m, carnage m. ◇ vt **1.** [animals] abattre - **2.** [people] massacrer.

slaughterhouse ['slɔːtəhaus] (pl [-hauzız]) n abattoir m.

slave [sleıv] ◇ n esclave mf. ◇ vi travailler comme un nègre ; **to slave over sthg** peiner sur qqch.

slavery ['sleıvərı] n esclavage m.

slay [sleı] (pt slew, pp slain) vt lit tuer.

sleazy ['sliːzı] adj [disreputable] mal famé(e).

sledge UK [sledʒ], **sled** US [sled] n luge f ; [larger] traîneau m.

sledgehammer ['sledʒ,hæmər] n masse f.

sleek [sli:k] *adj* **1.** [hair, fur] lisse, luisant(e) - **2.** [shape] aux lignes pures.

sleep [sli:p] ◇ *n* sommeil *m* ; **to go to sleep** s'endormir. ◇ *vi* (*pt & pp* **slept**) **1.** [be asleep] dormir - **2.** [spend night] coucher. ➡ **sleep in** *vi UK* faire la grasse matinée. ➡ **sleep with** *vt insep euph* coucher avec.

sleeper ['sli:pə˞] *n* **1.** [person]: **to be a heavy/light sleeper** avoir le sommeil lourd/léger *m* - **2.** [RAIL - berth] couchette *f* ; [- carriage] wagon-lit *m* ; [- train] train-couchettes *m* - **3.** *UK* [on railway track] traverse *f*.

sleeping bag ['sli:pɪŋ-] *n* sac *m* de couchage.

sleeping car ['sli:pɪŋ-] *n* wagon-lit *m*.

sleeping pill ['sli:pɪŋ-] *n* somnifère *m*.

sleepless ['sli:pləs] *adj* : **to have a sleepless night** passer une nuit blanche.

sleepwalk ['sli:pwɔ:k] *vi* être somnambule.

sleepy ['sli:pɪ] *adj* [person] qui a envie de dormir.

sleet [sli:t] ◇ *n* neige *f* fondue. ◇ *impers vb* : **it's sleeting** il tombe de la neige fondue.

sleeve [sli:v] *n* **1.** [of garment] manche *f* - **2.** [for record] pochette *f*.

sleigh [sleɪ] *n* traîneau *m*.

sleight of hand [,slaɪt-] *n* (U) **1.** [skill] habileté *f* - **2.** [trick] tour *m* de passe-passe.

slender ['slendə˞] *adj* **1.** [thin] mince - **2.** *fig* [resources, income] modeste, maigre ; [hope, chance] faible.

slept [slept] *pt & pp* ➡ **sleep**.

slew [slu:] ◇ *pt* ➡ **slay**. ◇ *vi* [car] déraper.

slice [slaɪs] ◇ *n* **1.** [thin piece] tranche *f* - **2.** *fig* [of profits, glory] part *f* - **3.** SPORT slice *m*. ◇ *vt* **1.** [cut into slices] couper en tranches - **2.** [cut cleanly] trancher - **3.** SPORT slicer.

slick [slɪk] ◇ *adj* **1.** [skilful] bien mené(e), habile - **2.** *pej* [superficial - talk] facile ; [- person] rusé(e). ◇ *n* nappe *f* de pétrole, marée *f* noire.

slide [slaɪd] ◇ *n* **1.** [in playground] toboggan *m* - **2.** PHOT diapositive *f*, diapo *f* - **3.** *UK* [for hair] barrette *f* - **4.** [decline] déclin *m* ; [in prices] baisse *f*. ◇ *vt* (*pt & pp* **slid** [slɪd]) faire glisser. ◇ *vi* (*pt & pp* **slid** [slɪd]) glisser.

sliding door [,slaɪdɪŋ-] *n* porte *f* coulissante.

sliding scale [,slaɪdɪŋ-] *n* échelle *f* mobile.

slight [slaɪt] ◇ *adj* **1.** [minor] léger(ère) ; **the slightest** le moindre (la moindre) ; **not in the slightest** pas du tout - **2.** [thin] mince. ◇ *n* affront *m*. ◇ *vt* offenser.

slightly ['slaɪtlɪ] *adv* [to small extent] légèrement.

slim [slɪm] ◇ *adj* **1.** [person, object] mince - **2.** [chance, possibility] faible. ◇ *vi* maigrir ; [diet] suivre un régime amaigrissant.

slime [slaɪm] *n* (U) substance *f* visqueuse ; [of snail] bave *f*.

slimming ['slɪmɪŋ] ◇ *n* amaigrissement *m*. ◇ *adj* [product] amaigrissant(e).

sling [slɪŋ] ◇ *n* **1.** [for arm] écharpe *f* - **2.** NAUT [for loads] élingue *f*. ◇ *vt* (*pt & pp* **slung**) **1.** [hammock etc] suspendre - **2.** *inf* [throw] lancer.

slip [slɪp] ◇ *n* **1.** [mistake] erreur *f* ; **a slip of the pen** un lapsus ; **a slip of the tongue** un lapsus - **2.** [of paper - gen] morceau *m* ; [- strip] bande *f* - **3.** [underwear] combinaison *f* ; **to give sb the slip** *inf* fausser compagnie à qqn. ◇ *vt* glisser ; **to slip sthg on** enfiler qqch. ◇ *vi* **1.** [slide] glisser ; **to slip into sthg** se glisser dans qqch - **2.** [decline] décliner. ➡ **slip up** *vi fig* faire une erreur.

slipped disc *UK*, **slipped disk** *US* [,slɪpt-] *n* hernie *f* discale.

slipper ['slɪpə˞] *n* pantoufle *f*, chausson *m*.

slippery ['slɪpərɪ] *adj* glissant(e).

slip road *n UK* bretelle *f*.

slipshod ['slɪpʃɒd] *adj* peu soigné(e).

slip-up *n inf* gaffe *f*.

slipway ['slɪpweɪ] *n* cale *f* de lancement.

slit [slɪt] ◇ *n* [opening] fente *f* ; [cut] incision *f*. ◇ *vt* (*pt & pp* **slit**) [make opening in] faire une fente dans, fendre ; [cut] inciser.

slither ['slɪðə˞] *vi* [person] glisser ; [snake] onduler.

sliver ['slɪvə˞] *n* [of glass, wood] éclat *m* ; [of meat, cheese] lamelle *f*.

slob [slɒb] *n inf* [in habits] saligaud *m* ; [in appearance] gros lard *m*.

slog [slɒg] *inf* ◇ *n* [tiring work] corvée *f*. ◇ *vi* [work] travailler comme un bœuf.

slogan ['sləʊgən] *n* slogan *m*.

slop [slɒp] ◇ *vt* renverser. ◇ *vi* déborder.

slope [sləʊp] ◇ *n* pente *f*. ◇ *vi* [land] être en pente ; [handwriting, table] pencher.

sloping ['sləʊpɪŋ] *adj* [land, shelf] en pente ; [handwriting] penché(e).

sloppy ['slɒpɪ] *adj* [careless] peu soigné(e).

slot [slɒt] *n* **1.** [opening] fente *f* - **2.** [groove] rainure *f* - **3.** [in schedule] créneau *m*.

slot machine n 1. [vending machine] distributeur m automatique - 2. [for gambling] machine f à sous.

slouch [slaʊtʃ] vi être avachi(e).

Slovakia [slə'vækɪə] n Slovaquie f.

slovenly ['slʌvnlɪ] adj négligé(e).

slow [sləʊ] <> adj 1. [gen] lent(e) - 2. [clock, watch] : **to be slow** retarder. <> adv lentement ; **to go slow** [driver] aller lentement ; [workers] faire la grève perlée. <> vt & vi ralentir. ➡ **slow down, slow up** vt sep & vi ralentir.

slowdown ['sləʊdaʊn] n ralentissement m.

slowly ['sləʊlɪ] adv lentement.

slow motion n : **in slow motion** au ralenti m.

sludge [slʌdʒ] n boue f.

slug [slʌg] n 1. [animal] limace f - 2. inf [of alcohol] rasade f - 3. US inf [bullet] balle f.

sluggish ['slʌgɪʃ] adj [person] apathique ; [movement, growth] lent(e) ; [business] calme, stagnant(e).

sluice [sluːs] n écluse f.

slum [slʌm] n [area] quartier m pauvre.

slumber ['slʌmbər] lit <> n sommeil m. <> vi dormir paisiblement.

slump [slʌmp] <> n 1. [decline] : **slump (in)** baisse f (de) - 2. [period of poverty] crise f (économique). <> vi lit & fig s'effondrer.

slung [slʌŋ] pt & pp ➡ sling.

slur [slɜːr] <> n 1. [slight] : **slur (on)** atteinte f (à) - 2. [insult] affront m, insulte f. <> vt mal articuler.

slush [slʌʃ] n [snow] neige f fondue.

slush fund, US slush money n fonds mpl secrets, caisse f noire.

slut [slʌt] n 1. inf [dirty, untidy] souillon f - 2. v inf [sexually immoral] salope f.

sly [slaɪ] adj (comp **slyer** OR **slier**, superl **slyest** OR **sliest**) 1. [look, smile] entendu(e) - 2. [person] rusé(e), sournois(e).

smack [smæk] <> n 1. [slap] claque f ; [on face] gifle f - 2. [impact] claquement m. <> vt 1. [slap] donner une claque à ; [face] gifler - 2. [place violently] poser violemment.

small [smɔːl] adj 1. [gen] petit(e) - 2. [trivial] petit, insignifiant(e).

small ads [-ædz] npl UK petites annonces fpl.

small change n petite monnaie f.

smallholder ['smɔːl,həʊldər] n UK petit cultivateur m.

small hours npl : **in the small hours** au petit jour OR matin.

smallpox ['smɔːlpɒks] n variole f, petite vérole f.

small print n : **the small print** les clauses fpl écrites en petits caractères.

small talk n (U) papotage m, bavardage m.

smarmy ['smɑːmɪ] adj mielleux(euse).

smart [smɑːt] <> adj 1. [stylish - person, clothes, car] élégant(e) - 2. esp US [clever] intelligent(e) - 3. [fashionable - club, society, hotel] à la mode, in (inv) - 4. [quick - answer, tap] vif (vive), rapide. <> vi 1. [eyes, skin] brûler, piquer - 2. [person] être blessé(e).

smarten ['smɑːtn] ➡ **smarten up** vt sep [room] arranger ; **to smarten o.s. up** se faire beau (belle).

smash [smæʃ] <> n 1. [sound] fracas m - 2. inf [car crash] collision f, accident m - 3. SPORT smash m. <> vt 1. [glass, plate etc] casser, briser - 2. fig [defeat] détruire. <> vi 1. [glass, plate etc] se briser - 2. [crash] : **to smash into sthg** s'écraser contre qqch.

smashing ['smæʃɪŋ] adj inf super (inv).

smattering ['smætərɪŋ] n : **to have a smattering of German** savoir quelques mots d'allemand.

smear [smɪər] <> n 1. [dirty mark] tache f - 2. MED frottis m - 3. [slander] diffamation f. <> vt 1. [smudge] barbouiller, maculer - 2. [spread] : **to smear sthg onto sthg** étaler qqch sur qqch ; **to smear sthg with sthg** enduire qqch de qqch - 3. [slander] calomnier.

smell [smel] <> n 1. [odour] odeur f - 2. [sense of smell] odorat m. <> vt (pt & pp -ed OR smelt) sentir. <> vi (pt & pp -ed OR smelt) 1. [flower, food] sentir ; **to smell of sthg** sentir qqch ; **to smell good/bad** sentir bon/mauvais - 2. [smell unpleasantly] sentir (mauvais), puer.

smelly ['smelɪ] adj qui sent mauvais, qui pue.

smelt [smelt] <> pt & pp ➡ smell. <> vt [metal] extraire par fusion ; [ore] fondre.

smile [smaɪl] <> n sourire m. <> vi sourire.

smiley ['smaɪlɪ] n smiley.

smirk [smɜːk] n sourire m narquois.

smock [smɒk] n blouse f.

smog [smɒg] n smog m.

smoke [sməʊk] <> n (U) [from fire] fumée f. <> vt & vi fumer.

smoked [sməʊkt] adj [food] fumé(e).

smoker ['sməʊkər] n 1. [person] fumeur m, -euse f - 2. RAIL compartiment m fumeurs.

smokescreen ['sməʊkskriːn] n fig couverture f.

smoke shop n US bureau m de tabac.

smoking ['sməʊkɪŋ] n tabagisme m ; **'no smoking'** 'défense de fumer'.

smoking gun n l'arme f du crime fig.

smoky ['sməʊkɪ] *adj* **1.** [room, air] enfumé(e) - **2.** [taste] fumé(e).

smolder *US* = **smoulder**.

smooth [smu:ð] <> *adj* **1.** [surface] lisse - **2.** [sauce] homogène, onctueux(euse) - **3.** [movement] régulier(ère) - **4.** [taste] moelleux(euse) - **5.** [flight, ride] confortable ; [landing, take-off] en douceur - **6.** *pej* [person, manner] doucereux(euse), mielleux(euse) - **7.** [operation, progress] sans problèmes. <> *vt* [hair] lisser ; [clothes, tablecloth] défroisser. ◆ **smooth out** *vt sep* défroisser.

smother ['smʌðər] *vt* **1.** [cover thickly] : **to smother sb/sthg with** couvrir qqn/qqch de - **2.** [person, fire] étouffer - **3.** *fig* [emotions] cacher, étouffer.

smoulder, *US* **smolder** ['sməʊldər] *vi lit & fig* couver.

SMS [,esem'es] (*abbrev of* **short message system**) *n* sms *m*, texto *m*, mini-message *m*.

smudge [smʌdʒ] <> *n* tache *f* ; [of ink] bavure *f*. <> *vt* [drawing, painting] maculer ; [paper] faire une marque OR trace sur ; [face] salir.

smug [smʌg] *adj* suffisant(e).

smuggle ['smʌgl] *vt* [across frontiers] faire passer en contrebande.

smuggler ['smʌglər] *n* contrebandier *m*, -ère *f*.

smuggling ['smʌglɪŋ] *n* (U) contrebande *f*.

smutty ['smʌtɪ] *adj pej* [book, language] cochon(onne).

snack [snæk] *n* casse-croûte *m inv*.

snack bar *n* snack *m*, snack-bar *m*.

snag [snæg] <> *n* [problem] inconvénient *m*, écueil *m*. <> *vi* : **to snag (on)** s'accrocher (à).

snail [sneɪl] *n* escargot *m*.

snail mail *n inf* poste *f*.

snake [sneɪk] *n* serpent *m*.

snap [snæp] <> *adj* [decision, election] subit(e) ; [judgment] irréfléchi(e). <> *n* **1.** [of branch] craquement *m* ; [of fingers] claquement *m* - **2.** [photograph] photo *f* - **3.** *UK* [card game] ≃ bataille *f* - **4.** *US inf* [easy task] : **it's a snap!** c'est simple comme bonjour! <> *vt* **1.** [break] casser net - **2.** [speak sharply] dire d'un ton sec. <> *vi* **1.** [break] se casser net - **2.** [dog] : **to snap at sb** essayer de mordre - **3.** [speak sharply] : **to snap (at sb)** parler (à qqn) d'un ton sec. ◆ **snap up** *vt sep* [bargain] sauter sur.

snap fastener *n esp US* pression *f*.

snappy ['snæpɪ] *adj inf* **1.** [stylish] chic - **2.** [quick] prompt(e) ; **make it snappy!** dépêche-toi!, et que ça saute!

snapshot ['snæpʃɒt] *n* photo *f*.

snare [sneər] <> *n* piège *m*, collet *m*. <> *vt* prendre au piège, attraper.

snarl [snɑːl] <> *n* grondement *m*. <> *vi* gronder.

snatch [snætʃ] <> *n* [of conversation] bribe *f* ; [of song] extrait *m*. <> *vt* [grab] saisir.

sneak [sni:k] <> *n UK inf* rapporteur *m*, -euse *f*. <> *vt* (*US, pt & pp* **snuck**) : **to sneak a look at sb/sthg** regarder qqn/qqch à la dérobée. <> *vi* (*US, pt & pp* **snuck**) [move quietly] se glisser.

sneakers ['sni:kəz] *npl US* tennis *mpl*, baskets *fpl*.

sneaky ['sni:kɪ] *adj inf* sournois(e).

sneer [snɪər] <> *n* [smile] sourire *m* dédaigneux ; [laugh] ricanement *m*. <> *vi* [smile] sourire dédaigneusement.

sneeze [sni:z] <> *n* éternuement *m*. <> *vi* éternuer.

snide [snaɪd] *adj* sournois(e).

sniff [snɪf] <> *vt* [smell] renifler. <> *vi* [to clear nose] renifler.

snigger ['snɪgər] <> *n* rire *m* en dessous. <> *vi* ricaner.

snip [snɪp] <> *n UK inf* [bargain] bonne affaire *f*. <> *vt* couper.

sniper ['snaɪpər] *n* tireur *m* isolé.

snippet ['snɪpɪt] *n* fragment *m*.

snivel ['snɪvl] (*UK & US*) *vi* geindre.

snob [snɒb] *n* snob *mf*.

snobbish ['snɒbɪʃ], **snobby** ['snɒbɪ] *adj* snob (*inv*).

snooker ['snu:kər] *n* [game] ≃ jeu *m* de billard.

snoop [snu:p] *vi inf* fureter.

snooty ['snu:tɪ] *adj inf* prétentieux(euse).

snooze [snu:z] <> *n* petit somme *m*. <> *vi* faire un petit somme.

snore [snɔːr] <> *n* ronflement *m*. <> *vi* ronfler.

snoring ['snɔːrɪŋ] *n* (U) ronflement *m*, ronflements *mpl*.

snorkel ['snɔːkl] *n* tuba *m*.

snort [snɔːt] <> *n* [of person] grognement *m* ; [of horse, bull] ébrouement *m*. <> *vi* [person] grogner ; [horse] s'ébrouer.

snout [snaʊt] *n* groin *m*.

snow [snəʊ] <> *n* neige *f*. <> *impers vb* neiger.

snowball ['snəʊbɔːl] <> *n* boule *f* de neige. <> *vi fig* faire boule de neige.

snowbank ['snəʊbæŋk] *n* congère *f*, banc *m* de neige *Québec*.

snowboard ['snəʊ,bɔːd] *n* surf *m* des neiges.

snowboarding ['snəʊˌbɔːdɪŋ] *n* surf *m* (des neiges).

snowbound ['snəʊbaʊnd] *adj* bloqué(e) par la neige.

snowdrift ['snəʊdrɪft] *n* congère *f*.

snowdrop ['snəʊdrɒp] *n* perce-neige *m inv*.

snowfall ['snəʊfɔːl] *n* chute *f* de neige.

snowflake ['snəʊfleɪk] *n* flocon *m* de neige.

snowman ['snəʊmæn] (*pl* -men [-men]) *n* bonhomme *m* de neige.

snowmobile ['snəʊməbiːl] *n* scooter *m* des neiges, motoneige *f Québec*.

snowplough *UK*, **snowplow** *US* ['snəʊplaʊ] *n* chasse-neige *m inv*.

snowshoe ['snəʊʃuː] *n* raquette *f*.

snowstorm ['snəʊstɔːm] *n* tempête *f* de neige.

SNP (*abbrev of* **Scottish National Party**) *n* parti nationaliste écossais.

Snr, snr *abbrev of* **senior**.

snub [snʌb] ◇ *n* rebuffade *f*. ◇ *vt* snober, ignorer.

snuck [snʌk] *US pt & pp* ► **sneak**.

snuff [snʌf] *n* tabac *m* à priser.

snug [snʌg] *adj* **1.** [person] à l'aise, confortable ; [in bed] bien au chaud - **2.** [place] douillet(ette) - **3.** [close-fitting] bien ajusté(e).

snuggle ['snʌgl] *vi* se blottir.

so [səʊ] ◇ *adv* **1.** [to such a degree] si, tellement ; **so difficult (that)...** si OR tellement difficile que... ; **don't be so stupid!** ne sois pas si bête ! ; **we had so much work!** nous avions tant de travail ! ; **I've never seen so much money/many cars** je n'ai jamais vu autant d'argent/de voitures - **2.** [in referring back to previous statement, event etc] : **so what's the point then?** alors à quoi bon ? ; **so you knew already?** alors tu le savais déjà ? ; **I don't think so** je ne crois pas ; **I'm afraid so** je crains bien que oui ; **if so** si oui ; **is that so?** vraiment ? - **3.** [also] aussi ; **so can/do/would etc I** moi aussi ; **she speaks French and so does her husband** elle parle français et son mari aussi - **4.** [in this way] : (like) **so** comme cela OR ça, de cette façon - **5.** [in expressing agreement] : **so there is** en effet, c'est vrai ; **so I see** c'est ce que je vois - **6.** [unspecified amount, limit] : **they pay us so much a week** ils nous payent tant par semaine ; **or so** environ, à peu près. ◇ *conj* alors ; **I'm away next week so I won't be there** je suis en voyage la semaine prochaine donc OR par conséquent je ne serai pas là ; **so what have you been up to?** alors, qu'est-ce que vous devenez? ; **so what?** *inf* et alors?, et après? ; **so there!** *inf* là!, et voilà! ► **so as** *conj* afin de, pour ; **we**

didn't knock so as not to disturb them nous n'avons pas frappé pour ne pas les déranger. ► **so that** *conj* [for the purpose that] pour que (+ *subjunctive*).

soak [səʊk] ◇ *vt* laisser OR faire tremper. ◇ *vi* **1.** [become thoroughly wet] : **to leave sthg to soak, to let sthg soak** laisser OR faire tremper qqch - **2.** [spread] : **to soak into sthg** tremper dans qqch ; **to soak through (sthg)** traverser (qqch). ► **soak up** *vt sep* absorber.

soaking ['səʊkɪŋ] *adj* trempé(e).

so-and-so *n inf* **1.** [to replace a name] : **Mr so-and-so** Monsieur Untel - **2.** [annoying person] enquiquineur *m*, -euse *f*.

soap [səʊp] *n* **1.** (*U*) [for washing] savon *m* - **2.** TV soap opera *m*.

soap flakes *npl* savon *m* en paillettes.

soap opera *n* soap opera *m*.

soap powder *n* lessive *f*.

soapy ['səʊpɪ] *adj* [water] savonneux(euse) ; [taste] de savon.

soar [sɔːr] *vi* **1.** [bird] planer - **2.** [balloon, kite] monter - **3.** [prices, temperature] monter en flèche.

sob [sɒb] ◇ *n* sanglot *m*. ◇ *vi* sangloter.

sober ['səʊbər] *adj* **1.** [not drunk] qui n'est pas ivre - **2.** [serious] sérieux(euse) - **3.** [plain - clothes, colours] sobre. ► **sober up** *vi* dessoûler.

sobering ['səʊbərɪŋ] *adj* qui donne à réfléchir.

so-called [-kɔːld] *adj* **1.** [misleadingly named] soi-disant (*inv*) - **2.** [widely known as] ainsi appelé(e).

soccer ['sɒkər] *n* football *m*.

sociable ['səʊʃəbl] *adj* sociable.

social ['səʊʃl] *adj* social(e).

social club *n* club *m*.

socialism ['səʊʃəlɪzm] *n* socialisme *m*.

socialist ['səʊʃəlɪst] ◇ *adj* socialiste. ◇ *n* socialiste *mf*.

socialize, *UK* **-ise** ['səʊʃəlaɪz] *vi* fréquenter des gens ; **to socialize with sb** fréquenter qqn, frayer avec qqn.

social security *n* aide *f* sociale.

social services *npl* services *mpl* sociaux.

social worker *n* assistant social *m*, assistante sociale *f*.

society [sə'saɪətɪ] *n* **1.** [gen] société *f* - **2.** [club] association *f*, club *m*.

sociology [ˌsəʊsɪ'ɒlədʒɪ] *n* sociologie *f*.

sock [sɒk] *n* chaussette *f*.

socket ['sɒkɪt] *n* **1.** [for light bulb] douille *f* ; [for plug] prise *f* de courant - **2.** [of eye] orbite *f* ; [for bone] cavité *f* articulaire.

sod [sɒd] *n* **1.** [of turf] motte *f* de gazon - **2.** UK *v inf* [person] con *m*.

soda ['səʊdə] *n* **1.** CHEM soude *f* - **2.** [soda water] eau *f* de Seltz - **3.** US [fizzy drink] soda *m*.

soda water *n* eau *f* de Seltz.

sodden ['sɒdn] *adj* trempé(e), détrempé(e).

sodium ['səʊdiəm] *n* sodium *m*.

sofa ['səʊfə] *n* canapé *m*.

Sofia ['səʊfjə] *n* Sofia.

soft [sɒft] *adj* **1.** [not hard] doux (douce), mou (molle) - **2.** [smooth, not loud, not bright] doux (douce) - **3.** [without force] léger(ère) - **4.** [caring] tendre - **5.** [lenient] faible, indulgent(e).

soft drink *n* boisson *f* non alcoolisée.

soften ['sɒfn] <> *vt* **1.** [fabric] assouplir ; [substance] ramollir ; [skin] adoucir - **2.** [shock, blow] atténuer, adoucir - **3.** [attitude] modérer, adoucir. <> *vi* **1.** [substance] se ramollir - **2.** [attitude, person] s'adoucir, se radoucir.

softhearted [,sɒft'hɑːtɪd] *adj* au cœur tendre.

softly ['sɒftlɪ] *adv* **1.** [gently, quietly] doucement - **2.** [not brightly] faiblement - **3.** [leniently] avec indulgence.

soft-spoken *adj* à la voix douce.

software ['sɒftweər] *n (U)* COMPUT logiciel *m*.

soggy ['sɒgɪ] *adj* trempé(e), détrempé(e).

soil [sɔɪl] <> *n (U)* **1.** [earth] sol *m*, terre *f* - **2.** *fig* [territory] sol *m*, territoire *m*. <> *vt* souiller, salir.

soiled [sɔɪld] *adj* sale.

solace ['sɒləs] *n lit* consolation *f*, réconfort *m*.

solar ['səʊlər] *adj* solaire.

sold [səʊld] *pt & pp* ► sell.

solder ['səʊldər] <> *n (U)* soudure *f*. <> *vt* souder.

soldier ['səʊldʒər] *n* soldat *m*.

sold-out *adj* [tickets] qui ont tous été vendus ; [play, concert] qui joue à guichets fermés.

sole [səʊl] <> *adj* **1.** [only] seul(e), unique - **2.** [exclusive] exclusif(ive). <> *n* **1.** [of foot] semelle *f* - **2.** (*pl* **sole** OR **-s**) [fish] sole *f*.

solemn ['sɒləm] *adj* solennel(elle) ; [person] sérieux(euse).

solicit [sə'lɪsɪt] <> *vt* [request] solliciter. <> *vi* [prostitute] racoler.

solicitor [sə'lɪsɪtər] *n* UK LAW notaire *m*.

solid ['sɒlɪd] <> *adj* **1.** [not fluid, sturdy, reliable] solide - **2.** [not hollow - tyres] plein(e) ; [- wood, rock, gold] massif(ive) - **3.** [without interruption] : **two hours solid** deux heures d'affilée. <> *n* solide *m*.

solidarity [,sɒlɪ'dærətɪ] *n* solidarité *f*.

solitaire [,sɒlɪ'teər] *n* **1.** [jewel, board game] solitaire *m* - **2.** US [card game] réussite *f*, patience *f*.

solitary ['sɒlɪtrɪ] *adj* **1.** [lonely, alone] solitaire - **2.** [just one] seul(e).

solitary confinement *n* isolement *m* cellulaire.

solitude ['sɒlɪtjuːd] *n* solitude *f*.

solo ['səʊləʊ] <> *adj* solo (*inv*). <> *n* (*pl* **-s**) solo *m*. <> *adv* en solo.

soloist ['səʊləʊɪst] *n* soliste *mf*.

soluble ['sɒljʊbl] *adj* soluble.

solution [sə'luːʃn] *n* **1.** [to problem] : **solution (to)** solution *f* (de) - **2.** [liquid] solution *f*.

solve [sɒlv] *vt* résoudre.

solvent ['sɒlvənt] <> *adj* FIN solvable. <> *n* dissolvant *m*, solvant *m*.

Somalia [sə'mɑːlɪə] *n* Somalie *f*.

sombre UK, **somber** US ['sɒmbər] *adj* sombre.

some [sʌm] <> *adj* **1.** [a certain amount, number of] : **some meat** de la viande ; **some money** de l'argent ; **some coffee** du café ; **some sweets** des bonbons - **2.** [fairly large number or quantity of] quelque ; **I had some difficulty getting here** j'ai eu quelque mal à venir ici ; **I've known him for some years** je le connais depuis plusieurs années OR pas mal d'années - **3.** *(contrastive use)* [certain] : **some jobs are better paid than others** certains boulots sont mieux rémunérés que d'autres ; **some people like his music** il y en a qui aiment sa musique - **4.** [in imprecise statements] quelque, quelconque ; **she married some writer or other** elle a épousé un écrivain quelconque OR quelque écrivain ; **there must be some mistake** il doit y avoir erreur - **5.** *inf* [very good] : **that was some party!** c'était une soirée formidable!, quelle soirée! <> *pron* **1.** [a certain amount] : **can I have some?** [money, milk, coffee etc] est-ce que je peux en prendre ? ; **some of it is mine** une partie est à moi - **2.** [a certain number] quelques-uns (quelques-unes), certains (certaines) ; **can I have some?** [books, pens, potatoes etc] est-ce que je peux en prendre (quelques-uns)? ; **some (of them) left early** quelques-uns d'entre eux sont partis tôt. <> *adv* quelque, environ ; **there were some 7,000 people there** il y avait quelque OR environ 7 000 personnes.

somebody ['sʌmbədɪ] *pron* quelqu'un.

someday ['sʌmdeɪ] *adv* un jour, un de ces jours.

somehow ['sʌmhaʊ], *US* **someway** ['sʌmweɪ] *adv* **1.** [by some action] d'une manière ou d'une autre - **2.** [for some reason] pour une raison ou pour une autre.

someone ['sʌmwʌn] *pron* quelqu'un.

someplace *US* = **somewhere**.

somersault ['sʌməsɔːlt] <> *n* cabriole *f*, culbute *f*. <> *vi* faire une cabriole OR culbute.

something ['sʌmθɪŋ] <> *pron* [unknown thing] quelque chose ; **something odd/interesting** quelque chose de bizarre/d'intéressant ; **or something** *inf* ou quelque chose comme ça. <> *adv* : **something like, something in the region of** environ, à peu près.

sometime ['sʌmtaɪm] <> *adj* ancien(enne). <> *adv* un de ces jours ; **sometime last week** la semaine dernière.

sometimes ['sʌmtaɪmz] *adv* quelquefois, parfois.

someway *US* = **somehow**.

somewhat ['sʌmwɒt] *adv* quelque peu.

somewhere ['sʌmweəʳ], *US* **someplace** ['sʌmpleɪs] *adv* **1.** [unknown place] quelque part ; **somewhere else** ailleurs ; **somewhere near here** près d'ici - **2.** [used in approximations] environ, à peu près.

son [sʌn] *n* fils *m*.

song [sɒŋ] *n* chanson *f* ; [of bird] chant *m*, ramage *m*.

sonic ['sɒnɪk] *adj* sonique.

son-in-law (*pl* **sons-in-law**) *n* gendre *m*, beau-fils *m*.

sonnet ['sɒnɪt] *n* sonnet *m*.

sonny ['sʌnɪ] *n* *inf* fiston *m*.

soon [suːn] *adv* **1.** [before long] bientôt ; **soon after** peu après - **2.** [early] tôt ; **write back soon** réponds-moi vite ; **how soon will it be ready?** ce sera prêt quand?, dans combien de temps est-ce que ce sera prêt? ; **as soon as** dès que, aussitôt que.

sooner ['suːnəʳ] *adv* **1.** [in time] plus tôt ; **no sooner... than...** à peine... que... ; **sooner or later** tôt ou tard ; **the sooner the better** le plus tôt sera le mieux - **2.** [expressing preference] : **I would sooner...** je préférerais..., j'aimerais mieux...

soot [sʊt] *n* suie *f*.

soothe [suːð] *vt* calmer, apaiser.

sophisticated [sə'fɪstɪkeɪtɪd] *adj* **1.** [stylish] raffiné(e), sophistiqué(e) - **2.** [intelligent] averti(e) - **3.** [complicated] sophistiqué(e), très perfectionné(e).

sophomore ['sɒfəmɔːʳ] *n* *US* [in high school] étudiant *m*, -e *f* de seconde année.

soporific [,sɒpə'rɪfɪk] *adj* soporifique.

sopping ['sɒpɪŋ] *adj* : **sopping (wet)** tout trempé (toute trempée).

soppy ['sɒpɪ] *adj* *inf* **1.** [sentimental - book, film] à l'eau de rose ; [- person] sentimental(e) - **2.** [silly] bêta(asse), bête.

soprano [sə'prɑːnəʊ] (*pl* **-s**) *n* [person] soprano *mf* ; [voice] soprano *m*.

sorbet ['sɔːbeɪ] *n* *UK* sorbet *m*.

sorcerer ['sɔːsərəʳ] *n* sorcier *m*.

sordid ['sɔːdɪd] *adj* sordide.

sore [sɔːʳ] <> *adj* **1.** [painful] douloureux(euse) ; **to have a sore throat** avoir mal à la gorge - **2.** *US* [upset] fâché(e), contrarié(e). <> *n* plaie *f*.

sorely ['sɔːlɪ] *adv* *lit* [needed] grandement.

sorrow ['sɒrəʊ] *n* peine *f*, chagrin *m*.

sorry ['sɒrɪ] <> *adj* **1.** [expressing apology, disappointment] désolé(e) ; **to be sorry about sthg** s'excuser pour qqch ; **to be sorry to do sthg** être désolé OR regretter de faire qqch - **2.** [poor] : **in a sorry state** en piteux état, dans un triste état. <> *excl* **1.** [expressing apology] pardon!, excusez-moi! ; **sorry, we're sold out** désolé, on n'en a plus - **2.** [asking for repetition] pardon?, comment? - **3.** [to correct oneself] non, pardon OR je veux dire.

sort [sɔːt] <> *n* genre *m*, sorte *f*, espèce *f* ; **sort of** [rather] plutôt, quelque peu ; **a sort of une** espèce OR sorte de. <> *vt* trier, classer. ◆ **sort out** *vt sep* **1.** [tidy up] ranger, classer - **2.** [solve] résoudre.

sorting office ['sɔːtɪŋ-] *n* centre *m* de tri.

SOS (*abbrev of* **save our souls**) *n* SOS *m*.

so-so *inf* <> *adj* quelconque. <> *adv* comme ci comme ça.

sought [sɔːt] *pt & pp* ► **seek**.

soul [səʊl] *n* **1.** [gen] âme *f* - **2.** [music] soul *m*.

soul-destroying [-dɪ,strɔɪɪŋ] *adj* abrutissant(e).

soulful ['səʊlfʊl] *adj* [look] expressif(ive) ; [song etc] sentimental(e).

sound [saʊnd] <> *adj* **1.** [healthy - body] sain(e), en bonne santé ; [- mind] sain - **2.** [sturdy] solide - **3.** [reliable - advice] judicieux(euse), sage ; [- investment] sûr(e). <> *adv* : **to be sound asleep** dormir à poings fermés, dormir d'un sommeil profond. <> *n* son *m* ; [particular sound] bruit *m*, son *m* ; **by the sound of it...** d'après ce que j'ai compris... <> *vt* [alarm, bell] sonner. <> *vi* **1.** [make a noise] sonner, retentir ; **to sound like sthg** ressembler à qqch - **2.** [seem] sembler, avoir l'air ; **to sound like sthg** avoir l'air de qqch, sembler être qqch. ◆ **sound out** *vt sep* : **to sound sb out (on** OR **about)** sonder qqn (sur).

sound barrier *n* mur *m* du son.

sound effects npl bruitage m, effets mpl sonores.

sounding ['saʊndɪŋ] n fig & NAUT sondage m.

soundly ['saʊndlɪ] adv **1.** [beaten] à plates coutures - **2.** [sleep] profondément.

soundproof ['saʊndpruːf] adj insonorisé(e).

soundtrack ['saʊndtræk] n bande-son f.

soup [suːp] n soupe f, potage m.

soup plate n assiette f creuse OR à soupe.

soup spoon n cuiller f à soupe.

sour ['saʊər] <> adj **1.** [taste, fruit] acide, aigre - **2.** [milk] aigre - **3.** [ill-tempered] aigre, acerbe. <> vt fig faire tourner au vinaigre, faire mal tourner.

source [sɔːs] n **1.** [gen] source f - **2.** [cause] origine f, cause f.

sour grapes n (U) inf what he said was just sour grapes il a dit ça par dépit.

south [saʊθ] <> n **1.** [direction] sud m - **2.** [region] : **the south** le sud ; **the South of France** le Sud de la France, le Midi (de la France). <> adj sud (inv) ; [wind] du sud. <> adv au sud, vers le sud ; **south of** au sud de.

South Africa n Afrique f du Sud.

South African <> adj sud-africain(e). <> n [person] Sud-Africain m, -e f.

South America n Amérique f du Sud.

South American <> adj sud-américain(e). <> n [person] Sud-Américain m, -e f.

southeast [ˌsaʊθ'iːst] <> n **1.** [direction] sud-est m - **2.** [region] : **the southeast** le sud-est. <> adj au sud-est, du sud-est ; [wind] du sud-est. <> adv au sud-est, vers le sud-est ; **southeast of** au sud-est de.

southerly ['sʌðəlɪ] adj au sud, du sud ; [wind] du sud.

southern ['sʌðən] adj au sud, du sud ; [France] du Midi.

South Korea n Corée f du Sud.

South Pole n : **the South Pole** le pôle Sud.

southward ['saʊθwəd] <> adj au sud, du sud. <> adv = **southwards**.

southwards ['saʊθwədz] adv vers le sud.

southwest [ˌsaʊθ'west] <> n **1.** [direction] sud-ouest m - **2.** [region] : **the southwest** le sud-ouest. <> adj au sud-ouest, du sud-ouest ; [wind] du sud-ouest. <> adv au sud-ouest, vers le sud-ouest ; **southwest of** au sud-ouest de.

souvenir [ˌsuːvə'nɪər] n souvenir m.

sovereign ['sɒvrɪn] <> adj souverain(e). <> n **1.** [ruler] souverain m, -e f - **2.** [coin] souverain m.

soviet ['saʊvɪət] n soviet m. ◆ **Soviet** <> adj soviétique. <> n [person] Soviétique mf.

Soviet Union n : **the (former) Soviet Union** l'(ex-) Union f soviétique.

sow¹ [saʊ] (pt -ed, pp sown OR -ed) vt lit & fig semer.

sow² [saʊ] n truie f.

sown [saʊn] pp ► **sow¹**.

soya ['sɔɪə] n soja m.

soy(a) bean ['sɔɪ(ə)-] n graine f de soja.

spa [spɑː] n station f thermale.

space [speɪs] <> n **1.** [gap, roominess, outer space] espace m ; [on form] blanc m, espace - **2.** [room] place f - **3.** [of time] : **within** OR **in the space of ten minutes** en l'espace de dix minutes. <> comp spatial(e). <> vt espacer. ◆ **space out** vt sep espacer.

spacecraft ['speɪskrɑːft] (pl spacecraft) n vaisseau m spatial.

spaceman ['speɪsmæn] (pl -men [-men]) n astronaute m, cosmonaute m.

spaceship ['speɪsʃɪp] n vaisseau m spatial.

space shuttle n navette f spatiale.

spacesuit ['speɪssuːt] n combinaison f spatiale.

spacing ['speɪsɪŋ] n TYPO espacement m.

spacious ['speɪʃəs] adj spacieux(euse).

spade [speɪd] n **1.** [tool] pelle f - **2.** [playing card] pique m. ◆ **spades** npl pique m.

spaghetti [spə'getɪ] n (U) spaghettis mpl.

Spain [speɪn] n Espagne f.

spam [spæm] (pt & pp -med, cont -ming) n inf pourriel m.

spammer ['spæmər] n spammeur m.

spamming ['spæmɪŋ] n (U) spam m, arrosage m offic.

span [spæn] <> pt ► **spin**. <> n **1.** [in time] espace m de temps, durée f - **2.** [range] éventail m, gamme f - **3.** [of bird, plane] envergure f - **4.** [of bridge] travée f ; [of arch] ouverture f. <> vt **1.** [in time] embrasser, couvrir - **2.** [subj: bridge] franchir.

Spaniard ['spænjəd] n Espagnol m, -e f.

spaniel ['spænjəl] n épagneul m.

Spanish ['spænɪʃ] <> adj espagnol(e). <> n [language] espagnol m. <> npl : **the Spanish** les Espagnols.

spank [spæŋk] vt donner une fessée à, fesser.

spanner ['spænər] n UK clé f à écrous.

spar [spɑːr] <> n espar m. <> vi [in boxing] s'entraîner à la boxe.

spare [speər] <> adj **1.** [surplus] de trop ; [component, clothing etc] de réserve, de rechange ; **spare bed** lit m d'appoint

- **2.** [available - seat, time, tickets] disponible. ◇ *n* [part] pièce *f* détachée OR de rechange. ◇ *vt* **1.** [make available - staff, money] se passer de ; [- time] disposer de ; **to have an hour to spare** avoir une heure de battement OR de libre ; **with a minute to spare** avec une minute d'avance - **2.** [not harm] épargner - **3.** [not use] épargner, ménager ; **to spare no expense** ne pas regarder à la dépense - **4.** [save from] : **to spare sb sthg** épargner qqch à qqn, éviter qqch à qqn.

spare part *n* pièce *f* détachée OR de rechange.

spare time *n* (U) temps *m* libre, loisirs *mpl*.

spare wheel *n* roue *f* de secours.

sparing ['speərɪŋ] *adj* : **to be sparing with** OR **of sthg** être économe de qqch, ménager qqch.

sparingly ['speərɪŋlɪ] *adv* [use] avec modération ; [spend] avec parcimonie.

spark [spɑːk] *n* lit & fig étincelle *f*.

sparking plug ['spɑːkɪŋ-] *UK* = **spark plug**.

sparkle ['spɑːkl] ◇ *n* (U) [of eyes, jewel] éclat *m* ; [of stars] scintillement *m*. ◇ *vi* étinceler, scintiller.

sparkling wine ['spɑːklɪŋ-] *n* vin *m* mousseux.

spark plug *n* bougie *f*.

sparrow ['spærəʊ] *n* moineau *m*.

sparse [spɑːs] *adj* clairsemé(e), épars(e).

spasm ['spæzm] *n* **1.** MED spasme *m* ; [of coughing] quinte *f* - **2.** [of emotion] accès *m*.

spastic ['spæstɪk] *n* MED handicapé *m*, -e *f* moteur.

spat [spæt] *pt* & *pp* ► **spit**.

spate [speɪt] *n* [of attacks etc] série *f*.

spatter ['spætər] *vt* éclabousser.

spawn [spɔːn] ◇ *n* (U) frai *m*, œufs *mpl*. ◇ *vt* fig donner naissance à, engendrer. ◇ *vi* [fish, frog] frayer.

speak [spiːk] (*pt* **spoke**, *pp* **spoken**) ◇ *vt* **1.** [say] dire - **2.** [language] parler. ◇ *vi* [general] parler ; **to speak to** OR **with sb** parler à qqn ; **to speak to sb about sthg** parler de qqch à qqn ; **to speak about sb/sthg** parler de qqn/qqch ; **speak now or forever hold your peace** parlez maintenant ou gardez le silence pour toujours. ◆ **so to speak** *adv* pour ainsi dire. ◆ **speak for** *vt insep* [represent] parler pour, parler au nom de. ◆ **speak up** *vi* **1.** [support] : **to speak up for sb/sthg** parler en faveur de qqn/qqch, soutenir qqn/qqch - **2.** [speak louder] parler plus fort.

speaker ['spiːkər] *n* **1.** [person talking] personne *f* qui parle - **2.** [person making speech] orateur *m* - **3.** [of language] : **a German speaker** une personne qui parle allemand - **4.** [loudspeaker] haut-parleur *m*.

speaking ['spiːkɪŋ] *adv* : **politically speaking** politiquement parlant.

spear [spɪər] ◇ *n* lance *f*. ◇ *vt* transpercer d'un coup de lance.

spearhead ['spɪəhed] ◇ *n* fer *m* de lance. ◇ *vt* [campaign] mener ; [attack] être le fer de lance de.

spec [spek] *n* *UK* *inf* **on spec** à tout hasard.

special ['speʃl] *adj* **1.** [gen] spécial(e) - **2.** [needs, effort, attention] particulier(ère).

special delivery *n* (U) [service] exprès *m*, envoi *m* par exprès ; **by special delivery** en exprès.

specialist ['speʃəlɪst] ◇ *adj* spécialisé(e). ◇ *n* spécialiste *mf*.

speciality *UK* [,speʃɪ'ælətɪ], **specialty** *US* ['speʃltɪ] *n* spécialité *f*.

specialize, *UK* **-ise** ['speʃəlaɪz] *vi* : **to specialize (in)** se spécialiser (dans).

specially ['speʃəlɪ] *adv* **1.** [specifically] spécialement ; [on purpose] exprès - **2.** [particularly] particulièrement.

specialty *n* *US* = **speciality**.

species ['spiːʃiːz] (*pl* **species**) *n* espèce *f*.

specific [spə'sɪfɪk] *adj* **1.** [particular] particulier(ère), précis(e) - **2.** [precise] précis(e) - **3.** [unique] : **specific to** propre à.

specifically [spə'sɪfɪklɪ] *adv* **1.** [particularly] particulièrement, spécialement - **2.** [precisely] précisément.

specify ['spesɪfaɪ] *vt* préciser, spécifier.

specimen ['spesɪmən] *n* **1.** [example] exemple *m*, spécimen *m* - **2.** [of blood] prélèvement *m* ; [of urine] échantillon *m*.

speck [spek] *n* **1.** [small stain] toute petite tache *f* - **2.** [of dust] grain *m*.

speckled ['spekld] *adj* : **speckled (with)** tacheté(e) de.

specs [speks] *npl* *inf* [glasses] lunettes *fpl*.

spectacle ['spektəkl] *n* spectacle *m*. ◆ **spectacles** *npl* [glasses] lunettes *fpl*.

spectacular [spek'tækjʊlər] *adj* spectaculaire.

spectator [spek'teɪtər] *n* spectateur *m*, -trice *f*.

spectre *UK*, **specter** *US* ['spektər] *n* spectre *m*.

spectrum ['spektrəm] (*pl* **-tra** [-trə]) *n* **1.** PHYS spectre *m* - **2.** fig [variety] gamme *f*.

speculation [,spekjʊ'leɪʃn] *n* **1.** [gen] spéculation *f* - **2.** [conjecture] conjectures *fpl*.

sped [sped] *pt* & *pp* ► **speed**.

speech [spiːtʃ] *n* **1.** (U) [ability] parole *f*

- **2.** [formal talk] discours *m* - **3.** THEAT texte *m* - **4.** [manner of speaking] façon *f* de parler - **5.** [dialect] parler *m*.

speechless ['spi:tʃlɪs] *adj* : speechless (with) muet(ette) (de).

speed [spi:d] ⬦ *n* vitesse *f* ; [of reply, action] vitesse, rapidité *f*. ⬦ *vi (pt & pp -ed* OR **sped)** **1.** [move fast] : **to speed along** aller à toute allure OR vitesse ; **to speed away** démarrer à toute allure - **2.** AUT [go too fast] rouler trop vite, faire un excès de vitesse. ⬗ **speed up** ⬦ *vt sep* [person] faire aller plus vite ; [work, production] accélérer. ⬦ *vi* aller plus vite ; [car] accélérer.

speedboat ['spi:dbəʊt] *n* hors-bord *m inv*.

speed bump *n* dos-d'âne *m inv*.

speed-dialling *UK*, **speed-dialing** *US n* (*U*) TELEC numérotation *f* rapide.

speeding ['spi:dɪŋ] *n* (*U*) excès *m* de vitesse.

speed limit *n* limitation *f* de vitesse.

speedometer [spɪ'dɒmɪtər] *n* compteur *m* (de vitesse).

speedway ['spi:dweɪ] *n* **1.** (*U*) SPORT course *f* de motos - **2.** *US* [road] voie *f* express.

speedy ['spi:dɪ] *adj* rapide.

spell [spel] ⬦ *n* **1.** [period of time] période *f* - **2.** [enchantment] charme *m* ; [words] formule *f* magique ; **to cast** OR **put a spell on sb** jeter un sort à qqn, envoûter qqn. ⬦ *vt (UK, pt & pp* **spelt** OR **-ed** *US, pt & pp* **-ed**) **1.** [word, name] écrire - **2.** *fig* [signify] signifier. ⬦ *vi (UK, pt & pp* **spelt** OR **-ed** *US, pt & pp* **-ed**) épeler. ⬗ **spell out** *vt sep* **1.** [read aloud] épeler - **2.** [explain] : **to spell sthg out (for** OR **to sb)** expliquer qqch clairement (à qqn).

spellbound ['spelbaʊnd] *adj* subjugué(e).

spell-check ⬦ *vt* [text, file, document] vérifier l'orthographe de. ⬦ *n* vérification *f* orthographique.

spell-checker [-tʃekər] *n* correcteur *m* OR vérificateur *m* orthographique.

spelling ['spelɪŋ] *n* orthographe *f*.

spelt [spelt] *UK pt & pp* ➤ **spell**.

spelunking [spe'lʌŋkɪŋ] *n US* spéléologie *f*.

spend [spend] (*pt & pp* **spent**) *vt* **1.** [pay out] : **to spend money (on)** dépenser de l'argent (pour) - **2.** [time, life] passer ; [effort] consacrer.

spendthrift ['spendθrɪft] *n* dépensier *m*, -ère *f*.

spent [spent] ⬦ *pt & pp* ➤ **spend**. ⬦ *adj* [fuel, match, ammunition] utilisé(e) ; [patience, energy] épuisé(e).

sperm [spɜːm] (*pl* **sperm** OR **-s**) *n* sperme *m*.

spew [spju:] *vt & vi* vomir.

sphere [sfɪər] *n* sphère *f*.

spice [spaɪs] *n* **1.** CULIN épice *f* - **2.** (*U*) *fig* [excitement] piment *m*.

spick-and-span [,spɪkən'spæn] *adj* impeccable, nickel (*inv*).

spicy ['spaɪsɪ] *adj* **1.** CULIN épicé(e) - **2.** *fig* [story] pimenté(e), piquant(e).

spider ['spaɪdər] *n* araignée *f*.

spike [spaɪk] *n* [metal] pointe *f*, lance *f* ; [of plant] piquant *m* ; [of hair] épi *m*.

spill [spɪl] (*UK, pt & pp* **spilt** OR **-ed** *US, pt & pp* **-ed**) ⬦ *vt* renverser. ⬦ *vi* [liquid] se répandre.

spilt [spɪlt] *UK pt & pp* ➤ **spill**.

spin [spɪn] ⬦ *n* **1.** [turn] : **to give sthg a spin** faire tourner qqch - **2.** AERON vrille *f* - **3.** *inf* [in car] tour *m* - **4.** SPORT effet *m*. ⬦ *vt (pt* **span** OR **spun,** *pp* **spun**) **1.** [wheel] faire tourner ; **to spin a coin** jouer à pile ou face - **2.** [washing] essorer - **3.** [thread, wool, cloth] filer - **4.** SPORT [ball] donner de l'effet à. ⬦ *vi (pt* **span** OR **spun,** *pp* **spun**) tourner, tournoyer. ⬗ **spin out** *vt sep* [money, story] faire durer.

spinach ['spɪnɪdʒ] *n* (*U*) épinards *mpl*.

spinal column ['spaɪnl-] *n* colonne *f* vertébrale.

spinal cord ['spaɪnl-] *n* moelle *f* épinière.

spindly ['spɪndlɪ] *adj* grêle, chétif(ive).

spin-dryer *n UK* essoreuse *f*.

spine [spaɪn] *n* **1.** ANAT colonne *f* vertébrale - **2.** [of book] dos *m* - **3.** [of plant, hedgehog] piquant *m*.

spinning ['spɪnɪŋ] *n* [of thread] filage *m*.

spinning top *n* toupie *f*.

spin-off *n* [by-product] dérivé *m*.

spinster ['spɪnstər] *n* célibataire *f* ; *pej* vieille fille *f*.

spiral ['spaɪərəl] ⬦ *adj* spiral(e). ⬦ *n* spirale *f*. ⬦ *vi (UK & US)* [staircase, smoke] monter en spirale.

spiral staircase *n* escalier *m* en colimaçon.

spire [spaɪər] *n* flèche *f*.

spirit ['spɪrɪt] *n* **1.** [gen] esprit *m* - **2.** (*U*) [determination] caractère *m*, courage *m*. ⬗ **spirits** *npl* **1.** [mood] humeur *f* ; **to be in high spirits** être gai(e) ; **to be in low spirits** être déprimé(e) - **2.** [alcohol] spiritueux *mpl*. ⬗ **spirit away** *vt sep* [carry off secretly] faire disparaître (comme par enchantement) ; [steal] escamoter, subtiliser.

spirited ['spɪrɪtɪd] *adj* fougueux(euse) ; [performance] interprété(e) avec brio.

spirit level *n* niveau *m* à bulle d'air.

spiritual ['spɪrɪtʃʊəl] *adj* spirituel(elle).

spit [spɪt] ⬦ *n* **1.** (*U*) [spittle] crachat *m* ; [saliva] salive *f* - **2.** [skewer] broche *f*. ⬦ *vi*

(UK, pt & pp **spat** US, pt & pp **spit**) cracher. ◇ *impers vb* (pt & pp **spat**) UK : **it's spitting** il tombe quelques gouttes.

spite [spaɪt] ◇ n rancune f. ◇ vt contrarier. ➠ **in spite of** prep en dépit de, malgré.

spiteful ['spaɪtfʊl] adj malveillant(e).

spittle ['spɪtl] n (U) crachat m.

splash [splæʃ] ◇ n **1.** [sound] plouf m - **2.** [of colour, light] tache f. ◇ vt [with water, mud] éclabousser. ◇ vi **1.** [person] : **to splash about** OR **around** barboter - **2.** [liquid] jaillir. ➠ **splash out** inf vi : **to splash out (on)** dépenser une fortune (pour).

spleen [spliːn] n **1.** ANAT rate f - **2.** (U) fig [anger] mauvaise humeur f.

splendid ['splendɪd] adj splendide ; [work, holiday, idea] excellent(e).

splint [splɪnt] n attelle f.

splinter ['splɪntər] ◇ n éclat m. ◇ vi [wood] - tear] se fendre en éclats ; [glass] se briser en éclats.

split [splɪt] ◇ n **1.** [in wood] fente f - **2.** [in garment - tear] déchirure f ; [- by design] échancrure f - **3.** POL : **split (in)** division f OR scission f (au sein de) - **4.** [difference] : **split between** écart m entre. ◇ vt (pt & pp **split**, cont **-ting**) **1.** [wood] fendre - **2.** [clothes] déchirer - **3.** [family & POL] diviser - **4.** [share] partager ; **to split the difference** fig couper la poire en deux. ◇ vi (pt & pp **split**, cont **-ting**) **1.** [wood] se fendre ; [clothes] se déchirer - **2.** POL se diviser ; [road, path] se séparer. ➠ **split up** vi [group, couple] se séparer.

split second n fraction f de seconde.

splutter ['splʌtər] vi [person] bredouiller, bafouiller ; [engine] tousser ; [fire] crépiter.

spoil [spɔɪl] (pt & pp **-ed** UK, pt & pp **spoilt**) vt **1.** [ruin - holiday] gâcher, gâter ; [- view] gâter ; [- food] gâter, abîmer - **2.** [over-indulge, treat well] gâter. ➠ **spoils** npl butin m.

spoiled [spɔɪld] adj = spoilt.

spoilsport ['spɔɪlspɔːt] n trouble-fête mf inv.

spoilt [spɔɪlt] ◇ pt & pp UK ➠ spoil. ◇ adj [child] gâté(e).

spoke [spəʊk] ◇ pt ➠ speak. ◇ n rayon m.

spoken ['spəʊkn] pp ➠ speak.

spokesman ['spəʊksmən] (pl **-men** [-mən]) n porte-parole m inv.

spokeswoman ['spəʊks,wʊmən] (pl **-women** [-,wɪmɪn]) n porte-parole f inv.

sponge [spʌndʒ] ◇ n **1.** [for cleaning, washing] éponge f - **2.** [cake] gâteau m OR biscuit m de Savoie. ◇ vt (UK, cont

spongeing US, cont **sponging**) éponger. ◇ vi (UK, cont **spongeing** US, cont **sponging**) inf **to sponge off sb** taper qqn.

sponge bag n UK trousse f de toilette.

sponge bath n toilette f d'un malade.

sponge cake n gâteau m OR biscuit m de Savoie.

sponsor ['spɒnsər] ◇ n sponsor m. ◇ vt **1.** [finance, for charity] sponsoriser, parrainer - **2.** [support] soutenir.

sponsored walk [,spɒnsəd-] n UK marche organisée pour recueillir des fonds.

sponsorship ['spɒnsəʃɪp] n sponsoring m, parrainage m.

spontaneous [spɒn'teɪnjəs] adj spontané(e).

spooky ['spuːkɪ] adj inf qui donne la chair de poule.

spool [spuːl] n [gen & COMPUT] bobine f.

spoon [spuːn] n cuillère f, cuiller f.

spoon-feed vt nourrir à la cuillère ; **to spoon-feed sb** fig mâcher le travail à qqn.

spoonful ['spuːnfʊl] (pl **-s** OR **spoonsful** ['spuːnsfʊl]) n cuillerée f.

sporadic [spə'rædɪk] adj sporadique.

sport [spɔːt] n **1.** [game] sport m - **2.** dated [cheerful person] chic type m /fille f.

sporting ['spɔːtɪŋ] adj **1.** [relating to sport] sportif(ive) - **2.** [generous, fair] chic (inv) ; **to have a sporting chance of doing sthg** avoir des chances de faire qqch.

sports car ['spɔːts-] n voiture f de sport.

sports jacket ['spɔːts-] n veste f sport.

sportsman ['spɔːtsmən] (pl **-men** [-mən]) n sportif m.

sportsmanship ['spɔːtsmənʃɪp] n sportivité f, esprit m sportif.

sportswear ['spɔːtsweər] n (U) vêtements mpl de sport.

sportswoman ['spɔːts,wʊmən] (pl **-women** [-,wɪmɪn]) n sportive f.

sporty ['spɔːtɪ] adj inf [person] sportif(ive).

spot [spɒt] ◇ n **1.** [mark, dot] tache f - **2.** UK [pimple] bouton m - **3.** [drop] goutte f - **4.** UK inf [small amount] : **to have a spot of bother** avoir quelques ennuis - **5.** [place] endroit m ; **on the spot** sur place ; **to do sthg on the spot** faire qqch immédiatement OR sur-le-champ - **6.** RADIO & TV numéro m. ◇ vt [notice] apercevoir.

spot check n contrôle m au hasard OR intermittent.

spotless ['spɒtlɪs] adj [clean] impeccable.

spotlight ['spɒtlaɪt] n [in theatre] projecteur m, spot m ; [in home] spot m ; **to be in the spotlight** fig être en vedette.

spotted ['spɒtɪd] *adj* [pattern, material] à pois.

spotty ['spɒtɪ] *adj UK* [skin] boutonneux(euse).

spouse [spaʊs] *n* époux *m*, épouse *f*.

spout [spaʊt] ◇ *n* bec *m*. ◇ *vi* : **to spout from** OR **out of** jaillir de.

sprain [spreɪn] ◇ *n* entorse *f*. ◇ *vt* : **to sprain one's ankle/wrist** se faire une entorse à la cheville/au poignet, se fouler la cheville/le poignet.

sprang [spræŋ] *pt* ➤ **spring**.

sprawl [sprɔːl] *vi* **1.** [person] être affalé(e) - **2.** [city] s'étaler.

spray [spreɪ] ◇ *n* **1.** (U) [of water] gouttelettes *fpl* ; [from sea] embruns *mpl* - **2.** [container] bombe *f*, pulvérisateur *m* - **3.** [of flowers] gerbe *f*. ◇ *vt* [product] pulvériser ; [plants, crops] pulvériser de l'insecticide sur.

spread [spred] ◇ *n* **1.** (U) [food] pâte *f* à tartiner - **2.** [of fire, disease] propagation *f* - **3.** [of opinions] gamme *f*. ◇ *vt* (*pt* & *pp* **spread**) **1.** [map, rug] étaler, étendre ; [fingers, arms, legs] écarter - **2.** [butter, jam etc] : **to spread sthg (on)** étaler qqch (sur) - **3.** [disease, rumour, germs] répandre, propager - **4.** [wealth, work] distribuer, répartir. ◇ *vi* (*pt* & *pp* **spread**) **1.** [disease, rumour] se propager, se répandre - **2.** [water, cloud] s'étaler. ➡ **spread out** *vi* se disperser.

spread-eagled [-,iːgld] *adj* affalé(e).

spreadsheet ['spredʃiːt] *n* COMPUT tableur *m*.

spree [spriː] *n* : **to go on a spending** OR **shopping spree** faire des folies.

sprightly ['spraɪtlɪ] *adj* alerte, fringant(e).

spring [sprɪŋ] ◇ *n* **1.** [season] printemps *m* ; **in spring** au printemps - **2.** [coil] ressort *m* - **3.** [water source] source *f*. ◇ *vi* (*pt* **sprang**, *pp* **sprung**) **1.** [jump] sauter, bondir - **2.** [originate] : **to spring from** provenir de. ➡ **spring up** *vi* [problem] surgir, se présenter ; [friendship] naître ; [wind] se lever.

springboard ['sprɪŋbɔːd] *n lit & fig* tremplin *m*.

spring-clean *vt* nettoyer de fond en comble.

spring onion *n UK* ciboule *f*.

springtime ['sprɪŋtaɪm] *n* : **in (the) springtime** au printemps.

springy ['sprɪŋɪ] *adj* [carpet] moelleux(euse) ; [mattress, rubber] élastique.

sprinkle ['sprɪŋkl] *vt* : **to sprinkle water over** OR **on sthg, to sprinkle sthg with water** asperger qqch d'eau ; **to sprinkle salt** *etc* **over** OR **on sthg, to sprinkle sthg with salt** *etc* saupoudrer qqch de sel *etc*.

sprinkler ['sprɪŋklər] *n* [for water] arroseur *m*.

sprint [sprɪnt] ◇ *n* sprint *m*. ◇ *vi* sprinter.

sprout [spraʊt] ◇ *n* **1.** [vegetable] : **(Brussels) sprouts** choux *mpl* de Bruxelles - **2.** [shoot] pousse *f*. ◇ *vt* [leaves] produire ; **to sprout shoots** germer. ◇ *vi* [grow] pousser.

spruce [spruːs] ◇ *adj* net (nette), pimpant(e). ◇ *n* épicéa *m*. ➡ **spruce up** *vt sep* astiquer, briquer.

sprung [sprʌŋ] *pp* ➤ **spring**.

spry [spraɪ] *adj* vif (vive).

spun [spʌn] *pt* & *pp* ➤ **spin**.

spur [spɜːr] ◇ *n* **1.** [incentive] incitation *f* - **2.** [on rider's boot] éperon *m*. ◇ *vt* [encourage] : **to spur sb to do sthg** encourager OR inciter qqn à faire qqch. ➡ **on the spur of the moment** *adv* sur un coup de tête, sous l'impulsion du moment. ➡ **spur on** *vt sep* encourager.

spurious ['spʊərɪəs] *adj* **1.** [affection, interest] feint(e) - **2.** [argument, logic] faux (fausse).

spurn [spɜːn] *vt* repousser.

spurt [spɜːt] ◇ *n* **1.** [gush] jaillissement *m* - **2.** [of activity, energy] sursaut *m* - **3.** [burst of speed] accélération *f*. ◇ *vi* [gush] : **to spurt (out of** OR **from)** jaillir (de).

spy [spaɪ] ◇ *n* espion *m*. ◇ *vt inf* apercevoir. ◇ *vi* espionner, faire de l'espionnage ; **to spy on sb** espionner qqn.

spying ['spaɪɪŋ] *n* (U) espionnage *m*.

Sq., sq. *abbrev of* **square**.

squabble ['skwɒbl] ◇ *n* querelle *f*. ◇ *vi* : **to squabble (about** OR **over)** se quereller (à propos de).

squad [skwɒd] *n* **1.** [of police] brigade *f* - **2.** MIL peloton *m* - **3.** SPORT [group of players] équipe *f (parmi laquelle la sélection sera faite)*.

squadron ['skwɒdrən] *n* escadron *m*.

squalid ['skwɒlɪd] *adj* sordide, ignoble.

squall [skwɔːl] *n* [storm] bourrasque *f*.

squalor ['skwɒlər] *n* (U) conditions *fpl* sordides.

squander ['skwɒndər] *vt* gaspiller.

square [skweər] ◇ *adj* **1.** [in shape] carré(e) ; **one square metre** *UK* un mètre carré ; **three metres square** trois mètres sur trois - **2.** [not owing money] être quitte ; **to be square** être quitte. ◇ *n* **1.** [shape & MATHS] carré *m* - **2.** [in town] place *f* - **3.** *inf* [unfashionable person] : **he's a square** il est vieux jeu. ◇ *vt* **1.** MATHS élever au carré

- **2.** [reconcile] accorder. ◆ **square up** *vi* [settle up] : **to square up with sb** régler ses comptes avec qqn.

squarely ['skweəlɪ] *adv* **1.** [directly] carrément - **2.** [honestly] honnêtement.

square meal *n* bon repas *m*.

squash [skwɒʃ] ◇ *n* **1.** SPORT squash *m* - **2.** UK [drink] : **orange squash** orangeade *f* - **3.** [vegetable] courge *f*. ◇ *vt* écraser.

squat [skwɒt] ◇ *adj* courtaud(e), ramassé(e). ◇ *vi* [crouch] : **to squat (down)** s'accroupir.

squatter ['skwɒtər] *n* squatter *m*.

squawk [skwɔːk] *n* cri *m* strident OR perçant.

squeak [skwiːk] *n* **1.** [of animal] petit cri *m* aigu - **2.** [of door, hinge] grincement *m*.

squeal [skwiːl] *vi* [person, animal] pousser des cris aigus.

squeamish ['skwiːmɪʃ] *adj* facilement dégoûté(e).

squeeze [skwiːz] ◇ *n* [pressure] pression *f*. ◇ *vt* **1.** [press firmly] presser - **2.** [liquid, toothpaste] exprimer - **3.** [cram] : **to squeeze sthg into sthg** entasser qqch dans qqch.

squelch [skweltʃ] *vi* : **to squelch through mud** patauger dans la boue.

squid [skwɪd] (*pl* **squid** OR **-s**) *n* calmar *m*.

squiggle ['skwɪgl] *n* gribouillis *m*.

squint [skwɪnt] ◇ *n* : **to have a squint** loucher, être atteint(e) de strabisme. ◇ *vi* : **to squint at sthg** regarder qqch en plissant les yeux.

squire ['skwaɪər] *n* [landowner] propriétaire *m*.

squirm [skwɜːm] *vi* [wriggle] se tortiller.

squirrel [UK 'skwɪrəl, US 'skwɜːrəl] *n* écureuil *m*.

squirt [skwɜːt] ◇ *vt* [water, oil] faire jaillir, faire gicler. ◇ *vi* : **to squirt (out of)** jaillir (de), gicler (de).

Sr *abbrev of* **senior**.

Sri Lanka [ˌsriːˈlæŋkə] *n* Sri Lanka *m*.

St 1. (*abbrev of* **saint**) St, Ste - **2.** *abbrev of* **Street**.

stab ◇ *n* **1.** [with knife] coup *m* de couteau - **2.** *inf* [attempt] : **to have a stab (at sthg)** essayer (qqch), tenter (qqch) - **3.** [twinge] : **stab of pain** élancement *m* ; **stab of guilt** remords *m*. ◇ *vt* [stab] **1.** [person] poignarder - **2.** [food] piquer.

stable ['steɪbl] ◇ *adj* stable. ◇ *n* écurie *f*.

stack [stæk] ◇ *n* [pile] pile *f*. ◇ *vt* [pile up] empiler.

stadium ['steɪdjəm] (*pl* **-diums** OR **-dia** [-djə]) *n* stade *m*.

staff [stɑːf] ◇ *n* [employees] personnel *m* ; [of school] personnel enseignant, professeurs *mpl*. ◇ *vt* pourvoir en personnel.

stag [stæg] (*pl* **stag** OR **-s**) *n* cerf *m*.

stage [steɪdʒ] ◇ *n* **1.** [phase] étape *f*, phase *f*, stade *m* - **2.** [platform] scène *f* - **3.** [acting profession] : **the stage** le théâtre. ◇ *vt* **1.** THEAT monter, mettre en scène - **2.** [organize] organiser.

stagecoach ['steɪdʒkəʊtʃ] *n* diligence *f*.

stage fright *n* trac *m*.

stage-manage *vt lit & fig* mettre en scène.

stagger ['stægər] ◇ *vt* **1.** [astound] stupéfier - **2.** [working hours] échelonner ; [holidays] étaler. ◇ *vi* tituber.

stagnant ['stægnənt] *adj* stagnant(e).

stagnate [stæg'neɪt] *vi* stagner.

staid [steɪd] *adj* guindé(e), collet monté.

stain [steɪn] ◇ *n* [mark] tache *f*. ◇ *vt* [discolour] tacher.

stained glass [ˌsteɪnd-] *n* (*U*) [windows] vitraux *mpl*.

stainless steel ['steɪnlɪs-] *n* acier *m* inoxydable, Inox® *m*.

stain remover [-ˌrɪmuːvər] *n* détachant *m*.

stair [steər] *n* marche *f*. ◆ **stairs** *npl* escalier *m*.

staircase ['steəkeɪs] *n* escalier *m*.

stairway ['steəweɪ] *n* escalier *m*.

stairwell ['steəwel] *n* cage *f* d'escalier.

stake [steɪk] ◇ *n* **1.** [share] : **to have a stake in sthg** avoir des intérêts dans qqch - **2.** [wooden post] poteau *m* - **3.** [in gambling] enjeu *m*. ◇ *vt* : **to stake money (on** OR **upon)** jouer OR miser de l'argent (sur) ; **to stake one's reputation (on)** jouer OR risquer sa réputation (sur). ◆ **at stake** *adv* en jeu.

stale [steɪl] *adj* [food, water] pas frais (fraîche) ; [bread] rassis(e) ; [air] qui sent le renfermé.

stalemate ['steɪlmeɪt] *n* **1.** [deadlock] impasse *f* - **2.** CHESS pat *m*.

stalk [stɔːk] ◇ *n* **1.** [of flower, plant] tige *f* - **2.** [of leaf, fruit] queue *f*. ◇ *vt* [hunt] traquer. ◇ *vi* : **to stalk in/out** entrer/sortir d'un air hautain.

stall [stɔːl] ◇ *n* **1.** [in street, market] éventaire *m*, étal *m* ; [at exhibition] stand *m* - **2.** [in stable] stalle *f*. ◇ *vt* AUT caler. ◇ *vi* **1.** AUT caler - **2.** [delay] essayer de gagner du temps. ◆ **stalls** *npl* UK [in cinema, theatre] orchestre *m*.

stallion ['stæljən] *n* étalon *m*.

stalwart ['stɔːlwət] *n* pilier *m*.

stamina ['stæmɪnə] *n* (*U*) résistance *f*.

stammer ['stæmər] <> n bégaiement m. <> vi bégayer.

stamp [stæmp] <> n 1. [for letter] timbre m - 2. [tool] tampon m - 3. fig [of authority etc] marque f. <> vt 1. [mark by stamping] tamponner - 2. [stomp] : **to stamp one's foot** taper du pied. <> vi 1. [stomp] taper du pied - 2. [tread heavily] : **to stamp on sthg** marcher sur qqch.

stamp album n album m de timbres.

stamp-collecting [-kə,lektɪŋ] n philatélie f.

stamped addressed envelope ['stæmptə,drest-] n enveloppe f affranchie pour la réponse.

stampede [stæm'piːd] n débandade f.

stance [stæns] n lit & fig position f.

stand [stænd] <> n 1. [stall] stand m ; [selling newspapers] kiosque m - 2. SPORT tribune f - 3. MIL résistance f ; **to make a stand** résister - 4. [public position] position f - 5. US LAW barre f. <> vt (pt & pp **stood**) 1. [place] mettre (debout), poser (debout) - 2. [withstand, tolerate] supporter. <> vi (pt & pp **stood**) 1. [be upright - person] être OR se tenir debout ; [- object] se trouver ; [- building] se dresser ; **stand still!** ne bouge pas!, reste tranquille! - 2. [stand up] se lever - 3. [remain] reposer - 4. [offer] tenir toujours ; [decision] demeurer valable - 5. [be in particular state] : **as things stand...** vu l'état actuel des choses... - 6. UK POL se présenter - 7. US [park car] se garer (pour un court instant) ; **'no standing'** 'stationnement interdit'. ◆ **stand back** vi reculer. ◆ **stand by** <> vt insep 1. [person] soutenir - 2. [statement, decision] s'en tenir à. <> vi [remain inactive] rester là. ◆ **stand down** vi UK [resign] démissionner. ◆ **stand for** vt insep 1. [signify] représenter - 2. [tolerate] supporter, tolérer. ◆ **stand in** vi : **to stand in for sb** remplacer qqn. ◆ **stand out** vi ressortir. ◆ **stand up** <> vt sep inf [boyfriend, girlfriend] poser un lapin à. <> vi [rise from seat] se lever ; **stand up!** debout! ◆ **stand up for** vt insep défendre. ◆ **stand up to** vt insep 1. [weather, heat etc] résister à - 2. [person, boss] tenir tête à.

standard ['stændəd] <> adj 1. [normal - gen] normal(e) ; [- size] standard (inv) - 2. [accepted] correct(e). <> n 1. [level] niveau m - 2. [point of reference] critère m ; TECH norme f - 3. [flag] étendard m. ◆ **standards** npl [principles] valeurs fpl.

standard lamp n UK lampadaire m.

standard of living (pl **standards of living**) n niveau m de vie.

standby ['stændbaɪ] <> n (pl -s) [person] remplaçant m, -e f ; **on standby** prêt à intervenir. <> comp [ticket, flight] stand-by (inv).

stand-in n remplaçant m, -e f.

standing ['stændɪŋ] <> adj [invitation, army] permanent(e) ; [joke] continuel(elle). <> n 1. [reputation] importance f, réputation f - 2. [duration] : **of long standing** de longue date ; **we're friends of 20 years' standing** nous sommes amis depuis 20 ans.

standing order n UK prélèvement m automatique.

standing room n (U) places fpl debout.

standoffish [,stænd'ɒfɪʃ] adj distant(e).

standpoint ['stændpɔɪnt] n point m de vue.

standstill ['stændstɪl] n : **at a standstill** [traffic, train] à l'arrêt ; [negotiations, work] paralysé(e) ; **to come to a standstill** [traffic, train] s'immobiliser ; [negotiations, work] cesser.

stank [stæŋk] pt ▶ stink.

staple ['steɪpl] <> adj [principal] principal(e), de base. <> n 1. [for paper] agrafe f - 2. [principal commodity] produit m de base. <> vt agrafer.

stapler ['steɪplər] n agrafeuse f.

star [stɑːr] <> n 1. [gen] étoile f - 2. [celebrity] vedette f, star f. <> comp [quality] de star ; **star performer** vedette f. <> vi : **to star (in)** être la vedette (de). ◆ **stars** npl horoscope m.

starboard ['stɑːbəd] <> adj de tribord. <> n : **to starboard** à tribord.

starch [stɑːtʃ] n amidon m.

stardom ['stɑːdəm] n (U) célébrité f.

stare [steər] <> n regard m fixe. <> vi : **to stare at sb/sthg** fixer qqn/qqch du regard.

stark [stɑːk] <> adj 1. [room, decoration] austère ; [landscape] désolé(e) - 2. [reality, fact] à l'état brut ; [contrast] dur(e). <> adv : **stark naked** tout nu (toute nue), à poil.

starling ['stɑːlɪŋ] n étourneau m.

starry ['stɑːrɪ] adj étoilé(e).

starry-eyed [-'aɪd] adj innocent(e).

Stars and Stripes n : **the Stars and Stripes** le drapeau des États-Unis, la bannière étoilée.

start [stɑːt] <> n 1. [beginning] début m - 2. [jump] sursaut m - 3. [starting place] départ m - 4. [time advantage] avance f. <> vt 1. [begin] commencer ; **to start doing** OR **to do sthg** commencer à faire qqch - 2. [turn on - machine] mettre en marche ; [- engine, vehicle] démarrer, mettre en marche - 3. [set up - business, band] créer. <> vi 1. [begin] commencer, débuter ; **to start with** pour commencer, d'abord - 2. [function - machine] se mettre en marche ; [- car] démarrer - 3. [begin journey] partir - 4. [jump] sursauter. ◆ **start off** <> vt sep [meeting] ouvrir, commencer ;

[rumour] faire naître ; [discussion] entamer, commencer. ◇ *vi* **1.** [begin] commencer ; [begin job] débuter **- 2.** [leave on journey] partir. ⬥ **start out** *vi* **1.** [in job] débuter **- 2.** [leave on journey] partir. ⬥ **start up** ◇ *vt sep* **1.** [business] créer ; [shop] ouvrir **- 2.** [car, engine] mettre en marche. ◇ *vi* **1.** [begin] commencer **- 2.** [machine] se mettre en route ; [car, engine] démarrer.

starter ['stɑ:tər] *n* **1.** UK [of meal] hors-d'œuvre *m inv* **- 2.** AUT démarreur *m* **- 3.** [to begin race] starter *m*.

starting point ['stɑ:tɪŋ-] *n* point *m* de départ.

startle ['stɑ:tl] *vt* faire sursauter.

startling ['stɑ:tlɪŋ] *adj* surprenant(e).

start-up *n* (U) **1.** [launch] création *f* (d'entreprise) ; start-up costs frais *mpl* de création d'une entreprise **- 2.** [new company] start-up *f*, jeune pousse *f*.

starvation [stɑ:'veɪʃn] *n* faim *f*.

starve [stɑ:v] ◇ *vt* [deprive of food] affamer. ◇ *vi* **1.** [have no food] être affamé(e) ; **to starve to death** mourir de faim **- 2.** *inf* [be hungry] avoir très faim, crever OR mourir de faim.

state [steɪt] ◇ *n* état *m* ; **to be in a state** être dans tous ses états. ◇ *comp* d'État. ◇ *vt* **1.** [express - reason] donner ; [- name and address] décliner ; **to state that...** déclarer que... **- 2.** [specify] préciser. ⬥ **State** *n* : the State l'État *m*. ⬥ **States** *npl* : the States *inf* les États-Unis *mpl*.

State Department *n* US ≃ ministère *m* des Affaires étrangères.

stately ['steɪtlɪ] *adj* majestueux(euse).

statement ['steɪtmənt] *n* **1.** [declaration] déclaration *f* **- 2.** LAW déposition *f* **- 3.** [from bank] relevé *m* de compte.

state of mind (*pl* **states of mind**) *n* humeur *f*.

statesman ['steɪtsmən] (*pl* **-men** [-mən]) *n* homme *m* d'État.

static ['stætɪk] ◇ *adj* statique. ◇ *n* (U) parasites *mpl*.

static electricity *n* électricité *f* statique.

station ['steɪʃn] ◇ *n* **1.** RAIL gare *f* ; [for buses, coaches] gare routière **- 2.** RADIO station *f* **- 3.** [building] poste *m* **- 4.** *fml* [rank] rang *m*. ◇ *vt* **1.** [position] placer, poster **- 2.** MIL poster.

stationary ['steɪʃnərɪ] *adj* immobile.

stationer ['steɪʃnər] *n* papetier *m*, -ère *f* ; **stationer's (shop)** papeterie *f*.

stationery ['steɪʃnərɪ] *n* (U) [equipment] fournitures *fpl* de bureau ; [paper] papier *m* à lettres.

stationmaster ['steɪʃn,mɑ:stər] *n* chef *m* de gare.

station wagon *n* US break *m*.

statistic [stə'tɪstɪk] *n* statistique *f*. ⬥ **statistics** *n* (U) [science] statistique *f*.

statistical [stə'tɪstɪkl] *adj* statistique ; [expert] en statistiques ; [report] de statistiques.

statue ['stætʃu:] *n* statue *f*.

stature ['stætʃər] *n* **1.** [height, size] stature *f*, taille *f* **- 2.** [importance] envergure *f*.

status ['steɪtəs] *n* (U) **1.** [legal or social position] statut *m* **- 2.** [prestige] prestige *m*.

status bar *n* COMPUT barre *f* d'état.

status symbol *n* signe *m* extérieur de richesse.

statute ['stætju:t] *n* loi *f*.

statutory ['stætjʊtrɪ] *adj* statutaire.

staunch [stɔ:ntʃ] ◇ *adj* loyal(e). ◇ *vt* [flow] arrêter ; [blood] étancher.

stave [steɪv] (*pt & pp* **-d** OR **stove**) *n* MUS portée *f*. ⬥ **stave off** *vt sep* [disaster, defeat] éviter ; [hunger] tromper.

stay [steɪ] ◇ *vi* **1.** [not move away] rester **- 2.** [as visitor - with friends] passer quelques jours ; [- in town, country] séjourner ; **to stay in a hotel** descendre à l'hôtel **- 3.** [continue, remain] rester, demeurer ; **to stay out of sthg** ne pas se mêler de qqch. ◇ *n* [visit] séjour *m*. ⬥ **stay in** *vi* rester chez soi, ne pas sortir. ⬥ **stay on** *vi* rester (plus longtemps). ⬥ **stay out** *vi* [from home] ne pas rentrer. ⬥ **stay up** *vi* ne pas se coucher, veiller ; **to stay up late** se coucher tard.

staying power ['steɪɪŋ-] *n* endurance *f*.

stead [sted] *n* : **to stand sb in good stead** être utile à qqn.

steadfast ['stedfɑ:st] *adj* ferme, résolu(e) ; [supporter] loyal(e).

steadily ['stedɪlɪ] *adv* **1.** [gradually] progressivement **- 2.** [regularly - breathe] régulièrement ; [- move] sans arrêt **- 3.** [calmly] de manière imperturbable.

steady ['stedɪ] ◇ *adj* **1.** [gradual] progressif(ive) **- 2.** [regular] régulier(ère) **- 3.** [not shaking] ferme **- 4.** [calm - voice] calme ; [- stare] imperturbable **- 5.** [stable - job, relationship] stable **- 6.** [sensible] sérieux(euse). ◇ *vt* **1.** [stop from shaking] empêcher de bouger ; **to steady o.s.** se remettre d'aplomb **- 2.** [control - nerves] calmer.

steak [steɪk] *n* steak *m*, bifteck *m* ; [of fish] darne *f*.

steal [sti:l] (*pt* **stole**, *pp* **stolen**) ◇ *vt* voler, dérober. ◇ *vi* [move secretly] se glisser.

stealthy ['stelθɪ] *adj* furtif(ive).

steam [sti:m] ◇ *n* (U) vapeur *f*. ◇ *vt*

CULIN cuire à la vapeur. ◇ *vi* [give off steam] fumer. ◆ **steam up** ◇ *vt sep* [mist up] embuer. ◇ *vi* se couvrir de buée.

steamboat ['sti:mbəʊt] *n* (bateau *m* à) vapeur *m*.

steam engine *n* locomotive *f* à vapeur.

steamer ['sti:mər] *n* [ship] (bateau *m* à) vapeur *m*.

steamroller ['sti:m,rəʊlər] *n* rouleau *m* compresseur.

steamy ['sti:mɪ] *adj* **1.** [full of steam] embué(e) - **2.** *inf* [erotic] érotique.

steel [sti:l] ◇ *n (U)* acier *m*. ◇ *comp* en acier, d'acier.

steelworks ['sti:lwɜːks] (*pl* **steelworks**) *n* aciérie *f*.

steep [sti:p] *adj* **1.** [hill, road] raide, abrupt(e) - **2.** [increase, decline] énorme - **3.** *inf* [expensive] excessif(ive).

steeple ['sti:pl] *n* clocher *m*, flèche *f*.

steeplechase ['sti:pltʃeɪs] *n* **1.** [horse race] steeple-chase *m* - **2.** [athletics race] steeple *m*.

steer ['stɪər] ◇ *n* bœuf *m*. ◇ *vt* **1.** [ship] gouverner ; [car, aeroplane] conduire, diriger - **2.** [person] diriger, guider. ◇ *vi* : **to steer well** [ship] gouverner bien ; [car] être facile à manœuvrer ; **to steer clear of sb/sthg** éviter qqn/qqch.

steering ['stɪərɪŋ] *n (U)* direction *f*.

steering wheel *n* volant *m*.

stem [stem] ◇ *n* **1.** [of plant] tige *f* - **2.** [of glass] pied *m* - **3.** [of pipe] tuyau *m* - **4.** GRAM radical *m*. ◇ *vt* [stop] arrêter. ◆ **stem from** *vt insep* provenir de.

stem cell *n* MED cellule *f* souche.

stench [stentʃ] *n* puanteur *f*.

stencil ['stensl] ◇ *n* pochoir *m*. ◇ *vt* (*UK & US*) faire au pochoir.

stenographer [stə'nɒɡrəfər] *n US* sténographe *mf*.

step [step] ◇ *n* **1.** [pace] pas *m* ; **in/out of step** with *fig* en accord/désaccord avec - **2.** [action] mesure *f* - **3.** [stage] étape *f* ; **step by step** petit à petit, progressivement - **4.** [stair] marche *f* - **5.** [of ladder] barreau *m*, échelon *m*. ◇ *vi* **1.** [move foot] : **to step forward** avancer ; **to step off** OR **down from sthg** descendre de qqch ; **to step back** reculer - **2.** [tread] : **to step on/in sthg** marcher sur/dans qqch. ◆ **steps** *npl* **1.** [stairs] marches *fpl* - **2.** *UK* [stepladder] escabeau *m*. ◆ **step down** *vi* [leave job] démissionner. ◆ **step in** *vi* intervenir. ◆ **step up** *vt sep* intensifier.

stepbrother ['step,brʌðər] *n* demi-frère *m*.

stepdaughter ['step,dɔːtər] *n* belle-fille *f*.

stepfather ['step,fɑːðər] *n* beau-père *m*.

stepladder ['step,lædər] *n* escabeau *m*.

stepmother ['step,mʌðər] *n* belle-mère *f*.

stepping-stone ['stepɪŋ-] *n* pierre *f* de gué ; *fig* tremplin *m*.

stepsister ['step,sɪstər] *n* demi-sœur *f*.

stepson ['stepsʌn] *n* beau-fils *m*.

stereo ['sterɪəʊ] ◇ *adj* stéréo (*inv*). ◇ *n* (*pl* **-s**) **1.** [appliance] chaîne *f* stéréo - **2.** [sound] : **in stereo** en stéréo.

stereotype ['sterɪətaɪp] *n* stéréotype *m*.

sterile ['steraɪl] *adj* stérile.

sterilize, *UK* **-ise** ['sterɪlaɪz] *vt* stériliser.

sterling ['stɜːlɪŋ] ◇ *adj* **1.** [of British money] **sterling** (*inv*) - **2.** [excellent] exceptionnel(elle). ◇ *n (U)* livre *f* sterling.

sterling silver *n* argent *m* fin.

stern [stɜːn] ◇ *adj* sévère. ◇ *n* NAUT arrière *m*.

steroid ['stɪərɔɪd] *n* stéroïde *m*.

stethoscope ['steθəskəʊp] *n* stéthoscope *m*.

stew [stju:] ◇ *n* ragoût *m*. ◇ *vt* [meat] cuire en ragoût ; [fruit] faire cuire.

steward ['stjʊəd] *n* **1.** [on plane, ship, train] steward *m* - **2.** *UK* [at demonstration, meeting] membre *m* du service d'ordre.

stewardess ['stjʊədɪs] *n dated* hôtesse *f*.

stick [stɪk] ◇ *n* **1.** [of wood, dynamite, candy] bâton *m* - **2.** [walking stick] canne *f* - **3.** SPORT crosse *f*. ◇ *vt* (*pt & pp* **stuck**) **1.** [push] : **to stick sthg in** OR **into** planter qqch dans - **2.** [with glue, adhesive tape] : **to stick sthg on** (**on** OR **to**) coller qqch (sur) - **3.** *inf* [put] mettre - **4.** *UK inf* [tolerate] supporter. ◇ *vi* (*pt & pp* **stuck**) **1.** [adhere] : **to stick (to)** coller (à) - **2.** [jam] se coincer. ◆ **stick out** ◇ *vt sep* **1.** [head] sortir ; [hand] lever ; [tongue] tirer - **2.** *inf* [endure] : **to stick it out** tenir le coup. ◇ *vi* **1.** [protrude] dépasser - **2.** *inf* [be noticeable] se remarquer. ◆ **stick to** *vt insep* **1.** [follow closely] suivre - **2.** [principles] rester fidèle à ; [decision] s'en tenir à ; [promise] tenir. ◆ **stick up** *vi* dépasser. ◆ **stick up for** *vt insep* défendre.

sticker ['stɪkər] *n* [label] autocollant *m*.

sticking plaster ['stɪkɪŋ-] *n UK* sparadrap *m*.

stickler ['stɪklər] *n* : **to be a stickler for** être à cheval sur.

stick shift *n US* levier *m* de vitesses.

stick-up *n inf* vol *m* à main armée.

sticky ['stɪkɪ] *adj* **1.** [hands, sweets] poisseux(euse) ; [label, tape] adhésif(ive) - **2.** *inf* [awkward] délicat(e).

stiff [stɪf] ◇ *adj* **1.** [rod, paper, material] rigide ; [shoes, brush] dur(e) ; [fabric] raide - **2.** [door, drawer, window] dur(e) (à ouvrir/

fermer) ; [joint] ankylosé(e) ; **to have a stiff back** avoir des courbatures dans le dos ; **to have a stiff neck** avoir un torticolis - **3.** [formal] guindé(e) - **4.** [severe - penalty] sévère ; [- resistance] tenace ; [- competition] serré(e) - **5.** [difficult - task] difficile. ◇ *adv inf* **to be bored stiff** s'ennuyer à mourir ; **to be frozen/scared stiff** mourir de froid/peur.

stiffen ['stɪfn] ◇ *vt* **1.** [material] raidir ; [with starch] empeser - **2.** [resolve] renforcer. ◇ *vi* **1.** [body] se raidir ; [joints] s'ankyloser - **2.** [competition, resistance] s'intensifier.

stifle ['staɪfl] *vt & vi* étouffer.

stifling ['staɪflɪŋ] *adj* étouffant(e).

stigma ['stɪɡmə] *n* **1.** [disgrace] honte *f*, stigmate *m* - **2.** BOT stigmate *m*.

stile [staɪl] *n* échalier *m*.

stiletto heel [stɪ'letəʊ-] *n* talon *m* aiguille.

still [stɪl] ◇ *adv* **1.** [up to now, up to then] encore, toujours ; **I've still got £5 left** il me reste encore 5 livres - **2.** [even now] encore - **3.** [nevertheless] tout de même - **4.** *(with compar)* **still bigger/more important** encore plus grand/plus important. ◇ *adj* **1.** [not moving] immobile - **2.** [calm] calme, tranquille - **3.** [not windy] sans vent - **4.** [not fizzy - gen] non gazeux(euse) ; [- mineral water] plat(e). ◇ *n* **1.** PHOT photo *f* - **2.** [for making alcohol] alambic *m*.

stillborn ['stɪlbɔːn] *adj* mort-né(e).

still life (*pl* **-s**) *n* nature *f* morte.

stilted ['stɪltɪd] *adj* emprunté(e), qui manque de naturel.

stilts [stɪlts] *npl* **1.** [for person] échasses *fpl* - **2.** [for building] pilotis *mpl*.

stimulate ['stɪmjʊleɪt] *vt* stimuler.

stimulating ['stɪmjʊleɪtɪŋ] *adj* stimulant(e).

stimulus ['stɪmjʊləs] (*pl* **-li** [-laɪ]) *n* **1.** [encouragement] stimulant *m* - **2.** BIOL & PSYCHOL stimulus *m*.

sting [stɪŋ] ◇ *n* **1.** [by bee] piqûre *f* ; [of bee] dard *m* - **2.** [sharp pain] brûlure *f*. ◇ *vt* (*pt & pp* **stung**) [gen] piquer. ◇ *vi* (*pt & pp* **stung**) piquer.

stingy ['stɪndʒɪ] *adj inf* radin(e).

stink [stɪŋk] ◇ *n* puanteur *f*. ◇ *vi* (*pt* **stank** OR **stunk**, *pp* **stunk**) [smell] puer, empester.

stinking ['stɪŋkɪŋ] *inf adj* [cold] gros (grosse) ; [weather] pourri(e) ; [place] infect(e).

stint [stɪnt] ◇ *n* [period of work] part *f* de travail. ◇ *vi* : **to stint on** lésiner sur.

stipulate ['stɪpjʊleɪt] *vt* stipuler.

stir [stɜːr] ◇ *n* [public excitement] sensation *f*. ◇ *vt* **1.** [mix] remuer - **2.** [move gently] agiter - **3.** [move emotionally] émouvoir. ◇ *vi* bouger, remuer. ◆ **stir up** *vt sep* **1.** [dust] soulever - **2.** [trouble] provoquer ; [resentment, dissatisfaction] susciter ; [rumour] faire naître.

stirrup ['stɪrəp] *n* étrier *m*.

stitch [stɪtʃ] ◇ *n* **1.** SEW point *m* ; [in knitting] maille *f* - **2.** MED point *m* de suture - **3.** [stomach pain] : **to have a stitch** avoir un point de côté. ◇ *vt* **1.** SEW coudre - **2.** MED suturer.

stoat [stəʊt] *n* hermine *f*.

stock [stɒk] ◇ *n* **1.** [supply] réserve *f* - **2.** (U) COMM stock *m*, réserve *f* ; **in stock** en stock ; **out of stock** épuisé(e) - **3.** FIN valeurs *fpl* US, actions *fpl* UK ; **stocks and shares** titres *mpl* - **4.** [ancestry] souche *f* - **5.** CULIN bouillon *m* - **6.** [livestock] cheptel *m* ; **to take stock (of)** faire le point (de). ◇ *adj* classique. ◇ *vt* **1.** COMM vendre, avoir en stock - **2.** [fill - shelves] garnir. ◆ **stock up** *vi* : **to stock up (with)** faire des provisions (de).

stockbroker ['stɒkˌbrəʊkər] *n* agent *m* de change.

stock cube *n* UK bouillon-cube *m*.

stock exchange *n* Bourse *f*.

stockholder ['stɒkˌhəʊldər] *n* US actionnaire *mf*.

Stockholm ['stɒkhəʊm] *n* Stockholm.

stocking ['stɒkɪŋ] *n* [for woman] bas *m*.

stockist ['stɒkɪst] *n* UK dépositaire *m*, stockiste *m*.

stock market *n* Bourse *f*.

stock phrase *n* cliché *m*.

stockpile ['stɒkpaɪl] ◇ *n* stock *m*. ◇ *vt* [weapons] amasser ; [food] stocker.

stocktaking ['stɒkˌteɪkɪŋ] *n* UK (U) inventaire *m*.

stocky ['stɒkɪ] *adj* trapu(e).

stodgy ['stɒdʒɪ] *adj* [food] lourd(e) (à digérer).

stoical ['stəʊɪkl] *adj* stoïque.

stoke [stəʊk] *vt* [fire] entretenir.

stole [stəʊl] ◇ *pt* ▶ **steal**. ◇ *n* étole *f*.

stolen ['stəʊln] *pp* ▶ **steal**.

stolid ['stɒlɪd] *adj* impassible.

stomach ['stʌmək] ◇ *n* [organ] estomac *m* ; [abdomen] ventre *m*. ◇ *vt* [tolerate] encaisser, supporter.

stomachache ['stʌməkeɪk] *n* : **to have stomachache** UK OR **a stomachache** US avoir mal au ventre.

stomach upset *n* embarras *m* gastrique.

stone [stəʊn] ◇ *n* **1.** [rock] pierre *f* ; [smaller] caillou *m* - **2.** UK [seed] noyau *m*

- 3. (*pl* stone OR -s) *UK* [unit of measurement] = 6,348 kg. <> *comp* de OR en pierre. <> *vt* [person, car etc] jeter des pierres sur.

stone-cold *adj* complètement froid(e) OR glacé(e).

stonewashed ['stəʊnwɒʃt] *adj* délavé(e).

stonework ['stəʊnwɜ:k] *n* maçonnerie *f*.

stood [stʊd] *pt & pp* ► stand.

stool [stu:l] *n* [seat] tabouret *m*.

stoop [stu:p] <> *n* [bent back] : **to walk with a stoop** marcher le dos voûté. <> *vi* 1. [bend down] se pencher - 2. [hunch shoulders] être voûté(e).

stop [stɒp] <> *n* 1. [gen] arrêt *m* ; **to put a stop to sthg** mettre un terme à qqch - 2. [full stop] point *m*. <> *vt* 1. [gen] arrêter ; [end] mettre fin à ; **to stop doing sthg** arrêter de faire qqch ; **to stop work** arrêter de travailler, cesser le travail - 2. [prevent] : **to stop sb/sthg (from doing sthg)** empêcher qqn/qqch (de faire qqch) - 3. [block] boucher. <> *vi* s'arrêter, cesser. ◆ **stop off** *vi* s'arrêter, faire halte. ◆ **stop up** *vt sep* [block] boucher.

stopgap ['stɒpgæp] *n* bouche-trou *m*.

stopover ['stɒp,əʊvə'] *n* halte *f*.

stoppage ['stɒpɪdʒ] *n* 1. [strike] grève *f* - 2. *UK* [deduction] retenue *f*.

stopper ['stɒpə'] *n* bouchon *m*.

stop press *n* nouvelles *fpl* de dernière heure.

stopwatch ['stɒpwɒtʃ] *n* chronomètre *m*.

storage ['stɔ:rɪdʒ] *n* 1. [of goods] entreposage *m*, emmagasinage *m* ; [of household objects] rangement *m* - 2. COMPUT stockage *m*, mémorisation *f*.

storage heater *n UK* radiateur *m* à accumulation.

store [stɔ:'] <> *n* 1. *esp US* [shop] magasin *m* - 2. [supply] provision *f* - 3. [place of storage] réserve *f*. <> *vt* 1. [save] mettre en réserve ; [goods] entreposer, emmagasiner - 2. COMPUT stocker, mémoriser. ◆ **store up** *vt sep* [provisions] mettre en réserve ; [goods] emmagasiner ; [information] mettre en mémoire, noter.

storekeeper ['stɔ:,ki:pə'] *n US* commerçant *m*, -e *f*.

storeroom ['stɔ:rʊm] *n* magasin *m*.

storey *UK* (*pl* -s), **story** *US* (*pl* -ies) ['stɔ:rɪ] *n* étage *m*.

stork [stɔ:k] *n* cigogne *f*.

storm [stɔ:m] <> *n* 1. [bad weather] orage *m* - 2. *fig* [of abuse] torrent *m* ; [of applause] tempête *f*. <> *vt* MIL prendre d'assaut. <> *vi* 1. [go angrily] : **to storm in/out** entrer/sortir comme un ouragan - 2. [speak angrily] fulminer.

stormy ['stɔ:mɪ] *adj lit & fig* orageux(euse).

story ['stɔ:rɪ] *n* 1. [gen] histoire *f* - 2. PRESS article *m* ; RADIO & TV nouvelle *f* - 3. *US* = storey.

storybook ['stɔ:rɪbʊk] *adj* [romance etc] de conte de fées.

storyteller ['stɔ:rɪ,telə'] *n* 1. [narrator] conteur *m*, -euse *f* - 2. *euph* [liar] menteur *m*, -euse *f*.

stout [staʊt] <> *adj* 1. [rather fat] corpulent(e) - 2. [strong] solide - 3. [resolute] ferme, résolu(e). <> *n* (*U*) stout *m*, bière *f* brune.

stove [stəʊv] <> *pt & pp* ► stave. <> *n* [for cooking] cuisinière *f* ; [for heating] poêle *m*, calorifère *m* Québec.

stow [stəʊ] *vt* : **to stow sthg (away)** ranger qqch.

stowaway ['stəʊəweɪ] *n* passager *m* clandestin.

straddle ['strædl] *vt* enjamber ; [chair] s'asseoir à califourchon sur.

straggle ['strægl] *vi* 1. [buildings] s'étendre, s'étaler ; [hair] être en désordre - 2. [person] traîner, lambiner.

straggler ['stræglə'] *n* traînard *m*, -e *f*.

straight [streɪt] <> *adj* 1. [not bent] droit(e) ; [hair] raide - 2. [frank] franc (franche), honnête - 3. [tidy] en ordre - 4. [choice, exchange] simple - 5. [alcoholic drink] sec, sans eau ; **let's get this straight** entendons-nous bien. <> *adv* 1. [in a straight line] droit - 2. [directly, immediately] droit, tout de suite - 3. [frankly] carrément, franchement - 4. [undiluted] sec, sans eau. ◆ **straight off** *adv* tout de suite, sur-le-champ. ◆ **straight out** *adv* sans mâcher ses mots.

straightaway [,streɪtə'weɪ] *adv* tout de suite, immédiatement.

straighten ['streɪtn] *vt* 1. [tidy - hair, dress] arranger ; [- room] mettre de l'ordre dans - 2. [make straight - horizontally] rendre droit(e) ; [- vertically] redresser. ◆ **straighten out** *vt sep* [problem] résoudre.

straight face *n* : **to keep a straight face** garder son sérieux.

straightforward [,streɪt'fɔ:wəd] *adj* 1. [easy] simple - 2. [frank] honnête, franc (franche).

strain [streɪn] <> *n* 1. [mental] tension *f*, stress *m* - 2. MED foulure *f* - 3. TECH contrainte *f*, effort *m*. <> *vt* 1. [work hard - eyes] plisser fort ; **to strain one's ears** tendre l'oreille - 2. [MED - muscle] se froisser ; [- eyes] se fatiguer ; **to strain one's back** se faire un tour de reins - 3. [patience] mettre à rude épreuve ; [budget] grever - 4. [drain]

passer - **5.** TECH exercer une contrainte sur. ◇ *vi* [try very hard]: **to strain to do sthg** faire un gros effort pour faire qqch, se donner du mal pour faire qqch. ◆ **strains** *npl* [of music] accords *mpl*, airs *mpl*.

strained [streɪnd] *adj* **1.** [worried] contracté(e), tendu(e) - **2.** [relations, relationship] tendu(e) - **3.** [unnatural] forcé(e).

strainer ['streɪnər] *n* passoire *f*.

strait [streɪt] *n* détroit *m*. ◆ **straits** *npl*: **in dire OR desperate straits** dans une situation désespérée.

straitjacket ['streɪt,dʒækɪt] *n* camisole *f* de force.

straitlaced [,streɪt'leɪst] *adj* collet monté *(inv)*.

strand [strænd] *n* **1.** [of cotton, wool] brin *m*, fil *m*; [of hair] mèche *f* - **2.** [theme] fil *m*.

stranded ['strændɪd] *adj* [boat] échoué(e); [people] abandonné(e), en rade.

strange [streɪndʒ] *adj* **1.** [odd] étrange, bizarre - **2.** [unfamiliar] inconnu(e).

stranger ['streɪndʒər] *n* **1.** [unfamiliar person] inconnu *m*, -e *f* - **2.** [from another place] étranger *m*, -ère *f*.

strangle ['stræŋgl] *vt* étrangler; *fig* étouffer.

stranglehold ['stræŋglhəʊld] *n* **1.** [round neck] étranglement *m* - **2.** *fig* [control]: **stranglehold (on)** domination *f* (de).

strap [stræp] ◇ *n* [for fastening] sangle *f*, courroie *f*; [of bag] bandoulière *f*; [of rifle, dress, bra] bretelle *f*; [of watch] bracelet *m*. ◇ *vt* [fasten] attacher.

strapping ['stræpɪŋ] *adj* bien bâti(e), robuste.

Strasbourg ['stræzbɜːg] *n* Strasbourg.

strategic [strə'tiːdʒɪk] *adj* stratégique.

strategy ['strætɪdʒɪ] *n* stratégie *f*.

straw [strɔː] *n* paille *f*; **that's the last straw!** ça c'est le comble!

strawberry ['strɔːbərɪ] ◇ *n* [fruit] fraise *f*. ◇ *comp* [tart, yoghurt] aux fraises; [jam] de fraises.

stray [streɪ] ◇ *adj* **1.** [animal] errant(e), perdu(e) - **2.** [bullet] perdu(e) - **3.** [example] isolé(e). ◇ *vi* **1.** [person, animal] errer, s'égarer - **2.** [thoughts] vagabonder, errer.

streak [striːk] ◇ *n* **1.** [line] bande *f*, marque *f*; **streak of lightning** éclair *m* - **2.** [in character] côté *m*. ◇ *vi* [move quickly] se déplacer comme un éclair.

stream [striːm] ◇ *n* **1.** [small river] ruisseau *m* - **2.** [of liquid, light] flot *m*, jet *m* - **3.** [of people, cars] flot *m*; [of complaints, abuse] torrent *m* - **4.** *UK* SCH classe *f* de niveau. ◇ *vi* **1.** [liquid] couler à flots,

ruisseler; [light] entrer à flots - **2.** [people, cars] affluer; **to stream past** passer à flots. ◇ *vt* *UK* SCH répartir par niveau.

streamer ['striːmər] *n* [for party] serpentin *m*.

streamlined ['striːmlaɪnd] *adj* **1.** [aerodynamic] au profil aérodynamique - **2.** [efficient] rationalisé(e).

street [striːt] *n* rue *f*.

streetcar ['striːtkɑːr] *n* *US* tramway *m*.

street lamp, **street light** *n* réverbère *m*.

street plan *n* plan *m*.

streetwise ['striːtwaɪz] *adj* *inf* averti(e), futé(e).

strength [streŋθ] *n* **1.** [gen] force *f* - **2.** [power, influence] puissance *f* - **3.** [solidity, of currency] solidité *f*.

strengthen ['streŋθn] *vt* **1.** [structure, team, argument] renforcer - **2.** [economy, currency, friendship] consolider - **3.** [resolve, dislike] fortifier, affermir - **4.** [person] enhardir.

strenuous ['strenjʊəs] *adj* [exercise, activity] fatigant(e), dur(e); [effort] vigoureux(euse), acharné(e).

stress [stres] ◇ *n* **1.** [emphasis]: **stress (on)** accent *m* (sur) - **2.** [mental] stress *m*, tension *f* - **3.** TECH: **stress (on)** contrainte *f* (sur), effort *m* (sur) - **4.** LING accent *m*. ◇ *vt* **1.** [emphasize] souligner, insister sur - **2.** LING accentuer. ◇ *vi* *inf* stresser. ◆ **stress out** *vt inf* stresser.

stress-buster *n inf* éliminateur *m* de stress.

stressful ['stresfʊl] *adj* stressant(e).

stress management *n* gestion *f* du stress.

stress out, **stress** *vt inf* stresser.

stretch [stretʃ] ◇ *n* **1.** [of land, water] étendue *f*; [of road, river] partie *f*, section *f* - **2.** [of time] période *f*. ◇ *vt* **1.** [arms] allonger; [legs] se dégourdir; [muscles] distendre - **2.** [pull taut] tendre, étirer - **3.** [overwork - person] surmener; [- resources, budget] grever - **4.** [challenge]: **to stretch sb** pousser qqn à la limite de ses capacités. ◇ *vi* **1.** [area]: **to stretch over** s'étendre sur; **to stretch from... to** s'étendre de... à - **2.** [person, animal] s'étirer - **3.** [material, elastic] se tendre, s'étirer. ◆ **stretch out** ◇ *vt sep* [arm, leg, hand] tendre. ◇ *vi* [lie down] s'étendre, s'allonger.

stretcher ['stretʃər] *n* brancard *m*, civière *f*.

strew [struː] (*pt* -ed, *pp* strewn [struːn] OR -ed) *vt*: **to be strewn with** être jonché(e) de.

stricken ['strɪkn] *adj*: **to be stricken by** OR **with panic** être pris(e) de panique; **to be stricken by an illness** souffrir OR être atteint(e) d'une maladie.

strict [strɪkt] *adj* [gen] strict(e).

strictly ['strɪktlɪ] *adv* **1.** [gen] strictement;

strictly speaking à proprement parler - **2.** [severely] d'une manière stricte, sévèrement.

stride [straɪd] <> n [long step] grand pas m, enjambée f. <> vi (pt **strode**, pp **stridden** ['strɪdn]) marcher à grandes enjambées OR à grands pas.

strident ['straɪdnt] adj **1.** [voice, sound] strident(e) - **2.** [demand, attack] véhément(e), bruyant(e).

strife [straɪf] n (U) conflit m, lutte f.

strike [straɪk] <> n **1.** [by workers] grève f ; **to be (out) on strike** être en grève ; **to go on strike** faire grève, se mettre en grève - **2.** MIL raid m - **3.** [of oil, gold] découverte f. <> vt (pt & pp **struck**) **1.** [hit - deliberately] frapper ; [- accidentally] heurter - **2.** [subj: thought] venir à l'esprit de - **3.** [conclude - deal, bargain] conclure - **4.** [light - match] frotter. <> vi (pt & pp **struck**) **1.** [workers] faire grève - **2.** [hit] frapper - **3.** [attack] attaquer - **4.** [chime] sonner. ◆ **strike down** vt sep terrasser. ◆ **strike out** <> vt sep rayer, barrer. <> vi [head out] se mettre en route, partir. ◆ **strike up** vt insep **1.** [conversation] commencer, engager ; **to strike up a friendship (with)** se lier d'amitié (avec) - **2.** [music] commencer à jouer.

striker ['straɪkər] n **1.** [person on strike] gréviste mf - **2.** FOOTBALL buteur m.

striking ['straɪkɪŋ] adj **1.** [noticeable] frappant(e), saisissant(e) - **2.** [attractive] d'une beauté frappante.

string [strɪŋ] n **1.** (U) [thin rope] ficelle f - **2.** [piece of thin rope] bout m de ficelle ; **to pull strings** faire jouer le piston - **3.** [of beads, pearls] rang m - **4.** [series] série f, suite f - **5.** [of musical instrument] corde f. ◆ **strings** npl MUS : **the strings** les cordes fpl. ◆ **string out** (pt & pp **strung out**) vt insep échelonner. ◆ **string together** (pt & pp **strung together**) vt sep fig aligner.

string bean n haricot m vert.

stringed instrument [,strɪŋd-] n instrument m à cordes.

stringent ['strɪndʒənt] adj strict(e), rigoureux(euse).

strip [strɪp] <> n **1.** [narrow piece] bande f - **2.** UK SPORT tenue f. <> vt **1.** [undress] déshabiller, dévêtir - **2.** [remove covering] enlever. <> vi [undress] se déshabiller, se dévêtir. ◆ **strip off** vi se déshabiller, se dévêtir.

strip cartoon n UK bande f dessinée.

stripe [straɪp] n **1.** [band of colour] rayure f - **2.** [sign of rank] galon m.

striped [straɪpt] adj à rayures, rayé(e).

strip lighting n éclairage m au néon.

stripper ['strɪpər] n **1.** [performer of strip-tease] strip-teaseuse f, effeuilleuse f - **2.** [for paint] décapant m.

striptease ['strɪptiːz] n strip-tease m.

strive [straɪv] (pt **strove**, pp **striven** ['strɪvn]) vi : **to strive for sthg** essayer d'obtenir qqch ; **to strive to do sthg** s'efforcer de faire qqch.

strode [strəud] pt > **stride**.

stroke [strəuk] <> n **1.** MED attaque f cérébrale - **2.** [of pen, brush] trait m - **3.** [in swimming - movement] mouvement m des bras ; [- style] nage f - **4.** [in rowing] coup m d'aviron - **5.** [in golf, tennis etc] coup m - **6.** [of clock] : **on the third stroke** ≃ au quatrième top - **7.** UK TYPO [oblique] barre f - **8.** [piece] : **a stroke of genius** un trait de génie ; **a stroke of luck** un coup de chance OR de veine ; **at a stroke** d'un seul coup. <> vt caresser.

stroll [strəul] <> n petite promenade f, petit tour m. <> vi se promener, flâner.

stroller ['strəulər] n US [for baby] poussette f.

strong [strɒŋ] adj **1.** [gen] fort(e) ; **strong point** point m fort - **2.** [structure, argument, friendship] solide - **3.** [healthy] robuste, vigoureux(euse) - **4.** [policy, measures] énergique - **5.** [in numbers] : **the crowd was 2,000 strong** il y avait une foule de 2 000 personnes - **6.** [team, candidate] sérieux(euse), qui a des chances de gagner.

strongbox ['strɒŋbɒks] n coffre-fort m.

stronghold ['strɒŋhəuld] n fig bastion m.

strongly ['strɒŋlɪ] adv **1.** [gen] fortement - **2.** [solidly] solidement.

strong room n chambre f forte.

strove [strəuv] pt > **strive**.

struck [strʌk] pt & pp > **strike**.

structure ['strʌktʃər] n **1.** [organization] structure f - **2.** [building] construction f.

struggle ['strʌgl] <> n **1.** [great effort] : **struggle (for sthg/to do sthg)** lutte f (pour qqch/pour faire qqch) - **2.** [fight] bagarre f. <> vi **1.** [make great effort] : **to struggle (for)** lutter (pour) ; **to struggle to do sthg** s'efforcer de faire qqch - **2.** [to free oneself] se débattre ; [fight] se battre.

strum [strʌm] vt [guitar] gratter de ; [tune] jouer.

strung [strʌŋ] pt & pp > **string**.

strut [strʌt] <> n CONSTR étai m, support m. <> vi se pavaner.

stub [stʌb] <> n **1.** [of cigarette] mégot m ; [of pencil] morceau m - **2.** [of ticket, cheque] talon m. <> vt : **to stub one's toe** se cogner le doigt de pied. ◆ **stub out** vt sep écraser.

stubble ['stʌbl] n (U) **1.** [in field] chaume m - **2.** [on chin] barbe f de plusieurs jours.

stubborn ['stʌbən] adj **1.** [person] têtu(e), obstiné(e) - **2.** [stain] qui ne veut pas partir, rebelle.

stuck [stʌk] ◇ pt & pp ▶ stick. ◇ adj **1.** [jammed, trapped] coincé(e) - **2.** [stumped] : **to be stuck** sécher - **3.** [stranded] bloqué(e), en rade.

stuck-up adj inf pej bêcheur(euse).

stud [stʌd] n **1.** [metal decoration] clou m décoratif - **2.** [earring] clou m d'oreille - **3.** UK [on boot, shoe] clou m ; [on sports boots] crampon m - **4.** [of horses] haras m.

studded ['stʌdɪd] adj : **studded (with)** parsemé(e) (de), constellé(e) (de).

student ['stju:dnt] ◇ n étudiant m, -e f. ◇ comp [life] estudiantin(e) ; [politics] des étudiants ; [disco] pour étudiants.

studio ['stju:dɪəʊ] (pl -s) n studio m ; [of artist] atelier m.

studio flat UK, **studio apartment** US n studio m.

studious ['stju:djəs] adj studieux(euse).

studiously ['stju:djəslɪ] adv studieusement.

study ['stʌdɪ] ◇ n **1.** [gen] étude f - **2.** [room] bureau m. ◇ vt **1.** [learn] étudier, faire des études de - **2.** [examine] examiner, étudier. ◇ vi étudier, faire ses études.

stuff [stʌf] ◇ n (U) **1.** inf [things] choses fpl - **2.** [substance] substance f - **3.** inf [belongings] affaires fpl. ◇ vt **1.** [push] fourrer - **2.** [fill] : **to stuff sthg (with)** remplir OR bourrer qqch (de) - **3.** CULIN farcir. ▸ **stuff up** vt sep [block] boucher.

stuffed [stʌft] adj **1.** [filled] : **stuffed with** bourré(e) de - **2.** inf [with food] gavé(e) - **3.** CULIN farci(e) - **4.** [toy] en peluche ; **he loves stuffed animals** il adore les peluches - **5.** [preserved - animal] empaillé(e).

stuffing ['stʌfɪŋ] n (U) **1.** [filling] bourre f, rembourrage m - **2.** CULIN farce f.

stuffy ['stʌfɪ] adj **1.** [room] mal aéré(e), qui manque d'air - **2.** [person, club] vieux jeu (inv).

stumble ['stʌmbl] vi trébucher. ▸ **stumble across**, **stumble on** vt insep tomber sur.

stumbling block ['stʌmblɪŋ-] n pierre f d'achoppement.

stump [stʌmp] ◇ n [of tree] souche f ; [of arm, leg] moignon m. ◇ vt [subj: question, problem] dérouter, rendre perplexe.

stun [stʌn] vt **1.** [knock unconscious] étourdir, assommer - **2.** [surprise] stupéfier, renverser.

stung [stʌŋ] pt & pp ▶ sting.

stunk [stʌŋk] pt & pp ▶ stink.

stunning ['stʌnɪŋ] adj **1.** [very beautiful] ravissant(e) ; [scenery] merveilleux(euse) - **2.** [surprising] stupéfiant(e), renversant(e).

stunt [stʌnt] ◇ n **1.** [for publicity] coup m - **2.** CIN cascade f. ◇ vt retarder, arrêter.

stunted ['stʌntɪd] adj rabougri(e).

stunt man n cascadeur m.

stupefy ['stju:pɪfaɪ] vt **1.** [tire] abrutir - **2.** [surprise] stupéfier, abasourdir.

stupendous [stju:'pendəs] adj extraordinaire, prodigieux(euse).

stupid ['stju:pɪd] adj **1.** [foolish] stupide, bête - **2.** inf [annoying] fichu(e).

stupidity [stju:'pɪdətɪ] n (U) bêtise f, stupidité f.

sturdy ['stɜ:dɪ] adj [person] robuste ; [furniture, structure] solide.

stutter ['stʌtər] vi bégayer.

sty [staɪ] n [pigsty] porcherie f.

stye [staɪ] n orgelet m, compère-loriot m.

style [staɪl] n **1.** [characteristic manner] style m - **2.** (U) [elegance] chic m, élégance f - **3.** [design] genre m, modèle m.

stylish ['staɪlɪʃ] adj chic (inv), élégant(e).

stylist ['staɪlɪst] n [hairdresser] coiffeur m, -euse f.

stylus ['staɪləs] (pl -es) n [on record player] pointe f de lecture, saphir m.

suave [swɑ:v] adj doucereux(euse).

sub [sʌb] n inf **1.** SPORT (abbrev of substitute) remplaçant m, -e f - **2.** (abbrev of submarine) sous-marin m - **3.** UK (abbrev of subscription) cotisation f.

subconscious [,sʌb'kɒnʃəs] ◇ adj inconscient(e). ◇ n : **the subconscious** l'inconscient m.

subcontract [,sʌbkən'trækt] vt sous-traiter.

subdivide [,sʌbdɪ'vaɪd] vt subdiviser.

subdue [səb'dju:] vt [control - rioters, enemy] soumettre, subjuguer ; [- temper, anger] maîtriser, réprimer.

subdued [səb'dju:d] adj **1.** [person] abattu(e) - **2.** [anger, emotion] contenu(e) - **3.** [colour] doux (douce) ; [light] tamisé(e).

subject ◇ adj ['sʌbdʒekt] soumis(e) ; **to be subject to** [tax, law] être soumis à ; [disease, headaches] être sujet (sujette) à. ◇ n ['sʌbdʒekt] **1.** [gen] sujet m - **2.** SCH & UNIV matière f. ◇ vt [səb'dʒekt] **1.** [control] soumettre, assujettir - **2.** [force to experience] : **to subject sb to sthg** exposer OR soumettre qqn à qqch. ▸ **subject to** prep ['sʌbdʒekt] sous réserve de.

subjective [səb'dʒektɪv] adj subjectif(ive).

subject matter n (U) sujet m.

subjunctive [səb'dʒʌŋktɪv] *n* GRAM : **subjunctive (mood)** (mode *m*) subjonctif *m*.

sublet [ˌsʌb'let] (*pt & pp* **sublet**) *vt* sous-louer.

sublime [sə'blaɪm] *adj* sublime.

submachine gun [ˌsʌbmə'ʃiːn-] *n* mitraillette *f*.

submarine [ˌsʌbmə'riːn] *n* sous-marin *m*.

submenu ['sʌbˌmenjuː] *n* COMPUT sous-menu *m*.

submerge [səb'mɜːdʒ] ⟨⟩ *vt* immerger, plonger. ⟨⟩ *vi* s'immerger, plonger.

submission [səb'mɪʃn] *n* **1.** [obedience] soumission *f* - **2.** [presentation] présentation *f*, soumission *f*.

submissive [səb'mɪsɪv] *adj* soumis(e), docile.

submit [səb'mɪt] ⟨⟩ *vt* soumettre. ⟨⟩ *vi* : **to submit (to)** se soumettre (à).

subnormal [ˌsʌb'nɔːml] *adj* arriéré(e), attardé(e).

subordinate ⟨⟩ *adj* [sə'bɔːdɪnət] *fml* [less important] : **subordinate (to)** subordonné(e) (à), moins important(e) (que). ⟨⟩ *n* [sə'bɔːdɪnət] subordonné *m*, -e *f*.

subpoena [sə'piːnə] ⟨⟩ *n* LAW citation *f*, assignation *f*. ⟨⟩ *vt* (*pt & pp* **-ed**) LAW citer OR assigner à comparaître.

subscribe [səb'skraɪb] *vi* **1.** [to magazine, ISP] s'abonner, être abonné(e) - **2.** [to view, belief] : **to subscribe to** être d'accord avec, approuver.

subscriber [səb'skraɪbər] *n* [to magazine, service] abonné *m*, -e *f*.

subscription [səb'skrɪpʃn] *n* **1.** [to magazine] abonnement *m* - **2.** *UK* [to charity, campaign] souscription *f* - **3.** *UK* [to club] cotisation *f*.

subsequent ['sʌbsɪkwənt] *adj* ultérieur(e), suivant(e).

subsequently ['sʌbsɪkwəntlɪ] *adv* par la suite, plus tard.

subservient [səb'sɜːvjənt] *adj* [servile] : **subservient (to)** servile (vis-à-vis de), obséquieux(euse) (envers).

subside [səb'saɪd] *vi* **1.** [pain, anger] se calmer, s'atténuer ; [noise] diminuer - **2.** [CONSTR - building] s'affaisser ; [- ground] se tasser.

subsidence [səb'saɪdns OR 'sʌbsɪdns] *n* [CONSTR - of building] affaissement *m* ; [- of ground] tassement *m*.

subsidiary [səb'sɪdjərɪ] ⟨⟩ *adj* subsidiaire. ⟨⟩ *n* : **subsidiary (company)** filiale *f*.

subsidize, *UK* **-ise** ['sʌbsɪdaɪz] *vt* subventionner.

subsidy ['sʌbsɪdɪ] *n* subvention *f*, subside *m*.

substance ['sʌbstəns] *n* **1.** [gen] substance *f* - **2.** [importance] importance *f*.

substantial [səb'stænʃl] *adj* **1.** [considerable] considérable, important(e) ; [meal] substantiel(elle) - **2.** [solid, well-built] solide.

substantially [səb'stænʃəlɪ] *adv* **1.** [considerably] considérablement - **2.** [mainly] en grande partie.

substantiate [səb'stænʃɪeɪt] *vt* *fml* prouver, établir.

substitute ['sʌbstɪtjuːt] ⟨⟩ *n* **1.** [replacement] : **substitute (for)** [person] remplaçant *m*, -e *f* (de) ; [thing] succédané *m* (de) - **2.** SPORT remplaçant *m*, -e *f*. ⟨⟩ *vt* : **to substitute A for B** substituer A à B, remplacer B par A.

subtitle ['sʌbˌtaɪtl] *n* sous-titre *m*.

subtle ['sʌtl] *adj* subtil(e).

subtlety ['sʌtltɪ] *n* subtilité *f*.

subtract [səb'trækt] *vt* : **to subtract sthg (from)** soustraire qqch (de).

subtraction [səb'trækʃn] *n* soustraction *f*.

suburb ['sʌbɜːb] *n* faubourg *m*. ⬥ **suburbs** *npl* : **the suburbs** la banlieue.

suburban [sə'bɜːbn] *adj* **1.** [of suburbs] de banlieue - **2.** *pej* [life] étriqué(e) ; [person] à l'esprit étroit.

suburbia [sə'bɜːbɪə] *n* (*U*) la banlieue.

subversive [səb'vɜːsɪv] ⟨⟩ *adj* subversif(ive). ⟨⟩ *n* personne *f* qui agit de façon subversive.

subway ['sʌbweɪ] *n* **1.** *UK* [underground walkway] passage *m* souterrain - **2.** *US* [underground railway] métro *m*.

succeed [sək'siːd] ⟨⟩ *vt* succéder à. ⟨⟩ *vi* réussir ; **to succeed in doing sthg** réussir à faire qqch.

succeeding [sək'siːdɪŋ] *adj* *fml* [in future] à venir ; [in past] suivant(e).

success [sək'ses] *n* succès *m*, réussite *f*.

successful [sək'sesful] *adj* **1.** [attempt] couronné(e) de succès - **2.** [film, book etc] à succès ; [person] qui a du succès.

succession [sək'seʃn] *n* succession *f*.

successive [sək'sesɪv] *adj* successif(ive).

succinct [sək'sɪŋkt] *adj* succinct(e).

succumb [sə'kʌm] *vi* : **to succumb (to)** succomber (à).

such [sʌtʃ] ⟨⟩ *adj* tel (telle), pareil(eille) ; **such nonsense** de telles inepties ; **do you have such a thing as a tin-opener?** est-ce que tu aurais un ouvre-boîtes par hasard ? ; **such money/books as I have** le peu d'argent/de livres que j'ai ; **such... that** tel... que. ⟨⟩ *adv* **1.** [for emphasis] si, tellement ; **it's such a horrible day!** quelle journée épouvantable ! ; **such a lot of books** tellement de livres ; **such a long time** si OR tellement longtemps - **2.** [in comparisons] aussi. ◇ *pron* : **and such (like)** et autres choses de ce genre. ▸ **as such** *adv* en tant que tel (telle), en soi. ▸ **such and such** *adj* tel et tel (telle et telle).

suck [sʌk] *vt* **1.** [with mouth] sucer - **2.** [draw in] aspirer.

sucker ['sʌkər] *n* **1.** [suction pad] ventouse *f* - **2.** *inf* [gullible person] poire *f*.

suction ['sʌkʃn] *n* succion *f*.

Sudan [suː'dɑːn] *n* Soudan *m*.

sudden ['sʌdn] *adj* soudain(e), brusque ; **all of a sudden** tout d'un coup, soudain.

suddenly ['sʌdnlɪ] *adv* soudainement, tout d'un coup.

suds [sʌdz] *npl* mousse *f* de savon.

sue [suː] *vt* : **to sue sb (for)** poursuivre qqn en justice (pour).

suede [sweɪd] *n* daim *m*.

suet ['suɪt] *n* graisse *f* de rognon.

suffer ['sʌfər] ◇ *vt* **1.** [pain, injury] souffrir de - **2.** [consequences, setback, loss] subir. ◇ *vi* souffrir ; **to suffer from** MED souffrir de.

sufferer ['sʌfrər] *n* MED malade *mf*.

suffering ['sʌfrɪŋ] *n* souffrance *f*.

suffice [sə'faɪs] *vi fml* suffire.

sufficient [sə'fɪʃnt] *adj* suffisant(e).

sufficiently [sə'fɪʃntlɪ] *adv* suffisamment.

suffocate ['sʌfəkeɪt] *vt & vi* suffoquer.

suffrage ['sʌfrɪdʒ] *n* suffrage *m*.

suffuse [sə'fjuːz] *vt* baigner.

sugar ['ʃʊgər] ◇ *n* sucre *m*. ◇ *vt* sucrer.

sugar beet *n* betterave *f* à sucre.

sugarcane ['ʃʊgəkeɪn] *n* (U) canne *f* à sucre.

sugary ['ʃʊgərɪ] *adj* [food] sucré(e).

suggest [sə'dʒest] *vt* **1.** [propose] proposer, suggérer - **2.** [imply] suggérer.

suggestion [sə'dʒestʃn] *n* **1.** [proposal] proposition *f*, suggestion *f* - **2.** (U) [implication] suggestion *f*.

suggestive [sə'dʒestɪv] *adj* suggestif(ive) ; **to be suggestive of sthg** suggérer qqch.

suicide ['suːɪsaɪd] *n* suicide *m* ; **to commit suicide** se suicider.

suit [suːt] ◇ *n* **1.** [for man] costume *m*, complet *m* ; [for woman] tailleur *m* - **2.** [in cards] couleur *f* - **3.** LAW procès *m*, action *f*. ◇ *vt* **1.** [subj: clothes, hairstyle] aller à - **2.** [be convenient, appropriate to] convenir à. ◇ *vi* convenir, aller.

suitable ['suːtəbl] *adj* qui convient, qui va.

suitably ['suːtəblɪ] *adv* convenablement.

suitcase ['suːtkeɪs] *n* valise *f*.

suite [swiːt] *n* **1.** [of rooms] suite *f* - **2.** [of furniture] ensemble *m*.

suited ['suːtɪd] *adj* **1.** [suitable] : **to be suited to/for** convenir à/pour, aller à/pour - **2.** [couple] : **well suited** très bien assortis.

suitor ['suːtər] *n dated* soupirant *m*.

sulfur *US* = **sulphur**.

sulk [sʌlk] *vi* bouder.

sulky ['sʌlkɪ] *adj* boudeur(euse).

sullen ['sʌlən] *adj* maussade.

sulphur *UK*, **sulfur** *US* ['sʌlfər] *n* soufre *m*.

sultana [səl'tɑːnə] *n UK* [dried grape] raisin *m* sec.

sultry ['sʌltrɪ] *adj* **1.** [weather] lourd(e) - **2.** [sexual] sensuel(elle).

sum [sʌm] *n* **1.** [amount of money] somme *f* - **2.** [calculation] calcul *m*. ▸ **sum up** ◇ *vt sep* [summarize] résumer. ◇ *vi* récapituler.

summarize, *UK* **-ise** ['sʌməraɪz] ◇ *vt* résumer. ◇ *vi* récapituler.

summary ['sʌmərɪ] *n* résumé *m*.

summer ['sʌmər] ◇ *n* été *m* ; **in summer** en été. ◇ *comp* d'été ; **the summer holidays** *UK* OR **vacation** *US* les grandes vacances *fpl*.

summerhouse ['sʌməhaʊs] (*pl* [-haʊzɪz]) *n* pavillon *m* d'été.

summer school *n* université *f* d'été.

summertime ['sʌmətaɪm] *n* été *m*.

summit ['sʌmɪt] *n* sommet *m*.

summon ['sʌmən] *vt* [send for] appeler, convoquer. ▸ **summon up** *vt sep* rassembler.

summons ['sʌmənz] ◇ *n* (*pl* **-es** [-ɪːz]) LAW assignation *f*. ◇ *vt* LAW assigner.

sump [sʌmp] *n UK* carter *m*.

sumptuous ['sʌmptʃʊəs] *adj* somptueux(euse).

sun [sʌn] *n* soleil *m* ; **in the sun** au soleil.

sunbathe ['sʌnbeɪð] *vi* prendre un bain de soleil.

sunbed ['sʌnbed] *n* lit *m* à ultra-violets.

sunburn ['sʌnbɜːn] *n* (U) coup *m* de soleil.

sunburned ['sʌnbɜːnd], **sunburnt** ['sʌnbɜːnt] *adj* brûlé(e) par le soleil, qui a attrapé un coup de soleil.

Sunday ['sʌndɪ] *n* dimanche *m* ; **Sunday lunch** déjeuner *m* du dimanche OR dominical ; *see also* **Saturday**.

Sunday school *n* catéchisme *m*.

sundial ['sʌndaɪəl] *n* cadran *m* solaire.

sundown ['sʌndaʊn] *n* coucher *m* du soleil.

sundries ['sʌndrɪz] *npl fml* articles *mpl* divers, objets *mpl* divers.

sundry ['sʌndrɪ] *adj fml* divers ; **all and sundry** tout le monde, n'importe qui.

sunflower ['sʌn,flaʊər] *n* tournesol *m*.

sung [sʌŋ] *pp* ▸ **sing**.

sunglasses ['sʌn,glɑːsɪz] *npl* lunettes *fpl* de soleil.

sunk [sʌŋk] *pp* ➤ sink.

sunlight ['sʌnlaɪt] *n* lumière *f* du soleil.

sunny ['sʌnɪ] *adj* 1. [day, place] ensoleillé(e) ; **it's sunny** il fait beau, il fait (du) soleil - 2. [cheerful] radieux(euse), heureux(euse).

sunrise ['sʌnraɪz] *n* lever *m* du soleil.

sunroof ['sʌnruːf] *n* toit *m* ouvrant.

sunscreen ['sʌnskriːn] *n* écran *m* OR filtre *m* solaire.

sunset ['sʌnset] *n* coucher *m* du soleil.

sunshade ['sʌnʃeɪd] *n* parasol *m*.

sunshine ['sʌnʃaɪn] *n* lumière *f* du soleil.

sunstroke ['sʌnstrəʊk] *n (U)* insolation *f*.

suntan ['sʌntæn] ◇ *n* bronzage *m*. ◇ *comp* [lotion, cream] solaire.

suntrap ['sʌntræp] *n* UK endroit très ensoleillé.

super ['suːpər] *adj inf* génial(e), super *(inv)*.

superannuation ['suːpə,rænjʊ'eɪʃn] *n (U)* pension *f* de retraite.

superb [suː'pɜːb] *adj* superbe.

superbug ['suːpəbʌg] *n* germe résistant aux traitements antibiotiques.

supercilious [,suːpə'sɪlɪəs] *adj* hautain(e).

superficial [,suːpə'fɪʃl] *adj* superficiel(elle).

superfluous [suː'pɜːflʊəs] *adj* superflu(e).

superhighway ['suːpə,haɪweɪ] *n* 1. US autoroute *f* - 2. = information highway.

superhuman [,suːpə'hjuːmən] *adj* surhumain(e).

superimpose [,suːpərɪm'pəʊz] *vt* : **to superimpose sthg (on)** superposer qqch (à).

superintendent [,suːpərɪn'tendənt] *n* 1. UK [of police] ≃ commissaire *m* - 2. [of department] directeur *m*, -trice *f*.

superior [suː'pɪərɪər] ◇ *adj* 1. [gen] : **superior (to)** supérieur(e) (à) - 2. [goods, craftsmanship] de qualité supérieure. ◇ *n* supérieur *m*, -e *f*.

superlative [suː'pɜːlətɪv] ◇ *adj* exceptionnel(elle), sans pareil(eille). ◇ *n* GRAM superlatif *m*.

supermarket ['suːpə,mɑːkɪt] *n* supermarché *m*.

supernatural [,suːpə'nætʃrəl] *adj* surnaturel(elle).

superpower ['suːpə,paʊər] *n* superpuissance *f*.

supersede [,suːpə'siːd] *vt* remplacer.

supersonic [,suːpə'sɒnɪk] *adj* supersonique.

superstitious [,suːpə'stɪʃəs] *adj* superstitieux(euse).

superstore ['suːpəstɔːr] *n* hypermarché *m*.

supertanker ['suːpə,tæŋkər] *n* supertanker *m*, pétrolier *m* géant.

supervise ['suːpəvaɪz] *vt* surveiller ; [work] superviser.

supervisor ['suːpəvaɪzər] *n* surveillant *m*, -e *f*.

supine ['suːpaɪn] *adj lit* [on one's back] couché(e) OR étendu(e) sur le dos.

supper ['sʌpər] *n* [evening meal] dîner *m*.

supple ['sʌpl] *adj* souple.

supplement ◇ *n* ['sʌplɪmənt] supplément *m*. ◇ *vt* ['sʌplɪment] compléter.

supplementary [,sʌplɪ'mentərɪ] *adj* supplémentaire.

supplementary benefit *n* UK ancien nom des allocations supplémentaires accordées aux personnes ayant un faible revenu.

supplier [sə'plaɪər] *n* fournisseur *m*, -euse *f*.

supply [sə'plaɪ] ◇ *n* 1. [store] réserve *f*, provision *f* - 2. [system] alimentation *f* - 3. *(U)* ECON offre *f*. ◇ *vt* 1. [provide] : **to supply sthg (to sb)** fournir qqch (à qqn) - 2. [provide to] : **to supply sb (with)** fournir qqn (en), approvisionner qqn (en) ; **to supply sthg with sthg** alimenter qqch en qqch. ◆ **supplies** *npl* [food] vivres *mpl* ; MIL approvisionnements *mpl* ; **office supplies** fournitures *fpl* de bureau.

support [sə'pɔːt] ◇ *n* 1. *(U)* [physical help] appui *m* - 2. *(U)* [emotional, financial help] soutien *m* - 3. [object] support *m*, appui *m* - 4. *(U)* COMPUT assistance *f*. ◇ *vt* 1. [physically] soutenir, supporter ; [weight] supporter - 2. [emotionally] soutenir - 3. [financially] subvenir aux besoins de - 4. [theory] être en faveur de, être partisan de ; [political party, candidate] appuyer ; SPORT être un supporter de.

supporter [sə'pɔːtər] *n* 1. [of person, plan] partisan *m*, -e *f* - 2. SPORT supporter *m*.

support group *n* groupe *m* d'entraide.

suppose [sə'pəʊz] ◇ *vt* supposer. ◇ *vi* supposer ; **I suppose (so)** je suppose que oui ; **I suppose not** je suppose que non.

supposed [sə'pəʊzd] *adj* 1. [doubtful] supposé(e) - 2. [reputed, intended] : **to be supposed to be** être censé(e) être.

supposedly [sə'pəʊzɪdlɪ] *adv* soi-disant.

supposing [sə'pəʊzɪŋ] *conj* et si, à supposer que (+ subjunctive).

suppress [sə'pres] *vt* 1. [uprising] réprimer - 2. [information] supprimer - 3. [emotions] réprimer, étouffer.

supreme [sʊ'priːm] *adj* suprême.

Supreme Court n [in US]: the Supreme Court la Cour suprême.

surcharge ['sɜːtʃɑːdʒ] n [extra payment] surcharge f ; [extra tax] surtaxe f.

sure [ʃʊəʳ] <> adj **1.** [gen] sûr(e) ; **to be sure of o.s.** être sûr de soi - **2.** [certain]: **to be sure (of sthg/of doing sthg)** être sûr(e) (de qqch/de faire qqch), être certain(e) (de qqch/de faire qqch) ; **to make sure (that)...** : **we made sure that no one was listening** nous nous sommes assurés OR nous avons vérifié que personne n'écoutait ; **I am** OR **I'm sure (that)...** je suis bien certain que..., je ne doute pas que... <> adv **1.** inf [yes] bien sûr - **2.** US [really] vraiment. **for sure** adv sans aucun doute. **sure enough** adv en effet, effectivement.

surely ['ʃʊəlɪ] adv sûrement.

surety ['ʃʊərətɪ] n (U) caution f.

surf [sɜːf] <> n ressac m. <> vt surfer ; **to surf the Net** naviguer sur l'Internet.

surface ['sɜːfɪs] <> n surface f ; **on the surface** fig à première vue, vu de l'extérieur. <> vi **1.** [diver] remonter à la surface ; [submarine, fish] faire surface - **2.** [problem, rumour] apparaître s'étaler au grand jour.

surface mail n courrier m par voie de terre/de mer.

surfboard ['sɜːfbɔːd] n planche f de surf.

surfeit ['sɜːfɪt] n fml excès m.

surfing ['sɜːfɪŋ] n surf m.

surge [sɜːdʒ] <> n **1.** [of people, vehicles] déferlement m ; ELEC surtension f - **2.** [of emotion, interest] vague f, montée f ; [of anger] bouffée f ; [of sales, applications] afflux m. <> vi [people, vehicles] déferler.

surgeon ['sɜːdʒən] n chirurgien m, -ienne f.

surgery ['sɜːdʒərɪ] n **1.** (U) MED [performing operations] chirurgie f - **2.** UK MED [place] cabinet m de consultation.

surgical ['sɜːdʒɪkl] adj chirurgical(e) ; **surgical stocking** bas m orthopédique.

surgical spirit n UK alcool m à 90°.

surly ['sɜːlɪ] adj revêche, renfrogné(e).

surmount [sɜːˈmaʊnt] vt surmonter.

surname ['sɜːneɪm] n nom m de famille.

surpass [səˈpɑːs] vt fml dépasser.

surplus ['sɜːpləs] <> adj en surplus. <> n surplus m.

surprise [səˈpraɪz] <> n surprise f. <> vt surprendre.

surprised [səˈpraɪzd] adj surpris(e).

surprising [səˈpraɪzɪŋ] adj surprenant(e).

surprisingly [səˈpraɪzɪŋlɪ] adv étonnamment.

surrender [səˈrendəʳ] <> n reddition f, capitulation f. <> vi **1.** [stop fighting] : **to surrender (to)** se rendre (à) - **2.** fig [give in] : **to surrender (to)** se laisser aller (à), se livrer (à).

surreptitious [ˌsʌrəpˈtɪʃəs] adj subreptice.

surrogate ['sʌrəgeɪt] <> adj de substitution. <> n substitut m.

surrogate mother n mère f porteuse.

surround [səˈraʊnd] vt entourer ; [subj: police, army] cerner.

surrounding [səˈraʊndɪŋ] adj environnant(e).

surroundings [səˈraʊndɪŋz] npl environnement m.

surveillance [sɜːˈveɪləns] n surveillance f.

survey <> n ['sɜːveɪ] **1.** [investigation] étude f ; [of public opinion] sondage m - **2.** [of land] levé m ; [of building] inspection f. <> vt [səˈveɪ] **1.** [contemplate] passer en revue - **2.** [investigate] faire une étude de, enquêter sur - **3.** [land] faire le levé de ; [building] inspecter.

surveyor [səˈveɪəʳ] n [of building] expert m, -e f ; [of land] géomètre m.

survival [səˈvaɪvl] n [continuing to live] survie f.

survive [səˈvaɪv] <> vt survivre à. <> vi survivre.

survivor [səˈvaɪvəʳ] n survivant m, -e f ; fig battant m, -e f.

susceptible [səˈseptəbl] adj : **susceptible (to)** sensible (à).

suspect <> adj ['sʌspekt] suspect(e). <> n ['sʌspekt] suspect m, -e f. <> vt [səˈspekt] **1.** [distrust] douter de - **2.** [think likely, consider guilty] soupçonner ; **to suspect sb of sthg** soupçonner qqn de qqch.

suspend [səˈspend] vt **1.** [gen] suspendre - **2.** [from school] renvoyer temporairement.

suspended sentence [səˈspendɪd-] n condamnation f avec sursis.

suspender belt [səˈspendəʳ-] n UK portejarretelles m inv.

suspenders [səˈspendəz] npl **1.** UK [for stockings] jarretelles fpl - **2.** US [for trousers] bretelles fpl.

suspense [səˈspens] n suspense m.

suspension [səˈspenʃn] n **1.** [gen & AUT] suspension f - **2.** [from school] renvoi m temporaire.

suspension bridge n pont m suspendu.

suspicion [səˈspɪʃn] n soupçon m.

suspicious [səˈspɪʃəs] adj **1.** [having suspicions] soupçonneux(euse) - **2.** [causing suspicion] suspect(e), louche.

sustain [səˈsteɪn] vt **1.** [maintain] soutenir - **2.** fml [suffer - damage] subir ; [- injury] recevoir - **3.** fml [weight] supporter.

sustenance ['sʌstɪnəns] n (U) fml nourriture f.

SW (abbrev of **short wave**) OC.

swab [swɒb] n MED tampon m.

swagger ['swægər] vi parader.

Swahili [swɑːˈhiːlɪ] n [language] swahili m.

swallow ['swɒləʊ] ⟨⟩ n [bird] hirondelle f. ⟨⟩ vt avaler ; fig [anger, tears] ravaler. ⟨⟩ vi avaler.

swam [swæm] pt ► swim.

swamp [swɒmp] ⟨⟩ n marais m. ⟨⟩ vt 1. [flood] submerger - 2. [overwhelm] déborder, submerger.

swan [swɒn] n cygne m.

swap [swɒp] vt : **to swap sthg (with sb/for sthg)** échanger qqch (avec qqn/contre qqch).

swarm [swɔːm] ⟨⟩ n essaim m. ⟨⟩ vi fig [people] grouiller ; **to be swarming (with)** [place] grouiller (de).

swarthy ['swɔːðɪ] adj basané(e).

swastika ['swɒstɪkə] n croix f gammée.

swat [swɒt] vt écraser.

sway [sweɪ] ⟨⟩ vt [influence] influencer. ⟨⟩ vi se balancer.

swear [sweər] (pt swore, pp sworn) ⟨⟩ vt jurer ; **to swear to do sthg** jurer de faire qqch. ⟨⟩ vi jurer.

swearword ['sweəwɜːd] n juron m, gros mot m.

sweat [swet] ⟨⟩ n [perspiration] transpiration f, sueur f. ⟨⟩ vi 1. [perspire] transpirer, suer - 2. inf [worry] se faire du mouron.

sweater ['swetər] n pullover m.

sweatshirt ['swetʃɜːt] n sweat-shirt m.

sweaty ['swetɪ] adj [skin, clothes] mouillé(e) de sueur.

swede [swiːd] n UK rutabaga m.

Swede [swiːd] n Suédois m, -e f.

Sweden ['swiːdn] n Suède f.

Swedish ['swiːdɪʃ] ⟨⟩ adj suédois(e). ⟨⟩ n [language] suédois m. ⟨⟩ npl : **the Swedish** les Suédois mpl.

sweep [swiːp] ⟨⟩ n 1. [sweeping movement] grand geste m - 2. [with brush] : **to give sthg a sweep** donner un coup de balai à qqch, balayer qqch - 3. [chimney sweep] ramoneur m. ⟨⟩ vt (pt & pp swept) [gen] balayer ; [scan with eyes] parcourir des yeux. ● **sweep away** vt sep [destroy] emporter, entraîner. ● **sweep up** vt sep [with brush] balayer. ⟨⟩ vi balayer.

sweeping ['swiːpɪŋ] adj 1. [effect, change] radical(e) - 2. [statement] hâtif(ive).

sweet [swiːt] ⟨⟩ adj 1. [gen] doux (douce) ; [cake, flavour, pudding] sucré(e)

- 2. [kind] gentil(ille) - 3. [attractive] adorable, mignon(onne). ⟨⟩ n UK 1. [candy] bonbon m - 2. [dessert] dessert m.

sweet corn n maïs m.

sweeten ['swiːtn] vt sucrer.

sweetheart ['swiːthɑːt] n 1. [term of endearment] chéri m, -e f, mon cœur m - 2. [boyfriend, girlfriend] petit ami m, petite amie f.

sweetness ['swiːtnɪs] n 1. [gen] douceur f ; [of taste] goût m sucré, douceur - 2. [attractiveness] charme m.

sweet pea n pois m de senteur.

swell [swel] ⟨⟩ vi (pt -ed, pp swollen OR -ed) 1. [leg, face etc] enfler ; [lungs, balloon] se gonfler ; **to swell with pride** se gonfler d'orgueil - 2. [crowd, population etc] grossir, augmenter ; [sound] grossir, s'enfler. ⟨⟩ vt (pt -ed, pp swollen OR -ed) grossir, augmenter. ⟨⟩ n [of sea] houle f. ⟨⟩ adj US inf dated chouette, épatant(e).

swelling ['swelɪŋ] n enflure f.

sweltering ['sweltərɪŋ] adj étouffant(e), suffocant(e).

swept [swept] pt & pp ► sweep.

swerve [swɜːv] vi faire une embardée.

swift [swɪft] ⟨⟩ adj 1. [fast] rapide - 2. [prompt] prompt(e). ⟨⟩ n [bird] martinet m.

swig [swɪg] inf n lampée f.

swill [swɪl] ⟨⟩ n (U) [pig food] pâtée f. ⟨⟩ vt UK [wash] laver à grande eau.

swim [swɪm] ⟨⟩ n : **to have a swim** nager ; **to go for a swim** aller se baigner, aller nager. ⟨⟩ vi (pt swam, pp swum) 1. [person, fish, animal] nager - 2. [room] tourner ; **my head was swimming** j'avais la tête qui tournait.

swimmer ['swɪmər] n nageur m, -euse f.

swimming ['swɪmɪŋ] n natation f ; **to go swimming** aller nager.

swimming cap n bonnet m de bain.

swimming costume n UK maillot m de bain.

swimming pool n piscine f.

swimming trunks npl maillot m OR slip m de bain.

swimsuit ['swɪmsuːt] n maillot m de bain.

swindle ['swɪndl] ⟨⟩ n escroquerie f. ⟨⟩ vt escroquer, rouler ; **to swindle sb out of sthg** escroquer qqch à qqn.

swine [swaɪn] n inf [person] salaud m.

swing [swɪŋ] ⟨⟩ n 1. [child's toy] balançoire f - 2. [change - of opinion] revirement m ; [- of mood] changement m, saute f - 3. [sway] balancement m ; **to be in full swing** battre son plein. ⟨⟩ vt (pt & pp swung) 1. [move back and forth] balancer - 2. [move in a curve] faire virer. ⟨⟩ vi (pt & pp swung) 1. [move back and forth] se balancer - **2.** [turn - vehicle] virer, tourner ; **to swing round** *UK* OR **around** *US* [person] se retourner - **3.** [change] changer.

swing bridge *n* pont *m* tournant.

swing door *UK*, **swinging door** *US n* porte *f* battante.

swingeing ['swɪndʒɪŋ] *adj UK* très sévère.

swipe [swaɪp] ◇ *vt inf* [steal] faucher, piquer. ◇ *vi :* **to swipe at** envoyer OR donner un coup à.

swirl [swɜːl] ◇ *n* tourbillon *m*. ◇ *vi* tourbillonner, tournoyer.

swish [swɪʃ] *vt* [tail] battre l'air de.

Swiss [swɪs] ◇ *adj* suisse. ◇ *n* [person] Suisse *mf*. ◇ *npl :* **the Swiss** les Suisses *mpl*.

Switch® *n* système de paiement non différé par carte bancaire.

switch [swɪtʃ] ◇ *n* **1.** [control device] interrupteur *m*, commutateur *m* ; [on radio, stereo etc] bouton *m* - **2.** [change] changement *m*. ◇ *vt* [swap] échanger ; [jobs] changer de ; **to switch places with sb** échanger sa place avec qqn. ◆ **switch off** *vt sep* éteindre. ◆ **switch on** *vt sep* allumer.

switchboard ['swɪtʃbɔːd] *n* standard *m*.

Switzerland ['swɪtsələnd] *n* Suisse *f* ; **in Switzerland** en Suisse.

swivel ['swɪvl] (*UK & US*) ◇ *vt* [chair] faire pivoter ; [head, eyes] faire tourner. ◇ *vi* [chair] pivoter ; [head, eyes] tourner.

swivel chair *n* fauteuil *m* pivotant OR tournant.

swollen ['swəʊln] ◇ *pp* ► swell. ◇ *adj* [ankle, face] enflé(e) ; [river] en crue.

swoop [swuːp] ◇ *n* [raid] descente *f*. ◇ *vi* **1.** [bird, plane] piquer - **2.** [police, army] faire une descente.

swop [swɒp] = swap.

sword [sɔːd] *n* épée *f*.

swordfish ['sɔːdfɪʃ] (*pl* swordfish OR -es [-iːz]) *n* espadon *m*.

swore [swɔːr] *pt* ► swear.

sworn [swɔːn] ◇ *pp* ► swear. ◇ *adj* LAW sous serment.

swot [swɒt] *UK inf* ◇ *n pej* bûcheur *m*, -euse *f*. ◇ *vi :* **to swot (for)** bûcher (pour).

swum [swʌm] *pp* ► swim.

swung [swʌŋ] *pt & pp* ► swing.

sycamore ['sɪkəmɔːr] *n* sycomore *m*.

syllable ['sɪləbl] *n* syllabe *f*.

syllabus ['sɪləbəs] (*pl* -buses [-bəsiːz] OR -bi [-baɪ]) *n* programme *m*.

symbol ['sɪmbl] *n* symbole *m*.

symbolize, *UK* -ise ['sɪmbəlaɪz] *vt* symboliser.

symmetry ['sɪmɪtrɪ] *n* symétrie *f*.

sympathetic [,sɪmpə'θetɪk] *adj* **1.** [understanding] compatissant(e), compréhensif(ive) - **2.** [willing to support] : **sympathetic (to)** bien disposé(e) (à l'égard de).

sympathize, *UK* -ise ['sɪmpəθaɪz] *vi* **1.** [feel sorry] compatir ; **to sympathize with sb** plaindre qqn ; [in grief] compatir à la douleur de qqn - **2.** [understand] : **to sympathize with sthg** comprendre qqch - **3.** [support] : **to sympathize with sthg** approuver qqch, soutenir qqch.

sympathizer, *UK* -iser ['sɪmpəθaɪzər] *n* sympathisant *m*, -e *f*.

sympathy ['sɪmpəθɪ] *n* (*U*) **1.** [understanding] : **sympathy (for)** compassion *f* (pour), sympathie *f* (pour) - **2.** [agreement] approbation *f*, sympathie *f*. ◆ **sympathies** *npl* [to bereaved person] condoléances *fpl*.

symphony ['sɪmfənɪ] *n* symphonie *f*.

symposium [sɪm'pəʊzjəm] (*pl* -siums OR -sia [-zjə]) *n* symposium *m*.

symptom ['sɪmptəm] *n* symptôme *m*.

synagogue ['sɪnəgɒg] *n* synagogue *f*.

syndicate *n* ['sɪndɪkət] syndicat *m*, consortium *m*.

syndrome ['sɪndrəʊm] *n* syndrome *m*.

synonym ['sɪnənɪm] *n :* **synonym (for** OR **of)** synonyme *m* (de).

synopsis [sɪ'nɒpsɪs] (*pl* -ses [-siːz]) *n* résumé *m* ; [film] synopsis *m*.

syntax ['sɪntæks] *n* syntaxe *f*.

synthesis ['sɪnθəsɪs] (*pl* -ses [-siːz]) *n* synthèse *f*.

synthetic [sɪn'θetɪk] *adj* **1.** [man-made] synthétique - **2.** *pej* [insincere] artificiel(elle), forcé(e).

syphilis ['sɪfɪlɪs] *n* syphilis *f*.

syphon ['saɪfn] = siphon.

Syria ['sɪrɪə] *n* Syrie *f*.

syringe [sɪ'rɪndʒ] *n* seringue *f*.

syrup ['sɪrəp] *n* (*U*) **1.** [sugar and water] sirop *m* - **2.** *UK* [golden syrup] mélasse *f* raffinée.

system ['sɪstəm] *n* **1.** [gen] système *m* ; road/railway system réseau *m* routier/de chemins de fer - **2.** [equipment - gen] installation *f* ; [- electric, electronic] appareil *m* - **3.** (*U*) [methodical approach] système *m*, méthode *f*.

systematic [,sɪstə'mætɪk] *adj* systématique.

system disk *n* COMPUT disque *m* système.

systems analyst ['sɪstəmz-] *n* COMPUT analyste fonctionnel *m*, analyste fonctionnelle *f*.

T

t [ti:] (*pl* **t's** OR **ts**), **T** (*pl* **T's** OR **Ts**) *n* [letter] t *m inv*, T *m inv*.

ta [tɑː] *excl* UK *inf* merci!

tab [tæb] *n* **1.** [of cloth] étiquette *f* - **2.** [of metal] languette *f* - **3.** US [bill] addition *f* ; **to keep tabs on sb** tenir OR avoir qqn à l'œil, surveiller qqn.

tabby ['tæbɪ] *n* : **tabby (cat)** chat tigré *m*, chatte tigrée *f*.

table ['teɪbl] <> *n* table *f*. <> *vt* UK [propose] présenter, proposer.

tablecloth ['teɪblklɒθ] *n* nappe *f*.

table lamp *n* lampe *f*.

tablemat ['teɪblmæt] *n* dessous-de-plat *m inv*.

tablespoon ['teɪblspuːn] *n* **1.** [spoon] cuiller *f* de service - **2.** [spoonful] cuillerée *f* à soupe.

tablet ['tæblɪt] *n* **1.** [pill] comprimé *m*, cachet *m* - **2.** [of stone] plaque *f* commémorative - **3.** [of soap] savonnette *f*, pain *m* de savon.

table tennis *n* ping-pong *m*, tennis *m* de table.

table wine *n* vin *m* de table.

tabloid ['tæblɔɪd] *n* : **tabloid (newspaper)** tabloïd *m*, tabloïde *m* ; **the tabloid press** la presse populaire.

tabulate ['tæbjʊleɪt] *vt* présenter sous forme de tableau.

tacit ['tæsɪt] *adj* tacite.

taciturn ['tæsɪtɜːn] *adj* taciturne.

tack [tæk] <> *n* **1.** [nail] clou *m* - **2.** US [thumbtack] punaise *f* - **3.** NAUT bord *m*, bordée *f* - **4.** *fig* [course of action] tactique *f*, méthode *f*. <> *vt* **1.** [fasten with nail - gen] clouer ; [- notice] punaiser - **2.** SEW faufiler. <> *vi* NAUT tirer une bordée.

tackle ['tækl] <> *n* **1.** FOOTBALL tacle *m* ; RUGBY plaquage *m* - **2.** [equipment] équipement *m*, matériel *m* - **3.** [for lifting] palan *m*, appareil *m* de levage. <> *vt* **1.** [deal with] s'attaquer à - **2.** FOOTBALL tacler ; RUGBY plaquer - **3.** [attack] empoigner.

tacky ['tækɪ] *adj* **1.** *inf* [film, remark] d'un goût douteux ; [jewellery] de pacotille - **2.** [sticky] collant(e), pas encore sec (sèche).

tact [tækt] *n* (U) tact *m*, délicatesse *f*.

tactful ['tæktfʊl] *adj* [remark] plein(e) de tact ; [person] qui a du tact OR de la délicatesse.

tactic ['tæktɪk] *n* tactique *f*. ➡ **tactics** *n* (U) MIL tactique *f*.

tactical ['tæktɪkl] *adj* tactique.

tactless ['tæktlɪs] *adj* qui manque de tact OR délicatesse.

tadpole ['tædpəʊl] *n* têtard *m*.

tag [tæg] *n* **1.** [of cloth] marque *f* - **2.** [of paper] étiquette *f*. ➡ **tag along** *vi inf* suivre.

tail [teɪl] <> *n* **1.** [gen] queue *f* - **2.** [of coat] basque *f*, pan *m* ; [of shirt] pan. <> *vt inf* [follow] filer. ➡ **tails** <> *n* [side of coin] pile *f*. <> *npl* [formal dress] queue-de-pie *f*, habit *m*. ➡ **tail off** *vi* [voice] s'affaiblir ; [noise] diminuer.

tailback ['teɪlbæk] *n* UK bouchon *m*.

tailcoat [ˌteɪl'kəʊt] *n* habit *m*, queue-de-pie *f*.

tail end *n* fin *f*.

tailfin ['teɪlfɪn] *n* dérive *f*.

tailgate ['teɪlgeɪt] *n* AUT hayon *m*.

tailor ['teɪlər] <> *n* tailleur *m*. <> *vt fig* adapter.

tailor-made *adj fig* sur mesure.

tailwind ['teɪlwɪnd] *n* vent *m* arrière.

tainted ['teɪntɪd] *adj* **1.** [reputation] souillé(e), entaché(e) - **2.** US [food] avarié(e).

Taiwan [ˌtaɪ'wɑːn] *n* Taiwan.

take [teɪk] (*pt* took, *pp* taken) <> *vt* **1.** [gen] prendre ; **to take an exam** passer un examen ; **to take a walk** se promener, faire une promenade ; **to take a bath/photo** prendre un bain/une photo ; **to take offence** se vexer, s'offenser - **2.** [lead, drive] emmener - **3.** [accept] accepter - **4.** [contain] contenir, avoir une capacité de - **5.** [tolerate] supporter - **6.** [require] demander ; **how long will it take?** combien de temps cela va-t-il prendre? - **7.** [wear] : **what size do you take?** [clothes] quelle taille faites-vous? ; [shoes] vous chaussez du combien? - **8.** [assume] : **I take it (that)...** je suppose que..., je pense que... - **9.** [rent] prendre, louer. <> *n* CIN prise *f* de vues. ➡ **take after** *vt insep* tenir de, ressembler à. ➡ **take apart** *vt sep* [dismantle] démonter. ➡ **take away** *vt sep* **1.** [remove] enlever - **2.** [deduct] retrancher, soustraire. ➡ **take back** *vt sep* **1.** [return] rendre, rapporter - **2.** [accept] reprendre - **3.** [statement, accusation] retirer. ➡ **take down** *vt sep* **1.** [dismantle] démonter - **2.** [write down] prendre - **3.** [lower] baisser. ➡ **take in** *vt sep* **1.** [deceive] rouler, tromper - **2.** [understand] comprendre - **3.** [include]

englober, couvrir - **4.** [provide accommodation for] recueillir. ➤ **take off** <> vt sep **1.** [remove] enlever, ôter - **2.** [have as holiday] : **to take a week/day off** prendre une semaine/un jour de congé - **3.** UK [imitate] imiter. <> vi **1.** [plane] décoller - **2.** [go away suddenly] partir. ➤ **take on** vt sep **1.** [accept] accepter, prendre - **2.** [employ] embaucher, prendre - **3.** [confront] s'attaquer à ; [competitor] faire concurrence à ; SPORT jouer contre. ➤ **take out** vt sep [go out with] emmener, sortir avec. ➤ **take over** <> vt sep **1.** [take control of] reprendre, prendre la direction de - **2.** [job] : **to take over sb's job** remplacer qqn, prendre la suite de qqn. <> vi **1.** [take control] prendre le pouvoir - **2.** [replace] prendre la relève. ➤ **take to** vt insep **1.** [person] éprouver de la sympathie pour, sympathiser avec ; [activity] prendre goût à - **2.** [begin] : **to take to doing sthg** se mettre à faire qqch. ➤ **take up** vt sep **1.** [begin - job] prendre ; **to take up singing** se mettre au chant - **2.** [use up] prendre, occuper. ➤ **take up on** vt sep [accept] : **to take sb up on an offer** accepter l'offre de qqn.

takeaway UK ['teɪkə,weɪ], **takeout** US ['teɪkaut] n [food] plat m à emporter.

taken ['teɪkn] pp ➤ take.

takeoff ['teɪkɒf] n [of plane] décollage m.

takeout US = takeaway.

takeover ['teɪk,əuvə^r] n **1.** [of company] prise f de contrôle, rachat m - **2.** [of government] prise f de pouvoir.

takings ['teɪkɪŋz] npl recette f.

talc [tælk], **talcum (powder)** ['tælkəm-] n talc m.

tale [teɪl] n **1.** [fictional story] histoire f, conte m - **2.** [anecdote] récit m, histoire f.

talent ['tælənt] n : **talent (for)** talent m (pour).

talented ['tæləntɪd] adj qui a du talent, talentueux(euse).

talk [tɔːk] <> n **1.** [conversation] discussion f, conversation f - **2.** (U) [gossip] bavardages mpl, racontars mpl - **3.** [lecture] conférence f, causerie f. <> vi **1.** [speak] : **to talk (to sb)** parler (à qqn) ; **to talk about** parler de - **2.** [gossip] bavarder, jaser - **3.** [make a speech] faire un discours, parler ; **to talk on** OR **about** parler de. <> vt parler. ➤ **talk into** vt sep : **to talk sb into doing sthg** persuader qqn de faire qqch. ➤ **talk out of** vt sep : **to talk sb out of doing sthg** dissuader qqn de faire qqch. ➤ **talk over** vt sep discuter de. ➤ **talk up** vt sep vanter les mérites de, faire de la publicité pour. ➤ **talks** npl entretiens mpl, pourparlers mpl.

talkative ['tɔːkətɪv] adj bavard(e), loquace.

talk show n TV talk-show m, causerie f télévisée.

talk time n (U) crédit m de communication.

tall [tɔːl] adj grand(e) ; **how tall are you?** combien mesurez-vous? ; **she's 5 feet tall** elle mesure 1,50 m.

tall story n histoire f à dormir debout.

tally ['tælɪ] <> n compte m. <> vi correspondre, concorder.

talon ['tælən] n serre f, griffe f.

tambourine [,tæmbə'riːn] n tambourin m.

tame [teɪm] <> adj **1.** [animal, bird] apprivoisé(e) - **2.** pej [person] docile ; [party, story, life] terne, morne. <> vt **1.** [animal, bird] apprivoiser - **2.** [people] mater, dresser.

tamper ['tæmpə^r] ➤ **tamper with** vt insep [machine] toucher à ; [records, file] altérer, falsifier ; [lock] essayer de crocheter.

tampon ['tæmpɒn] n tampon m.

tan [tæn] <> adj brun clair (inv). <> n bronzage m, hâle m. <> vi bronzer.

tang [tæŋ] n [taste] saveur f forte OR piquante ; [smell] odeur f forte OR piquante.

tangent ['tændʒənt] n GEOM tangente f ; **to go off at a tangent** fig changer de sujet, faire une digression.

tangerine [,tændʒə'riːn] n mandarine f.

tangible ['tændʒəbl] adj tangible.

Tangier [tæn'dʒɪə^r] n Tanger.

tangle ['tæŋgl] n **1.** [mass] enchevêtrement m, emmêlement m - **2.** fig [confusion] : **to get into a tangle** s'empêtrer, s'embrouiller.

tank [tæŋk] n **1.** [container] réservoir m ; **fish tank** aquarium m - **2.** MIL tank m, char m (d'assaut).

tanker ['tæŋkə^r] n **1.** [ship - for oil] pétrolier m - **2.** [truck] camion-citerne m - **3.** [train] wagon-citerne m.

tanned [tænd] adj bronzé(e), hâlé(e).

Tannoy® ['tænɔɪ] n système m de haut-parleurs.

tantalizing ['tæntəlaɪzɪŋ] adj [smell] très appétissant(e) ; [possibility, thought] très tentant(e).

tantamount ['tæntəmaunt] adj : **tantamount to équivalent(e) à.

tantrum ['tæntrəm] (pl -s) n crise f de colère ; **to have** OR **throw a tantrum** faire OR piquer une colère.

Tanzania [,tænzə'nɪə] n Tanzanie f.

tap [tæp] <> n **1.** UK [device] robinet m - **2.** [light blow] petite tape f, petit coup m. <> vt **1.** [hit] tapoter, taper - **2.** [resources, energy] exploiter, utiliser - **3.** [telephone, wire] mettre sur écoute.

tap dance n (U) claquettes fpl.

tape [teɪp] <> n **1.** [magnetic tape] bande f magnétique ; [cassette] cassette f - **2.** [strip of cloth, adhesive material] ruban m. <> vt **1.** [record] enregistrer ; [on video] magnétoscoper, enregistrer au magnétoscope - **2.** [stick] scotcher.

tape measure n centimètre m, mètre m.

taper ['teɪpər] vi s'effiler ; [trousers] se terminer en fuseau.

tape recorder n magnétophone m.

tapestry ['tæpɪstrɪ] n tapisserie f.

tar [tɑːr] n (U) goudron m.

target ['tɑːgɪt] <> n **1.** [of missile, bomb] objectif m ; [for archery, shooting] cible f - **2.** fig [for criticism] cible f - **3.** fig [goal] objectif m. <> vt **1.** [city, building] viser - **2.** fig [subj: policy] s'adresser à, viser ; [subj: advertising] cibler.

tariff ['tærɪf] n **1.** [tax] tarif m douanier - **2.** [list] tableau m OR liste f des prix.

Tarmac® ['tɑːmæk] n [material] macadam m. ⬪ **tarmac** n AERON : **the tarmac** la piste.

tarnish ['tɑːnɪʃ] vt lit & fig ternir.

tarpaulin [tɑːˈpɔːlɪn] n [material] toile f goudronnée ; [sheet] bâche f.

tart [tɑːt] <> adj **1.** [bitter] acide - **2.** [sarcastic] acide, acerbe. <> n **1.** CULIN tarte f - **2.** v inf [prostitute] pute f. ⬪ **tart up** vt sep UK inf pej [room] retaper, rénover ; **to tart o.s. up** se faire beau (belle).

tartan ['tɑːtn] <> n tartan m. <> comp écossais(e).

tartar(e) sauce ['tɑːtər-] n sauce f tartare.

task [tɑːsk] n tâche f, besogne f.

task force n MIL corps m expéditionnaire.

tassel ['tæsl] n pompon m, gland m.

taste [teɪst] <> n **1.** [gen] goût m ; **have a taste!** goûte! ; **in good/bad taste** de bon/mauvais goût - **2.** fig [liking] : **taste (for)** penchant m (pour), goût m (pour) - **3.** fig [experience] aperçu m. <> vt **1.** [sense - food] sentir - **2.** [test, try] déguster, goûter - **3.** fig [experience] tâter de, goûter de. <> vi : **to taste good/odd** etc avoir bon goût/un drôle de goût etc ; **to taste of/like** avoir le goût de.

tasteful ['teɪstfʊl] adj de bon goût.

tasteless ['teɪstlɪs] adj **1.** [object, decor, remark] de mauvais goût - **2.** [food] qui n'a aucun goût, fade.

tasty ['teɪstɪ] adj [delicious] délicieux(euse), succulent(e).

tatters ['tætəz] npl : **in tatters** [clothes] en lambeaux ; [confidence] brisé(e) ; [reputation] ruiné(e).

tattoo [təˈtuː] <> n (pl -s) **1.** [design] tatouage m - **2.** UK [military display] parade f OR défilé m militaire. <> vt tatouer.

tatty ['tætɪ] adj UK inf pej [clothes] défraîchi(e), usé(e) ; [flat, area] miteux(euse), minable.

taught [tɔːt] pt & pp ➤ **teach.**

taunt [tɔːnt] <> vt railler, se moquer de. <> n raillerie f, moquerie f.

Taurus ['tɔːrəs] n Taureau m.

taut [tɔːt] adj tendu(e).

tawdry ['tɔːdrɪ] adj pej [jewellery] clinquant(e) ; [clothes] voyant(e), criard(e).

tax [tæks] <> n ADMIN taxe f, impôt m. <> vt **1.** [goods] taxer - **2.** [profits, business, person] imposer - **3.** [strain] mettre à l'épreuve.

taxable ['tæksəbl] adj imposable.

tax allowance n UK abattement m fiscal.

taxation [tækˈseɪʃn] n (U) **1.** [system] imposition f - **2.** [amount] impôts mpl.

tax avoidance [-əˈvɔɪdəns] n évasion f fiscale.

tax collector n percepteur m.

tax disc n UK vignette f.

tax evasion n fraude f fiscale.

tax-free, US **tax-exempt** adj exonéré(e) (d'impôt).

taxi ['tæksɪ] <> n taxi m. <> vi [plane] rouler au sol.

taxi driver n chauffeur m de taxi.

tax inspector n inspecteur m des impôts.

taxi rank UK, **taxi stand** n station f de taxis.

taxpayer ['tæks,peɪər] n contribuable mf.

tax relief n allègement m OR dégrèvement m fiscal.

tax return n déclaration f d'impôts.

TB n abbrev of **tuberculosis.**

tea [tiː] n **1.** [drink, leaves] thé m - **2.** UK [afternoon meal] goûter m ; [evening meal] dîner m.

teabag ['tiːbæg] n sachet m de thé.

tea break n UK pause pour prendre le thé, ≈ pause-café f.

teach [tiːtʃ] (pt & pp **taught**) <> vt **1.** [instruct] apprendre ; **to teach sb sthg, to teach sthg to sb** apprendre qqch à qqn ; **to teach sb to do sthg** apprendre à qqn à faire qqch - **2.** [subj: teacher] enseigner ; **to teach sb sthg, to teach sthg to sb** enseigner qqch à qqn. <> vi enseigner.

teacher ['tiːtʃər] n [in primary school] instituteur m, -trice f, maître m, maîtresse f ; [in secondary school] professeur m, -(e) f.

teacher training college UK, **teacher's college** US n ≈ institut m universitaire de formation des maîtres, ≈ IUFM m.

teaching ['tiːtʃɪŋ] n enseignement m.

teaching aid n support m pédagogique.

tea cloth *n* UK **1.** [tablecloth] nappe *f* - **2.** [tea towel] torchon *m*.

tea cosy, US **tea cozy** *n* couvre-théière *m inv*, cosy *m*.

teacup ['ti:kʌp] *n* tasse *f* à thé.

teak [ti:k] *n* teck *m*.

team [ti:m] *n* équipe *f*.

teammate ['ti:mmeɪt] *n* co-équipier *m*, -ère *f*.

teamwork ['ti:mwɜ:k] *n (U)* travail *m* d'équipe, collaboration *f*.

teapot ['ti:pɒt] *n* théière *f*.

tear[1] [tɪə] *n* larme *f*.

tear[2] [teə] ⟨⟩ *vt* (*pt* **tore**, *pp* **torn**) **1.** [rip] déchirer - **2.** [remove roughly] arracher. ⟨⟩ *vi* (*pt* **tore**, *pp* **torn**) **1.** [rip] se déchirer - **2.** [move quickly] foncer, aller à toute allure. ⟨⟩ *n* déchirure *f*, accroc *m*. ◆ **tear apart** *vt sep* **1.** [rip] déchirer, mettre en morceaux - **2.** *fig* [country, company] diviser ; [person] déchirer. ◆ **tear down** *vt sep* [building] démolir ; [poster] arracher. ◆ **tear out** *vt sep* [page] arracher ; [cheque] détacher ; **to tear one's hair (out)** *lit & fig* s'arracher les cheveux. ◆ **tear up** *vt sep* déchirer.

teardrop ['tɪədrɒp] *n* larme *f*.

tearful ['tɪəfʊl] *adj* [person] en larmes.

tear gas [tɪə-] *n (U)* gaz *m* lacrymogène.

tearoom ['ti:rʊm] *n* salon *m* de thé.

tease [ti:z] ⟨⟩ *vt* taquin, -e *f*. ⟨⟩ *vt* [mock] : **to tease sb (about sthg)** taquiner qqn (à propos de qqch).

tea service, tea set *n* service *m* à thé.

teaspoon ['ti:spu:n] *n* **1.** [utensil] petite cuillère *f*, cuillère à café - **2.** [amount] cuillerée *f* à café.

teat [ti:t] *n* tétine *f*.

teatime ['ti:taɪm] *n* UK l'heure *f* du thé.

tea towel *n* UK torchon *m*.

technical ['teknɪkl] *adj* technique.

technical college *n* UK collège *m* technique.

technicality [,teknɪ'kælətɪ] *n* **1.** [intricacy] technicité *f* - **2.** [detail] détail *m* technique.

technically ['teknɪklɪ] *adv* **1.** [gen] techniquement - **2.** [theoretically] en théorie.

technician [tek'nɪʃn] *n* technicien *m*, -enne *f*.

technique [tek'ni:k] *n* technique *f*.

techno ['teknəʊ] *n* MUS techno *f*.

technological [,teknə'lɒdʒɪkl] *adj* technologique.

technology [tek'nɒlədʒɪ] *n* technologie *f*.

teddy ['tedɪ] *n* : **teddy (bear)** ours *m* en peluche, nounours *m*.

tedious ['ti:djəs] *adj* ennuyeux(euse).

tee [ti:] *n* GOLF tee *m*.

teem [ti:m] *vi* **1.** [rain] pleuvoir à verse - **2.** [place] : **to be teeming with** grouiller de.

teenage ['ti:neɪdʒ] *adj* adolescent(e).

teenager ['ti:n,eɪdʒə] *n* adolescent *m*, -e *f*.

teens [ti:nz] *npl* adolescence *f*.

tee shirt *n* tee-shirt *m*.

teeter ['ti:tə] *vi* vaciller ; **to teeter on the brink of** *fig* être au bord de.

teeth [ti:θ] *npl* ► **tooth**.

teethe [ti:ð] *vi* [baby] percer ses dents.

teething troubles ['ti:ðɪŋ-] *npl* *fig* difficultés *fpl* initiales.

teetotaller UK, **teetotaler** US [ti:'təʊtlə] *n* personne *f* qui ne boit jamais d'alcool.

TEFL ['tefl] (*abbrev of* **teaching of English as a foreign language**) *n* enseignement de l'anglais langue étrangère.

tel. (*abbrev of* **telephone**) tél.

telecom ['telɪkɒm] *n (U)* UK *inf* télécommunications *fpl*.

telecoms ['telɪkɒmz] *npl* = **telecom**.

telecommunications ['telɪkə,mju:nɪ'keɪʃnz] *npl* télécommunications *fpl*.

teleconference ['telɪ,kɒnfərəns] *n* téléconférence *f*.

telegram ['telɪgræm] *n* télégramme *m*.

telegraph ['telɪgrɑ:f] ⟨⟩ *n* télégraphe *m*. ⟨⟩ *vt* télégraphier.

telegraph pole UK, **telegraph post** UK, **telephone pole** US *n* poteau *m* télégraphique.

telepathy [tɪ'lepəθɪ] *n* télépathie *f*.

telephone ['telɪfəʊn] ⟨⟩ *n* téléphone *m* ; **to be on the telephone** UK [connected] avoir le téléphone ; [speaking] être au téléphone. ⟨⟩ *vt* téléphoner à. ⟨⟩ *vi* téléphoner.

telephone book *n* annuaire *m*.

telephone booth *n* cabine *f* téléphonique.

telephone box *n* UK cabine *f* téléphonique.

telephone call *n* appel *m* téléphonique, coup *m* de téléphone.

telephone directory *n* annuaire *m*.

telephone number *n* numéro *m* de téléphone.

telephone pole US = **telegraph pole**.

telephonist [tɪ'lefənɪst] *n* UK téléphoniste *mf*.

telephoto lens [,telɪ'fəʊtəʊ-] *n* téléobjectif *m*.

telescope ['telɪskəʊp] *n* télescope *m*.

teletext ['telɪtekst] *n* télétexte *m*.

televideo [telɪ'vɪdəʊ] *n* combiné *m* télémagnétoscope.

televise ['telɪvaɪz] *vt* téléviser.

television ['telɪ,vɪʒn] *n* **1.** *(U)* [medium, industry] télévision *f* ; **on television** à la télévision - **2.** [apparatus] (poste *m* de) télévision *f*, téléviseur *m*.

television set *n* poste *m* de télévision, téléviseur *m*.

telex ['teleks] ⟨⟩ *n* télex *m*. ⟨⟩ *vt* [message] envoyer par télex, télexer ; [person] envoyer un télex à.

tell [tel] *(pt & pp* **told**) ⟨⟩ *vt* **1.** [gen] dire ; [story] raconter ; **to tell sb (that)...** dire à qqn que... ; **to tell sb sthg, to tell sthg to sb** dire qqch à qqn ; **to tell sb to do sthg** dire OR ordonner à qqn de faire qqch - **2.** [judge, recognize] savoir, voir ; **could you tell me the time?** tu peux me dire l'heure (qu'il est)? ⟨⟩ *vi* **1.** [speak] parler - **2.** [judge] savoir - **3.** [have effect] se faire sentir. ◆ **tell apart** *vt sep* distinguer. ◆ **tell off** *vt sep* gronder.

telling ['telɪŋ] *adj* [remark] révélateur(trice).

telltale ['telteɪl] ⟨⟩ *adj* révélateur(trice). ⟨⟩ *n* rapporteur *m*, -euse *f*, mouchard *m*, -e *f*.

telly ['telɪ] *(abbrev of* **television***) n* UK *inf* télé *f* ; **on telly** à la télé.

temp [temp] *inf* ⟨⟩ *n (abbrev of* **temporary (employee)***)* intérimaire *mf*. ⟨⟩ *vi* UK travailler comme intérimaire.

temper ['tempər] ⟨⟩ *n* **1.** [angry state] : **to be in a temper** être en colère ; **to lose one's temper** se mettre en colère - **2.** [mood] humeur *f* - **3.** [temperament] tempérament *m*. ⟨⟩ *vt* [moderate] tempérer.

temperament ['temprəmənt] *n* tempérament *m*.

temperamental [,temprə'mentl] *adj* [volatile, unreliable] capricieux(euse).

temperate ['temprət] *adj* tempéré(e).

temperature ['temprətʃər] *n* température *f* ; **to have a temperature** avoir de la température OR de la fièvre.

tempestuous [tem'pestjʊəs] *adj lit & fig* orageux(euse).

template ['templɪt] *n* gabarit *m*.

temple ['templ] *n* **1.** RELIG temple *m* - **2.** ANAT tempe *f*.

temporarily [,tempə'rerəlɪ] *adv* temporairement, provisoirement.

temporary ['tempərərɪ] *adj* temporaire, provisoire.

tempt [tempt] *vt* tenter ; **to tempt sb to do sthg** donner à qqn l'envie de faire qqch.

temptation [temp'teɪʃn] *n* tentation *f*.

tempting ['temptɪŋ] *adj* tentant(e).

ten [ten] *num* dix ; *see also* **six**.

tenable ['tenəbl] *adj* [argument, position] défendable.

tenacious [tɪ'neɪʃəs] *adj* tenace.

tenancy ['tenənsɪ] *n* location *f*.

tenant ['tenənt] *n* locataire *mf*.

tend [tend] *vt* **1.** [have tendency] : **to tend to do sthg** avoir tendance à faire qqch - **2.** [look after] s'occuper de, garder.

tendency ['tendənsɪ] *n* : **tendency (to do sthg)** tendance *f* (à faire qqch).

tender ['tendər] ⟨⟩ *adj* tendre ; [bruise, part of body] sensible, douloureux(euse). ⟨⟩ *n* COMM soumission *f*. ⟨⟩ *vt fml* [apology, money] offrir ; [resignation] donner.

tendon ['tendən] *n* tendon *m*.

tenement ['tenəmənt] *n* immeuble *m*.

Tenerife [,tenə'ri:f] *n* Tenerife.

tenet ['tenɪt] *n fml* principe *m*.

tennis ['tenɪs] *n (U)* tennis *m*.

tennis ball *n* balle *f* de tennis.

tennis court *n* court *m* de tennis.

tennis racket *n* raquette *f* de tennis.

tenor ['tenər] *n* [singer] ténor *m*.

tense [tens] ⟨⟩ *adj* tendu(e). ⟨⟩ *n* temps *m*. ⟨⟩ *vt* tendre.

tension ['tenʃn] *n* tension *f*.

tent [tent] *n* tente *f*.

tentacle ['tentəkl] *n* tentacule *m*.

tentative ['tentətɪv] *adj* **1.** [hesitant] hésitant(e) - **2.** [not final] provisoire.

tenterhooks ['tentəhʊks] *npl* : **to be on tenterhooks** être sur des charbons ardents.

tenth [tenθ] *num* dixième ; *see also* **sixth**.

tent peg *n* piquet *m* de tente.

tent pole *n* montant *m* OR mât *m* de tente.

tenuous ['tenjʊəs] *adj* ténu(e).

tenure ['tenjər] *n (U) fml* **1.** [of property] bail *m* - **2.** [of job] : **to have tenure** être titulaire.

tepid ['tepɪd] *adj* tiède.

term [tɜ:m] ⟨⟩ *n* **1.** [word, expression] terme *m* - **2.** UK SCH & UNIV trimestre *m* - **3.** [period of time] durée *f*, période *f* ; **in the long/short term** à long/court terme. ⟨⟩ *vt* appeler. ◆ **terms** *npl* **1.** [of contract, agreement] conditions *fpl* - **2.** [basis] : **in international/real terms** en termes internationaux/réels ; **to be on good terms (with sb)** être en bons termes (avec qqn) ; **to come to terms with sthg** accepter qqch. ◆ **in terms of** *prep* sur le plan de, en termes de.

terminal ['tɜ:mɪnl] ⟨⟩ *adj* MED en phase terminale. ⟨⟩ *n* **1.** AERON, COMPUT & RAIL terminal *m* - **2.** ELEC borne *f*.

terminate ['tɜ:mɪneɪt] ⟨⟩ *vt.* *fml* [end-gen) terminer, mettre fin à ; [- contract] résilier - **2.** [pregnancy] interrompre. <> *vi* **1.** [bus, train] s'arrêter - **2.** [contract] se terminer.

termini ['tɜːmɪnaɪ] *npl* ▶ **terminus**.

terminus ['tɜːmɪnəs] (*pl* **-ni** [-naɪ] OR **-nuses** [-nəsiːz]) *n* terminus *m*.

terrace ['terəs] *n* **1.** [patio, on hillside] terrasse *f* - **2.** UK [of houses] rangée *f* de maisons. ◆ **terraces** *npl* FOOTBALL : **the terraces les gradins** *mpl*.

terraced ['terəst] *adj* [hillside] en terrasses.

terraced house *n* UK *maison attenante aux maisons voisines.*

terrain [te'reɪn] *n* terrain *m*.

terrible ['terəbl] *adj* terrible ; [holiday, headache, weather] affreux(euse), épouvantable.

terribly ['terəblɪ] *adv* terriblement ; [sing, write, organized] affreusement mal ; [injured] affreusement.

terrier ['terɪər] *n* terrier *m*.

terrific [tə'rɪfɪk] *adj* **1.** *inf* [wonderful] fantastique, formidable - **2.** [enormous] énorme, fantastique.

terrified ['terɪfaɪd] *adj* terrifié(e) ; **to be terrified of** avoir une terreur folle OR peur folle de.

terrifying ['terɪfaɪɪŋ] *adj* terrifiant(e).

territory ['terətrɪ] *n* territoire *m*.

terror ['terər] *n* terreur *f*.

terrorism ['terərɪzm] *n* terrorisme *m*.

terrorist ['terərɪst] *n* terroriste *mf*.

terrorize, UK **-ise** ['terəraɪz] *vt* terroriser.

terse [tɜːs] *adj* brusque.

Terylene® ['terəliːn] *n* Térylène® *m*.

test [test] <> *n* **1.** [trial] essai *m* ; [of friendship, courage] épreuve *f* - **2.** [examination - of aptitude, psychological] test *m* ; SCH & UNIV interrogation *f* écrite/orale ; [- of driving] (examen *m* du) permis *m* de conduire - **3.** [MED - of blood, urine] analyse *f* ; [- of eyes] examen *m*. <> *vt* **1.** [try] essayer ; [determination, friendship] mettre à l'épreuve - **2.** SCH & UNIV faire faire une interrogation écrite/orale à ; **to test sb on sthg** interroger qqn sur qqch - **3.** [MED - blood, urine] analyser ; [- eyes, reflexes] faire un examen de.

testament ['testəmənt] *n* [will] testament *m*.

test-drive *vt* essayer.

testicles ['testɪklz] *npl* testicules *mpl*.

testify ['testɪfaɪ] <> *vt* : **to testify that...** témoigner que... <> *vi* **1.** LAW témoigner - **2.** [be proof] : **to testify to sthg** témoigner de qqch.

testimony [UK 'testɪmənɪ, US 'testəməʊnɪ] *n* témoignage *m*.

testing ['testɪŋ] *adj* éprouvant(e).

test match *n* UK match *m* international.

test pilot *n* pilote *m* d'essai.

test tube *n* éprouvette *f*.

test-tube baby *n* bébé-éprouvette *m*.

tetanus ['tetənəs] *n* tétanos *m*.

tether ['teðər] <> *vt* attacher. <> *n* : **to be at the end of one's tether** être au bout du rouleau.

text [tekst] <> *n* **1.** [gen] texte *m* - **2.** TELEC mini-message *m*. <> *vi* TELEC envoyer un mini-message (à qn).

textbook ['tekstbʊk] *n* livre *m* OR manuel *m* scolaire.

textile ['tekstaɪl] *n* textile *m*.

texting ['tekstɪŋ] *n* (U) TELEC service *m* de mini-messages.

text message *n* TELEC mini-message *m*.

text messaging *n* (U) TELEC service *m* de mini-messages.

texture ['tekstʃər] *n* texture *f* ; [of paper, wood] grain *m*.

TFT [,tiːef'tiː] (*abbrev of* thin-film transistor) *adj* TFT ; **TFT screen** écran *m* TFT.

Thai [taɪ] <> *adj* thaïlandais(e). <> *n* **1.** [person] Thaïlandais, *m*, -e *f* - **2.** [language] thaï *m*.

Thailand ['taɪlænd] *n* Thaïlande *f*.

Thames [temz] *n* : **the Thames** la Tamise.

than (*weak form* [ðən], *strong form* [ðæn]) *conj* que ; **Sarah is younger than her sister** Sarah est plus jeune que sa sœur ; **more than three days/50 people** plus de trois jours/50 personnes.

thank [θæŋk] *vt* : **to thank sb (for)** remercier qqn (pour OR de) ; **thank God** OR **goodness** OR **heavens!** Dieu merci! ◆ **thanks** <> *npl* remerciements *mpl*. <> *excl* merci! ◆ **thanks to** *prep* grâce à.

thankful ['θæŋkfʊl] *adj* **1.** [grateful] : **thankful (for)** reconnaissant(e) (de) - **2.** [relieved] soulagé(e).

thankless ['θæŋklɪs] *adj* ingrat(e).

thanksgiving ['θæŋks,gɪvɪŋ] *n* action *f* de grâce. ◆ **Thanksgiving (Day)** *n* fête nationale américaine commémorant l'installation des premiers colons en Amérique.

thank you *excl* : **thank you (for)** merci (pour OR de).

that [ðæt] <> *pron* (*pl* **those** [ðəʊz]) **1.** (*demonstrative use: pl 'those'*) ce, cela, ça ; (*as opposed to 'this'*) celui-là (celle-là) ; **who's that?** qui est-ce? ; **is that Maureen?** c'est Maureen? ; **what's that?** qu'est-ce que c'est que ça? ; **that's a shame** c'est dommage ; **which shoes are you going to wear, these or**

those? quelles chaussures vas-tu mettre, celles-ci ou celles-là ? ; **those who** ceux (celles) qui - **2.** *(weak form* [ðət]*, strong form* [ðæt]*)* [to introduce relative clauses - subject] qui ; [- object] que ; [- with prep] lequel (laquelle), lesquels (lesquelles) *(pl)* ; : **we came to a path that led into the woods** nous arrivâmes à un sentier qui menait dans les bois ; **show me the book that you bought** montre-moi le livre que tu as acheté ; **on the day that we left** le jour où nous sommes partis. <> *adj (demonstrative: pl 'those')* ce (cette), cet *(before vowel or silent 'h')*, ces *(pl)* ; *(as opposed to 'this')* ce (cette)...-là, ces...-là *(pl)* ; **those chocolates are delicious** ces chocolats sont délicieux ; **later that day** plus tard ce jour-là ; **I prefer that book** je préfère ce livre-là ; **I'll have that one** je prendrai celui-là. <> *adv* aussi, si ; **it wasn't that bad/good** ce n'était pas si mal/bien que ça. <> *conj* [ðət] que ; **tell him that the children aren't coming** dites-lui que les enfants ne viennent pas ; **he recommended that I phone you** il m'a conseillé de vous appeler. **that is (to say)** *adv* c'est-à-dire.

thatched [θætʃt] *adj* de chaume.

that's [ðæts] = that is.

thaw [θɔ:] <> *vt* [ice] faire fondre OR dégeler ; [frozen food] décongeler. <> *vi* **1.** [ice] dégeler, fondre ; [frozen food] décongeler - **2.** *fig* [people, relations] se dégeler. <> *n* dégel *m.*

the *(weak form* [ðə]*, before vowel* [ði]*, strong form* [ði:]*) def art* **1.** [gen] le (la), l' *(+ vowel or silent 'h')*, les *(pl)* ; **the book** le livre ; **the sea** la mer ; **the man** l'homme ; **the boys/girls** les garçons/filles ; **the Joneses are coming to supper** les Jones viennent dîner ; **to play the piano** jouer du piano - **2.** *(with an adjective to form a noun)* **the British** les Britanniques ; **the old/young** les vieux/ jeunes ; **the impossible** l'impossible - **3.** [in dates] : **the twelfth of May** le douze mai ; **the forties** les années quarante - **4.** [in comparisons] : **the more... the less** plus... moins ; **the sooner the better** le plus tôt sera le mieux - **5.** [in titles] : **Alexander the Great** Alexandre le Grand ; **George the First** Georges Premier.

theatre *UK*, **theater** *US* ['θɪətər] *n* **1.** THEAT théâtre *m* - **2.** *UK* MED salle *f* d'opération - **3.** *US* [cinema] cinéma *m.*

theatregoer *UK*, **theatergoer** *US* ['θɪətəˌgəʊər] *n* habitué *m*, -e *f* du théâtre.

theatrical [θɪˈætrɪkl] *adj* théâtral(e) ; [company] de théâtre.

theft [θeft] *n* vol *m.*

their [ðeər] *poss adj* leur, leurs *(pl)* ; **their**

house leur maison ; **their children** leurs enfants ; **it wasn't THEIR fault** ce n'était pas de leur faute à eux.

theirs [ðeəz] *poss pron* le leur (la leur), les leurs *(pl)* ; **that house is theirs** cette maison est la leur, cette maison est à eux/elles ; **it wasn't our fault, it was THEIRS** ce n'était pas de notre faute, c'était de la leur ; **a friend of theirs** un de leurs amis, un ami à eux/elles.

them *(weak form* [ðəm]*, strong form* [ðem]*) pers pron pl* **1.** *(direct)* les ; **I know them** je les connais ; **if I were** OR **was them** si j'étais eux/elles, à leur place - **2.** *(indirect)* leur ; **we spoke to them** nous leur avons parlé ; **she sent them a letter** elle leur a envoyé une lettre ; **I gave it to them** je le leur ai donné - **3.** *(stressed, after prep, in comparisons etc)* eux (elles) ; **you can't expect THEM to do it** tu ne peux pas exiger que ce soit eux qui le fassent ; **with them** avec eux/elles ; **without them** sans eux/elles ; **we're not as wealthy as them** nous ne sommes pas aussi riches qu'eux/qu'elles.

theme [θi:m] *n* **1.** [topic, motif] thème *m*, sujet *m* - **2.** MUS thème *m* ; [signature tune] indicatif *m.*

theme park *n* parc *m* à thème.

theme pub *n UK* pub *m* à thème.

theme tune *n* chanson *f* principale.

themselves [ðem'selvz] *pron* **1.** *(reflexive)* se ; *(after prep)* eux (elles) - **2.** *(for emphasis)* eux-mêmes *mpl*, elles-mêmes *f* ; **they did it themselves** ils l'ont fait tous seuls.

then [ðen] *adv* **1.** [not now] alors, à cette époque - **2.** [next] puis, ensuite - **3.** [in that case] alors, dans ce cas - **4.** [therefore] donc - **5.** [also] d'ailleurs, et puis.

theology [θɪˈɒlədʒɪ] *n* théologie *f.*

theoretical [θɪəˈretɪkl] *adj* théorique.

theorize, *UK* **-ise** ['θɪəraɪz] *vi* : **to theorize (about)** émettre une théorie (sur), théoriser (sur).

theory ['θɪərɪ] *n* théorie *f* ; **in theory** en théorie.

therapeutic cloning *n* clonage *m* thérapeutique.

therapist ['θerəpɪst] *n* thérapeute *mf*, psychothérapeute *mf.*

therapy ['θerəpɪ] *n (U)* thérapie *f.*

there [ðeər] <> *pron* [indicating existence of sthg] : **there is/are** il y a ; **there's someone at the door** il y a quelqu'un à la porte ; **there must be some mistake** il doit y avoir erreur. <> *adv* **1.** [in existence, available] y, là ; **is anybody there?** il y a quelqu'un ? ; **is John there, please?** [when telephoning] est-ce que John est là, s'il vous plaît ? - **2.** [referring to place] y, là ; **I'm going there next week**

j'y vais la semaine prochaine ; **there it is** c'est là ; **there he is!** le voilà! ; **over there** là-bas ; **it's six kilometres there and back** cela fait six kilomètres aller-retour. ◇ *excl*: **there, I knew he'd turn up** tiens OR voilà, je savais bien qu'il s'amènerait ; **there, there** allons, allons. ➤ **there again** *adv* après tout ; **but there again, no one really knows** mais après tout, personne ne le sait vraiment. ➤ **there and then, then and there** *adv* immédiatement, sur-le-champ.

thereabouts [ðeərə'bauts], US **thereabout** [ðeərə'baut] *adv*: **or thereabouts** [nearby] par là ; [approximately] environ.

thereafter [,ðeər'ɑ:ftər] *adv fml* après cela, par la suite.

thereby [,ðeər'baɪ] *adv fml* ainsi, de cette façon.

therefore ['ðeəfɔ:r] *adv* donc, par conséquent.

there's [ðeəz] = there is.

thermal ['θɜ:ml] *adj* thermique ; [clothes] en Thermolactyl®.

thermometer [θə'mɒmɪtər] *n* thermomètre *m*.

Thermos (flask)® ['θɜ:məs-] *n* (bouteille *f*)Thermos® *m* ou *f*.

thermostat ['θɜ:məstæt] *n* thermostat *m*.

thesaurus [θɪ'sɔːrəs] (*pl* -es [-iːz]) *n* dictionnaire *m* de synonymes.

these [ðiːz] *pron pl* ➤ this.

thesis ['θiːsɪs] (*pl* theses ['θiːsiːz]) *n* thèse *f*.

they [ðeɪ] *pers pron pl* 1. [people, things, animals - unstressed] ils (elles) ; [- stressed] eux (elles) ; **they're pleased** ils sont contents (elles sont contentes) ; **they're pretty earrings** ce sont de jolies boucles d'oreille ; **THEY can't do it** eux (elles), ils (elles) ne peuvent pas le faire ; **there they are** les voilà - 2. [unspecified people] on, ils ; **they say it's going to snow** on dit qu'il va neiger.

they'd [ðeɪd] = they had, = they would.

they'll [ðeɪl] = they shall, = they will.

they're [ðeər] = they are.

they've [ðeɪv] = they have.

thick [θɪk] ◇ *adj* 1. [gen] épais (épaisse) ; [forest, hedge, fog] dense ; [voice] indistinct(e) ; **to be 6 inches thick** avoir 15 cm d'épaisseur - 2. *inf* [stupid] bouché(e). ◇ *n*: **in the thick of** au plus fort de, en plein OR au beau milieu de.

thicken ['θɪkn] ◇ *vt* épaissir. ◇ *vi* s'épaissir.

thicket ['θɪkɪt] *n* fourré *m*.

thickness ['θɪknɪs] *n* épaisseur *f*.

thickset [,θɪk'set] *adj* trapu(e).

thick-skinned [-'skɪnd] *adj* qui a la peau dure.

thief [θiːf] (*pl* thieves [θiːvz]) *n* voleur *m*, -euse *f*.

thieve [θiːv] *vt & vi* voler.

thieves [θiːvz] *npl* ➤ thief.

thigh [θaɪ] *n* cuisse *f*.

thimble ['θɪmbl] *n* dé *m* (à coudre).

thin [θɪn] *adj* 1. [slice, layer, paper] mince ; [cloth] léger(ère) ; [person] maigre - 2. [liquid, sauce] clair(e), peu épais (peu épaisse) - 3. [sparse - crowd] épars(e) ; [- vegetation, hair] clairsemé(e). ➤ **thin down** *vt sep* [liquid, paint] délayer, diluer ; [sauce] éclaircir.

thing [θɪŋ] *n* 1. [gen] chose *f* ; **the (best) thing to do would be...** le mieux serait de... ; **the thing is...** le problème, c'est que... ; **this is just the thing** US *inf* c'est exactement OR tout à fait ce qu'il faut - 2. [anything]: **I don't know a thing** je n'y connais absolument rien - 3. [object] chose *f*, objet *m* - 4. [person]: **you poor thing!** mon pauvre! ➤ **things** *npl* 1. [clothes, possessions] affaires *fpl* - 2. *inf* [life, situation]: **how are things?** comment ça va?

think [θɪŋk] ◇ *vt* (*pt & pp* thought) 1. [believe]: **to think (that)** croire que, penser que ; **I think so/not** je crois que oui/non, je pense que oui/non - 2. [have in mind] penser à - 3. [imagine] s'imaginer - 4. [in polite requests]: **do you think you could help me?** tu pourrais m'aider? ◇ *vi* (*pt & pp* thought) 1. [use mind] réfléchir, penser - 2. [have stated opinion]: **what do you think of** OR **about his new film?** que pensez-vous de son dernier film? ; **to think a lot of sb/sthg** penser beaucoup de bien de qqn/qqch ; **to think twice** y réfléchir à deux fois. ➤ **think about** *vt insep*: **to think about sb/sthg** songer à OR penser à qqn/qqch ; **to think about doing sthg** songer à faire qqch ; **I'll think about it** je vais y réfléchir. ➤ **think of** *vt insep* 1. [consider] = think about - 2. [remember] se rappeler - 3. [conceive] penser à, avoir l'idée de ; **to think of doing sthg** avoir l'idée de faire qqch. ➤ **think over** *vt sep* réfléchir à. ➤ **think up** *vt sep* imaginer.

think tank *n* comité *m* d'experts.

third [θɜ:d] ◇ *num* troisième. ◇ *n* UNIV ≃ licence *f* mention passable ; *see also* sixth.

thirdly ['θɜ:dlɪ] *adv* troisièmement, tertio.

third-party insurance *n* assurance *f* de responsabilité civile.

third-rate *adj pej* de dernier OR troisième ordre.

Third World *n*: **the Third World** le tiers-monde.

thirst [θɜ:st] *n* soif *f* ; **thirst for** *fig* soif de.

thirsty ['θɜːstɪ] *adj* **1.** [person] **: to be** OR **feel thirsty** avoir soif - **2.** [work] qui donne soif.

thirteen [,θɜː'tiːn] *num* treize ; *see also* **six**.

thirty ['θɜːtɪ] *num* trente ; *see also* **sixty**.

this [ðɪs] ◇ *pron* (*pl* **these** [ðiːz]) *(demonstrative use)* ce, ceci ; *(as opposed to 'that')* celui-ci (celle-ci) ; **this is for you** c'est pour vous ; **who's this?** qui est-ce? ; **what's this?** qu'est-ce que c'est? ; **which sweets does she prefer, these or those?** quels bonbons préfère-t-elle, ceux-ci ou ceux-là? ; **this is Daphne Logan** [introducing another person] je vous présente Daphne Logan ; [introducing oneself on phone] ici Daphne Logan, Daphne Logan à l'appareil. ◇ *adj* **1.** *(demonstrative use)* ce (cette), cet *(before vowel or silent 'h')*, ces *(pl)* ; *(as opposed to 'that')* ce (cette)...-ci, ces...-ci *(pl)* ; **these chocolates are delicious** ces chocolats sont délicieux ; **I prefer this book** je préfère ce livre-ci ; **I'll have this one** je prendrai celui-ci ; **this afternoon** cet après-midi ; **this morning** ce matin ; **this week** cette semaine - **2.** *inf* [a certain] un certain (une certaine). ◇ *adv* aussi ; **it was this big** c'était aussi grand que ça ; **you'll need about this much** il vous en faudra à peu près comme ceci.

thistle ['θɪsl] *n* chardon *m*.

thong [θɒŋ] *n* [of leather] lanière *f*.

thorn [θɔːn] *n* épine *f*.

thorny ['θɔːnɪ] *adj lit & fig* épineux(euse).

thorough ['θʌrə] *adj* **1.** [exhaustive - search, inspection] minutieux(euse) ; [- investigation, knowledge] approfondi(e) - **2.** [meticulous] méticuleux(euse) - **3.** [complete, utter] complet(ète), absolu(e).

thoroughbred ['θʌrəbred] *n* pur-sang *m inv*.

thoroughfare ['θʌrəfeər] *n fml* rue *f*, voie *f* publique.

thoroughly ['θʌrəlɪ] *adv* **1.** [fully, in detail] à fond - **2.** [completely, utterly] absolument, complètement.

those [ðəʊz] *pron pl* ► **that**.

though [ðəʊ] ◇ *conj* bien que (+ subjunctive), quoique (+ subjunctive). ◇ *adv* pourtant, cependant.

thought [θɔːt] ◇ *pt & pp* ► **think**. ◇ *n* **1.** [gen] pensée *f* ; [idea] idée *f*, pensée ; **after much thought** après avoir mûrement réfléchi - **2.** [intention] intention *f*. ◆ **thoughts** *npl* **1.** [reflections] pensées *fpl*, réflexions *fpl* - **2.** [views] opinions *fpl*, idées *fpl*.

thoughtful ['θɔːtfʊl] *adj* **1.** [pensive] pensif(ive) - **2.** [considerate - person] prévenant(e), attentionné(e) ; [- remark, act] plein(e) de gentillesse.

thoughtless ['θɔːtlɪs] *adj* [person] qui manque d'égards (pour les autres) ; [remark, behaviour] irréfléchi(e).

thousand ['θaʊznd] *num* mille ; **a** OR **one thousand** mille ; **thousands of** des milliers de ; *see also* **six**.

thousandth ['θaʊzntθ] *num* millième ; *see also* **sixth**.

thrash [θræʃ] *vt* **1.** [hit] battre, rosser - **2.** *inf* [defeat] écraser, battre à plates coutures. ◆ **thrash about, thrash around** *vi* s'agiter. ◆ **thrash out** *vt sep* [problem] débrouiller, démêler ; [idea] débattre, discuter.

thread [θred] ◇ *n* **1.** [gen] fil *m* - **2.** [of screw] filet *m*, pas *m*. ◇ *vt* [needle] enfiler.

threadbare ['θredbeər] *adj* usé(e) jusqu'à la corde.

threat [θret] *n* **: threat (to)** menace *f* (pour).

threaten ['θretn] ◇ *vt* **: to threaten sb (with)** menacer qqn (de) ; **to threaten to do sthg** menacer de faire qqch. ◇ *vi* menacer.

three [θriː] *num* trois ; *see also* **six**.

three-dimensional [-dɪ'menʃənl] *adj* [film, picture] en relief ; [object] à trois dimensions.

threefold ['θriːfəʊld] ◇ *adj* triple. ◇ *adv* **: to increase threefold** tripler.

three-piece *adj* **: three-piece suit** (costume *m*) trois pièces *m* ; **three-piece suite** canapé *m* et deux fauteuils assortis.

three-ply *adj* [wool] à trois fils.

thresh [θreʃ] *vt* battre.

threshold ['θreʃhəʊld] *n* seuil *m*.

threw [θruː] *pt* ► **throw**.

thrifty ['θrɪftɪ] *adj* économe.

thrill [θrɪl] ◇ *n* **1.** [sudden feeling] frisson *m*, sensation *f* - **2.** [enjoyable experience] plaisir *m*. ◇ *vt* transporter, exciter.

thrilled [θrɪld] *adj* **: thrilled (with sthg/to do sthg)** ravi(e) (de qqch/de faire qqch), enchanté(e) (de qqch/de faire qqch).

thriller ['θrɪlər] *n* thriller *m*.

thrilling ['θrɪlɪŋ] *adj* saisissant(e), palpitant(e).

thrive [θraɪv] (*pt* **-d** OR **throve**, *pp* **-d**) *vi* [person] bien se porter ; [plant] pousser bien ; [business] prospérer.

thriving ['θraɪvɪŋ] *adj* [person] bien portant(e) ; [plant] qui pousse bien ; [business] prospère.

throat [θrəʊt] *n* gorge *f*.

throb [θrɒb] *vi* [heart] palpiter, battre fort ; [engine] vibrer ; [music] taper ; **my head is throbbing** j'ai des élancements dans la tête.

throes [θrəʊz] *npl* **: to be in the throes of**

[war, disease] être en proie à ; **to be in the throes of an argument** être en pleine dispute.

throne [θrəʊn] *n* trône *m*.

throng [θrɒŋ] <> *n* foule *f*, multitude *f*. <> *vt* remplir, encombrer.

throttle ['θrɒtl] <> *n* [valve] papillon *m* des gaz ; [lever] commande *f* des gaz. <> *vt* [strangle] étrangler.

through [θruː] <> *adj* [finished] : **are you through?** tu as fini? ; **to be through with sthg** avoir fini qqch. <> *prep* **1.** [relating to place, position] à travers ; **to travel through sthg** traverser qqch ; **to cut through sthg** couper qqch - **2.** [during] pendant - **3.** [because of] à cause de - **4.** [by means of] par l'intermédiaire de, par l'entremise de - **5.** *US* [up till and including] : **Monday through Friday** du lundi au vendredi. <> **through and through** *adv* [completely] jusqu'au bout des ongles ; [thoroughly] par cœur, à fond.

throughout [θruː'aʊt] <> *prep* **1.** [during] pendant, durant ; **throughout the meeting** pendant toute la réunion - **2.** [everywhere in] partout dans. <> *adv* **1.** [all the time] tout le temps - **2.** [everywhere] partout.

throve [θrəʊv] *pt* ▶ **thrive**.

throw [θrəʊ] <> *vt* (*pt* **threw**, *pp* **thrown**) **1.** [gen] jeter ; [ball, javelin] lancer - **2.** [rider] désarçonner - **3.** *fig* [confuse] déconcerter, décontenancer. <> *n* lancement *m*, jet *m*. <> **throw away** *vt sep* **1.** [discard] jeter - **2.** *fig* [money] gaspiller ; [opportunity] perdre. <> **throw out** *vt sep* **1.** [discard] jeter - **2.** *fig* [reject] rejeter - **3.** [from house] mettre à la porte ; [from army, school] expulser, renvoyer. <> **throw up** *vi inf* [vomit] dégobiller, vomir.

throwaway ['θrəʊəˌweɪ] *adj* **1.** [disposable] jetable, à jeter - **2.** [remark] désinvolte.

throw-in *n UK* FOOTBALL rentrée *f* en touche.

thrown [θrəʊn] *pp* ▶ **throw**.

thru [θruː] *inf US* = **through**.

thrush [θrʌʃ] *n* **1.** [bird] grive *f* - **2.** MED muguet *m*.

thrust [θrʌst] <> *n* **1.** [forward movement] poussée *f* ; [of knife] coup *m* - **2.** [main aspect] idée *f* principale, aspect *m* principal. <> *vt* [shove] enfoncer, fourrer.

thud [θʌd] <> *n* bruit *m* sourd. <> *vi* tomber en faisant un bruit sourd.

thug [θʌg] *n* brute *f*, voyou *m*.

thumb [θʌm] <> *n* pouce *m*. <> *vt inf* [hitch] : **to thumb a lift** faire du stop or de l'auto-stop. <> **thumb through** *vt insep* feuilleter, parcourir.

thumbs down [ˌθʌmz-] *n* : **to get** or **be given the thumbs down** être rejeté(e).

thumbs up [ˌθʌmz-] *n* [go-ahead] : **to give sb the thumbs up** donner le feu vert à qqn.

thumbtack ['θʌmtæk] *n US* punaise *f*.

thump [θʌmp] <> *n* **1.** [blow] grand coup *m* - **2.** [thud] bruit *m* sourd. <> *vt* [hit] cogner, taper sur. <> *vi* [heart] battre fort.

thunder ['θʌndər] <> *n (U)* **1.** METEOR tonnerre *m* - **2.** *fig* [of traffic] vacarme *m* ; [of applause] tonnerre *m*. <> *impers vb* METEOR tonner.

thunderbolt ['θʌndəbəʊlt] *n* coup *m* de foudre.

thunderclap ['θʌndəklæp] *n* coup *m* de tonnerre.

thunderstorm ['θʌndəstɔːm] *n* orage *m*.

thundery ['θʌndərɪ] *adj* orageux(euse).

Thursday ['θɜːzdɪ] *n* jeudi *m* ; *see also* **Saturday**.

thus [ðʌs] *adv fml* **1.** [therefore] par conséquent, donc, ainsi - **2.** [in this way] ainsi, de cette façon, comme ceci.

thwart [θwɔːt] *vt* contrecarrer, contrarier.

thyme [taɪm] *n* thym *m*.

thyroid ['θaɪrɔɪd] *n* thyroïde *f*.

tiara [tɪ'ɑːrə] *n* [worn by woman] diadème *m*.

Tibet [tɪ'bet] *n* Tibet *m*.

tic [tɪk] *n* tic *m*.

tick [tɪk] <> *n* **1.** *UK* [written mark] coche *f* - **2.** [sound] tic-tac *m* - **3.** [insect] tique *f*. <> *vt UK* cocher. <> *vi* faire tic-tac. <> **tick off** *vt sep* **1.** *UK* [mark off] cocher - **2.** *UK inf* [tell off] enguirlander. <> **tick over** *vi UK* [engine, business] tourner au ralenti.

ticket ['tɪkɪt] *n* **1.** [for access, train, plane] billet *m* ; [for bus] ticket *m* ; [for library] carte *f* ; [label on product] étiquette *f* - **2.** [for traffic offence] P.-V. *m*, papillon *m*.

ticket collector *n UK* contrôleur *m*, -euse *f*.

ticket inspector *n UK* contrôleur *m*, -euse *f*.

ticket machine *n* distributeur *m* de billets.

ticket office *n* bureau *m* de vente des billets.

tickle ['tɪkl] <> *vt* **1.** [touch lightly] chatouiller - **2.** *fig* [amuse] amuser. <> *vi* chatouiller.

ticklish ['tɪklɪʃ] *adj* [person] qui craint les chatouilles, chatouilleux(euse).

tidal ['taɪdl] *adj* [force] de la marée ; [river] à marées ; [barrier] contre la marée.

tidal wave *n* raz-de-marée *m inv*.

tidbit *US* = **titbit**.

tiddlywinks ['tɪdlɪwɪŋks], *US* **tiddledywinks** ['tɪdldɪwɪŋks] *n* jeu *m* de puce.

tide [taɪd] *n* **1.** [of sea] marée *f* - **2.** *fig* [of opinion, fashion] courant *m*, tendance *f* ; [of protest] vague *f*.

tidy ['taɪdɪ] ◇ *adj* **1.** [room, desk] en ordre, bien rangé(e) ; [hair, dress] soigné(e) - **2.** [person - in habits] ordonné(e) ; [- in appearance] soigné(e). ◇ *vt* ranger, mettre de l'ordre dans. ◆ **tidy up** *vt sep* ranger, mettre de l'ordre dans. ◇ *vi* ranger.

tie [taɪ] ◇ *n* **1.** [necktie] cravate *f* - **2.** [in game, competition] égalité *f* de points. ◇ *vt* (*pt & pp* **tied**, *cont* **tying**) **1.** [fasten] attacher ; [shoelaces] nouer, attacher ; to tie a knot faire un nœud - **3.** *fig* [link] : to be tied to être lié(e) à. ◇ *vi* (*pt & pp* **tied**, *cont* **tying**) [draw] être à égalité. ◆ **tie down** *vt sep fig* [restrict] restreindre la liberté de. ◆ **tie in with** *vt insep* concorder avec, coïncider avec. ◆ **tie up** *vt sep* **1.** [with string, rope] attacher - **2.** [shoelaces] nouer, attacher - **3.** *fig* [money, resources] immobiliser - **4.** *fig* [link] : to be tied up with être lié(e) à.

tiebreak(er) ['taɪbreɪk(ər)] *n* **1.** TENNIS tiebreak *m*, jeu *m* décisif - **2.** [in game, competition] question *f* subsidiaire.

tiepin ['taɪpɪn] *n* épingle *f* de cravate.

tier [tɪər] *n* [of seats] gradin *m* ; [of cake] étage *m*.

tiff [tɪf] *n* bisbille *f*, petite querelle *f*.

tiger ['taɪgər] *n* tigre *m*.

tight [taɪt] ◇ *adj* **1.** [clothes, group, competition, knot] serré(e) - **2.** [taut] tendu(e) - **3.** [schedule] serré(e), minuté(e) - **4.** [strict] strict(e), sévère - **5.** [corner, bend] raide - **6.** *inf* [drunk] soûl(e), rond(e) - **7.** *inf* [miserly] radin(e), avare. ◇ *adv* **1.** [firmly, securely] bien, fort ; to hold tight tenir bien ; hold tight! tiens bon! ; to shut OR close sthg tight bien fermer qqch - **2.** [tautly] à fond. ◆ **tights** *npl* UK collant *m*, collants *mpl*.

tighten ['taɪtn] ◇ *vt* **1.** [belt, knot, screw] resserrer ; to tighten one's hold OR grip on resserrer sa prise sur - **2.** [pull tauter] tendre - **3.** [make stricter] renforcer. ◇ *vi* **1.** [rope] se tendre - **2.** [grip, hold] se resserrer.

tightfisted [,taɪt'fɪstɪd] *adj pej* radin(e), pingre.

tightly ['taɪtlɪ] *adv* [firmly] bien, fort.

tightrope ['taɪtrəʊp] *n* corde *f* raide.

tile [taɪl] *n* [on roof] tuile *f* ; [on floor, wall] carreau *m*.

tiled [taɪld] *adj* [floor, wall] carrelé(e) ; [roof] couvert(e) de tuiles.

till [tɪl] ◇ *prep* jusqu'à ; from six till ten o'clock de six heures à dix heures. ◇ *conj* jusqu'à ce que (+ *subjunctive*) ; wait till I come back attends que je revienne ; (*after negative*)

avant que (+ *subjunctive*) ; it won't be ready till tomorrow ça ne sera pas prêt avant demain. ◇ *n* tiroir-caisse *m*.

tiller ['tɪlər] *n* NAUT barre *f*.

tilt [tɪlt] ◇ *vt* incliner, pencher. ◇ *vi* s'incliner, pencher.

timber ['tɪmbər] *n* **1.** (*U*) [wood] bois *m* de charpente OR de construction - **2.** [beam] poutre *f*, madrier *m*.

time [taɪm] ◇ *n* **1.** [gen] temps *m* ; a long time longtemps ; in a short time dans peu de temps, sous peu ; to take time prendre du temps ; to be time for sthg être l'heure de qqch ; to have a good time s'amuser bien ; in good time de bonne heure ; ahead of time en avance, avant l'heure ; on time à l'heure ; to have no time for sb/sthg ne pas supporter qqn/qqch ; to pass the time passer le temps ; to play for time essayer de gagner du temps - **2.** [as measured by clock] heure *f* ; what time is it?, what's the time? quelle heure est-il? ; in a week's/year's time dans une semaine/un an - **3.** [point in time] époque *f* ; before my time avant que j'arrive ici - **4.** [occasion] fois *f* ; from time to time de temps en temps, de temps à autre ; time after time, time and again à maintes reprises, maintes et maintes fois - **5.** MUS mesure *f*. ◇ *vt* **1.** [schedule] fixer, prévoir - **2.** [race, runner] chronométrer - **3.** [arrival, remark] choisir le moment de. ◆ **times** ◇ *npl* fois *fpl* ; four times as much as me quatre fois plus que moi. ◇ *prep* MATHS fois. ◆ **at a time** *adv* d'affilée ; one at a time un par un, un seul à la fois ; months at a time des mois et des mois. ◆ **at times** *adv* quelquefois, parfois. ◆ **at the same time** *adv* en même temps. ◆ **about time** *adv* : it's about time (that)... il est grand temps que... ; about time too! ce n'est pas trop tôt! ◆ **for the time being** *adv* pour le moment. ◆ **in time** *adv* **1.** [not late] : in time (for) à l'heure (pour) - **2.** [eventually] à la fin, à la longue ; [after a while] avec le temps, à la longue.

time bomb *n lit & fig* bombe *f* à retardement.

time-critical *adj* critique en termes de temps.

time-expired *adj* périmé(e), obsolète.

time lag *n* décalage *m*.

timeless ['taɪmlɪs] *adj* éternel(elle).

time limit *n* délai *m*.

timely ['taɪmlɪ] *adj* opportun(e).

time off *n* temps *m* libre.

time out *n* SPORT temps *m* mort.

timer ['taɪmər] *n* minuteur *m*.

time scale *n* période *f* ; [of project] délai *m*.

time-share n logement m en multipropriété.

time switch n minuterie f.

timetable ['taɪm,teɪbl] n **1.** UK SCH emploi m du temps - **2.** [of buses, trains] horaire m - **3.** UK [schedule] calendrier m.

time zone n fuseau m horaire.

timid ['tɪmɪd] adj timide.

timing ['taɪmɪŋ] n (U) **1.** [of remark] à-propos m inv - **2.** [scheduling] : **the timing of the election** le moment choisi pour l'élection - **3.** [measuring] chronométrage m.

timpani ['tɪmpəni] npl timbales fpl.

tin [tɪn] n **1.** (U) [metal] étain m ; [in sheets] fer-blanc m - **2.** UK [can] boîte f de conserve - **3.** UK [small container] boîte f.

tin can n boîte f de conserve.

tinfoil ['tɪnfɔɪl] n (U) papier m (d')aluminium.

tinge [tɪndʒ] n **1.** [of colour] teinte f, nuance f - **2.** [of feeling] nuance f.

tinged [tɪndʒd] adj : **tinged with** teinté(e) de.

tingle ['tɪŋgl] vi picoter.

tinker ['tɪŋkər] <> n UK pej [gypsy] romanichel m, -elle f. <> vi : **to tinker (with sthg)** bricoler (qqch).

tinkle ['tɪŋkl] vi [ring] tinter.

tinned [tɪnd] adj UK en boîte.

tin opener n UK ouvre-boîtes m inv.

tinsel ['tɪnsl] n (U) guirlandes fpl de Noël.

tint [tɪnt] n teinte f, nuance f ; [in hair] rinçage m.

tinted ['tɪntɪd] adj [glasses, windows] teinté(e).

tiny ['taɪnɪ] adj minuscule.

tip [tɪp] <> n **1.** [end] bout m - **2.** UK [dump] décharge f - **3.** [to waiter etc] pourboire m - **4.** [piece of advice] tuyau m. <> vt **1.** [tilt] faire basculer - **2.** UK [spill] renverser - **3.** [waiter etc] donner un pourboire à. <> vi **1.** [tilt] basculer - **2.** UK [spill] se renverser. **tip over** <> vt sep renverser. <> vi se renverser.

tip-off n tuyau m ; [to police] dénonciation f.

tipped ['tɪpt] adj [cigarette] à bout filtre.

tipsy ['tɪpsɪ] adj inf gai(e).

tiptoe ['tɪptəʊ] <> n : **on tiptoe** sur la pointe des pieds. <> vi marcher sur la pointe des pieds.

tip-top adj inf dated excellent(e).

tire ['taɪər] <> n US = **tyre**. <> vt fatiguer. <> vi **1.** [get tired] se fatiguer - **2.** [get fed up] : **to tire of** se lasser de.

tired ['taɪəd] adj **1.** [sleepy] fatigué(e), las

(lasse) - **2.** [fed up] : **to be tired of sthg/of doing sthg** en avoir assez de qqch/de faire qqch.

tireless ['taɪəlɪs] adj infatigable.

tiresome ['taɪəsəm] adj ennuyeux(euse).

tiring ['taɪərɪŋ] adj fatigant(e).

tissue ['tɪʃuː] n **1.** [paper handkerchief] mouchoir m en papier - **2.** (U) BIOL tissu m.

tissue paper n (U) papier m de soie.

tit [tɪt] n **1.** [bird] mésange f - **2.** vulg [breast] nichon m, néné m.

titbit UK ['tɪtbɪt], **tidbit** US ['tɪdbɪt] n **1.** [of food] bon morceau m - **2.** fig [of news] petite nouvelle f.

tit for tat [-'tæt] n un prêté pour un rendu.

titillate ['tɪtɪleɪt] vt titiller.

title ['taɪtl] n titre m.

title deed n titre m de propriété.

title role n rôle m principal.

titter ['tɪtər] vi rire bêtement.

TM abbrev of **trademark**.

to (stressed [tuː], unstressed before consonant [tə], unstressed before vowel [tʊ]) <> prep **1.** [indicating place, direction] à ; **to go to Liverpool/Spain/school** aller à Liverpool/en Espagne/à l'école ; **to go to the butcher's** aller chez le boucher ; **to the left/right** à gauche/droite - **2.** (to express indirect object) à ; **to give sthg to sb** donner qqch à qqn ; **we were listening to the radio** nous écoutions la radio - **3.** [indicating reaction, effect] à ; **to my delight/surprise** à ma grande joie/surprise - **4.** [in stating opinion] : **to me,...** à mon avis,... ; **it seemed quite unnecessary to me/him etc** cela me/lui etc semblait tout à fait inutile - **5.** [indicating state, process] : **to drive sb to drink** pousser qqn à boire ; **it could lead to trouble** cela pourrait causer des ennuis - **6.** [as far as] à, jusqu'à ; **to count to 10** compter jusqu'à 10 ; **we work from 9 to 5** nous travaillons de 9 heures à 17 heures - **7.** [in expressions of time] moins ; **it's ten to three/quarter to one** il est trois heures moins dix/une heure moins le quart - **8.** [per] à ; **40 miles to the gallon** ≃ 7 litres aux cent (km) - **9.** [of, for] de ; **the key to the car** la clé de la voiture ; **a letter to my daughter** une lettre à ma fille. <> adv [shut] : **push the door to** fermez la porte. <> with infinitive **1.** (forming simple infinitive) **to walk** marcher ; **to laugh** rire - **2.** (following another verb) **to begin to do sthg** commencer à faire qqch ; **to try to do sthg** essayer de faire qqch ; **to want to do sthg** vouloir faire qqch - **3.** (following an adjective) **difficult to do** difficile à faire ; **ready to go** prêt à partir - **4.** (indicating purpose) pour ; **he worked hard to pass his exam** il a travaillé dur pour réussir son examen - **5.** (substituting for a relative clause) **I have a lot to do** j'ai beaucoup à faire ; **he told me to leave** il m'a dit de partir - **6.** *(to avoid repetition of infinitive)* I meant to call him but I forgot to je voulais l'appeler, mais j'ai oublié - **7.** [in comments] : **to be honest...** en toute franchise... ; **to sum up,...** en résumé,..., pour récapituler,...

toad [təud] *n* crapaud *m*.

toadstool ['təudstu:l] *n* champignon *m* vénéneux.

to and fro *adv* : **to go to and fro** aller et venir ; **to walk to and fro** marcher de long en large. **to-and-fro** *adj* de va-et-vient.

toast [təust] <> *n* **1.** (U) [bread] pain *m* grillé, toast *m* - **2.** [drink] toast *m* <> *vt* **1.** [bread] (faire) griller - **2.** [person] porter un toast à.

toasted sandwich [,təustɪd-] *n* sandwich *m* grillé.

toaster ['təustər] *n* grille-pain *m inv*.

tobacco [tə'bækəu] *n* (U) tabac *m*.

tobacconist [tə'bækənɪst] *n* UK buraliste *mf* ; **tobacconist's (shop)** bureau *m* de tabac.

toboggan [tə'bɒgən] *n* luge *f*, traîne *f* sauvage *Québec*.

today [tə'deɪ] <> *n* aujourd'hui *m*. <> *adv* aujourd'hui.

toddler ['tɒdlər] *n* tout-petit *m (qui commence à marcher)*.

toddy ['tɒdɪ] *n* grog *m*.

to-do (*pl* -s) *n inf dated* histoire *f*.

toe [təu] <> *n* [of foot] orteil *m*, doigt *m* de pied ; [of sock, shoe] bout *m*. <> *vt* : **to toe the line** se plier.

TOEFL [tɒfl] *(abbrev of* Test of English as a Foreign Language) *n* test d'anglais passé par les étudiants étrangers désirant faire des études dans une université américaine.

toenail ['təuneɪl] *n* ongle *m* d'orteil.

toffee ['tɒfɪ] *n* UK caramel *m*.

toga ['təugə] *n* toge *f*.

together [tə'geðər] *adv* **1.** [gen] ensemble - **2.** [at the same time] en même temps. **together with** *prep* ainsi que.

toil [tɔɪl] *lit* <> *n* labeur *m*. <> *vi* travailler dur.

toilet ['tɔɪlɪt] *n* [lavatory] toilettes *fpl*, cabinets *mpl* ; **to go to the toilet** aller aux toilettes OR aux cabinets.

toilet bag *n* trousse *f* de toilette.

toilet paper *n* (U) papier *m* hygiénique.

toiletries ['tɔɪlɪtrɪz] *npl* articles *mpl* de toilette.

toilet roll *n* rouleau *m* de papier hygiénique.

toilet water *n* eau *f* de toilette.

token ['təukn] <> *adj* symbolique. <> *n* **1.** [voucher] bon *m* - **2.** [symbol] marque *f*. **by the same token** *adv* de même.

told [təuld] *pt & pp* ⊳ **tell**.

tolerable ['tɒlərəbl] *adj* passable.

tolerance ['tɒlərəns] *n* tolérance *f*.

tolerant ['tɒlərənt] *adj* tolérant(e).

tolerate ['tɒləreɪt] *vt* **1.** [put up with] supporter - **2.** [permit] tolérer.

toll [təul] <> *n* **1.** [number] nombre *m* - **2.** [fee] péage *m* ; **to take its toll** se faire sentir. <> *vt & vi* sonner.

tollfree US *adv* : **to call tollfree** appeler un numéro vert.

tomato [UK tə'mɑ:təu, US tə'meɪtəu] (*pl* -es) *n* tomate *f*.

tomb [tu:m] *n* tombe *f*.

tomboy ['tɒmbɔɪ] *n* garçon *m* manqué.

tombstone ['tu:mstəun] *n* pierre *f* tombale.

tomcat ['tɒmkæt] *n* matou *m*.

tomorrow [tə'mɒrəu] <> *n* demain *m*. <> *adv* demain.

ton [tʌn] (*pl* ton OR -s) *n* **1.** UK [imperial] = 1016 kg ; US [imperial] ≃ tonne f (= 907,2 kg) - **2.** [metric] tonne f (= 1000 kg). **tons** *npl inf* **tons (of)** des tas (de), plein (de).

tone [təun] *n* **1.** [gen] ton *m* - **2.** [on phone] tonalité *f* ; [on answering machine] bip *m* sonore. **tone down** *vt sep* modérer. **tone up** *vt sep* tonifier.

tone-deaf *adj* qui n'a aucune oreille.

tongs [tɒŋz] *npl* pinces *fpl* ; [for hair] fer *m* à friser.

tongue [tʌŋ] *n* **1.** [gen] langue *f* ; **to hold one's tongue** *fig* tenir sa langue - **2.** [of shoe] languette *f*.

tongue-in-cheek *adj* ironique.

tongue-tied [-,taɪd] *adj* muet(ette).

tongue twister [-,twɪstər] *n* phrase *f* difficile à dire.

tonic ['tɒnɪk] *n* **1.** [tonic water] Schweppes® *m* - **2.** [medicine] tonique *m*.

tonic water *n* Schweppes® *m*.

tonight [tə'naɪt] <> *n* ce soir *m* ; [late] cette nuit *f*. <> *adv* ce soir ; [late] cette nuit.

tonnage ['tʌnɪdʒ] *n* tonnage *m*.

tonne [tʌn] (*pl* tonne OR -s) *n* tonne *f*.

tonsil ['tɒnsl] *n* amygdale *f*.

tonsil(l)itis [,tɒnsɪ'laɪtɪs] *n* (U) amygdalite *f*.

too [tu:] *adv* **1.** [also] aussi - **2.** [excessively] trop ; **too many people** trop de gens ; **it was over all too soon** ça s'était terminé bien trop tôt ; **I'd be only too happy to help** je serais trop heureux de vous aider ; **I wasn't too impressed** ça ne m'a pas impressionné outre mesure.

took [tʊk] pt ► take.

tool [tuːl] n lit & fig outil m.

tool box n boîte f à outils.

tool kit n trousse f à outils.

toot [tuːt] ◇ n coup m de Klaxon®. ◇ vi klaxonner.

tooth [tuːθ] (pl teeth [tiːθ]) n dent f.

toothache ['tuːθeɪk] n mal m OR rage f de dents ; **to have toothache** UK, **to have a toothache** US avoir mal aux dents.

toothbrush ['tuːθbrʌʃ] n brosse f à dents.

toothpaste ['tuːθpeɪst] n (pâte f) dentifrice m.

toothpick ['tuːθpɪk] n cure-dents m inv.

top [tɒp] ◇ adj **1.** [highest] du haut - **2.** [most important, successful - officials] important(e) ; [- executives] supérieur(e) ; [- pop singer] fameux(euse) ; [- sportsman, sportswoman] meilleur(e) ; [- in exam] premier(ère) - **3.** [maximum]- maximum. ◇ n **1.** [highest point - of hill] sommet m ; [- of page, pile] haut m ; [- of tree] cime f ; [- of list] début m, tête f ; **on top** dessus ; **at the top of one's voice** à tue-tête - **2.** [lid - of bottle, tube] bouchon m ; [- of pen] capuchon m ; [- of jar] couvercle m - **3.** [of table, box] dessus m - **4.** [clothing] haut m - **5.** [toy] toupie f - **6.** [highest rank - in league] tête f ; [- in scale] haut m ; SCH premier m, -ère f. ◇ vt **1.** [be first in] être en tête de - **2.** [better] surpasser - **3.** [exceed] dépasser. ► **on top of** prep **1.** [in space] sur - **2.** [in addition to] en plus de. ► **top up** UK, **top off** US vt sep remplir.

top floor n dernier étage m.

top hat n haut-de-forme m.

top-heavy adj mal équilibré(e).

topic ['tɒpɪk] n sujet m.

topical ['tɒpɪkl] adj d'actualité.

topless ['tɒplɪs] adj [woman] aux seins nus.

top-level adj au plus haut niveau.

topmost ['tɒpməʊst] adj le plus haut (la plus haute).

topping ['tɒpɪŋ] n garniture f.

topple ['tɒpl] ◇ vt renverser. ◇ vi basculer.

top-secret adj top secret (top secrète).

topspin ['tɒpspɪn] n lift m.

topsy-turvy [,tɒpsɪ'tɜːvɪ] adj **1.** [messy] sens dessus dessous - **2.** [confused] : **to be topsy-turvy** ne pas tourner rond.

top-up card n TELEC recharge f de téléphone mobile.

torch [tɔːtʃ] n **1.** UK [electric] lampe f électrique - **2.** [burning] torche f.

tore [tɔːr] pt ► tear².

torment ◇ n ['tɔːment] tourment m. ◇ vt [tɔː'ment] tourmenter.

torn [tɔːn] pp ► tear².

tornado [tɔː'neɪdəʊ] (pl -es OR -s) n tornade f.

torpedo [tɔː'piːdəʊ] n (pl -es) torpille f.

torrent ['tɒrənt] n torrent m.

torrid ['tɒrɪd] adj **1.** [hot] torride - **2.** fig [passionate] ardent(e).

tortoise ['tɔːtəs] n tortue f.

tortoiseshell ['tɔːtəʃel] ◇ adj : **tortoiseshell cat** chat m roux tigré. ◇ n (U) [material] écaille f.

torture ['tɔːtʃər] ◇ n torture f. ◇ vt torturer.

Tory ['tɔːrɪ] UK ◇ adj tory, conservateur(trice). ◇ n tory mf, conservateur m, -trice f.

toss [tɒs] ◇ vt **1.** [throw] jeter ; **to toss a coin** jouer à pile ou face ; **to toss one's head** rejeter la tête en arrière - **2.** [salad] fatiguer ; [pancake] faire sauter - **3.** [throw about] ballotter. ◇ vi [move about] : **to toss and turn** se tourner et se retourner. ► **toss up** vi jouer à pile ou face.

tot [tɒt] n **1.** inf [small child] tout-petit m - **2.** [of drink] larme f, goutte f.

total ['təʊtl] ◇ adj total(e) ; [disgrace, failure] complet(ète). ◇ n total m. ◇ vt (UK & US) **1.** [add up] additionner - **2.** [amount to] s'élever à.

totalitarian [,təʊtælɪ'teərɪən] adj totalitaire.

totally ['təʊtəlɪ] adv totalement ; **I totally agree** je suis entièrement d'accord.

totter ['tɒtər] vi lit & fig chanceler.

toucan crossing n passage m mixte piétons-cyclistes.

touch [tʌtʃ] ◇ n **1.** (U) [sense] toucher m - **2.** [detail] touche f - **3.** (U) [skill] marque f, note f - **4.** [contact] : **to keep in touch** (with sb) rester en contact (avec qqn) ; **to get in touch with sb** entrer en contact avec qqn ; **to lose touch with sb** perdre qqn de vue ; **to be out of touch with** ne plus être au courant de - **5.** SPORT : **in touch** en touche - **6.** [small amount] : **a touch** un petit peu. ◇ vt toucher. ◇ vi [be in contact] se toucher. ► **touch down** vi [plane] atterrir. ► **touch on** vt insep effleurer.

touch-and-go adj incertain(e).

touchdown ['tʌtʃdaʊn] n **1.** [of plane]

atterrissage m - **2.** [in American football] but m.

touched [tʌtʃt] adj **1.** [grateful] touché(e) - **2.** inf [slightly mad] **fêlé(e)**.

touching ['tʌtʃɪŋ] adj touchant(e).

touchline ['tʌtʃlaɪn] n ligne f de touche.

touchy ['tʌtʃɪ] adj **1.** [person] susceptible - **2.** [question] **délicat(e)**.

tough [tʌf] adj **1.** [material, vehicle, person] solide ; [character, life] **dur(e)** - **2.** [meat] dur(e) - **3.** [decision, problem, task] difficile - **4.** [rough - area of town] **dangereux(euse)** - **5.** [strict] sévère.

toughen ['tʌfn] vt **1.** [character] endurcir - **2.** [material] renforcer.

toupee ['tuːpeɪ] n postiche m.

tour [tʊər] <> n **1.** [journey] voyage m ; [by pop group etc] tournée f - **2.** [of town, museum] visite f, tour m. <> vt visiter.

touring ['tʊərɪŋ] n tourisme m.

tourism ['tʊərɪzm] n tourisme m.

tourist ['tʊərɪst] n touriste mf.

tourist (information) office n office m de tourisme.

tournament ['tɔːnəmənt] n tournoi m.

tour operator n voyagiste m.

tousle ['taʊzl] vt ébouriffer.

tout [taʊt] <> n revendeur m de billets. <> vt [tickets] revendre ; [goods] vendre. <> vi : **to tout for trade** racoler les clients.

tow [təʊ] <> n : **'on tow'** UK 'véhicule en remorque'. <> vt remorquer.

towards [təˈwɔːdz], US **toward** [təˈwɔːd] prep **1.** [gen] vers ; [movement] vers, en direction de - **2.** [in attitude] envers - **3.** [for the purpose of] pour.

towel ['taʊəl] n serviette f ; [tea towel] torchon m.

towelling UK, **toweling** US ['taʊəlɪŋ] n (U) tissu m éponge.

towel rail n porte-serviettes m inv.

tower ['taʊər] <> n tour f. <> vi s'élever ; **to tower over sb/sthg** dominer qqn/qqch.

tower block n UK tour f.

towering ['taʊərɪŋ] adj imposant(e).

town [taʊn] n ville f ; **to go out on the town** faire la tournée des grands ducs ; **to go to town on sthg** fig ne pas lésiner sur qqch.

town centre n UK centre-ville m.

town council n UK conseil m municipal.

town hall n UK mairie f.

town plan n UK plan m de ville.

town planning n UK urbanisme m.

township ['taʊnʃɪp] n **1.** [in South Africa] township f - **2.** [in US] ≃ canton m.

towpath ['təʊpɑːθ] (pl [-pɑːðz]) n chemin m de halage.

towrope ['təʊrəʊp] n câble m de remorquage.

tow truck n US dépanneuse f.

toxic ['tɒksɪk] adj toxique.

toy [tɔɪ] n jouet m. ◆ **toy with** vt insep **1.** [idea] caresser - **2.** [coin etc] jouer avec ; **to toy with one's food** manger du bout des dents.

toy shop n magasin m de jouets.

trace [treɪs] <> n trace f. <> vt **1.** [relatives, criminal] retrouver ; [development, progress] suivre ; [history, life] retracer - **2.** [on paper] tracer.

tracing paper ['treɪsɪŋ-] n (U) papier-calque m.

track [træk] <> n **1.** [path] chemin m - **2.** SPORT piste f - **3.** RAIL voie f ferrée - **4.** [of animal, person] trace f - **5.** [on record, tape] piste f ; **to keep track of sb** rester en contact avec qqn ; **to lose track of sb** perdre contact avec qqn ; **to be on the right track** être sur la bonne voie ; **to be on the wrong track** être sur la mauvaise piste. <> vt [follow] suivre la trace de. ◆ **track down** vt sep [criminal, animal] dépister ; [object, address etc] retrouver.

track and field n US athlétisme m.

track record n palmarès m.

tracksuit ['træksuːt] n survêtement m.

tract [trækt] n **1.** [pamphlet] tract m - **2.** [of land, forest] étendue f.

traction ['trækʃn] n (U) **1.** PHYS traction f - **2.** MED : **in traction** en extension.

tractor ['træktər] n tracteur m.

trade [treɪd] <> n **1.** (U) [commerce] commerce m - **2.** [job] métier m ; **by trade** de son état. <> vt [exchange] : **to trade sthg (for)** échanger qqch (contre). <> vi COMM : **to trade (with sb)** commercer (avec qqn). ◆ **trade in** vt sep [exchange] échanger, faire reprendre.

trade fair n exposition f commerciale.

trade-in n reprise f.

trademark ['treɪdmɑːk] n **1.** COMM marque f de fabrique - **2.** fig [characteristic] marque f.

trade name n nom m de marque.

trader ['treɪdər] n marchand m, -e f, commerçant m, -e f.

tradesman ['treɪdzmən] (pl -men [-mən]) n commerçant m.

trade(s) union n UK syndicat m.

Trades Union Congress n UK : **the Trades Union Congress** la Confédération des syndicats britanniques.

trade(s) unionist [-'juːnjənɪst] n UK syndicaliste mf.

trading ['treɪdɪŋ] n (U) commerce m.

trading estate *n* UK zone *f* industrielle.

trading standards officer *n* UK fonctionnaire *m* du service de la répression des fraudes.

tradition [trəˈdɪʃn] *n* tradition *f*.

traditional [trəˈdɪʃənl] *adj* traditionnel(elle).

traffic [ˈtræfɪk] ⬦ *n* (U) **1.** [vehicles] circulation *f* - **2.** [illegal trade] : **traffic (in)** trafic *m* (de). ⬦ *vi* (*pt & pp* -**ked**, *cont* -**king**) : **to traffic in** faire le trafic de.

traffic circle *n* US rond-point *m*.

traffic jam *n* embouteillage *m*.

trafficker [ˈtræfɪkə^r] *n* : **trafficker (in)** trafiquant *m*, -e *f* (de).

traffic lights *npl* feux *mpl* de signalisation.

traffic warden *n* UK contractuel *m*, -elle *f*.

tragedy [ˈtrædʒədɪ] *n* tragédie *f*.

tragic [ˈtrædʒɪk] *adj* tragique.

trail [treɪl] ⬦ *n* **1.** [path] sentier *m* - **2.** [trace] piste *f*. ⬦ *vt* **1.** [drag] traîner - **2.** [follow] suivre. ⬦ *vi* **1.** [drag, move slowly] traîner - **2.** SPORT [lose] : **to be trailing** être mené(e). ⬥ **trail away, trail off** *vi* s'estomper.

trailer [ˈtreɪlə^r] *n* **1.** [vehicle - for luggage] remorque *f* ; [- for living in] caravane *f* - **2.** CIN bande-annonce *f*.

train [treɪn] ⬦ *n* **1.** RAIL train *m* - **2.** [of dress] traîne *f*. ⬦ *vt* **1.** [teach] : **to train sb to do sthg** apprendre à qqn à faire qqch - **2.** [for job] former ; **to train sb as/in** former qqn comme/dans - **3.** SPORT : **to train sb (for)** entraîner qqn (pour) - **4.** [gun, camera] braquer. ⬦ *vi* **1.** [for job] : **to train (as)** recevoir OR faire une formation (de) - **2.** SPORT : **to train (for)** s'entraîner (pour).

trained [treɪnd] *adj* formé(e).

trainee [treɪˈniː] *n* stagiaire *mf*.

trainer [ˈtreɪnə^r] *n* **1.** [of animals] dresseur *m*, -euse *f* - **2.** SPORT entraîneur *m*. ⬥ **trainers** *npl* UK chaussures *fpl* de sport.

training [ˈtreɪnɪŋ] *n* (U) **1.** [for job] : **training (in)** formation *f* (de) - **2.** SPORT entraînement *m*.

training college *n* UK école *f* professionnelle.

training shoes *npl* UK chaussures *fpl* de sport.

train of thought *n* : **my/his train of thought** le fil de mes/ses pensées.

traipse [treɪps] *vi* traîner.

trait [treɪt] *n* trait *m*.

traitor [ˈtreɪtə^r] *n* traître *m*.

trajectory [trəˈdʒektərɪ] *n* trajectoire *f*.

tram [træm], **tramcar** [ˈtræmkɑː^r] *n* UK tram *m*, tramway *m*.

tramp [træmp] ⬦ *n* [homeless person] clochard *m*, -e *f*. ⬦ *vi* marcher d'un pas lourd.

trample [ˈtræmpl] *vt* piétiner.

trampoline [ˈtræmpəliːn] *n* trampoline *m*.

trance [trɑːns] *n* transe *f*.

tranquil [ˈtræŋkwɪl] *adj* tranquille.

tranquillizer UK, **tranquilizer** US [ˈtræŋkwɪlaɪzə^r] *n* tranquillisant *m*, calmant *m*.

transaction [trænˈzækʃn] *n* transaction *f*.

transcend [trænˈsend] *vt* transcender.

transcript [ˈtrænskrɪpt] *n* transcription *f*.

transfer ⬦ *n* [ˈtrænsfɜː^r] **1.** [gen] transfert *m* ; [of power] passation *f* ; [of money] virement *m* - **2.** UK [design] décalcomanie *f*. ⬦ *vt* [trænsˈfɜː^r] **1.** [gen] transférer ; [power, control] faire passer ; [money] virer - **2.** [employee] transférer, muter. ⬦ *vi* [trænsˈfɜː^r] être transféré.

transfix [trænsˈfɪks] *vt* : **to be transfixed with fear** être paralysé(e) par la peur.

transform [trænsˈfɔːm] *vt* : **to transform sb/sthg (into)** transformer qqn/qqch (en).

transfusion [trænsˈfjuːʒn] *n* transfusion *f*.

transient [ˈtrænzɪənt] *adj* passager(ère).

transistor [trænˈzɪstə^r] *n* transistor *m*.

transistor radio *n* transistor *m*.

transit [ˈtrænsɪt] *n* : **in transit** en transit.

transition [trænˈzɪʃn] *n* transition *f*.

transitive [ˈtrænzɪtɪv] *adj* GRAM transitif(ive).

transitory [ˈtrænzɪtrɪ] *adj* transitoire.

translate [trænsˈleɪt] *vt* traduire.

translation [trænsˈleɪʃn] *n* traduction *f*.

translator [trænsˈleɪtə^r] *n* traducteur *m*, -trice *f*.

transmission [trænzˈmɪʃn] *n* **1.** [gen] transmission *f* - **2.** RADIO & TV [programme] émission *f* - **3.** US AUT boîte *f* de vitesses.

transmit [trænzˈmɪt] *vt* transmettre.

transmitter [trænzˈmɪtə^r] *n* émetteur *m*.

transparency [transˈpærənsɪ] *n* PHOT diapositive *f* ; [for overhead projector] transparent *m*.

transparent [trænsˈpærənt] *adj* transparent(e).

transpire [trænˈspaɪə^r] *fml* ⬦ *vt* : **it transpires that...** on a appris que... ⬦ *vi* [happen] se passer, arriver.

transplant ⬦ *n* [ˈtrænsplɑːnt] MED greffe *f*, transplantation *f*. ⬦ *vt* [trænsˈplɑːnt] **1.** MED greffer, transplanter - **2.** [seedlings] repiquer.

transport ⬦ *n* [ˈtrænspɔːt] transport *m*. ⬦ *vt* [trænsˈpɔːt] transporter.

transportation [ˌtrænspɔːˈteɪʃn] *n esp US* transport *m*.

transport cafe *n UK* restaurant *m* de routiers, routier *m*.

transpose [trænsˈpəʊz] *vt* transposer.

trap [træp] ◇ *n* piège *m*. ◇ *vt* prendre au piège ; **to be trapped** être coincé.

trapdoor [ˌtræpˈdɔːr] *n* trappe *f*.

trapeze [trəˈpiːz] *n* trapèze *m*.

trappings [ˈtræpɪŋz] *npl* signes *mpl* extérieurs.

trash [træʃ] *n (U)* **1.** *US* [refuse] ordures *fpl* - **2.** *inf pej* [poor-quality thing] camelote *f*.

trashcan [ˈtræʃkæn] *n US* poubelle *f*.

trash collector *n US* éboueur *m*, éboueuse *f*.

traumatic [trɔːˈmætɪk] *adj* traumatisant(e).

travel [ˈtrævl] ◇ *n (U)* voyage *m*, voyages *mpl*. ◇ *vt (UK & US)* parcourir. ◇ *vi (UK & US)* **1.** [make journey] voyager - **2.** [move - current, signal] aller, passer ; [- news] se répandre, circuler.

travel agency *n* agence *f* de voyages.

travel agent *n* agent *m* de voyages ; **to/at the travel agent's** à l'agence *f* de voyages.

traveller *UK*, **traveler** *US* [ˈtrævlər] *n* **1.** [person on journey] voyageur *m*, -euse *f* - **2.** [sales representative] représentant *m*.

traveller's cheque *UK*, **traveler's check** *US n* chèque *m* de voyage.

travelling *UK*, **traveling** *US* [ˈtrævlɪŋ] *adj* **1.** [theatre, circus] ambulant(e) - **2.** [clock, bag etc] de voyage ; [allowance] de déplacement.

travelsick [ˈtrævlsɪk] *adj* : **to be travelsick** avoir le mal de route/de l'air/de mer.

travesty [ˈtrævəstɪ] *n* parodie *f*.

travolator [ˈtrævəleɪtər] *n* tapis *OR* trottoir roulant.

trawler [ˈtrɔːlər] *n* chalutier *m*.

tray [treɪ] *n* plateau *m*.

treacherous [ˈtretʃərəs] *adj* traître (traîtresse).

treachery [ˈtretʃərɪ] *n* traîtrise *f*.

treacle [ˈtriːkl] *n UK* mélasse *f*.

tread [tred] ◇ *n* **1.** [on tyre] bande *f* de roulement ; [of shoe] semelle *f* - **2.** [way of walking] pas *m* ; [sound] bruit *m* de pas. ◇ *vi (pt* trod, *pp* trodden) : **to tread (on)** marcher (sur).

treason [ˈtriːzn] *n* trahison *f*.

treasure [ˈtreʒər] ◇ *n* trésor *m*. ◇ *vt* [object] garder précieusement ; [memory] chérir.

treasurer [ˈtreʒərər] *n* trésorier *m*, -ère *f*.

treasury [ˈtreʒərɪ] *n* [room] trésorerie *f*.
➤ **Treasury** *n* : **the Treasury** le ministère des Finances.

treat [triːt] ◇ *vt* **1.** [gen] traiter - **2.** [special occasion] : **to treat sb to sthg** offrir *OR* payer qqch à qqn. ◇ *n* **1.** [gift] cadeau *m* - **2.** [delight] plaisir *m*.

treatise [ˈtriːtɪz] *n* : **treatise (on)** traité *m* (de).

treatment [ˈtriːtmənt] *n* traitement *m*.

treaty [ˈtriːtɪ] *n* traité *m*.

treble [ˈtrebl] ◇ *adj* **1.** [MUS - voice] de soprano ; [- recorder] aigu (aiguë) - **2.** [triple] triple. ◇ *n* [on stereo control] aigu *m* ; [boy singer] soprano *m*. ◇ *vt & vi* tripler.

treble clef *n* clef *f* de sol.

tree [triː] *n* **1.** [gen] arbre *m* - **2.** COMPUT arbre *m*, arborescence *f*.

tree-hugger *n inf hum & pej* écolo *mf*.

treetop [ˈtriːtɒp] *n* cime *f*.

tree trunk *n* tronc *m* d'arbre.

trek [trek] *n* randonnée *f*.

trellis [ˈtrelɪs] *n* treillis *m*.

tremble [ˈtrembl] *vi* trembler.

tremendous [trɪˈmendəs] *adj* **1.** [size, success, difference] énorme ; [noise] terrible - **2.** *inf* [really good] formidable.

tremor [ˈtremər] *n* tremblement *m*.

trench [trentʃ] *n* tranchée *f*.

trench coat *n* trench-coat *m*.

trend [trend] *n* [tendency] tendance *f*.

trendy [ˈtrendɪ] *inf adj* branché(e), à la mode.

trepidation [ˌtrepɪˈdeɪʃn] *n fml* : **in** *OR* **with trepidation** avec inquiétude.

trespass [ˈtrespəs] *vi* [on land] entrer sans permission ; **'no trespassing'** 'défense d'entrer'.

trespasser [ˈtrespəsər] *n* intrus *m*, -e *f* ; **'trespassers will be prosecuted'** 'défense d'entrer sous peine de poursuites'.

trestle [ˈtresl] *n* tréteau *m*.

trestle table *n* table *f* à tréteaux.

trial [ˈtraɪəl] *n* **1.** LAW procès *m* ; **to be on trial (for)** passer en justice (pour) - **2.** [test, experiment] essai *m* ; **on trial** à l'essai ; **by trial and error** en tâtonnant - **3.** [unpleasant experience] épreuve *f*.

triangle [ˈtraɪæŋgl] *n* [gen] triangle *m*.

tribe [traɪb] *n* tribu *f*.

tribunal [traɪˈbjuːnl] *n* tribunal *m*.

tributary [ˈtrɪbjʊtrɪ] *n* affluent *m*.

tribute [ˈtrɪbjuːt] *n* tribut *m*, hommage *m* ; **to pay tribute to** payer tribut à, rendre hommage à ; **to be a tribute to sthg** témoigner de qqch.

trice [traɪs] *n* : **in a trice** en un clin d'œil.

trick [trɪk] ◇ *n* **1.** [to deceive] tour *m*, farce *f* ; **to play a trick on sb** jouer un tour à qqn - **2.** [to entertain] tour *m* - **3.** [knack] truc *m* ; **that will do the trick** *inf* ça fera l'affaire. ◇ *vt* attraper, rouler ; **to trick sb into doing sthg** amener qqn à faire qqch (par la ruse).

trickery ['trɪkərɪ] *n* (U) ruse *f*.

trickle ['trɪkl] ◇ *n* [of liquid] filet *m*. ◇ *vi* [liquid] dégouliner ; **to trickle in/out** [people] entrer/sortir par petits groupes.

tricky ['trɪkɪ] *adj* [difficult] difficile.

tricycle ['traɪsɪkl] *n* tricycle *m*.

tried [traɪd] *adj* : **tried and tested** [method, system] qui a fait ses preuves.

trifle ['traɪfl] *n* **1.** *UK* CULIN ≃ diplomate *m* - **2.** [unimportant thing] bagatelle *f*. ▸ **a trifle** *adv* un peu, un tantinet.

trifling ['traɪflɪŋ] *adj* insignifiant(e).

trigger ['trɪgər] *n* [on gun] détente *f*, gâchette *f*. ▸ **trigger off** *vt sep* déclencher, provoquer.

trill [trɪl] *n* trille *m*.

trim [trɪm] ◇ *adj* **1.** [neat and tidy] net (nette) - **2.** [slim] svelte. ◇ *n* [of hair] coupe *f*. ◇ *vt* **1.** [cut - gen] couper ; [- hedge] tailler - **2.** [decorate] : **to trim sthg (with)** garnir OR orner qqch (de).

trimming ['trɪmɪŋ] *n* **1.** [on clothing] parement *m* - **2.** CULIN garniture *f*.

trinket ['trɪŋkɪt] *n* bibelot *m*.

trio ['triːəʊ] (*pl* -s) *n* trio *m*.

trip [trɪp] ◇ *n* **1.** [journey] voyage *m* - **2.** *drug sl* trip *m*. ◇ *vt* [make stumble] faire un croche-pied à. ◇ *vi* [stumble]. ▸ **to trip (over)** trébucher (sur). ▸ **trip up** *vt sep* [make stumble] faire un croche-pied à.

tripe [traɪp] *n* (U) CULIN tripe *f* - **2.** *inf* [nonsense] bêtises *fpl*, idioties *fpl*.

triple ['trɪpl] ◇ *adj* triple. ◇ *vt & vi* tripler.

triple jump *n* : **the triple jump** le triple saut.

triplets ['trɪplɪts] *npl* triplés *mpl*, triplées *fpl*.

triplicate ['trɪplɪkət] *n* : **in triplicate** en trois exemplaires.

tripod ['traɪpɒd] *n* trépied *m*.

trite [traɪt] *adj pej* banal(e).

triumph ['traɪəmf] ◇ *n* triomphe *m*. ◇ *vi* : **to triumph (over)** triompher (de).

trivia ['trɪvɪə] *n* (U) [trifles] vétilles *fpl*, riens *mpl*.

trivial ['trɪvɪəl] *adj* insignifiant(e).

trod [trɒd] *pt* ▸ **tread**.

trodden ['trɒdn] *pp* ▸ **tread**.

trolley ['trɒlɪ] (*pl* -s) *n* **1.** *UK* [for shopping, luggage] chariot *m*, caddie® *m* - **2.** *UK* [for food, drinks] chariot *m*, table *f* roulante - **3.** *US* [tram] tramway *m*, tram *m*.

trolley case *n UK* valise *f* à roulettes.

trombone [trɒm'bəʊn] *n* MUS trombone *m*.

troop [truːp] ◇ *n* bande *f*, troupe *f*. ◇ *vi* : **to troop in/out/off** entrer/sortir/partir en groupe. ▸ **troops** *npl* troupes *fpl*.

trophy ['trəʊfɪ] *n* trophée *m*.

tropical ['trɒpɪkl] *adj* tropical(e).

tropics ['trɒpɪks] *npl* : **the tropics** les tropiques *mpl*.

trot [trɒt] ◇ *n* [of horse] trot *m*. ◇ *vi* trotter. ▸ **on the trot** *adv inf* de suite, d'affilée.

trouble ['trʌbl] ◇ *n* (U) **1.** [difficulty] problème *m*, difficulté *f* ; **to be in trouble** avoir des ennuis - **2.** [bother] peine *f*, mal *m* ; **to take the trouble to do sthg** se donner la peine de faire qqch ; **it's no trouble!** ça ne me dérange pas! - **3.** [pain, illness] mal *m*, ennui *m* - **4.** [fighting] bagarre *f* ; POL **troubles** *mpl*, conflits *mpl*. ◇ *vt* **1.** [worry, upset] peiner, troubler - **2.** [bother] déranger - **3.** [give pain to] faire mal à. ▸ **troubles** *npl* **1.** [worries] ennuis *mpl* - **2.** POL troubles *mpl*, conflits *mpl*.

troubled ['trʌbld] *adj* **1.** [worried] inquiet(ète) - **2.** [disturbed - period] de troubles, agité(e) ; [- country] qui connaît une période de troubles.

troublemaker ['trʌbl,meɪkər] *n* fauteur *m*, -trice *f* de troubles.

troubleshooter ['trʌbl,ʃuːtər] *n* expert *m*, spécialiste *m*.

troublesome ['trʌblsəm] *adj* [job] pénible ; [cold] gênant(e) ; [back, knee] qui fait souffrir.

trough [trɒf] *n* **1.** [for animals - with water] abreuvoir *m* ; [- with food] auge *f* - **2.** [low point - of wave] creux *m* ; *fig* point *m* bas.

troupe [truːp] *n* troupe *f*.

trousers ['traʊzəz] *npl* pantalon *m*.

trout [traʊt] (*pl* trout OR -s) *n* truite *f*.

trowel ['traʊəl] *n* [for gardening] déplantoir *m* ; [for cement, plaster] truelle *f*.

truant ['truːənt] *n* [child] élève *mf* absentéiste ; **to play truant** *UK* faire l'école buissonnière.

truce [truːs] *n* trêve *f*.

truck [trʌk] *n* **1.** *esp US* [lorry] camion *m* - **2.** RAIL wagon *m* à plate-forme.

truck driver *n esp US* routier *m*.

trucker ['trʌkər] *n US* routier *m*, -ière *f*.

truck farm *n US* jardin *m* maraîcher.

truculent ['trʌkjʊlənt] *adj* agressif(ive).

trudge [trʌdʒ] *vi* marcher péniblement.

true ['tru:] adj **1.** [factual] vrai(e) ; **to come true** se réaliser - **2.** [genuine] vrai(e), authentique ; **true love** le grand amour - **3.** [exact] exact(e) - **4.** [faithful] fidèle, loyal(e).

truffle ['trʌfl] n truffe f.

truly ['tru:lɪ] adv **1.** [gen] vraiment - **2.** [sincerely] vraiment, sincèrement ; **yours truly** [at end of letter] je vous prie de croire à l'expression de mes sentiments distingués.

trump [trʌmp] n atout m.

trumped-up ['trʌmpt-] adj pej inventé(e) de toutes pièces.

trumpet ['trʌmpɪt] n trompette f.

truncheon ['trʌntʃən] n UK matraque f.

trundle ['trʌndl] vi aller lentement.

trunk [trʌŋk] n **1.** [of tree, person] tronc m - **2.** [of elephant] trompe f - **3.** [box] malle f - **4.** US [of car] coffre m. ◆ **trunks** npl maillot m de bain.

trunk call n UK communication f interurbaine.

trunk road n UK (route f) nationale f.

truss [trʌs] n MED bandage m herniaire.

trust [trʌst] ◇ vt **1.** [have confidence in] avoir confiance en, se fier à ; **to trust sb to do sthg** compter sur qqn pour faire qqch - **2.** [entrust] : **to trust sb with sthg** confier qqch à qqn - **3.** fml [hope] : **to trust (that)...** espérer que... ◇ n **1.** (U) [faith] : **trust (in sb/sthg)** confiance f (en qqn/dans qqch) - **2.** (U) [responsibility] responsabilité f - **3.** FIN : **in trust** en dépôt - **4.** COMM trust m.

trusted ['trʌstɪd] adj [person] de confiance ; [method] qui a fait ses preuves.

trustee [trʌs'ti:] n FIN & LAW fidéicommissaire mf ; [of institution] administrateur m, -trice f.

trust fund n fonds m en fidéicommis.

trusting ['trʌstɪŋ] adj confiant(e).

trustworthy ['trʌst,wɜ:ðɪ] adj digne de confiance.

truth [tru:θ] n vérité f ; **in (all) truth** à dire vrai, en vérité.

truthful ['tru:θfʊl] adj [person, reply] honnête ; [story] véridique.

try [traɪ] ◇ vt **1.** [attempt, test] essayer ; [food, drink] goûter ; **to try to do sthg** essayer de faire qqch - **2.** LAW juger - **3.** [put to the test] éprouver, mettre à l'épreuve. ◇ vi essayer ; **to try for sthg** essayer d'obtenir qqch. ◇ n **1.** [attempt] essai m, tentative f ; **to give sthg a try** essayer qqch - **2.** RUGBY essai m. ◆ **try on** vt sep [clothes] essayer. ◆ **try out** vt sep essayer.

trying ['traɪŋ] adj pénible, éprouvant(e).

T-shirt n tee-shirt m.

T-square n té m.

tub [tʌb] n **1.** [of ice cream - large] boîte f ; [- small] petit pot m ; [of margarine] barquette f - **2.** [bath] baignoire f.

tubby ['tʌbɪ] adj inf rondouillard(e), boulot(otte).

tube [tju:b] n **1.** [cylinder, container] tube m - **2.** UK [underground train] métro m ; **the tube** [system] le métro ; **by tube** en métro.

tuberculosis [tju:,bɜ:kjʊ'ləʊsɪs] n tuberculose f.

tubing ['tju:bɪŋ] n (U) tubes mpl, tuyaux mpl.

tubular ['tju:bjʊlər] adj tubulaire.

TUC n UK abbrev of **Trades Union Congress**.

tuck [tʌk] vt [place neatly] ranger. ◆ **tuck away** vt sep [store] mettre de côté OR en lieu sûr. ◆ **tuck in** ◇ vt **1.** [child, patient] border - **2.** [clothes] rentrer. ◇ vi inf boulotter. ◆ **tuck up** vt sep [child, patient] border.

tuck shop n UK [at school] petite boutique qui vend des bonbons et des gâteaux.

Tuesday ['tju:zdɪ] n mardi m ; see also **Saturday**.

tuft [tʌft] n touffe f.

tug [tʌg] ◇ n **1.** [pull] : **to give sthg a tug** tirer sur qqch - **2.** [boat] remorqueur m. ◇ vt tirer. ◇ vi : **to tug (at)** tirer (sur).

tug-of-war n lutte f de traction à la corde ; fig lutte acharnée.

tuition [tju:'ɪʃn] n (U) cours mpl.

tulip ['tju:lɪp] n tulipe f.

tumble ['tʌmbl] ◇ vi **1.** [person] tomber, faire une chute ; [water] tomber en cascades - **2.** fig [prices] tomber, chuter. ◇ n chute f, culbute f. ◆ **tumble to** vt insep UK inf piger.

tumbledown ['tʌmbldaʊn] adj délabré(e), qui tombe en ruines.

tumble-dryer [-,draɪər] n sèche-linge m inv.

tumbler ['tʌmblər] n [glass] verre m (droit).

tummy ['tʌmɪ] n inf ventre m.

tumour UK, **tumor** US ['tju:mər] n tumeur f.

tuna [UK 'tju:nə, US 'tu:nə] (pl **tuna** OR **-s**) n thon m.

tune [tju:n] ◇ n **1.** [song, melody] air m - **2.** [harmony] : **in tune** [instrument] accordé(e), juste ; [play, sing] juste ; **out of tune** [instrument] mal accordé(e) ; [play, sing] faux ; **to be in/out of tune (with)** fig être en accord/désaccord (avec). ◇ vt **1.** MUS accorder - **2.** RADIO & TV régler - **3.** [engine] régler. ◆ **tune in** vi RADIO & TV être à l'écoute ; **to tune in to** se mettre sur. ◆ **tune up** vi MUS accorder son instrument.

tuneful ['tjuːnfʊl] *adj* mélodieux(euse).

tuner ['tjuːnər] *n* **1.** RADIO & TV syntoniseur *m*, tuner *m* - **2.** MUS [person] accordeur *m*.

tunic ['tjuːnɪk] *n* tunique *f*.

tuning fork ['tjuːnɪŋ-] *n* diapason *m*.

Tunisia [tjuːˈnɪzɪə] *n* Tunisie *f*.

tunnel ['tʌnl] <> *n* tunnel *m*. <> *vi* (*UK & US*) faire OR creuser un tunnel.

turban ['tɜːbən] *n* turban *m*.

turbine ['tɜːbaɪn] *n* turbine *f*.

turbocharged ['tɜːbəʊtʃɑːdʒd] *adj* turbo (*inv*).

turbodiesel [ˌtɜːbəʊˈdiːzl] *n* turbodiesel *m*.

turbulence ['tɜːbjʊləns] *n* (*U*) **1.** [in air, water] turbulence *f* - **2.** *fig* [unrest] agitation *f*.

turbulent ['tɜːbjʊlənt] *adj* **1.** [air, water] agité(e) - **2.** *fig* [disorderly] tumultueux(euse), agité(e).

tureen [təˈriːn] *n* soupière *f*.

turf [tɜːf] <> *n* (*pl* -s *UK*, *pl* turves [tɜːvz]) **1.** [grass surface] gazon *m* - **2.** *US inf* [of gang] territoire *m* réservé - **3.** [clod] motte *f* de gazon. <> *vt* gazonner. **turf out** *vt sep UK inf* [person] virer ; [old clothes] balancer, bazarder.

turgid ['tɜːdʒɪd] *adj fml* [style, writing] pompeux(euse), ampoulé(e).

Turk [tɜːk] *n* Turc *m*, Turque *f*.

turkey ['tɜːkɪ] (*pl* -s) *n* dinde *f*.

Turkey ['tɜːkɪ] *n* Turquie *f*.

Turkish ['tɜːkɪʃ] <> *adj* turc (turque). <> *n* [language] turc *m*. <> *npl* : **the Turkish** les Turcs *mpl*.

Turkish delight *n* loukoum *m*.

turmoil ['tɜːmɔɪl] *n* agitation *f*, trouble *m*.

turn [tɜːn] <> *n* **1.** [in road] virage *m*, tournant *m* ; [in river] méandre *m* - **2.** [revolution, twist] tour *m* - **3.** [change] tournure *f*, tour *m* - **4.** [in game] tour *m* ; **it's my turn** c'est (à) mon tour ; **in turn** tour à tour, chacun (à) son tour - **5.** *UK* [performance] numéro *m* - **6.** *UK* MED crise *f*, attaque *f* ; **to do sb a good turn** rendre (un) service à qqn. <> *vt* **1.** [gen] tourner ; [omelette, steak etc] retourner ; **to turn sthg inside out** retourner qqch ; **to turn one's thoughts/attention to sthg** tourner ses pensées/son attention vers qqch - **2.** [change] : **to turn sthg into** changer qqch en - **3.** [become] : **to turn red** rougir. <> *vi* **1.** [gen] tourner ; [person] se tourner, se retourner - **2.** [in book] : **to turn to a page** se reporter OR aller à une page - **3.** [for consolation] : **to turn to sb/sthg** se tourner vers qqn/qqch - **4.** [change] : **to turn into** changer en, se transformer en. **turn around** *vt sep* = **turn round**. **turn away** <> *vt sep* [refuse entry to] refuser. <> *vi* se détourner. **turn back** <> *vt sep* [sheets] replier ; [person, vehicle] refouler. <> *vi* rebrousser chemin. **turn down** *vt sep* **1.** [reject] rejeter, refuser - **2.** [radio, volume, gas] baisser. **turn in** *vi inf* [go to bed] se pieuter. **turn off** <> *vt insep* [road, path] quitter. <> *vt sep* [radio, TV, engine, gas] éteindre ; [tap] fermer. <> *vi* [leave path, road] tourner. **turn on** <> *vt sep* **1.** [radio, TV, engine, gas] allumer ; [tap] ouvrir ; **to turn the light on** allumer la lumière - **2.** *inf* [excite sexually] exciter. <> *vt insep* [attack] attaquer. **turn out** <> *vt sep* **1.** [light, gas fire] éteindre - **2.** [empty - pocket, bag] retourner, vider. <> *vt insep* : **to turn out to be** s'avérer ; **it turns out that...** il s'avère que... <> *vi* **1.** [end up] finir - **2.** [arrive - person] venir. **turn over** <> *vt sep* **1.** [playing card, stone] retourner ; [page] tourner - **2.** [consider] retourner dans sa tête - **3.** [hand over] rendre, remettre. <> *vi* **1.** [roll over] se retourner - **2.** *UK* TV changer de chaîne. **turn round** *UK*, **turn around** *US* <> *vt sep* **1.** [reverse] retourner - **2.** [wheel, words] tourner. <> *vi* [person] se retourner. **turn up** <> *vt sep* [TV, radio] mettre plus fort ; [gas] monter. <> *vi* **1.** [arrive - person] se pointer - **2.** [be found - person, object] être retrouvé ; [- opportunity] se présenter.

turning ['tɜːnɪŋ] *n UK* [off road] route *f* latérale.

turning point *n* tournant *m*, moment *m* décisif.

turnip ['tɜːnɪp] *n* navet *m*.

turnout ['tɜːnaʊt] *n* [at election] taux *m* de participation ; [at meeting] assistance *f*.

turnover ['tɜːnˌəʊvər] *n* (*U*) **1.** [of personnel] renouvellement *m* - **2.** FIN chiffre *m* d'affaires.

turnpike ['tɜːnpaɪk] *n US* autoroute *f* à péage.

turnstile ['tɜːnstaɪl] *n* tourniquet *m*.

turntable ['tɜːnˌteɪbl] *n* platine *f*.

turn-up *n UK* [on trousers] revers *m inv* ; **a turn-up for the books** *inf* une sacrée surprise.

turpentine ['tɜːpəntaɪn] *n* térébenthine *f*.

turquoise ['tɜːkwɔɪz] <> *adj* turquoise (*inv*). <> *n* **1.** [mineral, gem] turquoise *f* - **2.** [colour] turquoise *m*.

turret ['tʌrɪt] *n* tourelle *f*.

turtle ['tɜːtl] (*pl* turtle OR -s) *n* tortue *f* de mer.

turtleneck ['tɜːtlnek] *n* [garment] pull *m* à col montant ; [neck] col *m* montant.

turves [tɜːvz] *UK npl* ▶ **turf**.

tusk [tʌsk] *n* défense *f*.

tussle ['tʌsl] <> *n* lutte *f*. <> *vi* se battre ; **to tussle over sthg** se disputer qqch.

tutor ['tjuːtə^r] *n* **1.** [private] professeur *m* particulier - **2.** UK UNIV directeur *m*, -trice *f* d'études.

tutorial [tjuːˈtɔːrɪəl] *n* travaux *mpl* dirigés.

tuxedo [tʌkˈsiːdəʊ] (*pl* **-s**) *n* UK smoking *m*.

TV (*abbrev of* **television**) *n* **1.** (U) [medium, industry] télé *f* - **2.** [apparatus] (poste *m* de) télé *f*.

TV movie *n* téléfilm *m*.

twang [twæŋ] *n* **1.** [sound] bruit *m* de pincement - **2.** [accent] nasillement *m*.

tweed [twiːd] *n* tweed *m*.

tweenage ['twiːneɪdʒ] *adj inf* préadolescence *f*.

tweenager ['twiːneɪdʒə^r] *n inf* préadolescent *m*, -e *f*.

tweezers ['twiːzəz] *npl* pince *f* à épiler.

twelfth [twelfθ] *num* douzième ; *see also* sixth.

twelve [twelv] *num* douze ; *see also* six.

twentieth ['twentɪəθ] *num* vingtième ; *see also* sixth.

twenty ['twentɪ] *num* vingt ; *see also* six.

twice [twaɪs] *adv* deux fois ; **twice a day** deux fois par jour ; **he earns twice as much as me** il gagne deux fois plus que moi ; **twice as big** deux fois plus grand ; **twice my size/age** le double de ma taille/mon âge.

twiddle ['twɪdl] <> *vt* jouer avec. <> *vi* : **to twiddle with sthg** jouer avec qqch.

twig [twɪg] *n* brindille *f*, petite branche *f*.

twilight ['twaɪlaɪt] *n* crépuscule *m*.

twin [twɪn] <> *adj* jumeau (jumelle) ; UK [town] jumelé(e) ; **twin beds** lits *mpl* jumeaux. <> *n* jumeau *m*, jumelle *f*.

twin-bedded [-'bedɪd] *adj* à deux lits.

twine [twaɪn] <> *n* (U) ficelle *f*. <> *vt* : **to twine sthg round** UK OR **around** US **sthg** enrouler qqch autour de qqch.

twinge [twɪndʒ] *n* [of pain] élancement *m* ; **a twinge of guilt** un remords.

twinkle ['twɪŋkl] *vi* [star, lights] scintiller ; [eyes] briller, pétiller.

twin room *n* chambre *f* à deux lits.

twin town *n* UK ville *f* jumelée.

twirl [twɜːl] <> *vt* faire tourner. <> *vi* tournoyer.

twist [twɪst] <> *n* **1.** [in road] zigzag *m*, tournant *m* ; [in river] méandre *m*, coude *m* ; [in rope] entortillement *m* - **2.** *fig* [in plot] rebondissement *m*. <> *vt* **1.** [wind, curl] entortiller - **2.** [contort] tordre - **3.** [turn] tourner ; [lid - to open] dévisser ; [- to close] visser - **4.** [sprain] : **to twist one's ankle** se

tordre OR se fouler la cheville - **5.** [words, meaning] déformer. <> *vi* **1.** [river, path] zigzaguer - **2.** [be contorted] se tordre - **3.** [turn] : **to twist round** UK OR **around** US retourner.

twit [twɪt] *n* UK *inf* crétin *m*, -e *f*.

twitch [twɪtʃ] <> *n* tic *m*. <> *vi* [muscle, eye, face] se contracter.

two [tuː] *num* deux ; **in two** en deux ; *see also* six.

two-door *adj* [car] à deux portes.

twofaced [,tuːˈfeɪst] *adj pej* fourbe.

twofold ['tuːfəʊld] <> *adj* double. <> *adv* doublement ; **to increase twofold** doubler.

two-piece *adj* : **two-piece swimsuit** deux-pièces *m inv* ; **two-piece suit** [for man] costume *m* (deux-pièces).

twosome ['tuːsəm] *n inf* couple *m*.

two-way *adj* [traffic, trade] dans les deux sens.

two-way street *n* rue *f* à circulation dans les deux sens.

tycoon [taɪˈkuːn] *n* magnat *m*.

type [taɪp] <> *n* **1.** [sort, kind] genre *m*, sorte *f* ; [model] modèle *m* ; [in classification] type *m* - **2.** (U) TYPO caractères *mpl*. <> *vt* [letter, reply] taper (à la machine). <> *vi* taper (à la machine).

typecast ['taɪpkɑːst] (*pt & pp* **typecast**) *vt* : **to be typecast as** être cantonné dans le rôle de ; **to be typecast** être cantonné aux mêmes rôles.

typeface ['taɪpfeɪs] *n* TYPO œil *m* de caractère.

typescript ['taɪpskrɪpt] *n* texte *m* dactylographié.

typeset ['taɪpset] (*pt & pp* **typeset**) *vt* composer.

typewriter ['taɪp,raɪtə^r] *n* machine *f* à écrire.

typhoid (fever) ['taɪfɔɪd-] *n* typhoïde *f*.

typhoon [taɪˈfuːn] *n* typhon *m*.

typical ['tɪpɪkl] *adj* : **typical (of)** typique (de), caractéristique (de) ; **that's typical (of him/her)!** c'est bien de lui/d'elle!

typing ['taɪpɪŋ] *n* dactylo *f*, dactylographie *f*.

typist ['taɪpɪst] *n* dactylo *mf*, dactylographe *mf*.

typography [taɪˈpɒɡrəfɪ] *n* typographie *f*.

tyranny ['tɪrənɪ] *n* tyrannie *f*.

tyrant ['taɪrənt] *n* tyran *m*.

tyre UK, **tire** US ['taɪə^r] *n* pneu *m*.

tyre pressure UK, **tire pressure** US *n* pression *f* (de gonflage).

U

u [juː] (*pl* **u's** OR **us**), **U** (*pl* **U's** OR **Us**) *n* [letter] u *m inv*, U *m inv*.

U-bend *n* siphon *m*.

udder ['ʌdər] *n* mamelle *f*.

UFO (*abbrev of* **unidentified flying object**) *n* OVNI *m*, ovni *m*.

Uganda [juːˈɡændə] *n* Ouganda *m*.

ugh [ʌɡ] *excl* pouah!, beurk!

ugly ['ʌɡlɪ] *adj* **1.** [unattractive] laid(e) - **2.** *fig* [unpleasant] pénible, désagréable.

UHF (*abbrev of* **ultra-high frequency**) *n* UHF.

UK (*abbrev of* **United Kingdom**) *n* Royaume-Uni *m*, R.U. *m*.

Ukraine [juːˈkreɪn] *n* : **the Ukraine** l'Ukraine *f*.

ulcer ['ʌlsər] *n* ulcère *m*.

ulcerated ['ʌlsəreɪtɪd] *adj* ulcéré(e).

Ulster ['ʌlstər] *n* Ulster *m*.

ulterior [ʌlˈtɪərɪər] *adj* : **ulterior motive** arrière-pensée *f*.

ultimata [ˌʌltɪˈmeɪtə] *npl* ▶ **ultimatum**.

ultimate ['ʌltɪmət] *adj* **1.** [final] final(e), ultime - **2.** [most powerful] ultime, suprême. ◇ *n* : **the ultimate in** le fin du fin dans.

ultimately ['ʌltɪmətlɪ] *adv* [finally] finalement.

ultimatum [ˌʌltɪˈmeɪtəm] (*pl* **-tums** OR **-ta** [-tə]) *n* ultimatum *m*.

ultrasound ['ʌltrəsaʊnd] *n* (*U*) ultrasons *mpl*.

ultraviolet [ˌʌltrəˈvaɪələt] *adj* ultraviolet(ette).

umbilical cord [ʌmˈbɪlɪkl-] *n* cordon *m* ombilical.

umbrella [ʌmˈbrelə] ◇ *n* [portable] parapluie *m* ; [fixed] parasol *m*. ◇ *adj* [organization] qui en regroupe plusieurs autres.

umpire ['ʌmpaɪər] ◇ *n* arbitre *m*. ◇ *vt* arbitrer.

umpteen [ˌʌmpˈtiːn] *num adj inf* je ne sais combien de.

umpteenth [ˌʌmpˈtiːnθ] *num adj inf* énième.

UN (*abbrev of* **United Nations**) *n* : **the UN** l'ONU *f*, l'Onu *f*.

unabated [ˌʌnəˈbeɪtɪd] *adj* : **the rain continued unabated** la pluie continua de tomber sans répit.

unable [ʌnˈeɪbl] *adj* : **to be unable to do sthg** ne pas pouvoir faire qqch, être incapable de faire qqch.

unacceptable [ˌʌnəkˈseptəbl] *adj* inacceptable.

unaccompanied [ˌʌnəˈkʌmpənɪd] *adj* **1.** [child] non accompagné(e) ; [luggage] sans surveillance - **2.** [song] a cappella, sans accompagnement.

unaccountably [ˌʌnəˈkaʊntəblɪ] *adv* [inexplicably] de façon inexplicable, inexplicablement.

unaccounted [ˌʌnəˈkaʊntɪd] *adj* : **to be unaccounted for** manquer.

unaccustomed [ˌʌnəˈkʌstəmd] *adj* [unused] : **to be unaccustomed to sthg/to doing sthg** ne pas être habitué(e) à qqch/à faire qqch.

unadulterated [ˌʌnəˈdʌltəreɪtɪd] *adj* **1.** [unspoilt - wine] non frelaté(e) ; [- food] naturel(elle) - **2.** [absolute - joy] sans mélange ; [- nonsense, truth] pur et simple (pure et simple).

unanimous [juːˈnænɪməs] *adj* unanime.

unanimously [juːˈnænɪməslɪ] *adv* à l'unanimité.

unanswered [ˌʌnˈɑːnsəd] *adj* qui reste sans réponse.

unappetizing, *UK* **-ising** [ˌʌnˈæpɪtaɪzɪŋ] *adj* peu appétissant(e).

unarmed [ˌʌnˈɑːmd] *adj* non armé(e).

unarmed combat *n* combat *m* sans armes.

unashamed [ˌʌnəˈʃeɪmd] *adj* [luxury] insolent(e) ; [liar, lie] effronté(e), éhonté(e).

unassuming [ˌʌnəˈsjuːmɪŋ] *adj* modeste, effacé(e).

unattached [ˌʌnəˈtætʃt] *adj* **1.** [not fastened, linked] : **unattached (to)** indépendant(e) (de) - **2.** [without partner] libre, sans attaches.

unattended [ˌʌnəˈtendɪd] *adj* [luggage, shop] sans surveillance ; [child] seul(e).

unattractive [ˌʌnəˈtræktɪv] *adj* **1.** [not beautiful] peu attrayant(e), peu séduisant(e) - **2.** [not pleasant] déplaisant(e).

unauthorized, *UK* **-ised** [ˌʌnˈɔːθəraɪzd] *adj* non autorisé(e).

unavailable [ˌʌnəˈveɪləbl] *adj* qui n'est pas disponible, indisponible.

unavoidable [ˌʌnəˈvɔɪdəbl] *adj* inévitable.

unaware [ˌʌnəˈweər] *adj* ignorant(e), inconscient(e) ; **to be unaware of sthg** ne pas avoir conscience de qqch, ignorer qqch.

unawares [ˌʌnəˈweəz] *adv* : **to catch** OR **take sb unawares** prendre qqn au dépourvu.

unbalanced [ˌʌn'bælənst] *adj* **1.** [biased] tendancieux(euse), partial(e) - **2.** [deranged] déséquilibré(e).

unbearable [ʌn'beərəbl] *adj* insupportable.

unbeatable [ˌʌn'biːtəbl] *adj* imbattable.

unbeknown(st) [ˌʌnbɪ'nəʊn(st)] *adv* : unbeknownst to à l'insu de.

unbelievable [ˌʌnbɪ'liːvəbl] *adj* incroyable.

unbending [ˌʌn'bendɪŋ] *adj* inflexible, intransigeant(e).

unbia(s)sed [ˌʌn'baɪəst] *adj* impartial(e).

unborn [ˌʌn'bɔːn] *adj* [child] qui n'est pas encore né(e).

unbreakable [ˌʌn'breɪkəbl] *adj* incassable.

unbridled [ˌʌn'braɪdld] *adj* effréné(e), débridé(e).

unbutton [ˌʌn'bʌtn] *vt* déboutonner.

uncalled-for [ˌʌn'kɔːld-] *adj* [remark] déplacé(e) ; [criticism] injustifié(e).

uncanny [ʌn'kænɪ] *adj* étrange, mystérieux(euse) ; [resemblance] troublant(e).

unceasing [ˌʌn'siːsɪŋ] *adj fml* incessant(e), continuel(elle).

unceremonious [ˈʌnˌserɪ'məʊnjəs] *adj* brusque.

uncertain [ʌn'sɜːtn] *adj* incertain(e) ; in no uncertain terms sans mâcher ses mots.

unchanged [ˌʌn'tʃeɪndʒd] *adj* inchangé(e).

unchecked [ˌʌn'tʃekt] *adj* non maîtrisé(e), sans frein.

uncivilized, *UK* **-ised** [ˌʌn'sɪvɪlaɪzd] *adj* non civilisé(e), barbare.

uncle ['ʌŋkl] *n* oncle *m*.

unclear [ˌʌn'klɪə] *adj* **1.** [message, meaning, motive] qui n'est pas clair(e) - **2.** [uncertain - person, future] incertain(e).

uncomfortable [ˌʌn'kʌmftəbl] *adj* **1.** [shoes, chair, clothes etc] inconfortable ; *fig* [fact, truth] désagréable - **2.** [person - physically] qui n'est pas à l'aise ; [- ill at ease] mal à l'aise.

uncommon [ʌn'kɒmən] *adj* **1.** [rare] rare - **2.** *fml* [extreme] extraordinaire.

uncompromising [ˌʌn'kɒmprəmaɪzɪŋ] *adj* intransigeant(e).

unconcerned [ˌʌnkən'sɜːnd] *adj* [not anxious] qui ne s'inquiète pas.

unconditional [ˌʌnkən'dɪʃənl] *adj* inconditionnel(elle).

unconscious [ʌn'kɒnʃəs] <> *adj* **1.** [having lost consciousness] sans connaissance - **2.** *fig* [unaware] : to be unconscious of ne pas avoir conscience de, ne pas se rendre compte de - **3.** [unnoticed - desires, feelings] inconscient(e). <> *n* PSYCHOL inconscient *m*.

unconsciously [ʌn'kɒnʃəslɪ] *adv* inconsciemment.

uncontrollable [ˌʌnkən'trəʊləbl] *adj* **1.** [unrestrainable - emotion, urge] irrépressible, irrésistible ; [- increase, epidemic] qui ne peut être enrayé(e) - **2.** [unmanageable - person] impossible, difficile.

unconventional [ˌʌnkən'venʃənl] *adj* peu conventionnel(elle), original(e).

unconvinced [ˌʌnkən'vɪnst] *adj* qui n'est pas convaincu(e), sceptique.

uncouth [ʌn'kuːθ] *adj* grossier(ère).

uncover [ʌn'kʌvə] *vt* découvrir.

undecided [ˌʌndɪ'saɪdɪd] *adj* [person] indécis(e), irrésolu(e) ; [issue] indécis(e).

undeniable [ˌʌndɪ'naɪəbl] *adj* indéniable, incontestable.

under ['ʌndə] <> *prep* **1.** [gen] sous - **2.** [less than] moins de ; children under five les enfants de moins de cinq ans - **3.** [subject to - effect, influence] sous ; under the circumstances dans ces circonstances, étant donné les circonstances ; to be under the impression that... avoir l'impression que... - **4.** [undergoing] : under discussion en discussion ; under consideration à l'étude, à l'examen - **5.** [according to] selon, conformément à. <> *adv* **1.** [underneath] dessous ; [underwater] sous l'eau ; to go under [company] couler, faire faillite - **2.** [less] au-dessous.

underage [ˌʌndər'eɪdʒ] *adj* mineur(e).

undercarriage ['ʌndəˌkærɪdʒ] *n* train *m* d'atterrissage.

undercharge [ˌʌndə'tʃɑːdʒ] *vt* faire payer insuffisamment à.

underclothes ['ʌndəkləʊðz] *npl* sous-vêtements *mpl*.

undercoat ['ʌndəkəʊt] *n* [of paint] couche *f* de fond.

undercover ['ʌndəˌkʌvə] *adj* secret(ète).

undercurrent ['ʌndəˌkʌrənt] *n fig* [tendency] courant *m* sous-jacent.

undercut [ˌʌndə'kʌt] (*pt & pp* **undercut**) *vt* [in price] vendre moins cher que.

underdeveloped [ˌʌndədɪ'veləpt] *adj* [country] sous-développé(e) ; [person] qui n'est pas complètement développé(e) OR formé(e).

underdog ['ʌndədɒg] *n* : the underdog l'opprimé *m* ; SPORT celui (celle) que l'on donne perdant(e).

underdone [ˌʌndə'dʌn] *adj* [food] pas assez cuit(e) ; [steak] saignant(e).

underestimate vt [ˌʌndər'estɪmeɪt] sous-estimer.

underexposed [ˌʌndərɪk'spəʊzd] adj PHOT sous-exposé(e).

underfoot [ˌʌndə'fʊt] adv sous les pieds.

undergo [ˌʌndə'gəʊ] (pt -went, pp -gone [-'gɒn]) vt subir ; [pain, difficulties] éprouver.

undergraduate [ˌʌndə'grædjʊət] n étudiant m, -e f qui prépare la licence.

underground ◇ adj ['ʌndəgraʊnd] 1. [below the ground] souterrain(e) - 2. fig [secret] clandestin(e). ◇ adv [ˌʌndə'graʊnd] : to go/be forced underground entrer dans la clandestinité. ◇ n ['ʌndəgraʊnd] 1. UK [subway] métro m - 2. [activist movement] résistance f.

undergrowth ['ʌndəgrəʊθ] n (U) sous-bois m inv.

underhand [ˌʌndə'hænd] adj sournois(e), en dessous.

underline [ˌʌndə'laɪn] vt souligner.

underlying [ˌʌndə'laɪɪŋ] adj sous-jacent(e).

undermine [ˌʌndə'maɪn] vt fig [weaken] saper, ébranler.

underneath [ˌʌndə'niːθ] ◇ prep 1. [beneath] sous, au-dessous de - 2. [in movements] sous. ◇ adv 1. [beneath] en dessous, dessous - 2. fig [fundamentally] au fond. ◇ adj inf d'en dessous. ◇ n [underside] : the underneath le dessous.

underpaid adj ['ʌndəpeɪd] sous-payé(e).

underpants ['ʌndəpænts] npl slip m.

underpass ['ʌndəpɑːs] n [for cars] passage m inférieur ; [for pedestrians] passage m souterrain.

underprivileged [ˌʌndə'prɪvɪlɪdʒd] adj défavorisé(e), déshérité(e).

underrated [ˌʌndə'reɪtɪd] adj sous-estimé(e).

undershirt ['ʌndəʃɜːt] n US maillot m de corps.

underside ['ʌndəsaɪd] n : the underside le dessous.

underskirt ['ʌndəskɜːt] n jupon m.

understand [ˌʌndə'stænd] (pt & pp -stood) ◇ vt 1. [gen] comprendre - 2. fml [be informed] : I understand (that)... je crois comprendre que..., il paraît que... ◇ vi comprendre.

understandable [ˌʌndə'stændəbl] adj compréhensible.

understanding [ˌʌndə'stændɪŋ] ◇ n 1. [knowledge, sympathy] compréhension f - 2. [agreement] accord m, arrangement m. ◇ adj [sympathetic] compréhensif(ive).

understatement [ˌʌndə'steɪtmənt] n 1. [inadequate statement] affirmation f en dessous de la vérité - 2. (U) [quality of understating] euphémisme m.

understood [ˌʌndə'stʊd] pt & pp ▶ understand.

understudy ['ʌndəˌstʌdɪ] n doublure f.

undertake [ˌʌndə'teɪk] (pt -took, pp -taken [-'teɪkn]) vt 1. [take on - gen] entreprendre ; [- responsibility] assumer - 2. [promise] : to undertake to do sthg promettre de faire qqch, s'engager à faire qqch.

undertaker ['ʌndəˌteɪkə'] n entrepreneur m des pompes funèbres.

undertaking [ˌʌndə'teɪkɪŋ] n 1. [task] entreprise f - 2. [promise] promesse f.

undertone ['ʌndətəʊn] n 1. [quiet voice] voix f basse - 2. [vague feeling] courant m.

undertook [ˌʌndə'tʊk] pt ▶ undertake.

underwater [ˌʌndə'wɔːtə'] ◇ adj sous-marin(e). ◇ adv sous l'eau.

underwear ['ʌndəweə'] n (U) sous-vêtements mpl.

underwent [ˌʌndə'went] pt ▶ undergo.

underworld ['ʌndəˌwɜːld] n [criminal society] : the underworld le milieu, la pègre.

underwriter ['ʌndəˌraɪtə'] n assureur m.

undid [ˌʌn'dɪd] pt ▶ undo.

undies ['ʌndɪz] npl inf dessous mpl, lingerie f.

undisputed [ˌʌndɪ'spjuːtɪd] adj incontesté(e).

undistinguished [ˌʌndɪ'stɪŋgwɪʃt] adj médiocre, quelconque.

undo [ˌʌn'duː] (pt -did, pp -done) vt 1. [unfasten] défaire - 2. [nullify] annuler, détruire.

undoing [ˌʌn'duːɪŋ] n (U) fml perte f, ruine f.

undone [ˌʌn'dʌn] ◇ pp ▶ undo. ◇ adj 1. [unfastened] défait(e) - 2. [task] non accompli(e).

undoubted [ʌn'daʊtɪd] adj indubitable, certain(e).

undoubtedly [ʌn'daʊtɪdlɪ] adv sans aucun doute.

undress [ˌʌn'dres] ◇ vt déshabiller. ◇ vi se déshabiller.

undue [ˌʌn'djuː] adj fml excessif(ive).

undulate ['ʌndjʊleɪt] vi onduler.

unduly [ˌʌn'djuːlɪ] adv fml trop, excessivement.

unearth [ʌn'ɜːθ] vt 1. [dig up] déterrer - 2. fig [discover] découvrir, dénicher.

unearthly [ʌn'ɜːθlɪ] adj inf [uncivilized - time of day] indu(e), impossible.

unease [ʌn'iːz] n (U) malaise m.

uneasy [ʌnˈiːzɪ] *adj* [person, feeling] mal à l'aise, gêné(e) ; [peace] troublé(e), incertain(e) ; [silence] gêné(e).

uneconomic [ˈʌnˌiːkəˈnɒmɪk] *adj* peu économique, peu rentable.

uneducated [ˌʌnˈedjʊkeɪtɪd] *adj* [person] sans instruction.

unemployed [ˌʌnɪmˈplɔɪd] <> *adj* au chômage, sans travail. <> *npl*: **the unemployed** les chômeurs *mpl*.

unemployment [ˌʌnɪmˈplɔɪmənt] *n* chômage *m*.

unemployment benefit UK, **unemployment compensation** US *n* allocation *f* de chômage.

unerring [ˌʌnˈɜːrɪŋ] *adj* sûr(e), infaillible.

uneven [ˌʌnˈiːvn] *adj* **1.** [not flat - surface] inégal(e) ; [- ground] accidenté(e) - **2.** [inconsistent] inégal(e) - **3.** [unfair] injuste.

unexpected [ˌʌnɪkˈspektɪd] *adj* inattendu(e), imprévu(e).

unexpectedly [ˌʌnɪkˈspektɪdlɪ] *adv* subitement, d'une manière imprévue.

unfailing [ʌnˈfeɪlɪŋ] *adj* qui ne se dément pas, constant(e).

unfair [ˌʌnˈfeər] *adj* injuste.

unfaithful [ˌʌnˈfeɪθfʊl] *adj* infidèle.

unfamiliar [ˌʌnfəˈmɪljər] *adj* **1.** [not well-known] peu familier(ère), peu connu(e) - **2.** [not acquainted] : **to be unfamiliar with sb/sthg** mal connaître qqn/qqch, ne pas connaître qqn/qqch.

unfashionable [ˌʌnˈfæʃnəbl] *adj* démodé(e), passé(e) de mode ; [person] qui n'est plus à la mode.

unfasten [ˌʌnˈfɑːsn] *vt* défaire.

unfavourable UK, **unfavorable** US [ˌʌnˈfeɪvrəbl] *adj* défavorable.

unfeeling [ʌnˈfiːlɪŋ] *adj* impitoyable, insensible.

unfinished [ˌʌnˈfɪnɪʃt] *adj* inachevé(e).

unfit [ˌʌnˈfɪt] *adj* **1.** [not in good health] qui n'est pas en forme - **2.** [not suitable] : **unfit (for)** impropre (à) ; [person] inapte (à).

unfold [ʌnˈfəʊld] <> *vt* [map, newspaper] déplier. <> *vi* [become clear] se dérouler.

unforeseen [ˌʌnfɔːˈsiːn] *adj* imprévu(e).

unforgettable [ˌʌnfəˈgetəbl] *adj* inoubliable.

unforgivable [ˌʌnfəˈgɪvəbl] *adj* impardonnable.

unfortunate [ʌnˈfɔːtʃnət] *adj* **1.** [unlucky] malheureux(euse), malchanceux(euse) - **2.** [regrettable] regrettable, fâcheux(euse).

unfortunately [ʌnˈfɔːtʃnətlɪ] *adv* malheureusement.

unfounded [ˌʌnˈfaʊndɪd] *adj* sans fondement, dénué(e) de tout fondement.

unfriendly [ˌʌnˈfrendlɪ] *adj* hostile, malveillant(e).

unfurnished [ˌʌnˈfɜːnɪʃt] *adj* non meublé(e).

ungainly [ʌnˈgeɪnlɪ] *adj* gauche.

ungodly [ˌʌnˈgɒdlɪ] *adj inf* [unreasonable] indu(e), impossible.

ungrateful [ʌnˈgreɪtfʊl] *adj* ingrat(e), peu reconnaissant(e).

unhappy [ʌnˈhæpɪ] *adj* **1.** [sad] triste, malheureux(euse) - **2.** [uneasy] : **to be unhappy (with OR about)** être inquiet(ète) (au sujet de) - **3.** [unfortunate] malheureux(euse), regrettable.

unharmed [ˌʌnˈhɑːmd] *adj* indemne, sain et sauf (saine et sauve).

unhealthy [ʌnˈhelθɪ] *adj* **1.** [person, skin] maladif(ive) ; [conditions, place] insalubre, malsain(e) ; [habit] malsain - **2.** *fig* [undesirable] malsain(e).

unheard-of [ʌnˈhɜːdɒv] *adj* **1.** [unknown] inconnu(e) - **2.** [unprecedented] sans précédent, inouï(e).

unhook [ˌʌnˈhʊk] *vt* **1.** [dress, bra] dégrafer - **2.** [coat, picture, trailer] décrocher.

unhurt [ˌʌnˈhɜːt] *adj* indemne, sain et sauf (saine et sauve).

unhygienic [ˌʌnhaɪˈdʒiːnɪk] *adj* non hygiénique.

unidentified flying object [ˌʌnaɪˈdentɪfaɪd-] *n* objet *m* volant non identifié.

unification [ˌjuːnɪfɪˈkeɪʃn] *n* unification *f*.

uniform [ˈjuːnɪfɔːm] <> *adj* [rate, colour] uniforme ; [size] même. <> *n* uniforme *m*.

unify [ˈjuːnɪfaɪ] *vt* unifier.

unilateral [ˌjuːnɪˈlætərəl] *adj* unilatéral(e).

unimportant [ˌʌnɪmˈpɔːtənt] *adj* sans importance, peu important(e).

uninhabited [ˌʌnɪnˈhæbɪtɪd] *adj* inhabité(e).

uninjured [ˌʌnˈɪndʒəd] *adj* qui n'est pas blessé(e), indemne.

uninstall [ˌʌnɪnˈstɔːl] *vt* désinstaller.

unintelligent [ˌʌnɪnˈtelɪdʒənt] *adj* inintelligent(e).

unintentional [ˌʌnɪnˈtenʃənl] *adj* involontaire, non intentionnel(elle).

union [ˈjuːnjən] <> *n* **1.** [trade union] syndicat *m* - **2.** [alliance] union *f*. <> *comp* syndical(e).

Union Jack *n* UK **the Union Jack** l'Union Jack *m*, le drapeau britannique.

unique [juːˈniːk] *adj* **1.** [exceptional] unique, exceptionnel(elle) - **2.** [exclusive] : **unique to** propre à - **3.** [very special] unique.

unison ['juːnɪzn] n unisson m ; **in unison** à l'unisson ; [say] en chœur, en même temps.

unit ['juːnɪt] n **1.** [gen] unité f - **2.** [machine part] élément m, bloc m - **3.** [of furniture] élément m - **4.** [department] service m.

unite [juːˈnaɪt] <> vt unifier. <> vi s'unir.

united [juːˈnaɪtɪd] adj **1.** [in harmony] uni(e) - **2.** [unified] unifié(e).

United Kingdom n : **the United Kingdom** le Royaume-Uni.

United Nations n : **the United Nations** les Nations fpl Unies.

United States n : **the United States (of America)** les États-Unis mpl (d'Amérique) ; **in the United States** aux États-Unis.

unit trust n UK société f d'investissement à capital variable.

unity ['juːnətɪ] n (U) unité f.

universal [ˌjuːnɪˈvɜːsl] adj universel(elle).

universe ['juːnɪvɜːs] n univers m.

university [ˌjuːnɪˈvɜːsətɪ] <> n université f. <> comp universitaire ; [lecturer] d'université ; **university student** étudiant m, -e f à l'université.

unjust [ˌʌnˈdʒʌst] adj injuste.

unkempt [ˌʌnˈkempt] adj [clothes, person] négligé(e), débraillé(e) ; [hair] mal peigné(e).

unkind [ʌnˈkaɪnd] adj [uncharitable] méchant(e), pas gentil(ille).

unknown [ˌʌnˈnəʊn] adj inconnu(e).

unlawful [ˌʌnˈlɔːfʊl] adj illégal(e).

unleaded [ˌʌnˈledɪd] <> adj sans plomb. <> n essence f sans plomb.

unleash [ˌʌnˈliːʃ] vt lit déchaîner.

unless [ənˈles] conj à moins que (+ subjunctive) ; **unless I'm mistaken** à moins que je (ne) me trompe.

unlike [ˌʌnˈlaɪk] prep **1.** [different from] différent(e) de - **2.** [in contrast to] contrairement à, à la différence de - **3.** [not typical of] : **it's unlike you to complain** cela ne te ressemble pas de te plaindre.

unlikely [ʌnˈlaɪklɪ] adj **1.** [event, result] peu probable, improbable ; [story] invraisemblable - **2.** [bizarre - clothes etc] invraisemblable.

unlisted [ʌnˈlɪstɪd] adj US [phone number] qui est sur la liste rouge.

unload [ˌʌnˈləʊd] vt décharger.

unlock [ˌʌnˈlɒk] vt ouvrir.

unlucky [ʌnˈlʌkɪ] adj **1.** [unfortunate - person] malchanceux(euse), qui n'a pas de chance ; [- experience, choice] malheureux(euse) - **2.** [object, number etc] qui porte malheur.

unmarried [ˌʌnˈmærɪd] adj célibataire, qui n'est pas marié(e).

unmetered [ʌnˈmiːtəd] adj illimité(e).

unmistakable [ˌʌnmɪˈsteɪkəbl] adj facilement reconnaissable.

unmitigated [ʌnˈmɪtɪgeɪtɪd] adj [disaster] total(e) ; [evil] non mitigé(e).

unnatural [ʌnˈnætʃrəl] adj **1.** [unusual] anormal(e), qui n'est pas naturel(elle) - **2.** [affected] peu naturel(elle) ; [smile] forcé(e).

unnecessary [ʌnˈnesəsərɪ] adj [remark, expense, delay] inutile.

unnerving [ˌʌnˈnɜːvɪŋ] adj troublant(e).

unnoticed [ˌʌnˈnəʊtɪst] adj inaperçu(e).

unobtainable [ˌʌnəbˈteɪnəbl] adj impossible à obtenir.

unobtrusive [ˌʌnəbˈtruːsɪv] adj [person] effacé(e) ; [object] discret(ète) ; [building] que l'on remarque à peine.

unofficial [ˌʌnəˈfɪʃl] adj non officiel(elle).

unorthodox [ˌʌnˈɔːθədɒks] adj peu orthodoxe.

unpack [ˌʌnˈpæk] <> vt [suitcase] défaire ; [box] vider ; [clothes] déballer. <> vi défaire ses bagages.

unpalatable [ʌnˈpælətəbl] adj d'un goût désagréable ; fig dur(e) à avaler.

unparalleled [ʌnˈpærəleld] adj [success, crisis] sans précédent ; [beauty] sans égal.

unpleasant [ʌnˈpleznt] adj désagréable.

unplug [ʌnˈplʌg] vt débrancher.

unpopular [ˌʌnˈpɒpjʊləʳ] adj impopulaire.

unprecedented [ʌnˈpresɪdəntɪd] adj sans précédent.

unpredictable [ˌʌnprɪˈdɪktəbl] adj imprévisible.

unprofessional [ˌʌnprəˈfeʃənl] adj [person, work] peu professionnel(elle) ; [attitude] contraire à l'éthique de la profession.

unqualified [ˌʌnˈkwɒlɪfaɪd] adj **1.** [person] non qualifié(e) ; [teacher, doctor] non diplômé(e) - **2.** [success] formidable ; [support] inconditionnel(elle).

unquestionable [ʌnˈkwestʃənəbl] adj [fact] incontestable ; [honesty] certain(e).

unquestioning [ʌnˈkwestʃənɪŋ] adj aveugle, absolu(e).

unravel [ʌnˈrævl] (UK & US) vt **1.** [undo - knitting] défaire ; [- fabric] effiler ; [- threads] démêler - **2.** fig [solve] éclaircir.

unreal [ˌʌnˈrɪəl] adj [strange] irréel(elle).

unrealistic [ˌʌnrɪəˈlɪstɪk] adj irréaliste.

unreasonable [ʌnˈriːznəbl] adj qui n'est pas raisonnable, déraisonnable.

unrelated [ˌʌnrɪˈleɪtɪd] adj : **to be unrelated (to)** n'avoir aucun rapport (avec).

unrelenting [ˌʌnrɪˈlentɪŋ] adj implacable.

unreliable [ˌʌnrɪ'laɪəbl] *adj* [machine, method] peu fiable ; [person] sur qui on ne peut pas compter.

unremitting [ˌʌnrɪ'mɪtɪŋ] *adj* inlassable.

unrequited [ˌʌnrɪ'kwaɪtɪd] *adj* non partagé(e).

unreserved [ˌʌnrɪ'zɜːvd] *adj* [support, admiration] sans réserve.

unresolved [ˌʌnrɪ'zɒlvd] *adj* non résolu(e).

unrest [ˌʌn'rest] *n* (U) troubles *mpl*.

unrivalled *UK*, **unrivaled** *US* [ʌn'raɪvld] *adj* sans égal(e).

unroll [ˌʌn'rəʊl] *vt* dérouler.

unruly [ʌn'ruːlɪ] *adj* [crowd, child] turbulent(e) ; [hair] indisciplinés.

unsafe [ˌʌn'seɪf] *adj* 1. [dangerous] dangereux(euse) - 2. [in danger] : **to feel unsafe** ne pas se sentir en sécurité.

unsaid [ˌʌn'sed] *adj* : **to leave sthg unsaid** passer qqch sous silence.

unsatisfactory ['ʌnˌsætɪs'fæktərɪ] *adj* qui laisse à désirer, peu satisfaisant(e).

unsavoury *UK*, **unsavory** *US* [ʌn'seɪvərɪ] *adj* [person] peu recommandable ; [district] mal famé(e).

unscathed [ˌʌn'skeɪðd] *adj* indemne.

unscrew [ˌʌn'skruː] *vt* dévisser.

unscrupulous [ʌn'skruːpjʊləs] *adj* sans scrupules.

unseemly [ʌn'siːmlɪ] *adj* inconvenant(e).

unselfish [ˌʌn'selfɪʃ] *adj* désintéressé(e).

unsettled [ˌʌn'setld] *adj* 1. [person] perturbé(e), troublé(e) - 2. [weather] variable, incertain(e) - 3. [argument] qui n'a pas été résolu(e) ; [situation] incertain(e).

unshak(e)able [ʌn'ʃeɪkəbl] *adj* inébranlable.

unshaven [ˌʌn'ʃeɪvn] *adj* non rasé(e).

unsightly [ʌn'saɪtlɪ] *adj* laid(e).

unskilled [ˌʌn'skɪld] *adj* non qualifié(e).

unsociable [ʌn'səʊʃəbl] *adj* sauvage.

unsocial [ˌʌn'səʊʃl] *adj* : **to work unsocial hours** *UK* travailler en dehors des heures normales.

unsound [ˌʌn'saʊnd] *adj* 1. [theory] mal fondé(e) ; [decision] peu judicieux(euse) - 2. [building, structure] en mauvais état.

unspeakable [ʌn'spiːkəbl] *adj* indescriptible.

unstable [ˌʌn'steɪbl] *adj* instable.

unsteady [ˌʌn'stedɪ] *adj* [hand] tremblant(e) ; [table, ladder] instable.

unstoppable [ˌʌn'stɒpəbl] *adj* qu'on ne peut pas arrêter.

unstuck [ˌʌn'stʌk] *adj* : **to come unstuck**

[notice, stamp, label] se décoller ; *fig* [plan, system] s'effondrer ; *fig* [person] essuyer un échec.

unsubscribe [ˌʌnsəb'skraɪb] *vi* : **to unsubscribe (from)** se désinscrire (de).

unsuccessful [ˌʌnsək'sesfʊl] *adj* [attempt] vain(e) ; [meeting] infructueux(euse) ; [candidate] refusé(e).

unsuccessfully [ˌʌnsək'sesfʊlɪ] *adv* en vain, sans succès.

unsuitable [ˌʌn'suːtəbl] *adj* qui ne convient pas ; [clothes] peu approprié(e) ; **to be unsuitable for** ne pas convenir à.

unsure [ˌʌn'ʃɔː] *adj* 1. [not certain] : **to be unsure (about/of)** ne pas être sûr(e) (de) - 2. [not confident] : **to be unsure (of o.s.)** ne pas être sûr(e) de soi.

unsuspecting [ˌʌnsə'spektɪŋ] *adj* qui ne se doute de rien.

unsympathetic ['ʌnˌsɪmpə'θetɪk] *adj* [unfeeling] indifférent(e).

untangle [ˌʌn'tæŋgl] *vt* [string, hair] démêler.

untapped [ˌʌn'tæpt] *adj* inexploité(e).

untenable [ˌʌn'tenəbl] *adj* indéfendable.

unthinkable [ʌn'θɪŋkəbl] *adj* impensable.

untidy [ʌn'taɪdɪ] *adj* [room, desk] en désordre ; [work, handwriting] brouillon *(inv)* ; [person, appearance] négligé(e).

untie [ˌʌn'taɪ] *(cont* **untying)** *vt* [knot, parcel, shoelaces] défaire ; [prisoner] détacher.

until [ən'tɪl] <> *prep* 1. [gen] jusqu'à ; **until now** jusqu'ici - 2. *(after negative)* avant ; **not until tomorrow** pas avant demain. <> *conj* 1. [gen] jusqu'à ce que (+ *subjunctive)* - 2. *(after negative)* avant que (+ *subjunctive).*

untimely [ʌn'taɪmlɪ] *adj* [death] prématuré(e) ; [arrival] intempestif(ive) ; [remark] mal à propos ; [moment] mal choisi(e).

untold [ˌʌn'təʊld] *adj* [amount, wealth] incalculable ; [suffering, joy] indescriptible.

untoward [ˌʌntə'wɔːd] *adj* malencontreux(euse).

untrue [ˌʌn'truː] *adj* [not accurate] faux (fausse), qui n'est pas vrai(e).

unused *adj* 1. [ˌʌn'juːzd] [clothes] neuf (neuve) ; [machine] qui n'a jamais servi ; [land] qui n'est pas exploité - 2. [ʌn'juːst] [unaccustomed] : **to be unused to sthg/to doing sthg** ne pas avoir l'habitude de qqch/de faire qqch.

unusual [ʌn'juːʒl] *adj* rare, inhabituel(elle).

unusually [ʌn'juːʒəlɪ] *adv* exceptionnellement.

unveil [ˌʌn'veɪl] *vt* *lit* & *fig* dévoiler.

unwanted [ˌʌnˈwɒntɪd] *adj* [object] dont on ne se sert pas ; [child] non désiré(e) ; **to feel unwanted** se sentir mal-aimé(e).

unwavering [ʌnˈweɪvərɪŋ] *adj* [determination] inébranlable.

unwelcome [ʌnˈwelkəm] *adj* [news, situation] fâcheux(euse) ; [visitor] importun(e).

unwell [ˌʌnˈwel] *adj* : **to be/feel unwell** ne pas être/se sentir bien.

unwieldy [ʌnˈwiːldɪ] *adj* **1.** [cumbersome] peu maniable - **2.** *fig* [system] lourd(e) ; [method] trop complexe.

unwilling [ˌʌnˈwɪlɪŋ] *adj* : **to be unwilling to do sthg** ne pas vouloir faire qqch.

unwind [ˌʌnˈwaɪnd] (*pt & pp* **-wound**) ◇ *vt* dérouler. ◇ *vi* *fig* [person] se détendre.

unwise [ˌʌnˈwaɪz] *adj* imprudent(e), peu sage.

unwitting [ʌnˈwɪtɪŋ] *adj* *fml* involontaire.

unworkable [ˌʌnˈwɜːkəbl] *adj* impraticable.

unworthy [ʌnˈwɜːðɪ] *adj* [undeserving] : **unworthy (of)** indigne (de).

unwound [ˌʌnˈwaʊnd] *pt & pp* ▶ unwind.

unwrap [ˌʌnˈræp] *vt* défaire.

unwritten law [ˌʌnrɪtn-] *n* droit *m* coutumier.

up [ʌp] ◇ *adv* **1.** [towards or in a higher position] en haut ; **she's up in her bedroom** elle est en haut dans sa chambre ; **we walked up to the top** on est montés jusqu'en haut ; **up there** là-haut - **2.** [into an upright position] : **to stand up** se lever ; **to sit up** s'asseoir (bien droit) - **3.** [northwards] : **I'm coming up to York next week** je viens à York la semaine prochaine ; **up north** dans le nord - **4.** [along a road, river] : **their house is a little further up** leur maison est un peu plus loin. ◇ *prep* **1.** [towards or in a higher position] en haut de ; **up a hill/mountain** en haut d'une colline/d'une montagne ; **up a ladder** sur une échelle ; **I went up the stairs** j'ai monté l'escalier - **2.** [at far end of] : **they live up the road from us** ils habitent un peu plus haut OR loin que nous (dans la même rue) - **3.** [against current of river] : **to sail up the Amazon** remonter l'Amazone en bateau. ◇ *adj* **1.** [out of bed] levé(e) : **I was up at six today** je me suis levé à six heures aujourd'hui - **2.** [at an end] : **time's up** c'est l'heure - **3.** *inf* [wrong] : **is something up?** il y a quelque chose qui ne va pas ? ; **what's up?** qu'est-ce qui ne va pas ?, qu'est-ce qu'il y a ? ◇ *n* : **ups and downs** hauts et bas *mpl*. ◆ **up and down** ◇ *adv* : **to jump up and down** sauter ; **to walk up and down** faire les cent pas. ◇ *prep* : **we walked up and down the avenue** nous avons arpenté l'avenue. ◆ **up to** *prep* **1.** [as far as] jusqu'à - **2.** [indicating level] jusqu'à ; **it could take up to six weeks** cela peut prendre jusqu'à six semaines ; **it's not up to standard** ce n'est pas de la qualité voulue, ceci n'a pas le niveau requis - **3.** [well or able enough for] : **to be up to doing sthg** [able to] être capable de faire qqch ; [well enough for] être en état de faire qqch ; **my French isn't up to much** mon français ne vaut pas grand-chose OR n'est pas fameux - **4.** *inf* [secretly doing something] : **what are you up to?** qu'est-ce que tu fabriques ? ; **they're up to something** ils mijotent quelque chose, ils préparent un coup - **5.** [indicating responsibility] : **it's not up to me to decide** ce n'est pas moi qui décide, il ne m'appartient pas de décider ; **it's up to you** c'est à vous de voir. ◆ **up until** *prep* jusqu'à.

up-and-coming *adj* à l'avenir prometteur.

upbringing [ˈʌpˌbrɪŋɪŋ] *n* éducation *f*.

update [ˌʌpˈdeɪt] *vt* mettre à jour.

upheaval [ʌpˈhiːvl] *n* bouleversement *m*.

upheld [ʌpˈheld] *pt & pp* ▶ uphold.

uphill [ˌʌpˈhɪl] ◇ *adj* **1.** [slope, path] qui monte - **2.** *fig* [task] ardu(e). ◇ *adv* : **to go uphill** monter.

uphold [ʌpˈhəʊld] (*pt & pp* **-held**) *vt* [law] maintenir ; [decision, system] soutenir.

upholstery [ʌpˈhəʊlstərɪ] *n* rembourrage *m* ; [of car] garniture *f* intérieure.

upkeep [ˈʌpkiːp] *n* entretien *m*.

uplifting [ʌpˈlɪftɪŋ] *adj* édifiant(e).

up-market *adj* haut de gamme *(inv)*.

upon [əˈpɒn] *prep* *fml* sur ; **upon hearing the news...** à ces nouvelles... ; **summer/the weekend is upon us** l'été/le week-end approche.

upper [ˈʌpər] ◇ *adj* supérieur(e). ◇ *n* [of shoe] empeigne *f*.

upper class *n* : **the upper class** la haute société. ◆ **upper-class** *adj* [accent, person] aristocratique.

upper hand *n* : **to have the upper hand** avoir le dessus ; **to gain** OR **get the upper hand** prendre le dessus.

uppermost [ˈʌpəməʊst] *adj* le plus haut (la plus haute) ; **it was uppermost in his mind** c'était sa préoccupation majeure.

upright ◇ *adj* **1.** [ˌʌpˈraɪt] [person] droit(e) ; [structure] vertical(e) ; [chair] à dossier droit - **2.** [ˈʌpraɪt] *fig* [honest] droit(e). ◇ *adv* [ˌʌpˈraɪt] [stand, sit] droite. ◇ *n* [ˈʌpraɪt] montant *m*.

uprising [ˈʌpˌraɪzɪŋ] *n* soulèvement *m*.

uproar [ˈʌprɔːr] *n* **1.** (*U*) [commotion] tumulte *m* - **2.** [protest] protestations *fpl*.

uproot [ʌpˈruːt] *vt* *lit & fig* déraciner.

upset [ʌp'set] <> adj **1.** [distressed] peiné(e), triste ; [offended] vexé(e) - **2.** MED : **to have an upset stomach** avoir l'estomac dérangé. <> n : **to have a stomach upset** avoir l'estomac dérangé. <> vt (pt & pp **upset**) **1.** [distress] faire de la peine à - **2.** [plan, operation] déranger - **3.** [overturn] renverser.

upshot ['ʌpʃɒt] n résultat m.

upside ['ʌpsaɪd] n [of situation] avantage m.

upside down [ˌʌpsaɪd-] <> adj à l'envers. <> adv à l'envers ; **to turn sthg upside down** fig mettre qqch sens dessus dessous.

upstairs [ˌʌp'steəz] <> adj d'en haut, du dessus. <> adv en haut. <> n étage m.

upstart ['ʌpstɑːt] n parvenu m, -e f.

upstream [ˌʌp'striːm] <> adj d'amont ; **to be upstream (from)** être en amont (de). <> adv vers l'amont ; [swim] contre le courant.

upsurge ['ʌpsɜːdʒ] n : **upsurge (of/in)** recrudescence f (de).

uptake ['ʌpteɪk] n : **to be quick on the uptake** saisir vite ; **to be slow on the uptake** être lent(e) à comprendre.

uptight [ʌp'taɪt] adj inf tendu(e).

up-to-date adj **1.** [modern] moderne - **2.** [most recent - news] tout dernier (toute dernière) - **3.** [informed] : **to keep up-to-date with** se tenir au courant de.

upturn ['ʌptɜːn] n : **upturn (in)** reprise f (de).

upward ['ʌpwəd] <> adj [movement] ascendant(e) ; [look, rise] vers le haut. <> adv US = **upwards**.

upwards ['ʌpwədz] adv vers le haut. <>> **upwards of** prep plus de.

uranium [jʊ'reɪnjəm] n uranium m.

urban ['ɜːbən] adj urbain(e).

urbane [ɜː'beɪn] adj courtois(e).

urchin ['ɜːtʃɪn] n dated gamin m, -e f.

Urdu ['ʊəduː] n ourdou m.

urge [ɜːdʒ] <> n forte envie f ; **to have an urge to do sthg** avoir une forte envie de faire qqch. <> vt **1.** [try to persuade] : **to urge sb to do sthg** pousser qqn à faire qqch, presser qqn de faire qqch - **2.** [advocate] conseiller.

urgency ['ɜːdʒənsɪ] n (U) urgence f.

urgent ['ɜːdʒənt] adj [letter, case, request] urgent(e) ; [plea, voice, need] pressant(e).

urinal [ˌjʊə'raɪnl] n urinoir m.

urinate ['jʊərɪneɪt] vi uriner.

urine ['jʊərɪn] n urine f.

URL (abbrev of **uniform resource locator**) n COMPUT URL m (adresse électronique).

urn [ɜːn] n **1.** [for ashes] urne f - **2.** [for tea] : **tea urn** fontaine f à thé.

Uruguay ['jʊərəgwaɪ] n Uruguay m.

us [ʌs] pers pron nous ; **can you see/hear us?** vous nous voyez/entendez ? ; **it's us** c'est nous ; **you can't expect US to do it** vous ne pouvez pas exiger que ce soit nous qui le fassions ; **she gave it to us** elle nous l'a donné ; **with/without us** avec/sans nous ; **they are more wealthy than us** ils sont plus riches que nous ; **some of us** quelques-uns d'entre nous.

US n abbrev of **United States**.

USA n abbrev of **United States of America**.

usage ['juːzɪdʒ] n **1.** LING usage m - **2.** (U) [handling, treatment] traitement m.

use <> n [juːs] **1.** [act of using] utilisation f, emploi m ; **to be in use** être utilisé ; **to be out of use** être hors d'usage ; **to make use of sthg** utiliser qqch - **2.** [ability to use] usage m - **3.** [usefulness] : **to be of use** être utile ; **it's no use** ça ne sert à rien ; **what's the use (of doing sthg)?** à quoi bon (faire qqch)? <> aux vb [juːs] : **I used to live in London** avant j'habitais à Londres ; **he didn't use to be so fat** il n'était pas si gros avant ; **there used to be a tree here** (autrefois) il y avait un arbre ici. <> vt [juːz] **1.** [gen] utiliser, se servir de, employer - **2.** pej [exploit] se servir de. <>> **use up** vt sep [supply] épuiser ; [food] finir ; [money] dépenser.

used adj **1.** [juːzd] [handkerchief, towel] sale - **2.** [juːzd] [car] d'occasion - **3.** [juːst] [accustomed] : **to be used to sthg/to doing sthg** avoir l'habitude de qqch/de faire qqch.

useful ['juːsfʊl] adj utile.

useless ['juːslɪs] adj **1.** [gen] inutile - **2.** inf [person] incompétent(e), nul (nulle).

Usenet® ['juːznet] n Usenet® m, forum m électronique.

user ['juːzə'] n [of product, machine] utilisateur m, -trice f ; [of service] usager m.

user-friendly adj convivial(e), facile à utiliser.

usher ['ʌʃə'] <> n placeur m. <> vt : **to usher sb in/out** faire entrer/sortir qqn.

usherette [ˌʌʃə'ret] n ouvreuse f.

USSR (abbrev of **Union of Soviet Socialist Republics**) n : **the (former) USSR** l'(ex-)URSS f.

usual ['juːʒəl] adj habituel(elle) ; **as usual** comme d'habitude.

usually ['juːʒəlɪ] adv d'habitude, d'ordinaire.

usurp [juː'zɜːp] vt usurper.

utensil [juː'tensl] n ustensile m.

uterus ['juːtərəs] (pl **-ri** [-raɪ] OR **-ruses** [-rəsiːz]) n utérus m.

utility [juːˈtɪlətɪ] *n* **1.** *(U)* [usefulness] utilité *f* - **2.** [public service] service *m* public - **3.** COMPUT utilitaire *m*.

utility room *n* buanderie *f*.

utilize, UK **-ise** [ˈjuːtəlaɪz] *vt* utiliser ; [resources] exploiter, utiliser.

utmost [ˈʌtməʊst] ⬦ *adj* le plus grand (la plus grande). ⬦ *n* : **to do one's utmost** faire tout son possible, faire l'impossible ; **to the utmost** au plus haut point.

utter [ˈʌtər] ⬦ *adj* total(e), complet(ète). ⬦ *vt* prononcer ; [cry] pousser.

utterly [ˈʌtəlɪ] *adv* complètement.

U-turn *n* demi-tour *m* ; *fig* revirement *m*.

v[1][viː] (*pl* **v's** OR **vs**), **V** (*pl* **V's** OR **Vs**) *n* [letter] v *m inv*, V *m inv*.

v[2] **1.** *(abbrev of* **verse)** v. - **2.** [cross-reference] *(abbrev of* **vide)** v. - **3.** *abbrev of* **versus** - **4.** *(abbrev of* **volt)** v.

vacancy [ˈveɪkənsɪ] *n* **1.** [job] poste *m* vacant - **2.** [room available] chambre *f* à louer ; **'vacancies'** 'chambres à louer' ; **'no vacancies'** 'complet'.

vacant [ˈveɪkənt] *adj* **1.** [room] inoccupé(e) ; [chair, toilet] libre - **2.** [job, post] vacant(e) - **3.** [look, expression] distrait(e).

vacant lot *n* terrain *m* inoccupé ; US terrain *m* vague ; [for sale] terrain *m* à vendre.

vacate [vəˈkeɪt] *vt* quitter.

vacation [vəˈkeɪʃn] *n* US vacances *fpl*.

vacationer [vəˈkeɪʃənər] *n* US vacancier *m*, -ère *f*.

vaccinate [ˈvæksɪneɪt] *vt* vacciner.

vaccine [UK ˈvæksiːn, US vækˈsiːn] *n* vaccin *m*.

vacuum [ˈvækjuəm] ⬦ *n* **1.** *fig* & TECH vide *m* - **2.** [cleaner] aspirateur *m*. ⬦ *vt* [room] passer l'aspirateur dans ; [carpet] passer à l'aspirateur.

vacuum cleaner *n* aspirateur *m*.

vacuum-packed *adj* emballé(e) sous vide.

vagina [vəˈdʒaɪnə] *n* vagin *m*.

vagrant [ˈveɪgrənt] *n* vagabond *m*, -e *f*.

vague [veɪg] *adj* **1.** [gen] vague, imprécis(e) - **2.** [absent-minded] distrait(e).

vaguely [ˈveɪglɪ] *adv* vaguement.

vain [veɪn] *adj* **1.** [futile, worthless] vain(e) - **2.** *pej* [conceited] vaniteux(euse). ⬦ **in vain** *adv* en vain, vainement.

valentine card [ˈvæləntaɪn-] *n* carte *f* de la Saint-Valentin.

Valentine's Day [ˈvæləntaɪnz-] *n* : **(St) Valentine's Day** la Saint-Valentin.

valet [ˈvæleɪ OR ˈvælɪt] *n* valet *m* de chambre.

valiant [ˈvæljənt] *adj* vaillant(e).

valid [ˈvælɪd] *adj* **1.** [reasonable] valable - **2.** [legally usable] valide.

valley [ˈvælɪ] (*pl* **-s**) *n* vallée *f*.

valour UK, **valor** US [ˈvælər] *n* *(U)* *fml* & *lit* bravoure *f*.

valuable [ˈvæljuəbl] *adj* **1.** [advice, time, information] précieux(euse) - **2.** [object, jewel] de valeur. ⬦ **valuables** *npl* objets *mpl* de valeur.

valuation [ˌvæljuˈeɪʃn] *n* **1.** *(U)* [pricing] estimation *f*, expertise *f* - **2.** [estimated price] valeur *f* estimée.

value [ˈvæljuː] ⬦ *n* valeur *f* ; **to be good value** être d'un bon rapport qualité-prix ; **to get value for money** en avoir pour son argent. ⬦ *vt* **1.** [estimate price of] expertiser - **2.** [cherish] apprécier. ⬦ **values** *npl* [morals] valeurs *fpl*.

value-added tax [-ædɪd-] *n* taxe *f* sur la valeur ajoutée.

valued [ˈvæljuːd] *adj* précieux(euse).

valve [vælv] *n* [on tyre] valve *f* ; TECH soupape *f*.

van [væn] *n* **1.** AUT camionnette *f* - **2.** UK RAIL fourgon *m*.

vandal [ˈvændl] *n* vandale *mf*.

vandalism [ˈvændəlɪzm] *n* vandalisme *m*.

vandalize, UK **-ise** [ˈvændəlaɪz] *vt* saccager.

vanguard [ˈvængɑːd] *n* avant-garde *f* ; **in the vanguard of** à l'avant-garde de.

vanilla [vəˈnɪlə] *n* vanille *f*.

vanish [ˈvænɪʃ] *vi* disparaître.

vanity [ˈvænɪtɪ] *n* **1.** *(U)* *pej* vanité *f* - **2.** US [furniture] coiffeuse *f*.

vantagepoint [ˈvɑːntɪdʒˌpɔɪnt] *n* [for view] bon endroit *m* ; *fig* position *f* avantageuse.

vapour UK, **vapor** US [ˈveɪpər] *n* *(U)* vapeur *f* ; [condensation] buée *f*.

variable [ˈveərɪəbl] *adj* variable ; [mood] changeant(e).

variance [ˈveərɪəns] *n* *fml* : **at variance (with)** en désaccord (avec).

variation [ˌveərɪˈeɪʃn] *n* : **variation (in)** variation *f* (de).

varicose veins [ˈværɪkəʊs-] *npl* varices *fpl*.

varied [ˈveərɪd] *adj* varié(e).

variety [vəˈraɪətɪ] *n* **1.** [gen] variété *f* - **2.** [type] variété *f*, sorte *f*.

variety show *n* spectacle *m* de variétés.

various [ˈveərɪəs] *adj* **1.** [several] plusieurs - **2.** [different] divers.

varnish [ˈvɑːnɪʃ] <> *n* vernis *m*. <> *vt* vernir.

vary [ˈveərɪ] <> *vt* varier. <> *vi* : **to vary (in/with)** varier (en/selon), changer (en/selon).

vase [*UK* vɑːz, *US* veɪz] *n* vase *m*.

Vaseline® [ˈvæsəliːn] *n* vaseline *f*.

vast [vɑːst] *adj* vaste, immense.

vat [væt] *n* cuve *f*.

VAT [væt OR viːˈeɪˈtiː] (*abbrev of* **value-added tax**) *n* TVA *f*.

Vatican [ˈvætɪkən] *n* : **the Vatican** le Vatican.

vault [vɔːlt] <> *n* **1.** [in bank] chambre *f* forte - **2.** [roof] voûte *f* - **3.** [in church] caveau *m*. <> *vt* sauter. <> *vi* : **to vault over sthg** sauter (par-dessus) qqch.

VCR (*abbrev of* **video cassette recorder**) *n* magnétoscope *m*.

VD (*abbrev of* **venereal disease**) *n* (*U*) MST *f*.

VDU (*abbrev of* **visual display unit**) *n* moniteur *m*.

veal [viːl] *n* (*U*) veau *m*.

veer [vɪər] *vi* virer.

vegan [ˈviːgən] <> *adj* végétalien(enne). <> *n* végétalien *m*, -enne *f*.

vegetable [ˈvedʒtəbl] <> *n* légume *m*. <> *adj* [matter, protein] végétal(e) ; [soup, casserole] de OR aux légumes.

vegetarian [ˌvedʒɪˈteərɪən] <> *adj* végétarien(enne). <> *n* végétarien *m*, -enne *f*.

vegetation [ˌvedʒɪˈteɪʃn] *n* (*U*) végétation *f*.

vehement [ˈviːɪmənt] *adj* véhément(e).

vehicle [ˈviːɪkl] *n lit & fig* véhicule *m*.

veil [veɪl] *n lit & fig* voile *m*.

vein [veɪn] *n* **1.** ANAT veine *f* - **2.** [of leaf] nervure *f* - **3.** [of mineral] filon *m*.

velocity [vɪˈlɒsətɪ] *n* vélocité *f*.

velvet [ˈvelvɪt] *n* velours *m*.

vendetta [venˈdetə] *n* vendetta *f*.

vending machine [ˈvendɪŋ-] *n* distributeur *m* automatique.

vendor [ˈvendər] *n* **1.** *fml* [salesperson] marchand *m*, -e *f* - **2.** LAW vendeur *m*, -eresse *f*.

veneer [vəˈnɪər] *n* placage *m* ; *fig* apparence *f*.

venereal disease [vɪˈnɪərɪəl-] *n* maladie *f* vénérienne.

venetian blind [vɪˌniːʃn-] *n* store *m* vénitien.

Venezuela [ˌvenɪzˈweɪlə] *n* Venezuela *m*.

vengeance [ˈvendʒəns] *n* vengeance *f* ; **it began raining with a vengeance** il a commencé à pleuvoir très fort.

venison [ˈvenɪzn] *n* venaison *f*.

venom [ˈvenəm] *n lit & fig* venin *m*.

vent [vent] <> *n* [pipe] tuyau *m* ; [opening] orifice *m* ; **to give vent to** donner libre cours à. <> *vt* [anger, feelings] donner libre cours à ; **to vent sthg on sb** décharger qqch sur qqn.

ventilate [ˈventɪleɪt] *vt* ventiler.

ventilator [ˈventɪleɪtər] *n* ventilateur *m*.

ventriloquist [venˈtrɪləkwɪst] *n* ventriloque *mf*.

venture [ˈventʃər] <> *n* entreprise *f*. <> *vt* risquer ; **to venture to do sthg** se permettre de faire qqch. <> *vi* s'aventurer.

venue [ˈvenjuː] *n* lieu *m*.

veranda(h) [vəˈrændə] *n* véranda *f*.

verb [vɜːb] *n* verbe *m*.

verbal [ˈvɜːbl] *adj* verbal(e).

verbatim [vɜːˈbeɪtɪm] *adj & adv* mot pour mot.

verbose [vɜːˈbəʊs] *adj* verbeux(euse).

verdict [ˈvɜːdɪkt] *n* **1.** LAW verdict *m* - **2.** [opinion] : **verdict (on)** avis *m* (sur).

verge [vɜːdʒ] *n* **1.** [of lawn] bordure *f* ; *UK* [of road] bas-côté *m*, accotement *m* - **2.** [brink] : **on the verge of sthg** au bord de qqch ; **on the verge of doing sthg** sur le point de faire qqch. ◆ **verge (up)on** *vt insep* friser, approcher de.

verify [ˈverɪfaɪ] *vt* vérifier.

veritable [ˈverɪtəbl] *adj hum & fml* véritable.

vermin [ˈvɜːmɪn] *npl* vermine *f*.

vermouth [ˈvɜːməθ] *n* vermouth *m*.

versa ► **vice versa**.

versatile [ˈvɜːsətaɪl] *adj* [person, player] aux talents multiples ; [machine, tool, food] souple d'emploi.

verse [vɜːs] *n* **1.** (*U*) [poetry] vers *mpl* - **2.** [stanza] strophe *f* - **3.** [in Bible] verset *m*.

versed [vɜːst] *adj* : **to be well versed in sthg** être versé(e) dans qqch.

version [ˈvɜːʃn] *n* version *f*.

versus [ˈvɜːsəs] *prep* **1.** SPORT contre - **2.** [as opposed to] par opposition à.

vertebra [ˈvɜːtɪbrə] (*pl* -brae [-briː]) *n* vertèbre *f*.

vertical [ˈvɜːtɪkl] *adj* vertical(e).

vertigo [ˈvɜːtɪgəʊ] *n* (*U*) vertige *m*.

verve [vɜːv] *n* verve *f*.

very [ˈverɪ] <> *adv* **1.** [as intensifier] très ; **very much** beaucoup ; **at the very least** tout au moins ; **very last/first** tout dernier/premier ; **of one's very own** bien à soi - **2.** [as euphemism] : **not very** pas très. ⬦ *adj* : **the very room/book** la pièce/le livre même ; **the very man/thing I've been looking for** juste l'homme/la chose que je cherchais. ➡ **very well** *adv* très bien ; **I can't very well tell him...** je ne peux tout de même pas lui dire que...

vessel ['vesl] *n fml* **1.** [boat] vaisseau *m* - **2.** [container] récipient *m*.

vest [vest] *n* **1.** *UK* [undershirt] maillot *m* de corps - **2.** *US* [waistcoat] gilet *m*.

vested interest ['vestɪd-] *n* : **vested interest (in)** intérêt *m* particulier (à).

vestibule ['vestɪbjuːl] *n fml* [entrance hall] vestibule *m*.

vestige ['vestɪdʒ] *n* vestige *m*.

vestry ['vestrɪ] *n* sacristie *f*.

vet [vet] ⬦ *n UK* (*abbrev of* **veterinary surgeon**) vétérinaire *mf*. ⬦ *vt UK* [candidates] examiner avec soin.

veteran ['vetrən] ⬦ *adj* [experienced] chevronné(e). ⬦ *n* **1.** MIL ancien combattant *m*, vétéran *mf* - **2.** [experienced person] vétéran *m*.

veterinarian [,vetərɪ'neərɪən] *n US* vétérinaire *mf*.

veterinary surgeon ['vetərɪnrɪ-] *n UK fml* vétérinaire *mf*.

veto ['viːtəʊ] ⬦ *n* (*pl* -es) veto *m*. ⬦ *vt* (*pt & pp* -ed, *cont* -ing) opposer son veto à.

vex [veks] *vt* contrarier.

vexed question [,vekst-] *n* question *f* controversée.

vg (*abbrev of* **very good**) tb.

VGA [,viːdʒiː'eɪ] (*abbrev of* **video graphics array/adapter**) *n* COMPUT VGA *m*.

VHF (*abbrev of* **very high frequency**) VHF.

VHS (*abbrev of* **video home system**) *n* VHS *m*.

via ['vaɪə] *prep* **1.** [travelling through] via, par - **2.** [by means of] au moyen de.

viable ['vaɪəbl] *adj* viable.

vibrate [vaɪ'breɪt] *vi* vibrer.

vicar ['vɪkər] *n* [in Church of England] pasteur *m*.

vicarage ['vɪkərɪdʒ] *n* presbytère *m*.

vicarious [vɪ'keərɪəs] *adj* : **to take a vicarious pleasure in sthg** retirer du plaisir indirectement de qqch.

vice [vaɪs] *n* **1.** [immorality, fault] vice *m* - **2.** [tool] étau *m*.

vice-chairman *n* vice-président *m*, -e *f*.

vice-chancellor *n UK* UNIV président *m*, -e *f*.

vice-president *n* vice-président *m*, -e *f*.

vice versa [,vaɪsɪ'vɜːsə] *adv* vice versa.

vicinity [vɪ'sɪnətɪ] *n* : **in the vicinity (of)** aux alentours (de), dans les environs (de).

vicious ['vɪʃəs] *adj* violent(e), brutal(e).

vicious circle *n* cercle *m* vicieux.

victim ['vɪktɪm] *n* victime *f*.

victimize, *UK* **-ise** ['vɪktɪmaɪz] *vt* faire une victime de.

victor ['vɪktər] *n* vainqueur *m*.

victorious [vɪk'tɔːrɪəs] *adj* victorieux(euse).

victory ['vɪktərɪ] *n* : **victory (over)** victoire *f* (sur).

video ['vɪdɪəʊ] ⬦ *n* (*pl* -s) **1.** [medium, recording] vidéo *f* - **2.** *UK* [machine] magnétoscope *m* - **3.** [cassette] vidéocassette *f*. ⬦ *comp* vidéo (*inv*). ⬦ *vt* (*pt & pp* -ed, *cont* -ing) **1.** [using video recorder] enregistrer sur magnétoscope - **2.** [using camera] faire une vidéo de, filmer.

video camera *n* caméra *f* vidéo.

video cassette *n* vidéocassette *f*.

videoconference ['vɪdɪəʊ'kɒnfərəns] *n* vidéoconférence *f*.

video game *n* jeu *m* vidéo.

videorecorder ['vɪdɪəʊrɪ,kɔːdər] *n* magnétoscope *m*.

video shop *UK*, **video store** *US* *n* vidéoclub *m*.

videotape ['vɪdɪəʊteɪp] *n* **1.** [cassette] vidéocassette *f* - **2.** (*U*) [ribbon] bande *f* vidéo.

vie [vaɪ] (*pt & pp* vied, *cont* vying) *vi* : **to vie for sthg** lutter pour qqch ; **to vie with sb (for sthg/to do sthg)** rivaliser avec qqn (pour qqch/pour faire qqch).

Vienna [vɪ'enə] *n* Vienne.

Vietnam [*UK* ,vjet'næm, *US* ,vjet'nɑːm] *n* Viêt-nam *m*.

Vietnamese [,vjetnə'miːz] ⬦ *adj* vietnamien(enne). ⬦ *n* [language] vietnamien *m*. ⬦ *npl* : **the Vietnamese** les Vietnamiens.

view [vjuː] ⬦ *n* **1.** [opinion] opinion *f*, avis *m* ; **in my view** à mon avis - **2.** [scene, sight] vue *f* ; **to come into view** apparaître. ⬦ *vt* **1.** [consider] considérer - **2.** [look at, examine - gen] examiner ; [- house] visiter. ➡ **in view of** *prep* vu, étant donné. ➡ **with a view to** *conj* dans l'intention de, avec l'idée de.

viewer ['vjuːər] *n* **1.** TV téléspectateur *m*, -trice *f* - **2.** [for slides] visionneuse *f*.

viewfinder ['vjuː,faɪndər] *n* viseur *m*.

viewpoint ['vjuːpɔɪnt] *n* point *m* de vue.

vigil ['vɪdʒɪl] *n* veille *f* ; RELIG vigile *f*.

vigilante [,vɪdʒɪ'læntɪ] *n* membre *m* d'un groupe d'autodéfense.

vigorous ['vɪgərəs] *adj* vigoureux(euse).

vile [vaɪl] *adj* [mood] massacrant(e), exécrable ; [person, act] vil(e), ignoble ; [food] infect(e), exécrable.

villa ['vɪlə] *n* villa *f* ; [bungalow] pavillon *m*.

village ['vɪlɪdʒ] *n* village *m*.

villager ['vɪlɪdʒə'] *n* villageois *m*, -e *f*.

villain ['vɪlən] *n* **1.** [of film, book] méchant *m*, -e *f* ; [of play] traître *m* - **2.** [criminal] bandit *m*.

vindicate ['vɪndɪkeɪt] *vt* justifier.

vindictive [vɪn'dɪktɪv] *adj* vindicatif(ive).

vine [vaɪn] *n* vigne *f*.

vinegar ['vɪnɪgə'] *n* vinaigre *m*.

vineyard ['vɪnjəd] *n* vignoble *m*.

vintage ['vɪntɪdʒ] <> *adj* **1.** [wine] de grand cru - **2.** [classic] typique. <> *n* année *f*, millésime *m*.

vintage wine *n* vin *m* de grand cru.

vinyl ['vaɪnɪl] *n* vinyle *m*.

viola [vɪ'əʊlə] *n* alto *m*.

violate ['vaɪəleɪt] *vt* violer.

violence ['vaɪələns] *n* violence *f*.

violent ['vaɪələnt] *adj* [gen] violent(e).

violet ['vaɪələt] <> *adj* violet(ette). <> *n* **1.** [flower] violette *f* - **2.** [colour] violet *m*.

violin [,vaɪə'lɪn] *n* violon *m*.

violinist [,vaɪə'lɪnɪst] *n* violoniste *mf*.

VIP (*abbrev of* **very important person**) *n* VIP *mf*.

viper ['vaɪpə'] *n* vipère *f*.

virgin ['vɜːdʒɪn] <> *adj lit* [land, forest, soil] vierge. <> *n* [woman] vierge *f* ; [man] garçon *m* /homme *m* vierge.

Virgo ['vɜːgəʊ] (*pl* **-s**) *n* Vierge *f*.

virile ['vɪraɪl] *adj* viril(e).

virtually ['vɜːtʃʊəlɪ] *adv* virtuellement, pratiquement.

virtual reality *n* réalité *f* virtuelle.

virtue ['vɜːtʃuː] *n* **1.** [good quality] vertu *f* - **2.** [benefit] : **virtue (in doing sthg)** mérite *m* (à faire qqch). ◆ **by virtue of** *prep fml* en vertu de.

virtuous ['vɜːtʃʊəs] *adj* vertueux(euse).

virus ['vaɪrəs] *n* COMPUT & MED virus *m*.

visa ['viːzə] *n* visa *m*.

vis-à-vis [,viːzɑː'viː] *prep fml* par rapport à.

viscose ['vɪskəʊs] *n* viscose *f*.

visibility [,vɪzɪ'bɪlətɪ] *n* visibilité *f*.

visible ['vɪzəbl] *adj* visible.

vision ['vɪʒn] *n* **1.** (*U*) [ability to see] vue *f* - **2.** [foresight, dream] vision *f*.

visit ['vɪzɪt] <> *n* visite *f* ; **on a visit en** visite ; **visit of a website** visite d'un site. <> *vt* [person] rendre visite à ; [place] visiter.

visiting hours ['vɪzɪtɪŋ-] *npl* heures *fpl* de visite.

visitor ['vɪzɪtə'] *n* [to person] invité *m*, -e *f* ; [to place] visiteur *m*, -euse *f* ; [to hotel] client *m*, -e *f*.

visitors' book *n* UK livre *m* d'or ; [in hotel] registre *m*.

visitor's passport *n* UK passeport *m* temporaire.

visor ['vaɪzə'] *n* visière *f*.

vista ['vɪstə] *n* [view] vue *f*.

visual ['vɪʒʊəl] *adj* visuel(elle).

visual aids *npl* supports *mpl* visuels.

visual display unit *n* écran *m* de visualisation.

visualize, UK **-ise** ['vɪʒʊəlaɪz] *vt* se représenter, s'imaginer.

vital ['vaɪtl] *adj* **1.** [essential] essentiel(elle) - **2.** [full of life] plein(e) d'entrain.

vitally ['vaɪtəlɪ] *adv* absolument.

vital statistics *npl inf* [of woman] mensurations *fpl*.

vitamin [UK 'vɪtəmɪn, US 'vaɪtəmɪn] *n* vitamine *f*.

vivacious [vɪ'veɪʃəs] *adj* enjoué(e).

vivid ['vɪvɪd] *adj* **1.** [bright] vif (vive) - **2.** [clear - description] vivant(e) ; [- memory] net (nette), précis(e).

vividly ['vɪvɪdlɪ] *adv* [describe] d'une manière vivante ; [remember] clairement.

vixen ['vɪksn] *n* [fox] renarde *f*.

VLF (*abbrev of* **very low frequency**) *n* très basse fréquence.

V-neck *n* [neck] décolleté *m* en V ; [sweater] pull *m* à décolleté en V.

vocabulary [və'kæbjʊlərɪ] *n* vocabulaire *m*.

vocal ['vəʊkl] *adj* **1.** [outspoken] qui se fait entendre - **2.** [of the voice] vocal(e).

vocal cords *npl* cordes *fpl* vocales.

vocation [vəʊ'keɪʃn] *n* vocation *f*.

vocational [vəʊ'keɪʃənl] *adj* professionnel(elle).

vociferous [və'sɪfərəs] *adj* bruyant(e).

vodka ['vɒdkə] *n* vodka *f*.

vogue [vəʊg] *n* vogue *f*, mode *f* ; **in vogue** en vogue, à la mode.

voice [vɔɪs] <> *n* [gen] voix *f*. <> *vt* [opinion, emotion] exprimer.

voice mail *n* COMPUT messagerie *f* vocale ; **to send/receive voice mail** envoyer/recevoir un message sur une boîte vocale.

void [vɔɪd] <> adj **1.** [invalid] nul (nulle), ► **null** - **2.** fml [empty] : **void of** dépourvu(e) de, dénué(e) de. <> n vide m.

volatile [UK 'vɒlətaɪl, US 'vɒlətl] adj [situation] explosif(ive) ; [person] lunatique ; [market] instable.

volcano [vɒl'keɪnəʊ] (pl **-es** OR **-s**) n volcan m.

volition [və'lɪʃn] n fml : **of one's own volition** de son propre gré.

volley ['vɒlɪ] <> n (pl **-s**) **1.** [of gunfire] salve f - **2.** fig [of questions, curses] torrent m ; [of blows] volée f, pluie f - **3.** SPORT volée f. <> vt frapper à la volée, reprendre de volée.

volleyball ['vɒlɪbɔːl] n volley-ball m.

volt [vəʊlt] n volt m.

voltage ['vəʊltɪdʒ] n voltage m, tension f.

voluble ['vɒljʊbl] adj volubile, loquace.

volume ['vɒljuːm] n **1.** [gen] volume m - **2.** [of work, letters] quantité f ; [of traffic] densité f.

voluntarily [UK 'vɒləntrɪlɪ, US ˌvɒlən'terəlɪ] adv volontairement.

voluntary ['vɒləntrɪ] adj **1.** [not obligatory] volontaire - **2.** [unpaid] bénévole.

volunteer [ˌvɒlən'tɪər] <> n **1.** [gen & MIL] volontaire mf - **2.** [unpaid worker] bénévole mf. <> vt **1.** [offer] : **to volunteer to do sthg** se proposer OR se porter volontaire pour faire qqch - **2.** [information, advice] donner spontanément. <> vi **1.** [offer one's services] : **to volunteer (for)** se porter volontaire (pour), proposer ses services (pour) - **2.** MIL s'engager comme volontaire.

vomit ['vɒmɪt] <> n vomi m. <> vi vomir.

vote [vəʊt] <> n **1.** [individual decision] : **vote (for/against)** vote m (pour/contre), voix f (pour/contre) - **2.** [ballot] vote m - **3.** [right to vote] droit m de vote. <> vt **1.** [declare] élire - **2.** [choose] : **to vote to do sthg** voter OR se prononcer pour faire qqch ; **they voted to return to work** ils ont voté le retour au travail. <> vi : **to vote (for/against)** voter (pour/contre).

vote of thanks (pl **votes of thanks**) n discours m de remerciement.

voter ['vəʊtər] n électeur m, -trice f.

voting ['vəʊtɪŋ] n scrutin m.

vouch [vaʊtʃ] ◆ **vouch for** vt insep répondre de, se porter garant de.

voucher ['vaʊtʃər] n bon m, coupon m.

vow [vaʊ] <> n vœu m, serment m. <> vt : **to vow to do sthg** jurer de faire qqch ; **to vow (that)...** jurer que...

vowel ['vaʊəl] n voyelle f.

voyage ['vɔɪɪdʒ] n voyage m en mer ; [in space] vol m.

vs abbrev of **versus.**

VSO (abbrev of **Voluntary Service Overseas**) n organisation britannique envoyant des travailleurs bénévoles dans des pays en voie de développement pour contribuer à leur développement technique.

vulgar ['vʌlgər] adj **1.** [in bad taste] vulgaire - **2.** [offensive] grossier(ère).

vulnerable ['vʌlnərəbl] adj vulnérable ; **vulnerable to** [attack] exposé(e) à ; [colds] sensible à.

vulture ['vʌltʃər] n lit & fig vautour m.

W

w¹ ['dʌblju:] (pl **w's** OR **ws**), **W** (pl **W's** OR **Ws**) n [letter] w m inv, W m inv.

W²1. (abbrev of **west**) O, W - **2.** (abbrev of **watt**) w.

wad [wɒd] n **1.** [of cotton wool, paper] tampon m - **2.** [of banknotes, documents] liasse f - **3.** [of tobacco] chique f ; [of chewing-gum] boulette f.

waddle ['wɒdl] vi se dandiner.

wade [weɪd] vi patauger. ◆ **wade through** vt insep fig se taper.

wading pool ['weɪdɪŋ-] n US pataugeoire f.

wafer ['weɪfər] n [thin biscuit] gaufrette f.

waffle ['wɒfl] <> n **1.** CULIN gaufre f - **2.** UK inf [vague talk] verbiage m. <> vi parler pour ne rien dire.

waft [wɑːft OR wɒft] vi flotter.

wag [wæg] <> vt remuer, agiter. <> vi [tail] remuer.

wage [weɪdʒ] <> n salaire m, paie f, paye f. <> vt : **to wage war against** faire la guerre à. ◆ **wages** npl salaire m.

wage earner [-ˌɜːnər] n salarié m, -e f.

wage packet n UK **1.** [envelope] enveloppe f de paye - **2.** fig [pay] paie f, paye f.

wager ['weɪdʒər] n pari m.

waggle ['wægl] inf vt agiter, remuer ; [ears] remuer.

waggon ['wægən] UK = **wagon.**

wagon ['wægən] n **1.** [horse-drawn] chariot m, charrette f - **2.** UK RAIL wagon m.

wail [weɪl] ⟨⟩ n gémissement m. ⟨⟩ vi gémir.

waist [weɪst] n taille f.

waistcoat ['weɪskəʊt] n esp UK gilet m.

waistline ['weɪstlaɪn] n taille f.

wait [weɪt] ⟨⟩ n attente f. ⟨⟩ vi attendre ; **I can't wait to see you** je brûle d'impatience de te voir ; **wait and see!** tu vas bien voir! ◆ **wait for** vt insep attendre ; **to wait for sb to do sthg** attendre que qqn fasse qqch. ◆ **wait on** vt insep [serve food to] servir. ◆ **wait up** vi veiller, ne pas se coucher.

waiter ['weɪtər] n garçon m, serveur m.

waiting list ['weɪtɪŋ-] n liste f d'attente.

waiting room ['weɪtɪŋ-] n salle f d'attente.

waitress ['weɪtrɪs] n serveuse f.

waive [weɪv] vt [fee] renoncer à ; [rule] prévoir une dérogation à.

wake [weɪk] ⟨⟩ n [of ship] sillage m. ⟨⟩ vt (pt **woke** OR **-d**, pp **woken** OR **-d**) réveiller. ⟨⟩ vi (pt **woke** OR **-d**, pp **woken** OR **-d**) se réveiller. ◆ **wake up** ⟨⟩ vt sep réveiller. ⟨⟩ vi [wake] se réveiller.

waken ['weɪkən] fml ⟨⟩ vt réveiller. ⟨⟩ vi se réveiller.

Wales [weɪlz] n pays m de Galles.

walk [wɔːk] ⟨⟩ n **1.** [way of walking] démarche f, façon f de marcher - **2.** [journey - for pleasure] promenade f ; [- long distance] marche f ; **it's a long walk** c'est loin à pied ; **to go for a walk** aller se promener, aller faire une promenade. ⟨⟩ vt **1.** [accompany - person] accompagner ; [- dog] promener - **2.** [distance] faire à pied. ⟨⟩ vi **1.** [gen] marcher - **2.** [for pleasure] se promener. ◆ **walk out** vi **1.** [leave suddenly] partir - **2.** [go on strike] se mettre en grève, faire grève. ◆ **walk out on** vt insep quitter.

walker ['wɔːkər] n [for pleasure] promeneur m, -euse f ; [long-distance] marcheur m, -euse f.

walkie-talkie [,wɔːkɪ'tɔːkɪ] n talkie-walkie m.

walking ['wɔːkɪŋ] n (U) marche f (à pied), promenade f.

walking shoes npl chaussures fpl de marche.

walking stick n canne f.

Walkman® ['wɔːkmən] n baladeur m, Walkman® m.

walk of life (pl **walks of life**) n milieu m.

walkout ['wɔːkaʊt] n [strike] grève f, débrayage m.

walkover ['wɔːk,əʊvər] n victoire f facile.

walkway ['wɔːkweɪ] n passage m ; [between buildings] passerelle f.

wall [wɔːl] n **1.** [of room, building] mur m ; [of rock, cave] paroi f - **2.** ANAT paroi f.

wallchart ['wɔːltʃɑːt] n planche f murale.

walled [wɔːld] adj fortifié(e).

wallet ['wɒlɪt] n portefeuille m.

wallflower ['wɔːl,flaʊər] n **1.** [plant] giroflée f - **2.** inf fig [person] : **to be a wallflower** faire tapisserie.

wall hanging n tenture f.

wallop ['wɒləp] inf vt [person] flanquer un coup à ; [ball] taper fort dans.

wallow ['wɒləʊ] vi [in liquid] se vautrer.

wallpaper ['wɔːl,peɪpər] ⟨⟩ n [for wall, computer screen] papier m peint. ⟨⟩ vt tapisser.

Wall Street n Wall Street m (quartier financier de New York).

wally ['wɒlɪ] n UK inf idiot m, -e f, andouille f.

walnut ['wɔːlnʌt] n **1.** [nut] noix f - **2.** [tree, wood] noyer m.

walrus ['wɔːlrəs] (pl **walrus** OR **-es** [-iːz]) n morse m.

waltz [wɔːls] ⟨⟩ n valse f. ⟨⟩ vi [dance] valser, danser la valse.

wan [wɒn] adj pâle, blême.

wand [wɒnd] n baguette f.

wander ['wɒndər] vi **1.** [person] errer - **2.** [mind] divaguer ; [thoughts] vagabonder.

wane [weɪn] vi **1.** [influence, interest] diminuer, faiblir - **2.** [moon] décroître.

wangle ['wæŋgl] vt inf se débrouiller pour obtenir.

wannabe ['wɒnə,biː] n inf se dit de quelqu'un qui veut être ce qu'il ne peut pas être ; **a Britney Spears wannabe** un clone de Britney Spears.

want [wɒnt] ⟨⟩ n **1.** [need] besoin m - **2.** [lack] manque m ; **for want of** faute de, par manque de - **3.** [deprivation] pauvreté f, besoin m. ⟨⟩ vt **1.** [wish, desire] vouloir ; **to want to do sthg** vouloir faire qqch ; **to want sb to do sthg** vouloir que qqn fasse qqch - **2.** inf [need] avoir besoin de.

wanted ['wɒntɪd] adj : **to be wanted (by the police)** être recherché(e) (par la police).

wanton ['wɒntən] adj [destruction, neglect] gratuit(e).

war [wɔːr] n guerre f.

ward [wɔːd] n **1.** [in hospital] salle f - **2.** UK POL circonscription f électorale - **3.** LAW pupille mf. ◆ **ward off** vt insep [danger] écarter ; [disease, blow] éviter ; [evil spirits] éloigner.

warden ['wɔːdn] n **1.** [of park etc] gardien m, -enne f - **2.** UK [of youth hostel, hall of residence] directeur m, -trice f - **3.** US [of prison] directeur m, -trice f.

warder ['wɔːdər] n UK [in prison] gardien m, -enne f.

wardrobe ['wɔːdrəʊb] n garde-robe f.

warehouse ['weəhaʊs] (pl [-haʊzɪz]) n entrepôt m, magasin m.

wares [weəz] npl marchandises fpl.

warfare ['wɔːfeər] n (U) guerre f.

warhead ['wɔːhed] n ogive f, tête f.

warily ['weərəlɪ] adv avec précaution OR circonspection.

warm [wɔːm] <> adj 1. [gen] chaud(e) ; it's warm today il fait chaud aujourd'hui - 2. [friendly] chaleureux(euse). <> vt chauffer. <> **warm to** vt insep [person] se prendre de sympathie pour ; [idea, place] se mettre à aimer. <> **warm up** <> vt sep réchauffer. <> vi 1. [person, room] se réchauffer - 2. [machine, engine] chauffer - 3. SPORT s'échauffer.

warm-hearted [-'hɑːtɪd] adj chaleureux(euse), affectueux(euse).

warmly ['wɔːmlɪ] adv 1. [in warm clothes] : to dress warmly s'habiller chaudement - 2. [in a friendly way] chaleureusement.

warmth [wɔːmθ] n chaleur f.

warn [wɔːn] vt avertir, prévenir ; to warn sb of sthg avertir qqn de qqch ; to warn sb not to do sthg conseiller à qqn de ne pas faire qqch, déconseiller à qqn de faire qqch.

warning ['wɔːnɪŋ] n avertissement m.

warning light n voyant m, avertisseur m lumineux.

warning triangle n UK triangle m de signalisation.

warp [wɔːp] <> vt 1. [wood] gauchir, voiler - 2. [personality] fausser, pervertir. <> vi [wood] gauchir, se voiler.

warrant ['wɒrənt] <> n LAW mandat m. <> vt 1. [justify] justifier - 2. [guarantee] garantir.

warranty ['wɒrəntɪ] n garantie f.

warren ['wɒrən] n terrier m.

warrior ['wɒrɪər] n guerrier m, -ère f.

Warsaw ['wɔːsɔː] n Varsovie ; the Warsaw Pact le pacte de Varsovie.

warship ['wɔːʃɪp] n navire m de guerre.

wart [wɔːt] n verrue f.

wartime ['wɔːtaɪm] n : in wartime en temps de guerre.

war-torn adj déchiré(e) par la guerre.

wary ['weərɪ] adj prudent(e), circonspect(e) ; to be wary of se méfier de ; to be wary of doing sthg hésiter à faire qqch.

was (weak form [wəz], strong form [wɒz]) pt ▶ be.

wash [wɒʃ] <> n 1. [act] lavage m ; to have a wash UK se laver ; to give sthg a wash

laver qqch - 2. [clothes] lessive f - 3. [from boat] remous m. <> vt [clean] laver ; to wash one's hands se laver les mains. <> vi se laver. <> **wash away** vt sep emporter. <> **wash up** <> vt sep UK [dishes] : to wash the dishes up faire OR laver la vaisselle. <> vi 1. UK [wash dishes] faire OR laver la vaisselle - 2. US [wash oneself] se laver.

washable ['wɒʃəbl] adj lavable.

washbasin UK ['wɒʃˌbeɪsn], **washbowl** US ['wɒʃbəʊl] n lavabo m.

washcloth ['wɒʃˌklɒθ] n US gant m de toilette.

washer ['wɒʃər] n 1. TECH rondelle f - 2. [washing machine] machine f à laver.

washing ['wɒʃɪŋ] n (U) 1. [action] lessive f - 2. [clothes] linge m, lessive f.

washing line n corde f à linge.

washing machine n machine f à laver.

washing powder n UK lessive f, détergent m.

Washington ['wɒʃɪŋtən] n [city] : Washington D.C. Washington.

washing-up n UK vaisselle f.

washing-up liquid n UK liquide m pour la vaisselle.

washout ['wɒʃaʊt] n inf fiasco m.

washroom ['wɒʃrʊm] n US toilettes fpl.

wasn't [wɒznt] = was not.

wasp [wɒsp] n guêpe f.

wastage ['weɪstɪdʒ] n gaspillage m.

waste [weɪst] <> adj [material] de rebut ; [fuel] perdu(e) ; [area of land] en friche. <> n 1. [misuse] gaspillage m ; it's a waste of money [extravagance] c'est du gaspillage ; [bad investment] c'est de l'argent perdu ; a waste of time une perte de temps - 2. (U) [refuse] déchets mpl, ordures fpl. <> vt [money, food, energy] gaspiller ; [time, opportunity] perdre. <> **wastes** npl lit étendues fpl désertes.

wastebasket US = wastepaper basket.

waste disposal unit n broyeur m d'ordures.

wasteful ['weɪstfʊl] adj [person] gaspilleur(euse) ; [activity] peu économique.

waste ground n (U) UK terrain m vague.

wastepaper basket, wastepaper bin UK [ˌweɪst'peɪpə-], US **wastebasket** ['weɪstˌbɑːskɪt] n corbeille f à papier.

watch [wɒtʃ] <> n 1. [timepiece] montre f - 2. [act of watching] : to keep watch faire le guet, monter la garde ; to keep watch on sb/sthg surveiller qqn/qqch - 3. [guard] garde f ; NAUT [shift] quart m. <> vt 1. [look at] regarder - 2. [spy on, guard] surveiller

- **3.** [be careful about] faire attention à. ◇ *vi* regarder. ◆ **watch out** *vi* faire attention, prendre garde.

watchdog ['wɒtʃdɒg] *n* **1.** [dog] chien *m* de garde - **2.** *fig* [organization] organisation *f* de contrôle.

watchful ['wɒtʃfʊl] *adj* vigilant(e).

watchmaker ['wɒtʃ,meɪkər] *n* horloger *m*, -ère *f*.

watchman ['wɒtʃmən] (*pl* **-men** [-mən]) *n* gardien *m*.

water ['wɔːtər] ◇ *n* [liquid] eau *f*. ◇ *vt* arroser. ◇ *vi* **1.** [eyes] pleurer, larmoyer - **2.** [mouth]: **my mouth was watering** j'en avais l'eau à la bouche. ◆ **waters** *npl* [sea] eaux *fpl*. ◆ **water down** *vt sep* **1.** [dilute] diluer ; [alcohol] couper d'eau - **2.** *pej* [plan, demand] atténuer, modérer ; [play, novel] édulcorer.

water bottle *n* gourde *f*, bidon *m* (à eau).

water closet *n dated* toilettes *fpl*, waters *mpl*.

watercolour UK, **watercolor** US ['wɔːtə,kʌlər] *n* **1.** [picture] aquarelle *f* - **2.** [paint] peinture *f* à l'eau, couleur *f* pour aquarelle.

watercress ['wɔːtəkres] *n* cresson *m*.

waterfall ['wɔːtəfɔːl] *n* chute *f* d'eau, cascade *f*.

water heater *n* chauffe-eau *m inv*.

waterhole ['wɔːtəhəʊl] *n* mare *f*, point *m* d'eau.

watering can ['wɔːtərɪŋ-] *n* arrosoir *m*.

water level *n* niveau *m* de l'eau.

water lily *n* nénuphar *m*.

waterline ['wɔːtəlaɪn] *n* NAUT ligne *f* de flottaison.

waterlogged ['wɔːtəlɒgd] *adj* **1.** [land] détrempé(e) - **2.** [vessel] plein(e) d'eau.

water main *n* conduite *f* principale d'eau.

watermark ['wɔːtəmɑːk] *n* **1.** [in paper] filigrane *m* - **2.** [showing water level] laisse *f*.

watermelon ['wɔːtə,melən] *n* pastèque *f*.

water polo *n* water-polo *m*.

waterproof ['wɔːtəpruːf] ◇ *adj* imperméable. ◇ *n* UK imperméable *m*.

watershed ['wɔːtəʃed] *n fig* [turning point] tournant *m*, moment *m* critique.

water skiing *n* ski *m* nautique.

water tank *n* réservoir *m* d'eau, citerne *f*.

watertight ['wɔːtətaɪt] *adj* **1.** [waterproof] étanche - **2.** *fig* [excuse, contract] parfait(e) ; [argument] irréfutable ; [plan] infaillible.

waterway ['wɔːtəweɪ] *n* voie *f* navigable.

waterworks ['wɔːtəwɜːks] (*pl* **waterworks**) *n* [building] installation *f* hydraulique, usine *f* de distribution d'eau.

watery ['wɔːtərɪ] *adj* **1.** [food, drink] trop dilué(e) ; [tea, coffee] pas assez fort(e) - **2.** [pale] pâle.

watt [wɒt] *n* watt *m*.

wave [weɪv] ◇ *n* **1.** [of hand] geste *m*, signe *m* - **2.** [of water, emotion, nausea] vague *f* - **3.** [of light, sound] onde *f* ; [of heat] bouffée *f* - **4.** [in hair] cran *m*, ondulation *f*. ◇ *vt* [arm, handkerchief] agiter ; [flag, stick] brandir. ◇ *vi* **1.** [with hand] faire signe de la main ; **to wave at** OR **to sb** faire signe à qqn, saluer qqn de la main - **2.** [flags, trees] flotter.

wavelength ['weɪvleŋθ] *n* longueur *f* d'ondes ; **to be on the same wavelength** *fig* être sur la même longueur d'ondes.

waver ['weɪvər] *vi* **1.** [falter] vaciller, chanceler - **2.** [hesitate] hésiter, vaciller - **3.** [fluctuate] fluctuer, varier.

wavy ['weɪvɪ] *adj* [hair] ondulé(e) ; [line] onduleux(euse).

wax [wæks] ◇ *n* (U) **1.** [in candles, polish] cire *f* ; [for skis] fart *m* - **2.** [in ears] cérumen *m*. ◇ *vt* cirer ; [skis] farter. ◇ *vi* [moon] croître.

wax paper *n* US papier *m* sulfurisé.

waxworks ['wækswɜːks] (*pl* **waxworks**) *n* [museum] musée *m* de cire.

way [weɪ] ◇ *n* **1.** [means, method] façon *f* ; **to get** OR **have one's way** obtenir ce qu'on veut - **2.** [manner, style] façon *f*, manière *f* ; **in the same way** de la même manière OR façon ; **this/that way** comme ça, de cette façon ; **try to see it my way** mettez-vous à ma place - **3.** [route, path] chemin *m* ; **way in** entrée *f* ; **way out** sortie *f* ; **to be out of one's way** [place] ne pas être sur sa route ; **on the** OR **one's way** sur le OR son chemin ; **to be under way** [ship] faire route ; [meeting] être en cours ; **to get under way** [ship] se mettre en route ; *fig* [meeting] démarrer ; **'give way'** UK AUT 'vous n'avez pas la priorité' ; **to be in the way** gêner ; **to go out of one's way to do sthg** se donner du mal pour faire qqch ; **to keep out of sb's way** éviter qqn ; **keep out of the way!** restez à l'écart ! ; **to make way for** faire place à - **4.** [direction] : **to go/look/come this way** aller/regarder/venir par ici ; **the right/wrong way round** [in sequence] dans le bon/mauvais ordre ; **she had her hat on the wrong way round** elle avait mis son chapeau à l'envers ; **the right/wrong way up** dans le bon/mauvais sens - **5.** [distance] : **all the way** tout le trajet ; *fig* [support etc] jusqu'au bout ; **a long way** loin ; **to give way** [under weight, pressure] céder ; **no way!** pas question ! ◇ *adv inf* [a lot] largement ; **way better** bien mieux. ◆ **ways** *npl* [customs, habits] coutumes *fpl*. ◆ **by the way** *adv* au fait.

waylay [,weɪ'leɪ] (*pt & pp* **-laid** [-'leɪd]) *vt* arrêter (au passage).

wayward ['weɪwəd] *adj* qui n'en fait qu'à sa tête ; [behaviour] capricieux(euse).

WC (*abbrev of* **water closet**) *n* W.-C. *mpl*

we [wi:] *pers pron* nous ; WE can't do it nous, nous ne pouvons pas le faire ; as we say in France comme on dit en France ; we British nous autres Britanniques.

weak [wi:k] *adj* 1. [gen] faible - 2. [delicate] fragile - 3. [unconvincing] peu convaincant(e) - 4. [drink] léger(ère).

weaken ['wi:kn] <> *vt* 1. [undermine] affaiblir - 2. [reduce] diminuer - 3. [physically - person] affaiblir ; [- structure] fragiliser. <> *vi* faiblir.

weakling ['wi:klɪŋ] *n pej* mauviette *f*.

weakness ['wi:knɪs] *n* 1. (U) [physical - of person] faiblesse *f* ; [- of structure] fragilité *f* - 2. [imperfect point] point *m* faible, faiblesse *f*.

wealth [welθ] *n* 1. (U) [riches] richesse *f* - 2. [abundance] : a wealth of une profusion de.

wealthy ['welθɪ] *adj* riche.

wean [wi:n] *vt* [baby, lamb] sevrer.

weapon ['wepən] *n* arme *f*.

weaponize ['wepənaɪz] *vt* militariser.

weaponry ['wepənrɪ] *n* (U) armement *m*.

weapons-grade *adj* militaire.

wear [weəʳ] <> *n* (U) 1. [type of clothes] tenue *f* - 2. [damage] usure *f* ; wear and tear usure *f* - 3. [use] : these shoes have had a lot of wear ces chaussures ont fait beaucoup d'usage. <> *vt* (*pt* wore, *pp* worn) 1. [clothes, hair] porter - 2. [damage] user. <> *vi* (*pt* wore, *pp* worn) 1. [deteriorate] s'user - 2. [last] : to wear well durer longtemps, faire de l'usage ; to wear badly ne pas durer longtemps. ◆ wear away <> *vt sep* [rock, wood] user ; [grass] abîmer. <> *vi* [rock, wood] s'user ; [grass] s'abîmer. ◆ wear down *vt sep* 1. [material] user - 2. [person, resistance] épuiser. ◆ wear off *vi* disparaître. ◆ wear out <> *vt sep* 1. [shoes, clothes] user - 2. [person] épuiser. <> *vi* s'user.

weary ['wɪərɪ] *adj* 1. [exhausted] las (lasse) ; [sigh] de lassitude - 2. [fed up] : to be weary of sthg/of doing sthg être las de qqch/de faire qqch.

weasel ['wi:zl] *n* belette *f*.

weather ['weðəʳ] <> *n* temps *m* ; to be under the weather être patraque. <> *vt* [crisis, problem] surmonter.

weather-beaten [-,bi:tn] *adj* [face, skin] tanné(e).

weathercock ['weðəkɒk] *n* girouette *f*.

weather forecast *n* météo *f*, prévisions *fpl* météorologiques.

weatherman ['weðəmæn] (*pl* **-men** [-men]) *n* météorologue *m*.

weather vane [-veɪn] *n* girouette *f*.

weave [wi:v] <> *vt* (*pt* wove, *pp* woven) [using loom] tisser. <> *vi* (*pt* wove, *pp* woven) [move] se faufiler.

weaver ['wi:vəʳ] *n* tisserand *m*, -e *f*.

web, Web [web] *n* 1. [cobweb] toile *f* (d'araignée) - 2. COMPUT : the web le Web, la Toile - 3. *fig* [of lies] tissu *m*.

web browser *n* COMPUT navigateur *m*.

webcam ['webkæm] *n* webcam *f*.

web designer *n* concepteur *m* de site web.

weblog ['weblɒg] *n* COMPUT weblog *m*.

webmaster ['web,mɑstəʳ] *n* webmaster *m*, webmestre *m*.

web page, Web page *n* page *f* Web.

website, Web site ['websaɪt] *n* COMPUT site *m* Internet OR Web.

wed [wed] (*pt & pp* wed OR **-ded**) *lit* <> *vt* épouser. <> *vi* se marier.

we'd [wi:d] = we had, = we would.

wedding ['wedɪŋ] *n* mariage *m*.

wedding anniversary *n* anniversaire *m* de mariage.

wedding cake *n* pièce *f* montée.

wedding dress *n* robe *f* de mariée.

wedding ring *n* alliance *f*.

wedge [wedʒ] <> *n* 1. [for steadying] cale *f* - 2. [for splitting] coin *m* - 3. [of cake, cheese] morceau *m*. <> *vt* caler.

Wednesday ['wenzdɪ] *n* mercredi *m* ; *see also* Saturday.

wee [wi:] <> *adj* Scot petit(e). <> *n UK inf* pipi *m*. <> *vi UK inf* faire pipi.

weed [wi:d] <> *n* 1. [plant] mauvaise herbe *f* - 2. *UK inf* [feeble person] mauviette *f*. <> *vt* désherber.

weedkiller ['wi:d,kɪləʳ] *n* désherbant *m*.

weedy ['wi:dɪ] *adj UK inf* [feeble] qui agit comme une mauviette.

week [wi:k] *n* semaine *f*.

weekday ['wi:kdeɪ] *n* jour *m* de semaine.

weekend [,wi:k'end] *n* week-end *m*, fin *m* de semaine ; on OR at the weekend le week-end.

weekly ['wi:klɪ] <> *adj* hebdomadaire. <> *adv* chaque semaine. <> *n* hebdomadaire *m*.

weep [wi:p] *vt & vi* (*pt & pp* wept) pleurer.

weeping willow [,wi:pɪŋ-] *n* saule *m* pleureur.

weigh [weɪ] *vt* 1. [gen] peser - 2. NAUT : to

weigh anchor lever l'ancre. ➤ **weigh down** vt sep **1.** [physically] : **to be weighed down with sthg** plier sous le poids de qqch - **2.** [mentally] : **to be weighed down by** OR **with sthg** être accablé par qqch. ➤ **weigh up** vt sep **1.** UK [consider carefully] examiner - **2.** [size up] juger, évaluer.

weight [weɪt] n lit & fig poids m ; **to put on** OR **gain weight** prendre du poids, grossir ; **to lose weight** perdre du poids, maigrir ; **to pull one's weight** faire sa part du travail, participer à la tâche.

weighted ['weɪtɪd] adj : **to be weighted in favour of/against** être favorable/défavorable à.

weighting ['weɪtɪŋ] n indemnité f.

weightlifting ['weɪt,lɪftɪŋ] n haltérophilie f.

weighty ['weɪtɪ] adj [serious] important(e), de poids.

weir [wɪər] n UK barrage m.

weird [wɪəd] adj bizarre.

welcome ['welkəm] ◇ adj **1.** [guest, help etc] bienvenu(e) - **2.** [free] : **you're welcome to...** n'hésitez pas à... - **3.** [in reply to thanks] : **you're welcome** il n'y a pas de quoi, de rien. ◇ n accueil m. ◇ vt **1.** [receive] accueillir - **2.** [approve of] se réjouir de. ◇ excl bienvenue!

weld [weld] ◇ n soudure f. ◇ vt souder.

welfare ['welfeər] ◇ adj social(e). ◇ n **1.** [well-being] bien-être m - **2.** US [income support] assistance f publique.

welfare state n État-providence m.

well [wel] ◇ adj (comp **better**, superl **best**) bien ; **I'm very well, thanks** je vais très bien, merci ; **all is well** tout va bien ; **just as well** aussi bien. ◇ adv bien ; **the team was well beaten** l'équipe a été battue à plates coutures ; **to go well** aller bien ; **well done!** bravo! ; **well and truly** bel et bien. ◇ n [for water, oil] puits m. ◇ excl **1.** [in hesitation] heu!, eh bien! - **2.** [to correct oneself] bon!, enfin! - **3.** [to express resignation] : **oh well!** eh bien! - **4.** [in surprise] : tiens! ➤ **as well** adv **1.** [in addition] aussi, également - **2.** [with same result] : **I/you etc may** OR **might as well (do sthg)** je/tu etc ferais aussi bien (de faire qqch). ➤ **as well as** conj en plus de, aussi bien que. ➤ **well up** vi : **tears welled up in her eyes** les larmes lui montaient aux yeux.

we'll [wiːl] = we shall, = we will.

well-advised [-əd'vaɪzd] adj sage ; **you would be well-advised to do sthg** tu ferais bien de faire qqch.

well-behaved [-bɪ'heɪvd] adj sage.

wellbeing [,wel'biːɪŋ] n bien-être m.

well-built adj bien bâti(e).

well-done adj CULIN bien cuit(e).

well-dressed [-'drest] adj bien habillé(e).

well-earned [-'ɜːnd] adj bien mérité(e).

well-heeled [-'hiːld] adj inf nanti(e).

wellington boots ['welɪŋtən-], **wellingtons** ['welɪŋtənz] npl UK bottes fpl de caoutchouc.

well-kept adj **1.** [building, garden] bien tenu(e) - **2.** [secret] bien gardé(e).

well-known adj bien connu(e).

well-mannered [-'mænəd] adj bien élevé(e).

well-meaning adj bien intentionné(e).

well-nigh [-naɪ] adv presque, pratiquement.

well-off adj **1.** [rich] riche - **2.** [well-provided] : **to be well-off for sthg** être bien pourvu(e) en qqch.

well-read [-'red] adj cultivé(e).

well-rounded [-'raundɪd] adj [education, background] complet(ète).

well-timed [-'taɪmd] adj bien calculé(e), qui vient à point nommé.

well-to-do adj riche.

wellwisher ['wel,wɪʃər] n admirateur m, -trice f.

Welsh [welʃ] ◇ adj gallois(e). ◇ n [language] gallois m. ◇ npl : **the Welsh** les Gallois mpl.

Welsh Assembly n Assemblée f galloise OR du pays de Galles.

Welshman ['welʃmən] (pl **-men** [-mən]) n Gallois m.

Welshwoman ['welʃ,wumən] (pl **-women** [-,wimin]) n Galloise f.

went [went] pt ➤ **go**.

wept [wept] pt & pp ➤ **weep**.

were [wɜːr] ➤ **be**.

we're [wɪər] = we are.

weren't [wɜːnt] = were not.

west [west] ◇ n **1.** [direction] ouest m - **2.** [region] : **the west** l'ouest m. ◇ adj ouest (inv) ; [wind] d'ouest. ◇ adv de l'ouest, vers l'ouest ; **west of** à l'ouest de. ➤ **West** n POL : **the West** l'Occident m.

West Bank n : **the West Bank** la Cisjordanie.

West Country n UK : **the West Country** le sud-ouest de l'Angleterre.

West End n UK : **the West End** le West-End (quartier des grands magasins et des théâtres, à Londres).

westerly ['westəlɪ] adj à l'ouest ; [wind] de l'ouest ; **in a westerly direction** vers l'ouest.

western ['westən] ◇ adj **1.** [gen] de l'ouest - **2.** POL occidental(e). ◇ n [book, film] western m.

West German <> adj ouest-allemand(e). <> n Allemand m, -e f de l'Ouest.

West Germany n : (former) West Germany (ex-) Allemagne f de l'Ouest.

West Indian <> adj antillais(e). <> n Antillais m, -e f.

West Indies [-'ɪndɪz] npl : the West Indies les Antilles fpl.

Westminster ['westmɪnstər] n quartier de Londres où se situe le Parlement britannique.

westward ['westwəd] adj & adv vers l'ouest.

westwards ['westwədz] adv vers l'ouest.

wet [wet] <> adj 1. [damp, soaked] mouillé(e) - 2. [rainy] pluvieux(euse) - 3. [not dry - paint, cement] frais (fraîche) - 4. UK inf pej [weak, feeble] ramolli(e). <> n UK inf POL modéré m, -e f. <> vt (pt & pp wet OR -ted) mouiller.

wet blanket n inf pej rabat-joie m inv.

wet suit n combinaison f de plongée.

we've [wiːv] = we have.

whack [wæk] inf <> n 1. UK [share] part f - 2. [hit] grand coup m. <> vt donner un grand coup à, frapper fort.

whale [weɪl] n baleine f.

wharf [wɔːf] (pl -s OR **wharves** [wɔːvz]) n quai m.

what [wɒt] <> adj 1. (in direct, indirect questions) quel (quelle), quels (quelles) (pl) ; what colour is it? c'est de quelle couleur? ; he asked me what colour it was il m'a demandé de quelle couleur c'était - 2. (in exclamations) quel (quelle), quels (quelles) (pl) ; what a surprise! quelle surprise! ; what an idiot I am! ce que je peux être bête! <> pron 1. [interrogative - subject] qu'est-ce qui ; [- object] qu'est-ce que, que ; [- after prep] quoi ; what are they doing? qu'est-ce qu'ils font? ; what are they doing? qu'est-ce qu'ils font?, que font-ils? ; what is going on? qu'est-ce qui se passe? ; what are they talking about? de quoi parlent-ils? ; what about another drink/going out for a meal? et si on prenait un autre verre/allait manger au restaurant? ; what about the rest of us? et nous alors? ; what if...? et si...? - 2. [relative - subject] ce qui ; [- object] ce que ; I saw what happened/fell j'ai vu ce qui s'était passé/était tombé ; you can't have what you want tu ne peux pas avoir ce que tu veux. <> excl (expressing disbelief) comment!, quoi!

whatever [wɒt'evər] <> adj quel (quelle) que soit ; any book whatever n'importe quel livre ; no chance whatever pas la moindre chance ; nothing whatever rien du tout. <> pron quoi que (+ subjunctive) ; I'll do whatever I can je ferai tout ce que je peux ; whatever can this be? qu'est-ce que cela peut-il bien être? ; whatever that may

mean quoi que cela puisse bien vouloir dire ; or whatever ou n'importe quoi d'autre.

whatsoever [,wɒtsəu'evər] adj : I had no interest whatsoever je n'éprouvais pas le moindre intérêt ; nothing whatsoever rien du tout.

wheat [wiːt] n blé m.

wheedle ['wiːdl] vt : to wheedle sb into doing sthg enjôler qqn pour qu'il fasse qqch ; to wheedle sthg out of sb enjôler qqn pour obtenir qqch.

wheel [wiːl] <> n 1. [gen] roue f - 2. [steering wheel] volant m. <> vt pousser. <> vi : to wheel (round) UK OR around US se retourner brusquement.

wheelbarrow ['wiːl,bærəu] n brouette f.

wheelchair ['wiːl,tʃeər] n fauteuil m roulant.

wheelclamp ['wiːl,klæmp] <> n sabot m de Denver. <> vt : my car was wheelclamped on a mis un sabot à ma voiture.

wheeze [wiːz] <> n [sound] respiration f sifflante. <> vi respirer avec un bruit sifflant.

whelk [welk] n bulot m, buccin m.

when [wen] <> adv (in direct, indirect questions) quand ; when does the plane arrive? quand OR à quelle heure arrive l'avion? ; he asked me when I would be in London il m'a demandé quand je serais à Londres. <> conj 1. [referring to time] quand, lorsque ; he came to see me when I was abroad il est venu me voir quand j'étais à l'étranger ; one day when I was on my own un jour que OR où j'étais tout seul ; on the day when it happened le jour où cela s'est passé - 2. [whereas, considering that] alors que.

whenever [wen'evər] <> conj quand ; [each time that] chaque fois que. <> adv n'importe quand.

where [weər] <> adv (in direct, indirect questions) où ; where do you live? où habitez-vous? ; do you know where he lives? est-ce que vous savez où il habite? <> conj 1. [referring to place, situation] où ; this is where... c'est là que... - 2. [whereas] alors que.

whereabouts <> adv [,weərə'bauts] où. <> npl ['weərəbauts] : their whereabouts are still unknown on ne sait toujours pas où ils se trouvent.

whereas [weər'æz] conj alors que.

whereby [weə'baɪ] conj fml par lequel (laquelle), au moyen duquel (de laquelle).

whereupon [,weərə'pɒn] conj fml après quoi, sur quoi.

wherever [weər'evər] <> conj où que

(+ *subjunctive*). <> *adv* **1.** [no matter where] n'importe où - **2.** [where] où donc ; **wherever did you hear that?** mais où donc as-tu entendu dire cela?

wherewithal ['weəwɪðɔːl] *n fml* : **to have the wherewithal to do sthg** avoir les moyens de faire qqch.

whet [wet] *vt* : **to whet sb's appetite for sthg** donner à qqn envie de qqch.

whether ['weðər] *conj* **1.** [indicating choice, doubt] si - **2.** [no matter if] : **whether I want to or not** que je le veuille ou non.

which [wɪtʃ] <> *adj* **1.** (*in direct, indirect questions*) quel (quelle), quels (quelles) (*pl*) ; **which house is yours?** quelle maison est la tienne? ; **which one?** lequel (laquelle) ? - **2.** [to refer back to sthg] : **in which case** auquel cas. <> *pron* **1.** (*in direct, indirect questions*) lequel (laquelle), lesquels (lesquelles) (*pl*) ; **which do you prefer?** lequel préférez-vous? ; **I can't decide which to have** je ne sais vraiment pas lequel prendre - **2.** [in relative clauses - subject] qui ; [- object] que ; [- after prep] lequel (laquelle), lesquels (lesquelles) (*pl*) ; **take the slice which is nearer to you** prends la tranche qui est le plus près de toi ; **the television which we bought** le téléviseur que nous avons acheté ; **the settee on which I am sitting** le canapé sur lequel je suis assis ; **the film of which you spoke** le film dont vous avez parlé - **3.** [referring back] [subject] ce qui ; [object] ce que ; **why did you say you were ill, which nobody believed?** pourquoi as-tu dit que tu étais malade, ce que personne n'a cru?

whichever [wɪtʃ'evər] <> *adj* [no matter what] quel (quelle) que soit. <> *pron* **1.** [the one that] celui qui *m*, celle qui *f*, ceux qui *mpl*, celles qui *f* - **2.** [no matter which one] n'importe lequel (laquelle).

whiff [wɪf] *n* [of perfume, smoke] bouffée *f* ; [of food] odeur *f*.

while [waɪl] <> *n* moment *m* ; **let's stay here for a while** restons ici un moment ; **for a long while** longtemps ; **after a while** après quelque temps. <> *conj* **1.** [during the time that] pendant que - **2.** [as long as] tant que - **3.** [whereas] alors que. <> **while away** *vt sep* passer.

whilst [waɪlst] *conj US* = **while**.

whim [wɪm] *n* lubie *f*.

whimper ['wɪmpər] *vt & vi* gémir.

whimsical ['wɪmzɪkl] *adj* saugrenu(e).

whine [waɪn] *vi* [make sound] gémir.

whinge [wɪndʒ] *vi UK* : **to whinge (about)** se plaindre (de).

whip [wɪp] <> *n* **1.** [for hitting] fouet *m* - **2.** POL chef *m* de file (*d'un groupe parlementaire*). <> *vt* **1.** [gen] fouetter - **2.** [take quickly] : **to whip sthg out** sortir qqch brusquement ; **to whip sthg off** ôter OR enlever qqch brusquement.

whipped cream [wɪpt-] *n* crème *f* fouettée.

whip-round *n UK inf* to have a whip-round faire une collecte.

whirl [wɜːl] <> *n lit & fig* tourbillon *m*. <> *vt* : **to whirl sb/sthg round** *UK*, OR **around** *US* [spin round] faire tourbillonner qqn/qqch. <> *vi* tourbillonner ; *fig* [head, mind] tourner.

whirlpool ['wɜːlpuːl] *n* tourbillon *m*.

whirlwind ['wɜːlwɪnd] *n* tornade *f*.

whirr [wɜːr] *vi* [engine] ronronner.

whisk [wɪsk] <> *n* CULIN fouet *m*, batteur *m* (à œufs). <> *vt* **1.** [move quickly] emmener OR emporter rapidement - **2.** CULIN battre.

whisker ['wɪskər] *n* moustache *f*. **whiskers** *npl* favoris *mpl*.

whisky *UK*, **whiskey** *US* (*Ir, pl* **-s**) ['wɪskɪ] *n* whisky *m*.

whisper ['wɪspər] <> *vt* murmurer, chuchoter. <> *vi* chuchoter.

whistle ['wɪsl] <> *n* **1.** [sound] sifflement *m* - **2.** [device] sifflet *m*. <> *vt & vi* siffler.

white [waɪt] <> *adj* **1.** [in colour] blanc (blanche) - **2.** *US* [coffee, tea] au lait. <> *n* **1.** [colour, of egg, eye] blanc *m* - **2.** [person] Blanc *m*, Blanche *f*.

whitecaps *n US* = **white horses**.

white-collar *adj* de bureau.

white elephant *n fig* objet *m* coûteux et inutile.

Whitehall ['waɪthɔːl] *n* rue de Londres, centre administratif du gouvernement britannique.

white-hot *adj* chauffé(e) à blanc.

White House *n* : **the White House** la Maison-Blanche.

white lie *n* pieux mensonge *m*.

whiteness ['waɪtnɪs] *n* blancheur *f*.

white paper *n* POL livre *m* blanc.

white sauce *n* sauce *f* blanche.

white spirit *n UK* white-spirit *m*.

whitewash ['waɪtwɒʃ] <> *n* **1.** (*U*) [paint] chaux *f* - **2.** *pej* [cover-up] : **a government whitewash** une combine du gouvernement pour étouffer l'affaire. <> *vt* [paint] blanchir à la chaux.

whiting ['waɪtɪŋ] (*pl* **whiting** OR **-s**) *n* merlan *m*.

Whitsun ['wɪtsn] *n* Pentecôte *f*.

whittle ['wɪtl] *vt* [reduce] : **to whittle sthg away** OR **down** réduire qqch.

whiz, whizz [wɪz] *vi* [go fast] aller à toute allure.

whiz(z) kid *n inf* petit prodige *m*.

who [hu:] *pron* **1.** *(in direct, indirect questions)* qui ; **who are you?** qui êtes-vous? ; **I didn't know who she was** je ne savais pas qui c'était - **2.** *(in relative clauses)* qui ; **he's the doctor who treated me** c'est le médecin qui m'a soigné ; **I don't know the person who came to see you** je ne connais pas la personne qui est venue vous voir.

who'd [hu:d] = who had ; = who would.

whodu(n)nit [,hu:'dʌnɪt] *n inf* polar *m*.

whoever [hu:'evər] *pron* **1.** [any person who] quiconque - **2.** [indicating surprise, astonishment] qui donc - **3.** [no matter who] qui que (+ *subjunctive*) ; **whoever wins** qui que ce soit qui gagne.

whole [həʊl] ⟨⟩ *adj* **1.** [entire, complete] entier(ère) - **2.** [for emphasis] : **a whole lot bigger** bien plus gros ; **a whole new idea** une idée tout à fait nouvelle. ⟨⟩ *n* **1.** [all] : **the whole of the school** toute l'école ; **the whole of the summer** tout l'été - **2.** [unit, complete thing] tout *m*. ➡ **as a whole** *adv* dans son ensemble. ➡ **on the whole** *adv* dans l'ensemble.

wholefood ['həʊlfu:d] *n UK* aliments *mpl* complets.

whole-hearted [-'hɑːtɪd] *adj* sans réserve, total(e).

wholemeal ['həʊlmi:l] *UK*, **whole wheat** *US adj* complet(ète).

wholesale ['həʊlseɪl] ⟨⟩ *adj* **1.** [buying, selling] en gros ; [price] de gros - **2.** *pej* [excessive] en masse. ⟨⟩ *adv* **1.** [in bulk] en gros - **2.** *pej* [excessively] en masse.

wholesaler ['həʊl,seɪlər] *n* marchand *m* de gros, grossiste *mf*.

wholesome ['həʊlsəm] *adj* sain(e).

whole wheat *US* = wholemeal.

who'll [hu:l] = who will.

wholly ['həʊlɪ] *adv* totalement.

whom [hu:m] *pron fml* **1.** *(in direct, indirect questions)* qui ; **whom did you phone?** qui avez-vous appelé? ; **for/of/to whom** pour/de/à qui - **2.** *(in relative clauses)* que ; **the girl whom he married** la jeune fille qu'il a épousée ; **the man of whom you speak** l'homme dont vous parlez ; **the man to whom you were speaking** l'homme à qui vous parliez.

whooping cough ['hu:pɪŋ-] *n* coqueluche *f*.

whopping ['wɒpɪŋ] *inf* ⟨⟩ *adj* énorme. ⟨⟩ *adv* : **a whopping great lorry/lie** un camion/mensonge absolument énorme.

whore [hɔːr] *n offens* putain *f*.

who're ['hu:ər] = who are.

whose [hu:z] ⟨⟩ *pron (in direct, indirect questions)* à qui ; **whose is this?** à qui est ceci? ⟨⟩ *adj* **1.** à qui ; **whose car is that?** à qui est cette voiture? ; **whose son is he?** de qui est-il le fils? - **2.** *(in relative clauses)* dont ; **that's the boy whose father's an MP** c'est le garçon dont le père est député ; **the girl whose mother you phoned yesterday** la fille à la mère de qui OR de laquelle tu as téléphoné hier.

who's who [hu:z-] *n* [book] Bottin® *m* mondain.

who've [hu:v] = who have.

why [waɪ] ⟨⟩ *adv (in direct questions)* pourquoi ; **why did you lie to me?** pourquoi m'as-tu menti? ; **why don't you all come?** pourquoi ne pas tous venir?, pourquoi est-ce que vous ne viendriez pas tous? ; **why not?** pourquoi pas? ⟨⟩ *conj* pourquoi ; **I don't know why he said that** je ne sais pas pourquoi il a dit cela. ⟨⟩ *pron* : **there are several reasons why he left** il est parti pour plusieurs raisons, les raisons pour lesquelles il est parti sont nombreuses ; **I don't know the reason why** je ne sais pas pourquoi. ➡ **why ever** *adv* pourquoi donc.

wick [wɪk] *n* [of candle, lighter] mèche *f*.

wicked ['wɪkɪd] *adj* **1.** [evil] mauvais(e) - **2.** [mischievous, devilish] malicieux(euse).

wicker ['wɪkər] *adj* en osier.

wickerwork ['wɪkəwɜːk] *n* vannerie *f*.

wicket ['wɪkɪt] *n* **1.** CRICKET [stumps, dismissal] guichet *m* - **2.** CRICKET [pitch] terrain *m* entre les guichets.

wide [waɪd] ⟨⟩ *adj* **1.** [gen] large ; **how wide is the room?** quelle est la largeur de la pièce? ; **to be six metres wide** faire six mètres de large OR de largeur - **2.** [gap, difference] grand(e) - **3.** [experience, knowledge, issue] vaste. ⟨⟩ *adv* **1.** [broadly] largement ; **open wide!** ouvrez grand! - **2.** [off-target] : **the shot went wide** le coup est passé loin du but OR à côté.

wide-angle lens *n* PHOT objectif *m* grand angle.

wide-awake *adj* tout à fait réveillé(e).

widely ['waɪdlɪ] *adv* **1.** [smile, vary] largement - **2.** [extensively] beaucoup ; **to be widely read** avoir beaucoup lu ; **it is widely believed that...** beaucoup pensent que..., nombreux sont ceux qui pensent que...

widen ['waɪdn] *vt* **1.** [make broader] élargir - **2.** [gap, difference] agrandir, élargir.

wide open *adj* grand ouvert (grande ouverte).

wide-ranging [-'reɪndʒɪŋ] *adj* varié(e) ; [consequences] de grande envergure.

widespread ['waɪdspred] *adj* très répandu(e).

widow ['wɪdəʊ] *n* veuve *f*.

widowed ['wɪdəud] *adj* veuf (veuve).

widower ['wɪdəuəʳ] *n* veuf *m*.

width [wɪdθ] *n* largeur *f* ; **in width** de large.

wield [wi:ld] *vt* **1.** [weapon] manier - **2.** [power] exercer.

wife [waɪf] (*pl* **wives** [waɪvz]) *n* femme *f*, épouse *f*.

wig [wɪg] *n* perruque *f*.

wiggle ['wɪgl] *inf vt* remuer.

wild [waɪld] *adj* **1.** [animal, attack, scenery, flower] sauvage - **2.** [weather, sea] déchaîné(e) - **3.** [laughter, hope, plan] fou (folle) - **4.** [random] fantaisiste ; **I made a wild guess** j'ai dit ça au hasard. ◆ **wilds** *npl* : **the wilds of** le fin fond de ; **to live in the wilds** habiter en pleine nature.

wilderness ['wɪldənɪs] *n* étendue *f* sauvage.

wild-goose chase *n inf* **it turned out to be a wild-goose chase** ça s'est révélé être totalement inutile.

wildlife ['waɪldlaɪf] *n* (*U*) faune *f* et flore *f*.

wildly ['waɪldlɪ] *adv* **1.** [enthusiastically, fanatically] frénétiquement - **2.** [guess, suggest] au hasard - **3.** [shoot] dans tous les sens - **3.** [very - different, impractical] tout à fait.

wilful *UK*, **willful** *US* ['wɪlful] *adj* **1.** [determined] obstiné(e) - **2.** [deliberate] délibéré(e).

will[1] [wɪl] ◇ *n* **1.** [mental] volonté *f* ; **against one's will** contre son gré - **2.** [document] testament *m*. ◇ *vt* : **to will sthg to happen** prier de toutes ses forces pour que qqch se passe ; **to will sb to do sthg** concentrer toute sa volonté sur qqn pour qu'il fasse qqch.

will[2] [wɪl] *modal vb* **1.** (to express future tense) **I will see you next week** je te verrai la semaine prochaine ; **when will you have finished it?** quand est-ce que vous l'aurez fini? ; **will you be here next week?** yes **I will/no I won't** est-ce que tu seras là la semaine prochaine? oui/non - **2.** [indicating willingness] : **will you have some more tea?** voulez-vous encore du thé? ; **I won't do it** je refuse de le faire, je ne veux pas le faire - **3.** [in commands, requests] : **you will leave this house at once** tu vas quitter cette maison tout de suite ; **close that window, will you?** ferme cette fenêtre, veux-tu? ; **will you be quiet!** veux-tu te taire!, tu vas te taire! - **4.** [indicating possibility, what usually happens] : **the hall will hold up to 1000 people** la salle peut abriter jusqu'à 1000 personnes - **5.** [expressing an assumption] : **that'll be your father** cela doit être ton père - **6.** [indicating irritation] : **she will keep phoning me** elle n'arrête pas de me téléphoner.

willful *US* = **wilful**.

willing ['wɪlɪŋ] *adj* **1.** [prepared] : **if you're willing** si vous voulez bien ; **to be willing to do sthg** être disposé(e) *OR* prêt(e) à faire qqch - **2.** [eager] enthousiaste.

willingly ['wɪlɪŋlɪ] *adv* volontiers.

willow (tree) ['wɪləu-] *n* saule *m*.

willpower ['wɪl,pauəʳ] *n* volonté *f*.

willy-nilly [,wɪlɪ'nɪlɪ] *adv* **1.** [at random] n'importe comment - **2.** [wanting to or not] bon gré mal gré.

wilt [wɪlt] *vi* [plant] se faner ; *fig* [person] dépérir.

wily ['waɪlɪ] *adj* rusé(e).

Wimbledon ['wɪmbldən] *n tournoi annuel de tennis à Londres.*

wimp [wɪmp] *n inf pej* mauviette *f*.

win [wɪn] ◇ *n* victoire *f*. ◇ *vt* (*pt & pp* **won**) **1.** [game, prize, competition] gagner - **2.** [support, approval] obtenir ; [love, friendship] gagner. ◇ *vi* gagner. ◆ **win over, win round** *UK vt sep* convaincre, gagner à sa cause.

wince [wɪns] *vi* : **to wince (at/with)** [with body] tressaillir (à/de) ; [with face] grimacer (à/de).

winch [wɪntʃ] *n* treuil *m*.

wind[1] [wɪnd] ◇ *n* **1.** METEOR vent *m* - **2.** [breath] souffle *m* - **3.** (*U*) [in stomach] gaz *mpl*. ◇ *vt* [knock breath out of] couper le souffle à.

wind[2] [waɪnd] (*pt & pp* **wound**) ◇ *vt* **1.** [string, thread] enrouler - **2.** [clock] remonter. ◇ *vi* [river, road] serpenter. ◆ **wind down** ◇ *vt sep* **1.** [car window] baisser - **2.** [business] cesser graduellement. ◇ *vi* [relax] se détendre. ◆ **wind up** *vt sep* **1.** [finish - meeting] clôturer ; [- business] liquider - **2.** *UK* [clock, car window] remonter - **3.** *UK inf* [deliberately annoy] faire marcher - **4.** *inf* [end up] : **to wind up doing sthg** finir par faire qqch.

windfall ['wɪndfɔːl] *n* [unexpected gift] aubaine *f*.

winding ['waɪndɪŋ] *adj* sinueux(euse).

wind instrument [wɪnd-] *n* instrument *m* à vent.

windmill ['wɪndmɪl] *n* moulin *m* à vent.

window ['wɪndəu] *n* **1.** [gen & COMPUT] fenêtre *f* - **2.** [pane of glass, in car] vitre *f* - **3.** [of shop] vitrine *f*.

window box *n* jardinière *f*.

window cleaner *n* laveur *m*, -euse *f* de vitres.

window ledge *n* rebord *m* de fenêtre.

windowpane *n* vitre *f*.

windowsill ['wɪndəusɪl] *n* [outside] rebord *m* de fenêtre ; [inside] appui *m* de fenêtre.

windpipe ['wɪndpaɪp] *n* trachée *f*.

windscreen UK ['wɪndskriːn], **windshield** US ['wɪndʃiːld] n pare-brise m inv.

windscreen washer n UK lave-glace m.

windscreen wiper [-ˌwaɪpəʳ] n UK essuie-glace m.

windshield US = windscreen.

windsurfing ['wɪndˌsɜːfɪŋ] n : **to go windsurfing** faire de la planche à voile.

windswept ['wɪndswept] adj [scenery] balayé(e) par les vents.

wind turbine n éolienne f.

windy ['wɪndɪ] adj venteux(euse) ; **it's windy** il fait OR il y a du vent.

wine [waɪn] n vin m.

wine bar n UK bar m à vin.

wine cellar n cave f (à vin).

wineglass ['waɪnɡlɑːs] n verre m à vin.

wine list n carte f des vins.

wine merchant n UK marchand m, -e f de vins.

wine tasting [-ˌteɪstɪŋ] n dégustation f (de vins).

wine waiter n sommelier m.

wing [wɪŋ] n aile f. ◆ **wings** npl THEAT : **the wings** les coulisses fpl.

winger ['wɪŋəʳ] n SPORT ailier m.

wink [wɪŋk] ◇ n clin m d'œil. ◇ vi [with eyes] : **to wink (at sb)** faire un clin d'œil (à qqn).

winkle ['wɪŋkl] n bigorneau m. ◆ **winkle out** vt sep extirper ; **to winkle sthg out of sb** arracher qqch à qqn.

Winnebago® [ˌwɪnɪ'beɪɡəʊ] n camping-car m, autocaravane f offic.

winner ['wɪnəʳ] n [person] gagnant m, -e f.

winning ['wɪnɪŋ] adj [victorious, successful] gagnant(e). ◆ **winnings** npl gains mpl.

winning post n poteau m d'arrivée.

winter ['wɪntəʳ] ◇ n hiver m ; **in winter** en hiver. ◇ comp d'hiver.

winter sports npl sports mpl d'hiver.

wintertime ['wɪntətaɪm] n (U) hiver m.

wint(e)ry ['wɪntrɪ] adj d'hiver.

wipe [waɪp] ◇ n 1. [action of wiping] : **to give sthg a wipe** essuyer qqch, donner un coup de torchon à qqch - 2. [cloth] lingette f. ◇ vt essuyer. ◆ **wipe out** vt sep 1. [erase] effacer - 2. [eradicate] anéantir. ◆ **wipe up** vt sep & vi essuyer.

wire ['waɪəʳ] ◇ n 1. (U) [metal] fil m de fer - 2. [cable etc] fil m - 3. esp US [telegram] télégramme m. ◇ vt 1. [ELEC - plug] installer ; [- house] faire l'installation électrique de - 2. esp US [send telegram to] télégraphier à.

wirefree ['waɪəfriː] adj sans fil.

wireless ['waɪəlɪs] n dated T.S.F. f

wiring ['waɪərɪŋ] n (U) installation f électrique.

wiry ['waɪərɪ] adj 1. [hair] crépu(e) - 2. [body, man] noueux(euse).

wisdom ['wɪzdəm] n sagesse f.

wisdom tooth n dent f de sagesse.

wise [waɪz] adj sage.

wisecrack ['waɪzkræk] n pej vanne f.

wise guy n inf malin m(e).

wish [wɪʃ] ◇ n 1. [desire] souhait m, désir m ; **wish for sthg/to do sthg** désir de qqch/de faire qqch - 2. [magic request] vœu m. ◇ vt 1. [want] : **to wish to do sthg** souhaiter faire qqch ; **I wish (that) he'd come** j'aimerais bien qu'il vienne ; **I wish I could** si seulement je pouvais - 2. [expressing hope] : **to wish sthg** souhaiter qqch à qqn. ◇ vi [by magic] : **to wish for sthg** souhaiter qqch. ◆ **wishes** npl : **best wishes** meilleurs vœux ; **(with) best wishes** [at end of letter] bien amicalement.

wishful thinking [ˌwɪʃful-] n : **that's just wishful thinking** c'est prendre mes/ses etc désirs pour des réalités.

wishy-washy ['wɪʃɪˌwɒʃɪ] adj inf pej [person] sans personnalité ; [ideas] vague.

wisp [wɪsp] n 1. [tuft] mèche f - 2. [small cloud] mince filet m OR volute f.

wistful ['wɪstful] adj nostalgique.

wit [wɪt] n 1. [humour] esprit m - 2. [intelligence] : **to have the wit to do sthg** avoir l'intelligence de faire qqch. ◆ **wits** npl : **to have** OR **keep one's wits about one** être attentif(ive) OR sur ses gardes.

witch [wɪtʃ] n sorcière f.

with [wɪð] prep 1. [in company of] avec ; **I play tennis with his wife** je joue au tennis avec sa femme ; **we stayed with them for a week** nous avons passé une semaine chez eux - 2. [indicating opposition] avec ; **to argue with sb** discuter avec qqn ; **the war with Germany** la guerre avec OR contre l'Allemagne - 3. [indicating means, manner, feelings] avec ; **I washed it with detergent** je l'ai lavé avec un détergent ; **she was trembling with fright** elle tremblait de peur - 4. [having] avec ; **a man with a beard** un homme avec une barbe, un barbu ; **the man with the moustache** l'homme à la moustache - 5. [regarding] : **he's very mean with money** il est très près de ses sous, il est très avare ; **the trouble with her is that...** l'ennui avec elle OR ce qu'il y a avec elle c'est que... - 6. [indicating simultaneity] : **I can't do it with you watching me** je ne peux pas le faire quand OR pendant que tu me regardes - 7. [because of] : **with my luck, I'll probably lose** avec ma chance habituelle, je suis sûr de perdre ; **I'm with you** [I understand] je vous suis ; [I'm on your side] je suis des vôtres ; [I agree] je suis d'accord avec vous.

withdraw [wɪð'drɔː] (*pt* **-drew**, *pp* **-drawn**) ◇ *vt* **1.** *fml* [remove] **: to withdraw sthg (from)** enlever qqch (de) - **2.** [money, troops, remark] retirer. ◇ *vi* **1.** *fml* [leave] **: to withdraw (from)** se retirer (de) - **2.** MIL se replier ; **to withdraw from** évacuer - **3.** [quit, give up] **: to withdraw (from)** se retirer (de).

withdrawal [wɪð'drɔːəl] *n* **1.** [gen] **: withdrawal (from)** retrait *m* (de) - **2.** MIL repli *m*.

withdrawal symptoms *npl* crise *f* de manque.

withdrawn [wɪð'drɔːn] ◇ *pp* ▶ withdraw. ◇ *adj* [shy, quiet] renfermé(e).

withdrew [wɪð'druː] *pt* ▶ withdraw.

wither [wɪðər] *vi* **1.** [dry up] se flétrir - **2.** [weaken] mourir.

withhold [wɪð'həʊld] (*pt & pp* **-held** [-'held]) *vt* [services] refuser ; [information] cacher ; [salary] retenir.

within [wɪ'ðɪn] ◇ *prep* **1.** [inside] à l'intérieur de, dans ; **within her** en elle, à l'intérieur d'elle-même - **2.** [budget, comprehension] dans les limites de ; [limits] dans - **3.** [less than - distance] à moins de ; [- time] d'ici, en moins de ; **within the week** avant la fin de la semaine. ◇ *adv* à l'intérieur.

without [wɪð'aʊt] ◇ *prep* sans ; **without a coat** sans manteau ; **I left without seeing him** je suis parti sans l'avoir vu ; **I left without him seeing me** je suis parti sans qu'il m'ait vu ; **to go without** se passer de qqch. ◇ *adv* **: to go** OR **do without** s'en passer.

withstand [wɪð'stænd] (*pt & pp* **-stood** [-'stʊd]) *vt* résister à.

witness [wɪtnɪs] ◇ *n* **1.** [gen] témoin *mf* ; **to be witness to sthg** être témoin de qqch - **2.** [testimony] **: to bear witness to sthg** témoigner de qqch. ◇ *vt* **1.** [accident, crime] être témoin de - **2.** *fig* [changes, rise in birth rate] assister à - **3.** [countersign] contresigner.

witness box UK, **witness stand** US *n* barre *f* des témoins.

witticism [wɪtɪsɪzm] *n* mot *m* d'esprit.

witty [wɪtɪ] *adj* plein(e) d'esprit, spirituel(elle).

wives [waɪvz] *npl* ▶ wife.

wizard [wɪzəd] *n* magicien *m* ; *fig* as *m*, champion *m*, -onne *f*.

wobble [wɒbl] *vi* [hand, wings] trembler ; [chair, table] branler.

woe [wəʊ] *n lit* malheur *m*.

woke [wəʊk] *pt* ▶ wake.

woken [wəʊkn] *pp* ▶ wake.

wolf [wʊlf] (*pl* **wolves** [wʊlvz]) *n* [animal] loup *m*.

woman [wʊmən] (*pl* **women**) ◇ *n* femme *f*. ◇ *comp* **: woman doctor** femme *f* médecin ; **woman teacher** professeur *m* femme.

womanly [wʊmənlɪ] *adj* féminin(e).

womb [wuːm] *n* utérus *m*.

women [wɪmɪn] *npl* ▶ woman.

women's lib *n* libération *f* de la femme.

women's liberation *n* libération *f* de la femme.

won [wʌn] *pt & pp* ▶ win.

wonder [wʌndər] ◇ *n* **1.** (U) [amazement] étonnement *m* - **2.** [cause for surprise] **:** **it's a wonder (that)...** c'est un miracle que... ; **it's no** OR **little** OR **small wonder (that)...** il n'est pas étonnant que... - **3.** [amazing thing, person] merveille *f*. ◇ *vt* **1.** [speculate] **: to wonder (if** OR **whether)** se demander (si) - **2.** [in polite requests] **: I wonder whether you would mind shutting the window?** est-ce que cela ne vous ennuierait pas de fermer la fenêtre ? ◇ *vi* [speculate] se demander ; **to wonder about sthg** s'interroger sur qqch.

wonderful [wʌndəfʊl] *adj* merveilleux(euse).

wonderfully [wʌndəfʊlɪ] *adv* **1.** [very well] merveilleusement, à merveille - **2.** [for emphasis] extrêmement.

won't [wəʊnt] = will not.

woo [wuː] *vt* **1.** *lit* [court] courtiser - **2.** [try to win over] chercher à rallier (à soi OR à sa cause).

wood [wʊd] ◇ *n* bois *m*. ◇ *comp* en bois. ◆ **woods** *npl* bois *mpl*.

wooded [wʊdɪd] *adj* boisé(e).

wooden [wʊdn] *adj* **1.** [of wood] en bois - **2.** *pej* [actor] gauche.

woodpecker [wʊd,pekər] *n* pivert *m*.

woodwind [wʊdwɪnd] *n* **: the woodwind** les bois *mpl*.

woodwork [wʊdwɜːk] *n* menuiserie *f*.

woodworm [wʊdwɜːm] *n* ver *m* du bois.

wool [wʊl] *n* laine *f* ; **to pull the wool over sb's eyes** *inf* rouler qqn (dans la farine).

woollen UK, **woolen** US [wʊlən] *adj* en laine, de laine. ◆ **woollens** *npl* lainages *mpl*.

woolly, US **wooly** [wʊlɪ] *adj* **1.** [woollen] en laine, de laine - **2.** *inf* [idea, thinking] confus(e).

word [wɜːd] ◇ *n* **1.** LING mot *m* ; **too stupid for words** vraiment trop bête ; **word for word** [repeat, copy] mot pour mot ; [translate] mot à mot ; **in other words** en d'autres mots OR termes ; **in a word** en un mot ; **to have a word (with sb)** parler (à qqn) ; **she doesn't mince her words** elle ne mâche pas ses mots ; **I couldn't get a word in edgeways** je n'ai pas réussi à placer un seul mot - **2.** (U) [news] nouvelles *fpl* - **3.** [promise] parole *f* ; **to give sb one's word** donner sa parole à qqn. ⟨> *vt* [letter, reply] rédiger.

wording ['wɜ:dɪŋ] *n* (U) termes *mpl*.

word processing *n* (U) COMPUT traitement *m* de texte.

word processor [-ˌprəʊsesə'] *n* COMPUT machine *f* à traitement de texte.

wore [wɔ:'] *pt* ▶ wear.

work [wɜ:k] ⟨> *n* **1.** (U) [employment] travail, emploi *m* ; **out of work** sans emploi, au chômage ; **at work** au travail - **2.** [activity, tasks] travail *m* ; **she put a lot of work** into that book elle a beaucoup travaillé sur ce livre - **3.** ART & LIT œuvre *f*. ⟨> *vt* **1.** [person, staff] faire travailler - **2.** [machine] faire marcher - **3.** [wood, metal, land] travailler. ⟨> *vi* **1.** [do a job] travailler ; **to work on sthg** travailler à qqch - **2.** [function] fonctionner, marcher - **3.** [succeed] marcher - **4.** [become] : **to work loose** se desserrer. ◆ **works** ⟨> *n* [factory] usine *f*. ⟨> *npl* **1.** [mechanism] mécanisme *m* - **2.** [digging, building] travaux *mpl*. ◆ **work on** *vt insep* **1.** [pay attention to] travailler à - **2.** [take as basis] se baser sur. ◆ **work out** ⟨> *vt sep* **1.** [plan, schedule] mettre au point - **2.** [total, answer] trouver. ⟨> *vi* **1.** [figure, total] : **to work out at** UK OR **to** US se monter à - **2.** [turn out] se dérouler - **3.** [be successful] (bien) marcher - **4.** [train, exercise] s'entraîner. ◆ **work up** *vt sep* **1.** [excite] : **to work o.s. up into a rage** se mettre en rage - **2.** [generate] : **to work up an appetite** s'ouvrir l'appétit ; **to work up enthusiasm** s'enthousiasmer.

workable ['wɜ:kəbl] *adj* [plan] réalisable ; [system] fonctionnel(elle).

workaholic [ˌwɜ:kə'hɒlɪk] *n* bourreau *m* de travail.

workday ['wɜ:kdeɪ] *n* [not weekend] jour *m* ouvrable.

worked up [ˌwɜ:kt-] *adj* dans tous ses états.

worker ['wɜ:kə'] *n* travailleur *m*, -euse *f*, ouvrier *m*, -ère *f*.

workforce ['wɜ:kfɔ:s] *n* main *f* d'œuvre.

working ['wɜ:kɪŋ] *adj* **1.** [in operation] qui marche - **2.** [having employment] qui travaille - **3.** [conditions, clothes, hours] de travail. ◆ **workings** *npl* [of system, machine] mécanisme *m*.

working class *n* : **the working class** la classe ouvrière. ◆ **working-class** *adj* ouvrier(ère).

working order *n* : **in working order** en état de marche.

workload ['wɜ:kləʊd] *n* quantité *f* de travail.

workman ['wɜ:kmən] (*pl* **-men** [-mən]) *n* ouvrier *m*.

workmanship ['wɜ:kmənʃɪp] *n* (U) travail *m*.

workmate ['wɜ:kmeɪt] *n* camarade *mf* OR collègue *mf* de travail.

work permit [-ˌpɜ:mɪt] *n* permis *m* de travail.

workplace ['wɜ:kpleɪs] *n* lieu *m* de travail.

workshop ['wɜ:kʃɒp] *n* atelier *m*.

workspace ['wɜ:kspeɪs] *n* COMPUT bureau *m*.

workstation ['wɜ:kˌsteɪʃn] *n* COMPUT poste *m* de travail.

worktop ['wɜ:ktɒp] *n* UK plan *m* de travail.

work-to-rule *n* UK grève *f* du zèle.

workweek *n* US = working week.

world [wɜ:ld] ⟨> *n* [gen] monde *m* ; **to think the world of sb** admirer qqn énormément, ne jurer que par qqn ; **a world of difference** une énorme différence. ⟨> *comp* [power] mondial(e) ; [language] universel(elle) ; [tour] du monde.

world-class *adj* de niveau international.

world-famous *adj* de renommée mondiale.

worldly ['wɜ:ldlɪ] *adj* de ce monde, matériel(elle).

World War I *n* la Première Guerre mondiale.

World War II *n* la Deuxième Guerre mondiale.

worldwide ['wɜ:ldwaɪd] ⟨> *adj* mondial(e). ⟨> *adv* dans le monde entier.

worm [wɜ:m] *n* [animal] ver *m*.

worn [wɔ:n] ⟨> *pp* ▶ wear. ⟨> *adj* **1.** [threadbare] usé(e) - **2.** [tired] las (lasse).

worn-out *adj* **1.** [old, threadbare] usé(e) - **2.** [tired] épuisé(e).

worried ['wʌrɪd] *adj* soucieux(euse), inquiet(ète).

worry ['wʌrɪ] ⟨> *n* **1.** [feeling] souci *m* - **2.** [problem] souci *m*, ennui *m*. ⟨> *vt* inquiéter, tracasser. ⟨> *vi* s'inquiéter ; **to worry about** se faire du souci au sujet de ; **don't worry!, not to worry!** ne vous en faites pas!

worrying ['wʌrɪɪŋ] *adj* inquiétant(e).

worse [wɜ:s] ⟨> *adj* **1.** [not as good] pire ; **to get worse** [situation] empirer - **2.** [more ill] : **he's worse today** il va plus mal aujourd'hui. ⟨> *adv* plus mal ; **they're even**

worse off c'est encore pire pour eux ; **worse off** [financially] plus pauvre. <> n pire m ; for the worse pour le pire.

worsen ['wɜːsn] vt & vi empirer.

worship ['wɜːʃɪp] <> vt (US & UK) adorer. <> n **1.** (U) RELIG culte m - **2.** [adoration] adoration f. ➡ **Worship** n : Your/Her/His Worship Votre/Son Honneur m.

worst [wɜːst] <> adj : **the worst** le pire (la pire), le plus mauvais (la plus mauvaise). <> adv le plus mal ; **the worst affected area** la zone la plus touchée. <> n : **the worst** le pire ; **if the worst comes to the worst** au pire. ➡ **at (the) worst** adv au pire.

worth [wɜːθ] <> prep **1.** [in value] : **to be worth sthg** valoir qqch ; **how much is it worth?** combien cela vaut-il ? - **2.** [deserving of] : **it's worth a visit** cela vaut une visite ; **to be worth doing sthg** valoir la peine de faire qqch. <> n valeur f ; **a week's/£20 worth of groceries** pour une semaine/20 livres d'épicerie.

worthless ['wɜːθlɪs] adj **1.** [object] sans valeur, qui ne vaut rien - **2.** [person] qui n'est bon à rien.

worthwhile [,wɜːθ'waɪl] adj [job, visit] qui en vaut la peine ; [charity] louable.

worthy ['wɜːðɪ] adj **1.** [deserving of respect] digne - **2.** [deserving] : **to be worthy of sthg** mériter qqch - **3.** pej [good but unexciting] méritant(e).

would [wʊd] modal vb **1.** (in reported speech) she said she would come elle a dit qu'elle viendrait - **2.** [indicating likelihood] : **what would you do?** que ferais-tu ? ; **what would you have done?** qu'aurais-tu fait ? ; **I would be most grateful** je vous en serais très reconnaissant - **3.** [indicating willingness] : **she wouldn't go** elle ne voulait pas y aller ; **he would do anything for her** il ferait n'importe quoi pour elle - **4.** (in polite questions) **would you like a drink?** voulez-vous OR voudriez-vous à boire ? ; **would you mind closing the window?** cela vous ennuierait-il de fermer la fenêtre ? - **5.** [indicating inevitability] : **he would say that** j'étais sûr qu'il allait dire ça, ça ne m'étonne pas de lui - **6.** [giving advice] : **I would report it if I were you** si j'étais vous je préviendrais les autorités - **7.** [expressing opinions] : **I would prefer** je préférerais ; **I would have thought (that)...** j'aurais pensé que... - **8.** [indicating habit] : **he would smoke a cigar after dinner** il fumait un cigare après le dîner ; **she would often complain about the neighbours** elle se plaignait souvent des voisins.

would-be adj prétendu(e).

wouldn't ['wʊdnt] = would not.

would've ['wʊdəv] = would have.

wound¹ [wuːnd] <> n blessure f. <> vt blesser.

wound² [waʊnd] pt & pp ➡ wind².

wove [wəʊv] pt ➡ weave.

woven ['wəʊvn] pp ➡ weave.

WP n (abbrev of **word processing, word processor**) TTX m.

wrangle ['ræŋgl] <> n dispute f. <> vi : **to wrangle (with sb over sthg)** se disputer (avec qqn à propos de qqch).

wrap [ræp] <> vt [cover in paper, cloth] : **to wrap sthg (in)** envelopper OR emballer qqch (dans) ; **to wrap sthg around** OR **round** UK **sthg** enrouler qqch autour de qqch. <> n [garment] châle m. ➡ **wrap up** <> vt sep [cover in paper or cloth] envelopper, emballer. <> vi [put warm clothes on] : **wrap up well** OR **warmly!** couvrez-vous bien !

wrapper ['ræpər] n papier m ; UK [of book] jaquette f, couverture f.

wrapping ['ræpɪŋ] n emballage m.

wrapping paper n (U) papier m d'emballage.

wrath [rɒθ] n (U) lit courroux m.

wreak [riːk] vt [destruction, havoc] entraîner.

wreath [riːθ] n couronne f.

wreck [rek] <> n **1.** [car, plane, ship] épave f - **2.** inf [person] loque f. <> vt **1.** [destroy] détruire - **2.** NAUT provoquer le naufrage de ; **to be wrecked** s'échouer - **3.** [spoil - holiday] gâcher ; [- health, hopes, plan] ruiner.

wreckage ['rekɪdʒ] n (U) débris mpl.

wren [ren] n roitelet m.

wrench [rentʃ] <> n [tool] clef f anglaise. <> vt **1.** [pull violently] tirer violemment ; **to wrench sthg off** arracher qqch - **2.** [arm, leg, knee] se tordre.

wrestle ['resl] vi **1.** [fight] : **to wrestle (with sb)** lutter (contre qqn) - **2.** fig [struggle] : **to wrestle with sthg** se débattre OR lutter contre qqch.

wrestler ['reslər] n lutteur m, -euse f.

wrestling ['reslɪŋ] n lutte f.

wretch [retʃ] n pauvre diable m.

wretched ['retʃɪd] adj **1.** [miserable] misérable - **2.** inf [damned] fichu(e).

wriggle ['rɪgl] vi remuer, se tortiller.

wring [rɪŋ] (pt & pp wrung) vt [washing] essorer, tordre.

wringing ['rɪŋɪŋ] adj : **wringing (wet)** [person] trempé(e) ; [clothes] mouillé(e), à tordre.

wrinkle ['rɪŋkl] <> n **1.** [on skin] ride f - **2.** [in cloth] pli m. <> vt plisser. <> vi se plisser, faire des plis.

wrist [rɪst] n poignet m.

wristwatch ['rɪstwɒtʃ] n montre-bracelet f.

writ [rɪt] *n* acte *m* judiciaire.

write [raɪt] (*pt* **wrote**, *pp* **written**) ⟺ *vt*
1. [gen & COMPUT] écrire - **2.** *US* [person]
écrire à - **3.** [cheque, prescription, will] faire.
⟺ *vi* [gen & COMPUT] écrire. ➡ **write
back** *vi* répondre. ➡ **write down** *vt sep*
écrire, noter. ➡ **write into** *vt sep* : **to
write a clause into a contract** insérer une
clause dans un contrat. ➡ **write off**
vt sep **1.** [project] considérer comme fichu
- **2.** [debt, investment] passer aux profits et
pertes - **3.** [person] considérer comme fini
- **4.** *UK inf* [vehicle] bousiller. ➡ **write up**
vt sep [notes] mettre au propre.

write-off *n inf* [vehicle] : **to be a write-off**
UK être complètement démoli(e).

writer ['raɪtər] *n* **1.** [as profession] écrivain
m, -e *f* - **2.** [of letter, article, story] auteur *m*,
-(e) *f*.

writhe [raɪð] *vi* se tordre.

writing ['raɪtɪŋ] *n (U)* **1.** [handwriting,
activity] écriture *f* ; **in writing** par écrit
- **2.** [something written] écrit *m*.

writing paper *n (U)* papier *m* à lettres.

written ['rɪtn] ⟺ *pp* ➡ **write**. ⟺ *adj*
écrit(e).

wrong [rɒŋ] ⟺ *adj* **1.** [not normal, not
satisfactory] qui ne va pas ; **is something
wrong?** y a-t-il quelque chose qui ne va
pas? ; **what's wrong?** qu'est-ce qui ne va
pas? ; **there's something wrong with the
switch** l'interrupteur ne marche pas bien
- **2.** [not suitable] qui ne convient pas
- **3.** [not correct - answer, address] faux
(fausse), mauvais(e) ; [- decision] mauvais ;
to be wrong [person] avoir tort ; **to be wrong
to do sthg** avoir tort de faire qqch - **4.** [mor-
ally bad] : **it's wrong to...** c'est mal de...
⟺ *adv* [incorrectly] mal ; **to get sthg wrong**
se tromper à propos de qqch ; **to go wrong**
[make a mistake] se tromper, faire une
erreur ; [stop functioning] se détraquer.
⟺ *n* mal *m* ; **to be in the wrong** être dans
son tort. ⟺ *vt* faire du tort à.

wrongful ['rɒŋfʊl] *adj* [unfair] injuste ;
[arrest, dismissal] injustifié(e).

wrongly ['rɒŋlɪ] *adv* **1.** [unsuitably] mal
- **2.** [mistakenly] à tort.

wrong number *n* faux numéro *m*.

wrote [rəʊt] *pt* ➡ **write**.

wrought iron [rɔːt-] *n* fer *m* forgé.

wrung [rʌŋ] *pt & pp* ➡ **wring**.

wry [raɪ] *adj* **1.** [amused - smile, look]
amusé(e) ; [- humour] ironique - **2.** [displea-
sed] désabusé(e).

WWW (*abbrev of* **World Wide Web**) *n*
WWW *m*.

x [eks] (*pl* **x's** OR **xs**), **X** (*pl* **X's** OR **Xs**) *n*
1. [letter] x *m inv*, X *m inv* - **2.** [unknown
thing] x *m inv* - **3.** [to mark place] **croix** *f*
- **4.** [at end of letter] : **XXX grosses bises.**

xenophobia [ˌzenə'fəʊbjə] *n* xénophobie
f.

Xmas ['eksməs] *n* Noël *m*.

XML [ˌeksem'el] (*abbrev of* **Extensible Mark-
up Language**) *n* COMPUT XML *m*.

X-ray ⟺ *n* **1.** [ray] rayon *m* X - **2.** [picture]
radiographie *f*, radio *f*. ⟺ *vt* radiographier.

xylophone ['zaɪləfəʊn] *n* xylophone *m*.

y [waɪ] (*pl* **y's** OR **ys**), **Y** (*pl* **Y's** OR **Ys**) *n* [letter]
y *m inv*, Y *m inv*.

yacht [jɒt] *n* yacht *m*.

yachting ['jɒtɪŋ] *n* yachting *m*.

yachtsman ['jɒtsmən] (*pl* **-men** [-mən]) *n*
yachtman *m*.

yam [jæm] *n* igname *f*.

Yank [jæŋk] *n UK inf* Amerloque *mf (terme
péjoratif désignant un Américain)*.

Yankee ['jæŋkɪ] *n UK inf* [American] Amerloque *mf (terme péjoratif désignant un Américain)*.

yap [jæp] *vi* [dog] japper.

yard [jɑːd] *n* **1.** [unit of measurement] yard
m (= 91,44 cm) - **2.** [walled area] cour *f*
- **3.** [area of work] chantier *m* - **4.** *US* [attached
to house] jardin *m*.

yardstick ['jɑːdstɪk] *n* mesure *f*.

yarn [jɑːn] *n* [thread] fil *m*.

yawn [jɔːn] ⟺ *n* [when tired] bâillement
m. ⟺ *vi* [when tired] bâiller.

yd *abbrev of* **yard**.

yeah [jeə] *adv inf* ouais.

year [jɪər] *n* **1.** [calendar year] année *f*
- **2.** [period of 12 months] année *f*, an *m* ; **to
be 21 years old** avoir 21 ans ; **all (the) year**

round toute l'année - **3.** [financial year] année f ; **the year 2002-03** l'exercice 2002-03.
➤ **years** npl [long time] années fpl.

yearly ['jɪəlɪ] ⬦ adj annuel(elle). ⬦ adv **1.** [once a year] annuellement - **2.** [every year] chaque année ; **twice yearly** deux fois par an.

yearn [jɜːn] vi : **to yearn for sthg/to do sthg** aspirer à qqch/à faire qqch.

yearning ['jɜːnɪŋ] n : **yearning (for sb/sthg)** désir m ardent (pour qqn/de qqch).

yeast [jiːst] n levure f.

yell [jel] ⬦ n hurlement m. ⬦ vi & vt hurler.

yellow ['jeləʊ] ⬦ adj [colour] jaune. ⬦ n jaune m.

yellow card n FOOTBALL carton m jaune.

yelp [jelp] vi japper.

yeoman of the guard ['jəʊmən-] (pl yeomen of the guard ['jəʊmən-]) n UK hallebardier m de la garde royale.

yer [jɜː] adj inf [e-mail] votre, ton (tates).

yes [jes] ⬦ adv **1.** [gen] oui ; **yes, please** oui, s'il te/vous plaît ; [expressing disagreement] si. ⬦ n oui m inv.

yesterday ['jestədɪ] ⬦ n hier m ; **the day before yesterday** avant-hier. ⬦ adv hier.

yet [jet] ⬦ adv **1.** [gen] encore ; **not yet** pas encore ; **yet again** encore une fois ; **as yet** jusqu'ici ; **yet faster** encore plus vite - **2.** déjà ; **have they finished yet?** est-ce qu'ils ont déjà fini ? ⬦ conj et cependant, mais.

yew [juː] n if m.

yield [jiːld] ⬦ n rendement m. ⬦ vt **1.** [produce] produire - **2.** [give up] céder. ⬦ vi **1.** [gen] : **to yield (to)** céder (à) - **2.** US AUT [give way] : **'yield'** 'cédez le passage'.

YMCA (abbrev of Young Men's Christian Association) n union chrétienne de jeunes gens (proposant notamment des services d'hébergement).

yoga ['jəʊgə] n yoga m.

yoghourt, yoghurt, yogurt [UK 'jɒgət, US 'jəʊgət] n yaourt m.

yoke [jəʊk] n lit & fig joug m.

yolk [jəʊk] n jaune m (d'œuf).

you [juː] pers pron **1.** [subject - sg] tu , [- polite form, pl] vous ; **you're a good cook** tu es/vous êtes bonne cuisinière ; **are you French?** tu es/vous êtes français ? ; **you French** vous autres Français ; **you idiot!** espèce d'idiot ! ; **if I were** OR **was you** si j'étais toi/vous, à ta/votre place ; **there you are** [- you've appeared] te/vous voilà ; [- have this] voilà, tiens/tenez ; **that jacket really isn't you** cette veste n'est pas vraiment ton/votre style - **2.** [object - un-

stressed, sg] **te** ; [- polite form, pl] **vous** ; **I can see you** je te/vous vois ; **I gave it to you** je te/vous l'ai donné - **3.** [object - stressed, sg] **toi** ; [- polite form, pl] **vous** ; **I don't expect YOU to do it** je n'exige pas que ce soit toi qui le fasses/vous qui le fassiez - **4.** [after prep, in comparisons etc - sg] **toi** ; [- polite form, pl] **vous** ; **we shall go without you** nous irons sans toi/vous ; **I'm shorter than you** je suis plus petit que toi/vous - **5.** [anyone, one] **on** ; **you have to be careful** on doit faire attention ; **exercise is good for you** l'exercice est bon pour la santé.

you'd [juːd] = **you had,** = **you would.**

you'll [juːl] = **you will.**

young [jʌŋ] ⬦ adj jeune. ⬦ npl **1.** [young people] : **the young** les jeunes mpl - **2.** [baby animals] les petits mpl.

younger ['jʌŋgər] adj plus jeune.

youngster ['jʌŋstər] n jeune m.

your [jɔːr] poss adj **1.** (referring to one person) ton (ta), tes (pl) ; (polite form, pl) votre, vos (pl) ; **your dog** ton/votre chien ; **your house** ta/votre maison ; **your children** tes/vos enfants ; **what's your name?** comment t'appelles-tu/vous appelez-vous ? ; **it wasn't YOUR fault** ce n'était pas de ta faute à toi/de votre faute à vous - **2.** (impersonal, one's) son (sa), ses (pl) ; **your attitude changes as you get older** on change sa manière de voir en vieillissant ; **it's good for your teeth/hair** c'est bon pour les dents/les cheveux ; **your average Englishman** l'Anglais moyen.

you're [jɔːr] = **you are.**

yours [jɔːz] poss pron (referring to one person) le tien (la tienne), les tiens (les tiennes) (pl) ; (polite form, pl) le vôtre (la vôtre), les vôtres (pl) ; **that desk is yours** ce bureau est à toi/à vous, ce bureau est le tien/le vôtre ; **it wasn't your fault, it was YOURS** ce n'était pas de sa faute, c'était de ta faute à toi/de votre faute à vous ; **a friend of yours** un ami à toi/vous, un de tes/vos amis. ➤ **Yours** adv [in letter] ➤ **faithfully,** ➤ **sincerely** etc.

yourself [jɔːˈself] (pl **-selves** [-ˈselvz]) pron **1.** [reflexive - sg] **te** ; [- polite form, pl] **vous** ; [after preposition - sg] **toi** ; [- polite form, pl] **vous** - **2.** [for emphasis - sg] **toi-même** ; [- polite form] **vous-même** ; [- pl] **vous-mêmes** ; **did you do it yourself?** tu l'as/vous l'avez fait tout seul ?

youth [juːθ] n **1.** (U) [period, quality] jeunesse f - **2.** [young man] jeune homme m - **3.** (U) [young people] jeunesse f, jeunes mpl.

youth club n centre m de jeunes.

youthful ['juːθfʊl] adj **1.** [eager, innocent] de jeunesse, juvénile - **2.** [young] jeune.

youth hostel *n* auberge *f* de jeunesse.

you've [juːv] = **you have**.

yrs (*abbrev of* **yours**) *pron* [e-mail] votre.

YTS (*abbrev of* **Youth Training Scheme**) *n* *programme gouvernemental britannique d'insertion des jeunes dans la vie professionnelle.*

Yugoslav = **Yugoslavian**.

Yugoslavia [ˌjuːgəˈslɑːvɪə] *n* Yougoslavie *f* ; **the former Yugoslavia** l'ex-Yougoslavie.

Yugoslavian [ˌjuːgəˈslɑːvɪən], **Yugoslav** [ˌjuːgəˈslɑːv] <> *adj* yougoslave. <> *n* Yougoslave *mf*.

yuppie, yuppy [ˈjʌpɪ] *n inf* yuppie *mf*.

YWCA (*abbrev of* **Young Women's Christian Association**) *n* union chrétienne de jeunes filles (*proposant notamment des services d'hébergement*).

Z

z [*UK* zed, *US* ziː] (*pl* **z's** OR **zs**), *US* **Z** (*pl* **Z's** OR **Zs**) *n* [letter] z *m inv*, Z *m inv*.

Zambia [ˈzæmbɪə] *n* Zambie *f*.

zany [ˈzeɪnɪ] *adj inf* dingue.

zap [zæp] *vi* **1.** *inf* **to zap (off) somewhere** foncer quelque part - **2.** *TV* zapper.

zeal [ziːl] *n* zèle *m*.

zealous [ˈzeləs] *adj* zélé(e).

zebra [*UK* ˈzebrə, *US* ˈziːbrə] (*pl inv* OR **-s**) *n* zèbre *m*.

zebra crossing *n UK* passage *m* pour piétons.

zenith [*UK* ˈzenɪθ, *US* ˈziːnəθ] *n lit & fig* zénith *m*.

zero [*UK* ˈzɪərəʊ, *US* ˈziːrəʊ] <> *adj* zéro, aucun(e). <> *n* (*pl* **zero** OR **-es**) zéro *m*.

zest [zest] *n* (*U*) **1.** [excitement] piquant *m* - **2.** [eagerness] entrain *m* - **3.** [of orange, lemon] zeste *m*.

zigzag [ˈzɪgzæg] *vi* (*pt & pp* **-ged**, *cont* **-ging**) zigzaguer.

Zimbabwe [zɪmˈbɑːbwɪ] *n* Zimbabwe *m*.

zinc [zɪŋk] *n* zinc *m*.

zip [zɪp] *n UK* [fastener] fermeture *f* Éclair®.
  ➤ **zip up** *vt sep* [jacket] remonter la fermeture Éclair® de ; [bag] fermer la fermeture Éclair® de.

zip code *n US* code *m* postal.

Zip disk® *n COMPUT* disque *m* zip.

zip fastener *n UK* = **zip**.

zipper [ˈzɪpər] *n US* = **zip**.

zodiac [ˈzəʊdɪæk] *n* : **the zodiac** le zodiaque.

zone [zəʊn] *n* zone *f*.

zoo [zuː] *n* zoo *m*.

zoology [zəʊˈɒlədʒɪ] *n* zoologie *f*.

zoom [zuːm] <> *vi inf* [move quickly] aller en trombe. <> *n PHOT* zoom *m*.

zoom lens *n* zoom *m*.

zucchini [zuːˈkiːnɪ] (*pl* **zucchini**) *n US* courgette *f*.

Achevé d'imprimer par l'Imprimerie
Maury-Imprimeur - 45330 Malesherbes en juin 2009
Dépôt légal : juin 2009 - N° d'imprimeur : 147145
Projet : 11008667 - 541016
Imprimé en France - (Printed in France)